CURRENT BIOGRAPHY

WHO'S NEWS AND WHY

1 9 4 5

EDITOR

Anna Rothe

ASSISTANT EDITOR

Helen Demarest

THE H. W. WILSON COMPANY

NEW YORK, N. Y.

SIXTH ANNUAL CUMULATION—1945

PRINTED IN THE UNITED STATES OF AMERICA

Copyright 1946
by
THE H. W. WILSON COMPANY

Preface

CURRENT BIOGRAPHY began publication a few months after the outbreak of World War II. And of this volume, its sixth Yearbook, it might be said that it presents the last of "the Captains and the Kings" whose records are an important part of the history of those war years. Also prominent among the thirty-one professions represented in this volume are the fields of politics, education, the arts, and science. In the last-named classification appear some of the names which, together with their "now-it-can-be-told" work, became headline news after the war.

All the biographies which have appeared in CURRENT BIOGRAPHY during the six years are listed in the "Cumulated Index—1940-1945" at the back of this volume. Users of this Yearbook should therefore consult that index if this annual does not contain the biographies they wish to read. The index will show, for example, that the biographies of the present Secretary of State, James F. Byrnes, and scientist Harold C. Urey appear in the 1941 Yearbook; and that General Eisenhower's biography is contained in the 1942 volume. Reference librarians will find the six-year index of even more value than before: it now includes references to the monthly issues as well as to the Yearbooks published since 1940.

Like the volumes of the past five years, 1945 CURRENT BIOGRAPHY Yearbook is a one-alphabet cumulation of the biographical articles and obituary notices that appeared in the year's monthly issues. However, before the articles were reprinted in the Yearbook, they were revised, when necessary, to include events that occurred in 1945 after the publication of those articles in the monthly numbers. While many biographies were thus rounded out as of December 31, 1945, that deadline of necessity left some matters pending at the close of the year.

The assembling of material for these biographies entails thorough-going research. Files of clippings are drawn upon when a name is selected for inclusion in CURRENT BIOGRAPHY. Indexes to magazine articles and books guide writers to a mass of information which is culled for biographical and background facts. Various "Who's Whos," encyclopedias, and other reference works contribute data. Information is also obtained from government offices and a variety of commercial and educational organizations. Whenever it is possible to get in touch with the subjects of the biographies, they are asked to confirm or correct facts; it should be pointed out, however, that these are not authorized biographies. The biographees, too, may send their photographs, although a number of the prints are procured from duly credited photographers. The Press Association, Inc., 50 Rockefeller Plaza, New York, is the source of those photographs not supplied by biographees or photographers.

The following members of CURRENT BIOGRAPHY's regular staff shared with the editors in the preparation of this Yearbook: Daisy Baum, Edith Faigman, Marian Prince, and Dana Rush; other writers and revisers who assisted were Ethel Ashworth, Ruth Lechlitner, Frances Rosenberg, Frances Wallace, and Alberta Worthington.

A. R.

Contents

Explanations

Authorities for biographees' full names, with few exceptions, are the bibliographical publications of The Wilson Company. When a biographee prefers a certain name form, that is indicated in the heading of the article. For example, "Nelson, (John) Byron (Jr.)" means that Nelson prefers to be called Byron Nelson; and when a professional name like "Pickford, Mary" is used in the heading, the real name—in her case Gladys Mary Smith—appears in the article itself.

The heading of each article includes the pronunciation of the name if it is difficult, date of birth (if obtainable), and occupation. The article is supplemented by a list of references to sources of biographical information, in two alphabets: (1) newspapers and periodicals, (2) books. Space limitation requires that these bibliographies be kept short, but an effort is made to include the most useful references.

References to newspapers and periodicals are listed in abbreviated form; for example, "Sat Eve Post 217:14-15 S 30 '44 por" means *Saturday Evening Post*, volume 217, pages 14-15, for September 30, 1944, with portrait. (See the section "Periodicals and Newspapers Consulted" for full names of the publications.) The books given as references are limited to those of a biographical nature, including such reference works as *Who's Who in America, Living Musicians,* etc. (See the section "Biographical References Consulted" for complete list.) Each obituary notice includes full dates when that information is available, and the reference is to the New York *Times.* When a name in the body of an article is followed by '40, '41, '42, '43, '44, or '45, the reference is to the CURRENT BIOGRAPHY Yearbook in which a biography of that person appears.

As indicated in the table of contents, this volume contains three name indexes, the purposes of which are self-evident. The all-inclusive index—the cumulated index to the biographies and obituary notices in the six volumes of CURRENT BIOGRAPHY published thus far—includes references to monthly issues as well as to Yearbooks.

Key to Pronunciation
(Based on Webster's Guide to Pronunciation *)

ā	āle	N	Not pronounced, but indicates the nasal tone of the preceding vowel, as in the French *bon* (bôN).	ū	cūbe
â	câre			û	ûrn; French eu, as in *jeu* (zhû); German ö, oe, as in *schön* (chûn), *Goethe* (gû'tĕ).
ă	ădd				
ă	loyăl				
ä	ärm				
à	àsk	ō	ōld	ŭ	tŭb
ȧ	sofȧ	ô	ôrb	ü	Pronounced approximately as ē, with rounded lips: French u, as in *menu* (mē-nü'); German ü, as in *grün*.
ē	ēve	ŏ	ŏdd		
ĕ	ĕnd	oi	oil		
ē	makēr	ōō	ōoze		
g	go	ŏŏ	fŏŏt		
ī	īce	ou	out	zh	azure
ĭ	ĭll			' = main accent
ᴋ	German ch as in *ich* (ĭᴋ)	*th*	then	" = secondary accent
		th	thin		

(* Exceptions: *th* in then; main and secondary accents.)

KEY TO ABBREVIATIONS

AAA	Agricultural Adjustment Administration
AAF	Army Air Forces
A.A.U.	Amateur Athletic Union
A.A.U.W.	American Association of University Women
ABC	American Broadcasting Company
A.C.L.U.	American Civil Liberties Union
AEF	American Expeditionary Force
A.F. of L.	American Federation of Labor
Ag	August
A.L.A.	American Library Association
A.M.A.	American Medical Association
AMG	Allied Military Government
ANT	American Negro Theatre
Ap	April
A.P.	Associated Press
ASCAP	American Society of Composers, Authors and Publishers
ASF	Army Service Forces
ASNE	American Society of Newspaper Editors
ATC	Air Transport Command
AVC	American Veterans Committee
AWVS	American Women's Voluntary Services
AYC	American Youth Congress
b.	business address
B.A.	Bachelor of Arts
BBC	British Broadcasting Corporation
B.D.	Bachelor of Divinity
BEF	British Expeditionary Force
B.L.	Bachelor of Letters
B.S.	Bachelor of Science
C.B.	Companion of the Bath
C.B.E.	Commander of (the Order of) the British Empire
CBS	Columbia Broadcasting System
C.E.	Civil Engineer
C.E.D.	Committee for Economic Development
C.E.M.A.	Council for the Encouragement of Music and the Arts
CIO	Congress of Industrial Organizations
C.M.G.	Companion of (the Order of) St. Michael and St. George
Com.	Commodore
cond.	condensed
C.P.A.	Certified Public Accountant
CWA	Civil Works Administration
CWS	Chemical Warfare Service
D	December
D.A.R.	Daughters of the American Revolution
D.C.L.	Doctor of Civil Law
D.D.	Doctor of Divinity
D.Eng.	Doctor of Engineering
D.F.C.	Distinguished Flying Cross
D.J.	Doctor of Jurisprudence
D.Litt.	Doctor of Literature
D.Mus.	Doctor of Music
D. Pol. Sc.	Doctor of Political Science
Dr.	Doctor
D.Sc.	Doctor of Science
D.S.C.	Distinguished Service Cross
D.S.M.	Distinguished Service Medal
D.S.O.	Distinguished Service Order
ed	edited, edition, editor
EDB	Economic Defense Board
E.N.S.A.	Entertainments National Service Association
F	February
FBI	Federal Bureau of Investigation
FCC	Federal Communications Commission
FEPC	Fair Employment Practice Committee
FERA	Federal Emergency Relief Administration
F.F.I.	French Forces of the Interior
FHA	Federal Housing Administration
FSA	Farm Security Administration
FTC	Federal Trade Commission
G.B.E.	Knight or Dame Grand Cross Order of the British Empire
G.C.B.	Knight Grand Cross of the Bath
G.C.V.O.	Knight Grand Cross of Royal Victorian Order
GHQ	General Headquarters
GSO	General Staff Officer
h.	home address
H.M.	His Majesty
HOLC	Home Owners' Loan Corporation
ICC	Interstate Commerce Commission
I.F.T.U.	International Federation of Trade Unions
il	illustrated
I.L.A.	International Longshoremen's Association
I.L.G.W.U.	International Ladies' Garment Workers' Union
I.L.O.	International Labor Office
INS	International News Service
I.W.W.	Industrial Workers of the World
J	Journal
Ja	January
J.C B.	Juris Canonici Bachelor
J.D.	Doctor of Jurisprudence
Je	June
Jl	July
K.B.E.	Knight of (the Order of) the British Empire
K.C.	King's Council
K.C.B.	Knight Commander of the Bath
L.H.D.	Doctor of Humanities
Litt.D.	Doctor of Letters
LL.B.	Bachelor of Laws
LL.D.	Doctor of Laws
LL.M.	Master of Laws
M.A.	Master of Arts
mag	magazine
M.B.A.	Master of Business Administration
M.C.	Military Cross
M.C.E.	Master of Civil Engineering
M.D.	Doctor of Medicine
MGM	Metro-Goldwyn-Mayer
Mgr.	Monsignor, Monseigneur
M.Litt.	Master of Literature
M.P.	Member of Parliament
M.P.P.D.A.	Motion Picture Producers and Distributors of America
Mr	March
MRP	Mouvement Républicain Populaire
M.Sc.	Master of Science
MVA	Missouri Valley Authority
My	May
N	November
NAACP	National Association for the Advancement of Colored People
NAB	National Association of Broadcasters
NAM	National Association of Manufacturers
N.A.N.A.	North American Newspaper Alliance
NBC	National Broadcasting Company
nd	no date
N.E.A.	National Education Association
NLRB	National Labor Relations Board
N.M.U.	National Maritime Union
no	number
NRA	National Recovery Administration
NRPB	National Resources Planning Board
ns	new series
NYA	National Youth Administration
O	October
OCD	Office of Civilian Defense
ODT	Office of Defense Transportation
OPA	Office of Price Administration
OPM	Office of Production Management
OWI	Office of War Information
OWMR	Office of War Mobilization and Reconversion
p	page
PAC	Political Action Committee
pam	pamphlet
P.C.	Privy Councilor
P.E.N.	Poets, Playwrights, Editors, Essayists and Novelists (International Association)
PGA	Professional Golfers Association
Ph.B.	Bachelor of Philosophy
Ph.D.	Doctor of Philosophy
pl	plate, -s
por	portrait, -s
POW	Prisoner of War
pseud	pseudonym
PWA	Public Works Administration
RAF	Royal Air Force
RCA	Radio Corporation of America
RFC	Reconstruction Finance Corporation
RKO	Radio Keith Orpheum
S	September
SEC	Security Exchange Commission
ser	series
SHAEF	Supreme Headquarters, Allied Expeditionary Force
S.J.D.	Doctor Juridical Science
SPA	Surplus Property Administration
SPAB	Supply Priorities and Allocation Board
S.T.B.	Bachelor of Sacred Theology
S.T.D.	Doctor of Sacred Theology
sup	supplement
S.W.O.C.	Steel Workers' Organizing Committee
SWPC	Smaller War Plants Corporation
TERA	Temporary Emergency Relief Administration
TNEC	Temporary National Economic Committee
tr	translated, translation, translator
TVA	Tennessee Valley Authority
TWA	Transcontinental and Western Air, Inc
U.A.W.A.	United Auto Workers of America
U.M.W.A.	United Mine Workers of America
UN(O)	United Nations (Organization)
UNRRA	United Nations Relief and Rehabilitation Administration
U.P.	United Press
USO	United Service Organizations
U.S.S.R.	Union of Socialist Soviet Republics
v	volume
V.F.W.	Veterans of Foreign Wars
w	weekly
WAC	War Assets Corporation
W.C.T.U.	Woman's Christian Temperance Union
WFA	War Food Administration
WLA	Women's Land Army
WLB	War Labor Board
WMC	War Manpower Commission
WPA	Work Projects Administration
WPB	War Production Board
YM(W)CA	Young Men's (Women's) Christian Association
YM(W)HA	Young Men's (Women's) Hebrew Association

CURRENT BIOGRAPHY

1945

ABDULLAH, ACHMED (äb-dōol'ä äk'-
mĕd) 1881—May 12, 1945 Author and adventurer, of Russian-Afghan parentage; many
of his short stories, novels, and plays were
based on his years of service in the British
Indian and Ottoman armies; the play *The
Grand Duke* (1921), the screen version of
The Lives of a Bengal Lancer (1935), and his
autobiography *The Cat Had Nine Lives*
(1933) are among his best-known works.

Obituary

N Y Times p20 My 13 '45 por

ACKERMAN, CARL W(ILLIAM) Jan.
16, 1890- Educator; journalist
Address: b. Pulitzer Bldg., Columbia University, New York City; h. Briar Patch, Lambert-
ville, N.J.

Dean of the Columbia University Graduate
School of Journalism since 1931, Carl W. Ackerman has been a vigorous champion of freedom of the press—in war and in peace—as an
expression of the will of the people in a democratic nation. In 1945 he was one of a committee of three men prominent in American
journalism chosen to tour the world on behalf
of a free press.

Carl William Ackerman was born in Richmond, Indiana, January 16, 1890. He is the
son of John F. and Mary Alice (Eggemeyer)
Ackerman. After attending the University of
Indiana for one year (1910), he entered Earlham College at Richmond, where he took his
B.A. in 1911. (He received his M.A. in 1917.)
In 1912 he went East to study at Columbia
University's new School of Journalism, and,
as a member of its first graduating class, received his B.Litt. the following year. He has
since been awarded LL.D. degrees by the University of Richmond, Northwestern University,
and Earlham College.

Ackerman's work as a journalist began in
1915, when he became a correspondent for the
United Press. After the First World War
began he was a special writer for the New
York *Tribune*, in 1917, and the following year
he became correspondent for the *Saturday
Evening Post*, covering Mexico, Spain, France,
and Switzerland. In 1918-19 he was correspondent for the New York *Times* with the Allied
armies in Siberia. On his return to the United
States in 1919 he became director of the Foreign News Service for the Philadelphia *Ledger*.

Ackerman left the newspaper field in 1921
for what was to be a period of ten years. Until 1927, as president of Carl W. Ackerman,
Inc., he handled corporations' public relations;
and in 1930-31 he served as assistant to the
president of General Motors. Then, in 1931,

CARL W. ACKERMAN

Ackerman was appointed dean of the nineteen-
year-old Columbia University School of Journalism, from which he had been graduated
eighteen years before. At the time the school
was founded (through Joseph Pulitzer's gift
of two and a half million dollars) it offered a
four-year undergraduate course leading to a
Bachelor of Literature degree; five years later
two years of college were made a prerequisite
of admission. The year after Ackerman became dean, plans were developed for its conversion into a graduate school. During the
transition period the Bachelor of Science degree
was offered to those students having three years
of college and two years of study in the school.
Since 1935, except in a few special cases where
students have had professional experience, a
baccalaureate has been required, and then
after completion of a one-year course students
receive the M.Sc. degree. Perhaps the most
widely known undertaking of the school is the
annual recommendation of its Advisory Board
of candidates for the ten annual Pulitzer Prizes,
awarded, in accordance with Pulitzer's will, in
the fields of journalism and letters.

In October 1943 Dean Ackerman announced
the establishment in Chungking of the graduate
School of Journalism, affiliated with the Central Political Institute of China. Columbia
University was sponsoring the school, in part
through two anonymous gifts to the trustees.
Ackerman had assisted in procuring funds and
materials, and Professor Harold L. Cross of

ACKERMAN, CARL W.—*Continued*

his faculty went to Chungking to head a staff of seven Americans and one Chinese. The school continued in operation until August 1945, when, upon the surrender of Japan, it was suspended.

By numerous addresses and articles during his years as dean, Ackerman has dealt with his major concern—freedom of the press. He has spoken, too, of the need for a journalism foundation in the United States "dedicated to the study of the daily newspaper and government. We need scientific studies of the press, by the press, and for the press," he said in 1936, "which will contribute to the progress of journalism as the great educational foundations have advanced medicine."

In April 1938 one of Ackerman's statements against censorship was made in an open letter to Otto Dietrich, then the Nazi press chief, who had proposed international treaties with Germany providing for government control of press and speech as a way to preserve peace. "No nation has ever been able to create confidence in its money by government decree," Ackerman wrote. "The same conditions apply to the printed and the spoken word as a medium of exchange between nations. . . .Good news, meaning truthful information, always has and always will drive bad news, meaning false information, out of circulation."

During the war years, too, Dean Ackerman spoke out strongly against what he described as attempts to "freeze" the press under the guise of preserving national security. To him such censorship was an attack upon America's traditional democracy, and he recalled that in 1933 he had "urged the newspapers of the United States to advocate and support a plan for the establishment of freedom of international news as a new approach to peace." He took a firm stand against any abrogation of the Bill of Rights in the war emergency, and he also declared in March 1941 that the Lend-Lease bill would give to President Roosevelt [42] the power to set up a censorship of news and opinion unjustified by any defense need. Ackerman saw the Wage-Hour Act as another danger to a free press, and when it came up for consideration in July 1940, he presented the plea of the American Association of Schools and Departments of Journalism for recognition of journalism as a profession rather than a trade under the act. The legislation, he said at the time, represented the culmination of "a long series of moves by the Federal Government to control the press of this country," and warned that newspapers must challenge every attempt to regulate the wages and working hours of their employees.

Late in 1941 Dean Ackerman left for Buenos Aires to study the South American press under war conditions. It was a fourteen-thousand-mile journey down the east coast of South America, with stops in Trinidad, Uruguay, and Brazil. "I traveled as an educator, not on a Government mission," he said. On his return in March 1942 Ackerman made a report, as a private citizen, to the Government. Summarizing the results of his observations, he said that Americans must recognize, as a nation, that they had a southern flank, which might become a southern military and naval front. He pointed out that delivery of supplies to these countries had been promised, but too many "cultural missionaries from Hollywood" were sent instead.

A committee of three editors was appointed in December 1944 by John S. Knight [45], president of the American Society of Newspaper Editors, to make a world tour in the interests of a free press. The appointees were Wilbur Forrest of the New York *Herald Tribune*, Ralph McGill of the Atlanta *Constitution*, and Dean Ackerman. The purpose of the trip, which was approved by the Government, was to urge the inclusion in peace treaties of a pledge that governments "will not censor news at the source; not use the press as an instrument of national policy; and permit a free flow of news in and out of signatory countries." It was the first time in history that such a mission had been undertaken. The committee visited England first, also interviewing there officials of three exiled governments—the Netherlands, Norway, and Czechoslovakia—who insisted upon the establishment of a free press in all enemy countries immediately after occupation. The Americans then went on to Paris, Brussels, Rome, Athens, Cairo, Jerusalem, Moscow, and Chungking. Ackerman remained in Chungking for a time to plan the schedule of the next academic year of the journalism school; on his return trip he visited the fighting fronts in the Philippines.

Having arrived in the United States in May 1945, the three-man committee of editors submitted on June 10 a fifty-thousand-word report on their survey of freedom of the press sentiment in other nations. In general, the committee found many governments "controlling the press politically under the guise of war security." It received pledges from government leaders for postwar press freedom, but some of these were described as "lip service." It found that people in Italy and Germany, as a result of a controlled press, knew little or nothing of the world around them. The committee also said that several editors abroad believed that the American press was dominated by advertisers; and that newspaper "trusts" directed much of American thinking along undemocratic lines. Further, said the Soviet editors, many articles in American journals were "not the truth." United States diplomatic and information officers complained to the committee of editors that American news services, such as the A.P., the U.P., and INS, were "screening" the news politically. In conclusion, Ackerman and his colleagues proposed that a postwar world conference on freedom of the press be held in Australia.

Dean Ackerman has lectured and participated in other activities in the journalistic field. He lectured on public opinion in 1935-36 at the Tokyo Imperial University, the University of the Philippines, and the Sorbonne. The following year he became an honorary professor at the Argentine School of Journalism, and the same year made a study of the press, radio, and motion pictures in seven Central and South American countries. In 1937 he also organized the system of Maria Moors Cabot Prizes which Columbia University awards annually to those publishers, editors, or writers in the Western Hemisphere who have contributed the most to understanding among the peoples of the hemisphere.

From his experiences as a correspondent during the First World War, Ackerman wrote three books: *Germany, the Next Republic?* (1917), *Mexico's Dilemma* (1918), and *Trailing the Bolsheviki* (1919). In 1924 came a biography, *Dawes, the Doer*, and in 1930 a study of George Eastman, the perfecter of film photography. The last named was called by the New York *Herald Tribune* critic "objective in the sense that it holds strictly to the drama of events in justification of its hero. This makes it eminently readable, even exciting at times, purely as an epic of success achieved . . . a sort of Pilgrim's Progress of business."

The "suave, self-reliant, businesslike" Dean Ackerman received the degree of Doctor *honoris causa* from the University of Havana in 1944. In 1914 he was married to Mabel Vander Hoof. They have one son, Robert Vander Hoof, assistant professor at the postgraduate school of journalism in Chungking.

References

Ann Am Acad 192:41 Jl '37
Literary Dig 117:13 F 3 '34 por
Who's Who in America, 1944-45

ADAMS, HERBERT 1858—May 21, 1945 American sculptor; founder and three times president of the National Sculpture Society; famous for his medallions and other works in relief, and his portrait busts of women; executed a number of public commissions throughout the United States; recipient of numerous awards in America and abroad.

Obituary

N Y Times p19 My 22 '45

ALBEE, FRED H(OUDLETTE) (ȧl'bē) Apr. 13, 1876—Feb. 15, 1945 American orthopedic surgeon of world renown; had been honored by many European and Latin American governments; was a consultant in United States on bone surgery to twenty-four leading hospitals, to railroads and air lines; his skill in grafting bones led fellow surgeons to call him "the Burbank of surgery"; his invention of instruments and development of intricate techniques opened new paths for bone surgery. See *Current Biography* 1943 Yearbook.

Obituary

N Y Times p23 F 16 '45 por

ALGER, ELLICE M(URDOCH) Dec. 26, 1870—Feb. 18, 1945 American ophthalmologist and professor; won the Leslie Dana Gold Medal in 1938 for "outstanding achievements in the prevention of blindness" and for his work in training hundreds of young physicians; a founder in 1915 of the National Society for the Prevention of Blindness.

Obituary

N Y Times p17 F 19 '45 por

ALLEE, MARJORIE (HILL) (ăl-lē) June 2, 1890—Apr. 30, 1945 American author of children's books; her last story, *The House* (1944), received the 1944 award of the Child Study Association of America; *A House of*

Her Own (1934) and *The Great Tradition* (1937) were two of her most popular books.

Obituary

N Y Times p23 My 1 '45

ALLEE, MRS. WARDER CLYDE *See* Allee, M. H.

ALLEN, FRANK A(LBERT, JR.) June 19, 1896- United States Army officer
Address: b. c/o War Department, Washington, D.C.; h. 1421 N. 12th St., Arlington, Va.

The United States Army's director of public relations in the European theater from August 1944 to August 1945 was Brigadier General Frank A. Allen. In his position as chief of the Public Relations Division of Supreme Headquarters, Allied Expeditionary Force, General Allen, who has had a long military career, was charged with great responsibility in the release of war news to the public. When he was appointed to this post one magazine remarked that Allied newspapermen "saw things change for the better." However, after the German offensive began in December 1944, Supreme Headquarters were the scene of stormy sessions between war correspondents and public relations officers on the subject of military censorship. Primarily concerned with safeguarding military security, Allen followed a strict course in releasing news.

An Ohioan, Frank Albert Allen, Jr., was born in Cleveland, June 19, 1896, the son of Frank Albert and Anastasia G. Allen. He attended Kenyon College in Ohio in 1916 and 1917, when his academic education was halted by America's entry into the World War. Young Allen attended the Officers Training Camp at Fort Benjamin Harrison, Indiana, for three months and was commissioned a second lieutenant in the Infantry Reserve on August 15, 1917. He was assigned to the Fifty-eighth Infantry and in September he went to the Fourth Machine Gun Battalion of the Second Division at Gettysburg, Pennsylvania. Within a month Allen had received his commission as second lieutenant in the Cavalry of the Regular Army, and simultaneously he was promoted to the temporary rank of first lieutenant. This appointment was made permanent in September 1919, and a year later he attained the permanent rank of captain. (During the following twenty-three years he held four successive ranks until his promotion to brigadier general [temporary] on September 11, 1942.)

In his long career in the Army, Allen has seen distinguished service both in the United States and abroad. He first left American shores in a military capacity in May 1918, when he went to France with the Seventy-seventh Field Artillery. With this regiment he served in the Aisne-Marne, Oise-Aisne, Saint-Mihiel, and Meuse-Argonne engagements. After the signing of the Armistice, Lieutenant Allen was assigned to the American Forces in Germany, stationed at Neuenahr. His next assignment came in July 1919, when he joined the Courier Service, which carried confidential documents between the scattered headquarters of Allied governments and armies in Europe. That

BRIG. GEN. FRANK A. ALLEN

November Allen served with the Typhus Relief Expedition in Coblenz and Warsaw.

On his return to the United States in December 1919 Lieutenant Allen was assigned to the Thirteenth Cavalry at Fort Clark, Texas. The following year he became a cavalry instructor at the Infantry School, Fort Benning, Georgia. He left Georgia after a year to become a professor of military science and tactics at Norwich University in Vermont. Then, resuming his advanced military education in 1923, Allen entered the Cavalry School at Fort Riley, Kansas. He was graduated the following May, at which time he was assigned to duty with the Operations and Training Division, G-3, of the War Department General Staff in Washington, D.C.

In 1926 Captain Allen became aide to Major General Dennis E. Nolan, then deputy chief of the War Department General Staff. In this capacity Allen accompanied General Nolan to three posts: Fort Hamilton, New York; Fort Hayes. Ohio, in 1927; and Governors Island. New York, in 1931, where he remained for two years. Allen was then ordered to Fort Myer, Virginia, for duty with the Third Cavalry, a post he held until his entrance into the Command and General Staff School, Fort Leavenworth, Kansas, in September 1935—a month after his promotion to the permanent rank of major. After his graduation a year later he went to Fort Riley, Kansas, where he served on the faculty of the Cavalry School until his transfer in 1938 to the Ninth Cavalry at the same post. In September 1939 Major Allen entered the Army War College in Washington, D.C.

After completion of the course Allen was assigned to the Public Relations Branch, Office of the Chief of Staff, and in February 1941 became chief of the Pictorial and Radio Branch of the War Department Bureau of Public Relations. Two months prior to this appointment he had been made colonel (temporary). (In August 1940 he had been made

lieutenant colonel.) August 1941 found Allen stationed at Fort Knox, Kentucky, on duty with the headquarters of the Armored Force. Here he served with the First Armored Division, and upon activation of the Fifth Armored Division in September he was given command of one of its units, the Eighty-fifth Armored Reconnaissance Battalion. He changed commands in February 1942, when he was assigned to the Thirty-fourth Armored Regiment of the Fifth Division. In August 1942 Allen assumed command of Combat Command A, Ninth Armored Division, Fort Riley, Kansas. A month later he was made brigadier general (temporary).

The General's first overseas assignment in the Second World War came in June 1943. He served as combat commander of the First Armored Division in the North African theater of operations until August 1944. At that time he was assigned to Supreme Headquarters, Allied Expeditionary Force, in the European theater, where the following month he was named chief of the Public Relations Division. In his Paris post Allen was confronted with serious public relations problems, for SHAEF had been sharply criticized for the handling of war news. One newspaper reported that "the difficulties appear to grow out of the fact that no satisfactory cooperative procedures for the handling of important news has been worked out by the United Nations or the United States." These difficulties culminated in early 1945 in the assignment of Stephen T. Early [41] to conduct a survey of the situation. At Allen's invitation, Early, as President Roosevelt's [42] aide, reviewed public relations affairs at SHAEF in Paris, acting in a civilian advisory capacity.

One of the major controversies in SHAEF's relations with the press occurred in December 1944 when the American war correspondents attached to SHAEF became indignant at the withholding of news of the Nazi offensive. *Time* Magazine, in discussing that affair, declared: "In the bitter confusion of the German break-through the Army clamped down a censorship thicker than the pea-soup fog that shrouded the great German counterattack. Communiques were as much as forty-eight hours behind the event. When they came they were meager and vague. Correspondents blew up." During those days of military secrecy Allen continued to assure the irate journalists that the Army's policy was based on security needs. He defended the news "blackout" and declared that the decision on policy had been made by the First Army and the Twelfth Army Group, supported by SHAEF and G-2 (Army Intelligence). However, it was reported that General Allen himself had tried to have the news restrictions lifted. Lively scenes between war correspondents and public relations officers were described in the press. One magazine in reporting the outcome of this situation wrote, "The wrangling bore fruit . . . . SHAEF decided to give a daily report of action which has taken place forty-eight hours previously. On December 23 the blackout was lifted."

There were further public relations difficulties on the active European front. Heated argument on the part of the press concerning the release of news followed the Allied counteroffensive. James F. McGlincy, writing from

Paris on January 5, 1945, said: "Both SHAEF and front-line correspondents protested bitterly that British Broadcasting Corporation broke a security blackout on news of the offensive, presenting the news eleven hours before a previously fixed deadline." Further confusion between SHAEF and the press resulted from the handling of the news of the shift in the commands of Field Marshal Sir Bernard L. Montgomery '42 and Lieutenant General Omar N. Bradley '43. The circulation of this news in the United States by *Time* Magazine and the United Press in advance of the official release of the story brought a storm of protest from correspondents. At this time Allen stated that the delay in the announcement of this news had been based entirely on military security. The affair resulted in an immediate investigation by SHAEF and the controversy was prominently featured in American newspapers. Discussing the war news on January 7, 1945, *PM* stated: "Another battle, the battle of SHAEF, continued at Allied Supreme Headquarters in Paris. The opponents were the American correspondents, who charged that SHAEF policy was giving the United States public a distorted and confused picture of the situation, and the Army press officers, carrying out orders from higher up, who continued to plead military security—if they defended themselves at all."

With the premature announcement of the German Government's unconditional surrender, made on May 7 by Edward Kennedy, chief of the Associated Press's Paris Bureau, the issue of freedom of the press and the public's right to the news as soon as it breaks again made considerable stir. Kennedy, without informing the other reporters assigned to the capitulation, flashed the momentous news to the world despite the pledge the newsmen had made to General Allen that they would not release their copy until sanctioned by SHAEF. Allen almost immediately penalized the A.P. by suspending its news filing privileges throughout the European theater, though the order was later rescinded for all A.P. personnel with the exception of Kennedy, after strong protests were received from the American press. A group of fifty-four SHAEF correspondents called Kennedy's scoop "the most unethical double cross in the history of journalism," and General Eisenhower '42 authorized Allen's statement that the A.P. newsman had placed the Supreme Commander in "the position of having broken an understanding" with the Russians concerning the announcement and imperiling the negotiations. Allen declared that Kennedy had deliberately violated security measures, involving possible loss of American and Allied lives. Kennedy contended that, "since it was conceded [by the chief American press censor] that no military security was involved" and that he "regarded the suppression as purely political censorship," he "therefore could not be bound by it." In the official investigation following, Kennedy was adjudged to have "deliberately violated the trust reposed in him by prematurely releasing through unauthorized channels and deliberately evading military censorship a news story concerning which he was pledged to secrecy."

The incident raised the question in SHAEF headquarters of the extent to which newsmen would have access to news of the most secret character. In the end, General Allen's recommendation of continuance of the past policy was approved by General Eisenhower, when Allen assumed personal responsibility for the good faith of each press representative permitted access to such stories. Friction between Army officials and the press continued, however, as several correspondents who made unauthorized visits to Berlin were placed on the suspension list. On May 28 Eisenhower awarded General Allen the Legion of Merit for "meritorious conduct in the performance of outstanding service"; "the sound judgment constantly demonstrated by this officer reflected great credit upon the United States Army," continued the citation.

When Supreme Headquarters, Allied Expeditionary Force, were dissolved on July 14, 1945, the United States, British, and French forces reverting formally to their own commands, General Allen became head of the public relations division of United States Forces, European Theater. In August he was assigned as acting commander of the Third Armored Division at Frankfort on the Main.

Square-jawed, battle-seasoned, he is called "Honk" for his "105-mm. larynx." The General and his wife, who was Ellen Gordon, were married May 10, 1922. They have four children, Walter Gordon, Laura Doan, Mary, and Frank Albert, 3d. Allen is a member of the Beta Theta Pi fraternity and his clubs are the Army Navy Club in Washington and the Army Navy Country Club in Arlington, Virginia. He has been called "a professional soldier who prefers combat to conferences."

References

Time 44:59 N 6 '44 por

Who's Who in America, 1944-45

ANDERSON, CLINTON P(RESBA) Oct. 23, 1895- United States Secretary of Agriculture

Address: b. Department of Agriculture, Washington, D.C.; h. Lazy V Cross Farm, R.F.D. No. 1, Albuquerque, N.M.; 6 Wesley Circle, Washington, D.C.

The vital food problems of the United States were the first important concern of the new Secretary of Agriculture, Clinton P. Anderson, after his appointment to the post by President Truman '45 in May 1945. This Democratic Congressman from New Mexico replaced Claude R. Wickard '40 and also assumed the duties of Marvin Jones '43, War Food Administrator. At the time he announced the Cabinet changes, the President revealed that the War Food Administration would be transferred to the Department of Agriculture in an effort to unify action on the food situation.

The Secretary of Agriculture has inherited a tradition of farming from his Swedish father, who immigrated to America to settle on the sloping plains of South Dakota. There, in the town of Centerville, Clinton Presba Anderson was born to Andrew Jay and Hattie Belle (Presba) Anderson on October 23, 1895. Clinton attended Dakota Wesleyan University from 1913 to 1915, after which he studied for a year at the University of Michigan. (Dakota

CLINTON P. ANDERSON

Wesleyan University conferred an honorary L.H.D. degree on him in 1933.) At the time of America's entry into the First World War, Anderson was engaged in prelaw studies. He applied for service but was rejected for officer training because of a lung condition. This illness also prevented the young man from being graduated and sent him south to New Mexico. Settling in Albuquerque, Anderson rapidly recovered his health and went to work for the *Journal* as a reporter and editor from 1918 to 1922. When a relapse forced him to spend more time outdoors he turned to selling insurance, later becoming manager of the insurance department of the New Mexico Loan and Mortgage Company. In 1925 Anderson acquired his own insurance agency, which he developed successfully; he is today president of the Mountain States Mutual Casualty Company.

Anderson first held public office in 1933 when, at the sudden death of New Mexico's State treasurer, the Governor appointed the insurance executive to fill the vacancy. He was again called to State service in 1935 when there was serious trouble in Albuquerque over relief problems. The Governor put Anderson in charge of the New Mexican Relief Administration, and order was soon restored. As relief administrator, he aimed foremost at equitable distribution of funds and required that the applicants work on public projects in return for assistance. His performance in this capacity led Anderson to the job of field representative of the Federal Emergency Relief Administration, a post he held for a time in 1935-36. From this position he advanced to become chairman and executive director of the Unemployment Compensation Commission of New Mexico (1936-38). The businessman also served as managing director of the United States Coronado Exposition for the year 1939-40, a celebration commemorating the Spaniard's explorations in the Southwest.

In 1940, for the first time, Anderson became a candidate for office, winning election as Democratic Representative at Large to the Seventy-seventh Congress. He was afterward re-elected to the House twice. (The last time he ran for office rather reluctantly, since he had planned to retire from public life.) In viewing his career, *PM* called him a "better-than-average Congressman," and the *United States News* refers to him as a "liberal in politics but not a New Dealer." Anderson gained prominence in the House in three principal issues: his support of the Federal soldier-vote bill, his investigation of campaign expenditures, and his food investigation.

A record of "mixed" votes characterized Anderson's Congressional career. In 1941 the Democrat registered his assent to amendment of the Neutrality Act, and after that he voted for UNRRA and extension of reciprocal trade agreements. On the domestic front, Anderson charged in a House speech in July 1942 that the President had failed to carry out his own seven-point program to prevent inflation. He voted in 1943 for the bill to increase the public debt limit and to revoke the $25,000 salary limit, and that year he also voted in favor of the Hobbs anti-racketeering bill, the anti-strike bill, and against subsidies and the Ruml '43 tax plan. Anderson led a House group in support of a pay-as-you-go tax measure. He voted to override the Presidential veto of the anti-strike bill, and to sustain the veto of the commodity credit bill. In 1944 he led a campaign to secure a record vote on the Worley Federal ballot bill: He drew up a petition which was signed by one hundred and twenty Democrats favoring a yea-and-nay vote on the issue of servicemen's votes. During that year he also voted against the ban on food subsidies, to sustain the veto of the anti-subsidy bill, to override the veto of the tax bill, against the compromise soldier-vote bill, and for investigation of Government seizure of Montgomery Ward's.

In early 1945 the Congressman voted against a permanent committee on un-American activities (formerly the Dies '40 Committee), for limited national service for men between eighteen and forty-five, and in March for the compromise manpower bill. In May Anderson voted against overriding President Truman's veto of the farm-draft deferment legislation. The New Mexican was given some significant committee assignments. In February 1943 he was named to a subcommittee of the House Appropriations Committee (of which he was then a member) to consider cases of subversive activities. In January 1945, at the first Democratic Party caucus of the new Congress, Anderson was elected to the powerful House Ways and Means Committee.

One of his most important committee assignments was in connection with the Campaign Expenditures Committee. As chairman of the committee Anderson led a thorough investigation of groups which influenced the elections of 1944. In September the committee investigated the activities of the CIO's Political Action Committee, visiting the group's New York headquarters. Anderson's committee also inquired into the affairs of the Constitutional Educational League and Gerald L. K. Smith's '43 "Committee of One Million." Reporting Smith's testimony at a committee hearing, one writer stated that Anderson "put Smith through one of the neatest jobs of police court cross-examination on record, leaving the self-styled nationalist leader spinning around in his chair and fumbling for answers to the most embarrassing questions— all asked with the utmost politeness."

In October Anderson charged that thirteen Republican Congressmen had mailed at Government expense over three million copies of a speech made by a Republican Representative. This fact was later cited in a radio speech by President Roosevelt and caused considerable comment. Subsequently, Anderson requested and was granted permission by the House committee to withdraw the report from the record. In the course of its investigation the Campaign Expenditures Committee examined the record of the Gallup '40 poll, listening to testimony by George Gallup and checking the figures of the poll. Chairman Anderson found "artificial coloring" and "dangerous adjustments" in the poll of Presidential votes and advised Gallup that it would be "wise to stick to the facts your poll reveals and let the people do their own interpreting." The investigation conducted by the Campaign Expenditures Committee resulted in some indictments, and in its final report the committee urged "remedial legislation to force purveyors of political propaganda to disclose the sources of their funds and their concrete objectives as distinguished from their abstract professions of faith." The committee's work was applauded in some quarters, but *PM* declared: "Despite the unbiased, thorough investigation conducted by Anderson, his committee's final report placed more heat on the CIO Political Action Committee than on the men and organizations who were held in contempt."

Early in 1945, when the House was discussing the organization of a food inquiry, Anderson insisted that they must get the facts, not only from the farmers but from the entire food industry and all Government agencies concerned. The New Mexican was put in charge of the House food investigation to conduct a complete survey of food conditions. At the outset he told agency chiefs: "We have no ax to grind. We're looking for no witches. Over facts there need be no dispute. Let's have your figures on farm goals and production, supply, stocks, and allocations." For five weeks hearings took place in Chicago, New York, Cleveland, Boston, Providence, and Washington, and a tour of the East and Middle West was made to get information on the meat shortage.

At a White House conference in April, Anderson urged that the Government open and operate closed meat packing plants throughout the Nation. The seven-thousand-word preliminary report of the committee to the President contained "alarming facts," including revelation of black market control of meat in New York and the danger of a black market in poultry and eggs in many other cities. The committee met again with the President on May 2 to discuss recommendations resulting from the meat investigation. The Anderson committee report strongly recommended consolidation of all War Food Administration and Office of Price Administration operations in food control.

The committee then proceeded to a study of the sugar situation. Its second report on this problem, revealing that twenty agencies now have a hand in sugar control, urged that one coordinating head be substituted. This report, termed "a fair and comprehensive picture", pointed to a growing sugar shortage. Anderson favors keeping the public informed on Government food exports to the United Nations. He once told a reporter how he would combat the menace of black markets: "The way to kill off the black markets and food-price inflation is abundant production, and the time to plan abundant production is now."

On May 22, 1945, Anderson was invited to lunch at the White House, where he was asked by the President if he would like to be Secretary of Agriculture. "I almost swallowed my grapefruit," Anderson later reported, adding, "But he gave me a job to do, and when Harry Truman gives you a job to do you do it." The nomination, announced on May 23, was warmly greeted in the House and on May 30 the Senate gave its approval. Press reaction to the appointment was favorable, with many commentators citing Anderson's vigorous food campaigns and noting that he would now have the opportunity to put into practice the recommendations of his committee. The *United States News*, commenting on the new Agriculture Secretary, said, "Food industry will find Mr. Anderson inclined to be 'practical.' Farmers will find that he has no formula for solving all of their problems, no really preconceived ideas on planning." Anderson has assured Congress that he will be "alert to the needs of the American farmer."

Until Anderson assumed his Cabinet seat in July, he continued his food inquiry, and during the month of June the committee schedule included hearings in Omaha, Minneapolis, Yakima, Seattle, San Francisco, and Southern California. During the Congressional debate over whether or not to turn OPA's food controls over to the prospective Secretary of Agriculture, who himself objected to the granting of such power, a conference committee of representatives of both the House and the Senate agreed upon a bill extending the OPA for a year, and giving Anderson the power to supervise regulations, orders, and price schedules applying to all agricultural commodities at the processor's level. In this decision to give the Secretary ultimate authority over food pricing, an earlier House decision to make him food "czar," capable of overriding even an Executive order, was reversed.

When Anderson assumed office on July 1, 1945, he outlined a four-point program for agricultural policy aimed to effect the consolidation of the War Food Administration with the Department of Agriculture, resulting in "an efficient organization serving agriculture and the people"; to coordinate food production and pricing policies for the attainment of maximum production; to obtain equitable distribution of food supplies meeting military, civilian, and foreign relief requirements; to restore food

ANDERSON, CLINTON P.—*Continued*

to legitimate channels of trade through rigid control of black markets and a strict policy of law enforcement. Leading interagency discussions began on plans to end food subsidies in 1946, thereby shifting one and a half billion dollars in food costs to consumer pocketbooks; the objective was to ease adjustment of farm prices to postwar conditions and to reduce Government expenditures. In August Anderson announced a thoroughgoing reorganization of the Department of Agriculture. An early New Deal bureau, the Agricultural Adjustment Agency, passed into history as a new super-agency, the Production and Marketing Administration, came into being. Consolidating the functions of fourteen other agencies, this top control unit will have broad powers to coordinate future governmental programs affecting marketing, price, and production policies.

Supporting Truman's legislative program, Anderson on August 23 endorsed the full employment bill, telling a Senate subcommittee that agriculture has a vital stake in the measure; full employment is essential if another farm depression is to be averted, he declared, and the bill's aim of maintaining full employment is "one of the greatest encouragements that Government can give" to businessmen. He went on record as favoring the sixty-five-cent minimum pay standard bill on September 27, noting it as "a step forward in the task of expanding the market for farm products." "For each increase of one billion dollars in the annual earnings of low-income workers there will be a corresponding increase in food expenditures of at least two hundred million dollars." At a conference with representatives of the American Farm Bureau Federation in September 1945, Secretary Anderson indicated that the Government's 1946 farm program will call for some reduction in over-all production in order to keep supplies in line with a prospective smaller peace-time demand.

Anderson headed the thirty-four-man delegation from the United States to the conference of the United Nations Food and Agriculture Organization, which, as the first permanent body to emanate from the UNO, met in Quebec in October. There he spoke on the major problem of the body—"to bring together countries which are desperately hungry and those which are concerned with finding markets for the food they produce"—this to be achieved by the application of scientific production and efficient distribution. For the last quarter of 1945 Anderson was able to predict a 50 per cent increase over the previous quarter's shipment of food to the United Kingdom and liberated Europe, and before the end of the year he had the satisfaction of seeing the lifting of the rationing of all foods except sugar.

The new Secretary of Agriculture is described as "tall, dark, and square of chin," soft-spoken, yet incisive. He weighs one hundred and eighty-five pounds, has brown hair and eyes. His favorite reading is history, particularly that of the Southwest. He belongs to Delta Theta Phi fraternity and is a Mason and an Elk. For many years he has also been an active member of the Rotary Club, in 1932-33 serving as president of Rotary International. The former newspaperman has contributed several articles to the *Rotarian,* the *American Magazine, Hygeia,* and others. Mrs. Anderson is the former Henrietta McCartney, to whom he was married on June 22, 1921. They have a son and a daughter, Sherburne Presba and Nancy. The family's New Mexico home is a 935-acre ranch near Albuquerque, where, according to *Time*'s statistics, Anderson has "450 acres of alfalfa, 135 milch cows, and 300 head of Rambouillet sheep." He owns additional land in South Dakota. He is fond of horseback riding, and a hint of one of his indoor recreations is given in the title of an amusing article he wrote in 1937—"Should We Abolish Bridge? No—Never!"

References

Bsns W p18 Ap 28 '45 por
Liberty 22:19+ Ag 4 '45 por
N Y Herald Tribune p12 My 24 '45; II p3 My 27 '45 por; VII p8+ S 2 '45 por
N Y Post Mag p5 Je 16 '45 por
N Y Sun p18 S 18 '44
Rotarian 67:26+ O '45 por
Who's Who in America, 1944-45

APPLETON, SIR EDWARD (VICTOR)
Sept, 6, 1892- Physicist; British Government official

Address: b. Department of Scientific and Industrial Research, Park House, 24 Rutland Gate, London; h. 39 Westleigh Ave., London

"The biggest single contribution by science to Allied triumph [in the Second World War]," in the opinion of many commentators, is that invention known in Britain as radiolocation and in America as radar. As revealed by Allied authorities, "it remains, despite the atomic bomb, an amazing contrivance, the reason behind countless Allied victories on land, on sea, and in the air, a weapon so formidable that it shortened the struggle against the Axis certainly by months, possibly by years." Defined by the highest-ranking physical scientist of the British Government, Sir Edward Appleton, as "the process of locating the position of an object in space by radio, without any active co-operation on the part of that object," radar has been worked out by the cooperation of many scientists, notably Sir Robert Watson-Watt '45 in Britain and Dr. A. Hoyt Taylor '45, with Leo C. Young, in the United States. Appleton himself originally made many of the discoveries in pure physics which have been applied in the development of radiolocation; and since the outbreak of the war he has been secretary of the British Government's Department of Scientific and Industrial Research.

Edward Victor Appleton, the son of Peter Appleton, was born in Bradford, Yorkshire, on September 6, 1892. After attending the Hanson School there, he went on to Cambridge University, where he was an exhibitioner and scholarship holder of St. John's College. At Cambridge he studied under the renowned physicists Sir Joseph J. Thomson and Lord Rutherford. He took the honors examination, or tripos, in natural science in 1913-14, specializing in physics, and won the Wiltshire Prize in 1913 and the Hutchinson research studentship in 1914. His studies were cut short by the outbreak of the First World War, however, and the young scientist joined Yorkshire's West Riding Regiment. Later he was transferred to the Royal Engineers, serving with the rank of captain.

After the war Captain Appleton returned to Cambridge, where he devoted himself to research on radio waves. For a time he was a fellow of St. John's College. In 1920 he was appointed assistant demonstrator in experimental physics at the Cavendish Laboratory, and two years later he became sub-lector at Trinity College of the university. In 1924 Dr. Appleton (he holds the M.A. and D.Sc. degrees) left Cambridge to become Wheatstone Professor of Physics at the University of London, where he remained for twelve years. Continuing his research, Appleton "repeated a variety of experiments on interference and polarization." Working with short waves in his laboratory and with long waves over distances of miles, to quote the *Encyclopædia Britannica,* "E. V. Appleton has shown that interference phenomena could be obtained with the Hertzian waves used in wireless telegraphy by reflection from the Heaviside layer," an atmospheric stratum.

Since 1896 it had been known that all electromagnetic waves were reflected by all objects; Appleton sought to prove the existence of this Kennelly-Heaviside layer, or "electrical roof of the world," by shooting radio waves at it to see if they bounced back. He worked, then and later, under the auspices of the Government Department of Scientific and Industrial Research. With the cooperation of the British Broadcasting Company, in late 1924 he used the Bournemouth transmitter for this experiment, which was successful. The Heaviside layer, or ionosphere, was identified in space and its height determined by measuring the time required for the waves to return. It was found to be sixty miles above ground; later research has shown that its altitude varies with the time of day.

In 1926 the young physicist discovered a second and electrically stronger nonconducting stratum, ninety miles higher than the ionosphere. The Appleton layer, as it is called, reflects short waves around the earth, and these experiments therefore proved the possibility of direct round-the-world broadcasting. Soon after this Appleton was honored with election as a Fellow of the Royal Society. In 1927 he was also awarded an honorary LL.D. by Aberdeen University, and in 1929 the American Institute of Radio Engineers voted him the Morris Liebman Memorial Prize for his research. In that year his investigations took him to northern Norway to study the aurora borealis. He is also an honorary D.Sc. of the universities of Oxford and Birmingham.

Continuing his study of the reflecting layers of the atmosphere, Appleton used a transmitter which sent out radio energy in bursts, and devised a way to photograph the invisible radio signals by means of a cathode-ray oscillograph. These theoretical findings became the basis for a practical military system of aircraft detection worked out by Robert Watson-Watt and his associates and by researchers who had worked with Appleton. The discovery that an airplane would also bounce back the Hertzian waves made it possible to find the plane's loca-

Walter Stoneman

SIR EDWARD APPLETON

tion before it could be seen. In 1933, when radiolocation was still in the future, Appleton was awarded the Hughes Medal by his colleagues of the Royal Society.

In 1936 Appleton returned to Cambridge as Jacksonian Professor of Natural Philosophy; three years later, when the Second World War began, he left to accept the secretaryship of the Department of Scientific and Industrial Research, which is described as the senior British Government post concerned with physical science. In addition to proceeding with pressingly important radio research, Appleton studied methods of civilian defense, dehydration, fuel economy, and improvements in items ranging from high-explosive bombs to building designs. Meanwhile, the radiolocation devices based on his findings were making it possible for Britain's outnumbered RAF to meet and conquer the German Luftwaffe. Commentators, in fact, have said that radiolocation won the Battle of Britain. In 1941 King George '43 created Professor Appleton a Knight Commander of the Bath. After the close of the war he was named to two Government committees on science—one to study atomic energy, the other, the use and development of Britain's scientific manpower and resources in the next ten years.

Sir Edward Appleton is president of the International Scientific Radio Union, chairman of the British National Committee for Radio Telegraphy, and a member of the Government committee on television. In 1932 he served as vice-president of the American Institute of Radio Engineers. A Londoner by adoption, Appleton is a member of the Athenaeum Club. He is described as "short, strong, and a tireless worker," and as having "the sturdy figure and balanced mind characteristic of Yorkshiremen." He is married to Jessie Longson, daughter of a clergyman, and has two daughters.

References

N Y Sun p17 Je 20 '41
Who's Who, 1945

APPLETON, ROBERT 1865 (?)—Jan. 19, 1945 American publisher; retired head of the former Robert Appleton Publishing Company, which he had founded to publish the *Catholic Encyclopedia*; previously a member of the publishing house of D. Appleton and Company, founded by forebears; a foe of corrupt city government, he wrote many articles demanding more effective powers for the grand jury.

Obituary

N Y Times p11 Ja 20 '45

ARGENTINITA (är-hän-tē-nē'tä) Mar. 25, 1905—Sept. 24, 1945 Spanish dancer; helped to organize the Madrid Ballet in 1932; made American debut in *The International Revue* in 1930; she and ensemble danced regularly as guest artists with Ballet Theatre at the Metropolitan Opera House; toured the United States and Central and South America. See *Current Biography* 1942 Yearbook.

Obituary

N Y Times p26 S 25 '45 por

ARMETTA, HENRY (är-mĕt'tä) July 4, 1888—Oct. 21, 1945 Sicilian-born stage and screen actor; specialized in the comedy character roles of an excited Italian; appeared in more than three hundred Hollywood motion pictures from 1923 until death.

Obituary

N Y Times p17 O 23 '45 por

ARMOUR, NORMAN Oct. 14, 1887-Diplomat

One of the most difficult posts for an American ambassador during the war years was in the Spain of dictator Francisco Franco '42. This ticklish assignment was given in late 1944 to career diplomat Norman Armour, who had been recalled in August 1944 from the Embassy in Argentina as a rebuff to Juan Perón's '44 military regime. Armour assumed his Madrid post in March 1945, but he was not to fill out the year there: In November he announced his wish to retire, after thirty years in the diplomatic service.

Norman Armour, who is not one of the meatpacking Armours, was born October 14, 1887, in Brighton, England, to American parents—George Allison and Harriette (Foote) Armour. Young Norman received his preparatory education at St. Paul's School in Concord, New Hampshire, and went on to Princeton University, from which he obtained his B.A. in 1909. Then, following his graduation from Harvard Law School four years later, he was admitted to the New Jersey bar in 1914. Resuming his studies at Princeton, he received his M.A. degree from that university in 1915.

At the age of twenty-eight, in 1915 Armour passed the State Department's Foreign Service examination and was appointed as attaché of the United States Embassy in Paris. Here he was a member of a neutral diplomatic staff in a country at war, as he continued to be when he was transferred in 1916 to Petrograd (now Leningrad) as third secretary of the Embassy. Before he left Russia Armour, who became

second secretary in 1917, was to see the disintegration of autocratic and military power in Russia, the two Revolutions of 1917, and, less than a year after the United States had joined the Allies, the signing in March 1918 of the Brest-Litovsk Treaty, which took Russia out of the war.

In revolutionary Russia, diplomat Norman Armour was also to have his share of adventure. He helped a young princess, Myra Koudacheff, flee the country. Then he himself was arrested at Moscow and detained for a month. According to the New York *Herald Tribune*, he escaped and, disguised as a Norwegian courier, made his way across the border into Finland. In 1919 he was married to the Princess, whose Russian title of Knyazna indicates relationship to one of the former ruling dynasties. Mrs. Armour, who looks more American than Russian, speaks unaccented English and three other languages, and loves to pack up and move. Since her marriage she has kept house in a dozen countries, and "never lost so much as a pin in the moving."

The first stop was Belgium, where Armour was second secretary of the American Embassy in 1919 and 1920. From there he was sent to the Netherlands as first secretary of the Embassy in The Hague. Next he filled the same post (1921-22) at Montevideo, Uruguay, from which he was recalled to Washington to assist the Under-Secretary of State. Sent to Rome in 1924 as first secretary, Armour had a box seat at the Fascist revolution and witnessed the emergence of Mussolini '42 as dictator of Italy. Armour's next assignment was to the Far East, to which he went in 1925 as counselor of the American Embassy in Tokyo, and in 1928 he returned to Paris where he remained for four years as Embassy counselor.

In October 1932 President Hoover '43 appointed the tall, aristocratic diplomat as Minister to Haiti; and after the inauguration of President Roosevelt '42 Armour negotiated the Executive agreement of August 7, 1933 which terminated the United States political and financial control of Haiti. Its terms were similar to those of the rejected treaty of September 3, 1932, but it advanced the date of American withdrawal from Haitian administration. In August 1934 the last of the United States marines who had been stationed in the island for nineteen years departed, and their barracks and administrative buildings were presented to the Republic of Haiti. When Armour left in June 1935, after he had suffered an attack of dengue fever, a reciprocal tariff agreement had been signed—marking the beginning of a new cooperative relationship between the two countries, and the end of United States intervention in the Caribbean.

The choice of Norman Armour as Minister to Canada in June 1935 "gave fresh assurance to Canada that we are sending a representative of our best," said the New York *Times*; and he was "met with the warmest welcome by the Canadian press." After a three-year term in that friendly Dominion, the fifty-two-year-old American was raised to the rank of Ambassador and accredited to Chile, where he was confronted with the problems brought about by a violent earthquake and a bloodless but revolutionary change of government to one based on the New Deal. In May 1939 Freda Kirchwey '42 wrote in the *Nation*: "Mr. Armour is a diplomat of long experience and a person of distinction and charm. For all that, he didn't belong in Chile." She explained that the Government of President Pedro Aguirre Cerda '41, supported by "a liberal-Left coalition of somewhat unstable composition, is trying to build up the wretched economy of the country and at the same time to repair the monstrous physical damage of the earthquake," which effort involved the United States particularly because "the necessary funds can come ultimately only from the wealth of Chile, which is largely in the capacious pockets of American financial interests." Nevertheless, Miss Kirchwey felt, Armour was slow in establishing rapport with the Aguirre Cerda administration.

But the *Nation*'s editor expressed approval of Armour's appointment to Argentina in early 1939. "For Argentina," she wrote, "Mr. Armour seems a safe choice. Relations between that republic and the United States are strained, and several ticklish problems are waiting to be solved. But the country is rich, its Government is strong and conservative, and the problems lie within traditional diplomatic boundaries, where Mr. Armour, by both temperament and experience, is equipped to do his best work." (It is, incidentally, considered a distinction to be appointed to Buenos Aires, the "gayest and most lavish of South American capitals," where "it is axiomatic in the Foreign Service that no man without a private income could hold down the post.")

In Argentina, Armour "rode the ups and downs of United States prestige like a veteran gaucho. . . . His dispatches continued to be unruffled, incisive, informative." In 1940 he was mentioned for the ambassadorship to Great Britain, but remained in Buenos Aires. The following April (1941) he reportedly made a deep impression on Argentine public opinion when he told the local British Society: "From this time forward your [Britain's] blood is our blood, your toil is our toil, your tears are our tears, your sweat is our sweat. . . . I want you to know how deeply our people are with you in this critical hour for democracy." Armour had had occasion earlier to protest anti-United States articles in various pro-Nazi and pro-Fascist newspapers such as the *Pampero*; he took no official notice, however, of the Argentine Government's ban on Charlie Chaplin's '40 *The Great Dictator* (1941), nor its approval of an anti-United States film, *Petroleo*. Some Americans thought the Ambassador should have taken a firmer stand; but *Time*, announcing the marriage plans of his only child, Norman Armour, Jr., in May 1941, identified the father as "Norman ('The Ideal Diplomat') Armour."

The position of the United States representative in Argentina became more difficult after his country had joined the United Nations in December 1941, for the Argentine Government was determinedly neutral; the population, largely of German and Italian origin, in addition to the descendants of Spanish settlers, included a large number of Axis sympathizers; and the United States high-tariff policy had created a certain amount of antagonism. A reciprocal trade agreement, sought by the United States since 1939, had, however, been

NORMAN ARMOUR

signed in October 1941. Two days after Pearl Harbor, Acting President Ramón Castillo '41 joined the other American republics in decreeing that the United States was not to be treated as a belligerent (and therefore not subject to the appropriate restrictions); but at the Rio de Janeiro Conference of Ministers of Foreign Affairs in January 1942 it was Argentina, with the assistance of Chile, which prevented the passage of a resolution calling for an immediate and unanimous break with the Axis powers. To quote the historian Graham H. Stuart, "Buenos Aires soon became the center of Nazi activities for all South America to such an extent that they endangered both lives and shipping in the Western Hemisphere. . . . In November 1942 United States Ambassador Norman Armour delivered three confidential memoranda on Nazi activities to the Castillo Government," which led to the dismissal of the German naval attaché for espionage.

Public sentiment seemed to be on the side of the United Nations, and on the first anniversary of Pearl Harbor, which was widely observed in Latin America, a mass meeting of "Homage to Roosevelt" was held in Buenos Aires. When Chile broke off relations with the Axis in January 1943, all the Argentine newspapers except German propaganda sheets greeted the news with "obvious pleasure and satisfaction." On June 4, 1943 the Castillo Government fell after a palace revolution, led by Generals Arturo Rawson and Pedro Pablo Ramírez, who became President. On Armour's recommendation, the new Cabinet was soon recognized by the United States, and also by twenty-one other nations. But the Ramírez Government proved a disappointment to the democracies, and in October Armour conveyed to it President Roosevelt's disapproval of the ban on Yiddish newspapers, which was soon lifted. In December 1943 a State Department document charged that Colonel Juan Perón '44, the power behind the Presidency, conspired in the pro-Nazi overthrow of the Bolivian Government. (He had already declared him-

ARMOUR, NORMAN—*Continued*

self as working to make Argentina a fascist state, although he did not use that term officially.)

According to *PM*'s Ray Josephs, Armour "was ahead of the State Department in wanting to crack down on the Argentine Government, but never fought publicly for his beliefs, and remained on friendly terms—in accordance with diplomatic tradition—with all groups in Argentina." In January 1944 the republic broke off diplomatic relations with the Axis; but one month later Ramírez was forced out, to be replaced "temporarily" by a "President delegate," General Edelmiro Farrell. In March the Acting Secretary of State of the United States, Edward R. Stettinius '40, stated that his nation could not resume relations with Argentina unless she proved by her actions that "groups not in sympathy with the declared Argentine policy of joining in the defense of the hemisphere" had not forced the change in the Government. The steps he suggested included interning Axis agents, cleaning up espionage, ending the smuggling of critical goods, and curtailing Axis communications. On March 28 Argentine Minister of the Interior, General Luis C. Perlinger, was reported to have denounced Ambassador Armour at a press conference, stating that all Argentinians should "look with an angry face at that gentleman"; previously, he had penalized American-owned companies on flimsy excuses. According to Pertinax (André Geraud '40), the General's remarks, thoroughly expurgated in a subsequent official version, were inspired by fear that his rival Perón was too friendly with Armour and the latter's close friend, Brazilian Ambassador Rodrigues Alves.

Armour himself was recalled to Washington in late June 1944, and on July 15 succeeded Lawrence Duggan as director of the State Department's reorganized Office of Latin-American Affairs, which left the United States without ambassadorial representation in Argentina. (On July 26 the Department published a summary of the situation, described as "one of the strongest documents, reflective of an irrevocable policy, that has emanated from the State Department in the eleven years Cordell Hull '40 has served as Secretary of State.") In his new State Department post the former Ambassador worked on implementing the security organization tentatively outlined at Dumbarton Oaks. Then, in December, he was appointed Ambassador to another trouble spot—Spain, succeeding the historian Carlton J. H. Hayes '42, who was criticized as an "appeaser." Most commentators called the appointment "a step in the right direction."

Armour presented his credentials to Generalissimo Franco on March 24, 1945. Possibly the most significant event during Armour's nine-month ambassadorship in Madrid was the publication in September of a letter the late President Roosevelt had sent to him at the time of his appointment, a letter which stated that a Franco Spain could not look for economic aid or friendship from the United States. The letter was made public by Under-Secretary of State Dean Acheson '41, but Franco censorship barred its publication in the Spanish press. Its printing in the United States Embassy's weekly bulletin, however, brought it to the notice of thousands of Spanish Government officials and leading citizens. Armour left Spain early in December after he requested to be relieved of the Madrid post. Upon his return to the United States he stated that Franco's changes in the direction of democratic government were not yet satisfactory to the United States. He said, too, that he had not seen signs in Spain of any organized opposition to Franco.

The former ambassador to Spain, who was fifty-seven at the time of his appointment, is tall and lean, and has wavy black hair. *Time* describes him as astute, aristocratic, popular, a top-flight diplomat; he is also described as having a straightforward manner and a magnetic personality. His church is the Episcopal, and his clubs are the University, Union, Princeton, Racquet and Tennis, and Brook in New York, and the Metropolitan in Washington. Norman Armour was, reputedly, the model for Ambassador Arnold Travis Spaulding in John Gunther's '41 *The Troubled Midnight* (1945)—a man depicted as happy and well-adjusted, somewhat old-fashioned, perhaps overly tolerand and disinterested, and leisurely; but incorruptible, selfless, Lincolnian. Gunther emphasizes his dignity, "his projection of a courteous good will no one could take advantage of. If he had been dressed in a pirate's costume, you would have known he was the American Ambassador. He gave an intense aroma of the best of the United States. He made you proud you were an American."

References

Lit Digest 119:11 Je 1 '35 por
N Y Herald Tribune II p3 Jl 9 '44 por
N Y Times p9 D 18 '40 por
Time 44:18 D 18 '44; 46:18 D 31 '45
Who's Who in America, 1944-45

ARNALL, ELLIS (GIBBS) Mar. 20, 1907-
Governor of Georgia
Address: b. State Capitol, Atlanta, Ga.

America's youngest state governor at the time he took office in 1943, Ellis Arnall of Georgia has set a liberal legislative record. The Democrat is an important figure in Southern political leadership and has been hailed for the reform program he has carried out in Eugene Talmadge's '41 old stronghold. Writing a new page in Southern history, Arnall led the fight which abolished the poll tax in his state. Again the Governor made national headlines when Georgia became the first state to lower the voting age to eighteen. Representative of the liberal movement in the South, his measures considered significant of "political things to come," Arnall looks forward to industrial expansion in Georgia and in the South generally.

A native of the state he now governs, Ellis Gibbs Arnall was born in the town of Newnan on March 20, 1907, into a wealthy family of mill owners and merchants. The son of Joe Gibbs and Bessie Lena (Ellis) Arnall, at the age of twelve the young man announced his intention of becoming governor. This early attraction to politics was probably the result of two factors: his grandfather was a member of the Alabama Legislature, and for a period young Arnall worked as a page in the Alabama House. He displayed his talents for leadership at school, where during four years at high school he was the leader of his class. At college, too, Arnall engaged widely in campus activities, first at Mercer University at Macon, Georgia (1924), and then at the University of the South at Sewanee, Tennessee. There he majored in Greek (which later proved of value in winning the Greek vote) and received his B.A. degree in 1928. Then, taking his legal training at the University of Georgia, he won high academic honors and was "top man" in extracurricular affairs: he served as president of his class, his legal fraternity, the interfraternity council, the general student body, and the campus Gridiron Club.

After receiving his LL.B. degree in 1931, Arnall won admission to the Georgia bar and began his legal practice. As a "county-seat lawyer" in his home town, he studied the political scene, and in 1933 entered the political arena as a candidate for the Georgia House of Representatives. Running against five opponents, the twenty-six-year-old attorney polled 2,546 votes to their combined 232 votes. Immediately after the election, as representative of Coweta County, he ran for speaker pro tem before he had taken his seat in the House. "They threw me the gavel," he comments. He served in the legislature until 1937, during which time he was prominent in civic affairs, winning the Distinguished Service Award of the Georgia Junior Chamber of Commerce as the outstanding young citizen of the community in 1934. In 1937 Arnall was appointed assistant State attorney general; in 1939 he entered the race for attorney general and was elected. As the youngest attorney general in the country, Arnall continued to grow in political stature. He became famous for his prosecution of certain asphalt contractors and for collecting damages for the State. Often he would hitchhike the forty miles from his home in Newnan to his office in the Capitol; it is said that motorists would compete to give him a lift. According to one columnist, he early adopted "the habit of dropping folks notes for one reason or another, a custom found useful by Jim Farley '⁴.'"

A firsthand knowledge of the Talmadge Administration reinforced Arnall's criticism of the Governor's power. Since the growing opposition to the regime of Eugene Talmadge needed a crusading leader, Arnall came to the front, organizing a blistering drive against Talmadge. "This State has been given a national black eye," he declared. "Georgia wants reformation and wants it quickly. I'm going to shake hands with every voter in the State and speak from every stump. I'm out to destroy forever the Hitler pattern." Shortly after announcing his candidacy for the Democratic nomination for Governor in early 1942, he conferred with President Roosevelt '⁴². In the gubernatorial election that followed he was backed by the President and liberals in and out of the State. The campaign raged for months, made bitter by the racial issue, which Talmadge emphasized. Campaigning vigorously "to restore decency and democracy in Georgia," Arnall exposed his opponent's demagogic use of this issue. While Talmadge ran on a program of "'white supremacy,' States' rights, and old-time religion," the young New Dealer pledged a broad pro-

ELLIS ARNALL

gram of reform, declaring, "Georgia now presents the worst type of dictatorship. . . .I now hope to be able to do something about it." When the votes were counted in the Democratic 'white primary' in September, Arnall had won a definite victory, with 162,889 votes to Talmadge's 117,731. (A primary victory is tantamount to election in the South.)

"The boy wonder of Georgia politics" was inaugurated in January 1943, at a ceremony attended by scores of proud relatives, a fact which aroused suspicion of continuing patronage in the minds of some Talmadge-weary persons. But suspicions were soon dispelled: Within twenty-four days after Arnall had taken office the legislature had unanimously adopted every campaign promise he had made. It required ten bills to accomplish his Georgian "revolution," in which he succeeded in removing every dictatorial statute of the Talmadge period without dissent in the legislature. Under his influence education was removed from the realm of politics and the State's institutions of higher learning were restored to their accredited standing. (Georgia's colleges had been suspended by the Southern Association of Colleges and Secondary Schools because of Talmadge's tactics in the schools.)

Further legislation drastically reduced the powers which Talmadge had acquired and brought the governor's authority within constitutional bounds. The pardon and clemency rackets were exposed, and the new governor set out to clean up Georgia's notorious prisons and to modernize its penal system. After shocking incidents in the State's work camps had been revealed, Arnall ordered public hearings and then called a special legislative session to take action. A comprehensive prison reform law abolished the Board of Prisons and set up a Department of Corrections. In an effort to get business back to Georgia, Arnall relaxed laws regulating corporations and pointed out the resources the State offers to manufacturers. Thus by encouraging capital, he hoped to see an industrial revival. Early in his ad-

ARNALL, ELLIS—*Continued*

ministration the Governor enlisted the Nation's best legal and administrative minds to assist in the formulation of a new constitution for the State. In August 1945 Georgia's citizens adopted the new constitution at the polls by an almost 3-to-1 vote, thus replacing the 1877 model with a "streamlined" charter. Left with a large State debt by his predecessor, Arnall worked to get Georgia "out of the red" and in the first two years reduced it.

In August 1943 Georgia became the first state to lower the voting age to eighteen. Georgians heeded the "fight at eighteen, vote at eighteen" slogan by ratifying the constitutional amendment by a popular vote of more than two to one. Georgia's youth had shown its strength in the fight against Talmadge, and Arnall returned their support by leading the way toward the lowered voting age. Proud of this accomplishment, the Governor, only twice eighteen himself, expressed the hope that other states and the Federal Government would follow Georgia's example. In an article in *Scholastic Debater* (March 1945) entitled "Admitting Youth to Citizenship," he explains his views on this issue. Accepting the validity of the argument favoring the vote for those who are "old enough to fight and die for their country," Arnall further believes that the idealism of youth is needed in public affairs and that young people should be given the opportunity to exercise their citizenship at the earliest possible time. His testimony on this issue before a subcommittee of the Committee on the Judiciary of the United States House of Representatives appears in the *Congressional Digest* for August-September 1944. Characterizing himself as a believer in dynamic government, one that changes with changing times, Georgia's chief executive declared: "No one can convince me that a young man or young woman of eighteen today does not have a power of understanding that transcends that of a twenty-one-year-old man or woman of a generation ago."

In January 1944 Georgia was first again in passing progressive voting legislation—the first state to pass a soldier-vote measure. In response to Arnall's plea, a bill was enacted to ease requirements and eliminate obstacles to voting by Georgia's citizens in service. The following year, in February, Arnall and Georgia were once more in the national spotlight on a franchise issue. At a joint legislative session the Governor declared that the poll tax must go, that if it were not eliminated by legislation he would do so by executive order. "I am tired of seeing Georgia kicked about in Washington and hearing our people called barbarians who hate democracy and prevent the citizens from voting," said Arnall. The previously reluctant legislature repealed the poll tax, winning for Georgia and Arnall applause throughout the country. *Time* Magazine commented that Georgia "would never have thrown off this feudal custom had it not been for its young and energetic governor," while Clark Foreman in the *New Republic* stated that Arnall "has done more to extend the franchise than any other American since women were given the vote." The Governor received the editorial congratulations of many publications, including the New York *Herald Tribune,* whose

article, noting with satisfaction that "when one Southern state discards a legalized pattern of prejudice, the pattern is weakened elsewhere," urged similar action in the seven remaining poll-tax states.

Despite these advances, it has been pointed out that Georgia does not yet have universal suffrage. The real elections are still seen as Democratic primaries, which remain "lily-white" by party decree. While a decision of the United States Supreme Court in April 1944 nullified the "white primary" in Texas, a decision which was held to apply in other states, Democratic party leaders in Georgia announced their intention of resisting the decision in every way possible. Arnall, too, disavowed the high court's ruling giving the Negro the right to participate in the primaries, when he labeled the decision "a blow to liberalism." On the Negro question, Arnall upholds the traditional Southern system of segregation as "conducive to the welfare of both the white and colored races." "We of the South do not believe in social equality with the Negro," he says. In Arnall's opinion, "the important thing for the Negro is not social equality but economic equality, the right to work and earn a decent living so that he will have enough to eat, a good home, and a good education." However, he has opposed the Government's attempt to guarantee such economic equality through the Fair Employment Practice Committee, rejecting FEPC as "unworkable" and as "an irritant to harmonious race relations." With a practical eye to the future, Arnall has said, "We want the Negro to get better wages, to have better homes, to improve his standard of living. It is foolish for anyone to think otherwise. The more prosperous the Negro is, the better off all of us are."

Associated with the late President Roosevelt and often termed a New Dealer, Arnall has voluntarily become involved in several national liberal issues. Late in 1944 he came out in opposition to the State Department appointments, and early the following year he was a firm supporter of Henry A. Wallace '40 in the debate that followed the latter's nomination as Secretary of Commerce. The Governor telegraphed the State's senior Senator, Walter F. George '43, urging him to drop his opposition to Wallace. As head of Georgia's delegation to the Democratic National Convention in June 1944, Arnall had kept his entire group solidly behind Wallace's nomination for the Vice-Presidency. Previously he had opposed a split within the Democratic Party when there was talk of a Southern "revolt" against the New Deal. Unlike many of his colleagues below the Mason-Dixon line, Arnall calls himself a "Federalist" who does not subscribe to "the moth-eaten doctrine of States' rights." Speaking at the Denver Conference of Western and Southern Governors in 1943, the Georgian emphasized that there has been "too much prattle about States' rights and not enough about States' responsibilities."

The Southern leader looks forward to a new era of revitalization for Georgia and the entire South as he predicts wide industrial expansion for that region. Discussing this theme at a meeting of the New York Southern Society in December 1943, he cited decentralization of industry and the removal of artificial restrictions on industry as signs of progress in this direction. For Georgia, Arnall seeks to keep "native talent" at home, to develop the State's rich resources and attract business. Writing in *Collier's* (July 28, 1945), the Governor declared, "The South has lived too much in the past." Afflicted by economic and political evils the South has stagnated, he continued; "but the new South is waking up and is going to work in a world of reality."

Arnall directed an attack on the railroads to break down freight rates "discriminatory" to the South. Charging conspiracy on the part of the railroads in their higher rates for the South, Arnall by-passed the ICC and went to the Supreme Court for action. The high court ruled to accept jurisdiction in the freight-rate controversy, and the Governor prepared to argue the State's (and thereby the South's) case against the railroads before that tribunal. An exponent of free trade, Arnall discussed "the freight-rate cartel" in an article in the *New Republic* (April 1945) in which he held the unequal freight rates were an obstacle to industrial development in the South and West. The ruling of the ICC the following month, which abolished higher rates for the South and West, was called a clear-cut victory for Arnall. In his New York *Times* article of July 15, 1945, the Governor hailed this decision, "which will make it possible for Southern industry to compete on the domestic market." This discussion of Southern economy names poverty the chief plague of that region and visualizes in the economic development of "Our Last Frontier" the hope of postwar America.

It was considered a rare tribute in the South when the Negro newspaper, the Atlanta *Daily World*, praised Georgia's governor in an editorial entitled "The People Want Arnall." A draft-Arnall movement in the State was defeated in 1945 when the legislature declined to remove the constitutional bar against self-succession. However, the Governor has been mentioned for various Federal posts and it is believed likely that President Truman '45 will offer him an office when Arnall's term expires in 1947. With his political finesse and bold, incisive speech, Arnall, according to one writer, "shows more signs of becoming another Hugo Black '41 or another Claude Pepper '41 than any other young progressive in the South today." To this Lowell Mellett of the New York *Post* adds: "Some think he dreams of smashing a more stubborn precedent than any he has tackled thus far—the precedent of the past eighty years against electing anyone from the South to our highest elective office." John Chamberlain '40 in an appraisal of Arnall in *Life* (August 6, 1945) declared: "But Arnall's concern for the common man is more of the head than of the heart and he is a little contemptuous of people like Pepper and Wallace who 'get themselves tagged.'" Chamberlain considers Arnall as differing from the true New Dealer in his "dislike of centralized Federal power and in his concern for balanced budgets, sinking funds, and 'pay-as-you-go' finance."

Arnall is a stocky figure, five feet six inches in height, weighing one hundred and ninety pounds. He has light, thinning hair, and dark brown eyes, and is given to wearing tweedy clothes. The Governor has been described as "a sort of class-reunion type—the fellow who was voted 'most likely to succeed' and then crossed them up by doing it." He is an avid reader of biography, fiction, and detective stories, preferring books with historical background. His sense of humor was evident when he appeared as guest on the *Information Please* program. A member of the American and Georgia State Bar Associations, he belongs to three fraternities, Phi Delta Phi, Kappa Alpha, and Phi Kappa Phi, and he is a Mason and a Woodman. Georgia's First Lady is the former Mildred Delaney Slemons of Orlando, Florida, to whom Arnall was married on April 6, 1935; they have two children: a son, Alvan Slemons, and a daughter, Mildred Delaney. Their official residence is the Executive Mansion in Atlanta, their home address Arnall's birthplace, about thirty-five miles from the capital. Georgia's governor has been characterized as "a genuine idealist-realist," and Thomas L. Stokes has said, "The young gentleman from Georgia is worth watching."

References

Life 19:68-76 Ag 6 '45 por
N Y Post Mag p7 O 10 '42 por; p29
  Ag 10 '44 por
Sat Eve Post 216:6 Ag 28 '43
Time 50:19-20 S 21 '42 por
America's Young Men, 1938-39
Who's Who in America, 1944-45

ARNE, SIGRID (ärn sē'grĭd) Journalist
Address: b. c/o Associated Press, Starr Bldg., Washington, D.C.; h. 1623 Mt. Eagle Pl., Alexandria, Va.

Considered one of the best Associated Press reporters in the international field, Sigrid Arne is the author of *The United Nations Primer*, published in September 1945. It is an attempt, according to her publishers, to make the world conferences from the Atlantic Charter meeting to the San Francisco conference clear to the average layman, without the use of propaganda. Miss Arne's reportorial assignments have varied widely: she has been sent to cover race riots and asked to pour tea at the home of a Supreme Court Justice.

Although she was born in New York City, Sigrid Arne (who adopted "Arne" as a pen name) spent only a short time in her mid-Manhattan home near Central Park. She is the daughter of Magnus Holmquist, a successful overcoat manufacturer, and Hulda (Larson) Holmquist. When she was four years old her father took the family to his native Sweden for a visit. Upon their return to the States, they decided to establish themselves in Cleveland. In that city Sigrid attended the Willard Grammar School and West High School. She received her B.A. from the University of Michigan in 1922 and began her career as a newspaper reporter four years later. Her talent for writing was evident from her earliest school days. Her first newspaper job was as a reporter on the Muskogee (Oklahoma) *Daily Phoenix*, for which she worked in 1926. She left the paper in the fall of that year, and for the next seven years, until she became a feature writer for the Associated Press in October

SIGRID ARNE

1933, she worked on the Oklahoma City *Times,* Detroit *News, Plain Talk* (a magazine), and the Cleveland *News.*

While gathering her newspaper experience, Miss Arne gained a reputation as a crusader for causes which she considered worth fighting for. In 1929, about ten years before the appearance of John Steinbeck's '40 best-selling novel, *The Grapes of Wrath,* Miss Arne wrote a series of fourteen articles on the plight of the "Okies," the migrant workers from Oklahoma. Her approach differed from that of Steinbeck's in that she actually reported facts and named names, reaching a limited newspaper audience, while Steinbeck, who based his novel on facts, made the entire nation suddenly conscious of the existence of the migratory worker. A few years later she discovered a flourishing black market in infants and bought a twenty-four-hour-old baby in order to expose the racket. She has also investigated and reported a great many facts about the Ku Klux Klan; and she succeeded in getting an aged convicted murderer's sentence commuted to life imprisonment because she was certain that extenuating circumstances warranted it.

In 1933, the year that followed the inception of the New Deal, Sigrid Arne joined the Washington Bureau of the Associated Press. In the years that followed it became one of Miss Arne's greatest responsibilities to analyze and interpret the intricacies of the New Deal. One of her most important assignments in Washington was the analysis of the Social Security Act. Her study brought to light many problems involved in the law. She constructed a chart and, using it for reference, presented her questions to many of the officials of the new bureau. After studying her chart, they, being unable to satisfactorily answer the questions, offered her the job of solving some of the problems she had discovered. Preferring her newspaper career, she refused the offer.

In 1941 Miss Arne went to Hollywood on her first assignment as a roving reporter for the A.P. She was not very fond of Hollywood, mainly because, with the world at war, she felt it an inappropriate place for herself, as a reporter, to be. During the three months she stayed there, nevertheless, she did turn up some good stories. For the next two years she wandered about the country, picking up stories about the war industries for the Associated Press. She also wrote two articles on different aspects of aviation, which were published in the magazine *Flying.* For this assignment she traveled up the Alaskan highway in a jeep. She wrote the first story on civilian defense, and made such difficult subjects as the Bretton Woods conference and UNRRA understandable to the average reader. Toward the end of the war Miss Arne pointed out that Germany was, even then, preparing for another war to come. She also broke a story disclosing secret German plans to accumulate a huge supply of raw materials to meet the needs of a new three-year war.

Miss Arne's postwar copy has been concerned almost entirely with production and trade problems. In spite of her supposed dislike for mathematics and inability to file her own income tax reports, she is interested in national and international economy. In Miss Arne's opinion, the great national debt will not have disastrous effects on the United States if production and, hence, taxes are kept at a high level until it is liquidated. She has stressed the need for full employment and discussed the employers' problems of reconverting their factories and of freeing cash for peacetime work. One of the interests closest to her heart is the growth of the United Nations organization. In her book, *The United Nations Primer,* she explains and interprets the complicated agreements reached at all the major United Nations conferences beginning with the meeting that produced the Atlantic Charter. She has covered United Nations conferences since they began, and told how she wore out a pair of brown suede oxfords in the marble lobby of the Veterans Building in San Francisco, getting from the various foreign ministers the story of the World Charter as it went together, piece by piece. While the New York *Times* reviewer called the volume "a miracle of crisp, compact report and analysis," it was added that "the need for condensation sometimes leads to the omission of vital material, which twists the pattern."

Sigrid Arne is described as a tall blonde, more handsome than pretty, who would make a perfect Isolde in Wagner's opera—at least pictorially. Observers say that she attacks a typewriter as though she has a personal grudge against its inventor, "spilling out stories like a crack stenographer bent on winning a time prize." Sailing is one of her recreations, and she likes to visit art museums. For ten years she wrote a serial fairy story for the A.P. that was published during the month of December. From friends in Shanghai, back in the thirties, she learned that these tales were very popular with young Chinese readers of the Shanghai *Times.*

ARTHUR, JEAN Oct. 17, 1908- Actress
Address: b. c/o Columbia Pictures Corp., Columbia Sq., Hollywood, Calif.

The least-known star in Hollywood off the screen, Jean Arthur has "more smash successes to her credit than any other movie person." She has been a top box-office attraction for ten years, having survived every movie epoch since the days of silent pictures. She has attained a stellar position on the screen on her own terms, refusing to play roles she dislikes, and she has studiously avoided the usual "intimate" Hollywood publicity.

A New Yorker, the actress was born Gladys Greene in the city's Washington Heights section, on October 17, 1908. She was a tomboy, liked to climb trees and fences, and her first ambition was to be a dancer. The young girl attended a New York City high school; then, after deciding against a teaching career, she became a model for Howard Chandler Christy. This work led her into the theater, where she appeared briefly. She started her film career in 1924, acting in two-reel comedies and westerns. In 1928 she played her first leading role, a part opposite Richard Dix in a Paramount baseball picture called *Warming Up*. The next year she appeared in two more Paramount films, *The Canary Murder Case* and *The Mysterious Dr. Fu Manchu*. For two or three years Miss Arthur acted in more than a dozen pictures, most of them for Paramount: *The Greene Murder Case* (1929), *Half Way to Heaven* (1929), *The Saturday Night Kid* (1929), *The Return of Dr. Fu Manchu* (1930), *Sins of the Fathers* (1930), *The Street of Chance* (1930).

But she was dissatisfied with her roles, and in 1932 the actress left Hollywood to return to the stage. In the next few years she played leading parts in several short-run productions: *Foreign Affairs* (1932) with Dorothy Gish [44]; *The Man Who Reclaimed His Head* (1932) opposite Claude Rains; *Twenty-five Dollars an Hour* (1933) opposite Georges Metaxa; her favorite, "a pleasant little comedy," *The Curtain Rises* (1933); and *The Bride of Torozko* (1934).

At the end of this period Miss Arthur accepted a contract with Columbia Pictures and resumed her film career. Eight or ten more pictures followed, including *Whirlpool* (1934), *The Whole Town's Talking* (1935), *Public Hero Number One* (MGM, 1935), and *Mr. Deeds Goes to Town* (1936), a successful comedy hit in which she was co-starred with Gary Cooper [41]. During 1936 she also appeared in *Adventure in Manhattan, More Than a Secretary,* and *The Plainsman* for Paramount. The following year the talented comedienne was starred in *History Is Made at Night* (United Artists), and *Easy Living* (Paramount). Then in 1938 she played a leading role in the celluloid adaptation of the successful Kaufman [41]-Hart [40] play *You Can't Take It With You*. The next year Miss Arthur appeared in *Only Angels Have Wings, Mr. Smith Goes to Washington,* and *Too Many Husbands*.

When Columbia Pictures filmed *Arizona* in 1940 Jean Arthur was given the leading feminine role in this rip-roaring western. The picture was released in Tucson, Arizona, as part of a tumultuous "revival" celebration of Pio-

JEAN ARTHUR

neer Week. Miss Arthur was present with other members of the film's cast and studio officials for the much-publicized première. Jerry Mason in *This Week* reveals that Miss Arthur likes to tell a story about this event, a story of a dinner given in her honor by the Mayor. "The *pièce de resistance* was to be the presentation to Jean of a beautiful hand-hammered copper plate. Dinner over, the Mayor rose, began his speech: 'It is indeed a pleasure to have here tonight the Sweetheart of Arizona. . . .We who had the honor to know her so very well came to love her. . . .So, on behalf of all her most intimate friends in Arizona, I'd like to present this plate to—Miss Gene Autry!' "

Miss Arthur's next film, *The Devil and Miss Jones* (1941), of which her husband Frank J. Ross, Jr., was co-producer, was hailed as a unique production. The story was a saucy comedy-drama of life in New York's "subway society," and Miss Arthur played a department store salesgirl. This success was followed by another fine comedy in 1942, *The Talk of the Town*, directed by George Stevens. *Time* Magazine commended Miss Arthur's "expert energy" in this hilarious comedy, and Bosley Crowther in his New York *Times* review said: "Miss Arthur is charming, as usual, in her bewilderment."

With her delightful portrayal of the harassed Washingtonian in *The More the Merrier* in 1943, Miss Arthur, again directed by George Stevens, added to her collection of fine performances. The New York *World-Telegram* applauded the film and found the charm of the picture in its "joyous nonsense," while another critic admiringly remarked that "Miss Arthur plays with spirit and charm." She next appeared in *A Lady Takes a Chance* (1943) opposite John Wayne, a part which *Variety* called one of her best roles. Miss Arthur, a native New Yorker herself, played the part of a New York bank clerk in this film. While making the picture, director William Seiter reports, Miss Arthur found herself becoming homesick

ARTHUR, JEAN—*Continued*

for her native city. (She delights in the cold weather of the Eastern winter and often spends vacations in New York.)

The Impatient Years, Miss Arthur's 1944 film, was a gay, amusing love story. She played the part of a young soldier's wife, a performance *Variety* described as "capital." The actress has entertained at Army camps and visited hospitals, but she dislikes receiving publicity for her war service activities. There have been rumors of Miss Arthur's decision to retire from the screen; but the Hollywood *Reporter* in September 1944 suggested that the star might change her mind since she can play the choice role in the adaptation of John van Druten's *The Voice of the Turtle* if she so desires. Then, in October the same paper revealed that for the first time Jean Arthur, at her own request, was not represented in the new edition of the *Players' Directory* (the Who's Who of the screen). In the 1945-46 Broadway season, Miss Arthur was one of several screen actresses to return to the stage. She was signed for the starring role of *Born Yesterday,* scheduled for out-of-town tryout in late December.

Miss Arthur studies her scripts carefully, and when she arrives on the set to work on a picture she knows her lines. She considers herself best in comedy roles and has made a success as a romantic comedienne. In 1944 she was nominated for an "Oscar" by the Academy of Motion Picture Arts and Sciences for her work in *The More the Merrier.* She has a distinctive, wistful voice, described by one writer as "clear, low, and sort of lilting." She is careful about her choice of roles, and when a part displeases her she refuses to accept it. Such actions by the star have resulted in her suspension by her studio on three occasions.

Her ideas about her motion picture work are definite. She explains: "You just go ahead and play each part as well as you can, and if movie audiences like you they'll keep on coming." Maintaining that publicity is not necessary to a successful career, the actress has stated: "If people don't like your work, all the still pictures in the world can't help you and nothing written about you, even oceans of it, will make you popular." Her aversion to publicity and her refusal to grant many interviews led the Hollywood Women's Press Club in 1942 to vote her one of the least cooperative actresses. But Miss Arthur has endeavored to explain her attitude: "I find it difficult to give interviews and let myself go to a person whom I have met for the first time. It is also difficult for that person to interpret correctly what I say on a first meeting." Hence there has been little authentic material published about this leading lady, for she prefers to live her personal life quietly. She pointedly states: "When I have something to say, I'll say it, but when I haven't, then I won't talk for publication."

The actress is married to Frank J. Ross, Jr., formerly a New York real estate broker. Since he is now a Hollywood producer, the couple's permanent home is in California, where Miss Arthur indulges in one of her hobbies—the collecting of fine china. Her other interests are books and symphonic music. A slim five feet four inches, she has gray-green eyes, and her brown hair is lightened for photographing. Unlike the comedienne's roles she plays so convincingly, Miss Arthur is known for her shyness—she is "a good talker, but a better listener."

References

Life 8:59+ Mr 11 '40 il pors
N Y Herald Tribune IX p10 N 1 '42 pors
N Y Post Mag p9 O 10 '42
Photoplay 21:49+ S '42 il por
International Motion Picture Almanac, 1943-44
Who's Who in America, 1944-45
Who's Who in the Theatre (1939)

ARTZYBASHEFF, BORIS (ärt-sĭ-bä'shĕf) May 25, 1899- Artist; author
Address: h. 524 E. 89th St., New York City

"I hate art for art's sake!" says Boris Artzybasheff, whose drawings have won almost unanimous critical praise; but he hates almost equally being pigeonholed as an illustrator, although he has decorated half a hundred books, has painted many covers for popular magazines, illustrated many advertisements, and is one of the four leading designers of book jackets. The explanation is that he looks on himself as a designer, "as every true artist is," whose field is "any object which is beautiful and useful," and resents having either the beauty or the meaning stressed at the expense of the other. As such, Artzybasheff has designed women's clothes, stage sets, portraits, murals, delicate and "startlingly lovely" initials, striking grotesques, a night club, and a cathedral altar. And he has made several distinct reputations—as an illustrator, editor, and author, particularly of children's books; as the creator of extremely useful charts and graphs; and as the painter of clever personifications of machines and other inanimate objects.

American by adoption, Boris Artzybasheff was born in Kharkov, Ukraine, Russia, on May 25, 1899, the centennial of the birth of Pushkin. His birth was not registered until June 5, however, and this is therefore given as his date of birth on his official papers and in certain reference works. He is a collateral descendant of Kosciusko through his father, Mikhail Petrovich Artsybashev (the name is transliterated in a number of ways), who began his career as a painter but became world-famous as the author of daring books and plays. Boris' parents separated when he was one year old, and the boy remained with his mother, Anna Vassilievna (Koboushko) Artsybasheva, in St. Petersburg; he saw his father twice a year, when passing through Moscow on his way to vacations in South Russia.

When he was eight Artzybasheff's mother entered him in Prince Tenishev's school, which he describes as "an extremely liberal and progressive school for the sons of the rich and powerful." "I wanted to be an artist ever since I stopped wanting to be a fireman," he says, and his work in art class was so far above average that the teachers did not even try to grade it. When Boris had been there for three years, his self-made father refused to continue paying the high tuition fees, but the school officials were so impressed by the boy's talent that they allowed him to continue on a scholarship. In 1917-18, after the outbreak of revolution, "the city starved and he starved with it," fainting on the street from hunger twice, although he was a fairly husky young man. Graduated in the winter of 1918-19, he had completed the equivalent of the first year of college; and he then enrolled in the University of Kiev's law school—not because he had any idea of becoming a lawyer, but because that was considered to offer the best-rounded education in Russia.

But Artzybasheff was drafted immediately into a German-sponsored Ukrainian army which was trying to carve an independent republic out of Russian territory—a movement with which he had no sympathy. He and the other upper-class youths were put in a machine-gun battalion, stationed behind their own lines to fire on retreating men. "Of course we didn't," the artist recalls. "We ran first." After this army's defeat five months later Artzybasheff made his way through the lines of the embattled Red and White armies on another man's passport; once he was captured and would have been shot, but managed to escape in the confusion. When he reached the Black Sea he signed on a vessel bound for Ceylon, hoping to get from there to Vladivostok—but the ship's destination turned out to be the United States.

The tall young sailor arrived in New York harbor with no knowledge of English, no friends or relatives in America, and his total assets consisted of a few cents' worth of Turkish money and the clothes he was wearing—Russian Army blouse, Russian Navy trousers, and boots which had split open. The immigration authorities detained him on Ellis Island for twenty-nine days, during which a visiting Russian priest gave him a suit at least twice too big, and a girl employee to whom he never spoke and whose name he never learned presented him with the shoes he needed so badly. After appealing to the Russian ambassador, Artzybasheff was released. The official who had committed him to Ellis Island had taken a fancy to him, and found him a job with an engraving firm. When it came to writing his name in the Latin alphabet, the Russian was persuaded by someone to spell it in its present form, Artzybasheff. He now thinks the name should properly be transliterated as Artsibashev, and regrets that he labeled himself as he did: "The zy frightens people."

After Artzybasheff had spent some time doing lettering, ornamental borders, and other hack work for fifteen dollars a week, the head artist failed to show up one day and Artzybasheff was given his assignment—a picture of three beer bottles. The firm was so pleased with the results that from then on they gave him all the bottles to draw. After he had been there three months the New York *World* accepted some of his caricatures, and the artist was emboldened to ask for a three-dollar raise in salary, and to leave when it was refused. The *World* published his drawings as "The Distinguished Russian Artist, Boris Artzybasheff . . . Impressionizing," and when the engraver saw it he asked Artzybasheff to return to his job, but he again refused. Rated an able-bodied seaman, the youth shipped on a Standard Oil tanker for South America. He made extra money by standing watch for his drunken shipmates at time-and-a-half, and re-

BORIS ARTZYBASHEFF

turned to New York after five months with about a hundred dollars. "As I had enlarged my English vocabulary by association with the sailors, most of whom were Swedes and Spaniards, the rest was comparatively easy," Artzybasheff has written.

Actually, as he told an interviewer, the years in which he was establishing himself as an independent artist were "complete hell. I established myself in a horrible house where several other young artists were living who later became well-known, and I lived largely on rice and I pretty near starved to death." A walk-up apartment, decorated by him entirely in fifteenth century Russian style, was, however, the subject of an article in the October 1921 *House Beautiful*. He was repelled by what he saw of America's "business civilization"; but, lacking a passport as well as money, he was unable to go to Paris, where he would have preferred to live, or to Turkey to see his mother before her death in 1923. It was the George S. Kaufman '41-Marc Connelly satire, *Beggar on Horseback* (1924), which finally reconciled Artzybasheff to life in the United States. "I was poor and hungry," he says, "but I saw it three times. It made me realize for the first time that there were Americans who saw the same things I did and made fun of them."

At about this time the artist happened to meet Jo Davidson's '45 sister, who commissioned him to do egg tempera murals for her Russian restaurant and supplied him with crates of eggs for the purpose. Only a few would have been needed, and Artzybasheff actually did the murals in an easier medium, anyway, but he found the eggs a welcome addition to his rice diet. Guy Pène Du Bois saw the murals and wrote an article about them for *International Studio*, illustrated with reproductions, which caused the president of E. P. Dutton to commission the artist to illustrate *Verotchka's Tales* (1922). After that Artzybasheff was considered as an illustrator of children's books. He had already illustrated an adult book, Ed-

ARTZYBASHEFF, BORIS—*Continued*

mund Wilson's [45] morbid *The Undertaker's Garland* (1922), although he was unable to read English. About 1922 Artzybasheff decorated a night club, the Russian Eagle, designed stage sets for Michel Fokine's ballets and others, but gave up stage designing when he had difficulty collecting payments for work done. He also designed dresses—"very cheap ones for two very cheap dress houses"—and even "twisted" himself to do realistic pictures for advertising agencies. The artist has continued to do commercial work, signed and unsigned, throughout his career.

In 1926 Artzybasheff, then twenty-seven, became a citizen of the United States, and with his precious new passport was enabled to spend much of that and succeeding years in Paris. These were not pleasure trips, however. Bruce Lockwood writes that "while abroad, the traveler toiled over book illustrations until hallucinations beset him." While in Paris he designed an altar for a Roman Catholic cathedral which was approved in toto by a consulting engineer; however, the prospective donor died before the altar could be built. The Russian-American held two one-man shows in Paris from 1926 to 1930; from 1923 through 1931 he also had six New York exhibitions. An interviewer who had been unable to find one unfavorable review of his pictures once asked Artzybasheff if he had ever received any. The only bad notice the artist could recall was from Westbrook Pegler [40] in 1932. "All the early praise made me feel I hadn't arrived," said Artzybasheff. "When they start pulling you down you know you have gotten there."

Artzybasheff's illustrations have received almost unqualified praise. He has designed some two dozen books, choosing their typography, size, binding, and decorations, and has illustrated as many more, among them three books by Padraic Colum, two by Dhan Gopal Mukerji, and others by Rabindranath Tagore, Margery Williams Bianco, Ella Young, William Allingham, and one by Balzac, *Droll Stories*. Boris Artzybasheff has edited and illustrated some old favorites, *The Arabian Nights Entertainments* and *Aesop's Fables*, and has written two well-received books. *Poor Shaydullah* (1931) is an original fable, and *Seven Simeons* (1937) is a retelling of a Russian fairy tale which won the *Herald Tribune* Spring Book Festival Prize for the best book for younger children. It was Artzybasheff's illustrations for Henriette Célarie's *Behind Moroccan Walls* to which Pegler objected, asserting that Artzybasheff had maligned the Arab race. The artist had, as it happened, done research for the pictures in North Africa.

For Padraic Colum's book of poems called *Creatures*, and for Mukerji's *Ghond the Hunter* and Jacques Dorey's *Three and the Moon*, during 1927-29, Artzybasheff employed an extremely rhythmical and decorative style of bold curves, black on white and white on black, which is said to have started a wave of imitations. A bookseller told Artzybasheff that the books were selling at a great rate to designers, especially of textiles, and Macy's department store admitted that they had used his pictures on their Christmas wrapping paper. The artist's friends could not understand why he took no action about this violation of

copyright. The style he employed in *The Circus of Dr. Lao* was termed surrealism by Clifton Fadiman [41], to Artzybasheff's annoyance.

Artzybasheff maintains that his work has no connection with surrealism, that he was employing his unrealistic "burlesque or grotesque" style long before Salvador Dali [40] came upon the scene, and that while it is intended to give emotion as design, it always has idea content. Therefore, he particularly enjoyed the making of statistical charts, maps, and graphs for *Fortune*, beginning about 1934. While making pictorially attractive designs, he built up a reputation for making complex relationships clear. As a result, during the Second World War he was engaged by the Office of the Geographer as a consultant, supervising graphic presentation of facts for use by the Department of State, and production of an atlas which was used also by the Army Training Command. Another Luce [41] publication, the news weekly *Time*, also began to use Artzybasheff's work; and the November 3, 1941, issue of *Life* reproduced five of his gouaches—works which fantastically but effectively showed war machines as men or animals. "The measure of his ability to put his point across in paint," *Life* commented, "is that the more closely the paintings are examined, the more clever their details become." (They were reprinted in South America, Sweden, and Germany—in the latter case without credit; his seventy-odd gruesomely amusing versions of the swastika were also reprinted in other countries.) His personifications appealed particularly to servicemen, as did the series of *Axis in Agony* caricatures he made for Wickwire Spencer Steel Company advertising after the United States entered the war. Several units of the armed forces asked him to design insignia for them, including a submarine's own flag.

Meanwhile, however, Artzybasheff was becoming known in still another connection. The first of his cover portraits for *Time* appeared in June 1941. It was a realistic portrait of Marshal Timoshenko [40]—against a background of the familiar profile of his friend and commander Joseph Stalin [42]. Artzybasheff says he had to fight to get *Time* editors to accept the idea of "expressive backgrounds"; but they did, and subsequently had all their cover artists employ this device. "Even then," writes P. I. Prentice of *Time*, "'Artzy' is likely to surprise us. . . . Often as not he works into his painting some dramatic animal-like machine. . . . They are almost his trademark today." Artzybasheff does as many covers as he chooses—they take him about a week each, working from photographs and when possible from notes. Private purchasers are charged "what I think it is worth," he says. Among them are a Texas museum which bought his Texans, including General Eisenhower [42] and Admiral Nimitz [42], and the Massachusetts Institute of Technology, which bought an anthropomorphized but accurate portrait of a B-29 radar set.

The "gentle-eyed and gentle-voiced" artist is six feet tall, dark-haired and light-complexioned. He wears rimless pince-nez, speaks with a slight Russian accent, and supposes that he should really weigh one hundred and seventy pounds instead of one hundred and eighty. Artzybasheff's extremely neat and workmanlike studio is in his house near New York's

East River. A good description of his working methods can be found in the December 1941 issue of *American Artist*: in general, he uses any method and material he thinks will create the particular line or tone he is after, and has devised several craft methods, including the use of thin celluloid sheets in lieu of paper, which "give his work a technical perfection that is unique." He seldom if ever uses a model, but may first sculpture a difficult object and draw from that. One of his woodcuts was chosen by the Kansas City Woodcut Society in 1937 for distribution to its members. Artzybasheff himself is a member of the Institute of Graphic Arts and the Society of Illustrators. His church is the Russian Greek Orthodox.

Artzybasheff is married to Elisabeth Southard Snyder, of an old New England family, who was working as a Wall Street secretary at the time of their marriage. That anniversary should be easy to remember—the date was Washington's Birthday, 1930. Mrs. Artzybasheff is even more enthusiastic than her husband about their East Haddam (Connecticut) farm, where the artist spends his free time working about the place. He is also fond of boating and of fishing and hunting. He has a contract with a publisher to do three book jackets each year at an "unprecentedly handsome" figure, but by the end of the first year he had not submitted one, probably because he was too busy preparing his own book on the travels of Marco Polo.

References

American Artist 5:11+ D '41 il por
Creative Art 12:11 Ja '33 il por
Golden Bk 9:4 F '29 il (cover and p40+)
Time 43:13 Jl 3 '44 il por
America's Young Men, 1938-39
Cooper, A. P., Authors and Others (1927)
Junior Book of Authors (1934)
Who's Who in America, 1944-45
Who's Who in American Art, 1940-41

ASQUITH, MARGOT (TENNANT), COUNTESS OF OXFORD AND ASQUITH *See* Oxford and Asquith, M.T.A.

ASTAIRE, FRED (*à-stâr'*) May 10, 1899- Dancer; actor

Address: b. c/o Metro-Goldwyn-Mayer, Culver City, Calif.; h. Beverly Hills, Calif.

The performer who is regarded as having revolutionized Hollywood's approach to film musicals and brought virtuosity and refinement to the distinctly American dance form, the tap dance, is Fred Astaire, of whom *Theatre Arts* wrote in 1936: "His proficiency . . . is the pure manifestation of modern tap dancing, in which the off-beat Negro rhythm has been combined with the old native clog dance of America's Irish and Lancashire immigrants. It has been whipped up to a frenzy of speed and precision . . . but it is charged with a dry wit that is purely Yankee heritage. It is as modern as the streamlined flier, and as sensitive as the rhythms of the old psalmists."

Fred Austerlitz—until he was seventeen Astaire used his family's name—was born in

FRED ASTAIRE

Omaha, Nebraska, on May 10, 1899. He is the son of Ann (Geilus) Austerlitz and Frederic E. Austerlitz, who was a traveling salesman. When Fred was four he began taking ballet lessons at the school where his sister Adele was already studying, and before many months had passed both of them were appearing in various local entertainments. By the time Fred was five and Adele six and a half, the Austerlitz' realized that the two children had unusual talent, and it was agreed that they should be taken to New York for further training.

For the next few years Adele and Fred attended a singing, dancing, and dramatic school near Times Square. This establishment was owned by Ned Wayburn, who is said to be the originator of modern tap dancing; and it was on his advice that they began studying the syncopated dance form which was to become their specialty. Mrs. Auterlitz tutored the children in elementary school subjects, for they had little time to attend a regular school, and she served also as their manager and promoter. Astaire has spoken of "her patient determination, her unselfish devotion, her fine diplomacy, her common sense."

Two years after their arrival in New York Adele and Fred began making vaudeville appearances, the first in New Jersey; not long after, touring on the Orpheum circuit, they made an appearance in New York itself. Their engagements during these next years were infrequent, however, for they were too young to be wage-earners under the State's child labor laws, and Adele's rapid growth had made them a badly matched dance team. But by 1916 they had reached the working age, and Fred was as tall as his sister. With an act entitled "Fred and Adele Astaire in New Songs and Smart Dances," they were given another opportunity to appear in New York, and by one reviewer, at least, they were praised as "the most talented youngsters who had yet graced the vaudeville stage." They toured the United

ASTAIRE, FRED—*Continued*

States and Canada with their act, and in 1917 were given their first show contract, parts in *Over the Top*.

Their success in this Sigmund Romberg '45 musical revue brought to an end the Astaires' vaudeville appearances. They were given dancing assignments in *The Passing Show of 1918*, and in 1919 they had parts in Fritz Kreisler's '44 operetta *Apple Blossoms*, which ran in New York and then toured until 1921. Although the brother and sister had no speaking roles in either of these shows, according to Lincoln Barnett (*Life,* August 5, 1941), "their adroit rhythmic comedy and liquid but precise teamwork made a profound impression on New York." Critics unable to determine the origin of their adopted surname decided that it was French and applauded "the Parisian chic of the young Astaires."

The team achieved stardom in 1922 in the musical *For Goodness' Sake,* in which they had speaking as well as dancing parts; and later that same year they played in *The Bunch and Judy.* The following season *For Goodness' Sake,* with the Astaires in the cast, was taken to London, where, retitled *Stop Flirting* for British audiences, it repeated its New York success. The American couple became established as international celebrities, causing even the staid London *Times* to write: "Columbus may have danced with joy at discovering America, but how he would have cavorted had he also discovered Fred and Adele Astaire!"

During the remainder of the twenties the Astaires danced through many more successful productions, both in New York and London. In 1925 it was the Gershwin-scored *Lady Be Good* in which they were starred, and two years later it was Gershwin's *Funny Face.* These shows in turn were each taken to London. In 1930 the dancers appeared in the Ziegfeld production of *Smiles,* and the following year they played the leads in *The Bandwagon.*

In this musical Fred Astaire not only received the customary praise for his dancing, but "an unexpected chorus of astonishment and delight at his newly revealed talents as a comedian." *The Bandwagon* was the last show in which Fred and Adele Astaire danced together. After the production closed in 1932 Miss Astaire retired from the stage to be married to Lord Charles Cavendish, the son of the ninth Duke of Devonshire. "She was a great artist," Astaire said of his sister, "incomparable and inimitable, and the grandest sister anybody could have."

The feeling was general after Adele's marriage that Astaire would never find the perfect partner his sister had been. Nevertheless, a few months later he appeared on Broadway with a new dancing partner, Claire Luce, in *The Gay Divorce* (1932). The critical consensus was that two Astaires were better than one, but the box office reception kept the musical going for eight months.

While *The Gay Divorce* was still running, RKO offered Astaire a contract. This surprised the dancer because, as he put it, "an inventory of my face would disclose no feature which could be hailed as what the successful movie star should wear." In the late spring of 1933 he nevertheless signed the contract, with the idea of becoming an actor, for he felt that

dancing would never be popular in films since "the flat surface of the screen seems to rob it of its three-dimensional quality." Although his first screen tests were not very favorable, he was assigned a featured dancing part opposite Ginger Rogers '41 in *Flying Down to Rio*; then, before production started, he was lent to MGM for a number in *Dancing Lady* (1933). Afterward he returned to RKO to make the *Rio* picture, in which he and Miss Rogers, with the colorful "Carioca," initiated the first of a long line of dancing vogues.

The "rushes" of the film convinced Astaire that his screen dancing appeared ponderous and his angular face grotesque. When he could not persuade the studio either to remake or delete his numbers, he left for London with *The Gay Divorce* before the opening, determined to forget motion pictures. But the release of the picture in New York in late 1933 changed his mind for him. Such reviews as "Fred Astaire is a new personality that should hit" and "the chief attraction is . . . the agile dancing of Fred Astaire" caused his studio to cable him to come back to Hollywood as soon as possible; and Astaire returned to begin the long series of pictures that was to make him the best-known and highest paid dancer in the world.

The first of these pictures was the celluloid adaptation of *The Gay Divorce* (1934), with both Miss Rogers and Astaire as the stars. (According to *Life,* the picture was renamed *The Gay Divorcée* by the Hays '43 office on the assumption that a divorcée might be gay, but a divorce should not.) Within a year after the release of the film, it was said that Astaire and Rogers had become the biggest money-making team in motion picture history, and RKO had Astaire's legs insured for a million dollars.

In the next five years the couple made seven pictures: *Roberta* and *Top Hat* (1935), *Follow the Fleet* and *Swing Time* (1936), *Shall We Dance?* (1937), *Carefree* (1938), and *The Story of Vernon and Irene Castle* (1939). The reviewers over the period were fairly consistent in their praise of the Astaire-Rogers dancing. For example, of his work in *Roberta,* considered one of their two best pictures (*Top Hat* was the other), the New York *Times* critic remarked, "Mr. Astaire's dancing is not only an esthetic excitement, but also comedy of a unique and lofty order." When in 1939 Miss Rogers abandoned musicals for straight roles, Richard Watts wrote, "No one has quite made me forget Adele Astaire, but Miss Rogers came closer to arranging any such forgetfulness than I had thought possible."

After Miss Rogers' departure Astaire was given a succession of partners: in the short space of six years six ladies danced through eight of his pictures. The first was Eleanor Powell, who appeared opposite him in *Broadway Melody of 1940*; and at the end of the same year, 1940, Paulette Goddard made *Second Chorus* with Astaire. Neither of these stars was considered the perfect successor to Miss Rogers, although Miss Powell, actually rated a good dancer, perhaps suffered from following so quickly after her predecessor. In 1941 Astaire was teamed with Marjorie Reynolds in the musical *Holiday Inn,* with Bing Crosby '41 singing the Irving Berlin '42 melodies.

His next and most popular partner was Rita Hayworth, who danced with him in *You'll Never Get Rich*. One enthusiastic reviewer remarked that she was able to match her partner "step for step," while Astaire himself declared that she is a born dancer. In 1942 Hayworth and Astaire were paired again, in *You Were Never Lovelier*—"another triumph for Miss Hayworth" and one more example of Astaire's "brilliant inventiveness" as evidenced by his choregraphy. The following year the dancer appeared opposite Joan Leslie in *The Sky's the Limit*. In this picture, a lesser success, he performed what is called the speediest dance ·of his career. Dancing on top of an ornate bar among glasses, bottles, and siphons, he moved so quickly that it was necessary to film the scene in twenty-second takes with a special camera and speed film.

In early 1944 Astaire made *Ziegfeld Follies*, a picture filled with numerous name stars, in which he danced for the first time with Gene Kelly '45, considered a potential rival, and a new dancer, Lucille Bremer. At the end of the year he made another film with Miss Bremer, the Technicolor fantasy *Yolanda and the Thief*. Released in November 1945, this Metro-Goldwyn-Mayer film was applauded for its rich and tasteful mounting by all the critics, most of whom complained, however, that it was too long and too slow-moving. All agreed that Astaire danced with his accustomed brilliancy, that he should have appeared oftener in the film, for it was his and his partner's performances that added excitement and gaiety. *Blue Skies*, a Paramount film on which Astaire was working in late 1945, will be his last: he announced he would retire from dancing, take a rest, and then become a producer.

Of Astaire's dancing Morton Eustis has written: "Out of an innate sense of form, of balance, and of rhythm complemented by a natural gift of showmanship, Astaire has created a diversified group of dance patterns . . . perfectly adapted to his own special capabilities as a dancer. . . .[They are] a blend of song and dance, sense and nonsense, beauty and agility with an almost universal appeal." According to *Life*, "Astaire dances to American rhythms and with an air of gay spontaneity that consummately reflects the folk origins of his art. Debonair, exultant, amused, he has imparted to the tap dance an elegance and mobility of which the cloggers and minstrels of the last century never dreamed. As the Astaire technique evolved, the American Dance washed off its black pigmentation and put on white tie and tails."

The success of the man with "the sophisticated toes" has not been achieved and maintained without a great deal of work and worry on his part. Concerned over the fact that as his own choreographer he may someday exhaust his supply of ideas, he will interrupt golf matches or week-end trips to put a sudden idea into action. He· is never completely satisfied with his dancing and, as a result, can never sit comfortably through a showing of his pictures. Two of them, he says, he has never seen at all.

Fred Astaire feels that dancing is not merely an exhibition of footwork, but also an expression of an idea—the rhythmical telling of a story in an effortless manner, which must be easily understood by the audience. He is also of the opinion that in both plays ·and motion pictures a dance must be an integral part of the plot, emerging as ·"the natural outcome of an action and not an insertion." For that reason, Lincoln Barnett says, when Astaire creates an original dance routine "it is roughly the equivalent in mental exertion to composing a sonata or writing a one-act play." In his motion picture work, Astaire, a perfectionist, spends several weeks practicing his numbers after he has completed the choregraphy. His final touch on a routine is to refine his body movements, gestures, and expressions before a mirror. His first teacher, Ned Wayburn, holds that Astaire is "the first American tap dancer to consciously employ the full resources of his arms, hands, and torso for visual ornamentation."

Astaire is considered not only a designer of dance routines, but also "a choreographer in terms of camera angles." Before his entry into motion pictures dancers were "photographed in pieces"—during a sequence the camera would shift its focus to different parts of the body, using trick shots taken from the floor, ceiling, or through lattice work. To reverse this process, to keep the flow of movement intact, Astaire has his numbers filmed "straight"—his entire body is kept in view during a dance. Each take is filmed with three cameras working simultaneously, and the best shots of each sequence are pieced together. The average dance is shot from six to ten times, each time in its entirety.

The dancer and Phyllis (Livingston) Potter were married in July 1933. They have three children (two sons and a younger daughter), the older son being the child of Mrs. Astaire's first marriage. The dancer is said to have. an aversion to publicity. He enjoys playing golf and tennis, fishing, and breeding and racing horses, and is considered an accomplished pianist and accordionist. A member of ASCAP, he has done some composing—of his five published songs three were popular for a time: "Just Like Taking Candy From a Baby", "No Time Like the Present," and "I'm Building Up to an Awful Let-down." In the fall of 1944 Astaire returned from a six-week USO tour of France, Belgium, and Holland. He had taken with him a number of his one hundred pairs of dancing shoes, but once, when there was a hitch in the arrangements, Astaire danced in heavy combat boots.

References

Am Mag 121:40-1+ Je '36 pors
Life 11:73-4+ Ag 25 '41 pors
Theatre Arts 21:371-86 My '37 pors
International Motion Picture Almanac, 1943-44
Who's Who in America, 1944-45
Who's Who in the Theatre (1939)

BABSON, ROGER W(ARD) July 6, 1875-
Statistician; economist
Address: Babson Park, Wellesley Hills, Mass.

The man who, it is said, has made more money out of statistics than anyone else in the United States is Roger W. Babson, known around Boston as "the seer of Wellesley Hills." Babson's Reports, Inc., sells his statistical serv-

ROGER W. BABSON

ice throughout the United States and Canada; the syndicated Publishers' Financial Bureau distributes his views to newspapers. He is the founder of Babson Institute, a business school; and of Webber College, exclusively for women interested in a business career. He is the author, also, of many books on money and investments—and on religion in relation to business and better living.

Roger Ward Babson, whom *Time* has called "a combination of Yankee piety and shrewdness," was born in Gloucester, Massachusetts, July 6, 1875. The son of Nathaniel and Ellen (Stearns) Babson, he is directly descended from Israel Putnam, the Reverend John Wise, and John Rogers: "I can see myself as a combination of these fighting, religious, and educational strains," he declares. Another strain, the commercial, he adds, comes from his sea captain ancestry. His father was the leading dry-goods merchant of Gloucester; as a boy Babson would go with him on his horse-and-buggy selling trips. Roger also spent much of his boyhood on his grandfather's dairy farm, of which he says, "I owe more to that farm than to any educational institution." In Gloucester he played mostly with children of the fishermen's families, and he organized a gang which would "periodically go to Nob Hill and lick the rich boys."

His mother, disapproving of the public schools, sent her young son to a private school; but he was considered an unruly youngster and dismissed. He then went to the Collins School for six years. After a rest following a nervous breakdown he entered the Gloucester High School in 1890. The school had a military training course, which he liked, and he became captain of his company. Because he did not take the regular scientific course (his father had insisted that he study bookkeeping) Roger got a diploma at graduation in 1894 marked "Special Course." Religion, during these years, was a major interest of young Babson. "The greatest event of my life was my conversion," he reports. After that he was a changed boy:

he taught a Sunday school class and joined the church organizations for young people. As a Congregationalist, Babson has throughout his life continued to be active in church work.

He had wanted to go to a Western college, but his father chose the Massachusetts Institute of Technology for him. It was all hard work, Babson says—there were no dormitories, recreation, nor sports, no religious instruction, no student aid. "I hated the place and all its courses." He took civil engineering, he says, because it was the first course listed in the catalogue and received his B.S. in 1898.

Apparently the various jobs he had held during his school years had interested young Babson more than his academic work. He earned his first money by carrying water for Chinese laundrymen—and for circus elephants. During high school vacations he was given his own tract of land where he raised vegetables, which he sold from house to house. His next job was installing doorbells and other electrical equipment in Gloucester; during the summers of his college years he worked, first as timekeeper, then as a State highway engineer. His father had always emphasized the importance of getting into a "repeat" business, like investment banking or insurance. So, when he was graduated, Babson first went to work for a small Boston investment house, but was discharged when he started making inquiries concerning profits in the sale of bonds. He then set up his own bond-selling business in New York, but left this to go into business with a public utility bond firm. He began to invest in various light and power companies, and became vice-president of the Adirondack Light and Power Company. "In the years which followed, my profits grew rapidly," he says, largely through consolidations with other companies. But when the profits from his own statistical business increased, he decided to retire from active participation in the utilities field.

In March 1900 Roger Babson was married to Grace Margaret Knight, the daughter of a New Hampshire preacher, and a student nurse at the time of her marriage. "I always liked bright, jolly girls, full of the dickens," he writes. But Grace Knight was of a different type. She was quiet, intelligent, did not talk much, but, he adds, "she let me tell her how wonderful I was. . . .I get the honors, but she has always been the real works." The Babsons' only child, Edith Low, was born in 1903.

When he became seriously ill with tuberculosis shortly after his marriage, Babson was told that he must spend most of his time out of doors, preferably in the West. He was determined to stay in the East, however, and moved to Wellesley Hills, Massachusetts, where he worked in an open-air bedroom. He learned to analyze and tabulate business reports for bankers. By 1904 he had incorporated the Babson Statistical Organization, with a capital of twelve hundred dollars, and himself and his wife, respectively, as president and treasurer, and as sole stockholders. "Our underlying purpose was to furnish protection to the investor in relation to his capital and income." As his business expanded he built an office building, where he continued to work in rooms with wide-open windows, wearing a special coat with an electrically heated pad in back; his secretary wore mittens and did her typing by striking the keys with rubber hammers—and Babson regained his health.

The panic of 1907 aroused in him an interest in making a study of stock exchange transactions—thus the "Babsonchart" was started. Babson's theory of depression and prosperity is based on Newton's law of "action and reaction." The Babson Reports Service (for which the Babsonchart is used) suggests to clients when to buy and when to sell. "Our forecast of future events," he explains, "is based on the assumption that the law of action and reaction applies to economics and human relations, en masse, as it applies to mechanics. Thus we assume that abnormal depression must follow abnormal activity; that lower prices must follow higher prices, or vice versa; and that we as classes or nations must ourselves get what we give and must prosper as we serve."

Babson states that his organization clearly forecast the 1925-35 business cycle. It was on September 5, 1929, that he made his most famous prediction—he foretold a drop in stock prices of sixty to eighty points. When, after three weeks, industrial shares dropped 50 per cent, Babson "soon became a lion among stock market prognosticators." He began a column, *Be Right With Babson,* for a New York newspaper. According to Ralph Robey, writing in the *Nation,* Babson had not always been so fortunate in his predictions. During 1926 the statistician had advised clients to "hold their funds in good liquid condition," while all the time the stock market moved upward. Even in 1927 he had urged his clients to stay out of the market. His blanket forecast for all of 1928 was: "Any major movement should be on the downward side." But as the market continued upward, "the Babson follower was more than 25 per cent worse off than the foolish speculator who tossed a coin." Babson explains, however, that his mistakes in forecasting business conditions have "usually resulted from being too early." In several articles for the New York *Times* in 1913 he forecast the First World War.

Other interests of Babson's, in the early part of his career, were the American Public Welfare Trust for promoting hygienic products (i.e., paper towels), and distributing rules for health; and the Gamewell Company, manufacturing red fire alarm boxes, installing fire prevention devices. The Babsons during these years also made several trips abroad to increase their clientele and to set up European services of the Babson agencies.

Upon the outbreak of the First World War, Babson became secretary of the Society to Eliminate the Economic Causes of War, which adopted a "Declaration of Independence" that foreshadowed the Versailles Treaty. During the war he worked in the Government as director general of information and education, under the Secretary of Labor. In 1917, with the approval of President Wilson, he wrote a booklet for the armed forces, entitled *Why Are We Fighting?* In 1920 he organized the various peace societies that sent delegates to the National Council for the Limitation of Armaments. Shortly after that he gave up active work in peace movements, but he believes that "world peace will be brought about only by extending equal opportunities to the people of all nations who meet a certain character test and observe certain rules."

The Babson "Experiment in Industrial Democracy" of 1916-24, a service established for Babson employees—free hospital service, dental clinic, community building, moving pictures, salary bonuses—was, said its originator, a failure. The trouble with "profit sharing," according to him, is that it works when the employer's profit goes up, but when it goes down in lean years the employees are dissatisfied because they can no longer get bonuses. "I am sure that the nation is not yet prepared for it." Babson once expressed himself as being against socialism as a form of government: "Any nation which now attempts to operate under a socialist system in competition with nations operating under private control would be licked to a frazzle." Once a Republican, but an independent since 1908, Babson is proud of his association with Theodore Roosevelt and his acquaintance with other Presidents; he admired Wilson for his peace principles; he approved of Coolidge, but not of Hoover.'[43]

In 1919 the Babson Institute near Wellesley Hills was founded, a school described as the first of its kind in the United States, and perhaps the first anywhere. The endowed school provides an intensive two-year course in business training for selected young men, with the idea that they would step immediately into responsible positions. Courses are given on finance, production, distribution, and personal efficiency, and students are taught to use dictaphones and to work with secretaries. There are no written examinations—"the test consists in whether or not the student has secured a position. If so, he gets a diploma; if not, his tuition is returned." Eight out of ten of the Institute's students are said to have succeeded. By 1935 two women were admitted to every class of twenty. The community of Babson Park, as the Babson Park Company, has its own post office, bank, radio station, movie house. The motion pictures are carefully censored; the radio never puts on the air any liquor, cigarette, patent medicine, or other so-called "objectionable" advertising. Babson owns a twelve-thousand-acre ranch in Florida (Babson Park in Polk County), where Webber College, a special training school for women, was started in 1927.

Lecturing, particularly before Chamber of Commerce meetings throughout the country, was a Babson occupation for several years. He started his long writing career in 1910 with an article in the *Saturday Evening Post* called "Mistakes of Investors." He did his first feature work for the Scripps Syndicate; and in 1923 started his own newspaper syndicate, Publishers Financial Bureau, which distributed its services to some four hundred newspapers.

By 1935, the year which saw the publication of his autobiography, *Actions and Reactions,* he had written thirty-eight books. *Washington and the Revolutionists* (1934), which discussed new personalities and policies in Washington, was commended as "brief, impartial, and interesting." *If Inflation Comes* (1937), was a discussion of possibilities of revolution as well as of inflation. Babson's suggestion was that ownership of a small farm was a good hedge against both. Also, he felt that one ought to learn the art of defensive war-

BABSON, ROGER W.—*Continued*

fare; and he advised young people to join a labor union, although in a later book he declared that in no case does labor union activity raise the real wages of workers. In *Looking Ahead Fifty Years* (1943) Babson anticipated developments in business, economics, and education. He declared that 20 per cent of the people are at times unemployable because of our faulty educational system. The book was chiefly criticized for its "general looseness of thought," its "many extreme views," and also for its "failure to come to grips with the momentous problems of the future." Babson has said that his purpose in writing all these books has been "to present great subjects so that the man on the street may understand and enjoy them."

Babson believes that the facts of religion are based upon and correlate with physical or scientific laws. "The study of the spiritual life is in the same condition in this twentieth century that the study of the physical sciences was in when Newton was born in 1642," the economist writes. He believes the Bible should be studied in school, and he himself presents a Bible to every new employee in his organization at Wellesley Hills. One of his books, *How To Increase Church Attendance,* was published in 1936. From 1936 to 1938 Babson served as moderator of the Congregationalist Christian Council. *Can These Bones Live?* was written in collaboration with Dudley Zuver and published in 1945. In its comment on the book, the New York *Times* said, "Mr. Babson is the *enfant terrible* of the churches, and in these pages he, with his collaborator, lashes the money-changers in the temple."

In the New Deal era Babson occasionally questioned certain of President Roosevelt's social policies. "Fundamentally," he wrote, "the only real security is high spiritual and intellectual character. . . .If the people do not have strong character, their Government insurance and security are useless." In 1940 Babson was unanimously nominated for the Presidency by the American Prohibition Party. In his convention speech he said that the party sought "a new mode of attack." While the main object was still to crush the liquor traffic, the goal could best be reached "by working for a spiritual awakening through churches, schools, movies, radio, and influential publications." The party, he said, should, furthermore, "work to keep this country out of war by insisting upon both friendly international relations and adequate defense."

In 1945 an idea Babson had conceived twenty years before became of unique importance in the future of American aviation. Having need for a good relief map of the United States with which to teach his students of business administration the material resources of their country, he organized a national advisory committee of educators and industrialists from each state to aid in the design of the largest relief map of the United States in the world. The map, costing two hundred thousand dollars and taking fifteen years to complete, shows every mountain, valley, river, prairie, and forest. On Babson's offer of the use of his giant map to the Government, Air Force technicians were dispatched to study it. It was reproduced, inch by inch, for use at the two hundred Government

airfields all over the country. Eventually, it is expected, each commercial airport will also have a replica of its own geographical section of the map at its briefing station.

Less active in church work and politics than in previous years, Roger Babson during the early forties has confined his interests to statistics, to his syndicated column, and to his various hobbies. His first hobby, some years ago, was a backyard garden—most of the profits of which came from articles he wrote about it for *Garden Magazine*. He collects old sailing maps as well as postage stamps; he collects and reads "good cheer" books. But Mrs. Babson, he says, is the real collector, her most valuable acquisition being her Newtoniana—all the works of Newton and the writings about him. Babson doesn't care particularly for the theater or music; but says he especially enjoys discussing new ideas and inventions: "I have always some prospective patent to work on." He is interested in air-conditioned beds, and a system whereby men may "subscribe" for clothing, the garments to be sent out periodically. "My chief hobby at the present time is trying to do things which will carry on after my death. This consists primarily in giving time to my grandchildren"—Babson's daughter, Mrs. Mustard, has five children. "All parents should give more time to their children, and all grandparents should give more time to their grandchildren. Children and grandchildren will remember us far more for the time we give them than for the money we leave them."

References

Christian Cent 55:725 Je 8 '38; 57:671 My 22 '40
Nation 130:359 Mr 26 '30
Review of Reviews 91:60 My '35
Time 27:27 Je 29 '36; 29:84 Mr 15 '37 por; 31:59 My 30 '38
Babson, R. W. Action and Reactions (1935)
National Cyclopædia of American Biography Current vol A p475
Who's Who in America, 1944-45

BAILEY, SIR DONALD COLEMAN
Sept. 15, 1901- British Government engineer
Address: b. c/o Experimental Bridging Establishment, Ministry of Supply, London

One of the military inventions of the Second World War that can look forward to a continued usefulness in peace is the Bailey Bridge, designed by British engineer Sir Donald Coleman Bailey. Called "the most remarkable bridge in the history of military operations," it proved its practicality and versatility in campaigns in Afria, Europe, and Asia, where it was used to span bomb craters, ravines and gorges, or rivers more than a thousand feet in width. A non-military usefulness is seen for it in the reconstruction of devastated Europe and in undeveloped regions of the world where slow ferries are the only means of crossing water barriers.

Born in Yorkshire in 1901, Donald Coleman Bailey later lived in Cambridge, where he took his first technical courses at the Leys School. Dams, reservoirs, and bridges filled his mind at an early age. This "water complex" once led the boy to expend three shillings for an old iron bedstead, which he then proceeded to carry down past the King's Parade in Cambridge to the River Cam. It was his intention to convert the bedstead into a boat by means of painted canvas, and to sail it on the river—but the outcome of that project is not recorded. When young Bailey was ready for college, an engineer friend of his father advised the elder Bailey to send the boy to Sheffield University, from which in due course Bailey received his engineering degree. And in the late twenties he was the engineer for a new reservoir in the city of Sheffield. At first attracted to railroad engineering, he remained in that field for only a short time. In 1929 he joined the Experimental Bridging Establishment of the Ministry of Supply as a civilian staff engineer, later being promoted to the position of assistant superintendent.

When the Second World War broke out Bailey had been working with experimental bridges for military use for about ten years. The British reverses suffered in the Battle of France which culminated in the disaster of Dunkerque in June 1940 had made it plain that bridging equipment would have to be improved to bear the armaments of a greatly increased mechanized warfare—the forty- and fifty-ton loads of, for instance, the British Churchill and Matilda tanks. But Bailey seems to have crossed his bridge before he came to it—he had been thinking of a new type of span for some time when, in late 1940, he drew a rough sketch of the bridge that was to be named after him. At that time chief designer of the E.B.E., the engineer was called to a conference to discuss the failure of a new bridge under test. On his way to the meeting he sketched the design he had in mind on the back of an envelope and showed it to his companion, an officer in the Royal Engineers.

The result was that Bailey was authorized to design his new bridge—a strong, comparatively light steel prefabricated sectional span that could be erected easily, quickly, and quietly (under fire if necessary), and whose interchangeable parts would simplify repair and permit variation in length and strength. Bailey completed his design within six weeks, and by February 1941 work had been started on a seventy-foot knock-down bridge. Within another three months the structure was ready for its first test.

The test bridge was put together in only a few hours. But when three heavy tanks were sent across it, the structure collapsed, whereupon Bailey sought and found the cause of the trouble. One of the tanks had veered into two of the main steel struts which had consequently given way. A truck was at once dispatched to a factory miles away for spare parts. By nine the next morning the bridge had been rebuilt and proved successful. Here was a practical demonstration, which Bailey had not scheduled, of the quick repair of the bridge and the easy replaceability of its parts. Quantity production was begun about four months later.

The girders of the Bailey Bridge are constructed from lattice-work panels or sections, each ten feet long, which are locked together with steel split pins. Between these girders,

British Official Photo.

SIR DONALD COLEMAN BAILEY

which resemble a child's Meccano toy, are laid transoms, and on them are placed wooden planks to form the roadway. The strength of the span may be increased by placing two, three, or more girders side by side on each side of the roadway, or by placing a second or third girder above the first. The notable feature of the bridge is its simplicity of erection and launching. The whole structure is put together on the near bank, its forward end equipped with an elevated false nose, the structure pushed over the gap on rollers, and the launching nose lowered on the far shore. In the war the launching rollers were brought across by men straddling the girders. Pontoons are only required for bridges more than two hundred and forty feet long. A pontoon bridge built across the flooded Maas in Holland measured four thousand feet, and even longer bridges were later built across the Rhine.

Bailey had designed a bridge that could be thrown across rivers in a short time. In one theater of war a 300-foot river was bridged in thirty-six hours, and in Burma five hundred men worked day and night for forty-eight hours to build the first bridge in history over the Chindwin River, more than a thousand feet in width. Since the basic method of erection is the same, regardless of the number of girders employed, and the parts are standardized, calculations required in the field were of the simplest. Panels were transported in three-ton trucks and hoisted in place by a squad of six men, who used only a few tools to join the parts, thus obviating the use of machinery. If necessary, the bridges could be strengthened while in position, and, if damaged, only the affected sections needed to be replaced.

By the end of 1944 an average of two of Bailey's bridges were being erected almost every day, so heavy was the demolition of existing bridges. Said Field Marshal Sir Bernard Law Montgomery [42]: "This bridge is quite the best thing in that line we have ever had; it does everything we want"; and the comment of a

BAILEY, SIR DONALD COLEMAN—
Continued

young American officer was that "the Bailey is really a marvelous gadget—you could make almost anything from a roller-coaster to an Eiffel Tower if you had enough pieces!" The United States forces adopted the Bailey as standard bridging equipment, and the Red Army was also given the plans.

To Bailey, who is characterized as modest and singularly unaffected, the designing of the bridge was all in the day's work. He is glad, he says, to have been able to "do something to help the troops." In recognition of his contribution to the victory, he was made an Officer of the Order of the British Empire, and later the engineer was knighted. Bailey and his wife live in Southbourne, in a house with a view of the English Channel. For relaxation he plays golf and reads detective stories. He is tall, slender, and blond, and, according to one description, has the "dome-like head of the deep thinker" and the "tenuous hands which bespeak the artist." He wears horn-rimmed glasses and is often seen in checked coat and cap. His young son Peter admires him particularly for his skill in assembling Meccano toy sets.

Reference

New Yorker 21:23 Mr 17 '45

BAILEY, JOSIAH W(ILLIAM) Sept. 14, 1873- United States Senator from North Carolina

Address: b. Senate Office Bldg., Washington, D. C.; h. 513 N. Blount St., Raleigh, N. C.

The senior Senator to the United States Congress from North Carolina and chairman of the powerful Senate Commerce Committee, Josiah W. Bailey, is a dignified but very vocal Democrat who has been called one of the old-school orators of the Senate. An outspoken critic of the New Deal, Bailey has been withal a party supporter from his earliest voting years.

The Southern legislator was born Josiah William Bailey in Warrenton, North Carolina, on September 14, 1873. Son of Virginia-born Christopher Thomas and Annie Sarah Bailey, the boy inherited a religious tradition from his father and grandfather, both Baptist preachers. As he grew older he himself participated in church activities. (This background, later reflected in many of his Senatorial speeches, caused the press to nickname him "Holy Joe.") He attended Wake Forest College in his home state, receiving his Bachelor of Arts degree from that college in 1893.

In the year of his graduation young Bailey became editor of the *Biblical Recorder*, the official organ of the Baptists in North Carolina. During part of his fourteen-year editorship, he studied law under S. F. Mordecai and at Trinity College (now Duke University). When he left the *Recorder* in 1907 he continued his law studies for a year at the Wake Forest Law School. In 1908, at the age of thirty-four, he was admitted to the State bar and began to practice law at Raleigh. That year he also served as Presidential elector-at-large for North Carolina; some years later, in 1913-14, he was a member of the State Constitutional Commission. From 1913 to 1921 he held the position of United States collector of internal revenue in his state, and at one time was director and vice-president of the Wake County Savings Bank.

Bailey's political ascendency began with his rebellion in the middle twenties against party dictatorship in Democratic North Carolina. Although he was then unsuccessful in upsetting the political machine, his biting, forthright language won him the label of "crusading rebel." In 1928 he campaigned in North Carolina in support of the Democratic Presidential ticket. Two years later, after his offer of assistance to several possible Senatorial candidates was refused, Bailey announced his own candidacy. The fighting Democrat swept the State in the primary, and was elected by the largest majority ever given to a North Carolina Senatorial candidate. When Bailey took office in 1931, Weimar Jones, discussing the new Senator in the *Nation*, described him as "a scholar whose devotion to abstract principles of right and wrong, and specifically to righteousness in civil and political affairs, borders on fanaticism." The North Carolinian was in 1945 serving his third term in the Senate, having been re-elected in 1943 by a ten-to-one majority over his Republican opponent.

Bailey took a strong stand on certain issues in legislative sessions. In 1935 he led a filibuster against an anti-lynching bill, promising the Senate, "We'll speak day and night if necessary." Two years later, when the bill was once more before the upper house for passage, Bailey said that while he did not like the measure itself, he approved of its objective, the extermination of lynching. In May 1944 the Senator again participated in a filibuster, when he was one of the Southerners to contribute to the defeat of the anti-poll tax bill on the Senate floor.

The Senator opposed the New Deal policy on several issues. He was one of those who helped to defeat President Roosevelt's [42] Supreme Court reorganization plan in the early days of the Administration. In March 1943 he helped to repeal the President's order limiting annual salaries to twenty-five thousand dollars after deduction of taxes. In May, with the majority, he voted against Presidential use of war emergency funds for the National Resources Planning Board. (This long-disputed war and postwar planning agency was ended two months later by Congress.) Bailey is on record as approving United States postwar participation in maintaining the peace; and in October 1943, in a poll taken by a news service, he supported the House's Fulbright [43] resolution for postwar collaboration.

An isolationist until 1941, Bailey repudiated his noninterventionist policies during Senate debate on the Lend-Lease bill. *Time* Magazine on March 3, 1941, reported: "Conservative Senator Josiah William Bailey of North Carolina, who has been 99 per cent against the Administration, except when campaigning for re-election, now recanted his onetime isolationism, ate his words with such solemn gusto that a hushed, impressed Senate clustered around his desk so as not to miss a syllable." Bailey stated his reversal of principle simply: "I have utterly changed my mind. . . . I am advocating intervention with all its implications. I am not hedging. All my life I have looked a thing in the face and argued it as it is." The New York *Times* editorially called his action "a brave change of mind."

The Senator upheld Administration policy in April 1943 when he urged Senatorial support of the President's veto of the Bankhead bill to increase farm prices, warning that price stabilization was imperative. The next year, in February, he contributed to the defeat of food subsidies by voting against an amendment to the Commodity Credit Corporation bill, providing for an appropriation for the subsidies. Again, supporting the Administration, at the end of 1944 Bailey voted for confirmation of the President's nominations to the State Department.

Bailey has been prominent in the dissension within the ranks of the Democratic Party, in 1943 proposing a resolution to amend the Constitution to prevent future Presidents from serving more than two terms. In December 1943 Senator Joseph F. Guffey '44, an Administration supporter, accused Southern Senators, including Bailey, of an "unpatriotic and unholy alliance" to defeat the soldier-vote bill. From the Senate floor Bailey answered with considerable heat, declaring that the "scorned" Southern Democrats could form a Southern Democratic Party of their own. Then, in March 1944 he was one of the principals in the Senatorial "revolt" against "Executive domination" which was set off by the resignation of Alben W. Barkley '41 as Senate majority leader.

In early 1945 Bailey once again demonstrated his rejection of New Deal philosophy. As chairman of the Commerce Committee, Bailey presided at the hearings at which Jesse Jones '40 and Henry Wallace '40 testified in the dispute over Wallace's appointment to Jones's Secretaryship of Commerce. Favoring the conservative Jones, Bailey pronounced former Vice-President Wallace a "dangerous" man. It was reported that Bailey had gone to the White House in January to urge the President to retain Jones as Commerce Secretary. Bailey was the leader of the opposition against Wallace's appointment and hence one of the central figures in the controversy that raged around the appointment. And it was Chairman Bailey who filed the Commerce Committee's reports to the Senate in which confirmation of Wallace was advised against. But when Wallace's nomination came to a vote, Bailey voted for confirmation of the appointment. He did this only after passage of the George bill had stripped the Commerce Department of all vital lending agencies. By a Senatorial vote of 56 to 32 Wallace became Secretary of Commerce. (Bailey attended the informal installation ceremony of the former Vice-President.) Shortly thereafter, in what the press called a "peace move," Bailey appointed a subcommittee headed by Senator Claude Pepper '41 to conduct with Wallace a survey of domestic commerce. The Commerce Committee chairman also named a subcommittee to work with the new Secretary on matters of foreign commerce.

The legislator's stand on States' rights and private industry has been clearly indicated in his Congressional record. In 1943 Bailey defended fire insurance companies against prosecution under the antitrust laws. The *Congressional Digest* of October 1944 carried Bailey's arguments for States' rights in the

JOSIAH W. BAILEY

control of the insurance business. In December 1943 he voted against the Federal soldier-vote legislation, favoring the State ballot. Bailey's amendment to the flood control bill in November 1944, which, he argued, was imperative for the "protection of private industry against a Government monopoly," was rejected by the Senate. As chairman of the Commerce Committee, Bailey attended the international civil aviation conference in Chicago in late 1944. His committee is expected to play an important part in planning policies for future commercial aviation. It is known that Bailey opposed Government ownership of transoceanic service. Another Federal project which was referred to Bailey's committee and to which he is opposed is the Missouri Valley Authority.

Senator Bailey has initiated some significant wartime legislation. The Bailey-Brewster bill, offered in 1944, provided for the assignment of 4-F draft registrants to work units. This measure was defeated, but 1945 saw the introduction in the House of a similar manpower measure designed to alleviate the critical manpower situation. This was the May-Bailey bill, which provided limited national service for deferred men between the ages of eighteen and forty-five. Jointly sponsored by Bailey and Representative Andrew J. May '41, the bill was referred to as the "work or fight" bill and had the support of Roosevelt, the military and naval Chiefs of Staff, and leading Government officials. However, the bill met the combined opposition of organized labor and industry. Both the CIO and the A. F. of L. were against the measure; and Ira Mosher '45, president of the NAM, voiced that group's disapproval. After lengthy debate in the House, the May-Bailey bill was passed February 1 and proceeded to the Senate. Here it was "bogged down" in the Senate Military Affairs Committee, and when the committee finally reported on February 22, it offered a drastically changed manpower bill. Thus the May-Bailey bill, as such, never came to a vote in the Senate. That body debated various manpower measures attacked from some quarters as "milk-and-

BAILEY, JOSIAH W.—*Continued*

water" cures. When Bailey endeavored to apply the principle of the May-Bailey bill to the legislation under consideration, he was "soundly beaten." The Senate finally passed the Kilgore '43-O'Mahoney '45 compromise bill.

In June 1945 Bailey supported President Truman's '45 fight to extend the reciprocal trade program by permitting a 50 per cent reduction in existing tariffs in exchange for concessions obtained by the United States. (Previously Bailey had proposed a modifying amendment to the reciprocal trade bill which would have forbidden reduction of duties on strategic metals and minerals.) Bailey's Senate Commerce Committee in early July rejected Senator Pat McCarran's bill to establish a single American company to handle international air commerce and also turned down an amended version which proposed to set international lines apart from domestic companies. Absent from the Senate during the history-making roll-call vote on the ratification of the United Nations Charter on July 28, 1945, Bailey, however, sent word that he would have voted "Yea" had he been present.

During September 1945 Bailey opposed an increase in state unemployment pay benefits; the Senate Finance Committee defeated the Kilgore bill in a vote of ten to eight. With Representative Brooks Hays of Arkansas, Bailey in the same month introduced a rural industrialization bill. Seen in utility circles as a forerunner of much anti-utility legislation if passed by Congress, the bill proposed a Commerce-Labor-Agriculture program to encourage the setting up of small businesses in rural areas and stressed the removal of "handicaps" for such business, including high electric and transportation rates and inadequate utility services. Bailey made known his stand on several important issues in the month of October. He supported the President's nomination of Raymond S. McKeough to the Maritime Commission (McKeough, ardent New Dealer and a Midwest regional director of CIO's Political Action Committee, was approved by the Senate committee); he declared himself in favor of universal military training, and supported the President on sharing scientific development of nuclear energy but retaining the secret of the atomic bomb's manufacture. In the Palestine crisis, Bailey threatened to fight in the Senate any move made by the United States toward assuming responsibility for the setting up of a Jewish state.

The Senator holds honorary Doctor of Laws degrees from Wake Forest College (1931), Colby College (1938), and Duke University (1941). He also received the Doctor of Letters degree from Elon College, North Carolina, in 1939. He is an honorary member of the Omicron Delta Kappa fraternity. Bailey has been married to the former Edith Pou since August 16, 1916; their five children are James Hinton Pou, Annie Elizabeth, Josiah William, Edith Pou, and Sallie. The family home is in Raleigh, North Carolina.

Bailey is an eloquent speaker, given to biblical and historical allusions. In a Senate debate he once spoke of John L. Lewis '42 as "that modern Catiline, unmatched by any Cicero so far, at the head of the mine workers." On one occasion, when answering an attack by Secretary of the Interior Harold L. Ickes '41,

Bailey delivered a sixty-eight-hundred-word oration on forgiveness. He has a resonant voice and emphatic manner, coupled with a habit of desk-pounding which has caused him "to split a knuckle at least once." Of medium build, the dignified Southerner has piercing eyes and a lean, angular face. While he has been described as "shrewdly amiable," he rarely smiles, and his sober demeanor is said to give little hint of talent for expansive expression. When Bailey asked Congress in early 1944 to appropriate twenty thousand dollars to survey the fishing resources of the country, the newspapers carried amusing reports of the session. One paper remarked: "Make no mistake about it—Bailey's a fisherman. He thinks nothing of inviting a dozen people out to his cabin at Beaver Dam for a fish dinner and not wetting a line until 5:00 P. M."

References

Nation 132:11-12 Ja 7 '31
Congressional Directory, 1945
National Cyclopædia of American Biography Current vol D p440
Who's Who in America, 1944-45
Who's Who in the Nation's Capital, 1938-39

BAKER, S(ARA) JOSEPHINE Nov. 15, 1873—Feb. 22, 1945 Noted physician and child-health specialist; director of Bureau of Child Hygiene of New York City's Department of Health (1909-23); the city's infant death rate was greatly reduced under her leadership; consulting director for the Children's Bureau of the United States Department of Labor and in 1917 served as consultant in child hygiene in the United States Public Health Service.

Obituary

N Y Times p17 F 23 '45 por

BALDWIN, WILLIAM H(ENRY) Sept. 17, 1891- Public relations counsel; social service leader

Address: b. National Urban League, 1133 Broadway, New York City; Baldwin and Mermey, 205 E. 42d St., New York City; h. New Canaan, Conn.

A descendant of a long line of public-spirited citizens of Colonial New England stock, William H. Baldwin is an active worker in the cause of the Negro and also one of the top public relations counsels in the United States. As president of the National Urban League, an organization devoted to social service among Negroes, he is carrying on a work inaugurated by his mother in 1910.

Born in Saginaw, Michigan, on September 17, 1891, William Henry Baldwin is the son of William Henry Baldwin, Jr., and Ruth Standish (Bowles) Baldwin. The first record of philanthropy in the Baldwin branch of the family is that of the publicist's grandfather, William Henry Baldwin, who gave up a prosperous business to devote himself to the Young Men's Christian Union, an organization in Boston. And William Henry Baldwin, Jr., while serving as vice-president of the Southern Railway, became interested in the Negro's problem in the South. He became a stanch supporter of

Booker T. Washington, and from 1897 until his death in 1905 acted as a trustee of the Tuskegee Institute. It is significant, too, that the present William Henry Baldwin's mother is the daughter of Samuel Bowles, who, as the owner and editor of the Springfield (Massachusetts) *Republican*, worked for the abolition of slavery in pre-Civil War days. The Springfield *Republican*, the first daily newspaper in Massachusetts outside of Boston, was founded in 1824 by the publicist's great-grandfather, a descendant of a Boston pewterer.

When William Baldwin was born his father was general manager of the Flint and Pere Marquette Railroad, whose offices were in Saginaw, Michigan. Young William attended the Hackley School in Tarrytown, New York (1906-08), the Phillips Academy in Andover, Massachusetts (1909), and then entered Harvard University, the alma mater of his father. Completing his undergraduate work in three years, he spent the next at the University of Wisconsin, returning to Harvard to take his B.A. with his class, that of 1913.

Choosing a newspaper career, in which his maternal ancestors had won distinction, Baldwin became a reporter in the city room of the New York *Evening Post* in August 1914. In June 1917 he resigned from that paper to enlist in the United States Naval Reserve. From chief yeoman he rose to the rank of an ensign in October of 1917.

Receiving his discharge from the Navy in 1919, Baldwin joined the staff of the American International Corporation. In 1922 he assumed his first big task for the Negro cause by directing a campaign to raise a million dollars for Fisk University, the Negro institution in Nashville, Tennessee. Upon the completion of that undertaking Baldwin became the first executive secretary of the American Arbitration Association, which was organized in 1926 by Jules S. Bache, John D. Rockefeller, Jr., Charles M. Schwab, and other prominent men for settling disputes out of court. Not only has the association saved millions of dollars in lawyers' fees for its clients, but it also has expedited adjustments. Cases brought before the board often have had a hearing one hour later and a decision in another two hours.

In June 1926 Baldwin resigned from the association to establish his own public relations office. In 1942 the firm name was changed to Baldwin and Mermey. *Coronet* Magazine reports that Baldwin's most outstanding accomplishment as a publicist was his work on the reorganization of the drug firm McKesson and Robbins. "In accepting that job," says *Coronet*, "he met one of the most dramatic challenges of the day." The reorganization was the outcome of a Government investigation of the firm which had led to the arrest in December 1938 of its president, Frank D. Coster, on the charge of violation of the SEC act. Further investigation disclosed that Coster's real name was Musica and that he was a former convict. With his brothers, Musica had been leading a dual existence, dealing in arms concealed in drug shipments, and violating other laws. Before Federal authorities could conduct him to trial, he committed suicide. The scandal made nationwide headlines. Continuation of the Government's investigation of the case, and the many suits brought by stock-

Bachrach

WILLIAM H. BALDWIN

holders of the drug company, kept the story in the news until 1941, while the business world believed that the firm could never survive the scandal. Much credit for the restoration of the firm's prestige and reorganization has been given to Baldwin and Mermey. The public relations firm also served in mobilizing public support for extension of the Reciprocal Trade Agreements Act in 1943 and again in 1945, and in counseling the National Association of Broadcasters in its fight with James C. Petrillo '40.

Two of the welfare organizations with which Baldwin has been associated were "inherited" from his parents. In September 1910 his mother called a conference in New York (to which the family had moved after the appointment of Baldwin's father to the presidency of the Long Island Railroad Company) of representatives of the Committee for Improving the Industrial Conditions of Negroes in New York and the League for the Protection of Colored Women. From this conference discussion of the urban social and economic conditions of the Negro sprang the National Urban League. Today the league has local affiliates in fifty-one cities throughout the country and more than two thousand active members of the Urban League boards and committees are attacking problems of employment, housing, health, recreation, education, and racial tension. The number of full-time employed staff members has risen to over three hundred. A sum of $100,000 expended by the national office in 1944 was supplemented by an additional $700,000 by local leagues. *Opportunity, Journal of Negro Life*, the league's official organ, completed its twenty-second year in 1944. The program of the organization outlines three goals: 1) Co-operation of welfare movements in an effort to apply to the Negro urban population the benefits of modern social service; 2) practical programs of amelioration of antisocial and destructive social and economic forces; 3) the training of Negro social workers so that they

BALDWIN, WILLIAM H.—*Continued*

themselves may not only accelerate social work among their own people, but pool their resources with those of white social workers for the good of society in general. It is stated in the league's 1944 annual report: "In the revulsion of public opinion against the disastrous race riots of 1943, hundreds of American communities organized official or unofficial committees to promote better race relations and public morale." Because of the geographical redistribution of Negroes to the North and the West, a movement which began after the First World War and has been accelerated since 1942, the problems of the Negro have become of greater National concern. The migrations have brought to light basic discriminations in the North and the West, for example, in the areas of employment and housing. These, in particular, "demand vigorous and constructive measures of national statesmanship."

Closely connected with the National Urban League since its beginning, young Baldwin became a member of its executive board in 1915. The following year he organized the Brooklyn Urban League, of which he subsequently became president, an office he held until 1927, except for his period of service in the Navy. In 1942 Baldwin became the president of the national body. Concerning the war effort of the thirteen million Negroes in the United States, Baldwin has said: "These millions of colored men and women are so thoroughly loyal that they not only seek but demand a real partnership in winning the war."

Baldwin was treasurer of the Committee of Fourteen, his inheritance in the way of civic work, when the organization went out of existence in 1932. (This group had succeeded the Committee of Fifteen which his father had headed but which was disbanded after he died in 1905.) The *Literary Digest* in 1932 reported that when the Committee of Fourteen "flamed into action against commercialized vice in 1905 . . . vice stalked, unafraid and unashamed." Much of the credit for vice suppression, the article stated, was due the committee. Later, however, the committee was to be criticized for incautious zeal which led to the arrest of innocent persons, a situation disclosed by the Seabury investigation of the thirties and by Raymond Moley[45] in his *Tribune of the People* (1933), a survey of the New York magistrate courts. "Unfortunately," said Baldwin, "there rose a public hysteria over the 'framing' of innocent women, and the impression developed in some quarters that the Committee of Fourteen either was a party to such methods, or was derelict in not having exposed them. In spite of all of this, however, the New York newspapers, upon learning all of the facts, re-established, with few reservations, their traditional confidence in the committee and its work." On its disbandment, because of lack of funds, the New York *Times* commented that the "single blemish" on the committee's record "should not outweigh the notable services it rendered this community [New York City] during the past quarter of a century."

In addition to serving as president of the National Urban League, Baldwin is a trustee of Fisk University; a director of Sydenham Hospital (New York), the country's first com-

pletely interracial hospital; a member of the finance committee of the Southern Education Foundation; treasurer of the American War-Community Services; director of the National Policy Committee. He has served as chairman of the National Association of Public Relations Counsel, as trustee of the New School for Social Research and of its Graduate Faculty, the "University in Exile." He is in 1945 in his third successive term as an elected member of the Board of Education at New Canaan, Connecticut, where he makes his home.

Baldwin has written *The Shopping Book* (1929), an aid to the housekeeper in judging and buying merchandise; and he contributed articles to the *Public Opinion Quarterly* during 1940, 1941, and 1944, and to the Harvard *Business Review* in 1942. His recreations are gardening and paddle tennis. Described as "faintly professorial in appearance," Baldwin wears glasses, has hazel eyes, brown hair, is five feet ten inches tall, and weighs one hundred and seventy pounds. In 1916 he was married to Cecilia Brewster. They have three children—William Henry, Walter Brewster, and George Lee.

References

Coronet 13:143 N '42 por
Who's Who in New York, 1938

BANNING, KENDALL Sept. 20, 1879— Dec. 27, 1944 American author and war veteran; editor of *Cosmopolitan* (1919-21), and *Popular Radio* (1922-28); attained rank of major in First World War and after 1922 was lieutenant colonel in the Signal Reserve; a few of his many books include, *West Point Today* (1937), *Annapolis Today* (1938), *The Fleet Today* (1941), *Submarine, the Story of Undersea Fighters* (1942), and *Our Army Today* (1943).

Obituary

N Y Times p19 D 28 '44

BARBEY, DANIEL E(DWARD) Dec. 23, 1889- United States naval officer

Address: b. c/o Navy Department, Washington, D. C.; h. 2810 N. E. 24th Ave., Portland, Ore.

Hailed by newsman Frazier Hunt as "Uncle Dan, the amphibious man," Vice-Admiral Daniel E. Barbey is credited with the development of amphibious type of warfare. Inventor of the "duck," a dual-purpose boat on wheels, he answered during the war years 1943-45 to the title of commander of the United States Amphibious Force, Seventh Fleet. In that capacity he was, in the words of *Newsweek*, the "key man who made General Douglas MacArthur's[41] island-hopping possible." Three months after V-J Day, in mid-November, he was made commander of the Seventh Fleet, succeeding Admiral Thomas C. Kinkaid[44]; and before the end of the year he was named commander of Atlantic Amphibious Forces.

Daniel Edward Barbey was born December 23, 1889 in Portland, Oregon, the son of John and Julia (Chlopeck) Barbey, and the grandson of Oregon pioneers. He was appointed to the Naval Academy from Oregon in 1908, and was commissioned an ensign in 1912. He saw service first in the armored cruiser *California*, from which he was transferred in July 1914 to the destroyer *Lawrence* as engineering officer; he assumed command of the vessel about April 1915 as an ensign. While serving as engineering officer of the gunboat *Annapolis*, 1916-17, he was awarded a letter of commendation by the Secretary of the Navy for services rendered in rescuing members of the crew of the grounded *Paddleford*. He was executive officer on the destroyer *Stevens*, when he was ordered to duty with the United States Naval Forces in Europe in December 1918. His first foreign duty was as naval port officer at Cardiff, Wales. Six months later he joined Naval Headquarters Staff in London. His next assignment was as aide on the staff of, and flag secretary to, and operations officer for, Rear Admiral Mark L. Bristol, commander of the United States Naval Forces in Turkish waters and High Commissioner to Turkey. Barbey was the American delegate on the Allied commission for control for trade with Turkey during his duty with Admiral Bristol.

During 1922-23 Barbey served as assistant engineer officer of the battleship *Oklahoma*. Then, after two years as officer in charge of the Navy Recruiting Station in his home town of Portland, he was married to Katharine Graham. Three years later, after serving as engineering officer of the cruiser *Cincinnati* and executive officer of the Navy oil tanker *Ramapo*, he was made aide and flag secretary to the Superintendent of the Naval Academy at Annapolis. He was also secretary to the Academic Board of the Naval Academy. In June 1931 he assumed command of the destroyer *Lea*. Two years later he was officer in charge of naval ordnance at the ammunition depot at Mare Island, California. In February 1935, a commander, he joined the battleship *New York* as damage control officer. In April a year later he was in the *Ramapo* again, this time as commanding officer. Then followed a period as commander of Destroyer Division No. 17, from June 1936 to 1937. He reported for duty at the end of that period to the Bureau of Navigation of the Navy Department, Washington, D. C., in charge of the War Plans Section. He was made captain during this period. In May 1940 he was in the *New York* again, as its commanding officer; and in January 1941 he became chief of staff and aide to Rear Admiral Randall Jacobs, commander of the Service Force and Amphibious Force, Atlantic Fleet.

Barbey was one of the few Navy men who possessed foresight about amphibious warfare. He became interested in it as early as 1937 when he was in charge of the War Plans Section, Bureau of Navigation, now known as Bureau of Naval Personnel. A small boat with a ramp used in the Sino-Japanese war had kindled his imagination. He studied pictures of it, and by late 1940 the Higgins boat, precursor of the craft technically called Landing Craft, Vehicle, Powered, but without a ramp, was being developed by the Navy. By that time, too, an amphibious force had been accepted as part of the Atlantic Fleet Service Force. In the summer of 1941, as chief of staff to Admiral Randall Jacobs, Barbey was ordered to organize a new amphibious force. With little information available, it was pioneering work. Barbey began by practicing amphibious maneuvers off the coast of North Carolina with

U. S. Navy

VICE-ADM. DANIEL E. BARBEY

fifty-foot, flat-bottom, front-door landing boats and "a little flock of lumbering, inefficient amphibious 'alligators.'" Then, named head of the Amphibious Warfare Section by Admiral Ernest J. King [42], he was given the job of organizing a workable unit "from scratch."

Barbey had a difficult and untried task ahead: the problem of lifting an army—the troops and all the interrelated parts that make up an army—to the objective, then getting it ashore and through the initial battle. The command was then to pass to the regular ground force chiefs. In one word, the amphibious force was to be the "starter" for all invasions. The value of this force has been pointed up by the losses in other wars. "At Gallipoli," said Frazier Hunt, "brave Aussies and New Zealanders, sent ashore in ordinary ships and boats, had jumped the surf, struggled through barbed-wire entanglements hidden below the water, and in the end were mowed down by Turkish machine guns."

As the work of organizing this new amphibious force got under way, odd-looking designs began to appear on drafting boards and odd-looking contrivances then emerged. One was the Landing Ship, Dock. A "long, lean ship, it could hold numbers of small craft, loaded in turn with 'alligators', 'buffaloes', 'ducks', troop barges, tank carriers, and bulldozers. Arriving at the scene of action, the LSD would intake water, sink into the sea, open its back doors, release its load, and shuttle back for another."

Barbey's "duck"—his invention—made a dramatic debut in the National Capital. As the account was printed in *Newsweek*—"A strange mechanical contrivance that looked like the ill-conceived offspring of a motor vehicle and a seagoing barge rumbled through Washington streets from the Navy Department." Crossing the Potomac bridge, the story went, the object slid gently into a lake while a policeman waved his hands impotently on the sandy shore. As soon as the nameless thing hit dry land again

BARBEY, DANIEL E.—*Continued*

all the occupants were promptly arrested for invading a bird sanctuary.

Another part of the task confronting Barbey was the problem of how best to load and unload Liberty ships, freighters, and troopships, as well as his new landing craft. Unloading was a precarious business, and five days was then the best record for unloading a big supply ship. Barbey reduced this to five hours. Speed could not be overstressed in amphibious operations. While shuttling to and from beaches the big vessels were invitations to enemy torpedoes and dive bombers.

Today, landings are almost a guaranteed success. A preliminary concentration of naval fire batters enemy defenses; simultaneously, the air arm bombs rear positions to break up enemy communications. As the landing craft near the beaches and come within range of their own fire, that suddenly changes and rocket tubes fired from deck tubes on the landing craft blast a clear path the rest of the way. It is this last send-off that instills confidence, according to Barbey: "When the fellows in the boats see those rockets it gives them a lot of encouragement." Before the Philippine invasion Barbey, by that time a rear admiral, advanced the claim that the Army could force landings on any given beachhead with sufficient men and sufficient air and naval preparation and support.

Toward the end of 1942, in reply to MacArthur's plea for an amphibious force, Barbey (in December 1942 appointed a rear admiral) was sent to the Southwest Pacific. There in January he took over the command of the Amphibious Force of the Seventh Fleet. But he had to wait three months for the necessary parts. Then, early in April 1943 they began to arrive "in twos and threes—in tiny squadrons and flotillas," and they were manned by inexperienced men. Time and trained reserves had been too short to find any alternatives for them. But Barbey was loud in their praise. "They were wonderful," he declared. Those who were not, found out that Barbey liked "starch" in his discipline and did not follow the Navy custom of easing the washouts, gradually and gently, out of command. But he promoted good men as fast as he weeded out the inefficient ones, and the results brought in dividends in the way of fighters, tough and excellent.

For his action on Lae on September 4, 1943, and at Finschhafen on September 22, 1943, Barbey was awarded the Navy Cross, with the citation: "You personally led your force to the beachheads, and in the face of repeated enemy air attacks, you successfully launched and directed the . . . landings which . . . resulted in complete victory for our forces." He received the Distinguished Service Medal "for exceptionally meritorious service to the Government . . . as commander of the Amphibious Forces of the Seventh Fleet from January 8, 1943, to May 12, 1944. Skillfully building and developing an organization from men and material untried in battle . . . Rear Admiral Barbey contributed immeasurably to the success of the campaigns in New Britain, New Guinea, and the Admiralties." In June 1944, just before the Normandy invasion, Barbey was called back to Washington to give his views as an expert

on the greatest landing ever planned. He was raised to vice-admiral.

Landing operations followed fast upon one another in 1945. After the Lingayen landing in early January, the largest of its kind yet made in the Pacific theater, Barbey's amphibious forces participated in the action at Subic Bay, Nasugbu, Bataan, Corregidor, Palawan Island, Lubang Island, Legaspi, Tawi Tawi, Masbate, and other points. In July Barbey took over-all command of the initial attack on the rich oil center in Dutch Borneo, Balikpapan. It was reported in that month that more than a million men and one and a half million tons of cargo had been landed in fifty-six amphibious operations in the Southwest Pacific under Vice-Admiral Barbey's command. With the "tremendous naval power" at America's disposal, asserted Barbey at this time, it is possible "practically to clear out any beachhead so that troops can go ashore with comparatively few casualties." When Japan's surrender the following month made the contemplated invasion unnecessary, Barbey's Seventh Amphibious Force was assigned to land Army occupation troops in Korea.

But the scene of Barbey's command soon shifted. By the middle of November, when he had been put in command of the Seventh Fleet, the landing of Chinese Nationalist troops from United States transports had been effected under his supervision at several North China ports. This use of American ships and personnel was criticized by those who saw the United States action as interference in China's factional strife, although Barbey followed a plan designed to keep American troops from becoming directly involved in hostilities. The Vice-Admiral suggested, too, that Chinese and Japanese nationals be used for transporting Chinese troops and repatriating Japanese from the territory so that American naval personnel might be sent home. Toward this end and to effect Japanese surrender terms, United States naval men began the training of Chinese crews to operate amphibious vessels. As the ranking American officer in North China he urged the Chinese Nationalists and Communists to reconcile their differences lest Manchuria secede and establish an independent state. (Barbey was scheduled to leave this post in January 1946 to take command of Atlantic Amphibious Forces.)

The successes attributed to Barbey are measured in part by his Yankee ability to "make it do." At first he had to use all his powers of persuasion to obtain even a tiny amphibious force, or "spit-kit" outfit, in Navy vernacular. He generally had to borrow equipment from Admiral William Halsey '42. Until Arawe he had not a single cruiser for prelanding bombardment. "But you can't keep Uncle Dan down," said Hunt once. "Give him a cluster of cans, a handful of small fighting craft, and he will try to lift MacArthur's men half around the world."

Stocky, gray-haired Daniel E. Barbey is an affable person, but, man of action that he is, the Admiral has no patience with red tape. A young commander once called Barbey's attention to the fact that one of the operational orders was contrary to a certain fleet training bulletin. The young man was gruffly told by Barbey to forget it and go ahead.

"But, Admiral, it simply isn't according to Bulletin 167." "To hell with Bulletin 167," roared the Admiral. "It's no good—I wrote it myself when I didn't know a damned thing about it. I know better now."

In addition to the Navy Cross and the Distinguished Service Medal, he has won a Gold Star in lieu of a second Distinguished Service Medal for "exceptionally meritorious service" as commander of the Amphibious Force, Seventh Fleet, during the period from July 2, 1944, to February 1, 1945. He also received the Grand Order of Orange Nassau (Netherlands) by Royal Decree in March 1945, and the Legion of Merit from the commander in chief of the United States Atlantic Fleet for his services in the period 1941-42.

Barbey's campaign medals include the following: Nicaraguan Campaign Medal, U. S. S. *California,* 1912; Mexican Service Medal, U. S. S. *Lawrence,* 1914; Victory Medal, Transport Clasp, U. S. S. *Stevens,* 1918; American Defense Service Medal, Fleet Clasp, 1940-41; American Theater Campaign Medal, 1941-42; Asiatic Pacific Area Campaign Medal, 1942-43; and Philippine Liberation Medal, 1944-45. MacArthur holds Admiral Barbey in high esteem: "Just about the No. 1 amphibious commander of the world," was his pronouncement.

References

Newsweek 24:31-2 O 23 '44 por
Sat Eve Post 217:24+ Jl 1 '44 por
U S News p68+ Ag 3 '45
Who's Who in America, 1944-45

BARBIER, GEORGE W. 1880(?)—July 19, 1945 American actor of stage and screen; appeared in several hundred roles during his stage career; entered motion picture field in 1930 and worked for all the major studios; known for his portrayals of "bombastic businessmen and flabbergasted fathers."

Obituary

N Y Times p11 Jl 21 '45 por

BARNARD, CHESTER I(RVING) Nov. 7, 1886- Corporation executive; USO official

Address: b. New Jersey Bell Telephone Co., 540 Broad St., Newark, N. J.; h. 333 Forest Rd., South Orange, N. J.

The president of the New Jersey Bell Telephone Company is Chester I. Barnard, chairman of the executive committee of the United Service Organizations, the wartime agency which provided recreational facilities for service personnel. As president of USO during the period of its greatest development (1942-45), he feels that it has work in the postwar years ahead in providing recreation for disabled servicemen in hospitals, and in assisting men and women in the service during the demobilization period. The USO will also provide a recreational outlet for American troops who must remain overseas for a time after the war. The son of Charles H. and Mary E. (Putnam) Barnard, Chester Irving Barnard was born in Malden, Massachusetts, on November 7, 1886. He worked his way through Mt. Hermon, one of the Northfield (Massachusetts) schools, whose students supplement academic studies with a daily work program. With scholarship aid, he spent three years at Harvard University, leaving college in 1909 to seek work.

Paul Parker Photo.

CHESTER I. BARNARD

His business career began with a clerk's position in the foreign language translation section of the statistical department of the American Telephone and Telegraph Company. Shortly afterward (1911) he was married to Grace F. Noera. (The Barnards have a daughter Frances, who is Mrs. C. Stuart Welch.)

During his early telephone career Barnard was sent to Europe by the American Telephone and Telegraph Company to make an exhaustive study of telephone practices there. In 1915 he became commercial engineer of the company, and in that capacity revised and developed the general commercial practices of the Bell system for greater efficiency. He became a recognized authority on telephone commercial practice and the economics of telephone rates, during the First World War serving as technical adviser on rates to the Rate Commission and Operating Board of the United States Telephone Administration. In 1922 he went to Pennsylvania as assistant vice-president and general manager of the Bell Telephone Company of Pennsylvania, and associated companies, becoming general manager of these companies in 1923, and vice-president in charge of operations in 1926, prior to going to New Jersey as president of the New Jersey Bell Telephone Company in 1927. This company was formed October 1, 1927, by merger of the New Jersey properties of the New York Telephone Company with the Delaware and Atlantic Telegraph Company, which operated in southern New Jersey.

Barnard has spent his entire business career in the telephone industry, although for a period he devoted all his time to the newly formed USO. Also, for many years he has participated actively in many civic affairs not connected with the telephone industry. In 1931, at the request of Governor Morgan F. Larson of New Jersey, he organized New Jersey's model Emergency Relief Administration and directed this organization for approximately two years; he served again in a reorganization

BARNARD, CHESTER I.—*Continued*
of the ERA in 1935. For a number of years
he served as a member of the board of managers of the New Jersey Reformatory for
Boys, and has been a member of the "Committee of One Hundred" sponsoring the National
Boys' Club movement. He is also a national
sponsor of Air Youth of America, and a
member of a special committee appointed by
the Secretary of Labor to study the problems
of children.

Chester Barnard represented New Jersey,
New York, Pennsylvania, and Delaware as a
director of the United States Chamber of
Commerce from 1931 to 1934; and he has
served on a number of special committees of
the Chamber of Commerce, one of which was
the committee on defense and business welfare.
In 1941 he was for a time an assistant to the
Secretary of the Treasury on a special assign-
ment. He is currently a member of the New
Jersey State Chamber of Commerce and of the
Chamber of Commerce of the State of New
York.

The USO was organized before Barnard became its president. After the passing of the
Selective Training and Service Act in Congress, social agencies felt that some provision
should be made for recreational facilities for
men and women in uniform. In October 1940
a group of people met to discuss this problem;
these people represented six agencies—the
Young Men's Christian Association, the Young
Women's Christian Association, the National
Catholic Community Service, the Salvation
Army, the National Jewish Welfare Board, and
the National Travelers Aid Association. These
agencies represented the dominant American
faiths, Protestant, Catholic, and Jewish. At
this meeting it was decided that, in order to
save duplication and waste, the six agencies
would combine to form one large organization.
(As the *Christian Science Monitor* expressed
it, " 'Let's do it together,' was the gist of that
meeting.") Less than four months later, on
February 4, 1941, the United Service Organizations for National Defense, as it was then
called, was formed, and plans were made for
approximately three hundred clubhouses for the
armed forces, to be built with Federal money
by the Federal Works Administration and
operated with USO funds. When, in October
1941, it was found that no buildings had been
erected, the project was transferred to the
United States Army's construction division
under Brigadier General Brehon Somervell [42],
and work on the clubhouses was started immediately in the nine Army corps areas.

In 1942 Chester Barnard came into the USO
picture when, on April 28, he was elected president of the United Service Organizations, Inc.,
to succeed Harper Sibley of Rochester, New
York, who had resigned because of the pressure of private business. By this time USO
had 692 units and was firmly established as a
vital force in the war effort. As Barnard became president, a campaign for thirty-two
million dollars to carry on its work was being
launched. So great was the enthusiasm for
USO that this campaign was oversubscribed;
in fact, USO has always had a good response
in its drives for funds. During the first two
years of its existence it conducted its own
money-raising campaigns, but in 1943 it became

a member of the National War Fund, which
unites the fund raising of many war-related
philanthropies in one annual nationwide campaign. In April 1945, after three years as USO
president, Barnard resigned from that office,
to continue as chairman of its executive committee.

After 1942, when Barnard assumed leadership
of the project, USO developed from an organization of less than seven hundred units to a
network of almost three thousand operations
(or units) serving the armed forces in the
continental United States, two territories, three
possessions, and fourteen overseas areas, with
USO-Camp Shows entertaining wherever men
and women in service were—in camp, hospital,
or at the front. It has been estimated that
thirty million service members each month
enjoyed the services of USO. Of the total
2,723 operations, 1,473 were conducted by USO
member agencies, 1,086 were community operated, and 164 were overseas units. Innovations
after 1942 included preparations to receive both
wounded and well servicemen at USO clubs; a
marked increase in the Hawaiian Islands units;
the organization of the National USO Council,
composed of volunteers from each state and
serving as an advisory group to guide changes
in USO policies made necessary by the shifting
course of the war; the establishment of regional
offices in Boston, New York, Richmond, Atlanta, Chicago, Kansas City (Missouri), San Antonio, and San Francisco; and the introduction
of a centralized accounting system.

USO clubs throughout the United States were
specially constructed or remodeled buildings
providing rooms for reading, writing, and
lounging; halls for dancing and entertainments;
Snack-Bars and other conveniences for servicemen and visiting wives and friends. Marcia
Davenport [44], writing in the New York *Times
Magazine,* described the USO club as a "fraternity house for a great fraternity" where,
on any night of the week, one might see homesick boys writing letters, disabled soldiers learning handicrafts, or ambitious ones studying languages—and where, of course, Boy Meets Girl.

The USO Mobile Service, sometimes called a
"Club-on-Wheels," served men at outpost stations and in maneuver areas. The Overseas
Division of the USO was composed of clubs,
lounges, and mobile units serving from Alaska
to Newfoundland to Brazil, and from Hawaii
to Bermuda; this division of the USO did not
go outside American territory (the American
Red Cross provided clubs for foreign areas),
but USO-Camp Shows, working closely with
the War Department, went wherever American
troops were stationed, and the actors and concert artists shared the discomforts and dangers
of the soldiers and sailors whom they entertained.

On February 4, 1945, this morale-building organization celebrated its fourth birthday with
special three-day Open House festivities in
clubs throughout the country, and a luncheon
meeting attended by one thousand at the Waldorf-Astoria in New York City. At the New
York meeting Major General Stephen G. Henry, Assistant Chief of Staff of the War Department, and Vice-Admiral Randall Jacobs [42],
Chief of the Bureau of Personnel of the United
States Navy, praised the work of the USO, particularly the entertainment of the USO-Camp

Shows, as being of "inestimable value" to the military success of the armed forces. Barnard also reported that one of the most difficult undertakings of the USO had been its wide service to Negroes and other colored races. "No matter what happens now," he said, "we have demonstrated that it is possible for us to perform a united service without relinquishing our special philosophy and points of view to make a total America. In the long run this accomplishment may be more important than anything we have done, for unity amid diversity is a fundamental problem of world peace."

The USO official is the author of *The Functions of the Executive* (1938) and numerous published addresses which he has made before university audiences and other groups. He is a trustee of the Northfield Schools and holds honorary degrees from Rutgers University in science, and from the University of Newark and Brown University in law. Barnard is a member of the advisory council to the department of politics at Princeton University and a Brackett Member (honorary) of the Princeton Engineering Association; a director of the Newark Institute of Arts and Sciences; and a member of the Newcomen Society of England. He was a member of the National Advisory Committee of the New York World's Fair in 1939; and late in 1945 he was appointed by President Truman '45 to a committee set up to coordinate Government medical services.

The telephone executive is a trustee and member of the executive committee of the Rockefeller Foundation; a Fellow of the American Academy of Arts and Sciences, and of the American Association for the Advancement of Science; a member of the American Philosophical Society; member-at-large of the Social Science Research Council; a director of the National Bureau of Economics Research, of the telephone company he heads, and of the Prudential Insurance Company of America, the American Insurance Company, and the Fidelity Union Trust Company, Newark, New Jersey.

Chester Barnard is a tall, well-built man who looks the part of the capable business executive. His hobby (aside from USO!) is music; he is a member of the Bach Society of New Jersey and the Newark Art Theatre, both of which he helped to found. His club memberships include the Essex Club at Harvard and the Harvard Club of New Jersey and New York, the Union League Club of New York, and the Harvard Faculty Club. In August 1944 Barnard received the Navy's Meritorius Civilian Service Award in recognition of outstanding service as senior civilian member of the Third Naval District Navy Manpower Survey Committee.

References

N Y Times p13 Ap 29 '42 por
National Cyclopædia of American Biography Current vol C p174
Who's Who in America, 1944-45
Who's Who in Commerce and Industry (1944)

BARNES, ALBERT C(OOMBS) 1872-
Art collector; educator; author

Address: Barnes Foundation, Merion, Pa.

The internationally known Philadelphian Albert C. Barnes is famous in the field of art by

ALBERT C. BARNES

reason of his fabulously valuable collection of modern art, which he has dedicated to the advancement of the educational and cultural interests of America. A wealthy scientist-manufacturer, with an unerring sense of future values of the work of new artists, he began to collect their work in the early nineteen-hundreds, many years before they became recognized by others in the art world.

Albert Coombs Barnes, born in 1872 in Philadelphia, is of American colonial stock. His father, a veteran of the Civil War, had been a butcher. Brought up in South Philadelphia, the boy attended the public schools in that city. After being graduated from Central High School, by tutoring and playing semiprofessional baseball, he was able to earn enough to pay his way through the medical school of the University of Pennsylvania.

In 1892 Barnes received the degree of M.D., following which he spent a year as resident physician in an institution for the insane so that he might study abnormal psychology. Much of what he has achieved, Barnes says today, he owes to his knowledge of psychology. In his youth he became a disciple of William James—later of John Dewey '44, who extended the James principle of pragmatism. In 1894 Barnes went to Berlin to study physiological chemistry, and in 1899 he entered the University of Heidelberg. While he completed his studies there for a Doctor of Philosophy degree, he did not take it. His thesis, however, won him an offer from Dr. Paul Ehrlich, discoverer of the famous "606" treatment for syphilis, to work as his assistant. Barnes declined. For a number of years he had been thinking of the possibility of evolving a silver nitrate compound which would have strong antiseptic powers without the burning quality of the nitrate. Returning to America, the young scientist began his experiments, many of which, it is reported, were made on the kitchen range in the Brooklyn home of Laura Leggett, who became his wife in 1901.

BARNES, ALBERT C.—*Continued*

The result of his work, called Argyrol, was put on the market in 1902. Endorsed by leading physicians of the United States and Europe, the product was an immediate success. The income from the sale of Argyrol increased steadily; Barnes at thirty-five, it is said, was a millionaire. He never patented Argyrol nor his other product, Ovoferrin. Theoretically, any other manufacturer could make and sell the compound under another name; practically, this is impossible because the formula of Argyrol is Barnes's secret.

Barnes's interest in things artistic and cultural was no sudden development. He had done a good deal of painting in his youth. In his maturity he looked at his canvases critically and burned the lot. The Barnes Foundation (which he established in 1922) may be said almost to have started in the first decade of the century, with an enrollment of ten. These ten were his employees in the Argyrol factory. Barnes established a six-hour day for his employees, and held daily informal seminars from twelve-thirty until one-thirty. The class discussed William James, then went on to Dewey, Bertrand Russell '40, and Santayana '44. Barnes's first art purchases adorned the walls of the workroom, and the student-workers discussed these, too. Barnes set up a trust fund for his employees and even after the company was sold to the Zonite Products Corporation in 1929, the employees continued to draw an income, and will continue to do so as long as they live. (The Foundation is endowed by Barnes for ten million dollars.)

Barnes began buying pictures in the early nineteen-hundreds. As his business flourished and needed less and less of his attention, he became a full-time connoisseur, going twice a year to Europe to make his purchases. He was one of the first to recognize the genius of Cézanne, Renoir, Picasso '43, Matisse '43, Monet, and Degas. He decided that they had not been recognized because of "politics" and conservatism among art officialdom, and he spent twenty thousand dollars to acquire paintings of these artists. Studying them, he became convinced that they and not the conventional painters of the times carried on the tradition of the old masters. He worked hard at what had become his life work, applying to the collection the same energy and business sense that had resulted in the success of Argyrol.

Pictures now valued in the thousands and even the hundreds of thousands of dollars Barnes "picked up" in pawnshops, garrets, and cafes for the proverbial song. He became not only a collector but a promoter in the sense that when word got about among the French artists that Barnes was taking an interest in anyone's work, that artist was "made." A dealer who had sold a Van Gogh to Barnes for six hundred dollars found that the same painting was valued at ninety thousand, twenty years later. Barnes's first Picasso cost him twenty dollars, his first Matisse fifty. He is said to have paid less than one hundred dollars for an El Greco now probably worth fifty thousand. In time Barnes became famous as the owner of the largest and best collection of French nineteenth and twentieth century art in the world. He has not, however, limited himself to one field. He has a fine collection

of the works of the old masters, considering them the ancestors of the moderns, whose cause he has espoused. And he is interested in sculpture (especially primitive Negro), furniture, and Pennsylvania handicrafts. Ker-Feal, a 177-year-old farmhouse, furnished in the period, is part of the Foundation.

For years the collector kept his acquisitions in the large house he and his wife occupied. Then, in 1921, Philadelphia became curious about modern art, and Barnes was asked to exhibit the paintings at the Pennsylvania Academy of Fine Arts, and did so. The public was aghast, and a group of alienists and psychologists pronounced the works the products of disordered minds. Barnes replied heatedly, and the next year announced his plans for the Barnes Foundation.

The gallery in which his famous twenty-million-dollar collection is housed is estimated to have cost Barnes a half million dollars. The walls of the twenty-six rooms are hung with pictures dating from 500 B.C. to the twentieth century. Barnes himself supervised their arrangement, works by moderns having been hung next to old masters so that the relationship in technique may be observed.

Barnes's idea was that the Foundation should offer free instruction in art to deserving students. At its inception he established a chair of modern art at the University of Pennsylvania and gave the students access to his gallery. Also, he announced his intention of leaving his art collection to the university. But the university officials hesitated at an association with the Foundation, with the result that Barnes "suspended" the university from further participation in his educational program.

From that time on the Barnes Foundation pursued its successful course. Its teachers, all of whom are graduates of the Foundation, select the students through personal interviews. There are now about two hundred students receiving free tuition in the art of understanding art, and there is always a waiting list of several hundred. Barnes bars sightseers—he says his students need peace and quiet. Some of the students are artists, some are studying to become art teachers in universities or colleges.

Barnes wants to teach his students an appreciation of art as related to life. Violette de Mazia, director of education at the Foundation, describes the institution as "a dream of John Dewey's—fifty years ago." (Dewey and Barnes have long been close friends. Dewey is adviser to the school, and his book, *Art as Experience*, was dedicated to Barnes.) "Stated in simple language," says Miss de Mazia, "the fundamental idea of our educational program is this: Art is not a phase of life apart from the workaday world to which one may turn in moments of leisure or perhaps in the name of so-called 'culture' or in a spirit of worship. In the Foundation's courses art is taken out of its usually detached, esoteric world and is linked up with life itself, because all the qualities which give painting its value are those which are found in various phases of everyday life, and art has value only because it expresses those qualities. In other words, 'art is a fragment of life presented to us enriched in feeling by means of the creative spirit of the artist.' We do not teach students how to paint, for that would be teaching a duck how to swim. We teach them how to learn to see; that is, to perceive the meanings in the events of everyday life, as well as in paintings, sculpture, music, furniture, objects in wrought-iron, trees, and flowers.

"We try to eradicate the almost universal, bad, confusing habit of looking at a painting for what it is not intended to be: information about subject matter, reminiscence, likeness to familiar objects, et cetera. We endeavor to create new habits of perception, that is, by observation of the component parts, the inter-relationships of which determine the form of a painting. We study the artist's language, that is, how he uses light, line, color, masses, and space, and how at all periods of time his use of these means is an index of his reaction to his particular environment; in short, we study great traditions of past and present. . . .

"The aim of the Foundation is not to defend the work of any particular school or work of art," Miss de Mazia continues, "but to provide for impartial and objective study of the art expressions of all periods, and to show the continuity of the traditions of great art throughout its history. The inherent attributes of human nature have remained the same throughout the ages; and this implies that there is no essential difference between the great art of the past and the great art of the present. . . .Unless the student grasps the meaning of these principles, and thereby acquires a new set of habits, he never arrives at the gateway of individuality or personal expression, which is the only factor that makes a man a creative artist."

In the early days of the Foundation Barnes used to lecture. He gave up this practice several years ago, but still talks informally to groups of students almost daily. They particularly enjoy his reminiscences of artists and art dealers. Barnes would also take a group of the most promising students to Europe every summer. His running commentary on the pictures in the Louvre often turned into lectures which excited the admiring attention of other visitors to the gallery. John Dewey in the summer of 1926 went along as a student. The art collector had studied with Dewey; in his late forties he became a member of Dewey's classes at Columbia, attending regularly for three years. The philosopher has said that in a lifetime spent with scholars he has not met Barnes's equal for "sheer brain power."

Barnes is an author, too, having written *The Art in Painting* (1926), which reached three editions; and, in collaboration with Miss de Mazia, *The French Primitives and Their Forms From Their Origin to the End of the Fifteenth Century* (1931), *The Art of Henri Matisse* (1933), *The Art of Renoir* (1935), and *The Art of Cézanne* (1939). The gist of much of the criticism of these books is that they are able, exhaustive, and systematic studies of their subjects. To some reviewers, the analyses in the book are lucid and sound. Other reviewers found the volumes ponderous, didactic or dogmatic.

A number of articles have been written about Barnes as an educator and an individual. Among these was a *Saturday Evening Post* series (published in the spring of 1942) which displeased him not a little. "The model

[for the articles]," declared Barnes, "is borrowed from Horatio Alger and adorned with the full and skillfully used bag of tricks of slick magazine reporting. . . . [The author] has constructed an elaborate series of fairy tales out of the record of my thirty years' efforts to advance the educational and cultural interests of America." (Other of Barnes's disagreements have been duly publicized, among them those with Alexander Woollcott [41] and Bertrand Russell.)

Albert Barnes is described as a man of good height, with a well-built, muscular body, gray hair, quick black eyes, ruddy complexion, and a firm jaw. "He looks more like an athletic coach than a student of aesthetics," it is said. In addition to his other interests, he is a thorough student of music (he played the violin in his youth) and an ardent admirer of Negro spirituals. He is an Officer of the Legion of Honor. Mrs. Barnes, "a gentle little person," is the director of the Foundation's courses in horticulture. The gardens of a twelve-acre aboretum are used as a laboratory for field study by the students. The Barnes live in an unpretentious home adjoining the gallery at Merion.

References

House & Gard 82:37 D '42 il por
Newsweek 8:26 S 12 '36 por
Outlook & Independent 154:634-5 Ap 16 '30
Sat Eve Post 214:9-11+ Mr 21 '42 il pors; 214:20-1+ Mr 28 '42 il pors; 214:18-19+ Ap 4 '42 il pors; 214:20+ Ap 11 '42 il pors

BARNES, WILLIAM R. 1867(?)—Feb. 8, 1945 American book publisher; chairman of the board of Barnes and Noble, textbook publishing house; a leading figure in promoting book selling and publishing interests throughout the United States.

Obituary

N Y Times p11 F 10 '45 por

BARTOK, BELA (bŏr'tŏk bā'lŏ) Mar. 25, 1881—Sept. 26, 1945 Hungarian composer; called one of most important composers of modern music; professor of the piano at the Royal Academy of Music at Budapest from 1907 until death; published collections of over six thousand Hungarian, Rumanian, and Arabian folk tunes; composed concertos, symphonic poems, operas, and orchestral suites. See *Current Biography* 1940 Yearbook.

Obituary

N Y Times p21 S 27 '45 por

BEACH, AMY MARCY *See* Beach, Mrs. H. H. A.

BEACH, MRS. H(ENRY) H(ARRIS) A(UBREY) 1867—Dec. 27, 1944 Celebrated American composer; produced musical settings for one hundred and fifty songs as well as composing eighty numbered works, the Mass in E Flat for chorus, orchestra, and organ, and the *Gaelic Symphony* for piano and

BEACH, MRS. H. H. A.—*Continued*
violins; before First World War made appearances as concert pianist.

Obituary

N Y Times p19 D 28 '44 por

BELLAMANN, HENRY Apr. 28, 1882–
June 16, 1945 American author and musician;
although first novel appeared in 1926, it was
not until publication of *King's Row* (1940)
that he scored a popular success; *The Floods
of Spring* (1942) and *Victoria Grandolet*
(1944) followed; chairman of examining
board of Juilliard Music Foundation (1924-
26) and dean of Curtis Institute of Music
(1931-32). See *Current Biography* 1942 Yearbook.

Obituary

N Y Times p26 Je 17 '45 por

BENAVIDES, OSCAR (RAIMUNDO)
(bä-nä-vē′thäs, ōs′kär rī-mōōn′dō) 1876—
July 2, 1945 Peruvian statesman and soldier;
President of Peru (1933-39); chief of military
junta during revolution (1914) and provisional
President (1915); Minister to Italy (1917-20),
Spain (1931), England (1932-33); Ambassador
to Spain (1940) and to Argentina (1941).

Obituary

N Y Times p13 Jl 3 '45 por

BENDIX, VINCENT 1882—Mar. 27, 1945
American inventor; founder of the Bendix
Aviation Corporation and president of Bendix
Helicopters, Inc.; was an international figure
in the field of aviation; founder and sponsor
of the Bendix Transcontinental Air Race and
donor of the Bendix Trophy.

Obituary

N Y Times p23 Mr 28 '45 por

BENTON, WILLIAM (BURNETT) Apr.
1, 1900- United States Government official
Address: b. Department of State, Washington,
D.C.; h. Southport, Conn.

Assistant Secretary of State in charge
of public affairs is William Benton, appointed
to this peacetime foreign information service of the United States by President Truman '45 in 1945. When the United States became a member of the United Nations Organization, Benton has stated, the American
people chose a policy of active participation in
world affairs and granted that security through
understanding, rather than force, was the aim
of America. "Yet the plain fact," continued
Benton, "is that as we enter this crucial period
of world history America is neither fairly nor
fully understood by the peoples of other nations." Although he has had no experience in
foreign relations, Benton is looked upon as one
of "America's busiest and most practical educators" and a "peerless sales and press agent."
After making his fortune in the advertising
business he became vice-president of the University of Chicago, where his special tasks
were the development of adult education by
radio and the improvement of classroom instruction by motion pictures.

Born on April 1, 1900, in Minneapolis, William Burnett Benton is the son of Charles
William and Elma Caroline (Hixson) Benton.
The first American Benton settled in Connecticut in 1638. Later generations of the family
have followed either the teaching profession
or the ministry. William's father was on the
faculty of the University of Minnesota for
thirty-three years, and his mother, after serving as a student assistant of secondary education (1917-18) became an assistant instructor
in the same department of Columbia University's Teachers College (1918-19). She was
also the head mistress of a St. Louis girls'
school. Before this, after the death of her
husband in 1913, Mrs. Benton had taken her
family to Montana where they lived during
four years of homesteading (1913-17).

Young Benton received his preparatory education at the Shattuck (military) School, in
Faribault, Minnesota, from which he was
graduated in 1917. Both his father and grandfather had graduated from Yale, and at his
mother's insistence young Benton took the examination for the Eastern university—but
flunked. His subsequent attendance at Carleton College in Northfield in the same state
(1917-18) was interrupted by the First World
War, during which he served in the Student
Army Training Corps at Yale. A campaign of
study was then planned by Benton and his
mother, which won his acceptance at Yale, and
in 1921 a B.A. degree. Moreover, he had maintained an excellent scholastic record, served on
the Yale *Record* as chairman of the board of
editors, and was offered a Rhodes scholarship
which he did not accept.

Benton's first effort in that direction was
made with the National Cash Register Company—selling cash registers from the tail of
a truck. Again his mother intervened, for
family tradition demanded that young Benton
follow a professional career. He agreed to
enter law, but before reaching Harvard Law
School he had secured a job as copywriter
with Lord and Thomas and later with the
George Batten advertising agency in New York.
That was in 1922. In the next five years he
attained the position of assistant manager of
the Lord and Thomas agency in Chicago, and
by 1929 that company was paying him twenty-
five thousand dollars a year, a salary they offered to double when he announced he was resigning to open his own agency.

A few months before the 1929 stock market
crash, Chester Bowles '42 and Benton formed
the advertising agency of Benton and Bowles
with a capital of eighteen thousand dollars.
The first big account was Certo for General
Foods Corporation. *Time* Magazine reports
that the two young men increased their knowledge of the market value of this gelatin product by ringing doorbells for four months and
asking housewives questions concerning it.
This preliminary survey enabled them to launch
an advertising campaign which proved so satisfactory to General Foods that the corporation turned over six additional food accounts
to Benton and Bowles in 1932, and the firm
became one of the leading advertising agencies.
Among the first to use radio as an advertising
medium, Benton and Bowles produced the Max-

well House *Showboat,* Palmolive *Beauty Box, Gang Busters,* and Fred Allen's '[41] *Town Hall Tonight.* In 1935 Benton, who had been president of the firm, became board chairman. His share of annual gross billings of $18,000,000 was $250,000. A year later, when only thirty-six, he retired from the business world.

Shortly thereafter, relates *Film and Radio Discussion Guide,* his classmate Hutchins, who had become president of the University of Chicago, asked Benton to make a survey of some of the university's problems. The erstwhile advertising man became so interested in the work that he accepted an offer of vice-presidency in the university on the condition that he would have a substantial amount of free time for related and outside activities. In his special assignment for the university, the development of adult education by radio and the improvement of classroom instruction by motion pictures, William Benton was very successful. "One result of his interest in educational broadcasting," says *Discussion Guide,* was "the very marked enlargement of the *University of Chicago Round Table.*" He was also responsible for *The Human Adventure* program which is produced by the university's radio department with the assistance of the faculty. The New York *Times* radio critic, Jack Gould, has defined the goal of the program as "bridging the chasm that ordinarily exists between the complexity of the scientist's work and the comprehension of the layman." The weekly program is now in its sixth year. It won the 1944 Peabody prize and in the summer of 1945 became one of the few educational programs to get a regular sponsor on a network basis. In late 1945 the program dealt with radar, the atomic bomb, and Einstein's '[41] theory of relativity.

When Sears, Roebuck and Company, which had acquired the *Encyclopædia Britannica* in 1920 when its owners went bankrupt, offered the publication to the University of Chicago in 1943 at Benton's suggestion, he agreed to provide the necessary working capital, to eliminate financial risk on the part of the university. (Today the university owns the preferred stock, Benton the common stock, and the university has options on his common stock at his death.) At the time of the transfer, Benton became board chairman of Britannica's United States, English, and Canadian companies. The publications issued by Encyclopædia Britannica, Inc., in addition to the encyclopedia, are *Britannica Year Book, Britannica Junior,* and *Britannica World Atlas.*

The only change of importance announced at that time was that the university faculty would become the official advisory staff of the publications, supervising the continuous revisions which the set of books undergoes. To insure "extreme vigilance in reading for revision, the Britannica company established fellowships at the University of Chicago. Fellows do the preliminary reading and make recommendations to faculty members, who in turn may recommend revision by experts." Among the group, besides Benton, who determined the policies of the Britannica project were Robert Hutchins, Henry R. Luce '[41], president of Time, Inc., and Paul G. Hoffman, president of the Studebaker Corporation. Another change in Britannica under Benton was the purchasing of contempor-

Rudolph H. Hoffmann
WILLIAM BENTON

ary American art. Then it was planned to exhibit the paintings throughout the United States in order to focus nationwide attention on American art. Accordingly, the Encyclopædia Britannica Collection of Contemporary American Paintings (117 paintings) held its first exhibition on April 12, 1945, at the Art Institute of Chicago. This collection, reported *American Artist,* is only the beginning—each year new paintings by known and new artists will be added to the collection. A champion of audio-visual education, Benton also negotiated Britannica's purchase of Erpi Classroom Films and the acquisition by the university through a gift of the Eastman Teaching Films, which have since been combined under the name, Encyclopædia Britannica Films, Inc.

The list of Benton's activities after retirement from business in 1936 continued to expand. He became vice-chairman of the non-profit organization, Committee for Economic Development, which he helped to found in 1942. (He was also chiefly responsible for proposing and stimulating the research side of C.E.D.) "In two years," stated *Fortune's* October 1944 issue, "C.E.D. has expanded to embrace 50,000 business men. . . .Its research division employs top-flight economists to study policies bearing on reconversion and prosperity. Its field development division gets individual business men to plan their postwar production now, so reconversion strains will be minimized and business' own sights set for high employment."

In his capacity of vice-chairman of C.E.D., Benton, with Eric Johnston '[43], made a trip to England in the summer of 1943 ·to study the possibility of "a friendly and profitable economic policy" between the two nations. Alarmed by the situation he found there, Benton, on his return to the United States, contributed articles on the subject to a number of leading magazines, including *Saturday Evening Post* and *Life.* He outlined five major areas of potential economic conflict between

BENTON, WILLIAM—*Continued*

the United States and Britain, namely, tariffs and other trade barriers, monetary stabilization, shipping policy, international aviation, and cartels. In fact, it was Benton's incisive comments on Anglo-American trade relations, reports *Business Week*, which drew attention to his qualifications for a post in the State Department.

In 1940 Benton gave his moral and financial support to Marshall Field [41] and others in setting up the paper *PM*. (His financial interest in the paper was disposed of shortly after its publication.) In 1938 he was made a trustee of the Shattuck School. He has acted on the Advisory Committee of the Office of Co-ordinator of Inter-American Affairs and as vice-chairman of the United States Commission of Inter-American Development Commission. He owns Associated Music Publishers, which holds the copyright on a high percentage of classical, chamber, and operatic music in America. It operates Muzak Transcriptions company which supplies music by wire to its subscribers. In 1938 Benton had a series of articles in the *Ladies' Home Journal* on education by radio, remedial reading instruction, and other related subjects in the field of education. Other articles by him on timely subjects have appeared in *Fortune, Reader's Digest, Life,* and the *Saturday Evening Post.*

After his appointment to Assistant Secretary of State in charge of public affairs, Benton resigned from his other positions. At his first press conference after assuming office (September 1945), his failure to say how he would discharge the heavy responsibilities of his new post disappointed newsmen. In addressing the New York *Herald Tribune* Forum on Current Problems in late October, however, Benton was more articulate regarding his plans. To remedy the fact that peoples of other lands do not know "the real America" (they regard us, says Benton, as either a "veritable Uncle Santa Claus" or an "Uncle Shylock"), radio, motion pictures, and information centers will be used as media of information. Referring to the *Voice of America*, a wartime Government radio broadcast which through thirty-eight shortwave transmitters operating in different parts of the globe broadcast news of the United States in forty languages, Benton said: "Today in the backwash of the war they [the *Voice of America* broadcasts] go out in eighteen languages . . . news untainted by special pleading or propaganda. . . .There should be Government information service abroad to strengthen America's voice." (For foreign service, the use of about four hundred information officers is contemplated.) As special assistant in his department, which at the time of his appointment was more or less in the embryonic stage, Benton has appointed John Howe, his former assistant at the University of Chicago. Among his consultants are Ralph McGill, editor of the Atlanta *Constitution,* Colonel John Hay Whitney [45], and Harold Lasswell.

Benton is an Episcopalian, a member of Zeta Psi, and of the clubs Fairfield Country and Pequot Yacht (Connecticut), Yale, University (New York), Chicago, Quadrangle (until 1945). In 1928 he was married to Helen Hemingway. The Bentons, who have a home in Southport, Connecticut, have four children, three of whom are adopted. They are Charles William, Helen Orr, Louise Hemingway, and John Hemingway. The half-smile Benton usually wears and "the whimsy that lurks in his eyes, bespeak the tolerance which happens to be one of his characteristics." Since assuming his State Department post he has worked twelve to fourteen hours a day.

References

Bsns W p8 S 15 '45
Film and Radio Directory Guide 11:5-6 My '45 por
N Y Herald Tribune IX p12 N 4 '45 por
N Y Sun p22 O 25 '45
Time 27:52 Je 29 '36 por
America's Young Men, 1938-39
Who's Who in America, 1944-45
Who's Who in Commerce and Industry (1944)

BERGEN, EDGAR Feb. 16, 1903- Ventriloquist

Address: b. c/o National Broadcasting Co., Hollywood, Calif.; h. 9876 Beverly Grove Dr., Beverly Hills, Calif.

"The art of ventriloquism is merely that of cultivating a 'grunt,' " says the ventriloquist Edgar Bergen, whose perfected "grunt" is the voice of lively, impertinent Charlie McCarthy, one of the most popular entertainers on the screen and the air waves. In the course of the Bergen-McCarthy partnership, which began about 1920, two other figures have been admitted to the "family," but Charlie maintains a comfortable lead. In fact, he has a way of reminding his creator that even the Bergen fame and fortune are of his making.

America's most successful ventriloquist was born Edgar John Bergren, February 16, 1903, in Chicago, where his Swedish parents, John and Nellie (Swanson) Bergren, had a retail dairy business for a time. While the boy was still small they also lived on a farm near Decatur, Michigan; and when he was four he was taken on a visit to Sweden, where he learned to speak Swedish—hence Charlie McCarthy's fluency in that tongue. The family then returned to America, to live in Chicago again.

It was there that the eleven-year-old boy discovered quite by accident that he could do strange things with his voice. Quentin Reynolds [41] described the event in an article in *Collier's:* One day, when Edgar was standing on the porch of his home he called a greeting to a passing friend, who, instead of returning the greeting to Edgar, called to another boy standing on a porch three houses away from Edgar's. At school that afternoon the future ventriloquist pondered over the phenomenon. Then, on his way home he tested his newly found gift by hailing another boy, who exclaimed, "Who was that calling me, anyhow?" Edgar continued to practice his vocal tricks, progressing so well that "his mother was forever answering the door in response to pleas of mysterious old men who begged to be let in." Before long Edgar's interests had extended to sleight of hand tricks and he was spending his small savings on boxes of magic paraphernalia. One of his purchases was a twenty-five-cent book on ventriloquism, with which he set about developing his talent for "voice diffusion." And when the famous ventriloquist Harry Lester played in Chicago, writes Don Drury in *Coronet* (March 1945), Edgar often watched his performances. When the boy was about fifteen years old he impressed Lester so much that Lester gave him, without charge, almost daily lessons for three months in the fundamentals of ventriloquism.

Meanwhile, young Bergen went on to high school, attending the Lane Technical and Lakeview schools. It was then that Charlie McCarthy was born. The inspiration for the impish dummy was a tough Irish newsboy, and the head was carved in white pine by a carpenter named Theodore Mack, who followed young Bergen's specifications. In gratitude Bergen added a Celtic suffix to the carpenter's name—and Charlie McCarthy was christened. While Charlie's head cost thirty-five dollars, Bergen himself made the body. The newly whittled brash youth was an immediate success, delighting Bergen's classmates and teachers. The dummy, incidentally, helped his master pass an important history course by completely charming the teacher. He continued to assist Bergen financially at Northwestern University, where the latter's first courses were in premedical subjects: Bergen earned his college expenses by giving a combination magic-ventriloquism act at private parties. During Lyceum circuits. Bergen's college activities the summer he appeared on the Chautauqua and also included dramatics, for it was his first ambition to be an actor. On this point the ventriloquist now comments: "The nearest I ever came to that was to work for the Little Theatre in Decatur. I played the piano before the show and during the intermissions. And to make it more degrading, it was a player piano."

Presently Bergen abandoned both his premedical study and his thoughts about an acting career to enter vaudeville. With Charlie he rose from the small-time circuits to two-a-day engagements. His popularity continued to grow, and from 1926 to 1936 the two toured America and went abroad to perform in Iceland, England, Sweden, and Russia. In Sweden they appeared in musical comedy, in an act in *Rolfe's Revue*, and gave a command performance before the Crown Prince. Bergen also played in South America; once he performed at a colony of lepers in Venezuela, where Charlie used the international idiom of song before an audience confined behind an iron grating.

With the eclipse of vaudeville, in the early thirties, Bergen polished his routine for night clubs. He was very successful with an act called "The Operation," in which he played the doctor, Charlie the patient, with a nurse in attendance. This act was based on reality: Bergen had recently undergone an operation— he had argued with the doctors and experienced the usual qualms of a patient—all of which he transformed into a satirical comedy. Again he was a hit in European capitals and in New York, where he was engaged by the de luxe Rainbow Room in Rockefeller Center. One night in 1936, on the invitation of Elsa Maxwell [*12], he performed at a party where one of the guests, Noel Coward [*41], congratulated Ber-

EDGAR BERGEN

gen on his fine dialogue. A week later, on December 16, Bergen was on Rudy Vallée's radio program, for which he received one hundred and fifty dollars.

That was the beginning of the radio career of Bergen and McCarthy. Instantly successful, they made frequent appearances on the Vallée show until Bergen signed a contract for his own program with Chase and Sanborn in May 1937. Since then he has received consistently high ratings in radio popularity polls. For two and one-half years he held first place. In December 1945, after eight years on the air, the Bergen-McCarthy team ranked fifth in the radio listeners' favor, as determined by the Hooper poll. The "magnificent splinter" has been joyously lampooning prominent personalities who appear as guests on the Bergen show. On one occasion he asked Orson Welles [*41], "Why don't you release a blimp for active service?"; and at another time he referred to Emily Post [*41] as a "vulture for culture." Such are the flippant verbal assaults, written by Bergen, which audacious Charlie expresses.

In the normal course of events Bergen and McCarthy went to Hollywood to engage in film work. (Before rising to radio stardom, Bergen had written and played in short films for Warner Brothers. Among these early shorts were *The Operation, Office Scandal, Donkey Business, The Eyes Have It, Free and Easy*, and *Africa Speaks English*.) In 1938 Bergen was featured in a two-million-dollar musical, *Goldwyn Follies*. That year he also appeared in Universal's *A Letter of Introduction*. Bergen received a special wooden "Oscar" from the Motion Picture Academy "for the outstanding comedy creation of 1938." The next year his ventriloquial talents were used in two more Universal pictures, *You Can't Cheat an Honest Man*, with W. C. Fields, and *Charlie McCarthy, Detective*. His next film was an RKO production, *Look Who's Laughing* (1941). In 1943 Bergen was one of the many stars in *Stage Door Canteen*. Reviewing this film, one writer

BERGEN, EDGAR—*Continued*

stated that when Bergen, "manipulates that fugitive from a picket fence, the show has great specialties." The next Bergen-McCarthy opus, in 1944, was *Song of the Open Road*, in which Charlie resumed an old feud with W. C. Fields. It was reported in October 1945 that Bergen, Charlie, and Mortimer Snerd would co-star in *Mickey and the Beanstalk,* a combined "live" action and animated cartoon feature, for Walt Disney '46.

With his radio and motion picture work, Bergen's finances have thrived. His sponsor in 1945 raised his weekly salary to ten thousand dollars, and he receives a hundred and fifty thousand for a motion picture. In addition, Charlie McCarthy toys, games, and jewelry, bring Bergen an annual seventy-five thousand dollars. In February 1945 *Variety* reported that Bergen's radio show was being offered to theaters for twenty-five thousand dollars a week, the "highest guaranty ever asked for a package show." Bergen's personal appearances have taken him into such de luxe spots as the Waldorf-Astoria Wedgewood Room. And other high places into which he will introduce Charlie are the Governors' mansions of the United States. The first of this series of broadcasts, which will run for two years, was held in Oklahoma in late 1945, when Governor Kerr of that state "guested."

Bergen maintains that the art of ventriloquisim cannot be taught since it is largely a matter of the structure of the vocal processes. His interest in his art is also scholarly—he wrote the *Encyclopedia Britannica* article on the subject. Explaining its history and technique one time in an interview, he said: "The word 'ventriloquism' comes from combining two Latin words, *'venter,'* meaning stomach, and *'loquor,'* meaning speak. Literally it is speaking from the stomach, instead of from the throat. It is a very old art, too. . . .The labials are the tough letters to get out without moving your lower lip. Letters like *m* and *p*, I mean. What I do is to make my tongue take the place of my lower lip in pronouncing labials. My tongue and the roof of my mouth really are substituted for my lips." Bergen does vocal exercises to sustain the ventriloquial quality, practicing high notes to keep Charlie's voice distinct from his own, which is naturally soft and fairly deep. Originating his own material, Bergen is considered one of the best comedy script writers in the business. In 1942 he was invited to lecture at the University of California on the subject of comedy writing. His originality was given wider scope when he added Mortimer Snerd, the yokel, to his "cast," and in 1944 he introduced the latest addition to his dummy family in the ample personage of Miss Effie Klinker. Bergen had been wary of feminine dummies since an eight-year-old wooden girl failed to please the public many years before. But Effie was the result of a Bergen performance on an NBC show for which he had no dummy and resorted to a falsetto voice he called "Ophelia." At the time he suddenly realized that "women can get into many more situations than men, particularly a bachelor maid." Hence the advent of Effie Klinker, a "ventrilowitch" of New England background and "spry libido."

In 1942 Bergen toured Army camps in Alaska with Charlie and Mortimer Snerd. The trio were a hit with the soldiers, who especially appreciated Charlie's military antics. The comedian returned impressed with the importance of entertainment in the war. In 1943 Bergen was again on tour, this time to Army and Navy bases in Newfoundland. For the trip he carried a racy two-reeler titled *The World's Greatest Lover and How I Became That Way*, starring Charlie McCarthy. Bergen filmed this vehicle himself, using the homes of Hollywood stars as background. He has long been an avid photography fan, and in his years of camera work has produced travelogues and newsreels. The entertainer's next tour, in 1944, covered Army and Navy hospitals. Bergen has also established a foundation for the training of student nurses, claiming he has been a "thwarted Dr. Kildare" since the days of his premedical work at Northwestern.

Bergen is considered as having done an excellent job in maintaining the pretense of Charlie McCarthy's individuality. Charlie's dominant personality, described as "saucy, lethally precocious, and irreverent," makes radio fans forget that he is of solid wood. Bergen keeps Charlie's age at fourteen, but Charlie's prodigious precocity often amazes his master. Sixty per cent of the voluminous Bergen-McCarthy mail is for the wooden charmer. Charlie has his own stationery inscribed with his motto: *E Pluribus Mow 'Em Downus.*

The lively fellow is manipulated by Bergen through a backflap in the figure. It is Bergen's view that "illusion is the mother of ventriloquism," and to many people Charlie is a strong illusion. Even at the radio studio his co-workers find it difficult to remember that Charlie is a dummy. Before Bergen takes his friend from his case Charlie is heard screaming profanely for release. Don Ameche, who has long worked with Bergen on the radio program, remarks, "I always have the feeling that he is a definite, living personality." Characterized by a New York *Times* writer as "a little vulgarian, a brassy, blustering, sniggering blockhead," Charlie McCarthy is nevertheless a favorite of the ladies, known as the "Casanova of Hollywood." The ogling "timber wolf" has played romantic scenes with some of filmdom's loveliest feminine stars, most often with Dorothy Lamour—"Dotty" to him.

Edgar Bergen is unlike the character he has created. He has said that Charlie's personality "is as opposite from mine as it can be, and I envy him. . . .To me it's quite remarkable that this carved piece of wood . . . should be so important. He can be invited to the White House, consulted by OWI, received by the royalty of Europe. . . .It's ridiculous, even, that my appearing any place without Charlie is a complete failure. I do think it's a case of the tail wags the dog." Bergen is really a shy, gentle man of meticulous habits and simple tastes, and is described as straightforward and nimble-witted. He is slender, five feet ten inches tall, weighing one hundred and forty pounds. He has blue-gray eyes and his receding blond hair occasions many a snide remark from Charlie. Charlie himself is thirty-eight inches tall and weighs forty pounds—a brown-eyed redhead whose top hat and tails cannot conceal the urchin heart.

In November 1945 it was revealed that Bergen had been married nearly five months. Frances Westerman, a Powers '45 model known as Frances Westcott, had become his wife in a ceremony in Mexico on June 28. The ventriloquist collects rare antiques, and for reading prefers serious music and books. He also enjoys tennis, riding, and working in his shop, where he turns out gadgets like his Electrical Ant Trap and keeps Charlie in fighting trim. (The Charlie of today, according to Drury, came from the workshop of Frank Marshall in Chicago.) Charlie lives regally in his own room, complete with well-filled closets and a private bath. His admirers will be glad to learn he has a stand-in for dangerous movie scenes and that he is insured for five thousand dollars and is provided for in Bergen's will. When he travels, his compartment is a plush-lined trunk.

Bergen is a member of the Screen Actors Guild, the Society of American Magicians, Delta Upsilon fraternity, and the Lambs :lub. Among Charlie McCarthy's honors is his appointment as first International Fire Chief. Bergen's alter ego also served as mayor of San Francisco for a day. In 1937 Northwestern University conferred an honorary degree on him, the degree of Master of Innuendo and Snappy Comeback. The citation, presented by Dean Dennis of the university's School of Speech, read: "Prince of Parasites, violent in company, churlish in behavior, acid in conversation, wooden-faced in all relationships, and thus in many respects a typical product of higher education in America." In 1944, when Bergen was decorated by King Gustav V '42 of Sweden with the Order of Vasa, First Class, for furthering American-Scandinavian relations, he immediately ordered a miniature of the decoration for his woodcrafty colleague.

References

Collier's 99:24+ Mr 20 '37 por
Read Digest 38:14+ Mr '41
Scholastic 43:19 S 20 '43 por
Time 44:54-7 N 20 '44 por
International Motion Picture Almanac, 1941-42
Who's Who in America, 1944-45

COUNT FOLKE BERNADOTTE

BERNADOTTE, FOLKE, COUNT (bĕr" nä"dôt' fôl-kĕ) Jan. 2, 1895 Swedish diplomat

Address: h. Dragongården, Djurgården, Stockholm

In the kaleidoscopic days before the actual surrender of Germany to the Allies the first week of May 1945, Count Folke Bernadotte played a brief, spectacular role as intermediary between Heinrich Himmler '41 and Great Britain and the United States, in what was the Nazis' most definite bid for peace up to that time. During the war years the Count, who is a nephew of King Gustav V of Sweden '42, had been known primarily as vice-chairman of the Swedish Red Cross and the man who had arranged for the exchange of thousands of war prisoners.

Oddly enough, kindness to war prisoners was instrumental in placing the first king of the Bernadotte dynasty on the throne of Sweden. In the course of his career as one of Napoleon's marshals, Jean Baptiste Jules Bernadotte (later governor of Hanover and Rome and Prince of Ponte Corvo), had shown leniency to Swedish war prisoners and had become friendly with Swedish officers. His resultant popularity in Sweden led, in 1810, to his election by the Riksdag as crown prince of Sweden, and in 1818 he succeeded, as Charles XIV, the childless Charles XIII.

Folke Bernadotte, Count of Wisborg (a title conferred upon his father by the Grand Duke of Luxembourg in 1892), was born in Stockholm on January 2, 1895. His father, of the fifth generation of the Bernadotte house, is Prince Oscar Carl August, second son of King Oscar II and brother of the present King. Prince Oscar renounced his rights to the throne when he was married to Ebba Henriette Munck of Fulkila, a lady of noble but nonroyal blood. Folke's boyhood was spent in Ostermalm, a section of modern Stockholm. The home life of Prince and Princess Bernadotte was characterized by a religious spirit; Biblical stories rather than fairy tales were told to young Folke, who is the second son and youngest of five children. An article written by Mac Lindahl for the *American Swedish Monthly* relates that during morning prayers he and his elder brother were not always able to maintain a fittingly solemn demeanor. The rebuke of the Prince, who for fifty years has acted as head of the Swedish YMCA, was characteristic of him: "Have a good time," he would say, "before we start being really serious."

This early religious emphasis at home brought Folke high grades in Bible study at school; English, too, was a study in which he excelled. After his early education was completed, he was entered at the officers' military school of Karlberg, the Swedish West Point. He did well in his studies there, graduating tenth in his class, and was next enrolled at the military riding school at Strömsholm. His excellent horsemanship won

BERNADOTTE, FOLKE, COUNT—*Cont.*

for him several prizes and trophies, and today he is a cavalry officer of the Royal Guards.

Count Bernadotte became known to Americans in 1928, when he was married to Estelle Romaine Manville, daughter of the late H. Edward Manville, former board chairman and president of the Johns-Manville Corporation, one of the largest asbestos concerns in the United States. The Count's introduction to the American heiress took place on the French Riviera, at a dinner given in honor of his royal uncle. "A toy balloon," relates Joachim Joesten '42, "came down near Miss Manville, who was seated next to Bernadotte, and exploded." They both laughed and from then on their acquaintance quickly developed into a romance, which led to their betrothal about two weeks later. "Pretty fast work," commented an American reporter when the Count arrived in America for the wedding, which took place on December 1, 1928. "You've got to work fast to get the best girl in the United States," quipped Bernadotte in reply.

Since his marriage Bernadotte has been a good-will ambassador to the United States on a number of occasions. In 1933 he represented his country at the Chicago Century of Progress exposition; during the New York World's Fair in 1939-40 he acted as commissioner general of the Swedish Pavilion, where he was often seen dining with his Countess. In his native land the Count is board chairman of *Det Bästa*, the Swedish edition of the *Reader's Digest*. During the Second World War he has served as head of an organization similar to the American USO; and it was due to his initiative as president of Sveriges Scoutförbund, or the Boy Scouts, that this youth group was closely linked with Sweden's defensive measures. The Scouts took an active part in the antiaircraft service of their country, and they were also trained as medical assistants.

Bernadotte's most significant war service, however, has been his work as vice-chairman of the Swedish Red Cross. In this capacity he has aided in the exchange of disabled German and British war prisoners, a service described by Britain's Foreign Minister Anthony Eden '40 as "a major humanitarian effort." The first exchange under his supervision took place by way of Sweden in October 1943. After that it was necessary for the Count to make frequent air trips to the capitals of the two belligerent countries. On one such mission he was caught in Berlin in the first heavy Allied raid over the city, in November 1943. In the course of the bombing all four of the Swedish Legation buildings were destroyed.

Early in 1945 Bernadotte arranged for the transfer of Danish and Norwegian political prisoners, held in several German camps, to a single camp operated under the supervision of the Swedish YMCA. It was while he was occupied with this work that he came into contact with Heinrich Himmler, the German commander in chief of the home front. In the opinion of Mac Lindahl, these meetings probably caused Himmler to think of the Swede in the role of an intermediary when

several months later the Germans were to seek an armistice with the Allies.

While working with the Red Cross in Germany, Bernadotte had been staying in the Swedish Legation's temporary headquarters in Friedrichsruh, near Hamburg. One day in April 1945, when all the world was anxiously awaiting signs of Germany's surrender, the Count received word that Himmler wished to see him. Hitler '42, the message said, was dying from a cerebral hemorrhage, and Himmler was therefore in the position of full authority. According to a release from the United States Department of State, the meeting arranged between Himmler and Bernadotte took place at one o'clock on the morning of April 24, in Lübeck in North Germany. The Gestapo chief proposed complete German surrender to Great Britain and the United States, with the condition that Germany be allowed to continue the resistance to the Russian armies in the East. When Bernadotte specifically asked whether the German troops in Norway and Denmark would be included in the capitulation, Himmler promised that these would also surrender, to the Americans, British, or Swedes.

With these terms, Bernadotte flew to Stockholm's Foreign Office, which, without revealing the peace emissary's name, relayed them to the British and American Ministers in Sweden. These representatives in turn notified Prime Minister Churchill '42 and President Truman '45. According to the story as it was later revealed, Truman went to the Pentagon Building in Washington on the afternoon of April 25 to hold a conference with Secretary of War Stimson '40, Acting Secretary of State Grew '41, General Marshall '40, and Admirals King '42 and Leahy '41. Transatlantic telephone conversations with Churchill resulted in the agreement to notify Stalin '42 of the Himmler offer and the British-American decision to accept only unconditional surrender to the three Allied Governments on all fronts. The next day the Swedish Foreign Office was informed, and on April 27 peace courier Bernadotte took off from Stockholm for Flensburg, Germany, just below the Danish border, to acquaint Himmler with the Allied rejection of his terms.

Up till April 28 no news of the closely guarded secret had leaked out, but on that day, a Saturday, news of the peace offer broke in all three Allied countries. The Moscow radio announced that the Tass agency had been authorized to state that reports of Himmler's offer had been confirmed in responsible Soviet quarters. Downing Street, while refusing either to confirm or deny the news, declared that the Allies would accept peace overtures only if they were made to all three Governments. That evening Senator Tom Connally '41, head of the Senate Foreign Relations Committee and delegate at the San Francisco conference, announced to an Associated Press reporter that Germany had surrendered unconditionally, with "no strings attached," after the United States and Great Britain had rejected a two-way surrender. Within a few minutes the A.P. had the scoop on the air, and a wave of celebration swept the excited country before the story could be denied. The Nazi-controlled Danish Radio, meanwhile, admitted that Bernadotte had been conferring with Reich officials. Later the American State Department announced that after the Swedish emissary had delivered the Allied Governments' reply, Himmler, refusing to accept it, had made no further offers.

It was not until April 30 that the world learned that Count Folke Bernadotte had been the unnamed individual who had relayed to the Allies the Himmler overtures for peace. Adding further drama to Bernadotte's errand was the report that he had narrowly escaped death when Allied planes bombed the Danish airfield from which he was about to take off on April 28. The Count, his chauffeur, and a companion had been forced to jump into a ditch for safety from Allied machine-gun fire. Bernadotte returned to Stockholm on May 1, the day Grand Admiral Karl Doenitz [42] announced the death of Hitler and his own succession as Führer. The Count's statement that he had not seen Himmler led the Swedish press to assume that Bernadotte had conducted peace negotiations with Doenitz, although the Admiral had announced that the war would continue, and the Swedish Foreign Office had stated that the Count had brought no message for the Allies. It was revealed, however, that he had arranged for the release of some fifteen thousand Norwegians and Danes, and of women of various other nationalities, from Nazi internment camps. Then, seven days later, on May 8, the world heard the official announcements that the unconditional surrender of the Germans to all the Allies was at last an actual fact.

Bernadotte's own account of his meetings with Himmler and other leaders of the Third Reich during the critical period from the middle of February to the end of May was published in Stockholm early in the summer. In October a translation of the Count's book was published in the United States under the title of *The Curtain Falls*. (It has also been translated into other European languages, and is to appear in Hebrew and Esperanto.) J. Raymond Walsh called it "a good little book, and George Harriss judged it "interesting not alone for the information it contains on negotiations and events, but for its picture of a nightmarish world." The book was considered valuable, too, for its portraits and glimpses of Nazi notables.

A New York *Times* dispatch on October 21 revealed that plans evolved by the Count and the Swedish YMCA for the revival of the YMCA in the American and British zones of Germany had been approved in principle by General Eisenhower [42]. Thus the program to replace the Hitler Youth by the YMCA may be in action by 1946. In an interview on November 20, the day of the opening of the Nuremberg war crimes trial, Bernadotte expressed his views on that subject. C. L. Sulzberger [44], New York *Times* correspondent, reported that while Bernadotte "agreed in principle with the theory of designating war criminals, he did not believe that high-ranking officers . . . should be tried if they were merely doing their duty and following military commands. Count Bernadotte said, however, that if an officer had violated the Hague Conventions, perhaps he could be classified as a criminal and that the officer should have considered risking death for mu-

tiny rather than obey such orders as those calling for the shooting of prisoners."

In the summer of 1945 the Count was honored for his Red Cross work: Norway awarded him the Grand Cross of the Order of St. Olav, and the Universities of Copenhagen and Uppsala gave him honorary Doctor's degrees. Later, a book containing the names of seven thousand men and women saved from Nazi concentration camps by the Swedish Red Cross was presented to him; and in November he was made a Commander of the French Legion of Honor. In November also he was appointed president of the Swedish Red Cross, to take office January 1, 1946. He succeeded his father, Prince Carl, who had been president since 1906.

Eh-ma-do-ye-na, or "He who is worshipped by everybody," is Bernadotte's honorary American Indian title. As this name suggests, the Count is considered a good diplomat, known for his integrity and his friendliness. Tall and handsome, he has smiling gray-blue eyes and a long, lean face. In his dress, he is partial to fedoras, and almost always wears a boutonniere on the lapel of his double-breasted suits. He is fond of horses, and likes bicycling —even in the prewar days of gasoline plenty he was seen every weekday morning peddling his way through the Stockholm streets to his office. With their two sons, the Count and Countess live in a park-like section of Stockholm not far from the Strand, one of the main streets of the city.

References

Am Swedish Mo 39:4 F '45 por
Mentor 17:58 Ap '29 por
N Y Sun p6 My 5 '45

BERRY, EDWARD WILBER Feb. 10, 1875—Sept. 20(?), 1945 American paleontologist; authority on classification and evolution of plants of southeastern North America, equatorial America, and South America; dean of Johns Hopkins University from 1929 to 1942; author of over five hundred articles on biology, geology, and paleontology for American and foreign scientific periodicals.

Obituary

N Y Times p21 S 21 '45 por

BERTRAM, ADOLF, CARDINAL 1859—July 12, 1945 German ecclesiastic; Archbishop of Breslau since 1914; dean of the German Catholic hierarchy; continually attacked Nazi tenets.

Obituary

N Y Times p11 Jl 13 '45 por

BIDAULT, GEORGES (bē-dō zhôrzh) 1899(?)- French Government official
Address: b. French Foreign Office, Quai d'Orsay, Paris

In the five years between the outbreak of the Second World War and September 1944 Georges Bidault had risen from the position of a history professor, who had never held a political office, to the rank of Foreign Minister of France, the second highest public office

GEORGES BIDAULT

in his country. After one year in office, Bidault was not only world known as a diplomat but had seen his party, the Mouvement Républicain Populaire or MRP, a moderately progressive group of which he is the leader, emerge from the October 1945 elections as one of France's strongest political parties. Although the Communists desired the important Cabinet post of Foreign Minister, De Gaulle [40] refused to replace Bidault, who was re-appointed to the post on November 22. "It took the imagination of history itself," declares Ernest O. Hauser, "to create this extraordinary character"—professor, editor, underground leader, and government official. In the last capacity he led the delegation that represented France at the United Nations Conference on World Organization, at San Francisco, in the spring of 1945.

Born about 1899 in Moulins, France, Georges Bidault is the son of middle-class parents. His father was a director of an insurance company in central France. After the death of his wife, when the boy was only two, the senior Bidault became so austere that the home life was "without much warmth or fun." At ten Georges was sent to a French Jesuit school in northern Italy, where he remained until he was sixteen. While there he was known as a brilliant scholar who preferred reading the classics and history to participating in sports, and even at that age it was felt that he would become a man of moment. His gift for leadership was displayed after he was elected president of the Catholic Youth Movement. Before he was drafted for service in the First World War at the age of eighteen, young Bidault had enrolled at the Sorbonne, to which university he returned after serving briefly with the French Army of Occupation in the Ruhr in 1919. Graduated with highest honors from the Sorbonne from which he received the degree of *agrégé*, Bidault began his teaching career as a professor of history at a lycée in Valenciennes. In his early thirties he was appointed to the Lycée Louis-le-Grand, France's most distinguished secondary school.

Establishing his bachelor home in the Latin Quarter of Paris, where the school was located, Bidault took up his professorial duties. In addition, he became foreign editor and columnist for the Catholic daily, *l'Aube*. In 1932 (an election year) he and a few young members of the Popular Democratic Party had founded this paper, "on a shoestring." The Popular Democrats, reports *Free France*, at that time were a group of Leftist Catholics who, despite their small representation in the Chamber of Deputies, had a strong appeal among young middle-class Catholics and Catholic workers throughout France. When the Popular Democrats joined the Popular Front in 1936 Bidault withdrew. He vigorously declared his opposition to the Munich pact and other prewar appeasement policies.

Bidault's daily column on foreign affairs in *l'Aube* (1932-39) made him somewhat of a national oracle. Although the circulation of the newspaper, described by him as "small but honest," never exceeded twenty thousand, and while he never enjoyed the popularity of a syndicated Walter Lippmann [40], he nevertheless left his impact upon the political thinking of the French intelligentsia. He never became a partisan politician either, and his only political activity was an unsuccessful try for the Chamber of Deputies in 1935. The main point of his editorials was that "national power and unity spring from a higher power and a deeper loyalty than mere party allegiance."

Ernest Hauser reports in the *Saturday Evening Post* that an examination of the issues of *l'Aube* during Bidault's column-writing days reveals the sanity and consistency of his views even in those pacifist prewar days. At the time of the Ethiopian crisis of 1935 Bidault wrote, "If Geneva allows aggression in Africa, what authority will she command to stop aggression in Europe?" The Austrian *Anschluss* to him was "a great misfortune from a viewpoint of civilization and peace." Franco's [42] Spanish rebellion was sharply criticized by the Catholic Bidault as "a pretense of saving Christian civilization and law and order with methods that violated both." In Hauser's opinion, the French editor's most brilliant series of articles were those written in condemnation of the appeasement policy toward Hitler's [42] Germany.

With the outbreak of the Second World War the life of the middle-aged editor and professor of history underwent a radical change. One day he was in the uniform of a sergeant in the French Army, and the next he was behind the barbed wire of a German prison camp. In 1941 he was free again, having been released with others of his age group and returned to France. He immediately enlisted with the underground, thereby beginning a precarious double life that was to last for two years. During the day he held a teaching post in Lyon in unoccupied France, and at night carried on the work of resistance. Thrice weekly he published the twenty-page underground *Bulletin de la France combattante*, and he also acted as liaison agent between the Resistance of Continental France and the Fighting France Headquarters in London. (His sister and two brothers worked for the underground also.)

Arrested in 1943, he succeeded in escaping and that year collaborated with a mysterious person known only as "Max," who had been smuggled into France with orders from General de Gaulle [40] to formulate into one group the three chief anti-Nazi groups (political parties, labor unions, and resistance groups). Max succeeded in uniting Communists and Catholics, aristocrats and proletarians, and also in creating the National Council of Resistance, an underground "government" which consisted of seventeen members. When the unoccupied zone was overrun by the Germans this council moved to Paris. In the summer of 1943 Max was arrested by the Gestapo, and Bidault, a member of the council, was chosen to succeed him as president. During the entire period of the ex-professor's leadership, says Hauser, not a single incident occurred which prompted any one of the divergent groups fighting under the Cross of Lorraine to threaten to secede from the council.

On his assumption of the highest but the most dangerous post in the underground, "Monsieur le professeur ceased to exist." In a pathetically simple disguise—a hat (something he had never worn before) and a mustache were added, eyeglasses removed—Bidault miraculously escaped recognition. The weekly meetings of the council (limited to five members at a time to escape detection) were held in different apartments, or sometimes in a publishing house or a doctor's office, but never twice in the same place. "The professor who had removed his spectacles knew how to elude the Gestapo." His dangerous job demanded that he give up all pretense of "pedantic regularity" to the life of the hunted. He lived on the Left Bank in a tiny bedroom intended for the maid in the apartment of a middle-class family. No one except "Fred," his secretary, ever came to see him. In the spring of 1944, however, despite all precautions, the Gestapo learned that Georges Bidault was the leader of the underground. From that time on "the bloodhounds were breathing down the professor's neck—but they never caught up with him." When asked later whether he had carried the customary death pill during his hunted days, Bidault, who is a devout Catholic, replied, "As a Christian, I reject suicide. The Lord preserved me."

Immediately after the liberation of Paris De Gaulle's Provisional Government was moved from Algiers to the French capital. On September 9, following several days of reshuffling and new appointments, the General announced his reorganized Cabinet. Eight of the original Algiers ministry were missing, and in their places were members of the Resistance. One of these was Georges Bidault, who succeeded René Massigli as Foreign Minister (or Commissioner). Alexander Uhl of *PM* commented, however, that the ratio of four Socialists and two Communists to fifteen members from other parties did not reflect the true political state of France, which he felt to be more to the Left.

Recognition of the Government by the Big Three nations, rumored at first to have been postponed until after a national election, came some six weeks after the formation of the Cabinet. On the afternoon of October 23 the Ambassadors of the United States, Great Britain, Russia, and Canada presented themselves at the Foreign Ministry in the historic Quai

d'Orsay to hand Bidault similar notes from their respective countries. Bidault, speaking with emotion, declared that France would enter, with her head high, the concert of great nations.

The next month the diplomatic triumphs continued for the new foreign minister. France was invited to become the fourth of the great-power members of the European Advisory Commission, which had been organized for the purpose of studying certain European questions. On November 21, in his first speech to the Consultative Assembly, Bidault announced his forthcoming visit to Moscow. He made it clear that France intended to maintain close relations with Russia and that she strongly disapproved of an exclusive bloc of nations in Western Europe. "France wants an alliance in the West and an alliance in the East," he said, adding that France would never agree to "belong only to the West." (After the United Nations conference "had approved of regional agreements as useful elements for the collaboration of peoples," Bidault came out in support of a Western European bloc, saying that he simply demanded for France "the right to do as others already have done.")

This visit of De Gaulle and Bidault to Russia resulted in a Franco-Soviet pact of alliance and mutual assistance. The first agreement made by the De Gaulle Government, it was signed in Moscow by Bidault and the General on December 10, 1944. The Paris press unanimously expressed satisfaction, calling it the starting point of an international organization and not the creation of a bloc excluding other alliances. Edgar Ansel Mowrer [41], New York *Post* columnist, welcomed the treaty, commenting that it prevented the zoning of Europe, which he considered "a divide-and-bully theory." Moreover, the dividing of Europe into an Eastern and Western zone, in the opinion of Mowrer, would place Germany in a pivotal position so that in the future she might play one against the other.

French representatives had not been asked to attend the Yalta conference of Churchill [42], Stalin [42], and Roosevelt [42] in February 1945, nor the Dumbarton Oaks security conference the preceding year. The French Foreign Office had at first expressed the Government's unwillingness to accept plans which it had had no part in formulating, but on February 12, before the publication of the final Yalta communiqué, the Provisional Government was officially informed of the results of the conference. The French Government was also asked to state its views on the conference declaration. Then, on February 20, Bidault, speaking before the Foreign Affairs Commission of the Consultative Assembly, stated that it was the Government's intention to cooperate to the fullest in the creation of an international system that would guarantee French and, consequently, European security. At the end of the month, on an invitation from Great Britain, Bidault visited London to discuss with Churchill and Anthony Eden [40] various matters of mutual concern. He had also signed an economic agreement with Belgium, Luxembourg, and the Netherlands, which the following October was renewed for another six months. The new

BIDAULT, GEORGES—*Continued*

agreement tripled commercial exchanges between the countries.

Bidault's views on a world organization follow closely those of another deeply religious man, another professor turned statesman, Woodrow Wilson, who desired a league in which all the nations of the world would be politically equal. Bidault has declared: "I do not believe in a five-power directorate for the affairs of Europe or the world. . . .There can be no prospect of wholehearted cooperation for peace unless a universal system is set up in which the smaller nations as well as the big powers are made to shoulder responsibilities in proportion to their means and power." His views on postwar terms for Germany also reflect those of Wilson, who said at the end of the First World War that the Allies must be just even to those to whom they did not wish to be. The Second World War statesman said in November of 1944, in an exclusive interview with the New York *Times*, "The peace with Germany should not be one of vengeance; it must be just and human. Germany will have to be controlled for years to come, but I am not for trying to make her harmless by dismembering her artificially." Bidault's statement that France did not want to incorporate any German territory nor want any German minority within her borders showed wisdom, commented the *Christian Science Monitor*.

Well in advance of the United Nations Conference on International Organization at San Francisco, France had stated her definition of security. At that time she said, "Above all, leave France, Russia, and any other powers allied in regional treaties against postwar Germany free to act without waiting the approval of the world organization. Abolish the right of veto now reserved to each of the Security Council's big-power members (including France). Give the world organization's parliament of nations, the General Assembly, some authority over the Security Council, which the Big Three would put completely beyond the Assembly's control." This attitude, in the opinion of *Time* Magazine, amounted to a bald declaration of "no confidence" in the Big Three design for peace. In short, France doubted that the "Big Three were big enough to run Europe and the world." On the other hand, General de Gaulle personally edited a statement which assured that France did not wish to wreck Dumbarton Oaks if nothing better were achieved, but that France "would be ready on her part to go even farther than Dumbarton Oaks and consent to greater limitation on her sovereignty in exchange for a more effective international organization than that proposed by this plan."

Foreign Minister Bidault, according to *Newsweek*, was responsible for having cleared the diplomatic atmosphere, and obtained De Gaulle's consent to send representatives to the San Francisco conference. Subsequently, however, France refused the invitation of Great Britain, Russia, and the United States to join them as sponsors of the conference. "In his quiet way," commented the magazine, "Bidault has followed the General in all his diplomatic forays, picking up the pieces." When the French delegation

first arrived at the conference it seemed as though the Government's refusal to act as a sponsor would handicap it in taking its place among big powers, but during the second week France joined their ranks. "Slowly but surely," reported Edwin L. James in the New York *Times*, "the French came to be invited to the meetings of the original inviting powers, and now the Big Four has definitely turned into the Big Five."

As head of his delegation, wrote the New York *Herald Tribune*, Bidault seemed resolved to "express the power and the stature of his country by reasonableness and French good sense rather than by oratory or impressive demands." According to Elsa Maxwell[43], he "completely captivated newsmen at his press conference [in early May] with his quiet way of talking, his head cocked sideways a bit, his quizzical smile. . . .He answered all questions swiftly," Miss Maxwell continued. "I felt, and so did others, that he was clever, but completely trustworthy . . . intelligent and honest."

In mid-May, as the situation in Syria and Lebanon became increasingly difficult, Bidault was forced to leave the conference, and Paul-Boncour[45] succeeded him. It was said that the Foreign Minister had considered resigning in protest against De Gaulle's policies in sending, in his absence, "more French troops to occupy the Val d'Aosta in Italy without the authorization of the Allies." In early July it was announced that the French Government would give Syria and Lebanon full sovereignty over their own armies, and in December both Great Britain and France formally agreed to withdraw their troops simultaneously from the two regions and to consult jointly on all Middle Eastern questions.

Despite the fact that France had been included in Big Power conferences at San Francisco, she was not invited to the Potsdam meeting of Russia, Great Britain, and the United States after Germany's surrender. The decisions taken at the meeting, in which France was asked to concur, were sent to the Foreign Ministry. France criticized these agreements, saying that they set up a new distribution of power, with the Soviet Union gaining the most. Sixteen days later Bidault and De Gaulle signed the ratification of the United Nations Charter. Shortly afterward the Minister accompanied the General to Washington to ask help from the United States in the reconversion period.

Subsequently, Bidault attended the London conference of the Council of Foreign Ministers, which had been set up by the Potsdam agreement to consider peace treaties with Italy and former satellites of Nazi Germany. After growing tension, the Big Five reached a deadlock on the Balkan question. The bone of contention, it was pointed out, was Russia's demand that all except the Big Three be excluded from drafting peace treaties with the Balkan nations. (Bidault, during the conference, succeeded in establishing an understanding between Italy and France.) "Despite the serious setbacks at London, we French," said Bidault, "do not despair of finding a formula for an accord among the Big Five. France and the United States both hope to see the creation of a permanent international organization." In referring to "Western bloc politics," the statesman said, "If people talk about the 'West' in connection with France, it is because geographically France belongs to the West, but she is equally in the world."

One of the surprises of the October 1945 French national election was the strength of Bidault's party, the Mouvement Républicain Populaire. This new party, organized in Algiers during the war, not only won 138 seats in the National Assembly, which placed it among the big three of France's political parties (the Communists elected 152 members and the Socialists 151 members), but also overwhelming approval at the polls on two questions of a referendum that they had supported. Their victory (shared with the Socialists) on these questions, the framing of a new constitution and the giving of more power to the Constituent Assembly, greatly increased the party's prestige.

The platform of MRP, reported the *Christian Science Monitor* at the time of the election, is "very similar to that of the Socialists, except that it is more vague and general in all planks. It is Roman Catholic of liberal trend. On only one issue does it split with the Socialists. . . . The Socialists are opposed to allowing any schools in France to be run by religious groups." Although the MRP approved of such schools in their party platform, Bidault, in a speech before his party in November, stated that the party would on no occasion make it an issue that could interfere with national coalition. His own description of the party of which he is the acknowledged spiritual head is, that in American terms, it "is the equivalent of New Dealism in the economic field." In his speech on MRP's willingness to form a coalition government with the Communists and Socialists, he said, however, that "the movement would refuse to be bound by the economic and political doctrines drawn up by the Delegation of the Left." Bidault's elaboration of the stand his party would take, commented the New York *Times,* was received with much interest because his views are said to be very close to those of De Gaulle. Concerning the nationalization called for by the National Council of Resistance, the statesman declared, "The method of nationalization is a matter of discussion and detailed work which we will not shirk. The MRP does not promise to any one that this or that industry will be nationalized within a given time. But we do promise to expedite the expropriation of private monopolies so that a more equitable regime can come into being, not only in distribution of profit but in division of authority."

Edgar Mowrer (New York *Post*) was of the opinion that the election results had justified the foreign policy of De Gaulle, now President, and Bidault. While seeking to remain "a bridge between the Soviets and the Western powers, France, if compelled to choose, will remain a Western power." The new Government, composed of twenty-two members, provided, in accordance with the wishes of the Constituent Assembly, for equal representation of the three main parties, with six of the ministries filled by lesser party groups and independents. Bidault remained in his post as Foreign Minister.

With the surrender of Germany, France had been given a share in the Allied administration of the occupied country. Her subsequent refusal to consent to the centralization of certain aspects of German economic life until Germany's western boundaries were determined, became the subject of strong criticism. According to Bidault, France feared the recreation of a German Reich. In December American Secretary of State James F. Byrnes [41] intimated that the Big Three might disregard the unanimity rule of the Allied Control Council in complying with the Potsdam pledge on unification. When it was announced that same month that the Foreign Ministers of Great Britain, the United States, and Russia would soon meet in Moscow, presumably to discuss the problem of Germany, Bidault was not asked to attend the meeting.

Bidault's accomplishments as a statesman have won for him acclaim from widely different sources. "The ablest French foreign minister I've ever dealt with," said Anthony Eden. He is different and much better than the traditional French minister, said a correspondent from *Free World* after an interview. "He has brought to the Government a new spirit, or even a new ideal, namely revolutionary Christianity or a dynamic Christian world order," commented the *Christian Science Monitor.*

In December 1945 Bidault was married to his assistant, Mlle. Suzanne Borel, France's only woman career diplomat. The Foreign Minister is short and slight, and has dark hair that is now graying and a striking face—"almost round, but unusually strong. It gives him a deceptive appearance of youthful robustness and sturdiness." His hobby studies are stamps and mushrooms, and he likes good wine, good food, and green apples. Although the duties of his office are arduous, Bidault says that he prefers making history to his former job of teaching it.

References

C S Mon Mag p9 Ap 14 '45 por
Free France 7:459 My 1 '45 por; 8:250 N-D '45 por
N Y Times p15 O 8 '44
N Y World-Telegram p22 Ap 25 '45
Newsweek 25:52+ Mr 5 '45 por
Sat Eve Post 217:17+ Ap 28 '45 pors

BLAIK, EARL H(ENRY) (blāk) Feb. 15, 1897- Football coach

Address: United States Military Academy, West Point, N. Y.

In December 1944, while American men in khaki faced the most formidable foe in all history, the West Point Cadets fought the most brilliant football game of their seventy-five football seasons against the best pigskin galaxy the Naval Academy had ever produced. Army's unbeaten "Black Knights" did it again in 1945. Only five years earlier football at West Point was in the doldrums, the team having been pulverized in 1940 by practically every squad it contested. Today Army is "the pride and joy of every heart in gray." The man credited with this resurrection is "metronomic drill-devil" Colonel Earl ("Red") Blaik, head coach at West Point since January 1941.

COL. EARL H. BLAIK

In three seasons from 1943 through 1945 his West Pointers won twenty-five games, tied one, and lost two, a record comparable to Tennessee's fabulous 27-2-1 record from 1929 to 1931. In 1944 and 1945 Blaik's boys ran up a winning streak of eighteen games, a total of 916 points and 135 touchdowns to their opponents' combined 81 points and 12 touchdowns. "It is nice to have such backs as Doc Blanchard and Glenn Davis and such linemen as Coulter, Green, etc.," commented Stanley Woodward, "but it takes a real job of handling to keep a winning team on its toes through a long season, to bring it up to full playing form each week, to give it enough poise to stand prosperity."

Earl Henry Blaik was born in Detroit, Michigan, February 15, 1897, the son of William Douglas and Margaret Jane Blaik. Graduating with a B. A. degree from Miami University at Oxford, Ohio, during the First World War, and entertaining thoughts of entering the war as an officer, Blaik secured an appointment to West Point. After completing the first two-year course in the Academy's history, he was graduated in 1920. Of his aptitude in sports Willis MacDonald, Blaik's barracksmate at West Point, has said: "Blaik was a good end. He made Army's kicking game go because he was very fast downfield under kicks. He was a deadly tackler and an unusually keen defensive player. As a football, basketball, and baseball player, he won the Army saber as the best athlete in his class." Although not very proficient in all phases of mathematics, Blaik was graduated from the Academy in the first third of his class.

Upon graduation Blaik was appointed a second lieutenant in the Cavalry of the Regular Army. Promoted to first lieutenant a month later, he was sent as a student officer to the Cavalry School at Fort Riley, Kansas, the following September, and in June 1921 he reported at Fort Bliss, Texas, for duty with the Eighth Cavalry. Less than a year later, discouraged by the Army policy of slow peacetime

promotions, the young lieutenant resigned in March 1922. Several days after having submitted his resignation he received a letter from Douglas MacArthur offering him a post greatly coveted by any young Army officer— that of personal aide to the General, who was about to leave for the Philippines. It is said that had Blaik received this appointment prior to his resignation from the Army he would undoubtedly have accepted the assignment.

From 1923 to 1934 Blaik joined his father in the building firm of W. D. and E. H. Blaik in Dayton, Ohio. The contracting business apparently did not absorb his whole attention, and with the passing of each year his longing for the gridiron grew. In the fall of 1926, taking time off, Blaik went to the University of Wisconsin to coach the ends and backs for a few months under George Little, who had been Red Blaik's coach at Miami in 1916. The next year Blaik worked for several weeks at West Point with Biff Jones, the Army coach, training more backs and ends. By 1929 Blaik's business had proved itself lucrative enough for him to devote more time to football.

In 1934, after serving as a part-time coach at West Point for seven years, he accepted the position of head coach at Dartmouth to try to rejuvenate a team whose only major victory the preceding season had been its defeat of Pennsylvania State College. Confident that the Indians could regain their high standing in the pigskin world, Red Blaik said, "We're going to bring home the bacon." His high hopes, however, were soon shattered. The herculean task of breaking in veterans to a new coaching regime resulted in a 7-2 defeat by Yale and a 21-6 "shellacking" by Cornell in the anticlimactic Cornell-Dartmouth encounter. Of that Blaik has recently said, "That was the worst nightmare I've ever lived. That night I needed no more than a gentle shove to steer me over those Cayuga cliffs." But by 1936 Blaik had produced a team that was almost invulnerable to scalpings. His record at Dartmouth reveals forty-five wins, fifteen losses, and four ties. Blaik's men won the mythical Ivy League Hat in 1936 and 1937, and tied Cornell for it in 1938. The Indians, now "a precisioned rock-and-sock team," were once again on the warpath.

In November 1940 Army suffered the most humiliating defeat in the history of Cadet football, when Penn State routed West Point by a 48-0 score. The new Superintendent of the Academy, Major General Robert L. Eichelberger '43, aware of the anomalous situation present in the existence of a poor Army team when the country was in the process of setting up the largest and most powerful army of all time, asked Red Blaik to consider Army before signing another Dartmouth contract, implying that it was Blaik's moral obligation to come to the rescue. Blaik, extremely happy with his work and environment at Dartmouth, was slow in accepting the offer. Finally, after much deliberation, he submitted his resignation at Dartmouth, saying that "in this national emergency I want to do something. . . . If I can make some small contribution toward our preparedness, I'm gratified. I'll say this, leaving Dartmouth was the hardest decision I've ever had to make."

Shortly after Blaik's arrival at West Point the United States entered the Second World War. The feeling arose among many Americans that what they called a "schoolboy's luxury" should be suspended for the duration of the war. Military and naval leaders asserted, however, that football inculcated into players a sense of strategy, leadership, teamwork, discipline, individual initiative, a will to win. The game was described as more analogous to warfare than any other. And since the start of the war Army and Navy authorities have continually requested more of "those football players."

Red Blaik was the first civilian coach West Point had had since 1911, when the Academy introduced the system of filling the post with an Army man. However, in December 1942 Blaik was back in the Army when he was commissioned a lieutenant colonel. Blaik's assignment at West Point was described as the toughest coaching job in the country. Intimate with the life and routine at West Point because of his past associations with it, Blaik was able to launch a sound rehabilitation program for Army football. "Our biggest job," said Blaik, "is to breed confidence into this squad. We must also blend the innate 'Kaydet' rigidity with the mental and physical elasticity with which the college player is better blessed."

In 1942 when Notre Dame substituted the T-formation for its own Rockne system, Blaik was slated for gridiron laurels, although completely unaware of it at the time. (The "T" is "an intricate system of cross-blocking and blind-angle blocking on the secondary, which produces devastating results when all the applicants carry out their assignments.") In order to set up defenses for this new formation, Blaik labored over its peculiarities. The more he studied it, the more impressed he became; and when finally certain of its potentialities, he scrapped the single-wing alignment, in which he had become recognized as a master, for the "T" plan. Red Blaik became enthusiastic about the modernized "T," "with its men-in-motion, flankers, and single blocks." Critics were dubious of the success of Blaik's switch and suggested he stick to something he knew. However, with the passing of each season, the record began to dispel the critics' doubts. Army was on the road to complete recovery. Each year the number of games that were won increased, and the games lost decreased.

In the 1944 season the Cadets had an all-winning season, inflicting a crushing 59-0 defeat on Notre Dame and a 62-7 one on Penn, avenging their gridiron defeats of 1942, when they were routed 13-0 and 19-0 by Notre Dame and Penn, respectively, and of 1943 when they were mauled 26-0 by Notre Dame. Ed McKeever '45, acting coach of Notre Dame, in commenting on the 59-0 rout inflicted by Army, said: "At least we got out of the game alive. We got it and got it good, but I think anyone who knows football knows we got it from a great team."

In December 1944 football fans were excited over the coming annual gridiron battle between the Cadets and their traditional foes, the Navy. There was a great deal of speculation as to the outcome of this game. Sport critics advertised Navy's mighty line, while they also extolled Army's speedy backs and the theoretical superiority of the T-formation. The game, in the previous two years staged in the semi-privacy of West Point and Annapolis, was given a metropolitan setting in Baltimore as a feature of the Treasury Department's Sixth War Bond Drive. To preclude any additional train traffic, the entire Cadet corps of twenty-three hundred men, with officers and instructors, traveled to Baltimore on a War Department troopship. Among the gridiron spectators were such notables as General George C. Marshall '40, Army Chief of Staff; Admiral William D. Leahy '41, Chief of Staff to the President; Admiral Ernest J. King '42, Commander in Chief of the Navy; General Henry H. Arnold '42, Chief of the Army Air Forces; and Admiral Jonas H. Ingram, Commander of the Atlantic Fleet. The game was relayed to the most advanced posts in the far-flung battlefields of the world so that twelve million other Americans could tune in.

Uncertain in attack in the early phases of the game, the Cadets unleashed their flashing T-formation in the fourth period and established their supremacy beyond doubt in the most discussed game in the history of this rivalry. Critics, formerly skeptical of Blaik's version of the "T," admitted that "it represents the highest perfection it has ever attained." Commander Oscar Hagberg, head coach at Annapolis, said: "Army simply gave us hell." Grantland Rice '41 wrote: "This is undoubtedly the best all-round Army team, ably coached in the "T" attack, that West Point has ever seen." Blaik, in very high spirits over the success of his team, said that he "couldn't single out any man. Everybody on the squad did a magnificent job."

Blaik's backfield was a powerhouse, with such figures as Felix Blanchard, "a fullback prize," Doug Kenna, "the 'T' quarterback of the war," and Glenn Davis, "the fastest back." Herman Hickman, Army's line coach, who had received All-American distinction as a guard at Tennessee, was responsible for producing a sturdy and rugged line that battered Navy's forwards. Blaik was voted into second place in 1944 and 1945 by college and football service coaches in the New York World-Telegram's annual poll to determine the favorite coaches in the United States. His Cadets were selected as the best football team in the collegiate world by one hundred and twenty-one sports writers, and for the first time they were awarded the Lambert trophy as the top eleven in the East.

Blaik's 1945 team was even more impressive. Blanchard and Glenn Davis were the two most talked-about players of the season, even appearing jointly on Time's cover as "Men of the Week," and other Army football names like DeWitt Coulter became familiar to the sports public. West Point won every game of a crowded season against all types of defense. "Any coach who has the misfortune to face the West Pointers," said one such unfortunate, "is utterly helpless. If he jams up the middle alley to check Blanchard, Davis murders him with his sweeps. If he spreads his defense to halt Davis, Blanchard pulverizes him on the outside with the charge of an angry water buffalo.

(Continued next page)

BLAIK, EARL—*Continued*

And if by some stroke of genius he can distribute his strength evenly enough to bother them both, Army passes him dizzy." On various occasions, moreover, Blaik gave his second team, and even his third and fourth-stringers, a chance to "play a little football, and toughen the fiber of their morale. . . .The way Blaik let the kids stay in there and find themselves" on one such occasion, wrote Joe Cummiskey, "the way they finally did stiffen and take the ball away on downs in the shadow of their own goal posts, actually seemed to afford Blaik more pleasure than the breakaway runs of his stars."

With a 32-13 score against Navy's hitherto unbeaten eleven to conclude the season, the West Point team was again named the top collegiate team by the country's sports writers, again awarded the Lambert trophy, and of its members, six were selected for the All-Eastern college team, five for the All-American. Also, one of the team, Doc Blanchard, won the Heisman Memorial Trophy as the Nation's outstanding football player. Recognized as one of the great football teams of all time, Blaik's team was to be augmented in the 1946 season by the two stars of Lou Little's '45 1945 Columbia Lions. Cadets-elect Lou Kusserow and Gene Rossides.

With Earl Blaik's promotion to colonel, the leaf has been displaced by a new silver eagle on each shoulder, "but nary a chip on either." Tall and thin, he has a personality which rallies the friendship of all his players. Although a "human dynamo" on the gridiron, with his "strict hours, pounding work, and meticulous timing," he also possesses a great deal of "Blaik the human" in realizing "that all work makes Jack a dull football player." The new master of the gridiron coaching craft is a member of the fraternities Beta Theta Pi and Tau Kappa Alpha. In 1924 he was married to Merle McDowell, his childhood sweetheart. Their elder son William, a hockey player with no football ambitions, was in 1945 at Dartmouth, "brushing up on his math" in preparation for entering the Military Academy in the summer of 1946. The Blaiks' other child, Robert, finished out the 1945 season as quarterback for the Highland Falls High School team, although a broken collarbone had put him out of the line-up for a month.

References

N Y Sun p33 N 15 '45
Sat Eve Post 214:16-17+ O 11 '41 il pors
Who's Who in America, 1944-45

BOCK, FEDOR VON (bôk fä′dôr fôn) Dec. 3, 1880—May (?) 1945 German field marshal who commanded the central army group in the German invasion of Russia in June 1941; had been relieved of command after the German failure to take either Moscow or Stalingrad; restored, as commander of German forces in southern Russia (1942). See *Current Biography* 1942 Yearbook.

Obituary

N Y Herald Tribune p5 My 7 '45

BOGERT, GEORGE H. 1864—Dec. 13, 1944 American landscape painter; represented by six works in the Metropolitan Museum of Art, New York, and by two in the National Gallery in Washington, as well as others in museums and galleries in the United States and Europe.

Obituary

N Y Times p23 D 14 '44 por

BOHR, NIELS (HENRIK DAVID) (bōr nēls) Oct. 7, 1885- Danish physicist
Address: b. c/o University of Copenhagen, Copenhagen

It has been pointed out that seldom do the scientists responsible for the elucidation of science's seeming enigmas play a large role in the technical application of their discoveries or theories. Thus, while the available data about Nobel Prize winner Niels Bohr, whose name has been connected with the atomic bomb, suggests that his part in the actual production of the bomb was small, the history of modern theoretical atomic physics begins, according to many scientists, with Bohr's atomic theory of 1913 and has been influenced by his leadership throughout the succeeding years.

Niels Henrik David Bohr was born October 7, 1885, in Copenhagen, Denmark, one of the sons of Christian Bohr, professor of physiology at the University of Copenhagen, and Ellen (Adler) Bohr. In 1903 Bohr entered the same university in preparation for a career in physics. By 1907 he had distinguished himself sufficiently to receive the gold medal of the Royal Danish Academy of Science. Two years later he received his degree of Master of Science in physics. And in 1911 the doctorate, for which he had investigated the electron theory of metals, was conferred upon him. Leaving Copenhagen, Bohr then crossed the North Sea to enter world-famous Cavendish Laboratory at Cambridge University, at that time directed by Sir Joseph J. Thomson, who discovered the electron nature of cathode rays.

In the spring of 1912, however, Bohr went to Lord (Ernest) Rutherford's laboratory in Manchester, arriving just at the time when, as he tells us, Rutherford and his students "were eagerly occupied with tracing out the consequences of his [Rutherford's] new view of the nuclear structure of the atom." It was this point of scientific contact which launched Bohr on his own career. As he modestly states, "enthusiastic for the great promises of the new theoretical outlooks," he came under the inspiration "of the unique friendliness and straightforwardness with which Rutherford [whom he elsewhere characterizes as a man of "powerful personality" and acute judgment] . . .was always prepared to listen to any student behind whose youthful inexperience he perceived a serious interest." It was during this stay in Manchester that Bohr formulated the theory which has since earned him the title of "the founder of modern atomic theory."

The atomic model which Rutherford proposed just before Bohr reached Manchester (as described by Bernard Jaffe in *Outposts of Science*) consisted of a positively charged nucleus around which revolved in orbits, like planets around the sun, electrons of a number to neutralize with their negative charges of electricity the corresponding number of positive charges in the nucleus. Almost at once, however, this theory encountered a fundamental difficulty, for observation showed that the emission of light accompanying the revolution of the electrons did not, as should be the case according to the older theories of electricity and magnetism, lead to a contraction of their orbits until the electrons fell into the nucleus.

The two papers which Bohr published in 1913 in the *Philosophical Magazine* of London not only solved this problem, and that by a revolutionary physical concept, but also provided the explanation for the characteristic spectra of the elements which had heretofore been known but not understood. As he pointed out years later in a radio address, Bohr realized "the impossibility of explaining many characteristic properties of atoms by means of the ordinary laws of physics, which apply to the behavior of matter in bulk." He was also aware of Max Planck's quantum theory, that the energy of radiation is discontinuous and occurs in minute exact measurable units called quanta.

The use Bohr made of Planck's theory is explained for the layman in George W. Gray's volume *New World Picture*. Retaining the nucleus and the revolving electrons of the Rutherford atomic picture, Bohr thereupon postulated a series of fixed orbits in which the electrons travel without emitting light and therefore without being drawn toward the nucleus. In these orbits the electrons are regarded as in "stationary states" because their energy content does not change and hence they travel at a uniform rate of speed. However, disturbance by an impact or by exterior radiation will cause a temporary displacement of the electrons, which will at once attempt to return to the home orbit by means of jumps. Each jump from an outer orbit to the adjacent inner orbit will be accompanied by the emission of a quantum of light, representing "the difference in energy between the higher [more distant from the nucleus] orbit just left and the lower orbit just occupied." This is the only time when light will be emitted. As Bohr phrased it, "For each atom there exists a number of definite states of motion called stationary states, in which the atom can exist without radiating energy. Only when the atom is disturbed and passes from one state to another can it radiate light."

With the exception of a brief lectureship at the University of Copenhagen in 1913, Bohr had remained in Manchester, where he formulated his theory, until 1916, first in the Rutherford Laboratory and from 1914 also as lecturer at the University of Manchester. In 1916 he returned to Denmark to become professor of theoretical physics at the University of Copenhagen. In 1920, when the university, largely at his recommendation, established the Institute for Theoretical Physics (with the aid of a Rockefeller Foundation endowment), Bohr became its director. Under his leadership (which was interrupted only during the Nazi occupation of Denmark), the institute has become world famous and has attracted some of the world's most renowned physicists. Bohr himself has been in constant demand on the lecture platforms of the leading universities

NIELS BOHR

of England and America and before the scientific societies of the world.

Bohr's frequent contributions to *Nature*, one of England's foremost scientific periodicals, show how active he has been in the development of quantum mechanics, to which his original atomic model gave the impetus. Gray has pictured him in this respect essentially as "a sort of elder brother of the youthful revolutionaries, encouraging and criticizing and sometimes interpreting through the contribution of a generalizing principle." And while, as he himself is the first to admit, scientific discoveries are the work not of one man but of many, his name is closely linked with two guiding principles which attempt to reconcile the two dominant trends of thought in contemporary physics—quantum, and wave, mechanics—and to integrate the modern conceptions of matter.

The first of these is the "correspondence principle," which (in the words of Hans Reichenbach in *Atoms and Cosmos*) "says that there must be a gradual approximation of the atomic model to the forms of macroscopic theory—that is, the theory of large-scale matter—when the electrons are at a rather great distance from the nucleus . . . it formulates the thought that only such a conception of the atom can be correct as goes continuously over into the old conception when dimensions are larger. For that the old conception holds good in the large is sufficiently attested by all experience, and a theory which takes no account of that fact is necessarily false." On this basis, Werner Heisenberg, a student of Bohr's, created a new mathematics for quantum mechanics, which has been called "an exact formulation of Bohr's Principle of Correspondence."

The second principle developed by Bohr springs from the experimental observations that a light ray at times presents the characteristics of wave motion and at other times of particle motion, but never both traits at the same time. The wave behavior and the particle behavior, therefore reasoned Bohr, "are complementary and mutually exclusive." With

BOHR, NIELS—*Continued*

recognition of this Principle of Complementarity, as with the Correspondence Principle, physics took another step forward.

In the winter of 1938-39, Bohr was working with Einstein [41] at the Institute for Advanced Study in Princeton, New Jersey, and it was through his presence there at that time that he was able to help set the Allies on the path to the manufacture of the atomic bomb. The immediate story goes back to 1938, when Otto Hahn, Fritz Strassmann, and Lise Meitner [45], in repeating an experiment in uranium atom bombardment performed earlier by Enrico Fermi in Italy, were obtaining the element barium in the results, where no barium should, by all known standards, have been. Forced to flee by the Nazis, Dr. Meitner reached Bohr's laboratory in Copenhagen with the tentative conclusion that the barium had resulted from the fission, or splitting, of the uranium into two new elements nearly equal in atomic weight, and that, according to an Einstein formula, a tremendous amount of energy should have been released. The news was at once transmitted to Bohr in America by his laboratory assistant Otto R. Frisch, who himself prepared to verify the experiment. Bohr for his part communicated the information to Fermi [45] and John R. Dunning at Columbia University and the results were quickly verified. At a meeting of theoretical physicists at George Washington University in Washington, D.C., a few days later, reported William L. Laurence [45] in the *Saturday Evening Post* in 1940, Bohr had the privilege of announcing to the world that the atom had been split. (This is the story according to the printed accounts of 1939 and 1940. The War Department report states that Lise Meitner gave the information directly to Bohr in Denmark, who took it to the United States with him, whence by indirect communication it reached Fermi at Columbia.)

The splitting of the uranium atom, however, had been expected to create a reaction of chain explosions. When this did not materialize, Bohr, at a meeting of the American Physical Society at Columbia University in February 1939, together with his Princeton colleague J. A. Wheeler, suggested that it was the rarer uranium isotope 235 which was responsible for the splitting and the more abundant U-238 which was inhibiting the process. This prediction was proved correct in 1940 after enough U-235 had been isolated to make the test.

Meanwhile, Bohr had returned to Denmark. And in April 1940 he halted work in the Institute for Theoretical Physics in protest against the Nazi invasion, devoting his time thereafter, according to a Scandinavian source, to "expounding the cause of liberty." (The institute was later raided by the Nazis, but nothing of value was found.) In September 1943 Bohr was forced to flee, taking with him, it is said, his precious atomic data. Landing on the Swedish coast from a fishing boat, he was taken into custody by the Swedish police—for his own protection at the request of the Danish underground—and nineteen days

later was flown to England in the bomb bay of a Mosquito bomber. His movements after that are still clouded in censorship, but it is known that he came to the United States, and that he made several trips between England and America. Henry D. Smyth in the War Department report states that Bohr "spent a great deal of time at Los Alamos [the atomic bomb laboratory in New Mexico headed by J. R. Oppenheimer [45]] and gave invaluable aid." It is Bohr's contention that atomic energy must be subject to international control. Once the secret of its manufacture was known, he has said, the sole advantage held by the United States would be that country's extensive engineering facilities.

Bohr received the Nobel Prize in Physics in 1922. He has also received the Hughes Medal from the Royal Society in London (1921), the H. C. Oerstad Medal from the Society for the Propagation of Natural Science (1924), the Norwegian gold medal from the University of Oslo (1924), the Barnard Medal from Columbia University (1925), the Mateucci Medal from the Societa Italiana della Scienze in Rome (1925), the Franklin Medal of the Franklin Institute in Baltimore (1926), the Faraday Medal from the Chemical Society of London (1930), the Planck Medal from the Deutsche Physikalische Gesellschaft (1930), and the Copley Medal from the Royal Society in 1938. He holds honorary degrees from the Universities of Oxford, Manchester, Edinburgh, London, and Oslo, among others. He is president of the Royal Danish Academy of Science and a member of more than twenty of the leading scientific academies of the world. He is the author of two volumes *Theory of Spectra and Atomic Constitution* (1922), and *Atomic Theory and Description of Nature* (1935), and of numerous scientific papers.

The physicist was married in August 1912 to Margrethe Noerlund, the daughter of a pharmacist of Slagelse, Denmark. They have four sons. Bohr, wrote one reporter, is "big and solid, with a strong, creased face overhung by the remnants of a once thick shock of hair. He speaks slowly through broad lips, and his platform manner is quiet. As often as not he stands with his hands shoved into his coat pockets. As often as not his coat could stand a pressing." Long ago Einstein said of him, "What is so marvelously attractive about Bohr as a scientific thinker is his rare blend of boldness and caution; seldom has anyone possessed such an intuitive grasp of hidden things combined with such a strong critical sense. With all his knowledge of the details, his eye is immovably fixed on the underlying principle. He is unquestionably one of the greatest discoverers of our age in the scientific field."

References

Commonweal 21:140+ N 30 '34 por
N Y Sun p16 Ag 9 '45
Sci Mo 44:285-6 Mr '37
Encyclopædia Britannica
International Who's Who, 1942
Who's Who, 1945

BOLTE, CHARLES G(UY) (bōl-tā) Jan.
19, 1920- Veterans' leader
Address: b. American Veterans Committee, 554
Madison Ave., New York City; h. 416 W. 20th
St., New York City

A disabled veteran of the Second World
War, Charles G. Bolté returned to the United
States in 1943 wondering how the ideals for
which he had fought could be realized and
safeguarded. He believed that military victory
would not automatically bring peace, jobs, and
freedom, but that positive steps would have to
be taken by those who won the war to preserve
the peace. Now, as national chairman of the
American Veterans Committee, an organization of Second World War veterans, he has become one of the most articulate spokesmen for
the new veteran.

A native New Yorker, Charles Guy Bolté
was born on January 19, 1920, to Guy Willard
and Marion (Stewart) Bolté. He received his
education at Greenwich High School and at
Dartmouth College, where he was elected to
Phi Beta Kappa and was associate editor of
The Dartmouth, the daily campus newspaper.
Like most of his generation, writes Bernardine
Kielty of *Book-of-the-Month Club News,* he
was a pacifist: "no more wars for democracy.
. . . In 1939 he still saw the European war as
'imperialist struggle.' Like most boys he hadn't
yet thought it through for himself, and was
accepting the slogans of the party line. Then
France fell, London was blitzed, and the truth
got through to him. His editorials now fought
for preparedness, for eventual American participation."

Immediately after his graduation in 1941,
Bolté and four of his friends decided not to
wait for the United States to enter the war.
They enlisted in the British Kings Royal Rifle
Corps, a motorized infantry regiment which
had originally been formed on American soil in
1756, at the time of the French and Indian War.
After nine months in the ranks, Bolté was sent
to Officers Training School and commissioned
as a second lieutenant. His outfit reached
North Africa in the summer of 1942, where it
fought with the British Eighth Army against
Rommel's '42 Afrika Korps. Four days after the
beginning of the British offensive at El Alamein, Lieutenant Bolté was shot in the right
leg while, as he describes it, "foolishly standing up." The leg was amputated above the
knee by an Australian surgeon in a field hospital. Of Bolté's four friends, two were killed
and two seriously wounded. Bolté himself was
awarded the Star of Africa.

After convalescing in a Cairo hospital for
eight months, Bolté was fitted with an artificial
leg, sent home, and discharged. He arrived in
the United States in June 1943, and was married a month later to Mary Brooks Elwell, a
girl whom he had known before he joined the
service and with whom he had been corresponding during his months of convalescence. Fulfilling his old ambition to have some sort of
a writing career, after his marriage the young
veteran procured a job as a military writer
with the OWI in New York. He stayed with
the Office ten months, leaving in 1944 to join
the Ziff Davis Publishing Company. He worked
there a short time before resigning to devote

David Pierce Studio

CHARLES G. BOLTE

all his time to the growing American Veterans
Committee.

The American Veterans Committee, Inc.,
whose "Statement of Intentions" emphasizes
full employment opportunities and a democratic
way of life in the postwar world as the primary
needs of its members, was the first organization
formed by and for the benefit of the veterans
of the Second World War exclusively. It was
started in January 1943 as a kind of committee
of correspondence among twenty-five servicemen, all old friends, who were worried about
their future in the postwar world. Gradually
their letters became bulletins mirroring soldiers'
thoughts in the various theaters of war. When
they realized that they all agreed upon the
need for veterans to work together after the
war, the AVC began to take form. As the
number of subscribers and contributors to the
bulletin grew, and because of their constantly
changing Army addresses, the group decided to
establish permanent headquarters with a veteran
in charge. By that time Bolté had joined the
organization and was suggested for the job.
In February 1944 he became editor of the
monthly publication, *Bulletin,* and general manager of AVC affairs. Bolté conducted all business from his own apartment until increased
funds from sympathetic persons enabled him to
give AVC an office address. The June 1944
Mediterranean edition of *Stars and Stripes*
printed a short account of the new committee.
Within two weeks Bolté received more than
three hundred V-mail letters of application. By
September 1945 the steadily growing membership had reached about four thousand. American men and women, of any race, creed, or
color, who are now serving with or have been
honorably discharged from the armed forces,
merchant marine or Allied forces are eligible
for membership. For veterans, the dues are $3
per year, and for members still in service, $2.

Until the time of complete demobilization
when it can elect officers and adopt a constitution, the AVC prefers to continue to function
in its present "formative" stage. The "State-

BOLTE, CHARLES G.—*Continued*

ment of Intentions" now acts as the basis of AVC thought and action, demanding for veterans: "Adequate financial, medical, vocational, and educational assistance. . . .A job . . . under a system of private enterprise in which business, labor, agriculture, and government work together to provide full employment and full production. . . .Thorough social and economic security. . . .Free speech, press, worship, assembly, and ballot. . . .Disarmament of Germany and Japan. . . .Active participation of the United States in the United Nations organization to stop any threat of aggression and to promote social and economic measures which will remove the causes of war. . . .An international veterans' council for the furtherance of world peace and justice among the peoples of all nations."

When the United Nations Conference on International Organization was being organized, Bolté, using the *Bulletin*, polled the AVC members on their opinions of a world organization. He did this in spite of an Army order which prohibited the polling of its personnel, but he was determined to give AVC members representation at San Francisco. Military authorities took no action against Bolté, however, and when he applied, he was given permission to send a committee of consultants to the American delegation at the conference. The committee included Bolté himself, Arthur W. Coats, Jr., the West Cost representative, and Private Alfred M. Lilienthal, who was the only enlisted man in uniform with official status at the conference. The three men reported to the delegation the results of the AVC poll, which had shown that the members favored the immediate formation of a strong United Nations organization and were willing to fight again, if necessary, to preserve the peace.

Since the success of his first poll, Bolté has made a practice of using the *Bulletin* (now published semi-monthly) to poll AVC members on questions of pertinent national legislation. He is working to destroy the public's stereotyped impression of "GI Joe." Bolté insists that GI Joe does not exist. "Beneath the collective idea of a division or a ship's company," he says, "the United States armed forces are composed of twelve million men who came from all the cities and towns and farms of America, taking with them every variety of experience and background." He feels that noncombatants who spent a few weeks in battle areas are not qualified to voice opinions of the soldiers' problems. Bolté is expressing the feeling of the AVC when he insists that no men except those who have served in the armed forces during the Second World War can presume to speak for the new veterans—particularly not Congressmen who toured the battle fronts, nor veterans' organizations of the First World War.

Bolté's book *The New Veteran: Hero or Problem?* excited wide interest when it appeared in November 1945, book reviewers giving much space to the presentation of his ideas and arguments, and the plans of the AVC With few exceptions the critics' judgments were much like these: "His is a stirring message and an inspiring book. . . .His arguments are logical and his voice is powerful" (Harry Hansen [42]) ; "this expression of ideals goes far deeper and will last considerably longer than the mere writing of a book" (Charles Hurd) ; "I am convinced that his book is a darned good thing, and so is his outfit" (Bill Mauldin [45]). The communist *Daily Worker,* however, did not approve of Bolté's deprecation of the American Legion: "We Communists," wrote I. Weise, "do not advocate that the veterans form any one organization."

Bolté has written articles on veterans' problems and military topics for numerous magazines, the *Nation, Harper's, Life, Mademoiselle,* New York *Times Magazine, American Legion Monthly,* and *Liberty.* (He is on the editorial staff of *Convoy.*) He has also been consulted by Congressional committees on such matters as permanent conscription and full employment legislation. He and the AVC strongly favor any legislation which they think will benefit veterans, directly or indirectly, believing that benefits to the veterans should also be benefits to the whole community. "What we want," Bolté has said, "does not mean the largest possible soldiers' bonus that can be pressured out of Congress." In late 1945 he was appealing for better medical care, a more efficient guidance and placement service for the returned soldier, and effective action to ease the veteran's housing needs. He was also in increasing demand as a public speaker.

Charles Bolté has dark brown hair and eyes and a bristling mustache which does not disguise his youth. He is six feet two inches tall and weighs one hundred and sixty-five pounds. His favorite forms of recreation are playing tennis, listening to music, and playing the piano—"a little," he adds.

References

N Y Herald Tribune p9 My 25 '44 por; p16 O 17 '44
N Y Post Mag p25 Jl 27 '45 por
PM p19 Ag 22 '45 il

BONCOUR, JOSEPH PAUL- *See* Paul-Boncour, J.

BONNELL, JOHN SUTHERLAND, REV. (bŏn-nĕl') Jan. 10, 1893- Clergyman

Address: b. Fifth Avenue Presbyterian Church, 7 W. 55th St., New York City; h. 1010 Fifth Ave., New York City

Dr. John Sutherland Bonnell, the Canadian-born pastor of the Fifth Avenue Presbyterian Church of New York City, for a decade has had an active career of unique social service. Well known as a platform and radio speaker, Bonnell has made an outstanding contribution to the life of the metropolis in which he now serves with the social service which he calls "pastoral psychiatry." Believing that there should be close cooperation between medicine and religion, Dr. Bonnell has made his study a consultation room, where since 1935 troubled people of "all shades of belief and disbelief" have received understanding and "spiritual prescriptions for mental ills." His method of psychotherapy, which has been called a venture in Christian helpfulness, is a combination of simple psychoanalysis and an invitation to call upon God in time of trouble.

The son of Abraham and Catherine (Cameron) Bonnell, John Sutherland Bonnell was born on Prince Edward Island in Canada, on January 10, 1893. Although not a physician, Abraham Bonnell was for forty-six years a member of the staff of, and for the greater part of that time supervisor of, the Falconwood Hospital, an institution for the insane, in Charlottetown, capital of the island. From the age of ten John accompanied his father on his daily rounds through the institution and thus, while still a boy, came to recognize the various types of mental illnesses. In his book *Pastoral Psychiatry,* written many years later, John Bonnell has painted a vivid picture of his father, describing the fine relationship that existed between father and son. The elder Bonnell was a kindly, patient, wise man, with a strong faith and a belief in the effectiveness of religion in mental cases. He had had no training in psychiatry, but he read widely on the subject. Looking on his patients as his children, he was always courteous and considerate to them. "My father had a sane respect for the insane," Dr. Bonnell has written. The kindly supervisor, who was to have such a strong influence on his son, was able to quiet even the most intractable of the patients, who would follow him as he walked about, holding his fingers or touching his arms. He had enough skill to take care of surgical cases when necessary, and he also acted as chaplain, often calming the restless inmates by his simple talks in the hospital chapel.

When he was seventeen John became an attendant at the hospital and went to the lectures given for the nurses. Later he was assigned the care of a former lawyer named Broadlawn. Although psychiatrists had pronounced Broadlawn a paranoiac, he was a brilliant scholar, and for two and a half years he prepared John for college, tutoring him in algebra, geometry, and Greek. Quarrelsome and suspicious with others, Broadlawn was calm and intelligent when with his pupil-nurse. The youth was resourceful in dealing with his patient's "sit-down strikes" and other vagaries, and the man and boy became fast friends. It was Broadlawn who first advised young Bonnell to go into the ministry. "If you can combine the knowledge you are gaining here [at Falconwood] with the power of religion to stabilize minds, you will blaze trails!" the lawyer used to declare. Today Dr. Bonnell feels that these early years at the hospital were, in a sense, his apprenticeship to the ministry.

At the outbreak of the First World War, John Bonnell was in Halifax completing his preparations to enter college as a divinity student. There Broadlawn, having escaped from the institution, sought the aid of his former pupil in enlisting in the Canadian artillery. Feeling that the lawyer had greatly improved in mental health, Bonnell helped him with his arrangements. Two years afterward, in 1916, Bonnell left college to enlist in the Army himself. On the troopship sailing from Halifax that September the young recruit met Broadlawn, now a sergeant; ten months later while fighting in France he learned that the friend whom he had helped to normal living had been killed in action, thus canceling what

REV. JOHN SUTHERLAND BONNELL

Broadlawn had always called his "debt to God and society."

On the front line in France with the Fifth Canadian Siege Battery (heavy artillery), Bonnell became the senior sergeant of his unit and was made acting sergeant major. At Falconwood he had learned that men could often be controlled by showing trust and gentleness toward them; at the front in 1917, when it became necessary to subdue men made obstreperous by drinking, he was to learn the necessity on occasion of unbending firmness in dealing with those who rebel against authority. The Canadian sergeant was wounded twice while in action and in 1918 was invalided home to Canada, where he resumed his studies for the ministry. He received his B.A. degree at Dalhousie University at Halifax in 1919, and on two occasions he took postgraduate work at the University of London. (At Pine Hill Divinity Hall in Halifax he received the B.D. degree in 1927, and in 1934 his D.D. degree.)

In 1922 John Bonnell was ordained a Presbyterian minister and took the pastorate of his first church, St. Andrews, in New Brunswick, Canada. He was married in 1923 to Bessie Louise Carruthers, and the couple remained at St. Andrews until 1929. Bonnell then became pastor of the Westminster Church in Winnipeg. After six years in Winnipeg, in 1935 he was called to the Fifth Avenue Presbyterian Church in New York City, where he has been pastor since that time.

Dr. Bonnell's psychiatric clinic was begun in 1935, the year he became pastor of the New York church. By 1941 six thousand men and women had come to him with their problems of futility, insecurity, inferiority, social failure, alcoholism, and emotional difficulties. Some of these people were definitely psychotic cases, beyond the minister's help, but most of them were people outwardly leading normal lives while inwardly carrying a burden of guilt or anxiety great enough to make them unhappy or unstable. In almost all the cases described in his

BONNELL, JOHN SUTHERLAND, REV.—*Continued*

book *Pastoral Psychiatry* Dr. Bonnell has found that his "pastoral psychiatry" has helped. He has found that confession of the problem to a sympathetic and patient listener—a counselor whose sixth sense is alert to hidden distress signals—gives the confessor much relief. Dr. Bonnell follows this with suggestions for prayer and spiritual reading. It has been said that he has introduced atheists to the Bible and taught doubters how to pray; he has prevented divorces, suicides, and nervous breakdowns; and he has cured functional disorders in the patients sent to him by physicians.

Bonnell points out that, according to the Greek derivation of the word "psychiatry" and the occurrence of the idea in the New Testament, the subject pertains primarily to the soul and secondarily to the mind. In his work as pastor and mentor, he directs his efforts to the healing of souls as medical psychiatrists direct their efforts to the regulating of feelings, emotions, and thoughts. He does not consider himself a psychiatrist in the medical sense, and warns clergymen to be wary of becoming fourth-rate psychiatrists, though he thinks they should study the methods of psychiatrists and psychologists to improve their own approach to their consultants. The pastor believes that there is some spark of religious instinct in everyone, even if he has not gone to church or prayed for years; he believes, too, that the spiritual urge needs only to be aroused to be of immeasurable help to the individual needing strength. The method employed by Bonnell is taking root and spreading among Prostestant churches, a number of which now have clinics similar to the one at the Fifth Avenue church. The *Reader's Digest* also points out that young men studying for the ministry are now studying and working in hospitals and penal institutions as part of their training to be physicians of the soul.

In May 1941, on the invitation of the Right Reverend J. R. Forgan, moderator of the Church of Scotland, Dr. Bonnell flew to Great Britain on a six weeks' good-will mission, representing the Presbyterian Church in the United States of America, the Federal Council of Churches of Christ in America, and other religious bodies. On this trip he went to Scotland, England, and Eire; he broadcast to America from England and delivered thirty addresses and sermons in churches, halls, air-raid shelters, shipyards, and soldiers' and sailors' barracks. As official delegate to the General Assembly of the Presbyterian Church of the United States of America, he attended the impressive meeting of the General Assembly of the Church of Scotland. Dr. Bonnell described the tour in his book, *Britons Under Fire* (1941), which critics considered a splendid contribution to the war effort in that it was an honest and inspiring report of the courage of the British people in wartime.

In addition to writing *Pastoral Psychiatry* and *Britons Under Fire*, Dr. Bonnell in 1936 compiled *Fifth Avenue Sermons*, a selection of twenty-one of his weekly sermons. (Each month one of his sermons is printed in the church bulletin and later in pamphlet form.) "These sermons," commented one reviewer, "explain why Dr. Bonnell is so universally acclaimed as one of the best present-day preachers." His "mind has been highly trained, and shows fruitful acquaintanceship with life and letters," wrote the critic of the New York *Herald Tribune*. ". . . This Fifth Avenue preacher knows the dangers of emotional evangelism, but he has not yet escaped them. His discourses are nonetheless readable and on occasion stimulating." Sunday morning sermons, delivered in "a forceful but restrained voice," draw an average weekly attendance of eighteen hundred persons to his Fifth Avenue church.

During the Second World War the pastor's sermons have frequently been on international topics, among them postwar problems. In October 1945 he suggested that a group of representative American religious leaders go to Russia to confer with the Patriarch of the Greek Orthodox Church, to serve as "ambassadors of Christian hopefulness and good will" and so arrest the "rapidly deteriorating" relationships between the United States and Soviet Russia. Declaring that "the world is big enough for different forms of government to exist without necessarily fighting each other," he added, "if the Governments are stalemated why shouldn't the churches act? . . . . The need of the hour is understanding and good will, and if we share some of the bountiful gifts that God has given to us with the suffering people of the world, we shall build up a good will that will mean much for international peace."

Since the year 1940 Dr. Bonnell and the Reverend Norman Vincent Peale, pastor of the Marble Collegiate Reformed Church, have conducted a weekly series of noon Lenten lectures under the auspices of the Greater New York Federation of Churches. In 1945 the subject was "Inner Strength for Wartime Living." From April 1942 to April 1944 the Fifth Avenue clergyman was a moderator of the Presbytery of New York City, and since 1938 he has been a lecturer at Princeton Theological Seminary. He received the honorary LL.D. degree from Washington and Jefferson College in 1943.

A popular preacher on the radio as well as in the pulpit and on the lecture platform, Dr. Bonnell has been broadcasting since 1943 over the American Broadcasting Company's network. For six months in 1943 he appeared weekly on the program *Our Spiritual Life*. Since then, beginning in January 1944, he has been appearing on an October-through-March schedule on the early morning program *Your Life Today*. Giving an eight-minute weekly address, Dr. Bonnell has alternated with other speakers on this daily program of religious talks. During these years and earlier, when the clergyman spoke over the Red Network, tens of thousands of listeners have requested copies of his talks.

The Bonnells have four children: a son, George Carruthers, and three daughters, Catherine Cameron, Elizabeth Louise, and Jessie Margaret. George Bonnell was studying for the ministry when he entered the service as a private in the Army of the United States; he was wounded in Italy in October 1944. Although the family are devoted to their Canadian homeland and maintain a summer home there on Prince Edward Island, Dr. Bonnell became a citizen of the United States in January 1945. In figure the clergyman is tall and slender; his face is sharp-featured, his hair dark. A quiet, yet warm and friendly person, he has been called a good "listening post."

References

Newsweek 17:74 My 12 '41
Read Digest 39:83-6 Jl '41
Bonnell, J. S. Pastoral Psychiatry (1938)
Religious Leaders of America, 1941-42
Who's Who in America, 1944-45

BONNET, HENRI (bô"ně' äN"rē') May 26, 1888- French Ambassador to the United States

Address: The French Embassy, Washington, D. C.

In keeping with his belief that "France cannot conceive a victory without a world organization," and that the United States will be of foremost importance in such an organization, General Charles de Gaulle [40] selected as his Government's first ambassador to the United States after its liberation from the Nazis a man who is a champion of strong international ties—Henri Bonnet. While Ambassador Bonnet is considered representative of the distinguished intellectuals whom the French traditionally appoint to important diplomatic posts, he also typifies the new generation of statesmen who are striving to widen the scope of international understanding. Not only has he devoted many years to the study of international problems, but in his post in the Secretariat of the League of Nations, he took part in many international conferences in Europe, Asia, and America. He is also the author of a number of books dealing with postwar plans for a world organization.

Henri Bonnet was born May 26, 1888, in Châteauponsac, in the mid-western department of Haute-Vienne. His parents, J. T. H. and Marie Thérèse (Lascoux) Bonnet, were of the intellectual middle class. They sent him to the University of Paris and in 1912 to l'Ecole Normale Supérieure in Paris, from which he was graduated with the degree of *agrégé,* an academic rank that entitled him to appointment to the highest teaching posts in lycées or on certain faculties of universities. Further study in history (the subject in which he had majored) was interrupted by the First World War, at the outbreak of which Bonnet was drafted, and from which he was discharged at its close with the rank of captain. He received several citations for bravery and was made a Chevalier of the Legion of Honor.

Re-entering civilian life Bonnet continued his work in history, specializing in foreign relations. By 1919 he had become the foreign editor of the Paris newspaper *L'Ere Nouvelle* ("The New Era"), and in another year, when the League of Nations came into existence, his knowledge of foreign affairs led to his appointment to a post in the Secretariat. Attached first to the Division of Press and Information, he later became the head of the cabinet of the Assistant Secretary-General of the League. Between 1920 and 1931 he attended international conferences of the League which were held in Geneva and other European cities as well as in China, Japan, Canada, and

HENRI BONNET

the United States. In 1931 he left Geneva to become the director of the International Institute of Intellectual Cooperation, a division of the League of Nations with offices in Paris.

Bonnet outlined the work and history of this division of the League in a chapter entitled "Intellectual Cooperation," which he contributed to a symposium on the League of Nations, *World Organization* (1943). The framers of the Covenant of the League, like the framers of the Constitution of the United States, included nothing about education or intellectual cooperation. The League had therefore no legal basis on which to form a technical organ for the important work of promoting better understanding among nations in intellectual and spiritual matters. During the first Assembly meeting in 1920, however, a committee was formed for the purpose of studying the problem. Among its very first members were Mme. Marie Curie, Albert Einstein [41], Robert Millikan [40], and James T. Shotwell [44]. In 1924 the Council and the Assembly of the League approved of the establishment of a technical organization (with the same status as other divisions), and in January 1926 the International Institute of Intellectual Cooperation was founded. The Institute was supported by funds provided by annual subsidies from forty governments and by grants from the Rockefeller and Carnegie foundations.

An important part of the work was the organization of "Conversations" and the publication of "Open Letters." Discussions at the Conversations or conferences, which were held in the countries of cooperating governments, were devoted to the exchange of information and drafting of plans on such subjects as reorganization of courses of higher study, the organization of international propaganda through radio and motion picture media, and scientific cooperation. Work of a more technical nature consisted of regular interchange of views and methods among libraries and institutes of arts and archeology; the establishment of inter-university relations and of a

BONNET, HENRI—*Continued*

uniform terminology in the sciences; and the introduction of instruction in schools on the aims of the League of Nations.

"It should be emphasized," says Bonnet, "that this machinery was an integral part of the League of Nations and at the disposal of the governments participating in its activities, among which were a certain number of non-member states." The most striking example of a direct request, says Bonnet, was that made by China (a member country) in 1931 for an educational mission to advise in the planning of the reorganization of Chinese schools. Bonnet, as Secretary-General of the International Conference of Higher Studies within the Institute, was selected for this work. During this period (1931-40) Bonnet also acted as vice-president of the Studies Center of Foreign Politics.

While never prominent in Parisian social circles, Bonnet during his residence there maintained an elaborate apartment and had an estate in Poitiers, where he gave hunting parties. In 1932 the statesman was married to Helle (Zervoudaki) Aghnaides, the daughter of a wealthy Greek tobacco merchant and former wife of Thanassis Aghnaides, the present Greek Ambassador to the Court of St. James. The Bonnets managed to escape from Paris to London with two suitcases before the Nazis conquered France.

During a month's stay in London Bonnet became active in the "Free French" movement. He carried on the work after his arrival in the United States, too, serving on the executive committee and as one of the vice-presidents of France Forever, which was associated with the Fighting French delegation. His decision to come to the United States was influenced by an invitation from the New School of Social Research in New York City. Later he became a member of the faculty of l'Ecole Libre des Hautes Etudes, or Free School for Higher Studies, which was set up after the fall of France by the French and Belgians, with the aid of the New School. He also served on the Council of the Free World Association and on the editorial board of that association's monthly magazine, *Free World*. Much of his time, however, was spent in Chicago as special adviser to the World Citizens' Association, which had been organized in December 1939 for the purpose of developing world-community awareness. Among its directors were Joseph E. Davies '42, Quincy Wright '43 and Anita McCormick Blaine. Working under the sponsorship of this organization, Bonnet edited or wrote a number of books.

The first of these volumes, *The World's Destiny and the United States*, written in 1941 before Pearl Harbor, contained the conclusions of thirty men and women on some of the important problems which are now confronting the democracies and will continue to confront them after the Second World War. *The United Nations, What They Are, What They May Become* (1942) reviews the existing means of collaboration and indicates how an organization might be created which would translate into reality the concept of the United Nations and make them a dynamic power for war and peace. In another study, *United Nations on the Way: Principles and Policies* (1942), Bonnet analyzed treaties and agreements of the United

Nations and the utterances of their leaders, indicating in some detail the social, economic, and political adjustments necessary for the achievement of a peaceful world. Supporting De Gaulle's opposition to blocs or European spheres of influence, Bonnet wrote in his *Outlines of the Future* (1943): "In order to prevent the return of these catastrophes which have twice loosed destruction on the world, the United Nations must continue to turn to new formulas. These formulas must assert that the distrust resulting from the spirit of political nationalism which the war—for a time at least —will have intensified, is no longer justified." In speaking of the United Nations, he said, "This is not a great alliance of a few powerful nations which tomorrow will control the world—continents or parts of continents. Any combination of powers not enjoying the full support and trust of all the peoples finally freed from fear and which possess only greater physical strength, would not even last as long as those after the Napoleonic Wars. . . .There likewise cannot be a return to the patchwork pattern of nations refusing to recognize their patent interdependence."

On June 3, 1943, the French Committee of National Liberation was formed under the joint chairmanship of De Gaulle and General Henri Honoré Giraud '43. Henri Bonnet was elected as Commissioner of Information after De Gaulle and Giraud had refused to accept each other's nominees. Bonnet was described as a "neutral" on the Giraud-De Gaulle question, although it was pointed out that his executive post with the Fighting France group indicated that his views were close to those of De Gaulle. Never having held any political office, Bonnet, at the time in Chicago engaged in research work, expressed surprise at his appointment. When interviewed by the American press he said that his only contact with De Gaulle had been in London just after the founding of the "Free French" movement (June 18, 1940). Regarding his sympathies, Bonnet declared: "Today the question of whether one is a Giraudist or a De Gaullist is not important. We have been appointed as a unit for France and we will serve as such." The new Commissioner of Information assumed his portfolio in Algiers on June 23, 1943.

A few days after taking office Bonnet announced his intention of unifying the De Gaullist and Giraudist press services which had been operating separately. He also soon gave evidence of wanting to give the press representatives the fullest information possible. In February 1944, following the resignation of Giraud as co-chairman of the Committee, Bonnet submitted a plan for a complete reform of the French press to the Provisional Consultative Assembly in Algiers in the form of a law. Its purpose was to keep the press from being influenced by commercial or financial interests or by foreign governments; and it proposed that a French information agency be created on the model of the American press associations, although it limited to some extent the American idea of the freedom of the press, at least for the period of transition between the liberation of France and the establishment of a regular government. The plan also included suggestions that relations among press associations of various countries be discussed at international conferences after the war; in the meantime an interchange of news among the "most important agencies" would be the sole basis of cooperation. Bonnet's plan also called for immediate reform of newspapers published in French North Africa and other French overseas possessions. It proposed that new papers be established in liberated France, that Nazi controlled papers be suppressed. The new papers would publish communiques issued by the temporary government but would be free to present the views of the political parties represented in the Higher Council of Resistance. Independent newspapers would be allowed to present news objectively.

The following summer the French news distribution decree was jointly criticized by American and British press representatives for giving a monopoly to the French agencies. To remove misunderstandings, Bonnet called a press conference at which he explained that the decree was merely temporary—that it did not imply continuing Governmental control after France was fully liberated. And in answer to the criticism that the ordinance bears no express provision that it is temporary, Bonnet contended that its very nature makes it so, since its stipulated purpose is to revive French newspapers and periodicals. "When this has been done," he said, "the ordinance will become obsolete." (Since assuming his Washington post, Bonnet, in addressing a meeting of the United Nations Information Board on January 4, 1945, stated that the French press encountered today no other restrictions than those imposed for military reasons.) Resigning his position as head of Information shortly after the French Provisional Government moved from Algiers to Paris, Bonnet gave as his reason: "Most key Government posts should be held by active members of the Resistance."

On New Year's Day 1945 Henri Bonnet presented his credentials to President Roosevelt [42] as France's first ambassador to the United States since the departure of Vichy's representative. Crossing to the State Department Bonnet then signed the document which made France the thirty-sixth member of the United Nations. In a brief speech he repeated the faith he so often had expressed in his books on the United Nations: "To this great cause France is prepared to devote herself wholeheartedly. . . .She knows that from now on, in a world where science and technology have surpassed distances, war, once begun, will spread over the entire world. Consequently she is convinced that any threat of attack must be met and, if necessary, curbed. She knows also that during this war the fraternal cooperation of the United Nations has proved that splendid results may be obtained in all domains through mutual aid, division of work, and the organization of a common effort toward the same goal." indicated that his views were close to those of

In other addresses delivered later in the year, Bonnet stated that the increase in markets for American goods in France and resumption of large-scale French exports to the United States depend on the speed with which America aids France in her economic recovery. When Georges Bidault [45] left the San Francisco conference in May, the Ambassador took his place as head of the French delegation. (He was the recipient of the honorary degrees of Doctor of Laws from Brown University in February 1945 and from Howard University in June 1945.)

The French Ambassador's scholarly background has not suppressed his sense of humor nor his "human touch." On Thanksgiving Day, shortly after his appointment to Washington, he entertained at dinner six American GI's. When all the possessions of the Bonnets were confiscated by the Vichy Government and they found themselves without money, they met with poise and ingenuity the task of earning a living in foreign surroundings—he as a teacher and she as a milliner. In a recent interview in the library of the big Tudor house that is the French Embassy, the tall, slender, dark-haired Helle Bonnet, who had been educated in a convent in Smyrna and at a finishing school in Lausanne, related how she had started the Helle Hat Shop in New York City in 1942 on a capital of only twenty-five dollars. (Elsa Maxwell [43] reported that the hats were in exquisite taste and that Mme. Bonnet, despite her straitened circumstances, continued to be chic during her three-year exile.) Although neither the new Ambassador nor his wife had moved in diplomatic circles before they came to Washington, it is predicted that their dignity and charm would win friends for themselves and France. Bonnet has a ready smile, is tall, slim, dark, and wears a closely cropped mustache.

References

Free France 6:487 D 15 '44
N Y Sun p16 Ja 2 '45

BONSAL, STEPHEN (bŏn'săl) Mar. 29, 1865- Author; journalist
Address: b. c/o Doubleday Doran & Co., Inc., 14 W. 49th St., New York City; h. 3142 P St., NW, Washington, D.C.

Perhaps "the most traveled of American reporters in the foreign field as well as the best and most readable literary stylist among journalists," is writer and historian Stephen Bonsal. As newspaperman and diplomatic aide he annotated virtually every conflict from the Bulgarian-Serbian War of 1888 to the First World War, visiting and surveying most of the countries of Europe, Asia, South America, and Africa. Bonsal's diary of the proceedings of the Versailles Peace Conference of 1919, where he served as interpreter for President Wilson and Colonel House, was published in 1944 under the title of *Unfinished Business*, and was awarded in May 1945 a Pulitzer Prize in the field of letters for 1944.

Born on March 29, 1865, in Baltimore, Maryland, Stephen Bonsal is the son of Stephen and Frances (Leigh) Bonsal. His father was a coffee importer and shipowner engaged in the Brazilian trade. Young Stephen attended St. Paul's School in New Hampshire until he was seventeen, when he became an *Ausserordentlicher* student, or auditor, at Heidelberg and Vienna universities. His work there earned him certificates in German and Italian literature. Afterward he returned to his Maryland home, where he lived until, as he puts it, he came a cropper with a mare. She was Lizzie Preston, owned jointly by Bonsal and Harry Harwood, the famous amateur steeplechase rider. One day she lost a race at a Sheepshead Bay (New York) track—and a portion of the Bonsal family fortune was lost with her.

STEPHEN BONSAL

The young man dallied briefly with the idea of joining the Foreign Legion, but in the end his good opinion of some of his own writing decided him on the field of journalism. He persistently plotted to secure a place on the New York *Herald*, and eventually succeeded in attracting the attention of one of its editors by an account of the thrilling escape of a Latin-American president from his ungrateful country. The reporting job Bonsal was given turned out to be as exciting as this introduction. He had the opportunity to report a riotous meeting of European revolutionaries, an experimental balloon flight, a trip in a submarine around New York Harbor, a Haitian revolution, and several sensational murders.

One of these stories appealed to the *Herald*'s owner, James Gordon Bennett, known as "the Commodore," who in 1887 sent for Bonsal to come to his London office. In London and on the Continent the new foreign correspondent moved entranced in an "ever-renewed and ever-changing gallery of important or fascinating people." He met Parnell, Gladstone, and Eleanor Aveling, the daughter of Karl Marx; and he himself came into the limelight with an exclusive story on the meeting of the uninhibited John L. Sullivan and the Prince of Wales. Later he scooped Arthur Brisbane with his article on the champion's fight in Paris with Charlie Mitchell.

Later in 1888 the Commodore assigned the twenty-three-year-old reporter to cover the "clouds over the Balkans . . . to be on hand whenever and wherever anything happens." In the course of the next few years Bonsal "crossed and recrossed the length and breadth of the Peninsula half a dozen times" on this beat between Vienna and the Bosphorus, as he observed the racial, political, and religious antagonisms that made the Balkans the powder keg of Europe. After three and a half years of this Bonsal was recalled to New York when he fell into disfavor with Bennett because of a dispute over his salary and expense account. The reporter who had mingled with royalty

and leaders in social and political circles in Europe now found himself in the humble position of "emergency man" on the city staff, at a salary of three dollars a day plus space rates.

From 1893 to 1897 Bonsal was in the diplomatic service of the United States—he served as secretary of the legation and chargé d'affaires in Madrid, Peking, and Tokyo. Meanwhile, having been reinstated at the *Herald*, he reported the Sino-Japanese War in 1894-95, traveled through Siberia in 1896, rushed to the scene of the Cuban insurrection of 1897, after which he remained in the Caribbean area to report the Spanish-American War. From this period the journalist drew upon his observations for three books: *The Real Condition of Cuba* (1897), *The Fight for Santiago* (1899), and *The Golden Horseshoe* (1900).

In 1900 Bonsal joined a China relief expedition, and the following year he was reporting on campaigns in the Philippines. The next decade took him to Venezuela, Russia, Japan, the Balkans, the West Indies, South America, and Mexico, where he covered uprisings, revolutions, and wars. The year 1912 found him writing his book *The American Mediterranean*; in 1913 he served as secretary to the Governor General of the Philippines, then as commissioner of public utilities for the Islands the following year. After a special mission in Mexico, Bonsal took up his reportorial duties again in 1915, covering the progress of Hindenberg's army on Germany's East Front in the First World War. After a chance meeting with Colonel House in Berlin the correspondent was pressed into service as interpreter in a series of important meetings with German political figures in which House was engaged. In 1916 Bonsal left Europe to assume the post of adviser to the American-Mexican Commission.

When the United States entered the First World War Bonsal was commissioned a major, serving first at the Army War College in Washington and then, in 1918, with the AEF in France. During the preparations for the Peace Conference following the Armistice, Colonel House cabled General Pershing, asking for the services of his former associate, who was at that time an officer at General Headquarters. Bonsal began his duties as adviser on Balkan affairs, soon becoming the close associate of House in all matters relating to the peace. During the secret meetings of the Big Four—Wilson, Clemenceau, Lloyd George '44, and Orlando '44—the erstwhile reporter sat with the President and Colonel House as their confidential interpreter. Since no stenographic notes of the proceedings were kept and no official translations were made, Bonsal at their request made a practice of daily transcribing his notes in the form of a journal, which was used for reference. Urged to publish his notes on the drafting of the Versailles Treaty and of the Covenant of the League of Nations soon afterward, Bonsal demurred, believing that this "might be indiscreet on the part of a professional writer who had been given access to confidential information." (President Wilson had, however, given his permission for publication of the journal.) Later that year Bonsal participated in the inter-

Allied mission to Austria-Hungary and the Balkan States under General Smuts [41] and in a special mission to Germany and Bohemia.

During the years that followed—except for a ten-thousand-mile tour through Soviet Russia in 1931 and a trip across North China and Manchuria in 1934—Bonsal's activities received little public notice. Much of his time he devoted to contributing sketches and short stories to magazines. In 1937 he set down his reminiscences of his early journalistic career, covering the period from 1885 to about 1892, in a volume he entitled *Heyday in a Vanished World*. Enlivened with countless anecdotes about its author, European princes, prime ministers, and "just common people," the account was pronounced "quite as lively and immediate" as the books of his younger colleagues.

In 1944, when Bonsal's friends, among them Arthur Krock [43], pointed out that it was the writer's duty to publish his notes on the 1919 Peace Conference because "we were beginning to repeat the same mistakes that led to the tragedy of Versailles," he submitted them to the public in *Unfinished Business*. Written "with a flourish, with wit, and many a neat characterization of the celebrities he saw daily," *Unfinished Business*, wrote the critics, is entertaining as well as historically revealing. "This is the first book to supply the missing links in the chain of events that led to Woodrow Wilson's failure to build an abiding peace structure and induce his own countrymen to be a part of it," stated Arthur Krock in the New York *Times*; "and it supplies as much news to President Roosevelt [42], to Marshal Stalin [42], and to Prime Minister Churchill [42] as to average readers of the present generation, although the three chiefs of state have had access to many secret documents." "A more timely book than this could hardly be imagined," commented Allan Nevins. "In the construction of a durable and effective fabric of collective security the world truly faces 'unfinished business'. . . .We find a strong light poured on the reasons why the first effort broke down." In May 1945 it was announced that Bonsal had been awarded one of the 1944 Pulitzer prizes in the field of letters for this "distinguished book on the history of the United States." (At the end of 1945 Bonsal was at work an another book relating to the Peace Conference. To be published in the spring of 1946 under the title of "Suitors and Suppliants at Versailles," it will consist of excerpts from the journal he kept of the secret conferences of the Big Four.)

The author in his next book, *When the French Were Here* (1945), recalled the story of the French Expeditionary Force of six thousand soldiers who assisted the American colonists in their war for independence. Bonsal, who before Clemenceau's death in 1929 had planned to collaborate with the statesman, wrote the volume from unpublished reports and letters made available to him in the National Archives of France and from documents in the manuscript division of the Library of Congress. While many critics rated this "narrative of the sojourn of the French forces in America, and their contribution to the Yorktown campaign" (the subtitle of the book) as "a delightful excursion into an eventful and interesting chapter of American history," at

least one (Virginia Kirkus) felt that Bonsal's book was "a concentrated phase of a war of the past studied in intimate detail—an objective and detached study for scholars, not for the general market."

The white-haired, mustached Bonsal, who is described as "a sardonic old realist" and "a brilliant raconteur," is a popular dinner guest. In his earlier years he enjoyed riding and fencing. He lives in Washington, D.C., with Mrs. Bonsal, the former Henrietta Fairfax Morris, to whom he was married in 1900. The Bonsals have four sons, Stephen, Philip Wilson, Dudley B., and Richard Morris; two are in Government work, and the other two have seen service in the Second World War. As if to sum up his long career, the veteran journalist introduced his autobiography with lines from an old English song which ends with, "This huntin' doesn't pay but we've prowli't up an' down a bit an' had a rattlin' day."

References

Bonsal, S. Heyday in a Vanished World (1937)
Who's Who in America, 1944-45

BOSE, SUBHAS CHANDRA (bōs shōōb-häsh' chŭn'drá) 1897—Aug. 18, 1945

Indian politician and nationalist; head of the Japanese-controlled Provisional Government of Free India; president of the All-India Trades Union Congress (1929-31); president of the Indian National Congress (1939); died in an airplane crash in Formosa; death confirmed at Japanese headquarters on November 21, 1945. See *Current Biography* 1944 Yearbook.

Obituary

N Y Times p3 Ag 24 '45

BOWMAN, ISAIAH Dec. 26, 1878-

University president; geographer

Address: b. Johns Hopkins University, Homewood, Baltimore; h. 108 W. 39th St., Baltimore

The development of the world's resources to offset the destruction of war is considered one of the most important aspects of postwar planning. Isaiah Bowman, president of Johns Hopkins University, believes that the Second World War has taught the American people that modern geography is no longer children's geography, to be finished in the seventh grade, and that geographic science has a significant part to play in postwar planning. Widely known as an author and educator and as America's "leading expert on geography," Bowman throughout his lifetime has correlated scientific study with practical experience by leading a number of fact-finding geographic expeditions to South America, and by serving on directorial boards of many educational, geographic, cultural, and peace institutions, including the Woodrow Wilson Foundation, and the Council of Foreign Relations. Since 1942 the university president had also served as an adviser on foreign affairs to President Roosevelt [42] and former Secretary of State Cordell Hull [42], Bowman's particular contribution being the application of his knowledge of politics and geography to territorial problems and to popula-

ISAIAH BOWMAN

tion pressures and world organization for peace and security.

Isaiah Bowman was born in Waterloo, Ontario, Canada, on December 26, 1878. His parents were Samuel Cressman and Emily (Shantz) Bowman. Within two months after his birth his parents had moved to Michigan. He was graduated from the State Normal College at Ypsilanti, Michigan, in 1902, and from Harvard University with a B.Sc. in 1905. The year 1903-4 was spent at the State Normal College at Ypsilanti as instructor in geography. He was assistant in physiography at Harvard in 1904-5, and then went to Yale as instructor in geography and for graduate work in that subject, receiving his Ph.D. degree there in 1909. He was special lecturer in geography at Wesleyan University from 1907 to 1909, and at the University of Chicago in 1908, and was assistant professor of geography at Yale during 1909-15.

While at Yale Bowman began his travels to South America. His first important field work was in 1907 as leader of the first Yale South American geographical expedition. He was geographer and geologist of the Yale Peruvian expedition in 1911, and in 1913 he was leader of an expedition to the Central Andes under the auspices of the American Geographical Society of New York. In 1915 he resigned his position at Yale University to become director of the American Geographical Society, a post he held for twenty years. During these years Bowman did much to increase the size of the library and the map collection of the society, while its chief publication, the *Geographical Review*, became a leading scientific journal. The chief project of the society during Bowman's administration was the preparation of a map of Hispanic America on a scale of 1:1,000,-000, in conformity with the standards of the Millionth Map of the World, sponsored by successive International Geographical Congresses. The preparation of this map cost over four hundred thousand dollars and required twenty years to complete. Two other notable enter-

prises which he developed were a systematic study of scientific objectives in polar exploration, and a world-wide study of possibilities of land settlement.

Bowman's career in foreign affairs began with his position as geographer for the Peace Conference in Paris following the First World War. In 1919 he was chief territorial specialist to the American Commission to Negotiate Peace; he also served on the Polish Commission, various territorial commissions, and the Polish-Ukrainian Armistice Commission. In 1920 he was physiographer for the United States Department of Justice in the dispute over the Red River boundary between Texas and Oklahoma. An amusing story is told of this period: Bowman seemed too sure of his facts to please the opposing lawyer, who said sarcastically: "May I inquire whether you consider yourself a major or a minor prophet?" Bowman replied: "I am called a major prophet; my name is Isaiah." (*Newsweek*, citing this story in 1944, called Bowman a "prophet without peer in the fields of geography and ethnology.")

Bowman was president of Social Science Abstracts, Inc., in 1929-31; in 1931 he was elected president of the International Geographical Union; and in 1934 he presided at the International Geographical Congress in Warsaw, at which forty nations were represented. He was director in 1933-35 of the Science Advisory Board appointed by President Roosevelt, and a member of the National Advisory Committee on National Parks and Monuments in 1932-36. He was elected a member of the National Academy of Sciences in 1930, and was chairman of the National Research Council in 1933-35.

In 1935 Isaiah Bowman was elected president of Johns Hopkins University to succeed Joseph Sweetman Ames. During the years he has been in office he is said to have proved himself an able administrator, many financial and academic improvements being credited to him. A new department of chemical engineering has been added to the School of Engineering; the work of the Walter Hines Page School of International Relations has been directed to special studies of Far Eastern problems; and "the university's unique tradition—emphasis upon advanced scholarly training and research" —has been fostered in every way possible.

His plans for geography in the postwar years and a delineation of his ideals were given in his annual report to the university (published in *Science* for December 24, 1943). In this report Bowman explained how the war had brought about an awareness of the importance of geography, formerly a neglected field in higher education, because that "imaginative grasp of space" which science shares with poetry had seemed impossible to attain until the United States Army, Navy, and Air Forces were scattered all over the world. Bowman feels that we shall be dealing for a long time to come with what was once considered the "outer world," and that we cannot escape corresponding educational demands. At Johns Hopkins geography was expanded quite suddenly, when the United States entered the Second World War, for the Army Specialized Training Program. Bowman also described the expansion of national research in his report, particularly the development of cartography, and meteorological and climatological research. Emphasis on scholarship has predominated under Bowman's regime; admission standards have been raised and all athletic scholarships eliminated. In 1937 Johns Hopkins became the first major institution in the country to attack the problem of overemphasis on and commercialism in intercollegiate sports; gate receipts in athletic contests have been eliminated, and the university now finances all intercollegiate sports as well as the intramural program.

Many provocative subjects, both national and international in scope, interested geographer Bowman in 1944. He took an active part in the controversy over the administration of the much discussed postwar program for Government-financed education for veterans, expressing the opinion that this program should be administered by educators, not by the Veterans' Administration, and that there should not be too much Federal control of the program. In January Cordell Hull, feeling the need of a reorganization of the State Department, appointed Bowman one of three men on the Advisory Council of Post-War Foreign Policy (the other two members being the late Norman H. Davis '40, chairman of the American Red Cross, and Myron C. Taylor '40, President Roosevelt's special envoy to the Vatican). The newspaper *PM*, commenting editorially on the State Department's "reorganization," pointed out that it was not exactly a "new wind" that had swept the Department but only the "gentlest of zephyrs," since the men appointed had for two years been advising the President, and all represented "pretty conservative thinking." (In December Bowman was appointed one of two special advisers to the new Secretary of State.)

In March Bowman was chosen by Edward R. Stettinius, Jr. '40, then Under-Secretary of State, to go to London for a series of conferences with the British Government. Four other experienced officials, each an expert in his field, accompanied Stettinius on this mission. *Time* Magazine, describing Bowman as a "front-rank political geographer," pointed out that there was a great deal of conjecture among reporters about the probable nature of the conversations. Bowman had helped Woodrow Wilson fix boundaries at the Paris Conference in 1919: Did his presence in the State Department group mean that postwar boundaries would be discussed in London? To these press representatives President Roosevelt replied that Bowman had been chosen because "he knows more about geography than everybody in this room, including myself." Later it was stated that the Stettinius mission had not made any definite decisions, but that it had helped to bring nearer to realization that complete unity of action among the big powers which foreshadowed the Dumbarton Oaks conference. In August 1944 Bowman was a delegate to the World Security Conference at Dumbarton Oaks in Washington, D.C., and in the spring of 1945 he served as one of the advisers to the American delegation at the San Francisco conference.

Bowman's writings and speeches make it clear that he feels that we must not make a failure of any part of the peace, now that the Second World War has come to an end. In a speech given in September 1944 in Cleve-land, Ohio, upon his retirement as president of the American Association for the Advancement of Science, he said: "Peace should be the business of every citizen, whatever his calling," and "we must all do something about it, now and hereafter, today and every day, down all the generations together." Of the part of science in the peace he said: "One of the roots of the tree of peace is science. . . .The creative powers of science can quickly make up some of the losses of war." On the question of compulsory military training, he urged the adoption of citizenship courses in the colleges to offset the military training "which inevitably includes indoctrination."

In discussing Bowman's work on territorial matters, *Newsweek* points out that his conception of geography embraces natural history, sociology, political science, and national and international relations, and it surmises that his advisory work on postwar problems has been concerned with "the knottiest geographical riddle that has yet risen to plague Allied relations," the future border of Poland. On the question of boundaries Bowman has said: "If every nation struggles uncompromisingly for the best strategic frontier, there can never be peace. . . .It is not the position of the line alone that is important; it is a whole group of economic, racial, ethnic, and religious factors that relate themselves to boundary location. Religion does not stop at a mountain crest, nor do marriages take account of ethnic majorities. A well-defined topographic feature may be too important to be neglected in favor of the ethnic considerations. The same may be said of any other line of defense, such as a river or a belt of marshes, as in eastern Poland."

Bowman is a director of Woods Hole (Massachusetts) Oceanographic Institution, the American Telephone and Telegraph Company, and a trustee of the Peabody Institute of Baltimore. He received an honorary M.A. degree from Yale University (1921); honorary M.Ed. degree from Michigan State College (1927); honorary Sc.D. degree from Bowdoin College (1931); and LL.D. degrees from Dartmouth, Charleston, and Dickinson colleges and the University of Pennsylvania (1935), University of Wisconsin and Harvard University (1936), Queens University, Ontario, Canada, and the University of Western Ontario (1937), and Washington College (1940). In 1941 he received honorary degrees from the universities of Cusco and Arequipa, Peru.

The university president is a Corresponding Member of the Geographical Society of London, the Swedish Society of Anthropology and Geography, and the Hispanic Society of America, and a member of foreign geographical societies. He is a member of the Association of American Geographers, the American Philosophical Society, the Explorers Club, and Century Association of New York City, and the Cosmos Club of Washington, D.C. He has been the American commissioner of the Permanent International Commission of China and the United States since 1940. He is a member of Sigma Psi (Yale, 1906), Phi Beta Kappa (honorary), Kappa Phi Alpha (Michigan Normal College), Delphi Society (Ferris Institute, 1900-1901). The Council on Foreign Relations of which he is a director is an

BOWMAN, ISAIAH—*Continued*

institution devoted to the study of international relations which was organized by men who attended the Paris Peace Conference in 1919. Early in 1945 the council plans to move into a new building, a mansion donated by Mrs. Harriet Pratt as a memorial to her husband. The directors feel that greatly increased demands will be made on institutions devoted to foreign affairs after the war, and they therefore plan to enlarge the activities of the council after moving into the new building.

Isaiah Bowman is the author of *Forest Physiography* (1911), *South America* (1915), *The Andes of Southern Peru* (1916), *The New World: Problems in Political Geography* (1921), *An American Boundary Dispute* (1923), *Desert Trails of Atacama* (1923), *The Mohammedan World* (1924), *International Relations* (1930), *The Pioneer Fringe* (1931), *Geography in Relation to the Social Sciences* (1934), *Design for Scholarship* (1936), and *Graduate School in American Democracy* (1939). He was co-editor and part author of *Human Geography* and editor and collaborator of *Limits of Land Settlement*. *The New World*, probably Bowman's most important work, has been a standard political geography text in colleges and universities in the twenty-three years since its publication.

For his services to science Bowman has been awarded gold medals by numerous societies (*Time* Magazine describes him as "many-medaled"), which include the Scottish, Paris, Chicago, and Philadelphia Geographical societies. The Civic Medal of the Geographical Society of Belgrade and the Patron's Gold Medal of the Royal Geographical Society of London were also awarded to him.

Bowman was married in Lynn, Massachusetts, on June 28, 1909, to Cora Olive, daughter of James Walter Goldthwait of Lynn. The Bowmans have three children: Walter Parker, Robert Goldthwait, and Olive (Mrs. Walter H. Gerwig). Judging from his photographs, the geographer is stocky, broadshouldered, and youthful looking. Though much of his work is scientific, he has combined a sense of beauty and idealism with his fact-finding; in one of his talks at Johns Hopkins he described the inspiration he derived from a book with beautiful engravings which he had picked up on his travels. "Whenever I turn to it," he said, "a magic begins to work. Presently I am on a mountain top, my compass needle points north again, and things big and little appear in true perspective."

References

Newsweek 23:86-7 Ja 10 '44; 23:98-9 Ap 3 '44
Sci Mo 59:95 Ag '44
Science 100:229-41 S 15 '44
Think 10:40 O '44
American Men of Science, 1938
International Who's Who, 1942
National Cyclopædia of American Biography Current vol F p458
Who's Who in America, 1944-45

BOYCE, WESTRAY BATTLE 1901- Director of the Women's Army Corps

Address: b. c/o War Department, Washington, D.C.

About halfway between V-E and V-J days approximately one hundred thousand members of the United States Women's Army Corps, who had served in every theater of the Second World War, were placed under the direction of Colonel Westray Battle Boyce. A veteran of overseas service, on July 12, 1945, Colonel Boyce replaced Colonel Oveta Culp Hobby'[42], who had served as director of the WAC since its organization in 1942. The de-

COL. WESTRAY BATTLE BOYCE

mobilization of the Corps, after three years of wartime service, was effected on a relative basis with that of the other components of the Army. Meanwhile, the Wacs continued with their regular assignments.

Like her predecessor, Westray Battle Boyce is a Southerner. She was born in Rocky Mount, North Carolina, in August 1901. The name Westray and her maiden name, Battle, are six-generation-old family names, and many members on the Battle side have, appropriately, been military men. Educated in her home state, the future WAC director attended the Women's Division of the University of North Carolina in Greensboro and Pell's Law School in Raleigh, but did not take a degree at either institution. For several years she worked in an administrative capacity in the home office of an insurance company in North Carolina's capital city. Then, for eight years the businesswoman worked for Government agencies in Washington, where she became well known. In this period she was employed by the Federal Works Agency and the National Recovery and the Rural Electrification Administrations. In the offices of the REA she served as chief of the Insurance Division.

Less than two months after the Women's Army Auxiliary Corps was created in May 1942, she relinquished this civilian status to enlist in the Corps, because she thought her joining "might make it possible for some father of small children to be able to stay at home." When the first WAAC Training

Center was opened at Fort Des Moines, Iowa, Mrs. Boyce was among the first to enter the Officer Candidates' School. Commissioned a second lieutenant on September 12, 1942, she then served for a period as a company officer at the Training Center.

Her next assignment brought the service-woman to New York City, where she acted as public relations officer in the Second Service Command for a brief time. Returning afterward to the South, Lieutenant Boyce became WAAC staff director of the Fourth Service Command in Atlanta, Georgia. In this post she was the first woman to serve on the staff of Major General William Bryden, commanding general of the Fourth Service Command. After a year in this position she was sent in August 1943 to the North African theater of operations as WAC staff director. (In early July 1943 President Roosevelt [42] signed Federal legislation making the Corps a part of the Army, thus eliminating "auxiliary" or one of the *A*'s from the name.) As director, Mrs. Boyce, now a captain, was Colonel Hobby's personal representative on the staff of General Dwight D. Eisenhower [42], and in this capacity she supervised the eighteen hundred Wacs in the North African theater. At the end of a year, during which she is said to have served with "special distinction," she was returned to the United States and assigned to the Personnel Division of the War Department General Staff.

A lieutenant colonel by 1945, she was named deputy director of the WAC on May 25, a few weeks after V-E Day. Two months later, on July 12, Lieutenant Colonel Boyce was appointed to succeed Colonel Hobby as WAC director when the latter resigned to devote her time to her family and business affairs. Under-Secretary of War Robert P. Patterson [41] announced the change in WAC command and at the same time pinned the resigning colonel's silver eagles on the shoulders of Westray Battle Boyce. At this ceremony the new WAC chief paid tribute to the retiring director and expressed her own feelings upon assuming command. "It is with great humility that I accept the assignment as director of the Women's Army Corps," Colonel Boyce declared. "I am grateful to the War Department for the confidence it has expressed in me and I shall endeavor to measure up to that confidence." The New York *Herald Tribune* editorially welcomed the appointment of Colonel Boyce to the chief WAC post and took the opportunity to congratulate the entire Corps for its wartime performance. According to this article, "Colonel Westray Battle Boyce appears well equipped in character and experience to carry on the Corps' traditions. . . . We can all be proud of these women and the record they have established. It can be safely predicted that henceforth military service in this country will remain a coeducational enterprise." By V-J Day enlistment of Wacs had been cancelled, and by November 1 the discharge score for enlisted Wacs had been reduced from 44 to 34, and that of officers to 37. In the over-all plan it was

expected that by July 1946 the Corps will have been reduced to thirty thousand or less. After V-J Day, in August, it was announced by the Veterans Administration that women veterans would receive the same benefits and preferences as those provided for ex-servicemen. To see to this, a WAC officer, Lieutenant Colonel Mary Agnes Brown, was appointed an adviser to General Omar Bradley [43], VA administrator.

At her first press conference it was reported that Colonel Boyce faced the roomful of reporters with confidence. A small, attractive woman with "an arresting combination of military erectness and Southern gentlewoman charm," she is described by her associates as "the velvet-glove-with-the-iron-hand type, but always feminine and charming." Blue-eyed and prematurely gray, she wears her hair combed high off her forehead. Her favorite reading is historical novels, and she collects silver, antiques, and pictures of her ancestors, which hang on the walls of her home. She also enjoys riding and swimming, and, domestically inclined, she likes to work about the home, sewing, cooking, and housecleaning. Colonel Boyce has one daughter, Westray Battle Boyce, Jr., who in 1945 attended Sweet Briar College.

References

N Y Herald Tribune II p3 Jl 22 '45 por
N Y Sun p16 Jl 13 '45 por; p18 Jl 26 '45

BOYLE, HAL Feb. 21, 1911- Journalist
Address: b. c/o The Associated Press, 50 Rockefeller Plaza, New York City; h. 110 Waverly Pl., New York City

A few days after the Allied invasion of Normandy in June 1944 General Omar N. Bradley [43], commander of the American invasion forces, held his first press conference. Bradley surveyed the group of correspondents, then asked, "Where's Hal Boyle?" The man about whom the General inquired had been reporting on the war since American soldiers first saw action in the North African campaign in November 1942. As Associated Press correspondent, this reporter followed the war in Europe from the front lines, advancing with the troops and sharing with them many of the dangers of war. He dispatched a steady stream of news from the war zone in his "spot" news reporting and in his feature column *Leaves From a War Correspondent's Notebook*. A favorite of GI's and newsmen alike, he received high praise in many quarters for his coverage of the human side of the fighting. Called the "American infantryman's Boswell," Boyle was awarded the Pulitzer Prize for distinguished correspondence in May 1945, one day before the official V-E Day.

The A.P.'s prize-winning correspondent, whose full name is Harold Vincent Boyle, was born February 21, 1911, to Peter E. and Margaret Boyle of Kansas City, Missouri. His first youthful ambition was to be a civil engineer, but his lack of mathematical ability caused him to change his mind. In high school he directed his studies toward a teaching career; then, after graduation he was attracted to newspaper work. His first job was

HAL BOYLE

with the organization for which he still reports —he was a night office boy in the Kansas City office of the A.P. After a brief period at this work, he left to go to college. He attended the University of Missouri, where, in 1932, he received his degree in journalism, with distinction in English. Awarded a scholarship by the university, he spent the next year doing graduate work in English. He had long wanted to write, although he now says that one of his teachers did not think highly of his literary efforts. Nevertheless he began his journalistic career in earnest, with his former employers, the Associated Press, where he advanced rapidly. He first worked as a reporter in the college town of Columbia, Missouri, writing sports and college news for about a year and a half. He then served successively in the A.P.'s Kansas City office and in the St. Louis office, where he was night editor for a year. His next position was with the New York bureau, where he was night editor at the time of his assignment to the American Expeditionary Force in 1942.

Boyle's career as a war correspondent had a baptism of fire at its very beginning. Landing with the invasion forces on the North African coast in November 1942, he was caught in the barrage of enemy cross fire as he stumbled through the surf toward the Moroccan shore. And Boyle's luck held as the campaign progressed: he pushed forward with the troops, gathering his stories from the fighting men and writing them from the soldier's angle. One day during the Tunisian campaign the reporter leaped into a slit trench as German shells crashed into the earth around him. He was greeted by a grinning soldier: "Come in. I've had all kinds of people in here today, but you're the first newspaper correspondent. What kind of news do you expect to find in a slit trench anyway?" But Boyle found a story wherever he went, and he usually wrote it in a soldier's own words, even adding the GI's name and address. In the first night assault on Sicily in July 1943, Boyle was with the invasion forces again. He accompanied

the troops to the beaches of Salerno and onward through Italy. Next, after being detained in England for a period of two weeks, Boyle landed in Normandy on D-Day plus twenty. From that time until V-E Day in May 1945 the correspondent covered the sweep across France and Germany.

According to a fellow reporter, Boyle was "famed along half-a-dozen fronts as the war's hardest working, self-proclaimed loafer." He once toured the Ninth, First, and Third Army fronts, advising A.P. newsmen not to overwork and declaring emphatically, "I'm absolutely through with this business of trying to write a bunch of spot news stories every day in addition to the column. We're just killing ourselves and not doing anybody else any good. . . . I'm a changed man. I'm going to take it easy." After lecturing his colleagues in this manner Boyle proceeded to ignore his own preachments, working practically day and night at the time of the Ardennes break-through in December 1944. During the period the Battle of the Bulge raged, he wrote from five to twelve spot stories a day, quick, eyewitness reports of news events. He visited scores of American outfits engaged in the fighting, filling his reports with the stories of the men he met. Going without much rest or sleep, the A.P. reporter tried to cover two-thirds of the break-through singlehanded. He maintained this pace, writing thousands of words daily, it is said, to the exasperation of rival reporters. Bad weather increased the difficulty of the situation, and Boyle now admits that he worked "pretty hard."

During the European campaign Boyle was often with the front-line troops as they entered captured towns, and his reports included accounts of life behind the German lines. Once the journalist hitchhiked four hundred miles to get a battle story. Ironically enough, after surviving the bombs and bullets of the battlefield, Boyle was injured during a military parade. This happened in August 1944 during a parade of American infantrymen down the Champs-Elysées in Paris. The reporter was gathering names in the crowd when a motorcycle policeman lost control of his machine; it spun into the crowd and hit Boyle, who suffered torn back ligaments. He continued his news gathering even on the X-ray table, taking down the names of the doctor and his assistants.

Boyle's human interest stories are considered his best work. He has described soldiers "with neither embellishment nor deprecation." In an issue of the *Quill*, the magazine of Sigma Delta Chi, the journalism fraternity, Boyle expressed his opinion on war reporting: "The terrible daily heroism and sacrifice of these men merely . . . doing the routine duties . . . are too barely sublime to be intensified by the imagination." Thus his column, *Leaves From a War Correspondent's Notebook,* followed closely the real GI pattern in speech and idea. This special A.P. feature was read by millions who were thereby brought closer to their fighting men. Through Boyle's "local" war reporting parents found news of their sons, and many a small town pointed proudly to a local man's name in print. In December 1944 *Newsweek* reported that over four hundred A.P.-

subscribing newspapers were running the Boyle feature column.

His distinguished reporting won him honorable mention in the awards of Sigma Delta Chi in April 1945. In May the trustees of Columbia University awarded Boyle the Pulitzer Prize for his reporting on the war. Informed of the award in Germany, the reporter expressed disbelief, accusing friends of playing a joke on him. "They must have made a mistake," said Boyle even when told again that it was true. A month later Boyle went back to the United States for a six-week furlough; except for one brief period, it was the first time he had been home in more than two years. After this vacation he continued his reporting from the Pacific theater, writing from Tokyo in late 1945 on various aspects of the American occupation of Japan. He was hoping when he returned home to have a "civilian" column, in which he would continue to write about people and perhaps occasionally on political matters.

Boyle is a modest man of simple, direct manner, more interested in writing about people than events. When he met Ernie Pyle [41], a man of similar tastes, on the North African front, the A.P. correspondent greeted him with: "So you're Ernie Pyle? Well, shake hands with Boyle, the poor man's Ernie Pyle." (In *The Story of G.I. Joe* [1945], the filmed story of Ernie Pyle, Boyle played himself along with other well known combat correspondents.) A big, agile man with blond, thinning hair and blue eyes, Boyle has "a prize fighter's face and a poet's soul." Riding to the front lines, he read the poetry of Emily Dickinson, whom he ranks "a shade below Shakespeare." (He collects early editions of Miss Dickinson's works.) The journalist's wife is the former Frances Young, to whom he was married on November 6, 1937. Their New York apartment, which also houses a cocker spaniel appropriately named Pencil, overflows with a variety of mementos collected by Boyle during his travels: brass, leather, and silver from Africa; books, bric-a-brac, and antique silver from London; chinaware from France; and laces from Belgium. Reporter friends relate with relish stories of shopping tours with Boyle in liberated towns, adding that "Boyle needed an extra jeep just for his gear."

Endowed with a hearty sense of humor, Boyle has been a continual source of amusement to troops and correspondents. One of his famous pranks had its setting in an African village which Boyle entered with the invading troops. The reporter addressed the cheering natives until they were enthusiastically repeating his words. The result of his oratory was heard a few days later when American officers entered the village—to be greeted by natives shouting, "Vote for Boyle, the son of toil. Honest Hal, the Arab's pal."

References

N Y Times p16 My 8 '45 por
Newsweek 24:79-80 D 25 '44 por

BOYLE, HAROLD VINCENT *See* Boyle, H.

BRADEN, SPRUILLE (brā'děn sprōō'ĭl) Mar. 13, 1894- United States Government official; diplomat

Address: b. c/o Department of State, Washington, D.C.

The man regarded as a symbol of militant democracy in South America is a Montana-born mining engineer, businessman, and diplomat who became Assistant Secretary of State in charge of Latin American affairs, at a time when the "Good Neighbor Policy needed a real instrument." Spruille Braden, appointed August 25, 1945, by President Truman [45] to succeed Nelson Rockefeller [41], is a diplomat who believes that frankness and fundamental honesty are the most effective and constructive instruments of diplomacy.

Spruille Braden apparently inherited his taste for the profession of engineering in which he earned early success. He was born March 13, 1894, in the mining town of Elkhorn, Montana, the son of William and Mary (Kimball) Braden. His father, who was associated with mining interests both in the West and in South America, founded the Braden Copper Company, a company which was later to be the indirect means of precipitating a major crisis in the son's diplomatic career. Young Braden obtained some practical experience in the mines before he entered Sheffield Scientific School, Yale University, and he spent vacations acquiring further knowledge in various concentrating and smelting plants as well as in mining camps.

Braden's work in South America began soon after his graduation in 1914, with a Ph.B. degree in mining engineering. For the five years that followed he occupied positions of growing responsibility: engineer and assistant to the general manager of Andes Exploration Company, 1914-16; acting manager of that company and of Santiago Mining Company, as well as general manager in South America of Anaconda Copper Mining Company interests, 1916-19; president and director of the Bolivia-Argentina Exploration Corporation, and associate-resident director of Errazuris, Simpson & Company, 1919.

During the First World War Braden's activities included the presidency of the American Red Cross Society of Chile. He was a member of the Inter-Allied Commercial Committee and Inter-Allied Central Committee for Chile, as well as president of the American Society of Chile. For a half-dozen years after the Armistice he was adviser to several South American governments in the negotiation of loans. He obtained a contract for Westinghouse Electric for electrification of Chilean state railways. In the United States he acquired control of the Monmouth Rug Mills at Englishtown, New Jersey, developed them into a prosperous business, and also became an official in other large industries. Throughout these years he was called into financial conferences, as a delegate to the Second Pan-American Financial Conference in 1920, and the Pan-American Commercial Conference at Buenos Aires in 1935. In 1932 he organized the Rehabilitation Corporation, financing income-producing properties.

Braden entered the diplomatic service as a delegate to the Inter-American Conference of

SPRUILLE BRADEN

American States in Montevideo in 1933. Later he played an important role in allaying the smoldering conflict between Paraguay and Bolivia, as chairman from 1935 to 1938 of the American delegation, with rank of ambassador, to the Chaco Peace Conference. In the latter year, President Roosevelt '42 appointed the forty-four-year-old financier United States Minister to Colombia. There Braden carried on an extensive investigation of Nazi activities during the early years of the Second World War, and short-circuited Nazi designs on the Panama Canal from air bases in Colombia. Shortly after Pearl Harbor he was nominated, on December 20, 1941, to be Ambassador to Cuba, where he presented his credentials with the following remarks: "Now we are allies in a great adventure to preserve the principles of liberty, justice, decency, and dignity for free nations and free men, irrespective of their size, wealth, or strength. . . .Under a test by fire the ideas of inter-American solidarity once again are being converted into effective co-operation for the benefit of all concerned and of civilization itself."

In these first important posts Braden is considered to have displayed qualities of statesmanship which identify him as outstanding among crusading democratic ambassadors. In Cuba he was influential in speeding the building of the gigantic Nicaro nickel-extraction plant. Begun in a jungle in 1942, this thirty-three-million-dollar Government project has produced enough nickel oxide to provide the United States with almost 10 per cent of its wartime nickel, which goes into heat-resistant steel for armor plate, gun forgings, and aviation engines. In addition, in the words of a report on the building of Nicaro (*Fortune,* July 1945), "He got the Cubans to run one American out of the country in handcuffs for corrupt practices and battled militantly against the ancient practice of United States firms of donating to Cuban Presidential campaign funds. Throughout Nicaro's building, the Ambassador publicized

among Cubans America's interest in quick production."

Speaking for the American Chamber of Commerce of Cuba, in April 1943, Ambassador Braden declared, "The principles of the Good Neighbor Policy are accepted and put into practice by an immense majority of our fellow citizens with conviction and enthusiasm. This policy has come to. stay. . . .No change in administration in our country will entail abandonment or neglect of the fundamental principles which now govern our relations with American nations." Inevitably there was certain opposition to Braden's attempts to put his policies into practice. In 1944 he was the storm center of a newspaper controversy in Havana, in the course of which a duel was fought in his defense. Eugenio de Sosa, Jr., director of Cuba's oldest newspaper, *Diario de la Marina,* charged that Braden sought to interfere with Cuban freedom of the press by opposing the newspaper's campaign for higher sugar prices. Sosa's attack resulted in a duel fought by Sosa and Guillermo Belt, a supporter of Braden in Havana.

What lay ahead for Braden became evident soon after President Truman nominated him to be Ambassador to Argentina in May 1945. In order of urgency, the first point to be established in any study of Argentina, a present festering spot of trouble for the United Nations, is the position of the present Argentine regime in the world-wide struggle against fascism. In the words of Roland Hall Sharp in the *Christian Science Monitor,* "The record speaks for itself. Argentina's Conservative and military dictatorship has steadily become more Fascist even while the cause of world democracy gained. The background of the crisis needs to be understood. On the stage of internal Argentine affairs, an economic and social revolution has been under way ever since the growth of industries and a middle class began to challenge the traditional wealth and privilege of the land-owning agricultural producers. . . . The new military rulers abolished Congress, decreed the dissolution of all political parties, choked the free press, arrested more than two thousand democrats and pro-Allied leaders, 'purged' the schools of independent professors, and began to militarize the nation. Nevertheless, Argentine public opinion stood in the preponderant majority with the Allies. . . .Such is the divorce between the Argentine people and the regime nominally headed by General Edelmiro J. Farrell, but actually controlled by Vice-President and War Minister Juan D. Perón '44 and other. Fascist officers."

In 1944 the United States had set up economic restrictions against Argentina, but these were removed in April 1945, after Argentina officially returned to the family of American nations by declaring war on the Axis, and by signing the Act of Chapultepec. Although her declaration of war gained Argentina's delayed admittance to the San Francisco conference, reports show that the Government used the state of war as an excuse to class every opposition to the Farrell-Perón regime as treason, and to intensify repression and censorship.

Before his departure for Argentina in May, Ambassador Braden said, "The Good Neighbor Policy is one of respect which begins with self-respect and then mutual respect. It is a two-way, not a one-way street to be traveled in dignity by both parties in full realization that they have rights and responsibilities. . . .I am not going to Argentina to re-establish friendly relations, but to establish new ones!" Proceeding to put these words into practice, according to an account in *Inter-American,* July 1945, "the day after he presented his credentials to the *Casa Rosada,* Ambassador Braden flatly told newspapermen that the United States would like to see democratic governments everywhere, and that recognition of Argentina was dictated by necessity alone. On May 29 it was announced that there would be no arms shipments to Argentina because of her failure to carry out the democratic terms of the Chapultepec declaration."

In the first months after he took his post Braden's investigations revealed that Nazis still held directorships in many Argentine firms. On June 20, 1945, according to a report in *PM,* "the American correspondents had complained to Ambassador Braden about the increasing censorship difficulties which were keeping them from telling the outside world what was really going on. The complaint was the straw that broke the back of Braden's patience. He picked up a telephone, known to be tapped, and dictated a cable to his secretary at his office, instructing him to dispatch it in plain language for all to read. The cable suggested to Washington that he, Braden, should be recalled, and the United States policy in regard to Argentina be revised, as Argentina was not fulfilling her Mexico City and San Francisco agreements. Within an hour Oscar Lumoto, Under-Secretary of Press and Propaganda, was at Braden's home, assuring him that complete freedom of the press, especially for foreign correspondents, was guaranteed in Argentina, and that instructions to that effect had been given by Perón."

While Braden's campaign for democracy thus brought results, the extreme nationalists counterattacked in a smear campaign. Posters appeared in Buenos Aires, denouncing Braden and attempting to connect his name with the death of some five hundred Chilean miners in a recent fire in the El Teniente mine of the Braden Copper Company in Chile. Although the latter company was founded by the Ambassador's father, another company bought it some years ago, and Braden was not connected with it. The attacks were considered by observers to be the result of official concern over the growing popular demand for democratic government in Argentina. Braden stated: "The campaign . . . against my country and me personally was apparently instituted by foreign Nazi elements totally alien to the truly noble feelings of the Argentine people."

Following the surrender of Japan in mid-August, new riots flared for four days between victory celebrants and pro-Government crowds. Then Braden, further denouncing Fascist regimes at a thanksgiving service held by the American community, said, "The peoples of the world have learned that Fascist militarists . . . will stop at nothing. . . .To defeat them we have paid a staggering price. . . .We shall not forget this lesson merely because petty tyrants are now assuming the disguise of spurious democracy. No longer can a self-respecting world . . . accept a government that rules through violence."

When President Truman ten days later named Ambassador Braden as Assistant Secretary of State in charge of American Republic Affairs, Secretary of State Byrnes [41] immediately announced that it would be Braden's duty to carry on "with unremitting vigor" the policies which he has "so courageously sponsored" in Argentina. At a farewell luncheon given Braden by Argentine and American cultural institutes, the new Assistant Secretary of State said, "Let no one imagine that my being transferred to Washington means the abandonment of the task I have undertaken. The voice of freedom makes itself heard in this land, and I do not believe anyone will succeed in drowning it. I shall hear it from Washington with the same clarity with which I hear it in Buenos Aires. . . .If, during my stay among you, I have faithfully reflected the feeling of the United States people, which is not different from that of their Government, I hope when I am in Washington to be able to interpret with equal fidelity the sentiment of the people of the Argentine Republic."

In the weeks before his departure for home the Ambassador stated that there were two conditions for a settlement of differences between his country and Argentina—complete elimination of Axis activities and restoration of democracy in Argentina. Shortly after this disclosure the Argentine Government made what one commentator called "an unabashed attempt to avert another rupture in relations with the United States and other American republics." First, a number of "belated" anti-Axis measures were adopted; later, in reply to accusations made by Nelson Rockefeller, a thirty-page document was released which undertook to show that Argentina was fulfilling her commitments under the Act of Chapultepec. (Braden rejected this document, stating that except for "one of the neutral countries adjacent to the struggle, there is no country in the world where the Nazis find themselves in such a strong position as they do in Argentina.") Braden himself received an apology from the Foreign Minister, Juan I. Cooke, for attacks made on him by the Argentine press.

In the wake of an abortive democratic uprising three days after Braden's departure, a state of siege was reimposed by the Farrell-Perón regime; all civil liberties were again suspended and press censorship was restored. On September 29 the State Department stated that it planned to continue the policy of non-intervention in Argentina, but to step up its campaign of moral pressure against its Government. Shortly afterward the Department announced the indefinite postponement of the Inter-American Conference on Peace and Security which had been scheduled for October 20, a move said to have been inspired by Braden.

Braden did not take the oath of office as Assistant Secretary of State for Latin American Affairs until October 29, two months after his nomination to that post, his confirmation having been held up in the Senate Foreign Relations Committee because of what some Senators saw as "meddling in Argentina's internal affairs." Braden denied that he was intervening in that country's domestic affairs, telling his critics that he had simply put an end to the

BRADEN, SPRUILLE—*Continued*

negative policy of silent acquiescence. Other Senators regarded Braden as a symbol of American desires for the introduction of democratic elements into Argentina. In one of the first speeches Braden made after taking his State Department post (at the National Foreign Trade Convention in mid-November), he again spoke his views on Argentina. United States, he said, would come to the aid of those democratic elements by "whatever means it had at its disposal," a statement on which he did not elaborate at the time. He also spoke strongly against the use of economic sanctions to bring pressure on Latin American neighbors. Of Braden's coming to Washington the *United States News* commentator wrote: "Mr. Braden is something new in the upper reaches of the State Department. He will be a much-watched and controversial figure for some time to come."

Described as big, jolly, and energetic, Braden finds recreation in swimming and playing handball with cronies. His exercise was more strenuous in college, where he played football and water polo. Collecting antique hand-wrought South American silver and rare books are now his favorite hobbies. In 1915 he was married to a prominent Chilean physician's daughter, Maria Humeres Solar. Their children are Maruja, Laurita, Isolina, William 2d, Patricia, and Spruille.

References

Collier's 116:11+ N 10 '45 por
Time 46:42+ N 15 '45 por

National Cyclopædia of American Biography Current vol F p532
Who's Who in America, 1944-45

BRICKELL, (HENRY) HERSCHEL
(brĭk'ĕl hûr'shĕl) Sept. 13, 1889- Editor; United States Government official

Address: b. c/o Department of State, Washington, D.C.; h. Ridgefield, Conn.

Since 1940 Herschel Brickell has been editor of the *O. Henry Memorial Prize Short Stories* series, an annual collection chosen from short stories published in the United States. Also assistant chief of the State Department's Division of Cultural Cooperation, in charge of the Latin American branch, and former cultural envoy to Colombia, Brickell has been journalist, book critic, essayist, and literary talent scout.

A native of Mississippi, Henry Herschel Brickell was born on the thirteenth of September, 1889, to Henry Hampton and Lula Johns (Harrison) Brickell. Herschel, as he was called, grew up in Yazoo City, where there was a good library: "When I wasn't going to school, riding horseback, or falling off a bicycle," he writes, "I was reading. I read a book a day in summer vacation time, sometimes two, thus preparing myself unwittingly for the life of a daily book columnist in New York." In 1906 the tall, slender youth entered the University of Mississippi, where for four years he did well in English courses and was active on the campus newspaper and literary magazine. However, as he says himself, he "flunked mathematics with perfect regularity," and therefore did not graduate with his class.

Brickell began his post-college life as reporter and sports writer for the Montgomery (Alabama) *Advertiser*, in which capacity, he says, he did very badly. At the end of four years, working on that and other Southern papers, he had risen to the editorship of a paper in Pensacola, Florida—and as editor he was rated good. For a few months in 1916, at the time of the Mexican border expedition, he served with the First Alabama State Guard as a battalion sergeant major; when Army food disagreed with him he was, as he expresses it, "sent home to die." He returned to Mississippi, as the medical authorities had ordered, but immediately went to work for the Jackson *Daily News*. For the next three years, while holding the position of editor, he subsisted on "Greek-made lemon pie and other Athenian delicacies beloved of newspapermen." In March 1918 he was married to Norma Long of Jackson, a pianist, who gave up her career of music to watch over her husband's diet.

Since Brickell now wanted to try for a job on a big metropolitan newspaper, the young couple moved to New York the year after their marriage. There the Southerner obtained a job as copyreader with the *Evening Post*, a position which he held until 1923. At this time he was made book columnist of the *Post*, and at intervals for twelve years he wrote the daily column *Books on Our Table*. In addition he contributed articles on literary subjects to several magazines. He left the paper in 1928 to become the general editor of the New York publishing firm of Henry Holt and Company. During the five years he remained with Holt he took courses at Columbia University, spent a considerable amount of time abroad in search of literary talent, and, on one of his trips, studied at the University of Santander in Spain. Spain, he says, Mrs. Brickell and he "loved beyond any country," and there they spent all their vacations. During this period Brickell also wrote reviews for the New York *Times* and the New York *Herald Tribune*, and for eight years contributed monthly essays to the *North American Review* under the title of *The Literary Landscape.*

In January 1934 Brickell resumed his column in the *Post*, becoming literary editor shortly after his return. He left the paper again in 1938, and that summer was one of the lecturers at the Bread Loaf (Vermont) Writers' Conference. He has since lectured at the writers' conferences of the University of New Hampshire and of the Blowing Rock (North Carolina) Summer School of English. In 1939, with the aid of a Julius Rosenwald Foundation award, he did research into the history of Natchez, Mississippi, and that same year received a Guggenheim fellowship for work on a book on Spain. The first project, Brickell reports, is "under way like a glacier," and the second "will have to wait for a happier time to get itself written." He has, however, written several articles for *Publisher's Weekly* on the modern literature of Spain, and has compiled a bibliography on the Spanish civil war.

The writer took up new duties in the field of criticism in 1940, when he assumed the editorship of the *O. Henry Memorial Prize Short Stories* series. (Muriel Fuller of Thomas Nelson and Sons, the New York publishers, became his assistant.) The plan for the anthologies, which are annual collections of stories selected from among those published in American magazines in a given year, originated with the New York Society of Arts and Sciences in 1918. The purpose was to "honor and preserve the memory of the master of the brief narrative, whose world-famous pseudonym is a part of the title." The first volume, edited by Blanche Colton William, appeared in 1920. Originally two prizes were awarded, for the two best stories of the year; in 1937 three awards were given; and when Brickell became editor the policy of awarding a fourth prize for the best first effort of an author was begun.

The critics' inspection of the first volume to appear under Brickell's editorship (1941) evoked favorable comments. The *New Yorker* reviewer wrote that the collection was "a much-better-than-average lot," and Milton Hindus observed that Brickell had "performed admirably his first job of editing" the story collection. In his introduction the editor stated that, although he believed the brief narrative must be entertaining and exciting, he attached "great value to originality in theme and treatment, and to style, which seems [to him] of supreme importance. . . .The very nature of the short story demands the best qualities of writing." (With the appearance of the 1945 volume of prize stories, Brickell himself said he believed it was the best to be published under his supervision.)

While continuing as editor of the *O. Henry* anthologies, Brickell in October 1941 assumed the duties of the State Department post of senior cultural relations assistant to Spruille Braden [45], who was then Ambassador to Colombia. His post, Brickell told reporters, was to "foment any kind of cultural work and to get things really started." During the two years he remained in Bogotá he helped to introduce American methods into Colombian libraries, to arrange for the interchange and translation of the books of the two countries, and to effect the opening of several free libraries. He believes that the progress made in the library field "will form a solid foundation . . . in the cultural interchange," since books are "cultural capsules."

In 1943 Brickell left his Colombian post for a position in Washington, D.C., as head of the Exchange of Persons Unit. When the division was later reorganized and its work divided into four geographical branches (European, Far Eastern, Near Eastern and African, and American Republic), he became the assistant chief of the Division of Cultural Cooperation, in charge of the Latin American branch. His responsibilities include formulating policies designed to encourage cultural contacts between the United States and Latin America through the exchange of students and experts in various fields, cooperating with private and Government agencies engaged in student and training programs, and aiding programs of a reciprocal nature in the intellectual, cultural, and technical fields.

Brickell has contributed numerous articles on Latin American subjects to a variety of magazines in the United States, and has had a collection of essays and speeches published in

HERSCHEL BRICKELL

Colombia, *Cosecha Colombiana* ("Colombian Harvest"). Several of his articles on library methods and on changes instituted in Latin American libraries appeared in *Publisher's Weekly* in 1942; and "Medillin, Valley Capital" and "Up to Manizales" are among the travelogues that were published (1943-45) in *Inter-American* and other periodicals. In 1945 Brickell wrote the Colombian and Venezuelan chapters for *What the South Americans Think of Us*. Harry Hansen [42], in reviewing the book in the New York *World-Telegram*, said that Brickell wrote his chapters with "judicial fairness—but then he is an employee of the State Department." Hansen added that Brickell is "the only contributor who feels that the Good Neighbor Policy will pay if continued." Working with Carlos Videla, Brickell translated Ricardo Rojas' *San Martín, el Santo de la Espada*, which was published in 1945 with the title *San Martín, Knight of the Andes*. He also contributed to the American literature survey of the *Encyclopædia Britannica Yearbook*.

The Brickells own a small house in Ridgefield, Connecticut, and have undertaken the "lifetime occupation" of doing it over. When they are in residence there they devote much of their time to gardening, especially to the growing of herbs. Another hobby is the raising of cats, their collection at one time numbering seventeen. In Bogotá Brickell's favorite pet was a black part-Persian named Federica García Lorca Uribe White Brickell after the Spanish poet Lorca, a close friend of the envoy's, and after White, director of the national library in Bogotá, whose black cats are famous. All in all, the Brickells know many amazing cat stories, all about their own felines, which Brickell claims were most remarkable.

References

R of Rs 93:4 Ja '36 por

Who's Who in America, 1944-45
Who's Who in New York, 1938

BROOKHART, SMITH W(ILDMAN)
Feb. 2, 1869—Nov. 15, 1944 Republican ex-Senator from Iowa; first elected in 1922 to fill vacancy, defeated in 1924, but re-elected in 1926; a spokesman for the farmer.

Obituary

N Y Times p 23 N 16 '44 por

BROWN, JOE E(VAN) July 28, 1892-
Actor

Address: b. c/o Russell Birdwell & Assocs., 200 S. Beverly Dr., Beverly Hills, Calif., h. 18 Oakmont, West Los Angeles, Calif.

The veteran entertainer Joe E. Brown can trace his appearances in the spotlight back through motion pictures, the theater, and burlesque to the circus, where he was an acrobat at the age of nine. Since the middle 1920's he has been a Hollywood figure famous on the screen for his wide-mouthed grin, his laugh, and other comedic qualities. During the Second World War he brought these morale-building talents to troops on the remotest fighting fronts.

Joe Evan Brown was born in Holgate, Ohio, July 28, 1892, the fourth of seven children. His father, Matthias Brown, was a house painter who worked hard to support his family on wages of from a dollar and a half to two dollars a day, and his mother, Anna (Evans) Brown, often had great difficulty making ends meet. It was not strange, therefore, that at the age of nine Joe was eager to earn some money himself. At that time the Browns were living in a two-family house in Toledo, and the neighbor's child, a boy about Joe's age, had got a job in an acrobatic act. When the act needed another boy, the neighbor thought of Joe, whereupon the nine-year-old was given a trial. In displaying his skill at back handsprings and somersaults, Joe slipped and cut his hand in a pile of cinders, but he got up and tried again. "O.K., kid," the leader said. "If you had quit I wouldn't have taken you." The act Joe went into was called The Five Marvelous Ashtons, and he found himself one of three boy marvels who were tossed back and forth forty feet in the air by two men. The act joined the Sells and Downs show in Kansas, and for four summers Joe Brown played circuses or county fairs with the act, returning home each fall to attend school until he had finished the eighth grade. By that time he was earning seven and one-half dollars a week.

In 1906 the troupe disbanded. The acrobats were playing San Francisco at the time, and Joe landed a job there with a vaudeville acrobatic act called the Bell and Prevost Troupe. Frank Prevost, though much older than Joe, became the lad's good friend, and one night when Joe was injured "Pre" said he would drop out of the act with him. Thus began an eleven-year association known as Prevost and Brown, with Joe the funnyman of the team. They often made as much as three hundred dollars a week—some weeks.

Brown has described his career as an acrobat as "thirteen years of merry hell . . . a glorious dream and a horrible nightmare mixed together." At first his only ambition was to be with a circus. The circus had got into his blood, and, no matter what happened to him, he has since said, "the glorious moments when I felt like a god, high up, whirling through

space, more than paid for the pain—and there was pain, cruel pain." In those days child entertainers were not protected by law. Injuries were taken as a matter of course—practically nothing short of a broken leg kept a boy out of an act. In his first performance Joe fell and cracked his jaw. For weeks he wore a sort of helmet to hold the jaw in place.

During the course of other performances he suffered sprained ankles, dislocated knees and shoulders, breaks in legs and fingers, and a snapped muscle in the calf of one leg. Every time he made a mistake he was punished—on the theory that this was the only way to train a boy. But when the young acrobat wrote to his parents he filled his letters only with accounts of his "triumphs" as "The Corkscrew Kid," never mentioning his hardships for fear of being made to leave the circus. His employers did teach him one thing, he says, that has helped him all his life. They never let him admit he was defeated.

Brown has always had a great enthusiasm for sports, especially baseball. He tried professional baseball and at seventeen was good enough to play with the St. Paul team. One spring he was actually taken south by the Yankees. He has explained why he did not stay on with the game he loved: "I had two idols at the time, Ty Cobb and William Jennings Bryan. Naturally, I tried to play baseball like Ty Cobb, but actually I played it like Bryan." (He is reported to have a photographic memory for baseball events.)

While Joe Brown was still in vaudeville he met his future wife, Kathryn Frances McGraw. One day in Duluth she stepped into the theater where he was appearing and heard him tell his now famous "Lil' Mousie" story. Miss McGraw thought it an extremely funny one and relayed it to her family. A few months later, when the entertainer was making a long jump to the West Coast, a pleasant, middle-aged woman sitting next to him on the train asked him whether he was the Joe E. Brown who told the "Lil' Mousie" story in vaudeville. He said he was, of course, and later he was introduced to her daughter. This meeting was the beginning of the couple's courtship, which ended in marriage in December 1915. Brown says they have quarreled just enough during their married life to make things lively; his wife says no woman ever had a more devoted or perfect husband. They celebrated their twenty-fifth anniversary in 1940 with another ceremony, their four children acting as attendants.

About a year after the Browns' marriage Joe felt he must take stock of himself. As an acrobat in vaudeville he had gone about as far as he could. As a comedian in burlesque he would have to start with less money, but, if he were successful, there was a chance he might be put into a Broadway musical. Encouraged by his wife, he made the break with his old life. He had to start at the bottom, and the best job he could get was in a burlesque show at seventy-five dollars a week. The Browns' first child, Don Evan, was born on Christmas Day, 1916, while the twenty-four-year-old father was in Boston giving his first performance as a comedian. In 1918 a second boy, Joe LeRoy, arrived. And the next year Joe E. Brown finally got his chance in a musical comedy, when he was added to the cast of

Listen, Lester. This was followed by more
parts—in *Jim Jam Jems* in 1920, two editions
of the *Greenwich Village Follies* (1921-23),
Betty Lee (1924), *Captain Jinks* (1925), and
Twinkle, Twinkle (1926), with vaudeville engagements between shows. It was while playing in the 1926 show in Los Angeles that Brown
was offered a contract in motion pictures.

Touring in vaudeville and musical comedy
did not offer much opportunity for the home
life the Browns wanted. Kathryn and Joe
Brown lived in hotels, and the boys went to
boarding schools. In 1927, therefore, the comedian and his family settled in Hollywood and
he began his film career. His first leading
role in silent pictures was in *Crooks Can't Win*
(1928). But it was the "talkies" that really
gave Brown his chance on the screen, and
audiences the opportunity to hear his famous
roar. His first leading role in talking pictures
was in *Painted Faces* (1930). *Going Wild*
(1931) was his first solo starring vehicle.
These were followed soon by such films as
Local Boy Makes Good (1931), *Fireman, Save
My Child* (1932), *You Said a Mouthful* (1932),
The Tenderfoot (1932), *Elmer the Great*
(1933), *Six Day Bike Rider* (1934), *The Circus Clown* (1934), *Alibi Ike* (1935), *Maybe
It's Love* (1935). As Frederick L. Collins
says in an article in *Liberty* Magazine, the
wide-mouthed comedian was "sitting pretty on
Hollywood's highest comedy roost." More re-
cent pictures include *A Midsummer Night's
Dream* (1935), *Sons o' Guns* (1936), *The
Gladiator* (1938), *$10,000 a Touchdown* (1939),
Shut My Big Mouth (1942).

Shortly after Joe E. Brown became established in Hollywood, his third child, Mary
Elizabeth Ann, was born (in 1930), and four
years later he and his wife adopted a girl and
named her Kathryn Frances after Mrs. Brown.
The boys went to public school first, then to
Urban Military Academy in Los Angeles. After
that they attended the Beverly Hills High
School. When Don wanted to postpone his
entering college a year to take a trip to China
(his parents had just returned from one), the
Browns heartily approved, on the condition that
the young man earn his own way. He did this,
as a cadet or bellboy on the boat, making the
trip twice and saving a goodly sum of money
out of his earnings. He then went to the University of California at Los Angeles. His
younger brother spent a year at Mercersburg,
an Eastern preparatory school, then he too entered U.C.L.A. The allowances of both Don
and Joe were always small, but there was always money saved. The Browns were proud
of their sons, for they were fine athletes—their
father had passed on to them his enthusiasm
for sports—and good students. Like their
father, too, neither smoked nor drank. No
college man himself, Brown is athletic patron
of his sons' university. He donates equipment
to the football team, awards an annual loving
cup to an outstanding player, frequently presides over athletic banquets. In 1938 he was
initiated as a regular member of Zeta Phi, to
which his sons belong, and he is the only non-
student ever to get a letter from U.C.L.A.
One of the finest athletes in U.C.L.A. history,
Mike Frankovich, has been "adopted" by the
Brown family.

Early in 1940 Brown narrowly escaped death
in an automobile accident in which his back

JOE E. BROWN

was broken. After spending six months in a
plaster cast, he was able to act again. In
August 1940, at the Cape Playhouse in Dennis,
Massachusetts, he was starred in a revival of
Elmer the Great, the Cohan and Lardner farce
about a rookie baseball pitcher in which he
had already played successfully, both on stage
and screen. The role was a "natural" for the
former acrobat-baseball player. Besides having played the game himself and having supported it as a fan, while at Warner Brothers
the actor had organized and coached a semi-
pro studio ball team and had seen to it in his
contract that all the players would be kept on
the payroll as long as he was. (Brown had
once been under long-term contract to the
Warners, but recently worked under a three-
picture-a-year arrangement with the independent
producer David Loew.)

In 1941 a soldier in Alaska wrote to the
actor to tell that servicemen overseas were
lonesome for a familiar face. This letter
started Brown off on his now famous trips to
the theaters of war. On his own initiative, in
February 1941 he went to Alaska. He was
the first and only entertainer the soldiers had
seen for many months, and their welcome convinced him of the need for more of this sort of
morale-building. He stayed until April, making a thirty-three-day tour of camps, outposts,
gun positions, and bases—the first Hollywood
star to visit the barren wastes of Alaska and
the Aleutians. To let him know how much his
visit meant to them, the citizens of the tiny
town of Gambell proclaimed March 17 (the
day of his arrival) Joe E. Brown Day and a
holiday thenceforth. Brown's will stipulates
that his children must carry on the tradition
by sending greetings in his name each March
17 to the citizens of Gambell. On his return
from the Aleutians, the actor toured in a revival of *The Show-off* and appeared at War
Bond rallies.

In January 1942 Brown left for the South
Pacific. That trip lasted four months, took him
everywhere it was possible to get an actor who

BROWN, JOE E.—*Continued*

was determined to bring a laugh to every serviceman he could reach. *Newsweek* Magazine reports there is even a Joe E. Brown Hill out there—"so named because the homely little comedian insisted on giving a show for four men out on the hill on patrol."

On October 19, 1942, Captain Don E. Brown was killed while on duty in the crash of an Army bomber near Palm Springs, California. After the funeral Brown threw himself wholeheartedly into a three months' entertainment tour for the men in service as a sort of memorial to his son. In April 1943, returning from the Pacific fifteen pounds lighter, his hair turned iron gray, he headed for his Hollywood home and a rest before leaving again for Alaska. He had been in the steaming jungles of New Guinea, the remotest Allied outposts in the South Pacific, and everywhere he had been impressed by the deep need for entertainment for the men. "Even when they couldn't hear me, they'd laugh," he reported. The participation in games by the men themselves he felt to be important, too. The sight of only one deck of playing cards in a base hospital in the Pacific had led him to establish the All-Pacific Recreation Fund, which supplies athletic equipment and games to servicemen in the various theaters of war.

In May 1943 Metro-Goldwyn-Mayer signed Brown to a contract, but in November he was off to entertain the men in service. This time he went to China-Burma-India and again was the first film entertainer to reach the servicemen in a distant war sector. The USO arranged for his trip, but he paid his own expenses. He went to India, Iran, Iraq, Arabia, Egypt, Italy, and North Africa—two hundred and two shows in all. On his return in February 1944 the "favorite pin-up boy of the Army," veteran of more than one hundred and fifty thousand miles of hazardous flying to the battlefronts, said there would be no more trips for a while because his family "insisted on eating." After an official reception in New York City under the auspices of Mayor La Guardia [40] and a dinner at the White House, at which he was the guest of honor, the traveling actor returned to Hollywood to do some picture work—*Casanova in Burlesque, Pin-up Girl*—and a radio quiz show over the Blue Network, *Stop or Go*, which went off the air in February 1945 after a year's run.

In October 1944 Brown's report of his travels appeared in print, as *Your Kids and Mine*. Reviewers called his "odyssey" a "little classic of World War II," and recommended it to civilians and GI's alike. Many agreed that, though Brown could not possibly have known when he wrote this report that he would be attacked by an Army paper for "running out" on the CBI area, the book constitutes a perfect defense and a "terrific tribute to our GI's and incidentally to Brown himself." L. L. Marchand said: "It is no literary epic . . . but he has dipped his pen in sincerity, even if with some sentimentality." In November, in celebration of his forty-fourth year in show business, the new author's life story was broadcast over WOR. Perhaps his philosophy has

been epitomized in these words: "The three R's are all right in their way, but the three L's—Love, Learn, and Laugh—are righter, especially right now. What we need to stop war is a crusade against hate—a crusade of laughter."

In April 1945 he left the United States again for a ten-week tour of the Pacific battlefronts, traveling thirty-eight thousand miles. In October Brown received the United States Army's highest award for a civilian, the Bronze Star, in recognition of his services as a civilian volunteer with the USO. Presented with the award at a surprise ceremony in Chicago, the comedian was deeply moved, but managed to say, "You are now seeing the raw edges of Joe E. Brown." The second civilian to be so honored by the War Department (the late Ernie Pyle [41] was the first), Brown gave his Bronze Star to his wife, to wear beneath the Gold Star she wears for their son. Late in October 1945 Brock Pemberton [45] announced that Brown had been signed to play the lead in the road company of the Pulitzer Prize comedy, *Harvey*. He will play Elwood P. Dowd, first enacted by Frank Fay [45], in the Mary Chase [45] Broadway success.

Joe E. Brown's screen popularity with children has long been second only to Shirley Temple's [45]. He is humble about his professional success, impressed rather with his responsibility than with his importance. He wants to be an all-round comedian and is "a little miffed" at times, as he expresses it, by studio emphasis on the size of his mouth. "I've seen a lot of funny looking people who were not comedians," he says. In a *New Yorker* profile of the actor, Alva Johnston pointed out that Brown's large mouth didn't make him famous—"Joe made the mouth famous." According to this writer, the comedian discovered his "million-dollar mouth" some twenty-five years ago while trying to enliven a dull scene he was playing. "Joe hit on the idea of opening his mouth as wide as possible and holding it that way until the audience was staring at it wtih concentrated attention, believing he had forgotten his lines and was petrified with fear. When he had perfect attention, he barely whispered his line."

Besides belonging to the Los Angeles High School Alumni Association as an honorary member, and to the Blue "C" Society of U.C.L.A., the actor is a Mason (Shriner) and an Elk. He also belongs to clubs in California and New York. His hobby is collecting sporting trophies, among which are the gloves Dempsey [45] used when he knocked out Willard, and the bat Babe Ruth [44] used when he knocked out his sixtieth home run in one particular season.

References

Am Mag 121:50-1+ My '36 pors
Liberty 17:25-6 S '28 '40 por
New Yorker 21:26-30+ Jl 7 '45 por
Photoplay 21:9-10 Jl '42 pors; 22:79
    My '43 pors; 24:12 My '44 pors
PM Mag p3-4 N 5 '44 por
Who's Who in America, 1944-45
Who's Who in the Theatre (1939)

BRUNNER, JEAN ADAM (brŭn'ĕr jĕn)
Oct. 31, 1893- Veterans' leader

Address: h. 99-43 Sixty-sixth Ave., Forest
Hills, Long Island, N.Y.

Allied victory in Europe and the Pacific
brought into sharp focus the problem of
the returning veterans, and with it consideration of the various organizations which represent their interests. Among the most important of these organizations is the Veterans
of Foreign Wars of the United States, whose
membership is composed of veterans of the
Spanish-American War and the two great
wars. Jean Adam Brunner, its commander
in chief from August 1944 to October 1945, in
speaking of the inadequate legislation and provisions for veterans at the end of the 1914-
1918 conflict, in which he served, has expressed
his and his organization's determination to win
proper provision for the veterans of the Second
World War.

A veteran of the First World War, Jean
Adam Brunner is French by birth. The son
of Marie (Layer) and Jean Adam Brunner,
he was born in Pont-à-Mousson in the department of Meurthe-et-Moselle, on October
31, 1893. When he was only a year old his
family emigrated to the United States, where
his father was to become the manager of the
New York restaurant Holland House. Young
Jean evidently became what is known as "a
typical American boy" for, when his family
returned to France for a visit twelve years
later, people frequently referred to him as
"that wild American." Jean's formal education was rather scanty; he was educated the
"hard way," through experience. During his
boyhood he sold newspapers on the streets
of New York, and before the First World
War he was employed as a clerk in the firm
of Peter McDonnell, transportation agents.

When he was twenty-four years old Brunner made another trip to France, this time
as a Yankee soldier in the Judge Advocate
General's Department. In July of 1919, eight
months after the Armistice had been signed,
Sergeant Brunner returned to the States, at
a time when the shouting that had earlier
greeted returning veterans had subsided, and
the soldier had become a man in need of a
job and advice. Brunner soon joined the
Veterans of Foreign Wars, becoming a charter
member of the Joseph A. Wynn Post 260
in Brooklyn. By 1923 he was commander of
that post, and two years later he headed the
Brooklyn Council of the V.F.W.

In less than twenty years Brunner worked
his way up from the Brooklyn Council to
the position of commander in chief of the
national organization. He was the head of
the New York Department of the V.F.W.
in the year 1927-28. Then from 1928 to 1936
he held no post in the V.F.W. In 1936 he
took a post again, for two years serving as a
member of the National Council of Administration of the V.F.W. Again for three years,
until 1941 when he became national chief of
staff, there was a gap in his executive activities. From 1942 until 1944, however, he was
junior and then senior vice-commander in chief
of the organization, and in August 1944, at the
closing session of the forty-fifth encampment,
Jean Brunner was elected national commander.

Strauss Peyton

JEAN ADAM BRUNNER

He served until October 1945, when he was
succeeded by Joseph M. Stack.

The Veterans of Foreign Wars of the
United States, an organization of eight hundred thousand members, second only in size to
the American Legion, was formed in 1913 by
the merger of the American Veterans of Foreign Service (1899) and the Army of the
Philippines. Together, the V.F.W. and the
Legion in their fight to win benefits for veterans, wielded tremendous power during the
period between the two world wars. Their insistence upon compensation rights and special
bonuses in a time of great instability caused
much bitterness among other groups struggling for economic security, and the two bodies
were accused of an antilabor, antinational welfare attitude. "If such sums must be taken
out of the Treasury," wrote the *Nation* when
the first bonus bill was introduced, "then let
them be appropriated as a whole to the general welfare in which the ex-soldiers share."

In the field of foreign affairs, the V.F.W.
held, as did other groups, that only by an
isolationist policy could the United States avoid
another war. The year that the Japanese occupied cities on the coast of northern China
(1937), the slogan of the V.F.W. was "Peace
for America"; in 1939 the organization called
for an eighteen-point neutrality program. Such
policies in a world armed for aggression were
gradually recognized as untenable, and by the
next year the V.F.W. had committed itself to
support of "an intensification of America's national defense program" by aid to Britain, and
"adoption of forceful policies that will convince potential enemies America is prepared
to meet the challenge of the dictators."

The attitude of the V.F.W. toward the
world organization for peace, although it has
not been isolationist, is felt by critics to display some of the former caution that characterized its policies in the twenties and
thirties. In 1943 it registered "unalterable
opposition" to the amalgamation of the United

BRUNNER, JEAN ADAM—*Continued*

States into a world organization or super-state; and in 1944, the year Brunner became commander, it adopted a resolution opposing "impractical and visionary charity" in distributing American relief to other nations after the war, since it considered that the primary obligation is to the people of the United States.

As part of its own postwar program, the V.F.W. has launched a training program to prepare discharged wounded soldiers as field workers in the fight for favorable veterans' legislation. It charged the Government's Veterans Administration in early 1945 with "red tape processes, undue delay and duplication of effort in handling beneficiaries." And, together with the American Legion, the V.F.W. earlier helped to enact the GI Bill of Rights.

With the war at an end, the problem now closest to the Veterans of Foreign Wars, as to the rest of the Nation, is the employment of returning veterans. Of the twelve million men again taking up civilian life, the majority will need work; many of these will find their former jobs no longer in existence, or filled by others. The question that arises is how to take care of these veterans without dislocating the national economy and ultimately creating even wider unemployment. Brunner himself, who has toured the fighting fronts and talked with or to thousands of soldiers, reports their concern over what the future holds for them. He has told them not to expect a "Santa Claus," but probable strikes; and he has suggested that they accept the first job opportunity offered, then later look for more attractive openings. The men overseas have already shown their ability and bravery, he says. "Now they must come home with the realization that America is again ready to judge them for their competence, their ability and desire to get to work and to a good job as workers and family men."

In an effort to make this possible, more than one solution has been advanced. Democratic Senators Robert F. Wagner [41] and James E. Murray [45] have drafted a bill, approved by President Truman [45], which aims at creating full employment by encouraging private industry to maintain full production. Only in the event that private industry is not capable of employing all the people who need jobs does the Murray-Wagner bill propose that the Government initiate a program of public works. The national legislative representative of Brunner's V.F.W., Omar Ketchum, has opposed this, declaring at a hearing on the bill that he had not been authorized to "endorse the principle that among constitutional rights shall be the guaranty of a gainful, suitable job for every American, even if the Government has to provide it."

The bill that the Veterans of Foreign Wars offers as an alternative to the Murray-Wagner full employment bill is one that the organization itself drafted, and which Republican Representative Knutson introduced into the House. This bill requires employers to credit veterans with job seniority equal to time spent in the armed forces. Another provision of the bill frees the veteran for one year from any obligation to join or pay dues to a union, irrespective of any law or contract. The view

of organized labor on the question of seniority is in profound disagreement with this latter proposal of the V.F.W. Union recommendations are that seniority rights be applied only after the returning veteran has got a job. If a layoff should occur, the new employee who came as a veteran would then have not only his months or years of actual work in the plant to his credit, but, in addition, the equivalent of the number of months or years during which he was in uniform.

The first major veterans' meeting after the Allied victory was the forty-sixth annual encampment of the Veterans of Foreign Wars in Chicago from October 1 to 4, 1945, when servicemen from at least seventeen countries gathered, ranging in rank from air marshals to enlisted men. Brunner remarked that the primary goal of this international gathering was that the delegates return to their countries "deeply impressed with our sincere desire to make the purposes of the United Nations Charter effective." He placed the organization on record as favoring a continuation of the draft until all overseas soldiers were released from the service, and also declared that the GI Bill of Rights could never benefit more than four or five million veterans (out of an estimated twelve million). Discussion at the conference included the suggestion of a bonus for veterans of the Second World War (to be called "adjusted pay") of three dollars a day for service in the United States and four dollars a day for overseas service. Brunner also stated that veterans would insist on labor-management-Government teamwork, and he asked that the first choice of new housing go to veterans.

At the same time that Jean Brunner has been working for the veterans he has been building a business career for himself. After the First World War Brunner worked in the export department of the Texas Oil Company for four years, until 1923, when he left to take a position in the Cross and Brown Company, real estate firm, where he has been ever since. He began there as a clerk, but his position in the firm, when he left for a leave of absence in August of 1944, was that of secretary. The tall heavy-set veterans' leader, who is unmarried, lives with his sister in Forest Hills, Long Island. He neither drinks nor smokes, and his favorite recreation, he says, is fishing.

Reference

N Y Post Mag p23 D 28 '44 por

BRYAN, CHARLES W(AYLAND) Feb. 10, 1867—Mar. 4, 1945 Former Governor of Nebraska, 1923-25 and 1931-35; had run seven times for the office; ran also for many other offices, one of them United States Senator; in 1924 was Democratic candidate for Vice-President of United States; brother of William Jennings Bryan.

Obituary

N Y Times p19 Mr 5 '45 por

BUCKNER, SIMON BOLIVAR, JR. July 18, 1886—June 18, 1945 Lieutenant General in command of American Tenth Army, Pacific campaign; killed in action by enemy artillery shell on Okinawa only a few days before its complete conquest; also has defense of Alaska and recapture of Aleutian Islands to his credit; a strong advocate of physical occupation of Japan. See *Current Biography* 1942 Yearbook.

Obituary

N Y Times p1+ Je 19 '45 por

BULL, JOHAN (bōōl jō-hän') Nov. 22, 1893—Sept. 12, 1945 Norwegian illustrator, cartoonist, portrait and landscape painter, and etcher; came to United States in 1925; contributed to *New Yorker, Collier's, Woman's Home Companion,* New York *Times,* and New York *Herald Tribune*; known especially for sport scenes.

Obituary

N Y Times p23 S 14 '45

BURKE, THOMAS 1887—Sept. 22, 1945 English novelist and essayist; wrote poetry, murder stories, and literary criticism; won acclaim for sketches based on his boyhood in the slum areas and Chinatown of London; author of *Limehouse Nights* (1916), *Whispering Windows* (1920), *The Wind and the Rain* (1926), *Flower of Life* (1929), and numerous other works.

Obituary

N Y Times p19 S 24 '45

BURTON, HAROLD H(ITZ) June 22, 1888- United States Supreme Court Justice

Address: b. c/o United States Supreme Court, Washington, D. C.; h. Hotel Cleveland, Cleveland

The first Supreme Court Justice appointed by President Truman '45 (on October 1, 1945) is Harold H. Burton, lawyer, ex-Senator, and thrice Mayor of strongly Democratic Cleveland. Republican Senator to the United States Congress from 1940 until his resignation in September 1945, Burton served on the Military Affairs and War Investigating committees and collaborated on the defeated B2H2 bill calling for United States leadership in a United Nations organization to maintain peace; he was also a co-sponsor of a Federal industrial relations bill which would modify many of the laws passed in recent years for the protection of labor, including the Wagner Labor Relations Act and the Norris-La Guardia '40 Anti-Injunction Statute.

Harold Hitz Burton was born in Jamaica Plain, Massachusetts, on June 22, 1888. His father was Alfred Edgar Burton, then dean of Massachusetts Institute of Technology, and his mother was the former Gertrude Hitz. After graduating from Newton High School in Newton, Massachusetts, young Burton attended Bowdoin College, in Maine (B.A., 1909), where he was a quarterback on the football team and a Phi Beta Kappa student. Eager to become a lawyer, he studied at Harvard University Law School and was graduated in 1912. Believing that New England was not the ideal location for an aspiring lawyer not fortunate enough to have inherited an established law business, he

HAROLD H. BURTON

moved to Cleveland, where his wife's uncle was living. (In June 1912 Burton had been married to Selma Florence Smith, whom he had known in high school. They now have four children, Barbara, William Smith, Deborah, and Robert Smith.) During the next five years the young attorney found the Middle West and West favorable territories for his law practice: in succession he was employed by the Gage, Wilbur and Wachner law firm in Cleveland (1912-14); as assistant attorney by the Utah Power and Light and the Utah Light and Traction companies in Salt Lake City (1914-16); and as an attorney by the Idaho Power and Boise Valley Traction companies in Boise, Idaho (1916-17).

With the outbreak of the First World War, the prospering attorney was commissioned a first lieutenant. He served (eventually as a captain) with the 361st Infantry, Ninety-first Division in the Army, receiving a citation and the Order of the Purple Heart, and the Croix de Guerre from Belgium, for his part in the Saint-Mihiel, Meuse-Argonne, and Ypres-Lys offensives. In 1919 his book *600 Days' Service*, a history of the 361st Infantry in the war, was published. In 1921-22 he served as a major with the Cleveland Grays.

From the close of the war until 1925 Burton was associated with the firm of Day, Day and Wilkin; and in 1925-29 with Cull, Burton and Laughlin. During 1923-25 he also served as an instructor in the law of private corporations at Western Reserve University Law School, Cleveland. In the late 'twenties a beginning interest in public affairs served as the springboard to his future political career. Having become concerned with plans for a regional government for Cleveland, Burton was made the unpaid research director of the citizens' committee which was promoting the idea. When the committee reached the point of drawing up a state constitutional amendment, it felt that Burton was the logical person to sponsor this measure in the State legislature. Consequently, largely through the efforts of the

BURTON, HAROLD H.—*Continued*

committee, Burton was elected to the Ohio House of Representatives in 1929.

That same year he accepted an appointment as director of law of the City of Cleveland, a post he held until 1932. In November 1931, when the city-manager system was supplanted by the mayor-council plan, Burton temporarily assumed the duties of Mayor until the mayoral election was held three months later. From 1933 to 1935 he then divided his time among his law firm, Andrews, Hadden and Burton, his chairmanship of the Cleveland Board of Education Committee on Citizenship Training, and the County Charter Commission of Cuyahoga County.

In 1935 Burton was nominated for Mayor of Cleveland, running as an Independent Republican. With the city overrun by gangsters, and 1935 a Democratic year, Burton's election on a reform ticket hinged on how strongly he could present his case to the voters. Although he did not have a gift for oratory, he campaigned sixteen hours a day in an attempt to contact as many diverse groups as possible, promising to make Cleveland "a happier place to live in, a better place to die in." These efforts were rewarded: he was elected (and re-elected twice) by the largest majority in the city's history. He chose Eliot Ness as his safety director, and together, with the help of the Cleveland *Press*, they "streamlined the city for swift, smooth law enforcement."

A major issue with which the Mayor was faced in his three terms in office was the problem of relief. Ever since 1935, when the Federal Government had turned relief measures over to the individual states to manage, Ohio had suffered a number of serious crises. By 1939 conditions were bad in Cleveland, as well as in other cities in the state. The rural-dominated State legislature, faced with the relief bill, had cut to fifteen million the eighty million dollars formerly allotted by the Federal Government. The estimated minimum need of the State was thirty million, and State laws made it almost impossible for the cities to levy taxes to raise the funds they needed. The cities of Ohio urged finally that a special meeting of the legislature be called to alleviate the situation, but Governor John W. Bricker [43] insisted that other means be found, saying that relief was essentially a problem for the big unemployment centers to handle locally and blaming the situation partly on WPA political manipulation.

In an address to the city's labor leaders, Mayor Burton said; "Labor can go to the Governor independently of the city. You can give him the devil far better than I can." In the end some state rulings were changed, the Federal Government contributed relief assistance, and Cleveland raised additional funds by the sale of bonds. When he relinquished his mayoralty in 1940, Burton was able to announce that the bonded debt of Cleveland had been slightly reduced. And, although a Republican, he claims credit for having obtained forty million dollars in WPA money in two years. During his period in office Cleveland reached a high level in civic morale—rackets were smashed, the racketeers imprisoned, and corrupt police officials ousted. The Mayor's emphasis on safety, public health,

and free speech and tolerance gained for his city the National Safety Award in 1939 and 1940, the National Health Award, and the National Civil Liberties Award.

In 1940 Burton, although opposed by the State machine and boss Ed Schorr of Cincinnati, was elected United States Senator. In March 1943 the Senator came into the limelight when he, in collaboration with three other Senators—Joseph H. Ball [43], Republican of Minnesota; Carl A. Hatch [44], Democrat of New Mexico; and Lister Hill [43], Democrat of Alabama—sponsored the B2H2 bill, as Senate Resolution 114 has been called after the surname initials of the four men. The resolution called for United States leadership in forming a United Nations organization which should convene immediately to discuss the prosecution of the war, postwar problems, and, particularly, the establishment of an international police force to maintain the peace. Burton was one of eighteen Congressmen, nine Senators and nine Representatives, who barnstormed the United States in an attempt to impress upon the people the importance of the bill. Said Burton: "To my mind to fail to recommend some constructive postwar foreign policy that will translate into action at least the primary lessons of the tragedies of the First and Second World War is to default in the leadership placed in our hands." Senator Tom Connally [41], Democrat from Texas and chairman of the Foreign Relations Committee, was, according to *Newsweek*, "miffed at the four Senators' intrusion into his bailiwick," and the B2H2 bill was eventually buried in the Foreign Relations Committee. It was superseded by the Connally resolution which, although it recognized the importance of a general international organization to maintain peace and security, was considered by many as far too vague. Burton himself attacked the Connally resolution as "an easy way out for those who may wish to retreat from any advanced position in foreign affairs in the postwar settlement." During the Senate debate the Connally resolution was amended so as to include the substance of the Moscow agreement of 1943. This conformed closely to the B2H2 proposal, and as amended the Connally resolution was passed by a vote of 85 to 5. It established the Senate's approval of a general international organization to maintain peace and security. In February 1944 Burton's booklet, *America's Road to Lasting Peace,* was widely distributed to Republicans in public office.

Burton is an ardent proponent of a constitutional amendment to authorize the approval of treaties by majorities of both houses of Congress, instead of by two thirds of the Senate. Declares the former lawmaker: "This two-thirds requirement violates the principle of majority rule, which is a foundation principle of self-government." The forces advocating the amendment contend that the two-thirds Senate ratification makes it possible for a minority in the Senate to override a policy important to the welfare of the nation, and generally approved by the people themselves. Burton also urges that private enterprise and not the Government be instrumental in providing jobs for returning servicemen.

In regard to the more important bills presented on the Senate floor after Burton became a Senator, he voted against the repeal of the Neutrality Act; and for the Lend-Lease bill; for the legislation empowering the President in 1941 to extend the active military duty of enlisted men, selectees, national guardsmen, and reserve officers. In 1943 he supported the continuation of the reciprocal trade agreements program; voted for the Fulbright resolution and for the compromise servicemen's vote bill. In 1945 he voted for the George '43 bill which removed the Reconstruction Finance Corporation from the jurisdiction of the Secretary of Commerce, but opposed the confirmation of Henry A. Wallace '40 as Secretary of Commerce. He urged legislation to make the Fair Employment Practice Committee permanent; and proposed, with Lister Hill, a bill calling for a nationwide hospital construction program to be financed by Federal grants-in-aid to states. This was approved by the Senate in December 1945. In 1944 Burton made an extended investigation of slum conditions in the Capital, and advocated an opportunity for private agencies to provide better housing.

In the 1944 Presidential campaign, Burton announced support of Bricker when the latter's name was entered in Ohio's primaries. When Dewey '44 and Bricker became the Republican Party's candidates, the Ohio Senator stated that his vote would go to them. Said Burton: "We're going to have an anti-Roosevelt Senate, so we need an anti-Roosevelt President." Burton voiced the opinion that Roosevelt's continuance in office was not necessary to the winning of the war or the establishment of sound international relations. With the promotion of accord between Congress and the President as his primary concern, Burton declared: "Regardless of party, any man who remains President for twelve years is bound to accumulate frictions, disappointments, and prejudices that handicap him in dealing with the Legislature."

Senator Burton and Senator James M. Tunnell, Democrat of Delaware, both members of the War Investigating Subcommittee, were sent in January 1945 to the Mediterranean and Middle East areas to examine American investments, to investigate American agencies operating in the region, and to determine the state of petroleum resources. Burton reported on his return that he was "particularly impressed with the resources for wealth and prosperity in the oil fields of Iran, Iraq, and Saudi Arabia." Some other conditions in the region were said to be less heartening. Cost records of air bases improved or constructed there were inadequate, the Senators said, with the result that American rights in installations built or improved by American funds were seldom "clear cut." Burton and Tunnell also stated that unless the United States made commercial agreements—almost nonexistent now—with the countries of the Middle East, and unless she established credit agreements to permit citizens of these areas to purchase American goods with American money, the Middle East market would be closed to American trade after the war. The need for an economic policy toward the Mediterranean and Middle East was immediate, these two Senators emphasized.

Joining the campaign which began in June 1945 to insure ratification of the San Francisco Security Charter, Senator Burton indicated that its opponents might use a "perfectionist" attack upon the Charter instead of viewing it with a "revisionist" approach. In a three-hour speech in the Senate on June 13 he defended the veto arrangement insisted upon by the Soviet Union whereby one of the Big Five powers could veto the use of collective force to prevent aggression; he declared that this was a necessary limitation and as much in the interest of the United States as of Russia. He added that the Charter "comes well within the policy outlined" by the Senate at the time of the passage of the Connally peace resolution. In view of Burton's support of international cooperation, it had been expected in many quarters that he would support to the utmost attempts to hasten approval of economic cooperation; in July, however, he voted for Senator Taft's '40 unsuccessful motion to postpone to November 15 action on the Bretton Woods agreements.

In June 1945 Burton, together with his fellow Senators Hatch and Ball, introduced a Federal industrial relations bill (S.1171), which the authors claimed was designed to remove management-labor strife in the postwar period. Drafted by a committee of citizens headed by former labor lawyer Donald R. Richberg, who avowedly had not consulted any representatives of either labor or management in its formulation, the bill immediately drew the united opposition of organized labor. The bill proposed to reorganize the Federal agencies by 1) setting up an independent five-man Federal labor relations board to take the place of the present NLRB, the Conciliation Service of the Labor Department, and ultimately the WLB; and by 2) the creation of a special board of three members to control, under machinery now used by the NLRB, unfair labor practices either by employers or employees. This feature of the program, it was said, assumed that labor had reached the point where it might be considered on terms of equality with industry before the law, although labor legislation had for years been based on the presumption that labor was the weaker party in industrial disputes and required the protection of the Government to preserve its rights in collective bargaining. Other major provisions of the Burton-Hatch-Ball bill would require compulsory arbitration in many cases, put curbs on the union shop, place restrictions on the right to strike, and impose other restraints. In the flood of criticism that ensued, Philip Murray '41 of the CIO denounced the measure as a "bald-faced attempt to destroy labor unions and nullify the basic constitutional rights of workers"; the A. F. of L.'s William Green '42 labeled it a "strait jacket" which would lead to the regimentation of labor and industry and would undermine free collective bargaining.

Senator Ball, in an article in the New York World-Telegram on July 9, 1945, indicated the four major reasons which had impelled the authors to propose the bill: 1) "there is grave danger of widespread stoppages of production as a result of labor disputes"; 2) "Federal labor policy on labor disputes today is confused, with jurisdiction scattered among many agencies"; 3) "many closed unions . . . monopolize for a privileged few the employment opportunities"; 4) "it is high time, if we want industry to expand, to afford employers some protection against arbitrary and coercive actions by employees." In another defense of the bill,

BURTON, HAROLD H.—*Continued*

Burton declared, "It will strengthen America's system of private enterprise in the interest of employer, employee, and the public."

The Republican Senator was elevated to the Supreme Court bench in October 1945, as successor to Justice Owen J. Roberts '41, who retired in July. The Senate, waiving its customary procedure of holding open hearings on judicial appointments, on September 19 unanimously confirmed Burton's nomination as an Associate Justice. Commentators for the most part agreed that President Truman had "revealed an innate fairness" in naming a Republican to the Court with only one member of that party left on the bench, Chief Justice Stone '41. The choice received praise from Senators of both parties, although there has been considerable speculation as to where Burton's economic and other views would place him in the tribunal. "Those who know him best," wrote Lewis Wood in the New York *Times* before the confirmation, "describe him as a liberal Republican of marked independence, who could never be accused of reactionary tendencies, but whose appointment would certainly not enlarge the 'advanced' wing of the Court as typified by Justices Hugo L. Black '41, William O. Douglas '41, Frank Murphy '40, and Wiley Rutledge '43." Burton himself commented: "My position is center. I hold to the belief that if folks get around a table and talk things through they usually can come to the right and fair answer." President Truman was present at the Supreme Court installation ceremony on October 1, thus becoming the first Chief Executive to appear in the courtroom while in office.

In May 1944 Burton was elected moderator of the Unitarian Churches of the United States and Canada for a two-year term. He is a member of the National Board of Incorporators of the American Red Cross, and is a member of the American Legion and the Veterans of Foreign Wars. The Justice also belongs to the American, Ohio, and Cleveland bar associations, and to a number of clubs.

Mild-mannered but energetic, Burton, since the beginning of his political career, has not missed a day of work because of illness. The Justice's lack of hobbies can be plausibly attributed to his busy life. However, his and Mrs. Burton's love of the out-of-doors brings them frequently to the parks in and near Washington. Their two daughters are married. Both sons and a son-in-law in 1945 served in the armed forces.

References

Cur Hist 49:22-4 O '38 por
Time 30:19 O 11 '37 por; 36:31 O 14 '40 por
Congressional Directory, 1945
Who's Who in America, 1944-45
Who's Who in Government, 1932-33

BYAS, HUGH (FULTON) (bī'ás) 1875(?)—Mar. 6, '45 Veteran Scottish-born newspaperman and leading authority on contemporary Japan; Tokyo correspondent for the London *Times* from 1926, and New York *Times* from 1927, to May 1941; watched and reported the critical years which led to the war in the Pacific and the period in which the Japanese

Army gained control of the Government. See *Current Biography* 1943 Yearbook.

Obituary

N Y Times p21 Mr 7 '45 por

CAILLAUX, JOSEPH (kà"yō' zhō"zĕf') Mar. 30, 1863—Nov. 21, 1944 French Premier before the First World War (1911-12) and Minister of Finance (1899-1902, 1906-9), and 1911); convicted of treasonable negotiations with the enemy during the war and imprisoned from 1920 to 1923; regarded an expert on finance.

Obituary

N Y Times p31 N 23 '44 por

CALDER, A(LEXANDER) STIRLING Jan. 11, 1870—Jan. 6, 1945 American sculptor; works are included in the permanent collection of the Pennsylvania Academy of Fine Arts, the City Museum of Art, St. Louis, the Smithsonian Institution, Washington, D. C., the Metropolitan Museum and the Museum of Modern Art in New York; recipient of many medals and awards; member of National Academy.

Obituary

N Y Times p17 Ja 8 '45 por

CALDER, WILLIAM M. Mar. 3, 1869—Mar. 3, 1945 Former United States Senator from New York (1917-23); leader in Republican politics; served in the House of Representatives from 1905 to 1915; Building Commissioner of Brooklyn (1902-05); credited with having done much in the development of the Brooklyn Borough.

Obituary

N Y Times p38 Mr 4 '45 por

CALLES, PLUTARCO ELIAS (kä'yäs plōo-tär'kō ā-lē'äs) Sept. 25, 1877—Oct. 19, 1945 Mexican general and political leader; as President (1924-28), carried out many reforms; "administration marked by struggle between church and state"; held other Government posts; fought throughout political career on side of "institutional" government; exiled to United States in 1936, but returned in 1941 after retirement of President Cárdenas.

Obituary

N Y Times p11 O 20 '45 por

CALLOWAY, CAB (căl'lō-wā) Dec. 25, 1907- Conductor; singer

Address: b. Cab Calloway, Inc., 1619 Broadway, New York City; h. Riverdale, N.Y.

Cab Calloway, the Negro orchestra leader, has been billed as "King of Hi De Ho" since the early thirties. He is famous for his individual style of singing, his voice having been described as containing "a joy and festive spirit which moves one to instant gaiety." Considered the "personality boy" among his colleagues, Calloway has been presented to the American public through almost every medium of entertainment—night clubs, the stage, the screen, and radio.

Cab (short for Cabell 3d) was born on Christmas night of 1907, in Rochester, New York. He was the second of the six children of Cabell and Eulalia (Reed) Calloway. When Cab was six years old the family moved to Baltimore, Maryland, where his father practiced law and conducted a real estate business. After school hours young Cab sold newspapers, and on Sundays he sang solos in the Bethlehem Methodist Episcopal Church, until he was graduated from Douglass High School at the age of seventeen. Although his father's fondest wish was to have Cab, the eldest son, study law, the boy had made up his mind to become an entertainer, and he turned to his older sister, Blanche, for advice and assistance when he finished school. She was his idol because she had gone to Chicago and was singing with a show.

Sister Blanche not only sent her brother the railroad fare for his trip to Chicago, but she got him a place as a singer with a quartet. Between performances he learned the fundamentals of acting under Blanche's tutelage and attended Crane College, purportedly in preparation for a law career. After a short period of drifting about from one South Side night club to another as a singer and master of ceremonies, Calloway found that he had a real talent for the drum. He had been spending most of his free time with musicians, and it was one night, while giving vocal assistance in an impromptu "jam session," that he tried his hand with the drumsticks and amazed himself as well as his friends by the results he obtained. A year of lessons on the drum followed, and in 1925 he secured the job that he looks back on as the beginning his career— that of drummer in the orchestra at the Sunset Cafe in Chicago.

When his musical apprenticeship was over Calloway organized his own orchestra and became both its leader and vocalist. "Cab Calloway and his Alabamians," as they called themselves, became very popular in Chicago, and within six months were on their way to New York to fill an engagement at the Savoy Ballroom in Harlem. At the Savoy the band was a dismal failure and the engagement was canceled. Calloway, becoming discouraged, dissolved the orchestra, and got himself a part in the all-Negro cast of a new Broadway musical comedy, *Connie's Hot Chocolates.* In it his rendition of the song "Ain't Misbehavin'" was a high spot and assured his success. Irving Mills, a Broadway manager, seeing Calloway's possibilities as an orchestra leader, became his personal manager and placed his discarded baton back in his hand. That same year, 1929, the Calloway orchestra joined Duke Ellington's [41] at the Cotton Club in New York, and for the next ten years the two musicians, who are good friends, played alternate engagements there. While the Ellington orchestra appeared at the Cotton Club, the Calloway band toured. It played in London and Paris as well as in numerous cities in the United States. It was during this long stay at the Cotton Club that Calloway developed the distinctive style of singing for which he is known today. One night, while introducing a new song, he forgot part of the lyrics. Forced to improvise quickly, he filled in the gaps with "skeeten, scaten, hi de ho." The enthu-

Cab Calloway, Inc.

CAB CALLOWAY

siastic reaction of the audience caused him to try it again, and before long the Calloway nonsense syllables had become a new style of jazz singing.

Early in his career the song "St. James Infirmary Blues" had become closely associated with the name of Cab Calloway. Shortly after he opened at the Cotton Club Calloway and his manager decided to find another song just as well suited to the singer's talents. After an unsuccessful search for a song the two sat down early one morning, when the club was empty of guests, and composed "Minnie the Moocher." The night he introduced the song Calloway was called back for six encores. His recording of Minnie's activities became internationally famous and a collector's item. The records have been sold in Bangkok, Sydney, and Shanghai, and in all the principal European cities. Whenever Calloway performs he includes these two songs in his program.

When the Cotton Club closed the Cab Calloway orchestra went on a tour of the United States. It appeared in such well known amusement places as the Casa Manana in California, the Panther Room of the Hotel Sherman in Chicago, and the Lookout House in Cincinnati. In theaters all over the country the Calloway troupe played to standing-room-only audiences, returning to New York just long enough to perform at the Strand and Paramount theaters. During a two-week engagement at the Paramount audiences paid $84,200 to hear him, a new summer record. In 1943 Calloway and the orchestra accepted an offer from the Park Central's Cocoanut Grove in New York, where they remained for an extended engagement. From there they went to Frank Dailey's Meadowbrook in New Jersey and finally back to Broadway for a prolonged stay at the Cafe Zanzibar, where Calloway heads the Negro group of entertainers.

In 1938 Calloway published the first edition of his *Hepster's Dictionary,* two million copies

CALLOWAY, CAB—*Continued*

of which were distributed. The pamphlet, which is the official "jive language" reference book in New York Public Library, is a collection of slang words and expressions used by entertainers and musicians—particularly in Harlem. In the foreword to the 1944 edition, which is the sixth, Calloway denies that any of the words are not actually used: he says they are authentic expressions which he discovered through careful research, or were contributed by people from all over the country. He has coined many of the phrases himself, being credited as the originator of the term "jitterbug." In Calloway's vocabulary "fortissimo" has become "sock it," and "scherzo" has been replaced by "medium bounce." Academic recognition has been given Calloway by New York University, which has awarded him the honorary title of Dean of American Jive.

Calloway has sung to fame many of his original musical compositions. His songs include "Chinese Rhythm," published in 1935, and "Jumpin' Jive," which appeared four years later. "Are You Hep to the Jive?" came out in 1940, and "Are You All Reet" in 1941. Three songs, "Virginia, Georgia and Caroline", "Geechee Joe," and "Mein Nein," appeared in 1942. Another novelty tune, the title of which is in deep "jive language", "Foo a Little Bally Hoo," was introduced the next year, with "If This Isn't Love" coming in 1945. In 1945 he is working on an operetta, tentatively titled *Rhapsody in Reverse*, which is based on the compositions of the old masters as they would be played in swing.

Calloway's unique brand of entertainment has been successfully adapted to the radio and screen. He has appeared in several song cartoons, including *Minnie the Moocher* and *Old Man of the Mountain*, and in the short subjects *Hi De Ho, Cab's Jitterbug Party,* and *Manhattan Merry-Go-Round.* Among the full-length motion pictures in which he has been featured are Paramount's *Big Broadcast* (1932), *International House* (1933), and *Roadshow* (1941), in which he was described as "a leader in the field of musical riot." In 1943 he was awarded an "Oscar" by the Negro Actors Guild for his performance in the Twentieth Century-Fox film *Stormy Weather*, in which Lena Horne [44] headed the all-Negro cast. In 1944 he returned to Hollywood to play a leading role in Andrew Stone's *Sensations of 1944.* Besides broadcasting regularly from the night club or hotel in which he happens to be playing, Cab has had his own program, *The Cab Calloway Quizzicale,* a satirical version of the question-and-answer radio shows. He has been a frequent guest on the *Fitch Bandwagon* and the *Coca-Cola Spotlight Bands* programs, and has made several test performances before television cameras. In his survey of jazz for *Esquire's 1945 Jazz Book*, Leonard Feather states that some critics acknowledge Calloway's important place as a hot jazz singer, while most "consider him more of a showman and entertainer . . . the leader of a consistently fine orchestra, combining swing, precision, and finesse in its ensemble work with a high standard of inspiration."

During the war the Calloway orchestra was among the leading units which entertained for servicemen. Calloway and the band were the first group of musicians from the United States to tour the Canadian Maritime Provinces, as well as the first to entertain the United States troops stationed in Nova Scotia. The orchestra played at the reopening of the Stage Door Canteen in New York, and Calloway's *Quizzicale* was the first radio show to be broadcast directly from an Army camp.

Calloway has said that he is so sensitive to the moods of his audiences that he can tell exactly what they want to hear. "If I feel that they seem to want faster tempos, I always step up my orchestra and revamp the schedule of the tunes to come. It is always the duty of a bandleader to be ready to give his audiences what *they* want, not what he wishes to dish out." He auditions hundreds of young musicians who write and call him for hearings, and, while he is unable to hire every talented hopeful he meets, he has helped numerous beginners to get jobs with bands.

Calloway and Wenonah Conacher were married in 1928 and have one daughter, Constance Wenonah. The musician weighs one hundred and eighty pounds and on the stage appears much taller than his five feet eight and a half inches. He achieves this effect by having his jackets and coat tails cut extra-long. Well known for his eccentricities of dress, Calloway is said to be the owner of forty suits and forty pairs of shoes. When working he makes as many as twelve changes in suits an evening, and he still frequently appears in the famous white zoot suit which he wore in the film *Stormy Weather.*

References

N Y Herald Tribune p14 Ag 11 '43
Who Is Who in Music, 1941

CANHAM, ERWIN D(AIN)   (kăn'ăm)
Feb. 13, 1904-   Newspaper editor

Address: b. c/o The Christian Science Publishing Society, 1 Norway St., Boston, Mass.; h. 72 Crofton Rd., Waban, Mass.

Widely regarded as one of America's outstanding journalists, Erwin D. Canham became editor of the *Christian Science Monitor* in 1945 after four years' experience as managing editor of the paper and many previous years of *Monitor* service as a national and foreign correspondent. A native of Maine and a former Rhodes Scholar with degrees from Bates College in Maine and Oxford University in England, Canham reported from Geneva in the years when it was the political center of the world and headed the *Monitor's* Washington news bureau during most of the nineteen-thirties. He has traveled extensively in Europe and the Orient, and has made many transcontinental tours of the United States with Presidential candidates. His column, *Down the Middle of the Road,* has appeared once each week since 1940 in the "dignified, intellectual, progressive" paper which is the only one of the eight Boston-published newspapers that has an international circulation. The *Christian Science Monitor* "shines like a bright star" among Boston newspapers, and is, in the words of Oswald Garrison Villard [40] in *The Disappearing Daily* (1944), "the sole remaining daily to recall the Hub's lost reputation for high intelligence and literary and intellectual taste."

The son of Vincent Walter and Elizabeth May (Gowell) Canham, Erwin Dain Canham was born into a Christian Scientist home in Auburn, Maine, on February 13, 1904, and he spent his youth in the general area of Auburn, which is thirty miles north of Portland. In this rural section many influences were to shape his future career. His father was agricultural editor of the *Lewiston Sun and Journal*, and the boy, in almost daily visits to the office of the country daily, early became familiar with printer's ink. In grammar school days he set type and folded and sold papers after school, and at the age of fourteen, while a student at high school, he worked during the summer on a local daily paper. The United States was fighting in the First World War at this time, and "because of the manpower shortage," he points out, he was a full-fledged reporter. Later, when the older men returned, he "reverted" to the composing room of the paper, working as galley boy and doing odd jobs. From that time he was occupied summer after summer with newspaper work of one kind or another, and there was never any question in his mind as to the choice of his vocation.

In 1921 young Canham entered Bates College in Lewiston. At the end of his junior year he was writing for a small paper, the *Hill-Top*, which was published in Poland Springs; "I sometimes managed to get in about twenty pages," he recalls with a smile. At this time he was also correspondent for eight metropolitan dailies and making more money than he did later as a full-time reporter. Debating was his chief extracurricular activity while in college. During his sophomore year he took part in the first debate with Oxford University to be held in America, and in the spring of his senior year he went to England with the college debating team, which competed with seven British universities. After receiving his B.A. degree from Bates in 1925 he worked as a reporter for the *Monitor* for a year and then went to Oxford as a Rhodes Scholar, studying there from 1926 to 1929 for the B.A. and M.A. he finally received in 1936. During all these years abroad Canham continued to report for the *Monitor*. His first important assignment was to cover American activities at the League of Nations Assembly in Geneva in the years 1926, 1927, and 1928. In 1929 he returned to America and reported Ramsay MacDonald's tour of the United States.

In 1930 Erwin Canham was married to Thelma Whitman Hart of Truro, Massachusetts. That year the young newsman was chief correspondent for the *Christian Science Monitor* at the London Naval Conference for three months, and then for two years he again reported the activities of the League of Nations from Geneva. In 1932 he was made head of the Washington bureau of the *Monitor*, a position which he held until 1939. During this period he frequently left Washington for *Monitor* news assignments: he attended the London Economic Conference with the American delegation in 1933 and was one of a group of twenty newspapermen to cover the inauguration of the Philippine Commonwealth Government in 1935. He wrote numerous articles on the Far East for the *Monitor* at this time. He also

Bachrach

ERWIN D. CANHAM

made several nationwide political surveys during these years and covered trips of American Presidents and Presidential candidates throughout the United States. By 1939 he was promoted from reporting to the general news editorship of his newspaper at the Boston publishing office, and in 1941 he was made managing editor. Since January 1945 Canham has been editor of the *Monitor*.

The *Christian Science Monitor* was launched in 1908 by Mrs. Mary Baker Eddy, the founder of the Christian Science Church. Feeling that the newspapers of the period were too sensational and that their emphasis on crime, disaster, and death was detrimental, she ordered her Board of Trustees to establish a daily newspaper whose principle would be "to injure no man but to bless all mankind." The first issue of the *Monitor* appeared on November 25, 1908. Mrs. Eddy directed the paper generally in its early beginnings until her death in 1910, and the news policy which she formulated has since governed the paper. This policy was set forth in an editorial in the first anniversary edition of the *Monitor* and has been republished many times since then; it is, in part: "It is not to be understood that the *Monitor* has stooped to a censorship so narrow or opinionated as to render its news service inadequate, inefficient, or incomplete. Far from it. Whatever is of public importance or affects the public welfare, even though it be news of what is ordinarily reckoned as crime or disaster, is printed in the *Monitor* in completeness sufficient for information but without unnecessary embellishment or sensational display. The emphasis, however, is reserved for the helpful, the constructive, the encouraging, not for their opposites."

The editors interpret this policy by mentioning disasters only when they are too big to be ignored or when they point a moral, and by printing stories of crime only when they are of social significance. Death and illness are mentioned as little as possible, and the verb "to pass on" is often used instead of "to die." The *Monitor* is owned by the Christian Science

CANHAM, ERWIN D.—*Continued*

Church, and the profit motive is secondary to the idealistic one. It does not accept advertisements for tea, coffee, liquor, tobacco, or any other products which it considers unwholesome. Ninety per cent of *Monitor* subscribers are Christian Scientists. Although its Boston circulation is small (15,000), and its entire circulation only approximately 155,000, its readers are said to live in ninety-six different countries and the paper reaches more than half a million people. "One of the most influential newspapers in the world, certainly one of the ten best in the United States," the *Monitor* is not popular, says *Time* Magazine, because it accents information, shuns sheer entertainment. And Kenneth Stewart [43], discussing in *PM* the weaknesses of the Boston press, says that the "limitations" imposed by the religious body prevent the *Monitor* from being "a complete newspaper, and from winning the complete confidence of many in Boston."

Because of the *Monitor*'s many unique aspects, Canham's work both as managing editor and editor has been difficult but challenging. As *PM* points out, he faces problems which most editors do not face. The *Monitor* must make its pages seem timely to the great mass of its readers outside Boston who receive the paper anywhere from one to thirty days late, at the same time that it keeps up with the hour-by-hour coverage of its local competition. Villard mentions another difficulty—the conflict between magazine and newspaper ideals which ensues because the *Monitor* is more of a daily magazine than a newspaper. *Time* feels that Canham's most important and difficult work on becoming editor lay in seeing that the paper passed theological as well as journalistic tests.

Local problems as well as those connected with war have tested Erwin Canham's ability as editor. In 1943 *PM* published an exposé of anti-Semitism in Boston and denounced the Boston papers for suppressing the news of these uprisings. When the *Monitor* was taken to task on this matter, Editor Canham met the issue, saying that the *Monitor* had been investigating anti-Jewish violence in Boston for many months but did not print a story about it because many responsible leaders in the Jewish community were disturbed at the prospect of publicity, feeling that it would do more harm than good. Later *PM* mentioned the *Monitor*'s fairness in dealing with racial minority group matters. In 1945 *PM* also commented on the fact that in Boston, which is seventy-five per cent Catholic, the *Monitor* is the only paper that comments unfavorably on any activities of the Catholic Church. In an article on the *Monitor* in the *Saturday Evening Post* (September 15, 1945) Marquis Childs [43] wrote: "*Monitor* correspondents are held accountable for a balanced insight into the situation they are assigned to cover"; and in holding to that policy the newspaper will sometimes delay the printing of an article on controversial issues until the discussion may be rounded out by material from other sources.

The *Monitor* has an editorial council of nine people. Canham is in executive editorial charge of the paper but responsible on matters of business policy to the *Monitor* business manager and the board of trustees of the Christian Science Publishing Society, and on editorial policies to the board of directors of the Mother Church. "High policy" decisions are made by this board of five. Although most of the editor's time is occupied in the editing of the paper and the supervision of its foreign correspondence, he does a considerable amount of writing for the paper he edits. In April 1945 the *Monitor* published an article by him, "The Continuity of American Government," and in May he reported from San Francisco on the United Nations conference. Some of the San Francisco columns were serious in nature and were signed by the editor; others were written in "human interest" style and in these he humorously called himself "our man."

Since 1940 his *Down the Middle of the Road* column has appeared four or five times a month. Usually editorial in style, this column deals in a forthright and pleasantly readable manner with domestic and international subjects, economics, current phases of the Second World War, and certain aspects of politics. The *Monitor* is generally independent in its politics, and the editor does not commit himself to any party in his column. Canham frequently uses the column to explain *Monitor* policies and to discuss freedom of the press and postwar journalistic plans. Some of the columns are extracts from speeches made to Rotary Clubs, the American Society of Newspaper Editors, and other groups. *Down the Middle of the Road* is popular with *Monitor* readers, many of whom write to the editor on some of the controversial matters discussed in the column. Speaking before the Rotary Club after the dropping of the atomic bomb on Japan in the summer of 1945, Canham emphasized that "power alone can never be the guaranty of peace." The fundamental need, he continued, "is to straighten out our thinking . . . to determine . . . to alleviate any friction spots which may develop in relations with other nations and—fundamentally—to learn to understand why other peoples have come to think differently on some questions. . . .In carrying out this determination, the press and radio have a very great responsibility and an equally great opportunity."

A great deal of press and literary comment on the *Monitor* has been made during Canham's editorial years, possibly because the Boston *Evening Transcript* ceased publication soon after he assumed his editorial duties, and attention focused on the *Monitor* and other Boston papers after the demise of the venerable *Transcript*, even though the *Monitor* is essentially an international, not a local paper. Most of this comment is favorable. The *Monitor* is called "an aristocrat in its field," a paper "published by intelligent people for intelligent people," and it is admired because it does not proselytize. (It confines its religious message to one daily article on the *Home Forum* page.) It is frequently noted that it is read by many people who are not Christian Scientists. *Time* speaks of its "clean, unruffled prose," and its fine typography, and *PM* likes its timeless, leisurely style. *PM* also feels that it is consistently international in viewpoint, and Oswald Garrison Villard thinks the *Monitor*'s conception of journalism is "the hope of the world." However, Villard criticizes the *Monitor* because it is too "soft-spoken" and does not crusade or strike out vigorously enough against wickedness and injustice. Villard also maintained that the *Monitor* supported the war, which he feels is inconsistent with its devotion to the teachings of Christ; he does point out, however, that the newspaper presented the Christian Scientist viewpoint about the war—that the victory of the democracies would mean a continuance of the slow but steady progress toward a world without war.

In 1942 the *Christian Science Monitor* received the fourth annual Maria Moors Cabot award for distinguished service in the field of inter-American relations. In 1943 the University of Missouri award for distinguished service in journalism was given to the international daily, and in 1945 it was chosen from among one thousand leading American papers for the thirteenth annual Francis Wayland Ayer award for typographical excellence. Also in 1945, the *Monitor* received the Helms Athletic Foundation award in recognition of noteworthy achievements in the realm of sports. Erwin Canham stopped in Los Angeles on his way to Boston from the United Nations conference at San Francisco to receive this award for his paper, saying at that time that it is the purpose of the *Monitor*'s sport pages to tell the world that it is possible to compete keenly without bitterness or hatred.

The *Monitor* and other periodicals and books of the Christian Science Church are published in a "block-big, sedate Boston palace" which cost four million dollars and is a constant source of amazement to visiting journalists, who comment on its landscaped gardens, its "hushed and palatial precincts," and its "unbegrimed" pressmen and linotypists who do not smoke, drink, or swear in the newspaper's unhurried and serene atmosphere.

The *Monitor* editor is well liked by his colleagues who call him "Spike" and describe him as "clean-cut," affable, competent, and conscientious. Oswald Villard considers Canham an able and experienced newspaperman who believes that the *Monitor* owes its strength not to any individual but to the ideals behind it. Canham is aware of public criticism of his paper but he is ever conscious of the mandate which rules its policies. He realizes, too, that there is great power in being freed of commercial control and for that reason is more eager to maintain its idealistic standards and at the same time to prevent the paper from becoming a house organ. He feels that the essential function of a newspaper is to give facts, and not "to sell the informational birthright for a mess of entertainment pottage."

Erwin Canham is a Mason, a member of Phi Beta Kappa and Delta Sigma Rho, the Gridiron Club (in whose shows he has acted), the Association of American Rhodes Scholars, and of the American Society of Newspaper Editors. He was president for two terms of the Overseas Writers' Club and is a trustee of Bates College. As American correspondent, he contributes an article every three months to the *Round Table,* a British quarterly. He frequently speaks on the radio, and in May

and June of 1945 broadcast over Mutual Network, substituting for Cedric Foster who was in the Pacific area. In December the editor began a weekly commentary over the ABC network. The program, under the sponsorship of the *Monitor,* also presented a dramatized documentation of special events headlined by the paper.

In appearance Canham is of medium height, broad-shouldered, with dark hair and eyes. He is described as a friendly man, relaxed in manner, and although of a serious, scholarly mien, he has a sense of humor that "lies just beneath the surface." His office resembles a spacious living room, and frequent callers are received there.

The *Monitor* editor and Mrs. Canham and their two daughters, Carolyn and Elizabeth, live in Waban, a suburb of Boston. The editor says that he has no hobbies, but while at home he spends much of the time out-of-doors, gardening and cutting wood on the acre of woodland behind his home. He does a great deal of his writing at home.

Reference

Who's Who in America, 1944-45

CANNON, WALTER BRADFORD Oct. 19, 1871—Oct. 1, 1945 American physiologist, widely known for work in fields of endocrinology and neurology; George Higginson Professor of Physiology at Harvard from 1906 until retirement in 1942; responsible for solving the problem of traumatic shock during First World War; discovered adrenalin-like hormone he called "sympathin."

Obituary

N Y Times p23 O 2 '45 por

CANTERBURY, GEOFFREY FRANCIS FISHER, ARCHBISHOP OF *See* Fisher, G. F.

CARAWAY, HATTIE W(YATT) Feb. 1, 1878- Government official; former United States Senator from Arkansas

Address: h. Jonesboro, Ark.; 100 Maryland Ave., N.E., Washington, D. C.

The only woman ever to be elected to the United States Senate in her own right is Hattie W. Caraway of Arkansas, who in December 1944 completed thirteen years of service in that chamber. A Democrat and a Methodist, she was born on a farm in the Deep South, near Bakerville, Tennessee. Her birthday was February 1, 1878. The daughter of William Carroll and Lucy Mildred (Burch) Wyatt, she was given the simple name of Hattie. At fourteen she entered the Dickson (Tennessee) Normal College, graduating with her B.A. in 1896. (Many Southern "colleges" of the day were what one would now term high schools.) The future Senator led a very rural sort of life; indeed, she has told reporters that she had never even seen a railroad train until her marriage. It was in 1902, when she was twenty-four, that dark-eyed Hattie Wyatt was married to Thaddeus H. Caraway, a thirty-

HATTIE W. CARAWAY

one-year-old lawyer, and went to live in Lake City, Arkansas.

From that time on, Mrs. Caraway was a housewife of the classic model, even keeping a kitchen garden and helping her husband run the cotton plantation he later acquired. She took little part in political or social activities, devoting her time to her homemaking and to the rearing of her children, Paul Wyatt and Forrest. (A third son, Robert Easley, is deceased. Brigadier General Paul Caraway, "an outstanding planner," *Time* was to report in 1945, served in the Second World War as deputy chief of staff to the Chinese Combat Command under Major General Robert Battery McClure.) "After equal suffrage in 1920," Senator Caraway now reminisces, "I just added voting to cooking and sewing and other household duties. Of course living in Arkansas helped a lot, for down there we don't have to bother about making a choice between two parties." Six years after their marriage Thaddeus Caraway was elected prosecuting attorney of the Second Arkansas Judicial Circuit—on the Democratic ticket, of course. After two terms as prosecutor he was elected in 1912 to the Federal House of Representatives in the Sixty-third United States Congress, and was re-elected at two-year intervals in the Sixty-fourth, Sixty-fifth, and Sixty-sixth Congresses. Mrs. Caraway continued for "a good many years" to do all her own housework in Washington, as at home in Jonesboro, and entered into little social activity.

In 1920 (the first election, incidentally, in which women might vote) Representative Caraway entered and won the race for a seat in the upper house. He was re-elected to the Senate in 1926 for another six-year term, serving in the administrations of Harding and Coolidge. During his ten years in the Senate, Caraway had a reputation for a sharp tongue (he made perhaps half a dozen public apologies in the course of a year), for keenness in Senate investigations, and for his hatred of lobbyists (he became chairman of the Lobbying Committee). His particular interests were flood control and air safety legislation. The Caraways' sons, meanwhile, were both appointed to West Point, graduated, and started on their careers as Army officers.

In September 1931, during the Hoover [43] Administration, Senator Caraway fell ill, and on November 6 he died. As a chivalrous gesture, and to give the politicos time to agree on a successor, Governor Harvey Parnell appointed Caraway's quiet widow to fill out the unexpired term, and she was duly elected in January 1932. (Her first official utterance on entering the Senate was, "The windows need washing.") Competition was keen for the nomination to replace Mrs. Caraway at the regular election; but, to everyone's surprise, she was persuaded by her fellow Senator Huey Long, the "Kingfish" of Louisiana, to campaign for re-election when her term expired in March 1933.

"To tell the honest truth," says Mrs. Caraway of Long's suggestion, "I was a good deal embarrassed, for, while the proposition had assets it was not without its liabilities." But she accepted his help and his advice—to doff her bright clothes for widow's weeds and to wear just one hat throughout the campaign. Then "down into Arkansas Long boomed with his sound trucks and Bible, and in the course of nine red-hot days he made exactly thirty-nine speeches in thirty counties," persuading the people of Arkansas (or as many as were white and had paid their poll tax) to send Mrs. Caraway back to the Senate. And they did, choosing her in preference to the wartime Governor of Arkansas, as well as a Democratic National Committeeman, a former commander of the American Legion, and three other opponents.

Assuming her seat in 1933, "Miss Hattie" was the first woman to be elected a United States Senator (Rebecca Latimer Felton of Georgia had been appointed in 1922 to fill out an unexpired term). A thoroughgoing supporter of President Roosevelt [42] since his inauguration, she devoted herself to voting as she thought her late husband would have done, and to furthering his ideas. Seldom did she make a speech (about once a year) or enter debate. "I haven't the heart to take a minute away from the men," she confided. "The poor dears love it so." But she worked hard at being a Senator: "Every morning I got down to the office at eight, an hour before the office force. I read every bill, every line in the *Congressional Record,* and every book I thought helpful. As for committee meetings, I don't think I've ever missed one, and that's where the important work of the Senate is really done. Thank heaven, I was fortunate enough to get on Agriculture and Commerce and also Forestry, for they were matters I knew something about and had a keen interest in. Just by looking at me you ought to be able to tell that I'm a farm woman, and as for flood control, Arkansas has more miles of streams than any other state in the Union."

Senator Caraway was placed also on the Library and Enrolled Bills committees, establishing a precedent by eventually becoming chairman of the latter, with Harry S. Truman [42] as the one other majority member. This is an undramatic but necessary committee which sees to it that every Senate-originated bill which has been passed is sent to the Government Printing Office in correct form, the proof checked for absolute accuracy, and an "enrolled" (official) parchment copy struck off, signed, and certified by the secretary of the Senate, the Vice-President, and the Speaker of the House of Representatives. After the President's signature is affixed, the enrolled bill is sent to the State Department, where it is kept for a year; then it is turned over to the National Archives.

During official sessions, Senator Caraway sat listening for hours, often bending over a crossword puzzle, while the men argued. "It's funny," she remarked at the close of debate on the Federal Land Bank Bill, "how they talk on after we've all made up our minds." "Conspicuously inconspicuous," without cosmetics and dressed in plain black, the Senator came to work by streetcar, often bringing her lunch; outside her office door there was often a row of milk bottles. Mrs. Caraway introduced a number of bills—forty-three on one memorable day, voted the regular Democratic line in an almost inaudible voice, and presided over the Senate for the first time in May 1932, in the absence of Vice-President Garner and the usual Senate president, pro tem. She was also the Senate's first woman committee chairman, first woman senior Senator, first woman to conduct a Senate committee hearing.

The Arkansan remained a stanch prohibitionist, anti-lobbyist, and defender of women's rights. (To the confusion of some, another Mrs. Caraway was president of the Women's National Republican Club during "Miss Hattie's" first full term.) Her one important defiance of the Administration, in January 1938, was in attacking the anti-lynching bill. Later that year Mrs. Caraway went back to Arkansas, without the help of her late friend Huey Long (whose widow Rose filled out his term from January 1936 to January 1937), and was re-elected for six more years, again the only woman Senator.

In her second elective term Mrs. Caraway continued to support the President in general, but joined other Southern Senators in November of 1942 to prevent closure of debate on the anti-poll tax bill. She voted with the farm bloc on several occasions: for overriding the veto of the inflationary Bankhead [43] farm price bill; for forbidding the Administration to use subsidies for food price rollbacks, while permitting them to encourage production of certain crops; for the Bankhead amendment to force a "readjustment" of the ceiling prices on cotton textiles. She voted also to repeal the Executive order limiting salaries to twenty-five thousand dollars after taxes; for a tax which fell more heavily on smaller incomes; for the Smith [43]-Connally [41] anti-strike bill, to override the veto; and for the Connally-Harness compromise anti-strike bill. Other Caraway votes in opposition to the Administration were for the McKellar bill to require confirmation of Federal appointments to most positions paying more than forty-five hundred dollars yearly, and for overriding the veto; she voted also to substitute the Rankin [44] "States-rights" voting qualifications bill for the Federal ballot bill.

In January 1943 Senator Caraway became co-sponsor of the Lucretia Mott Equal Rights Amendment to the Constitution, the first woman Congressman to endorse the measure, which had been presented to the Senate eleven times. (Margaret Chase Smith [45] of Maine and Winifred C. Stanley [43] of New York were the first women Representatives to sponsor it.)

The public interest aroused by "the lady Senator" often proved irksome. "Sometimes," Mrs. Caraway once chuckled, "I'm really afraid that tourists are going to poke me with their umbrellas! And yet there's no sound reason why women, if they have the time *and ability*, shouldn't sit with men on city councils, in state legislatures, or in the House and Senate. . . .Women are essentially practical because they've always had to be. From the dawn of time it's been our job to see that both ends meet. And women are much more realistic than men, particularly when it comes to public questions. Of course, having had the vote for such a short time is a distinct advantage, for we have no inheritance of political buncombe."

In 1944, after thirteen years in the Senate, Hattie Caraway did little campaigning for the renomination. But her four opponents did. One of them, former Governor Homer Adkins, had a powerful political organization behind him, and another was a colonel. A third, Representative J. W. Fulbright [43], was not only "young, well-educated, handsome, well-to-do, and friendly as an Arkansas hound pup"; he had also made a national reputation during his first term in Congress in connection with the short resolution which committed the Congress to international cooperation. In the Arkansas primary that summer Hattie Caraway was a poor fourth, and at the runoff primary Fulbright was chosen to succeed her. When the Seventy-eighth Congress held its last session, on December 19, 1944, Mrs. Caraway's voice was heard only at roll call; but, on the motion of Senator Carl A. Hatch [44] of New Mexico, the Senate rose in tribute to her, an act reporters described as "almost without precedent." Mrs. Caraway, who was then nearly sixty-seven, admitted later that when legislation "has been your whole life for thirteen years, you feel kind of lost" without it. She had, however, no intention of retiring, but hoped for a job, preferably in the Department of Agriculture or Commerce, where she could put her legislative experience to use. And in early 1945 President Roosevelt sent her nomination to the Senate as a member of the Federal Employees Compensation Commission, a nine-thousand-dollar-a-year position.

In spite of her years in the National Capital, ex-Senator Caraway remains the same conservative figure. To quote her admirer George Creel [44]: "Even without her own confession of domestic tastes, Mrs. Caraway would stand convicted on the strength of her looks: graying hair, parted in the middle and drawn back into a plain knot; a figure that scientific diet has never cabined, cribbed, nor confined; comfortable, roomy clothes, and a sense of complete capability, joined to an air of invincible placidity. While talking to her—as nice a way to pass an hour as could be imagined—one ex-

CARAWAY, HATTIE W.—*Continued*

pects her to start shelling peas at any moment, or else ask judgment on a batch of bread."

References

> Collier's 100:22+ S 18 '37 por
> Time 44:19 Ag 7 '44
> American Women, 1939
> National Cyclopædia of American Biography Current vol D p148
> Who's Who in America, 1944-45

CARLSON, JOHN F(ABIAN) May 4, 1875—Mar. 20, 1945 Noted Swedish-born American landscape painter who was one of the pioneer settlers of the Woodstock colony of artists in Connecticut; among the museums in which his paintings are to be seen are the Corcoran Gallery, Washington, D.C.; Carnegie Institute, Pittsburgh; and Baltimore Museum of Fine Arts; trees were the chief theme of his canvases.

Obituary

> N Y Times p23 Mr 21 '45

CASADESUS, ROBERT (MARCEL) (kä-sà-dà-zü' rô"bâr') Apr. 7, 1899- Pianist; composer

Address: b. c/o Arthur Judson, Inc., 113 W. 57th St., New York City; h. 32 Edgehill St., Princeton, N. J.

ROBERT CASADESUS

In France the name of Casadesus is renowned in the music world. In the United States it has become famous through Robert Casadesus, pianist and composer. He is "one of the most remarkable pianists of our day" and the "most self-effacing and honest of artists," says Jerome D. Bohm of the New York *Herald Tribune*; "one of the few virtuosos who have nothing in mind but the veracious conveyance of the composer's message."

Nephew of three famous musicians—Francis Casadesus, director of the American Con-

servatory at Fontainebleau (1918-22), Henri Gustave Casadesus, founder of the Société des Instruments Anciens of Paris, and Marcel Louis Casadesus, a cellist of international note —Robert Marcel Casadesus was born in Paris, April 7, 1899, the son of Varnay and Robert Casadesus. Since his mother had died at his birth and his father, an actor, was frequently on tour, he was brought up in his grandparents' home. His aunt, Rose Casadesus, the celebrated Parisian concert pianist, gave him his first piano lessons. Later, at the age of eleven, he began to study at the Paris National Conservatoire, winning the first medal in solfeggio the same year. In 1913 he was awarded the first prize in piano, and in 1919 the first prize in harmony. A year later he received the Prix Diémer and, with it, recognition as one of the foremost pianists of the day. At the conservatory he was the pupil of Louis Diémer, the famous pianist, and of Xavier Leroux, composer and former pupil of Massenet.

Casadesus says he began his career as a pianist in 1917, with a debut in Paris. Performances throughout Europe followed, and with each season he gave recitals in more distant lands, his tours taking him to Africa, Asia Minor, North America, and South America. In addition, he was professor of musical interpretation at the Conservatory of Genoa in 1929-30 and at the Conservatory of Lausanne in 1931-32. In 1935 he succeeded Isidor Philipp as head of the piano department of the American Conservatory at Fontainebleau, where he remained until the outbreak of the Second World War. Casadesus then brought his family to America. During the summers that followed he continued to teach—in 1940-41 at St. George's School, Newport, Rhode Island, and subsequently at the American counterpart of Fontainebleau at Great Barrington, Massachusetts, a school of music which Casadesus and his wife now conduct every summer.

On January 20, 1935, Casadesus made his American debut as a soloist with the New York Philharmonic Symphony, Hans Lange conducting. According to David Ewen, Toscanini '42 was in the audience and was so impressed by the performance that he urged Casadesus to appear as soloist with him the following season. Since that time the pianist has been soloist on numerous occasions with the Philharmonic and has appeared with the major orchestras all over the world.

Of a concert Casadesus gave after he came to the United States in 1940, a critic said: "Mr. Casadesus, one of France's foremost pianists, gave an admirable interpretation of the Mozart [*Coronation*] Concerto, possessing the clarity of style . . . essential for this music . . . as well as the combination of . . . delicacy and vitality." That same year, after a recital at Carnegie Hall, Howard Taubman of the New York *Times* observed that Casadesus is a mature musician who emphasizes what he thinks the music has to say rather than his own gifts as a virtuoso. "The Mozart Fantasie in D Minor was played with refinement of style that did not become artificial. . . . Perhaps the finest achievement of the evening was Schumann's *Kreisleriana* . . . the piano sang, and the tone glowed with the shifting hues that Schumann knew how to paint. Mr. Casadesus is a master of color, and this performance was the measure of his mastery." Olin Downes [43] has also written of the clarity, brilliancy, and taste of Casadesus' playing, and Louis Biancolli, in speaking of the pianist's flawless technique and tone, ranks him among the top five masters of the keyboard.

Although he is renowned for his interpretation of Mozart, Casadesus does not confine himself to a limited repertoire. In 1941 Irving Kolodin wrote in the New York Sun, "The recital by Robert Casadesus last night could be honored with the most telling of compliments . . . it was in a class by itself. . . . Mr. Casadesus started from the premise that this [the Sonata in B Minor] was the work of the manly genius of Chopin, rather than of the sick; and he had every resource of tone, technic, imagination, and scholarship to make that attitude the inescapable one for the work." Of his interpretation of Beethoven's Emperor Concerto, Virgil Thomson [40] observed, "Never an accent out of line; never a stress but for rhetorical reason. . . . His was an extraordinary performance . . . extraordinary for its beauty, its power, its physical perfection, its intellectual distinction." He again played this concerto with the New York Philharmonic Orchestra at a Red Cross benefit in April 1945, once more eliciting high praise from the critics—"beauty and poetry and vivid expression," "highly distinctive", "mellow and winning . . . and altogether competent in technical detail", "color gradations exquisitely modulated."

At a concert in Carnegie Hall in January 1945 marking the tenth anniversary of his first appearance in America, Casadesus brought high praise from the critics for his performance of the second book of Preludes by Debussy: "Here was pianism of the highest order. . . .It would be difficult to imagine a more exhaustive, magical mirroring of Debussy's fantastic creation." "He was never more fully a great master of the keyboard. . . . His absolute control of tone was above praise . . . marvels of technical skill . . . extraordinary insight and communicativeness." "He achieved so much beauty of texture, variety, delicacy, and subtlety of nuance as to make his performance thoroughly gratifying." Other concerts, too, have continued to receive equally high praise from critics. One of the great artists of our time," wrote a New York reviewer after a November 1945 concert. Another review at this time read: "Rarely does this pianist do anything but meritorious things. And rarely does he fail to bring the song measures of a number to the fore. Yet in his rendering of the concerto's solo part [Beethoven's Concerto in G Major], he 'threw' most of the lyrical passages away. . . . The only thing lacking . . . was the pulse of song to give the piece its complete life."

Casadesus' family share his deep love of music. His wife, the former Gaby L'Hôte, winner of a Prix Pagès of the Paris Conservatoire, is also a concert pianist. Both pupils of Professor Diémer, the couple met under musical circumstances: Casadesus, with a two-piano concerto he had just composed, arrived one day while Mlle. L'Hôte was receiving instruction. Professor Diémer suggested that the two students play the composi-

tion together. The friendship which developed later resulted in their marriage. Two of their three children are well along in their musical education. Jean, the oldest, who is studying the piano, has received a Paris award in recognition of his talent. Thérèse is still too young to choose her musical instrument, but Inez Foster of the Christian Science Monitor says that Guy plays both the violin and piano exceptionally well. Of all his performances, Casadesus anticipates most happily the recitals with his wife. Of one of these PM commented, "A thoroughly captivating evening of music was presented at Carnegie Hall by Robert and Gaby Casadesus who are both proficient and gifted artists. . . . The program was rendered with both energy and grace." Of the same concert the New York Times stated that they played the Mozart Sonata in D Major with a perfection of ensemble rarely heard in two-piano teams. "There were blendings and shadings of tone . . . that gave an individuality and personality to the duet almost never met with . . . except in solo playing."

Casadesus is the composer of many works, which include two violin sonatas, a sonata for piano and cello, three concertos for piano and orchestra, numerous preludes and etudes, two symphonies and two orchestral suites. His compositions are considered as having "positive merit." The etudes were called "worthwhile contributions to contemporary French piano music." Taubman considered five of them, premiered on Casadesus' fifth American tour, as "charming and brilliant . . . light, iridescent, and freshly felt; moreover, they do not take themselves too seriously." Casadesus wrote the Ballet for the Birth of a Dauphiness, an eight-part suite, in honor of the birth of his daughter Thérèse, who is called "La Dauphine." Employing a small orchestra in the eighteenth century manner, the Rochester (New York) Philharmonic Orchestra gave it its première in the 1943-44 season. It was called "witty and genial."

In 1937 Casadesus received a gold medal for a concerto for two pianos at the Paris Exposition. That same year he was made a member of the Order of Leopold of Belgium, in 1939 he was awarded the Légion d'Honneur star, and in 1944 an honorary D.Mus. degree from Lawrence College, Wisconsin. In August 1945 Casadesus was appointed honorary lecturer in the music department of Princeton University. His recordings include the C Minor Concerto of Mozart, the "Concertstück" by Weber and other works by Fauré, Scarlatti, and Mozart.

The five-foot-nine musician weighs one hundred and sixty-five pounds. His eyes are blue and his hair blond. Besides giving as many as sixty-five concerts in a year, he follows an intensive schedule of composing, teaching, and practicing, which may keep him at the piano more than eight hours a day. At such times an occasional brisk walk is his relaxation. With his family, he lives in The Barracks, Princeton's oldest Revolutionary house, where one of the neighbors and good friends is Albert Einstein [41]. When the physicist comes in for an evening he usually brings along his violin. Such gatherings as these, Mrs. Casadesus points out, show "how music

CASADESUS, ROBERT—*Continued*

binds not only the family but its friends close in a common interest and enjoyment."

References

C S Mon p10 F 11 '44 pors
N Y Times II p5 O 22 '44

Ewen, D. ed. Living Musicians (1940)
Thompson, O. ed. International Cyclo-pedia of Music and Musicians (1943)

CASSEL, KARL GUSTAV (kás′sěl) 1866
—Jan. 14, 1945 Swedish international economist and monetary expert; teacher, author, lecturer, and journalist; adviser to several European countries in financial crises precipitated by the First World War; delegate to numerous international conferences and recipient of many awards.

Obituary

N Y Times p19 Ja 16 '43 por

CHADWICK, SIR JAMES Oct. 20, 1891-
British physicist

Address: b. c/o University of Liverpool, Liverpool, England; h. Otterspool Bank, Aigburth Vale, Liverpool, England

The chief British scientist associated with the atomic bomb project was Nobel Prize winner Sir James Chadwick, who in 1932 discovered the projectile—the neutron—which made uranium fission possible. The eldest son of J. J. Chadwick, he was born in Manchester,

British Official Photo.

SIR JAMES CHADWICK

England, on October 20, 1891. He received his early education at a Manchester secondary school and in 1908 enrolled in the honors school of the Victoria University of Manchester.

It was in 1909, during his second year at Manchester, that the student first came under the influence of the famous English physicist Ernest Rutherford, when Lord Rutherford took over a course of lectures in electromagnetism. This proved a stimulating experience for him, he says, as did the research he entered upon in Rutherford's laboratory at the university the next year—"with great joy and, on occasions, alarm and terror." Rutherford was at this time continuing his studies, begun at McGill University in Montreal, Canada, of the properties of the alpha particle, and Chadwick's work for the next four years consisted of problems in this connection. Although the young physicist was awarded his M.Sc. degree in 1911, he elected to remain at the Rutherford laboratory and was thus present both when Rutherford announced his theory of the nuclear structure of the atom in 1911 and when Niels Bohr '45 perfected his quantum atomic model on the basis of Rutherford's and Max Planck's theories some months later.

Chadwick remained at the Rutherford laboratory until 1913. Then, on an 1851 Exhibition Science Scholarship, he went to the Physikalisch-technische Reichsanstalt at Charlottenburg, a surburb of Berlin, where he became associated in radioactivity experiments with Hans Geiger, whom he had met when the latter was Rutherford's assistant in Manchester. (These scholarships are administered by the Royal Commission for the Exhibition of 1851, which was "incorporated by supplemental charter as a permanent commission after winding up the affairs of the Great Exhibition of 1851. It has for its object the promotion of scientific and artistic education by means of funds derived from its Kensington Estate, purchased with the surplus left over from the Great Exhibition.") When the First World War broke out a year later Chadwick was interned in a civilian concentration camp in Ruhleben, Germany. The war years were not entirely lost for him, however, for he and several others managed to obtain permission to set up a makeshift physics laboratory in the camp, where they were able to carry out a bit of experimental work.

When Chadwick returned to Manchester in 1919 Rutherford had just demonstrated his history-making discovery that the nucleus of nitrogen could be disintegrated by alpha-particle bombardment. When a few months later Rutherford succeeded Sir Joseph J. Thomson as Cavendish Professor of Experimental Physics at Cambridge University, he invited his young assistant to accompany him to pursue further the artificial disintegration of elements by alpha particles. Chadwick, who had received the Wollaston Studentship at Gonville and Caius College, accepted, thus beginning a long and close association with his former mentor, whom he has called "the greatest experimental physicist since Faraday." In 1921 Chadwick received his Ph.D. from Cambridge University and was elected a Fellow of Gonville and Caius College. In the course of the next few years he was appointed university lecturer and assistant director of radioactive research in Cambridge's famed Cavendish Laboratory.

In the Cavendish Laboratory Chadwick worked with Rutherford on the artificial transmutation of elements by alpha-particle bombardment and on a series of experiments which probed the size and structure of the atomic nucleus. It was in the pursuit of the former line of attack that Rutherford and Chadwick first noticed the expulsion from the bombarded elements of what appeared to be hydrogen nuclei and thus discovered another of the fundamental constituents of the universe—named proton by Rutherford about 1922. In 1920 Chadwick's quantitative studies of alpha-particle scattering in the bombardment of selected elements provided experimental proof for Moseley's deduction that the electrical charge on the nucleus of the atom was the equivalent of the atomic number. "After the first rapid advances," Chadwick has however written of this period of his investigations, "progress became rather slow owing to difficulties inherent in the method of experiment. But Rutherford never lost his faith in the ultimate success of this work . . . [and about 1928] the development of electrical methods of counting particles enabled many striking advances to be made . . . and the subject of nuclear physics began to open up rapidly."

Chadwick's discovery of the neutron dates from the spring of 1932. For some months he had been following a line of investigation laid down by the German physicists Bothe and Becker of Giessen University and by Jean Frederic Joliot and his wife Irene Curie [40] (the daughter of Pierre and Marie Curie) at the French Institute of Radium. Bothe and Becker had found that the light metal beryllium, when bombarded with alpha particles, gave off an extremely penetrating radiation, which they had tentatively concluded to be akin to the therapeutic gamma rays emitted by radium. Varying the Bothe-Becker experiments somewhat, the Joliot-Curies had obtained even more astonishing results, which, assuming that the phenomenon obtained was a wave of radiation, could not be reconciled with known physical laws. With the aid of an old tube of radium emanation sent to him by the Howard Kelly Hospital of Baltimore—from which he extracted polonium which would give him alpha particles of known voltage—Chadwick repeated these experiments and devised others for purposes of comparison. His subsequent mathematical calculations convinced him that the results obtained could only be explained by the assumption of a particle of mass equal to the proton and having no electric charge—the neutron, the existence of which Rutherford had predicted several years before. Chadwick's discovery not only gave atomic physicists a powerful new weapon with which to explore the atom but also explained the mystery of the excessive weight of atomic nuclei in relation to the number of protons in their composition. In 1932 it brought him the Hughes Medal of the Royal Society and in 1935 the Nobel Prize in physics.

Chadwick left Cambridge University and the Cavendish Laboratory to accept the Lyons Jones Chair of Physics at the University of Liverpool in 1935—two years before he was to write of the death of Rutherford, "The world mourns the death of a great scientist, but we have lost our friend, our counselor, our staff and our leader." About November of 1941 he became associated with "Tube Alloys," the British atomic bomb project corresponding

to the American "Manhattan District," and two years later was appointed chief scientific adviser to the British members of the American-British-Canadian atomic bomb policy committee operating in the United States. Since the partial removal of censorship it has been revealed that many British scientists were reluctant to join with him in the project lest they be creating "a planet-destroying monster," and that others, including Chadwick himself, often hoped the bomb would not work.

Sir James, who was knighted in January 1945, has been characterized as a man of "unusual composure," habitually "austere" and reserved. He was married in 1925 to Aileen Stewart-Brown, the eldest daughter of H. Stewart-Brown of Liverpool; the Chadwicks now have twin daughters. Chadwick is a Fellow of the Royal Society, a Corresponding Member of the Sachsische Akademie der Wissenschaften of Leipzig, and a member of the Athenaeum Club in London. Together with Rutherford and C. D. Ellis he published *Radiations from Radioactive Substances* in 1930, and he is author of a number of papers on radioactivity and allied subjects, which have appeared in leading British scientific periodicals.

References

Nature 126:54-5 Jl 12 '30
International Who's Who, 1942
MacCullum, T. W. and Taylor, S. eds.
  The Nobel Prizewinners and the Nobel Foundation, 1901-1937 (1938)
Who's Who, 1945

CHARLOT, JEAN (shàr"lō' zhäɴ) Feb. 8, 1898- French artist; author

Address: h. Toledo 13, Apt. 301, Mexico City

When "master muralist" Jean Charlot went to Mexico in June 1945 he was entering upon the year's fellowship awarded to him in April 1944 by the John Simon Guggenheim Memorial Foundation. One of sixty-nine winners selected from applicants from the forty-eight states of the Union and three provinces of Canada, Charlot, whose fellowship was given in the Latin-American Studies group, will write a history of the beginnings of the modern Mexican school of mural painting, a movement in which he took an active part.

Born in Paris on February 8, 1898, Louis Henri Jean Charlot has a mixed heritage of Spanish, Russian, and French ancestry. His maternal grandfather, Louis Goupil, whose own father had settled in Mexico about 1820, was an officer in the retinue of the ill-fated Emperor Maximilian of Mexico. After his marriage in Mexico City to Sarah Meléndez, of Spanish-Jewish descent, Goupil took his bride to Paris. Their daughter, Anna Goupil, married Henri Charlot, a Frenchman from Russia. The parents of the future artist settled in Paris, but their young son, Jean, who began to draw at the age of three, grew up with the magic of Mexico implanted in his imagination by the art treasures from the New World in his family's possession. "I had," he said at a later date, "a stage country in my head: many feathers, blue, green, and tropical pantomime." Educated at the Lycée Condorcet, young Char-

JEAN CHARLOT

lot went on to the Ecole des Beaux-Arts, where the First World War interrupted his studies; in 1917 he was drafted into the French Army, becoming a lieutenant in the Artillery after he had gone to the officers training school at Fontainebleau. With the Army of Occupation at the close of the war, he remained in Germany until 1920. The paintings of the great German colorist of the sixteenth century, Matthias Grünewald, captivated the young artist, and became a definite influence in his later work. Released from the Army, Charlot, who earlier in his art career had made a number of wood carvings patterned on Breton polychromed folk sculpture, now turned to woodcut and engraving, exhibiting in the Salon d'Automne, in Paris.

In December 1920 the young artist left his native France and went to stay with an uncle in Mexico, where he was eagerly received because of his Beaux-Art training and his skill in the techniques of lithography and wood engraving. He helped to revive interest in "the lost art of wood carving," illustrated books and magazines, wrote critical essays for Parisian and Mexican *revues*, and worked in the openair atelier of Alfredo Ramos Martínez, "absorbing the country which had been so much a part of the tradition of his youth." Later he participated in the activities of the Syndicate of Technical Workers, Painters, and Sculptors, that short-lived artistic outgrowth of the Mexican revolution, which provided "an epochal opportunity" for an "extraordinary" group of talents—Charlot, Orozco '40, Rivera, Siqueiros, and others. Public works planned by the progressive Government of General Alvaro Obregón afforded wall space for murals. The Minister of Education, José Vasconcelos, directed the Government patronage of artists and in 1921 "a group of idealistic young men began to crystallize around the execution of the program . . . experimenting with the various techniques of encaustic and fresco painting." Freedom as to what and how they should paint was accorded to the artists, with one exception—the subject was to be Mexican. They were not

limited in time and were paid a regular daily wage. There ensued a "period of national reconstruction . . . aiming not at individual gain or glory but at the advancement of the group and nation . . . the first collective attempt at mural painting in modern art."

Jean Charlot painted the first fresco (since the colonial era), the *Fall of Tenochtitlán,* in 1922. Representing the sack of the ancient Mexican capital city by the Spanish conquistadors, this fresco occupies one side of the stairway in the Escuela Preparatoria Nacional in Mexico City. The success of the mural, which shows the influence of Uccello and of Leonardo da Vinci, has been attributed to Charlot's sophisticated and complex background. But critics have pointed out that the artist's use of a mixture containing cement, instead of the traditional pure lime, sand, and water, has resulted in a weak coloration because of the necessity of using very thin and watery paint, and that the chemical reaction of the cement has tended still further to reduce the color values. However, the composition is enormously effective, according to Laurence Schmeckebier, "fulfilling at once the requirements of its architectural setting . . . as well as that of a unified pictorial structure." The artist's next murals, painted for the Ministry of Education Building in 1923, are considered to be his best Mexican frescoes. Two panels—*The Washerwomen* and *The Pack Carriers* (a third, *The Dance of the Ribbons,* was destroyed to make room for Rivera's work)—decorate the second patio of the building. Dominated by opposing diagonals, these frescoes are based on a strictly mathematical framework. The influence of El Greco is seen in the decorative use of figures in a surface pattern, according to Schmeckebier, who notes the beautifully modeled forms and amazing brilliance of color, which ranges from shining white, yellow, red, blue, and green to rich purple and velvety black. It was this conception of "dynamic movement of figures crystallized into a decorative mural form" which, modified later by his studies of ancient Mayan art, finally became "the Charlot style."

When the Syndicate lost its patron, Vasconcelos, whose ministry terminated with the 1924 elections, Charlot's work for the Mexican Government came to an end. He continued in Mexico, however, painting and writing, and in 1925 became the art editor of *Mexican Folkways.* It was in this capacity that he attracted the attention of the head of the Carnegie Institution's archaeological expedition in Chichen-Itzá (Yucatán), Dr. Sylvanus G. Morley, who in 1926 engaged Charlot to copy to scale the bas-reliefs in the Temple of the Warriors. On his own account the artist copied frescoes in the Temple of the Tigers and the "Nunnery." This work . . . had considerable influence on Charlot's own stylistic development . . . not only in the use of a new Indian type—the continuous nose-and-forehead curve of the Mayan profile—but also in a decorative use of the twisted figure." He remained in Yucatán for three years, then went to Washington in 1929 to work on two monumental books dealing with the expedition. The first volume, *The Temple of the Warriors,* in which Charlot collaborated with Earl H. Morris and others, was brought out by the Carnegie Institution of Washington in 1931. This was followed by *Preliminary Study of the Ruins of Cobá, Quintana Roo, Mexico,* in which Charlot collaborated with John Eric Thompson and others, and was also published by the Carnegie Institution, in 1932.

Charlot now began a long series of teaching and lecturing engagements. The first of these was with the Art Students' League, where he lectured on fresco painting intermittently from 1931 to 1941. During this period he also lectured at the Chouinard School of Art, Los Angeles; the Florence Cane School of Art in New York City; the Walt Disney Studios, Hollywood; the University of California, Berkeley; the University of Iowa; Columbia University, New York; the University of Georgia, Athens; Black Mountain College, North Carolina; and Smith College, Northampton. Of these various connections, the most outstanding was the three years, 1941-44, spent as artist-in-residence at the University of Georgia, through a grant of the Carnegie Corporation. Charlot gave "informal art instruction" to the students, who also assisted in the preparation of the three murals the artist completed during his residence. The first of these, officially tagged WAlpb3661 and done in connection with the Government's Section of Fine Arts of the Public Buildings Administration, was the result of an "also-ran entry in a 1940 major mural contest." Done in oil on canvas, four and a half by eleven feet, for the Post Office at McDonough, Georgia, *Cotton Gin* portrays the cotton processing in the district. Charlot found the Negroes "blue . . . to an eye pitched to the terra cotta of Indian Mexico." He also felt inspired to record the date—October 9, 1941—when he "held live cotton in his hand." The next mural project, sponsored by the university, was a fresco, nine by forty-six feet, on the façade of the Fine Arts Building. It occupied three panels above the portico, the subjects being *Plastic Arts, The Theater,* and *Music.* Although several months were required for composition, preparation of the wall, and blocking-in of the design, the actual painting of the fresco took only eleven days—an average of thirty-six square feet per day. Lunch and dinner were served on the scaffolding to Charlot and his assistants, who had to work rapidly because of the quick-drying properties of the medium.

After the completion of the Fine Arts Building fresco, Charlot was invited by Dean John Drewry, of the School of Journalism, to decorate a wall in a corridor of a wing of the Commerce-Journalism Building. Sponsored jointly by the university and the Atlanta *Journal,* the general theme of the mural is the origin and history of reporting. The left panel of "the largest pencil sketch in the world," as the mural was called in its early stages, is entitled *Anno DMI 1519 Emperor Montezuma's Scouts Cover America's First Scoop* and depicts Cortés' landing in Mexico, while the Emperor's "fourthestaters" busily sketch the strange Spanish weapons and "hitherto unseen" horses. Charlot drew upon the findings of his previous researches for most of the Mexican detail but the steeds of the Spaniards were inspired by a farm horse named Pearl, sketched on the grounds of Black Mountain College in the fall of 1943. The right panel, *Anno DMI 1944 Press and Cameramen Flash on the Spot News, World War II,* shows a demolition squad going into action, with war correspondents jumping with the paratroopers, typing copy, and taking "candid" shots. For data Charlot visited a paratroop training school at Fort Benning, where he went to maneuvers every day for four days. In a smaller panel, placed over the entrance to the journalism reading room to connect the two murals on either side of the doorway, is the draped figure of a woman symbolizing Time. The results of Charlot's experiences in Georgia were set forth in a book, *The Charlot Murals in Georgia,* published by the university in the spring of 1945. In addition to the detailed account of daily activities, Charlot gives formulas, palettes, historical and technical discussion of fresco, the approach of the muralist as distinguished from that of the easel painter. The book is illustrated with photographs showing the murals in every stage of progress.

Although known chiefly as a muralist, Jean Charlot has had great success as an easel painter. His work was introduced to the North American public in 1923, when he exhibited with the Independent group in New York City. In 1925 he exhibited in the Mexican Section of the Pan American Exhibition at Los Angeles, and in 1928 the Mexican Government sent his paintings, together with work of other Mexican artists, to the group show held at the Art Center in New York. More than fifty one-man shows followed. *Parnassus* called an exhibition at the John Levy Galleries in 1931 "one of the most exciting shows of the season" and described certain paintings—*Bathers, Idol, Nude Reclining,* and *Luciana*—as "literally dazzling." An original and individual painter, Charlot was said to "combine the vitality of the baroque with the simplicity of the primitives." Carlyle Burrows noted the brusqueness and direct quality of his Mexican figure subjects in a later exhibition (1936) and the "curious grotesqueness" of his informal studies of women and children. A series of religious paintings, *The Mysteries of the Rosary,* in this exhibition had highly emotional color, but, according to James Lane, lack of religious sensitivity. In 1938 an exhibition of water colors at the Passedoit Gallery attracted attention for their monumental quality and resonant color. "His figures," wrote Martha Davidson in *Art News,* "seem chiseled out of rock of heroic scale, and they have the solidity, the magnitude, and the expressive force of their Mayan-Aztec ancestors." Outstanding papers included *Tortillera, Preparing for the Dance,* and *Philosopher.* Among canvases shown at the Bonestell Gallery in 1940 the critic of *Art News* singled out *First Steps* and *Market Place* for their experimentation in geometric form, and the "coloristic triumph" of *Interior* and *Nativity.* Father M. A. Couturier, of *Liturgical Arts* Magazine, pointed out, in an introduction to the catalogue, the impacted volumes, saturated colors, and mingling of violence and buffoonery in the religious paintings in the show, as well as the tender and childlike quality of the heroic *bambinos.* Charlot's last group of paintings at the Bonestell in April 1945 were mainly of folk festivals and biblical subjects. Maude Riley, in *Art Digest,* noted a "mural quality of flatness and carrying power" in two large canvases, *Dance of the Malinches* and *Mexican Kitchen.* The critic of the New York *World-Telegram*

CHARLOT, JEAN—*Continued*

considered a series of small paintings relating incidents on "The Flight Into Egypt" to be austerely and sophisticatedly put together, with rhythms established by repeated patterns and stirring harmonies produced by unrealistic colors. The informal subjects—*Rest on the Flight Into Egypt With Angels Washing, Rest on the Flight Into Egypt With Angels Cooking, Rest on the Flight Into Egypt With Joseph Unsaddling,* et cetera—give an idea of the "ingratiating" quality of this series. In October 1945 the Children's Room of the New York Public Library arranged a Charlot exhibition, stressing the artist's work in the juvenile field. In addition to paintings, colored lithographs and a number of books illustrated by Charlot were displayed.

Throughout his career the artist has been an enthusiastic print-maker. A portfolio of his black-and-white woodcuts, *Way of the Cross,* was brought out in France in 1920. Later, in collaboration with Albert Carman, he patented a color lithographic process. A collection of thirty-two of his chromolithographs, with inscriptions by Paul Claudel, was brought out in a second portfolio, *Picture Book,* published in 1933. Edward Alden Jewell found the forms bizarre and the message sometimes cryptic, but praised the "arresting and admirably orchestrated" color. He noted also that many of the social vignettes were "instinct with an understanding, a sense of human dignity and humor and pity that lift them into a realm of enduring significance." A third portfolio, of black-and-white process prints, also entitled *Way of the Cross,* appeared in 1938.

Charlot has been a fluent writer of critical and historical articles on art, contributing to many American and European periodicals. In addition to his books on the Mayan excavations and the Georgia murals, he is the author of *Art From the Mayans to Disney* (1939), a collection of essays, and *Catalogue of Prints* (1937). He has also illustrated twenty published books, among them *The Book of Christopher Columbus,* a lyrical drama by Paul Claudel, published in 1930; *The Sun, the Moon and a Rabbit,* by Amelia Martínez del Río (included in "Fifty Best Books of 1935"); *Characters of the Reformation* (1936), by Hilaire Belloc, with twenty-three portraits; *Tito's Hats* (1940), by Melchor G. Ferrer; Shakespeare's *Henry VI* and Prosper Mérimée's *Carmen,* published by Limited Editions in 1940; *The Story of Chan-Yuc* (1941), by Dorothy Rhoads; and *A Child's Good Night Book* (1943), by Margaret Wise.

Honors to Jean Charlot, besides the Carnegie Corporation grant in 1941 and the Guggenheim fellowship in 1944, comprise inclusion in "Among the Fifty Best Prints of 1929-1930" and "The Fifty Best Books of 1935." He is represented in the Uffizi Gallery, Florence; the British Museum, London; the Metropolitan Museum of Art, and the Museum of Modern Art, New York; the Phillips Memorial Gallery, Washington; the Walker Galleries, Minnesota; museums in Chicago, Philadelphia, and Rochester; and private collections.

On May 26, 1939, Charlot was married to Dorothy Zomah Day, of Brigham City, Utah. They have three children, Ann Maria, John Pierre, and Martin Peter Day. The slight, hazel-eyed artist, whose dark hair is now graying, prefers fresco painting to all other activities, and admits that the illustration of juvenile books is rewarding only when his own children approve the results. Although French by birth and training, and now an American citizen, Charlot is always associated with the modern Mexican movement in art.

References

Art News 44:25 My 1 '45
N Y Times VIII 13:2 F 9 '30

American Catholic Who's Who, 1942-43
Brenner, A. Idols Behind Altars (1929)
Charlot, J. Charlot Murals in Georgia (1945)
Mérida, C. Modern Mexican Artists (1937)
Schmeckebier, L. A. Modern Mexican Art (1939)

CHARNWOOD, GODFREY RATHBONE BENSON, 1ST BARON Nov. 6, 1864—Feb. 3, 1945 Former Liberal Member of British Parliament; claimed he entered politics solely because of his interest in Irish home rule; biographer of two American Presidents, *Abraham Lincoln* (1917) and *Theodore Roosevelt* (1923).

Obituary

N Y Times p19 F 6 '45

CHASE, MARY (COYLE) Feb. 25, 1907-Playwright; author

Address: h. 1364 St. Paul St., Denver, Colo.

Mary Chase, the author of the 1944-45 Pulitzer Prize comedy, *Harvey,* is a playwright with Celtic pookas and banshees in her pen. To provide the middle-aged protagonist of her play with a needed escape from reality, she invented Harvey, the perfect companion, an invisible white rabbit, six feet one and a half inches tall. One of the admirers of Mrs. Chase and Harvey has observed that the two have many attributes in common: "Both are genial, gentle, tolerant, and wise—and each share an Irish background."

Mary Chase, née Coyle, was actually born far from Ireland—in West Denver, Colorado, on February 25, 1907. However, her mother, Mary (McDonough) Coyle, had come from Ulster County at the age of sixteen to keep house for her four brothers, Peter, Timothy, James, and John, who in the eighties were trying their luck in the Colorado gold fields. Her father, Frank Coyle, had drifted to Denver after an unsuccessful attempt to reap a fortune in the Oklahoma land rush. After his marriage to Mary McDonough he became a salesman for a Denver flour mill. Although all of young Mary's four uncles were "men of talk and long memory," it was Timothy, who had attended Trinity College in Dublin, who captured her imagination with his tales of Irish folklore.

"I got the highest grades for studies and the lowest for deportment," the playwright has said of her years in Denver's elementary schools. She had the reputation of being a tomboy, and a book-lover, too. At the age of eight she read *A Tale of Two Cities,* at ten chose Thomas De Quincey for her favorite author (principally because his name attracted her), and at fifteen began Xenophon's *Anabasis* in the Greek. That year, 1922, she was graduated from the West Denver High School and entered the University of Denver, where she remained two and a half years before she went to Boulder to attend the University of Colorado. During summer vacations she served her apprenticeship as a reporter on the *Rocky Mountain News*, without salary.

At the end of a year at Colorado the future prize-winning playwright, who had completed a major in the classics in two years, gave up her formal schooling to accept a reporter's job on the *News*, this time with salary. John P. Lewis, then city editor of the Denver paper, has said of her work there: "Mary, like all girls on smaller papers around the country, did society and club notes and things like that, and finally was taken over on the city staff to be a sob sister. . . .In the sob sister's life, by the rules of this tradition, were the more infantile and more unpleasant chores in journalism . . . never being sane and normal but always writing highly artificial tragedy or forced humor. . . .Mary didn't take things very seriously on the surface, and we used to wonder if she would ever grow up. More recently some of us who knew her then have begun to suspect that maybe she grew up sooner than the rest of us." "She had the bland, amoral effrontery of a good aggressive cityside reporter," writes Wallis M. Reef, and a "flip, sharp tongue which contrasted nicely with her Madonna appearance." While she was with the paper the young reporter was fired three times, but co-workers say that this was nothing unusual; everyone on the *News* staff was fired at least twice.

Before her third departure from the paper Mary Coyle had been married, on June 7, 1928, to Robert L. Chase, "a tall serious-minded reporter" on the *News*, who is now managing editor. After she stopped working she found herself busy doing all the things she had always wanted to do, and she refused offers to return to the paper. Reef, radio news editor in Denver and a friend of the Chases, declares that in addition to her special interest, writing plays, she managed to "stay involved in about a half-dozen occupations, each of which would have been full time for anyone else. She aided in forming a chapter of the American Newspaper Guild, she handled publicity for NYA [a Government project of the depression period] and, with Mrs. Edward P. Costigan, widow of the late Senator from Colorado, fought for the rights of the Spanish-Americans in Denver, who had been getting kicked around. All this was done with a gaiety that astounded some of her dead-serious associates. She was likely to show up in a picket line wearing a fifty-dollar hat, fantastic earrings, and a dress best described as slinky. The effect on employers was amazing. At one time," continues her biographer, "she was running a quiet and effective lobby for an oleomargarine concern and writing a weekly radio program for the Teamsters' Union. The group of people whose activities seem to revolve about Mrs. Chase would, on a chart, be a sort of vertical section of Denver's social and economic life."

Mrs. Chase's interest in the theater had begun at the age of eleven. At that period, in order to attend a matinee at a Denver theater she would play truant from school and walk the five miles from her home to save the

MARY CHASE

carfare. Although her first writing took the form of the short story, her goal was always playwriting. When the New Deal added the Federal Theater to the WPA projects, Mary Coyle Chase, an ardent admirer of the late Franklin Roosevelt [42], saw her first play produced. The play, *Me Third*, was a comedy concerned with a Western politician whose campaign slogan was "God First, the People Second, Me Third." The WPA production attracted the attention of Broadway producer Brock Pemberton [45], and, in 1937 he brought it to New York under the title *Now I've Done It*. Although the play failed to win the support of either press or public, Pemberton encouraged Mrs. Chase to continue with her writing.

Among the plays that Mrs. Chase wrote after the political satire was *The Banshee*, a tragedy based on the legend of the Irish spirit who warns families of an approaching death. The manuscript was well thought of by critic friends, but Pemberton, who saw it after the beginning of the war, advised that production of the play be postponed until after the war. It was shortly after this that the playwright, seeking an escapist plot, conceived the idea of *Harvey* (originally *The White Rabbit*), which kept New York audiences smiling long after its première in November 1944.

Briefly, the theme of the play is: It is better to be zany and amiable than to be sane and disliked. Elwood P. Dowd, the central character (played by Frank Fay [45]), although "mildly potted all the time," is an inebriate of good morals, good taste, and good manners, as is also his pooka friend and drinking companion, Harvey, the white rabbit. The respect with which Mrs. Chase handled the psychotic Mr. Dowd may have been prompted by advice given to her by her mother: "Never be unkind or indifferent to a person others say is crazy. Often they have a deep wisdom. We pay them a great respect in the old country, and we call them fairy people, and it could be they are sometimes." It took Mrs. Chase two years to

CHASE, MARY—*Continued*

write the play, working after her three children, Michael, Colin, and Jerry, had gone to bed and her husband, whose hours are from 5:00 P. M. to 1:00 A. M., had gone to the office. (She works with a four-foot miniature stage.) "I rewrote it fifty times," says the author. "My pooka [spirit in animal form] was represented at first by a canary; when I changed it to a rabbit of man's size, although the change had its advantages, the situations required more delicate handling." Pemberton reports that Mrs. Chase never lacked faith in the play, and that she proved throughout its preparations for Broadway to be "an adroit playwright who knew her material upside down and inside out." The awarding of the Pulitzer Prize for *Harvey*, however, came as a surprise to Mrs. Chase. Her husband received the news over the wires at his office and hurried to a movie theater where he knew she was. When he told her, reports *Variety*, she screamed so loudly that she nearly started a panic in the theater.

Among the New York critics, on the other hand, the announcement of the award met with a divided reaction. A few felt that while *Harvey* was an extremely pleasant play, it was not an example of distinguished writing. The others who disapproved saw the comedy as condoning lunacy and drinking, or as a poor attempt to mix fantasy and farce. For the most part, however, the reviewers were enthusiastic over the story, even though many pointed out an unevenness in quality: "Its fresh and imaginative side," commented Louis Kronenberger [44], "is marred by much very routine farce-writing." "The wacky tale," wrote Howard Barnes of the New York *Herald Tribune*, "is certainly my choice for the most endearing and engaging play of the season." "It [Elwood Dowd's Harvey-inspired philosophy] is a boozy acceptance of reality, without complaint, without bitterness, without envy, hatred or ill will," said Burton Rascoe of the New York *World-Telegram*, while Lewis Nichols of the New York *Times* called it "one of the treats of the fall [1944] theater."

In 1941, for the entertainment of mountaineer infantrymen in training at Denver's near-by Camp Hale, Mrs. Chase had written a travesty on the old melodramas, with the addition of song and dance bits. This play, *A Slip of a Girl*, was enjoyed by the soldiers, says its author, "but for some unexplainable reason the USO failed to take it over." One of her short stories, "He's Our Baby," appeared in the April 1945 issue of the *Ladies' Home Journal*. In this story, described as subtly ironic and witty, Mrs. Chase introduced a new technique which enabled her to establish character and motivation with great economy. At the end of 1945 she was working on a book for children, based on *Harvey*.

In October 1945 Mrs. Chase's tragedy, *The Banshee*, was brought to New York, with Fay Bainter as the star. Although the play, re-entitled *The Next Half Hour*, had grossed nearly twenty-seven thousand dollars in a week's tryout in Washington, it met with adverse critical comment on Broadway, and producer Max Gordon [43] ended the run after eight performances. An expedition into Irish folklore, *The Next Half Hour* presented a tale of a superstitious mother who "hears the wail of the banshees, foresees impending disaster, and tries to circumvent it." While most of the critics found the play tedious and fruitless, Burton Rascoe wrote that it had "warmth, truth, and tension."

Mrs. Chase is described as "a beautiful woman with wide gray eyes, rich brown hair, and a white, imperious face." Her friends say that although most of the anecdotes told about her are amusing ones, she seldom smiles and there is a hint of melancholy in her eyes. One of the most frequently repeated stories is the one concerning the time the Chases decided they could at last afford to have the house redecorated and invited their three sons and a few friends to draw pictures in crayon on the old wallpaper. These murals were on exhibition longer than planned, however, for more pressing bills delayed the repapering for several months. Mrs. Chase, whose income from *Harvey* was to provide her with more than fifteen hundred dollars a week, says that around her house "money has never been anything you made; it has been merely something you owed."

References

PM p19 N 2 '44; p16 N 6 '44 por
Sat Eve Post 218:17+ S 1 '45 por

CHENEY, RUSSELL Oct. 16, 1881—July 12, 1945 American landscape and still-life painter; many of his paintings, which include *Skungimasug Morning, Ute Pass, Colleone*, and *Kittery Point*, portrayed scenes in vicinity of his home in Kittery, Maine; represented in such museums as Museum of Fine Arts in Boston and San Francisco Museum of Art.

Obituary

N.Y Times p11 Jl 13 '45

CHERNYAKHOVSKY, IVAN D(ANILOVICH) (chär"nyä-kŏf'skĭ) 1908 (?)—Feb. 18, 1945 Red Army tank commander whose Third White Russian Army was the first to invade Germany in Second World War; was the youngest general in Red Army, the youngest Army group commander, and one of Russia's outstanding strategists; died from wounds received on battlefield of East Prussia. See *Current Biography* 1944 Yearbook.

Obituary

N Y Times p8 F 19 '45 por

CHIFLEY, JOSEPH B(ENEDICT) Sept. 22, 1885- Prime Minister of Australia

Address: b. Parliament House, Canberra; h. Bathurst, Australia

After the death of Australian Prime Minister John Curtin [41] on July 4, 1945, the Australian Labor Party caucus, in what has been called by some observers an unexpected move, elected Joseph B. Chifley Prime Minister to succeed Curtin. Chifley, who entered politics from the ranks of the working class and was Prime Minister Curtin's closest friend in the Government, is a "solid Laborite," pledged to the socialist policies of the Curtin Ministry. Had Curtin been able to choose his successor, observers say he would have nominated "Ben" Chifley.

Joseph Benedict Chifley was born in Bathurst in the hilly western part of New South Wales, on September 22, 1885. His mother and his paternal grandparents were Irish, while his father, a blacksmith, was Australian. At an early age he left school and took a job with the New South Wales Railway, rising in time to the position of locomotive driver on the Sydney-Melbourne express. As a member of the Federated Union of Locomotive Engineers during these years, he developed an active interest in the Labor movement. But before entering Federal politics in 1928, he gave a large part of his time to the study of economics, finance, and industrial law, and he was an advocate for his union in the state and Federal industrial arbitration courts of Australia.

In 1928 Chifley was elected a Labor member of the House of Representatives for the Macquarie, New South Wales, constituency (of which his birthplace, Bathurst, is the center). This was the same election by which Curtin entered Parliament, and it is said that the friendship of the two newcomers began in the House, where they sat together on a back bench. In 1929 Chifley received his first Cabinet post, as Minister for Defense in James H. Scullin's Labor Government. During 1929-30 he was also a member of the Federal Accounts Committee. Then in 1931, together with Curtin and other Laborites, Chifley lost his seat in the general elections that were forced by defections from the Labor Ministry over its financial policy. After this defeat Chifley returned to Bathurst to become a shareholder of the Bathurst *Advocate,* a conservative labor newspaper and to contest, unsuccessfully, for several elective offices.

Although he failed to gain re-election to Parliament for some years, Chifley was not allowed to sever all connections wtih the Government, for non-Labor ministries requested his services. In 1935 Chifley was appointed by Prime Minister Joseph A. Lyons to the Royal Commission on Monetary Banking Systems. It was his investigation as a member of this body that gave him the practical experience on which he was to draw for his banking program while wartime Treasurer of the Commonwealth. In November 1939 Chifley was made a member of the Capital Issues Advisory Board. In 1940 Essington Lewis, then Director General of Munitions in the Cabinet of Prime Minister Robert Gordon Menzies '41 (United Australia Party), sought Chifley's advice on wartime labor problems, later having him appointed to the Ministry of Munitions as Director of Labor Supply and Regulation for New South Wales.

Resigning the last-named post near the end of 1940, Chifley again contested his former seat in the general elections. Branded "Communist" by opponents on the Right, and "Conservative" by the extreme Leftists, he nevertheless was victorious in the balloting, which brought many of his Labor colleagues back to Parliament for the first time since 1931. Although the Labor Party was not yet in power, Chifley's financial knowledge was once more utilized by the Government when it made him a member of the Board of Enquiry into Cash Order and Hire Purchase Agreement Systems of Trading in Australia in February 1941.

JOSEPH B. CHIFLEY

In the course of the next several months the Labor Party repeatedly refused to participate in the formation of a coalition Cabinet, and subsequently, on an amendment to the budget, supported by two independent members, succeeded in bringing about the resignation of the Government. Thus the Labor Party came into power, and with the formation of Curtin's first Labor Ministry in October 1941 Chifley was given the portfolio of Commonwealth Treasurer, for which his fiscal experience made him the obvious choice.

As Treasurer, Chifley designed and guided through Parliament what has been called "perhaps the most comprehensive system of wartime financial controls of any Allied government." His experiences in depression days had convinced him of the necessity for strict governmental regulation of all fiscal policies if economic security for the people as a whole was to be achieved. Hence, as wartime Treasurer, besides increasing taxes and adopting a stringent budget to meet the expenditures of a war economy, Chifley strengthened governmental control over banking and stock transactions and drastically extended price-control measures. In particular, he sponsored two bills which give the Commonwealth Bank, operated by the Government, supervisory powers over the entire banking system and authority to direct financial policies into Government-approved channels.

In 1942 Chifley received from Prime Minister Curtin the additional portfolio of Minister for Postwar Reconstruction, which he held simultaneously with the Treasury portfolio until a Cabinet reconstitution early in 1945 gave the post to John Dedman. As announced at the time of the appointment, Chifley's first task was to be the promulgation of a master plan for postwar reconstruction patterned after the Atlantic Charter. Influenced by his own reaction to the depression of 1929 and the succeeding years, he directed his platform toward the betterment of conditions for the "little man," advocating jobs for all who want work,

CHIFLEY, JOSEPH B.—*Continued*

social security measures, slum clearance, and other methods to raise the standard of living, all this to be financed by taxation based on ability to pay. But being a realist, Chifley said: "The Government will plan boldly but it has no starry-eyed dreams of a new world." Then he went to work and by mid-1943 had laid down a program calling for the rehabilitation of agriculture, the decentralization of industry, slum clearance and housing development, water conservation and expansion of electrification projects, improvement of hospital and medical services, and retraining of soldiers and war workers for peacetime employment. In the Labor Party, it has been observed, he leads a group which considered planning for social reform a wartime as well as a peacetime duty.

In the spring of 1945, with Prime Minister John Curtin ill and Deputy Prime Minister Francis Michael Forde out of the country representing Australia at the United Nations conference in San Francisco, Chifley became Acting Prime Minister. Reports agree that it was his capable leadership during these weeks before Curtin's death in July, as well as the Labor Party's hope that his conservative socialistic viewpoint would draw the independent votes to the party's standard in the coming 1946 general elections, which prompted the party caucus to pass over Forde and elect Chifley by a 3-to-1 vote. (In the Australian Labor Party a caucus is formed by representatives of the party from both the House of Representatives and the Senate, and its decisions are binding upon all Labor politicians.) To some persons the result of the election came as a surprise, as is evidenced by a pre-election report from a New York *Times* correspondent in Melbourne. "Expert observers," he wrote, "believe that against Mr. Forde, nobody will really be in the race."

The new Prime Minister, who had only reluctantly agreed to offer himself for party leadership at former Prime Minister Scullin's urging, retained the Treasury portfolio. He pledged himself to continue Curtin's socialist policies, many of which he had helped to frame, and to carry out his program for improving the Australian standard of living, for which he is said to have "concrete plans." In the sphere of international affairs, he believes in unity within the British Commonwealth and in Australo-American cooperation. "America," he says, "is the dominating Pacific power bound to keeping the peace in this vast area. Australia is a Pacific power. The people of the two countries will and must work side by side."

Chifley has a reputation for calm judgment and practical realism. As Commonwealth Treasurer, with the task of handling war finances and promoting a strict over-all economy, he won the respect of bankers, Treasury officials, and the Australian people. Parliamentarians say of him: "Give Ben time to light his pipe and take a few puffs and he'll solve any problem you put to him." In fact, problems during the last five years were solved as he and Curtin strolled, smoking the while, down Canberra's tree-lined streets. The man who now guides Australia toward socialism, in the belief that capitalists are merely "ordinary blokes" who will eventually accept socialism and even like it, has been described as a hard and conscientious worker, unflinching in his adherence to his convictions. Although "not an outstanding orator in the sense of brilliant rhetoric," he has a deep, somewhat rasping drawl which, with his deliberate manner and direct approach to the subject, holds his audiences. Tall and gaunt, with his pipe clenched between his teeth, he is a cartoonist's delight. His years on the railroad have left their mark in his complexion, in his eyes which show the effect of hours of gazing at glistening rails. He married in 1914 and owns a small home in Bathurst.

References

N Y Herald Tribune II p3 Jl 22 '45 por
N Y Times p1+ Jl 13 '45 por (p3)
Newsweek 26:54 Jl 23 '45 por

CHRISTIANS, MADY (mä-dē) Jan. 19, 1900- Actress

Address: b. c/o Michel Mok, 1545 Broadway, New York City

Since the early thirties the Viennese-American actress Mady Christian has enjoyed a well-established prominence in Europe and America, both on the stage and in motion pictures. In addition, she has appeared on radio programs and has lectured widely on the theater.

Marguerita Maria Christians was born January 19, 1900, in Vienna. Her father, Rudolph Christians, was well known in Europe as an actor and manager; her mother, Bertha (Klein) Christians, was an opera and concert singer. The family came to the United States in 1912, to New York, where the father managed a German repertoire company at the old Irving Place Theatre. Young Madi was educated privately. (Little Viennese girls are affectionately known as "Madi," and their brothers are "Bubi," like the American "Sis" and "Bud." The Christians continued to call their Marguerita "Madi," which was changed to "Mady" during subsequent tours of the Continent with theatrical companies.)

When she was sixteen Madi persuaded her father to allow her to play the heroine of one of his productions. Under the name of Eva Seetzen, she appeared in a one-act operetta, *Brüderlein fein*. After her first performance Christians said to his daughter, "Madi, I think you'd better get married." On the other hand, a reviewer who saw her in this difficult role (she played both an old woman and a seventeen-year-old bride) predicted that the young girl had a rosy future. "She is tall and slender, unusually pretty, vivacious in manner, sings charmingly in a sweet, well-trained soprano, and speaks English without an accent," he added.

In spite of her father's opposition, Madi was determined to become an actress. Her mother was sympathetic with this desire and did not allow her to become discouraged. In 1917, having given up her own career to devote her energies to her husband and daughter, Mrs. Christians took Madi to Europe, where she was enrolled in Max Reinhardt's school of acting. According to Elizabeth Valentine of the New York *Times*, "it was four years before anyone except Max Reinhardt and her mother thought there was any use bothering with her. . . .Mrs. Christians persisted; if her daughter wanted to be an actress so badly, then she would become one. Without her intelligent support, Madi would probably have quit."

Miss Christians made her professional debut under Reinhardt's aegis in Molière's *l'Avare,* at the Deutsches Theater in Berlin. Her performance was a failure, but Reinhardt encouraged her to continue as his student. After three years of discouragement, she suddenly blossomed into a full-fledged actress when she played opposite the great Italian actor Alexander Moissi in Tolstoi's *The Light Shines in the Darkness.* When Reinhardt refused to extend her contract in keeping with her new status, Miss Christians left his company and joined Ferdinand Bruckner's cabaret Schall und Rauch (Sound and Smoke). Within two weeks she was the star of the show, whereupon Reinhardt offered her a new contract on her own terms. The actress accepted, and remained under Reinhardt's management for five years, appearing all over Europe in as many as forty-five plays a year.

Appearing in both classical and modern works, Miss Christians soon became popular with Continental audiences. She acted in plays by Shakespeare, Lessing, Goethe, Molière, Lonsdale, Pirandello, and others. Gifted with a good soprano voice, the actress also played musical comedy roles. In Europe, too, she was the lead in almost sixty films, including *Glass of Water, Waltz Dream, Queen Louise, Burning Heart,* and *The Empress and I,* with Maurice Evans '[40]. She made German, French, and English versions of *Dich hab ich geliebt,* and in 1933 she was the star of the film *Friedericke,* which had a musical score by Franz Lehár. Lehár had known Miss Christians for many years, and had called her "my little fiancée" since she was four. *Who's Who in the Theatre* reveals that in 1931 the Viennese actress was touring the United States in *Marching By,* which she left before it reached Broadway.

The year 1933 found Miss Christians performing in Berlin as the Nazi tide began to rise. She says now that she became acquainted with the machinations of the Gestapo when the secret police dispersed a meeting of actors who planned to protest the Nazi domination of the theater. Later in the year she came to the United States. The newspapermen who interviewed her upon her arrival reported that this "luxuriantly blond Brünnhilde" told them she was "married fine" to Dr. Sven von Mueller, editor of a Hamburg newspaper. They have since been divorced, and Miss Christians has returned to Germany only once, to attend her mother's funeral in 1938. In 1939 she became an American citizen. "I am, first of all, an American actress," Miss Christian declared, "and I insist upon being listed and considered as one. Of European background, yes, but primarily and basically an American actress."

Back in the United States, the actress began a long unbroken streak of bad luck. She gave "a rich and sincere" performance in *The Divine Drudge,* adapted from a novel by her close friend Vicki Baum, but the play was a dismal failure. Reviewing Miss Christians' Broadway debut in this play, Brooks Atkin-

Lucas-Pritchard

MADY CHRISTIANS

son '[42] remarked, "It would be worth sitting through fifty bad plays to see her perform." As though to test him, there followed two more "quick flops," Rachel Crothers' *Talent,* and the Theatre Guild's *Races* (1934). In 1934 Miss Christians did radio work and appeared as the bedraggled mother of seven children in the motion picture *The Wicked Woman* (MGM), a story of misery in a Texas swamp "which since has caused Miss Christians to view all swamps and much of Texas with a feeling akin to a sharp attack of malaise."

Nevertheless, after 1934 she divided her time between the film capital and Broadway. In February 1936 she played the title role in *Alice Takat* (Ed Wynn's '[45] production "folly"), which ran for eight performances. That year also she played with Edward Arnold in the film *Come and Get It* for United Artists. In 1937 she appeared in *Seventh Heaven* (Twentieth Century-Fox)—as a street cleaner's wife—Paul Muni's '[44] *The Woman I Love* (RKO), and *Heidi* (Twentieth Century-Fox), in which she slapped Shirley Temple's '[45] face.

She returned to Broadway early in 1938 in George S. Kaufman's '[41] comedy *Save Me the Waltz,* another eight-performance failure. Later, in the spring, she had the important part of Hesione Hushabye in Orson Welles's '[41] production of Bernard Shaw's '[44] *Heartbreak House.* The actress found Welles a dynamic director with an intellectual approach to the play.

Then in October 1938 Mady Christians opened in one more queen's role, Gertrude in Margaret Webster's '[40] production of *Hamlet.* With Maurice Evans in the title role, this uncut version of the Shakespearean drama was very popular with Broadway audiences. The critics were unanimous in their praise of Miss Christians' performance, their reviews abounding in superlatives. John Mason Brown '[42] declared that Miss Christians gave to the part "a brand

CHRISTIANS, MADY—*Continued*

new tragedy which the text has always demanded in vain. She is warm . . . attractive, interested, and queenly . . . capable of tragedy in the closet scene and coquetry throughout." In complete agreement, Brooks Atkinson stated: "Mady Christians' frightened, tortured, grieving queen is the best one this theater-goer has ever seen."

Miss Christians' next play was also a Webster-Evans production: in early 1939 she opened in *Henry IV*, as Lady Percy—called "one of the most vivid characters that Shakespeare ever created in so small a compass." Her scenes with Wesley Addy as Hotspur were described as "an exquisite mixture of tenderness and humor . . . a charming interlude of domesticity almost in the Noel Coward [41] manner."

In 1939 also, the star played Hedda Gabler (one of her European roles) for Talking Book recordings of the Ibsen play, distributed by the Library of Congress for use by the blind. This was the first time that such recordings were done by theatrical stars instead of "straight readers." In 1941 the actress appeared in the brief run of the play *The Lady Who Came To Stay*.

When Lillian Hellman [41] wrote her powerful drama *Watch on the Rhine*, Miss Christians was given the leading role. This former favorite in the Berlin theaters was cast as Sara Müller, the American-born wife of a German anti-Fascist. The play opened on Broadway April 1, 1941. It was a triumph for the author and performers; with Paul Lukas [42], the male lead, Miss Christians earned high critical commendation. In the opinion of Brooks Atkinson, "Mady Christians' Sara Müller is full of womanly affection and a crusader's resignation to realities." *Watch on the Rhine* itself fared well, too, winning for its author the annual award of the New York Drama Critics' Circle. It was also listed among the best plays of the 1940-41 season by Burns Mantle [44].

In 1943 Miss Christians lectured on the theater in the hinterland. That year she also appeared in the motion picture *Address Unknown*, again playing opposite Paul Lukas. This was the film version of Kressman Taylor's best seller, another anti-Nazi drama which dealt specifically with Nazi corruption. While in Hollywood Miss Christians also played in *Tender Comrade* (1944), starring Ginger Rogers [41]. This picture, in which she had a small part as a housekeeper, received unfavorable reviews.

When Miss Christians read Kathryn Forbes's [44] stories about "Mama," titled *Mama's Bank Account*, she was enthusiastic about them. Then, when she heard that Richard Rodgers [40] and Oscar Hammerstein [44] were going to produce a play based on these stories, she wrote to each of them, asking for the part of Mama. It was somewhat of a coincidence, therefore, that John van Druten [44], after adapting the stories for the play, suggested Mady Christians for the part. (The playwright, incidentally, dedicated the play to Miss Christians.) *I Remember Mama* is a tender comedy-drama about a Norwegian-American family governed by the wise, simple mother. The actress prepared carefully for the role, developing a Norwegian accent by

studying with a Norwegian woman who did not realize how marked her accent was. Miss Christians says that she derived most of the feeling for the part from memories of her own mother. A short time after the very successful Broadway première in October 1944, the star remarked: "I'm still walking on air. This is the most beautiful part I've ever acted, except perhaps some of the classics, and to have the part in a beautiful play that is also a hit seems almost too good to be true. It will take me a few weeks to get used to believing it."

The critics were almost as enthusiastic about the play as Miss Christians, and they found many complimentary things to write about her performance, too. In the words of *Variety*, "Mady Christians has been outstanding before . . . but her Mama is superlative." "Most people who see the play will certainly remember Mama, and will be unable to think of her as anyone but Mady Christians," wrote another reviewer. And, as if echoing this, Elizabeth Valentine declared, "In fact, Miss Christians steps over the fine line between acting and being." Writing in the New York *Post*, Naomi Jolles declared that Miss Christians' portrayal of the sympathetic, understanding mother "has made her a truly dimensional figure and audiences have accepted Mama as real, sometimes to the eclipse of Miss Christians." Another critic commenting on the actress' triumph in the part observed that Miss Christians' performance "gets the lusty response it deserves." Burton Rascoe called her performance as Mama the finest of the year. The same critic also named Miss Christians as one of the ten most beautiful actresses of the year. She was awarded the Delia Austrian Medal by the Drama League of New York for the most distinguished performance of the season. The list of previous medal winners includes Katharine Cornell [41], Helen Hayes [42], Maurice Evans, Raymond Massey, Paul Muni, Alfred Lunt [41], Lynn Fontanne [41].

Miss Christians' contract for this play was for a period of at least two years. She studied singing again during that time, and she taught the theory and practice of acting in a course officially named "The Study of Roles and Scenes" at the Columbia University 1945 summer session, to the delight of a class of thirty. Professor Milton Smith, director of the University Theatre, has described Miss Christians as "a brilliant and thoroughly experienced practitioner of the art of the theater."

Questioned about her method of handling a part, Miss Christians has said, "I think it out intellectually first; I make careful research. . . . Little by little during the early rehearsals, I begin to feel it; there is one point there where I am overboard—all emotion—too much—this performance is terrible. After that I taper off; then once again during rehearsals I play it on feeling, and this time it is better. I begin to know how much to let loose. Finally the opening night I am playing mostly on feeling—controlled, of course—the mental understanding of the role acts as a brake and a guide. But once you've hit it right—after that you can do it from memory. It would be impossible to feel a part night after night for months."

Besides her stage and screen performances, Miss Christians has also done radio work, and she has made recordings of plays for the American Foundation for the Blind's Talking Books. She is a member of the Actors Equity council, the union's governing board. Her interests extend beyond the theatrical sphere: on April 18, 1945 she spoke at the International Security luncheon of the Independent Citizens Committee, and in September she joined a committee of Broadwayites backing Eugene Connolly for election to the City Council. In late 1945 she was reported to be working on her autobiography.

One writer has remarked that after seeing Miss Christians as Mama she found the actress' own, or offstage, personality a surprise, for, unlike Mama, Miss Christians has a "quick, rushing manner and talks eagerly and volubly." Radiant with vitality and enthusiasm, she has said: "I like life—the state of the world I do not like, naturally—but I think I am essentially a happy person." She enjoys her small farm in Connecticut, where she raises "too many beans and tomatoes." Long interested in directing, she hopes that some day she will direct young actors and actresses—"The older ones scare me. But the young ones—maybe I can do something for them."

An attractive, smartly tailored woman, Miss Christians has bright blond hair and gray-blue eyes, and has long been described as pretty and sometimes as beautiful. Because of her height (she is about five feet seven inches tall) and her "noble speech and regal bearing," Miss Christians has portrayed many queens: in addition to Gertrude of Denmark, she has played Anne of England, Louise of Prussia, Elizabeth of Spain, the Empresses Maria Theresa and Eugénie, and a number of fictional rulers. Possibly a disadvantage of her height has been that in playing romantic scenes opposite shorter leading men in Europe (where the average height is less than in America) she nearly always had to sit down or drape herself on a convenient piece of furniture. In fact, she claims to have played more scenes in this manner than any other actress.

References

N Y Herald Tribune VI p2 Jl 13 '41; IV p1+ N 12 '44 por
N Y Times II p1+ N 19 '44
PM p20 O 19 '44
International Motion Picture Almanac, 1939-40
Who's Who in the Theatre (1939)

CHRISTISON, SIR (ALEXANDER FRANK) PHILIP Nov. 17, 1893- British Army officer
Address: b. c/o War Office, London

One of the lesser known leaders of the Burmese campaign in the Second World War, Lieutenant General Sir Philip Christison commanded the first British force ever to win a major victory over the Japanese. In late 1945 he was in a more publicized role as commander of the Allied forces maintaining order in Java and the other Netherlands East Indies, where the Indonesian nationalists had risen in revolt against Dutch colonial rule and declared an Indonesian Republic in August.

Bassano, Ltd.

LT. GEN. SIR PHILIP CHRISTISON

Sir Philip's mother was English, but he comes of a distinguished Scottish family on his father's side. Christison's great-grandfather was Professor of Humanity at Edinburgh University. His grandfather, who also taught there, was Queen Victoria's senior physician in Scotland, and was created a baronet. His father, Sir Alexander Christison, was surgeon general of His Majesty's Bengal Army, one of the first Army doctors to use chloroform. The first of five children of Sir Alexander's second marriage, to Florence Elworthy, Alexander Frank Philip Christison was born on November 17, 1893, eleven years after his father succeeded to the baronetcy. He is now heir presumptive to his half-brother, Sir Robert Christison, twenty-three years his senior.

The future general attended Edinburgh Academy, where he was something of an athlete, and went on to study medicine at Oxford University. He played on the University College rugby team, and also refereed matches. Somewhere in his education, too, "Christy" Christison acquired a good knowledge of Gaelic and of ornithology. In 1914, after the First World War had begun, Christison joined the Royal Army Medical Corps. But, he says, "I was so horrified at the bad tactics of generals in France that I thought, 'Can't I save more lives by being a good soldier than by being a bad doctor?'"

Accordingly, Christison obtained a commission as second lieutenant in the Queen's Own Cameron Highlanders, and went to France with his battalion in August 1914. In the next three and half a years the young officer was mentioned in dispatches, wounded, and twice decorated, winning the immediate award of the Military Cross at Loos, and a bar, meaning a second award, at Arras. In February 1916 Captain Christison was married to Elizabeth Mitchell, daughter of the Bishop of Aberdeen and Orkney.

(Continued next page)

CHRISTISON, SIR PHILIP—*Continued*

Unlike most British officers, Christison has served in a number of infantry regiments. In 1919 he held command of the Seaforth Highlanders' Sixth Battalion, and from 1920 to 1923 and then from 1924 to 1927 he served, respectively, with the King's Own Borderers and the Camerons. In 1929-31 the infantryman had a staff job at the War Office, and was made brevet major in 1930. After two years as brigade major Aldershot Command, Christison was assigned to the Staff College as General Staff Officer 2. In 1937 he was given command of the Fourth Battalion of the Duke of Wellington's Regiment, with the rank of lieutenant colonel. Later that year he was promoted to colonel.

In 1938 Christison assumed command of the Fourth Indian Quetta Brigade in British Baluchistan, a land of deserts and rugged mountains. He is said to be a great admirer of the Indian soldiers, and he has familiarized himself with their traditions and addresses them in Urdu. While in Quetta the Colonel, an enthusiastic bird fancier, used to set out on a camel as a one-man bird-study expedition: his findings were published as *Birds of Northern Baluchistan* (1940). In 1940-41, with Britain engaged in the European war, he was commandant of the Staff College at Quetta; then the forty-eight-year-old officer was called back to England as brigadier to the General Staff.

Promoted to the acting rank of major general, the Scotsman was given command of the new Fifteenth Scottish Division. This was formed of the remaining battalions of the Highland and Lowland regiments which had been cut to pieces in the Battle of France in 1940. But in December 1941 Japan also declared war, attacked and captured Singapore and Lashio, and infiltrated the British lines in India. Christison was sent back to Baluchistan as general officer commanding. Then, in November 1942, he was given the new Thirty-third Indian Corps to prepare for the jungle campaign in Burma. "For a year," to quote an official release, "General Christison and his officers and men learned the geography of the country, its mountains, jungles, its climate, knowing that when the time came they would have to go 'against the grain'—over the mountains from west to east, not down the valleys running from north to south." In January 1943 he was made a Companion of the Bath, and in that year was promoted to three-star rank (temporary). The General had a special reason for wanting to beat the Japanese, for his only son, twenty-four-year-old Lieutenant John Anthony Alexander Christison, had been killed at the Hlegu Roadblock.

Next Christison was then transferred to command of the Fifteenth Indian Corps (it included the Fifth and Seventh divisions), which went into action against the Japanese in Arakan in November 1943, as part of General Sir William Slim's [45] Fourteenth Army. "When we go forward, we go forward to stay—and the hell with infiltration!" Christison told his men. At that time the Japanese held nearly all of Burma; it was Christison's corps which inflicted their first defeat by British forces. This was at Arakan, northeastern India, in February 1944.

His Seventh Division was cut off and surrounded by the enemy, but (to quote a later citation) "his cheerfulness . . . inspired his whole force," and division commander Messervy formed his troops into the famous British square and stuck it out. For eighteen days this "box" fought off the Japanese, living on supplies dropped by India-based planes. When Christison's Fifth Division came to relieve the beleaguered Seventh, the two joined forces under his leadership, hemmed the Japanese in between them, and hunted down the scattered enemies, killing ten thousand. Between battles in the Arakan jungle, the General found time to note two hundred and fifty different kinds of birds; each of his patrols was also instructed to watch for signs of rhinoceroses, as well as Japanese.

To quote the Southeast Asia theater commander, Admiral Lord Louis Mountbatten [42], "After that victory the Fifteenth Corps, fighting often in the worst conditions on the whole Burma front, secured the necessary air bases and ports from which the victorious advance of the Fourteenth Army over the Chindwin and down the center of Burma was sustained. [Perhaps the best known of these was Akyab, in January 1945.] Finally it was the Fifteenth Corps forces which made the amphibian and air-borne landings south of Rangoon [in May 1945] to capture that city, and set the seal of success upon the Burma operation."

When the Japanese surrender brought the war to an end in August 1945, Christison and the other English, Scotch, Irish, Welsh, Indian, East and West African, American, and Chinese soldiers, sailors, and airmen in the theater had liberated 85 per cent of Burma. That sweltering tropical jungle, incidentally, is host to every communicable disease, and infested also by leeches and poisonous snakes; during the first six months of 1944 there were more cases of illness in the Fourteenth Army than the entire strength of that army, and in the comparable period of 1945, there were six sick men for each battle casualty. When Lord Louis speaks of Christison facing the worst conditions on the front, therefore, it follows that those conditions were impressively bad.

Sir Philip—he was knighted on the field at Imphal in September 1944 as a K.B.E.—took command of the Allied Land Forces in Southeast Asia during the absence of General Slim. He was engaged in reoccupying Singapore and releasing the war prisoners and civilian internees there; later, when assigned the same task in the Netherlands East Indies, he had to cope with the Indonesian Nationalists' revolt against Netherlands rule in September 1945. His job of restoring order Christison described as "walking about a powder barrel, stamping on the fingers of those who are trying to touch a match to the powder."

In a situation where the solution depended to a considerable extent on the personality of the Allied occupying general, Christison, it was reported, seemed determined not to incite the Indonesians. He kept his men in the background as much as possible, and ordered them not to wear any weapons except when on duty. Christison emphasized that it was not his intention to pull Dutch chestnuts out of the fire. "Our only business is to disarm the Japs," he said, "release war prisoners, and, of course, maintain law and order, which is most desirable from our point of view. I expect to be treated as a guest." Ironically, however, the small British force found it necessary to use the available Japanese to help police the Indies, as choosing native or Dutch guards would, the General said, be playing politics. The end of October found Christison's men holding out against armed violence, in which a British brigadier was killed, and trying to arrange some peaceful settlement.

On October 31 General Christison announced: "These direct and unprovoked attacks upon British forces cannot in any circumstance be permitted, and unless the Indonesians who have committed these acts surrender to my forces, I intend to bring the whole weight of my sea, land, and air forces and all the weapons of modern war against them until they are crushed." (Prime Minister Attlee [40] had earlier charged that the Nationalist Movement had been sponsored by the Japanese for two or three years.) An ultimatum to the Indonesians in East Java, including the Surabaya naval base, to surrender their arms, expired on November tenth, and Christison's Java forces, under Major General E. C. Mansbergh, began to bomb and shell "known centers of extremist activity," in support of the Fifth Indian Division's advance toward Surabaya. Within a few days the Indians and Indonesians were locked in a bitter house-to-house struggle. The Indonesian president Achmed Soekarno charged the British and Dutch ex-prisoners with massacring an innocent civilian population, and the Allied field commanders stated that the rebels were employing surrendered Japanese weapons in a manner that suggested Japanese influence, and committing atrocities upon men, women, and children. Starvation and suffering were mounting among the Javanese population as a result of the disruption of communications.

In early December, according to United Press correspondent John Bower, the Indonesians controlled most of the communications, and British control in Java was limited to a few spots. Conferences among Christison, Premier Sutan Sjahrir of the Indonesian Republic, and Dutch Governor-General Hubertus Van Mook [42], failed to change the situation, and the (British) Allied commanders in the theater, Mountbatten and Dempsey [44], decided on a policy of employing whatever force might be necessary to overcome opposition. To this end, some of Christison's troops burned down two Indonesian villages, one in retaliation for the massacre of survivors of an airplane crash, and the other after snipers from the village had driven Indian troops from a rail crossing. By mid-December, however, the Allied troops were still outnumbered, although reinforcements were reported on their way to General Christison.

"Christy" to his friends, "The Smiling General" to his Indian troops, Sir Philip is considered by his officers "one of Britain's greatest generals." According to Darrell Berrigan of the New York *Post*, "graying, kindly, studious, unaffected," are the adjectives applied to the tall general. He is a member of the British Ornithologists Union and the Bombay Natural History Society, and one of the first questions he asked the Japanese general in Java was whether his soldiers had shot any of the local rhinoceroses. The versatile Scotsman is said to be "no mean performer" on the cello and bagpipes, a student of Celtic literature and music, a crack shot, an angler, a good athlete, a keen bridge player. His home is in Edinburgh. Sir Philip and Lady Christison have three daughters, Heather Cameron, Alison Ann, and Fiona.

References

Burke's Peerage (1936)
Who's Who, 1945

CLARK, TOM C(AMPBELL) Sept. 23, 1899- United States Attorney General
Address: b. Department of Justice, Washington, D.C.; h. 2101 Connecticut Ave., N.W., Washington, D.C.

The highest law officer of the United States Government is, since July 1, 1945, Attorney General Tom C. Clark. The Attorney General, who shares with one fellow Cabinet member (the Postmaster General) the traditional right to be addressed as "General," heads a department which has been described as "probably subject to more political pressure than any other. It is loaded at all times with potential political scandal." In addition to the classic functions of criminal detection and prosecution, law interpretation, prison supervision, and representing the Government in tax, claims, and customs cases, Clark's Department of Justice handles immigration and naturalization, antitrust prosecution, and is concerned with public lands. In time of war it enforces rationing, priorities, and other wartime controls, as well as prosecutes civil espionage and sabotage cases. And, as Arthur Krock [43] points out in the New York *Times*, "as the President's legal counsel as well as the chief law enforcement officer of the Administration, Attorney General Tom C. Clark will have a great deal to do with shaping legislation, with official courses toward industry, with the character of the Federal bench and bar, and with what may be termed the 'moral climate' of the Truman [45] regime. . . . The attitude and record of General Clark accordingly will have much to do with whatever score for high-mindedness is made by President Truman."

Tom Campbell Clark ("Tom" is not a diminutive, as many think, but his official name), whom President Truman nominated for the Cabinet in May 1945, was born about forty-five years earlier, September 23, 1899, on "the best residential street in Dallas, Texas." The son of Jennie (Falls) and William H. Clark, he is of Scotch-Irish ancestry. Tom's grandfather and father were well known lawyers, active in public affairs and Democratic politics. The boy did well at school and sports, worked on student publications, and attended Sunday school faithfully. (Clark is a Presbyterian.) After studying at the Bryan High School, where he edited the monthly publication, and won debating and oratorical honors, the youth entered the Virginia Military Institute, the private "West Point of the South," where he remained a year (1917-18); in this period he stood forty-sixth in his class of 242 cadets. He next served briefly as a sergeant in the 153d Infantry, and at the end of the First

TOM C. CLARK

World War went on to the University of Texas. At the university he won his B.A. in three years and his LL.B. the next year (1922). (In 1945 he received an honorary Doctor of Laws from the John Marshall College of Law.)

Admitted to the Texas bar in 1922, Clark joined his father and brother in their Dallas law practice. In November 1924 he was married to Mary Jane Ramsey (daughter of a State Supreme Court justice), who had lived in the sorority house next door to Clark's Delta Tau Delta house at the university. (The Clarks have one son, William Ramsey, and one daughter, Mildred.) The likable young attorney became active in Texas politics, and is described as a "political protégé" of Senator Tom Connally's '41 and of Representative Sam Rayburn's '40. With Connally's backing, Clark left private practice in 1927 to enter "that great political school, the D.A.'s office," as civil district attorney of Dallas County. *Newsweek* says that he did not lose a case during his five years there. "A good lawyer doesn't file a suit unless he's sure he'll win," Clark says; and *Time* reports that "among Washington legal eagles he is known for his bulldog tenacity in preparing cases."

In 1932 Clark resigned from his office to re-enter private practice, and spent two years as master in chancery in the Joiner oil litigation. In 1934 his earnings dropped because he spent a great deal of time campaigning for the election of his partner, William McGraw, as attorney general of Texas. According to the report of a Texas Senate investigating committee in 1937 (when McGraw was a prospective candidate for Governor), Clark experienced "a tremendous and startling increase in earnings" after his partner took office. Clark's friends explain that this was because he was again able to turn his full attention to his practice. In January 1935, according to the report, the Texas Petroleum Council engaged his services at a salary of twelve thousand dollars a year. Clark denies that this was for serving as a lobbyist, al-

though he did appear before the State legislature to speak against the chain store tax bill as representative of the Safeway grocery stores. The Texas investigating committee censured Clark for not being "willing and eager to make a full disclosure of his financial affairs," but his explanations proved satisfactory to the Judiciary Committee of the United States Senate when he was questioned, before the unanimous confirmation (on June 14, 1945) of his appointment as Attorney General.

With the sponsorship of Senator Connally and Representative Hatton Sumners, Clark was appointed to the Department of Justice in 1937, as special assistant to the Attorney General of the United States, Homer S. Cummings. First assigned to the Bureau of War Risk Insurance, the rangy Texan was transferred in 1938 to the revitalized Antitrust Division, where he specialized in cases concerning violations of the marketing and wage-hour acts. A year later the dynamic division head, Thurman Arnold '40, sent Clark to New Orleans to take charge of the field office there, and a few months after that made him chief of the division's West Coast offices, with headquarters at Los Angeles. There, according to *Newsweek*, Clark "won a reputation for ending price-fixing in the lumber industry."

One month after the Pearl Harbor attack and the entrance of the United States into the Second World War, Attorney General Francis Biddle '41 appointed Clark coordinator of alien enemy control in the Western Defense Command. The West Coast was alarmed by the presence of the many thousand Japanese (by birth or ancestry) and of the thousands of German and Italian citizens, and in February 1942 President Franklin D. Roosevelt '42 ordered them all to be evacuated from the Pacific Coast military zone. General John L. De Witt '42 was responsible for the evacuation, but Tom Clark was attached to his staff to handle the job and coordinate the work of all the Federal agencies concerned. The situation was a delicate one, for West Coast feeling ran high against the "alien enemies," while civil liberties groups were concerned with the protection of the rights of the sixty thousand racial Japanese who were American citizens, of whom many had relatives in the country's armed forces. Clark managed the job "with firmness and humaneness." Raymond Moley '45 writes, "I was in California when it was under way, and everyone concerned praised Clark's exemplary conduct." The lawyer organized the inland relocation centers, and established the legal machinery to handle the évacués' private affairs.

Clark's relocation work brought him, reportedly, an offer of a colonelcy, but apparently he preferred to return to the Department of Justice. Appointed first assistant to Assistant Attorney General Arnold in the Antitrust Division, the Texan was given charge of the War Frauds Unit in May 1942. There he worked closely with the Special Senate Committee Investigating the War Program, better known as the Truman Committee, often basing prosecutions on facts unearthed by Senator Harry S. Truman and his committeemen. At the end of March 1943, when Thurman Arnold left to become a Federal judge, Clark succeeded him as Assistant Attorney General heading the Antitrust Division. "There will be no witch-hunting, no uprooting of American customs or traditions," he told businessmen, "but there will be practical, swift, hard-hitting law enforcement." (When he became Attorney General two years later Clark again emphasized that the Government planned no program of persecution of business, but a strong enforcement program to maintain fair competition.) He was concerned particularly with preventing cartels (trade barriers set up by private agreement), from lowering the standard of living and from endangering the postwar peace by restricting production for their own profit.

During the five months Clark spent as head of the Antitrust Division the cases he prosecuted included a combination of some large New York department stores in an advertising boycott against a newspaper whose editorial policies they resented. Perhaps the most bitterly contested case was that of the motion picture consent decree, the agreement under which producers, distributors, and exhibitors operated, and under which the division had suspended its antitrust divorcement suits against Warner '45 Brothers, Paramount, MGM (Loew's, Inc.), Twentieth Century-Fox, and RKO-Radio Pictures. According to Moley, Clark "reached a settlement which quieted things, and all parties were sorry when Mr. Clark was transferred to other duties." On the other hand, *Variety*, the organ of show business, reported that after negotiating with the Big Five companies from mid-1943 until early 1944, Clark reported to Biddle that another consent decree could not be worked out, and recommended that the antitrust suit be resumed. This was done late in 1945.

Clark's War Frauds Unit meanwhile dealt with charges that followed the Truman Committee's revelations of the Wright Aeronautical Corporation's methods; of the Anaconda Wire and Cable Company, which admittted supplying defective wire and cables to the United Nations armed forces; and of the indictment, under the antitrust law, of the National Lead Company, its Titan Company, and E. I. du Pont de Nemours and Company "on charges of participating in a world-wide conspiracy to control the production and marketing of titanium compounds," of which 98 per cent of the supply was being used in war products. (In July 1945 it was announced that the Government had won the titanium cartel suit.) "Because cartels are, in effect, private economic super-governments, ruling over whole segments of our economy," said Clark in June 1943, "they were able to divide world markets, to undermine the Good Neighbor Policy by allowing South America to become in many instances the exclusive market of Axis economic interests, and to withhold processes and products necessary for the conduct of the war both from the United States and other members of the United Nations." (Statements like this caused the Assistant Attorney General to be accused by defendants of trying his cases in the newspapers.)

In August 1943, when Clark exchanged positions with Wendell Berge and became head of the Criminal Division, he took his War Frauds Unit along with him, and also the enforcement of priority orders, price control, rationing, and food allocation laws. Those who had hoped his appointment would mean

greater vigor in prosecution were not disappointed. Within a few months the Texan had completely reorganized his division to handle the more than fourteen thousand complaints it was receiving each month. *Newsweek* reported that Clark's telephone rang on an average of once every three minutes; "he occupied the hottest legal seat in the country. New York, Los Angeles, and What Cheer, Iowa, may be on the line at the same time with prosecution problems. . . . But no one in the department ever saw Clark get excited or heard him raise his voice."

Up to June 1944 his staff had reportedly won 92 per cent of its war frauds trials; by June 1945 his War Frauds Unit had won 250 convictions and $350,000 in fines. On occasion Clark himself argued cases before the Supreme Court, although only a stern order from his little daughter could make him discard his Western-style attire for the required formal morning dress. According to *Time,* he specialized in civil-rights and peonage cases. While working twelve hours a day ("I have to work long hours because I'm not as smart as some other fellows"), Clark found time to keep his Capitol Hill friendships in good repair, and to listen to the troubles of his division's five hundred workers, send them personal notes at Christmas, and encourage his less-experienced attorneys.

Clark also became president of the Federal Bar Association, which he helped to organize. Drew Pearson '41 writes that he "quit as its head after shocking Southern colleagues by demanding Negroes be admitted"; according to *Newsweek,* however, his enforcement of the wage-hour law in the South "gave due regard for regional conditions." In January 1945 Attorney General Biddle designated Clark, with two assistants, to conduct the prosecution of the spies William Colepaugh and Erich Gimpel, who had been landed from a U-boat on the Maine coast. The eight-day trial, which was conducted by a military commission behind closed doors, ended with the death sentence for both defendants (later commuted to life imprisonment by President Truman). Clark has said that this was his most interesting case.

A year earlier Charles Van Devander and William O. Player, Jr., in their column *Washington Memo,* had written that Tom Clark would succeed Francis Biddle as Attorney General within a month. Actually, it was fifteen months (May 1945) before Clark was appointed, by President Truman, to replace Biddle, and then the news was reported as coming as a surprise to everyone, including the new Attorney General. Commentators traced the appointment to the influence of Democratic National Chairman and Postmaster General Robert E. Hannegan '44, Senator Connally, Speaker Sam Rayburn, and also reminded their readers that Clark had worked with Truman when the latter had headed the investigating committee. Clark's appointment —coincidental with those of Lewis B. Schwellenbach '45 to replace Labor Secretary Frances Perkins '40, and Clinton P. Anderson '45, to replace Agriculture Secretary Claude Wickard '40 —was seen as a step toward replacing Eastern New Dealers by "organization Democrats"

CLARK, TOM C.—*Continued*

from the West, and the three were described as "mildly liberal . . . realists, not visionaries." All three had, however, supported much of the Roosevelt program.

Shortly after taking office on June 30 Clark announced plans for reorganizing the Justice Department and consolidation of some of its seven divisions, with contemplated annual savings of millions of dollars. One of the changes, announced several months later, was the assignment to the Federal Bureau of Investigation of all future investigations of antitrust cases, and of all criminal investigations to be undertaken by the Department. In the case of the antitrust suits, Clark indicated that bringing the FBI into the picture was not a move to produce more criminal indictments, although the Department intended to pursue a strong policy of antitrust enforcement during the reconversion period. Another plan announced by Clark was that of creating a new bureau on juvenile delinquency, headed by experts. In addition, he said that he would encourage Federal attorneys throughout the country to institute the "Brooklyn system," a method which has been used by Federal authorities in Brooklyn, New York, for several years. Under this system offenders under twenty-one are placed on probation before instead of after conviction. Their cases are investigated before they are brought to trial, and in many instances these persons are not prosecuted. Clark also recommended the establishment of youth centers to train young delinquents, these centers to be staffed by psychiatrists and other experts.

With the war not yet ended when he took office, the new Attorney General was faced with many pressing wartime problems. In July he was authorized by the President to order removal and repatriation of dangerous enemy aliens, and to this end he named a three-man board to hear cases of hundreds then in custody. He announced a coordinated campaign against black markets, to be prosecuted jointly by the Justice, Treasury, and Agriculture departments, and by the OPA. Cases of this sort and of tax evasion, he said, were to be heard first; with the coming of V-J Day he warned that the Justice Department did not propose to relax its vigilance.

After Japan's surrender the Attorney General's office was presented with new considerations—those of demobilization, the termination of war-derived authority, the protection of veterans' rights. In October Clark told reporters that the chief concern of the Department was then the prosecution of tax delinquents, while antitrust enforcement was the second big concern. Experience has shown, he told the Senate committee investigating the full employment bill, that the stifling of competition has "a pronounced effect on employment." It is the job of the Justice Department one commentator observed shortly after the end of the war, to see to it that during the reconversion period there is no promotion of monopoly while new enterprises are being formed and the Government is disposing of surplus war plants and other goods and properties. For his part, Clark emphasized in various speeches that it was not the intention of the Department to "make persecution out of prosecution."

One of the most complicated of the reconversion problems concerned the disposal of the fifty-two Government-owned aluminum plants, built during the war, in a manner that would insure fair competition in the industry. Involved in this was the question of the future of the Aluminum Company of America (Alcoa), declared a monopoly by the Federal courts in March 1945. In a report submitted to Congress in September, Clark recommended the reorganization and subdivision of Alcoa into a number of competing companies to bring about more efficiency, lower costs, and more jobs. This measure, the company claimed, would "destroy property values running into millions of dollars owned by thousands of small investors" and institutions, and prepare the way for Government subsidies.

The next month Congress was asked to "decide whether the Government should subsidize new producers of aluminum, both to carry out Clark's program for the dissolution into smaller companies of Alcoa and to fix a line of policy to be followed in the disposal" of the Government's seven-hundred-million-dollar plants. The difficulty of a solution lay partly in the fact that only Alcoa seemed to be in a position to buy and operate the plants without Government assistance. Another factor was that no peacetime consumer demand equaled that of the wartime aviation industry, with the result that large stockpiles of aluminum had piled up by the close of the war. Of the solution, the *Christian Science Monitor* wrote in October: "Whether it is measured in terms of dollars, of consequences on American industry, upon employment, or upon the pattern set between Government and private enterprise the issue now transcends any other reconversion problem that has come out of World War II." As put by W. Stuart Symington [45] of the Surplus Property Administration, Congress seemed to be faced with a choice between monopoly control of the aluminum industry by Alcoa and Federal subsidies, or Government interference in business, in the words of others.

Other monopoly cases with which Clark's Justice Department became concerned before the close of 1945 were those of the Permutit Company and of several companies engaged in manufacturing electrical goods. The Permutit Company was charged, with companies representing five foreign countries, of "dividing the world into six areas of operation with which each of the member companies would have the exclusive right to manufacture and sell the patented water-purifier equipment and process." The electrical companies, General Electric Company, Westinghouse Electric Corporation, two of their subsidiaries, and an export company controlled by them, were charged with having formed an international cartel in 1930 with leading German, British, and Swiss manufacturers.

Tom Clark is over six feet tall, dark, young-looking. He shows his Texas background by wearing a "ten-quart" Stetson hat, by colorful bow ties, of which he has scores, by his calm geniality, and by a soft Southern drawl. Clark is described as having graying hair, brown eyes, "a long nose with a slight bump to it, something of a double chin, a broad grin, and . . . a genius for making friends," particularly in Congress. A Mason (Scottish

Rite and Shriner), he belongs to clubs in Washington, Dallas, and Los Angeles. Before he became Attorney General he used to insist upon driving an ancient, dilapidated car. Now that he no longer has time for hunting and fishing, Clark depends on dieting and volleyball to keep his weight at one hundred seventy-five pounds; if he gets home before dark he plays ball with his son, and he likes to take young Mildred shopping. On Sunday mornings he cooks the household's hot cakes. He also claims a talent for frying chicken and concocting fruit salad; and he adds that he is "one of the greatest dishwashers in the country." Tom Clark's usual greeting to anyone he knows, a nice blend of Southern formality and Western breeziness, is "Hya doin', sir?"

References

N Y Post Mag p5 Je 9 '45 por
N Y Times p6 Mr 17 '43 por
N Y World-Telegram p19 My 24 '45
Newsweek 23:38 Je 12 '44 por; 25:37,
    116+ Je 4 '45 por
Time 45:22-3 Je 4 '45 por
Who's Who in America, 1944-45

CLARKE, JOHN HESSIN Sept. 18, 1857 —Mar. 22, 1945 Justice of the United States Supreme Court, retired; resigned from the high court in 1922 to take his fight for the League of Nations to the American people; while still a member of the Supreme Court, he advocated cancellation of war debts as a practical business move to stimulate world trade.

Obituary

N Y Times p19 Mr 23 '45 por

CLAY, LUCIUS D(UBIGNON) Apr. 23, 1897- United States Army officer

Address: b. c/o War Department, Washington, D.C.; h. 3900 Connecticut Ave., Washington, D.C.

The first man to direct civil affairs in the American zone of occupation in defeated Germany is the Army's "tough-minded" administrative expert Lieutenant General Lucius D. Clay. When President Roosevelt '42 in March 1945 announced Clay's appointment as deputy to General Eisenhower '42, then commander of the Allied military government in Germany, he said: "The task of developing an organization for occupied Germany and administering it is one for which General Clay is particularly qualified by reason of his splendid service in the civilian as well as in the military branches of government." A top-ranking engineer, Clay also became a leading production and supply specialist after Pearl Harbor. When General Joseph T. McNarney '44 became Eisenhower's successor, Clay remained as his deputy military governor.

A distant kinsman of the statesman Henry Clay, Lucius DuBignon Clay was born in Marietta, Georgia, to Sarah (Francis) and Alexander Stephens Clay. His date of birth is April 23, 1897, the year his father, a prominent lawyer, was elected to the United States Senate. (Alexander Clay held his Senatorial seat until

U.S. Army Signal Corps

LT. GEN. LUCIUS D. CLAY

his death in 1910.) In preparation for a military career, young Lucius was sent to the United States Military Academy. Immediately after his graduation from West Point in 1918, when the United States was at war, he received his commission as a second lieutenant in the Corps of Engineers on June 12, and on the same day he was promoted to first lieutenant and to captain (temporary). Three months later the young officer was married to Marjorie McKeown.

Clay's first assignment was as instructor at the Officers' Training Camp at Camp Humphreys, Virginia. In December 1918 he was assigned to the Engineers' School at the same post, and a year and a half later, in June 1920, he was graduated from the civil engineering course. In February of that year he had received his captain's bars (permanent). The following year he served as a professor of military science and tactics at Alabama Polytechnic Institute in Auburn, then returned to Camp Humphreys in August 1921 as engineering officer and instructor in the Engineers' School.

After a year in this teaching post, and another year during which he was engaged in preparing the training regulations at the camp, Clay was assigned to West Point as an instructor (August 1924). At the end of four years he returned once more to Camp Humphreys. In the course of his tour of duty there, in July 1930, he was graduated from the course for company officers at the Engineers' School. He was then assigned to Corozal, Panama Canal Zone, for service with the Eleventh Engineers. In September 1931 Clay was transferred to the Office of the District Engineer at Pittsburgh. In this post he was in charge of the construction of Lock and Dam Number Two on the Allegheny River until 1933, when he reported to Washington for duty in the River and Harbor Section of the Office of the Chief of Engineers. In 1934 Clay represented the United States at the Per-

CLAY, LUCIUS D.—*Continued*

manent International Navigation Conference at Brussels.

Clay joined General Douglas MacArthur's [41] staff in the Philippines in October 1937. With headquarters in Manila, he served as adviser on engineering projects and the survey of water power facilities. His next assignment took him back to the United States, to Texas, where he was appointed district engineer at Denison in August 1938. There he supervised construction of the Red River dam for two years. Engineering combined with aviation was to occupy him next, for in October 1940 he became secretary of the Airport Approval Board and assistant to the administrator of civil aeronautics. For his work in this position Clay was given the Legion of Merit award in April 1945. The citation reads: "For exceptionally meritorious conduct in the performance of outstanding service while in charge of the civil airport program of the United States from October 1, 1940, to December 16, 1941. Working in close cooperation with the War, Navy, and Commerce departments, General Clay organized and directed a construction program which included improving and enlarging 277 airports and constructing 197 new ones in the continental United States, Alaska, and certain Pacific islands. General Clay displayed unusual judgment, foresight, and energy in establishing a national system of airports which has proved to be of tremendous value to the United States in the war effort."

In March 1942, a few months after the entry of the United States into the war, Clay became deputy chief of staff for requirements and resources in the Services of Supply (later redesignated as the Army Service Forces). The following July he was assigned to the headquarters of the Army Service Forces in Washington, D.C., as assistant chief of staff for matériel, a title later changed to director of matériel. (At this post, in December 1942, he was advanced to major general [temporary].) In his capacity as director, the General was largely responsible for the procurement program of the Army Service Forces. As righthand man to General Brehon Somervell [42], commanding general of ASF, Clay dealt directly with top WBP officials and manufacturers. He studied the capacities and techniques of war plants, as well as their manpower and supply problems. The Army's hard-hitting matériel director "needled" manufacturers in filling contracts and contributed to the development of new weapons.

During this period Clay wrote a long and detailed article, "The Army Supply Program," which appeared in *Fortune* Magazine in February 1943. In this thorough survey the supply chief explained the Army's production policy and discussed the origin and operation of its supply program. This program, revised to meet wartime needs, was ready in February 1942. It was based on "the mobilization rate, and the composition of troops deemed desirable at that early stage of the war, and it included large quantities of matériel that our allies had ordered or requested the year before." Calling for sixty-two billion dollars, the program was gradually adjusted to changing requirements and supplies until the original cost was halved.

Clay discussed various phases of production, including scheduling and the problem of schedule breakdown. In plain language, using technical, explanatory illustrations, Clay painted the complex picture of the Army supply program and its numerous dependent factors. Emphasizing that "the requirements for all-out war are insatiable," Clay declared, "Production must be controlled by the necessities of war; it should never dictate requirements."

In April 1944 Clay headed a board of five officers assigned to investigate Army operation of the Breakers Hotel in Palm Beach, Florida. The decision of the Army to abandon this luxurious resort as a hospital provoked considerable public controversy. In its report the board of Army officers submitted its unanimous recommendation to relinquish the project as an "impracticable and financially unsound" venture. A month later Clay testified before the House Military Affairs Committee on the subject of surplus materials. He informed the committee that the War Department did not want the job of disposing of such supplies but rather believed that this task should be taken over by some outside agency. However, Clay pointed out that the War Department did want authority to determine what should be labeled surplus after the war and to select supplies to be held for national defense. He also added that some war plants must be held as "stand-by" equipment for five years or more after the war, certainly until it was known what the future military picture was likely to be. War plants recommended for prompt sale were those producing explosives and other types of manufacturing units whose rate of obsolescence of equipment and product is high. He also included those war plants equipped to serve civilian needs.

In August 1944 Clay appeared as a witness before the Senate War Investigating Committee, which considered production problems. He blamed the failure to reach certain production goals on manpower shortages, fatigue, and optimistic war news, which had the effect of "dulling the sense of urgency." Clay emphasized, however, that the general production picture was "magnificent." That same month *In Fact* reported a special press conference held by General Clay at which he denied an antilabor charge spread by press and radio. The supply director declared: "There has never been a case, so far as we have heard, where our men lacked ammunition due to any strike or other lag in production." Also in August, when the shortage of heavy-duty truck and bus tires became acute, Clay offered to the WPB the Army's plan to increase the output of these supplies. He outlined a furlough program for soldiers formerly engaged in the tire industry, providing leaves for such men over thirty stationed in the United States, and not in the infantry. In the fall of 1944, when there was trouble with supply lines after the Allied capture of Cherbourg, Clay, the Army's "prize troubleshooter," was sent to that French port. So successful was he in handling the difficulties in the wrecked city that one writer stated that in one day Clay "doubled the supplies shipped to the front, quintupled them before he left."

In December, when the Nazi offensive brought intensified production, the director of the Office of War Mobilization and Reconversion James Byrnes[41] requested Clay's assignment to his staff. Released temporarily by the Army from military service, Clay joined Byrnes as deputy director for war programs and general administration, retaining his uniform and rank. His primary responsibility was to coordinate the programs of all agencies concerned with war production and to "expedite the delivery of supplies from the assembly lines to the front lines." For the brief span of four months the General served as assistant to Byrnes, establishing a reputation for severe home-front policies. Some civilian officials resented Clay's tough "military-first" point of view, and it is reported that the OWMR advisory board desired the officer's dismissal.

But Clay's determined attitude remained unchanged; he was called "perhaps the most influential voice" in the Government's stern home-front policies. It is believed that he was responsible for many of the controversial "crack-down" measures, such as the racing ban, the ban on display lighting, and the curfew, reportedly adopted for their psychological effect on the home front. Acting as "buffer between the brass hats and the war agencies," Clay supported Byrnes's war measures and incurred the wrath of business-as-usual individuals. In the critical manpower situation he endorsed the May[41]-Bailey[45] bill for limited national service. He opposed reconversion experiments before V-E Day, insisting that the "need and demand for military supplies will be at their peak on the date the Germans quit." Throughout his activity in the OWMR Clay maintained that the important job was to supply the fighting forces—he was called the "conscience" of the home front.

Following his assignment as deputy to General Eisenhower, Clay went overseas in April 1945. (That same month President Truman[45] nominated Clay for promotion to lieutenant general, and the Senate later confirmed the nomination.) Knowing Clay's capabilities, Eisenhower had requested this assignment for his friend. (General Joseph T. McNarney succeeded Eisenhower late in 1945.) According to plan, following the surrender of Germany the administration of the country was placed under the direction of the Allied Group Control Council—later the Allied Control Council (France, Great Britain, the Soviet Union, and the United States); the policy the Council would follow was indicated by the Potsdam agreement. As deputy military governor, Clay was given the direction of civil affairs in the American zone of occupation in southern Germany. Clay was reported to be sensitively aware of the public relations part of his job, and of keeping the support of the American people while he dealt with the problems of German economy. A writer for Look's Washington bureau, in describing Clay's job of "driving an American twelve-horse team and keeping it in step with three similar teams," stated, "The horses of the team are the twelve divisions of the United States occupation government: ground army; naval; air; transport; political; economic; finance; reparation, deliveries and restitution; internal affairs and communications; legal; prisoners of war and displaced persons; and manpower."

The press welcomed Clay's appointment to this formidable job, calling him a strong believer in duty and principle. The appointment was consequently interpreted as a sign of stiffening AMG policy in Europe. The New York Herald Tribune editorially expressed its approval of the choice of Clay for the post: "Apart from his excellent personal qualifications, however, it is satisfying to know that an Army man has been selected for what is essentially an Army job. The occupation of Germany, quite possibly for some years to come, will mean extirpating the last vestiges of Nazism, of policing an anarchic state and providing direct control over German economy and public services." Analyzing Clay's past record as a severe administrator, most commentators agreed that "life will be hard for the German citizen, but things may be a little easier for the American." It was also pointed out that Clay does not belong to that group of persons who sympathize with the German people, as distinguished from their leaders. The United States News ventured the opinion that "the German civilian can expect a minimum of the things that make life more comfortable. But he can expect that as quickly as possible the debris of war will be cleared away and civil affairs set to moving on the basis of a solid organization."

Clay's first public statements on the planned military government of the Reich reassured those who had feared a policy of leniency might be adopted toward the conquered Germans. In an interview on May 17 the General outlined plans for Germany. He emphasized that the people would have a military government whose main purpose will be to de-Nazify the territory and restore the democratic processes. There was a fundamental split in the Allied Control Council, wrote Raymond Daniell[44] in September, between those who wished to continue the Anglo-Russian-American alliance and those who wished to preserve "a vestige of German industrial and military strength to defend Western civilization at the Elbe." This conflict, Daniell claimed, would come to a showdown on the issue of whether "reparations or the German standard of living was to be the primary consideration."

The question of how much industry Germany should be allowed to retain was answered from the American zone by General Clay, who stated, as Eisenhower did, that the Potsdam directives controlled American policy. His Government, he declared, interpreted these directives as "calling for the establishment in Germany of a standard of living equal to, but not above, that of surrounding countries." From American observers in Germany came the report, however, that the American Military Control Council under Clay was not carrying out the policy to eliminate Germany's power to make war. And the Stars and Stripes in December quoted a high-ranking officer to the effect that the American military government faced "complete collapse." Specialists of all kinds were desperately needed, he revealed; while William L. Shirer[41] indicated that hasty redeployment was responsible for an attitude of indifference.

Until General George Patton[43] was relieved of control of Bavaria after charges of laxness in removing Nazi officials from office, similar criticism was directed at other American of-

CLAY, LUCIUS D.—*Continued*

ficers. In response, Eisenhower had stated in October that Nazis were to be deprived of a vote in Germany, that the Army would "uproot Nazism in every shape and form." Several other positive steps could be seen by the end of 1945. Clay announced in October that the Allies had seized the three hundred German plants of I.G. Farbenindustrie. Of these, the war plants would be destroyed; the others would be dismantled and turned over to the Allies as reparations. (This issue of reparations was one on which the Russians had accused the British and Americans of being dilatory.)

In October the Allied Control Council formally proclaimed "the abolition of the National Socialist Party and the Nazi bureaus and subdivisions which had directed every phase of German life." Clay then announced that United States military government teams would be withdrawn from the administration of small towns and rural counties the next month, with transfer of this lower-level administration to non-Nazi Germans. By February 1, 1946, the General revealed, the first move would be made to increase this to state level, but American officers would be retained in a supervisory capacity, he added. (He has expressed the opinion that the Allies must remain in Germany for at least a generation.) At the end of the year he reported that German prisoners of war were being trained as administrators, policemen, and leaders of democracy. In explaining these moves, strongly criticized as premature, Clay said, "We are pulling out of a job that can best be left to the Germans. We believe we can better hold them responsible for administration if we give them a freer hand. In this way the German people will know that their own organs are responsible for the successes and failures of administration."

The food problem, another knotty question, was pointed up by Clay's statement in November that there was no food "in any substantial amounts" in Europe, and the request from the American zone for three hundred thousand tons of food to supply civilians in the area. The next month he assured the Council of State Minister Presidents (the chiefs of the German Government in each of the provinces in the American zone who "oversee and coordinate intrazone communications, trade, and finance), that the United States would not let the people starve, that food would be sent to them. The expenses, he explained, would be met when Germany was able to pay.

Clay's ninety-five-thousand-word official report on conditions in the American zone, issued at the end of the year, gave a gloomy picture. There was unrest and lawlessness among adult Germans, he pointed out, chiefly among displaced persons; and, although primary schools were slowly opening, teachers were scarce and juvenile unruliness was another problem. Without question, the Germans faced a cold, hungry winter, he said, for the scarcity of necessities, of adequate shelter and transportation, was becoming serious. Even such advancements as the return of religious freedom and an uncensored press were hampered by the difficult circumstances.

Throughout all the months of the Allied occupation it was becoming more and more obvious that the United States Army was anxious to turn over the control of Germany to civilians as quickly as possible. The problems caused by redeployment of Army personnel, and the feeling that the military are not properly prepared by training and experience for civil government were offered as reasons for a speedy transfer of duties. Finally, in November, while in Washington for discussions with the War Department, Clay disclosed that it appeared likely that this transfer would proceed rapidly during the early months of 1946. (Already such replacement had begun.)

From the beginning of the Allied occupation strong criticism was directed against the military government for its progress in de-Nazifying and deindustrializing Germany. The Allied Control Council itself by the end of 1945 had not determined on a unified program. The French, Clay reported on a visit to Washington in November, were opposed to any unification of Germany which might strengthen it industrially, and this stand, which hindered rehabilitation, was in opposition to Potsdam directives.

Blunt, tough, and thoroughly an Army man, General Clay is a trim military figure. He has coal-black hair, bushy brows, and a voice described as a "deceptively soft baritone." In April 1945 Clay received the Distinguished Service Medal for "exceptionally meritorious and distinguished service . . . as director of matériel." In September he was awarded the Russian Order of Kutuzoff, First Class for this same service and also for his work in demilitarizing Germany.

General Clay belongs to the American Society of Civil Engineers and the Society of American Military Engineers. He also is a member of the Permanent International Navigation Congress, while his clubs are the Army and Navy, and the Army and Navy Country Club. When Clay received his new assignment as director of German civil affairs he was frankly pleased, glad to leave his Washington desk for duties overseas. The General's two sons, Lucius Dubignon and Frenck Butner, were in Europe during the war, one in the Air Force and the other in a tank outfit.

References

N Y Times p1+ Mr 30 '45 por
Newsweek 25:48 Ja 1 '45 por; 25:52 F 19 '45 por
Time 45:77 Mr 19 '45 por
U S News 18:62-4 Ap 6 '45 por
Who's Who in America, 1944-45
Who's Who in Engineering, 1941

CLENDENING, LOGAN May 25, 1884— Jan. 31(?), 1945. American author; lecturer; physician; his column *Diet and Health* was popular syndicated newspaper feature; a few of his better-known books are *The Human Body* (1927), *The Care and Feeding of Adults* (1931), and *The Balanced Diet* (1936).

Obituary

N Y Times p25 F 1 '45

COLBERT, CLAUDETTE (kôl-bâr) Sept. 13, 1905- Actress

Address: h. Holmby Hills, Los Angeles, Calif.

One of Hollywood's most important box office attractions in the past decade, Claudette Colbert has won recognition for her portrayal of three types of characterizations—undiluted sex appeal (*Cleopatra*), light comedy (*It Happened One Night*), and mature drama (*Since You Went Away*). Born Claudette Chauchion in Paris on September 13, 1905, in 1910 she was brought to New York with her brother Charles by her parents, Georges and Jeanne (Loew) Chauchion. Lily, as she was nicknamed by her father, attended Washington Irving High School, where she studied art and designing with the hope of becoming a great fashion designer. Upon her graduation in 1923 she went to work as a general "handy" girl in a gown shop in order to learn more about designing. She supplemented her thin pay envelope by giving French lessons in the evenings.

But whatever ambitions she had in the field of dress designing evaporated when Anne Morrison, the playwright, not only suggested that she become an actress, but found her a three-line part in *The Wild Westcotts* (1923). Once Claudette Chauchion walked on the stage, she knew that she never wanted to do anything but act. (It was at this time that she changed her name to Colbert.)

After the tryout performance in Stamford, Connecticut, where the neophyte actress trod the boards in company with Cornelia Otis Skinner '42, Elliot Nugent '44, and Edna May Oliver, Miss Colbert's part was expanded. But the play soon closed, and then began the succession of small parts, short-lived engagements, and discouraging road tours, the school of most successful players. *We've Got To Have Money* (1923), *The Marionette Man* (1924), which closed in Washington, *The Cat Came Back* (1924), *High Stakes* (1924), and *Leah Kleschna* (1924) followed in quick order. Her luck turned when she appeared in the farcical comedy *A Kiss in a Taxi*, which ran for all of 103 performances. That opus (as well as several others of her earlier plays) was produced by Al Woods.

Then came the mysterious *Ghost Train* (1926), and the allegorical *The Pearl of Great Price* (1926), a spectacular production which died after thirty-two performances. Miss Colbert's first good opportunity to display her talent came in the role of Lou, the snake charmer, in Kenyon Nicholson's *The Barker* (1927). In that role, too, her nice legs attracted attention, and this led to her first part before the camera, playing opposite Ben Lyon in the silent film *Love O' Mike*, which was filmed during the 172-run performance of *The Barker*. Starring with her in *The Barker* were Walter Huston, and Norman Foster, to whom she was married in 1928. (The Fosters were divorced in 1934.) *Love O' Mike* proved a failure for her, however. "I'll never make another motion picture," she declared, and subsequently she graced Broadway's *Fast Life* (1928), *Tin Pan Alley* (1928), Eugene O'Neill's *Dynamo* (1928), which critics deemed the only bad play O'Neill ever wrote, and Elmer Rice's '42 *See Naples and Die* (1929).

CLAUDETTE COLBERT

Then Miss Colbert accepted a tempting offer from Paramount's New York studios. She made her "talkie" debut as the harassed heroine trying to elude Edward G. Robinson in the mystery thriller, *A Hole in the Wall* (1929). Paramount next cast her in *The Lady Lies* (1929), in which she was an instant hit. In 1930 Miss Colbert appeared in *The Big Pond* (with Maurice Chevalier), *Young Man of Manhattan*, and *Manslaughter*, for which she was dispatched to Hollywood. With the exception of the *Smiling Lieutenant* (1931), Miss Colbert's succeeding movies were a series of trivial pictures—*Secrets of a Secretary, Honor Among Lovers,* and *His Woman,* in 1931; and *The Wiser Sex, Misleading Lady,* and the *Man From Yesterday,* in 1932—in which she portrayed sweet, clinging, virtuous women. Finally, she boldly demanded the role of Poppaea, "the wickedest woman in the world," in DeMille's '42 *The Sign of the Cross* (1932), which depicted the persecution of Christians under Nero.

While Miss Colbert was now undisputably a star, until the revelation of her flair for comedy she was seen only in a string of comparatively undistinguished photoplays: *The Phantom President* (1932), *Tonight Is Ours* (1932), *I Cover the Waterfront* (1933), and *Three-Cornered Moon* (1933). Then Paramount loaned Miss Colbert to Columbia Pictures to play opposite Clark Gable '45 in *It Happened One Night* (1934), a highly diverting, lively comedy, skillfully directed, which concerned the adventures of a runaway heiress and a romantic newspaperman journeying by bus from Miami to New York. It was released by the studio with little fanfare, and immediately won for its director, Frank Capra, and the players a handsome collection of "Oscars." Now a veritable classic, it is still frequently revived.

Directly after her sensational success in *It Happened One Night*, she surprised her friends by accepting the *Imitation of Life* (1934) role, making her the mother of a grown daughter, in order to be able to do the same thing years later without being typed as a mother.

COLBERT, CLAUDETTE—*Continued*

It was she who chose the unknown Fred Mac-Murray to act with her in *The Gilded Lily* (1935), which made him a star. (Miss Colbert has made a practice of appearing in only two pictures a year, for which she is paid $150,000 each, and she regularly heads the list of high-salaried movie players, although her earnings are less than those of several actors who also have radio, recording, or other contracts.)

The actress was also to appear in a variety of films, ranging in mood from the allure of *Cleopatra* (1934) and the stark drama of *Private Worlds* (1935), to the expert comic artistry of *She Married Her Boss* (1935), *Tovarich* (1937), *I Met Him in Paris* (1937), *It's a Wonderful World* (1939), and *Midnight* (1939). Lesser successes included *Under Two Flags* (1936), a tale of life and love in the French Foreign Legion, the historical *Maid of Salem* (1937) and *Drums Along the Mohawk* (1939); *Bluebeard's Eighth Wife* (1938). *Zaza* (1939), the story of a French can-can dancer, was her one real failure.

In 1940, after the failure of *Boom Town*, a cavalcade of the oil industry which critics considered more as a parade of stars—Miss Colbert, Clark Gable, Spencer Tracy [43], and Hedy Lamarr—than a good play, the actress went back to the business of light comedy in *Arise My Love*. Set against the background of current events in Europe, this was a series of romantic scenes between a beauteous American reporter and an American aviator (Ray Milland) whom the girl has saved from a Spanish death sentence by pretending to be his wife. This was followed by *Skylark* (1941), with its slight plot about divorce; *Remember the Day* (1941), a sweetly nostalgic picture in which Miss Colbert appealingly portrayed a small-town, definitely gray-haired schoolteacher; and *Palm Beach Story* (1942), a wild slapstick farce written and directed by Preston Sturges [41].

In *No Time for Love* (1943) Miss Colbert, as a high-priced photographer, ventured deep into the mud usually braved only by the sandhogs who build tunnels under rivers. Next she relegated to the background her sartorial elegance and glamour as one of the exhausted young nurses wearing GI brogans and coveralls in *So Proudly We Hail* (1943), called an arresting, sincere war film, a tribute to the gallantry of Army nurses on Bataan.

For *Since You Went Away* (1944) Miss Colbert, giving perhaps the most notable performance of her career, became Anne Hilton, the successful wife and mother who upholds "that fortress—the American Home"—meanwhile graying perceptibly and learning to be a welder. While David O. Selznick's [41] first production since *Gone With the Wind* (1939) and *Rebecca* (1940) was considered a human document of the Second World War, charged with atmosphere and Americana, many critics felt that the two hours and fifty-one minutes running time of the film was marked by too many repetitive climaxes and too many heart-tugging sequences. After playing the mother of Jennifer Jones [44] and Shirley Temple [45] in Selznick [40]-International's *Since You Went Away*, Miss Colbert went back to a young role opposite Fred MacMurray in *Practically Yours*,

and was "admirably naïve, simple, and charming" in that lively comedy. Next came a less successful comedy, United Artists' *Guest Wife*, and then another mother role in the emotional drama *Tomorrow Is Forever*, opposite Orson Welles [41], in which she chose the co-star as well as her role. She was also reported to have signed with Sam Wood [45] of Columbia Pictures for *Jubal Troop*, having terminated her fourteen-year contract with Paramount in 1944.

A brown-eyed brunette who wears her reddish-brown hair in bangs, Claudette Colbert is five feet four and one-half inches tall and weighs one hundred and eight pounds. She is known in the film capital as the actress who will not present the right side of her face to the camera, because, she claims, that profile does not photograph well. When this preference was forgotten once by a director who had approved the construction of a set which necessitated the actress' entering a room with the right side of her face toward the audience, the set was dismantled and rebuilt.

At no time in her career, however, has the chic Miss Colbert relied upon beauty and physical appeal alone. These attributes are fortunate to possess, she believes, but a good story and a competent and showmanship-wise director are more important for a star. She has proved her theory that getting to the top does not depend upon having "connections" or a flashy "act," and that the so-called "breaks" are not mere accidents but the result of careful planning and knowing how to take advantage of opportunities. She is said to be friendly, completely untemperamental, and popular with cast and crew. She likes to dance and listens frequently to orchestral music, especially that of Tchaikovsky and Sibelius.

Miss Colbert and her husband, Joel Pressman, who is a physician and surgeon, live in a spacious house built at the time she achieved stardom. Working closely with the architects and builders, and concentrating on every detail, the actress spent weeks in New York shopping for incidental chairs, silver, lamps, and the original Manet which hangs over the drawing room fireplace. She says that one of the most important objects in the house, pinned over a mirror in the upstairs sitting room, is a little Silver Sun hanging from a pair of skis. Miss Colbert won the trophy at Sun Valley in the winter of 1939. She is proud of it because to get it a woman must cover the course in two minutes, fifteen seconds. Miss Colbert made it in one minute, forty-seven seconds.

References

Am Mag 120:58-9+ S '35 por
Collier's 103:11+ Ja 28 '39 por
Liberty 22:23+ O 27 '45 por
Photoplay 54:25-6+ D '40 il pors
International Motion Picture Almanac, 1943-44
Who's Who in America, 1944-45
Who's Who in the Theatre (1939)

COLE-HAMILTON, J(OHN) B(ERESFORD) Dec. 1, 1894—Aug. 22, 1945 Air Vice-Marshal of Royal Air Force; planner of fighter escort system for British bombers; joined the RAF in 1918 when it was amalgamated with the Royal Flying Corps; served in India, 1923-26 and 1934-38, and with the BEF in France, 1940.

Obituary

N Y Times p11 Ag 25 '45

COLIJN, HENDRICUS (kō-līn' hĕn-drē'kŭs) 1869—Sept. 16, 1944 Dutch statesman, Premier of the Netherlands in 1925-26 and again from 1933 to 1939; was head of the Calvinist Party; an outspoken anti-Nazi, he was held prisoner from the time of the German occupation of the Netherlands in 1940 until his death.

Obituary

N Y Times p19 N 13 '44 por

COMDEN, BETTY May 3, 1918- Playwright; actress
Address: h. 47 W. 68th St., New York City
GREEN, ADOLPH Dec. 2, 1918- Playwright; actor
Address: h. 240 Central Park South, New York City

BETTY COMDEN

"The theater is *jammed* with young talent," protests Adolph Green, in answer to Billy Rose's [40] contention that there is no scarcer commodity. And *On the Town* (1944), the musical ballet-comedy of which Green and Betty Comden are co-authors, is an even more effective answer. George Abbott [40], who directed the show, was the only person involved in its creation who is on the wrong side of thirty: Leonard Bernstein [44] (composer), Jerome Robbins (choreographer), Paul Feigay (producer), and Oliver Smith (stage sets, co-producer) are the other young talent responsible. On Broadway, *On the Town* has made theater history in at least two other respects: it is the first musical ever bought by Hollywood in a pre-production deal, and it is the first in which its authors are also actors.

The story of *On the Town*—"the daffiest musical comedy plot in years"—involves three sailors on a twenty-four-hour leave in Manhattan who are smitten by a picture of "Miss Turnstiles" on the subway and promptly set out to find her. The search takes them to Carnegie Hall, Central Park, Times Square, three quite identifiable night clubs, and Coney Island, all of which come in for their share of cheerful kidding in song, dance, and dialogue. It might be gathered that both of the young author-actors are New Yorkers—and they are. It might be added that they are fanatical New Yorkers, with no intention of ever becoming anything else.

Betty Comden is a product of Brooklyn, where she was born on May 3, 1918, the daughter of Leo and Rebecca (Sadvoransky) Comden. Her father was a lawyer, her mother a schoolteacher, and her brother (overseas in 1945) is a doctor. So far as she knows there were no writers or actors among her more distant ancestors either, but she has been writing and acting ever since she attended Brooklyn Ethical Culture School, where the students read books like Scott's *Ivanhoe* and dramatized them. And Betty continued to write while in Erasmus Hall High School, but by this time, having acquired the discouraging notion that an actress had to be "very beautiful," she spent her other creative moments at the Clay Club in Greenwich Village instead of trying out for high school plays. By the time she matriculated at New York University she had decided to major in dramatics, however.

Major in dramatics she did, with the idea of teaching it later. But teaching must have been an extremely half-hearted ambition. Guided by her unschoolteacherish subconscious, she never took quite enough teaching courses to get her license; and when she received her B.S. degree in 1938 she began patiently making the rounds of theatrical agents—with no luck at all. It was during that period that she met Adolph Green, who was doing exactly the same thing with exactly the same results.

Her collaborator-to-be was born in another New York City borough, the Bronx; the date was December 2, 1918, the parents Daniel and Helen (Weiss) Green. Adolph had written poetry and acted in school plays in grammar school and at camp, but his actual dramatic experience was even less impressive than Betty's at this point. Graduated from Clinton High School in 1934, he found Wall Street more eager to employ his talents than Broadway, and accepted a job as a Wall Street runner. By the time he met Miss Comden he had been "vaguely looking" for work as an actor for four unexciting but athletic years.

There were plenty of other young people in the same predicament in those semi-depression days. One of them, Judy Tuvin, knew the owner of the Village Vanguard, at that time the last stronghold of old Village bohemianism; he told her that he would like to put on some kind of a show there that would employ young talent. Judy Tuvin brought Adolph Green down to the Vanguard; Adolph Green promptly brought in Betty Comden and Alvin Hammer; Betty Comden introduced John Frank. The Revuers were being born, even if they didn't know it yet. It was only after the

ADOLPH GREEN

five of them had been putting on separate acts for a while that the idea came to them of doing a satirical show together. Fortunately all of them not only sang, danced, and acted, but were endowed with ingenuity and imagination—necessary qualities for a group of performers who had to write their own lyrics, music, and dialogue as well as provide their own backdrops and costumes. The Revuers' light-hearted kidding of advertising, journalism, American magazines, and Hollywood attracted all sorts of important theatrical people to the Vanguard, and from putting on one show every Sunday night they were soon playing three nights a week, then six. The Vanguard was rapidly becoming a popular night club, too: the owner was encouraged to install a telephone and to get a liquor license.

In everything but a financial sense The Revuers were already a success—and even twenty-two dollars a week apiece was some improvement over their original five dollars—but in September 1939 the mercenary five forsook the Vanguard for the Rainbow Room in Rockefeller Center. After a two months' engagement there they were invited to put on a weekly program over NBC—a program on which Dinah Shore '42 and the Basin Street boys also appeared. Engagements at Radio City's Music Hall, at Loew's State, at Spivy's, at Cafe Society (both Downtown and Uptown), and several television shows followed. It was while playing an engagement at the Blue Angel that they got their first movie offer—to play in *Duffy's Tavern*. That particular deal fell through, but in Hollywood they worked at the Trocadero until assigned by Twentieth Century-Fox to appear in *Greenwich Village* (1944).

The brief glimpse of The Revuers in *Greenwich Village* hardly made movie history. Only Miss Comden and Green returned to New York, however. Judy Tuvin (now Judy Holliday) and Alvin Hammer had succumbed to the lures of Hollywood; John Frank had dropped out of the group some time before, to go into defense work. The twosome that remained ended by accepting another engagement at the Blue Angel, and their satire did not seem to suffer from a depletion of their ranks. Then, one spring night, their friend Leonard Bernstein wandered in, with Paul Feigay and Oliver Smith in tow. The three young men asked the two remaining Revuers if they would be interested in doing the book and lyrics for a full-length show built around the idea of *Fancy Free*, the highly successful ballet by Bernstein and Jerome Robbins. There was no doubt that they would.

Soon, too, there was no doubt about what they wanted the show to be. In the first place, they wanted to make their characters three-dimensional—particularly the three young sailors, with their feeling of having to crowd everything into twenty-four hours. They wanted to capture the sailors' feeling about a big, strange city, too—not just any city, but New York, which is not quite like any other place in the world. They wanted everything in the show to be there for a reason, with no gags simply for gags' sake. Most of all, they wanted the music and the ballet to spring naturally from the story. "Integration" was the word they kept using while they worked.

The story, the character development, and the various numbers in *On the Town* were all Miss Comden's and Green's ideas, but neither of them is sure of who invented what—Miss Turnstiles, for example. Their collaborative technique was what it always has been—a matter of sitting down and talking, and writing down in longhand whatever came out of the interchange. As for the show's lyrics, some of them were written before Leonard Bernstein had composed the music for them; the music already existed for the ballads. It all sounded pretty hit-and-miss, but even before the book was in final shape RKO had seen the show's possibilities and had agreed to invest $31,500 in it on condition that it be the only film company involved. Then, before the first rehearsal, Metro-Goldwyn-Mayer offered to buy the film rights for $100,000 in cash, plus a percentage of the gross for another $150,000, plus an investment of $62,500 in the stage production. The president of RKO waived his company's condition, not wanting to hold up the deal—and that was how *On the Town* became the first musical comedy ever bought by Hollywood before it reached the boards. When *On the Town* opened in Boston late in December 1944 to almost unanimous "rave" notices, the reason for Hollywood's interest became obvious. The Boston *Post* critic predicted that the show would "probably do for New York what *Oklahoma!* did for that state in the wild West"; and the New York opening later that month found it doing something similar for the Adelphi box office, at least.

Not every New York critic "went completely overboard" for the show, but those who did went very far over. *PM*'s Louis Kronenberger[44] pronounced *On the Town* not only "much the best musical of the year," but "one of the freshest, gayest, liveliest musicals I have ever seen." Lewis Nichols of the New York *Times* called it "the freshest and most engaging musical show since the golden days of *Oklahoma!* Everything about it is right ... a perfect example of what a well-knit fusion of the respectable arts can provide for the theater." Ward Morehouse of the New York *Sun* ransacked his vocabulary of adjectives and came up with "brisk and festive," among others. E. C. Sherburne of the *Christian Science Monitor* described *On the Town* as "theatrical caviar, lifting caricature . . . one notch higher into a vein close to the ballet, which is nearer abstraction in entertainment than anything else now on the boards." The *New Yorker*'s Wollcott Gibbs found the whole affair so unlabored and effortless as to seem almost an improvisation. In *Variety*, however, these words appeared: "Not all the players are professional, and some appear to be semi-pros, if not amateurs. Not a real laugh was delivered at the debut and vocally the show is mediocre." The same reviewer pronounced the night club interlude "distinctly unfunny." Burton Rascoe did not go this far, but found *On the Town* only "pretty good fun," for those who are not "too exacting"; and the New York *Post* seemed to be somewhat reluctantly amused.

Those who didn't like the book were also in the minority. Here was "the best musical comedy book since *Pal Joey*," said Louis Kronenberger; Lewis Nichols found the book "coherent for a change," differing from most in that it speeded the action along instead of stopping it dead; the *Christian Science Monitor*'s critic also singled the book out for special compliments. But the New York *Herald Tribune*'s Howard Barnes decided that George Abbott's "shrewd direction" had made much of "scant material," while Wilella Waldorf talked in the New York *Post* of "proceedings" which "run all the way from slightly satiric tidbits to something approaching children's charades."

The parts that Betty Comden and Adolph Green wrote for themselves in *On the Town* are by no means the leading parts; if anyone could be called the star in a musical without starring roles it is Sono Osato '45, "Miss Turnstiles," who proves herself as ingratiating a comedian as she is a dancer. The sailor who finally acquires Miss Turnstiles and the predatory female taxi driver whose prey is the second sailor are almost equally fat parts. But Burton Rascoe has picked out as one of the high spots of the season's stage productions the scene in which Betty Comden (the lady anthropologist) pronounces Adolph Green (the third sailor, lost in the Museum of Natural History) "a rare specimen of the dolichocephalic skull." *Cue* says of Miss Comden that she "will remind you faintly, faintly of a young Fannie Brice," while Green "has that great showman quality, that indefinable cockiness that distinguishes a Joe E. Lewis or a Bob Hope '41 or even an Al Jolson '40 . . . which defies description, but is inherent in the way these men walk, talk, use their hands."

In the summer of 1945 the Comden-Green team, on leave from *On the Town*, wrote the book and lyrics for *Billion Dollar Baby*, for which Morton Gould '45 supplied the music and George Abbott '40 the directing. Smith and Feigay opened the production before the end of the year.

In private life dark-haired, attractive Betty Comden is part of another team: she was married on January 4, 1942, to Siegfried Schutzman, an artist who in 1945 is a sergeant in the Engineers, on detached service in connection with the Information and Educational Division. He was stationed in New York just in time for the opening of *On the Town*, which made everything "perfect." Mrs. Schutzman pronounces herself "just so happily married that there's nothing very colorful about my social life." She cooks, keeps house in a quite unpalatial apartment on West Sixty-eighth Street, owns no pets, and has no special eccentricities except a hatred of shopping (combined with a love for pretty clothes) and an equally violent distaste for being kept waiting. (She cannot cure herself of promptness.) Although she isn't on a diet she never eats chocolate; she didn't smoke even before the cigarette shortage; and she is no kind of parlor entertainer at all, if shows at the Stage Door Canteen and at veterans' hospitals can be excepted. As a member of the Independent Citizens Committee of the Arts, Sciences, and Professions, she makes sending telegrams to Congressmen one of her hobbies.

Adolph Green is unmarried, and interested in nearly everything—particularly the arts. Music is his special love—he whistles, can sing symphonic and rather unknown orchestral works from beginning to end and sound like a whole orchestra. Some day he would like to be a composer and conductor of symphonic music like his friend Leonard Bernstein. He also has a phenomenal memory, and as a student of the motion picture from way back amazes and sometimes annoys his friends by his ability to name the casts of every movie ever made. His chief dislikes, he says, are another Adolph —and "chi-chi."

CRABTREE, JAMES W(ILLIAM) Apr. 18, 1864—June 9, 1945 American educator; secretary emeritus of National Education Association since 1935; served as secretary to N.E.A. from 1917 to 1935, during which period membership grew from 10,000 to more than 200,000; secretary of former President Hoover's '43 Advisory Commitee on Education (1931-32) and World Federation of Education Associations (1935-38).

Obituary

N Y Times p15 Je 11 '45

CRAIG, MALIN (mā'lĭn) Aug. 5, 1875— July 25, 1945 United States Army officer; Chief of Staff of the United States Army (1935-39); served in Santiago campaign (1898), Boxer Rebellion (1900), First World War (1917-19); retired from active duty in 1939 after having commanded every type of military unit from cavalry troop to field army; recalled in 1941 to become head of War Department's Personnel Board. See *Current Biography* 1944 Yearbook.

Obituary

N Y Times p19 Jl 26 '45 por

CRAVEN, FRANK 1880(?)—Sept. 1, 1945 American actor, director, and playwright, well known in theater and motion pictures; appeared in *Bought and Paid For, New Brooms, Village Green,* and many other plays; author of *Too*

CRAVEN, FRANK—*Continued*

Many Cooks, The First Year, and *This Way Out*; scored great success in *Our Town* (1938).

Obituary

N Y Times p31 S 2 '45 por

CRAWFORD, CHERYL (chĕr'ĭl) Sept. 24, 1902- Producer

Address: b. 49 W. 45th St., New York City

"If you want to produce [plays]," says Cheryl Crawford, "you must go after playwrights, give them some of your ideas, work with them on their own." Then comes editing, changing, rewriting—and getting the author to accept necessary changes. "I've never seen a play that could be put into rehearsal from the original script, except something by Eugene O'Neill," she explains. The producer engages and supervises the director, designers, cast, and other workers, makes all the business arrangements, decides on billing, attends to the hundreds of incidental details, finds the financial backing—and pays the bills. Not many women have succeeded as producers, but Cheryl Crawford, Manhattan's one active woman producer, has presented such hits as the memorable revival of *Porgy and Bess,* the gay *One Touch of Venus,* and the record-breaking Margaret Webster '40 production of *The Tempest.* In association with Miss Webster and Eva Le Gallienne '42, Miss Crawford is also business director of the projected American Repertory Theatre, to open in September 1946.

Cheryl Crawford was born in Akron, Ohio, on September 24, 1902. Her father, Robert K. Crawford, was in the real estate business; her mother was the former Luella Elizabeth Parker. Miss Crawford's early ambition, not encouraged by her three brothers, was to be a missionary; but she became interested in the theater at fifteen, when she played Lady Macbeth in an amateur production. At Smith College, which she entered after a year at Buchtel College, her interest grew into an ambition in contact with Professor Samuel Eliot's drama courses. There Miss Crawford wrote a long play for which her professor gave her an "A," and two short ones which were produced at the college. ("They were rotten," she says now.) Cheryl Crawford is said to have been the first undergraduate to produce financially successful plays at Smith—Kyle Crichton describes them as "toga-mad tragedies"—and during junior vacation she built scenery and did some directing in Frank Shay's Provincetown company.

Miss Crawford was graduated with the B.A., *cum laude,* in 1925. Then, according to *Cue,* she "squeezed into the Theatre Guild's newly formed drama school." After a year of trying, not too successfully, to support herself in New York, she got a job with the Guild. *Theatre Arts* says that she began in a secretarial job, while other sources say she was engaged as third assistant stage manager. At any rate, in the fall of 1926 she was an assistant stage manager for the Guild production of *Juarez and Maximilian,* the cast of which included Alfred Lunt '41, Margalo Gillmore, and Edward G. Robinson, and she also understudied Helen Westley. From 1927 on Miss Crawford

shared in the Guild production of Dorothy and Du Bose Heyward's *Porgy* in New York, accompanied it on tour, and "played guardian to the company when it took the production to London," where it opened in April 1929. By 1930 twenty-seven-year-old Cheryl Crawford was casting director of the Theatre Guild, with the title of assistant to the Board of Managers. She was drawing a salary reported as $10,000 a year, and a place was being made for her on the Board.

The Theatre Guild was at the peak of its activity during these years. From 1926 to 1928 it produced fourteen hits in a row, a record never equaled by any other organization. But Cheryl Crawford felt, like many other younger members, that a permanent acting company should be established. Led by play-reader Harold Clurman, this group planned a noncommercial, experimental acting company. Miss Crawford obtained from the Guild Board their option on Paul Green's *The House of Connelly,* borrowed the services of young Franchot Tone '40 and Morris Carnovsky, and was given one thousand dollars toward production expenses. The group of about thirty actors, headed by the three directors (Crawford, Clurman, and Lee Strasberg), then spent the summer of 1931 as a sort of theatrical training camp, rehearsing *The House of Connelly.* At the end, the Theatre Guild agreed to put up half the production cost, Miss Crawford helped raise the remainder, and the play was presented. Notices were excellent and the backers broke even.

In early 1932 Miss Crawford and Harold Clurman resigned their Guild positions to become full-time directors, with Lee Strasberg, of the incorporated Group Theatre. They paid themselves fifty dollars a week, plus five hundred dollars apiece for each production (regardless of who actually directed it), thereby putting themselves in the middle pay bracket of the group. Established players like Tone, Carnovsky, and Luther and Stella Adler received several times that salary; but all the members were on regular salary, regardless of whether or not they were actually working on a current production, and regardless of the size of their current parts. There was a strong group feeling and an emotional intensity among the members which gave rise to a number of amusing stories, especially with regard to the "Stanislavsky system" which they employed in preparing roles. Cheryl Crawford devoted herself to what the others called "dirty jobs"— mainly raising money and shaping scripts into playable form; however, of *1931—,* Clurman quotes her in *The Fervent Years* as saying, "It is our theater's duty to produce such a play." The Group Theatre "supplied the New York stage in the 1930's with much of its vigor and excitement": it developed Clifford Odets '41, introduced William Saroyan '40 to the theater (with *My Heart's in the Highlands*), presented a number of important experimental plays, added luster to Tone, Carnovsky, and the Adlers, and trained many noted actors and directors, among them John Garfield, Elia Kazan, Robert Lewis, Roman Bohnen, Lee Cobb, Sanford Meisner, J. Edward Bromberg, and Alexander Kirkland. It actually had to suspend operations in 1933—and came back that fall with a smash hit, Sidney Kingsley's '43 *Men in White,* co-produced with Harmon and

Ullman '45. In 1935, incidentally, Clurman and
Miss Crawford went to the Soviet Union for
a five-week study of the Russian theater.

After six years with the Group Theatre,
which had been torn by dissension during the
last years, Miss Crawford resigned in April
1937. She announced her intention of becoming an independent producer, an unusual occupation for a woman. According to Kyle Crichton, her first undertaking was *Four Cents a
Word*, but she never brought it out of rehearsal.
"Slight doubts began to annoy me," is the way
Miss Crawford puts it. In early 1938, however, she presented *All the Living*, directed by
Lee Strasberg, a study of conditions in an
overcrowded, understaffed state institution for
the insane. *Theatre Arts* called it "a first production she may well be proud of"; the *New
Republic* came closer to the consensus by saying, "You have to do a good deal of shaking
down to get its best content quite clear of
drifting clutter, but that the result is worth
the effort." The public apparently did not
care to make that effort. "This was the time
of my dizzy spells," says the producer.

After this, writes Crichton, "it took her a
year to get her bearings. She mistrusted her
judgment, her health was affected, and she was
financially a cipher. A friend invited her to
stay in the country, and she left Broadway
with eagerness." The next Crawford production, Maxwell Anderson's '42 *Family Portrait*,
was presented in March 1939, with Judith
Anderson '41 as Mary, the mother of Jesus.
(Miss Crawford had deliberately "cast against
type," feeling that Miss Anderson's force and
power would save the role from insipidity.)
Staged by the well known Shakespearean director Margaret Webster, who also played Mary
of Magdala, *Family Portrait* was highly praised
by reviewers but was a partial financial loss.
Cheryl Crawford and John Wildberg next took
over the 1,400-seat summer theater at Maplewood, New Jersey—and lost $6,000 on their
first two productions there. "We decided we
were licked, anyway," says Miss Crawford,
"and brought in a play *we* liked: Tallulah Bankhead '41 in *The Second Mrs. Tanqueray*." This
was very successful, and the producers followed
it up with other Broadway-level plays for
week-long showings at half the Broadway
prices. The Maplewood playhouse, which continued to be their base of operations, flourished
and, in her words, Cheryl Crawford "stopped
being a neurotic mess." She began to work at
building up a future audience, holding discussions between the acts and giving lectures between shows.

In January 1942 Miss Crawford returned to
Broadway with her long-planned revival of
George Gershwin's "folk-opera," *Porgy and
Bess*. When produced by the Theatre Guild in
1935, it had been a critical success but a financial failure; but Miss Crawford, assisted by
John Wildberg, turned it into a resounding hit.
Spoken dialogue was substituted for Gershwin's
recitatives; the orchestration was thinned out
and generally clarified; various touches of pre-
tentiousness were eliminated. With most of
the original cast, under the baton of Alexander
Smallens and the direction of Robert Ross, the
revival moved "more confidently, more dramatically, and more honestly than ever before," to
quote Richard Watts, Jr. Despite the large

CHERYL CRAWFORD

orchestra required, Miss Crawford managed
to hold production costs down to $16,200—"an
astonishingly low figure," made necessary because of her difficulty in finding backers—and
made a reported net profit of $5,000 weekly. The
show ran nine months on Broadway, unprecedented for a revival, toured for a year and a
half, returned in September 1943 to let New
York have another look, toured the South and
West, returned in the spring of 1944 to do
"incredible things" to the box office of the City
Center, and went right on touring. But its producer was not immune to headaches. The season in which she launched *Porgy and Bess*
also saw her ill-fated revival of Barrie's *A
Kiss for Cinderella,* starring Luise Rainer, and
the unfortunate *The Flowers of Virtue,* which
she managed for Marc Connelly.

Although an average of fifteen scripts a week
came to Miss Crawford's office, none were satisfactory. For her next production (with Wildberg), she asked S. J. Perelman and Ogden
Nash '41 to write a musical comedy book based
on F. Anstey's story, "The Tinted Venus."
Then she got Kurt Weill '41 to do the music,
Agnes de Mille '43 to work out the dances, Mary
Martin '44 from Hollywood to play the title
role, Kenny Baker from radio and John Boles
from movies to co-star. The result was *One
Touch of Venus,* which took the town by storm
in October 1943. The selection of Mary Martin was especially praised: "Only Miss Martin,
I think," wrote Howard Barnes, "could get
away with being an animated statue of . . . the
top glamour girl of the Hellenic age." Ballerina
Sono Osato '45 was another hit of the season,
and Miss Crawford soon rewarded her with
featured billing. With a production cost of
$145,000 and a weekly salary list between four-
teen and fifteen thousand, *Venus* grossed a reported $1,650,000 during its first year in New
York, plus a $150,000 advance from Mary Pick-
ford '45 for the screen rights; two months later
it started its tour. After the production cost
was repaid, Crawford and Wildberg reportedly
shared the remaining 50 per cent of the gross.

CRAWFORD, CHERYL—*Continued*

Meanwhile, in October 1944, Miss Crawford's production of *The Perfect Marriage*, with Miriam Hopkins and Victor Jory, was called "singularly uninspired." It closed in January 1945, and shortly afterward Miss Crawford presented Margaret Webster's production of *The Tempest*, with the ballet dancer Zorina '41 as Ariel and the Negro actor Canada Lee '44 as Caliban. Its $50,000 cost was supplied by a reported twenty-seven backers. Played on a multilevel revolving stage, and with music scored by David Diamond, *The Tempest* was acclaimed by reviewers and ran for 101 performances, an all-time record (the previous high for performances of "this most difficult of Shakespeare's plays to stage" was thirty-two). It went on tour in September 1945, including an engagement at the New York City Center.

About this time Cheryl Crawford announced the result of many months of planning—a repertory theater supervised by Margaret Webster, Eva Le Gallienne, and herself, to be opened in September 1946. Miss Crawford, who is business manager, put a stock issue on the market late in September 1945, and by early November announced that two-thirds of the required $300,000 had already been raised. The American Repertory Theatre, Inc., as it is called, is to have a repertory of six plays to be prepared by a company of about thirty actors, under contract for a minimum of two seasons, and headed by Eva Le Gallienne and Victor Jory.

The Ohio-born producer is described as "brisk yet gracious, and comely with her blue eyes, tailored clothes, and short, wavy dark bob." Generally calm, she seldom attends her own premières because the strain is too great. Miss Crawford is said to have read "everything in poetry" and to remember all of it, and is credited with the most complete collection in existence of American popular sheet music since 1900. On the slightest encouragement, her friends say, she will sing any old popular song one can name with more enthusiasm than voice, and tell who wrote it. But Miss Crawford's main preoccupation is with the theatrical possibilities of anything she comes across: "In fact," wrote Mary Anderson in the New York *World-Telegram*, "it is her belief that everything, whether it's cooking her specialty of spareribs with an original sauce, delving into psychoanalysis, or listening to a symphony, bears on the theater." She seldom has lunch: "On light days," Miss Crawford says, "I sometimes have a double orange juice in a drugstore."

References

Collier's 110:48+ Jl 4 '42 por
Cue 10:17 Ag 2 '41 por
N Y Post p14 N 26 '41 por
N Y Sun p16 F 17 '42 por
N Y World-Telegram p28 F 11 '44 por
Theatre Arts 26:622-3 O '42 il
Clurman, H. The Fervent Years (1945)
Who's Who in America, 1944-45

CREGAR, LAIRD (krā-gär' lârd) July 28, 1916—Dec. 9, 1944 Hollywood character actor; *Blood and Sand* (1941), *Charlie's Aunt*

(1941), *This Gun for Hire* (1942), *Holy Matrimony* (1944), and *The Lodger* (1944) were some of his best-known pictures.

Obituary

N Y Times p54 D 10 '44 por

CRET, PAUL P(HILIPPE) (krā) Oct. 23, 1876—Sept. 8, 1945 French-born American architect; professor of design at the University of Pennsylvania (1903-37); consultant to Navy Department and to Army Engineer Office at Pittsburgh; designed war memorials of First World War in France, Folger Shakespeare Library and Federal Reserve Building in Washington, D.C., and Detroit Institute of Arts. See *Current Biography* 1942 Yearbook.

Obituary

N Y Times p9 S 9 '45

CREWE, ROBERT OFFLEY ASHBURTON CREWE-MILNES, 1ST MARQUIS OF Jan. 12, 1858—June 20, 1945 British statesman; leader of Liberal Party in the House of Lords until resignation seven months before his death; had held many Government offices, including those of Lord-Lieutenant of Ireland (1892-95), Lord Privy Seal (1908 and 1912-15), Secretary of State for India (1910-15), Ambassador to Paris (1922-28), and Secretary of State for War (1931).

Obituary

N Y Times p19 Je 21 '45

CRIST, WILLIAM E(ARL) (krĭst) Aug. 10, 1898- United States Army officer

Address: b. c/o War Department, Washington, D.C.; h. 1417 44th St., N.W., Washington, D.C.

The manifold problems involved in the occupation of Japan have been the subject of international concern since General Douglas MacArthur '41 first assumed control of the defeated Empire in early September 1945. Serving under the Supreme Commander as chief of the military government section is Brigadier General William E. Crist, who is charged with the responsibility of maintaining law and order in Japan. Crist's twenty-five-year Army career had taken him to the Orient twice before, when he served for periods in China. In the course of the Second World War the General has seen duty in the Soviet Union, Hawaii, and on Okinawa, as deputy commander of the military government.

A Pennsylvanian, William Earl Crist was born in the capital city, Harrisburg, on August 10, 1898, the son of Samuel Curtis and Emma Levina (Orr) Crist. He attended the United States Military Academy at West Point, earning his degree in 1920. Upon graduation Crist was commissioned a second lieutenant, on July 2, and on the same date promoted to first lieutenant. Two months later the young West Pointer entered the Infantry School at Fort Benning, Georgia, from which he was graduated in June 1921. Crist then remained at the Infantry School as an instructor for two years. His next assignment, in July 1923, took him to Tientsin, China, where he was stationed with the Fifteenth Infantry at the American Barracks. Returning home in 1926, he joined the Twenty-eighth Infantry, serving at Madison Barracks, New York, for a year. Following this, for an eight-month period he was instructor in the Infantry Unit of the R.O.T.C. at Cornell University. By the summer of 1929 the Lieutenant was back at West Point as an instructor, where he remained for three years.

Crist's next assignment took him back again to China, in October 1932. As a Chinese language student, the American officer was stationed at Peiping until the following July, when he became acting assistant military attaché at Nanking. Now a captain (he had been promoted on August 1, 1935), Crist returned to the United States in 1936 to join the Sixteenth Infantry at Fort Jay, New York. In August 1937 he enrolled in the Command and General Staff School at Fort Leavenworth, Kansas, from which he was graduated the following June. Assigned to Fort Benjamin Harrison in Indiana, he served with the Eleventh Infantry and in September 1939 became plans and training officer of this unit. In November of that year he was transferred to Washington, D.C., and assigned to the Military Intelligence Division of the War Department General Staff. On July 1, 1940, he was promoted to major. After the United States entered the Second World War the officer rose rapidly in rank. Made a lieutenant colonel (temporary) at the end of 1941, he was advanced to colonel (temporary) in August of the next year, and to brigadier general (temporary) in March 1943. Early in 1943 he went from his duties in the Capital to Camp White, Oregon, to serve as assistant division commander of the Ninety-first Division, with which he remained until the end of the year.

In December Crist was assigned to the Army Group in Washington, and shortly thereafter he became head of the Army division of the United States Military Mission to the Soviet Union. In Moscow the General participated in significant negotiations with the Russians: It was this mission which arranged for extension of the Anglo-American England-to-North Africa shuttle-bombing experiment to the use of bases in the U.S.S.R. This bold cooperative venture was first planned by Roosevelt '42 and Stalin '42 at the Teheran meeting, and was inaugurated in June 1944, when American Flying Fortresses, protected by fighter planes, bombed targets in Rumania, then continued on their route to land on secretly constructed American air bases in the U.S.S.R. After refueling and reloading, the planes made the reverse trip, dropping bombs over Germany on the way.

The General went from the European theater to the Pacific in November 1944, joining the Tenth Army in Hawaii as chief of the Civil Affairs Office. Under the command of Lieutenant General Simon Bolivar Buckner '42, the Tenth Army invaded Okinawa, the largest of the Ryukyu Islands, on April 1, 1945. Crist landed on the island with the invasion forces, and there served as deputy commander for the Okinawa Military Government—the first military government director to go ashore on Japanese-controlled territory. During the campaign he was faced with the problem of handling the natives in camps; when the main

U.S. Army Signal Corps

BRIG. GEN. WILLIAM E. CRIST

battle ended on June 21 his troubles multiplied. For then began the trek of the refugees from the caves—by July 2 more than two hundred and fifty thousand civilians were under American care. Crist was thus confronted with the largest hostile population yet encountered in the Pacific. According to reporters on Okinawa, his administration was stern but just, and while tight control on civilians was exercised, the people seemed to respect the Americans and to show confidence in them.

Discussing the American program on the island, Crist emphasized that the plan was based on the use of salvage. "We are determined to house, clothe, and feed the civilians from materials available on the island," he said, adding, "We will avoid the use of any article of which there is a shortage in the United States, and we will keep at an absolute minimum the use of American shipping in providing for civilians." Included in the regulation of scarce items were cigarettes and blood plasma. (Crist held that Okinawans could supply their own blood donors and not use American-donated plasma or whole blood.) On the whole, the military government sought to provide for the minimum humanitarian needs of the people "without pampering them." It was also pointed out that the military had no intention of raising the living standard of the natives, except in the matter of sanitation because of the presence of American troops on the island. John Beaufort, writing from Okinawa to the *Christian Science Monitor* in May 1945, noted that while Crist's handling of civilians had been strict, there was "no evidence of unfairness or undue harshness."

General Crist was reassigned in July 1945, this time to the Civil Affairs Division in Washington. Shortly after the Japanese surrender in August, he was fully instructed on military government policy and sent to join MacArthur's occupation forces in Tokyo. He became chief of the Military Government Division, responsible for the supervision of finance, public safety, health, utilities, and transportation. His forces consist of more than four thousand specially trained officers, including men with experience in the administration of various Pacific islands. Among his men are those trained in the military government schools of eight United States universities, plus the faculties of these schools, specialists in Japanese language, industry, law, and customs. In addition, specialists have been withdrawn from Europe for Japanese occupation service. Crist is considered well equipped for his present command, for it is believed that his service in China and with the Intelligence Division have provided him with valuable knowledge of Japanese mentality.

The wife of the Army officer is the former Margaret Koster, to whom he was married on May 14, 1921. They have a son, William Earl. The General is a Mason and belongs to the clubs Scabbard and Blade, and Sojourners.

References

N Y Sun p14 Ap 24 '45

Who's Who in America, 1944-45

CROW, CARL (krō) Sept. 26, 1883—June 8, 1945 American journalist and author of several widely known books on the Orient; *Four Hundred Million Customers*, the first of his popular books on China, was published in 1937 in six languages; he was Far Eastern representative of the Committee on Public Information (1916-18); owner of an advertising agency in Shanghai (1919-37); early advocate of aid to China after Japanese invasion in 1937. See *Current Biography* 1941 Yearbook.

Obituary

N Y Times p32 Je 10 '45 por

CROWNFIELD, GERTRUDE Oct. 26, 1877—June 2, 1945 Well-known American author of children's books; since appearance of her first book *The Little Tailor of the Winding Way* (1917), she had written almost a book each year until 1942.

Obituary

N Y Times p32 Je 3 '45

CURRAN, JOSEPH E(DWIN) Mar. 1, 1906- Labor leader

Address: b. National Maritime Union of America, 346 W. 17th St., New York City; h. 870 Riverside Dr., New York City

A rank-and-file seaman in the early days of the merchant marine in the United States, Joseph E. Curran was also a natural leader, aggressive in action, progressive in viewpoint. As president of the National Maritime Union since its organization in 1937, president of the Greater New York Industrial Union Council since 1940, and vice-president of the CIO since 1941, he has become an outstanding leader of American labor.

Joseph Edwin Curran was born on New York's East Side on March 1, 1906. His parents, Eugene and Ida (Cohan) Curran, were Irish Catholics. Eugene Curran died when Joe was two years old; and his widow,

who became a cook in Westfield, New Jersey, remarried. Joe's schooling was brief. After he was expelled from the seventh grade of the parochial school for his irregular attendance, he became a caddy, then a "factory monkey." At fifteen he went to New York City, where he took a job as office boy with the Gold Medal Flour Company. There young Joe could watch the ships on the near-by rivers, and it was not long before he had signed on his first ship as an ordinary seaman, in 1922 beginning a seventeen-year period at sea. He was paid thirty dollars a month, for which he often worked sixteen hours at a stretch.

At sixteen Joe was a "big, nervy kid who knew all the answers," in other words, a good talker and an aggressive leader. He soon compensated for his lack of education by reading—not fiction, but whatever else he could find in the ships' libraries or on shore, about world economic and labor conditions. He learned about ships and seamen primarily through firsthand experience: "Fo'c'sle" Joe sailed pretty nearly everywhere on the globe. And lurid stories are told of his early years, when living and working conditions in the merchant marine were tough. Today, Curran does not appreciate romances of the sea: "I've been to sea," he says laconically.

His background also accounts for the seasoned toughness of Curran that has earned for him the respect and loyalty of the men in his National Maritime Union. He first became a union man in 1935, when, in order to sign on the S.S. *California* sailing from New York, he joined the International Seamen's Union, affiliated with the A. F. of L. Even then, it is said, he did not think well of the organization: "Their officers were not seamen's officials, but shipowners' agents." He did not like the *California* either—the food and pay were bad, he said. When the ship docked in California, at San Pedro, her crew found out how much better the seamen's wages and conditions were on the West Coast, as the result of a strike of the previous year, and the men turned to Curran to lead them. He told the shipowners' agents that the *California* would not move unless her crew was given pay equal to that of West Coast sailors, and better conditions. When the newspapers reported the strike, it reached the attention of the Secretary of Labor, Frances Perkins[40], who informed Curran that if the crew would take the *California* back to New York there would be no discrimination against the men and their grievances would be given a hearing. Curran agreed to cooperate, but when the ship reached the East the owners discharged sixty-four of the crew.

This incident started the big East Coast strike in the spring of 1936: sailors began walking off ships and demanding the reinstatement of Curran and the rest of the ousted *California* crew. The officers of the International Seamen's Union threatened to expel those who joined the "outlaw" strike.

Meanwhile, while the strike was going on, the I.S.U. negotiated a contract giving pay raises to the crew. This agreement was challenged by Curran and the insurgents, however, because the terms fell short of the Pacific Coast wage scales which they had demanded. A request that the seamen be allowed to vote on the acceptance of the agreement was denied. According to Philip Taft in the *Political Science Quarterly*, "For the insurgents the strike was not only a struggle for higher wages, but a maneuver to embarrass the national officers of the seamen's union." The rank and file led by Curran, it is said, felt that men who were more recently sailors should replace the old-line incumbent officials. The strike dragged on for ten weeks. It was finally brought to a close upon the shipowners' promise that strikers would be reinstated, without discrimination. In October, nevertheless, a new strike broke out in another attempt to nullify the contract. Three months later it was formally ended, with no agreement having been reached. (The strikers claimed that the NLRB had assured them that elections would be held to determine collective bargaining representatives. Furthermore, it is pointed out, these insurgents were faced with financial difficulties.)

Out of this deadlock grew the National Maritime Union of America. Curran was determined to form a new body completely independent of the I.S.U. In May 1937 he led some thirty-five thousand members of the old union into his organization. (In June the right of the union to represent the men was decided by NLRB elections.) At the constitutional convention in July the new group voted to join the CIO. Curran was elected president, and he has been re-elected at each succeeding convention. With Joseph Kennedy [40], at that time head of the United States Maritime Commission, he was able to cooperate. When the Commission opened hearings in New York, Curran gruffly admitted: "This is the first time the seamen have ever had a chance to say what they really think at one of these things." They were allowed to state their complaints: lack of decent sleeping quarters, sanitation, good food, et cetera.

Curran soon became one of the most popular union heads in the country. As leader of the East Coast merchant mariners, he took a Left-wing stand similar to that of Harry Bridges [40], who headed the West Coast longshoremen. In contrast to the leadership of these men was that of the more conservative Joe Ryan of the International Longshoremen's Association and Harry Lundeberg of the Sailors' Union of the Pacific. Curran made friends quickly among the East and Gulf port employers with his long-term cooperative policies. As the majority bargaining agency for the ship and dock personnel of fifty-two major shipping lines on these coasts, Curran's N.M.U. negotiated contracts with many of them.

But Curran—independent, dramatic, outspoken—could not escape, from the beginning of his career, the charge of "Red," or "Communist," a charge the labor leader has repeatedly denied. However, all groups are welcomed by the N.M.U., and Communists have been among its most loyal members. Persons on both sides of the political fence have offered opinions on Curran's sympathy with, or awareness of, this radical element. Some declare that he is being "used" by the Communists for a "front"; others, members of the N.M.U., feel that he is aware of the Communists' influence, that when he is unable to cope with it he will oust these members. To the Dies [40] Committee's charges of commu-

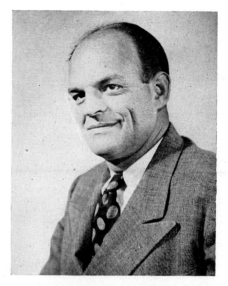

JOSEPH E. CURRAN

nism in 1939, as well as to later charges in which evidence was submitted, Curran and his spokesmen retorted that such evidence was forged.

In July 1940 the Greater New York Industrial Union Council was organized—an affiliation of one hundred eighteen local CIO unions that corresponded to the Central Trades and Labor Council of the A. F. of L. Joseph Curran was unanimously elected president of the council, which represented between three hundred fifty and four hundred thousand local union workers. One of the resolutions adopted stated that "labor has declared its willingness and desire to cooperate in a genuine and effective program of national defense, the true cornerstone of which is the protection of labor's rights of self-organization and collective bargaining." Curran now held a position of considerable influence in labor circles.

Soon, however, charges arose that Curran was "using his office in the CIO . . . council for partisan purposes." Some resentment against certain of his acts came from within the more conservative CIO membership. These members disapproved of a telegram sent by him asking local unions to support the emergency peace mobilization in Chicago in August 1940, before the United States entered the war. Curran then said: "In my opinion, the mobilization of peace sentiment in this country is by far the most important issue facing the labor movement today." Of the group protesting his stand he said: "If these unions were as quick to protest conscription as they are to protest against the Chicago peace mobilization, they would be working in the interests of organized labor. . . .If it wasn't the peace telegram it would be something else. There are certain forces at work in this city to hamper the organization of the unorganized and destroy the prestige of the CIO." Later in 1940 his endorsement of John L. Lewis [42] (when Lewis called for the defeat of Roosevelt [42]) and his opposition to Lend-Lease contributed to the split in the CIO, with Sid-

CURRAN, JOSEPH E.—*Continued*

ney Hillman[40] leading the faction that endorsed aid to Britain, and the Communists supporting the isolationist stand. Curran, it was argued, had been forced into his Lewis endorsement by the Communists. (Curran at this time was running for Congress on the American Labor Party ticket.) Curran, however, issued a call in May 1941 for seamen who had gone into other fields to return to merchant ships to assist during the emergency.

After the Nazi invasion of Soviet Russia, the N.M.U. reversed its isolationist stand, leaving Curran to answer a good deal of criticism. At the union's national convention in July 1941 he declared, "We recognize the present struggle of Great Britain and the Soviet Union against the forces of fascism to be sincere and requiring the full support of all liberty-loving people throughout the world." He declared that the N.M.U. would not abandon its drive for higher wages and improved working conditions. But his proposal that all seamen on the East and West coasts and on the Gulf unite under the banner of the N.M.U. was flatly rejected by an official of the Seafarers International Union of the A. F. of L. At its convention the N.M.U. also voted down a "Red inquiry" move—a proposal that an outside trial board be set up to investigate the charges of communism against Curran—and it adopted a resolution for discontinuance of the Dies Committee. Curran has also defeated other moves to investigate N.M.U. membership.

After the United States entered the war Curran devoted himself to the war effort. At the national council meeting of the N.M.U. in 1942 he said that everything must be subordinated to the one great task—that of defeating Hitler[42] and the Fascist aggressors: "As seamen, our major task is to man the ships, even at great personal sacrifice, and guarantee the delivery of the vital war materials and supplies to every part of the world where our forces and those of our allies are fighting." He was reported to be especially pleased when a Liberty freighter, the *Booker T. Washington*, was put in charge of a Negro captain, with both white and Negro officers serving under him: Curran had been the first maritime leader to welcome Negroes into his union. In March 1943 Curran announced to the State Department that his union had refused to man ships carrying goods to Spain. That same year, in July, he accused the War Shipping Administration of misinforming the public by its complaint that there were not enough vessels for wartime shipping. There were hundreds of vessels, Curran claimed, lying idle, or being used for unnecessary luxury shipping. There was no shortage of seamen either, he stated. He also demanded a second front in Europe.

The war years continued to be stormy ones for both Curran and his union, although Admiral Russell Waesche[45], Commandant of the Coast Guard, paid tribute to the work of the merchant marine in the war, and Anna Rosenberg[43], regional director of the WMC, commended the N.M.U. for keeping its wartime no-strike pledge. But charges and countercharges continued to come from other quarters. In early 1943 the N.M.U. faced the

charge—denied by the Army and Navy as well as by the union—that union seamen would not unload ships at Guadalcanal. Four million dollars' worth of libel suits were brought by the N.M.U. that year.

That same year, Curran and Westbrook Pegler[40], the well known columnist, "tangled." Part of the fireworks were set off over the union leader's draft status, Pegler raising the "fellow traveler" charge, and accusing Curran of draft-dodging. The union leader's draft board had deferred him as an essential worker whose job it was to keep American merchant ships manned. Curran claimed that he had not asked for this status, but had petitioned the board to let him serve as a merchant sailor. In September, while Curran was overseas investigating conditions of merchant mariners abroad, he was granted a new deferment, then the same month transferred to 1-A. (Curran had not notified his draft board before going abroad, and his deferment had expired in his absence.) Leon Henderson[40] came to his defense, declaring that the reclassification was motivated at least in part by "disagreement with Curran's policies and his extreme Leftist political views. . . .If the draft can be used to punish Joe Curran, none of us are safe." The newspaper *PM* also called the situation "an outrage," declaring, while "we don't agree with Curran, that isn't the issue here, and in this fight we're in his corner."

When Curran arrived back in the United States he appeared before his draft board, explaining that he had had no intention of violating the Selective Service Act. The local board considered his explanation satisfactory, and his union appealed his 1-A status to President Roosevelt. The President heeded the appeal, and on November 6 Curran was again reclassified as 2-A for six months, thus removing all possibility that he would be drafted, since by that time he would be over draft age. Commented Westbrook Pegler: "It was a foregone conclusion. . . .Thus the Navy Department protects the Navy's enemies." The Presidential order was also criticized by certain Congressmen, including Senators Harry F. Byrd[42] of Virginia and E. H. Moore of Oklahoma.

Curran's overseas trip also came under attack, while the labor leader himself made countercharges. He claimed that the State Department had delayed his request for a passport, so he had shipped out on his seaman's passport. "When we arrived at a North African port every member of the crew was given shore leave," he declared, "with one exception—Joseph Curran." He reported that he was told if he stepped down from the gangplank he would be shot on sight. "I can only think that some interests in the State Department wanted to keep me from seeing things." Nonetheless, he said, he learned enough to ascertain that merchant mariners were "not being treated as they should be, although they are delivering and working under adverse conditions." In various undisclosed ports he said he had found that ship survivors (merchant seamen) lacked proper medical care, or were neglected by consular officials.

Curran made more news early in 1944 when he was one of the few labor leaders to support President Roosevelt's call for a national service act. "There is no terror in a national service law," he said, "for ever since Pearl Harbor we have imposed one on ourselves, voluntarily." The more Right-wing groups of the CIO stood behind Philip Murray [41] in opposition. But by January 27 the Left-wing leaders reversed their stand, lining up solidly with the rest of the CIO and a resolution opposing the Austin [44]-Wadsworth [43] bill was unanimously adopted.

At the Truman [45] Senate committee meeting in Washington on March 8 Curran defended the Liberty ship as a sound cargo vessel, following a charge that they "cracked up" under stress of war service. Curran said in addition that certain groups and newspapers were trying to make political capital out of reports about Liberty ship failures. He joined with other progressives in the organization of the National Citizens Political Action Committee; and he was among those to demand a special session of the New York State Assembly to amend the State War Ballot Law to extend full voting rights to members of the merchant marine and other services outside the United States who could not vote under the State law. (Merchant seamen were not considered servicemen in the meaning of the act.) In April he joined with Basil Harris, president of the United States Lines, in urging for merchant seamen benefits such as those afforded war veterans by the GI Bill of Rights

In July 1945 Curran and the N.M.U. picketed the War Shipping Administration offices in Washington—Curran insisting that it was not a strike but a publicity campaign for a basic fifty-five-cent hourly wage. The war risks bonus paid to seamen on the Atlantic run, which had boosted the take-home wage from little more than twenty dollars a week to about fifty, had been cut by two-thirds by the Maritime War Emergency Board after the surrender of Germany. While Curran conceded that as the war risks went down the bonus would have to go too, he and his union had no intention of going back to prewar wages. In August 1945, when strikes and lay-offs followed close on the heels of victory over Japan, the Greater New York Council of CIO demanded in a rally that Congress adopt a full employment bill, a sixty-five-cent minimum hourly wage bill, and an unemployment insurance bill providing twenty-five dollars a week for six weeks. Early in September the WLB approved an increase of forty-five dollars a month in the base pay of seamen, to take effect immediately upon elimination of the war risks bonus on October first. During the New York strike of the International Longshoremen's Association in October the N.M.U. supported the rank and file committee of the A.F. of L. affiliate against the leadership of I.L.A. President Ryan. In the course of this controversial strike, the Greater New York CIO Council denied charges of interfering in the internal affairs of the I.L.A., while urging support of the strike for "improved wages and working conditions, and for their [the strikers'] right to a voice in their own affairs."

During the last months of 1945 Curran led an N.M.U. campaign for the speedy return of servicemen from overseas, urging the Government to use every available ship to bring the GI's home. This bring-the-boys-home-by-Christmas campaign was climaxed on December 3 by a twenty-four-hour work stoppage on commercial cargo ships in Atlantic, Gulf, and Pacific ports, excluding vessels carrying troops and relief supplies.

In February 1945 Curran was one of the delegates meeting in London for the purpose of organizing a new world labor body which (unlike the International Federation of Trade Unions) would include representation from the CIO and labor delegates from Russia. On their return to the United States the CIO delegates were prominent speakers at a world unity rally held on March 12 at Madison Square Garden, New York. Curran presided at the rally, which urged the A.F. of L. to join the new movement: "The formation of the new world labor movement provides ample opportunity for the A. F. of L. to come back into the international house of labor, which we strongly urge, and participate with other international labor organizations in the perfection of a peaceful and democratic world." As a CIO delegate to the World Trade Union Conference in October, Curran was present at the Paris sessions when the new World Federation of Trade Unions was formed. Shortly thereafter he was a member of the CIO delegation which visited Moscow, the first trade union delegation to go to that country since 1927. Curran and the entire delegation endorsed the proposal made by Soviet labor leaders to set up an American-Soviet trade union committee to facilitate co-operation between American and Russian workers. A month later, in November, the maritime leader was an alternate delegate of the CIO at the labor-management conference in the Capital.

In addition to his activities on behalf of labor unions, Joseph Curran also serves as a member of the regional board of the War Manpower Commission. He writes a weekly column for the *Pilot*, the official N.M.U. paper, and is the author of a number of pamphlets published by the union, including *Pork Chops and Politics, Take the Helm*, and *Listen, Brothers!* He was married to Retta Toble, a former "shipmate" on the Grace Line, in 1939, and has one son, Joseph Paul, born in December 1943. The busy union leader has never had much time for hobbies. One time, back in 1931, he thought he would like to raise prize dogs, feeling that might be more profitable than going to sea. He went so far as to buy eleven spitzes in Odessa, but after caring for the unhappy dogs and five new puppies in the ship's storeroom, he gave up the venture. His most recent hobby and recreation has been photographing his young son.

References

Bsns W p48 Ja 25 '41 por
Fortune 16:123+ S '37 il por
N Y Sun p22 O 29 '40; p21 O 5 '43
Time 42:23 S 27 '43 por

Who's Who in America, 1944-45

CURTIN, JOHN (kûr'tĭn) Jan. 8, 1885—July 5, 1945 Australian politician; member (1923-31, 1934-41) and leader of Labor Party (1935-41) in the Commonwealth Parliament; Prime Minister and Minister for Defense from 1941 to his death; editor of *Westralian Worker* (1917-28); Australian delegate to International

CURTIN, JOHN—*Continued*
Labor Conference at Geneva (1924). See *Current Biography* 1941 Yearbook.

Obituary
N Y Times p1+ Jl 5 '45 (por p13)

CURTIS, ANN Mar. 6, 1926- Swimmer
Address: b. c/o Crystal Plunge Pool, 775
Lombard St., San Francisco

Champion amateur swimmer of the United
States, Ann Curtis since mid-1943 has set
national and world records unequaled in the
history of women's competitive swimming.
Although commentators say that in 1945 she
has not yet reached the peak of her perform-

ANN CURTIS

ance (a woman swimmer usually reaches her
peak between nineteen and twenty-one), Miss
Curtis is already considered "the greatest
free-styler ever developed in the United States
—perhaps anywhere." Holder of seven national titles, two world records, and eighteen
American records, "the queen of the amateurs" has received the James E. Sullivan
award as the outstanding athlete of 1944.

Ann Curtis was born in San Francisco on
March 6, 1926, the daughter of Marvin Curtis,
Jr., and Florence Gertrude (Donohue) Curtis.
Ann became interested in swimming when
she was about nine years old. While the
girl was attending Ursuline Convent School at
Santa Rosa, California, one of the teachers
noticed her ease of movement in the water
and suggested that she swim at least an hour
each day, a pastime Ann found very pleasant.
After a year and a half at the convent, she
returned to San Francisco to continue her
elementary education at Commodore Sloat
Grammar School. These were busy days for
little Ann. Besides going to school, she
helped her mother at home, in their "guest
house," by waiting on tables and washing
dishes. "At one time," Miss Curtis says, "my

future interest in swimming was threatened
by an antipathy for water developed by association with sinks full of dirty pots and pans.
If swimming pools had suds on them, I'd
probably be a golfer or a soft-ball pitcher."

Ann spent her free time at the Jewish Community Center of San Francisco, receiving
instruction from the pool director, Charlie
Duhamel. Duhamel, impressed with her
prowess, entered the eleven-year-old swimmer
in the 1937 Amateur Athletic Union Championships in the city, in the free-style race for
girls under sixteen. With little effort, Ann
swam to victory. That fall she broke her first
authentic record, winning the 100-yard event in
the Pacific Coast Senior meet with a speed of
1:10. In the two years following she continued to win in minor competitions, but
threatened no other records. According to
Duhamel, she "lacked the imagination to be a
champion."

In 1939 the young girl began to study
aquatic ballet with Phil Patterson at the Fair-
mont Hotel in San Francisco, going to the
pool after her classes at the Roosevelt Junior
High School. After a year and a half of
these lessons she realized that she was more
interested in competitive swimming. In 1940
she therefore entered the 440-yard free-style
event in the West Coast Championships, but
in this race she finished seventy yards behind
the winner—"I was fat and short-winded,"
says Miss Curtis. On the advice of her mother
the discouraged future champion placed herself under the direction of Charles Sava, the
famous racing coach, at the Crystal Plunge
Club in the city.

Sava immediately set up a vigorous two-
hour daily routine for the young swimmer
to develop her arms and legs. ("I lost seven
pounds in the first ten days with Sava," she
says.) Realizing that her long arms might
handicap her in the shallow part of pools, the
instructor taught her a lateral arm stroke in
which her fingers are never more than two
feet beneath the surface of the water. He
also began intensive training on her knee action, since it is his belief that most girl swimmers rely too much on their arms. To develop
her leg power, "he looped a rope through a
pulley above the pool, attached a nine-pound
weight to that and lashed the other end to
her ankles. For thirty minutes [each day]
she kicked against this drag to force her way
through the water without using her hands.
After that Sava would bind her ankles and
dunk her, with only her arms between her
and complete immersion, something after the
manner of Jack Kearns in sending Jack
Dempsey[45] against bloodthirsty sparring partners with his right arm lashed behind him."

It was not until June 1943 that Sava, certain
that Miss Curtis was champion material, entered her in the Far Western Championships
in San Francisco. (Before the race Sava advised her to "just go in and get loosened up.")
Far from disappointing him, she broke Ann
Petty's eight-year-old record for 220 yards,
and won the 440-yard race by thirty feet. In
July she set an American woman's mark of
1:01.8 for the 100-yard event, defeating Brenda Helser, the reigning national champion.
During that month Miss Curtis also broke the
200-yard record, and in November the 500-

meter record. In December she was chosen by the Pacific Association of the A.A.U. as the outstanding woman athlete of the West Coast for 1943.

In 1944 Miss Curtis broke a record almost every time she participated in a swimming match. Competing in the National Indoor Championships at Oakland in May, the new aquatic star set marks of 2:30.2 for 220 yards, 2:28.3 for 200 meters, and 5:12.7 for 440 yards, but lost the 100-yard contest to Miss Helser. Two months later she broke her own records for 400 meters, 440 yards, and 500 yards established earlier that year. In July Miss Curtis achieved international fame. In the 880-yard free-style swim she finished in 11:18.6, lowering by seven and a half seconds the world mark established by Ragnhild Hveger in 1937. During that month she also set new American marks for the 800-meter and 880-yard races, (In the latter race she passed the 800-meter mark at a speed which broke the world record for the distance. Without stopping she finished the course, setting another record for the full distance of 880 yards.) In the three-day A.A.U. Women's National Swimming Championships at Kansas City, Missouri, in August, Miss Curtis became the third person in swimming history to score a "grand slam" by winning four national free-style titles—she won the 100-, 400-, 800-, and 1,500-meter free-style swims.

At the National A.A.U. Women's Indoor Swimming Championships held at Chicago's Town Club Pool in April 1945, the Crystal Plunge team, composed of Ann Curtis, her sister Sue, and four others, won with forty-seven points. Vying with Brenda Helser (considered one of the finest swimmers in the country) in the 100-yard event, Miss Curtis was behind her for most of the distance, but edged by her in the last fifteen yards to take the only important A.A.U. title she had not already held. She also defended her 220- and 440-yard titles, and finished the 440-yard event in 5:30.9, "loafing all the way." Miss Curtis' individual achievements, coupled with the team's victory in the 400-yard free-style relay, made the Crystal Plunge team the victors of this meet.

At the end of this swimming contest Miss Curtis was presented with the James E. Sullivan Memorial Trophy for 1944, which is awarded annually to the outstanding amateur athlete of the year. She is the first woman and also the first swimmer to receive the trophy in the fourteen years of its existence. The inscription on the trophy reads: "National A.A.U. Champion, 100, 400, 880, 1,500 meters outdoors, and 220 and 440 yards indoors. [She now also holds the 100-yard championship.] 1944-holder of two world and eighteen American records. The world records: 800 meters and 880 yards, 11:08.6. By reason of her qualities of leadership, strength of character, force of personality, high ideals of amateurism, and excellence of performance, she was selected by a tribunal of 800 sports leaders as the amateur athlete who did most in 1944 to advance the cause of sportsmanship."

The "Curtis Crawl," which is responsible for the swimmer's grace and speed, demonstrates her fine arm and leg synchronization. Her powerful legs produce a thrust when she dives into the water. She hits in a flat position, in order not to sink too low, with chin forward, water line at forehead, shoulder level with the surface of the water, and arms extended. Her movements in the crawl consist of eight leg beats to one complete arm cycle. The swimmer's speed in the water is attributed to her powerful shoulder muscles and this forceful leg drive. Says Sava: "Ann is just about the greatest girl swimmer this country has ever produced, and should there be postwar Olympics, she'll be in there splashing and winning."

Miss Curtis was graduated from Washington High School in San Francisco in June 1944, and enrolled in the University of California, where she began taking home economics courses. Pretty, with a well-proportioned figure, the swimmer has had several offers to appear in motion pictures, but she has refused them, for she does not like doing water ballets, which the movies usually feature, and she is eagerly waiting for the next Olympics.

In typical American schoolgirl fashion, she usually wears bobby socks, skirts, and blouses or sweaters, and ties a scarf over her short chestnut hair. When she is on dry land Miss Curtis will sometimes play badminton and table tennis, which she is said to do well. She also devoted some of her time during the war to volunteer work for the Red Cross. Her biggest problem in rubber-scarce 1945 was bathing caps. Early in the year she had only two left. "If anything happened to them," said the swimmer, "I'd be sunk."

References

Collier's 115:44+ Je 9 '45 por
Life 17:41+ S 18 '44 por; 18:94+ Ap 30 '45 pors
Look 9:56+ My 15 '45 il pors
N Y Herald Tribune (This Week) p13 Je 17 '45 por
Newsweek 25:85-6 Ja 15 '45 por
Time 45:53 Ag 28 '44; 45:66 Ap 23 '45 por

DALLIN, CYRUS EDWIN (dăl'ĭn) Nov. 22, 1861—Nov. 14, 1944 Dean of New England sculptors; creator of many widely known works on exhibit in museums and public buildings throughout the United States; two famous pieces are the statues of Paul Revere, in Boston, and of Sir Isaac Newton, in the Library of Congress.

Obituary

N Y Times p27 N 15 '44 por

DALTON, HUGH 1887- British Government official; economist

Address: b. House of Commons, London; h. West Leaze, Aldbourne, Wiltshire, England

The Chancellor of the Exchequer, the second highest Cabinet officer of the United Kingdom, has since July 1945 been the Right Honorable Hugh Dalton, M.P., P.C. A Socialist economist of high standing and an authority on international trade, Dalton had been a Labor Party member of Parliament for many years and had served in Winston Churchill's War Cabinet as Minister of Economic Warfare. As President of the Board of Trade, he had for three years controlled Britain's economy when the general election of 1945 swept

British Official Photo.

HUGH DALTON

the Laborites into power for the first time in sixteen years, and Prime Minister Clement Attlee^{'40} appointed Dalton to the exchequer post.

Hugh Dalton was born in 1887 at Neath, Glamorgan County, Wales. He is the only son of the Reverend Canon John Neale Dalton, K.C. V.O., C.M.G., and Catharine Alicia (Evan-Thomas) Dalton, of the Gnoll, Neath. (He has one sister.) Canon Dalton, himself the son of an Anglican rector, had served for six years as tutor to the future King George V and his brother Prince Albert Victor; at the time of Hugh's birth he was canon and precentor of St. George's Chapel at Windsor Castle; and during Hugh's childhood he was a chaplain in the royal household. "What a loud voice that child has . . . just like his father," Queen Victoria is reported to have said of Hugh—a sentiment shared, then and later, by many less exalted personages. When the boy was ten, incidentally, his uncle Cornelius Neale Dalton became Controller General of Patents, Designs, and Trade Marks, and was later knighted.

Young Dalton studied at Eton and went on to King's College, Cambridge, where he won the Winchester Reading Prize in 1909. He took his M.A. there, and from 1911 to 1913 he studied at the London School of Economics on a Hutchinson Research Studentship, winning his D.Sc. In 1914 he was a lecturer at the school. The same year the twenty-seven-year-old economist also passed the required legal examinations and was called to the bar at the Middle Temple; but he did not begin practicing law until after the First World War. He was married to Ruth Fox in the first year of the war.

Dalton served five years in the Army Service Corps and later in the Royal Garrison Artillery. He saw action on the French and Italian fronts; and in 1917 Italy awarded Dalton what he calls "a nice bit of blue ribbon"—the Medaglio al Valore Militare—for "getting

some guns across the Tagliamento River during an Italian retreat." In 1919 he returned to his economic studies, and at the same time set up his law practice. Dalton's war experiences resulted in a book, *With British Guns in Italy* (1919); they also resulted in a determination to prevent any future wars. The newly formed Labor Party seemed to him to offer the best hope of permanent peace. Its program called for the establishing of a minimum standard of living, and for "the use of surplus and idle wealth for the common good." Dalton "rapidly gained prominence in the party as an economist who wrote prodigiously in support of Labor policy." His books include *Inequality of Incomes in Modern Communities, The Peace of Nations,* and later, *Hitler's War Before and After* (1940). *Principles of Public Finance,* first published in 1923, had gone through ten revised editions by 1939, including a printing in the United States.

In 1914 Hugh Dalton had been attached to the Ministry of Labor for special investigations. In 1922, while he was the Sir Ernest Cassel Reader in Commerce at the University of London (a post which he held from 1920 to 1925), the tall, handsome economist stood for election to the House of Commons from Cambridge Town. According to the British Information Services, he "established something of a record by fighting five elections in thirty months, winning the fifth try in 1924 when he became member for Peckham," a division of Camberwell. (An M.P. need not live in the district which elects him.) In February 1929 Dalton was joined in Commons by his wife, the Labor member from the Bishop Auckland Division; they were said to be the third couple to serve in Commons at the same time. After the May 1929 general elections Dalton was returned to Commons from Bishop Auckland, which is a coal and iron district in Durham. (During this period, 1925-36, he was reader in economics at the University of London.)

When Ramsay MacDonald, the Labor Party leader, became Prime Minister in 1929, Dalton was chosen Parliamentary Undersecretary at the Foreign Office. "He is a highly talented linguist, which is unusual in a member of the British Government of any party," writes Patricia Strauss in *Bevin and Co.*; and he was "an able assistant" to Arthur Henderson, the Foreign Secretary, in the years between 1929 and 1931. He was Britain's representative at the League of Nations in 1929. "With Henderson he negotiated the evacuation of British and French troops from the Rhineland" in 1929-30. As Undersecretary for Foreign Affairs, Mrs. Strauss observed, he was "both able and happy, feeling he was laying the foundations of a foreign policy that would protect the world from war. Then came the MacDonald betrayal of 1931 [when the Laborite Prime Minister left the party]. Although Dalton is regarded as overwhelmingly ambitious, he refused MacDonald's blandishments and unhesitatingly stood with his colleagues in the Labor movement."

In the subsequent election he lost his seat, as did a large number of other Labor Party members. He then returned to the London School of Economics as a lecturer, and while there wrote *Practical Socialism for Britain* (1935), now a standard work in the field. Since 1931 he has also written widely on international relations, and is, says Mrs. Strauss, "the principal drafter of resolutions and pamphlets for the Labor Party on all matters of foreign policy. With all his Labor colleagues, except the convinced pacifists in the movement, he recognized that fascism was a menace which must be opposed even if it meant resisting with armed force." Dalton had an opportunity to see fascism at work in his travels, which took him throughout Europe and the United States. "From the time Adolf Hitler [42] came to power in Germany in 1933," says the New York *Times*, "Mr. Dalton strove to persuade the Parliamentary Labor group to abandon its opposition to rearmament, which was done in 1937." In 1935 he was again elected member from Bishop Auckland. Dalton is said not to have had great personal popularity, although his hard work and driving forcefulness made him "the strong man of the Party." (In 1936-37 he was chairman of its National Executive.)

The Second World War brought Dalton into the Cabinet. The economist, who had been "one of the most bitter critics of the Baldwin and Chamberlain governments and of the Ministry of Economic Warfare," was handed the latter portfolio in May 1940, when Conservative Winston Churchill formed his Coalition Government, in which Attlee became Lord Privy Seal. Dalton undertook a task which the Associated Press described as "much bigger than the Ministry of Blockade, which was the only comparable office in the . . . War Cabinet, since it takes in the whole field of closing the seas of the world to Axis commerce, fighting in world markets for essential supplies, and directing bomber squadrons to hit where the dictators' internal economy will be hurt worst." During the Battle of Britain he "slept in a basement shelter amid boiler pipes, where he was often found reading at 4 A.M.," and "often embarrassed his staff by appearing at his office before 8 A.M. . . . When an air raid was on, he was more likely to be found on the roof than in a shelter. He put out a number of incendiaries himself and had a close call when a bomb blew out the windows of his office and two of his staff were fatalities."

In 1942 Dalton became President of the Board of Trade, a post corresponding to the American Secretary of Commerce; as such, "the long sequence of decrees framed by him have had more effect on the lives of men, women and children in England than those of any other Minister, with the exception of Lord Woolton [40], the Food Controller." "Utility" and "austerity" were the key words in Dalton's program; he made shabbiness patriotic. "Not a box of tin tacks can be sold in a village store in the most obscure corner of Britain's countryside without the tacit permission of Mr. Dalton," wrote Augustus Muir. "He has a stranglehold upon everything save the contents of the pantry. . . . If anything is notable for its absence, it is a grumble about the Dalton austerity drive. . . .

"Mr. Dalton," continued Muir, "is not an easy man to work for. That is, he is out to win the war hell-for-leather, and he expects every member of his staff to keep pace with

him. He sleeps in a room next door to his office, and walks straight from an eight o'clock breakfast to his desk. You will find him back at the same desk after dinner at night, and he has a skeleton staff always on late-night duty. . . . Seldom does he see Mrs. Dalton, whose own hands are full with important war work in the Midlands." In July 1943, Dalton took an unprecedented action in denying J. Arthur Rank [45], who controlled a twenty-five-hundred-million-pound motion picture combination, any further extension of his interests in the film industry. Dalton based his stand on the War Time Emergency Powers Act, having no statutory power to prevent monopolies, and was said to have acted on the motion of the Trades Union Congress.

At the first general election in ten years, held in July 1945, the Labor Party had an overwhelming majority. Attlee, of course, became Prime Minister, and Hugh Dalton was given the second-ranking Cabinet post, Chancellor of the Exchequer. Herbert L. Matthews [43] cabled to the New York *Times* that Dalton was a compromise choice between Ernest Bevin [40], who became Foreign Minister, and his rival Herbert Morrison [40], who was named Lord President of the Council and Parliamentary leader. Sir Stafford Cripps [40], the brilliant "problem child" of the party's Left wing, replaced Dalton on the Board of Trade—two appointments which the conservative *Daily Mail* asserted were unpopular with finance, business, and industry. No doubt the editors were thinking of statements such as Dalton's 1936 pronouncement that the Labor Party program "must contain a substantial measure of socialization, enough to occupy usefully a Parliament five years long. The Bank of England and the armaments industry . . . would not, in my opinion, be enough. We should, I think, need to add coal, and some at least of its by-products, and electric power, and a large part of transport, and to provide for a rapid increase in the public ownership of land and for effective economic planning, including public control of new investment and the volume of credit. . . . Socialists could not claim less and still hope to deal with unemployment." The platform on which Labor had won the election included these points plus immediate broadening and increasing of social security, and Government control of housing, employment, and agriculture.

While the Labor Government at first moved slowly in its nationalization policy, it moved nevertheless toward "establishment of the Socialist Commonwealth of Great Britain"—not by confiscation, but through "fair compensation." To the Bank of England shareholders, for instance, the Government planned to issue four-hundred-pound securities at 3 per cent in exchange for each hundred-pound share of stock, thereby continuing the very high return stockholders had received for the preceding twenty-three years. Another pressing problem facing Chancellor Dalton was that the United Kingdom must "export or die." He took steps to cut down imports to "absolutely vital" food and raw materials, to conserve dollar balances. In late October Dalton stated that the Government intended to balance the budget only in periods of prosperity, deliberately creating Treasury deficits to stem depressions. That

DALTON, HUGH—*Continued*

November he said, "It is a necessary feature of any financial plan that we should control both priorities and timing of investment so that the projects of greatest national importance come first . . . to achieve our chosen ends—full employment and a balanced development, both for home trade and for export, of all our productive resources." After twelve weeks of negotiations, the United States and Britain signed an agreement providing for a loan to Britain of nearly four and a half billion dollars ($4,400,000,000), at 2 per cent interest over a fifty-year repayment period, to begin five years after the ratification of the agreement. (In December both Houses of Parliament approved the terms after some days of lively debate.)

The new Chancellor warned against "any extravagant hopes of relief from heavy taxation" (during the war even the lowest-paid workers were taxed half their incomes) and predicted a probable greater scarcity of food and clothing. When his budget was presented in October 1945, however, it proved to be an "almost miraculous" one, which "pleased the rapidly dwindling well-to-do by taking a shilling off the income tax when no relief was expected; pleased the poor by landing another leveling wallop on the rich with an increase in the surtax; and pleased big business by reducing the 100 per cent excess-profits tax by 40 per cent." Opposition Leader and former Chancellor Churchill praised it generously. In reading the budget, reported Mollie Panter-Downes, Dalton "introduced, for a Chancellor, a couple of pleasant innovations by sounding jolly and reasonable, which made the first Socialist budget sound more like the arguments of someone with a neat sense of humor and a good head for figures than like the involved, funereal economics through which in past years Britons have had to plow their gloomy way. Mr. Dalton has a mellow, booming voice which indoubtedly would have won him top honors in the church and which is a relief to correspondents. . . .His first budget has shown him to be one of his party's strongest ministers."

A reported later plan of his and Cripps's to devalue the pound, which had been pegged at $4.03, for the purpose of increasing Britain's export market, was said to have been dropped after the United States expressed opposition to it; and a plan to peg all Commonwealth money to the pound, leaving the pound free to fluctuate, was dropped as a result of Dominion opposition.

Dr. Hugh Dalton (who has D.Sc.'s from Sydney and Cambridge) is a powerfully built six-foot man with a bald head and unusually pale blue eyes. He has "a laugh like a high explosive" to match his voice, and is said to dress conservatively and expensively. (Dalton has a comfortable private income.) His favorite recreations, in addition to travel, are chess, tennis, long country walks, and digging in his Wiltshire garden. He has served on the council of the Royal Statistical Society.

References

C S Mon p5 F 19 '41 por
N Y Times p1 Jl 28 '45
New Republic 99:206 Je 28 '39
Strauss, P. Bevin and Co. (1941)
Who's Who, 1945

DAMASKINOS, ARCHBISHOP 1891-
Regent of Greece
Address: b. Scaramanga House, Athens

Since the end of December 1944 attention in the Greek political crisis has repeatedly centered upon Archbishop Damaskinos, the Primate of the Greek Orthodox Church, who has been likened by Pertinax [40] to those bishops "who in the Middle Ages, were as much at their ease storming enemy troops and capturing cities as officiating in their cathedral church." Appointed Regent of Greece on December 31, 1944, the Archbishop also found it necessary to undertake the duties of Premier for a period of two weeks in October 1945 in order to avert complete political chaos in his country. A month later he tendered his resignation as Regent but was persuaded to remain in office.

Damaskinos was born Dimetrios Papandreou in 1891 in Dobritza, in the hill country of Thessaly in Greece. He was one of the thirteen children of a peasant mountaineer family, reports *Time* Magazine, but he is not related to former Premier George Papandreou [44]. As a boy, villagers of Dobritza say, he used to range alone over the mountains. During one of these walks he paused before a picture of the Virgin outside a hillside monastery, put his last coin in the offering box, and vowed to become a priest of the Greek Orthodox Church. His uncle, a well-to-do-priest, continues *Time*, sent him to school at Karditza; and there the boy excelled as wrestler and javelin thrower. After his preliminary training, he entered the University of Athens, where he studied both theology and law. During the Balkan War of 1912 he had served as a private in the Greek Army. In 1917 he took holy **orders**.

The young priest first attracted public attention in 1918, when he was able to settle the nationalist quarrels among the Greek, Serbian, and Bulgarian monks in the monastic community on Mount Athos. In 1922 he was appointed Bishop of Corinth. In 1928 he paid his first visit to the United States in order to raise funds for the alleviation of the distressful conditions which followed the earthquake of that year. Two years later, as Metropolitan (a rank between bishop and archbishop in the Greek Orthodox Church), he again visited the United States, this time in order to mediate the selection of a leader who would satisfy the warring factions of the Greek Orthodox Church in America. Both incidents, notes *Time*, increased his status with the Greek clergy and public.

In 1938 Damaskinos was elected Archbishop of Athens and all Greece by the Holy Synod of the Greek Church. But his majority of only one vote provided Premier John Metaxas, who then ruled Greece with an iron hand, with an excuse to annul the election and appoint Damaskinos' opponent, Bishop Chrysanthos of Trebizond, in his stead. Exiled, Damaskinos sought refuge in a monastery, where much of his time, it is said, was spent with his pet dog and goat beside him, in learning to play Gregorian chants on a harmonium sent to him by a friend in Chicago. There he remained until the German invasion of Greece, when he was recalled by the Synod to replace Archbishop Chrysanthos, who had refused to swear in the first quisling premier, General George Tsolakoglou.

Far from being docile, Damaskinos fought the Germans with the natural weapons of his office. At one time when he attempted to save a group of hostages chosen to avenge the death of a German soldier, he was asked to name hostages. His response was to substitute a list of his bishops with his own name at the head, and the doomed men were spared. On visits to German military headquarters Damaskinos carried a length of rope to hand to irate Nazis with the words "If you wish to hang me, as the Turks did Gregorios, here is the rope." (This, notes *Time* Magazine, which prints the story, referred to Patriarch Gregorios who was hanged by the Turks before the Patriarchate in Constantinople during the wars of 1821.) By persuading Orthodox Greeks to conceal Jews, the Archibishop was instrumental in saving hundreds of lives. His relief work was widespread and included the organization of soup kitchens and the distribution of clothing and supplies to the poor. Through the EOCHA, or National Organization of Christian Solidarity, which he formed among his clergy, he was able to reach the men of the resistance movement in the hills. But for the wealthy who refused to help their fellow Greeks he had only criticism, and when the Greek quislings attempted to exploit the popular EOCHA he resisted fiercely. Finally, shortly before the liberation, the Nazis placed Damaskinos under house arrest.

With the liberation of Greece by the British in 1944, civil strife broke out between the forces of the Left, the EAM, or National Liberation Front, and the forces of the Government, represented by Premier George Papandreou. Papandreou was suspected of being a tool of the Royalists, who wanted King George II [43] restored to his throne at the earliest possible moment. While the rest of the world watched and Russia objected, British troops reinforced the Greek Government forces, quelling some of the insurgents, but the ELAS, the fighting arm of the EAM, refused to come to terms. Finally, toward the end of 1944, it was suggested that a regency be set up for the time being, with a plebiscite on the question of the return of the king to be held at a later date. When agreement on the first proposal— a three-man council with Damaskinos and a representative of the King as two of its members—was not forthcoming, a round table conference, attended by former Prime Minister Churchill [42] and presided over by the Archbishop, suggested that Damaskinos serve as sole regent until a plebiscite would be feasible. And, on December 31, 1944, after Churchill had persuaded King George II, whose consent was necessary in the unprecedented situation, to accept the solution, Damaskinos was sworn in on his "own sanctity."

At the time the new Regent was characterized as a lifelong liberal whose record showed him to have been habitually friendlier to the Left than to the Right, but it was added that he had "little taste for social revolution and no taste whatever for the brand of international communism that seems to thrive among the ranks of the EAM and ELAS forces," who are said to approve cession of Macedonia to Mar-

ARCHBISHOP DAMASKINOS

shal Tito's [43] Yugoslavia. However, reported A. C. Sedgwick of the New York *Times*, Damaskinos was "considered even in extreme Leftist circles to be a true follower of Christian precepts who is not hostile to the evolutionary advancement of their [the Leftists'] views, although unalterably opposed to efforts to seize the State by violence." It was his opinion, Damaskinos said, that Communist forces were acting on their own in the civil war rather than on orders from Moscow, and that in general in Europe there was no wish for revolution but "a great weariness over strife and endless turmoil." Moreover, he hoped that the coming plebiscite would mean the final unification of Greece. With the populace, correspondents pointed out, the Archbishop had won favor through his courageous opposition to the Nazis.

Despite his popularity, however, observers predicted difficult days ahead for Damaskinos. It had become his responsibility to find a premier who could form a Government uniting all or most of the hostile groups in Greece. "It will not be an easy job," commented Raymond Daniell [43], London correspondent of the New York *Times*. "Eight years of dictatorship in Greece [under Metaxas and later under the Nazis] have not tended to develop leaders untainted with the extreme political views of the Left or the Right." On the fourth day of his regency Damaskinos delegated the work of forming a Cabinet to his new premier, General Nicholas Plastiras, the man who in 1922 had forced the abdication of King Constantine by a military coup. Within two months, although the EAM remained suspicious and hostile to the Government, the Regent had succeeded in disbanding the ELAS. But by early April Plastiras had been dismissed. Well-informed British sources listed as reasons his attempt to impose upon Greece a strong military regime under his direction, his appointment of his former henchmen to important offices, and his

DAMASKINOS, ARCHBISHOP—*Cont.*

inability to handle the Greek economic situation.

This time Damaskinos called upon Admiral Petros Voulgaris, commander of the Greek Navy, to form a Cabinet. His administration is said to have "resulted in a definite amelioration of conditions generally," but it too was dissolved after the Regent returned from the meeting of the Council of Foreign Ministers in London. (Although he was excluded from sessions of the council by the objection of Molotov [40], "he had made his presence felt. . . . [and] dramatized the pivotal position of his country in the new geopolitics of the Mediterranean.") An Associated Press dispatch from Athens on October 9 gave as the reason for the downfall of the Cabinet the refusal of the large Liberal contingent to participate in the general elections scheduled for January 20, 1946, an event later postponed to March 31, 1946. This contingent, together with other Left-wing and Republican groups, had been "campaigning for postponement of the elections on the ground that registration lists were not completed." When eight days later (on October 17, 1945) no political leader had been able to form a Cabinet, the Regent himself took the oath of office as Premier and proceeded to form a Cabinet made up almost entirely of members of the previous one. He had acted, a communique from his office stated, because the political crisis could not be permittted to last any longer and because "the present situation in the country does not permit extemporaneous decisions." He would, he said, assume "personally the presidency of the Government until there was a definite settlement of the Government question on a sound basis." Two weeks later, on November 1, the Regent was able to relinquish the premiership to the "liberal and anti-Fascist" Panayoti Canellopoulos, former Greek Vice-Premier and leader of the Unionist Party, who formed a Cabinet preponderantly Republican but with Socialist leanings.

Like his predecessors in office, however, Canellopoulos failed to solve the economic situation, and on November 20 the formation of a new Government was entrusted to Themistocles Sophoulis. The next day a telegram from King George II, stating his opposition to the proposed postponement of the Greek plebiscite until 1948, precipitated a new crisis when Damaskinos interpreted the message as tantamount to abolishing his mandate as Regent. Fortunately for Greece, say observers, Damaskinos' letter of resignation was delayed and the Archbishop persuaded to remain. He is, wrote Derek Patmore to the *Christian Science Monitor*, "still the only moderating and stable influence in present-day Greek politics."

The Archbishop is a striking figure of a man, a "black-robed giant" standing six feet four inches tall, and towering seven feet in height in the head-dress of his clerical office. "Erect, stoutly built, and black-robed, his pectoral cross glittering on its chain, his pastoral staff pointing the way through argument, the magnificently bearded Archbishop has an overwhelming physical presence which seems to fill the room. Everything about him is very much alive. His Tartar-slanting eyes twinkle behind gold-rimmed glasses." During his visit to Greece Churchill found him "towering up mor-

ally as well as physically above the chaotic scene." And Delos Lovelace has written: "Greeks who remember their mythology, passing him on a dark night, might think that the woes of the land have drawn bearded Zeus down again from Olympus."

References

    Scholastic 45:8 Ja 22 '45
    Time 46:35+ O 1 '45

DAVIDSON, JO Mar. 30, 1883- Sculptor

Address: 80 W. 40th St., New York City; Lahaska, Pa.

Many years before Jo Davidson was called "the dean of United States sculptors," a fellow artist predicted that the time would come when "not to have been done by Davidson was not to have been a great man of the period." Since that time the American sculptor has become internationally known as "a biographer in bronze," whose works are seen in parks, public buildings, and homes all over the world. Envisaging his art as a plastic history of his era, Jo Davidson has gone wherever there was an "interesting head," and he has probably modeled more noted people than any other living sculptor. His Hall of Fame contains such a diversified group that a visitor to his studio in Paris once described it as "a 'pot-pourri' where John D. Rockefeller stood cheek by jowl with Charlie Chaplin [40], and Chaliapin gazed at Mrs. Harry Payne Whitney, while Owen D. Young, Samuel Vauclain and Reggie Vanderbilt clustered around Anatole France."

Accounts of Jo Davidson's early life vary— he himself is not interested in clarifying details, for he feels that chronological data are' unimportant; the past, he has told interviewers, has nothing to do with what he is at the present. However, it is known that he was born on the lower East Side of New York City on March 30, 1883, the son of Russian Jewish parents, Jacob S. and Haya (Getzoff) Davidson. As a boy Jo knew the cruelties of poverty, but from childhood he liked to paint and draw, and at fifteen he was studying at the Art Students' League, evidently on a part-scholarship, part-work basis. At nineteen he entered the Yale School of Medicine. Until this time he had never touched clay, but while in New Haven he experimented with modeling at the Yale Art School—and knew immediately what he wanted to do. He abandoned the idea of medical training and left Yale.

Meanwhile, to earn a living, he had become proficient in pyrography, which Richard Beer in an *Art News* article on Davidson described as "that unhappy art which once spread burnt leather sofa cushions over the land and made it pay." Davidson worked as a foreman in a shop where pyrographic articles were made and, by copying a photograph, he executed a burnt wood portrait of Arthur T. Hadley, then president of Yale. This portrait was purchased from an art dealer's window by W. S. Pardee, a New Haven lawyer, who became interested in the young artist and later encouraged him to go abroad to study.

By 1902, though still eking out his income by selling burnt-wood portraits, young Davidson had committed himself to sculpture and he began working with characteristic determination. From 1902 until 1904 he served as apprentice to Hermon R. MacNeil, who was then working on designs for the "Fountain of Liberty" for the World's Fair in St. Louis. In the beginning the young man earned less than a living wage for the rough work done in MacNeil's studio. In 1904 he spent eight precarious months at the St. Louis fair, living on a "strictly hand-to-mouth basis," but he was twenty-one and resourceful, says Richard Beer, and he sold enough pyrographic work at the fair to pay his way back to New York. There he became a pupil of George de Forest Brush, studied again at the Art Students' League, and at the Educational Alliance, an East Side community center. In 1904 he is said to have done his first striking piece of work, a head of his mother; and in 1905 he received his first commission—from W. S. Pardee, for a statue, *David*, which seems to have aroused no interest, though a later work, *Primitive Music*, gained Davidson some critical recognition. *The Faun*, which he modeled in 1906, was probably the last piece of sculpture that he made during this early American period, although he was drawing for the New York *World* at this time. In 1907 he was in Paris, having won a Hallgarten Scholarship.

Although he made frequent trips back to the United States, and his art-business trips took him to many countries (he even went as far afield as Japan), Jo Davidson lived in Paris from 1907 until the beginning of the Second World War. The early years in Paris were bleak ones: he found it difficult to live on a scholarship of thirty dollars a month, and he was unhappy at l'Ecole des Beaux Arts, and left there after only three weeks. "He appears next," wrote Beer, "on foot, with a knapsack on his back, tramping despondently across France in the direction of Switzerland, accompanied only by a Great Dane named Sultan."

On his return from the walking expedition, Davidson was pulled out of his slump by the artist John Duncan Fergusson and set going again. The sculptor did a bust of this new friend, a piece of work which was said to represent his first break with the conventional. The dog Sultan also proved to be a friend. One night when Davidson was sitting in a cafe in the Boulevard Montparnasse, Sultan wandered off among the tables hoping for some gifts of food. He stopped at the table of a solitary lady who became interested in the dignified animal and in the dark young man who, she learned, was his master. The lady was Gertrude Vanderbilt Whitney '41, and not long afterward she gave the young sculptor his first important commission. In 1909 he exhibited at the Salon d'Automne and had a show of sixteen statuettes at the Baillie Galleries. That winter he returned to New York to hold his first exhibition of work in America, in the basement of a Broadway store. This exhibition was successful, and Davidson was hailed by one critic as "a great impressionistic sculptor." A year later he was given the place of honor at the Paris Salon with his *La Terre*.

Although his work was now becoming known and admired, Davidson had still many years of struggle ahead of him. In 1909 he was married to Yvonne de Kerstat, a Frenchwoman of an old Breton family. Davidson, with a fam-

JO DAVIDSON

ily to support (the couple had two sons), was frank about his desire to receive the highest possible remuneration for his work. Guy Pène DuBois, in his autobiography, *Artists Say the Silliest Things* (1940) tells of working in a Greenwich Village studio just below one which Jo Davidson shared with Salvatore Billotti. ("It was Jo's when he was in New York and Bill's the rest of the time.") DuBois and Davidson would sometimes visit over a bottle and discuss their debts—Davidson's were always the more formidable. But the need for money which drove him on did not interfere with the development of his art, according to writers of the period, but rather matured and broadened it. Davidson's financial situation brightened when, in the years just before the First World War, he left France for England. In the words of one writer, "London fell for him." By 1914 he was showing portrait busts of such notable people as Lord Northcliffe, Rabindranath Tagore, Walter Hines Page, Israel Zangwill, Joseph Conrad, and Havelock Ellis; also included in the exhibition of this now-famous series of busts at the Leicester Galleries in London was a decorative bas-relief panel, which was enthusiastically praised by English critics.

The First World War years marked a new phase in Davidson's work. Back in France at the outbreak of the war, he posed as a war correspondent and entered the city of Ghent in advance of the British troops. At the peace conference he acted as messenger for a newspaperman. Later he went to Geneva to model the Soviet delegation. In 1916, when he was summoned to the United States to do a bust of President Woodrow Wilson at the White House, the Davidson home in France served as a hospital for French soldiers. In New York that year Davidson exhibited the portraits and drawings which he had made at the Belgian front. The winter after the Armistice he was given the commission of designing portrait busts of all the principal military leaders and peacemakers: Foch, Lloyd George '44, Lan-

DAVIDSON, JO—*Continued*

sing, Clemenceau, Baruch [41], Díaz, Tardieu, Joffre, Venizelos, Pershing, House, Balfour. In 1920 Davidson exhibited these busts, calling the exhibition "A Plastic History of the War."

In 1924 Davidson traveled through Russia, doing a series of busts of Soviet notables. During the late nineteen-twenties he did a portrait in oils of Andrew Mellon, then Secretary of the Treasury; a portrait bust of Mitchell Kennerley, publisher and at that time president of the Anderson Galleries in New York; and a statue of Senator La Follette, which is now in the Hall of Fame at the Capitol in Washington. Although he is generally known as a sculptor of men, Davidson has modeled some notable portraits of women, including Mrs. Whitney, Gertrude Stein, and Mme. Chiang Kai-shek [40].

Jo Davidson at forty-four was a "good-looking, dapper little fellow," according to a *New Yorker* writer who had known the artist in America and visited him in Paris in 1927. The Davidsons had by that time moved from musty Montparnasse to a Norman chalet in Auteuil, a suburb of Paris, and they also had a country home, an old manor house in Touraine. Davidson's wife, as "Yvonne Davidson, Champs Elysées," had become one of the fashionable dressmakers of Paris. The Davidsons had a large circle of friends and were now "cosmopolitans of note," who gave brilliant studio parties.

The writer of the *New Yorker* article quotes a French critic of this period who wrote of Davidson: "The man's art goes deep. There is a kind of primordial strength manifested in all his curves, his planes, and his masses. His work has not only strength and validity; it has the equivalent of color, form, and movement. His is a vital, impassioned utterance in stone, and alive—like himself—at every pore. . . . Yes, you feel the man is putting every ounce of himself into his work." Davidson expressed his own credo of art in this way: "It is a fallacy to set out with the assumption that there is a scale of values in art, 'bad' to 'good.' . . .My sculpture is neither good nor bad; it is mine because I did it, and it expresses something in me. Art is beyond good and evil. Let us say 'for better or worse, this art expresses us.'"

Before 1930 Davidson had finished a colossal bust of Adolf Zukor, which was later transported to the United States where it is now in the Paramount Building in New York City; he had also completed his statue of *The Pioneer Woman* and had modeled Mussolini [42] in Rome. In 1930 he was in London making busts of Frank Swinnerton, John Galsworthy, Bernard Shaw [44], and other "immortals of this day and age." In 1932 the sculptor returned to the United States for the first time in three years, but his subsequent visits were more frequent. On one such trip, in 1934, Mrs. Davidson died.

Greatly in sympathy with the Loyalist cause in the Spanish Civil War, Davidson spent the summer of 1938 visiting the Loyalist battle fronts and interviewing and sketching members of the people's army. Returning to Paris in January 1939, he completed his statue of Walt Whitman; in October, a month after the Nazis had invaded Poland, he flew to the United States to help obtain ambulance units

for France and to organize exhibitions of French artists called into service. Unable to return to France, Jo Davidson has since that time made his home in New York and Pennsylvania. All the work which he did in France, "thirty-three years of it," was left in Paris; the French Government sent packers from the Louvre, and sixty cases of his art work were taken to his country place in Touraine for safekeeping.

The Walt Whitman statue which was cast in France and sent to the United States in 1939 represented the fulfillment of one of Davidson's long-cherished dreams. "The Good Gray Poet" has always been a favorite of Davidson's (he can quote many of Whitman's poems), and he used Whitman's "Song of the Open Road" as the motif for the eight-and-a-half-foot statue, which was placed in New York's Bear Mountain State Park after being exhibited at the New York World's Fair.

One of Davidson's most successful "artistic head-hunting expeditions" was a six months' trip to South America in 1941, when he visited ten republics to model the heads of their Presidents. The tour was complicated by politics—in Venezuela, for example, Davidson found the Presidential situation so changeable that he "sculpted" both the outgoing and the incoming Presidents. In Caracas, Venezuela, the sculptor was married to a friend from childhood days, Florence G. Lucius, who is also a sculptor and painter.

Since his repatriation the sculptor has taken an active interest in American politics. A stanch admirer of Franklin Roosevelt [42], Davidson modeled a bust of him in 1933, and designed charm pieces and medallions to commemorate the Roosevelt inaugurations; in 1944 he was one of the organizers of the Independent Voters Committee of the Arts and Sciences for Roosevelt, a group formed by six hundred of the Nation's most prominent actors, musicians, and writers for the purpose of bringing about "united political action by participants in cultural activities." Davidson was temporary chairman of this organization (which came to be known popularly as the "Jo Davidson Committee") throughout its campaign for the re-election of Roosevelt. In September 1944 the committee sponsored a Wallace [40]-for-Roosevelt rally in Madison Square Garden. In early 1945 the committee was reorganized under the name of the Independent Citizens Committee of the Arts, Sciences and Professions with Davidson as chairman. (He was given a testimonial dinner in October.) When pianist Hazel Scott [43] was refused the use of Constitution Hall in Washington in October because of her race, Davidson on behalf of his group wired to the D.A.R.: "This indignity . . . is an insult not only to Miss Scott and the Negro people, but to all Americans of every race . . . who believe in the principles of freedom and equality. . . ."

Though he is said to be "downright and opinionated on everything from politics to petticoats," Jo Davidson is also considered a person of broad sympathies and understanding. Since his return to New York he has been active in many groups that have been organized since the beginning of the war, among them the Fund for Jewish Refugees from Germany, the Educational Alliance,

France Forever, and Lidice Lives. He is also active in American-Russian groups.

Davidson's *modus operandi* is interesting. His first approach to a new work is to study the subject for the most predominant characteristic; sometimes a miniature in clay is made before work is started on the actual bust. While the subject is posing Davidson entertains him so that the sitter does not feel the strain of posing. Usually a number of sittings are required for a portrait bust, but when necessary Davidson can do one from photographs or sketches, or even from memory. He did President Vargas [40] of Brazil in "six easy sittings," according to *Life* Magazine, and his bust of General de Gaulle [42] was made from sketches done in a ten-minute sitting during the General's short visit to New York in 1944. The cooperation of the sitter is an important factor in modeling; "it takes two to make a bust," the sculptor has pointed out. Some people, too, are more "sculptable" than others. He considers Franklin D. Roosevelt unique among his subjects, for he had no eccentricities. When Davidson modeled Ghandi [42] in London in 1930 the Mahatma dictated to his secretary during the sittings, but the sculptor refused to let Ambassador Dawes smoke his pipe during his sittings. When circumstances require lightning speed the work of modeling is more difficult, but Davidson has carved "grumpy marshals and nervy statesmen" while they worried and worked, orated, and even ate—though here discrimination was necessary, for the expression on the face of a prime minister eating a steak would not be the same as it would be if the gentleman were sitting at his desk weighing the fate of nations!

Although he has a studio in New York to which he goes several days in a week, Davidson does not do much work there because the "tonnage" of his material makes it necessary for him to have ample space and a workroom on the ground floor. In 1940 the Davidsons bought a one-hundred acre farm in Bucks County in Pennsylvania, and this is now their year-round residence. He has built a large studio on the grounds of this country place and does most of his work there, surrounded by his busts, which are lined against the walls "like head-hunters' trophies." Mrs. Davidson, who has both a professional and a wifely interest in her husband's work, says that he "works like mad until he has a thing finished and then never retouches it." She feels that this intensity of work gives his portraits a quality of aliveness that is often lacking in the work of artists who spend hours working on a small surface.

A colorful personality, Jo Davidson has always been good newspaper copy; reporters like to joke with him and draw him out; that cameramen find him photogenic is evidenced by the frequent appearances of his pictures—with his wire-haired terrier or his current portrait bust. Captions under these pictures describe him as "picturesque," "chunky", "booming-voiced," and, almost invariably, "gray-bearded or bush-bearded." A New York *Herald Tribune* reporter once commented on the fact that Davidson, who is always seeking notable heads to model, had himself one of the most interesting heads to be found anywhere: "massive and square with a heavy growth of curling hair, a full beard, smouldering eyes under thick black brows." Friends and critics never cease to be amazed at Jo Davidson's inexhaustible energy and enthusiasm. "He is so enormously vital that he fills to overflowing any studio he works in with his ideas, his energies, himself," wrote one magazine editor. A loquacious talker, Davidson is "apt to plunge at any time into a diatribe against conservatism, Puritanism, or the scholastic." At the time of the 1944 Presidential campaign he was vehement on the question of Roosevelt's continuation in office, saying "In these times of stress, when we are on the threshhold of a new era, it would be disastrous to break the rhythm." Of that epoch Davidson says, "It's the greatest in history. We are going through the birth pains of a new day." He voiced high hopes for the San Francisco United Nations conference, where he went to record the world peace makers in clay.

Davidson's busts have occasionally been criticized for being too impressionistic; Carlyle Burrows, writing in the New York *Herald Tribune*, said at one time that the First World War busts were "like so many postage stamps, struck off in a hurry"; and Leila Mechlin of the Washington *Star*, in describing the busts of the Spanish Loyalists, said that they were "rough externally." But unfavorable criticisms of Jo Davidson's art are seldom heard, praise by far outweighing adverse comments. "Jo Davidson has a Promethean gift for touching cold clay with fire," said *Life* Magazine; his bust of John D. Rockefeller was said to be "contemporary in any age"; he gave "Gertrude Stein's vast proportions a sort of bland, oriental significance." Of his own bust Paderewski said, "It is my truest portrait"; and when Gandhi's portrait bust was shown in London, English critics wrote that it conveyed "the power of quiet resistance," and " 'great art' would hardly be too high a praise for it." One writer has called Davidson's life "a fabled story of success." It would seem that Davidson has had few failures; but he did see his scheme for the erection of war memorials in Europe abandoned after the First World War—and still has a sixteen-foot statue of a doughboy, the product of two years' labor, as a relic of that conflict.

Davidson was made a Chevalier of the Legion of Honor in 1925 and was awarded the Maynard Prize of the National Academy of Design in 1934. In 1944 he was elected an Associate of the National Academy of Arts and Letters and a member of the National Academy of Design. The Newspaper Guild of New York selected him in 1945 for one of their Page One awards. Some of his most notable busts are: Dr. Abram Jacobi, in Mt. Sinai Hospital, New York City; John Purroy Mitchell, Columbia University, New York City; Senator Robert M. La Follette, Rotunda of the Capitol, Washington, D.C.; President Woodrow Wilson, Princeton University (presented in 1945). In his New York studio in 1945 were busts of Secretary of Commerce Henry A. Wallace, Helen Keller [42], and Ernie Pyle [41].

(Continued next page)

DAVIDSON, JO—*Continued*

References

Art N 32:13 Mr 17 '34 por
N Y Post Mag p35 My 4 '43 por
N Y World-Telegram p21 Jl 23 '43 por
Who's Who in America, 1944-45
Who's Who in American Art, 1940-41
Who's Who in American Jewry, 1938-39

DAVIS, JOAN, June 29, 1912- Actress

Address: b. c/o Lever Bros., 450 Seventh Ave., New York City; h. Laurel Canyon, Calif.

Often called the world's funniest woman, Joan Davis is the comedienne whose audiences laugh most loudly at her grimaces, her comic delivery, and her specialty of sitting down hard. She has been in motion pictures since 1937, and in 1941 first appeared on the radio. She has held high place both on the Crossley '41 and Hooper radio polls.

JOAN DAVIS

The only child of LeRoy Davis, a train dispatcher, and Nina Davis, Joan Davis was born Madonna Josephine Davis on June 29, 1912, in St. Paul, Minnesota. Although neither of her parents was connected with the stage, at the early age of three Jo, as she was called, was already singing, dancing, and reciting at various local gatherings. Three years later an unhappy experience started the child on her way professionally. While she was reciting a serious selection at an amateur contest in St. Paul, she was laughed at by the audience. Not one to be easily discouraged, the young entertainer appeared on the program again the following week with a different act. Presenting a comedy routine, she won applause. Vaudeville scouts were impressed with this precocious child, too, and persuaded the Davis family to allow Jo to tour the Pantages Theatre Circuit. Billed as "The Toy Comedienne," she had a fourteen-minute act.

A tutor accompanied the young trouper and her mother on the road, and whenever possible the child was taken back to St. Paul for a few months' schooling. Her parents realized, however, that as their daughter grew older it was better that she attend school regularly. After the completion of a successful tour of the Midwest, Jo therefore returned home to finish her elementary and secondary education. When she was graduated from the Mechanic Arts High School in St. Paul she was valedictorian of her class and a star of the school debating team.

With high school behind her, Miss Davis was now able to devote all her time to her developing career—improving her style and learning new routines. Certain that her métier was comedy, she studied the technique of various stage and screen comedians, concentrating particularly on the clownish antics of Charlie Chaplin '40. As often happens, recognition came the hard way. Miss Davis during her late teens, played almost every vaudeville circuit in the United States, as well as in amusement parks, summer camps, and Elks lodges. For a time she and her manager had been considering the addition of a "straight" man to her act, feeling that he might strengthen it. In March 1931 a young actor named Serenus (Si) Wills, who was also looking for a partner, was introduced to the comedienne, and that month Miss Davis, now "Joan," teamed up with him. Five months later the couple were married. As "Wills and Davis," the team evolved during the next few years into "a smart outfit." Their reward, after several years of barnstorming, was an appearance at the Palace Theatre in New York City, then the goal of all variety artists.

But vaudeville in the mid-'thirties was on the wane. Aware of this, about 1934 the prudent Miss Davis and her husband headed for Hollywood and motion pictures. (Their daughter Beverly had been born in 1933.) In early 1937, on the strength of Miss Davis' performance in a Mack Sennett hillbilly short called *Way Up Thar,* produced a few years earlier, she was given a featured comedy role in an RKO picture. Although that studio was pleased with her, it made no clamor for her services. Then, Twentieth Century-Fox, taking advantage of RKO's disinterest, signed her up for a long-term contract. From 1937 to 1941 she appeared in about twenty-five films for this company. Some of these were: *Thin Ice, You Can't Have Everything, Time Out for Romance, Wake Up and Live* (1937); *Sally, Irene and Mary, My Lucky Star, Hold That Co-Ed* (1938); *Tail Spin, Day-time Wife* (1939); *Manhattan Heartbeat, Free, Blonde and Twenty-one* (1940); *Sun Valley Serenade, For Beauty's Sake* (1941). Describing Miss Davis in her scene on the gridiron in *Hold That Co-Ed,* Kyle Crichton wrote, "Miss Davis makes flying tackles. . . .She takes off into space in an array of limbs and arms resembling nothing other than an octopus taking a flying test, she ends by falling on her caboose with a crash that not only shakes the stadium but shakes the inherent faith of man in the frailty of woman."

Realizing in 1941 that too many pictures are just as bad as too few, the actress secured a release from her studio. Freelancing in pictures for the next three years, Miss Davis appeared in *Yokel Boy* (1942) for Republic, *Sweetheart of the Fleet* (1942) for Columbia, *He's My Guy* (1943) for Universal, and *Around the World* (1943) for RKO. Of Miss Davis' performance in the last film, the *Christian Science Monitor* wrote: "Miss Davis keeps the laughter going in her athletic fashion, diving over the footlights at one point and being bounced out of a jeep at another. She can clown with the best of them in a comic song." In 1944 she signed a contract with RKO calling for two pictures a year over the period 1944-46, and giving her star billing. She also has a similar contract with Universal. Both of these studios allow Miss Davis to make one picture a year with another company. In 1944 her more important pictures were Columbia's *Beautiful But Broke* and Eddie Cantor's [41] production of *Show Business* for RKO. In his review of *Show Business*, Louis Kronenberger [44] of *PM* found that "Miss Davis in her tart, rueful fashion makes the most of her comedy lines." Miss Davis was co-starred with Jack Haley in *George White's Scandals*, a later 1945 release, in which the role of Miss Davis as a child was played by her twelve-year-old daughter Beverly Wills.

In early 1941 Miss Davis made her debut on the radio. Before this first appearance there had been apprehension as to how successful she would be, since her grimaces, pantomime, and angularity would be lost to the listening audience. Miss Davis, also skeptical about her reception, decided to introduce a new feature. On her first radio show she parodied the currently popular novelty ditty "Hey, Daddy," singing the first few lines, then changing to a monologue for the remainder of the song—"It was a new idea and it was good—and so was she." In August of that year she made a guest appearance on the Rudy Vallée program, *Village Store*. Her interpretation of the ballad "My Jim" was so enthusiastically received that Vallée invited her for another guest appearance within a very short time; in 1942 he engaged her as a regular member of the *Village Store*.

When Vallée entered the United States Coast Guard in 1943 Miss Davis took his place on the weekly half-hour show. Radio critics had doubted the comedienne's ability to handle such a responsibility. To their surprise, however, "the show not only survived, it developed." With the help of comedian Jack Haley, Miss Davis' show grew rapidly in popularity. At the end of the year she was voted radio's top comedienne of 1943 in polls conducted by the Scripps-Howard [40] newspapers and the Cleveland *Plain Dealer*. The same year and in 1944 she also won the *Motion Picture Daily*'s Fame Poll, which represented the votes of six hundred radio editors. According to Jack Gaver, as a result of her poll popularity she appeared as guest star on eight big radio programs within one week. The Crossley and Hooper ratings of January 1944 placed her show among the first five most popular programs on the air. By 1945 the comedienne's radio rating had climbed from the 19.7 of the previous year to 26.0, making her the biggest attraction in radio, with the exception of Bob Hope [41] and the team of Fibber McGee [41] and Molly.

In September 1945 she began a program for a new sponsor, with a staff of six top gag writers, one of the largest writing crews of any radio show. Moving from NBC to CBS, she replaced George Burns [40] and Gracie Allen [40] on their Monday night spot. This new contract is said to make Joan Davis the highest paid comedienne in radio. *Newsweek* reported that, weary of her customary man-chasing routine, she would substitute another characterization when she began her new show, but the New York *World-Telegram* reported after the first performance, "You probably won't even detect any difference. . . .We have Miss Davis . . . running a tearoom instead of a general store. . . .Modes in comedy may come and go but Miss Davis remains the good-humored lass, uneasy about having so much virtue so long. . . .Blessed with a sense of timing that is nothing short of sublime, Joan Davis remains one of the best comediennes in the business."

Five feet five inches tall, with reddish-brown hair and greenish eyes, Miss Davis is much prettier than she is made to appear on the screen. The comedienne is also considered one of the best-dressed women in Hollywood. Fond of sports, she rides, swims, golfs, and rarely misses seeing a Friday night boxing show at the American Legion Stadium in Hollywood. Always on the lookout for mirth-provoking material, she has a gag file that would fill more than a dozen volumes. And Miss Davis' radio program furnishes enough fun for the whole family—Beverly has played her sister on the show, and her husband is one of the writers of her scripts.

References

Collier's 102:11+ O 22 '38 por
Gaver, J. and Stanley, D. There's Laughter in the Air p266-8 (1945)
International Motion Picture Almanac, 1943-44

DAVIS, WATSON Apr. 29, 1896- Science editor

Address: b. Science Service, 1719 N St., Washington, D.C.; h. 1422 Rhode Island Ave., Washington, D.C.

"Science means, fundamentally, the ability to tell the true from the false, the effective from the ineffective, that which does work from that which does not. I'm not convinced the world at large is convinced, *emotionally*, that these truths are in fact truth. That's the big job of education." These words of Watson Davis, director of Science Service, express the purpose of his lifework. For the past twenty-five years he has devised methods for popularizing the study of science in general—"from sun, moon and stars to insects, and from the Maya civilization to United States paper money."

Watson Davis, the son of Allan and Maud (Watson) Davis, was born on April 29, 1896, in Washington, D.C., the city in which he was to pursue his vocation. In the Capital he attended George Washington University, from which he received his B.S. in civil engineering in 1918 and his C.E. degree in 1920. During these years the young student-scientist gave evidence of his capacity for diversified activities in his chosen profession. He entered the

Science Service

WATSON DAVIS

Federal service in 1917, as assistant engineer and physicist in the Bureau of Standards, a position which he filled until 1921, while from 1920 to 1922 he was science editor of the Washington *Herald*. In 1921 Davis also became news editor of Science Service, the organization established for the popularization of science, which was founded that year in Washington for the primary purpose of supplying science news daily to the Nation's press. Within another year Science Service began the publication of a weekly *Science News Letter*, and Davis was appointed its editor. He became secretary as well as managing editor of the organization in 1923. A decade later, in 1933, he was appointed director of Science Service, the position he now holds together with the editorship of *News Letter*.

The original purpose of Science Service has been greatly broadened under the guidance of its director. The documentation division, begun in July 1935 (implemented with grants from the Chemical Foundation and conducted with the cooperation of the United States Naval Medical School, Department of Agriculture Library, the Bureau of the Census, Works Progress Administration, Library of Congress and others), was the nucleus of the American Documentation Institute which was organized in Washington in March 1937. Davis, who became president of the new nonprofit corporation, announced that it had been created on behalf of some sixty national scholarly, scientific, and informational organizations "to attempt solution of some of the problems surrounding publication, bibliography, library facilities and other phases of documentation in fields of research, education and learning." He also stated that the institute would encourage, cooperate with, and in some cases operate services for transferring reading matter to microfilm for use in libraries.

A sponsor of science studies for young students, Davis is also director of Science Clubs of America, organized in 1941, another activity of Science Service, and he has done

much to develop this plan as "an educational force for the future." In the March 1945 issue of *Education*, he called attention to the fact that already the "150,000 boys and girls in these seven thousand clubs constitute the largest science organization in the world."

A co-project of Science Clubs was organized in 1944 for the purpose of finding jobs which boys and girls could fill while they studied science, a project in which organizations cooperated and thus assisted in lessening the labor shortage: the National Aeronautic Association needed surveys for future airports; the Forest Service needed deputy fire wardens and forest conservationists; the Federal Bureau of Investigation welcomed recruits who, by becoming informed, could offset the wave of juvenile delinquency. As a project for the United States Weather Bureau, boys and girls collect data on rainfall which, when compiled by the United States Weather Bureau, will help solve the mysteries of storms. Clubs have also been asked to study nutrition so they may educate their communities on better food habits.

An annual Science Talent Search is another activity of Science Clubs of America. Of an annual average of thirty-four hundred high school students who complete the requirements of this competition, three hundred are chosen for honorable mention. These students are recommended to colleges, universities, and technical schools for scholarships financed by various organizations. Forty students from this group are selected to go to Washington for five days at the Science Talent Institute, where they attend the lectures by outstanding scientists.

Davis believes that, "if the future belongs to youth and to science, there is a vastly more important place for science clubs in the scheme of things that are to be." He also believes the promise of FM radio offers possibilities for science clubs, in the operation and also in program production of science broadcasts. With the war at an end he is at work on plans for encouraging science activity on a local basis among students as young as ten years as well as in adult hobby groups. He also hopes to expand the number of clubs abroad and to effect the interchange of correspondence and equipment between clubs in United States and those in other lands. The age range for science clubs, he concludes, is "nine to ninety, and that may well give science its greatest educational force in future years." Writing in *School Science and Mathematics* (March 1945), Davis stressed the necessity for human beings "to think straight, to think scientifically, if the world is to be rescued from the plague of intolerance, emotional ignorance, and injustice that afflicts it."

In addition to making addresses before educational and other groups, as well as over the radio, Davis has been a prolific writer with a gift for easy and interesting expression. His first book, *The Story of Copper*, published in 1924, was a nontechnical account of its chemistry, history, and the many uses to which it is put in the world. In 1931 he edited an anthology entitled *Science Today*, which consisted of brief papers originally presented as radio addresses by men of science under the auspices of Science Service. His second anthology, published in 1934 under the title of *The Advance of Science,* summarized for the layman the recent findings of research workers in all branches of science. The book received favorable reviews, one of them appearing in *Industrial and Engineering Chemistry*: "We know of no other book of four hundred pages which carries an equal amount of authoritative scientific material in so many different fields." *Science Picture Parade* (1940) is a pictorial presentation of twenty different subjects, among them animals, atoms, electricity, mind, radio, weather. Of it the *Scientific Book Club Review* critic wrote: "Accompanied and preceded by his own [the author's] running comment, the pictures are informative and accurate; some are really beautiful; all are engrossing." Davis' articles in numerous educational and scientific magazines, as well as in Science Service publications, have covered topics such as "Living in a Scientific World", "Creative and Defensive Sciences", "Popularizing Research," and "Flying in the Sub-Arctic."

The scope of this scientist-editor's interest in research is indicated by his membership in the following organizations: American Eugenics Society, Seismological Society of America, Population Society of America, Philosophy Society of Washington, Washington Society of Eugenics, American Society for Testing Materials, American Concrete Institute, British Association for the Advancement of Science, History of Science Society, and Association Française Pour l'Advancement des Sciences. Since 1940 Davis has been a member of the National Inventors Council of the Department of Commerce, and he is also a member of the executive board of the National Child Research Center. He is a Fellow of the American Association for the Advancement of Science, and in 1939 was William L. Hounold lecturer at Knox College (Galesburg, Illinois). Among the scientific expeditions of which he was a member were the eclipse expeditions of the United States Naval Observatory (1925) and Science Service (1932). His clubs are the Cosmos, National Press, Torch, and Harvard. The science editor was married to Helen Augusta Miles on December 6, 1919. Their children are Charlotte and Miles.

Reference

Who's Who in America, 1944-45

DAVISON, F(REDERICK) TRUBEE

(trōō'bĭ) Feb. 7, 1896- Museum administrator
Address: b. American Museum of Natural History, New York City; h. Locust Valley, Long Island, N.Y.

F. Trubee Davison, president of the American Museum of Natural History, was formerly a member of the New York State Assembly and Assistant Secretary of War (for aeronautics) during the Coolidge and Hoover '43 Administrations; and in 1941 he again answered a summons from Washington to take part in the administration of the Army Air Forces during the Second World War, rising to the rank of brigadier general.

Born in New York City on February 7, 1896, Frederick Trubee Davison is the eldest son of Henry Pomeroy Davison, millionaire member of the House of Morgan, and Kate (Trubee) Davison. He received his early education

at a public school, where he was elected president of the student body, and he later was graduated from Groton School, where he was senior prefect. From Groton he went to Yale, which he left in his freshman year, in 1915, to drive an ambulance in France. He returned to the university the next year, however, and there organized an ambulance unit which was sent abroad before the United States entered the First World War. Davison remained in New Haven to continue his studies. That year he also organized the Yale Air Unit, for which he raised funds for the purchase of planes and payment of instructors. Peacock Point, the Davison estate at Locust Valley, Long Island, was the site of the unit's first lesson.

When the involvement of the United States in the war seemed inevitable, the members of the Yale Unit enlisted in the Naval Reserve Flying Corps. Davison was commissioned an ensign on March 24, 1917, and promoted to a lieutenant (junior grade) on May 1. He was ordered to active duty three days after his promotion and served as an instructor of aviation at West Palm Beach, Florida, and Huntington, Long Island, until 1918. The Yale Unit went overseas and distinguished itself in battle, but without Davison. During a practice flight his seaplane had crashed into Long Island Sound and he was invalided for months with badly broken legs and a fractured spine. The doctors predicted that he would never walk again without the aid of crutches, but in time Davison was able to discard his crutches for a cane. He was left with only a slight limp, and now walks without any aid. President Wilson awarded him the Navy Cross in 1920 for his services in the establishment of the flight school at Locust Valley. When he was discharged from the Navy a year later he had attained the rank of lieutenant commander.

Davison received his B.A. *honoris causa* and M.A. from Yale in 1918 and entered Columbia Law School the next year; he received his LL.B. in 1922. Then, before he had passed the bar examination, he was elected assemblyman from his district in Republican Nassau County. He served several terms in the State Assembly, where he was a member of a number of committees and chairman of the Committee on Taxation and Retrenchment. He also served on the National Crime Commission, formed under the auspices of Judge Elbert H. Gary to work for the prevention of crimes of violence in the United States. In a tour of the country Davison made a study of criminal legislation which influenced the adoption of the Baumes Laws in New York and similar legislation in other states. (The Baumes Laws are several statutes enacted in 1926 "providing for stricter prosecution and punishment of criminals. Especially well known is the statute providing life imprisonment for those under a fourth conviction for a felony or certain misdemeanors.") Davison was chairman of the National Crime Commission from 1925 to 1936.

Upon his father's death in 1923 Davison inherited the position of trustee of the American Museum of Natural History and more than half of an eight-million-dollar fortune. It is said that Henry Davison left the major portion of his money to his eldest son so as to allow him to engage in a career of public service unhampered by financial cares. In 1926 thirty-

U.S. Army Air Forces

BRIG. GEN. F. TRUBEE DAVISON

three-year-old Davison was called to Washington by President Coolidge to take the position of Assistant Secretary of War in charge of aeronautics, a post he continued to fill during the Hoover Administration. In 1927 he was commissioned a colonel in the Specialist Reserve Corps of the Army. Five years later, in 1932, he ran for the office of lieutenant governor of New York State on the Republican ticket. During the campaign he was considered a rather inept politician when, addressing an American Legion meeting, he called the Bonus Expeditionary Force "unpatriotic." Davison was among those candidates defeated in the overwhelming Democratic victories of that year.

After serving on the Board of Trustees of the American Museum of Natural History for ten years Davison was elected president of the museum in 1933. The board has been described as "the most exclusive club in the United States," membership being limited to those who are descendants of members, or who are prominent scientists or other specialists in similar institutions. Davison took the place of Henry Fairfield Osborn who declared that his successor possessed "in a large measure the qualities of public spirit, of museum-mindedness, of the love of nature, of determination to put things through, of tact, good judgment, of common sense which the museum needs in all its manifold relations." Franklin P. Adams [41] said humorously of Davison's appointment that he was "the only member of President Hoover's Cabinet to be put in a museum." That year Davison received the honorary degree of LL.D. from Syracuse University, and in 1935 he received the same honor from New York University.

The American Museum of Natural History, of which the main functions are education, research, exhibition, and publication, was founded in 1869 by a group of wealthy men, among whom was the elder J. P. Morgan. Inspired by the urging of a young naturalist, Albert Smith Bickmore, and by the theories of Darwin

and Huxley which had suddenly given a new interpretation to the origin of life, the group resolved to found a museum that would be the "means of teaching our youth to appreciate the wonderful works of the Creator." Unlike his predecessor, who had been in office for twenty-five years and was both an executive and scientist, Davison acts as an administrator, directing the policies and the finances of the institution. The executive duties are under the jurisdiction of Albert Eide Parr, director of the museum. When Davison first became president he gave the museum's exhibits more publicity than they had ever had before and began to develop its educational program, increasing public attendance by one hundred thousand people during his first year in his unsalaried post. In 1937 Davison started a ten-year development plan which called for an additional ten million dollars in endowments. The museum depends upon New York City for about one-fifth of its funds. The remainder is supplied by the endowment foundation and by the sale of publications and memberships. If there is a loss at the end of the year, the trustees make up the deficit. Since Davison has been in office, membership in the museum has more than doubled. It is visited by approximately 4,500 people each day.

On several occasions Davison himself has added to the institution's exhibits. It was through his friendship with Charles A. Lindbergh [41] that the museum procured the plane in which the famous flier and his wife flew around the world. In 1935 Davison with Mrs. Davison, Martin and Osa Johnson [40], went on an expedition to Africa. In Nairobi, Davison recalls, he had the "most exciting and dangerous two minutes" of his life when an elephant charged at him and he fell into a thorn bush. He fired one shot, but the animal was killed by other members of the party. That expedition succeeded in bringing home a group of five elephants to the museum. Some of Davison's letters to his sons written from Africa were published in the metropolitan press as front-page news.

In June 1941 Colonel Davison was called into active service and assigned to the headquarters of the Army Air Force Combat Command, Bolling Field, D.C. He was acting deputy chief of staff and aide-de-camp to General Delos C. Emmons, his duties consisting of choosing and training civilian and military personnel. In January 1943 he was transferred to the headquarters of the Army Air Forces, in Washington. Two months later he was made chief of the Special Projects Division, a division whose function was to prepare and have in readiness a workable plan for demobilization of the Army. Davison acted as representative for the Army Air Forces on the Interdepartmental Group on Material Demobilization Planning and served on the subcommittee on the disposal of transport aircraft under the Baruch plan. He also represented the Army Air Force on matters concerning contract termination and disposal of surpluses directed by the office of the Under-Secretary of War. Promoted to brigadier general on June 3, 1945, Davison expected to be discharged from the Army in the early part of 1946.

In addition to retaining his trusteeship of the American Museum of Natural History, Davison is a trustee of the New York Zoological Society, the National Recreation Association, and the Institute of Public Administration. He is also a member of the Board of Trustees of the New York Trust Company and the Mutual Life Insurance Company. He belongs to the Yale Club, the American Geographical Society, the American Legion, the Elks, and Masons.

In 1920 Davison was married to Dorothy Peabody, daughter of the late Reverend Endicott Peabody '40, who was headmaster and co-founder of Groton. The Davisons have three sons, Endicott Peabody, Daniel Pomeroy, and Gates. (Another child, Frederick Trubee, is deceased.) Davison has been described as an earnest and effective worker who dislikes writing and avoids interviews. He postpones the preparation of a speech until the last possible moment and rarely expresses himself for publication. A good friend of the late Houdini, Davison loses some of his reticence at private parties when he demonstrates the tricks the magician taught him. While once performing the famous mail-bag trick, he found himself so well locked in that his escape in the manner of Houdini was impossible. In his reading he prefers detective stories and biographies to novels, and although he does not care for bridge, he will play poker for small stakes.

References

Am Mag 115:45 Je '33 por
Cue 11:1 F 28 '42 por
Lit Digest 116:9 S 23 '33 por; 117:27 Ap 17 '34 por
Who's Who in America, 1944-45
Who's Who in Law, 1937

DAWSON, BERTRAND, 1ST VISCOUNT DAWSON OF PENN *See* Dawson of Penn, B.D., 1st Viscount

DAWSON, WILLIAM L(EVI) Apr. 26, 1886- United States Representative from Illinois; lawyer

Address: b. House of Representatives Office Bldg., Washington, D.C.; h. 1345 Franklin St., N.E., Washington, D.C.; 534 E. 42d St., Chicago

The second man of Negro blood to be elected to the United States Congress on the Democratic ticket, and one of the two Negro Representatives in the Seventy-ninth Congress, is William L. Dawson of Chicago, Representative from the First Illinois Congressional District. A successful lawyer, he was elected in 1942, and re-elected in 1944 with six and a half times his original plurality.

Born on April 26, 1886, in Albany, Georgia, William Levi Dawson is the son of Levi and Rebecca (Kendrick) Dawson. More fortunate than most Southern Negroes, he was able to attend the Albany Normal School in that state, and then went on to Fisk University at Nashville, Tennessee. He made an excellent record and was graduated in 1909 with his B.A. *magna cum laude*. Although he was twenty-three at the time, the future Representative had never cast a ballot: his Deep South birthplace denied this constitutional right, through the use of technicalities, to those of Negro blood. In 1912, therefore, Dawson left Georgia for Chicago, some seven hundred miles

WILLIAM L. DAWSON

away, a city second only to New York in the size of its Negro population, and therefore offering unusual opportunities to Negroes with professional training. He studied at Chicago-Kent College of Law and at the Northwestern University School of Law.

When the United States entered the First World War in April 1917 William Dawson was thirty-one. Nevertheless, he joined the Army, became a first lieutenant, and went overseas with the American Expeditionary Force, one of two hundred thousand Negroes to do so. Fighting with the 365th Infantry in the famous Meuse-Argonne offensive and in the Vosges Mountains, Lieutenant Dawson was wounded and gassed. On his return as a disabled veteran from the War, he was "greeted in his own country by news of the mobbings and lynchings of black boys because they had come home to the democracy they had helped preserve, wearing the uniform their heroism had glorified" (in the words of Karl E. Downs). (Sixty Negroes and four whites were lynched in the United States in 1918, seventy-six Negroes and seven whites in 1919, and fifty-three Negroes and eight whites in 1920.)

In 1920 Dawson was admitted to the Illinois bar, and began his legal practice in Chicago; two years later, in December 1922, the thirty-six-year-old lawyer was married to Nellie M. Brown. (They have two children, William L., Jr., and Barbara Ann.) It was in 1929 that Chicago first sent a Negro, the distinguished Oscar De Priest, to Congress. He was elected to fill out an unexpired term, and was re-elected in 1930 and 1932. De Priest was a Republican, the traditional political allegiance of American Negroes since the days of Lincoln; but his successor, Arthur W. Mitchell, also the son of former slaves, was the first Democrat of his race to be elected to Congress. (He sat in Congress from 1935 to 1943.) William Dawson was also a Democrat at this time. Although in his native South the all-powerful Democratic Party stood for "white supremacy," Dawson declared he saw liberalism in the national party which nomi-

DAWSON, WILLIAM L.—*Continued*

nated Alfred E. Smith[44] for the Presidency. He became active in local politics, with his eye on an eventual seat in Congress, and was elected State Democratic committeeman from the First Illinois Congressional District in 1930. Before the expiration of his term in this party organization post, he ran for alderman with the backing of Mayor Ed Kelly and was elected to represent Chicago's Second Ward in 1933. After six years in the city council, Alderman Dawson went back into the policy-forming branch of politics as Democratic National committeeman, which elective post he still holds.

In 1942, having won nomination for Representative in the Democratic primary election, Dawson won at the general election, polling 26,280 votes to his Republican opponent's 23,537. On taking the oath of office he said he had entered politics to do his part in "the enhancing of the American Dream [of fair treatment of, and equal rights for, all individuals]." As the only Negro member of Congress, the new Representative was prepared for many trying aspects of his position. On the Democratic side of the House and in party caucuses, he had to sit with Representatives from "white supremacy" states. Nor would a United States Congressman of Negro blood who passed over Jim Crow territory be exempt from the restrictions and discriminations inherited from slavery: Dawson's predecessor had on one occasion been ejected from a Pullman car when it passed through Arkansas. (When the case came before the Supreme Court that body ruled that the action was illegal; if states require separation of the races, they must furnish equal accommodations for all groups.) But Congressman Dawson shrugged off such discourtesy that came his way. "I've got a job to do," he explained, "and I don't want to be distracted from it." This attitude caused the Representative to be denounced by Communists and by those who felt that when prominent Negroes submit to Jim Crow laws they are thereby strengthening the very institutions which humiliate them.

In Congress, Dawson was one of the Roosevelt[42] Administration's most consistent supporters. He did, however, miss a number of votes while in Chicago campaigning for Mayor Kelly's re-election: no vote is recorded for him on repealing the President's order to limit salaries, on liquidating the Home Owners Loan Corporation, on the Hobbs anti-racketeering bill, or on legislation banning subsidies to keep food prices down. He did vote in June 1943 against an increased appropriation for rural electrification. The Chicago Representative used his vote against the Carlson-Ruml[43] plan bill, which "forgave" everybody a full year's taxes to bring them up to a current basis, and for the compromise Robertson-Forand bill in May; also for extending the Reciprocal Trade Agreements Act another two years. In June he voted against the conference income tax bill, which called for a proportionately heavier levy on those with smaller incomes; and against the Smith[41]-Connally[41] anti-strike bill, the compromise Smith-Connally-Harness anti-strike bill, and to sustain the veto. He voted in July to sustain the commodity credit bill veto; in September for the Fulbright[43] resolution fa-

voring the participation of the United States in the establishment of appropriate international machinery to establish and maintain a just and lasting peace; and in November against a rider outlawing the Administration's food subsidy program.

In October 1943 Dawson took the stand before the Senate Judiciary Committee to argue for the anti-poll tax bill. Pointing out that in the poll-tax states school expenditures are less than half the national average and the homicide rate is more than three times as high, he stated, "The passage of this bill will restore the right of participation in National Government to those who most need to raise their standard of living." From a constitutional viewpoint, he maintained, the Congress should act under its obligation to guarantee to every state a republican form of government, for in the poll-tax states "the reins of government are in the hands of a small minority which, by virtue of the control of all state government agencies, has entrenched itself in power, and is enabled to perpetuate itself in power by reason of corruption, fraud, and trickery."

During the 1944 session Dawson voted to sustain the President's veto of the tax bill; against the Eastland-Rankin "States' rights" compromise service vote bill; against an investigation of the Montgomery Ward seizure; and against freezing the Social Security tax at 1 per cent, which is said to be an actuarially unsound figure. That November he was re-elected to the Seventy-ninth Congress by 42,713 votes to his opponent's 26,204. No longer was he the only Negro Representative—for New York's Harlem had elected the Reverend Adam Clayton Powell, Jr.,[42] (Democrat-American Labor Party), who won a seat on the Labor Committee. Dawson himself was assigned by the party caucus to five lesser committees, those on Coinage, Weights, and Measures; Expenditures in the Executive Departments; Insular Affairs; Invalid Pensions; and Irrigation and Reclamation. He began his new term by introducing a bill for the establishment of a permanent Fair Employment Practice Committee to protect the right of every American citizen to employment "according to his knowledge and skill, regardless of race, religion, or national origin." He voted against reconstituting the (Dies[40]) Committee to Investigate un-American Activities as a standing committee; no vote is recorded for him on the May[41]-Bailey[45] bill to provide for limited national service (nonmilitary) for men from eighteen to forty-five, which came up in February. Later that February he had a chance indirectly to vote for the appointment of Henry Wallace[40] as Secretary of Commerce, when he helped defeat a motion to recommit the George bill (to separate the lending agencies of the RFC from the Commerce Department). This made Wallace's nomination acceptable to Senators who would otherwise have opposed it. In March 1945 Dawson voted for the drafting of nurses into the armed forces; no vote is recorded for him on the compromise manpower bill. On Federal full-employment legislation, he supported a strong bill.

Representative Dawson is a big, well-groomed man, with a thin slanting mustache; his voice is described as soft and musical. He is a thirty-second-degree Mason, an Elk, a member of

Alpha Phi Alpha, the American Legion, and the Disabled American Veterans. A 1943 visitor to his office found bookend figures of Lincoln on his desk, and a photograph of Vice-President Henry Wallace in the place of honor on the wall. The Representative sees his own particular mission as winning friends and developing understanding for his own group and for all underprivileged groups. Their particular grievances, he feels, "fade into insignificance in the light of the bigger questions raised by the war. America's enemies now are the foes of all minorities. There is no aristocracy in death."

References

PM p4 Ap 25 '43 por
Congressional Directory, 1945
Downs, K. E. Meet the Negro 1943
Who's Who in America, 1944-45

DAWSON OF PENN, BERTRAND DAWSON, 1ST VISCOUNT 1886(?)—Mar. 7, 1945 Physician to King George VI '42 of England; formerly Physician-in-Ordinary to King Edward VIII (Duke of Windsor '44), George V, and Edward VII; was regarded as "a spokesman in all that concerned the interests and activities of the British medical world."

Obituary

N Y Times p23 Mr 8 '45 por

DELAND, MARGARET WADE (CAMPBELL) Feb. 23, 1857—Jan. 13, 1945 American author for more than fifty years, who wrote short stories, poems, novels, and newspaper articles; although an extremely mild and serene woman, two of her writings were the subject of much controversy, *John Ward, Preacher* (1888) and an article dealing with the evils of war, "Beads" (1918); best-known books are the "Old Chester" tales.

Obituary

N Y Times p40 Ja 14 '45 por

DEMPSEY, JACK June 24, 1895- Restaurateur; former heavyweight boxing champion

Address: b. Jack Dempsey Restaurant, 1619 Broadway, New York City

The spotlight of public attention which is focused upon champions in the sports world usually shifts quickly to the new idols who supplant them. With few exceptions champions are retired into oblivion once they pass the peak of their performance. One of the exceptions is Jack Dempsey, for whom clamorous applause has subsided into quiet admiration. The heavyweight boxing champion of the world from 1919 to 1926, he is credited with "bringing boxing out of the small, smoke-filled clubs into the spacious arenas." Now a successful restaurateur in New York City, during the Second World War he was Commander Dempsey of the United States Coast Guard. But by old and young sports fans he is still called "The Champ."

William Harrison Dempsey, who took the name of Jack when he was twenty years old, was born June 24, 1895, of Indian, Irish, and Scottish ancestry. He was one of eleven chil-

JACK DEMPSEY

dren. When he was very young his parents, who were sharecroppers, made an effort to improve their lot by moving from his birthplace, Manassa, Colorado, to Utah. The boy went to the village school, where he showed little aptitude for learning, but excelled in competitive games: he would, for example, borrow boxing gloves which belonged to an older prize-fighting brother and box with classmates after school hours. His schooling, however, was not to continue beyond the eighth grade, for he then began to shift for himself by working at any job he could get—fruit picking, lumbering, or mining. He also found jobs in pool halls and shooting galleries, where, it is said, his practice in gauging an opponent's skill laid the foundation for his success as a boxer—a keenness in "sizing up the other fellow."

Determined to become a fighter, Dempsey trained tirelessly until punching and blocking became second nature with him. He saturated his hands, face, and neck with brine to toughen the skin. He practiced holding low-crouch positions to foil the punches of an opponent, and chewed gum incessantly to strengthen his jaw muscles and thus prevent a point-of-the-chin knockout. It was at this time that Dempsey changed his two prenames to Jack, his name thus becoming the same as that of the famous middleweight champion, Jack Dempsey, of the early 'nineties. (Young Dempsey's older brother had also been known by that name in his boxing days.) Fortified with a new name and a trained body, Jack Dempsey launched his fighting career. In two years—1915 and 1916—he knocked out practically every opponent he met, but he failed to gain recognition.

In 1917, when Dempsey was twenty-two, the turning point in his career came with the appearance of Jack Kearns, a fight manager. The promoter, appreciating the young fighter's pugilistic powers, teamed up with the promising boxer and set about to secure strong opponents that would develop Dempsey into championship material. The young boxer, just a little over six feet tall and weighing about one hundred and eighty pounds, fought such boxers

DEMPSEY, JACK—*Continued*

as Homer Smith, whom he downed in one round; Carl Morris, six feet four inches tall and weighing 235 pounds, whom he also knocked out in one round; and Fred Fulton, six feet five and one-half inches tall, whom he defeated in eighteen seconds. Newspapers began dubbing Dempsey "Manassa Mauler" and "Jack the Giant-Killer." By early 1919, when Dempsey's boxing record showed a score of victories and only one defeat in almost two years, the boxing world agreed that this hard fighter was headed for the heavyweight pugilist crown.

On the sultry Fourth of July of 1919, in Toledo, twenty-four-year-old Jack Dempsey reached the goal of every aspiring boxer—he won the world championship. The young fighter's adversary was Jess Willard, a huge man towering six inches over Dempsey's head and weighing about seventy pounds more. The fight was still in its early stage when Dempsey, standing on his toes to compensate for his shorter stature, drove his powerful right hand against Willard's midriff and his lethal left hand against his opponent's cheek bone, splintering it into thirteen pieces. Dempsey kept hammering away, until the seventh knockdown. Then Willard, exhausted and badly mauled, remained on the canvas after the count of ten, and Dempsey was pronounced the victor. However, a few seconds later the timekeeper announced that the round had ended before the count of ten, that the shouts of the crowd had drowned the clang of the bell. Dempsey returned to the ring, "finished the job" on Willard in the fourth round, and was crowned the new champion heavyweight of the world.

Even with his new title, however, Dempsey was described as not a completely happy man. The consuming concentration of his youth on becoming king of the ring had crowded out all other thoughts, depriving him of an appreciation of the many other interests of a rounded life. The limited schooling he had had, his rough exterior, and an inability to win personal popularity made him ill at ease with people. In addition, he was charged with draft evasion during the First World War while working in a shipyard. Although the court used his case as a test and acquitted him, there was still some criticism. Then Dempsey, who had little inclination for reading, began his program of self-education by observation and conversation. He became less shy and more interested in meeting people, and a transition set in. Dempsey began to win the regard and friendship of those who had previously shunned him.

Jack Dempsey's title was challenged six times in the seven years he was champion. In his match with Bill Brennan, the second bout for Dempsey's title, it took the champion twelve rounds to knock out his opponent. In the next title bout, the first million-dollar-gate fight in the history of the ring, the Manassa Mauler knocked out Georges Carpentier in the fourth round in Jersey City. In the two fights for the title in 1923 Dempsey no longer demonstrated quite the form that had rocketed him to the championship in 1919. It took him fifteen rounds to win by decision his combat with Tommy Gibbons, and on September 14 of the same year the "champ" fought his fiercest ring battle to retain his title. His opponent, Luis

Firpo, an Argentinean topping the champion's weight by twenty-five pounds, proved a most formidable ring enemy. In the first three minutes and fifty-seven seconds of a fight which brought forth pugilistic tactics in their most savage form, Dempsey hit the canvas twice, and the South American was floored ten times. After being knocked down by the impact of Firpo's powerful right, Dempsey came up fighting, although striking away in vain at Firpo. Dempsey himself has described this fight in New York City: "I never saw a man who could hit so hard and so fast at the same time." Just before the end of the first round Firpo's fearsome right catapulted the champion out of the ring, head first. Dragging himself to his feet, Dempsey, seemingly "through," leaped into the second round like a tiger and, with a powerful left synchronized with a right across, sent Luis Firpo down into defeat. The championship title was still Dempsey's.

On September 23, 1926, over one hundred thousand spectators (a number unparalleled at any other fight) came to Philadelphia to witness the Jack Dempsey-Gene Tunney match—the fight which dethroned the champion. "Jack the Giant-Killer" was no longer an apt description of Dempsey. Loss of form after three years of comparative inactivity, coupled with the fact that Kearns was harassing him with law suits, had reduced Dempsey's fighting skill, spirit, and ferocity. Dempsey was outboxed and, by decision, Tunney was declared the new champion heavyweight in the tenth round. Undaunted and reconditioned, a year later the ex-champion fought Tunney again in an attempt to retrieve his title. The seventh round of this Chicago bout is famous for the dramatic long-count which will probably pass down to posterity as a subject of much controversy in the boxing world. In this round Dempsey knocked down Tunney but was so befogged with fatigue that he failed to rush to the neutral corner as he was expected to do. Instead, Dempsey stood limply over the recumbent Tunney for about four seconds before he collected his faculties and retired to the neutral spot. Only then did the referee begin to count. Dempsey fans contend that his fighting time for the round was shortened so that he did not have an opportunity to inflict a final knockout in that round. After ten rounds, with Dempsey badly mauled, Tunney was named the victor. Commenting recently on the long-count, the ex-champion remarked: "The referee was not responsible; Tunney was not responsible. I should have been in the neutral corner." Dempsey feels the long-count was a stroke of good fortune for him. Had he regained the championship, the next title bout would have resulted in a more intense "shellacking" than the one he sustained in his 1927 encounter with Tunney.

During 1929 and 1930, when not busy with his numerous business enterprises, Dempsey refereed fights, announced matches, and advised aspiring young boxers. In 1931, when the depression made deep inroads into Dempsey's savings, the ex-fighter decided to re-enter the ring. At the age of thirty-six he began a vigorous workout to tone up his body, but found he could not live up to the regimen. Notwithstanding, he fought fifty-six exhibition bouts and gradually got himself into shape. However, a weakness resulting from a case of influenza contracted while on the boxing tour persisted throughout his attempted comeback period. In his fight with King Levinsky in Chicago in February 1932 Dempsey realized that the time to doff his boxing gloves had come. The ex-champ says, "It wasn't Levinsky who made me realize it; it was Old Man Time." Speaking from his own experience, Dempsey now says that champions should refrain from attempting comebacks because they usually are "punch-drunk" (not physically fit for the ring) and are inviting ring disasters.

During his years in the ring Dempsey fought sixty-nine professional bouts. Of these he won forty-seven by knockouts, seven by decisions, and one on a foul; he drew four, there was no decision in five, he lost four decisions, and was knocked out once. Over this period, according to his business manager, the fighter earned about five million dollars.

In evaluating the ex-champion's hitting power, some sports writers have referred to him as "the most powerful hitter of all time." Dempsey disagrees with that opinion. "It's *when* you hit the man that counts, not just how hard," he asserts. Dempsey's conviction is that once a fighter is in the ring he has to fight for all he's worth, every inch of the way. "That's what fans pay to see. . . .That's what makes fighting a good game. Take it easy and you let everybody down." When asked once by a heavyweight prospect how to become the world's champion, Dempsey simply said: "Keep your guard up, your chin down, and your seat off the canvas." According to Gene Tunney, the man who wrested the title from the Manassa Mauler, "Dempsey is the greatest fighter that ever lived."

After 1932 Dempsey continued with his referee work but devoted the major part of his time to his business interests. He became the proprietor of a clothing store, bought a large liquor house, purchased real estate in the form of hotels in Miami and Los Angeles, and opened two restaurants in New York City. The mural in one of these restaurants depicts a scene from the fight that gave Dempsey the championship title. In 1941, just before the entrance of the United States into the Second World War, Dempsey assumed a major job in the "Hale America" program. Appointed Deputy Director of Physical Training for Boxing under the Federal physical training program for civilian defense, Dempsey was responsible for conditioning boxers and getting a physical fitness message to the people of the United States. Said the assistant director of this program: "Not only is Jack a living example of health and physical perfection, but he stands unchallenged as a popular hero."

After Pearl Harbor, in early 1942, Dempsey tried to enlist in the American Army. Although in perfect condition, he was rejected because he was over-age and lacked military experience. He then joined the Coast Guard as director of its physical fitness program. With the rank of commander, he was a Coast Guard instructor and morale officer at Sheepshead Bay, New York. In July 1945 he was assigned to the Central Pacific as morale officer and went on a three months' flying tour of the various combat areas from Pearl Harbor to Australia to see what athletic and recreational training and equipment was needed. Dempsey says his greatest thrill of the whole trip came just before landing with the assault troops on Oki-

nawa. The boys, jittery and worried, relaxed when they saw the former champion and decided, "This can't be so tough if they send old men like Dempsey along with us."

Ending his Coast Guard service at the end of November 1945 with a Victory Bond tour, civilian Dempsey announced that he was signing a contract to head a newly formed fight promotion company at a salary of two hundred and fifty thousand dollars a year, for ten years. The company, he said, was the product of a large advertising concern and would promote prize fights in the United States and abroad. It would specialize in selling to advertisers the television rights to the fights.

Tall, heavily built, his soft eyes described as tiger-like when he was fighting, Jack Dempsey is known for his cheerful disposition and boundless energy. He comes in contact with countless people every day, when his keen faculty for remembering names and faces shows itself. He is also known for his generosity—he is said never to refuse a request from his friends for financial help. His second marriage, to the motion picture actress Estelle Taylor, ended in divorce, and in 1933 he was married to Hannah Williams, the singer. Divorced from her in 1943, he was given the custody of their two children, Joan Hannah and Barbara. His contentment with life nearly twenty years after he ceased being a world champion is expressed in his own words: "The best job I ever had was being champion. The next best is what I have now, being ex-champion."

References

Am Mercury 29:395-402 Ag '33
Collier's 103:16+ Ja 21 '39 il pors
Harper's 179:411-23 S '39
Fleischer, N. S. All-Time Ring Record Book 1944
Who's Who in New York, 1938

DEMPSEY, WILLIAM HARRISON *See* Dempsey, J.

DE ROCHEMONT, RICHARD (GUERTIS) (dĕ-rôsh'mŏnt gâr'tĭs) Dec. 13, 1903- Newsreel producer
Address: b. March of Time, 369 Lexington Ave., New York City

Richard de Rochemont is the producer of the March of Time documentary films which, in the United States, each month reach an audience of thirty million persons in nine thousand theaters.

Descendant of a Huguenot family forced to flee France in 1685 after the revocation of the Edict of Nantes, Richard Guertis de Rochemont was born on December 13, 1903, to Louis L. G. and Sarah Wilson (Miller) de Rochemont. A native of Massachusetts, having been born in Chelsea, he was educated in that state, at the Cambridge Latin School, Williams College, and Harvard University. From Harvard, which he attended during the year 1920-21 and from 1924 to 1928, De Rochemont received his bachelor's degree *cum laude* in 1928. While at Harvard he married Helen Bogart, a student from Simmons College, set up housekeeping, and secured a job as reporter on the Boston *Daily Advertiser*. This made the finding of time for study somewhat of a problem un-

RICHARD DE ROCHEMONT

til he read that the first two hours of sleep were more beneficial than all the succeeding four and his "obliging city editor" permitted him to choose his own hours provided they totaled forty-eight in the week. This arrangement permitted him to snatch his sleep in two hour shifts without disturbing the remainder of his schedule.

After commencement, De Rochemont and his wife sailed for a vacation in Paris financed by a relative. When they returned to the United States De Rochemont was hired by the New York *American*. For a time life proceeded smoothly and uneventfully until an executive remembered an article on tabloids which De Rochemont had written for the *American Mercury*, and the young man lost his job. Following a period (in 1929) in which he reported for the New York *Sun*, De Rochemont in 1930 began working for Fox-Movietone News of New York. In 1931, with only an inadequate command of high school French, he was transferred to Paris as editor of the French edition of the Fox-Movietone newsreels. This meant learning to speak French or quitting. The result was that De Rochemont learned enough of the language to occasion a friend's comment that he had the accent while De Rochemont had the vocabulary. Before De Rochemont resigned in 1934 he had risen to the position of director of the Actualities Fox Movietone.

In 1934, shortly after its establishment as a new production unit by Time, Inc., De Rochemont joined the March of Time as European manager. Shuttling back and forth between his Paris and London offices, he supervised during the next five years such March of Time features as *Croix de Feu, League of Nations, Revolt in France, The Maginot Line,* and *Crisis in the Mediterranean.* He was able to obtain the first newsreels ever made of the Paris executioner, Anatole Dieble, and of Sir Basil Zaharoff, the munitions mogul. For a film on the French grape and wine industry he was awarded the civilian decoration Chevalier du Merite Agricole in 1938. Always he was

"fiercely anti-Nazi." Always his principle of operations was "that truth makes the hardest anvil." The documentary approach to him was "essentially the hard-boiled approach." "Too many of the Hollywood efforts in that field," he asserts, "haven't had that attitude at the core. You've got to face facts."

But the events which finally forced De Rochemont home to the United States were already darkening Europe during the last prewar years, and an attempt to make a film about Poland gave him a foretaste of what was to come. He had found the Polish Government enthusiastic over the project and eager to cooperate. But when he attempted to get the necessary credentials to facilitate his group's progress through the country, he was told that there might be "some difficulty in getting proper credentials" for two of the men—Jews whom he had hired in Poland. Dramatically, it was in Warsaw that he learned of the opening of hostilities when a transatlantic telephone call from his brother Louis reached him with the information that Germany had invaded Poland that morning. With the Nazi invasion of France he was forced to evacuate the Parisian March of Time offices, first to Pont-Levoy and eventually to Bordeaux. At the same time, in 1939-40, he doubled as an accredited war correspondent with the French Army for *Life.* When Otto Dietrich, the German propaganda minister for France, arrived at De Rochemont's abandoned Paris quarters shortly after the capitulation, the producer, his wife and their dog were on their way to Lisbon "in a car so loaded with luggage that it was riding on the axle." "I see De Rochemont had the good sense to get out in time," Dietrich is said to have remarked.

Back in the United States, De Rochemont became managing editor of the main branch of the March of Time, of which his brother Louis was then producer and director. There followed a period in which he assumed increasing administrative responsibility because of his brother's ill health, and in 1943, when Louis departed for Hollywood, Richard de Rochemont was appointed producer. Asked at that time whether he contemplated any changes in policy, he replied: "I am not a reform administration, if that's what you mean. March of Time is a pretty well established institution and I have a good deal of respect for institutions—that is, as long as they behave themselves." During De Rochemont's tenure as editor-producer, the March of Time has filmed such highly praised reels as *Underground Report, What To Do With Germany, Report on Italy,* and *The New U.S. Frontier.* Under his direction it produced in 1941 *The Story of the Vatican* (released through RKO), the first officially sanctioned motion picture of the Papal State.

His concern for some time has been with the orientation of March of Time films in a postwar world; hence 1944 saw him concentrating on postwar themes such as the employment problem and in *Sweden Takes the Middle Road* dealing with a topic "that is at once international, contemporary, and has bearing on the future." A 1945 *March of Time* was *Palestine Problem,* an account of what the Jews had done toward establishing a homeland in Palestine. Envisioning an early and good market for his films in Europe, De Rochemont hopes to produce documentaries which, as New York *Times* interviewer Theodore Strauss phrases it, "see America in terms of the international horizons which have closed in upon it" and "see the international scene as an enlightened American would see it."

When not concerned with the March of Time, De Rochemont's thoughts are apt to turn to France, a country for which he has "acquired a terrific admiration." For several months in 1941—when he slipped into unoccupied France and came back with a strong indictment of the Vichy Government—and after the liberation in 1944, De Rochemont was again war correspondent in France for *Life* and the March of Time. A former vice-president of the French-American Club, he is now national president of France Forever, the Fighting French Committee in the United States, associated with the French Provisional Government of De Gaulle '40. On his first visit to France after V-E Day De Rochemont was decorated as an Officer of the Legion of Honor in recognition of his services to France. What he thinks of France and the French can be found in his articles in *Life* and the *Reader's Digest* and is summed up in his statement: "All the headaches I've had from them have never shaken my conviction that fundamentally we [France and the United States] get along. The French and the Americans share the same faults and the same virtues. I'd like to see France get back into business as a practicing democracy."

The March of Time producer is six feet in height, and his hair and eyes are brown. Called by Strauss of the *Times* "a hardheaded liberal with an ardent belief in the sanctity of the facts . . . [and] an instinctive distrust of conclusions based on anything else," he is said to have "a reporter's traditional inquisitiveness and . . . equally traditional skepticism." During the week he lives in a small apartment in New York City, but his real home, "where his wife is in charge of practical supervision," is the "strictly utilitarian" farmhouse "without a single panel of pine" on his seventy-acre farm at Flemington, New Jersey. He is fond of the movies but says he does not attend as often as he should. Somewhat of an amateur musician, he plays, by ear, a clarinet and an old valve trombone, both of which he picked up in Paris, but "strictly for home consumption and lease-breaking." Reading for the producer consists of material concerning his work, politics, and farming. "My wife reads the Government manuals and I read the theory," he says. "Then we fight about them and she wins."

References

N Y Post p7 O 23 '43

International Motion Picture Almanac, 1943-44

DICK, CHARLES Nov. 3, 1858—Mar. 13, 1945 Former United States Republican Senator from Ohio (1904-11); Ohio Representative to Congress (1898-1904); noted as the author of the Dick Militia Bill, forerunner of the National Defense Act.

Obituary

N Y Times p20 Mr 14 '45

DICKINSON, MRS. LAFELL Aug. 28, 1882- Clubwoman

Address: b. General Federation of Women's Clubs, 1734 N St., N.W., Washington, D.C.; h. 60 Roxbury St., Keene, N. H.

One of the oldest and largest women's organizations in the United States, the General Federation of Women's Clubs, is headed by Mrs. LaFell Dickinson (Lucy Jennings Dickinson), of Keene, New Hampshire. The executive began club work with her local group, broadening her activities through the years to become president of the Federation in 1944. A former business woman, the New England club leader has devoted herself to organization work for about twenty years.

Lucy Jennings was born in Winchester, New Hampshire, on August 28, 1882, to Willard Harvey and Jane (Buffum) Jennings, a descendant of the early settlers. She attended Oak Grove School in Amhurst, Massachusetts, and Brattleboro High School in Vermont. Then, following a family tradition, she entered Mount Holyoke College in South Hadley, Massachusetts, from which she received her B.A. degree in 1905. When her father died a few years afterward Lucy Jennings undertook the management of his lumber business. She also became a director of the Winchester National Bank, the first woman to serve there in that capacity. In the course of her business career, which had begun in 1907, she met LaFell Dickinson, and, she says, "I married my best customer."

After her marriage on October 28, 1911, Mrs. Dickinson retired from business. Later she became interested in club work, and by 1924 was president of the Keene Woman's Club, a position she held for two years. The mother of two children, Jane and Lucy, Mrs. Dickinson was also active in the Parent-Teacher Association movement, serving as State vice-president from 1928 to 1930. About the same time she rose to the presidency of the New Hampshire Federation of Women's Clubs (1929-31). In 1935 she became treasurer of the General Federation of Women's Clubs for a three-year period. Then, in 1941, the New Hampshire woman took over the post of first vice-president in the organization, a position which was followed by her election to the presidency in April 1944 for a three-year term. In assuming this office Mrs. Dickinson became the first president in the long history of the influential organization to come from a small town.

Founded in 1890, the General Federation of Women's Clubs consists of 16,500 clubs throughout the United States and in thirty foreign countries, with a membership of two and a half million. In 1930 its financial resources were more than $236,000. A nonpolitical, nonsectarian organization, it was one of the earliest groups to enter "the arena of political pressure." According to a study appearing in the *Annals of the American Academy of Political and Social Science* in May 1935, it is a potent molder of public opinion. In its many years of civic service, the Federation has worked on projects covering such fields as conservation, civil service reform, education, and world peace. According to its Constitution, "the object of the General Federation shall be to unite the

Underwood & Underwood

MRS. LAFELL DICKINSON

women's clubs and like organizations throughout the world for the purpose of mutual benefit, and for the promotion of their common interest in education, philanthropy, public welfare, moral values, civics and fine arts."

Mrs. Dickinson's program as president of the Federation has as its theme "Home as the Hub of World Affairs," building upon consultation, cooperation, kindness, and tolerance. Under her leadership a Post-War Planning Department had been created in the Federation even while the membership was actively engaged in war service. In a special war bond campaign during June 1944-June 1945 Federation members sold more than one hundred and fifty million dollars worth of bonds. The organization also conducted recruitment campaigns for the women's wartime auxiliary services as well as the United States Nurses Cadet Corps, and the Women's Land Army; it also made wide distribution of educational literature on all existing and proposed international organizations.

During a three-day meeting of the board of directors in October 1944 the Federation planned a broad youth program. Launching a national drive for postwar planning for the youth of the Nation, including co-ordination of all public and private resources, Mrs. Dickinson declared, "This is the most important thing we've ever undertaken." All of the units of the Federation were urged to enter actively into the youth campaign, which will be the organization's chief project for the next five or ten years. In April 1945 the Federation chief called a meeting of fifteen organization leaders to discuss the program and attempt to set up a clearing house, an agency for the integration of activities. Mrs. Dickinson pointed out that the aim was not to focus on juvenile delinquency but on aid to youth in the areas of education, health, and employment. In the early summer of that year she and Judge Anna M. Kross [45], chairman of the Federation's youth conservation committee, con-

ferred with Eleanor Roosevelt [40] on the subject. Soon afterward Mrs. Roosevelt wrote in her column: "I look with great hope on the interest of the Federation of Women's Clubs, which represents such a vast number of women throughout the country."

At the board of directors meeting in October 1944 a resolution was passed endorsing a proposed constitutional amendment providing for ratification of treaties by a majority of both houses of Congress. Another recommendation called for the training of psychiatric personnel as part of the national program for the demobilization of veterans. Early the following year the Federation joined other women's organizations in planning a reconversion blueprint for women in the state of Indiana. This project won the full approval of Frieda Miller [45], director of the Women's Bureau of the Labor Department, who indicated that women's groups "may well work together to develop a program dealing with the problems arising out of this extended wartime problem of women getting into new jobs." In March Mrs. Dickinson met with several other national women leaders to discuss the role of women in the postwar world. She stressed the need for action to get women appointed to policy-making positions, urging that public officers be reminded of the many women qualified for such positions. In April 1945 Mrs. Dickinson was named a consultant to the United States delegation to the United Nations Conference on International Organization in San Francisco. Upon her return from the West Coast she commented on the "immediate and friendly footing" on which North American and South American women came together at the conference. That same year the Federation supported the proposal for an international guaranty of human rights, and its president urged all clubs to send messages to this effect to the State Department. In August Mrs. Dickinson took part in a radio program in connection with the twenty-fifth anniversary of the Nineteenth Amendment, which gave the ballot to women. Another anniversary in which she took part was the November observance of the twenty-fifth birthday of radio, when she spoke of the challenge confronting it in winning the peace. With two other clubwomen, Mrs. Dickinson appeared that same month before the House Military Affairs Committee to speak of the controversial issue of universal military training. While she made it clear that she did not speak for her organization, she stated that she reflected the stand of thousands of American women in their support of draft in peacetime. The directors of the Federation seconded this stand in December by endorsing President Truman's [45] request for military training.

Mrs. Dickinson's wide organizational affiliations include membership in the American Association of University Women, the National Federation of Business and Professional Women's Clubs, and the League of Women Voters, of which she was the New Hampshire branch director in 1930. The New Englander belongs to the Daughters of the American Revolution, Daughters of Colonial Wars, and Colonial Dames. She also serves as a director of her state's Tuberculosis Society and Children's Aid and Protection Society. A member of the

Garden Club of America, Mrs. Dickinson is a fern enthusiast, her fernery containing more than fifty-some varieties from many states. In addition to gardening for recreation, she also likes to play contract bridge. The clubwoman is considered a good speaker and has addressed national and state meetings of clubs and other groups. A regular contributor to the organization's monthly publication, *General Federation Clubwoman,* she has also written for other magazines.

Lucy Jennings Dickinson is described as a plump woman, five feet five inches tall, with gray hair and brown eyes. A person of tact and "vast mental and physical vigor," she is said to have a lively sense of humor. The Dickinsons' fifteen-room summer home is located in Swanzey, not far from their permanent residence in Keene. The clubwoman commutes from her office in Washington to spend weekends with her family in New Hampshire. Her husband, president of the New England Box Company, is credited by Mrs. Dickinson with a large share of her success in club work, for, she has said, "At many points I should have given up if it had not been for his unfailing support." The Federation chief firmly believes there is a place for women in public life, intending herself to enter politics when her Federation term is ended. While she is enrolled as a Republican, Mrs. Dickinson states that she "votes for the best man regardless of party." Of her future political plans she says, "I shall start as a small-town politician just as I started as a small-town clubwoman."

References

N Y Herald Tribune p8 My 1 '44 por
N Y Sun p18 My 18 '44
American Women, 1939-40

DICKINSON, LUCY JENNINGS *See* Dickinson, Mrs. L.

DOBBIE, SIR WILLIAM (GEORGE SHEDDEN) (dŏ'bĭ) July 12, 1879- British Army officer (retired); writer; lecturer
Address: Bailey's Hotel, London

In 1943, when the Reverend Daniel A. Poling '43 ended a survey of armed services chaplains, he wrote of the high-ranking officers whom he had met: "Never before in any comparable area have I found so many ranking executives giving so much attention to religion." Typical and outstanding among these "sword and Bible" generals of the Second World War is Sir William Dobbie, who was called from retirement to become the hero of Malta, one of the most heavily bombed spots in the world and the island which "conceivably . . . saved the war." Dobbie, who is now again on the retired list, in 1945 made a lecture tour in America in which he brought home vividly to his audiences his sense of God's aid in the Battle of Malta.

William George Shedden Dobbie seemed destined at his birth for a military career. On the Dobbie side of the family he is of Crusader stock. Only his father, W. H. Dobbie, had broken with tradition, taking a post in the Indian Civil Service. Hence, it was in Madras that William was born in 1879. When he was only nine months old, his parents left

British Official Photo.

GENERAL SIR WILLIAM DOBBIE

him with relatives in England so that he might receive an education in keeping with his family's station. At Charterhouse, "one of the best of England's special preparatory schools," he became a top-ranking classical scholar and a keen student of ancient military campaigns. Upon completion of the course, by competitive examinations he proved qualified to continue his military career at the Royal Military Academy at Woolwich, from which, in due course, he went to the School of Military Engineering at Chatham. In 1899, at the age of twenty, he was commissioned a second lieutenant in the Royal Engineers. Dobbie first saw service in the Boer War in 1901 and 1902, winning the rare honor of the Queen's Medal with five clasps, indicating further awards. Thereafter, he was stationed for a time in Bermuda and later served in Ireland. In 1911 he entered the Staff College at Camberley for further training, and was graduated two years later. (In 1904 he had been married to Sybil Orde-Browne, youngest daughter of Captain Orde-Browne of the Royal Artillery. They are the parents of one daughter, who was with them on Malta, and of two sons who served in the British Army; they also have a grandson.)

During the First World War Dobbie served in France and Belgium, rising to the rank of brevet lieutenant colonel and becoming General Staff Officer No. 1 under Field Marshal Sir Douglas Haig. It was in this capacity that he acquired the distinction of composing, and issuing under his own signature, the "cease-firing" telegram of November 11, 1918: "Hostilities will cease at 11:00 hours today. Troops will stand fast at the line reached at that hour. There will be no fraternization with the enemy." When asked what he did in that war, Dobbie now answers that he ended it. Dobbie was also the officer who signed the order for the British occupation of Germany. *Life* reports that "he has since carried with him the originals of those two epochal orders." During those four years in battle Dobbie was the recipient of

DOBBIE, SIR WILLIAM—*Continued*

many honors: the Mons ribbon, the Croix de Guerre from Belgium, the Croix de Guerre with Palms from France. He was made Officer of the Order of Leopold by Belgium and was awarded the Distinguished Service Order (1916) and Companion of St. Michael and St. George (1919) by his Government. Seven times he was mentioned in dispatches. To his men he was a hero. Said one officer: "When things were blackest and one defeat had followed another, it was wonderful to see how the young officers and men admired the big fellow in the worn greatcoat who never revealed the slightest sign of fear." British officers still remember how, as a staff colonel in the operations section with Haig during the heavy German offensive in March 1918, Dobbie could not be disturbed by discouraging dispatches.

Even then he was a man of deep religious faith, and had been since his schooldays. "When I was a boy in my teens," he said once, "I heard it said that Christ came to earth to reveal the ways of God to man, but I had never taken it in. I got to thinking it might be a sensible thing to take the trouble to turn to the Bible and see for myself. I've read the Bible every day since then—always, if possible, before the day's work, and often before having to make decisions." Dobbie, who is a member of the Plymouth Brethren and the author of numerous pamphlets on religion for army use, finds that neither the progress of science nor war has disturbed his faith. Nor does he believe that the military profession is necessarily an evil. "It will . . . be seen," he has written, "that the Scripture indicates that the profession of arms is an honorable and lawful one: that the use of force and material weapons is not incompatible with faith in God: that God is a God of order who has ordained that human governments shall maintain order with force: that the time is not yet, though it will surely come, when 'the government will be on His shoulder' and man will be able to beat his sword into a ploughshare."

After the war Dobbie was promoted rapidly—to brevet colonel in 1922, lieutenant colonel in 1925, colonel in 1926. He served with the Rhine Army, in the Aldershot Command and, later, in the Western Command. From 1926 to 1928 he was general staff officer, first grade, in the War Office in London. In 1928, during the Arab-Jewish riots in Palestine, Dobbie was given the task of restoring order there. "This will be the easiest war we ever fought in," he was heard to remark on the trip out. "We will have to fight only four days a week. The Arabs won't fight on Friday, the Jews won't on Saturday, and Dobbie certainly won't on Sunday." During the next four years he was brigade commander in Egypt. Then, in 1933 he returned to England, a major general, to become commandant of the School of Military Engineering at Chatham and commander of the Chatham Area, officer commanding the Royal Engineers Depot at Chatham, and inspector of the Royal Engineers. Peculiar to his administration were the Bible classes he held each week for the officers and men of his command. In 1935 Dobbie was again sent overseas, this time as general officer commanding the British forces in Malaya, a post which he held until his retirement with pension in 1939.

When the Second World War burst upon Europe in the fall of 1939, Dobbie, though in retirement after a long and active military life, offered his services to his Government. The following April he was sent to command the strategic Mediterranean island of Malta, which was situated nine hundred miles in either direction from the nearest friendly base, Gibraltar to the west and Alexandria to the east. Once believed by some London officials to be a military liability, Malta is now credited with contributing largely to the downfall of the Axis power in the Mediterranean theater and elsewhere. Under General Dobbie's guidance, Malta became a constant threat to the Axis supply line, prevented thousands of Axis planes from reaching Europe and engaging in action in the Battle of Britain and on the Russian front, and provided a base for British submarines preying on Axis shipping. Serving first as acting governor and later as governor and commander in chief, Dobbie became the most popular leader the Maltese ever had, winning their respect and confidence by a belief in God and courage under fire which matched their own. When the initial attack occurred on June 11, 1940, the day after Mussolini [42] declared war on the Allies, Il Duce boasted that the taking of Malta would be only a matter of days, for the island was totally unprepared. With a garrison that numbered less than five thousand, General Dobbie, however, set out to defend the more than thirty miles of coastline of the island against overwhelming odds. For the first three months of the siege, he had only four nearly obsolescent airplanes, one of which was defective and unable to fly. Manned by some seaplane pilots who had never flown fighters, three of these planes—nicknamed "Faith", "Hope," and "Charity" by the islanders—together with a few antiaircraft guns, managed to keep off the swarm of Axis bombers and fighters during the months before aid came.

Malta did not fall, but its 270,000 people, huddled together in limestone caves honeycombing its ninety-one and a half rocky square miles, suffered greatly. Two-thirds of the island's food supply had to be imported and shipping of both food and matériel was paralyzed by the perils of enemy planes, submarines, and surface vessels. Yet the people and General Dobbie were equal to the situation, and together they firmly believe that it was God's help which brought them through the crisis. Typical of their spirit was one of Dobbie's orders of the day: "It may be that hard times lie ahead of us, but however hard they may be, I know that the courage and determination of all ranks will not falter, and that with God's help we will maintain the security of this fortress. I call on all officers and other ranks humbly to seek God's help and thus in reliance on Him to do their duty unflinchingly."

Dobbie is described as steadfastly calm and unflinching in the face of danger. During the worst air raids he could be found helping the wardens to rescue the wounded and helpless. (At one time he rescued a Persian cat, Maurice, which became his constant companion.) A young British officer, proud of his commander's courage, said: "Dobbie paid no more attention to bombs and machine-gun fire than to rain. He was in the tower of the palace roof when the Germans, trying to get the crippled *Illustrious* at the dockyard, concentrated more fire power on Valetta and Grand Harbor than has ever been released on any other spot on earth." Each day German and Italian planes were bombing and strafing the ship, which had limped into Malta for repairs, and for four successive days bombs were aimed at the crippled carrier but failed to inflict a mortal wound. "It was a wonderful sight," said Dobbie, "when on the evening of that fourth day the *Illustrious* steamed out of the harbor under her own power." During his command at Malta, Dobbie held nightly Bible classes and quoted the Scriptures in his War Office reports.

When Dobbie was relieved at Malta by the new governor, General the Viscount Gort [40], in May 1942, he had accomplished the complete fortification of the island and turned it into a bulwark which in March 1942 destroyed 275 German and Italian planes and badly damaged 600 others. Dobbie had also established cooperation of the chiefs of the Army, Navy, Air, and civilian forces through a central defense group and had, among other acts, exiled a boatload of Fifth Columnists. All this he did, say the island's defenders, "by his engineering skill, by his understanding of aviation, by making the most of the skills of many others—in a word, by personality and leadership." Prime Minister Winston Churchill [42], praising his work, said it "entitled him to release and repose." And for the gallant stand the Maltese made under General Dobbie, King George VI [42] awarded "to the fortress of Malta itself" the George Medal. In 1941 Dobbie, who had been elevated to the rank of temporary lieutenant general that year, had also been made Knight Commander of the Order of the Bath. In 1942 he was made Knight Grand Cross of St. Michael and St. George.

Sir William returned to England to rest, and to lecture on his experiences at Malta and his belief in the religious basis of this war. "If ever we have gone to war on a spiritual issue it is now," he wrote in 1942. "We are not only fighting for our existence and for the preservation of our institutions, we are fighting for the fundamental principles without which life, whether individual or national, will not be worth living. There can be no vestige of doubt that our cause is righteous, and that it must be in accordance with God's will." In January 1945 he began a similar lecture tour of the United States and Canada sponsored by the Moody Bible Institute of Chicago, during which, accompanied by Lady Dobbie, who had been with him at Malta, he traveled 15,000 miles, visiting forty cities and addressing audiences aggregating 150,000 persons. While in Ottawa he was entertained at Rideau Hall by the Earl of Athlone, Governor General of Canada, and Princess Alice. At Washington, Sir William and Lady Dobbie were guests of the White House. At City Hall in New York, the General was received by Mayor La Guardia [40].

General Dobbie, whose troops referred to him familiarly as "Old Dob Dob," has been described by a *Liberty* interviewer as "a huge, quick, but heavy-going man with thick gray hair, reddish eyebrows run wild, and a short gray mustache." "The most singular thing about him," says the same interviewer, "is the serenity of his deep-set gray-blue eyes." Like Field Marshal Sir Bernard Montgomery [42], Dobbie is a teetotaler, and does not smoke. Young men who have fought under him report that they will never be the skeptics they were before the war. Dobbie "did something" to them, they said. Added one young officer: "Old Dob is the simplest, humblest, gentlest of men. There never was a man with less vanity. I think that's one reason why after two years with him, I've found it so difficult to describe him to others. There's nothing to get hold of, no oddities. He was never excited in his life. There is in him an inner calm hard to explain." Dobbie, his men said, was always fair: it was a job done, not rank or position which mattered.

References

Liberty 19:10 D 26 '42
N Y Sun p8 Ja 25 '45
Newsweek 19:23 Ap 27 '42
Who's Who, 1945

DOBIE, J(AMES) FRANK (dō'bǐ) Sept. 26, 1888- Folklorist; author; college professor
Address: b. University of Texas, Austin; h. 702 Park Pl., Austin, Tex.

The man who "probably knows more about Texas folklore than any other man alive" is J. Frank Dobie, leading authority on the culture of the Southwest. The Lone Star State's colorful citizen, who refuses to be an academician, is known as "the maverick professor"— he teaches at the University of Texas, where his course "Life and Literature of the Southwest" has attracted students for more than fifteen years. Dobie is the author or editor of some thirty books on the subject, and his articles have appeared in a number of national magazines. He occupied the chair of American history, on an exchange professorship, at England's Cambridge University in 1943-44, a year that brought forth his book *A Texan in England* (1945). The Texan, who is also known for his outspoken liberalism, found much to admire in England, and book critics found much to admire about his book.

James Frank Dobie was born on a Texas ranch in Live Oak County, on September 26, 1888, the eldest of the six children of Richard Jonathan and Ella (Byler) Dobie. Heir to the old Texas traditions of a family long established on the range (his great-grandfather had come to Texas from Virginia in 1834), the boy lived on the family ranch of about seven thousand acres until his sixteenth year. Dobie tells the story of his childhood in *St. Nicholas* magazine, October 1933. His mother, who had been a teacher, gave him his first lessons—it was his parents, he said, who gave him his taste for literature; and it was the range country which taught him much besides—"the land

From a drawing by Tom Lea

J. FRANK DOBIE

on which I was reared and the brush growing on the land taught me more than schoolteachers have ever taught." For a time, with his brothers and sisters he went to the one-teacher schoolhouse built by several ranch families, and he had his share of chores to do. After going to high school in the town of Alice, forty miles away, he attended Southwestern University in Georgetown, Texas, where he received his B.A. degree in 1910. One summer before his graduation young Dobie studied at the University of Chicago, although he was drawn back to the ranch nearly every vacation. For one year (1910-11) Dobie was school principal in the Texas town of Alpine, after which he returned to Southwestern University as teacher of English and secretary to the president. During the summer of 1914 he worked on the Galveston *Tribune* as reporter, work he had done for one summer four years earlier on the San Antonio *Express*.

In 1914 Dobie received his M.A. at Columbia University and that year he joined the faculty of the University of Texas, where, except for a few absences, he has remained. During the First World War he served as a first lieutenant in the 116th Field Artillery and upon his return from France in 1919 he resumed his teaching career at the university. But after a year Dobie became dissatisfied with academic life and turned to his "earliest love," cattle raising. Accordingly, for the year 1920-21 he managed his uncle's quarter-of-a-million-acre ranch on the Nueces River. There he conceived the idea to which he has since devoted his life—to collect and retell the legends and folk tales of Texas.

In 1921 Dobie was back at the university, where he taught for two years before becoming head of the English department at Oklahoma Agricultural and Mechanical College. He held that position until 1925, when he returned to the University of Texas as adjunct professor of English. A year later Dobie became an associate professor and in 1933 a full professor, the first native Texan to receive a full pro-

fessorship in the university's English department. This was also unusual in that Dobie did not have a Ph.D.—of which he says: "I early learned that a Ph.D. thesis consists of transferring bones from one graveyard to another." During 1930-31 he held a research fellowship in the Laura Spelman Rockefeller Foundation and another in 1934-35. In the intervening time (1932-33), on a grant from the Guggenheim Memorial Foundation, he traveled two thousand miles on muleback gathering folklore. Much of his research has been done around camp fires, at trading posts, and in chuck wagons.

The folklorist has said that the only reason he teaches is to give his course, "Life and Literature of the Southwest," called the most popular course at the University of Texas. Labeled "a very unprofessorial professor," Dobie teaches through "windy, chatty yarns" and sings the ballads of the trail in his cowboy baritone. Class discussions on controversial subjects range from "a tirade against Pappy O'Daniel [Senator W. Lee O'Daniel] to a discourse on the race question." Dobie has called himself the outlaw of the campus, where he carries on a determined crusade to "keep Texas unique." His opposition to any attempt to standardize Texas has brought him into conflict with university officials, legislators, and politicians. When in 1936 the university's new twenty-seven-story, two-million-dollar building was opened, the professor was bluntly indignant. "It's like a toothpick in a pie," he declared as he refused to take office space in it. His acid remarks on a certain piece of campus sculpture brought admiring comments from Alexander Woollcott [41].

Dobie has also clashed with the university's board of regents. Late in 1943 he joined a faculty and student group in petitioning for the immediate reinstatement of three teachers who had been dismissed for their activities outside the school. This case eventually led to the dismissal of Dr. Homer P. Rainey, president of the university, who charged the regents with suppression of academic freedom. The Rainey case held national attention and resulted in the probation of the university in July 1945 by the Southern Association of Colleges and Secondary Schools. Actively supporting Rainey, Dobie said in his testimony at hearings that freedom was at stake in Texas.

When the Manford Act became law in Texas in 1943, to provide for strict regulation of unions and licensing of organizers, Dobie expressed his opinion in typically frank fashion. "A man can come to Texas and without interference invite all the people he wants to join the Republican Party, the Liar's Club, the Association for the Anointment of Herbert Hoover as Prophet, almost any kind of organization except one. If the Manford Law is an index of capitalism's future policy, the people had better begin digging cellars for the revolution." Dobie often uses his column in a Texas newspaper to express his opinions. The writer has a large progressive following in his state and in 1944 efforts were made to draft him to run for governor against Coke Stevenson, but Dobie declined. Describing himself as a liberal Democrat, he supported Roosevelt [42].

Dobie went to England in 1943 for the first time, to succeed Henry Steele Commager of Columbia as professor of American history at

Cambridge. (Commager was the first man to hold this position.) In commenting editorially on the Texan's appointment, the New York *Herald Tribune* said: "In Mr. Dobie the British will find a teacher different from any they ever saw before, and the impact upon them is sure to be considerable. . . .His venture into the halls of Cambridge promises to be one of the most happy of all our ambassadorships." In residence at Emmanuel College at the venerable British university, Dobie taught his own special kind of American history to RAF, Royal Navy, and civilian students. He also lectured for the OWI and the British Army Education Office. Dobie confessed that during the first term he "boned like any freshman." He explained that "he hadn't read the American Constitution since he was a boy and didn't understand it then, that he did know the length of the horns of longhorn steers . . . the music inherent in coyote howling . . . the smell of coffee boiled over mesquite wood."

In the course of his stay in England the "sombrero wearer among men in togas" wrote of his experiences for American magazines, and on his return to the United States these were incorporated in 1945 into a book, *A Texan in England*, filled with portrait sketches, anecdotes, descriptions, and "a fine appreciation of the best of England." Thus it abounds in word pictures of the English countryside, pubs, London under bombings, and many sorts of men and women in whom the author sees such qualities as casualness, patience, politeness, reticence.

While Dobie had written the final chapter of his book in England, on his return home he decided to write a new ending, which he calls "What England Did to Me." Oppressed by the atmosphere he found at the University of Texas, an atmosphere he termed "remote from the air of intellectual freedom enveloping Cambridge," he wrote: "Here on this campus, believers in the right as well as the duty to think are combating a gang of Fascist-minded regents: oil millionaires, corporation lawyers, a lobbyist, and a medical politician, who in anachronistic rage against liberal thought malign all liberals as 'Communists,' try with physical power to wall out ideas, and resort to chicanery as sickening as it is cheap. My mind is paralyzed by this manifestation of 'the American way of life.'" On a few other scores, too, Americans suffer from comparison with the English.

The critic J. A. Brandt thought that *A Texan in England* showed Dobie "politically alive, acutely sensitive to human rights and wrongs and making a hard-muscled stand for the right." Clifton Fadiman [41] wrote: "Though not deeply reflective nor particularly well organized, it is an honest and loving essay"; and Roger Pippett remarked that "no more lyrical account of the English countryside has been written by an American." In mild dissent, Englishman W. H. Hindle found Dobie's book "too much a picture of a gentlemanly, feudal England," and somewhat of an apology for this feudal way of life. Struthers Burt's opinion appeared in the New York *Times*: "At times, Frank Dobie can write carelessly and hastily, and in an odd and not too pleasing staccato fashion, although, as has been said, he can never write uninterestingly; but over and over again

his prose rises into something so translucent and starkly noble that it becomes Elizabethan." In the summer of 1945 Dobie returned to England to teach in the United States Army University organized near Oxford. At that time *A Texan in England* was going into its sixth printing.

The story-teller of the Southwest is the author of a number of other books, among them *A Vaquero of the Brush Country* (1929), *On the Open Range* (1931), *Tongues of the Monte* (1935), *The Flavor of Texas* (1936), and *Guide to Life and Literature of the Southwest* (1943). *Coronado's Children* (1931), a collection of legends of lost mines and buried treasures of the Southwest, was a Literary Guild selection. It was described by the *Saturday Review of Literature*'s critic as "a rich and fascinating volume, compiled with gusto." In his review of *Apache Gold and Yaqui Silver* (1939) Oliver La Farge declared: "Mr. Dobie's accounts are alive with the space and color of his setting." The writer's study of a vanishing breed of cattle, *The Longhorns* (1941), was greeted as a valuable, "full-bodied" work. Dobie's articles have appeared in such magazines as the *Yale Review*, *American Mercury*, *Atlantic*, and the *Saturday Evening Post*. In an issue devoted to the culture of the Southwest, the *Saturday Review of Literature* (May 16, 1942) carried the Texan's story of "Mister Ben Lilly," extraordinary bear hunter. The May 1943 issue of *Natural History* contains his lengthy study of "The Conquering Mesquite." Since 1922 Dobie has been editor and compiler of the annual publications of the Texas Folk-Lore Society, of which he is also secretary; and since 1924 he has been contributing editor of the *Southwest Review*.

Noted for his devastating frankness, Dobie is described as a "brash, blue-eyed scrapper" with a "wide Texas smile, a broad Texas hat, and a still wider Texas accent." A ruddy, stocky man of five feet eight inches, he is a vivid and versatile personality, known as "Pancho" to his friends. Dobie's wife, the former Bertha McKee, also a Texan, to whom he was married in 1916, at one time taught school after their marriage so that her husband might have time for writing. Her special interest in plants and gardens has been of value to Dobie—it is evident in what has been called as probably the best single chapter in *A Vaquero of the Brush Country,* a chapter on plant life in the brush country.

When Dobie works at his typewriter his hat is usually on his head, and he will read aloud what he has written, "tinkering" with sentences until they "sing like a fiddle." His hobbies are not far removed from his vocation—he collects literature on the range country and objects made of horn, and his favorite recreations are horseback-riding and deer-hunting. When Cambridge University awarded the Texan the honorary degree of Master of Arts, the citation read in part: *De bobus longicornibus quod ille non cognovit, inutile est alliis cognoscere.* In unacademic English that tribute reads: "What he doesn't know about longhorn cattle isn't worth knowing."

(Continued next page)

DOBIE, J. FRANK—*Continued*

References

N Y Sun p19 N 9 '43; p26 My 2 '45
Newsweek 22:102 O 25 '43 por
Sat Eve Post 216:14-15+ S 11 '43 pors
Time 37:96 Mr 17 '41
Rogers, J. W. Finding Literature on the
    Texas Plains (1931)
Texan Who's Who, 1937
Who's Who in America, 1944-45

DODDS, HAROLD W(ILLIS) June 28,
1889- University president
Address: b. c/o Princeton University, Princeton, N.J.; h. Prospect, Princeton, N.J.

As the academic year 1945-46 got under way,
Princeton University was preparing for its bicentennial in 1946. Under the leadership of
President Harold W. Dodds, whose competence
in many fields has earned him the appellation of
"best-known North American in Central and
South America" and "one of the foremost authorities on local government problems," the
university plans to highlight its celebration with
round-table conferences on postwar problems
affecting education, conferences to be attended
by the world's leading scholars. Princeton,
states a New York *Sun* editorial, is looking to
the future rather than to the past.

Harold Willis Dodds was born in Utica,
Pennsylvania, on June 28, 1889. His father was
Samuel Dodds, a descendant of James Dodds,
who came to settle in western Pennsylvania
in 1760 from County Down, Ireland; his
mother was Alice (Dunn) Dodds. The youth
attended Grove City College (Grove City,
Pennsylvania), where his father, a Presbyterian
minister, was Bible professor. Young Dodds
was graduated in 1909, a member of Phi Beta
Kappa. Twenty-six years after his graduation,
in his own words of guidance to the Princeton
class of 1937, President Dodds recalled the
teachers to whom he himself owed "the heaviest
debts of gratitude" as those "who had urged
young people to take chances rather than to
succumb to sure things." His own graduation
was followed by two years of teaching, after
which he began postgraduate work at Princeton University, receiving his Master's degree in
1914. From 1914 to 1916 Dodds was instructor
in economics at Purdue University, and in 1917
he took his Ph.D. degree at the University of
Pennsylvania. When defective eyesight caused
his rejection for military duty in the First
World War, Dodds offered his services to the
United States Food Administration and received
the post of executive secretary for Pennsylvania, which he held until 1919.

In that year Dodds accepted a position as
assistant professor of political science at Western Reserve University and for a year taught
courses in American government and in international law and politics. Then his steadily
growing interest in problems of local government determined his resignation from the Western Reserve faculty to accept the position of
secretary to the National Municipal League and
editor of its journal, the *National Municipal
Review*. Dodds remained as secretary of the
League through June 1928 and as editor of the
Review until 1933, at the same time engaging in

a number of other activities. In 1922 he lectured on a part-time basis on the subject of
municipal government at the University of
Pennsylvania; in 1924, on the same subject at
Swarthmore College; in 1925, on political science at New York University. Also in 1925, he
began lecturing on politics at Princeton University. And in 1922, in Nicaragua, he had
begun his career as electoral adviser to Latin
American governments. He was also technical
adviser to General John J. Pershing when the
latter was president of the Tacna-Arica Plebiscitary Commission acting during the dispute
over that province between Chile and Peru in
1925-26, and he acted as consultant on electoral
law and procedure to the Cuban Government in
1925.

In 1922, upon the recommendation of Secretary of State Charles Evans Hughes [41], Dodds
was selected as electoral adviser to the Nicaraguan Government, in which capacity it became
his task to formulate a new electoral law for a
nation which had not yet known a free or incorrupt election. The new law, known popularly as the Dodds Law, was adopted by the
Nicaraguan legislature in 1923, but with changes
which, according to Henry L. Stimson [40] and
others, "seriously weakened its integrity." It
was originally intended that the United States
supervise the ensuing presidential election of
1924, but the Conservatives in office, disagreeing with the Liberals, rejected the plan, and the
short-lived coalition incumbency of 1925 was
ousted by the *coup d'etat* of General Chamorro,
the defeated extreme Conservative candidate,
soon after the United States Marines were
withdrawn from the country in August 1925.
Although late in 1926 a reconstituted *de jure*
legislature elected Adolfo Diaz president-designate under the provisions of the Nicaraguan
constitution, civil war broke out between the
Liberals and Conservatives, and was not quelled
until Colonel Stimson was able to persuade
both sides to accede to a strict and complete
supervision by the United States of the
scheduled 1928 presidential election.

The American supervision was to be carried
out by a National Board of Elections of
Nicaragua, having as its chairman United States
Brigadier General Frank R. McCoy [45] and including one representative of each of the parties.
Dodds was appointed chief adviser to McCoy,
and the election was to be conducted under the
provisions of the Dodds Law. "This election,"
wrote Dodds afterward, "was not merely to be
'observed' by a few American representatives,
but an American was to sit as chairman of
every election board—national, departmental
and local—with a deciding vote in all electoral
matters and appropriate police powers to make
the supervision effective." It proved to be the
most successful and orderly election in Nicaragua's turbulent history, of which Dodds has
written: "Since the day of her independence
Nicaragua's story has been one of bitter feuds
between Liberals and Conservatives, with the
spoils of office and revenge the chief motivating
factors. With the possible exception of a slight
divergence in attitude toward the Catholic
Church, there are no appreciable differences
in principles or practices to provide a basis for
choice between the two parties, but the average
Nicaraguan is nevertheless a violent partisan of
one or the other. In reality the two parties are

much like two opposing gangs, and their political struggles can best be interpreted in terms of gang warfare." In 1935 Dodds was again asked to act as arbiter in an election dispute, this time in Cuba. In three days' time his compromise plan was completed and adopted.

In 1927 Dodds was appointed a professor of politics in Princeton University, and it was the added demands of this new post which caused him to resign as secretary of the National Municipal League the next year. In 1930 he was made chairman of the administrative committee of the newly established School of Public and International Affairs at Princeton, the purpose of which, in the words of former President John Grier Hibben of the university, was "to develop for the country each year a body of young men who will have not only a preliminary foundation for public and international careers but also a new sense of direction and responsibility for the affairs of their state and country." In 1932 Dodds was selected to direct a survey of New Jersey State administration undertaken at the request of Governor A. Harry Moore. "With twenty assistants [from the Princeton faculty]," noted William Lyon Phelps '43 at the conferring of the honorary Ph.D. degree on Dodds by Yale University in 1933, "Dr. Dodds worked four months without missing a class or a lecture and turned in a report of 150,000 words showing how the State could save $14,000,000."

In January 1933 the National Municipal League reluctantly accepted Dodds's resignation as editor of the *National Municipal Review* "because of increasing responsibilities at Princeton," at the same time appointing him chairman of the editorial council of the *Review*. (The following year the League elected him to its presidency.) A few months later it was announced that Dodds had been appointed fifteenth president of Princeton University to succeed John Grier Hibben. Statistically, Dodds became the youngest appointee to the office in 175 years, the third youngest in the history of the university, and the sixth to be appointed from the ranks of the faculty. Concerning the appointment, the *National Cyclopædia of American Biography* said: "His practical experience in governmental matters, chiefly as an adviser in state and municipal administration and finance . . . has given him a unique qualification for the post and his election seems to be a happy culmination of a long search which ended within the university's own walls."

In guiding Princeton Dodds has adhered to a basic and often-expressed formulation of the function of a university in a democratic state. "I suggest," he said at the opening exercises of the 1939-40 academic year, "that Princeton rededicate itself to its historic mission of making democracy work. By this I do not mean greater emphasis upon public affairs in the usual sense of the term. What I have in mind is far beyond politics or forms of government. Even as a form of government democracy is not an end as our forefathers supposed, but a means to an end, the good life. . . .A free society is an opportunity, not a guaranty of happiness. It exists to be used; if it is taken for granted, if its people are passive, uncultivated, or confused, it will be abandoned for some other instrumentality, promising a more automatic human perfectibility. A healthy democracy is

HAROLD W. DODDS

not a static thing. When functioning properly it is moving toward something. . . If we assume that it is mature, its power of survival is gone and the usual step from maturity to death will follow quickly. The basic truth here is that democracy must expand or perish. . . .The liberal arts college is the one most available agency to prepare young people to meet the human problems of an expanding democracy. There is no subject in the Princeton curriculum that can not be employed to contribute to this end." "Princeton firmly believes," he said on another occasion, "that trained intelligence, wide range of vision, discipline of mind and spirit, and the other related objectives of education in the liberal arts will continue to be of vital importance in the year 1943 and in all the years to follow." Princeton would continue to encourage original work on the part of its undergraduates "because original thinking toughens the muscles of the mind as no passively acquired information can do."

After more than three years of study, in December 1945 Dodds announced that, beginning in 1947, Princeton would inaugurate a new curriculum plan. Under the plan, which modifies the free elective system, freshmen will be required to "explore each of the four major areas of liberal learning—natural science, social science, arts and letters, and, finally, the trilogy of history, philosophy, and religion." Within each group the student may select his courses, and in his sophomore year he must choose the field in which he will concentrate. In his senior year he may expect to do original study, now often possible for only a graduate student.

Dodds is the holder of seventeen honorary degrees, including citations from Harvard, Yale, and Columbia universities. He is a member of the American Philosophical Society, the American Political Science Association; a director of the Council on Foreign Relations; a trustee of the Brookings Institution and the Carnegie Foundation for the Advancement of Teaching;

DODDS, HAROLD W.—*Continued*

and a member of the Rockefeller Foundation. In 1943 he was chairman of the American delegation to the Anglo-American Conference on the Refugee Problem held in Bermuda. In politics he is a Republican, and he has expressed his political creed thus: "I submit that democracy can not survive through trust in systems alone. Collective action demands greater competence on the part of the individuals acting than extreme individualism ever required. I have never accepted a philosophy which finds man's highest good in absorption by and subjection to any higher group in which his personality is supposed to be dissolved and then translated. I insist on an individual's right to kick and to persuade others to kick with him. I believe that in politics his majesty's opposition is as important as his majesty's government." In late 1945 Dodds became identified with two conferences concerned with postwar problems. He was named to a nine-member committee set up by President Truman [45] to coordinate Government medical services, of which the primary task "is to find ways of increasing the medical facilities of the United States Veteran Administration." He also became one of the sponsors of the conference for Safeguarding Wartime Savings, a movement fostered by the National Association of Better Business Bureaus to protect the American public from swindlers, who are anxious to dip into the billions of dollars the public saved during the war.

Princeton's president has written articles on governmental administration, foreign affairs and education that appeared in *American City, National Municipal Review, Foreign Affairs* and other periodicals; of a study, *Procedure in State Legislatures*, published by the American Academy of Political and Social Science in 1918; and of a book, *Out of This Nettle, Danger* (1943), which the New York *Times* characterized as a "concise compendium of reconstructive citizenship by one who believes that 'history is a spiritual achievement' and that 'the ethic of liberalism is the Christian ethic.'" Many of the university president's addresses are printed in the magazine *Vital Speeches of the Day.*

Dodds was married to Margaret Murray, of Halifax, Nova Scotia, on Christmas Day 1917. He is a member of the Century, Princeton (New York), and Nassau (Princeton) clubs, and has expressed a strong personal liking for life in the country. He stands five feet eleven inches tall, weighs one hundred and sixty pounds, has blue eyes and gray hair.

References

Sch & Soc 37:745 Je 10 '33; 38:12-13 Jl 1 '33
Sci Mo 37:474-5 N '33
International Who's Who, 1942
National Cyclopædia of American Biography, Current vol D p59
Who's Who, 1945
Who's Who in America, 1944-45
Who's Who in New York (1938)

DOUGLAS, EMILY TAFT Apr. 19, 1899-
United States Representative from Illinois

Address: b. House of Representatives Office Bldg., Washington, D.C.

As of 1945, Illinois is one of the two states in the Union to have two women Representatives in Congress. Like Connecticut, too, Illinois has a women Congressmen on each side of the dividing aisle in the House. On the Republican side sits Jessie Sumner [45] and on the Democratic, Emily Taft Douglas, Representative at Large from the Prairie State. Mrs. Douglas won a surprising victory in her first political candidacy, and an important committee assignment, the Foreign Relations Committee, in her first term in Congress.

Emily Taft Douglas was born in Chicago on April 19, 1899, one of the three daughters of the famous sculptor Lorado Taft and Ada (Bartlett) Taft. Her grandfather, Don Carlos Taft, was the first professor of science at the University of Illinois; William Howard Taft was a distant cousin. Her father was also an art teacher, writer, and a lecturer, often traveling twenty-five thousand miles in one year. From her childhood little Emily was internationally minded—her father made annual visits to the great European art centers—and she was also influenced by his work with the League to Enforce Peace during World War I. Despite her family's Republican tradition, she was impressed "terrifically" by Democratic President Wilson and his work for the League of Nations. "When he died," Mrs. Douglas recalls, "I remember I said to myself, 'If there's anything I can do to forward the things he stood for, I'm his man.'"

Meanwhile, the future Representative had her heart set on a stage career, but her parents insisted she must finish college first. So Miss Taft packed four years at the University of Chicago into three, receiving her B.A. in 1920. In 1922 she was given the lead in the mystery thriller, *The Cat and the Canary,* which she says scared her even in rehearsal. Two years later she was still playing the same role: "When it was over, I had had enough mystery to last me the rest of my life." Back she went to Chicago for graduate study in government and political science. In 1931, when she was thirty-two, Emily Taft was married to Paul Howard Douglas, professor of economics at the University of Illinois. Douglas has been described as "standing out like a landmark above the contemporary run of professors of economics." The couple have one daughter, Jean Taft, born in 1933. (Professor Douglas also has two sons and two daughters by an earlier marriage.) A specialist in industrial relations, Douglas is "a profoundly convinced and yet cheerfully optimistic nonviolent revolutionist," who believes firmly in the "family wage": inclusion in a worker's pay of an allowance for each dependent, a system already in operation in France and compulsory in Australia. (In the Second World War, Douglas enlisted in the Marines, rose to be a major, and was wounded on Peleliu and Okinawa. After his return to the United States he served as chairman of the planning committee for the Labor-Management Conference held in November 1945.)

In 1935 Paul and Emily Douglas spent a three-month vacation traveling through Europe. "Paul and I stood under the palace balcony in Rome on the day Mussolini '42 announced he had sent his troops into Ethiopia," Mrs. Douglas recalls. "I think out of all that wild and delirious multitude, we were probably the only ones who froze with fear and foreboding of what that meant. Suddenly, all the things we had seen and suspected that summer fell into place. It came crystal clear to us then and there that if Hitler '42 and Mussolini and the forces they represented were not stopped, the whole world would be engulfed."

On their return to Chicago, the Douglases took up the task of warning their fellow citizens of the impending catastrophe. In 1938 Professor Douglas won election as Democratic alderman from the Fifth Ward to the Chicago City Council. Mrs. Douglas became an organizer for the League of Women Voters and, in time, chairman of the Illinois League of Women Voters' department of government and foreign policy. "We wanted to strengthen democracy at the grass roots," says Mrs. Douglas, who therefore became active in local Democratic politics and "did ward work for a variety of local liberal candidates, some successful and others not." In 1942 she also became secretary of the Carnegie-endowed International Relations Center in Chicago, a clearinghouse for information, and took charge of its pamphlet shop.

In that year, when Paul Douglas still had one year to serve as alderman, he ran for Senator as an independent Democrat, but was defeated. Ten days later the fifty-year-old professor enlisted in the Marine Corps as a private. It never occurred to his wife that she might go to Congress in his stead, and when the Chicago Democratic leaders asked her to run for Representative at Large in 1944, she countered with, "Gentlemen, this is so sudden!"

The prospect was not a particularly encouraging one. To become Representative at Large from Illinois meant that she would have to win the support of a population of 7,897,241—the third largest state constituency in the country, and one traditionally Republican and isolationist. In her first campaign she would be opposed by a veteran incumbent, the Chicago *Tribune*'s candidate, Stephen Day. Paul Douglas, by then a captain, was on combat duty in the South Pacific, but his wife had no doubt of what his advice would have been. He had urged her to enter politics—therefore get into the campaign she did, at the time caring for little Jean and doing all her housework singlehandedly because she could not get a maid.

Apart from charging that Day had abused his Congressional franking privilege and was associated with the Nazi-minded George Sylvester Viereck '40, Mrs. Douglas campaigned entirely on a platform of support for President Roosevelt's '42 foreign policy and for world cooperation, stating that Day "by his voting record stands convicted as the worst obstructionist in Congress." The ultraconservative downstate districts were still sending to Congress Representatives who voted against Lend-Lease. The Republicans saw no threat to their usual solid majorities there from the shy, serious Mrs. Douglas; but small groups, who knew her work with the League of Women Voters, campaigned so effectively that even the rural districts gave her helpful pluralities. On Election Day, while Illinois elected a slate of Republican State officials, it sent to Congress

Corboy

EMILY TAFT DOUGLAS

Democratic Senator Scott Lucas, and Mrs. Douglas. She polled 2,030,573 votes to her opponent's 1,839,518, a margin larger than that accorded President Roosevelt '42 in the same territory. Said the new Representative-elect, "It was a clear-cut victory for the President's foreign policy."

Representative Douglas was an obvious choice for the House Foreign Affairs Committee, which is headed by Sol Bloom '43. Conservative Arthur Krock '43 calls her "an expert in the field, highly qualified to debate foreign policy questions in the House and estimate the binding actions of the Senate." It was thought, however, that she might not be placed on it, because it was a "prestige" assignment ordinarily given only to experienced Representatives, and because it already included two Illinoisans (Democrat Thomas S. Gordon and Republican Robert B. Chiperfield) and two women, Republicans Edith Nourse Rogers '42 of Massachusetts and Frances P. Bolton '40 of Ohio. Republican Clare Boothe Luce '42, Connecticut, had been refused a Foreign Affairs seat. But at the party caucus the Democratic membership was enlarged to fifteen so that Mrs. Douglas and Helen Gahagan Douglas '44 of California could be seated—a distinction comparable to that bestowed on Ruth Bryan Owen '44 sixteen years earlier. With the assignment of the third new woman Representative, Chase Going Woodhouse '45 of Connecticut, to the Banking and Currency Committee, it ceased entirely to be true that women, like Independents, were seldom placed on the major committees.

The first time Mrs. Douglas walked into the House she was stopped by a page who failed to recognize "all these dames"; the first time Speaker Sam Rayburn '40 gave her the floor, she failed to recognize herself as "the Gentleman from Illinois." (Women Representatives are traditionally referred to as "the Gentlewoman from. . ." but force of habit is strong even in Speakers.) But this inauspicious beginning was more than made up for when, on her third day in the House, Mrs. Douglas was invited to preside over its deliberations for a

DOUGLAS, EMILY TAFT—*Continued*

short time, a gesture which left her "a little trembly." To interviewers, the Representative from Illinois said: "In Congress, and especially in my work on the Foreign Affairs Committee, I am going to proceed on the thesis that the will to get along with the other nations of the world is of greater importance than the machinery. . . .We ourselves must have faith in the doctrine of collective security as a bulwark against another war and chaos. We must be prepared to make whatever compromises and sacrifices that security demands. And we must then persuade the other nations of our sincerity."

On the Seventy-ninth Congress' first roll-call vote, in January 1945, Mrs. Douglas said "Nay" to the reconstitution of the (Dies '40) Committee on Un-American Activities as a permanent standing committee; in February she voted for the May '41-Bailey '45 "limited national service" bill, and for immediate consideration of the George '43 bill to remove the RFC lending agencies from the Department of Commerce—an indirect vote for Henry Wallace '40 as Secretary of Commerce.

In March 1945 Mrs. Douglas came out for the drafting of nurses into the armed forces, and voted also for the compromise manpower bill. As befitted a freshman in Congress, she "kept her eyes and ears open and her mouth shut" at the Foreign Affairs Committee meetings and hearings on the extension of Lend-Lease and other momentous matters. She "accepted a few assignments" to speak in favor of the Dumbarton Oaks world security plan for the League of Women Voters. Her semi-monthly newsletter, *Window on Washington,* addressed to her Illinois constituents, drew praise from Henry Hoke, editor of the *Reporter of Direct Mail Advertising* and crusader against the abuse of the frank: he cited her and Augustus W. Bennet, Republican of New York, as examples of the worthiest use of the Congressional franking privilege. Among the information contained in the first few issues of *Window on Washington* was that Mrs. Douglas had decided to hold open competitive examinations for her appointments to West Point and Annapolis, although she pointed out that there would be only one such vacancy through 1946. In August Mrs. Douglas and several other members of a subcommittee of the House Foreign Affairs Committee went abroad to study the United Nations Relief and Rehabilitation Administration in Western Europe and the controversies which had arisen about it. Before the close of the year Mrs. Douglas and Representative Jerry Voorhis '41 of California introduced legislation to empower the United Nations Organization to control armaments and outlaw the atomic bomb.

In appearance Emily Taft Douglas is "little and cute." Five feet two inches tall, she weighs one hundred twenty-eight pounds. The blue-eyed and brown-haired Chicagoan uses little or no makeup, wears glasses for reading, and is described as "a quiet, housewifely person—an unusual type on the political rostrum."

Her chocolate cake is reported to be "awfully good," but with so many important things to be done she begrudges the time consumed in domestic tasks. Representative Douglas has had as much trouble as anyone else in finding a house in Washington and someone to take care of it. She is a voracious reader, especially of facts; she has "a passion for French pastry," likes to swim, and enjoys reading to her daughter and helping her with her stamp collection. The Representative delivers few addresses and gives little time to social affairs. "I'm niggardly with my evenings," she says with a smile.

References

N Y Herald Tribune p13 N 10 '44
N Y Post Mag p5 Mr 10 '45 por
N Y Times Mag p20+ F 18 '45 por
Congressional Directory, 1945

DUNNE, IRENE Dec. 20, 1904- Actress
Address: b. c/o Columbia Pictures Corp., Hollywood, Calif.

In the history of motion pictures, several women have been dubbed "First Lady of Hollywood." For years it was Norma Shearer; more recently it has been Greer Garson '42. Spanning the film cycles in which these two have reigned is a third "First Lady," Irene Dunne. In a profession and a community known for the well-publicized briefness of some careers and marriages, Miss Dunne has impressed observers by staying near the top in popularity since 1932, and by having been married to the same man since 1927. She has been equally successful in tragedy, comedy, and musical productions, and has seldom if ever scored a personal failure in more than twenty years of acting.

Of Irish descent, Irene Dunne was born in Louisville, Kentucky, on December 20, 1904. Her father, Joseph John Dunne, was a supervisory inspector of steamships for the United States Government; her mother, Adelaide Antoinette (Henry) Dunne, was an accomplished musician. The Dunnes were well-to-do, and little Irene had a pleasant childhood, attending Loretta Academy in Louisville and studying music with her mother. When the girl was eleven years old her father died, and the widowed Mrs. Dunne and Irene moved to Madison, Indiana, to live with the child's grandparents. During the next few years Irene studied voice and piano with private teachers and for the first time earned her own money by singing on Sundays in the church choir. After a year's study at a music conservatory in Indianapolis she accepted a position as music and art teacher in an East Chicago (Indiana) high school. While traveling to East Chicago, she noticed a newspaper advertisement of the annual scholarship contest held by the Chicago Musical College, and made a quick decision to stop in Chicago to enter the contest. Competing with singers who had had professional coaching, she won the scholarship which enabled her to study voice at the college for a year.

When her scholarship year was over, Miss Dunne headed for New York, determined to add her name to the roster of the Metropolitan

Opera Company. After auditioning, however, she was rejected for being "too young, too inexperienced, and too slight." Turning to musical comedy, Miss Dunne won the leading part in a road company of *Irene*, and after a five-month tour forgot opera and went on with other plays—*The Clinging Vine* (1922), *Lollipop* (1924), and *The City Chap* (1925). The next year she toured with *Sweetheart Time*, and also sang with light opera companies in Atlanta and St. Louis. She had continued to study intermittently at the Chicago Musical College, and in 1926 was graduated with high honors. (She is now an honorary member of the music fraternity Sigma Alpha Iota, and in July 1945 she received an honorary degree of Doctor of Music from the Chicago college.)

In January 1927 Miss Dunne opened on Broadway as Diana in *Yours Truly*, and in July of the same year she was married to Dr. Francis Dennis Griffin, a New York dentist. At the time of her marriage she planned to give up her theatrical work, but 1928 found her again behind the footlights, as Polly in *She's My Baby* and later as Arlette in *Luckee Girl*.

The year 1929 proved to be the turning point of her career. The story goes that Florenz Ziegfeld stood next to Miss Dunne in an office building elevator and was so struck by her beauty that he invited her to audition for a part in his forthcoming production of *Show Boat*. She enthusiastically accepted and was overwhelmed at being given the coveted leading role of Magnolia in the road company. An instantaneous success, she played to "standing room only" for seventy-two weeks in almost every large city east of the Mississippi. Soon motion pictures studios were competing for her services.

Finally Miss Dunne accepted an RKO contract, and in 1930 she said good-by to her husband and left for Hollywood. She and Dr. Griffin had decided that she would spend only as much time in California as her work necessitated, and that whenever possible she would return to New York, where Griffin had his practice. Nearly everyone has forgotten that Irene Dunne's unheralded debut was made in a minor film called *Leathernecking*; her second screen appearance was in *Present Arms*, in which she sang "Careless Kisses," a song by an unknown composer named Oscar Levant '40. Musical pictures were out of fashion at the time, so the prudent singer applied herself to dramatic lessons. After six months of study she felt confident enough to persuade RKO to let her test for the dramatic lead opposite Richard Dix in Edna Ferber's *Cimarron*, in competition with several experienced actresses—and she won it. The picture was released in 1931, and Irene Dunne was hailed as "a new dramatic star." After hearing her deliver Sabra Cravat's speech on election to Congress, the anti-women-in-politics Will Rogers declared, "If women like Irene Dunne would run for Congress, I'd vote for them." *Back Street* (1932), a "tearjerker" in which Miss Dunne appeared, brought in more money than the previous record-holder, *All Quiet on the Western Front*; and after that the star was typed in tragic or heavily sentimental roles. Among them were leads in *Symphony of Six Million* (1932), *No Other Woman* and *The Age of Innocence* in 1934,

Columbia Pictures

IRENE DUNNE

and *Magnificent Obsession* (1935), in which Robert Taylor was her co-star. Finally, after four years of shedding seas of tears, the soprano was given a singing role.

That opportunity came when the cycle of box-office favor brought film musicals back to the screen again. Thus, in 1935 Miss Dunne was presented in what proved to be her first important musical, Jerome Kern's '42 *Roberta* (adapted from the stage version), in which she shared honors with Fred Astaire and Ginger Rogers '41. She was described as "never having sung in richer voice or with as much feeling, warmth, and understanding. . . .She attains histrionic excellence." The next year she repeated for Universal her stage success in the film *Show Boat*, and was described by Regina Crew of the New York *American* as "the personification of grace and charm in the romantic character of Magnolia. She not only sings entrancingly but displays amazing versatility . . . as a singer and comedienne." Motion picture audiences saw for the first time Miss Dunne's comedic potentialities when the star went through a "shuffle-dance" and black-face song in a scene which "had the audience in stitches." In the words of another reviewer, "Miss Dunne in the role of Magnolia hits an all-time histrionic high. . . .She transcends all former virtuosity."

The vogue for "screwball" comedies in the mid-thirties brought Miss Dunne the offer of the title role in Columbia's *Theodora Goes Wild*—a prim New Englander who writes a daring book and then tries to live up to it. Miss Dunne, feeling certain that she could not play such extravagant comedy, refused the part and went off with her husband on a European vacation, hoping that by the time her holiday was over the story would have either been filmed or shelved. But apparently the studio had confidence in Irene Dunne as a comedienne, for upon her return to work she was once more offered the role of Theodora, opposite Melvyn Douglas '42. Reluctantly she

DUNNE, IRENE—*Continued*

agreed to play the part, and, much to her surprise, she was acclaimed "a comedienne of rare ability." This 1936 success was followed by another comedy, *The Awful Truth* (1938), with Cary Grant [40], of which Louella Parsons [40] wrote: "It is going to make Irene Dunne one of the most sought-after comedy players in filmdom." In 1938 Miss Dunne also appeared in a less successful comedy, *The Joy of Living*, in which she played opposite Douglas Fairbanks, Jr. [41].

Some critics and producers are still baffled by Miss Dunne's success as a comedienne, for, as one writer put it, "How can a woman with the aplomb of a duchess act the madcap so faultlessly?" The actress herself attributes the ability to a natural flair for comedy which she says she inherited from her father, "one of the most fun-loving people in the world." "The best way to be funny," she believes, "is to be cold-blooded and purely mental about it." Miss Dunne now prefers comedy roles, and she advises young actresses to study comedy first because it is more difficult to play than tragedy: "It demands more timing, pace, shading, and subtlety of emphasis. It is difficult to learn, but once it is acquired it can be easily slowed down and becomes an excellent foundation for dramatic acting."

Miss Dunne's appearance in early 1939 with Charles Boyer [43] in RKO's *Love Affair* established them as one of the most popular romantic teams in motion pictures. The film brought such great box-office returns that a few months later Universal costarred them in *When Tommorw Comes*. That year Miss Dunne also played opposite Fred MacMurray in *Invitation to Happiness*. In 1940 she appeared in the comedy hit *My Favorite Wife*, again with Cary Grant. One reviewer wrote, "No other star can be so nicely naughty as Irene Dunne, and in this film she neatly sidesteps the censorable." Alternating between drama and comedy in 1941, she next appeared in Columbia's *Penny Serenade*, with Bing Crosby [41], and in Universal's *Unfinished Business*. Of *Penny Serenade*, the story of a childless couple who adopt an infant, Miss Dunne remarked, "I don't think I've felt as close to any picture. It's very much the scheme of my own personal life." (In 1936 Miss Dunne and her husband had adopted a one-year-old baby girl.) The New York *Sun* reviewer found that Miss Dunne in *Penny Serenade* was "perfectly cast"; and Howard Barnes of the New York *Herald Tribune* wrote that she portrayed the role with "enormous warmth and conviction." In Gregory La Cava's [41] *Unfinished Business*, Miss Dunne, according to one critic, "combined the naïveté of Cinderella and the devastating wit of a Dorothy Parker charmingly," although the picture itself was called weak. (At about this time, in the 1941-42 season, Miss Dunne appeared as guest artist with the Chicago Symphony Orchestra.)

After the failure of Universal's *Lady in a Jam* in 1942, Miss Dunne waited for a good vehicle. She found it in *A Guy Named Joe* (1943), in which she played a Ferry Command pilot loved by both Spencer Tracy [43] and Van Johnson [45]. *Variety*, the organ of show business, said her performance was "tops," and the New York *Times'* Bosley Crowther called

her, "as lovely and fetching as we've ever seen her—maybe a little more so." Doffing her uniform for a hobble skirt, Miss Dunne next appeared in an adaptation of Alice Duer Miller's narrative poem, *The White Cliffs of Dover* (1944). The actress found a special significance in the story of an American, married to a titled Englishman, who comes to love England "dearly and deeply." "I don't think it smacks of propaganda," she said, "but if it does, then I'm glad. I feel everything possible should be done to cement friendship between the two nations that are most alike and speak the same language." Howard Barnes in his *Herald Tribune* review lauded Miss Dunne's performance for its "artistry and conviction . . . it becomes the rich core of the work." "One of her most eloquent performances," commented Eileen Creelman of the New York *Sun*. Capitalizing once again on the box-office attraction of Dunne and Boyer, MGM costarred them in the latter part of 1944 in the comedy-drama *Together Again*, in which she played a widowed small-town mayor who becomes romantically involved with a New York sculptor. The New York *Sun* declared that Miss Dunne was at her comedy best; and the New York *Herald Tribune* described her as "an accomplished artist." The actress' next picture was the celluloid adaptation of Ruth Gordon's [43] successful comedy, *Over Twenty-one*, released in August 1945. On the whole, critics felt that the film did not compare favorably with the stage production, and they were divided on the merits of Miss Dunne's performance, thus: "a delightful comedy performance"; "the strong urge to ape Miss Gordon . . . becomes monotonous and distracting after a time." One of her pictures scheduled for 1946, as announced in December 1945, was expected to be the lead in Margaret Landon's [45] *Anna and the King of Siam*.

In 1936 Miss Dunne's husband, Dr. Griffin, gave up his dentistry in New York in order to join his wife in California. The Griffins had had to deny continual rumors of estrangement in the nine years of their "long-distance" marriage, during which they had seen each other only on vacations. Miss Dunne believes that she has been able to combine a successful career with a happy marriage because she and her husband have different vocations. Hollywood and movie-making, for her, have "always begun and ended on the set." She has few intimate friends in the motion picture colony, makes few public appearances, and has been described as "hard on interviewers" because of her aversion to personal publicity. At the studio she is said to be hardworking and cooperative, and is considered a shrewd business woman; at home she is Mrs. Griffin, "the gracious, charming hostess" and "a devoted mother" to her adopted daughter Mary Frances, who is called "Missy." Jerome Beatty says that Miss Dunne is "the sort of person who is never caught with her hair rumpled or in the wrong dress." The Griffins live in Holmby Hills near Hollywood, in a nine-room French Provincial home which is called "the Griffins' home," not "the Dunne residence." On weekends the actress likes to golf with her husband at Santa Barbara or Palm Springs, or entertain his business friends. The Griffins own various enterprises, among them the Griffin Wellpoint Company.

Described as a "regal beauty," the classic-featured star is five feet five inches tall, has reddish-brown hair and "warm" gray eyes. A fine complexion is considered responsible for the unusually pleasing close-ups of the actress. Miss Dunne likes to write music, to garden, play golf and badminton, and cook. She is an ardent baseball and football fan, and she especially likes the plays of Shaw [44] and Barrie. Her extravagances are perfumes, some of which she blends herself, and shoes. She made regular hospital visits to wounded servicemen during the war, to chat and to write letters for them, and it is said she enjoyed their tribute of "Hiya, pal!" and admiring whistles. As for her plans for retiring, she has said, "I guess I'll go on acting until I'm old and feeble and nobody wants to look at me any more."

References

Am Mag 134:85 Ag '42 por; 138:29+ N '44 por
Look 4:32+ O 22 '40 il pors
N Y Post p10 My 21 '41 por
International Motion Picture Almanac, 1943-44
National Cyclopædia of American Biography Current vol F p465
Who's Who in America, 1944-45
Who's Who in the Theatre (1939)

DWYFOR, DAVID LLOYD GEORGE, 1ST EARL OF *See* Lloyd George of Dwyfor, D. L. G., 1st Earl

EASLEY, CLAUDIUS M(ILLER) (ēz'lĭ) July 11, 1891—June 19, 1945 American Brigadier General who was assistant commander of the Ninety-sixth Infantry Division fighting in the Pacific campaign; killed in action on Okinawa.

Obituary

N Y Times p2 Je 21 '45 por

EATON, CHARLES A(UBREY) Mar. 29, 1868- United States Representative from New Jersey
Address: b. House of Representatives Office Bldg., Washington, D.C.; h. P.O. Box 126, Plainfield, N.J.

New Jersey's Representative in Congress since 1925, Charles A. Eaton, was named by President Roosevelt [42] to serve with the American delegation at the United Nations conference at San Francisco in April 1945. The senior minority member of the House Foreign Affairs Committee, the Republican Congressman has taken an active part in foreign affairs problems for many years as a stanch advocate of international cooperation. Before election to Congress he was for twenty-six years a minister of the Baptist Church. The Congressman also has been a newspaper correspondent, an editor, and a sociologist, specializing in industrial relations. He is described as a man of "commanding personality" and broad human sympathies.

CHARLES A. EATON

The son of Stephen and Mary Desiah (Parker) Eaton, Charles Aubrey Eaton was born March 29, 1868, in Cumberland County, Nova Scotia, Canada. There he was educated in the high schools of Truro and Amherst and at Acadia University, where he received his B.A. in 1890 and his M.A. three years later. The young man then continued his studies at Newton Theological Institution in Massachusetts (graduating in 1893), and at McMaster University in Toronto, Ontario (M.A. 1896). (Eaton has received a D.D. degree from Baylor University in 1899, from Acadia University in 1907, and a LL.D. from McMaster University in 1916.) He was ordained in the Baptist ministry in 1893, becoming pastor of the First Church, Natick, Massachusetts, shortly thereafter. In 1895 Eaton assumed the pastorate of the Bloor Street Church in Toronto, where he remained for five years. It was in June 1895 that he was married to Mary Winifred Parlin. The couple had six children: Marion Aubrey, Margaret Evelyn, Frances Winifred, Charles Aubrey, Mary Rose, and Catharine Starr.

In 1901 Eaton's ministerial duties took him to the United States, to Cleveland, where he became pastor of the Euclid Avenue Church. From his Cleveland post Eaton was transferred in 1909 to New York's Madison Avenue Baptist Church. During these years, in addition to his clerical duties, Eaton indulged his liking for journalism. From 1896 to 1901 he was sociological editor of the Toronto *Globe.* In 1899 he also became associate editor of the *Westminster,* a monthly magazine published in Toronto. In addition, Eaton held the position of special correspondent for the New York *Tribune* and the Boston *Transcript* from 1897 to 1901. At one time the busy clergyman also acted as special correspondent for the London *Times.*

During the First World War Eaton won respect as a speaker and worker for the Allied cause. He served as head of the National Service Section of the United States Shipping Board, Emergency Fleet Corporation, engaged

EATON, CHARLES A.—*Continued*

in increasing the production of ships. This vital production role brought him into close contact with capitalistic and labor groups. During the stormy industrial era following the war Eaton endeavored to apply his knowledge of industrial relations toward improving living conditions. In July 1919 *World Outlook* published his article, "Labor's Stake in Capital." In a brief analysis of the relationship of capital and labor, Eaton declared: "The way to establish good will in industry is to make every man associated with that industry consciously and gladly a part of the entire organization." The pastor-sociologist made another significant statement that after some twenty-five years is still timely. "If the war has taught the world anything, it is that the destinies of men and nations are determined by what they are in their minds and hearts. If the war has decided any issue, it is that the whole world must adopt the principle of democracy in the entirety of its life."

Another article by Eaton appeared in the January 1920 issue of *World Outlook*, "What Is Wrong in the Industrial World." In his discussion of this theme, Eaton declared, "I have no theory to exploit and no party to advance. I interpret life from the point of view of its universal and spiritual aspect." He went on to consider the practical steps essential to improved industrial relations: "Industrial relations are human relations. . . .They are the vital moral relationships between living men described as capitalists and other living men described as laborers. . . .This man-to-man relationship . . . implies a sense of obligation toward each other." In his summation of the demands of the worker, he said that the American worker is aiming at "the betterment of his social and economic condition." Eaton is the author of two religious works, *Troubled Hearts* (1899) and *The Old Evangel and the New Evangelism* (1901). The pastor is also well known as a lecturer. He has visited England and the Continent many times and has preached several seasons in prominent London churches. His lectures were noted for their "beautiful imagery, clear reasoning, and brilliant wit."

Deeply interested in the problems of labor, Eaton resigned his pastorate of the Madison Avenue Baptist Church in 1919, to devote his time to this work. He became head of the industrial relations department of the National Lamp Works of the General Electric Company, in New Jersey; he has been editor of the company's publication, *Light*, since 1923. Eaton was first elected to Congress from the Fourth New Jersey District in 1925. From that time on he has retained his Congressional seat, representing the Fifth New Jersey District since 1933. The former minister is one of the leaders of the Republican Party, but in Congress his adherence to party lines has not been strict; he did not maintain an attitude of complete opposition to the Roosevelt Administration as did many of his party colleagues. On foreign policy Eaton followed the White House rather closely. This situation led one writer to call Eaton "something of an exception to the general run of violent anti-New Deal feeling among House Republicans."

Eaton occupies an important position as ranking Republican member of the powerful House Foreign Affairs Committee. In February 1943 the New Jersey Representative was among the Congressional leaders at the White House conference at which President Roosevelt revealed the secret offensive war plans for 1943 mapped at the Allied conference in Casablanca. In September of that year Eaton played a prominent role in Congressional debate on the Fulbright '43 resolution. He said tersely: "The question is just this, do we want to substitute law for force in world affairs? If we do, then the United States must participate. And if the United States is to participate, then Congress must say so." Thus Eaton strongly endorsed the Fulbright measure, declaring, "The problem is a challenge to the family of nations to do what the states of this Union have done." At one point during the lengthy debate on the resolution Eaton rose and told the half-empty House, "What are we fussing about here when we haven't enough interest to fill these seats and when we do fill them we sit around and gab and gossip like a bunch of old women at a sewing party? If we haven't enough interest, we should get out and give room for some decent people who have a sense of responsibility about these issues which will be here a hundred years from now." As the white-haired Republican continued his address the seats of the chamber were gradually filled, and when Eaton finished his speech the entire House rose in tribute.

The Republican Congressman voted for such measures as Lend-Lease, naval expansion, and the United Nations Relief and Rehabilitation Administration. During the debate on UNRRA Eaton was one of the vocal defenders of the relief measure, leading the Republican "cheering section" in its favor. Urging approval of the bill, he stated, "The object of this legislation—and do not forget it—is to help those people help themselves. . . .We cannot be a healthy nation surrounded by a sick world."

Eaton's Congressional record indicates, however, that his opposition to the New Deal's domestic policies was consistent. He voted against the WPA in 1939, the NYA in 1940, and against the rural electrification program in 1943. Also, in 1943 he voted to override the Presidential veto of the Smith '41-Connally '41 bill and the income tax bill. That same year he registered his opposition to the President's $25,000 income limit (after taxes) by voting for its abolition. The Republican also voted against the food subsidy program and the Federal ballot bill for servicemen.

As a prominent Republican leader, Eaton served on the committee which drafted that party's declaration of foreign policy at Mackinac Island, Michigan, in September 1943. The following July, Eaton conferred with Governor Thomas E. Dewey '44 in Albany, discussing politics and foreign affairs. After the meeting Eaton stated that he and Dewey agreed that America must take an active part in postwar world affairs. Voicing his opinion on this issue, Eaton declared, "My view all my life has been that this is the greatest, most powerful nation in the world economically, and the possession of that power involves responsibilities we must discharge, and whether we like it or not, this nation must take its place of leadership in world affairs." Eaton added that he and Dewey also agreed that the United States has the responsibility of aiding in European rehabilitation. But he qualified this opinion: "As soon as we have discharged our humanitarian duty to the starving and homeless—and that we ought to do as a free gift, as we always have done in times of great calamity elsewhere—then, after that, we ought not to be the world's Santa Claus." Eaton is a member of the American Post-War Association, described as an "organization of internationalists."

From the wealth of his experience Eaton wrote an article for the New York *Times*, published in the Sunday magazine section of that paper on March 4, 1945. Under the title "A Member of Congress Looks at Congress," Eaton discussed the composition and operation of the legislative body. Writing as a veteran of twenty-one consecutive years of Congressional service, he analyzed the functions of this body in American life. Pointing out the forces influencing Congress, he stated, "It must be kept in mind that Congress is always representative of actively warring political parties and, in these enlightened times, is further bedeviled by an army of predatory pressure groups who think and act only in terms of their own selfish advantage. It is inevitable that each of these power and profit-hungry parties and groups should have few kind words for members of Congress who refuse, as many do, to jump when they crack the whip." Eaton further declared that "the members of Congress, in character, ability, and patriotism, are representative of the people who elect them. Regardless of party labels, they constitute a true cross section out of the upper and middle strata of our national life." The article also treated plans for Congressional reorganization—efforts to "streamline" Congressional procedure.

On February 13, 1945, President Roosevelt announced the membership of the United States delegation that would attend the United Nations conference in San Francisco, starting April 25. Secretary of State Stettinius '40 was named chairman, while Cordell Hull '40 was appointed senior adviser. The other members besides Eaton were Virginia Gildersleeve '41, Senators Tom Connally and Arthur Vandenberg '40, Representative Sol Bloom '43 and Commander Harold Stassen '40. The New Jersey Congressmen went to San Francisco a strong advocate of international cooperation and American participation in world affairs. When the Teheran declaration of 1943 was first made public Eaton hailed it as "one of the most momentous documents ever penned."

He is credited with having done much hard work on the committee dealing with general provisions, including membership, of the United Nations Organization. As the conference approached its close Representative Eaton thus summed up the sentiments of the American delegation in particular: "There were times when I thought we were in danger of building for primeval chaos. Now I really think we're getting somewhere on the road to permanent peace." In his report to the House of Representatives in July, the legislator said, "In my judgment, the San Francisco conference and the Charter as created, regardless of whatever

imperfections it may develop in practice, is the greatest and most hopeful public event in history." Commenting on the American delegation, he added, "We represented as a sacred trust every white cross marking the burial place of every man and woman at every battle front who, like their Divine Redeemer, in saving others could not save themselves." Only a short time before he uttered these words the War Department had reported the death of his twenty-three-year-old grandson, Lieutenant Douglas Wilson Demler, Jr., of the United States Marine Corps, who was killed in action in May on Okinawa.

References

> Congressional Directory, 1945
> Who's Who in America, 1944-45
> Who's Who in the Nation's Capital, 1938-39

EDGE, WALTER E(VANS) Nov. 20, 1873- Governor of New Jersey

Address: b. State House, Trenton, N.J.; Press-Union Bldg., Atlantic Ave., Atlantic City, N.J.; h. Morven, Princeton, N.J.

Elected Governor of New Jersey on the Republican ticket in 1943, Walter E. Edge has attracted national attention for his sponsorship of progressive social legislation in that state, for his fight to secure a new State constitution, and for his vigorous opposition to the rule of Frank Hague, the Mayor of Jersey City and Democratic boss of Hudson County.

Walter Evans Edge is a Pennsylvanian, born in Philadelphia on November 20, 1873. His parents were William and Mary (Evans) Edge. He is a descendant of John Edge, who settled in the sixteen-seventies in Chester Valley, Pennsylvania, on a grant from William Penn. When he was a small boy Walter's family moved to Pleasantville, New Jersey, where he was graduated from grammar school at the age of fourteen.

His first job was as printer's devil on the Atlantic City *Review*, which he soon left for a position with the Dorland Advertising Agency, a small Atlantic City firm. (Later he was to become the owner of the agency and develop it into an international organization with offices in New York, London, Paris, Berlin, and Moscow.) When he was twenty-two Edge decided to return to the newspaper business. He started his own paper, the Atlantic City *Guest*, which later became the Atlantic City *Daily Press*. Subsequently he acquired the Atlantic City *Evening Union*, actively directing this publication and the *Press* for many years.

In 1897, when he was twenty-four, Edge began his political career by becoming a clerk in the New Jersey State Senate. After an interim, during which he fought in the Spanish-American War as a lieutenant in the Fourth New Jersey Volunteer Infantry, he became secretary of the Senate (1901-4). In 1910 he was elected to the New Jersey Assembly, becoming Republican leader in the State Senate (1911-16).

With his election to the governorship in 1917, Walter Edge brought his state into a position of national prominence. Progressive in outlook, he is considered as having instituted sound business and social legislation, and was respon-

Underwood & Underwood

WALTER E. EDGE

sible for the first workmen's compensation and employers' liability law in the State. He pioneered with the "pay-as-you-go" policy in New Jersey's public affairs, he consolidated State penal and charitable institutions, and he reorganized other departments for greater economy and efficiency in administration. He also sponsored the legislation which laid the basis for New Jersey's present State highway system, and for the construction of the Holland Tunnel and Delaware River Bridge.

Governor Edge resigned from his office in 1919 after his election to a seat in the United States Senate. (At the end of his six-year term he was re-elected.) During his years as Senator Edge backed much social legislation and adhered to the tenets of sound business practices in government. In 1929 he again resigned from an office, this time to accept the post of Ambassador Extraordinary and Plenipotentiary to France, a post he held until 1933. He is said to have won the admiration and respect of the French people, and he was instrumental in negotiating several trade treaties and economic agreements.

After some thirty years in public office Ambassador Edge retired to private activities. In the role of an elder statesman of the Republican Party, he continued his interests, however, in political affairs. His party regularly selected him as delegate at large to each national convention, and he took an active part in every campaign. In 1939, when repeal of the arms embargo was before the United States Congress, he insisted that all possible aid be given the Allies. He was keynote speaker at the New Jersey State Republican Convention in 1940, the year Charles Edison [40] was running for Governor on the Democratic ticket. "If Charles Edison is a good Secretary of the Navy," commented Edge, "he should stay in that post as a patriotic duty. If he isn't, he's not good enough to be Governor of New Jersey." Edge also defended the Republican Party from the charges of

President Roosevelt [42] that the party in 1933 had left the Army and Navy at its lowest ebb: he maintained that both parties had at that time directed every effort toward disarmament.

Three years later, with his country at war, the sixty-nine-year-old Edge found himself supported by New Jersey Republicans for the party's gubernatorial nomination of September 1943. He had emerged as the only candidate about whom most elements could rally, and he himself had expressed a desire to return to public office, prompted, he explained, by an aversion to being idle while great issues, raised by the war, were at stake. Leading Republican papers put themselves enthusiastically behind his candidacy, the New York *Herald Tribune* commenting that he possessed "initiative, energy, and the gift of leadership."

Mayor Hague and his supporters exerted every effort to find a strong candidate to oppose Edge. Mayor Vincent J. Murphy of Newark was finally chosen, but the campaign was one of Hague versus Edge. Said the Republican candidate: "I deprecate the effort being made by the opposition during this campaign to place labor on the bargain counter; to command labor to vote en masse for my opponent because he happens to be an official of a labor organization. . . .Those who seek to divide us here on the home front are guilty of a grave disservice to the Nation in the hour of its greatest crisis." Mayor Murphy, on the other hand, accused Edge, among other things, of appeasement and isolationist views. It was this charge which Wendell Willkie [40] called "ridiculous." He declared that as far back as 1919 Edge, in a speech in the Senate, had warned that the United States could not hold aloof from the problems of the world, that the airplane had destroyed America's isolation. Willkie recalled that the Republican had "fought vigorously [in 1940] against the attempts of noninterventionists to attach the so-called 'peace party' label to the Republican Party."

During his campaign Edge promised many social reforms, plans for State aid in the postwar employment of veterans, and revision of New Jersey's outmoded hundred-year-old constitution (a reform which he had helped Governor Edison push through the legislature). In addition, he stated his belief that "a new period of international cooperation is necessary to avert future world catastrophies."

Despite the big Democratic vote turned in by the Hague machine, Edge was elected to the governorship of New Jersey by an approximate plurality of 128,000 votes, the largest for a winning candidate since 1931. Moreover, the Republicans maintained their control of both houses of the legislature, with electoral approval of revision of the constitution for the first time in ninety-nine years. The Edge victory was hailed as a big blow to Hague—the worst defeat in his long career as political czar of the State. Former Governor Edison praised the large affirmative vote for constitutional revision as "proof that democracy works."

At his inauguration on January 18, 1944, Governor Edge, after stressing that the war program should not be impeded by strikes, outlined some of the desirable features proposed for the new constitution: a unified court structure; an extension of the governor's term to four years (to become effective with the next governor); the powers of the office strengthened to make the executive the actual head of the State government; a revised legislative section that would extend the Senate term to four years and the Assembly to two, with an increased compensation; and the improvement of fiscal procedures with a single State budget embracing all revenues and expenditures of the State.

The new Governor also promised speedy action to remedy the vote-getting irregularities in Hudson County. He recommended legislation requiring the installation of voting machines throughout all counties where such irregularities were reported. But it was a proposed drastic change in the State's judiciary system which would most affect Hague. A state-wide superior court would absorb the several existing district courts, all of which would considerably damage the prestige of Hague as a patronage dispenser. (In 1944 a bill for an independent grand jury was passed through the legislature at the behest of Edge. There still remained to be corrected, however, other recognized glaring defects of the antiquated judicial system.)

The new constitution, drafted by a committee of thirty members of the legislature, all Republican, was submitted to the legislature on January 25, 1944. Arrangements were made for public hearings to be held before a final draft was submitted to the people for ratification or rejection at the general election that November. In his annual budget message in February, Governor Edge proposed that a fund of $25,489,504 be set aside for postwar needs. Moreover, determined that his legislative program should be translated into law before he began distribution of patronage, Governor Edge "permitted the patronage log jam to continue," much to the disappointment of a large element in his party interested in political jobs.

On February 23 a soldier-vote bill, described as "much more liberal than that of any other state," was signed by Governor Edge. The law gave members of the armed forces and organizations such as the Red Cross, the merchant marine, and the USO an opportunity to vote for candidates for local, county, State and Federal offices. Edge did not wait for the Adjutant General's Department to compile the addresses of military personnel. Instead, he enlisted the aid of air-raid wardens and various organizations to make a house-to-house canvass to obtain the service address of every New Jersey resident in the armed services. And, although he believed two types of ballots would be confusing, he informed Roosevelt that New Jersey would authorize the use of the Federal ballot.

During the next few weeks the Governor worked for the passage of many important bills. He initiated a bill to reform the administration of State civil service. He signed bills to create a State department of taxation and finance; to provide State guaranties of loans up to three thousand dollars to veterans wishing to borrow funds to set themselves up in business or professions; to render illegal the practice of placing children for adoption on a commercial basis; to establish a State Department of Economic Development to deal with postwar problems. "During his first three

months in office," commented the New York *Herald Tribune,* he gave "new life to the government of his state and new spirit to his party." Edge also instituted a program to consolidate the government departments, a program which affected about one hundred State agencies.

Interest early turned to the role of New Jersey in the 1944 Presidential election. Republicans had high hopes that the State, Democratic in the last two elections, would return to Republican allegiance. Consequently, Governor Edge was boomed for the post of convention keynoter—an honor which he declined. He also said that New Jersey delegates to the convention would go unpledged to the support of any one candidate. But he was convinced, he said, that the Republican Party would carry the Nation. In several speeches he demanded a firm anti-isolationist stand. "We can't pussyfoot on international responsibilities," he said. "When this war is won we cannot drop our arms and run away unless we are prepared to invite a third world cataclysm." In an address at Drexel Institute he reiterated his advocacy of compulsory military training after the war. At the early sessions of the national convention he renewed his demand for the removal of "weasel words" from the tentative declaration favoring United States participation in a postwar security organization. Edge said he would challenge the platform on the floor of the convention if it was less than outspoken in behalf of world organization. But although the plank as finally drafted by Senators Warren Austin '44 and Arthur Vandenberg '40 did not meet with his full approval, Edge said that since the Republican nominee, Thomas E. Dewey '44, had accepted it, he also would. "I have every confidence that Governor Dewey will enlarge and amplify the party's position on this foreign policy plank." During the next few months Edge led the Republicans of New Jersey in an all-out campaign for his fellow Governor from New York State.

Domestic issues in New Jersey were a more difficult matter. The Hague machine had been rallying its forces for the forthcoming election. When Edge said, "The public interest in primary elections has become so apathetic they might as well be abolished," the Hague men accused him of plotting to end the open primary law. Hague also began his attacks on what he called the "unscrupulous railroad lobby with the power of the Edge administration behind it," which would "rob the people of every municipality in the State of railroad-tax interest which the high court has said is due and owing." Hague faced the possibility that the State might deny him Jersey City's ten-million-dollar share in the interest involved, on the basis of a two-year-old Supreme Court decision in another tax case.

Charging that the proposed new State charter was "loaded with tricks," Hague renewed his attack upon constitutional reform. Edge accused him of making the issue a political one. Altogether, the campaign was quite bitter. Hague's argument that war veterans would not receive a fair deal under the new constitution induced a number of veterans' organizations to go on record against it. His charge that the constitution did not protect labor influenced

EDGE, WALTER E.—*Continued*

both the CIO and the A.F. of L. to oppose it. Farmers were led to opposition, likewise the New Jersey Civil Service. When the Teachers Association of Jersey City took its stand against revision, Edge accused Hague of using "Hitler Gestapo pressure." He charged also that Hague was making misrepresentations designed to influence Roman Catholics to vote against constitutional reform. "A new falsehood, a new lie, a new appeal to a religious or racial group each day is Hague's answer to the many advantages for every citizen presented in this new constitution," said Edge in October. "During the last few weeks we have experienced one of the most vicious and unprincipled campaigns to sabotage a great public movement ever undertaken."

On November 7, 1944, the voters of New Jersey decided against the revision of the constitution. They also decided that they wanted President Roosevelt for another four years. It was a double triumph for Democratic Mayor Hague and his machine; and the rejection of the constitution was a keen disappointment to Governor Edge. The number of votes cast was larger than it had been in 1940, despite the fact that the Governor had declined the request of labor officials to extend the voting time. It was noted that in the wards in Jersey City, however, where voting machines had been installed for the first time, the Democratic vote was considerably lighter than it had previously been.

In spite of the November setbacks, Governor Edge was determined to carry on his reform program. When the New Jersey Legislature met in January 1945 he presented a fourteen-point program calling for broad reforms in the State government, and also promised that new plans for a revised constitution would be made. The new program included plans for much-needed improvements in the New Jersey highway system, liberalization of workmen's compensation and unemployment benefits, better regulation of migrant farm labor, strengthening of the Election Act, and adoption of a formula for suitable distribution of railroad-tax interest.

The stern warning of the Governor that he would not submit to legislative or other dictation in filling offices brought forth a good deal of criticism not only from the Democrats, but from some Republican members of the legislature. Indications were that, although the legislature was Republican-controlled, Governor Edge would find rougher sledding for his recommendations in 1945 than he had in 1944. Hague and his organization renewed the fight against Edge over the rail-tax funds; but the bills as proposed by him were passed despite Hague's opposition. When the matter of cheaper rates in transportation facilities by the Port of New York Authority (operating the Holland and Lincoln tunnels from Manhattan to New Jersey) came up, Hague supported the continuance in office of Frank Ferguson, president of the Hudson County National Bank, as Port Authority chairman. Under Ferguson, according to *PM*, pleas of motorists for a reduction in tolls have been ignored, "but, meanwhile, the Authority has continued to roll up surpluses tucked away in 'special reserves.'"

In the spring of 1945 the Governor signed other new laws: introduction into high schools of a required two-year course in American history and democracy; a reorganization of the State Board of Labor Mediation which increased the membership from five to seven; creation of a commission to deal with alcoholics as sick rather than as immoral persons; creation of a single general State fund and a single appropriations bill; placing in the general fund of the State treasury all interest on delinquent railroad taxes; liberalization of specific housing standards for migrant labor camps in regard to sleeping, health, eating, and recreational facilities. Said the president of the State Federation of Labor: "We have gotten more and better labor legislation during Governor Edge's term of office than we have under any other governor of New Jersey."

One measure which received divided comment upon passage that spring was the series of seven bills banning racial and religious discrimination in employment, schools, municipal hospitals, hotels, and places of entertainment. *PM* called the fair employment measure a crippled bill which incorporated "none of the amendments demanded almost unanimously by New Jersey civic, labor, political, religious, and Negro groups." The New York *Herald Tribune*'s comment was that the bills "translated vital principles of social justice into statutory form. Their weakness lies in the severity of their provisions. Under these laws discrimination would constitute a misdemeanor. Whether grand juries will indict . . . is questionable. The laws will prove of little practical benefit if unenforceable."

At the Governors' Conference which was held at Mackinac Island, Michigan, in July 1945, a committee of nine state governors was organized in an attempt to cope with the Nation's food shortage. Governor Edge was named chairman of the committee, and announced that the first move would be to get all figures on purchases, stocks, and requirements directly from the military agencies, Lend-Lease, United Nations Relief and Rehabilitation Administration, and the Maritime Service. In September, turning his attention to problems of reconversion after the fall of Japan, Governor Edge announced that New Jersey was ready to spend from seventeen to twenty million dollars in immediate public improvements to relieve unemployment. He added, however, that he expected private industry to do most of the work in absorbing unemployed workers. For the housing shortage, especially as it affects the needs of returning veterans, Edge, in October, recommended relaxation of municipal zoning restrictions to permit conversion of large dwellings into multi-family units.

Governor Edge was married to Camilla Loyall A. Sewall in 1922 (his first wife, Lady Lee Phillips, died in 1915). He has four children: Walter E. Edge, Jr. (by his first wife), in service with the Army Air Forces; Camilla Sewall, who in 1944 was married to Edward B. Lee, Jr.; Mary Esther, who has worked with the Women's Land Army; and Loyall Howard. In December 1944 Governor and Mrs. Edge moved from Ventnor, New Jersey, into Morven, an historic house near Princeton, which the Governor had purchased to present to the State for use either as a governor's mansion or an historic shrine. It was in 1944 that Governor Edge announced that New Jersey—in addition to progressive social legislation—had another improvement: The State, he said, need no longer be known as the "Mosquito State," because "almost miraculous progress" had been made by an extermination commission. By gubernatorial proclamation, New Jersey would again use its official name, the "Garden State," taking for its emblem the violet.

References

N Y Herald Tribune p4 Mr 29 '44 por
N Y Times p14 Ap 30 '43
National Cyclopædia of American Biography Current vol B p279
Who's Who in America, 1944-45
Who's Who in Government (1932)

EDWARDS, GUS Aug. 18, 1881(?)—Nov. 7, 1945 American actor, song-writer, and talent scout; stage performer for thirty years; motion picture actor since 1928; composer of the songs "Schooldays", "Orange Blossom Time", "When the Roses Bloom Again"; helped to discover and develop such comedians as George Jessel '43, Eddie Cantor '41 and Groucho Marx; *The Star Maker* (1939) was a motion picture based on his life.

Obituary

N Y Times p20 N 9 '45

EDWARDS, JOHN H(OMER) Sept. 10, 1869—Aug. 20, 1945 Former Assistant Secretary of the Interior during President Coolidge's Administration; elected to the Indiana House of Representatives in 1903, and served for three terms; was solicitor of the Post Office Department (1921-23): retired from Government service in 1933.

Obituary

N Y Times p21 Ag 21 '45

EICHER, EDWARD C(LAYTON) (ĭk'ĕr) Dec. 16, 1878—Nov. 30(?), 1944 Chief Justice of the United States Federal District Court for the District of Columbia; had presided over mass sedition trial since April 1944; was a member of the Securities and Exchange Commission (1938-42), chairman for the year 1941-42. See *Current Biography* 1941 Yearbook.

Obituary

N Y Times p16 D 1 '44 por

EKMAN, CARL GUSTAF 1872—June 15, 1945 Swedish politician and journalist; former leader of the Independent People's party; began his career as a stonecutter and a blacksmith; was the first workman to rise to the Premiership (1926-28 and 1930-32); called "the strong man in Swedish politics" till resignation in 1932.

Obituary

N Y Times p13 Je 16 '45

ELMAN, MISCHA (mē'shä) Jan. 20, 1891-
Violinist
Address: b. c/o Bernard R. La Berge, Inc., 119 W. 57th St., New York City; h. 101 Central Park West, New York City

Mischa Elman has been a violin virtuoso for more than three decades. Since making his musical debut as a boy of thirteen, the Russian-American artist has given more than three thousand concerts throughout the world. Today, with more than two million Elman records in circulation, it has been said that at every hour of the day this interpreter of Brahms, Beethoven, and Mendelssohn is being heard by music lovers somewhere. He is likewise acclaimed for his interpretation of a concerto by the Czech modernist Bohuslav Martinů '44.

Born in the ghetto of Talnoye in the Russian Ukraine, on January 20, 1891, Mischa Elman is the grandson of a concert violinist and the son of Saul Elman, a teacher of religion, who played the violin for diversion. Mischa's two sisters were also musical. The musician has said of his father, "He had more influence on me than any other human being. He traveled with me every minute until I was twenty-one, and, until he died [in 1940], was in complete sympathy with everything I did." At the age of four little Mischa began the study of the violin under his father's instruction. A year later the Countess Orosova invited him to give a private performance. Impressed by the boy's unusual talent, she engaged an experienced teacher for him. The first honor of his career came a few months later: He won a scholarship to the Odessa Imperial Academy of Music, where he was to study for five years under Fiedelmann.

In 1902 Leopold Auer, violinist to the Czar and Russia's most noted teacher of the violin, used his influence to gain the boy's admission as a free pupil to the St. Petersburg Conservatory, where he himself taught. Under Auer's guidance Mischa frequently played in the palaces of the nobility. On one of these occasions the Grand Duke of Mecklenburg-Strelitz gave the boy his first fine violin, an Amati.

Following a successful concert of Mischa's at the St. Petersburg Conservatory in 1904, Auer arranged for his thirteen-year-old pupil's debut in Berlin in October of the same year. It was an event that might not have taken place. "In my native Russia," related Elman in an *Etude* article, "we were quite definitely poor." When he went to the German capital he and his father had their first experience of living in a hotel. "That was the first time I had seen gaslight, and it was an event to have it in my own room, quite as rich people did." Not knowing how to turn off the gas completely, the boy almost fatally asphyxiated himself the night before his concert. When he stepped before the audience, Elman recalls, he felt giddy and ill, but he played with that "curious surcharge of energy that sometimes flames up in sick people." The program included Tchaikovsky's Violin Concerto, Bach's *Chaconne,* and other works of the classical concert repertoire. He got through all but the final group before he collapsed on the stage—but "the critical, discriminating audience of musical Berlin" acclaimed him one of the greatest of child prodigies. Concert dates in other German

J. Abresch

MISCHA ELMAN

cities followed. The great conductors Nikisch, Hans Richter, and Fiedler praised him; Joseph Joachim, the noted violinist, added his enthusiastic approval.

After a series of public appearances on the Continent, Mischa Elman soon made his debut in London. Acclaimed as a musical genius, the bushy-haired, blue-eyed youth became the idol of London society. It was at a command performance at Buckingham Palace that he met Caruso and their friendship began. At the concert King Edward had asked young Elman his opinion of London. To the amusement of the King and Caruso, who was standing near-by, the young violinist made no reference to his musical triumphs—it was the London bobbies who had delighted the boy. When Elman later went to the United States for his American debut, the two artists became close friends, and the phonograph records they made together are collectors' items today.

Elman's first American appearance, as soloist with the Russian Symphony Orchestra in New York on December 10, 1908, was a sensational success. The occasion, many critics said, marked his transformation from a child prodigy to a mature artist. Despite the fact that he was only seventeen, he impressed some of the critics to the extent that they classed him with Joachim and Ysaye. The connection, said Reginald de Koven in the New York *World*, "is obvious—marvelous and dashing interpretation is characteristic of all three of the artists." Critic James Huneker, while praising Elman's "amazing technical precision" and "still more amazing emotional temperament," was of the opinion that the violinist's conception of Beethoven was "neither as erudite as Kreisler's '[44]', nor as fascinating as Ysaye's."

After the Russian violinist's first recital at New York's Carnegie Hall the same month, Richard Aldrich, critic of the New York *Times,* observed that although Elman appeared to be trying to cast off his reputation as an infant curiosity and was demanding to be heard as an artist, "the shadow of his early exploitation as a prodigy lies upon his mature artistry, to its injury and disadvantages. There are serious defects in his playing," continued the critic, "that prevent him from taking the position of a truly great artist. He is too apt to force the note of pathos, of sentiment, of 'expression' generally." On another occasion the same critic commented, however, that there had been much to be admired in the performance: "the beauty and poignacy of the tone, the elasticity of the bowing, the clean precision of the left hand, the brilliancy that lightened it all."

Some years later James Huneker wrote of Elman: "United to an amazing technical precision there is a still more amazing emotional temperament all dominated by a powerful musical and mental intellect that is uncanny."

And later critics gave Elman a high standing; according to the distinguished critic Olin Downes '[43], "in several respects, there is no other violinist who rivals the magnificent stamina, breadth, and vitality of his art today," and none who gives certain music, specifically the Vitali-Charlier *Chaconne*, "a grander arch, a dignity, and distribution of detail." One reviewer complained that the violinist seemed "enamored of his own tone" and tried to improve on the work of a master; but Arthur Berger of the New York *Sun* holds that Elman's playing "continues to acquire new depth, directness, and musicality" after more than thirty years as a leading concert artist.

The veteran musician has appeared during his career as soloist with the major American and European orchestras. He has toured the world many times and was the first international artist to make concert appearances throughout the Far East. Generous in contributing his talent to benefit performances, in one year he made a coast-to-coast tour of the United States, giving twenty-six concerts to raise funds for the relief of refugees of all faiths. He also played frequently during the Second World War at service camps. His plans for the future include a tour of the Soviet Union and an appearance in Czechoslovakia to play a concerto which the Czech composer Bohuslav Martinů wrote expressly for him. Elman gave this work its première at a Boston Symphony concert at Carnegie Hall in January 1944—and the violinist's first essay into the field of contemporary music was acclaimed in the musical world.

The virtuoso does not object to "boogie-woogie." "To protest today against swing and jazz," he has said, "is as silly as it was for our grandfathers to protest against the waltz. Swing is just a social expression of our city youth and is a good outlet for their energies and emotions. It is no more to be deplored than the breakdown dances, let us say, in the country." He also pointed out that jazz supplies "the one remaining free improvisatory factor in the whole of music, and, as such, as every good musician knows, holds untold possibilities for the creative music of the future."

Since Elman has been continuously popular with American audiences (in his first season in the United States he played twenty-two concerts in New York and seventy throughout the rest of the country), he has made New York his home, and in 1923 became a naturalized citizen of the United States. Two years later he was married to Helen Frances Katten, whose wedding gift to him was the Madame Recamier Stradivarius (In addition to that instrument and the Amati, he also owns the Joachim Stradivarius.) The success of his marriage, says the violinist, is largely due to the fact that his American wife, although a music lover, "can't play a thing." Their daughter Nadia plays the piano but is ambitious for a theatrical career, while their son Joseph "fiddles strictly for fun." The Elmans live in a duplex apartment overlooking Central Park. Chess is one of Elman's hobbies. In appearance he is short, round-faced, and bald; and an outstanding trait of his personality is his rich sense of humor.

His days follow a businesslike schedule: He rises at eight-thirty, and, like many businessmen, he eats breakfast as he reads the paper. He begins practicing at nine and his accompanist arrives at ten. The rest of the morning is devoted to rehearsal of the next concert. (His repertoire consists of over six hundred numbers.) Afternoons are devoted to business appointments. "In a career of over forty years," the *New Yorker* reported in 1944, "Elman has had only five regular accompanists, and he regards it as a tribute to his lack of temperament that he has remained friends with all of them. 'I do not understand this raging and screaming that some artists do,' he has said. 'If I am uncertain, my accompanist is uncertain. It is better that I scream at myself. Not that I ever do, of course.'"

References

Etude 59:588 S '41
N Y Herald Tribune Mag p2 Ap 30 '44 por
N Y Post Mag p33 O 19 '44 pors
Opera News 8:9-10 Mr 6 '44 por
PM p20 O 18 '44 por
Baker's Biographical Dictionary of Musicians (1940)
Ewen, D. ed Living Musicians (1940)
Who's Who in America, 1944-45

EPSTEIN, JACOB (ĕp′stīn) 1880- Sculptor; artist

Address: 18 Hyde Park Gate, London

Probably the best-known contemporary sculptor as well as the most discussed artist since Rodin, Jacob Epstein was born in 1880 in New York's Hester Street. He describes the neighborhood, the lower East Side, as "the most densely populated of any city on earth . . . and the sight, sounds, and smells had the vividness and sharp impact of an Oriental city." The Epsteins were not poor, however; the sculptor tells "they had prospered, and I can recall that we had Polish Christian servants who still retained peasant habits, speaking no English, wearing kerchiefs, and going about on bare feet." The third of a large family of Russian-Polish Jews, Jacob was "the sick one," and took little part in family or religious activities. He was intensely absorbed in reading and drawing; at school, the teachers were so impressed by his talent that they disregarded his inattention to mathematics and grammar. Jacob was something of a trial to his non-artistic parents, however, "going off to the woods with a book, and not turning up at meals."

JACOB EPSTEIN

When the Epsteins moved uptown to "a more respectable and duller part of the city," Jacob stayed on Hester Street, where he could see and draw from "the most diverse life of many lands." Around the turn of the century Epstein entered the Art Students' League school. Although he "felt like a fish out of water" there, the youth was able to keep himself going by selling his drawings for small sums, and attended concerts, opera, and endless political meetings, always as a spectator rather than a participant. As a relief for his strained eyes, he turned to sculpture. In 1901 Epstein went to work in a foundry for bronze casting, at the same time studying sculptural modeling at night under the distinguished sculptor George Grey Barnard. Although he was greatly impressed by Barnard, the young East Sider was dissatisfied with the possibilities for further study, and determined to go to Paris as soon as he could manage it.

At this time Epstein met the writer Hutchins Hapgood, who chose him to illustrate *The Spirit of the Ghetto* (1902), for which the publishers paid him four hundred dollars. He sold some drawings, also, to the *Century Magazine,* and with this money bought passage to Europe. Epstein writes that he went directly to France; but, according to Arthur Strawn, it was in London, where he lived on rice and tea in an old stable, that the burning-eyed young artist was introduced to Mrs. Hamilton Fish. Mrs. Fish, a wealthy American patroness of the arts, financed his study in Paris. It was "a most interesting period artistically . . . the rebels were just beginning to gain recognition at the expense of the Academicians." Epstein shared a studio with an old friend, and "hurled himself at the clay," avoiding all the usual Bohemian distractions. The American soon applied for admission to the Ecole des Beaux-Arts where he spent his mornings modeling from life, and his afternoons carving in marble and drawing from casts. Foreigners, he writes, were few and unpopular. After six months

EPSTEIN, JACOB—*Continued*

his refusal to run errands, according to custom, for the students who entered a certain competition, aroused so much hostility that he went over to the Julien Academy. According to Strawn, Epstein won some important prizes in Paris. While there he "worked in a sustained explosion of energy," destroying each study after a week.

After three years, finding himself at a dead end in his work, Epstein went to London, attracted by the "easy and natural manners and great courtesy" of the English, and the riches of the British Museum; and after a visit to America (traveling steerage), he took up permanent residence in England, eventually becoming a British subject. The penniless twenty-six-year-old was still working hard at his studies when, in 1906, he married a "charming and forceful" Scotswoman, Margaret Gilmour Dunlop, whom he had met in Paris. According to Strawn, the couple "occupied two bare rooms, one serving as studio. . . . To earn money Epstein served as model at an art school, posing three nights a week from six to ten, earning a dollar and a half a night."

In 1907 Epstein won his first important recognition. Queen Alexandra, consort of Edward VII, purchased his bronze *Head of an Infant,* and he modeled three other major bronzes. That spring, on the recommendation of the etcher Muirhead Bone, the young sculptor was commissioned by the architect Charles Holden to decorate the new British Medical Association building at the corner of Agar Street and the Strand. "I thought I was wealthy," Epstein recalls, "and the future looked bright. I could now pay for models and get to work on large figures." He moved into a large studio in Cheyne Walk, Chelsea, and began work on the eighteen figures of "free decorative conception . . . imaginatively expressive of spiritual and physical energy, concerned in some way with the seven ages of man . . . conceived in the grave heroic mood of pre-Phidian sculpture." In "a task probably unequaled since the Renaissance," Epstein made full-size clay figures of which plaster casts were taken; two assistants roughly shaped the seven-foot blocks of Portland stone built into the third story of the building; and then Epstein mounted the scaffolding and carved his figures, working for fourteen months under a tarpaulin in all sorts of weather.

When the scaffolding was removed from the first five nudes in June 1908, the *Evening Standard and St. James's Gazette* looked through a telescope and was shaken by one of the "periodic English fits of morality." It began an editorial campaign of denunciation which made the young sculptor's name a household word. The result was that the Strand was soon crowded with Londoners anxious to draw their own conclusions, artists and critics rushed to Epstein's defense, censorship groups opposed him, and the controversy occupied much space in the press. But Epstein was "made": "this unexpected hubbub in 1908," he says, "ushered me into a publicity I have always detested." (In 1935

the statues were removed by a new tenant on the excuse that the stone had decayed.)

After the Strand statues were completed, Epstein determined to "train himself in a more intensive method of working," and began a series of portrait busts, some of them commissioned. Several busts of Mrs. Epstein are said to be among her husband's finest work. One of the earliest celebrities to sit for him was Lady Gregory, the Irish playwright. Later Epstein sculptured more celebrities than any other English artist, but he tells in his autobiography that "the history of those portraits is for the most part a story of failure to please the sitters or their relatives." In view of the sensations caused by Epstein's other works, it is not generally realized that he has done far more of these vivid bronze portraits, and that they are universally described as powerful and sometimes as great. "From the standpoint of the purist amateur of sculpture," wrote H. R. Wilenski, "these bronzes violate all canons; they suggest color, and qualities such as sensuality, intelligence, stupidity, breeding, and underbreeding, which from classical standards are no concern of the sculptor's art. But even the purist must bow down before Romantic art of this compelling intensity." By skillfully exaggerating the natural difference between two sides of a face, Epstein achieves "miraculous" portraits which "seem to breathe and to have the soft mobility of flesh." The sculptor's "mastery of light" is often compared to that of Rembrandt, and it is said that the rough "mud-pie" finish he affects "creates shadows and heights in the face so that the bronze becomes flesh." Critics place him in the very first rank of portrait sculptors, although some have thought him an exponent of "Art for the Devil's sake"—that is, with all defects and evil qualities exaggerated at the expense of comeliness, charm, and goodness.

But it is Epstein's larger works, his carvings in stone, with which he is usually identified. Soon after doing the Strand figures, he was commissioned to execute a tomb for Oscar Wilde, to be installed in the Père Lachaise cemetery in Paris. In June 1912, after nine months of labor on a twenty-ton monolith, Epstein received "singularly favorable" comments on his "flying demon-angel." The same *Evening Standard* which had attacked the Medical Association Building frieze began its review: "Seldom in this country are we permitted to see such a dignified piece of monumental sculpture as Mr. Jacob Epstein has carved for the tomb of Oscar Wilde." But once it was installed in the cemetery, the same story of attack and defense was repeated in a French version. While Epstein himself was in South Africa carving some granite lions for Pretoria in the Transvaal, Frenchmen of prominence in the arts took up the fight, with petitions and protests. Eventually, after remaining covered until the outbreak of the First World War, the statue was unveiled without arousing comment.

Epstein's autobiography contains no mention of his war service; he remarks merely that he became the object of official investigation because he lived from 1913 to 1916 on the seacoast at Pett Level, which the authorities could not understand in "an alleged sculptor." His biographers mention "a short period of war service," but there is little authoritative information as to its nature and duration. The manuscript of the first book about him was lost when its author, T. E. Hulme was killed in battle in 1917; and so the first of a number of such works to be published was Bernard van Dieren's *Epstein*, in 1920.

The sculptor continued to do portrait bronzes, including those of Iris Tree and Admiral Lord Fisher; and he also decorated the first London night club, Frida Strindberg's Cafe Royal. In general, however, this was a period of experimentation for Epstein; he was interested in the Vorticist movement and turned out a number of extremely simplified and abstract carvings, including his flenite works and some bird groups. The most discussed of these experiments was the *Rock Drill*, which was never completed but which is admired by those who have written books on Epstein. His large marble *Venus*, exhibited in 1917, differs radically from the classic conception, being a slender, faceless, and completely unrealistic figure. This, too, is well regarded by Epstein's admirers, although Thomas Craven [44], who considers him a great sculptor, calls the Venus "a monumental absurdity." At this first one-man exhibition of his work, as the London *Observer* reported, the Venus "brought a shower of abuse down upon his head, but attracted to the Leicester Galleries thousands of people who under other circumstances would not have crossed the street to see a newly discovered masterpiece by Phidias or Michelangelo. They came to scoff at the Venus, but remained to worship, not indeed at the shrine of the goddess, but before the busts and other works in which the great sculptor had expressed his forceful personality."

The next Epstein sensation was created by his bronze *Christ*, modeled from Van Dieren and exhibited in 1920. This gaunt, beardless figure, more than life-size, stands wrapped in its winding sheet, pointing accusingly with one huge hand to the wound in the other. "In this work," says Epstein, "I realized the dignity of man, his feebleness, his strength, his humility, and the wrath and pity of the Son of Man." To the sculptor's amazement, the statue was attacked by the press, the clergy, Royal Academicians, artists' associations, and social bodies, and it aroused the fury of "the man in the street." "Gross and grotesque thing . . . offending and hurting caricature" were the words with which one churchman condemned the figure. The defense was led by Bernard Shaw [44], while "critics and artists were giving it an unusual unison of approval as a noble and sincere and powerfully dramatic work of art." Eventually it was bought by Apsley Cherry-Garrard and removed from view.

Five years later similar excitement was caused by Epstein's design for a memorial panel to W. H. Hudson, author of *Green Mansions*. This stone carving, made in seven months, was set up in Hyde Park. Immediately the *Morning Post* and the *Daily Mail* demanded the panel's removal, and one shabbily clad man spent twelve hours a day before the memorial, denouncing it. "For a whole summer troops of Londoners and provincials wore the grass down into hard, beaten earth in front of the monument, seeking the obscenities that did not exist." Thirteen prominent persons signed a petition demanding its removal, which

was supported by many others, and the Home Under-Secretary was questioned about it in Parliament. The fight for keeping it was led and won by Sir Muirhead Bone, Bernard Shaw, and R. B. Cunninghame Grahame; but the work has several times been daubed with paint or tar by vandals.

Even Epstein's many portraits of his little daughter Peggy-Jean did not escape condemnation: some reviewers deplored the thought that so charming a child should grow up to be like Epstein's adults. The sculptor, who likes to work from children in spite of the strain of keeping them in pose, has also done a great many drawings and some statues of his son Jackie. Two of Epstein's large bronzes, *The Visitation* (1926) and *The Madonna and Child* (1927)—modeled from an Indian mother of the Moslem faith—were purchased by the National Art Collection Fund for the National Gallery of British Art. Epstein's drawings have always sold more readily than his sculptures—for thirty-odd pounds, as compared to two and three hundred pounds for a bust—and in 1929 seventy-five of his drawings of nudes and seminudes, made between July and October 1928, were printed in a limited edition selling for fifteen pounds. Epstein's drawings and paintings are made with great facility, and he has pointed out that he could earn much more if he were to devote himself to pictures instead of to the time-consuming labor and the expense of sculpture.

Epstein continued to make a sensation every few years. In 1929 it was again some architectonic sculptures commissioned by Charles Holden—groups called *Day* and *Night* for the Underground (subway) Headquarters Building. Again there was furious attack and ardent defense. In 1931 it was his *Genesis*, a huge nude marble mother, that shocked beholders, and in that year, too, his Old Testament illustrations were attacked as blasphemous. Like all his drawings, the illustrations sold well.

Epstein's *Primeval Gods, Sun God* panel, and fifty paintings of Epping Forest were well received in 1933; but his biennial sensation was provided by another carving of Jesus, the colossal *Behold the Man*, carved in stone so tough all Epstein's tools broke on it. This figure, which stands twice as high as its creator, is extremely simplified, with a huge head; and it aroused a storm of protest, extending not only to religious bodies but to Parliament and the Royal Navy. After this Epstein again turned to the graphic; asked to paint twenty flower pictures by some Dutch dealers, he painted three hundred and sixty. Some persons were outraged even by these gouaches: David Cohn writes that it is "because even the simple field-daisy under his hand glows with a strange light, and delphiniums become mauve-blue cathedral spires. His flower drawings are indeed shot through with some of the almost demonic vitality that appears in his bronze portraits, so that his sunflowers burn like a tropical noon, and his massed poppies seem warm to the touch." In 1937 Epstein also illustrated his jeweler friend Moysheh Oyved's *A Book of Affinity* with seven water colors.

In 1937 came his third sculpture of Christ, a recumbent pink alabaster figure called *Consum-*

EPSTEIN, JACOB—*Continued*

matum Est. Like the others, it drew bitter attack and high praise. Lesser denunciation was inspired by his sixty drawings for Baudelaire's *Les Fleurs du Mal,* commissioned by the Limited Editions Club. Then, after thirty years in the public eye, Epstein produced yet another shock, his seven-foot ape-like alabaster colossus, *Adam,* exhibited in 1939, which "pained the critics and maddened the coteries," although some found it "strangely impressive." *Adam* was purchased by an Australian collector for a reputed seven thousand pounds (Epstein says the price was less than a quarter of that amount for his fifteen months' labor) and exhibited at a seaside amusement place, where more than a million persons paid a shilling apiece to see it. When it arrived in the United States for a tour to raise money for bombers, one New York tabloid suggested, "Why not just bomb Berlin with *Adam?*" Up to 1946 Epstein had not produced another controversial piece—his *Jacob and the Angel* was well received.

Jacob Epstein had refused in 1931 to take time to write a book, although he had allowed Arnold Haskell to piece their conversations together into *The Sculptor Speaks.* But in 1940 he wrote an autobiography, *Let There Be Sculpture,* with a full account of the controversies aroused by his various works. The book makes it clear that Epstein, far from aiming to shock, was hurt and surprised each time by the reception accorded his work. "I have always sought the deeply intimate and human," he declares, "and so wrought them that they became classic and enduring. . . .I do not see myself as a martyr, but what has always astonished me was the bitterness of the attacks on my statues." Epstein feels that he has been deliberately neglected in many ways, pointing out that he has never been asked to teach, that he has never received any honor except an LL.D. from Aberdeen University in 1938, that he seldom has been commissioned by architects and never by public bodies. He says: "How superficial is the world of art, and what a wretched lot of logrollers, schemers, sharks, opportunists, profiteers, snobs, parasites, sycophants, camp followers, social climbers, and . . . 'fourflushers' infest the world of art—this jungle into which the artist is forced periodically to bring his work and live."

The sculptor detests "artiness," and in 1927 began listing prices in his exhibition catalogues, saying that his work became merchandise as soon as it was put on display. If he were free from the necessity of earning a living, the sculptor says he would choose to live in the country and model only from children; as it is, he must stay in London to be near the galleries and obtain commissions. He says that his sculptures of persons "who might mean something historically are few and accidental." These persons included the writers Bernard Shaw, Joseph Conrad, Emlyn Williams, Sir Hugh Walpole, and J. B. Priestley; stage personalities Paul Robeson [41], Dame Sybil Thorndike, Harriet Hoctor, and John Gielgud; and figures like Albert Einstein [41], Ramsay MacDonald, Lord Beaverbrook [40], John Dewey [44], and the Russian Ambassador Ivan Maisky [41].

After the British elections in August 1945 the War Artists' Advisory Commission commissioned Epstein to do a bust of the new British Foreign Secretary Ernest Bevin [40]. In September *Time* carried a photograph of the sculptor standing beside the clay model of his latest work, with the comment, "The head looked like a broad-ax approximation of the rough-and-ready Britain's Foreign Secretary, but, like all Epstein portraits, it had a lot of Epstein in it, too."

Epstein is described as short, bold-featured, carelessly dressed, "a big and powerful man radiating enormous vigor and the impression of almost inexhaustible physical energy. His torso is huge, his neck strong; his gray eyes are sad, his sensitive, tortured lips never quite still. He suggests at once Michelangelo and William Blake." The lack of humor with which he has been charged is refuted by his friends, who say he is "a superb talker and widely informed, but does not monopolize the conversation." He is keenly responsive to music, especially that of Bach and Beethoven. He works for long periods with intense concentration, says he does not know or care who is Prime Minister or what the weather is like at such times, and never answers his fan mail.

References

Atlan 164:751-8 D '39
Lit Digest 95:26-7 D 10 '27
Outlook and Independent 155:512-13 Jl 31 '30 il por
Black, R. The Art of Jacob Epstein (1942)
Bolitho, H. ed. Twelve Jews (1934)
Craven, T. Modern Art (1934)
Epstein, J. Let There Be Sculpture (1940)
Haskell, A. L. and Epstein, J. The Sculptor Speaks (1931)
Wellington, H. Jacob Epstein (1925)
Who's Who, 1945

ERTEGUN, MEHMET MUNIR 1883(?)—Nov. 11, 1944 Turkish Ambassador to United States from 1934 until his death; dean of the diplomatic corps in Washington; served as Ambassador to Great Britain and France prior to last appointment; was considered an authority on Turkish law.

Obituary

N Y Times p49 N 12 '44 por

EVANS, LUTHER H(ARRIS) Oct. 13, 1902- Librarian of Congress

Address: b. Library of Congress, Washington, D.C.

In June 1945 President Harry S. Truman [45] appointed Luther H. Evans, then Chief Assistant Librarian of the Library of Congress, the tenth Librarian of Congress. By this promotion Evans became the director of the 145-year-old institution, the holdings of which consisted (as of mid-1943) of more than six million books and pamphlets, one and a half million maps and charts, approximately the same number of volumes and pieces of music, more than half a million prints, and "uncounted millions of items of manuscript material." As the depository of all books copyrighted in the United States, through which its accessions grow annually by about one quarter of a million titles, the Library of Congress serves members of Congress and Government departments, offers rich research facilities, and provides bibliographic and interlibrary loan service to libraries throughout the country. More particularly, and recently, it supplied General MacArthur '41 with some of the information he needed for his contacts with the Philippine underground.

Luther Harris Evans was born October 13, 1902, the son of Lillie (Johnson) Evans and George Washington Evans, a maintenance of way section foreman for the Missouri, Kansas and Texas Railway. Luther was born at his grandmother's home on a farm near Sayers (or Sayersville) in Bastrop County, Texas, but very shortly afterward his father moved the family to a railroad section foreman's house near Sayers; later they moved to a house in the town. In the fall of 1908, when Luther was six, his father bought a farm (still in the family's possession) adjoining that formerly belonging to the boy's grandmother. On a piece of ground between the two farms the Cedar Grove School was erected, and it was there in 1908, in the one-teacher school, that he began his education, attending for six months of each year for the next twelve years. The remainder of his time was occupied by farm chores and in helping to care for eight younger brothers and sisters. After completing the tenth grade the youth entered Bastrop High School. He was graduated a year later, first in his class of seven.

In 1919 he enrolled at the University of Texas, where he majored in political science, took a minor in economics, and was a member of the Ross debating society. For a time he was assistant issue editor of the student paper. After receiving his Bachelor's degree in 1923, he continued his study of political economy at the university, and in 1924 he was awarded his M.A. Most of the money for college he had earned himself, and, while a senior and a graduate student, he had been a part-time instructor at the university.

The summer after he received his Master's degree Evans spent in Europe studying the governments of England, France, and Switzerland, and the activities of the League of Nations. Upon his return from the Continent he accepted an instructorship at Leland Stanford University, in California. For the next three years he alternately presented problems in citizenship to freshman orientation students and studied for a doctorate, which he took in political science, with modern history as his minor subject (Stanford, Ph.D. 1927). For his dissertation he wrote an examination of the mandates system of the League of Nations.

In 1927 the twenty-five-year-old Evans was appointed to teach government at New York University. The following two years he taught political science at Dartmouth College. Then, from 1930 to 1935 he was assistant professor of politics at Princeton University. (At all three institutions he is said to have been a popular instructor.) During these years he was also writing articles on colonial administration and international relations for political science periodicals. He was, in addition, working on his book *The Virgin Islands From Naval Base to New Deal* (published in March

Harris & Ewing

LUTHER H. EVANS

1945), which has been described as "a comprehensive study of the American administration of the Virgin Islands," and which the *Library Journal* points to as an example of "his painstaking concern about thoroughness in any search for facts." In the summer of 1935 Evans accepted the invitation extended by the Works Progress Administration to become director of its Historical Records Survey, a project calling for a nationwide inventory of historical source materials, including state and local archives and manuscript collections. Under his leadership several hundred guides to historical source materials were compiled and published. The results of the survey were acclaimed alike by historians, archivists, and librarians: the program was characterized as "the greatest single achievement of any nation in describing and interpreting the records of its people."

For Evans personally, the success of the WPA venture meant an offer from the newly appointed Librarian of Congress, Archibald MacLeish '40, to become director of the Legislative Reference Service of the Library of Congress. This position Evans accepted as of December 1, 1939, and held until he was promoted to the post of Chief Assistant Librarian, the principal executive office in the administrative setup of the Library. This appointment became effective November 1, 1940. Twice before his appointment as tenth Librarian of Congress in June 1945, Evans, as second in command in his capacity of Chief Assistant Librarian, had served as Acting Librarian: in 1942-43, when Archibald MacLeish took a leave of absence to direct the Office of Facts and Figures, and after MacLeish's resignation in December 1944.

Luther Evans' appointment as Librarian of Congress was confirmed on June 29, 1945. While this promotion meant little, if any, change for Evans, it has been observed that it marks the first time since the Civil War that the position has been filled from the ranks of

EVANS, LUTHER H.—*Continued*

the staff, and that, had members of the staff "been given the chance to select the next head by ballot, Evans would undoubtedly have been the person selected." *Library Journal* quoted this opinion: "Gifted with imagination and with a practical talent for getting things done, possessing through his background and wide professional experience an understanding of the problems of the people and institutions that the Library of Congress is called upon to serve, Luther Evans has the right qualifications for his new assignment."

During his previous five and a half years' association with the Library, Evans had participated actively in the reorganization made possible by an increased allotment of funds and the acquisition of an annex for its expanding services. "And," states the *Library Journal*, "one has but to read recent annual reports of the Librarian of Congress to realize how far advanced are technical skills [and] solution of library administrative problems." However, busy as his official responsibilities in guiding so large an institution keep him, and despite the scholarly and academic life he leads both in and away from the Library, Evans is always responsive to personal contacts. "Although he has been [since 1940] one of the busiest officials in the Library," wrote a Washington observer, "there is not one member of its staff who will not tell you that he has always been able to arrange an appointment, even on short notice, if requested. Be the staff member's problem official or personal, he has always been ready to discuss it fully."

As chief Librarian, Evans will make few changes in the Library's organization, because, he pointed out, he has been an active molder of its policies in the past. He will conduct the Library as a reference center, because he feels that it is a place from which to obtain information, not a reading room. He hopes, too, to be able to make its collections more easily available to other libraries through increased interlibrary loans, because he believes in the widest possible distribution of the library facilities which may furnish the country's political and military leaders with information capable of vitally affecting the destinies of the Nation. "The Library of Congress," he has said, "is a great factory on the frontier of knowledge. It is complete up to date." Above all, it is Evans' hope to make the Library of Congress to an even greater extent than it is today the active and acknowledged leader of the American library field. During the war the Library made every effort to have available any information which might be needed by any governmental department. "For instance," Evans told an interviewer while the war was being fought in Europe and the Pacific, "we receive by plane Russian and Japanese newspapers, probably brought into China by the underground. Important items are translated and furnished immediately to the State Department and other interested officials. . . .Maybe the War Department wants to know where in Osaka are the aircraft factories. We'll furnish the information. We even made a study of the manpower resources of Japan, the water resources of Morocco, rainfall in Burma, and manpower in Germany."

On behalf of the Library of Congress Evans, in September 1945, accepted the gift of Columbia Broadcasting System's complete files of foreign short-wave broadcasts from August 1939 to the end of the war picked up and recorded by CBS short-wave listening stations all over the world, in more than a dozen languages. When photographed on microfilm the ninety-six thousand pages of CBS records, which had filled forty filing cases, made only about eight thousand feet of film, or approximately the length of a single long feature picture. Copies of the microfilm are available to libraries throughout the United States through the regular interlibrary loan service, a service which Evans has always been interested in extending.

Evans is a member of the American Library Association, the American Political Science Association, the Society of American Archivists (of which he was vice-president for one year), and he has served as director of the reference libraries section of the Association of College and Reference Libraries, and on the Committee on War Devastated Libraries (for a time as acting chairman). In the fall of 1945 he was made one of the advisers to the American delegation to the London conference, which will frame a constitution for the United Nations Educational and Cultural Organization.

The Librarian of Congress has been described as "a brisk, businesslike executive" and as a man who "might be taken for a small-town merchant." An editorial in the Washington *Star* characterizes him as "a self-made success," a man who "came up the hard way, earning every advancement in terms of labors of mind and body." His dominant trait, says the *Library Journal*, is "an open frankness, tempered with a human idealism." The Librarian is five feet ten inches tall, weighs two hundred pounds, has blue-gray eyes and black hair. When reading and gardening do not claim his free time he may be found in a motion picture theater or canoeing. Mrs. Evans is the former Helen Murphy of Gainesville, Texas, to whom he was married September 12, 1925. Their son is Gill Cofer Evans.

References

Library J 70:641 Jl '45
Pub W 147:2439 Je 23 '45

FALL, ALBERT B(ACON) 1861—Nov. 30, 1944 Former United States Senator from New Mexico (1912-21); Secretary of the Interior in the Harding Administration; a central figure in the Teapot Dome oil scandal of 1922; convicted in 1929 for accepting bribe and imprisoned in 1931 for a year.

Obituary

N Y Times p23 D 1 '44 por

FAY, FRANK Nov. 17, 1897- Actor
Address: b. c/o Brock Pemberton, 244 W. 44th St., New York City; h. Savoy-Plaza Hotel, New York City

Frank Fay's style as a comedian in the musical variety field has given him a unique place in the theater. His talent for ad-libing not only has won him the title of America's

foremost Master of Ceremonies, but he is
given credit for originating that modern adaptation of the old minstrel-show interlocutor.
Seemingly without any preparation for a
dramatic role Fay in 1944 began his perfect
interpretation of Elwood P. Dowd, the genial
tipler, who consorts with an invisible rabbit
(height is exactly six feet one and a half inches) in Brock Pemberton's [45] production of
the Pulitzer prize-winning play *Harvey*. Fay
was not only acclaimed by the critics but at the
end of the 1944-45 season was given their prize
for the best dramatic performance of the year.
The Donaldson award, the result of a poll of
2,000 theater workers, went to Fay also.

Born on November 17, 1897, in San Francisco, Francis Anthony Fay (as he was christened) is the son of two stock-company
troupers of Celtic origin, Will and Molly
(Tynan) Fay. Fay recalls being introduced to
the footlights at the age of four, when he was
carried onstage by his father in the Chicago
company of *Quo Vadis* (1901). Two years
later the six-year-old child actor played the
Teddy bear in Victor Herbert's *Babes in Toy-
land*, an engagement that was terminated after
six performances when little Francis scattered
make-up over the scenery in a temperamental
outburst. However, Sir Henry Irving, who
was on his last American tour, promptly engaged the youthful Thespian for a bit in *The
Merchant of Venice* (1903). An appearance
in *The Catch of the Season* and a road tour
with Wilton Lackaye in *The Pit* followed in
1905. Somewhere in between these engagements in dramatic plays the boy trod the
boards in his first vaudeville act, as the Kid
in *O'Leary's Kid*. Then, at the age of eight
he made his debut on Broadway as Stephen in
The Redemption of David Corson (1906).
The play closed after sixteen performances,
but the following September young Master
Fay, "doubling in brass" as the Shrimp and
the Call Boy in the cast of *The Chorus Lady*,
was able to glory in his first long run (315
performances).

By the time he reached fifteen, reports *Life*
Magazine, Fay had traveled with all kinds of
stock companies and played in every Shakespearean drama except *Titus Andronicus,* and
in such plays as *A Kiss in Central Park* and
An Enemy of the People. Between engagements he attended the public schools in New
York City, where his father (whom he describes as an Indian fighter, actor, railroad
man, and poet by turns) made a home for the
family. "After briefly grappling with the
intricacies of fractions in the fifth grade,"
continues *Life,* Fay abandoned his formal
education. While the elder Fay was not enthusiastic about the theater as a profession
for his son, Frank would consider no other.

Although Fay had been eager to emulate
Sir Henry Irving as a Shakespearean actor,
he subsequently turned his attention to vaudeville. In 1914, among other acts, he appeared
in *Frank Fay and His Four Sweethearts*. It
was during this period that he began to frequent The Lambs clubhouse in New York;
listening to the conversation of Wilton Lackaye, Wilson Mizner, and other famous wits of
the time, he absorbed "their cruel but pertinent
observations on human foolishness." Though
he was soon to realize that the subtle, cynical

FRANK FAY

humor of these men, particularly that used in
their own annual show, *The Lambs Gambol,*
might be developed into a form more diverting
than the then-prevalent slapstick comedy, young
Fay joined a partner named Johnny Dyer in an
act that followed the timeworn pattern of clown
make-up, comedy falls, and gags in illiterate
verbiage.

Then in 1917 Fay used a new type of comedy technique in monologue. Meticulously
dressed in top hat and tails and discarding all
the traditional "business," the comedian used
an intimate type of patter which critics described as sophisticated. Depending on his
natural gifts for satire and wit, in time Fay
gained a reputation for never giving the same
performance twice. There is, however, a Fay
repertoire: the description of his uncle, the
string-saver; his Aunt Agatha, the putter-
awayer (especially of paper bags); an in-
ebriated gentleman doing a song and dance
turn; and his satire of John Charles Thomas [43]
singing the "Dark Town Strutter's Ball." In
recent years Fay's own particular method of
literal analysis of songs has become a great
favorite. "He is the one man," said a critic,
"music publishers should pay royalties not to
sing their songs, because when Fay gets
through he has sung a song right off the Hit
Parade."

In 1918 Fay temporarily left vaudeville and
brought his talents to the Broadway musicals
Girl o' Mine (1918) of which critics pronounced Fay and his partner, Marie Nord-
strom, the "undeniable hits"; *The Passing
Show of 1918,* in which Fred [45] and Adele
Astaire, Charles Ruggles, and Nita Naldi were
starred; *O What a Girl* (1919); and *Jim Jam
Jems* (1920). In 1922 the actor wrote, produced, and acted in his own musical show,
Frank Fay's Fables. The show, one of Fay's
first jobs as an "emcee," folded quickly; critic
Charles Darnton's verdict, "Not so good, not
so bad," was generally accepted by the public
and press. That same year saw Fay featured

FAY, FRANK—*Continued*

in *Pinwheel,* and in 1923 he had a successful run in the revue, *Artists and Models.*

For the next four years Fay was booked solidly in vaudeville, winning his first really notable success as a master of ceremonies. His first engagement at the Palace (New York City), the top theater of the vaudeville world, was held over for a second week, and later he was to break all records by playing at the Palace twenty-six weeks out of fifty-two. His rate rose to over the three-thousand mark as a single performer, and as high as seventeen thousand dollars when he carried a company. Fay "set a model to which all subsequent emcees are indebted," observes Maurice Zolotow in *Life* Magazine. "Besides introducing the acts, Fay would interrupt them to work in a gag, walk out onto the stage in each number, fill the time between acts with patter, and otherwise dominate the whole proceedings." "His cockiness and conceit," in those days, Zolotow wrote, "his rollicking sprees, his easy way with cash, and his weakness for pretty girls all made him a prominent figure in the Era of Wonderful Nonsense."

In August 1928, while playing a year's engagement as an emcee at the Missouri Theatre in Saint Louis, Fay was married to Ruby Stevens, who later changed her name to Barbara Stanwyck, whom he had met when she was a chorus girl in one of Texas Guinan's night spots. (Fay had previously been married to Frances White, well known singer of the period, and to the actress Lee Buchanan. Both marriages ended in divorce, and later they were annulled so that Fay and Miss Stanwyck might be married in the Catholic Church several years after their first marriage before a justice of the peace.) The following year Fay signed a contract with Warner Brothers '45 and the couple moved to Hollywood.

The New Yorker's first screen appearance was as master of ceremonies in *Show of Shows* (1929). Then he played the leads in *Under a Texas Moon* (1930) and *The Matrimonial Bed* (1930), his two most successful pictures. In the meantime Ruby, now Miss Stanwyck, was cast in *Locked Door* (1929) and *Mexicali Rose* (1929). When these pictures failed to click, Fay, on the strength of his prestige in the film colony, persuaded the president of Columbia Pictures and the director Frank Capra to put Miss Stanwyck into *Ladies of Leisure* (1930). Miss Stanwyck promptly began to climb to the top of the cinema ladder, while Fay began to descend the rungs. Fay subsequently appeared in the less successful *A Fool's Advice* (1932), the stage revue called *Tattle Tales* (1933), which he wrote with Nick Copeland, and the two motion pictures *Bright Lights* (1935) and *Stars Over Broadway* (1935).

This reversal of the Fays' professional standing, it is said, was one of the reasons for the couple's divorce in 1935. For many years their marriage had been considered one of the happiest of the film colony; Miss Stanwyck once told a reporter: "I was nobody until Frank came along. He taught me everything I know and I would have been nothing a great deal longer if he had not come along." Following their separation, the Fays engaged in several legal battles over the division of their property and the custody of an adopted son, Dion;

eventually Miss Stanwyck received the custody of the boy and was later married to Robert Taylor.

Fay remained in Hollywood, living on his huge Brentwood estate with his father. He secured a role in support of Carole Lombard and Fredric March '43 in Selznick's '41 *Nothing Sacred* (1937), and now and then he appeared in night clubs or on the radio. In 1939 he returned to Broadway in a lavishly staged vaudeville revival in which Elsie Janis and Eva LeGallienne '42 were also starred. In Hollywood again in 1940, Fay played a gambler in Paramount's *I Want a Divorce,* and the priest in RKO's picturization of the play *They Knew What They Wanted,* in which Charles Laughton and Carole Lombard were starred. *Laugh Time* (1943), a revival of vaudeville in the best tradition, returned Fay to Broadway as a master of ceremonies. "Frank Fay," wrote Burton Rascoe in the New York *World-Telegram,* "was in his best form and that is very excellent monologue form, indeed. He is a pleasing personality, a genuine wit, has perfect sense of timing, and good mimetic gifts. His speciality is the humor of anticlimax, which is a form of comedy that requires high technical precision to be effective. And he is expert at it." As Fay later told an interviewer, "The timing and technique in a thirty-minute act is the same as that used in a two-hour play."

Fay's engagement at New York's Copacabana night club in August 1944 caused one critic to point out that "when we laugh at Fay's disjointed and hilarious comment on life we are likely to overlook how well he puts across a song." Another reviewer described him as "a wild-eyed, wild-haired genius of song and patter." It was during this engagement that Brock Pemberton astutely cast Fay in the fantasy *Harvey.* So realistic is Fay's acting opposite the rabbit Harvey, said a typical review, "that grown-up people find themselves accepting as fact the definition that Harvey is a Celtic fairy spirit. . . .The role [of the philosophical alcoholic] demands subtlety of timing, an airy lightness of speech and gesture, and a general air of Gaelic magic." Even Wilella Waldorf of the New York *Post,* who differed sharply with her fellow critics on the merits of Mary Chase's '45 play, pointed out later that Fay was not included in her adverse opinion. *Variety* in April 1945 announced that Fay had signed a new contract with Pemberton which guaranteed him stardom in *Harvey* for two more years at a minimum salary of $1,250 a week or 12 per cent of the gross box office receipts, which during 1945 netted Fay over $2,000 a week.

Other contributions of Fay's to entertainment in 1945 included a twelve-week engagement on the *Trans-Atlantic Quiz* radio program and the writing of *How To Be Poor,* a book of his personal philosophy put in the form of monologues and illustrated by James Montgomery Flagg '40. This volume, published late in 1945, had been delivered to the publishers with "a solemn affidavit that the book was the product of Mr. Fay's own writer's cramp." "One man's humor is another man's poison," commented one critic, and in this fashion the reviewers were divided on the humor or lack of it in the book, the manner of Frank Fay's presentation being the leisurely style of his curtain speeches. "They [the monologues] are light and rambling in their humor, with here and there a sharp thorn of truth lurking among the buds of laughter," declared the New York *Herald Tribune*. Most of the other critics felt, however, that the humor suffered from not having the actor's particular stage delivery to project it, while Harry Hansen [42] observed that Fay's attempts to "get funny with the idea that money is corrosive, a bother, and a handicap," were pretentious and boring.

In October 1945 the governing council of Actors Equity Association censured Fay for statements, which, it was claimed, were "prejudicial to the welfare of the Association and its members." The censure followed Fay's public rebuke of five members for their alleged presence at a Spanish Refugee Appeal rally to which a speech was broadcast from London by Harold J. Laski [41] criticizing the role of the Catholic Church in Spain. The members, in preferring charges, had stated that they knew nothing of the speech, had not been present when it was made. After Equity's censure, Fay, who declared that he had made no charges but had asked for an investigation, prepared to ask the general membership to have the resolution recalled. In a subsequent closed meeting of Actors Equity the membership voted 470 to 72 to uphold their council's censure of Fay.

Described as easy-going and friendly, Fay is three and a half inches shorter than Harvey, and his one hundred and seventy-five pounds are "solid muscle"; his hair is red, his eyes light blue. His constant exercise has paid off in golf championship cups; he is also an excellent tennis player and an amateur boxer. Fay is of a religious nature, a devout Catholic. About six years ago he substituted coffee and more regular hours for his earlier love of stronger beverages and night clubbing. Known as a wit's wit, he has produced many often-quoted spontaneous comments. Once when Milton Berle, the radio comedian, challenged him to a duel of wits, he replied that it was against his principles to fight an unarmed man. The Fay delivery of his celebrated bons mots is "half the show—the gentle smile, the quizzical lift of the eyebrows, the sweet voice, his head cocked impudently."

References

Life 18:55-8+ Ja 8 '45 pors

Who's Who in the Theatre (1939)

FERMI, ENRICO (fär'mē än-rē'kō) Sept. 29, 1901- Physicist

Address: b. c/o University of Chicago, Chicago

When Britain's former Prime Minister Winston Churchill [42] spoke in the House of Commons after the announcement of the Allies' atomic bombing of Hiroshima in August 1945, he thanked the Axis powers for exiling, among others, Italy's most famous physicist, Nobel Prize winner Enrico Fermi: it was Fermi's work from 1934 to 1938 that paved the way for the atomic bomb, which he also helped to design.

Enrico Fermi was born in Rome, on September 29, 1901, the son of Alberto and Ida (de Gattis) Fermi. That he is today one of the few physicists "thoroughly at home in both

ENRICO FERMI

theoretical and experimental research" has been attributed by George B. Pegram (physicist and dean of the Graduate Faculties of Columbia University) to Fermi's boyhood interest in both physics and mathematics. The literature of experimental physics attracted Fermi as a schoolboy in Rome. Mathematics first claimed his attention when he was only thirteen, and, for the next four years, his mathematical reading was directed by an engineer friend. As a result, he had, before the age of seventeen, read and digested more of the subject than was required for a Doctor's degree in theoretical physics. It was with this equipment that Fermi entered the Scuola Normale Superiore of the University of Pisa on a scholarship in 1918. Graduating from Pisa in 1922, Fermi then went to the University of Göttingen, where for seven months he pursued his studies, principally with the famous mathematician Max Born, in an atmosphere thick with discussion of the quantum theory. (A fellow student at this time was Werner Heisenberg, who within a few years was to pioneer in the field of new quantum mechanics.) The following year Fermi studied at the University of Rome, and in 1923 he spent some time at the University of Leyden, where, says Pegram, he "matured and developed self-confidence."

In 1924 Fermi was appointed lecturer at the University of Florence, and it was there during the next two years that he made his first important contribution to theoretical physics, today known as the Fermi-Dirac statistics, although Fermi and Dirac arrived at their conclusions independently of one another. Extending "to the motions of the molecules of a gas the already known fact that in an atom no two electrons can exist in the same quantum state," and applying this principle also to an atomic model, the young theoretical physicist formulated the statistical theory underlying present-day work with the electron gas in metals.

In 1926 Fermi began his association with the University of Rome as professor of theoretical physics. There, in addition to making several

FERMI, ENRICO—*Continued*

important contributions to physical research while a member of the university's faculty, he was instrumental in promoting the growth and scientific stature of the university's school of theoretical physics. Until 1934 Fermi was still to be primarily the theoretical physicist, experimenting, of course, but more concerned with general physical laws. Notable in this connection is his perfection in 1934 of a theory of beta ray emission in radioactivity. Accepting the viewpoint that the beta particle (or electron emitted from the nucleus in radioactivity) is emitted as a result of the disintegration of a neutron (electrically neutral or uncharged particle) into its component parts of proton (positively charged particle) and electron (negatively charged particle), he postulated that along with the beta particle there must also be emitted a neutrino (neutral particle of mass comparable in minuteness to the mass of the electron), to account for the "distribution of energies in a continuous spectrum." This hypothesis has since formed the groundwork for further investigations.

The year 1934 was extremely important in Fermi's life not only because it was scientifically his most fertile year, but also because it foreshadowed his greater preoccupation with experimental physics in the succeeding decade. Moreover, the work Fermi began in 1934 led eventually to the invention of the atomic bomb. A few months earlier, toward the end of 1933, Jean Frederic Joliot and his wife Irene Curie '40, the daughter of Marie Curie, had succeeded in creating artificial radioactivity in elements normally exhibiting no radioactive qualities. This opened up a fruitful avenue of research which Fermi was not slow to travel. But, whereas the Joliot-Curies had used as their bullets the generally utilized alpha particles, Fermi determined to try bombarding the atom with the neutron, which had been discovered by Sir James Chadwick '45 two years before. Since the neutron, unlike the positively charged alpha particle, is electrically neutral, it would not, Fermi reasoned, be repulsed by the electric field of the atom and would therefore stand a much better chance of reaching its target and accomplishing its purpose of splitting the atom.

Experiments with the neutron at once proved Fermi correct, and within a short time he and his colleagues in the physical laboratory of the University of Rome had succeeded in inducing artificial radioactivity in approximately forty of the more than sixty elements which they bombarded with neutrons. Particularly important to future developments was Fermi's discovery during these experiments of the highly increased effectiveness of the slowed-down neutron. The neutrons which Fermi originally obtained by shooting alpha particles at beryllium powder he found were apt to speed past the nucleus without much effect. But when he happened to let these neutrons pass through paraffin on their way to the target he found them entering the nucleus in the same way that a slow golf ball will fall into the cup while a fast one rolls by. This effect Fermi attributed to the hydrogen nuclei in the paraffin which, he theorized, were able to hinder the neutron in its path because their mass is equivalent to the mass of the neutrons; and in 1935 Fermi wrote the equation of the probability of success in the use of slow neutrons. Recent newspaper accounts of the atomic bomb have made much of the slow neutron which is able to split U-235.

Fermi's experiments with artificial radioactivity during the period between 1934 and 1938 also presented a scientific problem which has not yet been satisfactorily explained. In 1934 Fermi announced the artificial creation of a new element—ekarhenium of atomic No. 93 —exhibiting radioactivity for thirteen minutes before disintegrating, which accounted for its nonexistence upon earth. Shortly thereafter he announced the creation of its transuranic—or heavier than uranium—twin, No. 94, and later confirmation of his results came from Germany and the United States. Many scientists, however, doubted these phenomena at the time, and Fermi himself said early in 1939 that his chemical analyses of the results did not enable him to state definitely whether he had proof that the new elements were heavier than uranium or whether some unusually complicated disintegration was taking place unrecognized. When uranium fission was announced in January 1939 many scientists leaped to the conclusion that Fermi's results had been identified as transuranic elements only because Fermi, not expecting fission, had not checked back far enough in the table of chemical elements to realize that his end products were in reality elements of half or less than half the weight of uranium. The manufacture of transuranic neptunium and plutonium—now respectively elements No. 93 and No. 94—for the atomic bomb, however, suggests that Fermi's original explanation may have been correct, even though he has said that possibly only the thin aluminum foil which prevented his completion of an experiment kept him from discovering uranium fission. (Indicative of the differing viewpoints is the official War Department report in which H. D. Smyth supports first the transuranic element interpretation of Fermi's results and later the uranium fission interpretation.)

In any case, it was in repeating Fermi's experiments that Otto Hahn and Fritz Strassmann performed the operation which was recognized by Lise Meitner '45 as uranium fission. Lise Meitner and Otto K. Frisch informed Niels Bohr '45 of their tentative conclusion in January 1939, just before Bohr left Denmark for America. (This is the story according to the War Department report; earlier accounts vary in details.) Fermi, who had received the Nobel Prize from, and lectured to, the Swedish Academy of Sciences in December 1938, had already arrived in the United States to take up his career, free from Fascist interference, as professor of physics at Columbia University. Bohr, who came to work for the next several months at the Institute for Advanced Study at Princeton, immediately told his Princeton colleagues, from whom the news went to Fermi. While Fermi left to attend the Conference of Theoretical Physics in Washington, John R. Dunning and George B. Pegram, working in a laboratory under the physics building of Columbia University, made the experiment which proved that the uranium atom had been split. Attending the meeting at George Washington University, Bohr and Fermi thus discussed, before the Columbia experiment had been completed, "the problem of fission, and in particular

Fermi mentioned the possibility that neutrons might be emitted during the process," making possible chain explosions. In March 1939 it was Fermi who was sent by Columbia University to interest Government officials in the possibility of an atomic bomb, and at that conference with the Navy Department "Fermi [first] suggested the possibility of achieving a controllable reaction using slow neutrons or a reaction of an explosive character using fast neutrons."

When the Government decided to attempt the production of an atomic bomb in early 1941, Fermi, who had been engaged in uranium research at Columbia, was one of the scientists summoned for the project: he was appointed chairman of the Theoretical Aspects Subsection of the Uranium Committee in the summer of 1941. Then, continues the Smyth report, in January 1942 physicist Arthur Holly Compton [40], in charge of chain reaction and plutonium research, "decided to concentrate the work for which he was responsible at the University of Chicago. The Columbia group under Fermi and its accumulated material and equipment . . . [was] moved to Chicago in the course of the spring." Under the protective name of "The Metallurgical Laboratory," researches in the manufacture of plutonium were begun and carried out. It was there on a squash court under the University of Chicago's stadium that the first plutonium "pile" was set up, with graphite used as a moderator or retarding agent to induce the chain reaction, as proposed by Fermi. The "pile" was "an oblate spheroid (doorknob shape), built up of graphite bricks with lumps of uranium . . . imbedded in their corners"—and at one point the material nearly got out of hand because the scientists had overestimated the "critical size" at which the chain reaction would begin spontaneously. After the first chain reaction had been obtained on December 2, 1942, and construction on plutonium plants had been started, Fermi was transferred to Los Alamos, New Mexico, as chief of the advanced physics department of the newly organized bomb production laboratory headed by J. Robert Oppenheimer.

In the summer of 1945 Fermi, who had won a Nobel prize in 1938, the Hughes Medal of the Royal Society in 1943, and who is the holder of several honorary degrees, was one of the first scientists to be appointed to a professorship in Chicago University's new Institute of Nuclear Studies, an atomic research foundation established as an outgrowth of the university's participation in the atomic bomb project. Fermi, together with Arthur H. Compton [40], J. Robert Oppenheimer [45], and Ernest O. Lawrence [40], was also made a member of the scientific panel set up to advise the interim committee on atomic energy control. A member of the Association of Los Alamos Scientists, Fermi believes with his fellow atom bomb workers that scientific information should be freely accessible to all, that military control of science is undemocratic.

Sir Henry Dale, president of England's Royal Society, has said of the physicist: "Professor Fermi's work is characterized throughout by profound insight and great experimental skill. In the fields which he has made his own he is universally acclaimed a leader." And George B. Pegram, chairman of the physics

department while Fermi was at Columbia, has written: "Very direct and clear in his thought and speech, sincere but not too serious, using few unnecessary words, he is recognized as an outstanding teacher. In experimental work also he achieves the direct and simple approach and in his discoveries he exemplifies well the fact that only the clearest minds can for the first time do the things that immediately thereafter are so simple and obvious for any one." It was in response to a long-standing invitation to live in America that Fermi, who had taught for a number of years at Michigan, Stanford, and Columbia University summer sessions, came to Pegram's physics department in 1939. (By 1945 he had become an American citizen.) He brought with him to America his wife, Laura (Capon) Fermi (to whom he was married in Italy in 1928), and their children, Nella and Giuglio. With a collaborator Mrs. Fermi has written a popular exposition of her husband's work.

References

Science 97:32 Ja 8 '43
Scientific Monthly 49:182+ Ag '39 por
Time 32:28+ N 21 '38 por
American Men of Science (1944)
International Who's Who, 1942
Who's Who in America, 1944-45

FERRIS, SCOTT Nov. 3, 1877—June 9, 1945 Former United States Congressman from Oklahoma (1907-21) ; served as Democratic National Committeeman for sixteen years; chairman of the Oklahoma State Highway Commission since 1935.

Obituary

N Y Times p32 Je 10 '45

FERRISS, HUGH July 12, 1889- Architect; artist

Address: b. 101 Park Ave., New York City; h. 35 E. Ninth St., New York City

To those who fear that functional architecture will always remain ugly, the president of the Architectural League of New York offers hope that the city of the future will combine beauty with utility. Hugh Ferriss, recipient of frequent prizes from the League before (and after) he was elected its president, consultant to achitectural planning commissions, and America's "No. 1 artist of architecture," whose drawings constantly appear in professional and general periodicals, believes that we are on the threshold of a new epoch in architecture.

Hugh Ferriss was born in St. Louis, Missouri, on July 12, 1889, the son of Franklin and Elizabeth Hall (Simon) Ferriss. He received his early education at the Manual Training School in St. Louis, and in 1911 he was graduated from the School of Architecture and Engineering of Washington University (St. Louis) with the degree of B.S. in architecture. From 1912 to 1915 he served his apprenticeship in the office of Cass Gilbert, New York architect, designer of the Woolworth Building in New York City and of the United States Supreme Court Building in Washington, D.C. Having been engaged as a draftsman by Gilbert, Ferriss spent these three years drawing from Gilbert's blueprints visualizations of the buildings and sections of

HUGH FERRISS

the buildings as they would appear when completed. In this way he had a small part in the construction of the Woolworth Building.

Then in 1915 Ferriss left Gilbert's office to establish a private practice. For the next fifteen years his time was unequally divided between much free-lance sketching of previews of structures about to be erected and an occasional essay at the preparation of original architectural designs. In the early twenties, for instance, when the new zoning laws (requiring that upper stories of tall buildings be placed back from the foundation line) were troubling other architects with supposed restrictions on initiative, Hugh Ferriss originated a fundamental skyscraper plan embodying the regulation's principles. This became the model for New York's Shelton Hotel, one of the first notable stepped-back skyscrapers, and for much of the city's skyline. Interspersed among these pursuits in Ferriss' program before 1930 were several series of lectures which he gave on architectural illustration and design at Columbia University in 1926 and at Yale University and the University of Pennsylvania in 1928. Also in 1928, his alma mater, Washington University, conferred upon him an honorary Master of Arts degree.

Ferriss was at that time, and still is, primarily an artist of architecture rather than a professional architect in the accepted sense of the term. Although his original designs and "grandiose" conceptions of the possibilities inherent in modern architecture are said to have profoundly influenced the profession in America, he has chosen to spend the larger part of his time in interpreting in mass and line the unrealized outlines of other architects' visions and in recording the best of the contemporary architectural scene. Technically designated "architectural rendering," Ferriss' craft is virtually unknown as such outside the precincts of the architect's office, or, if known, is considered merely "arty." Yet it is one of the most useful and important aids the archi-

tect can utilize. In an article for the *Encyclopædia Britaannica,* and elsewhere, Ferriss has defined it thus: "Architectural rendering is a pictorial art whose object is to visualize architectural conceptions." Architectural rendering is employed "to render clear—to make plain, record, report—some particular set of facts about some particular building project. Its aim is to communicate those facts which cannot readily be communicated in words."

The commonest use of architectural rendering is therefore to "convey advance realizations of proposed structures," particularly to the architect's clients. Equally important is its function in aiding to clarify ideas in the architect's own mind. "When an architectural conception first forms in the background of [the architect's] mind," Ferriss explains, "it has, of necessity, a certain nebulous character. But with the effort of expressing it on paper, in actual lines and tone values, it emerges, so to speak, and crystallizes. When so employed, rendering serves as a definite step in the evolution of architectural conceptions." Other uses for the graphic representations of architectural renderers include the interpretation of the architectural significance of existing buildings—the art which Ferriss himself has so successfully developed—guidance in city planning, assistance "in evolving new types of architecture" and the strengthening, through the medium of selected drawings, of the "psychological influence of · architecture on human values."

The technique of the skill varies, but Ferriss believes that the draftsman's "best procedure is first to delineate the essentials of his subject, then to build all indication of detail on his foundation." Ferriss sees the draftsman approaching his subject as though he were "facing a building which, although it exists in its entirety, is completely hidden from him in a mist or fog. As he approaches his subject, however, he begins to discern the principal outlines of its mass. Soon its secondary and tertiary features appear. He is free to continue to approach until the most minute details have become plain. Nevertheless, it is important that he halt at that point where his subject has revealed all that is essential to his inquiry." For above all, Ferriss maintains, the artist must always remember that the rendering is only the means toward the end, which is architecture.

In the preparation of his only book, *The Metropolis of Tomorrow* (1930), Ferriss employed the architectural rendering to illustrate his vision of the possibilities inherent in the still dim future of modern architecture. The volume pictures a planned city of wide open spaces with a few necessary huge buildings placed at infrequent and strategic intervals (another extension of the principles of the zoning laws). Each mammoth structure is the center of a particular functional district of the city: one houses the business center; another the science center; a third the art center; and so on. Each covers an area equal to three or four present-day city blocks and stands at least one-half mile distant from each of the others. Between them run avenues two hundred or more feet wide, and the roofs of all other buildings, which are low, provide areas for gardens. The style of these renderings, as comparison with others of his drawings readily establishes, is typical of the work of Ferriss, who, according to the *Saturday Review of Literature*, "is probably excelled by no draftsman practising today in indication, a sense of three dimensions, and monumental imagination." "He deals," the *Saturday Review* goes on to say, "with composition in mass and line, free from the preconceived dogmas of esthetics. He shows us the mountain, not each tree, stone, or waterfall on its slopes. Thus his designs are inspiring and awesome, perhaps too grand for immediate realization, but surely pointing the direction for our striving." And Albert Guerard of *Books* described the volume as "wise and generous in vision, cogent in thought, clear and strong in literary style, appealing as a work of art, magically stirring as a prophecy."

Ferriss' career since the publication of his book has brought him varied tasks and commissions and many rewards and prizes. He received his first prize—for rendering—from the Architectural League of New York in 1930. In 1934, for his rendering of the new Philadelphia Post Office, he was awarded the Birch Burdette Long Memorial Prize, given annually for architectural drawing by the same organization. Between 1936 and 1939 Ferriss served as one of the architectural consultants to the planning commission responsible for the New York World's Fair and drew many of the Fair's buildings as the plans were being worked out. In 1940 Ferriss and Leon V. Solon, artist, won the first Arnold W. Brunner award established to promote and encourage "accomplishment in the arts and professions represented in the membership of the Architectural League of New York, and to render such arts and professions of greater use to the community." Dividing the $2,000 in prize money between the two winners in such a way that both would be able to bring their projects to fruition, the League commissioned Ferriss to make a series of forty drawings of buildings erected in the United States since 1929 which, in his opinion, were "expressive of this Nation during this period, and worthy as combinations of usefulness and beauty to be recorded as masterpieces of contemporary architecture." Consequently, the year 1941 found Ferriss traveling a distance of 18,000 miles through forty states to record, within a period of six months, such architectural and engineering projects as a Curtiss-Wright plant, the Ohio Steel Foundry, the San Francisco-Oakland Bridge, the National Airport at Washington, D.C., and Boulder, Morris, Grand Coulee, and Shasta dams. The work was not easy, even after the selections had been made: "A peculiarity of Grand Coulee," Ferriss reported, "is the difficulty of grasping its magnitude . . . it was difficult to realize that the powerhouse . . . is as tall as the Architects Building in New York—eighteen stories." Upon completion of the drawings, the series was exhibited first at the League's headquarters in New York, and later at the Whitney Museum of Art, under the title "The Power of America in Buildings."

In 1941 Ferriss had also received the Allied Arts Prize (or President's Medal, as it is commonly called) from the Architectural League of New York, "for devotion to the League's welfare and especially for stimulating that interest in the arts for which the League stands by means of the panel exhibitions initiated and carried through this first year by his untiring efforts." He spent the year 1942-43 in making drawings of United States war plants with the official approval of the Secretaries of War, the Navy, and the Interior. Then in 1943 Ferriss was one of the ten recipients of one-thousand-dollar grants, given jointly by the American Academy of Arts and Letters and the National Institute of Arts and Letters, awards designed to aid creative artists in their work. In 1943, too, he was installed as president of the Architectural League of New York, to which post he was re-elected for the year 1944-45. And in 1944 he again won the Birch Burdette Long Memorial Prize.

The study occasioned by the fulfillment of the terms of the Brunner award impressed upon Ferriss certain trends and aspects of modern architecture and caused him to reach new, and reaffirm old, conclusions. Architecture, he had long felt, is history in stone and brick and steel. In that, he was not alone, he points out, for historians and sociologists have always seen the pyramids not merely as a "handsome mass" of stone but as a reminder of the slaves who dragged up the blocks from which they are built, and they have seen a medieval village nestling below the lord's castle not merely as a picturesque scene but as a symbol of feudalism. In 1941 this conclusion that architecture is history, which had occurred to him first ten years earlier, was brought home to him vividly once more. In 1930, standing on a parapet on the Architects Building in New York in the strange silence of empty offices and empty streets, he had become aware of a new meaning in the Manhattan skyline: then "those towering masses seemed monuments to the rugged individualism of the period; their topmost, unnecessary floors and gilded spires, to the conspicuous waste and rampant advertising; their long shadows across slums at their feet, to the exploitation." In 1941, however, he realized that that mushroom growth of skyscrapers had ended about the year 1930, for, with the exception of Rockefeller Center, he found almost no major skyscraper developments of recent date. In their stead America was building dams which give evidence "of a nation in its age of power," highway projects and airports which "record the stage of mobility," publishing plants, auditoriums and churches which "in their multiplicity and diverse character are the concrete signs of our Freedom of the Press, of Speech, of Assembly, and of Worship."

Ferriss wrote in 1942 that he had not been able to travel far in the United States "without realizing that this war, to a surprisingly large extent, is being waged in buildings." "It should be obvious," he was moved to add, "that we could have no aircraft without the aircraft plants; that factories could not operate without power plants, and could not be manned without the projects to house the men. . . . Yet one has to go through the country, seeing things at first hand, to realize the true enormousness of the war-construction effort. . . . To bring home a general, dramatic, and inspiring sense of it would be a national asset." Buildings, he asserts, indicate how we are fighting and what we are fighting to defend.

FERRISS, HUGH—*Continued*

They are records of civilization. "Our way of living is shown, in large measure, by the kind of buildings we build."

This same tour suggested to Ferriss that there was now hope that the reintegration in architecture between the artist and the engineer would come in the not too distant future. Before entering college Ferriss had taken the dictionary definition of architecture—"the science and art of building"—literally, believing that in the architect were blended the best of the artist and the best of the scientist. But at Washington University had come his rude awakening when he had seen the engineering and architectural students in the School of Architecture and Engineering housed on opposite sides of the campus and actually throwing stones through each other's windows. Consideration of the question during succeeding decades showed him that in the twenties the architectural "artists" dominated the scene, employing the engineers, so to speak, whereas in the thirties their positions were reversed, with the architectural "engineers" employing the artists, if the artists had anything to do with the matter at all. On his return from the Brunner trip, however, Ferriss was able to say, "I thought perhaps enough time had already elapsed for the first signs of beauty to appear in this new world of precise forms —for the reunion between scientist and artist to begin. I offer these drawings in evidence that a reintegration is well under way." The conflict has been, he says, "between those who find their chief inspiration in art, in forms of beauty," believing that a beautiful building is valid in any age solely because it is beautiful, and "those who find their chief inspiration in science, in truthful statements of actual functions," to whom an adaptation of the Parthenon erected today appears merely as an anachronism.

Early in 1945 Ferriss, addressing the Art Commission Association at its annual dinner, stated his own strong convictions "that architecture has two legs to stand on, science and art. That to be upright, it has to stand on both of them. That when this happened we got the 'grand epochs' of architecture, and only then. That it has not happened in the lifetime of anyone in this room. That in the younger generation, and their designs, are grounds for believing that it will happen within the predictable future. That the exact appearances of this future architecture cannot yet be delineated, except that we may confidently say it will resemble neither that of the twenties nor the thirties. That, meanwhile, we do well to keep an open mind; and do better if we lend a hand."

Hugh Ferriss is a man of medium height, dark complexioned, mustached. Mrs. Ferriss, to whom he was married in May 1914, is the former Dorothy Lapham. They have one daughter, Jean Elizabeth.

References

National Cyclopædia of American Biography Current vol B p97
Who's Who in America, 1944-45
Who's Who in American Art, 1940-41

FESTING, FRANCIS W(OGAN) Aug. 28, 1902- British Army officer
Address: b. c/o War Office, London

The three years after 1941, which saw such dramatic military history being made in the Pacific and European theaters of operations, meant to the Allied forces in Burma an endless "edging in from east and west at a right angle across the mountainous ridges of Burma." At last, when they had possession of the northern ends of the invasion routes, they were able to drive back an enemy which had held nearly all of that sweltering jungle land. One of the commanders who helped in that victory is British Major General Francis W. Festing, former leader of the Thirty-sixth Division in the Southeast Asia and China-Burma-India commands, who became in late 1945 general officer commanding the base of Hong Kong.

Francis Wogan Festing was born August 28, 1902, in England. Gazetted in December 1921, before the Second World War he had never served in combat. He was a lieutenant of rifles when, in 1926, he was appointed as aide-de-camp to a divisional commander, a post he held for four years. Upon graduation from the Staff College he was promoted to captain, and as an air liaison officer he served in the Eastern Command from 1936 to 1938. Transferred next to the War Office in London, he was promoted to the brevet rank of major, a commission giving an army officer a higher nominal rank but no increase in pay. In February 1939 Festing returned to his regiment as a lieutenant colonel.

When the war in Europe broke out in 1939 Festing, despite his desire to be posted to a combat area, was appointed liaison officer between General Headquarters in France and the War Office in London. In 1940, as the Germans invaded Norway, England dispatched a small expeditionary force to relieve the hard-pressed Norwegians. A company commander of this Allied force sent "to purge and cleanse the soil of Norway from the filthy pollution of Nazi tyranny," in the words of the then First Lord of the Admiralty, Winston Churchill [42], was Colonel Festing. The absence of artillery, antiaircraft batteries, air support, and antitank guns soon forced a hard-fought British withdrawal, and on June 10 Festing, and what was left of the British troops, re-embarked for England.

During the months which followed, when England was on the alert for an expected German invasion of the Isles, Festing was in command of units of the Home Forces, priming them for the defense. In this period he received two advancements, from lieutenant colonel to colonel, and next to brigadier (acting).

In 1942 the accelerated Japanese operations against Ceylon—coupled with Vichy's new rapprochement with Germany that brought Pierre Laval [40] to power—made the French island of Madagascar a possible target for Japanese attack. Since Madagascar formed one of the links in England's eastern supply line, it became necessary for the British to seize this island off the coast of eastern Africa. On May 5, with Festing in command of the assault landings, the occupation began, the British demanding the surrender of the French garrison. The demand was ignored. In the battle that ensued

Festing stationed himself in the most advanced line, engaging in personal reconnaissance and encouraging his men. Accompanied by his chief petty officer, he entered Antsirabe long before the struggle was over and accepted the personal surrender of the French Army's commander. The British were thus able to take possession of their key objective, the naval base at Diégo-Suarez, forestalling a possible Japanese landing on this strategically important east African island. Upon completion of this mission Festing was awarded the Distinguished Service Order. The citation reads: "While in command of the assault brigade he planned all details and carried his task through with great ability and dash, showing almost complete indifference to shelling and sniping."

By 1943 their strength in the Far East had grown sufficiently in men and steel for the Allies to attempt a counterthrust in Burma to open direly needed communications between India and China. The Japanese, intent upon invading India, bombed Chittagong, the Indian city over the Burma border, bombed Ceylon, and attacked ships in the Bay of Bengal. India seemed in imminent peril. To thwart this new Japanese aggression, the British embarked on a more intensive training program and sent Major General Festing to India to instruct and assume command of the Thirty-sixth Division. For nearly five months Festing drilled and trained his men in jungle warfare while General Orde Charles Wingate's Penetration Group (better known as the Chindits or Raiders), pressed farther into enemy-occupied territory. This group, comprised of British, Indians, and Burmese, had acquired under Wingate's leadership an unequaled reputation for jungle fighting.

In the autumn Festing and his Thirty-sixth Division joined the Fourteenth Army under General Sir William Slim [45], and by the early part of 1944 this contingent was pressing forward in the Arakan sector—"a wild, swampy noxious coast [in Western Burma] that experiences some of the heaviest rainfall in the world" —trying to keep the lines of communication open between the Fifth and Seventh Indian divisions that were advancing south. When the Japanese counterattacked, pinching in on the Seventh and on part of the Fifth, the Fourteenth Army held the Japanese at bay until the Twenty-sixth Indian Division and the unattacked portion of the Fifth Indian Division hacked down from the north through the jungle to relieve the oppressed troops.

In early 1944, when the Fifth Indian Division (part of General Philip Christison's [45] Fifteenth Corps) was flown north to Imphal in Assam, Festing's Thirty-sixth Division had to protect the battle area the Fifth had left, and also the incompleted Bawle-Razabil Road some distance away. Festing led his troops over the Mayu Ridge in Burma through Japanese positions, seized strategic points in the Mayu hills, and continued to advance with his division to secure the western tunnel of the Maungdaw-Buthedaung Road. Later the division was transferred to the command of General Joseph W. Stilwell [42], participating in the capture of the important Myitkyina airfields in Northern Burma. Then Festing started fighting his way southwest, along the Mogaung-Mandalay Railway, and achieved a link-up with the Chindits

MAJ. GEN. FRANCIS W. FESTING

under General Walter D. A. Lentaigne [44], Wingate's successor, in Central Burma. Health conditions in the sweltering, snake-infested Burmese jungle were such that in the Fourteenth Army there were more cases of illness in the first six months of 1944 than the number of its personnel; in the first six months of 1945 there were six cases of illness for each battle casualty.

By the time the Japanese surrendered in August 1945, the Allied forces had liberated 85 per cent of Burma. Shortly thereafter, British marines and navy men raised the white ensign over Hong Kong; and on September 16, 1945, Festing was present at the surrender of the Japanese commander to Admiral Cecil H. J. Harcourt. At this time he was assigned to Hong Kong as general officer commanding. In late November the General told reporters that his troops, which then numbered about eleven thousand, would probably be increased eventually to twenty-four thousand, and added that Hong Kong would supplement but not succeed Singapore as a naval base. In January 1943 the American and British Governments had renounced their extraterritoriality and other special rights in China. The British had, however, decided to retain Hong Kong as a Crown colony. The colony includes the island and city of Hong Kong, and the Kowloon peninsula.

The physique of the tall, broad-shouldered General is said to have once frightened an enemy garrison commander into surrendering. The story may be apocryphal, but there are several such stories told by the British about Festing, who, they say, carries with him on the battlefield an ash stick rumored to be four inches thick. And, indeed, his citation for the D.S.O. ends with this description: "His leadership was always an inspiration and forceful, as on the occasion when he applied his walking stick to the back sides of the few recalcitrants who appeared to have unnecessary interest in the rear areas." The General has

FESTING, FRANCIS W.—*Continued*

once or twice fought Japanese himself in single-handed combat, and, an inveterate souvenir hunter, he has in his collection some Japanese battle relics.

FIEDLER, ARTHUR (fēd'lĕr) Dec. 17, 1894- Conductor

Address: b. Symphony Hall, Boston; h. 28 Marshal St., Brookline, Mass.

At the close of the Boston Symphony Orchestra's winter season the black leather seats in Symphony Hall are removed and tables and chairs are set up in readiness for the food and drink "snacks" that will be served to audiences. Then the "Pop Concerts, a special spring prod-

ARTHUR FIEDLER

uct of Boston," entertain a full house almost every night from early May until mid-July, whereupon the Pop Orchestra moves to the Charles River Esplanade for its summertime free open-air concerts. The conductor of this popular—hence "Pop" or "Pops"—orchestra is Arthur Fiedler, who founded the Esplanade Concerts in 1929 and has conducted the Pop Concerts since 1930. A leader in many musical activities in and about Boston, Fiedler is said to have the distinction of being the only conductor whom everyone calls by his first name. Truck drivers who are Esplanade devotees hail him on the street, and servicemen write to him of their enjoyment of records and rebroadcasts of the Pop programs, which include everything "from Bach to Boogie Woogie."

Of Austrian ancestry and the son of Emanuel and Johanna (Bernfeld) Fiedler, Arthur Fiedler was born in the Back Bay section of Boston on December 17, 1894. "Music was in the Fiedlers' blood," writes the music critic of the Boston *Globe*, and Fiedler believes that the family's name derives from the German word *Fiedel*, meaning fiddle—for generations, he says, the Fiedlers were fiddlers. Arthur's grandfather was an orchestral conductor in

Sambor, the Polish town in which Emanuel Fiedler was born. Emanuel was brought to Boston by Wilhelm Gericke in 1885 to play in the first violin section of the Boston Symphony Orchestra, later becoming one of the original members of the famous Kneisel Quartet. Two brothers of Emanuel also were violinists and members of the same orchestra, and Arthur's three sisters are musicians.

Young Arthur attended the Prince School and Latin School, both in Boston, until 1910, when his father decided to return to Vienna with his family. Thus the Fiedlers lived in the Austrian capital for a while, and later went to Berlin. There the boy had a "brief exposure to business" while he worked in a publishing house. Business did not interest him, however, and he enrolled at the Royal Academy of Music of Berlin, where he studied the violin from 1911 to 1915 under Willy Hess who had once been concertmaster of the Boston Symphony. At this time he also studied the piano and conducting, at the age of seventeen being given his first opportunity of leading an orchestra at a concert when he conducted *Three German Dances* by Mozart and Mendelssohn's G-Minor Piano Concerto.

At the age of nineteen the young musician returned to America and became a member "in good standing" of the Boston Symphony Orchestra, playing in the second violin section under the direction of Karl Muck. In the words of the *Bostonian Magazine*, "the dark young man with the magnetic eyes and the thick hair occupied his modest chair until 1918, when he switched to the viola because it was more interesting." That year, when the United States was at war, young Fiedler served for a short time in the Army; upon receiving his honorable discharge he returned to his chair in the Boston orchestra, where he continued to play the viola until he became conductor of the Pop Orchestra in 1930. At times he also played the celesta, the piano, and the organ, and he frequently acted as accompanist for singers and as a musical coach. Not long after his discharge from the Army he organized the Boston Sinfonietta, an orchestra of twenty-five pieces which devotes itself to chamber music. Composed of members of the Boston Symphony, this small orchestra is said to be the first of its kind in America to use the name "sinfonietta." For years Fiedler toured the country with this group and directed it in many concerts in Boston. The music of the Arthur Fiedler Sinfonietta, as it is commonly called, is well known among those who enjoy the Victor albums of recorded music.

For a long time the "son of the Boston Symphony" had looked forward to a time when open-air concerts of symphonic music might be heard by the public without charge. Band concerts were the only form of music given out of doors when Fiedler began to talk to friends about his hopes. He received little encouragement, however, for the friends were politely skeptical and the police thought it would be too difficult to handle crowds. Nevertheless Fiedler persisted, a site was finally chosen on the bank of the Charles River in the heart of picturesque old Boston, and funds were provided to build a small wooden shell and to support the project for one year.

The first concert was given on the Fourth of July in 1929, on a night when a strong wind made the musicians' scores fly about like sea gulls. The concert was an unquestionable success. Later the state of Massachusetts supplied the money for the erection of a second shell, which proved acoustically good but inadequate in other respects. After Fiedler brought the Esplanade concerts to the attention of the trustees of the Hatch Fund, the Edward Hatch Memorial Shell, a permanent sounding board of granite lined with teakwood, was constructed at a cost of two hundred and seventy thousand dollars. "A long-cherished dream come true," the conductor said on the night of its dedication. In an article in the *Atlantic Monthly* entitled "Music Al Fresco," Fiedler has described the sky-and-water setting for the music, which is heard by a quarter of a million people in the course of one summer. While the programs of these concerts are shorter than the Pops offered in Symphony Hall, they are more serious, sometimes including a complete symphony. Their conductor finds particular enjoyment in his morning outdoor concerts for children, who usually attend in groups from playgrounds and settlement houses. For them his orchestra plays lighter music in programs on which youthful soloists often appear.

An audience estimated at forty thousand, the largest in the history of the Esplanade concerts, attended the closing concert on the evening of August 15, 1945. For that occasion a special program was arranged by Fiedler to celebrate the victory over Japan, and Massachusetts' Governor Maurice J. Tobin expressed his gratitude to the conductor and his orchestra for the concerts they had given in veterans' hospitals and for other contributions to the war effort.

At the indoor Pop Concerts in Symphony Hall, which in the spring follow Boston Symphony Orchestra programs directed by Serge Koussevitzky '40, the atmosphere is informal as listeners relax to the bright rhythms and flowing melodies and consume sandwiches and cold drinks between the numbers. These concerts have been compared to the English "Promenades," but the *Victor Record Review* considers them less serious in nature than either the "Proms" or the Stadium Concerts in New York City. Folk songs, overtures, ballet pieces, and marches are played, and among the composers on the programs are Richard Strauss '44, Gounod, Bizet, Offenbach, as well as the moderns, George Gershwin, Jerome Kern '42, Cole Porter '40. The Pops repertory includes several hundred works in a single season and is constantly augmented by popular hits and by new works of American composers, in whom Fiedler is always interested. "It is like mixing a salad," he has said in speaking of the preparation of the Pops programs. He studies his audiences, taking note of selections that please them, and the result may be a program of *Oklahoma!* selections, the introduction to the third act of *Lohengrin,* and the overture of *William Tell,* "a nice balance between the classical and modern." It has been pointed out that the direction of the Pops is a "large order," for the man with the baton must "understand and satisfy the symphonic purist and the jazz hound, each on his own ground."

Aside from his conducting of the Pop and Esplanade concerts, Arthur Fiedler is active in many enterprises, musical and otherwise. He is both orchestral and choral conductor, for he directs the Cecilia Choral Society, the Boston Male Choir, the University Glee Club of Providence, Rhode Island, the MacDowell Club Orchestra, and the Boston University Orchestra. He has appeared as guest conductor of the symphony orchestras of Boston, Minneapolis, Montreal, Toronto, and Guatemala, and with the Federal orchestras in New York and Philadelphia. His appearances on the radio have been numerous, and during the winter of 1945-46 he will resume the direction of the Boston Symphony Pop Orchestra on *Sundays at Four-thirty* on NBC.

The conductor is a member of the Boston University faculty and of the Harvard Musical Association. He is musical consultant to the Veterans Administration, and in 1940 he organized the Massachusetts National Youth Administration Symphony Orchestra, which he conducted until it disbanded in 1942. Active in bringing music to servicemen, Fiedler is on the entertainment committee of the USO-Greater Boston Soldiers and Sailors Committee, and in 1943 he served as chairman of the Victory Concerts held at the Museum of Fine Arts. During the war his defense duties included service as auxiliary policeman in Boston as well as membership in the Temporary Reserve of the United States Coast Guard. Among the honors bestowed upon the Boston conductor are: the Carnation decoration from the *Jewish Advocate* of his city; an honorary M.A. degree from Tufts College, and the Croix de l'Officier d'Academie for his interest in the music of French composers.

"The indefatigable Arthur Fiedler" is looked upon as a many-sided musician, a conductor who is also a master of the viola, the celesta, and the piano keyboard, and gifted with absolute pitch. He is regarded as a "quick-study" at score reading, with the ability to adapt himself to the music of any composer of any century. Although some critics find him, as a conductor, a very able technician rather than an interpreter, his popularity with the public is undisputed, and *Musician* finds his readings "always inspiring." Another critic has written: "He gives of himself freely and has won the admiration of musicians and devotees of music not only in Boston but wherever Pops recordings and broadcasts are heard." The conductor is also known to be a keen businessman who keeps an eye on the box office and publicity in behalf of his orchestra. He and his Esplanade orchestra arrived for one night's concert by boat from the opposite shore of the Charles River in time for a "chance meeting" with newspaper photographers, and at a Gay Nineties Evening of the Pops a barouche pulled up before Symphony Hall and Fiedler descended dressed as a dandy of the period, complete with stick and topper.

Fiedler is described as "a blend of Beacon Street, Europe, and the Stork Club." One of his greatest interests is travel—he has visited most of the conventional tourists spots of the world as well as less-traveled places. (As a young man he roamed the Black Forest of Germany and in one week walked the hundred and seventy-five miles between Paris and

FIEDLER, ARTHUR—_Continued_

Tours, his luggage consisting of a toothbrush.) An interviewer describes him as a handsome, distinguished-looking man of average height with dark eyes and graying hair. His manner is suave and urbane, and he speaks with the same energy and emphasis he puts into his conducting.

One of Boston's eligible bachelors for many years, the conductor was married in 1942 to Ellen M. Bottomley, a Boston society girl. The Fiedlers live in Brookline, the exclusive suburb of Boston, where Louise, the musician's housekeeper for many years, prepares the Austrian and Hungarian dishes he likes. His hobbies are collecting antiques, ship models, old woodwind instruments, and miniature scores. His musical library is known among musicians as a unique collection of editions published in Europe—it includes numerous first editions of Strauss waltzes and many of the one hundred and four Haydn symphonies. The Pops conductor can speak and "read his way around" in Germany, French, Italian, and Spanish. He can swear in Polish.

References

Bostonian Mag S '43

Thompson, O. ed. International Cyclopedia of Music and Musicians (1943)
Who's Who in America, 1944-45

FIELD, SIR FREDERICK LAURENCE Apr. 19, 1871—Oct. 24, 1945 British admiral; joined Royal Navy in 1884; fought in Boxer Rebellion in China; commander of H.M.S. _King George V_ at the Battle of Jutland in 1916; delegate to the Naval Disarmament Conference in Geneva; First Sea Lord of the British Admiralty and Chief of the Naval Staff (1930-33); was awarded the American Distinguished Service Medal.

Obituary

N Y Times p19 O 26 '45 por

FISCHER, HANS 1881—Apr.(?) 1945 German organic chemist; winner in 1930 of the Nobel Prize in chemistry for his discovery and isolation of hematin (the coloring matter of the red corpuscle); for many years a professor at Vienna and Munich universities.

Obituary

N Y Times p15 Ap 7 '45 por

FISHER, GEOFFREY FRANCIS, ARCHBISHOP OF CANTERBURY May 5, 1887- English primate

Address: Lambeth Palace, London

The hundredth Archbishop of Canterbury, the Right Reverend and Right Honourable Geoffrey Francis Fisher, was formally elected Primate of All England on January 22, 1945. In traditional manner Dr. Fisher's name was first suggested by Prime Minister Churchill [42] to King George VI [42], who then recommended the clergyman's election to the members of the Greater Chapter of the See of Canterbury. Duly elected, on February 2 Dr. Fisher was crowned Archbishop of Canterbury in St. Paul's Cathedral in London. Successor to the re-

nowned Dr. William Temple [42], who died suddenly in October 1944, the Archbishop was invested with the highest office of the Anglican Church and is spiritual leader of forty million people. With only twelve years of active clerical service, the Archbishop at his succession was not too well known by the British public. However, he has had a distinguished career and relinquished his bishopric of London after endearing himself to the people for his work in blitzed London.

Geoffrey Francis Fisher was born May 5, 1887, the youngest son of a parish Anglican priest, the late Reverend H. Fisher, Rector of Higham-on-the-Hill, Nuneaton. The young man attended Marlborough College and Exeter College. An outstanding scholar, he won First Class Honours in Moderations in 1908. The young man also participated in campus sports and he was a useful oarsman in Oxford's 1908 Trial Eights, in which the final crew is selected for the annual Oxford-Cambridge boat race. In 1910 Fisher received his degree in the ancient classics and the same year he was awarded the Liddon Studentship. He completed his theological training at Wells Theological College in 1911. (Dr. Fisher was made an Honorary Fellow of Exeter College, Oxford, in 1939.)

The churchman's career began in the educational field when, in 1911, he returned to his old school, Marlborough College, to assume the position of assistant master. Three years later, at the age of twenty-seven, he succeeded Dr. William Temple as headmaster of Repton School, a position he held for eighteen years. He is remembered by students as "conspicuously young and spry, a firm inculcator of the classics who gave tough examinations and prescribed traditional toppers and Eton jackets." Discussing Fisher's career in education, the New York _Herald Tribune_ remarked that he "had time to watch a steady stream of British youth come and go. His earliest students, from days before the First World War, have now turned fifty . . . his latest are in their twenties. To have been successful in his calling he must have learned much from them. Through them, and through his own sons . . . he must have a sense of personal contact with younger men throughout the nation. It is an unusual advantage for a man called to a position of great influence."

After twenty-one years as a schoolmaster Dr. Fisher became Bishop of Chester in 1932. In this capacity he established a reputation for efficiency and wisdom. The prelate prepared his sermons and church programs very carefully and made wise appointments. Thus he came to be considered by churchmen as an able and conservative administrator. When he became Bishop of London in 1939 Dr. Fisher was confronted with the complex problems of a great wartorn city. After his arrival at Fulham Palace, ancient home of the Bishops of London, war damage occupied much of his attention: he served as chairman of the Main Committee of Churches in cooperation with the Government War Damage Commission, a committee which has been concerned with the rebuilding of Britain's damaged churches. During the London blitz he sheltered three hundred persons nightly in spacious Fulham Palace, the home of Dr. Fisher and his family. In July 1943 _Time_ Magazine reported that the

Bishop had begun negotiations with the ecclesiastical commissioners to halve his salary (forty thousand dollars) and arrange Fulham Palace for service as a diocesan hostel. Through these new arrangements a large part of the palace passed from his personal control and he and his family lived in comparatively small quarters.

Special steps have been taken within the Church of England since the beginning of the war to re-plan parish boundaries in areas suffering war damage or affected by population changes. Recognized as a specialist in church management and legislation, Dr. Fisher was chosen in 1943 to present the planning measure before the Church Assembly, composed of clergy and laymen. This speech earned for him a reputation for "crystal-clear exposition." Later the Bishop was called upon to preside at the Convocation of Canterbury in the absence of the incapacitated Dr. Temple. On this occasion the American bishops were presented, and Dr. Fisher—considered a restrained but powerful speaker—addressed them, stressing the bond between Britain and America and their churches. He said: "For long now our two countries have stood together against the enemies of all that our two peoples hold dear and sacred. We go forward now to victory in the West together; together we shall go on to victory in the East. Then, please God, we shall go on together to establish among the nations those high principles of brotherhood which your President and our Prime Minister have proclaimed."

Dr. Fisher has also worked diligently for cooperation among the Christian churches and is known for his efforts on behalf of interdenominational understanding. He is chairman of the executive committee of the British Council of Churches, a post which enables him to maintain contact with the leaders of all Protestant denominations in Britain. He has written sympathetically, too, about the movement for church union in southern India. In his broad ecclesiastical activities he has been a leader in cooperative efforts between Protestants and Roman Catholics. He has presided at the Joint Committee which links the Protestant "Religion and Life" movement, and the Roman Catholic "Sword of the Spirit." In addition to his duties as headmaster and Bishop, Dr. Fisher was Select Preacher at Oxford University from 1925 to 1927 and at Cambridge University in 1937 and 1940. Since 1939 he has been Dean of the Chapels Royal and Prelate of the Order of the British Empire.

In succeeding a great churchman as Archbishop of Canterbury, Dr. Fisher does not feel he has inherited the gifts of the late Dr. Temple. After his election in January 1945 the new Primate received the press and expressed this tribute to his predecessor: "My great regret is that there should be this vacancy to fill. I knew Dr. Temple from the time when I was an undergraduate at Oxford and he a don, and I am not filling his place now; there is no man in England who could do that." The press discussed the appointment of the conservative Dr. Fisher as head of the Church of England. The Manchester *Guardian* declared: "His opinions on many great questions are still hidden, for he has spoken little and written less . . . Dr. Fisher has still to prove himself." In America,

British Official Photo.

GEOFFREY FRANCIS FISHER,
ARCHBISHOP OF CANTERBURY

Time Magazine declared: "Fisher has worked as hard as Temple for cooperation among the Christian churches. A better administrator, he may prove more effective than his predecessor in this respect. Another asset is his adroitness and tact. . . .And he is no stuffed shirt."

On April 19, 1945, in the war-scarred Cathedral which had withstood innumerable air raids, Dr. Fisher was enthroned as Archbishop of Canterbury before a throng of three thousand dignitaries. Urging Church and nation to stand together in the resurrection of a peaceful world, Archbishop Fisher said, "The Church has much to put in order if it is to serve the nation. The nation has much to learn and relearn if it is to heed what God says to it through His Church."

Dr. Fisher, who rarely enters into politics, has been called a "nonpolitical bishop." In general, however, he has supported social reform, expressing his approval of the Beveridge '43 plan and educational reform measures. On one occasion he praised the Soviet Union, declaring, "We owe Russia more than we can give and more than we can pay." On another occasion, in March 1945, he commended the Conference of Missionary Societies in Great Britain and Ireland for its appeal for the removal of the color bar in British colonies: "The only right course is that people of any race are given full opportunity of developing their proper characteristics and utilizing the opportunities that belong to all men without any barriers from outside." When the atom bomb was loosed upon Japan several months later, Dr. Fisher asserted, in an article in the *Diocesan Gazette,* that history "shows us mankind is ever accommodating its conscience to more deadly and inhuman forms of war, abandoning one restraint after another," and that "the only way of deliverance lies in the Charter of the United Nations." The unity achieved by Great Britain and the United States during the Second World War, he declared at another time, would make it possible for them "for all time" to "promote

**FISHER, GEOFFREY FRANCIS, ARCH-
BISHOP**—*Continued*

in all the world the principles of responsible
freedom and good neighborliness." At the end
of 1945 he criticized the limited aid Britain
was giving to Central Europe and declared that
it was the duty of Great Britain and other nations to save the Germans from freezing and
starving that winter.

The Primate has expressed disapproval of
Church participation in the peace conference
after the war. Interviewed by the American
Army newspaper *Stars and Stripes*, he said:
"Making the peace is a political job, a job for
statesmen. Inevitably it will involve compromise
and conniving at compromise in a sinful world.
All the church can do and should do is to keep
boldly before statesmen the inflexible principles
of right and wrong. That is one thing, anyhow, that all the churches of the world are
agreed on."

In the early summer of 1945 a commission
on evangelism which was appointed by the
Archbishop of York advocated an extensive
publicity campaign, calling for a fund of nearly
one million dollars for use in motion picture,
radio, newspaper, and commercial advertising.
Another unusual method of education was announced in July, when Dr. Fisher urged a
nationwide network of public bureaus, staffed
by clergy, doctors, psychologists, and lawyers,
to help adjust marital troubles and check an increase in the divorce rate, which he described
as "a grave national problem."

In 1917 Dr. Fisher was married to Rosamond
Chevallier Forman, daughter of the late Reverend A. F. E. Forman and granddaughter of
Dr. A. S. Pears, once headmaster of Repton.
The couple have six sons, of whom the four
eldest are serving in the British Army. One
son, Captain Francis Fisher, was taken prisoner at Tobruk, later escaped, and was awarded
the Military Cross. The two youngest Fisher
boys, Richard Temple and Geoffrey Robert
Chevallier, in 1945 are at school, the latter taking a medical course at Cambridge. A popular anecdote about the Fisher family reveals
that Dr. Fisher once organized a football team
called Lambeth United and played on it with
his six sons. Another story is told of the
churchman's appearance in the Chester town
square, "bishop's gaiters and all," grinding a
hand organ to help raise money for the Royal
Infirmary. Mrs. Fisher is also active in public affairs. In 1943 she broke precedent by being the first woman to make an address in St.
Paul's Cathedral. She is president of the largest women's organization in the United Kingdom. This group, the Mothers Union, is composed of five hundred thousand women who
crusade against divorce and immorality. During the Fishers' years at Fulham Palace, especially during the war, Mrs. Fisher often assisted with details of housekeeping.

For recreation the Archbishop goes walking
and reads thrillers, and sometimes he and Mrs.
Fisher attend the cinema. Fisher smokes a
pipe, insisting, "I can't work unless I smoke."
The Primate is considered "still in his episcopal
prime." Noted for his executive ability, he
has a tactful, magisterial manner. His democratic spirit has been evident in restrained but
powerful speech. He is a short man, has thin
lips, an aquiline nose, a long chin, and he

wears gold-rimmed spectacles. Called a "typical English clergyman," he assumes the heavy
responsibilities of his Augustinian seat fully
aware of the problems of the twentieth century
world.

References

Life 18:32-3 F 12 '45 il pors
N Y Sun p20 Ja 26 '45
N Y Times p1+ Ja 5 '45
Newsweek 25:75-6 Ja 15 '45
Time 45:49-50 Ja 15 '45 por

Who's Who, 1945

FITCH, AUBREY (WRAY) June 11,
1883- United States naval officer; aviator

Address: b. United States Naval Academy,
Annapolis, Md.; h. 2301 Connecticut Ave.,
N.W., Washington, D.C.

Vice-Admiral Aubrey "Jake" Fitch, appointed superintendent of the United States
Naval Academy at Annapolis in July 1945, has
been described as "the least publicized of all
the important military men" in the American
forces during the Second World War. An
article by Lawrence E. Watkin in *Flying* says,
"There is probably no other naval officer anywhere so genuinely liked and admired both by
Regular Navy and Reserve officers as Admiral
Fitch"; as for his professional standing, "except for Admiral King'42 . . . Admiral Fitch
has the longest sea duty record of any admiral
on the active list."

The Admiral's parents, Ernest and Emily
Louisa (Wray) Fitch, came from England to
St. Ignace, Michigan, where Aubrey Wray
Fitch was born on June 11, 1883. He attended
the public schools of St. Ignace, and at fifteen
entered St. John's Military Academy at Delafield, Wisconsin. When he later tried for the
Naval Academy, he failed one entrance examination, according to the Baltimore *Sun*, but
managed to pass the next year's. He entered
Annapolis in 1902, writes Watkin; one of his
fellow midshipmen "brought along with him
from St. John's the story that little Aubrey
had licked the class bully in defense of a Jewish kid named Jakey. They didn't believe it,
but they were convinced when he remained undefeated boxer of his class all through Annapolis. Thereafter, he was known as 'Jake.'" In
his first year Fitch was also on the crew and
track teams, and he played football throughout
the four years.

Fitch was graduated in February 1906, and
served with the Asiatic Fleet for the two years
of sea duty then required before commissioning, becoming an ensign in 1908. After torpedo
instruction and more sea duty, in September
1911 he was assigned to the Naval Academy,
where he served one academic year as discipline officer, and another as instructor in physical training. On his twenty-ninth birthday, in
June 1912, Lieutenant (j.g) Fitch was married
to Gwyneth Hungerford Conger. He was advanced to lieutenant the following year, while
on sea duty; and in August 1914 Fitch was
given his first command, the U.S.S. *Terry* and
the Second Division of the Atlantic Fleet's Reserve Torpedo Flotilla. The next month the
officer was assigned to the staff of the commander in chief of the Atlantic Fleet as aide

and fleet athletic officer; and he also commanded the *Yankton*, tender to the Admiral's flagship, until the United States entered the First World War in April 1917.

That September Fitch became gunnery officer in the *Wyoming*, which operated with the British Grand Fleet's Sixth Battle Squadron from December 1917 until the surrender of the German Fleet in November 1918. During the war he was promoted twice, to the temporary rank of commander; and after the war, while again on duty at the Naval Academy, he was commissioned as regular lieutenant commander. His four months at Annapolis were followed by two years as head of the Naval Ammunition Depot in Hingham, Massachusetts. Then the Commander went back to sea as skipper of a minelaying destroyer and commander of a minelaying division, comprising the *Luce* and *Mahan*. Next came diplomatic duty, with the future admiral a member of the United States mission to Brazil from December 1922 to March 1927, working with the Brazilian Navy. In November 1927, after six months as executive officer on the *Nevada*, Fitch assumed command of the *Arctic*.

At the age of forty-six Commander Fitch applied for flight training, and attended the famous naval air school at Pensacola, Florida, where his young classmates nicknamed him "The Gray-haired Ensign." The nickname is well remembered, as is the fact that he made a perfect landing on the flight deck of the carrier *Langley*—except for forgetting to lower his landing hook. After having won his wings in February 1930 and commanded the *Wright* for a time, Fitch went to the *Langley* as her skipper. In July 1931 he was advanced to the rank of captain, and a year later assumed command of the Norfolk Naval Air Station. From June 1935 to April 1936 Fitch was on the oldest and largest American aircraft carrier, the *Saratoga*, as chief of staff to the commander of the fleet's aircraft battle force, leaving this post to take over command of the *Lexington*. In 1937 Captain Fitch entered the Naval War College at Newport, completing the senior course in May 1938. (He has also taken its correspondence course in strategy and tactics.) He spent the next two years as commandant of the huge Pensacola station. Following this assignment, Fitch was given command of Patrol Wing Two in May 1940, made a rear admiral in July, and transferred in November to command of the fleet's Carrier Division One, with the *Saratoga* as his floating headquarters.

Less than four months after the attack on Pearl Harbor he was commanding a task force of Admiral Chester W. Nimitz' '42 crippled Pacific Fleet. As such, Fitch took part in the battle of the Coral Sea on May 7-8, 1942—perhaps the first step of that phase of the Second World War in which "the battered Allies, with meager equipment and great courage, managed by the skin of their teeth to bring the Japanese advance to a halt." His airmen outfought two Japanese task forces, but this battle, off the Solomons, northeast of Australia, cost the Americans the old *Lexington*. (Almost the only time Fitch's staff officers have ever seen him "blow up" was when his orderly offered to let the fifty-eight-year-old Admiral precede him off his doomed ship.) "I had the honor to be

U.S. Navy
VICE-ADM. AUBREY FITCH

sunk in that engagement" is the way Fitch puts it; but others say that the decision to abandon the crippled ship made it possible to save the lives of twenty-seven hundred members of the crew. Fitch's "outstanding leadership" and "the courageous devotion to duty of the units under his command resulted in the sinking of one enemy Japanese carrier, the serious damaging of another, and the sinking of one enemy cruiser." (This is quoted from the citation accompanying his Distinguished Service Medal.)

In September 1942 Fitch assumed duty as commander of the South Pacific Fleet's aircraft; and when, in December 1943, he was appointed vice-admiral (temporary), the promotion was made retroactive to December 1942. "Overcoming tremendous obstacles in the early phases of offensive operations, he skillfully coordinated Navy, Marine Corps, Army, and New Zealand air units during an extended period of intensive combat, striking fiercely at the enemy and causing terrific damage to Japanese shipping, aircraft, ground troops, and installations, with proportionally light losses to the forces under his command." At Fitch's headquarters there was not, reportedly, one single publicity officer or newspaper correspondent, with the result that the public hardly knew his name. Nevertheless, the accomplishments of those South Pacific fliers under the leadership of Admiral Fitch make "one of the most fascinating narratives of modern warfare," writes Watkin. "It had to be smart to succeed. With the decision to lick Germany first, and because Guadalcanal had been slow and costly, only a shoestring allotment was doled out to the continuing Solomons operation. Yet this handful of planes not only cut a swath all the way up from Guadalcanal to Munda to Ondonga to Barakoma to Stirling to Torokina to Green Island, but it managed to take on all the planes the Japs could send from the great supply center at Rabaul. When Rabaul was drained the enemy flew in fighters and bombers from the near-by Carolines, and finally all that could be

FITCH, AUBREY—*Continued* .

spared from the Empire itself. The Fitch fighters knocked them all down impartially. . . . Admiral Fitch himself disclosed that between September 1, 1942, and May 1, 1944, Americans and New Zealanders under his command shot down in aerial combat 3,031 Jap planes out of the Pacific skies."

Jake Fitch is credited by Watkin with the strategy behind the Solomons campaign of island bombardment, followed by invasion and immediate use of captured areas as the base for further air operations. Fitch himself, to quote the citation for the Distinguished Flying Cross, "performed numerous hazardous flights in the combat zone of the Solomon Seas area and the Coral Sea for the purpose of inspecting air activities and incident to the selection and development of bases for projected operations." "Throughout this many-sided land-based warfare," adds Watkin, "Admiral Fitch was an ever-present inspiring figure. . . .He was among the first ashore when Munda was seized. In the rough days at Guadalcanal he landed time after time on Henderson Field, while the Japs were firing mortars down the strip." At Green Island he landed the first plane ; and once, when he thought the fliers at his advanced outposts might appreciate a concert, he "bundled his band [a prerogative of three-star rank] into a Skytrain and took it along. . . .He made it a point to find out for himself if the men had enough handball courts, if the Ships Service was open at hours when they could best use it, if there was enough pogey bait—candy—for all. He saw to it that the ice-cream machine was putting out its three-ton maximum of gedunks every week." When Fitch was ordered back to Washington in August 1944 to become deputy chief of naval operations for air, he had won a D.F.C. from the Army, a Gold Star in lieu of a second D.S.M. from the Navy, and a placque of appreciation from the islanders.

Despite the importance of his new job, in which he supervised all Navy aviation, Fitch remained unknown to the public. The only news he made was his receipt in July 1945 of Brazil's National Order of the Southern Cross in the degree of Grand Officer, awarded in recognition of his services as a member of the American Naval Mission twenty years earlier. Another brief announcement appeared in the papers that August, when the Admiral became the thirty-fourth superintendent of the Naval Academy, the second of his rank. As such, he was also commandant of the Severn River Naval Command.

The first airman to head the Academy, Fitch announced: "After this year every man who graduates from the Naval Academy either is going to become an aviator or is going to have a lot of knowledge and a great respect for air power." He started the Academic Board working on plans for a department of aeronautics, construction of a landplane airport near Annapolis, and enlargement of the existent seaplane base. Midshipmen who wished to specialize in aviation would not, however, be able to win their wings at Annapolis, as Army cadets could at West Point, but would have to fulfill the required "hitch" of sea duty after graduation before flight training at Pensacola. At the end of the year (1945) he said that the Academy

hoped to increase its capacity to a possible seventy-five hundred midshipmen a year, double its wartime quota.

Superintendent Fitch is described as a kindly, quiet man, democratic and unpretentious. Of slight stature, he is nevertheless "barrel-chested," and at the age of sixty he demonstrated to his officers how to "lick the daylights" out of a punching bag. He can take "kidding" from his colleagues, or his three sons, all of whom were in the Naval Reserve in the Second World War. An Episcopalian, Fitch is a member of Delta Sigma Nu and of three clubs—the New York Yacht Club, the Racquet Club of Philadelphia, and the Chevy Chase Club of Washington. His favorite song is reportedly "God Bless America," and his favorite reading is Zane Grey's Westerns. Fitch is described, too, as the most avid football fan to head the Academy.

References

Flying 35 :49+ N '44 por
Liberty 21 :18-19+ Ja 8 '44 pors
Time 43 :66-7 Je 5 '44 por
Who's Who in America, 1944-45

FITZGERALD, BARRY　Mar. 10, 1888-
Actor

Address: b. Paramount Pictures, Inc., Hollywood, Calif.

Catapulted to cinema heights by his portrayal of Father Fitzgibbon in *Going My Way* (1944), Barry Fitzgerald is unmoved by his sudden rise to fame and fortune. A distinguished veteran of the renowned Abbey Theatre of Dublin, he had hitherto been given only supporting roles in motion pictures since his arrival in Hollywood. The new star, a fifty-six-year-old "nutcracker-faced" little Irishman, is no advertisement for celluloid romance or glamour. Shy and retiring by nature and wise through years of diversified experience, he is unaffected by the glitter of the Hollywood spotlight.

This Irish actor was born William Joseph Shields on March 10, 1888, in Dublin. His father, Adolphus William Shields, was a newspaperman of sober habits ; his mother was the former Fanny Ungerland. The family was large and, in the son's words, they were "always pretty hard up." Dublin-educated at Merchant Taylors Endowed School, and Skerrys College, young William Shields was trained for the British Civil Service. He explains this choice of profession : "It was the one into which most of the families of our grade in my young days tried to stow away their progeny, as it gave security, a fair living, and a certain social status." But he found the work dull and devoted his spare time to sports, to active participation in boxing, swimming, and football. The flowering Irish literary movement also interested him, an interest stimulated by an early acquaintance with James Joyce.

At the suggestion of his brother Arthur, who was attending the acting school of the Abbey Theatre, Fitzgerald often visited that famed Irish institution. Of this portentous period of his life Fitzgerald candidly comments : "I went frequently to the Abbey Theatre, of course, and once when I was invited backstage to meet some of the players, I was roped in to play a walk-on the following week. I played walk-ons frequently, never having the energy to go away and do something useful in my spare time. It became a habit. I got to know the players well and met many notable and interesting people. It was fun, but I didn't take it seriously and neither I nor anyone else thought I had the least talent for the stage." He spoke his first lines in Sheridan's play *The Critic*. He had four words to say: "'Tis meet it should." Terror twisted his tongue, and he recited: "'Tis sheet it mould." Thus through a ludicrous blunder, he says, was launched his career as the comedian Barry Fitzgerald—for he adopted this pseudonym for fear of losing his civil service job.

For twenty years Barry Fitzgerald played the dual role of civil servant by day and actor by night. To learn his parts he studied during lunch hours and in stolen minutes at his desk. Of this unusual initiation into the theater he remarks: "I had very short and scrappy rehearsals, but the regular players cooperated, and we did all right. Since those days I have rehearsed plays in London and New York for six weeks and nearly died of boredom before the plays opened." Playing many character types, he learned his art thoroughly and in time became a leading member of the Abbey Theatre group. He acted in the plays of the contemporary Irish masters, O'Casey, Synge, Yeats, Dunsany, and he played characters created by Pirandello, Molnar, and Strindberg.

This was the period of the Irish Easter Rebellion of 1916, and the revolutionary fervor of the times inspired many of the day's dramatic offerings. Thus Sean O'Casey's most popular plays, *The Plough and the Stars* and *Juno and the Paycock*, treated the tragic Irish theme with dynamic passion. Fitzgerald played leading roles in these productions and on occasion witnessed violent audience reaction. With the Abbey players he also appeared in a group of Bernard Shaw '44 plays. Later he accompanied the group on a tour throughout England.

The Abbey Theatre has long enjoyed an enviable reputation. The rigid and thorough apprenticeship demanded by its high standards and extensive repertoire commands critical admiration for its graduates. However, today Fitzgerald says that it was not the Abbey Theatre that made him a successful character actor. Insisting that character delineation cannot be learned by studying acting, he claims to have mastered his profession by studying people. When he studies a part he attempts to absorb the character instead of merely memorizing the dialogue. In his opinion pantomime is the best acting. Thus his screen characterizations are always distinctively animated by personality traits of face and figure.

In 1929 O'Casey wrote *The Silver Tassie* especially for Fitzgerald and persuaded the actor to play the leading role in London. It was a difficult decision for Fitzgerald to make. He was reluctant to discard the security of job and pension for the vagaries of the theater. But he chanced the leap and at forty became a full-time professional actor. Later he rejoined the Abbey players for their American tours. Following the Broadway seasons the company made extended road tours throughout the United States. In this way, playing in many cities and small college towns, Fitzgerald became familiar with the American scene. He

BARRY FITZGERALD

prides himself on this knowledge and claims to know the topography of the continent better than most Americans.

In 1936 the director John Ford '41 brought Fitzgerald to Hollywood to do RKO's film version of *The Plough and the Stars*. The money Fitzgerald earned from this venture was spent on a vacation. He was preparing to return home to Ireland when Mary Pickford '45 offered him a year's contract, which he accepted. Thereafter he remained in America, alternating his film career with periodic returns to Broadway. Working for the major studios, he appeared in several pictures, but his early film career was unspectacular. His talent helped sustain several undistinguished pictures wherein he made the smallest part significant. More recently Fitzgerald contributed memorable performances to such notable films as Walter Wanger's *The Long Voyage Home* (1940), based on a series of Eugene O'Neill's plays, Twentieth Century-Fox's *How Green Was My Valley* (1941), adapted from Richard Llewellyn's '40 book, and RKO's adaptation of another Llewellyn novel, *None But the Lonely Heart* (1944).

Returning to his first love, the stage, in 1939 Fitzgerald appeared on Broadway in Paul Vincent Carroll's *The White Steed*. In this play he first attracted the attention of Leo McCarey, future producer and director of *Going My Way*. Later Fitzgerald and Sara Allgood, his former colleague in the Abbey Theatre, revived their famous roles in *Juno and the Paycock*, to the delight of New York's drama critics. As Captain Jack, Fitzgerald tied with Alfred Lunt '41 for the critics' choice of the best performance of the 1939-40 season. Then again on Broadway in 1941, he and his brother Arthur Shields appeared in Jack Kirkland's presentation of *Tanyard Street*. Thus Fitzgerald's reputation as a first-rate artist of the stage had long been established before he won acclaim as a film actor.

With the advent of Paramount's *Going My Way* the middle-aged Dubliner became a phenomenal success. The critics were unanimous in their high praise of his profoundly human

FITZGERALD, BARRY—*Continued*
portrayal of the petulant old priest. One critic called it "one of the great performances of our time," and Archer Winsten offered this glowing testimony: "Fitzgerald's portrait of the aged priest is by far the best character work of his career, and he has not been without distinguished work in the past. It is so memorable that people will be harking back to it for years." The reviewers rejoiced that Fitzgerald had finally been given a role "worthy of his talent."

Going My Way was hailed as a "picture of rare excellence" and Fitzgerald shared the eloquent commendation with Bing Crosby '41 and producer-director Leo McCarey. This applause was a double victory for Fitzgerald, for the New York Film Critics voted his performance the best of the year and also voted *Going My Way* the best picture of the year. Lastly, in March, at the annual presentation of awards made by the Academy of Motion Picture Arts and Sciences, the film won nearly every major award, and the actor was named the best performer in a supporting role. (Because of the convincing characterization Fitzgerald gave of the Roman Catholic priest, people are often surprised to learn that the actor is actually a Protestant. His interpretation of kindly Father Fitzgibbon is based on a composite character drawn from several clerical friends.)

Until *Going My Way*, Fitzgerald had been given supporting roles in pictures, chiefly to supply comic color. Now he is in demand by the biggest studios and the choicest roles are sought for him. He was starred in the musical *Stork Club*, with Betty Hutton, and in the Agatha Christie '40 multi-murder *And Then There Were None*. Films announced as in preparation at the end of 1945 that would feature the Irish actor were *Third Avenue*, in which his brother Arthur was to portray his screen brother, and *California*, co-starring Ray Milland and Barbara Stanwyck. He was signed to a long-term contract by Paramount, and his salary was reportedly tripled. He also branched out into radio, in October 1945 beginning a series over NBC called *His Honor, the Barber*, written by Carlton E. Morse.

Fitzgerald has become a Hollywood legend overnight but he remains indifferent to the furor. In the wake of his rise to stardom the usual stories of his professional peculiarities arose. He quickly squelches such tales of his alleged idiosyncrasies which rumor breeds prolifically in imaginative movieland. Fitzgerald prefers to remain what he is—a simple man of humble tastes and modest desires. A bachelor, he lives in a rented bungalow with his Iroquois Indian friend and aide, Gus Tallon, who performs the divers duties of stand-in and houseman. The mainstay of the household, says the actor, is his cook Mrs. Cade, who, he hopes, will not "up and quit" as callers increase. Arthur Shields, Fitzgerald's brother, is now also a movie actor, and the two Abbey alumni often have dinner together. Fitzgerald is of small build, five feet three inches tall; he is blue-eyed and has graying blond hair and an aggressive jaw. The advancing years find him youthfully active and still riding to work on his motorcycle, despite the worried protests of studio officials. While his golf is admittedly way over par, it is never-

theless a satisfying source of relaxation. Fitzgerald's favorite hobby is music—he started piano lessons at fifty and still takes lessons twice a week. He enjoys practicing Bach, Beethoven, and Brahms, a habit that has not always pleased neighbors. Kyle Crichton reveals that on several occasions the actor "has been asked by other tenants to please pipe down. Hence, the present bungalow where he can play without being hated."

Barry Fitzgerald is given to a simple way of living. Characteristically, he prefers the quiet comfort of an evening at home with book and pipe to the livelier diversions that Hollywood offers. As a Hollywood star, he is deprived of much of the privacy he formerly enjoyed. He resents this intrusion on his mode of life and frankly declares that being a Hollywood celebrity is "downright boring." Fred Stanley, in his New York *Times* article of January 14, 1945, gives his impression after interviewing Fitzgerald: "He is surprisingly casual and relaxed. He impresses one as an intensely modest man gifted with a curious, searching mind. There are numerous clues that he and his characterizations, as many interviewers have noted, are cut from the same cloth." Fitzgerald's personality has shaped his art, for he likes people and enjoys making them laugh.

References

Collier's 114:12+ S 16 '44 por
N Y Herald Tribune IV p3 Mr 12 '44
N Y Times Mag p14+ Ja 14 '45 pors
New Yorker 21:16-17 Jl 28 '45
Photoplay 26:53+ Ja '45 pors
Time 43:90-1 My 1 '44 por

International Motion Picture Almanac, 1943-44

FLEMING, SIR (JOHN) AMBROSE 1849—Apr. 19, 1945 British electrical physicist, engineer, and inventor; widely known for his "Fleming valve", "one of the ancestors of the now great and complex family of vacuum tubes"; was associated with the introduction into Britain of the telephone, electric lighting, and wireless telegraphy.

Obituary

N Y Times p19 Ap 20 '45 por

FLESCH, KARL (flĕsh) 1873—Nov. 15, 1944 Noted Hungarian violinist and teacher; head of violin department of Curtis Institute, Philadelphia, from 1924 to 1928; founder of Curtis String Quartet; author of *The Art of Violin Playing* (2 vols., 1924-30), which has been translated into twenty-two languages.

Obituary

N Y Times p23 N 16 '44 por

FLEXNER, BERNARD Feb. 24, 1865—May 3, 1945 American lawyer; played a leading role in the organization in 1925 of the Palestine Economic Corporation, created to promote industry and commerce in Palestine; was president until 1931; keenly interested in social welfare, he co-authored *Juvenile Courts and Probation* (1914) and *The Legal Aspect of the Juvenile Court* (1922).

Obituary

N Y Times p19 My 4 '45 por

FLEXNER, JENNIE M(AAS) 1882—Nov.
17, 1944 Librarian and reader's adviser at New
York Public Library; devoted years to the
promotion of adult education and advisory service to readers; her books on the proper use of
libraries have been widely read in the United
States and translated into several languages.

Obituary

N Y Times p13 N 18 '44

FLORE, EDWARD F. (flôr'ē) Dec. 5,
1877—Sept. 27, 1945 American labor leader;
a vice-president of the American Federation of
Labor; international president of the Hotel and
Restaurant Employees International Alliance
and Bartenders International League from 1911
until death.

Obituary

N Y Times p21 S 28 '45 por

FOSDICK, RAYMOND B(LAINE) June
9, 1883- President of Rockefeller Foundation; lawyer

Address: b. Rockefeller Foundation, 49 W. 49th
St., New York City; h. 25 E. 83d St., New
York City

President of the Rockefeller Foundation,
which contributes some ten million dollars annually to "promote the welfare of mankind
throughout the world," is Raymond B. Fosdick, a New York lawyer and social thinker
who was the first under-secretary general of
the League of Nations. He shares with chairman of the board John D. Rockefeller, Jr.,'41
the major responsibility for allocating the funds
—funds used to wipe out a dreaded plague
in Brazil, to help in the reconstruction of China,
to assist institutions, to support the researches
of scholars the world over.

A descendant of Puritans, Raymond Blaine
Fosdick was born in Buffalo, New York, on
June 9, 1883, to Frank S. and Amie I. (Weaver) Fosdick. His father, the forward-looking
principal of a Buffalo high school, since 1870
had been a believer in evolution; his elder
brother (by five years) was Harry Emerson
Fosdick '40, later known as the Baptist pastor
of the Riverside Church in New York. Young
Raymond Fosdick studied at Princeton University, receiving his B.A. in 1905 and his M.A.
in 1906, and was elected to Phi Beta Kappa.
Then he went on to the New York Law School.
Graduated with his LL.B. in 1908, Fosdick became assistant corporation counsel for the City
of New York under Mayor George Brinton
McClellan. In 1910 he was made Commissioner of Accounts, a post he held for three
years. That December the twenty-seven-year-
old lawyer was married to Winifred Finlay of
Montclair, New Jersey; they had two children
Susan and Raymond Blaine, Jr.

Described by *Time* as "the sort of genial,
persuasive, energetic man who takes naturally
to public life without becoming a politician,"
Fosdick was asked by the Rockefeller Bureau
of Social Hygiene to make a comprehensive
study of European police systems, which he began in 1914. (The findings were published, as
European Police Systems, in 1915.) Then he
turned his investigating activity to the American police system; but wartime conditions
forced him to leave this task in 1916, to act as

RAYMOND B. FOSDICK

special representative of the Secretary of War,
Newton D. Baker, on the Mexican border.
(*American Police Systems* was finally published
in 1920.)

The day after the United States declared war
on the Central Powers in April 1917, Fosdick
was sent to Canada as chairman of the Commission on Training Camp Activities of the
War and Navy Departments. After studying
the Canadian methods, he made similar inspections in France and England, and then in
the United States. "We had to extemporize our
technique and our method of operation as we
went along," he says. "There was no recent
experience to guide us. It was all new and
untried to us, with the Civil War, fifty years
before, the last great war which we had
fought." *Keeping Our Fighters Fit,* written in
collaboration with E. F. Allen, came out in
1918.

In that year Fosdick was sent as special
representative of the War Department to
France, where he remained as civilian aide to
General Pershing. When the League of Nations was formed President Wilson assigned
the New Yorker to it, and Fosdick became the
first under-secretary general. To his disappointment, the Senate refused to ratify the
League Covenant, and in 1920 Fosdick resigned
from that office. Back in New York, he practiced law as a member of Curtis, Fosdick, and
Belknap. A constant supporter of the League,
he soon founded the League of Nations Association.

In the sixteen years of Fosdick's practice in
New York City, he was active in social and
philanthropic work, as well as in the promotion
of internationalism. A member of the national,
state, and city bar associations, he was on the
executive committee of the last; for a time
he served in the Phi Beta Kappa Senate; and
he was active in the American Institute of International Law and the National Institute of
Social Science. In 1925 he was awarded the
LL.D. degree by both Colgate University and
Colorado College. By 1930 Fosdick had been

FOSDICK, RAYMOND B.—*Continued*
elected trustee of seven important public service organizations: the Rockefeller Foundation (in 1924), the Rockefeller Institute for Medical Research, the Rockefeller General Education Board, the International Education Board, the Spelman Fund, the Brookings Institution, and the National Institute of Public Administration.

In 1928 a group of addresses given by Fosdick before various scholastic audiences was published as *The Old Savage in the New Civilization*. Here he sets forth the basic ideas of his thinking: "Modern science has revolutionized, not man, but his world. . . .He remains as he was and always has been—irrational, impulsive, emotional, inherently conservative to change, bound by customs and traditions which he will not analyze, the victim of age-old conventions and prejudices. . . .Suddenly armed to the teeth," this old savage "is asked to live in peace, crowded together with [international] neighbors whom he never knew before and for whom he has no particular liking. And all this has happened in a hundred years—happened so quickly, in fact, that it finds the race utterly unprepared in point of religion, ethics, law, philosophy, economics, politics, and government to meet the exigencies that have arisen. That is the challenge that we face in our generation. It is a challenge the answer to which must not be postponed."

In February 1933 Fosdick and Albert L. Scott undertook for John D. Rockefeller, Jr., a study of liquor control, which involved field investigation in twelve countries. Findings were published, as *Toward Liquor Control*, in that year, and the recommendation was for the establishment of state liquor authorities with a monopoly on liquor trade, plus the elimination of all but Federal taxation, which revenue could be shared with the states by prearrangement. Two years later Fosdick was elected president of the Rockefeller Foundation, on the retirement of Max Mason, and also president of the General Education Board, to succeed Trevor Arnett. (Widowed in 1932—his wife and their two children died under tragic circumstances—the fifty-three-year-old lawyer was married in April 1936 to Elizabeth Miner.)

Raymond Fosdick entered upon his two presidencies in July 1936, with the special duty of preventing the Board's activities from overlapping the Foundation's, and with the special problem of liquidating the Board over a period of years. (In 1945 it was still in the process of liquidation, with the prospect that the actual termination would be some years later.) "His first year as the Foundation's president," in the words of *Time*, "saw no sensational shifts of Rockefeller procedure but a continuation and broadening of traditional policy. His administration was proving quite satisfactory to his trustees, and there was a note of crispness and dispatch in the Rockefeller Center offices which would have gladdened the Baptist heart of old John D., Sr., who died during Mr. Fosdick's first year."

As president of the Foundation, of which he had been an adviser since its establishment in 1913, Fosdick was entrusted with assets totaling nearly two hundred million dollars—$185,000,-000, of which $11,300,000 were disbursed during his first year. Grants were made in 1936 to 130 agencies in fifty-four countries, including forty-one national or local governments, forty-four educational institutions, twenty research institutes, and twenty-three councils, associations, societies, and commissions. Fellowships were provided for seven hundred graduate students, and research funds for 222 scholars; while the Foundation's seventy public health experts, the International Health Board, carried on research against eight dangerous diseases. Some of its most important work was done against malaria; Foundation workers discovered the most dangerous carrier, the mosquito Anopheles gambiae of Africa, and a staff member, Dr. Fred L. Soper, directed the Brazilian Government's "offensive" against malaria, which by 1940 resulted in the eradication of the mosquito in that stricken country. Important work against yellow fever was also accomplished; Rockefeller researchers discovered and compounded the only prophylaxis against that scourge, a vaccine of which the Institute prepared a million units in 1940.

Fosdick was in the habit of making frequent visits to the Foundation offices in Europe, particularly those in Paris and London. The outbreak of the Second World War, which he had worked in vain to prevent by urging the establishment of a true world court to settle international disputes, curtailed his travel and the Foundation's work all over the world. In 1940 the Paris office had to be moved to Lisbon, and the Shanghai office (ironically, as later events proved) to Manila. "Our personnel," Fosdick reported for that year, "has had to be recalled from Egypt, where work was being carried on in malaria and schistosomiasis; from Turkey, where we were engaged in sanitary engineering; from Rumania, where scarlet fever studies were being conducted; and from Hungary, which was a station for influenza research However, Foundation personnel was still operating on the Burma Road, in India, in South China, in the Belgian Congo, in Uganda, Central Africa, in Spain, Portugal, and of course in Latin America"—as well as in the English-speaking countries.

Fosdick is acutely aware that "the condition of university life and standards on the Continent is now little short of appalling," and feels that the intellectual life of the world "cannot without disaster be broken up into separate parts. If . . . Europe freezes into an Arctic night," he has written, "we shall not easily keep the fires lit in the universities and laboratories of America." In 1940 alone the Foundation granted a total of $266,350 to further the work of fifty-six scientists, refugees from the Nazi terror in Germany and ten other countries; $100,000 to train selected British medical students in American institutions. Since the beginning of the war the Foundation "had had the privilege of keeping fundamental research alive," making grants to the great Swedish, Swiss, and British social science institutes, and to the research projects of individual chemists, biologists, and physical scientists. All this work in pure science is in addition to such practical applications by Foundation workers as the preparation of influenza and yellow fever vaccines for the Allied troops, and reconstruction in China. "That fundamental research can be maintained in countries where the shock of war is ever present," said Fosdick in 1944, "is in these dark days a refreshing reminder of the power and persistence of creative intelligence."

In the annual report of the Foundation for 1944, Fosdick disclosed that it had established an unusual number of scholarships and fellowships for returning veterans. He stressed the need for study of economics, sociology, anthropology, and other social sciences, explaining that, "because war tends to substitute fear for reason and propaganda for truth, imperative necessity requires the support of the agencies and the spirit which makes for nonpartisan understanding in the field of human relations."

As president of the General Education Board, Fosdick announced new appropriations during 1944 of $3,073,976, approximately two-thirds of which went to advance Negro education. He said the greatest need was to train better teachers and leaders in education, while he predicted that Negro colleges and universities would see a period of expansion unprecedented in their history. He cited Army examinations as revealing "a far from perfect record in simple literacy," and said American colleges face conversion problems as difficult as those of industry.

Since 1941 Fosdick has been a member of the Joint Army and Navy Committee on Welfare and Recreation, for which he again inspects camps and bases. A Wilson Democrat politically, he remains an advocate of that internationalism which he sees as the only way to a solution of man's inescapable problems. His experience with such world-traveling scourges as malaria and influenza "poses," he says, "a problem of larger significance which cannot be evaded. . . .The nations of the world face these enemies of mankind, not as isolated groups behind boundary lines, but as members of the human race living suddenly in a frightening propinquity. Some kind of regularized international cooperation is essential [to their control]."

Fosdick made a plea for success of the United Nations Conference when he wrote in the New York *Times Magazine* in April 1945: "Modern science has at last brought us face to face with a decision which we can no longer evade. Thanks to our chemists and physicists, war as a method of settling disputes between nations has become so monstrous in its destruction that it is now a vast canopy of death spread over a blackened and smoking world." In another *Times* article he wrote further that, while "our first defense must inevitably be the United Nations Organization," it "is not an automatic device. . . .[It] must be built on a realization of the common interests which bind men together everywhere and of the common dangers which confront us as members of the same human race. . . .In spite of the atomic bomb we are still the captains of our own destiny, and we can make that destiny anything we desire."

"War worker, peace advocate, internationlist, social science promoter," Raymond Fosdick is described by *Time* as "first and foremost a lawyer," and by *Newsweek* as "a good conversationalist, genial, witty, and generous . . . equally popular playing games with children or discussing international affairs with statesmen." His services have been rewarded with the Distinguished Service Medal, two doctorates, the rank of Commander of the French Legion of Honor, and election as a Fellow of the American Academy of Arts and Sciences and

as a member of the American Philosophical Society. His clubs are the Century and the Union Interalliée. In December 1945 he was made a member of a committee to study atomic energy which was appointed by the Carnegie Endowment for International Peace.

References

Newsweek 6:20 D 21 '35
Time 30:70 S 6 '37
International Who's Who, 1942
Who's Who in America, 1930-31; 1944-45

FOSTER, WILLIAM Z(EBULON) 1881-
Communist leader; author
Address: b. Communist Party, 35 E. 12th St, New York City

Veteran labor leader and long a prominent American Communist, William Z. Foster in 1945 was once again in the news spotlight, for in July, at the convention of the Communist Political Association, Earl Browder [45], long-time Communist leader, was deposed, and Foster became national chairman of the organization, now known once more to the world as the Communist Party. "America's foremost radical has played a militant part in struggles of the labor movement since 1894. Three-time Communist Presidential candidate, he has written scores of pamphlets and is the author of six books. Self-educated and well-traveled, he was for many years an industrial worker, a seaman, and, during the turbulent birth of industrial unionism, an organizer. Hard work and danger have filled his action-packed career as a revolutionary. Once termed "an engineer of the labor movement," Foster in his time has been "orthodox and outlaw, regular and rebel."

The Communist leader is a New England Yankee of humble origin. The son of an Irish railroad car washer, William Zebulon Foster was born in Taunton, Massachusetts in 1881. He grew up in the slums of Philadelphia, to which the family had moved when he was six, and there the boy joined one of the street gangs, the "Bulldogs." At the age of seven he began to work, selling newspapers to contribute to the meager family income. At nine he applied for a job at Wanamaker's department store, where he was advised to "grow up first." When he was ten he was apprenticed to an artist, from whom he began to learn such art crafts as modeling and stonecutting.

But after three years he gave up this work. "I felt no call to a life of art," he explains; "I wanted to become an industrial worker and was drawn as by a magnet to the shops." Thus, at the age of thirteen young Foster entered a period of more than twenty years during which he worked in seven different industries in various parts of the country. For three years he worked for the American Type Founders Company, where he became "saturated with lead." From 1898 to 1900 he worked in the fertilizer industry, at such jobs as laborer, steam fitter, fireman, engineer, and skilled fertilizer mixer. But this work was dangerous to health: the combination of garbage, dust and chemicals was a menace to the workers. He left, going to Havana, but finding economic conditions bad, he returned to look for work in Florida. After working in several Florida lumber camps,

WILLIAM Z. FOSTER

he traveled on to New York, where he spent some months working as a motorman on the Third Avenue Trolley lines. But when he joined the union he was again without a job. (At that time union membership meant dis- charge.)

Failing in health, the New Englander then signed on square-rigged merchant ships, work- ing as an able-bodied seaman. He sailed once around the world, and spent considerable time on the coasts of Africa, Australia, and South America. "Three years of knocking over the world in windjammers finally put me back on my feet again," he says. From this period, 1901-04, Foster has exciting tales to tell of the experiences of seafarers and of the prac- tice of shanghaiing men to make up crews. When he returned from his marine adventures in 1904 Foster found his way to Oregon where he became a homesteader with a claim high up in the rugged mountain country. During the period he owned this land he continued his work in lumber camps and on railroads, and after three summers he sold his land. He then took a "fling" at sheepherding in 1907, fol- lowed by another turn at railroading.

In these early years as a laborer, Foster says, he found the truth of the Marxist prin- ciples he was later to adopt, and his revolu- tionary ideology developed. He learned the theory of the class struggle and was con- vinced that "the way people get their living determines their social outlook." He had joined the Socialist Party in 1900 but was expelled nine years later when his ideas no longer conformed with the party line. In 1909 he was a member of the Wage Workers Party in Seattle and that year he joined the Industrial Workers of the World. This group aimed at socialism through industrial unionism, endeavoring to organize all workers, skilled and unskilled, into one great body. As a member of the I.W.W. Foster took part in many labor and free-speech fights and was a leading writer and orator of the organiza-

tion. He once participated in a secret organ- izing drive in a mining area and after a month he was driven out of the district by armed company guards.

In 1910 Foster went to Europe, where for thirteen months he studied the labor move- ments, principally in France and Germany. He was especially influenced by the French labor movement and learned much from the Confédération Générale du Travail. Return- ing to the United States, in the summer of 1912 he found work as canvasman for a tent show. He took this job with the traveling theatrical group in order to have time to write his first pamphlet, *Syndicalism*, in col- laboration with Earl Ford. The pamphlet outlined the principles and program of the Syndicalist League of North America which he had founded with Ford and of which he had become secretary. This radical group was active within the trade unions but took no part in political action. Its work was of considerable importance for a period, but after two years the organization ceased to exist. While working in various capacities as a rail- roader, Foster devoted all his spare time to reading and writing. His eyes became af- fected, almost to the point of blindness, and only after three years of trial remedies did an operation restore his sight.

During most of the years 1904-16 the wander- ing worker traveled around America "on the hobo." He covered thirty-five thousand miles on the railroads, becoming familiar with the life of migratory workers and the vast Amer- ican scene. Although it was his plan to find work and see the country, he traveled mainly for "revolutionary agitational purposes." Fos- ter found that "industrial workers as a whole react the same toward the basic problems that confront them in industry, yet they have con- siderable minor differences in psychology." In *Pages From a Worker's Life* he explains the causes for the different outlooks of the needle- worker and the steelworker, the sailor and the packinghouse worker.

As a vigorous partisan of labor, Foster played a vital part in numerous strikes in many industries, affiliated at various times with the I.W.W., the A.F. of L., the Railroad Brotherhoods, the Trade Union Unity League, the CIO, and independent unions. In 1915 he was the business agent of a Chicago railway union. The following year he again attempted to organize the radical element within the trade union movement by establishing the In- ternational Trade Union Educational League, an organization which acquired little influ- ence, however, and expired in 1917. This was the period of the rising tide of industrial unionism, which found Foster in the vanguard. In 1917-18 he was one of the leaders in the organization of the packinghouse workers, the first mass production industry to be completely organized on a national scale.

As an A.F. of L. organizer, Foster was a leader in the campaign in the steel industry, which culminated in the great steel strike of 1919, a bloody episode that held the Nation's attention for months. According to the *Jour- nal of Political Economy*, the organizer dem- onstrated "remarkable ability" in the steel cam- paign, and the *New Republic* called his work "a miracle of organization." This was the period of Attorney General A. Mitchell Palmer's "Red raids," when the strike was pictured by enemies as a revolutionary overture. Foster was attacked in the anti-labor press as a Red menace; his past affiliations and opinions, especially his pamphlet on syndicalism, were used to discredit him and the strike. When examined by a Senate investigating committee in connection with the strike, Foster revealed that his main source of opinion on social affairs was then the work of Lester F. Ward, pioneer American sociologist.

In November 1920 Foster founded the Trade Union Educational League, which carried on propaganda work designed to direct the trade-union movement toward industrial unionism and independent working-class political action. According to an analysis of the organization in the *Journal of Political Economy* in 1925, the T.U.E.L. considered the development of fascism an international menace to the labor movement. The group functioned as an auxiliary of the unions, with branches in the principal cities and industrial centers of the United States and Canada. Its ultimate goal was the abolition of capitalism and the establishment of a workers' republic. As national secretary of the T.U.E.L., Foster participated in many significant labor campaigns. In the summer of 1921 he and Earl Browder [44] attended the congress of the Red International of Labor Unions in Moscow as delegates from the T.U.E.L. The following year when the T.U.E.L. initiated a movement in the Chicago Federation of Labor for amalgamation of craft unions into industrial unions, Foster led the controversy with Samuel Gompers of the A.F. of L., a battle in which Gompers succeeded in keeping the craft status of the A.F. of L. In 1926-28 Foster was active on behalf of the United Mine Workers of America and participated in the 1931 coal strike, which he reports as "one of the severest strike tests" he ever witnessed.

On his return from the Moscow conference, Foster joined the Communist Party. The C.P. had been formed in 1920 after a split within the Socialist Party, and Foster had previously met with the executive council of the underground C.P. During the postwar "Red scare" era, Communist meetings were broken up and members arrested. Such action led to the formation of the milder-sounding Workers Party of America in 1921 while the Communist Party continued to function underground. In April 1923 this underground organization was dissolved and merged with the legalized Workers Party which later again became the Communist Party. During his many years of association with the Communist organization Foster has been "in the thick of all the bitter factional rows" and has always emerged successful. Internal party controversies, such as the Foster-Ruthenberg and the Foster-Lovestone disputes, have been widely publicized. Foster was arrested for his participation in a secret Communist convention in Bridgman, Michigan, in 1922. Indicted for criminal syndicalism, he was freed when the trial ended in a jury disagreement. The case attracted wide attention; according to Robert Morss Lovett [43], who reported the proceedings in the *New Republic,* "it may be that the result of the Michigan trial is after all a victory for the people."

After a futile attempt to organize a farmer-labor slate for the elections of 1924, the Workers Party ran their own candidates. As candidate for President on the first Communist ticket in the United States, Foster polled 33,000 votes. Running for the same office in 1928 he received 48,000 votes, and in the depression election of 1932 the Communist candidate polled 55,000 votes.

After a brief period as general secretary of the C.P., in 1930 Foster relinquished this position because of poor health and became chairman. That year he was his party's candidate for Governor of New York. During that same year Foster spent six months in a New York penitentiary for participating in a Union Square demonstration of the unemployed in March after the police had refused to issue a permit for the gathering. As a revolutionary, he tells of other experiences he had with armed guards, vigilantes, and police, including kidnapping by the Colorado Rangers and, he reported, the third degree at the hands of the Los Angeles police during the 1932 campaign.

The radical leader has attended several World Congresses and executive meetings of the Comintern and of the Red International of Labor Unions. He recalls the inspiration of first seeing Lenin in Moscow in 1921—in Lenin's teachings Foster found the basis for his lifework. In March 1941 the Communist Party filled New York's Madison Square Garden in celebration of Foster's sixtieth birthday.

The course of Foster's changing political ideology took him from the conservative stand to the most extreme radical wing within the labor movement. Thus, it was between the First and Second World Wars that he was often the target of bitter attack from critics within labor officialdom. In 1919 a writer in *Current Opinion* saw Foster as a leader who appealed "to men of foreign birth who have little or no conception of American ideals and institutions." In 1924 an editorial in the *New Republic* criticized Foster and his followers in their T.U.E.L. activities, which appeared "merely to have created dissension and have antagonized indispensable sections of the rank and file." Another writer in the same magazine said eight years later: "He veered about to the tactics of starting new labor organizations whenever the chance to control existing unions from the inside was denied. This was described by Foster's labor enemies as a 'rule or ruin' policy."

In May 1944 Foster presided at the national convention of the American Communist Party when, under Browder's leadership, the party dissolved itself and was immediately reconstituted as a non-party organization, the Communist Political Association. (In mid-1945 it once more became a party.) Previously Foster had expressed his disagreement with Browder's political course, but his arguments against the latter's theoretical theses had been rejected by most of the Communist leadership. At the time of the dissolution of the C.P. an article in *Nation's Business* expressed fear of the "infiltrative practice" of the Communists, while, on the other hand, a study in the *American Political Science Review* (February 1945) saw little danger from Communists since their party had not engaged in revolutionary propaganda for eight years and had "abandoned the last slight

FOSTER, WILLIAM Z.—*Continued*

remnant of revolutionary ideology in January 1944." This situation, however, was drastically altered in 1945 with the publication in America of the article "On the Dissolution of the Communist Party of the United States" by Jacques Duclos. Reprinted from the April issue of the theoretical organ of the French Communist Party, it appeared in the *Daily Worker* in May with a foreword by Browder in which the C.P.A. president admitted that the article "reflects the general trend of opinion of European Marxists in relation to America." In a lengthy analysis of the wartime policy of American Communists, Duclos sharply criticized Browder's course. Reverberations were immediate: on June 2 the National Board of the C.P.A. passed a resolution redefining the Communist program, which the anti-Communist press called another Communist somersault. The resolution paid tribute to Foster's part in the formulation of Communist policy: "We must recognize important contributions which Comrade Foster made in the struggle against opportunism." Besides scoring the opportunistic tendencies of the wartime Communist policy, Foster condemned Browder's "revisionist ideas" and further contended that the policies based on these ideas "violated many basic principles of Marxism-Leninism."

The resolution, as amended and approved by the National Committee on June 20 (with the one dissenting vote cast by Browder), is entitled, "The Present Situation and the Next Tasks." Analyzing the fallacies of past Communist policy, it sought to right the errors by stricter adherence to Marxist-Leninist principles. Hence the Communist "line" steers away from all-out cooperation with capitalism towards sharper struggle against monopoly capital and clearer focus on the "class nature of bourgeois democracy." While the program remained substantially the same, supporting "every effort of the Truman Administration to carry forward the policies of the Roosevelt-labor-Democratic coalition," it pointedly emphasized that the people must "sharply criticize all hesitations to apply these policies, and vigorously oppose any concessions to the reactionaries; for the camp of reaction must not be appeased—it must be isolated and routed."

Aiming to re-establish their organization as the "independent, Marxist party of the working class," a special national convention was called to open in July (1945) in New York. At the end of the three-day gathering, to which members of the press and the public were forbidden admittance, announcement was made that Foster had been named to head the party (no longer the C.P.A.), while Browder and Robert Minor had been dropped from active roles. A new constitution was adopted, which, together with the naming of Foster as the party's leader, was seen as "a complete repudiation of the views of Browder," who had been the target of bitter intraparty criticism for a number of months. Although the terms of the new constitution were not made public immediately, the preamble, which was published in the *Daily Worker,* stated that the Communist Party was "the political party of the American working class, basing itself upon the principles of scientific Socialism, Marxism-Leninism." When announcement was made later, in October, that

Louis F. Budenz, president and editor of the *Daily Worker,* had renounced communism to return to the Roman Catholic Church, Foster was quoted as saying it was "a most serious error" for the party to have promoted Budenz to responsible posts in past years. His statement that the promotions were "an example of political looseness and carelessness, which is related to the revisionism that characterized our party's policies in the more recent period" was seen as further criticism of Browder.

With the current reassertion of revolutionary principles, some observers see dangers in the altered Communist policy. This reaction was reflected in early June in an article by Eleanor Roosevelt[40], who observed that "certain actions of the American Communists in this country have added fuel to the general fear of communism as an international force." Along similar lines, a report submitted to the House Military Affairs Committee and unanimously accepted on June 29 stated that American Communists can now be expected "to plot such a revolution as they think will realize the Marx-Lenin dream." The New York *Times* carried Foster's denunciation of the report and his avowal that the Communists "remain steadfast to the objective of completing the destruction of fascism, and together with it Japanese militarism."

Late in the year, the war over, Foster was called before the House committee investigating un-American activities, and in his appearances at the hearings the committee drew forth his opinions on the Administration, strikes, the Soviet Union, United States imperialism. He accused President Truman[45] of leaning toward "aggressive imperialism," and said it was "a sorry day for world peace and world democracy" when James F. Byrnes[41] was appointed Secretary of State. Several weeks later, as conditions worsened in China's internal struggle between the Government and the Chinese Communists, Foster declared that the Administration would "precipitate civil war" in that country unless it removed American troops and withdrew its backing of Chiang Kai-shek's[40] "shaky regime." His warning was followed the next day in New York by a demonstration staged by the State committee of the Communist Party, at which Foster and a number of other speakers denounced "armed American intervention in China."

On another day in Washington a Syndicalist pamphlet written by the Communist leader in 1912 was introduced at the hearing, but Foster refused to answer questions pertaining to it, explaining that he had repudiated many years ago its revolutionary thesis. In references to the atomic bomb, he said that the retention of the secret of its manufacture was "the greatest political mistake" the United States had ever made, and he advocated turning it over to the United Nations Organization. Russia, the Latin American countries, and the new democratic countries of Europe, he declared, would not tolerate United States domination of the world. He denied that his Communist Party had any relation to that in the U.S.S.R., and that it received contributions from any groups outside the country. In regard to postwar reconstruction, he expressed the opinion that the United States should make loans to Russia and Great Britain, without dictating how the recipients should conduct their internal affairs. Strikes, he said on another day, were fomented by employers. (Before an audience of twelve thousand gathered in Madison Square Garden, New York City, in September in observance of the party's twenty-sixth anniversary, Foster "rededicated the party to a finish fight against capitalism," but said that "the limited economic program presented to Congress by President Truman must be adopted.")

A prolific pamphleteer, Foster has also written six books, *The Great Steel Strike and Its Lessons* (1920), *The Russian Revolution* (1921), *Misleaders of Labor* (1927), *Towards Soviet America* (1932), *From Bryan to Stalin* (1937), and *Pages From a Worker's Life* (1939). The last two are of an autobiographical nature and were well received by the critics. *From Bryan to Stalin,* according to the *Saturday Review of Literature,* is "a creditable piece of biographical writing, frank, clear, and complete." In reviewing *Pages From a Worker's Life,* Granville Hicks '42 wrote, "As a literary critic, I cannot help thinking how many proletarian novels might have come out of the experiences recorded in this book. Foster has seen so much, done so much, been so much. It is a modest book, characteristically impersonal, but you do feel the quality of the man." In one of his many pamphlets, *Your Questions Answered* (1939), Foster expressed the Communist views on political, economic, and social questions and declared, "We believe that a fundamental reorganization of society—socialism—is the only final solution of the workers' problems—unemployment, poverty, war."

Foster is described as "a tallish, thin Yankee with scanty hair, a slightly bulging forehead, a narrow chin, and mobile mouth." To a writer for *World Tomorrow* he looked like "a Presbyterian elder from the innermost hinterland," while he impressed *Current Opinion* as "a typical Western railroader." A mild-mannered man, Foster is, according to one source, "a hard fighter, whose zeal and self-sacrificial devotion to his cause cannot be questioned, but he is an incurable romantic." A seasoned orator, the Communist leader has a reputation for simple, forceful speech, with "little of the virtuosity of the politician or preacher who knows how to put over his personality." In a characterization of the American revolutionist, the writer George Soule wrote, "Ideas and movements are his food and drink, his work and play"

References

J Pol Econ 33:410-31 Ag '25
New Repub 21:163 Ja 7 '20; 72:196-9 O 5 '32
Foster, W. Z. From Bryan to Stalin (1937); Pages From a Worker's Life (1939)

FOUILHOUX, J(ACQUES) ANDRE

(foo-yoo') Sept. 27, 1879—June 20, 1945 French-born architect who was a leader of his profession in the United States; designed the trylon and perisphere at the New York World's Fair; one of the designers of Rockefeller Center, the *Daily News* Building in New York and the *Chicago Tribune* Building; president of the New York Building Congress; president of the American Relief for France.

Obituary

N Y Times p1+ Je 21 '45 por

FRANKENSTEEN, RICHARD T(RUMAN) Mar. 6, 1907- Labor leader

Address: b. 411 W. Milwaukee, Detroit, Mich.; h. 18685 Roselawn St., Detroit, Mich.

"One of the ablest leaders in any union in any part of the United States" is the New York *Sun's* description of Richard T. Frankensteen, whose unsuccessful campaign for election to the Detroit mayoralty in 1945 attracted nationwide attention. The UAW (CIO)—nobody ever calls it the United Automobile, Aircraft, and Agricultural Implement Workers of America—which he helped to found, has had as many as 1,236,580 members (in early 1944); but, although it is the world's largest union, its financial position is less secure than that of many others, for expenses tend to exceed the dues of a dollar a month. Officials stand for election each year, and "Big Dick" Frankensteen has weathered bitter factional fights since becoming one of the two vice-presidents in August 1942.

Richard Truman Frankensteen was born in Detroit on March 6, 1907, and was brought up in a Republican and Episcopalian household. His father, the late Harold L. Frankensteen, a singer, composer, and pianist, was soloist at Trinity Episcopal Church, and his mother, Grace (Smith) Frankensteen, still is. Dick and his brother Don, who is now a UAW official, sang in the Trinity choir. At thirteen, it is said, Dick weighed 185 pounds. Naturally, he played tackle on his high school football team, and he was selected as one of the All-State stars. During vacations the boy worked in the Chrysler automobile company's Dodge plant, beginning at the age of fifteen and continuing for six and one-half years. By the time he got to college, however (according to Joseph Driscoll of the New York *Herald Tribune*), Frankensteen is thought to have paid his way through the University of Dayton (Ohio) by playing professional football. While making an "enviable" scholastic record in the education course, he played tackle on the college football team and wrote and staged three musical plays. When Frankensteen was graduated in 1932, he was voted the most likely to succeed, and presented with a gold football and the Award of Honor as the best all-round man in his class.

The burly twenty-five-year-old was promised a job as teacher and athletic coach at the Noblesville (Indiana) High School, but the school board found itself bound by contract to keep the incumbent. Frankensteen had a wife to support—the former Grace Callahan of Dayton, to whom he had been married that April—and jobs were hard to get in those depression days. He therefore went back to the Dodge plant, working on the assembly line by day while he studied law at night at the University of Detroit. (He is a member of the Delta Theta Phi legal fraternity, as well as of Alpha Pi Chi.) During the three years Frankensteen worked in the Dodge trim department, he was elected employee representative and then presi-

RICHARD T. FRANKENSTEEN

dent of the bargaining council of the company union, and later became leader of the movement to reorganize it into an independent union. This was accomplished in 1935, and Frankensteen was elected president of the new Automotive Industrial Workers Association.

As president of this city-wide union, in 1935 Frankensteen led the first major organized industrial strike in the "open shop" city of Detroit. This was met with the violence characteristic of the period; in fights between union and anti-union forces tear gas, clubs, bricks, blackjacks, and similar weapons were used. From thousands of pickets, Frankensteen selected a few hundred as his "flying squadron" to meet the challenge; according to the UAW, this was the beginning of a standard practice. After his union amalgamated with the young United Auto Workers of America (CIO), Frankensteen was elected to the international executive board and assigned to direct organization in Detroit. When the thirty-year-old leader took over, the UAW had a few thousand members in Detroit plants; by the end of 1937, the membership was 250,000, and such companies as Midland Steel, Briggs, Packard, Murray, and Chevrolet, were forced to recognize the union as the workers' bargaining agent. During the widely publicized sit-down strike of April 1937, Frankensteen negotiated the first national contract with the Chrysler Corporation; the contracts he negotiated with Chrysler, then and later, were reported by his union as the best in the automobile industry, with the highest average wage rates.

In May of 1937 the union leader was halted and attacked by armed Ford company police when he attempted to hand out CIO leaflets in front of the River Rouge plant. This Battle of the Overpass, as it is known in UAW annals, was shown in newsreels, and a photograph of the battered and blood-spattered Frankensteen being comforted by fellow unionist Walter Reuther [41] was printed in newspapers in the United States and abroad. That

was not the only occasion on which he met violence: he has also been teargassed in line of union duty, his home has been bombed, and he has had occasion to use his pistol to defend himself in the city of Flint.

But it was the Ford incident which, to quote Newsweek, "projected his name into the national limelight, where it stayed through a series of violent factional battles within the union itself." In that year, with the backing of president Homer Martin, Frankensteen was elected vice-president of the international union. At this time dissatisfaction among the members, most of them new to unionism, was brought on largely by the business recession which meant layoffs and lowered working hours. Payment of UAW dues dropped so sharply that the union took all its organizers off the payroll temporarily. In addition, the leadership was split into opposing factions. In 1939 Martin was replaced as president by R. J. Thomas [42], and "Big Dick" was also out of office. He was appointed organizational director for the Chrysler department, which had come to terms with the UAW a few years earlier. (In 1939, too, Frankensteen ran unsuccessfully for the Detroit Common Council, polling 150,000 votes.) Then, in February 1941, CIO President Philip Murray [40] appointed Frankensteen national director of aircraft organization, to bring the workers of the Nation's expanding aviation industry into the CIO. When jurisdiction over aircraft was given to the UAW in 1942, Frankensteen retained the post. Since 1941, under his directorship, upwards of 450,000 aircraft workers have become union members, and the UAW thinks that Frankensteen's success in two separate organizational drives—automobile and aircraft— must set some kind of record.

Frankensteen helped negotiate a settlement of the Vultee and Ryan [43] aircraft strikes in Southern California, but in June 1941 he was put in an awkward position by the unauthorized strike of one of his locals at North American Aviation. Weeks of wrangling over wage demands had led to negotiations under the National Defense Mediation Board, during which the UAW had promised not to strike. Frankensteen left Washington, but his plea to the strikers failed (he suspended the local officials and fired five representatives of the international union for failing to carry out UAW policies), and President Roosevelt [42] ordered the Army to take over the plant. At the same time Frankensteen declared the right of aircraft workers to "win for themselves and their families a standard of living which is consistent with . . . an industry whose profits range among the top three American industries, and yet whose average hourly wages, according to United States Government figures, rank tenth, or next to last, among the first eleven American industries classified as vital to defense." Another important plant where labor disputes involved Frankensteen that year was the Bendix plant of Air Associates, Inc.

After Pearl Harbor, Frankensteen was appointed, along with UAW vice-president Reuther and secretary-treasurer George F. Addes, to the ten-man Committee on Labor and Management, which in January 1942 was reorganized as a seven-man committee of the Office of Production Management, to help develop the best methods of converting the automobile industry to war production. He also became a labor member of the National War Labor Board, and in March served on the fact-finding panel which heard the arguments in the "Little Steel" wage case. In the UAW elections that August, Frankensteen and Reuther, with the backing of Thomas, were elected to the newly created posts of vice-presidents, at an annual salary of $7,000. (According to Scripps-Howard '40 writer Charles T. Lucey, UAW officials' salaries are modest, compared to those of other union executives.)

Addes and Frankensteen reportedly led the group on the UAW executive board which upheld President Roosevelt's wage-freezing executive order and supported a wage incentive plan for their industry in April 1943, but they were overwhelmingly defeated in this instance by the Reuther faction. They joined the other board members in signing a demand for slashing prices; "equal pay for equal work" throughout industry; eliminating the "Little Steel" formula in favor of wage adjustments to "match the increase in the cost of living"; and the guaranty of forty hours' minimum pay for every worker in essential war work when "material shortages, changes in production scheduling, or military design" prevented him from working a full forty hours. That May of 1943, after Chrysler's failure to live up to its UAW contract had brought on strikes of two locals, union president Thomas assigned Frankensteen to share Leo Lamotte's duties as director of the Chrysler department. That September Frankensteen declared that the Byrnes '41 Office of War Mobilization had failed to meet the aircraft production emergency, and proposed a labor-management-Government conference to work on production problems and on the elimination of "wastage of materials, machines, and manpower on planes of doubtful military efficiency, equalization of wages with those paid in shipyards, and the writing into Government contracts of provisions for labor-management production committees."

In January 1944 Frankensteen wrote to the newspapers in favor of a Federal absentee ballot for soldiers. In March he was one of the CIO representatives who went to Washington to dispute charges by Navy Secretary Knox '40 and Under-Secretary of War Patterson '41 that the manpower shortage in the bearing industry evidenced the need for a national service act. The union men contended that the real reasons were low wages, bad working conditions, and "selfish and monopolistic practices": management refusing to sublet contracts to possible future competitors, failing to use entire production capacity for fear of being caught short by the end of the war, and in some cases diverting bearings to civilian customers. Later that month Frankensteen announced the calling of a conference of UAW members honorably discharged from the armed forces, to decide whether to form a new veterans' organization or to join one of the existing groups; they could, he said, be important in counteracting unfair antilabor propaganda which was being spread among servicemen. In July 1944 the labor leader was chairman of the Michigan delegation to the Democratic National Convention, of which his chief Thomas was a member. Supporting the renomination of Vice-President Henry A. Wallace '40, the huge delegate im-

pressed the crowd as he protested against the way Mayor Hague of Jersey City, boss Edward J. Flynn '40 of The Bronx, Mayor Kelly of Chicago, and Democratic National Chairman Hannegan '44 were directing the convention into choosing their candidate, Senator Harry Truman '45. Frankensteen's plea was unsuccessful but, says Newsweek, "he had stolen the show."

Later that month Frankensteen announced support of the Kilgore '43 bill for a central agency to handle cut-backs and reconversion to peacetime production, which would provide compensation, retraining and transportation costs of war workers moving to new jobs. He pointed out later that Congress had guaranteed industry against losses from reconversion, and declared that the Federal Government had "no more right to leave the eighteen million war workers unprotected during reconversion than it had to leave the marines stranded on Guadalcanal." In August, after a two-hour plea to strikers at the Wright Aeronautical Corporation in New Jersey, he brought their four-day wildcat strike to an end. At about this time his union petitioned the Federal Communications Commission to revoke the license of Station WHKC (Columbus, Ohio). The charges were that the station had unfairly censored and discriminated against the union by forcing Frankensteen and others on broadcasts for which time was paid for to rewrite speeches dealing with "controversial issues," yet permitting free expression to the political talks of Colonel Robert R. McCormick '42 and the anti-union and anti-Administration commentaries of Boake Carter '42 and Fulton Lewis, Jr. '42. The station's reply to the latter charge was that Carter and Lewis were network commentators and that an individual station could not control their utterances, while it could and should blue-pencil "controversial" discussion originating at its station. The station president also declared that the items eliminated from the union broadcasts "were not friendly or constructive, which was contrary to the contract between the union and the station." In October 1944, when Frankensteen was invited to address the National Association of Broadcasters' code compliance committee, he "pulled no punches" when he said that radio had completely ignored its legal obligation to permit unbiased presentation of controversial issues, and, in the case of labor relations, had flagrantly and conspicuously favored the employers.

In May 1944 Frankensteen denounced the Navy's sudden termination of contracts with the Brewster Aeronautical Corporation's Long Island and Johnsville plants without notice to the workers, as showing "a lack of concern on the part of Congress and certain Departments with effective war mobilization, and a complete disregard of labor's right to employment." As reported in the New York press, two days before the July termination, in an unprecedented move, 13,500 workers, of whom 7,600 had been dismissed, stayed in the plants to complete construction of remaining Corsair planes. They said they would continue without pay and thus give the company time to get other war contracts. (Frankensteen had made the offer to the corporation president.) This was done with the unofficial but cordial cooperation of the management, the workers camping in the plant without disorder, and in Johnsville the working

FRANKENSTEEN, RICHARD T.—*Cont.*

shift established a new record by doubling the average daily production of assembled airplanes. After a day's conference in Washington, Frankensteen called off the demonstration, as it had achieved his purpose of dramatizing the problems of abrupt contract termination and bringing about the President's intervention. The War Production Board made Brewster the first item on the agenda of a new Joint Contract Termination Board. The whole situation, Frankensteen declared, arose from the handling of manpower on "a fire-brigade basis: do nothing until you have a five-alarm fire; each emergency by itself"; and he called the termination at Brewster "the Pearl Harbor of labor."

Director of the UAW'S Political Action and Legislative Activities, Frankensteen was also one of the busiest PAC speakers in the national election campaign that year, traveling from coast to coast for the purpose. As the union political director, Frankensteen maintains a "very active" Washington office, "cooperating with Congress to bring the 'grass-roots' labor point of view to them on all current legislation," and keeping UAW members informed of the voting records of their Congressional representatives.

In March 1945 Frankensteen was involved in the ten-day series of Detroit strikes affecting six armament plants of the Chrysler Corporation and the Briggs Manufacturing Company. He and other UAW officials were booed by strikers whom they urged to return to work. Frankensteen said that a change in WLB policy was urgently needed to "avert collapse of Detroit area war production," and that prompt WLB action would prevent 90 per cent of work stoppages. In a prepared statement he charged Chrysler officials with provoking strikes in the hope of discrediting labor, the WLB, and the whole principle of collective bargaining. Not long afterward the Senate War Investigating Committee (the Mead [44] Committee) found low morale and questionable practices at the Packard plant in that area; and evidence given at its hearings revealed tension, suspicion, and alleged grievances on both sides throughout the area, which were causing a day-to-day loss in war production estimated at 25 per cent of capacity. In June Frankensteen again told strikers that they had "been misled into mobocracy, not guided by union principles of democracy," and that their waves of strikes was "bad and dangerous business in peace—in time of war it is tragic folly."

At this time he was a candidate for the nomination for mayor of Detroit, as the first prominent CIO official to run for public office. In addition to this campaign and to his executive problems of labor relations and finding jobs for displaced aircraft workers, Frankensteen campaigned for his re-election as UAW vice-president—never a sinecure—and was trying to raise the money to produce his operetta *Gypsy Moon*, on the music of which his late father had collaborated. (According to one report, CIO officials who saw a church production of the operetta in March contributed $60,000 of the necessary backing.) With the end of Frankensteen's aircraft duties he was free to devote his time to the campaign, during which he made ten to fifteen speeches a day.

The CIO executive board refused to allocate any funds for Frankensteen's campaign, but he had the support of the Political Action Committee and was president of Labor's Non-Partisan League of Wayne County. At the municipal primary in August Frankensteen ran first of the seven candidates, leading the incumbent Mayor Jeffries by 14,182 of the total 201,000 votes cast. (Detroit elections are on a non-party basis. The two highest candidates in the primary oppose each other at the general election.) Frankensteen declared that if he were elected he would resign from the UAW-CIO and "not only be mayor for all labor, but also for all Detroit," but the chief issue remained "labor in politics." The campaign was expensive and more than usually bitter, with Gerald L. K. Smith's [43] America Firsters among Jeffries' supporters, and Frankensteen finding it necessary to disavow the Communists. Frankensteen's cause was complicated, not only by A.F. of L. opposition to him as a CIO man, but by the unfavorable impression created by the UAW's demand for a 30 per cent wage increase from General Motors, although he had not been present at the executive session which made that decision. Out of an unprecedentedly high total of 492,000 votes, Frankensteen received about 44 per cent, losing to Jeffries by 57,000.

"A giant of a man," curly-haired Richard Frankensteen is very heavily built and is six feet tall. He has black hair, hazel eyes, is described as "a mild fellow who collects dolls for a hobby," and an ambitious amateur composer who sings baritone. There are three children in the family—Carol Lee, Marilyn Lee, and Richard, Jr. In public life, Frankensteen is "the glamour boy of the UAW—affable, engaging, charming, articulate. He has an invaluable radio voice, and he can turn in a rousing speech from any public platform." His committee memberships include the CIO's National Welfare Committee and the selection committee of UAW's nonprofit Labor Book Club (organized in early 1945), and he was appointed to Michigan's Emergency Relief Committee by Governor Murphy. Frankensteen is a member of the Pyramid Club, and a board member of the Michigan Red Cross. He was appointed by Roosevelt to both the WPB and the WLB, and perhaps his proudest possessions are letters on White House stationery, and a photograph inscribed "For Richard T. Frankensteen, from his friend Franklin D. Roosevelt."

References

N Y Herald Tribune p16 Ag 30 '45
N Y Sun p19 Ag 30 '45
Newsweek 25:38 Je 11 '45 pors
Time 46:24 O 29 '45 por
Who's Who in America, 1944-45

FRASER, LEON Nov. 27, 1889—Apr. 8, 1945 One of the leading financial figures of the United States and the world; president of the First National Bank of New York since 1936; former president of the Bank of International Settlements; in 1944 served as national chairman of the American Red Cross War Fund.

Obituary

N Y Times p1+ Ap 9 '45 por

FRICK, FORD C(HRISTOPHER) Dec.
19, 1894- Baseball executive; journalist

Address: b. National League of Professional
Baseball Clubs, 30 Rockefeller Plaza, New
York City; h. 16 Edgewood Lane, Bronxville,
N.Y.

As president of the National League of Professional Baseball Clubs, Ford C. Frick shares
with his opposite number, Will Harridge of
the American League, the second highest position in America's national sport, which is also
a big business. (The highest position is that of
Commissioner Albert "Happy" Chandler [43].)
Elected in 1934 and re-elected ever since by
the owners of the eight National League baseball teams, Frick presides over the destinies of
the Boston Braves, Brooklyn Dodgers, Chicago
Cubs, Cincinnati Reds, New York Giants,
Philadelphia Phillies, Pittsburgh Pirates, and
St. Louis Cardinals.

Ford Christopher Frick was born December
19, 1894, on a farm near the small town of
Wawaka in northeast Indiana. His parents,
Jacob and Emma (Prickett) Frick, moved to
Brimfield when Ford was five, and there he
attended the grade schools. "My ambition was
to be a major league first baseman," Frick
recalls, "and my idol was Cap Anson, Chicago's
great initial sacker. I read everything printed
about him—and about all the other famous
first basemen of the day—in the newspapers
and magazines." With this high resolve, Ford
tried hard to follow the same training methods.

After graduating in 1910 from the Consolidated High School in near-by Rome City, sixteen-year-old Ford got a job on the Fort
Wayne, Indiana, *Gazette*. In 1911 he entered
DePauw University, where he was on the baseball and track teams, was elected to Sigma
Delta Chi and Phi Kappa Psi, and made some
money as a correspondent for Indianapolis,
Terre Haute, and Chicago newspapers. (Frick
keeps in touch with college associates: he's an
active alumnus, for a time he was president of
the Alumni Association, and he is now president of the Alumni Fund Council and a trustee
of the university.)

Upon his graduation in 1915, the new B.A.
took his first step toward the major leagues:
he was signed as first baseman of the Walsenburg, Colorado, semi-professional baseball
team. A summer with them led to a position
teaching English in the Walsenburg high
school; and this, in turn, led to an assistant
professorship of English at Colorado College
that same year. In September 1916 the twenty-two-year-old professor was married to a
local girl, Eleanor Cowing. (They have one
son, Frederick Cowing Frick.) The next year,
1917, Frick's part-time work for the Colorado
Springs *Telegraph* blossomed into a full-time
job as reporter, which he left in 1918 to go
into war work.

During the First World War, Frick worked
for the War Department's rehabilitation division, supervising the training of rehabilitation
workers in Colorado, Utah, New Mexico, and
Wyoming. At the end of the war Ford Frick
joined the staff of the *Rocky Mountain News*
at Denver as a sports reporter; but later in
1919 he returned to Colorado Springs to form
an advertising agency, and soon found himself

FORD C. FRICK

writing a column for the *Telegraph*'s editorial
page. The *Telegraph*'s printer liked Frick's
column so much that he spoke of it to Arthur
Brisbane, editor of the New York *Evening
Journal*. Brisbane called the columnist to New
York for an interview, which led to a position
on the New York *American* staff in 1922.

A year later Frick moved to the *Journal*,
where for eleven years he wrote a sports-page
column of the Grantland Rice [41] school, sometimes putting his news and comments into verse
form. Assigned to cover the fabulous New
York Yankees baseball team, he "packed his
portable [typewriter] around the circuit" as
they toured the country each year. Besides
writing daily articles under his own by-line, he
"ghosted" those to which Babe Ruth [44] and
manager Miller Huggins signed their names.
The 1927 World Series between the Yankees
and the National League Pittsburgh Pirates
was particularly hectic for him, Frick recalls:
"Hug and Babe were regular assignments, but
they tossed in Lou Gehrig [40] in that Series for
good measure." In May 1930 the *Journal*'s
news editor missed his regular news broadcast
because of illness, so Ford Frick was called on
to substitute for him. Frick made such a good
impression that he was immediately signed for
a twice-daily sports broadcast, which he continued for four years, in addition to his newspaper work. In February 1934 Frick entered
upon the duties of manager of the Service
Bureau of the National League of Professional
Base Ball Clubs—publicity director of the
league, at a salary of ten thousand dollars.
("Base Ball" is now written as one word.)
He resigned his newspaper posts, but finished
out his broadcasting contracts, which expired
that December.

Less than ten months after taking over the
league's publicity, Ford Frick was unanimously
elected to its presidency, on the retirement of
John Arnold Heydler, who became chairman of
the board. Frick, who had just one month to
go before his fortieth birthday, was the young-

FRICK, FORD C.—*Continued*

est National League president and the second youngest in either league (the first being Bancroft Johnson, who in 1901 became president of the American League at thirty-six). President-elect Frick insisted that "but for the fact that Harvey [Traband, Heydler's secretary] absolutely refused this job, I don't think I would even have been considered."

In December 1934 Frick finished his radio chores and took over the league presidency. He was immediately confronted with a number of personality problems, centering in the World Series-winning "Gashouse Gang" of St. Louis Cardinals, which included such unrestrained enthusiasts as "Lippy" Leo Durocher '40, Dizzy Dean, Pepper Martin, Rip Collins, Joe (Ducky Wucky) Medwick, Bill (Kayo) DeLancey, and the umpire-baiting manager Frankie Frisch. Umpires are in the province of the league, which hunts for umpire talent as the clubs scout player talent; umpire trouble therefore had a way of making for Frick's office. Dizzy Dean was an extra problem, and some of Frick's former associates of the Baseball Writers Association "badgered him a lot" about letting the eccentric pitcher "walk all over him." Perhaps because a prophet is without honor among his colleagues, they "accused him of turning Rotarian and said the club owners were just using him as a 'front' man while continuing to conduct the league's business themselves." (At any rate, the owners reelected him at appropriate intervals and raised his annual salary from a reported twenty thousand dollars to an alleged thirty thousand.)

"During these early years," writes Al Laney in the New York *Herald Tribune*, "it is true that Frick was not impressive as a big executive. He seemed always to be sitting on the fence. But it now appears [after ten years] that he was feeling his way, gaining strength as he went along. After a while . . . he took charge, and he still is in charge. Now, if you look back over the years, you can see what Frick has meant to the National League and to baseball. The condition of the National League today testifies to that. It is a very strong organization, and Frick is entitled to most of the credit." When Frick took over, three of the eight National League clubs were on shaky financial ground: the Brooklyn Dodgers, the Boston Braves, and the Philadelphia Phillies. Observers credit Frick with putting them all back on their feet. To quote Laney again, "Frick cleaned it [the muddled Boston club] up and committed the league to putting up money to keep the club afloat until it could go under its own power. There also was the Brooklyn situation which, to put it mildly, had been a mess ever since Wilbert Robinson died." The club's debts amounted to $1,200,000. and the owners were split into two equal and opposed groups in 1938, when the Brooklyn Trust Company took over the club; it is said that Frick persuaded them to call in Larry MacPhail '45, who had built up the Cincinnati Reds to a winning team and who did even better for the Dodgers. As for the perennially last-place Phillies, they stayed at the bottom of the league but were brought up to a sound financial footing through the development and sale of players to more ambitious clubs.

One of the first problems confronting Frick was night baseball, which had been started by minor league clubs, and taken up by MacPhail in the early 'thirties. This change would make possible the attendance of thousands of persons who were at work during the afternoons; but many baseball men opposed the innovation, claiming that the reduced visibility by artificial light put an extra strain on the players. During 1935, therefore, Frick and his associates "examined the playing records of various minor leagues covering the performances of the last three years and found that the average ballplayer hit .004 worse and fielded .007 better under the stars than he did under the sun." The league therefore allowed evening games, which were, however, tentatively introduced into the schedule.

At the close of the 1935 season Frick directed another survey, this time of New Yorkers, "with a view to getting a representative cross section of metropolitan fandom's sentiments, desires, phobias, and ideas" on baseball, with particular reference to those of women. Other administrative problems concerned the total number of players to be allowed on one club's roster at any given time. During Frick's tenure this has risen from twenty-three to twenty-five and then to thirty. The first increase was made for purposes of efficiency, the second in order to provide jobs for men returning to baseball from the services. As of 1945, the permitted totals were forty-eight players per club in the off-season, thirty during the playing season, and twenty minor league players on option. A Frick innovation in 1935 was the issuance of lifetime passes to major league veterans, which was adopted by the American League a year later. Another Frick plan, in 1936, was reported by the *Literary Digest*: "To heighten National League competition and spectator interest this year, President Frick announced that rival baseball players 'fraternizing' on the field would be fined ten dollars." However, when Dick Bartell (Giants) and Van Mungo (Dodgers) fist-fought at Polo Grounds, he fined each twenty-five dollars and "served notice that the nonfraternizing restriction carries no license for free-for-alls."

Ford Frick was considered the moving spirit behind the celebration of baseball's hundredth anniversary in 1939, although the late Baseball Commissioner Kenesaw Mountain Landis '44 became chairman of the Centennial Committee. One of the founders of the ninety-thousand-dollar National Baseball Museum at Cooperstown, New York, which was opened in July 1938 and dedicated in 1939, Frick contributed several cherished National League mementos. These included the Temple Cup, a large silver bowl which the league had presented to the New York Giants for winning the national championship in 1888 and 1889, before the World Series was established as such. He even persuaded Johnny Vander Meer to part with the plaque he received for pitching two successive no-hit games in the 1938 season. That year, too, the National League produced a motion picture, *The National Game*, tracing baseball's hundred-year history.

After the United States entered the war in late 1941 Frick contributed his services to the war effort. He managed the Baseball Equipment Fund, supervised the distribution of playing equipment to the armed forces, and helped to organize the Camp Shows program. All National League players were advised to take war jobs during the off-season. This backfired on occasion, when players who took essential work found themselves "frozen" in their jobs and unable to return to the nonessential business of baseball. Commissioner Landis ruled that baseball not only would refrain from asking special consideration but would "stay out of Washngton" altogether. After the Judge's death in November 1944, however, Frick and Clark Griffith, president of the American League Washington Senators, went to the Capital and conferred with draft, manpower, and transportation officials to ascertain the prospects for their baseball clubs. In early 1945 War Manpower Commissioner Paul V. McNutt '40 ruled that men might leave war work for baseball during the season, when baseball was their "primary occupation."

To carry on the duties of the baseball commissionership, the club owners elected the triumvirate of Frick, American League president Will Harridge, and Landis' secretary-treasurer, Leslie O'Connor. The name of practically every United States executive who had or was thought to have or might be persuaded to take an interest in baseball was mentioned for the commissionership—including former Postmaster General James A. Farley '44, War Mobilization Director James F. Byrnes '41, dozens of assorted jurists, Generals Eisenhower '42, MacArthur '41, and Somervell '42, and even some baseball men. Ford Frick's candidacy had the reported backing of nine of the sixteen major league club owners; and in December 1944, re-elected president of the National League for four years, Frick sat in with the committee of club owners which drew up the new major league agreement defining the commissionership.

Commentators saw in Frick (the words are Joe Williams') a man who "has had a sufficiency of administrative experience to handle the job. The days when he'd let a Dizzy Dean run all over him in his office are far behind him. He knows how to get tough now; he is levelheaded, aggressive, and sensitive to the promotional needs of the sport. As a commissioner he'd do all right." Those who preferred a commissioner from outside the ranks of baseball had their way, however, and the commissionership finally went to Senator Happy Chandler of Kentucky.

Immediately after the news of Japan's surrender an unprecedented two-day meeting of baseball's postwar committee was held in Washington. Frick was appointed to a subcommittee to work out promotional plans; and on August 19 he announced that returning war veterans and younger players would get special attention by baseball in its peacetime expansion program. He further stated that baseball's postwar planning would be put into operation immediately, while new circuits and old reinstated organizations in the minor leagues would swell their activity threefold in 1946.

Ford Frick is, according to John Kieran '41, "a tall, dark gentlemen from Indiana with a clear head, a bright smile, a brisk Midwestern voice, and a large supply of energy always working in the right direction." An Episcopalian, he describes himself as "fifty-fifty" politically—half a Republican and half a Democrat. He and his wife live in the New York suburb of Bronxville, where he is a director of the Westchester County Children's Association. When the United States entered the war in 1941 the Fricks' son Frederick was in England doing postgraduate work at Cambridge; he went into psychological warfare work overseas, returning to the United States two years later, and entered the Army in 1943.

The senior Frick is a member of the Baseball Advisory Council, the National Journalistic Fraternity, the Advertising Club of America, the American Legion, and, since the late 'thirties, has served on the advisory committee of the National Dental Hygiene Association. Fond of golf, he belongs to three country clubs. The league president "likes to dunk rolls in coffee and doesn't care who knows it." Frick's enforced neutrality in the National League pennant race forces him to confine his rooting to the inter-league World Series and All-Star games, but has not affected his love for baseball: "I still feel like reaching for a glove and getting out there at shortstop when the sun sets the grass agleam and I hear a dozen and a half excited voices choosing up sides for the day's battle."

References

Lit Digest 118:12 N 24 '34 por
N Y Herald Tribune p32 N 9 '44 por
N Y Times p29 N 9 '34
Who's Who in America, 1944-45

FRYE, JACK   Mar. 18, 1904-   Air line executive

Address: b. Transcontinental and Western Air, Inc., Airlines Terminal Bldg., New York City; 101 W. 11th St., Kansas City, Mo.; h. Sedona, Ariz.

TWA, American, United, and Eastern are the "Big Four" of the nineteen American air lines that are already competing in the international struggle for postwar air leadership. Heading TWA (Transcontinental and Western Air, Inc.) is "big, burly, go-getting" Jack Frye, the youngest president of a major air-transport line in America and the only airline president to hold a transport pilot's license, having over six thousand flying hours in his own log. Active in aviation since the age of nineteen, Frye has been a pioneer in designing planes and establishing air lines, and believes that commercial aviation will be a primary factor in uniting the nations of the world in the future.

The son of William Henry Frye, Jack Frye was born March 18, 1904, in Sweetwater, Oklahoma. After his mother's death when he was eight years old, Jack spent much of his youth with his father and grandparents on the fifteen-thousand-acre family ranch near Wheeler, Texas. Texas has always seemed like home to him, and he is often referred to as a Texan. It might be said that Jack began his aviation career at the age of fourteen, when he ran errands for several stranded airmen who were forced down near his home. Jack almost immediately developed pneumonia and was ill for ten weeks, but his first vision of the romance of flying probably came to him at this time. After that his life pattern fol-

Transcontinental & Western Air, Inc.

JACK FRYE

lowed the popular American "success" tradition—he became known as a man with "a habit of making dreams come true."

Jack went to public school, leaving high school before graduation to spend a year in the Army Engineering Corps. In 1923 he went to California, where he worked as a soda clerk in Los Angeles. One day a friend drove young Frye past an airfield where a barnstorming pilot was taking passengers on fifteen-minute hops. The flier took Jack for a ride, with the result that the nineteen-year-old boy began taking flying lessons at twenty dollars an hour, paying for this first investment in the future with savings from his soda fountain earnings. After seven hours of instruction Jack was allowed to solo, and soon after that he took a passenger up with him. The passenger, incidentally, was not aware of the inexperience of his pilot.

His aeronautical novitiate completed, young Frye, together with his flying instructor, bought a battered old war-veteran plane, a Curtiss Jenny, put it in working order, and with it formed the nucleus of a flying school and aerial taxi service known as the Burdett Flying School. By 1926 Frye had become president of the Aero Corporation of California, which also operated a flying school as well as a service and maintenance base and an aircraft sales agency. (He was president of Aero until 1930.) In November 1927 the company launched a regular service between Los Angeles and Tucson, Arizona; a year later the route was extended to El Paso, Texas, with Fokker single-engine planes; in 1929 it was using Fokker three-engine F-10's.

Jane and Woodrow Wirsig, writing in *This Week*, tell a typical Frye story in connection with his next venture, the formation of the Standard Air-Lines for service between Phoenix and Los Angeles: It was a hot night in Phoenix in 1927. Bored and restless reporters were sitting around in the city room of the local newspaper when in strode a tall, gangling

stranger wearing grease-covered work clothes, with goggles pushed up under his flier's helmet. "My name's Jack Frye," he announced. "I'm going to start an air line here and I'd like to tell somebody about it." Frye and his partners, Paul E. Richter and Walter H. Hamilton, who had been his flying students, had established a one-plane subsidiary to the Aero Corporation to operate a scheduled air-transport service between Phoenix and Los Angeles. This subsidiary they named the Standard Air Lines.

Frye was president of Standard Air Lines until it merged with Western Air Express in 1930, when he became vice-president in charge of operations in the new company. This post he continued to hold when later that same year Western merged with Transcontinental Air Transport-Maddux, to become Transcontinental and Western Air, Inc. (One writer has compared Frye's merging of air companies with his youthful "ambidextrous merging of raspberry flips.") TWA immediately inaugurated the first coast-to-coast service to carry passengers entirely by air—thirty-six hours, with an over-night stop at Kansas City. In 1931 it acquired Northrop mail planes and took the lead in mail flying, while continuing passenger service in Fords and Fokkers. That same year TWA drew up specifications for a faster, larger, and more comfortable plane, which Donald Douglas [41], then a maker of military aircraft, built for the company and called the DC-1—the first Douglas plane designed exclusively for the commercial field. From this was developed the fourteen-passenger DC-2, which TWA was the first to fly. By the spring of 1934 it had thirty-one DC-2's in service and had reduced the cross-country flying time from twenty-four hours, which TWA had maintained since 1932 with DC-1's, to sixteen.

Jack Frye took over his present duties as president and director of TWA in 1934. (Walter Hamilton became a Douglas Aircraft executive, and Paul Richter an executive vice-president of TWA.) That same year all air-mail contracts with commercial lines were canceled by the Government and in February the Army Air Corps started flying the domestic mail. Later that same year, in June, following the deaths of ten Army mail pilots, the Government re-offered the contracts to the commercial lines on a bid basis. Frye had set a cross-country transport plane record in a DC-1 when he himself flew the last load of air mail under the old contract from Los Angeles to New York in thirteen hours and two minutes; then set another record under the new TWA-Government contract when he carried the first mail load in eleven hours and thirty-one minutes in a Northrop Gamma plane. In 1936 Frye made still another record when he flew from Chicago to Washington in two hours and twenty-two minutes. A "record" of a different sort was perhaps President Roosevelt's [42] use of TWA planes to cross the Atlantic on several history-making conferences of the Second World War. And in December 1945 a TWA Lockheed Constellation set a new commercial record of twelve hours and fifty-seven minutes from Washington to Paris.

In 1935 TWA began experiments in high-altitude flying in order to overcome one of the major dangers in scheduled flights. Frye has pointed out that pilots had trouble in clearing cloud formations which might be obscuring mountain peaks, and had difficulty in breathing above twelve thousand feet. TWA used the DC-1 for many high-altitude test flights, then in 1936 equipped a single-engine Northrop Gamma mail plane with a turbo-supercharger lent by the Army. On several occasions it was found that the Gamma, because of its higher ceiling flying level, could fly in safety in weather which necessitated the cancellation of regular lower flying transport service. By 1940 TWA had a fleet of thirty-three-passenger, four-engine Boeing Stratoliners, built to cruise at high altitudes. These were equipped with "pressurized" cabins in which atmospheric pressure was controlled so that passengers could enjoy low-altitude comfort while flying as high as twenty-two thousand feet. For eighteen months TWA operated five Stratoliners in domestic service; in the winter of 1941-42 Frye turned them over to the Army for use in the foreign courier service. But their use in commercial air service had been long enough to prove that high-altitude flying was acceptable to the traveling public.

In an article published in the *Commercial and Financial Chronicle* in January 1941, Frye listed the domestic transport service provided by the luxurious Stratoliners among the highlights of the year 1940, during which the air-transport industry "undertook one of the most rapid expansion programs ever to be carried out in one year." Other important projects of the year were the handling of capacity traffic at La Guardia Field, the opening of Philadelphia's new multi-million-dollar airport, the opening of Pan American Airways' new route across the South Pacific, and the completion in midtown New York of the world's first airline terminal building. TWA nearly doubled its personnel and office facilities that year, Frye pointed out. In addition to the introduction of five Stratoliners at a cost of two million dollars, (on which, according to *Newsweek*, they lost money), TWA placed orders for new twin-engine Douglas planes and a number of Wright engines. Applications for several new routes were filed with the Civil Aeronautics Board to provide new service into cities and regions without mail, passenger, and express air schedules.

In 1941 Frye with Howard Hughes [41], "the fabulous flier, movie producer, industrialist," began work on plans for the Lockheed Constellation, today considered TWA's most spectacular achievement. A triple-rudder transport, the Constellation, or "Connie," is said to be faster than a Japanese Zero, with a carrying capacity of from seventy-five to a hundred armed soldiers, or fifty-seven passengers and a crew. It has pressurized cabins, can fly at a ceiling of over thirty thousand feet, cruise for four thousand miles at more than three hundred miles an hour, and it has a wing spread three feet broader than the entire distance covered in the entire first flight of Orville Wright at Kitty Hawk in 1903. In discussing the Constellation, Jack Frye has pointed out that it has a range of flight and speed that would bring any capital in the Western Hemisphere within sixteen and a half hours of the United

States. Sydney, Australia, could be brought within forty flying hours of Dayton, Ohio, for example, as against twenty-three days by rail and steamer. In April 1944 a Constellation made a spectacular record when it was flown by Jack Frye and Howard Hughes from Burbank, California, to Washington, D.C., (2,663 miles) in six hours and fifty-eight minutes at an average speed of 355 miles an hour. Constellations, the largest land-based transports in full production in 1945 were, at the end of that year, in Government service, flying personnel and supplies out from fighting fronts and bringing wounded and about-to-be-discharged men home.

The question of international air routes is a controversial issue in 1945; tied up with it is the matter of postwar Atlantic fares, which *Time* Magazine calls "the battle of plane fares." Pan American Airways and American Export Airlines have had the only transatlantic air carriers operating in the Second World War. Pan American has taken the position that in order to meet foreign competition the United States must have only one air line operating internationally; Frye has consistently maintained that the United States was "large and powerful enough in relation to other countries to support a relatively greater number of international air lines." In April Frye told a Senate subcommittee that his company would have no part in a proposed cooperative international air line, feeling that a single monopoly for all United States international air transportation would lead only to Government ownership or failure. He thinks also that American competition would produce better service for the traveler.

In 1943 and 1944 TWA had applied to the Civil Aeronautics Board for commercial routes to the Azores and to Calcutta via London, Paris, and Cairo. By the end of 1944 there were more than a dozen air lines applying for transatlantic routes, but it was not until July 1945 that CAB authorized Pan American Airways, American Airlines (through its subsidiary the American Export Airlines), and TWA to fly to Europe. (Pan American is the only air line which had previously had permanent authorization for the North Atlantic service or for landing rights in the Azores, though TWA like many other domestic lines had been flying foreign routes for the Army.) The new CAB authorizations, limited to seven years to permit review by the Board, cover general routes instead of the usual point to point pattern, thus in effect giving permission to serve the general area through which the route passes.

Pan American strongly protested the new ruling, claiming "gross favoritism" to TWA and American. Frye in his counterargument claimed that he was in a better posiiton than anyone else to begin transatlantic service; that TWA had "operated more flights across the Atlantic than Pan American or any other carrier"; that the "only modern, high-speed, four-engine equipment that Pan American can get in the near future is the Constellation, which TWA developed and on which TWA has prior delivery rights. [TWA had in operation, in October 1945, five Boeing Stratoliners returned by the Army.] This leadership is the product of competition which Pan American seeks to extinguish. It explains that operator's con-

FRYE, JACK—*Continued*

stant effort for two years now to prevent the establishment of any United States foreign air route by anyone but Pan American." And the rate war was on. Frye announced a one-way fare from New York to London of $263.80, and the next day Pan American announced that it expected to drop its one-way fare to about a hundred and fifty dollars as soon as its new 128-passenger planes were available. At about the same time spectacular reductions in flying time schedules—ten-hour service from coast to coast and eleven-hour service between New York and London—were announced by the four major air lines, to take effect probably by January 1946.

A story illustrates Frye's plans for aviation: During the early days of his presidency of TWA he once was sitting at a directors' meeting when the bankers asked why the company was not paying dividends. "I'll tell you why," said Frye earnestly. "No airplane today is good enough. No air line flies often enough, or fast enough. Air lines shouldn't pay dividends for ten years—not until they reach the point where they can really serve the public." Today Frye thinks that vast merchant air fleets capable of transporting most of the world's cargo will emerge from the Second World War and may be the key to lasting peace. Aviation, which was a struggling young industry in 1932, has now a real record of achievement. The air line president thinks that the transport plane of tomorrow will be much larger than anything yet built, capable, perhaps, of carrying as much as two thousand tons vast distances on nonstop flights. American youth should be given a sound education in aviation, he thinks, to be prepared to carry on the enormous expansion in air routes that may be expected in the future. Before the end of 1946 Frye expects to triple the TWA fleet, and his goal is to make aviation both the fastest and the safest means of travel—but this he thinks will take another fifteen years.

Jack Frye is director of the Air Transport Association of America and a member of the advisory committee of the Institute of Aeronautical Sciences, the National Aeronautical Association, and the Air Lines Committee of United States Air Policy. He is a member of a number of clubs in cities not so far apart from an aviation expert's point of view: in San Francisco, Los Angeles, Kansas City, Chicago, New York, and Washington. In the Second World War he holds a commission as lieutenant commander in the United States Naval Reserve.

The air-line official is described as a dynamic person who knows his business "from swivel chair to cockpit." Over six feet tall, weighing close to two hundred pounds, he has brown eyes and dark brown hair peppered with gray. He is said to be meticulous about his clothes, liking red ties, tweeds, and dark worsteds "as snappy-looking as his planes." In 1941 he was married to Helen Warner Vanderbilt, who had formerly been married to Cornelius Vanderbilt, Jr. Mrs. Frye has told newspapermen that her interest in TWA advertising was partly responsible for their romance: she had told Frye that air-line advertising should portray the adventure of flying instead of emphasizing comfort and

speed. Mr. and Mrs. Frye spend as much time as possible on their ranch near Flagstaff, Arizona. Frye has written numerous newspaper and magazine articles on aviation and has other literary interests. His home library contains "practically everything from eighteenth century poetry to Saint Exupéry[40]."

References

Educa 63:80-5 O '42
N Y Herald Tribune VII p8+ F 11 '45 por
Who's Who in America, 1944-45
Who's Who in Aviation, 1942-43
Who's Who in Commerce and Industry (1944)

FUNK, CASIMIR (foöngk kăz'ĭ-mĭr) Feb. 23, 1884-   Biochemist

Address: h. 186 Riverside Dr., New York City

One of the world's most eminent biochemists, Casimir Funk is credited with the discovery of vitamins. Although he was born in Poland, he has been identified with important scientific institutions elsewhere in Europe, and in the States, of which he became a citizen in 1920. He has contributed his studies to various aspects of biochemistry and medicine, and has worked in the field of microchemistry. In addition to his contribution to the knowledge of nutrition, Funk has done important work with the hormones. He was the first to make adrenaline, one of the first to make salvarsan in the United States, and his was the first commercial vitamin concentrate accepted by the American Medical Association. Funk recalls with a smile that, while the A.M.A. once turned down his concentrate of Vitamin B-1 as unwanted, the American public spent a quarter of a billion dollars on vitamin capsules in 1943.

Born in Warsaw, Poland, on February 23, 1884, Casimir Funk is the son of Dr. Jacques Funk, a well known dermatologist, and the former Gustawa Zysan. Interested in biology from his early youth, Casimir nevertheless wanted to obtain a degree in medicine before going on with his chosen work. His father, who was influenced by the sensationally rapid advance that was being made in chemistry at that time, persuaded him to confine his efforts to biochemistry. Accordingly, at sixteen young Funk was sent to Berne University to study organic chemistry under Kostanecki, an authority on plant pigments. His thesis for his Ph.D. (Berne, 1904) on the derivatives of stilbene was a forerunner of important pioneer work that he and others were to do some twenty years later in the hormones. (A closely allied stilbene compound is now in use as a substitute for the female hormone.)

Following his graduation Funk spent two years in research at the Pasteur Institute in Paris, where Gabriel Bertrand was the biochemist and Elie Metchnikoff was doing his brilliant work in immunity and intestinal flora. Funk's work there made him collaborator of Emil Fischer and later assistant to Emil Abdehalden at the University of Berlin (1906-7, 1908-10). Under the guidance of Abdehalden, who like Fischer was considered a "master of protein chemistry," Funk received his foundation for the work he was to do in vitamins. During his stay in Germany he spent one year as a biochemist at the Wiesbaden Municipal Hospital (1907). In 1910, given the promise that he could carry on independent work, the young biochemist went to London to join the Lister Institute of Preventive Medicine. There he unexpectedly found his great opportunity. The director of the Institute, Charles Martin, wished research done on the causative factor of beriberi, which was highly prevalent in the Far East and which he believed was the result of inadequate protein in the natives' unvaried diet of polished rice.

The history of the discovery of the vitamin is like that of almost every scientific discovery. An army of other workers had done research in the field before Casimir Funk made public his findings. Each had profited from the experience of those who had come before him, had carried the study a little further. In 1757 James Lind's famous book on scurvy declared that experiments had demonstrated clearly the value of fruit in the treatment of the disease; in 1804, after his death, regulations enforced the consumption of daily rations of lemon or lime juice in the British Navy. In 1891 Bunge had announced to the world of science that experiments had demonstrated that while mice were unable to live solely on a diet of proteins, carbohydrates, fats, and salts, they survived when a small quantity of milk had been added to the diet. This proved that "other substances indispensable for nutrition must be present in milk besides casein, fat, lactose, and salts." In 1897 Christiaan Eijkman, the Dutch biologist, had produced a vitamin deficiency disease in fowl and had come to the conclusion that the disease was the result of a toxin present in rice. In 1905 the Dutch nutritionist Pekelharing expressed the opinion that an unknown substance of paramount importance occurs not only in milk but in vegetables and in meats. In 1906 Sir Frederick Hopkins undertook a series of experiments to establish the importance of certain amino acids in foods, particularly tryptophan (which he had isolated with S. W. Cole), and in a lecture he vaguely referred to the fact that "some hitherto unknown food elements must be present in a complete dietary."

Very early in his search for the cause of beriberi, Funk discarded Martin's theory that the disease was caused by inadequate protein in the diet and accordingly directed his research toward finding the unknown substance which, by experiments on pigeons, had led him to believe was present in rice bran but not in polished rice. It has been said that the needle-in-a-haystack is an appropriate simile for his search—rice bran and polishings yield as little as one-sixth ounce of Vitamin B-1 per ton. Finally, in 1911 his tedious work was rewarded. He isolated a minute crystalline fraction of material from rice bran capable of curing polyneuritis (a form of beriberi) in his birds. Later when he found the same mysterious substance in yeast he knew he had made an important discovery. Although the crystalline material Funk had discovered was not a pure form of the substance now known as thiamine, it was a far more potent concentrate of its kind than had hitherto been obtained, and his work paved the way for the isolation of thiamine.

CASIMIR FUNK

In his investigations he also found, in 1911, small amounts of nicotinic acid (now called niacine—a part of the B complex), the ingredient the lack of which is the causative factor in pellagra. Funk named these substances "vitamins": "vita," from the Latin, meaning life, plus "amine," the chemical compound, because he had the idea that they all contained nitrogen. The final e was later dropped from the name when it was found that not all vitamins contain nitrogen.

The scientist announced his findings in a paper (whose fame, it is said, "will outlast the pyramids") entitled "The Etiology of the Deficiency Diseases," published in the British *Journal of State Medicine* in July 1912. It immediately attracted world-wide attention. In it he presented conclusive evidence that a vitamin is a very definite chemical entity and that various vitamins—not just one—are necessary for normal health; the absence of any one of them would give rise to a characteristic "food deficiency" disease, namely, scurvy, beriberi, probably rickets and pellagra. Benjamin Harrow, the distinguished American biochemist, in a December 1944 article in the *Nation* pointed out how revolutionary the announcement was. It should be recalled, he wrote, that "with the exception of various metabolic disturbances, diseases were associated by physicians of the day with virulent micro-organisms," which Pasteur and others had so impressed upon the world. As in every discovery, there were challengers to Funk's title of "discoverer." The line of reasoning of this group followed that presented by L. H. Harris of the University of Cambridge, in his book *Vitamins* (1937). After describing Funk's 1912 findings as more the development of a theory, or the "systematization of knowledge," Harris conceded that an interpreter is "any man who is able to take a broad view of what has already been done by others, to collect the evidence and discern through it all some common connecting link."

As a warning to the American public, who consumed two hundred and fifty million dollars'

FUNK, CASIMIR—*Continued*

worth of vitamins during one single year, Funk says that it cannot be too strongly stressed that vitamins do not take the place of calories; an insufficient amount of fat, carbohydrate, and protein in the diet will cause starvation even if there is a superabundance of vitamins. "While theoretically it is possible," says the biochemist, "and certainly preferable, to obtain complete requirements from foodstuffs, under present conditions a diet intelligently selected may still be inadequate in vitamins and minerals because of a number of devitalizing factors." Devitalization of food may be caused by improper cultivation (a soil low in minerals will produce vegetation low in minerals and vitamins), transportation, over-processing, prolonged storage, and faulty cooking. As a supplement to a low-vitamin diet, the scientist says, "vitamin intake in synthetic form might often be useful and is sometimes indispensable."

Following his discovery, Funk was granted a Beit Fellowship and in 1913 acquired a doctorate in science. Resigning from Lister Institute, the twenty-nine-year-old scientist became head of the biochemistry department in London's Cancer Hospital, Research Institute (1913-15). The family fortune having had reverses in the first year of the First World War, Funk next accepted an assignment to do chemical research in cancer at Cornell Medical College (1915-16). In the course of his first American residence (1915-23), the scientist was connected also with H. A. Metz and Company as head of their research (1917-23) and was associate in biochemistry at the College of Physicians and Surgeons, Columbia University (1921-23). For the house of Metz, Funk developed, besides adrenaline, salvarsan and oscodol (a concentrate of vitamins A and D from cod liver oil); for another house he developed atophan-cinchophen, a compound used in arthritis.

Funk, who until 1923 had worked in almost every European country except his native Poland, accepted that year the directorship of the biochemical department at the State Institute of Hygiene in Warsaw. (Because the Institute was supported by the Rockefeller Foundation, he says his fourteen-room laboratory was the answer to a biochemist's dream.) It was while working there that he became interested in hormones. In 1924 he demonstrated that there is more than one hormone secretion of the posterior pituitary gland: one which acts on the muscles, and one on the water balance. Three years later Funk, who believed that Poland was politically an "unhealthy" place in which to live because of its unfortunate geographical position, left that country to set up his private laboratory, Casa Biochemica, in a Paris suburb. Later that year he made his second major discovery in collaboration with Harrow and Lejwa. The discovery, which Harrow describes in his article in the *Nation*, established the usefulness of the sex hormones in certain disturbances.

Funk is the author of *Die Vitamine* (1913), which he revised in 1914 and again upon its translation into English in 1922 by Harry E. Dubin. The work deals with the physiological import of vitamins as food components. Funk has also been a frequent contributor to *Science*

and other technical journals. The most recent article, written in collaboration with I. M. Chamelin, was "The Action of Liver Extracts in Counteracting the Toxic Effects of Diethystilbestrol Sulfamilamide" (*Archives of Biochemistry*, April 1943).

With the outbreak of the Second World War, Funk returned to the United States, of which he had become a citizen in 1920. He has since been research consultant of the United States Vitamin Corporation and is at present engaged in cancer research with Dr. Edward J. Jacobs in a New York laboratory, where they are working on the Otto Warburg (German Nobel prize winner in 1931) theory that the sugar metabolism of cancer cells differs from that of normal cells. This and other theories, particularly Funk's theory (first advanced in 1913) on the influence of diet on tumors, are now being subjected to rigid experimental and clinical tests. Funk is of the opinion that the study of stimulating and inhibiting factors of the cancer cell will develop new methods in the treatment of malignancy.

In speaking of Funk's work Harrow says the biochemist "has usually been ahead of the ideas warranted by established scientific work. Sometimes one feels that his imagination is more like that of a poet than a scientist." Funk, who is five feet six inches tall and weighs 129 pounds, has large blue eyes, and the flaxen-colored hair of his early childhood has darkened and is streaked with gray. He speaks English with an accent which has been described as a mixture of the five languages which he reads and speaks. He says he has no hobbies and no pet theories about his own diet.

In 1914 the biochemist was married to Alix Denise Schneidesch of Brussels, a handsome woman of French, Spanish, and German stock. Their son Ian, who was born in New York City in 1915 and who was studying medicine when the Second World War broke out, has worked with his father in cancer research. A captain in the Army Medical Corps, he was severely wounded in Europe. Doriane Jacqueline, the daughter, was born in Danzig in 1924; she is in 1945 a student at New York University and served as her father's laboratory assistant. Now living in a Riverside Drive apartment, the Funks have not yet decided if they will exchange the comforts of the New York home for the freedom of the suburban house and laboratory near Paris, where there is a garden with fruit trees and space for pets. Funk says they will doubtless choose the place that offers the best facilities for the completion of his work.

References

N Y Post p17 Mr 21 '40 por
Nation p741-2 D 16 '44
American Men of Science (1938)

GABLE, CLARK Feb. 1, 1901- Actor
Address: b. c/o Metro-Goldwyn-Mayer, Culver City, Calif.

In the Hollywood spotlight since 1931, Clark Gable has enjoyed an unbroken popularity with motion picture audiences. A onetime factory hand, oil-well driller, lumberjack, and stock

actor, his wide box-office appeal to women is
attributed to what the theater calls "sympathetic identification"—he is the sort of man
the American girl might meet in everyday life.
The gay adventurer of the screen won the
Academy Award in 1934 for his performance
in *It Happened One Night*; and the *Motion
Picture Herald*'s yearly surveys listed him
among the first ten money-making stars from
1932 to 1942, when he entered the United
States Army Air Forces. His subsequent three-
year absence from the screen did not decrease
this popularity either, for *Boxoffice*'s 1945 poll
placed him among the ten top male favorites
of motion picture audiences.

William Clark Gable (his first given name
was dropped when he entered the theater) was
born in Cadiz, Ohio, on February 1, 1901. He
was the only child of William H. Gable, an
oil contractor, and Adeline (Hershelman)
Gable, both of Dutch ancestry. After his
mother's death when he was only seven months
old, he was left in the care of his grandparents until he was five. Then his father
remarried, and the little family moved to Hope-
dale, another small town in Ohio. As a youth,
he was shy and awkward, shunning social activities. While in high school he had aspired
to be a doctor. Therefore, after graduation,
encouraged by his stepmother, whom he describes as one of the tenderest human beings
he has ever known, he left for Akron to take
premedical courses at Akron University in the
evenings—counter to his father's wishes. During the daytime he worked for the Firestone
Company, molding treads on tires.

Soon after his arrival in Akron, Gable was
introduced to two actors, members of a stock
company then playing in that city. Conversation about the theater aroused Gable's interest,
and the next evening he went backstage to
watch his new friends in the performance.
Immediately he was strongly attracted to acting. He spent all his leisure time at the
theater, learning all he could about the stage,
and within a very short time he had left his
job and studies to work as a nonsalaried callboy with the company. Occasionally he also
was given a bit part. Of those days Gable has
said: "I forgot all my ideas about becoming a
doctor when I made my first appearance on the
stage. I said only three words—'Good evening,
sir.' But those three words were enough.
They were hello to acting and good-by to medicine. They changed my entire life."

With an oil boom on in Oklahoma, Gable's
father urged him to join him there and try
oil drilling. But Gable, determined now to become an actor, left instead for New York. He
got a job on Broadway, but not before the
footlights. As a callboy, he rapped reverently
for nine months on the dressing room doors
of John and Lionel Barrymore '43, who in 1919
were co-starring in *The Jest*. Discouraged,
Gable left for Oklahoma, where he worked for
a year in the oil fields as his father had wished
him to do. Despite the fact that he was earning seventy-five dollars a week, he hated the
work. With the stage still uppermost in his
thoughts, he went from job to job until he had
saved enough money to try the theater again.
As general utility man with the Jewell Players,
a tent show repertoire company, Gable "drove
the stakes in the morning, played the cornet

CLARK GABLE

in the band before the show started, and then
dressed, made up, and became an actor." For
this wearing job he received, on an average,
the grand total of fourteen dollars a week. The
road company, very low in funds, closed after
two years, in the winter of 1922. Gable, almost
penniless, hopped a freight train to Portland,
Oregon. After working at odd jobs—as a
lumberjack, a timekeeper at a telephone company, a rodman with engineers, and a want-ad
clerk in a newspaper office, he joined a Little
Theater group in Portland which was under
the direction of Josephine Dillon. "For the
first time I learned about acting," says Gable.

In late 1924 Gable and his director were
married. Then, hearing that several plays
were to be produced in Los Angeles, they
went southward, for Gable hoped to gain
more stage experience before trying his luck
again on Broadway. Unsuccessful in his attempts to obtain work in the theater, Gable
reluctantly turned to the silent films. He made
his first appearance on the screen in a picture
starring Pola Negri. "I worked a few days
at that," recalls Gable, "and couldn't seem to
find out what it was all about. I was in a hot
uniform, held a sword, and got five dollars a
day." Deciding that his income as an extra
was too small and uncertain to warrant any
longer stay in Hollywood, Gable and his wife
were about to leave when he secured a part
as spearbearer in a Los Angeles stage production of *Romeo and Juliet* starring Jane Cowl.
When the same company hired Gable for a
minor role in *What Price Glory*, the actor had
his first bit of good fortune. The player originally intended for the important part of Sergeant Quirt left the cast, and Gable was given
the role.

Afterward, disheartened by an unfavorable
screen test, Gable worked for a while with a
Texas stock company and then headed for
Broadway. "Motion pictures," says Gable, "had
not begun to talk. In those days leading men
had to be Valentinos or John Gilberts, handsome fellows, great lovers, and pleasing to

GABLE, CLARK—*Continued*

behold. I didn't fit into those classifications. I was somewhat of a roughneck. Definitely, I could see no future for me in Hollywood." Fortified with several letters of recommendation, the actor got the part of the Young Man in Arthur Hopkins' New York production of *Machinal* (1928). The *Telegraph* described Gable as "young, vigorous, and brutally masculine." The *New Yorker* found him an "excellent lover," and, in the words of the New York *Time's* critic: "Gable played the casual, good-humored lover without a hackneyed gesture." Back in Los Angeles, three years later, he was given the role of Killer Mears in a local production of *The Last Mile*. This play had a twofold significance for the actor—his portrayal of Killer Mears was considered a minor triumph; and his impressive performance brought forth this comment from Lionel Barrymore: "I think you'd be good in pictures. I'd like to have a test made of you."

Gable, much influenced by Barrymore's opinion, decided to give motion pictures another try. He played his first role in the "talkies" as the villain in *The Painted Desert* (1931). "He wasn't a very good cowboy . . . but the lady fans liked him." Gable then returned to the theater for a while, but now he was only biding his time hoping for a second chance to get into pictures. At this time, after being divorced from his wife, he was married to Mrs. Ria Langham, a woman ten years his senior. Their marriage lasted only five years, but Gable says he will always be grateful to her for the encouragement she gave him during the early days of his motion picture career.

The introduction of the talking picture had brought with it a new demand for leading men. Talent scouts were eagerly searching for new faces, but, although Gable had been brought to their attention, there was no clamor for his services. However, there were some producers who were interested enough to experiment with various techniques of photographing the actor. They found that a certain type of lighting and "a three-quarters shot" of Gable softened his face and made his large ears less conspicuous. In fact, they even ventured to say that he might capture a few feminine hearts. Gable made his debut as a leading man in 1931, playing opposite Joan Crawford in *Dance, Fools, Dance*. Next, with Norma Shearer in *A Free Soul* (1931), he was described by one critic as "a fascinating villain" who had convinced the female customers that he was "naughty but nice." In the next few years his performances (mostly for Metro-Goldwyn-Mayer) in *Hell Divers* (1931), *Susan Lennox, Her Rise and Fall* (1931), *Possessed* (1931), *Polly of the Circus* (1932), Eugene O'Neill's *Strange Interlude* (1932), *Red Dust* (1932), *No Man of Her Own* (1932), *The White Sister* (1933), *Hold Your Man* (1933), *Night Flight* (1933), and *Dancing Lady* (1933) classed Gable as "just a good leading man"—opposite such top leading ladies as Greta Garbo, Marion Davies, Norma Shearer, Jean Harlow, Carole Lombard, Helen Hayes [42], and Joan Crawford. A victim of type casting, he was usually given the role of a "heavy" with redeeming traits. Gable asserts: "People were bored instead of delighted when I manhandled disagreeable women, and I was getting pretty sick of it myself."

In 1934 Clark Gable achieved stardom. Columbia Picture's still popular photoplay *It Happened One Night* "untyped" Gable and proved him to be a versatile actor. Gable, relaxed and casual, entered completely into the spirit of the story—a lively comedy about a runaway heiress and a newspaperman traveling from Miami to New York by bus. (A statistical item observed by the picture's publicity office was the 43 per cent increase in women bus travelers that year.) Both Gable and his leading lady, Claudette Colbert [45], received Academy awards for the best performances of the year. The following year Gable turned in another outstanding performance in the exciting film *Mutiny On the Bounty*, chosen by the Academy of Motion Pictures Arts and Sciences as the best film of 1935. Gable refers to this saga of the sea as his favorite film because "it was something you could get your teeth into, for it was history, a story of the struggle of real he-men with a refreshing absence of the usual load of love interest."

In the next seven years, as one of MGM's top stars, he appeared in over twenty-five pictures, prominent among which were *China Seas* (1935), *San Francisco* (1936), *Saratoga* (1937)—Jean Harlow's last film—*Test Pilot* (1938), *Idiot's Delight* and *Gone With the Wind* (1939), *Boom Town* (1940), *They Met in Bombay* (1941), and the last picture before his temporary retirement, *Somewhere I'll Find You* (1942).

In March 1939 Gable married Carole Lombard, Hollywood's "best screwball comedienne." Less than three years later, on January 16, 1942, she was killed in an airplane crash near Las Vegas, Nevada, while returning to Hollywood from a bond-selling tour. A week after his wife's death Gable announced that he would retire from the screen and made application for duty in the United States Army Air Forces. In August 1942 he was inducted into the Army of the United States as a private, and assigned to the Army Air Forces Officer Candidates' School at Miami, Florida. Indicative of his desire for action was his statement: "What I want is to be a machine-gunner on an airplane and be sent where the going is tough." Competing with classmates who had had a more extended formal education, Gable, only a high school graduate, was at a distinct disadvantage. But he graduated in the upper third of the class, explaining this accomplishment by saying: "I committed the manuals to memory." (His instructors are certain that the former actor had studied during many of the hours assigned to sleeping.) His classmates chose him to give the graduation address, on October 28, 1942. "Our job," Lieutenant Gable said then, "is to stay on the beam until—in victory—we are given the command 'fall out.'"

Sent over to England in April 1943, the new lieutenant was assigned by order of General H. H. Arnold [42], chief of Army Air Forces, to produce an aerial gunnery film designed to increase recruits for gunnery training. During six months of overseas service Gable, with the help of a six-man crew, "shot" fifty thousand feet of sixteen-millimeter color film revealing combat conditions over Antwerp, two unnamed targets near Paris, southern France, and the Ruhr Valley. This film, in which Gable is narrator and occasionally an actor, shows how air force men live, work, and fight. In November 1944 the Office of War Information announced that it would not be released for the general public since it is largely a duplication of the picture *Memphis Belle* (1944). The film is available for showing at bond-rally drives, war plants, and club meetings.

In October 1943, just prior to his return to the United States, Captain Gable received the Distinguished Flying Cross and the Air Medal, the latter for "exceptionally meritorious achievement while participating in five separate bomber combat missions." The citation said, "His courage, coolness, and skill in five missions reflect great credit on him and the armed forces." In May 1944 he was promoted from the temporary rank of captain to the temporary rank of major. The following month he returned to civilian life and was placed on the Army's inactive list, subject to recall. Finally discharged in 1945, by December of that year he had finished his first postwar picture, *Adventure,* with Greer Garson, and had begun work on *Lucky Baldwin.*

Of the Clark Gable who went to war Adela Rogers St. Johns wrote this observation: "The men liked him because he was literally one of them. . . .Yet when Gable talks about them you'd think every member of the [bomber] crew had done him a favor to accept him and approve him." And of the man who came back to America in 1945, after combat flying over Germany, she said: "The twinkle with which he'd always faced life until the death of his wife, Carole Lombard, was back." Clark Gable seldom discusses his "art" with anyone. Attributing his success to luck, he has hung his dressing room with mementos of the days when he was only a struggling actor. Across these mementos he has written the words: "Just to remind you, Gable." He plays excellent golf, likes to ride horseback, and is fond of long hunting trips. His favorite reading consists of adventure stories and mysteries.

References

Am Mag 122:35+ S '36 por
Collier's 94:17+ D 8 '34 por
Look 7:36+ Mr 23 '43 il pors
N Y Herald Tribune p7 O 28 '43 por
Sat Eve Post 212:23+ My 4 '40

International Motion Picture Almanac, 1942-43
Who's Who in America, 1944-45

GAFFNEY, T(HOMAS) ST. JOHN 1864 —Jan. 14, 1945 Irish-born United States Consul General at Dresden, Germany, from 1905 to 1911; Munich, 1911 to 1915; resignation requested in 1915 by Secretary of State because of his pro-Germanism and intense feeling against England; lifelong advocate of Irish nationalism.

Obituary

N Y Times p19 Ja 15 '43 por

GANNETT, FRANK E(RNEST) (găn-nĕt') Sept. 15, 1876- Newspaper publisher *Address:* b. 55 Exchange St., Rochester, N.Y.; h. 195 Sandringham Rd., Rochester, N.Y.; 5641 Collins Ave., Miami Beach, Fla.

FRANK E. GANNETT

A newspaper publisher since 1906, when he bought a half-interest in his first newspaper, Frank E. Gannett in 1945 is the owner of one of the largest newspaper groups in the United States. The newspapers, numbering twenty-one, are with three exceptions concentrated in middle-sized cities in upstate New York. Their combined circulation is more than half a million. Enlarging his activity in the field of information Frank Gannett has also bought an interest in several radio stations. In 1937 he founded the group now called the Committee for Constitutional Government. This committee is said to have been responsible in large part for the defeat of several New Deal measures and has earned for him from New Deal supporters the label of "economic royalist." This he forcefully resents. It has been pointed out that he "has arranged to perpetuate his newspapers as a foundation, excluding his family from control in the enterprise and insuring continued employment of those who helped him to succeed." Shortly after the establishment of the Foundation Gannett put into effect an employee profit-sharing plan.

Born on a farm in the New York State Finger Lakes district, near the town of Bristol, on September 15, 1876, Frank Ernest Gannett is the son of Joseph Charles and Maria (Brooks) Gannett. The first Gannetts to live in America emigrated from Dorsetshire, England, in the sixteen-thirties, settling in Hingham, Massachusetts. Warren Gannett, the publisher's grandfather, farmed a tract of land north of Syracuse, New York, which he had been granted as a veteran of the Revolution. The farm on which Gannett was born had been cleared from the wilderness by his

GANNETT, FRANK E.—*Continued*

father and uncles. Later, when it proved to be submarginal land and failed to support them, the Gannetts became tenants on a farm near Blood's Depot (now named Atlanta), New York. It was there, at the age of nine, that Frank Gannett began earning money. His newspaper career might be said to date from that time, for among his many odd jobs was delivering a Rochester newspaper to local subscribers—a paper he was to own years later. Tenant farming proving to be no more remunerative for Joseph Gannett than his first farming (a veteran of the Civil War, he was handicapped by ill health), he and his family moved to another village in New York, where he leased the small hotel, little more than an inn for mail coach travelers and freight wagon teamsters. Before young Frank was fifteen years old his father had failed to make much progress in the hotel business in three small towns in New York, and was planning to to another town for still another try.

This time the boy did not accompany his parents. The high school principal in Bolivar (the town in which the Gannetts were living at that time), encouraged Frank to continue his studies in Bolivar inasmuch as he had made a fine record there as a student. While attending high school the boy earned his living by doing chores in the Newton House, the successful rival of his father's former hotel. He waited on tables and on occasion substituted for the regular bartender. Graduated from high school at sixteen, but lacking the means to continue his education, young Gannett remained in Bolivar to work as a bookkeeper for two firms. In the New York State Regents' examinations he received the highest diploma that any high school student had then received. A Congressman offered him an appointment to the United States Military Academy. The four-year course at Government expense tempted him, but his mother, who had suffered so much as the wife of a disabled war veteran, dissuaded him. A few months after making his decision he won a Cornell University scholarship in a competitive examination conducted by the Department of Instruction of the State of New York.

Gannett, who arrived at Cornell with eighty dollars as his sole capital, during his college years not only succeeded in supporting himself, but, by his graduation in 1898 with a B.A. degree, he had accumulated a bank deposit of one thousand dollars. In his freshman year he supported himself by waiting on tables, running a laundry route, and doing other small jobs. By the end of that year he had been elected representative of the class of 1898 for the college newspaper, the Cornell *Sun.* It was his first writing job. Campus reporting at three dollars a week for the Ithaca *Journal* followed. Soon Gannett-written items were appearing in the Buffalo *News,* the New York *World,* and a dozen other newspapers. His first two summer vacations were spent in the rural districts of New York as a salesman for the *Cottage Physician,* a volume which undertook to tell people what to do before the doctor arrived. Although it was harder to sell a farmer something in those days than to "float a stock issue in

downtown New York," the energetic student earned enough money to spend six weeks of his third college vacation working without pay on the Syracuse *Herald* so that he might gain practical experience in his chosen field, journalism. Making good, he finally won from the *Herald* a ten-dollar weekly pay check for the rest of the summer.

When in 1899 the president of Cornell, Jacob Gould Schurman, became head of the first Philippine Commission, young Gannett accompanied him to the Islands as his secretary. (Gannett had been graduated the year before.) One achievement resulting from his residence there was his translation, from the Spanish, of *Friars and Filipinos* (1900). When the Schurman commission was recalled to the United States, Gannett, left in charge of the Manila office, learned enough about colonial problems to make him intensely anti-imperialistic. Consequently, when offered reappointment to his secretaryship by William Howard Taft, Schurman's successor in the Philippines, Gannett declined.

Upon his return to the States in 1900 Gannett became city editor of the Ithaca *Daily News* at a salary of fifteen dollars a week, and during the next five years rose to the positions of managing editor and business manager. For a part of this time he also acted as editor of the Cornell *Alumni News.* In 1905 he left Ithaca, working for a few months on *Leslie's Weekly* in New York City and for a few more months as editor of the Pittsburgh *Index.* The post failed to come up to his expectations, Gannett resigned, and shortly afterward bought a half-interest in the Elmira (New York) *Gazette.* This deal established Gannett's ability to obtain credit— the owner had asked twenty thousand dollars for the half-interest, but Gannett, having only three thousand in cash, paid the remaining amount in notes and money borrowed with only his good reputation behind him. The year was 1906—Gannett was twenty-nine years old and half-owner of a daily newspaper. In 1907 he bought the Elmira *Star* and merged it with the *Gazette* under the name of the *Star-Gazette.*

The Gannett chain of newspapers enlarged in 1912 when the thirty-six-year-old publisher bought the Ithaca *Journal,* which was later merged with the Ithaca *News* to form the Ithaca *Journal-News.* In 1918 the publisher took up residence in Rochester—location of his present home and business—when he and two associates, Erwin Davenport and Woodford J. Copeland, bought the Rochester *Union and Advertiser* and the Rochester *Evening Times,* which they merged into the Rochester *Times-Union.* By 1924 the publisher, who had bought his first newspaper on credit, was able to buy out his partners' interests in the *Times-Union* for two million dollars; by 1943, with the purchase of the Binghamton (New York) *Press,* he controlled a group of twenty-one newspapers located in sixteen middle-sized cities in four different states. Gannett is also chairman of the board of directors of the American *Agriculturist,* a semi-monthly publication. The publisher's only venture into metropolitan dailies proved to be unsuccessful—the Brooklyn *Eagle,* bought in 1929, was sold in 1932 after Gannett had decided that because of the growing depression it was wise to lessen his debt burden. He says he took a big loss on the sale of the paper.

Samuel T. Williamson's *Frank Gannett, a Biography* (1940) is the story of the publisher's rise from newsboy to newspaper owner, in which his interest in economic problems is given full exposition: Gannett operates his newspapers on "the autonomous policy" that publisher, editor, and employees of each should be local people who know the needs of their communities. With the exception of the Rochester *Times-Union*, none of Gannett's papers, says Williamson, editorially reflects Gannett's views. There has been no standardizing or rebuilding of Gannett's papers to a fixed plan. Gannett's only stipulation has been that the management give its city a "clean, fair, independent, constructive newspaper . . . fit to enter the home and be read by every member of the family." Before and after the repeal of the Eighteenth Amendment, Gannett's newspapers, at a loss in revenue estimated at one million dollars annually, refused all liquor advertisements. Although he is a total abstainer, Gannett is not a militant prohibitionist. His position is simply that such advertisements have no place in a newspaper read in the home. In the editorial sphere Gannett, who dislikes wordy articles, advises his staff to eliminate "lazy," useless words in writing.

In acquiring his group of papers Gannett has taken several financial risks. One of these was in 1929. The year before when he decided to buy two Albany newspapers, the *Knickerbocker Press* and the *Evening News*, he gave Archibald R. Graustein, president of the International Paper Company, four hundred and fifty thousand dollars' worth of stock in the papers as collateral for the loan. "It was understandable," said Gannett's biographer Samuel Williamson, "that Graustein [whose company was going increasingly into power utilities] should want more Gannett newsprint business," but, according to the writer, the transaction did not give the power trust influence in the editorial policy of the Gannett newspapers. (Later Gannett borrowed two million more to purchase the Brooklyn *Eagle*.) "As long as his borrowings from Graustein remained and International Paper Company held his securities," continues Williamson, "Gannett's papers continued to attack the power trust as they had before. Although he has changed his views since, Gannett then favored municipal ownership of city light and power plants, and supported ownership of power in wider fields."

When the Federal Trade Commission in 1929 began an investigation in Washington of the power trust's "machinations to control public opinion," the Hearst newspapers, "with which in Rochester and Albany Gannett had dared to compete, employed considerable black type in the exposure of Gannett's arrangement with International Paper. Gannett was pictured as bought by the power trust." When Gannett was called to Washington by the FTC for questioning (at which he was exonerated), he made what his biographer calls a characteristically audacious decision. Within a few hours he had borrowed from the Chemical National Bank of New York City two and a half million dollars, for which he gave the bank a four-month note, so that he might buy back his securities from Graustein. With this little matter settled between trains, Gannett went on to Washington. When his associates learned of his short-term note to the bank, however, they feared that for once Gannett had been foolhardy. But Gannett came through—half of the bank loan was paid by selling an issue of Gannett Company, Inc., preferred stock to employees. The *Christian Science Monitor* reported in 1940 that more than one-fourth of the four thousand employees owned one-third of the almost seven and a third million dollars of the preferred stock outstanding, representing the total indebtedness of the Gannett newspapers, with the properties conservatively valued at twenty-five million dollars.

"Gannett," says his biographer, "believes in the private competitive economic struggle. Yet he also believes with his whole heart that private property should respond to the call of general welfare. He has gone to considerable pains to see to it that Gannett newspapers, in their continued existence and in their profits in the days to come, shall heed that call." In September 1935 the publisher announced the formation of the Frank E. Gannett Newspaper Foundation, Inc. Ultimately the Foundation will own all of Class A common stock of the Gannett Company, Inc., and its resources will be devoted exclusively to "public, charitable, educational, and general philanthropic uses and purposes" in localities served by the Gannett newspapers. At least 75 per cent of its net income must be distributed in the year of its receipt. At least nine of its eleven directors must be experienced newspapermen. "These eleven self-perpetuating directors after Gannett's death will exercise control of the Gannett company by electing its board of seven directors, preferably from their own number; and the Gannett company board in turn shall elect a general manager." The *Christian Century* in commenting said, "What it means in a word, is that the responsible management of these influential newspapers will be in the hands of men thoroughly experienced in journalism but having no financial interest in the accumulation of inordinate profits . . . a control as disinterested as the control of a university."

Gannett first came into the political limelight in 1936—although he was not to win a public office—when he accepted an invitation of the Borah-for-President forces to run for Vice-President on the Republican ticket in the Ohio primaries. The Baltimore *Evening Sun* called the union of the two men "practically perfect," and the New York *World-Telegram* and other independent newspapers added their approval. That year Gannett took an active part in the Republican National Convention, and in September in the New York State Convention his name was put in nomination for governor. In 1940, after his candidacy for the Presidential nomination was launched, he toured the country in his private plane in a campaign reported to have cost several hundred thousand dollars. The New York *Herald Tribune* stated that the Gannett forces

GANNETT, FRANK E.—*Continued*

staked their hopes on a platform in defense of constitutional government and private enterprise. After Gannett lost the nomination to Willkie [40] many upstate New York Republicans advocated his candidacy for United States Senator. Appointed assistant chairman of the Republican National Committee in September 1942, Gannett resigned in November, but shortly afterward was in the race for the office of the chairman of the committee, a post to which Harrison Spangler was appointed.

In 1944, said *Editor and Publisher,* Gannett was one of the men upon whom Dewey leaned for advice; often in the company of the nominee, he came and went "much more frequently than any of the rest without the general public being aware of it." After the defeat of the Republican Party in the 1944 Presidential election Gannett proposed the formation of a national coalition party to "unite the Democratic Party of the South and the Republican Party of the North on national questions." Declaring that the Republican Party had failed to win the election because it "did not present a great burning issue," the publisher said that a vigorous effort had been made the previous summer to form such a coalition, "but the Republicans thought they could win without concessions to the South."

The Committee to Uphold Constitutional Government was founded by Gannett in 1937. (In 1939 he resigned as chairman of the committee, which was later succeeded by the Committee for Constitutional Government, of whose board he is now a member.) His committee is regarded as one of the strongest factors that brought about the defeat of four of the Administration's measures: Roosevelt's Supreme Court proposal, the Reorganization Bill, the attempt to purge the anti-New Deal Democrats in the 1938 elections, and the recovery (spending-through-lending) measures in 1939. Other New Deal measures attacked by the committee are the plans for food subsidies and the Wagner [41]-Murray-Dingell Bill for an expanded social and health security program. And, in addition, it has been working through the state legislatures for an amendment to the Constitution limiting the taxing power of Congress. The amendment it sponsors would prohibit Congress from levying an income, estate, or gift tax of more than 25 per cent. Thus far seventeen of thirty-two state legislatures required for the calling of a Constitutional Convention have approved the resolution. Opponents of the proposed amendment claim that, if passed, it would destroy the principle of progressive taxation and drastically reduce the Government's revenue.

In the fall of 1944 the Senate Special Committee to Investigate Lobbying Activities undertook to investigate the Committee for Constitutional Government under the Hatch Act. During the course of the hearing Edward A. Rumely, executive secretary of the committee, refused to submit its subscription list on the grounds that the founders considered the group "educational, and not political, and, therefore, outside the [House] committee's jurisdiction." When Rumely was

indicted for this refusal, Gannett issued a statement that officers and trustees of the Committee for Constitutional Government stood squarely back of Rumely. Contending that a great constitutional issue was at stake, Gannett declared that the committee was determined to bring the issue to a test in court. Although admitting that the committee had distributed many pamphlets and articles (reported to be more than eighty million) attacking the New Deal, Rumely said that it had "urged no one to support or defeat any candidate or party," and had confined itself to the "area of ideas." In its final report in January 1945 the House committee emphasized that "under the present law it is difficult to penalize such groups," because of their assertions of nonpolitical activity. They were therefore "not subject to the law requiring major parties to show their records and disclose the source of their funds to Congress." (Among the organizations under investigation at this time was the CIO Political Action Committee.) The Rumely trial (United States *vs.* Edward A. Rumely) in October 1945 resulted in a "hung" jury, largely over the definition of "politics," and a retrial was ordered. In August 1943 Gannet had come into public notice in connection with the discussion of the Committee for Constitutional Government by John Roy Carlson [43] in the latter's book *Under Cover.* The publisher of the book, E. P. Dutton, charged Gannett, among others, with attempting to curb sales of the book by warning booksellers of the possibility of libel suits.

When Roosevelt in his campaign speeches of 1944 described the Gannett newspapers as isolationist, the publisher assailed the statement as false, and pointed out that as early as 1935 he had urged the President to call a conference of leaders of important European nations to remove the causes "that were fast bringing on the present and greatest of all tragedies." "My attitude then," he said, "certainly was not that of an isolationist and never has been." In 1937 the *Rotarian* published an article by Gannett in which he declared that he believed "the one practical and effective step toward peace" is the establishment of a Department of Peace in the cabinets of the nations of the world, beginning with that of the United States, a proposal which, he adds, is not at all new. His 1940 stand on foreign policy was like the plank which both Democrats and Republicans later included in their platforms—for keeping America out of the war.

The publisher's interest in the problems of industrial relations led him to visit England in 1938 for a study of British industrial conditions, which he believed had much of value to offer both management and labor, "especially in the field of collective bargaining." The result of his study was published under the title *Industrial and Labour Relations in Great Britain* (1939), a symposium of the opinions of prominent Englishmen, which Gannett edited in collaboration with Benjamin F. Catherwood. *Management Review* recommended it to any student of the problem as "an exceedingly worthwhile treatment." *Survey Graphic,* on the other hand, thought that "on the whole the symposium hardly seems worth while," and that Gannett's introduction to the essays "is an expression of his personal views," which shows "no reflection of the hot fire of original work."

Another trait of Gannett's, says Williamson in his biography of the publisher, is his foresight. In 1920 for the first time in history the returns of a Presidential election were broadcast over the radio. "To most persons at the time this first radio news broadcast was a stunt of little significance—but Gannett heard about it and wondered." The following year Gannett, backing Lawrence G. Hickson, a student of the Mechanics Institute who had been experimenting for some time with wireless telegraphy, acquired an interest in WHQ, a Rochester radio station. He showed less foresight when he sold his interest in 1927 for six thousand dollars—the station is reported to be worth more than a million today. However, Gannett today holds an interest in eight stations in six different cities. He is also the promoter and director of a time-saving machine which is now being manufactured by the Teletypesetter Corporation.

Amidst his many activities the publisher has found time to support causes outside his immediate range of interests. In 1942 he was chairman of the Navy Relief Society's New York State Citizens' Committee and chairman of the Naval District of the relief society. In 1943 he was a speaker at the National Conference for Palestine, joining Chaim Weizmann[42] and other noted persons in condemning the 1939 White Paper issued by the British Government to restrict Jewish settlement in Palestine. In 1943 he served as chairman of the National Food Conference, which he called at the request of agricultural officials of sixteen states. For many years he has been active in newspaper associations: he was president of New York State Associated Dailies (1916-17), the New York Press Association (1917-18), and the New York State Publishers Association (1921-27). He was a member of the board of directors of the Associated Press from 1935 to 1940. As a member and president of the Cornellian Council (1925-26) Gannett has long served Cornell University and in 1926 was made a trustee. He is a member of the board of directors of the Rochester Institute of Technology, has been a trustee of Keuka College since 1924, and was for years a member of the Finger Lakes State Parks Commission. His honorary degrees include an M.A. from Wesleyan University (1929), LL. D.'s from Alfred University (1935), Hobart College (1937), and Hartwick College (1941), a Ph.D. from Oglethorpe University (1939), a Litt. D. from Keuka College (1939), and in 1937 he was made an honorary member of Phi Beta Kappa.

In 1920 the publisher was married to Caroline Werner, daughter of the late Justice William E. Werner of the New York State Court of Appeals. She is a native of Rochester but was educated abroad and in Rosemary Hall, Greenwich, Connecticut. The Gannetts have two children, Sally and Dixon. In speaking of her husband, Mrs. Gannett has said, "I've watched him grow from a little businessman to a big businessman without any show of growing pains." During his 1940 national campaign Mrs. Gannett addressed various women's organizations in his behalf. The Gan-

netts have two residences, one in Rochester and one in Miami Beach. Their recreations are golf and yachting. The publisher is five feet ten and one-half inches tall, and weighs one hundred sixty-two pounds. Although Gannett was born of a Methodist family, he is a Unitarian; and he succeeded William Howard Taft as director of the American Unitarian Association. Mrs. Gannett attends a Presbyterian church, their daughter is an Episcopalian, and their son, by his own choice, goes to a Reformed church Sunday school.

References

C S Mon Mag p3 F 24 '40 por
Liberty 17:39+ Ap 27 '40 pors
Newsweek 6:34-5 O 5 '35
Scholastic 36:10 Mr 11 '40 por
Time 35:22 Ja 22 '40
National Cyclopædia of American Biography Current vol E p496
Who's Who in America, 1944-45
Williamson, S.T. Frank Gannett (1940)

GANNON, ROBERT I(GNATIUS), REV.
Apr. 20, 1893- University president

Address: Fordham University, E. Fordham Rd. and Bronx Park, New York City

REV. ROBERT I. GANNON

Since 1936 the Very Reverend Robert I. Gannon, S.J., has been president of Fordham University, largest Catholic university in the United States. The son of well-to-do Catholic parents of Irish descent, Robert Ignatius was born in St. George, Staten Island, New York, on April 20, 1893. His father was Frank Stanislaus Gannon, at one time president of the Norfolk Southern Railroad, a director of the Metropolitan Street Railway Company and of the Emigrant Industrial Savings Bank. His mother was Marietta (Burrows) Gannon. (Dr. James A. Gannon of Washington, D.C., is a brother of Father Gannon, and a sister-in-law, Mrs. Frances Foley Gannon of Staten Island, is director of the Bureau of Consumer

GANNON, ROBERT I., REV.—*Continued*
Service and is known as "housekeeper to eight millions.") Robert, a "slim, curly-headed boy," attended the Loyola preparatory school in New York, graduating in 1909. He then went on to Georgetown University in Washington, D.C., from which he received a B.A. degree in 1913. In the same year he entered the Society of Jesus. He received an M.A. degree from Woodstock College in Maryland in 1919, and then began teaching as a Jesuit scholastic. (A "scholastic" in the Society of Jesus is one who has completed his novitiate and taken simple perpetual vows, after which he remains in the ranks for several years, teaching or studying in a Jesuit school until he is ordained.) From 1919 until 1923 Gannon was instructor and then assistant professor of English and philosophy at Fordham University. During this time he directed student dramatics and founded the Fordham Playhouse.

Father Gannon was ordained in 1926. The young priest went abroad after his ordination, receiving the degree of Doctor of Sacred Theology at the Gregorian University in Rome in 1927, and studying educational methods at the Sorbonne, Oxford, Cambridge, Perugia, and Louvain. At Christ's College, Cambridge, he received an M.A. degree. Back in the United States, in 1930 the Jesuit Father General sent him to Jersey City, New Jersey, to reopen St. Peter's College, which had been closed since the First World War. Four rooms, with an adjoining kitchen for a laboratory, were rented from the Chamber of Commerce, and the little college of eighty students opened with Father Gannon as dean. Three years later Father Gannon opened the Hudson College of Commerce and Finance, also in Jersey City, where he remained for three years. In June 1936, when Father Aloysius J. Hogan, president of Fordham, received orders from Rome to go to Georgetown University as dean, the Reverend Dr. Gannon became his successor at Fordham.

Fordham University was founded by the Right Reverend John Hughes, D.D. (who later became the first Archbishop of New York) upon the old Rose Hill farm in the borough of the Bronx of New York City. The new institution was formally opened with six students on June 24, 1841, and was called St. John's College. For five years the college was conducted by the diocesan clergy of New York; in 1846 it was placed under the direction of a band of Jesuits who came at Bishop Hughes's invitation from St. Mary's, Kentucky. Fordham has since then remained under Jesuit direction. In 1907, after the opening of the schools of Medicine and Law in 1905, an amendment to the charter of the college by the regents of the University of the State of New York changed the corporate name to Fordham University.

When Father Gannon became president in 1936 Fordham had an enrollment of almost eight thousand students. It was, in the words of *Time* Magazine, "an up-to-date university [noted for] a big-time football team, a world-famed seismograph station, a Nobel Prize winner . . . schools of law, business, social service, pharmacy." As Father Gannon began his presidency he made it clear that he had no ambitions

for further expansion of the university, but wanted to concentrate on its extracurricular activities. During his administration he has been responsible for many improvements. New buildings have been constructed, there have been administrative changes, scholarship and research facilities have increased, and he instituted the custom of publishing Fordham's annual accounts, an unusual procedure among Catholic college presidents. By 1945 Fordham University had twenty-six buildings on the Bronx campus, annexes in midtown and lower Manhattan. (The School of Adult Education is a recent addition to the university.)

In September 1941 Fordham held its centennial celebration and also commemorated the four hundredth anniversary of the arrival of the Jesuits in America. Delegates from more than five hundred colleges, universities, and learned societies in the United States and foreign countries gathered at Fordham for a three-day observance. At this time, with the entry of the United States into the war imminent, Father Gannon said, "Our lives are being lived for ideas, not for books, and we are not in an ivory tower. We are manning a lighthouse, and the darker the clouds, the more need there is for light. . . .The fact is, we have never felt more necessary."

At Fordham's ninety-fifth commencement in 1940 Father Gannon warned against "military armament without moral armament," and cited Fordham's chief responsibility to the United States as the cultivation of sound patriotism. Although he had been strongly opposed to the United States entrance into the Second World War, when the university opened in September 1942 Father Gannon admitted at the opening exercises that he thought he had been wrong in being an isolationist. "Today it is humiliating, but many of us are ready to stand up in meeting and confess that we were wrong. . . .It was our war from the first." Newspapers and magazines praised his honest stand at this time.

The years of the Second World War, described by him as "a brand new worry to sharpen her [Fordham's] wits," held many international interests for Father Gannon. In the spring of 1943 he accepted an invitation to preach a series of Lenten sermons at Westminster Cathedral in London and spent two and a half months in England. In the fall of that year, as a tribute to Poland, a room in Keating Hall on the Fordham campus was dedicated as the Lublin Room. In the dedication ceremony Fordham formally adopted the Catholic University of Lublin for the duration of the war, the room becoming symbolically the wartime home of the Polish university which had been taken over by the Germans. The honorary degree of Doctor of Laws was conferred on Wladyslaw Raszkiewicz, President of the Polish Government-in-Exile and received by the Polish Ambassador, Jan Ciechanowski. Later, in gratitude, President Raszkiewicz awarded to Father Gannon the insignia and diploma of the Grand Commander's Cross, with Star of the Order of Polonia Restituta.

In March 1944 Father Gannon participated in the St. Patrick's Day celebration in New York City, and at this time paid tribute to Eamon de Valera [40], Prime Minister of Eire, whom he described as "a man of principle and hence a conspicuous figure in world affairs." Annually the Feis of Tara, an ancient Irish festivity, is celebrated on the Fordham campus with songs, dances, and games. Father Gannon, honorary chairman of the twelfth (1944) annual celebration, asked that the day also be made one of prayer for loved ones fighting in the war. On February 18, 1945, the Fordham president presided at the "One World" dinner held at the Hotel Astor to honor the memory of Wendell Willkie [40]. Before the war, in 1938, the Catholic educator had visited Venezuela as a member of a cultural commission invited by President Lopez Contreras to advise the Government on educational matters. In 1945 he was again invited to South America, this time to help in the organization of the Institute of Brazilian Studies and to lecture in São Paulo on American education.

"The very square-jawed" Father Gannon received the 1942 award of the New York Academy of Public Education for "distinguished service in the field of education." Some of his convictions, which he has expressed in a fine dramatic voice and in a manner described as "urbanely dogmatic," are: "The college course should be reduced to three years, high school to three years, and grammar school to six. Then, if compulsory military training is introduced, the loss of a year will not be serious." Students should be taught obedience to the constituted authority simply because it is the constituted authority. ("We do not expect to argue with a Fordham freshman. We expect him to do as he is told.") "No one has any clear idea what it [academic freedom] means. . . .Men have been allowed in the academic world a license which is justly denied in every other. . . .For anyone in a cap and gown can hack away at the foundations of life, can rob our sons and daughters of all the principles on which civilization depends—but let him so much as whisper 'Academic Freedom' . . . and no professional educator dares to say a word of criticism." Father Gannon feels that there is much wrong with progressive education; he disapproves of the elective system. He emphasizes the importance of graduate study, and in January 1945 announced that two scholarships would be given by Fordham to cooperate in a plan for bringing students from the Netherlands to the United States for graduate study in subjects useful in postwar reconstruction.

At the end of the war President Gannon, with other college presidents, agreed that acceleration had been a necessary evil. Compressing four years of college into three was unpopular with students and faculty, and the impression, he said, was staleness on the part of the teachers and indigestion on the part of the students. Of Fordham's postwar football plans, Jack Coffey, the athletic director, announced in December 1945 that the university would resume its playing of intercollegiate games in 1946. Big-time football, however, he added, would probably not be seen at Fordham for several years. Father Gannon, one sports writer pointed out, is opposed to it and is not likely to change his position.

Father Gannon is the author of *The Technique of the One-Act Play* (1925) and has contributed numerous articles to periodicals. Honorary degrees have been conferred on him by Georgetown, Holy Cross, New York, and Rutgers universities, and by Columbia, Boston, Bowdoin, and Manhattan colleges. He is a trustee of New York Town Hall and of the New York Zoological Society, an elective manager of the New York Botanical Garden, an honorary life member of the Newcomen Society of England, and a director of the Pan American Society. He is also a director of the American Arbitration Association and the Netherlands-American Foundation, was a member of the Advisory Committee on Adult Education of the Columbia Broadcasting System until its demise, and was elected president of the Association of Colleges and Universities of the State of New York, in October 1945. In addition, the educator serves on the advisory committees of the Boy Scouts of America, the American Red Cross, and the Bronx Chamber of Commerce. He is a member of the Century Club of New York.

At the time of Fordham's centenary celebration *Time* described Father Gannon as a small, genial person who "had a wonderful time . . . bouncing among his guests, helping them to tea, conferring honorary degrees (in Latin) on bigwigs." He is noted for the "Irish wit and wisdom"—and sometimes irony—in his speeches and radio talks. Illustrative of his humor was the introduction to a talk which he once gave at a St. Patrick's Day celebration: "To speak of St. Patrick to the Society of the Friendly Sons of St. Patrick," he said, "is like a travel-lecturer preparing to tell his audience about a visit to Tibet and then looking down into his audience and seeing Marco Polo—or Eleanor Roosevelt."

References

Time 28:30-2 Jl 6 '36 por; 38:37 S 29 '41 por; 40:38-42 S 21 '42 por

American Catholic Who's Who, 1942-43

Who's Who in America, 1944-45

GARAND, JOHN C(ANTIUS) (găr'ănd kän'tsyüs) 1888- Inventor

Address: b. Springfield Armory, Springfield, Mass.; h. 25 Wilton St., Springfield, Mass.

Relatively few people have heard of John C. Garand, but nearly everyone knows of the Garand rifle, official arm of the United States Army and Marine Corps, which is generally considered the best rifle in the world. Like the Norden [45] bombsight, it was designed by a researcher born outside the United States who presented his invention to the United States Government royalty-free, drawing no profit from the millions of dollars expended for it.

John Cantius Garand was born in 1888 on a farm in the French-Canadian village of St. Remi, about twenty miles from Montreal. He does not remember the family statistics, but he does know he was the sixth or seventh child and that he had from eleven to thirteen brothers and sisters. When the boy was eight his mother died, and three years later the Garands moved across the border, to Connecticut. After only one more year of schooling, John went to work as a floor sweeper and bobbin boy in one of New England's textile mills. There he spent every free minute in the machine-repair shop, watching the mechanics. The foreman liked the curly-headed

JOHN   C.   GARAND

little boy and let him earn a bit of extra money by smoothing roughnesses off spindles with a piece of building brick. Before his fourteenth birthday John Garand had taken out a patent on an invention of his, a new type of jack screw. Another invention was called for by the rifle he and his brother owned jointly: a sort of deflector target which sent the bullets skyward so they would not hit the neighboring farmers as they passed by.

By the time Garand was eighteen he was a machinist at the textile mill. One summer, too, he helped his father and brother run a shooting gallery in Norwich, but, says Teale, "their enthusiasm for target practice ate up most of the profits." After John moved to Providence, Rhode Island, to be near his new job in a tool factory, he took up motorcycling, and designed an engine with which he won a number of races at New England tracks. For several winters he gave his free time to fancy ice-skating, but his main interest was firearms.

After the outbreak of the First World War, Garand, then in his thirties, went to New York to work in a micrometer plant. At the same time he took correspondence courses, studying in the evenings. Every Saturday he spent at Coney Island, using the shooting galleries as laboratories for studying the rifles as he shot them. Once, when he had shot at every target in the amusement park in the course of the day, his gallery fees came to one hundred dollars. "Luckily for his bank balance," writes Teale, "he discovered a gallery near Times Square, about this time, where the proprietor would let him shoot free. Firing a rifle from the hip so accurately that he could hit a swinging target seven times on a single swing, he always attracted a crowd that overflowed onto the sidewalk and kept the cash register ringing at the gun counter. . . .One evening before he sat down to his lessons he read in a newspaper that the Government was having difficulty finding a satisfactory machine gun. He couldn't see why there should be any problem

about that, so he sat down and designed a machine gun of his own."

Teale writes that Garand sent his plans to the Naval Board in Washington (another version has it that he merely wrote a letter to the War Department outlining his suggestions). At any rate, he was invited to the Capital to present his ideas in person. As a result, the officials offered to make him a master gauge and gun experimenter, annual salary eighteen hundred dollars, "turn him loose in a room at the Bureau of Standards, and let him prepare a model of his gun. The salary was just half of what he had been receiving as a skilled machinist, but he jumped at the chance. For eighteen months Garand buried himself in the room set aside for him. At the end of that time his gun was finished. But so was the World War, and the demand for machine guns was at a standstill."

Fortunately the Army was interested in developing a semiautomatic rifle that would combine the best features of a light machine gun and its famous bolt-operated Springfield rifle. In 1919 Garand was appointed as a consulting engineer at the United States Armory in Springfield, Massachusetts, which had turned out weapons for George Washington's army. Soon he began what was to be two decades of work on his rifle. Garand's basic design provided for expanding-gas pressure which would drive the bullet from its barrel, eject the empty shell, and throw the next cartridge into firing position. This not only made the firearm faster and easier to operate, but eliminated the Springfield's bruising kick after firing. He designed it, also, so that the user need touch only the wooden parts and not the heated metal. Garand's first rough model was submitted to the Bureau of Standards in 1923; but it was eleven years before his rifle was brought to a point where it met the Army standard in lightness, simplicity, and strength. The Ordnance Department held periodic competitions, at which designers submitted models of their guns. In 1929 Garand submitted one which, though too heavy, was "surprising." It enabled a man to fire eight times without taking his eyes from the target; it could be taken apart in the field within twelve seconds and reassembled with an ordinary cartridge as the only tool; it worked in heat or cold; and it could be fired successfully immediately after being immersed in water.

The inventor often felt that he could not possibly get his gas-operated rifle down to the required lightness. This was "in the back of Garand's mind night and day—when he was working, lying in bed, playing table tennis or badminton or pitching horseshoes. Often he came down to the Armory on week-ends," working over his plans in the deserted building, redesigning and again redesigning. He tried fifty different plans for the rear sight alone; and the final gun, according to Donald Wilhelm, contained nineteen different kinds of steel, worked out in consultation with metallurgists and machine-tool designers. To reduce the weight Garand had in most cases to reduce the number of parts. He eliminated an ounce here, a few grams there. Finally he designed one hammer spring that replaced five, saving a pound. In 1934, when the rifle was patented, it weighed nine and a quarter pounds, contained seventy-five parts—thirty-three fewer than the Springfield—and was "a precision instrument of rare ingenuity." The Army ordered eighty models for the "torture tests," which took months to produce, and Garand worked with both night and day shifts in the Armory model room, directing his eighteen workers and sleeping when he could.

In the tests, the Garand came out on top of a field of some fifty competing models. Then Chief of Staff Douglas MacArthur [41] changed the specifications from .276 caliber to .30, so its ammunition would be the same as for the Springfield and light machine guns, and again Garand redesigned his piece. Now at last he could have made a fortune in royalties —the Polish Government and a commercial munitions maker each offered him "literally millions"—but he chose to turn the patent over to the United States Government, royalty-free. He has the right to put the rifle into commercial production if the Army grants its permission, but he has never asked for it.

The next problem was to get the M-1, as the Ordnance Department termed it after it had been accepted in January 1936, into mass production. Fifteen hundred operations were required for this, and the Armory had to buy nearly a thousand different machines costing as much as twenty thousand dollars each, besides jigs and fixtures, writes Donald Wilhelm in *Forbes* Magazine. Later that year the first M-1's came off the assembly line, and the Infantry began to substitute them for the Springfields as fast as production permitted. After the rearming was well advanced the Marine Corps was under some pressure to make the Garand rifle also their official weapon. (Although the Marine Corps is under the Navy, its ordnance is supplied by the War Department, and it is naturally easier to supply one kind of rifle than two different ones.) The Garand did become the official Marine weapon in 1940, although the Corps' tests indicated that the arm, superior to any other semiautomatic rifle, was inferior to the Springfield in resistance to bad weather conditions. It was, however, three to three-and-a-half times as fast. Three million dollars were appropriated to supply the Marines with Garands, in addition to the Army's twenty-four million.

Gradually the complex operations required to produce Garands were cut down. In late 1940 the rifles were being turned out at the rate of seven hundred a day; in June 1941 the Springfield arsenal was producing a thousand a day: by August several factories were assembling them on a three-shift basis at more than one a minute, and more than a quarter-million had already been issued. Reporters who heard that this was the greatest advance in infantry arms since the beginning of the First World War had been amazed to find the inventor "an obscure civilian employee on the Government payroll at fifty-five hundred dollars a year—director of a staff of twenty men in the model room—who was bewildered by all the attention thrust upon him." "Did it ever occur to you," he was asked, "that the Garand rifle might kill a million men?" "I think," answered the designer, "that with this Government it will always be used for defense."

The Garand's value in that defense was proved when the Japanese attacked the Philippines in December 1941. General MacArthur praised the arm, and Garand was more pleased than surprised, for the Assistant Secretary of War had termed it the best shoulder rifle in the world, and several other generals had agreed. (In January 1945, General Patton [43] pronounced the M-1 "the greatest battle implement ever devised.") In March 1942, when the Japanese had captured some M-1's the weapon ceased to be a military secret. Garand estimated, however, that after individual models had been built it would take three years for a foreign power to put it in production. And he has continued to work out improvements, which have likewise been given to the United States Government, among them a new trigger mechanism patented in 1945 just before the Japanese surrender. According to General Marshall, America's chief advantages on the ground in the European war were the Garand semi-automatic rifle and multiple-drive motor equipment, principally the jeep and two-and-a-half-ton truck: "Our superiority in infantry fire-power, stemming from the use of the semi-automatic riffle, was never overcome."

Modest and reticent, John Garand does not discuss the various honors that have come to him. His four-line entry in *Who's Who in America* gives no biographical information except his receipt of the Holley Medal, which is given by the American Society of Mechanical Engineers to "one who, by some unique act of genius of an engineering nature, has accomplished a great and timely public benefit . . . meriting the highest honor within the gift of the mechanical engineering profession." (This award was made four days before Pearl Harbor.) Among his other awards is the medal of the Army Ordnance Association; in November 1943 he was one of three recipients of John Scott medals and premiums of one thousand dollars each awarded by the Philadelphia Board of City Trade; and in March 1944 he and the discoverer of radar, Dr. Albert Hoyt Taylor, received the first two Medals for Merit awarded to civilians for outstanding war services.

Garand is described as "alert, athletic, square-jawed," a short, dark-complexioned man with a mop of wavy black hair, and keen blue eyes framed by rimless eyeglasses. His speech shows traces of his French-Canadian origin, but he is a citizen of the United States, having taken the oath in 1920. The inventor is said to be an even better shot with a pistol than with one of his own rifles; "his idea of an exciting night's reading is to settle down in an armchair with a pile of machine-shop magazines beside him." Garand is puzzled when anyone unfamiliar with the customs of research workers suggests that he should have made money from his inventions instead of giving them away. His answer is that he has been able to support his wife and two children and has had "a lot of pleasure" out of his work. He does admit that he has never found time for the practicing necessary to make him a really good figure skater.

References

C S Mon p5 Mr 5 '42 por
Collier's 102:18-19 O 29 '38 il

GARAND, JOHN C.—*Continued*

N Y Sun p23 F 27 '42
N Y World-Telegram p7 Ag 7 '41
Newsweek 14:18 D 4 '39 il por
Pop Sci 137:68-71+ D '40 ils pors
Read Digest 37:33-6 O '40
Who's Who in America, 1944-45

GASSER, HERBERT S(PENCER) July 5, 1888- Physiologist

Address: b. Rockefeller Institute for Medical Research, 66th St. and York Ave, New York City

DR. HERBERT S. GASSER

The director of the renowned Rockefeller Institute for Medical Research is Dr. Herbert S. Gasser, a physiologist of international fame. In 1944 he shared with Dr. Joseph Erlanger, head of the department of physiology at Washington University in St. Louis, the Nobel prize in medicine. The award was made for fundamental research in muscle-nerve physiology demonstrating the reaction of nerve fibers to electrical impulses. Through their work, machines recording brain waves have been improved to the point where the extent of certain types of brain damage can be detected, and the extent of the repair of damaged nerves can be measured. Someday, scientists have ventured, this work may lead to the detecting of thought.

Herbert Spencer Gasser was born on July 5, 1888, in Platteville, Wisconsin. His father, Dr. Herman Gasser, had come to America from his native Dorbirn, in the Austrian Tyrol, with his parents in 1866. The mother of the scientist, Jane Elizabeth (Griswold) Gasser, is of old New England stock. During his boyhood young Herbert played the piano and violin. He was adept at handicrafts, too— painting china and making miniature furniture —and later at the State Normal School in Platteville he invented various contrivances.

He was graduated from the University of Wisconsin in 1910 with the Bachelor's degree, and the next year, after receiving his Master's, he began the study of medicine at the university. There he had the good fortune to study under A. S. Loevenhart, the pharmacologist. The Professor was so impressed with his student's ability that he called him his "scientific heir" and bequeathed him a medal, with the request that it be passed on to Gasser's own best pupil. While a student at the university's medical school, Gasser was an assistant instructor in physiology, from 1911 to 1913. Walter J. Meek, professor of physiology at the university, wrote in a 1935 issue of the *Scientific Monthly* that physiology had attracted Gasser's profound interest, and during the period of his instructorship he began his research career. He completed his medical studies at Johns Hopkins, where he received an M.D. in 1915.

The year 1916 Gasser spent as an instructor in pharmacology at the University of Wisconsin. He then went to Washington University in St. Louis, Missouri, as an instructor in the department of physiology, of which Joseph Erlanger, the co-winner of the 1944 Nobel Prize, was head. Erlanger, some years Gasser's senior, is also an alumnus of Johns Hopkins and had gone to Washington University after serving on the faculty of the University of Wisconsin.

In the course of the First World War, Gasser did research in the field of traumatic or wound shock, studying its nature and treatment; before the war ended he also worked as a pharmacologist in the research division of the Chemical Warfare Service at the American University Experimental Station in Washington, D.C. (In 1941, in the Second World War, he was made a member of the National Research Commission.) On his return to Washington University in 1918 he was promoted to associate instructor in physiology and in 1920 to associate professor. In 1921, at the age of thirty-three, he was made head of the university's department of pharmacology. Soon after his appointment he was granted a two-year leave of absence for study in London, Paris, and Munich.

"At no time," says Professor Meek, "has Dr. Gasser ever divorced himself for one instant from his laboratory researches. They began in his student days and have constantly increased in significance, volume, and importance. His earliest work was on cardiac nerves, coagulation, mechanisms of oxidation in the living body, blood volume, and traumatic shock." His research into the problem of muscle-nerve physiology began in 1919 with Dr. H. Sidney Newcomer, with whom he succeeded in demonstrating the nature of the discharge from the nervous system into the diaphragm during inspiration. The next step in his research on the subject was made with Erlanger. Ten years before the two physiologists were awarded the Nobel Prize for their work in this field, they were known as outstanding electrophysiologists. Gasser, says Meek, was already an international figure— his contributions to "the development of the cathode ray oscillograph for physiological purposes, nerve conduction as related to diameter of fiber, the refractory period of nerves, the nature of nerve conduction, heat production, and viscosity in muscular contraction, the effects of rapidly repeated stimuli to nerves and cord potentials," were known to all students of muscle-nerve physiology before 1935.

Gasser's technique for the study of man's nervous system was interpreted for the layman by *Newsweek* in 1935, as follows: "Mystery cloaks the process by which primary sense organs react upon nerve fibers and flash impulses to the brain. What goes on in a stimulated nerve? Why do some fibers communicate only cold, others heat, others pain? How do we become aware of sensations? These problems, keys to the mechanism of thought, would remain scientific blind spots. But Dr. Gasser perfected an apparatus [the cathode ray oscillograph] delicate enough to register the infinitesimal electric currents set up by the stimulated nerve. . . .To gain his end, Dr. Gasser harnessed electrophysics to physiology. He discarded the usual heavy string galvanometer, too crude to catch the tiny electric impulses accurately. From radio, just out of its infancy, he borrowed new technique. He got the required voltage with a vacuum tube that amplified the nerve current. . . .Upon a photographic screen the beam flashed a precise picture of nerve reaction."

In 1931 Gasser was invited to head Cornell Medical College's physiological laboratories in New York City, and he was given a full professorship in physiology. During the four years he occupied the post Gasser's lecture hall was usually filled to capacity, and foreign scientists often came to New York to consult with him. When he left the laboratories in 1935 it was to accept what is perhaps one of the highest posts in the field of medical research, the directorship of the Rockefeller Institute for Medical Research. "At his hand," wrote *Newsweek* at the time, "lie inestimable opportunities to improve mankind's condition." To all corners of the world "he may send white-clad armies against fever and plague. His decisions, encyclicals of medicine, have behind them a master corps of researchers, the world's best laboratory equipment, and three million Rockefeller dollars a year."

A number of medical men had been surprised when Dr. Gasser, a physiologist, had been appointed to succeed the resigning Dr. Simon Flexner, a pathologist, and director of the Institute since its founding in 1903. "I am wondering why we started with an expert in pathology (the study of what causes disease), and now we have one in physiology (the study of how the body works)," commented John D. Rockefeller, Jr.'[41], at a press interview after Gasser's appointment. "It is because we have to give more attention to the functions of the body," Gasser replied. "It is also because, in the last fifty years, in the field of conquest of infectious diseases, we have been very successful. . . . When one looks at the diseases that are decreasing and those that are increasing, one finds that those that are lethal because of deterioration of organs are increasing."

The announcement of the 1944 Nobel prizes in medicine was made from Stockholm in October 1944. In an interview Gasser said that he was surprised at the recognition given by the Nobel committee because "the device so far has had such limited practical application." In a *Science News Letter* he described the work as "a direct outgrowth of modern physics," which had made it possible through his development of the oscillograph to clarify "older observations and bring new ones to light." The future, he said, held "alluring prospects with respect to the unravelling of how the central nervous system works." As for the prize money, Gasser expressed his intention of devoting his share of the award (half of $29,500.07) to further research. "That was the spirit in which the money was given," he added, "and I think it would be a good way in which to spend it." The New York *Times* commented editorially that the year's prizes had been made "for determinations and measurements which demanded the finest equipment and finest skill. Such work is less spectacular than that which gave us the sulfa drugs and penicillin, but hardly less important."

In addition to the hundred or more papers Gasser himself has written, he has collaborated with Erlanger in *Electrical Signs of Nervous Activity* (1937), and is represented in *Symposium on the Synapse* (1939), which was published after a Toronto meeting of the American Physiologists Society, of which Gasser is an officer. He is a trustee of the Rockefeller Foundation, a Fellow of the American Association for the Advancement of Science, and a member of numerous scientific societies in the United States and abroad. He holds D.Sc. degrees from the University of Pennsylvania (1936) and the University of Wisconsin (1941), and LL.D. degrees from the University of Rochester (1940) and Washington University (1940).

The physiologist is a tall, slender man whose manner, his associates say, is modest and tactful. A bachelor, he lives in a New York City apartment, where one of his relaxations is playing the piano. Yachting and mountain climbing are his vacation pleasures.

References

N Y Times p15 O 27 '44 por
Newsweek 6:20 Jl 20 '35
Sci Mo 41:180-1 Ag '35 por
American Men of Science (1938)
National Cyclopædia of American Biography Current vol E p236
Who's Who in America, 1944-45

GAUSS, CHRISTIAN (gous) Feb. 2, 1878-
University professor

Address: Princeton University, Princeton, N.J.

One of the most popular persons on the campus of Princeton University is said to be the former dean of the college, Christian Gauss, who has won a wide reputation for wit and wisdom. Long a professor of modern languages, a position he still retained when he terminated his twenty years as dean in 1945, he has written half a dozen books and many articles, ranging from advice to parents of college students in the *Saturday Evening Post* to scholarly discussions on modern languages, history, philosophy, and literary criticism. It

CHRISTIAN GAUSS

is small wonder that Princeton seniors once composed a song that hailed him with:

> *Here's to Gauss, called Christian,*
> *A most encyclopedic man.*

Born in Ann Arbor, Michigan, February 2, 1878, Christian Gauss is the son of Christian and Katherine (Bischoff) Gauss. He received his B.A. in 1898 from the University of Michigan, where he had been a distance runner. After taking his M.A. the following year, he taught Romance languages for two years at the same university. In 1901 he went to Lehigh University as assistant professor of modern languages. Called to Princeton University in 1905, when Woodrow Wilson was its president, he was appointed assistant professor of Romance languages, then raised to full professorship in modern languages two years later. In 1913 he became chairman of the department, a responsibility he was to hold until 1936. During this period Gauss lectured at the University of Cincinnati (1913), New York University (1915-16), and Columbia University Institute of Arts and Sciences, and was literary editor of the Princeton *Alumni Weekly* (1914-20). In 1914 Gauss received a Litt.D. from Washington, in 1928 an L.H.D. from Lehigh, and 1933 an LL.D. from the University of Michigan.

Gauss has devoted some of his time to translating, editing, and writing. Among his books are *Selections From Jean Jacques Rousseau* (1914), *The German Emperor As Shown in His Public Utterances* (1915), *Through College on Nothing a Year* (1915), *Democracy Today, an American Interpretation* (1917), and *Why We Went to War* (1918). Of the latter volume, the New York *Times* observed: "If there is still left in this country any sceptic pacifist who cavils at our entrance into the war he should read Mr. Gauss's calm, well-reasoned, and convincing book. He will find it remarkably comprehensive, so logically and forcefully presented, and so interestingly written that he will surely be

compelled to surrender." A member of the editorial board of the *American Scholar* since its founding, Gauss is also associate editor of the *Journal of Education* and trustee of the Princeton University Press.

In 1925 Gauss began the practice of what he has humorously referred to as "an unhappy profession," for upon becoming dean of Princeton he was thus obliged to discipline young Princetonians for "offenses against a moral or social code not always entirely identical with their own." He continued his contact with them as professor, however, and as general supervisor of athletics; and when he resigned as dean of the college in 1945 he retained his position as teacher and chairman of the department of modern languages. (He was succeeded by Francis R. B. Godolphin.)

In his post as dean, Gauss drew upon his experience as campus father-confessor to discuss the problems and the life of the undergraduate as well as the errors of parents, in *Life in College* (1930). "If there is a wiser or kindlier dean of undergraduates anywhere than Dean Gauss of Princeton he has not yet written a book," commented the *Christian Century*. Wrote the *Saturday Review of Literature*: "This book is one of the few really good books on college life. First, because it is written not only by an expert, but by a sympathetic expert, and, secondly, because it rides no hobby. . . .It is a dignified, unexaggerated, and sincere presentation of the keen observations of an honest man." Gauss has continued these observations on college students in popular magazines, recognizing in 1935 the reorientation which was developing a socially minded college student who sought new standards of political and social thought.

In the list of the one hundred notable books of 1934 prepared by *New Republic*, Christian Gauss's *A Primer for Tomorrow* was listed as one of eleven notable volumes on philosophy and science. In this introduction to contemporary civilization, Gauss examined the modern spirit in order to explain the nature of events and the distinctive character of our culture, studying especially the effects of science, capitalism, and nationalism, and pointing to the decline of religion as a mark of national decay. The chief virtue of the educator's book, as of his others, is said to be its sanity. "Without any of the tricks manipulated by the journalist, Gauss is a lucid and attractive expositor," said the *American Review*. "His book may be commended to all who wish an unpartisan and mature guide to the modern mind and its imminent problems."

Much of Gauss's writing is done in the summer and after midnight. He once said that he had to write in self-defense, to reassure himself of his identity. "I was rapidly becoming a character in fiction," he says. "Day Edgar started it when he made me the dean in the stories *In Princeton Town* [1929]. Edmund Wilson '45 made it worse when he projected me as the professor in *I Thought of Daisy* [1929]. I became hopelessly confused when I was told that I was the comic-supplement dean in my old friend Edward Hope Coffey's *She Loves Me Not* [1933]. All this was very befuddling. Every now and then I have to write something and sign it with my own name to prove to myself that I am in my own person alive and kicking."

Christian Gauss has deplored the failure of American colleges to perceive the dangers of American nationalism and to "prepare the country for the ordeal it is now facing in common with other nations." As early as August 1933, writing in *Scribner's Magazine*, Gauss was among those who, recognizing the interdependence of nations, sounded a warning: "At a time when there are those who urge that we should carry our policy of nationalistic isolation farther than we have ever done in the past, we must bear in mind that in the past peace has not gone with faith in isolation and there is no guarantee that it will do so in the future. Quite the contrary. We cannot of course solve all of our problems at once, and those who prefer a continuing of, indeed even a stricter adherence to, the policy of nationalistic self-sufficiency must be warned that on this basis disarmament and the reduction of the risks of war are probably impossible. These can only be obtained by some form of international convention or union, which of course implies involvement."

To educate effectively for democracy, wrote Gauss in 1942, the colleges must impress upon their students that liberalism and nationalism do not go hand in hand, but are irreconcilably opposed to one another. There has been an "ever-increasing attempt to substitute the nation for mankind as the point of reference from which economic and political systems are to be judged."

This nationalistic spirit has had its impact on higher education, contends the educator. "In the past seventy-five years at an ever-accelerating rate we have been substituting the historical and the nationalistic standpoint for what may properly be called the humanistic or philosophical. No common human denominator is assumed to exist" in the humanities—languages and literature, the fine arts, music, philosophy, and history—since they are now studied with a chiefly analytical, historical approach. Although Gauss regretfully recognized that "the humanities are out for the duration" of the Second World War, he pointed out that "it will be a tragedy to allow this necessary diminution of college training in the liberal arts to be carried to reckless extremes," adding that "in time of war it is necessary that the secondary schools of a nation, even more than the colleges, take the long view of preparing those students whose abilities warrant, to become soundly and broadly educated men in a postwar world."

Gauss has served as honorary chairman of the American Association for a Democratic Germany, a group which proposed "to support and encourage democratic elements in Germany as a means of eradicating the danger of German aggression in Europe and the world." Gauss did not support Secretary of the Treasury Henry Morgenthau's [40] proposals for the reduction of Germany to an agricultural state. He holds that Germany's industry must be destroyed as a war measure, but that such action cannot make for a constructive peace. He urges "something constructive, creative," believing that wholesale wiping out of German industry would injure anti-Nazis as well as Nazis. He is now one of the co-sponsors of the re-formed Council for a Democratic Germany made up of former Germans, opponents of Nazism who came to the United States, whose unity in defining common objectives represents, the sponsors believe, a significant and encouraging development.

In addition to spending considerable time refusing offers of college presidencies, the educator's other activities have included membership in the executive committee of the National Committee for Democracy and Intellectual Freedom (1939-40), the senate of the United Chapters of Phi Beta Kappa, and the national committee of the American Civil Liberties Union. In 1935 Gauss was decorated by the Legion of Honor of France. Among his several enthusiasms are Vermont (where he owns a summer farmhouse), golf, bridge, baseball (both college and professional), and football. In 1902 he was married to the former Alice Hussey; their five children are Katherine, Dante, Christian, Natalie, and Hildegarde.

References

Leaders in Education (1941)
Who's Who in America, 1944-45

GAVIN, JAMES M(AURICE) (găv'ĭn) Mar. 22, 1907- United States Army officer
Address: c/o War Department, Washington, D. C.

"You are the pioneers of tomorrow's army." This statement of his belief in the importance and permanency of air-borne troops was the key sentence in the address Major General (then Colonel) James M. Gavin made to his regiment of paratroopers, the 505th Parachute Infantry, at the regiment's first battle-dress review, at Fort Benning, Georgia, in the fall of 1942. And it was General Gavin's command, the Eighty-second Air-borne Division, which, a little more than two years later, after playing an heroic part in repulsing the Germans in the December 1944 "Battle of the Bulge," won Field Marshal Montgomery's [42] tribute: "I take my hat off willingly to such men." Gavin's "All-American" Division, which General Sir Miles C. Dempsey [44] called the "best in the best Army in the world," was selected by the War Department to march in a four-mile parade in New York City, an event scheduled for January 12, 1946.

James Maurice Gavin is one of the youngest United States Army officers to command a division and probably the first parachute infantry officer to lead his division in combat. He was born in New York City on March 22, 1907, to Martin M. and Mary (Tearle) Gavin. His education was that of the average city boy—he went to the public schools, completing high school in 1924. Then, a week after his seventeenth birthday, he enlisted in the Coast Artillery Corps, in which, in the course of fifteen months, he served as private, private first class, and corporal with the Sixteenth and Second Coast Artillery regiments. On June 30, 1925, he received his appointment to the United States Military Academy.

After four years at West Point he was graduated on June 13, 1929, and was commissioned a second lieutenant in the Infantry. The twenty-two-year-old officer showed early an interest in aviation. In September 1929 he en-

MAJ. GEN. JAMES M. GAVIN

tered the Air Corps Primary Flying School at Brooks Field, Texas, where he remained until December. But he was not to use this training at that time, as he returned to an Infantry assignment with the Twenty-fifth Infantry at Camp Harry J. Jones, Douglas, Arizona, where he remained until September 1932. He then enrolled in the Infantry School, Fort Benning, Georgia, for an advanced course of military training, graduating in May 1933. He was next assigned to Fort Sill, Oklahoma, for duty with the Thirty-eighth Infantry, and was later transferred to the Twenty-ninth Infantry at the same post. Assuming the duties of a regimental plans and training officer in December of that year, he was promoted to first lieutenant the following November. Having requested foreign service he was transferred to the Fifty-seventh Infantry (Philippine Scouts) at Fort McKinley, remaining until October 1938. Upon returning to the United States he proceeded to Vancouver Barracks, Washington, for duty with the Seventh Infantry, serving with that unit until August 1940. While at this post Lieutenant Gavin received his captain's bars. After these varied assignments he returned to West Point, where he was instructor in tactics (1940-41).

With the threat of the Second World War drawing closer to the United States, the Army was experimenting at Fort Benning with a new type of soldier—the paratrooper. Anxious for an assignment which required daring to an unusual degree and offered him an opportunity to use his aviation training, Captain Gavin secured a transfer in September 1941 to the Provisional Parachute Group; then, after completing the course in "jump training," he became plans and training officer for the 505th Parachute Battalion, one of the first units of its kind in the United States Army. In October of that year he was promoted to the rank of major (temporary), and the following February, then a lieutenant colonel (temporary), he went to the Command and General Staff School, Fort Leavenworth, Kansas, to round out his training as a field officer. Upon the

completion of this course he returned to the Air-borne Command at Fort Bragg, North Carolina, where he served as plans and training officer.

The parachute troops were now being expanded rapidly. No longer were they organized as battalions, but had become full regiments. The 505th Parachute. Infantry was scheduled for organization and training at Fort Benning, and in August 1942 Lieutenant Colonel Gavin was given command. Under his guidance the regiment gradually grew from a handful of experienced officers and enlisted men to full strength. Requiring space for "jump training" and tactical exercises, the unit moved across the Chatahoochee River to the Alabama area of the post. There the men learned to jump with equipment and to hit the ground ready for combat. "Jumping is a poor means of transportation from the plane to the ground," he would often say to his men in an attempt to remove the false importance given to this phase of training over the greater importance of developing fighting ability as a military team. After the usual "growing pains" and the loss of several cadres to new units, the regiment completed preliminary training and "Ready"—the command given to paratroopers before the final word "Go" at which they leave the plane—was adopted as the motto for the regimental shield, a shield bearing a black panther emblazoned on silver.

Gavin was now a full colonel (temporary), a rank he had attained on September 25, 1942. His outfit had "come along" fast, and was transferred to Fort Bragg, where it became a part of the Eighty-second Air-borne Division. At this post the unit engaged in tactical exercises as part of a larger unit until January 1943, when it was given an unannounced overseas assignment. For the next six months its combat training exercises at Oudjda, one thousand miles west of Kairouan, North Africa, was a closely guarded military secret. At the edge of the Sahara Desert, living on canned rations, the division went through preparatory training on ground made to resemble the territory on which it was to fight in the approaching mission, the invasion of Sicily. As the day neared, a special feast was ordered by the commanding general, Major General Matthew B. Ridgeway, as a reward for the completion of rigorous training. Whole steers were roasted on spits, and the entire division had steak—a pound to a man.

The following night a combat team composed of infantry, artillery, engineers, and other branches of service dropped out of the sky upon enemy-held Sicily. "You will spearhead the landing of an American force upon the island of Sicily," had been their send-off order. In command of this hard-hitting force was Colonel Gavin. Under his direction the group was quickly organized after a hazardous landing in a high wind, and, although several groups had become separated, the larger part of the force got through to the objective, Viazza ridge. From this high ground they prevented the break-through of the Fifteenth German Panzer Division to the Gela-Vittoria road and its feeders, thereby ensuring the safe landing of the sea-borne forces which later struck the beaches of the south coast of the island on the morning of July 9, 1943.

This was not an easy accomplishment, for the Germans were equipped with Mark IV and the heavier Mark VI tanks. Against this array of strength the American combat team had three light parachute artillery pieces, and the potent bazooka. In Bunker Hill strategy the men were ordered to hold their fire until the last moment, making it more effective against the tanks. After breaking up several attacks they were finally reinforced with tanks and artillery from the beachhead. Their rear was now secure. The command to attack was given late in the afternoon of July 11, and they succeeded in driving the Germans from threatening positions on the flanks of the main American force. The next day the Germans had withdrawn and the beachhead was secured. Gavin, also in the action at San Margherita and Trapani, was awarded the Distinguished Service Cross and the Purple Heart for his services in Sicily.

After reorganization in Sicily the unit was called upon to reinforce the beachhead at Salerno, Italy, where the American forces were meeting with stiff opposition. This time the paratroopers were dropped behind their own lines, as reinforcements sharing in the victorious outcome of that bloody battle, which led to the capture of Naples and the advance to the Volturno River. They then dropped out of the news as quietly as they had dropped from the sky. Too valuable with their combat experience to be used as ground infantry, they were transferred to England, re-equipped, and trained for their most important mission, the invasion of Normandy.

Regretfully Colonel Gavin left his unit for a more important job. However, he did not leave the division, having taken over the task of assistant division commander of the Eighty-second in February 1944. In this capacity he took part in the landing on the French coast. In conjunction with the 101st Air-borne Division, the Eighty-second secured the causeways across the swamp lands of that shore, permitting the major forces to move quickly inland and mop up the Normandy peninsula.

In the Normandy invasion Gavin (made temporary brigadier general, September 1943) took part in the battles of Sainte-Mère-Eglise, Saint-Sauveur-le-Vicomte, and Hill 131. In this, his third major campaign, he added the Oak Leaf Cluster to his D.S.C. His fourth campaign was to take him into the Netherlands, where the Eighty-second Air-borne Division in conjunction with the 101st air-borne unit succeeded in making contact with the British ground forces and secured the Nijmegen bridge across the Waal (Rhine). A month prior to this, on August 15, 1944, Gavin became division commander of the Eighty-second after General Ridgeway had been promoted. In Holland, Gavin participated in the Grave, Mook, and Beek encounters before being sent into his fifth major campaign, the battle of the Belgian Bulge. Two days after the Germans' lunge into Belgium on December 16, the crack Eighty-second Air-borne Division made the first effort to blunt the German First Division's drive westward by going into action west of Saint Oumont. They were responsible for cutting off the vanguard of the First SS (Elite Guard) Panzer Division which attacked Habiemont on December 19 and later repulsed another attack

by the Twelfth SS Panzer Division, which eliminated the threat to Liege, the primary objective of the Nazi spearhead.

Following this they went to the rescue of other American units which had been by-passed and surrounded. General Gavin's troops advanced so rapidly that they not only broke through to permit the withdrawal of the trapped units, but also outdistanced other American divisions which were attacking on their right and left flanks. The Eighty-second was ordered to withdraw by Field Marshal Sir Bernard L. Montgomery, who had taken command of the Allied forces on the north flank of the German salient. Objecting at first, they finally complied with the order when they were convinced that they could withdraw with honor. In January, after the division cracked the Siegfried Line, it moved into Cologne, then followed the Second Armored Division into Berlin.

Gavin substituted for General Parks as chairman of the Allied Kommandantur in Berlin while Parks made a thirty-day trip to Washington, and was instrumental, during this interim command, in canceling the censoring of sports news in the American sector. In mid-summer 1945 the Eighty-second Air-borne Division was assigned to duty in the American zone of occupation. The men rolled into Berlin by train and jeep to relieve the Second Armored, except for ninety-nine "eager beavers" who had pledged themselves to "jump on Berlin"—in peace or war. At their special request they parachuted from transport planes, landing safely in nearby truck gardens. Later on, in the fall of 1945, the decision to disband the Eighty-second met with some disfavor. This was one of the proudest divisions of the United States Army—the division of Sergeant York, of General Wainwright, and of Lieutenant General John Lee—which had won distinction in both wars, matched by few other fighting units. Ironically, one of the reasons for liquidating it was that it had so many high-point men that it seemed simpler to disband it than to provide replacements. When its return to the States was scheduled for January 1946, New York City prepared to welcome it by what was predicted would be the biggest military parade since the end of the First World War. The Eighty-second was chosen for the victory parade, according to the War Department, because in the words of the New York *Times,* "it was felt that an airborne unit emphasizes the versatility of the common soldier, the modern-age American foot soldier."

Major General Gavin's Eighty-second Air-borne Division was given Belgium's red four-ragère military decoration on October 6, 1945, on the tenth received Holland's highest award, the orange cord of the Military Order of William, for its operations at Nijmegen the previous year. This is the second unit in Dutch history, and the first foreign unit ever to receive this honor. On the same occasion General Gavin was individually honored with the highest order which the Netherlands can confer, the Degree of Grand Officer with the Swords of the Order of Orange-Nassau. He is the first foreigner and the first person of non-royal blood to receive this order. Individual decorations were awarded to Gavin's men by the British, French, and Russian Gov-

GAVIN, JAMES M.—*Continued*

ernments, as well as three Congressional Medals of Honor, eighty Distinguished Service Crosses, nine hundred Silver Stars, fourteen hundred Bronze Stars, and ten thousand Purple Hearts.

While General Gavin speaks of himself as a comparatively uninteresting person, he cannot say too much or speak too highly of his pioneering paratroopers, whose training and combat technique are being studied by military experts everywhere: "The battle record of the Eighty-second is unique in our history for ground covered, losses sustained, continuous days in combat without relief, enemy killed, captured, and wounded, and over-all demonstrated eagerness and ability to destroy anything in the Wehrmacht." Gavin's coolness in jumping from planes was frequently the subject of comment among his men. Often, when he returned by plane from headquarters he would parachute to the ground rather than have the pilot land the plane. His quality of firmness is also well known. Any man under his command who did not "cut the mustard" was dropped from the unit. Tall and wiry Gavin, who looks more like a rugged Texan than a New Yorker, finds his chief peacetime recreation in athletics—tennis, handball, golf, and hunting. Married to Irma Margaret Baulair in September 1929, he has a daughter, Barbara Margaret.

GEIGER, ROY S(TANLEY) (gī′gēr)
Jan. 25, 1885- United States Marine Corps officer

Address: b. c/o Navy Department, Washington, D.C.; h. Box 98, Route 4, Pensacola, Fla.

In June 1945 the Headquarters of the United States Marine Corps, Department of the Navy, announced the appointment of Lieutenant General Roy S. Geiger, as Commanding General of the Fleet Marine Force in the Pacific. From the bloody battles in the Solomons to the invasion of Japan two and a half years later, General Geiger had led his amphibious marines with skillful planning and daring tactical leadership both on land and in the air. His record as aviator, graduate of the highest military schools of both the Army and the Navy, and combat veteran of two wars made him a "triple threat" to the Japanese.

Roy Stanley Geiger was born in Middleburg, Florida, on January 25, 1885, to Marion Francis and Josephine (Prevatt) Geiger. As a youth he was bent on becoming a lawyer, and after attending Florida State Normal School in Deland for four years (1900-4) he completed his studies at John B. Stetson University, where he received his LL.B. in 1907. At this point in his life Geiger made a sudden change in his plans. He enlisted in the United States Marine Corps on November 2, 1907, and a year and three months later, on February 5, 1909, he was appointed second lieutenant.

With platoons, companies, battalions, and on through the "chain of command," Geiger gained experience, training, and promotions. In 1912 he served in the first Nicaraguan campaign and was awarded a medal. He also

served in Cuba, Panama, the Philippines, China, and, following the First World War, in Haiti, and in the second Nicaraguan campaign, for which he received additional campaign awards.

When aviation had progressed far enough to become of military value, Geiger applied for training in flying. By 1916 he had completed the naval aviation course at Pensacola, Florida, becoming the fifth marine to receive his wings. With General Pershing in France, he flew on numerous bombing raids; and while serving with the First Marine Aviation Group he commanded Airplane Squadron No. 2, in recognition of which he was awarded the Navy Cross "for distinguished service in the line of his profession." (In 1916 he was married to Eunice Thompson; their two children are Joyce Renshaw and Roy Stanley.)

Returning from France, Geiger spent the 1920's as a military student and flier. He was graduated with distinction from the Command and General Staff School in 1925 and from the Army War College in 1929. In the interim he commanded aircraft squadrons in Haiti and at Quantico, Virginia. In 1930, when a hurricane struck Santo Domingo, Geiger was selected to pilot one of the three naval planes sent with medical supplies for the relief of the victims in that Republic. In April of the following year he flew on a similar mission to the victims of an earthquake at Managua, Nicaragua. In recognition of these flights he was awarded the Dominican Medal of Military Merit and the Nicaraguan Medal of Distinction.

The marine flier was appointed as Director of Aviation at Marine Corps Headquarters, where he served from 1931 until 1935. In 1940 Geiger completed the course of training at the Naval War College, and in 1941 the advanced course at the same school. He also attained his LL.D. in 1940 when he completed a postgraduate course in law. In May and June of 1941 he served as assistant naval attaché for air at the American Embassy in London and had an opportunity to observe the practical application of aviation in war. The following October he was appointed commanding general of the First Marine Aircraft Wing.

After Pearl Harbor and the first defeats the Americans suffered at the hands of the Japanese, the battle of Guadalcanal marked the turning point of the war in the Pacific. In the midst of this key campaign it was Major General Geiger who commanded the aviation units on that island from September 3, 1942 until November 4, 1942. Not content with commanding alone, Geiger proved to his airmen on one occasion that the much bombed airfield on the island was usable. Flying his own plane (at the age of fifty-seven) he took off with a 1,000-pound bomb which he dropped on a nearby Japanese headquarters, then returned to land his dive bomber on the pitted landing strip. During these operations the field was subjected to almost daily punishment, and on several occasions was the principal target for hostile naval gunfire and for harassment by shore-based artillery fire of the Japanese. Despite these conditions Geiger's men accounted for 286 enemy planes shot down, damage to a number estimated to be as great, destruction of twenty-three additional planes on the ground, the known sinking of six enemy ships including a heavy cruiser, the possible sinking of one other heavy cruiser and three destroyers, and damage to eighteen other ships. For his brilliant and daring leadership he was awarded a Gold Star in lieu of a second Navy Cross. "For extraordinary heroism and distinguished service . . . although personally endangered many times, [he] demonstrated a degree of fortitude and courage that served as an inspiration to all the officers and men under his command."

After Guadalcanal General Geiger was assigned to a tour of duty as Director, Marine Corps Aviation, and remained in that post until October 1943. He then returned to the fighting front which had shifted to Bougainville Island, where he succeeded Lieutenant General Alexander A. Vandegrift '43 as commander of the First Marine Amphibious Corps. From November 9 until December 15, 1943 Geiger pressed the attack. Despite difficult terrain, unfavorable weather, dense jungle, unhealthful climate, and fierce enemy resistance the First Corps seized and extended the important position on the west coast of Bougainville until necessary airfields could be constructed. "For exceptionally meritorious and distinguished service to the Government of the United States in a duty of great responsibility . . . due to his brilliant leadership, personal courage, and complete understanding of the task . . . skillful planning and daring tactical generalship displayed throughout this hazardous operation" Geiger was awarded the Distinguished Service Medal. A month and a half after marines had landed at Empress Augusta Bay, they were relieved by United States Army Forces under Lieutenant General Millard F. Harmon '42, December 15, 1943.

Elaborate preparations were under way to step up the tempo of the Pacific phase of the war. Two amphibious forces were organized. While one was engaged in a campaign the other was being supplied and trained for a new task. In July 1944 the two forces struck almost simultaneously, one against Tinian, while Major General Geiger led the other, the Third Marine Amphibious Corps, to Guam after the Americans had subjected that island to seventeen days of heavy bombing by carrier aircraft and a week of increasingly intensified shelling by all types of warship. By August 10 the island was secure. Signalizing the return of Guam to United States possession was the radio message received at Pearl Harbor, "This news is from Radio Guam. Nothing heard from you since 1941. Greetings." In a short time Guam became headquarters for the continued attack against Japan.

The following winter saw the consolidation of American gains in the Pacific, while Japanese island strongholds that had not been invaded were cut off from their supplies and rendered useless as a threat to continuing attacks by American forces. By the spring of 1945 an attack on the home islands of Japan was imminent; on the first of April the expected blow landed on Okinawa Island in the Ryukyu chain which extends south from the Japanese home islands. This was the largest amphibious assault in the Pacific, comprising the Tenth Army under Lieutenant General Simon Bolivar

U. S. Marine Corps

LT. GEN. ROY S. GEIGER

Buckner, Jr. '42, and supported by strong aerial and naval bombardment. Surprisingly, the initial resistance was light. The Twenty-fourth Army Corps after landing on the west coast of the island near the narrow waist in the middle pushed south against stiffening resistance. The Third Amphibious Marine Corps under General Geiger, who landed on the left of the Army Corps, drove north to secure the Ishikawa Isthmus, and found the going easy. As the favorable news continued to pour in on Geiger aboard ship, years seemed to drop from the General's shoulders and he grunted, "Looks good to poppa."

The strategy of the Japanese was a withdrawal to the southern extremity of the island, and between Naha, Shuri, and Yonabaru they had prepared elaborate defenses which stopped the initial assaults of the Army troops. In the north Geiger's marines mopped up the major portion of the mountainous Okinawa, and several of the near-by smaller islands. Soon after the completion of the drive in the north the marines were transferred to the southern front where the drive had been stalled before Naha. In this battle of attrition casualties were high. In the battle for Sugar Loaf Hill the marines were forced to retreat six times before they finally held this key to Naha. The high cost in dead to the enemy proved their eventual undoing, and after being driven back from their final defense line, they showed signs of weakening. General Buckner in a surprise move brought the Eighth Marine regimental combat team into the lines on the night of June 17-18, for an assault which began at dawn. With the attack, pressure was brought to bear all along the line and by late afternoon the beaches were reached. In the moment of final victory, General Buckner was killed by artillery fire. Succeeding to the command, General Geiger continued the attack to ultimate victory, and remained as head of the Tenth Army until relieved by Lieutenant General Joseph W. Stilwell '42. General Geiger's

GEIGER, ROY S.—*Continued*

formal appointment to General Bruckner's command gave him the distinction of being the first marine ever officially to head an army. He had in previous Pacific campaigns led combined Army and Marine Corps forces, notably at Bougainville when he won his D.S.M., and again at Guam when he was awarded a Gold Star in lieu of a second D.S.M. Subsequently he was awarded another Gold Star in lieu of a third D.S.M. for the invasion of the Palau Islands in 1944. In June 1945 Major General Geiger was promoted to lieutenant general and appointed by the Navy Department to the post of commanding general of the Fleet Marine Force in the Pacific, to succeed Lieutenant General Holland M. Smith '45.

Sixty-year-old, white-haired, stockily built General Geiger is one of the toughest men in a force known for its toughness. It is said that there is little that he does not know about aviation, that he is one of the best qualified officers in all three services for amphibious operations. A stickler for discipline, he has the "greatest respect for authority—and the greatest for his subordinates." And many anecdotes are told of his calmness. "Once, leading a formation into the teeth of a fierce tornado, Geiger received a message from a nervous Navy pilot: 'What about the storm?' Geiger's reply: 'Well, what about it?'" Among the peacetime pursuits he enjoys are golf, swimming, and poker.

References

Newsweek 20:21 D 21 '42 por
Time 42:65 N 22 '43 por

Who's Who in America, 1944-45

GEORGE, DAVID LLOYD, 1ST EARL LLOYD GEORGE OF DWYFOR *See* Lloyd George of Dwyfor, D. L. G., 1st Earl

GEROW, LEONARD TOWNSEND (jĕ-rō') July 13, 1888- United States Army officer

Address: b. c/o War Department, Washington, D.C.

The first commander of the United States Fifteenth Army, which went into action on the Western European front in March 1945 and for a time occupied the American zone of Germany, is known to his men as "General Gee," to his friends as Townsend, and to the newspapers as Lieutenant General Leonard T. Gerow. "Gerow" is a transliteration of Giraud, which was his Huguenot ancestors' name before they left France in the late sixteenhundreds to escape religious persecution.

Leonard Townsend Gerow was born July 13, 1888, to Leonard Rodgers and Eloise (Saunders) Gerow in Petersburg, Virginia; it was probably to avoid confusion with his father's name that the boy was called Townsend. He attended Virginia Military Institute, the private "West Point of the South," which includes among its graduates Stonewall Jackson and the future Chief of Staff of the United States Army, George C. Marshall '40. When Townsend Gerow was graduated in 1911 as honor man (he had been class president), his younger brother Lee, also a future general, still had two more years to go. On

his record, Townsend Gerow was appointed a second lieutenant of infantry in the United States Army that September, without examination.

Assigned to the Nineteenth Infantry Regiment at Fort Leavenworth, Kansas, Lieutenant Gerow began his service in January 1912, and accompanied his regiment to South Dakota, to Texas, and to Vera Cruz, Mexico. On his return to Texas, Gerow's work in the Galveston storm of August 1915 won him an official commendation. A year later he was promoted to first lieutenant and assigned to the Thirty-seventh Infantry, which got around in two years to five camps in Texas and one in New Mexico. Soon after the United States entered the First World War the Virginian was promoted to captain, and in April 1918 he sailed for France.

After two weeks of inspecting Signal Corps units in the field at Tours, Gerow was sent to Paris as assistant to the Signal Corps officer in charge of purchasing and disbursing, and soon became the officer in charge. Here he remained for the duration of the war, working with such "unusual ability and skill . . . tact, and energy," that he was rewarded with two temporary promotions, to major in June and lieutenant colonel in October; the Distinguished Service Medal; and the ribbon of a Chevalier of the French Legion of Honor. After the war the Colonel did equally well in disposing of the equipment he had purchased for the Army.

Returning to the United States in October 1919, Gerow spent a few days in the Office of the Chief Signal Officer. His next assignment was as commanding officer of the Signal Corps School at Fort Sam Houston, Texas. While there, on June 30, 1920, he reverted to his permanent rank of captain, and the following day was promoted to major. In February 1921 the future General was ordered to Washington for duty in the Office of the Chief of Infantry, and after two years became an assistant in the War Plans and Organization Section.

Leaving this post in September 1924, Gerow went to Fort Benning, Georgia, for the Infantry School's advanced course. Graduated in May 1925, he went right on to the Command and General Staff School in Kansas, from which he was graduated with honors in 1926. That August Major Gerow began a three-year tour of duty in the Office of the Assistant Secretary of War, as assistant executive officer. Then he enrolled at the Army War College, also in Washington, from which he was graduated in 1931. In addition to this highly advanced training, he took the field officer's course of the Chemical Warfare School at Edgewood Arsenal in Maryland, where he also served as assistant commandant.

After seven years behind various desks, Gerow was given a field assignment with the Thirty-first Infantry, serving in the Philippines and in the American Concession of Shanghai. The warring Japanese in China were inclined to be casual about respecting the rights of foreign nationals, but Gerow held them strictly to the letter of the law. In May 1934 he was appointed commander of Camp John Hay, in the Philippines, a post he held for seven months. In January 1935 he returned to the United States, and after completing an assignment at corps headquarters in

LT. GEN. LEONARD TOWNSEND GEROW

San Francisco and Atlanta, he entered the War Plans Division of the War Department General Staff. This was in April 1935. That August Gerow was promoted to lieutenant colonel, his first advancement of rank in fifteen years—a record typical of the under-budgeted United States Army between wars.

In May 1936 Colonel Gerow was appointed executive officer of the War Plans Division, a post he held until March 1939. Next he helped to develop the Army's tactical doctrine, as chairman of a special board with headquarters at Fort Benning. For a time he was also chief of staff of the Second ("Indian Head") Division. In July 1939 the fifty-one-year-old Colonel Townsend Gerow was married for the second time, to Mary Louise Kennedy of St. Paul, Minnesota, where the Gerows now have their home. They have no children. (The Colonel's first wife had been the former Mrs. Kathryn G. Urquhart of New York City.) During the May 1940 "war games," designed to prepare the newly expanded Army for the war its leaders felt to be inevitable, he was senior control officer with the sixty-five-thousand-man Third Army as it "fought flood and storm" in western Louisiana.

Assigned to the Infantry School as chief of section, Gerow served also as assistant commandant. In September 1940 he was promoted to colonel, and a month later appointed brigadier general (temporary). He was, therefore, a general officer long before such well-regarded leaders as Generals George S. Patton '43, Mark W. Clark '42, Carl "Tooey" Spaatz '42, and "Ike" Eisenhower '42. After two months with the Eighth Division at Fort Jackson, South Carolina, General Gerow was appointed acting assistant chief of staff in December 1940, and assigned to duty as chief of the War Plans Division of the General Staff. (His brother was also attached to the General Staff at that time.) Months before Pearl Harbor, President Roosevelt '42 instructed the War Department to work out strategic plans for the United States in case it should be drawn into the Second

World War; Gerow and his fellow officers labored long hours under high pressure to complete them.

Seventeen days after Pearl Harbor, Gerow was named assistant chief of staff, and continued to head the War Plans Division until February 1942, making "an invaluable contribution to our [United States] military effort through his foresight and sound planning." In a reorganization of the General Staff, Gerow was promoted to major general (temporary) and then replaced by a Brigadier General Dwight D. Eisenhower, who was described as "a recent associate of General Douglas MacArthur '41 in planning the defense of the Philippines." Gerow proceeded to Maryland to take command of the Twenty-ninth ("Blue and Gray") Infantry Division at Fort George Meade, Maryland. Here he was faced with serious shortages of personnel and equipment. ("You can't throw spitballs at the Germans and Japanese!" he is quoted as exclaiming on one occasion.) But with "tireless energy and rare acumen," Gerow "steadfastly held to his purpose of preparing his division for combat." The training was tough—Gerow believes in hard training to save lives—but morale was high. The General's work here and in the War Plans Division won him the Legion of Merit with the citation quoted above.

While the attention of the Western world was focused on the Mediterranean theater of war, General Gerow sailed for England, where he succeeded Brigadier General Russell P. Hartle as commander of United States field forces in the European theater. In July 1943 he was named commander of the Fifth Corps. At fifty-five he was one of the youngest generals appointed to a major command in the American ground forces. For eleven months Gerow displayed "great ability, energy, and initiative in the organization and training of the Fifth Corps for the amphibious assault on the European continent." Finally, on June 4, 1944, he embarked with his troops on Admiral Hall's amphibious flagship, which led the invasion fleet from Southampton to "Omaha Beach," the code name for the central Normandy beach on which Gerow was to land the first troops. "Next to Generals Eisenhower and Bradley '43," wrote correspondent Joseph Driscoll, "no American general on the Western front bore a heavier responsibility than Leonard Gerow. . . .One felt that he would be cool under any circumstances. He was a very quiet, unspectacular sort of person, with none of the color of a MacArthur or Patton.

"As commander of the Fifth Corps, it was Gerow's task to land the first troops on Omaha Beach and keep them moving toward Isigny and Carentan, the preliminary objectives. Nowadays [1945], when we have many corps on the Western front and scores of divisions, it is interesting to recall that Gerow had to accomplish his mission with two divisions [totaling perhaps twenty or thirty thousand men]." These were the famous old First Division, led by General Clarence Huebner, who had succeeded "Terrible Terry" Allen '43, and Gerow's old Twenty-ninth, led by General Charles H. Gerhardt. "General Huebner's First Division was to move in on the left," Driscoll continues, "and General Gerhardt's Twenty-ninth Division toward the right. The battle-tried First Division was handed the

GEROW, LEONARD TOWNSEND—
Continued

tougher mission, while the inexperienced Twenty-ninth had some marshlands as a natural bulwark against the Germans if the latter counterattacked to drive the Americans back into the sea. As it turned out, the Germans failed to counterattack, and, moreover, the well-trained Twenty-ninth demonstrated that even without previous battle testing our troops are able to more than hold their own."

Says the citation for Gerow's Oak Leaf Cluster (awarded in lieu of a second D.S.M.) : "On June 6, 1944, he brilliantly executed his plan of attack against the heavily fortified beaches, which were defended by strong and well-placed enemy forces. Under withering fire, sustained only by unlimited stamina and gallant leadership, his troops swept across the beach, overwhelming all opposition, and secured a firm lodgment from which further operations were launched." These further operations constituted the drive along the flooded, marshy Cherbourg peninsula, which Gerow planned and executed, and which made possible that city's liberation by the Seventh Corps under Major General J. Lawton Collins three weeks later.

General Gerow's First Army corps, in which the Second Division had also been identified, took part in the battle for Paris, along with Canadians, the famous French Second Armored Division, and the French Forces of the Interior. Gerow himself was the first American general to re-enter the capital, and was soon installed in Marshal Pétain's [40] old office, where he turned over military control of the city to French General Jacques-Philippe Leclerc [44]. On August 25 he was present in the Montparnasse railroad station as Leclerc and German General Dietrich von Choltitz signed the Nazi garrison's unconditional surrender order, an hour before General de Gaulle [40] entered Paris in triumph. (The North American troops in Paris were tactfully bivouacked near the city gates, letting the Frenchmen have the glory.)

First Army units continued their advance, crossing the historic Maas (Meuse) River six days later and reaching Belgium on the first of September, freeing Sedan on the 7th and Luxembourg on the 10th, while its spearheads pushed into Germany and breached the Siegfried Line on the 15th. In early October 1944 the First Army began its attack on Aachen (Aix-la-Chapelle), which was defended from street to street and from house to house, and which was finally cleared of German soldiers on the 21st. By November, when General William H. Simpson's [45] new United States Ninth Army swung into line between Sir Miles Dempsey's [44] British Second and the American First Army of General Courtney Hodges [41], Bradley's successor, they were opposite the northern section of the Siegfried Line, north of Aachen.

The First and Ninth joined in the battle of the Cologne plain against a background of snow, quagmiry mud, and almost unceasing rain. The German radio called this battle for the industrial Ruhr and Saar valleys "the most terrible and most ferocious in the history of all wars," and the New York *Times* described it as "fighting of unprecedented heat. . .enormous pressure against utmost resistance. . . white-hot war of attrition eating into the strength of both sides." The First Army continued to push on grimly, operating south of the Ninth. It joined with the other Allied armies in the Ardennes sector to beat back the powerful German counteroffensive which opened December 16 and proceeded unchecked for twelve days to form the so-called "Belgian bulge" in the Allied lines. At the beginning of January 1945 the Americans launched their own counteroffensive, and on January 12 the Germans began the retreat from their hundred-square-mile salient.

In January the President nominated Leonard Townsend Gerow for temporary promotion to lieutenant general, which was approved in February; and in March SHAEF announced that he had been succeeded in command of the Fifth Corps by Huebner. "I would have gone with them to hell or Berlin, were they ordered," said Gerow; but the General was ordered instead to form a new army of American soldiers who had debarked in Europe "anywhere from several months to two or three days" earlier, and he told reporters that he would cut through red tape to do so. With the activation of this new Fifteenth Army, commentators pointed out, General Bradley had in his Twelfth Army Group more than a million combat troops, more than any general in modern history had ever had under one field command. The Fifteenth's existence was announced at ceremonies in which General Gerow and seven other American generals were decorated, he with the rosette of Commander of the French Legion of Honor. Bradley, Gerow, and corps commander Collins had previously been decorated by Russia for their part in the Normandy campaign. They saw some heavy fighting before V-E Day, after which SHAEF assigned them to the American sector of Germany as the Army of Occupation. There Gerow was lauded by the Fifteenth as a writer of "the most beautiful prose," when he issued the order: "Pull your GI's off K.P. duty. . . . Let your men sit at table and let the Germans wait on them." In July the Fifteenth Army Group turned its sector over to the French, leaving itself wtihout a job. General Gerow was named president general of a board of American officers appointed by General Eisenhower to make a detailed study of the whole European war, with headquarters in Washington.

Near the close of the year Gerow appeared before the Congressional Committee Investigating Pearl Harbor. As chief of the War Plans Division in 1941 it had been his responsibility to inquire into the Hawaiian defenses. Concerning this, he told the Committee, he accepted full blame for the failure to realize, in November 1941, that Hawaii was not fully alerted against Japanese attack. "If there is any responsibility in the War Department for failure to make inquiry [as to Major General Walter C. Short's defense preparations]I accept that responsibility."

Although stern, "serious and almost retiring," brown-haired Townsend Gerow is described as "a man of intense energy." For recreation he likes hunting, fishing, and an occasional inexpert game of golf after Episcopal services on Sunday. According to Gault MacGowan [45] in the New York *Sun*, Gerow "has even sped up his native Southern drawl"; he has "personality-plus as a leader" and "a quick expressive turn of phrase which quickly endeared him to his new command."

References

N Y Herald Tribune p1+ Mr 10 '45
N Y Sun p26 Mr 7 '45; p4 Mr 13 '45
N Y Times p4 Mr 10 '45 por
Who's Who in America, 1944-45

GIBSON, CHARLES DANA Sept. 14, 1867—Dec. 29, 1944 Widely known American artist; won recognition in the early 'nineties with his creation the "Gibson Girl," a drawing which swept into public favor and greatly influenced fashions and the publication world; he gained prestige also for his paintings in oil.

Obituary

N Y Times p26 D 30 '44 por

GIFFORD, WALTER S(HERMAN) Jan. 10, 1885- Corporation executive

Address: b. American Telephone and Telegraph Co., 195 Broadway, New York City; h. 111 E. 70th St., New York City

The American Telephone and Telegraph Company is the largest single corporate body in the entire world. Its stockholders number 680,000, and its investment is estimated at $5,400,000,000. Heading this giant enterprise is Walter S. Gifford, who became its president in 1925, when he was only forty years old.

Walter Sherman Gifford, the son of Nathan Poole and Harriet Maria (Spinney) Gifford, was born in Salem, Massachusetts, on January 10, 1885. As a boy he did not participate in rough, competitive games, but spent much of his time with books and his hobby of collecting butterflies. His collection was "the epitome of the boy, just as his subsequent attainments are the epitome of the man," a *Literary Digest* article once pointed out. He did not gather butterflies haphazardly, in the usual manner of boys. "He wanted only the best and rarest specimens." Each was mounted and classified with its Latin name, as well as its complete history, which the young collector memorized.

Walter Gifford was fifteen years old when he completed high school. At sixteen he was enrolled at Harvard, and he was graduated three years later with a B.A. degree. While mathematics did not interest him particularly, the career of engineering did appeal to him, but his parents were not in a position to make further study possible. Young Gifford was therefore obliged to seek employment at the age of nineteen. Convinced that individual talent would be recognized in a big corporation, where the most active business minds were centered, the youth wrote two letters of application for a position—one to General Electric Company and the other to the Western Electric Company. "At this point," states French Strother in *World's Work*, "sheer chance enters the story. By accident he [Gifford] put the letter addressed to the General Electric Company into the envelope addressed to Western Electric. . . .Possibly the oddity of the

WALTER S. GIFFORD

mistake caused his letters to get more than usual attention when they were read. In any event, he got an offer from the Western Electric Company, and accepted." The job was in the payroll department and the salary about ten dollars a week. Young Gifford forgot his earlier indifference to mathematics and applied himself to the study of figures. He was soon promoted to assistant secretary and assistant treasurer, a dual post he held for three years (1905-8).

Not long thereafter the late Theodore N. Vail, then president of the Bell Telephone System of which Western Electric was a subsidiary, was greatly impressed by the graphic charts someone was using to supply information which he had requested from Western Electric. When it was brought to his attention that young Gifford was responsible for the organization of the facts, Vail offered him the newly created post of chief statistician of the American Telephone and Telegraph Company (of which the Bell System is a subsidiary). Vail had realized that here was not only "a device for preparing statistical information in a form of the utmost value to a busy executive," but also a capable young person with an original mind. Gifford spent the next five years (1911-16) as chief statistician in gathering facts for the use of the executives of A.T.& T. These facts were so presented that they were regarded as "essential to the decisions of questions of current management and of the problem of future expansion."

Early in 1916, when the First World War drew closer to America's shores, Gifford was called to Washington to become the supervising director of the Committee on Industrial Preparedness of the Naval Consulting Board. His task was "to prepare a statistical analysis of twenty-seven thousand manufacturing concerns whose facilities could be utilized in the national defense." The whole program was carried out with such skill that Gifford found himself with a new important assignment when the Council of National Defense was created

GIFFORD, WALTER S.—*Continued*

by Congress in December 1916. Gifford was made its director.

His task for the next two years was to assist in the subordination of productive enterprise "to the grand scheme of production of war materials." At the same time Congress authorized an advisory committee to the Defense Council, to which Gifford was also assigned as director. The Council itself consisted of Cabinet members, while the advisory committee consisted of representatives of industry and business generally. As the war drew closer, the Council created the Munitions Board on February 28, 1917. The following year, from July to September, Gifford represented the United States Government in Paris as secretary of the American section of the Inter-Allied Munitions Council. In October 1918 Vail wrote to Newton D. Baker, Secretary of War, requesting Gifford's release for the performance of urgently needed work for the telephone company. Gifford was accordingly released a month later, and upon his return to the A.T.& T. he was vice-president for four years, until 1923, when he became executive vice-president, serving for two years. In January 1925, a few days after his fortieth birthday, Gifford was elected the president of the American Telephone and Telegraph Company.

The famous "Telephone Investigation" by the Government was begun when Gifford had been president of the A.T.& T. about ten years. From time to time some Congressmen had suggested that the American Telephone and Telegraph Company, "the world's biggest monopoly," be investigated; but it was not until 1934, when the Federal Communications Commission was created, that Congress authorized a thoroughgoing study of the company. In his work *American Tel & Tel* (1939), Horace Coon summarizes the investigation: "Telephone officials say that the investigators were looking for loot and found none. Probably no corporation was ever asked so many questions by Government inquirers as was the A.T. & T. The company's files and correspondence were examined and significant portions quoted at length in the seventy-seven staff reports. The investigation was said to have cost the Government $2,000,000 and the A.T. & T. $1,500,-000." A preliminary report, by Paul A. Walker, was made public in April 1938, and his final report was issued about a year later. (The first report was not subscribed to by other members of the FCC. All members, however, approved the final report, which was then sent to Congress with recommendations for future regulation of the telephone industry.) "The A.T. & T. answered Mr. Walker's report with a 'Brief,' giving its reasons why the proposed report should not be adopted. However, it was accepted in principle and in substance." There were several general points of attack made by Walker. He criticized the company's methods of figuring depreciation, asserted that the telephone rates could be reduced without interfering with the standard of service, that the company had evaded effective State regulation, and that it was "treated as a unit for purposes of profit, and as a group of separate corporate entities for purposes of regulation."

Gifford replied that the investigation had been one-sided from the start: "We were denied not only the right to cross-examine investigation witnesses and to be heard in our own behalf, but also we were denied the right to have included in the record written material which we had prepared and considered necessary to point out serious and important errors affecting most of the investigators' reports. It became obvious that the telephone company's side of the story had not been told in the Walker report, and it became equally clear that the telephone company's story must be given thorough and fair-minded consideration in any discussion of the Walker criticisms."

In the preface to his book *A.T. & T.* (1939), N. R. Danielian replied to Gifford's criticism by pointing out that a Congressional investigation does not include a legal right of cross-examination. While two reviewers considered Danielian's work a penetrating study, another critic found it too full of biases to be favorably compared with Ida Tarbell's "poised and objective study" of the Standard Oil Company. Coon's book was judged not so scholarly as Danielian's, and its neutrality was both praised and condemned.

When war again threatened the United States, in 1939 Gifford became a member of the War Resources Board; and in 1941 he was made chairman of the Industry Advisory Committee of the Board of War Communications and a member of the executive committee of the New York State War Savings Commission. Active in the War Loan drives, he has also served as national chairman of the American Red Cross War Fund campaign. He heads the board of directors of the Greater New York Fund, which raised more than four and one-half million dollars in 1944, and he is chairman of the board of the Community Service Society, the largest private family welfare agency in the United States.

The Second World War greatly curtailed the expansion of the telephone company's installations for civilian needs: in the fall of 1944 Gifford announced that only one-third of the demands could be filled. In 1944, too, organized labor, for the first time in corporate history, made an attempt at the annual meeting of A. T. & T. stockholders to obtain direct representation on the company's board of directors. The attempt failed and union representatives' resolutions asking for revision of the pension system and for a halt of the sale of telegraph equipment to the Western Union Telegraph Company were voted down. The year before, on January 20, 1943, A.T. & T. agreed to lower its long distance telephone rate and to reduce its long line revenues by more than fifty million dollars per year.

The telephone executive has occupied a number of governmental posts during peacetime. In the winter of 1931-32 he directed President Hoover's '43 Organization on Unemployment Relief. He was a member of the Banking and Industrial Committee of the Second Federal Reserve District (1932), and of the Business Advisory Council for the Department of Commerce (1933-35). He has several business interests outside of A.T. & T. During the years from 1929 to 1939 Gifford was a member of the board of directors of the United States Steel Corporation, and he is also a director of the First National Bank of New York.

Numerous educational and philanthropic bodies engage Gifford's attention, too. In the first group, he is trustee of the New York School of Social Work, Johns Hopkins University, Cooper Union, General Education Board, Rockefeller Foundation, and the Carnegie Institution of Washington, D. C., and an overseer of Harvard University. In addition he is chairman of the lay council of the New York Academy of Medicine. Several universities have bestowed honorary degrees upon Gifford: Williams College an LL.D. in 1928; Colgate College the same degree in 1929; Oberlin College a D.Sc. in 1929; Union College a D.C.L. in 1939. He is a Fellow of the American Association for the Advancement of Science and of the American Statistical Association; a Gold Medalist of the National Institute of Social Science; and the third person to receive the Vermilye Medal of the Franklin Institute (1943), awarded every two years to a notable exponent of industrial management. In the fall of 1944 he announced that his own company had established a trust fund to finance five annual post-doctorate fellowships in physical science, the awards to be known as the Frank B. Jewett fellowships in honor of the president of the National Academy of Sciences and vice-president of A.T. & T.

A few magazine articles have been written by Gifford: "Does Business Want Scholars" (1928), "Pensions, Charity, and Old Age" (1930), "Can Prosperity Be Managed" (1930). In the second he set forth his objections to state old-age pensions; and a few years later, with the advent of the New Deal, he opposed the projected Communications Bill, holding that it would mean Government management rather than Government regulation of the country's communication services. A considerably modified Bill was finally passed. A champion of free enterprise, he has declared that it was the "basic privilege" upon which other freedoms would depend in the postwar era.

Gifford is described as "largish and strong;" in complexion sandy, hair thinning and graying; and he wears a small mustache. In 1916 he was married to Florence Pitman, now deceased. Their eldest son, Walter Sherman, a naval officer, was killed in the South Pacific in the summer of 1944. Another son, Richard Pitman, was also on active duty in the Navy during the war. On December 22, 1944, Gifford was married to Mrs. Augustine Lloyd Perry.

References

> Banking 34:75 F '42 por
> Bsns W 26+ S 9 '31 por
> Lit Digest 121:38 Ap 4 '36 por
> World's Work 52:164-5 Je '26
> National Cyclopædia of American Biography Current vol E p10
> Who's Who in America, 1944-45
> Who's Who in Commerce and Industry (1944)

GILDER, ROSAMOND Magazine editor; drama critic

Address: b. Theatre Arts, 130 W. 56th St., New York City; h. 24 Gramercy Park, New York City

Rosamond Gilder, the editor of *Theatre Arts,* "the international magazine of the theater," has devoted most of her adult life to writing about the theater and its people. Her articles,

Vandamm Studio

ROSAMOND GILDER

described as "scholarly, meticulous, and faintly romantic," have been an important part of the magazine for nearly twenty years; and one of her books, *John Gielgud's Hamlet,* has been recommended to all teachers and future producers of Shakespeare.

Born at her family's summer home in Marion, Massachusetts, Rosamond Gilder has lived in New York City all her life. Her father, Richard Watson Gilder, poet and editor, had begun his long editorial career in 1870 when he joined the staff of *Scribner's* as associate editor. When the magazine became the *Century* in 1881, he continued as editor, a post he held until his death in 1909. Miss Gilder's mother, Helena (de Kay) Gilder, was an artist and one of New York's best-known hostesses during the nineties. The child received a rich cultural heritage from others in her family, too, for her father's sister, Jeanette Leonard Gilder, was co-founder of the *Critic* and its editor from 1881 to 1906; and her uncles, William Henry Gilder and Joseph B. Gilder were well-known journalists.

In their home on East Eighth Street, the Gilders entertained the outstanding artists and literary figures of the day. With such notables as Walt Whitman, Henry James, Paderewski, and Eleanora Duse as Friday evening guests, the five Gilder children, of whom Rosamond was the youngest, grew up in a stimulating atmosphere. On the other hand, the girl's early formal education did not completely follow the pattern expected of the daughter of one in the Gilder's social position, for she received her first schooling at Public School No. 41. From there, however, she went to the fashionable Brearley day school, where she attended classes for two years. She was then forced to end her school days because of ill health, although she was graduated with her class. She and her family had withdrawn from the social limelight following Richard Gilder's death, but soon afterward Rosamond herself, enlisting the aid of her older sisters, began to entertain young

GILDER, ROSAMOND—*Continued*

people at Sunday night dances in the Gramercy Park apartment to which the Gilders had moved before the editor died.

In 1916 Miss Gilder made her first appearance in print, with a biography of her father which she had begun shortly after his death. The volume consists of a collection of Gilder's letters, for which his daughter had supplied the continuity. A year later, when the United States entered the war, she was on her way to France on a three-month assignment as confidential secretary to William Palmer Lucas, head of the Children's Bureau of the Red Cross. (Mrs. Lucas had been Miss Gilder's history teacher at Brearley.) Although her only qualification for the position was her knowledge of French, Miss Gilder remained in Paris for two years as executive secretary of the bureau. For her services the French Government awarded her the Médaille de Reconnaissance and the Médaille d'Epidemie.

Miss Gilder's first literary attempt after she returned from France was a translation of *My Life,* the autobiography of Emma Calvé. It was serialized in the *Saturday Evening Post* in 1922, and that same year the translation was published in book form. Two years later, in 1924, Miss Gilder went to work for *Theatre Arts Monthly* as a proofreader, substituting for a friend who was ill with the mumps. *Theatre Arts Monthly* had been established by Sheldon Cheney in Detroit in August 1916. When its office was moved to New York less than two years later, the magazine was without funds, but its purposes—"to represent all of the arts that go to the making of real theater" and to become "doubly international, in its content and subscribers"—were firmly established in the minds of its editors, who believed the theater to be "not only the most democratic, but the most international and illuminating of all arts." Miss Gilder's temporary position lengthened into twenty-one years of service as associate editor, in which capacity she wrote articles on all phases of the theater. (Edith J. R. Isaacs undertook the conduct of the magazine upon its removal to New York and has been its editor and publisher ever since.)

During the years 1932 through 1935 Miss Gilder was actively interested in the development of the little theater movement, giving much of her time to her duties as editorial secretary of the National Theater Conference. In 1935, when this organization became the basis for Hallie Flanagan's Federal Theater Plan, Miss Gilder left *Theatre Arts Monthly* to work on the Government project. After six months as director of the Bureau of Research and Publication (the Playwright's Bureau), she resigned from her WPA job. Returning to *Theatre Arts Monthly,* she resumed her position as associate editor. In 1938, upon the illness of Mrs. Isaacs, Miss Gilder assumed the additional responsibilities of drama critic, for which her apprenticeship years had prepared her. Her approach to the stage has been analyzed as scholarly. She evaluates a play on the basis of how it accomplishes its purposes, giving her readers an understanding of the play rather than a dogmatic opinion. Finally, in 1945, she became editor in chief of *Theatre Arts.* (In November 1939 the "Monthly" was dropped from the title.)

Besides reviewing plays, Miss Gilder has written many articles for the magazine on the theater, its personalities, history, and achievements. "La Nostalgilder, Some Letters of Eleanora Duse" appeared in *Theatre Arts* in 1926. The letters were written by the famous actress to Miss Gilder's mother, and in them La Duse used the word "nostalgilder," which she had coined to describe her feelings when she was separated from the Gilders. Some of Miss Gilder's other articles are "The American Theatre, 1916-1941," a brief history of the theater which she wrote for the twenty-fifth anniversary edition of the magazine; "The Fabulous Hart"; "The Federal Theatre, a Record," which was based on her experience with that agency; "Joseph Jefferson," a discussion of the noted portrayer of Rip Van Winkle; "Musical Comedy Between the Wars," an evaluation of that type of production; "An International Theatre: Made in America"; and "Theatre in the War Years."

The editor-critic's writing has not been limited to articles for *Theatre Arts,* although she remains within her main sphere of interests. Her book *Enter the Actress, First Women in the Theatre,* which was published in 1931, is composed of biographical sketches. The book is also a history of the part women have taken in the development of the dramatic art, for Miss Gilder highlights those women who have been innovators in their fields, tracing them as far back as Hrotsvitha, a tenth century nun credited with being the first feminine playwright. Miss Gilder was criticized by some for the omission of one or two actresses, but all critics agreed that the book was a valuable addition to the theatrical library. Her next two books were bibliographies published by Theatre Arts, Inc., which issues only those books considered essential to the field: *A Theatre Library, a Bibliography of One Hundred Books Relating to the Theatre* was published in 1932, and *Theatre Collections in Libraries and Museums, an International Handbook,* on which Miss Gilder collaborated with George Freedley, came out in 1936.

A year later Miss Gilder's *John Gielgud's Hamlet, a Record of Performance* appeared. The book includes the version of the play which Gielgud used and a description of every speech and movement made by the actor during the performance. It also includes some of Gielgud's notes on costumes, scenery, and stage business. In order to achieve what the critics considered a complete and invaluable record, Miss Gilder saw Gielgud's portrayal of Hamlet more than thirty times. During an interview with the actor she accepted his prompt book, but refused his offer of his personal notes on the characterization, because she felt that her study should be made entirely from the point of view of the audience.

Miss Gilder's activities, exclusive of *Theatre Arts,* have included her service as secretary to the American National Theatre and Academy, and to the New York Drama Critics Circle, of which she was once the only woman member. She has been a member of the board of governors of the Cosmopolitan Club (to which she still belongs) from 1925 through 1933, and president during the year 1932-33. She has overcome a phobia for public speaking, and her conversation is described as brilliant and witty, "but never at the expense of true scholarship. She is serious but not unduly academic; she has wit but no wisecracks. Her attack is so open and so gay that it is difficult to realize that she is really a shy person."

Five feet two inches tall, with brown hair and eyes, Miss Gilder has never allowed any ill health to interfere with her career as it did with her education. She budgets her strength carefully, seeming all the while to have much energy. She still lives at the Gramercy Park address (in a smaller apartment), where she entertains in the Gilder tradition, even borrowing the old apartment from her sister when the parties are too large for her own limited space. Her nieces and nephews are given the privilege of helping at many of her parties. She satisfies her love for gardening and sunbathing at the family farm in Tyringham, Massachusetts, and, although she professes to dislike writing, she spends five hours a day working at it even in the country.

References

Pub W 139:134-5 Ja 11 '41 por
American Women, 1939-41
Who's Who in America, 1944-45
Who's Who in the Theatre (1939)

GODDARD, ROBERT H(UTCHINGS) (gŏd′ẽrd) Oct. 5, 1882—Aug. 10, 1945 American physicist; internationally known pioneer in rocket propulsion; served as chief of Navy research on jet-propelled planes during war; was considered one of Nation's leading research workers in his field.

Obituary

N Y Times p13 Ag 11 '45 por

GOOSSENS, EUGENE (gōō′s′nz) May 26, 1893- Conductor; composer; violinist
Address: b. American Bldg., Cincinnati, Ohio

Eugene Goossens, conductor of the Cincinnati Symphony Orchestra, is not only one of the world's most important conductors, but a violinist, and a composer of note—"a musical personality of international repute." In England, his native land, he is considered "the bright and particular star of English contemporary composers," and since coming to America in 1923 he has not only succeeded in sustaining his Continental reputation, but has established himself securely in the "American way." He has entered wholeheartedly into the cause of the American composer, and has shown a special interest in the musical education of the younger generation.

One could scarcely picture Eugene Goossens as anything but an artist, for his father and his grandfather before him were well known conductors; thus, it is not surprising that as the most brilliant of the three he should possess an unusual array of musical gifts. He was born in London on May 26, 1893, of Belgian ancestry. Eugène seems to have been a favorite family name, since his father and his father's father bore the same name. Both were widely known in European musical circles and at different periods held the position of conductor with the Carl Rosa Opera Company. His grandfather conducted the first performance in England of Wagner's *Tannhäuser*. Goossens' mother also

EUGENE GOOSSENS

had something to contribute to his genius, for she was the former Annie Cook, daughter of Aynsley Cook, the operatic basso. In his immediate family the gift of musicianship was not confined to Eugene, for his younger brother Leon is a world-famous oboist, and two of his sisters play the harp, Marie being a member of the Royal Philharmonic Orchestra. His brother Adolphe also became a well known musician.

Eugene Goossens began his musical education at the Bruges Conservatoire. Later he entered the Liverpool College of Music, where in 1907 he won the scholarship that brought him to the Royal College of Music in London. Here he continued his studies—the violin under Serge Rivarde, composition with Sir Charles Stanford—graduating in 1911. The young musician began his professional career as a violinist with the Queen's Hall Orchestra, under the baton of Sir Henry Wood.

Goossens' progress from the violinist's chair to the podium was rapid, and it was not long before he was conducting regularly at the Drury Lane and Aldwych theaters, and in the provinces. He was now also composing prolifically. Once a year for a number of years he conducted one of his own compositions with the Queen's Hall Orchestra, and it is apparent that the first big opportunity of his career stemmed from the success of these performances. In 1915 he was invited by Sir Thomas Beecham to conduct a performance of Sir Charles Villiers Stanford's opera *The Critic*, an engagement which he fulfilled so well that he was chosen Sir Thomas' assistant, a position which he held until 1920. At the same time he became a familiar figure in Continental musical circles, accepting many invitations to conduct leading European orchestras. During this period he also conducted the Handel Society in London and the Royal Choral Society, at that time the largest choral society in England. From 1919 to 1923 he directed the Symphony Orchestra of the Diaghilev Ballet. In one of

GOOSSENS, EUGENE—*Continued*

those years (1921) he organized his own orchestra and gave concerts devoted to modern music, and in 1922 he conducted the Russian Ballet and opera performances at Covent Garden. "His work showed such remarkable musical insight and interpretive talent," writes David Ewen, "that he immediately impressed the English music world as a conductor of the first importance."

Goossens' reputation had preceded him to America. On his arrival in 1923 as conductor of the Rochester Philharmonic Orchestra, on the invitation of the Eastman School of Music (the parent body), he was commissioned by the Berkshire Festival authorities to write a string sextet. He remained for eight years in his Rochester post and was active also as a member of the faculty of the Eastman School of Music, teaching a class in conducting. He left Rochester in 1931 to succeed Fritz Reiner [41] as conductor of the Cincinnati Symphony Orchestra, a position which he still holds.

Goossens' activities in Cincinnati are not confined to the regular concerts of the Cincinnati orchestra, for the Cincinnati Orchestral Association Company also sponsors a series of young people's concerts, which include performances of opera. The leading roles in these operas, conducted by Goossens, have usually been sung by members of the Metropolitan Opera Company, supported by the Cincinnati Symphony Chorus. Whenever possible, the operas have been sung in English to increase their appeal to the music appreciation classes in the local schools.

Since coming to America Goossens has appeared as guest conductor with leading orchestras in the United States, including the Philadelphia, San Francisco, and Boston symphony orchestras, and the New York Philharmonic, with which he was a guest conductor during its centennial season in 1941. It was in that same year that he made his debut at New York's Lewisohn Stadium, with Mischa Elman as soloist. This was the first of a series of ten concerts for which he had been engaged.

It is interesting to note that Goossens, whose opinion of American composition up to this point had not been especially favorable, after careful scrutiny of many American scores composed over a period of years, selected five for inclusion in his Stadium concerts. His own words appearing in the New York *Times* of June 29, 1941, convey his attitude toward the rapid development of musical composition in America: "For how many years have we conductors prayed for a Grant Wood [40], a Steinbeck [40], or an O'Neill of American music? Our prayers are finally being answered. Imagine ten years ago my including five American works in a group of ten concerts, as I am doing in my series . . . at the Lewisohn Stadium!"

In an article in *Musician* of December 1927, Goossens has given his own analysis of the conducting art: "Conducting depends first and foremost on something that cannot be taught, an innate capacity to inspire players with personal thought and feeling," he writes. "Great conductors like Richter and Nikisch, under whose batons I played in early days, were not only superb musicians, but brought to their work a personality not to be acquired through teaching." According to more than one authority, Goossens himself possesses to a large degree this power to inspire his musicians.

A. Eagleford Hull has summarized Goossens' conducting art in a brief sentence: "For keenness, enthusiasm, sensitiveness, and sweet sanity, he is unsurpassed." Following Goossens' New York debut in 1926, Olin Downes [43] pronounced him "a definite personality" with "contagious enthusiasm." And he said, in referring to his reading of Stravinsky's [40] *Le Sacre du Printemps*, "He gave one of the clearest and most broadly effective interpretations of the score that has been heard here. . . .It was this performance that promised in him a new arrival with something of his own to say."

As a composer Eugene Goossens also ranks high, being considered one of the leaders of the contemporary British school. He has created music in every form, including opera, ballet, concerto, symphony, choral, and the various forms of chamber music. Ranking high among his compositions are his operas, *Judith* (1925) and *Don Juan de Mañara*. The latter was composed and given its first London performance in 1937, with Lawrence Tibbett [45] in the title role. (The libretto for this opera was written by Arnold Bennett.) *Newsweek*'s account of the première of the opera stated that Tibbett, "as the murdering, seducing, miracle-instigating Don . . . had to do some vocal gymnastics among Goossens' chromatic pitfalls and ever-changing rhythms. . . .In many instances he [Goossens] employed the human voice almost as if it were one of the musical instruments." Of the opera *Judith,* conceded by the majority of critics to represent Goossens' best work, Percy Grainger has said, "An amazing compositional and orchestral virtuosity pervades the score of *Judith*. Only a keen, vigorous mind could have conceived this music; in the main somewhat unbending in its extreme austerity and preciseness, though flowering forth occasionally into brief moments of luscious sensuousness."

In another analysis of Goossens as a composer, Oscar Thompson, in *Music and Musicians*, has written, "In his instrumental music, both for orchestra and for chamber combinations, he shows experimental tendencies united to a constant desire for formal perfection along semiclassical lines. There is also a marked element of humor in some of his music. His idiom is predominantly chromatic." Hull says that the best way to get acquainted with Goossens' music is through his piano pieces. The four contributions which "roughly correspond to the chief phases of his musical evolution are *Concert Study* (1915), the brilliant legerdemain stage; *Kaleidoscope* (1917-18), the French phase; *Nature Poems* (1919), the Stravinskian phase; and *Hommage à Debussy* (1920), a postimpressionist admiration of the great leader of French musical impressionism." Hull continues: "A love of other arts besides his own special one has kept him keenly alive to modern movements, and a genial and generous nature has enabled him to make the best of his operatic and orchestral experience in this much underrated land of ours, where others would have succumbed."

In criticism of the first New York performance (1941) of Goossens' Symphony No. 1, Opus 58, Olin Downes commented: "While his harmony is modern, and while his orchestration, formal procedure, and all that, can be described by the same term, the symphony is actually old-fashioned, conventional in spite of its advanced style, and not individual in invention." F. Bonavia, reviewing the first London performance of this work during the Promenade concert season two years later, wrote for the New York *Times*: "Perhaps the most ambitious of contemporary English works was the Symphony No. 1 of Eugene Goossens, whose performance had aroused expectations in those who remember his early essays and the hopes that their promise had kindled. Unfortunately the new symphony . . . aroused hopes only to disappoint them. His musicianship is never in question. He is a master of modern methods; his form, his color, his ingenious harmonic combinations proclaim great abilities, and his sense of rhythm is infinitely more intriguing than that of the composer who spends his time in whittling and dividing minute subdivisions. . . .What is missing . . . is the great theme, 'the *idée mère.'* "

In *Composers of Today* David Ewen comments on the reception which Goossens' earliest compositions received. The composer's "unorthodox style—his confusing rhythms, his sharp-pointed dissonances, and his strange melodic lines—puzzled the audience, but there were a few who could recognize the talent that flashed through these early works [two trios performed in the First World War period]. Since coming to this country [the United States] Goossens . . . has asserted himself as one of the most brilliant of modern English composers." The conductor-composer has made several wax transcriptions for posterity. Among these are his interpretation of Ravel's *Le Gibet* and the "Danse" from Debussy's two-piano suite *En blanc et noir*. Among the more important recordings of his own works is the ballet music from the opera *Judith*.

Eugene Goossens is deeply interested in the development of music among children, as evidenced by his frequent appearance with children's choruses. In an article by him appearing in November 1928 in the *Musician*, he said, "There is every reason to hope much from the reaction of children to music—indeed from the reaction of the child to all beauty and art, provided this contact is not subject to too much disciplinary interference."

In the summer of 1942, desiring to do something for the war effort, Goossens wrote to twenty-six composers asking for instrumental flourishes known as "fanfares," in which the spirit of the times would be represented. Nineteen responded. Six of the commissioned fanfares—those by Morton Gould, Henry Cowell, Paul Creston, Felix Borowski, Leo Sowerby, and Goossens himself (his *Fanfare for the Merchant Marine*)—were played by the National Broadcasting Company Orchestra in six weekly broadcasts of *Music at War*.

"Last summer," wrote the New York *Times* in March 1945, "when surveying the possibilities of new music for the fiftieth anniversary Jubilee season of the [Cincinnati Symphony] Orchestra, Mr. Goossens hit on the idea of submitting to several composers a theme, which he himself wrote, and asking each to write a variation on it. . . .He also sent out suggestions as to key relationships and matters of broad structure so that, when assembled, the variations would form a homogeneous unit. He himself wrote the finale for the work." This oddly fashioned composition, when played by the Cincinnati orchestra, contained single variations by Ernest Bloch, Aaron Copland [40], Paul Creston, Anis Fuleihan, Howard Hanson [41], Roy Harris [40], Walter Piston, Bernard Rogers, William Schuman [42], and Deems Taylor [40].

Goossens, an American citizen since 1943, is "very British," according to *Cue*'s description. "Tall and well-built, [he] talks [in clipped British accents] with that odd balance of friendly warmth and courteous reserve one finds in the cultivated Englishman." The composer has been married twice. After a divorce from his first wife, Dorothy Dodsworth, to whom he was married in 1919, he was married to Janet Lewis in 1930. There are three children by the first marriage, Annie, Jane, and Julia, and two by the second, Renée and Sidonie. The second Mrs. Goossens obtained a divorce in 1944.

In view of the fact that mathematics underlies the development of a musical composition, it is not surprising that Goossens once thought of being an architect and displays a special interest in design and decoration, and in sketching ships and Gothic churches. Says the composer: "Architecture has always absorbed me, and at one time I used to sketch every building I could find." He likes, too, an occasional game of golf, but is not what one could call a sports lover, although he formerly enjoyed fencing. His secretary in his pre-United States days once listed as his weaknesses "his London tailor and his Paris shirtmaker."

Goossens, who is not fond of club life, is happiest in rural or semi-rural surroundings. In his own words, he finds a Tudor house with some adjoining elm trees "more fascinating to keep company with than the club bore." As a climax to real contentment, he says that most of all he enjoys "being left alone . . . with a library of good books." Another unmusical diversion to which he will admit, according to *Cue*, is a passion for locomotives and steamships. The conductor-composer, who occasionally likes to "get away from music," is tremendously interested in locomotives, likes to ride in the cab, and once drove the Ohio State Express for ten miles, and that without accident. He spends his summers in Connecticut, composing in the morning and painting or sketching in the afternoon.

References

Lit Digest 72:30 F 18 '22 por
Time 42:76 Jl 26 '43
Ewen, D. Composers of Today (1936) ; Living Musicians (1940)
Thompson, O. ed. International Cyclopedia of Music and Musicians (1943)
Who's Who, 1945
Who's Who in America, 1944-45

GOSS, ALBERT S. (gŏs) Oct. 14, 1882-
Agricultural leader

Address: b. 744 Jackson Pl., Washington, D. C.; h. 2800 McKinley Pl., Washington, D. C.

The head of the oldest farm organization in the United States calls himself a "barnyard

ALBERT S. GOSS

economist." He is Albert S. Goss, who occupies a key position in the agricultural sphere as master of the National Grange. Since his election to this responsible post in 1941, Goss has effectively fostered Grange policies during the years of increased wartime agricultural problems. He has been an outspoken critic of the New Deal farm policies and has on occasion voiced strong opposition to the Administration's subsidy program. The National Grange is a highly influential body and boasts of a long history in American agricultural affairs. The power wielded by this conservative farm group has been felt with growing force in recent years. Writing in the New York *Herald Tribune* in February 1943, J. W. Johnston stressed the potential power of the farm bloc and ventured that a well-knit organization "might dominate Congress."

Albert S. Goss was born in Rochester, New York, October 14, 1882, to John W. and Flora M. (Alling) Goss. The family moved across the country when the boy was quite young, and from 1889 to 1898 they lived in Spokane, Washington. After attending high school and business college, Albert in 1901 began working as a bookkeeper. He left this occupation to learn the milling trade, and in time he was operating a flour mill. While he was engaged in this he bought a country store, which he owned for seven years, and later he became a farmer. For an interim he was also connected with a telephone company; then in 1914 he took up farming again.

Goss showed an early interest in farm organization and he has been actively identified with the Grange since 1920. He became master of the Washington State Grange in 1922, following a number of stormy years which culminated in the expulsion of the former master. Goss remained as head until 1933. Most of this time he was also chairman of the executive committee of the National Grange (1924-33). From 1928 to 1933 Goss was director of the Federal Land Bank in Spokane, Washington, a valuable preliminary to his next office, for, in

1933 came his appointment as Federal Land Bank Commissioner in the Farm Credit Administration. Goss held this position for seven years, leaving at the end of this period, he explains, in protest against the efforts which were being made to convert the system from a cooperative credit system to a Government-controlled system.

As Grange master, Goss strives to maintain the traditions of his long-established organization. The National Grange was founded at the end of the Civil War and still retains its secret ritualistic character. (The word "grange" is used in England to mean "farmstead" or "farm estate.") This rural fraternity provides social outlets as well as occupational organization, and draws its membership from the entire family group. It is the largest of the major farm associations—members attending its seventy-fifth convention came from forty different states. (The three other major agricultural organizations in the United States are the National Farmers Union, of which James G. Patton '45 is president; the National Council of Farmer Cooperatives, of which Homer L. Brinkley is president, and the American Farm Bureau Federation, whose president is Edward O'Neal.)

With its headquarters in Washington, D. C., the Grange pursues its principles and program in the Capital, frequently in Congressional chambers. However, the group has no political affiliations, and Goss appeared before both the Democratic and Republican national conventions of 1944 to express the views of the Grange. There is considerable interest in Grange opinion, since the organization is a large representative farm body. Dorothea Kahn in the *Christian Science Monitor* summarized Master Goss's speech to the Seventy-sixth Annual Convention of the Grange: "Increased farm production is needed not only to win the war but to insure a happier postwar world, and means must be found to make possible an international economy of plenty when the war is over."

In the past the Grange has confined itself to suggesting general peace proposals. But at its convention in November 1944 Goss emphasized to the farmers their stake in the peace, stating that the time had come for aggressive planning. He offered three "Grange Guideposts" as determinants in the formulation of foreign and domestic policy: (1) All prosperity springs from the production of wealth. (2) The compensation of each person should be based upon what he contributes to the general welfare. (3) The prime purpose of government is to protect its citizens from aggression. The Grange's endorsement of international cooperation was indicated in January 1945 when the organization approved, with specifications, the Dumbarton Oaks plan, the Bretton Woods conference (with reservations), and the International Food Conference. According to the New York *World-Telegram*, Goss made an important contribution to clear thinking on international trade and the Bretton Woods agreements in testimony before the House Committee on Banking and Currency in May 1945: "If any nation expects to preserve its credit, it must produce something to sell to pay for what it buys. If a nation sells as much as it buys, there is a demand for its currency because those who buy goods from that nation will have to buy currency to pay for the goods." At the meeting of the United Nations Food and Agricultural Organization at Quebec in October 1945, Goss joined with the presidents of the other large farmer organizations—the National Council of Farm Cooperatives, the American Farm Bureau Federation, and the National Farmers Union—in proposing an international commodity control body that would pool farm commodities from countries with surpluses, for distribution to countries with shortages.

The farm leader has been a vigorous opponent of the Administration's food program. The most heated campaign involving Government policy centered around the subsidy issue. Goss disapproved of the subsidy principle, and the Grange was firmly in the anti-subsidy camp. The *Christian Science Monitor* noted the importance of the fight and commented: "There is no doubt that the opposition of the Grange indicates not merely the position of a few leaders but of the rank and file." Goss was strong in his denunciation of subsidies, labeling them inflationary agents and arguing that "subsidies breed more subsidies." He took every opportunity to present the Grange's view on this vital issue and was widely quoted in the press. A typical example of his arguments follows: "In case of unavoidable shortage, rationing is the most practical course. . . . Subsidies may be justified as an aid or incentive to secure abnormal production in special cases where costs are too high to permit production normally. This is a very different principle from employing them to hold down the general price level to consumers. When so employed the effect is to pass on to the Government part of our normal living costs. This form of socialism is wholly unjustifiable."

Goss carried his fight into the Nation's legislative halls and expressed his views to President Roosevelt [42]. In 1942, when price control legislation was under consideration, the Grange leader appeared before the Senate Committee on Banking and Currency and presented his arguments and recommendations. Again in 1943 Goss appeared before this committee to argue against food subsidies. He testified at subsidy hearings in forceful, simple language and was termed "the strongest voice in the farm lobby." Goss attended a conference at the White House in April 1943 at which he expressed his ideas on subsidies and inflation to the President. In the course of his anti-subsidy campaign Goss also sent letters to every member of Congress. Finally, in March 1944, after his opposition to the subsidy program, Goss offered suggestions for a compromise. He advocated the "gradual abandonment of certain types of subsidies and retention of others." In the heat of the subsidy battle the farmers were accused of profiteering and conspiracy. Goss defended them as well as his organization against such accusations, producing statistics to prove the unsoundness of the charges. He introduced evidence of the low-income and sub-standard living conditions in many American farm homes.

In February 1944 Goss attended the national postwar conference at Atlantic City. This gathering was composed of sixteen organizations representing the entire range of the Na-

tion's economy. The Grange chief was a member of the temporary organizing committee and also served as chairman of the drafting committee. In this latter capacity he helped prepare the conference's statement of policy which affirmed the need for cooperative efforts to win the war and attain postwar plenty for the country. Later that same year, in November, President Roosevelt appointed Goss a member of the War Mobilization and Reconversion Advisory Board. Goss also served on the Labor-Management Committee of the War Manpower Commission. Thus the New Deal critic functions as agricultural representative in these essential Government agencies. In March 1945 he was assigned to a subcommittee of the Advisory Board to the Office of War Mobilization and Reconversion to study the problem of a guaranteed annual wage in peacetime, with Eric Johnston [43] of the United States Chamber of Commerce, Philip Murray [41] of the CIO, and Anna Rosenberg [43] of the Manpower Commission as the other members. On the question of compulsory military training in peacetime, Goss and his Grange were opposed to any action "until the terms of any international agreement are known and until the men at the front have ample opportunity to participate in the determination of policies so far-reaching."

Goss has been referred to as "a spare, gray, grim dissenter." Although his voice is soft, his manner carries conviction and commands attention. He is a friendly but reserved man and is reputed to look more like a professor than the master of eight thousand local granges. A slim one hundred and forty pounds, Goss is five feet seven and a half inches tall, has blue eyes and a white mustache. He and his wife, the former Minnie E. Hand, to whom he was married in 1907, live in Washington, D. C. They have three children—Ruth Dorothy Hanssen, Warren Hand, and Betty Jane (Mrs. Samuel J. Guill). Goss is now completing his second term as master of the Grange; he was re-elected to the office for a two-year term in 1943. His absorption in agricultural problems provoked this apt remark in a magazine characterization of Goss: "Farm credit remains his pet subject; subsidies are his main gripe."

References

N Y Herald Tribune p44 N 18 '41 por
N Y Sun p13 O 12 '43
N Y Times p21 N 18 '41
Who's Who in America, 1944-45

GOULD, MORTON (gōōld) Dec. 10, 1913-
Composer; conductor

Address: b. 30 Rockefeller Plaza, New York City; h. 77-35 113th St., Forest Hills, Long Island, N.Y.

One of the leading musical interpreters of the contemporary American scene is the youthful composer-conductor-pianist, Morton Gould, whom José Iturbi [43] has called "the most talented young composer in America." Gould's compositions have been conducted by Toscanini [42], Stokowski [41], Barbirolli [40], and Reiner [41]. As a conductor of note himself, he has led the New York Philharmonic-Symphony and for

MORTON GOULD

many years has been arranging and conducting music for radio programs.

Morton Gould is a native New Yorker, born in Richmond Hill, Long Island, on December 10, 1913, the eldest of the four sons of James and Frances Gould. His father was Viennese and it was his playing of waltzes that first influenced the boy musically. The band of the American Legion post across the street from the Gould home also had its effect on the young would-be composer, for one day at the age of four the child went to the piano and improvised a martial tune. As soon as his parents discovered his musical gift, he was sent to teachers—Abby Whiteside for piano and Vincent Jones for composition. The boy soon won a reputation as a prodigy and was engaged to play over station WOR. He played his first published piece over that station when he was seven, a composition composed at the age of six and aptly titled "Just Six." A year later he won a scholarship to the New York Institute of Musical Art. He attended Richmond Hill High School but left before finishing in order to concentrate on his music. At fifteen he had completed the courses at New York University's Music School.

In his early teens Gould's artistic efforts were divided between the piano and the palette, and it is said that his paintings showed great promise. For a period he was so fascinated by the bohemianism of a group of Greenwich Village artists that he persuaded his parents to allow him to join the artists for a summer at the artists' colony at Woodstock, New York. "My parents, hoping to discourage me, gave me only enough money to stay a week," he reveals. "However, I supported myself by giving music lessons and Sunday concerts. 'Stravinsky, Schoenberg, Hindemith, Gould,' the handbills read. You see, I modestly gave myself last billing." Incidentally, the musician continues, "I found myself supporting my friends while they sat around and talked art all day. Suddenly I realized that the real artists at Woodstock worked while my friends talked. When I got sick and they deserted me, I was through with bohemianism."

At seventeen Gould launched his career, with a concert tour, and later he gave an impressive performance of Ravel's Bolero during a vaudeville engagement in which "he thumped the keys with his arms to simulate the crashing drums at the climax." At eighteen he joined the music staff of New York's Roxy and Music Hall theaters, and the following year he accepted a position with the National Broadcasting Company, in which he did duo-piano work. When he was twenty-one his "break" came—in 1934 he was given his own program on WOR. He remained at NBC for nine years, conducting his large symphony orchestra in his own and others' music, ranging from the classics to swing. He has conducted an orchestra on CBS programs, among them Shower of Stars and the Cresta Blanca Carnival, in which he was co-starred with Alec Templeton [40]. Until mid-July 1945 he also conducted his own program, The Music of Morton Gould, each Thursday night over CBS. Variety reported on July 25 that an expanded Gould radio show, featuring him as a composer, is being prepared for a potential sponsor. (Since he does not have the time to practice, Gould no longer plays the piano professionally.) As guest conductor, he has directed the New York Philharmonic, the symphony orchestras of Los Angeles, St. Louis, Cincinnati, Minneapolis, and other cities, in addition to participating in high school and college musical affairs in different localities. He has also lectured at various universities.

Turning temporarily from his radio career, in 1944 Gould composed and conducted the music for the picture Delightfully Dangerous (1945). The Gould cinematic score included six songs and an arrangement of Strauss waltzes which were the "best recommendations" of the film, according to Variety's reviewer. The composer also had a small speaking role in the picture and he later told a reporter that his first experience before the camera as an actor was terrifying.

Gould's compositions have a definite American flavor, written, as they are, largely in the modern idiom on American themes, with frequent use of jazz rhythms. (He has acknowledged a debt to George Gershwin, and his work is also said to show the influence of the modern composer Dmitri Shostakovich [41].) "Blue-nose musicians," reports Mary Braggiotti in the New York Post, "have been known to call Gould the 'enfant terrible' of American music" because of this use of jazz rhythms in serious music. Critical estimates vary considerably—an ingenuity and versatility in his compositions are pointed out, while the intellectual content is frequently criticized. His works, nevertheless, are among the most frequently performed of serious modern American music, and many of his compositions have been recorded. (His ability as an arranger and orchestrator has received wide acknowledgment.) Leopold Stokowski once said that Gould's Chorale and Fugue in Jazz, composed at the age of eighteen, was "the most daring and creative work" ever submitted to him.

In April 1940 the twenty-six-year-old musician conducted the University of Michigan band in the première performance of his Cow-

boy Rhapsody, written in thirty-six hours especially for that band. This was Gould's first composition written specifically for band performance although many bands had used arrangements of his works. Presenting a melodic pattern of seven famous cowboy folk songs, among them "Bury Me Not on the Lone Prairee", "Git Along, Little Dogie," and "Home on the Range," the work became popular immediately. In commenting on the music after the first performance, Louis Untermeyer said, "It was brilliant—and exciting, too. It had an element of surprise. You knew the tunes, but there was such a new presentation that it was dynamite. I was on the edge of my seat, or was it my saddle?"

Earlier that year Gould's *Foster Gallery* and the *Pavane,* the second movement of his second *American Symphonette,* had been performed by Fritz Reiner and the Pittsburgh Orchestra. When Howard Barlow '40 conducted the New York Philharmonic in his reading of three pieces from this work in November 1942, Olin Downes wrote of them, "The pieces are not marvels of originality, but they are short and lively, in a generally jocose vein, with dashing instrumentation." In March 1941 after John Barbirolli conducted the Philharmonic in a performance of *Foster Gallery,* critic Henry Simon pronounced the work "as clever a piece of smart-aleckry as Carnegie Hall has heard all winter." This composition consists of thirteen short movements based on melodies by Stephen Foster; Simon remarked that, through Gould's orchestration, "Jeannie's light brown hair went to a barber shop, where it was torn out in fistfuls by a drunken barber." When the Pittsburgh Symphony gave its first performance of this work, one critic called it "a brilliant piece of orchestral writing, somewhat overweighted and too long, but daring and often skillful in its interweaving of well-known melodies."

Late in 1942 both Stokowski and Rodzinski '40 played Gould's *Spirituals for String Choir and Orchestra,* which was based on American spirituals. This composition was among five later chosen by the New York Music Critics' Circle for consideration as the best symphonic work of the year. Also, in November 1942, the musician achieved further recognition in his field when Toscanini conducted the first performance of his *Lincoln Legend.* Shortly thereafter the Soviet Government requested a copy of the score, which was sent by radio photo-film in exchange for new Russian music. During the summer of 1943 Gould was invited to conduct the Philharmonic at New York's Lewisohn Stadium. He devoted one concert to a United Nations program and on the Fourth of July conducted a holiday program of contemporary American works. The New York *Times* critic commented that Gould directed "in an alert, incisive manner, and invested his readings with ingratiating rhythmic precision, mood, and color," while another columnist remarked that he "certainly knows the orchestral checks and balances." During that summer his *Boogie-Woogie Etude,* played by José Iturbi, had its first performance on his own radio program. According to radio reporter Harriet Van Horne, the composition grew out of a luncheon discussion between the composer and the pianist; it was completed the same night and performed on the next. The response to the Etude was reportedly "sensational": orchestras throughout the country wired for permission to use the work, it was played by the noted Puerto Rican pianist Jesús María Sanromá and a symphony orchestra over the Blue Network, and soon Iturbi repeated his performance on another Gould show.

The première of Gould's *Symphony on Marching Tunes* in early June 1944 received generally unflattering reviews. Commissioned by the YMCA in commemoration of the organization's one hundredth anniversary and dedicated to "freedom-loving youth of the world," the work was considered as lacking in genuine symphonic quality. While *PM*'s critic noted earnestness and skill in the composition, he felt, nevertheless, "that a real musical talent has not yet found itself in spite of a serious effort." The critic of the New York *Herald Tribune* was more severe in his judgment, labeling the work "an eclectic product, wholly wanting in stylistic unity"; he singled out the last movement for special censure because of its "dreary application of Shostakovichian methods of harmonization and instrumentation, including the wide spacing of sonorities." Vladimir Golschmann conducted the Cleveland Orchestra in two performances of the Gould Concerto for Orchestra in February 1945. This symphonic "show piece" in three movements, "which "revels in swing rhythms and boogie-woogie," employs all the known percussion instruments and two saxophones. According to Elmore Bacon in *Musical America,* it is "ingenious, brilliant, colorful, and toe-tapping to the nth degree."

In the summer of 1945 Frank Black conducted the *General Motors Symphony of the Air* in the first performance of another Gould composition, the Concerto for Viola and Orchestra. Two months later the British pianist, Percy Grainger, played Gould's *American Concertette* at a Chicago concert. Reviewing the performance in the *Christian Science Monitor,* Felix Borowski declared, "The music as a whole was clever and ingenious, but there was little in it that was beautiful or eloquent." This music is used by Jerome Robbins in his ballet *Interplay,* which formed one of the principal and most popular acts of Billy Rose's '40 musical, *Concert Varieties,* and which was included in the Ballet Theatre's repertory at the Metropolitan Opera House during the 1945 fall season. Also in 1945, Gould wrote the music for, and appeared with his orchestra in, Charles R. Rogers' United Artists picture *Delightfully Dangerous.* And he contributed the "rich and varied" score to the Betty Comden '45-Adolph Green '45 musical *Billion Dollar Baby.*

In an interview published in *Etude* in January 1944, Gould gives advice to student musicians, stressing as of primary importance "the great, sweeping, structural lines" of creative ideas which are symbolized by notes in music. "The serious musician of tomorrow must familiarize himself with as many styles and 'schools' of music as he can. He must absorb not only the conventional classic repertory; he must be able also to read, feel, and express all contemporary American music. Jazz, for

GOULD, MORTON—*Continued*

instance, is important as a contemporary idiom."

In June 1945 Gould addressed the Conference of the Independent Citizens Committee of the Arts, Sciences and Professions, a body devoted to the study of employment problems and expansion in those fields. Speaking on "Music in Radio," the musician, while recognizing certain commercial considerations, urged advertising and broadcasting officials to devote part of their energies to encouraging contemporary music. Gould considers radio a potent force in American life, attributing a large measure of the Nation's musical growth to its influence. Radio columnist Arnold Blom says that Gould's specifications for his own program include a fifty-piece orchestra, the kind of music he prefers, and no comedian. Rather than compromise his principles, Gould has said that he would relinquish a position. While he has no political connections, Gould once told an interviewer, he considers it important for the artist to be politically conscious. It is the artist's responsibility, he maintains, to help in the betterment of humanity and thus work toward a "more meaningful art."

A slim figure of medium height, fair-haired and blue-eyed, the composer "seldom smiles among friends and absolutely never on the podium." "I'm not a glamour boy," he says. "When I'm out on the stage I'm there to do my work. There's nothing to smile about. In fact, it's usually pretty grim." Off-podium, he is a humorous man with a liking for golf and ping-pong, reading, and the theater. He was married to Shirley Banks of Minneapolis on May 22, 1944, and a son, Eric Franklin was born in 1945. The family lives in a Forest Hills apartment, where Gould composes, oblivious to neighborhood noises. In 1945 he was at work on a Concerto for Clarinet for Benny Goodman [42], a ballet, and an opera based on the Biblical story of Joseph. His belief is that "the outlook for the creative and interpretative future of American music is a heartening one."

References

N Y Post p21 My 1 '45 por
N Y Sun p10 D 24 '45
Newsweek 15:41-2 Ap 8 '40

Thompson, O. ed. International Cyclopedia of Music and Musicians (1943)
Who Is Who in Music, 1941

GRAHAM, GWETHALYN Jan. 18, 1913- Author

Address: b. c/o Monica McCall, Myron Selznick, Ltd., 610 Fifth Ave., New York City; h. 4129 Dorchester St., West, Montreal, Canada

One of the most timely and noteworthy novels of 1944 is Gwethalyn Graham's *Earth and High Heaven*, a thrust at racial bigotry and intolerance, specifically a story of anti-Semitism in Canada. "When people have asked me what my book is about," Miss Graham writes, "I have usually ended by saying that it is a plea for the individual, that he or she may be regarded and respected as such and not judged arbitrarily according to a category."

The daughter of Frank and Isabel Russell (MacCurdy) Erichsen-Brown, Gwethalyn Graham Erichsen-Brown was born in Toronto, on January 18, 1913, into a cultivated Canadian family of the Anglican, High Church faith. Her father is a lawyer and an enthusiastic amateur painter, and her mother, one of the leaders in the Canadian woman's suffrage movement, is "an unclassifiable individual whose interests range through people and books and music to too many organizations for which she does more work than is good for her." Miss Graham derived her strongly internationalist outlook from them and from her grandfather, a student of Oriental languages and "a genuine internationalist." "He was an individualist in the finest sense of the word," says Miss Graham, "and I remember that he would not tolerate the use of any of the derogatory slang words which label national or religious groups on this continent—such words as 'Wop', 'Mick', 'Hun,' or 'Chink.'"

Miss Graham lived in Toronto until she was sixteen, when she went to Europe to attend a girls' boarding school at Lausanne, Switzerland—Pensionnat des Allieres, where forty-eight girls represented twenty nationalities. Here she spent the year 1929. This experience was the background of her first novel, *Swiss Sonata*. (From the age of six she had taken it for granted that she would be a writer.) Published in the United States and England in 1938, it deals with the effects of the growth of Fascism and Hitlerism in that school, the action covering the three days immediately preceding the Saar plebiscite in 1935. Receiving the Governor General's Award for Fiction in 1938, it was added to the Nazis' blacklist.

After her Swiss schooling Miss Graham continued her education at Havergal College, Toronto, and then crossed the Canadian border to attend Smith College in Massachusetts (1931-32). She returned to Montreal in 1934 and has lived there since. In 1938 she spent six months in London, where she met many refugees. "Their plight sounded bad enough over here," she declared, "but there I saw them on the park benches." She hated to admit that she was a Canadian because her Government had refused to admit refugees unless they were wealthy or willing to become farmers. Back home, she devoted her energies toward circulating petitions and making speeches for the admission of refugees.

Miss Graham's deepening interest in sociological and human problems found expression in the writing of *Earth and High Heaven* with its problem of marriage between a Jewish man and a Gentile girl. Published in October 1944, it was the selection of the Literary Guild for that month. It was considered very daring when a month previously the popular periodical *Collier's* started serializing the novel, and the Writers' War Board went out of its way to praise the progressiveness of the weekly in so doing. The sale of the motion picture rights to Samuel Goldwyn [44] was considered another bit of evidence that the film industry, too, is willing to face basic issues.

Set in the city of Montreal, *Earth and High Heaven* is a novel "about two people in love who are confronted by almost insurmountable obstacles to their marriage—obstacles which arise directly from the way in which most of us have been taught to think," explains Miss Graham. It is the age-old conflict of racial and religious prejudices that separates Erica Drake, the daughter of a socially prominent English-Canadian family, and Marc Reiser, the young Jewish lawyer she loves. Their problem "actually turned out, in the end, to be simpler than either of them realized, because they both knew what they wanted; they knew what they would have to pay for it, and since in the course of their struggle against society, they had attained a certain degree of self-realization, they knew that they could afford to pay the price. And they were safe," Miss Graham concluded.

Critics lauded Miss Graham's treatment of the controversial theme, pointing out that the work is an expert blending of both a thesis and a novel. (One of Miss Graham's aversions is the "propaganda" novel, an epithet which reviewers found could not be hurled at her book.) "Her story has charm, romantic appeal, and dramatic force, as well as 'social significance,'" observed Orville Prescott in the New York *Times*. The smoothness and polish of her writing were noted. Rosemary Carr Benét commented in the *Saturday Review of Literature*: "It is skillful and mature work. Miss Graham has a good ear for conversation, a true flair for dialogue, and a saving sense of humor even when she is serious." It was pointed out, however, that *Earth and High Heaven* "does not penetrate very deeply beneath the outer surfaces of the characters, nor very deeply into the roots of anti-Semitism"; Bernard De Voto [43] noted that the emotional reconciliation at the conclusion of the novel is "hardly a solution to the problem originally posed." Perhaps the ultimate value of the book, as Prescott writes, is that "a book like Miss Graham's, a book which contains every element necessary for popularity, can help to dramatize for many the pity, the folly, and the injustice of race prejudice." In awarding the *Saturday Review of Literature* Anisfield-Wolf Prize for the best book on race relations (the 1945 award was divided between *Earth and High Heaven* and Gunnar Myrdal's *An American Dilemma*), the award committee stated, "Miss Graham's novel is one of the most sensitive and penetrating studies of the social relations between Jews and Christians in a long-established Anglo-Saxon community that has been written in our times. . . .Not only is this book an excellent study of Canadian racial relations, it is an admirable novel." It was given the Governor General's award for the best novel written by a Canadian in 1944. (Her *Swiss Sonata* had won the Governor General's award for 1938.) It was high on the best-seller lists for several months—in the first six months after publication 665,000 copies were sold. It has been printed in Braille, for the blind, and the movie rights were purchased by Samuel Goldwyn [44].

After the publication of the book it was reported that Miss Graham was working on a novel "dealing principally with English-French relations and the effects of monopoly capitalism working jointly with the church to maintain the status quo." Developing her philosophy of the individual, she writes: "At the

GWETHALYN GRAHAM

present time, the individual is recognized as the basis of our political system and there recognition ends, so that as yet democracy has only been partially realized. In order for it to be fully realized, the individual must be regarded as the basis of our *economic* system, which means production primarily for consumption, with profit the secondary motive rather than the other way round, and, finally, both in the national and international fields, he must be freed from the prison of judgments based almost entirely on so-called 'group, religious, or racial' characteristics."

Miss Graham believes that the French school of writers have influenced her work markedly. "If I could choose to write like anyone," she has said, "it would be Stendhal." Of the American and English novelists, she admires Ernest Hemingway, John Steinbeck [40], Thomas Wolfe, Willa Cather, Ford Madox Ford, and Somerset Maugham; the greatest novel of the last ten years, she believes, is Arthur Koestler's [43] *Darkness at Noon*.

In addition to her writing, Gwethalyn Graham spends a considerable amount of time in mothering her son Anthony. (She was married in 1932 and has since been divorced.) The tall, reddish-brown-haired writer likes sailing, skiing, and music.

References

Literary Guild R: Wings p5-10 O '44 il
　　por
N Y Herald Tribune II p8 O 1 '44

GRANT, HEBER J. Nov. 22, 1856—May 14, 1945 Mormon leader in the United States; elected the seventh president of the Church of Jesus Christ of Latter-Day Saints in 1918, a position he held until his death; many years before this appointment he earned a fortune in insurance business.

Obituary

N Y Times p19 My 15 '45 por

GREEN, ADOLPH *See* Comden, B. and Green, A.

GREEN, FLORENCE TOPPING 1882(?) —May 24, 1945 Internationally known British-born American portrait painter; was national director of American Art Week; represented United States in 1937 at the eighth annual Congress of Design and Applied Arts in Paris.

Obituary

N Y Times p19 My 25 '45

GREEN, MRS. HOWARD *See* Green, F. T.

GREGORY, EDMUND B(RISTOL) July 4, 1882- United States Army officer

Address: b. Office of the Quartermaster General, War Department, Washington, D.C.; h. 4401 Greenwich Parkway, N.W., Washington, D.C.

"If the United States Army were to advertise for a Quartermaster General," suggests Arthur Bartlett in the New York *Herald Tribune*, "the ad would have to run something like this: 'Wanted: Man to feed, clothe, house, and transport a million soldiers . . . business with yearly volume in the billions.'" The man the Army

U.S. Army Signal Corps
LT. GEN. EDMUND B. GREGORY

chose for this job in April 1940 is Lieutenant General Edmund B. Gregory, a veteran of the Quartermaster Corps since 1916. After the Second World War he was to turn from purchasing to selling when he was appointed chairman of the new War Assets Corporation.

Born at Storm Lake, Iowa, July 4, 1882, Edmund Bristol Gregory is the son of Frank Buckingham and Emily Hatch (Bristol) Gregory. He began his military career shortly before his twenty-second birthday, having been graduated from the United States Military

Academy on June 15, 1904, with a commission as a second lieutenant of Infantry. His first assignment was with the Fourteenth Infantry, which he joined at Camp Connell, Philippine Islands, on November 7 of that year. With the exception of a period as instructor in the department of English and history at West Point from July 1911 to December 1912, Gregory remained with the Fourteenth for eleven years. (In July 1911 he was married to Verna Ellsworth Green.)

Gregory's second assignment with his unit was at Vancouver Barracks, Washington, where he was stationed from April 24, 1905, until January 2, 1908. At the end of this period he again went to the Philippines, taking up station at Warwick Barracks. He remained with his regiment on that duty until February 15, 1910, when it was returned to the States and assigned to Fort William Henry Harrison in Montana. In Montana in March 1911 Gregory received his promotion to the rank of first lieutenant; four months later he was assigned to teach at West Point. When he rejoined his unit in December 1912 it was stationed at Fort Lawton, Washington. He remained with it until the end of 1915, when he returned for the third time to the Philippines. In this assignment he served with the Eighth Infantry at Cuartel de Espana for a year, until March 5, 1916, and with the Twenty-seventh at the same post until December 5. While with the latter group, in July 1916, he received his captaincy.

It was at this time that Captain Gregory was detailed to the Quartermaster Corps. He served first as assistant to the quartermaster at the headquarters of the Philippine Department in Manila, where he remained until July 15, 1917. After he returned to the States he received a promotion to major (temporary) that August and was assigned to duty at the General Supply Depot at Jefferson, Indiana. During the next four years, until March 1921, he served in a series of posts: he was assistant to the supply officer, officer in charge of the inspection division, officer in charge of the supplies division, zone storage officer, officer in charge of the supply service, and executive officer. In October 1918 he was promoted to lieutenant colonel (temporary). In May 1920 he reverted to his permanent rank of captain, and the following July he was given the permanent rank of major in the Regular Army.

Following a month and a half of duty as quartermaster supply officer at the Columbus Reserve Depot in Columbus, Ohio, Major Gregory was next assigned as assistant quartermaster supply officer at the Atlanta (Georgia) General Intermediate Depot. In July 1922 he was shifted to Washington, D. C., where he served for one month in the Sales Branch of the Office of the Assistant Secretary of War. In August he was ordered to the Orient as War Department representative, in connection with cooperative union contracts with the United States for sale of war supplies. He arrived at Shanghai on September 5 and remained until May 9, 1924.

After Gregory had returned to the United States he served for several months in the Office of the Assistant Secretary of War in Washington. Following that temporary assignment, from October to August 1927 he was an instructor in the New York National Guard. Then, in keeping with the Army's policy of periodic schooling for officers, the Major became a student at Harvard University's Graduate School of Business Administration. While there he was made a lieutenant colonel and in June 1929 he was graduated with the degree of Master of Business Administration. Taking up military duties again, for the next four years he served in the Office of the Quartermaster General in Washington. In August 1933 he became acting quartermaster at the headquarters of the Second Corps Area on Governors Island. He was later made executive officer and in August 1935 raised to a full colonel. In June 1936 he once more became a student, this time at the Army War College in Washington. After his graduation the following June he returned to the Office of the Quartermaster General in Washington, and on April 1, three years later, he was appointed Quartermaster General himself, with the rank of major general.

General Gregory was immediately confronted with the program of expansion which was under way for the Army. For the first time in history appropriations by Congress permitted large-scale maneuvers to test the plans and equipment. These maneuvers required long-range plans by the Quartermaster Corps. Estimates for food, billeting, transportation, and supplies which would be used in a real war had to be made well in advance and the logistics for their distribution prepared. The new QMG was getting a taste of the future in small doses. The same year the doses grew larger. The National Guard was called into active service for a year. The draft act followed and even before the attack on Pearl Harbor in December 1941 the Army began its climb toward astronomical figures in men and required matériel. Gregory's was considered the toughest job in the Army.

To begin with, extensive tests were made to develop vehicles suitable for the rigors of military transportation across all types of terrain. On the proving grounds of the Quartermaster Corps at Holabird, Maryland, many cars offered by manufacturers were shaken and pounded into wrecks. Some persons thought the tests were too severe, but Gregory stood by his demands. The results were the now famous "jeep" and other trucks and cars of capabilities fitted to their assignments, together rated the sturdiest motorized equipment in the world.

Probably the most important of the responsibilities of the Quartermaster Corps, however, at least to the individual soldier, was Army "chow." To back up his statement, "We've got the best-fed army in the world," Gregory detailed a group of enlisted men to find out what food the soldiers liked, and what food they ate only because it was served to them. In a twelve-month period the men examined meals served to 2,474,362 men in 500 Army mess halls, measured the uneaten food thrown into garbage cans, and noted eating habits. As a result of the investigation, new regulations were issued for the preparation of Army meals, and the food bill was lowered when a calculated percentage of absenteeism at meals was taken into account.

When stricter rationing on the home front brought charges that the Army was wasting

food, General Gregory said that investigations had already resulted in a drive to cut wastage from 21 to 11 per cent. In reply to charges of hoarding he declared, "The presence of . . . canned foods in the packing plant has caused critics to publish charges that the Army has purchased canned goods so far in excess of military needs that there was no place to store them. These published charges, whether innocently or selfishly inspired, simply are not and never have been true." "The real cause for food shortage," he told the Truman [45] Committee during an investigation in April 1943, "is the rising buying power of civilians in this country, which has caused food consumption to soar to record levels." The following May he struck at black market operators, disclosing that illegal markets in some districts continued to hinder Army procurement of food as well as equitable distribution, both civil and military.

In addition to feeding, clothing, and equipping the Army, the Quartermaster General was faced with the problem of housing this vast number of troops. It was his duty to procure and dispose of real estate and housing facilities, and to operate utilities for maintenance and repair. In August 1941 the construction program for the then rapidly expanding Army was sharply criticized by the Senate's Defense Investigating Committee. In a ninety-eight-page report prepared by Chairman Truman and Counsel Hugh A. Fulton, it was charged that as a result of poor judgment, misinformation, and lack of adequate plans for camps, one hundred million dollars was wasted. "We used that . . . figure because the Army admitted that much. It will run two and a half times that much, easily," stated Truman, who also conceded that some of the mistakes were due to Congressional politics. In answer to this criticism of the efficiency of himself and his Quartermaster Corps, General Gregory declared that if the Army wanted maximum speed it had to pay for it; that the Quartermaster Corps alone was not responsible for all the mistakes. According to his charts, 94.8 per cent of Army construction had been completed since his tremendous job of emergency building began the previous June.

The results of research to devise the best in equipment, food, and clothing for the Army during the war were pictured in an article by Gregory written for the January 23, 1944, issue of *This Week*. The Quartermaster General discussed many new products then in military use and, as the title of his article announced— "Army Miracles — for You!" — declared that after the end of the war civilians, too, would have such things as better glassware, crockery, soap, raincoats, antiseptics, and new products of plastics and nylon. As for the disposition of Government-owned surplus goods after the war, that was placed under the direction of Gregory when in December 1945, the President named the Quartermaster General the chairman of the new War Assets Corporation of the Reconstruction Finance Corporation. Gregory's responsibility for the disposition of nearly all war surpluses (the WAC will include the old Surplus Property Administration) will begin February 1, 1946.

Edmund Gregory is a squarish, graying man of medium height, with a quiet Middle Western voice. In the summer of 1945 he returned

GREGORY, EDMUND B.—*Continued*
from a tour of the fighting fronts without a
scratch. While resting after the trip, reports
Leonard Lyons of the New York *Post*, the
Quartermaster General ruptured a tendon in
his leg in an unmilitary accident when he attempted to avoid stepping on a snake on his
peaceful Maryland farm.

Reference

Who's Who in America, 1944-45

**GRIBBLE, HARRY WAGSTAFF (GRA-
HAM-)** Playwright; director
Address: b. 349 E. 49th St., New York City

"To review Harry Wagstaff Gribble's career
is to be impressed with his versatility." As
playwright or as director, and often in both
capacities on the same production, Gribble has
been successful with comedy, farce, melodrama,

George Karger
HARRY WAGSTAFF GRIBBLE

drama, musical—with Shakespeare and Shaw '44.
His 1944-45 hit, *Anna Lucasta*, is a comedy-
drama which he rewrote in part and directed.

Born around the turn of the century, in the
English town of Sevenoaks, Kent, the playwright-director was christened Harry Wagstaff Graham Gribble. Later his father, Theodore Graham Gribble, registered the family
name as Graham-Gribble. Young Harry's
mother, Mary Emilia (Soltâu) Gribble was
of Swiss (Huguenot) ancestry. "I think I must
have been born with a love of America," says
Gribble, who applied for American citizenship
shortly after his arrival in the United States.
His father, the construction engineer who built
Honolulu's first streetcar lines, brought back
from one of his American trips an alluring
verbal picture for a nine-year-old Harry. "His
description of the country, and especially of
New York City's sky line, fascinated me," recalls Gribble. America also represented to him
a land of fabulous fortunes. (His father's
brother, Henry Gribble had been married to

the daughter of Colonel Harry Wagstaff, millionaire associate of the Rockefellers in the
early days of the Standard Oil Company.)
Always a rebel against tradition, young Gribble
first asserted himself when he refused to become a missionary for the Plymouth Brethren, as other Gribbles had done, and announced
his conversion to Episcopalianism. Shortly
afterward he was confirmed by the Bishop of
London in Westminster Abbey.

After attending Clarence School, in
Weston super Mare on the Bristol Channel,
young Gribble entered Emmanuel College at
Cambridge in 1910. When a reversal of the
family fortune ended his college career two
years later, he joined a theatrical company going to South Africa. His meeting with the Ox-
ford-educated son of a Zulu chief on this tour,
explains Gribble, was the beginning of his interest in the Negro. "I have always found the
Negro," says the director of *Anna Lucasta*,
"vital and stimulating." On his return to England Gribble studied to be a chartered account-
ant, but the theater again captured his interest.
As actor he appeared in 1913 in the motion picture *Nellie's Ride*. Gribble still shivers when
he recalls his big scene in the film, in which
bound to a rock in a stormy sea—both storm
and sea the real things—he waited while Nellie
rode to his rescue. One of his experiments, an
attempt to lighten with a calcimine-like liquid
the shadows cast by the poor lighting system on
the actors' faces, caused audiences to wonder
whether they were watching white-faced clowns
or wraiths. In spite of this defect, however,
the picture won him a contract with a New
York film company.

"But when I arrived in New York," relates
Gribble, "I could not locate the company on
my important-looking contract." (There were
many fly-by-night film companies in those em-
bryo days of the cinema.) The young Englishman was rescued from his plight by Mrs. Pat
Campbell and her company, who engaged him
as stage manager for their New York engagement and transcontinental tour in Shaw's '44
Pygmalion (1914). Other small jobs in the
theater followed for Gribble before he finally
branched out as a playwright. This opportunity came while he was serving in the Twenty-seventh Division of the United States Army
during the First World War. *You Know Me,
Al*, written and produced by Gribble, was considered the Army's most successful play. His
Let's Beat It was also an Army production.

On his discharge from the Army, Gribble
wrote *The Outrageous Mrs. Palmer* (1919), a
sophisticated comedy centered around a temperamental actress. The play had a sixteen-
week run in Boston, but in New York, following, as it did, the earlier appearance of Brock
Pemberton's '45 *Enter, Madame*, also concerning
a temperamental star, Gribble's play was deprived of its novelty. Alan Dale, the famous
New York critic of the period, was the indirect cause of Gribble's writing his 1921 play,
March Hares, a forerunner of the type of
comedy which Noel Coward '41 and others were
to write. Annoyed because the critic had said
that he excelled in brilliant dialogue but was
weak in dramaturgy, Gribble had decided to
write a play without intricate plot development,
which in that day was considered necessary to
the success of a play. Despite the fact that

March Hares received a divided press on its opening and failed to achieve a long run, it has become a classic example of sophisticated comedy, produced frequently by art theater groups. On its London presentation six years later, British critics called it a masterpiece in "gay nonsense." The *Spectator*, after pointing out that the play had little substance and a negligible plot, said, "But it delightfully exemplifies the triumph of style over matter. . . . The matter is irradiated by a dainty touch of fantasy. Nobody does anything in the least probable; everybody, confronted with an improbable situation, says things that sound real or plausible. The author's dexterity in dramatic dialogue and a certain solidity of amusingly sketched character provide a sound basis for its unreality."

In 1922 Gribble turned to musical comedy. In collaboration with Harold Atterridge, he wrote the book for *Artists and Models,* a revue produced by the Shuberts, which he also staged. (Other musicals to his credit are *Topics of 1923, Artists and Models of 1924, Cherry Pie* [1926], and *Meet My Sister* [1930].) Two years later, in 1924, Gribble interrupted his writing of comedy to collaborate with Gertrude Purcell on the dramatization of the book *Stella Dallas,* which, however, because of casting complications, never reached Broadway. The play was nevertheless sold to United Artists while it was on the road, and later (1925) Gribble collaborated on its picturization, which was considered an outstanding film. (Since then he has written a number of other scripts. Chief among them are *A Bill of Divorcement* and *A Silent Witness,* both in 1932.)

The playwright's next directorial job was for the highly successful revival of the 1890 melodrama, *After Dark,* which Christopher Morley produced in 1928 in Hoboken, New Jersey. Aiming for travesty, Gribble, in staging the production, emphasized the "staginess" of acting in the eighteen-nineties. Its deep-dyed villain was made more sinister in his pursuit of the "pure-as-snow" heroine, all of which proved to be hilariously amusing to twentieth century New Yorkers. "It became the fad of the hour," reports Burns Mantle [44], "to take the tube to Hoboken and participate in hissing the villain and in cheering the heroine." Seats were booked weeks ahead at speculators' prices during the thirty-two-week run of the play. Encouraged by the success of *After Dark,* Morley leased another Hoboken theater and engaged Gribble to stage similarly a revival of *The Black Crook,* an 1890 musical. Not the least of this show's attractions was the feminine chorus, whose hour-glass figures "never had heard of a Hollywood diet." Gribble's manner of staging these revivals has been often imitated. *Hawkshaw, the Detective, The Drunkard,* and *The Fatal Wedding* are among the "mellers" presented by other producers.

Another of the outstanding plays of the thirty or more Gribble has directed since 1928 is *Cynara* (1931), adapted from the novel *The Imperfect Lover* by the author, R. F. Gore-Brown, and H. M. Harwood. In the opinion of *Outlook,* it was written and directed with such skill that it has none of the gaps or the literary flavor usually prevailing in dramatized novels; and Burns Mantle placed it on his list

of the season's ten best plays. Gribble was also the director of the memorable production of *The Taming of the Shrew* in 1935, in which the Lunts [41] were starred. Stark Young, pointing out that the aim of good staging is to have the production in harmony with the mood of the play, said that this had been "excellently devised" in the play. "Gribble has directed the whole affair," commented Brooks Atkinson [42], "with the versatility and dispatch of a musical comedy ringmaster."

In 1940 the playwright-director, tiring of the inconsequential plays which producers had assigned to him in the preceding years, became a producer on his own. In the era of plotless plays about everyday, undramatic people, Gribble, who had stimulated this school of writing, again bucked precedent. He selected for his first production Elmer Harris' *Johnny Belinda,* the story of an unmarried deaf mute who becomes a mother. The *Commonweal* critic, who found the theme fresh and poignant and the cast admirable, commented that Gribble had directed it "with his accustomed skill." "Sophisticated we may be," said the *Catholic World,* "but sentiment is not yet banished from the twentieth century breast. The audience is squarely behind the young mother, the same emotion which caused thousands to weep for the *East Lynne* mother, and will continue to do so—we hope—as long as the world spins on." (The audience supported the play for a year's run on Broadway.) Rosamond Gilder, on the other hand, regarded the play as a "stunt," although she considered Gribble's direction of the pantomime used by the deaf-mute heroine and her teacher as "the eloquence of free bodily movement," a much-needed lesson for "our muscle-bound theater."

It was about 1943 that Gribble became interested in the experimental group, the American Negro Theatre, organized by Frederick O'Neal and Abram Hill [45] in 1940. The group had become interested in a play by Philip Yordan about a Polish-American family and Gribble was asked to direct it. He saw possibilities in the "straggling" script, which had made the rounds of the Broadway producers for seven years without success. With Hill's and the author's permission, Gribble says, he "rewrote dialogue, situations, and re-characterized some of the characters. After seventeen weeks of this plus rehearsals the end product, *Anna Lucasta,* was presented in the group's tiny Harlem theater. Spirited bidding by Broadway producers followed, and in the summer of 1944 the play opened downtown. While the majority of the critics felt that it was not great drama, the production as a whole was acclaimed as "one of the most notable theatrical successes in many years," presenting as it did "a serious story of average human beings . . . who happen to have pigmented skins." A year after the opening, with the play still playing to capacity, Gribble was planning to direct a new version of Shakespeare's *Romeo and Juliet,* "based on the premise that the Capulets were of Moorish extraction, thereby injecting a note of racial antipathy into their feud with the Montagues." For his star, he hoped to have *Anna Lucasta*'s lead, Hilda Simms [44]. Another project on which Gribble was working in late 1945 is his autobiography.

GRIBBLE, HARRY WAGSTAFF—*Cont.*

Its title, "Some Days You Have," refers to the financial status of people of the theater.

Gribble is brown-haired and hazel-eyed, a slim-waisted five feet ten inches tall, weighs one hundred and sixty-five pounds. He often wears tweeds and dark blue shirts. In his New York City bachelor apartment overlooking the East River, the Broadway craftsman accumulates clippings on American art and nature. Someday he hopes to have these clippings bound and to donate them to a reference library.

References

International Motion Picture Almanac, 1936-37
Who's Who in the Theatre (1939)

GRONINGER, HOMER M. (grŏn'ĭng-ēr)
July 24, 1884- United States Army officer

Address: b. c/o War Department, Washington, D.C.; Port of Embarkation, San Francisco, Calif.

The commanding general of the San Francisco Port of Embarkation, United States Army Transportation Corps, which in turn is

U. S. Army Signal Corps
MAJ. GEN. HOMER M. GRONINGER

a unit of General Brehon Somervell's [42] Army Service Forces, is Major General Homer M. Groninger. The General, who was appointed to this post in June 1945, had previously spent four years and eight months building up the New York POE to the biggest military port in the world—a huge organization operating round the clock, seven days a week, to procure, process, and transport the several millions of men and scores of millions of tons of war goods needed to supply the entire Atlantic theater of war—operating "with never a mistake and never a halt . . . ever improving and ever expanding. . . .Yet, in the world's greatest city, he conducted his operations so expertly and so secretly that few realized this tremen-

dous port of war was running wide open before their very eyes." In San Francisco after midsummer of 1945 he commanded the transport of men through the Golden Gate as they sailed to and from the scenes of Japan's defeat.

Homer M. Groninger was born July 24, 1884, in Port Royal, Pennsylvania. The son of R. Elliott and Mary (McLaughlin) Groninger, he was brought up on his father's farm. Young Homer, or "Cy," as he is still known to his boyhood friends, studied at Airview Academy in Port Royal in 1901-2. While at Pennsylvania State College (1903-4) where he was an ardent baseball player, Groninger read a newspaper account of a game between Army and Navy teams and immediately decided upon a career as an officer. "I chose the Army," General Groninger says, "because I planned to marry some day, and a Navy man doesn't see much of his wife and home." He therefore asked his Congressman for and received an appointment to the United States Military Academy.

At West Point, from which he was graduated in 1908, Cadet Groninger was captain of the baseball team. A dashing polo player, he was commissioned a second lieutenant of Cavalry and assigned to the Fifth Cavalry at Fort Wingate, New Mexico. He accompanied his regiment to Schofield Barracks, Hawaii, where he stayed for a few years, a period broken by a course at the School of Musketry at Monterey, California, in 1912. Then, in early 1913 came service at Fort Huachuca, Arizona. In September 1913 the twenty-nine-year-old lieutenant was married to Gertrude Pomeroy from his home town, who had gone to Sunday school with him. Not long afterward Groninger was sent to Fort Myer, Virginia; his first promotion came a year later. In March 1916 he joined Colonel Pershing's punitive expedition into Mexico against Pancho Villa, whose bandits had raided American territory, and subsequently Groninger put in three months at a camp in Texas.

In May 1917 the Pennsylvanian was advanced to captain and appointed instructor at the Plattsburg (New York) Barracks Officers' Training Camp. Near the end of November he was promoted to major (temporary) and sent to Fort Sill, Oklahoma, to teach at the School of Arms, where he served until June 1918. Next, with the United States in the First World War, the thirty-three-year-old Groninger was transferred to the War Department General Staff in Washington, and in September 1918 he went overseas, wearing the silver oak leaves of a lieutenant colonel, to join General Pershing's AEF staff. During the Meuse-Argonne offensive he served as machine gun officer of the Second ("Indian Head") Division and from November to December in the Third Division, which won itself the nickname "The Rock of the Marne." After the surrender of Germany Colonel Groninger remained on the General Staff of the Army of Occupation in Germany.

In January 1919 Groninger returned to Washington and the War Department General Staff, serving also on the Small Arms and Machine Gun Board. In March 1920 he reverted to the permanent rank of captain, and three months later was promoted to major. From July 1921 to January 1922 he worked in the Office of the Chief of Cavalry, after which he went to the Cavalry School (Fort Riley, Kansas), graduating in June 1922. Then he entered the Command and General Staff School at Fort Leavenworth, Kansas, the second highest Army school. He had done some intermittent studying there from 1918 to 1922, and finished the course with distinction in 1923. In September the Major began a two-year tour of duty at the Cavalry School as instructor in tactics. After study at the Army War College in Washington, D.C., which gives the highest Army training, he was graduated in August 1926 and assigned to the faculty of West Point, where he spent four years.

Next came five years' teaching at the Command and General Staff School, during which Groninger was promoted to lieutenant colonel. In May 1935 the Pennsylvanian reported to Harrisburg, in his home state, as instructor of the Fifty-second Cavalry Brigade, Pennsylvania National Guard. In June 1938, as a colonel, Groninger was given a field command —the Eleventh Cavalry, stationed at the Presidio of Monterey—and in October 1940, when the Second World War was still in its European phase, the fifty-six-year-old cavalryman was made a brigadier general (temporary) and assigned to command the port of embarkation at Brooklyn, New York. He thus wore the stars of a general before such better-known leaders as Patton '43, Clark '42, Spaatz '42, and Eisenhower '42.

When General Groninger assumed command the New York POE consisted of one installation at the Brooklyn Army Base, and a "handful" (about 2,500) of military and civilian employees. Shortly after the Japanese attacked Pearl Harbor he was able to dispatch to the South Pacific an emergency mission of some 33,500 troops. POE activities were shrouded in secrecy "except," as one British naval commander put it, "for the two million New Yorkers who saw us from their office windows and kept quiet about it"; but it was later revealed that in four years Groninger built up his command to twenty times the number of men and women workers, handling the most extensive port of its kind in the world. It grew from the one original installation to "a massive array" including seven major port terminals, shipping centers scattered over a fifty-mile area in Brooklyn, Staten Island, Manhattan, and Queens, the New York Army Post Office, and three "staging areas" in New York and New Jersey, including the two largest in the world, Camps Kilmer and Shanks. Groninger's command also included "a massive network of rail lines, highways, waterways, piers, ships, and storage houses, all of them linked together so that operations could be maintained in the face of any possible catastrophe of nature or enemy action." By September 1944 cargo tonnage handled had risen to sixty-two times the amount of September 1940, and passengers were multiplied by thirty-five.

In the First World War, to quote Representative James W. Wadsworth '43, "freight bottlenecks developed at New York. Freight cars crammed with precious matériel were backed up far inland, lying idle. Troops sent to New York for embarkation sometimes languished in the area for weeks until the shipping was available for their transport. In this war there have been no delays and no traffic bottlenecks, despite the far greater volume of movement. This marvelous record is a tribute to the Army Transportation Corps, the largest transportation agency in the world, which operates the New York port and all other ports of embarkation for the Army." The port soon considered by its commanders to be in the first line of the war, as it filled the requisitions of theater commanders and maintained certain supplies at an automatic level, to make possible the Army boast of having the best-clothed, best-fed, and best-armed troops in the world. Perhaps the most dramatic filling of a requisition was in 1942, when a cargo ship was loaded with tanks and raced around the Cape of Good Hope and up the Red Sea to British Marshal Montgomery '42 in time to help him smash German Marshal Rommel's '42 Afrika Korps at El Alamein. The men and matériel remained officially under Groninger's command, through transport skippers and cargo security officers, until delivery. Altogether, 63,411,551 measurement tons of cargo were shipped from December 1941 through April 1945 to commanders in the entire Atlantic theater of operations; sending out bombers from bases in England; fighting in North Africa, Sicily, Italy, France, Luxembourg, Belgium, Holland, Germany.

Ninety-one per cent of all American troops in the North African and European campaigns passed through the New York POE—a total of 3,080,355 individuals from December 1941 through April 1945. At the staging areas they were housed while each soldier and all his equipment were thoroughly inspected, a routine involving checking of everything from teeth to watches, issuing of new equipment and an anti-gas outfit, and inoculations against diseases. These camps were also a huge school, with courses in subjects like abandoning ship, and a legal, business, and insurance office to handle personal problems for the outgoing troops. As part of General Groninger's program to "send them to Eisenhower in better shape than when they came to us," he established a unique school, soon dubbed "the GI Jam Session," at which about four successive groups a day were taught, in a one-hour session, how to entertain a GI audience in the inevitable waiting periods. According to Sergeant Robert Lieb's description in Liberty, the idea was a brilliant success. "Boredom among our troops is nearly as damaging as bullets," said the General, who emphasizes the importance of sports, "and if a soldier sticks a baseball glove or a football in his barracksbag and smuggles it overseas, more power to him! We'll never court-martial him for it."

Despite the size of these operations, effective secrecy was maintained. For many months, in fact, Groninger was not allowed to tell where he was stationed; and it was not until June 1945, when the General was relieved of his New York command, that the facts were released. Groninger, who had been given a second star in August 1942, then exchanged jobs with Major General Clarence H. Kells, commanding general of the San Francisco POE, as the emphasis shifted from an Atlantic to a Pacific war. Before leaving, how-

GRONINGER, HOMER M.—*Continued*

ever, he arranged to have the Statue of Liberty relighted on nights when troop transports entered New York Harbor, so as not to disappoint veterans eager for a glimpse of the famous symbol. Mayor Fiorello H. La Guardia [40] presented Groninger with New York City's certificate of distinguished service before he left to begin the task of staging the invasion of Japan. Before the lapse of two months, however, the tide had turned, and Japan's surrender converted San Francisco almost entirely into a port of disembarkation.

Homer M. Groninger is described by the artist-correspondent S. J. Woolf as "a general who can swear like a trooper and pray like a chaplain, a man who can be as tough as a top sergeant and as tender as a woman. . . .a tall, broad-shouldered, heavy-set, balding man with light blue eyes in which a gleam of humor seems to lurk." Others mention his "ready tongue and keen wit." He has no taste for fiction or for heavy drama, but likes to see an amusing movie every two or three months and to read history. The General has no preference in smoking—he likes cigars, cigarettes, and a pipe; he is still a baseball fan, although his own playing has been confined to softball for a number of years; and he likes to fish. He has never played bridge, and is saving that for the day when he retires to the farm where he was born. He still reads the Port Royal weekly newspaper, which arrives addressed to Lieutenant Groninger—in almost thirty years the General has not bothered to change his listing.

References

N Y Post Mag p33 Je 14 '44 por
N Y World-Telegram p4 F 17 '44 por
Who's Who in America, 1944-45

GROVES, LESLIE R(ICHARD)　Aug. 17, 1896-　United States Army officer

Address: b. War Department, Washington, D.C.

The explosion of one small bomb over the Japanese city of Hiroshima on August 5, 1945, ushered in for the Allies the last phase of the war against the enemy, and for the world the beginning of the Atomic Age. The invention of this bomb, the result of man's experiments in atom-smashing, cannot be attributed to any one person. Its history is one of research, planning, and production that involved thousands of men and years of work. In the last phase of its development, however, there were a few persons who were assigned special parts in the task. One of these was Brigadier General Leslie R. Groves, who headed the division of the United States War Department directing the production.

The son of Leslie Richard and Gwen (Griffith) Groves, Leslie Richard Groves was born August 17, 1896, in the manse of the First Presbyterian Church in Albany, New York, where his father was a minister. While Leslie was still a baby the Reverend Groves became an Army chaplain, and consequently for a time the family lived at Army posts all over the country, wherever the father happened to be stationed. At seventeen the youth entered the

University of Washington, but after a year he transferred to the Massachusetts Institute of Technology, where he remained for two years. At the end of this time he received an appointment to the United States Military Academy. At West Point young Groves was second-string center on the football team, and in 1918 he was graduated fourth in his class and commissioned a second lieutenant in the Corps of Engineers.

The twenty-two-year-old lieutenant was first sent to the Engineer School at Camp A. A. Humphreys, Virginia. After a year, in June 1919, he was sent to France with the American Expeditionary Force for a three months' observation tour; in September he returned to the Engineer School as a student officer. The following June he left the school again, this time to serve as the commander of a company in the Seventh Engineers. February 1921 found him back at the school once more, and in July he was graduated, having completed both the basic and the civil engineering courses.

From July 1921 until November 1922, when with the Third Engineers he was ordered to a tour of duty in Hawaii, Lieutenant Groves served with various engineering groups, at Camp Lewis and Fort Worden in Washington, and in San Francisco. He returned to the United States from Hawaii in 1925, and for the next two years he was assistant to the district engineer at Galveston, Texas. From 1927 to 1929 he was a member of the First Engineers, and as such was stationed successively at Fort DuPont, Delaware, Fort Ethan Allen, Vermont, and then again at Fort DuPont. When in October 1929 the Engineers were sent to Nicaragua for survey work on the proposed Nicaraguan interoceanic canal, Groves commanded a company from his regiment; subsequently he was awarded the Nicaraguan Medal of Merit for his work there.

When the Lieutenant returned to the United States in 1931 he was assigned to the Office of the Chief of Engineers in Washington, D.C., where he became chief of the Supply Section. It was while he held this post that he received his promotion to captain, in October 1934. A year later he left Washington for Kansas, to enroll in the Command and General Staff School at Fort Leavenworth. Upon graduation in June 1936 he was assigned as assistant to the division engineer of the Missouri River Division at Kansas City, Missouri, but September 1938 found him in Washington, receiving training at the Army War College.

Groves, after graduation the following summer, remained in Washington for service in the Operations and Training Division of the War Department General Staff. In July of 1940 he was promoted to major, and the following November, when he was raised to colonel (temporary), he was made a special assistant to Major General Edmund B. Gregory [45], the Quartermaster General. When Army construction program was transferred to the Corps of Engineers, Groves became a special assistant in General Eugene Reybold's [45] Office of the Chief of Engineers. In the capacity of deputy chief of Army construction, he assisted in the supervision of all military construction in the United States, work which totaled six hundred million dollars a month. Part of his job consisted of supervising the erection of the huge Pentagon across the Potomac from Washington. Grove's biggest assignment came in the summer of 1942, when he was made head of what was known for purposes of secrecy as the Manhattan Engineer District, the division of the War Department, it is known now, that was responsible for the production of the atomic bomb. The Colonel became a brigadier general (temporary) in September of that year, and a lieutenant colonel (permanent) in December 1942.

For years such world-renowned scientists as Niels Bohr '45, Sir James Chadwick '45, Enrico Fermi '45, and E. O. Lawrence '40 had been working on the problem of utilizing the tremendous force locked within the atom. Just before the Second World War began, the research in this field of atom fission—which is the principle upon which the atomic bomb works—was given immediate impetus by Lise Meitner '45, a woman scientist in Germany, who discovered that something that had previously seemed inexplicable was really an explosion of the atoms of metal uranium. (Uranium is a lustrous white metal that comes from pitchblende or carnotite.) At this point Miss Meitner left Germany for neutral Sweden and there released the news of her astounding discovery. Both Allied and Nazi scientists realized to what ends this information would lead—and the race was on to find the last steps in smashing the atom.

In the United States late in 1939, President Roosevelt '42 appointed a commission to investigate the problem and the possible use of atomic energy for military purposes. Until then only small-scale research with Navy funds had taken place. In two years' time the project was put under the direction of a group of eminent American scientists headed by Vannevar Bush '40, and turned over to a general policy group, including men like Henry A. Wallace '40, James B. Conant of Harvard '41, and Henry L. Stimson '40. British-American cooperation on the project was formally begun in October 1941. The following June it was decided to expand the work under the direction of the War Department, and it was then that Groves was called in to take complete executive charge. (He was made a major general [temporary] in December 1944.)

A complete city soon grew up around each plant. Oak Ridge, for example, ten miles from Knoxville in Tennessee, grew from almost nothing to the fifth largest city in the state. In 1943 a combined policy committee of English, American, and Canadian scientists was appointed to facilitate cooperation among the three countries. This was all done under the strictest secrecy. Only those people to whom it was essential that they know were informed of what was happening; even Groves's wife had no idea of what her husband was engaged in. The reports to Stimson had to be kept so secret that Groves used to deliver them orally to the Secretary of War.

When victory came in Europe in May 1945 the nerve-racking race came to an end, but, although the Germans were out of the running, the scientists in the United States did not slacken their pace. Finally, on July 16, 1945, the long-awaited solution was ready for the secret test. In New Mexico, near the special

U. S. Army Signal Corps
BRIG. GEN. LESLIE R. GROVES

laboratory set up under the direction of J. Robert Oppenheimer '45, theoretical physicist at the University of California, a speculative theory was projected into practicality as the test of the first atomic bomb succeeded almost beyond belief. According to the War Department release, those few who witnessed the shattering results felt that they "had been present at the birth of a new age—the Age of Atomic Energy." And they recognized, too, their "profound responsibility to help in guiding into right channels the tremendous forces which had been unlocked for the first time in history."

But the immediate purpose toward which Groves and the men under him had worked for three years had not yet been accomplished —the use of the bomb to hasten the end of the war. On the twenty-first day of the Atomic Age, therefore, August 5, an American B-29 dropped the first bomb on the enemy, on the Japanese city of Hiroshima. The next day President Truman '45 broke the news of the bombing to the public, which thereby learned for the first time of the release of a new force in the world. The effect of the power behind this force was demonstrated even more emphatically only a short time later, for on August 14, five days after a second bomb had been dropped on the city of Nagasaki, Japan surrendered unconditionally.

An interim committee was immediately provided to investigate the possibilities of the peacetime use of atomic energy, and to study postwar control of this force, for everyone realized that this phenomenal discovery has significance far beyond immediate comprehension, significance which shall depend upon what man chooses to make of man. The New York Times editorial comment on August 7, the day after the public announcement of the great discovery, was, in part: "A revolution in science and a revolution in warfare have occurred on the same day. . . .Civilization and humanity can now survive only if there is a revolution in mankind's political thinking."

GROVES, LESLIE R.—*Continued*

The subject of the development, use, and control of atomic energy continued to be widely discussed by the public, press, scientists, the military, and the national legislators during the remaining months of 1945. While the scientists pressed for the sharing of the secret and for world control, the Truman-Attlee-King meeting resulted in the Presidential announcement of their joint decision to share the bomb secret with other United Nations "just as soon as effective enforceable safeguards against its use for destructive purposes can be devised." Senator Ball introduced a bill to create a nine-man control commission, to include the Secretaries of War, Navy, State, Interior, and Commerce, which would set up three advisory boards for research, industrial, and military application of atomic energy. Late in October the Senate Committee on Atomic Energy was established as Congress looked forward to months of discussion on resolutions and bills. Groves himself appeared before the Senate Committee and also spoke publicly on the subject. It was his stand that "this weapon must be kept under the control of the United States until all of the other nations of the world are as anxious for peace as we are." He approved of the Truman-Attlee-King approach to the problem and envisioned the use of atomic energy in industry and medicine. In October Groves was promoted to Brigadier General (permanent) and nominated as assistant to the Army Chief of Engineers. The year closed with the setting up of a joint Army-Navy advisory to work with Groves.

The War Department has commended Groves highly for his performance in "securing the effective development" of the bomb in so short a period of time, and for his organization of an airtight security system. The General has been praised, too, for the job he did in organizing into an efficient working unity all the organizations and forces at work on the vast project. Groves himself has expressed appreciation for the cooperation he has received from scientists and technicians, A.F. of L. and CIO unions, who "in many cases buried jurisdictional difficulties of long standing so that work might be completed on schedule," contractors and industrialists, all of whom were essential to the successful execution of this two-billion-dollar enterprise. Happy over the success of the project, he has called the atomic bomb, according to a report in the New York *Herald Tribune*, a two-billion-dollar calculated risk which paid off. He said that some of the usual engineering procedures had had to be abandoned in the course of production, but that progress was made "through determination and the willingness to take a chance." Groves and a number of others were given Distinguished Service Medals or Distinguished Civilian Service Awards for achievements of "unfathomable importance to the future of the world" for their work in connection with the development of the atomic bomb. By the end of 1945 Hollywood was planning to record the history of the atomic bomb on celluloid, in which the role of General Groves might be played by Clark Gable '45.

The General and Mrs. Groves, the former Grace Hulbert Wilson, to whom he has been married since 1922, have two children: Gwen who in 1945 was at the National Catholic School for Girls in Washington, D.C., where the family makes its home, and Richard, who was graduated from West Point in June of 1945. The Lieutenant was assigned to Fort Belvoir, an engineering establishment in Virginia, the same post to which his father was assigned twenty-seven years before. Groves, whose organizing ability made possible the production of the atomic bomb, has been described as a heavy-set man, slightly under six feet in height, soft-spoken, and genial. A football player at West Point, he is still an athlete; his favorite sport, according to Mrs. Groves, is tennis, but for three years the General was kept too busy to find time for even one game.

References

N Y Herald Tribune p6 Ag 7 '45
PM p9 Ag 7 '45
Who's Who in America, 1944-45

GRUMMAN, LEROY R(ANDLE) (grŭm' mǎn) Jan. 4, 1895- Industrialist

Address: b. Grumman Aircraft Engineering Corp., Bethpage, Long Island, N.Y.; h. 77 Bayview Rd., Plandome, Long Island, N.Y.

When Rear Admiral John H. Towers in 1942 presented to the Grumman Aircraft Engineering Corporation its first Navy E, the first Navy E awarded in the industry, he told the Grumman employees: "Practically every airplane you turn out goes to an active combat area immediately. . . . Your products have been speaking for themselves." And Vice-Admiral John McCain '43 has said: "The name Grumman on a plane or a part is like sterling on silver." Aircraft planner and designer of the Wildcat, Hellcat, and Avenger planes, and reputed financial genius of the company, is its president, Leroy R. Grumman. In a decade and a half he has directed the corporation's growth from a plane repair shop employing sixteen persons to an industrial plant with twenty thousand employees who not only maintain the quantity and quality of their production but have a record of no strikes and very little absenteeism. On the strength of past performance, observers predict an important postwar future for Grumman.

Leroy Randle Grumman was born on January 4, 1895, in Huntington, Long Island. The family of his father, George Tyson Grumman, (according to Francis Sill Wickware in the *Saturday Evening Post*) generations earlier had given its name to the village of Grumman Hill, near Wilton, Connecticut. The elder Grumman was a carriage shop owner; his wife was the former Grace Ethel Conklin. Roy attended the Huntington High School, from which he was graduated in June 1911, the second highest in his class. Already interested in the technological developments in airplanes, he discussed the future of the then infant industry in his salutatorian address at the commencement exercises. Then continuing his education at Cornell, Grumman specialized in engineering, graduating in 1916.

He obtained his first job in the engineering department of the New York Telephone Com-

pany. When the United States entered the
First World War in 1917 Grumman became a
mechanics mate in the Navy and was sent for
special instruction to Columbia University.
Learning to fly at Miami and Pensacola in the
first months of 1918, he was promoted to the
rank of ensign and assigned as a pilot instructor to the Naval Air Training Station at
Pensacola. In 1919, after a second special
course, taken at Massachusetts Institute of
Technology, he was transferred to the Naval
Aircraft Factory in Philadelphia as a test pilot
and engineer. In 1920 he was retired as a
lieutenant, junior grade, to the United States
Naval Reserve. The experience thus gained
enabled him in 1920 to obtain the position of
general manager and aeronautical engineer with
the Loening Aeronautical Engineering Corporation of New York. For the succeeding nine
years Grumman remained with Loening.

In 1929, however, when mergers between aircraft firms were becoming increasingly frequent, the Loening Company announced its intention of combining with Keystone Aircraft,
and Grumman found himself confronted with
the alternative of accepting a less responsible
position in the new company or looking for another job. He decided to go into business for
himself, with Leon A ("Jake") Swirbul, factory manager at Loening and now Grumman's
vice-president and production manager, and
William T. Schwendler, a rising young engineer at Grumman Aircraft, as partners. On
December 6, 1929, they established the Grumman Aircraft Engineering Corporation with a
capitalization of thirty-two thousand dollars,
of which Grumman himself contributed approximately seventeen thousand. On January
2, 1930, the three young men opened their shop
for the repair of airplanes (especially the
Loening "Air Yachts" which rich private owners were always wrecking and which Loening
was no longer servicing) in a converted garage
in Baldwin, Long Island. Their first repair
job threatened to be their last—a motorist,
crashing into the projecting nose of an amphibian plane too large to fit into the workshop, threatened suit. But the matter was adjusted when Grumman agreed to repair the
car, and Grumman Aircraft was started on the
road to success.

Besides Grumman, Swirbul, Schwendler, and
two others on the office staff, the new company
employed sixteen men in its shop. As its reputation spread, work began to come in from
all over the country, with Pan American-
Grace Airways even shipping a plane all the
way from Panama to be repaired. Luck, too,
aided the new enterprise when an insurance
agent unfamiliar with aircraft allowed Grumman and Swirbul to buy a wrecked plane for
four hundred dollars which they were able to
sell for twenty-one thousand dollars after
replacing the motor and repairing the fuselage.
When work was slack, as at the end of 1930,
Grumman turned to other fields for employment, teaming up with C. S. Lyon's Motor
Haulage Corporation to produce a lightweight
but strong truck body for use on standard
chassis, and a chassis-less trailer for trucks.
Before the end of 1930 Grumman had also
begun work on a monocoque aluminum float
with a unique retractable landing gear which

LEROY R. GRUMMAN

was to convert Navy scout planes into amphibians. Although the Navy ordered two
floats merely from the plans, it afterward
balked when Navy engineers reported their inability to calculate the stresses of the revolutionary design, admitting that they were
unable to determine whether the float could
withstand the shock of a catapult launching.
Not to be daunted, Grumman and Swirbul
took their seats behind a Navy pilot in a
float-equipped plane, were catapulted from the
deck of a battleship, and proved their point.
A Navy contract for eight resulted.

Having conquered the first hurdle of manufacturing, Grumman redesigned his float and
added an arresting landing gear to facilitate
landing on a limited area such as a carrier
deck. The Navy responded with an order for
fifteen. The success of the retracting gear on
both models of the amphibian float suggested
to Grumman the employment of similar gear
construction on a military airplane. Conservative Navy men rejected the improvement, because expert opinion up to that time had
considered the advantages of the mechanism
offset by the disadvantages of extra weight
and complexity of construction. Grumman
found, however, that the Bureau of Aeronautics was interested, and, on the strength of
its encouragement, he moved his factory to a
larger building at Valley Stream, Long Island,
to begin work on a fighter plane embodying
his new landing gear principle. The XFF-1,
the ancestor of all Grumman planes, was delivered to the Navy at the end of December
1931. The craft's performance and remarkable speed, a convincing demonstration of
Grumman's theories, won an immediate Navy
contract and started Grumman on his career
as plane builder for the United States Navy.

The following years were occupied with the
improvement and modification of the XFF-1
and the amphibian floats. Expanding production forced Grumman in 1932 to move to still
larger quarters at Farmingdale, Long Island,

(Continued next page)

GRUMMAN, LEROY R.—*Continued*

Here the company specialized in building fighter and utility ships for the Navy, and developed "the stubby, teardrop-shaped fuselage that has become a virtual Grumman trade-mark." When the boom tapered off in the middle thirties Grumman placed in production two amphibians for private and commercial use, the G-21 selling for sixty thousand dollars and the smaller Widgeon selling for twenty-eight thousand. Owners soon included Marshall Field '41, Henry S. Morgan, Robert R. McCormick '42, and Lord Beaverbrook '40. So successful were these planes in navigating the inaccessible Georgia bayous and mountain fastnesses for oil companies and others that the Navy and the Army, too, were soon purchasing them. By 1937 lack of ready cash to complete the large number of orders on the books almost bankrupted the corporation, but the offer of a stock issue to the general public, underwritten in part by Bernard E. Smith, a Wall Street financier who wanted to buy an amphibian, averted the disaster.

When the Japanese attacked Pearl Harbor, Grumman, who had already been supplying the Navy with Wildcat carrier fighters for some time, swung into production on a large scale at his new plant at Bethpage, also on Long Island. While other manufacturers were still arguing over alterations in design, he consulted William S. Knudsen '40, then director of the Office of Production Management, froze his designs, and began to build planes wherever he could find space to convert into assembly lines. Wildcats quickly set records in the battle of the Pacific and, rechristened Martlets, for Britain in the Mediterranean, thus refuting the myth of the inferiority of carrier fighting planes to land-based fighters that was once presented by experts to Grumman as a basis for slighting quality on the former. Always interested in the improvement of his planes, Grumman soon perfected a folding wing, now installed on all his carrier planes, which made possible a 50 per cent increase in carrier capacity. (*Time* reports that, in his usual informal manner of working, Grumman worked out the construction principle by manipulating paper clips stuck into either side of an eraser.)

When Navy pilots reported trouble with Japanese Zeros, Grumman sent Swirbul to the Pacific for information and to the pilots' stipulations constructed the Hellcat to outdistance, outclimb, and outfight the Japanese plane. Says Grumman of the Hellcat—the first plane to be designed from pilots' specifications, the first to be produced in quantity before a test flight had been made, and a plane which set production records in the speed with which it was translated from blueprint to assembly line—"It is not right to think of the Hellcat as a sort of big brother of the Wildcat. It is a new plane, bigger, faster, more maneuverable." A Navy captain has called it "the answer to a fighter pilot's dream . . . the hottest thing in the air." Besides the Hellcat, which has superseded the Wildcat, Grumman has in production a torpedo bomber, the Avenger, design of which was begun in 1936 when experts predicted that the day of the fighter plane was over. Construction started in 1939, but the present Avengers owe their perfection to discussions with British military authorities after outmoded British Swordfish torpedo planes defeating the Italian Fleet at Taranto demonstrated the value of this newest weapon.

Production world records for these Grumman planes are said to be due to Grumman employment policies. (Grumman Aircraft was "the first plant to produce ten thousand planes of one model, designed and built after December 7, 1941"; and in one month, March 1945, completed 605 planes, 105 above its quota.) Swirbul and Grumman have found that it pays to hire local people instead of erecting temporary, barracks-like living quarters; and that employees will remain on the job if they are provided with satisfactory working conditions, an incentive wage plan, and recreation facilities; if they are able to consult the boss directly (Grumman's employees wander in and out of his office at will); and if their worries are mitigated by child-care nurseries and a little green emergency truck which can be sent to turn off a forgotten gas jet or to rescue a stranded motorist.

Immediately after V-J Day Grumman stopped production on the Hellcat and laid off its twenty-two thousand workers, then hired some five thousand back to work on pursuit models for the Navy; he plans to go into production of amphibians for private use. He has joined with other airplane manufacturers in urging a broad Government research program. In spite of reconversion problems, Grumman announced on October 27, 1945, that the company had just put into effect a new employee retirement plan, retroactive for five years prior to January 1, 1943, for which the company assumed all costs; at the same time the company carries group insurance for all employees, regardless of age or length of service.

Roy Grumman, as he is generally known, is described as a quiet, reflective small-town man who dislikes big cities—"pure counterpoint to the gusty Swirbul." He is reticent not only about himself but also about the company, declining to advertise, for instance, until his schoolboy son complained that no one had heard of his father's airplanes. Like Swirbul, however, he is informal and, according to *Time*, works in his shirtsleeves, often with his feet on the desk, in an office which he shares with his lieutenant. If the office becomes too crowded with workers, Grumman and Swirbul move into a second office, from the ceiling of which hang hundreds of model airplanes.

At home in the evenings—his white seventeen-room house with blue shutters overlooks Long Island Sound—Grumman reads, or he visits neighbors with Mrs. Grumman. He and Mrs. Grumman, the former Rose Marion Werther, to whom he was married in March 1921, have four children: Marion Elinor, Florence Werther, Grace Caroline, and David Leroy. Of medium height, Grumman is somewhat stoop-shouldered, has blue eyes and sandy hair, and a New England twang in his voice. He is a Presbyterian, and belongs to the North Hempstead Country Club, the Manhasset Bay Yacht Club, and the Hicksville Aviation Country Club. He is a Fellow of the Institute of Aeronautical Sciences and a member of the Society of Automotive Engineers. Grumman still likes to fly. "When you're alone five thousand feet in the air," he says, "lots of things about a plane become important that you can overlook on the ground."

References

Aero Digest 36:48-9+ Ja '40 il
N Y Herald Tribune p35 N '42 il por
Sat Eve Post 215:22+ S 5 '42 il por
Time 39:57-8 My 18 '42 por; 44:79-80+ S 11 '44 il por
Who's Who in America, 1944-45
Who's Who in Aviation, 1942-43

GUEDALLA, PHILIP (gwĕ-dăl'á) Mar. 12, 1889—Dec. 16, 1944 British biographer, historian, and essayist—a former lawyer turned writer; noted for his colorful style and dynamic phrases; some of his important works are *The Hundred Years* (1936), *Mr. Churchill* (1942), and *The Two Marshals, Bazaine and Pétain* (1943).

Obituary

N Y Times p37 D 17 '44 por

GULICK, LUTHER (HALSEY) (gū'lĭk) Jan. 17, 1892- United States Government official

Address: b. Institute of Public Administration, 684 Park Ave., New York City; h. 14 Sussex Ave., Bronxville, N.Y.

As director of the Institute of Public Administration, whose function is to render expert technical advice to governments, Luther Gulick is ranked by his colleagues as one of the top men in his field. His study of the New York State educational system and his work as a tax authority are also well known. Because of his special abilities in these fields, since 1941 Gulick has held important posts in various Federal Government war agencies.

Born in Osaka, Japan, January 17, 1892, Luther Halsey Gulick is one of the five children of Dr. Sidney Lewis and Cara M. (Fisher) Gulick. Because his father, an educator and missionary, was born in the Marshall Islands and his missionary grandfather in Hawaii, Gulick has to go back to his great-grandfather (also an educator) to find an American-born paternal ancestor. Before the outbreak of the Second World War members of the Gulick family were active in missionary work in Japan, China, India, Turkey, Iran, and Spain.

During his boyhood in Japan Gulick's education was acquired largely through tutors and from his parents. He later attended public schools in California and, for one year, in Germany. After his graduation from the Hotchkiss Preparatory School, he entered Oberlin College, where he received his B.A. in 1914. As an Oberlin undergraduate he was called "a fresh kid—talkative, boasting, energetic." He was an excellent student, staying on at Oberlin to take his master's degree in political science in 1915. (In 1939 Oberlin awarded him a Litt. D.) He then went to Columbia University to become a student of Professor Charles A. Beard's [41], and participated (1915-17) in the Training School for Public Service of the New York Bureau of Municipal Research, of which Beard was then director. The courses consisted of laboratory

LUTHER GULICK

work in public administration, affording Gulick a good deal of experience in the tax, police, fire, street cleaning, and other city departments.

With the outbreak of the First World War Gulick left Columbia to do statistical work for the Council of National Defense. Later he transferred to the War Department, becoming a captain in the statistical branch of the General Staff. After the war he returned to Columbia, where he received his doctor of philosophy degree in 1920.

In the early 'twenties Gulick taught classes in public administration at Columbia, and also became a staff member of the New York Bureau of Municipal Research, a private organization. He later became director of the bureau, which was renamed the Institute of Public Administration, in the service of which he currently continues as director. The Institute of Public Administration furnishes technical assistance to legislative commissions, tax departments, and the general administrations of state and local governments. At the time when Calvin Coolidge was Governor of Massachusetts it was Gulick who, as secretary of the joint special committee on the budget, helped Coolidge organize the Massachusetts budget system. Gulick was later called upon to work on the finances of other states, and he took part in several other reorganization studies with the staff of Bureau of Municipal Research. During these years he also lectured at various colleges, becoming Eaton Professor of Municipal Science and Administration of Columbia, and delivering special courses of lectures at Union College (1928-29), subsequently at the Universities of Buffalo, Chicago, and Pennsylvania. In 1933 he was Dodge Lecturer at Yale. His work in public administration thus functioned in two ways: through his own experiences in municipal research he was able to guide the academicians toward practical approaches to their studies; at the same time he brought to the public administrators themselves the theory and learning of the college professors.

(Continued next page)

GULICK, LUTHER—*Continued*

Gulick's first work of national importance began in 1933 when he was made the director of the Commission of Inquiry on Public Service Personnel, appointed by the Social Science Research Council. After a thorough investigation, his committee in 1935 submitted a seven-volume report of its findings. In an article in *Survey* for February 1935, Gulick discussed the major aspects of the situation. The Commission of Inquiry on Public Service Personnel had discovered that the most intelligent and ablest people do not go into government service. The situation exists, said Gulick, largely because of "the spoils system, the use of public payrolls for charity, and undiscriminating criticism of public employees." Gulick and his assistants recommended that the Government put the civil service on a career basis, recruiting young men and young women on the basis of capacity and providing for their advancement. It is said that many improvements in the Civil Service since 1937 have been due to this study on service personnel.

Having become increasingly active in the field of education, Gulick, as director of the Regents' Inquiry, began in 1935 a four-year study of the public school system of New York State. The findings and recommendations, published in eleven volumes, were considered "the most comprehensive study of an educational system ever made." For his share in it Gulick was awarded the Butler Medal by Columbia University in 1939, an award given annually to degree-holders of the university for the outstanding piece of work of the year. As a result of this survey Gulick was also offered more than one college presidency, but these offers he declined.

In "A New Hope for Education" (*Atlantic Monthly,* April 1939), Gulick described the investigations of the Regents' Inquiry Committee into the cost and character of education in New York State. Much of the school curriculum, he declared, was found to be outdated. Not enough was being done to provide adequate vocational education or knowledge of local government and civic problems. In his book *Education for American Life* (1938), Gulick recommended adding two more years to the high school course for those boys and girls who do not go into employment or to college. He would extend the preparation period of teachers and increase the salaries of rural teachers. He also recommended increased centralization of schools, a coordinator of adult education for every community, and increased student aid.

One of the most important undertakings of Gulick's career was his work on the President's Committee on Administrative Management, from 1936 to 1938. Serving on this committee with him were Louis Brownlow and Charles E. Merriam, together with a staff of specialists in government and administration. As early as 1933 Gulick had set forth his theory of taking politics out of administration: "The Government is becoming and is apparently destined to remain, at least to a degree, the super-holding company of the economic life of the Nation. The fundamental new function which government assumes in this process is that of devising and imposing a consistent master plan of national life. This will require a new division of actual work and therefore a new theory of the division of powers . . . concerned not with checks and balances or with the division of policy and administration, but with the division between policy veto on one side and policy planning and execution on the other."

The investigation of the Committee on Administrative Management became the basis of President Roosevelt's [42] reorganization of the administrative branches of the Federal Government. In his article "Making Democracy Work" (*Survey Graphic,* March 1937), Gulick reported that, for purposes of management, "boards and commissions have turned out to be failures. . . . Real efficiency must be built into the structure of a government just as it is built into a piece of machinery."

Among other measures the committee recommended were: (1) expansion of the White House staff by the addition of a number of administrative assistants to the President; (2) strengthening of the managerial agencies of the Government; (3) inclusion of independent agencies within the twelve major Executive departments; (4) establishment of the accountability of the Executive to Congress by the provision of a genuine independent post-audit of all fiscal transactions by an auditor-general. Of the committee program, Walter Lippmann [40] wrote: "It is a great document not because all of its specific proposals are necessarily great or wise or even well considered, but because the report has raised with such understanding, and would begin to remedy with such courage, the really great difficulties which have developed in the operation of the Government over a period of a hundred years."

Early in 1941 Gulick became a consultant on post-defense planning for the National Resources Planning Board. It was in this connection that he, with Professor Alvin Hansen [45] of Harvard, represented the United States at the International Conference on Science and the World Order held in London in September 1941. At this congress the problems of postwar reconstruction in the light of science were discussed. Afterward Gulick remained in England for three weeks to study special aspects of postwar planning. On his return home he stated his belief that "the most specific need in the postwar period in this country, whether you are optimistic, pessimistic, or realistic, will be that of urban reconstruction and transportation."

The post-defense division of the NRPB published an eighteen-page pamphlet, *After Defense—What?* The report discussed transition to a peacetime economy without depression and unemployment; and it was predicted that it would be read and re-examined as "a signpost to a new world." Two basic facts were pointed out: first, that any expansion of the economy can absorb only a few million workers in any given year; second, that when peace comes the United States must find peacetime jobs for all its manpower, otherwise the country would be "back in the valley of the depression." The report said that in postwar years the national income should be maintained at a level of a hundred billion dollars. Full employment could be accomplished, the report stated, through encouragement of a public works program, the development of new products, the expansion of public services, new forms of social security, and an end to isolationism.

In the year of 1941 Gulick served as a special assistant to the Secretary of the Treasury, was a member of the United States Census Advisory Committee, and president of the Tax Research Foundation. At this time he was also an expert consultant to the Secretary of War, and assisted his friend General Brehon Somervell [42] on supply reorganization problems.

In May 1942 Donald Nelson [41], then head of the War Production Board, appointed Gulick to direct a permanent office of organizational planning as a step toward decentralizing the WPB. The functions of Gulick's office, said Nelson, would include a continuous study of the responsibilities and operation of the various units of WPB in an effort to reduce duplications and overlapping of functions. A further duty was to study methods of achieving decentralization in order to concentrate as much authority as possible in the local offices. Gulick called his WPB assignment "the most difficult Government job in the world," and said he expected to stay with it for the duration of the war.

But in January 1943 Nelson announced with regret the resignation of Gulick from the WPB. Gulick had a new post—this time as chief of the Program and Requirements Division of the Office of Foreign Relief and Rehabilitation under Herbert H. Lehman [43]. He took a vigorous part in the organization of the United Nations Relief and Rehabilitation Administration, which he called "unique in the relief field." Its management, he said, "is sound, able, and humanitarian. The staff will be international and expert. The financing will be a joint world enterprise, of which our share at most will be a small fraction of what we are spending on the war." In an article, "Moscow, Atlantic City and Points Ahead" (*Survey Graphic*, December 1943), he wrote: "Don't let anybody tell you that the cost of rehabilitation is prohibitive. The truth is, the cost of any other policy is prohibitive. Relief without rehabilitation, in the economic shambles of present-day Europe, would cost five times as much as relief and rehabilitation together."

The Committee on Intergovernmental Fiscal Relations, consisting of Gulick and two professors of economics, Harold M. Groves of Wisconsin University, and Mabel Newcomer [44] of Vassar, submitted to Secretary Morgenthau [40] in March 1943 a plan for coordinating taxation in the three levels of government. It was called "a postwar fiscal system tailored to fit the new world envisioned by Roosevelt's National Resources Planning Board." The committee emphasized the need for the creation of a Federal-state fiscal authority to examine and suggest changes in the fiscal affairs which Federal, state, and local governments might well follow. The report, a six-volume work, contained sixty-nine recommendations, among the more important being: (1) Creation of a Federal-State fiscal authority; (2) public investment in such fields as public health, regional development, public housing, and nutrition to "underwrite the maintenance of a high level of economic opportunity and full use of resources and plant capacity in the United States"; (3) broadened Federal-aid programs

to include relief and public education, and maintenance of minimum standards of educational opportunity: any Federal program should control the division of educational moneys between whites and Negroes; (4) broader social security coverage to include groups now uncovered; (5) broadened Federal-aid programs, extended to relief and public education, providing for differential grants aimed to achieve national minimum standards; (6) Federal incorporation of companies doing interstate business; and (7) adoption of a more progressive tax system and elimination of tax loopholes. The committee recommended taxation of present tax-exempt securities and a complete overhauling of the death and gift tax structures.

Gulick's primary intellectual contribution has been in the development of the analysis and theory of administration. As a definition of "administration" he coined the word "Posdcorb," which stands for planning, organizing, staffing, directing, coordinating, reporting, and budgeting; these, according to Gulick, are the functional elements of administration. Gulick developed these theories in his best-known book, *Papers on the Science of Administration* (edited with L. Urwick), parts of which have been translated into French, German, Portuguese, Russian, Chinese, and Japanese.

During 1944, besides working with the UNRRA, Gulick continued in his own special field of public administration. He worked on plans to reorganize the Foreign Economic Administration Agency and various other Federal activities. He took a leading part, early in 1945, in a series of conferences on education sponsored by the New York *Times* and the Public Education Association. With several other educators he contended that Federal aid was a vital necessity to schools. Late in 1945, Gulick was one of fourteen advisers who accompanied Edwin W. Pauley [45] to Japan to survey "the amount and nature of assets held by the Japanese which should be used as reparations."

In addition to his posts in the fields of education, taxation, and administration, Gulick has held several other correlating positions. Since 1940 he has been chairman of the Educational Committee of the Office of the Coordinator of Inter-American affairs. He has been a member of the Social Science Research Council, and of the Liquor Control Commission. He is also chairman of the American Film Center and of the Public Affairs Committee. On May 15, 1945, Gulick was chosen as one of the twenty-one experts to assist Edwin W. Pauley [45], head of the American representatives to the Reparations Commission.

Gulick was married in 1917 to Helen McKelvey Swift. Mrs. Gulick has always taken an active interest in her husband's work, and on occasion has been of official assistance to him: when he was called to duty by the WPB she took over his desk with the National Resources Planning Board. (The Gulicks have two sons, Clarence Swift and Luther Halsey; one served in the Navy, the other in the Army.) "Of medium height, mild appearance, and wearing silver-rimmed glasses, Gulick affects no flourishes, dislikes publicity and usually avoids it. He keeps clear of politics [he himself is a Republican] and policy-making." He is "a lover of modern music and painting, a

GULICK, LUTHER—*Continued*

rather bad tennis player, an amateur mechanic, and a confirmed hiker." It is said that he once climbed mountains in Switzerland and the Rockies. One of his recreations now, when not working in his office from eight in the morning till ten at night, is hiking about the woods near his Westchester County home.

References

Newsweek 20:37 Jl 13 '42 por
Who's Who in America, 1944-45

HACHA, EMIL (hä′ĸá ĕ′mĭl) 1872—June 27, 1945 Former puppet Czech President of Bohemia and Moravia during the German occupation—elected in 1938 by German pressure; served as a state officer in the Austrian Empire (1898-1916); judge in the Austrian High Court of Administration (1916-18); made Senate president of the Czechoslovakian High Court in 1918 and president in 1925; died while awaiting trial on charges of collaboration. See *Current Biography* 1942 Yearbook.

Obituary

N Y Times p17 Jl 1 '45 por

HALSEY, EDWIN A(LEXANDER) Sept. 4, 1881—Jan. 29, 1945 Secretary of the United States Senate since 1933 and one of the most popular figures on Capitol Hill; served in various capacities as an employee of the Senate for nearly half a century; began career as page boy.

Obituary

N Y Times p19 Ja 30 '45 por

HANSELL, HAYWOOD S(HEPHERD, JR.) Sept. 28, 1903- United States Army Air Force officer

Address: b. c/o War Department, Washington, D.C.; h. 401 Wiltshire Ave., San Antonio, Tex.

The combination of abilities which makes a military man outstanding both in planning strategically and in executing that strategy on the field is found in Brigadier General Haywood ("Possum") Hansell. As chief of staff of the new Twentieth United States Air Force, he helped plan the bombing system used against Japan by the Boeing B-29 Superfortresses; as commanding general of the Twenty-first Bomber Command, Twentieth Air Force, he directed the operations of the Saipan-based "flying castles" which bombed Japan until V-J Day.

A fifth-generation Army man of English descent, whose grandfather and great-grandfather had fought against the Union in the Civil War, Haywood Shepherd Hansell, Jr., was born September 28, 1903, in the antebellum officers' quarters of Fort Monroe, Virginia. His father, Colonel Haywood S. Hansell, was an Army surgeon; his mother, the former Susan Wilson of Atlanta, was a belle in the old Southern tradition. Young Haywood's first language, it is said, was Chinese, which he has since forgotten: He learned it from his amah while Colonel Hansell was on duty in China during the Boxer Rebellion. When that officer

was transferred to the Philippines his three-year-old son started learning Spanish from his nurse, and it was not until then that his mother started to teach him English. This third language came in handy at the various Army posts where the Hansells lived after their return to the United States, and at Sewanee Military Academy, where Haywood was dubbed "Possum" for his alleged similarity to the opossum.

Nevertheless, in his senior year at Sewanee young Hansell was made captain of the cadet corps, and a very strict one he was—until his sudden demotion to buck private, the result of a sharp decline in grades. As a consequence, upon his graduation in 1920, he turned down an appointment to West Point in favor of studying mechanical engineering at Georgia School of Technology. At this time, says Sidney Shalett, the Possum's great ambition was to be a football player, although he barely tipped the scales at one hundred. However, Hansell recalls, "I had one of the most unusual football careers in the South. I played seven years without ever earning a letter. Neither at Sewanee nor Georgia Tech did I ever get off the bench in a major game." Graduated with his engineering degree in 1924, Hansell declined the offer of a second lieutenancy and rejoined his parents in San Francisco. In California the future General worked for the Steel Pipe and Tank Company at Berkeley as a helper, supplying his own tools out of wages of two dollars and sixty cents for a ten-hour day. After a year he was qualified as a journeyman boilermaker; after another year he was a draftsman and estimator; and in his fourth year Hansell was made chief engineer.

In February 1928 Hansell enrolled as a flying cadet, "just to learn something about planes so I could build them," he says. After training at March Field, California, and Kelly Field, Texas, he was graduated from the pursuit course with his wings in February 1929 and was commissioned a second lieutenant in the Air Reserves, entering active duty the following day. (His ratings are: command pilot, combat observer, and technical observer.) Three months later Hansell was given a commission in the Air Corps of the Regular Army and assigned to duty with the Second Bombardment Group at Langley Field, Virginia. While testing a P-12 fighter there one cold winter day, Lieutenant Hansell was forced to bail out over Chesapeake Bay; unable to wriggle out of his hastily adjusted parachute harness, he nearly drowned during the twenty minutes before he was rescued.

In September 1930, after three months' temporary duty with the Sixth Field Artillery at Fort Hoyle, Maryland, the twenty-seven-year-old Lieutenant returned to Langley Field as armament officer of the Air Corps Tactical School Detachment. He was sent to Maxwell Field, Alabama, in August 1931 for duty with the Fifty-first and later the Fifty-fourth School Squadrons as assistant operations officer. At this time Hansell was courting brunet Dorothy Rogers, a Texas belle whom he used to fly to Waco to visit. They were married in 1932, and have three children: Haywood, 3d (called "Tony"), Lucia, and Dennett, who, with their mother, live in San

Antonio, in which city the elder Hansells also have their home.

During this period, too, Hansell, a "hot pilot," joined Captain Claire Chennault [42] and Lieutenant Luke Williamson (Lieutenant William McDonald was alternate) to form the "Three Men on a Flying Trapeze," a team of aerobats who represented the Army Air Corps at the Cleveland National Air Races in September 1934. Chennault, with the daring ingenuity later to make him famous as head of the Flying Tigers, "used to sit up nights thinking up things that absolutely could not be done with an airplane; then he would take his team out next day and they would do them"—in perfect formation. "If we had kept at it long enough," General Hansell now says sedately, "we certainly all would have been killed."

"The only [other] thing that distinguished the pint-sized Lieutenant in those days," according to Shalett, "was the fact that he was the only shavetail at Maxwell who had a complete set of dress blues"—and those were thirty years old. But Lieutenant Colonel Harold L. George [42] was "immediately impressed that here was a man with a broad understanding of the proper utilization of air power—something not too many people had in those days." So George went to his friend Major Carl ("Tooey") Spaatz [42], who was in charge of tactical instruction, and got young Hansell assigned to study tactics and strategy under him (George) at the school from July 1934 to June 1935. In October 1934, nearly six years after his commissioning, Hansell was promoted to first lieutenant—par for the course in those depression days. On graduation he was appointed an instructor, one of the youngest at the school; his subject was called "air force." Here the officer distinguished himself at polo, tennis, and squash, as a tireless dancer, a tuneless baritone, and "the unofficial poet laureate of the Air Corps." A songbook published in 1937 by the Daedalians, an Army fliers' social group, boasts Hansell as the author of half its lyrics.

After three years the thirty-five-year-old Lieutenant was sent to the Command and General Staff School at Fort Leavenworth, Kansas, for advanced training. After his graduation in June 1939 Hansell was ordered to Washington, D. C., where he became assistant executive officer in the Office of the Chief of Air Corps. Then Colonel George discovered that "for some damn reason he doesn't know" his protégé was doing public relations work, and "yanked him back into planning, where he belonged." In November 1939, therefore, Captain Hansell (he had been promoted that May) was transferred to the Air Force Intelligence Division, and in July 1940 was made chief of the Foreign Intelligence Section's Operations Planning Branch. In March 1941 he was promoted to major (temporary), and in July he was sent to London as special observer to report on the air blitz.

In August 1941 Hansell returned to Washington for duty with the War Plans Division of the Air Staff. At that time President Roosevelt [42] instructed General H. H. Arnold [42] to draw up a strategic blueprint for the air forces in case of war. In ten weeks of sixteen-hour days, seven days a week, four future generals—George, his assistant Han-

BRIG. GEN. HAYWOOD S. HANSELL

sell, Kuter, and Walker—worked out a plan for the strategic long-range bombardment of Germany which was subsequently put into action and, "with necessary combat modifications, has stood up in Europe." It provided for an unprecedented force of more than 2,200,000 men and 88,000 planes; presumed that war would develop against Germany and Japan at the same time; and arranged for the European enemy to be dealt with first, by "a sustained and irresistible bombing offensive, deliberately aimed at Germany's vitals, [that] would make an invasion either unnecessary or . . . tremendously easier." All this was months before the Pearl Harbor attack hurled the United States into the Second World War.

The quality of Hansell's work brought him two promotions within three months—to lieutenant colonel (temporary) in January 1942, and to colonel (temporary) the following March. It also won him the Legion of Merit and, in August 1942, his promotion to brigadier general (temporary) and an assignment as General Ike Eisenhower's [42] air plans officer in the European Theater of Operations. In permanent rank, however, the new General was still a captain—a junior officer.

Feeling the need of more experience in the field, Hansell had himself transferred to the Third Bombardment Wing of the Eighth Air Force in December, as commanding general. At the beginning of 1943 he was given command of the First Bombardment Wing, composed of B-17 Flying Fortresses. On the third of January the flying General won the Silver Star for the "indomitable courage and superlative leadership" with which he led a bombing attack on the German U-boat pens at St. Nazaire against "terrific odds," bringing his planes to a friendly base without loss of life or equipment. Other missions won Hansell the Air Medal and the D.F.C.; and on March 13 he celebrated his elder son's birthday by flying his namesake Fortress, the *Tony H*, to occupied Amiens and "plastering hell" out of the freight yards there. Then in July he was recalled to London and a "chair-borne" job

HANSELL, HAYWOOD S.—*Continued*

as Air Marshal Sir Trafford Leigh-Mallory's [44] deputy commander in chief of the Allied Expeditionary Air Force in the Mediterranean.

In October 1943 Hansell was sent back to Washington for duty in the Office of the Assistant Chief of Air Staff for Plans. As an air planner on the joint planning staff of the Joint and Combined Chiefs of Staff, he was a member of the military delegation to the Roosevelt [42]-Churchill [42] conference in Quebec and to the three-power conferences at Cairo and Teheran. Returning from these, Hansell accompanied General George Marshall [40], United States Chief of Staff, on his globe-girdling thirty-five-thousand-mile inspection tour in December 1943.

Four months later General Hansell was promoted to the post of deputy chief of Air Staff, and was soon chief of staff as well to General Arnold in the General's capacity as commander of the secret global air force of super bombers which was then being developed. This Twentieth Air Force, composed of B-29 Superfortresses which dwarfed every other plane that had ever been built, was to operate as "an aerial battle fleet . . . wherever the need was greatest." Directly under control of the Joint Chiefs of Staff in Washington, it is in effect a separate air force, commanded personally by General Arnold and acting through bomber commands responsible to a deputy commander, Lieutenant General Millard F. Harmon [42]. The battle debut of the new force was made on June 15, 1944, when the Twentieth Bomber Command, then under Brigadier General Kenneth L. Wolfe, sent Superfortresses over Japan from West China bases—the first land-based planes to bomb the Nipponese islands, and the first raid since General James Doolittle's [42] daring strike at Tokyo in April 1942. From his headquarters in Washington's Pentagon Building, Hansell directed that first B-29 mission against the vast Yawata steel works on the island of Kyushu.

At that time initial elements of the still-secret Twenty-first Bomber Command, which had been activated in March, started for the Japanese-held Pacific islands in which they were to establish Superfortress bases. By the time they arrived the islands had been wrested from the Japanese. Hansell was placed in command on August 29, but not until September 1944 was it known that he was leaving Washington; later that month he was one of a group of American officers made Commanders of the British Empire for their distinguished service in the war. In mid-October the General landed the first B-29 to reach Saipan Island in the Marianas group. During the final training of his men, most of whom were veterans from other theaters of war, Hansell tightened up the Superfortress formations by taking up a P-47 fighter and himself "making passes" at the huge ships. That way he was able to tell the pilots just how their defensive positions could be improved. On November 24, when there was still "a sizable number of armed and desperate Japanese troops hiding in the hills" of Saipan, Superfortresses of Hansell's command made their first raid on Tokyo. Remarking on the "sheer grandeur of the remarkable assault," correspondent George Horne warned against forgetting that the men who planned the raid

themselves called it "in a sense experimental and tentative." Less than seventy-two hours later, Hansell's bombers "dramatically displayed the requisite ability to sustain an aerial offensive against the mainspring of Japan's war machine" by another attack. But the General himself was not along. As he ruefully told reporters, he was grounded—by higher-ups who thought him too valuable to risk.

General Haywood Hansell is described as slight of build, smiling, "brown-thatched," and of ruddy complexion. Speaking in a soft, rich baritone, he impressed the war correspondents assigned to him with the honesty and frankness of his statements, which are phrased in colorful terms. Formerly Hansell was one of three high air officers who, in his words, "might have been called the 'radicals' of the Air Force. We believed in a separate air force," he said, "and we believed without any compromise that air power could win a war alone. Now all of us believe that the proposal for a unified war department over all arms of the service is better. Air power, land power, and sea power should work together to win wars. That is the best way." And Hansell is, according to Sidney Shalett, "only slightly less difficult to dissuade than it is to shoot down a Superfortress with a kid's popgun."

References

N Y Herald Tribune II p3 D 24 '44 por
N Y Times p4 N 25 '44
N Y World-Telegram p21 N 24 '44 por
Sat Eve Post 217:17+ N 25 '44 pors

HANSEN, ALVIN H(ARVEY) Aug. 23, 1887- Economist; university professor

Address: b. Littauer Center, Harvard University, Cambridge, Mass; h. 56 Juniper Rd., Belmont, Mass.

Considered for many years the New Deal's ace economist, Professor Alvin H. Hansen, leading American exponent of the deficit spending theories of John Maynard Keynes [41] and of the "compensated economy" principle, has won an undisputed place in liberal economic circles. His postwar fiscal policies, set forth in such publications as *After the War—Full Employment* (1942) and *America's Role in the World Economy* (1945), are said to have greatly influenced proposed postwar legislation such as the full employment bill of 1945.

The son of Danish immigrant parents, Niels B. and Marie Bergita (Nielsen) Hansen, Alvin Hansen was born in Viborg, South Dakota, on August 23, 1887. He entered Yankton College, South Dakota, where he earned his board and tuition by waiting on tables; during vacations he milked cows and did other farm work. One winter he took care of a doctor's horse to earn his board and room. He participated in all the college debates, and one year won the debating competition. In 1910 he received his B.A. degree. He also holds an LL.D., from Yankton (1936).

In order to continue his college work Hansen took the post of principal, then superintendent, of the Lake Preston, South Dakota school system from 1910 to 1913. He received his M.A. from the University of Wisconsin in 1915, then became assistant instructor in economics at the university in 1915-16. Following this, for the next three years he taught economics at Brown University and in 1918 received his Ph.D. in economics from Wisconsin. He then continued his teaching at the University of Minnesota, where he was associate professor of economics (1919-23), then professor of economics for several more years. He still returns to Minnesota to give a course of annual lectures, and he was visiting professor in the summer sessions at Leland Stanford (1933) and Columbia (1937). Since 1937 he has also been the Lucius N. Littauer Professor of Political Economy at Harvard University, from which he received an honorary M.A. in 1942.

In 1933 Alvin Hansen began his career as an economic adviser in government, when he became research director and secretary to the Commission of Inquiry on National Policy in Economic Relations. In 1934 he was also appointed as a member of the Columbia University Commission on Economic Recovery. His first work in Washington was as an economist for the State Department in 1934-35. Hansen then became economic adviser to Prairie Provinces before the Canadian Royal Commission in Dominion-Provincial Relations; and he has been chairman of United States-Canada joint economic committees since 1941.

The economist began to be well known in Washington governmental circles when he testified before the Temporary National Economic Committee—testimony dealing with public investment and fiscal policy, and which was widely publicized. Hansen also was named a special economic adviser to the Federal Reserve System. Although the genial, quiet Harvard professor made no headlines, it has been said that he directed the economic policies of the Roosevelt '42 Administration. He was the friend and adviser of Marriner Eccles '41, chairman of the Federal Reserve System; and of Henry Wallace '40, Senator Robert Wagner '44, and other New Deal Congressmen. His influence increased when, during the early war years, he served as consultant to the National Resources Planning Board (abolished by Congress in 1943). In September 1941 he and Professor Luther H. Gulick '45 of Columbia University were the American delegates to the International Conference on Science and World Order held in London. Hansen also undertook, with Guy Greer, an extensive study of postwar urban redevelopment.

During these years Hansen had acquired his reputation as an economist of importance through his articles and such books as *Economic Stabilization in an Unbalanced World* (1932), *A New Plan for Unemployment Reserves* (1933) and *Full Recovery or Stagnation?* (1938). Of the last named the *Nation*'s reviewer wrote that "anyone who will cast aside his preconceptions and prejudices and study this book carefully will gain greatly in understanding of the world's problems." Several years later, when the immense war effort called forth "the biggest debt in the history of America"—an estimated one hundred and fifty billion dollars before the war's end—and Americans grew concerned over "the prospect of generations yet unborn shouldering the burden," Hansen, in what one reviewer called "one of the most discriminating and controversial fiscal books of the year," declared that

Harris & Ewing

ALVIN H. HANSEN

the Nation would be well able to carry this financial load. His book *Fiscal Policy and Business Cycles* (1941) bore directly on the deficit problem of the Roosevelt budget. In it Hansen set forth the theory that capitalism is gradually being modified into what he called "a dual economy," with increasing Federal projects existing on a side-by-side basis with private industry. This system will work, he said, as long as there is an expanding economy. He contended that a public debt is not like a private debt, it is an instrument to control national income. It should be increased as a means of fighting depression, and reduced if inflationary tendencies arise.

The book was called "the maturest analysis of the theory of a mature economy published so far" (*Commonweal*), and "the best expression of the compensated economy idea that has yet been produced" (New York *Times*). More conservative economists, on the other hand, disputed Hansen's theories. Henry Simons of the University of Chicago praised his "clarity of statement and excellence of style," but attacked him for his attitude toward private investment, "his disposition to write it off as technically hopeless or unpromising, and thus to evade and minimize what is our central policy problem." Nor did he favor Hansen's theory of debt expansion: The plan, he said, is "utterly defeatist if not utterly collectivist," and would "hasten the disintegration" of free exchange and free enterprise.

Hansen's pamphlet *After the War—Full Employment* (1942) became another focal point for a vigorous economic controversy. What is required, he said, is "a positive program of postwar economic expansion and full employment, boldly conceived and vigorously pursued." Disputing the theory that a postwar depression is inevitable, he wrote: "No country need be impoverished if its productive resources (both capital and human) are intact. The productive resources of this country will be on a considerably higher plane when this war is over

HANSEN, ALVIN H.—*Continued*

than ever before." Hansen's program called for, among other things, high corporate-income and excess-profits taxes; broadening of the individual income tax base, together with steeply graduated surtax rates; part payment of wages and salaries in defense bonds; major emphasis on the individual income tax and less reliance on the corporate income tax. He also advocated a program of public projects, including nationwide development of national resources, transportation facilities, and a public housing program; and expansion of public welfare expenditures and international collaboration to pursue internal policies designed to promote active employment. His plan was immediately attacked by the press, and by conservative Congressmen as a form of "economic dictatorship." Said the New York *Times*: "We must not forget that legitimate profits are the driving force of our whole system of private enterprise. . . . To place our reliance upon a scheme of perpetual Government borrowing and spending to circulate purchasing power . . . would mean that we were merely resigning ourselves to our own brand of economic totalitarianism after beating back the Nazi brand." But it was Hansen's program that underlay the full employment bill sponsored by Senators Murray '45, Wagner '41, and O'Mahoney in 1945.

In various articles published in 1942-43, Hansen continued to discuss aspects of his postwar economic program. The basic tasks confronting the world after the war, he stated, were the "elimination, or at any rate vast reduction of unemployment, the improvement of wide areas of low economic productivity, and the increase of consumption and its direction into more efficient channels. Together, they challenge the courage and creative genius of mankind." He advocated extensive international survey of resources, and the establishment of an international reconstruction finance corporation. "There will be need in the postwar years for three new international economic institutions: one to take care of monetary stabilization, a second to expand international capital investment, and another for the control of prices of primary products."

Writing for *PM* in April 1944, Hansen discussed three outstanding economic questions: 1) Can the United States escape chaotic financial conditions with a three-hundred-billion-dollar national debt? Yes, said Hansen, citing historical parallels in countries—like England following the First World War—employing orthodox financial methods, in contrast to the unsound financing in Germany at that time. The United States has enormous productive power based on vast resources, and enormous taxable capacity. "I think it may safely be asserted that the credit of such governments as the United States, Canada, and England surpasses by far that of any institution, public or private, in all history." Nor will vast holdings of bonds, contended Hansen, create an inflation, for less than twenty billion dollars' worth of these bonds are held by the general public— "This does not present any terrifying picture of a great spending spree." It was highly probable, too, that most people would hold these bonds against future need. The United States was actually in greater danger of not finding markets for its products than it was of infla-

tion. "But in the transition from war to peace, if we do not control prices we shall have chaotic conditions. We must continue the controls where they are necessary."

2) What may the Federal budget look like in the postwar period? First, it should be flexible, varying according to economic conditions. "It is sound finance to balance the budget only when private capital outlays are high enough to create full employment." The Federal budget must be planned ahead in order for it to act as a balance wheel to the nation economy. To avoid mass unemployment in the postwar period the Government must be ready with an adequate volume of useful and productive public investment, and with plans for public development projects.

3) What about postwar taxes? Hansen believes the main features of a postwar tax program should include: complete elimination of the excess profits tax; major reliance on individual income tax: raising exemptions and lowering the rates on personal incomes; sharp reduction in corporate income taxes; elimination of the nuisance war taxes and selective sales taxes, except the excises on alcoholic beverages, tobacco, and customs duties; generous loss offsets carried back and forward in order to induce risk taking and new investment. Above all, a compensatory fiscal program is necessary to cope with depression—a program which all democratic countries must undertake. In a compensatory program, if business conditions are good, government spending can be low, tax rates medium, borrowing at a minimum; but if business conditions are bad, government spending must be high, tax rates low and borrowing encouraged in order to maintain adequate family income.

In *America's Role in the World Economy* (1945) Alvin Hansen discussed the international machinery in the economic and financial fields indispensable and complementary to a world political organization. He emphasized throughout the book that it is impossible to promote international political security without, at the same time, promoting international economic security. He repeatedly stressed that the United States can make no greater contribution toward the solution of international problems than that of achieving a high level of internal stability, business activity, and employment. "Then we need no longer have any fear of imports. . . .It will be clear to everyone that goods imported are a net gain to our real income and to our consumption standards." Instead of trying to keep "backward" nations from competing, the United States should lend them money to develop their own railways, roads, and electric power in order to help raise their incomes and purchasing power. This will stimulate a demand for the typewriters, automobiles, and household appliances which America is in a favorable condition to supply. Although living standards in those countries rise, they will never reach such a point of self-sufficiency that they will stop buying. Hansen favored the Bretton Woods proposals for an international bank for reconstruction and development, and an international monetary fund. He said that these two institutions constitute "the cornerstone of the structure of international economic cooperation." He refuted opinion that opposes the Bretton Woods proposals, stating that, if the United States fails to enter these pacts, it will also remain aloof from other international economic institutions.

Critical opinion stood solidly behind Hansen's proposals in *America's Role in the World Economy*. "No one concerned to understand the basic economic issues underlying America's stake in the postwar world can afford to neglect it," said the critic of the New York *Times Book Review*. Herbert Morris pointed out in *PM* that Hansen has "displayed an immense capacity to change his thinking to correspond to the changes in our ways of work and wealth," that twenty years ago he was "an ardent apostle of Coolidge capitalism," but that today, in company with Keynes and Beveridge '43, he is a spokesman for a totally different view. His experience in the State Department and the Federal Reserve System has shown him that "the Good Neighbor Policy will be only a masquerade unless America puts its muscle into a positive program of world-wide economic collaboration." Hansen's book was praised not only for its timely theories, but for the clarity and simplicity of its writing. "Please don't ever complain again," commented a reviewer in the Chicago *Sun Book Week*, "that nobody bothered to tell you what the score is on the economic requisites for peace. Hansen did, and now the next move's up to you."

Hansen is a member of the American Economic Association (vice-president in 1937, president in 1938). He was associate editor of *Econometrica* from 1933 to 1938, and he has been a member of the board of editors of *Quarterly Journal of Economics* since 1937, and of the *Review of Economic Statistics* since 1938. In July 1945 he resigned from his position as special economic adviser to the Board of Governors of the Federal Reserve System, but he continues to serve as occasional consultant. Since September 1945 he has been acting as consultant to the Province of British Columbia on matters relating to the impending Dominion-Provincial fiscal agreements.

In August 1916 Hansen was married to Mabel Lewis; they have two daughters, Marian Grace and Mildred Jean. The professor-economist, who is said to have "upset more classical economic concepts than any other man in our era," and who has exerted much influence in Government circles, is described as "for the people because he is of the people." He is mild-mannered, square, and stocky, "with a little more than a suspicion of a middle-age droop. Yet he is fast on his feet," wrote one reporter. "His eyes are blue and somewhat sensitive to light, and the green eyeshade he habitually uses is known wherever economists gather. He is five feet six inches tall and weighs about one hundred and seventy pounds. A clearing runs down the middle of his head, flanked by somewhat disorderly light-colored and mildly fluffy individual hairs." Hansen has been too busy during the war years to take many vacations. But he likes to return occasionally to pitch hay and milk the cows on the South Dakota farm which was homesteaded by his parents, and which he now owns.

References

Am Mercury 61:55 Jl '45

N Y Sun p25 Ja 28 '43
Nation's Bus 32:34 Je '44
Scholastic 42:13 F 1 '43
Who's Who in America, 1944-45

HARBORD, JAMES G(UTHRIE) Mar. 21, 1866- Corporation executive; retired United States Army officer

Address: b. Radio Corporation of America, 30 Rockefeller Plaza, New York City; h. Dogwood Lane, Rye, N.Y.

Recipient of many honorary university degrees and American and European military decorations, author of three books and a prodigious number of articles, executive in a dozen business enterprises, chairman of the

JAMES G. HARBORD

Radio Corporation of America, James G. Harbord has spent most of his fourscore years in public service. A farm boy, he rose from the ranks of the United States Army to be a general in the First World War, and then advanced in civilian life to the head of one of the largest corporations in the United States.

James Guthrie Harbord was born March 21, 1866, in Bloomington, Illinois, the son of George W. and Effie Critton (Gault) Harbord. Young James's early days were spent on the prairies of Illinois; when he was six his father, a veteran of the Civil War, moved the family to Missouri and then to a farm in Kansas. Early in his teens the boy had set his heart on a military career. Accordingly, he studied at the Kansas State Agricultural College where military training was included in the curriculum. He earned part of his way by typewriting catalogue cards in the library, and was graduated in 1886 with a B.S. as senior captain of the cadet corps, the top student officer. With the idea of entering West Point, young Harbord took the competitive examination with twenty-six other aspirants, tying for first place with another candidate. Because of a circumstance, the other man received the

HARBORD, JAMES G.—*Continued*

appointment. Low in spirits but determined to enter the Academy, Harbord decided to wait for another opening, in the interim remaining to teach at the State College.

In 1889, aware that his age would soon bar him from the Military Academy even if a vacancy should occur, at the age of twenty-two the young teacher enlisted as a private in the Army, intent upon earning a commission. He was assigned to the Fourth Infantry and was sent to Fort Spokane, Washington, for his basic training. Young Harbord earned steady promotion; his rapid advancement, according to several stories, was the result of the kind notice a sergeant had taken of his college training, his proficiency at the typewriter, and his flair for writing.

After two and a half years in the ranks, Harbord, then a quartermaster sergeant, was permitted to take the officers' examination upon the recommendation of his colonel. In that competition he won first place. Commissioned a second lieutenant, he performed his "shavetail" chores while on duty with the Fifth Cavalry in Kansas, Texas, and the Indian Territory. In 1895 he was graduated from the Infantry and Cavalry schools with honors. (That same year he received a M.S. from Kansas State Agricultural College.) Three years later, when the Spanish-American War broke out, the young second lieutenant was commissioned a major (temporary) in the Second United States Volunteer Cavalry, commonly referred to as the Torrey Rough Riders. At the close of the war he was reverted to the permanent rank of first lieutenant in the Regular Army and was posted with the Tenth Cavalry.

With the acquisition of Guam, Puerto Rico, and the Philippines by the United States at the end of the war, American officers were transferred for duty in these possessions. Lieutenant Harbord's first position was in the Adjutant General's Department at Santiago, Cuba (then under military occupancy by the United States); this was followed by similar duty in Puerto Príncipe (now Camagüey), Cuba, and in Eastern Cuba. Promoted to captain in 1901 with the Eleventh Cavalry, he became assistant chief of the Division of Insular Affairs in the Office of the Secretary of War. In 1902 Captain Harbord was transferred to the Philippines, where he served as a cavalry officer until the following year. Then, upon the recommendation of Major General Leonard Wood (former Military Governor of Cuba), William Howard Taft (then Governor General of the Islands) appointed Harbord colonel and assistant chief of the Philippine Constabulary. Harbord was then detailed to the especially trying post of chief of the Moro Constabulary in the Philippines. His task was to subdue the Moros, who for centuries had been harassing the other natives with their sporadic raids. After serving in southern and central Luzon, Harbord was appointed chief of the Philippine Constabulary in 1904. In 1914, after a decade of service on the Islands, he returned to the United States in compliance with the American pledge to delegate greater powers of self-government to the Filipinos. While stationed with the First Cavalry in California and Ari-

zona, Harbord was given the rank of major; he saw service with Pershing on the Mexican border in 1916; then attended the War College in Washington from September to May 1917.

Prior to America's entrance into the First World War, ex-President Theodore Roosevelt, foreseeing the eventual involvement of the United States in the conflict, conceived the idea of organizing one hundred thousand volunteers for immediate action when war should be declared. For this task Roosevelt selected Harbord as a brigade commander. The plan was rejected, however, by the Secretary of War on the counsel of military leaders. But Harbord was to be called to a somewhat similar assignment not long after that: his course at the War College was interrupted in May 1917 when, soon after the United States declared war on Germany, General Pershing asked Harbord to accompany him to France as chief of staff of the AEF to assist in organizing, equipping, and training the American Expeditionary Forces for service. (That month he was made lieutenant colonel.) In record time an army of two million men was ready for trench warfare, and Colonel Harbord continued to serve under General Pershing until May 1918. He had been advanced to brigadier general of the National Army the preceding August—the National Army being that group of units composed of men obtained by the Selective Service Act, after Regular and National Guard quotas had been designated.

But Harbord was not content to remain in an administrative post, and in the critical spring of 1918, when the Allies were suffering severe setbacks, he asked to be transferred to the front. That March, April, and May the Germans had launched three great offensives which had succeeded in opening a wide breach in the British and French lines, bringing them by May 30 to the Marne River, within thirty-seven miles of Paris. At this point the Second Division of the AEF under General Omar Bundy was rushed up to assist the French Sixth Army. The American division was deployed across the Paris-Château-Thierry road facing Ludendorff's forces, who were concentrating northwest of Château-Thierry at Vaux and in the Belleau Wood, a forest tract less than a mile square. General Harbord was placed in command of the Fourth Marine Corps Brigade and given the task of dislodging the enemy from these positions. On the first attack the brigade penetrated the German lines but did not succeed in holding the wood. In the bitter two weeks of fighting that followed, however —the first time that trench warfare was supplanted by fighting in the open—the marines took Belleau, Bouresches, and Vaux, stopping the German advance toward the French capital. The Germans had lost 24 guns and 1,654 prisoners, but the Americans had suffered the loss of 285 officers and 7,585 men killed, wounded, and missing. In 1923 the Belleau Wood was dedicated as a permanent memorial to the United States officers and men who had lost their lives there, and the French Government changed its name to Bois de la Brigade de Marine. The engagement was the first in which the Americans had played a substantial role.

The marines' commander had been advanced to the rank of major general of the National

Army after the Belleau battle and given command of the Second Division, replacing Bundy. Four days after Harbord took command, Marshal Foch ordered a counterattack to meet Ludendorff's new attack west and east of Rheims, which had brought the German forces across the Marne. Under General Charles Mangin of the French Tenth Army, Harbord led his division in the battles of July 18 and 19, a part of the great Soissons offensive (or Second Battle of the Marne) which turned the tide against the enemy and gave Foch an initiative he never relinquished.

Then, while the Second was still pushing the Germans back, Harbord was recalled from the front by Pershing to take command of the Service of Supply. This meant the coordinated supervision of base ports, of the debarkation of men and cargoes, the overseeing of warehouses, hospitals, camps, and of various construction work—all representing a responsibility second only to that of Commander in Chief. In his book *The American Army in France,* Harbord says: "It was indeed farewell to arms for me. . . . But I felt I should go anywhere that General Pershing desired and attempt anything he thought me equal to perform." After relinquishing command of his "army" at the front, Harbord, it is unanimously agreed, "made the Service of Supply a fighting 'army' in the rear." In his World War memoirs Pershing comments, "Throughout the war Harbord never hesitated a moment to express his opinion with the utmost frankness, no matter how radically it might differ from my own, nor did he ever fail to carry out instructions faithfully, even when they were not in accord with his own views." In the words of Colonel Frederick Palmer, an official observer with the American Army in France: "I saw Harbord in command of troops and understood then that he went into the Army (instead of entering some other profession) because he was first of all by nature a soldier." Harbord was reappointed chief of staff of the AEF in May 1919 and served in this capacity until August. The preceding November he had been made a brigadier general in the United States Army. In September 1919 he was made a major general. In the Second World War Harbord was to give "invaluable advice" to the Services of Supply, for which he received the thanks of Lieutenant General John C. Lee '".

Harbord has written three books based on his war experiences. The first of these, *Leaves From a War Diary* (1925), is a collection of intimate memoranda and letters to Mrs. Harbord, originally not intended for public consumption. "It is full of pen pictures of the men and women who had a part in those stirring events," commented one reviewer, "and its informality is perhaps its greatest charm." Harbord "is a born letter writer," said the New York *Times*; but "perhaps the book would have been better with a judicious editing." His other two books are *America in the World War* (1933) and *The American Army in France, 1917-1919* (1936). The *Saturday Review of Literature* found that the latter contained "a seasoning of humor, dashes of tartness, deft and dry characterizations of sundry notables, touches of drama, sudden sorties of eloquence that are heightened by their very restraint."

In August 1919 Harbord set out for the Near East to study the Armenian situation. Since 1855 the Armenians had been the victims of massacres by the Turks which seemed to take on the shape of a systematic plan for the Armenians' extermination during the World War period. American pressure for some solution resulted in the sending of Harbord as chief of the American Military Mission to study the problem and to report the findings to the United States Government in the possibility that the United States might assume mandatory power over the area. That plan was abandoned, however, when a part of Armenia was incorporated into the U.S.S.R. in 1920, becoming the Transcaucasian Socialist Federated Soviet Republic.

Upon his return to the United States, General Harbord was assigned to command the Second Division of the United States Army at Camp Travis, Texas, until 1921, when he was appointed Deputy Chief of Staff of the Army. He held this post until December 1922, when his application for retirement became effective. (In July 1942 he was made a lieutenant general on the retired list.)

Taking stock of life in the Army, Harbord regards the profession of a soldier as a career with service, and service, in his opinion, is the yardstick of a career. He believes that "the heart of any true soldier must tell him that his is one of the noblest of professions." He has found the Army a "democratic place," but urges that more opportunities must be provided for advancement for those lacking West Point training. General Harbord maintains that the United States Army has always stood for peace, that the best means of preventing war is through preparedness, for "wars will occur while human nature remains the same and economic rivalries persist." He approved the Act of 1920, which provided the United States with its first fixed military policy, as a beginning of a gradual evolution of a citizen soldiery during peace. This act stipulated that the National Guard, Organized Reserve, and Regular Army should not be extemporized in an emergency, but that their organization should be set up and developed in time of peace. In 1939, in an address at the University of Virginia, Harbord urged that "a carefully planned selective service act . . . should be voted by Congress into permanent statute without delay. It should empower the President to augment our comparatively small Army and Navy by an application of the act immediately upon a declaration of war by Congress."

Harbord also advocated that Congress continue to reject the attempts of pacifists to make a referendum necessary before a state of war could exist between the United States and another nation. A few months before Pearl Harbor, Harbord pressed for the intervention of the United States in the war, stating that "the use of convoys to assure security of this country . . . must be done if equality of opportunity is to survive." He stressed also that "in our awareness of the totalitarian menace to our institutions lies the hope or despair of our country."

(Continued next page)

HARBORD, JAMES G.—*Continued*

When on January 1, 1923, James G. Harbord succeeded Edward J. Nally as the president of the Radio Corporation of America (three days after his official retirement from the Army), the Secretary of War made the statement: "The industry into which you are going is still in its infancy, and offers a large field for your activity. Being a gallant leader in the Army, there is no doubt that you will prove to be an equally great leader in the industrial and commercial field."

It was not until the close of the First World War that the United States Government realized that strides in the new field could only be made through directed research and a pooling of patents. In 1919, upon the Government's request for the formation of a company to prevent the acquisition of American patents by foreign interests, RCA was organized to take over all the patents controlled by General Electric, United Fruit, American Telephone and Telegraph, Westinghouse, and General Motors, these companies being compensated with shares in RCA commensurate with the value of their relinquished patents. Thus RCA was primarily set up as a "communication's corporation and patent-holder with the patent contributors manufacturing the communications equipment and RCA using it or acting as a seller."

RCA acquired about eight hundred wireless patents, including a dozen or more basic patents vital to the construction of all sending and receiving devices. According to Mauritz A. Hallgren, writing in the *Nation* in 1927, "these patents were made available to the members of the trust under what has become known as the cross-licensing system. . . . Further maneuvers gave the trust a virtual monopoly on the radio-engineering talent of the country so that today the individual members operate mammoth research laboratories, spend millions of dollars annually, employ hundreds of engineers, the fruits of whose labors, by means of another pooling arrangement, become the property of the trust as a whole."

Despite the fact that RCA was formed at the Government's suggestion, as early as 1923 the Federal Trade Commission began investigating the corporation as an alleged monopoly. RCA has asserted that "it was created primarily with a motive of carrying on, and it has since carried on, a patriotic service of making a world-wide communication system of radio, in which the most important influence rests in the United States and with the American citizens. . . . RCA was created in order to carry out the expressed desires and wishes of the United States, communicated by its officers and servants."

In 1930, the year Harbord assumed his new position of chairman of the board of RCA, the Department of Justice, pressed by the Senate and certain independent radio manufacturers, filed suit under the Sherman Antitrust Act. It was alleged "that the defendants, most of whom are competitors, by issuing patent licenses to one another have created a patent combination or pool through which they exercise joint control over the radio industry. . . . No outsider can obtain a license except on terms jointly prescribed by the chief defendants." Harbord maintained that during his incumbency radio apparatus sales had risen from eleven million dollars in 1922 to eighty-seven million in 1928. He argued that patents acquired by RCA were developed at great cost to the corporation, and that the granting of a license to radio manufacturers had been "based on their apparent ability to serve well the public." He defended license fees on the ground that they were payments to those whose energy and capital had made possible the development and purchase of inventions. Said Harbord, "Let this patent unification be at an end tomorrow, let each organization use only the radio patents it actually owns, let licensees operate only under their own inventions and not use those licensed to them by others, and on that day will topple the whole structure of service which radio is rendering for the benefit and entertainment of the American public."

In 1932 the Government's suit was finally settled by consent decree (a decree entered by consent of the parties concerned, upon agreement expressed in open court). Under it General Electric and Westinghouse had to give up their RCA holdings; interlocking directorates of the corporation were abolished; and the exclusive character of the RCA license was terminated. In 1942 the Department of Justice stated that "undisputed evidence has created an atmosphere and a public attitude which makes the decree an unworthy vehicle for the further enforcement of the law." Its appeal for termination was denied by the court, however, and the consent decree still stands.

Radio has grown by leaps and bounds since James G. Harbord entered RCA in 1923. His vision and pioneering spirit, in the opinion of many, were instrumental in developing radio from a medium intended for the exchange and delivery of messages, to its present manifold services. Harbord claims that not only is radio a servant of man in time of war (he has described the Second World War as "a radio war")—it has justified itself and, applied rightly, will assert itself even more strongly in the postwar period as a greater servant in peace. Harbord holds, too, that radio broadcasting will continue to knit the peoples of the world more closely together. Of the opinion that radio is both a science and an industry, he has said that the development of radar and television during the Second World War has predestined for the radio industry a period of greater achievement. In the words of the radio executive: "So long as invention, independent enterprise, and individual initiative are encouraged, it can never be said truthfully of the workers in radio: 'They've gone as far as they can go.'"

In addition to his RCA connections, Harbord has been a director or a member of the executive committees of several companies, including the National Broadcasting Company, Marconi Telegraph Cable Company, Bankers Trust Company, New York Life Insurance Company, Employers Liability Assurance Corporation, Ltd., Atchison, Topeka and Santa Fe Railway, and the Committee of Directors of Western Railroads. He is also a former chairman of the New York Chapter of the American Red Cross. The executive has received honorary degrees of LL.D. from Trinity College, Colgate College, Marietta College, Yale College, and Washington and Jefferson College. He has received the French Croix de Guerre, with two Palms, the D.S.M. from both the United States Army and Navy; he is a Knight Commander of St. Michael and St. George, a Commander of the French Legion of Honor; and he has been decorated with high honors by Belgium, Italy, Montenegro, Panama, and Poland. In 1937 he received the Ordnance Medal of Merit from the Army Ordnance Association. He is a member of several clubs and is a Mason, thirty-second degree.

A voracious reader, and prolific writer of magazine articles, Harbord is said to possess a keen memory and an ability to express himself succinctly. He was married to Emma Yeatman Ovenshine in January 1899, and in December 1938, a year and a half after her death, he was married to Mrs. Anne Lee Brown.

References

Cur Opinion 66:361-2 Je '19
N Y World-Telegram p15 My 26 '41 pors
National Cyclopædia of American Biography Current vol A p281
Variety Radio Directory, 1940-41
Who's Who in America, 1944-45
Who's Who in Commerce and Industry (1944)

HARDING, NELSON Oct. 31, 1879—Dec. 30, 1944 American newspaper cartoonist and humorist; winner of the Pulitzer Prize in 1927 and 1928, while with the Brooklyn *Eagle*, for the best cartoon published in an American newspaper during each of those years; veteran of the Spanish American War.

Obituary

N Y Times p19 Ja 2 '45 por

HARMON, MILLARD F(ILLMORE) Jan. 19, 1888—Mar. (?), 1945 United States Army officer, lieutenant general in command of the Army Air Forces of the Pacific Ocean areas since August 1944, and deputy commander of the Twentieth Air Force; reported missing in flight; assumed command of the Second Air Force in July 1941 and the next year was named chief of Air Staff. See *Current Biography* 1942 Yearbook.

Obituary

N Y Times p13 Mr 4 '45 por

HAY, CHARLES M(ARTIN) Nov. 10, 1879—Jan. 16, 1945 Deputy chairman and executive director of the United States War Manpower Commission since July 1944; lawyer; served in the Missouri House of Representatives (1913-14); counselor of St. Louis City (1932-35); part-time member of the Seventh Regional War Labor Board (1942-43); general counsel of the War Manpower Commission since 1943.

Obituary

N Y Times p21 Ja 17 '45

HAYEK, FRIEDRICH A(UGUST VON) (hī'yĕk frē'drĭĸ) May 8, 1899- Economist; author

Address: b. c/o London School of Economics, Houghton St., Aldwych, London; h. 8 Turner Close, London

Friedrich A. Hayek, Austrian-born English economist, educator, and lecturer, is the author of the controversial book *The Road to Serfdom*. The economist is considered qualified to write on what he considers the dangers in central planning, not only because he has probed the subject at length but because, as he points out in the preface to his book, he has had the unique opportunity of experiencing

FRIEDRICH A. HAYEK

conditions and a development of ideas in present-day England which are disturbingly similar to conditions he knew and views he himself held in his early manhood in Vienna.

Friedrich August von Hayek was born in Vienna on May 8, 1899. He is the son of the late August von Hayek, who was professor of botany at the University of Vienna. It was at this university that he received his own education, and he also holds the degrees of D.J. and D. Pol Sc. from that university, and the degree of D.Sc. (Econ.) from the University of London.

In 1921 Hayek entered the Austrian Civil Service. Two years later he went on leave to the United States, where he worked first for some months as research assistant to Professor Jeremiah W. Jenks at New York University and then, for the 1923-24 session, as a research fellow of the university. Hayek returned in 1924 to his post in the Civil Service, retaining this until 1926, the year in which he was married to Helen von Fritsch. (They have one son and one daughter.) The year after his marriage Hayek became director of the Austrian Institute of Economic Research, and in 1929 he accepted the post of lecturer in economics at the University of Vienna. This position he occupied simultaneously with the direc-

HAYEK, FRIEDRICH A.—*Continued*

torship until his eventual departure for England in 1931 to become Tooke Professor of Economic Science and Statistics at the University of London, a position in which he has since served as a member of the faculty of the London School of Economics. He is a member of the Council of the Royal Economic Society and since 1944 a Fellow of the British Academy. He became a British subject in 1938.

Professor Hayek's name first appeared on the title page of a book in 1927, when he edited the works of Herman Heinrich Gossen, the German economist, whose name has been given to the three economic theses he formulated. In 1929, while still in Vienna, Hayek published his own initial work in the field of theoretical economics, *Monetary Theory and The Trade Cycle* (the title is taken from the English edition, translated by N. Kaldor and H. M. Croome, which appeared in 1933). In this work he argues that the business cycle is caused not by variations in the value of money, but rather by fluctuations in the volume of money. In this same year Hayek also edited the works of Friedrich von Wieser, one of the leading exponents of the Austrian school of economics, in the atmosphere of whose doctrines Hayek had received his own early training.

In the two-year interval which preceded Hayek's next contribution to theoretical economic thought, *Prices and Production* (1931), he had gone to the University of London; his book, therefore, was appropriately published in English. The volume, a series of four papers read before the University of London in 1930-31, deals with, among other economic theories, the case for and against an "elastic" currency. Hayek next edited *Beiträge sur Geldtheorie* (1933), and in the same year, 1933, began editing the works of the founder of the Austrian, or "subjective," school of economics, Carl Menger, who considered primary in the study of economic phenomena "the values which men place on goods because of their utility." This task was not completed until 1936.

In the meantime, Hayek was also editing *Collectivist Economic Planning* (1935), his first appearance in print with the theme of *The Road to Serfdom*. The volume is a compilation of articles on the problem of central planning versus competition, written by leading twentieth century economists. These articles were selected by Hayek, who wrote for the book an introductory historical note and a concluding chapter setting forth the "Present State of the Debate."

During the year 1937 he had journeyed to Switzerland to lecture before the Graduate Institute of International Studies at Geneva, and upon his return to England in 1937 his lectures were published under the title of *Monetary Nationalism and International Stability*. Extending to the international field his belief in the cruciality of the volume of money, as propounded in *Prices and Production*, Hayek suggests as a cure for the great variability of liquidity of national currencies the amendment of present laws to permit 100 per cent coverage of bank deposits by paper money so that purchasing power shall hereafter move, in the words of Honor Croome, "not merely in proportion to gold but actually to the same extent."

Although theoretical or academic economics is Hayek's main interest, in April 1938 he again paused to sound a warning against the danger of dictatorship he saw in central planning. His article, "Freedom and the Economic System," which appeared in the *Contemporary Review* that month, was reprinted in enlarged form as a *Public Policy Pamphlet* by the Chicago University Press in 1939, and this became the core of *The Road to Serfdom*. Afterward, he returned to his university studies, producing in 1939 *Profits, Interest, and Investments,* an edition of the works of H. Thornton, and, in 1941, *The Pure Theory of Capital,* written to supplement the brief treatment of this subject in his earlier *Prices and Production*. At the same time the economist was contributing frequently to several English economic and general periodicals. In these he advocated, among other policies, a commodity reserve currency (in 1943), and (in 1939) a plan that Britain join France in an economic federation which would form the skeleton for a federation of all Europe. He also defended his theories against attacks.

In the early 1940's Hayek was mainly engaged in a comprehensive study of the interaction of social and scientific trends during the nineteenth and twentieth centuries, only parts of which have thus far appeared in the journal *Economica*; in connection with this he was also working on an edition of the letters of John Stuart Mill. But the dangers of totalitarianism seemed to him in the last years of the war with Germany to be increasing so alarmingly that he interrupted this work for an attempt at more popular exposition.

It was, in the economist's opinion, those concerned with the welfare of the laboring classes who in Great Britain were advocating the very policies which their counterparts had earlier advocated in Germany and which, according to Hayek, had made Hitler's [42] rise possible. Fascism, he believes, is not a reaction to collectivist and communist policies but grows out of them, because the administrator of a central plan, in order to be successful, must impose his aims and values upon the people and must exclude all ideas or policies which might jeopardize the proper functioning of the plan. "There can be no freedom of thought, no freedom of the press, where it is necessary that everything should be governed by a single system of thought. In theory," he says, "socialism may wish to enhance freedom, but in practice . . . totalitarianism is nothing but consistent collectivism, the ruthless execution of the principle that 'the whole comes before the individual' and the direction of all members of society by a single will supposed to represent 'the whole.'" Hayek believes that not only is central planning a potentially dangerous weapon but that it is also an inefficient and unwieldy tool as compared with free competition: he maintains it is impossible for one bureau or government leader to know at one time all the factors which will affect production and consumption, whereas, "this is precisely what the price system brings about if competition is functioning."

Although Hayek strongly favors world-wide free trade, he does not oppose all governmental regulation of business. He supports governmental control of industry to prevent monopoly and to provide a framework within which competition can operate—"the rule of law," as he calls it. He also endorses some forms of government investment and social security measures, but he insists that the individual must be left free to determine his own destiny in accordance with the laws of his country, unrestricted by the whims of one man or a minority in power. Competition, he writes, "is the only method which does not require the coercive or arbitrary intervention of authority."

The Road to Serfdom was published in England in early 1944, and in America in September of the same year. In the United States it made the nonfiction best-seller list almost at once, and on both sides of the Atlantic it evoked vociferous laudatory and condemnatory criticism in equal measure. Wrote H. J. M. of the Kansas City *Star,* "New Dealers will attack it and Right-wingers will praise it—but nobody can deny that it is an important book." From one side came a *New Republic* comment in a note entitled "Poor Mr. Hayek": Unrealistic, unhistorical, and pathetically ineffectual to restore "the economic theories of the eighteen-eighties." From the opposite side Henry Hazlitt of the New York *Times* declared, "One of the most important books of our generation," while the *Saturday Review of Literature* critic wrote, "Its thesis will come as a shock to many readers. It would be good if they would not refuse to read the book because it seems to run counter to many of the widely accepted and cherished slogans of the day, but accept the challenge and enter into the discussion." A shock of this kind was felt by Paul Hutchinson whose review in the *Christian Century* seems to carry out the injunction of the *Saturday Review*'s article. Hutchinson credits Hayek with having jolted him out of the complacency in which he saw himself as "left of center" while having only a vague notion of what a new socialist order would be. Hayek has not convinced him on all points, he says, but Hayek's argument seems to him "to demand serious and respectful consideration." (Hayek's ideas later became the subject of rebuttal in two books—Herman Finer's *The Road to Reaction* and Barbara Wootton's *Freedom Under Planning*.)

As a consequence of such reviews, in early 1945 the National Concert and Artists Corporation arranged a lecture tour of the United States for the author, during which he repeated and amplified his statements. He also appeared on the air on the *University of Chicago Round Table* in April, and his book was dramatized on the radio program *Words at War*. *Reader's Digest* printed a condensed version of the book in its April issue, and this condensation was reprinted in pamphlet form by the Book-of-the-Month Club, as well as in a series of ten daily articles distributed through Hearst's King Features Syndicate.

This success of course pleased Hayek. But it also embarrassed him somewhat, he declared in the Chicago *Sun,* to find that his arguments had become party weapons in the United States, because he had written *The Road to Serfdom* with very little thought of America. He explained that he had seen Britain selling

her birthright, her talent for adaptation and compromise, "the British capacity for muddling through," and he had set out to put his adopted country on her guard. "If in the growth of the social and political structure of Britain," he wrote in the *Spectator* of January 26, 1945, "the unforeseen and unintended has so frequently emerged, that is of course merely another way of saying that it has never been planned as a whole. In the piecemeal process of adaptation and change there has always been opportunity for the people to change institutions into something different from what they were intended to be, to create a society which was not the result of a single coherent plan but of innumerable decisions of free men and women."

Professor Hayek, who has brown eyes, is a man of commanding stature; he is over six feet in height and weighs nearly two hundred pounds. Book-collecting and mountaineering are his favorite forms of relaxation. One far-reaching effect of the economist's opinions was heard in his adopted land in June 1945 when Clement Attlee [40] remarked that Winston Churchill's [42] Parliamentary campaign speeches that year seemed to be merely "a second-hand version of the academic views of . . . Professor Friedrich August von Hayek."

References

N Y Times Book R p1+ S 24 '44 por
Who's Who, 1945

HAYTER, STANLEY WILLIAM Dec. 27, 1901- Artist

Address: b. Atelier 17, 41 E. 8th St., New York City; h. 247 Waverly Pl., New York City

Under the auspices of New York's New School for Social Research, an English painter continues in America his experiments in the graphic arts in his communal workshop. The studio, Atelier 17, which had its inception in Paris, is the outgrowth of his researches in an almost forgotten art. Between the Italian line engraver, Andrea Mantegna, and Stanley William Hayter lie five centuries during which engraving had been almost completely neglected except for a brief reappearance in the nineteenth century in the work of William Blake. Until Hayter became attracted by the possibilities of the powerful incisive line which can be cut directly into the metal, engraving had been relegated primarily to use in reproductions, and then photography pushed it out of that field, too. To Hayter's studio come mature artists as well as students who are interested in exploring with him all the possibilities of the rediscovered art.

The second son of William Harry and Ellen Mercy (Palmer) Hayter, Stanley William Hayter was born in London, December 27, 1901. (Later two daughters were born to the Hayters.) Although the painter's brush was a familiar object in this home—his father was an artist of no mean talent—the youth was persuaded to turn his back upon the art world. As if to escape the captiousness of the art critics and the coolness of the general public toward evolving art forms, he chose the career of a research chemist. After graduating from Whitgift, a secondary school founded by the

Rose Adler. Paris

WILLIAM STANLEY HAYTER

Archbishop of Canterbury at Croyden during the reign of Queen Elizabeth, young Hayter was enrolled at Kings College, London University. Apparently he was impatient to begin his career as a scientist, for at nineteen he was in possession of his degree. He was only twenty-one when he signed a contract as oil chemist in 1922, and for the next three years Hayter spent his working time in the oil fields of the Anglo-Iranian Oil Company in Albadan, Persia. His free hours he devoted to painting the Persian scene and to experiments in cubism. The first setback to the artist came not from the critics but from an attack of malaria which sent him home to London in 1925. There his company generously featured his paintings at a one-man show it arranged for him at its own expense. In doing this it unwittingly lost a chemist. The exhibition was successful beyond Hayter's expectations, and the newcomer to the art world headed for Paris, the mecca of the artists in the twenties.

The year was 1926. Montparnasse was seething with the bouts of the academicians and the cubists, and Hayter plunged into the fray. During the week he studied under Laurens the technique of certain Salon painters, which he disliked. After five days of this tethered conformity he would "lash out half a dozen savage cubisms" for the Saturday composition class. Invariably he was rewarded with a rise in Laurens' blood pressure. Despite his distaste for the type of training he was receiving, Hayter spent six months at this study of painting. Had the artist been content to remain just another participant in a Montparnassan battle in which paint and print flowed freely, his story might have ended there. The scientist's curiosity, coupled with the artist's need for the discovery of newer forms of expression, urged him on to explore the resources of the graphic arts. Since 1921, in fact, he had been experimenting, although not consistently, with etching. By 1927, when he had become quite proficient at it, he returned to it with intense

interest. Then one of the rare practitioners of the medium of Mantegna and Blake introduced him to it and Hayter quickly saw the creative possibilities it offered.

The significance of line engraving to Hayter lies in its being a perfect medium for the "integration of space and object," one of the problems which is the concern of the modern artist. In the March 1941 issue of the quarterly *Print* he defines engraving as "the production, by direct cutting, of grooves or irregularities in a surface. The surface may be of wood, stone or metal; and the incisions made in it can be designed to decorate or enrich the surface of the original, or to produce a surface from which one can print by either of two methods. In one of these methods, called 'intaglio,' ink is held in the crevices of the plate, the surface being wiped clean and the threads of ink transferred to damp paper by suitable pressure. It is obvious that such a line will stand up in relief above the level of the sheet, the paper being molded, or squeezed, by the pressure of the press, into the hollow of the plate. The alternative method of making a print from an engraved plate is to ink only the level surface with a composition roller, so that the cut-away parts of the plate remain clean. The print will be the negative of the intaglio print previously described, and the ink will lie on the *surface* of the paper. . . .The tools required are few and simple: a copper plate, a burin which must be extremely sharp, and a triangular section scraper, a burnisher, charcoal block and Scotch hone for corrections."

According to Hayter there is no routine method of handling line engraving, inasmuch as there are about twenty different ways of using the line engraving medium, and continuous experiments constantly disclose new procedures. It is all a matter of convenience to the individual artist. Line engraving as it is practiced by the artist is definitely not copy work but, as in painting and sculpture, he may find it necessary to draw about a dozen versions of his subject before he applies his burin, the cutting tool, to the copper plate. From then on he works directly from his original, preconceived idea. "You walk into your drawing like a map, instead of around it as you do in a pencil drawing," he said once in explanation of his technique. "Some prehistoric craftsmen saw drawings that way, too." Printing is done by the artist himself to insure a close relationship between the design on the copper plate and the one transferred from it to paper. In conjunction with line engraving, etching is often employed "to provide a concentrated mechanical element in contrast to the very flexible, expressive line of the burin, so that tension is not spread all over the plate." With the aid of a piece of silk, a skin, or an old gauzy stocking Hayter also varies the texture of his completed designs.

Hayter opened his Atelier 17, which takes its name from his Parisian address, 17 Campagne Premier, in 1927. Two American women had come to buy prints from him at his studio and became so enamored of his work that they persuaded him to instruct them in his methods. A few more pupils joined, and Atelier 17 was on its way. Later Pablo Picasso [43], Max Ernst [42], Marc Chagall [43], Jacques Lipschitz, Joán Miró [40], and Alexander Calder joined the artist in his studio. They came to learn the graphic process and to work with him in what became, in the truest sense, a communal workshop. In a sympathetic article on Hayter's work, the art critic Rosamund Frost (*Art News*, May 15-31, 1941) emphasizes that at the Parisian atelier "there were no trade secrets and any technical discovery was common property for the benefit of the group. Hayter made all tools, supervised all processes. . . .He first tried printing on plaster with astounding effects. . . .All in all, he assisted at the making of at least five thousand plates, or something like five times an average lifework, so it's not surprising that his technique is what it is."

For twelve years, from 1927 to 1939, Atelier 17 flourished in Paris. During that period Hayter had imparted his methods to some three hundred students. In addition to being shown annually at the galleries in Paris between 1934 and 1939, the prints were sent on group tours to Czechoslovakia and to Holland (The Hague and Maastrict) in 1936. In Paris they appeared at the Gallery Pierre, the Quatre Chemins, and the Gallery de Beaune. The last European exhibition was held in 1939 at the gallery of Peggy Guggenheim in London. The war which blacked out the lights of Europe also put a temporary halt to the explorations of Hayter and his co-workers. On the second day of the conflict, Hayter departed from France, leaving behind him one hundred copper plates and a press, all of which disappeared. Later he learned that the landlord had confiscated them "in default" of payment for the rent of the Paris studio occupied *in absentia*.

Back in England, Hayter accepted an invitation shortly before the fall of Dunkerque to transplant Atelier 17 to New York. In May of 1940 he arrived in the United States. That same summer, before the opening of his studio in New York, he conducted a summer course at the University of California. In conjunction with the course he held an exhibition of his works at the Museum of San Francisco.

In the fall of 1940 Hayter opened his workshop at the New School for Social Research in New York City. The American edition of Atelier 17 soon outgrew its quarters and its director was obliged to move it to larger headquarters in a loft building on East 8th Street. Reginald Marsh [41] and Abraham Rattner have frequented his New York studio to continue with him his renewed researches into the graphic mediums. Isabel Bishop and Douglas Gorsline have also sought to improve their technique through the experiments he conducts. Chagall and Lipschitz, who were with him in the original Atelier 17 in Paris, have rejoined him in America. In addition to his association with the New School where he has been instructor in etching and engraving, Hayter diverts part of his energy to a class he has been holding once a month since February 1945, at the Philadelphia Print Club.

Hayter, who reflects the inquisitive, creative faculties of the artist and the experimental, analytical mind of the scientist, has been "typed" as a line engraver. Despite his extensive work in the graphic medium he maintains that he is, and always has been, a painter. Like milestones his paintings mark the changes in his artistic life, particularly since the establishment of Atelier 17. Of his early paint-

ings he says that he did them "before things started to happen." He refers to them as "*décors*, empty settings." In 1927 he exhibited with the Salon d'Automne, the Salon de l'Escalier and the Indépendents in Paris. During 1928, paintings of his made their appearance at the gallery of the Surindépendents, together with works by Estève, Beaudin, and Lurçat. One of the provisos governing the artists who were permitted to hang their works with the Surindépendents was that they must not exhibit them at other galleries in Paris. Since many painters did not like this arrangement, the Surindépendents were able to exclude those who were content to participate in the exhibitions at the conventional salons. In 1929 Hayter's paintings were exhibited at the Brussels Palais des Beaux-Arts. Although the critics "vilified" them, the "more advanced" public was gratifyingly responsive to the artist's efforts.

The evolution of Hayter's work brought the founder of Atelier 17 closer to the surrealists. Instead of mere visual representation in his paintings he inclined toward images, "related to reality through a kind of dream process." Unlike dreams, however, they could be carefully selected. It has been his contention that, "by their persistence you can distinguish between valid and invalid images. Some fade quickly; others are just as insistent after three months. These, I then feel, are a kind of general image which is part of the collective human subconscious, not just my own subconscious." Hayter's preference for the presentation of what he believes is the "collective human subconscious" as opposed to the purely personal attitude of Dali [40] and his followers, explains the difference between the two major schools of surrealist thinking.

In the November 1944 issue of the *Magazine of Art*, Paul McPharlin [45] described Hayter's qualities as a painter in terms of the equipment of the modern artist. Today's artist looks out upon a world the dimensions of which have been enlarged with the aid of the telescope, the microscope, and the spectroscope of the scientist, as well as by the discoveries of the psychoanalyst. "A whole new dream world, its fringes scarcely parted by the surrealists, opens from the subconscious. A world of portentous shapes, some scarcely to be analyzed at all, arises from the unconscious." These ominous shapes, however, stem from reality. Hayter has shown that they can be the fruit of man's nightmarish physical experiences.

In 1937, when the activities of Atelier 17 in Paris were at their height, Hayter was invited to Spain by a liberal Ministry of Art. That country was in the agony of a civil war, a conflict which reverberated throughout the world. The six-foot *Man-eating Landscape*, which Hayter painted in Spain at this time, is an evocation of the horrors he witnessed as brother often fought against brother. In the surrealist manner he reminds the beholder of the grim extinction which ultimately awaits man in a war-torn world: the painting depicts a prostrate man clinging to the edge of a rock in a barren waste, and moving towards him is a giant molecule whose delicate fan-like skirt is a symbol of the refined cruelty with which it prepares to devour the broken man.

With few exceptions Hayter's prints have been cordially received. His paintings, how-

HAYTER, WILLIAM STANLEY—*Cont.*

ever, have often made him a storm center. In the United States the critics have reacted with varying feelings of enthusiasm, surprise, and dubiousness, and have not always shown themselves to be at ease in the presence of his startling and complex work. After his one-man exhibition of oils at the Bignou Gallery, New York, in April 1941, the art critic of *PM* remarked that "you felt the bombastic force of large broken color patterns strain against each other, the nervous movement of tangled lines. It was like a sea of breaking icebergs. And lurking somewhere was Hayter's subject matter." His prints which appeared in May of the same year at the Willard Gallery also puzzled the *PM* critic, who, however, found them "interesting in content and technique." In May 1943 the Willard Gallery in the same city featured a showing of his carved plaster abstractions and burin engravings. In the latter part of June 1944 the Museum of Modern Art gave over its entire auditorium galleries to a group showing of Atelier 17. At the close of the exhibition in September it was sent on a tour of other cities by the museum. Of this exhibition the art critic Howard Devree wrote on July 2 in the New York *Times*: "The graphics at the Museum of Modern Art reveal the excellence of the craftsmanship but leave me in doubt whether the technical proficiency is not the chief thing to come of the effort, and whether technique is not developed to a point at which science rather than art in some obscure way is served. Certainly my own interest in the work is largely mechanical rather than esthetic." Except for this dissenting voice the exhibition was warmly greeted and many critics commented on the modesty of Hayter, who often neglected to sign his name to his prints, which thus remained known only to the artists who had worked with him in his studio. When his paintings appeared in a one-man show at the Brandt Gallery in January 1945 the art critic of the New York *World-Telegram* stressed the brilliancy of his color and the success with which "both color and line are combined to make paintings of singular strength and power. . . .And the result is an organization in which color and line are so perfectly integrated that neither could stand alone. This is vibrant painting, alive with movement, faultless in taste."

Hayter's prints and paintings are in the permanent collections of the Bibliothèque Doucet in Paris, the British Museum and the Victoria and Albert Museum in London, and the Stockholm and Gothenburg museums in Sweden, as well as in private collections. In the United States his works, mostly prints and plasters, may be seen in the country's leading museums, chief among them the museums of Boston, Philadelphia, San Francisco, and Virginia, as well as the Brooklyn Museum, the Chicago Institute, the Museum of Modern Art in New York, the National Gallery in Washington, D.C., the Fogg Art Museum of Harvard University, and the Lessing J. Rosenwald collection.

The Philadelphia Print Club awarded Hayter the Alfred Noyes Prize in 1943 for his print *Laocoön*. In addition to articles written for publication in France, England, and America, he has been working on a book in his spare time since 1936. Hayter decided to undertake this project after he discovered that, since 1890, no book had been produced on the subject of original line engraving. His will be the history and technique of modern engraving as well as a speculation on its future possibilities, and considerable space will be devoted to Andrea Mantegna and William Blake.

Since 1940 Hayter has been married to the American sculptor Helen Elizabeth Phillips, who has exhibited at the San Francisco Museum. The Hayters now have two children, William and Julian. Of medium build, the artist has blue-gray eyes, light brown hair, and sensitive features.

References

Art N 40:13+ My 15-31 '41 il por; 43: 11+ Ag '44
Newsweek 24:89-90 Jl 10 '44 il por
PM p45 My 25 '41

HEAD, EDITH Fashion designer

Address: b. c/o Paramount Pictures, Inc., Hollywood, Calif.

Couturière to such film stars as Marlene Dietrich, Ingrid Bergman"[40], and Claudette Colbert '[45] Edith Head has created styles that have won wide popularity outside of Hollywood. As head designer for Paramount Pictures since 1938, she is the first woman to have been appointed to such a position in a major studio.

Born on the film industry's home grounds in Los Angeles, Edith Head was the only child of a mining engineer. Her father's work soon took the family to a Mexican mining town, where the child had no playmates and only a few toys. For amusement Edith, like other little girls, made dresses for her dolls, and even adorned uncomplaining burros. When she was eight years old the family moved back to the United States, living in mining camps in Nevada and Arizona. Thus it was during her childhood that Miss Head learned Spanish and also developed an appreciation of native Mexican and Indian costumes which was to influence her future designing.

Since there were no schools near the camps where the Heads lived, young Edith was tutored at home. When finally she was taken back to Los Angeles and enrolled in high school, she was shy and fearful about her recently acquired arithmetic and history. She continued her study of Spanish in high school, then specialized in languages in college, first at the University of California, where she earned her B.A., later at Leland Stanford University, where she received her M.A. degree.

When she had completed school Miss Head accepted a position as teacher of Spanish at the Bishop School at La Jolla, California. Her next job brought her a bit closer to her designing career—she transferred to the Hollywood School for Girls where she taught French and Spanish. Teaching left Miss Head some leisure time, which prompted her to study art. She had taken some art courses at college, and now she began to attend classes in sculpture, life drawing, and landscape and portrait painting. She studied at the Otis Institute and later at the Chouinard Art School in Los Angeles. An aptitude for drawing, combined with a strong interest in design, led her to do fashion sketches for her own enjoyment.

But, living in the environment of the motion picture (some of her pupils were the children of people in the films), she was attracted by the industry and eventually made her bid for entrance. In 1923 she took her fashion sketches to Howard Greer, then head fashion designer at Paramount. Greer immediately gave her a job as a sketcher. Her first task was to design an enormous waistband to support the palanquin on an elephant's back—she was back again to animal dressing!

There was, however, to be a vast amount of experience for Edith Head between the elephant's waistband and the sarong for Dorothy Lamour, a Head creation of 1936. That first assignment was in the period of spectacular C. B. DeMille [42] costume productions with huge mob scenes. Miss Head designed clothes for the extras of these scenes, costumes only visible for a moment on the screen but nevertheless important. From her experience with historical pictures she acquired skill with period costumes and special textiles. All of this experience impressed upon her the main principle of film designing: "That all clothes must suit the story and be subordinate to it." There was another period when Miss Head designed for "horse operas," clothing a stream of cowboys and cowgirls. Eventually her patience with boots and saddles was rewarded— when Travis Banton succeeded Greer at Paramount, she became his assistant. Then later, when Banton left in 1938 to do free-lance designing, Miss Head was made chief designer, the first chief woman designer in a major studio. By this time she was well grounded in the technique of film designing and ready for the considerable responsibilities of her new position.

The job of dressing the stars for their celluloid lives provides a crowded schedule for Miss Head. As chief designer her duties are broad: she reads the script of each picture under production in order to become familiar with the story and its costume requirements; she next confers with the producer, director, art director, cameraman, and the stars, and, if Technicolor is being used, she must also discuss that angle of the production with the color experts. While she is working Miss Head often has three hundred sketchers, drapers, cutters, and finishers carrying out her ideas. Supervising this large staff, she combines a knowledge of each individual job with the talents of executive and trouble-shooter.

A typical work day for the designer begins at nine, involves designing for various stars in different films, special emergency calls to sets, fittings for Ann Sheridan or Veronica Lake, the soothing of an irate director, and kindred tasks. Each day Miss Head also sees the daily rushes of every picture in production, all in all usually kept busy until after seven o'clock. When author Beryl Williams met Miss Head one day the designer was working simultaneously on "one picture with winter clothes, one with summer clothes, one war picture laid in England, one postwar picture, one musical laid in Mexico—not to mention one 1902 and one 1885 film." Each picture presents particular problems to the designer, historical films requiring special research, but in all pic-

EDITH HEAD

tures the clothes must always conform with the background and mood, not dominate. Miss Head believes that the clothes designer should seek to emphasize the particular beauty of the individual star, not to create fashion plates. Even though she is a designer, she has no wish to start fads, but she is frankly happy if something she has designed is suitable for many women and becomes popular. "Imitation," she observes, "is as pleasant a form of flattery in the designing field as it is anywhere else."

Recalling the early days of her career in Hollywood, a period when designing was "a cross between camouflage and costumes for Superman," Miss Head declares: "We dressed stars like nothing human." Discussing the ornate and often spectacular costumes of that time, she says: "After all, it was the fabulous era and the movies were very young." She credits the Government's war order ("L-85"), which limited the use of material, with curtailing lavishness in films. "L-85 was the greatest boon that ever came to fashion designers in Hollywood," she said in a New York interview in 1944. "It banished super-luxury and brought us all down to earth. . . .Today we create sensible styles for women—the kind they can actually wear." Paramount's sage of fashion believes that "good clothes are not good luck. They are the result of a pretty thoroughgoing knowledge of the people you are dressing." The designer must know, besides the measurements of the woman she is dressing, her coloring, facial contours, and her character. For, according to Miss Head, "what you do with clothes is counterbalance personality. Play it up or down." The September 1944 issue of *Screenland* Magazine carried her ideas on this subject in an article called "Dress Your Type." Using as examples Paulette Goddard, Veronica Lake, Dorothy Lamour, Betty Hutton, and Ginger Rogers [41], Miss Head described the kind of wardrobe she designs for these stars, then advised women of their types to pattern their clothes along the suggested lines.

(Continued next page)

HEAD, EDITH—*Continued*

She cautioned her readers, however, that "no two people can look alike in the same thing."

In the book *Fashion Is Our Business* (1945) Beryl Williams describes the careers of famous American designers, including Miss Head. In discussing this book, the *Saturday Review of Literature* called the story of Edith Head "one of the most challenging" in the volume. Miss Head's pet theory of design is simplicity. However, when the script demands a super-glamorous creation, she complies fittingly, as witness the mink gown worn by Ginger Rogers in *Lady in the Dark* (1944). The motion picture modiste likes Latin-American, Western, and Indian fashions, considering among her main contributions to Hollywood fashion her adaptations of the Spanish camisa (shirt), the rebozo (scarf), and the poncho (cloak). Actresses often buy their Head-designed costumes from the studio for personal use. Ginger Rogers and Barbara Stanwyck always have their clothes designed by Miss Head, regardless of where they are working.

The small, dynamic designer, who likes gardening and swimming, is reported to have one of the best figures among the many well-proportioned Hollywoodians. Her black hair and dark eyes complement her vibrant personality. Accentuating the Latin-American motif even in her own clothes, Miss Head prefers materials woven for her in Mexico, and she wears native Mexican costumes in her home whenever possible. Her basic wartime wardrobe, mathematically contrived, has consisted of four suits, converted into twelve outfits by the use of different blouses and skirts. Her favorite combination of colors is red and yellow; if she had to choose only one color to wear the rest of her life, she thinks now it would be white.

A collector of masks, porcelain cats and antique jewelry, Miss Head also owns one of the most complete collections of authentic Indian jewelry in the country, chiefly Navajo. The designer has retained her fondness for burros—these small animals are her pets on her ranch. She also likes to visit Mexico each year, as well as New York, which she considers the fashion center of the world today. Miss Head has retained her fluency in languages and broadcasts in Spanish via short-wave to South America, recognizing the benefits of closer relationships between the two continents. She also sends fashion sketches each month to Latin America because she believes there is a future there for southern California clothes. Paramount's fashion expert calls her work "the most exciting job in the world." Considering the lighter side of her designing days, Miss Head says she has had the most fun with Mae West, and with Charles Laughton, whom she once had to dress as Nero.

References

N Y Times p24 F 1 '44

Williams, B. Fashion Is Our Business (1945)

HEAD, WALTER W(ILLIAM) Dec. 18, 1877- President of the Boy Scouts of America; business executive

Address: b. 1501 Locust St., St. Louis, Mo.; h. 4931 Lindell Blvd., St. Louis, Mo.

With the Boy Scouts of America celebrating their thirty-fifth anniversary in 1945, Walter W. Head entered upon his twentieth year as president of the Scouts' National Council. His leadership is, however, only one phase of his activities. Widely known as a business executive, he has been a prominent figure in American financial and insurance circles for three decades, having been on the directorates of insurance companies, banks, and other corporations. In addition, he has been affiliated with numerous civic, charitable, and cultural organizations.

Of humble origin, Walter William Head was born on a farm near Adrian, Illinois, on December 18, 1877. Seven years later his parents, Alfred Walter and Margaret Jane (Lambert) Head, moved to a farm in De Kalb County, Missouri. The father made the journey in a covered wagon while the mother and children traveled by railroad. Young Walter was deeply influenced by his mother, a devout woman who imbued him with a warm, human philosophy of life. Educated in the rural schools of De Kalb County, Head worked his way through a Missouri normal school. He began his career as a teacher in a one-room rural school, and by 1901 he was principal of the public schools of the town of De Kalb, in Buchanan County.

At the age of twenty-six, after five years of teaching and school administration, Head was attracted to a business career. He resigned from a teaching post which paid one hundred twenty-five dollars a month to become acting cashier of the De Kalb State Bank for thirty dollars a month. But this proved a wise change, for the young man was successful in his new field. In 1906 he was appointed State and national bank examiner, a position he held for two years, until his election as cashier of the American National Bank at St. Joseph, Missouri. Endowed with business acumen, he progressed rapidly in the banking world. In 1917 he left the American National to become vice-president of the Omaha National Bank, and president in 1920. He was elected an officer of the National Bank Division of the American Bankers Association in 1918, became second vice-president in 1922, then first vice-president, and president in 1923.

Six years later he became president of the State Bank of Chicago, which was consolidated with the Foreman National Bank, to form the Foreman State National Bank, of which he was elected president. Head moved to New York in 1931, and was elected president of the Morris Plan Corporation of America. He resigned this position in 1933 to take over the presidency of the newly organized General American Life Insurance Company in St. Louis, which purchased the assets of the former Missouri State Life Insurance Company; they were then 50 per cent of the required legal reserve. Under Head's direction the General American Life Insurance Company developed rapidly. *Finance* in April 1944 reported: "In the ten years that have elapsed, Mr. Head and his associates have established a brilliant record in building a great new life insurance company in the heart of the Middle West, serving the holders of more than six hundred fifty thousand policies and certificates. The results he achieved in rehabilitating the business and assets of the former Missouri State Life for the benefit of its policyholders have won the acclaim of insurance executives throughout the Nation."

Since his early days as a schoolteacher Head has had a concern in the matter of community character-building, especially among young people. For twenty-seven years he has been active in the Boy Scouts of America, an organization without racial, religious, political, or class distinctions, having as its aim the mental, moral, and physical development of boys. Since 1926, as Scout president, Head has participated in Scouting activities in every state of the Union and in a number of foreign countries. (Every month he travels to New York to preside at the meeting of the council at National Scout Headquarters.) Late in 1941 the Boy Scouts offered to the Government the services of one and a half million members, who since have completed more than forty war projects requested by various Federal agencies. In early 1945 the organization established a World Friendship Fund, which will be raised among troop members throughout the United States to rebuild Scouting in liberated countries abroad. "For many years," wrote President Roosevelt [42] in a thirty-fifth anniversary message to the Scouts in February 1945, "the Boy Scout movement has been a real force among the democratic countries in helping to promote better understanding among the nations and international good will."

Head's war activities have extended beyond his work as Scout president. In the First War Loan Drive, he was general chairman of the United States Treasury Victory Fund Committee of St. Louis. When Chester C. Davis [40], president of the Federal Reserve Bank of St. Louis, was appointed War Food Administrator in 1943, Head succeeded him as chairman of the War Finance Committee of the Eighth Federal Reserve District. At the time of the First Victory Loan Drive the United States was divided into Federal Reserve Districts. Shortly afterward, when the drive was divided among states, Head became chairman of the Missouri War Finance Committee; in this capacity he led his state over the top by substantial margins in the second to seventh drives. In 1944 Head was elected chairman of the Citizens Committee for Postwar Improvement and Employment in the City of St. Louis. This committee will supervise the expenditure of sixty-three million dollars for a postwar municipal works project designed to provide necessary municipal facilities and employment for servicemen and war workers returning to civilian life. He is also president of the St. Louis USO council and State chairman of the Missouri USO.

Keenly civic-minded, Head has always participated in community affairs wherever he has lived. During his residence in Nebraska, in the years 1917 to 1929, he was a member of the State Capitol Commission which had charge of the construction of the ten-million-dollar Nebraska State Capitol. (He continued as a member during 1930.) He is now director of the St. Louis Chamber of Commerce, a mem-

George Dorrill

WALTER W. HEAD

ber of the board of the Missouri Social Hygiene Association, an elder in the Second Presbyterian Church, an endowment trustee of the Presbytery of St. Louis of the Presbyterian Church in the United States, and a teacher of a men's Bible class. Also consistent with his long interest in educational matters is his trusteeship of Grinnell College (Iowa), Presbyterian Theological Seminary (Chicago), and Westminster and Lindenwood colleges (Missouri). (He is chairman of the board of trustees of Westminster.)

The executive's numerous connections include his presidency of the Southern Ginning Company and the Missouri Mercantile Company, both of Kennett; his chairmanship or directorship in the Board of American Community Stores Corporation of Nebraska, the Navy League of the United States, and the United States Fidelity and Guaranty Company of Baltimore. He is also a member of the board of Governmental Research Institute, the St. Louis Convention and Publicity Bureau, chairman of the St. Louis branch of the Foreign Policy Association, and a member of the National Board of Directors and National Executive Committee of the National Conference of Christian and Jews, Inc.

Besides meeting his many business and civic responsibilities, Head has found time to write articles for several magazines. In the Hoover [43] Administration he wrote for the *Review of Reviews* on the subjects of Federal Reserve rates, agricultural problems, and politics, in which he militantly supported the right and responsibility of businessmen to participate in politics and government. A stanch Republican, he warmly supported President Hoover. In discussing the political situation of 1931 he said, "We have been idolizing individuals instead of idealizing principles."

The Boy Scouts' executive is six feet one inch tall, and his heavy working schedule has apparently not impaired his abundant energy. He used to devote much of his leisure time to horseback riding, hunting, fishing, and

HEAD, WALTER W.—*Continued*

camping, and he has traveled extensively in the United States, Alaska, Canada, Mexico, the British Isles, and Europe. For relaxation he now periodically visits his farm at St. Joseph, Missouri, where his agricultural pursuits are varied. He is a member of several clubs and societies, including the National Geographical Society and the Academy of Political Science. He is musical, has been a choral singer and pianist, and now serves as president of the St. Louis Grand Opera Association. In March 1900 he was married to Della Thompson; they have one daughter, Audrey Vernelle, now Mrs. Raymond A. Baur.

References

Finance 46:11-12+ Ap 10 '44 por
R of Rs 83:49 Mr 31 por
National Cyclopædia of American Biography Current vol A p485
Who's Who in America, 1944-45
Who's Who in Commerce and Industry (1944)

HERRING, CLYDE L(A VERNE) May 3, 1879—Sept. 15, 1945 Former Democratic Senator from Iowa (1937-43); member of Democratic National Committee (1924-28); Governor of Iowa (1932-36); assistant to Prentiss M. Brown [43] when Brown was head of the Office of Price Administration.

Obituary

N Y Times p42 S 23 '45

HERSHEY, MILTON S(NAVELY) Sept. 13, 1857—Oct. 13, 1945 American philanthropist and founder of the Hershey Chocolate Company; founded the Hershey Industrial School of orphan boys in 1905, and later set up trust fund of more than sixty million dollars; created Army "D" ration, for which he was awarded the Army-Navy "E" in 1942.

Obituary

N Y Times p44 O 14 '45 por

HERZOG, PAUL M(AX) Aug. 21, 1906- United States Government official

Address: b. National Labor Relations Board, Washington, D.C.

Among the important appointments President Truman [45] made in June 1945 was that of Paul M. Herzog to the chairmanship of the National Labor Relations Board. A prominent New York attorney, Herzog had been active in the field of labor relations since late 1933, serving both in Federal and State positions. He was on active duty as a lieutenant in the Navy from March 1944 to June 1945, when he was released so that he might assume his new office.

A native New Yorker, Paul Max Herzog was born on August 21, 1906, to Paul M. and Elsie (Loewenstein) Herzog. He received his early education in that city at the Lincoln School before going on to Harvard for advanced study. An honor student, Herzog earned his B.S. *magna cum laude* in 1927. He won the Bowdoin Prize that year at Har-

vard and was elected to Phi Beta Kappa. Beginning his career as a teacher, he was instructor in economics and government at the University of Wisconsin from 1928 to 1930. During this period he worked for his Master's degree which he received from that university in 1930. At this time Herzog returned to his alma mater as a teacher for a year (1930-31). He then entered the Harvard Law School, but his legal training was interrupted in 1933 when he was summoned to Government service in the early days of the New Deal.

Appointed as the assistant secretary of the National Labor Board by Senator Robert F. Wagner [41], he became known as one of the original labor relations "brain trusters." Herzog served on the board during its stormiest days until the dissolution of the NRA. In 1936 he completed his legal training at Columbia University. A Bachelor of Laws, he then joined the prominent New York law firm of Hays [42], St. John, Abramson, and Schulman. After a year of private law practice, however, the attorney was again called into public service upon the formation of the New York State Labor Relations Board in 1937.

After five years on the State board Herzog was named chairman by Governor Herbert H. Lehman [43], the appointment having been urged by the resigning chairman and the third board member. His colleagues recommended Herzog for the position because of his "unique knowledge of the substantive Labor Relations Acts, State and Federal, and because of his unswerving devotion to the democratic policy which inspired their passage, as well as for his warmhearted tact and natural honesty." He was optimistic when he discussed the achievements of the agency. In an interview in 1942 he remarked: "In neighborhood gossip, everybody hears about the couple who fight; no attention is paid to the happy marriages." The labor relations expert added pointedly: "Ninety per cent of cases the board handles are adjusted in informal conferences. There are hearings in one case in ten, but that one case is what the public hears about." The November 1942 issue of the *Annals of the American Academy of Political and Social Science* contains Herzog's article entitled "The Labor Relations Acts of the States," in which the writer presented an historical review of this type of social legislation in the various states, with statistical annotations. He discussed the procedural differences among the states and cited the advantages of such diversity in broad experimentation and experience.

In March 1944 Herzog resigned from the State board to join the Navy. At that time he was accorded the following tribute by Governor Thomas E. Dewey [44]: "Under your leadership the State Labor Relations Board has impartially, without fear or favor, built a great record in solving the problem of employers and employees. The board has served as a model of good administration in the settlement and adjudication of labor disputes." The labor relations authority was commissioned a Naval lieutenant and served in the Industrial Relations Section of the Navy Secretary's office in the Capital. Upon his appointment by President Truman to a five-year term on the NLRB in June 1945, Herzog was released by the Navy. The appointment was unanimously approved by the Senate Committee on Education and Labor on June 14 and was confirmed by the entire Senate the following day. *PM* reported the new chairman is regarded in labor quarters as an outstanding authority in the field of industrial relations.

Commenting on the change in the chairmanship of the NLRB, A.F. of L. spokesmen viewed it as signaling "an era of decreasing labor-representation controversies." The union leaders recalled Herzog's record as a member of the New York State Labor Relations Board and noted his success in avoiding conflicts between the CIO and the A.F. of L. It was further reported that the President's liberal supporters welcomed the choice of Herzog as NLRB chief. Editorially, the *World-Telegram* saw little likelihood of change in the board's policy on foremen's unions, since the writer had found indications in Herzog's record in support of the organizing of foremen. Another writer saw the appointment of Herzog to the board and of Lewis B. Schwellenbach [45] as Secretary of Labor as two important events in labor history. The Ives Committee, a New York group which is interested in industrial and labor conditions, expressed the hope that Herzog's new position "will make his unique abilities and experience available to the Nation in promoting, as he has in New York State, sound industrial and labor relations."

Sworn in as NLRB chairman on July 5, Herzog and other Government leaders took that opportunity to pay tribute to Senator Wagner on the tenth anniversary of President Roosevelt's approval of the National Labor Relations Act. "You can still recognize your child," Herzog remarked to Wagner on the occasion. At the ceremony the new chairman reminded the board staff that they should never forget that the board is a quasi-judicial body and "the servant of all the people of the United States." Herzog further emphasized the board's duty "to protect the rights of millions of wage earners to organize and bargain collectively through representatives of their own choosing." While relieved of his Navy commission, Herzog was "out of uniform but not out of the war"—more than half of the board's cases were from war industries.

It was considered significant that the first important issue on which the new chairman made his views known was the application of the Wagner Act to foremen's unions. Mark Sullivan considered Herzog's majority opinion, written in December, as "temperate in tone and close-reasoned." That opinion was that foremen are employees, not part of management, and as such constitute a bargaining unit. As to the fears of management that organized foremen would be inclined to be more loyal to other employees than to the employer, Herzog said: "Bargaining can only succeed if responsible unions representing supervisory employees, once their legal rights are established, recognize the validity of some of management's special fears and seek to dispel them by the terms of the ultimate bargain."

The industrial specialist is a handsome, six-foot figure, weighing 165 pounds, with blue eyes and light brown hair. A "chain pipe-smoker," he has a large variety of pipes. He was married on April 11, 1929, to Madeleine

Harris & Ewing
PAUL M. HERZOG

Straus Schafer, granddaughter of Oscar S. Straus, who was Secretary of Labor in Theodore Roosevelt's Cabinet. The Herzogs have two young children, John Paul and Andrea Elsie. A member of the Harvard Club of New York, he also belongs to Harvard's Signet Society, and the Cosmos Club of Washington. He likes classical music and indulges a fondness for photography and baseball.

References

PM p19 N 29 '42; p9 Je 8 '45
America's Young Men, 1938-39
Who's Who in American Jewry, 1938-39
Who's Who in New York, 1938

HICKMAN, EMILY (GREGORY) July 12, 1880- Educator
Address: b. c/o New Jersey College for Women, New Brunswick, N.J.; h. 27 Seaman St., New Brunswick, N.J.

The exclusion of women from the 1944 Dumbarton Oaks conference on postwar planning for peace prompted women's organizations throughout the United States to prepare a campaign for inclusion of their sex in all future international conferences. One of their first acts was to make public a list of American women qualified for membership in any international body. On this list was the name of Emily Hickman, veteran world peace crusader and professor of history at New Jersey College for Women, who in April 1945 was appointed an aide to John S. Dickey, public liaison officer at the San Francisco conference.

Born in Buffalo, New York, on July 12, 1880, Emily Gregory Hickman is the daughter of Arthur Washington and Alice (Gregory) Hickman. The Hickmans, their six children, and grandparents and aunts made a group of thirteen at the family dinner table—a table which creaked under its bountiful load in those lush, nonrationed days before the turn of the

Mabel H. Wells

EMILY HICKMAN

century. "A strawberry shortcake, the family's favorite dessert," recalls the professor today, "was so big that eating it was a rite." From this happy girlhood home in Buffalo, Emily Hickman went to Cornell University, where in 1901 she was granted a B.A. degree. In 1908-9 she studied on a fellowship at Cornell, in 1909-10 on a fellowship at Yale. The following year she was awarded her doctorate from Cornell, and the same year became a member of the history department at near-by Wells College (Aurora, New York). In 1927 she left Wells for a professorship in the history department of New Jersey College, the distaff side of Rutgers University in New Brunswick.

The professor's students have said that she is a teacher who succeeds in prodding the minds of the indifferent members of her classes, arousing them with her lectures on the development of Western thought, or by her terse comments on the subject which concerns her very much, American isolationism after the First World War and the failure of the United States to support the League of Nations. When there is opposition to her convictions on the organization of the nations of the world for peace, the customary twinkle in her eyes, it is said, disappears quickly. In keeping with this interest in world affairs is her direction of the International Relations Club at the college. Every two weeks she has been accustomed to entertaining at her home a discussion group of twelve girls from her classes. From the students' point of view, a feature of these evenings is the hot beverage served from the cups and saucers which are a part of the collection Miss Hickman has gathered in her world travels.

Miss Hickman's work on behalf of world peace began in 1925, when she became a member of the Committee on the Cause and Cure of War, founded by Carrie Chapman Catt [40]. Acknowledging that the well known feminist has influenced her more than any other person

has done, Miss Hickman says that she has followed the advice Mrs. Catt gave her at their first meeting—to "stick" to the peace movement. Since those days she has made two transcontinental lecture tours of the United States under the auspices of the Carnegie Endowment for International Peace (1938-39), and she has become associated with a number of organizations working for international cooperation. Among these are the Committee to Study the Organization of Peace and the United Nations Association of New Jersey. She is chairman of the commission on a world community of the National Peace Conference, and of the Committee on Participation of Women in Postwar Planning.

This last-named organization was brought into being by Mary E. Woolley [42], president emeritus of Mount Holyoke College, in Massachusetts. Realizing that women would not be asked to sit at any of the international conferences after the Second World War unless they forced the issue, Miss Woolley called a meeting in 1944 of representatives from thirty women's organizations. Twelve of these were represented at the first meeting of her Committee for the Participation of Women in Postwar Planning; sixty-one others soon became interested. This committee is now supported by such groups as the National Association of Women Lawyers, National Board of the YWCA, National Council of Jewish Women, National Council of Negro Women, Women's Action Committee for Victory and Lasting Peace, Federal Council of Churches of Christ in America, Women's International League for Peace and Freedom, Zonta International, Farmers' Educational Bureau, Women's Overseas Service League, and the National Council of Women of the United States. The membership represents millions of women; the YWCA alone has a membership of over a million.

Because Miss Hickman was influential in many women's organizations and a recognized authority on international affairs, she was given the chairmanship of the new committee. (Elderly Miss Woolley is living in retirement at her New York State home, although she attends meetings.) It has been a strenuous assignment for the New Jersey professor, a doubling of her already heavy schedule. Four or five days a week she regularly travels to New York City after teaching her classes at the college. Her long day ends near midnight.

When Miss Hickman first took over the chairmanship she explained: "What we are going to do specifically is to nominate women who will be qualified for membership in any international body. They will be able to sit with any international conference now being planned, for we are going to select those who are trained for such duties." To this end, a double committee was set up in Washington, D.C., to deal with the plans of the United States Government for international conferences and all phases of Pan American affairs. Miss Hickman has also pointed out that the task of getting women appointed to conferences in foreign lands has resulted in contacts with women in the governments-in-exile.

Women can note with satisfaction that members of their sex have already been recognized to some extent in postwar planning. Miss Josephine Schain '45 of New York was a delegate to the international food conference, Mrs. Ellen S. Woodward of Indianapolis and Mrs. Elizabeth A. Conkey of Illinois were delegates to the Atlantic City UNRRA conference, and Virginia Gildersleeve '41, dean of Barnard, Ruth Bryan Owen Rohde '44, and Miss Hickman herself were sent to the United Nations conference in San Francisco. As the two women members of a staff of six, Miss Hickman and Mrs. Rohde were named by John Dickey, director of the Office of Public Affairs of the State Department, to act as aides to the United States delegation. They were assigned to liaison work between the Government and forty-four civilian organizations. "Cooperation can prevent war," the New Jersey aide declares. "We'll have to establish an international law-making body and an international police force. . . .[And] women are going to help find the way."

In addition to holding membership in several peace organizations, Miss Hickman is a member of Phi Beta Kappa, the American Association of University Professors and the American History Association, and she is chairman of the Public Affairs Committee of the National Board of the YWCA. She has contributed articles to the *Dictionary of American Biography* and the *New England Quarterly*, and book reviews and editorials to the *Woman's Press*. For many summers the professor lectured at Cornell (1918-25), University of Colorado (1928, 1929, 1931), and Rutgers (1930). She is described as a small woman, with wide-set gray-blue eyes and graying hair frequently topped by perky hats. The internationalist likes to cook; she usually finds time to prepare her breakfasts and a week-end meal. For relaxation she works in the garden of her New Brunswick home.

References

N Y Post Mag p23 Mr 8 '44 por
American Women, 1939-40
Leaders in Education (1941)

HICKS, CLARENCE J(OHN) Mar. 7, 1863—Dec. 21, 1944 Industrialist; chairman of the executive committee of Industrial Relations Counselors, Inc., since 1933; held executive positions with Standard Oil, International Harvester, and other large corporations; lectured and advised on matters pertaining to industrial relations.

Obituary

N Y Times p13 D 23 '44 por

HILL, ABRAM Jan. 20, 1911- Theatrical director; playwright
Address: b. American Negro Theatre, 15 W. 126th St., New York City

Abram Hill, playwright-director of the important experimental American Negro Theatre, was born January 20, 1911, in Atlanta, Georgia. He is one of the five children of John and Minnie (Hill) Hill. Their identical surnames notwithstanding, his parents were not relatives. Mrs. Hill's maiden name stems from a family of slave-holding Hills who owned "about half" of Wilkes County, Geor-

ABRAM HILL

gia, and who had purchased Abram Hill's maternal great-grandmother in 1812, when she was only seven years old. She was more than a hundred years old when little Abram used to visit her and listen to her descriptions of her early days. From her he imbibed a respect for history which won for him the highest grades in his history courses. The boy's father was a fireman on the Seaboard Air Line Railroad. After the Government took over the railroads during the First World War, part of the Federal salary somehow found its way out of the Negro railroaders' pay envelopes before it reached them. John Hill led the successful protest to Washington, but after the war things were made so unpleasant for him by the local authorities that he left the railroad and became a house painter. Mrs. Hill for her part "did some sewing on the side."

Young Abram had been attracted to the stage when he made his first amateur appearance in the near-by Morehouse College chapel at the age of seven. But when he was fourteen pneumonia which kept him in the city hospital for eight weeks made the boy decide to become a surgeon. This pleased his parents, to whom success meant being a doctor, lawyer, or dentist, and it was by emphasizing the greater educational opportunities in New York that Abe persuaded his parents to move there in 1925. In New York he attended the Theodore Roosevelt High School for a time, but was graduated in 1929 from the De Witt Clinton High School. Then he went to work as an elevator operator in Macy's department store (1929-31). While taking a premedical course at the College of the City of New York (1930-32), he continued to work at Macy's and, in 1931-32 he was a photographer's assistant. He has supported himself also, according to Mary Braggiotti's article in the New York *Post,* as a hotel clerk, sandhog in the Westchester water tunnel, factory worker, and delivery boy. In his spare time Hill wrote a number of short stories and a

HILL, ABRAM—*Continued*

novel, "The Crystal Casket," but these were not published. In 1932, too, he became drama coach at St. Philip's Protestant Church and the Abyssinian Baptist Church.

In 1934 Hill entered Lincoln University in Pennsylvania to continue his medical course, but instead he was persuaded to take English and drama, and he won the Charles W. Conway Prize in English. Professor J. Newton Hill recognized student Hill's talent and "literally turned over the Little Theater" to him. And Hill spent all his free time writing, staging, directing, and experimenting. The professor gave him individual advanced work, and when Hill received his B.A. in 1937 he was retained for a semester as faculty assistant in drama. While he was at Lincoln the play production budget was quadrupled. During the summer vacations he served as dramatic director for the CCC unit at Camp Upton, Long Island. "In trying to find suitable material to stage for CCC camp shows," Hill recalls, "I had to turn to established plays, and soon adapted them to Negro life. . . .My drama group won the second highest honors in the Second Corps Area." (He had been made assistant State supervisor of CCC camps in 1935-36.)

After leaving the university the twenty-six-year-old director joined the Federal Theater Project; it had taken over the TERA State Board of Education program under which he had worked with the CCC. "It wasn't long before my talent was brought to the attention of Hallie Flanagan, national director," he says. He was assigned to her office and set to write the "case history of the Negro" in the Living Newspaper style originated by the Federal Theater. His first version, "Liberty Deferred," "created a mild furor in Federal Theater circles," but the eventual withdrawal of Congressional funds prevented it from reaching the stage. Plays involving Negro characters were turned over to Hill to read and review, and he claims to have prevented production of at least six, such as Octavus Roy Cohen's *Come Seven,* which he said gave a distorted picture of Negro life. Eventually all plays suggested were turned over to him for consideration.

Theresa Helburn [44] of the Theatre Guild had been greatly impressed by Hill's three-act play *Hell's Half Acre* (1937), inspired by his great-grandmother's reminiscences of slavery, and it was put on twice: by the Unity Players in the Bronx, and by Joseph Ornato. Another Hill play, a satire called *On Strivers' Row* (1939), was first produced in Harlem by the Rose McClendon Players and ran for sixteen performances; produced by the American Negro Theatre in 1940, it ran for 101 performances, the longest run thus far of any ANT play. (It is considered Harlem's favorite play.) Miss Helburn advised the young playwright to study his craft further, and he accordingly took courses at the New School and summer work in theater art at Columbia and Atlanta universities. Hill's work at the New School won him a scholarship from Miss Helburn to the same school, where he studied under John Gassner and in the same class with Tennessee Williams. Erwin Piscator nearly produced one of Hill's plays, but it had to be dropped because of casting difficulties.

After the dissolution of the Federal Theater project in 1939 Hill tried the commercial producers. "All said I was promising," he explains. "I got to a point where I couldn't live on promises. . . .In desperation I went to the National Association for the Advancement of Colored People and tried to interest them in doing something about the Negro theater." Acting on the suggestion of the NAACP's public relations counsel, he attempted to organize the Negro playwrights into a production company. After two months of work on this, however, Hill resigned, "quite brokenhearted over the Negro Playwrights Company's lack of vision and practical planning." In 1940-41 Hill was a researcher for the Federal Writers Project. He was accepted by the Yale School of Drama, but could not enroll because he lacked the tuition fee. Thereupon he decided to plan a theater group in New York City, and began to study the history of past efforts to organize a Negro theater and to analyze the reasons for their failure.

The result was that Hill made the first effort toward bringing about the organization of the American Negro Theatre by calling into session seven other interested persons. This body finally laid the plans for the organization's operation. In June 1940 the ANT was launched. "We had no money—only enthusiasm," Hill says. The company roster included a few professional actors, players of butler and maid parts, but most of the thirty were amateurs who rehearsed at night. Among them were teachers, typists, clerks, and domestic servants. Frederick O'Neal, founder of the Aldridge Players, the successful Negro community theater in St. Louis, was elected manager and Hill became director. The "ANTies," as Hill calls them, found a home in the small but new basement theater of the Harlem branch library; but library rules required that they leave by eleven each night.

Nevertheless, the company began rehearsals. Their first production was Hill's *On Strivers' Row,* written in 1939. But, like most experimental theater groups, the ANT's cooperative workshop felt the lack of suitable material. Hill therefore obtained permission to adapt certain plays to his needs. One of these was the Ephrons' *Three Is a Family,* where the only shift required was that of locale. Another was an unproduced play about Polish-Americans by Philip Yordan. Hill saw promise in it after forty-four Broadway producers had turned it down and took the script to Harry Wagstaff Gribble [45], who, upon Hill's request, accepted the directorial duties for its production; he and Hill added a prologue and epilogue and made a few other changes in Yordan's play. Under Gribble's direction, the company rehearsed for three months, and in June the ANT presented the play—*Anna Lucasta,* with Hilda Simms [44] in the title role. The budget for the production came from ANT's own treasury, the Rockefeller Foundation General Education Board's grant of ninety-five hundred dollars not having been available until two weeks after the opening. (In December 1945 another grant of twelve thousand dollars from the Board was announced. To be utilized over a two-year period, it provides for a full-time salary for Hill, thus allowing him time to raise funds for the building of ANT's own playhouse, a project he hopes will be realized in a few years.)

It is said that critics, motion picture representatives, and actors' agents had been visiting the ANT since its opening, but not until *Anna Lucasta* did the general theater-going public hear of it. Wilella Waldorf praised the play in the New York *Post*, and Burton Rascoe wrote in the New York *World-Telegram*, "I got one of the greatest thrills I have ever had in many years of playgoing [at the ANT's cramped basement playhouse]. . . .You have never seen better acting in your life . . . [but] the importance of *Anna Lucasta* is that . . . it is not the usual white theatrical exploitation of the Negro as a . . . 'colorful', 'quaint,' or 'charming' character, but is a serious story of average human beings (all highly individualized), who happen to have pigmented skins." *Anna Lucasta* was transplanted to Forty-seventh Street, minus the prologue and epilogue, under John Wildberg's aegis, and immediately established itself as a definite hit, with five members of the ANT cast playing their original roles (O'Neal was one of them). The ANT received 1¼ per cent of its weekly gross, which was earmarked for the theater the cooperative group intended to build in Harlem, near the source of its talent.

Meanwhile Abram Hill was working on the sixth ANT production, *Walk Hard,* which he had dramatized from Len Zinberg's novel *Walk Hard, Talk Loud.* It began a six-week engagement in November 1944 with a cast of nine Negro and nine white actors. Before the opening Hill told an interviewer he had already had many requests for the script from Broadway agents, but said, "It's a play with a message. Of course the audience won't get socked over the head with it, but it's there, so I'm not sure if *Walk Hard* is cut out for the $4.40 trade." *Walk Hard* was also produced in Providence. Other ANT productions, not directed by Hill, include *Natural Man, Starlight, Garden of Time,* and *Henri Christophe.*

The ANT is a cooperative group, sharing equally in the profits. "In directing," says Hill, "I strip actors of all their mannerisms, habits, and clichés, and drive them into the characters they are interpreting. Lines only serve to indicate the three dimensions of a character. Once they have been learned, they should literally be forgotten. I spend weeks helping the actor find the character—every detail of his background, the logic of his behavior, and the logic of the audience's emotional reaction. Then we drill and drill for character until the actor doesn't act, he's just naturally the person he is supposed to be. This may take months, but the results can be sensational. After we get a naturalness in the character, we become strictly technical—driving for rhythm, tempo, pace, movement, picturization, motivation, balance, focus, emphasis, overtones, undertones, meaning, mood, etc. In the end we get what ANT is widely known for: naturalness, rhythm, and vitality, which we are experimenting with. . . .As a director and a playwright, I have tried to bring about a balance in the Negro theater. Most

big-time commercial productions on race themes have dealt with only about 10 per cent of the Negro people—as a rule the exotic lower depths. All I'm trying to do is introduce a few of the other types who run the gamut from the professionals, middle class, and the everyday Dicks, Toms, and Harrys."

Hill has a regular job as drama editor of the *Amsterdam News.* Of his playwriting he says, "I hit out on any theme or situation or character that moves me. It is all inspirational—it comes to me when I least expect it." He has written several plays in addition to those mentioned, and in 1945 he was editing an anthology of ANT plays and writing a history of the group. In that year, too, Hill was given one of the Schomburg awards and one of the three Riverdale Children's Association awards for promoting interracial understanding.

Abram Hill is six feet tall and slender (his weight is one hundred and sixty-five pounds); his receding hair is close-clipped, his nose somewhat aquiline, and he wears a mustache. Besides his writing, which is "torture" but which he loves, Hill gives his interests as going to the theater (but not to musicals or motion pictures) reading, dancing to music, "hot, cold, and jitterbug," bicycling, horseback riding, good music, and conversation.

Reference

N Y Post Mag p25 D 29 '43 pors

HIMMLER, HEINRICH (hĭm'lĕr hīn'rĭk) Nov. 7, 1900—May 23, 1945 Leader of the German Storm Troops (SA) since 1929; chief of Gestapo or Nazi secret police since 1936; in 1944 became chief of the home front and commander of the Wehrmacht inside Germany; notorious for wholesale executions within Germany and in occupied countries; called the "evil genius of the German horror camps"; committed suicide upon capture by Allies after surrender of Germany. See *Current Biography* 1941 Yearbook.

Obituary

N Y Times p1 My 25 '45 por

HODGE, JOHN R(EED) June 12, 1893- United States Army officer

Address: b. c/o War Department, Washington, D.C.; h. 808 S. Illinois Ave., Carbondale, Ill.

"The six weeks after March 26, 1945, carried the Allied arms triumphantly from the Rhine to the Elbe, into Czechoslovakia, to the Brenner Pass, and to total victory over Nazism. The same six weeks barely brought the United States Tenth Army into the outskirts of Okinawa's obscure little capital city. . . .There have been struggles in Europe involving greater battlefields, greater concentrations of men and guns, and of greater strategic significance, but with the possible exception of Stalingrad there has been nothing to surpass the Okinawa battle in sheer fury." The greatest share of this fighting fell to the Twenty-fourth Corps of Lieutenant General John R. Hodge, a veteran of the South Pacific war and former leader in the first United States Army troops to take the offensive

LT. GEN. JOHN R. HODGE

against the Axis in any war theater. After the surrender of Japan he was made commander of the American Army of Occupation in Korea.

John Reed Hodge was born in Golconda, Illinois, on June 12, 1893. He is the son of John Hardin and Melissa Caroline (Steagall) Hodge. At nineteen he entered Southern Illinois Teachers College, where he studied in 1912-13. In May 1917, after having attended the University of Illinois, where he studied architectural engineering, he went to the Army Officers' Candidates School at Fort Sheridan, Illinois. Completing the course in August, Hodge was commissioned a second lieutenant in the Infantry Reserve and joined the Sixty-first Infantry at Gettysburg, Pennsylvania. That October Lieutenant Hodge was married to a Pennsylvania girl, Lydia Gillespie Parsons of Punxsutawney; and three weeks later the twenty-four-year-old Illinoisan was given a Regular Army commission and promoted to first lieutenant (temporary).

In February 1918 Hodge was transferred from Fort Greene, North Carolina (to which he had come in November of the previous year) and sent overseas to France the same month as a member of the advance detachment of the Fifth Division. After a two-month course at the Signal School at Langres he rejoined the Sixty-first Infantry as signal and liaison officer in May, later commanding a company. Hodge served in the First World War in the Anould and Saint-Dié sectors, and took part as an obscure junior officer in the Saint-Mihiel and Meuse-Argonne offensives. When the war ended he was a captain (temporary), and in April 1919, while his regiment was in Luxembourg, he was made a permanent first lieutenant, retaining his temporary grade of captain.

The Sixty-first returned to the United States in August 1919 and was assigned first to Camp Gordon, Georgia, and then to Camp Jackson, South Carolina. In October 1921 Captain Hodge (promoted to permanent grade in July 1920) joined the faculty of Mississippi

Agricultural and Mechanical College as professor of military science and tactics. Four years later the professor went back to school himself—at the Infantry School, Fort Benning, Georgia. After his graduation in May 1926 he was kept at Fort Benning for temporary duty, and in October 1926, he reported to Schofield Barracks, Hawaii, to join the Twenty-seventh Infantry. A year later Hodge was appointed plans and training officer of the Twenty-second Infantry Brigade.

In October 1929 the thirty-six-year-old captain returned to the United States and was assigned to the Eighteenth Infantry at Fort Hamilton, New York. Later he was chosen for intensive advanced training. From February to April 1932, Hodge was a student at the Chemical Warfare School, Edgewood Arsenal, Maryland; four months later he began the two-year course at the Command and General Staff School at Fort Leavenworth, Kansas. Next came a year at the Army War College in Washington, D.C. In August 1935, after a two months' leave, the Infantry officer was promoted to major and detailed to the Air Corps Tactical School, Maxwell Field, Alabama. The faculty there included the future Generals Lawrence S. Kuter, Harold L. George '42, and Haywood S. Hansell '45. Graduated in June 1936, Hodge had several months' duty commanding a battalion of the Twenty-third Infantry at Fort Sam Houston, Texas, before joining the War Department General Staff's Operations and Training Division, G-3, in late December.

That year of 1936 saw the founding of the Rome-Berlin-Tokyo Axis and the start of a world-wide armament race. The United States, as a traditionally nonmilitaristic nation, had cut its Army expenditures to the minimum, resulting in small and unbalanced armed forces. For over four years Major Hodge worked on a General Staff operating under this handicap, which had to integrate the greatest peacetime military expansion in American history and to prepare the country's military plans in case it should be drawn into the European war. Hodge was promoted to lieutenant colonel in 1940. In February 1941, already held past the normal four-year detail on the War Department General Staff, Hodge joined the newly organized Seventh Army Corps in Birmingham, Alabama, as plans and training officer, G-3, of Corps.

In December 1941 Hodge was promoted to colonel (temporary) and became chief of staff of the Seventh Army Corps, removed to the West Coast upon declaration of war, which means that he supervised all the routine work of personnel, intelligence, operations and training, and supply for the commanding general. Six months later, in June 1942, he was promoted to brigadier general (temporary) and made assistant division commander of the Twenty-fifth ("Tropic Lightning") Infantry Division, which was then in the Pacific area. This division moved to the South Pacific in November-December of 1942, coming under the command of Major General Alexander M. Patch '43, and relieved marines on the British-owned island of Guadalcanal. In the months since the marines had first reached Guadalcanal under Major General Alexander A. Vandegrift '43 in August 1942, they had written in blood a classic story of heroism. But Guadalcanal was still officially a "Navy show," and the troops were therefore under the over-all strategic command of Admiral William F. Halsey [42]. Finally on February 9, 1943, after careful preparatory measures and an intensive drive which lasted thirty days, General Patch's headquarters announced the "elimination of Japanese resistance" on Guadalcanal—the "complete rout and utter defeat of a Japanese army which executed a nonorderly withdrawal."

In late April 1943 John R. Hodge was promoted to major general (temporary) and was assigned to command the Americal Division. That July he was called for relief command of a division which had been in continuous action against the Japanese in New Georgia for almost thirty days and had suffered heavy casualties. "Under his aggressive leadership," says the citation for Hodge's Distinguished Service Medal, "the division was revitalized and continued the offensive with the zeal of fresh troops, taking its assigned objective in the minimum of time. General Hodge inspired his troops by his constant presence at the front and was primarily responsible for the forward drive of the division which brought the entire operation to a successful conclusion" in August.

After this, Hodge returned to command the Americal Division, which had been activated in May 1942 to hold off the Japanese on New Caledonia. This, the only American division organized overseas, was the first Army unit to take the offensive in the Second World War, and is the only one officially distinguished by name instead of by a number. ("Americal," a combination of "America" and "Caledonia," was originally suggested by an Infantry sergeant.) These men were veterans of Guadalcanal when Hodge assumed command. On Christmas Day 1943 the Americal landed on Bougainville Island, also in the Solomons group, and in January 1944 the Army commander in the South Pacific, Lieutenant General Millard F. Harmon [42], announced that Hodge's division had replaced the Third Marine Division fighting the Japanese Seventeenth Army on Bougainville. After beating back a major Japanese counteroffensive aimed at the destruction of the three Americal strategically important airfields near Bougainville's Empress Augusta Bay, the American troops achieved what was described on April 3, 1944, as a complete victory. Following this they remained in that area, continuing protection of the airfields and training for future operations.

In April 1944 Major General Hodge was transferred to the Central Pacific Command and was assigned to command the Twenty-fourth Corps. This included, among others, the Seventh Infantry Division, veterans of Attu and Kwajalein, and the newly activated Ninety-sixth recently from the West Coast. For five months Hodge supervised training and loading out of Army units for operations against the Marianas and Palaus and prepared his corps for the invasion of Yap Island in the western Carolines. Toward the end of the typhoon season, when troops assigned for this operation were actually on board the ships and leaving the island waters, there was a last-minute change of plans. The naval air attacks by Vice-Admiral Marc C. Mitscher's [44] fast carrier Task Force 58 had proved so successful that the leaders decided to invade the Philippines immediately. After a complete change in plans and several thousand miles of travel General Hodge and his men therefore found themselves in the largest Pacific convoy seen to that date, and commanded by Vice-Admiral Thomas C. Kinkaid [44]. After they hit the beach of Leyte Island early on October 20, theater commander Douglas MacArthur [41] was in personal command of the land forces, comprising "elements of [Lieutenant General Walter Krueger's [43]] Sixth United States Army, to which were attached units from the Central Pacific with supporting elements."

During the Leyte operations "General Hodge's dynamic leadership and constant bold extension of activity kept all elements of his command at a high pitch of aggressive effort" —to quote the citation accompanying the second-award Oak Leaf Cluster on his Distinguished Service Medal. General Hodge's drive west from Dulag-Tanauan beaches in the southern spearhead of the offensive was through dense banana groves, cornfields, and rice paddies, the latter described as chest-high swamps through which the men had to wade under Japanese sniper fire, and against heavy rains and strong winds which "turned the dirt roads into slick, treacherous traps for the motorized equipment." One twelve-mile march by spearheads of the Seventh Division, the longest one-day advance of the campaign, took ten hours and was described by newsmen as a test of endurance. The Ninety-sixth Division under Major General James L. Bradley accomplished what has been described as unbelievable feats in clearing the enemy from the coastal plains in the north part of the wide zone of action and destroying hostile forces which were driven into the mountains in north central Leyte. American losses in the bitter fighting were, however, less than one-tenth the Japanese casualties, General Krueger reported.

In mid-November the Eleventh Airborne Division commanded by Major General Joseph M. Swing joined Hodge's Twenty-fourth Corps, entering combat in the drive through the Jap infested mountains and meeting the Seventh Division. The airborne division "wrote new history in the annals of jungle and mountain warfare," supplying itself by parachute, evacuating wounded, and preventing the enemy reinforcements from reaching the Americans' vital airfield area.

In late November the Seventy-seventh ("Statue of Liberty") Division, veterans of Guam, under Major General Andrew Bruce, joined Hodge's command. It was almost immediately loaded for an amphibious assault and in early December landed south of the large port of Ormoc on the west coast of Leyte. The Seventy-seventh thus cut off the Japanese forces opposing the Seventh and the Eleventh Airborne Divisions to the south and pushed on toward Ormoc, capturing it three days later. This was the last important Nipponese base on Leyte Island, and with it the main enemy supply depots fell to Hodge's men. The Seventh closed the gap by strong attack to the north and four days later took over mopping up the Ormoc area, relieving the Seventy-seventh to drive on to the north end of Ormoc Valley and join forces with the First Cavalry Division under Major General Verne D. Mudge, trap-

HODGE, JOHN R.—*Continued*

ping many thousand of enemy troops. Meanwhile, the Eleventh Airborne Division completed cleaning out the enemy in the mountains to the south and the Ninety-sixth had destroyed all enemy in its zone. On Christmas Day 1944 the Seventy-seventh Division captured Palompon, a small Japanese port on the western peninsula of Leyte and the campaign was officially declared at an end. In the words of General MacArthur, "The completeness of this destruction has seldom been paralleled in the history of warfare. General Yamashita has sustained perhaps the greatest defeat in the military annals of the Japanese Army."

General Hodge was next heard of in connection with the invasion of Okinawa, chief of the Ryukyu Islands, on Easter Sunday, April 1, 1945. The Tenth Army of Lieutenant General Simon Bolivar Buckner [42], which went ashore from a fourteen-hundred-ship convoy after a ten-day sea and air attack, was made up mainly of Hodge's Twenty-fourth Corps and the Marine Third Amphibious Corps under General Geiger [45]. (The Kerama island group, eighteen miles west of Okinawa, had been cleaned up by Hodge's Seventy-seventh Division three days earlier.) Airfields taken during the first day were immediately put to use: Okinawa, nearly seven thousand miles from the United States, is but three hundred and sixty miles from Japan—two hours by bomber—and a similar distance from China and Formosa. In view of the island's obviously great strategic value, it was cause for wonder that the Japanese commander allowed an "incredibly easy" landing. By the second day some of General Hodge's troops were almost ten days ahead of schedule, meeting no strong or organized resistance, and had cut the island in two by driving to its east coast. "It is going far better than our wildest dreams," Hodge declared. "If they [the Japanese] had elected to hold in high ground in the middle of this area they could have given us plenty of trouble. I do not know why they gave us such a present but we are pleased to have it."

Within a week after the first landings Japanese resistance stiffened in a place where the narrowness of the island made it difficult for Hodge to maneuver his corps or to use its strength in any way but the costliest, frontal assault. There the Japanese fought with bitter tenacity from positions reported "as clever and intricate as anything devised by the Germans." Declared one high-ranking officer, "We've never seen a more elaborate organization of defense. It may take three months to clean up." For the first time in the Pacific war, also, the Japanese used massed artillery, although the Americans reportedly returned about ten shells for every one received. On April 15 the Twenty-seventh Division "New York's Own," veterans of Saipan and famous in the First World War, was identified in Hodge's corps, which was throwing back one counterattack after another as it continued a slow advance. One hill was taken and retaken eleven times before the Americans finally secured it. Even the weather had turned miserably wet with only short periods of sunshine. (Among the casualties was the war correspondent Ernie Pye [41], killed with Seventy-

seventh Division troops advancing on the little island of Ie Jima, off Okinawa.) On April 19 Hodge, after regrouping his forces and building up supplies, opened a grand offensive toward the capital, Naha, but after a month's fighting, in General Buckner's words, it was still necessary to root the Japanese out "with blowtorch and corkscrew" in a campaign described as one of "nagging slowness and brutal exhaustion."

By the end of May, by which time the Ninety-sixth Division had completed the capture of the enemy's eastern hold to the Shuri position, Hodge announced that the main Japanese defenses had been "busted" after sixty-one days of bitter fighting. It was then only a matter of time and a continued dogged advance until the Battle of Okinawa would be over. That fighting ended on June 22, when organized resistance on the part of the enemy ceased—all had been killed or captured, or had committed suicide. With victory in sight, Lieutenant General Buckner [42] was killed four days earlier while observing at the front. The cost of victory was high when compared to other battles in the Pacific, but the gain was considered tremendous—the enemy had lost well over one hundred thousand and the Americans had gained a strategic base on the threshold of the Japanese homeland. Near the end of the Battle of Okinawa General Hodge was officially informed that he had been promoted to the temporary grade of lieutenant general.

After the fall of Japan the task of bringing order out of chaos in southern Korea was assigned to General Hodge as commander of the American Army of Occupation. On September 9 he accepted the surrender of half of an estimated 375,000 Japanese troops in Korea, while the other half had in northern Korea, governed by Russia under the terms of the Potsdam agreement. The Koreans, who had been promised their independence at the Cairo conference "in due course", were especially bitter after the generation-long rule by the Japanese. Consequently, there was wide protest when Hodge, acting under directions to maintain existing Government machinery until the American occupation was completed, retained Japanese officials in administrative work. The press in the United States also voiced considerable opposition to the plan, although Hodge made it clear that the Japanese would have no independence of action, and that the political situation was chaotic with "many factions, each claiming the largest representation and pointing the finger of collaboration at the other." General MacArthur in Tokyo issued a proclamation, assuring the Koreans that their rights would be protected. However, street demonstrations in the Korean capital of Seoul continued until the Japanese governor general was removed on September 12. He was replaced by Major General Archibald V. Arnold, the American general, and Washington announced that all Japanese in governmental positions in Korea would be replaced as rapidly as consistent with safe operations.

In commenting on the difficulties with which Hodge was confronted, *Time* pointed out that occupation of Korea had had to be organized "in tearing haste, by combat-weary men driving themselves fifteen hours a day and more, trying to get a country of twenty-five million people rolling again." At the end of the first month Hodge was able to announce progress in putting occupation plans into effect. He stated that up to October 8 an estimated forty thousand Japanese Army and Navy personnel had been returned to Japan, and it was expected that Korea would be cleared of Japanese soldiers by November 1. He also reported that, although the American military governmental staff was still "seriously undermanned," there had been a revision downward in the number of occupation troops, due chiefly to the "speedy removal of the Japanese and the encouraging degree of Korean cooperation." The job facing Hodge, the New York *Times* pointed out, "was not one of restoring a government, but, with the help of the Koreans, of building an entirely new political structure from the ground up." The "enthusiasm and sincerity of the efforts being made by the Koreans," concluded the report, "is one of the most encouraging signs that this goal is now attainable. With little more than textbook understanding of what democracy really is, they are bravely facing the huge task." The more than one hundred political parties which were reported to exist when the Americans arrived were consolidated into twelve at the request of Hodge. He then interviewed two members of each of the twelve parties on their plans for Korean government, and asked them to submit recommendations for government bureau heads, the equivalent of cabinet ministers.

Meanwhile, Koreans continued to protest bitterly against the trusteeship set up by the Moscow Conference of Foreign Ministers. The problem was further complicated by conflict between the Korean Leftist and Rightist groups. Scattered rioting and strikes were the outward signs of the tense situation. Another aspect of the occupation problem was the division of the country into the industrial north and agricultural south, occupied, respectively, by Russians and Americans. By December, when efforts to eliminate the artificial barrier were under way, Hodge said: "Problems to be negotiated include the opening of communications, unification of the economic life of Korea and the exchange of goods and freedom of travel between the two zones." Before the end of the year, too, the Koreans had set up a provisional government headed by Kim Koo, and Major General Archer L. Lerch [45] had succeeded General Arnold as military governor.

Like other Army people, General and Mrs. Hodge have no permanent home, but live wherever he is stationed in time of peace, and she stays wherever she is stranded in time of war. They have one daughter, Barbara Anne (married to Air Force Lieutenant Hall, who piloted B-24 planes in Europe), and a grandson. Hodge is a member of the University of Illinois Chapters of Sigma Tau and Tau Beta Pi fraternities, and of the Triangle and Scarab, engineering and architectural societies, respectively.

Reference

Who's Who in America, 1944-45

HODGSON, JOSEPH V(ERNON) Jan. 2, 1899- United States Government official and Army officer; lawyer

Address: b. c/o War Department, Washington, D.C.; h. 2041 Kakela Dr., Honolulu

Lieutenant Colonel Joseph V. Hodgson, prominent lawyer and former Attorney General of Hawaii, is United States commissioner on the United Nations War Crimes Commission. Hodgson was appointed American representative on the war crimes body on May 12, 1945, by President Truman [45], after having served as acting commissioner from the first of January. Replacing Herbert C. Pell, whom he served as deputy, Hodgson assumed his seat on the Commission at a time when the eyes of the world were focused on that body. With the Allied military victory in Europe complete, the problem of punishment of war criminals was foremost on the agenda of European reorganization. There had been considerable speculation about the policy and operation of the War Crimes Commission since its formation. However, Hodgson indicated his policy soon after his assignment. "Justice will be done expeditiously," said the new commissioner.

Joseph Vernon Hodgson was born in Boyne Falls, Michigan, on January 2, 1899, the son of Joseph V. and Ada Delphine (Adams) Hodgson. Educated in his home state, Hodgson attended the University of Michigan, where his studies were interrupted by America's entrance into the First World War. The young man served as a second lieutenant in the Infantry, a commission he held from September to December, 1918. Having earned his B.A. degree in 1921, he decided on a legal career and continued his training at the university's law school, obtaining his LL.B. in 1925. Admitted to the California bar that same year, Hodgson then sought and won admission to the bar of Hawaii the following year. During the next three years he was associated in law practice with E. C. Peters, who later became a Justice of the Supreme Court of Hawaii, and Ray J. O'Brien, who later became a judge of the Tax Appeal Court of the Islands. From 1929 to 1931 Hodgson continued his legal work with Peters, after which he engaged in private practice until 1934. Then the thirty-five-year-old lawyer assumed public office, becoming Deputy Attorney General of Hawaii. In 1937 Hodgson rose to the post of Assistant Attorney General, and the following year he became Attorney General.

An active member of the Hawaiian community, Hodgson belonged to several of the Islands' legal and civic agencies. He was acting member of the Board of Public Lands in 1935, and from 1938 until 1942 the lawyer was a member of the Farm Loan Board. During that same period he also belonged to the Board of Bar Examiners of Hawaii, the Procedural Rules Committee of the Supreme Court, and the Board of Health. From 1940 to 1942 he was a commissioner of the National Conference of Commissioners on Uniform State Laws. He was also a member of the Governor's Special Advisory Committee on the Hawaii Defense Act (1941-42).

On May 29, 1942, Hodgson entered the Army of the United States with the rank of major, becoming assistant to the judge advocate at Fort Shafter, Hawaii. In July of the fol-

HODGSON, JOSEPH V.—*Continued*

lowing year he returned to the continental United States to attend the Judge Advocate General's School at Ann Arbor, Michigan. After three months he was assigned to the War Plans Division of the Judge Advocate General's Office in Washington, D.C. On May 9, 1944, Hodgson attained the rank of lieutenant colonel and at about the same time left for London to work with the United States representative on the War Crimes Commission. In December he was relieved from assignment in the European theater of operations and reassigned to the Judge Advocate General's Office in the Capital.

January 1945 found Hodgson in London as deputy to Herbert C. Pell, then American representative on the War Crimes Commission. At that time Acting Secretary of State Joseph C. Grew [41] notified Pell that he would not be retained in his post on the Commission because of Congressional failure to appropriate the thirty thousand dollars for his salary and expenses. As reported in detail in *PM*, sharp controversy arose after Pell's dismissal, vigorous protests coming particularly from liberal quarters. Pell, former Minister to Portugal and to Hungary, had been a leading figure on the Commission, pressing for swift, decisive action against war criminals. Following his dismissal he expressed the opinion that he had been dropped because some State Department officials were opposed to his proposal to punish the Nazis for crimes against their own nationals, including the Jews. In April Pell placed part of the blame for German atrocities on Department officials who had taken no action on the recommendations of the War Crimes Commission. Had the Nazis known that their savagery would bring certain punishment, they might have been deterred from such acts, Pell claimed. After Pell's dismissal, Hodgson represented the United States as acting commissioner until his formal appointment to the post by the President in May.

Plans for the establishment by the United Nations of a commission for the investigation of war crimes had been announced in London and Washington in October 1942. A week later V. M. Molotov [40] had revealed that the Soviet Union planned to set up a similar body. Thus, at present, the War Crimes Commission, which does not include the Soviet Union, represents sixteen nations. The Russian War Crimes Commission and the Red Army have been carrying on independent investigations in their own area of operations. The creation of an international tribunal to include the Soviet Union has been proposed, however. In February 1945 the Crimea Declaration reaffirmed the determination of the Big Three to "bring all war criminals to justice and swift punishment." The existing War Crimes Commission has no powers of investigation, but is only an advisory body. It deals with reports of war crimes referred to it by the member governments and other bodies, and from this evidence decides whether or not a prima-facie case exists. The Commission then compiles lists of criminals which it sends to the military authorities so that steps can be taken for the apprehension of the accused.

Hodgson was present at the meeting of the Commission on January 31, 1945, when Lord Wright [45], representative of Australia, was elected chairman. (The new chairman replaced Sir Cecil Hurst, who resigned.) The Commission has figured prominently in the news since then, as a result of the final military collapse of Germany and the capture of leading enemy figures. On May 16 it was stated that the Commission had indicted Hermann Göring [41] as a war criminal the previous November. His case, said one spokesman, would be regarded as a test of the speed and procedure applicable to subsequent trials of war criminals. On May 17 it was revealed that the Commission had completed indictments against all leading Nazis. In addition, the war crimes body announced that it was prepared to deliver its evidence to Justice Robert H. Jackson [40], chief United States prosecutor. According to Hodgson, the prosecution waited only on agreement between the Western Allies and the Soviet Union on the matter of trial by military tribunal, as proposed by the United States. The Colonel's views were made clear in a statement released on June 1, in which he charged the Axis leaders with responsibility for the crimes committed during their regime.

Hodgson was also a member of the War Crimes Conference on problems of detection and prosecution of war criminals, which opened on May 31 in London. Its chief object was to coordinate the work between national offices and the Commission in preparation for the first war crime trials. The Colonel proposed that a central recording office for all war crimes should be set up as the only means of tracing the pattern of Axis crimes committed throughout Europe. "While the evidence in the possession of one national office might be insufficient to identify the persons responsible for a crime," he said, "all the evidence, when collected, might well identify all of the persons."

Throughout the world public clamor for quick action on the accused was followed by intensified activity on the part of the Commission. On May 18 the New York *Times* reported that the biggest manhunt in history was tracking down war criminals from Norway to the Bavarian Alps. The report added that the United Nations blacklist of major German criminals was practically complete. The War Crimes Commission has also in its possession lists of Japanese war criminals, the first of which was given to the group by the Australian Government in March 1945. In August The War Crimes Commission in London announced a pact establishing an International Military Tribunal to try the major European Axis criminals. The Tribunal was to consist of four members—one each from Britain, the United States, Russia, and France. The greatest international trial in history opened before the Tribunal at the Nuremberg court house on November 20.

Hodgson is a member of the Hawaii, California, and American bar associations and he has also served on the executive committee of the Hawaii chapter of the American Red Cross. A Mason and an Elk, he belongs to the Pacific Club, Oahu Country Club, and Outrigger Canoe Club in Honolulu. He belongs to the American Academy of Political and

Social Science, and he holds membership in Sigma Phi Epsilon and Phi Alpha Delta. Colonel Hodgson is unmarried.

References

N Y Times p8 My 13 '45 por
Who's Who in America, 1944-45
Who's Who in Law, 1937

HOLMES, JULIUS C(ECIL) Apr. 24, 1899- Aviation executive; former United States diplomat and Government official

Address: b. c/o Transcontinental and Western Air, Inc., Airlines Terminal Bldg., New York City

After more than two years of overseas wartime service, which included an important part in dangerous and delicate missions, Brigadier General Julius C. Holmes was appointed by President Roosevelt to the office of Assistant Secretary of State in charge of the division of administration and personnel of the United States Department of State, with its Foreign Service. Holmes filled that post from January into August of 1945, and with the end of the war he became vice-president of Transcontinental and Western Air, Inc., which is headed by Jack Frye '45.

Julius Cecil Holmes was born April 24, 1899, in Pleasanton, Kansas, to James Reuben and Lou Jane (Trussell) Holmes. He studied at the University of Kansas intermittently, with time out for service in the First World War (he enlisted in the Student Army Training Corps in October 1918). In December 1919 Holmes was appointed a second lieutenant in the Infantry in the Kansas National Guard unit. Advanced to first lieutenant in March 1920, he enrolled for the National Guard course at the Infantry School, Fort Benning, Georgia, completing the course in February 1921. That June he was commissioned a first lieutenant in the Infantry Reserve. In 1923 the twenty-four-year-old future general went into the insurance business. In June 1924 he was appointed a first lieutenant in the Cavalry Reserve, resigning this commission in March 1925 to join the Department of State.

A graduate of the Foreign Service School, in April of 1925 Julius Holmes entered the United States Foreign Service, becoming the vice-consul at Marseilles. After two years in that post he was sent to Turkey as assistant delegate of the High Commission, remaining at Smyrna as vice-consul. In 1929 he was made secretary of the Legation at Tirana, in Albania, and Chargé d'Affaires; after ten months Holmes was moved to the Legation at Bucharest as its secretary. Here he stayed for four years; in 1932, at the age of thirty-three, he was married to Henrietta Allen. They have three children, Henry Allen, Elsie Jane, and Richard Peyton, and make their home in Washington, D. C.

In 1934 Holmes was recalled to Washington to become assistant chief of the Division of Protocol and International Conferences. In 1935 he was sent down to Rio de Janeiro as secretary general of the Inter-American conference which succeeded in ending the bloody five-year war of Paraguay and Bolivia for possession of the Gran Chaco region; and the next year he was secretary of an arbitration

BRIG. GEN. JULIUS C. HOLMES

commission. In October 1937 he resigned from the State Department to put his knowledge of protocol at the service of Grover Whalen's '44 New York World's Fair Corporation, where he was in charge of relations with all state and national governments. One of the most notable achievements of the Fair administration is that, after the outbreak of the Second World War in 1939, it persuaded all the warring nations (except Russia) to maintain their exhibits. About a month after the war had begun, Holmes was made vice-president of the Fair, and in January 1940 he went to Canada to negotiate for the appearance of the Dionne quintuplets. This offer was rejected by the Canadian Premier, Mitchell F. Hepburn '41—but not before it had secured some valuable publicity for the Fair.

After the closing of the Fair in 1940 Holmes accepted the post of president of General Mills do Brasil, General Mills South American subsidiary, which he filled from 1941 to 1942, at which time he was elected to the board of directors. In February 1942 the ex-diplomat, entered the Military Intelligence Service of the United States Army in which he had held a reserve commission as major since January 1936. Commissioned a lieutenant colonel (temporary) on February 1, 1942, he was ordered to "extended active duty" in the Office of the Combined Chiefs of Staff in Washington, D. C., as assistant secretary. In September 1942 Holmes was promoted to colonel (temporary) and sent overseas. There he had duty in the Office of the Assistant Chief of Staff for G-1 (personnel), serving in the Allied Force Headquarters in the European and North African theater of operations.

In October 1942 Holmes accompanied General Mark W. Clark '42 on a secret submarine trip from England to Algeria. There the party went ashore to meet by prearrangement with certain French officers, from whom they learned important facts about the disposition of the Vichy troops. Through an interpreter, Clark arranged with the Frenchmen for their surrender of the Algiers airfields as soon

HOLMES, JULIUS C.—*Continued*

as the Americans should arrive. Warned by some Arabs, the Vichy police raided the building, and the Clark party were forced to hide. When the police left, the party made their now famous escape.

The actual invasion landings, which Holmes had helped to plan, were made with relative ease, and "land resistance was not terrifically great anywhere," a fact which General Dwight Eisenhower'[42] attributed to "this modern Message to Garcia." Of Clark, Holmes, and their companions, he said, "I am exceedingly proud of all of them. They took great risks and accomplished their work." Holmes was present at the conferences with Vichy French Admiral Darlan'[41] which led to the surrender; in fact, he and Robert Murphy'[43] drew up the actual Franco-American agreement. For this reason Holmes was said to be unpopular with liberals and New Dealers, who considered that policy too generous toward the enemies of democracy and too careless of its friends; and *PM* charged Holmes with "frequently voicing hostility toward the resistance movements organized inside Fascist territory," and with urging the State Department, in the summer of 1943, to "assure Italian workers that the Allies were not warring on Fascism—that our only enemy was Germany." To the first of these charges, Holmes answered that "his part was to carry out the instructions which General Eisenhower received from the Joint Chiefs of Staff," and that he had nothing to do with American policy toward General de Gaulle'[40], leader of the Free French.

Colonel Holmes, named a brigadier general (temporary) by the President in June 1943, is generally credited with being the "father" of the Allied Military Government of Occupied Territory (formerly called AMGOT and later reduced to AMG). When the invasion of Sicily was mounted in North Africa, it was clear that some provision would have to be made for control of the civilian populations of what was then enemy territory. It was seen that civilian epidemics are no respecter of armies, that wandering refugees clutter the roads and impede military progress, and that disorder in general interferes with operations. Eisenhower's staff, of which Holmes was chief civil affairs officer from June 1943 to February 1944, devised a plan whereby British and American (and later French) civilian experts in the fields of government, law, finance, public health, and public safety should be put into uniform with appropriate ranks and given special training for administering occupied areas, once the conquering army moved on.

When an Allied army advanced AMG officers advanced with it. Their duty was to restore order and re-establish civilian life, usually in areas where the normal physical equipment has been badly damaged or perhaps completely destroyed. This task was, of course, made infinitely harder by the retreating armies' policy of destroying what they could and sabotaging the rest. There had been a constant stream of protest that AMG had put expedience above ideological considerations in getting the liberated areas back on their feet—had failed to root out the Fascists and collaborationists thoroughly, but had worked through and with the existent functionaries, except in the most flagrant cases. The military were, however, pleased with their free-

dom from, the burden of civil administration, and AMG has been extended to all areas occupied by the Anglo-American forces. In Italy its later form is known as the Allied Control Commission; and in Europe, as Supreme Headquarters announced in May 1944, a Civil Affairs Section has been added to the four traditional "G's" of the General Staff. In charge of this G-5 was British Lieutenant General A. E. Grassett, who had Holmes as his deputy, and Brigadier General Frank McSherry as Chief of Operations. In contradistinction to AMG, G-5 was to "assist and advise" the various liberated governments in restoring civilian life, rather than to control them, and was to represent to the governments the views of the Allied military commander.

To Holmes, his staff, and his superior fell the complex and difficult task of restoring life in France, in Paris itself, in Belgium and Luxembourg and Holland, as the Allied armies fought their way into Germany. As these were all United Nations, the civil affairs administration was "designed purely to assist those countries." But the situation was changed when a part of Germany came under Allied occupation. In October 1944 General Holmes made public the code of military laws and ordinances which had already been put into operation in a small area of Germany and which would be applied to all further territory captured by Eisenhower's command. As the troops entered, German sovereignty was suspended and authority became vested in the Allied commander. The scope and complexity of the code was described as "without parallel in history." "Germany," remarked correspondent David Anderson, "will revert to her 1932 way of life, as it was before Adolf Hitler'[42] attained power, if the scheme works out as planned. . . .The task of taking over a nation the size of Germany, lock, stock, and barrel, would be hard enough under the most favorable circumstances; with the country rebellious, bitter, and suffering from the shock of having familiar authority brushed aside, this undertaking will test the strength, patience, and ingenuity of the Allied command. It differs from Germany's [occupation] problem in 1940 in that no attempt will be made to employ quislings or foster the idea of normal life."

This code, which was to be enforced during "the rough-and-tumble period" before all hostilities ceased, and until the Allied powers including Russia devise a long-range program for Germany, was in effect the terms of unconditional surrender. Harsh but just—a trial according to accepted procedure was to be given each accused offender—these military laws were designed to eliminate Nazism; ensure the health and safety of the occupying forces; maintain public order; care for and repatriate recaptured Allied prisoners and other displaced persons; apprehend war criminals; protect Allied and United Nations property; control German Government property and public corporations; control foreign exchange assets; and to establish a suitable civil administration. Civilian activities were restricted; travel limited; discrimination based on race, religion, or political opinion forbidden; postal, telephone, and telegraph facilities closed; but the Germans, as those under Allied control had been astounded to discover, were allowed to keep their radios and listen to German broadcasts. Provision was made, also, for the punishment of war criminals, Nazi and Gestapo leaders.

On December 8, 1944, President Roosevelt [42] signed legislation creating two new assistant secretaries of state, in addition to the four already in existence, and then nominated General Holmes and James C. Dunn [43] for the posts. These appointments, considered jointly with those of Joseph C. Grew [41], William L. Clayton [44], Archibald MacLeish [40] and Nelson Rockefeller [41] (Dean Acheson [41] remained in the sixth assistant secretaryship), roused a storm of opposition in the Senate. Conservatives objected to MacLeish; many liberals joined with cotton Democrats to oppose Clayton; the name of Rockefeller was an anathema to some; while Dunn and Holmes drew the fire of liberals and New Dealers. "Every fairly progressive person who has had contact with Holmes in the European theater and in North Africa," wrote *PM*, "is appalled by his appointment," while the New York *Times*' Arthur Krock [43] described Holmes and Dunn as "very able career men [who] will fortify the Department."

The President stood firm behind his appointees, and the Senate finally held an unprecedented open hearing at which all the nominees were questioned. General Holmes flew in from Europe for the hearing the night before, was questioned for fifteen minutes, and then flew back to Allied Field Headquarters in Paris. All the nominations eventually went through, although with much criticism from Senators. And on December 29 the new Assistant Secretary of State in charge of administration and personnel of the Department and the Foreign Service received the Distinguished Service Medal for his exceptionally meritorious services as chief of the military government section at Supreme Headquarters the preceding year.

The duties of Holmes in his new State Department post included "budget and finance problems, personnel, communications, procurement of supplies, records and files, space problems, the coordination and review of correspondence . . . and the passport and visa division." (According to the *American Political Science Review* [April 1945], the two major organizational orders of January 12 and December 29, 1944, had provided the State Department "with a sound administrative pattern for conducting our foreign relations.")

The war over, Holmes resigned from Government service on August 17, stating that he had accepted his appointment by Roosevelt only as a war assignment and that he wished to return to private business. His vice-presidency of Transcontinental and Western Air dates from late 1945, in which capacity he takes an active part in the international relations of the airline's routes to Europe, North Africa, the Middle East, and Asia.

Julius C. Holmes was made an Officer of the Legion of Merit, and has been decorated with nine foreign orders: Commander of the Crown of Yugoslavia, Commander of the Greek Order of the Phoenix, Officer of the Southern Cross of Brazil, Chevalier of the French Legion of Honor, Commander of the Crown of Rumania, Commander of Oussam Alaouite (Morocco), Grand Officer of Nishan Iffticar (Tunisia), Companion of the Bath, and member of the Lebanese Order of Merit. The sandy-haired, mustached executive is a Fellow of the

American Geographic Institute, and a member of the American Foreign Service Association and the Academy of Political Science.

Reference

Who's Who in America, 1944-45

HOLSTI, (EINO) RUDOLF (WOLDE-MAR) (hŏl'stĭ ā-nō rōō'dŏlf wŏl'dĕ-màr) 1881—Aug. 3, 1945 Finnish Foreign Minister, 1917-19, 1936-38; served in Parliament, 1913-18, 1922-23; twice delegate to League of Nations and Minister to Switzerland; reports of friction with German Government at time of resignation from Foreign Ministry in 1938; at time of death lecturer in political science at Stanford University, California.

Obituary

N Y Times p37 Ag 5 '45 por

HOPKINS, NEVIL MONROE Sept. 15, 1873—Mar. 26, 1945 American engineer, inventor, and author; among his inventions are a super-submarine designed to carry a sixteen-inch gun, various long-range naval and anti-aircraft guns, and high-explosive antiaircraft shells; in 1942 he received the George Washington University Alumni Award for notable achievements in science.

Obituary

N Y Times p19 Mr 27 '45 por

HORROCKS, B(RIAN) G(WYNNE) Sept. 7, 1895- British Army officer
Address: b. c/o War Office, London

Lieutenant General B. G. Horrocks of the Twenty-first Army Group was regarded by many analysts, according to *Newsweek*, as probably the best corps commander in the British Army in the Second World War. Although, according to the magazine, Horrocks "won more victories for the Army than any other general," he was virtually unknown to the public until he was revealed as the commander who had led, in September 1944, the thrust of British ground forces toward Arnhem, the Netherlands, in support of General R. E. Urquhart's [44] First Air-borne Division. This had followed Horrocks' six-day march from the Seine to Antwerp and Brussels.

Brian Gwynne Horrocks was born September 7, 1895, the only son of Minna (Moore) Horrocks and William Heaton Horrocks, later a Royal Army medical officer and King's Honorary Surgeon. The Army career of Sir William's son started in 1914 when the nineteen-year-old soldier was sent to France as a second lieutenant with the Middlesex Regiment. Two months later, wounded and captured by the Germans, his grit showed itself through his repeated efforts to burrow his way under the prison walls, and won for him the nickname "Dog" from his fellow inmates. Finally escaping near the end of the war, Horrocks was awarded the Military Cross for his "perseverance and determination." In 1917 he was raised to captain, and, in February 1919, posted to Russia, where he remained until that fall. It was his last post abroad before the Second World War. In the Regular Army Horrocks served as an adjutant with the Territorial

LT. GEN. B. G. HORROCKS

Army, 1927-30; as a staff captain at the War Office, 1934-36; and as a brigade major, Aldershot Command, under General Sir Archibald Wavell '41, 1936-37. Having in the meantime also passed through the Staff College, he was made an instructor at Camberley in 1938. (His father had been an assistant professor at the Army Medical School at Netley before the First World War.)

The start of the Second World War found Major Horrocks still at Camberley. Made a lieutenant colonel that first October of the war, he was kept on at the college to train others until the following May, when he was given command of a battalion of his old regiment, the Middlesex. The succeeding steps from lieutenant colonel to lieutenant general were made in less than a year: A little more than a month after taking over the battalion he was made a brigadier and appointed to command an infantry brigade. In February 1941 he went to the Eastern Command as a brigadier on the General Staff, and four months later was made a major general. After a year spent in training a division in England, Horrocks was sent overseas as head of the Home Counties, Forty-fourth Division, which later won glory in the defense of Egypt and the victory of El Alamein. Another advancement made him lieutenant general (acting) and head of the Tenth Corps. Later he was transferred to the Thirteenth Corps of the Eighth Army, a corps made up of seven infantry brigades, two armored brigades, and a French flying column.

The British war correspondent, William Stapley, wrote in 1943 that Horrocks went secretly to Egypt in August 1942 at the special request of the British Eighth Army's commander, Field Marshal Sir Bernard Montgomery '42. "He was one of the key pieces on the Egyptian chessboard," reported Stapley; "a vital leader destined to pit his wits and tank-fighting genius against Rommel '42. He was a man of whom the German General Staff had no knowledge whatever."

During the battle of El Alamein in October 1942 the Thirteenth Corps made holding attacks in the south until Alexander '42 and Montgomery had forced a break-through in the north; then it moved up toward the coast and joined in the pursuit of Field Marshal Erwin Rommel and his Afrika Korps through Tobruk, Benghazi, El Agheila, and Tripoli to Tunis. For his services in Africa, Horrocks was recommended for the D.S.O. and the C.B. by Montgomery, who said that Horrock's handling of the Thirteenth Corps had contributed in a marked degree to the general success of the campaign. At Tunis the General had been seriously wounded in a forward area. Explaining his presence in the front line, he said: "Battles today are fought at thirty-five or forty miles an hour. Heading a division means you have got to be right up with your men. And it's a good thing." For a time it was feared that he would never be able to fight again, but, recovering gradually, he soon was spoiling for action, and when a corps commander had to be relieved in Normandy in 1944 Montgomery sent for Horrocks.

Soon after Horrocks took hold in Normandy the tempo of the campaign, according to Newsweek, was stepped up. In the last week of August British Army units were reported to have crossed the Seine, and by September 3 Horrocks' forces had completed the "mad dash" from the river through Amiens to take Brussels and Antwerp, a distance of over two hundred miles covered in less than a week. Horrocks, moreover, had had the satisfaction of driving forward over the same territory he had traveled in 1940 as commanding officer of a machine-gun battalion fighting part of the rear-guard action that had ended at Dunkerque.

From Antwerp Horrocks had then thrust on toward Nijmegen (the Netherlands) on the Waal River, in support of air-borne troops who had already been dropped at Arnhem ten miles beyond. Although Arnhem was lost to the Germans, the British were able to hold the Nijmegen bridge, "one of the biggest prizes in Holland." The failure to hold Arnhem, moreover, was not considered to be the fault of Horrocks' ground support, but was attributed to causes out of the General's control. As summed up by a New York Herald Tribune correspondent, these causes were: delays, forced by bad weather, in providing air-borne reinforcements and supplies for the air-borne division; interference with the overland flow of supplies—the Germans, considering the campaign a major attack against the Reich, had defended the sector with the best troops available.

Horrocks exposed himself to shellfire as readily as any soldier ordered to push forward. Almost completely cut off from his own tactical headquarters once during the Nijmegen battle, after he had been summoned back to Headquarters for a conference, the General had jumped into a Bren-gun carrier and, with a small platoon as a bodyguard, had slipped through Nazi positions in the early dawn.

Field Marshal Montgomery gave Horrocks almost carte blanche in planning battles, and he generally had his pick of divisions for specific attacks. He disliked paper work and as an alternative, used some of the best staff officers in the British Army as aides. His decisions were quick and final. A hard taskmaster, he still had a smile or friendly word for every-one, and his men were said to be devoted to him. His battle garb combined comfort with utility: brown corduroy trousers, a thick wool-en battle-dress jacket, and a peaked service cap. He never wore a helmet even when under heavy shellfire. Six feet tall, he is "slim and fit." His graying hair is "gently wavy," and "blue eyes peer around his thin hawklike nose." He speaks clearly and precisely and liked to carry on conversations in mid-battle. "If I'm too busy to talk to you," he said, "I'm not do-ing my job right."

References

Newsweek 24:27-8 O 16 '44 por
Who's Who, 1945

HOWARD, ALICE STURTEVANT Feb. 14, 1878—Oct. 7, 1945 Founder of the Amer-ican Merchant Marine Library Association (1921), an outgrowth of the Social Service Bureau of the United States Shipping Board Recruiting Service which she had also organ-ized (1918); author of *The Seaman's Hand-book for Shore Leave* (1942).

Obituary

N Y Times p15 O 8 '45

HOWARD, MRS. HENRY *See* Howard, A.S.

HOWE, C(LARENCE) D(ECATUR) Jan. 15, 1886- Canadian Government official; engi-neer

Address: b. 375 Wellington Rd., Ottawa; h. 7 Crescent Rd., Rockcliffe Park, Ottawa

Holding one of the key posts in the Cana-dian peacetime Cabinet is C. D. Howe, who, as Min-ister of Reconstruction, who, as Min-ister of Munitions and Supply, built up Can-ada's negligible industry into a major factor in the successful prosecution of the Allied war against Germany and Japan. Called by Ameri-can reporter Arthur Bartlett "the living sym-bol of our national cousinship to Canada," and by reporter Austin Cross "an assembly line in pants," Howe is said to wield greater influence over the lives of Canadians than anyone ex-cept Prime Minister Mackenzie King'40.

Clarence Decatur Howe was born in the United States, in Waltham, Massachusetts, in 1886, the son of William Clarence and Mary (Hastings) Howe. He was educated in Amer-ican public schools, and in 1907 he received his Bachelor of Science degree from Massa-chusetts Institute of Technology. After gradu-ation, although only in his twenty-second year, he became a member of the staff of M. I. T. In 1908 he was offered a post as professor of civil engineering at Dalhousie University, in Halifax, Nova Scotia. After teaching at Dal-housie for five years, he accepted a position with the Canadian Board of Grain Commis-sioners as chief engineer, at Fort William, On-tario (1913-16).

Howe in 1916 organized his own firm of con-sulting engineers, which designed and super-vised construction of grain elevators, pulp mills, coal docks, and other heavy engineering struc-tures. In a short time he became "the best

National Film Bd.

C. D. HOWE

known builder of grain elevators in the world," and the volume of his business in Canada and abroad swelled to the sum of one hundred mil-lion dollars. Between 1932 and 1934 he was also appointed by the Argentine Government as a special consultant on problems relating to the transportation and storage of grain.

In 1935 the engineer, who had been a Cana-dian citizen for some time, ran for Parliament. Elected to the House of Commons, he was at once appointed by Prime Minister Mackenzie King to the Cabinet as Minister of Railways and Canals, and later as Minister of Marine. Before the year was out Howe had stream-lined and consolidated the two ministries and he became Canada's first Minister of Trans-port. Said New York *Herald Tribune* inter-viewer Arthur Bartlett: "Fearless, even ruth-less, in accomplishing his objectives, he had chopped heads off first and apologized after-wards. 'There is nothing personal in this,' he had assured one big officeholder whose resig-nation was required. 'It is just one of the wretched things a man has to do when he takes on a responsibility such as I have.'" As Min-ister of Transport, Howe supervised the wide network of Government-owned Canadian Na-tional Railways, reorganizing its administra-tion, established the National Harbor Board, and founded the Canadian Broadcasting Cor-poration. In 1938 he opened for service Trans-Canada Airlines, Canada's first transcontinental passenger airline. It was his favorite project as Minister of Transport, reports Bartlett, and in order to organize its operating and ground services, "he flew all over the United States getting ideas and data; then went home and pushed the building of a string of airports and emergency landing fields across the continent."

In June 1939 Canada, anticipating war, set up its Defense Purchasing Board. When this bu-reau was replaced by the War Supply Board after the declaration of hostilities, C. D. Howe became its head. Then, in April 1940, Howe was appointed Minister of Munitions and Sup-

HOWE, C. D.—*Continued*

ply, or chief of the new department which superseded the War Supply Board. This was a job which called for the fullest abilities of the engineer, for Canada was not organized industrially for mass production of war supplies. During the First World War Canada's production had been limited largely to shells, and when the Second World War began in 1939 she had only one small munitions plant in operation, and had not launched a single seagoing merchant ship in twenty years. Two reasons for this retarded war production have been given by *Business Week*'s Ottawa Bureau: "Previous efforts to speed up industrial cooperation had been blocked from overseas, (1) through British industry's reluctance to furnish the standard specifications for the war equipment desired, and (2) through delays by the British Government in placing orders."

But when France fell in June 1940 England realized that for her own security Canada must be given the signal to produce for war. Receiving the "go ahead" signal in production that year, Canada, under Howe's leadership, threw into the struggle every economic resource that she possessed. Response to Howe's urging for constant day-and-night production was immediate, with strikers even canceling their walkouts to answer the call. Howe personally went to England determined to bring back the blueprints and specifications which Canadian industry required, and returned to Canada in February 1941 convinced that industry must speed up its operations still more. (On this trip he almost lost his life when the *Western Prince* was torpedoed and he spent twelve hours in a lifeboat.)

When there were complaints throughout Canada about Government delays, insufficient funds, and hampered production, especially in the airplane industry, Howe pointed out that Canada before 1940 had had no aircraft plants and that everything had had to be improvised. Production on the whole, he said, was up to schedule, although the maintenance of new contract obligations depended upon the amount of machine tools which could be obtained for the manufacture of guns, aircraft, tanks, and ships. And for these tools Canada depended to a large degree on cash, not Lend-Lease, purchases from the United States. With the cooperation of the Canadian Manufacturers Association and the Canadian Chamber of Commerce Howe then organized a census of available Canadian plant facilities and equipment and on the basis of the information obtained distributed production equally throughout the Dominion.

By 1941, according to Lord Beaverbrook,[40] Canada was producing more per unit of production than any other country in the world. Moreover, she was sending these arms and munitions to Great Britain and the Dominions, to the United States and China, and was preparing to fill orders for the Soviet Union. (The next year Canada became a member of the Combined Production and Resources Board, which hitherto had consisted only of representatives of Great Britain and the United States, and Howe was appointed Canada's representative.) Two years later the shipyards and factories reached an all-time peak in production. Some months before total victory in 1945 Howe summed up Canada's contribution to the war effort: "Generally speaking, the Canadian war output has been outstripped by that of the United Kingdom, the United States, and Soviet Russia. But in timeliness, variety, newness, and quality it has constituted a major factor in the Allied swing from desperate defense to victorious attack. Indeed, it is possible that without it in the earlier days of the war the United Nations might have been defeated."

Canada's part in the production of the atomic bomb was also under the supervision of C. D. Howe. In the early days of the war mines producing uranium were taken over by the Government, with extracting plants, in order to preserve this important material for the United Nations. Canada, according to a release of the Canadian Wartime Information Board, entered the field of uranium research at the suggestion of Great Britain, with whom she established a joint laboratory in Montreal. Canada played a very significant, if not a major role: she produced not the complete bomb, which was done only in the United States, but essential components of it. Canadian plants have also been producing plutonium, the newly evolved "fissil" substance derived from uranium and "heavy water." For the future the Dominion Government has proposed an extensive plan for exploration in the Northwest Territories to extend the known fields of uranium-bearing ore beyond those first discovered in Canada on the east side of Great Bear Lake in 1933.

In October 1944 Howe had been given the additional portfolio of Minister of Reconstruction. In March 1945, with a general election scheduled for the near future, Reconstruction Minister Howe presented the program for the postwar era on which the Liberal Party was returned to power on June 11, 1945. Placing emphasis on a free enterprise system, he recognized as the foremost of Canada's needs the necessity of providing jobs for the two million men then in the country's service or employed in war industry. To implement his program he planned to eliminate or at least to reduce wartime taxes as soon as feasible, to encourage private investment with low interest rates and loans from Government lending bureaus, to enlarge the export market and to expand the domestic market by finding private buyers to replace the Government in the purchase of more than half of Canada's production. He promised that there would be no large expenditure for public works and that emergency anti-inflation controls would be retained only for "a smoother, more rapid transition to a prosperous peacetime economy." A social welfare program was also on his agenda.

In late 1945, with reconversion getting under way, Howe was attempting to cope with a labor problem which threatened to bring about extensive unemployment in some areas while labor was needed in others. Labor, said Howe, is reluctant to go back to former jobs after being employed in war work; no one wants to perform the disagreeable tasks or to accept a reduced pay envelope. Critics of the Government, however, viewed the situation as an outgrowth of wartime labor policies, which, they said, favored the employers through "no strike" laws and the recognition of plant or unaffiliated unions. According to G. M. A. Grube, writing in the *Canadian Forum* in March 1941, labor even during the war was treated "as a potential enemy to be appeased instead of as a friend whose eager and invaluable cooperation could so easily have been enlisted." The Government, said Grube, put employers with violent hostility toward trade unions into positions of high responsibility. "Canadian labor," he continued, "needs a Wagner Act."

The Canadian has had honorary degrees conferred upon him, including one by Harvard University in June 1945. He is a member of the American Society of Civil Engineers and of Mechanical Engineers. Howe was married in September 1916 to Alice Martha Worcester. Their five children are William Hastings, Elisabeth, John Worcester, Barbara, and Mary Jeannette.

References

N Y Herald Tribune (This Week) X
p4-5+ N 23 '41 il por
N Y Sun p20 D 16 '43
PM p12 My 6 '41
Who's Who in America, 1944-45
Who's Who in Canada, 1940-41

HOWELL, WILLIAM H(ENRY) Feb. 20, 1860—Feb. 6, 1945 Internationally known physiologist and director emeritus of the School of Hygiene and Public Health of Johns Hopkins University; gained reputation for his research on the origin of red blood corpuscles, degeneration and regeneration of nerve fibres, mechanism of sleep, and similar studies; discoverer of heparin, a substance which prevents formation of blood clots.

Obituary

N Y Times p21 F 7 '45 por

HUGHES, HATCHER 1886?—Oct. 19, 1945 American playwright and university professor; associated with Columbia University as instructor or lecturer in English from 1910 until death; became assistant professor in 1928, specializing in dramatics; won Pulitzer Prize in 1924 for *Hell-Bent for Heaven*; among his other plays are *Ruint* (1925) and *The Lord Blesses the Bishop* (1932).

Obituary

N Y Times p11 O 20 '45

HUN, JOHN GALE Nov. 21, 1877—Sept. 15, 1945 American educator; teacher of mathematics at Princeton (1903-14); founder of Princeton Mathematical School 1914 and the Hun School, a preparatory school, in 1917; headmaster of the latter institution until his death; president of the Princeton Board of Education (1930-36); author of several mathematical textbooks.

Obituary

N Y Times p44 S 16 '45 por

IGOE, HERBERT A. (ī'gō) June 13, 1885—Feb. 11, 1945 Veteran American sports writer and cartoonist, known as "Hype"; often illustrated his own writings; was considered an authority on boxing; conducted a column *Pardon My Glove* in the New York *World*

for many years; had been with the New York *Journal-American* for eighteen years at the time of his death.

Obituary

N Y Times p19 F 12 '45 por

IRONSIDE, HENRY ALLAN Oct. 14, 1876- Clergyman
Address: b. Moody Memorial Church, 1609 N. LaSalle St., Chicago; h. Plaza Hotel, Chicago

"Archbishop of Fundamentalism" is the apt title once bestowed by a writer on Henry Allan Ironside, pastor of the Moody Memorial Church in Chicago. One of the best-known conservative expositors of the Bible in the United States, he has never been ordained and he belongs to no denomination. Yet, it is said, he has spoken from more pulpits than almost any other man in the United States. With more than fifty years spent as a home missionary, itinerant evangelist, Bible teacher, and pastor, Ironside has gained a place of great influence in Fundamentalist ranks.

Henry ("Harry") Allan Ironside was born in Toronto, Canada, October 14, 1876, of devout parents, John Williams and Sophia (Stafford) Ironside. Before young Harry was two years old his father, known throughout Toronto as the "Eternity Man," had died. His widow was forced to work hard to support herself and her two children, and in 1886, when Harry was ten years old, the family moved to the United States, settling in Los Angeles. There the home became a sort of haven for itinerant preachers and evangelists. By the time Harry was twelve he had read through the Bible ten times and was conducting his own Sunday school. Two years later the realization came to him that he must dedicate himself to evangelical Christianity. As he tells the story, he was attending a party one evening when, as he stood off by himself, he suddenly received the spiritual impact of certain verses from the Proverbs, those beginning, "Because I have called, and ye refused; I have stretched out my hand, and no man regarded." (Proverbs, Chap.1 :24-32)

Thus, after he had finished grammar school, the young convert had no desire to continue with his secular education. In his newly found zeal he joined the Salvation Army and soon was an officer. At the age of twenty-one he held the rank of captain, with the responsibility for a large corps territory in California. As a Salvationist, Ironside was a fervent street preacher, although he soon found himself unsure about his own spiritual qualifications for the evangelical calling. After much self-debate, he finally left the Salvation Army and joined a group commonly known as the Plymouth Brethren. The members of this section acknowledge only the title "Christians" or "Brethren." "They take the Scriptures as their sole guide, protest against sectarianism, and reject all ecclesiastical organization, creeds, rituals, and ordained ministry. They are Calvinistic . . . have no church buildings, and emphasize premillennialism," or the doctrine that the second coming of Christ ushers in the millennium.

Without definite means of livelihood, young Ironside continued to preach on street corners, in rescue missions, and in frontier towns. After about a year, in January 1898, he was married

HENRY ALLAN IRONSIDE

to Helen G. Schofield, the daughter of a Presbyterian minister. Ironside tells many stories of this period of his life. Once, he says, while preaching on a San Francisco street, he was challenged by an atheist to a debate on the subject of Christianity versus atheism. Before a crowd of several hundred people he accepted this challenge, adding, however, one condition— that the man present at least two bona fide witnesses who had benefited spiritually by following his belief; Ironside, on the other hand, would provide one hundred people who had been saved by the teachings of Christ. The atheist, says the preacher, refused these terms and walked away.

Mrs. Ironside accompanied her husband on his travels until Edmund, the first of their two sons, was born (their second son is John); then they established their home in Oakland, California. Ironside continued with his itinerant preaching, however. With the gradual recognition of the power of his preaching, his following spread until he was traveling continually from coast to coast conducting Bible conferences and evangelistic services in churches and other meeting places. As the years passed, his sermons reflected his gradual shift to a position of moderate Calvinism.

Early realizing his lack of formal education, Ironside had set about to educate himself. He studied Greek and Chinese. He became a voracious reader, often going through two or three doctrinal works in one day, until he is now a recognized authority in many fields of religion. His good memory has assisted him in remembering long poems and selections of the Scriptures, and it is possible for him to deliver a sermon without the aid of written notes. In 1900 he wrote his first book, entitled *Notes on Jeremiah*, and since then he has written many books and pamphlets on the Bible, some expository and others devotional volumes. The Western Book and Tract Company, a non-profit distributing organization for Christian literature, of which Ironside is president, was founded by him in California in 1912. Today

it distributes about seventy-five thousand dollars' worth of literature a year.

In 1930 the Moody Memorial Church, founded in Chicago by Dwight L. Moody in 1864, extended a call to Harry Ironside. He had never held a pastorate before, and now he was being offered the most influential Fundamentalist pulpit in the United States. After ten months of deliberation he finally accepted, although it meant breaking with a principle of the Brethren, who reject ecclesiastical organization. He became the tenth pastor of the historic Moody Church.

Fundamentalism is a twentieth century movement in Protestantism. It "re-emphasizes as fundamental to Christianity the inerrancy of the Scriptures, Biblical miracles, especially the virgin birth and physical resurrection of Christ, and substitutional atonement," which is the belief that "Christ took on himself the punishment due to sin, and by his sacrifice offered adequate satisfaction to the offended infinite majesty of God." In the church services the pastor seeks to secure conversions among the congregation, which involve "repentance, or turning from sin to God, and Christian faith, or turning to God . . . with a view to being turned more effectively from sin." In the psychology of religion conversion is a highly emotional experience, being "an abrupt rapid change to an enthusiastic religious attitude."

Ironside draws large audiences, and his simple, unspectacular method of preaching is said to win converts nearly every Sunday. His sermons are usually expository, but are sprinkled with humor. When he assumed the pastorate of the Moody Church, there remained a building debt of three hundred and nineteen thousand dollars on the structure, which had been built in 1925 at a cost of a million dollars. Under Ironside's leadership, the four thousand members had liquidated the debt by the end of 1943.

Ironside's sermons are broadcast on Sunday mornings from Moody Church, and electrically transcribed. In addition to his books—one of which, entitled *Except Ye Repent*, won the American Tract Society's one-thousand-dollar prize in 1936—Ironside writes a weekly commentary on the International lesson for the *Sunday School Times*, a magazine of evangelical Christianity. Nearly all his sermons and talks have appeared in print, so that many people know him as an author if not as a preacher. In conformity with an agreement whereby Ironside is at liberty to preach at other meetings during the week, he participates in as many as forty Bible conferences during a year, besides filling other preaching engagements. However, since these do not necessitate his traveling more than a thousand miles from Chicago, he is always in the Moody Church pulpit on Sunday morning.

Ironside has received two honorary degrees: a D.Litt. in 1930 from Wheaton College in Illinois, and a D.D. in 1942 from Bob Jones College in Florida. From 1925 to 1943 he was a visiting professor of Biblical literature at the Evangelical Theological Seminary in Dallas, Texas. He is also chairman of the board of directors of the Southern Bible Training School in Dallas, a school which prepares Negroes for the ministry. In 1942 he was elected president of the Africa Inland Mission.

During one of his several trips abroad, in 1936, he spoke from the pulpit of the St. Giles Cathedral in Edinburgh, the church of John Knox. In his free time, aside from collecting stamps (he has between twenty-five and thirty thousand), he finds relaxation, he says, in studying the Chinese language.

Bald and stout, Ironside is of medium height. He dresses conservatively, and is modest and friendly in manner. He declares he is uncomfortable in the presence of doctors of philosophy, and completely out of place in college academic processions. Like Dwight Moody, the noted American evangelist, Ironside is always happier when the "Reverend" is omitted in addressing him. His friends say that on special occasions he can be lured into singing, with appropriate gestures, the old Salvation Army songs of his youth, which, when contrasted with modern hymnody, he can make seem irresistibly funny.

Reference

Who's Who in America, 1944-45

ISAACS, GEORGE (ALFRED) 1883-
British Government official; labor leader

Address: b. Ministry of Labor, London; h. 13/16 Borough Rd., London

The British Labor Party, which in July 1945 formed its first Government in fourteen years, is made up basically of two elements. On the one hand it is a national party—pledged to the achievement of a basic standard of living—to which a number of peers and many middle-class persons belong as individuals, by conviction; this group is represented in the third Labor Government by such Ministers as Sir Stafford Cripps '40, Hugh Dalton '45, and Prime Minister Clement Attlee '40. On the other hand, the Labor Party is also an organ of the trade unions, and many of its M.P.'s arrived in Parliament through their activity in union affairs. The Right Honorable George Isaacs, Minister of Labor and National Service in the Attlee Government, is perhaps typical of this second group. "A powerful and popular labor leader," he holds one of the most difficult and responsible portfolios in the reconversion Ministry.

George Alfred Isaacs was born in London in 1883, the eldest of nine children. His father was a newspaper printer. At eleven, the future Minister was selling tea from door to door in Hoxton; at twelve, he got a job in a newspaper plant as office assistant. Later he was to work his way up through the various departments of the machine room. When married at the age of twenty-two, says Delos Lovelace of the New York *Sun*, Isaacs was earning two pounds two shillings (about ten dollars) a week as printer's assistant.

Isaacs was prominent in trade union activities, and became secretary of the National Society of Operative Printers and Assistants and editor of their *Natsopa Journal*. He was elected president, too, of the Printing and Kindred Trades Federation. In 1918, the year the Labor Party ceased to be an exclusively socialist-unionist movement and became a regular national political party, he contested for Parliament from North Southwark; and in 1919 the thirty-six-year-old printer became Mayor of Southwark for a two-year term. He was a can-

British Official Photo.

GEORGE ISAACS

didate in the Gravesend Division of Kent in 1922, and was elected to Parliament as a Laborite, serving in 1923-24. In the first Labor Government in 1924 Isaacs served as Parliamentary private secretary to J. H. Thomas, Secretary of State for the Colonies.

After five years' absence from the House of Commons, the unionist won election from the North Southwark constituency of London in 1929. When the second Labor Government was formed that same year, Isaacs again became Parliamentary private secretary to Thomas, then Lord Privy Seal. Like most Labor M.P.'s, Isaacs lost his seat in the general election of 1931 which followed Prime Minister Ramsay MacDonald's sudden defection from the Labor Party, and was not returned to Parliament until 1939. The next spring the Neville Chamberlain Government was forced to resign. When the Labor Party agreed to form a coalition wartime Government under Winston Churchill '42, Opposition Leader Attlee became Lord Privy Seal. In 1942 George Isaacs became Parliamentary secretary to the First Lord of the Admiralty, A. V. Alexander '40. (Isaacs has served on the Government's departmental committee on coroners and the departmental committee on workmen's compensations.)

Isaacs was a member of the Industrial Mission sent to the United States in September 1941. Apart from that, his most newsworthy appointment was 1944 chairman of the British Trades Union Congress, to whose Executive he had been elected ten years earlier. (Isaacs never actually became chairman for he soon attained ministerial rank.) Then came the general election of July 1945, which gave Labor an overwhelming majority in Commons. Prime Minister Attlee chose George Isaacs for the important Ministry of Labor and National Service, which was faced with the task of keeping the war industries and essential civilian production manned for the duration of the Second World War. He succeeded Bevin '40. Hardly had the new Ministers had time to get used

ISAACS, GEORGE—*Continued*

to their offices when the Japanese surrender hurled them into the equally formidable adjustments of the sudden peace. The "monumental task of demobilizing the armed forces and reallocating the nation's manpower for peacetime purposes" was before the sixty-two-year-old Labor Minister.

The end of the war found Britain in an unfortunate economic position. Deeply in debt to the nations which had furnished supplies during the war, she lacked the means to repay them after six years of a war economy, and yet she had to import food. Isaacs, who was in charge of the release of armed force personnel, told the House of Commons, "In this period of rapid readjustment, the orderly redistribution of workers is of greatest importance if the most urgent needs of the nation are to be satisfied first—if homes are to be built and furnished, household goods replenished, and exports raised in order to pay for raw materials and food." Outlining the Government's proposed scheme of controls, even more stringent than in wartime, Isaacs announced that, under Class B of the demobilization program (Class A was unconditional release), service personnel would be released if they went directly into certain industries where workers were needed. These included building textile mills, clothing and footwear factories, and laundries. As for releasing workers no longer needed for munitions making, he said, "where there is a choice, cuts in production will ordinarily be made first in those areas where the demands for labor for civilian production and services are most urgent." A difficulty was that those industries most in need of workers, such as textiles and mining, were the very ones to which workers were reluctant to return, because of lower pay, undesirable working conditions, and—especially in the Welsh mines—a long history of grievances. The Government hoped, however, that when the mines were nationalized the miners would be willing to return as public employees.

The British Government's long-awaited plan for a speed-up of demobilization was announced by Isaacs in early October 1945. The over-all plan called for the release of 1,500,000 men and women by the end of 1945 and another 1,500,000 by June 1946. During the longshoreman's strike in the same month the Labor Minister declared that, whatever the men's grievances were, they could not justify the strike because the regular machinery of governmental conciliation had not been consulted. As the strike continued, the Government refused to intervene because Isaacs said, it was the Government's policy to do nothing that would injure the constitutional machinery of collective bargaining. The strike ended early in November.

"Spectacled and serious" George Isaacs refrains from talking shop, to such an extent, it is reported, that his wife Flora did not know of his elevation to the Ministry until she read of it in a newspaper. The Isaacs, who have one married daughter and one adopted son (Mrs. Isaacs' nephew), live in Berryvil, an eight-room house in East Molesey, Surrey; the Minister's wife does the housework, with the assistance of a charwoman three times a week. Isaacs is a justice of the peace in Surrey County, chairman of the Kingston County Bench, and a Liveryman of the Worshipful Company of Stationers, a medieval guild, now mainly charitable. (The Liverymen elect the Lord Mayor of London and certain other officials.) He is also an alderman of the London Borough of Southwark. He has written one book, *The Story of the Newspaper Printing Press,* published by his union in 1931. For recreation Isaacs likes gardening and reading, especially tales of the Wild West; he likes to swim, when he gets the chance, and goes to the cinema once every month or so.

References

N Y Sun p6 Ag 18 '45
N Y Times p5 Ag 4 '45 por
International Who's Who, 1942
Who's Who, 1945

ITTNER, MARTIN H(ILL) (ĭt'nĕr) May 2, 1870—Apr. 22, 1945 American chemist; held honorary title of "modern pioneer" conferred by the National Association of Manufacturers in 1940; awarded Perkin Medal in 1942 by the Society of Chemical Industry for outstanding work in the field of chemistry; chief chemist for the Colgate-Palmolive-Peet Company since 1896. See *Current Biography* 1942 Yearbook.

Obituary

N Y Times p19 Ap 24 '45 por

IZAC, ED(OUARD) V(ICTOR MICHEL) (ē'zäk) Dec. 18, 1891- United States Representative from California

Address: b. House Office Bldg., Washington, D.C.; h. 5380 Cajon Blvd., San Diego, Calif.

Ed V. Izac, Democratic Representative from the Twenty-third Congressional District of California, in 1945 was in his fifth consecutive term in the House of Representatives. He is a member of the House Naval Affairs Committee and was one of the six Congressmen appointed, pursuant to General Eisenhower's request, to inspect the German concentration camps. A German prisoner of war during the First World War, he returned from the inspection tour firmly convinced that a harsh peace should be dealt the German people.

Edouard Victor Michel Izac was born on December 18, 1891, in Cresco, Iowa. He was one of the nine children of B. Michel Izac, who came to the United States from Alsace-Lorraine, and Mathilde (Geuth) Izac, a native of Philadelphia. He attended Iowa and Minnesota schools for his early education, going from high school in South St. Paul, Minnesota, to the United States Naval Academy in 1911. He received his Bachelor of Science degree from Annapolis in June 1915 and soon after commencement he was married to Agnes Cabell, daughter of General De Rosey Carroll Cabell of the United States Army. (The Izacs have six children—Cabell [Mrs. Robert Waller], Edouard Victor Michel, Jr., De Rosey Charles, Suzanne, Forrest René, and André.)

For nearly two years, until the United States entered the First World War, young Izac served on various men-of-war successively as an ensign, lieutenant (junior grade), and senior lieutenant. He was on duty in the battleship

Florida in 1917 when it trained the first gun crews for the merchant marine. By the time the United States was in the war, he had been transferred to the Transport Force. He was serving as first lieutenant aboard the transport *President Lincoln* when it was torpedoed in mid-Atlantic in May 1918. The young officer was captured by the German U-boat on which he took notes on submarine operations for the rest of the cruise, and planned to escape as soon as an opportunity presented itself. En route to Villingen, Baden, in a rapidly moving prison train, he jumped out of a window. He was recaptured and forced by his German captors to walk to camp at the point of a bayonet, although he had injured his head, knees, and feet in the leap from the train. Later he succeeded in escaping from the camp and, after swimming the Rhine, he passed through Switzerland and finally reached the Allied lines.

When the war was over Izac appeared before a claims commission to accuse the Germans of deliberate brutality. As witnesses he had American Army doctors who had been imprisoned with him and who testified that he was treated for one hundred injuries. As further evidence he produced a court-martial record of a German soldier convicted of destroying German Government property—the soldier had broken his rifle stock on Izac's head after recapture. Izac received $20,000 in damages, and the incident was cited as an example of one way of repaying American airmen who suffered cruelties at the hands of the Japanese during the Second World War. Isac published an interesting account of his experience in a book entitled *Prisoner of the U-90.*

In 1919 Isac became director of munitions at the Washington (D.C.) Navy Yard. He was then promoted to lieutenant commander, but he was forced to retire two years later because of his wounds. From 1921 until he entered politics thirteen years later Izac was engaged in newspaper work and free-lance writing. His articles covered a wide variety of subjects—history, the Nicaraguan Canal, his war experiences, veterans' problems, and English. In 1934 he was nominated by the Democratic and Progressive parties as Representative from the Twentieth Congressional District in California. He was defeated that year, but elected in 1936 to the Seventy-fifth Congress. He has been re-elected for each succeeding term, and in the Seventy-ninth Congress represents the Twenty-third District.

An Administration supporter, the Congressman voted for New Deal legislation and Roosevelt '⁴² win-the-war measures. His progressive record includes votes for appropriations for the United Nations Relief and Rehabilitation Administration, the anti-poll tax bill, and under the Truman '⁴⁵ Administration, for extending price control for another year. Izac has opposed the anti-strike bill, the anti-subsidy bill, and also voted against permanent status for the House Committee on Un-American Activities (Dies '⁴⁰ Committee).

Izac is a member of the Naval Affairs Committee of the House of Representatives. In January 1942 he signed the minority report of his committee's investigation of the ship-building industry. The report stated that "until there is conclusive evidence of either or both [capital and labor] having failed to keep faith

ED V. IZAC

with the Government and the people in this respect [settling differences by mediation and arbitration], we are of the opinion that Congressional committees should refrain from criticism of either or both." The opposing majority report stated that strikes were the "greatest single cause of delay in the defense program." In December 1943 Izac headed the Naval Affairs subcommittee investigating the congested areas on the West Coast, in San Diego, Los Angeles, San Francisco, California; Portland, Oregon; Seattle, Washington. The subcommittee's reports pointed out that the overcrowding was the result of the sudden rise in production without sufficient warning being given to the local authorities. The subcommittee found that racial minorities, particularly the Negroes, had the most serious housing and recreation problems. It was recommended that these areas be represented on the President's Committee for Congested Areas, and remedies were suggested for the food, transportation, child-care, and police problems. A month later, in January 1944, Izac headed the subcommittee on the transportation situation in the United States. His report charged the transportation industry and the War Production Board with causing the national crisis by their negative attitude. The committee felt that the WPB had neglected maintenance problems in its overemphasis on the manufacture of planes, tanks, ships, and armament. The committee held: "Certainly the transportation system of this country is so vitally an integral part of our war machine that its proper maintenance contributes more to the final victory than will a few planes or tanks."

In February 1944 Izac supported President Roosevelt's '⁴² veto of an income tax bill. It was the first time an important tax bill had ever been vetoed, but Izac remained firm in his conviction that "the bill proposed draining money from the little people and funneling it out to war profiteers." In June of that year the House tentatively adopted a proposal by

IZAC, ED V.—*Continued*

Representative Izac which provided for local authority on the part of the rent director to increase or decrease to a basis of comparability the rents on dwelling houses and apartments. A few days later he led in the defeat of a bill to allow women pilots to enter the Army until all the male aviators trained for the Army were employed although General Arnold advocated Army status for the Women Airforce Service pilots. Izac also opposed the motion to allow Waves to go overseas, insisting that there were enough men to do the work. In February 1945 Izac headed a subcommittee which visited the Naval oil installations in California. His comment on the investigation was: "We have seen at first hand what the Navy is doing toward fueling and powering the war in the Pacific, and we are thoroughly satisfied with the operations both at Elk Hills and the 100-octane plant at Richmond, California." He declared that the trip had been an "eye-opener."

Opposed to Representative Rankin's '44 proposal of a flat bonus to all veterans, Izac, with Representative Lesinski of Michigan, introduced a bill early in 1945 which would provide for a bonus of three dollars per day for home service and four dollars per day for overseas service. It would place a maximum of $3,500 on extra pay for home service and four dollars per day for men who went overseas, with an additional $500 for those who were wounded in action. The money would be paid in bonds maturing in ten years, the veterans being given the option of cashing them in at the rate of one-fifth of their face value for five years. Veterans who would keep the bonds for more than five years would get additional interest compounded annually.

In the spring of 1945, before the Allied victory in Europe, Izac was one of the six Representatives and six Senators appointed by the two Houses of Congress to investigate German atrocities and inspect their concentration camps. Izac, coauthor of the report on the trip, came back convinced that the German people themselves must be punished if a new war was to be discouraged. He advocated confiscating German goods and properties and distributing them to the people whose homes and farms had been looted by the Nazis. Izac felt that, with the camps situated on main highways, the people must have known of the atrocities being committed but did nothing to stop the crimes. He was indignant that the only people in Europe who wore leather shoes were Germans. He was very pessimistic about a harsh peace, however, because of the "forgiving hearts of the Americans."

A few months later, in July 1945, Izac headed a subcommittee of the Naval Affairs Committee which made the first comprehensive survey and study of the Pacific bases of the United States. The subcommittee recommended that the United States keep a string of islands regardless of who owned them before the war. In a House debate on a postwar Navy, Izac demanded that the United States keep control of Okinawa as the northern anchor of the Pacific arc of sea bases. He introduced a bill on September 3 to provide for an increase in the retirement and retainer benefits for Naval and Marine Corps reservists. The bill would allow them a salary amounting to half their former base pay plus all permanent additions. He was the author of the bill fixing the postwar Navy personnel at 500,000 enlisted men and 58,000 officers, an increase of more than 100 per cent over the prewar strength, with the reserves being incorporated in the Regular Navy.

Izac has been decorated by foreign countries as well as by the United States. He was awarded the Congressional Medal of Honor for "service above and beyond the call of duty" during the First World War, and his other decorations include the Croce di Guerra Italy and the Cross of Montenegro. Izac is a former post commander of the American Legion and the Diasabled American Veterans, a national aide-de-camp of the Veterans of Foreign Wars, and a member of the Legion of Valor. He belongs to the San Diego Club and the Catholic Club in the same city. Izac is five feet ten inches tall, and weighs one hundred and fifty-five pounds. He has brown eyes and silver-gray hair, and his favorite form of recreation is camping, hunting, and fishing.

References

Newsweek 21 :27 My 3 '45
Congressional Directory (1945)
Who's Who in America, 1944-45
Who's Who in the Nation's Capital, 1938-39

JELLIFFE, SMITH ELY (jĕl'ĭf) Oct. 27, 1866—Sept. 25, 1945 Neuropsychiatrist, and pioneer in field of psychoanalysis in America; former consulting neurologist at Manhattan State Hospital and Kings Park Hospital; managing editor of the *Journal of Nervous and Mental Diseases* from 1902 to death, and of the *Psychoanalytic Review* from 1913 to death; author of books and over four hundred papers.

Obituary

N Y Times p23 S 26 '45 por

JENSEN, OLIVER O(RMEROD) Apr. 16, 1914- Journalist; author

Address: b. c/o Life Magazine, 9 Rockefeller Plaza, New York City

Oliver O. Jensen was a lieutenant in the Navy when he wrote *Carrier War*, the story of Admiral Marc A. Mitscher's Task Force 58 and its combat record in the Second World War. Based partly on the author's firsthand observations of some of the historic engagements, his "free-running, easy-reading" account of the Navy's great sea-air offensive in the Pacific was hailed as one of the finest books to come out of the war.

Of English and Norwegian ancestry, Oliver Ormerod Jensen was born in Ithaca, New York, on April 16, 1914. He is, however, considered a New Englander, having lived in New London, Connecticut, for a number of years. Jensen attended Phillips Academy at Andover, Massachusetts, and then matriculated at Yale University. At Yale he studied government, and in the summer of 1935 took a bicycle trip through the German Rhineland to observe one type of government in action. Elected a Phi Beta Kappa student, Jensen was graduated from Yale in 1936.

He came to New York to start work on his first job, work which seemed slightly incongruous in view of his political science studies, for he began as a script writer, composing thrillers for radio. He was first employed by Phillips H. Lord, Inc., afterward working with other leading advertising agencies, among them J. Walter Thompson, and Benton and Bowles. There was another period of advertising work when he "counted hams on the shelves of Manhattan and Brooklyn butchers and acted as a spy for the dog-food interests." For a brief interlude the ex-government student also served as an editor of the humor magazine *Judge*. At one point in his career he had begun to contribute articles to *Life*, and in 1940 he joined the staff of that publication.

Jensen's articles in *Life* covered a wide variety of subjects, ranging from the Navy to the private life of film stars, stories written in a breezy, journalistic vein. In September 1941, in an article entitled "Lady of Sorrows," Jensen drew a word-picture of the popular adviser to the lovelorn, Doris Blake[41]. In another issue in 1941 a story, "880 Censors in Bermuda," revealed that "this little group of islands has been turned into Britain's Number One listening post, the chief Empire point, outside of England, for censorship and contraband control." This detailed article, giving a glimpse into the secret operations of censorship control in Bermuda, described the routine, personnel, and material handled at the island outpost. Jensen's story in *Life* about Ensign Weems, the top-ranking midshipman at the Annapolis graduation in 1941, was prophetic in some measure of what he was to report four years later in *Carrier War*. Discussing the Navy's requirements for leadership, Jensen remarked, "With the Naval Academy pouring thousands of men of the caliber of young Bee Weems onto a growing fleet of the best ships afloat, it is distinctly possible that the United States is going to have the best of each." Another of Jensen's stories, called "The Navy's Humor," discussed the slang and legends of the Navy, some of which appears in *Carrier War*. Jensen says one of the pieces of which he was especially proud was "The German Language," a humorous discussion widely reprinted.

In June 1942 Jensen took a duration-of-the-war leave from the staff of *Life* to enter the Navy with the rank of ensign. His first assignment was as a watch officer on a four-stack, First World War destroyer. On convoy duty in North Atlantic and Icelandic waters, the vessel fought U-boats through the winter of 1942-43. The severe weather of that winter did not improve life at sea; altogether, according to Jensen, "conditions were startlingly reminiscent of life inside a yo-yo." While on this destroyer duty he also made a few trips on the Caribbean and North African runs. He was later transferred to naval aviation. Then, as an unofficial naval correspondent, Jensen spent several months with a Navy search-plane squadron in England. After his return to the United States, he flew to the Pacific.

The ex-destroyer officer witnessed the landings at Hollandia in 1944 and saw also the raid on Truk. To supplement his personal observation, in order to obtain a complete and authentic picture of the entire Central Pacific campaign for the book he was planning, Jen-

LT. OLIVER O. JENSEN

sen consulted official battle records and interviewed hundreds of officers and men who participated in the engagements. Gathering his material from the pilots, crewmen, intelligence officers, commanding officers, and correspondents, Jensen assembled the details of battle while they were still vivid in the minds of fighters and observers. Hence, the text of his completed *Carrier War* retains the tone of informal reporting and the temper of on-the-spot excitement. His narrative pridefully traces the history of Task Force 58 from its first action in the Marcus Island raid of September 1, 1943, through the battles of Wake, Rabaul, the Gilbert and Marshall islands, Truk, Palau, Hollandia, and the epic battles of the Philippine Sea. (The book is based on the same material from which the documentary film *The Fighting Lady* was made.) In his account Jensen has revealed many significant details of the battles for the first time, including the identification of aircraft carriers and other ships which took part in some of the engagements.

Task Force 58, with its huge aircraft carriers, fast cruisers, big battleships, and destroyers, is "the greatest assemblage of naval might in the world," in his opinion. It has made naval history, administering devastating blows to the enemy with the "Spruance[41] Haircut" and the "Mitscher Shampoo." To Jensen, "everything about a carrier is thrilling, her lines, her impressive bulk, her speed, but the greatest thrill to the oldest hands remains the landing and take-off of her planes."

Life on a great carrier is described, too, with evident pleasure by Lieutenant Jensen. The commander of Task Force 58, Admiral Mitscher, the "fliers' favorite admiral," is depicted as "an astounding, gnomish man who has taken over most of the Pacific for his private duck pond." His fliers are known to the sailors as "airedales" or "birdmen." When one officer was promoted to commander his squadron held a party and presented him with a gift. Accord-

JENSEN, OLIVER O.—*Continued*

ing to Jensen, "There being no regulation caps or gold braid aboard, the gift was a baseball cap with yellow cotton scrambled eggs pasted on top of the long brim and a real stuffed bird pinned on to the spot customarily occupied by the Navy eagle." The author believes that "the American sailor or flier who goes into battle knows where he is going and why."

Jensen's *Carrier War* had been prepared as one of the "Battle Report Series" of the United States Navy, under the auspices of the Council of Books in Wartime. It was published simultaneously, early in 1945, by Simon and Schuster and Pocket Books, by the latter in an oversized "pocket" edition. Generally welcomed as an illuminating battle account, the book was sold out within a few days after publication. The March 26, 1945, issue of *Life* carried excerpts from the book.

Critical reaction to Jensen's book was good, with most reviewers recommending it as a magnificent story, well told. It was described as "lucid and stimulating," and the author was lauded for the "restrained language, a complete lack of melodramatic luridness, scrupulous accuracy, and a detailed knowledge of events." In dissenting tone, Hanson W. Baldwin '42 objected to one factor beyond the author's control, the "unmistakable evidence of rigorous and stupid censorship, so sweeping that one knows little more when he has finished this book than a careful student of the Pacific war knew before." Describing *Carrier War* as a paean of praise and a song of glory for the flattops, Baldwin called Jensen's style unfortunate for the serious intent of the book. "The reader feels a sense of motion, but not of emotion, the writing is graphic, but in too impersonalized a way." Still another critic, Lewis Gannett '41, primarily concerned with the substance of Jensen's story, commented that the "new semi-aerial Navy" disproved Major de Seversky's '41 theory of the superiority of land-based aviation. The collection of photographs in *Carrier War* was singled out for special commendation by most critics, who found them excellent complementary material for a "brilliant and highly readable" text. These photographs had been gathered from many sources, some of them taken by the author himself.

The foreword for Jensen's book, written by Artemus L. Gates, Assistant Secretary of the Navy for Air, states: "This proud story of America's new big carriers brings profound satisfaction to the Navy. *Carrier War* is an excellent account of their achievements in the Pacific and of the sights and sounds of battle as they actually exist." Included in the narrative are frank discussions of strategy and mistakes, and descriptions, for example, of thrilling rescues at sea and drama in the vivid details of the tragedy of the *Liscome Bay*. The author's concern for human detail and his keen sense of humor have been noted throughout. One critic remarked that while Jensen gives credit to the ship, "his heart is with the fliers."

Another comment, this on the young author himself, reveals that he is a tall man, six feet, four inches in height, and that he has sharp features. His resumption of civilian life will begin on January 2, 1946, the date for which his release from the Navy is scheduled. In the course of his duty on the *Yorktown*, he crossed the International Date Line several times, but only once, in April 1944, did it bother him: "The sixteenth simply disappeared, a disturbing matter personally since it happened to be my birthday."

References

N Y Times Book R p7 F 25 '45
Jensen, O. Carrier War (1945)

JOHNSON, HALL Mar. 12, 1888- Choral director; composer; arranger
Address: h. 5219 McKinley Ave., Los Angeles

Hall Johnson, composer and arranger, and founder and director of the Hall Johnson Negro Choir—which has been known throughout the United States since the twenties for concert, radio, and motion picture appearances—"came early under potent and religious influences." Johnson was born March 12, 1888, in Athens, Georgia. His father, the Reverend William Decker Johnson, was the minister of the African Methodist Episcopal Church; his mother, Alice Virginia (Sansom) Johnson, was a former slave—until she was a child of eight. His grandmother, too, had been a slave; and from this woman, Mary Hall Jones, the boy Hall learned the spirituals of his race. Many of those which his choir sing today he has never heard from any other source; and where she got them, he says, and how long ago, he often wonders.

Hall graduated from the Knox Institute in Athens when he was fifteen, then went to Atlanta University for a year. His father had meantime become president of Allen University in Columbus, South Carolina, and young Johnson was graduated from there in 1908. He had started to study the piano with an older sister while he was still a child, but not until he was a student at Allen University did he take up music in earnest. With a ten-cent self-instructor he taught himself to play a violin his mother had given him, and in a short time he was proficient enough to become a member of the dance orchestra of a local summer resort. By 1908 he had saved sufficient money to go to Philadelphia for his music lessons.

For the next five or six years the young musician worked and studied in Philadelphia. He took violin lessons at the Hahn School of Music, attended the weekly concerts of the Philadelphia Orchestra, and studied at the University of Pennsylvania's School of Music, from which he was graduated in 1910 with the Simon Haessler Prize for the best composition for orchestra and chorus. Two years later, in November 1912, he was married to Celeste Corpening, a friend from his days with the local Athens orchestra. (Mrs. Johnson died in 1935.)

The young couple went to New York City in 1914 because of the current demand there for Negro musicians in dance orchestras. Johnson became a member of the orchestra of Vernon and Irene Castle, he played in theaters, and toured the country with leading Negro attractions, including the revue *Shuffle Along*. During the war he was with Jim Europe's band. He studied, too: French and German with tutors, and music at the Institute of Musical Art in 1923-24.

Meanwhile Johnson, who already had had published transcriptions of several spirituals, conceived the idea, according to Karl E. Downs, of organizing a Negro choir that would be comparable to the Russian Don Cossack ensemble. In December 1925 his Hall Johnson Negro Choir of eight singers came into being in Harlem. It was not until February 29, 1928, however, that the choir, expanded by then to a mixed group of twenty voices, gave its first concert in a regular New York City auditorium—in the Pythian Temple. A month later, on March 20 in Town Hall, it gave its second concert. Other engagements followed quickly that first season; then for the next eight years the gradually expanding group was kept busy with radio, theater, and concert appearances, in both New York and on tour. For six consecutive seasons, beginning in August 1928, the choir made joint appearances with the Philharmonic Symphony at the Lewisohn Stadium in New York. John Mason Brown [42] once called the group "an all-American miracle."

The programs of the Hall Johnson choir are composed of both spirituals—"devotional songs, episodic songs, or songs of religious experience"—and the secular songs of the Negro— "the work songs of the levee, the rock pile, and the cotton field, the numerous lullabies and songs about animals, and . . . the social songs, the reels and ballads of the Negro in his hours of relaxation." "These traditional folk melodies," wrote Johnson for the first concert, "will be given in a manner which will reproduce the fervor of the camp meeting which gave them birth. . . .Beyond clarity of diction and fair precision of attack, no attempt is made to secure a perfect choral ensemble as generally accepted. We believe this enables us to preserve an emotional content that would be lost with greater refinement of method."

Critics at these early concerts found indeed that Johnson had not allowed his musical training to color his understanding of the essential simplicity of this folk music. Most of them found listening a new experience because, instead of following in the pattern of the small Negro ensemble that had been popular during the early twenties, Johnson attempted to re-create the effect of the old camp meetings with his larger group. His arrangements (the choir always use Johnson's arrangements) avoided the polished sophisticated form of other groups, thus enabling the choir to sing "as Negroes do when they do it spontaneously." "I have hardly ever heard such a direct expression of the source from which art is created," wrote conductor Willem van Hoogstraten in 1928.

Similar expressions of enthusiasm came from other critics. The group, declared Walter Damrosch [44], "sing with fine precision, beautiful tone quality, and, above all, with a deep inner emotion which fairly sweeps the listeners along." "They use the true Negro portamento suspected as the origin of jazz," commented W. J. Henderson of the New York Sun, "and they sing with the inexorable beat often lost by white singers." Others described the music as retaining its primitive appeal, elemental power, and, in the case of some songs, the deft humor. In a Stadium concert in 1938, however, during a return engagement in New York (Johnson and his group had been doing choral work in

HALL JOHNSON

Hollywood movies since 1935), there was evidence that some of the simplicity and depth that critics had formerly found praiseworthy was missing. Some of the arrangements, wrote the New York Times reviewer, seemed oversophisticated. "Johnson occasionally allowed himself harmonic elaboration and tricky effects in the accompaniments that are for one thing more instrumental than vocal and for another are entirely unsuited to the style of the Negro folk song."

Johnson's transference to Hollywood for such pictures as Lost Horizon (1937), Way down South (1939), Swanee River (1940), Cabin in the Sky (1943) had followed two Broadway presentations. The second, Green Pastures (1930), won for the choral director in 1931 the Harmon award for his arrangements and direction of the music, and an invitation to make the film version (released in 1936) of the play. The first offering, Run, Little Chillun (1933), for which he did the book and music, received a mixed reception. (It was produced in New York again in 1943, and in Los Angeles and San Francisco in 1938-39, following Federal Theater and other presentations throughout the country.)

The play had evoked much controversy. Its action revolved around the struggle between an itinerant moon-worshipping group, the New Day Pilgrims, and a Negro Baptist church over the soul of the Baptist minister's son, who had been seduced by a disciple of the nature cult. The two most discussed scenes in the music drama were the Pilgrims' religious orgy in the woods and the revival meeting of the Baptists. By many people, Run, Little Chillun was described as folk art. In contradiction Margaret Marshall of the Nation declared that, far from being such, it showed that the author had very confused ideas himself of what he was up to. The circumstances which produced the true Negro folk art no longer exist, she explained; and "any attempt to reproduce the forms of expression growing out of their [the Negroes'] experience as a folk can result only in senti-

JOHNSON, HALL—*Continued*

mentality, condescension, and bar art." On the laudatory side, critics referred to the play—in words summed up by Robert Garland of the New York *Sun*—as "noble and magnificent, superb and orgiastic, startling and ecstatic, savage and appealing, frenzied and moving, elemental and emotional"—some reviewers at the same time calling it a bad play.

"The exceptionally intimate association of speech and song, action and dance," wrote Olin Downes'[43], "gave an expression which is genuinely racial. . . . *Run, Little Chillun* is far from finished drama or opera . . . but it has real life and genuine musical qualities." Burton Rascoe declared that Johnson had shown, by "tremendous dramatic implication," how a new Negro religion—"developed out of the Negro's own essential nature and not grafted on through contact with other peoples"—"must inevitably fail as long as he is kept in a semi-slave state by the whites."

On the negative side the criticism was equally intense. The play is, wrote Louis Kronenberger'[44], "a crude tale of sex and religion in which, at times, it is hard to tell one from the other. Now and then a certain intensity overrides the general clumsiness, and here and there a certain naiveté is not unattractive in itself. But as drama, *Run, Little Chillun* is mostly inept or absurd, and the chief virtue . . . is a lot of good choral singing." Hall Johnson's "sense of what makes superlatively good theater has far outweighed his sense of what makes impressive drama, and has quite obliterated his sense of what makes for better understanding of the simpler and finer spiritual qualities of the Negro," wrote a *Commonweal* critic. "One could leave this play saying that the Negro's religious instinct is confined solely to emotional excitement. And that, I am convinced, is a serious calumny. It is quite as if we were to take the worship of Pan as the whole symbol of the civilization of Greece," the reviewer concluded.

Although Johnson and his choir continued to make radio and concert appearances outside of California after 1935 (in 1944 they were the summer replacement for the *New World A-Coming* series over WMCA, and in May 1945 they were in a vaudeville revue, *Blue Holiday*, with Ethel Waters), their film engagements for the most part confined them to concerts on the West Coast. In 1941 Johnson established the Festival Negro Choir of Los Angeles, a training group of two hundred. It is a nonprofit community effort, and all proceeds from the concerts go toward maintaining scholarships for talented young Negroes. Besides his directorial duties and his arranging and composing—he has completed the book and music for a Negro operetta to be entitled "Fi-yer"—Johnson contributes articles on Negro music to various magazines. He is the recipient of an honorary D. Mus. from the Philadelphia Musical Academy.

The tall, bespectacled choral director has, to quote one newspaperman, "the longest imaginable arms, the supplest imaginable fingers" (both called "necromantic" by another critic). After one concert a reviewer commented: Johnson "lead the choir by sign language of hands, arms, body, and head . . . that bore no conceivable relation to the . . . white man's art of conducting." As for his hobbies, Johnson once described them: "I still have my intense love for pictures, but it expresses itself through the camera. Next to that are my cigarette holders of all shapes, lengths, and materials. I play my unusual records [swing included] while smoking from my unusual holders while taking unusual photographs of my unusual friends."

References

N Y Post Mag p39 Ag 11 '43 pors
Downs, Karl E. Meet the Negro p90-1 (1943)
Who's Who in Colored America, 1941-44
Wier, A. E. ed. Macmillan Encyclopedia of Music and Musicians (1938)

JOHNSON, HIRAM (WARREN) Sept. 2, 1866—Aug. 6, 1945 United States Republican Senator from California from 1917 until his death; Governor from 1911 to 1917; a strong isolationist, who was instrumental in preventing the United States from entering League of Nations; voted against ratification of the United Nations Charter. See *Current Biography* 1941 Yearbook.

Obituary

N Y Times p 1+ Ag 7 '45 por

JOHNSON, J(OHN) MONROE May 5, 1878- United States Government official; civil engineer

Address: b. Office of Defense Transportation, Washington, D. C.; h. Marion, S. C.

The man charged with the formidable task of keeping the wheels of transportation rolling in the United States during the emergency created by the war is a veteran of military and industrial campaigns. As director of the Office of Defense Transportation, appointed April 4, 1944, J. Monroe Johnson was faced with unprecedented problems in maintaining the increased and accelerated traffic of military passengers and freight at the same time that civilian needs had to be met.

The son of John Monroe and Emma Crider (Richardson) Johnson, John Monroe Johnson was born May 5, 1878, in Marion, South Carolina. The elder Johnson was a lawyer and plantation owner who had served as an engineer in the Confederate Army. While he looked forward to a law career for young John, he also believed that a knowledge of engineering would be of value to a lawyer. The youth therefore took courses in two fields. He first attended the University of South Carolina for a year (1895-96), and then took a technical course the following year at Furman University in Greenville (1896-97). But his studies were interrupted by the outbreak of the Spanish-American War. Johnson volunteered for service and attained the rank of sergeant. Returning home from the war he opened an office as a civil engineer in Marion, South Carolina. Under the firm name of Johnson and Roberts this office has been maintained continuously since 1898. Thus established in business, the ambitious young engineer was married to Helen Barnwell in 1900. The couple had met in Charleston when Johnson was a soldier.

Johnson's career as a civil engineer progressed so successfully that at thirty he abandoned the idea of becoming a lawyer. He executed several large engineering jobs in various parts of South Carolina, building drainage systems, roads, and bridges. Among his principal projects were the Cow Castle Drainage District in Orangeburg and Godfreys Bridge in Gresham. From 1911 to 1914 he served on the Marion County Highway Commission. Two years later he was appointed chairman of the South Carolina State Highway Commission, a position he held for one year. In 1916, at the request of the Governor of his state, Johnson recruited a company of military engineers for service on the Mexican border. In 1917, with America at war, Governor Richard I. Manning again asked Johnson to recruit and head a battalion of engineers. Johnson accepted the assignment with the provision that the group be given immediate overseas service. In twelve hectic days Johnson organized the battalion. It became the First Battalion, 117th Engineers of the famous Rainbow Division, whose chief of staff was General Douglas MacArthur [41]. Johnson is a close friend of MacArthur's and holds him in high esteem, describing the General as a "great soldier."

In the course of the war Johnson rose from the rank of major to a colonelcy, and became chief engineer of his division. He participated in all its campaigns and later served with the Army of Occupation. His service in the field won him military honors—among his nine decorations are the Distinguished Service Medal, the Verdun Medal, the French Legion of Honor, and the Belgian Order of Leopold II. Johnson is a charter member of the American Legion and served on that organization's national executive committee from 1919 to 1936. He is also a member of the Military Order of the World War and the American Society of Military Engineers, which group he served as president in 1940-41. (Johnson also belongs to the American Society of Civil Engineers, and the American Association for the Advancement of Science. His fraternities are Sigma Nu and Omicron Delta Kappa, and his Washington clubs are Army and Navy, Chevy Chase, and Burning Tree.)

Upon his discharge from the Army Johnson resumed his engineering duties and in 1928 was appointed South Carolina's boundary commissioner. Until his first Washington appointment he was chiefly a consulting engineer. Then, in 1935 the South Carolinian became Assistant Secretary of Commerce. In this capacity he had jurisdiction over all the transportation activities of the Department, and made himself heard on many issues. Of his years as Assistant Secretary of Commerce, Delos W. Lovelace remarks: "Some corners of Washington still echo with the arguments he set forth then in favor of a transatlantic line of dirigible airships." But the irrepressible Johnson did not confine himself to expressing his views for the benefit of the Capital. His forthright arguments found their way into print in the form of articles devoted to different phases of transportation. The *Congressional Digest* of February 1936 carried a detailed article by Johnson entitled "The Plight of Our Merchant Fleet Today." The author urged immediate modernization of the merchant fleet. He illustrated statistically the inadequacy of

J. MONROE JOHNSON

the fleet and called for measures "to place the American Merchant Marine on a parity with the modern fleets of our foreign competitors." The May 1938 issue of the *American City* contains a portion of Johnson's address before the 1937 Annual Conference of the United States Conference of Mayors. In this speech, entitled "Municipal Airport Problems," he discussed the practical issues involved in aircraft transportation in the United States. Advocating the formulation of a national aviation plan, Johnson stressed the necessity of reaching a comprehensive airport program satisfactory to all interests concerned.

In May 1940 President Roosevelt [42] appointed J. Monroe Johnson a member of the Interstate Commerce Commission. At the time of the appointment White House spokesman Stephen Early [41] reported that the President had been urged by many Senators to choose a man familiar with the transportation problems of the Southern states, and, as Assistant Secretary of Commerce, Johnson had had jurisdiction over the Inland Waterways Corporation. At this time, Joseph B. Eastman [42], Johnson's predecessor at ODT, was also serving on the Commission. *Newsweek* reports that after his appointment to the ICC, Johnson "shared many an aspirin with Eastman as they struggled with transportation enigmas." Johnson had originally been appointed to the Commission to fill the unexpired term of resigning Marion M. Caskie. However, when Johnson's tenure expired in December 1941 he was reappointed for a full term, to expire December 1948. Shortly after Johnson took up his duties with the Commission he was placed in charge of the Bureau of Service, which supervised the use, control, supply, movement, exchange, and distribution of locomotives, cars, and other vehicles used in the transportation of freight. All this provided thorough grounding for the post that was to follow, the directorship of the Office of Defense Transportation.

President Roosevelt appointed Johnson to the ODT post on April 4, 1944. The selection was generally well received, *Newsweek* commenting:

JOHNSON, J. MONROE—*Continued*

"Railroad officials like the appointment of J. Monroe Johnson as ODT director. . . .They believe he will help heal the breach between the ODT and the Interstate Commerce Commission." In addition to serving in his new post, Johnson remained as a member of the ICC, but was relieved of routine duties. However, he continued to retain supervision of the Bureau of Service of the ICC, which enabled him to keep in touch with the operational problems of the railroads. Johnson swung into his new job with a strong warning: "There will be no shortage of military transportation. We will not hesitate to take any steps to provide it. If people take vacations, they may find themselves stranded away from home. We are on the eve of a great offensive. Watch out!"

Upon assuming the leadership of the Office of Defense Transportation Johnson was faced with the emergency conditions of the severely overburdened transportation system of mobilized America. He has worked consistently to ensure the movement of essential military freight and has on several occasions issued stringent orders. When transportation facilities were hampered by bad weather conditions in January 1945, Johnson instructed the railroads to discontinue passenger service wherever such action was required to keep wartime transportation moving.

Previously, when the pressure of troop movements and war freight reached record-breaking proportions, the ODT had requested the cancellation of all conventions and meetings not concerned with the war effort. The ban on nonessential conventions became effective in February 1945, and Johnson served as chairman of the War Committee on Conventions which considered requests for permission to hold conventions. On January 17, 1945, the White House made public a memorandum from Johnson to the President stating that the transportation of out-of-town guests not officially needed at the inaugural ceremonies would add "an alarming burden" to the transportation difficulties.

In is program of further curtailment of civilian travel, the ODT banned transportation for animal shows; ruled that coal-burning passenger trains operating at less than 35 per cent capacity cease "without exception"; asked New York City's millions to avoid traveling during rush hours when possible; appealed to state governors to enforce the wartime Federal speed limit of thirty-five miles an hour for motor vehicles. Big league baseball officials who were asked to consider curbs on transportation of their teams made two voluntary travel curtailments after conferences with Johnson.

Immediately after V-E Day on May 8, 1945, it was announced that, in view of the prodigious task of redeployment of men and matériel, no wartime controls over transportation could be relaxed. "Sports will be lucky to play out regular schedules this summer and fall unless Japan quickly folds up, relieving the burden on transportation," declared Johnson. A fifteen-point travel reduction program for college and high school athletics, including the elimination of post-season events, was announced a few days afterward. In late May Johnson recommended that the Army release fifty thousand experienced railroad men in uni-

form in order to help move members of the armed forces across the United States.

As the railroad crisis mounted, on June 29 the ODT decreed that reservations on passenger trains might be obtained no more than five days in advance instead of the usual thirty, and ordered four thousand soldiers furloughed for thirty days' work on the railroads to avert a breakdown in service. In July additional emergency measures were adopted: all sleeping car accommodations in use on trips between points 450 miles or less apart were banned; the transportation of race horses or show animals by railroads was prohibited; all Government agencies and departments were directed to make further reductions in travel. The country's entire supply of railway passenger coaches, express, and baggage cars was put at the disposal of the Army on July 17.

Testifying before the Mead '44 War Investigating Committee on July 23, Director Johnson placed responsibility for much of the growing congestion in redeployment on the Army and on the manpower shortage. Despite the ODT's responsibilities in the movement of all transportation in the United States, it was not consulted in advance on the redeployment plans, Johnson asserted. The information the agency had received, he added, was so incomplete that adequate preparation for the unprecedented traffic was defeated. Following Johnson's claim that the railroads required seventy-five thousand more men "right now," Chairman Mead proposed that the Army discharge or furlough servicemen working on railroads overseas. Although Army officials discounted Johnson's charges, claiming the railroad jam was not serious, on July 31, yielding to demands of Congress, Johnson, and other officials, the Army receded from its stand against releasing experienced railroad men with the necessary points for discharge.

After V-J Day on August 15, 1945, wartime restrictions began to be lifted gradually. Among the regulations swept out of existence were seven controls over commercial motor vehicle traffic; curbs on travel to sporting meets; limitations on wholesale and retail truck deliveries; the thirty-five-mile-an-hour speed limit; controls over local bus, trolley, coach, and streetcar services. In September bowling's major events were restored to the sports calendar for 1946. However, "wartime conditions" prevailed at the holiday season as ships brought more than a million servicemen to the ports on both coasts. With civilians also intent upon spending Christmas at home, Johnson warned that disappointment awaited many would-be travelers.

Johnson is a lean, gray-haired, ruddy-complexioned man who has retained the candid speech and manner of his youth. His direct approach to problems has been apparent throughout his Washington career. The press has commented on his bluntness, one magazine describing the reaction of the office staff at the ODT after the new director took over: "Five minutes after Colonel Johnson took office they knew the engineers had landed. They heard a voice that would have been audible to a deployed regiment. Orders came with a crispness and finality that only a veteran campaigner could produce." And Johnson is a busy man—

as transportation chief he finds little time to travel.

References

N Y Sun p22 Ag 30 '44
N Y Times p12 Ap 5 '44 por
Newsweek 23:40 Ap 24 '44 por
Railway Age 108:827-8 My 11 '40 por;
  116:683-4 Ap 4 '44 por
Who's Who in America, 1944-45

JOHNSON, VAN Aug. 25, 1916- Actor

Address: b. c/o Metro-Goldwyn-Mayer, Culver City, Calif.

One of Hollywood's newest and brightest stars, known only to a few movie-goers before 1944, is Van Johnson, who rose to stardom within a short year. Both men and women are counted among his admirers, it is reported, but he has also a special appeal for "female adolescent America," who see in his youth and vitality the ideal "boy next door."

The only child of Charles E. Johnson, a real-estate salesman, and Loretta Johnson, Van Johnson was born in Newport, Rhode Island, on August 25, 1916. Although he is often thought of as Irish, the actor is of Swedish descent. When Van was three years old his mother and father were separated. He was consequently reared by his father and grandmother, strict disciplinarians, who saw to it that the boy had a carefully supervised but pleasant childhood. Young Van received his elementary schooling at Calvert Grammar School, in Newport. After school hours he worked at odd jobs—mowing lawns, shoveling snow, delivering groceries, selling magazine subscriptions. Of those days Johnson recalls: "It wasn't that I loved work so much, but that I loved possessions more. Dad had one rule: I could have what I wanted if I earned the price of it myself."

Studying singing, dancing, and the violin, Van became stage-struck before he had even reached his teens. Specifically, Johnson says, that attraction began when he appeared for the first time in one of the annual shows presented by his music and dancing teachers. Wearing a straw hat and carrying a cane, the talented child went through a few Jack Donohue and Jack Whiting routines. With a zeal which Johnson now dismisses as "showing off," he and some friends turned all the unused barns in the neighborhood into theaters. And with that preliminary taken care of, Van proceeded to write the plays and cast himself in the leading roles. As Johnson now says, "Other small fry might be permitted to say 'Ouch' or 'Here come the girls,' but it was Master Johnson who played the extremely dashing heroes." While attending Rogers High School, the aspiring actor experienced his first bit of discouragement when he failed to "make" the dramatic club. He therefore turned his extra-curricular interests to playing the violin in the orchestra and to exhibiting his athletic skill on the basketball and baseball teams. Outside of school, in his free time Van performed at the Lions Club or the Kiwanis, attended Newport's Casino Theatre where such stars as Ruth Chatterton

VAN JOHNSON

and Alice Brady appeared in plays, and went to the circus or the movies.

Upon Johnson's graduation from high school in June 1935, his father urged him to enroll at Brown University to study law. Not interested in law as a vocation, Johnson tried, instead, to find a singing or dancing job. He was unsuccessful in his efforts the first summer and spent the season frying clams in a roadside restaurant which catered to tourists. While working here Johnson was urged to try his luck on Broadway by the manager of the restaurant—a young lady whom Johnson admired, and whom he describes as having "brains, breeding, beauty and courage." In September 1935 Johnson left Newport for Broadway, confident that he would be able to achieve success quickly and then marry his ex-employer, who however, married another suitor.

Life was very hard for Johnson during his first few months in New York and his confidence began to wane. He haunted the agencies, Johnson tells: "I tore the names and addresses of actors' agents out of the classified section of the phone book, starting with the A's and working down alphabetically." Finally, in December, the disheartened actor, exaggerating his experience, won a part in a revue called *Entre Nous,* which unfortunately had only a four-week run at the Cherry Lane Theatre in Greenwich Village. With his funds very low, he reluctantly accepted a job as a substitute dancer with a group that was touring New England, but after a short while he left the company. A few months later, in May 1936, almost a year after his arrival in New York, he got his first chance on Broadway. While watching a rehearsal of a new show called *New Faces* with a friend who was a member of the cast, Johnson was mistaken by the director for one of the performers and told to get on the stage. Bewildered for the moment, he nevertheless obeyed the order, and "knocking himself out," he was rewarded with a part in the show. He worked in *New*

JOHNSON, VAN—*Continued*

Faces for forty weeks, earning forty dollars a week, and when the show closed in early 1937 Johnson became a chorus boy at the Roxy Theatre. Shortly afterward he went on the road for several months as the third member of the comic team of Buster West and his wife, Lucille Page. In the summer of 1938 he entertained at hotel resorts, gaining diversified experience, in singing, dancing, playing the violin, and acting.

In early 1939 Johnson did his first bit of night club work, when he appeared as one of the *Eight Young Men of Manhattan*, an act written around Mary Martin '41 for the swank Rainbow Room. In 1940 Johnson was back in the theater again—this time in George Abbott's '40 *Too Many Girls*. As the understudy for the three male leads, Richard Kollmar, Desi Arnez, and Eddie Bracken '44, Johnson on several occasions had an opportunity to play one of the major roles. On the strength of these few performances he was given a fairly important part in another George Abbott production, *Pal Joey* (December 1940). In this he did a dance number with June Havoc and spoke about ten lines of dialogue. While *Pal Joey* was still running Columbia Pictures invited Johnson to Hollywood. Unimpressed with his subsequent screen test, however, the studio did not offer Johnson a contract, and the discouraged actor returned to New York and resumed his part in *Pal Joey*. But Hollywood had not completely rejected him. In early 1942 Warner Brothers '45 offered Johnson a six months' contract at three hundred dollars a week, and Johnson immediately went again to Hollywood. At the end of five and a half months he received four months' salary (his contract entitled the studio to release him for six weeks), but he had not been given an assignment. Two weeks before his contract was about to expire, Johnson was given the leading role in the picture *Murder in the Big House* (1942). Upon the completion of this "B" picture, which took all of twelve days to produce, the studio dropped Johnson's option.

With his future in motion pictures very uncertain, in the middle of 1942 Johnson decided to return once again to New York. However, while having dinner with Lucille Ball on his last night in Hollywood, Johnson was introduced by Miss Ball to Billy Grady, MGM talent scout. Grady was persuaded by Miss Ball to give the young actor a chance and asked Johnson to report to the studio the next morning. Almost immediately Johnson was given make-up tests, voice tests, and dramatic coaching—all in preparation for a *Crime Doesn't Pay* short. The result was that MGM signed Johnson to a contract. Playing the part of a soldier in a bit part, Johnson made his motion picture debut in *Somewhere I'll Find You* (1942), in which Clark Gable '45 and Lana Turner '43 were starred. Johnson then appeared before the year was over in *The War Against Mrs. Hadley*, *Skyway to Glory*, and in *Dr. Gillespie's New Assistant*, one of the series starring Lionel Barrymore '43.

In 1943 Johnson began to work steadily in Hollywood. He appeared as Marcus in *The Human Comedy*, as the reporter in *Madame Curie*, as a pilot in *Pilot Number Five*, and as the young pilot in *A Guy Named Joe*. The

production of *A Guy Named Joe*, in which Johnson had been given the coveted part of Ted Randall, was early interrupted by a near-tragedy—Johnson was badly injured in an automobile accident. Afraid that he would be replaced in the movie and thus lose his first good opportunity in Hollywood, he was overwhelmed when he learned that both Irene Dunne and Spencer Tracy '43, the stars of the film, had asked that work on the picture be suspended until he could recover. His three-month confinement in the hospital won him wide publicity, and his acting in the film, which was finally released in December 1943, won him the favorable notice of Howard Barnes of the New York *Herald Tribune*: "Van Johnson . . . contributes a superior performance to the film."

In 1944 Johnson achieved stardom. His performances in *The White Cliffs of Dover*, *Two Girls and a Sailor*, *Between Two Women*, and *Thirty Seconds Over Tokyo* established him as a versatile actor. In *Thirty Seconds Over Tokyo*, the story of Captain Ted Lawson's '43 Army bomber crew and the first American raid on Japan, Johnson (as Lawson) gave "a warm and brave performance and managed quite well to achieve a moving tenderness in love scenes and rigid strength in the action field," in the opinion of Bosley Crowther of the New York *Times*. *Time* found that Johnson played the role with "unusual heart and simplicity," while Pete Martin, writing in the *Saturday Evening Post*, said: "A few more opportunities like that and he may take the same grip on the grown-up public that he now has on the wearers of beanies, friendship rings, and charm bracelets." In May 1945 the actor appeared in the lavish musical *Thrill of a Romance* with the swimmer Esther Williams. Portraying an Air Force hero on furlough, Johnson, according to the critic of the New York *Herald Tribune*, "gives the type of performance that has endeared him to the younger set. He is the antithesis of the 'wolf' . . . clean cut, amiable, a little shy and needing aid and comfort." Eileen Creelman of the New York *Sun* found that "he makes a pleasant hero of the light comedy."

Another 1945 picture was *Week-end at the Waldorf*, in which Johnson's portrayal of the young Army captain was judged "boyishly appealing." Later that year he was working on the set for the film *No Leave, No Love*. Forthcoming films in which his appearance was announced are: *The Common Sin*, an episodic story by five authors; the film adaptation of Booth Tarkington's novel *The Image of Josephine*; *Till the Clouds Roll By*,' a screen biography of the late Jerome Kern; and a picture to be based on Cardinal Spellman's story "Risen Soldier." The year 1945 closed with Van Johnson occupying second place among the first ten "biggest money-making" stars of the year—the first time he could be included in that group.

The eight thousand fan letters Johnson receives each week from his admirers are a measure of his wide popularity. Much of the actor's mail reads: "Please don't get married, wait for me." In the hope that their idol is immune to Hollywood's beauties, Johnson's teen-age worshippers feel that "nabbing Johnson for a spouse" is a free race for all. As if answering their prayers, he has recently said, "I'd love to get married . . . but I don't think it will be an actress. One actor in the family is enough. . . .She should be an active person who plays tennis and rides horseback and has a sense of humor. She must like to dance but beauty is not essential." Concerned over the mass hysteria that greets the actor when he appears on the stage, his studio is refusing all requests for personal appearances. Pete Martin, who apparently had an eye-witness account from Hedda Hopper, describes a descent of a "bobby-soxers' blitz" upon Johnson: "The heat engendered by an opportunity to see and touch Johnson . . . shaped up very much like Pickett's charge at Gettysburg. A milling mob flowed around parked autos, climbed over them, and crawled under them, chasing a tall, reddish-blond guy with a determined grin on his face. Every now and then they caught up with him and engulfed him in a chorus of shrieks, shouts, and girlish giggles."

Van Johnson's reddish hair goes well with his blue eyes, freckles, snub nose, and "delayed action" smile. Picture magazines often show his six-foot-three, 185-pound figure clad in a bathing suit; and among his other recreations are roller-coasting, meeting other stars, and watching as many as five movies a week, although he shuns his own pictures. He still suffers from the severe headaches that followed the automobile accident and resulted in his classification as 4F. Shy, serious, and hardworking, he hopes to improve his acting and to play comedy parts "mixed with a little drama." Because of the numbers and persistence of his admirers, he moved from his Brentwood home, and in 1945 was living in a hotel hideaway in Los Angeles. Of his newly acquired fame he says, "I've been a very lucky guy."

References

Liberty 22:38-9+ O 13 '45 por
Life 17:47 N 13 '44 por; 19:115+ N 5 '45 pors
Look 9:34+ N 13 '45 por
Photoplay 25:45+ Je '44 il pors; 26:32-4+ F '45 il pors; 26:47+ Mr '45 il pors

JOHNSON, WILLIAM E(UGENE) Mar. 25, 1862—Feb. 2, 1945 Militant American prohibitionist; gave lectures all over the world; special agent of the Department of the Interior to enforce laws in Indian Territory and Oklahoma, 1906-7; chief special officer of the Indian Service, 1908-11; during this period became known as "Pussyfoot" because of his "catlike policies in pursuing lawbreakers," securing almost four and one-half thousand convictions.

Obituary

N Y Times p11 F 3 '45 por

JUDSON, ARTHUR (LEON) Feb. 17, 1881- Concert manager

Address: b. c/o Columbia Concerts Corp., 113 W. 57th St., New York City; h. 133 Woodrest Ave., White Plains, N.Y.

Ben Greenhaus

ARTHUR JUDSON

Throughout a career as violinist, professor, artist and orchestra manager, radio station and festival founder, Arthur Judson, president of Columbia Concerts Corporation, has been guided by one dominant motive: to bring the best of classical music, interpreted by the greatest artists, to as many people as could be reached. Once a music-hungry youth in a "musically ignorant" small town, he has earned through his subsequent efforts a reputation as "the dean of American concert managers and [the] architect of a vast democratic musical program for America." In the opinion of Olga Samaroff, he developed the possibility of the community concert series "with a skill and breadth of conception that is unequaled."

A native of Ohio, although he has for many years made his home in New York, Arthur Leon Judson was born in Dayton on February 17, 1881, to Francis H. and Mary M. (Myers) Judson. At the age of twelve he was introduced to the study of the violin and thereafter for a time had thought of becoming a violin virtuoso, an ambition he abandoned when he realized that he was less gifted than other violinists whom he heard. "I was a good violinist," he says now, "but no Kreisler '44 or Heifetz '44." However, after working his way through Denison University in Granville, Ohio, he decided that music in some form was what he wanted, and finding none to his satisfaction either in Dayton or Granville, he left for New York in 1900. "I wanted to hear good concerts," he explains, "but nobody ever came to Dayton, so I came to New York." In New York, where he remained for less than a year, Judson studied the violin with Max Bendix, violinist, conductor, and composer, and with Leopold Lichtenberg. He earned his living and gained experience meanwhile by playing the instrument in various small orchestras and by conducting, including one orchestra of one hundred men at Ocean Grove, New Jersey.

Within the year Judson returned to Ohio to become, despite his comparative youth, a pro-

JUDSON, ARTHUR—*Continued*

fessor of the history of music, and the dean of the Conservatory of Music, at his college, Denison University. Before he resigned from that position in 1907, notes *The International Cyclopedia of Music and Musicians*, he had built up the orchestra, sponsored concerts, instituted the annual Granville Music Festival, and developed the small conservatory into a progressive institution of musical education. During those years he had also written a guide to the study of musical history (*History of Music*, published by the Granville Festival Association in 1905) in which he discussed the relation of cause and effect in the history of music from the Crusades to modern times. Returning to New York in 1907, Judson joined the staff of *Musical America*, where he was to remain for nearly eight years, first in the editorial department, and later as advertising manager of the publication.

The year 1915 was the turning point in Judson's career. For the first time he was able to realize his ambition to become, as one interviewer has called him, a "salesman of fine music." In July 1915, having left the staff of *Musical America*, he was appointed manager of the Philadelphia Orchestra, then under Leopold Stokowski's [41] direction. At the same time, investing $250 of his savings, he launched his own musical booking agency, Concert Management Arthur Judson, Inc., in Philadelphia, soon following that venture with a second office in New York. His aim was twofold: he wanted to make American audiences more music-conscious, and he wanted to help artists of ability who might not become public successes without good management. Then, already dividing his time between Philadelphia and New York, Judson in 1922 took on the added duties of business manager of the New York Philharmonic-Symphony Orchestra, at that time known as the Philharmonic Society of New York.

In September 1926 the concert manager further expanded his activities when he organized a pioneer excursion into the sphere of radio entertainment at a time when radio was still thought of mostly as a means of communication with sinking vessels or polar expeditions and hardly as a medium for artistic expression. But Judson foresaw its inherent possibilities, and the Judson Radio Program Corporation was born to utilize them. "When we broadcast our first concert," he recalls, "we had to turn away hundreds of people. I knew then that radio could become the great common denominator, the instrument for bringing good music to the whole people." "It's a mass medium," he says today, "and, thanks to it, good music is becoming everybody's music."

Little more than a year after the formation of the Judson Radio Program Corporation, the aim of which was to present performances by great artists to a larger public than could be reached in the concert hall, Judson, in another move to popularize classical music, was instrumental in laying the foundation for the Columbia Broadcasting System, which "has made notable contributions to the cause of good music in the United States." In that year (1927) Judson, together with George A. Coats and Major J. Andrew White, established the United Independent Broadcasters, Inc., to make participation in chain broadcasts practicable for independent radio stations. Taking a year's lease on the facilities of Station WOR and utilizing its own station, WABC, the new company began operations under Judson's direction with sixteen stations. After a process of reorganization involving several changes of name and ownership of the new network, the Columbia Broadcasting System emerged in 1928. Although Judson's active share in the affairs of the Columbia Broadcasting System ceased in 1930, he is still one of that corporation's major stockholders.

Meanwhile, Judson expanded Concert Management. In October 1928 that organization, together with Judson's Radio Program Corporation, absorbed the Wolfsohn Musical Bureau, the oldest concert management bureau in the United States (having been founded in 1884). Another merger in 1930 united Judson's agencies with four of his prominent competitors—Haensel and Jones, The Metropolitan Musical Bureau, Evans and Salter, and the American Opera Company—to form Columbia Concerts Corporation. The Columbia Broadcasting System bought a half interest and Judson became president of the new organization. "The consolidation of these bureaus," Judson said at that time, "is a logical step on the part of concert managers to provide better music and more music for the public. There is no question about the fact that the public at large is interested in fine music and what has now been done will go far toward meeting the popular desire to hear and see the world's best musical artists, as well as developing the necessary talent and in other respects encouraging the popular appreciation of music as an art."

With a larger service made possible by the greater influence of Columbia Concerts Corporation Judson was able, also in 1930, to grasp the opportunity offered by Community Concert Service to accomplish his ambition of bringing good music not only to cities but to small towns. In December 1927, Ward French, a mid-western concert manager, had established Community Concert Service to promote his plan for underwriting concerts by means of prepaid subscriptions in towns eager for good music but unable to assume the financial risk of engaging high-salaried artists and unwilling to accept just anyone who would take a low fee. Believing in the practicality of the idea, Judson invited French to join Columbia Concerts in return for financial backing. The offer was accepted, and Judson, making Community Concert Service a subsidiary of Columbia Concerts Corporation (with the same administrators and board of directors), advanced nearly a quarter of a million dollars to put into operation the system by which towns throughout America may hear good music. Today this system makes it possible for towns to select each season from Community's lists the finest artists obtainable with the money raised and to present them to a new music public in a program on which the selections and not the visiting performers are the stellar attractions. Incidentally, the revocation of censorship surrounding atomic bomb activities was necessary to explain to Judson the origin of one such audience in

Richland, Washington. The town, now revealed as one of the chief manufacturing centers for the bomb, had come to be considered "the mystery town in music circles, because Community Concerts Service . . . was baffled by the sudden mushrooming of a large, receptive, and discriminative audience, and because artists scheduled to perform there had to sign a sworn statement agreeing not to talk of anything they had heard or seen in Richland."

Because the plan was instituted to benefit small-town music lovers, Judson says he regards the money he advanced in 1930 as a loan not to the communities but collectively to his artist clients. It is the artists, therefore, who are gradually decreasing the debt by paying a 20 per cent commission to Columbia Concerts on each engagement. A 1945 estimate of the plan's success states that Community Concert Service "has brought to nearly 400 cities and towns in the United States and Canada [none of which had previously known successful concert seasons] series of concerts aggregating 1,500 yearly artist engagements." And Judson himself reports that the artists are satisfied with the arrangement because they are reaping the benefits of added engagements. Today Judson's Columbia Concerts Corporation has only one large rival, NBC Artists Service, with which, in the small community sphere, it does not compete, but shares the field.

During these years Judson was still manager of both the New York Philharmonic-Symphony Orchestra and the Philadelphia Orchestra. Having been associated with the former since the season of 1914-15, he was not to relinquish control until 1935, when he resigned as manager, declining, however, to satisfy the press as to the reasons for his action. He was to be connected with the Philharmonic until 1943. A five-year period as advisory manager of the Cincinnati Symphony Orchestra made him at one time active in the concerns of three orchestras in addition to his concert management and radio work. While with the Philadelphia Orchestra Judson founded the Robin Hood Dell Concerts, and had brought the New York Philharmonic to play at the popular priced summer concerts in Lewisohn Stadium. His latest project extends the Community Service arrangement, with more than a hundred concerts scheduled in its first season, to Latin America, and, "awaits only the end of the war to embrace the five continents in a democratic exchange of American and foreign artists and audiences."

The major function of Columbia Concerts Judson deems to be the awakening of public interest in good music, the discovery of talent to promote this interest, and the "widest and most effective" distribution of this talent to the concert halls and radio auditoriums of the nation. He declares that this viewpoint, far from modifying his standards for performers, has resulted in a stiffening of them. For a successful musical career he cites three basic qualifications: technical mastery and an increasing repertory, individuality of interpretation, and personality. Because it takes fortitude to face a series of public appearances, life in hotel rooms and nights on Pullmans, constant change of circumstance and sur-

roundings, health, too, is an important consideration in Judson's estimate of a musician's possibilities. Relatively few musical amateurs meet his requirements, it is reported. Out of the thousands of candidates he interviews, he follows up only five or ten a year. For one thing, he says, too few people are willing to make an inventory of their assets as well as their desires. A "top genius," he maintains, comes along only after long and elaborate preparation. For instance, it took him ten years to make a public success of one musician whose talent he had recognized as worthy of promotion. Nor have critics much to do with an artist's success or failure, he adds, citing the example of Vladimir Horowitz's [43] New York debut, at which the critics were cool but the public clamored for more. Besides Horowitz, Judson has presented to American audiences for the first time José Iturbi [43], Bidu Sayao [42], John Barbirolli [40], Josef Szigeti [40], and others; and he has managed, among others, many of them personally, Jascha Heifetz [44], Lucrezia Bori, Nelson Eddy [43], Todd Duncan [42], Robert Casadesus [45], and Rudolph Serkin [40].

Judson, who holds an honorary Doctor of Music degree bestowed upon him in 1931 and who was elected an officer of the French Academy of Fine Arts in 1920, is an outdoor man as well as something of a scholar. He owns a summer place, Camp White Bear, on an island in Lake Timagami in northern Ontario, from which long canoe trips through the Canadian north woods are a favorite recreation. While he owns a home in the town of White Plains, New York, he is in 1945 landscaping a site for a future home in the neighboring town of Purchase, doing much of the manual work himself. But he is also an omnivorous reader, taking special interest in Elizabethan literature, and "his unique office with a high antique desk (at which he works standing up), with its steel engravings, comfortable chairs, shelves of books, antique furniture, and old pewter and Sheffield" reflects this side of his nature. Physically, he has been described as "a huge man, with a massive head, a rectangular, ruddy face, and great hands that have the strength of a lumberjack [he likes to chop wood] and the sensitivity of a violinist." On November 24, 1904, in Dayton he was married to Edna H. Bench, from whom he was subsequently divorced. His second marriage to Daphne Duquette of Montreal, Canada, took place in June 1941. He has one son, Francis Edward, by his first marriage.

References

N Y Post Mag p29 D 20 '44 por
Time 33:38-9 F 6 '39 por
Thompson, O. ed. International Cyclopedia of Music and Musicians (1943)
Who's Who in America, 1944-45
Who's Who in New York, 1938

KAHN, ELY JACQUES June 1, 1884-
Architect; designer

Address: b. 2 Park Ave., New York City; h. 970 Park Ave., New York City

The architect Ely Jacques Kahn is more than an architect of homes and buildings; he is a

ELY JACQUES KAHN

designer as well, for he feels that interior
decoration is an essential part of architecture.
He is interested in discovering new sources
of design and function through a study of
new materials and their adaptability to modern
usage, and he urges that craft schools give
students more of an opportunity to experiment
with new forms.

Ely Jacques Kahn was born June 1, 1884, in
New York, where he still lives. His parents
were Eugenie (Maximilian) Kahn, and Jacques
Kahn, a glass manufacturer who had come to
America in 1868 from the Austrian Tyrol.
Ely received his B.A. degree from Columbia
University in 1903 at the age of nineteen, and
a B.Arch. in 1907. Shortly afterward he went
abroad, there to continue his architectural
training in Paris. He studied painting and
decoration as well, and in 1911 the young
American won an award in painting given by
the Salon des Artistes Français. The following year he was graduated from the Ecole des
Beaux Arts with a diploma from the French
Government and the Prix Labarre.

Young Kahn began his career by working
for several years in the offices of well known
architects in Paris and New York. For a
part of this time, in 1915, he applied his
knowledge to the teaching field, as professor
of design at Cornell University. In 1917 he
became a member of the firm of Buchman and
Kahn, and twelve years later he established
his own office. Concurrent and subsequent
activities of Kahn's indicate that his interests
have extended outside the immediate field of
architecture, to interior decoration and to other
forms of the industrial and decorative arts.
From 1929 to 1934 he was on the staff of the
Metropolitan Museum Committee for Decorative Art Exhibitions, and he has lectured at
the museum on architecture. He is chairman
of the advisory commission of the School of
Industrial Design in New York and has
been vice-president of the National Sculpture
Society. In 1931 he was made director of the
department of architecture of the Beaux Arts

Institute of Design; the next year he was
made chief of the section of industrial arts
for the Chicago Centennial Fair of 1933.

Through his writing and his work Kahn
became known for his concern with the future
of American architecture and design. He felt
that an artist must combine a sense of beauty
with an appreciation of the functional aspects
of art; he emphasized a consideration of new
materials; and urged that designers break
away from outmoded conventions and a reliance European forms. The standard of design among students was low, he observed in
1932. He attacked the trivial brilliancy of
some "paper architecture," and said that
modern architecture must be a rational interpretation of new problems—simple, direct, and
honest.

In 1933 the New York architect was given
a ten-thousand-dollar grant by the Carnegie
Corporation to conduct an international survey
of industrial art progress and to compare American methods with those of other countries.
As a representative of the American Institute
of Architects, he was charged with finding the
answers to certain questions: Are American
craft schools doing their jobs in line with the
requirements of our mechanized civilization?
Are the studios producing works in metal,
glass, leather, and the like, imitating Europe
or Colonial America, or are they really designing? Are museums the morgues of salvaged
remnants, or are they stimulating the artist
and the public with interestingly staged shows?

The search for the answers took the architect around the world from east to west
through Hawaii, Japan, Korea, Manchuria,
China, the Celebes, the Philippines, Bali, Java,
Singapore, the Straits Settlements, Indo-China,
Cambodia, Siam, Burma, India, Ceylon, Egypt,
Italy and the rest of Europe, and then schools,
factories, and shops in the United States. The
results are in *Design in Art and Industry*
published in 1935. Kahn, the book revealed,
was dissatisfied with American craft schools.
He saw in them an academic inertia which he
had not found in the Orient. American schools,
he declared were not keeping up with the increasingly wide range of materials. Students
were taught traditional designs and experimented too little with new forms. He had
been able to find little genuine originality,
little freedom from outworn styles—a condition which he felt was better under the
apprentice system in Asia and Europe. The
public, however, was becoming aware of the
uses of glass, plastics, and rayon fabrics as a
result of large exhibitions.

American architectural schools, Kahn wrote
then, were guilty of imparting too much de-
rivative theory, which did nothing to help put
the student in contact with the great demand
for industrial designers. Technical schools, on
the other hand, tended to concentrate on machine technique and to encourage copying old
patterns instead of originating new designs.
Students in America, he said, must have more
practical experience. The architect must be a
designer as well, and must work in fields of
general design; he must try to improve public
taste, to establish high principles and live up
to them. He must have a knowledge of how
design develops from raw materials. The pub-

lic, in turn, must demand function and beauty in its buildings and in everything that is in them. Only by ridding itself of its present apathy can America expect to develop an art that is distinctive, vital, functional, and beautiful in the highest sense, and peculiarly her own.

"Design," Kahn has written, "is the basic element of all intellectual processes: music, drama, painting, architecture, mathematics, and engineering or science . . . an idea is a skeleton, the dynamic statement of which depends on amplification by a system of coordinated elements. This process of development is termed design." He sees buildings as units with carefully integrated parts. Architecture, he feels, unquestionably involves interior decoration. As a designer himself, Kahn is found by critics to be resourceful, striving always to express the essential character of his materials and to combine them for richness of texture and rhythm. He repeatedly urges decorators to study and make use of all available materials. His own interiors reveal an elaborate interplay of wood, glass, metal, stone, fabrics, tiling, and whatever else he chooses to include. The use of the grain in woods and the use of color, too, often play an important part in his interiors. In the homes he designs he attempts to eliminate waste space, to have as little complexity as possible. In designing office buildings he works on the principle that they must fulfill their intended purpose and be sound financial projects. He makes the most of lighting possibilities, and has advised whenever feasible the use of parking lots on either side of an office building to take advantage of the additional light and air—a plan which he feels would bring higher rents for otherwise dim bottom floors. For New York Kahn has designed such familiar buildings as the Jay Thorpe and Bonwit Teller stores, International Telephone and Telegraph, the Hospital for Joint Diseases, the Yardley Shop at Rockefeller Center, the Squibb Building, and the Continental Building. For the New York World's Fair he designed the Marine Building and the Ballantine Restaurant.

Aside from his book, the architect has written articles for *The Encyclopædia Britannica* and for several magazines, some of them outside the field of art and architecture. In 1928 and again in 1931 he wrote of the importance of coincident financing and planning. He stressed, too, the need for flexibility of plan in designing a new building. In a letter to the *New Republic* in 1931 he tried to arouse the New York public to investigate five aspects of a broad architectural program: housing, freight, traffic, park and playground, parking and vehicles. His writing, it is said, is characterized by rare energy, imagination, and sound judgment. He foresees problems and solutions which the public is sometimes slow to recognize. In 1935 Arthur Tappan North wrote of Kahn, "It is interesting to note the dates attached to the excerpts from the writings of Ely Jacques Kahn and relate them to the then current ideas and practices. Many of his ideas, as then expressed, are now accepted as correct and for that reason are a part of the true record of architectural developments." "Experiment is the soul of a civilized being,"

Kahn had said in 1930. (He does believe, however, that a genuine interest in archaic forms can help in the realization of natural artistic qualities.)

The architect has been president of the Peter Minuit Corporation, treasurer of Eray Securities Corporation, director of the Park Place Corporation, chairman of the board of the Beaux Arts Institute of Design, member of the Architectural League of New York, the Bund Deutscher Architekten of Berlin, and the Société des Architectes Diplômes par le Gouvernement Français, and Fellow of the A.I.A., and he was president of the Municipal Art Society (1942-45).

At present Kahn is an architect for Government housing projects. His interests range from the minutiae of decoration to Persian pottery, carpets, indirect lighting, comprehensive city planning, and the economics of skyscrapers, and he reads widely in English, French, and German literature. He is described as amiable and tolerant of the views of others, forthright and unaffected. He was married to Beatrice Sulzberger in November 1939. (His first wife, to whom he was married in 1913, was Elsie Plaut.) He has three children, Ely Jacques, Olivia, and Joan Plaut. His non-architectural memberships include the Sunningdale Country Club, the Iranian Institute, and the American Association for the Advancement of Science.

References

Ely Jacques Kahn (McGraw-Hill, 1931)
National Cyclopædia of American Biography Current vol D p160
Who's Who in America, 1944-45
Who's Who in New York (1938)

KANDINSKY, WASSILY (kŭn-dyēn'skû-ĭ vŭ-syē'lyû-ĭ) 1866—Dec. 17, 1944 Internationally known dean of non-objective painters; associated with the Moscow Academy and was director of the Museum of Pictorial Culture in Moscow; assisted in the establishment of museums in various parts of Russia and founded the Russian Academy of Artistic Sciences in 1921; worked in Paris after 1934.

Obituary

N Y Times p21 D 19 '44 por

KAN-IN, PRINCE KOTOHITO 1865(?) —May 21, 1945 Japanese field marshal and member of the Privy Council; former Chief of the Army General Staff (1931-40); served as president of the Japan-France Institute and the Japan-Russia Society.

Obituary

N Y Times p19 My 21 '45 por

KECK, GEORGE FRED May 17, 1895- Architect

Address: b. 612 N. Michigan Ave., Chicago; h. 5551 University Ave., Chicago

"The solar house can be counted on as a common denominator" in postwar home construction. Such is the considered opinion of three men who "have probably looked at more house plans than any other trio in the United

Hedrich-Blessing Studio

GEORGE FRED KECK

States," the editors of *Architectural Forum,
Architectural Record,* and *Pencil Points.*
Among the leaders of this development is
George Fred Keck, the creator of the original
solar house, today rated among the top ten
architects in the United States, whose work
for many years has been the planning of homes
orientated to the climate on solar principles and
to the occupants from the point of view of
sociological data.

George Fred Keck, whose prenames are the
reverse of those of his father, Fred George
Keck, was born in Watertown, Wisconsin, on
May 17, 1895. His mother, Amalia (Henze)
Keck, besides raising a large family, found
time to paint, and to teach him something of
that art before he was ten years old. The boy,
who was also handy with tools, was already
adept at drawing, but it was not until a number
of years later that he decided to become an
architect. In the meantime, he attended elementary and high school in Watertown. When
he enrolled at the University of Wisconsin he
chose a civil engineering course because he was
still undecided as to his career. A year later,
however, having made up his mind, he transferred to the University of Illinois because
Wisconsin had no school of architecture. When
the United States entered the First World War,
Keck became a lieutenant in the Coast Artillery
and served a year in France. Returning to the
University of Illinois afterward, he received
his B.S. in architectural engineering in 1920.

Until 1922 young Keck worked for William
Pruyn and then for D. H. Burnham, Chicago
architects. During the academic year 1923-24
he taught architectural design at his alma
mater, the University of Illinois. For the remainder of 1924 he and Mrs. Keck toured
England, studying its architecture. Upon the
Kecks' return to America the architect joined
the firm of Schmidt, Garden and Ernesen of
Chicago.

In 1926 Keck established his own architectural office, and he dates from this year the

dominant feature of his work—the application
to home architecture of the newest ideas and
inventions in building and decorating materials
to produce a more livable house. "An out-and-
out modernist"—as the *Architectural Forum*
characterizes him—Keck says, "Get rid of emotion and tradition and get to the facts and
needs of contemporary construction, and you
get good results." For the most part Keck has
specialized in single-family dwellings, although
he has designed apartment houses and commercial buildings. While most of these were cus-
tom-built, shortly before the war he was the
principal architect of a group of thirty solar
homes in Glenview, Illinois, built by a Chicago
firm on a built-for-sale basis. Recently he
has designed prefabricated solar homes for
erection by Green's Ready-Built Homes of
Rockford, Illinois. He has also acted as consultant to manufacturers in the development of
new building materials, and from 1940 to 1944
he was head of the department of architecture
of the Chicago School of Design.

Keck's rise to prominence is connected with
the Chicago Century of Progress Fair of 1933-
34 for two reasons: he was the architect of
the House of Tomorrow and of the Crystal
House; and it was there that he discovered
the solar principle with which his name has
since been linked. Because the House of Tomorrow was an exhibition house—"designed to
demonstrate mechanical equipment and new
building materials that are now on the market,"
a descriptive Chicago Fair brochure states—
"the chief concern of the architect was not to
give a specific form to his building, but rather
to find a solution to the many and varied new
requirements of a residence in a simple and
direct manner." The solution was entirely
functional and thoroughly modern. Keck built
the house literally as well as conceptually
around an air conditioning system which made
glass walls possible by eliminating the need
for window ventilation and which, together with
utility rooms, heating facilities, and the stairway, was placed in the central portion. The
unusual duodecagonal shape, to quote the brochure again, "resulted from the number and
sizes of the rooms required on the different
floors and from the fact that the glass walls
on each of these twelve sides would be of a
size that could be installed efficiently." And
the use of glass on all outside walls was made
possible by employing "store-front construction and a steel frame to carry floor and roof
loads." In the Crystal House this steel and
glass construction was carried out on a rectangular frame.

Keck's discovery of the solar principle was
an accident: One very cold day during the
construction of the House of Tomorrow, Keck
arrived at the scene to find the workmen indoors—behind the glass walls—in shirt sleeves
and perspiring, although the furnace had been
turned off for hours. Realizing the importance
of what he saw to housing improvement, Keck
thereupon set out to capture solar heat for
architectural purposes. Consultation with the
local weather bureau gave him the answer:
overhanging roof construction—mathematically
calculated in relation to the inclination of the
sun's beams throughout the year—which extends far enough to shade the house from the
almost direct rays of the summer sun high in

the heavens but not far enough to prevent the slanting rays of the winter sun from striking the windows beneath. To obtain maximum benefit, the house is orientated in the direction of the source of sunlight. Living areas of the solar house always face south, and the southern walls, almost entirely of glass, are made of thermopane, "the double plate glass pane with a metal-sealed dehydrated air space [an insulation against cold] in between." "Adjacent panels of adjustable louvers that claim the advantage of admitting air while keeping out the elements" provide the necessary ventilation. Service units (kitchen, pantry, etc.) are then placed on the north side of the house and furnished only with small windows so that they may serve as buffers against cold and storm. For added coolness in summer the roof is of flat construction and covered with a thin sheet of water in order to utilize the natural process of cooling, evaporation. Artificial winter heat is provided by conduits imbedded in the floor and walls. The results of this construction are better lighting and comfortable temperatures all year round, and a saving in fuel and light bills.

Design of the houses is extremely flexible. Keck has built solar houses in rectangular, crescent, or asymmetric shape, has used flat roof construction of one or several levels, and has solved the problem of privacy by careful orientation on the lot combined with the use of hedges and gardens or by the location of the north façade of the dwelling on the street side. His materials have been wood, glass and stone or brick for the exterior and a variety of new products, some soundproofed, for the interior. Some houses have been prefabricated. The houses themselves he designs around a basic unit, composed of a work area, a rest area, and a play area, generally of equal size, to correspond to the three divisions of the normal day. Living quarters may be increased in size at any time by the addition of transitional rooms or areas which are usually designed to be easily converted, for example, from nursery to study or for other use. Sliding walls between rooms supply additional flexibility.

Keck proceeds from the assumption that each individual is entitled to privacy and from the sociologic tenets that adults have fixed habits, that children today have more independence than formerly, that adolescents need space in which to entertain, that college students and young married couples often live with their families. To this architect, sociological and psychological considerations are as important in planning and improving housing as are mechanical considerations. "Biologically, the family unit does not change," he says. "But we Americans have progressed least up to now in our ability to provide proper living quarters for the family unit. The loose talk one hears about the disintegration of family life can quite properly be laid to the fact that our houses do not fit today's living conditions, and because they do not fit, there is a tendency to get away from them upon any provocation, and unless they soon begin to fit, disintegration will indeed occur. . . .More and more, the invention of accessories to the house more firmly establish the single-family unit; improvements in transportation, radio, television, airplane, all make it possible to bring the world and its goings-on to the house wherever it is situated.

All we have to do is design the house to take it."

Keck is six feet tall, weighs one hundred and sixty-eight pounds, and has brown eyes and graying hair. He still likes to paint, in water colors. In November 1921 he was married to Lucile S. Liebermann, whose family had lived across the street from his in Watertown. Mrs. Keck since 1932 has been librarian of the Joint Reference Library in Chicago. The Kecks now live in that city, in a house illustrating the architect's planning principles.

Reference

Coronet 8:106-14 il S '40

KELLEY, EDGAR STILLMAN 1857— Nov. 12, 1944 Dean of American composers; a scholarly musician who received many honors for his works, the best known of which were the *Gulliver* and *New England* symphonies, the orchestral suite, *Alice in Wonderland*, the choral work *The Sacred Choruses*, and the incidental music to the play *Ben Hur*.

Obituary

N Y Times p19 N 13 '44 por

KELLY, GENE Aug. 23, 1912- Dancer; actor, choreographer

Address: b. c/o Metro-Goldwyn-Mayer, Culver City, Calif.

An immediate hit in his first movie role in 1942, Gene Kelly has received critical approval since then as a choreographer, a dramatic actor, and a singer. But he usually is identified as a dancer "just a bit better than anyone else": Bob Hope '41 has quipped, "Every time Gene Kelly dances, Fred Astaire '45 starts counting his money."

Born in Pittsburgh, Pennsylvania, on August 23, 1912, Eugene Joseph Kelly is one of five children of Catholic parents. His Canadian-born father, James Patrick Kelly, was an executive with the Columbia Gramaphone Company; his mother, Harriet Kelly, had been on the stage as a young girl and after her marriage had continued her theatrical career with a Pittsburgh stock company. As a child Gene was sent to dancing school, much to his boyish chagrin. He attended St. Raphael's grammar school and Peabody High School, where he was a star halfback and played on the basketball and hockey teams. While in high school he also continued his dancing lessons and acted in school plays.

After his graduation from Peabody he entered Pennsylvania State College, but when the depression affected the family finances the student returned home. He found a job teaching gymnastics at Camp Porter, a YMCA camp near Pittsburgh. The following year he resumed his education, this time at the University of Pittsburgh, where he majored in journalism. Working his way through college for Kelly meant taking jobs as ditchdigger, concrete mixer, and carpenter's helper. Meanwhile, he continued to practice dance steps with his two brothers and two sisters. When brother Fred discovered that they could obtain engagements dancing in near-by night clubs, he and Gene turned to entertaining. "We made up a couple of jokes, stole a lot more, and paired up

GENE KELLY

as a team," Kelly says. Besides cafe appearances, the Kelly brothers won many amateur contests and thus helped to sustain the family income in the lean depression years.

Kelly's theatrical talent was well known on the university campus, for the student took part in the annual Cap and Gown shows, directing the production in his senior year. When his college friends became interested in his dancing, he offered to teach his terpsichorean art for fifty cents an hour. Soon the Kelly cellar was turned into a dancing school, and when that became crowded the family rented a hall and opened the Gene Kelly Studios of the Dance. (Meanwhile, Kelly was graduated from the university in 1933.) Directed by Mrs. Kelly, the dancing school was so successful that a second one was opened in Johnstown, where Kelly also taught tap and ballet. During the summers the instructor went to Chicago to attend the meetings of the Dancing Masters Association. In Chicago Kelly studied the dance, and now claims to have read every book on the ballet in the Chicago Public Library—including those in French. When his funds became low after such trips he took night club jobs, dancing and performing what he describes as "a beautifully corny master-of-ceremonies act." The Kelly schools made profits, but in a few years their owner decided to seek greener pastures in New York.

Leaving the schools in charge of his family, Kelly tried Broadway in 1938 and quickly won a small dancing part in *Leave It to Me,* in which Mary Martin [44] blossomed out with "My Heart Belongs to Daddy." Then followed a dancing and singing role in the Nancy Hamilton show *One for the Money,* which opened in February 1939. After a season of summer stock at Westport, Connecticut, Kelly won a dancing and acting part in the Theatre Guild-Eddie Dowling production of William Saroyan's [40] *The Time of Your Life.* The Pulitzer prize-winning play, for which Kelly staged his own dances, opened in the fall of 1939 and ran for twenty-two weeks. Then came another

period in summer stock before Kelly became dance director for Billy Rose's [40] Diamond Horseshoe. There he met Betsy Blair, a young chorus girl, to whom he was married, on September 22, 1941. (The Kellys now have a daughter, Kerry.)

Kelly's big chance in the theater came in late 1940, when he opened in the title role of *Pal Joey,* George Abbott's [40] production of the John O'Hara [41] stories. Playing opposite Vivienne Segal as the "heel-hero" of the musical comedy, Kelly says this part received laudatory criticisms. In a column devoted to a discussion of "Pal Kelly," John Martin (New York *Times,* June 8, 1941) wrote that in the play dancing and character were "far more closely united than in the majority of ballets." Martin pronounced the young leading man's work exceptional: "He is not only glib-footed, but he has a feeling for comment and content that both give his dancing personal distinction and raises it several notches as a theater art." That critic correctly predicted a Hollywood summons for the Broadwayite. But before he went west, Kelly turned to dance direction again, for another Abbott production, *Best Foot Forward,* which opened in October 1941. An outstanding musical success of that season, the show received good notices and Kelly's dance routines were commended. Meanwhile, the actor had been signed for films by David O. Selznick [41] as a result of his performance in *Pal Joey.* Thus he and Mrs. Kelly headed for California by way of Mexico, but once in the film capital, they found that Kelly's contract had been sold to MGM.

Kelly made his film debut in *For Me and My Gal* (1942) with Judy Garland [41] and George Murphy, in a role reminiscent of *Pal Joey.* According to *Newsweek,* he "progresses from heel to hero with a persuasiveness that scores a scoop for MGM's talent scouts." But Bosley Crowther in the New York *Times* declared that Kelly had been "pressed a bit too far in his first film role." Determined to avoid being typed as a dancer in motion pictures, Kelly next played a smaller dramatic part in *Pilot Number Five* (1943). This was followed by two musicals, *Du Barry Was a Lady* (1943) and *Thousands Cheer* (1943). His next picture again offered Kelly a dramatic role, as a Parisian taxi driver in *The Cross of Lorraine* (1943). Dealing with the tragedy of war prisoners under the Nazis, the film was well received and Kelly's performance was considered "moving."

Columbia Pictures then borrowed him for their Technicolor spectacle *Cover Girl* (1944), co-starring Rita Hayworth, for which Kelly devised his own dances. Termed by *Time* Magazine "the best cinemusical the year had produced, and one of the best in years," *Cover Girl* won high praise for Kelly. "Few cinemactors can match his reticence, exact evocativeness, and sincerity, or carry such acting abilities into dancing and singing," said one critic. Singled out for special attention was the "alter ego" dance. A New York *Herald Tribune* writer declared, "The human race has been having trouble with its conscience since time immemorial. It remained for Gene Kelly, however, to get his still, small voice out into the open and—dance with it." Equally enthusiastic was the *Times* critic, who said that "for once a dance on the screen is not merely a specialty but actually develops character and advances plot." This dance with his shadow, used by Kelly to express a mental struggle, entailed numerous technical difficulties in sound, photography, and timing, for the two Kellys threaten each other, pursue each other up and down a flight of stairs, leap over each other's heads— all in perfect rhythm and synchronization. Labeled "a psychic tour de force," it drew the following comment from the *Hollywood Reporter*: "Nothing finer in the way of a dance routine has ever been filmed."

Kelly was again cast in a dramatic role in *Christmas Holiday*, his next screen vehicle, an adaptation of Somerset Maugham's novel. The film was not too well received, and estimates of Kelly's performance varied. As Deanna Durbin's [41] reprobate husband, he "never ventures a tap," which vexed John T. McManus of *PM*, while the *Times*'s Crowther commented on Kelly's "breezy, attractive style, which is thoroughly confusing, considering the character that he is supposed to be." However, Alton Cook wrote in the New York *World-Telegram* that Kelly performed "superbly," while in the New York *Sun* Eileen Creelman complained that Kelly's part was "much too small." With Frank Sinatra [43] and Kathryn Grayson, Kelly next starred in the hit musical *Anchors Aweigh* (1944), for which he was also dance director. Cast as a sailor in the Technicolor romantic comedy, he tangoed with the leading lady, did a Mexican number with a seven-year-old child, a sailor routine with Sinatra, danced with an animated cartoon figure, and had a solo Spanish dance. His dancing, comedy talent, and even his singing were praised, and to one critic his performance was "an absolute climax to the brilliant start he had made on a career of dancing for the movies."

After seven months in the sailor role on the MGM lot Kelly entered the Navy in November 1944, taking his basic training in San Diego. A lieutenant (junior grade), near the end of 1945 he was stationed in Washington, D.C., in the Naval Photographic Science Laboratory. According to Kyle Crichton in *Collier's* (May 19, 1945), Kelly "has plans for revolutionizing dance treatments in the films" upon his return to Hollywood, and can experiment with them under his three-way contract as actor, director, and producer. For the forthcoming film *Ziegfeld Follies*, completed in 1945, Kelly danced for the first time with Fred Astaire. Their number is a double tap sequence to George and Ira Gershwin's "The Babbitt and the Bromide," written originally for Astaire and his sister Adele in *Funny Face*.

The dancing star has made several radio appearances, on the Frank Sinatra and Bing Crosby [41] programs. Known as a friendly, fun-loving person, Kelly is said to have "an American baseball personality." The brown-eyed, black-haired actor is five feet nine inches tall and weighs one hundred and fifty pounds. As evidenced by the many books in his home, Kelly's reading taste runs to modern biography, history, and economics. He is interested in politics and government and actively supported Franklin D. Roosevelt [42] in the 1944 campaign. A member of the wartime Hollywood Victory Committee, Kelly reported on the need for regular hospital entertainment (after a pioneer-ing Army hospital tour) and thus stimulated the organization of such a unit. In his concern for economic security for all, tolerance, and racial understanding, Gene Kelly believes that the actor should play his part as a citizen as well as a performer.

References

Collier's 115:20+ My 19 '45 por
N Y Herald Tribune VI p4 F 2 '41 por
N Y Post Mag p5 Ag 11 '45 por
N Y Times IX p3 Mr 2 '41
Photoplay 22:36-7+ My '43 pors; 24:54-
  6+ F '44 pors; 25:36+ Je '44 pors

KELLY, JOE May 31, 1901- Radio entertainer and script writer

Address: b. c/o Louis G. Cowan & Co., 8 S. Michigan Ave., Chicago; h. 4945 Washington Blvd., Chicago

Joe Kelly, quiz master of the *Quiz Kids* radio program since June 1940, is one of the most publicized members of the radio profession. Unlike others in the field, Kelly has risen to his present position not because of any formal educational qualifications, but because of his cheerful disposition, tact, and alertness in his conducting of the quiz program. According to Kelly, who started from "scratch," he now has twenty million listeners "waiting for him to go out on a limb and cut it off after him." To be sure, he has all the answers written on cards, but, as John Lear wrote in the *Saturday Evening Post*, "Few men since Solomon have braved so many confusions of the human mind. . . .Solomon had time to think. . . .Joe has to call them while they are still in the air. . . .He must say 'Right' or 'Wrong' before the next clock tick."

By birth, Joseph William Kelly is a Hoosier —he was born in Crawfordsville, Indiana, on May 31, 1901. His father, William Joseph Kelly, a brewery truck driver, died when eight-year-old Joe was about to enter the fourth grade at school. His mother, May Henrietta (Kepler) Kelly, an amateur poetess, was left without adequate means and was obliged to turn her son's fine soprano to the aid of the family exchequer. Joe was only six when he had won an amateur contest in an Indianapolis theater; then, at the age of eight he was engaged to sing for three dollars a night in the Crawfordsville Music Hall. It proved a windfall for the Kelly family when shortly afterward Edward Doyle, a leading stock-company manager, offered him fifty dollars a week as a featured member of his show. Joe quit school at once and joined the Doyle show at Huntington, Indiana, billed as "Master Joe Kelly, the Irish Nightingale."

The boy lived in dingy small-town hotels for the next three years, "with no one to comb his hair or patch his pants. But he made his own money—barrels of it, for a kid." He learned practical arithmetic by paying his hotel bills, acquired an ability to express himself by writing letters home to his mother, and, with the aid of a ten-cent-store dictionary, read stories of Horatio Alger boys, such as *Tom, the Bootblack, or, a Western Boy's Success;* and *Jed, the Poorhouse Boy, or, From Poverty to Title.* One day, Kelly says, he received word while on tour that his mother

C. M. Frank Studio

JOE KELLY

was dying. He hurried home, arriving in time to sing for her in the blue and white suit he wore in the show.

Joe arrived at the peak of his youthful singing career when, at the age of eleven, he left the Doyle show to join Neil O'Brien's minstrels at seventy-five dollars a week. He was advertised as the youngest minstrel in America, and had a sixteen-piece orchestra to support him, while, arrayed in a splendid purple satin suit, he lilted popular melodies. One woeful day two years later the boy's soprano broke suddenly in the middle of high C. It was then that he stepped from the world of footlights into the humdrum of everyday life, becoming an office boy in Indianapolis for the Singer Sewing Machine Company. The change was disconcerting, for although O'Brien's minstrels had some of the most famous names on its payroll—Lasses White, Bert Swor, Black-Face Eddie Ross, and Carol Norman, the Creole Fashion Plate—it was Joe who rode in the daily parade in a carriage drawn by two white horses, while everyone else in the company walked.

But young Kelly, it appears, was not the sort of person to become easily discouraged. Before long he was utilizing his noon hours to absorb some knowledge of piano playing. At the "five-and-ten" he listened to popular numbers being played in the sheet-music department. Thus inspired, although he couldn't read a note of music, he organized his own dance band, which he named Kelly's Klowns, and proceeded to conduct with evident success. At the age of seventeen he returned to the stage with the John D. Winninger Players, and later joined the Rex Players, an English troupe playing permanent stock in Kingston, Ontario. It was there that he fell in love with pretty Mary James (secretary of the Rex Company's office), to whom he was married on St. Patrick's Day, 1923, with the promise that he would quit show business forever.

When the Kellys arrived in Benton Harbor, Michigan, Lear relates, they had only thirty cents between them. As the mainspring of Kelly's life was music, it was not surprising, after they had pawned Joe's saxaphone and a ring of Mary's to set up housekeeping, that he first tried selling pianos and Victrolas. This did not develop into a very remunerative undertaking, for it was only in the evening that he could call on the farmers in the neighborhood. This meant stumbling about in the dark, encountering watch dogs and, on one occasion, a shotgun. Furthermore, writes Lear, "after the farmers heard him play their old pianos, they didn't think new ones could be half as good." In his final efforts to keep his promise to his wife, Kelly ran a railroad warehouse, managed a men's clothing store, and played with a dance orchestra in the evenings.

The radio career that led to the *National Barn Dance* and the *Quiz Kids* had its small beginnings some years ago when Kelly teamed up with Jack Holden in a comedy singing act, *The Two Lunatics of the Air*, broadcasting from Battle Creek, Michigan. They received twelve dollars a week, plus all the milk they could drink, from the sponsoring dairy company for six thirty-minute shows a week. Four years later Kelly left the act to join the announcing staff of Chicago's WLS, from which he was subsequently chosen for the role of master of ceremonies for *The National Barn Dance*, a position he has held since that time.

Kelly's much-discussed connection with the juvenile counterpart of *Information Please* began in June 1940. Because of his even disposition and down-to-childhood point of view, he was chosen in preference to any of the twenty-four college professors, news commentators, and quiz experts who had been auditioned. "The youngsters simply 'froze' with everybody else," explained Louis G. Cowan, owner of the *Quiz Kids* program. Kelly is fond of children (he has a son of his own, Joe, Jr., now in the Army), and his admiration for the Kids is returned by them. His motto is "Treat children as equals and never talk down to them." *PM* says a radio cynic once observed that "the Kids would drive Joe either to drink or encyclopedias." It is recorded that the children had the latter salutary effect—he now has several sets of the reference works in his Chicago apartment.

In his association with his juvenile phenomena Kelly has always been polite, although the effort it takes on occasion is said to cause him moments of acute nervous strain. According to *Cue*, "he was even polite the time one boy asked to sing 'Three Little Fishes,' swam over the dam and downstream for five minutes, and nothing could stop him." His easy laugh and casual jokes often conceal tense moments, as *Cue* has indicated in the following *Quiz Kid* incident:

"The question was: 'Define, respectively, a dodo, a dido, and a dado.' Eight-year-old Gerald Darrow answered confidently, 'A dodo is a prehistoric bird,' and added by way of color, 'I think he has a harsh call.'

"So Mr. Kelly said, 'I don't know about the dodo's harsh call, but otherwise you are O.K.'

"'Not exactly,' protested thirteen-year-old Van Dyke Tiers. 'The dodo is extinct but not prehistoric.'

"'Well,' Mr. Kelly drawled, stalling for time and hunting frantically through his notes. 'I guess there isn't much difference, eh?'

"'Mr. Kelly,' Van Dyke announced firmly, 'I would like to submit to you that all prehistoric animals are extinct, but all extinct animals are not necessarily prehistoric.'"

There was a moment in one of his opening broadcasts with the Quiz Kids that Joe Kelly will not easily forget. It was the day when he asked the question, "Whom might you expect to find on the master's end of the leash if you say each of the following three dogs?" —and then forgot the names of the dogs. There was friction in the studio later that night, and Kelly, who had never been "tossed out of a job in his life," thought that "this was it." But the sponsor of the show said "No" to all negative opinions, declaring that Kelly was at least human with the Kids. The result was that a research staff was hired to dig up all possible answers to future questions; this information was indexed on a set of cards which Kelly could take home with him on Saturdays to study. As a precaution against further endangering his pride and personal dignity, he bought an unabridged *Webster's International Dictionary*. With the help of that, together with his prodigious memory, he is said to have no more trouble in getting the answers down pat.

Working under pressure has proved beneficial to Kelly, for it is said that today in conversation he betrays no sign of limited education. According to Lear, he earns approximately six hundred dollars a week. Like many other untrained musicians, he has written several songs—*Kelly Blues, Lonesome and Grieving, Dear Little Girl, Gold Star Mother o' Mine, Just Ask the Quiz Kids, Jolly Joe's Official Birthday Song,* and *Hats Off to Old Glory.* In addition, he has done a cartoon strip, *Jolly Joe's Pet Pals,* and is a radio script writer. His screen appearances include one full-length feature, *The National Barn Dance* and six short subjects for Paramount, and one short subject with the Kids for the United States Department of Agriculture. He has a citation from the United States Treasury Department for his efforts on behalf of the National Defense Saving Program, and he is the possessor of a Merit Medal from Veterans of Foreign Wars.

Joe Kelly has an optimistic and effervescent personality. He is described as a plump and jolly five-foot-seven-and-a-half, weighing one hundred and seventy-five pounds. His eyes and hair are brown. He is a natty dresser, and his hobbies are collecting autographed photographs of famous people, swimming, golfing, and window shopping. He relishes making "involved" sandwiches and declares that some day he is going to open a chain of sandwich shops.

References

Cue 9:17-18 S 7 '40 por; 11:19 Ap 18 '42 por

PM p23 Ap 8 '42 por

Sat Eve Post 216:12-13+ Jl 8 '44 il pors

KELLY, JOSEPH WILLIAM *See* Kelly, J.

KERN, JEROME (DAVID) Jan. 27, 1885—Nov. 11, 1945 American composer of light operas; considered one of America's "foremost composers of music for the theater and screen"; among his musical scores are: *Showboat, Roberta, The Cat and the Fiddle, Music in the Air, Sunny,* and *Can't Help Singing.* See *Current Biography* 1942 Yearbook.

Obituary

N Y Times p21 N 12 '45 por

KIAM, OMAR (kĭ'ăm) 1894- Fashion designer

Address: b. c/o Ben Reig Company, 498 Seventh Ave., New York City; h. Hotel Plaza, New York City

"One of the most distinguished designers in the wholesale field," Omar Kiam of New York creates what he calls "distinctive clothes for the woman who would rather be smart than

Drawing by Plucer

OMAR KIAM

pretty." His dresses, some of which retail for hundreds of dollars apiece, are noted for their subtle details, and are designed to be worn for at least three years. Despite his use of fur and "fabulously rich" materials and trimmings, he holds that the most beautiful dress can be no more than a background for jewels, furs, and accessories, and that it is the ensembling which determines chic.

Born in 1894 in Monterrey, Mexico, Omar Kiam is the son of Alexander and Sarah (Block) Kiam, who gave him the name of Alexander. His parents, Alsatians by descent and Americans by citizenship, operated a hotel in the Mexican state of Nuevo León. After the death of his mother young Alexander went to live with his grandmother in Houston, Texas, where he began his elementary schooling. He then went East to attend the Riverview Military Academy, a preparatory school in Poughkeepsie, New York. It was here that his given

KIAM, OMAR—*Continued*

name was changed to Omar by his classmates when they studied *The Rubáiyát*.

At the age of eighteen Omar decided that he preferred a chance in the business world to years at college. Having a liking for the theater, he tried to get a position in some phase of theatrical work, but his lack of experience and his immediate need for money forced him to look elsewhere. He compromised by taking a job with a St. Louis millinery firm as a ten-dollar-a-week stock-boy in the baby-cap department. At first young Omar was very unhappy at his work, but he soon discovered the wire-frame hat department next to his own. As a result he spent his leisure moments decorating the frames with ribbons, bows, flowers, straw—all attached at what he considered artistic angles. The company manager was so much impressed with the aspiring designer's talent that he transferred the young man to the pattern department. Shortly thereafter (before the First World War) Kiam became "bored with bonnets," resigned his position, and went to New York City.

Omar Kiam's first job in the metropolis was as a raw skin sorter with Julius Klugman Sons, Inc., a retail fur company. "The work was so smelly," Kiam told a *World-Telegram* reporter, "that I begged for an errand boy's job and finally was given one." The firm was a conservative one, making coats from stock patterns only, and not accepting orders for original designs. One day Kiam stopped a disappointed customer and whispered to her that he would make up the canvas pattern in the style desired. The lady was pleased with the design, and the company thought well of the skill displayed in making it. This was the beginning of Omar Kiam's career in the designing field. Within a short time he was creating suits, gowns, and ensembles, as well as fur coats. During a seasonal slump in business, when women were storing their furs for the summer, he originated the summer fur vogue by putting silver fox on chiffon. When Kiam left this company to open a dress shop under his own name, he owned half of the firm, which by that time had gone into the wholesale fur business

When Omar Kiam "originals" became nationally known, the designer accepted Samuel Goldwyn's [44] invitation to work in Hollywood for United Artists Pictures. According to *Life* Magazine, Kiam created "lavish fur fashions and extravagant dresses" for the motion picture actresses. The designer went to the movie colony in 1935 with the expectation of remaining only a few months, but his designs received so much attention that he remained for five years. His clothes were worn by Janet Gaynor, appearing as a glamorous star for the first time is *A Star is Born* (1937), Loretta Young in *Call of the Wild* (1935), Ruth Chatterton in *Dodsworth* (1937), and Merle Oberon [41] in *Wuthering Heights* (1939). Other cinema favorites gowned by Kiam were Dorothy Lamour, Ann Sothern, Virginia Bruce, and Miriam Hopkins. The designer's talents, however, did not center upon women's clothing—he also won notice by his original "period" costumes in *Clive of India* (1935) and for his draping of Gary Cooper [41] in the *Adventures of Marco Polo* (1938). Although the designer's main purpose was to suit the physical characteristics and the

role of the player he was dressing, and to give special attention to the photographic effects of the colors and fabrics, it was not unusual for women to buy duplicates of these gowns for their personal wardrobes. While in Hollywood several of Kiam's designs were adapted for the popular market: the fur-lined coats which appeared in *Clive of India* are still used for spectator sports; the strapless evening gown designed for Virginia Bruce started the exposed shoulder fad for debutantes; and Cathy's wedding gown in *Wuthering Heights* appeared in the window of an upper Fifth Avenue store and was copied by several manufacturers.

In 1941 Omar Kiam was brought back to New York City to be the chief designer of the Ben Reig Corporation, a wholesale dress manufacturing establishment. Here Kiam creates garments which are neat, but dressy, and employs such transparent fabrics as chiffon or lace to make them rich without distracting from their simplicity. What he calls "cord eyelet" has often been regarded as one of the most important contributions to style within the past few years. "Fashions," the designer has said, "are born of necessity." The cord eyelet was developed during the Second World War when laces were unobtainable for dress trimmings. The designer then proceeded to combine several soft fabrics twisted or wound into a lace lattice work which could be placed on the yoke, peplum, skirt, or sleeves of dresses.

Kiam is happier working in the wholesale dress field in New York than he was when he designed for the Hollywood producers because, he says, "I prefer to and find it more interesting to design for a great many women than just a few." His method for creating a new dress is to drape the fabric on a model who stands before a mirror while an artist sketches it. Kiam then steps back, removes his tortoise shell glasses, and observes the effect.

Kiam, who is a stanch champion of American fashion, was one New York City designer to be disturbed when the WPB set forth L-85 regulation for saving fabrics during the war. He told a New York *Times* reporter that the new curb was drastic and would result in standardized clothing. "It's going to take a good deal of ingenuity to make clothes look unregimented," he said. In the fall of 1945, when the government decided to continue the wartime regulation, Kiam held that there was a "fifth column in fashion" which was trying to defeat the New York style and fashion leadership. "Paris," he said, "had no restriction on fabrics and no price controls. All we ask is to be permitted to go ahead on parallel lines with Paris. . .to silence those tongues that say we have no fashion initiative."

Kiam, who believes that "women dress for women," follows the theory that clothing should have simple lines and elaborate details. He and Elizabeth Hawes [40], American designer, author of *Fashion is Spinach*, once had a dispute on this subject. Omar Kiam declared: "The finer points of dress are for other women; the general effect of the whole ensemble is for men." He feels that women choose tailored dresses because of the hand-sewn seams and hem, feather-stitched button holes—details which only women will notice. On the other hand, Miss Hawes, who uses rich fabrics and unusual colors, stated: "Women dress for men.

In primitive days the primary motive in dressing was for decoration—to attract the opposite sex. . . .Passing centuries have changed the situation only slightly. . . .If a woman dresses to attract the attention of other women, she's only doing that to take away the other woman's man."

The designer has received several awards and honors: the Nieman-Marcus award in 1942; "one of the leading designers" selected by *Life* in 1944; and inclusion on the Al Rosenthal Honor List in 1945. He has had two exhibitions in the Metropolitan Museum of Art in New York, in 1941 and 1945. His designs have appeared with articles at various times in *Vogue, Harper's Bazaar, Photoplay,* the New York *Times,* and several other magazines and newspapers. In the thirties Kiam designed the costumes of the actresses Lynn Fontanne '41 and Ina Claire, and created the gowns for the two famous "dinner" plays, *Dinner at Eight* (1932) and *The Man Who Came to Dinner* (1939).

Bachelor Omar Kiam is six feet tall and massively built. He has hazel eyes, and his brown hair is receding slightly. His two main hobbies are interior decorating and antique furniture collecting. Although Kiam seems to be unconcerned about his own wardrobe, he was chosen by Custom Tailors of America as one of the best-dressed men in 1940. His usual outfit consists of a conservative pin-striped suit, one-color tie, and a blue or white shirt.

References

N Y World-Telegram p19 Ap 16 '40 por; p21 My 16 '45 por

International Motion Picture Almanac, 1943-44

KIRK, ALEXANDER C(OMSTOCK) Nov. 26, 1888- United States Ambassador to Italy

Address: b. c/o Department of State, Washington, D.C.; h. 3308 R St., Washington, D.C.

Diplomacy has been called America's first line of national defense. Hugh Gibson, former United States Ambassador to Belgium and author of *The Road to Foreign Policy* (1944), has said that a trained diplomat defends a nation's interests just as definitely as do its soldiers. One of the career diplomats in the United States Foreign Service is Alexander C. Kirk, a veteran of almost thirty years in that highly specialized profession, who was appointed United States Ambassador to Italy in November 1944. He is the first American ambassador to be sent to Rome since the severance of diplomatic ties between the United States and Italy upon Italy's entrance into the Second World War in 1940 as an ally of Nazi Germany. Ambassador Kirk's appointment not only re-established formal diplomatic relations between Italy and the United States, but confirmed United States recognition of the Government of Premier Ivanoe Bonomi '44 and brought the United States into the difficult problems of Italy and other unstable governments of liberated Europe.

Alexander Comstock Kirk was born in Chicago, Illinois, on November 26, 1888. His father was James Alexander Kirk, a successful soap manufacturer; his mother was Clara

ALEXANDER C. KIRK

(Comstock) Kirk. At the age of nine the boy studied a short time at the Chicago Art Institute. *Life* reports that he made an early business debut as order boy in the family soap factory, a job given with the understanding that he remain incognito. When his identity became known some months later, Kirk returned to his studies and traveling with his mother and young sister, who liked to spend several months each year in Europe. During the summers his reading was guided by an English tutor. Kirk had his first formal schooling at the University of Chicago; after a year he went to Yale, from which he was graduated in 1909. The future diplomat then went to Paris to study at l'Ecole Libre des Sciences Politiques, from which he received a diploma in 1911. He returned to America to study at Harvard Law School, received the degree of LL.B. from Harvard in 1914, and was admitted to the bar in Illinois.

Not caring for law, however, Kirk took the first step in his diplomatic career by becoming private secretary to the Third Assistant Secretary of State in March 1915. Then, after passing the State Department examination, he was assigned in August 1915 to his first post abroad, that of secretary at the American Embassy in Berlin. Following two years in Berlin, Kirk went to the American Legation at The Hague for a year; in 1918-19 in Paris he was attached to the American Committee to Negotiate Peace. Returning to America, he served as assistant to the Secretary of State in Washington from December 1919 to February 1920. From the Capital Kirk was assigned to the American Embassy in Tokyo. The two years in Japan (1920-22) were followed by one year in Peking (now Peiping). When he returned from the Orient, Kirk was sent to Mexico City in 1924 for a year as first secretary of the Embassy there. During the next three years he held various State Department positions in Washington: he was assistant to the Under-Secre-

KIRK, ALEXANDER C.—*Continued*

tary of State, vice-chairman of the Board of Review for Efficiency Ratings, and executive officer for the Department.

Kirk, who had seen the Russian Revolution and the collapse of the German Empire after the First World War, returned to Europe in 1928 to fulfill his assignment as first secretary of the American Embassy at Rome. By this time Mussolini [42] had formed the National Fascist Party and was reaching the height of his power as dictator, reviewing Fascist maneuvers with pomp and ceremony and celebrating the sixth anniversary of the March on Rome. Kirk was made counselor of the American Embassy in Rome in December 1929, and in 1936, the year of Mussolini's conquest of Ethiopia, he became consul general.

A year later Alexander Kirk went to Moscow as consul general, and counselor of the American Embassy there. During this period, when the nineteenth anniversary of the U.S.S.R. was celebrated and the Russians were working out their second Five-Year Plan, Joseph E. Davies [42] arrived in Moscow as American Ambassador to the Soviet Union. In his book *Mission to Moscow* (1941) Davies tells of the tasks for which he was sent to Russia—the negotiation of the Russo-American trade agreement, the settlement of the Kerensky debt question, and the broader matters of cementing friendly relations between the United States and the Soviet Union, and of gathering information on political, industrial, and military affairs. On June 6, 1938, Davies recorded in his diary: "Discussed the debt situation with Henderson [secretary of the Embassy] and Kirk, in an effort to get down to cases as to just what the proposition was and meant." A few days later he wrote: "Immediately following my talk with Stalin [42] I took the matter up with Loy Henderson and Kirk. Fortunately they were both familiar with the whole debt question."

When Ambassador Davies left Russia in June 1938 Kirk was still in Moscow, but in the fall of 1939, when Hugh Wilson [41] was recalled from Berlin, Kirk took his place there. As Chargé d'Affaires he was the chief representative of his Government in Germany for nearly two years—the crucial first years of the Second World War. William L. Shirer [41], who has written about this period in *Berlin Diary* (1941), tells of the meeting ("a fantastic show") in the Reichstag at which Hitler [42] eloquently offered peace, with the Nazis as masters of Europe. Shirer's account of the meeting—which was attended by gold-braided generals, Göring [41] pleased and pompous, and Count Ciano [40] in gray and black Fascist military uniform, "jumping up like a jack-in-the-box to give the Fascist salute"—includes this description of Kirk: "He sat there all evening, his face like a sphinx, breaking occasionally into an ironic smile when some of his diplomatic colleagues from the Balkans popped up to give the new slave salute."

On May 10, 1940, Belgium, the Netherlands, and Luxembourg had been invaded by the Nazis, and on May 28, Leopold III [44], King of the Belgians, had surrendered to Germany, an act for which he was bitterly criticized at the time. John Cudahy [43] had been Ambassador to Belgium during this period. In June Kirk returned to the United States to report on the

European situation, and in October 1940 he was formally recalled from Berlin. In November he was appointed to Rome as Chargé d'Affaires, with rank of Minister, to replace Ambassador William Phillips [40], who had been ill and had left the post in July.

The honorary rank of Minister, a designation not often used in the American diplomatic service, signified a promotion above the post Kirk had formerly held in Berlin and it lent prestige to his position. (Kirk had been promoted in July 1931 to Class 1, the highest class in the Foreign Service, which made him eligible for appointment by the President to the position of ambassador or minister.) At the time of Kirk's assignment to Rome several other changes were made in the Foreign Service in what *Newsweek* called a "diplomatic shuffle"; Joseph P. Kennedy [40] resigned his London post at this time, William C. Bullitt [40] resigned as Ambassador to France, Admiral William D. Leahy [41], retired, was appointed Ambassador to the Pétain [40] regime at Vichy, and John Cudahy resigned as Ambassador to Belgium.

From Rome Kirk went to Egypt in February 1941 to do double duty as Minister Plenipotentiary and Envoy Extraordinary to Egypt, and Minister to Saudi Arabia. In June 1943 he took on additional diplomatic duties when he was made Ambassador to the Greek Government in Exile then in Cairo. Later, in October 1943, James M. Landis [43], Director of Economic Operations in the Middle East, came to Cairo with ministerial rank to serve as assistant to Kirk. Kirk was relieved of one of his tasks when Lincoln McVeagh [41], former Minister to the Union of South Africa, became Ambassador to the Greek Government in Exile in December 1943. In April 1944 President Roosevelt [42] nominated S. Pinkney Tuck, former counselor of the Embassy at Vichy, to be Minister to Egypt, replacing Kirk, who was then assigned as the American member of the Allied Advisory Council for Italy, with the personal rank of Ambassador. In September he was appointed United States political adviser to the Supreme Allied Commander in Chief, Mediterranean theater. While serving on the Council he was appointed United States Ambassador to Italy in November 1944.

The political situation in Italy, which seemed to be approaching a crisis in December 1944, had become difficult after Italy's liberation from Axis domination and the formation of the Bonomi Government in June. In October Allied diplomatic relations were formally resumed with Italy when the United States, Great Britain, and the Latin American countries extended recognition to the erstwhile Axis partner. American commentators interpreted this action as a desire on the part of the United States to show appreciation for the sympathy of the Italian people during the Second World War, and as an attempt "to bring Italy back into the democratic way of life which she had abandoned for Fascism in 1922." The *Christian Science Monitor* pointed out that it was logical and gracious for America "to lift the military hand" at this time. However, it was also pointed out that in sending an ambassador to Rome the State Department was ignoring precedent, because a state of war declared by Congress on December 11, 1941, had not been officially ended, and that Italy was, therefore, still technically an enemy.

When the Bonomi Government was formed Count Sforza '42 was considered for the position of Minister of Foreign Affairs. His nomination in November, which was vetoed by Prime Minister Churchill '42 (who had supported the Badoglio '40 Government and the monarchy), almost precipitated an international crisis, for Secretary of State Stettinius' '40 declaration made at this time was considered a rebuke to the British Government for interfering in Italian affairs. This declaration stated that the United States had not in any way intimated that there would be any opposition on its part to Count Sforza, and that "it expected the Italians to work out their problems along democratic lines without influence from outside." The United States policy of "abstention" gave the Italian people some concern; according to the press, they were pleased that the United States would not meddle in their affairs, but felt that the Sforza incident had made it clear that they must choose men satisfactory to the British Government, and they wondered whether Italy would be left entirely to British influence if the United States was "washing its hands of Italian politics."

The New York *Times* pointed out that the reason for United States abstention at the time of the Sforza affair was partly a technical one, for, until an ambassador was appointed America could not take any part in the discussion. After his appointment Kirk discussed the situation with Count Sforza, prior to the Count's decision not to be Washington Ambassador. This incident, and many others, made it clear that Kirk would have need of all his diplomatic skill in Italy.

In January 1945 Kirk presented his credentials as American Ambassador to Italy to Crown Prince Humbert '43, Lieutenant General of the Realm, at a ceremony in the throne room of the Quirinal. He thus became the first ambassador to present his credentials since the armistice with Italy in September 1943. There were no formal speeches, but the ceremony, "possibly to show appreciation of the American action," was conducted in the traditionally regal style, except for the absence of the Italian cavalry escort which customarily attends an ambassador from the Embassy to the Quirinal. That month he conferred with Harry Hopkins '41, special assistant to President Roosevelt '42, who had come to Rome to arrange for the expected meeting of the President, Prime Minister Churchill '42, and Premier Stalin '42.

Along with editing and approving the several hundred reports which the American Embassy in Rome prepares weekly, Kirk's busy schedule includes, according to Noel F. Busch in *Life* Magazine, "keeping an eye on the local doings of AMG, OWI, PWB, UNRRA, and other semiautonomous agencies, discharging his obligations to the Allied Commission and the Allied Council, steering clear of epuration trials, integrating his activities with those of Myron Taylor '40 [American envoy] at the Vatican, and explaining United States foreign policy to interested but puzzled natives." While Kirk believes that a sharp line should be drawn between areas of United States and Italian responsibility in postwar Italy, he has urged, along with other Allied authorities, that American forces in Italy be retained during the winter of 1945-46, on the ground that they are required to "stabilize" the situation there. The

Ambassador participated in the five-power Council of Foreign Ministers, which met in London in September 1945. Later that year (November) he flew to Washington, where he presumably discussed the Italian interim peace settlement with President Truman '45 and Prime Minister Attlee '40.

With regard to diplomacy of the future, Ambassador Kirk believes that the United States should expand its diplomatic corps numerically and should train its members as technical experts, who would be chosen for "the ability not only to diagnose economic, industrial, and political trends, but also to adjust their dislocations before they can start wars." Suave, discreet Ambassador Kirk is described as "trim-rigged"—"he could not be better dressed if he had nine tailors." Mention of his personal affairs frequently includes references to his inherited "soap millions" and to his ability to buy a fine residence upon his arrival at a new post. He takes with him his collection of paintings, jewels, old furniture, and pipes—of the last-named he has about four hundred. "Kirk's conversation," wrote Busch, "is as witty as it is discreet. His manners are so good that they betray genuine friendliness."

References

Life 19:80-2+ Ag 13 '45 il pors
N Y Herald Tribune p34 Ap 9 '44
N Y Sun p6 Ap 8 '44
Newsweek 17:20 F 17 '41 por
Who's Who in America, 1944-45
Who's Who in the Nation's Capital, 1938-39

KNIGHT, JOHN S(HIVELY) Oct. 26, 1894- Newspaper publisher
Address: b. Chicago Daily News, 400 W Madison St., Chicago

In the dual role of editor-publisher of four leading newspapers, John S. Knight is a prominent figure in American journalism. Through Knight Newspapers, Inc., he controls a vital segment of the American press in one of the country's "smaller newspaper empires," dividing his time among his publishing enterprises— in Akron with the *Beacon-Journal*, in Detroit with the *Free Press*, in Miami with the *Herald*, and since the acquisition of his latest paper, in Chicago with the *Daily News*.

John Shively Knight was born in Bluefield, West Virginia, on October 26, 1894, to Charles Landon and Clara Irene (Sheifly) Knight. In 1900 the family moved to Akron, Ohio, where the father became advertising manager of the *Beacon-Journal*. By 1915 C. L. Knight had full control of the paper and was writing fiery editorials. As a militant foe of hypocrisy, the elder Knight minced no words in expressing his forthright opinions. Thus John S. Knight has a proud journalistic heritage. Today he enjoys discussing his father's newspaper career, his principles and practices. As a boy, young John worked in the newspaper office during the summer. He was educated at Central High School in Akron and at Tome School in Maryland (1911-1914). In 1914 he entered Cornell University but left college, when the United States declared war in 1917, to enlist in the Motor Transport Corps. Soon he was at the front lines in France, serving with the First and Twenty-sixth divisions. Shortly be-

JOHN S. KNIGHT

fore the Armistice he was transferred to the
Army Air Service.

Upon his return to the United States,
Knight went to California where for a time he
considered taking up cattle raising. His father
hoped he would join the newspaper staff, but
the young man was not sure that he wanted a
career in journalism. Finally, however, he
followed his father's wishes and went to work
for the *Beacon-Journal* in 1920, reading news
exchanges for a year, after which he turned
to sports writing. Knight used the pen name
of Walker, because, he now confesses, "I was
ashamed of the stuff. I didn't write well
enough." By 1925, however, he was managing editor, but he continued to work with
the "old hands." He wrote some editorials,
encouraged in this by his father. During 1925
he also became editorial director of another
Ohio paper, the Springfield *Sun*, a post he
held for two years. Then in 1927 when his
father purchased the Massillon *Independent*,
John Knight again became an editorial director. When his father died in 1933 Knight inherited the *Beacon-Journal*. At that time the
newspaper was struggling against the depression tide but the son proceeded cautiously in
his father's steps, building a solidly successful
business enterprise. In the words of one
writer: "John Knight has built methodically
upon the foundation which C.L. laid impetu-
ously." Extending his newspaper holdings,
Knight bought the Miami (Florida) *Herald*
in October 1937 for two million dollars. Two
months later he arranged to trade his Massillon *Independent* for the Miami *Tribune*, which
he then discontinued. (He had purchased it
with the intention of suspending publication,
for he felt there was not room in Miami for
three papers.) Thus the publisher of the
Herald became the owner of the only Miami
morning daily. Having firmly established his
publishing interests in Florida, Knight returned to Akron where, in 1938, he eliminated
competition to the *Beacon-Journal* by buying
out the Scripps-Howard *Times Press*. In this

way Knight achieved a press monopoly in
Akron, making that city and its suburbs "the
largest one-paper community in the country."

Still increasing his newspaper influence, on
May 1, 1940, Knight purchased the Detroit
Free Press, Michigan's oldest daily. He
promptly abolished outmoded production
methods, and his first order to the staff was
"Tell both sides of every story." The complete news coverage of the *Free Press,* circulating in one of the industrial "hot spots"
of the Nation, has earned praise from various
quarters. R. J. Thomas, president of the
United Automobile Workers, commended the
newspaper for the fairest labor coverage in
Detroit. The *Free Press* was also applauded
for its reporting of the race riots in Detroit
in 1943, its coverage of every angle of the
riots being regarded as "factually fair."

In April 1943 Knight temporarily left his
newspaper circuit to become director of the
United States Office of Censorship in London.
He was in England a year, as liaison man for
London and North Africa. For four months
after his agreed term had expired he stayed
at his post waiting for Byron Price '42, director
of the Office of Censorship, to find a successor.
Upon his return to the United States, Knight
discussed his London experience. Addressing
a group of Miami businessmen, he said: "To
anyone who has seen a bit of the war, the first
impression on coming back to America is one
of extreme unreality. I don't think anyone is
to blame for that, but our national thinking
just has not shaped itself to the point of realizing how grim the war really is over there."

Some months after his return from England,
Knight took another step in the newspaper
publishing field. In October 1944 he bought a
controlling interest in the important midwest
daily, the Chicago *Daily News,* from the estate
of the late Secretary of the Navy, Frank
Knox '40, a transaction involving more than
two million dollars. This acquisition presented
a certain challenge to Knight. According to
Time, the *News* had been losing circulation
and influence; its twenty-five-story building
had a mortgage of more than four million, its
financial structure was top-heavy (there was a
direct debt of more than one and a half million on the paper itself), and its profits had
fallen off greatly. On the other hand the
News still held prestige as the "New York
Times of the Midwest" because of its excellent
foreign coverage and its tradition of good
writing and independence. Knight immediately
instituted a number of changes. He appointed
as his executive editor Basil L. Walters, whom
he had hired in the spring of 1943 as executive
editor of the three other Knight papers. One
of Knight's specific orders was for "short
leads and short sentences." He announced
that the newspaper would remain politically
independent, adding that it would continue to
support the candidacy of Thomas E. Dewey '44
for the Presidency.

In a survey of journalism in *PM* Kenneth
Stewart '43 wrote: "With the Hearst and Howard domains past their prime, his [Knight's]
is generally regarded as the coming newspaper
chain of the Nation." Knight denies any ambition to own a national newspaper chain. Explaining his views he declared: "I don't like
chains. We try to maintain each paper's in-

dividuality, to present a cross section of the region in which it is published. Editorials are written locally and I think you get better ones that way than when they are handed out from Washington or Park Avenue." Knight's smoothly running and profitable papers are described as "a little daring journalistically, a little liberal politically." The publisher-editor has described himself as a "passionate believer in personal journalism." One of the few writing publishers in the country, he writes a weekly column, *The Editor's Notebook*, which appears in his four papers. He also writes editorials, which have been analyzed as "punchy . . .in short, snappy sentences."

In his plan of allowing each of his papers to keep its identity, Knight favors the printing of much local news. He is a strong advocate of factual, unbiased news columns. Editorially, he is opposed to machine politics, is independent, but not neutral—he says he has no wish to be a "straddler of issues, a do-nothing." In the 1944 Presidential campaign all four of Knight's papers supported Dewey. Knight was a warm admirer of Wendell Willkie [40], his good friend for twenty years. Until six months before Pearl Harbor the Detroit *Free Press* was counted among the isolationist forces, but in June 1941 the paper reversed its policy. In a front-page Sunday editorial Knight declared: "The *Free Press* has opposed every step leading toward involvement in a war which was not of our making. . . .But now the die is cast." Knight further pledged complete support of President Roosevelt as Commander in Chief.

As president of the American Society of Newspaper Editors, Knight has been fighting for world-wide freedom of the press. He appointed a committee of the organization to advance this aim in the platform committees of both the Republican and Democratic conventions in 1944. While he is aware that it will be a difficult goal to attain, the publisher believes that the access of the press to information should be guaranteed by treaty. Of freedom of the press he has stated: "It is one of the greatest challenges of our time. . . .The most powerful thing in the world is truth. If news moves freely, and if controls permitting systematic distortion are rigidly prevented, the people may have an abiding faith that truth will prevail. . . .A free and honest press in every country would contribute greatly toward lessening the chance of future wars." In December 1944 Knight appointed a committee of three editors to make a world tour in the cause of a free press. From January to April 1945 these emissaries of the ASNE traveled forty thousand miles around the world to a dozen countries, where they interviewed government officials and editors in the interest of journalistic freedom in the postwar world. Their report revealed that in practically all cases foreign editors subscribed to the society's views that there be incorporated in the peace treaties a pledge: "Governments not to censor news at the source; not to use the press as an instrument of national policy, and to permit a free flow of news in and out of signatory countries."

In March 1945 when the American Newspaper Publishers Association established a committee on press communications, Knight was appointed to serve on it. Several months later he accompanied six other American newspaper executives to the Pacific war theater as a guest of Secretary of the Navy Forrestal [42] and of Secretary of War Stimson [40], to observe military operations at first hand; their visit coincided with Japan's capitulation. This tour of Pacific bases, Knight stated, convinced him of the necessity of establishing a Government departmemnt of scientific research. Such a department would serve notice on the world that the United States was going to be ready for war if necessary, and it might, he suggested, be even more valuable in preventing war than some of the documents signed at the San Francisco conference. Shortly before the close of 1945 the publisher announced that the Chicago *Daily News* would establish a permanent fund to aid veterans "to relieve individual cases of distress . . . to obtain critically needed items for veterans' hospitals, for gifts or loans to help veterans establish themselves, and in other ways."

John Knight is described as frank and democratic, a manner said to have won him many admirers. Vigorous and energetic, he is a tall, slim, handsome man with graying hair and greenish eyes. He has two sons, Charles Landon and Frank McLain; his eldest son, John Shively, a lieutenant in the paratroopers, was killed in Germany in March 1945. (Their mother was Katherine McLain whom Knight married in 1921, and who died in 1929.) In 1932 Knight was married to Beryl Zoller Comstock. Together with Mrs. Knight's daughter Rita, they live in a large gray brick house in Akron. Knight finds recreation in fishing, swimming, and golfing—he excels in the last-named, for he has won the links championship of his golf club six times. Among his many clubs are the Portage Country Club in Akron, Tin Whistles in Pinehurst, North Carolina, Bath and Indian Creek in Miami, Detroit Economic, and the Burning Tree Golf Club in Washington, D.C. In Chicago he is a member of the Old Elm, Glenview and Tavern clubs. He also belongs to the Veterans of Foreign Wars and the American Legion. When questioned about the incentives to his achievement, he frankly replied that he believed it was pride that stimulated him, explaining that many people in his home town had considered him a rich man's son who would never amount to anything. Therefore, when his father died, Knight said, "I think I just resolved then that I would show them."

References

Newsweek 23:101-02 My 15 '44 por
PM Mag p6-9 O 29 '44 pors
Time 35:62 My 13 '40; 44:64-5 Jl 3 '44 por; 44:64-6 O 30 '44 por
Who's Who in America, 1944-45
Who's Who in Commerce and Industry (1944)

KNOBLOCK, EDWARD (nŏb'lŏk) Apr. 7, 1874—July 19, 1945 British playwright, scenarist, and novelist; also well known as a dramatist in his own right and as collaborator with Arnold Bennett, J. B. Priestley, and

KNOBLOCK, EDWARD—*Continued*
others; first great success was *Kismet* (1911);
his novels include *The Ant Heap* (1929).

Obituary

N Y Times p19 Jl 20 '45 por

KORNGOLD, JULIUS (kŏrn'gŏlt yōō'lē-
ōōs) Dec. 24, 1860—Sept. 25, 1945 Retired
dean of European music critics; writer on the
Vienna *Neue Freie Press* from 1902 until
the German invasion; came to America in 1938
to join his son Erich Wolfgang Korngold '43,
the composer; discovered the pianist Artur
Schnabel '42 and the violinist Nathan Milstein;
published several volumes of essays on contemporary opera.

Obituary

N Y Times p21 S 27 '45

KROSS, ANNA M(OSCOWITZ) July 17,
1891- Judge
Address: b. 130 E. 22d St., New York City;
h. 124 W. 79th St., New York City

Magistrate Anna M. Kross has been a
prominent member of the New York City
judiciary for more than a decade. Well known
for her sociological approach to the cases
brought into her court, she has been in the
forefront of the preventive battle against
juvenile delinquency for several years, speaking widely on this subject and on crime prevention in general. In 1945 Judge Kross was
chairman of the Youth Conservation Committee of the General Federation of Women's
Clubs, whose broad youth program aims at
coordination of all private and public resources
in planning for the youth of the Nation.

Weitzmann & Co.

ANNA M. KROSS

Anna Moscowitz was born in Nishwez, Russia, on July 17, 1891, to Maier and Esther Leah
(Drazen) Moscowitz. When she was about
two years old the child was brought to Amer-

ica, to which her Jewish parents immigrated
to escape persecution. There, in New York's
East Side, the girl grew up. With considerable struggle and sacrifice she earned the
money for her education: she graduated from
Wadleigh High School and then went on to
study at Teachers College of Columbia University. At seventeen she taught English to
foreigners at the Educational Alliance while
studying law at night on a scholarship.

Even as a young girl she was "struck by
certain injustices of the law toward children
and youth, and determined to do something
about it." Awarded her LL.B. by New York
University in 1910, she received her LL.M.
the following year and was admitted to the
bar in 1912. While subsequently engaged in
private law practice she became a special investigator for the Women's Night Court in
New York. This work won for her an invitation from the Prison Committee of the Church
of Ascension to head a group providing free
legal counsel for women brought into night
court, voluntary work which occupied her during the year 1914-17. In her private practice
in these years (1914-19) she also specialized
in labor work and acted as counsel for more
than eighty unions. Later she organized the
Building Trades Compensation Bureau, for
which she was legal adviser during the years
1923-25. From 1918 to 1923 she served in the
office of New York City's legal department,
the Corporation Counsel, when she was assigned to the domestic relations courts. While
there she made a significant nationwide survey
of family courts. Leaving her municipal post,
Mrs. Kross resumed private practice, which
she continued for ten years. In 1934 she was
appointed judge of the Magistrates Court of
New York City and has since established a
national reputation as "an outstanding, socially
minded member of the judiciary."

The jurist believes that the cases encountered
in the magistrates courts are essentially social
rather than criminal. In 1937 she sponsored
the organization of the Magistrates Courts
Social Service Bureau, "to socialize the administration of criminal justice." A voluntary
agency which provided assistance to those
brought into the courts, the bureau performed
a vital service. Another outgrowth of her
attitude toward crime and delinquency is the
Wayward Minors' Court, which she organized
and served for a year as its only judge. This
"experimental sociological" court handles the
problems of adolescent female delinquency.

In an address at a Teachers Union conference in 1938 Magistrate Kross outlined the
part schools can play in crime prevention.
Testifying at a hearing before the New York
City Board of Education in 1942, she urged
a higher school budget. The following year
she spoke to the conference of the American
Youth for Democracy on juvenile delinquency.
As chairman of the Department of Crime
Prevention and Social Adjustment of the New
York State Federation of Women's Clubs, the
judge was busy throughout the war years on
the problems of increased juvenile delinquency.
After a tour of her state late in 1942 she re-
ported that she had found no authority to cope
with this urgent problem. She then addressed
an appeal for action to Governor Thomas E.
Dewey '44. In March 1943 a committee of the

State Federation of Women's Clubs, headed by the Magistrate, conferred with Lieutenant Governor Wallace, and Judge Kross submitted a crime prevention plan. This plan was described by Albert Deutch of *PM* as an "over-all plan for reducing the existing confusion and waste in children's services."

In 1944 Magistrate Kross was in charge of a national survey conducted by the S.F.W.C. which studied juvenile delinquency. A *PM* article (August 6, 1944) reporting the findings of the study declared that some communities showed a 300 per cent rise in delinquency. Magistrate Kross compared the youth crime wave to the hoodlum-gangster period of prohibition after the First World War. Pointing out that the attempted cures have so far been ineffective, she declared, "Treatment itself is no cure. We need concerted national thinking, planning, and action for a prevention battle. We want a master-key plan, adaptable to the Nation's different patterns of delinquency— urban or rural—coordinating all prevention-treatment work at the local level, focusing responsibility in the community. We want a national youth conservation program." When the General Federation of Women's Clubs inaugurated their postwar youth program in October 1944, Judge Kross became chairman of the Youth Conservation Committee. In April 1945 she attended the discussions held in Washington, D.C., by fifteen organizations for the purpose of establishing a clearinghouse for youth activities. At that time she also conferred with Eleanor Roosevelt '40 on this subject. In July the Judge again met to discuss this issue with Mrs. Roosevelt and Mrs. LaFell Dickinson '45, president of the General Federation of Women's Clubs, and that fall Judge Kross and Mrs. Dickinson visited the White House to discuss the youth program with President Truman '45.

Magistrate Kross, who is a Democrat, has actively participated in many state and national campaigns. During Alfred E. Smith's '44 administration as Governor of New York, she served on his Committee to Remedy Defects in the Law and Its Administration. In 1938 she waged an unsuccessful campaign for a seat on the New York State Supreme Court. An American Labor Party candidate, she was supported by a group of organizations that included the Women's Bar Association and the National Lawyers Guild. She conducted her own campaign, without the aid of a manager, and was actively backed by Mayor La Guardia '40 and various citizens' groups.

The Magistrate's organization affiliations include membership in the National Association of Women Lawyers, in which she has been prominent. As first vice-president in 1940, she attended the association's convention in Philadelphia, where divorce conditions in the United States was one of the principal subjects under discussion. The New York judge later told a reporter, "Divorce conditions in the United States constitute a definite challenge to the women lawyers of this country, and I feel that they can render a fine service to American family life by using their legalistically trained minds in helping find a solution for the literally thousand-and-one complexities in our divorce laws. They can help educate the public." She reported agreement among members on the need for uniformity of divorce laws, but a division of opinion as to whether reform should be the responsibility of the Federal Government or the states. Judge Kross herself favors Federal legislation. In April 1945 the Magistrate presided at the North Mid-Atlantic Conference of the association. Urging that women participate in peace deliberations, she stated, "We women in America want to pledge ourselves that nothing will remain undone in order that unity may be brought about to insure future peace."

Judge Kross is co-author of a series of articles analyzing the scope, function, and procedure of the Magistrates Court. She has written other articles, for the *Journal of Educational Sociology* and the *Reader's Digest* discussion pamphlets. In addition to holding membership in various legal organizations, she belongs to the Women's Democratic Club and the Women's Civic Organization, and she has been a member of the national executive committee of the Zionist Organization of America (1927-29) and the national board of Hadassah (1930-33).

Magistrate Kross is the wife of Dr. Isidor Kross, the New York surgeon, to whom she was married in April 1917; and she is the mother of two daughters, Helen and Alice. She is an expert swimmer and enjoys horseback-riding, skating, and camping. The judge is a voracious reader. Small, with graying hair, she is a woman of great vitality. She impressed one interviewer as a woman who "walked and talked with the definite purposefulness of a person who knew where she was heading."

References

American Women, 1939-40
Who's Who in American Jewry, 1938-39
Women of Achievement (1940)

LAIDLER, HARRY W(ELLINGTON)

(lād'lẽr) Feb. 18, 1884- Economist; educator

Address: b. League for Industrial Democracy, 112 E. 19th St., New York City; h. 292 Garfield Pl., Brooklyn, N. Y.

Believing that the United States should aim to achieve for its people economic security, equal opportunity and genuine democracy, Harry W. Laidler has worked for social reforms and social reconstruction as executive director of the League for Industrial Democracy, as a frequent candidate for office, a city legislator, a lecturer, and an author. His most recent book, *Social-Economic Movements*, published in December 1944, is a comprehensive history of radical ideas and movements from the prophets of the Old Testament and the early philosophers and utopians to the current labor and socialist movements all over the world.

Born in Brooklyn, New York, on February 18, 1884, Harry Wellington Laidler is the son of William Ebenezer and Julia (Heary) Laidler. His grandfather, Stephen Laidler, was a Congregational minister who came to the United States from Manchester, England, in 1865 and worked in the South among the freed Negroes before holding several pastorates in the North. Harry Laidler received his early education in the public

HARRY W. LAIDLER

schools and before he was graduated from
Brooklyn Boys' High School he had read
much about social problems. He attended
Ruskin College for workingmen in Missouri
and the American Socialist College in Kansas, but he received his B.A. degree from
Wesleyan University in Middletown, Connecticut, in 1907. While at Wesleyan he
represented the university on its intercollegiate debating teams and was awarded the
Phi Beta Kappa key. Following his graduation he worked for three years as a reporter
on the Brooklyn *Daily Eagle*, also studying
during these years for the degree of LL.B.,
which was awarded to him in 1910 by the
Brooklyn Law School.

That same year he worked for six months
in the law firm of Henry A. Ingraham. He
was admitted to the New York bar in 1911.
In 1914 he was awarded the degree of Doctor
of Philosophy in political economy by Columbia University. His interest in socialism began
in high school. He joined the Socialist movement while attending college in the Middle
West in 1903, and during the next year and a
half combined college studies with lecturing
for socialism in Kansas and Oklahoma, as "the
boy orator." Returning to the East in the fall
of 1904, he entered Wesleyan University, and
the following year became one of the founders
of the Intercollegiate Socialist Society and
formed the Society's first chapter at Wesleyan
University. He became the executive of the
I.S.S. in 1910, which office he held until 1921.
He was editor of the *Intercollegiate Socialist*
from 1913 to 1919 and of the *Socialist Review*
from 1919 to 1921.

While Laidler has been a nominee for political office a number of times, he has not been
particularly successful in politics. As the New
York *Post* pointed out, he ran for every office
from borough president to governor in twenty
years as a Socialist Party stalwart (he was
the Socialist candidate for Governor of New
York in 1936 and a candidate for United States
Senator from New York in 1938), but he had
never held an elective office until he served in

1940-41 on the New York City Council as a
representative of the American Labor Party
and the Socialist Party. When the time came
for re-election, he was denied the endorsement
of the American Labor Party in Brooklyn, he
says, because of his "differences with the party
on national issues and because of pressures
from influential committee members to secure
the party's endorsement for relatives and
friends."

Laidler therefore ran for councilman again
on an independent ticket endorsed by the Citizens Non-Partisan Committee, the City Fusion
Party, the Socialist Party, and many trade
unions and civic organizations. Bishop Francis
J. McConnell, at that time Bishop of the Methodist Area of New York, was chairman of the
Laidler Independent Committee, and Mayor
Fiorello H. La Guardia '40, Freda Kirchwey '42,
editor of the *Nation*, John Dewey '44, and other
prominent liberals testified to Laidler's fine record as a councilman, his lifelong service to the
cause of labor, and his specialized knowledge
of public utilities. Laidler announced his determination to continue his fight for decent
homes for low-income groups, cheap electric
and telephone service, elimination of overcrowding in the schools, reorganization of an
"archaic" taxation system, more adequate relief, prevention of discrimination on account of
color, race, creed or religion, improvement of
transit facilities, and the guarantee of the right
of collective bargaining. (In 1945 Laidler
served as general consultant to the Municipal
Affairs Committee of the Liberal Party.)

In order to gain experience and a perspective
in his study of these social tenets, Laidler has
visited Europe six times to study labor, socialist, and cooperative movements. He was in
Prussia in 1929 and attended as observer the
Second Anti-Imperialist World Congress at
Frankfort, a meeting participated in by communists, socialists, and liberals. Numerous
speakers present protested against a capitalist
war in the proletarian struggle against imperialism.

Laidler then visited Vienna, where he was
greatly impressed by the new housing experiments and by the fact that this city, although
war- and poverty-stricken, had been able to
eliminate slums and build modern apartments
for its workers. By 1931 Laidler had twice
been in Russia, visiting the House of Culture,
the workingmen's college on the outskirts of
Leningrad, the clubhouses for industrial workers, the textile factories, and attending trade
union meetings. The intensity of the propaganda within Russia for the Five-Year Plan
impressed Laidler as being much greater than
the Communist propaganda abroad for world
revolution.

The League for Industrial Democracy, of
which Laidler is executive director and John
Dewey is honorary president, is a nonprofit
educational organization committed to a program of "education for increasing democracy
in our economic, political, and cultural life. It
has given particular attention to democracy in
industry. . . .It seeks to encourage every movement in the fields of labor, cooperatives, democratic public control and ownership, social legislation, civil liberties, education, and international organization which aims at the preservation and strengthening of the democratic way
of life."

During the Second World War the League has given much time to a "constructive postwar program for the full employment of the Nation's material and human resources for the common good, for an equitable distribution of the fruits of industry, and for international cooperation in behalf of a just and lasting peace." The work of the League consists of research in political, economic, social, and labor problems; of the issuing of pamphlets; and of conferences, lectures, and radio programs. It also acts as an information center on problems of industrial democracy, and in normal years conducts a summer school for students.

Writing in the *League for Industrial Democracy News Bulletin* for October 1944, Laidler, in preparation for the fortieth anniversary year (1945) of the League, described its inception and its development. It was officially born, wrote Laidler, in New York City in the early fall of 1905. At that time Upton Sinclair, then writing *The Jungle* (1906), sent out an appeal for the formation of a society "to promote an intelligent interest in socialism among college men and women." This appeal, which was signed by Jack London, Clarence Darrow Thomas Wentworth Higginson of Harvard, and others, met with a hearty response, and a large group of college graduates and undergraduates met that fall and formed the Intercollegiate Socialist Society. At this meeting London was chosen president; Owen R. Lovejoy, afterward secretary of the National Child Labor Association, became treasurer; and Harry Laidler, then an undergraduate at Wesleyan, was chosen one of the members of the executive committee.

The following year Jack London made a tour of colleges in behalf of the newly formed I.S.S., encouraging students "to think through the burning problems of the age," and not to be content with "the passionless pursuit of passionless intelligence." "Fight for socialism or fight against it," he urged. "Raise your voices one way or another; be alive."

The society continued, with desk space in the Rand School of Social Science in New York until 1910. In 1921 it was reorganized as the League for Industrial Democracy. Robert Morss Lovett '43, professor of English literature at the University of Chicago and an editor of the *New Republic*, was elected the first president, Stuart Chase '40 was made treasurer, and Norman Thomas and Harry Laidler were chosen executive directors. (Mark Starr is president of the League in 1944 and 1945.) Writing in 1944, Laidler said: "Of late the League has been greatly strengthening its ties with the organized labor movement—both A.F. of L. and CIO—and today represents a cross section of the progressive forces in all phases of our American life."

In his books and in numerous magazine articles, which have appeared since the year 1930 in the *New Republic, Current History, North American Review, Survey Graphic,* and the *Annals of the American Academy,* Laidler has defined his ideas of socialism and its significance in the social picture. In one article he explains that by socialism, Socialists do not mean rigid centralized industrial mechanism under which all industry is controlled by the state. Instead, they see it as an evolving social order in which the principal industries of a country are socially owned by municipal, state, national, or other

community units, and by consumers' and producers' cooperatives, with functional control and as much decentralization as is compatible with efficiency.

In another article Laidler traces the changes in American business and the growth of American monopolies. Business consolidation, Laidler points out, began about 1880 with the foundation of the Standard Oil Company and other "combines." The passage of the Sherman Antitrust Act in 1890 seemed to put an end to consolidation, but only momentarily, and in 1896 a new era came into bloom, a period which saw the formation of United States Steel. From 1904 to the First World War many mergers were achieved, but the movement was less intense. Then the war encouraged big corporations to pool their interests for war purposes, and immediately after the war the third major merger movement developed momentum, continuing until the Wall Street crash of 1929. Postwar development in concentrated control has taken place in the retail distributing businesses (the Atlantic and Pacific chain grocery stores, for example) and in the money trusts. The Federal Reserve System has kept these huge banking concerns under control, but powerful corporations, monopolies of utilities, and large trusts, such as the Ford Motor Company and General Foods have developed.

Laidler sees some good in these monopolies—conditions promoting more research, a better cost-accounting system, greater scientific management—but he feels that organized labor has no firm foothold in these big industries and that employment is not stabilized in them. These large corporations mean greater wealth to the inner group, he thinks, but no security for the worker or the businessman. In 1941 Laidler expressed his belief that there had been social progress in many fields in the United States, despite the crises then threatening in Europe; this was seen in the increasing progress of labor organizations in the basic industries, in the acceptance of the principles of collective bargaining among corporations, and the progress of consumer cooperatives, the decrease in unemployment and increase in minimum wages —and the failure of big business to elect its candidate in the 1940 Presidential election.

Laidler has been a director of the National Bureau of Economic Research since 1920; he was vice-president of the organization in 1928, president from 1930 to 1932, and chairman of the board of directors from 1932 to 1934. Other of his activities include membership since 1924 in the Christian Social Action Commission of the Federal Council of Churches, chairmanship from 1933 to 1936 of the economic committee of the National Advisory Council on Radio in Education, and directorship of the National Public Housing Conference since 1931. He has been a member of the American Labor Conference on International Affairs since 1943, and lecturer in economics at New York University (1942-43), at the College of the City of New York (1942-45), and at Brooklyn College (1943-44). He was awarded an honorary M.A. by Wesleyan University in 1933.

Laidler is the author of many books, among them *Boycotts and the Labor Struggle* (1914), *Socialism in Thought and Action* (1920), *A History of Socialist Thought* (1927), *Concentration of Control in American Industry* (1931), *The Road Ahead—a Primer of Capitalism and*

LAIDLER, HARRY W.—*Continued*

Socialism (1932), *Socialist Planning and a Socialist Program* (1933), *Socializing Our Democracy* (1935), and *A Program for Modern Americans* (1936).

Reviewers of Laidler's most recent book, *Social-Economic Movements*, have pointed out that it is the first comprehensive history of socialist movements (that is, groups advocating radical changes in society) ever published, and that an objective historical survey such as this book is warmly welcomed today when so many millions are searching for satisfactory solutions of the world's social, political, and economic ills. There have been some minor criticisms of the book, but in general it is considered a scholarly, well-organized work. In 1944 he was writing a book on European labor at work, a book dealing with trade unions, cooperatives, and political and educational phases of the labor movement in democratic countries of Europe.

Harry Laidler is a slight man (he is five feet three inches tall and weighs one hundred and twenty-two pounds), and has gray eyes and graying hair. He is considered an unusually lucid and forceful speaker. His favorite recreations are walking, swimming, and tennis. He is a Methodist and a member of Phi Delta Phi and Sigma Chi. In 1919 he was married to Agnes Fuller Armington. They have two children: John Armington and Rosamond.

References

N Y Post p6 O 28 '41 por

National Cyclopædia of American Biography Current vol D p346
Who's Who in America, 1944-45
Who's Who in American Education (1941-42)
Who's Who in New York, 1938

LAKE, SIMON Sept. 4, 1866—June 23, 1945 American Naval architect and engineer; known as father of the modern submarine, whose wartime use he did not foresee; invented even-keel type of submarine torpedo boats; built first experimental boat in 1894; also inventor of submarine appartus for locating and recovering sunken vessels and their cargoes, submarine apparatus for pearl and sponge fishing, heavy oil internal combustion engine for marine purposes, etc.

Obituary

N Y Times p22 Je 24 '45 por

LANDIS, KENESAW MOUNTAIN Nov. 20, 1866—Nov. 25, 1944 Baseball commissioner in the United States from 1920 until death; a joint committee of the two national leagues had, a week before his death, recommended his re-election for another seven-year term at expiration of his current term. See *Current Biography 1944 Yearbook.*

Obituary

N Y Times p56 N 26 '44 por

LANDON, MARGARET (DOROTHEA MORTENSON) Sept. 7, 1903- Author

Address: b. c/o The John Day Co., 40 E. 49th St., New York City; h. 4711 Fulton St., N.W., Washington, D. C.

MARGARET LANDON

When Margaret Landon, the wife of a Presbyterian missionary, was living in Siam (now Thailand) she happened upon two fascinating books, long since out of print, by a Mrs. Anna Leonowens. On these, the memoirs of a Welsh woman who became, in the eighteen-sixties, secretary to Siam's King Mongkut and governess to his sixty-odd children, Mrs. Landon based her story, *Anna and the King of Siam.* The July 1944 choice of the Literary Guild, the book was called startling, exotic, almost incredible, and is probably one of the most unusual first books ever to become a best seller.

Anna and the King of Siam is unusual, too, as the first publication of a woman who began her career as a teacher and missionary. The author was born Margaret Dorothea Mortenson in Somers, Wisconsin, on September 7, 1903, the daughter of Annenus Duabus and Adelle Johanne (Estberg) Mortenson. After attending the Evanston Township High School, she entered Wheaton College in Illinois, where she received her B.A. degree in 1925. For a year afterward she taught school at Bear Lake, Michigan.

In June 1926 she was married to Kenneth Perry Landon, an educational missionary. The following year, under the auspices of the Board of Foreign Missions of the Presbyterian Church, the young couple went to Siam. In the Far East they lived successively in Bangkok, Nakon, Sritamarat, and Trang—Mrs. Landon was principal of the Trang Girls' School for five years. The Landons returned to the United States in 1937. They have four children: Margaret Dorothea, William Bradley, Carol Elizabeth, and Kenneth Perry, Jr.

Mrs. Landon heard much in Siam of the strong-minded Welsh girl who had indoctrinated the royal court, in the eighteen-sixties, with Western ideals of freedom. She then read Anna Leonowens' two books (published in England in 1870 and 1872), *The English Governess at the Siamese Court* and *The Romance of the Harem.* Later she met Mrs. Leonowens' granddaughter, who gave her copies of several old letters; and in the Library of Congress in Washington, she found King Mongkut's letters, published in Siamese. Mrs. Landon based *Anna and the King of Siam* on this material, retaining in the process "something of Mrs. Leonowens' Victorian style, spicing it with her own very modern sense of humor."

The 1860 heroine of this best-selling book of 1945 was Anna Crawford, a young Welsh woman, who was married in India to a British Army officer, Major Thomas Leonowens. In a series of misfortunes she lost two of her children, her husband, and her money. But the twenty-eight-year-old widow had courage—she accepted the King of Siam's offer of one hundred dollars a month and a house to become his secretary and to teach his children and concubines the English language. During her five years in Siam, Anna, who became the "white angel" of the common people, was a one-woman liberalizing force in a feudal court. One of her young concubine pupils was able to translate *Uncle Tom's Cabin* into Siamese, and the Heir Apparent, upon his succession to the throne, abolished the custom of prostration before superiors and freed his slaves.

Although not fiction, *Anna and the King of Siam*, according to Harry Hansen [42], reads like a "refreshing historical novel." Sterling North [43] found the book "a 'natural,' drawing upon the richest vein of untapped material discovered in years. The author's prose lacks professional polish, but the facts of Anna Leonowens' life are sufficiently fascinating to camouflage this lack." William McFee felt that the re-creation of Anna was not successful. "Mrs. Landon has tried hard, but Anna has to a great degree eluded her. We get the external facts and Mrs. Landon's dialogue, but the essential Anna does not appear. . . .Research, like patriotism, is not enough. It takes something more to blow the breath of life into so strange a figure of history." To Lewis Gannett [41], however, it was "a refreshment and a delight" in the field of Victorian melodrama; and John Chamberlain [40] found the book "one of the most remarkable stories ever to be told about that most romantic of centuries, the nineteenth."

Following the success of its American appearance *Anna and the King of Siam* was also published in British and Swedish editions, and negotiations were under way for Spanish, Portuguese, and Dutch translations. The book was also transcribed by the American Red Cross into Braille, and both the American Foundation for the Blind and the American Printing House for the Blind are making it into a "Talking Book." The Theatre Guild in July 1944 acquired stage rights for a forthcoming dramatization. A film version of the book, with Dorothy McGuire portraying the role of Anna, was scheduled to be put into production in the fall of 1945.

Margaret Landon is five feet seven and one-half inches tall, of average weight, with attractive, regular features, deep-set blue eyes, and light brown hair. She and her husband, who serves on the Far Eastern staff of the State Department, have recently acquired a new house in Washington. Mrs. Landon is currently at work on a new book of non-fiction, "Pageant of Malayan History," in the Longmans Green "Pageant of History" series. She is also reported to have near completion a novel (ten-

tatively entitled "One Fainting Robin"), the background of which is again Siam.

References

N Y Herald Tribune p23 Je 29 '44; p32 O 25 '44 por
N Y World-Telegram p19 Je 29 '44

LANDOWSKA, WANDA (län-dôf'skä vän'dä) July 5, 1879- Harpsichordist and pianist

Address: b. c/o David Libidins, 113 W. 57th St., New York City; h. 50 Central Park West, New York City

"Since the beginning of my campaign in favor of the music of the past, I have always compelled myself to focus light on the fact that this so-called 'old music' is a living force, sometimes more modern than modern music itself," says Wanda Landowska, the leading harpsichordist in the world today. Her efforts to bring about a greater appreciation of the music of the seventeenth and eighteenth centuries have been almost unrivaled; and her interpretation of these early works, both on harpsichord and piano, is said to make them "sound frequently more contemporary than many written only yesterday."

Born on July 5, 1879, Wanda Landowska is a native of Warsaw, Poland. Her father, Marjan Landowska, was a lawyer and amateur musician; and her mother, Eve Landowska, was a linguist. Wanda began her piano instruction at the age of four. Old music, particularly that of Bach, fascinated the little girl, and her first teacher let her indulge her inclination. When a later instructor, a very "stern and tiresome" man, made her concentrate on Kalkbrenner and Thalberg, the unhappy young Wanda vowed she would someday devote an entire program to the music of Bach. Later her studies were continued at the Warsaw Conservatory, where her teacher was Michalowski, the well known interpreter of Chopin, and at fourteen she was graduated. She made her concert debut in Warsaw, then went to Berlin, where she studied composition under Urban, who was also the teacher of Paderewski, Josef Hofmann, and Rudolph Ganz. "I hardly knew Bach had any contemporaries," she has said, for as a young student she continued to be so devoted to the composer, who was not then very popular, that she was nicknamed "Bacchante" by the famous conductor Nikisch.

At the age of twenty-one Wanda Landowska went to Paris. That year also (1900) she was married there to Henri Lew, the folklorist, who later was to collaborate with her in preparing a book on music of the past. She was a good friend of Charles Bordes and Vincent d'Indy, directors of the Schola Cantorum in Paris, and Mme. Landowska often played in concerts at the school. In her subsequent European tours, writes David Ewen, "she achieved no small measure of fame" as a concert pianist. Meanwhile, the Polish musician since her arrival in France had become an enthusiastic student of the French, Flemish, and English music of the seventeenth and eighteenth centuries. As she studied further she gradually came to appreciate that these compositions should be played on the instru-

Lipnitzki, Paris

WANDA LANDOWSKA

ment for which they had been written, the harpsichord, the immediate precursor of the modern piano. She found that little or no technical material on the harpsichord existed and was thus forced to learn by experimenting how to interpret the old music, or, as she prefers to call it, the music of the past.

The musician commissioned Pleyel, the well known French piano maker, to build her first harpsichord, which was to be an authentic reproduction of the instrument as it was in the middle of the eighteenth century, at the time of its highest development; into the construction, however, would go the skill of the modern craftsman. (The harpsichord has seven medals, and two keyboards of five octaves each, which can be used singly or together.) When the instrument was completed Mme. Landowska began her campaign to reintroduce the classical music to audiences, and to win favor for the harpsichord itself. In 1912 she was called to the newly established Berlin Hochschule as professor of the harpsichord, a post created especially for her. During the war she was detained as an enemy alien, and when peace came she left Germany. After her husband's death in 1919 Mme. Landowska went to Basle, where she gave concerts, lectured, and held classes for advanced students of the piano, harpsichord, and other instruments, interpreting for them the old music. When she left Switzerland she returned to Paris and continued with her concertizing.

In 1925 Mme. Landowska established her own school in Saint-Leu-la-Forêt, a quaint little suburb of Paris, and she built a concert hall on the grounds. Students came from many places to hear her lectures on Bach and to study the piano and the harpsichord under her instruction, mastering the old music scientifically, as she believed was necessary. During the years until 1940, when Mme. Landowska was forced to flee from her adopted country, more than a thousand persons studied at her Ecole de Musique Ancienne, and Saint-Leu became known as a mecca for music lovers. "Her 'French Bayreuth,'" wrote Paul

Dambly, "has become a chamber of music in which . . . musical works, so young and so new, by the masters of old, are literally revived." (Mme. Landowska has also lectured on early music in Zurich, Geneva, Barcelona, and Philadelphia.)

Mme. Landowska did not discontinue her concertizing after the establishment of her school; she toured extensively in Europe, Africa, and North and South Americas. She made her North American debut in November 1923, as soloist with the Philadelphia Orchestra under Leopold Stokowski [41]. Three concertos were included in the program: one each by Handel and Bach for the harpsichord, and one by Mozart for the piano. "Her exquisite finish is beyond description," commented W. J. Henderson. "Its technical certainty—the sureness of the touch and the perfect suitability of the tonal response to the unerring artistic conception is something that only a musician or a very sensitive listener can perfectly appreciate. . . .She has so thoroughly saturated herself in the spirit of the seventeenth and eighteenth century music that she plays it back into vivid life and present actuality." Pitts Sanborn, writing for *Outlook* in 1930, declared: "Hasn't she even inspired dyed-in-the-wool modernists to compose for her?" Two of these were Manuel de Falla (Concerto for Harpsichord) and Francis Poulenc (*Concerto Champêtre*).

With the threatened occupation of Paris by the Nazis in 1940, Mme. Landowska, a naturalized French citizen, fled to southern France, and eventually to the United States. She left behind her famous collection of ancient instruments, a library of ten thousand volumes, and her dogs, Do, Re, Mi, Fa, Sol, Tempo, and Musette. All her possessions, she later learned, were confiscated by the Germans. Her harpsichord, too, was taken, but a Swiss friend of the musician's was able to secure it and ship it to New York. The harpsichordist's return to the New York concert stage was marked by a performance at Town Hall in February 1942, after an absence of fourteen years, and her audience, consisting largely of musicians, greeted her appearance with an ovation. In his review in the New York *Herald Tribune*, Virgil Thomson [40] wrote: "No matter what she plays it is one of the richest and grandest experiences available to lovers of tonal art. . . . A performance so complete, so wholly interpreted . . . is rarely to be encountered."

After a recital in Carnegie Hall in 1943 the New York *Times* critic pronounced her arrangements "exquisite," while Paul Bowles described her technique as "impeccable." The enthusiastic acclaim of the exacting New York reviewers continued during the next years also. "Bach got a break in Town Hall last night," Louis Biancolli declared after hearing a concert of four of Bach's sonatas for harpsichord and violin, which were performed by Mme. Landowska and Yehudi Menuhin [41] at the end of 1944. "The glory of the concert was Mme. Landowska's playing of Mozart," wrote Olin Downes [43] of a concert she gave in 1945, in which she performed on both piano and harpsichord. At this concert she also presented a work of Haydn's which she had discovered and edited.

Composer as well as editor of music, Mme. Landowska has written songs, piano pieces, and orchestral works. She is a radio as well as concert stage artist, and has made numerous harpsichord and piano recordings, solo and with orchestra, of the works of Scarlatti, Couperin, Rameau, Bach, Handel, Haydn, and Mozart. Since 1905, when she wrote a discussion of the works of Bach for the harpsichord, she has written many books, mostly in French, on the subject of music of the past. One of these, *La Musique ancienne*, was written in collaboration with her late husband. In 1937 the artist was awarded the Grand Prix of the Paris Exposition.

In 1943 Mme. Landowska composed *Liberation Fanfare*, which was arranged for band by Edwin Franco Goldman [42] and played many times in New York's Central Park and Prospect Park in Brooklyn. That summer she also attended the Goldman Band's summer concerts in Central Park, enjoying them so much that she postponed a two-week vacation in order to attend them all. Reporters who have interviewed the artist describe her as a "charming personality," friendly and cordial, and with a sense of humor. She likes to talk of her years in Saint-Leu-la-Forêt, which she considers the happiest of her life. Now in America she is again gathering together the things she cherishes—among them her forty-nine volumes of the works of Bach. "Everything begins now to blossom," she told a *Christian Science Monitor* reporter in 1943—"pupils, concerts, friends. Life for me is beginning all over in America."

References

Christian Sci Mon p11 N 19 '43 por
Musician 30:11+ Je '25 por
Baker's Biographical Dictionary of Musicians (1945)
Ewen, D. ed. Living Musicians (1940)
Thompson, O. ed. International Cyclopedia of Music and Musicians (1943)

LANGDON, HARRY June 15, 1884—Dec. 22, 1944 Veteran comedian of the American stage and screen; famous for his "dead-pan" expression; ventriloquist and cartoonist, once refused three thousand dollars a week to draw a daily strip, saying he was too busy and too successful; two of his best pictures were *Tramp, Tramp, Tramp* (1926) and *The Strong Man* (1926).

Obituary

N Y Times p13 D 23 '44 por

LANGLEY, ADRIA LOCKE Author

Address: b. c/o Whittlesey House, 330 W. 42nd St., New York City

Adria Locke Langley, author of a 1945 bestselling first novel *A Lion Is in the Streets*, has been a saleswoman for a mail order house, an organizer of civic groups, a relief investigator, and a war worker—work and interests which took her through the South, the Southwest, and into the crowded sections of New York City. The material of her travels—the study of Americans at work and out of work and in politics—became the substance of her book.

Zamouzakis, Hollywood

ADRIA LOCKE LANGLEY

Adria Locke was born in Iowa, the youngest of three children. When she was still a young child the family moved to Stanton, a small town in Nebraska, and there she grew up. Her father, William Locke, was the president of the Omaha livestock market. He was a Quaker, with a Quaker's idea of what a woman's place should be, and thus it was her maternal grandfather, Thomas Glendenning, modern despite his patriarchal years, who greatly influenced the girl in her future social consciousness. Grandfather Glendenning used to take his eager grandchild to visit and explore his native South. She was sent to Fremont College, in Nebraska, from which she received a teaching certificate after two years. Still too young to qualify as a teacher under the Nebraska laws, she instead entered Northwestern University, from which she was suspended, says interviewer Clip Boutell (New York *Post*), for holding a séance.

Miss Locke was married while still in her teens, and in 1929 she divorced her husband. With only $228.02 to support herself and her eight-month-old daughter, Adria Langley took a job selling a merchandise control system to department stores from Texas to New York. For almost a year she traveled through the South, selling the system so successfully that, on a salary-plus-commission basis, she earned eleven thousand dollars the first year. It was during this period of traveling that Mrs. Langley began attending town hall meetings wherever she happened to be. She became actively interested in a movement for prohibition reform and wrote an article about the work women were doing to combat the corruption of the dry era. As a result of her article she was invited to work with the Women's Organization for National Prohibition Reform in upper New York State, and she was personally responsible for signing up two hundred thousand women in the movement. Those were exciting days, which Clip Boutell describes: "Mrs. Langley was denounced by the local

LANGLEY, ADRIA LOCKE—*Continued*

gangsters as a Red and was jailed by the police in Cooperstown. She was shot at (the bullet smashed the windshield of her car) and she received a hundred and seventeen threatening letters in a single summer."

Her work with the Women's Organization for National Prohibition Reform led to field work for a group of anti-prohibition Congressmen, and by 1933 she was publicity director for the New York State Democratic Committee. Then in 1934 Mrs. Langley, by now a veteran crusader, took up the fight of the New York Dairymen for a price minimum on their products, and she saw to it that the case was brought to court in Albany. She herself appeared to testify in a wheel chair, having just been operated on for appendicitis. "I was just so burned up because no one would stand up for the farmers!" she said.

Her next job was as relief investigator in New York City. There her daily observations of the city's poverty so disturbed her that she wrote a series of articles for the New York *Post*, which evoked a "You can write!" from the editor. Mrs. Langley was convinced of the needlessness of the poverty she saw in the great city and elsewhere in rich America. "The trouble with America has never been overproduction. The trouble is obstructed consumption. When you see peaches being dumped . . . and oil being poured over lemons in California, and then you see hungry children, you know that something is wrong." But Mrs. Langley has also expressed her confidence in America, certain that it can right itself. "If we could solve the problems of money and distribution, we could get at the cause of war. . . .America ought to be able to solve these problems and it should be her destiny to show the answer to the rest of the world." The two great sores of America, Mrs. Langley feels, are poverty and demagoguery; and her novel *A Lion Is in the Streets*, aimed particularly at the latter, is the expression of the author's convictions.

A Lion Is in the Streets, published in the late spring of 1945, is a "first" novel in several respects: it is Mrs. Langley's first attempt at fiction; it was first on the best-seller list for a number of weeks; and it is the first novel to have its screen rights sold for as high as two hundred and fifty thousand dollars. The conditions under which the novel was written were unique. According to the author, the greater part of the book was written between the hours of twelve, midnight, and five in the morning. Her successive daytime jobs during that period were highly different: she worked in an advertising agency, taught psychology in a Long Beach (California) school, and worked as a riveter in a war plant at Santa Monica. For months she went to bed at nine, got up at midnight and wrote until five in the morning, when she would go to sleep again for two hours and then report for work. Since this schedule could not be continued indefinitely, five women friends managed to raise eight hundred dollars to enable her to devote full time to the book.

As the book took form, the author read the manuscript to groups of fellow war workers at one of the homes, where the friends would listen to the story of the rise to power of Hank Martin, "a robust tale, full of the un-tamed coarse eloquence of a backwoods spellbinder." Mrs. Langley, says Harry Hansen [42] of the New York *World-Telegram*, has put life into a novel of politics. "Her story shows how dictators rise on the feelings of the common people and fall when the honesty inherent in democracy catches up with them." Mrs. Langley's method of approach to this exploiting politician is not one of sharp denunciation. Sterling North [43] has written in his review of *A Lion Is in the Streets*: "The most unusual aspect of this novel is the extreme sympathy and understanding which the author shows for the leading character. . . .Her almost Tolstoyan understanding, her real love for people and for America are deeper wellsprings for effective fiction than sheer hatred of fascism." For nearly half of the book Hank Martin is presented as an admirable character. Even when he is only a peddler he is "a king among men," says N. L. Rothman writing in the *Saturday Review of Literature*. Various critics who think that Hank Martin is intended to represent Huey Long have criticized Mrs. Langley for not probing more deeply into the causes that have contributed to the making of such a man, but Mrs. Langley has denied that she intended to write a fictionized account of the career of Long. Martin, she says, is merely the universal demagogue.

Seldom has a book been received with such fanfare as Adria Langley's *A Lion Is in the Streets*. It ran in the *Saturday Evening Post*, eighty-five thousand copies of the book were ordered, and Mrs. Langley was feted by important literary figures before the book was published. In September it was dramatized on the air. To an editor who asked Mrs. Langley how it felt to be the object of so much attention, the author answered with good humor, "The critics haven't read the book yet. My position as an author being entertained before the book comes out is like that of a pet pig being fed and brushed and scrubbed—with all this lavish care, we both aren't sure whether it's for 'Show' or for 'Slaughter.'"

Mrs. Langley's favorite books are the Bible—from which she took the title of her novel (Proverbs, Chap. 26:13)—and the works of Francis Bacon. Described as a hearty, completely unaffected person, the red-headed author admits readily that she is thoroughly enjoying her success. In New York she and her teen-age daughter, Faith, live in a Park Avenue penthouse.

Reference

N Y Post Mag p25 Je 29 '45 por

LATTIMORE, OWEN (lă′tĭ-mōr) July 29, 1900- Orientalist; author; educator

Address: b. Johns Hopkins University, Baltimore, Md.

For the second time since he became director of the Johns Hopkins University Walter Hines Page School of International Relations in 1938, Owen Lattimore, in October 1945, was asked to take a leave of absence by the President of the United States. On the latter occasion the Orientalist and writer, a former adviser to Chiang Kai-shek [40], was appointed special economic adviser to Edwin W. Pauley [45], head of

President Truman's [45] economic mission to Tokyo. Since 1942 Lattimore's knowledge and understanding of the Far East—its people and problems—which he acquired in twenty-five years of travel and study in Asia, have proved of value to the United States Government. It has been reported that the only two books on the President's desk when he announced the surrender of Japan to the press were John Gunther's [41] *Inside Asia* (1939) and Owen Lattimore's *Solution in Asia* (1945).

Born in Washington, D.C., on July 29, 1900, Owen Lattimore until 1928 spent only the first few months of his life in his native country. The year of his birth his parents, David and Margaret (Barnes) Lattimore, moved to Northern China, where Lattimore's father was for twenty years in the educational service of the Chinese Government. When the boy was twelve years old he was sent to Europe to receive a western education. He spent two years at a school in Switzerland and then, in 1915, went to the St. Bees School in Cumberland, England. After being graduated four years later, Lattimore returned to China.

In 1920 he took a newspaper job in Shanghai. After two years he began work in Peiping and Tientsin for Arnhold and Company, Ltd., a firm that exported the produce of all of China's frontier dependencies, from Manchuria to northern Tibet and Turkestan. Four years later the young man resigned from his position and turned to exploring and writing about this territory, with which his work had made him familiar.

Before starting on his first long trip Lattimore was married, in 1926, to Eleanor Holgate, whose father, Thomas F. Holgate, was a mathematics professor, and acting president of Northwestern University in 1904-06 and in 1916-18. She had traveled in China with her parents in 1921 and had returned to Peiping three years later to teach in the Chinese schools. At the time of her marriage she was the secretary of the Peking Institute of Fine Arts. The Lattimores, who now have one son, David, spent their honeymoon traveling native style— on horseback, by camel train, and sled—across the hinterland of Mongolia through Chinese Turkestan. They were accompanied on the trip by Lattimore's Chinese servant, Moses. (Mrs. Lattimore's letters to her family were published in 1934 in book form under the title of *Turkestan Reunion*.)

In 1929 Lattimore traveled and studied in Manchuria on a fellowship from the Social Science Research Council; then, for the next three years he studied in Peiping and traveled in Inner Mongolia, first on a fellowship from the Harvard-Yenching Foundation and later on a John Simon Guggenheim Memorial Foundation fellowship, which was renewed for a second year in 1932. That summer he hired a Mongolian servant, Arash, with whom he wandered about intermittently for the next few years. In 1935 Lattimore, Arash, and a traveling companion were given permission to attend the annual memorial services held at the alleged repository of the bones (or ashes) of Genghis Khan. Lattimore and his friend were the first white men to view the shrine, from which they came away unconvinced that the remains of Genghis Khan were really there. Lattimore con-

OWEN LATTIMORE

tinued to live in Peiping and travel in China and Inner Mongolia until 1937 when the Japanese occupation made life in China difficult. He returned to the United States and the next year became director of the Walter Hines Page School of International Relations of Johns Hopkins University.

Lattimore, who is regarded as probably the only American with a thorough knowledge of the three frontier regions of China, Manchuria, Sinkiang, and Inner Mongolia, and who is equally at home in the Chinese, Mongol, and Russian languages, was recommended by President Roosevelt [42] in 1941 for the post of political adviser to Generalissimo Chiang Kai-shek. The Chinese leader accepted the President's recommendation, and Lattimore embarked for China for a six-month period.

In late 1942 Lattimore returned to the United States to take a post with the Office of War Information; he became deputy director of the overseas branch in charge of Pacific operations, with headquarters in San Francisco. Within two years, in June 1944, he was on his way back to China and Siberia as a member of Vice-President Wallace's [40] diplomatic party, which completed its mission in July of that year. In the early part of 1945 Lattimore resigned from the OWI post to resume his work at Johns Hopkins University, only to be called back into his country's service in October, when President Truman appointed him special economic adviser to Edwin W. Pauley, head of the economic mission to Japan. Of this appointment *PM* said: "In a long writing career, Lattimore has consistently expounded the cause of democracy in Asia. Acting as adviser to Generalissimo Chiang Kai-shek, he was not afraid to speak up against dictatorial tendencies, and in his new job he can be counted on to oppose the Zaibatsu, Japan's clique of industrialists."

Since 1926, when he resigned from the export firm, Lattimore has made important contributions to the literature on Asia. His first two books, *Desert Road to Turkestan* and *High Tartary,* published in 1929 and 1930 respec-

LATTIMORE, OWEN—*Continued*

tively, were written as a result of the year-long journey taken by the author and his wife. Both of these books were well received by the critics, the first being called "an interesting account" and the second "a fascinating and well-packed book." In 1932 he wrote *Man-churia—Cradle of Conflict*, a study of Man-churia's place in Chinese history and the significance of its relationship to the three types of civilization with which it comes in direct contact: the traditional culture of China, west-ernization as typified by Japan, and the new cultural influence of Soviet Russia. R. H. Tawney, in the *New Statesman and Nation*, said that the book was "the most learned and penetrating study [of its subject] available in English." Two years later *Mongols of Man-churia*, a supplement to his earlier work on Manchuria, was published. In 1940 he wrote *Inner Asian Frontiers*, a history of China's northern and western frontiers. The next year *Mongol Journeys*, the reminiscences of his years of wandering in Mongolia, came out. It was described in the New York *Times* as "an easily and sometimes beautifully written book." The author collaborated with Mrs. Lattimore on *The Making of Modern China* (1944), a short history of China.

In 1945 Lattimore's book *Solution in Asia* received enthusiastic reviews from the critics. In it the author discusses the future of the Asiatic countries as he sees it. He feels that they do not intend to become the victims of imperialism again and that the Allies must understand their drive towards self-expression and cooperate by helping them take their rightful places in a world of united nations. In an interview with a *PM* reporter, while he was still adviser to Chiang, he said, "Those people [Chinese, Indians and Indonesians] may be illiterate, but they know the kind of world they want to live in. They may not be able to read or write, but politically they are mature." Lattimore criticizes Joseph C. Grew's [41] plan to govern the Japanese people through the Emperor. He believes the Emperor and all his male heirs should be interned in China and a republic set up in Japan. Edgar Snow [41], authority on Far Eastern affairs, wrote in his review of the book: This book brilliantly illuminates the main questions of our time in Asia, and how they could be answered by an intelligent, vertebrate policy. . . . In order to win acceptance for such measures we need a new philosophy in Congress, which in turn (and alone) could impose it on the State Department." The book was also described as an "appeal to Chiang to free himself from the galling yoke [of the Kuomintang] and to set free the democratic forces which have proved effective in northwestern China." In its bulletin to librarians the East and West Association chose *Solution in Asia* as "the best recent book on Eastern peoples." It was also one of the three books selected by the Recommended Book Committee of the Council of Books in Wartime.

In addition to his books Lattimore has written articles on Asia, on such subjects as its geography, history, anthropology, and politics. They have been published in the *Atlantic Monthly*, *Asia*, *New Republic*, and *Virginia Quarterly Review*. From 1934 until 1941 the writer was editor of *Pacific Affairs*, the maga-zine published by the Institute of Pacific Affairs. Lattimore is a Gold Medallist of the Philadelphia Geographical Society and of the Royal Geographical Society of London, and a member of the American Geographical Society and the Royal Central Asia Society. He is five feet eight inches tall and weighs one hundred and seventy-five pounds. Interviewers have described him as tactful and self-effacing.

References

N Y Herald Tribune p9 Je 29 '41
N Y Herald Tribune Books p4 F 9 '41
N Y Sun p11 D 31 '44
America's Young Men, 1938-39
Who's Who, 1945
Who's Who in America, 1944-45

LATTRE DE TASSIGNY, JEAN (JO-SEPH MARIE GABRIEL) DE (là-tr tà" sĕ"nyĕ' zhäN) Feb. 2, 1889- French Army officer

General Jean de Lattre de Tassigny is not only one of the youngest five-star generals of the French Army, but was regarded by many as General Charles de Gaulle's [40] ablest field commander. With the United States Seventh Army, his French First Army formed the Allied Sixth Army Group in France.

Jean Joseph Marie Gabriel de Lattre de Tassigny was born February 2, 1889, at Mouilleron-en-Pareds (Vendée), birthplace of Clemenceau. Graduated from St. Cyr in 1910, he was a lieutenant in a cavalry regiment at the beginning of the First World War. In September 1914 he was wounded by a lance thrust in the chest but escaped from the enemy cavalry surrounding him, killing more than one German in hand-to-hand combat—slashing them down with a saber his grandfather had carried in the Napoleonic wars. The following year he was transferred to the infantry, and for three years he commanded a battalion of the Ninety-third Infantry Regiment. (By the end of the war he had been wounded four more times.)

After the First World War the young Frenchman participated in the Moroccan campaign at General Poeymiraud's headquarters, and afterward served as chief of staff of the Taza region. He was seriously wounded in the Riff campaign in 1925. A brevetted officer of l'Ecole Supérieure de Guerre, he then served as General Maxime Weygand's [40] chief of cabinet and later as chief of staff of the Fifth Army; before the outbreak of the Second World War De Lattre made himself popular as commander of the 151st Infantry at Metz—a regiment mainly composed of Parisian Communists. He is a Grand Officier de la Légion d'Honneur, and has received thirteen citations for bravery in action.

During the Second World War, De Lattre commanded the Fourteenth ("Iron") Division of Infantry, which distinguished itself at the defense of Rethel and on the Aisne from May 15 to June 11, 1940. His men threw the Germans back in the Aisne three times, and reached the Marne, then the Loire, still resisting heroically. On June 18, just before the conclusion of the armistice, De Lattre went to the French High Command to propose continuing the battle against the Germans by sending the Fourteenth Division either to England or to North Africa. With his plan rejected and the armistice concluded, De Lattre began devoting all his energy to "renovating" the Army of the Armistice and teaching modern methods of warfare. He was too successful to suit Vichy, and in September 1941 he was removed from his post and appointed commander of troops in Tunisia. Several weeks later came the British offensive in Libya; Rommel's [42] forces retreated before Montgomery [42], beside whom fought the Free French. By mid-December De Lattre had been informed that the German-Italian High Command was retreating from the region of Tripoli and, believing that Rommel might retreat to the Mareth Line, he ordered all troops under his command to resist any Axis attempt to penetrate into French territory. Once more Vichy apparently became alarmed, and on January 7, 1942, De Lattre was recalled to France and named commander of the Sixteenth Mechanized Division at Montpellier.

He was still military commander of the Montpellier region in France when on November 8, 1942, came news of the Allied landings in North Africa. Certain that the Germans would invade the Vichy zone (and perhaps believing that the Allied invasion of metropolitan France was at hand), he ordered dispositions for battle in an attempt to delay any German advance to the Mediterranean. He did succeed in allowing many anti-Nazis to escape to North Africa by way of the small port of Sète, which he succeeded in keeping open for a few hours with only two hundred men; but he ended in a Vichy military prison, accused of having attempted a personal *Putsch*. Haled before the State Court, on January 9, 1943, De Lattre was condemned to ten years in prison. At Riom fifty policemen armed with rifles and submachine guns were posted to prevent his escape, on the personal orders of Pierre Laval [40].

The detailed story of his escape has never been told; but it was accomplished on September 2, 1943, by his sawing the bars of his cell window and letting himself down by a rope. The French underground "railroad" helped him to reach London, and there he concealed his identity so successfully that as late as November the Paris press believed that he was leading a guerrilla force against the Germans in France itself. On December 22, 1943, however, he arrived in Algiers, and there he placed himself at the disposal of General de Gaulle. Later that month he was appointed to head all the French forces in North Africa.

May 1944 found General de Lattre with De Gaulle on a three-day inspection of victorious French troops with the Fifth Army at the front in Italy, and on June 17, 1944, units of French Army "B" commanded by him disembarked at Elba in the first all-French amphibious operation of the war. Then, on August 15, 1944, came the invasion of the French Mediterranean coast. The first assault troops to land were the Third, Thirty-six, and Forty-fifth divisions, veterans of the Italian campaign, accompanied by French troops under De Lattre's command. Their numbers were not large, for the southern landing was complementary and subsidiary to the northern operations, but they soon won glory for themselves in some of the bitterest fighting that had yet

GEN. JEAN DE LATTRE DE TASSIGNY

taken place. The original plan had been to assault the port area around Toulon and Marseille six days after D Day, but spies had brought information that the Germans had densely mined these ports and were planning to destroy them and then take up defensive positions in forts outside the towns. De Lattre therefore ordered an assault a day before schedule, in order to cut off the German garrison, with one-half of his forces still not ashore. In cleaning up the region 53,500 Germans were reportedly killed or captured—and at a cost of only one thousand French casualties. General Dwight Eisenhower [42] himself congratulated De Lattre on the "speed and brilliance" with which the French troops had broken German resistance at Toulon and Marseille, and General Alexander Patch [43], commander of the United States Seventh Army, called the action a "feat of arms which will go down as an epic in the annals of history." In September 1944 the daring French General was honored by De Gaulle with the Croix de la Libération. In France De Lattre was a hero who found mobs gathered at every town hall to cheer him, while passing French troops tossed out cans of American rations to villagers.

On September 22, 1944, it was announced that De Lattre's army, reinforced by elements of the F.F.I., was prepared for new operations. A week later the French First Army succeeded in breaking through the outer defenses of Belfort Gap in a wide swinging movement from the northwest. For many weeks after this, however, De Lattre's was an almost completely forgotten front. The fighting was bitter, and made more bitter because of bad weather and delay in the delivery of winter equipment. It was not until November 19 that the French First Army succeeded in crashing through Belfort Gap itself, in a sudden advance after weeks of pressure. De Lattre confided later that the French offensive had taken the Germans by surprise: "Our offensive was launched in such a snowstorm the Germans could not possibly imagine we would have the

LATTRE DE TASSIGNY, JEAN DE—

Continued

audacity to spring upon them." Belfort and Metz had been considered two of the strongest fortresses on the eastern border of France, Belfort being ringed by more than a score of formidable satellite forts which have never been taken by storm since their construction by Louis XIV. Actually Prime Minister Winston Churchill's '42 visit to De Lattre's army in the Vosges on November 13 had served as a pretext for moving a great number of troops and quantities of artillery "for the parade."

By December 1, 1944, the general Allied offensive had driven the Germans from all but about three thousand square miles of France—less than 2 per cent of the country's area. As for the American Seventh and French First armies, they were also pushing the drive on Alsace, of which the Germans still held a fifty-mile stretch. According to De Lattre's estimate, the equivalent of three German divisions had already been destroyed by his army alone, which, he claimed, had killed ten thousand Germans and captured fifteen thousand; two German divisions or their equivalent in manpower were still fighting on the French Army's front. By the end of December, however, the Germans were still trying to tie up the southern half of the Sixth Army Group by forcing some limited withdrawals, and by hanging on obstinately to a six-hundred-square-mile bridgehead across the Rhine around Colmar, apparently figuring that so long as they held this bridgehead the French could undertake no other major move.

Aware of the threat which the existence of a German bridgehead in Alsace meant to his army and to the whole Allied front, General de Lattre insisted on launching an attack to reduce the pocket of Colmar, in which he met with the full agreement of General Devers and General Eisenhower. The Twenty-first Army Corps, including such famous American divisions as the Third, the Twenty-eighth, the Seventy-fifth, and the Twenty-eighth Armored, were placed under his command as reinforcements. In the last days of January, despite bad weather, the attack against the German defenses was launched. A fortnight later Colmar was captured and the Nineteenth German Army thrown back on the right bank of the Rhine, leaving 23,000 prisoners in Allied hands. Won under the most difficult circumstances, this victory has been called the "Victory of the Will." Late in March De Lattre broke through the Siegfried Line, crossed the Rhine, and drove over the Danube more than three hundred kilometers into German and Austrian territory. Within twenty-five days the Nineteenth and Twenty-fourth German Armies were defeated, Baden and Württemberg invaded and occupied, and 175,000 Germans captured, among them thirty-four generals.

From September 1944 General de Lattre never ceased to welcome in the ranks of his Army the volunteers or the small units which had fought in the Maquis. Though poorly armed and equipped with parachuted or captured material, they were trained in front-line fighting. Like their ancestors, the volunteers of the French Revolution, they proved themselves to be gallant soldiers. The success of this newly amalgamated army is seen as a tribute to General de Lattre's leadership. The General, who had attended the signing of the surrender of Germany on May 9, 1945, was made commmander of the French occupation forces in Germany. Late in November of the same year the French Cabinet appointed him Inspector General of the Armies and Chief of the General Staff.

Long-faced, large-nosed General de Lattre has been described by Pertinax '40 as "a man of brilliant intelligence with a magnetic personality." Jacob L. Devers '42, the American general, paid a tribute to De Lattre when he called him the "Liberator of Alsace."

References

Lettre de la France au Combat 3:1-4 No 11
N Y Herald Tribune p3 D 24 '43; II p3 Ag 27 '44 por
N Y Sun p14 D 28 '43
N Y Times p4 Ja 9 '43; p1+ Ja 10 '43; p4 D 24 '43; p4 Ag 17 '44
Newsweek 23:28 Ja 3 '44 por

LAUGER, PAUL (loi'gĕr poul) Jan. 16, 1896- Swiss chemist; businessman

MULLER, PAUL (HERMAN) (mül'ĕr poul hĕr'män) Jan. 12, 1899- Swiss chemist

Address: b. c/o J. R. Geigy, S. A., Basle, Switzerland

"Soldiers have rarely won wars," said Hans Zinsser in his *Rats, Lice, and History.* "They more often mop up after the barrage of epidemics. . . . War is today, as much as ever, 75 per cent an engineering and sanitary problem, and a little less than 25 per cent a military one. Other things being approximately equal, that army will win which has the best engineering and sanitary services." In the Second World War, where Allied troops fought in all parts of the earth and Allied medical officers therefore had to cope with nearly every disease there is, one of the most powerful defensive weapons was the insecticide DDT, which became a peacetime staple. First used by the United States forces when the Japanese conquest of Malaya cut off supplies of the usual pyrethrum and rotenone, with a corresponding scarcity of copper and arsenic, DDT proved to be a "really phenomenal" insecticide. Developed in 1939 by the Swiss scientist Dr. Paul Müller, under the direction of Dr. Paul Läuger, it has been in commercial use since that time. "The public health potentials of DDT are enormous," writes Dr. Iago Galdston. "DDT will, for example, protect cloth against moths . . . will protect trees and plants against many insect pests. . . . But DDT more directly affects health in its extraordinary power to destroy disease-transmitting insects such as flies, fleas, mosquitoes, ticks, and other bloodsuckers."

Paul Läuger, who directed the research which produced DDT, was born in Basle, Switzerland, on January 16, 1896. He is the son of Lorenz and Emma (Dätwyler) Läuger. After attending the public elementary and high schools of Basle, he entered Basle University, where he majored in chemistry; he also studied physics, mathematics, zoology, and botany. In 1918 young Läuger became assistant in the department of organic chemistry. Majoring in that subject, he was graduated in 1919 with the Ph.D. *summa cum laude*, and he is described as the ablest student of chemistry ever to have studied there.

After graduation Dr. Läuger joined the firm of J. R. Geigy, also in Basle, an old company with branches all over Europe and in America, which manufactured and distributed dyestuffs and which was staffed with eminent scientists. For the next twelve years the chemist did research on azo-triphenyl-methane and chinonimid dyestuffs, and in that period invented what he modestly dismisses as "different groups of dyestuffs." In 1930-31 he began his research in the field of insecticides, working on mothproofing agents and also textile auxiliaries. Then Läuger drew up plans on which the company's future research in the entire insecticide field was to be based.

In 1933 Läuger was made assistant manager of the Geigy company and appointed chief of research in four new departments: synthetic tanning agents, insecticides, textile auxiliaries, and certain dyestuffs. Four years later he was promoted to chief of research of all departments, including dyestuffs, coloristic work, and biologicals; at the same time the forty-one-year-old chemist was elected to the board of directors. In 1939 (the year Dr. Paul Müller of his staff discovered DDT) Läuger added pharmaceutical research to his responsibilities. As of 1945, his staff of sixty-five research scientists is at work in two large laboratory buildings on organic synthesis, pharmacology, bacteriology, physiology, zoology, phytopathology, physics, and other research. Läuger has written extensively on sulfonamides, mothproofing agents, and insecticides, in collaboration with his co-workers in the field. In 1944, when DDT had become a household word, the University of Basle conferred an honorory M.D. upon its distinguished graduate for his direction of the Geigy research laboratory.

The actual inventor or rediscoverer of DDT, Paul Herman Müller, was born January 12, 1899, in Olten, Switzerland. His parents were Gottlieb Müller, an official of the Swiss Federal Railroads, and Fanny (Leypoldt) Müller. After attending the Free Evangelical Elementary School and Teachers College, he left college at seventeen and entered the employ of Dryfus and Company as assistant chemist in the Cellonite Society, where he worked a year in the testing laboratory of the Lonza Electric Works. Returning to Teachers College in 1918, he passed final examinations in 1919.

Next came postgraduate studies, first under Professor Fichter in the department of inorganic chemistry, and in 1922 in organic chemistry under Professor H. Rupe. During this period, in 1921-22, young Müller was assistant lecturer to Fichter on rare metals. Having passed examinations in inorganic, physical, and organic chemistry, Müller became third assistant to Fichter in the college's inorganic chemistry laboratory, while the Professor encouraged and directed his work (1923-25) on "The Chemical and Electrochemical Exidation of as.m-Xylidins and its Mono-and Di-methyl Derivatives."

In May 1925 Dr. Müller entered the Geigy firm as assistant manager of the dyewood department. Here he worked on developing synthetic tanning substances, which led in the

A. F. Sozio

PAUL LAUGER

period 1930-32 to the production of Irgatan G. Irgatan FL, and Irgatan FLT. Müller next turned his attention to disinfectants, and in 1936 worked on the problem of protecting plants against pests. Three years of work culminated in the discovery of a seed mordant, named Graminon, and of the insecticides Gesarol and Neocid, which contained the substance now known as DDT.

"The first compound found to have outstanding contact effectiveness," says Müller of his discovery, "was 2,2-diphenyl 1,1,1, trichloroethane. . . .While the Geigy Laboratories had for years been using the clothes moth for biological tests, I used flies chiefly. This compound was found to be very effective against flies. Many substances in which the phenyl group was substituted in para position were made, and finally amongst many other compositions I synthesized DDT"—dichloro-diphenyltrichloroethane, or 2,2 Bis (P-Chlorophenyl) 1,1,1, Trichloroethane. It was later found that a German student had synthesized DDT in 1874, but had not put it to any practical use.

Müller's experiments showed that DDT solutions and emulsions were effective, and that a powder formed of 3 to 5 per cent DDT in an inert carrier like talcum or chalk was more effective than pure DDT. A spray was made of water and extremely slight concentrations of a "wettable dust" of DDT, which were very effective against the imported cabbage worm and the Colorado potato beetle and its larvae. Tests showed that DDT was a contact poison of "astounding effectiveness," which remained lethal to insects for months after application, was unaffected by water, and could be removed with alcohol, oil, kerosene, or other organic solvents.

After extensive testing, Dr. Robert Wiesmann of the Government's Agricultural Experiment Station at Wädenswil, Switzerland, published the first important papers on the effectiveness of the DDT insecticide Gesarol. (Wiesmann later became the Geigy company's

LAUGER, PAUL, and MULLER, PAUL
—Continued

chief entomologist.) The first commercial use was in Switzerland in 1939, to combat the Colorado potato beetle. When bands of refugees from the Nazi invasion began streaming across the French border into Switzerland, the authorities used a DDT compound, Neocid, in delousing them.

In October 1942 J. R. Geigy's New York subsidiary notified the Washington officials of their insecticides. Their claims were verified by Department of Agriculture tests, and DDT manufacture was started in April 1943. That December its products were rushed to Naples for use by the Allied military governor, Brigadier General Edgar Erskine Hume '44, in checking a threatening epidemic of typhus. What made DDT famous, however, was its employment by the United States armed forces, who used airplanes to spray it over South Pacific islands and atolls before invasion, thus protecting the troops from malaria, typhus, dengue, filiarasis, and other insect-borne diseases. Such a development was obviously of the first importance; reported by war correspondents, it made DDT a household word and alarmed wildlife ecologists who feared its indiscriminate postwar use. Ninety per cent of all insects are beneficial, they pointed out, performing such functions as pollination, while the birds and animals which eat insects "make up one-half the base that supports the whole natural economy. . . .If DDT should ever be used widely and without care," said Richard Pough,

A. F. Sozio

PAUL MULLER

"we would have a country without fresh-water fish, serpents, frogs, and most of the birds we have now." The Geigy chemists therefore turned their attention to developing some means of immunity from DDT for the beneficial insects.

The United States Government invited Läuger, Müller, and Wiesmann to confer with American scientists and officials, and the three Swiss scientists arrived in July 1945. At a

press conference in late August, before their return, Müller answered questions through his colleague Läuger, who speaks fluent English; and the two posed for pictures, which show Müller as slight and dark, with a boyish smile, and Läuger as taller and broader than his colleague, silver-haired, and looking like a handsome and non-sinister Boris Karloff '41. Paul Müller is five feet ten inches tall and has brown hair and eyes; he is married and has three children, and spends his week-ends with his family in the mountains. Paul Läuger, his elder by three years, is an inch taller, with gray-blue eyes and fair complexion. When asked his hobby, he answers, "Work!"

LAURENCE, WILLIAM L(EONARD)
Mar. 7, 1888- Journalist

Address: b. c/o New York Times, 229 W. 43d St., New York City; h. 541 E. 72d St., New York City

The high point of a colorful career, which had its beginnings in a Russian political purge in 1905 and which has included during the last fifteen years the reporting of outstanding events in the world of science, came for William L. Laurence when the United States War Department chose him in 1945 to prepare the atomic bomb story for the public. Science reporter at large for the New York *Times* since 1930, in 1940 he had scooped the daily press with the first article on uranium fission.

William Leonard Laurence, as he has been known for most of his life, was born to Lipman and Sarah (Preuss) Siew, devout orthodox Jews, in Salantai, Lithuania, on March 7, 1888, when that country was politically a part of Russia. His intellectual tendencies showed themselves while he was still a young boy, and his resolve to come to the United States was taken during his early teens. The story, as told in the *New Yorker*, is that this decision resulted from the gift of a book dealing with a possible Martian civilization: it so kindled his imagination that he determined on establishing contact with Mars—which he thought could best be done from the United States. He soon had his opportunity. A political purge in 1905, when he was seventeen years old, forced him to flee Salantai. He finally landed in Hoboken, New Jersey, with, it is said, no more than fifty cents in assets. His destination was Boston, the fame of which city as an intellectual center had spread to Lithuania. To obtain the railroad fare young Siew found work in a Brooklyn textile factory. Arriving in the Hub, he secured a job with a florist and was soon sent on the errand across the Charles River which was to change his destiny, for it was while delivering a funeral wreath in Cambridge that he passed Harvard University and determined to study there. In 1906 he moved to Roxbury, a suburb of Boston, and lived on Lawrence Avenue, from which, changing the *w* to *u*, he took his surname at that time.

Having earned the money necessary for his tuition and expenses, the youth enrolled at Harvard in 1908. Majoring in philosophy, he studied under such eminent teachers as Palmer, Royce, and Santayana '44. While lack of funds forced him to drop out in 1911, he re-entered the university in the spring of 1914 and completed his course of study the next year. However, having neglected to fulfill all the university's requirements for graduation, he was not given a degree but was awarded the distinction of *cum laude* in philosophy instead.

Meanwhile, in 1913 Laurence had become a naturalized American citizen. The tutoring career which he followed for the next several years began during his final year at Harvard, when just before examinations two football players approached him for coaching in philosophy. When Laurence agreed they returned with forty-eight of their comrades and, grouped on the lawn below Laurence's window, listened to a six-hour lecture. So enthusiastic were the athletes that they insisted upon each paying him five dollars and receiving similar instruction the following day. Laurence's fame as a tutor soon spread, and shortly after commencement he was employed by the Roxbury Tutoring School, which was about to establish a branch in Cambridge. Until he joined the Army in 1917 Laurence tutored Harvard students in philosophy, psychology, and Russian literary history, and engaged brilliant Harvard undergraduates, notably chemistry student James Bryant Conant '41, to assist in other fields of learning.

Concluding a year's training course in the United States in 1917-18, Laurence went overseas in 1918 with the 301st Field Signal Battalion of the Seventy-sixth Division, United States Army. In France he intercepted and decoded German wireless dispatches and wrote the texts of surrender invitations which were dropped from the air behind the German lines. "After the Armistice," says the *New Yorker*, "he received fleeting attention when he went AWOL, informally liberated the city of Metz, and occupied it for five days, until Marshal Petain '40 arrived to relieve him." Then, during part of 1919, he studied at the University of Besançon in France at Government expense.

Returning to Cambridge that summer Laurence founded the Mt. Auburn Tutoring School with the soldier's bonus he received from Massachusetts. For two years he continued as its director and one of its instructors, but in 1921 he closed its doors and entered the Harvard Law School. Although he received his LL.B. in 1925 from Boston University, to which he had transferred, and passed his State bar examination, he did not practice but continued for a while one of the pursuits of his previous four years—free-lance writing and play adaptation. Three of the plays he adapted during this period have been produced: *Mr. Paraclete* (from the Russian of Evreinov) by the Harvard Dramatic Club in 1925; *At the Bottom* (from the Russian of Gorki) and *Devil in the Mind* (from the Russian of Andreyev) in New York in 1930 and 1931, respectively.

Laurence arrived in New York in 1926 with no job in sight. However, through a former student of his a chain of fortunate circumstances led to his inclusion in a party invited to the home of Herbert Bayard Swope '44, then editor of the New York *World*. There Laurence soon found himself engaged in a certain quiz game in which his host excelled. When he vanquished the hitherto invincible Swope, the editor demanded, "Who are you,

WILLIAM L. LAURENCE

and why?" Laurence apologized and explained, mentioning in due course that he was unemployed—whereupon Swope hired him as a reporter for the *World*.

Passed on to an unenthusiastic city editor, he nevertheless acquitted himself creditably on stiff assignments—often because he could call upon former students for aid. He located an obscure Russian spy within two hours, for instance, because he had the assistance of a former student who had become an FBI official. Laurence continued as general reporter for the *World* until 1930, supplementing those duties, from 1927 on, with the responsibilities of associate aviation editor; scientific assignments, which he preferred, were, on the other hand, few and scattered. Once, however, his erudition caused him to be assigned to cover a meeting of the American Philosophical Association at Columbia University, at which Professor James MacKaye of Dartmouth was scheduled to read a paper exploding the Einstein '41 theory. Unable to follow the Professor's involved mathematics, Laurence interviewed him after the lecture, obtained the general idea, and wrote the story for the *World*. The article later assured Laurence's appointment as science reporter for the New York *Times* when, in an interview with Laurence in 1930, acting *Times* managing editor Frederick T. Birchall remembered that the *Times* had been scooped on this event because none of its reporters had been qualified to handle it.

Since 1930 Laurence's roving commission for the *Times* has made it possible for him to report science exclusively. Not held to regular hours or deadlines, nor given specific assignments, he covers scientific meetings and culls scientific and technological periodicals for subject matter. He works independently of science editor and columnist Waldemar Kaempffert '43, producing scientifically accurate articles in laymen's language under such headlines as "Chemist Sees Age of Methusalehs" and "Life Is Created Without Parents." Many of his leads come from the letters-to-the-editor columns of prom-

LAURENCE, WILLIAM L.—*Continued*

inent scientific journals, such as the *Physical Review*, in which scientists present tentative theories and conclusions to their professional colleagues. It was a few lines printed in the *Physical Review* concerning the successful isolation of uranium 235 (which established as fact what Laurence had previously learned from the scientists concerned) that led him to write the story of atomic fission and potential atomic power with which he scooped the New York press in the *Times* of May 5, 1940. This account was afterward expanded for the *Saturday Evening Post* of September 7, 1940, causing the FBI to investigate would-be readers of the issue after censorship was imposed on atomic experiments. Laurence has also been first with the stories of the sulfa drugs and penicillin, and it was a hint of his which initiated the Squibb Company experimentation that produced sulfadiazine. It has been said that "perhaps his greatest contribution to human welfare is his reduction of the time lag between scientific discoveries and their useful application."

Gifted with a remarkable memory for scientific detail, Laurence has at times been able to correlate some of the accidental discoveries of scientists too immersed in their experiments to pay attention to happenings outside of their own laboratories. It may be that he recollects that someone to whom he had been talking was seeking information he has just heard. "While it is probable," Laurence once ended an article, "that some if not most of these suggestions are now under consideration, or are being tested, by others, they are hereby presented in the hope that they may prove useful in crystallizing an idea." At another time, his explanation in a *Times* article of iconoscope inventor Dr. Vladimir K. Zworykin's idea for a television supermicroscope made RCA officials realize the value of the invention then reposing in their files. His own chief contribution to scientific theory—the use of avidin to fight cancer—was the result of his correlation of isolated facts concerning cancer, erysipelas, the growth-promoting vitamin biotin, and the antivitamin substance avidin.

One day early in May 1945 Laurence failed to appear in the *Times* office, but only his wife and his managing editor, Edwin L. James, knew that the War Department had asked for his services on a top-priority project. Not until nearly three months later did his colleagues learn that Laurence had been chosen by the War Department to prepare the press releases on the atomic bomb. As the only newspaperman taken into the secret, Laurence during the spring and early summer inspected the various plans which made up the "Manhattan District," visited the Los Alamos, New Mexico, bomb laboratory and witnessed the test bombing on July 16 in the New Mexico desert.

On August 7 there appeared in the *Times* the War Department release beginning, "Mankind's successful transition to a new age, the Atomic Age, was ushered in July 16, 1945"— the *Times* had heard from its reporter. Before returning to his paper, Laurence flew with the airmen who dropped the bomb on Nagasaki and joined the group which investigated the possible persistence of dangerous radioactivity at the New Mexico testing ground. He began

in September a series of articles on the development and use of the atomic bomb, for which he received the annual award of the Silurian Society for the best editorial staff achievement in 1945 by a New York City newspaperman. Referring to Laurence's previous long silence, *Time* Magazine had lamented that "he had the story of his, or any newsman's life—but he couldn't write it"; however, Laurence will present this story in a book which he is preparing for publication in early 1946.

Laurence is "a small dark man . . . with a flattened nose," who speaks with a slight foreign accent. He was married on December 19, 1931, to Florence Davidow, daughter of the late Rabbi Joseph Anachowitz, of Lithuania; Laurence describes his wife, who is a graduate of the Pulitzer School of Journalism, "as an excellent cook and a very gracious hostess"; she writes poetry and is working on several novels. Because he has a great fondness for rivers, Laurence has installed in his New York apartment, which overlooks the East River, a series of mirrors arranged so that wherever one looks the water is visible—credit for which he says is largely due Mrs. Laurence. Among his numerous books are autographed first editions of two works of James Joyce, who hid the names of five hundred rivers in *Finnegans Wake*. Laurence also has a liking for gadgets and owns a dachshund which he has named Einstein. And among his possessions one will find a portrait by an Austrian refugee sportively depicting him as the universal mind.

Winner of the Pulitzer Prize in May 1937 for his reporting of the 1936 Harvard Tercentenary Conference of Arts and Sciences, and of a fellowship from the American Institute of the City of New York in 1940 for "a long-sustained pre-eminent record of reporting brilliantly to the daily press the achievements of science and technology," Laurence once humorously summed up his career: "I have been covering news in the realm of science, from astronomy to zoology and intermediate points. The infinitesimal and the infinite, from metagalaxies to microbes, constitute my present domain. I report news about the Einstein relativity and unified field theories, quantum mechanics, the cosmic ray, and the nucleus of the atom. I annihilate the universe with Eddington [41] and Jeans [41] and put it together again with Millikan [40]. If you want to know about genes and chromosomes, enzymes, hormones, vitamins, electrons, protons, photons, neutrons, and morons, read the New York *Times*."

References

New Yorker 21:26-30+ Ag 18 '45 por
Who's Who in America, 1944-45
Who's Who in American Jewry, 1938-39

LAVAL, PIERRE (lä"väl' pyâr) June 28, 1883—Oct. 15, 1945 French politician; became Premier of Vichy Government in 1942; leading exponent of collaboration with Germany; Premier (1931-32, 1935-36); Vice-Premier (1940); Minister of Foreign Affairs (1931-32, 1934-35, 1935-36); Minister of Labor (1932); Minister of Colonies (1934); tried for and convicted of treason before High Court of

Justice; executed by firing squad. See *Current Biography* 1940 Yearbook.

Obituary

N Y Times p1+ O 16 '45

LEE, BLAIR Aug. 9, 1857—Dec. 25, 1944 Former United States Democratic Senator from Maryland (1913-17); a leader in the organization that brought about the nomination of Woodrow Wilson for the Presidency.

Obituary

N Y Times p19 D 27 '44

LEE, WILLIS A(UGUSTUS, JR.) May 11, 1888—Aug. 25, 1945 Vice-Admiral in United States Navy; in 1942 appointed commander of a task force in the Southwest Pacific that sank a Japanese battleship and three cruisers off the Solomons; died of heart disease in Maine, where he had been for two months on a secret tactical assignment.

Obituary

N Y Times p43 Ag 26 '45 por

LEIGH-MALLORY, SIR TRAFFORD L(EIGH) July 11, 1892—Nov. 14(?), 1944 British air marshal; reported missing on flight to assume appointment as air commander in chief of the Southeast Asia Command; as commander in chief of the Allied Expeditionary Air Force he was responsible for the air offensive that preceded and accompanied the successful invasion of Western Europe in June 1944. See *Current Biography* 1944 Yearbook.

Obituary

N Y Times p1+ N 18 '44

LERCH, ARCHER L(YNN) Jan. 12, 1894- United States Army officer; lawyer

Address: b. c/o War Department, Washington, D.C.; h. 6416 31st Pl., N.W., Washington, D.C.

As of early 1945, the American Army's Corps of Military Police numbered more than two hundred thousand—more men than the entire United States Army six years earlier. Divided into small units, none larger than a battalion, and dispersed in most parts of the world, it performed "more diverse duties than any other branch of the Army." In addition to the always important disciplinary functions, the Second World War MP's acted as "a cross between an information bureau and a nurse"; as detectives, ferreting out spies, saboteurs, and black-market operators; as custodians of war prisoners; as riot control battalions; and as the traffic directors who made fast-moving mechanized warfare possible without breakdowns, or waded ashore on hostile beaches to direct the invading troops. This versatile Corps was headed during the Second World War by Major General Archer L. Lerch, the Provost Marshal General of the United States Army, who in December 1945 was reassigned to Korea as military governor of the American-occupied zone.

U.S. Army Signal Corps

MAJ. GEN. ARCHER L. LERCH

Archer Lynn Lerch was born in Sumner, Nebraska, on January 12, 1894, the son of Herman H. and Maud R. (Stevens) Lerch. His father was an Oakland (California) merchant. Young Lerch attended the University of California, graduating with the B.A. in 1917. Commissioned a second lieutenant of Infantry Section in the Officers' Reserve Corps when the United States entered the First World War in April, he was given a three-month training course in San Francisco, and then assigned to the Sixty-third Infantry there. That October Lerch accepted a commission in the Infantry of the Regular Army, and was immediately promoted to first lieutenant. In February 1918 he was married to Florence M. Wentworth, an Oakland girl.

Lieutenant Lerch spent two months in France with the American Expeditionary Forces, returning to America in January 1919. For the next two years he served at several Army posts, including three months as post adjutant at Fort Ontario, New York, and in July 1920 was promoted to the rank of captain. In May 1922, after an eight-month course at the Infantry School in Georgia, Lerch was stationed at Little Rock, Arkansas, as an instructor in the 153rd Infantry, Arkansas National Guard. After two years in Arkansas the thirty-year-old captain was sent to Cuartel-de-España in the Philippine Islands to join the Thirty-first Infantry.

In June 1926 Lerch returned to his old college, the University of California, where he remained five years as assistant professor of military science and tactics. After this, in September 1931, he went back to the tropics as legal adviser to General H. B. Wells at Hawaiian Department headquarters at Fort Shafter. His official title was Assistant Department Judge Advocate. In 1933 Lerch also became legal adviser to the Public Works Administration in the Territory, and in 1934 was named assistant deputy administrator and execu-

LERCH, ARCHER L.—*Continued*

tive officer for the National Recovery Administration in the Hawaiian Department.

The forty-year-old officer was promoted to major in August 1935. Typical of the United States Army at that time, it was his first advancement in fifteen years. In October he was sent to Fort Williams, Maine, for post and staff duties with the Fifth Infantry. Enrolled in the Command and General Staff School in Fort Leavenworth, Kansas, in August 1936, the future general was graduated in June 1937 and joined the University of Florida faculty as professor of military science and tactics.

In July 1938 Major Lerch transferred from the Infantry to the Judge Advocate General's Department, which handles courts-martial, military commissions of inquiry, and titles to lands owned by the War Department, and provides legal advice for various commands. Lerch's first assignment was to duty in the Military Affairs Section of the Judge Advocate General's Office in the Capital, as executive officer. From September 1938 to June 1939 he attended the George Washington University Law School as additional duty. In 1939 he successfully prosecuted Grover Cleveland Bergdoll, the First World War draft dodger, before a court-martial; and in 1942 the forty-eight-year-old officer received his LL.B. He has been admitted to practice before the bar of Florida and before the Supreme Court. During this period Lerch was promoted to lieutenant colonel in August 1940, and to colonel (temporary) in December 1941, seventeen days after Pearl Harbor. He had been ordered to the Army War College, which gives the country's highest military training, but these orders were revoked when the emergency was declared.

In November 1942 Lerch was appointed commanding officer of the Provost Marshal General Training Center and commandant of the Provost Marshal General School at Fort Custer, Michigan. A month later, with the temporary rank of brigadier general, he was assigned to duty in the Office of the Provost Marshal General in Washington. In May 1944 Lerch was made Acting Provost Marshal General, with the two stars of a major general, and in June became the Provost Marshal General.

As *Fortune* put it in June 1945, "the Provost Marshal General, Major General Lerch, has more major duties than the Pentagon has sides (actually his office is located in the War Department's shabby old Munitions Building). He is directly in charge of the Military Government Division; his other functions fall under three headings, each directed by an assistant provost marshal." The best known of these is that which General Lerch regards as the MP's primary job—to "keep the GI out of trouble." Besides checking on and enforcing military regulations and generally keeping order, the MP is told to "give information and advice, to help wounded veterans with their luggage, to see that soldiers get all reasonable breaks."

One of the MP's peacetime jobs which gained importance in war is "internal security," otherwise riot control, wherever Federal interests or property are threatened, or whenever

the President proclaims military intervention at the request of the Governor concerned. The Provost Marshal General, through his Security Intelligence Corps, also cooperates with the Treasury Department's Secret Service and the Justice Department's FBI in investigation, intelligence, and counterintelligence work.

One very important wartime development was the tactical use of MP's. For example, as *Fortune* states, "many a beachhead in New Guinea or on Pacific isles might have been lost if men and supplies plunging ashore out of charnel seas of landing barges had not been guided to their proper places for combat. . . . Many and many a convoy of men and weapons bound for the firing line would have come to grief in the mine fields or stalled before a dynamited bridge if they had not been signaled in time away from the wrong turning, by soldiers who knew the road nets and their conditions like the lines in the palms of their hands." General Patton's [43] spectacular drive across Germany would not have been possible had not MP traffic control made possible such maneuvers as two armored divisions crossing each other at right angles under combat conditions. "Many of these duties are performed not only under fire, but where fire is particularly sustained—at key road intersections and bridges and supply dumps and railroads. As a consequence the MP's in overseas service have acquired their share of combat decorations. Some 40 per cent of the MP's at Anzio, for example, got the Purple Heart."

But perhaps the most publicized and certainly the most unfavorably publicized task of General Lerch's command was the care of prisoners of war. All prisoners, including some taken by combat MP's themselves, were turned over to MP's directly behind the lines; in fluid fighting they could have been very dangerous if not quickly handled and efficiently guarded. It was those German, Italian, and Japanese soldiers in American prison camps whose reputed "coddling" roused a storm of protest in late 1944 and early 1945, brought to a head by the escape of twenty-five Germans from a camp in Papago Park, Arizona. (All were recaptured.) Discovery of the horrifying conditions in the Nazis' internment camps caused many persons to call for retaliatory measures. General Lerch admits that some of his PMG commanders may have erred in overleniency; an instance was the use of dining car facilities by prisoners on trains, which the General termed "a direct violation of our policy."

In answer to criticism, in April 1945 Lerch reported to the public on the entire prisoners-of-war picture. It was governed throughout, he explained, by the Geneva Convention, signed in 1929 and proclaimed as the law of the land in 1932: "If we want to break the Geneva Convention, then why have a Dumbarton Oaks?" He quoted Maurice Pate of the American Red Cross as stating, "The greatest single factor which gives us strength in getting relief and maintaining regular communication with our prisoner kin is the scrupulous attitude of the American Army in fulfilling the Treaty of Geneva toward enemy prisoners"—a conclusion agreed with by the House of Representatives Military Affairs Committee. Moreover, the treatment of war prisoners was known to have influenced many enemy soldiers to surrender, rather than fight to the death.

General Lerch's report revealed that there were twenty or thirty thousand American officers and enlisted personnel handling some 350,000 POW's. In late 1942 and early 1943, when manpower was desperately needed, the prisoners were put to work on nontactical duties at Army posts, on the roads, in the laundries, and so on. From June 1943 through January 1944 German reverses in Africa increased the flow of prisoners to America. The Army therefore allowed enterprisers who had been unable to find free labor to contract for POW labor, provided that the War Manpower Commission representative certified both the contractor's need for labor, and the prevailing wage for the work done. This wage was paid to the United States Treasury; the prisoners who worked received only the agreed amount of eighty cents a day in canteen coupons. In 1944, the General reported, private contractors paid the Government twenty-two million dollars, exclusive of transportation, housing, and subsistence, for a total 10,181,273 mandays of labor, more than half of it agricultural. The Army saved an estimated eighty million dollars by using prisoners for its own work, making a total of one hundred million dollars profit for that year. Despite the opportunities for escape afforded by work on farms, the escape rate was only one hundredth of one per cent higher than that from the heavily guarded Federal prisons (it was .45 per cent). As for the charges of Nazis dominating and terrorizing their anti-Nazi fellow prisoners, Lerch pointed out that the "uncooperative" prisoners were always kept in separate compounds or camps and stated that any prisoner who asked for protection would receive it, and that for the year ending April 1945 there had been no murders or suicides that could be attributed to Nazi methods.

Another aspect of the POW problem came to light in September 1945; the *Christian Science Monitor* reported that some months earlier General Dwight D. Eisenhower[42] had cabled a request for five thousand anti-Nazi German prisoners to be trained as supervisory and operational police for the American zone of occupation. General Lerch's office sent out ten "screening teams" to the POW camps in the United States. They came back with a list of fifteen thousand prisoners whose records were "thoroughly anti-Nazi," including some who had spent years in concentration camps, and some of Hitler's[42] personal enemies. The selected Germans agreed to give up the privileges of whatever rank they had held in the German Army, and were started through a special series of courses for the purpose at Fort Getty, Rhode Island. The aim was to prepare two thousand non-Nazis for use in the civil administration, in addition to the five thousand for police work, in the American zone. Another development, which was classified "top secret" up to September 1945, was put into operation in December 1944: a program of "general re-education in all camps by radio, newspaper, and entertainment." "We armed ourselves with the truth," said Assistant Provost Marshal General B. M. Bryan, Jr. "We did not compete with Goebbels[41]."

About four months after V-J Day, Lerch was to leave his Washington headquarters for assignment to a troubled area. In December he was ordered to southern Korea as military governor of the American-occupied part of that country, where General John R. Hodge[45] was in command of the American forces. (Bryan succeeded him as Provost Marshal General.)

The General responsible for the entire program was described as a quiet, spectacled soldier of scholarly manner. "The lawyer in General Lerch shows more than the soldier in the way he runs his shop. Every document that comes out of his office is drafted as meticulously as a legal brief. But his business is conducted with a rare informality and absence of red tape. Among his various memberships he values most an honorary one in the International Association of Chiefs of Police." A Methodist and a Mason, Lerch is a member of the Army and Navy Club in Washington. The Lerches' daughter, Janet, is married, and young Archer Lynn in 1945 is at West Point.

References

Am Mercury 60:536 My '45
Fortune 31:154+ Je '45 por
N Y Sun p22 Ap 20 '45
Who's Who in America, 1944-45

LEY, ROBERT (lī) Feb. 15, 1890—Oct. 24, 1945 Leader of German Nazi Labor Front after 1933; head of the Nazi Party Organization in 1932; appointed chief of the guerrilla forces in April 1945; noted for extreme anti-Semitism and ruthless disciplinary methods; captured by American troops; committted suicide while awaiting trial as a war criminal. See *Current Biography* 1940 Yearbook.

Obituary

N Y Times p1+ O 26 '45

LHEVINNE, JOSEF (lā-vēn' jō'zĕf) 1874—Dec. 2, 1944 Noted Russian-born pianist; won wide acclaim in United States as soloist and in joint recitals with his wife; renowned for his technical mastery of the keyboard and for tone quality of his music; made debut in Moscow at the age of fourteen.

Obituary

N Y Times p57 D 3 '44 por

LIEBLING, LEONARD (lēb'lĭng) Feb. 7, 1874—Oct. 28, 1945 American music critic, editor, librettist, and commentator; composer and pianist in Europe and the United States (1897-1910); joined staff of the *Musical Courier* in 1911 and had been editor since 1920; music critic of the New York *American* (1923-35); music editor of *Radio Guide,* 1937; composer of *The Balkan Princess* and *The American Maid.*

Obituary

N Y Times p19 O 29 '45 por

LILLIE, BEATRICE May 29, 1898- Actress

Address: h. Drayton Manor, Staffordshire, England

"Mistress of sophisticated slapstick," comedienne with the "Chaplinesque quality of wistful

BEATRICE LILLIE

frustration"—the British actress, Beatrice Lillie, has been an international star since the early 'twenties. Throughout these years, as surveys of printed comment indicate, she has remained, in the estimation of most drama critics, "one of the world's funniest gals." "With one dart of her eyes," wrote George Jean Nathan '45 in 1940, "she can spare a skit writer a dozen lines . . . [with] one little vocal squeak she can save the management royalties."

Beatrice Lillie was born Beatrice Lillie, on May 29, 1898. Her Irish-born father, John Lillie, and her Spanish-English mother, the former Lucie Shaw, had settled in Toronto, Canada, shortly before the birth of Beatrice Gladys, and there she and her older sister Muriel grew up. Mrs. Lillie, known in Toronto as a concert singer, envisioned a future for Muriel as a concert pianist, and for Beatrice as a soprano. The girls began their musical education early, and by the time the younger child was nine or ten a course in gestures was added to her lessons—rich gestures to accompany her singing, that would denote "sorrow and joy, birds flying, a bunch of grapes, farewell to summer, the ideas being subtly conveyed," explains Miss Lillie, "by delicate motions with the fingertips and outstretched arms."

The three Lillies frequently put their combined talents to the test, being addicted to entertaining their friends with "soireés." On Sundays Mrs. Lillie directed the choir in her church, Muriel played the organ, and Beatrice, until she became too liberal with her gestures, was a chorister. They appeared in local theaters, too, and once gave a tour of mining towns, accompanied by a small troupe. When the youngest member of the trio reached the age of fourteen she was sent to St. Agnes' College in Bellevue, near her home; but after a year of studying she concluded she preferred the stage. In 1914 she followed her mother and Muriel to England, and with great determination set about to establish herself as a serious singer of ballads, on the order of "I Hear You Calling Me" and "The Sunshine of Your Smile."

Time, and the whims of feature writers, have tended to confuse the details of Beatrice Lillie's final emergence as a comedienne, although the lady herself has described her London beginnings. After nearly a year of fruitless auditions she had the chance one day late in 1914 to be received by André Charlot, the thirty-two-year-old Frenchman who had introduced into England the so-called "intimate" revue, a small show that emphasized a clever cast rather than extravagant costuming and setting. Rather dispairing of her chance to impress this famous man, the young Canadian girl made up her mind to relax and at least enjoy herself. She tried out a few songs calculated to be amusing, for at home in Toronto she had found that, in a way she did not yet quite understand, she could convulse listeners, even church congregations when she was a chorister, by unconsciously interjecting a simple facial comment or gesture into a song or story. So, for the French producer that day in London, she sang such things as the ditty "The Next Horse I Ride On I'm Going To Be Tied On" and an Italian song with a few grapes and banana gesticulations. The net result of this venture, she says, was a three-year contract with Charlot for about fifteen pounds a week.

Beatrice Lillie started her career that October with a six weeks' tour of the provinces in the revue *Not Likely*, a production which eventually played in London, at the Alhambra, of which Charlot was then director. She sang, she says, "I Want a Toy Soldier Man," was embarrassed by her chorus costume, and failed to impress the reviewers. The producer next put the sixteen-year-old into his London production of *5064 Gerrard*, which opened at the Piccadilly in March 1915, almost simultaneously with the opening of the German Zepplin raids on England. She sang a number then new to Londoners, Irving Berlin's '42 song about wanting to go back to Michigan. It was with this song, theater chroniclers report, that Beatrice Lillie first "sparked" with audiences, although the young singer did not realize it that opening night until after she had gone back to her dressing room. For the next few war years she was "in everybody's act," in the Charlot revues *Now's the Time* (1915), *Samples* (in which she succeeded Mabel Russell in March 1916), and *Some* (1916).

Charlot had never given Beatrice Lillie any encouragement when she tried to be serious, and gradually she learned she was not very effective in straight roles, but was, in her own words, "a natural-born fool." On the last night of *Some* she gave expression to her inclination for deviltry, with the result that her antics in the chorus line caused her to be fined by an unsympathetic stage manager. Charlot, however, was pleased with the exhibition, and a part was written for Miss Lillie in his revue, *Cheep*, which opened in April 1917. After that Bea Lillie's clowning was a regular feature in Charlot productions: in *Tabs* (1918), *Oh, Joy* (a 1918 revue—revived in 1919—with music by Jerome Kern '42, originally called *Oh, Boy*), and *Bran-Pie* (a bright little 1919 revue in which, it was noted by *The London Times*, Beatrice Lillie was "as good as ever").

In October 1919 pictures of a slim languorous-looking girl appeared in newspapers over the announcement that "the popular Ontario singer," Miss Beatrice Lillie, had become engaged to the twenty-one-year-old Honorable Robert Peel, descendant of Robert Peel, Prime Minister to Queen Victoria and "creator" of London's famous police force, the "Bobbies" or "Peelers." The couple were married in January 1920, and the following December the actress gave birth to a son, named for his father.

The young bride's retirement from the stage was short-lived, however, for in April 1921 she reappeared in a non-Charlot production, the farce *Up in Mabel's Room*. This was followed by more Charlot: *Now and Then* (1921), *Pot Luck* (1921), and *A to Z* (1922). Then in October 1922 Beatrice starred in the *Nine O'Clock Revue*, of which her sister Muriel was the composer. Said to be the comedienne's best show up to that time, it ran about a year. At the end of the run in the winter of 1923, Charlot, in partnership with the American producer Arch Selwyn, decided to bring to New York what Noel Coward '41 has described as "a conglomeration of all the best numbers and sketches from the Charlot revues of the preceding few years." It was headed by three of Charlot's best-known stars, Miss Lillie, Jack Buchanan, and Gertrude Lawrence '40, who had got her start only a few years before by replacing Miss Lillie in a show when the star had been ill. (Also in this New York show was a comic named Eric Blore.)

Billed simply as *Charlot's Revue of 1924*, the show opened January 10, 1924, at the Times Square Theatre. There had been some skepticism as to how American audiences would react to British humor, but if there was any lack of appreciation after the show opened, it was not apparent in box office sales, and the performances of the leads skyrocketed them to international stardom. Dressed as Britannia, Queen of the Waves, Miss Lillie sang a song called "March with Me," a rowdy satire on Britain's sacred symbol of naval strength, in a manner that is still fondly recalled in play reviewers' columns today. Critics like Alexander Woollcott '41, Heywood Broun, and Percy Hammond wrote handsomely of the British comedienne. "She is slim, beautiful, and enormously funny, all at once," declared Broun the morning after; "I can think of no clown more comical than Beatrice Lillie," echoed Woollcott.

When the production closed several months later Miss Lillie returned to London to appear in the 1925 edition of the Charlot revues. After that, for the next fourteen years, she regularly moved back and forth between London and New York, a sort of transatlantic commuter. Theater histories and *Who's Who*'s list twelve productions for those years, as well as several seasons of cabaret work and appearances at London's Palladium. At the end of the 1926 run Miss Lillie remained in the States for the musical comedy *Oh, Please* (1926), in which Helen Broderick and Charles Winninger also played. (While only moderately successful in New York, the play had a prosperous run in Chicago.)

A revealing analysis of Miss Lillie's special comic talent was written by Stark Young while she was appearing in this play, generally considered to have been an indifferent musical. The play, wrote the critic "is a typical musical comedy. . . .But Miss Lillie takes it far otherwise; she gathers up all musical comedy and

guys it to exhaustion. She is wayward with its romance, comic with its sentiment. The trouble, then, with her in such a position begins with her not being on its plane. . . .Miss Lillie does not take the piece as it takes itself." There are those who "burlesque its [musical comedy's] sacred transitions from joy to wistful sweetness . . . from frail two-minute suspense to complete bliss with ensemble effects from the company." But those musical comedy "debunkers" who went as followers of Miss Lillie were confused as to what she really "did think of affairs." But, Young continued, although there was no opportunity for her to display her skill, "she was as astonishing as ever. Her absurdity, her wit, her variety were not diminished, the imps and inspirations of her art were the same. She evidently belongs in a revue; but wherever she is, her comic gift is one of the best in the world; our delight in her is endless." As if in response, Miss Lillie herself said several years later: "I'd be lost in a typical musical comedy. In the first place the audience would expect me to burlesque my part. I know my own limitations and realize that I am best in a sketch in which I can invent my own business and do whatever comes into my head."

Shortly before this, in February 1925, Miss Lillie's father-in-law died, her husband succeeding him as the fifth baronet. The actress thus became Lady Peel, a circumstance which was to provide many anecdotes for Lillie followers. About a year later she adopted the sleek coiffure which has become her trade mark.

Miss Lillie appeared in New York in January 1928 for the Rodgers '40 and Hart '40 musical farce *She's My Baby*, with Jack Whiting, Clifton Webb '43, and Irene Dunne '45. After a period at the Palladium in London, the comedienne returned to America and, with Noel Coward, played for several months in Coward's *This Year of Grace*. While in this their first show together the two friends performed for appreciative audiences, inside the theater and out. Whenever "Beattie" and Coward put in an appearance together, at fashionable night clubs, charity balls, select ladies' clubs, it was a signal for a flood of requests to sing one of the duets from the show, "Lilac Time," an *opéra bouffe* burlesque. "We sang it everywhere," Coward writes, except "at small convivial theatrical parties, to which we were invited on the strict understanding that in no circumstances would we sing 'Lilac Time.' "

The transatlantic commuting began again at the close of this play, in which, reviewers said as usual, Bea Lillie had "never been so brilliant." Back in London she appeared in *Charlot's Masquerade* (1930); in New York and Chicago the next year she appeared with Ernest Truex '41 in *The Third Little Show*, introducing "Mad Dogs and Englishmen." In 1932 she was Sweetie, the nurse, in the Theatre Guild production of Bernard Shaw's '44 good-natured poke at the human race, *Too Good To Be True*; and at the end of the year she appeared with the bespectacled Bobby Clark in the urbane *Walk a Little Faster*, as, among other things, a madcap coed of 1906. She went back to London for Charlot's *Please* in 1933; appeared at the Palladium the following year; then turned up in New York and in Chicago in 1935 for *At Home Abroad*, with Ethel Waters '41 and

LILLIE, BEATRICE—*Continued*

Reginald Gardiner and his sound-effect imitations of wallpaper and of trains. She herself, in one skit, was a Mrs. Blogden Blagg buying two dozen double damask dinner napkins, and a lady on a moon singing the somewhat naughty "Paree." At the end of 1936 she was starred in the long-run *The Show Is On* with Gardiner and Bert Lahr.

During the spring of 1938 Miss Lillie played in *Happy Returns* in London; then in January 1939 she appeared in the States with Richard Haydn in her second Coward show, *Set to Music*. She opened the show by riding on the stage astride a white horse, but many critics found the rest of the production dull and unspectacular. Bea Lillie, however, in the words of Brooks Atkinson [42], was "more iridescently witty than ever." The star returned to London just before the outbreak of the Second World War, and until December 1944 did not cross the Atlantic again. During the five-year interval she entertained Allied troops in England, Europe, and the Middle East. She was awarded the Africa Star and was decorated by General Charles de Gaulle [40]. In April 1942 her only child, Sir Robert Peel (the sixth baronet since his father's death in 1934), was killed in action with the Royal Navy near Ceylon.

After arranging details with Billy Rose [40], Miss Lillie, in December 1944, returned once more to the United States, to appear in the producer's *Seven Lively Arts*—and to receive on opening night a five-minute ovation from the audience. In addition to Miss Lillie, the play had been given all the trappings and build-up calculated to draw the public: the lushest first night since the start of the war—a twenty-four-dollar top for tickets, with champagne during the intermission—a reported production outlay of over a million dollars, including the money for refurbishing the old Ziegfeld Theatre, and a cast headed by Bert Lahr, Benny Goodman [42], Alicia Markova [43], Anton Dolin, and Doc Rockwell. The critics remarked that the general emphasis of the production seemed to have been on lavish mounting, rather than on the book, but they also found the show occasionally very witty and sometimes inspired. When otherwise, they wrote, it was pulled up by its bootstraps with each entrance of Miss Lillie, "not only the most expert comedienne on the stage, but by far the funniest." Miss Lillie was given the Donaldson Award (sponsored by *The Billboard*) for the best feminine lead in a musical show for her performance in *The Seven Lively Arts.*

Shortly after the opening of *Seven Lively Arts*, an English-made film of Miss Lillie's, *On Approval*, was released in New York—a reminder to American audiences that the comedienne also has made motion pictures. Her first one, *Exit Smiling*, was made in 1926, and in 1938 she played in an American movie, *Dr. Rhythm*, with Bing Crosby [41]. Also, although she feels inadequate without an audience before her, she has made, over the years, numerous guest appearances on the radio, and in 1935 she was on a sustaining program for Borden's Milk Company. While the Second World War continues Miss Lillie has no hobby other than that of entertaining servicemen after her performances.

In the years since Beatrice Lillie made her debut in London a great deal has been written about her and many attempts made to analyze her special talent. Yet, despite the abundance of words produced, a very small percentage of them has been used to criticize her adversely: "too fey" is perhaps the strongest comment. "Her range is limited," St. John Ervine pointed out in the 'twenties, "but," he added, "within that range she is superb." "She is at her worst," the *Literary Digest* explained, "when the producer of the moment goes stumbling in for art."

"To write that Miss Lillie is funny only because she has a superlative comedian's technique is, of course, foolish," wrote Morton Eustis for the *Theatre Arts Monthly* in 1939. "The light of real comic genius sparkles from beneath her dark eyelashes, radiates from each of the unexpected angles of her countenance, and illumines every motion and gesture she makes. But she would never be the Mistress of the Absurd if her technique were less sure. . . .Miss Lillie never delivers the comic thrust of a speech without reacting to it by some movement, however imperceptible. . . .Let her toss her hand absurdly forward and her back will respond (when the laugh has subsided) by a sudden stiffening which throws her posterior into relief, gaining another laugh, which she will top by a slight, but surely a refined, wiggle. The 'line' of her performance [physical or vocal] . . . always has contrast." In connection with this, a comment by Harrison Dowd in 1931 is interesting: "Breeding is always apparent in her. . . .Her refinement is positively sensational, considering she is primarily a grotesque. Perhaps it is the combination of these opposites that creates the sensation. . . .It is like entering a drawing room and beholding a duchess performing like a crazy downstairs maid."

Although Miss Lillie is but five feet three inches tall, she seems taller, for she is slender and lithe, once commented the artist and writer, S. J. Woolf. "One lock of her dark hair, which is short-cropped in back, sweeps across her forehead. . . .From it a nose none too small juts out suddenly, giving an inquisitive look to her face. She has large blue eyes, a full mouth with sparkling teeth, and a clear British complexion."

When asked the inevitable question of how she goes about getting laughs, Miss Lillie will reply, "By being myself—and relying upon my audience to coach me." "I see life painted in terms of humor," she said once; "unless things are funny they are apt not to exist for me at all."

References

    Collier's 27:10 Je 12 '26 pors; 104-21+ O 21 '39 por
    N Y Times Mag VI p13 N 26 '44 por
    New Yorker 20:15 Ja 20 '45
    Pictorial Review 27:2+ Ap '26 il por
    Stage Pictorial 2:5+ Winter 1945 por
    Coward. N. Present Indicative (1937)
    Who's Who, 1945
    Who's Who in America, 1944-45
    Who's Who in the Theatre (1939)

LINDSAY, SIR RONALD (CHARLES)
(lĭn'zĭ) May 3, 1877—Aug. 21, 1945 British diplomat since 1899; Minister at Paris (1920-

21) ; Undersecretary in British Foreign Office (1921-24) ; served in Constantinople for two years, first as representative, then as Ambassador ; Ambassador Extraordinary and Plenipotentiary to the United States from 1930 to 1939, during which time he was successful in cementing Anglo-American unity.

Obituary

N Y Times p23 Ag 23 '45 por

LITTLE, LOU(IS) Dec. 6, 1893- Football coach

Address: b. John Jay Hall, Columbia University, Morningside Hts., New York City; h. Barnstable, Mass.

"Teaching is a great art; and the best college teaching is usually found in the department of athletics," Professor William Lyon Phelps [43] wrote in an introduction to a book by Lou Little, Columbia University's veteran football coach. Hard-working Coach Little, who is said to be "the best-dressed, the best-informed, and one of the best-paid men in his business," kept his reputation as a teacher and strategist during a series of lean football years for Columbia. Now, in 1945, his Lions are again found among the leading teams in the United States.

The son of Michael and Theresa (de Dominick) Little, Louis Little was born in Boston on December 6, 1893, and brought up in Leominster, an industrial town of northern Massachusetts. He attended the Leominster High School and, in 1911-12, the Worcester Academy, and played on their football teams. According to *Look* Magazine, Lou was an iceman at sixteen and a brakeman at seventeen, and wanted to work in a bank. Entering the University of Pennsylvania in 1915, when he was twenty-one, the hawk-nosed six-footer played the 1916 season of varsity football as a tackle. His team was chosen to oppose the University of Oregon at the Tournament of Roses game in January 1917, but it traveled to California only to be thoroughly beaten. "Bob Folwell, Penn's head coach, was one of the sternest football disciplinarians I ever knew," Little recalls, "a fact for which I was frequently thankful during my Army career."

After the United States declaration of war in April 1917, Lou Little left school to enter an officers' training camp at Fort Oglethorpe, Georgia. On leave after being commissioned a first lieutenant, the New Englander was persuaded by Eddie Mahan, manager of the star-studded League Island Navy Yard football team, to join them for a game against the tough Boston Navy Yard squad. After three days of practice Lieutenant Little went onto the field as a tackle—and was brought off it unconscious. Later, as an officer of the Fifty-fourth Infantry, Little fought in France, taking part in the Meuse and Argonne offensives, and was promoted to captain. After the Armistice, General Pershing ordered the divisional teams to compete for the AEF football championship. Little and other stars of the past and future, without distinction of rank, joined in what he calls "the toughest football ever played anywhere"—in which a losing team stood in more danger of punishment from the buddies who had backed them with their entire pay, than from their opponents. The influence of

Bernard W. Goldman

LOU LITTLE

that season was reflected in the rough intercollegiate football playing of 1919, which found Little again playing on the Pennsylvania varsity. It is not true, as often stated, that Lou Little was chosen for the All-America "dream team" of the best players in the country, but he was definitely among the football heroes.

Graduated in 1920, Little planned to enter the university's dental school, but changed his mind when he discovered that all dental instruments were made for right-handed users, not "southpaws" like himself. "In those days," the coach recalls, "the general plan of action of well-known football players upon graduation was: When in doubt, sell bonds." So Little tried, without much success, to sell bonds in Philadelphia. Then he turned to something he knew better—football, playing and coaching with the Buffalo professional team. The tackle saved his money, and was soon owner, as well as player and coach, of the Philadelphia Yellow Jackets, which Quentin Reynolds [41] describes as probably the best team in the country at that time. "It isn't easy to coach a professional team," Reynolds adds. "To begin with, each player on the team has been taught a different style of football and it requires a lot of oiling to make a smooth-running machine out of several excellent but poorly fitting parts. Lou did it, however, and his Yellow Jacket teams were noted for the devastating power of their attack." According to the *Literary Digest*, Little played the last ten games of the 1921 season with a broken wrist, having insisted on remaining in the line-up.

Concurrently, the energetic Little was coaching several school teams—among them LaSalle Academy, Philadelphia, in 1920-21, Villanova College in 1921-22, and Abington (Pennsylvania) High School in 1922-23. He had as many as four teams under his wing at one time, and two of them he never saw play. This continued until 1924, when Little was called to Georgetown University, the Jesuit institution in Washington, D. C., as head football coach.

(Continued next page)

LITTLE, LOU—*Continued*

The Georgetown squad was very light, and obviously unsuited to the high-powered charging tactics the coach had been using with the Yellow Jackets. He therefore worked out what Reynolds calls "a flashy, bewildering, now-you-see-it-now-you-don't type of attack, employing a double wing back formation upon which he built spinners and double reverse plays and a lot of other devices designed to fool rather than to overpower. His backs weren't big or strong enough to provide effective interference for each other, so he brought linemen out to help." He developed the lateral pass (which had been confined mainly to use behind the line of scrimmage) as a down-field operation after a run or a completed forward pass. Little used it as an offensive maneuver to pull the defending players up and out of position, before trying for an extension of the gain. Another of his techniques has been dubbed "the muddle huddle," to hide the formation they were going to use. In general, it has been said, Little "thinks primarily in terms of offense and demands alert, precise play."

After a year at Georgetown, Lou Little was also appointed director of athletics. His 1928 team, incidentally, was one of the lightest he ever worked with—but, with the help of some smart quarterbacking, he maneuvered it to beat New York University 7-2, when that powerful team had an All-America running back, Ken Strong, "running wild behind the magnificent blocking of Ed Hill." In five years Little's teams suffered only eight defeats; and in February 1930 the New Englander accepted appointment as the head of the Columbia University coaching staff, at a reported salary of about seventeen thousand dollars a year. Columbia was known as a "coaches' graveyard" because of the lack of football material and interest, which even the great coach Percy Haughton had failed to overcome. During Coach Little's first season in New York there were only sixteen players on his blue-jerseyed squad, as compared with the usual forty or more. That fall they lost their first important game to Dartmouth, 52-0, and dropped three others; but for the next four years they won all except one game each season. In this first five years Little's boys won a total of thirty-four games and tied two. In 1932 Little's colleagues elected him chairman of the Football Coaches Rules Committee; and he has remained the chairman, and a tireless campaigner for changes which he believes would improve the game, especially those adopted by the professional football leagues.

While preparing his squad to meet Dartmouth in 1931, Little entered the scrimmage to demonstrate how to shake off two opposing tackles at once. After fifteen minutes he became tired, forgot his own advice to keep the head and shoulders up, and found himself demonstrating the consequences—a vertebral fracture which kept him in a plaster cast for two weeks, and in a leather and steel brace the rest of the season. From his hospital bed Little plotted strategy and directed the team through his five assistant coaches and then left the bed just long enough to watch Columbia win, 19-6.

At the close of the 1933 season, when Stanford University invited Columbia to oppose them in the Rose Bowl on New Year's Day, Little reportedly thought it was a joke. The choice of Columbia to represent the Eastern colleges was widely criticized and ridiculed; the Columbians were called the Little Lions as much for their size as for their coach, while the huge West Coast teams were considered almost invincible. Accepting the honor, Little so arranged the thirty-five-hundred-mile trip that his squad was able to get in a practice workout on a good field each afternoon as it made its way across the country, finally settling in Tucson, Arizona, for eight days of concentration. He even brought along three hundred gallons of New York's fine water. The final score was Columbia 7, Stanford 0—and Little's boys repeated it in New York in 1936, and held Stanford to a scoreless tie in 1937.

After carrying off the Rose Bowl game trophy, Lou Little was recognized as, "at a conservative estimate, one of the three best football coaches in the country." This reputation has endured, for his teams are "always outmanned, and usually outpowered, but seldom outfought and never outthought." In 1939 he was elected president of the American Football Coaches Association. *Look* reported in November 1942 that up to that time Little never had produced an undefeated team, "yet almost every month he is offered a new job at a larger salary. He always declines, graciously but firmly, saying, 'I have spent sixteen years at Columbia and they have all been happy ones. What more could any coach ask?'" 1943 may have strained the Little philosophy a bit, as the Columbians lost every game they played; but the coach was given the Touchdown Club award as the man who had done most for football in that year. Little's 1944 team was an improvement, to the extent of winning two games in the season; but his 1945 team, sparked by seventeen-year-olds Lou Kusserow and Gene Rossides, swept on from victories over Lafayette, Syracuse, and Yale to beat Colgate for the second time in thirteen tries. The 1945 campaign ended with victory over Dartmouth in November. Having bowed only to Pennsylvania, the Columbia Lions ran up a record score of 251 points, its highest total for a season since 1931, when 237 were tallied in ten contests.

Little is described as truly interested in football as a means of "making the boys better citizens," rather than as an end in itself. Not only does he insist that his players maintain a good scholastic standing and observe the amenities of a rounded social life, but, in his words, "I am in touch with the boy's instructors on the academic side. I know what subject he likes and in what subjects he is not so proficient. Frequently I take pains to look into his family history to find whether he is an only son or a member of a large family, what the financial circumstances of his boyhood have been, whether he has been popular or not with his mates in school. I have reports on his general make-up from the freshman coach. I observe him in spring practice or, if he has been with another squad during the spring, I get in touch with the other coaches. All of these point the way to the boy's general characteristics and personality."

This is quoted from *How To Watch Football* (1935), written by Little and Robert Harron, which sports columnist Bill Corum called "the most interesting and valuable" book on football that he had ever read. Little's ideas have also been expressed in another book, *Lou Little's Football* (1934), written with Arthur Sampson, and in lectures and articles in numerous magazines. In September 1945 he began a weekly series of televised football talks as NBC's *Friday Night Quarterback*, to continue through the Rose Bowl game.

The spectacled, strongly aquiline-nosed coach stands six feet tall and weighs two hundred pounds. He is said to roar like a reasonable imitation of the Columbia lion at practice sessions in Baker Field, criticizing sharply every movement of every man—and to talk like a friendly professor off it. "A football team isn't a machine," he has said. "It's a unit composed of eleven kids. . . .If a boy lost an important game for me, I wouldn't make him feel as if the world had ended." On the other hand, Little has expressed his disapproval of those who lose complacently. "Lose with a smile, certainly, but the smile should be a bit forced."

The coach and Mrs. Little, the former Loretta L. Donahue, live in a New York apartment and have a stock and produce farm in Massachusetts, where, besides farming, Little enjoys landscape gardening. He is a member of the Racquet Club of Philadelphia, the Oster Harbors Club of Cape Cod, and the Circus Saints and Sinners and Barnsbees Luncheon Club in New York. His church affiliation is Catholic, and he is not enrolled in any political party. A left-handed golfer, Lou enjoys "all activities of competition, particularly those of physical contact," and both Littles listen regularly to dozens of radio programs, including the *Lone Ranger*. According to *Look*, Little's hobby is buying clothes, and in November 1942 an inventory of his wardrobe listed forty suits, thirty pairs of shoes, and five hundred neckties.

References

Am Mag 118:49 S '45 por
Collier's 94:16+ O 13 '34 por
Look 6:62-5 N 3 '42 pors
Newsweek 4:15 S 1 '34
Who's Who in America, 1944-45

LLOYD GEORGE OF DWYFOR, DAVID LLOYD GEORGE, 1ST EARL
Jan. 17, 1863—Mar. 26, 1945 British statesman; "father" of the House of Commons; Britain's Prime Minister during the First World War and one of Big Four at Peace Conference; retired in 1944 as member of Parliament after having served fifty-four consecutive years as Liberal Party member from Caernarvonshire, Wales; called the "Welsh Wizard." See *Current Biography* 1944 Yearbook.

Obituary

N Y Times p1+ Mr 27 '45 por

LOESSER, FRANK (HENRY) (lĕs'ēr)
June 29, 1910- Song writer
Address: h. Hollywood, Calif.

"One of the brightest lights in Hollywood song writing," Frank Loesser collaborated on songs like "I Don't Want to Walk Without You, Baby," and "Jingle, Jangle, Jingle," and was known as a clever lyricist before joining the Army of the United States in the Second World War. Now he is better known as "the GI's own songwriter" and "the Army's one-man hit parade," the author of "Praise the Lord and Pass the Ammunition" and "Rodger Young."

Although he made his success in Hollywood, Frank Henry Loesser is a New Yorker by sentiment as well as by birth—that date is June 29, 1910. His parents, Henry and Julia (Ehrlich) Loesser, were natives, respectively, of Prussia and of Austria. Henry Loesser was a well-known piano teacher who had accompanied the famous soprano Lilli Lehmann. Frank's half-brother Arthur Loesser is a distinguished pianist and critic, former accompanist of Mischa Elman [45], and later head of the piano department of the Cleveland Institute of Music. Among the Loesser family and friends, Frank's songs are considered "very nice, but of course they're not music." He began being "different" at an early age: he never learned to read notes, although he plays the piano by ear, and he did not get along well in school.

Entering kindergarten with his older sister Grace, little Frank spent three years cutting out paper dolls before going on to the first grade. Later he entered the Speyer School and went on to the Townsend Harris High School, both of which were for "exceptionally gifted" pupils. He tells that he never studied or did homework, and was also addicted to practical jokes, with the result that he was dropped from Townsend Harris before graduation. Frank attended the commencement exercises, however, because one of his cousins was being graduated, and his surprise at discovering that he had won the art prize was no greater than the principal's when the boy came up to claim it. (Earlier, he had won the harmonica championship of New York City.) At fifteen young Loesser entered the College of the City of New York, the only institution which would admit him. But C.C.N.Y. soon dropped him, too, for "flunking everything but English and gym," and for polishing the nose of a bronze statue in the main hall. The dean was not impressed by the fact that Frank was on the swimming team and was writing the music for a college show.

Young Loesser designed and printed Christmas cards for sale to the people he knew, and combined his talents as a waiter-piano-player-caricaturist at a Catskill resort. With his eye on a newspaper career, he got a job taking classified advertisements for the New York *Herald Tribune*. Later he worked for *Women's Wear* as knit goods editor, and in early 1929 "F. H. Loesser" was signed to political cartoons in the Tuckahoe (New York) *Record*. That June Walter Winchell [43] recorded in his "Things I Never Knew Till Now" that "Frank Loesser, who writes special ditties for vaudevillians, is now city editor of the New Rochelle *News* and is only eighteen!"—an item that brought Loesser five hundred job applications, "mostly from old ladies." When this new little paper failed, the youth returned to New York and got a job as press agent for Tiffany Pictures, which starred Mae Murray. He thought

FRANK LOESSER

up a series of remarkable publicity stunts for them, most of which got him into trouble.

Concurrently, Loesser was writing song lyrics to music by his friend William Schuman [40], now a distinguished composer and director of the Juilliard School of Music in New York. Many were sold, but only one was published. Frank and a Joe Brandfon somehow got a year's $100-a-week contract with the music publisher Leo Feist, who never put out any of their works. Loesser and Schuman continued their collaboration on songs for night club and vaudeville routines. "No matter when I'd come home," Loesser's sister recalls, "he and Bill Schuman would be working on songs." Finally Frank got a chance to do lyrics for a musical, which was called the *Illustrators' Revue*. Opening in January 1936, it closed after four nights.

Until the depression, Frank's adventures and misadventures with jobs meant no real hardship, for his widowed mother was in comfortable circumstances. At that time, however, the family lost all their money, and Frank did any work he could get, including screwing the tops on bottles of insecticide. "There really seemed no place for me," he recalls. He got his meals by acting as a spotter for a chain of restaurants, which paid seventy-five cents plus the cost of a meal for reports on the food and service. "I used to eat twelve times a day," he says. "When you're poor, you're always hungry from walking around so much." Loesser did get a chance to do some vaudeville songs for Lita Gray Chaplin, and later he and Mrs. Chaplin's accompanist, Irving Actman, joined forces as a songwriting team. They arranged with Ann Minor, who owned the small Back Drop cafe, to sing and play their songs every night in exchange for dinner. One dull evening the owners brought in all available persons from a near-by theater to make the place livelier for the visit of the Japanese Ambassador. That night Loesser sang his love songs directly to one of the cast, a tall, striking blonde whose name turned out to be Lynn Garland—née Mary

Alice Blankenbaker, from the Middle West. She became Mrs. Loesser in October 1935.

Finally, in 1936, the lyric writer was put under contract by Universal Pictures and left for Hollywood. During this period he collaborated on several songs, such as "Junkman" and "I Wish I Were Twins," which his friend Fats Waller [42] liked and plugged. After Universal let him go, he free-lanced for a time, writing songs for *Oswald the Rabbit* cartoons and others, until he accepted a contract with Paramount. In 1937 the New Yorker did lyrics for Walter Wanger's *Vogues of 1938*, of which "Lovely One" was perhaps the most popular, and for Shirley Ross's songs in *Blossoms on Broadway*, for Paramount; according to the *International Motion Picture Almanac*, he also scored RKO's *Fight for Your Lady*, which meant he wrote one song.

The next year, Loesser teamed with Hoagy Carmichael [41] on some songs for *College Swing* and the novelty number "Small Fry" for Bing Crosby [41] in *Sing, You Sinners*, and for Bob Hope [41] and Shirley Ross in *Thanks for the Memory*, which featured their "Two Sleepy People" (Loesser did not, however, collaborate on the title song, which was taken from another picture). He also wrote lyrics that year for the Fred MacMurray-Harriet Hilliard *Cocoanut Grove*, and for incidental songs in the Joan Bennett-Randolph Scott *The Texans*, and the Henry Fonda-George Raft-Dorothy Lamour *Spawn of the North*. In United Artists' *The Hurricane*, Miss Lamour sang his "The Moon of Manakoora." "Says My Heart," from *Cocoanut Grove*, was one of his greatest successes of this period, and was for a time in the first place on *Your Hit Parade* as the most popular song of the day.

Frank Loesser and Hoagy Carmichael got together again in 1939 for *St. Louis Blues*, and the former also wrote music and lyrics for other films, including the Gene Krupa *Some Like It Hot*, and the Jack Benny [41]-Dorothy Lamour *Man About Town*. By this time Loesser was "in the big money." His 1940 credits include lyrics to Jimmy McHugh's music for another Benny picture, *Buck Benny Rides Again*, and others for two Lamour opuses, *Moon Over Burma* and Twentieth-Century-Fox's *Johnny Apollo*. Around this time, too, he spent a summer working on a full-length cartoon feature at Max Fleischer's studio in Miami.

In February 1941 Paramount executives called on Loesser, who chose as his collaborator the arranger Joe Lilley, to produce one song for the Fred MacMurray-Paulette Goddard thriller, *Forest Rangers*. The result of one Sunday night's work was "Jingle, Jangle, Jingle," a simple, catchy tune which made use of the round form on the second chorus. By July it was at the top of the Nation's record, juke box, and sheet music sales, although the picture itself was not released until October. According to *Newsweek*, "the two authors could pleasantly anticipate jingling upwards of $125,-000 for one hard night's work." (Later, General Elliott Roosevelt, whose Flying Fortress was named "Jingle, Jangle" and who used the song as the theme of his entire squadron, presented the lyricist with a pair of spurs which he had worn on his missions to carry out the theme. Loesser says that the song earned only some $50,000, and the promised spurs never arrived.) Concurrently, other Loesser ditties were hitting the hit parade. For *Kiss the Boys Goodbye,* to music by director Victor Schertzinger, he added five fresh and witty lyrics. One, "That's How I Got My Start," gave Mary Martin '44 the chance to do a version of the strip-tease which first brought her to public notice, and the other songs also won praise from reviewers.

Loesser's songs included several for Marlene Dietrich; singing his "The Boys in the Back Room" helped restore her box-office appeal. Others were rhythmic love songs, like "Dolores" and "Spring Will Be a Little Late This Year"; impudent novelty numbers, like "I Said No" (from the 1942 *Sweater Girl*); and still others were haunting torch songs, like "Can't Get Out of This Mood," and "I Don't Want to Walk Without You, Baby." A Loesser specialty was the "gripe song," both civilian ("I Get the Neck of the Chicken") and military ("In My Arms," from *See Here, Private Hargrove,* in which the soldier complains). Frank Loesser and McHugh wrote perhaps the first Calypso-type song for *Happy Go Lucky,* "Sing a Tropical Song." The lyric writer also tried his hand at collaborating on an original screenplay, *Priorities on Parade,* which fell with a dull thud in 1942. Perhaps his most outstanding assignment was the lyrics to Arthur Schwartz music for *Thank Your Lucky Stars,* which was not released until late 1943. Of the eight songs they wrote for performers ranging from Dinah Shore '42 to Bette Davis '41, Eddie Cantor '41 to Spike Jones, and Ann Sheridan to Hattie McDaniel '40 and Eddie (Rochester) Anderson, five became popular. The most notable was "They're Either Too Young or Too Old," the plaint of the girl back home about the shortage of men. "Love Isn't Born, It's Made" was also mentioned by reviewers, and three of more conventional type, "How Sweet You Are", "The Dreamer," and "I'm Ridin' for a Fall," as well as the title song, were heard from over the country's radios.

A month after Pearl Harbor, Loesser had been inspired by a chaplain's remark under fire to write "Praise the Lord and Pass the Ammunition," a war ballad for which the thirty-one-year-old lyricist did both words and music. Because he "didn't think the country knew what it was up against," he did not release the song until nine months later, when he felt that morale needed a boost, following this up by enlisting in the Army Air Forces. To prevent the song from being played to death, the OWI requested broadcasting stations to limit their use of it to no more than once every four hours; but by October 1942, nonetheless, more than 125,000 copies and 250,000 records of it had been sold, and its popularity continued to increase. Private Loesser, meanwhile, was applying himself so dutifully to his basic training that, according to Leonard Lyons, he did not look at a newspaper or magazine throughout that period. (Lyons adds that the writer Mark Hellinger was so shocked at Loesser's resultant ignorance that he presented him with five-year subscriptions to fourteen periodicals.) After his basic training, Loesser was assigned to write songs, which were published by regular music houses, with the profits going to Army Emergency Relief. To Army order, he turned out the official

Infantry song, "What Do You Do in the Infantry?" and songs for any other branch that wanted a new one; also "The Road to Victory" and about a hundred others. Some of them, including "First Class Private Mary Brown", "One Little Wac." and "Why Do They Call a Private a Private?" were for Army revues; and, while the two first-named were plugged for their recruiting value, other show songs were kept exclusively for GI use. Loesser avoided sloganeering: "I'm a pretty good propagandist," he said, "so I don't write propaganda." Orders being orders, he turned out good rousing marches when generals insisted, but left to himself wrote the "gripe" songs, like "Classification Blues," which he was convinced were what the soldiers wanted.

From January 1944, when he was transferred to New York, Loesser headed a three-man detail, turning out parodies for the Special Services' *Hit Kits,* song sheets of which nearly three million were distributed each month. "Loesser used to like to compose from 7 to 11 in the morning while being driven around in an auto. Incredible amounts of coffee and numerous friends also went into the recipe. Now," *Newsweek* continued, "he turns it out in an Army office from 8:15 to 5:15—whether his muse is with him or not." On his own time, Loesser joined Abe Burrows in creating "Leave Us Face It," a marvelously ungrammatical love song for Ed Gardner '43 on his Duffy's Tavern program—"Leave us not blush with no shame when people bandage our name, leave us face it, we're in love." A year later, Pfc. Loesser was inspired to compose a serious and stirring ballad. "Oh, they've got no time for glory in the Infantry," was the opening line of "Rodger Young," which is both a requiem for a hero and Loesser's tribute to "the everlasting courage of the Infantry." (*Variety* reported in October 1945 that the publisher, Bob Miller, had forbidden its use by dance bands and vocalists, restricting its performances to concert artists and folk-singers.)

Since his discharge from the Army in the fall of 1945, ex-Pfc. Loesser has developed a passion for collegiate clothes. He is, to quote Naomi Jolles, "a compact little guy whom you might describe as cute, an adjective which he uses pretty generously in his own speech." She mentions that he has "a bubbling personality," "moves with bounce and regards his surroundings with sharp, gleaming eyes." His eyes are brown, as is his receding hair, and some observers credit him with dimples. Loesser is an excellent rider. In his words, he "sings like an auctioneer," except that the words make sense. "I haven't cracked a book since *Beau Geste,*" he reports, and explains that it might cramp his literary style to do so. Frank and Mrs. Loesser have one daughter, Susan. The composer's wife is an ambitious singer and actress, and as a step up the ladder has served as stand-in for Zorina '41.

References

N Y Post p21 Jl 14 '44 pors
New Yorker 20:26+ D 9 '44
International Motion Picture Almanac, 1943-44

LOPEZ, ENCARNACION *See* Argentinita

MCCAIN, JOHN S(IDNEY) Aug. 9, 1884—Sept. 6, 1945 Vice-admiral in United States Navy; chief of the Bureau of Naval Aeronautics (1942-43); deputy chief of naval operations for air until he assumed command of the famous Navy Task Force No. 38 in 1944, succeeding Vice-Admiral Marc A. Mitscher [44]; took part in the official surrender ceremonies in Tokyo Bay; died of heart attack while at home. See *Current Biography* 1943 Yearbook.

Obituary

N Y Times p1+ S 7 '45 por

MCCARTHY, FRANK June 8, 1912-
Former United States Government official
Address: h. 1134½ West Ave., Richmond, Va.

One of the success stories of recent years is that of Colonel Frank McCarthy, who rose in five years from the rank of first lieutenant in the United States Field Artillery Reserve to, successively, the posts of Secretary of the War

U.S. Army

COL. FRANK MCCARTHY

Department General Staff and, in August 1945 when he was only thirty-three, of Assistant Secretary of State in charge of Administration. The youngest man to have held such an important post in the State Department, McCarthy resigned in October 1945 because of ill health.

Born in Virginia, on June 8, 1912, Frank McCarthy is the son of Frank Johnson and Lillian (Binford) McCarthy. He attended the Stonewall Jackson School, the Binford Junior High School, and the John Marshall High School in his native Richmond. In 1933, at the age of twenty-one, he was graduated with a B.A. from the Virginia Military Institute and commissioned a second lieutenant in the Field Artillery Reserve. As a high-ranking cadet in his class, the winner of several medals, and the man with a reputation as "a shark on tactics," McCarthy came to the attention of General George C. Marshall [40], who, as a distin-

guished alumnus of V.M.I., takes a prominent part at the institute's graduation exercises each year. After his graduation McCarthy stayed at V.M.I. as an instructor (1933-35), and his acquaintance with the future Chief of Staff of the War Department developed.

For an interval in 1935-36 the young instructor worked as a reporter for the Richmond *News Leader*, then returned to the institute again to teach. A short time after this change, the future Assistant Secretary became a Broadway press agent. Two playwriting fellow alumni, Fred F. Finklehoffe and John Monks, Jr., had sold *Brother Rat*, a farce-comedy with a V.M.I. background, to producer George Abbott [40], and at their suggestion McCarthy was engaged to do special promotional work on the play by publicizing it among the alumni. It was work that had at least two attractions for McCarthy—a better salary than he had ever received, and contact with the theater, in which, it is said, he had a strong interest. When he later expressed a desire to return to V.M.I., the Abbott office, showing as keen an appreciation of his abilities as General Marshall was later to display, offered him considerably more salary than the institute had. McCarthy therefore worked as advance agent for a road company of the popular show, later for a time in the New York office on other Abbott productions. When he finally resigned in 1939, his fellow publicists declared that he could have had a successful career on Broadway, although they admit now he seemed headed for better things.

In the summer of 1939 McCarthy returned to the South to enter the postgraduate school in government at the University of Virginia, which in 1940 granted him an M.A. degree. It was in July that he was called to active duty, with the rank of a first lieutenant, and, at the suggestion of Brigadier General John Magruder, the chief of G-2 and a former V.M.I. commandant, he was assigned to the Office of the Assistant Chief of Staff, as head of the dissemination section, Military Intelligence Division. (McCarthy had retained his status as a reserve officer, drilling in a New York City armory while working for Abbott.) In April of 1941 he was advanced to captain, and that June made liaison officer between the White House and the General Staff, assistant secretary to the General Staff, and military secretary to Marshall. His appointment to major came in February 1942, to lieutenant colonel in December. A year later he was made a full colonel, and in January 1944 appointed secretary to the General Staff. This promotion, coming when he was only thirty-two, made him not only the youngest man but the first reserve officer to reach such a high post.

"In the position," reports the New York *Times*, "Colonel McCarthy had a brilliant record in manifold duties which included the processing of problems requiring the action or concurrence of the President, the Secretary of War, the Chief of Staff, and other officials. Other duties that were under Colonel McCarthy's direction were the maintenance of an office of temporary record and recording, authentication and distribution of the decisions of the Chief of Staff, supervision of the War Department's confidential classified communications, collection of statistical information of military importance sought by the Secretary of War, the Chief of Staff, and Deputy Chief of Staff." In addition to these duties, during the whole time he retained his liaison post.

The citation accompanying the Distinguished Service Medal which was presented to McCarthy at a ceremony in General Marshall's office (August 1945) states that he had made a material contribution to the successful direction of the United States armed forces during his secretaryship (from January 15, 1944 to August 22, 1945) : "In the international conferences of the Chiefs of State and Staff of the United States, Great Britain, the U.S.S.R., and China, in which the strategic direction of Allied forces was accomplished, he accompanied the Chief of Staff of the Army as military secretary." The conferences to which the citation referred took place at London, Casablanca, Algiers, Cairo, Teheran, Yalta, and Potsdam. As an observer for General Marshall, McCarthy accompanied the assault forces ashore in the invasion of southern France. "His efficiency was exceptional. His devotion to duty was unusually wholehearted and unselfish," concludes the citation.

On August 21, 1945, following V-J Day, President Truman '45 announced the Colonel's appointment as Assistant Secretary of State in charge of Administration. The appointment filled the vacancy caused by the resignation of Brigadier General Julius C. Holmes '45, who had been the first person to hold the post, one of two new assistant secretaryships which President Roosevelt '42 had approved in December 1944. It had been expected that McCarthy, like his predecessor, would act as liaison man between the State and the War departments. His duties were to have included a large share of the responsibility in carrying out the expansion and reorganization programs of the State Department that were initiated by Cordell Hull '40, carried on by Edward R. Stettinius, Jr. '40, and completed by Secretary of State James F. Byrnes '41. However, McCarthy remained with the Department only until October 11, 1945, when he resigned because of illness.

Frank McCarthy is slender, five feet ten inches tall. His black hair recedes slightly from his forehead and his eyes are a blue-gray. He is boyish-looking, and some of his charm, admirers claim, is his smile and his soft Southern voice. According to one reporter, he likes tweed suits and noisy ties, and has "a nice diplomatic touch" in everything he does.

References

N Y Post p4 Ag 22 '45
N Y Sun p16 Ag 30 '45
N Y Times p23 Ag 22 '45
N Y Times Mag p24-5 S 9 '45 por
New Yorker 21 :19 S 8 '45

MCCORMACK, JOHN June 14, 1884— Sept. 16, 1945 Noted Irish tenor; made his American operatic debut in 1909 at the Manhattan Opera House; later sang with the Chicago-Philadelphia Opera Company, Chicago Grand Opera, and the Royal Opera, Covent Garden; especially popular as a concert singer; repertoire consisted of leading operatic tenor roles, Irish folksongs and ballads, and English, French, and Italian lyrics.

Obituary

N Y Times p21+ S 17 '45 por

MCCOY, FRANK R(OSS) Oct. 29, 1874- United States Government official; retired Army officer

Address: b. c/o Far Eastern Advisory Com., Washington, D.C.; Foreign Policy Assn., 22 E. 38th St., New York City; h. Lewistown, Pa.

"Frank McCoy is the best soldier I ever laid eyes on," President Theodore Roosevelt once told Edwin C. Hill '40; later, McCoy was generally referred to as one of the Army's leading diplomats. Of his forty-five years in the service, nearly a quarter-century was spent on diplomatic or quasi-diplomatic assignments which took him from the Western Hemisphere to the Far East, from supervising an election in Nicaragua to investigating Japanese aggression in Manchuria. After his retirement in November 1938 Major General McCoy became president of the Foreign Policy Association, served on various boards, and was appointed in October 1945 to represent the United States on the Far Eastern Commission on Japan.

Born in Lewistown, Pennsylvania, on October 29, 1874, of Ulsterite or Northern Irish descent, Frank Ross McCoy is the son of a soldier-lawyer father, Thomas Franklin McCoy, who rose to the rank of brigadier general in the Civil War. Frank's mother was the former Margaret Eleanor Ross. One of four children, Frank attended the Lewistown Academy and then Braden's Academy, where many officers' sons are prepared for West Point. He was appointed to the Military Academy in 1893, graduated in June 1897, and commissioned a second lieutenant of Cavalry. "As a West Point man," the General has written, "I have found Latin Americans who were fellow graduates, more than once the key to stiff situations encountered in Nicaragua and elsewhere."

When the Spanish-American War broke out in April 1898 the twenty-three-year-old lieutenant was transferred to the Tenth Cavalry, a Negro regiment, and took part in the Santiago de Cuba campaign. He won the Silver Star citation for gallantry in action at Guasimas on June 24, and won it again on July 1 at Santiago, where he was wounded in the charge up San Juan Hill. April 1899 found McCoy back in Cuba with his regiment, and in May 1900 the young officer was detailed as aide-de-camp to Major General Leonard Wood, the military governor of Cuba. In Wood's administration, which historians agree "stands as a model of fine trusteeship," Frank McCoy supervised the island finances. The Cuban Government was turned over to its new President in May 1902, and McCoy accompanied General Wood on his subsequent trip to Europe to witness the German Army maneuvers. On their way to the Philippines afterward, the Americans inspected the military establishments of other European and Asiatic countries, and their ways of administering their colonies. In England the American lieutenant broke precedent by becoming a friend

MAJ. GEN. FRANK R. MCCOY

of Field Marshal Lord Roberts, in spite of the great difference in rank.

About a year before the United States took over the Panama Canal Zone, President Theodore Roosevelt sent Frank McCoy on a secret mission to investigate several other proposed routes for the canal, on which he reported unfavorably. For three years the Pennsylvanian served as General Wood's aide in the Philippines, fighting against the hostile Moros and outlaws. In 1905 he led the Datú Ali expedition, which is said to be one of the classic exploits of American Army history: The tribal chief and his twenty thousand guerrillas had defied the American Army for two years, eluding pursuit in the swamps. Accompanied by a few men, McCoy surprised Ali, thus finally running him to earth. When not engaged in subduing the fierce Moros, McCoy held various offices in the civil government, serving as secretary of Moro Province in 1905, and province engineer in 1905-6.

Returning to the United States, McCoy was chosen military aide to the President. Later that year, when the Cuban President, Tomás Estrada Palma, asked Roosevelt's help in putting down an armed rebellion, the officer was sent back to Cuba as a member of the Peace Commission. As aide-de-camp to the Secretary of War, William Howard Taft, he arrived in Havana in September 1906 and served there for about a month while Taft was provisional governor of Cuba. Next McCoy commanded a cavalry troop in California before entering the Army War College. Graduated in 1910, he was placed on the initial General Staff Corps eligibility list and, after a period in New Mexico as a squadron commander, was detailed to the General Staff Corps in 1911. After four years on the General Staff, McCoy rejoined the Third Cavalry on the Mexican border, where he was charged with keeping order along five hundred miles of the Rio Grande, which Mexican bandits had been crossing to raid American territory. McCoy had successful engagements with them at Cavazas Crossings and Ojo de Agua. Besides human enemies, the Captain had to cope with the river, "a rebel stream that has the habit of changing its course and upsetting notions of where sovereignty abides," and he says that he once arrested an entire Mexican village and kept the villagers in his camp to save their lives. Later, in February 1917, the cavalryman was ordered to the American Embassy in Mexico City as military attaché, and in March he was promoted to major.

In June 1917 Major McCoy joined the American Expeditionary Forces in France, and served as General Staff secretary while Pershing's forces were being organized. (His *Principles of Military Training* came out in 1918.) In May 1918 he was assigned, with the temporary rank of colonel, to command the 165th Infantry Regiment of the Forty-second Division—better known as New York's Fighting Sixty-ninth, of the Rainbow Division. (Colonel Douglas MacArthur '41 was division chief of staff; McCoy said of him later, "He thinks of himself as a man of destiny, one of the few men I know who does. He is a man of destiny.") Colonel McCoy commanded his regiment in the Baccarat sector, in the Champagne-Marne defensive, and the Aisne-Marne offensive. In August 1918 he was appointed a temporary brigadier general, in charge of the Sixty-third Infantry Brigade, Thirty-second Division, which he commanded in the Oise-Aisne and Meuse-Argonne offensives. The General was awarded the Distinguished Service Medal for his staff work and his prominent part in what the citation terms "the difficult fighting east of Rheims." He has also been awarded a number of foreign decorations.

After the Armistice General McCoy commanded his brigade on its march into Germany, and was then ordered to Tours (France) in November 1918 as director of the Army Transport Service. Later he became director-general of transportation. When General James G. Harbord '45, the former AEF chief of staff, was named head of the American Military Mission to Armenia in August 1919, he chose McCoy to assist him in that investigating body. Harbord has been quoted as praising the younger general's "unvarying efficiency."

After twenty-eight months overseas McCoy was given a field command in Arizona and then two staff posts in Illinois. After reverting to his permanent rank of major, he was promoted to colonel. In 1921 "The McCoy" was again associated with Leonard Wood, as chief of staff of the Wood-Forbes special mission of investigation to the Philippines, and reportedly participated in the series of "heart-to-heart talks" which his chief had with Major General Baron Tanaka and other Japanese militarists on their way back through Tokyo. "The friendly understanding arrived at between the military leaders of America and Japan by the frank round table discussion of their irreducible minimum for peace" was said by the *Far Eastern Review* of July 1929 to have "cleared the surcharged atmosphere and made possible Japan's attendance at the Washington Conference and her acceptance of the American program for naval disarmament and the supplementary agreements concerning China." The great earthquake in Japan in September 1923 found McCoy in Shanghai, en route to Manila, but he returned to Japan to assume command of the American Relief Mission. To quote the *Far Eastern Review* again, "We know of no situation in the history of our Far Eastern relations which required such delicate handling as the one which sent the American Fleet and Army transports hurrying to Tokyo Bay laden with relief supplies. . . .His [McCoy's] splendid handling of this delicate mission . . . broke down and swept away all the remaining barriers between Japan and the United States."

McCoy returned to his duties in the Philippines as aide to Governor-General Wood. He and the future President, Manuel Quezón'⁴¹, were on terms of personal friendship. In January 1924 the forty-nine-year-old brigadier general (promoted in December 1922) was married to Mrs. Wood's niece, Frances Field Judson, whose grandfather had laid the first Atlantic cable. Ordered back to the United States in 1925, McCoy was assigned to duty in the Bureau of Insular Affairs. A course at the Infantry School (Georgia) in early 1926 was followed by command of an infantry brigade in Texas until March 1927. Similarly, after a short course at the Field Artillery School in Oklahoma, he was put in charge of a field artillery brigade in Maryland. But McCoy was soon back on diplomatic duty, as President Coolidge nominated him in August 1927 to supervise the Nicaraguan elections that November. (A condition of the armistice between the two warring Nicaraguan parties had been that the United States should guarantee the election which was to decide between them.) McCoy had under his command some five hundred of the seven thousand American marines distributed throughout the country to prevent riots and intimidation, and twenty airplanes flying over and communicating with the voting booths on election day and the day following, to prevent tampering with the ballots. McCoy was awarded an Oak Leaf Cluster to his D.S.M. for his "outstanding achievement in the face of seemingly insurmountable obstacles," and the fairness of the election was praised by the losing Conservatives as well as the winning Liberals.

In July 1928 the soldier-diplomat was appointed to represent the United States at the Pan American Conference in Washington, which was working out treaties for arbitration and conciliation. The deliberations were interrupted in December by an armed conflict between Bolivia and Paraguay over the much-disputed Gran Chaco boundary, and McCoy was selected as head of the seven-nation investigating commission. (Their efforts did not, however, avert the war, which broke out in 1933.) After two years and five months in command of the Fourth Corps Area at Atlanta, in February 1932 Major General McCoy was assigned by President Hoover'⁴³ to the League of Nations commission of inquiry into the Manchurian situation, headed by the Earl of Lytton; his fellow commissioners were an Italian count, a German doctor, and a French general. The Lytton Commission's report, issued in October 1932, stated that "it is a fact that without a declaration of war a large area of what was indisputably the Chinese territory has been forcibly seized and occupied by the armed forces of Japan, and has in consequence of this opera-

tion been separated from and declared independent of the rest of China." General McCoy's services on this delicate mission are officially described as "of the highest order."

Assigned to command the First Cavalry Division in Texas in March 1933, McCoy was ordered in October to Omaha to assume command of the Seventh Corps Area. In February 1935 he took over the Second Army and the Sixth Corps Area in Chicago, thus becoming one of the four most potent commanders in the country, after Chief of Staff Mac-Arthur—*Fortune* called them "the four big shots with the three Irish names," meaning Major Generals Nolan, McCoy, Hagood, and Malone, commanding the four armies. (McCoy's chief of staff in Chicago was Colonel George C. Marshall'⁴⁰.) As his last assignment before retiring, in May 1936 McCoy succeeded Nolan as commanding general at Governors Island (New York), which the *Literary Digest* called, "the Army's prize plum. . . .General McCoy might have climbed even higher," the magazine added, "to the four-starred shoulder straps of General and Chief of Staff, but he was in Scotland shooting grouse when the Army's top-notch billet was vacated. It was typical of him not to be in Washington, D.C., when commands were being shifted. He doesn't play military politics, or go out of his way to seek promotion."

For several years General McCoy headed a research group, in cooperation with Harold J. Tobin and Percy W. Bidwell; their findings, completed before the outbreak of the Second World War, were published as *Mobilizing Civilian America* (1940), with an introduction by McCoy.

On November 1, 1938, the sixty-four-year-old general went on the retired list, and the next February the board of directors of the Foreign Policy Association, a nonprofit and nonpartisan research and educational organization, elected him president. He was also elected to various other boards of directors or trustees, including the Equitable Life Assurance Society and a number of internationally and socially minded bodies.

The officer was selected in December 1941, with Justice Owen J. Roberts'⁴¹ and three colleagues, to investigate responsibility for the Pearl Harbor disaster. (Earlier, in 1931, he and three others toured Latin America in behalf of the Inter-American Escadrille, a membership organization.) In July 1942 President Franklin D. Roosevelt appointed McCoy to head the military commission of seven generals for the trial of eight Nazi spies and saboteurs who had been landed on the Atlantic Coast from German submarines.

He was called on again, in October 1945, when Secretary James Byrnes'⁴¹ announced the General's appointment to represent the United States on a projected Far Eastern advisory commission. This body was to report and make recommendations to the members' respective governments on carrying out the terms of the Japanese surrender.

Until the meeting of the Big Three foreign ministers in Moscow that December, the Russians refused to accept the commission, urging instead a division of authority in the control of Japan and the substitution of an Allied control council. As a result of the conference it

MCCOY, FRANK R.—*Continued*

was decided to revise the body, and Russia agreed to appoint a representative. Before the revision took place, however, the group, representing the United States, New Zealand, Britain, the U.S.S.R., the Netherlands, China, France, Canada, the Philippines, Australia, and India, left for Japan on December 26 to study the American administration of the country. Emphasizing that it hoped to become more of a policy-making body, the commission dropped the word "Advisory" from its original name of Far Eastern Advisory Commission. McCoy was unanimously chosen by the other delegates for chairman.

The mustached general from Pennsylvania, square-jawed and blue-eyed, is of average height and wiry build. He is said always to keep himself in the pink of condition, to be fond of shooting, a pretty good deep-sea fisherman, and able to "ride anything that has a saddle on it"; a friend says that he will take one drink during a social evening, but no more. McCoy's career has brought him many honors, including six honorary LL.D.'s and eight foreign decorations; he has returned one of them, the Japanese Order of the Rising Sun. He is a Presbyterian and belongs to two clubs in New York, one in Philadelphia, and three in Washington, and is president of the Philippine Club, a group of old-timers who meet to talk over island days.

References

Far Eastern R 25:293-4 Jl '29 por
Fortune 12:43 S '35 por
Lit Digest 121:22 Ap 25 '36 por
N Y Sun p7 Mr 6 '41
PM p3 O 11 '45 por
Columbia Encyclopedia (1935)
National Cyclopædia of American Biography Current vol E p514
Who's Who in America, 1944-45

MCCRACKEN, JOAN Dec. 31, 1922- Dancer; actress

Address: b. c/o Willard Keefe, 1545 Broadway, New York City; Warner Brothers Pictures, Inc., 321 W. 44th St., New York City

"Overnight successes" are fairly common in the New York theater; but on examination it usually turns out that the so-called "discovery" has been around for seasons without attracting any particular attention. An exception is bubbling Joan McCracken, an obscure ballet dancer who in 1943, on her first appearance in any play, stepped out of the *Oklahoma!* ballet line long enough to fall down, as required, and thereby win applause, publicity, a movie contract, and in 1944 a comedienne role in *Bloomer Girl.*

Joan McCracken was born December 31, 1922, in Philadelphia, where she attended grade and high schools. Her father, Frank McCracken, was a reporter who wrote sports news for the Philadelphia *Public Ledger.* For Joan's eighth birthday an aunt gave her tuition for dancing lessons. At first it was acrobatic dancing, but Joan ran into "trouble with flip-flops," and even her mother's offer of a dollar per flip-flop failed to inspire her. So Mrs. McCracken transferred Joan to the Catherine

Littlefield Ballet School, and was unmoved by her daughter's protests that all the other students were much better than she. According to the Warner [45] Brothers publicity office, Miss McCracken's own desire was to be an actress, and she was active in school dramatics, but she did well enough at ballet to attract the attention of Miss Littlefield's sister Dorothie, the noted dancer. In 1934 Dorothie Littlefield brought Joan, then twelve, to New York as one of an initial group of scholarship students at the School of American Ballet. There Joan studied under Miss Littlefield, George Balanchine [42], Muriel Steuart, and Pierre Vladimirovitch for several years. Her first public appearance was made with the American Ballet in the 1934-35 season.

When Joan was sixteen her father died, and her mother began to write the Pennsylvania Military Academy's publicity in return for young Frank's tuition. Joan, who had been studying dancing at the Littlefield School, left the West Philadelphia High School to join Catherine Littlefield's Philadelphia Ballet. Her first appearance with this group was at the Philadelphia Academy of Music; she then accompanied them on extensive tours, which reached England and the Continent, France and Belgium in particular. Catherine Littlefield, the choreographer whose company was later called the Littlefield Ballet, sought to have a young and thoroughly American sort of ballet, and her company has the distinction of never having danced *Swan Lake.* "When we did the classics," she says, "we did something that was not commonly done—the full-length *Sleeping Beauty, Daphnis et Chloé.* We started the Americana in divertissements. Then when I took the company abroad in 1937 I realized that what they would want to see there was not European but American ballet. That's how *Barn Dance, Terminal,* and later *Cafe Society* and *Ladies' Better Dresses* originated. The idea was: American themes, American composers, and American kids." And European audiences are said to have loved it.

After returning to the United States, Miss McCracken went back to the School of American Ballet (she earned some money as a model). In August 1941 the twenty-year-old brunette was engaged by the Radio City Music Hall Corps de Ballet to dance several times daily in the lavish stage show accompanying the motion picture presentations. Miss McCracken left the security and obscurity of this job in January 1942, after five months, to join Eugene Loring's Dance Players. This group of a dozen young dancers, with Janet Reed as the feminine star, made its New York debut in April 1942 and later toured the country with a repertoire of eight ballets, alternating roles. Joan McCracken's best part was as the Mexican sweetheart in Loring's *Billy the Kid,* which the *New Republic* calls "the most native and wonderful story ever danced." She was given the star role in Loring's new *Duke of Sacramento,* but this ballet never reached New York, which is to say that for all practical purposes it never really existed. After a year the Loring company broke up because of the difficulties of wartime touring.

Around this time, Agnes de Mille [43] was looking for dancers for *Away We Go,* a musical version of Riggs's *Green Grow the Lilacs* which the Theatre Guild was producing. For her ballets the choreographer wanted performers who were not only "dancers to their finger-tips" but actors as well, and "boys and girls you would remember . . . as friends you'd like to see again some time." Joan McCracken was chosen as one of them, to dance in four scenes. Although listed on the cast sheet as Sylvie, she had no real part in the dramatic portions, but Miss de Mille chose her to dance an awkward country girl who wobbled out of line and fell down, displaying her turn-of-the-century boots and drawers. She also had a real solo later, "all leaps and fillips," as one of two picturesquely dressed cancan girls.

On March 31, 1943, when the play opened in New York as *Oklahoma!* it immediately became a hit. The main attractions were, of course, the Rodgers '40-Hammerstein '44 score, the de Mille choreography, and the singing and acting of Alfred Drake '44, Celeste Holm '44, and Joan Roberts. But the surprise of the package was Joan McCracken, the "pixie ballerina," for despite the microscopic size of her part she "established herself on Broadway as an enchanting new talent with a flair for puckish comedy," attracting more attention than the ballet leads Katharine Sergava and Marc Platt combined. *Look* Magazine listed her as one of four "girls who have squirmed out of obscurity and are causing the paying customers to stamp their feet and callous their palms," and pointed out that at twenty-one she was younger than any of the others (Betty Garrett, Vera-Ellen, and Sono Osato '45). *Vogue* published her picture; *Life* gave "the girl who falls down" three pages; Chesterfield cigarettes spread her endorsement over the countryside; interviews became frequent; the Duke of Windsor '44, missing her when he saw *Oklahoma!* for a second time, came backstage to make inquiries. (She was suffering from jaundice.) And all the time Joan McCracken had so little to do onstage that many a far-off balcony patron left the theater without having decided which dancer was that McCracken girl he'd heard so much about.

Miss McCracken says she never daydreamed of an acting career. While appearing in *Oklahoma!* however, she "tried a few afternoons of it," appearing before invited audiences at the Neighborhood Playhouse in Tennessse Williams' *The Lady of the Larkspur Lotion.* The role she played had been written for Lillian Gish '44. "I loved playing the part, though," Miss McCracken is quoted. "It sort of gave me power I didn't realize I had before."

In April 1944 Warner Brothers picked Miss McCracken out of the *Oklahoma!* cast and sent her to Hollywood. There she worked on her singing, dancing, and acting, and spent seven weeks rehearsing and one week shooting a *Ballet in Jive* for *Hollywood Canteen.* This was one of the longer numbers in that "star-studded jumble," running a full five minutes on the screen, and was mentioned as a high spot by many reviewers. *Variety*, the bible of show business, wrote that the dancer "lenses excellently" and "terps for boff results." Director Lewis Milestone wanted her to play the model in the Hunt Stromberg production of *Guest in the House,* the part which finally went

JOAN MCCRACKEN

to Marie McDonald; but Miss McCracken got permission to return to New York for a featured role in another period musical, *Bloomer Girl.*

Bloomer Girl, which began its New York run in October 1944, had Celeste Holm and David Brooks in the leads and Joan McCracken as a singing and dancing comedienne. For her vocal numbers, a semi-strip to "T'morra, T'morra" and a play-within-a-play scene as Topsy, she sang in a raucous comedic voice which later proved useful in hailing cabs, although she was then studying with a voice teacher. Comments on it varied from "she handles her numbers beautifully," to "Miss McCracken is an excellent dancing comedienne who should not try to sing." In general, reviewers praised her "effervescent charm and humor." However, the New York *World-Telegram*'s intransigent Burton Rascoe complained that "Miss McCracken is cute, but last night she was so busy being cute that (to me) she was irritating." One scrivener added a wistful note: "It is a pity that Joan McCracken is kept so busy as a principal comedian that she has little time to dance, for she is a top-notch dancer." As the souvenir program remarked rather smugly, "Her emergence here as a singing and dancing comedienne has forced a violent shift of plans for her once she is back before the cameras. The studio didn't know her strength." She was given *The Billboard* Donaldson Award for the best feminine supporting performance in *Bloomer Girl.*

Miss McCracken left *Bloomer Girl* in September 1945. Three months later she opened in the title role of *Billion Dollar Baby,* sharing the spotlight with Mitzi Green. The authors of the musical comedy, Betty Comden '45 and Adolph Green '45, had conceived the idea of satirizing the "Terrific Twenties." The critics' reaction was that for the most part the two had fallen short of a good idea, while the part they had written for their heroine, "a feather-brained gold digger," was considered inconsistent. Reviewers wrote that Miss

MCCRACKEN, JOAN—*Continued*

McCracken disposed of this matter with "bouncing aplomb," that she was "beguiling," and "amiable," but that on the whole they were unable to unscramble the uncertainties of the character she was supposed to be.

Not long after *Bloomer Girl* opened, she proved her right to the term "trouper" by going on with her performance and a scheduled interview after receiving word of the death of Frank, her only brother, in the Pacific. That interviewer found the pert brunette and her mother living in an unpretentious little apartment full of Joan's paintings, which were described as striking primitives executed on barrel tops and crate ends, and showing a gift for likenesses. Miss McCracken's husband, Jack Dunphy, formerly of the *Oklahoma!* ballet, was an Army private on maneuvers at the time. (Warner Brothers report, incidentally, that when Joan and Mrs. McCracken were unable to get a painter for their Hollywood apartment, they painted the walls themselves.) The interviewer saw in Miss McCracken "everybody's older sister . . . the girl you never had to worry about because you never knew if she was sick or unhappy or had problems of her own . . . always sympathetic and always good for a laugh," and suggested that that quality communicated itself to an audience and was the basis for her popularity: "She has her audience in the palm of her hand every second."

Like most ballerinas, pretty Joan McCracken is a convenient size for a partner to lift: five feet one and one-half inches tall, she weighs one hundred and seven pounds. Her favorite color is red, which sets off her dark brown hair (naturally straight), gray eyes, and pert, childlike face. Besides painting, she collects antique furniture, writes, likes Russian and Irish literature, loves to ski, and is studying music seriously. Miss McCracken claims to be a contralto; but her teacher, a tenor with a preference for the higher registers, insists that she is a mezzo-soprano.

References

Life 17:78+ O 2 '44 il por
Look 8:54+ F 2 '44 pors; 8:38+ O 3
'44 pors
N Y Herald Tribune D 17 '44 p3 IV
PM O 29 '44 p m3+ por

MCCREERY, SIR RICHARD L(OU-DON) Feb. 1, 1898- British Army officer
Address: b. c/o War Office, London

The unconditional surrender of the German armies in Italy on May 2, 1945, brought to an end one of the hardest-fought campaigns of the Second World War. The British Eighth Army, under Lieutenant General Sir Richard L. McCreery, shares with the American Fifth Army of General Clark '42 and Truscott '45 the glory and the losses of the battle for Italy. Their campaign is described by the Allied Supreme Commander in the Mediterranean, Field Marshal Sir Harold R. L. G. Alexander '42, as one "which will long live in history as one of the greatest and most successful ever waged." A few months after V-E Day McCreery became commanding officer of the British Forces of Occupation in Austria.

Richard Loudon McCreery was born on February 1, 1898, the son of Walter A. and Emilia (McAdam) McCreery of Bilton Park, Rugby. After studying at Eton, he attended the Royal Military College at Sandhurst. At seventeen young McCreery joined the Twelfth Lancers, in August 1915, as a second lieutenant. He served with them in France until 1917, was wounded, and returned as a full lieutenant to fight from August to November 1918, when he won the Military Cross. His regiment was one of the first to be mechanized, and he "accepted the armored fighting vehicle without reserve."

Between wars McCreery spent most of his time on regimental duties, with time out for steeplechasing—he won the Grand Military Gold Cup at Sandown Park in 1923 and again in 1928. In 1921 he was chosen adjutant of the regiment, and was promoted to captain in 1923 and to major in 1927. He was married in 1928, to Lettice, daughter of Lord Percy St. Maur. In that year, too, the thirty-year-old Major entered the Staff College. In 1930 he was made brigade major of the Second Cavalry Brigade in the Southern Command, covering a number of regiments, and remained in this post until 1933. Two years later McCreery was raised to lieutenant colonel and given command of his old regiment, the Twelfth Lancers, which had become an armored car unit in 1928. In 1937 he was made a brevet colonel, and in July of that year was made a full colonel.

In 1938 Colonel McCreery was made General Staff Officer 1 of the First Division; his work in the desperate Dunkerque campaign of June 1940 won him the Distinguished Service Order and his promotion to brigadier in July (having first been made acting brigadier and then temporary brigadier). That December he was again promoted, to acting major general, and was given command of an armored division. General McCreery's work was mentioned in dispatches in 1941; he was "one of the young progressive generals to whom were entrusted the formation and training of the new armored divisions and the armored groups which came into existence in 1941." In the spring of 1942 he was in the Middle East as adviser on armored fighting vehicles at the General Headquarters. That summer General Sir Harold Alexander replaced Sir Claude Auchinleck '42 in command of operations, and General Sir Bernard L. Montgomery '42 was placed in command of the Eighth Army, after its loss of Tobruk. McCreery became Alexander's Chief of the General Staff. In this capacity he worked on the British counteroffensive which began on October 23, 1942, and was culminated at El Alamein; and he helped plan the North African landings in November 1942, the first large-scale amphibious operations the Allies had undertaken.

Like many armies, this "British" Eighth was made up of troops from various parts of the world, speaking various languages. In addition to the Englishmen, Irish, Scots, and Welshmen from the United Kingdom, it included New Zealanders, under Lieutenant General Sir Bernard C. Freyberg '40, and divisions from India, South Africa, and Australia, as well as Fighting French and Greek members of the Southern Division. Visiting the Eighth in Tripoli, Prime Minister Winston Churchill '[42] declared, "I have never in my life . . . seen troops who march with the style and air of the Desert Army. Talk about spit-and-polish—!" At the end of the Italian campaign, when the Allied forces in Italy included Canadian, Polish, and Brazilian units and the Jewish Brigade, Churchill was to term it "as gallant an army as has ever marched."

For his staff work in Tunisia and the Middle East General McCreery was made a Companion of the Bath, and later a Knight Commander of the same Order. (He had already received the decoration of the Order of the British Empire.) In 1943 his major generalcy was substantiated (made permanent); and late that August he was given a field command—the Tenth Corps, attached to General Mark W. Clark's American Fifth Army. This was just before the Allied invasion of Italy. In the battle for Salerno, McCreery's corps was so hard-pressed that at one time the Germans thought the Wehrmacht had won and announced its victory. But the British and Americans clung to their beachheads and battled their way inland. Later Sir Richard and his men "played a decisive part in developing a brilliant technique for the passage of swift mountain rivers in the face of violent opposition," to quote a British release, and in "employing armor with a decisive effect in what had previously been thought impossible ground and weather conditions."

The Allied forces liberated Naples on October 1, 1943, but their way to Rome was hampered by mountainous terrain and unfavorable weather conditions. While the British Eighth Army fought its way along the so-called "Hitler '[42] Line" of German defenses, the American Fifth and General McCreery's corps inched along toward the north. Rome was taken on June 4, 1944, and in July Alexander announced, "The Allied armies in Italy have driven a battered enemy a hundred and fifty miles to the north of Rome within one month in a campaign that must rank with the most vigorous and carefully planned campaigns in modern blitz warfare." With the fall of Florence in August 1944 the battle of central Italy was over, and the battle of northern Italy began.

In contrast to the movements of the Allies on the Western front, which began with the landings in Normandy in June 1944, the grim Italian fighting was slow and dull to the newspaper readers: *Time* aptly called it "the forgotten front." That November McCreery took over command of the Eighth when General Sir Oliver Leese [44] was transferred to India to head a new army group. Over the mountains and through the mud and rain his army pushed along the Rimini-Bologna highway. In December 1944 his Britishers and Canadians freed the Adriatic coastal city of Ravenna, putting McCreery in position to strike toward the flank and rear of the Bologna defenses; and the same month Faenza fell to the Eighth also. Then, on April 21, 1945, the Eighth and the American Fifth Army surged into Bologna from virtually all directions and gained the greatest victory in the Italian campaign since Rome was taken. The long and bitter battle of the Apennines had come to an end with the fall of the most important communications hub in the

British Official Photo.

LT. GEN. SIR RICHARD L. MCCREERY

Po Plain. With unabated speed the Allied armies pressed on toward the Brenner Pass, the Fifth capturing the important cities of Verona and Parma. The Italian Partisans rose in Milan and Turin and drove out the Germans, while McCreery's army took Venice.

On May 2, 1945, almost two years after the Allies made their first landing on the Italian mainland, the German armies in Italy surrendered unconditionally. The collapse was anticlimactic. The Fifth Army had already smashed to within thirty-five miles of the Austrian border for a junction with the American Seventh Army driving into the Austrian Alps under General Alexander M. Patch '[43], and it was reported in Rome dispatches that the British Eighth Army had joined with Tito's '[43] Yugoslav forces in a drive to crush the German troops still fighting in Yugoslavia. General Clark's statement, "The military power of Germany in Italy has . . . ceased, even though scattered fighting may continue," officially closed the Italian campaign. Sir Richard McCreery and his Eighth Army then went to work on Austria.

But McCreery's work in Italy was not finished. He sent his New Zealand Second Division two hundred and twenty-one miles in twenty-three days to cross the Isonzo River and seize the Istrian peninsula, to which Tito had laid claim. On the afternoon of May 2, 1945, General Freyberg accepted the surrender of the German garrison of Trieste to the Allied forces. The troops, which occupied the cities of Trieste and Gorizia, brought Allied Military Government units along, as usual, but they found that the Yugoslavs had already taken over the military government of the disputed area. There was, however (according to Milton Bracker of the New York *Times* staff), "on strictly military grounds not the slightest evidence of friction between the Yugoslavs, who now are administering the Adriatic city [Trieste], and Eighth Army New Zealanders," in ten days. (Since early April, inci-

MCCREERY, SIR RICHARD L.—*Cont.*

dentally, it was announced that General Mc-
Creery's old regiment, the Twelfth Royal Lancers, had "cooperated continuously" with the
New Zealand division.) The three cities of
Trieste, Gorizia, and Fiume were a long-standing sore point between Italy and the Slavs, having passed from hand to hand for hundreds of
years, but by mid-May 1945 the dispute seemed
to be on its way to a settlement. In July the
famous Eighth was disbanded, and McCreery
was appointed commander of the British Forces
of Occupation in Austria. It was a difficult assignment, for Austria was faced with scarci-
ties of fuel, food, clothing, and other necessities, and with an uncertain political future.

Sir Richard McCreery, K.C.B., K.B.E.,
D.S.O., M.C., is a thin, light-haired man.
Devoted to armored vehicles in the field, he
has an equal fondness for horses: his favorite
recreations are polo, hunting, and steeplechasing.
He is also a member of the Marylebone Cricket
Club. Sir Richard and Lady McCreery have
four sons and one daughter.

Reference

Who's Who, 1945

MACGOWAN, GAULT　Feb. 7, 1894-
Journalist

Address: b. c/o New York Sun, 280 Broadway, New York City

A veteran war correspondent who has lived
and traveled in many parts of the world, British-born Gault MacGowan has crammed more
dangerous adventures into his lifetime than
most men would care to experience. To top
them all, he was captured by the Germans on
August 14, 1944, while with the American
forces in northern France. After two weeks
as a prisoner MacGowan escaped "through a
series of adventures that would make a Hollywood scenarist bite his nails with envy," joined
the French Maquis in a forest near Champagne, and eventually returned to the United
States after five years of covering the war
fronts. At the end of 1945 he was director of
the European News Service for the New York
Sun.

Gault MacGowan was born in Manchester,
England, February 7, 1894, the son of Robert
Alexander Ernest and Marie (Hilton) Mac-
Gowan. He is the descendant of a long line
of Ulster Irish forebears who have been transatlantic commuters since the time of sailing
ships. The Gault name is Huguenot and is a
family name associated with the well known
Gault family of Montreal. MacGowan's grandfather was for many years a doctor near Belle-
fontaine, Ohio. "My grandmother was Elizabeth Gault, who fostered in me great respect
for and appreciation of the New England literary tradition," the correspondent says.

Young MacGowan went to the Manchester
Grammar School and to Manchester Univer-
sity; then to the Sorbonne for graduate work.
That was in 1914; when war broke out he
immediately enlisted. He was assigned to an
Indian cavalry regiment, the Lancers, rose to
the rank of captain, served in France, Italy, and
Mesopotamia, and was wounded several times.
On returning to India with his regiment in
1922 he became a correspondent for the Asso-

ciated Press, covering the disturbances on the
northwest frontier in India for a year. In
1923 he was married to Wendy Smith, daughter
of Mr. and Mrs. J. H. Corley Smith of Simla,
India. The couple have one son, Barry Alaric
Gault, born in Iraq in 1925.

Having decided on newspaper work for his
future career, MacGowan in 1924 accepted an
offer to become editor of the Mesopotamian
Times, which had been started after the war
for the officers and men stationed in that country. Then, in order to gain necessary experience on a large paper, he returned to London
to read copy for the London *Times*. In 1926-
27 he was a staff correspondent for the Paris
Daily Express, and two years later he left to
become assistant editor and editorial writer for
the Cardiff *Evening Express*. For a year he
also wrote a column, *Londoner's Diary*, for a
British syndicate.

Attracted to the West Indies, in 1929 Mac-
Gowan became managing editor of the Trinidad
Guardian, and until 1934 made his influence
felt throughout the West Indies. He represented those colonies at the Imperial Press
Conference in 1930, and from 1930 to 1935 was
the honorary secretary for the West Indies
on the council of the Institute of Journalists.
He was also the correspondent at Trinidad for
the London *Times*, the New York *Times*, and
other American and European newspapers.

In addition to journalistic recognition, Mac-
Gowan at various times since the war had won
attention by his travels and adventures. He
explored the wilds of northern India. He discovered a new pass through the Himalayas
into Little Tibet which was named for him.
He made aerial expeditions, too—the first
flight over Orinoco Delta and across Venezuelan llanos, between Trinidad and Maracay;
and the first flight between Trinidad and
British Guiana.

Two articles (later reprinted in pamphlet
form) resulted from these travels: "To the
End of the World and Beyond," and "My
Desert Dash to Damascus." The first told of
his discovery of the new pass into India:
"'The end of the world' was a real place in
Hindu mythology, but I proved it wasn't—
though there is no known road into Tibet
beyond the mighty cliff and shrine which gave
it its name." The Damascus trip was made via
motorcar across the desert from Kurdistan and
Mosul to Syria, the first trip of its kind. "The
desert was wild, lawless, and untamed," the
explorer related. "Holdups were frequent, and
an officer who tried it after me was stripped
of everything and had to walk naked into the
Lebanons!" MacGowan plans to incorporate
these two accounts into, he says, "the adventure book I plan to write when I stop having
adventures."

During his years as a "provincial" journalist,
and adventurer, Gault MacGowan received
honors from several foreign governments.
Among these were Officier de l'Instruction
Publique (1930), Officer of the Portugal Military Order of Christ (1933), and Chevalier
de la Légion d'Honneur (1934). He has also
been a Selfridge prizeman, a member of the
Company of Newspaper Makers, a Liveryman
of the Stationer's Company, a Freeman of the
City of London since 1937, and a Fellow of the
Royal Geographical Society of London. (He

was obliged to resign from the latter because of the time taken up by his newspaper work.)

It was in October 1934 that MacGowan joined the staff of the New York *Sun*. For that paper he covered the coronation of King George VI '42. He was on vacation abroad when the Spanish Civil War broke out, and was sent by the *Sun* to Spain. Among his articles at this time were "The Scarlet Pimpernels of Spain" and "Red Vultures of the Pyrenees," which appeared in the *Commonweal* in January and February 1938. In these two he told of some of the men and women who risked their lives to help the victims of the "Red Terror" escape to neutral lands. Condemning the Spanish Loyalists and their Left-wing sympathizers, MacGowan said that, on the fringe of the Pyrenees, "the crimson vultures of Sovietism hover for further pickings from the homes of civilization."

In the fall of 1938 MacGowan decided to visit England again, and was there when the war broke out. He represented his paper during the Battle of Britain and, early in 1941, during the Battle of the Atlantic, he began recounting his experiences aboard one of the American destroyers that had been transferred to England for convoy duty. Later he was press observer with the Commandos in the raid on Dieppe. MacGowan was particularly well qualified to cover Britain at war: as a former British Army man, he "talked the language" of the Tommies and their officers; he could well understand, also, the British civilian character and viewpoint. At the same time, from his long experience writing for an American paper, he could present what he saw in terms familiar to his American readers.

When the big news of the war shifted to North Africa, MacGowan was assigned as a correspondent to the American Army there. He was with the French on April 25, 1943, when they attacked Jabel Mansour in North Africa, where he received a leg wound. Despite the injury, MacGowan followed the attacking force through to the successful conclusion of the battle, and was awarded the Purple Heart by special order of President Roosevelt '42. For the same incident he was cited for bravery and awarded the Croix de Guerre by General Henri Giraud '42. In late 1943 he covered the action of the Royal Hellenic Navy, and reported on interviews with young seamen of Greek descent who had relatives in the United States.

In July 1944 MacGowan was with the United States forces in Normandy. To his paper he sent back stories not only of the progress of Allied troops, but of scenes following the German retreat. Some of MacGowan's own adventures were less heroic than humorous: He told how he had ridden to the front astride an old gray mare named Brünnhilde—actually a French horse who had been conscripted by the Germans. He had found her stampeding out of the German lines, pulling her cart behind her; since she had completely lost her gun-shyness, MacGowan mounted her and trotted off with the advancing infantry regiment. "It was a fantastic journey," he relates. "Men were sticking their heads out of tank turrets to shout such comments as 'Hi, ho, Silver'. 'Here comes Man-o'-War', 'Paul Revere,' and 'I'll trade you a tank for her,' as we ambled through the bomb-shattered countryside to sur-

N. Y. *Sun*

GAULT MACGOWAN

vey the damage." By the end of July MacGowan was moving with General Omar Bradley's '43 forces out of the hedgerow country into the Norman highlands, following the line of German retreat along miles of smashed vehicles. On the first of August the correspondent rode in the jeep with the first American to reach the historic island of Mont Saint Michel off the northwest coast of France.

Then, on September 1, the German radio reported that on August 15 one "Gowan," a correspondent for the New York *Sun*, had been captured. This was followed up by a cable to the *Sun* from MacGowan himself confirming the report but adding that he had managed to escape to Paris. Several days later the full story was made public. MacGowan and two British correspondents had heard a premature report of the capture of Chartres, and when they were captured near the city they were riding in a jeep ahead of the advancing American troops. After a night in a barracks with twenty American prisoners, the Captain (the rank accredited to correspondent MacGowan) was taken by two Nazi officer-correspondents on a tour of Paris night life—apparently to prove to him that Germans were not uncivilized. But it was the last night of German occupation: on the roads out of Paris the next day were "long, densely packed columns, the remnants of once proud regiments."

On his way to internment in Germany, the correspondent escaped from the train and, with clothes torn to shreds by barbed wire, made his way in the general direction of Patton's army. Guided by sympathetic French people he reached a Maquis camp, and there he witnessed the assault and capture of Châlons-sur-Marne, the hub of the German retreat from Paris. The F.F.I. had been mobilized in the woods, waiting to join up with General Patton's armored spearheads. They had excellent food, and "lived a life like Robin Hood's, not in Sherwood Forest, but in a Christmas tree land." When the Americans came the F.F.I. met them, led the way to Châlons, and took

MACGOWAN, GAULT—*Continued*

the town. On his own again, MacGowan made his way to Paris, where, on September 1, he walked into the bar of the Paris hotel which served as press headquarters. The rest of the reporters almost dropped their glasses. "For the usually immaculate MacGowan was dressed in borrowed French civilian clothes that fit him like Europe fits Hitler—too big in some places, too tight in others." He was a year later to visit concentration camps all over Germany in an effort to locate the prisoner-husband of one of the women who had supplied him with a farmer's overalls and helped him to escape.

Gault MacGowan went on to London for a few days to report the changing British scene, then sailed for New York in October 1944, for the first time in five years, looking "trim and fit in his correspondent's uniform, with a chest full of campaign ribbons and decorations from two wars." His associates decided that he deserved still another decoration, since the first act of the dauntless traveler and adventurer was to get lost in Brooklyn. He finally made his way "from the Brooklyn battlefront" to the *Sun* offices, where, for once on the other end of interviews, he recounted some of his experiences.

After his leave in the United States MacGowan returned once more to Europe. He covered the invasion with Patton's army, was in Paris for Easter 1945 and the first big military parade after the liberation, went to Berchtesgaden with the Americans and to Buchenwald with the French. He was in Potsdam for the Big Three conference in July and in London during the conference of Foreign Ministers in the autumn of 1945. At the end of December, after another brief period in America, his dispatches were again coming from the British capital. Shortly before that, MacGowan was one of a number of civilian war correspondents who received awards of campaign ribbons "for outstanding and conspicuous service with the armed forces under difficult and hazardous conditions."

The correspondent has received the warmest praise from one of his former fellow prisoners in German-occupied France. "With MacGowan there," the soldier wrote in a letter to the *Sun*, "you just couldn't help feeling good. He was always so darn cheerful and had such great stories to tell." The man also described MacGowan's prowess as a chess player: "It would take him only a few minutes to beat me; then he would try to teach me the tricks." Chess, it seems, is MacGowan's favorite indoor recreation. He plays the game, a colleague says, the way he goes for news: "All out to win and no quitting as long as a pawn is left." Other favored recreations of his are driving and horseback riding—although perhaps on something a little more elegant than the old gray mare on which he rode to the front in France.

Tall, dark-haired, with a "devil-may-care" look in his eyes, Gault MacGowan, according to his friends, seems to thrive on adventure. In appearance today he looks younger and more fit, if anything, they say, than he did when he left to cover the war in 1939. He declares that he isn't "ready for the carpet slippers yet. I have seen a lot, been through a lot, and I have enjoyed every minute of it.

Adventure keeps you young. Or maybe it's because I'm just a kid at heart. Anyway, I haven't had enough of it yet."

References

N Y Sun p3 Ap 5 '41 por; p11 Jl 3 '44 por; p1+ Ag 15 '44 por; p1+ O 12 '44 por; p10 O 13 '44
N Y Times p8 Ag 16 '44 por
Who's Who, 1945
Who's Who in America, 1944-45

McINTIRE, ROSS T. Aug. 11, 1889-

United States naval officer; physician
Address: b. c/o Navy Department, Washington, D.C.; h. 3637 49th St., N.W., Washington, D.C.

Surgeon General of the United States Navy and Chief of the Bureau of Medicine and Surgery since 1938, Vice-Admiral Ross T. McIntire was better known as the White House physician who for ten years had the vitally responsible job of looking after the health of the late President Franklin D. Roosevelt[42]. His administration of the Navy Medical Department during the time of the greatest expansion in its history won for him the rank of vice-admiral in 1945, the highest rank ever given a medical officer.

Born on August 11, 1889, in Salem, Oregon, Ross T. McIntire is the son of Charles Thaddeus and Ada (Thompson) McIntire. After attendance at Salem's public schools, he entered the Willamette University Medical School in 1907 (now merged with University of Oregon Medical School in Portland). He received his degree of Doctor of Medicine in 1912, and went into private practice in his native Salem. Ten years later, his country's neutrality threatened, the twenty-seven-year-old doctor joined the United States Naval Reserve in January 1917; in April he entered the Medical Corps of the regular Navy, as assistant surgeon, with the rank of lieutenant (junior grade). A course of instruction and indoctrination at the Naval Medical School, Washington, D.C., followed, and in July he was attached to the *New Orleans*. (During the war he rose to the rank of lieutenant commander, temporary.) After the war—he had decided to remain in the service—he was commissioned a regular lieutenant in July 1919. He remained with the *New Orleans*, which in the first postwar year operated in the Pacific with the Asiatic Fleet, and as a station ship at Vladivostok. Following his detachment from the *New Orleans* in January 1920, McIntire for a short time was on duty at the Naval Hospital in Canacao, Philippine Islands.

Returning to the United States, the young Navy doctor did postgraduate work at Washington University in St. Louis in 1920, and at the Washington Naval Medical School in 1921. After two years at the San Diego Naval Hospital he was assigned to the hospital ship, the *Relief*, in August 1923. His promotion to the rank of lieutenant commander came in June 1924. After detachment from the *Relief* in September 1925, he was assigned to duty at the Naval Dispensary and later at the Naval Hospital, both in Washington, D.C. In June 1929 he returned to his post on the *Relief*.

The physician's interest in the diseases of the eye and ear led him in 1929 to take further postgraduate work, this time at the University of Pennsylvania's School of Medicine. When he finished his course of studies he served for two more years on the *Relief* and then was appointed to an instructorship in ophthalmology and otolaryngology at the Naval Medical School in the Nation's Capital. At the same time he was on duty at the Naval Hospital.

In June 1934 McIntire, now a full commander, accompanied President Roosevelt on a cruise in the *Houston* to Panama and Hawaii; the following February he was appointed White House physician, at the same time continuing with his work at the Naval Hospital. With this appointment came his promotion to the temporary rank of captain, which was made permanent in July 1940. In the interim, on his appointment as Surgeon General of the Navy and Chief of the Bureau of Medicine and Surgery in December 1938, McIntire was given the temporary rank of rear admiral. This promotion raised him above one hundred and eighteen senior officers in the Medical Corps. (A precedent in jumping rank was established by Woodrow Wilson when he appointed Captain Cary T. Grayson as his personal physician. Roosevelt, in choosing an officer for his own doctor, had followed another long-established custom; Presidents Hoover and Wilson had Navy doctors, President Coolidge an Army doctor.)

McIntire's reputation as a specialist in diseases of the head (he is also a specialist in plastic surgery) greatly influenced his selection for the White House post. The new President was in good health, except for a minor but persistent sinus condition and a left ear which his physician has described as "a little down." No one, not excepting Mrs. Roosevelt '⁴⁰, saw more of Franklin Roosevelt during his occupancy of the White House than did McIntire. He accompanied the President on all trips (he was in the Presidential party at the conferences in the North Atlantic, Teheran, Africa, and the Pacific), and every morning and evening he visited him professionally. When the President was in Washington McIntire's car was parked before the White House, where he had an office equipped for everything from dentistry to radio therapy. While Roosevelt ate his nine-o'clock breakfast from a bedside tray McIntire and three other men joined him for a daily talk. McIntire has said that he could tell more about Roosevelt's condition by an appraisal of his mood than by any routine medical check-up.

In campaign years, in answer to the repeated charges that Roosevelt was not physically fit for the strenuous job as head of the Nation, McIntire was called upon to make public statements concerning the President's health. In October 1944, when the charges were again renewed, McIntire reported that the President was in good condition for his sixty-two years: "Nothing wrong—perfectly O.K. . . . .The stories that he is in bad health are . . . not true." The physician has been credited for the excellent health of his famous charge, which was maintained during his thirteen years in office. McIntire was in Washington when President Roosevelt died at Warm Springs from a cerebral hemorrhage. It was he, however, who directed Dr. James Paullin, the Atlanta specialist, to attend the President, and it

VICE-ADM. ROSS T. MCINTIRE

was he who later broke the news to Mrs. Roosevelt, by saying, "The President has slept away."

Between his morning and evening calls on the President, McIntire attended to his naval duties (instructor and specialist in ophthalmology and otolaryngology from 1931 to 1938, Navy Surgeon General since 1938). In a chapter, "The Navy Doctor at War," which he contributed to the book, *Doctors at War* (1945), McIntire told the story of how his department had carried on during the war. "It is no longer a new story," said McIntire, "that the size of the Medical Department of the United States Navy in 1944 exceeded the strength of the entire Navy as it existed at the outbreak of World War II in 1939. We grew accustomed to counting our medical and dental officers and our nurses in the thousands, and our hospital corpsmen in the scores of thousands, although it was only a few years ago that they ran only into the hundreds. . . . .Even before President Roosevelt's declaration of a state of national emergency in 1940, the Medical Department had begun to gear itself for any eventuality." Besides the increase in personnel, naval hospitals were built, Medical Department facilities were established at new bases in both the Atlantic and Pacific. Also, coincidental with the performance of this work was the research maintained in various branches of naval medicine in order to keep abreast of the rapidly changing developments brought about by war.

The destructiveness of total warfare demanded that Americans exercise their ingenuity, said McIntire. A great many gains were achieved, the treasury of medical knowledge enriched—all of which will be shared by the medical profession and the public at large. As a result of the tremendous progress, the great disparity between Navy-Marine casualties in the First World War and those in the Second "makes any comparison invidious." The mortality rate of wounded in 1917-18 was 12 per cent, in 1943 2.2 per cent. "As of March 31, 1944, more than 55 per cent of all sailors and

MCINTIRE, ROSS T.—*Continued*

marines wounded since Pearl Harbor—including the large number of casualties of that infamous day—had returned to active duty," reported McIntire. "Forty per cent were still under treatment, and a large portion of these could be expected to resume their regular duties in the near future. It was necessary to invalid less than 2 per cent from the service. Only three out of every hundred succumbed."

On December 1, 1942, McIntire was sworn in for a second term of four years as Surgeon General and Chief of the Bureau of Medicine and Surgery. Two years later, when President Roosevelt nominated McIntire and two other Navy Bureau chiefs for promotion from the rank of rear admiral to vice-admiral there was considerable opposition in Navy and Senate circles on the grounds that the rank was higher than any ever given officers serving on shore, primarily in administrative capacities. The New York *Times*'s prediction that the appointments would be confirmed by the Senate, because the appointees were "able men," was fulfilled on February 10, 1944.

In September 1945 McIntire resigned from his White House post to devote full time to his work with the Navy's Medical Department, which is still being expanded. (His term of office expires in December 1946.) The Vice-Admiral is described as "genial, but a stickler for medical and naval proprieties." He is stocky, broad-faced, full-mouthed, and bald. In 1923 he was married to Pauline Palmer. He is a Methodist, a Mason (Shriner), and a member of the Metropolitan and Burning Tree clubs in Washington. Besides holding a Fellowship in the American College of Surgeons, he is a member of the American Medical Association and the Association of Military Surgeons. The Navy physician has the Victory Medal with Escort Clasp, the American Defense Service Medal, and the Bronze Star. He has also received decorations from Brazil, Nicaragua, Sweden, Norway, Denmark, Belgium, France, Luxembourg, Poland, and French Morocco.

> *References*
>
> N Y Herald Tribune p1+ F 3 '44 por
> N Y Sun p24 Ja 19 '44 por
>
> Fishbein, M. ed. Doctors at War (1945)
> Who's Who Among Physicians and Surgeons, 1938
> Who's Who in America, 1944-45

MCKEEVER, ED(WARD CLARK) Aug. 25, 1910- Football coach

Address: b. Cornell University, Ithaca, N.Y.; h. 101 Delaware Ave., Ithaca, N.Y.

One of the most brilliant young college football coaches in the United States is Ed McKeever of Cornell, who led the "Fighting Irish" of Notre Dame through the 1944 season. After nine years as assistant coach at Texas Technological College, Boston College, and Notre Dame, and one year as acting athletic director and head football coach at the last-named, McKeever became head coach at Cornell in 1945. "An expert developer of passers," he is given credit for the training of Charley O'Rourke and Mickey Connolly at Boston College, and of Angelo Bertelli, Johnny Lujack, and Frank Dancewicz at Notre Dame.

Born in San Antonio, Texas, on August 25, 1910, Edward Clark McKeever is the son of Irish Catholic parents, Hugh and Mary Ellen (Clark) McKeever. Mrs. McKeever died when Ed was fourteen. The boy was a good athlete, participating in three major sports at St. Edward's University preparatory school in Austin. Notre Dame's great football coach Knute Rockne was his idol; but when young Tex McKeever entered the Indiana university in 1929 he was too light for the football team, although "smart and fast" on the field. At the end of his freshman year, however, Ed had to go back to Texas because of his father's illness. And later, with the death of Rockne in March 1931, McKeever lost interest in playing for Notre Dame. When the boy left Indiana, according to Arthur Daley of the New York *Times*, he had exactly thirty-five cents. Another player collected twelve dollars toward his fare, which took him to St. Louis, and McKeever rode freight trains from there to Texas.

After some time as a cowhand McKeever entered the Texas Technological College. Pete Cawthon, its football coach, had been told about Ed, and found him a dingy room in the gymnasium basement. Next day, says Daley, "the room was polished and spotless. So was McKeever." To support himself and his invalid father, the youth made snakeskin belts. "I'd go out with a rake and catch me as many as a hundred [rattlesnakes] in a day, cure the skins, and make belts out of them," he recalls. "Those belts would sell at a dollar apiece, and sometimes, when I caught too many rattlers, I'd even cut prices and let them go at seventy-five cents each. . . .All it cost me was a dime for buying salt to use in curing the skins." At Texas Tech McKeever played right halfback, although he weighed only one hundred and sixty pounds, and called the plays which in three years won thirty victories out of thirty-five games. When he was graduated with the B.A. in 1935 Coach Cawthon retained him as backfield coach. (That May McKeever was married to Gail Quinlan, his childhood sweetheart.) McKeever was backfield lecturer at Cawthon's "immensely popular" summer school for coaches, and in 1938 the line lecturer, Frank Leahy of Fordham, attended his classes regularly.

In early 1939, when Leahy was appointed head coach at Boston College, he sent for Tex McKeever to be one of his three assistants. In addition to their work with the team, the coaches made frequent appearances before various organizations, making as many as five speeches a week, showing films of the team's football games, and stirring up interest in a way new to B.C. The team finished undefeated in 1939 and 1940, and won the Sugar Bowl game from the Southern champion after the second year. Then Leahy moved to Notre Dame as head coach and athletic director, taking McKeever with him.

After a successful season in 1941 Coach Leahy decided to introduce the T-formation, used by the professional Chicago Bears, in place of Rockne's famous "Notre Dame shift." He and his assistants drilled themselves on the new system, working out on the handball

courts before introducing it at the 1942 spring
practice. The much-discussed and much-criticized innovation did not seem to work out
very well in the first two games of the season.
When Leahy was taken ill and had to go to
the Mayo Clinic for treatment, Ed McKeever
took over. "I was so scared . . . that, instead
of my calming the kids down, they calmed me
down," he says. After long telephone conferences with his chief, the Texan presided
over three games which everyone expected the
Irish to lose but which they won, beating Stanford 27-0, the Iowa Pre-Flight Seahawks 28-0,
and Illinois 21-14. This was the beginning of
a string of victories after Leahy returned to
Indiana. The next year, 1943, found Notre
Dame with a team weakened by the loss of
men inducted into the armed forces, and a
heavy schedule which included some of the
best teams in the country. Nevertheless, the
Fighting Irish won all except the last game
on their schedule, which went to the Great
Lakes Naval Training School. After the close
of the season Leahy entered the Navy as a
lieutenant, and Ed McKeever took over as
acting athletic director and head football
coach.

During the 1944 season McKeever's team
won eight of its ten games. The other two
were overwhelming defeats by Army and Navy,
but commentators praised the way the coach
"juggled his undermanned squad with consum-
mate skill, was a most gracious loser in crushing defeat . . . patched up a team that had
taken two terrific goings-over and got it gal-
loping again" to win three more games. One
of these three was the first Notre Dame victory over Great Lakes. McKeever's team, like
the other Notre Dame squads which sports
writers insist on calling "The Irish," included
names like Maggioli, Mergenthal, Adams,
Dancewicz, Szymanski, Schuster, Westen-
kircher, and Gasparella. Their coach was immediately popular with reporters, who described
him in such terms as "one of the ablest and
most genuinely liked young coaches to come
up in the game" and "that gay charmer from
Texas."

In December 1944 McKeever denied reports
that he was to be coach at Fordham University,
stating that he had signed a contract to continue at Notre Dame. In early 1945, however,
he accepted the post of head football coach at
Cornell University. In Ithaca (New York)
that March, he says, he found "a nice house
and three real football players waiting" for
him. By the time the season opened the coach
had lost all three of them, one to professional
football, one—Paul Robeson, Jr.—to the Army,
and one as a Navy trainee. His inexperienced
men averaged one hundred and eighty pounds
in weight, less than many high school players
in the South and Midwest. "We'll win some
games on our spirit, even if we are a little on
the small side," said McKeever. Newspapermen noted that "McKeever's enthusiasm has
fired the entire team," and remarked that after
twenty-five years of dour taskmasters, Cornell
finally had a likable and considerate football
coach. McKeever even agreed to let his players go out for track in season. In September
1945 Cornell's first game of the longest schedule in the Ivy League was a victory over Syracuse by 28-14. His men had been drilled in

ED MCKEEVER

the T-formation, which was new to Cornell.
"This 'T' stuff appeals to boys," the coach said.
"It's a lot more fun to play, as well as more
exciting to the spectators" than the single-
wing formation. "Those quick-breaking plays
practically guarantee a gain of three yards."

In the holiday between semesters of his first
Cornell season, McKeever had to take his team
apart and put it together again. The return of
Army men, including Robeson, the transfer of
Navy trainees, and wartime acceleration of college courses resulted in a situation where "total
strangers whom Ed McKeever never laid eyes
on were barging in to shake hands with their
new coach and, with the schedule already half
completed, stepping blithely into the first-string
line-up. A two-week training camp in mid-
season is uncommon enough in its own right,"
wrote Red Smith. "More curious still is the
spectacle of a college squad taking two long
workouts a day in October." With the single
exception of Allen Dekdebrun, all Cornell's
best backs were new or newly returned to the
team, and other players were coming in at
such a rate that, McKeever lamented, "as a
squad we'll be together only Thursday and Friday before the Yale game."

Green-eyed "Big Ed" McKeever, whose
speech is "pure Texas," has been described
as possessing great charm and organizing
ability, and as having "the same instinctive
knowledge of human nature and psychology
that made Rockne so great a coach." That
he can make friends of a crowd of a thousand as easily as of a team of eleven was
demonstrated in January 1945, when Mc-
Keever was inducted into the Circus Saints
and Sinners. The coach's pet superstition
is that he must wear a battered felt hat during games—it was on his head in 1942 when
his Notre Dame players upset all predictions
by winning from the Iowa Seahawks, and
he was not wearing it in 1944 when Army
beat Notre Dame 59-0. McKeever's twin
daughters, Susan Helen and Jane Anne,
were born in December 1940, just before the

MCKEEVER, ED—*Continued*

Sugar Bowl game, and their father gave the first two touchdown-scorers the privilege of naming them.

References

N Y Times p18 Je 29 '44; p14 O 20 '45
Scholastic 45:31 O 23 '44 por

MCLEAN, ALICE T(HROCKMORTON) (măk-lān') Mar. 8, 1886- President of the American Women's Voluntary Services
Address: b. AWVS National Headquarters, 345 Madison Ave., New York City; h. St. James, Long Island, N. Y.

When the board of directors of the American Women's Voluntary Services met in New York City in May 1945, President Truman '45 congratulated this organization of 325,000 women on its completion of "five years of helpful, constructive service to the Nation."

Virginia F. Stern

ALICE T. MCLEAN

At this time Alice T. McLean, founder and president of the AWVS, was re-elected to the presidency. Aside from her executive duties with one of the largest groups of uniformed women in America, Mrs. McLean is an expert horsewoman, the owner and manager of a large dairy and stock farm in upper New York State, and the mother of two sons in active service with the United States armed forces. She feels that the AWVS will best serve American communities in the postwar era by helping in the readjustment of the veteran and his family.

The daughter of James T. and Sara (Throckmorton) McLean, Alice Throckmorton McLean was born on March 8, 1886. The English family of Throckmorton, Alice McLean's maternal ancestors, had been in the ambassadorial service of Queen Elizabeth (the Elizabethan spelling of the name was "Throgmorton"). James McLean was of Scotch ancestry. His father, whose home was on the Island of Mull off the coast of Scotland, came to the United States with his wife in the middle of the nineteenth century to visit American relatives and decided to make America his home. After purchasing a large tract of land in the hills at the headwaters of the Delaware River at South Kortright in Delaware County, New York, he built a "huge, handsome mansion in the Palladian pillared style," and this house became the family's summer home. Alice's mother was one of the first New York matrons to be interested in infant welfare and was one of the founders of the Bethlehem Day Nursery. Alice was the youngest of three daughters born to James and Sara McLean, and with her sisters lived with the family in their New York town house on East Fifty-fifth Street and attended Miss Chapin's School and the Spence School. Summers spent at the Delaware County home alternated with those in which James McLean took his family to Syria, Persia, Egypt, Turkey, and Greece. But when they were in Europe the McLeans usually spent the month of August at French resorts such as Grenoble and Aix-les-Bains. Alice loved travel, but the summers spent on the farm at South Kortright were especially happy ones.

Many years younger than her sisters, Alice was her father's constant companion. She visited mining camps with him, became acquainted with Diaz and Villa in Mexico City, and, as a *New Yorker* writer expresses it, "saw a good bit of big business in the making." Her father taught her to ride, to play polo, and to drive tandem. When she was thirteen he took her to Paris to learn the fine points of four-in-hand driving from an expert teacher. She also studied languages and learned to speak fluently in French, German, and Italian. At the age of seventeen, Miss McLean married Edward Larocque Tinker, a New York lawyer who later became a literary critic and the author of *Lafcadio Hearn's American Days* (1924) and other books. Two sons were born to the couple. Partly as a tribute to her father to whom she was devoted, Alice McLean resumed his name when she got her divorce. Her two sons also use the name of McLean. During the war one son, James McLean, as a captain was aide to General Scott at Fort Knox, Kentucky; the other, Edward T. McLean, was a lieutenant commander with the Naval Air Forces in the Pacific. There are three grandchildren.

As part of her active life as a horsewoman, Alice McLean went to England every autumn in the years following her divorce and hunted with "the Pytchley pack" in Northamptonshire. In 1938 she became interested in the Women's Voluntary Services which had recently been formed in England, and her volunteer work with this group led her to make a study of other women's organizations—the Finnish and the Swiss. Becoming convinced that the war which had started in Europe would eventually involve the United States, she returned to America, and in the fall of 1939 designed posters intended to promote the things women could do in their communities for social and war relief. Friends helped her place these posters in restaurants and post offices. At this time she had no intention of founding an organization which would be completely dedicated to war work. "It seemed to me," she said in reviewing this period, "that an organization without creed or politics, giving community service, was needed—not to compete with other organizations but to help and stimulate them." Although she had previously worked with social agencies, this was her first attempt at organization, and the business training which her father had given her was of great help to her in this pioneer charting.

In 1940 the AWVS was founded, in a basement shop on East Sixty-second Street. By the end of the year the newly formed group had moved into an East Fifty-first Street mansion which was lent to it for headquarters. The aims of the organization during its first year were not so clearly formulated as they were to become later. In England at this time the W.V.S. had a membership of a million women, and every city and hamlet had its corps of uniformed ambulance drivers, evacuation clerks, and air-raid wardens. But, as the *New Yorker* points out, America not only was not at war at this time but was at the peak of its isolationism, and to the general "complacency" in regard to war in general was added the confusion of Army and Navy officials, municipal authorities, and politicians in the matter of what work volunteer women should do. Nevertheless, Mrs. McLean "got the AWVS going principally through her own tenacity and her belief in what she was doing." As these were the days of London's bombings by the Germans, American households following British example, were busy assembling sand buckets and water pails against the possibility of enemy bombs. When classes were offered by the AWVS in first aid and air-raid precautions, housewives joined them in order to learn new techniques which might be needed for war. Even before Pearl Harbor, AWVS membership had reached 18,362. When New York had its first false air raid alarms the AWVS sent its Civilian Protection Unit out into the streets, and when the *S.S. Normandie* burned, the AWVS canteen worked for twenty hours dispensing coffee and doughnuts to the firefighters.

In seven months after the entrance of the United States into the Second World War, fifty thousand new members were enrolled in New York alone. Mrs. McLean worked assiduously during this organization period. A story is told of a barbecue which she planned on her Delaware County farm for two hundred and fifty people; when three thousand neighbors appeared, she hastily added a steer and six hind quarters to the menu and sent a car with a loud speaker throughout the countryside inviting the whole valley to come. She then took advantage of the opportunity to tell about the AWVS with the result that ten new units were formed. By 1942 AWVS had "settled into its realistic stride," its aim at that time being to prepare women to serve the community in every way possible during the war, with long-range plans for training women in motor mechanics, emergency feeding, code practice, emergency switchboard operations, defense photography, and map reading.

In 1945 the AWVS has 325,000 volunteers enrolled from thirty-three states, the District of Columbia, and Alaska. The services are adapted from time to time to local communities, but in general they include child care, workshops, conservation and salvage, canteens, war service photography, rehabilitation work, and motor transport. In San Francisco AWVS volunteers have taught Braille to sailors blinded while swimming away through flames from sinking tankers; in Hollywood, nightly "chow trips" were made to Coast Guard stations and to air and fire watchers on remote posts; also, California AWVS obtained trained women fruit pickers to replace men called into service and Japanese farmers removed to relocation camps.

Between January 1940 and V-E Day, AWVS members sold over a billion dollars' worth of War Bonds and Stamps. Other outstanding activities of the AWVS War Service include: the taking of 30,000 pictures of men and women in the service and of servicemen's babies by AWVS War Service Photography and mailing the pictures all over the world; 1,033,964 articles turned out during a single year by AWVS workshops, including articles for the serviceman, layettes and children's clothes for his family, reconditioned and new garments and linens for hospitals and institutions; organization of over 200 Junior Auxiliaries with a specially planned program for over 32,000 teenagers; training of over 2,000 volunteers to operate salvage depots in cooperation with the War Production Board. The AWVS Motor Transport Service is on call twenty-four hours a day, seven days a week and drives approximately 350 Army and Navy vehicles each day in addition to its own fleet of cars.

Faced with a manpower shortage and curtailed yard goods for civilian use, the AWVS in May 1944 launched the National Clothing Conservation Program. Its purpose was to teach American women to conserve good materials in used clothing, enable women whose incomes were restricted to maintain their standard of living; help fight inflation and provide a wartime and postwar sewing project. Courses in pattern use, repair and care of clothing, and general sewing hints were sent to AWVS units and workshops. A group of leading American designers undertook to redesign worn and outmoded garments and these garments together with AWVS adaptations made in AWVS workshops formed the basis for a popular *Remake Revue* which has been presented more than eighty times in leading cities throughout the country. Over 200,000 of the AWVS "remake booklets" have been distributed to schools, colleges, clubs, store audiences, conventions, forums, and Government agencies, and are now being sent to foreign countries on request.

In November 1944, when twelve AWVS state chairmen met in New York City for a three-day conference, a nine-point program was adopted for the postwar era, in the fields of veteran rehabilitation, youth programs, job retraining for women, public health, conservation and salvage, thrift, motor transport service, canteens, and workshops. Governor Thomas E. Dewey [44] of New York has expressed his ap-

MCLEAN, ALICE T.—*Continued*
proval of the services of the AWVS and the hope of their continuation in the postwar period.

The organization is supported by the per capita fees of its members, and contributions. The organization is composed of local units which raise their own funds for their local activities in line with the over-all program. Wearing of the AWVS blue-gray uniform is optional. The organization is considered one of the most democratic in the country. Women of all races, creeds, and colors are welcomed to membership. It is nonpartisan and is engaged in recruiting, training, and placing volunteers for service to the country, community, and the American people. At one time one unit consisted of 1,200 office workers employed on Wall Street and lower Broadway in New York, and there are units in the International Ladies' Garment Workers Union and in the Milliners' Union. There are also three Chinese units.

Mrs. McLean's work with the AWVS is a purely patriotic effort. Since 1940 she has made several trips abroad, where she gathered first-hand information regarding the W.V.S. of Great Britain. (Correspondence is also carried on between the AWVS and women's voluntary organizations in forty-five countries.) In 1944 Mrs. McLean was chosen as one of the country's sixteen outstanding women from the viewpoint of interracial unity by Mrs. Mary McLeod Bethune [42], president of the National Council of Negro Women. In the words of the *New Yorker*, "sectarianism and politics seem to have passed her by. As a result her AWVS is a seething, super-democratic mixture of Jeffersonians, New Dealers, Fusionists, Father Diviners, Episcopalians, Fundamentalists, trade unionists, and Black Republicans."

The "lady squire" who directs the AWVS is a "small, personable, unmilitant" woman with dark brown hair, brown eyes, and "the iron hands of a horsewoman." On her farm are rare Galloway beef cattle brought over from Scotland, two dozen prize Jersey milch cows, a large kennel of pedigreed dogs, and horses of various breeds. Mrs. McLean used to breed her own hunters and was formerly assistant Master of the Hunt of the Smithtown Hounds at St. James, Long Island, where she has a home. In Delaware County she knows all the farmers for miles around and is admired by them for her practical husbandry—she is "as good as a man with crops, an absolute natural with horses." An indefatigable worker in her AWVS office, Mrs. McLean often telephones her staff in the middle of the night. She dictates her correspondence while walking about her office, and she has had to do most of the managing of her farm by telephone from her New York headquarters. In May 1945 Mrs. McLean cabled from England that the British Women's Voluntary Services "had not stopped for a vacation after V-E." Similarly, she and the AWVS are seen as facing America's postwar problems "with vision and gallantry." In August 1945 she again sailed for Europe to study relief conditions and the possible role of the AWVS in rehabilitation work there. In November Mrs. McLean sponsored a week-end conference at her home at South Kortright. A resolution was drafted urging President Tru-

man to appoint women to the United Nations Assembly which will meet in London in January 1946.

References

N Y Post Mag p25 N 28 '44 por
New Yorker 18:21-6+ Jl 4 '42 por

MCMAHON (JAMES O')BRIEN (măkmăn') Oct. 6, 1903- United States Senator from Connecticut; lawyer
Address: b. The Capitol, Washington, D.C.; h. Norwalk, Conn.

One of the most important chairmanships in the United States Senate, that of the Special Committee on Atomic Energy, was given in October 1945 to one of the youngest and newest Senators, Brien McMahon, Democrat of Connecticut. Although the Senate seat is McMahon's first elective office, he had earlier experience in a Federal office as an Assistant Attorney General, when he brought to trial the Harlan County Coal Operators Association. He is deeply conscious that atomic energy is "the most important question of our national history," but he is also "an effective operator, who can take care of himself in the rough-and-tumble of politics."

James O'Brien McMahon was born in Norwalk, Connecticut, on October 6, 1903. "My family's been living in Norwalk more than a hundred years," he told an interviewer. The son of William H. and Eugenie J. (O'Brien) McMahon, he was named James O'Brien after his grandfather, but he has whittled his prenames down to Brien. After attending the Norwalk public grammar and high schools, McMahon went to Fordham University, the Jesuit institution in New York, where his classmates prophetically nicknamed him "The Senator." Graduated at twenty, in 1924, McMahon studied law at Yale, and after receiving his LL.B. in 1927 was admitted to the Connecticut bar. Then he entered practice with the firm of Keogh and Candee in his native city.

After six years of private practice, young McMahon became a judge of the Norwalk City Court in 1933. Later that year he was appointed special assistant to Attorney General Homer S. Cummings, under whom his first work was the prosecution of tax cases. In 1935 McMahon was made acting Assistant Attorney General in charge of the Criminal Division, and in 1936 he became the head of that division. Here he worked on the prosecution of gangsters, and sent John Dillinger's attorney to prison for harboring the fugitive. In all, McMahon argued twenty cases before the Supreme Court, and did not lose one. He served also as chairman of the Attorney General's Committee on Survey of Release Procedures, whose findings were published by the Department of Justice in 1939.

McMahon handled the first prosecution under the Wagner [41] Labor Relations Act, that of the Harlan County (Kentucky) Coal Operators Association. Their coal fields had been known as "Bloody Harlan" since 1931, when the operators began to use measures which later resulted in charges that their workers were intimidated and unionism suppressed. The Federal indictment followed revelations before the National Labor Relations Board and the

Senate Civil Liberties Committee. Brien Mc-
Mahon directed the legal staff which aimed in
1938 at conviction of forty-four individuals.
Since the Wagner Act specified no penalties
for employers violating their employees' rights
to organize and bargain collectively, the Government also invoked the Civil Rights Statute
of 1870, aimed at the Ku Klux Klan, which
made it a crime to conspire to deprive citizens
of their constitutional or statutory rights. At
the trial, McMahon faced two main problems,
the first being to prove that the operators actually conspired to suppress the miners' rights
—not merely that such suppression occurred.
The second and perhaps more serious disadvantage was the nature of the jury, farmers and
storekeepers of that section of Kentucky where
persons from other States and agents of the
Federal Government itself were regarded as
"foreigners."

"The Irish Yankee speech of Brien Mc-
Mahon, chief prosecutor, apparently gave the
jury some difficulty at first," it was reported.
However, the jury was also "discovering that
there is no monopoly on courtliness and gallantry in the South" and noting "the calmness
and comparative gentleness of the Government
attorneys in handling witnesses." The eleven-
week trial in 1938 was marked by bomb-throw-
ing and fatal shootings. As the jury was dead-
locked, the case ended in a mistrial; but its
main objective, to establish the miners' right
to bargain collectively, was achieved, as twenty-
six days later the operators signed an agreement with the United Mine Workers (CIO).
The NLRB thereupon dropped the charges, although McMahon denied that such a commit-
ment had been made.

According to the New York Herald Tribune,
the Connecticut lawyer worked on the Mc-
Kesson and Robbins embezzlement case before
his return to private practice in 1939. Remaining in Washington, McMahon was married in
February 1940 to Rosemary Turner. When he
returned to public life more than four years
later, it was to run for the Senate from his
native state. In his first candidacy, McMahon
opposed the incumbent Republican, John Danaher, who was regarded as an ardent isolationist. Running on a platform of support for
President Roosevelt's '42 foreign policy, and denouncing all appeals to racial or religious
groupings, the lawyer delivered two hundred
campaign speeches. When Danaher denied that
he was an isolationist and countered that the
word was vague and undefined, McMahon "gave
him a fresh definition every day for the last
thirty days."

"With two Irishmen fighting it out," the
campaign was described as lively and spectacular. Out of 822,464 votes cast for Senatorial
candidates in Connecticut in November 1944,
McMahon was given 430,716 to Senator Danaher's 391,748. While election saw the replacement by internationalists of several Republican
isolationists, Brien McMahon's victory over
Danaher vied with that of Emily Taft Douglas '45 over Day of Illinois for the title of "biggest surprise."

Beginning his six-year term in January 1945,
McMahon was named at the Democratic caucus
to four standing committees: Claims, Expenditures in the Executive Departments, Finance,
and Interstate Commerce. He was also chosen

BRIEN MCMAHON

to sit on James E. Murray's '45 three-year-old
Special Committee to Study and Survey Problems of Small Business Enterprises. From the
first, Senator McMahon's record votes "went
down the line" of Administration support:
They included votes for confirming Henry Wallace '40 as Secretary of Commerce without removing the RFC lending agencies from his
jurisdiction; for ratifying the water treaty with
Mexico, participating in the Bretton Woods
monetary agreements, and ratifying the United
Nations Organization charter; and he made his
maiden speech, a fiery one, against any limitation
of the President's powers of tariff adjustment
under the Reciprocal Trade Agreements Act.
He voted against the automatic termination of
Lend Lease at the end of the war, an issue
which split the Senate 39-39, and on which
Vice-President Truman '45 broke the tie by casting his first vote since taking office against
the amendment. In September 1945 McMahon,
majority leader Barkley '41, and Hartley M. Kilgore '43 of West Virginia "battled with their
back to the wall" against requiring that the
US Employment Service be returned to the
individual states within ninety days after the
war. He voted for the O'Mahoney '45-Wagner-
Murray-Thomas '42 full employment bill, but
with the unopposed Taft '40-Radcliffe amendment which reversed its original philosophy by
requiring that the Federal budget for the peacetime years after 1947 be accompanied by a tax
program designed to "prevent any increase in
the national debt over a reasonable period."

Senate tradition holds that freshmen of that
body should be seen and not heard, but Brien
McMahon made his presence felt. Early in
the session he became a member of Senator
Pepper's '41 subcommittee on foreign trade. He
advocated complete removal of a surplus
disposal agency from War Mobilizer James F.
Byrnes's '41 jurisdiction in March; and in April
when it had been transferred to the Department of Commerce, introduced a bill to establish the board as a separate agency. In May he
supported a measure to apply the income tax

MCMAHON, BRIEN—*Continued*

to aliens living in the United States, who, he charged, were getting rich from speculation in Wall Street. Later that month McMahon was chosen chairman of the Small Business sub-committee of inquiry on labor-management re-lations. In late June the Senator introduced a bill to divorce the board of parole from the Department of Justice, having it appointed in-stead by the President. In August he asked President Truman to "propose to the United Nations the formation of a group, similar in scope and ability to that formed to work on the atomic bomb . . . in an effort to discover causes and cures for the deadly diseases of mankind." In September 1945, after a series of hearings behind closed doors, McMahon and three other Democrats considered to be pro-labor (Hayden of Arizona, Tunnell of Dela-ware, and Military Affairs Chairman Elbert Thomas), jointly introduced a bill for the peaceful settlement of labor disputes on a vol-untary basis. The chief provisions were for: impartial boards of inquiry for issues involving the public interest; a Division of Mediation and Conciliation in the Department of Labor, which would be freed from civil service restrictions on salaries in order to attract top talent; trans-ferring to the new Division the War Labor Board's Disputes Section, and a three-man board of arbitration, to be called on voluntarily but whose decisions would be binding (although subject to judicial review).

McMahon introduced the first bill dealing with atomic energy into the Senate. To prevent unlimited private exploitation, it called for a Government board (composed of six Cabinet members, the chairman of the Federal Power Commission, and a chairman appointed by the President) "to develop, control, and supervise the use and application of atomic energy," and to "license its use on an equal basis to all comers." McMahon further "adopted the prop-osition that we should turn over to the Se-curity Council of the United Nations what we know about atomic energy in return for every member of the United Nations making avail-able to us and to the other members of the Security Council all information and know-how that they might have on armaments and weap-ons of war. I also provided," he says, "that the Security Council would have the right to in-spect all plants and laboratories or operations in every country of the world to see whether the agreement was being kept, and that after the agreement was made it should not become effective until approved by the Congress of the United States." Introduced the first day after the Congressional recess, the bill was referred to the Foreign Relations Committee

In October 1945 the junior Senator from Connecticut offered a resolution, which was ap-proved by the Interstate Commerce Committee, to authorize a special committee of nine mem-bers to study the development, use, and con-trol of atomic energy. The Senate raised the number of committeemen to eleven and passed the resolution by unanimous voice vote. By Senate tradition, the sponsor of such a resolu-tion becomes chairman of the resultant com-mittee, but in this case there was opposition to giving so important a post to a first-termer who had just celebrated his forty-second birth-day. After a struggle marked by parliamen-

tary maneuvering, President of the Senate Ken-neth McKellar gave McMahon the chairman-ship. He was, however, exceeded in years and seniority by the other members: the Democrats were Edwin C. Johnson, acting chairman of the Military Affairs Committee and co-sponsor of the May '41-Johnson bill for military control of atomic research; Tom Connally '41, Foreign Relations chairman and member of the Mead '44 war investigating committee; and three from Naval Affairs—Richard B. Russell, Harry F. Byrd '42, and Millard E. Tydings '45. The Re-publican members were Senators Vandenberg '40, Millikin, Austin '44, Hart '42, and Hickenlooper. Altogether, it was what one columnist called "a group of the Senate's most conservative moss-backs."

Unlike the sponsors of the War Department-and Administration-backed May-Johnson bill, McMahon planned a full investigation of the problem before reaching any solution. "Within a few hours after his appointment was an-nounced," it was reported, "McMahon had dis-patched wires to key groups and individuals throughout the country in an effort to secure the services of an eminent atomic scientist who could work full time with the Committee on the May-Johnson atomic control bill." In early November the committee agreed to engage Dr. Edward U. Condon, director of the Bu-reau of Standards, as scientific adviser, and James R. Newman, whom *PM* described as a "prominent young liberal lawyer," as legal as-sistant. They planned to embark on a detailed inspection of the plants and processes involved in manufacturing the atomic bomb. Chairman McMahon's own bill was transferred to his committee for consideration. At the same time, as it happened, the Connecticut Senator moved into the historic Capitol suite formerly occupied by the isolationist veteran Hiram Johnson '41; McMahon got it on waivers from his seniors, none of whom cared to leave the Senate Of-fice Building.

Before opening the hearings, the Senator and his whole committee went to the Bureau of Standards and took a course in nuclear phy-sics in order to prepare themselves for the testimony of scientists. "In Senator McMahon's committee," wrote Nina Heidelberger in a League of Women Voters publication, "we see the first bright hope . . . that our legislators will be as willing [as the physicists] to change their political thinking to meet the challenge of the atomic age." Commentators remarked on the objectivity and purely factual tension of the hearings, contrasting them with the much publicized and strongly partisan Pearl Harbor investigation going on around the corner. "If there is ever an atomic Pearl Harbor," said Brien McMahon, "there won't be a coroner's jury of statesmen left to talk about it."

In the words of Anthony Leviero, writing in the December 15, 1945, New York *Times*, "the nature of the hearing is almost unprecedented in the annals of Congress. As yet there has been no partisan taint. . . .The current hear-ings of nuclear energy resemble a series of Platonic dialogues in which pragmatic politicians and empirical scientists think out loud, prepar-ing for a new code of international ethics by which the nations of the world may live in the atomic era. . . .The mental struggle that goes on as the committee and witnesses cope with so unusual a thesis often gets excruiating for the onlooker and must be painful occasionally for the participants." Other writers agreed, the *Christian Science Monitor*'s Richard L. Strout saying, "There was no politics at this Senate hearing. We were too much immersed in the future." Joseph and Stewart Alsop mentioned "the singular dedication which has overtaken Senator McMahon," whom they considered "an intelligent, somewhat paunchy, somewhat liverish politician of the type rarely given to crusades."

Just before the Christmas recess McMahon introduced a bill, milder than the shelved May-Johnson proposal and free of the latter's military-mindedness and rigid secrecy provisions. The new bill would establish a full-time paid commission (no dollar-a-year men), appointed by the President and confirmed by the Senate, to conduct research and development in nuclear processes, production of atomic energy, and the use of fissionable materials for health and industrial uses. This commission was to have exclusive control of all atomic-powered weapons and of the materials and natural resources necessary to produce them; and private ownership or exportation of fissionable materials was to be forbidden. No security regulations other than those of the existing Espionage Act were included in the bill, nor did it exempt military and naval officers from the operations of the statutes which would bar them from serving on the proposed board. The commission would be required to report to Congress on the economic, political, and social implications of any new developments and of applications for industrial licenses; and licenses for private industrial development could be granted only with Congressional approval. All bills thus far introduced provided for complete Federal control over "A-power" from mine to use, but the McMahon bill was preferred by the Federation of Atomic Scientists, who also seemed to prefer it as a model for future international controls. McMahon let it be known that he was working closely with Secretary of State Byrnes on the domestic and international phases of the question, and he proposed that foreign governments be invited to send observers to the planned naval tests of the atomic bomb at Bikini atoll.

The first Fordham alumnus to enter the Senate, Brien McMahon was elected first vice-president of its alumni association in March 1945, and was honored with a Doctorate of Laws in June. Blue-eyed, black-haired, and ruddy-complexioned, the Senator is described as "definitely on the handsome side," and also as "definitely chunky." He is of medium height and weighs about 200 pounds. His fraternity is Phi Alpha Delta, and he is a member of the American Bar Association. McMahon is said to be a better-than-average golfer; he belongs to country clubs in Connecticut and Maryland, and to the Burning Tree Club in Washington. He and Mrs. McMahon have one daughter, Patricia Rosemary. The junior Senator from Connecticut is said to read widely and is fond of broiling a steak over an outdoor charcoal fire.

References

N Y Herald Tribune II p3 N 12 '44 por
N Y Post Mag p5 D 9 '44 por

America's Young Men, 1938-39
Who's Who in America, 1944-45
Who's Who in Law, 1937
Who's Who in the Nation's Capital, 1938-39

MACPHAIL, LARRY Feb. 3, 1890- Baseball club president; businessman
Address: b. New York Yankees Baseball Club, 55 W. 42d St., New York City; h. Belair, Md.

In January 1945 the sports world was surprised by the announcement that "Loud Larry" MacPhail, who was being rumored for appointment as Federal sports coordinator, was quietly concluding negotiations to purchase the famous old New York Yankees Baseball Club. Larry MacPhail, known in the United States Army as Colonel Leland Stanford MacPhail, was born in Cass City, Michigan, on February 3, 1890, an immigrant Scottish storekeeper whose forebears had been neighbors of Robert Burns. During Larry's youth his father branched out into banking in Ludington, Michigan, and "as he traveled from one town to another, establishing banks, the family went along." Eventually there were twenty-one of these small-town banks, which the MacPhails liquidated without loss during the depression of the thirties.

Larry went to various Michigan schools, where he was an outstanding student and athlete; at fourteen he played the organ in the Scottville Episcopal Church. Entered in a military school at Staunton, Virginia, he continued to win scholastic and athletic honors. At sixteen he passed entrance examinations for the Naval Academy, but his parents advised against his going to Annapolis so young. He registered instead at Beloit College, Wisconsin, where he continued to be a good student and athlete, and became a member of Beta Theta Pi. Two years of success as "one of the loudest debaters in the history of Beloit College" determined him on law, rather than the Navy, and from Beloit he went to the University of Michigan Law School. With the idea of going into the consular service, Larry MacPhail transferred to George Washington University a year later. In 1910, when he was twenty, the tall, dynamic redhead completed the work for his LL.B. and that same year was offered a consular appointment to a French seaport, which he declined. Having passed the bar examinations of Michigan, Illinois, and the District of Columbia, MacPhail joined a Chicago law firm, and was married to Inez Thompson of Oak Park, Illinois, daughter of an American Car and Foundry Company vice-president. (There are three children, a daughter and two sons, both of whom were in the wartime Navy. Leland Stanford, Jr., is also a baseball businessman. Their father, after five years' separation from their mother, was divorced, and was married to Jean Bennett Wanamaker in May 1945.)

After six months, during which the Chicago firm failed to make him a partner, the impatient young lawyer left to become a junior partner in another, which thus became Fowler, McDonald, Rosenberg, and MacPhail. Given the assignment of reorganizing a tool company, MacPhail carried it out to such effect that, when the reorganization was completed,

LARRY MACPHAIL

MacPhail joined the tool company. A year later the twenty-four-year-old "boy wonder" was called to Nashville, Tennessee, to head a large department store. There he became friendly with Senator Luke Lea. When the country entered the World War in April 1917 the two young executives organized a volunteer regiment of hardbitten Tennessee backwoodsmen (Tennessee is known as the Volunteer State), with Colonel Lea commanding and MacPhail a mere private.

Private MacPhail rose rapidly, however, and when the regiment was taken into the Army of the United States as the 114th Field Artillery he was commissioned a captain. (The volunteers agreed, by the way, not to accept any decorations from foreign governments.) They served with the Thirtieth Division, better known as the Old Hickory outfit, and fought in the Saint-Mihiel and Argonne offensives, where MacPhail was wounded and gassed. (A result was the weakening of his eyes.) After the Armistice he and his colonel, accompanied by six of their men, celebrated the New Year with a lighthearted attempt to kidnap Kaiser Wilhelm from a castle in Amerongen, Holland, which involved cutting all telephone and fence wires. This caused a great furor and a formal inquiry, but Lea got off with an official reprimand, and MacPhail with one of the Kaiser's ashtrays, which he still has for a souvenir.

After MacPhail's discharge from the Army he settled in Columbus, Ohio, where he remained until 1933. "Among other things," writes Robert Lewis Taylor, "he took charge of the liquidation of several glass factories; refereed Big Ten [Midwestern state college and university] football games; traded in Columbus real estate; and obtained a controlling interest in a large automobile agency. As a result of these and earlier business activities, he was able in 1930 to put up about a hundred thousand dollars to buy the American Association baseball team in Columbus." Taylor continues: "It was when MacPhail became a base-ball magnate that he really began to find himself. . . .Once free of the taint of law and commerce, his personality unfolded like a morning glory. His clothing assumed such vivid variety that one of his Columbus acquaintances described it as a municipal eyesore. . . .He had never had his fill of airplane travel. As a result, he transported his baseball players solely by plane. A half hour before the game the team would drop down from the sky, with some of the players too airsick to lift a bat."

Eventually, MacPhail sold his team to the St. Louis Cardinals (National League), but their shrewd vice-president, Branch Rickey, persuaded him to stay on for three years as the Columbus club's president. (It was during this period that the Cardinal "front office" sent Billy Southworth [44] to MacPhail as manager for part of one unhappy season.) In 1933, with the "bedraggled" team established as a financial success, Larry MacPhail moved to the major leagues by becoming vice-president and business manager of the Cincinnati Reds (National League). The president, one of the principal financial backers, was Powel Crosley, Jr., the radio and refrigerator manufacturer. Crosley combined the first of these interests with baseball by summoning Red Barber [43] from Florida, where Barber was WRUF's leading announcer, to describe the Reds' games over the Crosley stations WSAI and WLW. Leaving no stone unturned in his promotion plans, Larry MacPhail repainted the ball park a gay orange, staffed it with pretty usherettes, made it the scene of all sorts of publicity stunts, and introduced a few night games into the schedule, an innovation much protested against by baseball men, but one which brought in many spectators who would not have attended an afternoon game. With such methods MacPhail established "a solid reputation for unpredictability." An explosive man, he was generous in money matters, causing his associates to conclude: "You can work for MacPhail forever—if you can stand him."

But MacPhail, with his sure instinct for flamboyant publicity, was not merely a sensationalist. A notably shrewd trader, behind the horseplay he was building the last-place Reds into a solid baseball organization. He left baseball in 1937, feeling that the strain was making him nervous, and the club went back that year from fifth place to eighth and last; but the farm system he founded for recruiting and training baseball talent is credited by observers with Cincinnati's two successive league pennants, the second followed by a World Series "killing," in 1939 and 1940. (The "farm club" method, which was initiated by Branch Rickey at St. Louis in 1919 and is now standard in baseball, is that by which the major league teams "get their players from the original source of supply—the Nation's sand lots—and develop them under capable supervision on the parent team's plentiful farms" or hierarchy of minor league clubs.)

Back in Michigan, MacPhail joined his father and brother in the investment business. A year later the Brooklyn Trust Company asked him to take over and "straighten out" the Brooklyn Dodgers. The fourth time they asked, he accepted. Perhaps the very difficulty of the task was a challenge; perhaps MacPhail felt himself drawn to a team whose reputation for colorful eccentricity went back to the days when they were the "Trolley Dodgers." Anyway, he found that he got "about seventeen summonses a week" at first, for the Dodgers management owed fully $1,200,000. The owners were neatly split into two mutually hostile groups, each of whose 50 per cent of the stock votes canceled out the other's, and the team itself was a serious rival of the Phillies for last place in the National League. Accepting the job on his own terms, MacPhail became vice-president and general manager, with full authority, plus the guaranty of working capital from the bank for improvements.

In Brooklyn Larry MacPhail really "went to town." After spending two hundred thousand dollars on refurbishing the ball park, including the provision of a luxurious free bar for newspapermen and hangers-on and of a drill-master for the gorgeously caparisoned ushers, he made his first step toward providing a team for it: For fifty thousand dollars he bought the right to sign up Dolph Camilli, star first baseman from the Phillies. MacPhail hired fifteen talent scouts and kept them busy; and he built up a farm system by buying six minor league clubs outright and establishing "working agreements" with six more (giving the Dodgers first choice of their promising players in return for financial support). He spent more than eight hundred and eighty thousand dollars to obtain the contracts of stars like Kirby Higbe, Joe Medwick, Mickey Owen, Pee Wee Reese, and Pete Reiser (who cost only one hundred dollars to get from one of the farms); also Tex Carleton, Whit Wyatt, Dixie Walker, Billy Herman, and others, including almost the entire roster of St. Louis Cardinal stars. He introduced night baseball, over the protests of the other New York teams, and played it with circusy "hoopla," from fireworks to footraces. And he brought in the crowds.

To build up the Brooklyn team's box office MacPhail succeeded in arousing borough patriotism in the denizens of that much-abused section, and in identifying the team with the town, though his administrative organization members had been brought almost intact from Cincinnati, and his players from St. Louis. Red Barber with his Southern dialect became known as the "Voice of Brooklyn." L. S. MacPhail himself was then living in Manhattan (his country home is a large Maryland stock farm, where he raises black Angus cattle). He and "Lippy Leo" Durocher [40], made manager in 1938, rivaled each other in picturesque language, and together they excelled in harassing umpires. This gave the Brooklyn fans a comforting certainty that they would not be "robbed"; it attracted patrons who came to see the fighting, and others who so disliked the Dodgers that they would gladly pay their money for a chance to see them beaten; it got reams of publicity, which in itself pays off at the box office.

At the end of the 1938 season the stockholders voted MacPhail a forty-thousand-dollar salary and the presidency; in 1939 and 1940 they voted him fifty-five thousand. In the 1939 season the Dodgers bounded from seventh place to third; in 1940 they were second to MacPhail's old team, the Cincinnati Reds; and in 1941 the roaring Brooklynites were up on top, winning their first pennant since 1920. Although they lost the post-season World Series championship to the "unbeatable" American League Yankees—4 to 1—the one game they did win was a moral victory: they broke up the other team's winning streak of ten Series games in succession. In 1942, however, the Dodgers were back in second place, to the disappointment of fans and stockholders. That year a full 45 per cent of all paid admissions to National League games was for Dodger games, and one million was the total attendance in relatively small Ebbets Field; but there were rumors that the Dodger owners, spoiled by a quick rise after a long depression, were dissatisfied with MacPhail. That fall the "Flatbush Firecracker," who was honorary Brooklyn chairman of the Committee to Defend America by Aiding the Allies, entered the Army with a temporary commission as lieutenant colonel. Reportedly, he was "hopeful that his fighting experience (World War I . . . and fisticuffs) would get him combat duty."

As special assistant to the Under-Secretary of War, Robert P. Patterson [41], Colonel MacPhail went to work at Lieutenant General Brehon Somervell's [42] Service of Supply (later Army Service Forces) headquarters in Washington. Although he did a serious job handling "public relations work on industrial conferences," and made inspection tours with his superiors on the French and Italian fronts, the old MacPhail cropped up now and then. There is, for instance, the story that reporters found him laying down the law to a two-star general—on a social occasion.

On January 26, 1945, when MacPhail was a full colonel, the sports world learned that he and two others had formed a syndicate and negotiated the purchase of the New York Yankees, baseball's most valuable and dignified organization. (The others were Captain Dan Topping of the Marine Corps, and Del Webb of Arizona.) Reportedly, "MacPhail just had to get a job somewhere, as he could not maintain his big Maryland stock farm on Army pay." This was nice work if he could get it—and he did. Ninety-eight per cent ownership of the Yankee "empire," never appraised at less than four million dollars, went for less than three million dollars ($2,800,000), as the syndicate had caught the owners short of cash to pay the high income taxes. This included not only the ten-time-champion Yankees themselves, but their three-million-dollar stadium, "the House that Ruth [44] Built"; the Newark Bears and Kansas City Blues, with their parks; and other minor league farm teams in Binghamton, Norfolk, and Wellsville—all of which showed a profit. The most interesting aspect of the situation was the question of what would happen when the flamboyant MacPhail (placed on reserve in February by the Army) began his contractual ten years as president and general manager of a great team whose conservative traditions he had often criticized for lacking in color.

Soon after taking over the Yankees, MacPhail brought pressure to bear on the big league powers to elect a successor to Kenesaw Mountain Landis [44] as baseball commissioner, a post left vacant by the death of Judge Landis

MACPHAIL, LARRY—*Continued*

in November 1944. James A. Farley [44] and Ford C. Frick [45], president of the National League, had been mentioned for the post, but with the backing of MacPhail, Senator Albert B. ("Happy") Chandler [43] of Kentucky was elected in April 1945 for a seven-year term, the second commissioner since the office was established in 1920. In November MacPhail signed up such prewar stars as Joe DiMaggio, Spurgeon Chandler, and many others for the 1946 season. A recent innovation at the Yankee Stadium has been the introduction of floodlights for night games, which had been a financial success at Ebbets Field.

A question on which MacPhail expressed himself was the use of Negro players in the major leagues. He was opposed to the color line in baseball: "I'd jump at the chance to sit down with anyone to see what could be worked out." He did meet with civic leaders, Negro and white, to discuss the matter, then went off to war and nothing came of it. A year later Mayor La Guardia, in August 1945, appointed a committee of ten prominent men of both races from various walks of life (among them MacPhail and Rickey of the Dodgers) to make a thorough survey and to submit recommendations to both major baseball leagues.

The Colonel himself, in MacPhail family tradition a Republican, is a colorful man literally, as well as figuratively. "He stands slightly over six feet in his socks, weighs a hundred and ninety-five pounds, and has the neck of a bouncer. His hair is bright red, and his face, which is about the same shade, is liberally freckled." His eyes are blue, and his expression, in rare moments of repose, is described as grim. Before he went into uniform, MacPhail's clothes were described as "a wild profusion of plaids." The new Yankee president is given to wearing dark glasses, to protect himself from autograph seekers and the sun; he plays the piano expertly, his favorite composer being Tchaikovsky, but he holds that the chirping of the wrens in his hundred and fifty birdhouses on the shores of Lake Michigan is the finest music on earth.

References

Liberty 19:25-6 Je 13 '42 pors
N Y World-Telegram p22 Ja 26 '45 por
New Yorker 17:20-3+Jl 12 '41 por;
　17:20-3+ Jl 19 '41 por
Time 40:40+ O 5 '42 por

MACPHAIL, LELAND STANFORD *See* MacPhail, L.

MCPHARLIN, PAUL Dec. 22, 1903- Designer; puppetry authority

Address: b. c/o J. Gordon Carr, 80 W. 40th St., New York City; h. 155 Wimbleton Dr., Birmingham, Mich.

"My urge toward the use of the pen whether for writing or drawing has taken me into the field of the book for authoring, editing, designing, illustrating, publishing, and complete production," says Paul McPharlin, who is also industrial designer and authority on puppetry, the latter from the point of both research and production. His contributions to the literature of these fields have appeared in art, theatrical, and publishing periodicals.

Paul McPharlin's native city is Detroit, Michigan, where he was born to William H. J. and Frances Christine (Lohmeyer) McPharlin on December 22, 1903. Moving East with his parents as a child, Paul was educated in New York City, first at Townsend Harris High School, and then at Columbia College, from which he was graduated in 1924. He was a student of John Erskine's at Columbia and has also studied under Gordon Craig, the noted English actor and stage designer. Later McPharlin returned to Michigan to work for his M.A. at Wayne University in Detroit (1938), and in 1940 he was awarded a Ph.D. by the University of Michigan. His thesis for this degree was a history of puppets in America since 1524.

Even before he left Columbia McPharlin began working in one of the two professions in which he was later to become prominent— from 1922 to 1928 he was employed in Cleveland and Chicago as a designer in the book and advertising fields. Since 1928 he has also been occupied intermittently with industrial design, part of his work being the making of models for machine production. In 1928, also, he turned to the other of the two major interests to which he has devoted most of his career. That year he became director of the Marionette Fellowship of Evanston, Illinois. Under his leadership this professional company for ten years produced a variety of plays with the stringed actors, plays that were often adapted from such works as Shakespeare's *Taming of the Shrew* and Henry Fielding's *The Tragedy of Tragedies; or, the Life and Death of Tom Thumb the Great.* For seven years, beginning in 1931, he also taught classes at Wayne University in puppetry and bookmaking.

The designer's activity in puppetry has yielded many books, pamphlets, and articles on the subject, besides his productions as manager of a puppet company. "I've collected all possible information on puppets," says McPharlin, who has the largest private library on the subject in the country. Among his friends he counts puppeteers throughout the world. In 1929 *A Repertory of Marionette Plays*, selected and translated by McPharlin, was published. The book, which includes works by Goethe, Bouchor, and Maeterlinck, was well received by the critics as "a useful and interesting book." The April 1929 issue of *Drama* contained McPharlin's article on Anton Aicher's Marionette Theatre in Salzburg, in which he described the work of the Austrian sculptor and puppeteer. Since 1930 he has edited *Puppetry, an International Yearbook* and has also published *Puppetry Imprints*, a series of handbooks. The year 1931 saw the publication of *Puppet Heads and Their Making*, followed by *Animal Marionettes* (1936), which prompted this tribute from one critic: "Mr. McPharlin's puppetry books are not only contributions by an expert to this large and rapidly growing literature, but beautiful in themselves." The artist's article in *New Outlook* in March 1935, entitled "He Still Hangs Around," presented an historical survey of puppetry, which detailed its diverse values. Successfully used for educational and advertising purposes, puppets also have a bright future in television, the author declared. According to McPharlin, "Puppets won't die because of their variety. Let people grow tired of the sort worked by strings, there are always hand-puppets, rod-puppets, shadow figures, and a score of types worked by various means from above, below, or on the stage plane, to be brought forward. Puppets may be tiny enough to be pulled by a baby, or so huge that they must be hoisted by cranes."

In 1936 McPharlin's *Puppets in America* was published, and the next year he organized Puppeteers of America and became its first president. The puppetry specialist toured England and the Continent in 1938, making a detailed study of European puppetry. *Theatre Arts* for July 1941 carried his article, "A Quarter-Century of American Puppetry," which was also a brief historical background of puppetry elsewhere in the world. "European puppeteers first started coming to America in 1524," he wrote, as he proceeded to assess the revival of American puppetry in the past twenty-five years. Emphasizing the wide scope of the medium and its varied utilization by puppet pioneers, he said, "Requiring little space, little money, and not much audience, it allowed them to create exactly as they pleased. They could go cubist or surrealist. They could revive the classics or stage their own scripts: satires, tragedies, combinations of the three-dimensional and the four-dimensional, of the panoramic and the microscopic." On the question of puppetry's worth, the author declared, "Educators have looked upon it as a developer of skills in handicraft, voice-production, social cooperation, and so on. Occupational therapists have liked it as a curative instrument. Psychiatrists have used it for analyzing children. Advertisers have capitalized upon its popular appeal to sugar-coat sales messages." But McPharlin pointed out the danger that "puppetry as entertainment and a minimal form of theater may be neglected," and expressed hope for its future in the work of experimenters.

In the realm of graphic arts, the other sphere in which he is particularly active, McPharlin is well regarded as creative artist and critic. Since 1944 he has been working in New York with the firm of J. Gordon Carr, industrial designer, specializing in typography and illustration. His book *Roman Numerals, Typographic Leaves, and Pointing Hands* was published in 1941 by the Typophiles, an organization which published books solely for the enjoyment of its own members. He has illustrated editions of Coleridge's *Ancient Mariner*, Gilbert and Sullivan's *Mikado*, and Rostand's *Cyrano de Bergerac*. Books designed by him include Poe's *The Raven, and Other Poems* and Franklin's *Satires and Bagatelles*. In October 1942 McPharlin began a series of articles for *Publishers' Weekly* devoted to epic works in the book publishing field, which ran through 1944. Inaugurated while the author was in the Army (he served in the Army Air Forces in 1942-1943), the series dealt with works like Benjamin Franklin's *Cato Major*, the *Nuremberg Chronicle*, and the Nonesuch Press edition of Dante's *Divine Comedy*. McPharlin's

Sauer Studios

PAUL MCPHARLIN

feeling for books was noted in his articles: Discussing Tonson's *Caesar*, he wrote, "Each line has tone color, tempo and expression, like a musical phrase or section in a melodic development, played on a particular instrument"; and then, writing of the Cranach *Hamlet*, McPharlin commented: "One likes beautiful books as one likes beautiful women . . . a good plain wife to cook and sew, and a pocket-edition of Shakespeare; a Hollywood beauty to adore from afar, and a Cranach *Hamlet*."

A detailed study by McPharlin called "Dimensions of Printed Line" appeared in the November 1944 issue of *Magazine of Art*. After a brief historical examination of printing the author surveyed the modern scene in the graphic arts field, treating especially the work of Studio Seventeen under Stanley William Hayter[45]. Dealing with such media as engraving and illustration, he outlined the new techniques in use. Of the vast sphere of art in the modern world, he stated, "Artists of today see much more than what meets the naked eye. They see with the telescope, the microscope, the spectroscope—with all the enlarged vision of science. They see with the interpretive perception of the psychoanalyst."

Other of McPharlin's activities have also been in the fields of books and art. For three years, 1935-38, he was publisher in Detroit of the Fine Book Circle. In 1941-42 he was State supervisor of the Michigan Art and Craft Project under the WPA. (One deviation from this pattern was a period of war work in Detroit following his discharge from the Army.) He is a member of the American Institute of Graphic Arts and the American Craftsmen and Designers, and is a contributor to such magazines as the *Mask, Players, American Artist, Spur*, the *Colophon*, and *American Printer*. His book *Paper Sculpture and Its Uses* was published in 1945.

Paul McPharlin once wrote that "big fellows have a compensatory fascination for the miniature," which may explain his own pen-

MCPHARLIN, PAUL—*Continued*

chant for puppets. He is more than six feet tall, weighs two hundred pounds, and has gray eyes and red hair. He collects books and as a hobby has done bindings for his own library. "My desire to make things well and beautifully," McPharlin explains, "has resulted in the development of handicraft skills in many crafts from ceramics to wood engraving." He has designed pewterware, textiles, and furniture, and, on a larger scale, a suburban house and a chain of candy stores in Chicago. The artist enjoys gardening and likes to travel. In 1945 he was editing the writings of the late William A. Kittredge, the typographic expert, and was also writing a full history of puppets in America.

Reference

Who's Who in American Art, 1940-41

MAGNUSON, WARREN G(RANT)
măg'nŭs-ŭn) Apr. 12, 1905- United States Senator from Washington; lawyer
Address: b. c/o Senate Office Bldg., Washington, D.C.; h. Olympic Hotel, Seattle, Wash.

The freshman Senator in Congress, from the state of Washington, is Warren G. Magnuson, who is a leading member of the Democratic bloc of progressives in the upper house. After seven years of service in the House of Representatives, during which he established "an excellent liberal record," Magnuson won a Senatorial seat in November 1944. Once called "a 1000 per cent New Dealer," he has supported the Administration both on the international and domestic fronts. The Western Senator is a veteran of the Second World War, having served as a lieutenant commander with the Pacific Fleet.

Warren Grant Magnuson is a native of the Midwest; he was born in Moorhead, Minnesota, on April 12, 1905. Of Scandinavian parentage, he was orphaned at an early age and adopted by a Swedish family; his parents were William G. and Emma (Anderson) Magnuson. While attending the high school in his native town, he ran a YMCA camp and worked in the fields during the summer. For a brief time he attended the University of North Dakota (1923-24), then for a period traveled through Canada. His Canadian adventures included working with threshing crews and "riding the rods" to Seattle. In that city he worked his way through the University of Washington, receiving his B.A. in 1925, and his LL.B. from the university's law school in 1929. He won admission to the Washington bar that year and began his law practice in Seattle. Magnuson was associated with the firm of Stern and Schermer from 1931 to 1932. In 1932 he served as special prosecutor for King County.

The attorney had first become active in Democratic politics during the Al Smith [44] Presidential campaign of 1928. Five years later he was elected to the State legislature, where he remained for a year, serving at the same time as a member of the State judicial council. According to a publicity pamphlet issued in Seattle, in the course of this legislative session Magnuson "wrote and put through the first unemployment compensation bill in the Nation." He was a delegate to the State Constitutional Convention in 1933 and that year became Assistant United States District Attorney. His next position brought him back to serve King County as prosecuting attorney, having been elected by the greatest majority ever given a candidate for that office. The Democrat was elected to Congress in 1936 and represented the First Washington District, Seattle, in the Seventy-fifth to Seventy-eighth Congresses, being re-elected three times by large majorities.

During his career in the House, Magnuson was generally consistent in his adherence to the policies of the Roosevelt [42] Administration, upholding, for example, most of the win-the-war measures. He voted against repeal of the measures limiting salaries to twenty-five thousand dollars, after taxes; against the anti-strike bill and the anti-subsidy bill; and twice he voted to sustain the Presidential veto, on the commodity credit and tax bills. (However, in 1938, on the issue of conscription, he called for a referendum and subsequently voted against the conscription bill.) From the time he entered Congress he championed the building of a highway joining the western United States and Alaska, working to get Congressional funds for such a project. His proposed measure got as far as the House Foreign Affairs Committee, which in 1938 approved his bill for a road through British Columbia and the Yukon. Magnuson studied the plan in detail, taking a plane trip over the territory in 1939, and thereafter, as chairman of the Alaskan International Highway Commission, he helped survey the terrain of the proposed route, a route he considered superior to that later chosen for the Alcan Highway. In 1940 he conferred with Canadian representatives on the plan, and the following year he toured Alaska. Returning from this trip, he emphasized the danger of Nazi penetration of Alaska through Siberia.

A lieutenant commander in the United States Naval Reserve, Magnuson went on active duty shortly after Pearl Harbor. After eight months with the fleet in the Aleutians and the South Pacific, he returned to the House, where he was subsequently active on the Naval Affairs Committee. When Congress investigated defense measures in the Aleutians in the summer of 1942, he represented the House in a tour of that area. The following year he was chairman of a subcommittee which worked with United States administrative agencies for the establishment of American island bases in the Pacific after the war

Early in 1943 he became chairman of a subcommittee to investigate the shipbuilding industry. In February the Washingtonian was chairman of the House committee that investigated the antilabor story that merchant seamen had refused to unload a ship at Guadalcanal on a Sunday. The committee's report condemned press usage of the story as "not based on fact." The next month the Representative from the Evergreen State took an active part in the drive for passage of the anti-poll tax bill. His name headed the list of the discharge petition to force a House vote on the measure, and it was Magnuson who controlled the bill on the House floor for the Democrats. About this time the Congressman, with a colleague, Representative John Coffee, requested a War Department investigation of alleged Army discrimination against veterans of the Lincoln

Brigade, who had fought on the side of the Loyalists in the Spanish civil war. Despite the evidence presented by the Congressmen, these charges were later denied by Under-Secretary of War Robert P. Patterson '41. Late that year the Magnuson bill repealing the Chinese Exclusion Act was passed. Previously, speaking in favor of the measure, Magnuson had said: "Exclusion has proved one of the most potent weapons the Japanese propaganda machine has had. Putting the Chinese on an equal quota basis will give Chungking a great weapon with which to fight it."

In April 1944, when the Special House Committee on Post-War Military Policy was formed, Magnuson was one of twenty-three Congressmen appointed by Speaker Rayburn '40 to serve with this group. The next month the report of Magnuson's Alaskan International Highway Commission branded the Alcan Highway "a stupendous blunder," while the chairman further charged that the Army and the La Guardia '40 Committee on Joint Defense had neglected to investigate an alternate route before building and had chosen the Alcan route "solely because it will help the Canadian Pacific Railroad."

In the 1944 elections Magnuson ran against Lieutenant Colonel Harry M. Cain for the Senatorial seat vacated by Homer T. Bone. In the course of the campaign for the re-election of Roosevelt, the Western Democrat, in a radio interview in September, delivered a "blistering" attack on Governor Thomas E. Dewey's '44 foreign policy statements and reviewed the record of Republicans in Congress. During this period he also signified his endorsement of a constitutional amendment providing for the ratification of treaties by a majority of the Senate. Magnuson won a decisive victory at the polls in November, and the following month Governor Langlie of Washington appointed him to the unexpired term of Senator Bone in order to place Magnuson ahead of other new Senators in seniority for committee appointments.

Shortly after taking his seat in the upper house, Magnuson cast his vote in favor of Henry Wallace '40 for Secretary of Commerce and Aubrey Williams '40 for Rural Electrification Administration head. In April, during a probe of the light metals industry sparked by the Alcoa case, he called for an investigation of all contracts negotiated by the RFC under the administration of Jesse Jones '40. Later Magnuson was on the bipartisan steering committee which worked, unsuccessfully, for passage of the anti-poll tax bill. In July he won applause from the Senate galleries when he interrupted a speech by Senator Burton K. Wheeler '40, who had called for a definition of surrender terms to Japan. Magnuson declared that the quickest way to defeat Japan was to "say that unconditional surrender means just that."

In late July the Democrat joined his Republican colleague Senator Joseph Ball '43 in sharp criticism of State Department policy in Spain and Argentina. Participating in a broadcast of NBC's University of the Air series, the Senators labeled the governments of these countries "clearly Fascist." "This bush league Axis ought to be cleaned up—now," Magnuson said, declaring that the State Department had fol-

WARREN G. MAGNUSON

lowed a policy of appeasement in Spain since the Spanish civil war, a policy that was "a mistake from the beginning." Voicing blunt anti-Franco '42 sentiments, both legislators urged American aid to the democratic forces of Spain and Argentina, and the breaking of diplomatic relations with those countries. On July 19 Magnuson introduced a bill providing for the establishment of a National Research Foundation and effecting the program previously suggested by the Office of Scientific Research and Development. Senator Kilgore '43, who had presented a similar measure, and Magnuson met with President Truman '45 in August to discuss these measures for Federal support of scientific research. Joint hearings on the combined bills began in October. Such leading scientists as Irving Langmuir '40 and Vannevar Bush '40 the National Association of Manufacturers, and the American Medical Association argued in favor of the operational plan proposed in Magnuson's bill, which would vest control of the new agency in a board of nine unsalaried members empowered to elect an administrator to carry out research projects. President Truman was among those who endorsed the Kilgore bill, which called for control by a single administrator, in consultation with an advisory board of scientists and government officials; another section of the bill provided that any invention, discovery, or patent rights produced in the course of Federally financed research or development become the property of the United States and would be generally available to all without royalty payments. The Magnuson bill lacks a patent policy.

Washington's new Senator has appeared on several radio programs, discussing domestic and international issues. Before the war ended he participated in a radio forum on Federal unemployment compensation during reconversion, stating, "The war worker is on the job because the Federal Government is waging war and he is under orders, just as the soldier is. We have already assumed the duty of protecting industry and property and the man in

MAGNUSON, WARREN G.—*Continued*

the service—surely the duty of the Federal Government extends to the war workers." In August 1945, on *America's Town Meeting*, he urged United States retention of Pacific island bases. When the atomic bomb was first used, Magnuson expressed what is believed to be the opinion of many statesmen. Commenting on the revolutionary character of the new weapon, he declared: "Either we must persuade all other powers . . . to institute true and universal democratic rights, or we must at once begin the race to win the Third World War—the war that would destroy every building above the surface of the earth and put us all into caves. Free people don't want wars. If they know what is going on and have the power, they will make their governments behave."

In 1945 Magnuson was a member of the Senate Committees on Commerce, Interoceanic Canals, Naval Affairs, and Territories and Insular Affairs. He began conducting a complete study of the postwar defense structure during the summer.

Measuring five feet eight inches in height and weighing one hundred and seventy pounds, the bachelor legislator has blue eyes, blond hair, and a "handsome Scandinavian face." His outdoor recreations are fishing and hunting, and he likes to collect books. He is a member of Theta Chi and a Fellow of the American Institute of Political Science. An Elk, Eagle, and a Moose, he also belongs to the Washington Athletic Club of Seattle; and he is a member of the Washington State and American Bar Associations. Popular with his constituents, Senator Magnuson is reported to have once donned kilts and marched down to Victory Square to greet a group of visiting bagpipers from a Vancouver shipyard.

References

N Y Sun p5 O 10 '42; p22 Ja 26 '44
America's Young Men, 1938-39
Congressional Directory, 1945
Who's Who in America, 1944-45
Who's Who in Law, 1937

MAHER, AHMED, PASHA (mä'hĕr ä'măd) 1888—Feb. 24, 1945 Egyptian Premier; assassinated after he had read a royal decree in Chamber of Deputies declaring war against the Axis; was head of the Saadist Party; had urged the Egyptian entry into the war as early as 1940 when Italian troops were massing at Libya; appointed Premier and Minister of the Interior by King Farouk '42 in October 1944.

Obituary

N Y Times p1+ F 25 '45 por

MALONEY, FRANCIS T. Mar. 31, 1894—Jan. 16, 1945 Democratic Senator to United States Congress from Connecticut, in his second term of office at time of death; rose from newspaperman to mayor, to United States Congressman (1933-35), to Senator in 1935; a gifted speaker and author of many bills which became laws.

Obituary

N Y Times p21 Ja 17 '45 por

MARCH, CHARLES HOYT Oct. 20, 1870—Aug. 28, 1945 Member of the United States Federal Trade Commission from 1929 until his death; organized the Fourth Regiment of Militia from Minnesota in the First World War; served as a delegate to the Republican National Conventions of 1920, 1924, and 1928.

Obituary

N Y Times p23 Ag 29 '45 por

MARRIOTT, SIR JOHN (ARTHUR RANSOME) 1859—June 7, 1945 English historian, and member of Parliament (1917-29); wrote many books on modern history and political science, including *George Canning and His Times* (1903) and *The Evolution of the British Empire and Commonwealth* (1939).

Obituary

N Y Times p19 Je 8 '45

MARTIN, EDWARD Sept. 18, 1879- Governor of Pennsylvania

Address: b. State Capitol, Harrisburg; h. 147 LeMoyne Ave., Washington, Pa.

Edward Martin, Governor of Pennsylvania since 1942, has had a long career, as soldier, lawyer, banker, and politician. As a soldier he has served in five wars; his business associations have been wide and varied; and his political life began in 1925. During the 1944 Presidential campaign he played an active role in Republican national politics—even being mentioned at various times as a possible candidate for the offices of both President and Vice-President—and he has been elected chairman of the National Conference of Governors for 1946.

The son of Joseph T. and Hannah M. (Bristor) Martin, Edward Martin was born on September 18, 1879, in the Pennsylvania township of Washington, in Greene County. At the outbreak of the Spanish-American War, Martin was a student at Waynesburg College in his home state. He left school to enlist in the Army, and, as a private and later a corporal, he served with the Tenth Pennsylvania Volunteer Infantry in the Philippines, both in the Spanish-American War and in the Philippine Insurrection. In August 1899 the nineteen-year-old sergeant was mustered out, but five months afterward he joined the Pennsylvania National Guard as a sergeant.

Martin returned to college at the end of the war and in 1901 he received his B.A. degree. Four years later he was admitted to the State bar, at which time he set up practice as a Waynesburg lawyer. Martin had meanwhile continued to serve with the National Guard. He received his commission as a first lieutenant in 1901, was made a captain in 1905, and a major in 1910. Six years later, at the time the expedition was dispatched to Mexico after Villa, Martin was assigned to border duty.

When the United States entered the World War in 1917, Martin went to France as major, subsequently serving with the 109th and 110th Regiments. In September 1918 he was promoted to lieutenant colonel, and before the war ended he was decorated four times. He received the Distinguished Service Cross, for commanding an inexperienced battalion in an attack against a strongly held position. ". . . advancing with the front line, [he] raised the morale of officers and men by his coolness under heavy fire and utter disregard for personal danger." His citation for the Oak Leaf Cluster read: ". . . extraordinary heroism in action near Courmont, France, July 30, 1918. Although painfully wounded when regimental headquarters was destroyed by shell fire, he went with a battalion commander and directed the successful attack against a strong enemy position, remaining in command of the regiment until its relief." He was also awarded a Purple Heart with an Oak Leaf Cluster. Two years after the end of the war, Martin was promoted to a full colonel and placed on the Initial General Staff Eligibility List; in August 1922 he was raised to brigadier general.

In June 1939, just before war began again in Europe, Martin was made a major general and given command of the Twenty-eighth Division of the Pennsylvania National Guard. In 1941 the division was federalized and sent on maneuvers in the South; for his command of the unit at this time, Martin was cited by the Second Army Corps. Early the next year, having been relieved of his command because of his age, the sixty-two-year-old general was assigned to the headquarters of the Fifth Corps Area, at Fort Hayes, Ohio. In April he was placed on the Army's inactive list. (He has written a history of the Twenty-eighth Division.)

In peace years Martin had served as director or president-director of several companies— Washington County Fire Insurance Company, Dunn-Mar Oil and Gas Company, Chartiers Discount Company, and Citizens National Bank of Washington (Pennsylvania)—and in 1925 he entered politics. His first political position was that of auditor-general of Pennsylvania, a post he held for four years, and then State treasurer for four years. During the years between 1928 and 1934 he was the chairman of the Republican State Committee of Pennsylvania. From 1939 until 1943 he was adjutant general of Pennsylvania except for the period between February 17, 1941, and April 1, 1942, when he was in military service.

Immediately after his release from the Army in 1942 Martin was offered the Republican nomination for governor by the political machine of Joseph Newton Pew, Jr. '41, and a former Pennsylvania Senator, Joseph R. Grundy. Campaign posters showed Martin wearing his uniform, and his platform was based on the argument that Pennsylvania needed a governor familiar with "the terror and tumult of war." In the Republican primaries, with a majority of 94,000 votes, he sent Senator James J. Davis down to defeat. In November he was again the victor, defeating Democrat F. Clair Ross for the governorship.

As Governor, Martin has remained, for the most part, a loyal Republican. During the 1944 Presidential campaign he was among the party leaders who formed the platform for the Republican's candidate, Thomas E. Dewey '44. He served on the committee, headed by Senator Arthur Vandenberg '40, which introduced the foreign policy resolution at the Republican Governors' Conference at Mackinac Island in 1943. The resolution, which was later incor-

EDWARD MARTIN

porated into the party platform, approved "responsible participation by the United States in a postwar cooperative organization among sovereign nations to prevent military aggression and to attain permanent peace with organized justice in a free world." It was one of the few points raised on which all Republicans, isolationist and internationalist, could agree, since its loose terminology was seen as permitting a wide variety of interpretations. (In July 1945, at the next Governors' Conference on Mackinac Island, the World Charter was endorsed at the urging of Commander Harold Stassen '40.) Martin campaigned vigorously for Dewey, declaring that a young man should now be elected to the White House. He denounced Roosevelt '42 as being unprepared for and mismanaging the war, and maintained that the United States would win the war in spite of President Roosevelt's methods, not because of them. Earlier that year Martin himself was criticized for extravagance in his capacity as host to the Governors' Conference in Hershey, at a time when wartime conservation was being stressed.

In 1943 Governor Dewey urged the five states bordering on New York to support the Office of Price Administration with State legislation in order to keep black markets from flourishing. According to Governor Martin, Pennsylvania would have liked to have cooperated, but he was not sure of the procedure. In April 1944 Governor Martin advocated an increase of fifty cents a barrel in the cost of oil "to stimulate production and keep the industry healthy by insuring necessary good wages to employees."

In his annual message to the Pennsylvania State Legislature, in January 1945, Governor Martin surprised both his political enemies and friends. He broke with party tradition by demanding legislation providing larger unemployment compensation and liberalized compensations for occupational diseases. He recommended larger appropriations for safety inspections of mines and factories, to give Penn-

MARTIN, EDWARD—*Continued*

sylvania workers "as safe a place to work as possible." He advocated new low-cost housing and denounced racial discrimination as un-American. In September, however, he again stood with his party when he opposed the Kilgore '43 bill, which would have raised total unemployment compensation benefits to a maximum of twenty-five dollars per week for twenty-six weeks, by supplementary Federal payments. In addition, it would have given travel payments to unemployed war workers to enable them to return to their homes. Governor Martin announced that he was opposed to "any bill or plan designed to federalize the administration of unemployment compensation." He also stated that he was in favor of full employment, not "coddling," for returning veterans, and also for much less "interference" by Washington in State affairs.

The tall, white-haired Governor was married to Charity Scott, a Waynesburg girl, in December 1908. They have two children, Edward and Mary (Mrs. James B. W. Murphy). Martin holds numerous honorary degrees: LL.D. degrees from Washington and Jefferson College (1938), the University of Pittsburgh (1941), Temple University, Pennsylvania Military College, Villanova College, Drexel Institute of Technology (all 1943), Gettysburg College (1944), and Grove City College, Lebanon Valley College, and Westminster College (all in 1945). He has a Doctor of Military Science degree from Waynesburg College (1940), of which he is a trustee; a Doctor of Humane Letters from the Hahnemann Medical College and the Hospital of Philadelphia (both in 1945); and in 1937 he was awarded the Pennsylvania Reilly Medal for his military services.

Among the veterans' organizations to which he belongs are the American Legion, the Veterans of Foreign Wars, and the Legion of Valor. Because he saw service before the First World War, he is a member of the Military Order of the Carabao and the Spanish-American War Veterans. Since the beginning of his forty-four-year career as a soldier, he has been collecting military books. This library, which consists of nearly six hundred volumes, is divided into three classifications: basic textbooks on various branches of service, histories of military campaigns, and biographies. One part of the collection is housed in his home, the other in the library of the Indiantown Gap Military Reservation, where the books were used by servicemen during the Second World War. Martin belongs to the Elks and is a thirty-third-degree Mason. He is an elder in the Presbyterian Church, a member of the board of directors of the Department of Church Cooperation and the Union of the Presbyterian Church in the United States, and vice-president and director of the Pennsylvania State Sabbath School.

References

Hobbies 49:104-5 My '44 il
N Y Sun p24 O 4 '44
Who's Who in America, 1944-45
Who's Who in Law, 1937

MARTIN, GEORGE BROWN Aug. 18, 1876—Nov. 12, 1945 Former United States Democratic Senator from Kentucky; appointed as a member of the United States Senate in 1918 to succeed Ollie M. James, and served until 1919; judge of Boyd County, Kentucky, (1904); delegate to the Democratic National Convention in 1928; Democratic elector, 1932 and 1936.

Obituary

N Y Times p21 N 13 '45

MARTINELLI, GIOVANNI (jō-van'nē) Oct. 22, 1885- Singer
Address: b. c/o Michael DePace, 1270 Sixth Ave., New York City

The vigorous and versatile Giovanni Martinelli of the Metropolitan Opera Company has not only played a record number of seasons but is regarded as one of the best-loved Metropolitan tenors of all time. This singer, whose snowy hair "seems to rise by sheer electricity" from his temples, made his first appearance at the Metropolitan in 1913. He has sung more than fifty roles in the past thirty-two seasons. Many people in today's opera audiences have never known a time when the Italian tenor was not singing in New York.

Giovanni Martinelli was born in Montagnana (near Padua), Italy, on October 22, 1885, the son of Antonio and Lucia (Bellini) Martinelli. His father was a cabinetmaker; and Giovanni, the eldest of fourteen children, was ambitious to become a master craftsman like his father. He sang as a boy in the village church choir—but "his thirteen brothers and sisters sang, too, and so, for that matter, did most of the other Montagnana villagers." To be able to sing wasn't enough to distinguish a boy in a town of music-lovers. But Giovanni could also play the clarinet; and at twelve he became clarinetist in the town band.

At the age of twenty Martinelli was drafted for three years of military service. It is said he likes to reminisce about those years in the army: "My ability to play the clarinet," he recalls, "was the means of procuring [for] me a life of comparative ease. I applied for membership in the regimental band and was accepted. Bandsmen had the privilege of officers, so I was very well off. One day some of my companions and I were spending our recreation time together singing and joking. I was one of the most enthusiastic vocalists, and had just finished a selection, sung fortissimo, when our bandmaster came out into the enclosure where we were. . . . I thought I had been guilty of some breach of discipline. Imagine how the world changed when instead . . . the bandmaster spoke the magic words: 'You have a wonderful voice. You should study.' . . . That was all that was needed to fire me with ambition. The bandmaster and my colonel were good friends. The latter gave me permission to go with the bandmaster to the homes of the prominent families of Piedmont to sing and, as they were pleased, I was granted leave to go to Milan for an audition. There . . . I was advised to take lessons." Young Martinelli's friends then proceeded not only to win his father's permission to let him study, but to help him secure wealthy patronage. When his military service ended, the singer therefore began his lessons.

It was in December 1910 that Martinelli made his concert debut in Rossini's *Stabat Mater*. Two weeks later his opera debut took place in a Milan production of Verdi's *Ernani*. According to one account, the singer "dropped his sword and flubbed his lines" in his stage role. But he had a voice. Furthermore, Puccini was in the audience and engaged him for the European première of his *The Girl of the Golden West* with Toscanini'⁴² conducting, in Rome in 1911. Following this came a rapid succession of engagements in Milan, Monte Carlo, Genoa, Naples, Turin, Budapest, and Brussels. London first heard the new tenor at Covent Garden in 1912. There he sang in *Francesca da Rimini* and *The Jewels of the Madonna*. Since then Martinelli has been one of the most popular Italian tenors with the English public: they have frequently requested his return, and in the spring of 1937 gave him the honor of opening the coronation opera season in the title role of *Otello*. (In 1913, just before coming to America, Giovanni Martinelli was married to Adele Previtali. They have three children: Bettina [Mrs. Mario Libotte], Antonio, and Giovanna.)

The young tenor, not yet thirty, was almost unknown to the American music world, and no stir heralded his debut at the Metropolitan in a performance of *La Bohème* on November 20, 1913. When the curtain rose the applause for Rodolfo was "only perfunctory." The new tenor was nervous and forced his voice to be heard above the orchestra. But his performance became increasingly moving, and at the end of the third act he was greeted with tumultuous applause. Critical opinion was divided, however, ranging from the unqualified commendation for the voice of "a real lyric tenor, intense and peculiarly vital in timbre," to the regret that "his strongest conviction seemed to be that force meant feeling." But it was in general agreed that the Metropolitan had added a valuable member to its company, and it was also predicted that the newcomer would win a place for himself.

In the course of time Giovanni Martinelli came to be regarded as the best all-round Italian tenor on the Metropolitan roster. His repertoire included a great number of roles, some of the best-known being *Aïda, Carmen, Samson et Dalila, Tosca, Faust, Rigoletto, La Juive, Pagliacci,* and *Otello*. The two extremes in his repertoire are the lyrical role of Riccardo in Verdi's *A Masked Ball*—and the much heavier title role in *Otello*. He has been the incomparable Rhadames of more than three hundred and fifty performances of *Aïda* alone: but he did not attempt the role of Otello until 1937.

On March 20, 1938, his twenty-fifth consecutive season as a Metropolitan singer was celebrated by a gala performance. Eighteen of the leading singers of the Metropolitan participated, and Martinelli himself sang three important arias from *La Bohème, La Juive,* and *Otello*. It was on the occasion of this jubilee celebration that the late Metropolitan president, Paul D. Cravath, remarking on the singer's elasticity of temperament, his strength and vigor, said that the fifty-two-year-old Martinelli had surely "bathed in the Fountain of Youth." In 1939,

GIOVANNI MARTINELLI

in the Chicago opera season, Martinelli satisfied one of his most cherished ambitions—to sing a major Wagnerian role. This he did, in *Tristan und Isolde*.

The year 1940, because of the war, was a critical one for the Metropolitan Opera Company, in so far as its Italian singers were concerned. Several who had been on vacation in Italy, or otherwise engaged abroad, had had their passports canceled. Martinelli, however, was protected by his United States citizenship; and he was thus in New York in October of that year to sign his twenty-eighth consecutive contract, so "establishing a new record for longevity of service at the House for a first-string singer." The season proved to be one of the Metropolitan's most successful in recent years. Martinelli was one of the three top box-office stars, the other two being Kirsten Flagstad and Lily Pons'⁴⁴.

On September 17, 1941, Martinelli was appointed artistic director of the Chicago Opera Company for the 1941 season, to work with Fortune Gallo as general director. R. H. McCormick, chairman of the Chicago Opera, said that the new assignment would not interfere with Martinelli's own singing career, that he would sing with the Chicago company, as well as at the New York Metropolitan, and also make a nationwide concert tour. Most of the repertoire had already been chosen, and most of the company assembled. But Martinelli had to make final supervision of the casts and find last-minute solutions of emergencies. It is evident that Martinelli held those singers under his direction to a rather strict code. According to him, a singer must be familiar not only with his role, but with the language, the libretto, and the psychology of the part he portrays, and the tradition, also, of playing the part. "I am eager to find singers who are also actors, who feel their parts with intense sincerity, and have the ability to stimulate such feeling in others through a wholehearted giving of self; who are willing to begin at the bottom in order to ascend to the top."

(Continued next page)

MARTINELLI, GIOVANNI—*Continued*

Regarding opera in general, Martinelli has said that in large cosmopolitan cities opera may be safely given in its original language. But "in small cities of native, homogeneous population, opera should be given, I believe, in the language of the audience." Opera will be further improved, he said, when the public realizes that "voices" and "names" are not enough to make characters live. "The first requisite for operatic work is not a name, but a dramatic ability." Martinelli believes that one great handicap to the American artist is lack in the United States of sufficient opera companies in which a singer may acquire practice in public.

In February 1943 Martinelli began, with Verdi's *Il Trovatore*, his thirtieth consecutive year as a Metropolitan artist. According to the New York *World-Telegram*, for the past couple of years the noted tenor's voice had not been "all that he himself might have wanted it to be, let alone the opinions of others. But, like the experienced trouper that he is, he stayed with the music, pacing himself wonderfully well. What he lacked in tonal purity or volume he made up in finesse and operatic 'savvy.' . . .Not the least effective side of his impersonation was his stage deportment, his adherence to the tenents of the role at all times." In 1945 Martinelli sang Manrico in *Il Trovatore* and Polione in *Norma* in two of a series of farewell appearances.

Martinelli's skill and versatility throughout his long career have been accompanied by unusual good health and good nature. In his fifty-sixth year, when he was director of the Chicago Opera Company, he also learned to drive a car. He went at the latter venture with the same energy he puts into learning a new role. "Within a few months of his first lessons at the wheel of the Buick he rolled up seventeen thousand miles." Martinelli has the actor's usual superstition. His friends say that there is a backstage ritual to be followed by him before every operatic performance. There is a little holy relic that must be saluted; and photographs of his wife and three children must "be placed carefully on the dressing-room table, and a kiss given each."

Martinelli's equanimity and cheerfulness account for his popularity. He is not only the "youngest, happiest, most ebullient performer to bow at any curtain," but the gayest figure at the speaker's table. the man with the brightest smile at a party. He is a gourmet and makes a hobby of cooking: he "rewards a properly appreciative guest with his own prized recipe for a *risotto*, or for spaghetti done after a favorite method of his old friend Enrico Caruso." It is said, too, that Martinelli has had amazingly few disagreements with his Metropolitan fellow artists. The most memorable was an intense but short-lived quarrel with the great Scotti over the exact amount of salt required to bring a spaghetti sauce to perfection.

References

Metropolitan Opera Program p6 D 27 '39 por
Musical Am 61:4 O 10 '41 por
N Y World-Telegram p6 F 6 '43
Newsweek 11:26 Mr 21 '38

Opera N 4:16 Mr 25 '40; 6:5 N 3 '41; 8:29 N 15 '43 por
Time 31:40 Mr 28 '38
Variety p3 O 9 '40
Ewen, David, ed. Living Musicians (1940)
Thompson, O. ed. International Cyclopedia of Music and Musicians (1943)
Who's Who in America, 1944-45

MASCAGNI, PIETRO (mäs-kä'nyē pyâ' trō) Dec. 7, 1863—Aug 2, 1945 Composer considered one of the most popular of contemporary Italian musicians; composed *Cavalleria Rusticana* and several less successful operatic works, including *Iris, Le Maschere,* and *Isobel*; his last opera, *Il Nerone* (1935), was given popular acclaim; also composed various symphonic works, chamber, and church music.

Obituary

N Y Times p17 Ag 3 '45 por

MATTHEWS, H(ARRISON) FREEMAN May 26, 1899- United States Government official

Address: b. c/o Department of State, Washington, D. C.; h. 3224 Woodlawn Dr., N.W., Washington, D.C.

In the service of the United States Department of State since 1923, H. Freeman Matthews is one of those men who have risen steadily if unsensationally in their chosen field. His appointment as director of the State Department's Office of European Affairs on December 20, 1944, occasioned no surprise among his confrères; nor did fanfares of publicity attend his appointment. It was to be expected in the natural course of events. Matthews was then forty-five, but in terms of his position he was considered one of the more promising young men in public life.

Harrison Freeman Matthews was born in Baltimore, Maryland, on May 26, 1899. The son of Henry Clay and Bertha (Freeman) Matthews, he attended the Gilman Country School, Princeton University (B.A. 1921, M.A. 1922), and l'Ecole Libre des Sciences Politiques in Paris in 1922-23.

Matthews began his career as a Foreign Service officer on December 12, 1923, as secretary of embassy or legation, class four, assigned to the State Department. In February 1924, he was sent to Budapest, where on July 1 of the same year he attained the rank of third secretary. A little over two years later, on September 2, 1926, he became third secretary at Bogotá. On August 19, 1929, he was reassigned to Washington, appointed assistant chief of the Division of Latin American Affairs on November 1, 1930, and sent on special detail to El Salvador the following year. On October 4, 1933, he was appointed second secretary of the Embassy at Havana, and on November 27 was made first secretary.

After his six and a half years of experience in Latin American affairs, Matthews returned to the European scene. On July 13, 1937, he was made first secretary at Paris, and a month later consul, combining his duties as consul with those of first secretary after April 21, 1938.

April 4, 1939, saw him as first secretary at Madrid. He returned to Paris as first secretary on July 1, 1939, then was sent to Vichy in 1940. He went to London as counselor of the Embassy late in 1941, and in 1942 was made counselor with rank of Minister. In August of 1943 he was made chief of the Division of European Affairs in the Department of State. In January 1944 he became deputy director, and in December of the same year director of the Office of European Affairs.

Thus Matthews has had experience in both Latin American and European affairs. Furthermore, he has served his Government in various embassies at times when relations of the United States and those countries were anything but smooth. He has seen diplomatic relations at their most complicated. Much still remains to be ironed out between the United States and Latin America, Spain, and France, as a review of United States relations with these countries before and during the war reveals. Logically, Matthews would seem to be one of the men fitted by interest and experience to help with the improvement of those relations. The United States-Vichy relations during the latter half of 1940 (when Matthews was on duty in Vichy) were more complicated than the general public suspected at the time. In 1943 the State Department published six documents covering the period from June 17 to December 20, 1940. (Matthews was at Vichy from June 10, 1940, until October of 1941.) The State Department documents reveal that a diplomatic breach between the United States Government and that of Marshal Pétain '40 almost occurred in November 1940, thirteen months before Pearl Harbor. The documents included instructions from Secretary of State Cordell Hull '40 to Anthony J. Drexel Biddle, Jr., '41 the American Ambassador then serving with the French Government at Bordeaux, and to Matthews, as well as their replies. Also included among the documents was one containing President Roosevelt's '42 instructions to Admiral William D. Leahy '41 as he was assuming his duties as Ambassador to France.

On June 17, 1940, with the fall of France, Hull instructed Biddle to obtain assurances that the French fleet would not fall into German hands. If it did, France was warned, she would lose the friendship and good will of Americans and risk the loss of their help in restoring her independence and autonomy. Ambassador Biddle obtained the required assurances from Paul Baudoin, the French Foreign Minister. Later, on October 25, after Dakar and other British naval operations, another warning was sent. President Roosevelt gave a note to Ambassador Gaston Henry-Haye '40 and sent one to Marshal Pétain through Matthews, again warning about the French fleet, this time with respect to its possible use against the British. The message also warned that if France provided assistance to Germany she would not have American influence in retaining her overseas possessions. In his reply to this message Marshal Pétain showed resentment, but gave his word once more that the French fleet would "never be surrendered."

Obviously the situation was one of the utmost delicacy. The United States was suspicious—as events later proved, justifiably so—not only of the intentions of Pierre Laval '40,

H. FREEMAN MATTHEWS

but also of the intentions of the Vichy Government as a whole. That Pétain and the late Admiral Jean Darlan '41, the French Navy Minister, kept their word and did not permit the French fleet to fall into the hands of the Axis powers was a victory for the United States, a victory which must have been due, at least in part, to the competence of the American diplomatic corps in Vichy.

Matthews first came to the foreground at the time of his appointment as chief of the European Division of the State Department in 1943 (succeeding Ray Atherton, who became minister to Canada). The New York Herald Tribune styled him a "career diplomat" who had first come into the limelight in the autumn of 1940, after the fall of France, "when he was Chargé d'Affaires of the American Embassy in Vichy during the interregnum between the departure of Ambassador William C. Bullitt '40 for the United States and the arrival of Admiral William D. Leahy as Ambassador in January 1941. Even after the advent of Admiral Leahy," continues the Herald Tribune, "Mr. Matthews was an important figure in American diplomatic circles in Vichy because he always accompanied the American Ambassador on his calls on Marshal Henri Pétain, Admiral Jean Darlan, and other leading Vichy officials. Admiral Leahy spoke little French, and it was up to Mr. Matthews to act as interpreter." PM has called Matthews "one of the younger men of the State Department who have been rising to the top in recent years," adding, "he is regarded as an extremely capable man, rather on the conservative side but by no means a reactionary. Ambassador Winant '41 is understood to have thought highly of him."

In March 1944 Edward Stettinius, Jr., '40 then Under-Secretary of State, made a trip to London for high-policy talks with the British Government. Matthews was one of Stettinius' aides on this mission. The others were Wallace S. Murray, director of the Office of Near-Eastern and African Affairs; Isaiah Bowman '45, president of Johns Hopkins University

MATTHEWS, H. FREEMAN—*Continued*
and geographer and postwar planner; John Lee
Pratt, consultant on commercial affairs and
former Lend-Lease official; and Robert J.
Lynch, secretary to Stettinius and executive
secretary of the mission.

On April 26 it was announced that the work
of the mission was almost over. The members left London "satisfied that their visit,
while it had settled nothing finally, had helped
to bring nearer to realization that complete
unity of action among the big powers that the
conferences at Moscow, Teheran, and Cairo
had foreshadowed." The talks resulted in no
final decisions but did help clear away many
points on which there had been misunderstanding. While the mission was in London there
arose the urgent problem of how to deal with
neutral governments which persisted in trading
with the enemy. In a note to Sweden, Britain
and the United States appealed to that country
to stop shipping ball bearings to the Nazis.
Also, an appeal was made to Spain that she stop
exporting wolfram to Germany. (Both of those
countries subsequently stopped most of the shipments of these materials to Germany.)

In July 1945 Matthews accompanied President Truman to the Potsdam conference and
in December he attended the Moscow meeting
of the Big Three Ministers together with Secretary of State Byrnes. It is said that Matthews, as chief of the Division of European
Affairs, was an important figure at these meetings.

Matthews was married on September 15,
1925, to Elizabeth Luke. He has two sons, H.
Freeman Matthews, Jr., and Thomas Luke
Matthews. His church affiliation is Presbyterian. Among his recreations he lists tennis
and mountain climbing.

References

N Y Herald Tribune p4 Jl 3 '43
PM p9 Jl 14 '43
Who's Who in America, 1944-45

MAULDIN, BILL Oct. 29, 1921- Cartoonist

Address: b. c/o Henry Holt & Co., 257 Fourth
Ave., New York City

Up Front With Mauldin, a series of realistic
sketches of two war-weary, unkempt GI's of
the Second World War, has been compared
to Bruce Bairnsfather's *The Better 'Ole* of the
First World War. The creator of this now
famous pair of infantrymen, Joe and Willie,
is Bill Mauldin from Arizona who understands the grim humor of combat troops because he himself has been in combat. His cartoon series, which appeared in the pages of
the Army overseas newspaper the *Stars and
Stripes,* and was syndicated in seventy-nine
United States daily papers. Mauldin was
awarded the Pulitzer Prize in 1945 "for distinguished service as a cartoonist."

William Henry Mauldin has lived his short
life "the hard way." He was born on October
29, 1921, in Mountain Park, New Mexico, and
seems to have spent part of his boyhood there
and the rest in Phoenix, Arizona. His father,
Sidney Mauldin, had been badly gassed in the
First World War and afterward "found the

going tough." He tried dry farming on his
homestead near Phoenix, worked as a hired
hand, then for a while was a tire-changer at a
bus station in Phoenix. As a boy Bill had
rickets and thus was forced to spend most of
his sickly, lonesome childhood in bed, looking
out of the window and watching the other
children at play. The countless pictures that
he drew of himself riding ponies in cowboy
chaps and ten-gallon hats, or shoveling coal
into a locomotive firebox, expressed his childhood dreams. When he was graduated from
grammar school as valedictorian of his class,
however, he finally received the horse for which
he had longed.

In 1938 the parents of the "scrawny, cocky"
seventeen-year-old artist were divorced, and he
and his brother Sidney went back to Phoenix
from New Mexico, where they had been living. There Bill joined the ROTC and was
made a corporal. The first public recognition
of his art had come while he was in high
school and had sold his first drawing for ten
dollars, to the La Luz Pottery Company in
New Mexico. When he sold his next drawing
he invested the five dollars he had received
for it as a down payment on a correspondence
course in cartooning. Then he initiated a
wolf-from-the-door routine which was to continue for many months. He painted posters, he
"even painted the white sidewalls of aristocratic tires," he told Frederick Painton in
1945. But because of this extracurricular work,
he found himself a half-point short at graduation, and did not receive his diploma.

Determined to be a professional cartoonist,
Mauldin wanted formal training. From "Grandma Callie Bemis," his maternal grandmother,
he procured the three hundred dollars necessary to enter the Chicago Academy of Fine
Arts. Again he worked his way—washing
dishes, painting signs, illustrating menus. (He
thinks that the permanent impairment of his
eyesight began at this time, for he would work
all day and often most of the night.) After
the period of work and study in Chicago he
returned to Phoenix in his usual financial condition—"broke." His next attempt at a moneyraising venture was to draw "gag" sketches for
national magazines; he drew many hundreds
in the course of a year, sending them out
regularly and as regularly getting them back.
But he sold some cartoons to Arizona Highways; then, finding himself in the midst of the
1940 gubernatorial campaign, he helped a local
political cartoonist with sketches for "smear
posters"; he got twenty-five dollars a sketch,
which paid for his room and meals. But, according to *Life* Magazine, he almost got into
trouble when it was discovered that he was
drawing similar posters for the rival aspirants
for office. In September he enlisted in the
Arizona National Guard. Volunteers to this
organization did not have to pass a physical
examination, but, ironically, five days after
Mauldin enlisted, the Arizona Guard was federalized, and the young cartoonist, who "couldn't
have passed the first doctor," found himself
in the Army.

"I was in this man's army when it was an
infant," Mauldin says, "and we kinda grew up
together—me being only eighteen. All I know
—grown up—is Army life." He began his infantry training with the Forty-fifth Division

at Fort Sill, Oklahoma—drilling, patrolling, marching all day and spending most of the night in the division *News* office drawing pictures for the paper. Later these *News* cartoons were printed by the Oklahoma University Press in a volume called *News of the 45th.*

While at Camp Barkeley, in Texas, the young soldier-artist met Norma Jean Humphries from Toyah (Texas), an eighteen-year-old junior at Hardin-Simmons University. His courtship interrupted her academic career as well as a romance with a Royal Canadian Air Force suitor. When she became engaged to Mauldin, the artist drew a cartoon for the *Daily Oklahoman* for the down payment on a diamond ring costing twenty-seven dollars and fifty cents. The young couple were married in February 1942, and after their wedding Bill did more art work for the *Oklahoman* to add to his soldier's pay.

With his division Mauldin moved about the country: Camp Barkeley, Fort Devans, Pine Camp, Camp Pickett, and Camp Patrick Henry were stops along the way to Italy. "There was little home life for the bride and the boy trying to be a soldier," writes Painton, "but he could still draw cartoons of doughboys pitching pup tents beside the bus terminal and setting up housekeeping while waiting for room on the bus." His second book of cartoons, *Mud, Mules and Mountains* (1943), which was published by the *Army Times,* eased the Mauldin's financial burden when their son, Bruce Patrick was born, shortly after the artist's arrival in Sicily. *Sicily Sketchbook,* printed in a shop in Palermo, brought in eighteen hundred dollars more. (Seventeen thousand copies of the book were bought by members of the Forty-fifth Division alone.)

After Mauldin became a sergeant the editors of the *Stars and Stripes* arranged to have him transferred to their staff. On July 13, 1943, three days after Sicilian D-Day, they had brought out the first edition of an American Army newspaper to be printed on European soil. Several weeks later Mauldin was in the hospital with sandfly fever; when he was discharged he found that some of the troops had already left Sicily for Salerno. Not wanting to be left behind, he left the replacement center unceremoniously and caught up with his division just as the last boats were leaving for Salerno.

At Salerno the cartoonist was wounded and awarded the Purple Heart. During that hard winter of 1943-44 he traveled between the two bitterest fronts of the Italian campaign, Cassino and Anzio, seeing tired men of the Fifth Army go back day after day with courage and endurance to "the dogged slugging that finally beat the best the Germans had." When his old outfit landed in France, Mauldin stowed away with his jeep aboard an LST and went with them. After two months in France he returned to Italy, and after that he made frequent trips to the Fifth Army front.

Mauldin says that it is difficult for him to remember just how or when his cartoon character Joe was created. "He didn't appear suddenly," he wrote from Italy for *Life* Magazine in 1944, "and we were never formally introduced. He hung around for years, and I suspect that, like Topsy, he just grew." In

SGT. BILL MAULDIN

1940, he recalls, when he was a private at Fort Sill, Oklahoma, he used to give expression to his rebellious feelings under Army discipline in cartoons for the division newspaper. After a year "the kind gods with brass on their shoulders" decided that the sketches were a morale factor, and Mauldin was given a full-time job on the paper, in which he continued "hammering blows at the Army system." "It never fell," comments the young artist, "but sometimes I felt convinced it was tottering and was content."

Joe, in those early days, was a youthful, clean-shaven anonymous recruit. When he got to Sicily he acquired the name Joe because Sicilian children called out to the Americans as they pushed through their little villages, "Hey, Joe! Candy? Cigarette?" (Mauldin has pointed out that "GI" is an authentic soldierism, except in combination with "Joe"; "GI Joe" is a strictly civilian expression.) With the acquisition of a name and some campaign experience, Joe and his comrades began to age. After the fighting in Italy their metamorphosis was complete; they had become the tired, dirty, dull-eyed, unshaven foot soldiers of the current cartoons. To the civilians who complain that they look more like hobos than like any familiar conception of the American soldier, and to women who write protesting that "our boys don't look like the way you draw them— bearded and horrible looking," Bill Mauldin answers, "I draw our guys like that because that's the way they are." "I was eighteen when I joined the Army," he explains in *Life.* "I knew a lot of these kids then. Now, after they've been through a couple of campaigns, after being in the line for weeks, they're old men. They've aged ten or fifteen years, have beards, their eyes have bags underneath, and they wear a dopey expression like they need a lot of sleep. . . . The poor guys have changed so that I hardly recognize them."

"The foot soldier is unhappy most of the time," write two Mauldin defenders in *Life.*

MAULDIN, BILL—*Continued*

"Saddled with the grimmest, most wretched job in the Army, he is tired, wet, and scared most of the time. . . .He feels friendless and forgotten." This misery of the infantryman is expressed in one of the Mauldin sketches depicting a little dog shivering in the rain outside a cave where several doughboys have sought shelter. "Let him come it," says one of the men from the darkness inside. "I wanna see a critter I kin feel sorry for." "In these hollow-eyed, unshaven infantry characters," writes Frederick Painton of Mauldin's soldiers, he has "immortalized the misery, the grandeur, and the godlike patience—as well as the grim humor—of the front-line fighting man." The late Ernie Pyle '41, too, has defended his artistic counterpart in Italy, captioning a picture release of a weary soldier on Okinawa with, "So you at home think Cartoonist Bill Mauldin's 'GI Joe' doesn't look that way. Well, he does, and here's proof."

During his Army career Mauldin has drawn hundreds of cartoons. His own favorite is a sketch of an old cavalry sergeant pointing a revolver, in grief, at the radiator of his broken-down old jeep. That drawing, he says, is really funny. The artist has several taboos for his work: he does not use sex as a subject; he did not portray Germans as funny or ludicrous—the enemy in mortal combat is never comical, he declares; and he does not portray fear or death. He cannot be "cute" about war, he feels; he can only try to make something out of the humorous situations which accompany misery.

Since his cartoons have continually satirized the military hierarchy, Mauldin has frequently been reprimanded. His contention is that the long-suffering doughboy should be allowed the pleasure of "tossing an occasional tomato" at "a brass hat." Some officers agree with this theory; others feel the cartoons are disrespectful or objectionable for other reasons. At one time on the verge of military arrest, Mauldin was championed by General Mark W. Clark '42. Later Mauldin clashed with General George S. Patton '43 on the subject of the cartoons. Patton considered them injurious to morale and threatened to ban *Stars and Stripes* from his area unless Mauldin made his men less grimy. At the suggestion of General Eisenhower who enjoys the cartoons himself, the Sergeant and General Patton met to discuss the matter. After the conference Mauldin reported: "I came out with all my hide on. . . .I don't think we changed each other's opinions. . . .A soldier's mind is his own property." Mauldin's GI's remained unshaven and unwashed, but an April 1945 cartoon depicted Joe attempting to carry out Army orders to shave off his tough beard. The caption under the sketch reads: "By gad, sir, I *tried*!" Patton continued critical of Mauldin and his cartoons: "He's the Bairnsfather of this war and I don't like either of them." Hanson Baldwin's '42 comment was: "As long as Regular Army officers . . . think that Bill Mauldin's cartoons are destructive of morale, just that long will there be an officer-enlisted man problem."

But the soldiers find no fault with Bill Mauldin. His second book, *Mud, Mules and Mountains*, sold three hundred thousand to the Fifth Army in Italy, where GI's put it in their rucksacks. Further evidence of his popularity was a six-foot reproduction of his infantryman on the Fifth Army float at the big Fifth Army-Twelfth Air Force football game on New Year's Day 1945. Tom Meany, reporting the game for *PM*, described Joe as "the raggedy hero of every soldier in Italy." In March the *Army Times* proposed that Bill Mauldin be sent to the San Francisco conference in April 1945 to represent the "Foxhole Fraternity." His fourth book of cartoons, *Up Front*, containing a hundred and sixty drawings and thirty thousand words of text, was published in June and chosen by the Book-of-the-Month Club for July distribution. The original publishers completely exhausted their stock within two weeks after publication; with no paper available they disposed of the publishing rights to a reprint house which sold a million copies in the first month. (International Pictures bought the motion picture rights and Mauldin is scheduled to go to Hollywood to help write the screen version.) Mauldin had been awarded the Pulitzer Prize in May 1945 for a particular cartoon in his *Up Front With Mauldin* series, captioned "Fresh, spirited American troops, flushed with victory"—a drawing of American bedraggled soldiers in pouring rain.

In Europe the artist had a jeep assigned to him by General Clark. This vehicle, which he named Jeanie, was a traveling pin-up gallery of pictures of his wife and son, and had portraits of Joe and Willie painted on the outside. The back seat was made into a locker in which rations and drawing materials were packed, and Mauldin used the top of the seat for a bed. The entire jeep could be blacked out so that he could work at night by light supplied by built-in batteries (he often went two or three days without sleep). He never tired of talking with soldiers and was a stickler for accuracy of details in his drawings—spending hours sketching new uniforms, equipment, and weapons. If he missed a point, he said, he was mercilessly "kidded" by the GI's.

With sufficient discharge points to his credit, Mauldin came home in June 1945, two days before *Up Front* was published, to his wife and Bruce, their twenty-month-old son in Los Angeles. (In October, however, he filed a divorce suit against his wife, asking for the custody of the child). Willie and Joe have come home, too, cleaned up and shaved, in the new series, at first called *Sweatin' It Out With Mauldin*, and later superseded by individual titles. According to *Time*, Mauldin does not think Willie and Joe are going to be a problem: "They are so damned sick and tired of war that their only ambition will be to forget it. They don't need pity . . . they simply need bosses who will give them a little time to adjust their minds and their hands, and women who are faithful to them, and friends and families who stay by them until they are the same guys who left years ago." At the fourteenth New York *Herald Tribune* Forum in November Bill Mauldin made a spirited speech against racial intolerance: "One of the greatest foundations upon which our country is built is the creed that every citizen shall have the right to freedom of expression, and worship, and of life, liberty, and the pursuit of happiness. Anything designed to deprive any citizen of any of these rights is the greatest un-American activity of all."

According to his *Saturday Evening Post* biographer, Frederick Painton, who interviewed the young cartoonist on the Anzio beachhead in late 1944, Bill Mauldin has "jug-handle ears, big brown eyes with a satyr expression, and a boyishly smooth complexion that only requires a razor—to his secret sorrow—once a week. His uncombable shock of black hair, his youthful grin, and his slim, eager walk make him appear some high school kid not quite dry behind the ears. He is twenty-three, and when he is tired he looks all of sixteen."

References

Life 16:8-10 Ja 17 '45 il; 16:11-14 Mr 27 '44; 18:49-53 F 5 '45 il pors
P M p7-9 My 27 '45
Sat Eve Post 27:22-3+ Mr 17 '45 il pors

MAULDIN, WILLIAM HENRY *See* Mauldin, B.

MAYS, BENJAMIN E(LIJAH) Aug. 1, 1895- College president

Address: Morehouse College, Atlanta, Ga.

The president of Morehouse College in Atlanta, Georgia, an outstanding Negro institution for men, is Benjamin E. Mays, prominent leader in education and religion. Mays has contributed widely to educational and religious publications concerned with the problems of the Negro people. On February 19, 1945, on the occasion of the seventy-eighth anniversary of the college, Mays delivered a radio address which expressed the purposes of Morehouse and at the same time gave a glimpse into the character and life work of the speaker. He said: "It will not be sufficient for Morehouse College, for any college, for that matter, to produce clever graduates, men fluent in speech and able to argue their way through; but rather honest men, men who can be trusted in public and private life—men who are sensitive to the wrongs, the sufferings, and the injustices of society and who are willing to accept responsibility for correcting the ills."

Benjamin Elijah Mays was born in Epworth, South Carolina, August 1, 1895, to S. Hezekiah and Louvenia (Carter) Mays. He attended the high school of South Carolina State College, completing the course in three years and graduating as class valedictorian (1916). He went North for his higher education, first to Bates College in Maine and later to the University of Chicago. At Bates the young man was a leading campus figure, scholastically as well as in extracurricular activities. He was an honor student (Bates College elected him to Phi Beta Kappa in 1935) and served as president of the debating council, of Bates Forum, and of the Phil-Hellenic Club; he was also a member of the YMCA cabinet and a star intercollegiate debater. After receiving his B.A. degree in 1920 he prepared for the church and was ordained a Baptist minister two years later. His first pastorate at the Shiloh Baptist Church of Atlanta was close to Morehouse College, where he taught higher mathematics until 1924. The following year he received

BENJAMIN E. MAYS

his M.A. from the University of Chicago and in 1935 he was awarded his Ph.D. degree. In 1925 he became instructor of English in the State College of South Carolina at Orangeburg.

His first wife was Ellen Harvin. On August 9, 1926, he was married to Sadie Gray, teacher and social worker, who had also received her M.A. from the University of Chicago. The couple have since worked together wherever Mays's work has taken them. In 1926 he was appointed executive secretary of the Tampa (Florida) Urban League. After two years at this post he became national student secretary of the YMCA. From 1930 until 1932 he directed a study of the Negro churches in the United States under the auspices of the Institute of Social and Religious Research in New York City. Out of this work grew his book *The Negro's Church*, written in collaboration with J. W. Nicholson and published in 1933. This volume is an exhaustive survey of the Negro church in America, based on a firsthand study of 609 urban and 185 rural churches in twelve cities and four rural areas. Carefully documented, the book treats of various aspects of the Negro church with scholarly thoroughness. In later years Mays discussed this subject in magazine articles.

The educator's next position took him to Washington, D.C., where he became dean of the Howard University School of Religion in 1934. During his six-year administration the school attracted national attention and was rated Class A by the American Association of Theological Schools. During this period Mays represented the United States at various world conferences. In 1937, with twelve other Americans, he attended the World Conference of the YMCA in Mysore, India. That year he was also present as America's delegate at the Oxford Conference on the Church, Community, and State at Oxford University, England. In the course of these years of travel Mays's opportunity to observe foreign countries and peoples was extensive: in 1937 he and his wife traveled in England, Scotland, Holland, Ger-

MAYS, BENJAMIN E.—*Continued*

many, Switzerland, and France. Two years later he again represented the YMCA, this time at the Plenary Session of the World Committee in Stockholm. That same year he was a leader at the Youth Conference in Amsterdam.

Mays became president of Morehouse College in July 1940. The school, a fully accredited liberal arts college for men, is part of the Atlanta University system. Rated Class A by the Southern Association of Colleges and Secondary Schools, Morehouse is the alma mater of many leading Negroes of the nation. During Mays's wartime presidency, a period of difficulty for all colleges, the school's enrollment has "remained satisfactory." In the 1945 spring issue of the Morehouse College *Bulletin* the president stated the school's educational aims: "To improve the quality and quantity of our work to the end that our graduates will improve the quality of their leadership in their respective communities. . . .We should strive to produce men superior in poise, social imagination, integrity, resourcefulness, and superior in possessing an all-embracing love for all peoples irrespective of race or color." The Negro should see, he also has said, that "his sufferings and his ills are fragmentary parts of the sufferings of all peoples in history from the dawn of man up to the present." He has lectured in some seventy colleges in the past few years. Notable among these addresses was his "The Crisis in Race Relations: Which Way for the Church and Democracy?" at Vassar in September 1944.

Mays's many writings include articles in such publications as the *Crisis, Christian Century, Journal of Negro Education* (of which he is a contributing editor), *Missions,* and *Woman's Press.* He has also contributed book reviews to various magazines, and 1938 saw the publication of his second book, *The Negro's God.* This volume traces the development of the idea of God in Negro literature from 1760 to 1937. Delving into the history of the Negro in America, the author examines the literary expression of the Negro's conception of God from its early roots in slavery to the modern atheistic tendencies. All theses are illustrated by excerpts from original sources. Mays discusses the literature of the Negro masses as seen in spirituals, sermons, and prayers, proceeding further to an analysis of classical Negro literature. In the latter category the writer includes the early poets and the work of Booker T. Washington. Developing his theme, Mays reviews the work of leading modern Negro writers, including W. E. B. Du Bois '40, Claude McKay, James Weldon Johnson, Countee Cullen, and Langston Hughes '40. Summarizing his subject in historical perspective, Mays declares: "The Negro's firm faith in God has saved him, up to this point, from violent revolutionary methods of achieving his rights. His faith in God has not only served as an opiate for the Negro, but it has suggested and indicated that pacific and legal methods are to be used in achieving them. It is not too much to say that unless liberal prophetic religion moves more progressively to the Left in the effort to achieve complete citizenship rights for the Negro, he will become

more irreligious and he will become more militant and communistic in his efforts to attain full manhood in American life."

Mays devoted himself to the struggle for interracial understanding early in his career. In March 1931 the *Christian Century* published his article "Realities in Race Relations," called a frank and objective discussion of the complex problem. He emphasized the need for white and Negro people together to face the issues sincerely and honestly, thus gradually eliminating the barrier of distrust between them. He cited as progressive steps toward interracial improvement the development of genuine student friendships on a Christian basis, the awakening of the public mind, and the creation of a public opinion against mob violence and anti-Negro political campaigning. However, on the debit side remains the concrete fact of the injustice and discrimination in the administration of public funds for the Negro in education, recreation, health, dependency, delinquency. In addition, economic and cultural conflicts exist; especially obvious is the competition for jobs. Mays further pointed out that the Negro resents "patronage, paternalism, and condescension" on the part of the white man. Patience and tolerance are essential to good relations between the two groups, he declared.

Mays discussed another aspect of the same theme in an article entitled "The American Negro and the Christian Religion," published in the July 1939 *Journal of Negro Education.* Examining the Negro within the framework of Christianity, he found him discriminated against in every area of American life, a policy, he states, that is sanctioned for the most part by religious groups and administered by so-called "Christians." However, Mays stressed the valuable charitable contributions of Christian groups on behalf of the Negro in the educational field. Emphasizing the need for a crusade to abolish all dualism in American society, he called for a strong Christian endeavor for the realization of Christian ideals in race relations. In another article in the same publication for July 1940, he wrote on the topic "The Religious Life and Needs of Negro Students." In this lengthy analysis, statistically annotated, Mays stated that "the Negro church is the most completely owned institution" of the Negro race. Again on the subject of the Negro church, Mays's article in the 1940 Summer number of *Christendom* discussed its origin, development, and problems. The Negro church has played a significant role in American life, "keeping one-tenth of America's population sanely religious in the midst of an environment that is, for the most part, hostile to it."

In July 1942 the *Journal of Negro Education* carried Mays's discussion of "The Role of the Negro Liberal Arts College in Post-War Reconstruction," in which the special problems of the Negro student were given attention. Mays also considered the issue of the Negro soldier, fighting for democracy on foreign battlefields, only to return home to be denied the rights of democracy. Enlarging on Lincoln's view, Mays declared: "If years ago this country could not exist half slave and half free, it cannot continue to exist now half democratic and half totalitarian." The keystone of the college president's policies can be seen in his article in the *Christian Century,* called "Negroes and the

Will to Justice" (October 28, 1942). Here he declared, "Truth is seldom, if ever, found in extremes." He advocated the peaceful, sane road to justice for the Negro, aware, however, that "social changes come slowly and deepseated prejudices die hard even when civilization hangs in the balance." Contending that certain steps can be taken now "within the present structure of society" to promote interracial adjustment and democracy, Mays outlined a brief program: (1) Give the Negro equal opportunity to earn a living; (2) abolish all devices which deprive him of the right to vote; (3) give the Negro equal opportunity in education; (4) improve his health conditions; and (5) give him justice in the courts. These measures, for which all legal bases already exist, can be accomplished through the concerted efforts of the nation's officials, editors, teachers, and labor leaders, Mays believes. According to *Time,* he is a "firm believer in education and patience as cures for racial discrimination."

In December 1944 Mays was elected vicepresident of the Federal Council of the Churches of Christ in America, the first member of his race to hold that office; he will serve with Bishop G. Bromley Oxnam '44. The distinguished educator belongs to several organizations, including the Commission on Interracial Cooperation, the Southern Regional Council, the Commission on Basis of a Just and Durable Peace, and the Commission on Christian Strategy for Post-War Planning. Mays is a member of Phi Beta Kappa, and of three fraternities, Delta Sigma Rho, Delta Theta Chi, and Omega Psi Phi; and he is also a member of the national board of the YMCA. A well known lecturer, he is frequently called to speak before Southern white audiences, as well as Negroes, and he has lectured at more than eighty colleges in the United States. In a New York interview in December 1944 Mays called education the Negro's "number one problem," followed closely by suffrage restrictions, especially the "white primary." He added that the racial policies of the South, determined by the minority ruling class, will never be reformed by the South alone. Mays was in 1944 named on the Schomburg Honor Roll of Race Relations as one of twelve Negroes who have done outstanding work in building better race relations in America.

Mays is a handsome, dignified figure, nearly six feet tall and weighing one hundred and sixty-three pounds. A quiet, earnest man, this Baptist minister is so tolerant that it is said he has never thought of proselytizing his Methodist wife. The Negro leader has stated that his belief in man, based on Christian faith, governs his behavior, and his own life, he says, has been enriched by the friendships of people of many nations and religions.

References

N Y Herald Tribune p29 D 17 '44
Religious Leaders of America, 1941-42
Who's Who in America, 1944-45
Who's Who in American Education, 1941-42
Who's Who in Colored America, 1941-44

MEITNER, LISE (mīt′nĕr lē′zĕ) Nov. 7, 1878- Austrian physicist
Address: b. c/o Nobel Institute, Stockholm

When the dream of utilizing atomic energy was finally realized with the release of the atomic bomb in the summer of 1945, public attention was focused on several scientists whose long years of research had brought civilization to the threshhold of the Atomic Age. Among those internationally recognized pioneers in science is Lise Meitner, Austrian physicist and mathematician. Her research in atomic physics, especially her work in uranium fission, played a significant part in the development of the greatest scientific achievement in centuries.

A Viennese, Lise Meitner was born on November 7, 1878, the daughter of a lawyer and one of a family of seven children. She began her science studies in Vienna, where she became interested in atomic physics during her first year of work, and as an aspiring scientist she was fascinated by the newspaper accounts of the discovery of radium by Pierre and Marie Curie in 1902. In 1908 her advanced studies brought her to Berlin, where she studied theory with the renowned German physicist, Dr. Max Planck. (Planck originated the quantum theory and won the Nobel Prize for physics in 1918.) At this time she also began her experimental work with Dr. Otto Hahn which gave her the opportunity to study further the radioactivity of the atom.

Dr. Meitner became assistant to Planck at the University of Berlin, in which capacity she served for three years, at the same time continuing her work with Hahn. While Germany was at war, in 1917, she was charged with the organization of a department of physical radioactivity at Berlin's famous Kaiser Wilhelm Institute. There, as a professor and leading member of the institute, Dr. Meitner's research facilities were much enlarged by the addition of a staff of assistants and students, and she was able to concentrate on the study of the natural and artificial transmutation of the elements.

In Berlin, the center of scientific research, Dr. Meitner studied the developments in the field of atomic physics while conducting experiments with Hahn and with Dr. Fritz Strassmann. She won a distinguished reputation for her work on the products of the disintegration of radium, thorium, and actinium, on the behavior of the beta rays, and on the physics of the atomic nucleus. In 1918, together with Hahn, she discovered protoactinium, a radioactive element which, by disintegration, yields actinium.

In 1938 the three scientists, Meitner, Hahn, and Strassmann, announced the creation of a trans-uranium element (heavier than uranium), produced by bombardment of uranium with neutrons. Meitner and Hahn were repeating the experiment of Enrico Fermi, also a Nobel prize-winner, to liberate the energy within the nucleus of the atom. For this work the two scientists at the Kaiser Wilhelm Institute had devised an "atomic microscope", a very delicate instrument, for the observation of chemical action. Firing slow-speed neutrons (electrically neutral particles) at the uranium nucleus, they were startled to observe the appearance of barium, an element which had not been present

LISE MEITNER

at the beginning of the experiment. Before the mystery of the barium was solved, Dr. Meitner, who is a Jewess, left Germany. (According to a report in the New York *Sun,* she had been dismissed from her teaching post at the University of Berlin in 1933.) A confirmed anti-Fascist, the scientist chose to leave the country, although the Nazis were willing to overlook their anti-Semitic laws to compel her to remain in the Reich to continue her work. She escaped with the assistance of Dutch colleagues who had obtained permission for her to enter Holland without a visa, since her Austrian passport had become invalid. Thus, in 1938, traveling via Holland and Denmark, Dr. Meitner arrived in Sweden.

By the time Dr. Meitner had reached Stockholm she had solved mathematically the supposed barium mystery, and she made known her findings in a report for a scientific journal. (In an article for the Overseas News Agency in August 1945 she wrote that her report was actually an interpretation of an experiment done by Hahn and Strassmann in connection with experiments made before she had left Germany.) Her report revealed that the unexplained appearance of barium indicated the fission of the uranium atom, one part being the barium, the other krypton. This was an astounding discovery. Although scientists in the past had succeeded in chipping off small pieces of the atom, none had split it into halves. According to her interpretation, the uranium atom, the heaviest of the elements, having an atomic weight of 92, was split into two nearly equal parts—barium (56) and krypton (36). She calculated that the atomic energy released by thus splitting it amounted to two hundred million electron volts per atom. William L. Laurence, in an article describing Dr. Meitner's work (*Saturday Evening Post,* September 7, 1940), wrote, "She was experiencing sensations that must have been akin to those of Columbus. . . .She and Dr. Hahn had accidently stumbled upon one of the greatest discoveries of the age. They had come upon the

trail of what might lead to the shores of the Promised Land of Atomic Energy."

Through the efforts of Dr. Otto R. Frisch, Dr. Meitner's nephew, the results of the experiment were transmitted to Dr. Niels Bohr [45] in America in January 1939, and he immediately made known the information to the scientific world. In releasing the report, Dr. Meitner and her co-workers had had no thought of the destructive use to which their discovery would be put, but both Germany and the Allies saw the possibility of utilizing it for military purposes. In the United States the production of an atom bomb became a project of the War Department, under the direction of General Leslie R. Groves [45], while in Germany scientists worked feverishly at the problem—until the Allies won both the military and the scientific race.

The news that the Allies had dropped an atomic bomb on the Japanese city of Hiroshima on August 5, 1945, came altogether as a surprise to the physicist as she rested at a summer hotel in Dalarne province in central Sweden. Thrust suddenly into the world spotlight, she was reluctant to discuss her part in the development and a few weeks later released only a modest description of her work through the Overseas News Agency. The American press carried glowing tributes to Dr. Meitner, pointing out that the Nazis had deprived themselves of her work. In a New York *Times* article Harry M. Davis declared, "Generations millenniums hence may look back upon these years when atomic energy was first put to work in the same spirit in which we now think of the less well-documented occasion when man first learned the use of fire."

Speaking from Leksand in Sweden, Dr. Meitner participated in a joint NBC transatlantic broadcast with Eleanor Roosevelt [40] on August 9. Mrs. Roosevelt congratulated the scientist and compared her to the great Marie Curie, adding the wish that Dr. Meitner might some day visit America as did the Polish physicist. (She has been invited to join the faculty of the Catholic University of America in Washington in February 1946 as a visiting professor and to lecture in the physics department.) Expressing her hopes for world cooperation and peaceful use of science's tremendous discovery, Dr. Meitner stated, "Women have a great responsibility and they are obliged to try, so far as they can, to prevent another war. I hope that the construction of the atom bomb not only will help to finish this awful war but that we will be able, too, to use this great energy that has been released for peaceful work." On the question of use of the discovery, she has said, "I think it should be controlled very carefully, internationally."

The scientist was active on the political front, working with the Democratic Austrian Society, an organization which resisted Nazism during the war. She declared that she had no intention of returning to Germany. In Sweden she has been associated since 1938 with the Nobel Institute in Stockholm. Dr. Meitner was elected a foreign member of the Swedish Academy of Science in October 1945. The honor has been conferred on only two other women in the two hundred years of the academy's existence—a Swedish woman, elected in 1748, and Mme.

Curie, elected in 1910. In addition, Dr. Lise Meitner lectures at universities and clubs. She has continued her work on uranium fission at the Research Institute for Physics and plans to carry on her work with Professor Karl Manne Siegbahn of the Academy of Science. The March 16, 1940, issue of *Nature* carried her report on her work on the "capture cross-sections for thermal neutrons in thorium, lead, and uranium 238." Dr. Meitner contributes to scientific journals and is the author of various works, including *Beiträge zur Physik der Atomkerne* (1926), *Der Aufbau der Atomkerne* (1935, with Max Delbrück), and a study "on the products of the fission of uranium and thorium under neutron bombardment" (1940, with Frisch).

Scientist Lise Meitner is described as a small, dignified woman with a quiet voice and rather a shy manner. When speaking to people she will at times "employ a friendly sympathetic smile that begins quickly about the mouth and fades slowly and reluctantly from her brown eyes." She resides with a sister in Stockholm, while two other sisters live in the United States, in New York and Washington.

References

N Y Herald Tribune p6 Ag 12 '45
N Y Post p28+ Ag 22 '45 por
N Y Sun p5 Ag 6 '45

MELCHER, FREDERIC G(ERSHOM) Apr. 12, 1879- Magazine publisher, editor; author

Address: b. Publishers' Weekly, 62 W. 45th St., New York City; h. Montclair, N.J.

"Zeal is an old-fashioned word," wrote Christopher Morley in a tribute to Frederic G. Melcher, editor of *Publishers' Weekly* and president of the publishing house of R. R. Bowker Company, "but I can't think of anyone more zealous than Fred Melcher. The number of books, schemes, ideas, transactions, ceremonies, speeches, promotions, dinners, awards, conferences, editorials, articles, that have passed through his mind, leaving, apparently, no trace of erosion or corrugations on his brow, staggers me to contemplate, even with only one finger on the keyboard of my typewriter." The occasion for Morley's words was the celebration of the fiftieth anniversary of the publisher-editor's entrance into the book trade. And to that encomium Mildred C. Smith added that Fred Melcher "has made the *Publishers' Weekly* an exciting place to work; he has made publishing, bookselling, librarianship, work with children's books and with the graphic arts seem a more exciting occupation in all the fifty years in which he has been connected with them."

Books are among Frederic Gershom Melcher's earliest memories. Born in Malden, Massachusetts, six miles from Boston, on April 12, 1879, he is the son of Edwin Forrest and Alice Jane (Bartlett) Melcher. The Bartletts were Bostonians, the Melchers New Hampshiremen. When Fred was four his family moved to a lakeside house at Newton Center, about fourteen miles away. From Melcher's reminiscences, his youth must have been extremely happy, for he writes, "A lake shore is a fine place to grow up, for there is,

Bachrach

FREDERIC G. MELCHER

of course, swimming, boating, fishing and skating, with the pleasant industry of ice-cutting going on near-by"; he tells, too, that he "had the good luck to grow up in a congenial crowd of twenty or thirty resourceful young people." "As we grew beyond the little home parties of childhood, we had our dances, husking bees, sleighing parties, and canoeing trips." A "busy reader of almost anything that came to hand," the boy read five weekly and three monthly magazines, as well as all the books he could find. At the Mason Public School he skipped one grade and took two others at once ("they must have been getting a little crowded"), thus enabling him to catch up to his sister, Mabel, and older cousin. Fred entered the Newton High School at twelve (he was exempted from military drill because he was too small to handle a gun) and took a course intended to prepare boys for the Massachusetts Institute of Technology. At school he was more attracted to literature than to chemistry or mathematics; but the "Institute Course" did not include enough Latin and Greek to satisfy college entrance requirements, and sixteen-year-old Fred Melcher decided to go to work instead of studying further.

"Jobs were as scarce after the panic of 1893 as they were to be forty years later," but his grandfather found Fred a position with one of his tenants, the Boston booksellers Estes and Lauriat. The tall, gangling boy was hired at the "going rate" of four dollars for a six-day week, and he began to work as soon as his school closed for the summer in 1895. Young Melcher first worked in the mailing room, where he is recalled as "alert, inclined to seriousness, and not unduly given to skylarking with other boys." Next he was promoted to the receiving department, where he opened bundles and cases for two years; then he was assigned to handle library orders. (On occasion, too, Melcher carried a spear as supernumerary in "many a grand opera of the

MELCHER, FREDERIC G.—*Continued*

de Reszke and Nordica days" around the turn of the century.) In Boston young Melcher came under the influence of the famous printer Daniel Berkeley Updike, who first aroused his enthusiasm for beautiful books and his appreciation of the craftsmanship of bookmaking.

By 1906 Frederic Melcher was a popular salesman with a large personal following: he "studied to know his customers as he knew his books, and he matched one to the other with an almost incredible accuracy." He took time also to study book classification, stock arrangement, and store routine, and to suggest improvements; as assistant to the Lauriat buyer, he persuaded that conservative gentleman to accept new ideas. In 1908, when publisher George H. Doran had written off Arnold Bennett's *The Old Wives' Tale* as a failure, Melcher read a laudatory British review and so thoroughly impressed his clientele with the book's value that he sold five hundred copies in two weeks. (The total sale up to that point had been three hundred and fifty copies.) Doran calls Melcher "the first among bookmen the world over to discover the essential potential classic quality of Arnold Bennett's *The Old Wives' Tale.*" When the Boston Booksellers' League was organized he was an active member, as well as of the American Booksellers Association, and he attracted considerable attention by maintaining that, while the book buying problems under discussion were of importance, "we should go forth . . . chiefly resolved to concentrate on book*selling.*" A year later, in 1912, Melcher became the Boston Booksellers' League president.

In 1913 W. Kerfoot Stewart asked Melcher to manage his Indianapolis bookstore. The thirty-three-year-old bookman moved to Indiana that March with his wife, the former Marguerite Fellows, whom he had married in 1910, and their son Daniel. (Melcher's two other children are named Nancy and Charity.) Three weeks later came the "Dayton flood." The next January (1914) the bookstore was destroyed by fire, but within three days Melcher had found temporary quarters, acquired a new stock, and had opened for business. The store prospered under his direction, and was patronized largely by artists and writers. "Everyone who has lived in Indianapolis in the second decade of this century and who bought books owes a debt of gratitude to Frederic Melcher," writes Booth Tarkington. Others who often dropped into the bookshop were Vachel Lindsay, Albert Beveridge, George Ade, and James Whitcomb Riley, while Melcher often discussed the making of fine books with the great printer, Edwin Grabhorn. A member of the Indianapolis Literary Club, and the Portfolio Club of artists, musicians, writers, and assorted literati, Melcher is remembered for "the breadth of his knowledge and the delightful energy of his participation in whatever topic came up for discussion." A lay reader at a Unitarian church, the New Englander led the church children in carols each year, and he "could make them sing like all get-out." Melcher also took an interest in librarianship, beginning "those inspiring talks to library

groups which have been one of his greatest contributions to the book world." When the First World War came, he started two branch stores at Fort Benjamin Harrison, and these, too, prospered.

According to Harry Hansen [42] of the New York *World-Telegram*, while in Indianapolis Melcher wrote to the *Publishers' Weekly* in praise of Robert Frost's book of poems, *North of Boston*. This won him the gratitude of Frost's publisher, Alfred Harcourt, the firm friendship of the poet, and the attention of the magazine. In 1918 Melcher went East to New York to become coeditor of the *Weekly*. (He is now president of the R. R. Bowker publishing company, which puts out *Publishers' Weekly* and the *Library Journal*.) The next year the new editor recognized the importance of the making of books by giving that subject a full column, which grew into a critical department, *Book Clinic,* seven years later.

Children's Book Week, which he and Franklin K. Mathiews, the Boy Scouts' chief librarian, evolved in 1919, is now observed annually from coast to coast by librarians, bookshops, and schools, and its influence is spreading to other countries. In 1920 Melcher began to devote special issues of *Publishers' Weekly* entirely to juvenile literature; he is credited with a share in persuading the Macmillan Company and Doubleday, Doran and Company to set up departments for publishing such books; and in 1921 he established the Newbery Medal, given annually for the most distinguished contribution to American literature for children. It is named for the first seller of juvenile books in English, and was first awarded to Hendrik Willem van Loon's *Story of Mankind*. In 1937, Melcher also established the annual Caldecott Medal (named for the nineteenth-century illustrator) for the most distinguished American picture book for children; the first award went to Dorothy Lathrop's *Animals of the Bible*. Selections are made by the Children's Librarians Section of the American Library Association.

Melcher's years of editorship are summed up by Hansen: "The possibilities of making books better, more useful, more widely distributed, more fairly sold, were always on the editor's mind. He neglected nothing. Religious books, technical books, war books—all had his attention, and his comment led the special issues. He supported all progressive measures, whether copyright law revision or fair trade practices. He gave librarians a voice in his journal and endorsed attempts to interest new groups, advocating the extension of libraries in secondary schools and even challenging architects to serve culture—and the book trade—by building bookcases in new houses. There is no phase of publishing that has not received its just attention in the *Publishers' Weekly*. And all this comment came from a man who put on his hat and coat and left the office to keep himself informed. There were many hours of legwork, of rides on trains, of patient meetings with long-winded committees behind these editorials."

In his first year in New York Melcher became secretary of the American Booksellers Association, and is now an honorary fellow. He served as head of the copyright committee of the National Associaton of Book Publishers, and later the Book Publishers Bureau, and helped to draft the NRA code. From 1920 to 1924 he was executive secretary of the National Association of Book Publishers; in 1924-25 he was president of the New York Booksellers' League; two years later he became president of the American Institute of Graphic Arts; and in 1935-36 he served as president of the New York Library Association. Melcher's other memberships are in the P.E.N. Club, Authors' League of America, American Antiquarian Society, Grolier Club, Bibliographical Society of America, American Library Association, American Library Institute, and the National Council of the Boy Scouts of America. It has been said that "wherever there were committees, there you were sure to find Fred Melcher working." He has endowed a number of awards in the book field, and attended International Congresses of Publishers in Paris and London. In the summers of 1927, 1928, and 1932 he gave a course at the Library School of Columbia University on practical aspects of bookselling, and he has delivered many other lectures, especially to librarians.

It was Melcher who initiated the quadrennial A. B. A. gift of two hundred books to the White House Library. (Having discovered that there were "practically no books" there, the Association in 1929 had presented the White House with the five hundred basic books with which a good private library should begin.) Melcher, again chairman of the selection committee in 1945, reported that the year's fiction list would be very thin and that history, current affairs, and biography would furnish most of the titles. He "rounded up" the National Council on Books in Wartime in June 1942, and, in the opinion of War Production Board chairman J. A. Krug '44, his complete cooperation and wide following have made his editorials "of inestimable value . . . in creating a better understanding of, and cooperation with, those of our [WPB] programs entailing a reduction in use of the materials consumed by the book industry and in critically short supply." In March 1937 the *Atlantic Monthly* had identified him as, "for close to twenty years . . . the best-trusted referee in American publishing." In the days between the two World Wars, when the Leipzig Book Fair and other international meetings of publishers were instruments of good will and understanding, Melcher represented the American publishers at Leipzig and at the International Congress of Publishers in Paris in 1931 and in 1936 in London. In June 1945 he again went to London, this time for six weeks, at the invitation of the new National Book League of England, founded in 1944 with John Masefield as its first president. The trip was sponsored by the OWI.

In May 1945, his fiftieth year in the book trade, Melcher was given a testimonial dinner by its leading members. Guests were presented with a small book, *Frederic G. Melcher: Friendly Reminiscences of a Half Century Among Books and Bookmen,* published by the Book Publishers' Bureau for the occasion. Chapters in the book are by the reviewer Harry Hansen, the rare-book seller Charles Goodspeed, the librarian Harry M. Lydenberg '41 and seven other authors. One of them, Marion E. Dodd, more or less

summed up the tribute of the others when she wrote that Melcher "now stands as number one liaison man to all the branches of the book world. His specific knowledge of publishing, of the graphic arts, of the problems of libraries, and of the distribution of the printed word by booksellers has rolled up into great authority . . . . Whatever he has done, wherever he has been down through these fifty years, Fred Melcher is first and foremost a creative bookseller, a master in the art of the distribution of books." The same month the bookman was awarded the Gold Medal of the American Institute of Graphic Arts. At the mid-winter meeting of its Council in Chicago, Melcher was elected an honorary member of the American Library Association. This rarely-bestowed distinction was held in 1945 by six persons who, the association felt, had given especial service to the cause of books and reading.

Lean, bespectacled Melcher was once described as "informal as his red tie, direct, cheerful, optimistic, interested . . . unhurried and unobtrusive in manner . . . a quiet-spoken, friendly man who had the beginnings of a smile curling at the corners of his mouth when he talked. . . . I have never known a man to be so well informed, so ready to lend what help he could and make so little fuss in doing it." His home, an old New Jersey farmhouse around which the town of Montclair has grown up, "has abounded with the Melchers, their children, dogs, friends, bridge tables, and books these many years, notably the friends and books." He enjoys swimming, skating, sailing, and all the work entailed in serving huge beach suppers at his summer place on Cape Cod. Melcher's particular treasure is his collection of beautiful books, especially Pickerings and some Grabhorn editions. His test for a well-made book is simple: "It *feels* right and you feel right about it." Himself a Unitarian, Melcher feels, as he said in one of his editorials, that "no one can be satisfied with the world as we have built it. No one nation, race, or religion can have by itself the complete solution of the problems ahead. . . . There is need to resolve that all denominations work together. There is need not only for solidarity on military and political fronts, but also on the fronts which face the big problems of life."

References

Library J 70:507-9 Je 1 '45
Frederic G. Melcher; Friendly Reminiscences of a Half Century Among Books and Bookmen (1945)
Who's Who in America, 1944-45

MELTON, JAMES Jan. 2, 1904- Singer
Address: c/o Evans and Salter, 113 W. 57th St., New York City; h. Westport, Conn.

The popular artist of radio, concert, and opera, American tenor James Melton, was born in Moultrie, Georgia, on January 2, 1904. Both his parents were amateur musicians: His father, James Wilburn Melton, a lumberman, was a singer and a musician in the Moultrie band; his mother, Rose (Thornton) Melton, was an organist. Soon after James's birth the family

JAMES MELTON

moved to Citra in northern Florida, where the elder Melton owned and operated several large lumber mills. As he grew up, it was young James's delight to do some of the company's errands in his father's car, driving even at the early age of twelve; for then, as now, he loved automobiles. One of the most enjoyable of the assignments he was given was to pick up the Negro millhands in town to drive them out through the woods to the mill, and it was from these workers that he learned many of the spirituals he now sings.

Upon graduation from high school in 1920 Melton entered the University of Florida to prepare for a career in law. To pay his expenses, he sang with the college band and led a dance orchestra which he had organized. It was these musical activities rather than his work in the prelaw courses which brought Melton to the attention of the university's president, Albert A. Murphree, who, discerning the latent talent of the young student, helped him to revise his plan of study to further his potentialities and personally guided his development during the two years he remained at the university. After his sophomore year Melton left Florida to attend the University of Georgia, where he studied for a year, earning his living expenses meanwhile by playing the saxophone in the college band. In 1923 he entered Vanderbilt University in Nashville, Tennessee, and began grand opera studies with Gaetano de Luca.

After leaving Vanderbilt University in 1924, Melton continued to study with De Luca in Nashville, having been assisted by three businessmen friends who lent him the necessary funds. (The money he later paid back, with interest, in one year's time.) Then, when he arrived in New York in 1927 the Southerner besieged "Roxy" Rothafel for an audition, singing outside the manager's door, it is said. Melton's approach was successful, and so was the audition: Rothafel hired him as a member of his Roxy Gang, the well known group of

entertainers who gave frequent performances over the Columbia Broadcasting System. This work brought him an engagement with the Revelers Quartet, "an outstanding radio quartet and one of the earliest groups of 'precision' singers."

Since that time Melton has become one of the most popular singers on the radio: From 1928 to 1931 he sang on the *Seiberling Singers* program; in 1933, the *Voice of Firestone*; in 1935, *Ward's Family Theater*; in 1936, *Sealtest Sunday Night Party*; in 1937, *Palmolive Beauty Box Theater*; in 1938, the *Song Shop*; in 1940, the *Telephone Hour*. Of one of Melton's performances on the *Telephone Hour*, *Etude* wrote: "James Melton has not sung better at any time during his radio musical career than in the Telephone shows." In July 1944 the tenor took over Fred Allen's [41] show *Star Theater* as the summer replacement. When the comedian decided not to return to radio in the fall, Melton then became the full-time star of the program. Jack Gould of the New York *Times* has since praised Melton for "turning in a fine job. . . .Being the presiding officer [of the musical program], Mr. Melton naturally stands out, as well as he might. His lyric tenor encompasses both the operatic and popular with complete aplomb and, as with others who have had to make themselves heard in the balcony, he really sings, leaving to crooners et al. the substitution of a mike's amplifying qualities for vocal versatility." Another reviewer wrote that Melton in his radio role of star and master of ceremonies of *Star Theater* "manages to provide a pleasing and well-balanced musical fare." In August 1944 Melton was rated in sixth place in the Hooper poll of radio popularity. (He is also a recording favorite.)

Radio was, however, only the first field in which he was to become an established star. His voice teacher, Enrico Rosati, he says, soon opened his eyes to his bigger vocal possibilities. In 1932, therefore, Melton made his concert debut with a recital in New York's Town Hall, and favorable reviews encouraged him to continue with concert work. His first tour was with George Gershwin in 1934. In the succeeding years he built up a repertoire of more than twenty-two hundred selections—arias, *Lieder,* folk songs and traditional melodies, Negro spirituals, modern songs, ballads, and light operatic numbers. The tenor believes that a concert program "can be built with a solid foundation, but every number, whether it is a classic or an English or American song, should be on the program for one purpose; it should have audience appeal and entertain."

After his concert debut Melton in 1936 decided to pursue his earliest singing ambition— opera. The singer explains: "I knew that if I applied myself, the roles could be learned, together with stage technique." He bought a dozen scores and chose as his first opera for study *Madame Butterfly*. After two years of intensive study, in 1938 the tenor made his operatic debut as Lieutenant Pinkerton at the Zoo Opera in Cincinnati, and three months later he repeated this performance with the San Carlo company at the Center Theatre in New York. The New York *Times* reviewer wrote that Melton's "steady tones had all the needed volume for the part and were projected with convincing eloquence and ardor in an interpretation that was natural, sincere and convincing." His second operatic role was that of Alfredo in Verdi's *La Traviata,* which he played in the fall of 1938 with the St. Louis Opera Company. He was awarded a contract with the Chicago Civic Opera Company that same year, and was soon singing opposite such divas as Licia Albanese in *Madame Butterfly,* Josephine Antoine '44 in *Martha,* and Lily Pons '44 in *Lucia di Lammermoor.*

Until 1942 Melton divided his time between radio work and operatic performances with the St. Louis, Cincinnati, and Chicago opera companies. Then in September 1942 he auditioned for New York's Metropolitan Opera Company, singing arias from *Don Giovanni* and *Lucia di Lammermoor* for conductor Bruno Walter '42. "I would like to hear you in *The Magic Flute,*" said Walter, and Melton set about learning the role of Tamino for his second audition. He committed it to memory within five days, and after this second audition won a contract. Three weeks later he made his debut on the Metropolitan Opera House stage, singing his audition role. According to Henry Simon, writing in *PM,* "Melton has a clean way of turning a phrase that most critics would call far more genuinely Mozartean than some of the Puccini-Mozart we get from older hands at the business. His voice is light, a little hard, but well placed, and he uses his six feet of good looks with grace and conviction. . . .His debut made him sound like a thoroughly useful acquisition for the lighter tenor roles and for disillusioning that part of the public which imagines a career in popular music and an engaging, thoroughly American personality disqualify one for the Metropolitan."

Melton's association with the Metropolitan has been described on the whole as "a most valuable addition to the roster of international singers." During the 1944-45 opera season his appearance as Tamino was described by Jerome D. Bohm of the *Herald Tribune* as "Melton's best role, although his agreeable voice would sound still better if less openly projected. His enunciation of the English words, however, might easily serve as a model for the rest of the cast." Olin Downes '43 of the New York *Times* lauded his "fresh and youthful voice, his intelligence and sincerity in whatever he did." Some reviewers liked the singer's portrayal of Wilhelm Meister in *Mignon,* although the *Herald Tribune*'s critic complained, "Mr. Melton is never very happy with Wilhelm Meister's music, and . . . his singing, aside from its customary 'whiteness,' was taut and thin in the upper reaches."

During a performance, an interviewer reports, Melton drinks one pint of pineapple juice, "for energy." Through his years of experience in studying opera, the singer finds that it is best to learn the score of the last act first, since, he says, "Quite often singers learn the first act of an opera with a fresh, inspired feeling . . . but are sometimes apt to slight the last act." In speaking of the libretto, Melton says, "[It] is much more difficult for me to learn than the music, and since we often hear operatic recitatives performed uninterestingly,

I learn them in strict rhythm, and exactly as they are written, but during the performance I try to expand them and make out of them a real, interesting conversation."

During March and April 1945 Melton toured the United States and Canada, and in June he made an appearance as soloist with the New York Philharmonic-Symphony Orchestra at Lewisohn Stadium, New York. Noel Straus, reviewing the performance for the New York *Times,* said, "Mr. Melton displayed his usual musicianship in all of his selections, adhering strictly to true pitch. But his tones were pushed and often quavering, as a result of attempting to give them more than their inherent amount of volume." According to the critic of the New York *Sun,* "Mr. Melton, though often tight, pleased many of the five thousand listeners with his appealing native vocal gifts." Then featured on the screen in the all-star musical revue, *Ziegfeld Follies,* Melton was scheduled to appear in the leading role of a musical version of Edna Ferber's *Cimarron,* which was first produced in 1931 with Irene Dunne '45. Earlier, in the thirties, Melton appeared in *Sing Me a Love Song* and *Melody for Two,* both released in 1937.

James Melton is described as "handsome, genial, and easygoing, boyish and brown-eyed", "a good-looking six-foot-two with a pug nose, an ear-to-ear grin, and a cavernous laugh." The singer likes to hunt, and he collects pewter and old glass, but he is best known for his collection of ancient automobiles. Since 1935 he has accumulated about eighty cars, which date back to 1893. A good mechanic, he keeps all the motors in running condition, and during the wartime gasoline shortage he used to drive to New York from his Westport, Connecticut, home in "a little ole 'lectric" or a Stanley Steamer. A prize item is a 1900 Rockwell hansom cab, which is said to be the first taxi used in New York; another is Diamond Jim Brady's 1908 Fiat, with sterling silver fittings. Melton wears on his lapel a diamond miniature, formerly owned by Brady, of another of the financier's cars, a 1906 ("#16") Locomobile which once won a Vanderbilt Cup race. Melton's Rockwell, incidentally, was entered in a benefit race against a horse and buggy in 1943, and lost. The state of Connecticut, proud of being the location for what is claimed to be the largest collection of old automobiles in the world, has appropriated a hundred and fifty thousand dollars to build a museum for them at Stamford. Melton is vice-president of the Veteran Motor Car Club of America.

Melton frequently assists young singers. Two of his protégés are Lawrence Brooks, star of the 1945 operetta *Song of Norway,* and a crippled Negro tenor, Pruth McFarlin, who, Melton says, has "one of the greatest voices" he has ever heard. Since June 1929 Melton has been married to Marjorie Louise McClure, daughter of Marjorie Barkley McClure, novelist. The singer is a member of the Delta Tau Delta fraternity and the New York Athletic and Fairfield County Hunt clubs. In speaking of success, he says, "My real happiness comes from the fact that I have solved many of life's problems by learning how to work."

(Continued next page)

MELTON, JAMES—*Continued*

References

Etude 61:12+ Ja '43 por
N Y Times II p5 Je 17 '45
Opera News 7:10-12 D 7 '42 por
Ewen, D. ed Living Musicians (1940)
Who's Who in America, 1944-45

MENNINGER, WILLIAM CLAIRE
(měn'ĭng-ẽr) Oct. 15, 1899- United States
Army officer; psychiatrist

Address: b. c/o Surgeon General's Office, 1818
H St., N.W., Washington, D.C.; h. 2260
Cathedral Ave., N. W. Washington, D. C.

U.S. Army Medical Museum

BRIG. GEN. WILLIAM CLAIRE MENNINGER

Because of the large number of neuropsychiatric casualties in the United States Army (43
per cent of all medical discharges), Surgeon
General Norman T. Kirk '44 placed psychiatry
on an equal footing with medicine and surgery,
and in December 1943 appointed Brigadier
General (then Colonel) William Claire Menninger as director of the Neuropsychiatry Consultants Division in the Office of the Surgeon
General. Co-founder of the Menninger Clinic
in Topeka, Kansas, Menninger has long
been regarded as one of the country's foremost psychiatrists. His management of the
Army's neuropsychiatry division not only has
won him the first annual Albert and Mary
Lasker Award in 1944 for "outstanding service
in the field of mental hygiene," but has done
much toward the settlement of "the forty-year
feud between old-time psychiatrists and the
'upstart' psychoanalysts who follow, with varying degrees of fidelity, the theories of the old
master, Sigmund Freud."

On both sides of his family William Claire
Menninger is of German-American stock. His
father, Charles Frederick Menninger, was a
teacher at Campbell University, a pioneer college in Holton, Kansas, until five years after
his (the father's) marriage, when he resigned
to study medicine. His mother, Flo V. (Knise-
ly) Menninger, of Pennsylvania Dutch origin,
worked as a hired girl in order to put herself
through Campbell, where she met and was married to Professor Menninger. After her marriage she taught school, too, and although her
husband later became a successful Topeka physician, she continued to teach until before the
birth of her third son, William Claire, on
October 15, 1899. The story of those years,
the couple's early financial struggles and later
prosperity, she has recounted in her book, *Days
of My Life* (1940).

With his two elder brothers, Karl Augustus
and Edwin, Claire, as his mother calls him,
had an unusually healthy and happy childhood.
There was a clubroom for the boys and their
friends on the lower floor of the large house
the Menningers occupied in Topeka. There
were evenings of singing together around the
piano, and a string orchestra in which Karl
played the piano, Edwin the violin, and Claire
the cello. They were the first family in Kansas to have a sleeping porch, the first to grow
peonies, and the first to hold a meeting of Boy
Scouts. This third "first" had come about
shortly after the organization of the Boy Scouts
of America, when the group of boys who played
and sometimes camped in the Menningers' large
back yard became the nucleus of a Boy Scout
troop. Today William Claire Menninger is
still actively associated with this troop.

When the United States entered the First
World War, nineteen-year-old Menninger interrupted his studies to enlist in the Army, becoming a second lieutenant in the Infantry.
When the war ended he returned to receive a
B.A. degree in 1919 from Topeka's Washburn College, later an M.A. from Columbia in
1922, and an M.D. from Cornell in 1924. From
1924 to 1926 he then served an internship in
medicine and surgery at Bellevue Hospital in
New York City. Upon the completion of his
internship, young Dr. Menninger joined his
father and brother Karl in a psychiatric clinic
which they had founded six years earlier in
1920. Charles Menninger had long been convinced of two things about medicine: "first,
that physicians should practice in groups so that
they could support and complement one another; and, secondly, that the psychological aspect of disease (psychiatry) was the most
rapidly developing and important field." The
Menninger Clinic, "the psychiatric equivalent
of the Mayo Clinic," was based on these principles. William Menninger's first work there
was in the field of internal medicine, but in
1927, after postgraduate study in psychiatry
at St. Elizabeth's Hospital in Washington, D.C.,
he began specializing in psychiatry at the clinic.
Later, in 1934-35, he attended the Chicago
Psychoanalytic Institute for further study of
psychoanalysis.

The Menninger Clinic, meanwhile, has had
"great influence on psychiatric practice in
America." (Karl Menninger, through his books
and his articles published in the leading popular magazines, has done much toward popularizing "the most abstruse points of psychiatry.")
Since 1930 William Menninger has been a

member of the board of directors, medical director of the Menninger Psychiatric Hospital, secretary of the Menninger Foundation, and a member of the editorial board of the monthly *Bulletin of the Menninger Clinic*. Among his other professional duties in Topeka is that of neurologist and psychiatrist for the Southard School for Handicapped Children. To his credit are some one hundred and fifty scientific papers, chief among which is the monograph *Juvenile Paresis* (1936).

The entrance of the United States into the Second World War brought Menninger into the Army in November 1942 as a lieutenant colonel in the Medical Corps. Appointed neuropsychiatry consultant for the Fourth Service Command (the seven Southeastern states) the following year, he soon won recognition for his work. Since his appointment in December 1943 as chief of the Neuropsychiatry Consultants Division in the Office of the Surgeon General, he has directed the expansion of the Army's neuropsychiatric work, "an expansion made necessary by the ever-increasing number of casualties returning from the war front." His personality—"modest, quietly good-humored, warm, frank, and tolerant—together with his pronounced professional ability," wrote Albert Deutsch in *PM*, "has helped him break down many walls of hostility and suspicion against psychiatry that impeded proper treatment of mental cases in military service. . . . Army psychiatry, which was in an almost scandalous state of neglect and confusion in the early months of the war, has been markedly improved under Menninger's efficient handling of the neuropsychiatric division. From induction center to battle station, the soldier has a better chance of being protected against a possible mental crackup and of getting prompt and efficient treatment if he does crack up."

On his return from a six-week inspection survey of the European theater of war in the fall of 1944 Menninger, then a Colonel (a year later he became Brigadier General), stated that he had observed a direct relationship between Army morale and mental hygiene. "When morale is good the rate of mental crackups goes down, and vice versa." To make up for the shortage of trained psychiatrists during the war, Menninger's division conducted special intensive three-month courses for young Army doctors. It also operated lecture programs for doctors so that they could better recognize incipient and actual psychiatric cases, and give emergency psychiatric treatment when necessary.

Menninger, in reporting in July 1945 on the expansion of psychiatric service, stated that at that time there was an outstanding psychiatrist in each of the five large overseas war theaters, a consulting psychiatrist with each army, and a division psychiatrist with each division. In the United States there was a leading Army psychiatrist serving as consultant to each of the nine service commands, and psychiatrists were attached to all Army hospitals. In addition, mental hygiene consultation units had been opened and were functioning in thirty-seven United States training camps. Menninger pointed out also that there was a closer relationship between psychiatry, medicine, and surgery in the army than in most civilian institutions.

One of the most telling arguments for the full-employment bill was made by Menninger in testimony before the Senate Committee hearings on the measure in September. He described the dangerous effects of continued unemployment on family life and on human personality, should the bill be rejected. Chronic unemployment during the last depression affected the mental health of two generations, as the effect on the children of the jobless workers was "beyond calculation." "When a family is plagued with unemployment", he said, "it is impossible to conceive of the children maturing without some degree of warp in their personality structure and, consequently, difficulties in their relations to people and to the community—evidence of mental ill health."

The fact that 39 per cent of all men rejected for military service in the last war—1,825,000 out of 4,650,000—were suffering from some type of personality disorder gives an idea of the emotional end results on "depression kids." Furthermore, 300,000 men had to be discharged from the Army for neuropsychiatric reasons, constituting the amazing total of 43 per cent of all discharges for medical reasons." Still another 130,000 men had been discharged, he said, on an administrative basis because of inadaptability or ineptness. Many of these persons, the psychiatrist pointed out, will have difficulty in obtaining and in holding jobs. "Of all the obligations we owe," he said "none is greater than to our disabled veterans, including the neuropsychiatric casualties." If these men do not obtain work, many of them may become confirmed invalids. In conclusion, Menninger called for a program of maximum employment opportunities plus a social security system that would not affect the morale of the temporarily unemployed but would serve as an insurance against the hazards of wide-spread mental ill health.

In an article, "The Mentally or Emotionally Handicapped Veteran," written for the *Annals of the American Academy of Political and Social Science* (May 1945), Menninger stated that in the postwar world it will be up to each community to develop a mental health department in its public health program to assist veterans with psychoneurotic scars. "Many Army misfits," wrote the psychiatrist, "could have been prevented [the United States Army had a greater number of neuropsychiatric casualties than any other army in the Second World War] if there had been greater use of psychiatric and mental hygiene services in the educational system of the country. . . . Just as our tuberculosis incidence was reduced by long years of public education, so can the frequency of psychoneurotic illness be affected by public education which can be planned and directed by the community agencies and the medical profession. One phase of such education," he suggests, "might be concerned with the changeover of community agency responsibility from charitable welfare to service to all in the area who can profit from its workers' training and experience—for fee as well as for free."

The psychiatrist's professional affiliations include Fellowship in the American Psychiatric

MENNINGER, WILLIAM CLAIRE
—Continued

Association, the American College of Physicians, and the American Medical Association. He is a member of the American Orthopsychiatric Association, the American Psychoanalytic Association, the American Psychopathological Association, the Central Neuropsychiatric Association (secretary since 1937), the Association for Research in Nervous and Mental Disease, the Central Society for Clinical Research, and the Kansas Psychiatric Society.

His work has not prevented the psychiatrist from following his avocation as a "Scouter." During the period of his internship in New York he served as assistant district commissioner of the Queens Council of the Boy Scouts of America, and following his return to Topeka in 1925 he became Scoutmaster of his boyhood troop. While Scout leader he developed in nine years seventy-five Eagle Scouts, the highest Scout rank. (During his own Eagle Scout days Menninger had qualified for eighty-seven Merit Badges out of a possible hundred offered for Scout electives.) In 1928 he organized a Sea Scout Patrol as an experiment. A year later this patrol was converted into a regular Scout ship, the S.S.S. *Kansan*, which, with Menninger acting as Skipper, was three times awarded first place in nationwide competitions. He has served on the National Executive Board of the Boy Scouts since 1937, and for three years (1938-40) he acted as president of the Jayhawk Council for Boy Scouts. In addition to contributing frequently to the magazine *Scouting*, Menninger has written *Handbook for Skippers* (1934).

Menninger's other non-professional affiliations include membership in the American Ornithological Union, the American Philatelic Society, the Collectors Club of New York, and the American Legion. He is a Mason and a Presbyterian. In 1925 he was married to Catharine Wright of East Orange, New Jersey. The Menningers have three sons, Roy Wright, Philip Bratton, and William Walter. The psychiatrist has been described as "tall, clean, and wholesome, like the wheat of his native Kansas."

References

Lit Digest 119:19 F 9 '35 il por
Menninger, F. V. Days of My Life (1940)
Who's Who in America, 1944-45

MERRIAM, JOHN CAMPBELL (mĕr'ĭ-ăm) Oct. 20, 1869—Oct. 30, 1945 American paleontologist, educator, and administrator; president of the Carnegie Institution of Washington (1920-38), and president emeritus since 1939; directed several archaeological expeditions in the western United States; found fossils which helped to prove the theory of evolution; prolific scientific writer.

Obituary

N Y Times p23 O 31 '45 por

MILAM, CARL H(ASTINGS) (mĭ'lăm) Oct. 22, 1884- Librarian

Address: b. American Library Assn., 520 N. Michigan Ave., Chicago; h. 2608 Orrington Ave., Evanston, Ill.

The record of the past quarter of a century of the American Library Association has been one of steady expansion. The fact that the organization is the effective body it is today is considered the result of the unifying and directing force of Carl H. Milam, its executive secretary since April 1920.

Carl Hastings Milam, the son of George Lee and Florence Amanda (Burch) Milam, was born in Harper County, Kansas, on October 22, 1884. Upon the completion of his secondary education he entered the University of Oklahoma, receiving his B.A. degree there in 1907. While at the university he had his first taste of library work as a student assistant in the library under Milton J. Ferguson, who was to become chief librarian of the Brooklyn (New York) Public Library in 1930. He liked it so well that immediately upon graduation he enrolled in the New York State Library School in Albany, stopping first in Chicago for a few months of experience in the John Crerar Library. He obtained his library certificate the following year. His first position was as an assistant in the Purdue University Library, Lafayette, Indiana.

Milam was at Purdue for a year, obtaining experience in the organization and direction of library service, then became secretary and State organizer of the Public Library Commission of Indiana. The foundation for his future work in the library field was now being laid. In this position he acquired an understanding of library needs on a state-wide basis. He held this post until 1913, when he took over the directorship of the public library in Birmingham, Alabama. In this capacity, according to Louis R. Wilson (*Library Journal*, April 15, 1945), Milam became acquainted with "the relation of public libraries to the population of a region largely unserved by libraries and confronted with the difficult problems of race relationships." Added to this, Milam's membership on various State committees and on the Council of the American Library Association developed to "a national level" his knowledge of libraries and their various types of service. He was president of the League of Library Commissions in 1912-13.

Herbert Putnam, Librarian of Congress, had been appointed director general of the A.L.A. Library War Service, and in October 1917 Milam became his assistant while still retaining his Birmingham library post. In the next three years Milam often came in contact with officials in Washington, contacts later to prove beneficial in his work as executive secretary. He assisted in the collection and distribution of millions of books and in the raising and expenditure of five million dollars for library service to the armed forces. He observed as well as directed "libraries on the march" wherever American soldiers were assigned. "All of which," states Louis Wilson, "served as a training ground for the following twenty-five years of leadership, which have been characterized by his national as well as his international point of view."

Milam succeeded George B. Utley as executive secretary of the A.L.A. in April 1920. At that time the association's "enlarged program" was under consideration. This plan called for the expenditure of three million dollars for the extension of library service and the improvement of existing libraries. Many progressive and farsighted librarians were behind the project. They strove to interest people in the idea, but it was received with little enthusiasm. The scope of the enterprise and the fact that America wanted to settle down to the prewar status was felt to be largely responsible for this lack of interest. Although his first efforts as executive secretary of the A.L.A. met with apparent failure, Milam was not discouraged. To him, the ideas contained in the defeated program were a goal to be attained by America's libraries if they were to justify their position in American life. From that time on he continued to work for their adoption in a modified form, and his efforts have contributed in a great measure to the establishment of the Boards of Adult Education and of Education for Librarianship, the A.L.A. Survey, and the Committee on International Relations. Embodied in these organizations are the aims of the enlarged program, although slightly altered to meet the needs of today.

In his first year of service with the A.L.A. Milam began his campaign to educate the public to the potentialities of library service. In an article written for *Public Libraries* in April 1920, he advocated the preparation and wide distribution of reading courses for adult education, such courses eventually to cover all vocations and reach the thousands who could not hope to have the personal attention of a librarian. He stressed the importance of interesting books on the reading lists. "They must tell enough of the subject in such a way as to entice the prospective student to start the reading course and, so prepared, to keep him interested in completing it." Milam wrote also of the need for the creation of public sentiment that would demand the establishment of libraries in communities lacking such facilities and the adequate financing of libraries then in operation.

In December 1934 Milam advised all librarians to be ready with constructive proposals for the reorganization of library service within their respective states. He was of the opinion, as were many others, that, under the new Federal Administration, changes would take place in the national and state responsibilities of library administration. At that time the executive secretary was far from satisfied with existing library conditions. That same year he decried the slash in library budgets which had been made despite the tremendous rise in the demand for library service, a result of the increase in the number of persons with enforced leisure. The public's opinion of libraries was gradually being lowered because of the depleted book stocks, the less efficient service on the part of overworked librarians, the poor condition of books, and the reduced hours of service.

Still hopeful of educating the public to the importance of "libraries for civilized living," Milam urged the establishment of a system of public and school libraries which would make books and competent guidance in the use of books easily available to every person in the United States. In the October 1934 issue of *School and Society* Milam wrote, "If, as I believe, it is the business of democracy to provide opportunity for individual development to the highest possible levels, then

Stadler Studios

CARL H. MILAM

our National Government also has some responsibility for the institutions of education, recreation, and culture." As one method of reaching isolated populations, he suggested the federation or reorganization of public libraries into large systems; the maintenance of these units on a minimum basis by state funds; the cooperation of the Federal Government with the states in planning for their development.

In an address at the Cleveland Public Library in 1938 Milam discussed the public library of the future. Because of the growing importance of pamphlet material, Milam predicted the development of a special open-shelf pamphlet room, presided over by a special pamphlet librarian. He prophesied an increase in music records and music scores, both in quantity and quality, to be available in all libraries; and he foresaw, above all, an expansion of educational services to the public. He advocated that librarians employ subject specialists; open special rooms; and then, through exhibits, posters, newspapers, radio, and moving pictures, stimulate reading interest. When duplicates are needed, he urged that they be purchased by the hundreds or the thousands, if the demand required them, not by the customary threes or fours.

Nor did Milam hesitate to discuss the obvious shortcomings of American public libraries. He stated that they still suffer from tradition. Years ago books were assembled for preservation and for the use of scholars; today, he said, they should be made accessible to everyone. Milam agrees with many of the younger librarians that in order to make the cataloging and classifying of books more useful to the public, the methods should be restudied and improved. And if librarians wish to encourage those who are not attracted by the grandeur and formality of the large library, more thought should be given to architecture, color, and comfort. In his final remarks he recommended cooperation among counties to form regional libraries, a procedure

MILAM, CARL H.—*Continued*

long advocated by many librarians. It is the only method known which will render service to sparsely populated areas. "There are forty million Americans who today have no access to public libraries. Not a healthy situation," he remarked, "for a country which believes in equal educational opportunity for all."

The outbreak of the war in Europe in September 1939 was a danger signal for American libraries to be prepared for readjustment to meet national emergency. In July 1940 Milam, as executive secretary of the A.L.A, outlined special duties for librarians. It was important, he said, for them to speed up book and pamphlet acquisitions to meet new and prospective requests, such as in vocations related to war industries; to help make democracy work by encouraging reading on all current problems; to forego, temporarily, their efforts to obtain well-rounded collections but instead to buy choice books which would be most useful during the war emergency. Moreover, realizing the necessity for an organization which would unite the committees assigned to various phases of war library service, both national and international, the A.L.A. executive board appointed a Committee on International Cultural Relations to study the whole problem of library participation in international cultural cooperation, a project to which Milam has since given much of his time and effort. The librarian believes that the restoration of libraries throughout the world is fundamental to the re-establishment of world intellectual activity, and that a more systematic and thorough interchange of books and journals between countries will increase respect for the nation which produced them. He is confident that the resultant understanding and esteem will contribute immeasurably toward maintaining a permanent peace. As one suggestion to assist in procuring such publications, Milam recommends a revision in copyright, tariff, and postal agreements by the various nations.

For years the executive secretary of the A.L.A. has worked for a closer relationship in library activities with Latin America. He has urged the interchange of library students and librarians in addition to the establishment of library schools and scholarships which will afford a better mutual understanding. In 1939 funds granted by the Rockefeller Foundation made it possible to investigate conditions and plan a program of activities. In 1940 several hundred thousand dollars were expended in the administration of libraries in Managua, Mexico City, and Montevideo, and in the shipment of books to Latin American libraries. Carl Milam and Harry M. Lydenberg '41 of the New York Public Library visited Latin America in the summer of 1944. They had the cooperation of the State Department and financial assistance of the Rockefeller Foundation in making their observations. The recommendations as the result of their study were responsible for the formation of the International Relations Board which now handles the A.L.A. activities related to foreign libraries and librarians from an office in the Annex of the Library of Congress.

Since 1926 Carl Milam has been an officer of the American Association for Adult Education. He is a member of the Cleveland Conference; a consultant to the Joint Army and Navy's Educational Advisory Council; a member of the National Board of Consultants of the Columbia Broadcasting System and of the Liaison Committee for International Education. He has been a consultant of the Division of Cultural Relations of the State Department since 1938 and has worked closely with the Coordinator of Inter-American Affairs. He was a delegate to the first International Library Congress, held in Rome in 1929, and again at its session in 1935 at Madrid. On both occasions he played an important role in the organization and development of the International Federation of Library Associations. He is an honorary member of the Asociación de Bibliotecarios y Bibliógrafos de España and a fellow of the American Library Institute. He is a Congregationalist and a Democrat. His clubs are the Cliff Dwellers (Chicago), University (Evanston, Illinois), and Cosmos (Washington, D.C.).

Of the many characteristics which have contributed to Carl Milam's success, four are said to be predominant: his abundant physical energy; his equally sustained mental ability; his ability to work with others; and his breadth of view. During his term of office Milam has thus far served under twenty-five A.L.A. presidents and worked with twenty-five executive boards. William Warner Bishop considers the executive secretary's constant search for new and unrevealed ability, his insight into possibilities not at first evident, his ability to interpret libraries to persons not engaged in the profession, and his quality of friendliness as his greatest contributions to the advance of librarianship. Bishop also points out that Carl Milam has had much help from other librarians in most of his endeavors, which, he says, is in itself all to his credit: "A lesser man would have tried to do it all himself." On the occasions librarians have disagreed with the policies of the executive secretary, they have been unanimous in their respect for the man and for his work.

In 1910 the librarian was married to Nellie Watson Robinson. They have two daughters, Margery Robinson and Mary Virginia. "Milam is not always to be found in the board room, on the conference platform, or on the national or international front," a writer once observed. "Sometimes he cannot be found at all. He is a fisherman and, once the annual conference is over, he is apt to disappear into some remote region where the fish are supposed to be biting best. If not there, one might find him busily setting out a thousand new trees on his recently acquired farm in northern Illinois."

References

ALA Bul 39:131-2 Ap '45 por
Ann Am Acad 235:100-6 S '44
Library J 70:331-3, 334-5, 348 Ap 15 '45 por
Who's Who in America, 1944-45
Who's Who in Library Service (1943)

MILLER, FRIEDA S(EGELKE) Apr. 16, 1890- United States Government official

Address: b. c/o Women's Bureau, United States Department of Labor, Washington, D. C.

The new director of the Women's Bureau of the United States Department of Labor since August 1944 is Frieda S. Miller, former industrial commissioner of New York State's Labor Department. Miss Miller, who in public office has worked for the improvement of labor conditions in both the economic and social aspects, has had an impressive career in labor activities. Frances Perkins '40, when she was United States Secretary of Labor, paid tribute to Miss Miller's work as a practical administrator who understood the economic problems of both New York employers and employees.

Frieda Segelke Miller was born April 16, 1890, in La Crosse, Wisconsin. Her grandparents brought her up after the early death of her father and mother, James Gordon and Erna (Segelke) Miller. In 1911 Miss Miller was awarded a bachelor's degree by Milwaukee-Downer College in Wisconsin. She spent the next four years in graduate work at the University of Chicago, three of them (1912-15) as a fellow in economics. In 1916-17 Miss Miller taught social economy in Bryn Mawr College in Pennsylvania and in 1918 accepted the post of secretary of the Philadelphia Women's Trade Union League, which she held until 1923. In this position she participated in the organization of the Trade Union College later established in Philadelphia, serving as secretary and teaching a number of classes in economics. She had a part also in the founding of the Workers' Education Bureau of America and was one of the original members of the Joint Executive Committee of the Bryn Mawr Summer School.

"I began as a highbrow," Frieda Miller says, explaining that she entered labor activities through the "intellectual back door": "If you're interested in labor problems, you find more interesting material if you go out into the world where those problems exist rather than pondering them behind the protection of a charming campus." Her experiences broadened in the years she spent with the Philadelphia Women's Trade Union League. Young but ingenious, she wore a badge that looked like a state inspector's; she says it helped considerably as she frowningly inspected fire buckets and sanitary facilities.

In the spring of 1923 Miss Miller sailed for Europe as delegate to the International Conference of Working Women which was held in Vienna. She spent a year abroad studying labor conditions in Austria, England, and Germany, where she adopted a German baby named Elizabeth (in 1945 a talented and energetic young woman, a senior at Vassar).

Back in New York in 1924, Frieda Miller worked as a factory inspector and for the fact-finding Joint Board of Sanitary Control of the ladies' garment industry until 1926. Her experiences were further broadened in her survey of the city homes for the aged on Welfare and Staten islands for the New York City Committee of the State Charities Aid (1926-27) and the Welfare Council (1927-29).

FRIEDA S. MILLER

Miss Miller's next post in the New York State labor field came with her appointment in 1929 as director of the Division of Women in Industry in the Empire State's labor department. She served in that capacity for nearly a decade. In the years 1936, 1938, and 1941 she was the United States delegate to the International Labor Organization conferences in Santiago (Chile), Geneva, and New York.

According to the *Christian Science Monitor*, Miss Miller's competence as director of the Division of Women in Industry marked her as the logical appointee for the position of New York State industrial commissioner to effect the solution of the problem that developed after unemployment insurance benefits became payable in the State in January 1938. When the business slump early that year threw many workers out of jobs, more than half a million claims were filed during the first month. In August 1938 Governor Lehman '43 appointed Miss Miller the second woman labor commissioner in New York State, the first in the post having been Frances Perkins. Climaxing nine years in the State Labor Department, Miss Miller undertook an office which embraced an almost unlimited range of activities, including not only the administration of the State labor and the workmen's compensation laws, but also the acts relating to unemployment insurance, minimum wages, State labor relations, wage claims, and the mediation board. Other ramifications extended to the administration of the laws governing general business, education, domestic relations, civil rights, and social welfare.

Taking the long-range view that the chief problem of the Employment Service was to discover ways and means of conquering unemployment, Miss Miller turned her attention to the problem of re-employment at the same time that she was solving the critical unemployment insurance problem by the decentralized payment plan. As the immediate result of her efforts, placement of men and women in industry increased by 50 per cent in 1939—before defense industries had started rolling. By

MILLER, FRIEDA S.—*Continued*

1940 she had put unemployment insurance in functioning order after a period of two years. In the year 1940 sixty-five million dollars' worth of unemployment insurance checks had been mailed, 98 per cent of them on time.

Throughout her administration a fundamental principle asserted itself: "Labor standards are themselves a basic part of national defense"; reducing labor standards would decrease individual productivity and efficiency. Citing the experiences of industry in Europe and in the First World War, she warned against the lengthening of working hours, except under emergency dispensations in critical war industries.

The passage of the Schwartzwald and Washburn bills gave Industrial Commissioner Miller the authority to enforce the already existing State Civil Rights laws opposing discrimination in industry on the grounds of race, religion, or national origin, by using the powers of administration, investigation, inquiry, subpoena, and hearing. As chairman of the Committee on Discrimination in Employment of the State War Council, Miss Miller was empowered to require the submission of information, records, and reports pertinent to discriminatory practices in industry at any time she saw fit; and in October 1942 she revealed that many employers engaged on war contracts had voluntarily recognized the need for relaxing discriminatory employment specifications, and that "the use of appeal and persuasion by the committee had brought tangible results in some cases and promises of complete cooperation in others."

This 1942 analysis had covered one hundred and twenty employers with nearly two hundred thousand employees who had been investigated by field representatives following complaints by individuals and groups. Although this "implementation for persuasion" applied only to employment in public utilities and in war industries, Miss Miller was not discouraged, believing that public education is far more effective than laws in ending discrimination. "We must make the public understand that it is humanly bad for them to discriminate, that it's bad for their community, that the relief problem is a direct reflection of discrimination."

On December 31, 1942, Miss Miller resigned her office before the incumbency of Governor Thomas E. Dewey '44, who felt that the administration of workmen's compensation had been badly handled. While an investigation by William F. Bleakley and Herman T. Stichman, counsel to Mr. Bleakley, later charged Miss Miller with contributing to the establishment of a "cumbersome bureaucracy," Charles Poletti '43 paid tribute to her: "Both industry and labor attest to your splendid service"; and he also stated that she had met the problems of four and one-half years "with understanding, courage, and intelligence."

In 1940 when she was fast becoming an internationally known expert in labor law administration, Miss Miller had been president of the International Association of Government Labor Officials at the twenty-sixth annual convention in New York. In that year Russell Sage College awarded her an honorary Doctorate of Humane Letters. Then, in March

1943 she was appointed special assistant on labor to United States Ambassador John G. Winant '41 at London. As a result of her English experience, she uses the "buzz bomb" as a favorite simile for the destructive effect of legislation lacking social vision. Miss Miller returned to the United States in the spring of 1944 to play an important role in the I.L.O. Conference held in Philadelphia. One of the significant recommendations of that conclave was the equal-opportunity, equal-pay principle for men and women workers. Miss Miller, herself a strong supporter of this recommendation, believes that passage of the equal-pay measure will not only assure women their rights, but will prevent their becoming "wage cutters and depressors of men's earnings."

In August 1944 Miss Miller went to Washington as head of the Women's Bureau of the United States Department of Labor. She succeeded Miss Mary Anderson, director of the bureau for twenty-five years and long a co-worker with Miss Miller in international labor relations. The new director enlisted in a quiet campaign to oppose the proposed equal-rights amendment. Frances Perkins and a number of national women's groups agree with the head of the Women's Bureau that the pending amendment "sounds nice" but would actually "take away from women hard-earned industrial gains which have led to a better standard of living." "No amendment can give women consideration at the hands of the employers who hold the jobs in this country," Miss Miller declares. "It is a matter of prejudice and I have fought that prejudice." During the first ten months of 1945 Miss Miller's Women's Bureau interviewed thirteen thousand women workers, 75 per cent of whom expected to continue work, chiefly from necessity; nine out of ten contribute to the family budget, a substantial number as the only breadwinner. "Their purchasing power," said Miss Miller, "is an inextricable part of . . . national welfare. Their employment is not a war phenomenon, but a long historical development growing out of mass-production techniques. . . .The answer to the question of women in industry should be sought in the direction of a full-employment program."

The most pressing problem facing the Women's Bureau, Miss Miller believes, is the readjustment of women workers during postwar conversion. She urged that women trade union members, housewives in women's civic groups, and Government representatives from both local and Federal agencies should cooperate after the war in solving such problems of community welfare as health, housing, and employment for women. In December 1944 Miss Miller made public a Reconversion Blueprint for Women drafted by representatives of thirty-one national and women's labor organizations. The suggestions included the need for the making of analyses of future job possibilities for women war workers; the establishment of anti-discrimination policies, sufficient public employment service facilities, training and retraining facilities; the advance planning of public works programs; the extension to all states of the collective-bargaining, minimum-wage, and equal-pay for equal-work laws; the extension and improvement of social security measures; the improvement of conditions in major women-employing fields; the analyzing of job shifts; and establishment of seniority rights.

This "mistress strategist of the office and factory feminists" is a robust, cheerful woman with greenish eyes and natural color in her cheeks. She clings to a few old-fashioned tastes: thus her face is guiltless of cosmetics, her long sandy-colored hair remains straight, and she leans to cameos and lace at the throat. Although the emphasis in her career has been in helping women who have sought a livelihood away from home, Miss Miller has typical domestic interests, delighting in experimental cooking and gardening on her ten-acre farm in West Redding, Connecticut. She particularly enjoys sidestroke swimming in her "good little New England pond." Miss Miller is a member of the Academy of Political Science, of the American Association for Labor Legislation, and a Fellow of the American Geographical Society.

References

C S Mon p9 N 22 '40 por
Ind Woman 22:201 Jl '43 por; 23:296 S '44
N Y Herald Tribune p19 Je 22 '44 por
N Y Post Mag p5 O 14 '44 por
N Y Sun p16 Je 30 '44
PM p22 My 11 '42 por

MOLEY, RAYMOND (CHARLES) (mō′lĭ) Sept. 27, 1886- Editor; author; college professor

Address: b. c/o Newsweek, 152 W. 42d St, New York City; h. 2 E. 55th St., New York City

The associate editor of *Newsweek*, Raymond Moley, is a nationally known editor, writer, teacher, and lecturer. He has taught public law at Columbia since 1923 and is the author of books on government and citizenship, as well as of *The Hays Office* (1945). Chief of the prominent members of President Roosevelt's '42 "brain trust," Moley served as Assistant Secretary of State and mentor to Government officials and agencies during the President's first term; subsequently he became one of the most outspoken critics of the New Deal.

Of French and Irish descent, Raymond Charles Moley was born September 27, 1886, in the small Middle Western town of Berea, Ohio. He is the son of Felix James and Agnes (Fairchild) Moley. After attending the public schools he entered the small Baldwin-Wallace College in Berea, where he received the degree of Ph.B. in 1906. Twenty-year-old Moley then became superintendent of schools for the village of Olmsted Falls, Ohio, a position which he held until 1910. After a siege of tuberculosis had sent him to New Mexico and Colorado for two years, Moley returned to Ohio in 1912 to teach history in Cleveland's West High School, where he remained until 1914. Meanwhile, he studied at Oberlin College and obtained his M.A. degree in 1913. Then he became an instructor and, in 1918-19, assistant professor of politics at Western Reserve University. In that year (1916) he was married to Eva Dall. (The Moleys have twin sons, Malcolm and Raymond, born in 1925.)

Raymond Moley was thirty-two when, in 1918, he became director of Americanization

RAYMOND MOLEY

activities, under Governor Cox, for the Ohio State Council of Defense. The following year he took charge of the Cleveland Foundation, and began a five-year survey of organized crime, *The Cleveland Crime Survey* (1922). His work was so successful that he was called upon as consultant for crime surveys in several other states, including Illinois, Pennsylvania and Virginia. During these years Professor Moley published six factual books, one of which, *Lessons in American Citizenship for Men and Women Preparing for Naturalization,* went through ten editions from 1917 to 1930.

In 1923 Moley moved East to become an associate professor of government at Columbia University, where he had received his Ph.D. degree in 1918; five years later he became professor of public law, a position he still holds. At the same time he continued his work in criminology, publishing his findings in *Politics and Criminal Prosecution* (1929); *Our Criminal Courts* (1930), a "most useful" volume which was said to clarify the crime situation and "offer reassurance to those who are beginning to be dismayed by it"; and *Tribunes of the People; the Past and Future of the New York Magistrates' Courts* (1932), which resulted from Moley's study of the magistrates' courts when he assisted Judge Samuel Seabury in an investigation of the tribunals. He has also assisted Seabury in an investigation of the district attorney's office. In 1926 New York's Governor Alfred E. Smith '44 had appointed Moley as director of research on the New York State Crime Commission, on which he served for approximately three years, and in 1930 he was a member of a committee which drafted a model State parole system for Governor Franklin D. Roosevelt. Recognizing Moley's abilities as criminal investigator, Roosevelt appointed him his chief representative on the New York State Commission on Administration of Justice (1931-33).

In that capacity, Moley came into close contact with Governor Roosevelt, whom he assisted in all State matters relating to the ad-

MOLEY, RAYMOND—*Continued*

ministration of justice and criminal law. He was the first of the group of confidential advisers on economics and public policy whom Roosevelt began to gather around him in the months before he received the Presidential nomination. This group, later designated as the "brain trust," soon included, among others, Rex Tugwell [41], Adolf A. Berle, Jr. [40], General Hugh S. Johnson [40], and Felix Frankfurter [41]. During the campaign Moley acted as coordinator for the growing group, forwarding to Roosevelt those of the experts' suggestions which merited consideration. Moley is credited with having suggested William Sumner's famous phrase, "the Forgotten Man," and with having originated the term "New Deal" to keynote the campaign.

After the election Moley accompanied the new President to Washington in 1933. There he served as Assistant Secretary of State under Cordell Hull [40] during the famous "hundred days" of history-making legislation, and as liaison officer between Roosevelt and the American delegation to the abortive Economic Conference held in London later that year. In Washington the economist was the brunt of incessant waves of criticism. To accusations that he was an impractical theorist he replied, "I am essentially a conservative fellow," and "I tilt at no windmills." Moley worked hard, and he had a blunt, outspoken manner that often got under the skin of his opponents; practical and realistic, still he was "never so happy as when poking a portly tradition in the nose." Moley had intended to remain only a short time in Washington, and in September 1933 he resigned. However, before leaving Government service he accepted an assignment in the Department of Justice to organize a Federal program for the curbing of racketeering, kidnapping, and other forms of organized crime.

In the meantime Moley had been commuting weekly to New York to lecture to his classes at Barnard College of Columbia University, had been writing a syndicated weekly column of comment for the McNaught Newspaper Syndicate since June 1933, and had been making plans for the launching of a new national weekly magazine. Financed by Vincent Astor, W. Averell Harriman [41], and Mary Harriman Rumsey, this new journalistic venture, *Today,* was to be "primarily concerned with public affairs, independent in its political affiliations, presenting opinion as well as fact, liberal in outlook"—as editor Moley outlined its scope. The first number appeared in October 1933, and within three years the periodical had a circulation of one hundred thousand. Ultimately, early in 1937 *Today* was merged with the magazine *Newsweek,* then merely a weekly digest of news, "in order to incorporate in one periodical signed opinion, a compendium of the news, and an appraisal of the significance of the news," explained Moley. He and his friend Ralph Robey [41] became associate editors of that magazine, each contributing a weekly column of opinion. In 1945 Moley was the main survivor of the original staff, and by the end of that year he had submitted his column of comment every week without a break for twelve years, in six of which he was the only signed commentator.

Between 1933 and 1937 Moley's editorial opinion in *Today* reflected the changing course of his feeling toward Roosevelt and New Deal policies. The backers of *Today* were deeply sympathetic with the objectives of the New Deal, "objectives which we felt any enlightened American government, Democratic or Republican, must strive for," and even after Moley's resignation from his State Department post he did not disappear from the councils of the Administration. During 1934 and 1935 he saw Roosevelt frequently in Washington, and "there was scarcely a message or major speech in whose preparation I took no part," he says. He was also asked to help draft bills, and it was he who suggested the appointments to the Securities and Exchange Commission. As time went on, however, Moley became strongly critical of new Presidential proposals, such as the "soak-the-rich" tax and the plan to "pack" the Supreme Court by enlarging it; he condemned Roosevelt's "less and less neutral" policies, such as breaking off trade relations with Italy, and he admonished him for his dislike of business in general. The man in the street, observed Moley, while he believes in the New Deal, does not at the same time believe that businessmen are all devils, and "we must all see how unsatisfactory, how intolerable the relations of business and government have come to be." He began to view the President as one endowed "with a conviction of personal rectitude that would brook no dissent, suffer no challenge." It was at the close of Roosevelt's first term in office that the erstwhile ardent New Dealer decided to sever completely his relations with the Administration.

In 1939 Moley's criticism of Roosevelt and the New Deal, *After Seven Years,* "an account of political events as I saw them," was published. Based upon his "notes, memoranda, documents, daily journal, and other firsthand material," the volume was published immediately, Moley wrote in his preface, because "an obligation to give to the public that which belongs to the public rests upon anyone who is privileged to participate in public affairs." Most reviewers recognized *After Seven Years* as first-rate writing and absorbing reading and conceded that it is "an important contribution to contemporary political history in its inside phases." It was said also that it was far from being an objective book. Wrote the *Yale Review*: "To read it is to stir your blood; to criticize it is to take sides in a political debate that will last as long as the United States maintains the ballot box." Moley declared in 1945, however, that "no fact in the book has been successfully controverted, and only one fact has been controverted at all."

Moley's weekly column on the last page of *Newsweek,* under the title of *Perspective,* as well as his coast-to-coast lectures and talks and his syndicated newspaper column, have brought him prominence as a political analyst. His syndicated column, distributed through Associated Newspapers, Inc., was begun in 1941. It appears thrice weekly and reaches sixty-four papers, with an aggregate circulation of over six million.

Since the death of Roosevelt Moley has looked with favor upon President Truman [45], predicting that the new Administration would be unfavorable to extremists and that the Democratic Party would swing toward the Right. At the same time he asserted that the Republican Party would show a trend toward the Left. In January 1945 Moley had made news by setting forth, in a speech before the Indiana State Bar Association, a program of "twelve commandments" for the Republican Party to follow. No. 1 was "Stop hating Roosevelt." "Thou shalt not covet Roosevelt's ideas," continued Moley. "It is quite possible to build a set of principles that are progressive and anti-New Deal." Among the other precepts were that party members stop fighting among themselves and try to learn from Sidney Hillman[40] and the PAC how to get out the votes.

Moley became the newest addition to the ranks of radio commentators in March 1945. It was said that the American Broadcasting Company chose Moley for his "middle-of-the-road" stand to offset its other commentators who seemed to "hang a little heavier on the New Deal side because of the predominant audience appeal of [Walter] Winchell[43] and [Drew] Pearson[41]." Moley, who is on the air on Sunday evenings, says that he is not a reporter, but that, basically, he will try to explain why things happen and what may logically happen as a result. In October he left ABC, stating that "after six months of lush news there wasn't going to be enough to talk about on the air."

Back in 1936 Moley began collecting material for his history of the Motion Picture Producers and Distributors of America, *The Hays Office*, a volume he completed in 1945. A study of the activities of Will H. Hays[43] since he assumed the presidency of the M.P.P.D.A. in 1922, the book is, Moley wrote in his foreword, "an account of what one industry has learned about governing itself." Expressing unqualified admiration for Hays as a politician and businessman, Moley believes that the Hays Office represents an experience in self-regulation by which business in general can learn how to avoid "the paralyzing hand of government bureaucracy and politics." *Variety* and the *Saturday Review of Literature* rate *The Hays Office* as an objectively written, reportorially dispassionate "capsule history of the motion picture business." The motion picture trade papers, too, received the book with approval, as did most newspaper critics. Some reviewers, however, noted an over-adulatory attitude toward the benefits of the Hays Office. "In short," commented Bosley Crowther in the New York *Times*, "the author has successfully failed to make the dispassionate analysis of the Hays Office that we sorely need."

Twelve years ago Moley was described as "a youngish man of medium height, broad-shouldered, with fat cheeks but no jowls, a low voice, wide forehead, black brows and thinning gray hair." Although he is heavier in figure in 1945, his appearance has changed little. He is said to be an approachable, likable man who laughs easily. While he takes no exercise if he can avoid it, he does like an occasional game of billiards.

References

Collier's 91:17+ Je 17 '33 por
Scrib Mag 94:257-66 N '33 por

Moley, R. After Seven Years (1939)
National Cyclopædia of American Biography Current vol D p21
Who's Who in America, 1944-45

MORRISON, HENRY CLINTON Oct. 7, 1871—Mar. 19, 1945 University of Chicago professor emeritus of education; inventor of the Morrison unit plan of teaching as a substitute for lesson assignments in high school; an advocate of the wider adoption of the junior high school and junior college systems, and the abolition of report cards; author of a number of books on education.

Obituary

N Y Times p19 Mr 20 '45

MOSES, GEORGE HIGGINS Feb. 9, 1869—Dec. 20, 1944 Former United States Republican Senator from New Hampshire (1918-33); during term of office he opposed the World Court, the League of Nations, and the London Naval Limitation Treaty of 1930; Minister to Greece and Montenegro (1909-12).

Obituary

N Y Times p21 D 21 '44 por

MOSES, JOHN June 12, 1885—Mar. 3, 1945 Democratic Senator to the United States Congress and former Governor of North Dakota; first Democrat ever elected to represent North Dakota in either house of Congress; served as Governor for three consecutive terms, 1939-45; defeated Gerald P. Nye[41] in 1944.

Obituary

N Y Times p38 Mr 4 '45 por

MOSHER, IRA (mō'zhĕr) Nov. 15, 1887- Manufacturer

Address: b. Russell Harrington Cutlery Co., Southbridge, Mass.; h. 56 Everett St., Southbridge, Mass.

The president of the National Association of Manufacturers for 1945, Ira Mosher, is a small businessman, head of the Russell Harrington Cutlery Company in Massachusetts and director of several other organizations. Born in Melrose, Massachusetts, on November 15, 1887, Mosher is the son of Ira and Cordelia (Sweet) Mosher, who had emigrated from St. John, New Brunswick. He is a graduate of the Melrose high school and a school of accounting.

At the age of twenty-six young Mosher became one of the first certified public accountants in Massachusetts. Twelve years later, in January 1925, the C.P.A. became director and treasurer of the Russell Harrington Cutlery Company, a small manufacturing concern in Southbridge, Massachusetts, employing three hundred persons. After another twelve years Mosher, in January 1937, was elected president, a post he has held since that time. In the last years he has also been part-owner. His office has never been a full-time one, however. In addition to it he has held directorships in the Southbridge National Bank, the British branch of the American Optical Company, the McLaurin-Jones Company, the

IRA MOSHER

G. C. Winter Company; the presidency of Canada's Consolidated Optical Company; and he has been treasurer and director of the Better Vision Institute. His principal work, however, has been with the American Optical Company of Southbridge. Since 1922 he has been successively comptroller, treasurer, vice-president, and general manager and trustee of the concern, but in November 1944 he severed all connections to devote more time to his other work.

Mosher had had several other organization leadership jobs before his election as NAM president. In 1941 he was elected president of the Associated Industries of Massachusetts; he served on the NAM's Relation of Government to Industry Committee the same year; and he helped to organize the first regional War Labor Board of New England.

Up until a few weeks before the forty-ninth annual convention of the NAM in early December 1944—when Mosher was chosen to succeed Robert Gaylord [44] in the nonpaying post of president—business leaders had held the optimistic opinion that reconversion would be the most discussed subject before the convention. By convention week, however, it was found that war production still had undisputed precedence. Returning from a tour of the European battlefronts, Frederick C. Crawford [43], chairman of the Association's executive committee, reported that the American industrialist must make an unprecedented number of bombs, shells, and other war materials to win the European war. And from General Brehon Somervell [42], chief of the Army Service Forces, came the warning that production was lagging behind consumption, that, although present shortages were local and largely due to transportation difficulties, the concern was for the future, when battles would become heavier. This, said *Time*, was "the first official word to United States business that cutbacks in war production after V-E Day had shrunk from the 40 per cent which WPB once promised to a slim 15-20 per cent.' "In some confusion," continued the magazine, "the NAMsters hastily

armed their full support to the war. Then the ponderous convention machinery, which had been geared up to reconversion . . . rolled on into the postwar world."

One of the most important tasks before Mosher is that of directing the six-point program drafted by the convention. In it, according to *Time*, were generalities against cartels, in favor of free enterprise, good government, a sound currency system, but no mention of a protective tariff for postwar business. The *Christian Science Monitor*'s interpretation of these resolutions is that they say in effect: "Private enterprise *is* the American economic system, and given truly free competition the system would be automatically self-regulating. There should, therefore, be no restriction on regulation of the system, 'except to protect the public health and safety.' Government is instrinsically bad; it is a necessary evil, which should be limited to the performance of its protective functions." The *Monitor* article declared that the "chief trouble with the NAM credo is that it is unrealistic. Private enterprise . . . never has been the whole of the American economic system. . . .'.Competition has never been altogether free, nor wholly self-regulating, nor self-regulating altogether for the common good. . . .In fact, wholly unrestricted competition implies such a cost in waste and distress that neither capital nor labor has ever been willing to try it out."

To explain how free private enterprise proposes to provide jobs and a higher living standard for all, NAM launched a million-dollar advertising campaign after the convention. The key advertisement, according to *Newsweek*, "called on working men and women to support tax policies that leave sufficient funds for expansion, laws that prevent unregulated monopoly, labor policies that establish responsibilities of both labor and management, and business operation under law instead of under unpredictable Government directive." In speaking of the campaign the financial editor of the New York *World-Telegram*, Ralph Hendershot, wrote: "Association officials are aware that the very best logic in the world presented in the prettiest package will not, of itself, get the job done. . . .If American economic leadership is to be intrusted to businessmen in the future, these leaders must demonstrate by performance that they have what it takes."

Mosher says he is aware that he faces no easy task. "He believes that domestic differences must first be resolved if the country is to win complete victory in the war and be strong enough to contribute to something better than political chaos abroad. In his first public statement he discussed labor relations, saying, "I can only speak for myself, but too many businessmen are content to limit their concern to the four walls of their own plants. It's past time that they got out and talked to people. We'll get understanding the same way we always got it. That's by sitting down and talking things out in the public's interest, not in any group interest. Personally, I'm willing to sit down right now with any recognized labor leaders to work out ways and means of resolving differences to establish an effective, coherent national policy that respects rights and defines responsibilities for both sides."

Following the public announcement that an industry-labor charter designed for postwar unity had been signed on March 28, 1945, by Eric Johnston [43], president of the United States Chamber of Commerce, Philip Murray [41], president of the CIO, and William Green [42], president of the A. F. of L., Mosher stated that he would offer wholehearted cooperation, provided certain points in the code were clarified. He also said, "We must find some way of resolving the issues which divided labor and management in recent years, some way of minimizing the industrial strife which paralyzes production and prevents attainment of true prosperity. . . .The proposed charter is a significant step in this direction. If certain shortcomings can be eliminated, it will provide an important foundation for further progress."

As the May-Bailey bill (amended from a "work-or-fight" to "work-or-else" measure) was being debated in Congress, the *NAM News* said: "Management and labor must solve the problem—manpower—for themselves." (Labor generally is regarded as also being against the bill.) As reported in the *Christian Science Monitor* on February 1, Mosher predicted that the bill would become a "fight-or-work" law "by rewarding conscript workers and penalizing the free workers in our war plants." In another statement he contended that the measure would become the "national slowdown bill."

Mosher has joined with the resolutions committee of the Association in attacking the development of government-sanctioned cartels, and he has urged that Congress consider immediate passage of legislation which will "reflect what the people want." The NAM's attack on cartels, commented *Newsweek* "had the force of novelty," since the question had been "left in the air" by the International Business Conference, the National Foreign Trade Council, and the Bretton Woods conference of 1944. Although the question of protective tariffs was not covered at the convention, Mosher has since stated that he favors "progressively lower tariffs as economic events make them possible."

In May 1945, when the NAM mailed to its membership the reprinted condensation by *Reader's Digest* of Friedrich Hayek's [45] controversial book, *The Road to Serfdom,* Mosher wrote an accompanying letter in which he said, "This condensation will, in my judgment, do much to arm businessmen to effectively analyze the dangers of government planning and the soundness of a system based on individual and free enterprise." In June 1945 Mosher urged the Nation's business leaders to unite in a ten-year postwar prosperity plan, and proposed that delegates from manufacturing, retailing, banking, transportation, the utilities, and other economic interests hold a "National War-to-Peace Council" as soon as Office of Defense Transportation regulations would permit, to chart an all-business postwar program.

Fully realizing the necessity of a speedy reconversion to peacetime production on the part of industry, Mosher declared in a symposium prepared for the New York *Herald Tribune* that reconversion problems were confined to a very small segment of industry, and that, according to an NAM survey, the solving of those problems would not be "as prolonged as the pessimists would have the public think." He added that this survey of more than seventeen hundred NAM companies showed that 61 per cent of manufacturers had practically no reconversion problems, and only 11 per cent of them would require more than thirty days to get started on peacetime production. He concluded: "All that is needed to write a thrilling sequel to the 'Miracle of War Production' is the necessary materials, the go-ahead from Washington and the cooperation of labor." Ten days after the fall of Japan Mosher attended the White House meeting at which representatives of business and labor organizations agreed to participate in a management-labor conference under Government auspices. It was opened on November 5 by President Truman. Philip Murray [41], backed by Henry Wallace [40], pleaded for inclusion of wage increases in the discussions, but Ira Mosher declared that this was not a national collective bargaining conference. At another meeting he said that industry was ready to "forego lockouts and unfair labor practices" but that labor is unwilling to forego "strikes, boycotts" and other "weapons of industrial warfare." Until labor was willing to accept responsibility under the law, he added, there was little hope for real accomplishments at the parley.

As an alternative to the Murray [45] full employment bill, Mosher urged Congress to adopt "a national policy of eliminating special favors and special privileges." This would include vigorous enforcement of antitrust statutes and overhauling of the national labor policy. He outlined the plan in testimony prepared for the House Executive Expenditures Committee, and urged sharp reductions in corporation taxes to a level that would assure a free flow of capital into jobmaking activities.

In June 1912 Mosher was married to Grace Howard. The couple have three sons—Howard, Jack, and Paul, the first two of whom in 1945 are in the armed services. In Southbridge Mosher serves as trustee for the YMCA and the Universalist Church, and he takes an active interest in the Southbridge Manufacturers and Merchants Association. His greatest source of relaxation is found working in the machine shop he has built in the basement of his old-fashioned house in Southbridge. He also owns a house in the woods near the Connecticut border. "Both he and his wife are familiar figures on the golf course, and they frequently entertain week-end groups in their summer home." Mosher is described as being "chunky" and as having sharp features, bushy black eyebrows over rimless glasses, and a wide smile. He is considered forceful and blunt-spoken, and a good mixer. "Business associates," reports *Newsweek*, "rate him as a keen, quick-witted, aggressive executive, bubbling with ideas."

References

Bsns W p16 D 9 '44 por
Newsweek 24:68 D 18 '44 (por p66)
Time p79 D 18 '44 por

Who's Who in Commerce and Industry, 1940-41

MOTT, JAMES W(HEATON) Nov. 12, 1883—Nov. 12, 1945 United States Republican Representative of Oregon from 1933 until his death; served in the United States Navy (1918); city attorney of Astoria, Oregon (1920-22); elected to Oregon House of Rep-

MOTT, JAMES W.—*Continued*

resentatives in 1922, serving for three terms, and again from 1930 to 1932; member of House Naval Affairs Committee.

Obituary

N Y Times p21 N 13 '45 por

MULLER, PAUL (HERMAN) *See* Läuger, P. and Müller, P. H.

MUNSEL, PATRICE (mŭn-sĕl' pätrēs') May 14, 1925- Singer

Address: b. c/o Hurok Attractions, Inc., 711 Fifth Ave., New York City

The "baby coloratura" of the Metropolitan Opera is Patrice Munsel, who startled the musical world in December 1943 with her debut at the age of eighteen. "Princess Pat," as she is affectionately called, began her swift flight to operatic stardom when she won a

PATRICE MUNSEL

Metropolitan contract on the *Metropolitan Auditions of the Air* only a few months before her debut. Since that event she has sung leading roles in the world's greatest opera house and has won an even larger audience through her appearances on the concert stage and on radio programs.

The Metropolitan's youngest singer was born Patrice Munsil on May 14, 1925, in Spokane, Washington, the only child of Dr. Audley J. and Eunice Munsil. Her father is a successful Spokane dentist, and her mother, who is her constant companion, is musically inclined and plays the piano. Patrice attended Lewis and Clarke High School, where she was captain of the girls' football team and star of the school's theatrical productions. Not so long before her Metropolitan debut she was singing the lead in the high school's version of Gilbert and Sullivan's *The Pirates of Penzance*. The athletic schoolgirl took ballet and tap-dancing

lessons and also studied "rhythmic whistling." Before she studied singing seriously Patrice was a "virtuoso at artistic whistling" and she now claims that whistling was valuable in her singing career for the training it gave her in breath control and phrasing. At twelve Patrice began taking singing lessons with Charlotte Gramis Lange and Mrs. Paul Kennedy. Her voice soon attracted attention in Spokane, and it was suggested that she sing for Vladimir Bakaleinikoff, associate conductor of the Pittsburgh Symphony Orchestra. Bakaleinikoff, who was then in the West, was greatly impressed with the young girl's voice and advised intensive study. Her mother therefore took her to New York for lessons, but after two months they decided they had been premature in their plans—the adolescent voice was not yet ready for professional development. Two years later the sixteen-year-old girl and her mother were back in New York, embarked on a rigorous training schedule for the young singer. Miss Munsel still adheres to this program, which includes voice lessons with William Herman and Renato Bellini, acting and Italian with Antoinette Stabile, French with Maria Savage, and coaching in operatic roles with Giacomo Spadoni.

Opera News reports that it was Spadoni who brought his young pupil to the attention of Wilfred Pelletier [44], program conductor of the *Metropolitan Auditions of the Air*. Miss Munsel entered the *Auditions* and in the finals in March 1943 sang the "Mad Scene" from *Lucia di Lammermoor*. As the youngest winner in the history of the radio series, Miss Munsel attracted special notice in the press. Her prize in this operatic contest was a thousand dollars and a silver plaque, in addition to the cherished contract with the Metropolitan. The Spokane soprano thus was the youngest singer ever signed by the Metropolitan and the second youngest of operatic debutantes, only the famed Adelina Patti having made her debut at an earlier age. But there were still new triumphs in store for Miss Munsel. She received another thousand-dollar award from a fund established for the education of young singers by the late Madame Anna Schoen-René. Then, in November 1943 she signed a contract with S. Hurok [41] for a minimum guaranty of one hundred and twenty thousand dollars for concert appearances during the following three years. (About this time the young star changed the spelling of her name to "Munsel" to simplify the pronunciation.) There were radio and film offers the aspiring singer refused in order to sing at the Metropolitan.

Before her much-heralded debut at the Metropolitan Opera in 1943, Miss Munsel went home to Spokane in June to give her first professional concert. The recital, a benefit for the Red Cross, was a great success. It was considered a civic event in the star's birthplace, being described as "unique in the history of that city." Miss Munsel later repeated this concert for a large soldier audience, which accorded her a warm reception. Before leaving Spokane she was made honorary Base Commander of Geiger Field, in Washington, by courtesy of the commanding officer "in recognition of her musical achievements and her devotion to her country and the armed forces." Since then the singer has frequently entertained servicemen, singing operatic as well as the lighter popular music.

Patrice Munsel's first professional engagement with an orchestra came in August 1943 in Salt Lake City, where she sang with the Utah State Orchestra and drew flattering press reviews. In the fall Miss Munsel was back in New York preparing for her operatic debut, an event keenly anticipated by the operatic world. In her few years of musical study the soprano had mastered ten operatic roles. But for her debut she had to learn a new role, that of Philine in *Mignon*. On December 4, 1943, the self-assured young girl sang grand opera for the first time from the stage of the Metropolitan. She was an immediate favorite with the audience, her rendition of the aria "Je suis Titania" provoking an eight-minute ovation. However, she did not fare so well with the critics, most of whom considered Miss Munsel miscast in the sophisticated courtesan's role. Several critical reviews noted the newcomer's dramatic ability, poise, and vocal agility, at the same time contending that she was not yet ready for the Metropolitan. Virgil Thomson's '40 review in effect summarized the general opinion: "Miss Munsel, though a young woman of phenomenal talents, is far from being prepared for present glory."

Soon after her debut Miss Munsel again sang in *Mignon*, this time for a high school audience at a Junior Performance of the Metropolitan Opera Guild. On this occasion the youthful star remarked: "It thrills me no end when my own age group burst out in whistles and cheers, yet there is nothing in the world to compare with the feeling I get when I hear the 'bravos' of that wonderful Metropolitan audience." Since her appearance in *Mignon* Miss Munsel has sung other leading coloratura roles. Her second part was the mechanical doll Olympia in *Tales of Hoffmann*, which was followed by the role of Gilda in *Rigoletto*. As Gilda, she was considered lacking in operatic technique and consistent vocal quality. When the young prima donna sang the title role in *Lucia di Lammermoor* the critics pronounced her immature for this taxing role, which has been sung by such notables as Melba, Galli-Curci, and Pons '44. Her voice was called "schoolgirlish" by some, while her musical intelligence and natural stage presence were commended by others. The New York *Post* critic declared that her voice was much more lovely in quality than it had been the previous season, and that she handled it much better. "It is a large voice for a coloratura," the reviewer continued, "and happily much more emotional in quality than the usual bird imitation characteristic of so many voices of this type."

In December 1944, in *The Barber of Seville*, the "baby diva" earned her most favorable critical comments. In the comic Rossini opera, the critics found the soprano very acceptable and decidedly promising. The critic of the New York *Times* called the performance "by far the most proficient singing of her Metropolitan career so far," and Jerome D. Bohm in the New York *Herald Tribune* spoke of the singer's "native vocal flexibility and wide range." Miss Munsel's rendition of the famous aria, "Una voce, poco fa" was especially singled out for praise of its brilliance. On March 1,

1945, the soprano sang the difficult role of the Queen of Shamakhan in Rimsky-Korsakoff's operatic fantasy, *The Golden Cockerel*, presented by the Metropolitan for the first time in English. A later part was that of Juliet in the Metropolitan's revival of Gounod's *Romeo and Juliet* in December.

The soprano in early 1945 started out on her second concert tour, with an itinerary of thirty cities, of which one was Chicago. C. J. Bulliet of the Chicago *Daily News,* in reviewing Miss Munsel's rendition of the spectacular and difficult "Echo Song" by Eckert at one of her early concerts, observed that the work illustrated as well as anything could the singer's merits and defects: "Her merits are overwhelmingly in the ascendant—a voice with a warm and human charm duplicating the incomparable witchery of her magnetic personality. . . .Her defects are the defects of youth and inexperience. She hasn't quite mastered her miraculous native talents. . . .Patrice's voice is one that may cause her to be pursued through life by critical purists. But such purists will indicate that she has other attainments so rare that the attention she gets will be tribute to her challenging personality."

Miss Munsel enjoys concert work and finds travel exciting. In addition, since August 1944, replacing Gladys Swarthout '44, she has been the featured artist on the *Family Hour* over the Columbia Broadcasting System. In March 1944 the *Cavalcade of America* program presented a radio adaptation of Patrice Munsel's biography entitled *Song From Spokane*. In the Second Annual Radio Poll, conducted by *Musical America,* Miss Munsel ranked among the three most popular woman singers for 1944-45. Miss Munsel has a contract with RCA-Victor for a series of recordings. (The Victor *Record Review* considers her voice "unrivaled for thrilling precision and clarity.") In 1945 she is also under contract to Warner Brothers '46. Miss Munsel still works and studies, guided by her mother who keeps shorthand notes of the instructions of directors to aid her daughter in studying her operatic roles. The energetic singer can sing high G in alt above high C in practice, but in performances she has not sung higher than F above high C.

This slender young woman stands five feet five and a half inches tall and weighs one hundred and nineteen pounds. She has large deep-brown eyes, and her oval face is framed by shoulder-length dark hair. Her brunet beauty has been pictured prominently in the press, and her flashing smile has graced the cover of *Life*. She is a fun-loving, vivacious girl, fond of sports, especially skiing and riding. Her favorite drink is a chocolate soda, and like most of her contemporaries she likes boogie-woogie music and dancing.

References

Life 16:48-52 F 21 '44 il pors
N Y Post Mag p43 Ap 9 '43 pors
N Y Times Mag p47 N 21 '43 por
Opera N 8:10 D 20 '43 por
Time 42:49 N 22 '43 por

MURDOCK, VICTOR Mar. 18, 1871— July 8, 1945 Former United States Congressman from Kansas (1903-15); member of Federal Trade Commission (1917-24); chairman

MURDOCK, VICTOR—*Continued*
of Progressive National Committee; editor in
chief of Wichita Eagle from 1924 until death.

Obituary

N Y Times p11 Jl 9 '45 por

MURRAY, JAMES E(DWARD) May 3,
1876- United States Senator from Montana
Address: b. Senate Office Bldg., Washington,
D. C.; h. 321 Broadway, Butte, Mont.

James E. Murray, proponent of many progressive measures, has been less well known
to the general public than his fellow Senator
from Montana, the anti-New Deal Burton K.
Wheeler [40]. But during recent years the
Democratic Senator Murray has come forward as the sponsor of much of the Administration's most far-reaching legislation.

JAMES E. MURRAY

Emerging as the protector of small business,
he has had a firm hand in such important
matters as war contracts termination, surplus
property disposal, and the extension of the
social security system. At least two of his
major projects—a bill for the independent development of the Missouri Valley Authority
and the full employment bill of 1945—have
been called "foundation stones in the postwar
plans of Left-wing Democrats."

James Edward Murray was born in Canada,
near St. Thomas, Ontario, on May 3, 1876.
His parents were Andrew James Murray and
Anna Mary (Cooley) Murray. In 1897, when
the Murrays moved to Butte, Montana, the
boy's uncle, a wealthy miner for whom James
was named, sent him to New York to study
law. The young Canadian became an American citizen and took his LL.B. at New York
University Law School in 1900, his LL.M.
a year later. He then returned to Montana
and, settling down under the wing of his
colorful and influential uncle, proceeded to
build up a comfortable law practice.

Murray's first elective office was that of
county attorney of Silver Bow County (1906-
08), to which he was elected at thirty. For
the next two decades Murray lived a quiet
life: To the citizens of Montana he was "a
comparatively drab figure," while his uncle
remained the outstanding Murray of the State.
It was not until 1933 that he again entered the
political scene, becoming chairman of the
State Advisory Board for the PWA. On
November 6, 1934, Murray was elected to the
United States Senate to fill the unexpired term
of the late Thomas J. Walsh. With little opposition, he was re-elected for the 1936 and
1942 terms. A faithful New Dealer, during
these years he backed the majority of the
Administration's legislative measures, and
soon became known as one of the most progressive Senators.

In the early months of 1941, when problems
of national defense became a paramount concern, Senator Murray, as head of the Special
Senate Committee on Small Business, became
the champion of these small enterprises in
their competition with big business for the
major defense production contracts. In September 1941 he asked for an appropriation of
one million dollars to study their problems.
For some months things moved slowly for the
Murray Committee. But by the end of 1942
small business found a firm backer in Donald
M. Nelson [41], chairman of the War Production
Board, who assured Murray that the WPB
sub-agency, the Smaller War Plants Corporation, would make a number of surveys.

The Murray Committee was able to bring to
light, in December 1943, examples of discrimination against small business when General Brehon Somervell's [42] Services of Supply
overloaded large plants with its orders but
overlooked the facilities of small companies
"crying for a part in the war program." The
Anaconda Wire and Cable Company was particularly named by Murray—the company had
been charged with supplying defective communication wire to the Army and was also
seen as opposing the Government through the
many newspapers it owned in Montana. (The
former charge was dealt with by the Department of Justice's War Frauds Unit under
Tom C. Clark [45].)

Early in 1943 Senator Murray warned that
growing giant corporate monopolies would lead
to "a complete abandonment of free enterprise
and the building in its place of a totalitarian
system like that of Germany" unless something
were done to "tide smaller firms over the war
period." Although the Smaller War Plants
Corporation Act, devised to aid smaller companies to get war contracts, was finally passed,
Senator Murray charged a lack of coordinated
aid to small business bungled the whole problem. In 1944 the SWPC was renamed the
Small Business Corporation.

The Montana Senator in July 1943 introduced his war contracts termination legislation,
terming this "one of the prime tasks before
the present session of Congress." His bill
provided for permissive loans by the Government up to 75 per cent of a contractor's
claims at the time his contract was canceled.
There was, however, considerable pressure for
redrafting, and Murray came forward with a

recommendation for an "omnibus" war contracts termination law.

On February 22, 1944, Murray joined with conservative Democratic Senator George '43 of Georgia to introduce into Congress an industrial demobilization bill which embodied some of the Baruch '41-Hancock plans for terminating war contracts, together with disposal of surplus Government property. The Murray-George bill was passed by the Senate on May 4. Harley Kilgore '41 of Virginia in turn offered an amendment (which the Senate rejected) to establish a central planning board, and fought to get the Senate to consider such "human" things as unemployment compensation for workers who lose jobs when contracts are canceled. Foreseeing the possibility of "nineteen million idle" at the close of the war, Murray urged that legislation meeting the best features of both proposals be enacted at once. But the new Kilgore-Murray bill, drafted in August was defeated by supporters of the George bill, the latter advocating not Federal but state-controlled compensation plans. Kilgore, however, supported by Murray, reintroduced his bill into Congress in July 1945.

Tied in with all this was the problem of the disposal of many millions of dollars in surplus war properties. Murray explained that the Small Business Act of 1944 was devised to authorize the Small Business Corporation to "acquire these surpluses for disposal through it to small concerns." A bill providing for civilian rather than military control over surplus properties was introduced in August 1944 by Senators Murray, Steward, and Taft '40. The bill would further empower the Attorney General to prevent sale of plants to monopolies. But a deadlock soon arose between the Murray supporters and Presidential right-of-center advisers, including "assistant president" James Byrnes '41 and Baruch. In 1943 Will Clayton '44, Southern "cotton baron," had been named Surplus Property Administrator. At that time the Murray-led liberals had succeeded in passing a bill that would provide instead for a three-man board, which Clayton called unworkable. But when it was reported that Clayton, backed by Secretary of Commerce Jesse Jones '40, had moved to place on the board men who had "big business" interests, Murray warned the President that such appointments would be a betrayal of the New Deal, and the Jones-Clayton appointees were ruled out. In January 1945 Murray's Small Business Committee was liberally represented on the newly created Surplus Properties Board. Public hearings for disposal of approximately two hundred billion dollars' worth of surplus were held by the Murray Committee, and the scramble to negotiate acquisition of large Government war plants began.

Shortly after the defeat of the Murray-Kilgore bill, the Senator from Montana turned his attention in September 1944 to President Roosevelt's '42 request for early legislation to create a Missouri Valley Authority for most of the country west of the Mississippi, to be patterned after the Tennessee Valley Authority. The proposed legislation for the MVA was opposed by the Army Engineers (who are in charge of river and harbor work) and the Reclamation Service, and the lameduck Congress of November tried to scuttle the Administration's plan for an independent MVA by introducing piecemeal legislation. But on November 28 the Senate voiced unanimous opposition to a substitute plan for turning the river's resources into various projects favored by Western states.

Early in 1945 Murray introduced a revised bill for the MVA, the project to affect large areas in Missouri, North and South Dakota, Nebraska, Iowa, Kansas, Montana, Wyoming, and Colorado. "The full development of the resources of this great region," he said, "might well rank as the most important national development since the Louisiana Purchase. But Vice-President Truman '45, although a Missourian, committted the bill to the Senate Commerce Committee, headed by Josiah Bailey '45, who was known to be opposed to Government-owned power projects. Secretary of the Interior Ickes '41 further complicated matters by proposing that the MVA be put under control of the Department of the Interior. By September 1945 a strong lobby, said to be, "the first large-scale power lobby since the National Electric Light Association, controlled by the Samuel Insulls," was doing everything possible to defeat the MVA bill. A national association of electric companies, representing a large number of private power companies and the utility holding company interests, was heading the lobby, aided by the Mississippi Valley Development Association and the National Reclamation Association. President Truman, in the meantime, had come out in support of the bill, and thousands of residents of the states affected had petitioned Congress for its early passage.

It was in connection with a bold program for postwar security in America that the name of the Montana Senator began to appear most often before the public. Jointly with Senator Robert Wagner '41 of New York and Representative John Dingell of Michigan, Murray on June 3, 1943, introduced into Congress a bill designed to eliminate the economic hazards of unemployment, sickness, and old age for every American. It would extend the social security system to fifteen million citizens not yet covered, broaden old age and unemployment benefits, and set up medical and hospital insurance to cover all workers and their families.

The bill's most popular feature—and the one also subject to most attack—was the proposal of a broad Federal system for postwar medical and hospital insurance for all. This program would be financed by setting aside one fourth of the total social security collections under the proposed system—an estimated two to two and a half billion dollars a year. Among its provisions were: Each person would be entitled to choose his own doctor; doctors would be free to go in or stay out of the plan, and those who went in would be free to select their patients; doctors would be paid from the insurance fund; hospital care would be limited to thirty days a year, and include all illnesses except tuberculosis and mental cases. While the program for medical care received the immediate support of some organizations, strong opposition came from the powerful American Medical Association and certain large commercial interests. In a series of speeches in November 1943, Senator Murray charged these groups with "waging a political fight" to destroy the health provisions of

MURRAY, JAMES E.—*Continued*

the proposed social security plan. "It is tragic," he said, "that a bill introduced solely in order to bring more adequate medical care to all the people in the United States should be so misinterpreted by a group which professes to represent the medical profession."

For more than a year the Wagner-Murray-Dingell bill lay in committee, receiving no hearings. Then, with the drafting of a new bill in April 1945, further provisions for national health were made in a program to meet practically all family medical costs except the purchase of patent medicines. Dental care was included, and provisions made for grants to states for maternal and child-health service, and for the extension of health insurance to independent farmers, professional persons, and small businessmen, although the measure was attacked as one aimed at "centralization and socialization of the Federal Government." In November a five-point national health program, including the first plan for compulsory health insurance in the history of the United States was presented to Congress by President Truman. Bills by Senators Wagner and Murray were immediately introduced in the Senate to support the President's recommendations. The bills were again sharply attacked by the A.M.A. It unanimously adopted a statement which declared that positive proof existed from experience in other countries that inferior medical service resulted from compulsory health insurance.

In December 1944 the War Contracts Subcommittee of the Senate Committee on Military Affairs, with Senator Murray as chairman, had drawn up a basic plan for farreaching legislation intended to guarantee a job for every employable American after the war. The program, designed to provide sixty million postwar jobs (the figure cited by President Roosevelt in a campaign speech), came to be called the full employment bill of 1945. Cosponsored by Senators Wagner, Elbert D. Thomas [42], and Joseph C. O'Mahoney [45], it was introduced by Murray into the Senate in January 1945. The bill would set up a "new type of budget to carry out the policy of necessary investment and expenditures—a national production and employment budget." Each year the President would furnish Congress with an estimate of the number of persons willing to work for whom employment would be needed; an estimate of the total investment of and expenditure by private business, state, local, and Federal governments needed to provide this employment; and an estimate of the amount of such expenditure in prospect. If, when his suggestions were accepted, there was still prospect of unemployment, he would be directed to offer a program of public works. A joint committee of the House and Senate would be set up to study the President's proposals so that Congress would be prepared to take action before a depression came. "This is not just a bill to take up the slack through public works," said Murray. "It is founded on the premise that we can't just sit around and wait until people are out of work before we do something about promoting employment." The legislation looked toward the cooperation of industry, agriculture, labor, and state and local governments

for the free competitive enterprise which would provide full utilization of the country's resources.

Early hearings on the full-employment bill were promised. But the measure, called the "fool employment bill" (*Newsweek*, June 18, 1945) by its opponents, brought forth considerable attack from the supporters of big business. The *Saturday Evening Post* called it "The Sixty-Million-Jobs Myth." Others said it was an "undemocratic" move: "No democratic government can manage the national economy and remain the government of a free people." Anti-New Dealers saw in the bill the beginning of a "new" New Deal for the postwar period. Senator Murray, for his part, warned business leaders against adopting the position that business needs and wants a floating number of unemployed in order to operate "to the better advantage of business." America cannot survive, he said, unless "business wholeheartedly adopts the goal of jobs for all who are able and willing to work."

Strong support for the bill came with its endorsement in June by War Mobilization Director Fred M. Vinson [43], known as a conservative Southern Democrat. President Truman, who as a Senator had been on the Murray subcommittee which originated the bill, could be counted on, it was said, to make it one of the major objectives of his Administration. "Virtually every Government agency dealing with labor and postwar economic problems, as well as the A. F. of L and CIO, stood behind the full employment bill. It was passed by the Senate late in September 1945, but only after it had been amended to read that any expenditure "shall be accompanied by a program of taxation . . . to prevent any net increase in the national debt." When the Attlee [40] Labor Party won in Great Britain, Senators Murray and Wagner declared that it was the unemployment issue that contributed to the political upheaval in Britain and "turned it toward socialism."

During 1943, 1944, and 1945 Senator Murray had lent active support to other Administrative progressive legislation. He urged that the Government take the public into its confidence in planning price control and rationing. The enactment of a bill to take the Office of Civilian Supply away from the WPB and establish it as an independent administration was seen as a victory for Murray's Small Business Committee. During the debate over Secretary Stettinius' [40] selections for his State Department staff, Murray approved all except Will Clayton. He led the opposition against the Social Security Tax freeze which the Senate passed in December 1944. In January 1945 he introduced, with Senator Wagner, a bill to liberalize the unemployment sections of the GI Bill of Rights. In March he introduced a bill to prohibit large tire manufacturers from distributing their products through company-owned outlets. In April he suggested the use of idle textile mills in France to help take care of the huge Army textile requirements. Throughout the war years he assailed as "traitors" those who he said were "trying to strike terror into the hearts of our people with false tales about Russia's plan to communize the world and desert the United Nations." He cosponsored a resolution to persuade Great Britain to allow establishment of refugee centers in Palestine, and declared in regard to developments there in the fall of 1945, "There is hardly another instance in the memory of our generation where promises have been so lavishly made and so consistently violated." At a dinner given in New York for Yugoslav relief, he lauded Marshal Tito '43 as a "great leader." In early 1945 he headed a committee of nationally known Catholics to urge the Big Three at their conference to discuss a world-wide ban on racial discrimination.

In January 1945 he succeeded to the chairmanship of the Senate Committee on Education and Labor. He reported at that time that organized labor was not asking for any new legislation on its own behalf. In May 1945, as chairman of the Small Business Committee, Murray ordered a broad study of labor-management relations, including the question of consolidating the Government's scattered labor agencies. Hearings were scheduled for June to discuss in particular the role of labor organizations as related to small business. It was on May 23 that the Senate Committee on Education and Labor voted for the Chavez bill to establish a permanent statutory Fair Employment Practice Commission to succeed the wartime FEPC created by President Roosevelt in 1941. New work loomed before the Labor Committee when, in June, stiff labor opposition rose against the new Ball '43-Burton '45-Hatch '44 bill for a proposed Federal industrial law. Murray was also a supporter of President Truman's plan to establish fact-finding boards empowered to make recommendations in major labor disputes. Murray has consistently opposed any further extension of the draft and has frequently gone on record for repeal of the Act passed in 1940. When the question of further investigation of the Pearl Harbor situation was brought up in the Senate in the autumn of 1945, Murray lead the opposition.

James E. Murray is said to be one of the wealthiest members of the Senate. His thin, sensitive face, with a broad brow, is offset by a determined mouth and chin. He has been described as "a soft-spoken, gentle, and modest (one might say shy) soul utterly devoid of the bluster and brass one finds on Capitol Hill." Another writer has said, "You catch an angry glint in his eye and a firmer set to his jaw" when he fights opposition to the social measures he has sponsored. Murray was married in 1905 to Viola Edna Horgan; they are the parents of five sons: James, William, Edward, Howard and Charles. The youngest son, Charles, who is an economist and secretary to the Senate Labor Committee, is said to be "the chief confidant of his father, who makes few decisions without consulting him."

References

Bsns W F 10 '45 por
N Y Times p25 O 20 '43
PM p17 Mr 9 '44 por; p8 My 10 '45 por
Sat Eve Post 218:9 D 8 '45
Congressional Directory, 1945
Who's Who in America, 1944-45

MUSSOLINI, BENITO (AMILCARE ANDREA) (moo"so-lē'nē) July 29, 1883—Apr. 28, 1945 Former Italian dictator; organized first Fascio di Combattimento at Milan in 1919, the beginning of Fascism in Italy; organized Fascism as political party in 1921; by 1922 he had demanded and received dictatorial powers, and in the following year he had created a powerful Fascist militia; removed from office and made prisoner by the decision of the Fascist Grand Council in July 1943; executed by Italian Partisans. See *Current Biography* 1942 Yearbook.

Obituary

N Y Times p1+ Ap 30 '45 pors

MYDANS, CARL M(AYER) (mī'dàns) May 20, 1907- Photographer; journalist

MYDANS, SHELLEY SMITH May 20, 1915- Journalist; author

Address: b. c/o Time, Inc., 9 Rockefeller Plaza, New York City

In June 1938 *Life* Magazine's first photographer-reporter team was formed by the marriage of two staff members, Carl M. Mydans, photographer and reporter, and Shelley Smith, researcher and writer. Throughout the war the Mydans, working jointly or independently, reported in words and pictures from almost every

Alfred Eisenstaedt
CARL M. MYDANS

fighting front. And as internees in the Santo Tomás camp in Manila, and in the Shanghai International Settlement, for twenty-one months in 1942-43 they experienced another phase of the war, as prisoners of the Japanese. The story of these months has been told in novel form by Shelley Smith Mydans in her book *The Open City* (1945).

The son of David J. Mydans, an oboist, Carl Mayer Mydans was born in Boston on May 20, 1907, eight years, to the day, before the birth of his future wife and co-worker, Shel-

SHELLEY SMITH MYDANS

ley Smith. A native of Palo Alto, California, she is the daughter of Everett W. Smith, professor of journalism at Leland Stanford University. After being graduated from Boston University in 1930 with a B.S. in journalism, young Mydans spent the next five years on the city desks of various newspapers and, during the major portion of this period, as news editor of the *American Banker*. An enthusiastic photographer, the young editor spent his leisure time improving his technique, and in 1935 he became a photographer for the United States Resettlement Administration.

Unlike Carl Mydans' early training, Shelley Smith's preparation for a career was no springboard to her journalistic future. Eager to be a dancer and an actress, she was for a while a member of a stock company in San Francisco, before going to New York to pursue her career on Broadway. But, as circumstances would have it, she went to work instead as researchist for the now defunct *Literary Digest*. Meanwhile, a year before she was to transfer to *Life*'s research staff, Carl Mydans joined *Life* as a photo-reporter. Mydans' peacetime assignments were unusually scattered: photo-reports on Hollywood studios, sailors in submarines, Mexican cattle ranches, transcontinental trucking, High Mass at St. Patrick's Cathedral in New York City. Then, at *Life*'s Christmas Eve party in 1937, Mydans and Shelley Smith were introduced, and six months later (June 1938) the couple were married. For the next two years Mrs. Mydans worked in *Life*'s New York office, while her husband carried out assignments in the field.

At the outbreak of war in September 1939, the Mydans were sent to Europe as correspondents for their magazine. The couple didn't reach Paris till the latter part of October because of an emergency appendectomy Mydans underwent in Bermuda, their first stop en route. France, still in the deceptive "phony" state of war, was not an exciting spot for correspondents eager for action, so the team left for England. In December Carl Mydans set

out for the Finnish-Russian front, while his wife went to Sweden. For two and a half months Mydans photographed, in sub-zero weather, the hardships of Finnish civilians during Russian bombings, the Kemi River battlefield, Viipuri under fire. The cold was so intense that he carried two cameras inside his sheepskin coat, alternating their use so as not to expose one camera too long to the cold. Says the photographer: "Pictures lay at every glance, but never have I suffered more in getting them."

Joining his wife in Stockholm, he next photo-reported an article on Sweden's possible course of action in the event of a German invasion. After a short stay in London, Mydans then returned to the Continent to cover the capitulation of France in June 1940. Coincidental with his stay in Paris, was Shelley Mydans' assignment in Portugal, where she collaborated on an article with *Life* photographer Bernard Hoffman. A few days before the Germans entered Paris, Mydans and his colleagues of the *Life-Time* staff started south for the Spanish border. Mydans' repeated attempts to photograph the panicky exodus of civilians to the south were frustrated. Frenchmen, angry, frightened, and tired, found a ready-made scapegoat in this reportorial staff of twenty-five Americans and Britishers. The people shouted "Capitalist robbers" at *Life*'s automobiles; the Britishers were refused service at restaurants; some of the staff, including Mydans, were mistaken for German parachutists and almost hanged; and when Mydans photographed a group of Frenchmen at a gas station he was mobbed by the crowd and rescued only by the intervention of a soldier attached to *Life*'s employees by the French Ministry of Information. The staff finally reached Lisbon on June 24 and boarded a clipper for the United States.

Back in the States, Shelley Mydans was assigned to the National Defense Departments of Time, Inc., in New York and Washington, D.C., while her husband, after two weeks in Washington, embarked for Hawaii. Two months later he covered maneuvers of the Pacific Fleet, then headed for Mexico to report on the inauguration of President Avila Camacho '40. While in Mexico, Mydans was attacked by an anti-United States, anti-Camacho mob.

With the Far East their next joint assignment, the Mydans left California in December 1940 on the S.S. *President Taft*. Leaving the ship at Hong Kong, they continued by plane to Chungking. In an article in *Life* entitled "The Backwoods Capital of China," they described the Chungking of 1941 as a blockaded city filled with poverty, dirt, and disease, but inhabited by an undaunted people. According to the Mydans, "It must be discouraging to the Japanese to see China make great strides in health, education, and modern living under the steady rain of bombs. . . .And it must cause consternation in Tokyo to realize that if a Chinese farmer's house is destroyed by a bomb, and his horse and pig killed, the collected metal of the destructive missile will pay for a new home, horse, pig, and set him up anew."

Life in China was hard for the Americans, too, becoming more unsafe for the Mydans with the gradual destruction of their hotel by bombings, but Carl Mydans kept right on photographing, in the sweltering heat, life in wartorn China. From Chungking the couple headed for Singapore on a photo-reporting assignment embracing the social, economic, and military conditions of the British colony. Following their return to China, they visited the Yellow River front, Chengtu, Langchow, and Sian, then turned eastward to Hong Kong.

In these travels through the Orient prior to the bombing of Pearl Harbor, the Mydans found Japan's efforts at fraternization under the banner "Asia for the Asiatics" almost ineffectual, reactions varying with the locality. Inhabitants of the hot regions of Malaya, Java, and Sumatra were less antagonistic to Japanese rule than the subjugated peoples farther north. But, contended Mydans and his wife, in the long run, Japanese slogans and sporadic gestures of good will would be outweighed in all the conquered areas by the hunger and maltreatment they brought.

In September 1941 the couple flew from Hong Kong to Manila to gather information on the defenses of the Philippines. They wrote two articles—one on Corregidor and one called "Defenders of the Philippines." The latter, illustrated by Mydans' photographs of the United States Army's preparations for the defense of the Philippines, was based on Shelley Mydans' research. Traveling on the last clipper leaving Manila prior to December 7, 1941, the manuscripts arrived in New York on Pearl Harbor day.

Choosing to remain in burning Manila while Time's correspondent in the Philippines, Melville Jacoby, followed the American retreat toward Bataan and Corregidor, Carl and Shelley Mydans shortly afterward, on January 2, 1942, were interned with about thirty-five hundred American and Allied nationals at Santo Tomás University in the Philippine capital. Describing the internment, the Mydans say: "At dusk on January 2, 1942, the Japanese advance forces entered the city. . . .With a minimum of contact and good order, they separated us from the Filipinos interned with us, confiscated our property and business, then moved on toward Bataan, leaving Manila a breadless, inert city."

In September 1942 the Mydans were fortunate enough to be transferred by the Japanese from Manila to the Chapei Civil Assembly Center in Shanghai, where they had more liberty. In December 1943, they were repatriated on the Gripsholm. In a letter to Life's executive editor, Wilson Hicks, written soon after they boarded the Gripsholm, Shelley Mydans said: "Despite our anticipation, none of us was quite prepared for the emotions that suddenly choked us as we stepped onto the deck." Freedom to the fifteen hundred men, women, and children after twenty-two months of imprisonment felt like a new experience. Describing the Japanese repatriates, Shelley Mydans commented on the fact that they looked healthy and well-dressed in comparison to the pitifully thin and raggedly clothed Allied repatriates. She described their first meal aboard the Gripsholm—jokes and casual conversation did not very well camouflage the longing looks in the people's eyes as each dish was set before them. They had two years' hunger to appease,

but had been advised to eat sparingly. In the words of Mrs. Mydans, "Our shrunken stomachs are easily satisfied, as are our hearts. They were both filled to discomfort—a little bit of food and the feeling that we were welcome." Greeted by the press upon their arrival in New York, Mydans said, "This is the first time I have ever been on the receiving end of this kind of business."

Mydans' first important undertaking after his return to the United States was a photo-report on the Tule Lake Segregation Camp—a relocation center for Japanese considered disloyal to the United States. His pictorial report of the camp contained illuminating photographs of a community run on a cooperative basis. After a week's stay at the center, Life's correspondent noted that "the Japanese at Tule Lake have everything they need for happiness except the one thing they want most—liberty."

Mrs. Mydans was kept busy, too. After answering with her husband the large number of letters from relatives and friends of the internees at the Manila camp, she wrote two articles for the April 1944 issue of Fortune, "When the Jap Came to Manila" and "Asia for the Japanese." In the first article she pointed out the difficulties the Japanese encountered in the Philippines after December 1941 in trying to eradicate the islanders' concepts of personal freedom and their deep-seated Occidentalism. In "Asia for the Japanese," she wrote a study of Japan's growth during the Second World War from a "have not" nation to one of the great "have" nations of the world.

In February 1945, after the liberation of Manila, Shelley Smith Mydans' book The Open City was published. Written as a novel, The Open City portrays, through fictional characters, life as experienced by the internees at the Santo Tomás camp. She tells of the camp's organization into committees—education, purchasing, sanitation, disciplinary, recreation, work assignment, and insect control—a division of work which produced an efficiently run community bent on maintaining order and justice. Its reputation for being "the best camp in Asia" was attributed to the fact that the internees handled most of their own affairs. The author asserts that anxiety more than physical privations were responsible for the distress of many of the prisoners. (Mydans worked in the camp clinic and his wife was on the sanitation committee, cereal cleaning detail, and was monitor of the women's room.) The book also discusses such details as "the rumors from Bataan; the clogged drains; the weevily rice; the brutalities of the gendarmes, only worsened by complaint; and the heroisms and hesitations of Americans." Said Lewis Gannett [41], "Her book is a novel, and perhaps because it is a novel it is more desperately real than any factual account of life in such a camp could dare to be." James Fuller, reviewing the book in the New York Times, found The Open City an ingenuous novel written . . . with sympathy and sincerity. . . .Mrs. Mydans, for all her keen observations, is not a natural story-teller. . . . A factual journal by Mrs. Mydans would almost certainly have been impressive."

The next few months after their return from Manila found Mrs. Mydans at Life's New York news office, and her husband in Italy as an accredited correspondent with the United States

MYDANS, CARL M. and MYDANS, SHELLEY SMITH—Continued

Army in the Mediterranean theater of war. He accompanied the Fifth Army in the Cassino fighting, and later covered the invasion of southern France and the drive north.

Then, as one of three correspondents on board General MacArthur's [41] ship, Mydans returned to the Philippines in October 1944 with the invasion forces. His wife joined him there about a month later. Assigned to the Second Squadron of the Eighth Cavalry Regiment of the First Cavalry Division, Mydans accompanied a motorized column in a sixty-mile dash through Japanese-held territory to free the internees of Santo Tomás. By February 4, 1945, the camp was in American hands. Mydans, describing the raising of the American flag over the camp, said, "The internees stood by breathlessly. . . .Some started singing 'God Bless America,' and the entire camp picked it up. I have never heard people singing 'God Bless America' and weeping openly. And these people have never seen soldiers—hard-bitten youngsters such as make up the First Cavalry—stand unashamed and weep." Carl Mydans was officially commended by Major General Verne A. D. Mudge, commanding general of the First Cavalry Division, for coverage of the "flying wedge" attack on Manila. Husband and wife are back in the United States again. Shelley Mydans will become a radio commentator for Time Magazine, beginning January 1946. She will do newscasting on a program called Time for Women. Carl Mydans is based in the New York home office of Life as a photographer.

Shelley Mydans, slim and pretty, is said to possess much patience in tracking down facts. Carl Mydans is short and dark, and has an amiable disposition, plus an adeptness for getting out of difficult situations. In 1939 he won the United States Camera Magazine's award.

References

Life 12:8-9+ F 23 '42 il pors
N Y Herald Tribune p17 F 15 '45 por

MYDANS, SHELLEY SMITH. See Mydans, C. M. and Mydans, S. S.

NATHAN, GEORGE JEAN Feb. 14, 1882-
Critic, author, editor

Address: The Royalton, 44 W. 44th St., New York City

Although there is a popular legend to the effect that George Jean Nathan, the drama critic, is a thoroughgoing skeptic who writes with "bitter scorn and contemptuous cynicism," it is generally conceded that no other American critic has so greatly influenced public taste or played a more important part in raising the standards of the American theater during a third of a century. A master at lampooning, Nathan has penned "annihilating waggeries" that have laid low many objects of his barbs. On the other hand he has stanchly and consistently supported those who have contributed originality, honesty, and dignity to the theater. He is credited with the introduction into the American theater of the best of the European modern dramatists, with the encouragement of young native playwrights like Eugene O'Neill

and William Saroyan '[40], and with a reformation of the general critical attitude toward the theater. In the past Nathan has been associated with a great many leading American and European periodicals. In 1945 he was conducting the drama departments for the *American Mercury* and *Esquire* as well as doing a weekly (Monday) drama report for the New York *Journal-American*. He is the author of thirty or more books, most of which are devoted to the theater. He was co-editor with H. L. Mencken of the *Smart Set* magazine (1914-23), and in 1924 helped Mencken found and edit the *American Mercury*.

George Jean Nathan was born in Fort Wayne, Indiana, on February 14, 1882, to Charles Naret and Ella (Nirdlinger) Nathan. His father, born Charles Naret, the son of Jean-Jacques and Renée (Callot) Naret, was given his stepfather's name (Nathan) when his mother remarried. Charles Naret Nathan, a Parisian lawyer, was a graduate of Heidelberg. A linguist, a skilled fencer, and the owner of French vineyards and a Brazilian coffee plantation, he had lived in almost every civilized country of the globe. On a visit to Fort Wayne, Indiana, he met and was married to Ella Nirdlinger, whose family had settled there when it was little more than a frontier fort. Of German origin, the Nirdlingers made the journey to Fort Wayne from Chambersburg, Pennsylvania, in a covered wagon. Although Nathan's father never engaged in business in Indiana the family continued to live there until George Jean was four years old, when they moved to Cleveland.

In Cleveland George attended the public school and received private instruction in Spanish, German, and French, as well as piano lessons. As early as eleven the future critic showed interest in the theater; he wrote dramas which were acted by the neighborhood children in the Nathan barn. "Love: A Scientific Analysis," his first long piece, was written at the age of sixteen. The flippancy with which he dealt with "poor Cupid on the dissecting table," foreshadowed the writing of Nathan, the man: it was the "protoplasmic ancestor" of his books *The Bachelor Life* (1941) and *Beware of Parents* (1943), inspired, he says, by his own unmarried state at the age of sixty.

Graduated from the Cleveland High School, young Nathan chose to go to Cornell because it seemed to him the one of all American universities to approach most closely the European universities which he had come to know during three summers spent abroad in his high-school days. His record as an undergraduate shows that he was active in extracurricular activities. He was a member of Kappa Sigma; Quill and Dagger, senior honorary society; the Masque, the dramatic club; and the fencing team. He was also editor of the college daily, the *Sun*, and of the *Cornell Widow*. In addition to fencing (for which he won the Amsler Gold Medal) he was excellent at tennis. Upon obtaining his B.A. degree from Cornell (1904), Nathan went to Italy where he attended the University of Bologna for a year. He returned to the States and, through the influence of his uncle, Charles Frederic Nirdlinger, playwright and well known critic of his day and a friend of James

Gordon Bennett, editor of the New York *Herald*, young Nathan became a cub reporter at fifteen dollars a week on the *Herald* (1905-06). The writing of murder stories, sports, and Sunday feature stories followed in the succession named. In between his feature stories Nathan, as third-string drama critic, occasionally turned in a play review. Irked by the many "don'ts" of Bennett's editorial policy, Nathan left the newspaper to become associate editor and drama critic on two magazines, the *Outing* and the *Bohemian* (1906-08). Nathan's biographer, Isaac Goldberg, in *Theatre of George Jean Nathan* (1926), says that Nathan has too much imagination and "caprice in the face of facts" to have been happy as a newspaperman. (Nathan has consistently refused to accept the post of drama critic on any daily newspaper because, he says, he could not conscientiously turn in a play review immediately after seeing a performance; to him it seems that critical opinions should be given after longer consideration.)

One of the best pieces of advice Nathan ever received on free-lance writing came from Finley Peter Dunne, creator of the popular cartoon character, Mr. Dooley. "Don't ever bother about the dignity or importance of the medium for which you write," said Dunne. "It doesn't matter where your stuff appears, so long as it is good. If it is good, the right people are sure to see it." In his career Nathan has been associated with more than thirty publications as drama reviewer. By 1925 he had become the most widely read and the highest paid dramatic critic in the world. At that time, besides holding a staff position on *Judge*, he contributed a weekly drama review to the New York *Telegraph* which was widely sold throughout the United States and in other countries by the Wheeler Syndicate. During the same year he also contributed articles on the theater to English, German, Italian, and Dutch journals. Although the victims of his diatribes attempted reprisals, no one disputed his thorough knowledge of the world theater and its literature, his catholicity of taste, and his independence of judgment. His fight to raise the American theater from its low estate of over two decades ago to its present artistic heights as seen in the productions of the Theatre Guild, Arthur Hopkins, Guthrie McClintic '43, Brock Pemberton '45 (to name only a few), was carried on alone through what has been called the most searching and illuminating sort of criticism—burlesque. "This method," wrote Mencken in a defense of Nathan, "of course, makes for broken heads. . . . There is so far as I know no one on Broadway who has not tried, at one time or another, to dispose of Nathan *attentat*." Nathan's criticism, Mencken pointed out, is founded on the Benedetto Croce '44 doctrine, "that every work of art is at bottom unique, and that it is the business of the critic, not to label and pigeon-hole it, but to seek for its inner intent and content and to value it according as that intent is carried out and the content is valid and worthwhile. . . . It lets in every theatrical work that has an honest aim and achieves that aim passably and is presented frankly for what it is. Bear this theory in mind," Mencken continued, "and you have a clear explanation of his [Nathan's] lampooning and his ardent championing of such widely diverse men."

GEORGE JEAN NATHAN

In the second decade of the century Nathan championed Max Reinhardt's *The Miracle*, the early plays of George Bernard Shaw '44, "the daring nobodies of the Grand Guignol, such divergent originals as Lord Dunsany, Ziegfeld, George M. Cohan, and Arthur Schnitzler; the farces of Avery Hopwood, the whimsey humor of Clare Kummer and Ferenc Molnar, the simple and unaffected writing of Eleanor Gates in *The Poor Little Rich Girl*." Mencken continues, "He distinguished what was sound in the Little Theater movement from what was mere attitudinizing and pseudo-intellectuality. He refused to recognize Belasco as a profound artist or Augustus Thomas as a great playwright or Maeterlinck as a great thinker. Coming upon the scene at the height of the Ibsen mania, he ranged himself against its windy pretenses from the beginning. He saw the high merit of Ibsen as a dramatic craftsman but he also saw how platitudinous was the ideational content of his plays and announced the facts in terms highly offensive to the Ibsenites." To the less discerning, Nathan's destructive methods are most frequently remembered, although he has supported many a "lost" play. He very early recognized O'Neill as a playwright of "size," a term Nathan reserves for genius. Although O'Neill had had his first plays produced by the Provincetown Players, he has said that Nathan's publication in *Smart Set* of three of his one-act plays, the *Long Voyage Home, Ile,* and *Moon of the Caribbees,* presented him to a wider and more general public, and that recognition from Nathan meant a disinterested and critical approval. (Nathan was also instrumental in the production of O'Neill's first long play, *Beyond the Horizon.*) Later Nathan was to welcome the Abbey Players to the American stage, and to see the special qualities in the playwrights, Sean O'Casey, Paul Vincent Carroll, and William Saroyan.

Edith R. Isaacs of the *Theatre Arts* Magazine said that when Nathan sees quality in an artist, he becomes at once not only his champion

NATHAN, GEORGE JEAN—*Continued*

but his salesman to the public. "He trumpets alone, and long, if need be." Eleanora Duse was one of the few actresses whom the critic respected enough not to want to touch with a satirical pen. Although John Barrymore's *Hamlet* had received the highest acclaim from the critics, Nathan declared that his performance was so critically precise "that it is at times histrionically defective."

According to Isaac Goldberg the close friendship between Nathan and Mencken began when they were engaged to edit *Smart Set* in 1914. Over their first cocktail, following a conference, they discovered that they had many opinions and attitudes in common. "That night," recalls Nathan, "we met again over the beer table." The friendship thus begun had a profound effect on American culture. Under their editorship *Smart Set* "projected new attitudes, campaigned for a free, virile, open-air joy in the arts." While some of its humor was regarded as verging on vulgarity, it was "Rabelais rather than barbershop." The co-editors contributed, in addition to book reviews (by Mencken) and drama reviews (by Nathan), a department (written jointly) called *Répétition Générale*, which contained ideational patter and their observations on the human comedy. The magazine thrived, becoming "a focus of intellectual rebelliousness, a rally-ground for disaffected youth, a forum for the new talents." Some of the new talents discovered or fostered under the Mencken-Nathan guidance of *Smart Set* were F. Scott Fitzgerald, Theodore Dreiser, James Branch Cabell, Aldous Huxley, Ben Hecht '42, and James Joyce. However, despite its pleasing of the intelligentsia, *Smart Set* was not a financial success, earning for each of the erudite pair, who were given stock in the publication in lieu of salary, less than fifty dollars a week. When Alfred Knopf '43, the publisher, offered to back them in a new venture, they accepted, resigning from *Smart Set.*

The new venture was the *American Mercury*, which Nathan and Mencken founded in 1924. In this they owned an equal share of the stock. They also shared in the job of editing, Mencken writing the book reviews and a monthly editorial, and Nathan being responsible for the drama department and, to a larger degree than Mencken, for *Clinical Notes*, the successor to *Smart Set's Répétition Générale*. In a 1925 *Bookman* article Nathan wrote: "A magazine, to me—and to my associate, friend, and partner Mencken no less— is a toy, something with which to amuse ourselves and also, perhaps, a sufficient number of similarly minded readers to keep the mechanism of the toy from running down. It provides us with the pleasure of unloading certain of our ideas upon the world, and sensing the reaction of other men to those ideas." A professed hedonist, Nathan has repeatedly stated that he had "no itch to make the world a better place to live in," and that he had never indulged in either "messiah" editing or writing. When the *Mercury* under the more socially conscious Mencken veered toward politics and considerations of a non-aesthetic nature, Nathan announced his resignation as co-editor (August 1925) and his continuance as a contributing editor. This change, however, did not affect the friendship of the two men. After the *Mercury* went into other hands (it had been a financial and literary success from the beginning) Nathan with Theodore Dreiser, Eugene O'Neill, James Branch Cabell, and Ernest Boyd founded the American *Spectator* (1932-37), a "literary newspaper," patterned after the London *Spectator.*

In 1913 Nathan interrupted his duties as a critic to write *The Eternal Mystery*, a one-act play, which was presented on Holbrook Blinn's distinguished program of short plays at New York's Princess Theatre. Dealing with "an illusory agnostic element in religion" (Nathan is an avowed agnostic) the playlet was called sacrilegious, and when it met with the same criticism on its production by tributary theaters in Philadelphia, Pittsburgh, and Detroit, Nathan withdrew it from American production. With the exception of three scenarios for plays which he and Mencken had planned to write but did not finish, this was Nathan's only attempt at serious creative writing for the theater. The play *Heliogabalus* (1920), written in collaboration with Mencken, was never intended for production. Published in a private and limited edition it was pronounced by James Gibbons Huneker, the art and music critic, "a brilliant farce. . .a hell-broth of wit, humor, fantasy, and downright idol-smashing," with a Roman rather than a Christian moral. Nathan's third play, also a product of his impishness, was published under the title *The Avon Flows* (1937). In it he "orchestrated" three of Shakespeare's plays into a "comedy of modern marriage." The opening act is taken from *Romeo and Juliet*, the second and third acts are transposed scenes (dialogue intact) from *Othello* and *The Taming of the Shrew*. The re-identification of the leading characters from the last named plays with the characters Romeo and Juliet and added stage directions resulted in an amusing play.

The critic's series of books on the contemporary theater, published annually since 1916, have met with diverse reviews. *The Popular Theatre* (1918), the first to receive wide acclaim, won from Gordon Craig the tribute that Nathan was greater than Shaw in the art of criticism: "He sees . . . Shaw tries to see. He feels . . . Shaw thinks." *Comedians All* (1919) drew so many adverse reviews that Alexander Woollcott '41, then drama critic of the New York *Times*, came to his colleague's defense: "Many popular misconceptions and dislikes begotten by the Nathan mannerisms should not betray his not inconsiderable public from profiting by the soundness of much that he writes." Nathan's prolific output of books on the theater is seen as taxing his ingenuity at titling. *Encyclopædia of the Theatre*, the title given his 1940 volume, was called a misnomer, inasmuch as it is not an encyclopedia except in the alphabetical arrangement of subjects. The *New Yorker* pronounced it "good standard Nathan"; the New York *Times* reviewer pointed out what he considered Nathan shortcomings as repetitiousness, lack of clarity and "a style too breezy." In 1943 when he used the title *Theatre Book of the Year 1942-1943* and announced a projected series of yearbooks under that title, there was a general protest from reviewers. "A misleading title," said Burton Rascoe of the New York *World-Telegram*. "It is in no sense a completely rounded survey," or a "book of record." The *Library Journal* warned that "in no way is it a rival of Burns Mantle's'[44] justly famous annual volume." The subtitle, *A Record and an Interpretation*, was considered more appropriate. These yearbooks contain an honor list of "bests" in different fields of theatrical accomplishment, critical essays on the season's plays, some statistics, and an index. The New York *Times* review of Nathan's second yearbook (1943-1944) proclaimed him to be "still the nimblest spirit in the narrow row of world dramatic criticism." In his third yearbook (1944-1945) Nathan remained as "jubilantly dizzy" as ever, although for the first time he arranged his impressions chronologically and even provided an index. John Mason Brown wrote of Nathan in the *Saturday Review of Literature*: "The energy of the man is unfailing and incredible . . . his critical headwork at sixty-three amazing . . . his joy in his job undiminished, his precision unerring."

Possibly the two most important books Nathan has written on subjects other than the theater are *The American Credo* (1920), written in collaboration with Mencken, and *The New American Credo* (1927), which he wrote alone. The first-named, a book of 193 pages, contains a preface of 103 pages. This disproportion was justified by the authors by, "Having read it [the preface], one need not read the book." In their book the authors held that "deep down in every man there is a body of congenital attitudes, a corpus of ineradicable doctrines and ways of thinking, that determines the reactions to this ideational environment." The book's preface consists of ratiocinations on those attitudes and doctrine, the book itself is a collection of maxims and traditional tenets of the modern man. The Boston *Transcript*'s critic wrote of the book: "The truth about America and its inhabitants is told as it has not been for some time." Disagreeing, the *Survey* commented: "The stringing together of widely held fallacies does not constitute an American credo." *The New American Credo* was pronounced a "more significant book" than the first *Credo* but "still far from a complete corpus of the current superstitions, prejudices and platitudes which help to render literature and conversation deadly."

The Borzoi Reader (1936), selections from Knopf publications, contains Nathan's "Three Friends: Lewis, O'Neill, and Dreiser." These intimate recollections of the three famous men reveal the author's keen insight into character and his ability to do "exquisite" word caricatures. They also reveal Nathan and Mencken in the lighter moments of their *Smart Set* days. Dreiser, painted as a somber individual, was the butt of their practical jokes, such as filling his mail-box with Black Hand threats, sending him letters purportedly from the President urging him to visit the White House, a photograph of the Czar bearing the inscription: "To Theodore Dreiser, gentleman and scholar—well, anyway, scholar." In 1945 Nathan edited a collection of seven *Pulitzer Prize Plays*.

Nathan's facial characteristics are eyes "like the middle of August," a sensitive mouth, a "nice" nose; his hair, originally dark, is gray. Five feet and seven and one-half inches tall, he weighs 130 pounds. Nathan's favorite form of exercise is now "walking to the nearest taxicab," his favorite recreation, "sitting and

smoking." His voice is pleasing. He has a "seductive" collection of walking sticks, and of his many overcoats, one (of Russian wolf) Broadway says he has trained to bark. On special first nights he wears a silk hat and Inverness cape. He has lived in a three-room apartment in The Royalton for thirty years. Through the years of his bachelorhood the rooms have become filled with books and manuscripts. They line the walls, are stacked ceiling-high on chairs, tables, and on the floor. His favorite restaurants are the 21 Club, the Colony, and Fourteenth-Street Luchow's. Elsa Maxwell'[43] says that he is one of a "strange, ill-assorted, but charming group of people who dine with Dumpa" (the Fifth Avenue and Newport Mrs. Hermann Oelrichs) every Christmas. "Nathan under a Christmas tree," says the columnist, "giving and receiving presents . . . his eyes swimming with sentimental and true affection for his friends," is not the man his public confessions would lead you to expect.

References

Sat R Lit 25:12-13 Ja 24 '42
Goldberg, I. Theatre of George Jean Nathan (1926)
Kunitz, S. J. and Haycraft, H. eds. Twentieth Century Authors (1942)
Mencken, H. L. Prejudices p208-23 v 1 (1924)
National Cyclopædia of American Biography Current vol C p108
Who's Who in America, 1944-45
Who's Who in the Theatre (1939)

NAZIMOVA, ALLA (na-zĭm'ō-va) June 4, 1879—July 13, 1945 Russian-born actress; since debuts in St. Petersburg (1904) and New York (1905) she has acted on the stage continuously both in the United States and Europe; best known for her interpretation of Ibsen roles; was also one of the most popular actresses of the silent films; shortly before death appeared in *Since You Went Away* (1944), *In Our Time,* (1944) and other movies.

Obituary

N Y Times p11 Jl 14 '45 por

NEAGLE, ANNA (nēg'l) Oct. 20, 1904-
Motion picture actress
WILCOX, HERBERT Sept. 19, 1892-
Motion picture producer and director
Address: b. Pathé Films, Film House, Wardour St., London; h. Hartfield House, Deacons Hill, Elstree, Hertfordshire, England

"The culmination of the longest professional association in the British film industry," is the way the Irish-born British producer and director, Herbert Wilcox, described his marriage to the English film star, Anna Neagle, which took place at a London registry office in 1943. Since 1932 in their respective capacities they have made nineteen pictures together, including the memorable *Nell Gwynn* (1934), *Victoria the Great* (1937), and the 1945 release *A Yank in London*. In addition to discovering Miss Neagle, who, under his direction, rose from an unstarred role in musical comedy to "England's first lady of the screen," Wilcox is credited with introducing to the screen Charles Laughton, Herbert Mar-

Swarbrick studios, London

ANNA NEAGLE

shall, Sir C. Aubrey Smith '44, John Loder,
Jack Buchanan, and Dame Sybil Thorndike.
He is one of the few British producers who
have made films in Hollywood and whose
English-made pictures have been widely dis-
tributed in the United States.

Anna Neagle was born Marjorie Robertson
in Forest Gate, near London, on October 20,
1904 (*Who's Who in the Theatre*). She is
the daughter of Herbert William Robertson,
then a captain in the British Merchant Marine,
and of Florence (Neagle) Robertson, whose
surname the actress later took for the stage.
"Of all the good fortune I've had," Miss
Neagle once told an interviewer, "the greatest
was a happy home life during my childhood."
With her two elder brothers she played cricket,
and when on occasional cruises with her father
swabbed down decks and cooked in the ship's
galley. Pretty, blond Marjorie was a "natural"
for heroine roles in school plays, but a shyness
which she did not overcome for many years
made her refuse everything except ensemble
work. At ten she began taking dancing lessons
and at sixteen entered a school for advanced
dancing. A *Collier's* article reports that while
at dancing school the future star became a
dance instructor or a dance hostess at a West
End London hotel. But, being stepped upon
by portly gentlemen did not please her, and
she soon left. It is also recorded that she
had been a gymnasium teacher as well as
dancing teacher, and that in the days before
entering the theater world she reached the
finals in a world championship dance contest
held in Queen's Hall. Later, when forced to
add to the family income because of her
father's illness, Miss Neagle became a chorus
girl.

"Dangerously contented" is the expression
the star has used to describe her attitude during the six years she spent in the choruses of
different London musicals. Her first engagement was in the 1925 edition of André Charlot's famous revues, the revues that introduced
Beatrice Lillie '45, Gertrude Lawrence '40, and

other stars to London audiences. Other musicals of Miss Neagle's chorus days were the
London presentations of American productions,
Rose Marie (1926) and *Desert Song* (1927),
and Noel Coward's '41 *This Year of Grace*
(1928). It was while she was working in the
cabaret at the Trocadero Restaurant that she
entered the cast of *Wake Up and Dream*
(1929), a revue with Cole Porter '40 music and
lyrics. The success of this London production,
in which Jack Buchanan, Jessie Matthews, and
Tillie Losch '44 were starred, brought it and
Miss Neagle to New York for 136 performances on Broadway.

It was the American chorus girls who jolted
the English chorine out of her dangerous contentment. Under that stimulus, Miss Neagle
set out to promote herself. She began visiting
Hollywood agents, took tap dancing and singing lessons. Nevertheless, although the agents
told her she was lovely to look at, she failed
to secure a contract. Her luck was not much
better when she returned to London. For four
months she tramped from office to office, securing only bit parts in two motion pictures,
Should a Doctor Tell? and *The Chinese Bungalow,* the latter described as "an early English
movie which even the British are trying to
forget."

Then one day she received a tryout notification for Buchanan's first show as a producer,
Stand Up and Sing. A place in the chorus
with the star of the show that had taken her
to New York was hers for the asking, but she
requested the feminine lead. And, surprisingly
enough, she received it, for Buchanan had felt
that his own drawing power was sufficient to
carry the show and that an unknown lead
would save him many pounds in salary. During the out-of-town tryout the new leading
lady suffered from the shyness which had
made her content with chorus work for six
years. But Buchanan was kind—he "built her
up in her own estimation, and London [in
1931] was a cinch." Moreover, she proved
a "great success," and the musical ran for
more than three hundred performances.

While the show was still running Buchanan
took Miss Neagle to meet producer Herbert
Wilcox. Actually, it was not their first introduction. Earlier, the actress had tried to
get a part in a Wilcox film starring Madeleine
Carroll, but at that time Miss Neagle's future
husband, the man with whom she was to
become internationally famous, gave her a perfunctory dismissal. On this second occasion
their long association began when Wilcox decided to use the young actress in a picture he
was directing.

Herbert Wilcox had been producing pictures
for more than ten years before he met Miss
Neagle. A dozen years her senior, he was
born in Cork, Ireland, on April 19, in the year
1891 (*International Motion Picture Almanac*).
His parents, Joseph John and Mary (Healy)
Wilcox, moved to England while he was still
a boy, and he was educated in the Brighton
schools. He worked for a time on a newspaper, but when England entered the war he
enlisted, and served as pilot in the RAF until
1919. Wilcox's connection with the motion
picture field began, one source records, with
his sale of a number of original stories to
several film companies. In another account it

is told that in 1919 he began producing pictures independently, having accumulated funds through working as a film renter in Leeds. His initial offering as a producer seems to have been *The Wonderful Story*, called a masterpiece of the early days of the silent film. Numerous other silent pictures followed: *Chu Chin Chow, Madame Pompadour, The Only Way, Paddy the Next Best Thing, The Triumph of the Scarlet Pimpernel*, the production in which Miss Neagle had tried to get a bit part. After the advent of the talkies, Wilcox organized the British and Dominion Productions, and his debut as a producer of talking pictures was made with *Black Waters*, which starred James Kirkwood and Mary Brian.

The first picture that Wilcox was to make with Miss Neagle in the cast was *Good Night, Vienna* (1931) (released in the United States in 1932 as *Magic Night*). The actress was now calling herself Anna Neagle, for Marjorie Robertson was too well known as a member of the chorus line. Her first important picture in the Wilcox studios was the adaptation of Noel Coward's *Bitter Sweet* (1933), but her first big hit was in Wilcox's remake of *Nell Gwynn* (1934), which the producer had made originally with Dorothy Gish[44] in the title role. English reviewers called the new star "vivacious", "alluring," and "an admirable actress." Although there were dissenting voices on Wilcox's direction of the famous love story of Charles II (played by Sir Cedric Hardwicke) and Nell, orange-seller and actress, the film was popular with the English public. Before it could be released in the United States, the Hays[43] Office demanded drastic changes in the script. *Time* Magazine commented that these changes had "made it one of the more genteel specimens of British historical cinema," but that its lack of *esprit*, and the frequently forlorn comedy scenes were compensated for by the sympathetic acting of Hardwicke and Neagle.

Other motion pictures by the Neagle-Wilcox team followed, for a time a series of historical films. One of the greatest successes was *Victoria the Great*, which opened in London in September 1937. Before the première the film had won the "Cup of all Nations" award at an international contest held in Vienna, and Wilcox, who has been called the P. T. Barnum of the cinema, allowed this news to "slip out." Piccadilly on opening night was "jammed with swells in toppers and ladies in sables": British society for the first time was honoring the lowly flickers. After expressing regret over the omission of many historically important issues in the sixty-year reign of Victoria, the *Spectator* concluded that, "if the limits are too narrow, the excellence of the portrayals . . . the authenticity of the settings, and the beauty of the photography make up for much." The London *Mercury and Bookman* said, "Judged by the average standards of screen entertainment, *Victoria the Great* is an unusually good picture. Judged as a piece of craftsmanship, it is not brilliant but very skillful." American critics hailed it as the best film yet to come out of England. It was considered so satisfactory a story of Great Britain's queen, played with noteworthy distinction by Miss Neagle, that Hollywood did not film Laurence Hous-

HERBERT WILCOX

man's *Victoria Regina*, in which Helen Hayes[42] had captivated American audiences a season before.

Victoria was the actress and producer's first big financial success. In fact, so low had the Wilcox coffers been previously that Miss Neagle, it is said, was forced to add her personal savings to tide him through production. When RKO rewarded them with a contract for several pictures to be released through the Hollywood company, Miss Neagle remarked that it was a great relief to know that in the future they would be able to do a picture "without the cashier and the sheriff playing tag among the sets."

Shortly before the release of *Victoria*, the Imperator Film Productions, Ltd., was organized, and Wilcox became chairman and managing director. A unit of this syndicate was Wilcox Productions. One of the earlier pictures to be made under this new setup was *Sixty Glorious Years* (1938), which Miss Neagle and Wilcox made as a sequel to *Victoria the Great*. "Anybody who possesses even a small acquaintance with the history and the personalities of the nineteenth century," wrote the reviewer of the *New Statesman and Nation*, "must recognize that the thing is a travesty of the truth." Nevertheless, the film received "a shower of praise," "even in the most respectable press," in the words of the *New Statesman* critic.

In 1939 another biographical picture was released by Wilcox, *Nurse Edith Cavell*. The story of the English nurse who was executed by a German firing squad for espionage during the First World War, had been produced in 1920 under the title *Dawn*, with Dame Sybil Thorndike as Nurse Cavell. *Sociology and Social Research* hailed Miss Neagle in the role as England's finest actress, the story "a reminder to the civilized world that the military code at its worst reads, 'No mercy to be shown.'" The *Spectator* found Wilcox's new version of the story "all exactly as you would expect: Belgians sing Anglican carols . . . .

NEAGLE, ANNA, and WILCOX, HERBERT—*Continued*

Germans . . . . all brutes in boots (except for the one regulation officer who is always inserted in such films to show the measure of our impartiality)." Miss Neagle looked nice as the nurse, continued the review, but "she moves rigidly on the set, as if wheels were concealed under the stately skirt: she says her piece with flat dignity and trolleys out again." The blame for this lack of "life, character, and truth" was placed on the "slow and ponderous" production.

On the Hollywood RKO lot the English pair in 1940 decided to shelve *Queen of Destiny,* a third play about Victoria, in favor of a musical comedy. *Irene,* a 1919 American hit, was selected. American critics were warm in their praise of the actress' beauty and "her smart dancing legs," but found the Wilcox adaptation "stiffly British." Vincent Youmans' '44 *No, No, Nanette,* which Wilcox put before the camera in 1940 fared no better with the American press. *Sunny,* based on an old Otto Harbach and Oscar Hammerstein 2d '44 musical, had, in the opinion of the New York *Sun,* "the snap" that was missing in the previous musicals. "After two years [1940-41] in Hollywood," it was commented, "Wilcox has picked up a brisker technique."

"Wilcox has fashioned an honest and timely biography," wrote *Time* of *Wings and the Woman* (1942) in which Miss Neagle played Amy Johnson Mollison, the world-renown English aviator who lost her life in 1941 when the plane she was ferrying for the Air Transport Auxiliary broke up over the Thames estuary. Wilcox this time had given the story a slow pace and a minimum of fictional embroidery. *Newsweek* called Miss Neagle's performance "a restrained, sympathetic, and always creditable characterization of the flier." The next year Miss Neagle and Wilcox both worked on *Forever and a Day* (1943), a screen play made in Hollywood by seven well known producers and directors, some twenty writers, and an all-star English-born cast. The picture was conceived in 1941 as a tribute to English courage in the war, and was made cooperatively by both Britons and Americans, who gave their services free of charge. Profits went to charitable organizations.

The first picture that Miss Neagle and Wilcox made upon their return to England after America's entry into the war was *The Yellow Canary* (England, 1942; United States, 1944). A spy story of the Second World War, it revealed to critics that Wilcox had not forgotten his Hollywood lessons in faster tempo. And Miss Neagle, one reviewer declared, "gives a good account of herself as a British lady of quality who isn't as bad as duty (in her role of a counterspy) forces her to be." When the producer-director visited the United States again, in July 1945, he signed a contract with Twentieth Century-Fox for a series of pictures scheduled for world-wide distribution. The first of these is expected to be *A Yank in London,* originally entitled *I Lived in Grosvenor Square.* "It is the best bet on Anglo-American relations build-up the screen has yet offered," was *Variety's* preview comment on the film, which is based on an actual story of a heroic American Air Corps crew in England. Miss Neagle, another reviewer wrote, gives her "most convincing performance to date."

Since becoming a film actress Miss Neagle has occasionally returned to the stage. In 1934 the former chorus girl played Rosalind in *As You Like It* and Olivia in *Twelfth Night.* A few years later, while *Victoria the Great* was drawing record crowds to a Piccadilly film house, the actress was appearing in person in another Piccadilly theater in the title role of Barrie's *Peter Pan.* In 1945, besides touring Army camps on the Continent in *French Without Tears,* Miss Neagle played London and the provinces in Jane Austen's *Emma.*

The star is five feet five inches tall and weighs one hundred and eighteen pounds. To these statistics one male reporter has added that she has red-gold hair, deep blue eyes, "teeth that reduce tooth paste models to shuddering defeats," and a smile that could "make a Romeo out of a woman-hater." In addition, in 1940 the Fashion Academy of New York voted her the best-dressed woman on the international screen. For exercise, the actress walks and bicycles to offset the effects of the lemon pie she likes so well. She has been described as modest and sensible, and when a guest on *Information, Please* one evening in 1941 she acquitted herself with "such charm and wit" that she was invited to participate in the movie short made of the radio program. Part of the acquitting consisted of spotting a Chopin waltz before music expert Oscar Levant '40 did, and correcting the Shakespearean authorities on a quotation from *King Lear.*

In a July 1945 interview with the New York *Herald Tribune,* Miss Neagle's husband, in comparing the film products of the United States and England, that he believes that the chief difference is the matter of pace. In his opinion (contrary to critical opinion on some of his films), "English films have a faster, more provocative pace . . . mostly because Hollywood chooses to slow down its films by abusing the use of the close-up." The producer-director rarely makes a change in his shooting script, rarely shoots more than thirteen takes of any action, never acts out a scene for his carefully chosen cast, and is one director who never raises his voice.

Wilcox, who wears glasses, is described as blondish, inclined to be stocky, and not much taller than Miss Neagle. A superstition of the Irish-born producer is centered on the number thirteen. Since his World War days in the RAF, when several incidents involving the number made him regard it as a lucky one, his life has been quite wittingly interspersed with thirteens—today all his important business undertakings are begun on that day of the month. When traveling, he is usually accompanied by his manservant, Taylor, who is distinguished by his birthplace, Windsor Castle, and by his mixing of Wilcox's favorite drink, the English version of a mint julep (gin substituted for whisky). Wilcox frequently talks in superlatives, particularly when speaking of his favorite star, Mrs. Wilcox. Shortly after his marriage to the actress in August 1943, the British Broadcasting Company dramatized the romance, with the principals playing themselves. The Wilcoxes have a country home near London, and from there, until gasoline rationing, traveled to every soccer game within reasonable motoring distance. Taylor's opinion is that the couple are "real people."

References

Collier's 101:13+ F 5 '38 por
Life 8:59-61 Ap 8 '40 pors
N Y Times p14 Ag 10 '43 por
Time 35:82 My 6 '40 por
International Motion Picture Almanac, 1943-44
Who's Who, 1945

NEGRIN, JUAN (nä-grēn' hwän) 1892(?)- Spanish Republican leader; scientist

With the growing international opposition to the Franco [42] dictatorship in Spain, Juan Negrín, the last Premier of the Republic, has become a cohesive force among Spanish Republicans within the country and in exile in England, France, the United States, and Mexico. The Socialist Negrín has been working throughout his own exile toward the re-establishment of a democratic Spain and, in the opinion of Freda Kirchwey [42], he "will succeed in drawing together all groups except the die-hard irreconcilables."

Juan Negrín was born in the Canary Islands, the Spanish possession in the Atlantic Ocean off the coast of Africa; one source gives the date as 1892. Educated largely on the Continent, he studied medicine at several German universities. It was in these student years that he came into contact with the leaders of German socialism and his political ideology developed. When he had completed his studies in Germany, Negrín studied in other European capitals. Returning finally to Madrid, he became one of the youngest professors in Spain. (Negrín was one of the founders of University City, which was later reduced to rubble in the fight for the capital.) He served as professor of physiology at the Medical Faculty of Madrid University, and was also at different times director of the Physiological Institute and director of the Madrid Chemical Laboratory. In addition to his scientific prominence, the Spanish intellectual gained a reputation as an expert in economic and financial affairs and as a political philosopher. The professor's practical ability was also demonstrated, as for example, in his formation of *Editorial España*, described as "that great nursery of Spanish contemporary thought." A member of the Socialist Party for many years, he actively entered politics in September 1936 when he became Minister of Finance in the Largo Caballero Cabinet. One of his first acts upon assuming office was to reassure American investors concerning their holdings in Spain.

In April 1931 the people of Spain had voted for a republic and King Alfonso had fled into exile. Thus by a bloodless revolution the Bourbon monarchy was replaced by moderate Republican leaders, with a new constitution which provided for universal suffrage, sweeping social legislation, the separation of Church and State, and cooperation with the League of Nations. As Minister of Finance Negrín survived many Cabinet changes in the swiftly flowing current of Spanish politics. In May 1937 the professor-politician was made Premier, a fact which is said to have caused some surprise

JUAN NEGRIN

since he was considered a mediator rather than a leader. Jacques Ambrun, writing in *Living Age* (October 1938), pronounced Negrín's election "a good thing in many respects, and, indeed, [it] marks a new era in Spanish politics." He emphasized that Negrín, "the leading spirit of Republican Spain," was a man whose "patriotism is not marred by overexcessive, foaming-at-the-mouth nationalism and to whom Europe is a reality. . . .By education and conviction, he is primarily a European."

Negrín retained the portfolio of Minister of Finance and Economy in his own Cabinet, and in April 1938 assumed the added responsibility of the Ministry of National Defense. Spain, in the grip of a bloody civil war since July 1936, was ravaged as the Loyalists fought for the Republic against German and Italian arms under Franco's command. For almost three years the struggle raged. William C. Atkinson, writing in the British *Fortnightly* in January 1939, stated that the Republican resistance "belied all the prophets, even the dictators; it will be remembered when the history of human values in the twentieth century comes to be written." To the claim of Franco sympathizers in the United States that he was fighting bolshevism, one reporter stated, "There was not a single Communist in the Popular Front Government when the Franco forces launched their rebellion," and *Time* Magazine pointed out that Negrín's Cabinet was "no more and no less Red than that of French Premier Léon Blum [40]."

Negrín and the Republicans appealed to the world for help, but the non-interventionist policy of the democracies and increasing German and Italian aid to Franco doomed the Republic. At Geneva in 1938 in one of his many calls for action by the League of Nations, the Spanish Premier stated, "Once foreign intervention in Spain has been eliminated, I can assure you a policy of national conciliation, conducted under the firm, energetic direction of an authoritative government, will make it possible for

NEGRIN, JUAN—*Continued*

all Spaniards to forget these years of conflict and cruelty and will rapidly re-establish the domestic peace." Negrín also announced at that time the evacuation of foreign volunteers from the Republican ranks—those men who had come from many countries to fight in the international brigades beside the Loyalists. Treatment of Spain's case by the League was described by one reporter as "power politics in the raw and at their worst." In those stormy years Negrín once told reporters, "Gas masks today are worth more than all the protests to Geneva. We will fight in the language the enemy understands."

On May 1, 1938, Negrín announced a long-term program, addressed to all Spaniards on both sides asking them to cooperate in the building of a new, peaceful Spain. Among the Premier's "Thirteen Points" were: 1) the absolute independence and territorial integrity of the country; 2) the ejection of all foreign elements, military and economic, "who since July 1936 have invaded Spain and sought to dominate her economic life in their own interests"; 3) a republic of the people, based on the principles of pure democracy, with a strong executive power dependent at all times on the will of the people, plus provisions for social legislation, agrarian reform, and amnesty of prisoners. But Franco's troops continued their advance, and the closing phase of the struggle was marked by upheavals within the Loyalist regime itself. When President Manuel Azaña resigned in February 1939 Negrín became active head of state. A month later Madrid was delivered to the Nationalists by a military coup d'état, and the Government leaders fled to France. There Negrín remained until June 1940 when he went to live in England.

Living in exile in London, Negrín has maintained contact with his ministers, many of whom are in Mexico. (Meanwhile, in Madrid in 1941 a Franco court stripped him of his citizenship and imposed a fine of one hundred million pesetas.) The Spanish leader is said to have retained the optimistic confidence which distinguished him even in the hopeless days of the civil war as he now plans for the restoration of the Republic. In 1941, in his first speech after the end of the civil war, Negrín told a group of Loyalists in London of the continuing resistance within their country. He called for an end to "squandering precious energies in back-room recriminations and personal knife-play," and urged all to join in the common struggle against fascism and nazism. Early in 1942 the press carried reports of Negrín's fight on another front, the scientific—he assisted in experiments carried on by the eminent British scientist J. B. S. Haldane [40], among them, the testing of the effects of gases on submarine crews.

With the military defeat of fascism in Europe the anti-Franco forces have gained power, and predictions are made of impending trouble for the Falangist leader. In January 1945, writing in *PM,* Alexander H. Uhl declared, "The battle for Spain is going on right now." That same month a meeting in New York's Madison Square Garden under the sponsorship of Nation Associates and other liberal groups urged the United States to break relations with Franco Spain. The rally was scheduled to hear an address by Negrín broadcast from London, but British authorities refused the Spaniard permission to use the radiotelephone service, an action which caused adverse comment in Britain and America. Negrín's speech was, however, read at the meeting and was thereafter reprinted in various periodicals. The Spanish Premier, who had broken his five-year silence, self-imposed because he "did not want to add fuel to the political bickerings within the Spanish emigration," emphasized his belief that the Spanish people were ready and able to conduct their own affairs without intervention, but would welcome the help of friends.

In February Ted Allan in a *Collier's* article, "Battle For Spain," wrote that he found Spain industrially under German "occupation" and that more people died from starvation and disease in Spain from 1941 to 1944 than in any other country in Europe. Allan told of the underground movement directed by a broad anti-Franco group, the Junta Suprema de Unión Nacional, whose leaders still repeat their war slogan, "Madrid will yet be the tomb of fascism." Negrín, Allan stated, "may be the hope of Spain—for he alone may be able to unite all the various factions. Once before all the anti-Franco factions fought under his leadership during the civil war, and Spain's underground is hoping that he will again emerge to head a national coalition." In March Negrín spent five weeks in conference with Spanish leaders in France, winning the support of the Communists. A few months before that he had conferred with anti-Franco political groups in Paris, where the French press had welcomed him. In March Clifton Daniel reported in the New York *Times,* "Dr. Negrín's prestige has grown enormously in the past six months."

In May 1945 Negrín arrived in America, stopping in Washington and New York on his way to the United Nations Conference on International Organization. His presence in San Francisco at that time was interpreted by the liberal press as a hopeful sign for Spain. A *PM* editorial lauded the San Francisco rejection of the Franco regime and applauded Negrín's plan for establishing a government-in-exile. By July Negrín was in Mexico working with Republicans there. Meanwhile, anti-Franco sentiment continued to grow on an international scale. The Potsdam conference decision on Spain was considered a major blow to Franco's reign. The joint communique of the Big Three barred the admission of Spain to the United Nations organization because the Spanish Government, "having been founded with the support of the Axis powers, does not, in view of its origin, its nature, its record, and its close association with the aggressor states, possess the qualifications necessary to justify such membership."

The New York *Herald Tribune* carried a series of articles in August 1945, "Spain Under Franco," in which the author, John Chabot Smith, stated, "It is said in Spain that 95 per cent of the people are opposed to the Franco regime." J. Alvarez del Vayo, last Republican Foreign Minister, discussed Negrín's plan for Spain in the *Nation* (July 21, 1945). "His dominating concern," said del Vayo, "is to bring about the restoration of the Republic with a minimum of violence and to establish rapidly the peace and order necessary for reconstructing the country." In August he told a Republican meeting in Mexico City that he would be willing to resign to expedite unity. Later that month when Diego Martinez Barrio was installed as provisional President of the Spanish Republic before the exiled Cortes (Parliament), Negrín urged a government of all parties to work toward the restoration of the Republic, and he and his Cabinet resigned, according to custom. A few days later when José Giral became Premier, it is reported that his first act was to call on Negrín to induce him to join the new Cabinet as Foreign Secretary. Negrín's refusal caused considerable speculation as to dissension within the Republican bloc. However, Negrín is not opposed to the Giral Government; and according to an article by Owen Roche (*PM*, September 5, 1945), his absence is due to the following reasons: "1) to remove any cause for red-baiting; 2) to eliminate the fears of British and other investors in Spain; 3) to enable him and his followers to return to Spain in the best position to accept a mandate from the Spanish people themselves." In her book *Smouldering Freedom,* published in early September 1945, Isabel de Palencia [41] stated that there can be no doubt that Negrín "has the support of the majority of Spanish Republicans in exile and probably of those within Spain also."

After having consulted with Under Secretary Dean Acheson at the State Department in late December 1945, Negrín proceeded to Paris where members of the Spanish republican Government-in-exile were gathering. He has steadfastly insisted on the legitimacy of the present Government-in-exile, but in the opinion of many observers he will use his influence to make it more representative of the Spanish resistance groups than it has been.

The Spanish democrat, a man of vigor and "exceptional versatility," is described by one writer as "that strange phenomenon, an active scholar, a curious mixture of scientist and businessman, an intellectual and an organizer." A fluent linguist, Negrín speaks English, French, and German, and understands Russian. He writes little, but did contribute an article to *Free World* in January 1943, "Science and Statesmanship," in which he stressed the necessity for a union between science and statesmanship in order to achieve reconstruction and a lasting peace. A man of modest manners with a lively sense of humor, Negrín is reported to have appeared to Churchill [42] as "one of the ablest statesmen in Europe." Negrín's family has been in America since 1939; his wife María and son Miguel were in New York City to greet him when he arrived in May 1945. Another son, Juan, is a brain specialist in a New York hospital.

References

Liv Age 355:138-40 O '38
PM p12 D 18 '42 por
International Who's Who, 1942

NELSON, (JOHN) BYRON (JR.) Feb. 4, 1912- Professional golfer

Address: b. c/o Haas-Jordon Co., 1447 Summit St., Toledo, Ohio; h. Route No. 2, Denton, Tex.

BYRON NELSON

Voted the outstanding golfer in the United States in 1943 by fifteen leading fellow professionals, and named in December 1944 the male athlete of the year by seventy-nine sports writers throughout the country, Byron Nelson broke golf records in 1944 by averaging less than seventy strokes on eighteen holes in seventy-eight competitive rounds of big-time tournament. Called "the master of the iron shot," Nelson succeeded Gene Sarazen as the second golfer who won first place in the fourteen years' history of the sports writers' poll. Biggest golf money-maker in 1944, he won more than forty thousand dollars in war bonds in prizes. He played even better golf in 1945. Winner of the national professional golfers' championship and of eighteen other tournaments, he was named the world's No. 1 male athlete of 1945 in the annual Associated Press poll for the second consecutive year.

The son of John Byron and Madge Marie (Allen) Nelson, John Byron Nelson, Jr., was born February 4, 1912, near Fort Worth, Texas. Young Byron's at-homeness on the golf greens dates from his early teens, when he caddied after school hours on the local courses, and also managed to play a few rounds of golf with the other boys when the backs of the club overseers were turned. From the time it became clear to him that "practice makes perfect" he spent all his spare hours on the links. After his graduation from the Polytechnic High School he got a job as a file clerk in the accounting office of the Fort Worth and Denver Railroad. Although his job left him much less leisure time, Nelson nevertheless worked in a lot of golf practice. He played over week-ends and after office hours, concentrating on his drives and long shots until sundown and then putting on the green until it became dark, using a white handkerchief to spot the cup.

In 1930, during the depression, eighteen-year-old Nelson was released by the railroad com-

NELSON, BYRON—*Continued*

pany. He then found employment on a bankers' magazine, a job which fortunately gave him more free time for the links. Within a year Nelson reached his first milestone in the golfing world when he entered the 1931 National Amateur at Beverly, in Chicago. Although his practice in Texas had perfected his skill in playing in a wind, it had not prepared him for working on wet fairways. Yet he missed qualifying by only one stroke. The following year, with jobs scarce and golfing more to his liking than any other occupation, Nelson turned professional in the latter part of 1932 to play in the five-hundred-dollar Texarkana Open (held in the city on Texas-Arkansas border), where he finished third with a prize of seventy-five dollars. Then, touring the tournament circuit in California in the winter of 1932, Nelson accumulated winnings reaching the grand total of twelve dollars and fifty cents, a share of the last money prize in one of the tournaments. With his lean reserve ebbing away and his winnings small, Nelson embarked on a rather stringent diet, making many meals of bars of chocolate. Ironically, he came to be known as the "Kandy Kid" by friends who, ignorant of his dire straits, thought he had an extremely sweet tooth. Nelson attributes his poor playing at that time to an unbalanced diet. Often playing through the early stages of tournaments under seventy, he would lose control of the necessary body coordination and clarity of mind as the session wore on. Some said he had "lack of heart"; he knew it was "lack of stomach."

In 1933 the Kandy Kid accepted the Texarkana Club's offer of the job of club "pro," a position which promised a steady salary. With three regular meals a day and few financial worries, good fortune began inching toward Nelson. During 1934-35 his winnings jumped from $924 to $2,708. In that year, too, he was married, to Louise Shofner, also a golfer. Later that season he became affiliated with the Ridgewood Country Club in New Jersey. In his last year with this club (1936) he won his first major tournament, the Metropolitan Open at Quaker Ridge in New York State. From 1937 to 1939 he was pro of the Reading Country Club in Pennsylvania; from 1940 to 1944 he was pro at the Inverness Golf Club in Toledo.

It is the opinion now of most golf experts that although "some can output him, some out-drive him, and some exhibit prettier form, Byron Nelson is 'King of Golf' because he hits his peak just when you think you have him licked." In almost every instance, either when apparently defeated or confronted with a difficult shot, he emerged a victor. In the 1939 National Open at Spring Mill, Philadelphia, Nelson lagged behind six strokes after the first thirty-six-hole play of the tournament. There were twelve men ahead of him as the final two rounds began. At the end of the two rounds Nelson was tied with Craig Wood and Denny Shute for a total of 284.

In the play-off for the championship the contestants had been whittled down to Nelson and Wood. At the end of the first eighteen holes they broke even. In the next round Nelson picked up a two-stroke lead on the third

hole by pitching a long approach shot to within a yard of the pin for a birdie three. On the fourth, where he was outdriven by Wood, Nelson put the ball right into the pin from a downslope position 215 yards from the green. According to Robert M. Yoder and James S. Kearns, in the *Saturday Evening Post*, "Nelson was gambling heavily on his ability to hit the exact shot the situation demanded. What he produced was a good example of the Nelson Emergency Special, the kind of shot he performs best when the situation is tough. . . . With a brisk cross-wind blowing, he hit a low-line drive, drawing it through the wind with just enough hold to curve over the front corner of the green, right into the hole." Nelson finished the round with a seventy and the championship. He had played the seventy-two holes in 277, four strokes under the best golf ever played for the regulation four rounds of a National Open. (That same year he also won the Western Open.)

In 1940 Nelson won the top golf tournament, the Professional Golfers' Association match at Hershey, Pennsylvania, only to lose it the following year to Victor Ghezzi. According to Nelson's own analysis, he had played the game "too safe." In the 1942 Professional Golfers' Association match in Atlantic City Nelson lost the game on a twenty-inch putt. Had the putt been a twenty-foot one, his followers claim, the "Crisis Kid" would have made it. He also lost the P.G.A. match in 1944, but won again in 1945.

That same year, 1942, Nelson won his second Masters' championship at Augusta, this time defeating Ben Hogan. (In 1937 he had also been a winner.) This second match forced Nelson to use every bit of skill and good judgment he possessed. At the end of thirty-six holes he was eight strokes ahead of Hogan. After seventy-two holes they were tied at 280. Handicapped by a recurring digestive ailment which especially "acts up" when his nerves are taut, Nelson was the answer to his opponent's dream. On the first hole he had a right hook which settled under a scrub pine. The only way to get at it was to play the ball left-handed with the back of his putter. Before he finished the hole he had a six, Hogan four. Ralph Guldahl, a former Masters' winner and two-time National Champion, commented: "This is Nelson's kind of a spot, when he's chasing you, he's really tough." And he was. On the sixth Nelson, now trailing Hogan by three strokes, cut his opponent's lead two strokes by sinking a ten-foot putt for a deuce. In the eight holes following this deuce Nelson was six under par. As Yoder and Kearns put it, "it was one of the Nelson runs that break an opponent's heart."

In the 1942 Tam O'Shanter Open in Chicago —a rally which drew one of the largest galleries in the history of golf—Nelson again displayed some of the tactics which make him "one of the hottest golfers of the day." After achieving a 4-3-1 score against a par of 5-5-3, and finishing the third round at sixty-five, seven under par, Nelson on the next thirty-six gave the game back to his opponent, Clayton Heafner, by chalking up a seventy-seven score against Heafner's seventy-two. In a depressing, discouraging situation and with two thousand dollars at stake, Nelson responded as expected. On the fourth hole on a muddy and soggy fairway, he landed the ball ten feet past the pin, then putted in for a birdie three. On the next hole Heafner's second shot landed near the cup for a sure birdie, but Nelson was in a heavy rough. He lifted the ball out of the shaggy grass with his wedge and bounced it into the cup for an eagle two. With the next hole, a birdie for both contestants, Nelson won the prize money.

According to Tommy Armour, who has held every major open title in the world, "Even when Nelson is only half-way putting, he can't be beaten. He plays golf shots like a virtuoso. There is no type of problem he can't handle. High shots, low shots, with the wind, or across it, hooks or fades, he has absolute control of all of them. He is the finest golfer I have ever seen." This is an almost unanimous opinion of Nelson's playing that perhaps can be attributed to his five requisites for top-notch golfing. Nelson asserts that interminable practice, plus stamina, coolness, unflinching courage in a precarious moment, and a competitive spirit are essential to successful golf play. Says Nelson: "They aren't discovered suddenly; they're developed through long and earnest training and practice." According to him, no golfer gets results on the course unless he keeps regular hours and good diet. Nelson also urges the development of a "golf temperament"—"play the shot you're playing," he says, "not the preceding one." Nelson has learned through experience that golfers harassed by previous mishaps throw the subsequent shots away. He still indulges in pep talks to himself during a tense moment, on the order of, "All right, Nelson, old kid, take it easy. So you've made a bad one. So what? Another bad one won't make it good. Take it easy."

Sport fans are of the opinion that Nelson is a master of the iron shots but is weak in putting, this weakness being ascribed to a tendency to strike short putts with too much force. However, there is much controversy over, and many explanations for, Nelson's alleged "unorthodox cocking of the wrists on the down swing." Tony Longo of the Inwood Country Club finds that Nelson on a swing leads so sharply with his left side that his wrists and hands, with relation to the club head, result in a wrist-cock. All professionals agree that the style is unusual. According to Phil Turnesa of the Metropolis Country Club, "Nelson, tall of stature, and possessed of powerful hands, doesn't need a full back-swing, and the fact that he takes less than a three-quarter arc accounts for his unerring direction from tee to green." Very few golfers attempt to imitate Nelson's peculiar swing because of the unfavorable results they get.

In the first two months of 1945 Nelson played in six open tournaments, in which he won three of them, tied for second in one, and came in second in two of the others. In the Los Angeles Open tournament, a $13,333 war bond event, Nelson lost first prize to Sam Snead, missing a chance to tie his opponent when he faltered on a twenty-foot putt. In this match he tied with Harold McSpaden, winning sixteen hundred dollars in bonds instead of the top prize of $2,666. In the same month Nelson won the Phoenix Open with a score of 274, ten strokes under par for the seventy-two holes. In February Nelson was "a par-

cracker" in the Corpus Christi (Texas) Open, scoring sixteen under par, with McSpaden gaining second place. In one of the most interesting tournaments of the winter season, Nelson shot a seven under par when he defeated McSpaden by five strokes in a play-off round for the New Orleans Open. In the Gulfport (Mississippi) Open, golfer Nelson tied with Sammy Snead for first place, but lost the tournament to him in the play-off by missing a sixty-foot putt by two inches on the last hole. The Pensacola (Florida) Open he lost to Snead by seven strokes. This defeat put him one game behind his opponent in the fourteenth tournament of the 1944-45 winter golf circuit.

During the first week in April Nelson set a seventy-two-hole scoring record of 263 on the Capitol City links at Atlanta, Georgia. The match for the mythical world championship of golf opened at Fresh Meadow Country Club, Flushing, Long Island, on May 26, with thirty-six holes of medal play. Defeated by a single stroke, Nelson came back the next day at the Essex Country Club, West Orange, New Jersey, and defeated Snead, four up and three to play. Actually, as the New York *Sun* pointed out, "Snead and Nelson broke even, Snead winning stroke-play laurals at Fresh Meadow and Nelson taking match-play honors at Essex." The big event of the season was the Professional Golfers' championship held at Dayton, Ohio, on July 15. Nelson capped a brilliant season of open tournament play by winning in a test that showed him to be as good a match player as he was a medal player. Although he was hard pressed twice during the match play the Texan made good, sweeping the honors from qualifying to final. In the latter he defeated Sam Byrd, coming from behind to win comfortably under windy and difficult conditions after being down early in the afternoon round of the crucial test. The PGA tournament raised $51,000 for the veterans' hospitals. (Nelson has played numerous matches for the benefit of the Red Cross, the USO, and Bond-selling campaigns.)

On July 30, at the Tam O'Shanter Country Club in Chicago, Nelson won the seventy-two-hole All-American Open, nineteen strokes under par and eleven strokes ahead of his nearest rivals. His award was a $10,500 check, "the richest golf pay-off in the country." In September, while seeking his seventeenth major victory of 1945, Nelson lost the Nashville Open when Ben Hogan, former Air Forces lieutenant, won with the record-approaching score of 265. Then in October Nelson broke his own world competitive record for par-seventy golf courses when he shot a sixty-six for a seventy-two-hole mark of 259, beating par by twenty-one strokes in the final round of the Seattle Open. This feat won him $2,000 in war bonds, the first prize in the $10,000 tournament. The day following the tournament the Professional Golfers' Association announced plans to classify golf courses as to championship or nonchampionship qualities, in order to protect scoring records set by its members. The tournament manager, Fred Corcoran, explained, "This is not to detract anything from Nelson's remarkable victory, but there is a difference in courses, and some method must be determined to protect records made on the tougher ones."

(Continued next page)

NELSON, BYRON—*Continued*

Nelson closed out the year in golf on December 16 with his nineteenth tournament victory. He swept over the icy Glen Garden Country Club course with a sixty-six, 77-136 for the final thirty-six holes, giving him a total of 273, eleven under par. The prize of $2,000 in Victory Bonds brought his golf earnings up to $66,000, the largest gains ever made by any player in a twelve-month period. At the end of the year Nelson was named the world's No. 1 male athlete of 1945 by sports writers throughout the country in the annual Associated Press poll. In the words of *Life*, "Nelson has made golf the only sport in the United States that is better than it was before the war. The great Bobby Jones has said, 'At my best I never came close to the golf Nelson shoots.'" As 1945 drew to a close, the sports authority, Grantland Rice, commented on Nelson's victories, and said "the Toledo-Texan should crowd Babe Ruth's[44] top baseball mark of $80,000 before another New Year's arrives." Actor Bing Crosby[41] commented humorously in *Pic*, "If Byron could putt, they wouldn't have to play any tournament. They could just send him the money because he'd win 'em all." Crosby was also quoted as saying that putting is "entirely mental," and that Nelson "thinks he is a bad putter and so he is."

Over six feet tall and weighing one hundred and eighty pounds, Nelson is a large man, has blue eyes and brown hair. He neither drinks nor smokes; he says that such abstinence has been a tradition in his family since the time of his great-grandparents. He enjoys the movies, bridge, and baseball, but is particularly fond of hunting—deer, elk, and quail. In the latter part of 1943 Nelson became vice-president of Toledo's Haas-Jordan Company, umbrella manufacturers. This American golfer, who has held every major title except the British Open, has had the honor of playing on two Ryder Cup teams, an international golf competition between Americans and Britons. Each team consists of ten players, and to be selected a golfer's record and scoring are considered over a two-year period. When Nelson played in 1937 his score was the lowest of the Americans competing in the British Open. In the tournament he placed fifth; but with the war's end he hopes to do something about that score.

References

Sat Eve Post 216:15+ Je 10 '44 pors
Time 44:86-7 O 23 '44 por
Who's Who in America, 1944-45

NEWBERRY, TRUMAN H(ANDY)
Nov. 5, 1864—Oct. 3, 1945 American industrialist and politician; largely responsible for founding of Packard Motor Car Company; Assistant Secretary of Navy (1905-8), and Secretary (1908-9); Republican Senator from Michigan from 1919 until resignation in 1922; convicted in Michigan courts for corruption in obtaining nomination, but case dismissed in Supreme Court; exonerated by Senate committee.

Obituary

N Y Times p23 O 4 '45 por

NEWTON, CLEVELAND ALEXANDER
Sept. 3, 1873—Sept. 17, 1945 Republican Representative from Missouri to United States Congress, 1918-27; member of the State House of Representatives, 1902-4; special assistant to Attorney General, 1911-13.

Obituary

N Y Times p24 S 18 '45 por

NOCK, ALBERT JAY 1873(?)—Aug. 19, 1945 American critic and essayist; former associate of the old *Freeman*; his most widely read literary publication was the column *The State of the Nation*, which appeared in the *American Mercury*; principal works include *Jefferson* (1926), *Our Enemy, the State* (1935), *Free Speech and Plain Language* (1937). See *Current Biography* 1944 Yearbook.

Obituary

N Y Times p19 Ag 20 '45 por

NORDEN, CARL L(UKAS) Apr. 23, 1880- Inventor; consulting engineer

Address: b. Carl L. Norden, Inc., 80 Lafayette St., New York City

"Delicate as a pharmacist's balances, fine as a thoroughbred colt, closely-guarded as a sultana—but sturdy as a stone barn"—the Norden bombsight is, in the words of Kurt Rand, "the most discussed yet least known of all the tools of today's war." And its designer, Carl L. Norden, is perhaps the least known of the Second World War's celebrities.

Carl Lukas Norden, who has devoted twenty years to the service of the United States Navy and Air Forces, was born a citizen of the Netherlands in Semarang, Java, on April 23, 1880. When he was five his father died, and the widowed Mrs. Norden took her children back to Holland. Young Carl attended the schools at Nijmegen, a name to be made famous sixty years later by a great battle of the Second World War, and later at Apeldoorn. In 1893, when Carl was thirteen, his family moved to Dresden, Germany, and three years later to Zurich, Switzerland. There the sixteen-year-old boy went to work as an apprentice in a machine shop, where he spent about three years. Then he left the shop and went back to school to prepare for the entrance examinations of the Federal Polytechnical School. He passed them, and was admitted in 1900.

Graduated in 1904 with a degree in mechanical engineering, Norden sailed for the United States, where he was employed by the H. R. Worthington Pump and Machine Works in Brooklyn, New York. Part of the next two years he spent upstate and in Ohio working for affiliated companies, but in 1906 the young Hollander was back in Brooklyn, designing and estimating special equipment for the J. H. Lidgerwood Manufacturing Company. After five years, in the fall of 1911, Norden was engaged by the famed Sperry Gyroscope Company to design the first gyro-stabilizing equipment ever produced for ships in the United States. After its successful test on the United States destroyer *Worden*, the engineer was given a number of similar assignments, including work on the transport *Henderson*.

In 1915, when the First World War was already raging in Europe, the thirty-five-year-old designer set up his own establishment in Brooklyn as a consulting engineer. During the next years he furnished the United States Navy with many advanced instruments and devices, such as the radio-controlled target airplanes. Although he devised practical robot flying bombs, these were not put into use because they were considered an inhuman and undiscriminating weapon. It was Norden, too, who designed the catapults and arresting gears for the aircraft carriers, the *Lexington* and *Saratoga*. For these he worked out the first hydraulically controlled landing gears ever made.

The Navy Bureau of Ordnance entrusted Norden with the study of precision bombing problems in 1921. Two years later he was joined by another consulting engineer for the Navy, Theodore H. Barth, who is listed in *Who's Who in America* as "co-inventor of U.S. bombsight." The two formed a partnership, with Barth "putting Norden's ideas into metal." In 1927, after six years of work, Norden's laboratory turned out "a practical timing sight, incorporating optics directly stabilized on three axes," which reduced the usual radial error by 83 per cent. The following year the partnership was succeeded by a corporation, Carl L. Norden, Inc., of which from 1928 to 1938 Norden owned one-half of the stock and was an official. Barth was president of the corporation, and attended to the business and production aspects, while Norden devoted all his time to laboratory research. Their company had only one customer: the United States Navy, which in turn supplied the Army Air Forces. From its beginning on one floor of a New York building, the corporation had by 1943 two entire buildings and also operated other offices, and plants in Indianapolis, Indiana, Easthampton, Massachusetts, and Danbury, Connecticut. When the United States entered the Second World War the company also began to subcontract, supervising production of the Norden bombsight in other factories.

In 1928 Carl Norden was joined in his experiments by the assistant research chief of the Navy Bureau of Ordnance, Captain Frederick I. Entwistle. From that time on the inventor devoted himself to designing and improving aviation equipment, particularly for bombardment purposes. From his laboratory came glide bombing devices, automatic erectors, sights for dive bombing, and radar (radio aircraft detection and range-finding) sights and equipment. (Norden was not, however, the originator of the radar principle.) In 1938 the bombsight now in general use was completely designed and available for subsequent large production. Working in a field where items sometimes become obsolete while in production, Norden had turned out an instrument which was still to be in use years later. This, the most secret and the best known of all his devices— is called simply the Norden precision bombsight, although Captain Entwistle shares the patents and the credit.

Until 1945 this valuable mechanism was "surrounded with the most elaborate and spectacular secrecy, such a ritual of hiding, with armed escorts and oath-swearing guardians, that the forms of protection became a legend, and the bombsight's mere existence a propa-

Underwood & Underwood
CARL L. NORDEN

ganda." To some observers, it is in itself responsible for the Army Air Forces technique of high-altitude daylight precision bombing. "Around the Air Forces schools, where thousands of young men have been taught to use the bombsight," someone wrote while the war was going on, "one of the ancient but favorite jokes is the mock-solemn prediction that, any time now, the Army is going to start giving commissions to the bombsights and leave the bombardiers at home." To a layman, certainly, "bombsight" seems an inadequate word for a handy ninety-pound gadget which can take over complete control of a huge Superfortress, make a series of complicated calculations with lightning speed, and drop the ship's bombs squarely on the distant target. To the bombardier, however, some credit must be given: it takes a man four hundred and eighty-two hours, in an eighteen-week course, to master the use of the instrument.

What is the Norden bombsight? Among other things, it's a device which costs the taxpayers nearly ten thousand dollars, can be carried by one man, is standard equipment on all United States multi-engined bombers, and contains some two thousand parts—"a bewildering confusion of gears, mirrors, cams, lenses, wires, prisms, bearings, and a myriad of tiny parts," all machined to extremely fine tolerances. The lower half, usually fixed permanently into the plane, is a stabilizer. In the one-half cubic foot space in its castings there is a horizontal gyroscope, with azimuth control. The upper part—the sight proper—was carried aboard the plane, during the war in a crate, under guard, never uncovered while on the ground, and returned to the bombsight officer after the mission. One unit is a vertical gyroscope; the other includes a telescope, to sight through, and the computing apparatus. As the target is approached the human bombardier adjusts the sight for the weight of the bombs, the airspeed, and the altitude; sets the gyroscope spinning with its axis perpendicular to the ground; lines up the target through the

NORDEN, CARL L.—*Continued*

cross-hair sight, which turns the plane automatically in the right direction. This last operation, by means of the Norden automatic pilot, keeps the plane on the proper course. All compensation for the plane's forward motion, for its drift, and for motion of the target, is made automatically. Then "Bombs away!" and the bombsight gives the plane back to the pilot, while the bombardier reflects that with it he could "drop a dime into a pickle barrel at fifty thousand feet."

The engineer who made all this possible was honored for his "valuable devices which should hasten the peace" by the American Society of Mechanical Engineers in November 1944. He was awarded the Holley Medal, given annually to "one who, by some unique act of genius of an engineering nature, has accomplished a great and timely public benefit . . . meriting the highest honor within the gift of the mechanical engineering profession." Norden, who emerged from his self-imposed obscurity just long enough to accept the honor and then went right back to his laboratory, revealed in his brief acceptance speech that all patent rights, models, and designs for his immensely valuable inventions were turned over to the United States Government for the nominal payment of one dollar apiece. "These many individual dollars," Norden added, "I never received. But it occurred to me that this very evening, through your great kindness, they have indeed been paid with compound interest."

Less than a month later the name of Carl L. Norden, by virtue of the Carl L. Norden firm, was again in the news, in connection with a Federal indictment, although the engineer himself was specifically excluded from the charge of conspiracy to restrict production of the Norden bombsight to the Norden concern. (The defendants involved entered pleas of not guilty.)

Although a first-grade notable, Carl L. Norden is hardly known outside the intimate circle of Army, Navy, and aviation engineers. His private life is nearly as well kept a secret as what makes his devices tick. His name is not to be found in any of the *Who's Who*'s, and few know that he is married and has a son and a daughter. In appearance Norden fits the stereotype of a Hollander. A big, heavy-set man, fair-haired, short-nosed, thin-lipped, and heavy-lidded, he has light eyebrows and a thick, blond mustache. Norden has retained his Netherlands citizenship, but he is said to be selflessly devoted to the adopted country he served so well.

Reference

Flying 33:37+ Jl '43 il

NORRIS, CHARLES G(ILMAN) Apr. 23, 1881—July 25, 1945 American novelist; best known works include *Brass* (1921), *Bread* (1923), *Seed* (1930), *Bricks Without Straw* (1938), and *Flint* (1944); husband of Kathleen Norris and brother of Frank Norris, both novelists.

Obituary

N Y Times p17 Jl 26 '45 por

NORTON, W(ILLIAM) W(ARNER) Sept. 17, 1891—Nov. 8, 1945 American book publisher, president and editor of W. W. Norton and Company, Inc., New York, since 1924; president of the National Association of Book Publishers (1933-35); chairman of the Council of Books in Wartime for servicemen during the Second World War; originated the plan of publishing scientific treatises which had been presented by adult-education projects.

Obituary

N Y Times p19 N 9 '45 por

NYE, RUSSEL B(LAINE) (nī) Feb. 17, 1913- Author; educator

Address: b. c/o Michigan State College, East Lansing, Mich.; h. 540 Glenmoor Rd., East Lansing, Mich.

In 1945 a young teacher of English was awarded the Pulitzer Prize in American biography for a work that originated as a doctoral thesis. The prize winner is Russel B. Nye, whose first book, *George Bancroft; Brahmin Rebel,* was welcomed as a scholarly study of the nineteenth century historian. Described as an "intelligent, well-organized, superior" biography, the book was considered by the *Christian Science Monitor* "far more than the life of one man, but instead a history of Bancroft's times." The author, an associate professor at Michigan State College of Agriculture and Applied Science, has been teaching college English since 1935. In 1942 he won the second annual Knopf '43 Fellowship in Biography to assist him in completion of the Bancroft study which was then in progress.

Russel Blaine Nye is a native of Wisconsin. He was born in the town of Viola on February 17, 1913, to Charles Henry and Zelma (Schimeyer) Nye. He received his early education in Viroqua, a town not far from his birthplace. Going to Ohio for further study, Nye attended Oberlin College, where he won his B.A. in 1934. The next year he took graduate work at the University of Wisconsin and earned his Master of Arts degree. At that time he obtained a position as instructor at Jordan College, where he remained for a year. In 1936 he returned to the University of Wisconsin, joining the faculty as an assistant instructor. Nye accepted a similar position three years later at Adelphi College in Long Island, a post he left in 1940 for his present professorship at Michigan State College. During much of this period he had been working on his doctoral thesis, a study of the life and times of George Bancroft, and in 1940 he received his Ph.D. from the University of Wisconsin.

After having completed this thesis, Nye became even more deeply interested in his subject and planned to continue his research. His interest in the American historian-diplomat, who founded the Naval Academy and ordered the occupation of California, dates back to Nye's childhood, when he spent hours browsing in his grandfather's library where a large set of Bancroft's writings was a venerated possession. In 1942 the Knopf Fellowship assisted him in the completion of his project. He won the twelve-hundred-dollar grant on the merits of the incomplete manuscript, with the understanding that Knopf would publish the book. Two years later, after the author had spent many months in further research work, studying the Bancroft material in New York, Cambridge, Boston, and the Library of Congress, *George Bancroft; Brahmin Rebel* was published. The writer has remarked that the Bancroft records are "disconcertingly voluminous," for George Bancroft's life covered a long and eventful span in America's history: from 1800 to 1891 Bancroft lived and worked in a growing Nation; educator, diplomat, and politician, he also wrote history—his *History of the United States* was the standard text for two generations of Americans. In the words of his biographer, "he was much more than a writer of history. He was a maker of it as well."

In the preface of his book Nye has explained his method of treatment of the famous nineteen century figure: "I have thought it proper to allow Bancroft, as much as possible, to tell his own story, supplemented by the accounts and impressions of his acquaintances." Most critics admired the scholarship of Nye's biography; according to the *Weekly Book Review,* "it takes its place at once as the definitive biography of the great historian." Comment was also made on the work's panoramic view of the historical, political, social, and educational currents of Bancroft's day. Agreeing that the book was "meticulous and scholarly," Orville Prescott found it written "directly and well, but without any particular grace or charm to lure the reader on," an opinion concurred in by a few reviewers. "Perhaps, however," wrote one of them, "Bancroft is better served by pedestrian lucidity than by epigram." There was some critical discussion about Nye's designation of Bancroft as a Brahmin—a member of the highly cultured and exclusive New England society. Gerald W. Johnson in the New York *Herald Tribune* questioned the author's accuracy in this case, as Bancroft's father was a "slightly heretical minister" and the son "turned Democrat when all the rest of Beacon Street was Whig, which would seem to rule the son out of the caste." To Nye, Bancroft represented "the culmination of the Brahmin tradition of New England, the tradition of Concord, Cambridge, and Boston at its highest, yet he was a rebel against it and could not make his peace with it." While any estimation of Bancroft's place in history is regarded as debatable, his influence as a historian is generally admitted. Most critics also agree that he presents a diverse and interesting study in character. Nye found him "a fascinating, many-sided, paradoxical personality. He was shrewd and realistic, yet a visionary and a dreamer."

On May 7, 1945, Nye received the Pulitzer Prize for the year 1944 for his biography, "teaching patriotic and unselfish services to the people." At the time the Pulitzer awards were announced the book had sold about five thousand copies and another printing was reported a few weeks later. There was some surprise in literary circles when the book was chosen by the Pulitzer board. Previously the

RUSSEL B. NYE

annual advance poll conducted by the *Saturday Review of Literature* among thirty-seven critics and editors had given Catherine Drinker Bowen's *Yankee From Olympus* twenty-four votes, and Nye's book two votes.

The teacher-writer in 1945 was working on three projects: a sketch of the American abolitionist, Theodore Weld, and two studies, "Civil Liberties and Abolition" and "Theology in American Poetry." Nye was awarded a Rockefeller Foundation Fellowship for the year 1944-45. The blue-eyed, brown-haired biographer is five feet eleven inches tall and weighs one hundred and seventy-five pounds. He was married to Mary Kathryn Chaney on August 6, 1938; the couple have a son, Peter William. Nye is an independent in politics. For recreation, he prefers golf and baseball.

References

N Y Herald Tribune p13 My 8 '45 por
Pub W 140:1905 My 23 '42 por

O'CONNOR, JAMES FRANCIS May 7, 1878—Jan. 15, 1945 Democratic Representative to United States Congress from Montana since 1937; had begun his fifth consecutive term at time of death; special counsel for the Federal Trade Commission in 1918; member of the State House of Representatives in (1917-18); chairman of the Indian Affairs Committee.

Obituary

N Y Times p19 Ja 16 '43 por

OLMSTEAD, ALBERT TEN EYCK (ŏm'stĕd) Mar. 23, 1880—Apr. 11, 1945 Professor of Oriental history at the University of Chicago and an outstanding historian; two of many works are *History of Assyria* (1923) and *History of Palestine and Syria* (1931); his contributions to New Testament history and his book *Jesus in the Light of History* have been called monumental.

Obituary

N Y Times p23 Ap 12 '45

O'MAHONEY, JOSEPH C(HRISTO-PHER) (ō-mă'hŏ-nĭ) Nov. 5, 1884- United States Senator from Wyoming
Address: b. Senate Office Bldg., Washington, D.C.; h. 502 E. 22d St., Cheyenne, Wyo.

For more than a decade Senator Joseph C. O'Mahoney has been one of the leading progressive members of the upper house of Congress. A former newspaperman and lawyer, the Democratic Senator from Wyoming is a crusading antimonopolist, having, as the chairman of the Temporary National Eco-

JOSEPH C. O'MAHONEY

nomic Committee, conducted an exhaustive survey of the American economy. Among the significant measures he has initiated is the "epoch-making" O'Mahoney-Murray[45]-Wagner[41]-Thomas[42] full employment bill, which was the subject of Senatorial debate in the fall of 1945.

The Western Senator is a New Englander by birth. Born in Chelsea, Massachusetts, on November 5, 1884, Joseph Christopher O'Mahoney is the son of Irish immigrant parents, Dennis and Elizabeth (Sheehan) O'Mahoney. The boy attended the Cambridge Latin School in his home state before going to New York, where he studied at Columbia University from 1905 to 1907. He then began a ten-year period in journalism, taking a job as a reporter on the Cambridge *Democrat*. In 1908 young O'Mahoney went West, to Boulder, Colorado, where he became city editor of the *Herald*. After eight years he moved again, this time to Cheyenne, Wyoming, where he took over the city editor's desk of the *State Leader*. He served in this capacity until March 1917, when he was appointed secretary to Wyoming's United States Senator John B. Kendrick, who was also owner of the *Leader*. In the Capital, O'Mahoney took the opportunity to continue his studies. He attended the law school of Georgetown University, winning his LL.B. degree in 1920. (He has since been awarded an honorary LL.D. by Columbia

[1938] and Georgetown [1941].) He then returned to Cheyenne to set up his law practice.

While O'Mahoney had joined Theodore Roosevelt's Bull Moose campaign in 1912, since 1916 he has been a member of the Democratic Party. He rose rapidly through the party ranks and by 1922 was vice-chairman of the Democratic State Committee, a position he held for eight years. During the year 1925-26 he represented Wyoming at the conference on uniform state laws, and in 1929 was elected Democratic national committeeman. In the crucial 1932 Presidential campaign, as a delegate to the national convention, he helped formulate the party's platform and served as vice-chairman of the campaign committee. After this initial Roosevelt[42] victory O'Mahoney was appointed first assistant United States postmaster general in March 1933. But the following December he resigned to accept an appointment as member of the Senate, designated by Wyoming's governor to fill the vacancy caused by the death of Senator Kendrick. Since first assuming office in January 1934, O'Mahoney has retained his seat, having been re-elected for another six-year term in November 1940.

According to Raymond Moley[45], O'Mahoney, once in the Senate, "neatly telescoped the usual two- or three-year-long novitiate, emerging after a few months as one of the most respected young members." He was a member of the committees on appropriations, Indian affairs, irrigation and reclamation, post offices and post roads, and public lands and surveys. Although once known as "a 100 per cent New Dealer," he came into the national spotlight when he fought against the President's Supreme Court reorganization plan. An article in the *Nation's Business* (September 1938) reported that the Wyoming Senator "wrote the bitter and more acid part of the report of the Judiciary Committee in which the President's plan for reorganizing the Supreme Court was denounced." Long opposed to monopolistic and bureaucratic practices, he has spoken on such issues both in and out of the Senate. It is said that a favorite quotation of the legislator's is a statement from Wyoming's constitution, which reads: "Arbitrary power exists nowhere in a republic, not even in the largest majority." In 1938 his bill requiring Federal licensing for corporations engaged in interstate commerce received wide support. In a radio discussion of this measure, O'Mahoney analyzed the evils of unregulated corporations and called for enactment of a Federal law which "shall clearly define the corporate powers of all interstate corporations." The *Literary Digest* called the bill pro-labor, pointing out that it would grant charters only to corporations which did not practice discrimination against women workers, did not employ child labor, and recognized collective bargaining.

In 1938 Congress created the Temporary National Economic Committee, composed of six Executive and six Congressional members, and headed by O'Mahoney. The chairmanship of the TNEC was called the biggest job of his political career, and the long investigation aroused much discussion and controversy. In the stormy aftermath of the great depression, TNEC, also known as the Monopoly Investigation, studied the concentration of wealth in American industry, seeking to discover why there is "poverty in the midst of plenty." Under the leadership of O'Mahoney and such Administration figures as Leon Henderson [40], Robert H. Jackson [40], and Thurman Arnold [40], the probe was carried on for almost three years, during which time such matters as industrial monopoly, unemployment, life insurance, corporation methods, and technology were examined, and a steady stream of monographs was issued. The *Christian Science Monitor* saw the committee as a "springboard for the advocacy of a wide variety of economic reform ideas and the source of numerous significant economic studies." Shortly before the expiration of the committee in 1941, O'Mahoney proposed the following program: 1) national charters for corporations doing business on a national scale; 2) effective and thorough enforcement of antitrust laws; 3) encouragement of new business and small enterprise by revision of tax laws; 4) a national conference of representatives of business, labor, agriculture, and consumers to concentrate public thought on objectives on which there is general agreement.

With the conclusion of the TNEC inquiry, various estimates of its work were offered. *Business Week,* in an article entitled "TNEC—Magnificent Failure," reported that the committee's monographs had become almost "best sellers" by establishing sales records at the Government Printing Office. A writer for the National Association of Manufacturers attacked the TNEC reports, seeing no reason for "all the fuss over concentration of economic power." One article named as TNEC's one achievement the direction of legislative and business attention to "the choice between two correctives for monopolistic conditions: either tighter antitrust laws to compel increased competition or more Government regulation of individual industries." Writing in the *Nation* (March 22, 1941), I. F. Stone declared that the investigation "will rank with the great inquiries of the past," and called O'Mahoney's summary "a document which deserves to be read by every American." According to this writer, TNEC showed the extent to which the Nation and its institutions "no longer belong to the people who inhabit it." In April 1941 the *United States News* predicted that the TNEC "blueprints for the next reform era" would be laid aside for the duration of the war but were "likely to provide the basic design for numerous postwar reorganization plans."

O'Mahoney's antimonopoly activities include a long fight against the insurance lobby, which won him commendation in liberal quarters. In 1943 he led the investigation of the fire insurance industry's effort to block Federal antitrust legislation by the attempted passage of the Bailey [45]-Van Nuys [44] bill. In May of the following year a writer in the *New Republic* stated that the legislator deserved "a Congressional Medal of Honor for statesmanship" for his diligent work in the public interest. In the Senate Judiciary Committee he blocked passage of the bill "almost single-handedly," giving evidence that the insurance industry was "monopoly-ridden." In 1943, as

chairman of the Subcommittee on Industrial Reorganization of the Post-War Planning Committee, he again stressed the danger of concentrated economic power. The following year O'Mahoney urged the abolition of the two-thirds Senate vote on treaties, favoring instead a majority vote "which would more nearly approximate the will of the Nation."

Called a "middle-of-the-road" politician, the Senator generally supported the Roosevelt Administration, but voted against it on some vital issues. In 1943 he voted for repeal of the Executive order limiting salaries to twenty-five thousand dollars after taxes; for the anti-strike bill, and then for overriding the Presidential veto of this measure. In 1944 he again voted to override a Presidential veto, this time on the tax bill. Each time anti-poll tax legislation has been under consideration O'Mahoney has signified his opposition: in November 1942 he voted against adoption of closure to limit debate on the bill and prevent filibuster, and since then in the Judiciary Committee he has voted against the bill. However, he believes that the poll tax should be abolished by constitutional amendment, a method which has been criticized as "cumbersome"; in September 1945 he introduced a resolution to submit the question to the States as a constitutional amendment.

On the manpower problem during the war, he favored some controls but not stringent Government control of the worker. The Senate accepted the O'Mahoney-Kilgore [43] manpower bill as a substitute for the stronger May [41]-Bailey work-or-fight bill in 1945. During that year the Senator conducted hearings before the Senate Patents Committee and the Senate Petroleum Committee in an investigation of cartels, and introduced a bill requiring registration of international cartel agreements by American firms. In the early summer of 1945 O'Mahoney's subcommittee of the Senate Military Affairs Committee began investigating the operations of the Surplus Property Board, headed by W. Stuart Symington [45].

Columnist Thomas L. Stokes has remarked that O'Mahoney pursues a progressive course on a broad national and international scale, "but he goes Wyoming on the tariff." Noting the possibility that the Wyoming cattle industry is fearful of the Argentine cattle interests, that writer pointed out the Senator's desire for Congressional approval of every trade agreement. In early June the Senate rejected his amendment to this effect, and later that month he voted against the Trade Agreements Law, which nevertheless passed, becoming the first Congressional victory of the Truman [45] Administration. In the fall strong Administration support was being given the full employment bill, sponsored by the senior Senator from Wyoming and his colleagues, Wagner, Murray, and Thomas. This measure, which would establish a national production and employment budget, has been called "the most far-reaching proposal for Government planning that has ever been seriously advanced" in the United States. Testifying on behalf of his bill in August, O'Mahoney warned that only full employment could avert economic crisis. "We cannot afford to drift," he declared. "We dare not take a chance that the soldiers returning from this war will be unable to find jobs. We

O'MAHONEY, JOSEPH C.—*Continued*

dare not risk mass unemployment, for without full employment the capitalistic system will be rocked to its foundation."

The Senator has voiced his opinions widely, through press and radio, and in speeches before various groups. An article in the magazine *Flying* (April 1944) contained his views on aviation's fuel supply. In a radio broadcast in 1943 O'Mahoney predicted that Congress would try to curb the "growing Federal bureaucracy," and, while suggesting no "invasion of Executive authority," he called for judicial review of administrative decisions. In similar vein was his article in *Reader's Digest* (August 1943), entitled "America Is Being Made Over—And We Won't Like It." Here he again objected to the current use of Executive authority, stating: "Policies are no longer being determined by the people or their representatives but through Executive order by employees of the Executive arm of the Government." O'Mahoney has a reputation as an incisive fact-finder and a courteous but thorough inquisitor.

His committee assignments in 1945 include Appropriations, Indian Affairs, of which he is chairman, Judiciary, Military Affairs, Patents, and Public Lands and Surveys; he is chairman of the special committees to investigate the wool situation and petroleum resources, and is a member of the Special Committee on Post-War Economic Policy and Planning. As a member of the subcommittee of the Senate Irrigation and Reclamation Committee he voted against the Truman-sponsored bill for the creation of an MVA because it "delegated to a distant board power over the intimate lives of the people of the region." In October 1945 he introduced a resolution asking Congress to support American participation in a "universal international agreement to outlaw the use of the atomic bomb."

The senior Senator from Wyoming is a member of the American Bar Association, and his fraternity is Phi Kappa Sigma. Mrs. O'Mahoney is the former Agnes Veronica O'Leary of Massachusetts, to whom he was married on June 11, 1913. The legislator is described as a "welterweight" with sandy hair and penetrating gray eyes. A well-liked Washington figure, he is known for his unaffected warmth, sincerity, and good humor, one "who speaks for the wide open spaces of Wyoming with a Boston accent."

References

Lit Digest 116:11 D 2 '33 por
Nation's Bus 26:15+ S '38
Congressional Directory, 1945
International Who's Who, 1942
National Cyclopædia of American Biography Current vol D p391
Who's Who in America, 1944-45
Who's Who in Law, 1937
Who's Who in the Nation's Capital, 1938-39

OPPENHEIMER, J. ROBERT Apr. 22, 1904- Physicist

Address: b. c/o University of California, Berkeley, Calif.; h. Eagle Hill, Berkeley, Calif.

In 1942 a young physicist then unknown to the general public, J. Robert Oppenheimer, was called from his laboratory at the University of California by the War Department to play a leading part in solving the problems of building the first atomic bomb. In 1945, after he had served for two and a half years as director of the atomic bomb laboratory at Los Alamos, New Mexico, the War Department credited him with "the implementation of atomic energy for military purposes."

J. Robert Oppenheimer was born on April 22, 1904, in New York City, to Julius and Ella (Freedman) Oppenheimer. Educated at Harvard University, which he had entered in 1922, the youth received his B.A., *summa cum laude*, in 1926 as a member of the class of 1925. At the same time he was elected to membership in Phi Beta Kappa. The year 1925-26 Oppenheimer spent as a student at Cambridge University; the following year the Ph.D. degree was conferred upon him by the University of Göttingen. Then, in 1927-28, as a National Research Fellow, and in 1928-29, as an International Education Board Fellow, Oppenheimer studied at Harvard University, the California Institute of Technology, and in Leyden and Zurich. His fellowship years spanned a period of rapid development in the quantum theory stimulated by Werner Heisenberg's formulation of the "uncertainty principle" and his new quantum mechanics based thereon; and Oppenheimer worked on many problems deriving from the quantum theory, "both to see what the implications of the quantum mechanics would be," he says, "and to try to extend it into the field of electromagnetic phenomena." In 1928 the physicist was appointed an associate professor at the California Institute of Technology. He was made an assistant professor of theoretical physics at the University of California in 1929 and became an associate professor the next year.

When the positron (a particle equal in mass to the electron but opposite in charge) was discovered in 1932 by the American scientist Carl D. Anderson, Oppenheimer's interest in the general questions of the quantum theory and atomic physics led him to an investigation of the new particle and especially to a study of the creation and disappearance of electron-positron pairs. On the basis of these investigations, Oppenheimer evolved a new theory of cosmic ray showers and drew the conclusion that the bulk of these cosmic rays must be composed of still unknown particles—particles which have since been discovered and named mesotrons. In nuclear physics his experimental work during succeeding years concerned, among other questions, deuteron reactions (now called the Oppenheimer-Phillips Reaction), the peculiarities of the reaction of light nuclei, and artificial radioactivity induced by deuteron bombardment. Shortly before the war began the connections between mesotrons and nuclear forces had come under his investigation. Meanwhile, at the University of California he had risen to the position of professor in 1935, and in 1937 he was promoted to the rank of professor at the California Institute of Technology. Both in Berkeley, where the University of California maintains a large school of theoretical physics, and in Pasadena at the institute, Oppenheimer's work was done, he says, in collaboration with research associates,

National Research Fellows, and graduate students—the training of physicists coordinating naturally with the research programs of the laboratories.

In the summer of 1942 (as far as can be gathered from the H. D. Smyth report), Oppenheimer joined the atomic bomb project. Succeeding G. Breit, who had been directing various physical studies which were necessary preliminaries to the designing of the bomb, Oppenheimer was brought into the "Metallurgical Project" of the University of Chicago at that time to expand and coordinate the work begun by Breit—most of which was now transferred to the laboratories of the University of California. "By the end of the summer of 1942, when General L. R. Groves[45] took charge of the entire project," states Smyth, "it was decided to expand the work considerably, and, at the earliest possible time, to set up a separate laboratory." By November the site at Los Alamos, New Mexico, "located on a mesa about twenty miles from Santa Fe," had been chosen because of its isolation and the large area available for proving grounds. Oppenheimer was appointed director, and he arrived at Los Alamos in March 1943.

Despite the handicap of a location devoid of usable buildings and accessible only by a winding mountain road, the task of assembling the necessary equipment—which included "three carloads of apparatus from the Princeton project . . . a cyclotron from Harvard, two Van de Graaff generators from Wisconsin, and a Cockcroft-Walton high voltage device from Illinois"—was completed in short order and the first experiment was performed early in July. Oppenheimer now had under his control "probably the best-equipped physics research laboratory in the world" and "an extraordinary galaxy of scientific stars," in addition to an auxiliary force of nearly six thousand scientific and military employees. "Established," summarizes Smyth, "for the purpose of investigating the design and construction of the atomic bomb, from the stage of receipt of U-235 or plutonium to the stage of use of the bomb, the new laboratory improved the theoretical treatment of design and performance problems, refined and extended the measurements of the nuclear constants involved, developed methods of purifying the materials to be used, and, finally, designed and constructed operable atomic bombs."

Both the War Department and Oppenheimer's colleagues at Los Alamos have praised the physicist's handling of the laboratory, which has been termed by one of the scientists concerned the "true nerve center" of the "Manhattan Project." "The main decisions," this scientist continues, "were made by Oppenheimer, and all proved to be correct. . . .The amazing thing about . . . [his direction of the laboratory was] his ability to keep in touch with detailed developments in every part of the project. It has been my own experience on more than one occasion to see 'Oppy' come down to our office . . . ask to see some piece of work, glance at it for a few seconds, and then make some pointed suggestion." Former Secretary of War Henry L. Stimson[40] cited Oppenheimer's "genius and leadership," and the War Department described him as a leading teacher and a man of "boundless energy, rare common sense

J. ROBERT OPPENHEIMER

. . . possessing tremendous organizational abilities." Another associate has said, " 'Oppy' is smart. No one can fool him for a second—he knows more about most of our specialties than we know ourselves. In fact, he's the smartest of the lot in everything."

Oppenheimer's resignation as director of the Los Alamos laboratory was announced in October 1945. Although "a little scared of what he had made," he has stated that he has no regrets, believing that in wartime "it was necessary and right for us to make bombs" and that in peacetime atomic energy will be capable of transforming and enriching man's existence. "It is fair to say," he said in an interview, "that no scientist would be honestly or conscientiously a scientist if he believed that the advancement of human knowledge were a bad thing. A scientist cannot hold back progress because of fears of what the world will do with his discoveries." Oppenheimer believes that scientists are primarily humanists, reports Peter Edson, New York *World-Telegram* columnist. "People are inclined to forget that. Scientists aren't interested in the things they do in a narrow sense. It is the effect of what they do on humanity and everyday life that counts. . . .It is the next job given to atomic fission that is important. Dr. Oppenheimer finds it difficult to understand why this subject isn't being debated constantly."

Oppenheimer was a member of the scientific panel advising the committee that drafted the May[41]-Johnson Bill, which proposed to set up strict domestic control of atomic energy on the ground that the United States could not otherwise keep its prospective international commitments to control or outlaw the bomb. While he felt that the bill granted a great deal of power to the nine-man commission and administrator who would control atomic energy and that under the bill science could be "stopped in its tracks," he declared that he could see no alternative to such a bill; it was impossible to limit the commission's powers in a field changing so rapidly and so unpredictably. As discussions continued, Oppenheimer stated that a

OPPENHEIMER, J. ROBERT—*Continued*
nation might now set itself up in the business
of manufacturing atomic bombs at a cost in the
neighborhood of $2,000,000, instead of the
$2,000,000,000 it cost the United States.

In an interview in November 1945 the scientist recommended that the United States offer
Russia joint control of atomic weapons; saying
that "we could afford to put a great deal into
the pot" in exchange for the cooperation of all
nations, he added that "if the United States and
Russia can collaborate on atomic weapons then
the back of the problem of world federation is
broken." "Let us in this field not insist on
national sovereignty," he concluded. "The
deadliest danger for all mankind lies in an
atomic armament race." In December two
hundred scientists, including Oppenheimer,
made public a statement offering to cooperate
in drafting national science legislation. Their
purpose is to serve the national interest by
securing the collaboration of the maximum
number of qualified scientists in a united attack
on the scientific problems confronting the nation.

Oppenheimer was described after the successful conclusion of his part in the war as
"terribly tired after three years of the most
intense mental strain any man ever had to
undergo. Yet he does not show it. His blue
eyes sparkle and his smile is human and warm
He is nervously tense, but he has probably
always been that way. High strung like a race
horse." He is of slender build and medium
height, has somewhat unruly brown hair,
and wears "youngish," almost collegiate
clothes. The scientist was married to Katherine
Harrison in November 1940 and is the father
of a son, Peter. He is a keen horseman and
owns a ranch in the Pecos Valley near Santa
Fe. Some of his papers appeared in the *Proceedings* of the National Academy of Sciences.
He is a member of the National Academy and
a Fellow of the American Physical Society
and of the American Academy of Arts and
Sciences.

References

American Men of Science, 1944
Who's Who in America, 1944-45

OSATO, SONO (ō-sàt′ō sō′nō′) Aug. 29,
1919- Dancer; actress
Address: b. c/o Herman Levin, 5 E. 57th St.,
New York City; h. 234 E. 52d St., New York
City

The dancer-actress co-star of *On the Town*,
Sono Osato, says that her favorite review is
one of Wolcott Gibbs's, written after her debut
in *One Touch of Venus* in 1943: "I can only
pay my deep respects to Sono Osato," Gibbs
wrote, "a marvelously limber girl . . . who led
the dancers and alarmed and fascinated me
almost unbearably." For this part, which
"kidded the ballet slippers right off the ballet,"
Miss Osato was prepared by eight years with
classical ballet groups.

The dancer's nationality, which Gibbs found
"cryptic," is American by birth, but her father,
Shoji Osato, was born in Japan, and her
mother, Frances (Fitzpatrick) Osato, is of
Irish-French extraction. The young couple

had met in Omaha, Nebraska, in 1918, when
Osato, as the society photographer of the local
newspaper, was sent to take pictures of Miss
Fitzpatrick, who was visiting the city with her
father, Francis W. Fitzpatrick, a Washington,
D.C., architect. Fitzpatrick continued on his
way to California, but his daughter remained behind to marry the young photographer.

The Osato's first child, Sono (the name
means "in a garden"), was born August 29,
1919, in Omaha. In 1923 they took her and
her sister Teru to Japan, where her paternal
grandparents were still living; in September,
after only a short visit, they were forced to
flee from the earthquake that devastated Japan
that year. Four years later the girl went with
her mother, sister, and brother Mitsuru
("Timmie") to France, where they lived until
1929. The Osatos' next home was in Chicago;
there the father established his own photographic studio and Sono, at the age of ten,
began ballet lessons with Berenice Holmes
and Adolph Bolm. She had "always danced
about everything," she explains, but adds that
she was extremely lazy and disliked to practice. In 1934, when she was fourteen, Colonel
Wassily de Basil and his Ballet Russe came to
Chicago. On his last evening, as was his custom, the Colonel saw several promising dancers, and that season Sono was one of those
asked to come backstage at the end of the
Ballet's performance. The conversation that
the ballet director had with Mrs. Osato after
Sono danced has been variously reported, but
the result of it was that the first-year high
school student joined the Russian troupe as
its youngest member.

Among the Russians, Scandinavians, Germans, Italians, and other members of the
Ballet Russe, the Japanese-Irish-American
girl was called "Osatchka." Arnold L. Haskell wrote at this time that she was "the most
fascinating of Japanese dolls, but with a mind
and a will to lend interest to her work." Her
first bit part was in Massine's [40] *Union Pacific*,
which was given its initial performance in
Philadelphia the year Miss Osato joined the
group. In this ballet, the first American one
to be produced by de Basil, she danced the
part of the Assistant to the choreographer's
Barman.

For the next six years Miss Osato toured
with the company, dancing six months of each
year in the United States and six months
abroad. She soon discovered that a ballerina
lives no "toast-of-the-Continent" existence, but
an unglamorous, exhausting routine of rehearsals and performances, with only occasional evenings of leisure. In her own case,
at the time Miss Osato left the company she
was appearing in thirty-one out of the thirty-
five ballets in its repertoire. Her work in
these had given her a standing in the dance
world—in the opinion of *Dance*, her most important part was probably as the Siren opposite David Lichine in the *Prodigal Son*.
However, notwithstanding her reputation, in
her own words, she was "fed up" with working as hard as she had done for fifty dollars
a week. Feeling that she could advance no
further artistically, she left the Ballet Russe
in December 1940.

Miss Osato spent the next six months studying at the American Ballet School in New York. In the fall of 1941 she returned to a paying job, signing with the Ballet Theatre for a reported sixty dollars a week. During the next year and a half she danced a variety of parts. Among them were the queen in *Bluebeard*, Aphrodite in *Helen of Troy*, and one of the three graces in *Romantic Age*. According to *Dance*, she received particular notice in the ballets of Antony Tudor '45, *Lilac Garden*, *Pillar of Fire*, and *Romeo and Juliet*. In the last, continues the magazine, she danced the part of Rosaline, which Tudor had created specially for her, for it is a character who does not appear but is only discussed in Shakespeare's play. Of her share in the ballet, John Martin of the New York *Times* wrote, "One of the most delightful things . . . was Sono Osato as Rosaline. Though she had no more than two scenes of any moment, she made them one of the best-realized characters in the whole work." When she left the theater to be married in April 1943 to the Moroccan-born designer, Victor Elmaleh, Martin observed, "Too bad, indeed, that Miss Osato has turned her back upon the ballet in favor of domestic life; it is a serious loss to the field."

The reason that Miss Osato gave for leaving ballet was that she did not wish to be always on tour while her husband remained in New York. The summer following her marriage she learned that Agnes de Mille '43 was preparing the ballet numbers for the forthcoming *One Touch of Venus*; this she felt presented the opportunity to dance in a New York production. When she asked the choreographer, whom she knew, for a part in the musical, she was given the leading dancing assignment. The show opened on Broadway that October, with Mary Martin '44, Kenny Baker, and John Boles as the stars.

Miss Osato's work consisted of three numbers, one of which was a satire on classical ballet ("Foolish Heart") that "stopped the show cold" each performance and caused critics to hail the young dancer as a new star. Said Lewis Nichols of the New York *Times*, "As the première danseuse . . . she is, to be brisk about it, wonderful." "In the first act," wrote the New York *Herald Tribune* critic, "she dances with a precise sharpness in every limb and a rhythmic punch that startles: she is a galvanic comedienne. In the second act she [is] glamorous, alluring . . . quite serious and beautiful." Previously Miss Osato had usually danced either sultry roles or the part of a so-called "bad woman." For *One Touch of Venus*, Miss de Mille had brought out a hitherto undisclosed comedic sense. "Agnes is the most exciting choreographer I've ever worked with," says Miss Osato, "and I've worked with most of them. Her kind of ballet is so much more alive and meaningful than classical ballet. Here you're making tradition instead of adhering to it." For her dancing in the play, Miss Osato won the Donaldson award of 1944, and shortly after the opening was given featured billing. She remained with the play until the summer of 1944, when she retired for a rest.

When plans were being made to produce Betty Comden '45 and Adolph Green's '45 musical comedy, *On the Town*, Miss Osato was selected for a leading role, and her part, according to the authors, was designed to suit her particular talents. The dances made use of her abilities, also, for choreographer Jerome Robbins had known her since her Ballet Theatre days, having, for one thing, danced with her in *Romeo and Juliet*. The resultant tailored role, a speaking as well as a dancing one, was that of Miss Turnstiles, one of the monthly poster queens of the New York subways, whom three sailors are trying to meet while on twenty-four-hour passes. The play, which opened in December 1944, received divided comment on its satiric and other values, but the critics were on the whole very enthusiastic about Miss Turnstiles' interpreter. "Miss Osato," wrote Edwin Denby of the New York *Herald Tribune*, "danced in the dream [sequence] and everywhere else with brilliant rhythm and a brilliant sense of shades of character. . . . She is an impish and a warmhearted comedienne, completely natural in the general New York hometown atmosphere [of the play]." She "proves once again," said the *PM* critic, "that she is more than just a good dancer; she . . . is full of the right kind of personality."

Marcus Blechman

SONO OSATO

After her success in *On the Town* Miss Osato felt that she would like to do more acting in the future. (After leaving *One Touch of Venus* she had studied voice and diction.) In September 1945 it was announced that she would leave the musical to appear in a straight part that season, in the title role of *Undine* by Jean Giradoux. The adapter, Schuyler Watts, Arthur Stanton, and the dancer's husband, Victor Elmaleh, were listed as producers.

The extra-professional activities of Miss Osato, who is a member of the American Labor Party, have included campaigning for Roosevelt '42 in the 1944 election, assisting relief groups during the war, and, in 1944, conducting dancing classes for a teen-age group at the Harlem Youth Center of the American Theatre Wing. "Let me assure you," she once told a New York *Post* columnist, "it's not enough just to dance and sing. After all, just because you

OSATO, SONO—*Continued*

are an artist does not mean you are not a citizen, too." Miss Osato was one of the five Broadway performers involved in the controversy that arose when actor Frank Fay '45 was "censured and reprimanded" by the council of Actors Equity Association.

Sono Osato and her husband live in a New York City apartment that is uncluttered by knickknacks. One of the few decorations in her living room is a Fiji tapa cloth which she acquired on a round-the-world tour; she also has a head of herself by the sculptor Noguchi '43. Her favorite colors are yellow and gray-green, and she likes both severe and exotic clothes. For her reading she prefers modern books and plays, and she enjoys swimming and going to the theater or motion pictures for relaxation. The slender five-foot-five dancer has an ivory complexion, and a heart-shaped face, with large brown eyes. She wears her black hair bound close to her head and dressed with bows or flowers.

Miss Osato has a warm personality, her friends say. Her mixed parentage, she states, has never presented a problem to her because she and her brother and sister were reared like other American children. "We were never taught to think of ourselves as different," she once told a *PM* interviewer, "and, nobody treated us as different. People were always curious about us, but that was all." The foreign languages that the dancer speaks are French and Russian, but she does not understand Japanese. On one of her tours the Japanese consul in Melbourne presented her with a bouquet of flowers and made a long speech. "All I could think of to say," she reports, "was, 'Thanks, loads.'"

References

Cue 14:6-7 Ja 13 '45 il pors
Dance 19:8-9 F '45 pors
Look 8:56-7 Ag 8 '44 pors
N Y Post p3 N 27 '40 por
N Y Post Mag p29 Ja 26 '45 pors
PM Mag p10-11 D 5 '43 pors

O'SHEA, WILLIAM F(RANCIS), BISHOP Dec. 9, 1884—Feb. 27, 1945 Vicar apostolic of Heijo, Korea, and former secretary general of Maryknoll Seminary in New York State; consecrated Bishop in 1939 by Pope Pius XII '41 at the Vatican; interned by the Japanese after Pearl Harbor, released in 1942.

Obituary

N Y Times p24 F 28 '45 por

OUMANSKY, CONSTANTINE (ALEXANDROVICH) (ōō-mȧn'skĭ kŏn'stȧn-tēn ŭ-lyĭ-ksȧn'drŭ-vyĭch) 1902—Jan. 25, 1945 Soviet Ambassador to Mexico since June 1943; was killed in plane crash on way to Costa Rica, where he was to have been Foreign Minister from the U.S.S.R.; Ambassador to the United States from 1939 to 1941; was instrumental in stirring up strong anti-Nazi sentiment in the States. See *Current Biography* 1941 Yearbook.

Obituary

N Y Times p1+ Ja 26 '45 por

OXFORD AND ASQUITH, MARGOT (TENNANT) ASQUITH, COUNTESS OF (mär'gō) 1864—July 28, 1945 British author; widow of Prime Minister Herbert Henry Asquith; her autobiography, published in 1920, gave her a reputation for "wit and biting candor"; author of *More or Less About Myself* (1934) and *Off the Record* (1944).

Obituary

N Y Times p39 Jl 27 '45

PALÉOLOGUE, (GEORGES) MAURICE (pȧ"lä"ô"lôg' zhôrzh mô"rēs') June 13, 1859—Nov.(?) 1944 French diplomat; Ambassador to Russia from 1914 to 1917; Director-General of French Foreign Office from 1921 to 1925; author of many critical studies, biographies, and histories.

Obituary

N Y Times p19 N 22 '44 por

PAPASHVILY, GEORGE (pȧ-pȧsh-vē'lĭ) 1895(?)- Author
PAPASHVILY, HELEN (WAITE) Author

Address: b. Moby Dick Bookshop, Allentown, Pa.

The true story of one immigrant's delightsome discovery of America and his adjustment to the strange customs of his chosen land is the theme of a 1945 best seller aptly titled *Anything Can Happen*. The authors of this light-hearted little book of "wonder, innocence, and spontaneous wit" are George and Helen (Waite) Papashvily, an obscure couple who suddenly found themselves literary celebrities.

George and Helen Papashvily, products of distinctly dissimilar backgrounds, live in an old Dutch farmhouse in Bucks County, Pennsylvania. The story of how they happen to be living there, of how an American girl and a Russian man met and married and eventually migrated to a Pennsylvania farm, is part of the story of *Anything Can Happen*. George Papashvily was born in Kobiankari, a small village in Caucasian Georgia, sometime between 1895 and 1900. He is proud of his peasant parentage and the fact that his mother was the only person in the village who could read and write. But his mother died tragically in a fire when little George was three years old, and his father could not afford the small fee needed to send the boy to the local school. George's education is described by Roger Butterfield: "He used to follow the other children and sit outside the school door with his dog, trying to catch a few words. The teacher found this out and shut the door. Later George's father gave a precious bag of grain to the local prince (in Georgia then almost anyone who owned much land or property was a 'prince') to teach his son to write his own name. The prince gave him two quick readings of the alphabet and that was the end of his schooling."

George's father was a practical man, however, and had his son trained for two trades—making ornamented riding crops and swords. The boy's apprenticeship to the swordmaker was a hard period in his life; his heavy labor in the unfriendly employer's house was relieved only by his friendship with "Uncle" John. (The latter, George's devoted friend, is one of the most colorful characters in *Anything Can Happen*. He was a great, zestful man, gifted in the art of preparing Russian delicacies.) In the First World War George Papashvily was a sharpshooter on the Turkish front, later becoming an aviation mechanic. He served in the Czar's army for six years and during the Revolution he was in the Georgian national army. Afterward he went to Constantinople, where he "dug wells, drove a taxicab, and hunted wild pig on the Anatolian plains."

Anything Can Happen begins George Papashvily's life story with his entry into the United States in 1923 in the steerage of a Greek ship. During the passage he spent most of his money on extra food but he managed to flash a roll of rented bills to convince the immigration officials of his financial security. On his first day in New York the young man found and lost a job. An employment agency, after convincing him that ornamenting crop handles and making swords were not thriving trades in America, found him a job as a dishwasher. But breaking too many dishes and eating the proprietor's best caviar brought prompt dismissal. There then followed in swift succession jobs in a silk mill, a garage, and a statue factory. When Papashvily tried to improve the statues he found himself again at leisure. He then turned to house painting and later worked in a cleaning factory where the gas fumes bothered him. Sundays found him and his friends in New York's Van Cortlandt Park, enjoying the outdoors and making fires to roast their beloved *shashlik* (a Russian dish made of cubed lamb). On one of these Sunday picnics a flower-picking episode led to a police summons, an incident which makes one of the most hilarious chapters of the book. In court to plead his innocence, Papashvily caused much amusement by addressing the judge as "Your Honesty."

In time New York's cement vistas became oppressive to the Georgian. Consequently, when he overheard some favorable references to Pittsburgh in a subway conversation, he decided to go to that city. There, after a two-month search for work, he found a job in a glue factory, but that lasted only three days. Then the immigrant found himself employed in a strike-bound factory, unknowingly working as a scab. Learning of the true situation, he protested to the employer and eventually joined the picket line. This significant incident in the book has been singled out for special comment by the critics. It is one of the few serious notes in the story.

Papashvily next went to Ambridge, Pennsylvania, where he worked in a railroad yard and a garage. His wanderings began again when he decided to accompany a friend to Detroit. There he worked for several automobile companies and devised schemes to get rich quickly. Once he invested his savings in real estate, only to discover that the lots he had bought were under water. But nothing disillusioned the irrepressible Papashvily. In 1929 when the depression descended upon Detroit, Papashvily and his Russian friends sought to escape from it. They started on a memorable

J. Loving

GEORGE and HELEN (WAITE)
PAPASHVILY

journey to California—in the words of the *Christian Science Monitor* this "trek across the country is irresistible reading." Papashvily found little choice of jobs in Hollywood, and after playing a Cossack in films for some time he decided he could have stayed in Russia and have practically been one. However, he was soon managing a lunchbox business, in the course of which, while selling sandwiches to soldiers on a rifle range one day, the ex-sharpshooter found himself joining the National Guard.

George and Helen Papashvily first met in California in 1930 when a mutual friend introduced them. At that time California-born Helen Waite was a senior at the University of California and manager of a small bookshop. Her ancestors, cabinetmakers by trade, had come from England and settled originally in Vermont. But her father, Herbert Waite, gave up the family trade and became a contractor in California. When she left the University of California, she joined the staff of Creeds Bookshop in Berkeley, and later managed two other bookshops in that city.

Miss Waite came to New York in 1933 to do bibliographical work and free-lance collecting for two private libraries. She had already been writing for some years, having contributed to several magazines for children. When Helen Waite and George Papashvily announced their intention of marrying, both her family and his friends doubted the wisdom of such a venture. His Russian friends warned him about marrying an American girl, but they were somewhat reassured of George's happiness at the impressive Georgian wedding feast arranged by Uncle John and the bride's bewildered family. The bride was secretly advised on the ways of happy married life by one of her groom's friend: "At least once a day say to your husband 'I love you.' And whenever you set a table for Georgians, remember—only too much is ever enough." The bridegroom was delighted with his newly ac-

PAPASHVILY, GEORGE and PAPASHVILY, HELEN (WAITE)—*Continued*

quired family, declaring with a Russian twist to his English: "Should have everybody a grandmother to make a dignified ornament for the house."

Since Papashvily discovered that in America "they're crazy about any kind of inventions, especially those that work," he has been inventing things. When he was experimenting with some sort of duplicating paper after his marriage, the couple moved to Virginia to be near the place where the necessary material was made. Papashvily imported some chemical from Germany for the ink used in the process until his disapproval of Hitlerism caused him to stop buying German material, which put an end to the experiment. At another time he invented a waterproof cement which he used successfully. During the second year in Virginia, Papashvily entered a contest and, for his brief letter on the qualities of a certain salad oil, won a furnace, stoker, and eight tons of coal. Since the winner had neither the need nor the space for his prize, the oil company presented him instead with a refrigerator. When the Papashvilys moved to Pennsylvania in 1939 and bought their farm, their friends helped them set the house and land in order. (These friends add to the fun of *Anything Can Happen*.) Papashvily forthwith became a farmer, raising successively chickens, goats, bees, corn, sheep, pigs, flax, and finally tomatoes. All this netted the Papashvilys much fun but little profit. But meanwhile, Mrs. Papashvily had the happy thought of writing down some of her husband's accounts of his twenty-year Americanization process, just as he told them. The short pieces, which first appeared in the magazines *Common Ground* and *Direction*, later became part of *Anything Can Happen*. Published in January 1945, the book met an enthusiastic critical reception and became the Book-of-the-Month Club's co-selection for January. That same month *Anything Can Happen* was purchased for a motion picture by RKO-Radio for thirty thousand dollars, plus an arrangement for additional editions sold.

The amazing adventures of George Papashvily form the backbone of the book, and its flesh and blood are the warmth of friendship and optimism, the courageous spirit, and the love of life of the people in it. For these human qualities the book received glowing critical tribute. The critics also called the volume "rollicking entertainment", "tender and funny and deeply perceptive"; and there were those who also considered it an effective force toward the better understanding of immigrants. Several reviewers noted a Saroyan touch in the book, and many appreciated especially this Georgian's love of America and his feeling of good fellowship for all men. John K. Sherman saw in *Anything Can Happen* a "vision of democracy," while Sterling North [43] declared it "a book to make you love America as only an immigrant can love her and to cringe for her brutal aspects as only a citizen with a social conscience can cringe. From the reception of this starry-eyed Georgian (cheated and hoodwinked in the very shadow of the Statue of Liberty) to the mov

ing toast to the United Nations on the last page, this is a story destined to promote international tolerance." The Springfield *Republican* called *Anything Can Happen* "America sunny side up"; Isabelle Mallet in the New York *Times* expressed the same view, declaring that Papashvily "brushes aside with philosophic calm the details of hunger, cold, discouragement, and unemployment." But Miss Mallet also adds: "When we want the Four Freedoms of America poignantly outlined by a poet and philosopher, we'll let George do it."

The language of the book, delightful to some critics, provoked the following remark in the *Library Journal*: "The foreign idiom is not always consistent and the author sometimes takes advantage of it to accentuate his points." Helen Papashvily dealt with this question on a February radio broadcast of *Author Meets the Critics* on which the Papashvilys were guests. On this occasion Bennett Cerf [41] criticized the "phony accent" of the book, which he found apparent in the change from the Georgian-type speech to pages of pure literate English. Mrs. Papashvily explained that she had had no wish to write a "dialect book," that she had endeavored to capture the rhythm and flavor of her husband's language rather than his exact speech. Critic Harry Hansen [42] found some of the situations in the book "obviously synthetic," but the consensus of critical opinion applauded its "naïve humor" and "essential good nature." To those who doubt the veracity of George Papashvily's more unusual adventures, both husband and wife offer firm reassurance of the truth of the story. George Papashvily repeats his belief that in America "anything can happen."

The Papashvilys still live on their Pennsylvania farm, not far from Allentown. There Mrs. Papashvily runs the Moby Dick Bookshop, which they bought in 1939. Not long ago she forced her husband to read English by refusing to read the newspapers to him, but he still does not write English. In his spare time he carves animals in limestone, sandstone, or wood. His work is said to have an interesting, primitive quality. Typical of their natural simplicity was the couple's reaction to their success. Helen Papashvily reveals this in a letter written after they were informed that *Anything Can Happen* had been chosen by the Book-of-the-Month Club: "Your wire came yesterday. Fortunately George was at home because his factory had a holiday. Only he was sitting on top of the ridge pole and I was afraid if I told him he might fall off. So I said, come down and I'll tell you something nice, but he went on pounding shingles and saying, tell me from there. Finally, I got him down and, of course, he was very glad and we sat under the tree being happy for an hour. But then he said I might as well put the other side of the roof on now . . . so he went back on his ladder and I decided I might as well finish making peach jam as long as I was half-way through."

George Papashvily, who has a quick smile, "looks a little like an eagle," has thinning grayish hair, a black mustache under a prominent nose. He calls his wife Elena Gerbertovna, in Russian style. (The second name means daughter of Herbert—the H, which does not exist in Russian, becomes a G sound.) Helen Papashvily is a plump, dark-haired, sweet-faced woman. She has learned to make several Russian dishes, which the Papashvilys serve bountifully to their friends. Their latest plan for the farm is an artesian well, since the "present flow of water is not equal to their Georgian hospitality."

References

Book-of-the-Month Club N p7-8 D '44
    pors
N Y Sun p18 Ja 5 '45
N Y Times Book R p5 D 31 '44
Pub W 147:454-5 Ja 27 '45

Papashvily, G. and H. W. Anything Can Happen (1945)

PARRI, FERRUCCIO (păr-rē fä-rōōt′chō) 1890(?)- Former Premier of Italy

Probably the most distinguished record of anti-Fascist and anti-Nazi activity in Italy is that of Ferruccio Parri, Italy's Premier from June to November 1945. Like France's Georges Bidault '45, Parri was a mild-mannered history teacher who has served the cause of freedom as a writer, editor, and general of guerrillas; his underground activities continued unbroken for more than twenty years, of which nine were spent in Fascist prisons. Unlike his predecessors, Parri is from the more advanced and articulate northern section of Italy, where Fascism never attained quite the acceptance it did in the poor and semifeudal south. It was north Italy that was occupied by the Nazis after Italy's surrender to the Allies on September 1943, and it was in Milan and Turin that the patriots rose in April 1945 and drove out the invader.

The future Premier was born in Turin about 1890. In 1915, writes Gaetano Salvemini '43 in the *Nation*, "Parri was an instructor in history in a high school. [Other sources give his field as classical literature.] Tall, pale, with beautiful dark eyes and a great shock of black hair, as severe with himself as with others in the fulfillment of duty, Parri was adored by his pupils." He was in favor of Italy's entrance into the First World War, on the side of the Allies, which he saw as a war to obtain justice for all and to complete the unification of Italy. Entering the Army as a lieutenant, Parri participated in nine offensives, was wounded four times, and received four decorations for valor, among them the Croce per Merito di Guerra and the French Croix de Guerre. Afterward, to quote Salvemini, Major Parri "followed President Wilson's work with enthusiasm. When Leonida Bissolati resigned from the Orlando '44-Sonnino Cabinet because he would not associate himself with its demands for Dalmatia and openly defied the Nationalists and Mussolini '42, Ferruccio Parri took sides with him, while Ivanoe Bonomi '44, who had been Bissolati's follower and friend, betrayed him by taking his place in the Cabinet."

An anti-Fascist from the first, after his discharge from the Army Parri became assistant editor of the liberal newspaper *Corriere della sera* ("Evening Messenger"). In 1925 he resigned because the editor in chief, Senator Albertini, had been replaced by a Fascist; and from that time on Parri devoted himself to

FERRUCCIO PARRI

secret counterrevolutionary activities against the Fascist dictatorship. In 1926 he was Italian correspondent for the emigré newspaper *Corriere degli Italiani*, published in France by Giuseppe Donati and other anti-Fascists. This work ended for Parri in November of that year, when he and Carlo Rosselli managed to effect the escape of seventy-year-old Filippo Turati, leader of the Socialist Party in Italy. "When . . . all remnants of resistance were suppressed in Italy," Parri wrote in explanation, "I felt it my duty to make a protest which should declare my faith in a better Italy. This protest could only be made public abroad. . . . Signor Turati is well fitted to present to civilized Europe our protest against the darkness that has fallen upon our country and our faith in an Italy which will give equal liberty to all Italians."

Returning to Italy, Parri and Rosselli were stopped by customs guards at Tuscany, and admitted their complicity in "unauthorized expatriation." Under Fascist law they were entitled to be set free while awaiting trial, but the police interned them on the island of Ustica for a month. Salvemini has given in his article a graphic description of the "conditions of torture" with which the future Premier and his fellow internees were treated. At the trial Parri took the offensive, rousing the courtroom to wild applause, it is reported, by his ringing accusations that the Fascist Government itself had made the step necessary by treating Turati illegally and unjustly. This was the first real challenge anyone had dared offer the Blackshirts, and caused a sensation. The two patriots were given the minimum sentence of ten months' imprisonment, after which Rosselli was again seized and interned. Parri was freed, but the Milan police kept an eye on him, and, says Delos Lovelace, the newspapers on which he worked after that "were generally seized by Mussolini's agents as soon as an issue began to run off the presses."

In all, the future Premier spent nine years in Fascist prisons, of which three years were

PARRI, FERRUCCIO—*Continued*

in detention while awaiting trial. Mrs. Parri, the former Ester Verrua, also served one term. Toward the end of 1930, when other leaders of the underground Justice and Liberty movement were seized and sent to a penal island where they remained until 1943, Parri miraculously escaped arrest, and, "amid the general hopelessness, steadfastly refused to make any compromises with the victorious Fascist regime." (The founding of the Rome-Berlin Axis added to the danger for his Jewish wife.) The coming of the Second World War and the occupation of north Italy by the Germans after the fall of Mussolini only intensified the work of the underground and Parri. "Week after week," to quote *Newsweek*, "he went to bed at 2:00 or 3:00 A.M., rose again at eight, and worked through the day without lunch. When hiding from the Germans Parri sometimes shaved off his black, gray-flecked mustache or changed his glasses." As a leader of the fighting Partisans, or guerrillas, he was best known to the Germans as "General Maurizio," and was also heard of as "Lo Zio" ("The Uncle"). Other war pseudonyms used by Parri were Milanesi, Pozzi, and Pazzolini. He always carried his own bag of secret documents, rather than entrust them to someone else whom the Nazis would be less likely to suspect, as underground leaders did. "An electrical expert and former research director of the Italian Edison Society," *Newsweek* adds, "he organized an elaborate system of radio communication with the Allies in Rome."

More than once Parri slipped across to southern Italy for conferences. Picked up by the Gestapo after one such visit, Parri identified himself frankly as "chief organizer of warfare against Nazism and Fascism." He expected to be executed, but was set free in Switzerland. In one version of the incident, a quick-thinking American major, in the name of General Mark Clark [42], ordered the release of a German general in exchange for that of the white-haired Partisan—or the General's death if Parri were killed. According to Colonel Edward J. F. Glavin of the Office of Strategic Services, the German delivered "Maurizio" and another Italian prisoner in Switzerland for return to the Allies, as proof of their good intentions in asking for surrender terms. At any rate, Parri went back to Milan and the Partisans—he was one of the highest commanders of this underground, which was said to be one of the most efficient in all of Europe. Later "Maurizio" and several of his colleagues were decorated by General Clark with the Bronze Star, which some Americans considered ridiculously inadequate for the value and difficulty of their services to the Allied cause.

The anti-monarchist and mildly socialistic Action Party, which Parri helped found in northern Italy, is not one of the largest parties, but it is one of the most influential. According to the New York *Post* correspondent Thomas Healy, "Parri's Action Party has always adopted the mediating role" between the Leftists and the parties of the Right, which include the Christian Democrats and the so-called "Liberals"; and the Actionists "may be truly said to be the party without 'isms,' whose principles give homage to democracy and

permit its expression. Its members—membership costs about a dime—total 120,000 in north Italy and 80,000 in the south. It raised more members of the fighting Partisan armies of the north than any other single party: seventeen divisions, or one-third of the total Partisan forces." In June 1945, when fifty days of crisis had found none of the six parties in Premier Bonomi's Government willing to succeed him, Parri was called to Rome for consultations. A few days later Prince Humbert [43], Lieutenant General of the Realm, designated him to form a new Cabinet. Conservatives had agreed to his selection, reportedly, as the least radical of the Left-wingers and as the most distinguished anti-Fascist.

"I would sooner have been shot by General Kappler," was Parri's reaction, although he accepted the task. As Anne O'Hare McCormick [40] put it, "Nobody wants a job that carries responsibility without power and depends on outside powers who don't know what they want. . . . Nearly half the territory is still under military government, and the rest is only nominally under Italian rule. The regime remains subject to the still-unpublished terms of the armistice, which restrict its political authority and give it almost no economic power. The cupboard is so bare, moreover, that economic control means very little. Italy has no ships, no material for reconstruction, no access to Lend-Lease, no assistance from UNRRA except to a limited number of children and displaced persons."

As President of the Council of Ministers, Parri abolished the title of "Excellency," and was usually addressed as "Professor." After stormy interparty sessions, he took over the important and much-disputed portfolio of the Interior, which controls elections and all local government, appointed the Socialist Pietro Nenni to make plans for a constituent assembly to vote on keeping or rejecting the monarchy, and formed a Cabinet of three members of his Action Party, the same number from each of three others, one admiral, and four of the (Roman Catholic) Christian Democrats—a compromise to reconcile the last-named to a Socialist Minister of Education.

Premier Parri broke Italian precedent by giving the people a frank and dispassionate statement of the facts: "We are still far from the status of a great nation, which our history, importance, and numbers should give us. We must merit that status. It won't be given to us as a gift." The Italians, he said, must work to gain the trust of the Allies: "their trust means bread, coal, raw materials, and credits, . . . the very possibility of our livelihood. This trust will be the base of our ability to govern ourselves." In July Italy declared war on Japan. Despite the Premier's efforts, he was unable to get the Allies to terminate or even to make public the reputedly harsh and hampering terms of the 1943 armistice, under which Italy was still technically considered an enemy nation. It was against this background of uncertainty and of unemployment and the threat of famine that the first free assembly of Italian representatives (designated by their parties) in twenty years opened, in September 1945.

The Premier labored for five months to keep his six-party coalition government united. When the Liberal party, ranked among conservatives, became alarmed at Parri's resolute purge of officials who were tainted with Fascism, two Liberals and one Independent resigned from the coalition. Thus on November 24, 1945, Italy's third national government since the liberation of Rome in June 1944 was dissolved under the weight of conservative attacks when the Premier resigned. Parri warned of a renascence of Fascism and the threat of civil war, eight large Italian cities staged protest strikes, and the United States asked all the political parties to subordinate their own aims to the national interest. Although the Rightist politicians who had forced Parri's resignation waged a high-pressure campaign to replace him with Vittorio Orlando, eighty-five-year-old former Premier, who in 1935 had published a letter praising the Fascist aggression in Ethiopia, on December 4 Alcide de Gasperi, Christian Democratic leader, was elevated to the Premiership. His government retained the coalition of liberation, six parties sharing equally in the new cabinet. It was reported on December 14 that the new government had not altered the course of the Parri regime.

Ferruccio Parri is described as a tall, lean man, spectacled and weather-beaten. He has thick silvery hair, and dark eyebrows and a mustache. The Premier is soft-voiced and, unlike most of his countrymen, he makes few gestures when he talks. He enjoys mountain climbing when he has time, and he smokes about thirty cigarettes each day. Correspondents described Parri at first as "the harassed, poorly dressed professor in politics," but several months as Premier seem to have changed his appearance and personality to that of "a perfect aristocrat." His own description of himself is "an average man—just anybody (*'uomo de strada—uomo qualunque'*)." Thomas Healy, one of his most enthusiastic American admirers, writes, "I have read everything about Parri. He is Italy's great man and will become much greater. He has the qualifications—good sense, intellect, honesty, respect for his given word —and is a true democrat." Another American, Philip Hamburger of the *New Yorker*, calls Parri "a man of pure intelligence. . . .It's wonderful to hear a man . . . use words like 'morality' and 'democracy' and know that they mean something in his mouth."

References

N Y Sun p10 Jl 11 '45
Nation 161:59-61 Jl 21 '45
Newsweek 26:40 Jl 2 '45
Scholastic 47:10 O 15 '45 por
Time 46:34-6 Jl 2 '45 por

PARTRIDGE, SIR BERNARD Oct. 11, 1861—Aug. 9, 1945 British illustrator for *Punch* from 1891 until few months before death; considered one of the world's foremost political cartoonists; preferred realism to extravagant emphasis.

Obituary

N Y Times p13 Ag 11 '45 por

PASVOLSKY, LEO (päs-vŏl'skĭ) Aug. 22, 1893- United States Government official; economist

Address: b. c/o Department of State, Washington, D.C.; h. 3641 R St., N.W., Washington, D.C.

One of the lesser known officials at the United Nations Conference on International Organization, in the spring of 1945, was Leo Pasvolsky, special assistant to the Secretary of State of the United States. An "old hand at conferences," he is considered "one of the principal architects of the Dumbarton Oaks proposals for world peace." He is also credited with drafting the plan for international trusteeships of such conquered territory as is not ceded outright to the victorious United Nations, a plan to which President Roosevelt [42] had committed the United States.

The son of Michael and Maria Pasvolsky, Leo Pasvolsky came into the world on August 22, 1893, in the Black Sea town of Pavlograd, Russia. His father, an anti-Czarist journalist, took part in the attempted revolution of 1905, then sought refuge in the United States after its failure, becoming a teacher of Russian literature. Twelve-year-old Leo learned English as he went along in the New York public schools; he became an American citizen in 1911. Intending to become an electrical engineer, he entered the College of the City of New York, but soon discovered that he lacked mathematical aptitude and therefore concentrated on political economy. In his student days, according to Josef Israels 2d, Pasvolsky lived in "a ratty Greenwich Village apartment above a laundry . . . [but] he served caviar and cheese to cronies and sought out exotic restaurants for a gourmet's appetite."

Since the age of fifteen Pasvolsky had been contributing to Russian-language publications and to those concerned with Russian subjects, and after his graduation from C.C.N.Y. in 1916 he became editor of a monthly, the *Russian Review*. In 1917 he also began to edit a Russian-language daily, the *Russkoye Slovo* ("Russian Word"), and a monthly, the *Amerikanskii Viestnik* ("American Messenger"); and from 1916 to 1918 he pursued graduate studies at Columbia University. Pasvolsky found time also to do some translations from the Russian, notably a selection of eleven of Aleksandr I. Kuprin's short stories, published as *The Bracelet of Garnets and Other Stories* in 1917, with an introduction by his friend William Lyon Phelps [43]. That year saw the publication, too, of *Economic Russia*, which he helped to prepare. When *Mentor* Magazine devoted its July 1917 issue to the Russian Empire, it turned to Pasvolsky for an expert summary.

In 1918 Pasvolsky left the *Russian Review* and the *Amerikanskii Viestnik* and joined the War Work Extension of the United States Department of the Interior. He was also a member of the New York City Mayor's Committee on National Defense. Pasvolsky covered the Versailles Conference in 1919 for the Brooklyn *Eagle* and the New York *Tribune*. He remained editor of the *Russian Word* until 1920, after which he worked as a free-lance writer. In this capacity Pasvolsky covered the Wash-

LEO PASVOLSKY

ington Naval Conference of November 1921-February 1922 for the Baltimore *Sun*.

After a study of the official Soviet statistics covering the period from the beginning of the Russian Revolution to the end of 1920, Pasvolsky wrote *The Economics of Communism, With Special Reference to Russia's Experiment*, published in 1921. In his view, the Soviet Union faced the fundamental dilemma that "Communism is impossible without the application of compulsion in the economic life of the country; but economic production is impossible with the application of such compulsion. . . .Either the Soviet regime must give up its Communism in the processes of production and distribution, or else it will be overthrown."

In Pasvolsky's next book, *Russia in the Far East* (1922), he pursued the idea that Soviet Russia "is bound to be, by its very nature, insatiably aggressive and . . . violently imperialistic." A democratic regime, such as the short-lived Kerensky Government of 1917 which was overthrown by the Bolsheviks, was, he felt, "bound to emerge from the suffering country's present tragic trials." He reported the U.S.S.R. "ready to spare no efforts for the consummation" of a disabling war between Japan and the United States, but predicted an economic partnership of those nations with a future democratic Russia in the development of Siberia. He recommended also that the United States exert a stabilizing influence, which would be possible only through "an idealistic international policy."

In 1922 the author joined the research staff of the Institute of Economics in Washington (which was to become part of the famous Brookings Institution by a merger five years later) and assisted in preparing its studies. With Harold G. Moulton[44] he wrote *Russian Debts and Russian Reconstruction* (1924) and *World War Debt Settlements* (1926). In November 1926 the thirty-three-year-old economist was married to Irish-American Christine Mc-

Cormick of Pittsburgh, who makes even fewer social appearances than her shy husband.

Pasvolsky worked on the Brookings Institution's *Economic Nationalism of the Danubian States* (1928) and *Bulgaria's Economic Position* (1930). His *War Debts and World Prosperity* (1932), written with Harold G. Moulton, presented with "admirable lucidity" the substance of all previous discussions of the topic. Translated into several languages, it became an international best seller; Walter Lippmann[40] called it "the indispensable source book" on the subject. In 1932-33 Pasvolsky studied at the University of Geneva. At this time he was the American member of the International Chamber of Commerce's special committee of economists to prepare the draft report for the World Monetary and Economic Conference. He was a member also of the subcommittee on finance of the Permanent Bureau for Study of Danubian Problems, and acted as special observer for the Brookings Institution. At the conference he presented a paper, *The Necessity for a Stable International Monetary Standard* (1933), advocating an international gold standard (not to be confused with an international currency), based on "international cooperation to maintain stable relationships," and managed in the same sense as a managed-paper currency.

Pasvolsky developed this idea further in writing an Institution report, *Current Monetary Issues* (1933), on the Washington, London, and Geneva economic conferences. This book met with almost unanimous praise, a typical reaction being this (from the *New Republic*): "One is impressed throughout with his [Pasvolsky's] fairness and competence in the analysis of issues and in the interpretation of conflicting positions. While leaning obviously toward a cautious conservatism on questions of monetary policy, he has not allowed his own convictions to distort his reporting." Pasvolsky's belief was that "the only practical means of maintaining stable foreign exchanges is through the operation of an international gold standard based upon fixed gold ratios, unlimited redemption of paper currency in gold at a fixed rate for purposes of international payments, an unlimited market for gold at a fixed price, and free exports and imports of the metal."

In 1934 Pasvolsky was appointed economist in the United States Bureau of Foreign and Domestic Commerce under the Franklin D. Roosevelt Administration. The following year he entered the Department of State as an economist in the Division of Trade Agreements. Politically, according to Israels, Leo Pasvolsky's early record "placed him well to the Left. As he progressed in influence and position, he headed toward center. About 1936 his ideas began to coincide with those of the New Deal, which he had often opposed." In that year he collaborated on Brookings' *The Recovery Problem in the United States* (1936), and was awarded a Ph.D. by the Institution. In that year, too, he was alternate American member of the League of Nations economic committee. And in that year he was appointed special assistant to the Secretary of State, Cordell Hull[40]. "Since that time," says *Newsweek*, "very few diplomatic matters have arisen in which he has not had a finger. He is an unobtrusive figure, but the force of his decisions is felt, and the extent of his influence understood, in foreign embassies and legations."

Pasvolsky's position on the official State Department organizational chart is on the same level as the six Assistant Secretaries of State. The reason for his title of special assistant, according to Israels, was to spare the White House "possible wrangling in Congress over a Russian-born expert with a political past as varied as a zebra's stripes." At any rate, the Russian-born expert became one of Secretary Hull's closest advisers and editor in chief of his speeches and diplomatic memoranda. "A spade becomes 'an agricultural implement,'" wrote *Newsweek*, "and the Secretary's picturesque vernacular is transposed into English acceptable for family publications."

In 1939, when the State Department became convinced that war was inevitable, Pasvolsky "was quietly put on the job of organizing new sources of knowledge about foreign countries. . . .Since 1939 hundreds of experts on the nations of the world, both in and out of government, have made contributions to this board, working together under Pasvolsky's general coordination. Millions of facts and opinions on people and nations and politics have been refined through many minds into the over-all knowledge contained in its documents. Pasvolsky has been their human funnel." He is said to be particularly proud of the exactness of his analysis of the long-range trends for the Secretary and the President. (Pasvolsky came in for some criticism in February 1941, in a series of articles Tabitha Petran and William Walton wrote for *PM* on the State Department: "The only one in the economics division who approaches adviser Herbert Feis in do-nothingism is . . . Leo Pasvolsky, special assistant to the Secretary of State on economic affairs. [Salary $8,500]. . . .Mr Pasvolsky clings to pre-World War economics, opposes any regulation of international trade.")

In 1941 Pasvolsky was officially named chief of the Division of Special Research and given larger appropriations. Intensive study groups were set up by him, Under-Secretary of State Sumner Welles '40, and Isaiah Bowman '45, the noted geographer who had helped President Wilson fix post-World War boundary lines. Pasvolsky then turned his attention to postwar problems. He became executive director of the Department's Committee on Postwar Problems, composed of the Secretary, Under-Secretary, Assistant Secretaries, and division directors. According to *Newsweek*, "Functioning as a clearinghouse, the committee farmed out for special study the questions that must be settled at the war's conclusion." Its findings were prepared by Pasvolsky as a formal basis for United States policy on postwar questions.

In August 1943 Leo Pasvolsky accompanied President Roosevelt to his Quebec meeting with Winston Churchill '42. That September columnist Drew Pearson '41 complained that the State Department was "consistently needling" its Russian allies by failing to give them certain information, "cold-shouldering" Soviet and pro-Soviet officials, and conspicuously favoring anti-Soviets; and was also trying to build up buffer states around the U.S.S.R. In these decisions, Pearson declared, Secretary Hull relied heavily for advice on Pasvolsky and As-

sistant Secretary of State Adolf A. Berle '40, both of whom Pearson classified as anti-Soviet.

Friction developed between Pasvolsky and Sumner Welles, as it had between Hull and the forthright Under-Secretary; and on Welles's resignation, he was replaced by Lend-Lease Administrator Edward R. Stettinius, Jr. '40. When Stettinius succeeded Hull in November 1944, the youngest Secretary of State since George Washington's day found in Pasvolsky "a mind alert to the complex details of international economics and security organization, combined with a skillful anonymity." In addition to his role as Special Assistant to the Secretary, Pasvolsky supervises the activities of the Office of Special Political Affairs. Prior to the January 1944 reorganization the work of this office was organized on a study basis, and as such was fairly well removed from the day-to-day operations of the Department. During 1944, however, it rapidly became a more vital part of the Department's working mechanism. With the time rapidly approaching for the establishment of the United Nations Organization and the Permanent Court, and postwar settlements, in general the work of this office was to become even more important than in the past.

Pasvolsky is credited with an important share in the proposals for a world security organization formulated at Dumbarton Oaks in August 1944 by representatives of the Big Four among the Allies. There, it is said, he answered Stettinius' every question, from his photographic knowledge of hundreds of documents dated even as far back as a quarter of a century. Josef Israels wrote that he also turned out to be a valuable liaison man with the Soviet delegates. "Russians think like Asiatics," one observer commented, "and it takes a Russian to do business with a Russian." In February 1945 he attended the Inter-American Conference at Mexico City.

New York *Times* columnist Arthur Krock '43 stated that the "trusteeship" plan proposed for adoption at the United Nations Conference on International Organization at San Francisco in April 1945 was also credited to Pasvolsky. Under its terms, "a special committee of the Assembly would provide international administrative machinery for conquered enemy territory that will not be, or has not been, given to members of the United Nations; for areas that were mandated [under the old League of Nations] to enemy and neutral nations; and for colonial possessions which may be ceded to the international trusteeship by the victorious powers." The trustee "would have full rights to establish [military] bases and administer the civil affairs of the population. But it would be responsible to the Assembly committee, and be required to give full access to members of the new security league and to assist the inhabitants to independence." This plan, opposed by the War and Navy Departments for strategic reasons, and by Allies with colonial possessions, was designed to prevent the "no-territorial-aggrandizement" clause of the Atlantic Charter from becoming a dead letter and a mockery, and no one, up to that time, had suggested anything better. At the conference where he headed the technical staff sent by the Administration, Pasvolsky was one of a five-man subcommittee to study proposals

PASVOLSKY, LEO—*Continued*

for amendments to the Dumbarton Oaks agreement submitted by the countries which had not participated in its formulation. When the United Nations Charter was presented to the Senate Foreign Relations Committee on July 9, 1945, it was Pasvolsky's task to detail line by line the meaning of the one hundred and eleven sections of the Charter. A recognition of his work was the Townsend Harris Medal, awarded to him in 1945 by New York City College for outstanding post-graduate achievement.

The mustached and bespectacled Pasvolsky, "a ball of energy," is "easily distinguishable from any direction by his bald pate, stubby, egg-shaped figure, and a long trail of pipe smoke." A shunner of publicity he lives unpretentiously. He puts in brief appearances at the required diplomatic parties, but prefers to spend his free time playing billiards at the Cosmos Club (he belongs also to clubs in London and Geneva). He is said to be a "shark" at bridge for one-twentieth of a cent a point. His fondness for Polish food, especially *zrazy* with *kasha*, has led indirectly to one of his nicknames—"Humpty Dumpty"—in recognition of the two hundred pounds which once covered his five-foot-five-inch frame. A year of reducing brought the Pasvolsky weight down forty pounds. The economist's beatific expression has inspired some Washingtonians to call him "St. Leo," while others, struck by his academic speech, refer to him as "The Brain That Walks Like a Man." The one photograph in his office, that of Cordell Hull, is autographed, "With esteem."

References

N Y Herald Tribune (This Week p9+)
  Ap 15 '45 por
Newsweek 23:37 My 1 '44 por
Who's Who in America, 1944-45

PATTEN, GILBERT Oct. 25, 1866—Jan. 16, 1945 Author, known to most Americans as Burt L. Standish, creator of the hero of boys stories, the fabulous Frank Merriwell from Yale; for twenty years he was one of the most popular authors in the world; a prolific writer, he wrote an estimated forty million words in his lifetime.

Obituary

N Y Times p21 Ja 17 '45 por

PATTON, JAMES G(EORGE) Nov. 8, 1902- Agricultural leader

Address: b. National Farmers Union Service, Inc., Denver, Colo.; h. 954 Bonnie Brae Blvd., Denver, Colo.

The National Farmers Union, one of the four major agricultural organizations in the United States, has during recent years played a more vigorous and progressive part in the national scene than any of the other groups. Credit for this is given to its young, forward-looking president, James Patton. The membership and influence of the National Farmers Union has grown particularly since the outbreak of the war, when the mobilization of food production became an important part of the national program.

James George Patton, the son of Ernest Everett and Jane Alice (Gross) Patton, was born in Bazar, Kansas, November 8, 1902, the year the Farmers Union was founded by a liberal farm-minded printer and ten farmers in a barn near Point, Texas. During Jim's boyhood the family moved to Colorado, where his father became a mining engineer, and also operated a small farm with indifferent success. The boy went to the Grand Junction High School, from which he was graduated in 1921. He then entered Western State College, at Gunnison, Colorado, where he worked to pay his expenses. Before Patton had finished college his father died, and he was left with a mortgaged farm on his hands, a mother and three younger sisters to support. To add to his responsibilities, he was married in June 1925 to Velma Adeline Fouse. (The Pattons now have two children: Marjorie Jane and Robert Lyle. Two others, James George and George Everett, are deceased.) With his own family to support, Jim Patton's attendance at college was intermittent. He worked at various jobs—he was an athletic director and instructor in physical education in Colorado and Nevada, 1921-26; assistant business manager of Western State, 1927-29; a general agent for a life insurance company in 1931; and organizer of cooperative insurance for the Colorado Farmers Union, 1932-34. He did not get his college degree; but in 1941 Western State College gave him the honorary degree of LL. D.

From first-hand experience Patton knew the difficulties of the small farmer; he had also grown up in a community where there was a thriving cooperative movement among farmers. In 1934 he began his career as an agricultural leader when he became secretary of the Colorado Farmers Union. Three years later he was made a member of the board of directors of the National Farmers Union, and that same year he became president of the National Union Security Association (Fraternal Life Insurance Society), of which organization he is still president. From 1938 to 1943 he was a member of the advisory committee of the National Youth Administration; in 1942 President Roosevelt '42 appointed him a member of the Economic Stabilization Board; and in December 1944 Patton was assigned by the President to serve on the War Mobilization and Reconversion Advisory Board.

It was in 1940 that Jim Patton became president of the National Farmers Union—on a trial basis at first, because he was considered rather young for the post. But the probationery basis soon changed to a fairly permanent status: at the end of each term since then Patton has been re-elected to the presidency. The other three major agricultural organizations in the United States are: the National Grange, of which Albert S. Goss '45 is master; the National Council of Farm Cooperatives, guided largely by secretary Ezra T. Benson; and the American Farm Bureau Federation, whose president is Edward A. O'Neal. Unlike these three organizations, the National Farmers Union has always stood for the "family type" farm, as opposed to the very large farm of the "corporate" type. Unlike them, also, it is friendly toward organized labor, and has worked in close relationship with the CIO and the A.F. of L. It was at its 1941 convention in Kansas that the Farmers Union formalized the understanding between its own objectives and those of organized labor. The Farmers Union has stood behind the New Deal aims and policies from the beginning; and, though the New Deal by 1944 had yielded considerable ground to various pressure groups, Patton still held inflexibly to the New Deal program and on several issues went even further than the New Deal. In 1943, according to Paul Sifton, head of the Washington office, under Patton's leadership the National Farmers Union had a membership of 300,000 representing 125,000 low-income farm families, and was rapidly increasing. The Union has member-owned cooperatives in twenty-six states, with assets of $100,000,000. They handle oil, insurance, crops and farm supplies, and are organized along Rochdale plan lines—one stockholder, one vote (the principle of the cooperative store established in Rochdale, England, in 1844). The headquarters of the Union are Denver, Colorado.

In 1942, when food production was being mobilized to meet the needs of a country at war, the stand of the Farmers Union was initially taken when Patton decried the demand for higher farm prices. The war effort, he said, required national unity and not "partisan hog-trough tactics by farmers, labor, or big business." He particularly criticized President Edward O'Neal of the American Farm Bureau Federation for having complained that agriculture was not getting parity prices. In September of that year President Roosevelt called the spokesmen of the four big farm organizations to Washington to get their views on farm prices and procedures. O'Neal, representing the higher-income farm families, was not on good terms with labor, but knew that Patton had the labor union support. When Patton said that organized labor and the farmers could be brought together on wages and fair ceiling prices, O'Neal contested the statement. The dispute between the two men was by no means their last battle. Patton early took up the cudgels in support of the Farm Security Administration, as opposed to the desires of the large-scale commercial farmers, led by O'Neal, who had a powerful lobby in Washington. According to *Time* (September 14, 1942): "If a workable form of inflation control is developed, Jim Patton, the only farm leader who was willing to play ball, may well turn up as a much bigger figure against the background of plowed fields."

In a speech on December 29, 1942, Patton further stated his stand. "Such political democracy as we have—and few nations have as much—is threatened by stubborn refusal to accept economic democracy in agriculture and in industry. . . .And, solely as peace assurance, leaving aside all altruism or humanity, we must attend to the distribution of minimum abundance throughout the world. . . .Have our people's organizations, farmers, labor unions, civic, welfare and religious groups slipped into the habit of expecting the New Deal or the Administration to do our jobs for us? Were we, perhaps, in danger of contracting a 'company union' attitude? If so, that's over. From here on, we're on our own."

Speaking in January 1943, of the necessity of expanding food production, Patton said that Congress had ignored the warning of the Farmers Union and turned down its proposals

JAMES G. PATTON

that three and one-half million dollars be appropriated to expand food production by assisting hundreds of thousands of low-income, under-employed farm families. He said the only way to prevent oncoming shortages was for consumers, farmers, administrative agencies, and Congress to act swiftly to (1) improve and extend rationing machinery and operations; (2) increase the 1943 food production goals by 20 per cent; and (3) pass immediately a special war appropriation of one billion dollars to be used by the Food Production Administration in expanding American agriculture as the "first leg on a three-year program." The National Farmers Union had pointed out that two and one-half billion dollars (roughly equal to the cost of running the war for eighteen days) was necessary 'not only to assure minimum food supplies to the United States and its allies, but also to make good on its promises of food to the liberated nations. . . .A ton of food delivered to liberated peoples is worth its weight in ammunition."

At a meeting of the National Economic Stabilization Board on March 6, 1943, Patton urged that the Government give war contracts to farmers as well as industry. Prices must be thought of as directives rather than as goals, he said. "Total war will call for much greater individual responsibility and discipline in what has been an almost unorganized industry." Among the specific proposals Patton made to the Board were the simplification of milk collection and distribution, to save rubber and manpower, complete enforcement of draft deferment of skilled farmers, and the unrestricted use of wheat supplies for feed.

In April 1943 Congress was expected to open a drive to abolish the Farm Security Administration, the agency that had been set up to help small farmers. The National Farmers Union pledged itself to save the FSA, joining with a coalition that included the CIO, the A.F. of L., the Catholic Rural Life Conference, the Federal Council of Churches, and other groups. The Farmers Union Council said that the proposals to do away with the FSA by trans-

PATTON, JAMES G.—*Continued*

ferring its functions to other agencies was an admission that "continuance of its work is vital in production of food to meet our rising war needs. . . .A general who won a brilliant battle for greater food production is going to be shot, virtually without a trial." But the House Appropriations Committee proposed FSA abolition, with transfer of its credit functions to the Farm Credit Administration—an agency that would receive most of its appropriations from the Reconstruction Finance Corporation. Patton was upheld in his protests against this move by Representative Hampton Fulmer, Agriculture Committee chairman, who said that those who approved the fund measure had been influenced by "big farmer" lobbying organizations; and James B. Carey [41] of the CIO said the whole thing was designed to "extend commercialized agriculture and the plantation type of farming." On April 15 a House bloc was formed to save at least the framework of the FSA so that the agency's program could be restored in the Senate. In November the fight to save the FSA moved to the Senate following House action which would force the FSA to reduce the number of employees and country officers by half and restrict itself to servicing old loans. Then in May 1944 the National Farmers Union attacked the amended Cooley bill, which would create the Farmers Home Corporation as successor to the FSA. Patton charged that the bill "has not strengthened provisions for rehabilitation loans and supervision above a bare family subsistence level."

On July 25, 1943, Patton again urged that the Government should make war food production agreements with farmers on the same terms as those that have produced world records in industrial war production. Farmers, he said, should be furnished with credit, have assured prices, crop insurance, and priorities in such things as machinery and fertilizer. He charged that the organizations and men who fought the Economic Stabilization Act were now against the President's anti-inflation program. He also held that it was organized labor and consumers who supported the proposed stabilization of prices and wages and endorsed the Farmers Union proposals for increasing food production.

President Roosevelt again called in the leaders of the four farm organizations on September 15 to discuss a program calling for increased "support prices" to farmers. It was reported that the farm leaders, with the exception of Patton, gave no assurance that they would not oppose all, or part, of the program which the President had in mind. Patton pointed out after the meeting that "support prices" was only another name for consumer subsidies—although the other three farm leaders denied this. O'Neal, Goss, and Benson said that labor was getting too much in ratio to the farmers; and Patton pointed out that although farm income is the highest in history, the lion's share of farm income went to the top third of the farmers. He said that four million small farmers might be squeezed out of production unless credit and aid could be given them, and he particularly voiced his concern over the wheat growers, who had planted without parity payments and with no crop insurance.

A further meeting of the agricultural leaders and the President on October 19 resulted in

a "hammer-and-tongs" session. Patton accused the leaders of the farm lobby of "sponsoring starvation" for forty million American citizens by their opposition to food subsidies and advocacy of rising farm prices. He also accused O'Neal and his associates of clearly favoring inflation by their tactics. O'Neal claimed that farmers opposed subsidies because "the Government handout system is neither economic nor conducive to production."

Concerning another angle of the farm problem, Patton charged in 1943 that "the most glaring of wartime wastes of manpower is in agriculture." He said that no national farm organization would defend the labor freezing provisions of the Pace bill, which resulted in farm labor shortages in many areas and a surplus in others. Manpower is also wasted because over a million farm families, according to Patton, are underfinanced, underequipped, and consequently underemployed "from producing war foods at the maximum." He urged immediate restoration of crop insurance and provision for 1944 parity payments, appealing to Congress to "move with all speed to increase food production by at least 20 per cent in 1944."

Early in 1944 Patton, as a representative of the small farmers, expressed concern over the new tax bill, and urged President Roosevelt to veto it as an inadequate measure. "The farmers I represent are buying bonds—as many War Bonds as they can afford. They want those War Bonds to be worth after the war as much as they are worth today. This tax bill will not contribute to that end. With an inflationary gap of twenty-five billion dollars or more, a tax bill that brings in at most only eight hundred million dollars more than the present law is a fraud on the holders of War Bonds." He further attacked Bernard Baruch's [41] plan for postwar reconversion.

There was evidence that Patton was becoming increasingly critical of Administration programs. His newspaper, the *National Union Farmer*, gave front-page space to Wendell Willkie's [40] farm program; and in March 1944 in Chicago Patton said he would advise Republicans to make Willkie their nominee. At the same time there were hints of a split between the Farmers Union and the leaders of labor unions. Patton continued to defend the unions, however, as "people's organizations" when he attacked the National Association of Manufacturers' Postwar Conference as "a pincers movement threatening Congress and democracy." The Administration was also criticized by Patton for relaxing the rationing of meats and other foods in May 1944. Patton regarded this as "surrender to farm bloc isolationists and a serious threat to postwar rehabilitation."

Will Clayton [44], former Surplus Property Administrator, came under attack when it was charged that he had placed the disposal of surplus Government-owned real estate into the hands of the big real estate interests. Patton and others felt that Clayton's setup was "geared to make the operation a speculative land grab for the real estate interests." Patton said that it had been recommended that the disposal of farm land be vested in the Department of Agriculture, but that Clayton declined to do this. On September 19, however, the House of Representatives decided to adopt the Senate's measure of a three-man board for the disposal of surplus Government property. There was a rumor that Clayton might resign, and that, if he did, Patton could "take much credit for forcing him out." But Patton still had a fight on his hands when on November 13 it was announced that the three new appointees to the Surplus Property Board would be under the controlling thumbs of Jesse Jones '40 and Will Clayton. This, Patton said, "would represent a victory for the big business interests which have just finished a bitter fight to prevent the re-election of the President."

The National Farmers Union submitted on August 4, 1944, a five-point program to the War Food Administration, the OPA, and the Office of Economic Stabilization: (1) authorize the writing of an annual agreement between the Government and the individual farmer on what he should raise, and, in return, what he would receive in farm income, technical assistance, and credit for the year; (2) assure the payment of support prices to farmers; (3) establish a two-year support price, at parity, for cattle; (4) coordinate cattle and hog marketing facilities; (5) provide sufficient funds to enable the payment of whatever subsidies are needed.

Several other activities besides those pertaining directly to agriculture have been on Patton's roster. He served on a committee to help underground German labor organizations; he urged President Roosevelt to give serious consideration to the establishment of free ports in the United States as temporary havens for refugees from Nazi Europe. He was active in Russian War Relief work, including the "Write to Russia" campaign. The American Council on Race Relations is one of Patton's interests; and he supported the demands of Negro voters for an antidiscrimination plank in the Democratic Party platform. He was one of the original members of the National Citizens Political Action Committee formed by liberals outside the CIO. It was a Dies '40 subcommittee in Congress that branded Patton's Farmers Union as a "communist-front" organization. During the labor controversy involving Montgomery Ward and Company, Patton served as chairman of the national committee to protect labor rights of Montgomery Ward workers in their efforts to secure compliance with War Labor Board orders by the company. Early in 1945 Patton was also a member of the board of Americans United for World Organization, Inc., which opened a national campaign to rally support for establishment of an international organization to enforce the peace. When President Roosevelt's nomination of Aubrey Williams '40 to be Rural Electrification administrator was rejected by the Senate in March 1945, Patton indicated that the Senate's action would be used as the starting point of an intensive national organizing and political campaign by the union in the South.

In connection with hearings of the Senate Food Investigating Committee in April 1945, Patton warned the chairman, Senator Elmer Thomas, of the "extremely dangerous threat to economic stability involved in the tone of the investigation and the resultant delay in extension of price control legislation." Patton said further that the "unreasoning fear of hunger aroused by the character of the Senate hearings could have a highly undesirable effect upon our international relations at this most critical time."

He declared the only real problem to be distribution, "because farmers, by their magnificent efforts during the war, have broken all production records."

After the war's end Patton again stressed the necessity of sending supplies to war-stricken people. "If we are interested in preventing the growth of any type of totalitarian government," he stated in Look, "one way to do it is to see that genuine free democratic processes are available to all citizens." However, he declared that America's principal weapon against radical action—Right or Left—was to furnish "much more food, clothing, fuel, and shelter than we now seemed prepared to do." In November the National Farmers Union recommended a program intended to give "adequate credit" to the Second World War veterans. Patton estimated that one million members of the armed forces would be seeking farms or farm employment.

Perhaps the most far-reaching proposal made to date by Patton was that offered on August 7, 1944, in connection with the Kilgore '43 Demobilization bill. The proposal submitted through the Farmers Union, was in the nature of an amendment to the Kilgore bill to authorize the Government "to invest and spend the amount by which prospective investment and construction expenditures in each year fall short of forty billion dollars, the annual volume required to maintain full employment." This plan would permit the Government to spend money, when necessary, to make up the gap between the amount invested by private enterprise and the amount necessary for full employment. This would be done by offering, through the Reconstruction Finance Corporation, loans to private industry at low rates, and, if industry did not absorb the balance, the slack would be taken up by a public works program. It was called "the first concrete plan advanced by a prominent and influential political figure to bring about the goal of full employment." Said Patton: "The National Farmers Union believes the American people prefer to go forward to full employment, prosperity, free enterprise for all, security and peace." Favorable comment on the plan came from Chester Bowles '43, Frances Perkins '40, Michael Straus, and Leo Crowley '43.

The president of the National Farmers' Union, in the words of a writer for the New York Post, "has one curious extravagance: buying oil paintings, particularly marines and mountain views." His reading is said to consist largely of technical books on farming and theoretical volumes on the nature of American culture.

References

N Y World-Telegram p22 Mr 11 '43 por
Newsweek 22:59 O 11 '43 por
Time 40:22 S 14 '42 por
Who's Who in America, 1944-45

PAUL-BONCOUR, JOSEPH (pôl'bôn″ koōr' zhō-zĕf') Aug. 4, 1873- French statesman

Address: b. Consultative Assembly, Paris; h. Saint-Aignan, Loir-et-Cher, France

"A gentleman of the old school with an oratorical manner," Joseph Paul-Boncour was sent to San Francisco in April 1945 as a member of the French delegation to the United Na-

JOSEPH PAUL-BONCOUR

tions Conference on International Organization. For more than three decades he has been a familiar figure in French politics and international affairs. An outstanding lawyer, former Socialist Deputy and Premier, in 1940 he was leader of eighty former parliamentarians who voted in Vichy against plenary powers for Marshal Henri-Philippe Pétain '40. Shortly after his appointment to the Consultative Assembly in November 1944, Paul-Boncour was made chairman of the commission for the study for France of the Dumbarton Oaks plan, a post for which he had been well prepared by his many years at Geneva as a delegate to the League of Nations Assembly.

Born in Saint-Aignan, in the department of Loir-et-Cher, on August 4, 1873, Joseph Paul-Boncour is the son of middle-class parents. After making a brilliant university record and receiving the degree of Doctor of Laws, young Paul-Boncour was admitted to the Paris bar. He was to become one of France's most famous lawyers—his clients included notables like Queen Marie and her son Carol '40. His political career began in a sense when he served as private secretary to Waldeck-Rousseau during the latter's premiership, from 1899 to 1902, and later to René Viviani when the Socialist was Minister of Labor (1906-9). "In an atmosphere still charged with the emotion roused by the Dreyfus case, young Paul-Boncour became an opponent of militarism, nationalism, and reaction in all its forms"; it is a fight he has waged consistently throughout his career.

He was thirty-six when in 1909, as an independent Socialist and a follower of Paul Painlevé, he left Viviani to take a seat in the Chamber. His success in that turbulent assembly was instantaneous, and two years later, in 1911, he became Minister of Labor himself in the Radical Monis Cabinet. This promising political career was interrupted a few years afterward by the First World War. As commander of an infantry battalion, the French statesman won the Croix de Guerre and was made a

Chevalier of the Legion of Honor. But in spite of these honors, on his discharge from the Army he renewed his fight against militarism with greater ardor.

In 1919 he had joined the Socialist Party as fulfillment of a promise he made to the Socialist leader Jean Jaurès a few months before the latter's assassination in 1914. His friends had warned him that by declaring himself on the side of the Socialists Paul-Boncour was throwing to the winds his chances of ministerial promotion. (Even at this point in his career it was realized that he was a potential Premier). Their warnings were not heeded, however; for twelve years, until he was fifty-eight, he was to remain as a member of the Socialist Party, pleading its cause in his "organ-like tones" in the Chamber and the tribunals. His socialistic ideas, in the words of *The Columbia Encyclopedia,* "resemble those of Jean Jaurès; he expressed belief in a gradual evolution of democracy out of the superficial realm of politics into administrative, economic, and social realities. Thus his socialism was based on faith in the ideas of the French Revolution rather than in Marxian theories."

In November 1919 Paul-Boncour was returned to the Chamber as an independent Socialist. (For some time he was to be head of the Foreign Affairs Committee of the Chamber.) He at once joined Léon Blum '40, then chairman of the Socialist Party's executive board and a fellow Deputy, in the Left's struggle against the conservative, anti-Communist National bloc, which had won a decisive victory in the latest elections. Under the successive premierships of Clemenceau, Millerand, Briand, and Poincaré, historians point out, France instituted a policy of anti-Sovietism (despite what Sumner Welles '40 calls "an overwhelmingly 'Marxist' working class" in France), a foreign policy which alienated Britain, and a policy of force in dealing with Germany, which meant a "cordon sanitaire" around that country and, in 1922, a nine-month occupation of the Ruhr. (Briand is described as more of a moderate in his policies.) The Left, on the other hand, demanded in part, "a reversal in foreign policy which should lead to greater cooperation with Great Britain, recognition of the Russian Soviet Government, conciliation rather than force in dealing with Germany." A Leftist bloc was formed to defeat the Nationalists, and in the elections of 1924 the National bloc lost more than one hundred seats, while the parties of the Left were returned in a majority.

Paul-Boncour had been one of those returned as a Deputy, and for the next seven years he remained in the Chamber. In the course of his years in the Assembly, while ministries rapidly succeeded each other, France suffered and recovered from a severe fiscal crisis. Her foreign policy underwent a change: she indicated a willingness to collaborate more closely with Britain; the Russian Government was recognized; cordial relations with Germany were established and a more friendly attitude toward the League of Nations was adopted.

A stanch supporter of the League of Nations himself, Paul-Boncour was sent to Geneva soon after its founding, as a member of the French delegation. His appointment came at a time when the League was trying to carry out one of the most pressing tasks imposed by its Covenant—that of world armament reduction. It was early realized, however, that the member Powers required further guaranties of security. The temporary commission appointed by the Assembly in 1921 to make general proposals for disarmament therefore drafted a treaty which provided for mutual security to be given in exchange for the reduction of armaments. Under this treaty groups of States could enter into regional agreements to support each other if attacked. At the same time they must agree to proportional disarmament. In case of war the Council of the League was to decide which State was the aggressor. This last point was criticized because it did not define aggression, nor give a clear-cut indication of the aggressor. The regional aspect of the pacts was criticized, too, on the grounds that detailed plans for reciprocal military support not only would not encourage disarmament but would authorize the grouping of friendly States against prospective enemies—the latter result in direct conflict with the essential spirit of the League. A month after the rejection of the proposed treaty by the States, a second plan was drawn up—the so-called "Geneva Protocol," adopted by the League Assembly in October 1924.

Paul-Boncour not only gave the Geneva Protocol his vigorous support in 1924, but the spirit of its plan has governed all of his subsequent crusades to establish a potent world organization. This protocol proposed unlimited arbitration among the fifty-four member States of the League; an aggressor was defined as any State resorting to war in violation of the League Covenant or the protocol itself; and provision was made, in accordance with the Covenant, for the use against an aggressor of the economic boycott and possible military action. The defeat of the protocol, F. Lee Benns shows, was due to the fact that most of the States felt in general that it increased the international obligations of the members, a factor which was not seen as desirable in Europe after the First World War.

In 1926 Paul-Boncour proposed the adoption of a resolution which would commit to the League Council the question of defining its own duties and the means of convening for action in case of war. This measure—also defeated—further provided that the permanent consulting commission of the League should consider the means necessary to securing the peace of Europe and, in case of war, the means of placing military aid at the command of the attacked nation.

The role which Paul-Boncour had played at Geneva made him the target of attacks from many members of the Socialist Party, who reproached him with having been at Geneva as the official delegate of a bourgeois government, and who tried to force on him the choice between this role and membership in their party. Following the withdrawal of the Radical Socialist Party's support from the Government in 1928, Paul-Boncour resigned his appointment as head of the French delegation to the League and shortly afterward, in November 1931, resigned his membership in the Socialist Party. (In September he had been elected Senator.) Although the Socialists were bitter over his resignation, many admitted later that he had broken with them chiefly because the party's rigid discipline forbade taking office. After his resignation from the Leftist group, Paul-Boncour did not join another party, but remained an independent of the Left.

After the fall of the conservative Laval[40] and Tardieu governments in 1932, the rise and fall of ministries in the succeeding years, says Benns, was "generally connected with some phase of the Republic's perplexing budgetary, fiscal, or economic problems." In June 1932 Paul-Boncour became Minister of War in the Herriot Government, and on December 19, 1932, he was asked to form a Cabinet, which lasted until the following January 31. (He also served as Foreign Minister.) His appointment as Premier was called inevitable by the London *Spectator*, which considered that he had "every qualification that French politics require." Without great wealth, powerful connections, or social position, Paul-Boncour had risen to the premiership largely because of his League activities. The *Spectator* predicted that he would be governed by the Geneva Protocol slogan: "Arbitration, Security, Disarmament"; the British *New Statesman and Nation* declared that Paul-Boncour was incapable of international thinking because he was "essentially national and patriotic in his outlook."

During the middle 'thirties France was divided between two bitter factions, the Right and the Left. "There was no France any more," says Sumner Welles; "there were two nations." In November 1933 Paul-Boncour was again named Foreign Minister, this time in the Left Government of Camille Chautemps. When this Government resigned in the middle of the Stavisky scandal, Paul-Boncour remained as Foreign Minister in the new Daladier[40] Government, formed in January, which lasted less than ten days. He did not return to the Government again until 1936, when he became Minister without Portfolio in the Radical Socialist Government of Albert Sarraut.

This was the period which saw the beginning of Hitler's[42] rearmament and the triumph of the Popular Front in Spain. In France itself the Popular Front of Leftist parties had been formed against the threat of fascism within the country, and Léon Blum became Premier (June 1936 to June 1937). During his second, much briefer term in office in early 1938, Paul-Boncour served as his Foreign Minister. That spring the sixty-five-year-old statesman resigned his presidency of the Socialist-Republican union, of which he had been head since its formation in 1935, and retired from public life, not returning to the service of his country until after the De Gaulle[40] Government re-entered liberated France in September 1944. After the liberation of Paris Paul-Boncour was made chairman of the Committee of Twenty who selected the sixty members of the Paris Parliament to be sent to the Consultative Assembly. He himself has been a member since November 7, 1944. (During that month it was reported from Paris that an attempt had been made upon his life.)

French representatives had not been present at the Dumbarton Oaks conference nor the Yalta meeting of Roosevelt[42], Churchill[42], and Stalin[42]. Foreign Minister Georges Bidault[45] therefore appointed Paul-Boncour as chairman

PAUL-BONCOUR, JOSEPH—*Continued*

of the commission for the study of the proposed world peace organization. The commission was made up of prominent jurists, experts on international affairs, members of the Consultative Assembly, and officials of the Foreign Affairs Ministry. It was the conclusions drawn from this study that prompted France to announce she would not attend the San Francisco conference as one of the sponsoring powers, a refusal reported to be based on her request that the Dumbarton Oaks plan be considered as a basis for discussion and not as a definitely settled project.

Paul-Boncour's analysis of the proposals drawn up at Dumbarton Oaks was published in *Pour la victoire*, a New York French-language newspaper, on March 18, 1945. After expressing his relief at Churchill's assurance that the new peace organization would not be founded on a big-power dictatorship, he pointed out that the small nations, "and, we must admit, not without cause," have shown anxiety over some of the plans, "which are in conflict with the Atlantic Charter and which seem to strike a blow at international democracy. . . . I might say that peace guaranties will henceforth rest exclusively on agreement among the great powers. . . . It is a fact which one may regret, but it must be acknowledged that in the present state of affairs such common action is requisite to peace and that any decision against the wishes of a great power is unlikely to be carried out." He expressed the hope that the time would come when it would be possible to restrain any power, no matter how great. He added: "Nevertheless, evolution is determined by certain principles laid down at the start. It is these principles which give cause for anxiety." Another salient criticism from the man who fought so many years to try to make the League of Nations a potent and effective custodian of world peace is that some of the methods proposed by the Dumbarton Oaks plan are similar to those which the Holy Alliance of 1815 used to crush democracy, "which it is now sought to maintain."

Paul-Boncour's fear in this instance was that the great powers might develop a practice of using their vetoes with a misplaced reciprocity which would paralyze the peace organization. "It may be," Paul-Boncour continued, "that, in view of the chaotic conditions in which the cataclysm will leave the world, nothing else can be done. I sincerely believe this to be the case. . . . Then, by tenacious action, in which I can assure them they will have the support of France, let the small nations endeavor to instill democracy in the somewhat arbitrary institution we are trying to build. The great nations themselves will be forced to help them. Finally . . . let us make sure that democracy will be an irresistible force; that, after preserving it within the nations themselves, it will seem contradictory not to support it throughout the world."

The ex-Premier announced himself on his arrival at the San Francisco conference as an advocate of a permanent international armed force to avoid the fatal weakness of the old League—its "lack of punch." "Peace is impossible," he said, "without a permanent big stick which the Big Five must be ready to use at the first sign of aggression." Paul-Boncour

was as good as his word. Following Bidault's return to France, Paul-Boncour became head of the French delegation and drew up the report outlining a practical working program for the United Nations military arrangements for keeping the peace. His report, presented in June 1945, provided "teeth" in its significant amendments of the original Dumbarton Oaks proposals and won the unanimous approval of the conference. The spokesman for France, a land twice the victim of German aggression within a quarter of a century, insisted that the new world organization's forces have "the right of passage." Failure to have this right frustrated France's efforts from 1935 to 1939 to save the peace. Belgium, the Netherlands, and Luxembourg had stood on their rights as sovereign powers not to permit or even to consider French "right of passage" through the strategic areas of their territory which Germany would have to invade to reach France. Similarly, Poland had refused such right of passage to the Soviet Army. Because of the stand of Paul-Boncour and his equally eloquent compatriot, Leon Bourgeois, the Charter specifically mentions this "right of passage."

Two world wars taught France that promise of help is not synonymous with assistance itself. Paul-Boncour succeeded in persuading the other nations that in addition to pledging national armed forces to the Security Council their "degree of preparation and general location" must be specifically mentioned and fixed. Of the nations, Australia, Canada, and Peru principally aided France in improving the Dumbarton Oaks draft. In the most dramatic commission meeting of the conference the French delegate supported with an impassioned address the proposal of Luis Quintanilla, former Mexican Ambassador to the Soviet Union, that Spain be barred from membership in the new world organization as long as it remained under Franco's [42] Fascist domination. James Dunn [43], the American Assistant Secretary of State, joined in this statement to Madrid. It was approved by acclamation by the Commission on General Principles meeting in public session on June 19.

Summing up in his speech during the final plenary session, Paul-Boncour accented the differences between the old League and the new United Nations organization: "The Covenant of the League merely provided for the recommendation of military sanctions involving air, sea, or land forces, and consequently left the nations the option of backing out. . . . In the Charter sanctioned by this plenary assembly, the obligation of all member states to help in suppressing aggression is plainly established. An international force is to be formed and placed at the disposal of the Security Council in order to insure respect for its decisions. This force will consist of national contingents arranged for in advance by special agreements negotiated on the initiative of the Security Council. . . . If called upon to do so by the Security Council, the entire force will march against a State convicted of aggression, in accordance with the provisions for enforcement as laid down for the Security Council." "The United Nations, and more especially the great nations with a permanent seat on the Council, must remain truly united," he further declared. "The whole efficacy of the Charter depends on this unity. In the hour when immense hope rises from our hearts, let us swear to remain faithful in peace to this unity which was our strength in war."

The veteran statesman is the author of several works on government and law. Pictures show him to be lion-headed and somewhat stoop-shouldered. His personality is described as likable and magnetic, and he is said to have no prejudices. Once married to a member of the Menier family, the chocolate manufacturers, he is now divorced. He maintains a country home in his native Loir-et-Cher. One of his favorite forms of amusement is attending the Comédie Française; according to Elsa Maxwell [43], this theater was robbed of a star when Paul-Boncour chose the law and politics for his profession.

References

Free France 7:461 My 1 '45 por
Liv Age 343:500-1 F '33
International Who's Who, 1942
Qui etes-vous? 1924
Who's Who, 1945

Blackstone Studios
EDWIN W. PAULEY

PAULEY, EDWIN W(ENDELL) Jan. 7, 1903- United States Government official; businessman

Address: b. Allied Reparations Commissioner, c/o The White House, Washington, D.C.; Petrol Corporation, 756 S. Broadway, Los Angeles, Calif.

The American member of the Allied Reparations Commission is Edwin W. Pauley, President Truman's [45] special representative with the personal rank of Ambassador, a self-made multimillionaire and treasurer of the Democratic National Committee.

Edwin Wendell Pauley was born on January 7, 1903, in Indianapolis, Indiana. When he was six weeks old he was taken to live in Alabama. For his secondary education he was sent to Georgia Military Academy. After his graduation in 1918 sixteen-year-old Ed went West and entered Occidental College, transferring a year later to the University of California's College of Commerce and Business Administration, where he won his letters in football and rowing. He received his B.S. in 1922, and his M.S. in 1923, working his way by selling encyclopedias (whose contents he is said to have "mastered, more or less") and by working as a laborer in the California oil fields. Lowell Mellett [42] writes that Pauley began as a mucker, was promoted to "roughneck," and then, successively, to derrick man, driller, buyer, and refinery evaluator. But what he wanted to do was to teach economics at the university, which he did, until an airplane crash broke his neck, his back, and thirty-two other bones. During his year of hospitalization, Pauley accumulated doctors' bills amounting to nine thousand dollars, which he realized he would never be able to pay on an instructor's salary.

As soon as he was able, therefore, Pauley persuaded some others to join him in leasing an oil refinery. This became the Petrol Corporation of Los Angeles, which branched out into oil production, transportation, and marketing, as well as refining. Pauley became its president. As an independent oil man, he battled established companies on production allotments, emerged unscathed from price wars, and built up what *Time* calls "a sizable business." In fifteen years he had made a fortune of several million dollars, and become president also of the Fortune Petroleum Corporation and Golconda Petroleum Corporation. Some of his business methods have been called into question by political opponents. His salary from Petrol was reported in 1945 as eighteen thousand dollars a year.

Besides holding oil interests, Pauley was a founder of the People's Bank of California, and served for a time on its board of directors. He is a partner in the John S. Griffiths building firm which developed Lakewood City in California, and is a director of the Griffith and Legg Construction Company. The oil man retained his interest in the University of California, particularly the economics department, and was active on the finance committee. He found time also to enter various yacht races and to win some of them, including the 1939 Trans-Pacific Yacht Race from San Francisco to Honolulu.

Pauley was a supporter of Franklin D. Roosevelt [42]; Mellett says that the New Yorker's fight against infantile paralysis had inspired Pauley when he himself was in the hospital. Active in the Presidential campaign of 1932, he was on the NRA's Planning and Coordinating Committee in 1933 as representative of the independent oil men; from 1934 to 1938 he was president of the Independent Petroleum Association. When Roosevelt was campaigning for re-election in 1936 Pauley was particularly active in his behalf; and in 1940 Democratic chairman Ed Flynn [40] asked him to take over the raising of campaign funds in eleven Western states. (Pauley had, meanwhile, been elected a regent of the university to serve until 1955, had served as vice-chairman of the 1938 Los Angeles Community Chest Drive, and had represented the Governor of California at the Pan-American Highway Conference of 1939, on the Natural Resources Commission, and on the Interstate Oil and

PAULEY, EDWIN W.—*Continued*

Compact Commission.) Pauley did such a good job for Flynn that the Bronx leader made him a regional director of the Democratic Party.

Ed Pauley helped organize the California Defense Council in 1941 and was finance chairman of the Los Angeles China Relief. To quote Mellett, when the British were in desperate need of gasoline "Pauley wired the President that one hundred tankers carrying gasoline for domestic use could be released to serve Britain if our rail shipments were properly routed. (His postgraduate thesis at the university had been on the subject of transportation.) The President asked him to report at the White House the next day. Pauley arrived and laid down a plan that would enable the railroads to do more of their job than they had been doing. [Pauley was appointed special representative to act as liaison with Britain on the use of oil tankers.] His plan worked. [With similar status] he promoted, then, the creation of the Petroleum Administration for War with Harold Ickes [41] heading it. That also worked." Pauley helped select the PAW staff of oil men. (In 1941 he became secretary of the Democratic National Committee.)

Pauley was drawn into the operations of Lend-Lease as special representative on petroleum supplies for Britain and Russia, and to work with the British in reporting on enemy petroleum supplies. Mellett says that the Californian "persuaded Sir Arthur Salter, top British shipping man, to revise the wasteful routing of that country's own tankers," and that he also dealt with the Soviet Ambassador, Ivan Maisky. The Russians had requested a large amount of hundred-octane gasoline through Lend-Lease, but Pauley considered it would be preferable for them to adopt certain processes which would enable their own refineries to produce the valuable fuel. As Mellett tells it, Maisky demurred, but Pauley had his way. "The results were what he had promised," and led to "a perfect understanding between Pauley and Maisky." The American spent August and September 1941 in Europe, working on the British oil supply problem.

In 1942 President Roosevelt asked secretary Ed Pauley to become treasurer of the Democratic Party and get rid of its $750,000 debt. The Californian did that: by January 1944 the party was solvent, for "nearly the first time in its history," and Pauley turned his attention to raising a campaign fund. "We will have to spend a lot of money on registering the workers who have migrated because of war work from one community to another," he told reporters. "These workers are our people. Unfortunately they don't pay much attention to registration or registration laws. We will have to get to work on that right away."

Pauley succeeded Ambrose O'Connell as director of the July 1944 Democratic National Convention when the latter resigned in June to accept a Federal judgeship. Each party was allotted fifty thousand dollars for convention expenses by the Chicago Citizens Committee, and the stadium expenses were underwritten by the committee and the City Council. This gave the arrangements committees only half of the amount they had had to work

with in 1940; the Republican chairman, Walter S. Hallanan, explained to reporters that this meant perhaps one-third their 1940 buying power. The opposing parties, incidentally, worked together closely on arrangements, in the interests of economy and efficiency.

At the Democratic convention Pauley was described as aggressively backing the nomination of Senator Harry S. Truman as vice-president on the Roosevelt ticket. *Time* described his "sales talk" (in the May 7, 1945, issue) as: "We're not nominating the Vice-President; we're nominating the next President." Truman, who also had the powerful support of Democratic National Chairman Robert E. Hannegan [44], proved an acceptable compromise candidate, midway between the incumbent Henry A. Wallace [40] and the Southern conservatives' choice, the Presidential assistant Justice James F. Byrnes [41].

After the election, rumor had Pauley in one appointment after another. Columnist Leonard Lyons alone mentioned him, at different times, for Assistant Secretary of the Navy and head of the Reconstruction Finance Commission, and quoted him as saying, "The President knows of my desire to return to private life." After Vice-President Truman succeeded to the Presidency *PM*'s Max Lerner [42] wrote that the appointment of Pauley as Federal Loan administrator was being "powerfully urged" on him.

In April 1945 Edwin Pauley was named to represent the United States on the three-power Allied Reparations Commission to sit in Moscow. President Roosevelt had already appointed a former "braintruster," Isador Lubin [41], to that post, but Truman designated Lubin to assist Pauley, with the rank of Minister. Pauley's appointment was regarded by some as a payment for his labors in the political vineyards—*Time* said flatly, "There had been little to qualify him for the task ahead" —but the *United States News* saw the matter differently. In its view, when Lubin was appointed "the reparations question was considered a matter of statistics and economics. . . . This country's [United States] interest was confined primarily to making certain that Germany is so stripped of productive capacity that she will be unable to go to war for many decades to come. Dr. Lubin, a quiet, capable, and clearheaded statistician and economist, was considered well chosen for the job he was expected to do. But he is no dickerer, no driver of hard bargains. But, as matters have developed, bargaining among the victors is expected to be a principal characteristic of the reparations settlement. Russia wants to strip most of the industrial machinery from German areas to be occupied by the Americans and British, and install it in Soviet factories. America and Britain want food from the usually productive fields of eastern Germany and Poland, occupied or strongly influenced by Russia. A bargain must be struck on that and other points. So President Truman replaced Dr. Lubin with Mr. Pauley, the shrewd, practical oil operator."

Columnist Lowell Mellett also pointed out that Pauley had had successful diplomatic encounters with his future fellow commissioners Salter and Maisky. "Being a member of the Allied Reparations Commission isn't a job that anybody would ask for if he were merely seeking an honor," Mellett pointed out. "It's a job of hard, disagreeable work for which a man is unlikely to receive any recognition, whether he does it well or otherwise. . . .So Ed Pauley has taken the job and had the dubious pleasure of reading that his appointment is a political pay-off by President Truman." Forrest Davis, who wrote that the President had first offered the post to retiring Postmaster General Frank Walker [40], considered that, "actually, Dr. Lubin, while nominally No. 2, was looked upon as the mainstay of the mission, his equipment and background qualifying him for dealing with the essentially economic nature of the day-to-day decisions."

Pauley himself said of his new post, "I am not a soft-peace man. I have no reluctance in making that fact known. Whether we have a hard peace or a soft one is a question for all the United Nations and their governments to decide. What I can promise in my new position is that once the peace is made I shall do everything in my power to prevent it from becoming a brittle peace: that is, one that may be hard in the making but will not hold together under the strain of postwar economics. That is the mistake that was made at the end of the First World War. . . .I make my pledge that it will not happen again." Before leaving for an inspection tour of Germany with Mrs. Pauley and twenty staff members, the reparations commissioner expressed the opinion that the Germans should be permitted "enough light industry to maintain a civilian economy. Otherwise they will be a burden on us."

The American plan presented by Commissioner Pauley called for deindustrializing Germany to the point where she could not make war. War industries which could be moved out of the country were to be taken as reparations in kind. (At the Potsdam Conference, Allied leaders had agreed to divide all reparations on a percentage basis, with about half of the total going to Russia and Poland because of their great loss in life and property.) Immovable war plants were to be destroyed entirely. The Ruhr industrial center was to be broken up, the steel mills and factories being dismantled and distributed to neighboring countries as reparations. Coal from the Ruhr mines was to go to Belgium and France, where new steel centers were planned to utilize the iron ore produced by Sweden, Spain, and France. The whole of Europe was considered as an economic unit, with the inland waterways (the Rhine, the Danube, and various canals) to be under international control. The British and Soviet commissioners agreed to the American plan to make the postwar Germany economically self-sufficient as soon as possible by using the proceeds from German exports to pay for necessary imports, rather than applying the money to payment of past debts or reparations. It was hoped that this plan would enable the United Nations to avoid the mistakes of the period after the First World War, when the demand for reparations produced a need for foreign credit and for the rebuilding of German industries.

Following a Commission meeting in Moscow in August 1945 Pauley disclosed the official American stand on "human reparations." "Compulsory labor service should be required only from those who have been judicially determined to be war criminals, including individuals determined to be members of European Axis organizations, official or unofficial, which themselves have been adjudged criminal organizations," Pauley announced in a statement framed with the help of Associate Justice of the Supreme Court Robert H. Jackson [40], the United States prosecutor for the war criminals trials. The Gestapo, the SS, and possibly the Nazi Party might be so adjudged and their members sentenced to rebuild devastated areas, clear mine fields, and remove tank barriers left after the war. After his return to New York in October 1945, before starting off to Japan (without Dr. Lubin) for similar work, Pauley made several speeches in which he assailed those who attacked the program as "unrealistic." "Can it be," he asked, "that an attempt is being made behind the scenes to preserve vast investments within Germany and to set up anew at the old stand business which proved so profitable to the few and so disastrous to the many?"

In November Pauley flew to Tokyo to make preliminary surveys on material penalties to be imposed on Japan for her war guilt. After a survey of her assets, Pauley said that Japan would be able to pay little to the United States in reparations, much less the "staggering" cost of the occupation. "Our reparations policy will be stern but fair," the Presidential envoy stated. "The final bill will be a bill that we expect to collect. In neither Germany nor Japan are we going to make the mistake that we made after the last war—that of assessing a fantastic sum that is uncollectible." On his return, Pauley recommended to President Truman that part of Emperor Hirohito's personal fortune, estimated at more than one hundred million dollars, be claimed to pay war reparations to the Allies. Pauley further recommended that Japan be stripped of all assets abroad, virtually all chemical, steel, and shipbuilding facilities and half her electric power and machine tool industries. "Only in this way can any possibility of Japan ever waging war again be destroyed, and the countries she victimized be reimbursed," he added.

Inventories of seven of the twenty-three principal Japanese industries, prepared by Allied headquarters for the reparations commission on a twelve-day rush order, indicated that contrary to previous Japanese government reports there was still considerable "fat" on Japan's industrial economy, especially in steel; and she was within 18 per cent of self-sufficiency in food. Pauley was unable to survey Japanese assets in northern Korea and Manchuria, however, as the occupying Russians refused him entry, and in December 1945 he therefore left for Washington, stopping for two days in the Philippines to inspect war damage and confer with Government officials about reparations.

After Pauley's return to Washington, the dollar-a-year man's name was again mentioned for appointment to important posts, mainly that of Secretary of the Navy. The St. Louis Post-Dispatch ran a series of articles opposing this possible appointment, because of the Navy's connection wtih oil reserves and Pauley's connection with an oil company. His lobbying for passage of certain bills affecting the oil industry, both before the California legislature and

PAULEY, EDWIN W.—*Continued*
the national Congress, was cited as something legitimate in itself but dangerous in a future Navy Secretary.

Pauley is married to the former Barbara Jean McHenry of California. The couple, whose home is in Beverly Hills, have three sons, Edwin, Jr., Stephen McHenry, and Robert Van Petten, and a daughter named Susan Jean. "Big, bulky, and energetic, a ready talker, a man who attracts people and gets along easily with them," the Californian looks like a man who has gotten where he is the hard way. Despite his untough enthusiasm for economics, which is said to be his favorite reading subject, and for sailing boats of any size, Pauley, who is six feet three inches tall, has impressed at least one observer as "a convincing detective for a Dashiell Hammett movie."

References

    Look 9:49 D 25 '45 por
    N Y Post Mag p22 My 8 '45
    Time 45:21 My 7 '45 por
    U S News 18:62+ My 11 '45 por

PEABODY, ENDICOTT, REV. May 30, 1857—Nov. 17, 1944 Clergyman; founder and headmaster of Groton School, Groton, Massachusetts; taught many notable men, among them Franklin D. Roosevelt '42, Sumner Welles '40, W. Averell Harriman '41, and Joseph C. Grew '41. See *Current Biography* 1940 Yearbook.

Obituary

    N Y Times p13 N 18 '44 por

PEMBERTON, BROCK Dec. 14, 1885- Producer; director
Address: b. 244 W. 44th St., New York City; h. 455 E. 51st St., New York City

A dramatic critic who has turned producer, Brock Pemberton during his twenty-five years in the theater has not only contributed more than his quota of good plays, but has helped to bring new talent into the theater. He presented the first plays of Maxwell Anderson '42, Sidney Howard, Paul Osborn, Zona Gale, and gave Preston Sturges '41 his first Broadway success. The list of players he has introduced is equally imposing—Walter Huston, Miriam Hopkins, Claudette Colbert '45, Fredric March '43—and in 1944 he brought vaudeville and night club performer Frank Fay, the star of *Harvey*, to the fore as a top-flight actor.

Brock Pemberton, born in Leavenworth, Kansas, on December 14, 1885, is the son of Albert and Ella (Murdock) Pemberton. The Murdocks were pioneers who traveled from Morgantown, West Virginia, by boat down the Ohio River, finishing their journey in Kansas in a covered wagon. On the Murdock side the family became prominent in Kansas newspaper circles, owning at one time five newspapers in that state. (The present owner of the Wichita *Eagle* is a cousin of Brock Pemberton's; and the late William Allen White '40 once worked on the El Dorado *Republican*, a Murdock paper.) Pemberton's own father, a Kentuckian, established a mercantile shoe business in Leavenworth after learning the business of shoemaking from a Cincinnati bootmaker.

One feature writer has pictured Pemberton's first encounter with the theater at the age of fourteen. On one afternoon, the story goes, the boy carried coal into the basement of the local "opery" house in order to earn a pass to that night's performance. Then he went home, washed off the coal dust, and presented himself and his pass to the ticket-taker. But the Scrooge at the door only looked at him and said, "You never carried any coal in your life," and tore up the pass.

Graduating from the Emporia (Kansas) High School in 1902 Pemberton entered the Student College of Emporia, a Presbyterian school. His stay there was turbulent, for he was much given to playing pranks, and—although on two occasions William Allen White interceded for him—it came to an end in 1905 when the prankster was finally advised to continue his education elsewhere. White, perhaps counting on the steadying influence of work, again offered help and printed a feature story of Pemberton's, "The Floods of Neosho Valley," in the Emporia *Gazette*. This article won Brock the offer of a reportorial job on the Philadelphia *Bulletin*. Later he entered the University of Kansas, where, with the guidance of White, he succeeded in obtaining a B.A. degree in 1908.

Reporting and play reviewing on the Emporia *Gazette* followed. In 1910, however, young Pemberton came East to obtain experience on the metropolitan dailies. His first job (1910-11) was with the New York *Evening Mail*, reporting ship news. The drama desk then became vacant, and the managing editor asked Pemberton to become drama critic. In 1911 he became assistant drama editor to Louis Vincent DeFoe on the New York *World*, where he remained for three years; three more years were spent in a similar position on the New York *Times* during the Alexander Woollcott '41 reign as dramatic critic. Finally in 1917 Pemberton deserted the critics' circle to apprentice himself to producer Arthur Hopkins, who subsequently entered the most distinguished period of his career through his productions starring John Barrymore.

In 1920 Pemberton became an independent producer with *Enter Madame*. The play was an immediate success. Although some of the play reviewers called it "a standardized Broadway play," it won "a sustained chorus of applause" from the rest of the critics. The success of the play actually was fourfold—in road, London, and stock company productions, in addition to the Broadway run.

Miss Lulu Bett introduced novelist Zona Gale to Broadway as the adapter of her own best-selling novel of the same name. Although the play captured the Pulitzer Prize for the season of 1920-21, Pemberton's erstwhile fellow newspaper drama critics were divided in their opinion on the merits of the play. Most of the reviewers on the periodicals were kinder, with the exception of George Jean Nathan, who suggested "there was a booky flavor to the play that will not down." Heywood Broun in *Vanity Fair* thought the play contained the "most amusing dialogue of the season"; and Dorothy Parker commented that Pemberton's production of the popular novel was "truthful, interesting, and amusing." Burns Mantle '44, however, failed to include *Miss Lulu Bett* among his seasonal "ten best plays." (He had included *Enter Madame* in that list).

The most distinguished productions of Pemberton's career are said to be the Italian grotesques by Luigi Pirandello which introduced the playwright to American audiences. The first of these, *Six Characters in Search of an Author* (1922), was called a "document in esthetic theory which makes clear the difficulties under which the artist works in dealing with life, the material of art . . . the reality of created characters, the differences between the realties of art and the realities of life, together with the falsification of both when they are represented through the personalities of actors bound by the conventions and tied to a theory of illusions." As the play opens, on a stage on which a play is about to be rehearsed suddenly step six characters, who explain that they were abandoned by the author who created them, and that they will be wretched if not permitted to finish the tragedy in which they were involved. The director decides to allow them to enact the drama of their lives. The story which these characters unfold was considered so daringly frank when Pirandello's play was performed in Italy that there resulted a storm of protest. The American reviewers, however, were concerned only with its intellectual value. One critic wrote, "Amazing that such deep stuff comes off almost too perfectly"; another declared that Pemberton's "plausible casting and excellent direction partly account for the high level that we get throughout the performance."

The second Pirandello produced by Pemberton, *The Living Mask* (1924), also won the plaudits of the critics, but it failed to achieve the fame of the first production. It has a thematic resemblance to *Harvey*, the play which captured the fancy of theatergoers in 1944-45—"in wackiness lies the greatest wisdom and the truest happiness." *The Living Mask* concerns a man who believed he was Henry IV, Emperor of the Holy Roman Empire. For many years this insane man lived the part of Henry, surrounded by men dressed as attendants to humor him. One day he regains his sanity, but goes on living the masque, simulating his insanity so as not to have to return to the world of reality.

In the past Pemberton has followed his pioneering instinct not only in producing authors' first plays, but in daring to depart from conventional dramatic forms. In 1921 when he presented *Swords*, Sidney Howard's poetic drama, the modern writers' version of that form was more or less new to the Broadway theater. Maxwell Anderson's *White Desert* (1923), written in the rhythmic prose which was later to bring this playwright high praise, is still regarded by Pemberton as a fine play. He believes its failure was due to the fact that it was ahead of its time.

The Ladder, a 1926 production of Pemberton's, does not seem to fit into the Pemberton record of good plays. It made theatrical history because it remained on Broadway for 264 performances, despite an all-time low in critical reviews and in attendance. It has been reported that as many as a thousand passes were given out for a single performance; but after a time even the free seats were not used, and the actors played to empty seats. There

BROCK PEMBERTON

were all sorts of explanations for its continuance; the most plausible was the explanation that the backer, Edgar B. Davis, as a believer in reincarnation (the subject of the play), was willing to spend the half a million the play cost him to win converts to his belief.

"Fortunately," says Pemberton, "producers are remembered for their successes, their failures are interred with their bones. More often than not, that's all there is to throw in." Although the producer has had his failures, he has a high average for hits among the thirty or more plays he has produced since 1920. His pet failure, Ransom Rideout's *Goin' Home* (1928), was a Longmans, Green and Company prize play. Despite the unanimous acclaim it received from the reviewers, and the forced three months' run at a cost of forty thousand dollars to Pemberton, the play failed to "click" with the public. (Its subject, miscegenation, belongs on the "Don't Touch" list of producers.)

The failure of *Goin' Home* marked a turning point in Pemberton's career. "My policy," he says, "had been to do a play if I liked it—now I wouldn't do a play unless I was convinced that it would sell to an audience." The following year, 1929, *Strictly Dishonorable,* Preston Sturges' first successful play, became the biggest box office attraction of Pemberton's career. Described by *Outlook* as a "light-as-air comedy of love and adventure, produced and directed with almost flawless taste and artistry," the play ran from September 18, 1929, to January 1, 1931.

A contract gave the owner of the theater where it was housed disposition of the tickets. With the law limiting the number of tickets allotted to brokers and restricting their surcharge to seventy-five cents still in the future, seats for such hits as *Strictly Dishonorable* often brought as much as twenty dollars. "A conservative estimate of the amount paid by the public above box office price to see *Strictly Dishonorable* would be between five hundred thousand and one million dollars," Brock Pem-

PEMBERTON, BROCK—*Continued*

berton has said, adding, "and not a dollar of this reached the producer." Although the ticket code, sponsored by the League of New York Theatres and Actors Equity, and the provisions of the Mitchell Act serve as partial restraints, the racket continued. "Scalpers are happy because they can still get tickets somehow and sell them at a handsome premium for all the smash hits," Burton Rascoe wrote in the *World-Telegram* in 1945. "In spite of all the indignant to-do about their activities, no one, as yet, has found a way to put the finger on them . . . nobody has been jailed yet for tending the harvest while it is good."

The profits from *Strictly Dishonorable* sustained Pemberton through a series of failures. *Three Times the Hour* (1931) ran twenty performances, *Christopher Comes Across* (1932) seven performances, *Personal Appearance* (1934) 501 performances. One critic said that the chorus of hallelujahs which had greeted Pemberton's production of the latter, a farce-comedy, was perhaps overdone, but it was understandable as the play was "hilariously funny." A first play by Lawrence Riley, *Personal Appearance* brought Gladys George stardom through her interpretation of the Hollywood queen who played havoc in a small town when stranded there on a personal appearance tour.

Ceiling Zero of the following year played 135 performances—a moderate success. But Pemberton's three productions in 1937, *Now You've Done It, Chalked Out,* and *Red Harvest,* had runs "as short as a bicycle race." In 1938 *Kiss the Boys Goodbye* by Clare Boothe Luce '42 not only had a successful run, but was listed by Burns Mantle in his seasonal "ten best plays." *Out From Under, Lady in Waiting* (based on Margery Sharp's novel *Nutmeg Tree*), and *Glamour Preferred* were unsuccessful productions of 1940. *Cuckoos on the Hearth* (1941), "a completely mad but quite exciting satire on most of the mystery yarns was considered by some as great, others found it silly. Pemberton nursed the play along for 129 performances before calling it a failure." "A serpent's tooth is a blunt instrument compared to an unsuccessful play," Pemberton wryly observed after one of his productions flopped. *Janie,* opening on September 10, 1942, was still playing to packed houses on Broadway when Pemberton closed it in February 1944 so that it might reap the larger road profits before the motion picture made by the Warners '15 (who had paid one hundred thousand dollars for the rights) was released. His next production, *Pillar to Post* (1943), closed after twenty-seven performances. The consensus of critical opinion was that not only was it a poor play, but that it had been miscast and poorly directed.

Harvey, the producer's 1944 production, is an "essay in whimsy," announced Lucius Beebe '40 and "has restored Brock Pemberton to his accustomed luster as one of the first showmen of Broadway." Not only has the play won enthusiastic reviews from the press, but Park Avenue, according to Beebe, has decreed seeing the play "the thing to do." Critics have distributed "orchids" evenly among the producer, director, author, and Frank Fay, the actor, whom Pemberton "plucked from the night club and

radio world to play the most difficult part given out in many a year." Fay plays Elwood P. Dowd, a bachelor given to sociable drinking who has without regrets traded the reality of the world which irked him for the reality of a rabbit (a rabbit over six feet, named Harvey)—to the dismay of his family. Antoinette Perry, who has been associated with the producer since 1928, had the difficult task of directing the play. Mary Coyle Chase '45, the author, is a onetime Denver newspaperwoman. Producer Brock Pemberton, who says "playwrights do not stick to the producer who has given them their first chance," is grateful to Mrs. Chase for giving him the first reading on *Harvey.* He had produced her play *Now You've Done It* in 1937 and, although the play failed, he had encouraged her to continue writing.

"I'd give *Harvey* five years—and up," Pemberton told Ward Morehouse, critic of the New York *Sun,* in April 1945, calling *Harvey* a bigger hit than *Strictly Dishonorable.* With the play grossing nineteen thousand dollars weekly at the end of 1945, its author earning sixteen hundred a week as her share, London and Paris productions in the offing, and translation and production of the play in many other foreign countries being planned, *Harvey* had "hit the bell."

In addition to his work as producer, Pemberton has also in the past assumed that of the director. Known as a patient director, he seldom corrected an actor's reading of a line during rehearsals. One author watching him direct one of her plays said that her first impression was that Pemberton was doing nothing to guide the actors, and to her suggestions on how certain lines should be read, Pemberton would say, "Give them time—it means so much more when they find out a thing for themselves." After the opening night the author concluded that the production of her play had run smoothly because Pemberton was more intent on getting out of every member of the company his creative bit than in remembering that he himself was the director.

Although Pemberton never asks for a credit as a collaborator, he has had a hand in the writing of many of the plays he has produced. Today he says, "I will not accept a play unless the author is willing to make revisions under my direction. In my whole career I have found only one or two plays which did not require changes before they were ready for production." Pemberton is credited with a flair for comedy. With almost as big a reputation for silence as Calvin Coolidge, in writing (he has written many articles for the New York *Times Magazine, Theatre Arts* and other magazines) author Pemberton finds that words seem to flow spontaneously into pungent sentences. A lecture tour he made through the United States during the first three months of 1944 was considered a great success because of his wit and humor on the subject of Broadway. And Pemberton, as an opponent of the New Deal, is said to have supplied Representative Clare Luce with a remark she used effectively in her speeches during the 1944 Presidential campaign.

Pemberton finds his greatest recreation as a football and tennis spectator. He is six feet, weighs one hundred and seventy-six pounds, has blond hair which recently has taken on a platinum sheen, gray-blue eyes, which can be kind and are usually merry. In 1915 he was married to Margaret McCoy of East Orange, New Jersey. The Pembertons live in a spacious apartment overlooking New York's East River. Margaret Pemberton, like her husband, spent her summers since Pearl Harbor at the Stage Door Canteen and the Merchant Seamen's Club. Pemberton is a member of the board of directors of the American Theatre Wing War Service, organizing and laying the groundwork for canteens all over the country. Pemberton spent ten weeks in the summer of 1944 (at his own expense and without salary) in establishing a canteen in San Francisco. He was one of the organizers of the USO-Camp Shows and of the Merchant Seamen's Club and he holds executive posts in the New York Theatre League, the Stage Relief Fund, and the American Theatre Council. Mrs. Pemberton has done the costuming of all her husband's productions and at one time was head of a department for theatrical costuming at Saks Fifth Avenue in New York City.

References

N Y Post p6 Ap 20 '40; p7 D 25 '41 por
N Y Sun p29 My 15 '40 por
Who's Who in America, 1944-45
Who's Who in the Theatre (1939)

PENDERGAST, THOMAS J(OSEPH)

July 22, 1870—Jan. 26, 1945 Former Kansas City (Missouri) Democratic political boss; a powerful figure in city and state for many years; during his regime participated in important conferences at every Democratic National Convention, where he controlled Missouri's bloc of votes; sentenced to a fifteen-month term in Leavenworth Penitentiary in 1939 for income-tax evasion.

Obituary

N Y Times p11 Ja 27 '45 por

PIATIGORSKY, GREGOR (pyä″tĭ-gôr′skĭ grĕg′ĕr) Apr. 17, 1903- Cellist

Address: b. c/o Columbia Concerts, Inc., 113 W. 57th St., New York City; h. 1830 S. Rittenhouse Sq., Philadelphia, Pa.

Internationally recognized as a leading cello virtuoso, Gregor Piatigorsky is, in the opinion of Serge Koussevitzky '40, "the greatest cellist of our day." After a brilliant youthful career in Europe, the musician came to the United States in 1929 and has become well known to the American concert-goer. Piatigorsky has played more concerts in the United States and Canada than any other cellist, appearing with the principal symphony orchestras and conductors, and he has done considerable recording. Author of several compositions himself, he has added much to the repertoire of the cello through transcriptions of classical and modern works.

The Ukrainian town of Ekaterinoslav is the birthplace of Gregor Piatigorsky. He was born there on April 17, 1903, to Paul I. and Maria (Amchislawsky) Piatigorsky. Paul Piatigorsky was a violinist and began teaching his son when the boy was six years old. To contribute to the struggling family's support, "Grisha" went to work at the age of nine, playing the

GREGOR PIATIGORSKY

cello in the local motion picture theater. He attended school during the day, worked at night, and practiced whenever there was time. He advanced so rapidly that by the age of fifteen he was launched on a promising career: he became first cellist of the Imperial Opera Orchestra in Moscow. At this time he also played in the string quartet at the Conservatory while studying under Alfred von Glehn. Meanwhile, the Revolution had begun, and the musician tried to leave the country. He finally entered Poland in 1921 after a series of mishaps. There followed a period of hunger and suffering for the refugee which ended with his appointment to the Warsaw Opera Orchestra. After about a year, however, he decided to go on to Berlin, where for a time he again met bad luck and was forced to support himself by playing in cafes and theaters. In Berlin he continued his studies with Julius Klengel, who considered him already a master.

At about this time Artur Schnabel '42 heard Piatigorsky play, and that, in the opinion of David Ewen in *Living Musicians*, proved to be the turning point in the cellist's career. According to Ewen, Schnabel invited Piatigorsky to perform a work by Arnold Schoenberg '42, and at this performance another musician introduced the cellist to the important German conductor, Wilhelm Furtwängler. The latter urged Piatigorsky to compete for the position of first cellist in the Berlin Philharmonic, and in 1923 the Russian won the appointment. Thereafter, his rise was swift; Furtwängler had him play many concertos, and European engagements mounted. In 1926 Piatigorsky became a professor at the Scherwenka Conservatory of Music in the German capital. Two years later he resigned from the Berlin Philharmonic to devote himself to solo appearances. "However," writes Ewen, "as a sign of gratitude to the conductor who discovered him, Piatigorsky always returned to his first desk in the Berlin Philharmonic whenever Furtwängler conducted."

(Continued next page)

PIATIGORSKY, GREGOR—*Continued*

The cellist now toured Europe as soloist with the leading orchestras and also with chamber music groups—for a period he was a member of a trio with Schnabel and the violinist, Karl Flesch. Then, in 1929 he came to the United States, making his American debut in Oberlin, Ohio, on November 5, 1929. The next month he gave his first New York performance, with the Philharmonic under Mengelberg, playing the Dvořák concerto. Of this performance Samuel Chotzinoff '40 wrote: "In his hands the instrument shed its reputed limitations. The lower register yielded beautiful sounds, as did the higher. . . .He is one of the most poetic and sensitive performers now before the public." Since then the musician has made several American tours, sometimes playing for audiences who had never before heard a solo cellist. A writer in *Newsweek* once declared: "His playing has brought about a cello renaissance."

During a tour of the British Isles in 1934 Piatigorsky chanced to meet in London an American patron of the arts, Ernest B. Dane, then president of the trustees of the Boston Symphony, and to him the Russian complained, "My cello is sick." Before he returned home, Dane had presented the musician with a rare and beautiful Montagnana, made in 1739 and valued at thirty thousand dollars. Piatigorsky allows no one to play this cello, feeling strongly about the rapport between the artist and his instrument. He first played it for an American audience in January 1935, when, with the Philharmonic under Toscanini '42, he introduced a cello concerto composed for him by Castelnuovo-Tedesco. This concert grew out of a shipboard friendship between the cellist and the conductor, a former cellist, when both were traveling to Italy in the spring of the previous year. Other composers who have dedicated cello concertos to Piatigorsky are Prokofiev '41, Stan Golestan, and Paul Hindemith '41.

In a concert at Carnegie Hall in March 1940 with the Boston Symphony under Koussevitzky, the cellist played a new Prokofiev concerto for cello, and Richard Strauss's '44 tone poem, *Don Quixote*. In his review in the New York *Sun*, Irving Kolodin pronounced the cellist in "top form" but added parenthetically, "save for an odd disposition to play out of tune every so often." In the Strauss work, this critic went on to say, Piatigorsky "gave himself over wholly to the unpredictableness of the creature's nature." That summer the musician again played *Don Quixote* under Koussevitzky's baton, this time at the Berkshire Symphonic Festival. When he recorded this work late in 1942 with Fritz Reiner '41 and the Pittsburgh Symphony, the critics were unanimous in their approval. In the New York *Times*, Howard Taubman wrote: "He contributes a beautiful job," while in *Etude,* Peter Hugh Reed pronounced it better than Emanuel Feuermann's rendition of the work, "more expressive and more poetically sensitive." After a New York benefit recital in October 1943 a New York *World-Telegram* writer reported: "Gregor Piatigorsky turned poet and seer at the cello," and the *Times* critic called it "an exhibition of cello playing at the peak of perfection." When in November of the following year he played Haydn's D Major Cello Concerto, Oscar Thompson found "its plentiful technical skill

blemished by some poor intonation on higher notes—particularly in the first movement." After his concert with the Philadelphia Orchestra under Eugene Ormandy '41 in February 1945, several critics commented on the sentimentality of his reading of the Schumann cello concerto; while the critic for *Musical America* wrote praisingly of the artist: "Mr. Piatigorsky, at the top of his magnificent form, played the solo with a plangent, voluminous tone, faultless taste, and a depth of intimate feeling untouched by the slightest trace of shallow virtuosity. The great cellist has done nothing finer in this city."

Piatigorsky's concerts have taken him on world-wide tours and he has taught in several conservatories. In June 1942 he joined the faculty of Philadelphia's Curtis Institute of Music as head of the violoncello department, but resigned that position two years later to devote himself to concert work. He has also been the head of the chamber music department at the Berkshire Symphonic Festivals. In February 1944 the cellist temporarily left his instrument for the podium, to conduct the Denver Symphony Orchestra. His radio work includes performances with the Philharmonic under John Barbirolli '40 over CBS, with the NBC Symphony, and as guest artist on the *Telephone Hour.*

On the subject of modern music—he plays both modern and classical works—Piatigorsky has commented that "contemporary music is not necessarily modern. It may be classic, romantic, anything at all. It may be melodic or it may be atonal." In his opinion, "Beethoven's last quartets are as modern as anything ever written, in that they are new. They will always be new for they say that which was never said before and never will be repeated." "The cellist's choice of selections is small," Piatigorsky has declared. As a director of the Koussevitzky Music Foundation, he stressed the need for such compositions, and in 1945 special grants were awarded to encourage composers. Interested, also, in promoting American music, Piatigorsky is one of the sponsors of the American Youth Orchestra and has established a scholarship fund for American composers at the University of Chicago. The Russian-born musician, who became an American citizen in 1942, believes that his native and adopted lands have much in common. "There is a vastness of territory, a variety of climates, a mixed population in these countries that shows itself in the personality of their people," he says. "No two countries in the world reflect the breadth of the masses as Russia and the United States."

Once chosen by sculptress Katharine Ward Lane as one of the ten handsomest men in the United States, the brown-haired, dark-eyed cellist was described as "marvelously proportioned, though massive"—he is over six feet tall and weighs one hundred and eighty-five pounds. He has been a frequent subject for artists, and in 1943 his portrait, painted by Wayman Adams, won first prize in the annual Carnegie Institute Exhibition in Pittsburgh. His hobby is writing poetry—in Russian—and he enjoys bridge, chess, boating, and swimming. An honorary member of many musical institutions and clubs, Piatigorsky holds a citation from the United States Treasury Department and honorary life membership in the Pension

Fund of the Philadelphia Orchestra. He was married to Jacqueline de Rothschild, daughter of Baron Edouard de Rothschild of Paris, on January 26, 1937, and the couple have two children, Jeptha Maria and Joram Paul. Mrs. Piatigorsky, who is said to be a good amateur musician, plays the piano and bassoon. A number of stories are told of Piatigorsky's sense of humor. When Columbia Concerts advised its artists to travel light because of wartime restrictions the cellist wrote to his manager that he was changing to the piccolo.

References

N Y Post p17 Mr 27 '43 por
Baker's Biographical Dictionary of Musicians (1940)
Ewen, D. ed Living Musicians (1940)
Who's Who, 1945
Who's Who in America, 1944-45

PICKETT, CLARENCE E(VAN) Oct. 19, 1884- Social service leader
Address: b. c/o American Friends Service Committee, 20 S. 12th St., Philadelphia; h. Wallingford, Pa.

Representing the Society of Friends in the international social service field, the American Friends Service Committee is a widely known organization whose projects encompass whatever activities can help human beings in distress. The executive secretary of this committee since 1929 has been Clarence E. Pickett, a former minister and teacher of biblical literature. A director of the United States Committee for the Care of European Children and president of the American Council on Race Relations, he has done constructive Quaker service in relief and rehabilitation work in America, as well as directing the European relief work of the Service Committee.

The youngest of the eight children of Evan and Huldah (Macy) Pickett, Clarence Evan Pickett was born on October 19, 1884, on an Illinois farm in Cissna Park, eighty miles south of Chicago. When he was two years old his parents moved to Kansas, where Clarence was brought up on a prairie farm "in a Quaker colony in the middle of nowhere," to use his words. He received his early education in the local district school and village high school. After teaching for a year in the local community school he "pulled up stakes" and went to Penn College at Oskaloosa, Iowa, from which he was graduated with a B.A. degree in 1910. "On the campus," one writer observes, "he was untraditional, the liberal, the social action leader, proving his unenterprising nature by going to Europe directly after college."

After college Pickett's choice of a career seemed to be limited to farming, teaching, or the ministry. Despite his background, however, Pickett never wanted to be a farmer, and though he was not "overwhelmingly convinced" that he should be a minister, he entered Hartford Theological Seminary in Connecticut. He studied there from 1910 to 1913, receiving the B.D. degree. During this period of theological study he spent one summer traveling and studying in Europe and another summer as a social worker at the Spring Street Neighborhood House in New York City. In 1913 he was married to Lilly Peckham of Oskaloosa, the

CLARENCE E. PICKETT

marriage being the culmination of a courtship begun in college.

The year of his marriage young Pickett became the minister of the Friends Church in Toronto, Canada. He remained there until 1917, when he went back to Oskaloosa to become leader of the College Church, a position which he held for two years. From September 1919 to September 1922 he was secretary of Young Friends in America, with one period of a few months' study in Europe as a part of this service. This work dealt particularly with the development of personnel study and placement work in colleges and universities. Then for a year he studied at Harvard University's Divinity School, afterward going to Earlham College at Richmond, Indiana, in 1923 to be professor of biblical literature. This position, which he held until 1929, involved teaching religion and conducting courses and experiments in the application of ethical principles to social problems. In 1929 he accepted his present post of executive secretary of the American Friends Service Committee, in Philadelphia.

From the time of the founding of their sect in England in the seventeenth century, the Society of Friends, or Quakers, have believed that their religious faith must go hand in hand with action. Quaker service, they feel, must go further than charitable relief; it tries to strike at the core of social ills. Thus, it "engages in war relief or aids the victims of industrial dislocation, rather than being drawn to relieve natural disasters which present no problems of human conflict and in which other agencies can operate effectively." The American Friends Service Committee, an incorporated body under the laws of the State of Pennsylvania, was formed in 1917 by Friends who wanted to make "a constructive and nonmilitary contribution to the world." Under the leadership of Rufus Jones '41 (who in 1945 at eighty-two still headed the Committee), this active organization of "wearers of the red and black star" received world-wide recognition for their

PICKETT, CLARENCE E.—*Continued*

relief work in Europe during the First World War, and later for their humane enterprises in almost all quarters of the globe.

In a foreword to *Quakers Take Stock,* a book compiled by Anna L. Curtis in 1944 giving accounts of recent developments in Friends' relief and refugee work, Clarence Pickett compares the American Friends Service Committee to "a river that is forever old and forever new." "Its projects change," he writes, "but its purpose remains the same. Sometimes the emphasis is on relief work overseas for suffering victims of war or persecution. At other times grave problems in our own country, such as industrial unrest and racial antagonisms, claim our chief attention, but always the Service Committee is seeking to create the kind of a world that should grow out of a Christian faith—a world in which men, women, and children can live in peace, security, and self-respect, and in friendly accord with one another regardless of racial, religious, or political differences."

Since becoming secretary of the Committee, which has a staff of two hundred, Clarence Pickett has been in charge of the European work of the Committee, spending several periods abroad studying conditions. At the end of the First World War, however, he concentrated his activities to some extent on relief and rehabilitation work in America. As early as 1922 the Service Committee had started to feed the children of unemployed miners in the bituminous coal fields. As the distress of these people deepened, this relief work grew to major proportions. Aggravated by the depression, by 1931 the need for immediate relief had spread to the coal fields of many states. With funds largely furnished by the American Relief Administration Children's Fund, the Friends fed a maximum of forty thousand children daily in schoolhouses throughout the coal fields of Pennsylvania, West Virginia, Kentucky, Maryland, Illinois, Ohio, and Tennessee.

As an outgrowth of this emergency feeding, several experiments were made to find a solution to large-scale unemployment and to develop new skills for displaced workers. Miners have been trained in carpentry, handicrafts, and subsistence farming, and several communities and factories have been organized. From 1933 to 1935 Pickett served part-time in the Division of Subsistence Homesteads, under the Department of the Interior, working with the problem of stranded mining and industrial populations. In 1935-36 he served part-time as a consultant in the Resettlement Administration in Washington, D.C., and then as a consultant in the Farm Security Administration (later the National Housing Agency).

According to the Boston *Transcript,* in 1940, when the United States had no ambassador in Berlin, Clarence Pickett was considered as a possibility for the post. Eleanor Roosevelt '40 and Myron C. Taylor '40 (he was then peace negotiator at the Vatican), both friends of Pickett's, were said to have favored his appointment because the United States would thus have an envoy who would be in touch with the German people. Since Pickett had for several years maintained Friends Centers in Berlin and Vienna, he seemed a logical choice. However, the United States did not

send an envoy at that time, and Alexander Kirk '45, who as Chargé d'Affaires had been the only representative of the United States in Germany during the opening years of the Second World War, was recalled in October 1940.

In 1942 in New York, at the yearly meeting of the Society of Friends, Pickett declared that in his opinion relief for people in distress throughout the world should be placed on a basis similar to Lend-Lease war aid, pointing out that "relief in reconstruction is beyond the capacity of a private organization. If the United States could build a structure whereby the relief needs of the peoples of the world could be supplied," he said, "fundamental thinking might be directed toward a combination of practical economics and spiritual expression."

In July 1944 Clarence Pickett, writing in the *Annals of the American Academy,* described conditions in occupied Europe as "grim" and "deteriorating." In Poland and Greece people had died of starvation, he said; in Belgium, Yugoslavia, France, the Netherlands, and Norway there had been few such deaths, but the mortality rate had increased because of general susceptibility to disease, and there was widespread distress, particularly among the middle classes and the poor who could not afford the high prices of the black market. The American Friends Service Committee would continue to ask the United States Government to permit relief supplies to be sent through the Allied blockade to Europe, he said, because in no other way could the Allied people be kept from starvation, and the way be prepared for the full functioning of the United Nations Relief and Rehabilitation Administration. "We have not suffered as have the people of Europe," he wrote, "and our desire to be helpful will not be enough. They will see in us a people who are well-fed, well-clothed, insulated in a security which they have long ago lost or discarded. They will resent us or turn away unless we can give them understanding instead of moral judgments, unless, sharing their pain, we can find spiritual strength for a ministry of humility and dedication."

At the end of the year Pickett went to England and France on the invitation of the Committee on Anglo-American Collaboration of the Meeting for Sufferings. He discussed with the Meeting for Sufferings, the Friends Service Council, the Friends ambulance units, and other groups how American and English Friends could join forces in relief enterprises and "efforts to carry the message of peace to a world which has largely lost faith." Mrs. Roosevelt, who had talked to Pickett on his return from France, was greatly moved by his report of conditions and wrote of it in her daily newspaper column. Later the secretary told interviewers that the Friends were caring for two thousand Spanish children in the south of France, though the French were beginning to adopt some of them.

In his report of the year's activties, presented to the meeting of the American Friends Service Committee in January 1945, the secretary reviewed the accomplishments of the Committee in the fields of peace education, work camps, foreign service, interracial fellowship, and civilian public service. Quaker forums for adults and college students discussed the Dumbarton Oaks proposals and permanent compulsory military training. Work camps for young volunteers handled projects varying from aid to village clinics in Mexico to the repair of Kentucky mountain schoolhouses. The foreign service organized visits to French prison camps, operated ambulance units in China and India, assisted refugees in Portugal, Spain, Switzerland, Italy, North Africa, and the Middle East (in some sections working under UNRRA), and sent tons of clothing, food, medicine, and household articles abroad.

At the close of 1944, according to the Pickett report, there were 1,733 men enrolled in Friends Civilian Public Service, a department organized in 1941. (Conscientious objectors are enrolled in this branch.) Some of these men are on assignment to work camps, others care for the mentally ill in state hospitals or for children in state training schools. Other activities include agricultural experiments, public health, and medical research.

Quakers have always been opposed to violence or coercion, even though the end of certain actions appears admirable. In 1944 Clarence Pickett was one of twenty-eight clergymen and other leaders who signed a much-criticized appeal against "obliteration bombings" of German cities. This appeal was published as a foreword to "Massacre by Bombing," an article by Vera Brittain published in the March issue of *Fellowship,* the monthly organ of the Fellowship of Reconciliation, a pacifist organization. Though in general there is great respect for the Quakers' point of view and admiration for their practical and valuable work, there is also criticism of their pacifism. The Dumbarton Oaks proposals have been approved by the Friends Service Committee in general although they were considered inadequate. Some Friends supported the war as individuals, but all Quaker bodies reaffirmed their pacifism. However, it was pointed out that the Quaker peace testimony was more difficult to maintain in the Second World War than in preceding wars because of the variance with Quaker beliefs of Hitler '42 standards and because of the inescapable involvement of civilians in the war.

Alarmed at the increasingly critical food situation in Central Europe, Pickett asked that foodstuffs be carried to the starving children of that area and that the Allied Control Council policy which prevents American voluntary relief agency operation in Germany and Austria be changed at once if famine and wholesale death were to be averted during the winter. He pointed out that the American Friends Service Committee was well aware of the fact that re-education of the children was as necessary as actual food was to them, but, he continued, "you cannot educate children who are starving."

The Service Committee secretary is a director of the National Planning Association, National Refugee Service, Celo Community, Inc., of North Carolina, Field Foundation, Inc., New School for Social Research, and United China Relief. Although it is not connected with the American Friends Service Committee, the American Council on Race Relations, which was formed in 1944 and of which Clarence Pickett is president, shares a main common interest with the Friends—the field of race relations in the United States. As one writer has said, "helping minorities in trouble is an old, established habit of Mr. Pickett's." The Council concerns itself with all sorts of minority tensions, the president has pointed out, not only the problems of Negroes, but those of Mexican-Americans, Japanese-Americans, and other minorities as well.

Mr. and Mrs. Pickett live in Wallingford, Pennsylvania, in a house "surrounded by an acre of flowers and vegetables," according to a New York *Post* interviewer. The work of the "genial, wiry" secretary necessitates a great deal of traveling, but when he is at home he enjoys gardening, an occasional game of golf, or walking with his two cocker spaniels. He collects walking sticks but seldom carries one. The Picketts have two daughters and a granddaughter. Pickett considers himself a Kansan, pointing out that he cannot call himself a Philadelphian since he has lived there "only sixteen years—not two hundred and fifty."

References

N Y Post Mag p21 My 22 '45 por
Religious Leaders of America, 1941-42
Who's Who in America, 1944-45

PICKFORD, MARY Apr. 8, 1893- Actress; producer

Address: h. Pickfair, Beverly Hills, Calif.

Today Mary Pickford, whose motion picture career was the talk of the world, heads her own producing company and wears the title of "America's Sweetheart, Emeritus." Her golden curls have given way to a modish coiffeur, but she still looks many years younger than her age. As "Queen of the Movies"—both on the screen and in Hollywood society—she has reigned a long time, for no one has seemed to take her place, although many were groomed for it. A child actress before the age of six, Mary Pickford reached phenomenal success, acquiring millions and winning international fame. A capable business woman, she is also admired for her quiet charm and sincerity.

Mary Pickford was born April 8, 1893, in Toronto, Canada. Her name then was Gladys Mary Smith, becoming Gladys Pickford when she was about nine years old, and Mary Pickford a few years later. Her father, John Smith, died when she was four. Her Irish Canadian mother, Charlotte Smith, struggling to make ends meet, did sewing and played small parts in stock companies to provide for her three small children. In 1898, when Mrs. Smith was with the Valentine Stock Company of Toronto, the company decided to produce a whimsical play entitled *Bootle's Baby*. One day Mrs. Smith brought Gladys, her eldest child, to a rehearsal. The manager had been searching for a child to play the baby role but had been unsuccessful. That day he was bewailing his predicament when, to his amazement, five-year-old Gladys solemnly volunteered to play the part. She played it so well that she was given other child roles in the same company.

(Continued next page)

MARY PICKFORD

The roles which little Gladys Smith played in the Valentine Stock Company in the course of the next year or so were simple parts. Nevertheless, she came to all the rehearsals, for her mother was playing regularly. Her thin shoulders wrapped in a shawl, she moved about the drafty stage, watching the world of make-believe come to life, quietly absorbing the atmosphere of the theater, playing with the ubiquitous backstage kittens. When Gladys was nearly seven, a wealthy doctor and his wife offered to adopt her. Upon the insistence of her aunt that she be allowed to decide for herself, Gladys chose to remain with her mother. Miss Pickford has said she never regretted it, although it meant years of struggle for her at an age when most children are not compelled to work.

After another year Mrs. Smith was offered a part in a road production of *The Little Red Schoolhouse*. There were parts for Gladys and sister Lottie, too, so the family left Toronto to go on tour. In 1902 they became members of a company which presented *The Fatal Wedding*, in which Gladys played the role of Jessie. She attracted attention even at this early age by the "utter naturalness" of her acting. Other melodramas followed in which Gladys appeared: as Eva in *Uncle Tom's Cabin* and as Willie Carlyle in *East Lynne*. Chauncey Olcott then engaged the family as members of his company. It was while touring with Olcott in *Edmund Burke*, in 1906, that Mrs. Smith decided to take a new stage name for her family. That name was Pickford, after the children's paternal grandmother. As Pickford, then, the whole family acted in *Edmund Burke*, for brother Jack had now joined the trouping family. After the Olcott engagement Gladys Pickford was the child in many more blood-and-thunder melodramas. For several years the family kept together, playing in small road companies which made one-night stands. Gladys was the official packer for the family and, when not acting, she mothered the two younger children. At one time their mother was under-

study for all the women in the cast, Lottie understudied Gladys, and Jack played a minor part—all for the combined salary of twenty dollars a week and railroad fare.

During all this period of gypsying on the road, Gladys kept her eyes and ears wide open, absorbing the "tremendous trifles" of the actor's art so essential to stage success. She learned what to do with her hands and feet, how to control the muscles of her face, how to look grave and gay by turn, how to interpret ideas and emotions to the audience through pantomime. Her face began to assume the look of "sweet and questioning seriousness" that was one of her chief charms. This and the dimpling smile made her a favorite with audiences everywhere.

Gladys was now earning most of the money the family received and, always a serious child, she felt the responsibility of being the chief breadwinner. Finally, after tours through the Middle West and South, the bright-haired, sunny-tempered little actress, now about thirteen, reached a New Jersey town across the Hudson from Manhattan. Intent upon becoming a star on Broadway, according to one tale, she took a ferry across the river one morning and presented herself at the stage door of the Belasco Theatre, where the first rehearsal of *The Warrens of Virginia* was being held. When she asked to see the producer Belasco, the doorkeeper told her it was impossible. She insisted, and the doorkeeper, charmed by the intensity of the slight girl with the golden curls, took the request to Belasco. The rehearsal was not going too well—the child part of Betty Warren was not well cast and Belasco had no time to interview an unknown. The doorkeeper broke the news as gently as possible to her and she gave vent to one of the outbursts of temper which became famous because of their rare occurrence. She rushed through the door to the stage. Breathless and flushed with indignation, she confronted Belasco with an irresistible smile. "Oh," she exclaimed delightedly, "I know you from your picture." The situation intrigued Belasco. Amused by her naïveté and impressed by her sincerity, he gave her a tryout. After that, rehearsals went smoothly, for Mary Pickford was playing the part of the child well enough to please the famous producer.

Thus, the fourteen-year-old Miss Pickford made her first appearance in New York at the Belasco Theatre on December 3, 1907 as Betty in *The Warrens of Virginia*. Belasco later said it was a pleasure to direct her. "She was a hard worker, always first at rehearsals and last to go. . . .On the first night she was the most composed of the entire company. . . .From the first she gave promise of the ability that made her the greatest motion picture artist in the world." Mary spent two seasons with Belasco in New York and on tour. They were invaluable years to her, although both her part and salary were small. By the time she returned to New York, at the close of the second season, however, she had saved $250. Most of it went for clothes and to help her mother. It was summer now and the regular theaters were closed, but Mary had to work, so she decided to try the movies.

The old Biograph Motion Picture Company had its studios on Fourteenth Street at that time. The young actress was taken on as an "extra" at once. That night she was paid for her work and told to return the next day. She continued as an "extra" for several weeks, playing short, unimportant parts. She was always on time, obedient, quiet, and unobtrusive. Her first screen appearance was in *Her First Biscuits* with Florence Lawrence and William Courtwright, who again appeared with her in *My Best Girl* in 1927 when she was famous. Her first leading role was in *The Violin Maker of Cremona*, directed by D. W. Griffith. Then she went to Independent Motion Picture Company for a while, and then returned to Biograph. At first she was known as "The Biograph Girl with the Curls." The names of players were not announced in those days; advertisements gave the titles and short synopses of the pictures but no mention whatsoever of the actors. Then the public learned her first name and she became "Our Mary" and "Little Mary." In the course of time, she was cast for leading roles opposite a good-looking young leading man named Owen Moore. The unusual occurrence of a large company of film players being sent to Havana and the news of the secret marriage of Miss Pickford and Owen Moore brought her name into the newspapers. For the first time hundreds of thousands who had seen her knew who she was.

When Mary Pickford's star began to rise, she was under contract to Zukor who had founded The Famous Players Film Company in 1912. Her first real hit was to be *Hearts Adrift* in 1914. Between her and Adolph Zukor there has existed a working friendship of long standing. His pictures made her famous; her popularity brought him more and more money. They were just enough alike to understand, just different enough to admire each other, as one feature magazine article put it. Zukor recognized and admired her intelligence and shrewdness. "I always liked his ideas," says the star. "She taught me a great deal," says Zukor. When other firms began paying lesser stars more than she was getting, she told Zukor. "All right, let's be happy," said he and made it one thousand dollars a week.

In January 1913 Miss Pickford returned to Belasco to be starred as Juliet in *A Good Little Devil*. When she had left the theater to go into movies, she had promised to return if he ever needed her. Her success in the difficult role of the little blind girl was phenomenal. Belasco himself said that nothing like her remarkable performance in the child's part had ever been seen in New York or elsewhere. As a result, she was sought eagerly by moving picture managers for their companies. In the spring of 1913 she made a film of the play for Famous Players and after that rose rapidly to her subsequent eminence in pictures. Zukor advanced her salary to $2,000 a week and then in 1916 to $4,000, an unprecedented salary for that time.

In the summer of 1916 her contract with Famous Players expired. The whole motion picture industry knew it and the larger companies prepared for spirited bidding. At that moment Miss Pickford outshone all other stars, for the rise of Chaplin '40 came later. Any firm could afford to lose money on her for the prestige she would give its other productions. She was working in Hollywood at the time, but she arranged to come to New York between pictures. Offers from other firms began

to come even before she left Hollywood. She saw Zukor and told him frankly she was worth more money. He agreed with her but he made no offer, and she promised to see him before she signed with anyone else. The first to raise the bidding was an agent of the American Tobacco Company—he offered $7,000 a week. Vitagraph raised that. Mutual laid before her a contract which meant virtually a million a year. There the bidding stopped. Miss Pickford had kept Zukor informed as to the status of the negotiations; and when she faced him, he said, "I'm going to give you half of the profits of your films and a voice in the selection of them. And a guaranty of $10,000 a week. And, Mary, that's my limit. Others may offer you more. But it is as much as I can afford." She knew he meant it. After a little discussion of details, she signed the contract, much to the wonder of the motion picture business. "I like to work with him," Miss Pickford explained. "We have the same ideas. We've been down in the world and up in the world together and I'm sure of him. And $10,000 a week is enough. Besides, he's established. I don't have to worry about getting my money."

After signing with Zukor, Mary Pickford returned to Hollywood while he remained in New York, absorbed in business. The lot at Hollywood had grown into a veritable factory; the management became complex and impersonal. The intimate touch of the old days when they thrashed out scenarios in Frohman's apartment were gone forever. Aware of all this, the newly organized First National approached Miss Pickford with an offer as her Zukor contract was about to expire—an offer of a share of the profits, certain powers of decision, and a guaranty of $250,000 for each picture. After another talk with Zukor, Miss Pickford chose not to sign with him. Thus ended a five-year association during which the young actress had risen from a "nobody" in a new medium of entertainment to the world-famous "America's Sweetheart." In 1918 she became an independent producer, making pictures for release through First National. Early in 1919 Miss Pickford became one of the organizers of United Artists Corporation, which releases her productions today. Among Mary Pickford's best known silent films were *Hearts Adrift* (1914), *Tess of the Storm Country*, first produced in 1914, with a second version in 1922, *Stella Maris* (1918), *Daddy Long Legs* (1919), *Pollyanna* (1920), *Rebecca of Sunnybrook Farm* (1917), *Poor Little Rich Girl* (1917), *Little Lord Fauntleroy* (1921).

Though successful in her career, Miss Pickford had not found happiness in her marriage. She obtained a divorce from Owen Moore and in March, 1920, married Douglas Fairbanks '40, the popular film star. "Mary and Doug" were both at the height of their popularity, and their marriage was considered an ideal love match. They had a quiet wedding and came East on business. While in New York, they decided to give themselves a six-week vacation in Europe. The honeymoon, as Alexander Woollcott described it, was the most conspicuous in the history of the marriage institution. They were mobbed by people, wined and dined by the aristocracy and artists in England and on the Continent. Everywhere they went they caused

PICKFORD, MARY—*Continued*

a near-riot. The police had to protect them from over-enthusiastic admirers. The press discussed it all at great length, in serious and satiric vein. The recipients of all this acclaim were the least surprised of all, for letters had been pouring in to them for years from all over the globe—Miss Pickford's mail had often reached ten thousand letters a week.

Returning to America, the couple resumed their respective roles of king and queen of motion pictures and of Hollywood society. They bought Pickfair, a luxurious showplace in Beverly Hills to which invitations were sought avidly by all Hollywoodites and visitors from all corners of the world. Fairbanks bore the household expenses, and Mary Pickford took care of her mother's home. Together they shared the studio expenses. In 1928 her mother died, a loss the actress felt deeply. They had been very devoted all their lives, and Mrs. Pickford had been her daughter's business manager for a large part of her career.

Mary Pickford brought Ernst Lubitsch to America to direct her in *Rosita* in 1923, thus introducing the now famous "Lubitsch touch" to Hollywood. In 1927 she was one of the sponsors, with Cecil B. de Mille ['42], Irving Thalberg, Jesse Lasky, Douglas Fairbanks, and others, of the Motion Picture Academy of Arts and Sciences, a nonprofit organization which has become famous for its annual award of "Oscars" for excellence of acting, production, and scenario.

It was early in 1929 that Miss Pickford cut off her curls and "faced the facts of life on the screen." She made her first talking picture—*Coquette.* Some time later, she and Fairbanks made their first appearance together in an all-talking version of *The Taming of the Shrew.* In 1932 she appeared in *Kiki* for United Artists. The year 1934 saw her debut as a writer. *Why Not Try God* was published that year, *My Rendezvous with Life* appeared in 1935; both of these books set forth her philosophy of life. Miss Pickford is also the author of a novel, *The Demi-Widow* (1935).

Miss Pickford and Douglas Fairbanks were divorced early in 1935 after a separation and repeated rumors of reconciliation. With the passing of years her interest in picture production increased. In 1935 she became first vice-president of United Artists, producing *One Rainy Afternoon* (1936) and *Gay Desperado* (1936). She also appeared in a series of radio sketches over CBS, and in 1937 she formed the Mary Pickford Cosmetic Company.

Miss Pickford continues to be part-owner, with David O. Selznick and Charles Chaplin, of United Artists. Late in 1944 she set up an independent production company after signing up Sam Coslow to participate on a percentage basis. Three productions were on the 1946 schedule—*There Goes Lona Henry,* to be released through United Artists; *One Touch of Venus,* a three-million-dollar production; and *Champagne for Everybody,* starring the Mexican screen actor Armen Daris, formerly known as Pedro Armendariz. In November 1945 Mary Pickford announced the formation of a new production unit to make six moderate budget pictures during 1946 for United Artists. Most of the films will be limited to sixty minutes running time. Miss Pickford will be presi-

dent of the new company, her husband, Charles Rogers, vice-president and treasurer, and Edward J. Peskay executive vice-president.

In December 1943 and again in 1944 Miss Pickford was appointed head of the women's division of the National Foundation for Infantile Paralysis. Pickfair, her home, was still serving in 1945 as a de luxe branch of the USO, with weekly swimming parties and other entertainment for servicemen. Pickfair was on the "must" list of GI's from all over the world. Charles ("Buddy") Rogers, to whom Miss Pickford was married in 1937, served during the war as a lieutenant commander in the Navy. They have two adopted children, Ronnie and Roxanne.

References

Am Mag 77:64 Ap '14 pors; 85:34+
    My '18 por; 95:34+ My '23 por
Good H 91:37+ O '30 por
Ladies' H J 40:9+ S '23
Lit Digest 99:58-63 N 3 '28
N Y Sun p6 S 9 '44
N Y World-Telegram p3 F 11 '44 por
Overland 86:73 Mr '28 por
International Motion Picture Almanac,
    1940-41
National Cyclopædia of American Biography Current vol A p92
Who's Who in America, 1944-45
Who's Who in the Theatre (1939)

PIPPIN, HORACE Feb. 22, 1888- Artist
Address: b. c/o Robert Carlen Gallery, 323 S. 16th St., Philadelphia

"The most important Negro painter to appear in America," is Albert C. Barnes's ['45] evaluation of Horace Pippin, primitivist painter whose artistic rise has been swift and sudden. Since he was "discovered" in 1937, Pippin has had one-man exhibitions in leading art galleries, and his paintings are now part of the permanent collections of the Nation's art museums and private collections. Hailed as "one of the rare figures in contemporary American art," he is completely self-taught, having had neither artistic training nor contact with the work of other artists. The painter has hurdled the obstacles of poverty, the strain of heavy labor, physical disability, and racial handicap to attain his present position of distinction in American art.

The son of Negro laborers, Horace Pippin was born on Washington's Birthday, 1888, in West Chester, Pennsylvania. When the boy was very young the family moved to Goshen, New York, and there he frequented the race track, sketching the trotters on scraps of paper. In elementary school he found drawing objects easier than writing words, and one of his early prizes was a crayon and watercoler set. Once graduated from grammar school, he had to go to work, and during the next fifteen years he held a number of jobs: he was a farm hand, coal unloader, junk dealer, and moving man. Pippin also tried to get jobs crating paintings in order to be able to touch and study oils. For seven years he worked as a warehouse porter, a job which left him little leisure for painting. When the United States entered the First World War in 1917, the twenty-nine-year-old Negro enlisted in the

New York National Guard, going overseas later that year with the 369th Infantry. In the front-line trenches in France, Pippin kept a full diary of his impressions and experiences in five-cent copy books. These notes he saved, and in later years they supplied him with considerable material for his canvases. Severely wounded in the right shoulder in September 1918, he was hospitalized for several months and finally sent home in May of the following year with an honorable discharge and the Croix de Guerre. When Pippin was released from the Army, the doctors pronounced him unfit for work. Twenty-six years later, in a notification dated September 13, 1945, Pippin learned from the Army that he had been awarded the Purple Heart for wounds received in action on September 29, 1918.

In 1920 Pippin married Ora Giles of South Carolina and settled in his home town of West Chester, where the couple lived simply on his disability pension and Mrs. Pippin's earnings as a laundress. In the long years of his convalescence the veteran always wanted to paint but was unable to raise his right hand to shoulder level. He finally hit upon an idea: with a hot iron poker he burned an outline on an oak panel which he held in his lap. Later he filled in the design with color and in this way his first picture was created. After a year of patient, painful work in this fashion, the artist's wrist and arm grew stronger and he decided to attempt working at an easel. Supporting his right hand with his left, he began his first canvas in 1931, inspired by still-vivid war memories. For three years he worked on this first large picture, a powerful war scene called *The End of the War—Starting Home*, which depicted enemy soldiers surrendering amidst bursting shells. The picture was painted in the heaviest impasto, like others of Pippin's early period, for, according to a writer in *Art News*, "in his eagerness to convey the depth and texture of the bomb-torn earth he frequently built up his surface with nearly fifty coats of house paint." (This work is now in the collection of the Philadelphia Museum of Art.) These first works revealed the intensity of war experiences that Pippin had stored up within himself; his early canvases were "strange and compelling" war scenes.

For several years the artist's work was unknown except to his friends; then, in 1935, Dr. Christian Brinton of the West Chester Art Center became interested in Pippin's paintings. In May 1937 Dr. Brinton arranged an exhibition for him at the West Chester Community Center. By this time Pippin had been supplied with proper painting equipment and his technique had begun to change. In 1938 the New York Museum of Modern Art included four of his pictures in the exhibition, "Masters of Popular Painting." In this, his first New York showing, Pippin attracted considerable attention. There followed successful one-man shows in Philadelphia, New York, Chicago, and San Francisco. Pippin's first exhibition at the Carlen Gallery in Philadelphia in early 1940 created somewhat of a furor in that city's art circles. The introduction to the catalogue for the show, written by Dr. Barnes, the noted art critic reputed to own the finest

Carl Van Vechten

HORACE PIPPIN

private collection of modern art in the country, stated: "The facts that the work seemed crude in the sense that it lacked skill and finesse in the use of paint, and that it showed no evidence of borrowings from any old or modern artist, bore out the claim that Pippin had had neither academic training nor contact with the work of other painters. It was as primitive as the drawings of the prehistoric cave dwellers and it had the ruggedness, stark simplicity, vivid drama, naïveté, accentuated rhythms, and picturesqueness characteristic of the spirituals of the American Negro." Dr. Barnes considered Pippin's closest artistic kinship "with the group of natural, untaught painters to be found at all periods and in all nations, and to which custom has attached the word 'primitive.'" Reaction to the Carlen exhibition was discussed at length in the local press and is summed up by the headline of one such article: "Pippin's Paintings Create Sensation in Philadelphia." Dorothy Grafley, writing in the Philadelphia *Record*, declared: "What many an artist spends years learning Pippin knows by instinct. He is a remarkable designer, and a master of black, white, blue, and green contrasts. He holds pattern to simple essentials; yet has a grasp of perspective that baffles academicians."

In the fall of 1940 Pippin made his long-awaited Fifty-seventh Street debut when the Bignou Gallery in New York held an exhibition of his work. Pennsylvania's modern primitive won critical commendation for his sincerity, naïveté, and boldness with colors. One critic was especially impressed by "the variety in his arrangements with regard to the interrelationships of mass, line and color," while the general consensus agreed that the show was "extremely interesting." Critic Bryan Holme found Pippin's work reminiscent of the famous French painter, Henri Rousseau, and also noted "a tinge of Matisse '43." Previously Barnes had compared Pippin to the noted American painter, John Kane, an opinion which Holme enlarged upon, declaring:

PIPPIN, HORACE—*Continued*

"Of all American painters Pippin comes closest to John Kane, but at times his painting definitely has more charm than any of Kane's canvases can boast." Robert M. Coates of the *New Yorker* judged Pippin's work "precise, sharply drawn, and minutely detailed," boasting "a kind of natural sophistication in the use of color that is at times surprising." Through the Bignou show the artist's development could be traced, both in technical growth and thematic change. The change in subject matter from war to peace and in color from "a gray, restricted palette to one more vivid and varied," was noted by one writer. While Pippin's early works were usually limited to three or four dominant tones, his later pictures use many intense colors, such as saturated greens and fiery reds.

In 1941 Pippin's works were exhibited at the Art Club of Chicago and the following year at San Francisco's Museum of Art. Commissioned to paint a picture for the Capehart series in 1943, he produced *I'se Comin'* which appeared in color reproductions in various magazines including *Life, Time,* and the *New Yorker.* In March of the next year the Downtown Gallery in New York held an exhibition of Pippin's recent works after having previously included the artist in their show, "American Negro Art." Margaret Breuning, who reviewed the Pippin exhibit in the *Art Digest* (March 1, 1944), noted the vitality and charm of Pippin's canvases, and found that he had "gained in power of expression as well as subtlety of color relations." This critic was especially impressed by the genre scenes and the flower paintings which "display great lushness of color and richness of textures resolved in a harmonious soundness of simplified statement." The Downtown Gallery reported the Pippin exhibition "close to a sellout." In October 1944 the artist was represented in the Carnegie Institute exhibition, "Painting in the United States, 1944," at which his landscape, *Cabin in the Cotton,* won fourth honorable mention and one hundred dollars in the competition judged by prominent art experts. Widely exhibited and reproduced in several magazines, it caused some controversy in artistic circles.

Horace Pippin's painting *The Holy Mountain* was chosen in 1945 for inclusion in the *Encyclopædia Britannica* collection of twentieth century American art. The artist's humbly eloquent letter about his picture (published in the *Art Digest,* April 1, 1945) reveals its biblical inspiration and the passionate hope for peace which motivated Pippin. Of the series of white crosses in the background of the painting, Pippin says: "Now my picture would not be complete of today if the little ghost-like memory did not appear in the left of the picture. As the men are dying, today the little crosses tell us of them in the First World War and what is doing in the South today—all of that we are going through now. But there will be peace."

In January 1941 one critic expressed the hope that Pippin's contact with other art "will not cause his painting to become less fresh and stimulating in the future." However, it has since been noted that the Negro artist's development "has not been arrested by copying traits or techniques individual to particular painters or traditions," but rather that his artistic growth has been evidenced in a more comprehensive knowledge of how to apply paint and how to use and coordinate color, line, light, space and pattern. Generally classed as a primitive, an instinctive painter, "with an inner vision of burning intensity," Pippin is said to possess an "extraordinary sense of design, color, and perspective." One writer believes that the artist's sophistication has gradually eliminated the "primitivist" label and Edward Alden Jewell has suggested his classification as a neo-primitive. N. C. Wyeth's appraisal of Pippin finds "a basic African quality" in his work while another critic pronounced Pippin's art "distinctly American." To a writer for the New York *Sun* in 1944, "His colors have the boldness and the clarity of a flower garden seen after a rain and his instinct for decoration is unfailing," and another admiring critic declares: "Perhaps Pippin's outstanding distinction is the fertility of his ideas in compositional arrangement." Edward Alden Jewell, noting the painter's technical progress, found "solid artistic virtue" in *Birmingham Meeting House in Late Summer,* but termed *Lady of the Lake* "no more than quaint—quite sincere, no doubt, but obscurely fanciful rather than creatively imaginative." Margaret Breuning has described *Sunday Morning Breakfast,* "with its excellent give and take of rhythms and fine integration of figures in the design" as outstanding, commending also the remarkable vividness of the John Brown series by Pippin.

Pippin canvases are included in the permanent collections of the Whitney Museum, the Philadelphia Museum, the Pennsylvania Academy of Fine Arts, Barnes Foundation, Phillips Memorial Gallery, Albright Art Gallery, Rhode Island School of Design, and the Wichita Art Museum. Among the art collectors who own his works are Averell Harriman [41], Mrs. Plunkett Stewart, John D. Hamilton, and Alain Locke [44]. Theatrical people are reported to be among his most ardent collectors and according to one source in 1944, thirteen were waiting to purchase forthcoming Pippin paintings. Describing his personal artistic process, the artist has said: "Pictures just come to my mind. I think my pictures out with my brain and then I tell my heart to go ahead. If the idea is worthwhile, I paint it. I go over the picture in my mind several times. Then I start painting." Pippin works from the more distant objects to those in the foreground. "This throws the background away from the foreground," he explains. His ideas come from magazines, books, and his own memory and imagination. He still paints with his right hand propped up by the left and after six hours of work he is very tired, but he has worked as long as seventeen hours without a stop. Painting mostly at night, he still spends months on one picture. He works in the dining room of his small frame house.

A tall, broad, "open-faced" man with a flashing smile and a hearty laugh, Pippin has been described as a warm, religious person. In the words of one writer, "his sole reason for painting is his own satisfaction in his work." He himself has said, "My opinion of art is that a man . . . paints from his heart and mind. To me it seems impossible for another to teach one of art."

References

American Artist 9:17 Ap '45 il
Art News 43:21 Mr 1-14 '44 il por
Friday 2:22-3 Ja 17 '41 pors
Time 35:56 Ja 29 '40 por
Who's Who in American Art, 1940-41

PORTER, PAUL A(LDERMANDT) Oct. 6, 1904- United States Government official; lawyer

Address: b. New Post Office Bldg., Washington, D. C.; h. 6001 Broad Branch Rd., N.W., Washington, D. C.

Appointed chairman of the United States Federal Communications Commission in December 1944, Paul A. Porter, has, in a short span of a decade, been lawyer, newspaperman, college professor, radio counsel, and government official. A "Porter competence," coupled with wit and genuine fondness for all sorts of people, has helped him ride out numerous storms in different posts without losing the friendship of an opponent.

Paul Aldermandt Porter was born October 6, 1904, in Joplin, Missouri. He is the son of John J. and Dolly (Carpenter) Porter. The family moved to Winchester, Kentucky, when he was three months old. Paul started working at fourteen to help support his widowed mother and the eight children. She got the fifteen-year-old boy a job as a reporter on the Winchester *Sun* where he clocked in at 5:00 A.M. for work before reporting for classes at the Clark County High School. He continued this schedule after he entered Kentucky Wesleyan College in his home town in 1921.

Three years later Porter determined to study law at the Law College of the University of Kentucky, from which he received his LL.B. in 1927. In 1925, while still at the university, the young student became city editor of the Lexington *Herald*, remaining with the paper until 1928, when he left to enter private law practice. Then in 1929 he was able to combine his two professional interests, law and journalism, by accepting a position as general attorney for Oklahoma Newspapers, Inc. He left this job in 1931, and for a year held a similar position with General Newspapers, Inc. Both of these legal posts involved contacts with southern and southwestern farm newspapers and gave to Porter an appreciation of the problems confronting the farmer.

While editing the chain's La Grange (Georgia) *News,* Porter took the bold step of throwing into the waste basket the "canned" editorials set up in type for small-town newspapers. Then he wrote his own. This led to his first Government job, for several of the columns he wrote on cotton in 1933 so impressed Secretary of Agriculture Henry A. Wallace [40] that he summoned Porter to Washington as a special legal assistant; and in 1935 he was made executive assistant to the head of the Agricultural Adjustment Administration.

His lawyer-editor mind and familiarity with agricultural problems and his strong sympathy with the principles of the New Deal made him the person for this position. Under his di-

PAUL A. PORTER

rection the AAA organized a publicity staff whose setup was comparable in design to a daily newspaper office, replete with reporters, copyreaders, rewrite men, and editors. Their output was distributed to correspondents in the form of mimeographed "handouts," skeletons of the fuller reports found later in the newspapers. A good number of the AAA's radio addresses were ghostwritten by Porter. Through his efforts an amendment which circumvented a 1926 restriction was adopted, making it possible to publicize price and production predictions. Porter's Amendment, as it is sometimes referred to, helped to boost the prestige of the publicity department. And Porter, weathering the 1935 "purge" within the AAA, when several key men of the agency were ousted, remained in office for two more years.

In 1937 the young publicity man left the Department to become Washington counsel for the Columbia Broadcasting System, a position he held until 1942. Then in 1940, when the entrance of the United States into the war was becoming inevitable, Porter, on leave from CBS, became legal adviser and assistant to Chester C. Davies [40] on the National Defense Advisory Commission, a commission formed for the purpose of formulating a food program for an America at war. However, since very few people at this time recognized the possibility of there being a food problem in the impending conflict, the endeavor was short-lived (June to December).

The following year Paul Porter lectured on administrative law at the Catholic University College of Law in Washington, D. C., then left in 1942 to accept the position of deputy administrator in charge of rent control in the Office of Price Administration. During Porter's term in office the (Howard W.) Smith [41] Committee of the House of Representatives, investigating practices of executive agencies, attacked the rent office for "arbitrary, capricious" operations outside the "expressed mandates of Congress." One of the complaints

PORTER, PAUL A.—*Continued*

heard during the inquiry was that the office had been unfair to small owners on fixed rentals. Porter submitted figures to prove that, on the contrary, a survey of twenty cities showed that income from rentals had increased since the start of the war. At the end of the inquiry the committee reported that, on the whole, OPA rent control had been effective, although it criticized OPA methods, charging that the office had discriminated between landlord and tenant and had disregarded state and local laws. The CIO and the A.F. of L. for their part both voiced appreciation to the office for executing its responsibilities so successfully.

Porter resigned as OPA deputy administrator on June 1, 1943. Thirty days later he was shifted to the War Food Administration as associate administrator under Marvin Jones[43], to aid in the budgeting of the Nation's military, foreign, and civilian food requirements. Porter's short tenure of office (one month) with the WFA has been ascribed, according to Gardner Jackson of *PM*, to his opposition to various practices employed by Assistant Secretary of Agriculture, Grover B. Hill. It is believed that Porter felt that some of Hill's policies conflicted with the principles of price control and with effective food production. In August, therefore, he was free to assume the associate directorship of the Office of Economic Stabilization, as first assistant to Fred M. Vinson[43]. He framed the Vinson directive aimed at forcing manufacturers to make more cheap work clothes and fewer luxury garments.

When, in February 1944, Charles Michelson[40] resigned from the post of public relations director of the Democratic National Committee, Stephen Early[41], President Roosevelt's secretary, suggested Porter for the vacancy. Harry Hopkins[41] seconded the choice: Porter knew the press and radio, had a good political sense, could write or make a good speech. Porter thus became publicity director for the Democrats in their 1944 Presidential campaign. The election won, Porter was named to a Federal post near the end of 1944: James L. Fly[40] had resigned as chairman of the Federal Communications Commission before the expiration of his seven-year term of office; and on December 21 President Roosevelt appointed Porter the new chairman. This was an interim appointment, "to give Porter experience" before the convening of the new Congress. In January the President's choice was approved by the Senate.

Paul Porter's post entails the issuing of licenses to radio stations and operators, and the regulation of interstate and foreign communications by telephone, telegraph, cable, and radio. The FCC is also engaged in promotion of safety at sea through the use of communication facilities. In addition, the responsibility which Porter inherited has been for the past few years the storm center of controversy among naval officers, the National Association of Broadcasters, the networks, and Congress, which in mid-1943, through a House committee (whose original chairman was Eugene Cox[43]), had begun an investigation of the Commission. The subject of the investigation (occasionally labeled a "star-chamber" probe) was the power of the FCC to regulate broadcasting chains (upheld by the Supreme Court in May 1943) and its withholding of licenses for newspaper ownership of stations. In January 1945 the House committee submitted a majority report stating that it believed the Commission had functioned with "reasonable satisfaction" in almost every instance scrutinized during the inquiry. "The committee believes that this entire matter of newspaper ownership and the monopoly angle should be reviewed by the Congress with a view of providing the necessary new or clarifying legislation that should settle this problem." The minority report disagreed on almost every count, charging the FCC with assuming powers not granted to it by Congress.

In February Porter advised Director of War Mobilization and Reconversion James F. Byrnes[41] that nineteen thousand miles of leased wire circuits, with seven hundred extensions, and a large number of telephone sets previously used for the dissemination of racing information had been made available for essential civilian use as a result of Byrnes's ban on horse and dog racing the month before. Then a really complicated problem was presented to Porter. Late in March Navy Secretary Forrestal[42] told Congress that the United States had no stated policy governing international communications, that anyone could set up a radio, telephone or cable company, and that this sort of free competition was out of date. Forrestal advocated a monopolistic "chosen instrument"—that is, a merger sanctioned by Congress of all United States companies engaged in international communications into one big Government-backed corporation so that the United States could compete with similar foreign companies and send secretly its diplomatic and commercial messages. Porter too has urged a consolidation of overseas services but does not believe the Forrestal idea feasible because the FCC would have the job of regulating a corporation that included five Cabinet members among its directors, and in any question of national policy the Secretaries of War, State, Navy, Commerce, and Post Office could overrule the fifteen directors from private business. The taxpayer's stake is enormous, Porter told the Senate Interstate Commerce Committee on International Communications. The total cost of combined plant and equipment of the thirteen American companies now in the field is $133,500,000, and with book depreciation subtracted, $52,000,000. Compared to this is the Navy budget expenditure of $480,000,000 for purchase and maintenance of communications equipment for 1945 alone; and the Army investment is higher, Porter pointed out.

The Senate Committee desired to obtain all possible information before determining policy, according to Lowell Mellett[42], who endorsed its pivotal point: the conviction that any enduring peace must be based on the fullest understanding among nations and that this can be achieved only through the freest communications. Porter told the committee that cable rates were preposterously high, that the actual transmission cost by radio is about the same for a message traveling from New York half way round the globe as it is from New York to Boston. If a merger were enforced, then one big company could use either cable, radio telegraph, or radio telephone for sending messages most satisfactorily, Porter maintained, at the same time requesting permission for the FCC to withhold any recommendation until all the evidence was in. This included testimony from the thirteen companies concerned. The International Telephone and Telegraph Corporation and Radio Corporation of America generally favored a merger but the "American Telephone and Telegraph Company, which does not want anyone to cut into its telephone monopoly, and lusty, young Press Wireless, Inc., which now carries over half of all press dispatches in and out of the United States," are lined up against the one big company idea, according to *Time* (April 2, 1945). Both *Time* and *United States News* believed that a Government-controlled merger brings up the question of censorship and that this is the issue on which it may principally be fought.

Realizing that clear channel stations are now primarily serving metropolitan areas instead of the rural America they were originally intended to serve, Porter pointed out in April 1945 that nearly 57 per cent of the population got only inferior radio reception—a situation he called intolerable and which the FCC proposed to deal with shortly. Porter also warned broadcasting stations that "the spirit of the Communications Act of 1934 requires radio to be an instrument of free speech." Organized labor and cooperative organizations have long protested that the code of the National Association of Broadcasters is prejudicial to them and favors big business. The refusal of some stations to sell time on the air to unions and cooperatives has elicited Porter's warning that the NAB code "is inconsistent with the concept of public interest established by the Communications Act, as a criterion of radio regulation."

The swelling volume of complaints about "over-commercialism" of radio today brought Porter to the microphone and into print in a fatherly but fighting mood, admonishing both the public and the broadcasting stations of their responsibilities. "Radio Must Grow Up" was the warning title of Porter's article in the *American Magazine*, October 1945. "It must be clear to the radio industry that if it is to avoid legislative intervention to certain phases of its operation it should undertake to discontinue practices which are making the public angry," wrote Porter—and then addressed the public: "The air waves do not belong to the Government, or to the FCC, or to the broadcasting stations. They belong, by law, to you—the public. It is right and necessary for you to debate and seriously consider the nature of the guest who comes into your home." Urgent as this was before, it is doubly so now because radio has come to a turning point in its history, Porter continued, highlighting the scientific advances, especially FM (Frequency Modulation) which will open up a vast new empire.

The FCC has no power to censor the radio but it can revoke licenses in the public interest. When application is made for a permit to build a station, specific pledges are given that "time will be available for civic, educational, agricultural, and other public service programs." In the past the FCC has renewed licenses automatically for a three-year period,

although the record showed that some licensees had not fulfilled the promises originally made to the commission. This practice, Porter said, would not continue in the future. Radio was operating under a statute drafted eighteen years ago when there were no nationwide networks and less than six and a half million receivers in homes. Today there are 933 stations licensed, four national networks, and upward of sixty million receiving sets. In 1944 advertisers spent $285,000,000 for air time, and net profits before taxes, as reported to the FCC by 836 stations, were 125 per cent over 1942. By revising the old Radio Act of 1927 Congress would, Porter believes, "doubtless take up questions of whether news should be sponsored at all, and consider proposals that certain hours of good listening time be withheld from sale entirely in order that stations would have no alternative but to broadcast sustaining public-service programs during that period."

In 1940 a FCC ruling had opened the air lanes to commercial stations using FM. (Frequency Modulation [FM], in contrast to the ordinarily used Amplitude Modulation [AM], signifies changing the length of the radio wave and thus eliminating static, as radio waves and static have the same electrical characteristics. This method of conquering static by means of a wide band Frequency Modulation was found by Edwin Howard Armstrong [40] as early as 1928.) The fact that any number of properly spaced FM stations could operate in the same air channel solved FCC's difficult problem of satisfying a greater number of license applicants. By September 1940 there were twenty-two experimental stations licensed, many applications for FM commercial stations pending. The war, however, put a temporary stop to their increase.

The prediction of a swift reconversion of the radio manufacturing industry from a wartime to a peacetime basis after V-J Day was not fulfilled. The delay was a result of both technical and economic issues peculiar to radio in general and to FM, the newest and most contested broadcasting art in particular. It was with virtually all phases of FM that there existed much controversy and confusion. The differences took in engineering factors (disagreement as to the width of the FM band), Government regulations, transmitter and receiver manufacturing, programing, Petrillo's demand that a double crew of musicians be hired if a musical program were duplicated on both FM and standard outlets, and also purely economic and competitive considerations. In spite of being temporarily unfavorable, however, the prospects of FM remained undimmed. In November, when the FCC scheduled hearings to allocate hundreds of channels available for FM stations, an intensive struggle for new broadcasting licenses set in. More than seven hundred applicants filed for permission to operate FM stations, the newest applicants being labor unions who up to that time had been barred from the air. Porter declared that the decisive factor in judging applications would be "public interest." He then added: "I can see nothing in the Communications act . . . that would discriminate against labor unions." Among other applicants there were educational and non-commercial groups as well

PORTER, PAUL A.—*Continued*

as major set manufacturers with large economic resources. At the end of 1945 Porter predicted that there would be one thousand FM stations on the air within three years and that they would supplant AM stations except in rural areas.

Late in November the United States and the nations of the British Commonwealth opened a telecommunications conference in Bermuda with an agreement that radio and cable rates should be cheaper and more uniform in the future. Porter, in his capacity as chairman of the FCC, demanded elimination of British monopolies in Greece, Saudi Arabia, and Iran, and maintenance of United States circuits to British nations and the Near East. At the close of the twelve-day conference all eight participating Governments signed an executive agreement cutting international communications rates, abandoning communications monopolies in other countries, and giving the United States the right to maintain direct radio circuits with the United Kingdom, Australia, New Zealand, and India.

In June 1930 Paul Porter was married to Bessie Edgar Benton, and now has two daughters, Betsy Goodloe and Ann Covington. Tall, six feet three, and weighing one hundred and ninety-five pounds, "lanky, affable" Porter has a medium complexion, wears rimless glasses. His favorite recreation is golf. The FCC chairman is a member of Sigma Alpha Epsilon and Phi Alpha Delta, the New York Bar Association, the Federal Communications Bar Association, and the National Press Association. His church affiliation is Baptist. He is known in Washington as "the story-teller with an inexhaustible stock pile of yarns" which "always have a point and more often than not emphasize an argument he is trying to register."

References

Bsns W p7 Jl 17 '43 por
N Y Times p36 N 17 '44 por
New Outlook 164:29 Jl '34
Newsweek p36 Ja 8 '45
PM p14 F 14 '44 por; p13 N 17 '44 por
Who's Who in America, 1944-45

PORTER, WILLIAM N(ICHOLS) Mar. 15, 1886- Former United States Army officer
Address: b. c/o American Cyanamid Co., 30 Rockefeller Plaza, New York City

In the Second World War searing, probing fingers of flame reduced impregnable pillboxes and strong points of the enemy when other means failed; incendiary bombs burned out the manufacturing centers and arsenals of the Axis, reducing their means of waging effective warfare; and smoke that screened landing operations had the effect of greatly reducing losses among Allied invasion forces. Such developments of modern warfare are the charge of the United States Army Chemical Warfare Service, of which Major General William M. Porter was wartime chief.

William Nichols Porter was born in Lima, Ohio, on March 15, 1886, to William Harley and Ilva (Nichols) Porter. In 1909, at the age of twenty-three, William was graduated from the United States Naval Academy. He was assigned to the U.S.S. *Connecticut*, but

after less than a year of service the young ensign in February 1910 resigned from the Navy. The next month he entered the United States Army, with a commission as second lieutenant in the Coast Artillery Corps. In July 1911 he was married to Gladys Baxter, the daughter of a naval officer.

Porter's first tour of duty was with the Forty-first Coast Artillery Company at Fort Monroe, Virginia; then after two months, in July 1910, he was transferred to the 168th Company. The following year, in September, he was shifted to the 145th Company at Fort Moultrie, South Carolina, where he remained until February 1913. (The previous September he had been made a first lieutenant.) His next duty was in Galveston, Texas, but five months later he was returned to his first post, Fort Monroe, and then in September of the same year served at Fort Andrews, Massachusetts. Two years later he went to Fort Mills in the Philippine Islands as assistant adjutant and adjutant of coast defenses of Manila and Subic bays, returning to the United States on July 15, 1918, after the United States had entered the war. During his stay in the East he had received two promotions: to captain in May 1917, to major (temporary) a year later.

During the remainder of the First World War Porter was stationed in the United States. For a brief period he first served at Fort Monroe, Virginia. In September 1918, when he was raised to the rank of lieutenant colonel (temporary), he was assigned as camp adjutant to Fort Eustis, and in October he was given the command of the Thirtieth Coast Artillery. He remained with the Thirtieth until January 1919, when he was transferred to San Francisco and given the command of Fort Miley. In May he reverted to his permanent rank of captain. In July he became coast defense adjutant at Fort Winfield Scott, where as a major he remained until September 1920. His last tour of duty as an artillery officer was at Camp Lewis, Washington, for on June 30, 1921, he was assigned to the Office of the Chief of Chemical Warfare Service, Washington, D.C., as the assistant executive officer.

The Chemical Warfare Service was set up as a temporary expedient in the First World War to meet the Germans' use of gas, flame-throwers, and aerial incendiaries. At the end of the war, in July 1920, a year before Porter's assignment, the department was made a permanent branch of the Army. During the next twenty-four years, while the CWS developed the equipment and methods of gas warfare, Porter kept pace with the technical and tactical advancement by his attendance at Army schools.

He first left the Office of the Chief of Chemical Warfare Service to take a five-month course at the Army Industrial College in Washington, from which he was graduated in January 1926. The following year he took the course at the Command and General Staff School, Fort Leavenworth, Kansas, and upon graduation in June 1927 became chief of the Training Division in Washington; two years later he was made executive officer of the department. Third on his list of Army schools was the Chemical Warfare School, Edgewood Arsenal, Maryland. Following graduation in August 1931 he was made assistant commandant of that school. In September 1933 he went to Maxwell Field, Alabama, as an instructor in and later director of the Department of Ground Tactics of the Air Corps Tactical School. While at this station he received his promotion to the rank of lieutenant colonel, in October 1934. Finally, in August 1937, he enrolled in the Army War College, the highest Army training school, and was graduated the following June.

Appointed as chemical officer of the Ninth Corps Area at San Francisco after graduating from the War College, Porter, now a colonel (December 1938), remained on the West Coast until April 28, 1940. He was then assigned as chemical officer of the General Headquarters Air Force at Langley Field, Virginia. On June 2, 1941, six months before Pearl Harbor, he was appointed Chief of the Chemical Warfare Service, with the rank of major general, effective from May 1.

America's entry into the Second World War at the end of 1941 presented the Chemical Warfare Service with many problems. At that time it seemed quite likely that the Germans would use poison gas. Under General Porter's direction the country's facilities for manufacturing equipment as a defense against chemical attack were expanded. However, the General did not stop at providing defense equipment. To Porter, "defense" was a "weasel word." Backing up this statement made to the American Chemical Society on September 10, 1941, he instituted a program for manufacturing poison gas in quantities far greater than it was thought the Axis countries could provide for their own use. Edgewood Arsenal, home of the CWS, was expanded; new plants were constructed at Huntsville, Alabama, Pine Bluff, Arkansas, and Denver, Colorado. The best scientific minds in the nation were mobilized under the direction of the National Defense Research Committee, headed by James B. Conant [41], president of Harvard University, and Roger Adams, head of the department of chemistry at the University of Illinois.

Out of these efforts came many innovations and improvements. One of these is the "Goon" gun, a 4.2-inch rifled mortar with an effective range of 3,200 yards. It can fire phosphorus shells, high explosives, gas, or smoke; a chemical battalion equipped with thirty-eight of the mortars can build a smoke wall three miles long and nearly 1,000 feet high, and maintain that wall for eighteen hours. In the European war the weapon was successful in tank attacks and in artillery battles with the famed German 88's (88-millimeter guns), which are thirty times heavier than the mortar. Developed by the CWS in 1942, it was called "America's secret weapon" by the Germans.

Rapid strides were also made in the employment of smoke as an aid in the attack as well as the defense. Smoke pots and smoke shells were improved, including a pot that will float on water. But the best "smoker" of all is considered to be the generator, resembling the old-fashioned horse-drawn fire engine, which can blanket an area one mile square in ten minutes. This smoke generator was developed by Irving Langmuir [40] and Vincent Schaefer at the General Electric Company's research laboratory; the first one was designed

MAJ. GEN. WILLIAM N. PORTER

and made by the Standard Oil Company, from which it gained its nickname, "Esso."

The flame-thrower and incendiary bomb, introduced by Germany during the First World War, have been developed by the CWS to a point of "tremendous effectiveness." There are seven distinct types of aerial incendiaries, which range in size from the four-pound firesticks to the five-hundred-pound "factory burners." The fuels in these bombs can be magnesium, thermite, phosphorus, or oil. Of all the varieties, the most spectacular is known as "fire-roe," a thickener for gasoline that resembles fish roe in appearance. It can also be used as fuel in the flame-thrower and produces an extremely high heat; it has the added advantage of sticking like glue to the places it touches when the container explodes or the flame is spurted from the flame-thrower. The Chemical Warfare Service during the war had stores of poison gas, too, which were held in reserve. These stocks, which were described as far greater than any supply available to either the Germans or the Japanese, were kept for retaliatory purposes only, for the United States refused to take the initiative in employing them.

The Chemical Warfare Service is by no means devoted entirely to offensive and defensive warfare, but includes research in preventive and curative medicine, sanitation, food and water contamination, and the effect of various gases on men and animals. Developed by Dr. Paul Müller [45], under the direction of Dr. Paul Läuger [45], the new insecticide DDT was improved for use by CWS in collaboration with the Department of Agriculture; and the medical division has made great strides in combating respiratory diseases, and in treating burns and heavy metal poisoning, to name a few. "There is no section of the Army," said Porter, "where plowshares and swords run so closely together." The CWS decontamination apparatus can be used to spray crops; smoke generators can economically protect fruit trees

PORTER, WILLIAM N.—*Continued*

against frost; the flame-thrower can be used remove ice and snow from airport runways, to throw back forest fires, or to destroy water plants which impede navigation; and the protective clothing can be used in dangerous chemical operations or to protect against cold and moisture. With the end of the war the Army was faced with disposal of enormous stocks of unused gases. Some will be broken down and used in industry, others will deteriorate in time and can be allowed to disperse in the air, and still others will be cast into the sea in non-rustproof casks where they will gradually leak out and do no harm.

William Porter is an Episcopalian, a member of the Army and Navy clubs and the Army and Navy Country Club in Washington, D. C. His son, William Baxter, followed in his early footsteps, becoming a lieutenant commander in the United States Navy, while his daughter, Margaret Baxter, is married to a Navy man, Lieutenant Commander L. M. Stevens. For his services in the First World War, General Porter was awarded the Belgian Order of Leopold. In February 1945 he was made a member of the executive committee of the Research Board for National Security, established by the National Academy of Sciences. Upon his retirement from the Army in November 1945 he became an executive of the American Cyanamid Company, in New York City.

References

N Y Sun p25 Ja 6 '43
Who's Who in America, 1944-45

POWERS, JOHN ROBERT Dec. 1896-
Model-agency director
Address: b. 247 Park Ave., New York City

"Can you imagine," asks the *Yale Record*, "a job of which the prime duty is to merely look after the most beautiful and shapeliest girls in the world? Can you imagine a profession which entails just sitting behind an office desk and interviewing daily between thirty and forty of the comeliest girls this side of heaven?" The man whose occupation fits this description is John Robert Powers. Owner of the largest and best-known model agency in New York and therefore in the world, Powers chooses from among the one hundred and fifty thousand mail and in-person applicants a year the three who will be added each month to his register, and then helps them to develop into successful models. Although his agency schedules appointments for persons of both sexes, and from the age of six months, he is usually identified with young beauties nationally known as "the Powers Girls," of whom there are one hundred and fifty at any one time.

Of Irish ancestry, John Robert Powers was born in Easton, Pennsylvania, in December 1896. Like many prominent Americans, he started life on a farm. After completing his secondary education, John made what he calls "a temporary halt" at Lafayette College, after which he managed to get small parts with various theatrical stock companies and in some silent films. "Though I played with Elsie Ferguson and other talented actors," Powers

recalls, "I never had my entrances greeted by a burst of applause. Producers and audiences alike were unimpressed. Kindly producers told me that I was wasting my talents; the rest told me bluntly I was wasting their time." But Sir Herbert Beerbohm Tree hired the young Pennsylvanian as assistant manager and understudy in his touring company. "While the pay checks were still coming in regularly," Powers was married to blond Alice Hathaway Burton, who gave up her work on the stage to become Mrs. Powers.

Powers stayed with Sir Herbert for two years (Tree died in 1917), but after the First World War he found himself jobless again. After making the rounds of all the theatrical agencies in New York, "more from force of habit than with any real hope," he answered a newspaper advertisement calling for models for a commercial photographer. The photographer needed eight men to pose for clothing advertisements, whereupon Powers rounded up seven of his unemployed actor friends, and they got the job. ("Today most of them are famous stars," he says.) Commercial photography by 1921 was only about three years old, and not very well organized. When an artist or photographer needed a model, he advertised for one. What he got was usually out-of-work actors or chorus girls, and "with the best will in the world" the latter "were unable to make themselves look like anything but chorus girls," which was no help in posing as housewives or debutantes. And there was no organization for bringing photographers together with prospective models.

Powers gives his wife credit for the idea of creating such an agency. His method was simple: "I got in touch with everyone I knew, friends, acquaintances, and their friends and acquaintances, had their pictures taken, made up a catalogue containing their descriptions and measurements, and sent it to anyone in New York who might be a prospective client—commercial photographers, advertisers, department stores, artists. There were not more than forty people listed in that first catalogue, but the idea was a new one. Not only the photographers but the advertisers began to see its possibilities. . . .While I had started with the idea of supplying a demand, I began to discover that I was creating one. The advertisers were quick to see the tremendous sales possibilities represented by lovely girls whose youth and beauty appealed to everyone, men and women, old and young alike. A beautiful girl's smile sold more tooth paste than the most telling copy that could be devised. A photograph dramatized a product more effectively than columns of words. Dresses worn by an attractive girl were more interesting than the same dresses hanging on a rack or draped on a wax figure"—and Powers got 10 per cent of each model's fees.

The Powers agency was not the only one to be set up—Walter Thornton was an early rival, and others came later—but it became the largest. Powers encouraged his models to go on to other fields. In 1924 he had to persuade the future Barbara Stanwyck to accept a tiny movie role at the Cosmopolitan studio. "Anyone who can pose, can act," he told her. Powers estimates that about fifty of his men and girls have gone on to success in Hollywood and on Broadway; the number includes Joan Bennett, Joan Blondell, Georgia Carroll, Dolores Costello, Kay Francis, Paulette Goddard, Anita Louise (a child model), Marie MacDonald, Norma Shearer, Gene Tierney, and Helen Vinson. Before they became famous Rosalind Russell '43 and Jennifer Jones '44 filled some assignments through the Powers agency, as did Henry Fonda, Tyrone Power, and Fredric March '43. Other Powers graduates have become stylists, fashion editors, clothes designers, and a number of Powers Girls have made wealthy marriages, among them to Woolworth Donahue, Marshall Hemingway, and Winthrop Gardiner.

John Powers takes a personal pride in the "social acceptability" of his models, in contrast to the exclusion of the earlier mannequin. He attaches importance to their "looking and acting like ladies"—for advertising and illustration models must appeal to women even more than to men. After the financial crash of 1929 many young ladies of prominent families found it necessary to earn money to pay for their debuts. The first to become a model was Elsie Little of New York; she was followed by other debutantes, including Halldis Prince of Boston, Pat Plunkett, Mimi Richardson, and Ridgely Vermilyea. Some, like Babs Beckwith (Mrs. Winthrop Gardiner), continued their modeling after marriage, as do more than half the Powers Girls.

During the depression of the 'thirties Powers prospered, for when buying was slow advertising became even more important. In 1930 the photographic modeling field was still so little known to those outside it that when Marie Beynon Ray wrote an article tracing the history of the mannequin for the April 1930 *Mentor*, the only contemporary model she mentioned was "the minx who parades the dressmaking establishments." By 1935 magazine writers were beginning to tell the public that "in New York about a hundred and fifty men and women are earning an average of more than twenty-five dollars a week as photograph models [in addition to several hundred part-time models]. About one hundred and twenty-five of them are girls. Men usually take it up only until they can get a job at something else. Perhaps twenty-five or thirty of these girls make around seventy-five dollars a week, and an additional eight or ten who demand at least ten dollars an appointment—and get it—average one hundred dollars or more." At this time there was also a great demand for babies, particularly with curls and dimples à la Shirley Temple, or in batches of five as popularized by the Dionnes.

In 1937 Harry Conover, a model whose picture is still being used in hair-tonic advertisements, left Powers and opened his own agency, with the help of top-flight model Anita Colby. In contrast to Powers, Conover introduced the star system into modeling, playing up individual girls and thinking up such names are Candy Jones, Dusty Anderson, Choo-Choo Johnson, and Melody Thomson. Since then Conover has built up the identification of his clients as Conover Cover Girls, while Powers began to place somewhat more emphasis on the individual "Long-stemmed American Beauty" (phrase by the illustrator Arthur William Brown).

JOHN ROBERT POWERS

In 1937 there were fifteen telephones incessantly ringing in Powers' inner office; by late 1940 the number had risen to twenty-three, on which appointments were made for the four hundred models registered with Powers. All ages and both sexes were included, but as always the main attention was focused on the pretty girl, who by then was known around New York simply as "a Powers Girl." Powers Girls, as such, had become a decided feature of cafe society; Powers quotes Elsa Maxwell '43 as saying that she could give one of her famous parties without debutantes, but not without at least half-a-dozen Powers Girls. Wrote E. J. Kahn, Jr., in the *New Yorker,* "Gossip writers, who would rather be specific than otherwise, occasionally mention a male night-club habitué by name and say that he was seen out with 'a Powers model.' This . . . is merely an admission that columnists simply cannot tell Powers models apart. Few people can." From photographs and fashion shows, the Powers Girls branched out into other forms of promotion. Manufacturers of all sorts of products, from automobiles and luxury cruises to international good will, hired professional beauties to travel across the country or even to other countries to demonstrate their products.

The name John Robert Powers became better known to New Yorkers in 1940, when the New York Subways Advertising Company asked him to make monthly selections of "Miss Subways" for one of their eleven car-card features. And the bookshops began in 1941 to carry his *The Powers Girls,* a detailed guide to the modeling field which also includes a bit of autobiography. The author mentions, too, the Powers School, which gives a ten-week course (tuition, $200) of private instruction in charm —health, poise, posture, grooming, "makedown," voice and diction, patience, responsiveness, grace, and the proper choice of coiffure, clothes, and accessories. The course in "Vitality and Grooming" is taught by Powers' wife, Alice Burton Hathaway. The Powers

POWERS, JOHN ROBERT—*Continued*

School training differs from the pioneer charm course, the DuBarry Success School of the Richard Hudnut salon, in that it covers more ground and concentrates more on how the student acts, as opposed to how she looks. In February 1943 an individualized correspondence course (seven weeks, $25) was added, which has been taken by thousands of women. "Students are urged to write to the school for information on individual problems that arise during the course," reports Juliet Bridgman in *Liberty*. "They all get answers, too. This has brought on a lot of overtime work for the faculty. One woman wrote fifteen letters, and some of her questions perplexed the faculty until she explained that her husband was taking the course with her, exercises and all. Did him a world of good, she said."

Powers bears little or no resemblance to Alan Mowbray, the actor who portrayed him on the screen in *The Powers Girl* (1943). He is a solidly built, young-looking man, long-nosed and thin-lipped, with wavy black hair and very heavy eyebrows above eyes which almost disappear when he smiles. A 1936 interviewer reported that Mr. and Mrs. Powers were given to four-o'clock-in-the-morning horseback rides near their Huntington (Long Island) home. From nine-thirty on, however, Powers is generally to be found at the reception desk in his Park Avenue office. He does not quite trust anyone else to choose the potential Powers Girls from the scores of self-conscious, badly dressed, over-made-up applicants. "In one week, by relying entirely on the estimate of someone else," he says ruefully, "I lost several girls who later became very successful."

References

Am Mag 121:58 Ja '36 por
Powers, J. R. The Powers Girls (1941)

PRATT, FREDERIC BAYLEY Feb. 22, 1865—May 3, 1945 Retired president (1923-37) of Pratt Institute in Brooklyn, founded by his father, Charles Pratt; served fifty-seven years with the institute; in 1937 became chairman of the board; was a leader in civic and cultural affairs.

Obituary

N Y Times p19 My 4 '45 por

PRICE HARRISON J(ACKSON) Apr. 3, 1868—Sept. 16, 1945 Brigadier general in United States Army, retired; served in Cuba (1898), the Philippines (1900-3, 1906-7, 1915-17), and in France during the First World War as commander of the 154th Infantry Brigade, Seventy-seventh Division.

Obituary

N Y Times p24 S 18 '45

PRINCE, JOHN DYNELEY Apr. 17, 1868—Oct. 11, 1945 American diplomat and world renown linguist; professor of Semitic languages at New York University (1892-1902); professor, at Columbia University, of Semitic languages (1902-15), of Slavonic languages (1915-21), of East European languages

(1935-37); became professor emeritus in 1937; Minister to Denmark (1921-26) and to Yugoslavia (1926-33); also served in New Jersey Assembly and Senate, and (1912) as Acting Governor; author of a number of works on philology.

Obituary

N Y Times p23 O 12 '45 por

PUEYRREDON, HONORIO July 9, 1876—Sept. 23, 1945 Argentine politician and diplomat; stormy career as Minister of Foreign Affairs during First World War and Ambassador to United States, 1923-28; election to governorship of Province of Buenos Aires in 1931 voided by revolutionary government; defeated again in 1935 when police and Conservatives barred opposition voters from polls.

Obituary

N Y Times p19 S 24 '45 por

PUGMIRE, ERNEST I(VISON) Mar. 4, 1888- Social service leader

Address: b. Salvation Army Headquarters, 120 W. 14th St., New York City; h. 186 Boulder Trail, Yonkers, N. Y.

Since its inauspicious beginnings in the slums of London in 1865, the Salvation Army has become a widely known international organization whose blue-uniformed workers are serving in ninety-seven countries and, in 1945, on twenty-five war fronts. Never deviating from their own rigid standards of conduct and their purpose of spiritual regeneration accompanied by practical social service, the Salvationists have marched on, indifferent to the smiles their bonnet hats, jangling tambourines, and street-corner bands may provoke. Heading this "soul-saving" army in America and directing its many useful activities is Ernest I. Pugmire, National Commander and also Commissioner of the Eastern Territory. A vigorous and active person, Commander Pugmire grew up in the Army and has served in four countries.

Son of Joseph and Marian (Ivison) Pugmire, Ernest Ivison Pugmire was born in Kansas City, Missouri, on March 4, 1888. Major Pugmire (who later became Colonel) came from Penrith, England and had at one time been known in Salvation Army circles as the "Singing Evangelist." He was one of the pioneers of the Salvation Army in America, helping in the organization of Salvation Army corps in eight states. Soon after the birth of his son, Ernest, he was recalled to England and during the next ten years was transferred successively to Canada, Bermuda, Canada, then England and back to Toronto where he and his family stayed for the next seventeen years. Before Ernest was ten he had crossed the Atlantic four times.

Ernest attended public schools in Toronto. He experienced a religious conversion at the age of ten, and while still in school he was an active member of the Salvation Army Cadet Corps and played the horn in the Salvation Army band. However, at about the time he finished school he began to question his religious faith—for the son of a Salvation Army officer, an extremely serious matter. He considered leaving the Army to prepare for a career which would give more scope to his business ability, but he was dissuaded by two Salvation Army officers for whom he had a strong personal admiration. One of these men, whose secretary he became, was Commissioner Coombe of the Eastern Canadian Territory. Soon after this Ernest entered the Salvation Army Training School for officers. In 1906 he received his commission as captain and was appointed to the finance department at Toronto headquarters.

Five years later, in 1911, Pugmire was married to Captain Grace Vickers, a corps commander who had also been commissioned at the Training School in Toronto. Born in London, she had done Salvation Army work in St. Albans and Southsea, England, before coming to Canada with her parents in 1905. A few years after his marriage, in May 1914, Pugmire had a narrow escape from death when the *Empress of Ireland,* on which he was sailing for England, sank in the St. Lawrence River with the loss of more than a thousand lives.

In 1915 Pugmire received his first important advancement when he was called to Winnipeg as financial secretary in the Western Canada Territory which had just been opened by the Salvation Army. From there, in 1918, he was transferred to China to serve again as financial secretary, and a year later he was moved to Japan. Here he acted first as financial secretary under Commissioners Johannes de Groot, Charles D. Duce and William E. Eadie, then as chief secretary under Commissioner Gunpei Yamamuro, the first native-born commissioner of the Japanese territory.

Before Commissioner Pugmire arrived in Japan, the Salvation Army had become strong enough to march into Tokyo's geisha district and attempt to free some of the geisha girls. Though the attempt was met with some violence, it focused public attention on some of the worst conditions and resulted in slight improvement in the situation. At the time of the Tokyo earthquake in 1923, Commissioner Pugmire was away from the city but after great difficulty he was able to return to it. The Salvation Army headquarters had been destroyed and there had been considerable loss of life, but the Army survivors were already starting to organize relief, which included shelters, especially for women and children, nurseries for very small children, and food centers. Comparatively few meals were given free as the Japanese did not wish to accept food as a gift from the foreigners, although they were content to pay a fraction of the cost price. It was after this, while Commissioner Pugmire was still in Japan, that General Evangeline Booth [41] visited the country and had an audience with the Emperor at which she appeared in her Salvation Army uniform—the only occasion on which a woman had appeared at a court function in anything except a formal court dress.

While in China, before going to Japan, the Pugmire's first child was born, and a second child was born in Japan. But although she had these small children to care for, Mrs. Pugmire carried on active social work among the women, according to Salvation Army custom. Both Commander and Mrs. Pugmire felt that the Salvation Army work in Japan was very successful; not only were converts made among the under-privileged but also among middle-class Japanese. The Pugmires believe that at

Salvation Army

ERNEST I. PUGMIRE

the termination of the Second World War those of the Japanese Salvation Army who survive will emerge still loyal to the religion to which they were converted.

In 1931, after twelve years in Japan, the Pugmires returned to Canada, this time to Winnipeg. A year later the Commissioner was at long last transferred to the country of his birth and became chief secretary for the United States Central Territory. Less than two years later he was appointed territorial commander for the Southern States, and in 1939 he was made commander of the more important Central District. Having served as colonel and lieutenant commander, he was made a commissioner in 1939. In 1942 he was appointed Commissioner of the United States Eastern Territory, which includes the New England states and New York, New Jersey, Pennsylvania, Delaware and Ohio, and is, next to London, the largest and most influential command in the Salvation Army. In this territory are 1,770 officers of the Salvation Army, 1,979 employees and 205 Salvation Army-operated social service institutions. In 1944 Commissioner Pugmire was appointed Commander of the Salvation Army in the United States, still retaining his position as Eastern Commissioner, and this yearly appointment was renewed for 1945. In his dual role of National Commander and Commissioner of the Eastern Territory, Commander Pugmire is second in command to the international leader of the Salvation Army. General George Carpenter [43] who succeeded Evangeline Booth in 1939 as the fifth general to be elected.

The Salvation Army has a system of government organized on a quasi-military basis, which requires unquestioned obedience from its members. Each country is divided into territories, under a commissioner, and each territory is divided into provisions. divisions, and corps, the latter being under the direction of a captain and a lieutenant. From its inception the Army has tried to improve social conditions in order to pave the way for evangelization, believing

PUGMIRE, ERNEST I.—*Continued*

that bad physical and environmental conditions make it difficult for people to apprehend the spiritual message. "The surest way to lead a needy person back to God is first to serve him when he is in need," the Salvationists say. The Salvation Army maintains homes for unmarried mothers, day nurseries and infant hospitals, settlement homes and summer camps for children, and clubs for boys. It also operates employment bureaus, hotels and cafeterias, clinics and rehabilitation centers and gives prisoners' aid service, immigration and citizenship service, and conducts missing persons bureaus. Under Commissioner Pugmire's leadership the Salvation Army entered the battle against juvenile delinquency, which had increased considerably during the war, and in 1945 opened the first of a group of psychiatric clinics serving both servicemen and civilians.

The record of the Salvation Army's service in the Second World War is impressive. Reporting on it in September 1945, Commissioner Pugmire disclosed that the work, carried on in ninety-seven countries and territories, took its diversified activities to all the Allies on twenty-six fighting fronts. "Invasion canteens" rolled down the ramps of LST's along with jeeps, trucks, and tanks, and improvised huts were set up on beachheads, in jungles, and desert outposts. The soldiers called the beachhead Salvationists "strictly first-line operators"; there were casualties, beginning with Dunkerque, when only two of the score of canteens returned to England. In the United States the Salvation Army clubs, some operating in conjunction with the USO, provided sleeping accommodations for a million and a half men on leave or furlough; almost a million soldiers asked for and received individual counsel and 260,000 soldiers had voice recordings made to send back home in addition to those made in hospitals. Other war-related services included a home in France where children returned from Germany might remain until their parents were found, a refugee boys' home and "warphanage" in China, soldier and sailor rest homes in South America and the Middle East, homes for evacuées from England's bombings, grocery stores in Canada for stranded families in boom towns, dining rooms in the United States for children of war workers, restaurants in Belgium for child and adult refugees, and hostess houses throughout the United States for families and friends of enlisted men. Salvation Army chaplains served with all armies of the Allied nations, adapting religious observances to circumstances and location—religious guidance and consolation were given to all requesting them, regardless of creed, race, or color.

Discussing the servicemen's clubs, Commander Pugmire said: "What servicemen want in their free time is to get out somewhere—get away from authority. We don't try to proselytize. We don't try to coerce them into enjoying themselves. We don't try to make them dance if they happen to be in the mood to write a letter home. We don't insist on their hearing popular music if they prefer—and you'd be surprised how many do—Beethoven or Tchaikovsky."

Toward the close of 1945 the Salvation Army adopted an expanded program designed to give five types of aid to veterans. It had been carefully planned to avoid overlapping or duplication of Government or other programs for veterans. The five types of assistance include family aid, emergency assistance, aid of an informational nature, vocational-rehabilitation aid, and spiritual help. The program, according to the Commissioner would be carried out in 1,867 cities and towns in the United States.

Commander Pugmire is described as a fluent and effective speaker, a man with a photographic memory; he rarely forgets a thing which he has seen written down. He has always been fond of exercise and of outdoor sports, particularly tennis, although he regards sports more as a means of keeping fit than as recreation. He reads widely, especially biography, history, and economics. Although the Pugmires have five children, Mrs. Pugmire has been a leader in women's work wherever they happened to be stationed. (Salvation Army officers are permitted to marry only "under the flag"; after marriage the wife shares her husband's title and as far as possible his work.) A woman of unusual charm and an experienced leader, she is now territorial leader of the League of Mercy which was organized for the purpose of visiting prisoners, sick persons, and others needing attention or sympathy.

PYLE, ERNEST TAYLOR *See* Pyle, E.

PYLE, ERNIE (pīl) Aug. 3, 1900—Apr. 18, 1945 American journalist and war correspondent; killed by Japanese machine-gun fire on the island of Ie, west of Okinawa, where he was covering the front; his two books *Here Is Your War* (1943) and *Brave Men* (1944) were best sellers; admired by public, GI's, and officers alike. See *Current Biography* 1941 Yearbook.

Obituary

N Y Times p1+ Ap 19 '45 pors

RAMA RAU, SANTHA (rä'mä rou sän'thä) Jan. 24, 1923- Author

Address: b. c/o Harper & Bros., 49 E. 33d St., New York City

For its refreshing, readable contrast to serious and weighty works on the complex problem of India, an autobiographical book by Santha Rama Rau, a Hindu girl educated at Wellesley, has won the unanimous approval of American critics. Informal, humorous, honest, and explicit, *Home to India* (1945) should— according to reviewers—do a great deal toward clarifying and interpreting India to the West. In midsummer 1945 the book was on the nonfiction list of best-sellers.

Its author is entitled by birth to wear on her forehead the distinguishing mark of "one of the most rarefied subdivisions of the Brahman caste." Santha Rama Rau was born January 24, 1923, in Madras, India. Her Cambridge-educated father, Sir Benegal Rama Rau, had married Dhanvanthi, daughter of Pandit R. K. Handoo, and was serving in the Finance Department of the Government of India when Santha and her sister Premila were little girls. The girls traveled with their parents to their father's various stations in India. When he was appointed a member of the Round Table Conference in London, Santha was taken to England and sent to primary school in Weybridge, Surrey, then to St. Paul's in London. Later, when he was Deputy High Commissioner for India, her father remained in the London headquarters. Since he had to attend a good many conferences in European capitals, during vacations Santha and Premila joined their parents and saw a good deal of Europe. Then, in 1938, her father was appointed Indian High Commissioner in South Africa, and the following year the family visited him there. When war broke out in Europe it was impossible for them to get return passage to England. Accordingly, her mother took the girls back to India with her.

It was then, at sixteen, and with her viewpoint shaped by her life and education in England, that the young Indian girl saw her native land after years of absence. Santha Rama Rau wanted to understand India, to understand also the complex differences between Eastern and Western cultures, between the ruling and the ruled, between herself and those who had never left India. Her mother gave her this advice: "Feeling at home here and, as you put it, understanding Indians, is mostly I think a matter of having something to contribute to Indian life—something, that is, that Indians want—and of having or acquiring the technique of contributing it."

In order to learn what she might contribute, Miss Rama Rau traveled through her native land, accompanied by several servants. Her travels included an interlude of camping in the Himalayas, which was recorded by a staff photographer from *Life* Magazine. But Miss Rama Rau managed to see a good deal of the poverty and misery, the ignorance and filth that were the ordinary lot of many Indians. She talked also with the younger Indians in the Congress Movement, and she decided that she stood with Gandhi [42] and Nehru [41] on the question of political independence.

Because she had crossed water, eaten beef, and neglected to wear her caste mark, Santha Rama Rau had lost the privileges of her religion and caste, but she was still forbidden to marry outside her Brahman caste. She had not only to grapple with these problems, but with those of color and of race prejudice. No Indian, whatever his caste, was allowed to enter the British clubs in India (in South Africa she had seen signs, "Indians, natives, and wild dogs not allowed"). There were social and other conventions which Miss Rama Rau and her sister felt were "not only retrogressive and socially crippling to the country, but also a little ridiculous." When she inadvertently invited an English boy to her grandmother's house, she had to forestall his arrival by meeting him at a club: Europeans are not received in strict Brahman homes.

But the sympathies of the British-educated girl were nevertheless with India—and she wanted to join other young Indians working to better conditions there. "Here things were just beginning," she felt. "Here anybody could be a pioneer." Most of all, she felt the need of a working knowledge of the "mechanics of democracy." Since British intentions were distrusted in India, Miss Rama Rau decided to go to America to study, and Wellesley was the college her mother chose for her.

SANTHA RAMA RAU

At Wellesley, which she entered in 1941, Miss Rama Rau specialized in English while learning what she could about the workings of American democracy. She put her education to practical use by writing for the News and Features Bureau of the Office of War Information in New York during college vacations. After her graduation with a B.A. degree in 1944 she worked for several weeks with the Commission to Study the Organization of Peace. She then began her book, *Home to India*, which was published in May 1945.

Her experiences and impressions have been written—as Orville Prescott noted—from a point of view that is "partly that of a tourist and partly that of an initiate of Indian affairs." Lewis Gannett [41] called the book the only one about India that he had read which was "young and gay." Other reviewers, too, gave it a warm reception. The New York *Herald Tribune* book reviewer said that it was "worth one battleship, two cruisers, and three regiments in the difficult business of making one world. . . .A more delightful, more honest little book it is difficult to imagine." The New York *Times'* critic found it a calm, sincere plea for Indian nationalism. According to the *Christian Science Monitor*, it "may succeed in interpreting India to the West in a way which more weighty volumes often fail to do."

Santha Rama Rau is described as tall, slender, and attractive, fond of tennis and dancing. She has traveled in New England and has lived in New York City, where she had a studio apartment in a modernized brownstone house. There an interviewer found her wearing not her usual Indian sari, but "a white jersey dress, with bobby socks and white sandals." In fact, the writer commented, "she looked as if she'd just stepped off a nice cool tennis court." Speaking of the Indian people, Miss Rama Rau said many were tenant farmers and sharecroppers, and she thought a project like the TVA and a planned agricultural economy would be the sort of New Deal India wanted—provided the British withdrew and

RAMA RAU, SANTHA—*Continued*

gave India independence. In July 1945 she returned home, planning first to spend a long vacation with her family in Kashmir, then to find some way to participate usefully in Indian affairs.

References

PM Mag p3+ Jl 29 '45 por
Rau, S. R. Home to India (1945)

RAMSAY, SIR BERTRAM (HOME)
1883—Jan. 2, 1945 British admiral, supreme Allied naval commander in chief under General Dwight Eisenhower '42; killed in a plane crash; considered the world's foremost expert on planning and organizing vast naval expeditions; responsible for engineering the Dunkerque rescue; planned the naval phase of the landings in North Africa, Sicily, Italy, and Normandy. See *Current Biography* 1944 Yearbook.

Obituary

N Y Times p1+ Ja 3 '45 por

RANK, J(OSEPH) ARTHUR Dec. 23, 1888- British motion picture producer; industrialist

Address: b. 49 Park Lane, London; h. Heathfield, Reigate Heath, Surrey, England

J. ARTHUR RANK

Admirers of J. Arthur Rank, Britain's film czar, prophesy that Hollywood producers, long accustomed to dominating the world film market without appreciable opposition, may soon have to exert themselves to meet his competition. For the ambition of this British industrialist, owner of 60 per cent of British film production facilities, is to create a market for English films where American films have heretofore held unchallenged sway and, incidentally, to recapture some of the money which has been drained out of the Empire.

Joseph Arthur Rank was born into the Methodist background which has colored his entire life on December 23, 1888, in Hull, Yorkshire. His mother was Emily (Voase) Rank. His father was the unobtrusive but fabulous Methodist industrialist and philanthropist Joseph Rank, who transformed the inheritance of a Yorkshire grain mill into a hundred-million-dollar flour industry which today (under the management of his sons J. Arthur and James Voase) supplies an estimated one-fifth to one-third of England's total requirement of that commodity. The boy attended the Leys School in Cambridge, and Western College, West Riding, Yorkshire. But at the age of seventeen he left school to enter the family business—by now the industrial empire of Ranks, Ltd.—as a thirteen-hour-a-day junior clerk. After serving his apprenticeship, Rank was appointed manager of Peterkin's Self-Raising Flour, a Rank subsidiary—and proceeded to lose, according to *Fortune*, a million pounds. It is said, however, that this is the only time that Rank has lost money and that his father attributed the incident to lack of experience. During the First World War Rank served with a field ambulance unit in France, and in 1919 he returned to the management of his father's flour mills. Until 1935 the milling industry continued to be his primary concern and he remained a familiar figure in "the City" (the Wall Street of London).

In the middle thirties, however, Rank's zeal for Methodism determined his investment of some of his fortune in an effort to raise the standard of religious films then being shown to Methodist Sunday school children. Forming the Religious Films Society together with his father and others, Rank began his connection with the motion picture industry by financing several religious shorts. At the same time he helped finance a film of life in Yorkshire fishing villages entitled *The Turn of the Tide*. Although this picture achieved third place at the International Film Exhibit held in Venice, it received few showings in Britain, and Rank turned to the box office to find out the reason. While he was "still poised on the threshold looking at it," continues *Fortune*, "and deliberating whether to gamble his extra energy and his money on [the industry]. . . Lord Portal and the banking firm of Japhets pushed him into it." Acting for the Board of Trade, Lord Portal had singled out Rank—who had both the capital and the apparent interest—to rescue the British motion picture industry from imminent collapse.

Since its beginnings the British film industry had operated at a loss because of its inability to meet the competition of Hollywood, which was accounting for as much as 87 per cent of Britons' screen fare. In an attempt to remedy the situation, the Government had established film quotas in 1927. But this move had resulted only in a scramble for the new market on the part of small, inexperienced British producers and American companies incorporated in England, all producing poor films. Hollywood products continued to dominate the English screen, and a ten-million-dollar loss in a cinema investment, such as that sustained by the Prudential Assurance Company, became not uncommon. In the marketing of Alexander Korda's *The Private Life of Henry VIII*, however, Lord Portal had seen a corrective for the existing conditions. A good picture, it had made money not only in England but in the United States. If, therefore, Britain could produce more pictures which would make money in the United States and use the profits realized to finance other pictures, these pictures could compete in the world market, especially in the United States market, which constituted 65 per cent of that market—and the problem of the film industry would be solved. This was the idea Portal broached to Rank.

In 1935, when Rank was not yet ready to risk alone the millions necessary for such a venture, assistance came from C. M. Woolf, veteran movie man and organizer of Gaumont-British's theater chain. Together they established General Film Distributors, Ltd., and Rank acquired several small theater circuits and began production on a small scale. Then, in 1936 he created the holding company General Cinema Finance Corporation and increased the scale of his operations. His first big opportunity came when a group of American bankers were seeking a purchaser for a 25 per cent interest at two million dollars in Universal Pictures Corporation stock. Buying through General Cinema Finance Corporation, Rank entered into an agreement whereby he obtained distribution rights to Universal pictures in Britain and production and distribution rights to the newsreel the company had been placing on the British market. Next he was able to buy into the extensive Odeon Theatre Chain, of which he was to get control in 1941. When Gaumont-British ran into financial difficulty, Rank by fiscal maneuvering was able to acquire 5,100 of the 10,000 voting shares of the holding company, the Metropolitan and Bradford Trust, which controlled that organization and its numerous subsidiaries. He "achieved control," notes *Fortune*, "with the assistance of bankers who regarded him as one of the best risks in England for psychological credit" because of his "Methodist rectitude."

Rank was now in control of two of the three major British theater chains, a major producing company and a growing distribution organization. And he set out to complete what he called the "rationalization" of the industry. Having already built a studio at Pinewood, he prevailed upon Alexander Korda and Prudential Assurance to sell him their studio at Denham, the best in England. He also bought from Korda a film and print laboratory near the studio and acquired G.B.-Kalee, Ltd., the purveyor of nearly 90 per cent of British theater and studio equipment. "Rank," comments *Fortune*, "did all this in eight years [1935-43] and at exactly the right time. He bought at the bottom and was in possession at the time of the movies' greatest boom. During the war Britons could spend their money on practically nothing but films, and Arthur Rank's theaters took a little less than a third of all the admissions. Profits were so plentiful that most of them were in danger of being drained away in excess-profits taxes. Rank realized the hour to take the big gamble had struck."

Rank wanted, continues *Fortune*, "to use his theater profits to produce expensive pictures that would really put Britain on the movie map." But he was not to be allowed to do so. Before he could get started on his objective, he ran into opposition in the form of a Cinematograph Films Council monopoly investigation for the Government. In the late spring of 1943 the Trades Union Congress, acting for the cinema industry unions, lodged with the Board of Trade a protest concerning the growing monopoly in the industry. In a letter from Hugh Dalton '45, president of the Board, Rank was told: "The Government, which desires to see the development of a vigorous and successful film industry, and which looks to you to play an important part in achieving this aim, lately has been much concerned at the appearance of certain monopolistic tendencies." The Government would allow him to complete several deals then pending, Dalton continued, but further extensions of his film interests in Britain would not be tolerated. With these directives Rank complied.

As the protests continued, however, the Films Council, an advisory body of the Board of Trade, was delegated to investigate—despite active defense of and commendation for Rank in Parliament, and especially in the House of Lords, for his rehabilitation of and leadership in the industry. The Film Council's report established the existence of monopoly not solely by Rank but by Rank and his largest rival, Associated British Pictures. Of Britain's 5,000 cinemas, observers pointed out, 2,000 are first-run, and only 600 of these were under Rank's control. Of the 30 production stages active in early 1945, only 15 were Rank-owned. Thus, they noted, 1,400 first-run houses and 15 active production stages did not belong to Rank. But if the Associated British Pictures holdings were included in the total, only 950 first-run theaters, including only one-third of their number in the remunerative London area, and only 10 active production stages were found to be independent, thus indicating, in the words of one critic, "an almost complete stranglehold" by the two combines. No action was taken against Rank, however, first, because there is no statutory provision for the prevention of monopoly, and, secondly, because the beneficial effect of a strong competitor against Hollywood was recognized.

The agitation about monopoly having lessened, Rank turned once more toward expansion in a world market. While the British film industry had been considerably rehabilitated through the efforts of Rank, the original problem of enlarging the British market for British films and of securing global sales remained. (Statistics show that American producers earned eighty-three million dollars in Britain in 1944.) In June 1945, therefore, the producer made a business trip to the United States, on which he was royally feted by Hollywood moguls. His aims were to study Hollywood movie-making technique, to initiate or complete negotiations with Hollywood producers which might prevent the reoccurrence of such releasing troubles as he had had with Twentieth Century-Fox on *The Way Ahead*, and to determine the reasons for the limited appeal of English movies for American audiences, a problem which he had already been investigating by means of judi-

RANK, J. ARTHUR—*Continued*

cious questioning of GI's in England and through the agency of special investigaters mingling with American movie audiences. Before he returned to England Rank had arranged for the interchange of stars and technicians between England and the United States, had formed a company with David O. Selznick '41—Selznick International Pictures of England, Ltd.—"for the joint production of super-colossal features in Britain," had made a similar arrangement with RKO, and had agreed to finance the leasing of New York's Winter Garden by United Artists as a showcase for Rank pictures. (The first picture to be shown in the theater was the film Adaptation of Noel Coward's '41 *Blithe Spirit*, photographed, as the advertisements proclaimed, in "blushing Technicolor.") Earlier, Rank had set up Eagle-Lion Films, Inc., as an American distributing, and ultimately producing, unit for his films. He had also bought a half-interest in Odeon Theatres of Canada, Ltd., and was believed to have made advantageous deals in both Russia and France.

Rank realized that his only hope was to produce films of such quality that American exhibitors would wish to present them. He believes that quality counts in film making and that adult pictures will sell. "Your people have a low opinion of the American public," he told Hollywood skeptics on his American visit. "I don't. I think if Shakespeare is done properly, they'll like it." Despite the American box-office failure of *Colonel Blimp* (1945) and *Mr. Emmanuel* (1945), he is confident that his *Henry V* (costing $2,000,000) and *Caesar and Cleopatra* (costing $5,000,000—to *Gone With the Wind*'s $3,800,000) will make money in the United States. But he also realized that he would have to glamorize British stars and to key both material and method to American audiences, as he had done in *Way to the Stars*, in order to accomplish his objective. As to a possible film war between Britain and the United States, Rank said: "Our growing up does not create a conflict between the American and British film industries. Rather it creates a most healthy condition of fair competition, good for all concerned—and the best films will attract the widest audiences when they are given an opportunity to be exhibited. All we ask is that, if our films are entertaining enough and good enough, a fair proportion of the audiences of the world shall be given a chance to see them. Where Britain's films are given a chance to be tested at the box office, they usually stand the public test well and will do better and better as we progress." To a colleague in England he wrote while in the United States: "In my heart I have a great desire to cooperate with our American friends. I believe we can give more to the world if we work together than if we each go our own way. Whatever rebuffs I get I shall stick to this policy and return to the charge again and again."

In his latest move to achieve wider world circulation for British films, Rank, in November 1945, established United World Pictures Company in association with Universal Pictures Corporation and International Pictures, both of Hollywood. Forming a second unit for the reciprocal distribution of British and American motion pictures three weeks later, Rank joined with Pathé Industries, Inc., in the organization of Eagle Lion Films, which will become operative in September 1946.

A normal working day for Rank, whose business interests also include such companies as the B.I. Transport Company, Ltd., Sunbeam Milk Bars, Ltd., and Methodist Newspapers, Ltd., begins at 8:30 A.M. and rarely ends before one or two o'clock the next morning. "He works," writes Francis Sill Wickware in *Life*, "even while being driven from office to office and has the door open and is ready to leap out while the car is still moving. . . . [He] keeps the details of his enterprises under close personal scrutiny and does not delegate much to others. . . . His 'office' consists mainly of four heavy brief cases which he carries with him wherever he goes. Somehow he can find immediately any paper he wants, even though the documents in the brief cases pertain to the intricate affairs of no fewer than sixty different companies." Rank made himself equally at home in "fairyland" Hollywood and grain center Minneapolis. At Hollywood parties, as a teetotaler, he drank fruit juices or ginger ale—in addition to his tea. *Life* tells that he kept his watch on British time while in the film colony. Rank was married to the Honorable Laura Ellen Marshall, daughter of Lord Marshall of Chipstead, in 1917. The couple have two daughters; Ursula and Shelagh. They own, in addition to their Reigate home, a fifteen-thousand-acre estate, Sutton Manor, in Hampshire, where Rank has constructed an intricate practice golf course. His recreations are golfing and shooting. He is a powerfully built man, six feet tall, weighing 184 pounds, with brown eyes and black hair. Said one observer: "His shrewd brown eyes are set close to a long, hawklike nose, and his forehead is ridged with wrinkles that come from intensive scrutiny of the motives and maneuverability of men."

References

Fortune 32:149+ O '45 por
Life 19:106+ O 8 '45 pors
Time 42:86+ D 20 '43 pors
Who's Who, 1945

RAWLINGS, SIR (HENRY) BERNARD (HUGHES) May 21, 1889- British naval officer

Address: b. c/o British Admiralty, London; h. Lancarffe, Bodmin, England

At the time of the surrender of Japan in August 1945, Vice-Admiral Sir Bernard Rawlings was in command of the carrier force which bombarded Japan, second in command under Admiral Sir Bruce Fraser '43, commander in chief of the British Pacific Naval Forces. In at the kill, Rawlings' units were supporting the larger American fleets in the Allied attacks on the Japanese mainland. Sir Bernard has been in the Royal Navy for more than forty years, and has seen service in all parts of the world. He spent three years in Tokyo itself as naval attaché, and he is determined, he says, to destroy the Japanese military caste and see it discredited in the eyes of the Japanese.

The son of W. J. Rawlings, Henry Bernard Hughes Rawlings (always called "Bernard" to avoid confusion with Rear Admiral Henry Clive Rawlings, his older cousin) was born in Hayle, Cornwall, on May 21, 1889. He went to school at Stanmore Park, and at the age of fifteen entered the Navy as a cadet in the H.M.S. *Britannia*. He was graduated as a torpedo officer, and received his first assignment as a lieutenant two months after the outbreak of the First World War. From August 1915 to April 1917 he was in the *Antrim*, and until the end of the war, nineteen months later, he carried out paravane and torpedo duties on the H.M.S. *Undaunted* and *Coventry*, with the Harwich Force. (A paravane is a safety device against moored mines.) One month after the Armistice Rawlings, then a lieutenant commander, was assigned to accompany a mission to Poland. In 1919 he was appointed naval liaison officer to the British military mission at Warsaw, at which post he remained for three years, receiving the Order of the British Empire in 1920 in recognition of his services there.

The year 1922 found Rawlings as torpedo officer in the *Diomede*. Then he became an instructor in H.M.S. *Vernon*, the torpedo school at Portsmouth, took the staff course at Greenwich, and in 1927 was back again as fleet torpedo officer in the *Revenge*. Rawlings received a promotion to captain three years later, when he was forty-one, and was given the commands, successively, of the *Curacao, Active,* and the *Delhi*, after completing a senior officers' tactical course. In 1935 Captain Rawlings was graduated from the Imperial Defence College, where he had received advanced training, and was sent to Japan as naval attaché in the British Embassy in Tokyo. The officer was in Japan during the years from 1936 to 1939, crucial ones both in Europe and the Far East. It was during Rawlings' service in Tokyo that the Japanese captured Shanghai, Nanking, Hankow, and Canton. The capture of these cities greatly affected British sentiment towards Japan, for England had large commercial interests particularly in Canton and Shanghai.

Rawlings returned to England in March 1939, and in August of the same year, just before the outbreak of the Second World War, he was put in command of the battleship *Valiant*. When France fell in the summer of 1940 many ships were ordered to the Mediterranean in order to strengthen Britain's position in those strategic waters, and among them was the *Valiant*. In company with the aircraft carrier *Illustrious* and two cruisers, she was sent to Alexandria. In that same year Rawlings, who had already been mentioned in dispatches for "successful operations against the enemy," was promoted to rear admiral, and was assigned to the command of the First Battle Squadron. In 1941 his squadron engaged the Italians at Matapan and sunk five ships of the Italian Fleet and damaged others at a cost of only one British aircraft.

In the spring he was given command of the Seventh Cruiser Squadron. With the *Warspite,* and the *Valiant,* Rawlings lay off the west coast of Crete, the rumor of his presence keeping the Italians out of those waters. A week later, when the German air force had

British Official Photo.

VICE-ADM. SIR BERNARD RAWLINGS

invaded the island, Admiral Rawlings was called upon to evacuate the Heraklion garrison. He accomplished this mission, but not without encountering serious difficulties: One destroyer was lost and another crippled; the captain of the *Orion,* Rawlings' flagship, was killed, and the Admiral himself was wounded. In this action Rawlings made manifest his "fearless judgment and gallant bearing," and it was said that he extricated his squadron with great determination in the face of the gravest dangers. Later in January 1942 he was made a Companion of the Bath "for gallantry, leadership, and skill during the Battle of Crete." When he recovered from his injuries Rawlings resumed command of the Seventh Cruiser Squadron, which consisted now of only two cruisers, and took part with the addition of two destroyers in the defense of Malta by blowing up an ammunition ship in the face of superior Italian forces, and sinking a destroyer and tanker, all in one day.

In March 1942 the Admiral returned home to receive an Admiralty appointment, serving in England for one year as Assistant Chief of Naval Staff. But in 1943 Rawlings, now acting vice-admiral, was back again in active service, this time as flag officer in West Africa during the Tunisian campaign. In November of the same year he received his promotion to vice-admiral, and two months later it became known that Vice-Admiral Rawlings was back in the Eastern Mediterranean, with a force of cruisers, carriers, submarines, flotillas of mine sweepers, and coastal craft, as well as a contingent of the Greek Navy, and French and Polish vessels. He supervised the harassing of German ships and transports, and the routing of them from that area. Shortly after that Rawlings was relieved of his Mediterranean command, knighted by King George VI[42], and then given another command at sea.

It was in March 1945 that the first reports of joint British-American action in the Pacific

RAWLINGS, SIR BERNARD—*Cont.*

were received in dispatches on the battle of the Ryukyu Islands. Admiral Nimitz issued a communique to the effect that British forces had destroyed twenty enemy aircraft on the ground, shattered one coastal vessel and wrecked several others, and had left the town of Ohama in flames. It was reported that at the beginning of the Allied attack on the Ryukyu Islands (directed by an American, Admiral Raymond A. Spruance [44]) Commodore Worrall R. Carter of the United States Navy sent the English flagship this message, blinked from his ship: "Good hunting, good luck, and Godspeed to you, British brothers." And Rawlings made the reply, "Thank you very much, I hope we meet again, Commodore—nearer Tokyo."

By July 17 Admiral Rawlings and the British task force were nearer Tokyo, together with the American Third Fleet under the command of Admiral William F. Halsey [42]. In fact, the combined British and American fleet was so near to the general area of Tokyo that they were able to shatter it with shells. In these midsummer battles in the Pacific, the British naval forces showed themselves to be highly adaptable to changed circumstances, for they had to depart from century-old tactics and adopt new ones. For years the British Navy had fought from bases spaced no more than a thousand miles apart, but in the Ryukyu Islands battles it had to operate from the nearest British base in Australia, four thousand miles away. These new tactics have made obligatory the use of a fleet train, an American invention, a kind of floating naval base. A dispatch to the New York *Times* on April 19, 1945, reported that the British sea forces had shown a finer grasp of long-range fighting in every new operation in which they participated.

The British force under Sir Bernard included the 35,000-ton battleship *King George V,* the 23,000-ton carrier, *Formidable,* two cruisers, and five destroyers. This British force accompanied the American Third Fleet when Admiral Halsey began his attack on the Japanese mainland, steaming within ten miles of the coast of Honshu, northeast of Tokyo, under a black and heavily overcast sky. (The British attack was the first strike against the Japanese homeland, in retaliation for the Japanese sinking of the *Repulse* and the *Prince of Wales* off Singapore early in the Pacific war, in December 1941.) These history-making attacks led by Admiral Halsey resulted for the Japanese in the loss of 1,278 airplanes destroyed or damaged, and a total of 1,035 Japanese surface craft sunk in the Honshu waters, according to the announcement of Admiral Nimitz on August 1, 1945. The Allied forces also succeeded in shelling and bombing industrial centers in the Tokyo area, but perhaps even more important, British-American cooperation was said to be something of a psychological blow to the Japanese, who had hoped to benefit from any British-American disunity.

Sir Bernard Rawlings is said to possess the stout courage and ready judgment of the warrior, and a gift for friendliness in his relations with the men of his ships. Off duty he is known as "a first-class international mixer." The Admiral's own personal postwar plans are to return to his family, at least for a time; his wife, Eva Loveday, to whom he was married in 1922, and their three children, two sons and a daughter, await him in their home in Lancarffe, Bodmin, where Sir Bernard has been accustomed to enjoy his favorite recreations of fishing and gardening. In September 1945, as if to mark the official surrender of Japan, Vice-Admiral Rawlings became a Knight of the British Empire in recognition of his services in command of the British task force.

References

N Y Sun p20 Ap 4 '45
Who's Who, 1945

RAY, (JACKSON HARVELLE) RANDOLPH, REV. June 11, 1886- Clergyman

Address: Church of the Transfiguration, 1 E. 29th St., New York City

Rector for the past twenty-three years of New York's Episcopal Church of the Transfiguration, more popularly called the Little Church Around the Corner, is the Reverend Dr. Randolph Ray, who is also known as an author and lecturer.

Jackson Harvelle Randolph Ray was born June 11, 1886 in Madison County, Mississippi, the son of Jackson H. Ray and of the former Alice More Spottswood Tidwell. On his father's side he is a descendant of Sir Christopher Wray, Lord Chief Justice in Queen Elizabeth's reign, and of William Wray, who came to America at the time of the Restoration of Charles II. Through his mother his most famous American antecedent is Governor Alexander Spottswood of Virginia. Randolph's father, a veteran of the Confederate Army, was a gentleman farmer, owner of a cotton plantation. Young Randolph received his early education at private schools and through governesses. His mother, a devout person, encouraged the boy's study of religion, hoping that he might some day enter the clergy. One of Randolph's childhood delights was to put on a white apron and preach to the fowl in their coops.

In 1905 young Ray received his B.A. from Emory and Henry College, Virginia, and came to New York intending to study medicine at Columbia University. According to Dr. Ray, his brief inspection of the various laboratories on his first day at medical school was enough, and he turned almost immediately to the study of law. After a year (1906) at law school journalism attracted him. He therefore abandoned law to take post graduate work in English at Columbia University. While at Columbia, the late Dr. Brander Matthews of the English Department was enough impressed with Ray's writing ability to introduce him to Frank Andrew Munsey, then publisher of several magazines and owner of the New York *Evening Sun* and *Evening Telegram.* Ray wrote articles for Munsey's publications as well as thrillers for the pulp magazines while at Columbia, but devoted the major part of his time to writing for and editing trade magazines. He also worked briefly as a reporter for the Brooklyn *Eagle.*

Ray's vocational experiments had apparently not been satisfactory. In 1908 the once aspiring doctor-lawyer-writer entered the General Theological Seminary in New York City. Three years later he was ordained deacon, and a year later priest of the Protestant Episcopal Church. From 1911 to 1914 he was curate of the Church of Zion and St. Timothy in New York; then he assumed the rectorship of St. Andrew's Church in Bryan, Texas, and was at the same time chaplain at the near-by Texas Agricultural and Mechanical College. Rejected by the Red Cross for services overseas during the First World War, he became dean at St. Matthew's Cathedral in Dallas, Texas, and civilian chaplain at an adjacent air-force station. In April, 1923, he became rector of the Church of the Transfiguration, The Little Church Around the Corner, in New York City.

The Church of the Transfiguration, founded in 1848, was built at 29th Street and Fifth Avenue— a section of New York City then referred to as Lovers' Lane. Its founder and first rector, Dr. George Hendric Houghton, has been described as the First Saint of the American Episcopal Church. A supporter of the most conservative viewpoints, Dr. Houghton was also an upholder of unconventional action "when he believed it to be right." Under Dr. Houghton's pastorate the church gained a reputation for kindly, liberal acts. It first broke with conservative tradition during the last year of the Civil War when it offered refuge to Negroes.

In 1870, paradoxically for the church that was to become known for weddings, the funeral of an actor made it famous. The widow of the well known English actor, George Holland, sought with the help of Joseph Jefferson to have her husband buried from a church on near-by Madison Avenue. The minister of that church said it would be impossible to hold services for an actor, but suggested that they go to the "little church around the corner." Jefferson's explanation to Dr. Houghton of the Church of the Transfiguration brought the reply: "I only know that your friend is dead and my services are asked. That is quite enough." Since that day the influx of theatrical folk as parishioners has increased steadily. Actors were the first to make it popular as a church from which to be married, and today the church contains memorial windows to such actors as Joseph Jefferson, Edwin Booth, John Drew, and Richard Mansfield. The once tiny edifice is now a small cathedral with world-wide fame. Says Dr. Ray: "First the brides came from New York City and its vicinity; then from the Middle West and Far West; later from Europe and the distant corners of the earth. Continuously, children and grandchildren of people married in this church come here to be married."

More than a hundred thousand bridal couples have been married in the church during its ninety-five years of existence. Yet the church is not a Gretna Green, in the sense that couples can be married there easily, at a moment's notice. In the words of Dr. Ray, "Because the Little Church was started under the influence of the Oxford Revival, it adopted the Catholic idea of marriage. The sacramental aspect was emphasized; the bridal couple must not be divorced, they must be baptized, they must enter upon their marriage with the understanding that it is to be for life." Because of these tenets, the church has had to refuse marrying approximately five hundred couples each year. As a young curate, Dr. Ray observed that the

REV. RANDOLPH RAY

wedding service was often badly read. He therefore studied diction with the veteran actor Philip Ben Greet to improve his delivery of the marriage lines. In his twenty-two years of rectorship at the Church of the Transfiguration, he has approved the holding of fifty thousand weddings and has performed more than half of them himself. Although weddings play such a vital role in the work of the church, other services are not neglected. The sick are visited and the needy looked after. In the depths of the depression the church fed seventy-five thousand unemployed in the course of a few weeks.

Dr. Ray's *Marriage Is a Serious Business*, published early in 1944, is in the opinion of the *Churchman* "helpful to the clergy who perform marriages, to the young people who contemplate them, to the mothers who wish to manage them, and even to those who are already married. The book is full of wise advice, kindly humor, deep insight." The clergyman is basically opposed to wartime marriages because a couple are not apt to know each other very well. Before he performs a marriage he poses four questions to the couple: (1) Do you really know each other? (2) Have you similar backgrounds and interests? (3) Are you both really in love? (4) Does the girl realize that when her husband returns home he may be a stranger to her? Dr. Ray urges a war bride not to follow her husband to his various posts, but to set up a home of her own, to keep in touch with her husband's family, and to live within the bounds of her husband's financial scale. He also advises her to keep busy; "to try to grow in understanding with her husband even though he is away, and to cultivate faith in God and in each other."

The rector feels that romance is the best assurance for a happy marriage. His familiar bit of advice to newlyweds is: "Now don't both get mad at the same time." According to Dr. Ray a successful marriage requires as much concentration as a career. Marriage is not, in his opinion, a part-time job, but one that

RAY, REV. RANDOLPH—*Continued*

requires maximum effort throughout one's life. Says the rector of The Little Church Around the Corner: "Marriage is the rock on which our civilization is founded. . . .It has floundered and gone down not on big obstacles but, for the most part, on little ones. And yet there is no one who cannot, if he will, solve the little things. Happiness is in reach and we let it go for an absurd triviality, for a selfish impulse, from an inability to recognize it when we see it." *Marriage Is a Serious Business* has been listed as prescribed reading for social relations courses at Vassar College.

With men returning from overseas to begin anew their civilian and family lives, Dr. Ray feels that "marriage is still a serious business." But he has added three words: "So is divorce." Referring to the tremendous rise in divorce statistics after the war's end, he cautioned young couples to take time to think things over before making the final decision. "Give yourselves time to get reacquainted. . . .Try a second courtship if you feel like strangers. . . . Forget your hurts, your fears, and cooperate toward rescuing your marriage. . . .Only with patience, tolerance, and understanding from both sides will you succeed in re-establishing a good relationship," is his parting advice to young people seeking his help.

Dr. Ray believes the war has given the clergy a wider understanding of the needs of mankind. He believes, too, that "the human being must cultivate himself today precisely because war has a tendency to take human life cheaply and make it seem of slight importance. In wartime we must find God somewhere, and religion must rally people to the old standards and help them keep up their morale." The rector feels the hope of the world lies in the breaking down of prejudices and in the practice of the simple teachings of religion in everyday life. On Armistice Day in 1942 Dr. Ray dedicated the church's Victory Shrine, before which daily prayers are held for victory and peace on behalf of six thousand servicemen who have visited it. Celebrating the end of hostilities with the Japanese, Dr. Ray said in the V-J sermon on September 2, 1945, that peace cannot be imposed by laws, by treaties, or by "the immemorial methods which resort to the sword. We can no longer depend on the means of warfare to defend our inalienable rights. We have come to our last chance and the knowledge that the world's only resort is brotherhood in the sense of these things in which we are alike and in which we have a common interest."

The rector of the Little Church Around the Corner has told of his interest in astrology and the theater. For many years he was a close friend of Evangeline Adams, the astrologer, and he recalls her prediction that he would some day be rector of the Little Church. His interest in the theater resulted in his establishing the Dallas Little Theatre in the deanery of St. Matthew's Cathedral, and later in his founding of the Episcopal Actors Guild at the New York church. He is an officer of the Guild, and a member of the Lambs and the Players clubs. The clergyman declares that, contrary to general opinion, the actor is "incurably religious" since the artist is inherently spiritual. In his many years of contact with people of the theater, he has found most of

them applying their faith not only in religious and moral problems but also in their profession. He urges ministers to become affiliated with the different actors' guilds to increase mutual interest between the clergy and members of the theatrical profession. That the rector has helped carry out this self-imposed task is indicated by the words of Frank Gillmore, president of the Association of Actors and Artists of America: "It is here that we actors have been married, have christened our babies and buried our dead—the church that Joe Jefferson made ours when he gave it the most caressing and gentle nickname, the Little Church Around the Corner." To preserve the Little Church on 29th Street has, of course, been one of the rector's important concerns. With the constant leveling of buildings and new construction in the neighborhood, he felt that nothing would save the structure except human sentiment. "Money alone will not do it," he said in 1930 when he organized the "Family of the Little Church Around the Corner." "I am attempting to organize this sentiment for the purpose of perpetuating this church as a national shrine for generations to come as a medium of God's love to men." Some 40,000 persons keep in touch with Dr. Ray and the church by mail and personal contact, even when their church attendance is irregular.

Dr. Ray received the D.D. degree from the University of the South in 1925, and he was a member of the General Conventions of the Protestant Episcopal Church in Detroit (1919), Portland (Oregon) in 1922, Kansas City since 1940, and Cleveland (1943). The rector is a tall, dignified man with an ingratiating smile. Golf and gardening are his favorite means of relaxation. In July 1922 he was married to Mary Elmendorf Watson, a descendant of the Van Cortlandt, Schuyler and Livingston families and of Edward Winslow, early governor of the Plymouth colony. Her death in 1939 was a great loss to Dr. Ray, who describes his late wife as a woman "of beauty, intelligence and poise." His only child, Kathryna Hoffman, was married in 1944 to Lieutenant Courtlandt Nicoll, also a descendant of old New York families. Dr. Ray hopes to write an article on the influence of the three women in his life— his mother, his wife and his daughter.

References

N Y Post Mag p25 N 9 '43 pors
Newsweek 23:86 Mr 13 '44 por
Time 43:49-50 Ap 24 '44 por

Ray, R. Marriage Is a Serious Business (1944)
Who's Who in America, 1944-45
Who's Who in the Clergy, 1935-36

RECKORD, MILTON A(TCHISON)
Dec. 28, 1879- United States Army officer
Address: c/o War Department, Washington, D.C.

Provost Marshal General of the United States Army Forces in the European theater of operations—the chief of the military police units—was Major General Milton A. Reckord. Born December 28, 1879, in Harford County, Maryland, Milton Atchison Reckord entered upon his military career shortly after his twenty-second birthday, when he enlisted on

February 15, 1901, in Company D of the First Infantry of the Maryland National Guard. His aptitude for soldiering was soon recognized: on December 28, 1903, he was appointed captain in the Infantry, Maryland National Guard, after serving as private and first sergeant. In another three years he was promoted to major, on September 27, 1906; and on June 28, 1916, in the same rank, he was mustered into Federal service, serving on the Mexican border with the First Infantry, National Guard, until November 4, 1916.

When the United States entered the First World War not many months after the Mexican expedition, Major Reckord was again called into service for duty with the First Infantry, Maryland National Guard, on May 29, 1917. He was immediately assigned as a student to the School of Fire, Fort Sill, Oklahoma, where he stayed from May until August of that year. Promoted to lieutenant colonel on August 5, 1917, he was transferred to the Fifth Infantry of the National Guard. Soon thereafter that unit was renumbered the 115th Infantry, Twenty-ninth Division, and was stationed at Fort McClellan, Alabama. Reckord was next assigned to the Brigade and Field Officers School at Fort Sam Houston, Texas. After his graduation, he received his promotion to colonel on May 1, 1918, when he assumed command of the 115th Infantry.

The following month Colonel Reckord and his unit sailed for France with the American Expeditionary Forces, where they participated in the action north of Verdun. For his part in this battle Colonel Reckord was awarded the Distinguished Service Medal as well as the French Croix de Guerre with Palm. His citation for the D.S.M. read in part: "Inspiring his men by his aggressive spirit and fervent devotion to his task, he led them with noted success through three weeks of constant action against the enemy." After the Verdun engagement Reckord attended the Line Officers School at Longeau, France, and, upon the completion of the course, he was assigned to command the Fifty-seventh Infantry Brigade. The brigade, after defending the Center Sector (in Alsace) under Colonel Reckord, took part in the Meuse-Argonne offensive, America's greatest battle of the war.

Honorably discharged on June 26, 1919, a month after returning to the United States, Reckord continued his military service with the Officers Reserve Corps, accepting an appointment as colonel in the Infantry on September 1, 1919. During the peacetime years he served in several important posts with the Maryland National Guard. The first of these was as Adjutant General of the State of Maryland in March 1920, followed by three periods of active duty with the War Department General Staff during the years from 1920 to 1924. Appointed a colonel, Adjutant General's Department, Maryland National Guard, on April 30, 1921, Reckord was promoted to brigadier general three months later. After this promotion and service with the War Department General Staff, on March 21, 1924, he was reappointed from the Adjutant General's Department to the rank of brigadier general of the line, and on the same day he assumed command of the Fifty-eighth Infantry Brigade of the Maryland National Guard. During that

U. S. Army Signal Corps
MAJ. GEN. MILTON A. RECKORD

year and in 1925 he also served as president of the National Guard Association.

On April 14, 1934, he was promoted to major general in the National Guard of the United States and assumed command of the Twenty-ninth Division, serving in this capacity through the induction of the division into Federal service on February 3, 1941, until January, 1942, when he was transferred to the headquarters of the Third Corps Area, in Baltimore. The following May he was assigned as commanding general of the Third Corps Area (redesignated Third Service Command), and served with distinction in that post until December 1943. For his ability in reorganizing the Third Service Command, he was awarded the Oak Leaf Cluster to the Distinguished Service Medal in 1944.

In December 1943 General Reckord was ordered to duty in the European theater as Provost Marshal General. In this position the General is responsible for criminal investigation activities, custody and disposition of offenders, as well as duties relating to prisoners of war, stragglers and deserters, traffic control, policing and supervision of civilians in combat areas, and the over-all command of military police units in his theater of operations. At the time of his appointment Reckord was concerned with the discipline, morale, and protection of the American soldiers waiting in England for the imminent invasion of France. His interest was to aid rather than hinder the American soldier in his search for excitement while on furlough. "For in this war," he wrote in *This Week*, June 25, 1944, "the MP isn't so much a cop as a cross between an information bureau and a nurse. We have even put them in white helmets, white leggings, and white gloves, so it will be easier for the men to find them." To the soldiers of the First World War, this is a far cry from the "Who won the war?" wisecrack so freely used then in referring to the MP's.

(Continued next page)

RECKORD, MILTON A.—*Continued*

Once the invasion began the Office of the Provost Marshal was burdened with expected, but fast multiplying, duties. Soldiers lost from their units in the confusion of battle had to be routed through prepared straggler lines. "AWOL's" and deserters apprehended in the rear areas were returned to their units for punishment or confinement. At one time their number was estimated at eighteen thousand, but this number was cut to eight thousand when General Reckord showed that the original figure had been arrived at by adding six hundred to the total each day without deducting the number of men who had been returned to their outfits. Nor were these the only snarls that had to be untangled. Soon after the freeing of Paris in August 1944, the headquarters of the Provost Marshal were moved to that city and the staff immediately set about controlling traffic through the bicycle jams and narrow streets. Supplies to the front were routed through with utmost speed despite the Parisians who, having been used to automobile-free streets, became a hazard to the American and British drivers.

At the end of 1944 the cigarette shortage on both the battlefront in Europe and the home front in the United States reached headline proportions—a shortage which was discovered in part to be due to black market operations among American soldiers in France. In November 1944 General Reckord detailed over one hundred undercover agents to specific areas throughout France. Through these efforts the first arrests were made simultaneously at sixteen places between Cherbourg and Paris on November 27. Two officers and two hundred enlisted men who were arrested by the Army confessed receiving more than two hundred thousand dollars from the sale of stolen American cigarettes in the black market. Courts-martial sentences of those proven guilty ranged from a few months to as much as thirty years.

The duties of the Provost Marshal include supervision of prisoners of war. During the victorious campaigns in France and Germany, when great numbers of prisoners were taken, they were housed and fed as were the American troops in base areas in accordance with the Geneva Convention, and "also in the hope that the hardships of American prisoners in Germany might be eased as a result." The maintenance of order and the distribution of food among civilians in liberated areas were also the tasks of the Provost Marshal until the Allied Military Government was established and had taken over. The rehabilitation of liberated Allied prisoners of war was another responsibility of General Reckord.

Reference

Who's Who in America, 1944-45

REID, FRANK R., SR. Apr. 19, 1879— Jan. 25, 1945 Lawyer; former Illinois Republican Representative to United States Congress (1923-35); served six consecutive terms before retirement; was chief civilian counsel for the late Brigadier General William Mitchell at the latter's court-martial in 1925; became prominent as chairman of the House Flood Control Committee in 1927.

Obituary

N Y Times p21 Ja 26 '45

RENNER, KARL (rĕn'ĕr kärl) Dec. 14, 1870- President of Austria

Address: Vienna

Karl Renner, President of the newly liberated Austrian state, has been a leading figure at the several key points of his country's history over the last thirty-odd years. Born three years after the *Ausgleich* which established the Dual Monarchy, he was the first Chancellor of the Austrian Republic and signer for defeated Austria of the treaty of 1919 which made her a small, powerless state. Later he was one of the Socialist leaders who was jailed in early 1934, when events foreshadowed Austria's annexation by Nazi Germany; he became the first Chancellor of the Provisional Government set up after her liberation, and in December 1945 was elected President of Austria.

The son of peasants, Matthias and Marie (Habiger) Renner, Karl Renner was born in Dolní-Dunajovice, Moravia, on December 14, 1870. He studied law at the University of Vienna, where he was introduced to Neo-Marxist thought, and before his graduation with an LL.D. he became a Social Democrat and leader of the Neo-Marxist movement. (The Neo-Marxists sought to make Marxian socialism evolutionary rather than revolutionary.) In 1907 he was elected a deputy to the National Assembly, and, as a leader of the Social Democrats, he was in the vanguard of the opposition to the Hapsburg monarchy. The Government was notorious for suppression of its heterogeneous minority groups, and in the years leading up to the outbreak of the First World War the spirit of nationalism within the empire became very strong. Renner himself is the author of *Das Selbstbestimmungsrecht der Nationen* ("The Nations' Right to Self-determination"), published in 1918.

This rising and disruptive nationalism in Austria-Hungary was an expression of the feeling prevalent throughout the whole of Europe on the eve of the war. It was particularly strong among the Serbs, Croats and Slovenes—known collectively as the Yugoslavs—within and without the empire. Consequently, when the Dual Monarchy acquired the predominantly Croatian and Serbian provinces of Bosnia and Herzegovina in 1908, the nationalistic fervor of the Serbian Yugoslavs exploded, setting off a series of events that eventually led to the assassination in 1914 of the Archduke Francis Ferdinand, the heir to the Hapsburg throne. In a tense Europe, where the "engrained competitive nationalism [of the great powers] proved to be stronger than the more recently awakened ideal of international conciliation," this event was only the last of the crises that plunged the world into war, and ended in the dissolution of the Austro-Hungarian empire.

The end of Austria-Hungary as a unit came on November 12, 1918, when German Austria was proclaimed a republic and a temporary Cabinet formed with Renner as its head. Attempts were made by Communists to bring Austria into the ranks of the Soviet republics, but Renner thwarted all demands of the Communists made with the object of overthrowing the Provincial Government. In the first republican elections, in February 1919, the Social Democrats won the largest representation in the new National Constitutional Assembly, and Renner, the moderate Socialist, became the first State Chancellor of the Austrian Republic, in a coalition Government composed predominantly of Social Democrats and the conservative Christian Socialists. That summer the Chancellor went to Paris to accept Allied peace terms, and when Foreign Minister Otto Bauer resigned rather than accept certain provisions of the treaty, Renner took over his portfolio. In September, as head of the Austrian delegation, he therefore signed the Treaty of St. Germain with the victorious Allied powers. A second coalition Government was formed the next month, in which Renner retained both the Chancellorship and the Foreign Affairs portfolio. When the coalition was dissolved the following June he remained as Foreign Minister, until his resignation that October.

The establishment of a republic was, however, not to be the solution to Austria's postwar economic and social problems. Under the terms of the Treaty of St. Germain she had been forced to recognize Czechoslovakia, Yugoslavia, and Poland as independent states, and to cede to them and to other states large portions of her land. As a result, she was deprived of three-fourths of her territory and people, and reduced to a small landlocked state. This left the country without sufficient food and raw materials, and trade was cut off by the tariff barriers erected at the end of the war by the succession states of central Europe. To many Austrians at this time, including the Social Democrats, the only way out of this situation was *Anschluss* or union with Germany, a move forbidden by the terms of the treaty and vigorously opposed by the Allies and by the monarchists and clericals within Austria itself. Renner, a member of the National Assembly in 1922 (president from 1931 to 1933), was one of those who supported the union. "Of course we all know," he said, "that as things are now, Austria has no future. We can keep ourselves alive just until the hour of liberation strikes, that is, until we as Germans can decide in favor of the state to which we belong by the nature of things."

The League of Nations, by arranging for loans and supplying financial supervision, came to the aid of the young Republic in the early twenties, and again at the time of the world depression; notwithstanding, a desire for union with Germany remained. With the rise of Hitler [42], however, the *Anschluss* question developed complications, for *Anschluss* now meant union with a Nazified Germany. A subdivision of Hitler's National Socialist Party was established in Austria, and a concerted effort was made by the Nazis to bring about annexation by Germany. Nazism spread rapidly among the conservatives in Austria, and Dollfuss decided to rule by decree in order to maintain the country's independence.

Meanwhile, Austria was disturbed as well by the antagonism between the radical urban proletariat and the conservative rural classes, rep-

KARL RENNER

resented, respectively, by Renner's Social Democrats and the Christian Socialists. (In Vienna, where the Social Democrats were strong—after 1919 they never again gained a majority in the National Government—the city passed legislation providing for social welfare, public health, housing, education, recreation, and city improvements.) The result of this hostility was the formation of two militant organizations, the Schutzbund of the Socialist workers, now opponents of the *Anschluss* movement, and the Heimwehr of the peasants, described as "a type of Fascist organization, strongly anti-Socialist." In February 1934 Dollfuss, seeking the aid of these Austrian Fascists and Mussolini [42] against Germany, began raiding Social Democratic headquarters—the price of Fascist support. When leaders of the party (among them Julius Deutsch [44]) declared a strike, it was put down with accompanying bloodshed by the Army. In the end the party was outlawed and Renner and other leaders jailed. Renner was released the following June, however, there being insufficient evidence to hold him.

Shortly after the suppression of the liberal elements in the country, Austria, by a new constitution, became an authoritarian corporate state like Italy, and universal suffrage was abolished. In July the Nazis made an abortive attempt at a coup d'état that ended with the assassination of Dollfuss. During the next four years Austria, under Chancellor Schuschnigg, became merely an appendage of Germany. On March 13, 1938, this relationship was made official; Austria no longer existed as a nation. Earlier in the month, when there was a faint chance that there might be a plebiscite on the question of *Anschluss*, Renner made this statement: "As a Socialist and as an adherent to the principle of self-determination of nations. . . .I will vote 'Yes.'" Whether this was delivered under pressure is not known.

After Austria's extinction as a state, those democratic forces who did not leave the coun-

RENNER, KARL—*Continued*

try went underground. Renner, too, it is reported by Selwyn James in *PM*, is believed to have worked in the underground movement during the war. Shortly after the Red Army reached Vienna in April 1945 Moscow announced the formation of a Provisional Government headed by the seventy-four-year-old Renner, and consisting of Social Democrats, Communists, and People's Party and nonparty representatives. This government, wrote Ernst Karl Winter, an Austrian political refugee, for the *Nation*, is the kind of government political realists have wanted for Austria since 1930. Renner's Government (Renner himself is anti-Communistic and anti-Soviet) has been recognized by the Soviet Government, but has still to be officially authorized by the British and American governments through their representatives on the Allied Control Council for Austria. In the meantime, it is faced with the problem of feeding a starving population and providing fuel for the winter.

In September the issue of Allied recognition of the Austrian and other provisional governments in Europe was placed before the meeting of the Big Five Foreign Ministers in London. The question seemed to be one of "British-American anxiety over the spread of Communism and Russia's insistence that governments of neighboring states must be friendly to her for security reasons if nothing else." In the case of Austria, it was felt that Renner's Government was more representative of radical Vienna than of the whole of Austria, a condition, according to the Chancellor, that was due to the fact that all of the country had not been liberated when the Government was formed. (Of fourteen Ministers, three were Communists.) In a letter to the *Times* of London, Renner pointed out that Austria had turned for guidance to the League of Nations in 1920, to Rome in 1934, and to Berlin in 1938. Now, he concluded, Austria was turning, not to Moscow, but to the United Nations organization and nothing else. "I hope," he wrote, "to have succeeded in having at least explained that the guaranty for Austria's existence and her future does not rest solely, nor even in the first instance, with the people of her soil, but that it rests, to a higher degree, with the world outside."

Delegates from Austria's nine provinces met in Vienna on September 24, 1945, for the first time since the Anschluss of 1938 to construct a representative Government acceptable to the Allies. The new broadened and strengthened provisional Government, headed by Renner, which came into being as an outgrowth of the three-day conference, was formally recognized by the United States, Great Britain, Russia, and France on October 20. Action was taken in behalf of the four occupying powers by the Allied Control Council, on orders from the members' respective capitals; one of the principal conditions enumerated was that free elections were to be held "as early as possible and no later than December 31."

The first national elections in fifteen years were thus held on November 25. Leopold Figl's Rightist Volkspartei (Catholic People's Party) won more than 51 per cent of the seats. Upon resigning, Renner was designated as acting chancellor of the interim provisional government, pending the meeting of the new National Assembly on December 12. In a joint meeting on December 20, 1945, both chambers unanimously elected Renner Austria's President, to serve six years. Future Presidential elections are expected to be by popular ballot. According to the Constitution of 1929, which has been restored with slight modifications, Renner will have limited powers; he can dissolve Parliament but has no power to veto bills passed by the Lower House.

The elderly Renner, who has spent most of his life in Government service, was once General State Librarian of the National Assembly. He has been president of the International Association for Social Progress in Basle, and a member of the International Cooperative Alliance in London. Since 1901, when his first publication appeared, *Staat und Parlament*, he has been a prolific writer, chiefly in the fields of economics, government, law, and socialism. Some writings were published under the pseudonyms of Rudolf Springer and Synopticus. As head of the Austrian Government he is believed to be the lowest paid chief of state in Europe. With his wife Luise, he lives in an old house in the American zone in Vienna, with which his Government provides him.

References

Encyclopædia Britannica (1929)
International Who's Who, 1942
Who's Who in Central and East-Europe, 1935-36

REYBOLD, EUGENE (rī'bōld) Feb. 13, 1884-   Engineer; Delaware State official; former United States Army officer

Address: b. c/o Delaware State Highway Department, Wilmington, Del.

"Of all [United States] Army units," said *Life* in February 1942, "the Engineers are perhaps best known to the peacetime populace. For, in addition to their concern with military establishments, they obtrude often on the civilian consciousness through such matters as flood control, harbor improvement, public works. Army Engineers built the Washington Monument, the Capitol, and the Library of Congress. But it is in war that the Corps becomes the Army's most resourceful, versatile, and valued property. In the Second World War the Engineer Corps was commanded by Major (later Lieutenant) General Eugene Reybold.

"If there is a tough, dirty job to be done in any combat operation, the Engineers will do it. They are at the head of every attacking force—crossing unfordable rivers in assault boats, establishing bridgeheads, reducing bunkers, pillboxes, and road-blocks, building pontoon bridges and gun emplacements under enemy fire. And they are at the rear of every retreating army—laying mines, demolishing communications, seeking by every deadly means to retard the advancing foe. When, as happens, they are overtaken, they pick up their guns and fight. They are proud of the skills and hazards of their calling. For they know that without the Engineers, no modern army could roll." Or, as General Douglas MacArthur '[41] told General Reybold, "this is distinctly an Engineer's war."

The Engineer chief was born February 13, 1884, in Delaware City, Delaware, the son of John Franklin and Lydia Maxwell (Tybout) Reybold. The first Chief of Engineers not to attend the Military Academy at West Point—which was founded in 1802 as a school for engineers—Eugene Reybold got his civil engineering degree from Delaware College in 1903, when he was nineteen, and went to work for the United States Engineering Department. At twenty-two Reybold was married to Margaret Eyre Moore, now deceased. (Their daughter Elizabeth Tybout—Mrs. Paul F. Yount—is married to an Army officer, and the Reybold's son Franklin Bell, a West Point graduate, is a Coast Artillery officer.)

It was in the United States Coast Artillery Corps that Gene Reybold was commissioned a second lieutenant in September 1908. After two years at Fort Mott, New Jersey, in the course of which he was advanced to first lieutenant, Reybold was ordered to the Philippines for three years of construction quartermaster duties. On his return to the United States, Lieutenant Reybold was stationed at Fort Banks, Massachusetts, while he worked on the coast defenses of Boston Harbor. Completing this assignment in December 1915, the engineer was sent to Fort Monroe, Virginia, to study at the Coast Artillery School, where he remained as instructor and then director of the Department of Enlisted Specialists. His rank became captain in July 1916, major (temporary) at the end of 1917, lieutenant colonel (temporary) on September 5, 1918, and colonel (temporary) two weeks later. Stationed at Monroe throughout the First World War, Reybold never saw combat, then or later; but the "excellent judgment, energy, and foresight" he displayed there won him the Distinguished Service Medal.

At the end of June 1920 Colonel Reybold reverted to the permanent rank of captain, and was promoted to major the following day. At this time he was on quartermaster duty at Fort Monroe, supervising construction there and at Langley Field, Camp Eustis, and a number of other Army posts in Virginia. In February 1922 the thirty-eight-year-old major returned to the Coast Artillery School for a four-month field officer's course, after which he spent the summer on duty with the 202nd Antiaircraft Artillery Regiment of the Illinois National Guard at Camp Custer, Michigan.

Next Major Reybold was ordered to the Command and General Staff School at Fort Leavenworth, Kansas, where he completed the course in June 1923. Remaining at Fort Leavenworth, he spent three years teaching at the General Service Schools. While at the Command and General Staff School he was transferred in April 1926 from the Coast Artillery to the Corps of Engineers, which is said to include the most brilliant graduates of West Point.

After this Reybold was sent to the Army War College in Washington, D.C., which gives the service's highest training. From August 1927 to October 1932 he served at Buffalo, New York, as assistant district engineer and then as district engineer. In this capacity Reybold directed all the engineering works on

U. S. Army Signal Corps
LT. GEN. EUGENE REYBOLD

Lakes Huron and Erie, and on the Niagara and St. Lawrence rivers, and was a member of the National Control Board for Niagara Falls, as well as having some additional duty with the Second Corps Area's organized reserves. In November 1932 Reybold was given his first promotion in twelve years, to lieutenant colonel, and assigned to the Board of Engineers for Rivers and Harbors in the office of the Chief of Engineers.

After a year Reybold was sent to Wilmington, North Carolina, as district engineer, transferring to Memphis, Tennessee, in April 1935. (The widowed colonel was remarried in October 1933, to Ruth Wineow Lord.) In 1937 he successfully fought the tremendous Ohio-Mississippi Valley floods which swept the South and Middle West from Pittsburgh to Memphis. That July he was promoted to colonel and ordered to Little Rock, Arkansas, to become division engineer of the Southwest division.

Three years later Chief of Staff George C. Marshall [740] appointed Reybold to the War Department General Staff as acting assistant chief of staff for supply (C-4), which "oversees most of the household details of Army life, from buying soldiers' underwear to building barracks." (That October, 1940, he was promoted to brigadier general, temporary, and named assistant chief of staff.) "In the greatest peacetime Army expansion in United States history," wrote Time, "the General Staff is as busy as beavers in a springtime flood. . . . True to a custom in Washington (a supposed sop to pacifistic civilian taxpayers), Gene Reybold sat down at his desk in shirtsleeves and mufti, a pair of tortoise-shell spectacles camouflaging his military nose. Like most Army men out of uniform, he managed to look more like a country doctor than like the top-flight soldier he is." Assigned to the Office of the Chief of Engineers as acting chief in September 1941, he was appointed Chief of Engineers in October, with the rank of major general.

(Continued next page)

REYBOLD, EUGENE—*Continued*

Only two months after entering on his four-year term General Reybold was faced with directing construction for a global war. As General MacArthur, himself a former Engineer, said to him two years later, "Reybold, this is an air and amphibian war; because of the nature of air and amphibian operations, it is distinctly an Engineer's war." First the Engineers had to put up the largest office building in the world, the War Department's giant Pentagon. Begun in September, 1941, on a design by David J. Witmer and G. Edgar Bergstrom, its five sections were built clockwise in a record-breaking fourteen months by the Engineers under Lieutenant Colonel Clarence Renshaw, and J. Paul Hauck. The first employees moved in in May 1942. The seventy-million-dollar building, of which its architects boast that no two offices on the same floor are more than a half-mile apart, soon caught the public fancy, and stories began to circulate about it—from the true statement that the Great Pyramid of Cheops could be set within the Pentagon, with a few hundred feet to spare, to the apocryphal report that strangers entering the building were invariably lost for days, including one telegraph messenger who finally emerged as a lieutenant colonel.

When Reybold became the Chief of Engineers one soldier in sixteen, or a total of eighty-five thousand, was an Engineer, and it was estimated that the proportion would double in case of war, especially as the combat Engineer troops of the German Army had been responsible for storming fortresses formerly considered impregnable. Even with a war on his hands, Reybold still had to handle flood-control work, bridges, and the care of rivers and harbors throughout the United States. (At the port of New York, for instance, the crew of an Engineers' fleet of three dredges worked seven days a week from March 1941 through November 1942 to cut new anchorages, deepen some channels for the use of huge troop transports, and generally keep the harbor free of mud, silt, sand, and clay.) Like any housekeeper, the Engineers have to sweep the navigable streams constantly, in war or peace. Other Engineer functions of which the public is generally not aware include camouflage, photography, water purification, the testing, developing, and improving of special devices, and contracting for those approved, and the immense task of map making for an army fighting on both sides of the world. (During Reybold's tenure, incidentally, the research section of the Army Engineer School at Fort Belvoir, Virginia, adopted a system of requesting suggestions for devices and methods from any source, which is unique in the armed forces. About 11 per cent of the suggestions had been put to use up to February 1943, and the originators were given full credit and a report on the subsequent development of the ideas.)

"Every battle begins on a map," wrote Reybold in the May 1945 *Popular Science*, "and the Engineers literally had to remap the world for air and amphibious assaults on America's foes. For information about some Pacific islands that are well known steppingstones to Tokyo now, we had to begin by ransacking the memories of old shipmasters and missionaries. For the invasion of France we had to prepare 5,625 tons of maps, which is well over two hundred freight-car loads. The one hundred and sixteen million maps in this single order were approximately four times the total prepared and printed for all of the First World War.

"At the same time that these miles of paper plans were being made, however, the Engineers had to make it possible to move millions of men and billions of tons of matériel over supply lines twice as long as the equator. By June 1942 the United States Army Engineers were directing construction in this country at a rate of twenty million dollars a day. . . . The world's biggest factories and the training camps throughout this country were but a base from which shafts had to be run to spearheads in Africa, Europe, and Asia. And these 'shafts' were no mere lines on a map, but such tangible things as airfields, roads, bridges, ports, railroads, pipelines, and more bases.

"The roads include the sixteen-hundred-mile ['Alcan'] Alaska Military Highway from Dawson Creek, Canada, to Fairbanks, Alaska; the completed portions of the Pan-American Highway from Mexico to the Panama Canal; and the thousand-mile Ledo-Burma Road from India to China. These three new roads run through parts of the world where it previously was impossible to travel by truck. In France alone, Army Engineers have put into operation a road network of four thousand miles, involving the construction of one hundred and forty-five major highway bridges; nearly seven hundred bridges had to be strung over treacherous, snake-filled rivers for the Ledo-Burma Road. But those are only a trifling percentage of the bridges that the Engineers have built during this war," perhaps the most difficult being over the Volturno. Among the other facts General Reybold discloses are that "in France, an Engineer pipeline crew was only thirty-five miles behind the first Americans to enter Paris . . . one and a half million gallons of gasoline a day flowed through the pipes from Normandy"; and "there were more Engineers than infantry or troops of any other service invading Leyte on D-Day. When the Engineers land they stay until an old-timer can no longer recognize the place."

General Reybold, who spent five weeks in 1943 inspecting British and North African installations and who returned in December from a thirty-thousand-mile tour of inspection in the Pacific, reported that his men and the Navy's famous Seabees (Construction Battalions) "get on well together, and either lend or steal equipment from one another." As correspondent Robert Sherrod [44] has pointed out, "the Seabee is an expert before he joins up. The Army Engineer is just an average guy named Joe who got drafted. But Joe learns, and he, too, has accomplished some near-miracles of construction and of fighting in this war. I just hate to see him neglected [by the writers]." As for the Regulars, to quote their chief, "To men trained in the Army Engineers' river-and-harbor and flood-control work, the war is just a somewhat bigger job of shoving earth around."

According to reports, the German High Command was well informed about the Engineer Corps and by no means underestimated its competence. Captured German documents stressed that the redoubtable Engineers who did the manual labor for the combat soldiers often were ten times more efficient than the enemy had estimated. The German Army concentrated forces at important coastal ports in the belief that their possession was essential to the Allies. But American Engineers developed captured minor ports to unheard-of capacities. They built "from scratch" 306 railroad bridges, rebuilt 1,563 miles of rail lines, and restored 237 shattered road bridges. And it was the Engineers who worked out with the British the intricate problem of making the Normandy invasion possible by inventing a way to construct artificial harbors permitting the landing of troops and materials on a hostile shore. Had that been unsuccessful, experts state, the early termination of the war would have been impossible. It was the Engineers, too, who built the vital airfields on every continent. Some of the most dangerous work of the war was performed by them in removing sunken and mined ships from harbors. Working with British material and with Indian and Chinese workmen, the Engineers built the new telephone line along the Ledo Road in Burma.

The spectacular performance of the Corps has not, however, given it immunity to Congressional investigation. The continued construction by the Army until November 1943 of the 905-mile stretch of the 1,600-mile Pan-American Highway through six Central American republics at a cost of $42,715,591—against the original estimate of $14,714,000—although the military necessity for the work had ended in 1942, was criticized by the Senate War Investigating Committee in July 1945. General Reybold testified that he had reported to the Director of Requirements Division of the Army Service Forces on April 9, 1943, that "it is not believed that work already done has been carried out without interference to the war effort, or that work remaining to be done can be accomplished without such interference." His report, however, which would have closed work on the Pan-American Highway, was filed away, and not until August 1943 was a study of the highway project begun and revisions of the military program concluded.

When in April 1945 Reybold was made a temporary lieutenant general, he became the first Chief of Engineers to wear three stars. Up to that date his Construction Division had handled eleven and a half billion dollars' worth of building; his Supply Division had spent six and a half billion dollars since the attack on Pearl Harbor; while his flood-control and waterways experts had outlined a postwar program involving an estimated four and a half billion dollars. But General Reybold did not supervise the postwar project because, on October 1, 1945, he retired as chief of the Army Engineers to join the staff of the Delaware State Highway Department on November 1 as director of the Delaware River crossing division which, following authorization by the Delaware General Assembly in 1945, was scheduled to construct a Delaware River crossing near Wilmington.

The bespectacled general is referred to by *Time* as "husky, golfing (middle seventies) Gene Reybold . . . a crack administrator." In April 1943 he became director of the War Artists Units of military and civilian painters,

who were to record war scenes (no official portraits). He was to be assisted by a War Department Art Advisory Committee, of which George Biddle [42] was a member, and by a consulting committee. Reybold, who is a member of the American Society of Military Engineers and the American Society of Civil Engineers, has received honorary doctorates since 1940 from the Universities of Delaware and Arkansas, and the Drexel Institute of Technology. He feels a certain superiority to Omar Khayyám, for the poet's yearning to "grasp this sorry scheme of things entire" and "remold it closer to the heart's desire" has been, he feels, "almost literally" fulfilled by the Army Engineers.

References

N Y Sun p17 F 19 '42
N Y Times p26 Ap 29 '45 por
Who's Who in America, 1944-45

RICKEY, BRANCH (WESLEY) Dec. 20, 1881- Baseball executive
Address: b. Brooklyn National League Baseball Club, 215 Montague St., Brooklyn, N.Y.

"No man in baseball in the last quarter of a century, with the possible exception of Judge Landis [44] and Babe Ruth [44], has left so deep an impress on the game as Branch Rickey," writes Frederick G. Lieb. Rickey, now president of the Brooklyn Dodgers, "devised a method whereby the poorer clubs could cope on equal terms with the more opulent ones." Generally considered the best judge and shrewdest trader of baseball talent in the world, "The Brain" invented the "farm system" for developing players, and incidentally earned for himself what is said now to be the highest salary in baseball.

A descendant of pioneers, Branch Wesley Rickey was born on a farm in Stockdale, Ohio, on December 20, 1881, the second of three brothers. His parents, Jacob Franklin and Emily (Brown) Rickey, known to everyone as Uncle Frank and Aunt Emma, were farmers, not very well off financially but distinguished for their piety and for Frank Rickey's ability as a wrestler. "Weck," as young Rickey was called, was brought up in the strict Wesleyan discipline, and has never been known to drink, use profanity, or work on Sunday, although he now smokes cigars. After completing the course at the local school, he was hired to teach in another country schoolhouse. From a salary of thirty-five dollars a month, the youth bought a bicycle on which to travel the eighteen miles to school from his home, books from which he taught himself Latin, rhetoric, and higher mathematics, and managed in two years to save sixty- or seventy-odd dollars toward college expenses. Two local educators encouraged him, lending him additional books and coaching him for the entrance examination to Ohio Wesleyan University. As a trial, Rickey took the West Point examinations, but did not seek appointment when he passed.

Young Rickey was a good athlete, organizing baseball and football teams on which "he was always the manager and always the catcher," the position from which he could see the entire picture and give directions. He paid his way through the university as a professional athlete,

BRANCH RICKEY

playing baseball in summer and football in the fall and winter. According to Lieb, Rickey got "as high as a hundred and fifty dollars a game for playing the backfield for the strong Shelby (Ohio) professional football club. A broken leg closed his gridiron career in 1902. His leg healed by the following spring and he started the 1903 season as catcher for the Lamar (Wyoming) baseball team. Rickey went up quickly that season; by July he was with Dallas in the Texas League, and a month later Branch had the first taste of the major leagues when he was purchased by the Cincinnati Reds." The Cincinnati manager released him, however, because of his refusal to play on Sunday, the most profitable day of the week. His contract reverted to Dallas, and in 1904 (the year he received his Litt.B. degree) he caught for the Dallas team. Late that year he returned to the major leagues via the Chicago White Sox, who traded him to the St. Louis Browns.

Meanwhile, Rickey continued his studies, earning his B.A. from Wesleyan in 1906. That June the twenty-four-year-old Ohioan fulfilled another long-standing ambition by marrying Jane Moulton, daughter of the proprietor of the Lucasville general store, after proposing more than a hundred times. According to Lieb, after getting his degree Rickey coached for a time at Alleghany College and then at Delaware College, both in Ohio. He continued to play baseball during the season, although it was considered a rough and rowdy game, but in 1907 began to show signs of strain. For the New York Yankees (then the Highlanders), who had him that season, Rickey made the lowest average in the league both as catcher and outfielder, and failed to prevent the Washington Senators from stealing thirteen bases in one game—an all-time record in the American League. In the 1908 off-season, incidentally, Rickey toured as a prohibition lecturer; later that year he entered the University of Michigan law school. There he took a three-year course in two years and went on to his doctorate, at the same time coaching the Michigan baseball

squad. (It was there that he discovered the great George Sisler.) By the time Rickey had his J.D. in 1911, his health gave way completely. He lost fifty pounds, and was forced to go to Saranac Lake to recuperate from tuberculosis. Upon his return he went to Boise, Idaho, and opened a law office.

In 1913 the owner of the St. Louis Browns, Colonel Bob Hedges, invited Rickey to become one of his scouts, covering the Pacific coast teams. Accepting, the lawyer later became club secretary and still later succeeded to the managership. (Burt Shotton was the Sunday manager for Rickey, then and later.) In 1914 and 1915 Rickey's team finished in fifth and sixth places, respectively, whereas for the preceding four years the Browns had not been better than seventh. When Hedges sold the club to Phil Ball, Rickey remained as vice-president and business manager. Meanwhile, most of the important St. Louis businessmen had combined to purchase the St. Louis National League club, the Cardinals. In *The St. Louis Cardinals* (1944), Lieb tells how in early 1917 the instigator of the campaign asked St. Louis sports editors and baseball writers whom they would recommend for club president, and found only one name on all the ballots—Branch Rickey. Rickey accepted the offer, for he "never was happy under the blustering Ball with his high voltage adjectives." Ball refused to release his business manager, and the latter had to go to court to prove that his contract permitted him to change jobs if a better one was offered. Later, when Don Barnes purchased the Browns from the Ball estate, Rickey represented both parties and received a reported commission of twenty-five thousand dollars.

Branch Rickey's first year as club president saw the Cardinals rise from a tie for seventh place in the league to third, but most of the credit went to manager Miller Huggins. (Rickey also introduced Ladies' Day to St. Louis.) When the War Department issued its "work-or-fight" order on Labor Day 1918, the thirty-six-year-old executive joined the Army, and was soon a major in the new Chemical Warfare Service. On his return after the Armistice, Major Rickey also assumed the duties of field manager, and acquired his former assistant Burt Shotton from the Washington Americans to act as outfielder and Sunday manager. Rickey also found some other good players: his "uncanny ability to pick baseball material" was in evidence; and "the famous Rickey notebook, in which the names of many great players of the future were noted, already was a fixture. They used to laugh a lot about that notebook . . . yet that notebook gave St. Louis fans hundred-thousand-dollar ballplayers for the price of a railroad ticket." But the club was $175,000 in debt and could hardly meet operating expenses. "We didn't even have money enough to send the club south for spring training," Rickey recalled a quarter-century later, "so we trained at home. We even wore the same uniforms at home and on the road. . . .I had to pass up my salary to meet the payroll. It was really rugged." On one occasion the president-manager sneaked a rug from his own home, without his wife's knowledge, to brighten his bare office when business visitors were expected.

As a result, minor league officials whom Rickey approached would often wire to richer teams, saying that if Rickey wanted a certain player that player must be good, and the other club would be in a position to make a better offer for him. Or, if Rickey turned a discovery of his over to a minor league team for seasoning, the minor manager might "double-cross" him and sell his discovery to a rival club. "That kind of thing drove me mad," says Rickey. "I pondered long on it, and finally concluded that, if we were too poor to buy, we would have to raise our own." By 1919, therefore, the Cardinal boss took a step which was eventually to change the entire minor league setup by establishing the "farm system," with the major-league team owning a hierarchy of minor clubs. He began modestly enough, by buying 18 per cent of the stock of the Houston club (Texas League). Then he acquired Fort Smith (Arkansas) in the Western Association, a Class C team. In 1920, when Sam Breadon had replaced Rickey as president, leaving him as manager and later as business manager, Rickey continued to expand the Cardinals' holdings. Part ownership proving unsatisfactory, they bought out their partners. "Rickey even went so far as to back entire leagues," says Lieb, "and at one time he controlled the entire player supply in the Nebraska State and Arkansas-Missouri leagues. But this was too much for Commissioner Landis, opposed to Rickey's idea from the start, and the Cardinals were limited to one club in each of these leagues, Farmer Branch finding big-league sponsors for the other teams."

The farm system was first ridiculed and then bitterly attacked as "Rickey's chain gang," but it produced players whose listing "reads like a World Series Who's Who." Within a few years the very clubs which had scoffed at Rickey's farm system were establishing their own —and were paying fancy prices for home-grown Cardinal players. As for the Cardinal empire itself, by 1940 the Redbirds owned thirty-two clubs outright and had optional agreements with eight others, there being some six hundred players involved. The only Class D league in organized baseball in which the St. Louis club was not represented was in Canada.

But, after the first few years, Rickey was less successful on the field than off. In 1920 the Cardinals turned down an offer totaling $350,000 from the New York Giants for the star Rogers Hornsby, but the team ended in a tie for fifth place. The next year they were third, and led both leagues in batting averages. Rickey's team was third again in 1922, and President Breadon signed the manager to a five-year contract. Things went wrong in the 1923 season, however; there was trouble between Rickey and Hornsby, climaxed by a fist fight between the manager and his star player, and the latter worked in only 106 games, while the rest of the team "slipped perceptibly." After the Cardinals had ended two seasons in fifth and sixth places, respectively, and had drawn very poor attendance at the beginning of a third, Breadon replaced Rickey with Hornsby, keeping the former as vice-president and business manager. Chagrined, Rickey sold all his Cardinal stock to his successor, making a profit of twenty thousand dollars; less than two years later, the

same stock went for several times what Rickey sold it for.

"Too much theory and too little practical baseball" seems to be the consensus as to why Rickey failed as manager; his readiness to sell or trade experienced players and replace them by younger men is also cited. "There wasn't anything wrong with Rickey's baseball theories," Roy Stockton says. "Major league managers still use many Rickey innovations— blackboard talks, sliding pits, plays to catch runners off base. [But] Rickey's players could not understand his ideas or execute them." After he took charge of the front office, with complete charge over all personnel except the manager, the Cardinal organization showed a profit for every year but three. "Rickey, gathering thousands of young prospects, found enough stars to win pennants in 1926, 1928, 1930, 1931, and 1942—and world championships in four of those years. . . . It is no reflection on Rickey's over-all ability that he touted many players as sure-fire stars, only to have them flop out without leaving an imprint on the majors. Besides getting publicity, that also demonstrated another Rickey asset—unbounded enthusiasm and steadfast devotion to his job. And it didn't hurt the Cardinal sale of players either." In that sale of players, the Ohioan demonstrated his ability to tell almost without exception when a star player had passed his peak, and to sell him while his drawing power still surpassed his playing power, and while baseball executives were willing to pay high prices for that drawing power.

Despite his own strict conventionality, Rickey showed a great feeling for "color," even to the point of eccentricity. It was he who created "the most colorful, picturesque club of modern baseball," the Series-winning Gashouse Gang of 1934, composed of players like Dizzy Dean, Pepper Martin, Lippy Durocher '40, Muscles Medwick, and Showboat Orsatti, and managed by the umpire-baiting Frankie Frisch. It was typical of the mad but successful team that, at Leo Durocher's request, Rickey successfully appealed to a certain Miss Grace Dozier, as an old friend and a Cardinal fan, to marry his shortstop at once and clear his mind for the World Series. Later, when most of the Gashouse Gang stars were sold to Larry MacPhail '44, much of that reputation went with them to the Brooklyn Dodgers.

Less than a month after the Cardinals had won the 1942 World Series, Breadon notified Colonel Rickey (who was military aide to Governor Forrest Donnell) that his contract would not be renewed. One reason was his large salary and profit-sharing arrangement, totaling $88,000 for 1941 and $65,000 for 1942 —the highest income in baseball, and perhaps disproportionate in wartime for a club whose salaries are said to be less than average. Rickey immediately signed a five-year contract, at a reported salary of $85,000, as president and general manager of the Brooklyn Dodgers, succeeding his friend and "prize pupil" Larry MacPhail. After thirty-eight years in baseball, Rickey remarked that "it will be gratifying not to worry about the money involved in player deals." The Brooklyn farm system, in-

RICKEY, BRANCH—*Continued*

cidentally, had been headed by Branch Rickey, Jr., since 1939. (Rickey, Sr., also has five daughters.) A three-man syndicate headed by Rickey purchased 25 per cent of the Dodger stock, which Frank Graham, the team's historian, termed "a tangible expression of confidence on the part of a man who doesn't make bad investments." After a year *Look* reported that the new boss had "ironed out many a Dodger wrinkle—umpire-baiting, bean balls, and high-stake card games have been replaced by seriousness and esprit de corps." After two years Rickey had made himself unpopular by "payroll paring," which included his "selling down the river" favorites like Dolph Camilli, Medwick, Bobo Newsom, and Johnny Allen. The Dodgers were in seventh place in 1944, but Rickey continued his long-range program, and at the end of the 1945 season they were third in the league.

During 1945 Rickey advocated the appointment of a national sports coordinator, and announced his intention of "putting a football team on the field as soon as practicable." He extended the Dodgers' farm system by purchasing the Fort Worth club (Texas League), and enlarged his own holdings by increasing his syndicate's share of the stock to 75 per cent by acquiring an additional 50 per cent through the purchase of the stock of the Ebbets estate. The sixty-three-year-old executive was appointed by Mayor Fiorello H. La Guardia [40] of New York as one of a ten-man committee, to make recommendations on eliminating "the color line in baseball." This was of particular interest because Rickey had in April been the first major league president approached for tryouts for Negro players, and in May he had announced the formation of a new Negro baseball league, the United States League, and the renting of Ebbets Field for games by the Brooklyn Brown Dodgers. Sports writers expressed puzzlement over the move, while Joe Bostic of the *People's Voice* declared that Rickey's interest was in "widening the outposts of segregation."

Then, in October 1945, Rickey made baseball history with the signing of Jackie Robinson, the first Negro player ever to be signed by any club in the history of modern organized baseball, by the Dodgers' Montreal farm team of the International League. The opportunity afforded Robinson represented the first success scored by all the organizations and individuals who have been clamoring for big league baseball to end its traditional discrimination against Negro players. Some quarters who protested the signing declared that since organized baseball derived substantial revenues from the operation of Negro leagues, these leagues would fail if they were "raided" of their players, as Robinson had been taken from the Kansas City Monarchs. The Chicago *Defender*, national weekly newspaper published for Negroes, placed Rickey on its annual honor roll of leading Americans who distinguished themselves in 1945 by improving race relations.

Rickey is a trustee of Ohio Wesleyan, a member of the board of Westminster College and of the Methodist Board of Temperance, Prohibition, and Public Morals, alumni secretary of Delta Tau Delta, and belongs to two

bar associations, three veterans' associations, and various civic clubs, social organizations, and fraternal orders—and makes speeches before all of them. In 1928 McKendrick College gave him an LL.D. A Republican, he was mentioned by the New York *Post* of December 20, 1944, as one of "a group of Governor Dewey's [44] closest friends and political supporters."

The "Mahatma," as sports columnists like to call Rickey, now "chunky and bespectacled," is described by *Time* as looking "like Lionel Barrymore [43] playing Thaddeus Stevens" and talking "like an evangelist, in a voice that exploits the whisper as aptly as the roar." He has, in fact, a reputation as a lay preacher and is known among sports writers for a pontifical manner, the length and intricacy of his statements, the ease with which he obscures the answer to an unwelcome question, and his fine feeling for the colorful and humorous details which add human interest. He has kept up all his contacts, and "those friendships constitute a valuable chain, stretching from coast to coast, and provide an effective voluntary scouting system."

References

Look 7:70 Je 15 '43 pors
N Y Herald Tribune X p6 Ag 31 '41 il por
N Y Post Mag p15 N 14 '42 pors
N Y Times p24 O 24 '42 por
Time 39:65 Ap 13 '42
Lieb, F. G. The St. Louis Cardinals p61 ff. (1944)
Stockton, J. R. The Gashouse Gang and a Couple of Other Guys p220-39 (1945)
Who's Who in America, 1944-45

RINGLING, ROBERT E(DWARD) Aug. 16, 1897- Circus executive; singer

Address: Sarasota, Fla.

The world's largest circus, Ringling Brothers and Barnum and Bailey Combined Shows, Inc., has become an American institution whose arrival each year is eagerly awaited in cities and towns throughout the Nation. The president of this circus since 1943 has been Robert E. Ringling, the first Ringling to head the "Big Show" since the founding family lost control in 1933. Returning after many years on the opera stage to the circus world which he had left as a young man, the former baritone of the Chicago Civic Opera Company has brought a good business sense as well as a rich musical background to the "Big Top."

The son of Charles Edward and Edith (Conway) Ringling, Robert Edward Ringling was born in the little town of Baraboo, Wisconsin, on August 16, 1897. The story of his parents and the beginnings of the circus is inherently a part of Robert Ringling's story. His mother was the daughter of the local Methodist minister; his father was the youngest of a family of eight children—seven sons and a daughter—of a Baraboo harness-maker who made a comfortable living from his small business. The Ringlings were a music-loving family, and Robert's father and uncles taught themselves to play various musical instruments; when they were young men, five of them formed a family orchestra at home, later earning money by playing for local concerts and dances.

By 1880, when Charles was eighteen, the group had developed into the Ringling Brothers Classic and Comic Concert Company. The brothers themselves provided the entertainment for the *Carnival of Fun*, as the musical program was called. Later, when the young men began to accept one-night stands around Baraboo, they added a comic sketch or two to enliven the show. Mrs. Charles Ringling, still a very lively person known as "The First Lady of the Circus," never tires of talking of these early days and the development of this "small company of small-town boys." The world's greatest circus, she points out, grew out of a love of music. In 1884, thirteen years after P. T. Barnum had started his circus, the young impresarios had saved enough money to invest in a small wagon show, which consisted of a few circus acts, some animal acts, and a band. It was a great day when an elephant joined their trained horse and the dancing bear, even though the elephant was rather knock-kneed, and the animals mangy. In 1890 the old wagon show had been changed to a railroad show.

Charles Ringling and Edith Conway were married in these exciting days; after their son Robert was born in 1897 he spent his early years with the circus caravan. His mother recalls that there was a five-octave piano in the private car which was the family's living room for eight months of the year, and almost every evening a group gathered around it, Charles Ringling playing the piano, Mrs. Charles singing and playing the cello or some other instrument. Mozart sonatas, Strauss waltzes, and popular and classical songs were a daily part of Robert's childhood. Later he went to school in Baraboo and traveled with the circus during the summer. When he was seven he began the study of the violin and took singing lessons. After several years, realizing that he did not have the hands of a violinist, he gave up the instrument to concentrate on singing. All this musical training was an excellent foundation for the work of the future circus executive, for music is an integral part of any circus.

When Robert was nine years old his parents took him abroad, where in London he was fascinated by the Coldstream Guards. For years he was to hold a vivid memory of the changing of the guard and to cherish a dream of using the colorful ceremony as the basis of a circus act. After returning to America he developed an enthusiasm for playing punchboards. At one time when the circus train stopped at Redding, California, to feed the animals, Robert was given permission to play a few games in the town, but he was cautioned to return in fifteen minutes. With two members of the company he played his favorite gambling game until he had won forty dollars in gold pieces; then the trio went back to the feeding stop to find that the train had left. Robert's forty dollars were spent in hiring an automobile to take them to the next town, forty miles away —and his interest in punchboards ceased after this adventure.

Intensely fond of all sports, Robert was particularly devoted to sand-lot football; when he was twelve he broke both hips in a game

ROBERT E. RINGLING

and was unable to walk for four years. Seventeen months of this period were spent in bed in a plaster cast. According to his mother, the boy turned the painful interval into a profitable time by spending most of the days listening to phonograph records, learning songs, arias, and various roles, and perfecting himself in languages. "He emerged from this ordeal with a background of musical knowledge that was most helpful to him when his own career began."

In circus vernacular, one who loves the circus and cannot live away from it is said to have "sawdust in his nose"; outsiders and amateurs are called "gillies." Judged by circus standards, Robert did not have sawdust in his nose, for he entered the Evanston (Illinois) Academy of Fine Arts when he was about sixteen, graduating from there in 1914. He then entered Northwestern University, but left it when he found he could not do justice to both his university work and his singing. He was married on December 8, 1920, to Virginia Elizabeth Sullivan. (Four sons were born to the couple. Two of the sons and Mrs. Ringling are now deceased.)

The young singer made his debut as an operatic baritone in Tampa, Florida, in 1922, then toured the United States with the San Carlo Opera Company for a year. Another tour followed with Josephine Lucchesi in the Middle West and South. By this time he had left the circus definitely, or so he thought, and in 1924 he went abroad to study. He first became a member of the State Opera Company in Ulm, Germany; a year with that company was followed by a year in Munich with the National Opera Company, and a year with the State Opera at Darmstadt. After his return to America in 1927 he became a member of the Chicago Civic Opera Company, and during the summer for the next three years he sang with the Cincinnati Zoo Opera Company.

On November 17, 1927, the young baritone of the Civic Opera Company made his debut

RINGLING, ROBERT E.—*Continued*

in the role of Tonio, the heartbroken clown of *Pagliacci.* It is said that he received a dozen curtain calls after this performance, and today many critics consider the role to have been his most successful one. The singer also won distinction as Faninal in Richard Strauss's [44] *Der Rosenkavalier,* as Mephistopheles in *Faust,* and in many Wagnerian parts; he had an extensive repertoire of more than a hundred roles in French, Italian, and German. Dr. Ringling, as he was called in musical circles after receiving the honorary degree of Doctor of Music from Rollins College in 1930, remained with the Chicago Civic Opera Company until 1939 when he retired from the professional opera stage. In 1940 he was married to Irene Bauernfeind.

In 1907 Ringling Brothers had bought the Barnum and Bailey Circus for four hundred and ten thousand dollars. Soon afterward the organization took the double name by which it has since been known: Ringling Brothers and Barnum and Bailey Combined Shows, Inc. John Ringling, the last of the five founders of the Ringling contingent to direct the combined enterprise, also bought other smaller circuses. Under his long leadership the business prospered, and by 1924, forty years after the first Ringling wagon show appeared, John Ringling was rated one of the thirteen richest men in the world. So vast was the enterprise that the payroll included five thousand persons and it took two hundred and forty railroad cars to move his shows.

By 1929 circus profits had reached an all-time high of a million dollars. But that spring Ringling borrowed over a million dollars to buy the American Circus Corporation, which owned Sells-Floto and several other circuses, putting up Ringling Brothers-Barnum and Bailey stock as security. By this elaborate business deal he kept alive the tradition of the spring opening in Madison Square Garden (which Sells-Floto had previously engaged). His attempts to keep his circus going were useless, however, for the Wall Street crash of 1929 "froze his wealth solid," to use the words of the *Saturday Evening Post.* Some writers have pointed out that circus profits probably would have dropped considerably at this time anyway because of indirect competition with radio and motion pictures, and direct competition with a swarm of smaller circuses "which nibbled away at the Greatest Show on Earth." By 1932 John Ringling had paid off part of his debt, but later he was forced to give so much additional circus stock for collateral (he also gave his entire personal estate, including railroads, oil wells, and art collections) that the Ringling family lost control of the circus. In 1936 John Ringling died, technically bankrupt. But the following year his estate borrowed nearly a million dollars from the Manufacturers Trust Company of New York to buy the note held by the Allied Owners Corporation which had acquired control. This organization continued to operate the circus but critical opinion said the Big Show became so dull during its period of control that the public had almost lost interest in it.

With control once more in Ringling hands, the Greatest Show on Earth staged a comeback under the direction of John Ringling North (the son of John Ringling's sister Ida), who had become president of the organization as executor of his uncle's estate. John Ringling had been a good showman; he had had sawdust in his nose. North was also a good showman, but to circus people he was a "gillie," or an outsider, because he had left the circus when a young man to become a broker. They were critical of him when he returned to the circus world, blaming labor troubles and other difficulties on the jinx which a gillie is apt to cause. However, John Ringling North made the circus pay profits during the period—less than three years—of his directorship. He believed that the circus needed streamlining, and under him it received a Norman Bel Geddes '40 modernistic setting, a Stravinsky '40-Balanchine '42 ballet, and Gargantua, the gorilla, in a twenty-thousand-dollar, air-conditioned cage. North's first season, 1938, was cut short by strikes, but 1939 showed a profit, and 1940 a record profit. In October of that year the estate paid off its note to the bank, and in September 1942 the note to the estate was paid off.

In January 1943 there was a shakeup at a directors' meeting, a disagreement that occurred because North did not want to take the circus on the road that year. Other members of the group felt that the circus might never go on again if it were allowed to be idle for a year. As a result of this meeting, active managership of the Greatest Show on Earth passed from the hands of John North to Robert Ringling, his mother, and Mrs. Aubrey Ringling; Robert became president, his mother and aunt became vice-presidents, and James A. Haley, a circus official for many years, became first vice-president. The Ringlings now own all except a few shares of the circus stock.

When the managership of Ringling Brothers-Barnum and Bailey was "thrown into Robert's lap," he was not unprepared for the position, despite his years in the opera, for during his boyhood summers with the circus he had been instructed by his father in circus management. In 1937 he had assumed the duties of senior vice-president, in addition to the presidency of the Ringling Trust and Savings Bank. When he took over the direction of the circus in 1943, the modernistic *décor* was dropped and, according to *Time* Magazine, "once again everything was traditional, absurd, and gaudy." One of the most successful numbers was a spectacular pageant of elephants built around the idea of the changing of the guard, which had been in Ringling's mind since boyhood. The year 1943 presented many wartime difficulties, but June 1944 found the circus winding up its "longest, biggest indoor run of all time and completely out of hock financially." Then, in July 1944, occurred the Hartford (Connecticut) fire in which the death toll was a hundred and fifty-eight. The circus resumed its tour a month later, playing in open-air theaters. On its tour the following spring it carried with it seventy-five thousand yards of new canvas which had been flame-proofed under a process used for Army and Navy tenting. As a result of the tragedy six of the circus officials received prison sentences on charges of involuntary manslaughter. One of them, James Haley, was removed from the board of directors, but remained as one of the vice-presidents. All six were endorsed by the directors at their annual meeting in the spring of 1945 in a resolution commending them for having "unselfishly" pleaded "no contest" to the charges for the benefit of the circus corporation, "notwithstanding their sincere belief in their own innocence." Had the six elected to stand trial, the successful operation of the circus might have been prevented, the resolution set forth.

The forty-six-day engagement at Madison Square Garden in 1945 broke all New York records as to gross profits and attendance in the history of Ringling, Barnum & Bailey, exceeding the previous year's record of $1,500,000 by $100,000. No dividends were to be paid, however, until the Hartford fire claims were liquidated, *Variety* reported on May 23. By the end of November of 1945 it was announced by Attorney Edward S. Rogin, receiver of the Ringling Brothers and Barnum & Bailey Combined Shows, Inc., that cash and assets in the amount of $755,000 were available for the benefit of the estates of those who had died or were injured in the circus fire.

Robert Ringling is five feet eight inches tall and stockily built. He has blue eyes and thinning gray hair, and is described as a quiet, unostentatious, but self-assured person. Though he frequently carries a cane, it is not for effect but because of his childhood accident. His employees like him, calling him "Mr. Bob." His attractive wife and his two sons, James Conway and Charles Joseph, are frequent visitors to the circus. Ringling is interested in yachting and powerboat racing, and is a member of numerous sports clubs in and around Chicago and in Florida. Although he has retired professionally from opera, he "keeps his baritone in trim" by frequent appearances on church and concert programs. He does not feel that the transition from opera to circus has been difficult. Both are lavish spectacles, he has pointed out, depending to a large extent on staging, costumes, colors, lighting, and broad gestures for effectiveness. "They're very much alike," he has also remarked; "they're both crazy."

References

Etude 62:438-9 Ag '44 il pors
N Y World Telegram p15 Ap 23 '43 il pors
Thompson, O. ed. International Cyclopedia of Music and Musicians (1943)
Who's Who in America, 1944-45

RIPLEY, ROBERT L(EROY) Dec. 25, 1893- Cartoonist; author

Address: b. 2 W. 67th St., New York City; h. Taylor's Lane, Mamaroneck, N.Y.

"Believe It or Not, this is Ripley," says the road marker before a certain American town—a bow to Robert L. Ripley, probably the best-known "disseminator of the incredible truth," whose daily audience numbers some eighty millions. A nationwide survey showed that, with the single exception of front-page news pictures, Ripley's *Believe It or Not* cartoon was the greatest reader-interest feature in newspapers, exceeding even the front-page headline news; and its creator has also been successful on the radio, in writing books, as a lecturer, and in producing "Odditoriums."

LeRoy Ripley, who added the name Robert twenty years later, was born in the small town of Santa Rosa, California, on Christmas Day, 1893. His mother, Lily Belle (Yocka) Ripley, whose parents were Western pioneers, had been born in a covered wagon; his father, Isaac Davis Ripley, was a carpenter. At eleven, Roy was graduated from grammar school and entered the Santa Rosa High School, where his English teacher recalls him as "a dear, shy boy." She noticed his skill in drawing and, aware that he disliked composition, offered to accept an illustration in place of each assigned paper. Young Ripley therefore illustrated nearly all the classics studied, doing research to ensure the accuracy of his drawings. When the boy was twelve his father died, and he had to help support his mother, younger sister, and brother Douglas, whom he looks on as more a son than a brother. Roy got a job after school polishing gravestones for a tombstone company, and later left high school to go to work; but although he never graduated he drew the cover of the graduation number of the school publication.

When Ripley was fourteen he sold his first commercial drawing to the old *Life* Magazine for eight dollars. Titled *The Village Belles Were Wringing*, it showed three girls wringing clothes over a washtub. During the summers the boy pitched on a semi-professional baseball team, receiving anywhere from seven to fifteen dollars a week for pitching and drawing a weekly baseball poster for the team owner. His baseball career was to be cut short by an arm injury sustained while trying out for the New York Giants, but his posters brought him to the attention of the editor of the San Francisco *Bulletin*, who hired the sixteen-year-old boy as sports cartoonist for eight dollars a week, later raised to ten dollars. When Ripley asked for another raise he was fired, went over to the San Francisco *Chronicle,* and repeated the process, this time getting up to twenty dollars a week before being discharged. In 1913, when Ripley was twenty, he left the West Coast for New York, where he was hired by the New York *Globe* for twenty-five dollars. The *Globe* insisted that their sports cartoonist should have a more athletic-sounding name than LeRoy, so the Californian became Bob Ripley, demoting LeRoy to a middle initial, L.; his old friends still call him Roy, however. Here Ripley drew one or two sports cartoons a week, spending most of his free time playing handball at the New York Athletic Club. He also did some wrestling, and in 1916 he and "Bugs" Baer put on a wrestling match at the old Lexington Opera House.

In December 1918, Ripley had a deadline to meet and no idea as to subject. At last he "hurriedly gathered together a few athletic oddities," drew cartoons of seven men who had set records for running backwards, hopping, broadjumping on ice, and so forth, and grouped them under the heading "Believe It or Not!" Reader response was so favorable that Ripley was encouraged to devote himself to athletic oddities, and then to oddities of all kinds, making a regular weekly feature of it. In 1919 he was married to a *Follies* girl named Beatrice Roberts, who had been

ROBERT L. RIPLEY

a beauty contest winner in Massachusetts. (They were divorced some years later.)

When the *Globe* ceased publication, in 1923 Ripley joined the staff of the New York *Evening Post,* with which he remained until 1928. (His two books on travel, one on handball, and another on boxing had been published before this time.) His feature was syndicated in about thirty papers, and Ripley also drew pictures for *Collier's,* but, as Geoffrey T. Hellman remarked in the *New Yorker,* "he never made as much as ten thousand dollars a year" until 1928, when the publisher Max Schuster '41 finally persuaded him to put *Believe It or Not* into book form.

Simon '41 and Schuster sent a copy to William Randolph Hearst, who instructed his gigantic King Features Syndicate to sign Ripley to a contract paying over one hundred thousand dollars the first year. By the beginning of the forties Ripley's *Believe It or Not* was appearing in nearly three hundred American newspapers and was being translated into seventeen languages for publication in thirty-eight other countries. It is said that no newspaper had ever canceled its subscription to *Believe It or Not,* even in the depths of the depression, until the Second World War; and that the cartoon brings its creator a gross income of half a million dollars. From this amount, however, he has to pay a staff of sixty-six, including the researchers who unearth his material and a dozen secretaries—this in addition to the nine persons King Features assigned to the Ripley mail, which is said to be the heaviest received by any individual in the world. In 1930 the Post Office finally refused to attempt to decipher the many trick addresses of letters to him.

Another consequence of the first *Believe It or Not* book was a three-hundred-fifty-thousand-dollar contract to make twenty-six movie shorts for Warner '45 Brothers-Vitaphone in 1930 (he has done more since); and in April of that year Ripley put his feature on the air

in dramatized form, under the sponsorship of Colonial Beacon Oil Company. Ripley's voice is not "radiogenic," but he took diction lessons to such good effect that he no longer stutters, and received the honorary degree of Doctor of Oratory from Staley College of the Spoken Word in 1940. After completing his first radio series, Ripley was sponsored successively by Standard Oil, the Hudson Motor Car Company, Standard Brands, and Nehi Company (for Royal Crown Cola). *Believe It or Not* is described as the first commercial program to use remote pick-ups consistently; Ripley used them for interviews with persons who spoke from the rapids of Colorado River, an iron lung, the North Pole, underneath Niagara Falls, and from the air. One of his two-way interviews from New York was with Douglas "Wrong-Way" Corrigan in Dublin; another time Ripley gave a "play-by-play" description of fire-walking. On the program which began in 1940, *See America First with Bob Ripley,* he went further, transporting his entire program staff, including the vocalist, agency representative, and all the writers and engineers, in order to broadcast from such unlikely places as the bottom of the Grand Canyon, a snake pit, and an underwater garden. In November 1940 Ripley's program was described by *Radio Guide* as "consistently, the most interesting and thrilling program on the air." In 1945 he went on a CBS program, *Romance, Rhythm, and Ripley.*

Not only has *Believe It or Not* gained wide popularity through Ripley's writings and radio work but also through his "Odditoriums," or exhibits. His first large-scale exhibit was shown at the Chicago World's Fair in 1933; it is estimated that more than two and a half million people visited the display. At both the New York World's Fair and the San Francisco Exposition, the "Odditorium" was one of the most successful displays. Ripley's later books, devoted to oddities, include *The New Believe It or Not Book* (1931), *Believe It or Not Omnibus* (1934), *Believe It or Not Big Book* (1939). Several disclosures in *Believe It or Not* have historical importance. He revealed, for instance, that "The Star-Spangled Banner" had never been officially recognized as the national anthem of the United States. More than five million people signed a petition urging Congress to rectify this lapse, and Congress complied in 1931.

For the educational value of his work, Ripley has received honorary degrees from Dartmouth and Missouri Valley College; Oglethorpe University selected him as "the outstanding cartoonist of the age," and put some of his work into the repository of contemporary civilization which they are leaving for future generations. He has kept out of politics, although the local Democrats offered him their nomination for mayor. He is a member of the Circumnavigators, Explorers, Lotus, and Adventurers clubs, of the American Geographical and National Geographic Society, and of the British Royal Geographical Society.

Ripley has a passion for traveling, and intends to visit all countries of the world which, he has calculated, number two hundred and fifty-three. When the United States entered the Second World War, he still had fifty-three more to go—his entry in *Who's Who in America* says he has traveled in two hundred countries. (This makes no allowance for territorial changes resulting from the war.) Ripley claims also to have employed every known method of transportation. When traveling by air he likes to take along a batch of his unanswered mail (he says he has a million unanswered letters) and write replies, tossing the old letters casually out of the plane. He enjoys the thought of people receiving his answers "several years late, and postmarked from Sarawak or Cambodia."

Bion, his island home (the name is formed from the initial letters of *Believe It or Not*), lies off Mamaroneck in Long Island Sound. It also houses a museum of curios whose worth the owner estimates at two million dollars. "My home is my hobby," he says, pointing out that it is his first real home—he bought it in 1930, fifteen years after his mother's death. A big, energetic man with dimples and a receding hairline, Ripley has not allowed his protruding front teeth to be completely corrected because he felt they were familiar to millions of people. The cartoonist draws from seven to eleven in the morning, and his assistant fills in details and lettering. He spends much of his time arranging new acquisitions (he is said to have three agents covering the auctions for suitable curiosities) and rearranging old totem poles, Buddhist shrines, instruments of torture, and other "oddities." He never eats lunch, making up for it by frequent snacks, and he maintains a steam room to keep his weight down. Ripley believes that people grow old by relaxing too frequently, and his own motto is, "Keep going."

References

Am Mercury 31:60-4 Ja '34
Lit Digest 123:28-9 Je 26 '37 por
New Yorker 16:2-4 Ag 31 '40 por; 16: 27-30 S 7 '40 por
Who's Who in America, 1944-45

RIVES, AMELIE. *See* Troubetzkoy, A. R.

ROBESON, ESLANDA (CARDOZA) GOODE Dec. 15, 1896- Anthropologist; author

Address: h. The Beeches, Enfield, Conn.

"Africans are people," says Eslanda Goode Robeson in the closing sentence of her story of a trip across the Dark Continent. What she learned about these people and their lives is graphically told in *African Journey*, published in August 1945. An American anthropologist and author, Mrs. Robeson is the wife of the internationally known Negro actor and singer, Paul Robeson '41. Active in the cause of the Negro people, she is a lecturer on race relations and other aspects of democracy.

Born in the Nation's Capital on December 15, 1896, Eslanda Cardoza Goode is an American of the type her husband sings of in the *Ballad for Americans*. Questioned by reporters once on the subject of her ancestry, she replied "mischievously but truthfully" that she

ESLANDA GOODE ROBESON

had "some Spanish, English, Scottish, Jewish, American Indian, with a large majority of Negro blood." Her father held a clerical position in the War Department, while her maternal grandfather, Francis Lewis Cardoza, well known for his early awareness of the problems of his people, served during Reconstruction days as South Carolina's Secretary of State as well as of the Treasury.

Brought up in a prosperous, intellectual atmosphere, the girl was deeply influenced by the family's strong interest in politics and racial questions. After studying for a period at the University of Chicago she decided on a career in chemistry. She came East to New York, where at the Teachers College of Columbia University she earned her Bachelor of Science degree in chemistry in 1923. Two years previously, on August 17, she had been married to Paul Robeson, then a student at Columbia Law School. During her student years she began to work as surgical technician and chemist at the Presbyterian Hospital, a position she held until 1925. (She believes that she was the first Negro ever engaged by the hospital.)

After her husband became a concert singer and actor Mrs. Robeson often toured with him, and has lived for periods in Paris, Vienna, Kitzbuehl in the Austrian Tyrol, Moscow, Barcelona, and London. In the summer of 1925 the Robesons left America for London, where the Negro actor was starred in *Emperor Jones*. Living in Chelsea, they enjoyed the unsegregated, easy atmosphere of London, which reminded them of their "beloved" Greenwich Village in New York. When the play closed they went to the Riviera, and there in a little French-Italian town they spent much time with American friends—Glenway Westcott, Emma Goldman, Claude McKay, Max Eastman. After their return to America for a concert tour, their son Pauli was born on November 2, 1927. Six months later Robeson's engagements again took the family to London, where the singer appeared in *Show Boat*. This time they re-

ROBESON, ESLANDA GOODE—*Cont.*

mained in Europe for more than ten years, returning home finally late in 1939.

Throughout these years Eslanda Robeson led a busy life, attending to the details of her husband's work and pursuing several studies that interested her. In 1930 her first book, *Paul Robeson, Negro*, was published. Critical reaction to this biography was varied, most reviewers remarking upon the naïveté and simplicity of the narrative. Langston Hughes [40] called it a book that "couldn't have been bettered by the best press agent," while Stark Young mentioned the volume's "mediocrity." Mrs. Robeson has also done research on the theater, films, and radio at Cambridge and Malvern in England, and at Columbia in the United States. But most fascinating to her has been her work in the field of anthropology.

Specializing in the subject of Africa, the Negro and, later, all colored peoples, Mrs. Robeson studied anthropology at London University and at the London School of Economics from 1935 to 1937. She read all the pertinent material she could find in the libraries of these institutions and in the British Museum and House of Commons libraries while studying under such teachers as Malinowski [41], Firth, Perry, and Hocart. This work stimulated her latent desire to visit Africa—even as a child she had wondered about the "old country"— and finally in 1936 she decided to undertake the pilgrimage to the homeland of her ancestors. Thus she set out on a kind of anthropological field trip to observe for herself the peoples and countries which had been loosely labeled "primitive" and "backward." Since she quickly discovered that visas for Negroes to visit Africa were difficult to obtain, Mrs. Robeson cited her studies and desire for practical research as the reason for her journey. Accordingly, with her young son she boarded the S.S. *Winchester Castle* and started on the travels which were to cover a continent and result in *African Journey*, published about nine years later, in 1945.

After her eventful trek through Africa Mrs. Robeson and Pauli returned to England. During the Spanish civil war Mr. and Mrs. Robeson visited Spain as guests of the Loyalist Government, and the Negro sang for the soldiers on the battle lines near Madrid. In November 1939 the Robesons returned to America, where Mrs. Robeson continued her studies at the Hartford Seminary Foundation. August of 1945 saw the publication of *African Journey*.

African Journey was accorded a favorable critical reception, with the reviewers in general agreement with Ernestine Evan's description of the book as "an excellent tourist account as well as a treatise on the color line." The *Library Journal* states that Mrs. Robeson "shows that, for the first time since the colonization of Africa, the peoples of the world must take account of the people of Africa." "She writes as a wife and mother," comments Lewis Gannett [41], "which gives her story a kind of warmth and intimacy rare in travel reports from Africa." In an otherwise favorable review, John Latouche [40] (*Saturday Review of Literature*) says, "Sometimes the points she makes are extreme, and occasionally her statements are traditional rather than exact." The New York *Times* critic found the book "an extremely attractive and natural book," while Stuart Cloete declared, "She has written a very interesting book—the first, I think, of its kind, and one which should make the white South African wonder sometimes, if he never did before, what those whom he calls his servants think of him." Cloete mentions that the book is "biased in favor of the black man. But almost every other African book is biased in favor of the white."

In *African Journey* the author depicts the oppressive yoke under which the millions of black Africans live. In the words of one writer, "the evidence of manipulation and exploitation is exposed by her as any Jeffersonian might have exposed it. . . .Her book may not be the most tactful and diplomatic ever written, but through its lively travelogue it transmits a clear and ringing denunciation of capitalism's tendency to rob the blind of their pennies." Mrs. Robeson found the Africans "far more politically aware" than her fellow Negroes in America. These people were eager to learn about interracial progress in the Soviet Union, a subject which the anthropologist discussed from first-hand experience. Mrs. Robeson is convinced that racial inequality all over the world is part of one and the same problem, "not a black problem, but a white problem, created by the behavior and attitudes of white people toward the darker races." One critic noted her belief that "what educational and economic advantages have done for her they will do for other Negroes." (Several reviewers spoke of the impressive photographs, taken by the author herself to illustrate her book.)

Living in Enfield, Connecticut, Mrs. Robeson has been an active worker in the Red Cross Motor Corps and, as always, a militant partisan in the cause of the Negro. She has lectured widely on race relations and in late August of 1945 joined the staff of the Council on African Affairs. Her articles on the Negro and Africa have appeared in *Asia and the Americas*. Engaged in the summer of 1945 in the preparation of a new book, Eslanda Robeson was also planning two projects with Pearl Buck. She recently told New York *Post* writer Mary Braggiotti of her hopes in this connection: "First, we are going to work for a Federal bill for a minimum standard of education in this country. Education is not universal; it isn't free. Americans were shocked at the Army statistics of illiteracy. Second," continued Mrs. Robeson, "we would like to get a Federal bill to the effect that any public service must be really public or else it cannot have a public license."

Eslanda Robeson is described as a woman of great vitality and warmth, "vivacious, spirited, bubbling with ideas." She is accounted an excellent swimmer and at one time was a star basketball forward. When she has the time she enjoys bowling with her son and his friends in the recreation house of their large Colonial home, The Beeches. Pauli was educated largely in England and the Soviet Union and in 1945 was a student at Cornell University.

References

Am Mag 137:29+ My '44 por
N Y Post Mag p37 Ag 22 '45 por

Robeson, E. G. African Journey (1945) ;
    Paul Robeson, Negro (1930)

ROBESON, MRS. PAUL *See* Robeson, E. C. G.

ROBINS, MARGARET DREIER 1869(?) —Feb. 21, 1945 American social economist; an international leader in the movement to improve the condition of women and children in industry; co-founder of the Women's Municipal League of New York; president of the National Women's Trade Union League (1907-22); president, chairman, and member of numerous labor and social committees; held many honorary positions.

Obituary

N Y Times p27 F 22 '45 por

ROBINS, MRS. RAYMOND *See* Robins, M. D.

ROBINSON, HOLTON D. 1863 (?)— May 7, 1945 American bridge engineer; played a prominent part in the design and construction of many of the world's largest spans, including the George Washington and the Triborough in New York City; an authority on bridge-cable construction, held many cable invention patents.

Obituary

N Y Times p19 My 8 '45 por

ROCKWELL, NORMAN Feb. 3, 1894- Artist

Address: Arlington, Vt.

If the American public were asked to choose their best-loved painter, it has been said that they would vote "either for Norman Rockwell or, through error, for Rockwell Kent '⁴²." (Another illustrator, Douglass Crockwell, avoids being mistaken for Norman Rockwell by signing his pictures "Douglass.") Unlike the artist-explorer Kent, Norman Rockwell has no interest in landscapes; his tremendously popular illustrations have led one writer to remark, "In reality Mr. Rockwell is a portrait painter, although he never has styled himself such. . . . He paints his portraits for millions to see and enjoy rather than for the occasional visitor to a stately drawing room."

Norman Rockwell was born in New York City on February 3, 1894, the elder of two sons. His father, J. Waring Rockwell, an amateur artist, was what his son calls "an old retainer" of a Philadelphia cotton-goods concern whose New York office he managed; Norman Rockwell is quoted as saying that his father's salary was "so small he was ashamed of it and he never told us how much it was, but I've never in my life seen anyone more devoted to a business firm." Norman's mother, Ann Mary (Hill) Rockwell, was the daughter of William Hill, an English portrait painter who lived in Yonkers, New York, where he put his twelve children to work on landscapes, in assembly-line fashion.

When Norman was ten the Rockwells moved to Mamaroneck, New York. He early showed his love of drawing, and at thirteen he was allowed to enroll at the Chase School of Art for lessons twice a week. (At the same time, of course, he continued his ordinary schooling.)

NORMAN ROCKWELL

Later Norman was sent to the National Academy of Design, where he and two other boys signed in blood a vow never to make more than fifty dollars a week and to strive for the highest in art. At sixteen Rockwell left the second year of high school to enter the Art Students' League, where he won two scholarships and studied under George Bridgeman and Thomas Fogarty. His fellow students soon nicknamed him "The Deacon" for his solemnity. (According to Rufus Jarman in the *New Yorker*, Rockwell and a friend had their first studio when he was sixteen, but had to move to another when Norman's father came visiting and saw the dubious nature of the building.)

Through Fogarty, the seventeen-year-old painter got some assignments from Condé Nast to illustrate McBride and Nast publications. The first of these was an historical work on Champlain; next came a children's book, *Tell-Me-Why Stories*, and a volume on camping by Edward Cave, editor of the Boy Scout magazine, *Boy's Life*. According to Jarman, this latter won him a canoe and, shortly afterward, a fifty-dollar-a-month position as Cave's art editor. This meant that he painted most of the covers and illustrated two or more stories each month. Young Rockwell added to this income by doing illustrations for *St. Nicholas, American Boy*, and a children's monthly, *Everyland*, as well as for some books by Ralph Henry Barbour, including *Onward and Forward, The Crimson Sweater,* and *Four Afloat.* After a rest, he moved to New Rochelle, New York, to devote all his time to free-lance illustrating. In those days, he recalls, "you offered your stuff to the *Saturday Evening Post* first, then to the old *Life* Magazine, *Leslie's*, and the others in regular order. If we couldn't sell a drawing anywhere else we shipped it out to Des Moines to the *People's Popular Monthly*. They bought everything, and paid fifty dollars for each drawing, good or bad."

After five years of free-lancing Rockwell seemed not to be making very much progress.

ROCKWELL, NORMAN—*Continued*

It was the cartoonist Clyde "Vic" Forsythe, with whom he shared a studio, who persuaded Rockwell in 1916 to submit a magazine cover to the *Saturday Evening Post*. Forsythe vetoed Norman's first sketch, of a gracious prima donna, as "not his kind of work." Then, as later, Rockwell found himself unable to draw any but homey women. ("Lord knows I used to try to be sexy," Jarman quotes him, "but when I'd finished they all looked like fine wives and mothers." "I can draw a pretty girl," he has said elsewhere, "but I've never had to.") So Rockwell put some of his "kid stuff" into cover form and took the results to Philadelphia, where George Horace Lorimer accepted all four for about seventy-five dollars each. Lorimer is said to have been so impressed by Rockwell's work that he issued an order that all would-be contributors should be made welcome. Since his first sale to the *Post* Rockwell has sold them an average of ten covers every year, in addition to numerous drawings for the inside pages.

As soon as his pictures were accepted the artist wired his fiancée, a girl from upstate New York, and they were married. The first cover by Rockwell appeared in May 1916. It showed a disgusted boy pushing a baby carriage while his jeering friends went off to play baseball. Since then Rockwell has specialized in such "subject pictures" of the more endearing ages of man (babies, children, "the calf-lovers, the young gentleman, and the codger"), drawn with great and realistic detail. Over the first hurdle, the twenty-two-year-old illustrator gave up the regular income from his other illustrating to devote himself entirely to developing the more remunerative magazine covers for the *Post, Literary Digest,* and the old *Life,* and similar pictures for advertising. A year later, when the United States entered the First World War, Rockwell enlisted in the Navy, becoming a first-class painter and varnisher; but the commandant of the Charleston Navy Yard kept him there working on naval portraits. The magazines also got special permission for him to continue his work on "timely subjects of strong patriotic appeal," so that his income was considerably larger than the commandant's. When the Armistice was signed Rockwell procured an immediate discharge on the one possible ground—inadaptability.

In 1922, when Rockwell was twenty-eight, he took his first trip abroad and had his first chance to study the masterpieces in European galleries. Several friends of his student days tried unsuccessfully to convert him to the New Art, for they were scornful of the "commercialization to which he had descended"; but before he left (because there were not enough typically American subjects for him to work on) several of the scorners asked him whether he thought there would be a good market for them in advertising art back in the States. On several later trips to Paris, Mr. and Mrs. Rockwell engaged in "a mad social whirl." Rockwell's income, mainly from advertisements, was then about forty-five thousand dollars a year. He built an expensive house in New Rochelle and an eighteen-thousand-dollar studio, which he describes as "a mess." "I built it," he says, "at the height of the antique craze, and it was patterned after the Wayside Inn

at Sudbury. Everything was imitation antique." Others were less critical, including *Good Housekeeping* Magazine, which published an article on the Rockwell home entitled "A House With Real Charm."

The Rockwells were divorced in late 1928, and Norman moved back to New York. In 1929 his friends persuaded the thirty-five-year-old artist to take up dynamic symmetry, which is based on a theory that all paintings can be reduced to converging straight lines. Rockwell experimented with it for two years before deciding that it was unsuited to the cover dimensions of the *Saturday Evening Post*. After the 1929 crash he went to California for a vacation and was introduced to Mary Rhodes Barstow, a twenty-year-old schoolteacher of San Gabriel. Ten days later they were engaged, and in April 1930 they were married and went to live in New Rochelle.

In 1932, when their son Jerry (Jarvis Waring Rockwell) was six months old, Rockwell suddenly decided to study in Paris, and two weeks later they sailed. "I was about thirty-eight at the time," the painter recalls, "and thought I ought to get into abstractions, whatever they are." This attitude "bewildered the instructors at several Paris art schools, some of whom said frankly that they didn't know what they could teach a man who got as much for two or three magazine covers as they made in a year. He stayed in Paris seven or eight months, painting, among other things, two abstract covers for the *Post,* which the editors gamely printed. 'My best efforts,' he recalls, 'were some modernistic things that looked like very lousy Matisses[43].' . . .To the great relief of the *Post,* he then settled back into his old groove."

That groove included "standing head and shoulders above almost all others in depicting scenes from his country's Colonial days," to quote the *Ladies' Home Journal* of February 1939. A year earlier *Judge* Magazine had given its High Hat Award to "Norman Rockwell, artist, illustrator, raconteur," for eleven reasons, including "having become, while still a young man, a tradition in art . . . for having painted one of the country's finest murals in the Nassau Tavern at Princeton; for having . . . proven that careless modernization is not a part of good craftsmanship; for having been the inspiration for a school of drawing . . . for his encouragement given to aspiring young artists . . . for his youthful enthusiasm for and curiosity about all things." Rockwell has never liked to paint advertisements, and nowadays extra-*Post* work is confined mainly to the official Boy Scout calendars, which he has painted for Brown and Bigelow nearly every year since 1920 and which have been the Nation's best-selling calendars since the beginning of the 'forties. By 1945, however, Rockwell was running out of good deeds to portray.

Rockwell has illustrated some books, notably de luxe editions of Mark Twain's *Tom Sawyer* and *Huckleberry Finn* in the mid-'thirties. It was while doing research for these in Hannibal, Missouri, that the artist first began to use photographs instead of relying entirely on sketches from the model. Rockwell claims to be the first illustrator to admit that he was using photographs, a nearly universal practice. "I don't suppose anyone will follow my advice," he says, "but it is better not to use photographs until after you have proved your ability to get along wholly without them," and Rockwell himself makes one illustration out of every four or five without the camera, to make sure that he still can. After the preliminary sketches comes a complete full-size charcoal drawing from life, and a smaller color sketch. Then Rockwell traces the charcoal drawing on to the final canvas and is ready to begin the painting, a stage lasting anywhere from two weeks to two months, during which he sometimes gets stage fright. When painting Rockwell wears bifocal lenses divided perpendicularly so that he can look alternately at the models and the easel. During this stage Mrs. Rockwell reads to him, and they have thus gone through "most of the best sellers published in the last thirty years, besides the complete works of Tolstoi, Dickens, Henry James, Voltaire, and Jane Austen." Then, says Rockwell, "I wrap the picture up and send it in and pray."

Seldom is a Rockwell picture refused. Jarman reports that nothing else in the *Saturday Evening Post* draws as consistently large a public response as Rockwell covers; that in 1945 the editors were still receiving requests for copies of a picture published sixteen years earlier; and that the first of his annual April Fool covers, in 1943, brought in a hundred and forty thousand letters. Rockwell attributes much of his appeal to his realism, based on the use of genuine models and properties. His home in Arlington (Vermont) is furnished mainly with Victorian and early American items he has used in his pictures. (Rockwell moved to Arlington, where he had been spending the summers, after having more or less used up his New Rochelle neighborhood as a model source.)

The artist finds many potential models at the weekly square dance of the West Arlington Grange (he is a Grange officer) and has had so many of the townspeople pose for him that "the feeling in town is that a person hasn't arrived until he has posed for a Rockwell painting or at least served as a critic for one. When the artist is having trouble with a picture, he is likely to call in anyone who happens by and ask what is wrong with it. . . . 'If they don't understand the story I'm trying to tell,' he explains, 'I figure that I haven't made it clear enough and that a lot of other people around the country won't understand it, either.'" When Rockwell's studio burned down in 1943, destroying a huge and irreplaceable collection of costumes, paints, brushes, reference materials, old guns, prints, and paintings, the artist "put it all down." *My Studio Burns Down* appeared in the July 17, 1943, *Post* as a double-page spread; but his next studio was equipped with several fire extinguishers and a fireman's hat and ax, and his new house (he sold the old one) has a sprinkler system. The studio, incidentally, is kept with a neatness phenomenal among painters.

Despite his immense popularity, Rockwell is dismissed rather lightly by the "art artists," who look down on illustration and on "pleasing the public." *Time*'s critic holds that "Rockwell would probably be incapable of portraying a really evil human being, or even a really complex one—perhaps even a really real one.

Though he paints and composes exceedingly well, it is questionable whether any of his work could be seriously described as art. Even the celebrated Four Freedoms posters fall short of artistic maturity through their very virtue as posters: they hit hardest at first sight. But as a loving image of what a great people likes to imagine itself to be, Rockwell's work has dignity, warmth, value." The New York ~~Times~~ has compared his work to the writings of Mark Twain and Booth Tarkington. George Grosz, a "serious" painter, says firmly that Rockwell has "excellent technique, great strength, and a clearness of touch that the old masters had. His things are so universal that they would be appreciated anywhere." And one admirer demanding to know why *Time* said Rockwell's paintings were not art, wrote: "Is it because Rockwell is commercial? . . . If so, would you say that the work of Michelangelo, Franz Hals, and Velásquez is also not art? They did their stuff to order for the Popes, Medici, burghers, and princes. . . . Is it because Rockwell enjoys detail? If so, where does that put Vermeer, Dürer, and Holbein? Is it because he puts the light of beauty ('sweetness,' if you like) into the tired and commonplace? And if so, where does that leave Raphael, Corregio, Botticelli, and Company?" In a defense of his brother illustrators and himself, as presented in a *New Yorker* "Profile," Rockwell declared illustration to be as much an art as any other form of painting, one which presented the artist with even more limitations and difficulties. He finds particularly confining the necessity to present the story clearly, within the limits dictated by the size and shape of a magazine page.

Norman Rockwell, six feet tall and dark, is described as "stringy, boyish, only moderately craggy . . . with a long nose, an active Adam's apple, deep-set, melancholy brown eyes, and a good-natured air." His only recorded vanity is buying his shoes too small. The Rockwells rise at six-forty-five, and Norman keeps regular "office hours" at his studio. He works himself to the edge of a breakdown, then snatches an immediate vacation, normally in Europe. "Handsome, charming" Mrs. Rockwell learned to bicycle and to play baseball so that she could join her husband and their sons, Jerry, Tommy, and Peter, at their play, and she is said to "pitch a mean curve." Rockwell seldom returns to his native New York except to deliver a picture and see a play; a succession of untoward events discouraged each of his past attempts to re-enter its "sophisticated chaos." He does address the annual meeting of the Society of American Illustrators, and is said to be its most popular speaker. He is a member also of the Free Lance Artists of America, and during the Second World War, of the local Civilian Defense Unit and of a War Artists Unit sketching sick and wounded men in service hospitals. Asked by an interviewer what he would rather do, see, and be than anything else, Rockwell answered succinctly, "Paint", "Fine Paintings," and "Great Painter."

References

Am Artist 4:11 My '40 por
Good H 116:31 F '43 por
International Studio 77:519-22 S '23 il
Ladies' H J 56:2 F '39 por

ROCKWELL, NORMAN—*Continued*

N Y World-Telegram p21 Je 6 '40 il
pors
New Yorker 21:34-8+ Mr 17 '45; 21:
36-40+ Mr 24 '45 pors
Time 41:41 Je 21 '43 il por
Who's Who in America, 1944-45

ROLLAND, ROMAIN (rô″län′ rô″män′)
Jan. 29, 1866—Dec. 30, 1944 Noted French
author, internationalist, and socialist; his works
include plays, biographies, historical and critical works, and political and social pamphlets;
awarded the Nobel Prize in 1915; best known
for his novel *Jean-Christophe* (1911-15); his
death in a German concentration camp was reported in October 1943, but report was denied
by DNB, the German news agency.

Obituary

N Y Times p19 Jan 2 '45 por

ROMBERG, SIGMUND July 29, 1887-
Composer; pianist
Address: b. c/o ASCAP, 30 Rockefeller Plaza,
New York City; h. Beverly Hills, Calif.

Often called the American successor to Johann Strauss, Hungarian-born, Viennese-edu-
cated Sigmund Romberg brings a nostalgic
flavor to his lilting melodies which Americans

SIGMUND ROMBERG

have been humming for a quarter of a century.
One of the most prolific writers of popular
music, he has composed, in thirty years, the
scores for more than seventy musical shows, a
total of some two thousand songs. In the history of the New York stage he is the only
composer who has had three shows which
have each seen more than five hundred performances on Broadway, namely, *Blossom
Time* (1921), *The Student Prince* (1924), and
The New Moon (1928). *Up in Central Park*,
the 1945 musical with a Romberg score, has

made the hit class largely because the music
is "lush and singable."

Szegedin, in Hungary, is the birthplace of
Sigmund Romberg. He was born there July
29, 1887, to Adam and Clara Romberg. In his
family were musicians and writers: his father,
a chemical manufacturer, was an amateur
pianist of no little ability, while his mother,
under the name of Clara Berg, was a well-
known novelist; the world-famous Alfred
Grünfeld was a cousin of his father's, as
was Adela Strauss, wife of Johann. At the
age of seven Sigmund began to take violin
lessons; he was taught by his father to play
the piano, and before long he was able to play
several other instruments, including the cello,
trumpet, and drums.

After attending schools in his native Hungary, young Romberg went to Vienna to finish
his education. There his work in school orchestras and bands attracted the attention of
Richard Heuberger, conductor of the noted
Wiener Männergesangverein, a men's choral
body. Under Heuberger's guidance the fourteen-year-old Romberg, who had never attended a school of music, began the study of
theory, harmony, and counterpoint. At sixteen
he wrote his first composition, a march called
"Soldiers of Mercy," which he dedicated to
the Grand Duchess Clotilde, Red Cross patroness in Austria. His pronounced talent for
music notwithstanding, Romberg enrolled in
the Vienna Technische Hochschule to study
civil engineering—but his leisure hours were
spent in Vienna musical circles. In 1907 Romberg's engineering course was interrupted
by Austria's compulsory one-year army training. At the end of the period a Balkan disturbance occurred, and for nine months Romberg was on border patrol duty. At the end
of his military service it was decided, in
family conference, that he might go to the
land of "boundless opportunity"—America.

The three hundred dollars which his family
had provided for the venture were soon gone,
and Romberg, who spoke very little English,
was glad to accept a seven-dollar-a-week job
with the Eagle Pencil Company in New York
City. Penniless on his fourth day at work, he
borrowed twenty-five cents for a meal at a
Second Avenue cafe, which in that year of
1910 offered a heaping plate of Hungarian
goulash, a stein of beer, and music by a string
quartet. While there the young foreigner engaged the orchestra leader in conversation, the
result of which was a pianist job for Romberg
at fifteen dollars a week, plus all the goulash
he could eat during a working day.

The cafe was a rendezvous for musicians.
Three weeks later the manager of Pabst's
Harlem Restaurant, after hearing the young
pianist play, offered him twenty-five dollars a
week, and fried chicken in place of goulash.
Before the year was out Romberg, who still
could not speak English well, was earning
forty-five dollars a week and had had his
first composition, "Memories," published.
After playing in a number of other cafes and
restaurants, he decided to organize his own
orchestra. At that period the most tiring
job on the New York cafe circuit was that
of entertainer in the famous Bustanoby's,
whose doors were open from noon to five in

the morning. Romberg, leading his own orchestra, not only survived the seventeen-hour grind of playing dance music, but while there composed three dance tunes: "Leg of Mutton," a turkey trot; "Some Smoke," a one-step; and "The Poem," a waltz.

J. J. Shubert, of the famed Shubert family, heard Romberg's work and immediately engaged him to write the musical score for the first Winter Garden show, *The Whirl of the World* (January 1914). The revue, starring Willie and Eugene Howard and the Dolly Sisters, ran for 161 performances on Broadway—establishing the reputation of Romberg and the Winter Garden shows. (In that era several prominent showmen produced annual revues: Florenz Ziegfeld did the *Follies,* George White, the *Scandals,* and the Shuberts, the *Passing Show,* which was always presented on the Winter Garden stage.)

Romberg contributed to, or was solely responsible for, the scores of the *Passing Show* of 1914, 1916, 1917, 1918, 1919, 1923, and 1924, and before he left the Shuberts in 1925 he had written scores for twenty-three other musical shows which the brothers had produced. Among the stars who appeared in these productions were Al Jolson '40, Ed Wynn '44, John Charles Thomas '43, Clifton Webb '43, Nora Bayes, Marilyn Miller, Vivienne Segal, Eleanor Painter, Peggy Wood '42, Leon Errol, DeWolf Hopper, the Dolly Sisters, and the Howard brothers. The composer's first major triumph came with his first operetta, *Maytime* (1917), a story of New York City in the early eighteen-hundreds. Although the press was divided on the merits of the production, the operetta proved so popular with the public that it remained on Broadway for 492 performances.

In 1919 Romberg formed his own producing firm with Max R. Willner, but the actors' strike that same year proved to be the undoing of this venture. As a result, the composer returned to the Shuberts, under whose banner in 1921 he wrote what has been the most successful production of his career so far—the operetta *Blossom Time.* In its first Broadway presentation it played 509 performances, and it was revived in 1926, 1931, 1938, and 1943. In between and during these Broadway engagements numerous companies brought the operetta to the four corners of the earth. Its book, written by Dorothy Donnelly, concerned the love story of Franz Schubert; the score was Romberg's modernization of Schubert melodies, and included his adaptation of Heinrich Berté's operetta *Das Dreimäderlhaus* (1916), which was also based on Schubert music.

Another major hit of the Romberg-Shubert association was *The Student Prince* (1924), the Americanization of *Alt Heidelberg.* It ran for 608 performances on Broadway, and has been revived a number of times in the United States and other countries. After the 1943 revival, Howard Barnes of the New York *Herald Tribune* reported that its most popular numbers, "The Drinking Song," and "Deep in My Heart, Dear," were as excitingly stirring as they had been two decades before. In October 1945 *Variety* noted that the "tuneful perennial drew $22,000" in Detroit the previous week. Shortly after the *Student Prince* Romberg left the Shuberts. His first smash hit under new management was *The Desert Song,*

produced in 1926 by Lawrence Schwab and Frank Mandel. This operetta had been written in collaboration with Mandel and its book and lyrics were by Schwab, Otto Harbach, and Oscar Hammerstein 2d '44.

The peak of Romberg's prolific output came in the year 1927. With *The Desert Song* still playing on Broadway, *My Maryland* was presented. (This work Romberg calls his favorite, although it never achieved the long run that some of his other operettas did.) In addition to these two, in the year 1927 Broadway audiences heard Romberg scores in *My Golden Girl, Cherry Blossoms, Bonita, My Princess,* and *Rosalie.* The last, a Ziegfeld musical written for Marilyn Miller, was "tossed off" by Romberg in collaboration with George Gershwin, while both composers were engaged in doing the scores for other productions. Romberg was in the midst of working on *The New Moon* and Gershwin was doing *Funny Face,* which starred Adele and Fred Astaire. *Rosalie* opened the same day as the other two shows, although in a different city, leaving the composers "up in the air trying to keep track of them."

The show with which *Rosalie* competed, *The New Moon,* was another Schwab and Mandel production with Hammerstein lyrics. It was produced in 1928 and turned out to be the composer's third show to pass the five-hundred mark on Broadway. On its revival at the New York City Center in 1944 critics called the Romberg score the show's greatest asset. "There is no denying," declared the New York *Times,* "that when he set it down he was writing the Hit Parade of 1928, and as well writing songs which have not been forgotten." These were "Softly as in a Morning Sunrise", "One Kiss", "Wanting You," and the song Romberg has called his favorite, "Lover, Come Back to Me." When this 1928 hit was played in between national anthems at the San Francisco Conference, according to a report in the New York *Times,* "everyone rose to his feet in fitting tribute." (*Oklahoma!* the 1943 Richard Rodgers '40-Oscar Hammerstein show, is the first musical to equal *The New Moon* in its number of hit songs.) The 1944 critics pronounced the book, with its pirates and revolutions, "drearily out of date." Hammerstein and Romberg collaborated on nine other productions after *The New Moon.* Among these were *East Wind* (1931), which closed after only thirty-one performances; *May Wine* (1935), a comedy about Hollywood which ran for 213 performances; and *Sunny River* (1941), the music of which was described by the New York *Times* as "ponderous and pedestrian."

With the advent of musical motion pictures, Hollywood sent for Romberg in 1929. It was to be a happy collaboration, for, although the composer has continued to contribute to Broadway musicals, he has established his home in Beverly Hills and casts his vote in California elections. Among the screen musicals on which he has worked in the succeeding two decades are *Viennese Nights* (1930), *The Girl of the Golden West* (1930), *Children of Dreams* (1931), and *The Night Is Young* (1935), as well as the adaptations of three of his operettas, *Maytime* (1937), *The New Moon* (1940), and *The Desert Song* (1943). In 1933 Romberg went to Paris to write the

ROMBERG, SIGMUND—*Continued*

music for an original operetta, *Rose de France*, which was produced by the Société Anonyme Française Chappell.

Although the composer has often appeared on the radio, until 1945 he had only one sponsored air series, a program for Swift and Company in 1934. In an interview with *Newsweek* at that time Romberg confessed about he preferred movie to radio work. "In Hollywood," he said, "if you ask for three military bands, they give them to you—in radio it's hard to create an effect. All you get is four blank walls." Moreover, he found that his weekly broadcast demanded all of his time—two new tunes a week and five-hour weekly rehearsals. In the summer of 1945, however, Romberg returned to radio, and "An Evening with Romberg," sponsored by Raleigh Cigarettes, was a weekly half-hour feature, offering twenty minutes of his own selections. The program was continued, except for a brief vacation, until the late autumn when Romberg planned an extensive concert series. He has said that he finds the preparation of a radio program, with its problems of timing and of gratifying the sponsor's mood, to be "infinitely more exertion than a cross-country concert tour."

In 1942 Romberg began a new venture. Acting on his theory that people were a little tired of hearing jazz or serious music at concerts, he contracted to conduct six concerts in Eastern cities, a program called *An Evening With Sigmund Romberg*. The program naturally contained much Romberg music, but there were bits of Jerome Kern [42], Gershwin, Lehár, and other "standards" in the "pop" concert repertoire. The six concerts, scheduled for the last months of 1942, had become 277 in 128 cities by January 1944, and had made over seven hundred thousand dollars. Louisville, for example, heard the program five times. On his tours the composer was accompanied by a forty-five-piece orchestra and several soloists. His conducting was described as unorthodox, "everything geared to a nice relaxation." In concerts he gave at Army and Navy camps, Romberg says, he sang some of his own tunes, although he has no singing voice. The presence of the composer seemed to please the men, he felt. The wide appeal of his work was again evident in July 1945, when Romberg, leading the Philharmonic-Symphony Orchestra, attracted an audience of fifteen thousand to the Lewisohn Stadium in New York City, to enjoy "an evening of music in the old Vienna manner."

Up in Central Park (January 1945), Romberg's first Broadway production in many seasons, became a "sellout" in its first weeks on Broadway, despite a diversity of critical opinion as to its merits. It is the story of how New York's "ugly Back Yard" became the famous Central Park of today only because its development offered "Boss" Tweed of Tammany a rich opportunity for swindling the taxpayers. Like Romberg's first operetta, *Maytime*, it is set in the eighteen-hundreds— a blend of fiction and history. The book (by Dorothy and Herbert Fields), Lewis Nichols of the New York *Times* said, "plods where it should dance," while the score, though pleasant enough in a nostalgic fashion," with several good songs, "It Doesn't Cost You Any-

thing To Dream", "Close as Pages in a Book," was not varied enough. Ward Morehouse [40] pronounced the score "first rate" and the comedy "weak." The New York *World-Telegram* reviewer, Burton Rascoe, put the show on the "must list," hailing Romberg as "the master melodist." According to Diana Gibbings, in the New York *Times*, Romberg says that it takes him about ten to twelve weeks to write a score. "My wastebasket is full of discarded tunes, but one has to shake off a failure like a dog shakes off water."

In the past ten years the composer has given much of his time to organization work. He is a member of the ASCAP board of directors and is president of the Songwriters Protective Association. During the time he has held the latter post (1932 to 1936 and since 1942), he has worked to establish a closed shop for the songwriters. A closed shop for free-lance composers is maintained through an agreement between a songwriters' association and a publishers' association in which each has agreed to do business only with members of the other association on minimum basic terms for all song rights. Romberg has also worked for better copyright protection for the members of SPA. He has stated, "We want the same protection that England gives its writers—a copyright which does not expire until fifty years after the death of the owner." He is also working for 50 per cent royalties on television rights, because, he explains, "there's no telling how far this new medium will go."

Romberg was married to Lillian Harris in 1925. The Rombergs, who have maintained New York apartments at different times, regard Beverly Hills, California, as their permanent home. The most prominent feature in their house is the library, which holds more than five thousand volumes—original manuscripts, first editions, operas, and operettas—one of the most important libraries of its kind in the world. A combination organ-piano greatly aids the composer in his work, for which he finds most of his inspiration in the early hours of the morning. Stoutish, bald, and genial in manner, he was once described by a writer as a "Viennese burgher." Romberg requested that the characterization be changed to "Viennese boulevardier," which, considering the composer's keen sense of humor and the dancing quality of his melodies, seems a more fitting description.

References

N Y Sun p20 Ja 12 '45
Newsweek 4:28 D 1 '34 por
Time 26:61 D 16 '35 por
International Motion Picture Almanac, 1943-44
Who's Who in America, 1944-45
Who's Who in the Theatre (1939)

ROOSEVELT, FRANKLIN D(ELANO)
(rō'zě-vělt děl'á-nō) Jan. 30, 1882—Apr. 12, 1945 Thirty-first President of the United States, seventh President to die in office, and the only Chief Executive in American history to be elected for more than two terms; was stricken by a cerebral hemorrhage on the eighty-third day of his fourth term, "in an hour of high triumph," as Allied victory in Second World

War seemed near; during political life was member of New York State Senate (1910-13), Assistant Secretary of the Navy (1913-20), Governor of New York (1929-33), President of the United States since 1933; initiated administrative and legislative reforms known collectively as the New Deal; met at sea with Winston Churchill '42 August 1941 to draw up joint statement of American-British international policy now known as the Atlantic Charter; took part in momentous conferences with Allied leaders at Casablanca (January 1943), Quebec (August 1943), Teheran (November 1943), and Yalta (February 1945), in which he made vital contributions to decisions affecting broad military strategy and the postwar world. See *Current Biography* 1942 Yearbook.

Obituary

N Y Times p1+ Ap 13 '45 pors

ROPER, ELMO (BURNS, JR.) July 31, 1900- Marketing consultant; public opinion analyst; United States Government official

Address: b. Elmo Roper, 30 Rockefeller Plaza, New York City; h. West Redding, Conn.

Blackstone Studios

ELMO ROPER

The closest estimate of the popular vote in three United States Presidential elections has been that of Elmo Roper, market researcher and public opinion analyst. In the words of *Fortune* Magazine, whose monthly surveys he conducts, "Not only has Mr. Roper been one of the first to create a technique for the scientific sampling of the public mind, but he has also contributed perhaps more than any other individual to the development of a rationale for that technique. . . .Today, thanks largely to the thinking of Mr. Roper, public opinion research holds an important place among the social sciences."

Like his friends and closest rivals, George Gallup '40 of the Gallup Poll and Archibald Crossley '41 of the Crossley Rating, Elmo Burns Roper, Jr., was born in a small town. His birthplace was Hebron, Nebraska, and the date was July 31, 1900. The son of Elmo Burns and Coco (Malowney) Roper, young Elmo spent a fair portion of his early years asking people not to call him Elmer—still his "pet peeve." Graduated from Hebron High School in 1918, Roper attended the University of Minnesota for one year. Urged by a Scottish grandmother, he went to Scotland to study moral philosophy at the University of Edinburgh. But the youth never got his degree, for in 1921 he returned to the United States and opened a jewelry store in Creston, Iowa. By June 1922 he was sufficiently well established to be married to Dorothy C. Shaw. (The Ropers have two sons, Burns Worthington and James Jeremy.) A member of the local businessman's associations, Rotary, the Chamber of Commerce, and the Iowa Retail Jewelers' Association, in 1927 Roper became president of the latter.

Nevertheless, the young jeweler's store was not quite so successful as he thought it should be. Analyzing the situation (as Beverly Smith tells it in the *American* Magazine), the jeweler discovered at twenty-seven that he was trying to sell jewelry he liked, instead of the kind his customers liked. Roper investigated his neighbors' preferences and then decided he did

not want to sell "the kind of jewelry the Iowa farmers liked." So he gave up his store in 1928 and took a job as salesman for the Seth Thomas Clock Company, later becoming associated with the New Haven Clock Company, and then with the Traub Manufacturing Company of Detroit, Michigan.

Remembering his Iowa experience, Roper constantly quizzed his customers as to their likes and dislikes in clocks. With this information as a basis, he continued to make a fine sales record throughout the depression, and was promoted to sales supervisor and assistant sales manager. In 1933 he gave up selling to enter marketing research in New York, where he went into partnership the next year with the marketing expert Paul T. Cherington and the writer Richardson Wood—establishing themselves as Cherington, Roper and Wood, distribution consultants. Roper devoted himself to taking polls of public taste for the firm's clients in private industry, and developed a sampling technique which utilized a relatively small number of subjects, carefully selected to be a representative cross-section of the group surveyed.

In 1935 Henry Luce '40 engaged Roper's firm to conduct the *Fortune* surveys of public opinion, to be published that July and quarterly thereafter. (Since July 1938 the surveys have appeared in nearly every issue.) The next year Cherington, Roper, and Wood parted company, Cherington and Roper remaining partners until November 1, 1937, when Roper went on alone. The 1937 Presidential election first brought Elmo Roper to the public's attention, as it did Gallup and Crossley, who had independently worked out "economical and apparently scientific methods of polling a small, representative cross-section of the population." That year the celebrated *Literary Digest* straw vote showed an easy prospective victory for Alf Landon '44 in his Presidential race against Franklin D. Roosevelt '42. Gallup and Crossley each predicted that the Republican would win about 54 per cent of the popular vote, and listed a num-

ROPER, ELMO—*Continued*

ber of states for Landon, while Roper's findings
led him to predict a Roosevelt victory, with 61.7
per cent of the popular vote, opposed only by
the northeast section of the country. But Democratic National Chairman James A. Farley '44,
hit the bull's-eye when he announced that
Landon would carry only Maine and Vermont.
Roosevelt won with 60.7 per cent, a result which
differed from the *Literary Digest*'s figure by 19
per cent, from Crossley's and Gallup's by nearly 7 per cent, and from Roper's *Fortune* survey by only 1 per cent. This had two effects:
it contributed to the decline of the *Literary
Digest*, and established the three poll-takers as
national oracles.

Forecasting elections is perhaps the least important aspect of survey work; Roper himself
calls it "a socially useless function," admitting
ruefully that "those of us who have stuck our
necks out in election predictions are expected
to keep on doing so." Yet such forecasts have
an importance in that the whole world is interested in a Presidential election, while much
opinion research is necessarily private, even
secret; market research is at best dull to the
outsider. Even a local election offers a chance
to measure the surveyor's accuracy, test new
techniques, and demonstrate his trustworthiness.
In 1940 his was the most accurate forecast in
the Presidential election, with a statistical error
of one-half of 1 per cent. (Gallup's was 3
per cent; Wall's missed by 2 per cent; and
Emil Huria and William L. Crum each predicted a Willkie '40 victory.) In that election,
for the first time, CBS had Roper analyzing
voting trends over the air. The prestige
of the surveys had reached such heights
that at least one Congressman (Walter M.
Pierce of Oregon) claimed that the surveys
influenced elections by creating a "bandwagon
vote," thus opening a way for "private manipulation of public opinion for profit." This all
three leading researchers deny, although they
agree that their survey results probably (and
properly) influence legislative votes. Roper
goes further; he thinks the Federal Government should establish its own poll, on much
the same basis as the Supreme Court, to determine the public's opinion on the issues before it.

Roper's surveys—which, like most leading
statisticians', are considered "absolutely honest
and scrupulously impartial"—are made in a
somewhat different manner from most others.
He has the smallest staff of interviewers
(one hundred and fifty-six, to Gallup's eleven
hundred and Wall's four thousand). He polls
the smallest number of people. His interviewers, however, are intensively trained,
while Gallup employs business and professional people who work for him only a few
hours a week. Each Roper worker in a given
area is assigned to interview a given number of
men and women, of whom an assigned number
is to be in each age group, each income group,
and each occupational group, plus whatever
other factors the survey may call for. As
Dorothy Dunbar Bromley comments, "Interviewers have to be good at acrostics." In
addition to the monthly *Fortune* survey, Roper's
staff carries on research for an impressive list
of private clients, which includes the Columbia
Broadcasting System, the Standard Oil Com-

pany of New Jersey, Spiegel, Inc., and the
American Meat Institute.

In February 1941, ten months before Pearl
Harbor, Elmo Roper became a dollar-a-year
man as a member of the Advisory Committee
to Donald M. Nelson '41 in the Purchases Division of the Office of Production Management,
which later became the War Production Board.
In addition, that July Roper was appointed
deputy director under Colonel William J.
Donovan '41 of the Office of the Co-ordinator
of Information; and when the Office of Facts
and Figures was formed in October, with
Archibald MacLeish '40 as head, Roper was
made a member of the Board of Governors.
At the same time, the remaining services
of Donovan's COI were assigned to the
new Office of Strategic Services, of which
Roper was deputy director. (This office, which
operated under the Joint Chiefs of Staff, was
so secret that, alone among Government agencies, its accounts were not subject to auditing.
With the war's end, its functions were transferred to the State Department.) Roper, whose
research activities continued full blast, was
made a director of Spiegel, Inc., at about this
time, and was also elected to the board of
Traub Manufacturing Company a few months
afterward. Later that year Williams College
awarded him an honorary M.A. degree. For
several years Roper has also been on the faculty
of Columbia University's Graduate School of
Journalism as an assistant professor, giving
occasional lectures.

During the pre-election period, beginning
October 9, 1944, a large number of newspapers
subscribed for Professor Roper's semi-weekly
column *What People Are Thinking* through
the New York *Herald Tribune* syndicate. The
Fortune survey forecast a 53.6 per cent vote
for Roosevelt, missing by only two-tenths of
1 per cent, to Crossley's 1.3 per cent statistical
error, and Gallup's 1.8 per cent. (On Election
Day night, in what promised to become a network tradition, CBS had Roper analyzing election trends, Blue had Gallup, and WOR-Mutual
had Crossley.) Roper also delivered to the
newspapers a post-election column not called
for in his contract; and one week later he
began a weekly series, under the same title, to
be published in the *Tribune* and eight other
newspapers.

The researcher had already written several
magazine articles on public opinion, in which
he stated several conclusions from his years
of poll-taking. One is that, when intensity of
opinion is measured, the women usually tend
to take a moderate position, while the men
usually choose the violent or extreme positions. (This fact contradicts the popular
impression on the subject.) Perhaps Roper's
most significant finding is that the common
working-class man is often disappointingly uninformed about vital matters, but that "he is
fundamentally possessed of a vast store of
common sense." "Moreover," says Roper, "it
has been my observation that when the public
has enough of the facts to judge the probable
result of any given action, it is likely to steer
just as wise and fair a course as that plotted
by any of its leaders. For this reason, I think
the emphasis in public opinion research has
been largely misplaced. I believe its first duty
is to explore the areas of public ignorance."

Its second great function is "to report the opinions of the majorities on such matters as the public is, because of its knowledge, equipped to judge. For on such subjects the people have a sovereign right to be heard and to be heeded by their representatives."

His other conclusions Roper reported in a February 1942 *Rotarian* Magazine article, "What Americans Believe." "The second major conclusion I have arrived at," he wrote, "is that a way must be found, under some form of capitalistic society, to redistribute earning opportunity. The United States cannot continue to go forward with a system of dividing the rewards of industry [which involves] . . . a cumbersome system of taxes and organized charity [to rectify its injustices]. A more equitable distribution by industry itself is essential. This should be kept in mind as a postwar objective." And in February 1944 a Roper article stated that "in ten years of sampling the opinions of workmen—organized and unorganized, in all parts of the country and in all income brackets—we have discovered some remarkable common denominators of opinion. . . .From the answers to a great variety of questions we have been asking almost continuously since 1933, it is fair to assert that the American workman wants, first of all, *security*," which includes the right to work continuously at reasonably good wages, and also various additional forms, such as better education, pension plans, home ownership, etc. The second main desire is *a chance to advance.* "In this connection," Roper comments, "it would not be surprising if industry seriously considered the idea of educating its employees and their children." The third main demand is for treatment *"like human beings"*—that is, with politeness, friendliness, and consideration. And the fourth is the desire to feel that one is making a real contribution: 70 per cent of American workers say they feel a definite obligation to pass something on to the next generation. "Having set down these four great basic desires of the people in America who work for a living," says the analyst, "there seems very little left that cannot properly be included in one of these groupings. . . .The four desires are not in any sense mutually exclusive. . . . Yet it should be pointed out that in order to have some of each, the average workman seems willing to give up some of each." "In describing what labor wants," Roper concludes, "perhaps I have only been describing what everyone, everywhere, wants."

Early in 1945 one of Roper's columns in *What People Are Thinking,* which summarized results of surveys in recent years, caused Eleanor Roosevelt to comment in the New York *World-Telegram*: "He tells some of the curious quirks which illustrate our lack of information, or our complete misinformation on many things that most of us assume everybody knows about. One of the items which Mr. Roper picks out is that 51 per cent of our high school students, tested in one survey, were unable to name either of the United States Senators from their state." There are many other obvious things cited by Roper, concluded Mrs. Roosevelt, "which make one wonder whether the great majority of people really read their newspapers and whether, when they listen on the radio, they take in much of what they hear." *Time* called attention to Roper's own conclusion that many

United States citizens were uninformed even about our closest Allies. Nevertheless, reports on polls during past months reflect an unusual degree of enlightened thought in general upon such immediate questions as a World Security Organization, Truman's handling of domestic problems, labor's strike record during the war, disposal of surplus property, use of the atomic bomb, Americans' attitudes towards Russia, and the United States Jews' stand on Palestine.

On the eve of the San Francisco Conference, Roper participated in a special radio broadcast and announced that his poll, just completed, of American opinion on the question of a World Security Organization revealed that 72 per cent of the population want to see the United States take an active part in an international organization. On the crucial problems involving the atomic bomb, Roper's poll reported in November that the majority of Americans approved of the use of the bomb, but believe they cannot keep the secret of the bomb for as long as five years. Almost 50 per cent of the people were of the opinion that the discovery had decreased the possibility of a future world war.

From the public opinion surveys he has conducted Roper has found that better informed persons were less liable to have strong prejudices resulting from misconceptions. "Racial and religious intolerance," he maintains, "can best be fought and overcome through facts. . . . The opportunity to attend school must be extended to an ever-increasing number of people, and more and better newspapers, magazines, radio broadcasts, motion pictures, and forums must be encouraged and supported."

This marketing-consultant-statistician-professor-columnist-official is a lean, quiet six-footer with curly brown hair parted in the middle, brown eyes behind rimless glasses, and a pleasant, thin-lipped face. Photographs seldom show him without one or more pipes, but he denies that he has a collection, or any other hobby or favorite recreation. "One might do me good," he smiles, "but I haven't got any." (This, according to psychologist Johnson O'Connor of the Human Engineering Laboratories, means that Roper is completely fulfilling himself in his work.) A Presbyterian and a Democrat (although he voted for Norman Thomas [44] in 1932), Roper is a member of several professional and social organizations, including the Masonic Order, and he was president of the Market Research Council in 1942-43. He is a member of the New York Housing Authority's Committee to Review Tenant Selection Procedure. Roper is described as an agreeable, frankly spoken man, who thinks of his work as an infant science about which there is still much to learn. He frequently meets with his chief competitors, Gallup and Crossley, for friendly shoptalks.

References

Am Mag 130:31 N '40 por
Rotarian 60:56 F '42 por
Time 36:67 N 18 '40 por
Who's Who in America, 1944-45

ROSE, MAURICE Nov. 26, 1899—Apr.(?) 1945 Major General in the United States Army; commander of the Third Armored Division in the Second World War; met death while leading his division in spearheading the

ROSE, MAURICE—*Continued*

advance of United States troops in Germany; distinguished himself many times during African and French battles; awarded Distinguished Service Medal.

Obituary

N Y Times p10 Ap 3 '45 por

ROSENTHAL, JOE . Oct. 9, 1911- Photographer

Address: b. c/o The Associated Press, Chronicle Bldg., San Francisco

Joe Rosenthal's photograph of the flag raising atop Mount Suribachi on Iwo Jima in February 1945 so stirred the American people by its drama that it became the official poster of

JOE ROSENTHAL

the Seventh War Loan Drive, was reproduced millions of times in newspapers and magazines, was selected for the design of a commemorative postage stamp, and was awarded a Pulitzer Prize.

Born in Washington, D.C., on October 9, 1911, Joe Rosenthal is one of five sons of David and Lena Rosenthal, Russian immigrants to America. His father was in the clothing business. Much as any American boy, he became a Boy Scout and played with a Brownie camera, although he was not then interested in photography as a career. When his small size barred him from the football team at McKinley Technical High School in Washington, his interest in athletics made him join the track team. A pole vaulter who could vault eleven feet, he won his letter and several medals. Upon graduation in 1930, he left Washington to join his brothers in San Francisco, intending to work his way through the University of California. However, at this time he got no further than registering, because his job as office boy with the Newspaper Enterprise Association proved too interesting to give up. "When I got that job,"

he says, "N.E.A. might have meant National Education Association, for all I knew. I guess if it had been a grocery company, I'd be distributing groceries now." But his interest in photography had been aroused during his high school days, and N.E.A.'s San Francisco office became his training ground.

Two years later, wishing to attain the prominence of an occasional by-line at the head of a newspaper story, he became a reporter and photographer for the San Francisco *News,* covering police headquarters, the civil courts, and hospitals. In 1935 he became chief photographer of the Acme News Pictures' San Francisco bureau, and a year later he accepted the position of bureau manager with Wide World Photos, which he grinningly describes as "janitor and vice-president in charge of licking stamps." When in 1941 the Associated Press bought the Wide World from its owner the New York *Times* (the sale was effective August 1), Rosenthal became an Associated Press cameraman. By this time the photographer had won recognition at least twice: In 1934 he made newspaper headlines all over the country when, despite injuries which sent him to the hospital for eight days and the smashing of his camera, he managed to obtain a photograph of the San Francisco water front strikers. In 1936, in its first annual national competition for the best photograph of the year, *Editor and Publisher* gave Rosenthal's picture of Max Baer taking a shower first honors in the sports division and designated it the best news photograph of 1936.

After the attack on Pearl Harbor, Rosenthal did his best to get into the armed forces, but one after another the Army, Navy, and Marine Corps rejected him because of his vision, which has been described as about one-twentieth of normal. (He wears thick bifocal lenses, but even with these he has to squint at times.) Finally, however, through the agency of a friend, the eye test was waived for the photographer and he became a warrant officer in the United States Maritime Service. Assigned to a convoy bound for England in July 1943, he took pictures of the ships and of life on shipboard in the Atlantic, of British ports when he arrived in England, and of the North African theater before returning to the United States in January 1944. He went back to the A.P. when that organization offered him what he considered a better chance to see more action. From March of that year, when he was made an accredited war photographer in the Pacific area and sent out on an assignment with the Wartime Still Pictures Pool, Rosenthal was at Guadalcanal and covered invasions of New Guinea, Hollandia, Guam, Palau, Peleliu, and Angaur islands. Landings on the last three named were made, he says, within a period of only three days. In addition, he recorded action on carrier bombing missions against Formosa, Ryukyu Islands, including Okinawa, at Manila, and during the second battle of the Philippines. Before he won fame with the flag-raising photograph, he had taken another highly praised shot of the marines of the Fourth Division, "digging in on Iwo Jima, after wrecking an 'impregnable' Jap pillbox," and he has referred to himself as the man who spent a month at General MacArthur's [41] headquarters without taking a picture of the General.

The now famous picture was taken on February 23, 1945, at the second unofficial flag raising on Iwo Jima, about three-quarters of an hour after the marines had hoisted, also unofficially, a smaller banner on a staff of lead pipe. The official ceremony occurred on March 14, when Admiral Chester W. Nimitz[42] formally took military possession of the island and unfurled the Stars and Stripes at the base of Mount Suribachi. Rosenthal was not present at the first flag raising. He got the opportunity to take the photograph of the second more or less by chance when a companion pointed to the marines starting up the hill with the flag (a six-foot banner on a twenty-foot staff). Together with two Marine Corps photographers, one of whom was Sergeant William Genaust who took the movie sequence of the flag raising which was incorporated in the official film *To the Shores of Iwo Jima,* Joe Rosenthal toiled up the sandy volcanic slope, side-stepping hastily marked mines, dodging snipers' bullets, and avoiding American demolition squads. Arrived at the summit, he piled rocks and a Japanese sandbag on the crater's rim in order to gain a wider range for his camera. He took three shots, the famous one with the staff halfway up, a second with the marines surveying their accomplishment, and a third, frankly posed, with the men standing around the flag cheering.

Because he sent the film straight to Guam for developing, Rosenthal did not know until he arrived on Guam five days later, which picture was meant in the radio message "Fine pix flag raising." He thought the words referred to the one for which he had posed the marines. About the picture Rosenthal said, "It wouldn't have been any disgrace at all to figure out a composition like that. But it just so happened I didn't. Good luck was with me, that's all—the wind rippling the flag right, the men in fine positions, and the day clear enough to bring everything into sharp focus." "The shot was taken," said the *New Yorker* after an interview with Rosenthal, "with a Speed Graphic, between f/8 and f/11 at 1/400th of a second, on an Agfa Ansco Superpan Press filmpack against an overcast sky, with camera visibility about five miles."

The appearance of the scene on the front page of newspapers and coloroto magazine sections won Rosenthal nation-wide acclaim and, after his return to the United States on March 17, a round of banquets and interviews planned by the Associated Press. Besides being interviewed by reporters and appearing on the radio program *We, the People,* he was asked to select a group of his Pacific photographs for publication in *U. S. Camera* and was dined by A.P. President Kent Cooper[44]. He told a *New Yorker* interviewer that he would like to see the Statue of Liberty but did not expect to get the chance before being rushed to Washington. When his photograph, in the form of an oil painting by C. C. Beall (who says that the painting is an exact reproduction in color), became the official poster of the Seventh War Loan, Rosenthal was sent on a War Bond tour together with Rene Gagnon and Ira Hayes, two of the survivors of the episode. Another oil painting reproduc-

tion of the photograph, executed by Major J. Capolino, M.C.R., was presented in September to the Senate Naval Committee by General A. A. Vandegrift, Marine Corps commandant, who said Rosenthal's photograph is "the highlight of Marine Corps history in this war."

The photograph has won Rosenthal many honors, including the Pulitzer Prize of five hundred dollars for news photography in May 1945. He received one plaque from the New York Photographers Association. In April he received another from the recently organized Catholic Institute of the Press at its first public function, a Communion breakfast at the Waldorf-Astoria Hotel. (He has been a Roman Catholic since 1939.) This plaque bears on a scroll below a reproduction of the flag-raising photograph the inscription: "Faith in God was his armor, his weapons valor and skill. He served in the best traditions of the American press photographer." (Rosenthal presented the plaque to the A.P.) The A.P. itself gave Rosenthal the largest bonus it had ever given a photographer—shortly before this he had received a raise. At a dinner given in his honor by *U.S. Camera* in June, he received a thousand-dollar War Bond and a medallion. In announcing the award, *U.S. Camera* wrote: "The Editors of *U.S. Camera* were guided in making their selection by the conviction that the Iwo picture fully accomplished the ultimate purpose of photography, which is to make the viewer relive the events recorded. The Iwo picture caught the event so effectively that one who looks at it can virtually feel and hear the breeze which whips the flag. In a sense, in that moment, Rosenthal's camera recorded the soul of a nation." He also received the Graflex Camera award.

It has been estimated that for the Seventh War Loan Drive Rosenthal's flag picture appeared on 3,500,000 posters, 15,000 outdoor panels, and 175,000 car cards, not counting its appearance in simplified form in countless newspaper advertisements. It has been proposed as a model for war memorials by committees all over the country. A fifty-foot reproduction of the photograph, with lifelike twelve-foot figures posed by six marine veterans of the South Pacific, was set up by the war activities committee of the motion picture industry in the Times Square area in New York. At its unveiling, the three survivors of the flag raising hoisted the original battle-scarred banner to the top of the statue's flagstaff. The statue stood in Times Square through the summer months, and on October 26 it was presented to the United States Naval Hospital, St. Albans, Queens, New York, at a ceremony attended by more than three hundred patients and members of the hospital staff. In accepting the statue from the organization which erected it, Captain Edward D. McMorries, medical officer in command of the hospital, said, "I hope that every patient who enters the hospital may see this statue and get from it the inspiration to continue his fight back to normal health." Another statue, also modeled after the famous photograph, stands in front of the Navy Building in Washington, D.C. It was unveiled on November 10 in observance of the Marine Corps' one hundred and seventieth anniversary. In addition, the picture was used as the central design

ROSENTHAL, JOE—*Continued*

of a commemorative postage stamp honoring the achievements of the Marine Corps. The three-cent postage stamp broke all post office records for first-day cover cancellations, according to a report of the Post Office Department. A total of 400,279 covers or envelopes were canceled. (The previous record was reported to have been set by the Roosevelt Memorial three-cent stamp June 27, when 391,-650 covers were canceled.)

Interviewers have found Rosenthal amiable, but shy and inclined to belittle his accomplishment, but those who know his work think his success was due as much to a keen sense for photographic possibilities as to luck. Secretary of the Navy James V. Forrestal '42 considered his action in obtaining the photograph as gallant as that of the men raising the flag. Asked about his work in the Pacific area, Rosenthal replied, "I like to go ashore during the early hours of the morning because you get better action shots. Scared? Sure, I'm scared. But there's one thing about an invasion —it's all one-way traffic and you can't get a ride going the other way." In a dispatch from Guam, Malcolm Johnson wrote: "Joe is the kind of fellow who will return from a hard day's work to find his room overflowing with acquaintances, or even strangers, engaged in an endless session of shooting the breeze. More often than not they have appropriated Joe's liquor as well as his room. Instead of remonstrating that he's tired and wants to go to bed, Joe will retire modestly to a corner, usually sitting on the floor, grin good-naturedly and then nod and doze while the session continued far into the night."

Rosenthal is short, about five feet five inches. He has a mustache and smokes cigarettes through a holder. *Time* Magazine reports that after the publication of his photograph his San Francisco draft board changed his draft status from 4-F (because of defective vision) to 2-AF (essential deferment), explaining that he now deserved "a classification better than 4-F." After spending a four-week vacation in California, he was assigned to the A.P.'s San Francisco office.

References

N Y Post Mag p21 Mr 29 '45 por
N Y Sun p13 Mr 26 '45 por
N Y Times p16 My 8 '45 il por
New Yorker 21:17-18 Ap 7 '45
Newsweek 25:82 Ap 16 '45 il por
Scholastic 46:29 My 7 '45
Time 45:60 Mr 26 '45 por
U S Camera 9:16-17+ Je '45 por

ROSS, CHARLES (GRIFFITH) Nov. 9, 1885- Journalist

Address: White House, Washington, D.C.

In what was then hailed as a master stroke in cementing relations between the White House and news disseminating agencies, President Harry S. Truman '45 in April 1945 appointed Charles Ross, leading Washington newspaperman and his lifelong friend, to the post of Presidential press secretary. Ross, in relinquishing his connection with the St. Louis *Post-Dispatch*, for which he specialized in po-

litical and economic reporting from Washington, made one proviso: that he be allowed to cover the San Francisco conference for his paper before assuming his new duties; hence, the appointment, although made on April 19, did not take effect until May 15.

Charles Griffith Ross was born in Independence, Missouri, President Truman's home town, on November 9, 1885; he is the son of James Bruce and Ella (Thomas) Ross. He and Truman received their secondary education at the same high school, which Bess Wallace, now Mrs. Truman, also attended, she being in the class below. Although Ross is nearly two years younger than the President, he was graduated with Truman in the class of 1901 and, more scholarly than his friend, he was the class's valedictorian. A contemporary, recently quoted by Cabell Phillips in a feature article for the New York *Times*, recalls that Truman and Ross were the two brightest boys in the class, and that "they spent their afternoons for a month whittling out a model bridge made exactly to the specifications of one of Caesar's bridges described in the Commentaries." After commencement their paths diverged, Truman going into business and politics and Ross to the University of Missouri at Columbia. He was graduated in 1905, a member of Phi Beta Kappa. While still at the university, Ross in 1904 joined the staff of the Columbia (Missouri) *Herald*, which position he held until 1906, when he moved to the Victor (Colorado) *Record*. During the year 1906-7 he was with the St. Louis *Post-Dispatch*, and in the following year, with the St. Louis *Republic*.

In 1908 Ross joined the faculty of the newly organized School of Journalism at the University of Missouri, the first school of its kind in the United States. Here he was with an old associate, for the dean was the late Walter Williams, editor of the Columbia *Herald*. While with the university, Ross in 1911 wrote *The Writing of the News*. On August 20, 1913, he was married to Florence Griffin. Their two sons were both in active service during the war—John Bruce was a lieutenant in the Medical Corps, Walter William a lieutenant in the Navy. In 1916-17, on a year's sabbatical leave from the University of Missouri, Ross was in Australia as sub-editor of the Melbourne *Herald*.

In 1918, ten years after his appointment to the university faculty, Ross began his long career with the St. Louis *Post-Dispatch*, on which, back in 1906-7, he had already served a year's apprenticeship. He became chief correspondent of the *Post-Dispatch*'s newly formed Washington bureau, with which he remained for a record sixteen years. In 1932 Ross won the Pulitzer Prize in journalism for an article written for his paper in 1931, "The Country's Plight—What Can Be Done About It?" an inquiry into the causes of the depression and the remedies administered by President Herbert Hoover '45. In 1933 he received a medal of honor from the University of Missouri "for his thorough intellectual background, practically motivated; for reporting significant current history; for his scholarly interpretation, lucidly and interestingly expressed, of the great efforts of the day; for his unfailing efforts to promote among the people a better understanding of government and finance, and of the whole economic fabric of the present crisis. As an extraordinary reporter of facts and ideas, he has faithfully fulfilled his public trust."

Ross left Washington for St. Louis in 1934 to become editor of the *Post-Dispatch*'s editorial page. In 1935 he was awarded an honorary Doctor of Laws degree from George Washington University (Washington, D.C.) for his contribution to journalism, and in 1936 he received the same degree from the University of Missouri. He returned to the Capital in 1939 in the capacity of contributing editor of his newspaper. During his last two years in this post he concentrated on a series of articles entitled *Men and Jobs After the War*, a study in peace and postwar problems.

According to a report in *Newsweek,* Truman had proposed the secretariat to Ross as early as April 13 (1945), the day after he became President, although the New York *Times* implies that the date was somewhat later. Ross is known to have been reluctant to exchange his eminently satisfactory contributing editorship for the governmental post; nevertheless, the President prevailed upon him to accept and upon his publisher, Joseph Pulitzer (a son of the late Joseph Pulitzer of Pulitzer Prize fame), to grant him a two-year leave of absence. The appointment was made on April 19, and was supposed to be kept secret until Ross took office. The news, however, leaked out when Truman and Ross telephoned their former high school English teacher in Independence to tell her the good news that "Harry and Charlie were working together once more." Miss Matilda Brown, or Miss Tillie as she is known to all Independence, quickly spread the news throughout the town, as Stephen T. Early [41], who was present when the call was made, predicted she would, and the Independence *Examiner* was able to offer a scoop to the country's newspapers, including the St. Louis *Post-Dispatch.* The next day, while Ross was speeding to San Francisco aboard the "Correspondents' Special," President Truman confirmed the appointment at a hastily summoned press conference. On May 15, after his return from San Francisco, Ross was sworn in as Secretary to the President, in charge of press relations, by Associate Justice Wiley Rutledge, Jr. [43], of the United States Supreme Court. The ceremony took place in Truman's office in the White House, with the President and Mrs. Ross looking on.

The position to which Ross had been appointed might be, as it was for Early during President Roosevelt's [42] last years, a difficult one, because the press secretary has to carry out the Executive's wishes without incurring the displeasure of the press; he is the "buffer" between the President and the reporters. But Ross's job was made immeasurably easier by the high esteem in which he was held by the Nation's newsmen. The news policy formulated for the new administration included one Presidential news conference a week, which Ross hoped to be able to announce well in advance. Aside from that, Ross intended to see that news emanating from White House sources would come from his office so that everyone would get a "square deal." Since President Truman approved the "fullest possible flow

CHARLES ROSS

of information to the press and radio," Ross planned to answer all the questions he could, to admit his ignorance if he did not know the answers, and to say when information could not be disclosed. With his industry, "cool judgment," and knowledge of Washington, he was expected to be an invaluable Presidential aide. According to a feature article in the *United States News* in October, the early months of the Truman administration provide evidence that these expectations were justified. "Far more important in the shaping of general policies than he is generally given credit for," said the magazine, "is Charles G. Ross . . . [He] works quietly in the background, but his activities are considerably broader than the simple disclosure of White House news. . . .His advice [as one of the President's inner advisory circle] has carried great weight."

Ross is a tall gray-haired, stoop-shouldered, scholarly-looking man. Commentators agree that he brings to his new post the personal qualities of intelligence, courage, integrity, and a sense of responsibility, and that his years in Washington have given him a profound understanding of national political and economic problems. His colleagues expect Ross to succeed not merely to Early's post as press secretary but also to take Early's place as Presidential adviser, especially since Ross has more than once advised Truman in the past. Ross is not only respected but well liked by his associates for his "winning personality" and good fellowship. He is a member of the Gridiron Club, of which he was president in 1933, of the Overseas Writers, of which he was chairman in 1927, and of the fraternities Sigma Chi and Sigma Delta Chi, the latter having made him honorary national president in 1935. Described as "a man of great personal dignity but no solemnity," he enjoys the lively talk which characterizes the luncheons at the National Press Club, at which, metaphorically speaking, "no holds are barred."

(Continued next page)

ROSS, CHARLES—*Continued*

References

N Y Times p14 Ap 21 '45
St. Louis Post-Dispatch p1+ Ap 20 '45
    por
Time 45:19 Ap 30 '45 por
U S News 18:64+ My 25 '45 por
Who's Who in America, 1944-45

ROTHENSTEIN, SIR WILLIAM (rō'-thĕn-stīn) Jan. 29, 1872—Feb. 14, 1945

Noted British artist, teacher, writer; his work, which includes lithographs, etchings, landscapes, portraits, and interiors in oil, is represented in the principal public galleries of Great Britain; also in the Musée du Jeu de Paume, Paris, and the Metropolitan Museum, New York; his extensive writings include the first book in English on Goya, *Life of Goya* (1900), and the two-volume work, *Men and Memories* (1931-32).

Obituary

N Y Times p19 F 15 '45 por

ROUAULT, GEORGES (rōō"ō' zhôrzh)

May 27, 1871- French painter, etcher, writer
Address: 14 rue de la Rochefoucauld, Paris

A "medieval modern," Georges Rouault, "laid bare the raw wounds of the human soul" in a large retrospective exhibition at New York's Museum of Modern Art from April 3 to June 3, 1945. Called the most brilliant exhibition

Pierre Matisse

GEORGES ROUAULT

ever held at the museum, this panorama of "mundane turbulence" which is the art of Rouault, ranged the full gamut of his work, from 1893 to 1939. "Concerned passionately and consistently with human drama . . .Rouault is neither a genre painter nor a chronicler of contemporary manners. He revolts with iconoclastic rage against the evil that he sees everywhere." Thus his work is a diatribe against, rather than a record of, society. Margaret

Breuning in *Art Digest* described the exhibition as a torrential outpouring of an intense nature, and singled out three canvases for comment—the early *Clown* (1907) "with its magic of loosely washed color and broken lines of calligraphy"; the monumental *Old King* (1916-36) with its "varied impastos of color"; and the "terrible satire" of *Three Judges* (1913) "which possesses a certain cosmic grandeur in its completeness of expression."

The tragic destiny of Rouault was foreshadowed at his birth, which occurred in Paris on May 27, 1871, during the Commune, while the city was being bombarded by the Versaillais. When a stray shell struck the family home in the Belleville quarter, the young mother was taken to the cellar and it was there that the future painter was born. His father, of Breton and Celtic origin, was a cabinetmaker and varnisher for the Pleyel piano company. His Parisian mother was the daughter of Alexandre Champdavoine, whose penchant for collecting reproductions of the artists he admired—Rembrandt, Courbet, Manet, Daumier—probably influenced his grandson. The child used to draw with chalk on the tiled floors of his grandfather's apartment in the rue de Sévigné, or to play with the paints belonging to his aunts, who decorated china and fans. Young Georges was sent to a Protestant school, because of the anti-clerical views of his father. But at the age of fourteen he was apprenticed to a stained-glass maker named Hirsch, with whom he worked for the next half-dozen years.

Although Rouault regarded this period of his life as one of drudgery, he was unconsciously acquiring, as he sorted the medieval blood-red and noctural blues of the bits of twelfth- and thirteenth-century windows to be repaired, the smoldering color that was to be a distinctive feature of his art. Persisting in his desire to become a painter, young Georges, after his twelve hours' daily work in the Hirsch studio, would walk to the Ecole des Arts Décoratifs, on the other side of Paris, to draw from casts and from life, in the evenings. His Sundays were spent at the Louvre, or at home sketching himself from a mirror. After some years of this arduous existence, his ability was recognized and in 1891 he enrolled in the Ecole des Beaux-Arts, where he studied with Elie Delaunay. On the death of Delaunay soon after, Rouault became the pupil of Gustave Moreau, whose "mysticism and glowing palette" were to influence him for the rest of his life. Among other students in Moreau's classes at this time were Henri Matisse '43 and Raoul Dufy.

Rouault soon became the favorite pupil of Moreau, who understood the melancholy youth and recognized that he should be permitted to follow his own vision. In 1892 Rouault won a student prize for a series of religious paintings, and the following year he was encouraged by his teacher to compete for the Prix de Rome with *The Ordeal of Samson*, a composition whose subject matter presaged the theme of all Rouault's later work—"man's inhumanity to man." He failed to win the prize, but in 1894 the Prix Chenavard was awarded to him for *Infant Jesus Among the Doctors*. A second entry for the Prix de Rome, which also failed to achieve that honor, *Christ Mourned by the Holy Women*, was later awarded the Prix Fortin d'Ivry in 1895 and also received honorable mention at the Exposition Universelle the same year. Advised by his teacher to leave the Beaux-Arts, Rouault forsook academic subjects and began to paint dramatic landscapes in the blue tonality then in vogue. These somber canvases, which were not representations of nature but "fabulous, legendary *décors* of imaginary locations," were exhibited in the Salon des Beaux-Arts where by virtue of the influence of Moreau Rouault showed from 1895 to 1901.

In 1898 Rouault entered upon a critical period of his life. Moreau died; and at about the same time Rouault's brother-in-law also passed away. His parents went to Algeria to stay with their bereaved daughter, and Rouault was left alone. Deprived of the advice and support of his master, and separated from his devoted family, he experienced a period of solitary sorrow that led to a moral crisis. It is to the sufferings endured at this time that Rouault attributes the bitter quality that has permeated all his subsequent work. Moreau had willed his home and his paintings to the City of Paris. When the Musée Gustave Moreau was established, Rouault was made the curator, a position he still holds. But this honor did not dispel the gloom that shadowed the artist. He has never ceased to mourn his friend and teacher. Rouault had been influenced by the Catholic writer, Ernest Hello; and also by the novels of Léon Bloy, who later became a friend of the painter, though never an admirer of his art. Another friend was Joris-Karl Huysmans, who tried to form a group of Catholic artists at the Trappist monastery at Ligué in Poitou, where Rouault sometimes went on short visits. Here he had a resurgence of faith and thought of taking monastic vows, but was restrained by the advice Moreau had given him against retirement from the world. Always energetic, Rouault worked with such intensity that he became ill, and was obliged to go to Switzerland to recuperate. The beauty of the country and, above all, the quality of light acted as a tonic, and when he returned to Paris he discarded the browns and heavy blues of his former tonality and began to paint in a lighter key, remarking that the rest, the sky, and the snow had cleansed his eye.

Rouault had now broken completely with the conventional style of religious art and had begun to paint what André Malraux calls his "trinity of parodies, the harlot, the buffoon, and the judge," introducing to the public a "world of tragedy." In 1902 he became one of a coterie of artists who founded the Salon d'Automne the following year, to provide artists not welcome at the national Salon an opportunity to exhibit. The 1905 Salon d'Automne, held in the Grand Palais, had a room set aside for a group of youthful painters, including Rouault, Matisse, Derain, Dufy, and Braque. Their canvases shocked visitors to the exhibition, who called the artists the Fauves, the "wild beasts" of Paris. Rouault himself, on seeing for the first time one of his new canvases hung in an exhibition, had exclaimed, "What a terrible thing I have done!" Later these painters became known as the School of Paris. Rouault also exhibited in the Salon des Indépendants, from 1905 to 1912, and in addition appeared at the Berthe Weill gallery from time to time. But he was never closely identified with any

group, "he has followed his own path, keeping quietly clear both of limelight and controversy." Wilenski, writing in *Apollo*, called him "one of the few individual artists in Europe," and commented that "in a way that defies analysis this artist pours a passionate temperament into his plastic creations." Outstanding among the water colors of this period are the defiant *Circus Woman* (1906) in pastel and gouache, whose caricatural grandeur recalls Goya and Daumier; *Woman at a Table* (1906); and *Red Haired Woman* (1908). The rose, blue, and orange tones derive from Cézanne. Sometime during 1906 Druet became the first dealer to handle Rouault's work; the E. Druet Galleries organized the first big Rouault exhibition, comprising one hundred and eighty-three items—paintings, drawings, and ceramics—in 1910. Druet was succeeded by Ambroise Vollard, who became Rouault's dealer in 1916.

There now began Rouault's intense preoccupation with illustration, which has earned him the title of "master of black." Before the war he had experimented with monotypes, and had published a color lithograph, *Les Chevaux*. His work for Vollard at first consisted of etchings and wood engravings for the dealer's *Réincarnations du Père Ubu* (1932), a sequel to Alfred Jarry's *Ubu Roi*. It is in this series of plates that Rouault is considered to have realized most fully his talents. Other series of etchings and lithographs were made for *Les Clowns* (1922), with text by Henry Church; *Paysages légendaires* (1924), with poems by Rouault; *Le Cirque de l'étoile filante* (1930), with text by Rouault; *Passion* (1939), with text by André Suarès; and *Divertissement*, with poems by Rouault, brought out by *Verve* in 1943. According to Venturi, there is a pictorial freedom in Rouault's lithographs that is absent in his paintings. In the medium of print-making he is influenced by Goya as well as by Rembrandt. A powerful colorist, he attains dramatic effects of velvety texture, depth, and chiaroscuro when working with his favorite color—black. Carl O. Schniewind observes that Rouault has "brought new life into the time-worn methods of traditional etching." Employing the "same copious ingenuity and disrespect for all conventions," he "uses almost every instrument known to the engraver, and every acid known to the etcher in order to render to his satisfaction the tones and values of his unique images." In his color etchings Rouault has had expert assistants. He has also made no attempt to master the technique of wood engraving. For his series of woodcuts he has had the collaboration of Georges Aubert, considered "the most skillful technician of our time." Together they have supplemented the etchings and lithographs in his books with several hundred wood blocks whose variations of blacks are so liquid and so luminous that they "achieve the effect of black and white reproductions of oil paintings."

During Rouault's protracted activities for the Vollard publications, he did not entirely neglect his oils. Progress on the enormous number of sketches he had made prior to 1916—after which date no new themes appeared—still continued. The series of types he had created for his "human comedy" served as a basis for his subsequent output. As he worked over these

ROUAULT, GEORGES—*Continued*

sketches in an endless search for perfection, his canvases became overlaid with thick coatings of pigment which deepened in luminosity. An example of this method is *The Old King*, in which the magic richness of color is superimposed "like a sensual veil." Frank Crowninshield considers that the "indescribable note of grandeur and energy" in Rouault's painting is the result of "spreading pure colors . . . over fairly sizable areas . . . of avoiding muted, or dirty, effects by refusing to mix his paints . . . and of giving his color blocks ['emerald greens, mineral blues, van Gogh yellows, blood reds'] an added importance by the blackest, broadest, and most dramatic of outlines." As for distortion, Wilenski contends that Rouault does not distort nature because the figures in his pictures only exist within the concept in the artist's mind. Critics agree that it is "far-fetched to attempt to assign any progenitors to Rouault. That he has no followers is, according to Jan Gordon, "the natural result of an artist who insists upon personality; he becomes inimitable."

A decade of exhibitions included a one-man show at the Gallerie La Licorne in Paris in 1921; an important retrospective at the Gallerie E. Druet in 1924, when his first museum sale was made (to the Musée de Grenoble, for the early *Christ Mourned by the Holy Women*); and at various galleries in Berlin, Munich, Zurich, and London. In 1930 Rouault's first one-man show in New York was held at the Brummer Gallery. Royal Cortissoz found "not a trace of beauty in the exhibition," but noted the brute force, energy, and expressiveness in the artist's work. *Art Digest* considered that the group of religious subjects revealed the heart of Rouault's genius, while the critic of *Art News* found Rouault a strangely aloof personality curiously self-sufficient and single-minded, and noted that the bitterness and scorn that emanated from most of his work was softened in the deeply felt tragedy of *L'Enterrement* and in the portrait of the charming young girl in *Qui est vrai et simple.* After the Brummer exhibition, Rouault's work appeared at various other galleries in New York, including the Julien Levy Gallery in 1933, where the superstylized plates for his illustrations for *Les Réincarnations du Père Ubu* were considered "exciting documents for those who have come to enjoy Rouault's strange and often violent art"; and in November of that same year the Pierre Matisse Gallery exhibition of twenty paintings, "macabre, melancholy, often grotesque," which embodied his "protest against the existing social order."

It has been asked why the work of so Christian a painter as Georges Rouault should not find favor with the Roman Catholic Church. This is explained by Waldemar-George, who states in *La Renaissance* (1937) that the church, accustomed to a more conventional art, objects to the "violence, the brutal and figurative language, the mixture of heresy and sacred and profane elements which are characteristic of Rouault's art," and "accuses the painter of the *Christ mort* of spreading despair, distorting the legend of the Saviour, and of disseminating terror." According to Waldemar-George, the only Catholic writers who understand the meaning and significance of Rouault's religious pictures are Jacques Maritain and René Schwob. Rouault himself says, "A Christian, I believe only in these threatening times in Jesus on the Cross."

In 1938 New York's Museum of Modern Art held an exhibition of Rouault's prints, an event of especial significance in that it was the first museum-sponsored show of his work. Included were nearly one hundred and fifty lithographs, wood engravings, and etchings from his books, and from the *Miserere et guerre* series, as well as various portraits—"the first comprehensive showing of his graphic work in America." *Art Digest* noted that "the prints smolder with the same fire that burns in the paintings and the same stylistic characterizations are evident in both." This exhibition was followed by an important retrospective of Rouault's work at Boston's Institute of Modern Art. Alfred Frankfurter, in *Art News*, described it as "a broad, rich panorama of a man's art," showing the three phases of the painter's development. He cited the *Calvary* (1891), with its perfect draftsmanship and influence of Rembrandt and Rubens, as an outstanding example of his first and academic period; the *Woman With a Hat* (1908), with its pure blue and red dominants, and *Clown* as examples of the middle period, contemporary with his Fauve days; and *Three Judges, Circus Trio,* and *The Old King* (considered one of Rouault's most important paintings, with its burning reds, golds, and nocturnal blues) as examples of his late period. Later this exhibition was seen at the Phillips Memorial Gallery in Washington, the San Francisco Museum of Art, and in abbreviated form at the Marie Harriman Gallery in New York.

Although the bulk of Rouault's work is in painting and illustration, he has experimented with other forms. Early in his career he became interested in ceramics, making a number of decorations for pottery which were carried out by Albert Metthey, the master potter of Asnières-sur-Seine, who collaborated with many of the Fauve group. Metthey also assisted Rouault in various circular ceramics, the most noted being the *Head of Christ,* a liturgical work. In 1929 Rouault supplied the *décors* for Prokofiev's ballet, *Le Fils prodigue,* which was produced in Paris in May 1929, by Diaghilev. According to Michel Georges-Michel, Rouault accepted the commission for these sets because he thought it would be like painting immense stained glass windows. But he had to make a careful study of lighting—necessary in stage designing—and to work with "tumultuous" speed, something quite foreign to his nature, for he often spent five years on a single canvas. Henry Prunières, in his Paris column of the New York *Times,* called this ballet the "great event of the Russian season" and added that "the very beautiful *décors* by Georges Rouault, which can only be criticized as being a picture rather than a *décor,* contributed to the success of the production." Another medium in which Rouault succeeded was tapestry. He painted a number of "cartoons" which were executed in low-warp Point de Beauvais under the supervision of Mme. Marie Cuttoli, who, in an attempt to revive the art of tapestry weaving, had persuaded seven famous modern painters—Dufy, Braque, Rouault,

Picasso, Léger, Lurçat, and Matisse—to make some designs for her. The most striking of the Rouault tapestries are *The Dancer, Wounded Clown,* and *St. Veronica's Veil.* Mme. Cuttoli's collection of modern French tapestries was exhibited at the Bignou Gallery in New York in April 1936.

In contrast to the "hell Rouault has created and filled with grim, gloomy figures, saints and whores, sinister clowns of the circus and grotesque politicians and magistrates," his writings are "full of allusions to music, theology and classic poetry—one finds in them scarcely a reference to modern history, or class injustice or the ghastly alternatives of European war and peace." His first poems appeared in *Les Soirées de Paris* in 1914. Later he wrote frequent articles and poems for *Verve, La Revue universelle,* the *Journal des Beaux-Arts, Mercure de France, L'Amour de l'art,* and other publications. His first book, *Souvenirs intimes,* which appeared in 1926, is concerned with various figures of the art world—Moreau, Degas, Cézanne, and others, and contains a number of portraits by the author. In addition, Rouault wrote text and poems to accompany his books of etchings—*Paysages légendaires, Le Cirque de l'étoile filante, Divertissement.* These volumes, all of generous size, are intended to be read on lecterns.

Examples of Rouault's work are in the museums of Avallon, Colmar, Copenhagen, Frankfurt, Grenoble, Moscow, London, Paris, New York, Pittsburgh, and in many private collections in the United States and Europe. In 1924 the artist was decorated with the Legion of Honor, in recognition of his services as curator of the Musée Gustave Moreau.

Rouault, who has been described by Raïssa Maritain as having a long face with ivory paleness, thin lips, clear blue eyes, and a melancholy air, is married to the former Marthe Le Sidaner, of the painter family. They have four children—Géneviève, Isabelle, Michel, and Agnès. Georges Rouault has been a victim of three wars—the last days of the Paris Commune, which cast a shadow over his birth, the First World War; and the Second World War. The First World War unsettled the artist's financial condition, his income from the museum shrank, Mme. Rouault was obliged to give piano lessons to help defray the expenses of the children's schooling, and Rouault sold many of his canvases for small sums. When the Germans began to shell Paris in 1918 Vollard became alarmed for the safety of his collection and begged Rouault, who had gone to L'Isle-sur-le-Serein with his family, to care for his treasures. A house at Saumur, on the Loire, was found and Rouault became the custodian, until the end of the war, of seventy packages of the works of Cézanne, Degas, Gauguin, and Renoir. In 1940 Rouault was at his country home, in Beaumont-sur-Sarthe, when the first fugitives from the Nazis appeared. Persuaded by his daughter Géneviève to join the stream of refugees, Rouault, his wife, his two daughters, and his grandchildren drove across the Massif Central to Grasse. Later, at Golfe Juan, on the Riviera, the artist and his family lived in a small apartment; he wrote at night and painted during the day. But he was not happy in this environment, and after a time

returned to Beaumont, in occupied territory, where he was unmolested by the Germans, although his anti-Nazi sentiments were well known. He made "pitiless caricatures of the German General Staff, called 'vons'" and his expressions of hatred for the Nazis were "like the imprecations of the prophets." Now back in Paris, the painter, who is regarded as "the great tragic artist of our time," is reported to be "working with freshness and freedom and may yet give new proof to the world of his innate gifts."

References

L'Amour de l'art 14:138 Je '38
La Renaissance Oct-Dec '37
Town and Country 100:68 My '45
Tricolor p65 My '44
Charensol, G. Georges Rouault: l'homme et l'œuvre (1926)
Georges-Michel, M. Peintres et sculpteurs que j'ai connus (1942)
Maritain, R. We Have Been Friends Together (1942)
Soby, J. T. Georges Rouault (1945)
Thieme-Becker Künstler-Lexikon v29 (1935)
Venturi, L. Georges Rouault (1940)
Wheeler, M. The Prints of Georges Rouault (1938)
Who's Who, 1945

ROWE, L(EO) S(TANTON) (rō) Sept. 17, 1871- Director-general of the Pan American Union

Address: b. Pan American Union, Washington, D.C.

For more than two decades L. S. Rowe has been director-general of the Pan American Union. His work in the interest of Pan Americanism has been reflected in the Union's record of constantly expanding influence and activities, in which every opportunity to foster cooperation among the governments and peoples of the American republics has been utilized. For these services as a Good Neighbor, Rowe himself has received recognition from many of the countries of Latin America.

Leo Stanton Rowe, the son of Louis and Katherine (Raff) Rowe, was born in McGregor, Iowa, on September 17, 1871. He received his early education in Pennsylvania, and in 1887 was graduated from Central High School in Philadelphia with that school's degree. Three years later he received the degree of Bachelor of Science from the University of Pennsylvania. The nineteen-year-old Rowe then went abroad, and after several years in France, Austria, and Germany, he received his Ph.D. from the University of Halle, in Germany. He returned to the United States to continue his studies at the University of Pennsylvania, and in 1895 received his LL.B.

Although he was admitted to the Pennsylvania bar after receiving his law degree, Rowe turned to teaching. He became an instructor in municipal government at the university, and the following year was advanced to assistant professor of political science; in 1904 he was made head professor. During the years immediately preceding the outbreak of the First

L. S. ROWE

World War, he occupied the chair of international law at the Wharton School of the University of Pennsylvania.

While at the University of Pennsylvania, Rowe several times served on Government committees or was the United States delegate on international commissions. His first assignment took him to Puerto Rico in 1900-1 as a member of the commission appointed by President McKinley to revise and compile the laws of the island. The report of the commission, which appeared in 1901, was compiled by Rowe, Judge Daly, and Juan Hernandez-Lopez. The next year, in 1901-2, the professor was chairman of the Insular Code Commission. His report, drawn up with J. M. Keedy, was published in eight volumes in 1902. The findings of these two commissions were adopted substantially as the law under which the island is now governed. Rowe's own book, *The United States and Puerto Rico, with Special Reference to the Problems Arising out of Our Contact with the Spanish-American Civilization*, was published in 1904.

Rowe resumed his work in the international field in 1906, when he went to Rio de Janeiro as the United States delegate to the Third International Conference of American States. Since that time he has attended most of the important inter-American scientific, economic, and political meetings, activity which has given him a knowledge of the two continents considered second to none in the diplomatic service. (In 1945 he represented the Pan American Union at the United Nations Conference on International Organization, in San Francisco.) He was chairman of the delegation to the First Pan American Scientific Congress at Santiago, Chile, December 25, 1908 to January 5, 1909; and when the second congress was held in 1915 he was again the delegate from his country. In 1913 he was a member of the United States-Panama Mixed Claims Commission in Washington, D.C.; in 1915 he served as secretary-general of the First Pan American Financial Conference in Washington; and

later (1915-17) he was secretary general of the United States section of the Inter-American High Commission. At this time he also prepared a study on municipal government, *Problems of City Government* (1908), and a book in Spanish entitled *Problemas Americanos Conferencias*, which appeared in 1915.

In 1917 Rowe was appointed Assistant Secretary of the United States Treasury, and in order to accept the post he resigned from the university faculty. He served two years in the office and a year as chief of the Latin American Section of the Department of State, an appointment which *Pan American* Magazine characterized as a tribute to his judgment and statesmanship. His studies of the effects of the war on Latin American countries appeared as *Early Effects of the European War Upon the Finance, Commerce, and Industry of Chile* (1918) and *Early Effects of the European War Upon the Finance, Commerce, and Industry of Peru* (1920).

Rowe's work in the field of inter-American affairs led to his election in 1920 as director-general of the Pan American Union, the oldest organized expression of the Good Neighbor Policy. The Union was formed in 1890 as a result of the first Pan American Congress, which was held in 1889-90 on the invitation of the United States. (It was originally called the International Bureau of American Republics; in 1910 its present name was adopted.) The governing board is made up of the United States Secretary of State and the diplomatic representatives in Washington of the other American states. The management is in the hands of the director-general (with headquarters in Washington). As the official international organization of the twenty-one republics, the Union is maintained to disseminate information, promote understanding, and advance peace and arbitration among the nations. To this end, it periodically issues bulletins giving commercial, economic, political, and cultural information on the republics. "The Pan American Union," the Director-General has said, "is the outward symbol of an American continental system, rooted in the idea of international cooperation, good will and mutual helpfulness, dedicated to the ideals of peace, and laboring day in and day out to strengthen the bonds of friendship and understanding between the nations of the Western world."

Rowe contends that "whether we like it or not, we have been thrust into a world situation that has placed a great responsibility on our country. Never again will it be possible for us to withdraw from our obligations, as was the case at the close of the First World War. Not only shall we be called upon to play an important part in the final settlement, but we shall have to accept heavy responsibilities in making that settlement work for the benefit of all mankind as well as for ourselves." He believes that the Americas have learned the principles on which the future peace of the world depends. These he states are as follows: (1) no matter how difficult or delicate the controversy, it can be settled peacefully; (2) any menace to one is a menace to all; (3) principles of economic and financial cooperation which have proved so fruitful on the American continent must be applied in world affairs; (4) every resource must be used to secure for all peoples freedom under law and enjoyment of the fundamental civil rights; and (5) the vast resources of the Americas must be used in rehabilitation of the economic and financial structure of the devasted sections of the world.

Rowe's contributions to the cause of Pan Americanism and peace have been recognized by numerous allied organizations, and by many of the countries of Central and South America. In addition, he has received honorary Doctor of Laws degrees from the National University of La Plata in Argentina (1906), the University of San Marcos in Peru (1906), the University of Chile (1907), the University of Pennsylvania (1931), Georgetown University (1933); and in 1942 he received a Doctor of Laws from Catholic University of America. In honor of his twenty-fifth year as director-general of the Pan American Union, a dinner was given in Rowe's honor. Tributes were paid him by Senator Tom Connally, Frederick E. Hasler, president of the Pan American Society, and Dr. George William McClelland, president of the University of Pennsylvania. President Truman sent a message of congratulation in which he said: "Dr. Rowe's contribution to the cause of Inter-American friendship and understanding is deserving of the highest honors. His belief in the ideals of Pan Americanism, his qualities of statesmanship and leadership and his ability to overcome obstacles to unity and cooperation among the twenty-one American republics have been of major importance."

The Director-General of the Pan American Union is a slight man, several inches under six feet in height and weighing one hundred and thirty pounds. He has blue eyes and brown hair. His interests are broad, his activities include membership, some honorary, in numerous cultural, historical, scientific, and legal societies in both the Americas. For twenty-eight years he was president of the American Academy of Political and Social Science. From 1921 to 1926 he was in charge of the Latin American Round Table at the Institute of Politics in Williamstown, Massachusetts. And, in addition to his activities at rostrum and round table, he has contributed articles, monographs, and reports to numerous economic, political, and scientific journals, including the *Annals of the American Academy of Political and Social Science,* and he is the author of a number of books and pamphlets dealing with Latin-American affairs.

When the 1940 gold medal of the Inter-American Commercial Arbitration Commission was presented to this veteran worker in the cause of hemisphere solidarity, Spruille Braden, then the United States Ambassador to Colombia and honorary chairman of the commission, said: "Quietly and unremittingly you have labored for more than twenty years to advance the principle that all differences, large or small, may be accommodated pacifically."

References

Agriculture in the Americas 2:99 My '42

Who's Who in America, 1944-45

Who's Who in the Nation's Capital, 1938-39

ROYAL, FORREST B. 1893(?)—June 18, 1945 American Admiral in command of the Seventh Amphibious Force in Pacific theater of war; died on high seas of natural causes shortly after he had completed a most successful landing on northwest Borneo; received the D.S.M. for his performance as commander of amphibious group operating against Leyte and Luzon in the Philippines from July 1944 to January 1945.

Obituary

N Y Times p19 Je 21 '45 por

RUBINSTEIN, ARTUR (roo'bĭn-stĭn är'toōr) Jan. 28, 1886- Pianist

Address: b. c/o Hurok Attractions, Inc., 30 Rockefeller Plaza, New York City; h. 12921 Marlboro St., Brentwood, West Los Angeles, Calif.

The internationally known Polish pianist, Artur Rubinstein, who has traveled over a million miles, is a favorite of American concert-goers and "the adopted son of all Spanish-speaking countries." He has toured the world as a concert artist and during the two World Wars he was looked upon as an unofficial ambassador for his freedom-loving country.

The youngest of the seven children of Ignace and Felicia (Heyman) Rubinstein, Artur Rubinstein was born in Lodz, Poland, on January 28, 1886. The child showed his musical talent at the age of three, when he was given his first lessons on the piano. Within the next three years he had given two public solo performances for charity, one at Warsaw. When Artur was eight years old he began to study in the Polish capital, but in a few months he had exhausted the teaching of his instructor. At that time, however, the prodigy's sister was leaving for Berlin to prepare for her marriage, and it was decided that the boy accompany her so that he might perform for Joseph Joachim, the violinist. Joachim was so much interested in the boy's musical gift that he assumed responsibility for the development of Artur's talent, a relationship which was to last for eight years. The protégé was sent to Heinrich Barth for piano technique, and to Robert Kahn and Max Bruch for instruction in theory, harmony, and composition. When Joachim sent his charge to Paderewski, the Polish pianist and statesman was so greatly impressed by the youth's ability that he asked young Artur to remain with him for three months.

At eleven young Artur made his formal debut in Berlin, when he performed the Mozart A Major Concerto with Joachim conducting the Berlin Symphony Orchestra. This concert is considered as marking the beginning of his career. From that time until his twentieth year, he performed in his own country, Germany, Russia, and France. In Poland Rubinstein, then fifteen, played with the Warsaw Symphony Orchestra under the baton of Emil Mlynarski, whose daughter Aniela, as yet unborn, was later to become the wife of the piano virtuoso. When in Russia, he toured with Serge Koussevitsky [40], who was then conducting his own orchestra. Rubinstein's talent received greater recognition with each concert, and he became renowned for his interpretation of Chopin,

ARTUR RUBINSTEIN

Beethoven, and Liszt. After meeting the young pianist in Paris, Saint-Saëns introduced him to the Concert Society of Paris (a fraternal organization of musicians) as one of the greatest artists he knew. "I foresee for him an admirable career....He is worthy of the great name he bears." (Artur Rubinstein, however, is not related to the Russian composer and pianist Anton Rubinstein.)

Twenty-year-old Artur Rubinstein made his first American appearance in January 1906 in Philadelphia, where he played with the Philadelphia Orchestra; and he made his New York debut in Carnegie Hall a few days later with the same orchestra, Fritz Scheel conducting. Richard Aldrich, in a review (reprinted in his book *Concert Life in New York, 1902-1923*), said that the young artist displayed "a crisp and brilliant touch, remarkable facility, and fleetness of technique," but he added that "there is little worth of beauty in Rubinstein's tone and little variety in his effects. It would be interesting to know whether he can express some of the deeper things there are in music." One week after his Carnegie Hall appearance Rubinstein gave a recital of Bach, Beethoven, and Schumann at the old Casino Theatre. He was acclaimed again for his technique, although the critics were dubious about his interpretative abilities—"then, naturally, not fully developed." Rubinstein gave seventy-five concerts in the three months he spent in the United States, and he then returned to Europe, where he went into temporary retirement. He lived in Paris and devoted himself to further study, in order, he explains, to "hurdle the greatest obstacle in the path of a prodigy, that of shedding my immaturity."

In 1910 Rubinstein made his first re-appearance in Berlin, and during the next six years he concertized throughout Europe. (For his St. Petersburg's performance he chose Anton Rubinstein's Concerto in D Minor.) With his return to concert work, "he was unanimously acclaimed as a mature artist," David Ewen writes in *Living Musicians*. For his tour of

Italy, which he made immediately before the First World War, Rubinstein was given a diplomatic passport by the Italian government. His native Poland had granted him a similar document with the inscription: "On a mission of art for Poland."

Rubinstein was in London at the outbreak of the First World War. Although he wanted to enlist with the Polish Legion, his knowledge of eight languages made him more valuable as an interpreter at the Allied Headquarters. He served in this capacity for a few months; he then went out on tour for the Allied cause with the violinist Eugène Ysaye, on which they played a series of nine concerts. Shocked by the Germans' treatment of Belgians and Poles, Rubinstein vowed then that he would never perform in Germany again, a vow he has kept.

Rubinstein's first visit to Spain in 1916, where he played the music of Spanish composers like Manuel de Falla and Albéniz, won him a reputation as the leading interpreter of their music. Scheduled to give four concerts, he remained to give one hundred and twenty. This success brought invitations to visit the Spanish-speaking countries of South America. That tour was so prolonged that Rubinstein did not reach the United States again until the 1919 concert season.

His return concert in North America was given in Carnegie Hall on February 20, 1919. The pianist had given two recitals in the United States thirteen years previously, but this second appearance was considered his official North American debut. The New York *Times* reviewer called him "a pianist of great charm and technical finesse," and one whose tone was "light" and whose style was "casual." The critic summed up the concert thus: "It may be said of Rubinstein that he came, played, and was liked. But a miniaturist." During the next ten years the artist gave concerts in the United States, South America, and Europe. While in the United States he appeared with the leading orchestras and such conductors as Walter Damrosch '44, Leopold Stokowski '41, Pierre Monteux, and Willem Mengelberg. The American concert stage did not see Rubinstein for almost another decade: he toured Europe, South America, and in Australia alone gave twenty-four concerts.

Appearing again in the United States in 1940, Artur Rubinstein gave a number of concerts in New York in Carnegie Hall, Town Hall, and Lewisohn Stadium. After hearing the pianist in Carnegie Hall in the late spring of 1940, Irving Kolodin of the New York *Sun* wrote: "Mr. Rubinstein plays Bach seriously, Beethoven intelligently, and Brahms earnestly," while the music critic of the New York *World-Telegram* reported that the audience was "gaping in wonder" as the virtuoso "outdid himself" at the recital. When Rubinstein gave a program of the compositions of Beethoven, Schumann, Chopin, Ravel, Rathaus, Shostakovich '41, and De Falla on November 26, 1942, Robert Laurence felt that the artist, "when at his best ranks among the greatest pianists of the day," and Henry Simon of *PM* expressed the feeling that a "Rubinstein recital becomes not only a fine musical experience, but an Event." The following year Artur Rubinstein gave his only concert of the season, when the New York critics found him not in "top form." When he gave an all-Chopin program in honor of his compatriot in 1944, the critics acclaimed him for playing the works with "surpassing sensitivity."

The Polish pianist has made numerous recordings. These include solos and concertos with the London Symphony Orchestra, and albums of the music of Chopin, Brahms, Franck, Bach, Tchaikovsky, and of Heitor Villa-Lobos'[45], whose music Rubinstein made popular. His recording of the Brahms D Minor Sonata, made with the late violinist Paul Kochanski, is a collectors' item. It has been estimated that his record albums gross over $500,000 annually. In discussing the album of Villa-Lobos music, a New York *Times* critic called the interpretations "authoritative and highly effective"; Rubinstein "can usually be counted on for a vigorous, colorful reading, and this album is no exception to the rule." The pianist's recording of the Tchaikovsky Concerto in B Flat Minor, which sold over 200,000, so appealed to bandleader Freddie Martin that he made an arrangement of the compostion for dance orchestras. Supplied with a lyric and a title, "Tonight We Love" started a "national furor"—it was played in juke boxes from coast to coast and eventually became the Number One song on *Your Hit Parade,* a radio program devoted to the ten most popular songs of the day. In October Rubinstein signed a contract with Republic, one of the smaller Hollywood studios, to record the entire musical score for the Technicolor film *Concerto* for which he was to receive a reported $85,000. He will play Rachmaninoff's Second Concerto and Beethoven's Sonata Appassionata. The artist will not be seen in the motion picture, as he believes it would be "an egregious folly" to allow himself to be photographed for the screen.

In addition to being recognized as a fine interpreter of Brahms and Chopin, Rubinstein has also been acclaimed, by modern composers, for his interpretation of their own works. "The two toughest keyboard workouts of all time" were dedicated to him by their composers: Stravinsky's Sonata from the ballet score of *Petrouchka,* and Villa-Lobos' *Rudepoêma.* Rubinstein has received decorations from several countries: the Legion of Honor from France, the Cross of Alfonso XII from Spain, the Commander of the Crown and Officer, Order of Leopold I from Belgium, the Polonia Restituta, his native Poland's highest decoration; and the Commander of the Crown from Italy, which he returned in 1938.

Artur Rubinstein has been described as a loquacious, "small, dapper, pink-cheeked man," a connoisseur of wine, cigars, and fashion. The pianist ended his bachelorhood at the age of forty-six when he was married to Aniela Mlynarski in Paris. They have three children, a son and two daughters, Eva, Paul, and Alina. Although the Rubinsteins are now living in California, they have a home in Paris which they vacated shortly before the Nazi occupation of France. There the pianist had a valuable library of rare musical objects and first editions, many art treasures, and toys, which he had collected during his trips around the world. The pianist has composed several piano compositions and chamber music, and has written articles on the piano for *Etude.* As friends he prefers writers to musicians, and one of his closest friends is Ernest Hemingway. At one time he was commissioned to write his autobiography, of which, however, he said: "I cannot write it. My life is too naughty. I am too shy about telling it."

References

Time 38:39-40 D 8 '41
Baker's Biographical Dictionary of Musicians (1940)
Ewen, D. ed. Living Musicians (1940)
Thompson, O. ed. International Cyclopedia of Music and Musicians (1943)
Who Is Who in Music (1941)
Who's Who in America, 1944-45

RUPERTUS, WILLIAM H(ENRY) (rōo-pĕr'tŭs) Nov. 14, 1889—Mar. 25, 1945 Major general in United States Marine Corps; won the Navy Cross and Distinguished Service Medal for his command of the First Marine Division in the Solomons and New Britain campaigns of the Second World War; personally led the marines who captured Tulagi, Gavutu, and Florida islands; died in Washington, D. C., of a heart attack.

Obituary

N Y Times p9 Mr 27 '45 por

RUSSELL, JAMES EARL July 1, 1864—Nov. 4, 1945 American educator; dean of Teachers College (Columbia University) from 1897 to 1927; dean emeritus since 1927; European agent for the Bureau of Education in Washington, D.C. (1904-27); his writings include *The History, Organization and Methods of Secondary Education in Germany* (1899) and *Trend in American Education* (1922).

Obituary

N Y Times p9 N 5 '45 por

RYAN, JOHN (AUGUSTINE) MSGR. May 25, 1869—Sept. 16, 1945 Theologian; a leading liberal of the Roman Catholic Church in America; authority on labor and social welfare; helped bring about such social reforms as minimum wage laws and collective bargaining; author of *A Living Wage* (1906), *Distributive Justice* (1916), and *A Better Economic Order* (1935).

Obituary

N Y Times p19 S 17 '45 por

SABIN, FLORENCE R(ENA) (sā'bĭn) Nov. 9, 1871- Anatomist
Address: h. 1333 Tenth Ave., Denver, Colo.

"A time will come when men and women will live their alloted span quietly, peacefully, without illness, free from pain, until they pass gently, as a tired child closes sleepy eyes, from this world to the next." These words of Dr. Florence R. Sabin embody her credo, an aim toward which she has devoted her life, tirelessly and fruitfully. Dr. Sabin ranks among the world's most distinguished scientists, her research work on the lymphatics, the blood cells and vessels, bone marrow, and tuberculosis, having won for her the highest recognition of her profession.

DR. FLORENCE R. SABIN

Florence Rena Sabin was born in Central City, Colorado, November 9, 1871. Her father, George Kimball Sabin, had come from Vermont to go into mining and there had met and married Rena Miner, also of Vermont, who had come to teach school in the rugged West. They sent their young daughter, Florence, to be educated in Vermont where she prepared for college. She then attended Smith College, from which she was graduated with her B.S. in 1893. While at Smith, Miss Sabin became interested in zoology and, after learning that the new Johns Hopkins Medical School was open to women, she decided to become a doctor. (The founders of Johns Hopkins, which was opened in 1893, had provided for the admission of men and women on equal terms.) To earn money for her medical education, Florence Sabin taught school for three years—mathematics at Wolfe Hall in Denver, and zoology at Smith. Finally she entered the fourth class of the Johns Hopkins Medical School, one of fifteen women in a class of forty-two. As a student, she attracted the attention of her professors by her enthusiasm for laboratory work and her accuracy in detail. Her professor of anatomy, Dr. Franklin P. Mall, suggested that she make a model of the brain stem of the newborn child, which had never been done before. This she did, producing a model of such precision that new light was shed on the general structure of the lower brain area. Reproductions of this model are still in use in medical schools throughout the world.

Florence Sabin received her medical degree from Johns Hopkins in 1900 and remained as interne at the hospital for a year. The following year she was granted a year's fellowship by the Baltimore Association for the Advancement of University Education of Women. Again, at Dr. Mall's suggestion she began a special study of the lymphatics (the vessels that conduct the lymph through the body), making discoveries that overturned the accepted medical theories on the subject. For her paper on the development of the lymphatic system,

Dr. Sabin received the thousand-dollar award of the Naples Table Association. After this year of research the objections to the presence of a woman in the laboratory were soon forgotten, and the scientist joined the faculty of Johns Hopkins in 1902 as assistant in anatomy. She continued her research work while teaching, enriching her lectures with reports on her own experiments. By 1905 she was an associate professor, a post she held until 1917, when she was appointed a full professor of histology.

Of Dr. Sabin's work at that time, Alice Booth wrote: "The research on lymphatics led her to restudy the old problem of how blood vessels arise and develop, and, working with the blastoderms of chicks . . . to follow the development of the veins and capillaries in the living specimens." Dr. Sabin and her collaborators then devoted years of research to the study and observation of the red and white corpuscles, a monumental scientific task, requiring skill and perseverance. In an article in a 1926 issue of *World's Work,* Frances McMullen described this research: First, they had to establish a post of observation whence they might effectively scrutinize the territory. This involved perfecting a technique whereby they might study a living blood specimen under the microscope. Next they had to count the forces that came within their range of vision, listing the number of red corpuscles and of the seven different kinds of white corpuscles in every drop of blood. As the numbers were never the same in two successive counts, they decided to stick at the census work by the day. Every fifteen minutes Dr. Sabin would take a fresh drop of blood from her finger, mount it on a slide and slip it under the microscope. From morning until night and sometimes far into the night, often going without lunch, the group took records, on different days, of the numerical strength of the corpuscle regiments. After such a day, weeks were needed to chart and interpret the data. During her years of work on the blood, Dr. Sabin perfected a technique of her own, establishing basic methods for a new system of studying the corpuscles. By 1919 she had determined the origin of the red corpuscles. Her work was then judged of great promise for the future control of diseases of the blood.

In 1925 Dr. Sabin terminated a long and mutually rewarding association with Johns Hopkins by joining the staff of the Rockefeller Institute for Medical Research in New York. Here she continued her work on the blood, concentrating on the relationship of her studies to tuberculosis. Supervising a group working on the problem of tuberculosis, Dr. Sabin studied the tubercle bacillus for several years. Firmly convinced that the fight against tuberculosis could be won, she declared: "If I didn't believe the answer could be found, I wouldn't be working on it." Four years after Dr. Sabin joined the Institute, Dr. Simon Flexner, then head of medical research, called her "the greatest living woman scientist and one of the foremost scientists of all time." In 1939, in compliance with the rules of retirement of the Rockefeller Foundation, Dr. Sabin and four other scientists turned over their administrative duties to younger colleagues but continued their important research in the laboratories. According to *Time,* these scientists were "five of the keenest scientific brains on earth."

When Dr. Sabin left Johns Hopkins she had ended a teaching career of twenty-six years. In her presidential address before the American Association of Anatomists in 1925, she discussed the general principles of teaching in relation to the teaching of anatomy. This detailed address was published as the leading article in *Science*, May 15, 1925. In it the scientist declared: "I have ceased to be a professional teacher, but remain a professional student." She expounded her views of scientific education, offering as basic principles "liberty of thought in education and cooperation in research." These principles have served Dr. Sabin well throughout her career. As a teacher, she was undogmatic, vigorous, always alive to growth and change within her field. "Books are merely records of what other people have thought and observed," she would tell her students. "The material is a far safer guide." She favored dynamic teaching methods, and encouraged complete freedom within the course for the teacher and the student. Another tenet was one Dr. Mall had impressed upon her when she taught her first class: "Never make your directions for students so specific as to rob them of the pleasure of discovering things for themselves." Two of her former pupils who were to become her associates in her work on the blood were Dr. R. S. Cunningham and Dr. Charles A. Doan. "Dr. Sabin," wrote Frances McMullen, "has always believed in the efficacy of group work for science and points out that such investigations as hers could not have been undertaken otherwise." Of research Dr. Sabin has said: "Research lifts teaching to a high plane. No one can be a really great educator unless he himself is an investigator." She also has definite views about making known the progress of research. "The investigator who holds back his conclusions until he is absolutely sure, never progresses far. When I reach certain conclusions, I do not hesitate to publish them, even though, after further study, I may find I was wrong; then I do not hesitate to say that I have changed my mind."

Articles by Dr. Sabin have been widely published in medical journals, and she has been called upon to speak on numerous occasions. In both her speech and writing, the stamp of the scientist is apparent. Logical sequence of thought and vivid clarity of diction distinguish her expression. In an address at Bryn Mawr College in 1936, entitled "Women in Science," Dr. Sabin paid tribute to the early fighters in the cause of women's rights in the educational field. She also discussed the significant contributions made by women to scientific progress. In 1934 Dr. Sabin's biography of her old professor, Dr. Mall, was published, under the title *Franklin Paine Mall; the Story of a Mind.* Previously Dr. Sabin had written a sketch of Dr. Mall's life for *Biographical Memoirs,* compiled by the National Academy of Sciences. The full biography of Dr. Mall was called "a model of its kind," the New York *Times*' critic writing: "Dr. Sabin has written a vivid life of Dr. Mall. She was well equipped for the task; herself a distinguished teacher and investigator, an associate and pupil of Mall for twenty years, no one understood so well the gifted and somewhat whimsical personality, or followed more closely his scientific work, or could better render its meaning in non-technical language."

Dr. Sabin's career has included several prominent "firsts." In December 1944 she was elected to honorary life membership in the New York Academy of Sciences. She was the first woman to teach at Johns Hopkins Medical School, the first woman member of the Rockefeller Institute (of which she is now member emeritus), the first of her sex elected to the National Academy of Sciences, and the first to serve as president of the American Association of Anatomists. In March 1945 the American Cancer Society announced the appointment of Dr. Sabin to a committee of five leaders in the cancer field who will direct a comprehensive program of research on cancer.

Dr. Sabin is a member of the board of John Simon Guggenheim Memorial Foundation and Finney-Howell Research Foundation; and she is a member of several scientific organizations, including the National Tuberculosis Association and the American Association for the Advancement of Science. She also belongs to the Cosmopolitan Club, the American Women's Association, and the Society of Colonial Dames. Dr. Sabin holds honorary degrees from a dozen leading universities and has also received the National Achievement Award (1932) and the M. Carey Thomas Prize (1935). In June 1945 she was awarded the Trudeau Medal of the National Tuberculosis Association; it is given annually for "meritorious contribution to the cause, treatment or prevention of tuberculosis."

Florence Sabin has been described as a woman with a "marvelous personality," a kindly face, keen eyes, and a warm smile. Possessing a wide vision, she has not kept her imagination within the walls of the laboratory but has recognized the necessity for large-scale application of medical science to all people through endowed hospitals, hospitals for group nursing, and group medical insurance. "Dr. Florence Rena Sabin," wrote Alice Booth, "is the only person I have ever known who—if she had the power of choice—would live her life over again exactly as it was, trying to do just the same things."

References

Good H 92:50+ Je '31 por
Lit Digest 124:18 Jl 10 '37 por
Time 33:54 Ap 24 '39
World's Work 51:417-21 F '26 por
American Women, 1939-40
National Cyclopædia of American Biography Current vol C p288
Who's Who in America, 1944-45

SAINT EXUPERY, ANTOINE DE (săn″ tăg″zü″pā″rē′ än″twàn′) 1900—Aug.(?) 1944
French aviator and author; reported missing since August 1944 after a mission over southern France; from his experiences as a French mail pilot he wrote *Night Flight* (1932) and *Wind, Sand and Stars* (1939); his two latest books were *Flight to Arras* (1942) and *The Little Prince* (1943). See *Current Biography* 1940 Yearbook.

Obituary

N Y Times p4 Ag 10 '44 por

SALTEN, FELIX (zäl'těn fē'lĭks) Sept. 6, 1869—Oct. 8, 1945 Austrian author of essays, plays, and novels; books for children include *Bambi* (1928), of which he made adaptation for Walt Disney[40] film, *Florian, the Emperor's Stallion* (1934), *Perri* (1938), and *Bambi's Children* (1939); two books on Palestine and United States have not been translated into English; fled from Austria to Switzerland after Nazi occupation.

Obituary

N Y Times p22 O 9 '45 por

SALTER, ALFRED 1873—Aug. 24, 1945 British physician; Labor Member of Parliament in 1922-23, and from 1924 until his death; ardent prohibitionist; wrote numerous articles on bacteriology and pathology for scientific publications; in 1897 won both the Gold Medal Scholarship in Public Health and the Gull Research Scholarship in Pathology.

Obituary

N Y Times p11 Ag 25 '45

SARGENT, (HAROLD) MALCOLM (WATTS) Apr. 29, 1895- Conductor

Address: 20 Chesham Place, London, S.W.1., England

Malcolm Sargent has been called Britain's "ambassador of music" because he has brought British music to such widely separated places as Australia, Sweden, and America. His most recent journey brought him, for the first time, to the United States in the spring of 1945 as guest conductor of the National Broadcasting Company Symphony Orchestra, of which Arturo Toscanini[42] is conductor. He first gained international recognition in the early thirties when he was chosen by Artur Schnabel[42] as conductor for the pianist's recording of the five Beethoven concertos.

Harold Malcolm Watts Sargent was born in Stamford, Lincolnshire, England, on April 29, 1895. His father was Henry Edward Sargent, a church organist. At the age of six the boy was singing alto in the church choir and had said he wanted to be a musician. By the age of ten he had become an organist. "He bought his first piano score of *Messiah* for a penny," relates British critic C. B. Rees, "and knew it backwards at an age when most people have never heard of it at all." Sargent was educated at Stamford School, where he also studied music, and he became an Associate of the Royal College of Organists and won the Sawyer prize in 1910, while still a pupil at the school. In 1911 he was articled to the organist of Peterborough Cathedral, Dr. Keeton, with whom he remained until he received his B.Mus. degree in 1914. In that year he became organist of the parish church of Melton Mowbray in Leicestershire. Although the First World War, during which he served with the Twenty-seventh Durham Light Infantry, seriously interrupted his musical activities, Sargent, already a noted organist, was able to take his D.Mus. degree in 1919. From 1919 to 1921 he studied with Benno Moiseiwitsch, famous Anglo-Russian pianist, and is said to have played remarkably well for his limited experience.

Sargent's introduction to the conductor's podium was accidental. At the last moment a rehearsal of *The Gondoliers* in Stamford was jeopardized when the conductor failed to appear, and young Sargent was urged to take the baton. In 1921 the late Sir Henry Wood, one of Britain's foremost musicians and founder and conductor of the Queen's Hall Promenade Concerts, heard Sargent conduct his own composition, *Impressions of a Windy Day*, in Leicester and invited the young conductor to present it at Queen's Hall. Wrote violinist Bernard Shore in *The Orchestra Speaks* of the Queen's Hall rehearsal of this work: "A vivid memory remains of an extremely thin and wiry young man with flying arms, crashing with a breathless orchestra through . . . the piece. . . .His stick moved so fast that it could scarcely be seen but seemed to make a blur like the spokes of a fast-moving wheel. And all the time he was rehearsing he never stopped talking." In 1922 Sargent went back to Leicester to become musical director and conductor of the Leicester Symphony Orchestra, still one of his many activities. In 1923 he was appointed junior orchestral conductor and musical instructor at the Royal College of Music in London, where today he is a professor of music. In 1924 he conducted the premier of Vaughan Williams' opera *Hugh the Drover* for the Royal College of Music and the British National Opera Company. A year later in Manchester he conducted the first performance of Gustav Holst's opera *At the Boar's Head,* and thereafter conducted the standard repertory with the British National Opera Company.

In rapid succession at about this time Sargent also became conductor of the Lord Palmer's Patrons Fund Concerts (from 1924), the British Women's Symphony Orchestra (from 1925), the Llandudno (North Wales) Orchestral Seasons (1926-28), the annual pageant production of Coleridge-Taylor's *Hiawatha* at Royal Albert Hall (from 1926), the Diaghilev Ballet Russe's London season (from 1927), and the Gramophone Company's orchestra (H.M.V. Records); musical director and conductor of the London season of Gilbert and Sullivan operettas given by the D'Oyly Carte Opera Company (from 1926), and musical director for British International Pictures (from 1931). (Except where indicated, he is still, in 1945, connected with these enterprises.) In 1929, in collaboration with the late Mrs. Samuel Courtauld, he established the Concert Club in London which annually presents the Courtauld-Sargent Concerts.

It was also in 1924 that Sargent began his long association with the Robert Mayer Concerts for Children. For these, relates Bernard Shore, he begins with a brief rehearsal immediately before the performance. "Then . . . the orchestra assembles again and he introduces to the children the particular section of the orchestra with which he is dealing, whereupon the whole vast audience of the Westminster Central Hall becomes as quiet as in church. He holds them fast in his hand while in an effortless and brilliant little lecture he describes the orchestral instruments, and gives a concise and imaginative explanation of the program. Sargent has blessed this generation of children with something unknown to the children of the past. His power lies in his ability to express himself in terms any child can understand. Then after the talk, he does what few other conductors could achieve with so little time, giving a first-class performance of the program. . . . His understanding of the child-mind is perfect, and even hardened orchestral players enjoy seeing happy relations between him and his Saturday morning audience."

Beginning with the Royal Choral Society, of which he was appointed conductor-in-chief in 1928, Sargent has likewise made a name for himself as a choral conductor. Today, in addition to conducting the Royal Choral Society in London, he is the regular conductor of the Bradford Festival Choral Society, the Huddersfield Choral Society, and the Leicester Philharmonic Choral Society. Much in request by choral as well as symphonic societies all over the country, Sargent has also shared the direction of several Leeds choral festivals with Sir Thomas Beecham [41] and led the first performance of William Turner Walton's [40] *Belshazzar's Feast* at the Leeds Festival in 1931. "As a choral conductor," says C. B. Rees, "he has no superior and few equals. His clear, vigorous beat, his communicable energy, his mingled charm and discipline make him an ideal interpreter and trainer where large choral forces are concerned." "To see him at work with a choir at a country festival is, perhaps, to see him in his most inspired moments," wrote Bernard Shore in 1938. "He is able to instill into the singers a life and efficiency they never dreamed of. You have only to see the eyes of a choral society screwing into him like hundreds of gimlets, to understand what he means to them. He is hypnotic with the choir—he plays upon the imagination and minds of the singers like a mesmerist. The Royal Choral Society is a wonderful instrument in his hands."

In 1936 Sargent went to New Zealand and Australia to give a series of concerts for the Australian Broadcasting Commission. In 1937 he conducted the Coronation concerts of the Palestine Orchestra in Jerusalem. Again in 1938 and 1939 he made his second and third Palestinian and Australian tours. At the beginning of the Second World War he returned to England to offer his services to his government but was told that his most valuable contribution was his music. During the War, therefore, he conducted in blitzed towns and cities, during air raids, before workers on their lunch hour, "doing much to sustain morale and keep alive the love of music in circumstances of great trial and continuous strain." Typical of his spirit was an incident which occurred in a northern provincial town when the air-raid siren sounded: he turned to his audience with the words, "Anybody who wants to go can do so now. But the orchestra will carry on. We may be killed, but we shall play something that Hitler [42] can never kill." Then lifting his baton, he signalled to the players, who crashed into the opening bars of Beethoven's Fifth Symphony. Needless to report, the audience remained. Since V-E day Sargent has given concerts in Sweden, Portugal, and the United States, as well as in England, where, in addition to his standard routine, he has guest-conducted with the London, Liverpool, Bristol, and Portsmouth Philharmonic Orchestras, with the Scottish Orchestra and at the Brand Lane and British Museum Concerts.

"You wonder when he ever stops and why," says C. B. Rees. "That is your first impression of Malcolm Sargent, slim, wiry, alive and tin-

British Official Photo.
MALCOLM SARGENT

gling in every nerve, immaculate too, and with his thick black hair shining and undisturbed in the most frenzied climax. His frame looks too frail for the energy it contains—but he is one of the hardest working conductors in the world, and this despite a long and trying illness some years ago. . . . He rushes from one end of the country to another, takes an orchestra in hand at rehearsal in the morning, say, in the North of England; then immediately after the concert at night he is in the train speeding south, studying his score [he always uses a score] for, perhaps, a performance of Bach's mighty B minor Mass, before an audience of five thousand people at the Albert Hall, London. He is a non-stop worker [and] on Sunday afternoon you may hear him as a guest in the now famous radio *Brains Trust* [the British equivalent of *Information Please*]. . . . With orchestra and chorus he is efficient and unfussy. He knows what he wants and how to get it. His tastes are wide and generous, [ranging through both modern and classical works] and his versatility is a thing to wonder at." In 1942 he was awarded an honorary Doctor of Music degree by Oxford University.

Sargent was married in 1923 to Eileen Laura Harding, daughter of Frederic Horne of Drinkstone, Suffolk, and they are the parents of a son, Peter. When not serving the cause of music, Sargent relaxes at the theater or zoo, or rides. His clubs are the Garrick, Beefsteak, and Pratt's.

References

Newsweek 25:87-8 F 26 '45

Ewen, D. ed. Living Musicians (1940)
Grove's Dictionary of Music and Musicians IV p524; suppl. vol. (1940) p565
International Who's Who, 1942
Macmillan's Encyclopedia of Music and Musicians (1938)
Thompson, O. ed. International Cyclopedia of Music and Musicians (1943)
Who's Who, 1945

SCHAIN, JOSEPHINE (shān) Consultant on international relations; social worker; lecturer
Address: h. 3 Mitchell Pl., New York City

In the words of the *American Magazine,* Josephine Schain is "one of the most versatile women in the world. Organizer, businesswoman, diplomat, cook, geologist, basketweaver . . . calm, decisive, she can tie knots, cook 'slum,' or crack a diplomatic whip over

JOSEPHINE SCHAIN

a conference of internationally minded ladies." The first woman appointed to represent the United States at a conference of the United Nations, she has attended more international conferences than most people can call to mind, has served as national director of the Girl Scouts of America, and has spent thirty years working through dozens of organizations for woman suffrage, disarmament, permanent peace, and international organization.

The daughter of Jacob Theodore and Irene (Burdick) Schain, Josephine Schain was born in Brown's Valley, "up where Minnesota juts into South Dakota." Brown's Valley is bounded, according to Delos Lovelace, by two lakes, one flowing into the Gulf of Mexico and the other into Hudson Bay, symbolic, it would seem, of Miss Schain's future internationalism. Her mother was "advanced," and Josephine, a tall, rosy-cheeked brunette, studied law at the University of Minnesota, where she was elected to Pi Beta Phi, and received her LL.B. in 1908. She never practiced law, however, but became a social worker in Minneapolis. A member of the International Alliance of Women for Suffrage and Equal Citizenship, Miss Schain was active as a speaker in the 1915 campaign for the passage of the Nineteenth Amendment, which provided that the vote could not be denied anyone on the ground of sex, and which became a part of the Federal Constitution when finally ratified in 1920.

In 1916 Miss Schain went into settlement work; two years later she went to New York to work in a settlement house on the teeming, polyglot lower East Side. But she had a strong interest, also, in international affairs, and in 1924 she became director of the Department of International Relations of the five-year-old League of Women Voters, which Carrie Chapman Catt [40] had founded in 1919. While in this post Miss Schain helped Mrs. Catt organize the National Committee on the Cause and Cure of War in 1925; attended the Institute of International Relations at Geneva in 1926; won her M.A. in International Law; and attended several sessions of the League of Nations. Her term as director ended in 1928, but Miss Schain continued her activities for international good will. She was one of a deputation of three women sent to the London Naval Conference in 1930 by the National Committee on the Cause and Cure of War.

An enthusiastic camper who pitched her tent in the Arabian Desert and South Persia as casually as in the Rocky Mountains, in 1930 Miss Schain was elected national director of the Girl Scouts of America, with her office in New York. In this position, to quote the *American Magazine,* she was for five years "the head of a family of 333,840—all girls"—and "controlled a million-dollar organization." At the same time she continued her internationalist activities. In 1931 she was one of the two United States delegates to the Geneva meeting at which the Women's Peace and Disarmament Committee was formed, and two years later Miss Schain became a member of the board of the International Alliance of Women for Suffrage and Equal Citizenship. She was the only American woman observer at the Geneva Disarmament Conference in 1933. In May 1935, her second year as chairman of the National Committee on the Cause and Cure of War, Miss Schain headed the American delegation to the International Alliance's triennial conference at Istanbul, and also led its Peace Committee. The thirty-year change in women's status was highlighted at this conference, where the largest delegations were from India and Egypt, when the recently emancipated Turkish women joined in denouncing the Nazis' curtailment of the rights of German women. (The principles for which the Alliance stood were equal political, moral, economic, and legal rights for both sexes, and peace and support of the League of Nations.)

Miss Schain returned to America in 1935 convinced that there was a real desire for peace in every country, including the dictatorships. The next year, however, saw the founding of the Rome-Berlin Axis and the beginning of a world-wide armament race. This was the background for the Universal Peace Congress of October 1936, at which Miss Schain was one of fifty-eight United States delegates. (Earlier, she had made some speeches for the re-election of President Franklin D. Roosevelt [42].) Among the five thousand delegates from every country in the world were six hundred women, representing women's organizations with a total membership of forty-five million. The Congress decided to attempt to coordinate the work of all the peace forces in the world, and Miss Schain was given the "unprecedented honor" of heading the Commission on Women's Organizations, made up of their six hundred representatives.

The next month Miss Schain represented the National Committee on the Cause and Cure of War at the People's Conference in Favor of Peace, and came into conflict with Doris Stevens, chairman of the International Commission on Women, which was set up by the sixth Pan-American Conference. Miss Stevens, who had the advantage of Miss Schain in being able to address the Latin-Americans in Spanish, drew up a resolution to be presented to the Inter-American Conference for the Maintenance of Peace, at Buenos Aires, urging all member nations to make laws guaranteeing women unqualifiedly equal rights with men. In the recurrent debate as to whether or not such laws would defeat their own purpose, Miss Schain held the latter opinion, and declared that all the United States delegates were pledged to support it, having been "hand-picked" by Carrie Chapman Catt for the purpose. The Stevens resolution was passed by acclamation, however, with the support of all the United States delegates except Miss Schain and Helen Hayes '42, who represented the YWCA. The controversy was carried to the Buenos Aires conference in December 1936, where it occupied the entire attention of all delegates for a time. (Miss Schain was one of a large United States delegation headed by Secretary of State Cordell Hull '40 and Under-Secretary Sumner Welles '40, and joined by President Roosevelt.) Here she opposed the resolution on the ground that woman suffrage in its international aspect was already under study by the International Labor Office at Geneva, and that all discussion should await its findings. The situation was finally resolved by a compromise.

As war approached, Miss Schain gave lectures on the need for a stronger State Department and a stronger United States foreign policy, as well as on the need for educating children for peace. (She was a member of the executive committee of the Committee for Non-Participation in Japanese Aggression.) In 1937 she was a delegate to the Conference of the Women's Pan-Pacific Association in Vancouver. In that year Miss Schain's services to women and to the world were recognized by Smith College, which awarded her an honorary LL.D. In addition to serving on committees and associations directly concerned with international affairs, Miss Schain has also energetically aided the work of other organizations, including the General Federation of Women's Clubs, the American Association of University Women, the YWCA, and the National Council of Jewish Women, as consultant in international relations. Between conferences she lectured and traveled widely, having by 1943 run up a score of nine trips on the Continent, two journeys through the Near East and Russia, and one visit to South America. In 1940 she was chairman of the executive committee of the Women's Centennial Congress.

Josephine Schain became in May 1943 the first woman to represent the United States at a United Nations conference, having been appointed by Secretary Hull, with the President's approval, as one of six delegates to the Conference on Food and Agriculture at Hot Springs, Virginia. (The United States advisers and technical secretariat included five other women, all doctors specializing in food and nutrition.) Miss Schain was there as representative of the Commission to Study the Organization of Peace; the other American delegates were all experts on health, commerce, and agriculture, and she was the only woman delegate of any of the forty-five nations represented.

In January 1944 Miss Schain undertook to conduct a department, *Invitation to Information*, in the *Independent Woman*, organ of the National Federation of Business and Professional Women's Clubs. In it she gave a series of outlines and bibliographies for international questions. That October the Federation's new president, Margaret A. Hickey '44, appointed her to a two-year term as chairman of the Committee on International Relations, which she had headed from December 1931 to November 1934. In 1945 the State Department invited forty-two civic, social, labor, agricultural, and professional groups to send two consultants each to the American delegation at the United Nations Conference on World Organization, which opened in San Francisco in April 1945. The Federation sent Josephine Schain. A member of the executive committee of the Committee on Participation of Women in Postwar Planning, Miss Schain expressed satisfaction at the representation of women at the conference. "Besides the official women delegates from ten countries," she told reporters, "there are innumerable women at San Francisco as advisers, technical people, consultants, et cetera, including important women representatives from France, Norway, and Colombia. Don't you think that's pretty good?"

At the nine-week conference Miss Schain and the other women were divided on the question of including in the Charter of the new world organization a provision "guaranteeing and serving to establish the eligibility of women, as well as men, to serve as representatives of their nations in these organs and agencies where membership is accorded nations." This proposed provision, set forth by "a strongly united and articulate bloc of Latin-American women," was opposed by women from countries where their rights were more extensive, particularly by the British Ellen Wilkinson '41 and Florence Horsbrugh; but the Latin Americans finally convinced them that such a provision was indeed necessary to establish opportunities for women of the Latin nations. Later in the year Miss Schain was sent as a delegate to the United Nations Conference on Food and Agriculture at Hot Springs, Virginia, the purpose of which was to study the nutrition needs of the world.

Josephine Schain is described as a tall, handsome woman of full figure, with strong features, dark brows which contrast with her silvery white hair—and unexpected dimples when she smiles. "Her blunt words," according to Gledhill Cameron, "are leavened by good sense and good humor." In her spare

SCHAIN, JOSEPHINE—*Continued*

time she likes to write poetry; she is fond of gardening, and "can ride, swim, hike, and camp with the best of the Girl Scouts." In addition to Miss Schain's membership in innumerable committees and associations, she is a member of the Cosmopolitan and Pen and Brush clubs of New York, and the Women's University Club of Washington, D.C. Miss Schain is unmarried, and makes her home in New York.

References

Am Mag 118:48 S '34 por
Ind Woman 22:200 Jl '43 por; 23:324
O '44 por
N Y World-Telegram p17 Je 7 '45 por
American Women, 1939
Who's Who in America, 1944-45
Who's Who in New York, 1938
Women of Achievement (1940)

SCHLEICH, MICHEL, REV. 1863—Apr. 26, 1945 American Catholic educator and inspector general of all Marianist schools throughout the world, a post he held since 1911; directed activities of the four thousand schools from headquarters in Belgium.

Obituary

N Y Times p15 Ap 28 '45

SCHREMBS, ARCHBISHOP JOSEPH (shrĕms) March 12, 1866—Nov. 2, 1945 Bavarian-born Archbishop of the Roman Catholic Diocese in Cleveland (Ohio) since 1939; established a record as a builder of church edifices in Ohio.

Obituary

N Y Times p15 N 3 '45 por

SCHWELLENBACH, LEWIS B(AX-TER) (schwĕl'ĕn-bäk) Sept. 20, 1894-United States Secretary of Labor; lawyer
Address: b. Department of Labor, Washington, D.C.

Six weeks after Harry S. Truman[45] was sworn in as President of the United States he announced the appointment of a new Secretary of Labor—Lewis B. Schwellenbach. Successor to Frances Perkins[40], who had been the target of much criticism in the twelve years she held that key Cabinet post, Schwellenbach was a Federal district judge and former Democratic Senator from the State of Washington. A fighting liberal closely identified with the policies of Franklin D. Roosevelt[42], he is generally well regarded in labor quarters.

As his name indicates, Lewis Baxter Schwellenbach is of German descent, the son of Frank William and Martha (Baxter) Schwellenbach. He was born September 20, 1894, in Superior, Wisconsin, but when he was a small child the family moved to Spokane, Washington. When the child was still quite young his father died, and at the age of eight Lewis was selling newspapers to contribute his small bit to the family's support. He attended Washington Grade School and South Central High

School, where he developed a taste for debate. He was ambitious for a legal career, and after high school worked his way through the University of Washington, earning his LL.B. in 1917. During his university days he had demonstrated a flair for debate and politics and had organized the Woodrow Wilson Club on the campus.

Schwellenbach began his professional career as an assistant instructor in the university's department of liberal arts, but after the United States declared war on Germany he entered the Army as a private in Company M of the Twelfth Infantry Regiment. When the war was over he did not return to teaching. He was admitted to the Washington State bar in 1919 and became associated with the Seattle law firm of Roberts and Skeel, with whom he remained for two years. As an Army veteran he was also an active member of the American Legion, serving as a department commander in 1922-23.

In 1924 the rising attorney became chairman of the Democratic State Convention. The following year, with two other men, he formed the law firm of Schwellenbach, Merrick and Macfarlane, an association that lasted for six years. It was also in 1925 that he helped organize the North Coast Bank and Trust Company, of which he became president in 1930. In 1931 Schwellenbach decided to carry on his legal practice alone. For the next few years he represented several financial institutions in the Pacific Northwest affiliated with the Brotherhood of Locomotive Engineers. In that period, also, his prestige on the political scene increased. He had been chairman of the King County Democratic Committee from 1928 to 1930, and in 1932 he was the party's candidate for Governor in the primaries. The liberal lawyer ran on a platform of State operation of idle farms and factories for the benefit of the unemployed. Although unsuccessful in his candidacy, he continued his political activities, in 1934 becoming a candidate for the United States Senate from the Evergreen State. With the help of the American Legion, Schwellenbach carried on a victorious campaign under the slogan "End poverty in Washington."

Succeeding Senator Clarence C. Dill, who had coached him in oratory in high school, Schwellenbach took his seat in the Senate early in 1935. Even as a freshman Senator he made his presence felt (contrary to customary Senate procedure), in his first session leading a group of other newly elected Senators in an attempt to force a showdown on Huey Long's filibustering. His voting record soon demonstrated that he had liberal and labor leanings. He supported liberal relief expenditures during the depression, anti-lynching legislation, the utilities holding-company bill, reciprocal trade agreements, the wage-hour and the Wagner[41] labor acts, expansion of old-age pensions, and the Hatch[44] clean politics bills.

As a member of the Foreign Relations Committee, from 1937 he campaigned in and out of the Senate against the sale of scrap iron to Japan, sponsoring legislation to prevent its shipment. He was an active member of the Senate Lobby Investigating Committee headed by Hugo L. Black[41], and on occasion conducted committee hearings, demonstrating his ability in prosecuting the investigations. According to one writer, Schwellenbach, Black, and Sherman Minton '⁴¹ were the "Three Musketeers of the Senate." In the course of his career in the Senate Schwellenbach was also a member of the Robert La Follette '⁴⁴ Civil Liberties Committee, chairman of the special committee on conservation and utilization of aquatic life, and a member of the regular committees on Agriculture and Forestry, Claims, Immigration, and Pensions.

Early in his Senatorial career Schwellenbach had indicated strong sympathy with President Roosevelt's policies. Another Senator who had entered the legislature at the same time that Schwellenbach had was Harry S. Truman from Missouri, and the two freshmen became close friends. Together with Carl Hatch and Sherman Minton, they were known as the "four young Turks" in the Senate vanguard of the New Deal battle line. The Washington Senator attracted attention with his denunciation of the "Economic Royalists"; in 1937 Carlisle Bargeron in the *Nation's Business* called him the chief denouncer for the New Deal in the Senate. He "revels in the fight," wrote Bargeron, "and in bitterness and acrimony he has no worries about coming out second best." In the course of Schwellenbach's five years as New Deal stand-by in the Capital, Delos Lovelace reports, he was usually around when things were happening, "especially if the heads were rolling."

Among Administration measures which Schwellenbach supported was the hotly contested Supreme Court reorganization bill. Later he rallied to the Administration's defense when Roosevelt policies were under attack by the American Liberty League, a conservative organization largely supported by big business interests. In February 1936 he declared, "I am not one who holds the theory that the businessmen are in themselves public enemies who should as a group be condemned in the discussion of political problems. My criticism of American business is its inconsistency. It is constantly asking for governmental assistance, either financial or in the form of legislation which will assist the particular branch or industry in which the particular proponent of the particular legislation may be interested. At the same time American business is constantly criticizing the financial policy of the Government and the regulatory acts adopted by the Government." Again the militant Senator clashed with a scion of big business when, in March 1936 he devoted two days in the Senate to an "exposé" of the career of William Randolph Hearst. Some weeks later the Hearst newspapers carried a series of articles entitled *Lewis the Laundryman*, dealing with alleged manipulations of a Seattle concern, Superior Service Laundries, Inc., of which Schwellenbach was president. The Senator replied that this matter had been completely "thrashed out" during his Senatorial campaign.

In March 1938, in a discussion of the subject "Depression or Recession," Schwellenbach suggested that small business should be helped by making available adequate credit facilities. Analyzing the reasons for the country's depressed economic condition, he said, "But it seems to me that the most adequate explanation

LEWIS B. SCHWELLENBACH

of the present business condition is to be found in the undeniable fact that private enterprise failed to take up the slack occasioned by the curtailment of the Government's spending program." He appealed to industrialists to cooperate with the Government in bringing about a business revival. Also treating current labor conditions, he talked of the effect of controversy between labor groups: "I feel that in most fights between employees and employers the scales of public opinion are weighted in favor of those who work. That same favorable public reaction does not exist when organized labor fights within itself. . . . We need and we must have cooperation between government, industry, and labor. The preservation of American democracy justifies it, and demands it."

During his term of office Schwellenbach made several radio addresses, discussing such topics as tolerance, relief, the evils of dictatorship, Roosevelt's recovery program. One of his talks, "The First Seven Years of the New Deal," was reprinted by *Vital Speeches* in March 1940. Recalling the President's actions when he took office in the depths of the depression, the Senator declared, "Never in our history has one man accomplished what Roosevelt did then." He weighed the assets and liabilities of the New Deal, answering its critics with facts and figures. On the labor issue, he commented, "So long as we have the Weirs '⁴¹ and the Girdlers '⁴⁴ dominating our industrial scene, just so long will we have labor controversy."

In May 1940 President Roosevelt appointed Schwellenbach to the post of Federal district judge of the Eastern District of Washington State. In line with Senate tradition, his colleagues gave the appointment immediate confirmation without referring it to the Judiciary Committee for hearings. As it was, Schwellenbach did not don his judicial robes at once, preferring to wait until the end of the Congressional session in December. The judgeship was considered in some quarters a reward for the outspoken New Deal Senator.

(Continued next page)

SCHWELLENBACH, LEWIS B.—*Cont.*

Before he left the Senate, however, Schwellenbach was to oppose the Administration on a vital issue. In September 1940 he voted against conscription, the first time he had ever opposed the Administration on a major issue. In a speech on the Senate floor on August 28 he explained his decision to vote against the conscription measure and the Russell amendment (an amendment to the Selective Service Act providing for conscription of industry under certain conditions). Pointing out that peacetime conscription is an historical departure for America, Schwellenbach added that if one accepts the principle of conscription of men, then, logically, it must be extended to industry, and "when the time comes and we reach the logical conclusion of the course which this bill proposes, necessarily the system of free economics in this country must be destroyed."

In the first weeks after Truman had taken office as President rumors persisted that there would be a shakeup in the Roosevelt Cabinet. Among those mentioned for replacement was Secretary of Labor Frances Perkins, who had held her post for the twelve years of Roosevelt's Administration; and as early as April 26 the New York *Times* reported that Judge Schwellenbach was a prominent possibility for the Labor secretaryship. On May 23, less than a month later, Truman announced the first of his Cabinet changes, naming the jurist for Miss Perkins' post. A few days later the Senate Education and Labor Committee unanimously approved the nomination and on May 31 the full Senate seconded it by unanimous vote. Marquis W. Childs '43, pronouncing the choice excellent, added that the President had informed Schwellenbach that he "intended to restore to the Labor Department all the powers that had slipped away during the long tenure of Secretary Perkins. This was one of the arguments he used in persuading his friend to give up a Federal judgeship to come to Washington."

Columnist Thomas L. Stokes, in discussing the appointment of the Washingtonian, noted that the Pacific Coast was taking its place in the Cabinet and the "West gets a break." *PM* had referred earlier to his "splendid" Congressional record. Editorially the New York *World-Telegram* praised the appointment, looking forward to coordination within the Labor Department. Along similar lines, the New York *Herald Tribune*'s editorial hailed the change in the Labor secretaryship and expressed the belief that Schwellenbach would make a good Secretary. The reaction of labor was favorable, A.F. of L President William Green '42 enthusiastically greeting the new Secretary. *PM* indicated that it was understood that CIO sentiment also favored the Presidential appointee. (Schwellenbach's labor standing was demonstrated during the last general election when both A.F. of L. and CIO leaders in his state urged him to run for Governor or the Senate.) Announcing the new Cabinet members (Secretary of Labor, Attorney General, and Secretary of Agriculture), White House officials made it clear that the appointees were to have a free hand in reorganizing their departments. It was reported that the WLB and various independent labor agencies would be consolidated within the Labor Department and former powers of the Department would be restored. Commenting on the apparent shift in labor policy, the *United States News* pointed out that, while in recent years the Labor Department had become "principally a statistical agency, Judge Schwellenbach's idea is that it should be run impartially, as a court is run."

The new Secretary of Labor took office on the first of July. In his first "general order," approved by President Truman and issued through the White House, Schwellenbach directed all Labor Department employees to execute the laws as they stood, and explained that the order was sent out because, "after six years in the Senate and four and a half years on the Federal Bench, I know there is a tendency in the executive branch to interpret the law the way an administrative officer thinks it should be instead of following the law as written by Congress and interpreted by the courts. I am not going to allow that in my department."

Schwellenbach's first direct approach to the public was a speech over the radio, in which he warned both labor and management that industrial peace and creation of jobs were a joint responsibility. He also made it clear that he considered his Department as "obligated to protect the welfare of all workers, unorganized as well as members of trade unions." In a Labor Day radio address from Washington, Schwellenbach further warned organized labor to assume responsibilities for the public good or risk Federal controls. Schwellenbach early made known his appointment of Edgar L. Warren, chairman of the War Labor Board in Chicago, as chief of a reorganized United States Conciliation Service. Commenting on plans to strengthen the Conciliation Service, Schwellenbach stressed his belief in collective bargaining. (The size of the Government's conciliation task was indicated in a wartime report of the Conciliation Service which revealed that from December 7, 1941, to August 1, 1945, it handled 75,653 disputes, and of this number 57,537 cases were settled by the service through processes of arbitration.)

After a series of conferences with the three top labor leaders Schwellenbach indicated that the Bureau of Labor Statistics would be reorganized "because its work is too academic and not realistic enough." Early indication that other important changes were in order was confirmed when President Truman disclosed on September 18 that he had transferred all the powers and operations of the War Labor Board, the War Manpower Commission, and the United States Employment Service to the Labor Department. Eventually all labor functions of the Government were to be centralized within the Labor Department as far as possible.

In the midst of a threatened resumption of the prewar labor-industry conflict, plans were accelerated for a management-labor conference which President Truman had announced shortly after V-J Day, to be held in Washington beginning November 5. Weeks before the meeting could take place, however, the nation was faced with a record number of strikes or impending strikes involving such basic needs as coal, steel, oil, telephones, shipping, and motors. Leading industrialists as well as labor chiefs were called to Washington as a preliminary to the labor-management conference for consultation in the creation of a new wage and labor policy. In October Schwellenbach also testified in behalf of important pending legislation affecting labor. He commended the Pepper-Morse equal pay bill, "not only as a matter of fairness to women but also from the standpoint of preserving wage standards and consumer purchasing power." Schwellenbach also strongly advocated legislation to raise the legal minimum wage to 65 cents an hour, declaring that price control could be maintained without danger to industry. In urging adoption of the full employment bill, he condemned the views of those who wanted a "cheap labor" pool which would reduce production costs. However, Schwellenbach took occasion, in an address before the New York *Herald Tribune* Forum on October 31, to blame both sides in strikes, declaring that "collective bargaining is not collective bludgeoning."

In the first week of November, when he appeared at the final hearing on full employment legislation, Schwellenbach said the Administration had withheld suggestions on labor legislation so that it could not be accused of interfering or prejudging the labor-management conference then in session. Secretary of Labor Schwellenbach and Secretary of Commerce Henry Wallace were the Administration's two representatives in the conference. Limited in number so that it would be a real working group, it was composed of thirty-six delegates, who had been chosen by spokesmen for labor and industry. After four weeks of intensive discussion, the labor-management conference adjourned on November 30, having failed to set up a plan to avert work stoppages when collective bargaining and mediation failed.

Acting with speed President Truman recommended fact-finding by a Government board as a possible solution to end strikes which interfered with the public interest. On certification of the Secretary of Labor that a dispute would vitally affect the public interest, the President would be authorized to appoint a fact-finding board within the next five days. Earlier in the year Schwellenbach had already warned oil-industry heads and labor leaders when summoning them to Washington for a parley that "the time was rapidly approaching when the American people as a whole were going to take some stand on these questions." President Truman asked Congress for fact-finding legislation with the idea in mind of trying to force both sides to come to some sort of agreement or else risk stronger Government interventions later. By the end of the year fact-finding boards were engaged in the attempt to settle two of the country's most important disputes, those in the oil refineries and in General Motors' plants. Although their efforts were not very successful, the President wanted to give the fact-finding idea a thorough trial before taking other measures. His main concern was that Congress would "quickly" enact the necessary legislation. At his press conference on December 20 President Truman stated that one of his main purposes in asking Congress to vest fact-finding boards with power of subpoena was to enable them to examine the books of an employer "to determine the ability of the employer to pay an increase in wages." Secretary Schwellenbach

the next day said that fact-finding boards "must necessarily inquire into the issue of the employer's ability to pay," and moreover that they might "inquire into production and other costs where relevant."

Lewis Schwellenbach has taken an active interest in educational affairs. In 1933 he was appointed president of the board of regents of the University of Washington; he served as president of the board of Washington State College from 1941 to 1944, and in September 1944 he was appointed dean of the Gonzaga University Law School in Spokane. The jurist also served as president of the alumni association of his alma mater in 1928-29. Schwellenbach was a delegate to the Inter-parliamentary Union at The Hague in 1938. He is a member of the American Bar Association, the American Society on International Law, and the Regional Board of Legal Examiners in Spokane. His extensive organizational affiliations include membership in the American Council of the Institute of Pacific Relations, the American Academy of Political and Social Science, the Rotary Club of Spokane, and the advisory board of the Salvation Army in that city. A member of three fraternal orders, Schwellenbach is an Elk, an Eagle, and a Woodman. In 1945 he received an honorary LL.D. degree from the State College of Washington.

His Senate friends agree in their description of him as "able, independent, brilliant intellectually, and a liberal at heart." A friend of two Presidents, Schwellenbach is regarded as a sober, hard-working man, endowed with "tremendous force and energy." During the early and middle years of the Roosevelt Administration, when the Washington Senator was called upon to act as Administration trouble shooter, the late liberal Senator George W. Norris said of him, "Schwellenbach is the coming hope of the United States Senate." The Secretary is a large figure, six feet tall, and he weighs about two hundred pounds. He has dark hair and wears horn-rimmed glasses. During his first year as a Senator (1935) he was married to his secretary, Anne Duffy, in Chicago on December 30. For recreation the Westerner likes to spend evenings at home with books and cigars.

References

N Y Herald Tribune p32 My 4 '45; p12 My 24 '45
N Y Sun p20 My 4 '45
N Y World-Telegram p19 My 24 '45
PM p4 My 24 '45
Congressional Directory, 1945
Who's Who in America, 1944-45
Who's Who in Law, 1937
Who's Who in the Nation's Capital, 1938-39

SCOBIE, RONALD M(ACKENZIE) June 8, 1893- British Army officer

Address: b. c/o War Office, London; h. Cleeve Hill, N. Cheltenham, Gloucestershire, England

On a day in December 1944, while the Greek civil war was raging in the streets of Athens, a British Army officer, wearing a red-banded general's cap and many medals, stood calmly erect in the front seat of a scout car as he

British Official Photo.

LT. GEN. RONALD M. SCOBIE

drove through snipers' bullets. This officer was Lieutenant General Ronald M. Scobie, commander of the British Land Forces of the Adriatic, and, after the beginning of the Greek uprisings, commander in chief of Allied forces in Greece. Not one of Britain's headline commanders, according to the press, but "one who has never flopped," General Scobie is a veteran of the First World War and, in the Second World War, the former commander of the besieged fortresses of Tobruk and Malta. He was thought by many to have been in the "toughest" spot in his career during the forty-day fighting in Greece.

Ronald MacKenzie Scobie was born June 8, 1893. Though little information about his early life is available, one may assume that he spent it in Scotland as he is known to have played for Scotland in international rugby football matches against England, Ireland, and Wales in 1914. He entered the British Army in February 1914 and was commissioned a second lieutenant in the Royal Engineers in August, soon after he was twenty-one. In October young Scobie landed in France and, though wounded shortly after, remained at the front during the four years of the First World War, being mentioned twice in dispatches and winning the Military Cross. He was promoted to captain in 1917, and was made a brevet major in 1919, giving him the nominal rank but not the pay of a major.

Scobie continued to hold that rank in France until September 1920, when he returned to England to take command of a company at Woolwich. He was stationed at the Royal Military Academy from 1920 to 1924; then at Aldershot where he was first a staff captain from 1927 to 1929, and later a brigade major, serving in the command of Field Marshal Lord Archibald Wavell '41. Scobie's next duty was overseas. A graduate of the Staff College and later also of the Imperial Defence College, he was sent to the Australian Royal Military College, where he was director of military artillery from 1932 to 1935.

From Australia Scobie returned to England, and in January 1938 he received another staff appointment—that of assistant adjutant general. His days in the field seemed almost as irretrievably in the past as those when he had played rugby for Scotland, for his next post was again administrative, this time one of high importance: he was Deputy Director of Mobilization from September 1, 1939, to May 8, 1940. He is said to have been a skillful, resourceful administrator in this post. For eight months he worked at the War Office and then, just before Italy declared war, he went out to the Middle East as deputy adjutant general. Scobie had been a brevet lieutenant colonel in 1934, a lieutenant colonel and colonel in 1937, and in 1941 he was made a major general. In August the Italians invaded British Somaliland; Scobie was with the British troops in the Sudan and a brigadier on the General Staff from August 18, 1940, to October 16, 1941.

Throughout the Abyssinian campaign the General was on the staff that planned the gigantic north-to-south pincer movement which broke Italian military power in East Africa. The southern arm of the forces based in Kenya was under General Sir Alan Cunningham '41; brother of Admiral Sir Andrew Cunningham '41; the northern was under General Sir William Platt, driving in from the Sudan. Scobie was under General Platt advancing in February 1941 to take Agordat, to break the core of Italian resistance in East Africa by the capture of Keren in March 1941, and finally to conquer the whole of Eritrea.

Succeeding General Moreshead as general officer in command of the "beleaguered sandy fortress of Tobruk," Scobie led the British Seventieth Division in by sea to relieve the Australians in October 1941. The Seventieth Division held the fortress, even attacking from it to meet the relieving forces advancing under General Sir Claude Auchinleck '42. This was the second British offensive of the Western Desert, and the advance reached El Agheila. For his campaign in Eritrea and at Tobruk, Scobie was twice decorated, with the Order of the British Empire in 1941 and with the Order of the Bath in 1942.

Marshal Erwin Rommel's '42 counteroffensive followed Auchinleck's advance, and except for a month of the six months that it lasted—from January to July 1942—Scobie was once again on the staff as deputy adjutant general (from February 17, 1942 to August 5, 1942). His next post, as general officer in command or operational commander of what has been called "the still more durable island bastion" of Malta, combined in many ways the work of the last two appointments. He was commanding the troops on the Mediterranean island when it was under siege.

During these months in the summer and autumn of 1942 the fortress of Malta was under continual attack by Nazi and Italian planes. The blockade by sea was also intensified at this time, and the subsequent shortage of food and equipment caused Lord Gort '40 to institute such measures as putting the island on half rations, and cutting fuel consumption to the extent of forbidding the use of light or power all summer. Finally, however, the siege was lifted as the Eighth Army moved swiftly west from El Alamein and the Allied Forces landed in North Africa in November 1942.

After the relief of Malta, Scobie was again given a new appointment, this time as chief of the General Staff in the Middle East, but he had held it only for a few months when he was given "special employment," in preparation for the invasion of Greece in October 1944. It was only after British troops had landed in Greece that it became generally known that Scobie was leading this invasion.

In his address of January 18, 1945, to the House of Commons, Prime Minister Churchill [42] explained, in answer to criticism of Britain's actions in Greece, "We went on the invitation of the Greek Government in which all parties, even the Communists, were represented, and as a result of a military conference at which the generals of ELAS and of EDES were equally present. We brought food, clothing, and supplies. We came with a small force of troops. We took up our positions from no military point of view, spreading our troops in a number of places on the coast and at small points inland, where we hoped to be able to pour in the largest number of supplies as quickly as possible to a very hungry people." (At Caserta, in September, the generals had declared "their full acceptance of the orders of the Greek Government and of the Supreme Allied Commander," under whose orders the Greek Government had placed all Greek forces operating in the country.)

By "small force of troops" Churchill meant the Land Forces of the Adriatic, which, according to *Time* Magazine, are a "small unit of British Commando troops, paratroops, and special service forces under the command of a British Army officer." The group was organized formally during the summer of 1944 and placed under the Allied Balkan Air Force, continued *Time*. It was based in Italy and worked closely with the Navy and Air Force in order to move back and forth across the Adriatic, operating over a front about seven hundred and fifty miles long.

Before the liberation of Greece the Greek Government in Exile had announced that Greek guerrilla factions had agreed to act together under Allied command in the fight against the Germans. Scobie was named commander of Allied operations in Greece, and in October British Commandos were reported to have landed on three Greek islands.

But in October 1944, when Greece was liberated from Axis domination (George Papandreou [44] was Premier and the exiled King George II [43] was waiting in London for a plebiscite on the question of his return to the throne), EAM, the Leftist guerrilla organization, had been growing in power. After the liberation of Greece and the return of the Government to Athens, ELAS, the military arm of EAM, was in almost complete control of the city, where festive celebrations had led to street riots. Said *Newsweek*, ELAS troops held much of Athens and the surrounding countryside by the middle of December, and it became obvious that Lieutenant General Scobie faced a full campaign unless some political solution were found.

In November, after a conference with Scobie, Papandreou ordered all guerrilla groups to disband, and the Greek Communist Party and the EAM resistance organizations agreed to this Government order. On December 1 Scobie broadcast to the Greek people to remind them that the British troops had come, first, to drive out the invader, secondly, to bring relief, and, thirdly, to help restore prosperity. He said that he would stand by the side of the constitutional Government headed by Papandreou until it could be established with a legal armed force behind it and was able to hold free elections, and that he would protect the Greek Government from a coup d'état. Millions of copies of Scobie's proclamation were dropped by planes all over Greece, and the British Government issued a statement approving Scobie's declaration and giving full support to the Papandreou Government. But the unrest and uncertainty continued. *Newsweek* described the Greek situation as "a witch's brew of internal discord and foreign interventions" which was slowly reaching the boiling point.

The crisis did reach the boiling point when a general strike was declared in Athens on December 4, and the British troops disarmed over three hundred Left-wing supporters who had marched into Athens in defiance of the British military rule. Orders were sent to Scobie to take over military command of Athens and to restore and maintain order by whatever measures were necessary—in the words of one commentator, "the normal life of the city came to a halt."

For a while the task of clearing the city of ELAS partisans progressed steadily. British troops supported by strafing planes, tanks, and field artillery continued to hold the center of the Greek capital. By December 11, however, ELAS partisans had filtered back, and bloody street fighting raged in Athens, with over twenty thousand armed Leftist troops sniping and shelling British and Greek Government positions in the heart of the capital. "If I did wrong," Churchill afterward told the House of Commons, "I take the full responsibility. . . . For three or four days, or more, it was a struggle to prevent a hideous massacre in the center of Athens."

Churchill insisted that it was necessary for the British to maintain order by force because the EAM was seeking to seize power and terrorize the country, a charge which the EAM vehemently denied. The EAM leaders also proclaimed that the struggle would continue until the resignation of Papandreou. Scobie was bitterly denounced during these tense days. At one time leaflets addressed to British soldiers containing strong criticisms of him were distributed by the EAM; in these leaflets Scobie with his "murderous orders" was contrasted with Lord Byron, who "gave his life for the liberty of Greece [while] General Scobie supplies arms for its slavery."

On December 12 Scobie informed EAM delegates that under the Caserta agreement they must leave Attica, cease fighting, and surrender their arms before any settlement could be made. Airplanes again dropped leaflets containing this warning. According to *Newsweek*, the reluctance of the EAM leaders to disband was based upon what they considered the fundamental issue of the civil war (the same issue which split other liberated countries of Europe), which they questioned: the Government's right to disarm all soldiers outside the Regular Army. By retaining their arms ELAS leaders declared that they retained their only chance of

SCOBIE, RONALD M.—*Continued*

participating in a new Greek Government and preventing the installation of a monarchist dictatorship.

The next day British headquarters reported two determined ELAS attacks, one on a Greek brigade and the other on British troops. While British reinforcements arrived, ELAS forces shelled the center of the city, especially the headquarters, during that night and the following day. On Christmas Day Prime Minister Churchill and Foreign Secretary Anthony Eden '40 arrived in Athens. A regency was demanded, and King George issued a proclamation naming Archbishop Damaskinos '45 as Regent. General Nicholas Plastiras was made Premier to replace the "British puppet" Papandreou, who had resigned, and, with the formation of a new Cabinet, the strife in Athens seemed to have come to a close. Scobie and four ELAS delegates signed a truce on January 11, 1945, halting hostilities and, although there were some difficulties concerning the question of hostages, the forty-day civil war was considered at an end.

However, Great Britain received little credit, although Scobie was said to have done well with what little he had. There were comments that the British, in the words of the New York *World-Telegram,* "badly underestimated the depth of the situation and arrived with far too little force." In January, reports of the release of a large proportion of the hostages held by ELAS lightened the political situation. ELAS central committee men had authorized the chief of the International Red Cross committee mission there to take possession of all hostages except those considered by ELAS to be responsible for the Greek crisis. Scobie had authorized the chief of the Red Cross mission to arrange for an exchange of prisoners. In January, too, Scobie, in the report of Leland Stowe in the New York *Post,* "forbade correspondents to have any contacts with 'the enemy' (EAM and ELAS representatives), even interviews supervised by British officers. Eleven out of twelve American correspondents appealed to the United States government to intervene so that the American public, 'without any infringement of British military security,' might hear occasionally 'a part of the EAM view of the present conflict.'"

Reports of violence and unrest continued to come from Greece through succeeding months. In July, according to an account in the New York *Times,* "a long document charging that the British had severely abused Greek Left Wingers detained in North Africa since the mutiny of Greek armed forces was made public by Maritpress, recently established in London as a news agency for EAM and ELAS." Following criticism of the official British position made by a delegation of Labor Members of Parliament who visited Greece, and who contended that "free elections were impossible in Greece under present conditions," announcement was made from London on November 6 that Foreign Secretary Ernest Bevin would send Under-Secretary for Foreign Affairs, Hector MacNeil, to Athens. The Foreign Office stated that MacNeil would consult with the new Greek government on "certain aspects" of the problem of speeding reconstruction. There was

official denial, however, that there was any intention of withdrawing General Scobie.

General Scobie—who, according to *Newsweek,* is unsuitably known to the Greek press and public as "Mr. Scobie"—is described as a typically soft-spoken, steel-willed British Army officer with a long, ruddy face, slightly aquiline nose, minute mustache, and graying chestnut hair. Tall and lean, with erect military carriage and quick, dignified steps, he has retained a youthful appearance. His official manner is quiet, almost diffident, but his dignity is impressive. *Newsweek* says that his tall, attractive wife and his daughter Jane live at Cleeve Hill, near Cheltenham in Gloucestershire. In 1945 Jane was attending the Cheltenham Ladies' College, and Mrs. Scobie, who before the war traveled with her husband to his posts, was working at a nonprofit restaurant operated by the British Government.

References

N Y Sun p14 D 28 '44
Newsweek 24:47 D 25 '44
Who's Who, 1945

SCRUGHAM, JAMES GRAVES (skrŭg'-am) Jan. 19, 1880—June 23, 1945 United States Senator (Democratic) from Nevada since 1943; Representative in Congress (1933-43); Governor of Nevada (1923-27); an engineer by profession, he was professor of mechanical engineering at the University of Nevada (1903-14) and Dean of the Engineering College (1914-17); editor and publisher of *Nevada State Journal* (1927-32); one of the incorporators of the American Legion.

Obituary

N Y Times p22 Je 24 '45 por

SEABROOK, WILLIAM B(UEHLER) Feb. 22, 1886—Sept. 20(?), 1945 American author and explorer; in 1934 had himself committed to institution for alcoholism; his book *Asylum* (1935) based on experiences there; other books include *Adventures in Arabia* (1927), *The Magic Island* (1929), and *An Analysis of Magic and Witchcraft* (1940). See sketch *Current Biography* 1940 Yearbook.

Obituary

N Y Times p22 S 21 '45 por

SEIBOLD, LOUIS (sī'bōld) 1864(?)—May 10, 1945 Retired New York newspaperman; winner of the Pulitzer Prize for reporting in 1920; responsible for a number of exposés and reforms through his newspaper stories; author of *Japan and Its Expansion* and two other books.

Obituary

N Y Times p19 My 11 '45 por

SHAPOSHNIKOV, BORIS (MIKHAILOVICH) (shä'pôsh-nyĭ-kôf myĭ-κĭ'lŭ-vyĭch) 1882—Mar. 27, 1945 Russian Army officer; credited with devising most of Bolshevik military strategy during Revolution; chief of General Staff of Red Army, 1928-31; made marshal of Red Army following successful attack on Mannerheim Line (Finland) in 1940; appointed commander in chief of Russian Army in 1942; became ill and retired same year.

Obituary

N Y Times p19 Mr 27 '45

SHAW, LAU (lō) 1898- Chinese author
Address: b. c/o Reynal & Hitchcock, 8 W. 40th St., New York City

One of the leading literary interpreters of contemporary Chinese life has won wide attention in America with the appearance in English of one of his books, *Rickshaw Boy* (1945), under the pseudonym Lau Shaw. He is Shu Ch'ing-ch'un, popular in his native China as a prolific novelist, playwright, and poet. As a writer he has been compared to the great Western classicists who faithfully transcribed the social scenes of their day into vivid indictments of the evils within those societies. According to Lewis Gannett '41, *Rickshaw Boy* "belongs to something more than a Chinese tradition; it reminds one of Gorky and Nexö; it is part of the great stream." This story of a Peking coolie, the first of Lau Shaw's works to appear in America, was the August 1945 selection of the Book-of-the-Month Club, and it was also the subject of a radio dramatization.

Lau Shaw, or Shu Ch'ing-ch'un, is of Manchu descent. He was born in Peking about 1898. (In Chinese calculation a person is one year old when he is born, and a year older after each New Year's Day.) Since the author rarely writes or talks about himself, there is little information about his early life. What is known is that he studied at a provincial normal school where he later taught, and that he also attended Peking University, during which time he wrote stories. Whether he received a degree from the university is unknown, for, in the words of Kay Yang, "The truth is, he never cared to make certain whether he had received one or not. All he had in mind at the time was to go back to teach in his own province and continue to write stories." He devoted several years to teaching until he accepted an opportunity to go to Oxford University to study education.

In London Lau Shaw became acquainted with the late Professor Hsu Ti-shan, a well known scholar and short story writer, who saw promise in the young man's literary efforts. Encouraged by the Professor, Lau Shaw began to write his first novel, *Chao Tze Yueh* ("Mr. Chao Said"). When the book was published about 1928, it was an immediate success. It has been called a keen satire of Chinese students "caught between the tide of Western culture and the old Confucian tradition, imagining themselves successors to Confucius in setting up new traditions, while actually they were little more than buffoons." The writer also collaborated with Clement Egerton in his translation of the great Chinese novel *Chin P'ing Mei* ("King Ping Mei"), which was published in England in four volumes under the title *The Golden Lotus*.

In the late twenties Lau Shaw returned to China and his teaching. He taught at the Cheeloo University (formerly Shantung Christian University) at Tsinan and the National

LAU SHAW

Shantung University at Tsingtao, both in the province of Shantung, while continuing his own writing. Since that period he has written several novels, collections of short stories, plays, and humorous sketches. His best-known works are *The Philosophy of Lao Chang, Camel Happy Boy* (the title of *Rickshaw Boy* in China), and the play, *The Problem of Face*. Lin Yutang '40 has said that Lau Shaw enjoys an established reputation in China, as a writer of "genuine, unimpeachable Peking dialect."

Like so many of his countrymen, the author moved inland in 1937 in the face of the advancing Japanese, leaving Northern China after the Marco Polo Bridge incident that July. (Marco Polo Bridge or Lukowkiao is a railway junction near Peking where a minor incident was seized upon by the Japanese as a pretext for further aggression in that area.) He arrived in Hankow in 1938 but soon left that doomed city for the Nationalist capital at Chungking. Trips to the northwest during this time provided material for two narrative poems, each of about five thousand lines, descriptive of his journeys to Sian and Lanchow. Then, in collaboration with Soang Chih-ti, he wrote a four-act play concerned with Mohammedan and Chinese unity, *The Nation Above All.* He also wrote stories to be sung in the popular "Big Drum" form. Written in the traditional style, his narrative poems and plays are designed to reach the common people. Professor Chi-Chen Wang of Columbia University believes that the writer was considerably influenced by Western satirical writers, especially Dickens. According to Professor Wang, "In *Lao Niu P'o Ch'e* ("Old Ox Cart"), a volume on his own experience as a writer, he states that it was after reading Dickens' *Nicholas Nickleby* and *Pickwick Papers* that he had the courage to offer his 'Old Chang's Philosophy' to the public."

When the National Anti-Japanese Association of All Chinese Writers was organized in 1938, Lau Shaw became its president and

SHAW, LAU—*Continued*

by repeated re-elections has retained that position. During the war, in addition to pursuing his literary work, he was active in the organization and direction of Chinese writers in the cause of their country. Under his auspices the association sent young writers to homes and the front and to the enemy rear to visit Chinese soldiers and write of their experiences. The resulting stories, sketches, poems, plays, and critical articles were published in the organization's monthly organ, *Resistance War Literature,* edited jointly by Lau Shaw and Mao Tun. At frequent meetings the writers read and discussed new poems and stories, and their discussions dealt with social as well as literary questions. Lau Shaw succeeded in establishing branches of the association in practically all the large cities, activating the literati of those metropolitan centers. However, the growing political control of the press greatly reduced the organization until it became "an almost empty name, with most of the active writers in hiding." In spite of Lau Shaw's effort to keep the publication going, *Resistance War Literature* has appeared only about twice yearly.

The author's devotion to the people is evident in *Rickshaw Boy,* whose hero represents the universal common man. Happy Boy is a young, naive, and inarticulate country boy who comes to the city of Peking and is quickly caught in the web of slum life. The book is the story of his misfortunes—"a series of those fateful perversities that are part of the whole tragic pattern of poverty." The boy learns that "the poor have only one way of deciding any issue that confronts them, and that is on the basis of dollars and cents." Yet, with all his sufferings, he also learns, slowly and vaguely, that "he is not alone in his wretchedness, that he is one of many striving for a better world."

Rickshaw Boy has been called "a devastatingly honest novel which tells more about modern China and its tragic pattern of life than any other book thus far available in America." As a social document, it has been compared with the work of Dickens and the great Russian novelists, Gogol and Dostoevski. Mai-mai Sze found "something Swiftian in the passionate anger of the author's attitude against the system that begets such conditions of unrelieved misery." However, it was pointed out by several critics that the author never uses his characters as "mouth-pieces." "Without a word of propaganda," said Richard Watts, Jr., in the *New Republic,* "it is a most valuable propaganda work for the idealistic theory that all men of good will are brothers." Recognized as a significant contribution to American understanding of modern China, the book, according to Harrison Smith, teaches us about the Chinese people, "their hearts, the comradeship of their multitudinous poor, and the injustice that rules their living and dying." In his review in the New York *Post,* Clip Boutell declared, "*Rickshaw Boy* will make you wonder on what basis peace will be established in the Far East."

General critical opinion commended the vigorous, pungent language of the book and the absence of melodrama in the realistic treatment of the theme. The expert use of the ancient city of Peking as a background was emphasized; Peking, "symbolic of antiquity's massive legacy of stagnation and oppression," is described in all moods and weathers until "it becomes as real as any character." The people of the book were called universal types, "admirably drawn," and especially singled out for praise was the searching analysis of Happy Boy himself. In a dissenting tone, however, William Du Bois [40] wrote that "symbols are poor substitutes for people," and called the book "a worthy try, but a dull novel."

Lau Shaw's novel was translated from the Chinese by Evan King, an American who has lived in China for many years and who some years ago brought another Chinese novel to American readers, *Village in August* by T'ien Chun. Complications arose over the question of royalties on *Rickshaw Boy,* since there are no copyrights on American books in China, and vice versa; King and Lau Shaw are both in China, which further confuses the matter on the issue of taxes. Sweden has already bought publication rights for the book, and it will soon be available to other European readers upon completion of negotiations for the sale of publication rights in France, England, Spain, and Switzerland. Before the book was published in America, some of the author's short stories had appeared in *Contemporary Chinese Stories.* In late 1945 Lau Shaw was working on a novel about wartime China, entitled "Cremation," to be the longest he has ever written.

The Chinese writer is a spectacled man of medium height with brown eyes and "an open, candid gaze." Described by Lin Yutang as an individualist who can not be classified in any school, Lau Shaw is a liberal with no political inclinations, "except for the liberty of his country, and the welfare and freedom of the people." Commenting in an article on the current lack of freedom of expression in his country, he stated, "When I write I feel myself a thief, constantly watching around to see whether there is somebody sneaking behind, watching over what I am writing. How can a writer work when he has to watch over every word he puts down just like a thief watching his every action?" The author has suffered much, and his poor health, caused by undernourishment, hard work, and mental strain, confined him to a hospital for some time in 1944. Living in poverty with his family in Peipei, near Chungking, he refused to accept financial aid, which he felt would compromise his ideals. When a large assemblage paid tribute to him in June 1944 on the occasion of his twentieth anniversary as a writer, he said, "I pledge that while I breathe I won't desert my pen and the honesty of it."

References

Book-of-the-Month Club N p5-6 Jl '45
    por
N Y Times p17 Jl 30 '45

SHAWCROSS, SIR HARTLEY (WILLIAM) Feb. 4, 1902- British Government official; lawyer

Address: b. Ministry of Justice, London; h. Peckhams, Halland, near Uckfield, Sussex, England

Late in the year 1945 international attention was focused on the long-awaited war-crimes trials in Nuremburg, Germany, conducted by the United States, the United Kingdom, the Soviet Union, and France. The chief United Kingdom prosecutor is Sir Hartley Shawcross, K.C., M.P., appointed to the post on August 13, 1945. Shortly before that the relatively young barrister had become Britain's Attorney General, following the Labor Party victory.

Hartley William Shawcross was born on February 4, 1902 to John and Hilda Shawcross. Educated at Dulwich College near London, he also attended the London School of Economics for a brief period. The Englishman then went abroad, spending some time in Geneva, where he studied at the University. Shawcross had become interested in politics at an early age and at sixteen had joined the Labor Party. While he was in Geneva, where the second Socialist International Conference was in session, he assisted in the secretariat and also met many delegates from various countries. Back in England, Shawcross served as election agent for Lewis Silkin during the 1922 General Election when the latter waged an unsuccessful battle for a Conservative district. (Silkin is the present Minister of Town and Country Planning.) As Shawcross gained experience in the Labor movement, he became determined to remain active in its work.

At about this time Shawcross began his legal studies, in which he won first class honors in all examinations, and came out highest in the Bar Final. Called to the Bar at Gray's Inn in 1925, he then practiced law in London for two years. In 1927 he moved from the capital to Liverpool where, until 1934, he was senior law lecturer at Liverpool University. (He received an honorary LL.M. degree from that institution in 1932.) During these years he also practiced law on the Northern Circuit. At a trial at Manchester, Shawcross was junior counsel for the prosecution of a Lancaster murderer. At one time, the barrister led an inquiry into the Gresford Colliery disaster. Conducting the investigation on behalf of the coal owners, he was matched with his friend, Sir Stafford Cripps '40, on the miners' side. It is believed that his conduct of this inquiry considerably aided his career. In 1939 Shawcross became a bencher (one of the senior and governing members who control calling to the bar) of Gray's Inn, and that year "took silk"—received letters patent as a King's Counsel. In 1940 he left his private practice to accept a Government assignment, and a year later, while engaged in important government work as independent chairman of the Kew District Board on coal mining, he was appointed recorder of Salford, in Lancashire. About that time he was also appointed deputy regional commissioner for the South Eastern Region, one of the many zones into which the country had been divided for purposes of defense, and he was a Justice of the Peace for Sussex and assistant chairman of the East Sussex Quarter Sessions. The fol-

Barratts, London

SIR HARTLEY SHAWCROSS

lowing year Shawcross was promoted to the post of commissioner of the North Western Region. Charged with the responsibility of the region's entire defense organization, he traveled constantly in his district. In public speeches he repeatedly warned of the probable resumption of large-scale air attacks and urged mutual aid plans among small traders, to become operative during raids, which would benefit storekeepers and the community alike.

The lawyer's work as regional commissioner was a valuable prelude to his duties as chairman of the Catering Wages Commission, established in July 1943 by the Ministry of Labor and National Service. This Commission was set up to investigate wages and to suggest methods of developing the catering, restaurant, and hotel industry in the postwar period in order to meet the needs of the domestic public and foreign visitors. Shawcross served on the commission until July 1945, at which time he resigned to run for Parliament. However, at the time of his resignation most of the Commission's investigations had been completed and its report was published in September. It has been said that this report, when implemented, will "stabilize wages and conditions throughout the previously unorganized industry, and pave the way for an improved standard of hotel accommodation."

Active for many years in Labor Party work, Shawcross had been asked to stand for election in 1924 but at that time had declined. In July 1945 he was a successful candidate for Parliament in the General Election which swept the Labor Party into power. Shawcross won a majority of about 17,000 over his Conservative opponent, quadrupling the former Labor majority in his constituency. Under Prime Minister Clement R. Attlee's '40 new Labor Government, the new M.P. was appointed Attorney General and shortly thereafter was named chief prosecutor of the war crimes trials for Britain. A few days later, on August 15, Shawcross was knighted. His appointment to these vital

SHAWCROSS, SIR HARTLEY—*Cont.*

offices was welcomed in both legal and non-legal circles, with the press describing him as one of the country's "most highly-regarded young attorneys." The new Attorney General was in the headline news barely a month later as prosecutor of William Joyce in the treason trial at Old Bailey. Joyce's defense, based on the contention that he was an American citizen, was shattered when the judge accepted the prosecutor's view that "A person who enjoys the effective protection of the British Crown is under duty of allegiance so long as the protection continues." (The defendant had a British passport, issued in 1939). Found guilty by the jury, Joyce was sentenced to be hanged for his broadcasts as "Lord Haw-Haw."

Less than a week after he became chief prosecutor Shawcross flew to Nuremberg with his American, French, and Russian colleagues to inspect the facilities for the trial. The basis for the case against the major war criminals had been established by the four Powers in the formal agreement made in London on August 8, 1945. At that time an historic new code of international law was adopted, defining aggressive warfare as a crime against the world. The agreement established a four-Power international military tribunal and three classifications of war crimes: 1) crimes against peace, involving the planning, preparation, initiation, or waging of aggressive war; 2) war crimes, defined as violations of the laws or customs of war; 3) crimes against humanity. Pursuant to this agreement, the four United Nations representatives prepared a lengthy indictment against the twenty-four major Nazi war criminals, which was released in October, bearing the signatures of Robert H. Jackson [40] for the United States, Shawcross for the United Kingdom, François de Menthon [44] for France, and R. A. Rudenko for the Soviet Union. Proceedings began on November 20, 1945. Each person in the courtroom was supplied with earphones which could be tuned to the verbatim proceedings or to any of four translations, and twelve interpreters were also in attendance. Two hundred and fifty newsmen had arranged to cover the trials, and Justice Jackson had announced that there would be no censorship. Sir Hartley's deputy in the prosecution, incidentally, is Sir David Maxwell Fyfe, who was Attorney General in the coalition Government of Winston Churchill [42].

In his thirty-thousand-word address which opened the British presentation of the case against the twenty Nazi defendants on December 4, 1945, in Nuremberg, Sir Hartley reviewed the international treaties and agreements since the 1899 Hague Convention to prove that the world had outlawed aggressive war. Thus, it is not correct, he declared, to regard punishment for aggressive war as retroactive justice. As to the individual responsibility each defendant bore, he contended: "There comes a point when a man must refuse to answer to his leader if he is also to answer to his own conscience." The British prosecutor was one of the four delegates the House of Commons chose later in December to accompany Prime Minister Attlee to the United Nations General Assembly scheduled to convene early in January 1946.

Both in his legal and political activities Shawcross has expressed his convictions strongly. An ardent Socialist, he made his first political speech as a youth at a public meeting in Birmingham. The Attorney General has expressed himself forcibly against some British prison and punishment methods. In discussing the Penal Reform Bill in 1939, he condemned flogging: "A punishment which makes strong men sick cannot be a good thing," he said. "If flogging is a good thing, why not go back to the thumb-screw, the rack, and other systems of medieval torture?" Known as a hard worker, Shawcross is said to study every brief himself, never passing on his work to juniors.

The Chief Prosecutor is described by Margaret Armour as "a tall, spare, at once dignified and athletic-looking man, with high cheekbones and the healthily weather-tanned complexion of the sportsman." He has dark eyes and hair and a quiet voice. After the death of his first wife, who was Rosita Alberta Shyvers, he married Joan Winifred Mather whom he met while serving as regional commissioner when she was assigned to drive him through the area. They live in a small old country house near Uckfield in Sussex. When he has time for recreation Shawcross likes reading, golfing, or riding. A yachting enthusiast, he belongs to four yacht clubs, Royal Thames, Royal Cornwall, Royal Mersey, and Royal Motor. Sir Hartley is a member also of the Reform Club.

Reference

Who's Who, 1945

SHEAR, T(HEODORE) LESLIE Aug. 11, 1880—July 3, 1945 Internationally known American archaeologist; lecturer on art and archaeology (1912-27) and professor of classical archaeology (from 1928 to death) at Princeton; directed four major excavations of the ancient world: Cnidus (1911) and Sardis (1922) in Asia Minor, Corinth in Greece (1925-31), and the marketplace of ancient Athens (1931-39); field director of American School of Classical Studies in Athens.

Obituary

N Y Times p13 Jl 5 '45 por

SHEEHAN, WINFIELD R. (shē′ǎn) Sept. 24, 1883—July 25, 1945 American motion picture producer; organized Fox Film Corporation studios (1914); vice-president and general manager of the studio until 1935; produced *In Old Arizona* (1929), first feature picture with sound, and was also identified with development of sound recording on the screen; among other films he is known for are *What Price Glory* (1926), *Seventh Heaven* (1927), *Cavalcade* (1933), and *Captain Eddie* (1945); he was the husband of opera star Maria Jeritza.

Obituary

N Y Times p19 Jl 26 '45 por

SHELLABARGER, SAMUEL (shĕl'a-bär'gẽr) May 18, 1888- Author; educator
Address: b. c/o The Blakiston Co., 1012 Walnut St., Philadelphia, Pa.; h. 631 E. Town St., Columbus, Ohio

Samuel Shellabarger is the author of one of the 1945 best sellers, *Captain From Castile,* called "one of the most exciting novels of the cloak-and-sword variety to come along in years." No literary novice, Shellabarger has written nine mystery and adventure novels under two pseudonyms, in addition to two scholarly biographies. Combining teaching and writing ability, he has also had a long career as an educator.

A native of Washington, D. C., Samuel Shellabarger was born on May 18, 1888. The son of Robert Rodgers and Sarah Rivera (Wood) Shellabarger, young Samuel was educated in Washington private schools and at the Hill School in Pottstown, Pennsylvania. He entered Princeton University in 1905 when Woodrow Wilson was in the zenith of his career there. Of these decisive years Shellabarger remarks, "Long before then I had decided to make writing either my profession or my avocation, and during the undergraduate years at Princeton I took, I believe, all the various prizes offered in English. In order to secure greater leisure for writing, I decided to enter the academic career rather than to follow the profession of law, which had been my first ambition."

Awarded his B.A. degree in 1909, Shellabarger took a year of graduate work at Princeton and then went to Germany with the intention of taking his doctor's degree at Munich or Leipzig. However, after a year of study at Munich University (1910-11), he returned to America to complete his graduate work at Harvard under such popular men as Professors Kittredge, Neilson, Baker, and Robinson. He received his Ph.D. in 1917. While in Europe on a visit to Sweden in the summer of 1914, he had met Vivan Georgia Lovegrove Borg (the daughter of a Swedish cavalry officer), to whom he was married on June 14, 1915. The Shellabargers have three children: Ingrid Rivera (Mrs. William H. Rea), whose husband served during the war with the Pacific Fleet; Marion, who worked with a Clubmobile unit of the Red Cross in England; and Eric, who was killed in Germany in May 1945.

At the time of his marriage Shellabarger was teaching in the English department of Princeton, a position he had accepted in the autumn of 1914. His teaching career was interrupted by America's entry into the First World War. In 1917 he served as a first lieutenant in the Ordnance Department of the Army. The next year he was transferred to Military Intelligence, promoted to a captaincy, and appointed assistant military attaché at the United States Legation in Stockholm.

When the war ended Shellabarger returned to Princeton as assistant professor of English. After four years of teaching he decided to leave the university to devote more time to writing. In 1923 the Shellabarger family went abroad to live, and for the next five years, the author says, he and his family had their headquarters in Lausanne, Switzerland,

SAMUEL SHELLABARGER

although they traveled widely in Italy and France. During this period he prepared the biography of Chevalier Bayard and wrote a novel, *The Black Gale* (1929) and a mystery story *The Door of Death* (1928). Upon his return to America in 1928 *The Chevalier Bayard* was published.

After another two years at Princeton the writer returned to his travels, residing for a time in France and England. Back in America again in 1931, Shellabarger devoted himself to writing for several years. In 1935 his biography of Lord Chesterfield was published. Under the pen name of John Esteven (which he had used for *The Door of Death*), he next wrote mysteries of the "shudders and chills" variety. They bore the suggestive titles: *Voodoo* (1930), *By Night at Dinsmore* (1935), *While Murder Waits* (1937), *Graveyard Watch* (1938), and *Assurance Double Sure* (1939). Using the name of Peter Loring, Shellabarger wrote *Grief Before Night* (1938) and *Miss Rolling Stone* (1939). The writer has also contributed fiction to magazines, including *McCall's* and *Cosmopolitan*.

Shellabarger returned to the educational field when, in 1938, he accepted the position of headmaster at the Columbus School for Girls in Ohio's capital. The educator now declares that he has found in secondary school work "a much keener appeal and a much more varied scope than university work provided." His students approve highly of their headmaster's 1945 novel, *Captain From Castile*, agreeing with the American reading public, which kept the book at the top of best seller lists for weeks after its publication in January.

A picaresque novel of the early sixteenth century Spanish conquest of Mexico, the book was chosen by the Literary Guild for distribution among its three hundred and fifty thousand members. Before publication, *Captain From Castile* was purchased for a motion picture in November 1944 by Twentieth Century-Fox for one hundred thousand dollars. The

SHELLABARGER, SAMUEL—*Continued*
film will be produced in 1946, with Tyrone
Power in the role of the romantic hero. It is
estimated that cinema production of this swashbuckling saga will cost three million dollars.
Most critics agreed that the romantic tale is a
"natural" for films—its action and glamour are
"tailored" for a grandiose Technicolor setting.
The book was in its twelfth printing in March,
and English, Norwegian, Swedish, Danish,
Dutch, French, Spanish, German, and Portuguese rights to the book have been sold.

Shellabarger has written, in the Dumas tradition, a colorful melodrama of epic proportions.
The story concerns the handsome young Spanish nobleman Pedro de Vargas, whom Sterling
North [43] described as "the Three Musketeers
and Rudolph Valentino rolled into one sixteenth
century package." He joins Cortes in his Mexican adventures and is thus involved in the
violent and varied fortunes of the Spaniards in
the New World. It is a story brimming with
romance and action, set in the period of the
Spanish Inquisition. From the heart of Spain to
the Mexico of the Aztecs, Shellabarger's bright
tapestry of the dramatic Renaissance is considered to be skillfully woven. (The author's
historical accuracy was commented upon by the
critics.)

Time Magazine considered *Captain From
Castile* "among the best popular fictional accounts of the conquistadors that has appeared,"
a book that is not slowed down by "philosophical pauses, such as clogged the pell-mell
action of [Hervey Allen's] *Anthony Adverse*."
The work was also commended by other critics,
including Orville Prescott, who wrote: "As
an example of sheer yarn spinning, of keeping
a brew of exciting action constantly at the
boiling point, *Captain From Castile* is excellent." Harrison Smith of the *Saturday Review
of Literature* stated: "His narrative style is
lively and simple, his characters, although they
are necessarily stereotyped, are not period costumes with sawdust insides, but something resembling flesh and blood." On the other hand,
Prescott declared, "The characterization
throughout is rudimentary and superficial, which
are faults of its kind." William Du Bois [40]
agreed with him that the characters are "a bit
on the wooden side." However, most reviewers
liked the vivid pageantry of this period romance. To hold the reader spellbound and
convinced, said Robert Root, faculty dean of
Princeton, "called not only for the art of the
story-teller, but also for the reconstructive
imagination of the historical scholar. . . .But
the antiquarian learning never obtrudes itself
on the reader. . . .The scholar and the story-
teller are perfectly fused." The book is "a fine
literary achievement," declared Root.

A fluent linguist, Shellabarger speaks and
reads French, German, Swedish, Italian, Dutch,
and Spanish; he is also a Greek and Latin
scholar. The collection of the classics of all
these languages has been his lifetime hobby.
Discussing the job of a writer, Shellabarger
once said: "I don't feel a writer should just
write, he should be out in the world." The
author has also expressed his belief that the
historical novelist "could often do better work
from contemporary chronicles than through seeing a place at the present time." For this rea-

son Shellabarger wishes he had not lived so
long in Italy, since he is now working on a
novel dealing with Ferrara and Rome in the
year 1500.

The professor-turned-novelist is a cheerful
white-haired, ruddy-faced man. Fencing, riding, and tennis are his favorite sports. He
is a member of Phi Beta Kappa, the Tower
Club at Princeton, and Columbus' Crichton and
Review clubs. The world traveler has especially enjoyed hunting and camping in the
Canadian Rockies, visiting ranching friends in
Arizona and the borders of Mexico, and climbing in the Alps and Norway. Shellabarger is
interested in the historical and social backgrounds of the great European capitals, and his
favorite cities are Stockholm, Munich, Paris,
and Rome. Significantly, the author of a book
laid in the Spanish scene says, "One of my
favorite ranges of mountains is the Pyrenees,
with their gateways into the distinctively different Spanish world."

References

N Y Post p13 F 21 '45
N Y Times p13 Ja 5 '45 por
Leaders in Education (1941)
Who's Who in America, 1944-45

SHREVE, R(ICHMOND) H(AROLD)
(shrēv) June 25, 1877- Architect
Address: b. Shreve, Lamb and Harmon,
Architects, 11 E. 44th St., New York City; h.
50 Euclid Ave., Hastings-on-Hudson, N.Y.

The senior member of the firm of Shreve,
Lamb and Harmon, the architects who designed New York's Empire State Building, is
R. H. Shreve. Long a well known figure in
the architectural world, Shreve concentrates
on the operational and administrative problems
of building, his associates assuming responsibility for the design.

Richmond Harold Shreve was born in Cornwallis, Canada, on June 25, 1877, and went to
the United States with his parents, Richmond
and Mary C. P. (Hocken) Shreve, when he
was eight years old. The family made their
home in Albany, New York, where the youth
attended Albany High School and then went
to work to earn the money for his college tuition. The job he obtained was in the office of
the New York State architect in Albany, for
whom he was hired as an office boy; before
he entered Cornell University he had worked
himself up to the position of junior draftsman.

After receiving his degree of Bachelor of
Architecture in 1902, Shreve was able to satisfy his desire to do graduate work in structural design and special engineering problems
by taking a post on the faculty of the College
of Architecture at Cornell. While teaching
and studying at the university he became associated with the firm of Carrere and Hastings, prominent New York architects, who at
that time had a contract for a million-dollar
building project on the campus. Shreve was
given the job of superintendent and inspector
of construction, and when the buildings were
completed in 1906 he accepted the offer of a
position in the firm's New York office. (He
was naturalized that year.) In 1920 the firm
became Carrere, Hastings, Shreve and Lamb.

Four years later the two junior partners, Shreve and William Frederick Lamb, branched out on their own, and in 1929 they were joined by Arthur Loomis Harmon, becoming the present organization of Shreve, Lamb and Harmon.

In its field, Shreve, Lamb, and Harmon are noted for their ability to function as a well-integrated team. When commissioned to do a building two or all three of the executives meet the client in a conference. Shreve is always present at these conferences, in which the needs and wishes of the client are discussed; the responsibility for the actual design is taken by either Lamb or Harmon. When the design is ready for approval Shreve criticizes it from the client's point of view, emphasizing utility and practicability rather than the esthetic qualities of the building. In the actual construction Shreve is particularly concerned with planning operations, in which his special talent is recognized among his colleagues. His main task in the office is now business administration, but he still cherishes a bronze medal he won for an original design, and he likes to remember that one of his life drawings hung for many years on the wall of an instructor's office at Cornell.

The firm of Shreve, Lamb and Harmon, Architects, has designed several New York City skyscrapers, the most famous of which is the 102-storied Empire State Building. (Since 1931, when the tallest building in the world was completed, six million people have visited the observation tower, more than four hundred thousand each year.) For its work, the firm has been awarded the Gold Medal of the Architectural League of New York and the Gold Medal of the Fifth Avenue Association, both given in 1931. Among the firm's other designs in New York are 500 Fifth Avenue, an office building of fifty-eight stories, the forty-storied Lefcourt Building, and the block-sized General Motors Building, which is used for offices and showrooms.

The firm which Shreve heads has not confined its work to New York City, however, having designed buildings such as the R. J. Reynolds Tobacco Company plant in Winston-Salem, North Carolina, and the Acacia Mutual Life Insurance Company in Washington, D.C. Nor has it limited its commissions to offices—buildings for Hunter College in New York City being only a few of its many designs for educational institutions. The firm was responsible for several buildings at Connecticut College for Women, Williams College, Wesleyan University, and for the buildings which house the School of Engineering at Shreve's alma mater, Cornell University.

During the Second World War the firm was commissioned by the Government to handle several wartime projects. It designed the Outlying Defense Base in Newfoundland, in collaboration with the engineering company of Fay, Spofford and Thorndyke, and the United States Coast Guard Academy Building at New London, Connecticut, which was designed to serve as a combination hospital, infirmary, and classroom building. It planned additional housing at Mitchel Field, the Army Air Force base on Long Island, and designed the Naval Training Station at Sampson, New

R. H. SHREVE

York, where thirty thousand trainees and staff members were accommodated at one time.

Shreve's firm has been the recipient of many awards in addition to the medals for the Empire State Building. For 1930 it was awarded the Fifth Avenue Association's Gold Medal by a jury of architects for the L. P. Hollander Company Building, and two years later it received the Medal of Honor of the New York Chapter of the American Institute of Architects for "distinguished work of high professional standing." In November 1937, at the Paris Exposition, the Grand Prix in Architecture was given to Shreve, Lamb and Harmon. The company was awarded the Gold Medal of the Fifth Avenue Association again in 1939 for the Lily Daché building in New York, on which it collaborated with Georges Letelie of Paris. The design was judged the best one made for a Fifth Avenue building in the years 1932 through 1938.

Each year, upon the recommendation of the faculty of Cornell University's School of Architecture, an outstanding graduate of the school is given an apprenticeship with Shreve, Lamb and Harmon, which assures the winner of a year of varied experience. At the end of the year the graduate is offered a permanent position on the staff if his work has been satisfactory.

Although his firm specializes in office and other commercial buildings, Shreve himself has a deep interest in housing problems, and since 1934 has been director of the Slum Clearance Commission of New York City. He was the chief architect of the Williamsburg Housing Project in Brooklyn, which was completed in 1938 after three years of work by a group of associated architects. In 1939 he held a similar position with the Vladeck Houses, a housing project in Manhattan which was also planned by a group of architects. During the years 1938 and 1941 Shreve was the chairman of the Board of design and chief architect of Parkchester, a low-rent residential

SHREVE, R. H.—*Continued*
community built by the Metropolitan Life Insurance Company in the Bronx, New York.

Shreve is an active member of the Real Estate Board of New York, having served on the Board of Governors from 1930 to 1932, from 1935 until 1937, and from 1940 to 1942. He is a member of the New York Building Congress, of which he was elected president in 1927, and he remained in office until 1930, for three consecutive terms. In 1939 he became a member of the Board of Design for the New York World's Fair, for which Shreve, Lamb and Harmon designed the Johns-Manville building. He is a member of the Advisory Board of Architects of Goucher College and of the Advisory Council of Architects of Cornell University. A member of the American Institute of Architects, Shreve has not only served as the New York chapter president, but as president of the national organization for two terms, from 1941 until 1943. He belongs to the Cornell Club, of which he was president from 1924 until 1927, and to the Union League Club in New York. He is an honorary Corresponding Member of the Royal Institute of British Architects.

When interviewed after his election to the presidency of the A.I.A., Shreve gave reporters his opinions of the changes occurring in his profession. He thinks that the opportunity which the architect of the twenties had to earn money through the patronage of the rich will never return, that government, community, and business have replaced the rich art patron as the architect's employer. In the future, Shreve continued, the designer will build for utility and economy rather than for "pride, display, and self-gratification. . . .We shall undoubtedly see outdated, inefficient, uneconomical structures torn down to make way for new and efficient and economical buildings, in tune with the time and meeting our constantly growing needs." Shreve feels that, rather than suppressing originality, this type of architecture will require even more ingenuity and skill than has been required in the past.

The architect was married in 1906 to Ruth Bentley. They have three sons, Richmond Bentley, Robert Wilton, and Thomas Charles, none of whom has turned to architecture as a profession. Shreve spends most of his vacations fishing in the northern part of the United States. He is very methodical, planning even his fishing trips as carefully as he would the operations chart of a building.

References

Arch Rec 90:73, 77-8 Ag '41 por
Who's Who in America, 1944-45

SHU, CH'ING-CH'UN *See* Shaw, Lau, pseud.

SIMMS, RUTH HANNA MCCORMICK
Mar. 27, 1880—Dec. 31, 1944 Daughter of Mark Hanna; Republican national committee-woman, Illinois (1924-28); Representative-at-large (1929-31); in 1930 was nominee for United States Senate seat of late husband, Medill McCormick, publisher of the Chicago *Tribune*; active in political, industrial, and

civic affairs; publisher of two Rockford, Illinois, newspapers.

Obituary

N Y Times p21 Ja 1 '45 por

SIMPSON, WILLIAM H(OOD) May 19, 1888- United States Army officer
Address: b. c/o War Department, Washington, D. C.

Like several other top-ranking United States Army officers, Lieutenant General William H. Simpson, who led the Ninth Army to victory in Europe in the Second World War, comes from a family of Civil War rebels. The son of a Confederate veteran, Edward James Simpson, and of the former Elizabeth Amelia Hood, William Hood Simpson was born May 19, 1888, in the town of Weatherford, Texas. "As soon as he could walk," it is said, "he was toddling around in parts of his father's old Tennessee Cavalry uniform." Young Bill attended Weatherford schools and reportedly starred on the high school football team. At fifteen he entered the Hughey and Turner Training School, and at seventeen he traveled from Aledo, Texas, to West Point, New York, where he had won appointment as a Military Academy cadet. Robert H. Shoemaker writes that Simpson had a hard time keeping up with the work because his scholastic background was inadequate; at one time he "conveniently became sick and spent his time in the hospital studying" for examinations. The Texan played football at the Academy until a knee injury put him out of the game. At his graduation in June 1909 he was the youngest man in his class, and the lowest in grades. Since then, however, Shoemaker adds, he has been an honor student at each of the Army Schools in which he enrolled.

Commissioned a second lieutenant, Simpson was sent to Fort Lincoln, North Dakota, to join the Sixth Infantry Regiment. At the end of that year his regiment left for the Philippines, where he served until July 1912, at which time he was assigned to the Presidio of San Francisco. Two years later "Texas Bill" Simpson was back in Texas, on border patrol duty at El Paso. After duty at the Panama Pacific International Exposition at San Francisco from February to December 1915, the Lieutenant returned to Texas and rejoined his regiment for the more serious business of the punitive expedition into Mexico, which General Pershing led against the bandits of Pancho Villa in 1916.

Back in Texas with a promotion to first lieutenant, Simpson was chosen by General George Bell, Jr., as his aide, and accompanied the General on a tour of observation with the British and French armies from February to December 1917. Afterward the twenty-nine-year-old captain (promoted in May) was made assistant chief of staff of the Thirty-third Division, which embarked for France in May 1918. Arriving in Europe, Simpson was sent to the AEF's Army General Staff College; later he rejoined his unit, on which duty he won the Distinguished Service Medal for his staff services, and the Silver Star for his personal gallantry. The French Government honored him also with the Croix de Guerre and the Legion of Honor. Six days before the Armistice, Major Simpson was given a second temporary promotion, to lieutenant colonel. At this time he was division chief of staff, which meant that he was responsible for all the commanding general's routine work and for the operation of the four staff sections—personnel administration, intelligence, operations and training, and supply. As chief of staff, in short, it was Simpson's duty to know everything about everything pertaining to the fifteen thousand men of the division, and to the enemy forces as well.

Returning to the United States in May 1919 Colonel Simpson became chief of staff for the Sixth Division at Camp Grant, Illinois. On June 30, 1920, he reverted to his permanent rank of captain, and the following day was promoted to major. At the beginning of 1921 he was assigned to duty in the Office of the Chief of Infantry. That December the thirty-three-year-old major was married to Jean Ruth (Webber) Krakauer, a London-born widow who lived in El Paso with her two children: Syble Kight (Mrs. Robert H. Stevenson) and Ralph Krakauer. "When we were first married," Ruth Simpson says of her husband, "he had a difficult time speaking in public. So we set up a private speech class in our home in Washington." Later Simpson taught the first War Department classes in public speaking. Until 1923, it is said, Simpson was one of the Army's best polo players. But in that year, when he was captain of the Fort Benning team, his polo days were ended when he fractured his hip on the field.

After two years in Washington, he was sent to the Infantry School at Fort Benning, Georgia, and then to the Command and General Staff School at Fort Leavenworth, Kansas. Completing the course at the latter on June 19, 1925, he was described officially as a "distinguished graduate." Then the Texan was given command of the Third Battalion of the Twelfth Infantry Regiment, first at Fort Meade and later at Fort Washington, Maryland. Reportedly, the future general distinguished himself in maneuvers; and in August 1927 he was enrolled for the highest United States military training, at the Army War College. While there the Major headed a committee on decorations. When the present General of the Army George C. Marshall '40 learned that Simpson's idea was to "take a barrel of decorations and hand them out right after a battle," he agreed heartily. A liberal system of awards, much joked about by the less liberal British Army, has prevailed ever since Marshall became Chief of Staff.

Graduated in 1928, Simpson became a member of the War Department General Staff in Washington, where he served until 1932. Next he taught military science and tactics at Pomona College, California, returning to the Army War College as an instructor in 1936. (Advanced to lieutenant colonel in October 1934, he was made a colonel in September 1938.) He remained at the War College until 1940. In August of that year he was given command of the Ninth Infantry Regiment, headquarters at Fort Sam Houston, Texas. On October 1, 1940, Colonel Simpson, who is said to have acquired an expert knowledge of tanks and field artillery, was promoted to brigadier general

U. S. Army Signal Corps
LT. GEN. WILLIAM H. SIMPSON

(temporary) and named assistant division commander of the Second Division, at the same station. Seven months later he was assigned to command the replacement center at Camp Wolters, Texas, and in September 1941 he was advanced to major general (temporary). On October 14, 1941, he became commanding general of the Thirty-fifth Infantry Division at Camp Robinson, Arkansas, and a few days after the United States entered the Second World War took that division to California. In May 1942 he was transferred to Fort Jackson, South Carolina, and assigned as commanding general of the Thirtieth Infantry, the Old Hickory Division.

When the Twelfth Army Corps (a corps is two or more divisions strong) was activated at Fort Jackson, South Carolina, in September 1942, Simpson was designated as commanding general. In October 1943, with the rank of lieutenant general (temporary), he was appointed commanding general of the Fourth Army at San José, California. This army, until recently part of the Western Defense Command, had been separated from it, and it was Simpson's task to shape it into a combat unit. As leader of one of the few full United States armies—at least two corps—he reorganized the armored divisions and increased the number of infantrymen in them "so they can play a greater part in work with tanks." "With victory assured," he said in April 1944, "earlier victory is the issue." The General called for "more spiritual preparation as well as mental and physical preparation for the ordeal of battle," and quoted with approval British General Sir Harold Alexander's '42 dictum that the Allied soldiers should be indoctrinated, not with hatred, but with "the willingness to give their lives for a way of life they know to be superior."

In May 1944 Simpson arrived in England in command of the United States Eighth Army. General Dwight D. Eisenhower '42 changed its designation to the Ninth Army two days later, to avoid confusion with the famous British

SIMPSON, WILLIAM H.—*Continued*

Eighth Army; and thereafter all United States forces in the European theater were given odd numbers. Like other armies, the Ninth includes representatives of other Allied nations, members of the Royal (British) Armored Corps having served in it with particular distinction. The original plans were to keep it in England until October—meanwhile shifting its component units around so as to confuse the enemy Intelligence; but things were speeded up after the success of the Normandy breakthrough, and on September 13, 1944, SHAEF announced that the United States Ninth Army had gone into action on the western front in France. It was the fourth American army there, the others being the First, under Lieutenant General Courtney H. Hodges '43, the Third, and the Seventh, commanded by Simpson's old friends Lieutenant General George S. Patton '43 and Major General Alexander M. Patch '43, respectively. (Mark Clark's '42 Fifth was still fighting in Italy.) Also fighting the Germans on French soil were the British Second Army under Sir Miles C. Dempsey '44 and the Canadian First under Lieutenant General H. D. G. Crerar '44. The Ninth's location was not announced, nor was it made clear whether that army came under Lieutenant General Omar N. Bradley's '43 Twelfth Army Group, Field Marshal Sir Bernard L. Montgomery's '42 Twenty-first Army Group, or some other, as yet unknown. (Actually, the Ninth was under Bradley.) For this reason newspaper writers referred to it as "the mystery army."

Something of a mystery general too, Simpson was "known to the Nazis only through his reputation as a genius at military organization," the United Press reported, "and as the onetime ace trouble shooter for the late Lieutenant General Lesley J. McNair '42, architect of American ground forces . . . a firm advocate of thoroughgoing infantry tactics." His army "took over the job of cleaning up Brittany" on the fifteenth of September, accepted the surrender of some twenty thousand fully equipped German troops on the sixteenth, and besieged the port of Brest, which fell on the twentieth.

After this successful debut Simpson and his army dropped out of the news swiftly and completely; apparently the German Intelligence was as much in the dark as the American public as to its whereabouts. To achieve this secrecy the Ninth "leap-frogged almost eight hundred miles across the paths of other armies," through Luxembourg, France, Belgium, and Holland for two months, until it entered Germany. In October it swung into line between the British Second and American First Armies. Meanwhile, Simpson "ordered up a minimum of forty complete plans" for the forthcoming operations, the drive against the steel and concrete Westwall which began November 16, just north of Aachen, otherwise Aix-la-Chapelle. Simpson was constantly with his troops in the field, personally inspecting every freezing, muddy, snowed-on sector of his command and visiting nearly every unit by plane or jeep.

Ninth Army progress was slow and full of "desolation, difficulty, danger, and discomfort." The Germans, fighting in defense of their homeland, were strongly entrenched and had to be blasted from house after house. They employed several V-weapons ("V" for vengeance) against Simpson's men, including flying bombs, robot tanks, and rockets. Dictating the painful character of the advance was the weather, a combination of snow with almost unceasing rain which turned the flat open Aachen region into one huge quagmire. Air coordination was sharply reduced; tanks and other heavy tracked vehicles were useless in the thick mud through which the doughboys waded, sometimes up to their ankles, sometimes to their knees, sometimes to their hips. This battle of the Cologne plain, fought by the First and Ninth armies, was described by the German radio as "the most terrible and most ferocious in the history of all wars." Wrote the New York *Times*: "The whole front, four hundred and fifty miles from Switzerland to the Netherlands, was ablaze, but on the approaches to the industrial Ruhr and Saar [valleys] the fighting was of unprecedented heat. Enormous pressure against utmost resistance was generating white-hot war of attrition, eating into the strength of both sides."

Grimly the Ninth pushed on through thickly-sown mine fields. Gains were counted in yards rather than in miles, and the Germans were reported to have 30 to 40 per cent of their forces, including most of their best troops, holding the Ninth's 15 per cent of the entire Allied western front. On February 23, 1945, the First and Ninth armies surged across the flooded Roer River, the last natural barrier before the Rhine, and crossed the Cologne plain with such speed as to reach the Rhine sixty hours later. On March 24 they crossed the Rhine and completed the encirclement of the Ruhr. So many thousands of prisoners surrendered that they constituted a serious inconvenience. Members of the Volkssturm (People's Army) were usually sent home and told to behave themselves. More of a problem were the many thousands of displaced persons—liberated slave laborers and concentration camp victims—clogging the roads; Simpson received constant appeals for help from his combat units in caring for these usually mistreated and needy Allied nationals as well as people who had been persecuted by the Germans. Little preparation had been made for them. The General had to designate increasingly large combat units for the purpose. After the surrender, his Sixth Corps set four infantry divisions to the task of collecting and caring for the displaced persons, with the aid of UNRRA teams.

Simpson's men were apparently in a position to take Berlin, but Supreme Headquarters halted them on the Elbe. After the surrender photographers did not fail to catch the "superb spectacle" of General Simpson's dignified and immaculate figure being tossed in the air three times, as a mark of honor, by a group of Red Army entertainers whose performance at a victory banquet he had praised. Another honor accorded the American general was his investiture by King George '42 as a Knight Commander of the Order of the British Empire.

June 24 found Simpson one of a group of twelve generals who flew back from the ETO to the United States. Less than a month later the fifty-eight-year-old general arrived in Chungking. With the commander of American forces in China, General Albert C. Wedemeyer '45, he made a five-thousand-mile tour of

Chinese provinces by plane and jeep in ten days. In October of that year, two months after the Japanese surrender ended the Second World War, "Texas Bill" Simpson assumed command of the Second Army at Memphis, while his wartime Ninth Army was being disbanded.

The Doughboy General, as Simpson is sometimes called, is lean and hard—some say cadaverous—sharp-featured, soft-spoken, and completely bald. A close student of military tactics, he is reportedly one of the best raconteurs in the Army, and likes to relax after duty by taking a long walk or watching a movie at his headquarters. He seldom raises his voice even when angry; Hanson Baldwin [42] calls him "the sort of fellow who you feel instinctively would make a good friend." Others sum him up as "a Texas cowboy who got into the Army and never got out." He is a Mason, but not a very active one. An excellent horseman, he is fond also of golf, and up to 1943, Shoemaker writes, he used to take a twenty-five-mile hike under full pack every Saturday. "I doubt if there's a military history or biography he hasn't read," says his wife. The six-foot-one-inch soldier is noted for his smartness of dress. Gault MacGowan [45], interviewing him on the Cologne plain, at a time when the General had not had more than four hours of nightly rest since the opening of an offensive, gave this description: "Smooth-shaven, spotlessly clean, with his high shoes brilliantly polished and his chest dazzling with resplendent rows of ribbons, he might just have stepped off the West Point parade grounds." Another correspondent, the dramatic critic Howard Barnes, remarked, "Simpson is no actor, but he has the dynamic power of a great man in his field who relies on underacting to make his point."

References

N Y Herald Tribune p5 S 14 '44 por; VII p9 Mr 25 '45 por
N Y Sun p15 N 16 '44 por; p18 N 27 '44
N Y Times p1 S 14 '44 por; p4 N 17 '44
N Y Times Mag p10-11+ O 22 '44 por
PM p19 N '44 por
Who's Who in America, 1944-45

SLIM, SIR WILLIAM JOSEPH Aug. 6, 1891- British Army officer

Address: b. c/o War Office, London

The British Fourteenth Army, after three extremely hard years of large-scale guerrilla fighting, captured the Burmese port of Rangoon on May 3, 1945, thus bringing to a close the most forgotten of all "forgotten wars," the Burma campaign of the Second World War. At the head of this army, composed of British, Indian, and West African troops, was Lieutenant General Sir William Joseph Slim, who led them through one thousand miles of Japanese-infested mountain and jungle, from Imphal to Rangoon. After the surrender of Japan the General was appointed commander of Allied land forces in Southeast Asia and at the end of the year commandant of the newly reopened Imperial Defence College in London.

British Official Photo.

LT. GEN. SIR WILLIAM JOSEPH SLIM

Born on August 6, 1891, William Joseph Slim is a veteran of two wars. He received his schooling at King Edward's Grammar School in Birmingham, and by his twenty-third year had tried his hand at clerking, teaching, and as a foreman of a testing gang in an engineering plant, but when the First World War began he found that he was best suited to be a soldier. Commissioned on August 22, 1914, in the Royal Warwickshire Regiment, he first served as a junior territorial N.C.O. He was soon sent to Mesopotamia; later he was shifted to "bloody" Gallipoli, where he suffered his first wound. At this point the young officer's military career might have ended. He was discharged from an English hospital as permanently unfit for service, but, by what he calls "undivulged means," he got back into the Army and fought in France and Belgium. Then, returning to Mesopotamia, he took part in the capture of Bagdad, was again wounded, and was awarded the Military Cross.

Between wars Bill Slim served with the famous Sixth Ghurka Rifles. He was attached to the General Staff of the Indian Army from 1917 to 1920, and again from 1929 to 1933. He was also graduated from and later instructed at the Staff College, and he completed a course at the Imperial Defence College. In 1919 he was promoted to captain, and eleven years later to brevet major. Before the Second World War began, Slim, in June 1939, was appointed commandant of the Senior Officers' School at Belgaum, in the province of Bombay.

In August 1940 General Slim led the Tenth Indian Infantry Brigade of the Fifth Indian Division into the Anglo-Egyptian Sudan where his men aided in the recapture of Gallabat on the Abyssinian border. By the following January he was fighting in Eritrea on the Red Sea. While on a reconnaissance in the vicinity his party was attacked from the air, and Slim was severely wounded. This injury prevented him from taking further part in the campaign that secured the Red Sea as a channel of communication for the Allies. However, he was returned to duty in March of the same year, and took up a staff post in Iraq. Shortly afterward

SLIM, SIR WILLIAM JOSEPH—*Cont.*

he assumed command of the Tenth Indian Division, marching these troops across Iraq into Syria, where they assisted in the Allied campaign which in June of that year successfully ended the resistance fomented by the Vichy Government, thereby preventing the acquisition of airports by the Germans. Slim next took part in the Anglo-Russian operations in Iran, assaulting the powerful enemy positions at Kermanshah, then driving north to Aveh for the first juncture of British Imperial troops with their new Russian allies. One of the results of these operations was to make possible the southern supply route to Russia. For his part in the campaign, General Slim was awarded the Distinguished Service Order.

By this time (December 1941) Japan had entered the war and was threatening the British forces in Burma. Slim was transferred to this theater in March 1942 and given command of the newly formed First Burma Corps, under the command of Field Marshal Sir Harold L. Alexander.[42] The British, being greatly outnumbered by the Japanese, were forced to withdraw from Burma to the Indian frontier. By June, however, British forces in this area had been strengthened, and Slim took command of the Fifteenth Indian Corps in India. In December a limited operation was undertaken by this corps in the Arakan district of Burma as a diversionary move to offset the Japanese thrust toward the American transport base at Kunming, China. In recognition of his services in this campaign, Slim was made a Commander of the British Empire.

In August 1943 Admiral Lord Louis Mountbatten[42] took the over-all command in the southeast Asia sector, and Allied forces soon reached great strength. The newly formed Fourteenth British Army, composed of the Fifteenth Army Corps in Arakan, and the Fourth Corps in Assam, was put under the command of General Slim in October of that year. Despite 237,000 cases of illness in the first six months of 1944, the Fourteenth was maintained at a strength of more than a quarter of a million men. Its divisions were formed from men of the United Kingdom, East and West Africa, India, and Burma.

No large-scale operation was started, however, because the Allied supplies and landing craft were channeled into the European invasion. When spring came the Japanese struck, moving toward the vital Ledo Road. By June Slim's men had flung them back, by August they had cleared the Nipponese from India— a victory for which their general was made a Knight Commander of the Bath. Slim's forces went on the offensive, racing against the monsoons which turn the country into a quagmire. After two months of attack and counterattacks, in weather stifling by day and bitter cold by night, important Mandalay was captured in March, 1945. Rangoon fell in early May. All supplies used in the year-long offensive were dropped by parachute, totaling some six hundred thousand tons. Burma had been secured for the Allies by Slim's flood warfare, but not conquered: "one of the dirtiest clean-up jobs of the Pacific war remained to be accomplished," and "the ceaseless, drenching monsoon rains, the knee-deep muck, and the menace of tropical disease contributed to the particularly

ugly and difficult character of the fighting." This continued until the end of the war with Japan, despite the annihilation of the Japanese Imperial Twenty-Eighth Army which was announced at the end of July.

After the surrender of Japan General Slim was appointed commander of Allied land forces in Southeast Asia. Describing the situation in Indo-China between released Frenchmen and native Annamites as "tense," Sir William said, "We have no political aims whatever except for dealing with the danger arising." With the outbreak of hostilities in Java in September Slim was sent to Batavia to help the Dutch quell the Indonesian nationalist movement in Java. In December the British Government decided to reopen the Imperial Defence College in London, and General Sir William Slim was called back to England to head it as commandant. That month he was decorated with the American Legion of Merit.

A sturdy, strong-jawed man who looks more like an English farmer than a general, Slim is shy of publicity. Reading is his favorite diversion, and he has written articles under a pen name. During the war Lady Slim worked as an assistant in hospitals in Shillong in Assam; their son in 1945 was studying at Dehra Dun Military College in India, and their daughter was attending school.

Reference

N Y Sun p6 Mr 18 '44

SLOAN, SAMUEL 1905(?)—Mar. 30, 1945 American book publisher and editor; vice-president and treasurer of Duell, Sloan and Pearce; formed present company with C. Halliwell Duell and Charles A. Pearce in 1932.

Obituary

N Y Times p19 Mr 31 '45

SMITH, SIR BEN 1879- British Government official; labor leader

Address: b. Food Ministry, London; Transport House, Smith Square, London

The important post of the Minister of Food in the Attlee[40] Labor Government of the United Kingdom was given in July 1945 to one of the most colorful Members of Parliament, Sir Ben Smith. A former sailor, merchant seaman, cab driver, dockyard worker, and union organizer, "Big Ben" Smith had been knighted in June for his work during the wartime coalition Government of Winston Churchill.[42]

Born in 1879 to Mr. and Mrs. Richard Smith, the future M.P. was named simply Ben. Like many boys of working-class families, he left home at an early age, in his case eleven, to enter the Royal Navy. While serving as ship's boy on the training ship H.M.S. *Warspite* for fifteen shillings (less than four dollars) a month, the tall young boy was for a year middle-weight champion of the Royal Navy lower-deck. Soon afterward he turned to the Merchant Navy, becoming cook on a topsail schooner, in the days when, as he recalls, "We had to float our biscuits on top of the hot tea so as to frighten off the weevils."

At twenty, Smith was married to Mildred Ellen Edison of Peckham and left the sea. (The Smiths now have two sons.) "Necessity rather than choice" forced him to become a cabby. In 1906 Smith gave up his horse for an automobile, which was one of the first taxis in London. "In those days," says George Darling of the BBC, "the taxi-men were not only exploited by hard hire-purchase [installment buying] terms and low fares, but they made the exploitation worse by cutting each other's livelihood. Altogether the conditions were such an offense to Ben Smith's practical common sense that he started organizing his fellow cabbies to cooperate for standard fares and agreements and the promise of a decent living." He became an official of the new union, and in 1920, when it was merged with several others to form the huge Transport and General Workers' Union, he continued as an organizer.

To quote Darling again, "Ben Smith worked among the dock workers on London's riverside and the men who run London's ubiquitous bus services, for dockers and road transport operators are the backbone of the union. He did more organizing than negotiating. His job was to make the union strong and make the members aware of its strength. He suited London's transport workers.

"He looked like a union organizer, tough, bluff, and strong, but the men he worked with learned also to respect his mind. He has a surprising grasp of industrial technique and organization and like most of Britain's trade union officials he is keenly interested in local government. The dockers elected him to the Bermondsey Borough Council. Bermondsey is a poor district on the south side of the Thames, stretching from London Bridge down below the network of the Surrey Commercial Docks. Waterside workers, mechanics, railwaymen, workers in London's markets, warehouses, and back street factories live there, and Ben Smith has served them well. He is still an alderman of the borough."

In 1923 Alderman Smith was elected to Parliament from the Rotherhithe Division of Bermondsey, and continued to serve there for eight years. In 1925 he was chosen Labor Party whip, thus making him responsible for party discipline and attendance; the party whip is also responsible, usually, for obtaining pairs for members who cannot be present when a vote is taken. In 1924 he led a procession of hired vehicles through Hyde Park, which had been reserved for private carriages for three hundred years. Later he became general manager of his union, which has been described as probably the largest in the world. In the Ramsay MacDonald Labor Government of 1929-31, the unionist was Treasurer of the Royal Household—a post in which he, like two fellow Laborites, wore a resplendent uniform, complete with ceremonial sword and wand of office. King George V allowed Smith and the others to keep the wands for souvenirs when the Government resigned, and also presented them with photographs of himself and Queen Mary. During a vacation, incidentally, the Smiths toured Egypt and Palestine, in company with another Labor M.P., traveling both ways by tanker.

SIR BEN SMITH

Smith lost his seat in the Conservative landslide of 1931, after Prime Minister MacDonald left his party. While out of office Smith contested the Clay Cross, Derbyshire, by-election, but without success. In 1935 he won back his seat for Rotherhithe, defeating Nora Runge. Back in Parliament, he entered vigorously into debate on his subjects of shipping, railways, and road haulage. (Smith is vice-chairman for roads of the Safety First Association, an executive member of the Roads Improvement Association, a member of the London Traffic Advisory Committee, and an associate of the Institute of Transport.) In 1937 the Laborite was in the news as he led an unsuccessful deputation of protest to the Home Secretary, Sir Samuel Hoare '40, asking him not to permit the British Fascists to march through South London. Later that year the M.P. charged that he had been enrolled as a constable of West Hartlepool, without his consent, in an attempt to curb his trade union activities, a charge denied by the mayor and town council.

When the Second World War broke out Smith, then sixty, took an active part in recruiting drives. After Lord Beaverbrook '40 became Minister of Aircraft Production in the all-party War Cabinet headed by Winston Churchill '42, he "looked round for the toughest trade union leader he could find to . . . smooth out all the appalling labor difficulties," and chose Ben Smith. In July 1940, when Smith entered on his unpaid duties as honorary labor adviser to the Aircraft Ministry, the Germans had smashed through Belgium, the Netherlands, and France, had driven the Allied armies into the Dunkerque retreat, and only the ill-equipped RAF and the English Channel stood between Britain and an enemy astride the Continent. When Beaverbrook undertook to speed up the production of Spitfires and Hurricanes, "the speed and urgency of the job created a welter of labor problems. Green labor, mostly conscripted women and girls, had to be trained, billeted, settled into jobs, put on a ten-hour day, seven-day week schedule. New wage rates

SMITH, SIR BEN—*Continued*

had to be fixed somehow, and canteens provided in the factories; shop committees had to be set up, and a thousand other jobs done." In the Cabinet shuffle of March 1942 Smith's two years of work on these problems were recognized, and he was elevated to the junior ministry as Parliamentary secretary to the Ministry of Aircraft Production. "Since then," says Darling, "he has repeatedly surprised everybody with his clear understanding of the complex technical organization of the aircraft industry. He became a big-business executive, helping to direct at the top an industry which now [1944] produces thirty-five hundred aircraft a month." Smith also did some work in Civil Defense, and in 1941 he obtained from the Ministry of Health redress for the captured British seamen who had been freed from the prison ship *Altmark* by Captain Philip Vian [44], only to find that they were asked to make up the insurance payments they had missed or lose their pension rights.

In 1943 Smith was made a member of the Privy Council, and in November of that year was appointed Minister Resident for Supply in Washington, D.C., to succeed Colonel John Llewellin. After he had been in the United States for eleven weeks, working hard at four jobs (chairman of the British Supply Council in North America and of the Principal Commonwealth Supply Committee, British member of the UNRRA Committee on Supply, and senior alternate member on the UNRRA council), a London *Daily Express* correspondent asked Americans what they thought of Smith. Said the columnist Marquis Childs [43]: "He speaks straight from the shoulder, more than any other man you have sent here. He is tremendously shrewd. He has worked very quietly, but effectively." Smith had impressed a group of editors of industrial publications with his knowledge of technical trade matters; and an unidentified official was quoted as saying, "Ben Smith is the finest shipment of reverse Lend-Lease ever sent here from the Old Country." After Smith resigned in May 1945 in order to campaign for re-election, and was knighted (K.B.E.) in June for his services, he was mentioned as the most likely choice to succeed Lord Halifax [40] as Ambassador to the United States, should the Attlee Government be unable to resist pressure to remove the Conservative appointee. Sir Ben was, however, chosen for the difficult and important post of Food Minister, again succeeding Colonel Llewellin.

"In his first press conference," to quote an American reporter, "Sir Ben was faced with the task of telling the British that, although the war is over, the sacrifices are not." Postwar rationing in Britain became even more severe after V-J Day. There was less meat, fats, and cheese; and the supply of dried eggs, which had largely replaced shell eggs in the British menu, was cut after the termination of Lend-Lease. Serious as Britain's economic position was, it was better than most of the rest of Europe, and her leaders felt the need of dipping into their own depleted rations to help maintain life on the Continent. One of the Food Minister's first announcements was that Britain would lend France fifty thousand tons of refined sugar and ten thousand tons of margarine, to be repaid later in raw sugar and ground nuts.

Sir Ben Smith's most obvious quality is said to be his toughness. "He stands well over six feet and in spite of his years his back is straight and broad, like a Guardsman's. He looks aggressive, although he is really a mild-mannered good fellow, one of the most popular members of the House of Commons, ever ready to entertain his friends with a never-ending flow of good stories and personal anecdotes." He is described as looking much younger than his years, and as being one of the best boxers and jujitsu artists among men of his age. Smith is a member of the City Livery and Royal Automobile clubs, and is a Liveryman of the City of London: he belongs to the Bakers' and Carmens' companies, two of the medieval guilds, which in these days carry on charitable work and elect certain officials, including the Lord Mayor. The Food Minister is given to wearing somber clothes and a wide-brimmed black hat, and has what the British call "a distinctive taste in stickpins."

References

N Y Herald Tribune II p3 D 19 '43 por
N Y Times p14 N 12 '43
International Who's Who, 1942
Who's Who, 1945

SMITH, C(YRUS) R(OWLETT) Sept. 9, 1899- Air line executive

Address: b. American Airlines, Inc., 100 E. 42d St., New York City; h. 322 E. 57th St., New York City

"Aviation is the architect of a changing world," says C. R. Smith, the chairman of the board of American Airlines. The significance of this belief can be easily appreciated when considered in the light of the history of the airplane. Forty years after the appearance of the Wright brothers' first plane, the Office of War Information issued a report stating that in the postwar world an airplane trip from Washington to Paris will take only eleven hours, to Moscow sixteen, and to Tokyo twenty-two. Smith, a former deputy commander of the Air Transport Command, has been a leader in this growing industry since the twenties.

Cyrus Rowlett Smith (he now uses only the initials of his first and middle names) was born on the "wrong side of the tracks" in the city of Minerva, Texas, on September 9, 1899, the son of Roy Edgerton and Marion (Burck) Smith. During Cyrus Smith's early childhood the Smiths wandered over a wide area of Texas and Louisiana, stopping wherever the head of the family found work. When Cyrus was nine (according to a *Saturday Evening Post* article) his father, an "erratic religionist," left the family. There were seven children, and Cyrus was the eldest son. By cooperative effort and Mrs. Smith's expert management, the family was able to support itself: Mrs. Smith herself alternately taught school and kept boarders; and each child, as he or she became old enough, was sent to work, the earnings going into a common fund which in the end put all seven children through college.

When Cyrus himself was only nine he got a job as office boy to a cattleman in Amarillo, and from that time until he was sixteen he held various poorly paying jobs. His first important position came in 1915, when the First National Bank of Whitney hired him as a bookkeeper and spare-time teller at thirty dollars a month. The following year the enterprising seventeen-year-old moved on to greener fields and more money as bookkeeper in a cotton mill in Hillsboro. In three years time Smith was earning two hundred dollars a month, but in 1919 he left the mill in order to work in the franchise-tax department in the office of the Secretary of State in Austin. By 1920 he felt that he had had enough business experience, and now needed a formal education. At the age of twenty-one he therefore entered the University of Texas, in the School of Business Administration and Law. Besides attending school and working part time as an examiner with the Federal Reserve Bank, the industrious student conducted a one-man advertising agency, belonged to two fraternities, Alpha Kappa Psi and Kappa Sigma, and served as president of his junior class and the public speaking club.

When Smith was graduated in 1924 he took a regular position as a junior clerk in an accounting firm in Dallas for one hundred and fifty dollars a month, half of what he had earned through his advertising agency. In a short time he became known in his firm as an expert in business management. In that capacity Smith met A. P. Barrett, the Texas utilities magnate, who offered him the post of assistant treasurer in the Texas-Louisiana Power Company. Smith worked for the power company for three years. At the end of that time, in 1928, when the power company purchased Texas Air Transport, an air-mail line from Dallas and Fort Worth to Brownsville and Houston, Barrett persuaded Smith to assume the management of the line. In a short time it was consolidated with other lines, forming Southern Air Transport, which carried some passengers besides the mail. Smith, as treasurer of this enterprise and later as vice-president, was closely associated with the development of passenger service in Texas. During this period, too, Smith earned his transport pilot's license.

In 1929 Aviation Corporation bought a large share of the stock of Southern Air Transport, which developed into a nationwide airway. Smith as vice-president aided in the development of the southern transcontinental route which linked Atlanta and California. In 1930 American Airways, predecessor of the American Airlines, was created by Aviation Corporation as a means of coordinating several operating units into one, and Smith remained as vice-president of the new company, in charge of the southern division. This sprawling network of badly articulated air routes was losing money, and in 1934 when the Post Office Department canceled its mail contracts, reorganization of the entire company became necessary. In February 1934, therefore, a new company named American Airlines was created, and in October of the same year C. R. Smith became its president. Recalling those days, when at thirty-five he was called upon to devise some way to save the failing company, Smith has said: "One of the first things that we did as soon as possible after 1934 was to go back to system operation and control, as against divisional operation and control," which

Harris & Ewing

C. R. SMITH

change eliminated criss-crossing and duplication in routes.

Immediately after the reorganization a five-year plan was initiated: Equipment was brought up to date and standardized to reduce costs and confusion in maintenance; Condor sleepers and day coaches were put into use, along with Vultee transports, making air travel swifter and more comfortable. When Smith became president of the lines he continued this policy of re-equipping and standardization, making American Airlines by 1945 the largest user of Douglas air equipment in America and the leading domestic air line in the country.

In April 1942 Smith resigned as president and director of American Airlines to enter the Army with a commission as a colonel in the Air Corps Ferrying Command. (Two years before, in July 1940, he had become adviser to Ralph Budd, president of the Burlington Railroad, who in the months before Pearl Harbor was in charge of coordinating all forms of transportation for the national defense.) The Ferrying Command had been established in May 1941, before the United States entered the war, to fly Lend-Lease planes bound for Britain to take-off points in America and Canada. After December 7 it became necessary to rush supplies as well as planes to American and Allied war theaters. In June 1942 the Command was therefore reconstituted and redesignated the Air Transport Command, with two divisions, Ferrying and Air Transportation. Major General Harold L. George '42 became commanding general and Smith chief of staff.

The ATC as reconstituted was charged with providing "all air transport for the War Department of cargo, personnel, and mail to, from, and between theaters of operations and within the continental United States." Through its ferrying division it was to ferry planes from factory to using locations both in the States and overseas. In addition, it was to provide air transport services for other Government agencies and for governments of the United

SMITH, C. R.—*Continued*

Nations. One of its outstanding operations proved to be the supplying of vital material to the China theater after the Burma Road was closed in 1942.

As chief of staff and later as deputy commander, the former air-line official mapped many of ATC's new routes, and located and developed many of its airdromes. By the end of 1943 the Command was operating over air routes in the United States totaling 35,000 miles and overseas air routes totaling more than 95,000 miles. According to the *Official Guide to the Army Air Forces*, "a number of civil carriers entered into contracts with the Government under which they operated scheduled transport services with planes allotted to them by the AAF." American Airlines was the largest of these commercial companies to operate transatlantic ATC aircraft.

Major General Smith (he was made a brigadier general in October 1942, a major general in September 1944) retired from the service after V-E Day in May 1945. While in the Army he had received the Distinguished Service Medal, with a citation from General Henry H. Arnold '42 calling him "one of the world's greatest contributors to the development of military and global air transportation"; the Legion of Merit for his services as chief of a special mission to French West Africa charged with eliminating custom duties; and the Air Medal for rescue operations in Burma. He shared, too, in a Distinguished Unit Citation for ATC transportation of supplies to China.

On July 12, 1945, American Airlines announced the election of Smith to the newly created position of chairman of the board, and the election of Ralph S. Damon, formerly of Curtiss Wright Airplane and Motor Company, as president. Plans for the expansion of American Airlines have proceeded rapidly. On July 5 the Civil Aeronautics Board, with President Truman's '45 endorsement, approved a policy of allowing domestic airlines to enter the overseas field. The next month the Civil Aeronautics Board granted seven-year transatlantic operation certificates to Pan American, Transcontinental and Western Airlines, and American Airlines. (Previously Pan American had held exclusive rights to such operations.) American Airlines with the approval of CAB is going ahead with plans for a transatlantic route with stops in Newfoundland, Labrador, Greenland, Iceland, Glasgow, Foynes, London, Berlin, Copenhagen, Amsterdam, Stavanger, Oslo, Helsinki, Leningrad, Stockholm, Moscow and Warsaw. The company which now employs ten thousand people, four thousand of whom Smith is said to know, has plans for increasing its staff to fifty thousand.

The comment has been made that if there were an award for the model executive, tall, square-jawed C. R. Smith would win it: He is easy-going and slow-spoken, friendly in his relations with his employees, a good listener who weighs carefully the smallest detail before coming to a decision. Divorced from the former Elizabeth Lewis Manget of Dallas, Texas, he lives in a twelve-room house on a large estate at Sands Point, Long Island. The interior has been described as resembling "the Great American Southwest wing of

a natural history museum." There are paintings of the West on the walls, wood carvings of cowboys and horses, mounted animal heads, Navaho rugs, and a phonograph with records of doleful cowboy songs. In this setting, and in his office, he thinks, lives, and talks aviation. "We are all proud of the eighty-six planes we have," he said of American Airlines in 1945," and we will be prouder of the one hundred planes we will soon have. But any employee who can't see the day when we will have one thousand planes had better look for a job somewhere else!"

References

N Y Sun p15 Je 11 '40
Sat Eve Post 213:9+ F 1 '41
Who's Who in America, 1944-45
Who's Who in Aviation, 1942-43

SMITH, LADY ELEANOR (FURNEAUX) (fûr'nō) 1902—Oct. 20, 1945 British novelist; considered an authority on the Russian ballet, circuses, and gypsy life and traditions; among her books are *Red Wagon* (1930), *Ballerina* (1932), *Tzigane* (1935), *Portrait of a Lady* (1936), *Life's a Circus* (autobiography, 1939), *The Man in Gray* (1941).

Obituary

N Y Times p46 O 21 '45 por

SMITH, E(LLISON) DURANT Aug. 1, 1864—Nov. 17, 1944 Dean of the United States Senate, he served from 1909 to defeat in 1944; although a Democrat (South Carolina), he was a bitter critic of the New Deal; known as "Cotton Ed," he favored legislation for the cotton farmer; also spoke out for "white supremacy," maintenance of poll tax, and States' rights, and opposed anti-lynching laws.

Obituary

N Y Times p13 N 18 '44 por

SMITH, HOLLAND M(CTYEIRE) (mäktēr') Apr. 20, 1882- United States Marine Corps officer

Address: b. c/o United States Marine Corps, Washington, D.C.; h. 24 Virginia Ave., Montgomery, Ala.

Makin, Tarawa, Saipan, Iwo Jima—historic battle stops on the road to Japan in the Second World War—were American victories made possible to a great extent by the work of Lieutenant General Holland M. Smith. As second in rank to the Commandant of the Marine Corps, General A. A. Vandegrift '43, General Smith was commander of the Fleet Marine Force in the Pacific, where he commanded marine forces in action from the Gilbert Islands through Iwo Jima. General Smith is known as the "father of modern amphibious warfare," having undertaken to drill marines in ship-to-shore operations long before the United States entered the war. Shortly before the surrender of Japan he was made commanding general of the Replacement Training Command at San Diego, California.

This "Pacific Cyclone" is a Southerner, born in Seale, Russell County, Alabama, on April 20, 1882, and named Holland McTyeire Smith.

His mother was Corrie E. (McTyeire) Smith, and his father was John V. Smith, a Montgomery lawyer. Young Smith followed his father's profession: after graduating from Alabama Polytechnic Institute in 1901 with a Bachelor of Science degree, he went to the University of Alabama for legal training (LL.B. 1903). He was admitted to the Alabama bar in 1903, but after two years of clerking in a Montgomery law office, the twenty-three-year-old Smith was finished with his law career. He went to Washington, D.C., to ask his Congressman for help in obtaining an Army commission. There were no Army vacancies at the time, but there was an opportunity in the Marine Corps, whereupon young Smith asked: "What are the marines?" He has spent his life since then finding out.

On March 29, 1905, Smith was commissioned a second lieutenant in the Marine Corps. He attended the School of Application at Annapolis, after which he was sent to the Philippines. It was while Smith was training at Annapolis that he had met Ada B. Wilkinson of Phoenixville, Pennsylvania, at a dance. He was married to her when he returned from the Philippines in 1909, despite the "anti-Yankee doubts of the Alabama Smiths." The couple's roving existence has led them to such scattered points as Bremerton, Manila, Shanghai, Puerta Plata, Newport, Quantico, and New Orleans. Once within a two-year period the Smiths moved fourteen times. Smith's nickname is "Howlin' Mad," and neither he nor his close associates recall when and where it originated. But somewhere in the Philippines it emerged, and it has clung to him ever since.

After Smith's return from the Islands he was placed on expeditionary duty in Panama. In 1916 he was sent to Santo Domingo, where he saw service in several engagements. With the outbreak of the First World War, Smith left for France aboard the U.S.S. *Henderson,* June 14, 1917. He was then in command of the Eighth Company, Fifth Regiment of Marines, but as adjutant he later joined the Fourth Brigade of Marines, Second Division. During his two years of service in France, Smith participated in the battles of Château-Thierry and Soissons, the Champagne-Marne defensive, and the Oisne-Aisne and Saint-Mihiel offensives. For his "fine courage and remarkable ability," he was awarded the Croix de Guerre, with Palm. General Smith holds numerous other awards and citations, among them the Mexican Service Medal (1916), Purple Heart (1918), Meritorious Service Citation Certificate (1918), Victoria Medal (1918), Distinguished Service Medal (1943) with two Gold Stars (1944). But this growing accumulation of decorations one never sees except on the most formal occasions.

After his return to the United States, Smith was given successive posts at various Marine Corps stations. He then attended the Naval War College, and after completion of his course served on several plans and training boards. In 1924-25 he was chief of staff of the Brigade of Marines in Haiti, and later was on the staff of the commander of the Pacific Fleet Battle Force. By 1934 Smith was a colonel. The next year he became chief of staff and personnel officer in the Department of the Pacific, a post he held until his assignment as director of the Division of Operations and

LT. GEN. HOLLAND M. SMITH

Training in 1937. He remained in the operations division, where he became a brigadier general in 1938, until 1939.

In 1939, with the United States awakening to the growing war menace, it was seen that the need for procuring adequate equipment for the armed forces was a pressing one. General Holland Smith in April was called to Marine Corps Headquarters to become assistant to his old friend, Major General Thomas Holcomb[42], Commandant of the Corps. Smith recognized too the problem of lack of adequate equipment. In his early amphibious drills he had had to use two old, unsuitable launches. He started experimenting with Andrew J. Higgins[43] on landing boats, working with the shipbuilder on specially designed, fast, shallow-draft craft for landing both men and tanks. According to Josef Israels 2d in the New York *Herald Tribune,* Smith also experimented with a weird amphibious tractor which had been built by Donald Roebling for use in the Florida Everglades. These and other experiments resulted in today's amphibious tank and "the whole breed of landing craft" which carried our men ashore on the Pacific islands. (Rear Admiral Daniel E. Barbey[45] of the Navy is also one of the pioneers in this phase of amphibious warfare.)

Along with new equipment and methods, new blood poured in, and the strength of the Marine Corps increased to approximately five hundred thousand men. In September 1939 Brigadier General Holland Smith was given command of the First Marine Brigade. About a year later he took these troops to Cuba for training as amphibious fighters, but not until he and Holcomb had overcome the objections of Washington officials who were concerned over the lack of housing for the marines near Guantánamo.

After six months of training, during which it was enlarged, the First Brigade came back in May 1941, more than doubled in numbers, as the First Division, USMC, eight thousand strong. Their commander, "ruddier than ever,

SMITH, HOLLAND M.—*Continued*

had the two stars of a major general on his shoulder straps." He also had, in *Time*'s words, "a story of training to tell that will be required reading for other officers, if General Smith ever calms it down to writing." The pioneer work of Smith and his marines in Guantánamo is a story of hard labor and even harder training. When the First Brigade arrived at this Cuban outpost they were faced with the job of clearing swamps and building living quarters before they could start any training. Smith worked his men seven days a week, twelve hours a day. They cleared five hundred acres—twenty minutes to the acre—and constructed the necessary buildings at record speed. When ready for the special training which had brought them there, they were then put through their paces by the General. Day and night they practiced using small boats to get on and off transports, did landing party exercises, and seized beachheads, using special combat techniques. So successful were Smith's methods of training that he was afterward asked to teach the Army the fundamentals of amphibious warfare. With Vice-Admiral R. Kelly Turner[44] of the Navy he shares the credit for shaping the tactics of the forces that stormed Guadalcanal, North Africa, Sicily, and the Aleutians.

During the early stages of the war, while the General was training his men for combat, he had become eager to see active service himself. In October 1942 he joined Headquarters Company of the Amphibious Corps, Pacific Fleet, which later became known as the Fifth Amphibious Corps. In July 1944 he was appointed to his post as frontline commander of the Fleet Marine Force in the Pacific. That year he was also advanced to lieutenant general. In his post with the Central Pacific combat corps, Holland Smith had a hand in strategic and tactical planning and the supervision of the final training of the island invasion troops. (He was also commander in 1943 of the Amphibious Corps, Aleutian Islands.)

The "Old Man of the Atolls" has won fame on the battle-scarred beaches of the Pacific. Smith was in command of the landings on Makin and Tarawa in the Gilberts. The marines landed on Tarawa in November 1943 and seventy-six hours later that atoll fortress was taken. Smith, addressing the American families at home, aghast at the losses in battle, revealed that the marines on Tarawa had killed four Japanese for each marine lost; that Tarawa was taken only because of their "willingness to die." He admitted that mistakes were made in the first phase of the attack, but added that valuable lessons were learned in that battle which were applied in later operations. In the opinion of many high-ranking officers, the campaign was the toughest in the history of the battle-seasoned Marine Corps up to that time. The impatient, explosive General declared: "It took Europe nineteen years to learn how to fight Napoleon. . . .It took the marines just three days to learn how to storm an atoll fortress and dig the Japs out. . . .We've got the toughest and smartest fighting men in the world. But as long as the war lasts some of them somewhere will be getting killed. We have got to acknowledge that or else we might as well stay home."

Led by their pugnacious commander, Smith's leathernecks blazed a trail over the Pacific beaches, writing into American battle history the names of Kwajalein, Saipan, and Iwo Jima. Smith was on the command ship of Vice-Admiral R. Kelly Turner when the landing on Iwo Jima began on February 19, 1945. This eight-square-mile fortress was called by correspondent Robert Sherrod[44] "probably the world's most heavily defended island." The battle for the small lamb chop of rock, the costliest assault in the history of the marines, raged for weeks with unrelenting fury, costing as many American lives as Tarawa and Saipan combined.

And volcanic Iwo, "the nightmare of fire," was taken, after twenty-six days of the bitterest, costliest battle of the Pacific war up to then: Americans were in Japan's "backyard." Commanded by Smith, marines of the Third, Fourth, and Fifth divisions paid a high price for a victory which he called "incomparable in all our history as to completeness." During the fierce fighting Smith himself narrowly escaped a sniper's bullet while viewing the battle. Said one reporter, "Imagine Wallace Beery, clad in a spotted jumper, grasping a carbine, jumping up and down, alternately swearing and beaming over his spectacles, and you have Lieutenant General Holland Smith." "Howlin' Mad" is the traditional leatherneck, "outwardly hard-boiled, inwardly soft-hearted."

Holland Smith is a short, heavy man with a mustache. He wears glasses, and his eyes are described as "mild blue." He is a constant cigar smoker and a light eater; when he finds time for sports he plays tennis and golf. His fraternity is Alpha Tau Omega; his clubs are the Bohemian in San Francisco, Army and Navy in Washington, D.C., and Army and Navy Country Club in Arlington, Virginia.

In discussing the General, said to be of mercurial temper, kind but often profane, one writer declared, "Perennially truculent, Holland Smith would have been busted out years ago if he had not been the man and the marine he is." *This Week* has reported that "those who live closest to Smith describe his concern for the lives of his men as almost spiritual." He is very Marine Corps-conscious, warmly defending his service in the traditional interservice rivalry. On this score he argues with his blond, six-foot-tall son, John Victor (Annapolis 1934), who in 1945 was serving as aide to Admiral William D. Leahy[41]. (Two of the General's favorite conversation topics are his grandchildren, Marion and Holland 2d.) Considered a military liberal, the elder Smith is constantly seeking improved techniques for amphibious warfare. And it is reported that he once sent General Holcomb a list of Marine Corps generals he thought should be retired to give younger officers a chance. The first name on the list was Holland Smith. On October 12, 1945, when he was in charge of the San Diego area, it was announced officially that Smith would request retirement the following spring, when he would be sixty-four years old.

References

N Y Herald Tribune VII p4-5 O 22 '44 por
N Y World-Telegram p30 N 15 '41
Time 37:23 My 5 '41 por; 43:25+ F 21 '44 por
Who's Who in America, 1944-45

SMITH, MARGARET CHASE Dec. 14, 1897- United States Representative from Maine

Address: b. House of Representatives Office Bldg.; h. 2745 29th St., N. W. Washington; Skowhegan, Me.

The first woman member of the United States House of Representatives' Naval Affairs Committee and the first woman to represent Maine is Margaret Chase Smith, who was elected in September 1944 to her fourth term in Congress. (Maine holds its Congressional elections two months earlier than the rest of the country.) Mrs. Smith, a Republican, has a record of progressiveness in labor legislation, and has on occasion bolted her party to follow her convictions.

The daughter of George Emery and Carrie (Murray) Chase, Margaret Chase was born in Skowhegan, Maine, on December 14, 1897. After attending the local grammar school she was graduated from Skowhegan High School in 1916 and obtained a teaching post. She set out to achieve success, it is said, via "a variety of occupations from telephone operator to ghost writer." A business executive for the Maine Telephone and Telegraph Company at twenty-one, Miss Chase then went to work in the executive office of the local country newspaper, the *Independent Reporter.*

After eight years there, she became in 1928 treasurer of the New England Waste Process Company at Skowhegan, and at the same time she became connected with the Daniel E. Cummings Woolen Company. In May 1930 Miss Chase was married to former State senator Clyde H. Smith, president of the Steward Goodwin Company at Bangor, Maine. Smith, then fifty-four, had been the youngest man ever elected to the State legislature, where he backed the old-age pension system, and was in 1930 chairman of the State Highway Commission and a Skowhegan selectman. (In forty-eight assorted candidacies during his lifetime, Smith was never once defeated.)

Mrs. Smith became active in politics, doing "a thousand thankless party tasks," and was elected to the Republican State Committee of Maine, on which she served from 1930 to 1936. She is also past president of the Maine Federation of Business and Professional Women's Clubs. From 1932 to 1936 her husband was a member of the Governor's Council; and in September 1936 he was elected to the Seventy-fifth Congress as Representative from the Second Maine District. Congressman Clyde Smith worked on the House Labor Committee, on which he helped formulate the Wages and Hours Act which Chairman Mary T. Norton '44 successfully steered through the House, while his attractive wife put in fifteen hours a day as his secretary. She took care of all the Congressman's routine office work, personally handled his mail, and did research on the subjects of various bills. The Smiths always kept open house at their home in the Washington suburb of Chevy Chase, Maryland (later in Cleveland Park), and during the summer in their thirty-room Skowhegan residence. Margaret Smith found time also to serve as treasurer of the Congressional Club, composed of the wives of Congressmen and Cabinet members, and to bake the beans which, in the New England tradition,

MARGARET CHASE SMITH

always graced the Smith table on Saturday evening.

In April 1940, in his last illness, Clyde Smith appealed to the Maine voters to preserve their social gains and ensure the continuance of his liberal policies by electing his "partner in public life" to succeed him. At the special election on June 3 the tall, gray-haired widow was chosen to fill the unexpired term; and in September 1940 she was re-elected to the Seventy-seventh Congress by 57,152 votes out of 88,486 —nearly three times her late husband's 1938 plurality. As the representative of an industrial district, the first woman Congressman from Maine requested a seat on the Labor Committee on which her husband had distinguished himself. She was assigned, however, to three lesser committees: Education, Invalid Pensions, and Post Offices and Post Roads. (It is in committee that "the real work of Congress" is done, as the committees determine what bill shall be brought to the floor for a vote, and in what form—and which bills shall be pigeonholed and left to die.) A quiet, conscientious legislator, Margaret Chase Smith generally voted along regular Republican lines, but cast an occasional vote for Administration measures. From the beginning, however, she voted 100 per cent for the Administration's foreign policy. Daughter of a seaboard state, Mrs. Smith has always been interested in maritime affairs, and advocated naval expansion in the neutral days of 1938.

Re-elected to the Seventy-eighth Congress, Mrs. Smith asked in January 1943 if she might fill a vacancy on the Naval Affairs or the Appropriations Committee: "The reason why I'm asking to be on the Naval Committee," she said, "is Maine's long coastline, shipbuilding, and Navy Yard interests." This was done, "in recognition of the services of the Navy's women reserves, the Waves, Spars, and Marines." In this capacity the Maine Representative was given "good" assignments, such as the investigation of destroyer production; she is believed to be the first woman ever to sail on

SMITH, MARGARET CHASE—*Continued*
a United States destroyer in wartime. Mrs.
Smith is the author of the bill raising the maximum Wave rank from lieutenant commander to
captain, entitling Waves to dependents' allowances (except for husbands), and allowing the
assignment of Waves to duty overseas. The
bill was passed by the House without debate
on June 8, 1943, although a similar proposal
by Melvin Maas several weeks earlier had been
defeated. The overseas clause was, however,
stricken out by the Senate Naval Affairs Committee.

Reintroduced a year later, after Admiral
Nimitz '42 had reported a pressing need for 5,000
Waves, 1,535 Marines, and 150 Spars at Pearl
Harbor, it was requested by Secretary Forrestal '42 and high-ranking officers of the Navy.
For reasons not entirely clear, action was postponed until after the Congressional summer
recess: and it was not until September 1944,
when Mrs. Smith withdrew her bill in favor
of Senator David Walsh's "watered-down version," that the Senate finally allowed volunteers
to go overseas, and sent that bill to the House,
where it went through in less than sixty seconds. At this time Mrs. Smith reported that
women's naval services totaled 103,872 members. During this time and up to December
she was conducting an exhaustive inspection of
their installations. In December, before leaving with other committeemen for a tour of advance South Pacific bases, she recommended
that plans be made for the demobilization of the
women; that housing arrangements needed
modification; and that at least a skeleton
organization should be continued after the
war. Upon returning from her 25,000-mile inspection tour, Mrs. Smith submitted recommendations for improvement of morale and living
conditions at the bases. They were adopted and
put into effect by Navy Secretary James Forrestal, who praised her work.

Mrs. Smith and Winifred Stanley '43 of New
York were the first women members of Congress to declare for the Equal Rights Amendment, sponsored by the National Woman's
Party and the National Federation of Business
and Professional Women's Clubs, which has
been introduced at every session since the suffrage amendment. (This proposed amendment,
which states that men and women shall have
equal rights in the United States and all places
subject to its jurisdiction, was defeated because
it could be so construed as to invalidate existing health legislation.)

In Congress Mrs. Smith followed the party line. She voted against the twenty-five-
thousand-dollar (after taxes) limit on salaries;
for the income tax bill which broadened the
tax base to include more people with small incomes; for the Ruml '43 "pay-as-you-go" tax
plan, which "forgave" rich and poor alike a
full year's taxes; for the Carlson-Ruml bill,
and against the Robertson-Forand compromise.
On farm affairs, she opposed incentive payments to farmers; voted against increasing the
appropriation for soil conservation, against any
funds for crop insurance, and against spending
any more on rural electrification. Her vote
was cast for the liquidation of the Home Owners Loan Corporation; against the use of appropriations to subsidize price rollbacks, to
override the veto of the Commodity Credit

Corporation bill which carried that rider, and
in February 1944, to ban such food subsidies
outright. On the record, she voted to abolish
the OWI's domestic branch; to investigate the
Government seizure of Montgomery Ward's
Chicago facilities in May 1944; to create the
Smith Committee, under an Administration
critic, Howard W. Smith '41 of Virginia, which
would investigate any alleged overstepping of
authority by the executive branch; and to continue the Dies Committee to Investigate un-
American Activities. In January 1945, however, when Martin Dies '40 was no longer in
Congress, she was one of the thirty-four Republicans and one hundred and fifty Democrats
who unsuccessfully opposed the establishment
of the committee as a standing body.

On certain points the Republican leadership
was in accord with the Administration: extending Lend-Lease, which they had opposed before
the war; passing the Fulbright '43 resolution
pledging the country to join in a world peace
organization; passing the anti-poll tax bill.
In addition, Mrs. Smith also voted to support
the Administration by opposing the [Howard]
Smith-Connally '41 anti-strike bill (she had
previously helped vote down more stringent
ones), and used her vote, unsuccessfully, against
overriding the President's veto. She also voted
with the Administration to increase the pay of
Federal employees in view of the increased cost
of living, and against the reduction of OPA
funds, although she had had to make representations to the OPA for her lumbermen constituents. In addition, she was one of a half-
dozen Republican Congressmen, led by Representative Charles LaFollette of Indiana, and
Charles Wolverton of New Jersey, who broke
away from the party to vote for the George
demobilization bill.

In March 1944 she joined with the House's
six other women to beat by 64-59 the Taber
proposal to cut in half the appropriation for
community facilities. Representative Smith,
who seldom enters debate, told the House that
on her trips with the Naval Affairs Committee
she had found war workers' children locked in
automobiles because their parents had nowhere
else to leave them, and declared that Congress
had already waited too long in meeting this
emergency. In December 1944 the Maine Representative was one of six Republicans voting
against freezing the Social Security tax at its
present and allegedly inadequate level, a measure carried by 262 votes to 72. Earlier she
voted against the bill to punish absenteeism
from war work. Representative Smith helped
to defeat a roll-call vote on the Worley Federal soldier-vote bill, which would have recorded each Representative's stand. (The bill
itself was later defeated in a teller vote.) In
the subsequent passage of the compromise bill,
the Eastland-Rankin '44 (States' rights) soldier-
vote bill, Mrs. Smith voted "Yea."

Mrs. Smith's record was acceptable to her
constituents, for in September 1944 she was
re-elected to the Seventy-ninth Congress, with
the endorsement of A.F. of L. leaders and the
support of the railway unions. No desk-bound
Congressman, the Maine Representative had
returned from an investigation to issue a report in February 1944, had served in April as
one of thirteen advisers to the United States
Government delegation at the International
Labor Organization in Philadelphia, and had

led the Maine delegation to the Republican National Convention in July. And in December she left for the South Pacific, returning in time for the opening of the Seventy-ninth Congress in January 1945.

After the fall of Germany, Mrs. Smith proposed that wives be permittted to join husbands assigned for an indefinite stay or a period of one year or more in occupied Europe. She said, according to a report in the New York *Herald Tribune,* that her "proposal was prompted by her desire to prevent further disintegration of the American home and the American family life." This is reported to have brought a promise from the War Department that families and fiancées of service men in occupied Europe would be allowed to join them "when conditions permit." In addition to her study of more complicated problems, the Congresswoman is also "mindful of details." Josephine Ripley, in the *Christian Science Monitor,* pointed out that Mrs. Smith "has gone to bat repeatedly for the bell-bottom-trouser boys with urgent pleas for redesigning of their pocketless uniform, and she now has word that action may be taken in this direction as soon as textiles are in normal supply again."

"Hardworking" and "well-liked" are the adjectives applied to Margaret Chase Smith. Delos Lovelace calls her "a sturdy Mainite, tall, assured, and pleasant to look at." Her short gray hair is streaked with white, perhaps the only dramatic touch about the "quiet and unassuming" Representative, and she is described by an NEA correspondent as having a trim figure and "a well-turned ankle." Like most women in public life, she feels that women Congressmen "must be treated like the men treat each other. We women represent all the people in our districts," she points out, "just as the men do." As for the duties of citizenship, Mrs. Smith declared, in a speech at the seventy-fifth anniversary celebration of Wilson College in October, that good citizenship calls for independent thinking and translating thought into action at the polls. She added, according to the New York *Times,* that when we accept the statements and proposals of demogogues "because we are too lazy to think and test their statements and proposals," we can blame no one but ourselves for subsequent events.

References

Collier's 112:22 Ag 28 '43 por
Ind Woman 19:379 D '40 por
N Y Sun p20 Ja 14 '44
Congressional Directory, 1945
Who's Who in America, 1944-45

SNYDER, JOHN W(ESLEY) June 21, 1896-   United States Government official

Address: b. Office of War Mobilization and Reconversion, Washington, D.C.; h. Wardman Park Hotel, Washington, D.C.

By the end of the first quarter-year of President Harry S. Truman's[45] Administration, John W. Snyder, a relatively unknown Missouri banker, had been twice elevated to new office in the Government. Snyder was Truman's first major appointee when in April 1945 Truman gave him the post of Federal Loan Administrator which had remained vacant after Fred M. Vinson[43] had resigned to become Director

JOHN W. SNYDER

of War Mobilization. In July Snyder again succeeded Vinson, becoming chief of the expanded Office of War Mobilization and Reconversion when his predecessor received the Treasury post. Three weeks later the sudden ending of the war in the Pacific plunged the new Director of War Mobilization and Reconversion into the midst of the problem of guiding the nation's economy back to a peacetime basis.

John Wesley Snyder was born on June 21, 1896, in Jonesboro, Arkansas, the son of Jerre Hartwell Snyder, a druggist, and Ellen (Hatcher) Snyder. He received his early schooling in Jonesboro, attending the Jonesboro High School from 1910 to 1914. In 1914 he entered Vanderbilt University (Nashville, Tennessee), but withdrew in 1915 without obtaining a degree. The year and a half between the fall of 1915 and the spring of 1917, when he entered the Army, Snyder spent on business trips with his uncle, Judge E. A. Rolfe, in connection with the latter's farming, timber, and banking interests. During the First World War Snyder served as a captain in the Fifty-seventh Field Artillery Brigade of the Thirty-second ("Red Arrow") Division. Contrary to popular report, he did not serve in the same army unit with Truman, nor did they train together before going overseas. Snyder met Captain Truman by chance in 1918 when both were with the AEF in France. For several summers after the Armistice, however, Snyder and Truman trained together in the Officers' Reserve Corps (Snyder is now a colonel, Field Artillery Reserve) at such Army posts as Fort Riley in Kansas, Fort Sill in Oklahoma, Camp McCoy in Wisconsin, and Fort Ripley in Minnesota.

Between 1919 and 1930 Snyder served in various banks in Arkansas and Missouri, learning his profession. Then in 1930 he became national bank receiver in the Office of the Comptroller of the Currency, Washington, D.C., a position in which he supervised the liquidation of bankrupt financial institutions.

SNYDER, JOHN W.—*Continued*

In 1937 he was appointed manager of the St. Louis Loan Agency of the Reconstruction Finance Corporation. In July 1940, although retaining control of the St. Louis RFC, he was brought to Washington by Jesse Jones [40] to be executive vice-president and director of the new Defense Plant Corporation and assistant to the directors of the Reconstruction Finance Corporation.

As director of the Defense Plant Corporation, a subsidiary of the Reconstruction Finance Corporation, Snyder handled between five and eight billion dollars in expenditures for war plant expansion; and he earned the respect of his colleagues for his ability to get things done despite red tape and occasional sharp differences of opinion with Jesse Jones, then head of the RFC. Whereas Jones believed in cautious, orthodox financing for the war plants, Snyder was convinced of the necessity of speedily augmenting the nation's armament program to the fullest extent. Accordingly, he brought to bear on Jones all the pressure he could muster, including persuasion from the War Department, in order to expedite the task of arming the country.

While DPC head, Snyder was also one of the few men well aware that the allocation of contracts during the emergency would determine the existence or non-existence of monopoly in postwar commerce. His associates in the Defense Plant Corporation say that he fought vigorously and constantly for a program which would leave final disposition of the Government-financed plants under governmental control and would deny to the industries concerned the option of "scrapping the wartime plants so that they could limit production, prices, and employment."

In January 1943 Snyder returned to private banking, resigning from his Washington office on the first to accept the vice-presidency of the First National Bank of St. Louis, Missouri. On February 15 of that year he also resigned from the managership of the St. Louis RFC, which post he had, during the latter part of his tenure, held simultaneously with the DPC directorship. He thus severed, at least for the time being, all official relations with the Government. Early in 1945, however, Snyder's name was suggested to President Franklin D. Roosevelt [42] for the office of Federal Loan Administrator by both Truman and Jones, and, when Truman himself became President, this was one of the first nominations he sent to Congress. Thus on April 30, 1945, Snyder again found himself installed in a Federal post. On the appointment, Jesse Jones, former incumbent of the office, commented, "The President could not have made a better appointment for Federal Loan Administrator than John W. Snyder. Mr. Snyder's long experience with the RFC, both in the field and in Washington, has made him thoroughly familiar with the activities of the loan administration." (From April 1939, when it was created, to February 1942, the Federal Loan Agency had been administered independently of the Department of Commerce. At that time, Jesse H. Jones being already both Federal Loan Administrator and Secretary of Commerce, Executive Order 9071 had transferred its functions to the Commerce Department. When early in 1945, however, Henry A. Wallace's [40] name was suggested as Secretary of Commerce, Congress, not wishing to grant Wallace the extensive powers of the combined post, passed the George bill to redivorce the two agencies. Wallace then received the Commerce post; Fred M. Vinson the Loan post. In April Snyder succeeded Vinson.)

As Federal Loan Administrator Snyder became principal adviser on economic and monetary policies to the Truman Administration. The post, furthermore, placed him directly in charge of a large part of the reconversion program, because the RFC, as the parent corporation, exercises general supervision over the management of its otherwise autonomous subsidiaries, such as the Rubber Reserve Company, the Metal Reserve Company, the Defense Plant Corporation, the Defense Supplies Corporation, and the Disaster Loan Corporation. All together, these agencies, during the past thirteen years, have made loans to the extent of forty-five billion dollars. And on the one hand the Surplus Property Board made the RFC its agent in disposing of the surplus Government-owned war plants in such a way as to promote the Government's full employment program; on the other, business interests looked to the RFC "to pump needed reconversion credits through the banks." Snyder's first act in the post was to request Congress to pass legislation enabling the RFC to absorb its subsidiaries in the interests of economy and efficiency. The simplification of the agencies, merely organizational in nature, involved no changes in policy or personnel, but was directed towards reducing operating costs and was influenced by Snyder's ultimate aim to restore to private industry economic activity temporarily undertaken by the Government.

During his association with the Defense Plant Corporation Snyder had demonstrated that he was essentially a "profit-system man" and a good friend of small business by his retention of control over surplus plant disposal in order to discourage future monopoly. When Henry Wallace as Secretary of Commerce wanted to gain the support of small business early in 1945 by appointing a committee to consider its welfare, he chose from among others on the Commerce Department's Business Advisory Council John W. Snyder. At a banker's seminar at the University of Missouri in 1941, Snyder had explained his views: "The defense program," he said then, "is designed to protect a democratic system, founded upon private initiative and individual liberty. Sacrifices of certain privileges will be only the legitimate means to a vital end . . . defending our ideal of democracy . . . and the system of private initiative which is its very foundation. Bankers can . . . serve as guides in pointing out the way back after difficult days." Hence, he emphasized in a news conference that the RFC was not entering into competition with private banks in making loans but "was supporting the banks themselves to enable them to make loans beyond their normal lending limit and to take risks that they might not otherwise be prepared to take." Direct loans by the RFC, he said then, would be made only when it was determined that local credit was not available after "reasonable efforts" had been made to obtain it. The loan policy of the RFC through the banks, however, he said would be a liberal one, intended to speed the successful conclusion of the war with Japan and the resumption of normal private enterprise.

"With or without banking participation," depending upon the degree of cooperation he received, Snyder indicated that the specific program of the Federal Loan Agency would embrace five main points: "(1) To make loans against terminated contracts and subcontracts for the purpose of making funds available for other war production. (2) To make loans for civilian production, and for reconversion and other purposes. (3) To finance plant and equipment reconversion, to finance new equipment and plant purchases, and to finance surplus property and surplus equipment purchases. (4) To make business loans to returning veterans under its own veterans' loan program, and to perform its present functions as well as others which the Veterans Administration may request under the Servicemen's Readjustment Business Loan Program. (5) To make commitments now for future loans so that industry may proceed with plans for rehabilitation and reconversion." Loans were to be made strictly on a business basis: credit to be extended "to those people who have demonstrated that they deserve it." "It is my opinion," Snyder told the House Small Business Committee, "that together the banks and the RFC can solve the financial problems of small businesses which are capable of and entitled to solution during the reconversion and postwar periods."

In mid-July 1945 Snyder was promoted from the Federal Loan Agency to the Office of War Mobilization and Reconversion. That agency was created by Executive order in 1943 "to develop and establish programs for the maximum utilization of the nation's natural and industrial resources for military and civilian needs, the effective use of civilian manpower, and the maintenance and stabilization of civilian economy . . . [with] power to unify the activities of Federal agencies and departments concerned with production, procurement, distribution, or transportation of military or civilian supplies and materials." (The definition is by Smith and Zurcher in *A Dictionary of American Politics*.) Once in office Snyder had the heads of the various agencies under his control prepare their programs for the transition period. When the Japanese surrender offer came just three weeks later, therefore, he was ready to direct the reconversion plan. His first report to the President, "From War to Peace: a Challenge," issued on August 15, predicted "considerable but temporary unemployment" and set forth full peacetime production and a steadily rising standard of living as objectives which if achieved would tide the nation over the transition period of heavy demand and short supply. Then, with the Presidential announcement of surrender, he began canceling all military contracts above a minimum necessity and abolishing many of the wartime production, distribution, price, and wage controls. By the middle of September even most of the curbs

on the crucial construction industry had been lifted. In fact, he moved so fast that his opponents charged that he was paving the road for runaway inflation. (Snyder has been both praised and criticized for the manner in which he has handled reconversion.) In addition, during the first weeks of peace, he was called upon to solve the redeployment transportation crisis, passed on to him by the Senate's Mead committee, and to arbitrate the dispute between the armed services and the fuel control agencies over manpower to operate the coal mines. At the end of September Snyder spent two weeks in Europe surveying the surplus and lend-lease property situation. In December he drew up the housing program adopted by the President and placed under the administration of Housing Expediter Wilson W. Wyatt.

In guiding the nation back to a peacetime economy Snyder advocated larger unemployment benefits and passage of President Truman's full employment bill. In his first quarterly report he predicted that there might be as many as eight million unemployed by the spring of 1946 and called for a 40 to 50 per cent increase in the supply of goods and services to absorb these expected unemployed. He also advocated repeal of the normal and excess profits taxes, reduction of the excise taxes, and an increase in the 40-cent legal wage floor. While he declared himself in favor of raising wages when such rise would not affect prices, Snyder went on record as a supporter of continued price control for essential items until supply could catch up with demand. "Untimely removal" of such war curbs, he believed, would "delay reconversion" as much as the removal of restrictions on production would hasten it. A lifelong foe of bureaucracy, Snyder expects that his last measures as Director of Reconversion will be the abolition, in accordance with a specific Congressional directive "to plan to simplify, consolidate, or eliminate the emergency war agencies," those numerous war-born bureaus which have of necessity interfered with the functioning of the competitive enterprise system during the last five years.

Snyder, who was often consulted by Truman while the latter was still a Senator, is described by *Business Week* as a realist. His former associates in the Defense Plant Corporation point out that he knows when to fight and when to retreat and that he never opposed Jesse Jones when he knew that defeat was certain. He is known as a hard worker who frequently spends ten to twelve hours at his desk. An avid reader, he tries to find time for four books—two of biography, one of history, one novel—each week. Like many of Truman's friends, he plays a close game of poker. He collects United States coins and airplane pictures, and his favorite sport is baseball. The most common adjective used of Snyder physically is "rotund." He is five feet nine inches in height, weighs 170 pounds, has gray eyes, and dark brown hair which is turning gray and receding at the temples. He uses gold-rimmed spectacles and, unlike most people, wears his watch on his right wrist, where it is always in front of him. He is an Episcopalian and a Democrat. A charter member of Rotary, he is also a member of Alpha Tau Omega and president of the Missouri Athletic

SNYDER, JOHN W.—*Continued*

Club (of which he was vice-president in 1944-45 and has been on the Board of Governors since 1940). In addition, he is a director of the Chase and Coronado hotels in St. Louis. On January 5, 1920, he was married to Evlyn Cook; the Snyders have one daughter, Edith Cook, who in 1945 was a college student.

References

Liberty 22:19+ O 20 '45
Newsweek 25:46 Ap 30 '45
N Y Herald Tribune II p12 S 16 '45
N Y Times VI p13+ S 23 '45
Time 45:19 Ap 30 '45
Who's Who in America, 1944-45
Who's Who in Commerce and Industry (1944)

SOULE, GEORGE (HENRY, JR.) (sōl) June 11, 1887- Editor; economist

Address: b. New Republic, 40 E. 49th St., New York City; h. South Kent, Conn.

"Anyone who reads Mr. Soule puts himself in touch with one of the sanest and most civilized minds now at work on man and his problems," H. D. Lasswell has written of George

Arni

GEORGE SOULE

Soule. A leading liberal economist, Soule has written several books of social theory, his latest being *America's Stake in Britain's Future,* published in October 1945. For more than twenty years the social scientist has been an editor of the *New Republic,* in which his articles on the problems of modern society have appeared since 1914. Soule has been associated with important economic research agencies and has taught at Yale Law School, Columbia, and the University of North Carolina.

A descendant and namesake of a signer of the Mayflower compact, George Henry Soule, Jr., was born in Stamford, Connecticut, to George Henry and Ellen (Smyth) Soule on June 11, 1887. His American heritage includes one ancestor who participated in the Boston Tea Party and several who fought in the American Revolution. According to Soule, his "most prized progenitor was Robert Calef, who wrote a book satirizing Cotton Mather and the Salem witchcraft persecutions—a book banned by the conservatives of the time and sold from under the counter in Cambridge, Massachusetts." After attending Stamford High School, where he was editor of the school paper, young Soule entered Yale University, where he became editor of the *Yale Literary Magazine.* Soule's major studies in college were English and economics. After earning his B.A. in 1908, he joined the New York publishing firm of Frederick A. Stokes, of which he later became advertising manager. While with this company Soule became editor of the first publishers' cooperative bulletin on books, "an attempt to present bona fide news of new books without praise of them." Of this venture Soule says, "My interest in the success of the esthetically meritorious books came into constant collision with exploitation of so-called 'popular' taste, and I began to believe that something better than a commercial civilization was necessary if cultural values were to be well served."

Soule joined the staff of the *New Republic* soon after its founding in 1914. In those early days of the liberal weekly his duties ranged from proofreading and make-up to editing art criticism and writing articles. He became increasingly interested in public affairs, and began combining the economic with the literary in his work. After the First World War began, Soule enlisted in the Coast Artillery and soon became a corporal. In August 1918 he was detailed to study antisubmarine devices at New London, Connecticut, and in his new post achieved the unique military grade of "First Class Listener." In September he was sent to Officers Training School at Fort Monroe, Virginia, and after two months was commissioned a second lieutenant, just as the Armistice was declared.

Discharged from service, the writer rejoined the *New Republic,* becoming its Washington correspondent. Early in 1919 he became a member of the editorial staff of the New York *Evening Post.* Soule also served in that year as an investigator for the Inter-Church World Movement Commission on the steel strike. The war had reinforced his belief in the need for social and economic reform. With Stuart Chase '40 and others, therefore, he founded the Labor Bureau, Inc., in 1920, to carry on technical and professional work for labor and cooperative organizations. He has since been a director of the bureau, winning recognition for his economic research.

For the first three months of 1921 Soule was a statistician for the *Nautical Gazette.* Since 1922 he has been director-at-large of the National Bureau of Economic Research. On January 1, 1924, he became an editor of the *New Republic,* and in his long association with the magazine he has been concerned in his writings with socio-economic topics. In 1927 he was special adviser to the Secretary of the Interior on reclamation and rural development in the South. His articles have appeared in many magazines, including the *Independent Woman,* the *Virginia Quarterly Review, Current History,* the *Dial,* the *Nation,* the *Saturday Evening Post,* and the *American Economic Review.* He has also written pamphlets and various reports and scientific papers, and his articles are included in several essay collections. He has been called "the first person to have introduced case methods into industrial economics."

Following the First World War many of Soule's writings were on the seething labor situation, with attention centered on the unions. In the February 1924 issue of the *Atlantic Monthly* his "Unions and the Public" was a lengthy study with factual, statistical data. During the depression period the economist discussed its causes and cures in the pages of the *New Republic* always urging economic planning to avoid such disaster. With the advent of the New Deal Soule focused his study on its economic program, analyzing the Administration measures instituted. In an article in *Harper's* (June 1938) entitled "Capitalism Without Capital," the economist declared that such measures were "buttressing capitalism and renewing confidence in it." Turning his attention in 1937 to political affairs, Soule in a radio address urged that the Neutrality Act be invoked in the Sino-Japanese war.

After the outbreak of the Second World War, when America was gearing itself for national defense, the economist offered this reminder in March 1941: "Everybody knows, as a result of what happened last time, that war prosperity is fallacious and fickle." A *New Republic* article in March 1943 dealt with Soviet-American relations and the problem of the Prussian military caste. On the first-named subject Soule pointed out that a large segment of America feared and distrusted the Soviet Union because "it is the living representative of a socialist state." On the other topic the writer declared that "those who believe that Europe can have no assurance of peace until the Prussian military caste is finally liquidated are talking sense."

Seeing little danger of communism in a flourishing economy, Soule advocated the closest cooperation between the Soviet Union and the Western powers. In *Foreign Affairs* in April 1944 ("Labor and the Peace"), the economist contended that "Labor knows how to preserve private enterprise far better than does an organization like the National Association of Manufacturers. It continually presses for those modifications which can make private enterprise tolerable to workers who might otherwise wish to abolish it." Previously, in a *New Republic* article, Soule had stated, "If private enterprise were the flexible and efficient system which those who praise it say it is, there would be little trouble." In 1945 he wrote several articles on British and American economic policy, coincidental with his book on the subject. The *Annals of the American Academy of Political and Social Science* contained such a study of Anglo-American economic relations, in which Soule concluded that "basically, the questions about future British trade and exchange policy must be answered in the United States." Again advocating planning for full employment, he declared, "The ultimate alternative to stabilized full employment in the United States is likely to be economic isolation

enforced upon us by other and more progressive nations."

Soule is the author of more than ten books on social theory, which have commanded the respectful attention of critics. *Planned Society* (1932), which discussed the possiblities of a planned system in the United States, received divergent but largely favorable reviews. Typical were the remarks of the *Saturday Review of Literature* critic: "Whether one agrees with Mr. Soule's conclusions or not, both his arguments and his assertions of fact are, almost without exception, sound, accurate, and illuminating." Two years later, in *The Coming American Revolution,* Soule found the United States in the midst of a great social revolution, far from its climax. According to the economist another breakdown of capitalism, such as the depression, is likely to come; if accompanied by certain revolutionary conditions, "at such a time, probably by peaceful and possibly even by constitutional means, the control of production and exchange may easily pass to one of the more moderate movements opposed to the profit system." E. H. Walton, in reviewing this book in *Forum,* stated, "Mr.Soule is one of the ablest and most clearheaded of our more advanced writers on economics, and this, so far, is the best of his books." In the New York *Herald Tribune* Lewis Gannett [41] wrote, "Mr. Soule, if less brilliant than Stuart Chase at his best, less lucid than Walter Lippmann [40], has more courageous realism than either."

In *The Future of Liberty* (1936) the writer presented an historical analysis of liberty in America, concluding with a reasoned advocacy of socialism as true liberty for the greatest number. Soule stated his own credo in this book. "My bias is democratic and liberal," he declared. "I believe in the right of the individual to seek his own fulfillment, in equality of status, in the attempt of man to control his own destiny....I believe in the right to question all creeds and institutions in the light of reason, in a continually recurring need to reject and build anew. I believe in the legitimacy of revolution: not merely the revolution that my forefathers helped to make in the eighteenth century, but any new revolution that may be justified by the interest and reason of the common man." Soule considers his faith rooted in American soil by the Declaration of Independence and the Bill of Rights. While opposed to Soule's theories, Henry Hazlitt in the New York *Times* nevertheless found the author "intelligent, well read, and restrained in tone. He is one of the most persuasive of the planners. But his replies even to the criticisms that he cites seem to be often feeble and evasive."

Combining biography and sociology, Soule's next book, *Sidney Hillman, Labor Statesman* (1939) was called "an exciting and altogether important chronicle, clearly and factually set down." That year also saw the publication of *An Economic Constitution for Democracy,* a compilation of lectures he had delivered at Yale Law School in an analysis of the economic aims and achievements of the New Deal. Soule's next study in social theory, *The Strength of Nations* (1942), urged a "psycho-social approach" to world problems. Critical opinion agreed that it was a significant and provocative work, but Frank Kingdon [44] considered the book "weakened by the fact that it is the brief

SOULE, GEORGE—*Continued*

of an advocate for science rather than an in-
clusive attempt to mobilize all the methods and
motives that operate in men's conduct."

In collaboration with David Efron and Norman Ness, Soule wrote *Latin America in the
Future World* in 1945, after two years of research. Prepared under the supervision of Alvin H. Hansen '45 for the National Planning
Association (of which Soule was a founder),
the book was hailed as a valuable, scholarly
work, and Allan Chase declared that it could
well become "the economic *Uncle Tom's Cabin*
of the Western Hemisphere." After a visit to
England in December 1944 and January 1945 on
an unofficial research mission, Soule wrote
America's Stake in Britain's Future, which was
published in October 1945. This "significant
and useful economic tract" advances the theory
that the economic future depends upon whether
the United States averts unemployment and depression. Soule contends that "the cornerstone
of Anglo-American cooperation, which is regarded as essential, must be the adoption by
both countries of a policy aimed at maintaining
full employment within each. In one sense this
is a matter for domestic decision within each
of the nations, and yet upon it depends the
gravest of international consequences." Norman
Angell remarked that Soule's "useful contribution comes at precisely the right and urgent
moment," while another reviewer pointed out
that "it is dangerous both for the United States
and Britain to place the whole, or the basic,
case for Anglo-American cooperation on economic grounds."

According to *Time* Magazine, Soule is known
in liberal circles for "his antiseptic aloofness,"
while in the opinion of Professor Carl Beck he
"belongs with those Socialists of the Norman
Thomas '44 brand who believe that it is necessary
to socialize the means of production, but differ
from the Communists in believing that the
means of production can be socialized by peaceful democratic procedure." Soule is a Fellow
of the American Association for the Advancement of Science and a member of the American
Economic Association. He is married to Dr.
Flanders Dunbar (his third wife), a member of
the faculty of the College of Physicians and
Surgeons and managing editor of *Psychosomatic
Medicine*. They have a daughter named Marcia
Winslow Dunbar-Soule. In late 1945 the ed-
itor-economist is writing an economic history
of the United States covering the twelve years
from 1917 to 1929.

References

Kunitz, S. J., and Haycraft, H. eds.
Twentieth Century Authors (1942)
Who's Who in America, 1945

SPAAK, PAUL-HENRI (späk pôl än″rē′)
Jan. 25, 1899- Belgian Government official;
lawyer

Address: b. Ministry of Foreign Affairs, Brussels

The Belgian Foreign Minister, Paul-Henri
Spaak, was born in Brussels on January 25,
1899. His father Paul Spaak, a well known
poet, was director of the Brussels opera, the
Théâtre Royale de la Monnaie; his mother, an
active Socialist, was Belgium's first woman Senator. Former Prime Minister Paul Emile Janson
is his uncle. Paul-Henri was only fifteen when
the Germans invaded Belgium in August 1914.
Two years later, at seventeen, he was caught
trying to cross the Dutch border in order to
rejoin the Belgian Army on the Yser, and was
therefore interned until the end of the war.
After the war young Spaak studied law at the
Université Libre de Bruxelles, a liberal-minded
institution which became important when the
Belgian Relief Commission under Herbert
Hoover '43 presented it with their thirty-million-
dollar surplus. The gift was made to the non-
sectarian University of Brussels, rather than to
one of the more prominent universities, because
of political considerations. To this day, it is
reported, there are annual street fights between
students of Brussels and those of the Catholic
University of Louvain.

Spaak received his LL.D. and was called to
the bar at Brussels, where he practiced "brilliantly." He was an outstanding tennis player,
too, and in 1922 was a member of the Belgian
team in international competition. A Socialist
like his mother, an eloquent speaker, and "a
bit of a firebrand," in 1932 the thirty-three-
year-old lawyer was elected Socialist Deputy for
Brussels to the Chamber of Representatives of
the Belgian Parliament, in which he has served
ever since. Two years later he joined the staff
of a revolutionary weekly, *l'Action civique*;
he became co-editor. In March 1935 he accepted the post of Minister of Transportation,
Posts and Telegraph in the Cabinet of progressive Paul van Zeeland—a coalition government, like most Belgian cabinets, which
lasted until June. When Van Zeeland again
became Prime Minister in 1936 Spaak was
chosen Minister of Foreign Affairs. At thirty-
seven he was one of the youngest foreign ministers in Belgian history.

The year 1936 was one of universal rearmament, the year of the founding of the Rome-
Berlin-Tokyo Axis. "As in the hectic prewar
days," to quote the historian F. L. Benns, "the
vicious cycle of national fear and resultant increased armaments was once more present to
undermine the peace of the world." In October Belgium announced her determination to
resume a policy of neutrality, while at the
same time increasing her military establishment
to protect her neutrality. Both Britain and
France promised Belgium their military support in case of unprovoked aggression. Foreign Minister Spaak and King Leopold '44 conducted the negotiations which resulted, in April
1937, in those two powers releasing Belgium
from her obligations under the Locarno Pact
of 1925 and the Anglo-Franco-Belgian Agreement of 1936, while reaffirming their protection
of her neutrality.

In 1937 Spaak was chairman of the Nine-
Power Conference in Brussels on Far Eastern
questions. In November 1937 the Van Zeeland
Government was succeeded by that of Spaak's
uncle, the Liberal Paul Emile Janson, described
as "something of an isolationist in foreign policy and a reformer in internal affairs." When
this Government fell Paul-Henri Spaak became
Premier; his Government lasted from May 1938
to February 1939, when he was succeeded by
the Catholic Conservative Hubert Pierlot '43.

According to Lemuel F. Parton in the New York *Sun*, "as Spaak rose in politics, he moved more to middle ground, admitting the need for organization and discipline and pioneering authoritarian democracy," what Spaak himself termed "adapting democratic institutions to modern realities." Says Parton, "He has been effective against both the Communists and Fascists [Leon Dégrelle's Rexists], although his political enemies insisted that his allegiance was shifting to the latter when he aided in severing Belgium's old alliance with Britain, as he urged a defensive alliance of small neutral countries. This, it would appear, has been elaborately disproved."

On September 3, 1939, the day Britain and France declared war on Germany, Deputy Spaak was again appointed Minister of Foreign Affairs. Eight months later, on May 10, 1940, German troops marched into Belgium, Luxembourg, and the Netherlands, "in defiance of solemn engagements which Germany had renewed a few days before the invasion"; four hours later German Ambassador Bülow-Schwante called on Foreign Minister Spaak to notify him of the fact. At the end of the eighteen-day battle of Belgium, Spaak and the other Cabinet ministers went to France, where they were interned. After France was attacked Spaak and Prime Minister Pierlot escaped across the Spanish border on their second try. In Spain they were again kept in "enforced residence," reportedly on the demand of Nazi agents. After two months Spaak and Pierlot made their escape, and dodged the Gestapo for the five days it took them to reach Lisbon. On October 22, 1940, the two reached London, where Spaak took up the duties of Foreign Minister and Minister of Labor in the Belgian Government-in-Exile.

In June 1942 Paul-Henri Spaak and British Foreign Secretary Anthony Eden '40 signed two treaties, formalizing the agreements by which Belgian forces in Africa were to operate under the Supreme Command of the United Nations, and by which the British were to purchase all the gold, copper, and rubber produced in the Belgian Congo. At this time the Belgians had one squadron in the air and another forming. "They have contributed an extraordinarily large percentage to the fight against Germany," cabled a New York *Times* reporter. "The Germans would love to know the number of Belgians who are fighting against them in proportion to the number of Belgians at home; the Germans would love to know this because they would base their atrocities accordingly." Later, in February 1943, Spaak broadcast to the Belgian people the news that the Government "would continue her economic understanding with Luxembourg and would be ready to join in new and closer ties with the Netherlands and France, as well as endeavoring both in Europe and Africa to tie up her interests with Britain." That November Spaak headed the Belgian delegation to the United Nations Relief and Rehabilitation Administration Conference at Atlantic City, New Jersey, where he presided over the first meeting of the Committee on Organization and Administration.

In September 1944 Belgium was liberated, and later Spaak returned to London to "talk Western power bloc" with Anthony Eden, as *Time*

Belgian Inf. Center

PAUL-HENRI SPAAK

put it. "The benefits of such a West European power bloc were chiefly political, but there were others: (1) Belgium and Holland have planned a trade agreement which is virtually a customs union, specifically designed with collaboration of France and Britain in mind; (2) Belgium hopes to coordinate her military policy with Britain's, pool her air force with the RAF." At this time Spaak was described by *Newsweek* as "the most popular and respected member of the Government." In London, in November 1944, he told newsmen that he had discussed "immediately equipping a Belgian Army so that it can participate in the occupation of Germany next spring." According to reports of the projected "Western bloc" (a term Spaak deprecates), France would maintain a strong army, Britain a powerful fleet and air force, while "Belgium and Holland would waive their former [prewar] attitude of neutrality to provide air bases near Germany's borders. After the Allied forces have been withdrawn entirely from Germany, this arrangement would give the Western alliance a combination able to act quickly in concert by sea, land, and air." Belgium made known, too, her reservation of the right to demand portions of former German territory. Wrote Homer Metz, "A coterie of extreme Belgian nationalists has agitated for a frontier on the Rhine for generations. Yet very few Belgians now believe that this would provide more than a tissue-paper bulwark against the renascent German militarism. If certain reports coming out of Europe are to be credited, Belgium is talking about extending its hegemony eastward chiefly because it wants a diplomatic weapon to counter what it fancies are threats to its independence in the collective security envisaged by the United Nations." This writer cites a dispatch from Brussels to the effect that "the Belgians also are somewhat apprehensive over what they believe may be imperialistic ambitions on the part of France. . . .The Belgians still remember

SPAAK, PAUL-HENRI—*Continued*

Napoleon . . . and the spread of communism in France also worries them."

Like other swiftly liberated countries, Belgium was suffering from a completely disorganized economy after the fighting had moved on past her borders, which led to a four-day uprising at the end of November. André Visson, describing Premier Pierlot as "honest, tired, and weak," stated that the two strongest men of the Cabinet were Spaak, who had the confidence of the trade unions, and Camille Gutt, the Conservative Minister of Finance. Alexander H. Uhl wrote in *PM*: "This crisis has all the characteristics of the late nineteen-thirties—the demonstrations in the streets, the placards denouncing the Government, the gendarmes too handy with their rifles, and the scared little men in Parliament seeing the revolution around the corner. Actually what you have is a Parliament whose mandate expired more than a year ago coming back to power as though the war and the occupation hadn't happened, and a Communist and working-class resistance group beating its head in frustration against what it feels is a stone wall of Belgian reaction."

A *PM* editorial by Blair Bolles headed "The People Can't Win Without Some Help" complained that "Belgian Socialists, represented in the Government chiefly by Foreign Minister Paul-Henri Spaak, have the name but not the inclination of radicals. It is a watered-down party, and Spaak dispenses reactionary dogma out of a book with a Socialist cover." Uhl pointed out, however, in a later article that the Socialists were in an intolerable position, forced to support a Government whose policies they could not approve, because no other was available. As Spaak retorted to Uhl, it was true that the Pierlot Government did not reflect accurately the true feelings of the Belgian people—but neither did the Communists. At the same time, however, Spaak was reportedly working to create a Leftist bloc. And in February 1945 the Pierlot Cabinet finally replaced by that of the Socialist Labor Minister, Achilles van Acker. Spaak, who was on the way to Paris at that moment, was retained as Minister of Foreign Affairs.

It was expected that a stronger Government would "help to clarify the Belgian international position," and later that month announcement was made of four international agreements Spaak had negotiated with General de Gaulle [40] and French Foreign Minister Georges Bidault [45]. Belgium announced also that she would support the French proposals for separation of the Ruhr Valley and the Rhineland from Germany; France had offered to let the Belgian Army take over part of the territory which, it was thought, might be the French zone of postwar occupation of the Rhineland. And in April Spaak headed the nine-man Belgian delegation to the United Nations Conference on International Organization at San Francisco, which included a "former political enemy and now fast friend," the Communist, Albert Marteaux. On his departure Spaak defined the role of the small nations at the conference as "to do nothing to make more difficult an agreement between the great powers and to defend at the same time the essential interests, moral and

material, which they represent." At the conference Spaak was chairman of one of the four commissions, that on general provisions. "M. Spaak is becoming one of the important voices in the conference," reported Anne O'Hare McCormick [40]. "He is eloquent, active, and conciliatory. He was one of the half-dozen who voted with Russia on [refusing to admit] Argentina, and in the Steering Committee he supports the view of one of the Big Four on this issue and another on that. M. Spaak will be worth watching."

Back in Brussels Spaak addressed the Socialist Party Congress in June, pointing out that the formula of a government of national unity was no longer sufficient. To this he added, "We must find a government in which all members are agreed on structural reforms. I believe that at the present time only socialism is possible. Thousands of people are unconsciously tending toward the socialist solution." The Minister also said that Belgium's food situation was better than that of other liberated countries and that his country would enter an extraordinary period of prosperity if it could solve the coal problem.

On the question of what King Leopold's position in his homeland should be following his liberation from German detention, Spaak spoke in no uncertain terms. He told the Belgian Parliament in July that the King, his former friend, leaned in Hitler's [42] direction as early as 1940 when the monarch pronounced the Allied cause lost, differing radically with the Government. "If Belgium survives today it is because we disobeyed the King at that time," said Spaak. "All those who carried out sabotage during the occupation or worked against the Germans likewise disobeyed the king. Leopold can no longer be accepted as a symbol of unity."

Spaak went to London as Belgian delegate to the Preparatory Commission of the United Nations Organization which opened its sessions on November 25, 1945. Contrary to the opinion of many delegations he was elected second vice-chairman—not chairman of the commission. It was understood, however, that the British delegation headed by Philip J. Noel-Baker was pressing behind the scenes to achieve the election of Spaak as chairman of the General Assembly of the United Nations and that this was an important factor in the election of Dr. Zuleta-Angel of Colombia as chairman. Spaak favored a European site for the United Nations' headquarters, his main argument against choosing the United States for its future home being that the equality of the Big Five would thus be upset. Pleading against the concentration of international life in one country, since most of the other big international organizations had American headquarters, the Belgian Foreign Minister continued: "The placing of the headquarters in Europe would be an act of faith and confidence in the old Continent, which has been stricken by war. It would be a way of bringing her back to life and of showing that you believe in her resurrection to become the balance between the Old World and the New."

Photographs show Paul-Henri Spaak to be a chubby, cherub-faced man, partly bald. He is described as "a brilliant lawyer, an excellent organizer and campaigner, and an eloquent orator," who "considers Marxism obsolete." He is still a better-than-average tennis player.

References

N Y Sun p22 O 24 '40
Who's Who of the Allied Governments, 1943

SPEAKS, JOHN CHARLES Feb. 11, 1859 —Nov. 6, 1945 Former Republican Representative from Ohio to United States Congress (1921-31); served in the Ohio National Guard for forty years, advancing from private to brigadier general; saw action in the Spanish-American War, the Mexican border campaign, and the First World War.

Obituary

N Y Times p23 N 7 '45

SPEARMAN, CHARLES E. 1863—Sept. 17, 1945 British psychologist; professor emeritus of psychology at the University of London; discoverer with associates of the psychological ingredient, "G," which has been described as "person's general mind power"; author of *The Abilities of Man* and *The Principles of Cognition* in 1927, *Creative Mind* (1931), and *Psychology Down the Ages* (1937).

Obituary

N Y Times p25 S 19 '45

SPROUL, ROBERT GORDON (sproul) May 22, 1891- University president

Address: h. President's House, University of California, Berkeley, Calif.

"An educational convention on the Pacific Coast without Mr. Sproul would be like a performance of *Hamlet* with the title role omitted. I know of no man whose views in this vital field will present more of interest and challenge to our profession." In 1942 those words, spoken by President William Howard Pillsbury of the American Association of School Administrators, served to introduce to the Association one of the speakers of the day, Robert Gordon Sproul, the president of the University of California, who occupies his high office without benefit of a Doctor's degree (although he has been the recipient of eleven honorary degrees) and who earlier had refused a lucrative bank presidency because he felt that the path of highest service lay in the educational rather than the financial sphere. "To preserve and strengthen higher education in a world of brutal war and revolutionary change," he said in 1943, "may prove, in the long record of time, to have been the most fundamental even of our immediate and urgent necessities."

Robert Gordon Sproul was born in San Francisco on May 22, 1891. His father, Robert Sproul, an auditor of the Southern Pacific Company, was a native of Scotland and a graduate of the University of Glasgow. His mother, Sarah Elizabeth (Moore) Sproul, was a New Englander. Sproul received his B.S. in 1913 from the University of California, where he divided his time between books and athletics. Of his prowess in the latter, the story is told that in 1910, while running his

ROBERT GORDON SPROUL

two miles against Stanford on the California oval in a driving rain, he was handed an umbrella by a sympathetic onlooker and came in far ahead of the field holding the umbrella over his head. His record in scholarship is attested by his membership in Phi Beta Kappa. "He began his career," according to the *National Cyclopædia of American Biography,* "in the efficiency department of the city of Oakland, California." But soon thereafter, in 1914, he became cashier of the University of California, thus beginning his long and unbroken association with that university. On September 6, 1916, in Oakland, Robert Sproul was married to Ida Amelia Wittschen, and the next July their first child, Marion Elizabeth, was born. (The Sprouls have two other children, Robert Gordon and John Allan, born, respectively, in 1920 and 1924.)

In 1918 Sproul was made assistant comptroller of the university, advancing in 1920 to comptroller and secretary to the Regents of the university. In 1925, while still retaining his post as comptroller, he was named vice-president. In this dual position Sproul was in one year (1929-30) responsible for expenditures amounting to $15,253,000, of which $4,725,000 went for land, buildings, and improvements. On July 1, 1930, having been comptroller for ten years and comptroller and vice-president for the last five of them, Sproul succeeded William Wallace Campbell in the presidency of the University of California, becoming at the age of thirty-nine one of the country's youngest university presidents and, like Chicago's Robert Hutchins [40], one of the few without a doctorate. On October 22, 1930, the inauguration ceremonies took place amid general acclaim, although, as *Time* put it, some "scholars winced at this raising of administrative talent over learned distinction."

Sproul assumed the presidency at a time when the University of California was both expanding and consolidating, when one of the aims of its administrators was to make it in

SPROUL, ROBERT GORDON—*Continued*
purpose and scope not merely the University
of California but of the entire Pacific Coast.
The division between the two main centers of
the institution, one for the south and one for
the north of the state, indicated in the official
designations of the University of California
at Los Angeles and the parent University of
California at Berkeley, was rapidly being supplemented by the six other campuses which
complete the eight of the university today.
The need was for one university to serve the
large and populous state of California, in the
words of President Sproul, "on the principle
of home rule—autonomous working parts like
those of the British Empire, commonwealths
working toward a common end." Under
President Sproul, who has been described as
business executive, politician, and lover of
scholarship, the goal was reached, for the
University of California is today considered
one of the foremost universities, and the foremost state university, in America.

President Sproul conceives of the role of a
university in terms of democratic citizenship.
"It is the schools," he told the American Association of School Administrators, "which give
substance to the ideals of democracy; it is the
schools which are most potent in keeping those
ideals alive." The objectives towards which
university training should be directed, he feels,
are: "(1) the laying of a cultural foundation on
which one may build a rich, abundant, useful
life; (2) the development of civic consciousness and of the capacity to meet the responsibilities of a democratic citizen; and (3) the
acquisition of the knowledge and skills essential to vocational and professional success in
specific fields." The products of a university
should be able leaders and intelligent followers,
the mainstays of a democratic republic. In this
work the quality of the teacher is of prime
importance. "No system of teaching and no
curriculum plan is better than the persons who
administer it," he said in 1942. "If I had to
choose between a model curriculum and teaching procedure administered by a mediocre
teacher, and any old kind of curriculum or
teaching procedure with an intelligent, highly
qualified teacher, I should unhesitatingly take
the latter."

Sproul believes that the role of the university is not confined to peacetime, that the universities, in addition to training specialists for
the immediate demands of war, have in times
of conflict a sacred trust and obligation to preserve and defend "those ideals which are essential to the dignity of the human spirit
[which is the center of the arch of democracy]:
that men may read and teach the truth unafraid;
that even the least of them may have an un-
smothered voice in the determination of his
destiny; that youth may be trained as free citizens not as janissaries; that the state may exist
for men, not men for the state; that honor and
decency and justice may prevail." He further
points out that the best hope for international
cooperation lies in following along paths which
the universities have long traveled. "Elsewhere
brotherhood may seem an idle and utopian
dream," he says, "but in the world-wide fraternity of universities, where scholarship is the
password, it has long been an established and

accepted fact. . . .Thought never has been successfully nationalized." He envisions the universities in the postwar world to be the beacons
which will lead to the realization of the ideals
for which the United Nations are fighting.

The university president declares that the
present system of "so-called progressive education" has not accomplished this purpose. It
has failed, he says, to train disciplined citizens
imbued with democratic ideals, has produced instead "helpless victims" of all sorts of "educational dyspepsia and malnutrition", "rampant
adolescents" who are undermining "the long-
time interests of the race." He predicts that
"catastrophe lies ahead" unless the schools return to the "disciplined education of their students . . . as citizens."

Sproul's course as president of the University of California has not always been easy or
clear cut. In 1940, for instance, two thousand
of his students demonstrated in protest against
the draft. That in 1941 they reversed their
stand and voted heavily for conscription and
aid to Britain, at the same time disbanding the
local branch of the allegedly Communist-domi-
nated American Students Union, has been attributed to the influence of President Sproul.
At one time when the University was attacked
as a Communist-influenced institution, Sproul
found it necessary to tour the state to win
friends. In 1942, when Sproul, sympathizing
with three hundred Nisei students (Americans
of Japanese descent) who were to be moved
away from the Pacific Coast, asked thirty-two
inland colleges to take them, he received only
fourteen favorable replies, three of which were
afterward withdrawn by the colleges concerned because of the local opposition the idea
aroused. As late as 1943 Sproul had to contend with the adverse criticism directed
against the Writers' Congress held on his
campus, a gathering attackers labeled "communistic." A personal problem involving the
University also had to be solved. In 1939
Sproul (whose salary in 1939 was stated to be
$13,500 plus expenses) was offered the $50,000-
a-year presidency of the Anglo California National Bank of San Francisco, a position he
refused when a student demonstration "confirmed [his] belief that being the president
of a university is the greatest way to high
service." *Time* (March 29, 1939) was of the
opinion that Sproul, who is said to have political aspirations (he is a Republican), might
have paved the way to governmental office had
he accepted the bank presidency.

Sproul has been awarded numerous honors.
He is the recipient of eleven honorary Doctor
of Laws degrees: from Occidental College, the
universities of Southern California and San
Francisco, Pomona College, University of Oregon, University of Nebraska, Yale University,
University of Maine, University of New Mexico, Harvard University, and Mills College;
and he has received the Doctor of Letters degree from Columbia University. In 1934 his
own institution gave him the Benjamin Ide
Wheeler Distinguished Service Award, and in
1941 he was made an honorary fellow of Stanford University. He has been honored by foreign governments, having been made Chevalier
of the Legion of Honor by France in 1932,
Commander of the Order of the Crown by

Rumania in 1936, and Knight of the Order of Iron Crown by Italy in 1938.

Because of active concern with civic and social welfare and his wide interests, he has officiated on numerous boards and committees. During the decade of his comptrollership (1920-30), he was general manager of the Bear Gulch Water Company and he served on the California State Committee on Agricultural Education (1921-23), the California State Board of Social Welfare (1928-31), the commission on the revision of the California State Constitution, as director of the Berkeley Chamber of Commerce, and as treasurer of the Save-the-Redwoods League (which post he has held since 1921). At present, in other posts not connected with the University of California, he is a member of the Pan American Trade Association, the president of the American Council of the Institute of Pacific Relations, a trustee of the Carnegie Foundation for the Advancement of Teaching, the Rockefeller Foundation, and the General Education Board, a member of the radio advisory committee of America's Town Meeting of the Air, and vice-president and director of the Berkeley Guarantee Building and Loan Association. His war activities included membership on the advisory committee on the utilization of colleges and universities of the War Manpower Commission, membership on the National Child Refugee Committee and the American Red Cross Advisory Committee, the Joint Army-Navy Board for Training Unit Contracts, the Special Committee of the Veterans Administration, the Board of Visitors to the Naval Academy for 1945, the Naval Academy Centennial Commission, the Northern California Books for Russia Committee, and he served as special consultant to the Office of Scientific Research and Development. In 1945 he was made adviser "on the human aspects of reparations" to Edwin W. Pauley [45] of the Allied Reparations Commission. He is a member of the Committee for Economic Development.

Together with seven other college presidents, Sproul in November 1945 wrote to President Truman requesting that "a system of deferments for college students majoring in science on a quota basis, which was abandoned at the height of the war emergency," be reinstated. Declaring that the United States was the only one of the Allied nations that had adopted a policy of drafting all able-bodied men from universities regardless of the profession for which they were training, the appeal stated that we "face an alarming dearth" of doctors, dentists, trained industrialists and scientists.

Sproul has been described as big, blond, and "booming." He is still an athlete and finds much of his recreation in such sports as hiking, mountain climbing, skiing, tennis, swimming, and fishing. He is popular with his students, and with the residents of Berkeley, who frequently hail him as "Bob" Sproul. His good nature and tact, observers say, have helped him over rough spots with the California State Legislature. Especially well read in history and political science, he enlivens his addresses by his gift for humor. While he has written no books, his many speeches and the few articles he has written have appeared in educational periodicals and in the magazine *Vital Speeches of the Day*. He is a member of the Presby-

terian Church. Some of his clubs are the Rotary, Bohemian, Claremount Country, Berkeley Country, and University (of New York).

References

World's Work 59:68-72+ Jl '30 ils por
America's Young Men, 1936-37
National Cyclopædia of American Biography Current vol C p387
Who's Who in America, 1944-45
Who's Who in American Education, 1929-30

STANDISH, BURT L., pseud. *See* Patten, G.

STANFIELD, ROBERT NELSON July 9, 1877—Apr. 13, 1945 Former United States Republican Senator from Oregon (1921-27); headed the Senate Public Lands Committee in 1927; in 1920 he was said to be the largest sheep owner in the world.

Obituary

N Y Times p23 Ap 16 '45 por

STANTON, FRANK Mar. 20, 1908- Radio executive

Address: b. Columbia Broadcasting System, 485 Madison Ave., New York City; h. 25 E. 83d St., New York City

In June 1945 Vice-President Frank Stanton of the Columbia Broadcasting System added to his already numerous responsibilities the position of general manager of CBS, to become one of the youngest and best-known major executives in the radio industry in the United States. Recognized as one of the chief authorities in the field of radio research, he rose to his present position through his technical and psychological work in that field.

Frank Stanton was born in Muskegon, Michigan, on March 20, 1908, the elder of two sons of Frank Cooper and Helen Josephine (Schmidt) Stanton. Later the Stantons moved to Dayton, Ohio, where the father became a teacher in the city schools. A graduate of Steele High School of that city, in 1930 young Stanton received his Bachelor's degree from Ohio Wesleyan University, and two years later his Master's degree from Ohio State University. Having been appointed an instructor in the psychology department of Ohio State in 1932, Stanton then combined teaching with study until he received his Ph.D. in psychology from Ohio State in 1935. As part of the work for that degree, Stanton had, in 1934, written for a relatively obscure scholarly journal a paper establishing by means of experimental data "the novel thesis" that aural impressions are more powerful than visual. This paper attracted the attention of Columbia Broadcasting System executives, and the young college instructor was brought to New York to to serve as a consultant to Columbia on listener research. Later, in 1935, Stanton resigned from the faculty of Ohio State University to become a member of the research staff of the radio network.

In 1937 researcher Stanton turned his attention to program analysis and together with Paul F. Lazarsfeld, now director of the Office

FRANK STANTON

of Radio Research of Columbia University, he developed the Stanton-Lazarsfeld Program Analyzer. In testing program reactions with this invention, listeners at the studios, identified only by numbers, are asked to listen to a particular program while holding push button controls in their hands: to push the right-hand, a green, button for preference; the left-hand, a red, for aversion. In this way likes and dislikes are indicated at intervals as the program progresses. "Each button," explains *Time* Magazine, "is electrically connected with a [separate] pen which draws a continuous line on a moving paper tape pulled under it at a constant speed of approximately one inch every five seconds. When a button is pressed an electric magnet jogs the pen a quarter of an inch [so that the reaction is recorded in the relative color], keeping it off the apathy line until the button is released." At the conclusion of the test program, interviewers, working from scripts with time notations, probe for the cause of likes and dislikes both of the entire program and of single numbers and episodes.

In 1938 Stanton was given the position of director of research. Another promotion in 1942, after he had doubled as advertising director for the preceding year, made him one of the youngest vice-presidents of the corporation. Concurrently, from 1937 to 1940, he had been associate director of the Office of Radio Research at Princeton University, and in 1940 he had been appointed a member of the advisory council of the Office of Radio Research at Columbia University. During his years in radio research, in addition to developing the Program Analyzer, he had been the first to develop and use an automatic recording device which can be placed in home radio sets to record accurately the operation of the sets. This project (1931-35) formed the basis of his doctoral dissertation. To Stanton, notes a reporter, radio research was always only "one of many means to an end, an instrument of administration, not a substitute for creative and imaginative thinking."

As an administrative vice-president at CBS, Stanton was responsible for the operation of the research, reference, press information, and sales departments, and of the department of building construction, maintenance, and operations. He also supervised the functioning of Columbia stations WABC and WABC-FM (New York), WBBM and WBBM-FM (Chicago), WCCO (Minneapolis-St. Paul), WEEI (Boston), KMOX (St. Louis), KNX (Los Angeles), and WTOP (Washington). In 1941 his services were requested by the Office of Facts and Figures in Washington, and in 1942 he was made a consultant to the Office of War Information and to the Secretary of War. His promotion to the vice-presidency and general managership of the Columbia Broadcasting System dated from June 4, 1945. He has also been elected a member of the board of directors of the organization.

Besides discharging his regular duties at CBS, Stanton acts as a member of the board of directors of the American Film Center, Inc., the Audio Electronics Company, the Columbia Recording Corporation, and the National Association of Broadcasters, Broadcast Measurement Bureau, Inc., Cooperative Analysis of Broadcasting, Inc.; of the governing committee of the Bureau of Applied Social Research of Columbia University; and of the editorial board of *Sociometry,* and the *Public Opinion Quarterly.* He also holds memberships in the American Psychological Association, the American Statistical Association, the American Marketing Association, and is a member of the Market Research Council, in addition to being a Fellow of the American Association of Applied Psychologists and a member of six Greek-letter fraternities. He contributed sections to *Students' Guide—the Study of Psychology* (1935), and *Experimental Foundations of General Psychology* (1938). In addition, he was co-editor with Lazarsfeld of *Radio Research, 1941,* and *Radio Research, 1942-1943,* and he produced two films: *Some Psychological Reactions to Emotional Stimuli* (1932) and *Factors in Visual Depth Perception* (1936).

Stanton was married on December 31, 1931, while he was a graduate student of psychology at Ohio State University, to Ruth Stephenson. He is a photography enthusiast. One reporter has described him as "big, blond, burly, looking more like a college fullback than the scholar he is."

References

Bsns W p102 Je 9 '45 por
Who's Who in America, 1944-45
Who's Who in Commerce and Industry (1944)

STARK, LOUIS May 1, 1888- Journalist
Address: b. c/o New York Times Bureau, Washington, D.C.; h. 1921 Kalorama Rd., Washington, D.C.

Veteran journalist Louis Stark has been the New York *Times* labor news specialist in Washington, D.C., since 1923. Winner of the Pulitzer Prize in journalism and letters for the year 1941, Stark has covered national and international labor affairs during a momentous era of the labor movement. His newspaper career, begun after a brief period in the teaching and publishing fields, covers more than a quarter of a century of news reporting for the *Times*.

Louis Stark, a native of Tibold Daracz, Hungary, was born in 1888 on Europe's Labor Day, May 1, a significant day for a man who was to devote himself to the affairs of labor. A son of Adolph and Rose (Kohn) Stark, the child came with his parents to the United States at the age of three. The family lived in New York City, where Louis attended the public schools and was graduated from De Witt Clinton High School in 1907. During the next two years he studied at the New York Training School for Teachers. Upon completion of this course in 1909 he was given a teaching post at Public School No. 75 in Manhattan. After six months of teaching he left this position to enter the publishing business; for the next year and a half he served as a book agent for a New York publisher.

At the end of this time Stark then turned to the newspaper field, joining the advertising department of the New York *Times* in 1911. While writing advertisements for the *Times*, he also began to take assignments for the New York City News Association. Offered a full-time job by the association late in 1913, Stark accepted, thus beginning his reporting career. During the next few years, a period of struggle and growth within the labor movement, he gained his first experience reporting labor news, including the activities of the I.W.W. (Industrial Workers of the World). In the summer of 1917 Stark left the association to work for the New York *Evening Sun*. After a few months, on October 1, 1917, he gave up this position to transfer once more to the staff of the New York *Times,* where he has remained ever since. The reporter covered varied assignments until 1923, when he began to specialize in economic affairs, particularly labor news and views. In recent years Stark's writing has been entirely devoted to this field.

In the course of his career Stark has covered numerous labor conventions in the United States and abroad, as well as strikes and industrial disputes in different parts of the Nation. He went to Basel, Switzerland, in 1931 to report the proceedings of the World Zionist Convention. During that year his series of articles for the *Times* on the Harlan (Kentucky) coal strike caused considerable comment. In 1933 he was sent to Washington to cover certain aspects of the NRA, and since then most of his work has been done in the Capital. Since the outbreak of the Second World War, Stark has covered almost all of the major industrial issues. He reported the railroad workers' strike threat late in 1943; the activities of the United Mine Workers in January 1944, when they sought readmission to the American Federation of Labor; the important decisions of the War Labor Board; and the International Labor Conference held in Philadelphia in April 1944. On more than one occasion Stark has called attention to the inequalities in the national wage program, noting that the increased earnings of industrial workers are in no way balanced by the almost stationary incomes of unorganized white-collar workers who have had no appreciable income rise.

LOUIS STARK

In September 1944 Stark was present at the United Mine Workers' convention in Cincinnati, reporting fiery sessions involving intra-union disputes. In addition, the convention was stirred by violent political differences, heightened by the approaching Presidential election. Stark's dispatches from the scene revealed the attack on President Roosevelt '42 by an opposition group led by John L. Lewis '42. January 1945 found the journalist in London attending the sessions of three international organizations. First, he reported the meetings of the governing body of the International Labor Office, at which Robert J. Watt '45 represented the United States. Then, on February 1, Stark was present at the opening of the International Federation of Trade Unions, a meeting marked by a bitter attack by the French delegates on the organization's inactivity during the war. A week later the reporter was covering the proceedings of the World Trade Union Conference. His dispatches in the *Times* detailed the conference's stormy sessions on the question of admission of delegates from former enemy countries. While in London Stark also took part in a radio program, the *BBC Guest Book*, heard in America over station WQXR.

Stark's widely published articles have appeared in such publications as the *Atlantic Monthly*, the *Yale Review*, *Current History*, and the *Nation's Business*. Throughout the depression period his work bore the mark of the crisis with such titles as "All I Want Is Work", "Old at Forty," and "Sit-Down Strikes." Discussing the question "Are Labor Unions Destructive?" in the *Outlook* in 1930, Stark said that while no labor organization is utopian, the features of many point to increasing harmony between the employer and the wage earner. The labor analyst covered "The Crisis in the Labor Movement" in the *New Republic* (March 25, 1936), discussing the formation of the CIO and its ensuing struggle with the A.F. of L. This same theme was more fully developed in "Your Stake in Labor's War," which appeared in *Nation's*

STARK, LOUIS—*Continued*

Business in February 1938. The *Survey Graphic* of November 1941 carried the journalist's article "Tares in the Wheat," described as an analysis of "subversive activities by Nazi and Communist sympathizers behind the union front," an article confined almost entirely to a discussion of Communist activity within the labor movement.

In January 1942 Stark's essay on "The Press and Labor News" appeared in the *Annals of the American Academy of Political and Social Science*. Treating the subject in historical perspective, the writer traced the attitude of the press toward labor from the earliest days of American trade unions to the present, when labor is front-page news. First, with the passage of the NIRA, and later, with the Wagner '41 act and the NLRB, labor came into the headlines. "Today," wrote Stark, "labor news has come into its own as a feature of American newspaper coverage." Regarding the future of labor news, the *Times* correspondent declared, "So long as freedom of the press in the United States remains one of the Four Freedoms, and democratic institutions prevail, the men and women who work . . . and join unions of their own choosing will make front-page news, because their organizations are participating more and more in vital decisions of national policy."

Stark was one of thirteen *Times* correspondents who collaborated on the book *We Saw It Happen: the News Behind the News That's Fit To Print* (1938). The chapter written by the labor reporter, called "A Case That Rocked the World," dealt with the Sacco-Vanzetti case, one of the most famous issues in the annals of labor. Stark had previously written on this case; his article in *Survey* (October 1927), "The Grounds for Doubt," was based on his coverage of the controversial case in Boston during the three weeks before the execution of Sacco and Vanzetti, political radicals accused of murder and theft. Another article in the July 1943 issue of *Survey Graphic*, entitled "What's the Matter With Labor?" offered an extensive evaluation of the labor scene since the Japanese attack on Pearl Harbor, ending on a note of warning against inflation.

The reporter's writings in the *Times* have included several feature articles in the magazine section of that paper on his special field and related subjects. He has devoted articles to prominent personalities such as William H. Davis '41, "Labor Catalyst," John G. Winant '41, "A New Kind of Envoy to a New Kind of Britain," and "The Militant Mr. Lewis," the U.M.W.'s president. In July 1944 Stark wrote a series dealing with manpower and production conditions in the foundry industry, a detailed study which involved various Government agencies. In July and August of that year the *Times* also carried his series on the role of the CIO in American politics. Calling political action "something new in American political life," Stark discussed Chairman Sidney Hillman's '40 views and activities and presented criticism of PAC from various sources. Another article on labor's campaign role weighed the issues and found PAC emerging as a potent political force. Considering labor's stake in the election, Stark stated,

"While the Roosevelt Administration has not been a 'labor government' in the British sense of that term, it has nevertheless been as close to a labor government as any this Nation has ever had."

Stark stated his views on the cause and cure of industrial unrest in general and, specifically, in relation to the crucial period of reconversion following the cessation of hostilities in an article written for the New York *Times Magazine* on September 30, 1945. "The basic cause of what are usually called 'labor troubles,' but which may also be classed as 'management troubles,' are economic, social and psychological. . . .The economic system under which we live stresses profits, prices and wages. These factors are in disequilibrium. . . .Workmen, when they find their income inadequate to keep their families in comfort and decency, will fight the employer who seeks to reduce wages. . . .Feeling confused and helpless, the workman looks about and finds that 'in union there is strength.' . . .Nevertheless, there are still social troglodytes who see in unions a menace, a snare, and delusion. . . .Our frontier heritage of violence has not disappeared. The picket line disturbance is the firing line on the industrial battlefield. . . .No single employer or industry can cope with these kaleidoscopic transformations. Therefore social legislation is indicated. . . . On the organizational side, both management and labor may improve their relations by establishing methods of cooperation that will eliminate many of the recurring frictions. . . .The Government itself should be responsible for improving its conciliation machinery. Since . . . [the adoption of the National Labor Relations Act] the Government has done little to complete the structure, for the Nation still lacks a rounded-out national labor policy. . . .Legislation, however, would be futile if it embraced compulsory arbitration, since neither labor, industry, nor the public desire such drastic control. . . .It is to be hoped that Congress may enact whatever minimum legislation may be necessary during this early reconversion period and not defer action until the Nation's industries are geared to full production. . . .Finally, when one is tempted to despair over the recurrence of industrial disputes, it may be well to remember that the right to strike, the right of employers and employees to disagree, is in essence a guaranty of the democratic freedoms which we cherish. But the possession of such rights does not mean license to use them irresponsibly . . . to interfere with the common good."

Subject to criticism, like most journalists, Stark has come in for his share of bouquets and brickbats. He has been variously charged with distortion and partiality in the reporting of labor news. However, fellow newspapermen have pointed to his knowledge and integrity. When Stark won the Pulitzer Prize in 1942 colleague James A. Wechsler of *PM* paid tribute to him in the *Guild Reporter*, official organ of the American Newspaper Guild. Wechsler said of Stark: "There are few reporters as universally respected by all sides. . . .All of us who cover labor owe him much, if only because it was largely through his work that news of labor unions became page-one news." Once described by the editors of *Current History* as "fair, honest, and objective," this observer of the labor scene is generally considered a distinguished authority in the industrial field.

The gray-haired journalist is five feet five inches tall and weighs one hundred and forty-eight pounds. His wife is the former Jennie House, to whom he was married on August 17, 1916; they have one son, Arthur. The politically independent newspaperman lives in Washington, D.C., where he is a member of the National Press Club. In 1937 Stark was awarded an honorary Doctor of Laws degree from Reed College in Portland, Oregon, with a citation which said in part: "Never seeking publicity for himself, he has brought distinction to a great newspaper by living up to his ideal of searching for and presenting the whole truth."

References

N Y Times p14 My 5 '42
Who's Who in America, 1944-45

STEBBINS, GEORGE COLES Feb. 1846 —Oct. 6, 1945 American hymn writer; wrote and directed music for the evangelical team of Moody and Sankey for nearly twenty-five years; composer of fifteen hundred hymns, including "Evening Prayer", "There's a Green Hill Far Away", "Take Time To Be Holy," and "Have Thine Own Way, Lord."

Obituary

N Y Times p44 O 7 '45 por

STOKES, I(SAAC) N(EWTON) PHELPS Apr. 11, 1867—Dec. 18, 1944 American architect, historian, and housing expert; designer of notable public buildings; helped to lay the groundwork for the formation of the United States Housing Corporation; held many honorary positions.

Obituary

N Y Times p21 D 19 '44 por

STRAUSS, ANNA LORD Sept. 20, 1899- Civic leader

Address: b. National League of Women Voters, 726 Jackson Pl., N.W., Washington, D.C.; h. 2500 Q St., N.W., Washington, D.C.

Among the most influential women's organizations in the United States is the National League of Women Voters, whose president, Anna Lord Strauss, has devoted many years to civic work. In her capacity as leader of some sixty thousand American women, Miss Strauss plays a prominent role in nonpartisan American politics. She rose to head the League after six years of service as president of the New York City branch of the organization. Her active career has included national and state government posts in addition to literary and personnel work.

Anna Lord Strauss was born in New York City on September 20, 1899. Through her mother, Lucretia Mott (Lord) Strauss, she traces her ancestry back to America's pioneer feminist, the Quaker Lucretia Mott. Her father, Albert Strauss, began work as an errand boy and eventually became a partner in a banking house, his wealth enabling his daughter to devote much time to volunteer civic work. Miss Strauss was educated at the Horace Mann School and attended Miss Marshall's classes in New York City. She was interested in sports as a girl, she explains, partly because she had two brilliant sisters and could "shine better that way than in any other activity."

When she was ready to enter college America was in the First World War and she therefore decided to take a secretarial course. After completing her studies at the New York School for Secretaries, she was employed by Government agencies during the remainder of the war. She served in a secretarial capacity in the New York office of the Federal Reserve Board in 1918, and in that year also worked for the United States Shipping Board. In 1919 Miss Strauss was employed by the War Trade Board and then worked in the State Department. When her father went to the peace conference as a financial adviser, she accompanied him on the European mission.

In 1923 Miss Strauss began a six-year literary adventure which brought her from the position of office secretary to that of managing editor of the *Century*. (She also edited a children's book on ships.) Her next position was as librarian for the Employment Service of the New York Department of Labor, from 1931 to 1933. Then followed a year of service as consumer representative on the New York City Compliance Board of the NRA. In 1934 she became a member of the board of directors of the National League of Women Voters, and three years later was elected president of the New York City division. Under her leadership this group was conspicuously active in the field of voters' education and in various local campaigns. Working for county reform, the League sought to have the five county sheriffs replaced by one such officer for the city and to have him appointed by civil service examination; and they similarly sought to have the four county registers replaced by one. Supporters of the campaign for county reform included Mayor La Guardia [40] and many civic organizations. In an interview in 1941 Miss Strauss described the existing county situation as "political patronage of the most blatant sort," and at the same time pointed out that "each citizen must learn his power and, having learned, must participate." The campaign for county reform resulted in a "notable victory" in 1941, following which the reform leader was made Special Civil Service Examiner for the Office of Register for the City of New York.

Two years later, in 1943, Miss Strauss, after having served several terms as head of the New York City group, retired for the summer to rest on her Connecticut farm. But America was again at war, and in the fall she accepted a position at the Chance Vought division of the United Aircraft Corporation in Stratford. Here she was engaged in personnel work, which largely concerned the problem of absenteeism. However, she was soon called back to League duties, for, at the Chicago convention in April 1944, the National League of Women Voters elected her president by a vote of 269 to 120, rejecting the official candidate of the nominating committee in favor of the

Harris & Ewing

ANNA LORD STRAUSS

New York woman. At this convention the delegates also adopted a broad program: On the legislative front they favored Federal aid to education, to be administered through state departments of education; they pledged support of the preservation of civil liberties and protection of minority groups against discrimination. On the question of foreign policy, they supported United States participation in international relief and rehabilitation, and membership in an international organization to prevent aggression. Dorothea Kahn pointed out in the *Christian Science Monitor* that the League's recognition of the need for the use of military and economic force to maintain peace was a new position for the organization. The convention also voted to press for a constitutional amendment to change Senate procedure on treaty ratification to a more democratic method.

The League of which Miss Strauss became head had been organized at the victory convention of the National American Suffrage Association in 1920 "to finish the fight by teaching women to wield ballots wisely." Professor Bessie Louise Pierce, in a survey of women's organizations in the *Annals of the American Academy of Political and Social Science* for May 1935, concluded that the League is "a force with which lawmakers reckon." Consisting of six hundred local units in thirty-five states, with headquarters in the Nation's Capital, the League is reported to be "a much greater factor in national affairs than its membership figures [sixty thousand] suggest." According to Volta Torrey, in an article in *Liberty* (September 2, 1944), "Some members wear mink, and some wear shoddy coats. But most of them are public-spirited, middle-class housewives and business and professional women who often are the molders of public opinion." This writer also states that many of the leagues of the major cities are "the most reliable and least partisan sources of information available to a citizen."

Several prominent women politicians are said to have "learned the ropes" in the League, among them Eleanor Roosevelt [40], who credits it with having taught her much about her country and her government. While the organization does not discourage partisanship, it considers its own job beyond the realm of party politics. It sets for itself the task of explaining government and political questions and encouraging people to "become active participants in government."

In a *Reader's Digest* article (July 1940) entitled "Women Voters on the Job," Stanley High wrote, "Primarily, what the League stands for is digging up facts. . . .I doubt whether any organization in America is so effective a force for good government." Trying to present all sides of issues, the League is active the year round, especially at election time. Its reports on candidates and issues, based on extensive research, personal interviews, and questionnaires, are widely used. In 1945 the League's publications included the pamphlets "The Story of Dumbarton Oaks", "The Story of Bretton Woods," and a study of the United Nations Charter. One of its pamphlets reminded the reader: "Your time and thought, your considered convictions, your discussion of the problems of peace with others, and your letters to those responsible for the acts of our government, are all essential to winning the peace." In early 1945 the women's group initiated its drive to promote support of United States participation in the United Nations security organization, an undertaking endorsed by the Secretary of State, Edward R. Stettinius [40]. On the twenty-fifth anniversary of the League Miss Strauss spoke of the contributions of women's groups to the cause of world peace. (Other speakers included Senators Tom Connally [41] and Harold Burton [45].)

The League president endorsed the reciprocal trade agreement bill when the Administration measure was being considered by the Senate Banking Committee in June 1945. In July Miss Strauss testified on the United Nations Charter before the Senate Foreign Relations Committee, and urged the Senate to "proceed with all possible speed" to ratify the Charter. The following month she was one of several women leaders who visited President Truman [45] to voice their support of the Pepper [41]-Morse [42] "equal pay for equal work" bill. Again in September she met with other leaders of women's groups who had sent consultants to the United Nations conference, to consider "how the representation so effectively done at San Francisco can be carried on." Later that month the head of the League appeared before the Senate Foreign Relations Committee to voice her views on the Senate's treaty ratification power. Critical of the existing method, she said that some Senators "automatically vote against a treaty presented by the opposite party regardless of the merits of the treaty." This remark drew a sharp rebuke from Chairman Tom Connally. In October the President appointed Miss Strauss a member of the United States delegation to the first session of the Conference of the Food and Agriculture Organization of the United Nations at Quebec, Canada.

Anna Lord Strauss once told a reporter that she was shy, but added that "the individual can forget herself in the necessity of persuading others." An attractive brown-eyed, gray-haired woman, she is five feet five inches tall, weighs one hundred and thirty pounds, and, it is reported, "obvious physical fitness gives her a youthful appearance." One of the first women to sail her own racing boats on Long Island Sound, she has represented her native city in squash matches and has figure-skated in New York Skating Club carnivals. She likes to read biography, history, and government. She also enjoys traveling and has seen much of her own country, Central and South America, and Europe. Her Quaker heritage shows itself strongly and, according to one writer, "She and her sisters use 'thee' and 'thou' to one another, even though she has found harder pronouns more effective in politics." Not domestically inclined, when asked what dish she prefers she replies, "The nearest." Miss Strauss is a trustee of Connecticut College, and her clubs include Cosmopolitan, Town Hall, and the Women's City Club of New York. The executive rarely goes to the theater or professional games, for, she says, "I'd rather do things than watch them."

References

N Y Post Mag p5 S 9 '44 pors
N Y Sun p26 Mr 14 '45
American Women, 1939-40

STUART, KENNETH Sept. 9, 1891—Nov. 3, 1945 Lieutenant General in the Canadian Army; former Chief of General Staff at Canadian military headquarters in London from December 1943 until his resignation in late 1944; served as commander of a company of engineers during the First World War; director of Military Operations and Intelligence (1938-39); holder of Distinguished Service Cross. See *Current Biography* 1944 Yearbook.

Obituary

N Y Times p19 N 5 '45

SUGIYAMA, HAJIME (soō-gē-yä-mä hä-jē-mě) 1880—Sept. 12, 1945 Field marshal general in Japanese Army; commander of First Imperial Army and Japan's home defense army; attended Disarmament Conference in Geneva (1926-28); member of Supreme War Council in 1935; War Minister in 1937-38 and in Premier Koiso's Cabinet until resignation in 1945; killed himself after United States occupied Japan.

Obituary

N Y Times p1-2 S 13 '45 por

SULTAN, DANIEL I(SOM) Dec. 9, 1885- United States Army officer
Address: b. c/o War Department, Washington, D. C.

The first Army man to receive four Distinguished Service Medals, Lieutenant General Daniel I. Sultan was originally known as a United States Army Engineer in the Philippines, Nicaragua, and continental United States. In November 1944 he was appointed comman-

U. S. Army

LT. GEN. DANIEL I. SULTAN

der of the strategic India-Burma theater of operations and on August 14, 1945, was awarded the third Oak Leaf Cluster to the D.M.C. for "exceptionally meritorious and distinguished service as commander of the United States forces in the India-Burma theater." His promotion to Inspector General of the Army preceded this honor: President Truman '45 nominated him to that office on July 9.

Born Daniel Isom Sultan on December 9, 1885, in Oxford, Mississippi, he is the son of Daniel Isom and Emma Linda (Wohlleben) Sultan. His Southern drawl betrays his birthplace, but he has not been back there, except to visit, since he left the University of Mississippi. His appointment to the United States Military Academy came while he was still studying at the university (1901-3), and he left before graduation to enter the Point. While there he played football, and was chosen an all-American center. Upon his graduation in June 1907 he received a commission as a second lieutenant in the Engineer Corps.

After serving for a year at Fort Leavenworth, Kansas, with the Third Battalion of Engineers, young Lieutenant Sultan was ordered to Washington Barracks (now Fort Humphreys) in the District of Columbia, where he remained until 1912. During this period he attended the Engineers School at the post, and upon graduation was made a first lieutenant. He was next stationed at West Point, as an instructor in the department of engineering. He remained in that post from 1912 until 1916 and during that time, in February 1914, was advanced to the rank of captain. In September 1916 he left the Academy for the Philippine Islands, where he served successively with the Engineer troops as the officer in charge of construction and maintenance of fortifications on Corregidor and Caballo islands in the Philippine group; and as engineer of the Philippine Department in charge of all fortification work in the Islands. With the entrance of the United States into the war in April 1917, the thirty-

SULTAN, DANIEL I.—*Continued*

one-year-old engineer was advanced rapidly, in May to the rank of major, and in August to the temporary rank of lieutenant colonel.

From March 1918 to June 1919 Sultan served in Washington, D.C., on the War Department General Staff. In July 1918, he was again advanced, to the temporary rank of colonel. Then in 1919 he was ordered overseas for duty on the General Staff of the American Expeditionary Forces in France. But in August of the same year he returned to the United States for further duty with the War Department General Staff in Washington, where he remained until the summer of 1922. For his work with commissioned personnel under the Chief of Staff during the World War and the demobilization period, Colonel Sultan was awarded the Distinguished Service Medal. The citation reads: "His work was characterized by conspicuous breadth of vision and keen foresight. His splendid judgment and the sound policies initiated by him contributed in a large measure to the successful handling of the commissioned personnel of the Army. He rendered service of signal worth to the Government in a position of great responsibility." In March 1920 he reverted to his permanent rank of major.

When his duties with the General Staff had ended in 1922 Major Sultan returned to Fort Leavenworth, where he had served before the war, to attend the Command and General Staff School there. He was graduated in 1923 and was assigned, as district engineer, to Savannah, Georgia, where he remained until August 1925, supervising river and harbor improvements and fortifications in the district. When the assignment was completed he entered the Army War College in Washington, from which he was graduated in 1926. He remained in the Capital until August 1929, however, as resident member of the Board of Engineers for Rivers and Harbors.

Sultan's next assignment took him to Nicaragua, where he remained for two years. While there he was in charge of the interoceanic canal survey and in command of United States Army troops in the Central American country. On October 1, 1930, he was advanced to the rank of lieutenant colonel. During the Nicaraguan earthquake in March 1931 he was in charge of the Army's relief activities, and for this he was awarded the Oak Leaf Cluster. The citation for this award reads: "For exceptionally meritorious and distinguished services. While serving as commanding officer of United States Army troops in Nicaragua, Colonel Sultan conducted an investigation of the interoceanic canal route with efficiency and maintained high morale among his troops under conditions of unusual hardship and difficulty. By his tact and diplomacy in handling intricate problems he maintained cordial relations with the people of Nicaragua. Following the disastrous earthquake in Nicaragua in March 1931 Colonel Sultan by his prompt and effective relief work evoked the appreciation and gratitude of the afflicted people. In the performance of these duties, he demonstrated marked ability, sound judgment, and untiring zeal in a position of great responsibility, thereby rendering services of great value to his Government." The

Nicaraguan Government also presented him with its Presidential Medal of Merit and Congressional Medal of Distinction.

Sultan returned to Washington after his Nicaraguan assignment and was assigned to duty in the Capital, from July 1931 to January 1932, with the Interoceanic Canal Board in the Office of the Chief of Engineers. After this he was ordered to Chicago as district engineer. He remained in this post until the summer of 1934, when he was reassigned to the District of Columbia, this time as engineering commissioner. In October 1935 he was advanced to the rank of colonel.

In August 1938 Colonel Sultan was transferred to Fort Logan, Colorado, to command the Second Engineers, and on his advancement to brigadier general in December assumed command of the Fort. He was relieved of this command in June of the following year and assigned to command the Twenty-second Infantry Brigade at Schofield Barracks, Hawaii, where he stayed until April 1941. During the last month he was commanding general of the Hawaiian Division, and in April, just before he left the Islands, his rank was advanced to major general (temporary). He was then named to command the Thirty-eighth Division at Camp Shelby, Mississippi. This post he held from May 1, 1941, through the entrance of the United States into the Second World War, until April 6 of the following year. *Time* Magazine characterized this appointment as a "small but hopeful sign that the United States Army might be on the way to getting tough—tough enough to face modern military competition." Sultan, it is said, was the first Regular Army officer to replace the National Guard commander of a Guard division after the start of the war. He subsequently became commanding general of the Eighth Army Corps (later redesignated the Eighth Corps), serving in this capacity until November 1943, when he was made deputy commander in chief of the China-Burma-India theater of operations under General Joseph Stilwell. In September he was made lieutenant general (temporary).

Upon General Stilwell's recall in October 1944 this Far Eastern theater of operations was divided into two sectors—one to be known as the China area, now commanded by Major General Albert C. Wedemeyer[45]; the other the India and Burma area, under Sultan. On assuming command Sultan told the American troops that the recent events, such as the recall of General Stilwell, had changed "neither our mission, nor our strategy. . . .Our job is to open the Burma Road so heavy equipment . . . can be gotten to the Fourteenth Air Force, so that artillery may be gotten to the Chinese armies. . . .This Chinese Army," he continued, "has tied up numerous Japanese divisions which could have been used and could still be used against our forces in the Pacific."

The General took official command of the Chinese armies in Burma on November 12, 1944, under direct deputization from Generalissimo Chiang Kai-shek[40]. This northern combat group included the Chinese First Army, the Chinese Sixth Army, the British Thirty-sixth Division, and what General Sultan described at a press conference as a "considerable force" of Americans. Within a short time after assuming his command Sultan saw his troops inflict ten-to-one casualties on the Japanese, but the General declared, "I have seen no indication that the Japanese intend to give up Burma."

Nevertheless, in early December it was announced that more Allied supplies were flowing into Burma than ever before—more than twice as much as a year before. Chinese-American and British troops pushed deep into Burma and during a ten-week campaign won half as much territory as Allied forces were able to take from the enemy throughout the previous year. By the end of the month Sultan's combat area command in Burma announced that Chinese troops had crossed the border into their own country. The loss of the Burma Road, closed by the Japanese capture of Lashio in Burma in April 1942, was not remedied until the road-building and counter offensive campaign by the Chinese, American, and British forces were finally completed on January 28, 1945, when the first convoy of American supplies rolled into Wantung, on the border of China. Honoring "Vinegar Joe," Generalissimo Chiang Kai-shek named the new Ledo-Burma highway "Stilwell Road." The road partially relieved the Air Forces of the task of carrying gasoline and trucks over "the hump" to China; and bulldozers, graders, and other heavy equipment that could not be sent by air, could now reach China. Lashio itself was captured in March by the American-trained Chinese First Army troops under Sultan, who remained in command until July 1945, when he was appointed Inspector General of the Army. On August 14 he was signally honored by a third Oak Cluster to his Distinguished Service Medal—the first time an Army man had received four such medals. The *United States Government Manual* defines Sultan's Washington post: "The Inspector General assists the Chief of Staff in keeping the Secretary of War informed as to the state of the Army and makes such inspections, investigations, and reports dealing with the efficiency and economy of the Army as may be prescribed by law or directed . . . or requested" by specified officials or officers.

In 1916 Daniel Sultan was married to Florence Bracen. He has two daughters and one stepdaughter. (Two of them are married to Army officers.) The General is a member of the American Society of Engineers, Sigma Chi, the Army and Navy, and the Washington Army and Navy Country clubs. He is fond of mystery stories and is an ardent admirer of the fictional Chinese detective, Charlie Chan.

References

N Y Herald Tribune p7 Ja 4 '44 por
N Y Sun p16 N 28 '44
Time 39:22 My 12 '41
Who's Who in America, 1944-45

SUMNER, JESSIE United States Representative from Illinois; lawyer
Address: b. House of Representatives Old Office Bldg., Washington, D. C.; h. Milford, Ill.; Mayflower Hotel, Washington, D. C.

One of the most thoroughgoing anti-Administration legislators in the United States Con-

JESSIE SUMNER

gress is Jessie Sumner of Illinois, who was re-elected in November 1944 for her fourth term. The only woman Representative to be found at the extreme Right, she has been a consistent opponent of the New Deal, Great Britain, Russia, the war and the conduct of the war, and home front Administration measures.

Jessie Sumner was born in the little town of Milford, Illinois, eighty-eight miles south of Chicago. Her parents were A. T. and Elizabeth (Gillan) Sumner. Her pioneer grandfather had acquired thousands of acres of rich corn land; her father founded the Sumner National Bank at Sheldon, Illinois. (Today Miss Sumner is a large landowner and a director of the bank.) After her graduation from a private school in 1916, Jessie attended Smith College, where she studied economics under her future colleague, Chase Going Woodhouse '45, receiving her diploma in 1920, and then went on to study law at the University of Chicago. One of the first American women to take law at Oxford University, Miss Sumner spent two terms there, acquiring a British manner of speech which remained long after her return to the Middle West. (When she first ran for Congress the press associations referred to her as "the old Oxonian" and pointed out that, if elected, she would be the first Midwestern Representative with a British accent. In 1943, Jack Steele pointed out in the New York *Herald Tribune*, the Chicago *Tribune* published lists of Rhodes scholars and other Americans educated at Oxford, whose loyalty to the United States was therefore questionable; the lists, he reported, did not include Miss Sumner's name.) Continuing her study, she attended Columbia University Law School in New York, the New York University School of Commerce, and the University of Wisconsin summer school.

In 1923 Miss Sumner was admitted to the Illinois bar and practiced in Chicago; she joined the Chicago Bar Association, the Illinois Women's Bar Association, and the National Women Lawyers' Association, as well as the Business and Professional Women's Club,

SUMNER, JESSIE—*Continued*

the National Women's Republican Club, and the National Federation of Women's Clubs. Miss Sumner is also a member of the Farm Bureau, and manager of the South Side (Chicago) Legal Bureau; she belongs to two Greek-letter societies and the Order of the Eastern Star, and she is a member of the Methodist Church.

During the boom years of 1928-29 Jessie Sumner was employed by the Chase National Bank of New York; in the depression year of 1932 she returned to Milford and took up the practice of law there. Then melodrama entered the picture: her brother was kidnapped by bank robbers. Miss Sumner was active in securing their conviction, and was inspired to run for State's attorney. She was, however, defeated in the Republican primary election. When her uncle the county judge died in 1937, she was elected to fill out his term. The first woman judge in Illinois, Judge Sumner was most cooperative with the gentlemen from the Chicago press, who soon gave her a reputation as a wit.

Miss Sumner's judicial county was one of six (Clark, Cumberland, Edgar, Iroquois, Kankakee, and Vermilion) stretched out along the Indiana border and forming the Eighteenth Illinois Congressional District. A normally Republican area, the Eighteenth was represented at the time by a Democrat, James Meeks, an ailing old gentleman who was said to be late even for his own campaign rallies. Miss Sumner announced that she would run against him in 1938, and then, after some well-publicized indecision, did so, winning the election with an anti-New Deal platform by 56,587 votes to 45,691.

Entering the Seventy-sixth Congress as Illinois' youngest female Representative, Congressman Sumner was placed on the Banking and Currency Committee (the same assignment as her predecessor), for which she was qualified by her banking and legal experience. Amy Porter of *Collier's* says that the Representative has offered "to-the-point amendments" to such bills as the Commodity Credit Corporation and Little Business acts. At a 1941 hearing, however, Miss Sumner expressed surprise on hearing that the WPA had retained consulting economists, and said she saw no reason why WPA should have any.

About one thing there was no doubt, however; that was Representative Sumner's condemnation of "Papa Roosevelt," as she called the President, and of his policies. She is an isolationist and Anglophobe who believed that the United States could and should refuse to expend blood and treasure in the recurrent wars of a quarrelsome Old World. At the time of her election isolationism was still the majority sentiment; radicals and conservatives alike demanded that America stay out of war. "As the rise of Hitler'[42] and the truculence of Japan presaged new wars," in the words of historian Allan Nevins, "the obsessing idea of the American public was to stay out. . . .The Neutrality Act of 1937 registered the high-water mark of isolationist power and sentiment in the United States."

Jessie Sumner was with the majority when, as a freshman in Congress, she helped defeat the proposed improvement of Guam Harbor in February 1939; but the public opinion shifted in response to outside events, and after the beginning of the Second World War she was in a minority as she voted against lifting the arms embargo in favor of cash-and-carry, against expanding the Navy, and against making international reciprocal trade agreements. In 1940, after the fall of France, Holland, and Belgium, when the United States was already committed to an effective defense alliance with Canada, the Illinois Representative demanded of the House, "What reason have you to think that that [defense] program, begun only a month or two ago, will be any less extravagantly administered than the tragic, futile efforts at [economic] recovery? Look at what that outfit in Germany has done and is doing to build up a strong, efficient, trained military force—an outfit which has never wasted a dollar or a pint of oil, or even a pat of butter!" In the light of this belief, she voted against the Burke '[40]-Wadsworth'[43] Selective Service bill for military training.

Miss Sumner returned to Illinois for the 1940 campaign, in which she continued to have the backing of Colonel Robert McCormick's'[42] isolationist, strongly anti-British and anti-Roosevelt Chicago *Tribune*. Winning again over her 1938 opponent (by a vote of 64,409 to 56,744) on the Willkie'[40] ticket, she began her second term by opposing Lend-Lease and then attempting to cut out the appropriation to support it, and she voted against the arming of merchant ships, which were then being attacked by the Nazis.

On August 12, 1941, Miss Sumner voted against extending the Selective Service System another year. In explanation of her opposing vote, the Illinois Representative said she was "just against war," as a woman. "She says," reported one interviewer, "that she thought long ago that, if a committee had been sent to see Hitler'[42] at the right time, all of this trouble might have been avoided." With the United States in the war, Miss Sumner voiced her criticism of military operations, the allies of the United States, the President, and wartime Federal bureaus. Upon the expiration of her term, her Illinois district returned her for a third term in November 1942.

The following January, stating that "New Dealers have been sending up so many trial balloons concerning peace plans that they have created a balloon barrage which prevents rather than facilitates our penetrating their designs," Congressman Sumner introduced a resolution to appoint a special committee of the House to "investigate the cause and prevention of wars likely to involve the United States," and to investigate and recommend peace offers. That February Miss Sumner joined the House's other women legislators in demanding of the Appropriations Committee how women could be expected to work in war factories unless care were provided for their children—an instance in which the few gentlewomen of Congress acted as a bloc. Usually they split along party lines and on the basis of individual beliefs, ranging from Miss Sumner's militant Republicanism to Representative Mary T. Norton's'[44] strong support of the Administration. It was also one of the few occasions when the Illinois Representative was in agreement with House liberals.

Another such occasion arose in March 1943, when Miss Sumner and Clare Boothe Luce [42] were two of the twenty-eight Republicans who helped defeat the Ruml [43]-Carlson plan for "pay-as-you-earn" taxes, brought up to a current basis by "forgiving" one year's taxes. (One hundred twenty-eight Republicans voted "Aye.") "I feel," said Miss Sumner, "that it is absolutely New Dealish. . . .We are giving a Christmas present to those remaining at home at the cost of our soldiers overseas and those soldiers' children." In May she again helped defeat it, 206 to 202, and later voted the same way on a similar bill passed by the Senate.

During the four-hour argument over the Fulbright [43] resolution in September 1943, Jessie Sumner opposed it vigorously, calling it a "Machiavellian" scheme to make permanent the policy of "handouts across the sea." She charged further that British influences were trying to oust General George Marshall [40] from his post as Chief of Staff and have him sent to a field command "because he stands up for American rights. . . .For the same reason," she claimed, "they keep General MacArthur" [41] from heading our warfront." This information she had on "the right kind of authority." In spite of her condemnation of the fifty-four-word Fulbright resolution as "the most dangerous bill ever presented to an American Congress," the House declared itself overwhelmingly, 360 to 29, as "favoring the creation of appropriate international machinery with power adequate to establish and maintain a just and lasting peace among the nations of the world, and as favoring participation of the United States therein, through constitutional processes."

A meeting of four thousand Poles and Polish-Americans in New York on the twenty-fifth anniversary of the Republic of Poland applauded Miss Sumner when she called the Churchill [42]-Stalin [42] Moscow meeting "another Munich—only worse." She quoted unidentified "Washington officials" as saying that Stalin was more to be feared than Hitler, "because Hitler is already doomed to defeat by overwhelming Allied forces, while Stalin will rule Europe after his own fashion, with his rule guaranteed by the new Allied organization." And in December 1943 her suggestion that the foreign policy of Latin American nations was influenced by financial considerations brought immediate reaction in Buenos Aires, where the extreme Rightist, "anti-Yanqui" newspapers, such as the *Pampero* and *Cabildo*, played it up as a blow at the Good Neighbor Policy, and the democratic-minded *Prensa* protested.

In January 1944 Miss Sumner spoke against funds for UNRRA, and warned that Stalin will become "a successor to Hitler," backed, it might be, by UNRRA funds. She was against the bill for a soldier ballot; early in March she reversed her position on child care and was then the only woman voting for a drastic cut in its funds. In April she was one of twenty-one Representatives, nineteen of them Middle West Republicans, opposing the extension of Lend-Lease for another year; in June she voted for a bill to free insurance firms from the provisions of the antitrust laws; in

September she helped defeat the demobilization bill, which included unemployment compensation for wartime Government and war plant workers. But the high point in her isolationism had been reached in the spring, when Congressman Sumner demanded Congressional action to postpone the imminent invasion of Europe. "The difference between these two ambitious tyrants [Hitler and Stalin] is not worth the life of a single American boy !" she declared. A month later she reiterated that if the invasion "comes as scheduled, it is premature," explaining that "the Luftwaffe has not yet been destroyed." She therefore introduced two bills, one to postpone the invasion ("many of our keenest military experts," she declared, "call this invasion costly and stupid"), and the other to provide that "all of the American land, sea, and air forces now being employed in the war against Japan shall be coordinated" under General MacArthur, who was to receive whatever forces and equipment he might request.

In 1945 Miss Sumner continued to oppose Administration measures, even voting in committee to forbid the President the power to reorganize the Executive agencies. In May she attempted to block the reciprocal trade treaty bill; in March she denounced the United Nations Charter as leading to a "world super-state"; and in June she was one of the eighteen Republicans who alone voted against participation in the Bretton Woods World Bank and World Fund. She was not able, however, to muster more than twenty-nine votes for, to 328 against, her proposal to join only the Bank and not the Fund—a procedure impossible under the terms of the agreement. That month she also opposed the tax-free twenty-five-hundred-dollar expense account the House voted its members; she voted for consideration of the anti-poll-tax bill, but against the bill itself, and also against the extension of price control. In December the Illinois Congressman voted for repeal of the Smith [43]-Connally [41] Act in favor of more stringent controls on labor, and later that month she was one of fourteen Republicans and one Progressive to vote against American participation in the United Nations organization, which she attacked as "the new plunderbund." "We have joined the dance of death on the European and Asiatic battlefields," she said when the act passed by 344 to 15.

Jessie Sumner, according to Delos Lovelace, is popular with her fellow Representatives, who like her breeziness and quote her quips. Blue-eyed and blond, she wears her hair short and has a ready smile—even for the photographer who catches her under the hair drier. Miss Sumner, who is judged to be in her forties, has never married. "If a woman has neither husband nor children," she has said, "she wants to do something to serve her generation."

References

Collier's 112 :22 Ag 22 '43 por
N Y Sun p17 S 23 '43
PM p3 Jl 10 '42 por
American Women, 1939-40
Congressional Directory, 1945
Who's Who in America, 1944-45

SURLES, ALEXANDER D(AY) Aug. 14, 1886- United States Army officer

Address: b. c/o The Adjutant General, War Department, Washington, D.C.; h. 1870 Wyoming St., N.W., Washington, D.C.

War Department relations with Congress and the public, and information and education for the troops, the responsibility of Major General Alexander D. Surles, who served as head

U.S. Army Signal Corps

MAJ. GEN. ALEXANDER D. SURLES

of the War Department Bureau of Public Relations from August 1941 to September 1945, made him the supreme court of appeal on American military censorship. As might be expected, this resulted in much criticism from some newspapers on specific points, but it also brought praise for his fairness and honesty.

Alexander Day Surles was born in Milwaukee, Wisconsin, on August 14, 1886. His parents were William Henry Surles, a life insurance man, and Caroline (Pascoe) Surles. After studying at the University of Michigan in 1906-7, young Surles received an appointment to the United States Military Academy from Wisconsin in June of 1907. At West Point the future general immediately made the varsity football, baseball, and basketball teams, and acquired a reputation as "one of West Point's all-time athletic greats." "I was just good enough to make the varsity," is the way he puts it. Graduated in June 1911, he received his B.S. and was commissioned a second lieutenant of Cavalry.

Lieutenant Surles joined the Fifteenth Cavalry in Virginia in September 1911, and after a year accompanied his regiment to Texas, where they were stationed for three years. While in Texas, the twenty-eight-year-old lieutenant was married to Anna Lee Gaines, the daughter of an El Paso banker. Eight months later Surles embarked for the Philippine Islands, where he served two years at Fort William McKinley, returning in September 1917 with the rank of captain.

After six months of duty in California, Arizona, and New Jersey, the thirty-one-year-old captain sailed for France, where he served with the Fifteenth Cavalry and received a temporary promotion to major in June 1918. In July Surles was given command of the Remount Depot at Bayonne and Camp Souge, and the next year had a succession of staff posts. A month as staff athletic officer at Tours under the Service of Supply was followed by two with the Personnel Section and then four with the Training Section of the AEF General Staff. Somewhere along the line Surles was made an officer of the French Order of the Black Star.

Reverting to the permanent rank of captain in August 1919, the cavalryman returned to the United States and was assigned to West Point as an instructor; a year later he was advanced to major. (According to Lemuel F. Parton in the New York *Sun*, in 1919 Surles was staff athletic officer and later football representative of the Third Corps Area, with headquarters in Baltimore.) Leaving the Point in September 1923, Major Surles enrolled for the Cavalry School's advanced course, which he completed in June 1924, and was then ordered to the Command and General Staff School, also in Kansas. Upon his graduation from the latter in June 1925, the Major joined the Seventh Cavalry in Texas, where he spent two years as a regimental officer. Next he moved up to the First Cavalry Division staff as assistant chief of staff for military intelligence.

Three years in Intelligence were followed by a period with the Third Cavalry near Washington, and then Surles was ordered to the Army War College in the Capital, which gives the service's highest schooling. Graduated in June 1935, he was soon promoted to lieutenant colonel and was assigned to the War Department as chief of the public relations branch, Military Intelligence Division. This press section consisted of two small offices inhabited by the Colonel and two assistants, and its main problem at the time was answering the chorus of pacifist and isolationist disapproval, which reached its maximum in 1937, when the Neutrality Act was passed. According to *Time,* "newsmen rated him the ablest question-answerer ever to hold down the job" during his four-year stay.

In June 1939 Surles got a field assignment with the Seventh Cavalry—but it was mechanized cavalry, guarding the country's hoard of gold bullion at Fort Knox, Kentucky. While there he was given command of a light tank regiment, the First Armored. In March 1940 Surles was promoted to colonel, and in July he was ordered to duty with the First Armored Division. A year later, in the Army expansion, the popular officer was made a brigadier general (temporary) and appointed director of the War Department Bureau of Public Relations, succeeding a major general. "Frankly regretful to leave Fort Knox, which shared his disappointment," General Surles was described by *Time* as "characteristically modest about his plans for tackling the big headaches ahead": "I'll let the newspaper boys do the writing. I'll furnish the facts. That's my idea of the job. There is definitely no idea of censorship."

In contrast to its earlier modest establishment, Surles found the Bureau to consist of eight departments, manned by "a dozen lieutenant colonels, fifteen majors, ten captains, twenty-five lieutenants, twenty civilian writers, picture and radio editors, assorted experts of all shades, plus more than one hundred and fifty clerks, typists, stenographers, mimeograph operators, and so forth." And this was while the country was still at peace. Four months after taking over the job, the fifty-five-year-old general had to deal with the accounts of the surprise attack on Pearl Harbor; and from that time on the pressure of his duties increased with the need for censorship, the number of war correspondents, the size and diversity of the Army, and the tempo of its accomplishments. In February 1942 he was given his second star (temporary). That October, after a press agent's stunt had started a spy hunt, a departmental reorganization placed him in charge of all public relations work for the War Department. This was organized in four divisions—news, war intelligence, industrial service, and executive, the last-named including Army Emergency Relief for soldiers' dependents.

Surles accompanied President Roosevelt '42 and Secretary of State Cordell Hull '40 to the Quebec conference with Winston Churchill '42 and Anthony Eden '40 in August 1943; his Navy equivalent also attended, together with an OWI representative and the President's press secretary, Steve Early '41. The General also accompanied Secretary of War Henry L. Stimson '40 on his inspection trip to Europe in July 1944, and was one of the galaxy of generals present when the flag that had flown over the Capitol on Pearl Harbor Day was raised in triumph over Mussolini's '42 palace. But there were less pleasant aspects of his job, stemming mainly from the inevitable cross-purposes of publication and censorship. One occasion which found the General in "no-man's-land between the public and the armed forces" was that of the incomplete and conflicting reports of American losses after Colonel Jimmy Doolittle's '42 famous air raid on Japan in April 1942. Another was the Alton Levy case in October 1943, when the War Department refused to make public its report of the court-martial of the former I.L.G.W.U. organizer, whose union claimed that he had been "railroaded" for protesting against discriminatory practices against Negro troops at one air base. Perhaps the "hottest" one to handle was the Patton '43 soldier-slapping incident, which Drew Pearson '41 revealed that November.

Other occasions when Army officials either censored or edited material to conceal alleged errors or mishaps (such as antiaircraft guns firing on friendly planes) found Surles in the line of editorial fire. One of the bitterest and most consistent protesters in such cases was the newspaper *PM* which editorialized: "We have had many occasions to appeal directly to the General against attempts by lesser officials to use the power of military censorship to suppress or alter stories or facts to protect individual officers or the Army itself from criticism. In no single case where General Surles has passed on such an appeal have we found that he has permitted any factor save military security to influence his decision. . . . We think there are lots of holes in the Army treatment of news. There are lots of things

the people are not finding out that they should find out. But what passes through General Surles's hands . . . comes out straight and honest." In April 1945 *PM's* editor, John P. Lewis, again declared, "I can't think of a case in which appeal was made from misuse of the censor's pencil that was not cleared up satisfactorily and censorship limited to security."

When all the Army publicity and information services were to be reorganized on a postwar basis, General Surles was named Director of Information. As announced in September 1945, he was to exercise "over-all policy direction" over three divisions: To his Bureau of Public Relations were added the Legislative and Liaison Division of the War Department special staff, to deal with Congress, and the Information and Education Division of the Army Service Forces, devoted to the troops. In December the General was assigned to special duty on the staff of General Dwight D. Eisenhower, Chief of Staff. Lieutenant General Joseph L. Collins succeeded him as Director of Information for the War Department.

The tall, lanky general (five feet eleven inches, one hundred and fifty-five pounds) is said to "fancy himself a yellow-legged cavalryman rather than a press agent," and to look the part from head to heels. He is described as having an affable manner, tact, and a talent for making friends—the qualities which presumably won him the post of wartime censor-in-chief. Surles is a member of the Army and Navy Club and the Army and Navy Country Club. He and Mrs. Surles have two sons, Alexander Day, a Regular Army officer, and William Gaines Surles.

References

N Y Sun p5 O 24 '42; p28 O 3 '45
Time 38:42 Ag 18 '41 por
Who's Who in America, 1944-45

SUZUKI, KANTARO, BARON (sōō-zōō-kĭ kän-tä-rō′) Dec. 24, 1867- Japanese statesman

The Japanese Premier who was in office during the last fateful months of Nippon's defeat is Admiral the Baron Kantaro Suzuki. The first son of Yutetsu Suzuki (Suzuki is perhaps one of the commonest names in Japan), he was born December 24, 1867. His birthplace is usually given as Osaka, but *Who's Who in Japan* gives Chiba-ken (near Tokyo). The Japanese Empire (Nippon) was at that time under the rule of the Tokugawa Shogunate, hereditary dictatorship of great feudal lords—literally, generals—who since 1598 had kept the sacred Imperial family in enforced retirement. Only ten days after Suzuki's birth, on January 3, 1868, came the Meiji Restoration, when "a combination of out-of-power Shoguns, merchants, lesser Samurai [knights], and loyal court nobles" succeeded in overthrowing the Shogunate and placing the Emperor Meiji on the throne.

Thus Suzuki grew up in an essentially feudal society, strictly disciplined and theocratically based; yet one which was in the process of industrialization and material Westernization. The Japanese, who never questioned their own inherent divinity and superior culture, were shocked to learn that the Occident regarded

SUZUKI, KANTARO, BARON—*Continued*

them as backward and inferior; and Suzuki grew up, also, in a nation seeking to prove its greatness by territorial aggrandizement. Suzuki himself, when his views came to be of importance, was a moderate; but, as the New York *Herald Tribune* wrote editorially, "a moderate in Japan often is a person just as devoted to the idea of conquering the world as anyone in the Empire. The difference between a moderate and an extremist frequently has been that the extremist believed the Japanese could enslave the world in a year or two, while the moderate was of the opinion that it might take several decades."

According to Maurice Crain in *Rulers of the World,* Japanese naval officers are drawn from the Samurai and rich merchant classes. Young Suzuki entered the Imperial Naval College at seventeen and began in 1887 forty years of active service. He was "an up-and-coming naval officer" during the war with the Chinese Empire in 1894-95, which was fought for the ostensible purpose of freeing Korea. However, three great powers—France, Germany, and Russia—brought pressure on the victorious Nipponese and forced them to accept Formosa, renamed Chosen, and an indemnity in place of Liaotung Pennisular in Manchuria. Three years later, thirty-year-old Kantaro Suzuki became a lieutenant commander, and in 1903 he was promoted to commander. The second war in which he served against Czarist Russia (1904-05), ended in a naval victory which not only won Japan "treaty rights" in southern Manchuria and led to the annexation of Korea five years later, but brought the Empire its first recognition as a power in world affairs.

Suzuki avoided identification either with the "Army clique" which favored expansion on the Asiatic continent, or the "Navy clique" which looked toward conquest in the South Seas, and rose eventually to the supreme naval command. In August 1913 he was in command of the Second Squadron, and that December became chief of the Navy's Personnel Bureau. In September 1917 he left this important shore duty to assume command of the training squadron. On one training cruise which took the squadron to the United States in 1918, Suzuki made a speech at a San Francisco reception; he quotes himself as saying, "The Pacific Ocean is a peaceful ocean, true to its name, which the gods favor for peaceful trade between Japan and the United States. . . . If the Pacific Ocean should be used for the transportation of armed forces, both Japan and the United States would never escape Heaven's punishment." The years which followed brought Suzuki many high posts. He served for a time as Vice-Minister of the Navy (the War and Navy ministers are always named to the Cabinet from the officer corps); he commanded the Kure Naval Station, was commander-in-chief of the combined fleet, then chief of the Navy General Staff, with a rank equivalent to that of a five-star admiral in the British and American navies. In 1927, when Suzuki was nearly sixty, he retired from the Navy and was appointed to the Supreme War Council.

In 1929 the elderly admiral succeeded the famous Admiral Togo as Grand Chamberlain (and Privy Councillor), a post in which he was a member of the Imperial household, literally and figuratively close to the "Son of Heaven," young Emperor Hirohito '42. *Time* says he "walked a few respectful paces behind Hirohito at public functions, helped name the Emperor's first-born son [Tsugu-no-maya Akihito]. Most important, he served as the door through which the war lords had access to the throne." (The Army and Navy heads and members of the General Staff have direct and immediate access to the Emperor and can appeal any decision over the Premier's head.) Suzuki's "moderate" counsels enraged the Kwantung Army group of "young officers" bent on quick conquests in Manchuria in 1931; and on February 26, 1936 he was one of the victims of their "Showa Restoration" mutiny. (Showa, literally "radiant peace," was the designation Hirohito had chosen for his reign.) As *Time* tells the story, "the Grand Chamberlain had just come through Tokyo's snowy streets from dinner and movies at the United States Embassy—a 'happy evening,' Ambassador Joseph Grew '41 noted in his diary. The young officers had just come from their barracks, with swords and submachine guns [they succeeded in killing twenty-four venerable dignitaries and the Premier's brother-in-law, whom they mistook for the Premier]. . . .The Grand Chamberlain, confronted by a hundred wild-eyed soldiers, argued with them for ten minutes. When words failed, he straightened up, commanded, 'Then shoot me!' They did, and he crumpled in a pool of blood. The rebels burned incense over his body, saluted, and hurried off. The incense and the salute were premature." Other accounts say that Suzuki was shot at three times but hardly injured; that he received several sword wounds; that his life was despaired of. All these accounts may be true; even a slight injury could be extremely serious to a seventy-year-old man. At any rate, Admiral Suzuki resigned the Chamberlainship, and the Emperor rewarded his services with a peerage. The rebellion had been called off at the Emperor's order, or, as John Gunther '40 reports in *Inside Asia,* the rebels surrendered bloodlessly because they had no positive program, no place to go from there.

In August 1944, upon the death of the President of the Privy Council, Baron Suzuki was elected to replace him; and in April 1945, on the resignation of Premier General Kuniaki Koiso, the seventy-seven-year-old peer was appointed to succeed him. Adding to the rapidly deteriorating war situation which confronted Suzuki, the Soviet Government chose that same day to denounce its neutrality pact with Japan. The Empire's military situation was also critical, with every indication that it was about to become worse: a "mounting series of disasters" had been capped by the American invasion of Okinawa, only three hundred and sixty miles from the home islands. This island in the Ryukyus chain, nearly seven thousand miles from the United States, was only two hours by bomber from Japan, which was already under bombardment by American Superfortresses based in China and the Marianas. *Time* reports that while making up his

Cabinet, Suzuki was forced to take shelter from an hour-long air raid.

Suzuki's Cabinet, which contained fewer military men than his predecessor's, was by no means the "peace cabinet" which some foreign observers expected, and included several "violently anti-American" ministers. "While shunting the more reckless but incompetent militarists into the background," commented the New York *Times*, "the new Cabinet is really a Cabinet of national concentration formed for the purpose of an even more vigorous prosecution of the war . . . [comprising] the Elder Statesmen, the Manchuria Gang [i.e., the Kwantung Army group], and the Navy, big business, the old political parties, the new and supposedly more dynamic 'Sure Victory' party, and above all the Court." The Associated Press also reported the Suzuki Cabinet "a strong one, composed of some of the Empire's best production experts, with emphasis on the development of the war potential in Korea and Manchuria." Later that month, on the death of the American President, Franklin D. Roosevelt '42, Suzuki broadcast his "profound sympathy" for the "great loss his passing means to the American people"; but he did not bother to congratulate his ally, Reichsführer Adolf Hitler '42, on the latter's fifty-sixth birthday. In May, as a result of the German and Italian surrender, Suzuki's Cabinet abrogated all treaties with European countries, and in June it asked for and received dictatorial powers. Within another two months, on August 14, 1945, Nippon's crisis, after repeated bombings by American and British planes, the Russian advance in Manchuria, and the climactic dropping of the two atomic bombs, ended in unconditional surrender. Suzuki thereupon tendered the resignation of his Cabinet because of "the new situation created by Japanese acceptance of the Potsdam declaration." His successor was Prince Naruhiko Higashi-Kuni, a cousin of Emperor Hirohito and the first member of the Imperial family ever to head a Japanese cabinet. By the end of the year Suzuki's resignation as President of the Privy Council was predicted by the Tokyo correspondent of the New York *Times*.

Admiral Baron Suzuki is a white-haired, heavy-browed old courtier with a "soup-strainer" mustache. Photographs show him wearing a number of decorations, although not nearly so many as, for instance, Premier General Tojo '41. Suzuki was married in 1915, when he was forty-seven. He was said to have much influence with the Emperor. As befits a Japanese official, he is a devout worshiper at the shrines of the state religion, Shinto. As Premier, Suzuki had an extraordinary official residence, which John Gunther describes in *Inside Asia*. "Like Frank Lloyd Wright's '41 Imperial Hotel, which withstood the 1923 earthquake, it is built on a kind of floating foundation to resist seismic shocks, and is full of bewildering passageways, interior bridges, and rooms within rooms. It contains, too, various devices to impede assassins, including secret exits and bombproof doors; one legend—the Japanese scoff at it but not very convincingly—is that the Prime Minister, if he is in danger at night, can push a button, whereupon he disappears, bed and all, into a steel vault." These precautions lose much of their comic quality when it is recalled that the post of Premier of Japan is beset with occupational hazards; that from 1918 to 1936 more than a quarter of the Premiers were murdered; and that, as Gunther comments, "among modern peoples only the Arabs have such an instinct to consider assassination as an acceptable political weapon."

References

N Y Times p1+ Ap 6 '45
Time 45:45 Ap 16 '45 por
Who's Who in Japan, 1937

SYKES, EUGENE OCTAVE (sīks) July 16, 1876—June 21, 1945 American jurist; former justice of the Supreme Court of Mississippi (1916-24); an original member of the Federal Radio Commission (1927-33) and of the later Federal Communications Commission (1934-39); solved many of the legal problems affecting the radio, telephone, and telegraph industries; became known as "American radio's international walking delegate."

Obituary

N Y Times p15 Je 22 '45 por

SYMINGTON, W(ILLIAM) STUART (3D) (sī'mǐng-tǔn) June 26, 1901- United States Government official
Address: b. Surplus Property Administration, 811 Vermont Ave., N.W., Washington, D.C.; h. Route 2, Creve Coeur, Mo.

One of the key jobs on the reconversion scene in the United States was entrusted to a young, liberal-minded businessman when W. Stuart Symington was named chairman of the three-man Surplus Property Board in June 1945, and several months later administrator of the superseding Surplus Property Administration. In 1945 he thus held "one of the toughest administrative jobs in Washington"—disposal of billions of dollars' worth of surplus war property. He early indicated the course of his plans—the promotion of full employment and local enterprise in disposing of surplus material. Well known as an industrialist, Symington won a reputation for himself in the business world for rehabilitating small businesses. His cooperation with labor and the labor record of the Emerson Electric Manufacturing Company under his management brought him wide recognition as a forward-looking executive.

The son of William Stuart and Emily Haxall (Harrison) Symington, William Stuart Symington 3d was born into a wealthy family in Amherst, Massachusetts, on June 26, 1901. Brought up in Baltimore, he joined the Army while still in his teens in the last year of the First World War. After his military service Symington completed his education, attending Yale University from 1919 to 1923. He participated in campus affairs, was associate editor of the *Yale Daily News*, and a member of the Dramatic Association, the University Club, and D.K.E. When he left Yale in 1923 he entered one of his family's concerns, Symington Company (now Symington-Gould), a railroad equipment plant. But the young businessman found fault with the company product

W. STUART SYMINGTON

and was discharged. According to one writer, "the family gave him another chance at a drafting board." This work, however, did not satisfy Symington. He soon bought a clay products company which within a short time became a successful enterprise. In 1927, entering another branch of the family interests, he became president of the Gould Car Lighting Company and vice-president of the Gould Storage Battery Company. Of the latter experience he remarks, "The family fired me again, this time because I told the president no one on the lot knew how to make batteries."

In 1928 the blunt-tongued industrialist sold Gould Car Lighting and began to manufacture radio loudspeakers under the name of Valley Appliances, Inc. Merging this concern with the Colonial Radio Corporation in 1930, Symington became president of Colonial Radio in Rochester, New York, in which capacity he served for five years. Under his direction this company grew into a "big-set" manufacturer, equipped to ride out the storm of the depression. But in 1935, when he was offered the job of reorganizing the Rustless Iron and Steel Company, Symington accepted. Thus he returned again to Baltimore, where, as president of the iron and steel company for two years, he succeeded in his reorganization of the firm.

The executive was "dabbling" in new inventions when in 1938 he became interested in the Emerson Electric Manufacturing Company. In assuming the presidency of this St. Louis concern, Symington was again faced with a difficult industrial situation. Emerson was in bad financial straits, with labor troubles rife. The executive proceeded to untangle the financial affairs, then set to work on the labor problem. His solution of this was to work with the representative of the CIO's United Electrical and Radio Machine Workers of America, which covered Emerson. The St. Louis U.E. organizer was William Sentner, who also happened to be a Communist. The story of Symington's dealings with Sentner in working out amicable labor relations is told in a lengthy

Fortune Magazine article, "A Yaleman and a Communist" (November 1943).

Symington's decision to cooperate with his employees through the union is said to have been based on his desire to make the company profitable as well as a good place to work. The industrialist assisted in the consolidation of the union at Emerson, saying, "If I'm going to have a union, I'm going to have a good union." A profit-sharing plan was instituted and the employees rallied to the support of the company, with the result that the plant maintained a high production record and was labeled "the only big war plant in St. Louis that has had no labor trouble." One report found that within two years Symington had "converted Emerson from a thing fit for the flies into a robust small business." The executive pointed out that the union-company relationship was "balanced industrial democracy that works." It is his belief that under the Wagner [41] Act industry must deal with the workers' elected representatives without regard to personal politics.

While in the beginning some St. Louis businessmen condemned Symington's attitude toward the union, especially his cooperation with a Communist, his success was rapidly apparent and he was soon approved by business leaders. He became a member of the board of directors of the Chamber of Commerce and vice-chairman of the Committee for Economic Development. Serving also in various community groups, he was a member of the Mayor's Interracial Committee. At his St. Louis club, it is reported that he "often startled the old elite with his unconventional views on labor, his quick, nervous energy, his thoroughly Eastern glibness." In the course of his work at Emerson, his handling of war contracts necessitated Washington conferences and in 1941 a trip to England to study British experience in the manufacture of bomber turrets, as an observer for the Office of Production Management.

Following his appointment to the chairmanship of the Surplus Property Board on June 7, 1945, which was confirmed by the Senate on July 12, Symington resigned from his post at Emerson. The Presidential choice of the Missouri executive to replace Senator Guy M. Gillette was said to have been based on Truman's acquaintance with Symington's labor record at Emerson, which was revealed in a Congressional war contracts investigation when the President was a Senator. Press reaction was generally favorable, his industrial experience and labor record receiving special stress. In the New York *Times* C. F. Hughes wrote, "With the appointment of a businessman to head the Board, it is possible that political considerations will play a smaller part in guiding its policies." Most commentators pointed out the difficulties of Symington's new job, while *Time* declared that the disposal of approximately ninety billion dollars of surplus war property is dependent upon his use of the "confused" Surplus Property Act of 1944. On July 17 President Truman in a message to Congress urged revision of this law, calling for a single administrator instead of the three-man board. This action was interpreted by Arthur Krock [43] as a move toward more efficient government. On September 12 Congressional approval was given this revision. Symington became the head of the powerful Surplus Property Administration in October and thus "the first person in history to run a one-hundred-billion-dollar secondhand store."

W. Stuart Symington had listed as a first objective the creation of jobs and aid to small business. "If we do not promote local, independent business," Symington said, "we will end up with a few great companies. That would be most unfortunate for the economy." Symington is willing to dispose of material at a loss in order to attain these objectives. He favors continuation of the Pacific Coast steel industry, in which Henry J. Kaiser [42] has shown considerable interest. In early September Symington was named as a member of a delegation who would visit Europe to investigate the surplus property situation.

The Surplus Property Administration chief made a good impression in liberal quarters when he ruled, with the approval of Congress and the courts, that the seven hundred million dollars' worth of Government war-built aluminum plants should not be sold or leased to ALCOA because that firm already had a monopoly. However, would-be competitors of ALCOA claimed that they could not operate without government subsidies in some form, and ALCOA, on the other hand, protested that subsidies would mean "government in business" and "government competition." The issue drifted into a stalemate. Senator Hugh D. Mitchell, chairman of a special subcommittee of the Senate War Investigating Committee on Surplus Property, in November 1945 criticized the Surplus Property Administration and the Office of War Mobilization and Reconversion, which, he said, were furthering the ALCOA monopoly by "do-nothing" tactics. In December 1945 Symington moved to alleviate the veterans' housing shortage by formally authorizing Federal agencies to turn over to New York and other state and local governments without charge surplus land, materials, and equipment for conversion to emergency housing projects.

While the end of 1945 found Symington still in his SPA office, the possibility of change was seen in a *United States News* comment on December 28: "W. Stuart Symington . . . is coming around to the idea that his job should be liquidated and the functions of the office shifted to the War Assets Corporation now organized inside the Reconstruction Finance Corporation to handle surplus disposal in this country."

Described as "no proletarian," Symington is nevertheless also said to be keenly aware of trends on the labor scene. He was reported as studying proposals for an annual wage, one of the objectives of organized labor. *PM* has stated that this business leader believes in the right of the worker to his job. He also believes that postwar cooperation between industry and the Government is essential, "unless they both want to kick the whole system over." On the political scene, he supported Thomas E. Dewey [44] in 1940, but eventually voted for Wendell L. Willkie [40]. In the 1944 campaign he backed President Roosevelt [42], serving on a committee for his re-election. The executive denies having any personal political ambitions.

His contacts in the world of big business are vast and he is said to possess an "uncanny intuition." One writer has said, "He is not an explicit fellow who consciously charts a course and sticks to it. Rather his actions are instinctive and emotional." Another writer has described him as a "smart, energetic industrialist."

Handsome "Stu" Symington is over six feet tall and weighs one hundred and ninety pounds, "a lanky, loose-jointed" man who "canters around with the exuberant energy of a well-bred horse." Square-jawed, with blue eyes and "taffy-colored" hair, he is often called "charming." The affluent executive was married to Evelyn Wadsworth, the daughter of Republican Congressman James W. Wadsworth [43], on March 1, 1924; they have two sons, William Stuart and James Wadsworth. As Eve Symington, Mrs. Symington was at one time a popular "society chanteuse." The new Government official enjoys tennis, golf, and an occasional game of bridge. In the words of one reporter, "he either works hard and enjoys it, or quits in favor of long sabbaticals."

References

Fortune 28:146-9+ N '43 por
N Y Sun p17 Jl 30 '45 por
N Y World-Telegram p25 Je 8 '45 por

SYMONS, ARTHUR Feb. 28, 1865—Jan. 22, 1945 British poet and literary critic; best known for his work in familiarizing Europeans with English works and the British with the literature of France and Italy; although not widely read in America, he gained a place in college anthologies and among students of recent European literature; two of his works are *Studies in Prose and Verse* (1904) and *The Romantic Movement in English Poetry* (1909).

Obituary

N Y Times p21 Ja 26 '45

SZELL, GEORGE (sĕl) June 7, 1897- Conductor; composer; pianist

Address: b. c/o Columbia Concerts. Inc., 113 W. 57th St., New York City; h. 7 Park Ave., New York City

One of the most distinguished of the younger opera and concert conductors in the United States, George Szell has at one time or another appeared as conductor or guest conductor with almost every leading orchestra in Europe and America. The Hungarian-born conductor-pianist-composer is, in the opinion of Olin Downes [43], "a leader of stature and widely eclectic understanding . . . a conductor of high rank." Although Szell himself states that he has conducted more operas by composers other than Wagner since his debut in the United States in 1940, he has become best known for his interpretation of the works of the noted German. "It is my specialty," the conductor is said to have declared, "not to have any specialty."

While sometimes thought of as a Czechoslovakian because of his long residence in Prague, George Szell is a Hungarian, born in Budapest on June 7, 1897. He is the only child of George Charles and Maragarethe

GEORGE SZELL

(Harmat) Szell. George spent most of his childhood in Vienna, to which his parents had moved soon after his birth. At the age of four the boy knew when a wrong note was played in a piano piece, and within another year or so, it is said, he wrote from memory thirty measures of a musical selection he had heard the day before. Shortly thereafter the enthusiastic parents turned their son over to Richard Robert, "one of the greatest teachers of the keyboard," for a month's trial. Robert was impressed enough to accept the boy as his pupil, and George remained with him for about ten years. At the same time these lessons were supplemented by the study of composition and theory with Eusebius Mandyczewski, the famous Brahms scholar; he also studied with Joseph Bohuslav Förster and Max Reger.

At the age of ten George made his first public appearance, playing with the Vienna Symphony Orchestra at the Grosse Musikvereinssaal, the largest concert hall in Vienna. His playing of the Mozart Concerto in A Major, Mendelssohn's B Minor *Capriccio brillante,* and his own *Rondo* was climaxed by the orchestra's performance of an overture George had composed. This concert was so successful that he received invitations to play in other cities of Europe. His parents decided, however, that it was unwise to allow the abnormal life of the child prodigy to endanger his future. He therefore studied with private teachers in Vienna until he was sixteen, and also (in the same city) at the State Academy of Music, from which he was graduated. The young musician appeared publicly only for occasional performances in Prague, Dresden, and at Albert and Queen's halls in London, in concerts under the baton of Sir Landon Ronald. During these early years his own ideas about his musical future were taking shape; although the emphasis in his training had been upon the piano, young Szell soon declared his preference for conducting. His first opportunity to display his latent talent came when the regular conductor

of the Vienna Symphony, having sustained an arm injury, asked him to take the baton.

In 1914, at the age of seventeen, Szell made his debut as a guest conductor, appearing with the Berlin Philharmonic Orchestra. The program consisted of Beethoven's "Emperor" Concerto, Richard Strauss's [44] tone poem, *Till Eulenspiegel,* and a symphonic composition of his own which he had written at the age of fourteen. A year later Szell was appointed assistant conductor at the Royal Opera in Berlin. There he worked under Strauss, his duties ranging from the most insignificant chores to the conducting of Strauss's *Ariadne auf Naxos.* It was during this period that the future interpreter of Wagner received his first insight into the works of the composer of the Ring cycle, for Strauss was an ardent admirer of Wagner.

When Otto Klemperer (now a conductor in the United States) left his post in 1917 as first conductor of the Strasbourg Municipal Theater, Szell, who had been recommended by Strauss, replaced him for a season. For the next six years the young conductor filled the post of conductor in several cities: the German National Theater in Prague, 1919; the Court Theater in Darmstadt, 1921-24; the Municipal Theater at Düsseldorf, 1922-24. From 1924 to 1929 Szell was the principal conductor for the Berlin State Opera House and the Berlin Broadcasting Symphony Orchestra. During these years his prestige was growing—he was acclaimed for conducting music that displayed "intriguing zest and force." (At this period he was also teaching at the Berlin State Academy of Music.)

For the next eight years, commencing in 1929, Szell's life was centered mostly in Prague, where he was general musical director of the Philharmonic Concerts and the German Opera House, and where he taught at the Academy of Music and Dramatic Arts. In these years he took temporary leaves to appear as guest conductor with the Vienna, Berlin, and London philharmonic orchestras, and with the symphonic orchestras at Leningrad, Amsterdam, The Hague, Brussels, Stockholm, and Copenhagen. In 1931 he came to the United States for three months, appearing as guest conductor with the St. Louis Symphony. Of one of his concerts, "a typical balance between the classic and modern," the St. Louis *Times* (March 28, 1931) wrote, "It was one of the few really great concerts."

In 1937 Szell succeeded John Barbirolli [40] as general conductor of the Scottish Orchestra of Glasgow, at the same time accepting appointment as semi-permanent conductor of the Residentie Orkest of The Hague (he held both posts for two years). Twice in the next two years he flew to Australia to conduct the Celebrity Concerts of the Australian Broadcasting Commission in Sydney and Melbourne, and when the Second World War broke out he was in New York. Since the Scottish Orchestra had been disbanded when the war began, Szell decided to make the United States his new home.

Because of other commitments Szell had the previous spring he declined Toscanini's [42] invitation to conduct the newly formed National Broadcasting Company Symphony Orchestra. His first concert in America since 1931 therefore took place at the Hollywood Bowl when he appeared as guest conductor with the Los Angeles Philharmonic Orchestra. (He was to return for four years.) In 1941 he made his first public appearance in New York, directing four concerts of the National Broadcasting Symphony Orchestra over the period March 1941-January 1942. His programs included Strauss's *Till Eulenspiegel*, "a presentation displaying great technical virtuosity"; the "Eroica" Symphony by Beethoven, "an accomplishment of a musician whose knowledge and sincerity are never in question"; Schumann's Fourth Symphony, "an example of clean, clear articulation of phrase"; and Mozart's Piano Concerto in C Major, "an expression of noble interpretation." He also conducted during this year the Chicago Symphony Orchestra at the Ravinia Festival, and the Detroit Symphony and the Los Angeles Philharmonic orchestras. In 1942, in addition to fulfilling other engagements, he appeared as guest conductor of fifteen performances at the Metropolitan Opera House, and in early 1943 he made his first appearance with the Boston Symphony Orchestra.

Upon the opening of the 1944-45 season of the Metropolitan Opera House Szell assumed the status of permanent conductor. His interpretations of Wagner during the season were widely acclaimed in the musical world, Louis Biancolli of the New York *World-Telegram* declaring that "Wagnerism is in the man's blood." Robert Bagar found Szell's conducting of *Götterdämmerung* "of commanding brilliance," and in the opinion of Oscar Thompson, Szell's direction of *Die Walküre* demonstrated "musical leadership of a distinguished order." According to Jerome D. Bohm of the New York *Herald Tribune*, "the cogency and justly paced melos" of the performances of *Das Rheingold* and *Siegfried* must go to Szell." *PM*, discussing the four operas of the Wagner Ring, commented that Szell was "the star of each performance." His masterly conducting of Wagner are attributed to his imaginative readings and thorough knowledge of the scores, which bring out sonority of sound and subtleties of tempo. In the words of a critic for *Musical America*, "George Szell is absolutely the life and soul of what Wagnerian opera he directs." During the 1944-45 season Szell also received very favorable reviews for his conducting of *Die Meistersinger*, Mozart's *Don Giovanni*, and Strauss's *Der Rosenkavalier*.

Szell's direction during 1944-45 of four performances by the New York Philharmonic-Symphony revealed a virtuosity in the reading of symphonic music equal to his operatic interpretations. Some of the works performed were Beethoven's "Eroica" Symphony, played with "a certain unaccustomed sweetness of sound"; Brahm's Fourth Symphony, conducted with "warmth, breadth, and virility"; Schumann's Fourth Symphony in D Minor, described as "admirably integrated"; and Haydn's C Major Symphony, "vitally conceived." In February 1945 Szell made his first New York appearance as a pianist, performing with the Budapest String Quartet in a program presented by the New Friends of Music at Town Hall. His playing of Mozart's G Minor and E-flat Major piano quartets evoked praise comparable to

that describing his conducting. Mark A. Schubart of the New York *Times* said early in 1945, "It would be no exaggeration to say that of late no conductor in New York has received such universally—and almost monotonously—laudatory comments and public acclaim. He has joined that very small circle of truly authoritative conductors." The second annual poll of *Musical America*, announced in May 1945, confirmed this estimate by giving to Szell a place as an opera conductor second only to Bruno Walter.[42]

Szell, in discussing his art, contends that "since a conductor draws his expression from a manifold and complex human instrument, he requires a manifold and complex preparation." Conducting, asserts Szell, calls for aptitude and extensive training. A good conductor must possess the inherent qualities of good memory, a sense of rhythm, fairly absolute pitch, and confidence. In addition he must have a thorough grounding in the mechanics of music, such as theory, counterpoint, form, orchestration, and score reading, as well as a knowledge of different instruments. Since interpretation plays a very important part in conducting, Szell feels that a conductor must not only understand the work but must "re-create it for himself if he is to re-create it for others." The absence in America of a counterpart of the musician's apprenticeship in state opera houses in Europe is of much concern to Szell. This apprenticeship, he points out, gives the European musicians several years of varied musical experience—from the coaching of singers to the conducting of the orchestra. Some plan will be established, he hopes, whereby funds from American institutions and individuals will enable the management of the Metropolitan Opera House to create a number of such "internships" for aspiring conductors.

The armchair listener can hear George Szell's conducting on numerous recordings, and servicemen were able to hear him at the USO concerts he gave during the war. Szell is a tall man, has blue eyes, thinning blond hair. In January 1938 he was married to Helene Schulz, a Czechoslovak. He is attracted by widely different fields of knowledge, while among his hobbies are cooking, golf, bridge, and collecting amusing stories and odd journalistic misprints. Among his compositions are numerous works for the piano, the *Lyric Overture*, and variations on an original theme for orchestra. His happiest moments, Szell says, are those in which he succeeds in doing some justice to the works he conducts.

References
Etude 62:139+ Mr '44 pors
N Y Herald Tribune p8 S 21 '42 por
N Y Times VIII p17 Ja 17 '43
Time 43:44-6 Ap 17 '44 por

Ewen, D. ed. Living Musicians (1940)
Grove's Dictionary of Music and Musicians, Suppl vol (1940)
Thompson, O. ed. International Cyclopedia of Music and Musicians (1943)
Who's Who in America, 1944-45

SZOLD, HENRIETTA (zōld) 1860—Feb. 13, 1945 American-Jewish women's leader; founder and president of Hadassah (1912-26), United States women's Zionist organization; in

SZOLD, HENRIETTA—*Continued*

1909 conceived the idea of district nursing in the Holy Land, to which she devoted the remainder of her life; often described as the "most brilliant Jewish woman in America." See *Current Biography* 1940 Yearbook.

Obituary

N Y Times p19 F 14 '45 por

TAFT, CHARLES P(HELPS, 2d) Sept. 20, 1897- United States Government official; lawyer

Address: b. Dixie Terminal Bldg., Cincinnati, Ohio; Department of State, Washington, D. C.; h. 16 Garden Pl., Cincinnati, Ohio

The Second World War brought Charles P. Taft, younger brother of Senator Robert A. Taft [40], of the notable Taft family, to Washington from his activities in law and politics in Cincinnati. As a lawyer, author of two books, and as one of the founders of Cincinnati's highly successful city-manager government, Taft in 1945 served as director of the Office of Wartime Economic Affairs and of the Office of Transportation and Communications, both of the State Department. His championship of the Truman [45] Administration's 1945 reciprocal tariff program emphasized the distinction between him and his Senator-brother, who led the opposition to the measure. It has been said that this difference "symbolizes the differences within the Republican Party itself today—Charles Phelps representing the progressive wing of his party, and Robert the conservative."

When Charles Phelps Taft 2d was born in Cincinnati on September 20, 1897, his father William Howard Taft, who was to become twenty-seventh President and tenth Chief Justice of the United States, was a circuit judge and professor of law at the University of Cincinnati. William Howard was the third generation of Tafts to serve as a judge. His grandfather, Peter Rawson Taft of old Vermont farm stock, won distinction in his home state as a probate and county court judge. Peter Taft's son Alphonso attended Yale and, after obtaining his degree in law, migrated to Cincinnati, there to achieve renown but no wealth—rising from a local judgeship to a place in President Grant's Cabinet and to ambassadorial posts in Vienna and St. Petersburg. The mother of Charles Phelps, Helen Herron Taft, was the daughter of a lawyer. When the boy was three years old, his father was appointed president of the Philippine Commission, and a year later he became the first Civil Governor of the Islands. During their residence in Manila, the family spent summers in Yokohama and took a trip through China.

In 1905 William Howard Taft accepted the office of Secretary of War in Theodore Roosevelt's second term as President, and Washington became the home of the Tafts for the next eight years. With his brother Robert, young Charles was sent to the Taft School in Watertown, Connecticut, from which he was graduated in 1913. (This school had been founded and was directed by Horace Taft, the boys' uncle.) In 1909 the Tafts moved into the White House when William Howard Taft was elected to succeed Roosevelt.

Like his grandfather, father, and brother Robert, Charles attended Yale University. As an undergraduate he won the Gordon Brown prize for "manhood . . . scholarship . . . leadership"; he was also made a tackle on the football team and was captain of the basketball team. Then the entrance of the United States into the war interrupted his schooling. (He received his B.A. degree *in absentia* in 1918.) He enlisted in the Army in May 1917 and was assigned to the Twelfth Field Artillery of the Second Division. In October of the same year the twenty-year-old soldier was married to Eleanor K. Chase, daughter of the president of the Ingersoll Watch Company. Young Taft served in France for a year, for a month at the front as a sergeant major before entering the Saumur Artillery School, from which he was graduated in August 1918; two months later he was commissioned a first lieutenant. Taft's military connection continued until March 1939 when he allowed his commission as a reserve officer to expire because of his inability to take any active training.

On his return to the United States Taft entered Yale's law school—he served as coach while there—and received his LL.B. degree in 1921. In 1922 the young man was admitted to the Ohio bar and with his brother Robert formed the law firm of Taft and Taft in Cincinnati. Their one-room law office expanded rapidly into one of the biggest and most profitable in the city. Two years later, Charlie Taft, as he is known in Cincinnati, became a member of the firm of Taft, Stettinius, and Hollister. Not the least of his assets as a successful lawyer is said to be his infectious smile. "Charlie smiled me out of court," has been the complaint of more than one legal opponent.

Taft has been in the thick of Cincinnati politics from the beginning of his legal career, when he was elected Hamilton County prosecuting attorney (1927-28), an office his father had held in 1881. He has generally backed "fusion" reform parties in local politics. Taft led and won a fight for charter revision in Ohio counties and for "a general cleanup of Cincinnati's government." *City Management* (1933) is Taft's story of how he and other citizens fought and won their battle against political misrule and bossism, and succeeded in establishing what is considered one of the best governed cities in the United States under the city-manager plan and charter. The New York *Times* called it "a rattling good tale." Told informally, the account is also a statistical and detailed report. From 1938 to 1942 the author-lawyer served as member of the Cincinnati Council.

You and I—and Roosevelt (1936), a small book, won for Taft praise as an author and caused Alf Landon [44], the 1936 Republican Presidential nominee, to make him chief of a three-man advisory board to serve during the campaign. (This board was facetiously dubbed "the Brain Trusters," because it acted as a fact-finding body in the same way that Raymond Moley [45] and others, similarly named, had served Roosevelt [42].) Landon had been attracted to Taft when he heard him speak at a Republican meeting the winter before on the subject of a progressive Republican program. After Taft had expanded that address in the book, *You and I—and Roosevelt,* he sent a copy to the Kansas Governor. On the flyleaf he had written: "To the man who fits the blueprint set forth in this little book." Landon liked the volume so much that he adopted it as a sort of campaign primer. The *Christian Science Monitor* said: "The great value—and it is great—of Taft's brief discussion of campaign issues is as a moderate's appeal to moderates." The *Saturday Review of Literature* prophesied that it would appeal to young Republicans but not to the Old Guard, and *Newsweek* credited Taft with forming the planks in the 1936 Republican platform on relief, social security, and civil service.

The Cincinnati attorney in 1941 assumed the responsibility of war duties in Washington. In March of that year he became one of a new three-man committee, headed by Joseph E. Davies '42, the President's Committee on War Relief Agencies, to handle and coordinate organized drives for both foreign and domestic relief funds. (This committee became known as the President's War Relief Control Board in July 1942.) In 1941 Taft was appointed also to the Office of Defense Health and Welfare Services of the Federal Security Agency. As assistant director of its health and welfare section Taft supported the war-area child-care bill of 1943 and programs for efficient handling of juvenile delinquency, and joined with the Public Health Service in a campaign to cut down the rate of venereal disease. He resigned in late 1943 to become special adviser to the State Department. He served there in the capacity of chairman of the Area Committee for Coordination of the Planning of United States Agencies, to assist in the economic rehabilitation of the East Indies, and as chairman of a similar committee for Malaya.

Since January 1944, when Secretary of State Cordell Hull '40 announced a reorganization of the State Department in accordance with the coordination plan of President Roosevelt, Taft has served as the director of the newly created Office of Wartime Economic Affairs. He supported extension and expansion of the ten-year-old Reciprocal Trade Agreements Act when the issue came before Congress in May and June 1945. In a "dramatic conflict of view," his Senator brother was among those who led the fight against the Administration-requested program. Charles P. Taft, wrote New York *World-Telegram* columnist Thomas L. Stokes, "is taking on the tariff—as in other issues—a broad and international viewpoint," while his brother "is taking the narrow, backward glance of the standpat G.O.P. based on localism and economic isolationism." "Time," stated Charles Taft, "is waiting for no man these days. Without prompt action to stabilize currencies, to finance reconstruction, and to stop the threat of spiraling tariffs and preferences and trade barriers abroad, the chances for expansion of private trade to supply needs and raise the standards of living in the world are slim indeed." On June 19, 1945, the Senate protectionists were defeated when the upper chamber voted (47 to 33) to give the President the right to cut 1945 tariff rates up to 50 per cent for nations making concessions.

Taft also served as director of the State Department's new Office of Transportation and

CHARLES P. TAFT

Communications Policy in 1945. On May 11 his office announced that an agreement had been signed with the United Kingdom, France, Belgium, the Netherlands, Norway, and Luxembourg for the rehabilitation and operation of Western Europe's railways, highways, and canals. This seven-nation pact, which had a six-month tenure though a more permanent organization was contemplated, operated pending acceptance of a draft agreement for broader jurisdiction by Russia and other countries. Taft served, too, as an adviser to the American delegation to the San Francisco conference. Like his father, Taft favors a world organization; he has stated that "the real explanation of our failure in the [First World] War and in the peace is that having put our hand to the plow we—the United States —turned back. . . .Our influence for peace might have accomplished the dream of centuries," had we supported the League of Nations.

On July 26, 1945, Taft resigned from his State Department office, effective September 1, to return to Cincinnati and city politics. Joseph C. Grew '41, Acting Secretary of State, thanked him for the signal work he had done with the Department in various phases of economic activity. "We are particularly grateful," the Secretary said, "for the part he played in successfully achieving the extension of the Reciprocal Agreements Act, which is among the many valuable services he rendered." Taft continued as a member of the War Relief Control Board, working under President Truman, and as a member of the Army-Navy Committee on Education and Recreation.

Charles Taft is described as a tall, well-built man. He is active in the Episcopalian Church and has served as a member of the provisional committee for the World Council of Churches. From 1937 to 1939 he was chairman of the National Committee of Community Mobilization for Human Needs; he is a trustee of the Twentieth Century Fund and

TAFT, CHARLES P.—*Continued*

the Carnegie Institution of Washington. He also is a member of the Cincinnati and Ohio State bar associations, and of Beta Theta Pi and Phi Delta Phi. The Tafts have six children: Eleanor Kellogg (Mrs. Donald T. Hall), Sylvia Howard (Mrs. William Lotspeich), Seth Chase, Lucia Chase, Cynthia Herron, and Peter Rawson.

References

Christian Cent 58:11 Ja 1 '41
N Y World-Telegram p13 Je 12 '45
Newsweek 8:13-14 Jl 25 '36
Pringle, H. F. The Life and Times of William Howard Taft (1939)
Who's Who in America, 1944-45
Who's Who in Law, 1937

TARDIEU, ANDRE (tàr"dyû' äN"drā') Sept. 22, 1876—Sept. 15, 1945 French diplomat, statesman, and historian; outstanding political writer before First World War; head of French War Commission in the United States during the First World War; member of Paris Peace Conference and supporter of Clemenceau at the Versailles Conference; Premier of France from 1929 to 1930 and again in 1932; four times a Minister in Government.

Obituary

N Y Times p23 S 18 '45 por

TASSIGNY, JEAN (JOSEPH MARIE GABRIEL) DE LATTRE DE *See* Lattre de Tassigny, J.J.M.G. de

TATEKAWA, YOSHITSUGU (tä-tĕ-kä-wä yō-shē-tsōō-gōō) 1880—Sept. 10, 1945 Japanese diplomat; retired (1936) lieutenant general in Army; former military attaché in London and Nanking; military representative to Disarmament Conference in Geneva in 1932; commander of the Tenth Division and the Fourth Division (1935); Ambassador to U.S.S.R. (1940-42).

Obituary

N Y Times p25 S 12 '45

TAYLOR, A(LBERT) HOYT Jan. 1, 1879- Physicist; United States Navy consultant; radio engineer

Address: b. c/o Naval Research Laboratory, Washington, D.C.; h. 2910 Pennsylvania Ave., S. E., Washington, D.C.

"If the atomic bomb was the most powerful weapon evolved by the scientists [in the Second World War]," writes Dexter Masters, "radar was the most versatile. . . .It was taking on new jobs right up to the end, and at its older jobs it had become a staple of combat operations long before the end." Radar guided the aiming of guns, the navigation of ships and planes, the dropping of bombs, the control of bomber missions or the movements of a single paratrooper, penetrating darkness, distance, camouflage, and bad weather. Thousands of research workers in several countries had a hand in this electronic miracle, but one, Dr. A. Hoyt Taylor, chief physicist

for the United States Navy, is regarded by many as the "father of radar." As he points out, radar was a development rather than a discovery; but his was perhaps the most important role in developing American radar.

Albert Hoyt Taylor was born in Chicago on the first day of 1879; his parents were Albert H. and Harriet (Getschell) Taylor. By the age of twenty he had begun research in the new field of radio, investigating the high-frequency waves, up to two hundred megacycles per second—frequencies which were to occupy the attention of scientists decades later. Taylor published his first report of findings in 1902, the year of his graduation from Northwestern University. In 1903 he joined the University of Wisconsin faculty as instructor in physics, and was promoted to assistant professor two years later.

In 1908-9 the young physicist studied for his Ph.D. in Germany, at the University of Göttingen. There, to quote a Navy release, he "associated with such pioneers as Simon, noted for his work in high-frequency arcs and analysis of alternating current phenomena by dynamical characteristics; Hilbert, the noted mathematician; and Voight, recognized for his work in mathematical physics." On his return to the United States, Taylor became professor and head of the physics department at the University of North Dakota, where he remained for eight years. In 1911 he was married to Sarah E. Hickman. (They have four children, Albert, Barbara, Harriet, and Margaret.)

After the United States entered the First World War, Taylor was commissioned a lieutenant in the Naval Reserve, becoming district communications superintendent of three naval districts. Later he organized and directed the Navy's transatlantic radio communication system. The scientist was afterward placed in charge of the experimental division of the naval air station at Hampton Roads, Virginia, and then of the Naval Aircraft Laboratory. At the time, this laboratory was in the Bureau of Standards, but it was moved to the Washington naval air station. Commander Taylor went on the USNR retired list in 1922, but remained with the Navy in a civilian capacity.

In September 1922 he and an assistant, Leo C. Young, were conducting experiments on the use of short waves in plane-to-plane and plane-to-ground communications. While attempting to measure signals transmitted from across the Potomac River, they were annoyed to find that the passing ships caused "a definite interference pattern." This gave them an idea, and the two researchers suggested to the Navy Department that "possibly an arrangement could be worked out whereby destroyers located in a line a number of miles apart could be immediately aware of the passage of an enemy vessel between any two destroyers in the line, irrespective of fog, darkness, or smoke screen"—the germ of the radar principle.

When the Naval Research Laboratory was established Taylor headed its radio division. To quote the Navy's official history of radar (released May 23, 1943), Taylor and his assistant superintendent Young experienced "almost unbelievable equipment difficulties, but . . . despite the pressure of their other work and the discouraging factors which face the pursual of most research work, Dr. Taylor and Mr. Young continued their trail. Between 1925 and 1930 the reflection phenomenon observed in 1922 was used to measure the height of the Kennelly-Heaviside layer, an atmospheric formation which acts as a reflector for certain beams [proving that the transmitter and receiver could be at the same place]. Dr. Taylor and Mr. Young did this work in conjunction with Dr. Gregory Breit and Dr. Merle A. Tuve, of the Carnegie Institute. . . .During this period, Dr. Taylor and Mr. Young also measured the time required for radio signals to go around the world by reflection from the Kennelly-Heaviside layer. For this purpose extremely brief radio signals were employed, and apparatus was developed to both transmit and receive such brief signals." (Articles reporting this work were said by members of a British technical mission in 1940 to have furnished the base on which Sir Robert Watson-Watt [45] and other British scientists had erected an independent system of radiolocation during the following years. The American development came to be called radar, the short name for radio detection and ranging.)

In January 1931 the Naval Research Laboratory was officially assigned to investigate the use of radio to detect the presence of enemy vessels and aircraft, with special emphasis on "the confidential nature of the problem." (A year later the Navy began to share its findings along this line with the Army, which went to work on its own forms of radio detection.) In July 1932 Taylor reported that moving airplanes had been detected at a distance of nearly fifty miles, and called for instruments to record and correlate data to show the position, angle, and speed of approaching planes. These were developed by Robert M. Page, with the assistance of Robert A. Guthrie. The Naval Affairs Committee of the House of Representatives, then headed by a former engineer, became "intensely interested" in the development of radar, and in 1935 it allotted the Naval Research Laboratory a hundred thousand dollars for its research.

The next problem was to adapt radar equipment to shipboard use. The first radars to go on board ships were put on the destroyer *Leary* in April 1937 and were followed in 1938 by an improved installation on the battleship *U.S.S. New York*. The ship's commander and the admiral in charge of the battleship division were enthusiastic about the results. The first contract for radar equipment—six sets—was awarded in 1939 to the Radio Corporation of America, which, with Bell Laboratories, had been cooperating in the research. That September the Americans exchanged technical information with a British technical mission which included Sir Robert Watson-Watt, developer of British radar. In August 1940, when the United States began to look uneasily at its defenses, General Electric became the first company to transfer all its radio engineers to radar work.

As Barbara Klaw wrote in the New York *Post*, "Dr. Taylor and his closest associates, Leo C. Young and R. M. Page, found themselves saddled with the multiple duties of launching a great new science. For a few furious years they taught students, organized industry, designed and installed equipment,

A. HOYT TAYLOR

while carrying on their still incomplete research at the same time." Finally, in 1941, radar went into quantity production. A radar set, operated by an Army private, actually detected the Japanese planes approaching Pearl Harbor on December 7; the warning went unheeded, however, as the technician's superior assumed that the planes were a scheduled flight of American B-17's. Once the United States was in the war, radar underwent spectacular development under conditions of greatest secrecy.

As explained by Taylor, "radar is simply an echo of light. In the old days of river steamers the ship captain would toot the horn on foggy days and by judging the length of time it took for an echo to return from the river banks he would judge the position of his boat in the stream. The principle of radar is the same. We send out pulsating streams or beams of electric impulses. When these impulses strike an object they rebound. When the rebound is recorded we can compute the distance and in most cases the size and nature of the object which sent the impulse echo back to us." These radio waves travel at nearly the speed of light, 186,000 miles per second; by means of a modulator, they are sent through the antenna in bursts of about one-millionth of a second duration with pauses of a few thousandths of a second to allow the receiver to handle the returning impulses. A 'scope (oscilloscope) or viewing screen transforms the invisible radio signals to visible patterns of dark and light which can be easily interpreted by a skilled operator. These are the essentials. There were many modifications for different uses, ranging from small sets for fighter planes to hundred-man installations occupying an acre or more. One of the special devices was IFF—identification of friend or foe —carried by each American ship and plane, which automatically gave out an identifying code signal when struck by radar waves. American radar was generally acknowledged to be the best in the world, and to have contributed immensely to victory. The funds allotted the

TAYLOR, A. HOYT—*Continued*

Naval Research Laboratory for 1945, incidentally, were estimated at nearly nine million dollars—almost three thousand times its average annual budget up to 1942.

In July 1945 Taylor, until then superintendent of the radio division of the laboratory, became the laboratory's chief consultant and chief coordinator for electronics. He has to his credit about fifty patented inventions concerning radio, "the development of theory and practice of propagation of high-frequency energy, the development and application of the quartz crystal oscillator, and the development of high- and super-frequency radio communication systems, which have seen wide application, not alone in the Navy, but in all Government and commercial service."

In March 1944 Taylor was awarded one of the first two United States Medals for Merit, awarded to civilians for outstanding services in the war, in recognition of his work in developing radar (the other medal went to John C. Garand '[45] for the Garand rifle). Secretary of State Cordell Hull presented the medal to Taylor with a citation ending with these words: "His [Taylor's] foresight, technical skill and steadfast perseverance contributed in large measure to the timely introduction of a scientific device which has yielded the United States Navy a definite advantage over her enemies during the present war."

The Institute of Radio Engineers had awarded Taylor the Morris Liebmann Memorial Prize for his "important contributions to radio communications" in 1927. In 1929 he was president of the I.R.E.; and in 1941 the institute awarded him its Medal of Honor. The next year he was honored by the Philadelphia Board of Trade with a John Scott Medal and a prize of money. Taylor is a member of Sigma Xi fraternity, a fellow of the American Physical Society and of the Institute of Electrical Engineers. He is a member also of the American Geophysical Society and the American Association for the Advancement of Science. The elderly physicist is described as slight and baldish, and as "still working at top speed to improve radar." One thing he would like to do something about is making the radar beam curve with the earth so that its low-level usefulness may continue beyond the horizon line. Another of his postwar projects is to send straight-line radar impulses to the moon.

References

American Men of Science, 1938
Dunlap, O. E.   Radio's 100 Men of
    Science (1944)

TAYLOR, LAURETTE Apr. 1, 1884- Actress

Address: b. c/o Harry Davies, 701 7th Ave., New York City

As if with one accord, reviewers of *The Glass Menagerie* wrote the word "magnificent" in 1945 in describing Laurette Taylor's interpretation of a former Southern belle who has become a frowzy but fiercely ambitious mother. "A really magnificent performance," wrote Wolcott Gibbs (the *New Yorker*)— "The magnificent art of her performance is all but incredible," said Lewis Nichols (New York *Times*)—these were two exclamations. When

one critic compared Miss Taylor to the great Duse, Wilella Waldorf (New York *Post*) promptly asserted that she was "too interesting to be compared to anyone." And later in the season the members of the Drama Critics Circle unanimously accorded the star the award for best actress of 1944-45. Those of her own profession were equally enthusiastic. The second annual Donaldson Award for outstanding achievements in the theater, decided by a poll of 2,000 theater people, gave Miss Taylor the largest number of votes in any category. A star in 1910, she is one of the few actresses to have been equally successful in youthful and mature parts, in comedy and tragedy.

The actress was born April 1, 1884, in New York City, to James and Elizabeth Cooney. A Roman Catholic, little Miss Cooney on her confirmation added Magdalene to her baptismal names of Helen Laurette. "It was intended to be Margaret, not Magdalene at all," the actress says, "but I was an imp as a little girl . . . and quite a ham, too. Those colored pictures of Mary Magdalene with her long golden hair in repentant postures had been too much for me. I didn't bother about what made her so tragic; all I knew was I wanted to be like her, so when I was confirmed, I took the pen and, when I was sure nobody was looking, wrote 'Magdalene' and let 'Margaret' slide." The "ham" of those early years expressed itself in recitations of "The Curfew Shall Not Ring To-Night," and other favorites. The little girl was featured in school entertainments and at twelve was commanding five and ten dollars a performance for semi-professional appearances. It was but a step to her debut as "La Belle Laurette," child impersonator, in a small-time vaudeville house at Gloucester, Massachusetts. Her repertoire included imitations of Eddie Foy, Anna Held, George M. Cohan, and other "old reliables" of that era. Not a success as an impersonator, at the age of fourteen she returned to school.

Miss Cooney made another vaudeville appearance as La Belle Laurette, at the Boston Athenaeum in 1903, when she was nineteen; and before the year was out she was launched on her career as a dramatic actress with the title role in *The Child Wife*. For her second role in the theater, she was cast in that epic melodrama of the "ten-twent'-thirt'" theater, *From Rags to Riches*, also in 1903. The author, Charles A. Taylor, the "king of the mellers," who was twenty years older than the young heroine, fell in love with her, and they were married. The new Mrs. Taylor became Miss Taylor on the stage. She and Charles Taylor (from whom she was divorced in 1910) had two children, Marguerite and Dwight. (Dwight Taylor, a Hollywood writer since 1930, has written, among many screen plays, the successful *Gay Divorcée, The Thin Man Goes Home*, and *Conflict*.)

A Western tour of *From Rags to Riches* brought the Taylors to Seattle, where they established their own stock company, with Laurette as the leading woman. Added to the usual stock company plays of that period—*Uncle Tom's Cabin, Camille*, and *Faust*—were melodramas by Taylor. In the soubrette roles, which were a part of the time-worn pattern of the "mellers," Laurette Taylor not only provided the comic relief but on occasion substituted something more human for her husband's stilted lines—for the actress was outgrowing the sentimentality and staginess of that type of play. After two years a nervous breakdown interrupted her stock-company grind. And though her illness forced her to spend two months in a hospital, later she came to regard it as an escape—it brought her to New York City. However, before making her bow in the more sophisticated Broadway plays she appeared in another Taylor melodrama—*Yosemite*, a Shubert production which toured Eastern cities and played in Chicago. A Buffalo critic observed that Miss Taylor was "charming, graceful, and unique." The year was 1908. It was shortly after this that Taylor went to Alaska to establish another stock company while Laurette began a long trek of job-seeking on the Great White Way. "I was shabby, I was anxious—and an actress should never look either," says Miss Taylor of her struggle to establish herself in the Broadway theater.

There was one failure before she began her triumphant journey to stardom. Cast as Jolan in *The Devil* (1908), a part which had been originated by another, Miss Taylor again failed as an imitator. She was discharged during rehearsal because she was unable to interpret the part as her predecessor had. Her first Broadway role was a minor one in J. Hartley Manners' play, *The Great John Ganton* (1909). However, the part had one big scene and the newcomer, playing it "naturally but with force and finesse," won the critics. It is significant that one reviewer announced that "the fine quality of her histrionic intelligence and imagination, her power to communicate moods amounts to genius." The Shuberts placed Miss Taylor under a three-year contract. *The Ringmaster* and *Mrs. Dakon,* two Shubert productions of 1909, increased the actress' prestige but failed as plays.

The Girl in Waiting (1910), although far from being a successful play, gave Miss Taylor star billing, and also marked the growth of a new friendship that was later to result in her second marriage. One of the most successful Broadway playwrights of that period was J. Hartley Manners, a handsome Englishman who was an established actor on the London stage before he made his American debut as Lily Langtry's leading man in *The Crossways* (1902), a play the two stars had written in collaboration. Miss Taylor and Manners were married in 1911. To Manners she has given much credit for her mastery of the technique of acting, Manners having been a director as well as a playwright.

Miss Taylor's first substantial success came as Rose Lane in *Alias Jimmy Valentine* (1910), a play adapted by Paul Armstrong from an O. Henry story. Although the distinguished H. B. Warner played the title role it was Miss Taylor who received the greater praise from the critics. Following a year's run in New York and on the road the star appeared in the short-lived *The Seven Sisters* (1911), a play translated from the Hungarian. Another major success for the actress was as Princess Luana, a Madame Butterfly type of role, in Richard Walton Tully's *The Bird of Paradise* (1912). The high point of this part of her career, which might be called the soubrette or ingenue period, was reached in Manners' *Peg o' My Heart,*

Lucas-Pritchard

LAURETTE TAYLOR

which Miss Taylor called her husband's wedding gift. It won her international stardom and made them both financially independent.

Opening on Broadway in December 1912, the play broke all records by playing 603 performances. After a successful road tour Miss Taylor made her London debut in 1914 as Peg, the Irish-American colleen from Brooklyn. "The most delightful actress America has sent us" in "the most delicious play of all the ages," were comments in enthusiastic reviews which greeted the star and play. It became one of the fourteen plays in London's theater history to run more than 700 performances, and there were successful revivals in 1916, 1918, and 1920. There was, however, some unfavorable criticism of the play: One critic pronounced it "stilted and, when Miss Taylor is not on the stage, a ridiculous play."

Although Miss Taylor appeared in ten or more of the twenty-two plays written by her husband, none ever approached the popularity achieved by *Peg*. Among the more important of these was *The Harp of Life* (1916) which, with Lynn Fontanne [41] and Philip Merivale in supporting roles, played 136 performances on Broadway. *Happiness* (1917), developed by Manners from a one-act play of the same title, caused Charles Collins (Chicago *Evening Post*) to announce in a valedictory to Miss Taylor at the end of her Chicago run that he had been converted from a "hardened dramatic reviewer into an idolater." Capable of "the most poignant tragic acting . . . she is the most interesting creature that now walks on the American stage."

It was in Manners' *One Night in Rome* (1919) that the star played her first serious role. Burns Mantle [44] hailed the play as the best of Manners' works and Miss Taylor's acting the most satisfying of her career. *The National Anthem* (1922) won from Alexander Woollcott [41] the tribute of being good, direct, vigorous drama brilliantly played by Miss Taylor. George Jean Nathan [45], on the other

TAYLOR, LAURETTE—*Continued*

hand, was of the opinion that Manners' contribution to the success of his plays was negligible—that it was Miss Taylor's talent that invested them with those qualities that made them distinguished. Other memorable performances of the actress' career include Sarah Kantor in Fannie Hurst's *Humoresque* (1923), Young Pierrot in *Pierrot and the Prodigal* (1925), and Rose Trelawny in *Trelawny of the Wells* (1925).

A vulnerable spot in the star's career proved to be Shakespeare. At a matinee in April 1918 she appeared with a distinguished cast in leading scenes from *Romeo and Juliet, The Taming of the Shrew,* and *The Merchant of Venice.* The consensus of the critics was that Miss Taylor's Katharine was "vulgar," her Juliet "too coquettish," and her Portia "too prosaic." In the New York *World,* in reply to her critics, she protested "against inclosing Shakespearean characters in rigid molds of precedent, to which all interpreters are supposed to adjust themselves." Her interpretations, she said, had been "modern." "If you are to make a family Bible of Shakespeare," she continued, "do so by all means. But put him on the parlor table and don't put him on the stage."

The death of Manners in 1928 ended a marriage which had been called "a perfect union." After twenty-five years of uninterrupted activity in the theater, she retired and did not appear again for four years. Then her revival of two of Sir James Barrie's plays, a condensed version of *Alice Sit-by-the-Fire,* and his one-act *The Old Lady Shows Her Medals,* won hosannas from the critics. Her transition, on the same evening's bill, from the cultured young mother of *Alice* to the elderly Cockney charwoman in *The Old Lady* was made "with the ease that stamps one who loves her art. She is superb in both roles," Benjamin De Casseres wrote. She repeated the bill thirty-two times on Broadway before she again went into retirement, although in 1934 she appeared in a tryout of a play from her own pen, *At Marian's,* in the Ogunquit, Maine, summer theater, and in 1938 she played on the straw-hat circuit in *Tomorrow's Sunday, Mary, Mary, Quite Contrary,* and *Candida.*

In December 1938 Miss Taylor returned to Broadway as the "charlady" in a revival of Sutton Vane's *Outward Bound.* As excellent as Beryl Mercer's interpretation of that role had been in the original production, "it did not equal Miss Taylor's, which in subtlety, pathos, and power has rarely been equaled on any stage."

Notwithstanding the high praise given her, the star did not return to Broadway for four more years. There were offers from producers but most of the parts, says the actress, "were terrible old hags." When she read Tennessee Williams' *The Glass Menagerie* she knew Amanda was the part for her. "One of the ways I judge a play," said Miss Taylor in an interview, "is whether I can see things about the people in it that aren't in the lines—bits of their lives. . . .If I can, I know the play has substance. I learned that from Hartley." In *The Glass Menagerie,* which has been called a character sketch without much plot, Miss Taylor plays a shabby-genteel Southerner whose anxiety to marry off her crippled daughter (played by Julie Haydon) and set right her discontented son (played by Eddie Dowling) leads her to nag them both incessantly. Burton Rascoe called them three "creatures caught in the most ordinary but most terrible of tragedies—that of trying to live when they have no sensible reason for living," and described Miss Taylor's Amanda as "a simple, sanely insane, horrible mother, pathetic and terribly human and terribly real. She succeeded in destroying every vestige of hope and beauty and joy in the lives of the two people who loved her, her son and her daughter." Laurette Taylor herself sees the matter differently: "She nags her children, but it's because she wants to pull them out of their poverty. She loves them. For them she has strength and tenacity. And I don't believe our play ends as unhappily as some people tell you it does. Why, with a mother like Amanda that daughter is going to get a chance in life somehow. By hook or by crook, Amanda will see to it. Besides, the girl has found that she can dance and she's been kissed. She's lovely. She'll dance and be kissed again."

When the play opened in Chicago on Christmas Eve 1944, the critics were enthusiastic, but the public stayed away for several weeks. Finally, however, the critics succeeded in "hypoing" public interest and *The Glass Menagerie* was still playing to crowded houses when producer Eddie Dowling decided to bring it to New York in time to become a candidate for the Pulitzer and Drama Critics awards. Tennessee Williams won the Critics Award on a divided vote, whereas the vote for Miss Taylor was unanimous. Several of the reviewers agreed that "without the magnificent art of Laurette Taylor it might not seem the marvelous and memorable play that it is."

During the heyday of her fame and celebrity the star is said never to have forgotten friends of humbler days. At every social event given by her and Manners the numerous Cooney clan was not only well represented but "well up in front" at the gathering. Her charm and vivid imagination are said to be distinctly Celtic. She is titian-haired, with "eyes like brown pansies," a figure more rounded than in her younger days but still "on the good side" for her five feet five inches. As of 1945, she has never acted before the camera, and her only appearance on the radio was a memorial program honoring President Roosevelt '42. Her chief interest, other than the stage, is in writing. Her play *Enchantment,* which came near production in 1933, has been revised, and Billy Rose '40, on George Jean Nathan's recommendation, is considering it. In July 1945 Miss Taylor finished another play, *Fun With Stella,* as well as the draft of a book, to be called "Stars That Have Crossed Mine," a book "more about people I've met than about me," Miss Taylor said in an interview. To this she added, "If I can prove to be a successful writer I'm not going to act any more."

References

N Y Times II p1 Mr 25 '45
Who's Who in the Theatre, 1939

TEMPLE, SHIRLEY Apr. 23, 1928- Motion picture actress

Address: b. c/o David O. Selznick Productions, Culver City, Calif.; h. 227 N. Rockingham Rd., Brentwood Hts., Calif.

A star at five, a leading box-office money-maker at seven, a retired millionaire at twelve, "professionally reborn at seventeen"—such is the record of Shirley Temple, America's most famous child actress.

Shirley Jane Temple was born in Santa Monica, California, on Shakespeare's birthday, April 23—the year was 1928, not 1929 as Twentieth Century-Fox's original publicity stated. Her parents were bank clerk (later bank manager and business counselor) George Francis Temple, a native of Pennsylvania and a resident of California since 1903, and Chicagoan Gertrude (Creiger) Temple. Shirley was the third child—the Temples already had two half-grown sons. "She looked like a little dancer, even as a baby," Mrs. Temple reminisces. When Shirley began to walk at the age of one, she walked on her toes, Mrs Temple says. "From the time she took her first step, she ran on her toes, as if she were dancing." But dancing lessons, the fulfillment of Gertrude Temple's hope that her daughter could have the instruction she herself had been denied, were merely a part of Shirley's general education, and began in 1932 when she was about four. Hollywood, although only ten miles from Santa Monica, was then far from her parent's thoughts.

Hollywood, specifically Educational Pictures, was well aware, however, of the possibility of latent talent in dancing school children, and in 1932 sent director Charles Lamont to Shirley's neighborhood school as a talent scout. The official account of Shirley's first encounter with the movies states merely that the reluctant Mrs. Temple was persuaded to let her four-year-old daughter perform for Lamont, that Shirley did what she was told, and that Lamont, in due course, selected her along with several other children for a screen test. Shirley's story is that she hid under the piano at Lamont's approach. "He stood around for a while watching," she says, "and then he said, 'I'll take the one under the piano.'" Somewhat skeptical about a movie career for their daughter, George and Gertrude Temple were scarcely pleased when the company telephoned three days later, but finally agreed to a screen test to see how Shirley would photograph. The pictures to be made were *Baby Burlesk* short subjects intended to satirize important feature films. Because the first of these, *War Babies,* was a comic miniature edition of *What Price Glory,* the first words Shirley uttered before the cameras were in French. "Oui, mon cher," she spoke into the microphone overhead before she answered Lamont's questions about her pets and dolls and the little playhouse in the backyard—while, unobserved, the cameras were recording the scene.

In the next twelve months Shirley played in seven of these one-reelers, earning approximately three hundred dollars. A few bit parts in full-length pictures, such as *Red-haired Alibi* and *Out all Night,* also came her

Columbia Pictures

SHIRLEY TEMPLE

way, and Zasu Pitts, then at the height of her career, prophesied a shining future for the budding star. In the spring of 1933, however, the studio terminated the *Baby Burlesk* series because the children were growing too large. (Shirley herself was nearly forty inches tall, four inches taller than the desired thirty-six.) When Educational Pictures asked for Shirley's services again at the end of the summer, Shirley joined the cast of the two-reel *Frolics of Youth.* Meanwhile, Mrs. Temple also took Shirley to answer the Fox call for several children to do a singing and dancing number in George White's *Scandals.* While nothing ever came of this studio idea, the interview served to introduce Shirley to assistant director Leo Houck of Fox, who already had his eye on the child, and who was to give Shirley her chance. It was at a preview of the second of the *Frolics of Youth* that Houck introduced the Temples to Jay Gorney, the song writer, who was seeking a child to play the part of James Dunn's daughter in the Will Rogers-Vincent Sheean '41 musical *Stand Up and Cheer.* Shirley was taken to Lew Brown, the discoverer of Jackie Coogan, auditioned, and signed for the part.

Filmed in early 1934, *Stand Up and Cheer* provided Shirley with the "Baby, Take a Bow" song-and-dance sequence which, in the opinion of exhibitors, at once established her as "a full-fledged star in her own right." "She's stolen the picture," it is reported that Vincent Sheean had shouted at the preview. And back in his office a short while later he is said to have told Shirley: "You're going to be the most loved little girl in the whole world." But stardom did not come overnight for the child. Fox gave her small roles in two now forgotten pictures, *Now I'll Tell* and *Change of Heart,* released almost simultaneously with *Stand Up and Cheer* in 1934. They next loaned her to Paramount for *Little Miss Marker,* in which she was hailed as "sensational," featured her in *Baby, Take a Bow,*

TEMPLE, SHIRLEY—*Continued*

and then reloaned her to Paramount for *Now and Forever,* with Carole Lombard and Gary Cooper '41. Before the end of the year, however, *Bright Eyes* had made Shirley—now given star billing by Fox—a box-office favorite, and the Academy of Motion Picture Arts and Sciences Award banquet had seen her honored with a special "Oscar" as "the outstanding personality of 1934."

From 1934 through 1939, Shirley Temple remained at the top in box-office appeal—singing and matching Bill Robinson '41 tap for tap in *Dimples* and *Rebecca of Sunnybrook Farm;* singing again in *Curly Top* and *Poor Little Rich Girl;* and interpreting story-book characters in *The Little Colonel, The Littlest Rebel,* and *Heidi.* In Kipling's story *Wee Willie Winkie* became a girl so that Shirley could play the role. Her popularity was world-wide; in South America she was known as "Ricito de Oro", "Golden Curls." Thousands of fans wrote to her each day. Her salary rose from one hundred and fifty dollars a week to several thousand; for the year 1937 it came to $307,014, the seventh highest income in the country; and she is said to have made more than fifteen times as much from "by-products" like Shirley Temple dolls, advertising, and so forth, as from her acting.

The public and experts alike sought the formula for her phenomenal success. Was it genius? On the Pintner-Cunningham intelligence test—on which an IQ of above 135 is rated "genius"—Shirley had scored 155. Lionel Barrymore '43 characterized her work in *The Little Colonel* as a reasoned rather than imitative performance, and Jack Donahue, her dance director, found himself teaching a little girl who learned dance steps "by ear" without looking at his feet and remembered them for weeks after rehearsals had ended. Was it acting ability? She was "one-take Temple," the child who always knew her own lines perfectly and frequently those of the rest of the cast as well. Amazed at her knowledge of acting technique, Adolphe Menjou had called her an "Ethel Barrymore '41 at four" after the first day's shooting of *Little Miss Marker.* Lyle Talbot, describing a scene in *Our Little Girl,* in which Shirley screams at him, "I hate you!" recalled: "There was something heartbreaking in the emotion she displayed—half rage, half childish dismay. She made the scene so real with her little eyes flashing and her baby's voice breaking with rage, that the entire troupe was impressed, and very quiet, when the scene was finished." In *Captain January,* when the script called for her to tap dance down a forty-five-foot lighthouse stairway, delivering a line at each turn of the stairs, Shirley, to everyone's astonishment, did it the first time with perfect timing. Was it personality? From the time that James Dunn, who played with her in four pictures, credited Shirley with a new influence for good in his life, all who knew her pointed out the readily flashing smile, the alertness and responsiveness, which set apart the little girl. However, like other children, she made mudpies, raced her tricycle, listened to *Gang Busters,* and sent in her boxtops for make-believe detective badges.

But work before the cameras—more play than work to Shirley—consumed no more than three hours a day, in accordance with California laws. Three more hours constituted Shirley's school day, dictated by these same regulations and provided for in Shirley's contract. While the Los Angeles Board of Education supplied the books, supervised the curriculum, and assigned the teacher, Twentieth Century-Fox paid the teacher and furnished the schoolhouse. "School" was held in Shirley's bungalow on the studio lot or in a trailer schoolhouse which followed Shirley for the day, the teacher clocking her in and out to make certain that she received her full three hours of instruction daily. Such irregular lessons did not trouble Shirley, however, declared her teacher, who had been authorized by the Child Labor Board to halt production if Shirley's welfare were endangered. "Shirley possesses marvelous powers of concentration," she said. "She throws herself into a scene for all she's worth, then instantly centers upon her studies the moment she sits down at her table." She learned about China when making *Stowaway* and about India while acting in *Wee Willie Winkie,* and picked up part of her arithmetic as she operated the cash register of a make-believe grocery store. French by the conversational method, dancing, and piano were also part of her education. At night there were the next day's lines to be learned with her mother—who was paid a reported several hundred a week by the studio to be Shirley's private director and coach and who has generally been considered responsible for Shirley's screen success.

The first sign that Little Miss Marker was growing up came in 1938, when Shirley made *Rebecca of Sunnybrook Farm*—her mass of curls was parted and tied back. Although her name still made headlines when that spring she crossed the country on a vacation trip, thereafter both her publicity and her box-office drawing power began gradually to decline. Partially withdrawn from pictures in 1939 in order to have the companionship of other girls at a nonprofessional school, Shirley scored only minor successes in her next films. Then, in 1940 *The Blue Bird,* based on the Maeterlinck fantasy, failed to make a profit, and the studio, as Jack Oakie put it, gave "the kid who had coined millions for the industry . . . a chill to go down in movie history." Fox maintained that Shirley had merely lost her appeal, but Mrs. Temple blamed the unvarying Cinderella themes of the Temple vehicles, and in 1940, after *Young People* had been filmed, bought Shirley's release from the remainder of her contract. Eight months later schoolgirl Shirley was again under contract—this time to MGM. After making *Kathleen* on loan to Edward Small in 1941 and *Miss Annie Rooney* for her new home studio in 1942, and starring on a radio program series, Shirley again retired—to emerge in 1944 under the aegis of David O. Selznick '41. But *Since You Went Away,* with Claudette Colbert '45 and Jennifer Jones '44, and *I'll Be Seeing You,* with Ginger Rogers '41 and Joseph Cotten '43, afforded the former child actress only minor roles, which were not considered an index to her capabilities.

(She did, however, receive two citations for her work on the former film.)

A real test of her ability was left for *Kiss and Tell*, Shirley's first starring vehicle in three years and a comedy in which Hollywood previewers hailed her as Selznick's biggest potential money-maker. Reviewers were enthusiastic about the picture. Wrote Bosley Crowther in the New York *Times*: "You've got to hand it to Miss Temple—she's superb in the leading role, a compound of girlish innocence and female perversity. The leap from her former saccharine didoes into this mildly terrifying 'teen-age' role is one that required uncommon talent. The lady has got it—plus looks." "Miss Temple is quite extraordinary," was Howard Barnes's comment in the New York *Herald Tribune*. "She is as aware as she is adult in a new phase of acting." Shirley Temple's next role will be in *Suddenly It's Spring,* opposite Joseph Cotton.

Besides her film and school work, Shirley Temple found time to prepare her autobiography. It was published in October 1945 under the title *My Young Life*. On the whole, reviews were favorable: The Chicago *Sun*'s *Book Week* observed that "there is much of the pertness and sureness of the Temple personality in the story and several of those chuckles and humorous touches that put the 'Baby Bernhardt' ahead of all rival screen moppets." A reviewer in the New York *Herald Tribune* pointed out that "her personal comment is friendly and commendably untemperamental, and her language a happy medium between adult English and that widely used by her generation."

The Shirley Temple who was graduated from the Westlake School for Girls on June 13, 1945, and who on September 19, 1945, was married to Sergeant John Agar, Jr., of the Army Air Forces, son of the late Chicago packer, has been described as "just like the girl next door—provided, of course, you live in heaven." At the New York *Herald Tribune* Forum in 1945, she said that she regards motion pictures as "the biggest single factor in shaping young minds" and considers them a potent force for the spread of democratic concepts in former Axis nations. They teach by example, she has also said, and have made history, geography and even the absorption of moral concepts an interesting and exciting experience. Motion pictures, Miss Temple predicted, will largely replace books in future educational programs, and particularly fairy tales usually read by young children. She considers her years in the studios as having given her an object lesson in democracy in the give and take of picture-making. Now a slim five-foot-three with reddish-gold hair, brown-eyed Miss Temple enjoys horseback riding, badminton and swimming, and calls herself a born collector—of autographs, knickknacks, and the dresses from her baby pictures.

References

Am Mag 119:26+ F '35 pors
Look 9:81 Ag 21 '45 pors
Sat Eve Post 211:10+ Jl 9 '38 pors
Time 27:36+ Ap 27 '36 pors

American Women, 1939-40
International Motion Picture Almanac, 1943-44
Temple, S. My Young Life (1945)
Who's Who in America, 1944-45

TENNANT, WILLIAM GEORGE Jan. 2, 1890- British naval officer
Address: b. c/o The Admiralty, London; h. The Eades, Upton-on-Severn, Worcestershire, England

Until June 1944, in the fifth year of the Second World War, the Americans and British had been coping with the herculean task of transporting and landing the huge tonnage of equipment necessary for fighting a modern war of machines on foreign shores. Not until they planned for the invasion of the Continent, however, did they face their greatest test. To meet the stupendous problem of disembarking men and gigantic stores of material on the beaches of Normandy with a maximum of speed, American and British engineers and technicians conceived the ingenious idea of fabricating harbors—constructed in sections—which they could tow across the Channel and set up on the French coast. One of the experts responsible for this feat was Vice-Admiral William George Tennant, a navigation specialist who helped in the planning and was in operational control of the undertaking.

William George Tennant was born January 2, 1890, the son of Lieutenant Colonel E. W. Tennant of Upton-on-Severn, Worcestershire. At the age of fifteen young William became a midshipman on the training ship *Britannia,* and after completing the required five years of professional and general education he received his commission as a sub-officer in the British Royal Navy. As a lieutenant of twenty-three he later entered Portsmouth to take advanced courses in navigation. Upon completion of this two-year course he was posted for duty in the Dardanelles as navigation officer in H.M.S. *Chatham.* Shortly afterward, while serving in the cruiser *Nottingham,* the young officer participated in the most important naval engagement of the First World War, the 1916 Battle of Jutland that destroyed the German threat to British naval superiority. The cruiser survived this battle, in which England suffered great material losses, but three months later she was torpedoed by a German U-boat in the North Sea while Tennant was still aboard.

For the next decade Tennant served in several battle cruisers, including the famed *Renown* and her sister ship, the *Repulse,* which he was to command in the Second World War. In 1925 the thirty-five-year-old officer was promoted to the rank of commander, and in 1932, having completed the two-year course at the Staff College, Greenwich, he was given his captaincy. After a year's course (1934-35) at the Imperial Defence College, Tennant was placed in command, as flag captain and chief staff officer, of the new cruiser *Arethusa,* a ship in the Third Cruiser Squadron. Transferred to shore duty in 1937, he was next an instructor for two years at the Imperial Defence College.

At the outset of the war in Europe in 1939 Captain Tennant was at the Admiralty, serving as chief staff officer to the First Sea Lord, the

British Official Photo.

VICE-ADM. WILLIAM GEORGE TENNANT

late Admiral Sir Dudley Pound '41. Less than
a year later he was participating in the Dunkerque evacuation, as beachmaster. On May
26, 1940, he had been sent to Dover, with two
hundred officers and ratings, to take part in
what was then called "Operation Dynamo." On
the order of Vice-Admiral Ramsay '44, Tennant
and his party had proceeded to Dunkerque, under heavy fire, to investigate possible areas of
embarkation from a coast known for its treacherous shoals. Tennant had reported back that
a narrow mole or breakwater running out from
the harbor could be used for removing the
troops, and on this report evacuation plans were
organized.

As senior staff officer ashore Tennant worked
with his men on the beach throughout the subsequent operations, directing the evacuation under a rain of German bombs. Dunkerque was
a defeat for the Allies, but it has been considered one of the most efficiently executed
operations of its kind. On June 6 Captain
Tennant was created a Companion of the Bath,
"for good services in organizing the withdrawal
to England, under fire and in the face of many
and great difficulties, officers and men of the
Allied armies . . . between May 27 and June 4."

Shortly afterward, Tennant was put in command of the 32,000-ton battle cruiser, the *Repulse*, and he commanded her until that fateful
day in December 1941 when she was sunk in
the South China Sea by Japanese torpedo planes
and dive bombers—in the first action the ship
had seen since the start of the war. Cecil
Brown '42, the American correspondent, was
aboard the *Repulse* at the time of the sinking,
and he has written a full and graphic account
of it in his book *Suez to Singapore* (1942).
The cruiser, accompanied by what Tennant
called the more "glamorous" *Prince of Wales*
and by four destroyers, had left Singapore December 8—before the radio had brought word
of the attack on Pearl Harbor—on a four-day
assignment. "We are off to look for trouble,"
wrote Tennant to the ship's company. "I expect we shall find it. . . .We are going to

carry out a sweep to the northward to see what
we can pick up and what we can roar up. We
must all be on our toes."

On the morning of December 10 they found
the "trouble." A Japanese landing on the Malayan coast, a hundred and fifty miles north of
Singapore, had been sighted, and, although
already spotted themselves by enemy reconnaissance, the small British force had turned
westward to encounter the Japanese ships.
Shortly before noon the attack came—from
enemy aircraft—and in a little over an hour
both the *Prince of Wales* and the *Repulse* were
sinking, hit by torpedo bombs. Almost at the
end, Brown reports, the officers and men of
the bridge were forced to push Captain Tennant into the sea because he refused to leave
his ship of his own volition. The men of the
two ships were rescued, after a short period in
the water, by the destroyers which had escaped
destruction, and taken back to Singapore.

Two months after this action, in February
1942, Tennant was promoted to rear admiral
and placed in command of a cruiser squadron
in the Eastern Fleet. (In April Admiral Sir
James Somerville '43 was named commander of
this fleet.) This was an important assignment for Tennant, in the face of the continued
strength of the Japanese in the Pacific, and,
indeed, the next two years were to be difficult
ones for the Allies. Striking down from Thailand, the Japanese slashed through Malaya, captured Singapore that February, pressed on
through Burma; farther East they took Java
and Sumatra in the late winter and spring.
That April the Admiralty announced that during the first part of the month England had
suffered serious losses in the Bay of Bengal
off the coast of Ceylon, when Japanese carrier
planes had sunk two cruisers and an aircraft
carrier. In addition, nearly all the torpedo
planes, fighters, and bombers engaged in an
attack on Japanese ships off the naval base of
Trincomalee had been shot down or damaged.

With the Japanese now supreme in the Indian Ocean, the British, in order to forestall
an attack from Ceylon on Madagascar, in May
seized Diégo-Suarez, the naval base on the
French island off the coast of eastern Africa.
(The British forces were led by General
Francis W. Festing '45.) The Germans made
advantageous use of the areas left under the
control of the Vichy Government, however, and
this prompted the British later in the year to
send Admiral Tennant, as joint commander
with General Robert Grice Sturges, to effect a
second invasion of Madagascar. Part of the
troops disembarked on the west coast of the
island and worked their way inland, while another column advanced south from the British-
held region of Diégo-Suarez. The campaign
was successfully completed in less than two
months, and Admiral Somerville has paid tribute to Tennant for his skill in conducting the
operations.

By the end of 1943, with the Allied invasion
of Europe in the offing, Tennant was recalled
from his sea command (from January to November he had been second-in-command of the
Eastern Fleet under Somerville), and was made
responsible for the operational control of prefabricated harbors, to be used in the imminent
landings on the Continent in June 1944. The
scheme had been decided on by the British and
American commanders at a meeting in London

in June 1943, and approved at the Quebec conference. Later detailed proposals had been submitted to the Combined Chiefs of Staff in Washington in September, and in November, with the blueprints completed, Tennant had been put on the job.

The fabricated harbors each consisted of several components: the "mulberry," of British design and the most impressive portion of the harbor, was a three-thousand-foot floating bridge; the "phoenixes" were the breakwater sections; and the "lobnitz" piers were the floating piers which were raised on giant steel columns or stilts. In addition, there were thousands of feet of floating bridges. In its entirety, the harbor gave the impression of a "vast walled city floating on the water." About one hundred and fifty "phoenixes," twenty "lobnitz" piers, and twenty thousand feet of floating bridge were towed across the Channel for two ports—one built by the Americans and one by the British—and assembled on the French coast. The wharf of the British prefabricated harbor on the Normandy coast consisted of seven "spud pierheads" or steel pontoons, displacing a thousand tons. Each pierhead was a complete "ship," with crew quarters and pier roadways leading to the shore.

At Admiral Tennant's suggestion, blockships were sunk off the beaches to provide immediate shelter in the unlikely event of a northerly gale's springing up during operations. General Dwight Eisenhower '42 had had the choice of two dates from which to chose the day of the Normandy invasion, the weather expert having offered June 6 or June 19. The date the General chose is now history, but the invasion might have been an historic disaster if Eisenhower had decided on the latter. The worst storm in eighty years struck the Channel in the afternoon of the nineteenth and raged for three days. Although the towing job was over by then, the storm cost the Allies five days, during which time they could not unload any supplies.

The British harbor during this time was protected by a shoal and thus remained intact, although damaged in part by some five hundred landing craft and small boats, "which tossed like chips and bounced into wreckage on the steel structure and the beachheads." The American harbor, less sheltered from the gale, was largely destroyed. It was decided, therefore, to repair the British port with some of the salvaged parts from the American-made one, and to extend, strengthen, and double-bank the American blockship breakwater so that it could be used as a shallow-water harbor. At these two ports were deposited many thousands of tons of stores upon the French shore.

Five months after the invasion Tennant said, "They have done their job. One day now, along will come a normal winter gale, and that will be the end of it all." In November Tennant became naval commander in the Levant, with acting rank of vice-admiral.

Tall and thin, with graying hair, Admiral Tennant, according to Cecil Brown, has "an open pleasant face, pinkish, smooth skin with wrinkles around the eyes." In 1919 he was married to Catherine Blount, the daughter of a British Army officer.

Reference

Who's Who, 1945

TERBOVEN, JOSEF (tĕr-bō'vĕn yō'zĕf) May 23, 1898—May 11, 1945 Reich Commissioner for Norway since 1940; committed suicide to escape capture by the Allies. See *Current Biography* 1941 Yearbook.

Obituary

N Y Times p5 My 12 '45

TEYTE, MAGGIE (tāt) Apr. 17, 1889- Concert singer

Address: b. c/o Austin Wilder, 745 Fifth Ave., New York City

Setting a record by having two concerts sold out within hours of their announcement, English lyric soprano Maggie Teyte, the first European artist to visit the United States since V-E day, took New York musical circles by storm on October 31, 1945, in a welcome which one reviewer irreverently compared to a Sinatra reception. Miss Teyte, who is considered the foremost living interpreter of modern French songs, was making her first appearance in New York since the early 1920's.

Maggie Teyte was born Margaret Tate on April 17, 1889, near Wolverhampton, Staffordshire, England. Of English-Irish-Scotch extraction, she is the daughter of a hotel owner, an amateur pianist; and her mother was a singer. Miss Teyte received her formal education at St. Joseph's Convent in Wolverhampton, where she had what she calls the usual training. She does not remember when she first began to sing, but at the age of twelve it was recognized that her voice was of unusual quality, and her parents decided to send her to the Royal College of Music. Although Sir Hubert Parry at first refused to accept the application because of her extreme youth, the talented young singer was finally admitted to the college, where she studied piano and voice until she was fourteen. Then in 1903, notes *Opera News*, when she sang Tosti's "Goodbye" at a church fete in London, she so impressed Walter Rubens, a musical patron in the audience, that he raised a purse among his friends to send the girl to study with Jean de Reszke, the noted Metropolitan tenor who in 1902 had settled as a teacher in Paris. At the audition De Reszke predicted a brilliant career for Miss Teyte and immediately took her under his wing. It was at his suggestion, too, that she changed the spelling of her name at her debut so that French audiences might have no difficulty with its pronunciation.

The musical foundation which in 1945 still causes critics to marvel at her voice, Miss Teyte says she owes solely to De Reszke. "I studied voice production only with De Reszke," she told Noel Straus of the New York *Times* in 1945, "and I form my tones today according to the identical precepts of his that I followed at my debut. He had a real method of his own, taken from many sources and singularly free from complications. It was based on a dozen exercises, every one for a special purpose, which covered every phase of vocalism. One exercise, which I practiced daily, afforded complete mastery of pianissimo singing and consisted of a passage from the Queen's aria from the last act of Verdi's *Don Carlos*. Another exercise enabled me to sing Brünnhilde's 'Ho-yo-to-ho,' from *Die Walküre*, like a dramatic

MAGGIE TEYTE

soprano, though I knew I would never use music of that type in public." Special stress was laid on Mozart by De Reszke, and by Reynaldo Hahn, Venezuelan-French composer and conductor who coached her in dramatic routine, but she also had to learn every important coloratura aria in the operatic repertory.

Miss Teyte made her first public appearance at the age of seventeen as Zerlina in a concert version of *Don Giovanni* given at a Mozart festival in Paris under Reynaldo Hahn's direction. She next appeared with Paderewski at a concert in Monte Carlo. In February 1907, with the Monte Carlo Opera Company, she made her official debut, again as Zerlina, under the direction of Hahn. Two years, during which she sang minor roles, followed at the Opéra Comique, until on June 12, 1908, she excited Paris with her interpretation of Mélisande in Debussy's *Pelléas et Mélisande*, a role which Marguerite Carré had insisted Miss Teyte take when Mary Garden left for the United States. Of this performance the critic of the Paris *Temps* wrote: "Miss Maggie Teyte took it upon herself to teach them that youth, grace, a pure and supple voice of a soft and melodious timbre, could accomplish wonders. . . .She added to Maeterlinck's drama an entirely new charm, and enriched the poetry of Debussy's music with her loving and tender touch." (Miss Teyte sang the role seventeen times that season.)

For the role of Mélisande Miss Teyte had been prepared by nine months of instruction with the composer himself. An audition with Debussy had been requested for her by De Reszke, and the story of the little girl in pigtails whom Debussy refused to identify with Miss Maggie Teyte until he had heard her sing is famous. She worked with Debussy on both the opera and his songs three hours each day. "No other song composer," Miss Teyte is quoted by Noel Straus on Debussy's methods, "has marked his lyrics with so many definite and detailed indications of his intentions, and he insisted that one and all of them be meti-

culously heeded. Every note had to be given its exact time-duration, even in measures that in other composers might be considered rhythmically rather free. And each slightest stress and other marking had to be positively observed, in order to bring out the true colors of the text."

Miss Teyte made her London debut in October 1909 at a concert in Queen's Hall. She made her first appearance on the London operatic stage with the Beecham [41] Opera Company at His Majesty's Theatre on May 25, 1910, singing Melka in *Muguette*; and in that season she also appeared in *Hansel and Gretel*, as Antonia in *Tales of Hoffmann*, as Blonda in *Il Seraglio* and as Cherubino in *The Marriage of Figaro*. In October of the same year, with the same company, she appeared as Nuri in *Tiefland*, Marguerite in *Faust*, Zerlina in *Don Giovanni* and Mélisande in *Pelléas et Mélisande*. The following year she went to the United States, making her American debut as Cherubino with the Chicago-Philadelphia Opera Company on November 4, 1911, at the Philadelphia Metropolitan Opera House. Two days later, opposite Mary Garden as Prince Charming, she created the role of Cinderella at the American première of Massenet's *Cendrillon*. Other roles with the Chicago-Philadelphia Opera Company during her first American season, were Marguerite and Antonia, Lygia in *Quo Vadis*, Dot in *Cricket on the Hearth*, Mignon, and Mimi in *La Boheme*. On November 16, 1911, she gave her first song recital in New York at Carnegie Hall, and on February 20, 1912, she made her only appearance on the stage of the Metropolitan Opera House in New York in *Cendrillon* under the sponsorship of the Chicago-Philadelphia management.

In the summer of 1913 Miss Teyte toured England and the Riviera, returning in October 1913 to the United States for her third American season in Chicago and Philadelphia. And after March 1914 she again toured England, this time with the Czech violinist and composer Jan Kubelik. She joined the Boston National Grand Opera Company in 1915, remaining with the organization for the next two years and participating in its summer engagement in Paris. In 1917 she began an extensive two-year concert and recital tour of the United States which ended when she returned to England to take leading roles in operetta. At the Prince's Theatre, London, on April 19, 1919, the young singer created the role of Lady Mary Carlisle in the première of *Monsieur Beaucaire*. The operetta had a six months' engagement and was followed by Miss Teyte's appearance for another six months' run, beginning in December 1920, as Princess Julia in Emerich Kalman's *A Little Dutch Girl* at the Lyric Theatre.

As a leading operatic soprano Miss Teyte had been warmly applauded by the critics. As Mimi, said *Musical America*, she "gave a truly touching and absolutely convincing portrayal of that attractive and very unfortunate heroine. She looks the part, dresses the part, and acts the part. . . .It should be added also that Miss Teyte sang the role and did so with plenitude and sweet quality of tone, modulated at all times to the appropriate emotional aspects, and directed invariably by exquisite taste and deep sense of artistic proportions." Her Marguerite, wrote A. Scheinfeld of Milwaukee, "is one of appealing beauty and wistfulness. She sang the role in a voice of peculiar beauty, responding easily to its demands, and invested it with a simplicity, a gentleness and truth, wholly devoid of apparent stage craft." In *Mignon*, wrote the Philadelphia *Public Ledger* reviewer, "Miss Teyte clearly apprehended the distinctive characteristics of Goethe's heroine, her passionate fervor, her wayward, impetuous impulsiveness, her capacity for a self-sacrificing devotion, and she expressed them with a fine sincerity and an eloquently appealing art."

Miss Teyte's concert work was likewise highly praised. "Her voice," wrote the late Richard Aldrich of the New York *Times*, "is an almost startlingly powerful one to come from a person of her diminutive stature. . . .In its best tones, which are heard in her *mezzo voce*, the voice has real beauty, though it has not great range of color and expressiveness....She is a singer of exceeding intelligence, of fine taste and musical feeling, of a commanding temperament that produces results sometimes unlooked for." To Henry Taylor Parker it was "a distinctly French voice . . . . a very bright voice that has been polished into a kind of dry clearness. . . . It falls on the ear much as the light of a very clear, dry, cool, still autumn day falls on the eye. There are glints in Miss Teyte's tones; they are transparent, prismatic, catching many reflections from the music and the mood of the songs.... It is a voice for connoisseurs." And the *Ohio State Journal*: "With a voice like a thrush, eyes as roguish as a March wind, and a smile like a breath of spring, in her concert in Memorial Hall last night she revealed a singing art that was a delight, supplemented by a personality as winning as can be imagined. This diminutive prima donna sings as if singing were the best fun in the world, and there is a freshness and spontaneity about the way she does it that makes her most captivating."

Her marriage to W. S. Cottingham in 1921 sent Maggie Teyte into semi-retirement for nine years, although in 1923 she returned for a while to grand opera with the British National Opera Company, to sing in *Hansel and Gretel, La Bohème, Madame Butterfly,* and to create the role of the Princess in Holst's *The Perfect Fool* (May 1923 at Covent Garden). Then, in June 1930 she reappeared as Mélisande. In 1932 she toured Australia, established a vocal school in England and joined the British Broadcasting Company as a radio artist. During the Coronation opera season in 1937 she appeared in *Orpheus, Hansel and Gretel, Madame Butterfly* and as Eva in *Die Meistersinger* at Covent Garden, appearing there for the last time as Cio-Cio-San on October 29, 1937. Her favorite roles had been Mélisande, Butterfly, Mimi, Cherubino, and Hansel. During the Second World War she drove ambulances, spent some time in a mechanical school and on the assembly line, and then, forced by an aggravated sinus condition to give up that form of war service, toured army camps throughout England under the auspices of E.N.S.A. and C.E.M.A. (British equivalents of the USO), singing both classic and popular songs.

Miss Teyte is known to the present generation of American music lovers primarily through her recordings of French art songs by Duparc, Chausson, and Fauré, with the pianist Gerald Moore, and especially Debussy, with the pianist Alfred Cortot. Of the Debussy songs she has said: "Though exceedingly *raffiné,* complex and subtle, Debussy was essentially a primitive, one might almost say savage, person. Reticent and a man of few words, he seemed always striving for an unattainable goal with such intensity that he gave the impression of being ill, and like a soul in Purgatory, breathing heavily and never at peace with himself. The widespread notion that Debussy, whose music faithfully reflected his personality, intended his compositions to be projected in a vague, nebulous and primarily atmospheric manner is wide of the mark. A fierce power was basic in his nature. When he played the piano, he infused the accompaniments of his songs with this elemental strength. But it was invariably held in leash. This forcefulness under curb he asked of the singer as well as of the accompanist, and it is a fundamental requirement in the interpretation of his music. His songs demand exceeding warmth of temperament, but ever firmly controlled."

It was with these modern French songs that Maggie Teyte scored a fresh triumph on October 31, 1945, in New York's Town Hall, when after an absence of approximately twenty-five years (which led to the belief that she had died) she returned to America, thus becoming the first European artist to cross the Atlantic since V-E day. Two scheduled recitals (October 31 and December 19, the second later postponed to December 28), her manager reported, were each sold out within one day after their announcement. The audience at the first received her tumultuously, with a welcome, noted *PM*'s Robert A. Hague, beside which "a Sinatra demonstration at the Paramount is a feeble thing indeed." Wrote Jerome W. Bohm, who had attended the concert with misgivings: "Miss Teyte proved beyond dispute that a voice which has been properly produced can be of service even after its owner has passed the prime of life. It was a great pleasure to hear her clearly attacked, firm tones, and her ability to color them to suit the inflection of each and every word of her songs was worthy of great admiration. . . .[She] brought to her interpretations an enkindling imagination, a blending of impassioned musicality and intimate poetic insight which suggested unerringly the widely variegated moods of the songs." Olin Downes[43] found that, "For a lesser artist the evening would have been an unmitigated triumph. For a Maggie Teyte it was something less." But for Robert Bagar "an artist in the great tradition" had returned: "The utterly musical manner of her phrasing, her coloring, her rhythms and rubatos left one a little speechless. . . .Those who believe in music as something to be shared by performer and listener saw last night the ideal exemplification of it. Miss Teyte does not merely sing a song; she lives it, acts it when necessary, breathes movement in it by the potent humanity of her understanding." Her second reception in New York, following a tour of San Francisco, Los Angeles, Portland, and Seattle, in which she received ovations such as are rarely heard, was equally enthusiastic.

Maggie Teyte, who is just over five feet in height, is a "sprightly woman with reddish curly hair and blue eyes," who enjoys motoring, golf,

TEYTE, MAGGIE—*Continued*

tennis, and other out-door sports. She has been married twice, to Eugene Plumon and to W. S. Cottingham, and both marriages were dissolved. For her services to French music she was awarded the Croix de Lorraine by General Charles de Gaulle '[40]. Allene Talmey of *Vogue* found her "a small, quick, witty Englishwoman, with . . . eyebrows that she uses the way the French do their hands. She talks with them. . . .She laughs with a low, crumpled laugh that is not at all soprano. Though her pastel quality, her paleness, her accent are thoroughly English, her crystal chandelier sparkle is pure French." Said the *Opera News* interviewer recently: "The crystalline beauty of Maggie Teyte's recordings, their sublety and restraint should prepare one for the birdlike charm of her personality. But they don't . . . what baffles one is that irrepressible vivacity, the prodigal flow of wit and gaiety, the gestures, the constant *mot juste*. How can a woman past middle life spend herself so generously and still safeguard her classic art? How can a babbling, sparkling brook still keep its depth pellucid?"

References

N Y Times II p4 S 30 '45
Newswk 26:71 S 3 '45
Opera News 10:6-7 N 19 '45
Time 46:60 Jl 23 '45
Baker's Biographical Dictionary of Musicians
Grove's Dictionary of Music and Musicians, Am. suppl. (vol. 6)
Pratt, W. S. ed. The New Encyclopedia of Music and Musicians
Taylor, D. & Russell, K. eds. Music Lovers' Encyclopedia
Thompson, O. ed. International Cyclopedia of Music & Musicians
Who is Who in Music (1941)
Who's Who, 1945
Who's Who in the Theatre (1939)

THACKREY, DOROTHY S(CHIFF)
Mar. 11, 1903- Newspaper publisher

Address: b. 75 West St., New York City; h. 133 E. 64th St., New York City

At the helm of New York City's oldest daily newspaper, the *Post,* is Mrs. Dorothy S. Thackrey, its owner since 1943. One of the few women newspaper publishers in the United States to own a metropolitan paper, she has expanded her interests by acquiring a New York community paper and three radio stations, and by establishing a European edition of her paper in Paris. The publisher has also given much of her time to social welfare and civic work.

A grandchild of Jacob Schiff, philanthropist and founder of the banking house of Kuhn, Loeb and Company, Dorothy Schiff Thackrey is the daughter of Mortimer and Adele A. (Neustadt) Schiff. Born to wealth, in New York City on March 11, 1903, she was educated at the fashionable Brearley School in that city; and she spent much of each year traveling abroad with her mother. In 1920, at the age of seventeen, she entered Bryn Mawr College, but upon the completion of her freshman year, she says, she was told not to

return because her grades were too low. She therefore studied alone, concentrating on history, psychology, horticulture, stenography, and cooking. In 1921 Miss Schiff was introduced to society, and two years later she was married to Richard B. W. Hall, a broker. (Divorced from her husband in 1931, she was married to George Backer; and following a second divorce, she became the wife of Theodore Olin Thackrey in 1943.)

In 1931, following her divorce, Mrs. Thackrey first entered the social service field. As a member of the Social Service Committee of Bellevue Hospital for four years, she gained an insight into the plight of the poor. The work of the committee, says Mrs. Thackrey, "was a sincere attempt to help, but of course it seemed a pretty feeble effort. It seemed to me that what we were doing was simply putting a little salve on the sore; not curing the disease." While in Florida that year, she was told by George Backer (who became her husband) that a lunch club was being formed in New York to provide noon-day meals for girls who were looking for employment. Enthusiastic about the plan, upon her return to New York she became one of the sponsors of the club, which functioned for several years during the thirties.

A stanch Republican, Mrs. Thackrey nevertheless began to question the policies of her party during the years of President Roosevelt's '[42] first term. In early 1936, already a member of such organizations as the Women's City Club, the League of Women Voters, and the Women's Trade Union League, she joined the School of Politics of the Women's National Republican Club to study more closely the tenets of the Republican Party and its criticism of the New Deal and the Roosevelt Administration. After viewing the unemployment situation from both Republican and Democratic angles, she arrived at the conclusion that "the Administration was trying to solve this problem in an honest, sane, American way" through Government intervention.

If she was still undecided as to whether or not to bolt the Republican Party, President Roosevelt's acceptance address—"Rendezvous with Destiny"—which he delivered at the 1936 Democratic National Convention, made the decision for her. Mrs. Thackrey was so impressed with this speech in which Roosevelt assailed the "economic royalists" for "concentrating into their own hands an almost complete control over other people's property, other people's money, other people's labor . . . making free enterprise privileged enterprise" that she immediately enrolled in the Democratic Party and was appointed radio chairman of the women's division of the Democratic State Committee. Commenting on New Deal legislation, she said: "Taxes seem to me to be far less demoralizing than private charities. I am glad to be taxed because it is the least devastating way to meet social needs both for the underprivileged and overprivileged."

Continuing with her social welfare work (in 1934 she had become a member of the Ellis Island Investigating Committee and a director of the board of Mt. Sinai Hospital), in January 1937 Mrs. Thackrey became secretary-treasurer of the New York Joint Committee for the Ratification of the Child Labor

Amendment. Not one to mince words, she said: "Child labor is economically stupid, socially unjust, and morally wrong." Later that year she was appointed by Mayor La Guardia [40] as a member of the Board of Child Welfare, on which she served until 1939. The Board of Child Welfare, before it was absorbed by the Department of Welfare in 1941, provided funds for destitute mothers whose husbands had deserted them or were deceased or disabled. Mrs. Thackrey was chairman of two of the board's committees, Case Policy and Appeal from Clients, and Medical Care.

In June 1939 Mrs. Thackrey bought the New York *Post* from J. David Stern. The *Post* was founded by Alexander Hamilton in 1801. Some of its stands on important issues during the 1800's were: support of the Jacksonian principles, advocacy of labor organizations, support of the abolition of slavery, defense of free trade as opposed to protective tariffs. In the first three decades of the 1900's the paper followed the *laissez faire* policy. But with the advent of the Roosevelt era in 1932 the *Post* "has become a vital organ, frankly progressive and demanding a greater share in the resources and productive machinery of the nation for the benefit of all people and not for a select and fortunate few."

As director, vice-president, and treasurer of the New York *Post* from 1939 to 1942, Mrs. Thackrey took an active part in managing the newspaper's affairs. A newcomer in the journalistic field, she studied every department of the newspaper plant. In 1942 she was elected president and publisher of the *Post* to succeed her husband who resigned because of ill health. On assuming her new post she immediately announced important changes. She appointed Theodore Olin Thackrey, the executive editor, as the *Post's* editor and general manager. Thackrey's wide experience in the newspaper field was seen as a guiding influence in the subsequent development in the paper's editorial and business policies—it was converted to tabloid size, and its price increased from three to five cents. The new tabloid format was not entirely an innovation for the *Post,* since it had been published in that size for a few weeks in 1934 and on Saturdays during the month before Mrs. Thackrey's change. Although the new publisher said she was "a little afraid intellectuals might feel it a vulgarization to present the news in tabloid," she was influenced by the ease with which a tabloid can be handled, especially in crowded subways. (Following her divorce from George Backer the publisher was married to her executive editor in July 1943.)

As the head of the New York *Post,* Mrs. Thackrey stated that the newspaper's most important job "was to help win the war by supporting the Government's policies. However, the paper will not hesitate to criticize that which seems to be detrimental to the public good." She pointed out that the *Post* is an independent paper and that it is not "pro anything" except pro-American, emphasizing that the paper is not an Administration paper and that it "would back a Republican if he would support such things as social legislation." Interested in making the *Post* colorful as well as factual, Mrs. Thackrey said she would increase its number of features and

DOROTHY S. THACKREY

strengthen the woman's page. One of the regular *Post* features, *Ideas on the March,* is an outgrowth of her own busy day. Unable to find the time to read the news in all the important newspapers and magazines, she had her secretary condense the information. Soon her husband realized that such a summary would be appreciated by many *Post* readers. As it exists today, *Ideas on the March* is a digest of editorials and columns which appear in the leading newspapers throughout the United States; it also includes abstracts of radio commentaries on world events. One of its constant readers, it is said, is Eleanor Roosevelt [40].

Although much occupied with the editorial and business policies of the paper, Mrs. Thackrey is also concerned with "inner-organization" relations work. She is greatly interested in her staff and says she derives her greatest satisfaction from giving young people a chance in the field and "watching them grow at their work." She is of the opinion that newspapers should present more of the background reporting of facts because readers are interested in the "whys and wherefores" of a happening. (With the formation of the Post Syndicate in September 1944, several *Post* columnists and cartoonists are now writing for a wider audience). Mrs. Thackrey hopes the newspaper will some day attain the largest circulation in New York City, a goal she says it may reach within ten years. May 1945 Mrs. Thackrey took one step in her expansion plans when she bought the *Home News,* a daily and Sunday paper published in the Bronx borough of New York. Since its founding in 1907, it has been known for its civic spirit. In marking the occasion, Mrs. Thackrey said: "We have admired and respected the high standard of community newspaper service set by the *Home News,* the outstanding community newspaper in America for many years. Our chief interest in assuming the duties and responsibilities of ownership is to make certain the newspaper's service is not impaired, but that its facilities and services shall

THACKREY, DOROTHY S.—*Continued*

continue to expand in the future as in the past with the community itself."

A milestone in the history of the *Post* was the launching of the Paris *Post*, the second American newspaper to be published in the French capital. (Thus far the New York *Herald Tribune*'s Paris edition was alone in the field.) The Paris *Post*, it was announced by *Time*, is "wholly independent of the New York *Post* but voices the same New Dealish views." Its editor is Paul Scott Mowrer, formerly of the foreign staff of the Chicago *Daily News*; and Herbert Pell, former American member of the United Nations War Crimes Commission, is general manager.

Mrs. Thackrey, of the opinion that "there is a wide and hitherto unexplored field of co-operation between radio and newspaper service to the community," bought in July 1944 station WLIB in Brooklyn, New York, for a reported $250,000. News, new features, and discussions of vital topics by known authorities compose about half of the station's program, while the other half is devoted to recorded music programs so diversified as to appeal to listeners of different musical tastes. Postwar plans for this station included added power and the installation of frequency modulation and television. Mrs. Thackrey also owns two radio stations on the West coast—KMTR in Los Angeles and KYA in San Francisco.

The owner of the New York *Post* has backed two successful Broadway plays—*Dead End* and *Abe Lincoln in Illinois*. She was particularly interested in having *Dead End* produced because of the social significance it had for her in the light of an experience she had had. She was living at that time in Beekman Place on the East River (the locale of the play) when her apartment was robbed by street urchins (also an incident in the play). Anxious at first that these boys be caught and punished, after reading the play she felt more kindly toward the delinquents. She has also helped finance the Playwrights Producing Company which in 1945 was composed of four of America's foremost writers—Robert E. Sherwood '40, Maxwell Anderson '42, S. N. Behrman '43 and Elmer Rice '43. Mrs. Thackrey has said of her judgment of plays: "I have average taste, and what pleases me is fairly sure to please a wider public."

An attractive youthful-appearing woman with hazel eyes and dark hair, Dorothy Thackrey is the mother of two grown children—Mortimer Hall, and Adele (Hall) Gray, who in 1944 was married to Lieutenant Arthur Gray, Jr., of the Army Air Forces—and of a younger child Sarah Ann Backer. Outside the office Mrs. Thackrey enjoys trying out the recipes concocted by the *Post* food editor; and in the evening she listens to the radio, particularly to mysteries and political speeches, while she works at her needlepoint. She is described as one of those smokers who can gracefully manipulate a long cigarette holder. "I used to enjoy night-clubbing but now I don't care for it much any more," the publisher has said. "I am happier and more lively when I am working."

References

Time 46:59-60 Jl 16 '45 por
Who's Who in America, 1944-45

THOMAS, JOHN W. Jan. 4, 1874—Nov. 10, 1945 United States Republican Senator; from Idaho from 1928 to 1933, and again from 1940 until his death; chairman of the Idaho Republican State Committee (1922-24); member of the Republican National Committee since 1925; active on the Banking and Currency, Finance, and Military Affairs Committees.

Obituary

N Y Times p42 N 11 '45 por

THOMPSON, OSCAR Oct. 10, 1887—July 3, 1945 American music critic, author, editor, lecturer; successively music critic, associate editor, and editor of *Musical America* (1919-43); on staff of New York's *Evening Post* (1928-34), *Times* (1935), and *Sun* from 1937 to death; books include *How To Understand Music* (1935); editor in chief of the *International Cyclopedia of Music and Musicians* (1943).

Obituary

N Y Times p13 Jl 4 '45

TIBBETT, LAWRENCE (tĭb'ĕt) Nov. 16, 1896- Singer

Address: b. c/o W. Colston Leigh, Inc., 521 Fifth Ave., New York City; h. Honey Hill Farm, Wilton, Conn.

The world-famous operatic baritone, Lawrence Tibbett, has gained a wide audience both on the opera stage and through other entertainment mediums, serious and popular. His appearance for seven months in 1945 on the popular-music radio program *Your Hit Parade* caused much comment in the musical world—only Tibbett seemed to see no reason for the flurry. In fact, he considered it only another pioneering job, for he had been the first opera singer to appear in motion pictures and the first to go on a commercial radio series.

Lawrence Mervil Tibbett inherits his interest in new ventures from forebears who were California pioneers in the 'forty-nine Gold Rush. He was born November 16, 1896, in Bakersfield, California, to William Edward and Frances Ellen (Mackenzie) Tibbet. (The singer added another *t* to his surname when an early Metropolitan program spelled it "Tibbett" in error.) His grandfather, father, and uncles were sheriffs. When Lawrence was only seven years old his father was killed by Wild Jim McKinney, a "bad man" of the West, whom Sheriff Tibbet had ordered out of the locality.

"My father had ten thousand dollars in life insurance," Tibbett wrote in his autobiography for the *American Magazine* in 1933, "and my mother took us to Long Beach, California, where she tried to support her four children by running a hotel." Lawrence was twelve when his mother sold the hotel at a loss and moved her family to Los Angeles. "Kindly but inaccurate biographers," says the singer, "have said that I helped to support the family by working as a bellhop and by selling papers. I did both, but we were not so poor that my efforts were any help. The most I ever made in one day by selling papers was fifteen cents, and I was so proud of myself that I spent it all on a banana split." In Los Angeles his mother bought a large house and took in lodgers; and she also worked as a practical nurse to eke out a living and pay for her son's piano lessons. When he became a student at the Manual Arts High School in Los Angeles, young Lawrence began to appreciate the sacrifices his mother was making for him. "I tried to help out by working Saturdays in the office of a Los Angeles paper, stuffing comics and magazine sections into Sunday newspapers, and counting classified ads." In high school he sang in the glee club and acted in a score of plays. "Although I liked to sing," recalls Tibbett, "my ambition was to become an actor."

Young Tibbett's campus hero at Manual Arts High School was an all-round athlete who was to make history in the Second World War as General James Doolittle '42. As a result of their first meeting in the school gymnasium the tall, gangling Tibbett began to give more attention to physical training. The meeting came about when someone suggested that Tibbett "take on" Doolittle, and the two boys faced each other in a test of fisticuffs. "There was a slight sound of a current of air being stirred up— then a bump and silence—as Doolittle advised, 'Stick to singing.'" Later Tibbett learned that an operatic singer—especially a baritone—must have the "diaphragm of a heavyweight prize fighter." (To keep fit Tibbett exercises on a rowing machine and bicycle machine, swims, works on his farm, and occasionally stands on his head before singing—performing the last-named not as a superstition, but to promote good circulation.)

By the time Tibbett was graduated from high school in 1915 he was beginning to earn small fees by singing in church choirs and at funerals. He also obtained a few professional engagements in Los Angeles, with the Civic Repertory Company and with a company headed by Tyrone Power, father of the film star, which gave selected scenes from Shakespeare. But the First World War cut short these beginnings on the stage—Tibbett joined the Navy when the United States declared war.

Four days after his discharge from the Navy, on May 19, 1919, the twenty-two-year-old Tibbett was married to Grace Mackay Smith, who had boarded for several years with his mother. With five hundred dollars he had saved and a car received as a wedding present, the young Tibbetts drove to Portland, Oregon, on their honeymoon. "Although," says Tibbett, "our marriage did not last forever [they were divorced in 1931], it was an adventure and an important event in my life. When I was married I was a dreamer and wanted to sit under a palm tree and philosophize. If I had had no responsibilities I probably would still be sitting under that same palm tree." A year after his marriage twin sons, Richard Mackay and Lawrence Ivan, who served in the Second World War, were born.

The early years of the Tibbetts' marriage were not easy ones. He had a family to support and singing engagements were not exactly plentiful nor well-paying. There is a story about the time when the rent was six months in arrears, the automobile tank empty, and a singing engagement to be kept at a funeral in Los Angeles seventeen miles away. A kind tow came to the rescue, however, so that Tibbett was able to keep the date—he sang two songs, and was paid five dollars. (In 1945 his Hit

LAWRENCE TIBBETT

Parade contract called for three songs at a sum estimated at anywhere from twenty-five to forty-five hundred weekly.) Recalling the hardships Tibbett says, "I did not suffer at all, I had a magnificent time." Or in the words of one writer, Lawrence Tibbett believes in "traveling wide open to all that life has to offer. There is a surging, splurging, lunging, plunging vehemence to his spiritedness." The major landmarks in this part of Tibbett's career were a fifty-dollar-a-week position as a prologue-singer in a Los Angeles motion picture house and the role of Iago with a small opera company. But he had already begun to study with voice teachers, one of whom was Basil Ruysdael, a basso at the Metropolitan Opera House before he went to Los Angeles, and who years later was to be announcer on Your Hit Parade. (Tibbett has said since that the instruction he received from Ruysdael was most important to him because the teacher caught him in the formative period when he was about to build "pompous-singer" habits.)

The turning point of Tibbett's life came when Rupert Hughes, the novelist and musician, convinced him that a successful singing career lay before him and advised him to go to New York to study. In Los Angeles Tibbett was a member of the Orpheus Club, a men's choral society, of which James G. Warren, a wealthy businessman, was president. With money borrowed from Warren, Tibbett left for New York. There his first teacher was Frank La Forge, who at that time was coaching Frances Alda and accompanying Margaret Matzenauer and other famous singers in concert work.

The baritone had been studying six months in New York when La Forge suggested an audition at the Metropolitan. The surprised Tibbett protested that he did not know any opera roles, that he sang only in English, and, moreover, that he did not believe his voice good enough for that distinguished opera company. Three months later, however, he stood on the stage of the opera house prepared to sing the Prologue from Pagliacci for his audition. At

TIBBETT, LAWRENCE—*Continued*

the mention of the well-worn audition favorite a sigh of weariness escaped from the impresario seated in the darkened auditorium. La Forge recognized the cue and therefore began playing "Eri tu" from Verdi's *A Masked Ball*, in which the nervous singer's voice cracked on a high F sharp. Three weeks later, through the good offices of Mme. Alda, then the wife of Gatti-Casazza, who was the general director of the Metropolitan at that time, Tibbett was given a second audition. For his singing of Iago's "Credo" from *Otello*, he was engaged at sixty dollars a week. Tibbett has described that first contract with the company in 1923 as "an option affair by which, if they chose, they could keep me for four years, at one hundred dollars a week for the second season, one hundred and twenty-five for the third, and one hundred and fifty for the fourth." It gave him permission to sing in concerts, but "no radio. no musical comedy, no movies" without the Metropolitan's permission. When he appeared in motion pictures in 1929 he paid the Metropolitan a percentage of his earnings.

Before his debut at the Metropolitan, however, Tibbett sang in the Hollywood Bowl (September 1923) in *Aïda*'s Amonasro role. After he had reached the pinnacle of his career and was regarded as America's greatest baritone, Tibbett confessed that he had given *Who's Who* inexact information about his debut role in the Metropolitan on September 24, 1923, because he had not cared to admit that it was an inconspicuous part, sung mostly in the wings. That role was one of two monks in *Boris Godunoff*. His first name role, Valentine in *Faust*, came four days later.

Tibbett was still a comparatively unknown young man who sang brief roles in the Metropolitan when, on January 2, 1925, he won one of the most overwhelming ovations ever given a singer in that company. It was the old, old story of the understudy who makes good. *Falstaff* was being revived as a tribute to Antonio Scotti, and the singer cast in the role of Ford became ill. "The night of the opera," recalls baritone Tibbett, "I . . . let go with all I had. In my aria in the second act I tore my heart out. Some subconscious force lifted me up." The applause that followed lasted sixteen minutes. Twenty years later (1944) critic Oscar Thompson, in discussing the ovation, said that demonstrations in the Metropolitan are a part of the usual order of things and that there is no official record of their length or volume. The only person Thompson knew who could speak with authority on the subject was the late Tom Bull, who had been doorman of the opera house for almost a half-century. Bull had told the critic that there had been only one other demonstration in his memory that topped the one that acclaimed Tibbett. It was the 1900 ovation for Jean de Reszke when he returned in *Lohengrin* after a season's absence. Tibbett's triumph was hailed on the New York *Times* front page as an "unprecedented event," and Olin Downes[43] wrote in praise of his singing: "Exemplary in its sincerity and dramatic feeling, its justness of accent, and its excellent vocal quality." For the first time in opera history an American without European training won stellar honors in one of the world's most important opera companies.

The public was beginning to call Tibbett a one-role singer when a year later he again scored a triumph, in the première of Umberto Giordano's *Cena delle Beffe*. And soon after, he gained stature in the original productions of Howard Hanson's[41] *Merry Mount*, Deems Taylor's[40] *The King's Henchman* and *Peter Ibbetson*, and Louis Gruenberg's *Emperor Jones*. The last, which was written expressly for Tibbett, revealed him as a singing-actor (musical shorthand for the combination of a great voice with the power to create dramatic characterizations). When Tibbett stole the honors from Scotti in *Falstaff* his repertoire consisted chiefly of Italian and French roles, but he soon mastered almost every type of opera, including Wagner. He has a repertoire of nearly fifty complete operas—some five hundred songs—and he has appeared in more than one thousand concerts. His favorite role is Simon Boccanegra in Verdi's opera of the same name. The *Opera News* gives credit to Tibbett for making this opera a success. It had failed on its European première, some seventy-five years before the Metropolitan revived it in 1932. "So inspiring and powerful" was the baritone's singing of that role that critical opinion called it a signal triumph. For several seasons the Metropolitan honored Tibbett by making it the opening opera.

In the spring of 1937, twelve years after his rise to stardom, the baritone made his first opera appearance in Europe. London "mildly condemned him for his melodramatic tendencies," but he "won all hearts" in the première of Eugene Goossens'[45] new opera, *Don Juan de Mañara*, the libretto of which was written by Arnold Bennett. Tibbett's seven-month tour of European capitals brought him new honors: in Stockholm, for example, he received the Litteris et Artibus medal from King Gustav[42]. Previously he had received (in 1933) the gold medal of the American Academy of Arts and Letters in recognition of his good diction, and honorary degrees were bestowed upon him: the Master of Music by the University of Southern California in 1928, and Doctor of Music by New York University in 1934.

The artist's first appearance before the microphone was made in 1922 over the Los Angeles station KHJ. His commercial series—over the big networks CBS and NBC—have since included: the *Atwater Kent Radio Hour* (1921-31); *Voice of Firestone* (1932-33); *Packard* (Motor Car) *Presents* (1934-36); *Chesterfield Presents* (1937-38); *The Circle*, for the Kellogg Company (1939); and the *Ford Sunday Evening Hour* (1937-40). After a throat condition prevented him from singing for part of 1940, the baritone appeared on the *Telephone Hour*. Radio audiences have heard him sing also as guest star on numerous broadcasts as well as on the Saturday afternoon broadcasts from the Metropolitan stage. He has recorded his entire repertoire of concert songs, as well as many operatic arias. The Prologue of *Pagliacci*, one of his first records, totaled nearly ten thousand dollars in royalties during its first year.

When it was announced in January 1945 that Tibbett would replace Frank Sinatra[43] on the popular-music program *Your Hit Parade* over the Columbia Broadcasting System, "a small series of shocks ran through musical strata and was registered on operatic and concert seismographs," in the words of *Musical America.* Lovers of the opera deemed it undignified for a Metropolitan star to move into the "crooner's" domain, and Sinatra's "bobby-socks" followers registered their disapproval. *Opera News,* the magazine of the Metropolitan Opera Guild, honored the singer, however, by placing his picture on the cover of its issue for January 15. The contract, announced the magazine, was "the biggest radio deal ever made."

Many listeners expressed dislike of the exceptionally fast rendition of the tunes played on *Your Hit Parade* (called "an outmoded conception of jazz"), a kind of trade-mark of the program. And after Tibbett's debut performance in January 1945 the New York *Times* wrote that the singer "seemed seriously handicapped by the predetermined regimentation of melody." In general, however, his "Don't Fence Me In" and "I Got Plenty o' Nut'in'" pleased listeners. After his final broadcast on *Your Hit Parade* on July 21, 1945, Tibbett left for an overseas USO tour.

Tibbett's announcement in 1929 that he would sing in Hollywood motion pictures created almost as much of a stir as that following his 1945 contract with *Your Hit Parade.* But his venture soon paved the way for the appearance of other operatic stars in films. *The Rogue Song* (1930), which he made with Catherine Dale Owen, played for five months at the Astor Theatre in New York. His other pictures include: *New Moon* (1930) with Grace Moore [44], *The Prodigal* (1931), *The Cuban Love Song* (1931) with Lupe Velez and Jimmy Durante, *Metropolitan* (1935), and *Under Your Spell* (1936).

Throughout his career Tibbett has campaigned for the recognition of American composers and performers—he has been openly scornful of what he has called "the flapdoodle of European prestige." He declares that English-speaking audiences are the only ones patient enough to listen to opera sung in a foreign tongue, and strongly advocates the translation of foreign operas into English for American audiences. Apropos of this, he likes to tell the story of how once during a Metropolitan performance the Russian basso Chaliapin was able to convey a message to his valet in the wings, in the language of the opera—"Go home and get me a suit of underwear."

The famous baritone has given generously of his time toward promoting the welfare of his fellow artists. In 1933 while on a week-end of golf, he and Frank Chapman, the husband of Gladys Swarthout [44], and others formed a society later called the American Guild of Musical Artists. Formally launched in 1936, its one hundred and fifteen charter members include Lily Pons [44], Jascha Heifetz [44], Alma Gluck, and Grace Moore. This organization of eighteen hundred members has succeeded in reducing agents' commissions for concert engagements from 33⅓ to 20 per cent, and commissions for radio engagements have been lowered from 25 to 10 per cent. Tibbett has been president of the Guild since its founding, and in 1940 he was elected president of the American Federation of Radio Artists, a post to which he has been unanimously re-elected ever since. He has also been active in USO camp shows and in Red Cross and war bond drives. He participated in a Carnegie Hall concert devoted to Russian music for the benefit of war orphans of Stalingrad; and, together with Leopold Stokowski [41], Jose Iturbi [46], and the New York Philharmonic Orchestra, he has contributed his services gratis to the New York Center of Music and Drama, which makes concerts, ballets, and plays available at moderate prices.

Divorced in 1931 from his wife, on whom he reportedly made a generous settlement, on January 1, 1932, Tibbett was married again. His second wife is the former Jennie Marston Burgard, the daughter of the late Edgar L. Marston, a banker. A son, Michael Edward, was born in 1933, and the family includes Mrs. Tibbetts' sons by a former marriage. Before the war they lived in an apartment overlooking the East River; their annual New Year's party was a high point in musical circles. In the summer the family lives on Honey Hill Farm in Connecticut, which yields bumper crops of apples. Lawrence Tibbett is a lively conversationalist and is known for his friendliness. He is over six feet tall and weighs one hundred and ninety pounds, and his light brown hair has taken on a gray tinge about the temples.

References

Am Mag 116:11-5+ Ag '33 pors; 116:32-5+ S '33 pors; 116:26-9+ O '33 pors; 116:56-9+ N '33 pors
N Y World-Telegram p10 Ja 3 '42 pors
Opera N p7 N 29 '39; 7:5 Ja 11 '43
Ewen, D. ed. Living Musicians (1940)
International Motion Picture Almanac, 1943-44
National Cyclopædia of American Biography Current vol F p295
Thompson, O. ed. International Cyclopedia of Music and Musicians (1943)
Variety Radio Directory, 1940-41
Who's Who in America, 1944-45

TISDEL, ALTON P. 1880(?)—June 1, 1945 United State Government official; Superintendent of Documents of the Government Printing Office for almost a quarter of a century.

Obituary

N Y Times p15 Je 2 '45

TOBIAS, CHANNING H(EGGIE), REV. (tō-bī′ăs) Feb. 1, 1882- YMCA executive

Address: b. The National Council of the YMCA, 347 Madison Ave., New York City; h. 35 W. 110th St., New York City

A distinguished Negro social worker and religious and civic leader, Dr. Channing H. Tobias has long been a vocal champion of his people's cause. For twenty-two years he has served as Senior Secretary of the Colored Men's Department of the Young Men's Christian Association of the United States, participating in national and international YMCA affairs. Long active in the crusade for interracial understanding and cooperation, Tobias' broad organizational affiliations afford him a wide range of expression and action.

Channing Heggie Tobias was born in Augusta, Georgia, on February 1, 1882, to Fair J. and Clara Belle (Robinson) Tobias. His mother, who was a domestic servant, died when

Bachrach

REV. CHANNING H. TOBIAS

the boy was twelve years old; there was an Indian strain in her ancestry, which is apparent in the facial characteristics of her son. Channing Tobias' father, whose mother had some French blood, had attended Atlanta University. He liked horses, however, and became a coachman. The boy attended the Augusta public schools and then studied for three years at the academy connected with Paine College preparatory to entering the college itself. He received a B.A. degree in 1902.

In 1900 he was ordained a minister of the Colored Methodist Episcopal Church. For further religious training he studied at the Drew Theological Seminary in Madison, New Jersey, where he received his B.D. degree in 1905. During the next six years he was professor of biblical literature at Paine College, taking time out in 1908 for special work at the University of Pennsylvania. Stepping from his role as classroom teacher, Tobias then entered YMCA work, thus carrying on his educational mission on a broader plane. He became student secretary of the International Committee of the YMCA's, a post he held for twelve years. Elected senior secretary of the Colored Men's Department of the National Council in September 1923, Tobias has since retained that position. From 1935 to 1942 he also served as associate director of the Commission on Interracial Cooperation.

In 1921 the Negro leader was a member of the Pan-African Congress in Paris and of the student deputation visiting European relief areas. During the year 1926 he was a delegate and speaker at the World Conference of the YMCA's at Helsingfors, Finland, where he led group discussions on race relations. In 1926 he also lectured at Riga, Latvia, and visited YMCA centers there and in Estonia, Poland, and Czechoslovakia. Two years later he served on the executive committee of the National Interracial Conference in Washington, D.C. The year 1934 found Tobias in the Capital again, as a member of the Planning Committee of the

National Conference on the Fundamental Problems in the Education of Negroes. Tobias and Benjamin E. Mays [45] were the two Negro members of the twelve-party United States delegation to the World Conference of the YMCA's in Mysore, India, in 1937. The Senior Secretary spent considerable time before and after the conference traveling in the Near East and the Far East; his pamphlet *Travel Notes*, covering the period from December 1936 to March 1937, reveals his impressions and opinions of peoples and places observed. From Cairo he wrote of the thrill of viewing the contributions of the Negro to the great ancient civilizations, adding: "What a tonic it was to live for a few days in a land where color carried no opprobrium with it." India's vastness impressed the YMCA executive and he was especially pleased to see the lack of color prejudice among the Indians. He was sympathetic with their struggle for independence under the leadership of Gandhi [42] and of Nehru [41], whom he termed "the coming man of India."

At the YMCA World Conference Tobias held a vital assignment as chairman of the Commission on Race Relationships under whose sponsorship a resolution was passed unanimously by the Conference stating that "national movements request their local associations to do away with racial exclusion policies in membership." Tobias points out that "America and South Africa are practically the only countries in the world where racial exclusion is practiced in YMCA's." At the conclusion of the Conference, the delegate proceeded to visit YMCA's in various parts of India before continuing his journey to Ceylon and thence to China. Tobias found the Chinese people deeply interested in the Negro problem in America; and his university and church addresses were cordially received. Visiting the large cities of Japan next, the American tourist then continued his journey through the Pacific, arriving finally at Hawaii. "As attractive as it is for natural beauty," Tobias remarked, "it is more attractive as a social laboratory in which problems of race relationships are being worked out satisfactorily. I felt pride in my American citizenship as I mingled with the people of Honolulu, for at least I had found a spot under the American flag that seemed to be devoid of color consciousness."

Besides his YMCA work, the social worker's interest in youth has been further channeled through educational and community activities. Tobias is a member of the board of trustees of Howard University, Paine College, Hampton Institute, and Palmer Memorial Institute; he serves on the joint advisory council of the Harlem Educational Projects and belongs to the board of directors of Youth House, Forest House, and the Wiltwyck School for Boys. Prominent in civic affairs in New York City, he belongs to the City-wide Citizens Committee on Harlem and is on the board of directors of the Citizens Housing Council. He is a veteran adviser of youth, and has delivered numerous commencement addresses, including sermons at Morehouse College, Fisk University, and Tuskegee Institute. In 1942 he spoke before the American Association for Adult Education on the topic "Training and Job Opportunities for Negroes in Postwar America." Again in 1943 he dealt with this problem in his speech, "The

Larger Task of Education for Negroes," delivered at the tenth annual conference of the Association of Colleges and Secondary Schools for Negroes.

In a speech at Hampton Institute in 1940 entitled, "Let Negroes Work," Tobias, recommending vocational training, declared: "We have come finally to see that while our professional classes are indispensable to our ultimate progress and success, they are absolutely helpless without the support of the laboring masses." Broadcasting that year in the eighth vocational opportunity campaign conducted by the National Urban League, the YMCA leader treated the topic "Prepare Today for Tomorrow's Job." He decried the limited employment sphere open to Negroes and cited unemployment, which falls heaviest on the Negro, as "the one great shadow that darkens the pathway of his progress."

Tobias' activities during the war kept the leader busy as a member of the National Advisory Committee on Selective Service, the Joint Army and Navy Committee on Welfare and Recreation, the Negro Service Committee of the United Service Organizations, and various war fund groups. His interest in the deeper problems of war and peace is evidenced by his affiliation with the Committee on Overseas Relief and Reconstruction and the committee of direction of the Commisison on a Just and Durable Peace. His religious ties are wide: he belongs to several committees of the Federal Council of Churches of Christ in America, the Universal Christian Council for Life and Work, the board of managers of the American Bible Society, and the Commission on the Church and Minority Peoples.

Especially concerned with the problems of the Negro people and harmonious race relations, Tobias serves with several groups devoted to such work. He is a member of the board of directors of the National Association for the Advancement of Colored People, the Council on African Affairs, the (New York) Mayor's Committee on Unity, and the American Council on Race Relations. Tobias is also cochairman of the executive board of the New York Chapter of the Southern Conference on Human Welfare. In an address to this assembly, Tobias stated: "I have greater confidence in this group than any other in the South because it has had the courage from the beginning to say that we cannot have wholesome relations across racial lines as long as those lines remain intact." Late in 1940 Tobias, together with Walter White '42 and A. Philip Randolph '40, conferred with President Roosevelt on the status of the Negro in the armed forces and war industries.

A popular speaker on race relations, the Negro leader has addressed many organizations and colleges, among them Vassar College and Columbia University, and local YMCA's throughout the United States. His broadcasts have included OWI shortwave programs and three appearances on the *New World A-Coming* series. At a Cooper Union forum in March 1943 Tobias discussed "The Negro in Our Democracy." While acknowledging signs of progress in race relations, he stated the problems confronting the Negro as the victim of a "double standard of citizenship." There have been only faint efforts to make democracy work

for this one-tenth of the Nation. Tobias contended. Aware that much of the resolution of the difficulties of race relations depends on slow educational processes, he believed, nevertheless, that it was "possible under the stress and pressure of war to move forward immediately and effectively in bringing about changes in certain fixed practices without which changes it would be impossible for America to push ahead rapidly to the winning of the war and the achieving of a just and lasting peace." Five suggestions for such action were proposed by Tobias: (1) a Presidential order for the abolition of segregation in the armed forces; (2) full compliance with Government Order 8802 (FEPC) barring discrimination by industries holding war contracts; (3) the abolition of the segregated blood plasma policy of the Army and Navy as practiced by the Red Cross; (4) newspapers to stop their policy of "associating race with crime in the case of the Negro, as is done with no other racial group"; (5) the motion picture industry to abolish its code restrictions "that confine Negroes to roles of menial service and buffoonery."

Speaking before the Foreign Missions Conference in 1944 on "World Implications of Race," Tobias considered British and American foreign policy as it affects race relationships, and declared: "I am absolutely certain that there will be trouble down the road if the victorious nations, following this war, insist upon holding unbroken the ring of white dominance that now encircles the darker peoples of the earth." Expressing hope for all peoples despite difficulties ahead, the speaker, however, went on to qualify his faith. "Blueprints alone, though backed and implemented by all the combined material resources of the Allied nations, cannot change deeply rooted prejudices into mutual trust and good will," he said. "That is a spiritual task, and leadership and direction for such a task can only be provided by an institution that is spiritually motivated. That is why I pin my hope for future good will and peace among the races of mankind on the Christian church."

The end of the war, which brought with it problems of reconversion and unemployment, spurred Tobias to renewed activity in behalf of his people. He helped to draft New York State's fair employment act, aimed at eliminating discrimination in employment because of race, creed, color, or national origin. That measure, known as the Ives-Quinn bill, became effective in July 1945; it was the first law of its kind to be passed by any State. Tobias was also active in the fight for the continuation of the Federal Fair Employment Practice Committee. In a speech in Washington he told of widespread bias against minority groups and of organized attempt to block FEPC legislation. He also "pointedly warned" both major parties that their action or inaction on that legislation would be reflected in votes cast by minority groups for Senators and Representatives in the 1946 elections. Another example of racial discrimination that brought vigorous protest from Tobias was the denying of the use of D.A.R.'s Constitution Hall to Hazel Scott '43. In his letter to President Truman, Tobias particularly expressed regret that the Hall had been "honored by the presence and patronage"

TOBIAS, CHANNING H. REV.—*Cont.*

of Mrs. Truman on the day after the D.A.R. had barred the Negro musician.

In the political field, Tobias' activities have placed him generally on the liberal side. According to Roi Ottley [43] (*New World A-Coming*), Tobias, as the Fusion Party's candidate for the New York City Council in 1941, withdrew from the election in favor of the Reverend Adam Clayton Powell, Jr. [42]. Designated for the same office in 1943 by the New York County Executive Committee of the Republican Party, Tobias declined the nomination. In September 1944 Tobias, together with the Negro leaders Walter White and Mary McLeod Bethune [42], conferred with President Roosevelt [42] and won his renewed promise of support in the struggle against racial discrimination. During the 1944 presidential campaign, Tobias, a lifelong Republican, worked vigorously for the re-election of Roosevelt. His many campaign appearances included speeches at the rally for Roosevelt sponsored by the Independent Voters Committee of the Arts and Sciences for Roosevelt, at the Liberal Party rally for the President, and for the National Non-partisan Committee for the Re-election of Roosevelt.

Tobias was twice chairman of the Negro Freedom Rally held in New York's Madison Square Garden in 1943 and 1944. In January 1945 he hailed the nomination of Henry A. Wallace [40] as Secretary of Commerce, and at a Wallace rally at Town Hall the following month he spoke in support of confirmation of the appointment. In January he also addressed a Madison Square Garden meeting which urged the United States to break relations with Franco [42] Spain. At a CIO rally for labor unity in March, Tobias was a principal speaker. Elected to the National Committee of the National Citizens Political Action Committee in May, he is also on the executive board of the New York chapter of the Union for Democratic Action. An admirer of the late Wendell L. Willkie [40], Tobias was on the Sponsors Committee of the Willkie Memorial Building Fund of Freedom House, and he is a member of the honorary committee for the Wendell L. Willkie Awards, prizes for distinguished writing published in Negro newspapers and magazines.

Articles by Tobias have appeared in various magazines. His address to the Hartford YMCA on the occasion of the hundredth anniversary of the Association in June 1944 (printed in pamphlet form) contains his eight-point program for improvement of the YMCA. Significant in this outline are proposals to encourage members to participate in public affairs, to increase democracy within the organization, and to remove race and color bars. Tobias is a member of the board of editorial advisers of the *Protestant Digest* and also belongs to the editorial board of the *Protestant Voice*.

In November 1945 Tobias was made director of the Phelps-Stokes Fund, which is concerned with national interracial relations and Negro education and with housing for Negroes in New York City. Recipient of the Harmon Award for Religious Services in 1928, the clergyman was named on the Schomburg Honor Roll of Race Relations in 1943 and the following year he received the citation of the Chicago *Defender* Honor Roll. Tobias holds an honorary D.D. degree from Gammon Theological Seminary (1924) and an honorary LL.D. from Morehouse College (1942).

In 1910 Channing Tobias was married to Mary Pritchard, whom he had met as a fellow student at Paine College. One daughter, Mary, directed arts and crafts in the USO. Another daughter, Belle, a graduate of Barnard College with a Master's degree from Wellesley, is deceased. A picture of Mary, now Mrs. Dean, and her two small children hangs on the wall behind Tobias' desk. They are, he says, his "hobbies."

References

N Y Post Mag p34 S 20 '45 por
Religious Leaders of America, 1941-42
Who's Who in America, 1944-45
Who's Who in Colored America, 1941-44

TOBIN, DANIEL J(OSEPH) 1875- Labor leader

Address: b. International Brotherhood of Teamsters, Chauffeurs, Warehousemen and Helpers, 222 E. Michigan St., Indianapolis, Ind.

Since 1907 Daniel J. Tobin has been president of the International Brotherhood of Teamsters, Chauffeurs, Warehousemen and Helpers, one of the most powerful labor organizations in the United States. Commonly known as the Teamsters Union, this labor group is considered as occupying a crucial position in relation to the Nation's economy, for, according to Tobin, who is regarded as a moderate in aims and methods, it touches every trade and industry in the country. The union is the largest affiliate in the American Federation of Labor, of which "the fighting Irishman" has been a vice-president since 1933. A vigorous supporter of the late Franklin D. Roosevelt [42], he has represented labor at international meetings and in Government posts, and he has been active in the drive to achieve unity within the labor movement.

Daniel Joseph Tobin, the son of John and Bridget (Kennelly) Tobin, was born in Ireland in 1875. When the boy was only fourteen he journeyed alone to the United States. At first he attended grade school and evening high school classes in Cambridge and Boston, but later he continued his studies at home. Tobin has vivid recollections of his early working days in Boston, where he drove a team of horses for a trucking concern, and was paid eleven dollars for a sixty- or seventy-hour work week.

He soon joined the local teamsters' union and, as its Boston representative, became active in its struggles. This was a stormy period for America's developing labor movement, and Tobin, so to speak, grew up with it, a friend and follower of the A.F. of L. founder and president, Samuel Gompers. In 1903 the Team Drivers' International Union and the National Teamsters of Chicago were merged to form the International Brotherhood of Teamsters, an affiliate of the A.F. of L., and four years later Tobin became the president of the new body, the position he still holds. Since 1903 the union has grown into an organization of almost a thousand locals in the United States and Canada, with a membership of seven hundred thousand, encompassing almost every category of the trucking field. According to an article in *Fortune* in May 1941, the Brotherhood that year had funds amounting to more than six million dollars and paid its president a yearly salary of thirty thousand dollars, plus expenses.

The Teamsters have acquired over the years a reputation for rough tactics, but one writer reports that "nothing will infuriate 'Uncle Dan' so much as a slur on the character or conduct of his Teamsters." Considerable discussion has centered on the internal operation of the union, and charges of racketeering and abusive practices have been leveled against certain locals. However, in the words of one writer in *Fortune* (1941), "No responsible person has ever challenged the personal honesty of Uncle Dan Tobin, and undoubtedly the great majority of Teamsters' locals are thoroughly honest. But some of the strongest ones have been under suspicion." *Business Week* (July 1942) noted an emphatic "crime-must-go" attitude in the union's publication, although Tobin appeared to the *Fortune* writer as "far more interested in proceeding against Communists, representing the new militant members, rather than against corruption." (The Teamsters' constitution bars Communists from membership.)

Fortune describes Tobin as a conservative exponent of the "old-line" philosophy who has shown a cautious use of power in his leadership. He favors arbitration, but forsees dangers to labor if it is made compulsory. He has warned his membership against "excessive demands that might result in driving employers out of business," and he is opposed to strikes except as a last resort. He sees in industrial unionism (CIO), as contrasted to craft unionism (A.F. of L.), "an attempt to destroy the very foundations upon which this Federation [the A.F. of L.] has been builded and upon which it has succeeded for years." In 1942 *PM* reported that the union chief objected to the issue of Negro A.F. of L. membership being raised at that year's convention. Tobin as an individual has also been the target of sharp criticism by writers whom some regard as pro-CIO: Edward Levinson in *Labor on the March* (1938) sees Tobin as skillful in "swathing his dictation in sentiment and blarney," while Herbert Harris in *American Labor* (1938) describes the Teamsters' head as "hard-boiled and autocratic."

During the war Tobin cooperated closely with the war effort. In November 1941 he called off a Detroit strike of railway express drivers in deference to the wishes of the President; the next year he rebuked a Pittsburgh local for a sympathy strike. The June 1945 issue of the *International Teamster* printed his injunction to his men to disregard picket lines unless otherwise ordered by union officials. The union leader is proud of the Teamsters' war record and boasts that the union observed the no-strike pledge "almost 100 per cent."

The January 1945 issue of the union magazine included an article by Tobin's executive assistant calling for repeal of the Wagner [41] National Labor Relations Act and abolition of the National Labor Relations Board, which, he said, had "become nothing more than a standing committee of the CIO." This article

DANIEL J. TOBIN

occasioned a flurry of comment in the press and in labor circles, until Tobin declared his sentiments in the February issue, affirming his approval of the Wagner [41] act but condemning the work of the NLRB. In March Tobin repudiated an editorial in the magazine (of which he is editor) urging support of the "Little Steel" wage formula. He appeared before the Senate Finance Committee in June to endorse the Reciprocal Trade Agreements Act, emphasizing that the United States must play a part in the rehabilitation of Europe. The year before he had stated his refusal to participate in the World Conference on Labor in London because he would not deal with organizations which he felt were not free—"whose wages are set by the government."

Since the split within labor's ranks and the subsequent formation of the CIO in 1935, labor leaders, Tobin among them, have been trying to mend the breach. In December 1942 he was a member of the six-man committee of A.F. of L. and CIO representatives who engaged in a labor peace conference. The committee deliberations resulted in a public declaration of a mutual desire to work toward unity and to cooperate in the installation of machinery toward this end. The Teamsters' chief supported these sentiments, observing, "Remember, this is the first time we have ever made such an agreement." Serving on a joint committee to handle jurisdictional disputes the following year, Tobin's optimism was seen as waning. "We have just enough men on both sides who look at today and fail to look for tomorrow, and who are anxious to make a mountain out of a molehill," he declared. "Lawmakers and politicians and other enemies are most certainly taking every advantage of us, because and only because of the division of labor—a division that should never have been, and a division that now should and could be eliminated if leaders of labor sincerely and unselfishly desired it."

Tobin was active in the negotiations between the A.F. of L. and John L. Lewis [40], head of

TOBIN, DANIEL J.—*Continued*

the United Mine Workers. In 1943 Tobin was chairman of a three-man committee which conferred with Lewis on his application for readmission of the U.M.W. into the Federation. In August of that year Louis Stark [45] reported a session of the A.F. of L.'s executive council at which Tobin made a motion to refer Lewis' application to the A.F. of L. convention. Another reporter remarked that "foxy" Dan Tobin was an "active wire-puller" against Lewis' readmission into the Federation. According to William Green [42], the convention instructed the executive council to resume negotiations with Lewis, and in 1945 deliberations were still going on. The New York *Times* reported in February that Tobin opposed the reaffiliation of the U.M.W., except on condition that all jurisdictional disputes between the miners and the A.F. of L. first be settled.

During four successive Presidential election campaigns Tobin has served as chairman of the labor division of the Democratic National Committee. In October 1944 the Teamster leader criticized the nonpartisan stand of the A.F. of L. executive council, refuting the argument that the Federation is traditionally nonpartisan by recalling the positive political activities of Samuel Gompers. In the stormy political climate of the 1944 elections, the New Deal laborite waged a vigorous campaign aimed at unifying the labor vote for Roosevelt, Truman [45], and, in New York, for Senator Robert F. Wagner. President Roosevelt, moreover, opened his campaign for a fourth term with an address to the Teamsters at the Statler Hotel in Washington, D.C. The much publicized "Battle of the Statler" followed the speech, involving some Teamsters and two Navy men. The press carried conflicting accounts of the incident, which was seized upon as "campaign fodder." A preliminary inquiry into the case by the Senate Campaign Expenditures Committee quickly resulted in dismissal of the entire matter. After the election the Teamsters Union claimed credit for Roosevelt's victory, asserting that the union had done more than any other organization in America to bring it about. In 1945, together with most of the labor movement Tobin strongly supported the appointment of Henry Wallace [40] as Secretary of Commerce.

During Roosevelt's tenure of office Tobin several times served in Government posts, or in an advisory capacity. Appointed administrative assistant to the Chief Executive in July 1940, he held this post until October, when he resigned to take up election duties. In 1942 Tobin was one of the A.F. of L. members of a special advisory board to the President. In August of that year Roosevelt sent the labor leader to England to investigate labor conditions and to report his findings to the American people. Upon his return from this assignment Tobin delivered a radio report which was printed in the *Congressional Digest* in March 1943. An outspoken New Dealer, Tobin was offered a position as regional administrator under the PWA in 1933, a post which he declined. Twice, in 1933 and again in 1945, his name was mentioned for the position of Secretary of Labor. In January 1933, it is reported, a petition was signed by "every leading labor man

in the United States, including John L. Lewis, on behalf of Tobin."

The Teamsters' president has also seen service as treasurer of the A.F. of L., from 1917 to 1928, when he resigned; as vice-president of the Federation since 1933, in which capacity he has sat on the organization's executive council. He has also been vice-president of the National Building Trades Department since 1933. Active on the international labor scene, Tobin represented the A.F. of L. at the British Trades Union Congress in 1911, 1938, and 1942. In 1918 the Teamster chief was a delegate to the International Federation of Trade Unions at Amsterdam. He was also present at the conference called by the International Labor Office at Geneva in 1939, having been delegated by the Government to attend. In the First World War Tobin was a member of President Wilson's Industrial Conference and also served on various labor mediation boards.

Hard-hitting, burly "Big Dan" Tobin is an orator of the old school, whose eloquence has won him a reputation as somewhat of a spellbinder. He is five feet eight inches tall, has a fair complexion and wears his gray hair parted in the middle. His first wife was the former Annie Reagan, by whom he has five sons. After her death, in 1923 Tobin was married to Irene Halloran. The Tobin children are John, Frank, Frederick, Edmund, Joseph, and Katherine.

References

Fortune 23:97-100+ My '41 il pors
N Y Sun p5 N 28 '42
Who's Who in America, 1944-45

TOLBUKHIN, FEDOR I(VANOVICH) (tôl-bōōк'ĭn fyô'dĕr ĭ-vä'nŭ-vyĭch) 1895(?)- Russian Army officer

Address: b. c/o Commissariat for Defense, Moscow

The victorious defense of Stalingrad in the fall and winter of 1942, and the accompanying annihilation of the German Sixth Army under Field Marshal Friedrich von Paulus, brought to the attention of people outside the Soviet Union many able leaders among the officers and men of the Red Army. Prominent among them is the commander of the Third Ukrainian Army, Marshal Fedor I. Tolbukhin, whose encircling tactics in this campaign were highly rated by military experts.

There are few facts available on the early life of Fedor Ivanovich Tolbukhin. It is known that he was born about fifty years ago, and that his father was a peasant who had served as a private in the Czar's Army. At the time of the First World War the twenty-year-old Tolbukhin enlisted in the Army as a motorcyclist. After being wounded he went to an officers' training school, from which he went back into combat, eventually becoming commander of a battalion. When the Revolution broke out the young officer joined the Red Army.

The Marshal's military accomplishments meant repeated disasters for the Nazi forces that opposed his army on the southern flank of the great Eastern front. Pacing the entire Russian offensive that was initiated after the heroic defense of Stalingrad, the Fourth

Ukrainian Army by a brilliant and daring thrust under Tolbukhin pierced the German lines north of Taganrog in August 1943 for a distance of twenty-eight miles. While shock troops drove on that strategic prize from the east, he closed the northern arm of his pincers on the Sea of Azov. Caught in this trap, the German forces were disposed of, group by group. Greater than the physical losses of the Nazi forces (35,000 killed, 5,100 prisoners), however, was the threat to the entire German Army in the Donets Basin, whose flank was now exposed. From this time on, the Germans were unable to make a successful stand short of the Dnieper River.

The fall of Taganrog made Stalino, another important city in the Donets Basin, untenable by the Germans. On September 8 this great mining and manufacturing center fell to General Rodion Y. Malinovsky's [44] Red Army shock troops. Two days later Colonel General Tolbukhin's tanks and cavalry south of Stalino swept along the coast of the Sea of Azov to seize Mariupol, port of the Donets Basin. These victories were hailed in Moscow by twenty salvos from two hundred and twenty-four guns, and Marshal Stalin [42] announced in an order of the day, "The troops of the southern and southwestern fronts have torn from the Germans and returned to our country the Donets Basin, the most important coal and industrial region of our country."

With the German forces in this area completely demoralized, Tolbukhin pressed his advantage. His army raced along the north shore of the Sea of Azov, and by November 1943 had sealed off the Crimean peninsula by taking Genichesk and Perekop, and had reached the lower Dnieper River with the capture of Kakhovka. In this operation large forces of Nazis were trapped on the shores of the Sivash Sea, while far to the west of the Perekop isthmus Tolbukhin's hard-riding cavalry rapidly cleared the Nogais Steppe, forcing the fleeing Nazis back across the Dnieper. Even though supported by artillery and mortar fire from the west bank of the river, the Germans found the crossing a costly one.

Consolidating his gains, Tolbukhin prepared his Fourth Ukrainian Army for the next phase of the offensive. In February 1944, in conjunction with General Malinovsky's Third Ukrainian Army, his forces cleared the Germans from their Dnieper bridgehead east of Nikopol, capturing that great manganese center in one of the bloodiest battles in history. By the time the commander of the Fourth Ukrainians had ordered his guns to cease firing, tens of thousands of Germans had fallen.

While the Nikopol bridgehead was being eliminated, General Tolbukhin was making extensive preparations for the drive into the Crimea. Early in April he sent one force driving down the Perekop bottleneck, while his other troops drove across the shallow, salt marshes of the Sivash Sea. Overrunning the antitank ditches and thick mine fields on the isthmus, he breached the German lines, and both arms of the attack joined to capture Simferopol, capital of the Crimea, on April 14, while eighty miles to the east General Andrei Yeremenko's Independent Maritime

MARSHAL FEDOR I. TOLBUKHIN

Army forced the Kerch Strait. Combining forces in the Crimea, both armies drove on Sevastopol the next month, and after a three-day assault captured the "jewel of the Crimea." The fall of the great naval base was hailed as a strategic victory of primary importance, for with it went control of the Black Sea.

General Tolbukhin was now ranked among the eleven top officers of the Red Army. These eleven men had two things in common: all were unknown outside the Red Army before the German attack in 1941, and all were relatively young men. In recognition of his able and courageous leadership of military operations and for successes achieved as a result of these operations in the fighting against the Nazi invaders, General Tolbukhin was awarded the Order of Suvorov, First Class, shortly after the fall of Sevastopol. In September 1944 he was again honored, by promotion to the rank of marshal. He was now in command of the Third Ukrainian Army, and Malinovsky had assumed command of the Second.

While Tolbukhin was freeing the "Florida" of Russia, Malinovsky drove into Odessa, completing the liberation of southern Russia, east of the Dniester River. Then, in late August, the two armies combined forces to retake the province of Bessarabia, which had been ceded to Rumania by the Germans. Along the Black Sea flank raced the Third Ukrainian Army. It stormed Kishinev, while below the city a noose was closed around sixty thousand Germans. Then the Third Ukrainian Army sped down the coast. In a few days Tolbukhin's troops were deep within the sprawling, muddy Danube Delta, having captured Ismail and Galati, eastern anchor of the gap leading into greater Rumania. Within a week the Russians had advanced 125 miles, overrun 18,500 square miles, recovered all of Bessarabia, and killed or captured 300,000 enemy troops. Strategically, the Carpathian line was turned, Rumania was tactically and politically tied to Russia, the great wheat fields were

TOLBUKHIN, FEDOR I.—*Continued*

available to feed Russia's population, and the Ploeşti oil fields, last major source of German fuel, were exposed to capture.

With this major Russian victory the German stand in the south collapsed. Within a few days Ploeşti fell, Bucharest capitulated, and the German puppet governments in the entire Balkan area crumbled. Bulgaria, which had only recently become a belligerent by Russia's declaration of war, made a complete turnabout and on September 8 declared war on Germany, exposing the German forces in Greece to capture. By October Marshal Tolbukhin had driven into Yugoslavia, where he joined with the Yugoslav National Liberation Army of Marshal Tito '43 to liberate the charred ruins of Belgrade, capital of Yugoslavia.

Added to the military responsibilities of Marshal Tolbukhin were the political concerns of the Russian Government in the Balkans. While his army pushed into Hungary to threaten Budapest, he negotiated for the surrender of Bulgaria, and on October 28, 1944, he signed the terms as the representative of the Soviet Union. (Lieutenant General J. A. H. Gammell signed for the Allied Supreme Command in the Mediterranean theater.) Russia's influence in southeastern Europe had reached a point never before attained by any government in the complicated history of that area. Charges were made, however, that Tolbukhin had unduly suppressed the efforts of a democratic group in Bulgaria to challenge other political parties for control, and much was written about the Communistic influence in the uprising in neighboring Greece. In carrying out the interests of his own Government, Tolbukhin deferred the claims of Bulgaria and Greece for postwar arbitration. For the present, it was said, civil affairs would be conducted by a provisional administrative committee of one Bulgarian, one Greek, and one Turk.

Meanwhile, the drive into Hungary, last ally of the Germans, continued; Budapest was threatened by Tolbukhin's flanking drive through southwestern Hungary and northern Yugoslavia. Pushing through the area flanked by the Danube and Drava rivers, the Third Ukrainian Army reached the shore of Lake Balaton on December 5 and surrounded the northern and southern ends of the fifty-mile-long lake. Capturing Székesfehérvár, strategic city on the northern end of Balaton, Tolbukhin then drove northward to cut the main escape route from Budapest to Vienna. By Christmas Day the Hungarian capital was virtually encircled, and on December 30 an ultimatum was sent to the German commander in the besieged city, who, instead of accepting the offer, had the Russians shot who delivered it. For the next forty-nine days Tolbukhin and Malinovsky drove on the city, which finally fell on February 13, 1945. The cost to the stubborn Nazis in men, food, and equipment was terrific; they had suffered the greatest manpower disaster since Stalingrad—110,00 soldiers captured and 49,000 killed. This high cost was followed by an additional loss of 16,000 men in the German counterthrust northwest of Vienna.

These terrific losses dismayed the Germans. War industries in Austria and Czechoslovakia, the last the Nazis had for the defense of the "inner bastion," were threatened. To throw back the oncoming Russians, a desperate counterattack was begun. Eleven tank divisions were thrown into the battle, and, for a few days, Marshal Tolbukhin's troops were hard-pressed. Despite the critical state of the battle, however, the Russian General held out his reserves until the German armor had been over one-half destroyed. When he did send forth his operational reserves, they were able to advance forty miles on a sixty-mile front. By March 30 they had crossed the Austrian border and captured Köszeg. On the southern end of Lake Balaton another arm of Tolbukhin's army drove into the Hungarian transport hub of Nagykanizsa, then on toward the Italian border, for the Germans had not yet evolved a defensive strategy to combat the Red Army's technique of taking bastioned cities by complex, encircling attacks. As they did at Budapest, the two big armies of Marshals Tolbukhin and Malinovsky struck swiftly at the sides of Vienna. After crossing the Morava River, the Red raiders leapfrogged ashore at night to attack from the rear. Through the woods to the west infantrymen crossed the main roads leading from the city, then cut swiftly to the Danube north of the city. On April 13 the Russians burst through, and the capital fell—seven years, one month, and a day after Adolf Hitler '42 had sent his legions into the capital of Austria for the forced *Anschluss* of 1938.

On the 8th of May President Truman '45 and Prime Minister Churchill '42 simultaneously announced the end of the war in Europe. On the Russian front the fighting continued where Germans refused to surrender. Ten hours after the official V-E Day proclamation Moscow announced the German surrender to the Russians. Yet on the 10th of May German forces in Czechoslovakia had still refused to surrender, and in Austria Tolbukhin's Third Ukrainian Army mop-up squads were still busy. Shortly afterward Tolbukhin's troops linked up with the British Eighth Army west of Graz. On May 16, at a spontaneous ceremony near Linz, Austria, Tolbukhin pinned the Order of Kutuzoff First Class on General George S. Patton, Jr. '43, on behalf of the Soviet Government.

Tolbukhin is often referred to as a rotund man with a heavy, calm face. When viewed from certain angles he bears a striking resemblance to Winston Churchill. Regarded as an expert horseman, he is known, incidentally, as one of the "Four Horsemen of the German Apocalypse," the others being Konstantin Rokossovksy '44, Ivan S. Konev '43, and Rodion Y. Malinovsky. In April 1945 Tolbukhin received the diamond-studded Order of Victory, the Soviet Army's highest award.

TOLSTOI, ALEKSEI NIKOLAEVICH, COUNT (tŭl-stoi' ŭ-lyĭ-ksyā'ĭ nyĭ-kŭ-lā' yĕ-vyĭch) 1882—Feb. (?) 1945 Soviet Russia's greatest contemporary writer, so called by many critics; left Russia during the Revolution in 1917, but returned in 1922; abandoned his nonpolitical attitude when his country became menaced by Nazi Germany, taking an active part in the Soviet propaganda front; one of his major works was *Peter the Great,* translated into English in 1932.

Obituary

N Y Times p11 F 24 '45 por

TROUBETZKOY, AMELIE (RIVES) PRINCESS (trōō′bĕts-koi a′mä-lē rēvz) Aug. 23, 1863—June 15, 1945 Popular American novelist of the nineties; achieved a sensational literary success on publication of her first novel, *The Quick or the Dead?* (1888); she was also a playwright, poet, and essayist.

Obituary

N Y Times p26 Je 17 '45

TRUMAN, HARRY S. May 8, 1884- President of the United States

Address: The White House, Washington, D.C.

NOTE: This biography of Harry S. Truman supersedes the one which appeared in *Current Biography* in 1942, when he was United States Senator from Missouri.

Harry S. Truman, who succeeded to the Presidency of the United States on the death of Franklin D. Roosevelt '42 on April 12, 1945, is considered "a real United States American." His grandparents, Kentuckians of Scottish and English ancestry, had settled in Jackson County, Missouri, in 1842. One Truman, Harry's cousin, did eventually become a general in the United States Army, but all the other Trumans were plain, solid citizens. Both of Harry Truman's parents, John Anderson and Martha Ellen (Young) Truman, took the Confederate rebels' side in the Civil War, and were therefore forced to leave their homes for a time; years later, aged Martha Truman still corrected reporters with a sharp "I'm no Yankee." Their son Harry, the first of three children, was born May 8, 1884, nineteen years after the conclusion of the war, in Lamar, Barton County, Missouri. When it came to giving him a middle name, they could not agree on either Shippe, for his Truman grandfather, or Solomon, in honor of his maternal grandfather. They compromised on simply "S."

When Harry was four the Trumans moved to Grandview, six hundred rolling acres of bottomland, eighteen miles from the county seat of Independence, which four generations of Trumans had farmed. Three years later (1891), they moved to Independence, where John Truman carried on his business in livestock. At nine Harry entered the Independence school. A shy, quiet boy who wore glasses from the age of eight, the future President "made books his sport," while his classmates were racing their horses around the countryside. By fifteen he is said to have read every one of the books in the local library. Mrs. Truman discovered that her son had some musical talent, and compelled him to take piano lessons from the age of nine. "In Independence, Mo., in 1893 this was tough," comments Gerald W. Johnson in *Life*. "All the young Tom Sawyers in public school regarded a boy who studied music as a terrible sissy, and the music roll that Harry Truman carried through the streets was a stigma that evoked merciless ridicule. However, it was easier to defy the gang than his mother, so he stuck to it until approaching manhood and the necessity of earning a living deprived him of the necessary time." He is still fond of playing the piano, and wishes he could perform the Chopin études better than he does.

Blackstone Studios

HARRY S. TRUMAN

Young Truman, a diligent student of military history, obtained an appointment to West Point after graduating from the three-year Independence high school, but was rejected because of his defective vision. The Trumans had suffered financial reverses, and while in high school Harry had worked part-time: a year in a drugstore for three dollars a week, and six months at seven dollars a week wrapping papers in the mailing room of the Kansas City (Missouri) *Star*. Now the seventeen-year-old boy went to work for thirty-five dollars a month and board as timekeeper for the construction crews building local Santa Fe railroad trackage. After six months he went to Kansas City and got a job at the same salary with the National Bank of Commerce, where his brother Vivian was already employed. After a year the youth changed to the Union National Bank as a bookkeeper. He remained in their employ three years, eventually earning $125 a month—"a heck of a high salary." When the future President was twenty-two, the bachelor uncle for whom he had been named retired and turned over to the Trumans the farm where Harry was reared, whereupon the family went back to the country.

For twelve years Truman was a farmer, and although he had not chosen that occupation he calls them the happiest days of his life. "That boy could plow the straightest row of corn in the county," his mother recalls. "He could sow wheat so there would not be a bare spot in the whole field. He was a farmer and could do anything there was to do just a little better than anyone else." President Truman is still joint owner, with his sister Mary Jane and brother Vivian, of the Grandview farm, now somewhat smaller, and operated by his brother, who is assistant director of the Federal Housing Administration's Kansas City office. Vivian Truman also carries on the family's livestock business.

According to *This Man Truman* (1945), Harry Truman's father had always taken an

TRUMAN, HARRY S.—*Continued*

active part in local politics as one of the Pendergast Democrats. From 1906 he served as elections judge in Grandview precinct, usually with his son Harry as clerk, and for the four years before his death he was road overseer for the southern half of Washington township. Young Truman, whose brother had moved away a few years earlier, succeeded his father as road overseer, his first political appointment. This required him to spend his spare time collecting taxes, repairing culverts and bridges, and dragging dirt roads after the rain with an eight-mule grader, for a salary of five dollars a day. In spite of its humble nature, the road overseer system was (to quote a Missouri newspaper) "the backbone of the Jackson County Democratic organization," and when Truman resigned this post because of a disagreement with his superiors over the need for improvements, he was appointed postmaster at Grandview with the support of Democratic Congressman William P. Borland. However, Truman turned over both the duties and the fifty-dollar monthly salary of this post to his assistant, Ella Hall.

Harry Truman had joined the National Guard in 1905, when he came of age, and had been honorably discharged as a corporal at the end of his second enlistment in 1911. "After reading all the books I could obtain in the Independence and Kansas City public libraries on history and government, from early Egypt to the United States of America," he once explained, "I came to the conclusion that every citizen should know something about the military, finance or banking, and agriculture. All my heroes or great leaders were somewhat familiar with one or the other or all three." A few days after his country entered the First World War, the thirty-three-year-old farmer was sworn in as a first lieutenant, passing the physical examination, it is said, by arranging to have the examining sergeant prompt him on the eye chart.

He attended the Field Artillery School at Fort Sill, Oklahoma, and helped organize the Second Missouri Field Artillery, which became the 129th. At Fort Sill, according to the New York *Herald Tribune*, "he started a canteen by collecting two dollars from each of the eleven hundred men in his regiment. With the aid of a buddy, Eddie Jacobson, who had had mercantile experience, he built up the canteen until in six months it not only refunded the two dollars apiece but accumulated fifteen thousand dollars in dividends for the regiment."

Thirty-three-year-old Truman was sent overseas in March 1918 with the Thirty-fifth Division as captain and adjutant of the Second Battalion, and after further training was given command of Battery D, 129th Field Artillery in the same division. This battery was known as "a hardboiled bunch of Kansas City Irish" who had worn out five previous captains and greeted this one with marked skepticism. But the quiet, bespectacled farmer won their respect and affection, as he led them through the Saint-Mihiel, Vosges, and Meuse-Argonne offensives. Two specific incidents are remembered of him. Once he ignored a colonel's ill-advised order to move his men in double time to another sector, and once, when his panicky battery was on the verge of a disorderly retreat, he gave

them a "bawling-out in no-man's land" which restored their morale. Truman's battery fired their last volley of the war at Herneville, France, fifteen minutes before the start of the Armistice. He returned to the United States and was discharged with a reserve commission in the rank of major and appreciable skill in ju-jitsu. On the trip home his men had put aside a percentage of each dice game to buy Captain Truman a ten-gallon loving cup which stands four feet high and is too big for his mantel. (Truman was a founder of Officers Reserve Corps Number 1 at Kansas City. In 1927 he was raised to the rank of colonel in the Reserve.)

In June 1919, six weeks after his return, Truman was married to Bess Wallace, the schoolteacher daughter of a farmer, and granddaughter of a well-known flour miller. Bess, one year younger than he and "the only girl he ever went with," had been a blond tomboy in the days when they went to the same Presbyterian Sunday School. After their marriage the couple lived with her mother. (The Trumans have one daughter, Mary Margaret, born in 1924 and usually called "Baby." Margaret, like her mother, is an Episcopalian, although Truman lists himself as a Baptist.) Then Harry Truman went into partnership with his friend Eddie Jacobson in a Kansas City haberdashery shop. "The store made out well for a while," says the New York *Herald Tribune*. "But its earnings were plowed back into inventory; its contracts were at boom levels; and when business sagged, the haberdashery was squeezed to pieces in [the deflation of] 1921." Truman, who lost his entire savings of fifteen thousand dollars and twenty thousand more, refused to file a bankruptcy petition, and saved for fifteen years to pay off his debts.

Meanwhile Truman had been active in the American Legion; during the postwar reaction of disillusionment with all things military, he urged "preparedness," and he helped frame the Legion policy of unifying the armed services under a single Cabinet Secretary—a change he still advocates. A thirty-second-degree Mason, he was for a time Grand Master of the Kansas City lodge. His family were stanch Democrats, and he had many friends among both farmers and townspeople. These qualifications appealed to Boss Tom Pendergast of the local Democratic machine, when they were presented to him by a nephew who had served with Truman in the war. Pendergast nominated Truman as one of the three judges of the Jackson County Court—not a judicial body despite its title, but an administrative one, corresponding to the county commissioners or boards of supervisors in other States. Elected in 1922, the future President took office in 1923. Coming to the conclusion that "knowing a little law wouldn't hurt," he enrolled for evening courses at the Kansas City School of Law, where he studied from 1923 to 1925, taking about half of the course required for a law degree and making a "B" average. After Truman's defeat for reelection in 1924, he helped organize the Kansas City Automobile Club, and within less than two years he "ballooned the membership to more than three thousand."

Truman's connection with Pendergast has drawn much criticism. In the light of a thorough Federal investigation which sent the boss to jail on an income tax charge in 1939, there is no doubt that the Pendergast machine was thoroughly corrupt. His henchmen won elections by "voting the ghosts"—registering votes for persons dead or nonexistent—and then used their power for their own profit. Far-reaching and most unsavory underworld connections were revealed by the investigation. But there is no doubt that Harry Truman himself was scrupulously honest at all times. According to Johnson, "The record of the Pendergast gang in Kansas City is such that any man who could work with that crowd and remain honest is honest indeed. But this means financial honesty alone. . . .Of course the [future] Senator was not acquainted with all the appalling details, but he must have known that some pretty rough stuff was going on." Some commentators point out that Pendergast gave efficient and relatively honest government at the time Truman became associated with him, and that these abuses developed about nine years later, when Truman was in Washington. When Boss Tom acquired a bad name, Truman's strong sense of loyalty caused him to stand by his friend, as he did until Pendergast's death in January 1945.

At any rate, Truman was swept out of office during the split between the Pendergast and Shannon Democrats in 1924; but two years later, having failed of nomination to the twenty-five-thousand-a-year county collectorship, he was elected Presiding Judge of the County Court, an important post, as Jackson County includes Kansas City. "I had charge of the spending of sixty million dollars for highways and public buildings in Jackson County" for the eight years from 1927 to 1935, Truman recalls. "Nobody ever found anything wrong with that, and it wasn't because they didn't look hard either. We built more miles of paved roads in Jackson County than any other county in the Nation, with two exceptions." Once, however, he did have a thirty-six-thousand-dollar surplus left over from four and a half million appropriated for the Jackson County courthouse. "Instead of returning the surplus to the treasury," the President confesses, "I spent it on a statue of Andrew Jackson." During these years Truman became an important figure in the County Judges Association, one of the most powerful political organizations in the State. Missourians remember Judge Truman as "harping day and night on cutting taxes and preaching constantly his theory of economy and value received in government expense, as in business." He realized fully that "the costs of government can be cut only by eliminating some services and equalizing the burden. It is an economic problem and must be handled in an economic manner." In 1930 the Odessa County *Democrat* started a gubernatorial boom for him, but he was overwhelmingly re-elected to the County Court. According to Cyril Clemens' *The Man From Missouri*, Truman leaned over backward to be honest, to such an extent that he refused to pay his mother for the eleven acres taken from her farm for a county boulevard, although she was entitled to eleven thousand dollars in compensation.

After eight years in that sixty-three-hundred-a-year post, Truman asked Pendergast to nominate him for a more lucrative one. According to the story most prevalent, he asked for the tax collectorship, but received instead a United States Senatorship at ten thousand dollars. Truman himself says he asked for nomination to represent a new Congressional district which had just been formed, but found that the machine's support had already been pledged to C. Jasper Bell. Some weeks later, while Judge Truman was touring the State in support of a bond issue, the Democratic State chairman persuaded him to accept the nomination for the higher chamber.

Elected to the Senate in 1934 by a plurality of 262,000 votes over his nearest opponents, Truman followed Pendergast's advice to work hard, to keep his mouth shut until he knew the ropes, and to answer his mail. As his secretary, Mrs. Truman assisted in the carrying out of the last-named directive—at an annual salary of forty-five hundred dollars. (This practice of employing a member of one's family is not uncommon among Government officials without large private incomes. The salaries of Federal public servants are customarily inadequate for expenses of the office, one of the reasons being that they were usually determined long ago.) The modest four-line biography with which he furnished the *Congressional Directory* was less than one-tenth the length of that given by his friend Bennett Champ Clark [41], senior Senator from Missouri. Truman differed from Clark in other ways, too, for Clark was an isolationist and an opponent of many of President Roosevelt's New Deal policies. Truman, on the other hand, "went down the line for the Administration" when it came to a vote for the original AAA Act, the Wagner [41] Labor Relations Act, the Social Security Act, the TVA, joining the World Court, and building the Florida Ship Canal and the Passamaquoddy Dam. He did vote to override the veto of bonus payments to World War veterans.

In 1937 Senator Truman first came into national notice: he presented a bill for the Federal licensing of operators of motor vehicles used in interstate traffic, and he served as chairman of two Interstate Commerce subcommittees. One of these subcommittees drafted the Civil Aeronautics Act which brought all nonmilitary aviation under control of the Civil Aeronautics Authority. The other subcommittee under Truman's chairmanship drafted a bill which became the Railroad Transportation Act of 1940. This was preceded by an extensive investigation of railroad financing. "When it came to digging into the Missouri Pacific," writes Charles T. Lucey of the Scripps-Howard [40] staff, "names of politicians and others in Missouri began to bob up. Telegrams and telephone calls poured in on Senator Truman asking him to ease up on that home-state stuff. Boss Pendergast was one of those who turned on the heat. But Mr. Truman told his committee investigators, 'I don't want you to ease up on anything. Treat this investigation just as you do all the others.'" Investigator Max Lowenthal told a St. Louis *Post-Dispatch* reporter that in his opinion "there were not two other Senators who would have withstood such local political pressure as Senator Truman did."

During the investigation of the Pendergast regime by United States District At-

TRUMAN, HARRY S.—*Continued*

torney Maurice M. Milligan, Truman was referred to as "Boss Pendergast's errand boy," but he refused to "desert a sinking ship." When the Senate was asked to confirm President Roosevelt's renomination of Milligan in 1938, Truman "fought it tooth and nail," says George Creel '44, "branding Milligan as 'personally obnoxious,' and going so far as to intimate that his investigation of election frauds in Kansas City was inspired by political animus. True," comments Creel, "this was a full year before the indictment of Tom Pendergast, and only small fry were involved, but the Senate majority regarded the attack as unfair and rebuked it by an overwhelming vote." (Five years later Vice-President Truman was to succeed in preventing Milligan's reappointment. Truman, however, has a reputation of not holding grudges.)

By the time Senator Truman was up for re-election in 1940, the Democratic registration had lost some forty-seven thousand names of nonexistent voters. Truman seemed to have no chance to win. But his two opponents for the nomination, District Attorney Milligan and Governor Lloyd C. Stark, each claimed the credit for ridding Missouri of the Pendergast gang. They split the anti-machine vote and "killed each other off," allowing Truman to win the primary election by the slim margin of 7,000 votes, and the general election by 40,000. Nevertheless, he is quoted as saying. "I could have won if only one of them was running."

Back in Washington, the Senator began getting letters from Missourians complaining about waste in construction at Fort Leonard Wood, and stating that defense contracts were going almost exclusively to the large corporations connected with members of the War Department's Construction Advisory Board. In February 1941, after a personal tour of investigation, Truman submitted a bill creating a Senate committee to look into the situation; and in March that body created the Special Committee to Investigate Contracts under the National Defense Program, which soon became nationally known as the Truman Committee. It set something of a record by probing controversial matters, yet always emerging with a unanimous report.

In view of the committee's fame and accomplishments, the modesty of its establishment is not generally realized. Truman was given five first-term Senators: Democrats Carl A. Hatch '44 of New Mexico, James M. Mead '44 of New York, and Mon C. Wallgren of Washington; and Republicans Joseph H. Ball '43 of Minnesota and Ralph O. Brewster of Maine. One Senate veteran, Tom Connally '41 of Texas, was added to keep the freshmen under control. Every member was serving also on other committees, Truman himself on six others: the important standing committees on Appropriations, Military Affairs, and Interstate Commerce; and the Enrolled Bills, Printing, and Public Buildings and Grounds committees. Later additions to the Truman Committee were Clyde La Verne Herring of Iowa, Harley Kilgore '43 of West Virginia, Harold H. Burton '45 of Ohio, and Homer Ferguson '43 of Michigan, bringing the membership to six Democrats and four Republicans. (Photog-

raphers were never able to catch the entire committee together.)

The first appropriation was only fifteen thousand dollars. The entire staff, housed in four offices, consisted of fifteen investigators, eighteen stenographers, clerks, and the well-thought-of committee counsel, Hugh A. Fulton. Truman had appointed him on the recommendation of Attorney General (later Justice) Robert H. Jackson '40, who knew Fulton's work as an assistant district attorney in New York. The Truman Committee's first report was issued in August 1941. It presented sensational facts in ninety-eight completely unsensational pages. After studying nine Army camps, the committee outlined the "needless waste of one hundred million dollars" in Army construction and "fantastically poor judgment" in various matters. General Brehon Somervell '42, whose Services of Supply frequently was brought up short by the Truman Committee, estimates that this inquiry alone saved the Government two hundred million dollars.

Truman Committee reports were responsible for causing President Roosevelt to abolish the bumbling Supply Priorities and Allocation Board in favor of the one-man Office of Production Management in January 1942; and then when Truman, among other revelations, showed how many of the dollar-a-year men were lobbyists for their own businesses, caused the OPM to be reorganized as the War Production Board. Later reports exposed the cartel agreement between Standard Oil of New Jersey and the German I. G. Farbenindustrie; the responsibility of the big steel companies for the scrap shortage; Army-Navy rivalry and duplication of facilities; "negligence or willful misconduct" in the Navy's Bureau of Ships; imperfections in fighter aircraft; malpractice by labor unions; and the lack of central authority in coordinating the war program. (In the meantime, Reserve Colonel Truman had applied to Chief of Staff Marshall '40 for active service and been refused.) By September 1943, according to Stanley High, the committee had received appropriations of only two hundred thousand dollars, "doled out by the Senate in driblets"—a small fraction of that given Martin Dies '40 for his Committee to Investigate Un-American Activities. So effective was the Truman Committee as "the public's most accessible court of appeals, the sharpest prod, and one of the most powerful action-getting agencies in the Government," that much of its work became preventive. "To insure quick action on Truman facts, numerous war agencies, among them the War and Navy departments, the Maritime Commission, and the War Production Board, have representatives attached, full time, to the committee." Altogether, the Truman Committee (which was to become the Mead Committee when Truman left the Senate) was considered a model of its kind.

At the Democratic National Convention in July 1944 there was little doubt that President Roosevelt would be renominated for a fourth term, and interest centered on the selection of a Vice-Presidential nominee. The CIO-PAC and the liberals and Leftists generally were strongly for the renomination of Henry Wallace '40. The Southern conservatives backed Presidential assistant and former Supreme Court Justice James F. Byrnes '41, and other segments of the party had other candidates. Soon it became clear that each of the possible candidates, with the exception of Truman and Justice William O. Douglas '41, had heavy political liabilities. Truman had no desire for the honor ("I've got the best job a man could have," he said), and he had in fact agreed to make a speech nominating Byrnes. But he was the choice of Democratic National Chairman Robert Hannegan '44. The A. F. of L. leaders and the railway brotherhoods were for him rather than Douglas, and all other groups found him acceptable as "the second Missouri Compromise."

Liberals approved his voting record, and conservatives felt that "at heart he was an old-fashioned Missourian, not a 'Pink' or reformer." Southerners liked his Confederate background; Negroes and anti-discrimination groups recalled that he had consistently voted their way. The machine bosses knew him as an organization man. But the defect of his virtue was also in evidence: if Truman inspired no denunciation, neither did he inspire wild applause—even at the convention at which he was nominated, the defeated Henry Wallace outshone him. During the campaign it was charged that Truman had belonged to the terroristic Ku Klux Klan in 1922, but his categorical denial was generally accepted. Apart from that, he was frankly the tail to Roosevelt's kite and was elected as such.

As students of government know, the Vice-Presidency of the United States carries few real duties. The Vice-President is supposed to preside over the Senate, but in practice this is usually done by a president pro tempore; the incumbent himself serves as an "understudy" for the President. Truman's plan, according to Luther Huston, was to "be the politician's Vice-President. . . .He will have a hand in shaping legislation and steering it through the Senate; will operate behind the scenes to keep fences patched and curb feuds, and may even be more zealous at times than [former Vice-President John N.] Garner in championing the programs of the Administration." In his spare time Truman continued his study of history and military strategy. For the first time, the Trumans began to take a noticeably active part in the Washington social scene, although the women continued to do housework in their modest five-room apartment. Margaret was attending George Washington University and singing during the summer in Denver Opera Company productions. "She's getting what I never had, a college education," her proud father told people. (Truman's mother-in-law, a Missouri pioneer, was also a member of the household.)

But Truman was to serve as Vice-President only eighty-three days before he was catapulted into the highest office in the country. One of his official actions in those few months, a move which puzzled some observers, was his committing of the bill for a Missouri Valley Authority on the order of the TVA to the Senate Commerce Committee, where Chairman Josiah W. Bailey '45 was known to be hostile to the proposal, rather than to the Agriculture Committee, as the author of the bill had requested. He himself was considered favorable to the proposal, however. For the immediate future, Truman was preparing to lead the Senate fight on accepting the world monetary stabilization plan proposed at Bretton Woods. Then, on April 12, 1945, Franklin Delano Roosevelt died,

and sixty-year-old Harry Truman succeeded to the Presidency. As such, he had one privilege never accorded Roosevelt: unlike an elected President, a Vice-President who succeeds to the White House can designate his own "heir apparent," for the Presidential succession after him (in case of his own death) is made up of the Cabinet members in the order of their Departments' seniority. Observers therefore watched with particular interest to see whom, if anyone, Truman would choose to replace Secretary of State Edward R. Stettinius '40, the first in the line of succession. His eventual choice was Judge Byrnes, appointed June 30, but in a special message the President asked Congress to pass an act establishing a new order of Presidential succession. He recommended that the Speaker of the House and the President of the Senate precede the Cabinet members, so that the country might have an elected rather than an appointed heir-apparent.

President Truman took office at "surely one of the most unpropitious moments in history" for a change of leaders; he himself had pointed out the dangers of a change of Presidents in his campaign speeches against Dewey '44. The nearness of the San Francisco Conference of the United Nations, scheduled to open thirteen days later, threw into sharp relief the problems facing the new President. He must of necessity take a leading part in winning the war, making the peace, dealing with the enemy nations, reconverting from a wartime to a peacetime economy, helping the wartorn lands, and putting into concretion the overwhelming desire of his people that "this must be the last war." Millions of plain people, who had felt that "you could leave things to Roosevelt," realized anew the immensity of the task confronting the American President, and wondered what might be expected of Truman. One comment was that he had inherited a whirlwind.

"An awful, awful lot of GI's never heard of Harry Truman, who among other things is now their Commander in Chief," said CBS reporter Bill Slocum, from Paris. Curiosity about the little-known new President was world-wide, and mingled with the grief at Roosevelt's passing. There was even some question about his number in the succession of Presidents (caused by the fact that Grover Cleveland had served two nonconsecutive terms, and was therefore counted by some as two Presidents). Truman is the thirty-second man to hold the office. The questioning public learned, too, that he was the first President, as he had been the first Vice-President, from Missouri, and the second President from west of the Mississippi. From Missourians, such as Roy Roberts of the Kansas City Star, they heard such descriptions as this: "Humility probably would be the first characterization. Then loyalty, perhaps excessive loyalties that sometimes get high officials into trouble; common sense; deep patriotism; and above all an abiding faith in his country and its democratic system. Harry Truman couldn't go in for personal government under any circumstances. He doesn't believe in it and wouldn't know how to operate it."

The new President's first official announcement after being sworn in was that the San Francisco Conference on International Organization would convene as scheduled; and within two days he had won praise by successfully re-

TRUMAN, HARRY S.—*Continued*

questing Stalin '42 to send Foreign Commissar Molotov '40 to the Conference, instead of having the U.S.S.R. represented by the regular Ambassador to the United States. At his first press conference Truman endorsed Bretton Woods, continuance of the reciprocal trade policy, and American participation in the United Nations organization. Truman's first appointment, after members of his personal staff, was that of the St. Louis banker and RFC director John Snyder '45 as Federal Loan Administrator. Later, in July 1945, he was to appoint Snyder to the over-all planning post of Director of the Office of War Mobilization and Reconversion—"Secretary of Domestic Policy."

Other much-publicized appointments were: April 27, Edwin Pauley '45, California oil and real estate man and Democratic treasurer, to the Allied Reparations Commission; May 2, Supreme Court Justice Robert H. Jackson as chief American prosecutor at the German war criminals' trials; May 7, Democratic National Chairman Hannegan of St. Louis as Postmaster-General; May 23, Assistant Attorney General Tom C. Clark '45 of Texas as Attorney-General, Judge Lewis B. Schwellenbach '45 of Washington State as Secretary of Labor, and New Mexico Representative Clinton P. Anderson '45, chairman of the House Food Investigating Committee, as Secretary of Agriculture; June 7, liberal young businessman W. Stuart Symington '45 of St. Louis as chairman of the Surplus War Property Board, and General Omar N. Bradley '43 as head of the Veterans Administration. Twenty days later Truman named Stettinius to the United Nations Security Council and then replaced him in the Secretaryship of State with Judge Byrnes. Economic Stabilization Director Fred M. Vinson '43, six-term Representative from Kentucky who had established himself as a tax expert before appointment to the Federal bench, was named Secretary of the Treasury on July 16; Senator Burton was nominated to succeed retiring Justice Roberts '41 on the Supreme Court September 18. A significant appointment was that of Judge John C. Collett of the Missouri Supreme Court as Stabilization Administrator in September, after Truman had lost the well-regarded William H. Davis '41 by a removal, which he later reconsidered, of all price, rationing, and production control. After the dramatic resignation of General Patrick J. Hurley '44 in November, Truman named ex-Chief of Staff Marshall as special envoy to China (Marshall, Bradley, and Vinson were his only appointees to important posts who were already well-known to the country in their fields). In December he chose Wilson W. Wyatt the dynamic young mayor of Louisville, as housing expediter to deal with the acute housing shortage.

The President's executive method was described as "pick a man and let him run his own job." It was praised as a return to Cabinet government, an end to "one-man rule," and it was condemned as drifting and as lacking an over-all policy—failure to recognize that all Federal offices were dealing with different aspects of a few basic situations, not with independent problems. Truman's Cabinet, which included some hold-overs from the Roosevelt regime, was summed up by *Fortune* at the end of the year as: "five able administrators: [Secretary of the Navy] Forrestal '42, [Secretary of the Treasury] Vinson, [Secretary of War] Patterson '44, [Secretary of the Interior] Ickes '41, and [Secretary of Commerce] Wallace '40; two hard-working question marks, at present swamped by their responsibilities, Byrnes and Schwellenbach; two politicians, Hannegan and Clark; and one unknown quantity, Anderson."

Less than a month after Truman was sworn in, the war in Europe ended on May 8. In less than four months he saw his country ratify the United Nations Charter (July 28), and he joined with Churchill '42, Attlee '40, and Stalin at the historic Potsdam Conference (July-August) which determined certain frontiers, set the Allied reparations policy, and announced that Spain was not wanted in the United Nations. Four days later he announced the existence and first use of the atomic bomb, and on August 14 he proclaimed the surrender of Japan. Meanwhile, of course, he continued the endless Presidential routine of choosing subordinates, receiving their reports, granting pardons and commutations of sentences, dealing with Congress, hand-shaking, mending political fences, creating and awarding medals, accepting gifts and honors, making speeches, conferring with diplomats, greeting distinguished visitors—including Herbert Hoover '43, with whom he discussed the food situation in Europe, and Alf M. Landon '44, 1936 Republican nominee for President, who said Truman had an "excellent" foreign policy. Other invitations to the White House went to former Vice-president John Nance Garner and 1944 Republican candidate Thomas E. Dewey; and it was observed that labor leaders ceased to be frequent visitors. Before the end of 1945 the President found it necessary to order the seizure and operation of more than a dozen petroleum refineries, machine works, coal mines, textile mills, rubber plants, railroad and truck lines (including the entire Chicago trucking industry) to keep these basic facilities from being shut down by industrial disputes; and he was asked to take over many more. Truman's generally "hands-off" labor policy was in contrast to that of the preceding twelve years, in which the Government acted as an interested party; and it has been suggested by *Fortune* that this factor was responsible for the failure of the labor-management conference the President called in November.

The man from Missouri had an unprecedentedly high degree of popularity during the "political honeymoon"—the classic hundred days' grace before a President's opponents settle down to opposing his policies and criticizing his personality. His popularity with the people, as indicated by surveys, remained high throughout the year: Elmo Roper's '45 December 1945 survey found 75.6 per cent classifying his conduct of foreign relations as excellent or good, 64.7 per cent (including more Republicans than Democrats) saying the same of his handling of Congress, and 58.9 per cent approving his handling of home problems. Four months earlier, approval of his internal and Congressional relations had been about five points higher, but approval of his relations with foreign countries had been 3.3 per cent lower.

Truman's legislative program—enough, it was said, to keep Congress busy for several sessions—was in the New Deal tradition on most or all points. His twenty-one-point message of September 6 included requests for increases in the minimum wage and unemployment benefits, a permanent FEPC, early action on the full employment bill, continuation of Federal control of the employment service, a single agency for Government scientific research and for promotion and support of science, and protection and encouragement of small business. It backed the "revolutionary" Wyatt housing program for ten to fifteen million houses in ten years, and asked for a program of regional development of the Nation's river valleys, crop insurance, research on agricultural problems, and the use of five hundred surplus Lend-Lease millions for the Commodities Credit Corporation to support prices. His viewpoint on public works and provision for veterans were in line with Roosevelt's, and he went further than his predecessor in recommending a five-point program for the country to "safeguard the health of all its citizens" by making provisions for adequate medical care for all. Despite the economies Truman had effected and the further decreases he had promised, he recommended the raising of Federal salaries—to twenty thousand a year in the case of Congressmen—and an "adequate" retirement system. He was not New Deal, however, when he approved a bill to place the hundred and one Government corporations, such as the TVA, RFC, HOLC, SWPC, under "annual scrutiny by Congress and . . . current financial control thereof," thereby ending the flexibility and quick action which were the corporations' reasons for being, and opening them to Congressional patronage. Unlike Roosevelt, too, Truman left the disposal of his proposed laws to Congress, engaging neither in political maneuvering for their passage nor in head-on fights with Congress.

Of the President's more than two dozen major proposals to Congress, five were passed: one-man administration of the huge job of surplus property disposal, funds for UNRRA, the formula for disposing of surplus ships, and participation in Bretton Woods and the United Nations. Five were drastically revised by the legislators: a "high level" employment planning program, retention of wartime Executive powers, lowered taxes, and authority to reorganize the Executive branch (thirteen agencies were wholly or partially exempted, contrary to the President's request). At the end of 1945, the rest had not been passed. This was in contrast to most people's expectations, as Truman had gone out of his way to maintain friendly relations with Congress. On the first day of his Presidency he had gone to the Capitol for an unprecedented luncheon conference with Congressional leaders, and eight days later he had invited the president pro tempore of the Senate, Southern Democrat Kenneth D. McKellar, to occupy the Vice-presidential seat at Cabinet meetings. Nevertheless, the same Republican-Southern Democratic coalition which had hampered Roosevelt seemed to have Truman's program blocked.

A striking difference was noticed between the President's public popularity and the tone of published comment after the first three months. Apart from ordinary partisanship, certain of his policies and actions brought unfavorable comment: the sudden removal of price control and rationing after V-E Day, and their restoration in September; the legally correct but undiplomatically and, for the borrowers, uneconomically, abrupt termination of Lend-Lease seven days after the Japanese surrender, a move approved by 49.4 per cent of the Nation, and by 19.6 per cent fewer Democrats than Republicans. His expressed hope that labor and management would "cut out all this foolishness and strikes and get back to work," did not endear him to either side; his oft-cited remarks that he had not wished to be President, and "sometimes I forget I'm President," drew ironic comment. The latter quotation might perhaps summarize the main faults found with him: that he appointed men who were too small for their jobs ("Truman's midgets") and leaned too heavily toward fellow-Missourians; that he lacked regard for his personal safety; that he offended important Congressmen by keeping in much closer touch with the clerk of the Senate, Leslie Biffle; that, although known to be a hard, long, and efficient worker, he took days off in a time of crisis for recreation; that he had continued Roosevelt's policies, but failed to fight for them, and had appointed men not in sympathy with their objectives to carry them out; that he was neither dynamic nor inspiring; that, in short, he was not a leader. General opinion seemed to agree with the *New Republic* estimate of him as "a well-intentioned, politically minded middle-roader, of higher caliber than some feared and of weaker leadership than some hoped."

Harry S. Truman is five feet ten, and "can still get into his World War uniform if the buttons are well anchored" (he weighs one hundred sixty-seven pounds). His hair is gray, with traces of black still remaining, and he has a bald spot; his eyes are hazel, and the spectacles he wears tend to magnify them. The President, who "never has a sick day," says he has no hobby or favorite sport; his only exercise is walking and calisthenics after he rises at six-thirty. Truman never smokes, and dislikes seeing women smoke. He drinks moderately, plays the piano—and a much better game of poker than he admits. One Missouri reporter solemnly told his readers that Harry Truman "cusses, but you notice that he avoids blasphemous profanity." He is a student of history, and can discuss past military campaigns in "astonishing" detail. Since becoming President, he has added, to his studies in American history, research on the life and times of Andrew Johnson, the former tailor who succeeded Abraham Lincoln just eighty years before Truman succeeded Roosevelt. President Truman calls himself a politician. "Government is politics," he has said, "and government which is not in the hands of skilled and honest politicians is less likely to be good government."

References

Collier's 114:24+ S 9 '44 pors
Life 17:75-9 Ag 21 '44 pors; 17:103+ N 6 '44 pors
N Y Herald Tribune p1+ Ap 13 '45 pors

TRUMAN, HARRY S.—*Continued*

N Y Sun p6 Ap 13 '45 por
N Y Times IV p4 Ap 15 '45
N Y Times Mag p13+ Ja 21 '45 por
New Republic 112:577-9 Ap 30 '45; 112: 635-8 My 7 '45 por
Newsweek 24:29-30 Jl 31 '44; 25:27-33 Ap 23 '45 pors
Read Dig p32-6 Je '45 por
St. Louis Post-Dispatch p6A Ap 13 '45 por
Time 41:13-15 Mr 8 '43 por; 44:14 Jl 31 '44; 45:21-4 Ap 23 '45 pors
Clemens, C. The Man From Missouri (1945)
Congressional Directory, 1945
McNaughton, F. and Hehmeyer, C. This Man Truman (1945)
Who's Who in America, 1944-45

TRUSCOTT, LUCIAN K(ING, JR.)
Jan. 9, 1895- United States Army officer
Address: b. c/o War Department, Washington, D.C.; h. Charlottesville, Va.

Lieutenant General Lucian K. Truscott, once called by *Time* "the ablest sea-to-land commander in the United States Army," succeeded General George S. Patton '43 in command of the Third Army occupying Bavaria in October 1945.

Born in Chatfield, Texas, on January 9, 1895, Lucian King Truscott, Jr., is the son of Lucian

U.S. Army Signal Corps
LT. GEN. LUCIAN K. TRUSCOTT

King Truscott, a country doctor, and Maria Temple (Tully) Truscott. On his mother's side he is of Irish descent; on his father's he is English. Lucian spent his early childhood in Chatfield, then moved with his family to Oklahoma when he was six. In 1911 he received a certificate from the normal school in Norman, Oklahoma; afterward, for six years he taught school in one-room Oklahoma schoolhouses during the winter and studied at various teachers' institutes during the summer, receiving certificates from schools in Sapulpa (1912) and

Eufaula (1913). Lucian's grandfather, for whom the town of Truscott is named, had helped found the Texas Agricultural and Mechanical College.

Enlisting in the United States Army during the First World War, the former schoolteacher was assigned to Officers Training Camp at Fort Logan H. Roots, Arkansas. Commissioned a second lieutenant of Cavalry in the Officers Reserve Corps on August 15, 1917, he was assigned to the Seventeenth Cavalry at Douglas, Arizona. On October 26, 1917, he was commissioned a second lieutenant of Cavalry in the Regular Army and on the same day was promoted to first lieutenant (temporary). Two months later his lieutenancy was made permanent.

Young Lieutenant Truscott in March 1919 was transferred with his cavalry unit for duty at Schofield Barracks, Hawaii, where he was stationed for the next two and a half years. During this period he was promoted to captain. Returning to the United States in October 1921, Captain Truscott was assigned to duty at the Presidio at San Francisco. His assignment there was short-lived, for within two months he was transferred to the First Machine Gun Squadron at Douglas, Arizona. Transferred again almost immediately, in February 1922 he was assigned to the First Cavalry at the same post, where he stayed for three and a half years. At the end of this time he was assigned to Fort Bliss, Texas, for service with the Eighth Cavalry.

In October 1925 the Captain entered the Cavalry School at Fort Riley, from which he was graduated the following June. One year later, having completed his course in the Advanced Class, Truscott became an instructor at the school. His next assignment was to the Third Cavalry at Fort Myer, Virginia, where, beginning in June 1931, he served for a little less than three years. In March 1934 he went to Mexico as a member of the United States Army polo team. An expert player, he helped to defeat the Mexican Army team, then in May returned to his former duties at Fort Myer. Three months later he enrolled at the Command and General Staff School at Fort Leavenworth, Kansas, completing his course in June 1936. While at the school he was promoted to major.

After graduation Major Truscott remained at the school as an instructor, a post he held until September 1940. At this time he was appointed executive officer of the Second Battalion of the Thirteenth Armored Regiment at Fort Knox, Kentucky, and a few months later he became operations officer of the regiment. In July 1941 he went to Fort Lewis, Washington, joining the Ninth Corps General Staff as assistant to the plans and training officer, G-3. Three weeks after the bombing of Pearl Harbor he became a colonel (temporary), and in May 1942 he was promoted to brigadier general (temporary).

That same month the new general was sent to England and attached to Admiral Lord Louis Mountbatten's '42 combined operations staff of the British Army, Navy, and Air Force. Assigned to organize an American counterpart to the British Commandos, Truscott visited every Commando training unit in England and Scotland. The outcome of this inspection tour was an American Ranger unit, the first of its kind, which he organized and trained. These Rangers of Truscott's took their name from Rogers' Rangers—crafty frontiersmen who in Colonial days had fought the French near the Canadian border under their leader, Major Robert Rogers. (Later, in the American Revolution, Rogers fought on the side of the British.)

All of Truscott's Rangers were volunteers, chosen for their adeptness in using mortars, daggers, grenades, or tommy (submachine) guns. Describing the intensive training which the Rangers had to undergo, Rice Yahner of the Associated Press has written: "The men drilled at double time until their feet blistered and their lungs were bursting. When their legs were ready to fold, they started again. . . . Then they got climbing and diving and crawling over obstacles and crossing a bridge made of the seven-foot ropes which each man carries. . . . Then a thirty-six-mile hike over bleak, trackless mountains, with only half-rations and what the men could forage from the countryside." Truscott, their leader, was "hard as hell, drove the men, but outdid the best of them." When the Rangers were ready for action, Truscott, as the ranking American officer, joined in the planning of the Dieppe raid. In August 1942 American Rangers, Canadians, Free French, and Mountbatten's Commandos launched a land, sea, and air raid on the little French town. Although the attackers suffered heavy casualties and the operation was unsuccessful, the Allies learned much about invasion technique that was useful in later landings.

In the invasion of North Africa in November Truscott led a special task force to capture Port Lyautey in French Morocco. That same month he was made a major general (temporary). On December 15 he was awarded the Distinguished Service Medal. The citation, in part, said: "For exceptionally meritorious service in a duty of great responsibility. General Truscott organized a wholly strange command . . . and planned operations in a manner that demonstrated organization and administrative ability of the highest order. His conduct of the landing operations . . . resulted in the capture of Port Lyautey, with its harbor, against superior enemy opposition. He exhibited tireless activity and devotion to duty and complete scorn of personal danger."

During the battle of Tunisia in the winter of 1942-43 Truscott was field deputy to Allied Commander Dwight D. Eisenhower [42]. At the close of the North African campaign, Truscott became commanding general of the Third Infantry Division—the "Rock of the Marne Division" of the First World War, which had existed as a Regular Army unit between the two wars. Truscott at once established a rigorous training program for his Third Division. Intent on making his soldiers the "fastest, toughest marchers in the Army," he increased the infantry marching speed of two and a half miles per hour to five miles per hour the first hour, four miles per hour for the next two hours, and three and a half miles an hour for the remainder of the distance. The men soon referred to these exhausting "hikes" as the "Truscott Trot." However, it was this trot and Truscott's driving hatred of the Germans that helped to make the Third Infantry Division a powerful fighting unit.

In the battle of Sicily in July 1943, Truscott's Third Division found that their weeks of intense training had been very profitable. Landing at Licata on the southern coast of Sicily, they fought northward towards Agrigento. After a week's battle in Agrigento, they marched a hundred miles in five days from that city to Palermo. *Life* Magazine refers to this operation as one that is already "classic in military annals for speed and success." For his "extraordinary heroism . . . intrepid direction . . . heroic leadership . . . superior professional ability," Truscott received the Distinguished Service Cross. From Palermo men moved eastward through mountainous terrain, in record time; in September they made two amphibious landings on the Italian mainland to capture Messina. In the words of one Army officer, "What Truscott did in Sicily was to turn his infantry into a cavalry." Truscott was awarded the Legion of Merit in August of the same year.

From Messina the Third Division was rushed to Salerno to reinforce the battered troops of General Sir Oliver Leese's [44] British Eighth Army. Pushing northward, the Allies then took Naples in October. At the Volturno River, north of Naples, a stubborn German Army found Truscott a determined adversary. In a desperate effort to get his tanks across the river to an unprotected regiment of men who had worked their way across the Volturno in advance of the armored mobile units, the General appeared at the most advanced post, shouting to the engineers, "You've got only picks and shovels, men, only your hands, but right now they're better than guns. Let's get this job done! We've got a whole regiment over there. They'll get wiped out unless you get those tanks across." The engineers finished the bridge that day, and the tanks were able to go to the aid of the vulnerable regiment. Pressing forward, the division fought a bitter battle, which drove the enemy to the Liri Valley, thus providing a toehold for later Allied attacks. After this battle, Truscott's men were given well-deserved furloughs.

In January 1944 Truscott was appointed deputy commander of the Sixth Army Corps (of which the Third Division was a component). This division was one of the two divisions that made the original landings at Anzio. Immediately after the second German counterattack in March, which almost pushed the Allied troops into the sea, Truscott was promoted to commander of the corps. The new commander so successfully smashed a third enemy offensive that the Germans limited their action to holding the area. After the few months' Anzio stalemate the corps finally broke through to take part in the capture of Rome. According to one source, the corps has a signed certificate from Rome's chief of police stating that it was the first unit to reach the capital.

When plans for the invasion of southern France were completed, Truscott and his men were withdrawn from Italy in August 1944 to take part in the amphibious landing. Leading the assault forces, the General directed what has been called one of the outstanding operations in amphibious warfare. What is not generally realized is that more troops were put ashore in southern France at

TRUSCOTT, LUCIAN K.—*Continued*

H-Hour than had been landed earlier in Normandy at H-Hour. The early capture by Truscott's troops of three ranking German officers, one a divisional general and another in charge of invasion defenses, upset the enemy's communications and command. Attached to General Alexander M. Patch's [43] Seventh Army, Truscott employed surprise attacks and fast flanking movements to catch the enemy off guard. Consequently, the Allied forces drove through southern France with incredible speed. Within nineteen days they had taken Lyon. Truscott planned for an early junction at the Belfort Gap, near the French-German-Swiss border, with American troops driving southeast from Normandy. The speedy and successful carrying out of this plan cut off thousands of Germans in southern France. On September 2 Truscott was promoted to lieutenant general (temporary).

At the end of the year, in December, General Truscott was sent back to Italy and made commanding general of the Fifth Army, succeeding General Mark Clark [42] who was given command of the Fifteenth Army Group. Under Truscott's command the Fifth Army continued its push north on a seventy-mile front, from the Ligurian coast of western Italy to Imola, a city about twenty-five miles south of Bologna. Progress was greatly impeded by bad weather and the mountainous terrain, and it was not until April 21, 1945, that Bologna, communications hub of the Po Plain, fell to the Allies. On April 30 General Mark Clark said, "The German armies in Italy have been virtually eliminated as a military force by the shattering onslaught of the Allies." A few days later, on May 2, the German armies in Italy surrendered unconditionally.

The Fifth Army "became unoperational" on the second anniversary of its landing at Salerno; the men were sent home for discharge in September 1945. The next month, their commander was given charge of the Third Army and the Eastern Military District (more than half the American zone of occupation), succeeding the spectacular General Patton, who had expressed disagreement with Supreme Commander Eisenhower's denazification policy. This appointment placed Truscott in military control of Bavaria, and on October 26 President Truman [45] made him a permanent brigadier general. "Truscott has made a very good impression on his own men and on the press representatives here generally," reported Victor Bernstein of *PM*. "And in place of the clerico-fascist Friedrich Schaeffer, the new government of Bavaria now has a mild Leftist cabinet headed by [returned exile] Wilhelm Hoegner, Social Democrat, as prime minister, and including three other Social Democrats and one Communist minister without portfolio who has been given the key job of denazification. The new Cabinet," he added, "is not pure red, or even pure pink. At several spots it smells, if not of brown cloth, at least of black."

Truscott saw his first task of reform as educating his own soldiers to the realities of the situation. There was a constant flux and shift of personnel, with resulting confusion; but beyond that was the problem of men without combat experience, who had never encountered the Germans except as a defeated nation and were therefore open to "a widespread attitude of laxness and cordiality toward all Germans" without distinction. Bavaria had a normal population of eight million; but despite the absence of its young men, the total was increased to a million and a half more Germans —by refugees from bombed areas and deportees from Czechoslovakia—plus half a million displaced persons of other nationalities, housed by December in two hundred and twenty UNRRA camps. Truscott reported that disorder in general was less than in a comparable area in the United States, and stated that the closest watch discovered no sign of an underground movement, no attempt at sabotage, and no concerted opposition to American authority. Commenting on the vastness of the occupation problem, Anne O'Hare McCormick [40] wrote, "a great many officers are performing an unprecedented and supremely difficult job with impressive competence and devotion."

"Gray-haired, with a jutting jaw and squinting gray eyes," the General is described as a handsome man. Unorthodox in his military dress, he wore a shiny, enameled helmet, a weather-stained jacket, a white silk scarf, and his "lucky" faded dress cavalry breeches and boots. Even in the field, *Life* said he insisted that flowers be put in his tent every day and that his meals be prepared by a Chinese-American cook. His men were said to admire and respect him. General Truscott was awarded two foreign decorations in 1943—the Legion of Honor in the degree of Officer, from General Giraud [42], and the Honorary Companion of the Most Honorable Order of the Bath, from Great Britain's King. In 1919 Truscott was married to Sarah Randolph, a descendant of the Thomas Jefferson branch of Virginia's Randolph family. They have three children, two sons (one of whom in 1945 was studying at West Point), and one daughter. Polo is the General's favorite peacetime sport.

References

Life 17:96-111 O 2 '44 il pors
N Y Herald Tribune II p3 O 7 '45 por
N Y Sun p18 D 6 '44 por
Newsweek 20:21 Ag 31 '42
Who's Who in America, 1944-45

TUCKER, SOPHIE 1884(?)- Entertainer
Address: b. c/o William Morris, 1270 Sixth Ave., New York City

The "Last of the Red-hot Mamas," Sophie Tucker, has been booming her throaty tones for almost two score years: she began her career in 1906 in the heyday of American vaudeville, and has, through night-club appearances, survived its decline and fall. Endowed with the determination, stamina, and spirit of a good trouper, and with a personality and voice which match her generous proportions, this vaudevillian has won audiences not only in the United States, but in the British Isles and on the Continent. Her autobiography, named for her theme song, "Some of These Days," and published in the spring of 1945, gives a hearty account of her full life.

Sophie Tucker was literally born "on the road." In 1884 her mother was traveling by wagon out of Russia on her way to join her

husband in America, when the child was born.
The family name was originally Kalish, but
on his journey to America, the father took the
name of a dead friend. Miss Tucker describes
the circumstances: "Papa, who had a terror
of the Russian authorities reaching out and
grabbing him and shipping him to Siberia for
life, prudently helped himself to the Italian's
papers and moniker. Don't ask me what the
United States immigration officers made of an
Italian who couldn't speak anything but Russian and Yiddish; but it was as 'Charles Abuza'
that Papa got into this country, and found a
job in Boston."

Hence, in 1884, at the age of three months,
Sophie Abuza arrived in Boston, where the
family lived for eight years—Miss Tucker remarks regretfully that nobody has ever admired her "Harvard accent." They moved to
Hartford when the father bought a restaurant
there. With her brothers, Philip and Moses,
and her sister, Anna, young Sophie enjoyed the
excitement of the city streets near the Connecticut River. The children had to help in the
restaurant, which Sophie disliked. She hated
especially the endless dish washing but obedi-
ently followed her mother's stern orders. Because she rose early to finish kitchen chores
before going to school, the girl sometimes fell
asleep in class.

While working at her job at the tables
the young girl listened to the talk of the actors
who frequented the Abuza Restaurant. She had
a strong voice and would often sing popular
songs in the restaurant, after which the customers would tip her. Once her mother saved
enough money to buy a second-hand piano, but
when Sophie neglected her piano practice, the
instrument was sold. Hoping to draw customers, the girl began to sing regularly in the restaurant, winning some applause. She went to
vaudeville matinees and learned the songs in
the shows. But while actors complimented her
singing, her parents warned her against show
business. Miss Tucker recalls how thrilled she
was when she served the great Jewish actors
Jacob Adler and Boris Thomashefsky, who had
come to eat Mrs. Abuza's cooking. These celebrities urged the girl's family to permit her to
join one of the Jewish theatrical companies,
but the parents firmly refused. Soon after her
graduation from school, when she was sixteen,
Sophie Abuza eloped with Louis Tuck. She
had hoped to escape the drudgery of the kitchen, but the joy of her own small apartment
was short lived. When their son Bert was
born, the couple moved back with the Abuza
family to ease their financial difficulties. Once
more Sophie was back in the restaurant. She
started singing there again, and was told her
voice was better than before. About this time
she was separated from her husband, eventually
obtaining a divorce.

The ambitious young woman, determined to
get away from restaurant chores, saved all
her money and, on the pretext of going on a
vacation, left home to become an entertainer.
She went first to New Haven to see Willie
Howard, who had advised her to try the entertainment field. The comedian told her to
go to New York to try her luck. She spent
her first weeks in the big city looking for work
as a "song plugger" in Tin Pan Alley, with
no success. When her money ran low she

SOPHIE TUCKER

"sang for her supper" in restaurants. Meanwhile, she continued to frequent the offices of
the music publishers, making friends and becoming known to the song writers. In 1906 she
changed her name to Tucker.

In November of that year she obtained a
job at a popular cafe, the German Village,
singing for fifteen dollars a week. She worked
herself up to leading entertainer in this place,
all the while continuing to visit the music publishers for new songs. Throughout her career
she has been careful about her songs, seeking
new tunes continually, especially those suited
to her robust style of singing. She auditioned
for an amateur show at the 125th Street Theatre and overheard the manager give orders for
her to appear in blackface, saying she was
"too big and ugly." Thus she started her stage
career in disguise, wearing blackface make-up.
Joe Woods booked her on a small-time vaudeville circuit, billing her as a "World-renowned
Coon Shouter." Later she played on the Park
Circuit, performing in the smaller cities of
New York, New Jersey, Pennsylvania, and
Ohio, where she began to acquire a following.
Her first New York date was at the Music
Hall on 116th Street on December 9, 1906.
Thereafter she played her blackface act on the
New England circuit, learning from other per-
formers and developing her technique.

Tony Pastor's Theatre in New York was
then one of the city's famous entertainment centers. Miss Tucker obtained an engagement
there and made elaborate preparations for her
appearance. When she came on the stage, a
noisy audience entering the theatre paid little
attention to her. She shouted at the audience,
won their attention and, soon, their approval.
After seeing her act at Pastor's, a burlesque
manager offered Miss Tucker a contract. She
accepted, having heard that burlesque work
was good theatrical training. Her first part
in burlesque was a cranky old wife, and although she learned dialogue quickly, she had
difficulty with the character. But despite the

TUCKER, SOPHIE—*Continued*

bad rehearsals, she was a success when the show opened.

One day while playing the burlesque circuit her trunk containing her make-up and costumes was lost, forcing her to perform without blackface. It was a triumphant moment for her when she realized she could hold an audience without the benefit of disguise. In 1909 a talent scout saw Miss Tucker in one of these shows and she was offered a part in the current Ziegfeld *Follies*. Nora Bayes was the star of this particular production, a lavish production with the usual abundance of beautiful girls. During rehearsals nobody seemed to notice Miss Tucker, who was doubtful until the last minute that she would actually appear in the show.

Finally she was assigned to a jungle scene, and at the time of her first and only rehearsal, a cold prevented her from singing. In this show she was also scheduled to fill in time between acts with songs selected by her old friend Irving Berlin [42]. Opening night was a gala event, with an audience of celebrities including "Diamond Jim" Brady, Lillian Russell, George M. Cohan, and Sam Harris. Miss Tucker stopped the show with her inter-act specialty. The star objected, and Ziegfeld decided that Miss Tucker was to do only the jungle song. Years later Miss Tucker became a close friend of Nora Bayes's, but neither of them ever mentioned this incident. When the *Follies* came to New York, Miss Bayes had left the show and was replaced by Eva Tanguay, who wanted the jungle number herself. So Miss Tucker was fired. During her trying times with the *Follies*, she was befriended by a Negro maid, Mollie Elkins, who became her lifelong friend.

Back in New York, without work or money, the singer suffered a temporary loss of voice. With Miss Elkins' help she managed to start again after a brief rest. It was then she began her long association with William Morris, whose agency still manages her. Morris organized his own vaudeville circuit of American Music Halls, for which he brought to America such English entertainers as Sir Harry Lauder and Charlie Chaplin [40]. Miss Tucker played this circuit with great success; she had finally attained a sense of security in her work. In Chicago, where she was especially popular, billed as "The Mary Garden of Ragtime," Ashton Stevens wrote: "Miss Tucker can move an audience or a piano with equal address. Don't miss any of her." During this period of her career, she started to use the double-entendre songs which have become closely identified with her style. She explains that she sings "hot numbers" to entertain, not to shock, insisting that all of these songs have as themes something real in people's lives. She says: "The innocents couldn't find a thing in it to object to, and the others would find a belly laugh in every line." (Jack Yellen has been writing this type of song for her for over twenty years.) Miss Tucker first saw her name in lights at an Atlantic City theater—she was a headliner at last. She made recordings for the Edison Company and sent the money she earned home to her mother. All these years she had been contributing to her family's support and had sent her brother through college.

When she was booked on the Pantages Circuit, the singer traveled West, increasing her popularity. Once in Dayton she tried a costume publicity stunt which failed because people were more interested in the airplane the Wright brothers were trying out. Back in Chicago in April 1911, after her Western tour, she accepted a part in the show *Merry Mary*. This was a failure, but her next venture, *Louisiana Lou*, was a hit. Her earnings were high but gambling took its toll. However, whenever she was in financial difficulties she would sign for a road tour and wipe out the deficit. In 1911 the Negro composer Shelton Brooks brought her his song "Some of These Days." She made it her trade mark and it has remained popular ever since.

Miss Tucker delights in telling of her return in triumph to her home town to headline the show at Poli's Theatre in Hartford. The joy of her return was increased by the presence of her son who was vacationing from military school. (Whenever she was in New York, Miss Tucker always sent for the boy.) During her next engagement she met Frank Westphal, who had a piano act, and the two became a team. In August 1914 she attained the pinnacle of vaudeville success—a date at the Palace Theatre in New York. For this engagement she earned one thousand dollars and the plaudits of both audience and critics. One critic stated, "She just walked out and owned the place." Miss Tucker married Westphal in Chicago, where the wedding party was treated to the Lohengrin *Wedding March* played by Paderewski, who happened to be in the restaurant in which they were celebrating. The couple's strenuous vaudeville schedule, Miss Tucker says, was not exactly conducive to matrimonial harmony—they played two shows daily, six or seven days a week for several seasons of "big-time" vaudeville. During the years of the First World War Miss Tucker introduced the famous song "M-o-t-h-e-r, the Word That Means the World to Me." She was changing her singing style, abandoning "coon shouting." In 1916 she toured in the show *Town Topics*. During her tours she met the great celebrities of the time, as well as many struggling vaudevillians who later rose to fame. On one bill she played with Gus Edwards' school act; among the child actors were Eddie Cantor [41], George Jessel [43], and Walter Winchell [43].

When Miss Tucker found her marriage failing she set her husband up in the garage business and continued alone. She organized a jazz band, named it "The Five Kings of Syncopation" and called herself "The Queen of Jazz." The new act was a success; Miss Tucker started dramatizing songs, an innovation which became popular. Then her father's death brought about another change in her style: she began to sing ballads—"tearjerkers"—and discovered that she could sing them effectively. This new act entailed greater responsibility for the singer, charged with the supervision of the men in the band. In December 1916 they opened at Reisenweber's, one of the leading restaurants of the day. That was the beginning of the Jazz Era and Miss Tucker and her band were a smash success. Her "Bohemian Nights" at Reisenweber's became famous; she introduced new songs and new performers. On Sunday nights she sang in concerts at the Winter Garden Theatre, where she was the hit of the 1919 season. That year she also appeared in the show *Hello Alexander*. After a summer at her Freeport (Long Island) home, among theatrical friends, Miss Tucker and Westphal were divorced. Following frequent changes in the personnel of her act, it was disbanded. Miss Tucker hired a new pianist, Ted Schapiro, who has been with her since. After playing Reisenweber's for five years she decided to try something new. Morris arranged her booking in the British music halls (equivalent of vaudeville in America), and the singer sailed for England on March 25, 1922.

Upon her arrival in England she noted the differences between the technique of the English music hall and American vaudeville and set about adapting her material to her new audience. She slowed her tempo down to British tastes and also changed some of the lyrics to follow British colloquialisms more closely. Overcoming her nervousness and becoming accustomed to the sloping British stages, Miss Tucker was a hit with the English. At a Jewish benefit at the Palladium in London, she used a duo-piano team for the first time and also delighted the audience by her remarks in Yiddish. Her tour included Glasgow, Edinburgh, Cardiff, Nottingham, Manchester, and the provinces. Everywhere she was well received, and Miss Tucker says simply: "The British are just folks, same as those in the U.S.A." Dramatic critic Hanan Swaffer expressed the British view, describing Miss Tucker as "a big, fat blond genius, with a dynamic personality and amazing vitality." While in England the singer played in the show *Round in Fifty* for three months. She made many friends in London, entertaining for "high society" and royalty. But her proudest memory of London is the reception she received at the Rivoli Theatre in Whitechapel from London's Jewish population. Before returning home, Miss Tucker visited Brussels, Berlin, and Paris.

After a triumphant return to the Palace Theatre in New York, she began a new tour, this time on the Orpheum Circuit. There was a brief stop in Hollywood for work in silent films, which was unsuccessful. The next two years were filled with steady vaudeville work, highlighted by her acquaintance with Helen Keller [42] (who appeared on the stage), and by a performance at San Quentin Prison, where the singer met Tom Mooney. In August 1925 Miss Tucker again sailed for England to fill an engagement at the fashionable Kit-Kat Klub in London. In addition to her night-club performances, the singer played in the music halls and appeared with Beatrice Lillie [45] and Gertrude Lawrence [40] in *Charlot's Revue*. One of her most popular songs in England was "My Yiddisha Mama," which audiences always demanded. Her stay in England was halted by news of her mother's illness. She broke contracts to return home, but during the voyage was notified of her mother's death. It was three months before Miss Tucker was able to sing again. She lost her self-confidence and her desire to be amusing. Finally, with the assistance of

Morris, she began to sing again, first at benefits and then in her own cafe, Sophie Tucker's Playground. Eventually, fully restored, Miss Tucker went back to vaudeville. She was offered a part in Earl Carroll's *Vanities*, but after ten days among the "beauties" she left the show. At another appearance at the Palace she was billed as the "Last of the Red-hot Mamas"—and that title has stayed with her.

In 1928 Miss Tucker was once more back in London, playing at the Kit-Kat Klub, the music halls and touring the provinces. She was persuaded to take a part opposite Edmund Brean in a Greek play, *Socrates*, which thereby was transformed into an uproarious farce. In 1929, back in America, she made her first talking film, *Honky Tonk,* for Warner Brothers, but found motion pictures a difficult type of work. Returning to London in 1930 she played in a musical comedy, *Follow a Star.* (In the intervening years she had been married to Al Lackey.) After this London engagement Miss Tucker attempted performances for Continental audiences, but the language bar was a handicap. At Ostend the audience did not understand any of her songs; at her Paris opening her only knowledge of French was one chorus of "Some of These Days," which she had had translated. So she returned for a tour in England, after which she and her husband vacationed in Europe. In Vienna she discovered that her records were popular—the best seller was "My Yiddisha Mama." Miss Tucker was invited to broadcast this song in Berlin in 1931; after Hitler [42] came into power her records were ordered smashed and their sale banned in the Reich.

The singer returned to the United States to find vaudeville in its last days. The years 1931 and 1932 saw the death of vaudeville—a painful episode for the "oldtimers" who had to step aside for the new motion picture idols. But although her pride suffered, the singer continued her active career. In 1934 she played at the Hollywood Country Club in Florida. (At about this time she was divorced from Al Lackey.) Cafe business was bad; besides films, there was now radio competition. In 1934 Miss Tucker was back in England, performing in the big cities and provinces. That year she gave a command performance for King George V and Queen Mary. On her return to America she was given a gala home-coming party by the American Federation of Actors. During the winter of 1934-35 she played at the Hollywood Restaurant in New York, and at many benefit performances. Next she appeared at the Hollywood Trocadero, making a new bid for motion pictures but without success. In 1936 she returned to London in time to witness the strained weeks leading up to the abdication of King Edward VIII (Duke of Windsor [44]). Miss Tucker was acquainted with the former Prince of Wales and was deeply touched by the entire affair.

In 1937 Miss Tucker was in Hollywood, trying the films again, under contract to Metro-Goldwyn-Mayer. Anxious for success in the new medium, she took acting lessons from Laura Hope Crews. In *Broadway Melody* Miss Tucker played with Eleanor Powell, Robert Taylor, and Judy Garland [41]. Then in *Thoroughbreds Don't Cry* she played a straight character part without singing. But she was dissatisfied with her career in motion pictures

TUCKER, SOPHIE—*Continued*

and left Hollywood. She does not recommend the pictures she has made, declaring: "That is not Tucker you see on the screen." From Hollywood she went back to night-club work, appearing in 1938 at Ben Marden's Riviera in New Jersey. In that same year she was elected president of the American Federation of Actors, the first woman to hold that office.

In November 1938 she opened in the musical comedy *Leave It To Me*, which was a success on Broadway and later on tour. While performing in this show she did cafe and radio work, also participating actively in the affairs of the A.F.A. Her next show, in 1941, was George Jessel's *High Kickers*. It received bad critical notices much to Miss Tucker's indignation. In March 1944 "The Durable Tucker" opened as star of a brilliant revue at New York's Copacabana. Discussing the show, the New York *Sun* stated: "Sophie Tucker isn't cooling off any, and for that matter neither is her doting audience. . . .Miss Tucker, magnificently turned out, gives utterance to hardy aphorisms and characteristic laments with all of her raucous sincerity, and her audience loves it." In April 1944 *PM* paid tribute to Miss Tucker for canceling a Boston night-club engagement to entertain wounded servicemen at Halloran General Hospital in New York. The singer is as popular with servicemen in the Second World War as she was in the First.

The sixty-one-year-old trouper was given a write-up in *Variety* in October 1945, a report of her engagement at the Mayfair in Boston: "Headlining at $3,500-a-week salary, an accepted invitation to speak at the Boston Book Fair, and sell-out dinner tables every night, Sophie Tucker is doing very well by herself. Time has not changed nor custom withered the marvelous trouper's 'Honey Boy', 'Some of These Days,' and 'How You Gonna Keep 'Em Down on the Farm?' which have the same wow reaction as when Soph was here three years ago. . . .She still has the spirit of youth, and now and then carries out the promise of a hit song, 'Red Hot Mama Is a Jitterbug Now.'" *Variety* added that only Miss Tucker could put the rowdy "Tax on Love" across under Boston censorship—and that she did it with a "cosmic bang." On the occasion of her engagement at the Martinique, New York newspaper reviews were equally enthusiastic.

For a number of years Miss Tucker had been writing down her own account of her long life in show business. In March 1945 the finished book, *Some of These Days*, was published. The autobiography, as one might expect, was full of anecdotes of Miss Tucker's famous friends in the entertainment world, as well as being a lively, hearty tale of struggle and success, with no mistake about the success. Stanley Walker described it as one of the "pleasantest, most ingratiating and unpretentious autobiographies ever turned out by anybody in show business." The *Library Journal* called it "frank and racy," written "entertainingly and with engaging honesty." Dissenting opinion was voiced by Bernard Sobel, who wrote in the *Saturday Review of Literature*: "As an autobiographer Sophie Tucker is—to use her own idiom—a 'flop.' But as an entertainer she is still 'tops' . . . international goddess of off-color laughter and

song." But *Variety*, the "showbiz" paper, called the book "real, earthy, honest. Soph takes pride in herself, her work, and her profession. . . .Her cavalcade of names reads like a who's who out of *Burke's Peerage* and the Ellis Island steerage, with a very imposing array of Equity, NVA, Hollywood, and Côte d'Azur names in between." Jo Ranson in the New York *Times* said pungently, "This is a sharp, honest, and frequently uncorseted tale. . . . Sophie herself has gone right on, singing the 'hot numbers' which, she explains, are all very moral because 'they have to do with sex, but not with vice.'" "She does not gloss over or apologize for anything, not even her love life, which she admits 'set her back a million,'" the *Book-of-the-Month Club News* commented. And when Miss Tucker arrived in New York in July 1945 after a run at the Chez Paree in Chicago, *Variety* reported she "sliced a $34,200 melon to theatrical and other charities gained through sales of fifteen hundred of the twenty-five-dollar de luxe editions of her autobiog. Beneficiaries on an even split are Actors Fund, Catholic, Episcopal, and Jewish Theatrical Guilds, Home for the Aged, Hartford, Connecticut, and the Sophie Tucker Playground Camp Fund."

The fair-haired, blue-eyed entertainer is "big in voice, heart and beam." Disarmingly frank about her appearance, Miss Tucker has capitalized on her unglamorous aspects in song. When performing she has always been elaborately gowned and gorgeously bejeweled. Past sixty, the personable performer is still an audience favorite and still "good old Sophie" to the admiring members of her profession. Called by one critic "an institution" in the entertainment world, Miss Tucker has a formula for success in show business: "Above all, the performer must look ahead. You can't grow stale or cling to a period. You must belong to your time." She firmly believes in organization in the theatrical profession; her experiences in unionism form an interesting part of her autobiography. She states: "I am convinced that the actor needs his union. But he needs to be an active, vigorous part of it." High-spirited, philanthropic Miss Tucker is proud of her profession and its great tradition. "Show business has been my life. I wouldn't have had any other. It is the life I always wanted."

References

N Y Post p20 Mr 24 '44
N Y World-Telegram p13 S 22 '41; p15 Ap 17 '44 pors
International Motion Picture Almanac, 1937-38
Tucker, S. Some of These Days (1945)

TUDOR, ANTONY Apr. 4, 1909- Choreographer; dancer

Address: b. c/o Ballet Theatre, 25 W. 45th St., New York City; h. 52 W. 52d St., New York City

Antony Tudor, as dancer and "one of the most significant choreographers of this century," has been a leading member of the Ballet Theatre in America since 1938. Previously his career in the ballet comprised eight years as dancer and choreographer in his native England; and he has won distinction in the United States for his creation of works ranging from tragedy to satire.

Born in London on April 4, 1909, Antony Tudor (the dancer's professional name) was brought up in the British capital, where his family was in business. The young man began his career as a clerk, but a few visits to the ballet determined his future—for in 1928 he saw Anna Pavlova dance, and he attended the ballets presented by Serge Diaghilev. "These experiences changed the whole course of his life," writes Cyril W. Beaumont in the *Complete Book of Ballets*. Tudor became deeply interested in the dance, ambitious to become the director of a ballet company. He therefore decided to study the technique of the classical ballet and subsequently studied with Mme. Marie Rambert, Pearl Argyle, and Harold Turner.

Meanwhile he continued to earn his living in business, and in 1930 he joined a firm of real estate assessors. The position, however, required traveling and thus interfered with his ballet studies. For this reason, when Mme. Rambert founded the Ballet Club later that year and offered him a two-year contract as secretary and dancer, Tudor accepted. The young dancer soon tried his talents at choreography, going to Shakespeare's *Twelfth Night* for the theme of his first ballet, *Cross-gartered*. Produced in 1931, this work won praise from Massine '40. It is reported that Tudor had very little money during this period; when part of his research for his first work involved a trip to its original setting in Italy, his father supplied the funds as a gift for his twenty-first birthday.

In 1932 Tudor's contract was renewed for another year and when, in September 1933, he joined the Vic-Wells Ballet, he maintained his connection with the Ballet Club. During two years with Vic-Wells he danced many roles, including Eusebius in *Le Carnaval*, the Man in *La Création du monde*, and the Man in *Hommage aux belles Viennoises*. Tudor also arranged the ballets in the operas *Carmen* and *Faust*, while continuing to produce his own works at the Ballet Club. In 1932 he composed the ballet *Lysistrata* or *The Strike of Wives*, with music by Prokofiev '41, and that year also saw the production of *Adam and Eve* (Lambert) for the Camargo Society. The next year brought *Atlanta of the East* (Seelig), which, with Tudor's first two works, was pronounced by A. L. Haskell (*Balletomania*, 1934) "the most interesting yet produced by an Englishman." In 1934 *The Planets* (Holst) was presented, and Tudor also produced *Castor and Pollux* for the Oxford University Opera Club. In 1935 came *The Descent of Hebe* (Bloch) and during the opera season at Covent Garden the choreographer arranged the dances for *Schwanda*, *La Cenerentola*, *Carmen*, and *Koanga*. His next ballet, in 1936, *Lilac Garden* (Chausson), with "a Maupassant-like plot," was later to become an American favorite. *Dark Elegies* (Mahler), too, first presented at the Duchess Theatre in 1937, was destined for American popularity. In 1937 Tudor also produced *Gallant Assembly* (Tartini) at the Playhouse at Oxford. In each of his ballets the choreographer danced a principal role. During

Shelburne Studios

ANTONY TUDOR

those years of his London career Tudor arranged the dances for musicals and once coached movie actress Vivien Leigh for a dancing part in *The Happy Hypocrite*.

When the Ballet Theatre invited Antony Tudor to come to America in 1938, the Englishman brought with him his most popular works, which rapidly won approval and became part of the company's active repertoire. Critics of the dance generally acknowledge Tudor as one of the most original choreographers in the contemporary ballet. His work is judged part of the modern idiom, like the ballets of Agnes de Mille '43 and Jerome Robbins, which have revitalized the dance. Mark Schubart has said that of all choreographers Tudor "manages best to utilize the modern idiom in a way that people understand; to have new ideas and get them across to his audience." Another critic, noting the Tudor traits of simplicity and understatement, has commented that his ballets have "a dreamlike, nostalgic, heavily perfumed quality." Edwin Denby, in his article "Tudor and Pantomime" (New York *Herald Tribune*, July 11, 1943), remarked that "Tudor succeeds as a storyteller, using ballet images." In *Dance* (June 1945), Dorothy Barret in discussing the choreographer's scholarly treatment of themes declared, "There is more than meets the eye in Tudor's ballets."

Lilac Garden, presented during the 1940 season, won the praise of New York *Times* critic John Martin, who commented that the sentimental, poignant drama made good use of the academic tradition. Four years later the *Sun*'s Arthur V. Berger called this ballet "a work which is among the best contemporary ballets." At New York's Lewisohn Stadium in August 1940 the Ballet Theatre presented Tudor's "lighthearted little ballet," *Goya Pastoral*, set to the music of Granados' *Goyescas*. February 1941 saw the American première of *Gala Performance*, a spirited burlesque of ballet in "the most Russian-Russian manner," which became an immediate box-office success.

TUDOR, ANTONY—*Continued*

After a performance in April 1943 Burton Rascoe called this satire "a delight."

With the première of *Pillar of Fire* in April 1942, another facet of Tudor's creative ability was revealed, a talent for psychological probing. Set to Arnold Schoenberg's '42 *Verklaerte Nacht*, this dramatic study of a young girl's frustration elicited praiseful superlatives. Martin found it "magnificent," while a performance two years later prompted Berger to place it among the "most solid and inspired" works in the repertoire. When *Dim Lustre* was first performed at the Metropolitan Opera House in October 1943, Louis Biancolli wrote in his review that "nostalgia and fine-shaded nuance are still Mr. Tudor's forte, and smooth, interweaving patterns his secret." Called another "psychological episode," this ballet, danced to the Richard Strauss '44 *Burleska*, was welcomed for its charm and spontaneity. However, to a critic reviewing a performance in 1944, it seemed "a shabbier and emptier piece each time it is seen again."

Tudor considers *Dark Elegies* his best work In the ballet, according to a critic in 1942, the choreographer has created "a visual counterpart of Mahler's affecting *Kindertotenlieder*." After viewing it in April 1944 Edwin Denby remarked that the actual dance detail is "willfully spare, but it is also of a remarkable elegance in its arrangement." In April 1943 Tudor's *Romeo and Juliet* made its debut at the Metropolitan, danced by Hugh Laing and Alicia Markova '43, with a production cost of about twenty thousand dollars. In this work the choreographer ventured into the major tradition of the narrative ballet, thus, according to one critic, "abandoning the erotic in favor of a tender lyricism." Tudor had first become interested in this theme three years earlier, when listening to Prokofiev's ballet suite. Although this music inspired the idea, Tudor sought another score, trying the *Romeo and Juliet* music of Tchaikovsky, Berlioz, and Gounod before he selected various suites of Delius arranged by Antal Dorati. The ballet's libretto follows closely the Shakespearean text, but moves about four times faster than the play. Called "a wonderful stage piece" and "a consistently poetic medieval story," the ballet was given a reception summed up by *PM*'s headline as "Romeo and Juliet in Dance Is Shakespeare As You Like It." Tudor, who danced the part of Tybalt, was, in the opinion of one writer, "an epic and malevolent Tybalt."

Besides dancing in his own works, Tudor also appears in other productions. His dancing in Massine's *Aleko* was called "first rate" by Harriett Johnson, while Margaret Lloyd considered him "a very fine dancer." The latter especially singled out for commendation his interpretation of the Dummy in *The Great American Goof*, the Lover in *Lilac Garden*, the Mourner in *Dark Elegies*, and his jitterbug *pas de deux* in *The Raymond Scott Quintet*. While Tudor did not dance in his 1945 offering, *Undertow*, it was agreed that he did dominate the stage through his story. First presented in April, *Undertow* excited much controversy, although the critics felt that the work displayed strength and brilliance. The story, based on an idea of John van Druten's '44 and danced to music especially composed by Wil-

liam Schuman '42, depicts childbirth, murder, depravity, and corruption, unusual materials for the ballet. To John Martin it appeared as "a kind of Greek tragedy in terms of the London slums," and he praised Tudor's courage in having created and produced it. The ballet's theme drew columns of discussion: *Newsweek* predicted that the graphic treatment would "shock and repel many people"; Harriett Johnson in the New York *Post* regretted that it presented "an ignoble side of life"; while Margaret Lloyd in the *Christian Science Monitor* reminded those who found the subject matter revolting to consider the actual world scene as reported in their newspapers. Combining the real and the symbolic, *Undertow* was called "complex and confused" but at the same time a challenging, absorbing ballet. In an otherwise favorable review, Robert A. Hague noted "a feeling of unfulfillment at the end which is not aesthetically satisfying." Margaret Lloyd found it especially significant that two of America's greatest choreographers, Antony Tudor and Martha Graham '44, "must go to the grim depths of psychological torment for their material. Their technical methods are different, but it is 'out of the hurt heart' of humanity that they compose."

Some critics remarked on the absence of program notes for *Undertow*, which reduced understanding of the work to a completely personal basis. "To everyone in the audience it meant something quite different, which I think is good," Tudor has remarked. The choreographer does not like to use long synopses of ballet plots, but prefers that suggestive character titles and the action of the dance tell the story. (His works are thought to require as much acting as dancing.) "If audiences are to gain the fullest enjoyment," says Tudor, "they must be trained as well as the dancers to do some of the work." Hugh Laing, who has danced the parts of many of Tudor's heroes, believes that the choreographer translates life movements into dance movements, blending all elements—music, setting, costumes, lights—"into a perfect whole."

In 1943 Tudor was honored by the Ballet Theatre with an all-Tudor program and then presented with gifts by the entire company and by impresario S. Hurok '41—"the first time in modern ballet history that an artist has been publicly so honored by his associates." Another "evening of Tudor" at the Metropolitan in 1945 brought praiseful notices. That year Tudor turned to musical comedy again, creating the ballet *Success Story* for the ill-fated show *Hollywood Pinafore*. Using only four dancers, this "dramatic and inspiring little masterpiece stopped the show every night." Tudor staged the ballets for John C. Wilson's production **T**he *Day Before Spring* which opened in New Haven on October 25 and in New York four weeks later. Burton Rascoe of the New York *World-Telegram* spoke of the "superb ballets portraying dream fantasies," while Lewis Nichols in the New York *Times* thought that, although the informal dances were "unpretentious and easy," the two ballets lacked the light touch. As a regular member of the Ballet Theatre company Tudor appeared with the group in performances on the West Coast in the summer of 1945 and that fall was dancing with them in New York.

Antony Tudor is described as a charming and unassuming person, serious and quiet-spoken. Each year the choreographer appears less frequently as a dancer. He plans eventually to stop dancing in order to devote himself entirely to creative work—"My best performances are in the rehearsal studio."

References

Christian Sci Mon p9 F 24 '40 por
PM p23 Mr 25 '43 por
Time 42:75-6 N 15 '43 por

Beaumont, C. W. Complete Book of Ballets (1941)

TYDINGS, MILLARD E(VELYN) (tī' dǐngz) Apr. 6, 1890- United States Senator from Maryland

Address: b. Senate Office Bldg., Washington, D.C.; h. Havre de Grace, Md.

One of the most prominent anti-New Deal Southern Democrats in the United States Senate is urbane Millard E. Tydings, who in 1944 was re-elected to his legislative post for a fourth consecutive term—and with 29,000 more votes from Maryland than President Roosevelt [42] himself received in that state. An eminently successful lawyer, he is the senior partner of the Baltimore firm of Tydings, Sauerwein, Levy and Archer.

Born in Havre de Grace, Maryland, on April 6, 1890, Millard Evelyn Tydings is the son of Mary B. (O'Neill) Tydings and Millard F. Tydings, a government clerk. The future Senator received his B.S. in mechanical engineering from the Maryland Agricultural College in 1910 and then he went on to the University of Maryland, which gave him his LL.B. three years later. Admitted to the Maryland bar the same year, he began his law practice in Havre de Grace; and in 1916 became a member of the Maryland House of Delegates, serving for a two-year term. Neither law nor politics claimed most of his attention during those two years, however, for in 1916 he served as a private on the Mexican border, and when the United States entered the First World War a year later he was an officer with the AEF, advancing to the rank of lieutenant colonel in the Twenty-ninth Division, Machine Gun Units. He participated in the Haute Alsace, and Meuse-Argonne offensives, and when he returned to the United States it was with a D.S.M., a D.S.C., and three citations. The Senator is a member of the American Legion and the Veterans of Foreign Wars.

Tydings resumed his public life after the war. From 1920 to 1922 he served as speaker of the Maryland House of Delegates, and was then elected to the Maryland State Senate. In 1923 he went to the United States House of Representatives from the Second Maryland District, and in 1927 he was sent to the Senate. Since that time no opponent has succeeded in displacing him.

In the early days of the New Deal, Tydings voted against unemployment relief, farm relief, low-cost housing. He may have been a candidate for Roosevelt's attempted "purge" of 1938, but was nevertheless returned to the Senate in that year. In the foreign policy field Tydings opposed the Administration as often as not. In August 1940 he voted for Selective

MILLARD E. TYDINGS

Service, but in December he suggested that the United States ask Great Britain and the Axis for a statement of conditions under which each would agree to end the European war, so that the United States could determine if there was any basis for the negotiation of a "just peace." (According to Joseph Alsop and Robert Kintner, this proposal followed a talk with Ambassador Kennedy [40].) In 1941 the Senator voted against the extension of the draft law and, a month before Pearl Harbor, against relaxation of the neutrality law to permit American ships to carry munitions to Great Britain and Russia. In 1943 he proposed that Great Britain transfer its island possessions in the Western Hemisphere to the United States, protesting that the American people were naïve and overgenerous in regard to Lend-Lease.

A member of the Senate Appropriations Committee, Tydings has always been particularly concerned about Federal expenditures, and in February 1942 he became head of a special subcommittee of the Appropriations Committee authorized to promote economy and efficiency in the Government. Equally concerned about Government deficits, as early as November 1940 he called for a broadening of the income tax base on the theory that those with small incomes must help to pay the deficit. Late in 1942 he introduced a proposal for a constitutional amendment providing that in peacetime Congress could not appropriate funds by less than a three-fifths majority of each house, unless at the same time it levied taxes sufficient to cover the appropriation. Other phases of the domestic front during the war—strikes in war plants, Government participation in business, unemployment relief, the National Youth Administration, price rollback subsidies—were targets of his attacks in the Senate.

In March 1944, announcing his candidacy for renomination to the Senate, Tydings said he would "work for government by law, and, in

TYDINGS, MILLARD E.—*Continued*
accordance with true Democratic principles,
against the establishment of government by
bureaus." At about the same time Harry H.
Woodring, organizing anti-New Deal forces
for a convention fight against a fourth term
for Roosevelt, listed Tydings as among the
Democrats who he believed would be available
for a third party Presidential nomination; but
in the spring of 1944 Tydings was reportedly
receiving National Democratic Committee aid
in his fight for re-election. It was not a difficult fight. Running against four opponents,
in May he was renominated by better than
3 to 1 in the Maryland primaries, and in November Roosevelt himself ran behind him on
the Democratic ticket. The Senator uses radio
transcriptions to keep himself before his con-
stitutents. The 1944 vote was 344,725 to
213,705.

One of Tydings' first record votes of 1944
had been against Federal handling of ballots
for servicemen in the forthcoming elections;
but later, in February, he cast his vote for the
Federal-ballot amendment to the "States'
rights" bill. Another was for freezing the
Social Security tax at 1 per cent, and a third
was to require labor unions, farm cooperatives,
and other nonprofit organizations to file yearly
financial reports. He was against any further
payment of subsidies to keep down food prices;
for the "ripper amendment" to bring the TVA
under the immediate control of Congress;
against closure in the antipoll tax bill filibuster; for the George [43] Reconversion bill, as
against an Administration-backed measure; but
against the Bankhead [43] amendment to raise
cotton textile price ceilings. In 1945 he voted
for the confirmation of Henry Wallace [40] as
Secretary of Commerce after the RFC lending
agencies had been removed from his control.
Tydings favored a limited national service bill
for deferred men of draft age (backed by the
Administration but opposed by industry and
unions); he called Congress cowardly for preferring the compromise Kilgore [43]-O'Mahoney [45] bill, voted against it and for the Ball [43]
amendment, which imposed penalties on employers violating War Manpower Commission
orders, and he introduced an amendment to fine
deferred agricultural workers who left their
farm jobs.

Senator Tydings voted against confirming
former NYA head Aubrey Williams [40] as Rural
Electrification Administrator. He was paired
for ending Lend-Lease automatically with the
end of hostilities, saying, "I do not want to
sign any blank checks for the postwar era";
he was for the "high level" employment bill,
as amended, and voted to have Federal control of the Employment Service extended. His
foreign policy vote record for 1945 included a
vote for confirming the Mexican Water Treaty,
a pair for extending the Reciprocal Trade
Agreements Law without lessening the President's tariff-reducing powers, and a pair for
entering the world bank and world fund agreed
upon at Bretton Woods. He sought unsuccessfully to get President Truman [45] unqualified
Congressional authorization to reorganize all
the Executive agencies and departments. In
September 1945 the *Christian Science Monitor*
classed Millard Tydings with George of Geor-

gia and Byrd [42] of Virginia as leaders of the
conservative Southern wing of the Democratic
Party.

Tydings, in turn, has been the target for
attack by New Dealers. In 1939 Drew Pearson [41] and Robert Allen [41] charged that he had
called upon the WPA to construct a road and
yacht basin on the Tydings estate in Maryland. Actually the improvements had not been
made on Tydings' property; a road had been
built up to the estate and a yacht harbor constructed adjacent to it. Attorney General Robert H. Jackson's [40] refusal to prosecute Pearson and Allen for libel caused Tydings to vote
against confirming Jackson's nomination as Associate Justice of the Supreme Court in June
1941. The Tydings-Miller amendment to the
Antitrust Act, an amendment which went into
effect in 1939 and permitted price-fixing by
manufacturers, was criticized by the Federal
Trade Commission as "economically unsound
and undesirable in a competitive economy . . .
a cloak for many conspiracies in restraint of
trade . . . inconsistent with the purposes of
the antitrust laws."

As chairman of the Senate Committee on
Territories and Insular Affairs, Senator
Tydings has more than once found himself
working side by side with New Dealers. He
is joint sponsor of the 1934 Tydings-McDuffie
Act by which the Philippines were promised
their independence in 1946, and in September
1943 he presented a resolution to give independence to the Philippines then rather than
in 1946. Shortly afterward Roosevelt called
on Congress to give him authority to grant
independence to the Philippines before 1946,
and Tydings' resolution was revised to grant
power to the President to proclaim Philippine
independence when he considered the moment
propitious. The Tydings-McDuffie Act was the
result of Roosevelt's request that the Filipino-
rejected Hare-Hawes-Cutting Act of 1932 be
revived and amended. The amended Act contained one change looking toward the removal
of United States military establishments from
the Philippines after a ten-year period. The
Philippine Government accepted the new terms
on May 1, 1934, the thirty-sixth anniversary
of Dewey's victory in Manila Bay, although the
Act still contained the tariff provisions which
had been found objectionable.

In 1945 Tydings became chairman of the
Philippine Rehabilitation Commission, composed of Congressmen and Philippine representatives, and in early June he returned from
a Presidential mission to the islands to report
on the "indescribable" situation there. His
recommendations, presuming the grant of independence on the scheduled date of July 4,
1946, included: the gift of one hundred million
dollars, administered by American Army Engineers, toward reconstruction and rehabilitation
of the devastated islands; liberal loans to tide
the new republic over the acutely difficult postwar years; continued low tariffs on Philippine
products for the next few years, followed by
a gradual increase to normal tariff levels.
Many persons held that at least twenty years
inside the American tariff walls would be
needed by the Filipinos, but Tydings reminded
critics that political independence necessarily
meant the eventual loss of protection. Later,
urging passage of a bill to turn over imme-

diately some seventy-one million dollars which were being held in trust for the Philippines until independence, he told the Senate it would probably obviate the need for a loan. In response to a request from President Truman, Tydings introduced legislation to authorize a prompt general election in the islands. Other problems of the Committee on Territories and Insular Affairs concerned Puerto Rico, and the Senator from Maryland announced that a bill was being drafted to let Puerto Ricans choose between independence and greater local self-government under the American flag. It was, he thought, doubtful that Congress would authorize either statehood or dominion status for the Spanish-speaking tropical island.

As of 1945, Tydings was not only chairman of the Senate Committee on Territories and Insular Affairs, but was assigned to five other committees, where the real work of shaping legislation is done. He had a place on the Appropriations Committee, was ranking member of the Naval Affairs Committee; and he served also on three of lesser importance, District of Columbia, Public Buildings and Grounds, and the Committee to Audit and Control the Contingent Expenses of the Senate. In October 1945 he was one of the ten Senators who were appointed to the Special Committee on Atomic Energy, of which Brien McMahon [45] was chairman. One of the three Naval Affairs members on that committee, he, with other members, took a course in nuclear physics at the Bureau of Standards before making investigations and hearing testimony on atomic research. Observers commented on the quiet tension and lack of partisan feeling at the committee meetings, which were described as unique in the annals of Congress. "It is up to the United States," Tydings said, "to find ways of creating friendships between nations to prevent a push-botton war that will be over before most people will know it began."

Long one of Washington's most eligible bachelors, he was married in 1935 to Eleanor Davies Cheseborough, daughter of Joseph E. Davies [42] and stepdaughter of Marjorie Post Close Hutton Davies, General Foods heiress. Senator and Mrs. Tydings have two children, Joseph Davies and Eleanor. The Tydings are among the Capital's most notable "diner-outers," and their country estate at Aberdeen, Maryland, makes Tydings the "squire of Harford County." A tall, lean, muscular man, his favorite recreations are athletic—golf, fishing, and boating—but he is also an accomplished pianist. He is the author of *The Machine Gunners*; *Before and After Prohibition* (1930), an argument against national prohibition, and of *Counter-Attack, a Battle Plan To Defeat the Depression* (1933). The "four horsemen" of the depression were seen as tariff and embargo, depreciated currency, war debt, and armaments. Tydings urged whole-hearted cooperation with other nations to defeat depression through renewal of the trade of the world, final settlement of war debts, stabilization of national currencies, and disarmament to a peacetime basis. Of the book the New York *Times* reviewer said: "It has the value . . . of vivid dramatic presentation."

Tydings is an Episcopalian, a Mason, and an Elk; his clubs include the Havre de Grace Yacht Club, the Maryland Club (Baltimore), the Chevy Chase (Washington), and the Burning Tree. He has received honorary degrees from St. John's College and Washington College.

References

N Y Sun p14 Jl 28 '44
P M p7 Ja 15 '41 por; p9 F 16 '41 por
Congressional Directory, 1945
National Cyclopædia of American Biography Current vol F p203
Who's Who in America, 1944-45

ULIO, JAMES A(LEXANDER) (ū'lĭ-ō) June 29, 1882- Former United States Army officer
Address: b. c/o Food Fair Stores, Inc., Elizabeth, N. J.

"Personnel director" for an army of 8,300,-000 men—that was the job of Major General James A. Ulio, the Adjutant General of the United States Army. His responsibilities covered the procurement and disposition of all personnel, from the time men reported to their draft boards for induction until their discharge or death. He was also responsible for the service records of these men, which were vitally important in the adjustment of claims through the Veterans Administration, or as a basis for personal history required by the discharged soldier or his family. Whether it was the date and severity of a wound received in action, or simply the number of typhoid shots received while in service, the Adjutant General's Office could furnish the information. As the officer whose responsibility touched the American public most closely—recording, as he did, the service history of its soldier relatives—the Adjutant General became an unofficial liaison officer between the Army and the civil population, explaining and, when necessary, defending Army policy before the bar of public opinion.

Despite his Latin-sounding name, Ulio is the son of an Irish immigrant who was born in Belfast, became an Army man in the United States, and rose to the rank of major. The son, James Alexander Ulio, was born in Walla Walla, Washington, on June 29, 1882. He, too, chose a military career, enlisting in the Regular Army in September 1900, a few months after his eighteenth birthday. While an enlisted man he served as private, corporal, and battalion sergeant major; then, in October 1904 he won a commission as a second lieutenant in the Infantry.

Before the First World War Ulio's assignments were divided between service in the States and in the Territories. His first duties as an officer were with the First Infantry, with which he served at Fort Brady, Michigan, from November 1904 until January 1906. He was then ordered to the Philippine Islands and later back to Vancouver Barracks, Washington, in May 1908. He was promoted to first lieutenant while at the latter station, in March 1911, and went to Hawaii in May of the following year, serving with the First Infantry until August 1916. (He had been raised to the rank of captain in July.) He next joined the Thirty-

U.S. Army Signal Corps

MAJ. GEN. JAMES A. ULIO

second Infantry stationed at Schofield Barracks, also in the Islands, but before the year ended America had entered the First World War, and Ulio returned to the States. He was assigned to the Twenty-third Infantry at El Paso, Texas, in May 1917, and the same month he accompanied the regiment to Syracuse, New York. In August he received a promotion to major (temporary) and was transferred to Camp McClellan, Alabama, to take up the post of adjutant of the Twenty-ninth "Blue and Gray" Division.

Ulio is said to have revealed marked ability as adjutant. He was sent to France in March 1918, and after attending the Army General Staff College for two months was made assistant chief of staff for personnel, with the Thirty-fifth Division. In June he was given a similar post with the Fourth Corps, with which he remained until November. (In September he had been made lieutenant colonel, temporary.) While with the corps Ulio received the Distinguished Service Medal for showing "marked organizing and administrative ability. By his tireless efforts and ceaseless energy he contributed in a large degree to the success achieved by the Fourth Corps in the Toul sector and in the battles of the Saint-Mihiel salient. Later he handled with great success the evacuation and feeding of French civilians in the occupied territory recovered from the enemy, rendering invaluable service to the American Expeditionary Forces." He was also made a Chevalier of the French Legion of Honor.

From the end of 1918 until the following August Colonel Ulio was chief of the statistical division and in charge of the Central Records Office at General Pershing's AEF Headquarters. At this time, because of his efficiency in caring for civilians in war-stricken areas, and because of his administrative skill, he was chosen as assistant chief of staff for William Haskell's relief mission to Armenia, a position he held until May 1920. For the

next three years Ulio served in the Adjutant General's Office in Washington. At the end of this time he was again selected for the job of aiding a distressed nation, when in January 1923 he was sent to Greece for several months as chief of the Administrative Division of the American Red Cross. For his services, Ulio was made a Knight of the Greek Order of the Redeemer and a Commander of the Montenegrin Order of Prince Danilo. He has also received the Serbian Order of the White Eagle, with Swords, third class, and the Panamanian medal of La Solidaridad, second class.

The following years contributed their share to Ulio's training for his present post. After returning from Greece he served until June 1926 as assistant to the adjutant general at the headquarters of the Second Corps Area, Governors Island, New York. He then returned to Washington to serve for three more years in the Adjutant General's Office. In November 1928 he was raised to the permanent rank of lieutenant colonel. Two years later, after his graduation from the Command and General Staff School at Fort Leavenworth, Kansas, he resumed his duties in Washington, also serving for a time as an aide to President Herbert Hoover '43 at the White House. He next attended and in June 1934 was graduated from the Army War College in Washington, and then functioned as executive officer in the Adjutant General's Office until February 1935.

In March 1935 General Ulio went to Hawaii for his second military assignment there, this time as aide to Major General Hugh A. Drum '41, commanding general of the Hawaiian Department. In June Ulio became chief of the Service Command Section at the headquarters of the Department (in August he was made colonel), remaining in that post until September 1936, when he assumed the post of chief of staff. In November 1937 he returned to the United States, where from March to May, 1938, he served as assistant adjutant general of the Second Corps Area. He was then ordered to Washington as executive officer in the Adjutant General's Office, a post he held until December 1939, when he was appointed, for a term of four years, as Assistant Adjutant General of the Army, with the rank of brigadier general.

The Assistant Adjutant General assumed no easy task. His major job was maintenance of the Army's morale, and he was confronted by political ramifications growing out of the extension of draft and National Guard service, by the soldiers' disgust with extemporized equipment, by the ineffective leadership of certain "stuffed-shirt" officers, and by the boredom of first-class fighting men without a fight. Fully aware of the conditions, General Ulio analyzed the causes and gave this definition of what morale is: "It is when a soldier thinks his army is the best in the world, his regiment the best in the army, his company the best in the regiment . . . and that he himself is the best damn soldier-man in the outfit." In early 1941 this quality was conspicuously lacking in a large part of the United States Army. Said one old sergeant: "Give us a shooting war and there won't be a morale problem." In December 1941, he got his wish.

Three months after the attack on Pearl Harbor Ulio was promoted to the rank of major general and raised to the post of the Adjutant General of the Army. His task was tremendous. The Army mushroomed from nearly two million to over eight million. Each man required a separate and distinct record. He was classified, reclassified, assigned, paid, promoted, transferred, retired, or discharged. The Chief of Staff, General George C. Marshall [40], had adopted a replacement system by means of which battle losses were to be made up by sending trained replacements into the depleted units, rather than withdrawing the entire unit for regrouping, as was customary. He also believed in a generous policy of awarding decorations for courage and ability, and it was up to Ulio to work out the details. Leaves and furloughs had to be handled, too. The incompetent were to be weeded out, the unruly punished. Mail and welfare facilities were expanded to serve the need of a rapidly expanding and far-flung army. Guiding these manifold efforts and supervising the many details was the Adjutant General, James A. Ulio. On the home front, it was Ulio's duty to notify the family of a soldier of his injury or death or capture by the enemy. On the political front he had to explain War Department policy whenever it affected votes in Congress or diplomatic relations with the Allies.

Before the Presidential election of 1944, in answer to a charge that politicians were plotting to deprive the servicemen of their vote, Ulio published a statement through the various service commands to the effect that all induction centers specifically provided that no draftee should be deprived of his vote by reason of induction. There was also a political hullabaloo over the appointment of Communists as commissioned officers. Ulio clarified the change of Army policy, stating, "Restrictions on soldier Communists were relaxed in justice to the individual and fairness to the Government." The receipt of commissions was based on individual attitudes and actions. Congressmen questioned the matter and appointed an investigating committee. These situations were complicated by the possibility of offending an ally, the Soviet Union. Upon the victorious culmination of the war in Europe an outcry immediately arose, demanding quick furloughs and discharges for soldiers who had been away from their homes and families a long time. To meet this problem of national morale, General Ulio forecast a reduction in the strength of the Army to 6,968,000 men within a year. He disclosed that 40,000 to 50,000 front-line soldiers were being sent home each month, and indicated that the number of furloughs would be increased during the months ahead. Liberated prisoners and movable wounded were given top priority, while soldiers who had not as yet seen foreign service were slated for such assignment before discharge.

Ulio, who had been on terminal leave from the War Department after September 21, 1945, was elected vice-president of Food Fair Stores, Inc., in October. In his civilian post, one of his duties will be the direction of re-employment and retraining of the more than one thousand employees who had served in the armed forces. The General's retirement becomes effective in January 1946.

General Ulio has been described as a pleasant-faced, white-haired soldier. It is said that his Latin name and appearance have caused strangers to think him an Italian. Delos Lovelace reports that old acquaintances remember him as the best piano player in his regiment. "The General does not lean too heavily on entertainment, or athletics either, for building up morale, however," the writer continues. "Make a man believe his army is the best in the world," Ulio says, "and his own outfit is the best in the whole army and you won't have to worry about shows or ball games."

References

N Y Herald Tribune p20 F 26 '42 por
N Y Sun p22 F 18 '44
Who's Who in America, 1944-45

ULLMAN, JAMES R(AMSEY) Nov. 24, 1907- Author

Address: 109 W. 11th St., New York City

Playwright, essayist, and short story writer, James R. Ullman produced his first novel with *The White Tower* (1945). This story of a hazardous ascent is the outcome of twin interests—his long-time avocation of mountain climbing and his profession of writing.

A native New Yorker, James Ramsey Ullman was born on November 24, 1907. His parents, Alexander F. and Eunice (Ramsey) Ullman, in comfortable financial circumstances, sent him to the Ethical Culture School in New York and to Phillips Academy in Andover, Massachusetts. He received his B.A. from Princeton University in 1929, and his prize-winning senior essay, "Mad Shelley," was published in book form the year after his graduation. Although the author was criticized for being "too much in love with his subject," it was also considered that this first literary attempt was "an able and thoughtful essay."

From Princeton Ullman went to work on a Brooklyn (New York) newspaper as a reporter and feature writer. He tried playwriting also, turning out, among other things, *Is Nothing Sacred?*. (Two of these plays were produced.) In 1933 he left the newspaper and began his short but eventful career as a theatrical producer. His first Broadway production, *Faraway Horses*, opened the same day the banks closed; two days later the play followed suit. The next year he scored a huge success with Sidney Kingsley's [43] *Men in White*, the Pulitzer Prize play for 1933-34, which his new firm, Harmon and Ullman, co-produced with the Group Theatre. Lesser hits that followed were the drama *Blind Alley* and the comedy *The Milky Way*. His ten productions also included failures, the year 1936 having a record of four of these in succession. Shortly after the appearance of such press notices as "*So Proudly We Hail* doesn't amount to a hoot in Joe Leblang's bargain basement," and "*The Laughing Woman* has the dramatic content of a hole in a doughnut," this bit of news appeared in Winchell's [43] column: "James R. Ullman, the theatrical producer, is leaving for the Amazon Jungles next week."

The Other Side of the Mountain, which was published in 1938, was the diary Ullman kept during his trip to the Amazon region. It concerned his ten-day journey across the Andes and down the Amazon River in the company of Herman Lord, a former Iowa mayor, who

Cromhard

JAMES R. ULLMAN

had answered Ullman's advertisement in a Lima paper for a traveling companion. (In the book Ullman quotes some of the adverse citicism of his plays and chides the drama critics of New York for causing his departure for South America.) In general, the criticism of *The Other Side of the Mountain* seemed to agree with the Springfield *Republican*'s comment that it was "an undistinguished work with the distinction of getting close to its subject."

Ullman returned to the United States in 1937 and took a job with the Federal Theater, where, he says, he was so busy solving administrative problems that he never had a chance to produce a play. He worked for the project for two years in New York and California, resigning in 1939, just a few months before Congress dissolved the whole program. From that time on he devoted himself to free-lance writing, and has contributed short stories to the *Saturday Evening Post, Story, Collier's, Esquire,* the *American Mercury,* the *American Magazine,* and other "class", "mass," and "quality" publications; several of his articles on mountain climbing have also been published.

In September 1939 Ullman began his attempts to enlist in the Army, but he was rejected several times because of near-sightedness. Finally he joined the American Field Service and spent fifteen months in 1942 and 1943 with the British Eighth Army in Africa, from the Battle of El Alamein through the Tunisian campaign. Most of the time he was an officer in charge of the American ambulances with the Seventh Armored "Desert Rat" Division. Subsequently he was given assignments that took him as far afield as Bagdad and Gibraltar. He was awarded the Star of Africa by Great Britain.

The unrecorded periods in Ullman's life were devoted mainly to mountain climbing, which he did for the first time in 1927 while vacationing in Switzerland as a Princeton undergraduate. He has climbed Mt. Olympus in one hundred and ten degrees of heat, Ixtaccihuatl, the Mex-

ican volcano, through six-foot snow drifts, Popocatapetl, the Jungfrau, the Matterhorn, some of the Andes "foothills" (sixteen and seventeen thousand feet), and the mountains of the Tetons and Canadian Rockies. The most difficult climbing he has ever done is up Breakneck, on the Hudson, opposite West Point. It is also the place where he came closest to death when he suddenly encountered a snake on a high, narrow precipice. On another occasion he was standing on a six-inch footing high on the side of a Wyoming Teton when a large knapsack dropped from above and muffled his head. Ullman has, however, yet to fulfill his ambition to make an expedition to the Himalayas and climb Mt. Everest. He belongs to the inner circle of American mountain climbers —the American Alpine Society, which limits its members to those who can prove that they have climbed certain peaks.

The author's enthusiasm for mountain climbing led him to write *High Conquest* in 1941. In it he deals with mountaineering all over the world, particularly the history of climbing in the Swiss Alps, from the beginning of the development of the sport to the point it had reached in the prewar period. He familiarizes the reader with many facts about famous mountains and mountaineers and traces the growth of competitive climbing among various nationalities. The book was well received by the critics—more for the information it contained than for its literary style. Clifton Fadiman [41] in his *New Yorker* review considered it "among the finest popular histories (at least in English) of its subject" that he was familiar with, and George Barker in the *New Republic* said that the style was "unassuming and just awkward enough in the right places to give the impression that the author climbs mountains better than he manipulates words."

Ullman's *The White Tower,* which was selected by the Book-of-the-Month Club for September 1945, is his first novel. The critics for the most part agreed that, granting the author's unlikely premises concerning his remarkably representative group of characters, everything else in the novel seems real. The mountain, the Weissturm, which these characters climb, is probably a combination of several mountains Ullman has known. Symbolically, it is made by the author the goal in life toward which the world is constantly striving. The reviewers found that Ullman's thorough knowledge of mountain climbing enabled him to make the sections concerning the ascent so vivid that, during these passages of sustained suspense, the reader almost becomes one of the climbers himself. Some of the characters, all symbolic of a world at war, are never realistically developed, reviewers observed, but are allowed to remain as symbols throughout. As part of the plot, all are motivated by different forces, and although no one is sure of what he will accomplish by making the dangerous climb, each feels a compulsion to try it. At the end they have either been frustrated by their inability to reach the top or killed in the attempt—here it was generally felt that Ullman's philosophy becomes indistinct—but the mountain remains the unconquerable protagonist.

In June 1930 the author was married to Ruth Fishman. The couple, divorced in 1945, have two sons, James Ramsey and William. James Ullman is five feet ten inches tall, and has brown hair and eyes and a bronzed complexion. He reports that his method for writing is to proceed slowly and carefully, seldom rewriting anything. His next novel, he says, will be "very flat—geographically."

References

Book-of-the-Month Club N p5-6 Ag '45 por
Read Digest p112 F '42
Who's Who in America, 1944-45

VAIL, ROBERT W(ILLIAM) G(LENROIE) Mar. 26, 1890- Librarian

Address: b. New York Historical Society, 170 Central Park West, New York City; h. 270 Riverside Dr., New York City

"America on Review" might be a fitting title for the collection of Americana housed in the library-museum of the New York Historical Society in New York City, the second oldest society of its kind in the United States. Its collection of historical literature, manuscripts, paintings, folk art, and other objects is considered one of the finest in the world. From such exhibits as Washington's camp cot, to a display of Army and Navy "E" awards, the visitor may conveniently review the history of America. In addition, the Society has probably the best collection of New York and State reference material available. The director of this rich collection, which draws historians from all over the country, is Robert W. G. Vail, former Librarian of New York State.

Robert William Glenroie Vail was born in Victor, New York, on March 26, 1890. His parents were James Gardiner and Mary Elizabeth (Boughton) Vail. After completing his early education, he entered Cornell University on a State scholarship. Although he worked his way through college, he managed to complete the course in three and one-half years, receiving his B.A. degree in 1914. That same year he joined the staff of the New York Public Library as an assistant in the reference department, and, combining study with his work, he obtained his certificate in librarianship in 1916 from the school then conducted by the library. He continued as an assistant until the outbreak of the First World War, when he enlisted in the Student Army Training Corps at Columbia University. Shortly after he volunteered for this service, he was assigned to Fort Totten, New York, as a private in the Coast Artillery Corps. He had been stationed at this post six months when the Armistice was signed. In June he had been married to the former Marie Rogers. They now have two children, Robert William and Mary Elizabeth.

Returning to his former position at the New York library, he continued his studies, taking graduate work in history at Columbia University. Before he was able to complete his course, however, he was offered in 1920 the post of librarian at the Minnesota Historical Society in St. Paul. During the time Vail held this post he was able to continue his studies in historical research, this time at the University of Minnesota. He had been with the So-

Blackstone Studios, Inc.

ROBERT W. G. VAIL

ciety only a year when he was asked to head the Roosevelt Memorial Association Library in New York City. The idea for such an association had been conceived at the funeral of Theodore Roosevelt by a group of Roosevelt's intimate friends who had felt that an effort should be made to perpetuate the President's memory and ideals. After the organization of the library was begun the Association moved into the restored Roosevelt birthplace on East Twentieth Street in New York.

In addition to recording and procuring all the writings of Theodore Roosevelt, Vail got in touch with every cartoonist, photographer, author, and publisher in the world who might have produced material about Roosevelt. Two results of this enterprise were the publication of the *Memorial Edition of the Works of Theodore Roosevelt* (1923-26) in twenty-four volumes, for which Vail himself compiled the bibliographies, and the establishment of the first historical film library known to be in existence at the time. The accumulated slides, photographs, and newsreels provided material for over a dozen films revealing various phases of the President's life, and these films have been in continuous demand since their first release. (In this period, too, Vail found time to begin an elaborate bibliography of all Roosevelt's writings, including reprints and translations. Although now complete, publication will be postponed until after the end of the Second World War.) By 1928 the Roosevelt Memorial collection was considered virtually complete. From a nucleus of only twelve volumes the library-museum's collection had attained the valuation of over a half million dollars. However, to make the library more accessible to scholars, it has since been given to Harvard University.

His work for the Roosevelt collection finished, Vail was asked to return to the New York Public Library as general assistant. In this new capacity he selected and purchased rare books, suggested and prepared exhibits, wrote articles for the *Library Bulletin*, and supervised the library publicity. Six months

VAIL, ROBERT W. G.—*Continued*

after his return he was again approached in regard to a new project, this time by members of the Bibliographical Society of America which sought his help in its completion of Sabin's *Dictionary of Books on American History.* This tremendous undertaking had been started in 1867 by Joseph Sabin and was continued until his death in 1881. Three years later Wilberforce Eames took over the task, and spent eight years in gathering data on publication on all phases of American history. Other duties forced Eames to discontinue his research in 1892, and nothing more was done for almost thirty years. The Society, aware that such a project should not be permitted to remain uncompleted, finally raised the necessary funds to proceed with the research. Vail was asked to estimate the approximate research required to complete the compilation of the dictionary. Satisfied with his report that it would take six compilers about seven years, the Society offered him the editorship.

It had been Sabin's original intention to include in his volumes everything concerning the political, governmental, military, economic, social, and religious history from America's discovery to the date of the dictionary's publication. Later, when it was found impossible to follow this plan, the titles were restricted to material published not later than 1876. This date was selected because the *American Catalogue* came into being that year and would record material published after that date. After leaving his post at the New York Public Library, Vail undertook what he considered his greatest achievement. When the twenty-nine volumes were completed seven years later, in 1936, they included references to well over a quarter of a million different publications, in addition to the location of almost a million publications in libraries all over the world.

But Vail was able to give this project his undivided attention for only one year. In 1930 the American Antiquarian Society, in Worcester, Massachusetts—a society devoted to the collection and publication of American history, offered him the post of librarian. It was a tempting offer, for this collection was considered the greatest library of American history in the world, and the librarianship would give him an opportunity to develop many of his ideas. Since the Bibliographical Society did not object to his continuing the research on the dictionary in Massachusetts, Vail, taking some of his staff with him, moved to Worcester to assume his new post.

While at Worcester, Robert Vail was able to encourage students in near-by universities to use the reference material made available by the Society. That was one of his many goals, and he had the satisfaction of observing the results. "One professor from Harvard," Vail has remarked, "would bring his entire history seminar to the library. The plan would be to make an extensive study of one year in America's history, and each student would be assigned a different phase of the year's happenings. Almanacs, newspapers, broadsides, diaries, manuscripts, letters, etc., were examined, with the resultant amazement of the students that so much information might be discovered.

"I was surprised myself," he continued, "to find a wealth of material relating to the early American circus in the antiquarian collections. After an investigation I discovered that very little had ever been written on the subject. This prompted me to write a monograph entitled *The Early History of the American Circus* (1934). I had a lot of fun gathering the facts, and later I put on a circus exhibition in one of the New York museums. Since then I've acquired quite some notoriety as a circus fan."

One project Vail was very glad he followed through to completion while at Worcester was concerned with the drawings of the French artist Charles Alexandre Lesueur. In 1937 the librarian came upon a reference in the library's records that Lesueur's sketches of America, drawn in the early nineteenth century, were at the National History Museum at Le Havre in France. This famous French naturalist and artist, who had come to America in 1816 to collect zoological specimens, had been so impressed with the country that he had remained for a number of years as art instructor in New Harmony, Indiana. During this time he had drawn sketches of hundreds of American towns and landscapes—many of them the only historical representations of that period.

With these drawings in France and their purchase impossible, Vail concluded that even photographs of the pictures would be a valuable acquisition for the United States. He then set about to obtain the permission of the Le Havre authorities to photograph Lesueur's work. Permission granted, he next procured the services of a friend, who traveled extensively, to supervise the work. When the photographs arrived at Worcester, Vail proceeded to prepare a monograph under the title *American Sketchbook of Charles Alexandre Lesueuer* (1938), with a biography of the artist and references to, and identification of, the known locales pictured. The Le Havre library was destroyed in the Second World War; therefore, unless the original sketches were removed to safety, the photographs now at the Antiquarian Society are the only complete record of Lesueur's drawings. There are a few partial duplicate sets in Western historical societies.

In 1939 Vail was offered the post of Librarian of New York State by the New York State Department of Education. After nine years with the American Antiquarian Society the decision to leave was a difficult one for him to make, but it was a challenge to his abilities since much constructive and corrective work was needed. He accepted the offer and was appointed State Librarian in December 1939. His responsibilities included the supervision of the work of a dozen departments; direction of the State medical, law, legislative reference, manuscript, history, and educational libraries; supervision of the services for the blind, the functions of the inter-library loans, the work with the Board of Regents, and the traveling libraries. He was also directly responsible for the selection and acquisition of material relating to New York State history and the replacement, wherever possible, of all books, maps, prints, and manuscripts destroyed by fire in 1911. In addition, it was also his duty to weed out and replace books in all the departments.

When Vail left Albany to assume the directorship of the New York Historical Society in September 1944, the problems at the New York State Library had been tackled and the library's functions redirected toward more constructive purposes. The traveling libraries had over a half a million up-to-date volumes in their collection, with postwar plans to serve those rural areas not covered before. Additions were made to the State historical material, and people were encouraged to donate valuable reference matter. All the book collections have been improved, and inter-library loans expanded. Students were urged to make the most of the source material, and Vail himself took such a personal interest they would often ask his advice in selecting subjects for their theses. Authors and historians also frequently came to him for the assistance which he gladly gave.

As director of the New York Historical Society, Vail retains the same fundamental aim —to acquaint the public with the wealth of material available at the Society so that readers and researchers will make use of it. This collection differs from the usual library in that it consists of paintings, furnishings, folk art, and other historical materials, in addition to the vast printed and manuscript resources in the reference library. It is this combination of museum and library which makes the institution unique.

It is the ambition of the director to work closely with schools and colleges and to reach professors as well as the graduate students, who will be the historians of tomorrow. "So often," remarks Vail, "we find that a book is published on a certain subject without the author knowing of the wealth of facts which were obtainable here at the Society." When asked once what exhibit seems to hold the greatest interest for the public, he replied, "With the diversified interests of our visitors, each has his favorites. American textiles or old advertisements may appeal to some, early American furniture or utensils may appeal to others, and ships might be the fancy of many. In fact," he chuckled, probably thinking of his own experience in Worcester, "quite a few enjoy an exhibit of old circus posters."

Vail's other activities are closely related to his work. In 1942 he was president of the New York State Library Association. For a number of years he represented the Antiquarian Society and the Bibliographical Society at the National Council of Learned Societies. He is a member of the American Library Association Council, and one of the consultants for the Library of Congress. In 1945 he was compiling a bibliography, "American Indian Captivities."

Six-foot, two-hundred-pound Robert Vail has a light complexion and silver-gray hair, which is receding slightly from the temples. His voice is soft and his speech calm and deliberate. Deeply interested in people and world affairs, he feel strongly that education is one of the answers to the problem of maintaining a permanent peace. If the resources of the Society can contribute to this knowledge, he says, his work and that of the staff will have been well worth the effort. "I used to collect rare books and manuscripts," he said once when asked about his hobby. "At one time I had one of the finest collections of material on western New York history in private hands, but I was competing with my own profession

and livelihood so I had to give up my hobby. My favorite pastime now," he continued, "is my job here at the Society."

References

Who's Who in America, 1944-45
Who's Who in Library Service (1943)

VALERY, PAUL AMBROSE (và″lā″rē′) Oct. 30, 1871—July 20, 1945 French poet, philosopher, and critic; his production small and somewhat obscure, but has won high critical acclaim for its classic beauty; among his books of verse are *Le jeune parque* (1917) and *Le cimitière marin* (1920); his prose writings include *L'âme et la danse* (1924) and *Regards sur le monde actuel* (1931); a member of the French Academy.

Obituary

N Y Times p11 Jl 21 '45

VANDENBERG, HOYT S(ANFORD) Jan. 24, 1899- United States Army Air Forces officer

Address: b. c/o War Department, Washington, D.C.; h. 4000 Cathedral Ave., N.W., Washington, D.C.

Of all the great Allied air fleets on the European continent, the largest was the United States Ninth Army Air Force, which gave tactical cooperation to ground commanders in their fight against the Germans. The Ninth's commander, a brilliant but little known flier and planner, was Lieutenant General Hoyt S. Vandenberg. He is called "one of the chief architects of the system of air and ground cooperation." In July 1945 he was appointed assistant chief of the Air Staff in the Army Air Forces.

A descendant of the early Dutch settlers of New York, Hoyt Sanford Vandenberg was born in Milwaukee, Wisconsin, on January 24, 1899. His parents were William Collins and Pearl (Kane) Vandenberg, and Michigan's influential Republican Senator Arthur H. Vandenberg [40] is his uncle. After some study at the Columbian School, young "Van" Vandenberg obtained a Michigan appointment to the Military Academy, where he was a hardworking but not brilliant student, graduating in the bottom tenth of his class. The tall, handsome twenty-four-year-old "made the air grade," however, "by reason of his superb physical condition" (to quote *Time*), and was commissioned a second lieutenant in the Air Service in June 1923. That September he entered its Primary Flying School at Brooks Field, Texas, and was graduated from the Advanced Flying School at Kelly Field a year later. At this time Lieutenant Vandenberg was married to Gladys Rose of Tuxedo, New York, whom he had met at a West Point dance. The couple, whose home is in Washington, have a daughter, Gloria Rose, and a son, Hoyt Sanford.

On the completion of his training Vandenberg joined the Third Attack Group at Kelly Field, transferring with it to Crockett Field, Texas, in August 1926, the year the Air Service became the Air Corps. One of the Army's best attack pilots, the Lieutenant was chosen

U. S. Air Forces

MAJ. GEN. HOYT S. VANDENBERG

to be an instructor at the Air Corps Primary Flying School, March Field, California, in October 1927. His promotion to first lieutenant came through ten months later. Next Vandenberg was sent to Schofield Barracks, Hawaii, in May 1929, to join the Sixth Pursuit Squadron, and was placed in command after he had been there six months. Back in the United States in September 1931, the thirty-two-year-old lieutenant again became an instructor, teaching flying at Randolph Field, Texas, where he was made a flight commander in March 1933. Then he himself went back to studying, attending the Air Corps Tactical School at Maxwell Field, Alabama, from August 1934 to June 1935, and entering the Command and General Staff School (at Fort Leavenworth, Kansas) as a captain the following August. After about two years on the faculty of the Tactical School, Vandenberg was enrolled for the Army's highest training at the Army War College on March 28, 1938. Graduated in April 1939, he was assigned to duty in the Plans Division of the Office of the Chief of Air Corps, where he served until July 1941, when he was placed on the staff of the AAF chief, General H. H. Arnold '42, and advanced to the permanent rank of major.

At this time, when the involvement of the United States in the Second World War was imminent, President Roosevelt '42 instructed General Arnold to prepare the strategic plans for the air forces. Working under high pressure, the air staff formulated its plans, to which Vandenberg contributed a "wise evaluation of the situation created by the requirements of air power set against the national matériel and personnel resources." He had the delicate task of balancing defense and training needs against the need of planes to carry the fight to the presumptive enemy, and then supervised the carrying-out of his allotment program, all on a hitherto undreamed-of scale. In March 1942 Colonel Vandenberg (raised to the temporary rank of lieutenant

colonel one month before Pearl Harbor and to temporary colonel in January 1942) became operations and training officer (A-3) on the Air Staff. His work in Washington and in Britain, where he worked on air plans for the North Africa operations under General Dwight Eisenhower '42, won him the Distinguished Service Medal with a citation for "exceptional ability, energy, judgment, and brilliant professional knowledge."

While in Britain, Vandenberg was given, in October 1942, the job of organizing the Twelfth Air Force as its chief of staff, under General James Doolittle '42. "In the face of almost insuperable difficulties due to lack of time, experienced personnel, and equipment," he and Doolittle whipped together an "excellently organized" tactical air force to cover the Allied ground troops fighting in North Africa. (The quotation is from the document accompanying Vandenberg's Legion of Merit.) The Twelfth included bombers, fighters, air support units serving under ground commanders, a troop carrier wing, and service commands. Its fighters and bombers took on the Luftwaffe in November 1942, and proceeded to account for more than four hundred enemy planes in the next three months, wreaking ground and air destruction on the Germans equal to many times their own losses. The citation above calls this accomplishment "a tribute to his [Vandenberg's] organizational and administrative ability." In February 1943 all the Allied air forces in the theater were merged into the Northwest African Air Forces, under Lieutenant General Carl Spaatz '42, which was subdivided into five service units and three air forces, the Coastal, Tactical, and Strategic. Vandenberg was chief of staff of the last-named, planning and supervising the air operations over Tunisia which largely prevented the Germans from bringing in needed supplies and reinforcements.

At the same time the dashing colonel, who became a brigadier general (temporary) in December 1942, used to "sneak off on combat missions" with or without Doolittle, winning the Silver Star by his "display of gallantry and courageous leadership." Flying as copilot, gunner, or observer, he took part in all types of bombing attacks over Tunisia, Sardinia, Sicily, Italy, and Pantelleria. Vandenberg, it seems, had a lot of fun—and then came back with recommendations about tactics, techniques, and discipline which "added immeasurably" to their improvement. This "achievement far above and beyond the requirements of his position" won him the Distinguished Flying Cross, as well as the Air Medal with four Oak Leaf Clusters (indicating that he had made at least twenty-five sorties). Vandenberg wears the wings of a command pilot, and is rated a technical observer and aircraft observer.

In August 1943 the Wisconsin-born flier was ordered back to the United States and assigned to AAF headquarters in Washington as one of the four deputy chiefs of Air Staff. After six months in this post he was made a major general (temporary) and sent overseas to join "Ike" Eisenhower's Supreme Headquarters staff in London as deputy commander in chief of the Allied Expeditionary Air Forces. Here he impressed the British with his tactical planning, which they described as "outstanding." A natural diplomat, Vandenberg was on the President's military staff at the Quebec, Cairo, and Teheran conferences; *Time* states that he "helped persuade the Russians to give the Allies air bases." His work in this post and as deputy commander of the Ninth United States Air Force, the largest on the Continent, won him a Cluster (indicating an additional award) to his D.S.M.

Beginning in early 1944 the Ninth, which was composed of tactical air commands, was engaged in a campaign against enemy fortifications on the Channel coast and in occupied areas; it also provided fighter protection on the long missions of Major General Frederick L. Anderson's [44] Eighth (Strategic) Air Force heavy bombers. When the Ninth's commanding general, Lewis Brereton [43], was picked in the summer of 1944 to head the newly formed First Allied Airborne Army, Eisenhower chose Van Vandenberg to succeed him.

As a tactical air force, the Ninth's job was first to destroy the enemy air force, and secondly to isolate the field of battle. Unlike the strategic bombing units, which were charged with breaking down enemy production on a long-range basis, the tactical forces were concerned with the immediate situation: with paving the way for ground advances, preventing the enemy from bringing in supplies and reinforcements, blocking his retreat, and knocking out specific positions and vehicles. The Eighth faced losses from flak and enemy air attacks; but the planes of the Ninth, constantly engaged in dive bombing and strafing (gunning ground positions from the air), came under concentrated antiaircraft fire. Often they flew within range of rifles and even pistols. As a result, the "rate of attrition" which had been worked out on a basis of the Eighth's experience proved too low: *Newsweek* reported in December 1944 that "some Ninth groups have suffered casualties of almost 50 per cent. At times squadrons of twenty-five planes have had only eight or nine planes in operation....Changes were made just in time to avert serious consequences."

The General has reportedly "wielded the weapon of his big air force with skill and devotion," working with various Allied armies as they dashed forward or inched grimly along in Western Europe. "If other top airmen had any criticism of the Ninth," wrote one reporter, "it might be that its forces had got to working too closely with ground force commanders," thus running the risk of "giving extra ground support at the expense of sound tactical air doctrine." (This would be the case if, for example, the fighter-bombers were too busy themselves knocking out tanks to such an extent that they failed to attack enemy communications.) But hard-driving General George S. Patton [43] declares that the Third Army's amazing drive through France in August 1944 would have been impossible without the Ninth Air Force's help. "I make the German armies move so fast they have to use the roads," explained Patton in more colorful wording, "and the Ninth bombs and strafes them off the roads." New York *Times* correspondent Clifton Daniels called Vandenberg's force "specialists in routing armies," and said

its planes were piloted by "some of the keenest gunners on any front."

General Vandenberg, who was given his third star in April 1945, issued this summary of his air force's work in May. The Ninth, which was reported by Leland Stowe [40] to be almost as large in personnel as Patton's Third Army, made its last flight against Germany on May 8. Its final score stood at nearly four hundred thousand flights in nineteen months; to a loss of fewer than three thousand planes, mostly fighters, and less than five thousand personnel killed, wounded, or missing, they had destroyed more than four thousand German planes in the air and on the ground, and more than three thousand "probables." Other destruction wreaked on the enemy included: more than thirty-six hundred motor vehicles and sixty-seven hundred horse-drawn vehicles; seven thousand locomotives and sixty thousand railroad cars, plus "uncounted thousands" of others smashed in attacks on railroad yards; sixty-five hundred tanks and armored vehicles; and seventeen thousand gun positions and fortified buildings. That March Vandenberg had been made a commander of the French Legion of Honor; and that July, after his return to the United States, he was appointed assistant chief of Air Staff in charge of operations. In October he was one of three air officers (the others were Major Generals Curtis E. LeMay [44] and Lauris Norstad) to be nominated by President Truman [45] for permanent brigadier generalcies for which they lacked the years of service required by law. Special legislation was therefore needed to permit their appointment.

Hoyt Sanford Vandenberg, Sr., is a general whom movie audiences would approve on sight. Six feet tall and slim (one hundred and sixty-five pounds), he has gray eyes, streaked iron-gray hair, and an impeccably groomed sort of good looks, with charm to match. *Time* reported that he "seems always to be in action . . . usually flies his own Thunderbolt in hops to staff headquarters . . . combines the energy of an athlete with mature judgment. He is dead serious and fluent about anything having to do with aviation, reasonably interested in such lesser matters as golf (low eighties), tennis, gin rummy, Scotch highballs, and good panatelas," beating his aircrewmen and enlisted men at volleyball and ping-pong, and forcing his reluctant staff to join him in quartets in the evening. The General, it is reported, cannot carry a tune.

References

Time 45:26-8 Ja 15 '45 pors
Official Guide to the Army Air Forces: AAF (1944)
Who's Who in America, 1944-45

VELEZ, LUPE July 18, 1910—Dec. 14, 1944 Mexican-born Hollywood film actress whose real name was Guadaloupe Velez de Villabos; first important motion picture part in *The Gaucho* (1927) with Douglas Fairbanks [40]; other well known pictures were *The Squaw Man* (1931), *The Cuban Love Song* (1931), and a series named for her, including *Mexican Spitfire at Sea* (1942) and other "Spitfire" titles; death was by suicide.

Obituary

N Y Times p26 D 15 '44 por

VILLA-LOBOS, HEITOR (vē'lä-lō'boos
ä'tôr) Mar. 5, 1884(?)- Brazilian composer

Address: b. Departamento de Educação, Rua
São Cristovão, 18, Largo Estacio, Rio de
Janeiro

The leading South American composer, "a
sort of Berlioz of the New World"—individualist, innovator—Heitor Villa-Lobos is one of the
most prolific composers of all time, being
credited with fourteen hundred compositions
ranging from simple songs to intricate musical
works. One of the first truly national composers of Latin America, a Brazilian writing
true "Brazilian music," he has had a decided
influence on other Latin American composers,
and is, according to Olin Downes'[43] "one of
the greatest creative figures in the field of
contemporaneous composition."

Heitor Villa-Lobos was born in Rio de
Janeiro on a certain March 5. But, as Nicolas
Slonimsky writes, "among other things Villa-
Lobos does not know about himself is the
year of his birth. Friends of his family say
. . . that he was born in 1881, but Villa-Lobos
prefers 1888. He is also experimenting with
the years 1886, 1887, and 1890. There is no
chance of finding documentary evidence . . .
for the registries of birth were not established
in Rio de Janeiro until the 'nineties of the
last century." The records are clearer, however, in regard to the composer's parents. His
father, Raul Villa-Lobos, was an author of
historical works and an amateur cellist of
some repute; his mother was the former
Noemia Monteiro. The boy's father taught
him the rudiments of music and gave him
some instruction on the cello, but he was
largely self-taught. Although some sources
state that he was forced to leave school at
eleven, following his father's death, to take
work in restaurant and third-rate theater orchestras, there is also evidence that his education extended beyond this early age. *Who's
Who in America* lists the schools that he
attended as Colegio Pedro II, 1897-1901;
Colegio São Bento, 1900; and Institute of
Music in Rio, 1901, where he is said to have
studied briefly with Agnello França and Francisco Braga, although he was always impatient
with accepted musical forms. Nevertheless,
before he was very old it is believed he had
become proficient in playing several instruments, including the piano, the guitar, and a
number of wind instruments.

Meanwhile, too, the youth was making friendships among prominent Brazilian musicians and
composers, "reveling," writes Andrade Muricy,
"in the great musical orgy in which the music
of Rio de Janeiro was assuming a definite
character. . . .Popular music flourished then
with complete spontaneity," and was not "flattened into the banality of a standard type.
Villa-Lobos," continues Muricy, "listening
somewhat absent-mindedly with one ear to
classical music, absorbed with the other . . .
the fundamentals of the popular style." Then,
within a few years, he had discovered another
world, the world of native Brazilian music. He
made several trips through the northeastern
part of his country—Espírito Santo, Bahia,
Pernambuco, Manaus—(in 1912 with a scientific expedition), and there he absorbed the
elements of Portuguese, African, and Indian
folklore among the tribes, becoming familiar
with the ceremonials of the natives. At
first he composed waltzes and schottisches, and
only a few folk songs, aware that music imbued with the rustic and pagan elements of the
hinterland would be given a cold reception in
sophisticated Brazilian society. But "at length,"
says Muricy, "Villa-Lobos arrived at the critical and decisive epoch of his life when the
necessity of asserting himself coincided with
the need for defining the music of his race."

"It would be very convenient for the critic
and for the historian," wrote Muricy in 1945,
"if Villa-Lobos' work had developed in a measured and balanced way, but his production was
not cast in a definite mold. . . .What Villa-
Lobos did try to express was the Brazilian
nebula with all its vagueness, but also with the
power to persist and strengthen. The Brazilian
soul is an inchoate world where moments of
pure sensuous delight and the astringent savor
of our tropical fruits alternate or mingle with
the surges of primitive barbarism."

By studying the folk-songs and rituals of
the Negroes and Indians, Villa-Lobos had become intimate with native folklore, melodies,
and rhythms, and now could re-create them in
new forms, with color, sentiment, design,
rhythm. He was equipped with "a new technique and musical prowess so novel and exotic
in its use of weird harmonic innovations and
chordal progressions that the musical world was
rocked to its foundations." His absence of
formal education, writes Nicolas Slonimsky,
was not a handicap, for he was "not bound by
conventional ideas of Western harmony, utterly unsuitable for the melodic inflections of
Brazilian song. . . .Inasmuch as drums make
up the only native orchestra of primitive tribes,
the compositions in which Villa-Lobos embodied the product of his research are rich in
percussion of all kinds. In public performance
these native instruments are of the essence, and
cannot be replaced by kettle-drums or any other
percussion instruments of European origin."

In 1914 Villa-Lobos wrote his first big orchestral composition, a set of three dances exhibiting the primitive influence, which he entitled *Dansas dos Indios Mestiços* ("Indian
Mestizos"). Prior to this, in 1912, he had also
written an opera in three acts, *Agláia,* and in
1914 a four-act opera, *Izaht.* In 1915 he gave
a concert of his own works, principally chamber music, then, in the next few years, turned
out "a flood of music" of varied types. Since
the symphonic form is a favorite of Brazilians,
it is not surprising that the work produced in
this period included a number of symphonies
and about ten symphonic poems. At the close
of the war, 1919, his third symphony ("The
War") was heard. "Hyperromantic and
hauntingly descriptive," it is said, it conveyed
the anguish and foreboding of prewar days,
and the violence of the ensuing war.

Recognition outside of Brazil first came to
the composer in 1919 when Artur Rubinstein[45],
during a concert tour of South America, happened to hear one of Villa-Lobos' compositions
played in a motion picture theater. Rubinstein
sought out the composer, who was playing in
the orchestra, and who seemed incredulous
when the foreign artist expressed his pleasure.
Nevertheless, Villa-Lobos a little later, accompanied by a whole orchestra, appeared at the

pianist's hotel prepared to play more of his own works. After listening to an hour's performance, Rubinstein was even more enthusiastic, and the result was that he saw to it that an influential Brazilian arranged for Villa-Lobos to go to Paris on a Government fellowship. Said Rubinstein, "Villa-Lobos creates with force and facility of a genius; from the viewpoint of fecundity and facility of expression, he reminds me of Schubert."

Villa-Lobos remained in Paris until 1926. He had already become acquainted with the work of the Impressionists and other French composers through Darius Milhaud [41], who was at the French Embassy in Rio de Janeiro from 1917 to 1919. In France the Brazilian came into contact himself with this young school of musicians. "He was a composer already formed when he came to Paris," wrote Burle Marx in 1939; "his musical compulsion was more powerful and rich than that of most Europeans. He arrived with curiosity but supreme confidence; his attitude was, 'I didn't come to study with you, I came to show what I've done.'" However, comments Slonimsky, "there is no mistaking the influence of French impressionism and early neoclassicism on Villa-Lobos' music of the Paris period." His success abroad was almost instantaneous. Since that time Paris, then the musical capital of the world, has considered him one of the major modern composers. Discussing his years in Paris, Villa-Lobos himself has said: "I was there, and I listened attentively, but never allowed myself to be influenced by any of the novelties I heard."

When the composer returned to Brazil he found that the acclaim abroad had elevated him in the esteem of his countrymen. Before going to Paris he had begun work on a series of compositions, a type of sentimental folk serenade called *"chôros"* by Brazilian street musicians. From 1920 to 1929 he composed fourteen of these serenades, each entitled *Chôros* (and numbered), which were written for various instruments. *"Chôros,"* says Villa-Lobos, "represents a new form of musical composition in which a synthesis is made of different types of Brazilian music, Indian and popular, reflecting in its fundamental elements the rhythm and characteristic melodies of the people." "The harmonic treatment," he continued, "represents a stylization of the original material." The first of the group is a simple guitar solo, but each successive piece becomes more elaborate, the fourteenth calling for full orchestra, fanfare, and mixed chorus. The two most important groups of Villa-Lobos' works are considered to be these *Chôros* and his *Serestas,* which are Brazilian songs patterned after the serenade, but freer in style, written for cello and piano. The *Serestas* form the most noteworthy group of Brazilian songs since those of Nepomuceno, while the *Chôros* are the "backbone of his [Villa Lobos'] work and, taken together, his masterpiece."

In classifying the prolific composer's other works, musical catalogs list them as vocal works, suites, concertos, chamber music, and songs, and works for piano, orchestra, and the theater. (He has written several operas and eighteen ballets for the theater.) One critic in the early 'forties calculated that if all of Villa-Lobos' works listed in catalogs were played "end to end," seventy-five hours and

HEITOR VILLA-LOBOS

fifty-seven minutes would be required for the performance. (Two of the artists who have recorded a number of the composer's works are Bidu Sayao [42] and Jennie Tourel, of the Metropolitan Opera Company.)

Villa-Lobos' work reveals that he is a programist in that all of his works present a story. His métier is the transmutation of folk tunes. He takes a folk tune or a primitive rhythm, re-creates it, building it into his own composition. Emphasizing that he is not a folklorist, but a creative artist inspired by folklore, he says: "I compose in the folk-style; I utilize the themes in my own ways and subject them to my own development."

The music of Villa-Lobos is considered unorthodox—"a musical dialect made from aboriginal shouts and strummings," an orgy of color, a diversity of novel sonorities and pungent rhythms. North Americans describe his style as "a dazzling, ingenious mixture of jungle boogie-woogie, sophisticated orchestration, five-sixteenth rhythms, Latin dance tunes, and instrumental oddities." The rendering of an effective interpretation of his music requires a comprehension of his independent technique of composition which capitalizes on the resources of the piano (though "sometimes doing them violence") and an appreciation of his compelling and intricate rhythms. In spite of Villa-Lobos' indifference to an orchestra's powers, his compositions are not unplayable. One of the reasons often given for the neglect of his work in North America is the problems his scores present to non-South American orchestras, usually lacking in a "kitchen" section. His scores call for unusual instruments such as gourds, rattles, notched sticks, box-like drums, and the caxambu (a gravel-filled bottle).

Of Villa-Lobos' scoring, Olin Downes says, "One scents as well as hears the forest, sees the play of lights, is aware of the tropical night and its strange enchantment." Oscar Thompson's over-all impression of Villa-Lobos' compositions is that they are too loosely woven, "risking monotony through their

VILLA-LOBOS, HEITOR—*Continued*

waste spots and repetition of accompaniment figures. But the color of what he writes is always interesting."

As an adjunct to his musical qualifications, his love of children made him the natural choice in 1931 for the position of director of Brazil's Department of Musical Education. The story is told that he persuaded President Vargas [40] to establish such a department by pointing out that people interested in listening to music and singing together would have little desire to instigate revolution. Villa-Lobos has given choral singing in the schools unprecedented attention: "Mass singing is the best and simplest way to make a nation musical," he declares. He drilled schoolteachers in a method of notation of his own devising (by raising or lowering the fingers to signify the notes), thus establishing a means of musical communication to great numbers of children, and used it to spread through Brazilian schools an enjoyment of both classical music and folk tunes. He also established a training school for teachers called the Orfeão de Professores. Each year on Brazil's Independence Day, September 7, he conducts a chorus of some twenty thousand school children, directing from a tower in the center of Rio's largest stadium.

Choruses of a thousand or more voices have often sung under the direction of Villa-Lobos. In 1931, at São Paulo he led the most impressive musical presentation in the history of Brazil up to that time when he conducted a chorus of one thousand voices and an orchestra of four hundred pieces through a sweeping program of native music. When the National Education Congress met in Rio de Janeiro in 1935 Villa-Lobos directed an even larger group—thirty thousand singers and an orchestra of one thousand. In that same year he had a contract with the Teatro Colón in Buenos Aires to direct ten concerts and four ballets, and the next year he was delegate to the International Congress of Musical Education at Prague, and to the International Meeting of Melody and Piano at Vienna.

One of the most unique devices for teaching children to write music is by means of Villa-Lobos' "millimetric music chart." A sentimental idea that the Corcovado and Sugar Loaf mountains had been "waiting for millions of years for people capable of reading and expressing the music of their unique lines" inspired Villa-Lobos' creation of this chart. It is set up in the form of a graph having "in vertical columns on the left side the diatonic, chromatic, and other scales, with one note for each horizontal line." Using photographs of Brazil's major mountains, he traces their outlines along the graph with the base of the mountain on any note that suits his whim. The rhythm is arbitrary and the melody may be harmonized in any style.

From a photograph of Manhattan's skyline Villa-Lobos, in 1940, set down on a graph the pinnacles of the buildings in relation to one another, and sketched a melody based on the C-minor scale, explaining that "the feeling the photo gives me is distinctly minor, though I know that the interior of the city is distinctly major." (He had then not been in New York.) In a little less than two hours the composition was completed. In its final form, harmonized for voice (without words) and piano, it was recorded as the *New York Sky Line Melody*, which had its initial international broadcast from Rio de Janeiro to New York on the opening of the Brazilian Building at the New York World's Fair in 1940. On seeing New York for the first time five years later, he proudly remarked that the *New York Sky Line Melody* needed no alterations.

In 1940 the Museum of Modern Art in New York, with the Commissioner General from Brazil to the World's Fair, presented a five-day festival of Brazilian music, devoting the greater portion of the program to the works of Villa-Lobos. Among the selections played were the *Nonentto,* written in 1923 and considered his chief chamber music composition. The critic of the New York *Times* found it had "intensity and cumulative power. . . . It contains an almost brash interplay of colors, harmonies, and rhythms." The composer's *Bachiana Brasileira* No. 1 (one of the five suites revealing Villa-Lobos' interest in Bach, and his desire "to transmit the spirit of Bach . . . into the soul of Brazil," though never trying to imitate him) proved to Olin Downes that Villa-Lobos is a composer of "extraordinary force, originality, and fertility." The highlight of the festival was the playing by Artur Rubinstein of the Brazilian's *Rude-poêma* ("Savage Poem"), one of the most difficult piano compositions ever written. It was dedicated to Rubinstein, of whom it is a musical portrait. The pianist has also popularized Villa-Lobos' *Prole do Bébé* ("Child's Family")—three sets of piano pieces about dolls. Paradoxically, few children are advanced enough to play or understand these difficult selections.

In December 1944 South and North America saw a bond of friendship in the first visit of Villa-Lobos to the United States. He conducted the Janssen Symphony of Los Angeles at his initial American public appearance; then made his New York debut by conducting the Philharmonic-Symphony Orchestra in the playing of his *Chôros* Nos. 8 and 9. Virgil Thomson [40] stated that these were "excellent tunes; their varied instrumentation, their abundance of fancy in general, and their easy but perfectly real modernity of thought have placed them in a repertory as valid musical creations of this century." *Musical America's* judgment was: "One of most stimulating evenings of music that New York has enjoyed in many a moon was afforded by this wildly heterogeneous program. Mr. Villa-Lobos also appears to be a much better conductor than most composers are; at least, the orchestra performed the fiendishly intricate scores for him splendidly."

A week later, sharing the podium with Leopold Stokowski [41], Villa-Lobos conducted the New York Symphony Orchestra in his symphonic poem *Uirapura,* and his seventh *Bachiana Brasileira*. Again *Musical America*: "His gift is basic, luxuriant, and tremendously vital. It has about it the naïveté and simple childlike directness of that true genius which is so strong in its own right as to have no need of pose, cleverness, rhetoric, or any of the other mechanisms commonly employed to bolster slender talents." The musician also made guest appearances in Chicago and Kansas City.

On invitation from Serge Koussevitsky '40, Villa-Lobos next appeared as guest conductor with the Boston Symphony Orchestra. During his stay in the United States the Brazilian composer wrote a new Fantasia for cello and orchestra, which he dedicated to Koussevitsky; a ninth Bachiana, dedicated to Aaron Copland '40, the American composer; and a Concerto for harmonica and orchestra for Larry Adler '44, of whom he is an ardent admirer. He also studied pictures of the mountains in America in preparation for his next work, his seventh symphony. In February 1945 the United States League of Composers set aside the week of the nineteenth as "Villa-Lobos Week," in honor of the composer's first visit to the States. Another honor was given to him when he received in 1945 the Koussevitzky Music Foundation commission for a symphonic work. In the same year, together with Lorenzo Fernandez, another Brazilian composer, Villa-Lobos founded the Brazilian Academy of Music, which is modeled after similar institutions in Europe. Its membership will be fifty, forty composers and ten musicologists.

Author of several literary works among which are *Alma do Brasil* and *Programa de Musica* (an official publication of the Department of Education, 1934), this "plump, gay, and bouncy Latin," is a member of many musical organizations, most of them in Brazil, Mexico, and France; and he is honorary director of various musical institutes in Brazil and abroad. He has conducted orchestras in Paris, Brussels, and Barcelona; and is a recipient of honorary decorations from Belgium, Spain, and Portugal. In 1910 he was married to a well known Brazilian concert pianist, Lucilia Guimarães. An enthusiastic billiard player, Villa-Lobos is Rio's three-cushion billiards champion. His favorite bit of tribute to himself as a musician is, "Better bad of mine than good of someone else."

References

Etude 54:498 Jl '41
Inter-American 3:25-7+ Ja '44 por
N Y Times 11 p7 D 17 '44 por
New Yorker 20:16 F 10 '45
Pan Am Union Bul 79:1-10 Ja '45 pors
Time 35:44 Ja 29 '40 por; 45:63 F 19 '45 por
Victor Record R 7:3-4 Je '44 por
Thompson, O. ed. International Cyclopedia of Music and Musicians (1943)
Who's Who in America, 1944-45
Who's Who in Latin America (1940)

WAESCHE, RUSSELL R(ANDOLPH) (wā-shē) Jan. 6, 1886- United States Coast Guard officer

Address: b. c/o Coast Guard Headquarters, 1300 E St., N.W., Washington, D.C.; h. 7005 Rolling Rd., Chevy Chase, Md.

The least known of the armed forces of the United States is also the oldest—the Coast Guard, established in 1790 by Alexander Hamilton to prevent smuggling. Civilians, who refer to Coast Guardsmen as Coast Guards, usually fail to recognize the insigne on a Coast Guardsman's sleeve or lapel, and as-

ADM. RUSSELL R. WAESCHE

sume that the wearer is a Navy man; and the confusion is increased by the fact that the Guard, a Treasury service in peacetime, does operate under the Navy in a war. It is, however, a separate service, like the Marine Corps, with its own proud traditions; when the marines land, in fact, the Coast Guard is there to direct them. Heading its diverse services is Admiral Russell R. Waesche, who has been the Commandant longer than his opposite number in any of the other branches (Army General Marshall '40, Fleet Admiral Ernest King '42, and Marine General Thomas Holcomb '42). Waesche's feeling about his Service is reflected in his booklet, *Deeds of Valor From the Annals of the Coast Guard*, which bears the Guard's secondary motto, "You have to go out, but you don't have to come back."

Russell Randolph Waesche was born in Thurmont, Frederick County, Maryland, on January 6, 1886. The son of Leonard Randolph and Mary Martha (Foreman) Waesche, he attended the Maryland public schools. At fifteen he enrolled in the electrical engineering department of Purdue University, where an elder brother was an instructor. "I didn't have too much dough," the Admiral says. "With my brother teaching at Purdue I figured on saving some of my board bill." After a year Waesche's brother told him that he was too young to appreciate a college education, and should get "a little military training" first. As it happened, the competitive examinations for the Coast Guard Academy were announced just then, and young Russell took them. Appointed a cadet, he completed his Academy training and was then commissioned an ensign in October 1906, beginning twelve years of service as a line officer aboard cutters and destroyers in Atlantic, Pacific, and Arctic waters. "When I woke up," says Waesche, "I found I liked the Service too much and was too old to get back to electrical engineering."

The future admiral began his rise through the grades with promotion to lieutenant (junior grade) in 1907. He was married in 1911 to Dorothy Duke, by whom he had three sons.

WAESCHE, RUSSELL R.—*Continued*

During the Second World War, one of them, Harry Lee Waesche, was to serve as a lieutenant colonel in the Army Air Forces, while Russell Randolph, Jr., and James Mountford Waesche were in the Coast Guard—the former as a lieutenant commander, the latter as a petty officer (noncommissioned). The Waesches were divorced in 1926.

Advancement to full lieutenant came to Russell Waesche in 1917, when he was serving a three-year term as first head of the Division of Communications. When he assumed this post in 1916, with Europe already at war, the Guard's coastal communications system consisted of about 1,435 miles of overhead telephone wire and sixty-five miles of under-sea cables—far from the complete coverage desired. Waesche "organized, modernized, and extended" the system, supervising the placement of many miles of new line and acquiring others. By the end of the war, due to Waesche's efforts, the Coast Guard controlled and operated some three thousand miles of communication lines, connecting the Coast Guard stations with each other and with other points, such as lighthouses, and operating in conjunction with naval radio stations. As a by-product, Waesche made a name for himself as "a man with ideas for solving tough Navy problems."

After the passage of the widely violated Eighteenth Amendment, the Lieutenant was assigned to the offshore patrol to prevent rum-running, commanding a destroyer division. Promoted to lieutenant commander in 1923 and to commander three years later, in 1928 Waesche left the sea to become chief ordnance officer at Coast Guard headquarters in the Treasury Department in Washington. In 1931 he effected a reorganization of the Guard's field forces, with time out to serve as harbor master at the Yorktown Sesquicentennial, and a year later was assigned to four months of liaison work with the Navy's War Plans Division, in the Office of the Chief of Naval Operations. Then the forty-six-year-old officer was honored by being chosen aide to the Coast Guard Commandant, leaving this duty when appointed chief of the Finance Division. In June 1936 President Roosevelt [42] passed over many senior officers to appoint Commander Waesche Commandant of the entire Coast Guard for a four-year term, elevating him two ranks to rear admiral.

The new Commandant "streamlined the administrative setup" of the Service, of which the personnel then numbered between nine and ten thousand, and originated the Coast Guard Institute and correspondence school for warrant officers and enlisted men. He is responsible also for the extensive gunnery practice given Coast Guardsmen. At the Yorktown Sesquicentennial he had made the acquaintance of various Congressmen and dignitaries and had impressed Representative Schuyler Otis Bland of Virginia with his "splendid services." Bland was chairman of the House Committee on the Merchant Marine and Fisheries, which has jurisdiction over Coast Guard legislation, and this was the beginning of Admiral Waesche's enviable relations with the Congress. He was said also to be popular with his subordinates and to work well with his civilian superior, Assistant Secretary of the Treasury Herbert E. Gaston, who had charge also of the Customs and Narcotics Bureaus, the Secret Service, and Treasury law enforcement generally.

The enforcement at sea of Federal laws is one of the Coast Guard's two basic civilian functions; the other is service to the seagoing public. The first of these functions involves such diverse details as the apprehension of smugglers, the protection of seal herds, the policing of harbors, and the prevention of illegal whaling. The Coast Guard is charged with safeguarding life and property on inland waterways as well as at sea, which involves every service from inspecting merchant ships to manning an iceberg patrol and a weather survey, and from providing lighthouses and other navigational aids to supervising the training of merchant mariners. During the J. Edgar Hoover [40] headline era, the Guard activities won it the nickname "the G-men of the sea." In peacetime, too, Coast Guardsmen make an average of fifteen sea rescues every day, maintaining nearly two hundred lifeboat stations for the purpose, and provide relief in stricken areas. At the same time, the Commandant has to see that the Guard is kept in good military order, ready to become an effective part of the Navy whenever it may be necessary.

As the war in Europe became ever more certain, Waesche's duties became more complex and demanding. With the effectuating in 1939 of the Neutrality Act of 1937, his command was charged too with neutrality patrol: preventing the shipment of war materials to any of the belligerent nations. Quick anti-sabotage work was called for in regard to foreign ships in American ports. To quote an official report: "Along the Nation's forty thousand miles of seacoast and inland waterways, the officers and men, the cutters, boats, and planes of the Service maintained a constant lookout, guarding against the illegal entrance and activity of belligerents. Gradually, they extended their activities several hundred miles offshore—as far north as Greenland, where the cruising cutters not only carried out routine patrols, but aided the United States Army in establishing air bases in that strategic region. It was during this time that the cutter *Northland* aided in seizing a Nazi weather station set up in northeast Greenland....At the same time, the Service found itself responsible for new types of duty. One of these was the assignment of cutters to weather ship stations in midocean to supply meteorological data for the safe passage of transoceanic surface and air craft. The technique for this duty had been perfected during the international ice patrols which the Coast Guard maintains on the Grand Banks. But weather ship operation did not begin until early in the year of 1940—when European hostilities forced all ships at sea to maintain radio silence for their own protection."

At the request of the Service, in June 1939 Congress authorized it to organize a voluntary nonmilitary fleet of amateur yachtsmen for auxiliary duties. In addition to this, Waesche was engaged in the expansion of the Coast Guard proper, bringing it up to twenty-five thousand officers and enlisted men by December 1941, more than twice its strength at the time he took office. Reappointed for a second four-year term in 1940, the Commandant was authorized in February 1941 to create a Coast Guard Reserve, toward which end a Coast Guard Reserve Cadet School was established at the Academy in New London; the Coast Guard Auxiliary to organize and train owners of yachts and motorboats; and a Coast Guard Temporary Reserve, composed of civilian men and women who volunteered their services for at least twelve hours each week. By early 1945 there were over fifty-three hundred Temporary Reservists, of whom eighteen hundred were members of the Volunteer Port Security Force, on security patrol in twenty leading ports.

In November 1941 Roosevelt ordered the Coast Guard transferred from the Treasury to the Navy service, where it is a separate arm like the Marines, thus placing the Service on a wartime footing. At this time, two thousand Coast Guardsmen were already operating five Navy transports and manning lifeboats on twenty-two others; some of the expert surfmen were teaching the art of small-boat landings to the Army-Navy-Marine amphibious forces at landing-craft training stations; about forty cutters had been converted to minesweepers, and nearly one hundred fifty were armed and armored for combat. When the Japanese attack on Pearl Harbor brought the country into war, the Coast Guard immediately went on a combat footing.

Admiral Waesche's men established "a constant day-and-night patrol on foot, on horseback, and in jeeps, [including the use of sentry dogs], at almost every point where the Atlantic, the Pacific, and the Gulf touched the United States." Records are hardly a fair measure of any preventive agency, but it was the beach patrol who discovered the two parties of Nazi saboteurs put ashore from submarines in the spring of 1942; and it was the beach patrol, at the time when merchant ships were being torpedoed offshore, who saved scores of the seamen escaping from their sinking ships. Waesche's command also had to take care of "port security"—more than five million linear feet of wharfage had to be protected, most of which had been built "with an almost complete disregard of the fire hazard." For this purpose, Waesche directed the assembling of a fireboat fleet eventually to number more than two hundred fifty, and of a system of surveillance over every ship in every port of the United States, its territories, and later its invaded and liberated foreign areas. Coast Guardsmen were even assigned to supervise the loading of all munitions and other explosives. So successful was this captain-of-the-port system, which at its peak involved more than forty thousand officers and men, including the Volunteer Port Security Force, that in two years no serious waterfront mishap had occurred. The President described this as an achievement exceeding his most optimistic expectations.

One month after Pearl Harbor the first German U-boat struck in American waters. To meet this emergency, the Coast Guard borrowed, chartered, and purchased more than two thousand civilian vessels, many with their owners as temporary reservists, to take patrol stations alongside the regular patrolships. These, operating under the Naval Sea Frontier Command, aided in the coastal convoys, while larger Coast Guard cutters traveled back and forth across the Atlantic, shepherding their convoys of merchant ships and fighting the enemy whenever he showed himself. When the Nazi submarines moved to the Caribbean area the "makeshift fleet" followed, as the Guard laconically puts it, with success. Meanwhile, in March 1942, the President transferred to the Service certain functions of the Bureau of Marine Navigation and Inspection, which meant that it had to regulate and inspect literally everything and everybody concerned with the huge wartime shipping. That July some of the burden was taken off, when the President transferred the Merchant Marine Training Program from Waesche's command to Admiral Emory S. Land's [42] War Shipping Administration.

On August 7, 1942, when the Americans launched their first land offensive of the war at Guadalcanal in the Solomon Islands, Coast Guard officers and men took the marines ashore, manned the attack transport *Hunter Liggett*, and supplemented the crews of a number of Navy ships. Coast Guard beachmasters and beach parties directed the invasion traffic—incoming replacements and supplies, outgoing casualties, and tanks, trucks, jeeps, guns, bulldozers, munitions, food. They have continued to do so in subsequent invasions, manning more and more of the attack transports, as well as the huge troop transports—at Fedala, Casablanca, Safi, Algiers, Oran in North Africa, and at Scoglitti, Gela, Licata in Sicily, the entire Pacific area, and again at Salerno, Anzio, Normandy, and southern France. Army and Navy vessels manned by Coast Guard personnel include troop transports, destroyer escorts, frigates, barges, tankers, tugs, freight ships, and landing craft from LST's to LCI's, to which Admiral Waesche estimated in March 1945 that more than fifty-four thousand men and Coast Guard officers had been assigned. The assignment was made possible by the decreased need for coast and antisubmarine patrol, by the assistance of the temporary reserves, and, after November 1942, by the women's reserve, the SPARS or Spars, so named for the Coast Guard motto "Semper Paratus"—"Always Ready." Under the command of Captain Dorothy C. Stratton [43], former dean of women at Waesche's old university, Purdue, these ten thousand officers and enlisted women served in all except combat capacities. Civilians who never learned to tell a Coast Guardsman from a sailor could distinguish an enlisted Spar from her Wave counterpart; she wore "U.S. Coast Guard" on her hat, a white shield on the right sleeve of her jacket, and the Coast Guard insignia on her jacket lapel.

In March 1942, when Russell R. Waesche was made the first Coast Guard vice-admiral, his command numbered forty-two thousand. By January 1945 it had increased more than four times (more than fifteen times prewar strength) to approximately one hundred seventy thousand, plus fifty thousand temporary reservists added since 1943. In view of "the size and accomplishments of the Coast Guard,"

WAESCHE, RUSSELL R.—*Continued*

a bill was introduced into the House of Representatives and favorably reported on to establish the grade of full admiral for the Coast Guard Commandant. A laudatory Washington *Post* editorial had been placed in the *Congressional Record* by Representative Gordon Canfield of New Jersey the preceding June, and Representative Bland inserted an "extension of remarks" in which he declared, "Admiral Waesche is one of the most efficient, capable, conscientious painstaking, informed officials in the United States Government today." This was on the occasion of Waesche's swearing-in for a third term as Commandant. In March 1945 the bill was passed. The next month Waesche was raised to the rank of admiral, thereby becoming the first Coast Guard full admiral. Because of ill health, however, Waesche's retirement was announced for January 1946.

The Admiral, who has received little personal publicity, is five feet ten inches tall, lean (weighing one hundred and forty-five pounds), ruddy-complexioned, nearly bald. His gray eyes have the sharpness of the expert marksman he is—especially with a rifle. He is described as highly likable. Purdue honored him in February 1944 with the degree of Doctor of Engineering, and that May he was elected president of the Society of American Military Engineers. An Episcopalian and a Mason, Waesche is a member of the Newcomen Society, the National Sojourners, the Propeller Club, and the Society of Naval Architects and Marine Engineers, as well as the University and Army and Navy clubs, the American Legion, and the Military Order of the World War. In 1933 he married Agnes (Rizzuto) Cronin; they have one son, William Alexander Waesche.

References

Congressional Record (Extension of Remarks) Je 23 '44
Time 41:64 My 3 '43 por
U S News 10:48-9 Ap 18 '41 por
The Generals and the Admirals (1945)
Who's Who in America, 1944-45

WAKE-WALKER, SIR W(ILLIAM) FREDERICK Mar. 24, 1888-Sept. 24, 1945 British admiral; Third Sea Lord and Controller of the British Navy at time of death; saw action during the evacuation of Dunkerque; aided in the sinking of the *Bismarck* as Admiral of the Cruiser Squadron which first sighted the battleship in the Denmark Straits and then trailed her.

Obituary

N Y Times p23 S 26 '45

WANG CHING-WEI (wäng' jĭng' wā') 1884—Nov. 10, 1944 Chinese politician; was a hero of the Chinese Revolution in 1911 and one-time high official in Central Government, only to become later his nation's traitor; was President and Premier of the Japanese-sponsored puppet Government of China at Nanking at time of death. See *Current Biography* 1940 Yearbook.

Obituary

N Y Times p11 N 13 '44 por

WANG SHIH-CHIEH (wäng shĭr jĭ'ĕh') 1891- Chinese Government official; diplomat; educator

Address: b: Foreign Ministry, Chungking

Any resumé of the career of Wang Shih-chieh, China's Minister of Foreign Affairs, is an account of modern China as well. During his lifetime, which has spanned the past half-century, his country has been in an unsettled political and economic state. China "has been almost continually harassed by civil strife, revolution, and international trouble . . . not to mention disastrous earthquakes, floods, famines, pestilence, inflation, and nationwide starvation." After his appointment in July 1945 the new Foreign Minister was faced with the additional danger that China might try to settle the long-standing hostility between the Government and the Chinese Communists by force of arms, "precipitating a crisis which would involve not only the peace of Asia but the whole world's efforts at recovery from war." In September Wang went to London, where, together with the Foreign Ministers of the other of the Big Five Nations, he began the additional task of "translating into workable and lasting agreements the maze of problems" arising out of the war.

Wang Shih-chieh brings to his new work not only a wealth of experience in law and education (two "arms of civilization" so desperately needed in the settlement of China's problems), but a first-hand knowledge of revolutionary methods. Born in 1891 in the northeastern province of Hupeh, Wang grew up during the period when Sun Yat-sen was attempting to overthrow the Manchu Dynasty, and in 1911 the twenty-year-old Wang took part in the Wuhan revolt which forced the last Manchu emperor to abdicate. His studies at the Paiyang University were followed by special work in economics and political science at the University of London, from which he was graduated in 1917 with a Bachelor of Science degree. He finished his postgraduate work in 1920 at the University of Paris, receiving the degree of Docteur en Droit.

Upon his return to China he was on the faculty of the Peking National University from 1921 to 1927, first as a lecturer of comparative constitutional law and then as dean of the faculty of law. In 1927 he was appointed director of the Bureau of Law Codification in Nanking, and a year later he became a member of the Permanent Court of Arbitration at The Hague. In 1928 Wang was also appointed a member of the Legislative Yuan, the law-drafting and research body of the Chinese Government, which advises on matters of legislation, budgets, and important international affairs. Members of the Legislative Yuan are appointed by the chairman of the National Government, on the suggestion of the president of the Legislative Yuan, for a term of two years.

While he was still a member of the Yuan, in 1929 Wang became president of the National Wuhan University at Wuchang, in his native province. The university is composed of three colleges—arts, science, and law—and is said to be the most beautifully and sumptuously housed of all Chinese universities. (To prevent the university from falling into Japanese hands, it has since been moved, with other refugee colleges, farther inland to Loshan, near Mount Omei in the province of Szechwan.) As a result of his work at Wuhan University, in 1933 Wang was appointed Minister of Education, thereby becoming the highest authority on education administration in China.

The next year Wang's Ministry called a national conference on vocational education, which submitted plans for the organization of specialized vocational schools. As for the university, in May 1934 Wang issued provisional regulations for the organization, financing, and staffing of a postgraduate school, stating that "the underlying motive has been to combine the greatest amount of academic freedom with the minimum of supervision from the Ministry of Education." In 1934, too, Wang reversed a previous ruling which banned private evening schools. "Adult schools," he said, "are not only supplementary to university education but also a means of social reform and social revolution"; and in 1936 he began a campaign to popularize the radio and motion pictures as mediums for social education. Further, he reduced the number of hours of class instruction, to give students more time for free development—a departure from the rigid Chinese tradition in education; and he also established summer research sessions for secondary school-teachers. On the other hand, he abolished the elective system, and in 1935 approved a standardized curriculum and a Ministry final examination for the universities. In 1935 the National Government took the unprecedented step of establishing a five-year plan for compulsory education to end illiteracy; but the outbreak of hostilities forced it to suspend this program.

In 1939, while Wang was serving as Minister of Education, he was also appointed Minister of Information. He held this position until 1942, and was reappointed in November 1944. During these years he worked to improve Chinese relations with Great Britain, the United States, and other countries. In February 1944, he was head of the Chinese Good Will Mission to Great Britain. That November he began to liberalize the censorship considerably. A leader in China's constitutional movement, in 1938 Wang had become secretary-general of the People's Political Council, China's wartime advisory assembly, which was formed to "utilize the best minds in national affairs and to rally all elements in the country in time of war." A year after the Central Planning Board was established in 1941, Wang also became its secretary-general. Among important measures formulated while he held the latter position was the five-year National Defense and Economic Reconstruction Plan and the ten-year plan for the development of the northwestern provinces.

In 1944 Wang, who is described as one of Generalissimo Chiang Kai-shek's [40] most trusted advisers, became the Central Government's chief negotiator in dealing with the Chinese Communist problem—"without doubt the thorniest of China's internal political questions." It is the general opinion that his dealings with the Communists, who controlled the entire Northwest Region, led to his appointment as Foreign Minister in July 1945. "The struggle between Chungking and the Communists dates back to 1926, when Chiang took the lead in expelling them from the Kuomintang, the po-

WANG SHIH-CHIEH

litical party which controls China, and then led his armed forces in driving them from the cities they controlled in South China, notably Canton [and in waging an avowed war of extermination against them]." The conflict between Chiang and the Communists, moreover, was only partly submerged while both factions concentrated on fighting the Jap invaders. Upon his return from Yenan, the capital of Red China, in December 1944, Wang said, "One of the most encouraging signs is that the atmosphere is calm and that there has been a marked diminution of recrimination on either side." However, the collapse of Japan in August 1945 brought into sharp focus the long-standing conflict, and the threat of further conflagration was only allayed when the text of the thirty-year Sino-Soviet treaty was made public on August 27. Then it became evident that Moscow formally recognized Chiang's Government as supreme in China, thus withholding by inference any support of the Communist regime in Yenan. Indications that the treaty might end the threat of civil war were seen in the belated acceptance by the Chinese Communist leader, Mao Tse-tung [43], of Chiang's third invitation to visit Chungking to discuss differences.

The month after the defeat of Japan the Foreign Ministers of China, France, Great Britain, the United States, and the U.S.S.R.— Wang, Bidault [45], Bevin [40], Byrnes [41], and Molotov [40]—began the period of "drawing the framework for the peace." The principles guiding them, said the New York Times, "had been laid down in the series of Allied statements and Big Three conferences declarations beginning with the Atlantic Charter in August 1941." China's personal concern in the meeting was with settling the problem of her sovereignty and territorial independence in Asia. After three weeks of almost continuous meetings, however, the first peace conference of the Second World War ended in a deadlock, the Foreign Ministers being able to agree only on terminating their session. Wang returned to

WANG SHIH-CHIEH—*Continued*

Chungking to continue his activity in the negotiations between Chiang Kai-shek and Mao Tze-tung on a plan for a unified government for China. In December 1945 he participated in the all-party People's Consultative Council, composed of representatives of other parties and nonpartisans, in addition to the Kuomintang and the Communist party.

References

China Handbook, 1937-43
Who's Who in China (1936)

WARNER, ALBERT July 23, 1884- Producer
WARNER, HARRY M(ORRIS) Dec. 12, 1881- Producer
WARNER, JACK L. Aug. 2, 1892- Producer
Address: b. Warner Brothers Pictures, Inc., 321 W. 44th St., New York City; Warner Brothers Studios, Olive Ave., Burbank, Calif.

Warner Brothers Pictures, Inc., one of the largest film organizations in the United States, and the company to introduce sound to the screen, is headed by three brothers, Harry M.,

ALBERT WARNER

the president, Jack L., the vice-president and executive producer, and Albert Warner. Harry Morris, the eldest, was born in Poland on December 12, 1881; Albert was born there several years later, on July 23, 1884; while Jack L., the youngest of the twelve Warner children, was born in London, Ontario, Canada, on August 2, 1892. According to one source, their Russian parents, Benjamin and Pearl (Eichelbaum) Warner, emigrated from Poland with their children in 1890. They lived for a time in Canada before moving in 1894 to Youngstown, Ohio, where Benjamin Warner became a butcher.

Each of the several sons was expected to contribute a share to the family's income. Harry worked for a time as a cobbler's apprentice, then with Armour and Company, the meat packers. Albert ("Abe") and Samuel, another brother, worked, in turn, at odd jobs before undertaking a new enterprise—the exhibition of moving pictures. The early programs consisted of several pictures, fifty to two hundred feet in length. They used a projection machine they had obtained by pawning Sam's treasured birthday gift from his father, a gold watch and chain. Then Harry, who in later life was to display a sixth sense for business, began to realize the possibilities of the projection machine and soon joined Abe and Sam. The family had always exemplified the motto "One for all and all for one," so Jack, too (who had begun as a singer in minstrels and operettas at the age of twelve), and Rose, their sister, entered the venture. They held showings in the neighboring towns, moving on when there were no people left who had not seen the film. Sam handled the projection machine, while Harry and Albert supervised the advertising and the business ends, very much as they do today. Jack's part was to sing before and after the picture, and to dance while the rest of the family rewound the film. Rose sold tickets and played the piano accompaniments for illustrated song slides, an added attraction. From Youngstown, Ohio, they moved to Newcastle, Pennsylvania, and about 1903 opened their first theater in an empty store—a building with a seating capacity for exactly ninety-nine persons. Any more than this would have made the theater subject to local and state fire regulations. Business was good, except when there was a death in the community; then the brothers had to dash over to the funeral parlor with the ninety-nine chairs.

However, the motion picture business was then a precarious one, and the Warners were beset with numerous obstacles. There was no guaranty of film delivery. Sometimes it was necessary to improvise a program because delivery was held up, or they had three or four films on hand simultaneously and had to juggle them ingeniously around among the four or five theaters they had acquired, in order to live up to their advance billing. Surveying the situation, Harry Warner conceived the idea of a group of exhibitors and theater owners forming an exchange to facilitate the acquisition and showing of films. The result was the Duquesne Amusement Supply Company, the first organization of its kind in the country. It was established in Pittsburgh and, while it won the support of exhibitors throughout the region, it was short-lived. The producers, discovering that the exchange company was making more money on their products than they were, did everything in their power to discourage the project: they raised the rental rates, delivered poor prints, and often included unwanted or unordered films. The Warner brothers continued the company until 1912, then sold out to the General Film Company. The result of this exchange idea convinced the Warners that if they were to be sure of having pictures to distribute, they must make them themselves. They gathered in New York and began turning out what the trade came to know as "Warner Features" at the old Vitagraph studios. Then in 1917 Ambassador James W. Gerard published his book *My Four Years in Germany*. Aware of the possibilities in it for an excellent movie, Harry Warner secured the rights by offering Gerard a share in the prospective profits. The resulting film grossed almost a million dollars—and the Warner brothers were "on their way."

A few years before the beginning of the First World War, Jack Warner had established a studio in Santa Paula, California, but this production unit was discontinued in 1914. In 1918, however, the Warners again shifted their production headquarters to California. This time they built their studio, a larger one, on Sunset Boulevard in Hollywood, where a number of years later they were to pioneer with talking pictures.

In 1923, although they were incorporated now as the Warner Brothers Pictures, Inc., they were still selling their pictures through franchise holders—powerful independent distributors who advanced them money to make their pictures, but not enough. It was obvious that the solution to the problem would be to control their own distribution network. In 1925 the financier Waddill Catchings met the brothers and, impressed by their business sense and frugal private lives, helped them to raise eight hundred thousand dollars. With this they were able to purchase the Vitagraph Company, which had a nationwide system of exchanges. That freed them from the independent franchise holders. By 1928 they were a sixteen-million-dollar corporation, and within two more years they were worth two hundred and thirty million. This was something unheard of then, even in the movie industry.

During this period the brothers had secured the services of John Barrymore, Lenore Ulric, Ernst Lubitsch, and the great animal star, the dog Rin-Tin-Tin. They had also added to their equipment an invention which united speech with the action in a picture, Vitaphone synchronization. The idea of using sound had started when Sam persuaded Harry to listen to a device the Bell Laboratories had invented and which other studios had turned down. Harry was impressed, and Sam, assisted by the telephone company engineers, conducted the work which made the device practical for motion pictures.

In the summer of 1926 the first Vitaphone picture was released—a John Barrymore vehicle entitled *Don Juan*. Although the voices of Barrymore and the rest of the cast were not recorded, the picture contained a full synchronized musical score by the New York Philharmonic Orchestra. It was soon followed by other Warner films, each offering opportunity for improvement in the sound track. With the release of Al Jolson's '40 *The Jazz Singer* in the fall of 1927, the once wary competitors began to realize that talking pictures were here to stay. This film was the official debut of modern movie history because Jolson's voice was heard—the first time spoken dialogue had been used in a feature picture, for the singing voice had been recorded. But in making *The Jazz Singer* Jolson, by accident before launching into his song "Blue Skies," had said, "Come on, Ma, listen to this." The

HARRY M. WARNER

line was left in, once it was recorded, along with his singing, and the audience was electrified. A new, living, breathing medium of entertainment had come into being.

But for the Warners the joy of accomplishment was marred by bereavement: the day before the showing Sam Warner died. The weeks of work and worry had taken their toll, a cold he had contracted had developed into a fatal case of pneumonia. The brothers, although cheered by their success, could not forget the price paid by one of them in making it possible, and they sailed for Europe for a rest. Fate, however, played into their hands. During their absence members of the staff decided that the material in a short then in production, *Lights of New York*, warranted development into a full-length film. They added additional scenes and dialogue to the script and managed to wheedle more funds than the original budget had provided. When the Warner brothers returned from Europe they found that they owned the first all-talking motion picture ever made. Costing forty thousand dollars, it grossed more than two million.

Realizing the head start it had on the others in the film industry, the company proceeded to press its advantage. It brought "big names" to the screen—George Arliss, Leslie Howard, Paul Muni '44, Edward G. Robinson, James Cagney '42—and it devoted the new medium to entertainment of a sort hitherto unknown to film audiences. Warner's produced *Kismet* (1930), *Little Caesar* (1930), *Five Star Final* (1931), *I Am a Fugitive From a Chain Gang* (1932), and many other pictures. The acquisition of the Stanley Company of America, which controlled some two hundred and fifty motion picture houses and also owned a third of First National Pictures, a top-notch studio, put Warner Brothers once and for all on its financial feet. These theaters were a guaranteed outlet for its pictures, no small item when other producer-distributor groups were

JACK L. WARNER

keeping competitors out of the houses they controlled.

By selling their share of the company's stock, plus debentures and common stock, the brothers acquired a chain of some five hundred theaters. Harry bought out the balance of shareholders of First National (its studio became the present home of Warner's, the largest producing unit anywhere); bought up radio companies, music publishers, foreign sound patents; and "raided" other studios for such stars as William Powell, Ruth Chatterton, and Kay Francis, whose contracts were limited only by their agents' imaginations. In short, the Warner company was a "big-timer" now and was able to hold its own. It set the pace in the field of musicals with the lavish *Gold Digger* series. It established an unequaled reputation for the production of "headline pictures" built around the most important news stories of the day—pictures like *G-Men* (1935), *China Clipper* (1936), and *Marked Woman* (1937). It made "spectacles," too— *A Midsummer Night's Dream* (1935), *Anthony Adverse* (1936), *Green Pastures* (1936), *The Adventures of Robin Hood* (1938).

For years, too, Warner Brothers has considered the screen a medium for presenting social issues of contemporary concern. Through such pictures as *Black Fury* (1935), which dealt with labor problems in the mines, *The Story of Louis Pasteur* (1935), *The Black Legion* (1936), which involved racial and religious bigotry, and *The Life of Emile Zola* (1937), Warner's has maintained a high record in film artistry and proved that educative films can be entertaining—and a box office success.

As a film corporation Warner Brothers has had its share of problems, too. There have been theatrical union strikes; charges of monopoly on the part of independent theater owners; salary and contract feuds with some of the leading stars; and, in December 1944, a break with the association Motion Picture Producers and Distributors of America,

attributed to dissatisfaction with the Association's handling of labor relations and wage negotiations with the A.F. of L. Screen Actors Guild. Six months after its notification of withdrawal, Warner Brothers Pictures resigned from the M.P.D.A. (June 1945), of which Will H. Hays [43] was then president. By September Hays had been succeeded by Eric A. Johnston [43], former president of the States Chamber of Commerce of the United States of America. About two months later, the bitter eight-month strike of from three to seven thousand employees of various Hollywood studios (in which the Warner studio had been the scene of clashes) was settled. The agreement was reached between the A. F. of L., Johnston, and Donald M. Nelson [41], president of the Independent Motion Picture Producers. Following this, in early November, Warner's was again a member of M.P.D.A.

In the face of growing reports in film trade circles that the American public was becoming bored with pictures concerning the war, Harry M. Warner was the first producer to make a definite statement on the course the motion picture industry in the United States should take during the war. "This is a time for the movies to tell the public what it is fighting for and about," he said in May 1943. "If we fail to recognize this obligation to inform as well as entertain, there would be little justification for our existence." Jack Warner later reiterated: "Obviously the screen is able to reach millions who cannot be reached by any other means," he wrote, at the same time emphasizing a few of the vital services the screen has and will be able to contribute towards the maintenance of peace by "the exposure of the sinister aims and ruthless methods . . . of totalitarianism . . . the promotion of international amity through honest . . . sympathetic presentation of the peoples of the United Nations to each other. . . .These purposes we have sought to serve," Warner continued, "through the production of entertainment which serves simultaneously the not inconsiderate function of bolstering public morale throughout the free world."

After the start of the Second World War, in an attempt to keep audiences abreast of events, Warner's produced such films as Lillian Hellman's [41] *Watch on the Rhine* (1943), *Destination Tokyo* (1943), Irving Berlin's [42] *This Is the Army* (1943), *Casablanca* (1942). (Shortly before the war it made a series of patriotic shorts, "preparing America for the crisis ahead.") In its "win-the-war" effort, Warner's produced films that were rewarded with eight "Oscars" for the year 1944—the gold statuettes awarded annually by the Hollywood Academy of Motion Picture Arts and Sciences. In the case of Warner's the awards were for the best film of the year, best actor, best director, the two best screenplays, best musical scoring, best film editing, and best produced—*Princess O'Rourke, Air Force, Casablanca, Watch on the Rhine,* and *This Is the Army* winning the awards. (Harry Warner had announced that it was not the ambition of the studio to make the best musical film in a war year.) Before the statuettes were awarded the entire proceeds from *This Is the Army*—totaling some ten million dollars—had been turned over to the Army War Relief. In December 1944 the film *Hollywood Canteen* was released. A large portion of the profits from the picture went directly to the real canteen.

Among the most popular of Warner's 1945 releases were the war pictures *Objective—Burma, Hotel Berlin, God Is My Co-Pilot,* and *Confidential Agent;* the comedies *Roughly Speaking* and *Christmas in Connecticut;* the dramas *To Have and Have Not* (with Bogart and Bacall), *The Corn Is Green* (with Bette Davis), and *Mildred Pierce* (with Joan Crawford); and the picture based on the life of George Gershwin, *Rhapsody in Blue.* The company in the same year acquired the rights to the Broadway successes *Life with Father* and *The Voice of the Turtle,* and for the best seller, *The Fountainhead,* by Ayn Rand. Altogether, announced Jack Warner in December 1945, forty-six new feature films were on the Warner program for the coming year.

It is reported that Warner's is planning to collaborate with other major companies in the production of educational films, which will deal largely with social and political issues. During the war, on a nonprofit basis it made many training films for the armed forces, and also short subjects for the Government. For its efforts in the past Warner Brothers received the annual award of the New York Teacher's Union in April 1944. The president of the union, in announcing the award, pointed to the excellent record of "distinguished contributions to the education of America," through Warner Brothers' ability to combine good citizenship with good picture-making. Special mention was also made of the educational bureau recently established by Warner under the direction of Charles S. Steinberg.

Something about the future production policies of the three brothers may be gathered from a statement made by Jack Warner at a studio meeting in December. He emphasized the need for "reconverting the products of the mind as well as the factories" in the direction of a lasting peace. He said that the motion pictures (which his brother Harry had two days before declared as coming "as close to being a universal language as we are likely to get in our time")) "have an implicit responsibility in the prevention of future wars by demonstrating democratic ways of life among peoples, in small groups as well as in national groups. Honest exchange of information and ideas is the primary function of motion pictures as well as of newspapers and the radio." In conclusion he stated that his company would continue its policy of blending entertainment with information.

Harry Warner, the president, is a short, wiry, gray-haired man, and, it is said, he has a vague resemblance to George Arliss. He is said to be a worrier, constantly preoccupied with his own thoughts, and he often fits that Hollywood definition of a producer: a man who asks a question, gives the answer, then tells the other person he's wrong. "Nothing about his appearance, manners, habits, or conversation," says one writer, on the other hand, "suggests a motion picture magnate. In a crowd he would pass for a retired businessman living on a modest income." He has never forgotten that he started at the bottom, and that it was hard work, an iron will, and

courage which account for his success. Harry has been the head of the Warner household since its earliest days. According to *Fortune,* that responsibility having been relaxed a little, he is now merely the court of appeals, or trouble department. "They never bring anything to me," he explains, "until it's already wrong." In addition to "managing" the family, Harry has the role of the undisputed boss of Warner Brothers, Inc., and he is regarded as one of the most influential men in the motion picture industry. He has been married since August 1907 to Rea Levinson, which he considers quite a record in Hollywood. They have three children, Lewis, who died when he was twenty-one, Doris Ruth, and Betty.

Albert Warner, treasurer and head of sales and distribution, is often referred to as "honest Abe." Harry claims that Albert is the most popular man in the movie industry, while he (Harry) is probably the most disliked. Albert is not so active in the industry as he used to be, but he is still addressed as Major Albert Warner, a rank given to him by the Army during the First World War for his propaganda work. Abe likes to think of Warner Brothers as the "Ford of the Movies," since Warner films lead in the low-cost field, the profit to the company being due to volume of sales rather than to an occasional smash hit. Of Albert's personal life, little is known. He seldom appears in public, leaving statements of company policy to Harry and Jack.

Jack, vice-president in charge of Warner Brothers' production, is the youngest of the brothers. Like Harry, he looks upon the movie industry as any other kind of factory production, requiring discipline and order rather than temperament and talent. He "personally supervises selection of story material, the assignment and over-all guidance of producers and directors, the discovery and assignment of acting talent as well as the general supervision of all production details. Every device to effect economy is used: repeated use of material, preassembled sets, anticipation of future needs, and a minimum of wasted time and space. However, Jack's real economy consists of the way in which he handles talent and ideas—the really expensive ingredients of a movie, according to *Fortune.* Nor is he blind to the merit of providing opportunities for new directorial talent, and he has faith in his system of creating opportunities for young men. *Princess O'Rourke* (1943), *Watch on the Rhine,* and *Destination Tokyo* were all "firsts" for three young directors. Jack also is aware that roles must be cast on the basis of suitability of the players, and has not hesitated to employ outside talent. Such stars as Cary Grant '41, Ingrid Bergman '40, Robert Cummings, Miriam Hopkins, Michele Morgan, Philip Dorn, Paul Lukas '42, C. Aubrey Smith '44, and Fredric March '43 were engaged from other studios to play those parts which Warner Brothers felt they alone were suited to fill.

However, Jack has not confined his interest to the immediate problems of production. He and Harry have spent much time studying and expounding the future possibilities and obligations of the screen. In August 1944 the Canadian Government presented Warner Brothers with a plaque as an expression of appreciation for the film *The Shining Future,* which

WARNER, ALBERT; WARNER, HARRY M.; and WARNER, JACK L.—*Cont.*

Warner produced for use in Canada's Sixth War Loan. In his acceptance speech Jack declared that after the war "motion pictures must have the same freedom of expression as is guaranteed to the press and the spoken word." Later Jack called for representation of the film industry at the peace conference "because of the increasingly important role the screen will be required to play in the postwar world." He spoke, also, of the necessity for authenticity in foreign themes. "People in other countries will want to see their own modes and customs accurately portrayed . . . and they will no longer be willing to accept an American version of an Englishman, Frenchman, or Russian." In October Jack warned both producers and theater owners against making the mistake of offering "cheaper pictures" during the readjustment period. He stated that the industry had educated the public to expect better pictures and that it was the producers' and exhibitors' duty to supply them.

Immediately after the United States entered the war Jack offered his services to the Army. He was commissioned a lieutenant colonel in the Air Forces. Then, after a year of duty, he was placed on the inactive list; this permitted him to devote his time to the war work the studio was doing. His son Jack, formerly associate producer for Warner's, also served as an officer in the Army during the war. In June 1944 the last Liberty ship from the Richmond Shipyard in California was named *Benjamin Warner* in honor of the brothers' father.

> *References*
>
> C S Mon Mag p10 S 2 '44 por; p9 O 7
>   '44 il
> Fortune 16:110-13+ D '37 il por
> Liberty 19:14+ O 31 '42 pors; 19:32+
>   D 12 '42 pors
> N Y Sun p6 Ag 12 '44
> International Motion Picture Almanac,
>   1943-44
> National Cyclopædia of American Biography Current vol D p230
> Who's Who in America, 1944-45

WATERLOW, SIR SYDNEY P(HILIP) Oct. 22, 1878—Dec. 4, 1944 British diplomat; acting first secretary at the Paris Peace Conference in 1919; served as Minister to Siam (1926-28), to Ethiopia (1928-29), to Bulgaria (1929-33), and to Greece (1933-39).

> *Obituary*
>
> N Y Times p25 D 7 '44 por

WATSON, EDWIN M(ARTIN) Dec. 10, 1883—Feb. 20, 1945 Military aide (major general) and secretary to President Roosevelt [42], appointed in 1933 and 1939, respectively; chief of the military section of President Wilson's personal staff at the peace conference in Paris; military attaché at the American Embassy, Brussels (1927-31).

> *Obituary*
>
> N Y Times p23 F 28 '45 por

WATSON-WATT, SIR ROBERT (ALEXANDER) Apr. 13, 1892- Physicist; British Government official

Address: b. c/o Air Ministry, London; h. 287 Sheen Lane, London

The man acclaimed in Britain as the developer of the radiolocator, the British equivalent of the American radar, is Sir Robert Watson-Watt, who is regarded by many as the hero of the Battle of Britain. His radiolocator, produced and operated in secrecy, was probably the most effective defense mechanism against the overwhelming air strength of the Germans during the grim months of 1940. When the Luftwaffe flew over the island daily to drop cargoes of bombs, it was radiolocation that enabled the then outnumbered RAF to concentrate its forces at the proper time and place to meet the enemy. It was radiolocation, too, that directed the antiaircraft fire and planes accurately and effectively through darkness and fog. Without the aid of this device, Britain, it is believed, might not have emerged unconquered from that early battle. Sir Stafford Cripps [40] has said of radiolocation: "It contributed to the winning of the war more than any other single factor."

Robert Alexander Watson-Watt was born in Brechin, Scotland, on April 13, 1892, to Patrick and Mary (Matthew) Watson Watt. He received most of his education in schools near his home, going from Brechin High School to University College, Dundee, a college of the University of St. Andrews. He was graduated from University College with a B.Sc., with special honors in electrical engineering. Later he was awarded the honorary degrees of LL.D. by St. Andrews (1943) and D.Sc. by the University of Toronto.

The twenty-year-old engineer began his career in 1912 as assistant professor of physics at his alma mater, University College. Four years later he met and was married to Margaret Robertson, one of the students at the college. In 1915 he was appointed to the first of his many civil service posts as Senior. From 1917 until 1921 he held the position of meteorologist-in-charge at the Royal Aircraft Establishment. It was while employed as a weatherman that he patented his first radiolocation device, in 1919—a contrivance "useful for meteorological purposes such as the location of atmospheric discharges." In the years that followed Watson-Watt concentrated more intensely on radio research, receiving fourteen patents for improved radio direction finders, more sensitive and accurate than the first. (The theoretical findings of Sir Edward Appleton [45] on the reflecting layers of the atmosphere formed a basis for his work in this field.)

In 1921 Watson-Watt became superintendent of the radio research stations of the Government's Department of Scientific and Industrial Research. From 1933 to 1936 he was superintendent of the radio department of the National Physical Laboratory. Then, on April 2, 1935, the Scotsman received his eleventh patent relating to wireless direction and position—a landmark in the history of the radiolocator. For months before he had been carrying on experiments in an old truck parked on a country lane near Daventry, with an RAF plane flying overhead constantly. He had been working on a new type of radiolocator, an instrument which could detect the approach of the flying plane and follow it on its course of flight. This was the real birth of radiolocation, the secret weapon of the Battle of Britain. (Similar work was carried on in the United States by Dr. A. Hoyt Taylor '45.) The first radiolocator was crude, but Watson-Watt and his associates worked on it constantly, and within a year he was granted three new patents. The improvements intensified the sensitivity of the radiolocator, provided it with one device for checking its accuracy and another for increasing the visibility of the warning signals. During the years between 1936 and 1938 Watson-Watt was superintendent of the Bawdsey Research Station of the Air Ministry, where he led the intensive study of radiolocation that was being carried on in Britain.

In 1937 the radio engineer's research took him away from the laboratory into what might be termed "field work." At this time, when the British radiolocation researchers were preparing the first large-scale trial of their devices, there had been a report about a place in East Prussia that appeared dangerously similar to the British radar experimental station at Bawdsey. Watson-Watt and his wife were sent to Germany to investigate the rumor and to observe, if they could, to what extent the Germans had progressed in the field of radar. They traveled as ordinary English tourists, equipped with the familiar walking shoes and Baedeker—plus a pocket telescope which appeared to be a flashlight. They visited many ancient churches, observing the views from the steeples. Mrs. Watson-Watt sketched the landscapes while her husband hunted about in old churchyards for signs of a radar station—signs he would have been quick to recognize since he had personally taken part in the construction of every radiolocation station in England. (The events of the next few years proved that Germany had lagged far behind the Allies in the development of radar. Flushed with their early victories in the war, the Nazis abandoned the study of radiolocation, and later, when they needed it, found themselves two years behind the Allies in their development— a gap not easy to bridge in the realm of science.)

A year before the outbreak of the Second World War Watson-Watt was made director of the Communications Development of the Air Ministry. After 1939 he was appointed to, and still holds, the posts of scientific adviser on telecommunications to the Air Ministry (1940) and vice-controller of Communications Equipment in the Ministry of Aircraft Production (1942). He is also deputy chairman of the Radio Board of the War Cabinet. In 1941 Watson-Watt was sent to the United States to consult with United States Army and Air Force chiefs and to reveal to them the full extent of British discoveries in the field of radiolocation. American scientists A. Hoyt Taylor '45 and Leo C. Young had developed a device based on the same principles as Wat-

British Official Photo.

SIR ROBERT WATSON-WATT

son-Watt's radiolocator, but from that time radar, as the device was officially renamed, became a joint project of the United States and Great Britain.

Sir Robert's lectures and writings have been in the fields of meteorology and radio engineering. In collaboration with J. F. Herd and L. H. Bainbridge Bell he wrote *Application of the Cathode Ray Oscillograph in Radio Research*, showing the value of the cathode tube, which is used in television receivers and in radar, for research into the behavior of radio waves. In 1935 he collected a series of broadcasts into book form under the title of *Through the Weather House*, in which he presented much technical information about weather for popular consumption.

Described as a genial, modest Scot who looks younger than he is, spectacled Sir Robert has a reputation among his associates for his habits of hard work and little relaxation. He has been honored several times by his country for his scientific achievements. In the New Year's Honors of 1941 he was made a Companion of the Bath, and in March of the same year was elected to Fellowship by the Royal Society for his "contribution to radio engineering, particularly in relation to aerial and marine navigation." He was knighted at the King's birthday celebration the next year. As president of the Association of Scientific Workers, he has always advocated the employment of women in science and industry. His wife has assisted him with many of his important experiments, and early in the war he trained three of his WAAF typists as one of the first radiolocation crews.

References

Collier's 111:16 My 22 '43 il
N Y Herald Tribune p1+ Ap 25 '43
  por
Who's Who, 1945

WATT, ROBERT J. July 16, 1894- Labor leader; United States Government official

Address: b. c/o A.F. of L. Bldg., Washington, D.C.; h. 1421 Massachusetts Ave., Washington, D.C.

The workers' delegate from the American Federation of Labor to meetings of the International Labor Organization, Robert J. Watt has for many years been an outstanding labor union man in the United States. President Roosevelt '42 appointed him the sole workers' delegate to the I.L.O. meeting in Philadelphia in 1944, and in February 1945 he attended the meeting of the International

ROBERT J. WATT

Federation of Trade Unions in London. In 1942 he was made an alternate on the National War Labor Board.

An immigrant who came to the United States at the age of eighteen, Robert J. Watt was born in Scotland, July 16, 1894. "I was one of twelve children [of Alexander and Helen (Robertson) Watt]," he says, "and the passing of my father when I was a boy left my mother with seven children under her wing." Since the boy was compelled to go to work when his father died, his schooling did not go beyond the sixth grade. For four years young Watt served as an indentured apprentice, learning the trade of painting, paper hanging, and house decorating. At sixteen his apprenticeship was over, and, in his words, he was "all through."

"Landing in the United States on January 1, 1912," he says, "I went to work in a paper mill in Lawrence, Massachusetts, at fifteen cents an hour. For sixty-five hours a week—thirteen hours a night and five nights a week—I drew nine dollars and seventy-five cents." His activities as a labor union member in the United States began in 1915. (He had been an apprentice union member in Scotland.) And two years later he was married to Janet Learmonth; the Watts have two children, Janet and Robert.

When the First World War broke out Watt immediately enlisted as a private in the infantry of the Canadian Army and served for two years. On his return to the United States in 1919, the year he took out his citizenship papers, he became active in the Lawrence Central Labor Union, of which he was president from 1925 to 1930. In 1932 he was elected vice-president of the Massachusetts State Federation of Labor (he remained in office five years); later he became secretary-treasurer of the organization, a post which he held in Boston for nine years. He was also labor member (1936-38) of the Massachusetts Unemployment Commission. During these years he was called "the most influential labor leader in Massachusetts."

Meanwhile, in 1934 America had joined the International Labor Organization. This body, the largest international organization in existence, was established at Geneva in 1919 to investigate labor problems everywhere and to draft model laws for acceptance by member states. Its main objective is to see that reasonable, comparable standards for labor are made the basis for international trade. Every country which is a member of the League of Nations must be a member of it—there are fifty-three members—but the United States, Brazil, and other non-League members also belong to it. Its delegates are representatives of government (two), labor (one), and capital (one).

In the United States the A. F. of L. was to send the worker delegate, a different one each year. (The CIO was not formed until the year after the United States joined the I.L.O.) Since the first two worker representatives knew very little about international labor conditions, the American representation was not very effective. But in 1936 Robert Watt was chosen as the A. F. of L. delegate. He showed immediately such a grasp of international labor affairs at the Geneva meetings that the A. F. of L. made him its permanent delegate to the I.L.O., with headquarters in Washington. His duties took him to Europe for the quarterly I.L.O. meetings from 1936 to 1940. In addition, he was in 1938 the only labor member of a commission appointed by the President to study labor legislation in Britain and Sweden. In 1939 he represented American workers at I.L.O. meetings in Chile and Cuba.

Over the years, in articles and speeches, Robert Watt has stated the position and convictions of organized labor in the United States. "American labor today," he said in 1938, "wants to be recognized as the partner of capital in production, as the customer of capital in distribution, as the majority voice in a political democracy, and as the substantial center of our community life." He said that it should be a responsibility of business to refuse to use sweatshop materials; that unemployment compensation and old-age insurance are legitimate expenses of business, to be regarded, not as a tax, but as a labor cost.

In January 1942 Watt was appointed by President Roosevelt as an alternate on the National War Labor Board. Speaking on the issue of union labor and the war, he said that "the records of the Bureau of Labor Statistics show that during the first three months of 1941, 53 per cent of all strikes were for the purpose of securing union recognition." He criticized the emphasis placed on loss of man-hours resulting from strikes, since losses following injuries in accidents were six times as large. In another speech he called for the establishment of machinery of representation for organized labor, industry, and agriculture that would be invested with responsibility and authority essential for "real defense and security now and after the war. . . .Failure to establish the machinery of economic self-government for labor and industry has been the greatest failure of our Nation." The next year Watt led the A. F. of L. bloc on the Board in denouncing the new wage ceiling program issued under order of President Roosevelt. The order, they declared, was "detrimental to the war effort" and a violation of the "no-strike, no-lockout" agreement. The order would wreck the wage stabilization program, they also charged, and seriously imperil the Board.

In the spring of 1943 Bob Watt expressed himself as pleased with the establishment of friendly relations between labor and the United States Chamber of Commerce. Invited to address it at its annual convention, he said: "Coming to a Chamber of Commerce meeting is an adventure for a labor representative. He is bound to feel a bit like Daniel in the lion's den." The changed attitude of business, he felt, was due "to the spirit of the national chamber as led by its president, Eric A. Johnston"[43], who has done more to remove the barriers of suspicion and hostility which used to exist between labor and industry than anyone would have believed possible a few years ago." He saw further evidence of collaboration between labor, business, and other organizations when, at a national conference on postwar problems held early in 1944, such groups as the NAM, the A. F. of L., and the CIO were equally represented. In analyzing the importance of the charter drawn up by this conference Watt said, "The war has developed a progressive wing of American industry which is ready and willing to cooperate with labor in doing a good job for the benefit of the country as a whole." "We stand with management," he continued, "in opposition to Government interference and labor interference in the performance of the task of management."

On the international labor front certain bitter conflicts of opinion developed when the I.L.O. held its 1944 meeting at Philadelphia. The trouble began with conflicting claims of the CIO and the A. F. of L. for representation in the United States delegation. Under the I.L.O. agreement each nation was entitled to only one delegate representing labor; heretofore the United States delegate had always been Robert J. Watt of the A. F. of L. When the A. F. of L. refused the President's pre-convention request that the two American labor groups share the vote, the CIO withdrew its claim for equal representation, and Roosevelt named Watt as the sole representative of the workers. Watt was elected a member of the governing board.

But the Scottish-born labor leader immediately ran into difficulties over the question of labor representation from the Soviet Union. Since 1939 his opinions on the subject of Communism were pretty well known. "I believe Communism can inspire hope only in the most exploited and downtrodden people," he has said. The Russian leaders, according to Watt, "ignored the spiritual needs and human appetites of the individual. They did not realize that man can be happy only as a man, not as a mechanical unit." Although Russia had not been represented at an I.L.O. meeting since her withdrawal from the League of Nations in 1939, she was asked—following Germany's attack upon her in 1941—to return to the I.L.O. But Watt's proposal that "delegates from any nation that did not have a free democratic government and a free responsible trade-union movement be barred" would have automatically prohibited the return of Russia. Later, on a renewed invitation, Russia replied she would join only if the organization were made an agency of the United Nations, indicating through *Izvestia* her disapproval of the invitations extended by the I.L.O. to one or more Fascist nations.

The right of one of these Fascist nations to a seat at the Philadelphia conference was challenged by Vicente Lombardo Toledano, workers' delegate from Mexico, acting as spokesman for the Latin American group. In a debate with him, Watt, as reported by the New York *Post*, implied that the Mexican's anti-Fascist sympathies dated from Hitler's attack on Russia. (According to a New York *Herald Tribune* writer, Paul Tobenkin, Watt considers Toledano a Communist.) Watt said further that if Argentina were ousted because its labor was subject to Government interference, and therefore was not free, there were "certain other countries" to which the same principle might be applied. With a vote of 14 to 3 the I.L.O. labor delegates barred Argentina (American, British, and Australian representatives cast the negative votes). Later the Argentines were seated by vote of the full conference.

The American workers' delegate encountered more opposition and considerable verbal attack when the question arose concerning the kind of administration to be set up by the United Nations for Germany. Watt demanded that freedom of association be restored in Germany as quickly as possible. He said: "As regards the responsibility of the whole German people, I am in something of a quandary. In all humility, I confess that I should find it difficult to hold peoples always responsible for all the crimes committed by their governments. I doubt if peoples differ as greatly from one another as some . . . seem to believe. I do not believe that any people is naturally and inherently cruel." At this Sir Walter Citrine[41], British worker delegate, was aroused: "Would you say that of the Japanese?" After an exchange of words, Watt replied: "I agree that the Japanese are cruel. So are the Germans. But does that mean that peoples are always, under all circumstances, responsible for their governments? . . .If the whole people is responsible, each individual should be punished for the cruelties and the acts of barbarism that have been committted. Speaking for myself, I cannot lightly accept that conclusion."

(Continued next page)

WATT, ROBERT J.—*Continued*

However, all representatives of the British Government and labor at the conference, and the members of the Czech, French, and Norwegian delegations, refused to consider any resolution on the treatment of Germany and other Axis nations with Soviet Russia absent from the conference. By a vote of 9 to 2 a hands-off attitude was adopted, Watt and the Australian worker representative dissenting. Watt, though defeated, made every effort to reopen the issue to reverse the decision.

Later in 1944 the delegate appeared to have won some concession from the International Federation of Trade Unions, which resolved that "the reconstruction of trade-union organizations and restoration of trade-union rights in all countries is one of the first steps toward human liberties and democratic institutions." The conference accepted a plan drafted by American industry for postwar world-wide economic reconversion, reconstruction, and expansion. A committee was appointed to recommend the plan, which had been given Watt's approval, to the United Nations. Recommendations were also made by the conference for an international economic policy designed to promote full employment and better living standards for the workers of all nations; and a resolution was signed by the worker delegates calling for the immediate rescue of victims of the Nazi terror.

Robert Watt was given a place on a committee of nine appointed at the final session of the I.L.O. conference by the governing body to stand ready at all times to present the social viewpoint of the I.L.O. at any international meetings prior to the next international labor conference. The governing body also created a tripartite committee of eighteen to wage a world-wide fight against unemployment in concert with other agencies that have been or are to be set up by the United Nations.

The veteran A. F. of L leader was heard often in connection with various labor issues during 1944-45. At a conference on Inter-American Development, called by representatives of Government and business, Watt and James B. Carey [41] of the CIO were the only two speakers representing labor. In his speech Watt said that the success of international cooperation and collective security would depend upon the ability of labor to participate with management in evolving economic democracy and keeping it free from political control. He was named chairman of the press committee at the May meeting of the National Post-War Conference. He said that the first meeting, held in February, had shown that diverse interests could get together in "recognition of their joint responsibility to establish a postwar economy of plenty and prevent mass unemployment." Referring to the Montgomery Ward case, he said that "it is utterly wrong to have to go to the President with a labor controversy"— the first union leader to state this opinion publicly. During the 1944 Presidential campaign Watt, viewing the activities of the PAC of the CIO, said that "in every instance where the labor movement has become a front for

a political party, it has eventually died." He said it was difficult to keep the wage question out of politics; but noted that in the drive to smash the "Little Steel" formula, labor organizations friendly to Roosevelt's re-election were "unanimously opposed to this Administration policy, while it was being defended by industrialists presumably opposed to a fourth term."

A leader in labor's dissatisfaction with existing legislation for returning war veterans, Watt said that the re-employment provisions of the Selective Service Act were glaringly deficient. He stated that the problem of providing steady jobs at decent wages and good conditions for returning servicemen could be solved only if industrial and commercial activity could be maintained at a rate that would provide such jobs for all who wanted to work. "It will take more than a GI Bill of Rights to do the job." He decried a program set up to discharge a debt owed to servicemen, while "at the same time legislation to meet readjustment needs of industrial workers has been just as promptly defeated. We hope the program will not divide the Nation into mutually antagonistic classes each seeking privileges at the expense of others."

As a member of the Federal Advisory Board for Vocational Education, Watt has suggested utilizing the specialized program of the armed services in developing a broader project relative to the requirements of trade and industry. The vocational schools, he said, should have the active aid and advice of representatives of labor, industry, agriculture, and other organizations in "training the citizens of tomorrow." In an article, "Responsibilities of Vocational Education" (*Education for Victory*, February 3, 1944), he also wrote that "public vocational schools under the framework of Federal cooperation should be at the foundation of the proposed program of vocational training for servicemen."

In January 1945 Watt went to London to attend the meeting of the governing board of the I.L.O. Its object was to discuss the future relationship of the organization with the projected world peace organization. The next month he attended the meeting of the International Federation of Trade Unions. Led by the A. F. of L. representative, the general council of the Federation refused to go on record as favoring a change in the constitution to permit the entrance of the CIO and the Soviet trade unions.

Close on the heels of the I.F.T.U. meeting came a conference called by Sir Walter Citrine, president of I.F.T.U., for the formation of a new World Labor Congress to meet in San Francisco simultaneously with the United Nations conference in April 1945. To it came two hundred and forty delegates from thirty-eight Allied nations and several neutral countries. Russia was among those represented—by a group of thirty-five delegates. The CIO, headed by Sidney Hillman [40], was represented by more than a dozen delegates; but Watt, the sole A. F. of L. representative, refused to attend with Russia present, saying that, as the A. F. of L. has consistently maintained, "the labor unions in Soviet Russia are not free trade unions, but are dominated by the Kremlin." The new World Labor Congress asked for direct representation on the economic and social council of the San Francisco conference; but here again Watt disagreed, saying: "I believe the major social and economic agency . . . should be the I.L.O., through which for twenty-five years governments, employers, and workers have successfully endeavored to define standards and improve conditions of labor." President Truman ['45] reappointed Watt as labor's delegate to the I.L.O. conference held in Paris in October 1945. The attempt of four Argentine delegates to take their seats in this convention aroused sharp protest from Robert Watt and other delegates.

The Scottish-born labor leader, who for more than thirty years has devoted his life to the cause he believes in, is short in stature, has heavy shoulders and an aggressive chin. During the First World War he weighed only one hundred and seventeen, he says, but a good deal of desk work has added more flesh to his frame, and the pressure of labor problems has put quite a bit of gray in his blond hair. As a writer and speaker, he is considered straightforward, prosaic. Occasionally, however, Watt's language is vivid, as in his comment: "I think we would rather spend large sums of money each year to deliver milk to the Hottentots . . . than to expend tens of thousands of lives periodically delivering explosive eggs to free the Hottentots from aggressor nations."

References

C S Mon p6 My 9 '44 por
N Y Herald Tribune X p18 N 22 '42
Who's Who in America, 1944-45

WEAVER, ARTHUR J. Nov. 18, 1873—Oct. 18, 1945 Republican Governor of Nebraska (1929-30); served in several local elective posts, including that of Mayor of Falls City (1915), and in party offices; an orchardist, he helped to established southeast Nebraska's fruit industry.

Obituary

N Y Times p23 O 19 '45 por

WEBSTER, H(AROLD) T(UCKER)
Sept. 21, 1885- Cartoonist
Address: h. Shippan Point, Stamford, Conn.

The "Mark Twain of cartoonists," H. T. Webster, has been amusing American newspaper readers for over forty years. Creator of comic characters with a broad appeal, his syndicated cartoons enjoy a vast national audience, appearing in the New York *Herald Tribune* and eighty other daily papers. During his long and prolific career his drawings have ranged from militant political cartoons to homely human-interest sketches. His famous creation Caspar Milquetoast, hero of the *Timid Soul* series, has become a nationally known character whose name is a popular term of mild reproach. A Webster cartoon that caused especially favorable comment was titled "Collaborationist." This humorously stabbed at the French method of treating women transgressors during the war. *Newsweek* in December 1944 applauded the car-

H. T. WEBSTER

toon and its creator, stating that fans rate Webster "perhaps the Nation's sharpest and most sophisticated cartoonist."

Harold Tucker Webster, son of James Clarence and Fannie Marsh (Tucker) Webster, was born September 21, 1885, in Parkersburg, West Virginia. His boyhood was spent in Tomahawk, Wisconsin, where he grew up happily, fishing and hunting and listening to the discussions of the men who gathered in his father's drugstore. He was "an average student," Webster confesses, "talented at playing hooky."

Throughout his school years from the age of seven, when he first started to draw, the boy made sketches of "everything and everybody." When Frank Holmes started a correspondence school of illustration, young Webster took the course. He studied elementary drawing, perspective, composition, lettering, portraiture, and cartooning. His aim at this time was to be an assignment artist, and he wanted to go to Chicago to study art. During the summers the youth took odd jobs to earn enough money for his art education. He worked in a brickyard, a railroad station, and later drove a delivery wagon for a year, studying and drawing cartoons for the village weekly at night. His first published cartoon, for which he was paid five dollars, appeared in a magazine called *Recreation.* At seventeen Webster had completed his third year of high school and saved one hundred and fifty dollars. With this money he set out for Chicago to attend Frank Holmes's School of Illustration. But twenty days later the school closed.

Webster's next step was to make the rounds of the newspaper offices with his sketches. This search for a job was unsuccessful, but quite unexpectedly he was offered the chance to submit drawings to the Denver *Republican,* although he was to receive no payment for those accepted. The young man, it seems, had sent some of his drawings to an aunt in Denver who, in turn, had showed them to the editor of the paper. Webster saw the offer

WEBSTER, H. T.—*Continued*

as an opportunity to get something in print and in 1902 went to Denver. It was an unproductive move, however, for few of his things were actually printed. When a vacancy occurred on the Denver *Post*, he therefore applied and was hired at fifteen dollars a week. Very soon afterward the teen-age Webster resigned: learning that an artist of some reputation was joining the staff, he had felt sensitive about his own inexperience.

He returned to Chicago and again applied at the editorial offices of the newspapers without success. When his funds ran low he decided to go to Milwaukee to find a job. But again his efforts were futile, and before long he was back in Chicago. After his return he wrote and illustrated some jokes which were accepted by the Chicago *Daily News* and the Chicago *American*; and he sold cartoons to both papers regularly for several months. Then he went home for a rest. While there he accepted an offer from the Chicago *Daily News* and was soon working for that paper at seven dollars a week. He held a job there as comic artist for two years (1903-05), until he was earning twenty dollars a week. In those days his heroes were John T. McCutcheon, George Ade, and Charles Dana Gibson— Webster confesses that he once aspired to be Gibson's office boy.

In 1905 Webster joined the staff of the Chicago *Inter-Ocean* at the "phenomenal" salary of thirty dollars a week to draw front-page political cartoons. Of the subsequent three-year period with the paper Webster remarks: "Two noteworthy events occurred while I was drawing political cartoons for the *Inter-Ocean*. One of them was when a reporter came in and told the editor that a man had laughed so hard at one of my cartoons while riding on the Elgin Electric that he had suffered a stroke and had to be carried off the train in a dangerous condition. The second was when a member of the State legislature waved one of my cartoons before the House and introduced a bill making it a crime for cartoonists to ridicule that solemn and august body."

When a friend urged Webster to take a job with the Cincinnati *Post* the cartoonist could not resist the salary—seventy dollars a week. Although on this job Webster was kept busy drawing political cartoons, it was here that he first began to draw his human-interest sketches. From this period dates the series *Little Tragedies of Childhood*, which was the forerunner of another of his famous series, *Life's Darkest Moment*. It was also during his days at the *Post* that the "infamous M. Huc du Boisdieu hoax" was perpetrated. This incident involved an imaginary French cartoonist whom Webster and his editor invented to supply cartoons during Webster's vacation. The *Post* published accounts of the Frenchman's arrival in the States; Webster's face, disguised with whiskers, appeared in news photos; and the nonexistent M. du Boisdieu, registered at a local hotel, mystified everyone by always being out when callers came. The hoax was later exposed, Webster reports, to the embarrassment of those who had declared they had really met the foreign visitor.

In 1911 Webster fulfilled an old desire by taking a trip around the world. The artist visited Italy, the Near East, China, and Japan. Back in the United States, he was determined to try his luck in New York. On his first night in that city he took a political cartoon to the New York *World*, which was used the following day. The Associated Newspapers signed Webster on a year's contract, with the result that once again he was drawing political "editorials." But now he was more interested in drawing sketches of everyday life; he began to believe that he could accomplish more by depicting the minor events and details that fill people's lives. Gradually then, more and more of his human-interest sketches were used; newspaper readers began to demand "more boys and dogs and funny husbands."

Finally, in 1915, Webster's first book of collected cartoons, *Our Boyhood Thrills and Other Cartoons*, was published, and two years later came *Boys and Folks*. Four years later Webster joined the staff of the New York *Tribune*, where he remained until he changed to the New York *World* in 1923. When Webster and his wife (who was Ethel Worts when they were married in 1916) wanted to spend some time in Europe in 1927, the artist undertook to draw enough cartoons in one month for his paper to use for three and a half months. While working at this task his right hand, his drawing hand, began to hurt, but he continued to draw. On his return from Europe the hand still pained him, and the doctors pronounced the affliction writer's cramp. Webster tried every known remedy, but the paralysis continued. In spite of the pain, the cartoonist delivered his drawings regularly. Undiscouraged, every day he would practice drawing with his left hand. Finally, after four months he triumphed—he was able to do his cartoons as well with his left hand as he had with his right, although he could not and still cannot write with that hand. A few years after this experience, in 1931, Webster began his present association with the New York *Herald Tribune*.

As "America's most talented producer of newspaper comics for adults," Webster has created several series, including *The Thrill That Comes Once in a Lifetime, The Boy Who Made Good, They Don't Speak Our Language, How To Torture Your Wife*, and *Poker Portraits*. The inspiration for his work has been the small dramas of daily life and he has very often drawn from his own childhood memories. His humorous contemplation of life and human nature has earned him a leading place among nationally recognized cartoonists. Bridge and poker players are delighted by Webster's cartoons on their games: he has published several collections—*Webster's Bridge* (1924), *Webster's Poker Book* (1925), and the *Culbertson Webster Contract System* (1932). His book *The Timid Soul* was published in 1931, and met warm critical approval. (Its introduction is by Ring Lardner.) The New York *Times* commended the book for its delineation of human nature and remarked that Webster "catches virtually all of humanity at one time or another in its most spineless moments." Discussing the origin of the hero Caspar Milquetoast, Webster remarked that the well known character "slipped into the world almost unnoticed, apologetically, you might say." The cartoonist created Caspar to fill space in the New York *World,* and it was several days after his initial appearance that Webster decided to keep him. In his latest series, *The Unseen Audience,* Webster has sharpened his pencil in behalf of long-suffering radio listeners afflicted with inescapable, too-oft-repeated commercials.

Webster wrote a diverting article which appeared in *Forum* (December 1933) on his series *They Don't Speak Our Language.* In his discussion of this series Webster revealed that it was directly inspired by a conversation he overheard in which two young girls talked in a language beyond his comprehension. The article proceeds to illustrate the caste marks of speech, offering amusing examples of the jargon of the underworld, the stage, and of Webster's favorite argot, circus talk. The humorous vein of the discussion reinforces the cartoonist's claim that language is kept vital by corruptions, vulgarisms, and slang, that new situations and objects constantly require new words and phrases.

Webster's most famous cartoon was first published in 1918, on Lincoln's Birthday, and it is still reprinted by newspapers on the anniversary. Entitled "Hardin County—1809," it shows two old farmers who have met on the road exchanging the following remarks:

"Any news down t' th' village, Ezry?"

"Well, Squire McLean's gone t' Washington t' see Madison swore in, an' ol' Spellman tells me this Bonaparte fella has captured most o' Spain. What's new out here, neighbor?"

"Nuthin' a tall, nuthin' a tall, 'cept fer a new baby down't Tom Lincoln's. Nuthin' ever happens out here."

Jerome Beatty reports that Webster's own favorite cartoon is one of Caspar Milquetoast, The Timid Soul. It shows Caspar "standing on a street corner in a drenching rain without an umbrella, his collar turned up, hands in his pockets, clothes soaked, and water trickling down his neck. Pedestrians in raincoats and rubbers, carrying umbrellas, splash briskly past, but Caspar stands there shivering. Finally, however, he declares, 'Well, I'll wait one more hour for him and if he doesn't come then he can go and borrow that one hundred dollars from somebody else.'"

In 1945 two series of cartoons by Webster were published in book form, *Webster Unabridged* and *To Hell With Fishing.* C. V. Terry wrote in the New York *Times Book Review* that "he who has yet to make the acquaintance of H. T. Webster has only himself to blame: faced with two new cartoon anthologies by that acerb (but always kindly) commentator on human foibles, the critic can only pass the word along." "To add anything to the tributes which the cartoons of H. T. Webster have garnered through the years would be carrying Newcastle to coal," was the comment of Lisle Bell in the New York *Herald Tribune Weekly Book Review.* "Mr. Webster is a beloved fixture of the American scene which he so joyously records."

Webster works about four hours every afternoon and, needless to say, enjoys his work. The cartoonist is six feet three inches tall, has blue eyes, clearly defined features, and a gracious manner. He has described the circumstances of his marriage: "On one important evening in 1916 R. M. Brinkerhoff introduced me to a young lady who was then studying at Columbia University. We went to dinner, and from there, by easy stages, up to the altar. I was very deliberate and cautious about it. It was all of two weeks before I married her." (They were married August 2, 1916.) Webster calls his wife his "severest critic." The Webster home in Connecticut is a replica of a New England farmhouse, and the artist has his own workshop. He is a member of the Society of Illustrators and his clubs are Dutch Treat, Players, and Coffee House. The artist likes the games he depicts so humorously —they are bridge and poker. Nowadays he restricts himself to bridge, however, having given up poker after his marriage. An expert fisherman, he frequently goes fly-fishing in one of the Maine lakes, where he owns an island. He has many fond recollections of his early boyhood, and when he receives letters from children he always answers them. Webster's sympathies are also with the timid soul, the Caspar Milquetoast, who, he insists, is a self-portrait.

References

Am Mag 98:50-1+ S '24 il por
Lit Digest 116:9 N 25 '33 por
Read Digest 32:100-3 Ap '38
Who's Who in America, 1944-45

WEDEMEYER, ALBERT C(OADY) (wĕd'ē-mī-ēr) July 9, 1897- United States Army officer

Address: b. c/o War Department, Washington, D. C.; h. 2118 Wyoming Ave., N.W., Washington, D. C.

Lieutenant General Albert C. Wedemeyer came to the fore in October 1944 as the commanding general of the United States Army Forces in the China theater of war, and Chief of Staff to Generalissimo Chiang Kai-shek [40], serving in one of the most bitterly divided countries in the world.

Albert Coady Wedemeyer was born in Omaha, Nebraska, on July 9, 1897, the son of Albert Anthony and Margaret Elizabeth (Coady) Wedemeyer. His grandfather had emigrated from Germany, organized a band for the Union Army, and marched it through Georgia; his father was a bandmaster in the Spanish-American War. Albert was appointed to the Military Academy at West Point and was graduated in the class of 1918, which finished in a year and a half and was then brought back for six months' "polishing." He was commissioned a second lieutenant of Infantry on November 1, 1918. Until June 1919 he was stationed at the Academy. He then went to Europe for an observation tour of battlefields in Belgium and France, returning to the United States in September, when he entered the Infantry School at Fort Benning, Georgia. On February 27, 1920, he was promoted to first lieutenant. Upon graduation that June he was assigned to the Twenty-ninth Infantry at Fort Benning, where he remained for two years. At the end of that time Lieutenant Wedemeyer became aide to Brigadier General Paul B. Malone, commandant of the Infantry School. He

U. S. Army Signal Corps

LT. GEN. ALBERT C. WEDEMEYER

accompanied the General to Fort Sill, Oklahoma, in December 1922, and later that month to Fort Sam Houston, Texas, where he remained until September 1923. The Lieutenant then was sent to the Philippines for duty with the Thirty-first Infantry at Manila. In December he was transferred to the Fifty-seventh at Fort McKinley, also in the Islands.

In October 1925 he returned to the United States and was assigned to the Twelfth Infantry at Fort Washington, Maryland. In December 1927 he was assigned as aide to the commanding general of the District of Washington, in which post he remained until 1930. In January of that year he went to Tientsin, China, for duty with the Fifteenth Infantry. While there he studied Mandarin. In March 1932, Wedemeyer was reassigned to the Philippines, as aide to Major General C. E. Kilbourne on Corregidor. In June of the following year, still on that island, he was assigned as aide to Major General Stanley D. Embick, his father-in-law, Wedemeyer having been married to Elizabeth Dade Embick in February 1920 while at Fort Benning. At about this time he became interested in the study of economics, history, foreign affairs, and air power.

Wedemeyer returned to the United States in June 1934 and entered the Command and General Staff School at Fort Leavenworth, Kansas. On August 1, 1935, he was advanced to the rank of captain. Upon graduation from the difficult two-year course in June 1936, he went to Washington, D. C., for a brief tour of duty with the Intelligence Division, G-2, of the War Department General Staff. Because he had graduated with such high honors from the Command and General Staff School, he was chosen to go abroad in July 1936 to continue his studies, becoming the first American officer after the First World War to attend the German General Staff School, the Kriegsakademie. He remained at the German war college until August 1938, and during the two years he had an opportunity to witness the growth of the Nazi war machine. The New

York *Sun* says Captain Wedemeyer returned "with a suggestion of the monocled aplomb which distinguishes the best of the German General Staff." Upon his arrival in the States he was assigned once more to the Twentyninth Infantry at Fort Benning, Georgia. In January 1940 he was transferred to the Ninetyfourth Antitank Battalion there, serving as executive officer. On July 1 of that year he was promoted to the permanent rank of major, and in September he went to Washington, D. C., to serve in the Training Section of the Office of the Chief of Infantry.

Eight months later Major Wedemeyer became a member of the Plans Group of the War Department General Staff, serving under General Dwight D. Eisenhower [42]. On September 15, 1941, he was promoted to the temporary rank of lieutenant colonel, and on February 1, 1942, to colonel (temporary). While with the Plans Division he served as a member of the Joint Strategic Committee and the Combined Subjects Committee, continuing in that assignment when the War Plans Division became the Operations Division in March 1942. In June he became assistant to Major General Thomas Handy, the assistant chief of staff of the Operations Division. On July 7 of that year the Colonel was raised to the temporary rank of brigadier general, and on December 11 his permanent rank was raised to lieutenant colonel. He is regarded as an expert in war plans and during the war went with General Marshall [40] on most of his trips abroad. In February 1943 Wedemeyer represented the United States Chief of Staff at a conference with Chinese and British leaders in the war against Japan.

In 1943 Wedemeyer was awarded the Distinguished Service Medal. The citation for the award reads: "For exceptionally meritorious and distinguished service in a position of great responsibility as chief of the Strategy Section and subsequently as chief of the Strategy and Policy Group, Operations Division, War Department General Staff, and as the War Department representative with the Joint and Combined Staff Planners. By his outstanding ability, resourcefulness, tact, initiative, and profound strategical judgment, he contributed in large measure to the adoption by the United States and by the United Nations of sound strategical plans which have formed the basis for the successful prosecution of the war on all fronts."

In September 1943 Wedemeyer was advanced to the temporary rank of major general, and in October the War Department announced his appointment as American deputy chief of staff of the Southeast Asia Command under Admiral Lord Louis Mountbatten [42], who was said to have been extremely pleased with the selection. In the differences which developed during the following spring between Mountbatten and Stilwell, with regard to the proposed Burma campaign, Wedemeyer was reported to have been a little inclined to agree with the British admiral in his wish to postpone until after the monsoon season the launching of a large-scale campaign to retake Burma. The difficulty of mounting such a campaign, with the prior claims of the European theater on Allied shipping and supplies, was an additional reason in favor of postponement.

At the end of October 1944 it was unexpectedly announced that General Stilwell had been relieved of his command in the China-Burma-India theater in response to a demand from Generalissimo Chiang Kai-shek. The theater was to be divided into two areas, with the forty-seven-year-old Major General Wedemeyer in command of United States Army Forces in the China area (including French Indo-China), and Lieutenant General Daniel I. Sultan '45 in command of the India-Burma theater. Concurrently, Wedemeyer was named chief of staff to Chiang. (In January 1945 Wedemeyer received his promotion to lieutenant general [temporary].) At the same time announcement was made of the resignation of Ambassador Clarence Gauss '41, who, it was believed, had supported Stilwell. According to reports, Chiang and his chief of staff had disagreed on practically every vital issue, including the relative merits of air power versus the combined use of ground and air forces, which Stilwell recommended; the American's attempts to get Chiang to cooperate with the Chinese Communists in the war against Japan; and his desire to modernize the Chinese Army. According to a summary in a New York *Herald Tribune* editorial, indications were that the Chiang dictatorship had been getting increasingly reactionary, autocratic, and inefficient in war—having diverted thousands of its best troops to blockade the Chinese Communist forces in the north, who were putting up the more aggressive battle against the common enemy.

In his first interview with the press, the new American commander in China, faced with these difficult problems, described the military situation as "unfavorable, but not irretrievable," and he made it clear that his job was to serve the Chinese in the war against Japan, that he would not interfere in Chinese politics. By November Wedemeyer was able to report some progress. The plans he had offered to Chiang for disposing of Chinese forces to meet possible Japanese moves in the near future had been accepted. Toward the end of the month long-demanded extensive changes in the Chinese Cabinet were announced. According to a New York *Times* analyst, "taken together, they seemed to point to a more effective conduct of military and political affairs."

Wedemeyer was in an equivocal and difficult position as administrator of an American foreign policy which seemed to many ill-defined and to some, ill-advised. From the military viewpoint, however, his work drew favorable press comment. "General Wedemeyer has improved American aid by installing an improved supervisory system over American equipment and supplies delivered to the Chinese," wrote Henry J. Taylor in June. By insisting on American supervision over the local food purchases with Lend-Lease funds, he is said to have improved the Chinese soldiers' typical diet greatly. He obtained planes from the Joint Chiefs of Staff. "He has increased the quick and effective use of American materials against Japan. . . .He has improved the understanding of China's problems within the Joint Chiefs of Staff and has stayed clear of Chinese politics. He has stuck to Washington's order to support militarily only Chiang Kai-shek," Taylor wrote further. The American troops under Wedemeyer's command were not primarily combat forces, the General said, but were there to train the Chinese ground forces and keep the all-important supply lines open. They did, however, go into action with their pupils "in an advisory capacity"; and in November 1945 he announced that the advisers were withdrawn from all troops engaged in "fratricidal strife."

Left-of-center commentators, notably the newspaper *PM,* charged that instead of Wedemeyer carrying out the orders of the Joint Chiefs of Staff, in many cases they were simply backing up the policies he made on the spot—policies which interfered in the undeclared civil war by giving aid and comfort to one side. The General also found it necessary to explain that the use of American Lend-Lease weapons in factional battles was due to their being stolen or otherwise diverted from their assigned use against the common enemy; but he remained the target of daily attacks in the Communist Chinese press. The relations of his troops with the Chinese population also deteriorated to a low level, Dixie Tighe reported. He finally issued orders forbidding military personnel to engage in outside business activities, because of black market sales by American soldiers. He admitted that some of his men had been drawn into "little isolated clashes" with Communist Army troops, and reported that on certain occasions Americans had been fired upon, although denying that they had ever taken the offensive. Altogether, however, it was pointed out that Wedemeyer had come to China at the low ebb of her Government's morale and military power and had built them both up to effectiveness. After consultations in Washington, he returned to his Chinese duties in the fall of 1945, and it was reported that Chiang looked with favor upon having him head the projected military mission which was to replace the wartime troops in that country.

Handsome General Albert C. Wedemeyer has been described as having a profile suggesting George Washington's. "His high, gray pompadour tops a lean body over six feet. He is quiet, yet friendly; frank, yet modest and unselfseeking"; honest, but shrewd; clever, aggressive, and full of typical American energy. He is an infantryman, but air-minded. Thomas M. Johnson, in an article in the New York *World-Telegram,* says that Wedemeyer would probably be happiest commanding one of the air-borne divisions which he considers the units of the future. He strongly favors triphibious training and helped organize the new Joint Army and Navy Staff College. The General has two sons, Albert Dunbar and Robert Dade. In January 1945 he was honored with the British Order of Commander of the Bath, and in November 1945 he was given the Distinguished Flying Cross for "flying over some of the most rugged terrain in the world, often in treacherous weather, to take an active hand as commander of the China theater."

References

N Y Herald Tribune p3 O 16 '43; pl N 24 '44
N Y Sun p22 N 3 '44
N Y World-Telegram p22 N 16 '44
Who's Who in America, 1944-45

WERFEL, FRANZ (vĕr'fĕl fränts) Sept. 10, 1890—Aug. 26, 1945 German-Czech novelist, dramatist, and poet; has been described as the master of the Expressionist school; his novels called "spiritual"; most important works, in English translation, include: *Juarez and Maximilian* (1926); *The Pure in Heart* (1931); *The Forty Days of Musa Dagh* (1934); *Embezzled Heaven* (1940); and *The Song of Bernadette* (1942); was forced to flee from the Nazis, and reached the United States in 1940, where he remained until his death. See *Current Biography* 1940 Yearbook.

Obituary

N Y Times p19 Ag 27 '45 por

WESTMORE, PERC (pĕrs) Oct. 29, 1904- Cosmetician; businessman

Address: b. c/o Warner Brothers Studios, Olive Ave., Burbank, Calif.; House of Westmore, Inc., 6638 Sunset Blvd., Hollywood, Calif.; h. 1416 Bluebird Dr., Los Angeles, Calif.

Perhaps the best-known and best-paid make-up artist in the world is Perc Westmore, the president of the House of Westmore, who was chosen by the editors of the *Encyclopædia Britannica* to write the article on motion picture make-up for the current edition. Westmore and three of his brothers have supervised costume and make-up for several film companies. Perc is head of the make-up and hair styling department of Warner '45 Brothers studios, Wally has the same post at Paramount Pictures, Bud is director of make-up and hairdressing for Producers Releasing Corporation Studios; and the three brothers together constitute "The Royal Family of Make-up," whose influence on American standards of beauty and indirectly on economic life was sharply demonstrated in the late thirties. At that time Perc Westmore became annoyed with a certain permanent-wave company and therefore devised a coiffure for his stars which required no wave, the pageboy bob. "I learned my lesson," he says. "Women stayed away from beauty shops all over the country. They didn't have permanent waves. They didn't have anything. They just rolled up their hair and let it go at that. Shops closed up by the score. . . . Anything we do is reflected in other businesses all over the country, wherever pictures are shown. We've learned to remember that."

The make-up trio and their cosmetician brothers Frank and Ernest are the only ones of George Westmore's nineteen children who are living. Perc, who does not reveal the rest of his prenames, was born to Ada Florence (Savage) Westmore on October 29, 1904, in the historic town of Canterbury, England, where his father was a wigmaker. When he was four, the family moved to Canada, where they lived in Montreal and in Toronto. After living in Buffalo, St. Louis, Cleveland, New Orleans (where Bud was born in 1916), San Antonio, Washington, and Pittsburgh, they finally settled in Los Angeles. George Westmore believed that children should learn a trade early, and began teaching Perc wigmaking when the boy was nine. Perc had

only four years in two Cleveland schools, and while going to school as well as later he helped his father in the latter's wig shops and salons.

Perc began his career as an apprentice wigmaker in 1916. At fourteen he was employed as a skilled wigmaker. Later, according to the *American Magazine*, the Westmore brothers started out in California as rabbit ranchers, but when the furs failed to bring a fortune, they went back to their father's profession. Perc joined the Maison Cesare in Los Angeles as assistant wigmaker and janitor; while there, he read widely in the fields of skin, hair, and anatomy, and experimented with cosmetology and make-up.

Seventeen-year-old Perc got the chance to make a half-mustache for Adolphe Menjou, who had accidentally shaved his off; and its naturalness so impressed Douglas Fairbanks '40 that he ordered Westmore to remake all the hairpieces for *The Three Musketeers*. Perc and his father worked night and day to fill the order, and the latter was asked to report to the studio each day to put them on the actors, a revolutionary innovation. Inspired, George Westmore began to hold nightly classes for his sons at home in "making ourselves indispensable on sets," and he was the first to put his ideas into practice. However, this work for United Studios in 1921 also led to a job for Perc at the First National Studios. Their close-ups, Westmore recalls, "were always terrible." One day in 1923 or 1925—accounts differ—he suggested that the problem was not one of lighting or of film development, but of make-up. As a result, he was authorized to organize a make-up department, the first of its kind in any studio, and saw to it that the make-up was applied in exactly the same way each day.

After First National was merged into Warner Brothers', "Jack and Harry Warner pioneered the way in supplying the tools and materials for research on a comprehensive scale." In 1929 they consented to Westmore's joining the Max Factor Company as a make-up adviser, while remaining head of their make-up and hair styling department. "Many outstanding and revolutionary improvements in the motion picture industry and the cosmetic and wigmaking fields were the result of his connection with this organization," to quote a House of Westmore release, and he "played an important part in the development of the widespread popularity of the Factor cosmetic line. Probably one of the most impressive contributions of Perc Westmore's to this company was the founding of the Hollywood Art School of Make-up." Among the Westmore innovations is the principle of "corrective make-up," by which "the make-up itself accepts and reflects or rejects [and absorbs] light to retouch the planes of the face, much on the same principle as retouching the proof of a portrait study."

Like any make-up director, Perc Westmore was responsible for various kinds of *maquillage*: to make male players, including such "tough guys" as Humphrey Bogart '42, James Cagney '42, Errol Flynn, George Raft, and Edward G. Robinson, look natural and unmade-up on the screen; to accentuate the best points of actresses like Olivia de Havilland '44, Ann Sheridan, Merle Oberon '41, and Lauren Bacall; to make any player look older or younger; and to transform an actor into some other character, often one of whom the audience already has a clear mental picture—for example, making Bette Davis '41 into Queen Elizabeth for *The Private Lives of Elizabeth and Essex* (1939). Pete Martin, the *Saturday Evening Post* writer, who was made up by Westmore on successive days as Will Rogers, Benjamin Franklin, and Dick Tracy, has given a description of the process involved in the March 11, 1944, issue.

In 1935 Perc, Wally, Bud, and Frank Westmore opened a Hollywood beauty salon which, because of their lack of business sense, threatened to turn out a failure. Realizing this, they hired a businessman, S. Willard Isaacs, owner of a beauty-shop chain, to run it. In 1945 it had a staff of one hundred operators caring for an estimated eight thousand patrons a week. A few years later they put House of Westmore make-up on the market. MGM's Max Factor had long had a line of cosmetics, but whereas Factor's were in the expensive category, Westmore's cosmetics, in a box decorated with a gold coat-of-arms, sold at prices satisfactory to the average buyer. In addition to rouge, lipstick, and face powder, Westmores' original line included a tinted, waterproof foundation cream, which they claim was the first of its kind and is still the largest-selling. Later developments were a liquid cream base, Overglo, and a non-chromatic powder for use with tinted foundation.

Perc Westmore's proudest make-up achievement was transforming Fredric March '43 into Mark Twain; when he walked into the executive lunchroom at his studio with "Twain," everyone present, it is reported, rose in spontaneous applause. This was the expert's last assignment before induction into the Army, which he liked. "Maybe it was because I'd never had time to be a Boy Scout, or to go camping or hunting or anything like that," he has said. "The Army was my Boy Scout camp." After some months, however, Westmore was discharged, because of chronic sinus trouble and an attack of pneumonia. The first picture on which he worked after his return was *Mr. Skeffington* (1944), which he considers his worst job, although he was working on his favorite subject, Bette Davis.

Westmore has given much time to improving the appearance of the disfigured. He and his brother Wally Westmore experimented with artificial jaws, ears, and limbs made of a latex rubber material on which he holds the patent, and which he had been using instead of putty since 1939. By late 1944 they had worked out objects which would last three months under rough handling. Another of Westmore's inventions is the hairlace wig, which is said to be undetectable. Perc Westmore's invention of the hairlace wig and other developments were recognized by the Motion Picture Make-up Artists Association with a scroll of appreciation. (The cosmetician was president of the Association for five years between 1924 and 1931.) In 1936 Westmore wrote a series of syndicated articles on make-up, and he has also lectured and written other articles on the subject. In 1939 he wrote the *Encyclopædia*

PERC WESTMORE

Britannica article, which he revised in 1945; in 1945, too, he wrote a chapter, "The Principles of Stage Make-up," for the textbook *Navy on Stage*. During the war he made technical short features for the Army and appeared in skits presented at Army camps.

The head of the House of Westmore is tall, hazel-eyed, olive-skinned, with curly dark hair and a boyish face. He is said to be "volatile and extroverted . . . the reverse of poker-faced." According to the Warners publicity office, he is "roundly (self-)educated, a competent sketcher, a student of anatomy and prosthesis." Westmore has collected a library of rare books on his subject: he points out that the essentials of make-up are the same as those of the ancient Greek masks—upturned lines for cheerfulness, downward lines for gloom—and says that women's brows and lips should therefore have an upward tendency. Perc Westmore has been married four times; his present wife is the former Margaret Donovan, whom he married in May 1943. By earlier marriages he has a grown daughter, Norma Elizabeth, and a younger child, Virginia Paula. The cosmetician, who lives in Beverly Hills, is an amateur cabinetmaker, pointing with especial pride to one doghouse of his making—a miniature Swiss chalet of two stories, connected by a stairway, and complete with cornices and a shingled roof. Because of the danger from his electrically run lathes and saws, Westmore has had his hands insured. His favorite sport is deep-sea fishing.

References

Am Mag 133:90-1 Mr '42 il por
N Y Sun p27 Ap 20 '45
Sat Eve Post 216:16+ Mr 11 '44 il pors

WEYERHAEUSER, FREDERICK E(D-WARD) (wī'ēr-hou"zēr) Nov. 4, 1872—Oct. 18, 1945 Lumberman; reported to be the largest owner of timber lands in the United States; in 1930 included by James W. Gerard in a list of fifty-nine men who "rule the United States";

WEYERHAEUSER, FREDERICK E.—
Continued

president of the Weyerhaeuser Timber Company, Tacoma, at time of death.

Obituary

N Y Times p23 O 19 '45

WHITE, HELEN C(ONSTANCE) Nov.
26, 1896- Educator; author

Address: b. c/o University of Wisconsin, Madison, Wis.; h. 417 Sterling Pl., Madison, Wis.

Through a nationwide mail ballot of its members, the American Association of University Women, largest women's organization in the United States, in June 1945 re-elected to its presidency Helen C. White. Novelist, scholar, and one of a small number of women in the country who are full professors, Miss White places her main interest, as borne out by both her fiction and nonfiction writings, "in the field of the history of ideas."

Helen Constance White was born on November 26, 1896, in New Haven, Connecticut. Reared in the Catholic faith, she is one of several daughters of John and Mary Josephine (King) White. She attended Girls' High School in Boston and Radcliffe College, the woman's branch of Harvard University, in Cambridge, Massachusetts, where she majored in English. In 1916 she received her Bachelor's degree from Radcliffe and was elected to Phi Beta Kappa. The next year, after receiving her Master's degree from Radcliffe, she joined the faculty of Smith College as assistant in English, a post which she held until 1919. Prior to 1919—the year of the promulgation of the Nineteenth Amendment—she had become interested in the woman's suffrage movement during her sophomore year in high school. In 1919 she accepted a position as instructor of English at the University of Wisconsin, where she has taught since, when not spending a leave of absence on research abroad or at home. Always interested as much in research as in teaching, she found time during those first years in the West to study for her Ph.D. degree, and in 1924 the University of Wisconsin conferred that degree upon her. The following year the university promoted her to the position of assistant professor of English. And in 1927 her Ph.D. thesis was published in book form under the title of *The Mysticism of William Blake.*

Miss White's life has been an exceptionally crowded one. She once commented that her teaching schedule included "everything from freshman English to a graduate seminar in the seventeenth century," forgetting at the moment to specify that it also included classes in creative writing. Her general schedule includes, besides her teaching and critical research, novel writing, committee membership, and travel. The year 1928-29 she spent abroad as a Guggenheim Fellow, studying English religious literature of the early seventeenth century at the British Museum and at Oxford's Bodleian Library in England. In the summer of 1930, an additional grant from the Guggenheim Foundation made it possible for her to return to England to check her manuscript which was published in 1931 under the title *English Devotional Literature: Prose 1600-1640.* In 1930 she also served as coeditor with Finley M. K. Foster of a volume of selections of Victorian prose.

The professor-author's first work of fiction, *A Watch in the Night,* appeared in 1933 and was chosen as a book-of-the-month by the Catholic Book Club. It was also the first choice of the Pulitzer Novel Committee, but the General Committee chose *Lamb in His Bosom!* by Caroline Miller because it was laid in an American scene. The novel's conception (it is the story of a thirteenth century Franciscan) dates back to Miss White's vacation in the Umbrian hill country of Italy during her year of study abroad (1928-29), the vacation during which in all probability, says one reviewer, she absorbed much of its background. Critical opinion of the book varied. Though all critics agreed on the novel's amazing richness of detail and luxuriance of language, some approved and some condemned these traits. One reviewer considered *A Watch in the Night* "an entrancingly beautiful narrative, one that has a majestic sweep like a mighty river . . . a story that lives and is vital." Another found the book's greatest asset in that it is "first and last and all the time . . . a story." A third wrote, however: "Miss White's Jacopone is a conventional figure; and the events that convert him from a worldly young lawyer of the Renaissance into a very holy man are also conventional. The appeal in this story is of a nature that would tend to please a simple audience with a taste for melodrama." And the reviewer of *Catholic World,* attempting to evaluate the novel's position in American literature, concluded: "*A Watch in the Night* is an important historical novel, a distinguished piece of literary prose, and, besides, an interesting and vivid story. Were the author successful in her attempt as scholar, artist, and novelist, the volume would have to be classed as indeed a great book. But, in trying to accomplish a feat which means achieving greatness on three levels all at once, Miss White has not reached full measure on any."

In 1935 Miss White—who had now been associate professor of English at the University of Wisconsin for almost two years—published her second novel, *Not Built With Hands,* the story of Pope Gregory VII and Matilda, Countess of Tuscany, during one of the crucial periods in the history of the Roman Catholic Church. It was the philosophical conclusion of this book, says the author, which came first to her mind, the resumption of the "little life of the world . . . when the great who had striven with the mightier issues of existence were defeated and dead." She does not know exactly when she first became interested in Gregory VII, but she remembers that he attracted her in her freshman history course at Radcliffe. As for Matilda, she exercised on Miss White the same attraction as had the suffragettes. Thus slowly the novel was born, to be written during the summer of 1934.

Chosen as a book-of-the-month by the Catholic Book Club, as was its predecessor, *Not Built With Hands* in general received more entirely favorable reviews than *A Watch in the Night,* although Catholic critics failed to agree on the accuracy of its Church history and some commentators felt that the later chapters fell below the narrative standard set by the author. The novel's prose style was praised by nearly all. Pointing out the core of Miss White's literary talent, one reviewer commented: "Helen White's two novels fall outside the customary categories of fiction today . . . [because she deals] with subjects which transcend the usual fictional preoccupations. Her concern is with philosophical, or, if you like, religious significance in the life of man, with the profounder seekings of the human heart. So it is very natural that she should set her conflicts back in those centuries when men and women met their inevitable problems and dealt with them . . . as signs and warnings on a road that should be leading to God."

In the spring of 1935, Miss White was at Harvard University gathering material for another scholarly book, "a critical study," she said before she had decided upon its title, "of the religious thought and feeling of a group of five poets—Donne, Crashaw, Herbert, Vaughan, and Traherne, who are usually known in English literature as the metaphysical poets." A grant from the University of Wisconsin enabled her to complete her researches at the British Museum in the summer of that year. Entitled *The Metaphysical Poets; a Study in Religious Experience*, the book came out in 1936. Critics praised its precise and careful scholarship and deplored or applauded her cautious and unemotional approach to a degree commensurate with their academic leanings. It was in the year this volume was published that Miss White received her third promotion, becoming one of the comparatively few women to hold a full professorship and the only woman full professor in the University of Wisconsin's College of Letters and Science.

In 1939 Miss White's *To the End of the World* was published, a story of the French Revolution as seen through the eyes of a young priest of Cluny Monastery, "who valiantly played his part in maintaining the stability and piety of the Church through the period of the Terror." Critics wrote: "Though the story is somewhat slow moving at first, due to the vast amount of detail involved, and though, in the last chapters, Michel's path may perhaps seem to smooth out too swiftly and easily, the reader is left with an impression of a rich and colorful picture of a gallant struggle," and "Miss White writes with distinction and consideration. Her picture of the time is powerful and convincing, and the great panorama she draws . . . gives a comprehensive view of a churning era. In a way, there is a pageant here, but it is a pageant that serves as a backdrop for the one central character who commands the stage at all times. . . . [This] is a book for those who desire to understand what leveling revolution can do to the ideals enunciated by Jesus Christ."

The year 1939-40 Miss White spent as a Research Fellow at the Henry E. Huntington Library in San Marino, California, studying that institution's collection of popular sixteenth century literature in order to determine whether religion was a socially stabilizing or socially upsetting influence in sixteenth century life. Her conclusions—that there is evidence to support both contentions and that the emphasis seems to be on the stabilizing effects toward the end of the century—were published in 1944 in her latest scholarly treatise *Social Criticism in Popular Religious Literature of the Sixteenth Century*. Reviewers considered the book a work of "impeccable scholarship" and "sureness of vision," one which "the most exacting student

HELEN C. WHITE

of social history may use with confidence" and one which might well be of interest to a wide circle of lay readers.

In 1941 Miss White was first elected president of the American Association of University Women, in which she had long been an active member, serving on the Committee on Membership and Maintaining Standards from 1933 to 1938, and on the Committee on Fellowship Awards from 1937 to 1941. As president, Miss White, who was re-elected to the post in 1945, has urged the organization to carry on in the tradition of "practical work in education" which its founders mapped out and to use their college-trained minds to study and investigate all issues before passing judgment or taking action. "In the press of immediate questions," she told a meeting of A.A.U.W. state presidents, "we must not forget that the great problem of the world is the replacement of force as the arbiter of man's destiny. Persuasion by appeal to reason is the essence of that substitute, by whatever name it is called. And the great instrument of persuasion is education, democratic education with its faith in man's reasonableness, with its confidence in man's intellectual and moral freedom."

Helen White has been awarded honorary degrees by Mount St. Scholastica College (LL.D., 1939), Mount Mary College (Litt.D., 1941), and Rockford College (LL.D., 1942). In 1942 she was the sixtieth recipient, and the thirteenth woman recipient, of the Laetare Medal given annually by the University of Notre Dame (Indiana) to an outstanding Catholic layman. For the fall semester of 1943-44 she accepted the invitation of Columbia University to be visiting professor of English in Barnard College. She is a member of the executive council of the Modern Language Association and of the Executive Committee of the American Council on Education, and she was formerly president of the University of Wisconsin Teachers Union and the first woman to become president of Wisconsin's University Club. "Her humor, keen analytical power, and gift for beautiful

WHITE, HELEN C.—*Continued*

expression," announced an A.A.U.W. press release, "have made her much in demand as a speaker."

Miss White enjoys "doing things with people," which accounts for both her teaching and her frequent committee work. But she complains that she has "one of those inconvenient minds that can really take in only one thing at a time" and that "the result is a very jerky tandem effect" and, she is afraid, more than her "due contribution to the saga of the absent-minded professor." She likes to travel, to see architecture, scenery, and people, "just the look and feel of it all." She revels in history, she says, but would write only poetry, if she could write poetry at all. For relaxation, her recipe is a detective story. "When I am too tired or lazy to cope with the vast sense of things undone," she says, "and haven't enough sense to go to bed, I like a good detective story; you know the sort—foggy night on the Thames, corpse number one quite cold, to be followed by about two spares—not much sentiment, and still less psychology. I can't stand many in a row, and I don't very often have a chance to indulge. So I hardly belong to the honorable company, but it is a proper vice for my profession."

References

Kunitz, S. J., and Haycraft, H. eds.
Twentieth Century Authors (1942)
Who's Who in America, 1944-45

WHITE, PORTIA June 24, 1917- Singer
Address: b. c/o Hope Associates, 40 E. 49th St., New York City

When Portia White made her debut at the Town Hall in New York in March 1944, critics hailed the event as "the unheralded birth of a star." Since then, at recitals in many United States and Canadian cities, her rich contralto voice has been compared to that of the late Sigrid Onegin, and she has been called the "Marian Anderson of Canada." The first Canadian singer to be officially sponsored by her native province and city, Miss White was aided in her studies by the Portia White Trust which was established for her by the citizens of Halifax.

One of the six daughters and four sons of the Reverend and Mrs. William Andrew White, Portia White was born in Truro, Nova Scotia, on June 24, 1917. A month before, her father had sailed for Europe, where he served in England and France as the only Negro chaplain in the British forces in the First World War. When Portia was two years old the White family moved to Halifax, Nova Scotia, where the Reverend Mr. White had been appointed pastor of the Cornwallis Baptist Church.

The Whites were a "singing family," and the singer can hardly remember a time when she was not enjoying music in her home. When Portia was five her mother began giving her piano lessons, and when the child was six she joined the choir of her father's church. The White children represented their school in numerous competitive music festivals: Portia appeared at one of these festivals in Hali-

fax when she was eight years old, singing with one of her sisters a duet arrangement from *Lucia di Lammermoor*. On Sundays, especially on rainy ones, she and her brothers and sisters were the mainstay of the choir at the Cornwallis Church—where some of the Whites still sing.

As Miss White tells it, she was always a bit discontented as a child. "I don't know why," she once said to a New York *Post* interviewer. "I had lots of freedom and lots of company, and I should have been happy. But I was always very tense and used to go around with a heavy heart. Perhaps it was because I wanted to express myself but didn't know how. Well, that heavy heart's one thing I've outgrown!" While attending public school in Halifax she won many prizes for her singing, and for three consecutive years was awarded the music festival's silver cup. While she was in high school she won a scholarship to the Halifax Conservatory of Music. This scholarship, awarded by a ladies' musical club, only paid for her voice lessons, and to help pay other expenses she found a position as a primary school teacher in a Halifax public school. She also attended the Dalhousie University of Halifax.

Portia White admits now that life has flowed smoothly for her and that she has never really had to struggle. As one writer expressed it, "Time after time when she has poured forth her rich dramatic voice, the right people have heard it, appreciated it, and done something about it." During her conservatory days she was in constant demand as soloist for music clubs and entertainments. One day in 1941 she sang at an afternoon tea, and afterward was asked to sing for a visitor, Edith Read, principal of the Branksome School in Toronto. Miss Read was so impressed with Miss White's talent that she promised to arrange a concert for her in Toronto, one of Canada's leading musical centers. The Toronto concert proved to be the turning point in the young contralto's career, for the papers gave such enthusiastic reviews of it that she was encouraged to give up her teaching position and to begin earning her living with her voice.

Another friend and counselor was the singer's voice teacher, Ernesto Vinci, who in 1939 was appointed head of the vocal department of the Halifax Conservatory on the recommendation of Arturo Toscanini '42. Under Vinci's direction, and encouraged by Miss Read's interest, the young singer worked diligently at her musical studies and appeared in numerous recitals in Canadian cities. Vinci is one of the committee who administer the trust fund which was created in Halifax by public subscription to enable Portia White to further her career. This fund has been made a permanent institution and will be used to aid other gifted Canadian musicians when Portia White has no further need of it.

In 1943 arrangements were made through Miss Read for the Nova Scotia girl to sing for Edward Johnson '43, manager of the Metropolitan Opera Company. He was interested in Miss White's voice, but urged her to return for another year of study with Ernesto Vinci to build up a larger and more varied repertoire. This she did, returning to New York the next year to make her debut in March at New York's Town Hall.

"She has one of the finest contralto voices to reach New York since Marian Anderson '40," wrote Henry Simon of *PM* after Portia White's first recital in New York. "It is a large voice with a firm, slightly metallic quality that gives a peculiar ring of authority to everything she sings." He also mentioned her ability to vary her tones, a gift displayed when she sang Verdi's aria "O Don Fatale" in a dramatic manner, and Purcell's "I Attempt From Love's Sickness To Fly" with light and delicate charm. A New York *Times* critic described her voice as "deep and impressive in the low registers, full and clear in the middle, and strong and vibrant on the top notes." Both critics felt that more time and experience were needed for the voice of the young Canadian singer to reach its full development. Others have commented on her clear diction and gracious stage presence.

After the Town Hall debut Portia White was recognized as a singer of importance, and when she returned to Canada she appeared at a command performance in Ottawa before the Earl of Athlone and Princess Alice. Her repertoire had been built up to include opera, *Lieder,* ballads, and spirituals. In October 1944 she returned again to New York and sang once more at Town Hall, this time in a concert sponsored by the New York chapter of the National Council for Negro Women. Again she was warmly received, critics describing her as "an artist of high rank," and "a singer with a future"; one writer wrote that she made "a hauntingly tender thing of Schubert's "Death and the Maiden"; another liked her singing of Saint-Saëns' arias and other French songs. But there was criticism, too, particularly of her breathing and the uneven tones of her voice. To quote from *Musical America*: "Miss White is indisputably sincere and earnest and can lay claim to fine vocal material. . . . But it will do her no service to pretend that she has fully laid her artistic and technical groundwork....At present Miss White's pitch is not as secure as it needs to become; and to equalize her scale she should rid herself of her habit of forcing her low notes to the inevitable detriment of her medium ones. It ought then to become plain whether she is indeed a contralto or a mezzo-soprano."

In December Miss White sang with Alexander Kipnis '43, the basso, donating her services at a dinner given by the Emergency Committee to Save the Jewish People of Europe. Through the winter of 1944-45 she sang at many concerts for Canadians and for United States servicemen in Canada, and she appeared as a soloist at the Promenade Symphony Concert in Toronto under the baton of Andre Kostelanetz '42. In February 1945 a spring concert tour of South America was being planned. That same month it was announced that Miss White had been chosen by the National Film Board of Canada to appear in a motion picture entitled *This Is Canada*, to be distributed throughout the United Nations by the Dominion Government.

Her third Town Hall appearance on December 5 again brought the young singer favorable reviews. "Miss White's voice is rich and full

Hope Associates

PORTIA WHITE

and vibrant with many lovely tones," was the comment of a New York *Times* critic. "One could carry away a very satisfying memory of beautiful tone," wrote a reviewer in the New York *Sun*. But they were both of the opinion that her vocal technique was not adequate for the proper exploitation of her natural voice.

Portia White is said to have charm and to be handsomer than her pictures show her to be. She is described as self-effacing and soft-spoken. She enjoys sports, books on philosophy, psychiatry, and on fantastic and imaginative subjects; and she likes to crochet and to listen to the radio and her brother's jazz band. Miss White hopes some day to sing in grand opera; a more immediate concern is her interpretation of spirituals, in which she feels she needs some coaching, for, as she has pointed out, Nova Scotia has never had the tradition of spirituals. Before a concert, nervousness prevents her from sleeping, and on such a night, after she has retired, her whole program runs through her mind—"complete with encores."

References

Musical Am 64:12 N 25 '44 por
N Y Post Mag p29 O 24 '44 pors
PM p20 O 27 '44 por

WHITEMAN, PAUL   Mar. 28, 1891- Conductor

Address: b. c/o American Broadcasting Co., 30 Rockefeller Plaza, New York City

After a quarter of a century of prominence in music, Paul ("Pops") Whiteman, the man who popularized jazz in America and Europe and won for himself the title "King of Jazz," remains a bright star on the entertainment horizon. The fabulous Whiteman career helped to develop a school of musical composition in the jazz idiom and gained for it the serious consideration of musicians all over the world. Through vaudeville, night clubs, rec-

PAUL WHITEMAN

ords, concerts, films, and radio, the conductor has brought music to millions, introducing new works and new personalities. Among the Whiteman alumni are George Gershwin, whose *Rhapsody in Blue* Whiteman commissioned, Bing Crosby '41, Dinah Shore '42, Ferde Grofé '40, Mildred Bailey, Morton Downey, and the Dorseys '42.

Paul Whiteman is a native of Denver, Colorado, born there on March 28, 1891 into an affluent and artistic family. His father, Wilberforce James Whiteman, was supervisor of music in the public schools and reputed to have organized the first high school orchestra. His mother, Elfrida (Dallison) Whiteman, and his sister, Ferne, were both vocalists. Thus, in a household resounding with melody, young Paul developed an early love for music. His father presented him with a violin, but the boy's reluctance to practice caused him to be locked in his mother's sewing room each afternoon with only his violin for company. Finally Paul decided to end his woes by smashing the violin, only to discover that he would be forced to earn the money to replace it. After mowing innumerable lawns, the boy had saved enough money to buy an instrument, but according to Ring Lardner, "he spent it on a viola because it was bigger than a regular fiddle and no more expensive, and didn't seem quite so unfair for a boy his size to pick on." In high school, he joined the school orchestra and received training in classical music.

While still in his teens the young musician was first viola in the Denver Symphony Orchestra. Later he played in the San Francisco People's Symphony, in the orchestra at the San Francisco World's Fair in 1915, and in the Minetti String Quartet. The conductor has often expressed gratitude for these years of classical music which, he claims, prepared him for the work he was to do in jazz. During the First World War Whiteman served in the Navy, as bandmaster at Bear Island, California, with an orchestra of fifty-seven men. "The Navy sent me to radio school, too,"

Whiteman adds, "so that later, when I started recording with the orchestra, I knew what that microphone was thinking about us. It made a lot of difference."

Whiteman recalls that he first encountered jazz in a dance place on the Barbary Coast and was impressed with the effect the raucous music had on people. He finally abandoned the symphony orchestras to take a job in Tait's Cafe, but after one day he was fired because he could not play jazz. The musician then formed his own orchestra in 1919, organizing what has been called the first "dance orchestra." Playing at a hotel in Santa Barbara, Whiteman introduced his "symphonic jazz." Later in November 1919, he played at the Hotel Alexandria in Los Angeles, where such stars of the motion picture colony as Charlie Chaplin '40 and Douglas Fairbanks '40 were among his most ardent admirers, sometimes joining him in "jam sessions."

While Whiteman was "scandalizing the profession" by "jazzing" the classics, he was also being favorably mentioned in musical circles. Asked to play at the Ambassador Hotel at Atlantic City, the bandleader introduced his new musical style on the East Coast with great success. According to one writer, "Jazz à la Whiteman was a revelation to the Boardwalk. Jazz had been blatant and raucous. Whiteman's nine-piece ensemble whispered its heresies." Soon the orchestra was making records for the Victor Talking Machine Company, gaining national popularity—their first recording of "Whispering" sold slightly under two million, while one writer has remarked that enough Whiteman recordings of "Meditations" from *Thaïs* were sold "to pave the country." In 1920 came an invitation to play at Broadway's famous Palais Royale, and in the opinion of some critics the "Jazz Age" began with Paul Whiteman's arrival at that night club.

The bandleader's earnings soared; he organized orchestras for other night clubs, theaters, and ships—by 1924 there were fifty-two Paul Whiteman orchestras in the United States, Europe, and Mexico. In that period he also appeared on Broadway in George White's *Scandals,* while some time later he played in Ziegfeld productions. Ignoring the warnings of experts that a dance band could not possibly be successful in vaudeville, the "master showman" nevertheless essayed that medium next, making jazz history in five packed weeks at the Palace Theater, the mecca of vaudeville. In 1923 Whiteman introduced his music to the applauding British. He also gave a command performance in London. There, in the front line of his following were the Prince of Wales (now Duke of Windsor '44), Lord Louis Mountbatten '42 and Lady Mountbatten.

On his return home Whiteman announced plans for a jazz concert, part of his campaign to win a wider hearing and recognition for jazz. The concert was to be held on Lincoln's Birthday, 1924, in New York's "sanctum of the Symphonic Muse," Aeolian Hall. According to Alton Cook, Whiteman was motivated by fear that his arch-rival, Vincent Lopez, planned to beat him to this artistic punch. Calling his program an "experiment in modern music," Whiteman played a varied concert, including "Livery Stable Blues", "Yes, We have No Bananas," and compositions written especially for the occasion by Victor Herbert and George Gershwin. The first performance of the latter's hastily written *Rhapsody in Blue* proved to be "one of the major milestones in the history of jazz." The mixed audience of jazz devotees and serious musicians heard this first concert of its kind with mixed emotions. According to Deems Taylor '40, "jazz came out of the kitchen and moved upstairs into the parlor," while Henrietta Straus, writing in the *Nation*, found in the music "a distinctive and well-developed art having obvious kinship with world-thought of today." The eminent writer, Carl Van Vechten, wrote in *Vanity Fair*: "February 12th, 1924, a date which many of us will remember henceforth as commemorative of another event of importance besides the birth of our famous President: George Gershwin's *Rhapsody in Blue* was performed for the first time by Paul Whiteman's orchestra with the composer at the piano." With the Aeolian Hall concert jazz came into its own. Thereafter Whiteman played in the leading concert halls of the country, often conducting famous symphony orchestras. He toured the United States and in 1926 again brought his music to Europe, winning applause in London, Paris, Vienna, and Berlin.

Controversy over jazz raged for many years in the musical field. General critical opinion gives to Whiteman the lion's share of credit for its present form and status. Whiteman found jazz a noisy, haphazard kind of music played largely by untrained musicians and transformed it into an influential and internationally popular idiom. Critics differ concerning the origin of jazz. Writing in *Collier's* in 1925, Robert Haven Schauffler contended that the first jazz piece was written by Beethoven as a scherzo for his sixth string quartet, which Schauffler labeled "worthy of the loftiest and latest traditions of Paul Whiteman"; and Ernest Newman, distinguished English music critic, once likened jazz to some British music of the fourteenth century. However, in his book *Jazz*, written in 1926 with Mary Margaret McBride '41, Whiteman claims that "jazz came to America three hundred years ago in chains." With the Negro slaves the new music came to America and flourished in the South, Whiteman continues. Tracing the history of jazz through its growth in New Orleans, the musician declares, "All I did was to orchestrate jazz. The time was ripe for that." The first to arrange music for the jazz orchestra, Whiteman also developed many style effects, such as muted horns, which have become part of the medium. He accepts John Philip Sousa's explanation of the origin of the term "jazz"—as derived from the minstrel show where performers "jazzboed" or improvised upon a melody. Books were written in English, French, and German on the new music, and critical columns often ranged from frigid to fervent comment on the subject.

To critic Lawrence Gilman, Whiteman's band in 1924 was representative of the best in jazz, while Virgil Thomson '40 considered jazz impossible for use in serious composition. In 1925 the critic of *Musical Life and Arts*, reviewing Whiteman's Boston concerts, declared:

"This is music for the feet, not for the head or the heart." The following year, when Whiteman played Gershwin's one-act jazz operetta at his Carnegie Hall concert, critic Samuel Chotzinoff '40 said: "Musically, I believe it has immense significance." Henry Osborne Osgood in his book, *So This Is Jazz*, written in 1926, stated that Whiteman has "the largest and best jazz orchestra and in the repertoire especially arranged for him are practically all the pieces that have interested serious musicians in jazz and gained for it recognition as a legitimate element in standard music." The *British Musician* in June 1929 carried an article entitled, "Paul Whiteman—The Reformer of Music," in which the musician is described as "a man with an iron energy, with an extraordinary sense of music, and a positive belief that jazz can be beautiful." Determined to "cure" the experts of prejudice against jazz, Whiteman demonstrated its musical possibilities by introducing several serious jazz compositions. Among these works in addition to the now-famous Gershwin *Rhapsody*, are Deems Taylor's *Circus Days*, and the *Grand Canyon Suite* by Ferde Grofé, who served for many years as orchestrator for Whiteman.

Always experimenting with music, the jazz master in addition to playing new works often tried new effects. Reporting a Whiteman concert in 1933, a writer for the New York *Herald Tribune* stated: "Typewriters were among the instruments employed." In a *New Yorker* profile of the bandleader (November 27, 1926), Niven Busch, Jr., declared: "He is directly responsible for the artistic recognition of jazz and for many of its instrumental methods; his influence is obvious in numberless orchestras." Many of the Nation's leading jazz musicians have played in Whiteman's orchestra, including the famous cornettist, Bix Beiderbecke, who played under his baton in the late twenties, Tommy and Jimmy Dorsey, Red Nichols, Lennie Hayton, Henry Busse, Jack Teagarden, and Roy Bargy. The high artistic caliber of Whiteman's musicians has often been remarked—Rachmaninoff once termed the band "an orchestra of virtuosos." Whiteman considers jazz the folk music of modern America. Writing in the *Rotarian* (June 1939) on the topic, "This Thing Called Jazz," he stated: "Jazz is, first of all, a way of playing any music." In 1936 Whiteman established a Museum of American Music at Williams College at Williamstown, Massachusetts, contributing musical collections and scholarships to what he hopes will become a center of research in American music.

Whiteman has brought his music to the public through all the entertainment channels. His concerts have drawn capacity audiences to such well-known places as New York's Lewisohn Stadium, Madison Square Garden, Metropolitan Opera House, and Philadelphia's Robin Hood Dell. Whiteman has conducted in the leading hotels and theaters in the country and in 1936 he appeared in Billy Rose's '40 spectacle *Jumbo*. As guest bandleader at the Roxy Theater in 1943 he received $6,500, a record figure for a conductor without a band. Among the first bandleaders in films, he has appeared in short pictures for Vitaphone and 20th Century-Fox and features for the major studios. In the

WHITEMAN, PAUL—*Continued*

words of one writer, Whiteman's picture *King of Jazz* (Universal, 1930), "sent him hastily back to the dance floors." His other films include *Thanks a Million*, with Dick Powell, (20th Century-Fox, 1935), *Strike Up the Band*, with Mickey Rooney '42 and Judy Garland '41, (Metro-Goldwyn-Mayer, 1940), and *Atlantic City* (Republic, 1944). In 1945 Whiteman played his real-life role in the cinematic biography of George Gershwin, *Rhapsody in Blue* (Warner Brothers). A popular radio personality, he has been conducting music on the air since 1932, featured on programs over the Columbia Broadcasting System and the National Broadcasting Company. In March 1943 he was appointed musical director of the Blue Network, a position which enables him to carry out his musical ideas and plans. One such project was undertaken in 1944 when thirteen leading contemporary composers were commissioned to write compositions for radio presentation in a series entitled, *Music Out of the Blue*. Directing the series, Whiteman declared its purpose to be the attempt to find another *Rhapsody in Blue* or *Park Avenue Fantasy*. The composers chosen on a non-competitive basis included Igor Stravinsky '40, Roy Harris '40, Leonard Bernstein '44, Paul Creston, and Morton Gould '45. Whiteman's executive duties have not curtailed his musical activities—since 1943 his music on the popular Philco *Radio Hall of Fame* has been frequently commended by *Variety*.

So that he might devote more time to radio work Whiteman in the fall of 1945 decided to refuse all future theater engagements (with the exception of his annual appearance at the Capitol Theater in New York). On November 7 the American Broadcasting Company put on a special anniversary show, "The First Twenty-five," built around the bandleader's music. It showed how the taste in popular music had changed through the years. For early 1946 Whiteman was planning a "mammoth event" at Carnegie Hall to celebrate his twenty-first year as a maestro.

Whiteman's broad proportions and tiny black mustache are well known. The man whom Olin Downes '43 once called "Jazz Jelly" has earned more money than any other conductor in America. The genial maestro is the author of many magazine articles on jazz and has often given advice to aspiring young musicians and has held auditions in numerous towns. His book, *How To Be a Bandleader*, written with Leslie Lieber in 1941, gives practical advice to jazz enthusiasts. Declaring that showmanship, tact, and business ability are primary requisites, he recommends a thorough grounding in the classics for the jazz musician.

"Man of many comebacks and no retirements," Whiteman once complained, "There's no time for golf or any real social life for a band leader." However, he does manage to spend some time with his family on his productive six-hundred-acre New Jersey farm. Whiteman was married for the fourth time on August 18, 1931, when film actress Margaret Livingston became his wife after having persuaded him to shed more than one hundred pounds. (The story of this slimming process is amusingly told by Mrs. Whiteman in her book, *Whiteman's Burden*, written with Isabel Leighton in 1933.) He has a daughter, Margot, and a son, Paul, Jr. Known as "Pops" to his friends, Whiteman is said to have a "horror" of heights, boats, and elevators. The man who "put jazz in a dress suit" believes that good music "does something to you. It makes your feet tap or else it stretches your soul."

References

Am Mag 97:74-5 Je '24 il por
Collier's 75:38 Ja 3 '25 por
N Y Post Mag p30 N 2 '43 pors
National Cyclopædia of American Biography Current vol E p30
Ramsey, F. Jr. and Smith, C. E. eds. Jazzmen 1939
Thompson, O. ed. International Cyclopedia of Music and Musicians 1943
Variety Radio Directory, 1940-41
Who's Who in America, 1944-45

WHITNEY, JOHN HAY Aug. 17, 1904- Financier; United States Government official; sportsman

Address: b. 630 Fifth Ave., New York City; h. 972 Fifth Avenue, New York City

Colonel John Hay Whitney, better known as "Jock" Whitney, millionaire sportsman and financier, occupies the post of Special Adviser and Consultant on Motion Pictures in the United States State Department. Before he was appointed to that position Whitney had had a successful career in the film industry. He was board chairman of Selznick '41-International, the company which produced, among others, the Academy Award-winning films *Gone With the Wind* and *Rebecca*. From 1940 to 1942, before he entered the Army as a public relations officer, Whitney was director of the motion picture division of the Office of the Co-Ordinator of Inter-American Affairs, whose "good will" work in cultural and commercial relations between the United States and Latin America has been praised by diplomats.

Born on August 17, 1904, in Ellsworth, Maine, to Payne and Helen (Hay) Whitney, John Hay Whitney is a member of one of the most distinguished of the Nation's wealthy families. The Whitneys are descended from John Whitney, who came from England to Watertown, Massachusetts, in 1635. The first Whitney to figure in history was Brigadier General James Scollay Whitney; his son William C. Whitney not only founded the family fortune but was a person of great influence both in New York City and Washington political circles. In New York he worked with Samuel J. Tilden to destroy the "Tweed ring," and as Secretary of the Navy during President Grover Cleveland's first Administration he reorganized the Navy, introducing armor-plated ships. The Whitney millions were accumulated through this astute politician's investments in street railways and through his marriage to Flora Payne, daughter of Henry B. Payne, noted railroad builder, who also was a United States Senator. Through his mother, John Hay Whitney is a grandson of John Hay, statesman and author, who was assistant private secretary to President Abraham Lincoln, Ambassador to the Court of St. James, and Secretary of State under Presidents William Mc-Kinley and Theodore Roosevelt. During John Hay's regime in the State Department he became known as "a maker of policies," responsible for the Open-Door policy in China and for the Hay-Pauncefote treaty.

Friends of Colonel Whitney, an athlete noted for his "gladiator-like" build, like to recall that his formal education began at Miss Chapin's select school for young ladies. Little John was in the school's kindergarten class which, at that time, admitted equally select young men. In 1916, at the age of twelve, young Whitney was sent to Groton, where he remained until 1922. There he distinguished himself in baseball and football, won the heavyweight boxing championship, and in his senior year was elected president of his class. "But, from the time he saw Forbes-Robertson in Shakespearean roles at the age of six," relates an *American* Magazine article, "his private ambition was to get into theatricals." Soon after entering Yale (1922), the university of his father and grandfather, Jock, as he has been called since his knee-trousers days, "wangled a small role in Bernard Shaw's "*Caesar and Cleopatra.*" In the scanty tunic of a Roman soldier young Whitney's physique, rather than his histrionic ability, was praised. After that, says Whitney, although "I was busy as possible in dramatics, I knew better than to think I could ever be an actor." As his father before him, he excelled in Yale athletics. He was on the varsity crew and was also adept at squash and tennis.

In 1926 Whitney left Yale to enter Oxford University, but upon the death of his father in 1927 he returned to America to take up the management of his estate, which has been variously reported as the interest on $27,000,000 or a fourth share of $240,000,000. (On the death of his mother in 1944 he and his sister are said to have divided another fifty millions.) To prepare himself for this part in his many-sided career the young heir clerked for a brief period, at a salary of fifteen dollars a week, in the Wall Street house of Lee Higginson.

In addition to the fortune founded by his grandfather and greatly increased by his father, John Hay Whitney inherited their interest in horses. His grandfather had won the 1901 English Derby. His mother, known internationally for her charm and intellect, had after her husband's death divided her time between her many philanthropies and her turf enthusiasm. She owned the famous Greentree Stables and her colors, candy-striped black and cherry, were carried to victories in both hemispheres. Among the horses in the Whitney stables are Twenty Grand and Shut Out. *Country Life* reported in 1935 that Jock Whitney, as owner of the largest string of horses in America, had horses in England, Ireland, Virginia, and Kentucky, and kept polo ponies at his Long Island estate. "Recognized in his own right as a breeder and judge of horseflesh," Whitney was one of the youngest members of the Jockey Club, president of the American Thoroughbred Breeders Association, and vice-president and stockholder in the Westchester Racing Association, which operates Belmont Park. One honor to come to him in this field was his appointment by Governor Herbert Lehman [43] to the three-man New York State Racing Commission. His greatest disappointment on the race courses was

COL. JOHN HAY WHITNEY

in 1929 when his pet horse, Easter Hero, after leading a record field of sixty-six in the Grand National, cracked one of his shoes and limped in second.

Whitney has carried on the family tradition in polo, too. His uncle, Harry Payne Whitney was captain and chief strategist of the "Big Four," which *Fortune* magazine credits with being "the finest polo team ever assembled." In 1924, when Harry Payne Whitney dropped out of the game in which he had been prominent for twenty years, young Whitney, with his "Greentree Team," took over. Under his captaincy and with Tommy Hitchcock, Jr., "the greatest poloist the world has yet seen," the team achieved during its life (it was disbanded in 1940) the record of winning two United States Open championships in succession and the Waterbury Cup (1935). Although Whitney became internationally famous as a polo player it was not known to polo fans that he was forced to wear contact lenses because of faulty vision. "Yet, Jock never hesitated," says Tom O'Reilly, *PM* sports writer, "to stick his head in where the mallets flew thickest, and he had a surprising habit of playing like a world-beater when the chips were down." Whitney, upon his retirement in 1940, had a six-goal handicap rating. In describing Whitney the sportsman, Daniel Fosdick Parker said: "He is just about one of the physically strongest sportsmen in the country. . . . He stands six feet one and weighs almost 200 pounds. . . . He is built like an old-time gladiator."

"I love the theater," is the explanation the millionaire-sportsman gave when asked why he had become one of the biggest investors in Broadway plays. Although his theatrical attorney, John Wharton, has said that Whitney will finance an almost certain failure if he thinks "the play has something to say that should be said," his investment in some thirty plays from 1929 to 1945 has netted a nice profit, which is devoted to Whitney charities. The Whitney money (his sister, Mrs. Charles

WHITNEY, JOHN HAY—*Continued*

Payson, and his cousin, Cornelius Vanderbilt Whitney, often are represented in Jock's theatrical and movie enterprises) has been in the following hit plays: *Broken Dishes, Post Road, Whistling in the Dark, Kind Lady* (original production), *Gay Divorce,* and *Life With Father.* His worst wrong guess, he says, was Peter Arno's [42] musical, *Here Goes the Bride,* which is reported to have lost him $100,000. Although Whitney's own dramatic judgment has been reliable, he had by 1940 formed the Wharton-Gabel Corporation, which is headed by two experienced theatrical people. One instance of his dramatic sense is the story of how he relied upon his own judgment in investing in *Life With Father.* The late Robert Benchley [41], actor-humorist and one-time dramatic critic, who, as one of Whitney's closest friends, often advised him on plays, sent back the script of "Father" with the comment: "I could smell this alleged comedy you want to back, before the mailman got it up to the door. If you don't want to lose your shirt, lay off." Despite Benchley's advice, Whitney placed his money in the show. *Life With Father* began its history-making run in 1939, and in its sixth year, after grossing nearly eight million dollars from its Broadway and road company runs, was sold to the movies for the highest price ever paid for a play—a down payment of $500,000, with royalties on the film's gross.

"When Socialite Whitney invaded the motion picture industry, which had long been monopolized by a small clique of specialists," reports *Time* Magazine, "Hollywood veterans smirked, knowingly predicting he would singe his fingertips." But by 1940, when he sold out some of his Hollywood interests because of world conditions, Whitney had made a profit of over a million dollars. His first venture in the film industry was the organization of Pioneer Pictures to produce pictures in Technicolor, a process which at that time no one in Hollywood "would touch with a ten-foot pole." In return for Pioneer's use and publicizing of the new medium, Whitney received a bonus of 100,000 shares of stock at below market price from its inventor, Herbert T. Kalmus. The initial production, *La Cucaracha,* grossed more than any other short in film history, including Walt Disney's [40] *Three Little Pigs,* but the next production, *Becky Sharp,* a full-length film with Miriam Hopkins in the star role, suffered a series of mishaps during its making and cost more than it earned in box-office receipts. "But the film proved the worth of the color technique—Jock's ace in the hole—and in the long run with its stock shooting up from three to thirty, more than repaid the cost of the film."

In 1935, Whitney, with David Selznick and others, formed Selznick-International, the motion picture company which made such "four-star" hits as *A Star Is Born* (1937), *The Prisoner of Zenda* (1937), *Rebecca* (1940), and *Gone With The Wind* (1940). With the last named, Whitney again showed his ability to judge the dramatic value of a story from a script. Selznick had been "cold" to the story when an agent sent him a synopsis of the then unpublished *Gone With The Wind.* Nevertheless, Whitney took it with him on a plane trip to Hollywood. "Two hours later," relates *American* Magazine, "he leaped out of the ship at the Pittsburgh airport to send a wire back to New York. 'If Selznick won't purchase the book for company, I'll buy personally.'" His quick decision enabled the company to buy the film rights for this best of best-sellers for the very low sum of $50,000—a month later Selznick-International turned down an offer of $350,000 for the story. Its filming, made at a cost of $4,250,000, not only won the Academy award of 1940 but has proved to be one of biggest box-office attractions in film history. In 1943 when Metro-Goldwyn-Mayer (one of the investors) bought outright Whitney's interest in "GWTW," it had grossed in domestic rentals $31,000,000 and it was expected to gross another $10,000,000 to $15,000,000 with the reopening of foreign markets after the Second World War.

Although Whitney is proud of his wise investments, he does not deny that he has made some unwise decisions. Among these is his investment in "some weird tree which was supposed to corner the hemp market," and his backing with Marshall Field, 3rd [41], William Benton [45], and others, of the New York paper, *PM.* (Three months after the founding of *PM* Whitney sold Field his interest at twenty cents on the dollar, plus a fifteen per cent interest in the voting stock.) Whitney also owned a considerable share in the magazine *Polo* and the old *Outlook.* His other business connections include the board chairmanship of the Freeport Sulphur Company, which during the war produced 130,000 tons of manganese annually; directorship of the Great Northern Paper Company, the Publications Research Corporation, and the Pan American Airways, Inc. This last-named in 1940 had already won him a profit of 50 per cent on his investment. He is also a trustee of the United States Trust Company and of the New York Hospital. His philanthropies include a gift of five million dollars to Yale University, made by himself and his mother for the erection of a new gymnasium in memory of Payne Whitney.

The Whitneys have long been patrons of art and Whitney has shown much pride in his connection with the Museum of Modern Art. A member of the board of trustees since the museum's establishment in 1931, and president of the Film Library since its beginning in 1935, he became the museum's president after the resignation of Nelson A. Rockefeller [41] in 1940. After the United States entered the War, Whitney announced that the museum, in cooperation with the Federal Government, would open a new program "to improve relations between the United States and the Latin American republics, through the interchange of art and culture." The most famous paintings in Whitney's personal collection are Renoir's *Le Moulin de la Galatte* and a Gilbert Stuart portrait of George Washington.

When the United States public became aware of the fact that organized "fifth columns" throughout the Americas threatened the harmony existing between the Americas, Nelson Rockefeller, John Whitney, and a number of other energetic young men decided to do something about it. In August 1940 President Franklin D. Roosevelt [42] approved an organization which they had planned and through an executive order made it a branch of the Council of National Defense with the title, Office for

Coordination of Commercial and Cultural Relations Between the American Republics. This title was later changed to Office of the Coordinator of Inter-American Affairs. "The State Department," said *Time*, "which cherished the professional's distaste for the amateur . . . developed toward it an attitude of chilly reserve." By June 1941, however, "the reserve had noticeably thawed." The State Department and the rest of Washington as well observed that the new organization "had accomplished a good deal, seemed on the way to accomplish more." Whitney, in charge of the motion-picture division, had persuaded Hollywood producers to rid their films of sequences offensive to Latin Americans, to send Hollywood stars on good-will tours of Latin American countries, and to produce pictures with sympathetic Latin-American backgrounds.

After two years of service with the office of Inter-American Affairs, Whitney, in May 1942, entered the Eighth United States Army Air Force as a captain in the Combat Intelligence Division. Sent to England in August of the same year, he was made public relations director of the Eighth and subsequently promoted to the rank of major. Then, in February 1943 he accompanied General Ira C. Eaker [41] to the Mediterranean theater, where he rose to the rank of, first, lieutenant colonel and, later, full colonel. Four days after his fortieth birthday, Whitney was captured by the Nazis while riding in a jeep with four companions through southern France. With shaved heads, the prisoners were put aboard a train carrying German units out of France. They were dive-bombed and shelled by Allied artillery and the French underground, and the journey, Whitney later related, "was a veritable hell." But the confusion from the attacks which destroyed three locomotives during an eleven-day journey enabled him and his companions to escape. Eighteen days after his capture Whitney had made his way back to his base.

In March 1945 Whitney was decorated with the Legion of Merit—the citation read "for exceptionally meritorious conduct in the performance of outstanding services from February 15, 1943, to January 1, 1944." His appointment as special adviser and consultant to the State Department's Public and Cultural Relations division under the directorship of William Benton and the International Information Service under Ferdinand Kuhn was announced on October 15, 1945. He advises on relations with the motion picture industry, "growing out of the activities not only of the Office of War Information and the Office of Inter-American Affairs, but also of the past and present interest of the State Department." Information and documentary pictures "aimed to give peoples of other countries a better idea of Americans," also come under his supervision.

In 1930 Whitney was married to Mary Elizabeth Altemus, Philadelphia socialite who has been described by Elsa Maxwell [43] as "a hard-hitting, swashbuckling, hard-riding gal who took many a tumble but never came a cropper," and who shared her husband's interest in the theater-world. Ten years later the Whitneys were divorced, with Whitney reportedly settling three million dollars on her. In 1942 Whitney was married to Betsy Cushing Roosevelt, former wife of James Roosevelt, eldest son of the late President. The brown-haired Mrs. Whitney has two daughters, Sara Delano and Kate, by her former husband. During the War Mrs. Whitney and her sister, Mrs. Vincent Astor, created Ship's Service, "one of the best volunteer organizations for naval aid in New York." The Whitneys have a Fifth Avenue house, a Georgia plantation, and a Long Island estate, "Greentree." At "Greentree" there is a polo field and for the benefit of guests, a field house has been equipped with all kinds of sports clothes in almost every size. Whitney's Radio City office has a kitchenette and a "Romanesque" marble bathroom. In an inner, sound-proof office the "zestful giant" conducts the affairs of his many-sided career. Dark-haired, with hazel eyes, he has been described as "quiet-spoken, almost embarrassingly modest."

References

Am Mag 129:27+ My '40 por
Country Life 67:41-3+ Mr '35 pors
N Y Herald Tribune p5 S 14 '44 por
N Y Sun p18 S 18 '44
N Y World-Telegram p10 F 15 '41 pors
Who's Who in America, 1944-45

WHITTLE, FRANK June 1, 1907- Royal Air Force officer; inventor

Address: b. c/o British Air Ministry, London

"I am completely embarrassed. Damn it, I wish I had been a doctor." With these words Air Commodore Frank Whittle, R.A.F. group captain and inventor of the first successful jet-propulsion engine for aircraft, stepped right into the tradition of the shy man of science who quietly sets the world on end and then runs like the hare from publicity. In October 1944 Whittle's invention brought him the highest award of the Council of the Royal Aeronautical Society, the gold medal that had been awarded on only seven previous occasions in thirty-five years, the first time, in 1909, to the Wright brothers.

Dark and slight, Air Commodore Whittle, whose invention inspired wary gentlemen of the press to talk blandly in terms of space ships and interplanetary travel, was born in Coventry, England, on June 1, 1907. Whittle, senior, was an inventor himself, and his boy showed very early an interest in tinkering: the family album shows a snapshot of four-year-old Frank holding a model plane in his hand. At sixteen he became an apprentice with the Royal Air Force. He showed such an unusual talent for designing model planes that he was awarded a cadetship and began flying in 1926. In the two years which followed he studied at Cranwell, the RAF College, receiving at the end of his course the Abdy-Gerald-Fellowes Memorial Prize for aeronautical sciences.

After the cadetship, in 1928 he became a pilot officer in No. 111 Fighter Squadron. In 1929, while in the instructors' class at the Central Flying School, he began work on his jet-propulsion idea. The next year he was promoted to flying officer and assumed the position of instructor at No. 2 Flying Training School, Digby. (He was married that year and now has two sons.)

"By 1930 he was probably the most brilliant pilot in the RAF," says George Peyton, of

British Official Photo

AIR COMMODORE FRANK WHITTLE

the New York *Herald Tribune*. "Like many great men he is an amazing mixture of cold deliberation and crazy daring." Friends and observers thought, however, that it was simply crazy daring that impelled him to perform a "bunt" (an outside loop that stumped experts) in a plane considered unsuited for the purpose. Emerging from the feat he remarked with complete *sang-froid*: "It wasn't difficult or even dangerous. You see, I'd worked it all out on a slide rule."

In 1931-32 the airman was a test pilot on float seaplanes, specializing in catapult work. After that there was a year's study of engineering at Henlow, and in January 1934 he was promoted to flight lieutenant. He then spent three years at Cambridge University, where he obtained a First Class Honors Mechanical Science Tripos. Squadron leader and group captain successively in 1937, he became a wing commander in June 1940 and air commodore in October 1944.

"The idea of a jet-propelled aircraft first came to me as a cadet at Cranwell," Whittle admitted in a rarely communicative moment. "When we had to write a science thesis I chose as my subject the future development of aircraft. I am delighted it has worked out so well, and it is only the beginning."

In an embryonic state, jet propulsion has existed for centuries. According to *Newsweek* Magazine, its principle dates back to a hundred years before Christ, when the Alexandrian mathematician Hero demonstrated an aeolipile, which *Webster's* defines as "an apparatus such as a globe or cylinder with one or more projecting bent tubes from which steam is ejected, causing the cylinder to move." This "action against reaction" is quite simply explained by a demonstration with a toy balloon: release the neck of an inflated balloon and the expulsion of air will shoot it quite a distance. This principle is applied to jet planes through a "power plant" that sucks in air, compresses it, mixes it with gasoline, and then ignites the mixture. This causes a tremendous

expansion, and the combustible gases pass through turbine blades and are expelled through a tailpipe nozzle. The thrust of the compressed gases against the atmosphere sends the propellerless airplane forward.

Replacing the propeller, Whittle's jet propulsion eliminates some of the most retarding features of a propeller-driven plane. Functioning as a screw, the propeller "bites" into the air. At heights where the air is thin it has little to take hold of. On the other hand, the "jay-pee" (its abbreviated name) reacts more favorably at a high altitude; its expelled gases expand in a rarified atmosphere, thus increasing the plane's drive. The actual speed of the jay-pee has never been announced, but it is known that the jet leaves the tail of the plane at 740 miles per hour. While this fast, highstepping little craft will obligingly perform on kerosene, crude oil, or even powdered coal, it consumes fuel at an extremely high rate, thereby cutting down its operating range. Dynamite on the ground as well as in the air, the jay-pee acts as an oversized vacuum cleaner, swallowing whole whatever chances too near its air intake. Legend has it that unwary birds, sporting in the heavens, are suddenly sucked into the jet to emerge at the tail "skewered, cooked, and ready for the table."

The jay-pee might never have been completed, one of its original supporters has stated. Commodore Whittle might have been peddling a worthless invention for shelling peas for all the attention his jet engine received from the big industrialists of England. He became so discouraged that for five years he did not even bother to pay the renewal on the original patent taken out on the engine in 1930. Four classmates at Cambridge lent him their moral support. Two of them, Tinling and Williams, former RAF men and partners in business, scraped up enough to finance Power Jets, Ltd., and bring up the "Squirt" to maturity.

By 1937 Whittle's first engine actually ran, and in 1939 the British Air Ministry placed an order for the first jet-propelled airplane. The Gloster Aircraft Company was appointed to design and build a plane, and Power Jets, Ltd., was to make the engine. Whittle prepared to perfect his brain child. Recruiting three talented men to form a crew, he moved his work into an old disused foundry on the outskirts of a Midlands town. (The local people thought they were making sausage machines and complained of the noise.) It was a willing crew. One of the "back room boys," Bozzoni, alias "Old Bozzy," had a particular talent for turning marvelous machines out of scrap and his imagination, obligingly sweeping the factory floor as well. When the engine was ready for its first test the employees, by then numbering forty, stopped just long enough to toast their success with a bottle of champagne and affix their signatures to the bottle. English countryfolk became frightened and mystified by sporadic appearances of the strange plane that sounded "like a giant whistling teakettle on the boil," then was gone before they could draw another breath. They soon got so used to it, however, that they began to give it nicknames: "Putt-Putt", "Hush-Hush", "Siberia", "Super-Secret," and "Squirt," which in time became the favorite one.

In July 1941 the British Air Ministry turned all information on the jet plane over to General Henry H. Arnold [42], and in September, Whittle and his colleague "Bozzy" flew to America with the engine's parts. There they took assumed names, moved from place to place to avoid attracting notice. The Bell Aircraft Corporation contracted to manufacture the P-59 body in the United States, and General Electric Company, the Whittle engine. The American jay-pee is a two-motor plane, in contrast to the single-engined Gloster that is manufactured by the British. For military purposes both types could serve either as interceptors of enemy bombers or as high-altitude reconnaissance crafts. What the Mosquito plane was to the bomber, the jay-pee could be to the fighter command. The details of its further development and actual use, however, remained secret. Jet propulsion has been adapted to take-off equipment for use on propeller-driven planes to enable a plane to carry a heavier load than it would ordinarily be able to lift from the ground. Robot bombs were also equipped with jet propulsion engines before the war was over, and the principle has been applied to helicopters.

If a "super secret," it was asked, why let it out before the new weapon could be sprung as a surprise on the Germans and the Japanese? For one reason, jet propulsion was actually no secret. Major European powers had been experimenting with the idea, although the results were not revealed. The announcement of the jay-pee at a time when German morale was toppling, suggested observers, was all part of the Allied war of nerves. On the other hand, Brigadier General B. W. Chidlaw, chief of the matériel division of the United States Army Air Forces and one of the first to test the plane, offered an entirely different reason. As he broadcast on the *Army Hour* program: "While the German technique of propaganda in announcing new and secret weapons of war is to terrorize and frighten the enemy, our reason, however, for making it public now is prompted by a motive only a free people can understand. . . . Your sons will some day fly these planes. You are entitled to know, within the bounds of national security, that all our resources are still at work to turn out better planes and better equipment to make our Allied air forces the best air forces in the world."

References

N Y Herald Tribune VII p14-15 Jl 9 '44 por
N Y Times p6 Ja 8 '44; p6 O 3 '44 por
Newsweek 23:52+ Ja 17 '44 por
PM p8 Ja 9 '44
Time 43:62 Ja 17 '44 por

WHITTY, DAME MAY June 19, 1865- Actress

Address: c/o Metro-Goldwyn-Mayer Studios, Culver City, Calif.

With the opening of the play *Thérèse* in October 1945 and the première of the film *My Name is Julia Ross* in November 1945, Dame May Whitty, eighty-year-old trouper of the English stage, joined the envied company of those who find their names in lights simultaneously on both theater and movie marquees. When in 1936 and 1937 she first became familiar to large American theater and movie audiences

DAME MAY WHITTY

with the portrayal of Mrs. Branson in *Night Must Fall*, she was already a veteran of almost a hundred roles, the listing of which filled more than three columns in the 1936 *Who's Who in the Theatre*. In 1945 Dame May can celebrate the sixty-fifth anniversary of a distinguished career on the stage.

May Whitty, daughter of Alfred and Mary (Ashton) Whitty, was born in Liverpool, England, on June 19, 1865. Her paternal grandfather, Michael James Whitty, was for a time the owner and editor of the Liverpool *Journal*, and in 1855 he founded the Liverpool *Daily Post*, the first penny daily issued in Great Britain. Journalism was likewise her father's profession, and Miss Whitty's childhood was consequently passed in what has been called a "typical newspaper atmosphere." She was privately educated, and recalls that by the time she was ten years old she had read much of Dickens, Scott, Thackeray and other English authors. This, she thinks, has done her more good than any other part of her early education. As a child she loved the theater. She used to sit breathless, she says, as the footlights went on and the green baize curtains went up behind the proscenium arch, "revealing the painted drop with the formal garden and pool, with a troubadour leaning against a marble pillar and cupids flying all about." The stage was fairyland, and May Whitty's ambition was to become a part of it.

Her opportunity came at the age of fifteen, when her mother, who knew Madge Kendal, obtained an interview for her with the famous actress. Mrs. Kendal gave the stage-struck but awed girl a note of introduction to the manager of the Court Theatre in Liverpool, the result of which was Miss Whitty's first appearance on the stage, in *The Mountain Sylph*, an adaptation of the ballet *Les Sylphides*. That was in 1881. There followed several other appearances in Liverpool, and on April 22, 1882, she made her London debut as Fillippa in *Boccaccio* at the Comedy Theatre. The next year John Hare of the Hare and Kendal

WHITTY, DAME MAY—*Continued*

(William Hunter Kendal, husband and leading man of Madge Kendal) management at the St. James' Theatre engaged May Whitty as understudy to the then much publicized Miss Webster, granddaughter of the famous London actor and manager Benjamin Nottingham ("Ben") Webster. A frequent visitor at rehearsals of the company at that time was Miss Webster's young brother Ben, then a law student, whom young May Whitty thought the handsomest man she had ever seen. It is interesting to note that both Miss Whitty and her future husband, who in 1887 was to desert the bar for the stage, made their initial recorded appearances under Hare and Kendal in the same play, *A Scrap of Paper*, in December 1883. (May Whitty and Ben Webster were married in August 1892, and celebrated their golden wedding anniversary in 1942. They have one daughter, the noted Shakespearean director and actress, Margaret Webster '⁴⁰.)

Until 1885 Miss Whitty remained at the St. James, chiefly as an understudy. Then, at the age of twenty, she went on tour with a repertory stock company, an engagement of which Margaret Webster relates: "My mother played fourteen parts in two weeks, with one rehearsal for each—parts such as Lydia Languish and Kate Hardcastle, [Lady Teazle, Lady Gay Spanker], plus some meaty old melodramas and a farce or two. Between rehearsals and performances she made her own costumes." In the next decade May Whitty appeared in such plays as *Harbor Lights, The Monk's Room, Linda Grey, Beauty's Toils,* and others; she toured in *The Candidate* and *Hoodman Blind*. Sometime between 1885 and 1887 she was a member of Ben Greet's original Shakespearean company. (Her earlier experiences with the Bard's plays included roles in the rarely produced *Two Gentlemen of Verona* and in the Kendals' production of *As You Like It*.) In 1888 she played with Richard Mansfield in *Prince Karl* and with Kate Vaughan in *She Stoops to Conquer* and *School for Scandal*. In 1894, she toured with Forbes-Robertson as Comtesse Zicka in *Diplomacy* and as Irene in *The Profligate*. On May 8, 1899, she played the Countess Cathleen in William Butler Yeats' play of that name at the opening performance of the Irish Literary Theatre, the unit later to become famous as Dublin's Abbey Theatre. Along with repertory stands in the 1890's, appearances in two or even three plays a year was accepted practice, and melodramas formed a considerable portion of the fare. Melodramas of those days, reminisces Dame May, "were dramas of situation with big scenic effects. In *Harbor Lights* the hero climbed down over the cliff to rescue the heroine. *Hoodman Blind* was about twin sisters, and I played both of them. One was good and the other bad, the bad one throwing herself over the Thames embankment."

In June 1895 the actress joined the Lyceum Company of Sir Henry Irving and Ellen Terry, then the giants of the English stage. But, unfortunately, she recalls, she "never had a chance to see Sir Henry building up his roles. He was hard to work with, because he was dreadfully remote, as was the rule with

most of the great actors of that school and period. Long before I ever knew him to work with he had mastered all the lines and business and technique of every play he produced, so that I could never see a representation being evolved." "Ellen Terry," Dame May told an interviewer, "was the kindest and grandest woman I have ever known" and one of the few actresses who acted with "grace and simplicity" in an age which, judged by modern histrionic standards, was given to declamation and excess emotionalism. Dame May thinks herself fortunate in having been asked to assist Ellen Terry in the preparation of new roles, reading the lines of them to her. Thus the younger actress was able to observe the star's characterizations developing. Miss Whitty's roles with the Lyceum Company, as given in *Who's Who in the Theatre*, were Marie in *Louis XI*, Julie in *The Lyons Mail*, Emilie in *The Corsican Brothers*, the daughter in *The Bells*, and the Gentlewoman in *Macbeth*. From September 1895 to May 1896 she toured with the company in the United States. It was her first visit—though Irving's fifth—and it was marked by the presence of her husband, Ben Webster, in the company.

While Ben Webster remained with Irving at the Lyceum until 1898, May Whitty left the company shortly after the conclusion of this American tour because she was not receiving suitable parts. At various theaters in London for the next several years she played such roles as Edith Varney in *Secret Service*, Rosamond Pilliner in *Cupboard Love*, Mrs. Grace Tyrrell in *The Heather Field*, Katherine Blake in *The Last Chapter*. At the Vaudeville in August 1903 Miss Whitty began an engagement as Susan Throssell in Sir James M. Barrie's *Quality Street*, afterwards touring with the play. Early in 1905 she accompanied Ben Webster to New York where he was to play opposite Ellis Jeffreys in *The Prince Consort* and at the end of the year with Grace George in *The Marriage of William Ashe*. (It was during the run of the former play, on March 15, 1905, that Margaret Webster was born.) In December 1907 she took the role of Carrie Hardinge in the Viola Allen production of *Irene Wycherly* in Baltimore and New York.

Returning to London Miss Whitty joined Charles Frohman's repertory company at the Duke of York's, playing Dame Dresden in George Meredith's *The Sentimentalists,* Amelia Madras in Harley Granville-Barker's *The Madras House,* and Mrs. Trafalgar Gower in Arthur Wing Pinero's *Trelawney of the Wells*. During rehearsals of the latter two plays, says Margaret Webster, Miss Whitty encountered her first real specimens of the genus director, vintage twentieth century. (When she began to act there were no directors, only stage managers to distribute the meticulously marked prompt copies dictating moves laid down by actor-managers.) Pinero, relates Miss Webster, was a "martinet who drilled his actors in every detail of movement and inflection. Sometimes . . . imposed mannerisms supposed to indicate character. I remember my mother sedulously practising a high screech demanded by Pinero, half giggle and half snort, till people on the streets turned round to stare, and the cook gave notice." And Granville-Barker, she adds, "gave [my mother] a long dissertation on the history, habits, idiosyncracies and antecedents of a character in *The Madras House,* all of which she was to convey to the audience by the significance with which she said her first line. The line was 'Good afternoon.'"

In the second decade of the century Miss Whitty still generally acted in several plays a year. She portrayed Peg Woffington in *The First Actress*; took roles in *Ready Money, The Grand Seigneur, Iris Intervenes*; was Mrs. Sharp in *The Passing of the Third Floor Back.* Although not a star as Ellen Terry was a star, she was seldom off the boards for any length of time. English critics who habitually paid more attention to the play than to the players, characterized her performances as "admirable," "splendid," "superb," and, as she grew into the portrayals of older personalities (she was over fifty when she played in *The Passing of the Third Floor Back* in 1917), delighted in pointing out that, no matter how bad the play, Miss Whitty always gave the excellent performance expected of her.

Between performances during the First World War the actress, as a prominent member of the Actresses Franchise League, helped to organize the Women's Emergency Corps, devoted to placing women in war work in hospital and factory. As the head of the W.E.C. she was instrumental in organizing workrooms for the disabled and conducted a successful campaign to raise funds for the Star and Garter Home for Disabled Sailors, Soldiers and Airmen. In recognition of her services, on January 1, 1918, King George V decorated May Whitty with the silver star and gold cross of the Order of the British Empire, conferring upon her the title of Dame Commander of the Order (equal in rank to Knight Commander).

At the age of seventy-five Dame May is said to have exclaimed, "Quit? Only the aged and infirm quit, and I am neither! So long as I can do my bit, I'll keep right on doing it!" It is not surprising, therefore, to find her in 1928 at the age of sixty-two touring South Africa in repertory with Zena Dare and later, in 1937, beginning a movie career at the age of seventy-one. (Ben Webster, who had previously acted with his wife in a number of plays, joined her in both ventures.) In 1920 she had toured as Lady Marsden in *Mr. Pim Passes By.* In 1921 she had undertaken the management of the Florence Etlinger Dramatic School. (This she relinquished about 1926.) And her successes in this period both before and after the South African tour included roles in Pinero's *The Enchanted Cottage,* Charles Pollock's *The Fool,* Frederick Lonsdale's *The Last of Mrs. Cheney,* Barrie's *Dear Brutus,* John van Druten's [44] *There's Always Juliet* (which she also did in New York), Granville-Barker's *The Voysey Inheritance,* and Ronald MacKenzie's *The Maitlands* with John Gielgud, who particularly commended her performance in his autobiography. Wrote a New York reviewer of *There's Always Juliet*: "Dame May Whitty, as Leonora's disapproving maid, catches with sure technique the exact degree of acid dignity needed to set a background to the cavortings of the lovers. This favorite English actress deserves to be seen in parts which offer a larger range for her matured skill." Ivor Brown said, "Dame May Whitty as the mother [Mrs. Surrege in *The Lake*] once more reveals her

charming ability to get under the skin of the English middle class. Most actresses would have tidied up the part of Mrs. Surrege and given it a quite unbourgeois polish and lacquer of theatrical smartness. Instead, it is played with extraordinary fidelity to the woolly-minded fact." Concluded the (London) *Saturday Review* concerning *The Ringmaster*: "Dame May Whitty, of course, could not put a wrong foot as the dear devoted mother who always appeared at the wrong moment and ventured the most tactless remarks."

Dame May's roles had changed since her first years in the theater, but they had changed to her liking. "I rather like playing terrors," she told an interviewer, "I really prefer playing taciturn, self-centered, fatuous individuals. I find they are fascinating to create, although they are much harder to act than docile, sweet types. And it amuses and compliments me to hear persons remark about such a performance: 'She certainly reminded me of Aunt Cora or Jim's sister,' showing that a really acid role gets far more attention than an old knitting grandmother." And the theater, too, was altered from the days of Irving and Terry, of Mansfield and the Kendals, she commented in 1932. "The individual giants of the stage when I first knew it were far more god-like and impressive than any actors and actresses of today, but the average of technical competence and professional accomplishment wasn't nearly so high. . . .In general, I believe that there is far more good acting on the English stage today than ever before. For one thing, the whole method of expression has changed. Emotion is now expressed by concealing it. The technique is far more difficult and calls for greater adroitness just as it calls for far more intelligence on the part of audiences to follow a modern play."

In 1935 Dame May scored one of the biggest triumphs of her career as Mrs. Bramson in Emlyn Williams' [41] *Night Must Fall.* Her performance, said the London critics, was "superb", "a masterpiece of subtlety." Brought to New York in 1936, it drew from the New York *American* reviewer the plaudit: "It has been the better part of a year and a half that Dame May Whitty has been paralyzed by fear of being assassinated some misty twilight by that ruthless psychopathic, Emlyn Williams, in his own evil invention, *Night Must Fall,* and for the better part of a year and a half, she has been going on giving that same admirable performance of the acidulous, miserly and fright-crazed hypochondriac, Mrs. Bramson." "Her performance," wrote the New York *Herald Tribune* critic, "might give many a younger and more languid actress pause. The scene in the last act where she finally rises from the wheel chair she has occupied all evening, strides vigorously around the stage and then bursts into wild hysterics, amazes those who know she is seventy-two years old." Of this same scene—and testifying to her vitality—Dame May said, "It leaves me breathless and a little gaspy for the rest of the act, but otherwise I feel no strain. I did it for a year in London, and my vocal chords seemed to take to it with ease. I never even had a touch of laryngitis. I don't think another year of it would bother me."

In 1937 the role of Mrs. Bramson launched the veteran actress on a film career with a

WHITTY, DAME MAY—*Continued*

performance which one critic called "a masterpiece that loses nothing in its transition from familiar stage to unfamiliar screen." Once before, in 1914, Dame May had appeared in a film, in the British-made *Enoch Arden* with Ben Webster and Gerald Lawrence. Since 1937 she has appeared on the screen in *Thirteenth Chair, The Lady Vanishes, Raffles,* the remake of *Bill of Divorcement, Suspicion, Mrs. Miniver, Slightly Dangerous, Lassie Come Home, Mme. Curie,* and others. (Most of the films were made under her MGM contract.) In 1945 she is a featured player in *My Name is Julia Ross,* in which, " a past master of the matronly facade hiding stark villainy," as Otis L. Guernsey, Jr., put it, she gives a "matchless performance." For her performance as Lady Belden in Mrs. Miniver she was nominated for an Academy Award, and in several of these films Ben Webster has played with her. Of the new medium Dame May said in 1938: "In a play you build brick by brick for your effect, slowly pyramiding to a climax, both in character and situation. In pictures you build bit by bit and these you do over and over again, first your close-ups and then for attitudes and camera angles. In a sense films are an unnatural medium, from the stage's point of view of logical development. It surprised me that I could step in after a lifetime of stage training, and have so little difficulty in portraying a character. I should have thought this was because I had already played the part on the stage if it were not that I played three other picture roles entirely new to me."

The 1945-46 season brought Dame May, now an octogenarian, again to the stage after an absence of five years. (She had last been seen as the nurse in Laurence Olivier's New York production of *Romeo and Juliet* in the spring of 1940.) *Thérèse* also marked the first professional alliance of May Whitty and Margaret Webster. In the early thirties mother and daughter had been associated non-professionally in a production of Thornton Wilder's '43 *The Long Christmas Dinner* for a Sunday night membership society in London; in August 1939 again in a tryout production of *Viceroy Sarah* for Bela Blau's theater in Deertrees, Maine; and in 1941 in the Experimental Theater's first production, Euripedes' *The Trojan Woman,* in which Margaret Webster both directed and acted the part of Andromache and Dame May played Hecuba. For this venture, recalls Margaret Webster, her mother, knowing how much she wanted "to establish the principle of experimental shows on the lines of the English membership societies . . . volunteered to come from Hollywood at her own expense to rehearse and play the tremendous part of Hecuba for two performances for nothing." In *Thérèse,* the Thomas Job adaptation of Emile Zola's *Thérèse Raquin,* Margaret Webster directs her mother (and Eva Le Gallienne '42 and Victor Jory) in what most of the critics considered a mediocre play but another May Whitty acting triumph, and a role which demands, in one entire scene, that Dame May "express herself only by the blazing hatred in her eyes." "Her performance" wrote Howard Barnes of the New York *Herald Tribune,* "makes this contemporary version of a theatrical antique something more than a clever and entertaining stunt. No matter what convolutions the plot takes in relating dark deeds, remorse and confession, she towers through the production with all the serenity she might have had in playing a great classic or modern tragedy. She quickens every scene of *Thérèse* with dramatic overtones which are not always discernible in the script." "She is so wonderful," said Burton Rascoe, "that tears of gratitude came into my eyes that I was privileged to see such art."

Since 1939 Dame May and Ben Webster have lived most of the time in Hollywood, where the actress is chairman of the British Actor's Orphanage and vice-president of the Los Angeles Branch of British War Relief. "In talking with the beloved couple," said one interviewer recently, "one gets the impression that their life together—their interest in the English children they have had brought to this country, their friends, the career of their daughter—all come before movie work. Wherever they go, they establish in their hotel rooms an air of hospitality with the inevitable teapot and cake and crumpets. They like to take quiet rooms overlooking a park. With typical English love for atmosphere and places, they can gaze for hours at a park whether it is covered in pale gray mist or splashed with sunshine. New York, says Dame May, has everything except fireplaces. Not near enough fireplaces. She loves America too—thinks its dentistry and architecture and fresh fruit are wonderful. But she doesn't understand women's clubs and is appalled by the funnies."

References

Christian Sci Mon p6 D 17 '43
N Y Herald Tribune V p3 O 10 '43; IV p1 O 7 '45
N Y Times II p1 O 7 '45
International Motion Picture Almanac, 1943-44
Who's Who, 1945
Who's Who in the Theatre (1939)

WILBY, FRANCIS B(OWDITCH) Apr. 24, 1883- United States Army officer
Address: c/o War Department, Washington, D.C.

In January 1942, when Major General Francis B. Wilby became wartime head of the United States Military Academy at West Point (known to the less rigorous Naval Academy as "Hell on the Hudson") he assumed command of a military school unique in the world. West Point is the only one in any major country, probably the only one in the world, which gives a full collegiate education, leading to a bachelor's degree as well as to an officer's commission. Another factor distinguishing the Academy from similar ones in other countries is that it is a general training school, rather than one for a specific branch of service; with one exception (Air Force officers), its graduates are expected to get such training at the special service schools, and, in as many cases as possible, at the Command and General Staff School, Army War College, and perhaps Army Industrial College. Still a third difference between the USMA and, for example, the Royal Military College of Canada and its British forerunners, is that West Point cadets are chosen from every class of society and are paid by the Government. To prevent any distinction by income, cadets are not allowed to handle any money, not even small change. (Oddly enough, the Japanese army training schools are similarly free and open to those physically and mentally qualified.) The thirty-ninth in a line of superintendents which includes Sylvanus Thayer, Robert E. Lee, and Douglas MacArthur '41, General Wilby was given the responsibility of directing the 143-year-old Academy during the Second World War.

Francis Bowditch Wilby was born in Detroit, Michigan, on April 24, 1883, the son of Richard Clark and Margaret Ann (Ingersoll) Wilby. *Who's Who in the Regular Army* gives his father's occupation as minister. After a year of study at Harvard University, eighteen-year-old Francis was appointed to the Academy from Massachusetts. At graduation in 1905, he stood third in his class, and as such was commissioned a second lieutenant in the Corps of Engineers. Wilby began service in September 1905 at Fort Leavenworth, Kansas. Next he worked on a survey in Wyoming; and after a pause at Fort Riley, Kansas, he sailed for four months' duty in Cuba, at the end of which, in June 1907, he was promoted to first lieutenant.

In September 1907, Wilby was sent to the Engineer School at Washington, D.C., from which he was graduated in 1908. After a land survey project in Rhode Island, he was stationed briefly at Washington Barracks, and then, in February 1909, went on duty in the Philippines. Wilby remained overseas for two years, including five months in Peking with the Military Information Division. Returning to Washington in March 1911, he was married that May to Dorothy Langfitt, whose father, William C. Langfitt, was an engineer lieutenant colonel in charge of river and harbor improvements and water supply. (The Wilbys have one son, Langfitt Bowditch.)

Wilby's second promotion, to captain, came in September 1912, when he was twenty-nine. At thirty-four he was a major, serving with the Ohio River Board in West Virginia; promoted one month after the United States declaration of war, he was raised again to the rank of lieutenant colonel (temporary) in August 1917, and sailed for France with the First Engineers. (At this time his father-in-law was General Pershing's AEF chief of staff.) After a short course at a French school, Colonel Wilby assumed command of the First Corps Engineer School. Leaving this post in February 1918, he was advanced to colonel (temporary) and assigned to the Office of the Chief Engineer overseas as assistant in charge of military operations. He spent five months there, another month at the front with the First Engineers, attached to the famous First Division, and then six months at Allied General Headquarters at Chaumont writing for and editing *Engineer Field Notes.* Wilby went to the First Army front in September and spent three weeks assisting the chief engineer in the Saint-Mihiel offensive. Then he was given command of the First Engineers and became division engineer, participating in the Meuse-Argonne offensive.

U. S. Army Signal Corps

MAJ. GEN. FRANCIS B. WILBY

Battles in which he participated include Cambrai and the Aisne-Marne. In all of these positions, Colonel Wilby "displayed unusual ability and professional attainments of a high order. . . . By his rare technical skill and knowledge, keen adaptability to all conditions, he contributed materially to the success of the First Division . . . in times and circumstances of the gravest importance," and was rewarded with the Croix de Guerre with Palm, the First Division's fourragère, and the Distinguished Service Medal with the citation quoted.

After the Armistice, Wilby served with the American forces in Germany. Returning to the United States in March 1919, he served in the National Guard Bureau, and then in September was assigned to the Office of the Chief of Engineers. In June 1920 Wilby reverted to his permanent rank of major, and in late 1921 he entered the School of the Line at Fort Leavenworth. Graduated with honors in June 1922, the thirty-nine-year-old officer went right on to the Command and General Staff School and then to the Army War College at Washington—taking the Army's highest training at one sitting, so to speak. After graduation from the War College in June 1924, Major Wilby worked four years on the War Department General Staff. Then he was promoted to lieutenant colonel and sent to Memphis, Tennessee, where he remained three years, as district engineer in charge of river and harbor work on the Mississippi River. Back in the Office of the Chief of Engineers, Colonel Wilby served three years, to June 1935, as chief of the military division; and then went back to river and harbor work as chief of the Gulf of Mexico Division, stationed at New Orleans, and member of the Mississippi River Commission. In November 1938 the Colonel assumed command of the North Atlantic Division Engineers, with headquarters in New York City.

(*Continued next page*)

WILBY, FRANCIS B.—*Continued*

In October 1939 Wilby was designated chief of staff of the First Army, under General Hugh A. Drum [41], with headquarters on Governor's Island in New York harbor. A year later, when the Army was being expanded by the induction of draftees, he was made a brigadier general (temporary)—at a time when many outstanding generals of the Second World War were still wearing eagles and oak leaves on their shoulders. In this post, his "brilliant planning, remarkable ability for organizing . . . supplemented by resourcefulness and ingenuity" won him the Legion of Merit (awarded five years later, in March 1945).

In June 1941, General Wilby was given command of the First Corps Area, with headquarters in Boston, and that September he was made a major general. In January 1942, with the United States at war, Wilby relieved Major General Robert L. Eichelberger [43] as superintendent of the United States Military Academy—abbreviated officially as USMA, and informally as West Point or simply the Point.

"In theory," writes Henry F. Pringle in *Collier's*, "the Academy is run by the superintendent and his staff under the supervision of the War Department. Actually, I am convinced, it is run by a permanent group of officers called the Academic Board. This is composed of the heads of the various collegiate departments, [all colonels], the superintendent, and two or three other officers. Their devotion to West Point is sincere and complete. So, I suspect, is their control. I don't think any superintendent, whose assignment to the institution is normally for four years, would cross swords with the Academic Board [of which most members are appointed for life]. I doubt that the War Department would oppose its will." "Is West Point any good?" Pringle had asked in 1940, and answered himself, "That depends on what you want. If it is an institution which turns out men of honor, men of intelligence, men who believe in tradition, men who are brave—why then, West Point is very good indeed . . . If you want a West Point tuned up to immediate combat, to tanks and parachute troops and totalitarian efficiency and lightning thrusts and mechanization and horror and death—why then, West Point is not much good." This objection, which has been raised by others, arises partly from misunderstanding of or disagreement with the basic policy governing West Point—that it is, to quote *Life*, "a college for the training of next war's generals, not a training camp for this war's shavetails." Superintendent Eichelberger, however, began a program of modernization which was carried further under Wilby.

In 1942 Wilby invited criticism of the shortened curriculum from a board of consultants which included Ernest M. Hopkins [44] and Karl T. Compton [41], the presidents, respectively, of Dartmouth College and the Massachusetts Institute of Technology. The board reported that it was "greatly impressed by the thoroughness of the instruction, the alertness of the students, and the excellence in balance between the discussion allowed the students . . . and the more formal aspect of recitation and instruction. . . . There is no justification for the popular conception that West Point instruction is rigid, steryotyped, and regimented." In August of that year, 1942, Stewart Field, the "Wings of West Point," was dedicated; and although "still in the turmoil of excavation, grading, and building," it went into immediate operation. Since then, to quote the commanding officer, "Flying instruction continued, flying officers were graduated, and flying in general proceeded normally even though contractors, heavy trucks, shovels, and graders were as numerous as planes on the airfield scene." At Stewart, which is larger than New York's LaGuardia [40] Field, certain enlisted men were trained; all cadets were required to fly at least five hours as air observers; and those cadets who chose to specialize in flying were given a complete and rigorous training. "Of the 514 officers who graduated from the Military Academy on June 1, 1943, there were 206 who wore the silver wings of the Army Air Forces. These were the first men to wear wings earned in training received entirely at Stewart Field." "In order to spare the time for the necessary hours of advanced flying training," General Wilby explained, "this class took a concentrated one-month course covering academic subjects for the entire year. These included military history, economics, government, law, ordnance, and some engineering." Another long-standing need was met in June 1943, when construction was finished at Camp Popolopen, "several thousand acres of rugged country" adjoining the Academy grounds.

In September 1945 Wilby was made commanding General of Fort Belvoir, Virginia. Toward the end of the year it was announced that the General was planning to retire early in 1946.

Reference

Who's Who in America, 1944-45

WILCOX, HERBERT *See* Neagle, A. and Wilcox, H.

WILSON, EDMUND May 8, 1895- Critic; author

Address: b. c/o The New Yorker, 25 W. 43d St., New York City

Edmund Wilson, author of several distinguished books of social and literary criticism, has for several years been considered one of America's leading critics. He has been called the foremost "intellectual's intellectual" in the United States, his reputation overshadowed only by that of T. S. Eliot. Dissenting opinion has termed him negative rather than dynamic, "of the second order of attainment rather than the first," accused him of confusions and reversals of judgment. In answer to this, his admirers have upheld him as "independent" and "a character in continuous evolution."

Edmund Wilson, who has called himself a "typical specimen of the current American bourgeoisie," was born in Red Bank, New Jersey, May 8, 1895, the son of Edmund and Helen Mather (Kimball) Wilson. His family for several generations on both sides belonged to the learned professions. None were rich, but all were comfortably well off. His grandfather's family, of Puritan stock, had emigrated from Massachusetts to Talcottville in upstate

New York, where the Wilson children used to go for summer vacations.

Edmund's father was a lawyer, at one time Attorney General of New Jersey, whose independence and "distrust of big business" confined his practice to local clients. The boy grew up in moderate prosperity: "I have been put through the same sort of mill as all the other young bourgeois Americans of my generation," he says. He went to Hill School, Pottstown, Pennsylvania from 1909 to 1912. "At boarding school and college," he writes, "I used to react violently against this mill, but except by expressing heretical opinions I never tried to revolt against it." His literary and critical talents were early evident. He was one of the editors of the school magazine, and later edited the literary magazine at Princeton University, which he entered in 1912. At Princeton (he took his B.A. there in 1916) his close friends were F. Scott Fitzgerald and the poet John Peale Bishop.

After his graduation the young man went to New York to work and to write. There he became a reporter on the New York *Evening Sun* (1916-17), but, he has said, "It seemed to me that my life in New York was college all over again." Consequently, when the First World War broke out, he enlisted. "Not because I cared much about the war," he says, "but because—aside from the social pressure— I wanted to get away from my old life." For this reason, too, he enlisted as a private instead of going to an officers' training camp, as most of his friends did. Although he disliked Army life intensely, he felt that his relations with others at least were real in a way they had not been in school and college. He served in France with Base Hospital Unit 36, and with the Intelligence Corps from August 1917 to July 1919. "One day in France, sick in bed," he tells, "I swore to myself that when the war was over I should stand outside society altogether. I should do without the comforts and amenities of the conventional world altogether, and I should devote myself to the great human interests which transcend standards of living and convention: Literature, History, the Creation of Beauty, the Discovery of Truth."

After the war Wilson returned to New York to become managing editor of *Vanity Fair* (1920-21). With John Peale Bishop he wrote *The Undertaker's Garland* (1922)—satiric and humorous descriptions of deaths and funerals, written in both verse and prose. "Nothing in the book," wrote Gilbert Seldes [41], "gives evidence of haste or indolence or contempt for the practiced art."

In 1926 Wilson joined the editorial staff of the *New Republic*, writing for the book review section. He resigned as an associate editor in 1931 to devote himself to his own writing, but remained as a contributing editor. He had, meanwhile, published three books. In *Discordant Encounters* (1927), a group of plays and dialogues concerning the battle between the old and the new in our social forces, Clifton Fadiman [41] discerned "wit and lucidity and sweetness." A book of lyrics with a few prose sketches, *Poets, Farewell* (1929), won little attention, but some praise for its "swift, slashing satire."

By 1931 Edmund Wilson had turned his attention to social and literary criticism. While

EDMUND WILSON

some reviewers have felt that his viewpoint and conclusions with regard to social criticism have been less objective, less consistent than his work in the field of letters, his study of social, economic, and political happenings has contributed a background of understanding to the work of contemporary writers. In his preface to *Axel's Castle* (1931) he stated his ideas of what literary criticism ought to be: "A history of man's ideas and imaginings in the setting of the conditions which have shaped them."

Axel's Castle established Edmund Wilson as one of America's important literary critics; Henry Hazlitt said that the book was "destined to exercise a deeper influence on American criticism than any volume since *A Book of Prefaces*" (Mencken, 1918). With "an intelligence that is alert, informed, and catholic to a degree rarely found in contemporary criticism" (William Troy in the *Nation*), Wilson's essays in this volume were studies of the effect of the Symbolist movement on Yeats, Valery, T. S. Eliot, Proust, Joyce, Gertrude Stein, Villiers de l'Isle-Adam, and Rimbaud. Symbolism, a reaction against naturalism, first appeared in poetry: each poet sought the special language or symbols peculiarly suited to his individuality. Poetry, indeed, became so much a "private concern" that it was often incomprehensible to the reader.

The American Jitters—a Year of the Slump (1932), the first of Wilson's social surveys, covered the months from October 1930 to December 1931. It was in the main a study of moral and ethical standards in the United States during the depression. The author discovered that "class antagonism, conflicts, and injustices are real, that they rarely get any publicity, that the class on top virtually controls the organs of publicity, that the capacities of human nature for remaining blind to the consequences of its actions where its comfort and prestige are concerned are so great that it cannot usually be induced even to notice what it is up to without a violent jolt from below, and that there is no hope for genuine decency and fair play

WILSON, EDMUND—*Continued*

except from a society where classes are abolished." For these reasons, Wilson concluded, there was not much hope for a "liberal" solution. He turned instead to Russia, where he saw "a great new movement of creative thought and culture in a classless society." He admired the Russian leaders because they "are men of superior brains who have triumphed over the ignorance, the stupidity, and the shortsighted selfishness of the mass." He advised writers that it was bad for their art to try to adapt themselves to capitalism, the enemy of art; that it was healthier for them to contribute their talents to Communist aims than to be content to express a purely personal viewpoint.

Growing enthusiasm for Russia took Edmund Wilson on a visit to that country from May to October 1935. His impressions were set down in his book, *Travels in Two Democracies* (1936). A study in contrasts, the first part was a continuation of the American scene during the depression years. The Russian half of the book was considered by such critics as Malcolm Cowley "more favorable to the Soviets than anyone would guess from the separately printed extracts." Edmund Wilson liked the Russian people: "It is much easier to establish friendly relations with Russians than with the people of any other country I know." In the cities he found the people badly dressed, but earnest and enthusiastic. "The crowds moved . . . as if the whole city belonged to them." Wilson was much impressed, too, by the prestige which literature and writers commanded. "Literature is one of the things for which the Russians have a special national genius. . . .Nowhere else in the world does a writer receive so much honor."

One trying but illuminating experience was the six weeks Wilson spent, ill with scarlet fever, in a free but poorly kept hospital in Odessa. The attendants were courteous and kind, but, he discovered, if one wanted anything done, he "had to go to a Communist for action." The strongest impression he got in Russia was "one of extraordinary heroism. . . . You feel you are at the moral top of the world where the light never really goes out." Many critics felt that America, pictured too darkly, came off second best in the study of the two democracies. "It is assuredly not a fair comparison of the systems and the countries," wrote R. L. Duffus.

Back home, Wilson turned to literary concerns again. *This Room and This Gin and These Sandwiches* (1937), a book of three "experimental" plays, was followed in 1938 by *The Triple Thinkers*. These essays included an attack on the critic Paul Elmer More; a discussion of verse as a "dying technique"; a eulogy of the Russian poet Pushkin; an analysis of the work of Henry James; praise for Shaw [44] as a dramatist, but not as a social and political philosopher; and a concluding essay on Marxism and literature. In the latter Wilson reversed his former dicta, including some of the statements made in *Travels in Two Democracies*. There was literature in the Soviet Union, he now said, when "Lenin and Trotsky worked sincerely to keep literature free." But, under Stalin [42], "unliterary and uncultured himself," literature was "a means of manipulating a population." The practice of the deliberate

falsification of social and political history "has attained fantastic proportions." Harold Strauss found *The Triple Thinkers* "stimulating from cover to cover," while T. C. Wilson felt that "Mr. Wilson has spent his time trying to prove a thesis which both the examples he cites and the more representative ones he ignores, refute. For critical inquiry and judgment he has substituted the easier labors of irresponsible prophecy."

During the middle 'thirties there were indications that Edmund Wilson's readers were discovering conflict, contradiction, and change in his social, political, and literary judgments—a reversed political viewpoint reflected in his various writings. In 1932 he had greatly admired the Russians, had found Stalin "running Russia fairly and sensibly." In 1937 he declared that "one of the worst drawbacks of being a Stalinist is that you have to defend so many falsehoods." Among those intellectuals who, like himself, were undergoing disillusionment with regard to Russia's role in world affairs, Wilson was praised for his "integrity of character, his refusal to swallow any political faith or formula." Other critics expressed themselves less certain of the stability or independence of his judgments. Wrote John Abbot Clark: "In view of Wilson's critical confusions, his about-faces . . . his exhortations first to this and then almost immediately to its diametrical opposite, many of his readers have just about given up all expectations of finding in his writings either 'an intelligent basis of taste' or 'an intelligible point of view.'"

To the Finland Station (1940) was a study of the European revolutionary movement: its beginnings with Vico and Michelet; its decline in Renan, Taine, and Anatole France; its socialistic period with Babeuf, Saint-Simon, Fourier, and Owen; its theoretical apogee in Marx and Engels; its anarchist deviation in Bakunin; its activist phase in Lenin and Trotsky. Wilson upheld Trotsky as "the successor of Lenin, pursued from country to country, hounded and persecuted," and bitterly condemned the Stalin regime. "We have seen the State that Trotsky helped to build in a phase combining the butcheries of the Robespierre Terror with the corruption and reaction of the Directory." Said Lewis Gannett [41]: "As brilliant and muddled a book as one may meet." Louis Hacker found it "the most discerning guide to the faith and vision of communism that we have." Howard Mumford Jones called the work "ponderous and even sluggish. For once Mr. Wilson is erudite and solid rather than erudite and brilliant."

Leaving Russia, Wilson turned to the California group of American writers, *The Boys in the Back Room* (1941). Of this group, which stemmed "originally from Hemingway," he found James M. Cain the best. John O'Hara [41] was less successful, his *Pal Joey* being "a little amoeba-monster." Saroyan [40], he said, also derived from Hemingway (Saroyan in an essay later denied this, saying his influence was Shaw), that he had real merit, but must avoid the danger of becoming merely a columnist. He praised Hans Otto Storm's earlier work; found Nathanael West the first writer to catch "the emptiness of Hollywood" and to "make this emptiness horrible"; said that F. Scott Fitzgerald had written before his death "a substantial part of what promised to be by all odds the best novel ever devoted to Hollywood." Wilson found in Steinbeck'[40] only one thing constant: his "preoccupation with biology," his presentation of life in animal terms, which was at the bottom of his relative unsuccess in representing human beings. Clifton Fadiman praised in particular this essay as an "illuminating job of literary criticism."

The Wound and the Bow (1941) had the best critical reception of any of Wilson's books since *Axel's Castle.* "Seven of the most resourceful, and among them four of the best essays that Mr. Wilson has yet written," and "its solid virtues will enhance his fame as one of the best literary critics now writing," were among the comments. The book's title was derived from the legend of Philoctetes, who was equipped with an invincible bow, but also handicapped by an incurable wound. From this premise Wilson psychoanalytically interpreted the dualism of certain writers: Dickens and Kipling at length; with briefer glances at Casanova, Edith Wharton, Hemingway, and Joyce.

A collection of verse and some prose pieces, *Notebooks of Night,* appeared in 1942. Robert Penn Warren said the verses were of "uneven quality," with patches of conventional and sentimental writing, but Mary Colum, one of Wilson's most unwavering admirers, considered "practically every poem" in the volume interesting. John Chamberlain'[40] found the prose pieces adept: "Mr. Wilson's subconscious mind is prolific of strangely beautiful stuff." In 1943 Wilson edited an anthology, *The Shock of Recognition,* pieces selected to show the development of literature in the United States, excluding all criticism and comment "which is not written by men who themselves have contributed to our literature." In 1945 he edited a volume of Scott Fitzgerald's unpublished sketches, notebooks, letters, and doggerel, entitled *The Crack-Up,* which Wilson characterized as "an autobiographical sequence which vividly puts on record his [Fitzgerald's] state of mind and his point of view during the latter years of his life." Wilson's *Memoirs of Hecate County,* a book of short stories, was announced for publication early in 1946.

In January 1944 Edmund Wilson succeeded Clifton Fadiman as literary critic of the *New Yorker.* Fadiman's urbane wit and ebullient brilliance had set a precedent which, some readers felt, would be difficult for any incoming critic to match. Characteristically, Wilson made no effort to give *New Yorker* readers what they thought they wanted. He meant to say exactly what he wished to say about a book, whether a best seller or by a little known writer. In his first three reviews he dismissed with firm scorn Harold Nicholson's *The Desire To Please;* he found *Cannery Row* the one book by Steinbeck he most enjoyed; he called Joyce's *Stephen Hero* "the most important document on Joyce's life yet made public."

Best sellers in general throughout 1944 were to feel the Wilsonian ax: Kay Boyle's'[42] *Avalanche,* "nothing but a piece of pure rubbish"; of Louis Bromfield's'[44] *What Became of Anna Bolton:* "He has gradually made his way into the fourth rank, where his place is now secure." He had good words, however, for Van Wyck Brooks's'[41] *The World of Washington Irving,* Joseph Wood Krutch's *Samuel Johnson,* and Jan Karski's *Story of a Secret State.*

Wilson occasionally singled out for comment work by writers almost unknown. Anaïs Nin's'[44] book of experimental surrealist short stories, *Under a Glass Bell,* printed by the author herself, he praised as "really beautiful little pieces." Salvador Dali's'[40] *Hidden Faces,* however, he called "one of the most old-fashioned novels that anybody has written in years."

In his *New Yorker* department Wilson aroused the greatest reader interest through his series, *Why Do People Read Detective Stories?* The first of these, condemning detective fiction, including that of Rex Stout, Agatha Christie'[40], Ngaio Marsh, Dorothy Sayers and Dashiel Hammett, brought letters, he says, "in a volume and of a passionate earnestness which had hardly been elicited even by my occasional criticism of the Soviet Union." Most of these mystery fans said he had not read the right ones. Their preferences were most divergent, but Dorothy Sayers was at the top, whereupon Wilson read *The Nine Tailors:* "It seems to be one of the dullest books I have ever encountered in any field." Bernard De Voto '[43] (in *Harper's* for December 1944) lamented Wilson's "patronizing and academic approach: Will Mr. Wilson be so good as to stop asking Mr. Stout to be Proust?" Wilson went on to criticize Ngaio Marsh, "whom Mr. De Voto says writes excellent prose. . . .This throws for me a good deal of light on Mr. De Voto's opinions as a critic." His final conclusion: The reading of detective stories is simply "a kind of vice that . . . ranks somewhere between crossword puzzles and smoking. . . .There is no need to bore ourselves with this rubbish." Toward the end of the controversy he admitted that he had turned his attention to A. Conan Doyle and had succeeded in finding pleasure in Sherlock Holmes because it is "literature on a humble but ignoble level, whereas the mystery writers most in vogue are not."

The critic-author is described as quiet, shy, absent-minded, as having reflective brown eyes under a wide brow, and a small, gentle mouth. In 1938 he was married to Mary McCarthy, his third wife, also a writer and critic, whose reviews and articles have appeared in the *Nation* and other periodicals. They have a "polysyllabic" son, Reuel, and live in a Cape Cod house in Wellfleet, Massachusetts.

References

New Repub 81:133 D 12 '34
Wilson Lib Bul 5:484 Ap '31 por
Who's Who in America, 1944-45
Wilson, E. American Jitters (1932);
Travels in Two Democracies (1936)

WILSON, EUGENE E(DWARD) Aug. 21, 1887- Aircraft executive; author

Address: b. United Aircraft Corp., East Hartford, Conn.; h. 1844 Albany Ave., West Hartford, Conn.

The aviation executive, Eugene E. Wilson, who is author of *Air Power for Peace* (1945), believes that the world is on the threshold of the "Age of Flight." As vice-chairman of the United Aircraft Corporation and president of the Aircraft Industries Association, he is a leading spokesman for the American aircraft

John Haley

EUGENE E. WILSON

industry. In 1930 Wilson terminated a twenty-five-year naval career, which had covered the pioneering stages of naval aviation, to enter the manufacturing field of aeronautics. He has since been associated with significant engineering developments, including the controllable pitch propeller, the two-seat dive bomber, the long-range fighter-bomber, and the high-powered, air-cooled radial engines.

Eugene Talmadge and Clara (Pomeroy) Wilson were pioneers of the Northwest who finally settled in the small town of Dayton, Washington. There, on August 21, 1887, their son Eugene Edward Wilson was born. Eugene and his father, who was a great sportsman, were "inseparable in and out of doors." When the boy was ten the family moved to Helena, Montana, where he spent the summers on a ranch, learning to handle a rifle and absorbing the spirit of the old West. During this period he became a photography enthusiast, using the then new Brownie camera for nature studies.

In 1902 the Wilsons moved back to Seattle, where Eugene Wilson made the acquaintance of Captain Dorr F. Tozier of the United States Revenue Cutter Service. As the Captain's summer guest, the young man cruised in the waters of Puget Sound and southeastern Alaska. Wilson believes that this experience influenced his choice of a career, for, upon graduation from the Seattle High School in 1904, he entered the United States Naval Academy at Annapolis. "I felt a Western boy should go East and vice versa, and this looked like a good school," he has remarked. At Annapolis Wilson joined the rifle team, which won the national championship at Camp Perry in 1909. His class was the last required to go to sea for two years as passed midshipmen before being commissioned as ensigns. In the class were three candidates named Wilson, which caused confusion in the records of the promotion examination, and Eugene Wilson was left off the list of those passing. But this was quickly corrected; he was graduated twenty-first in a class of two hundred and twenty, and awarded the "Class

of 1871" prize sword for excellence in practical and theoretical ordnance and gunnery.

Wilson joined the destroyer flotilla, in which he was soon given command of the *Truxton*. But in 1913 he was ordered to Annapolis for postgraduate training, after which he attended Columbia University. There he studied engineering under Charles Edward Lucke, who, says Wilson, "set out to teach us to think." After winning his M.A. in 1915 (Columbia gave no scientific degrees at that time), Wilson was assigned to the *Arkansas.* In short order he became the ship's chief engineer, in which capacity he developed a new system of distilling sea water through waste auxiliary exhaust steam. This economical process gained wide usage, but its inventor narrowly escaped punishment for "unauthorized alteration of the power plant."

During the First World War Wilson served in the United States Sixth Battle Squadron of the British Grand Fleet and was present when the Germans surrendered to this unit at Rosyth on November 21, 1918. His book of verse, *Comrades of the Mist and Other Rhymes of the Grand Fleet,* was published early in 1919. On his return from the war zone that year the officer was given command of the Aviation Mechanics School at the Naval Training Station at Great Lakes, Illinois. Here he met Captain William A. Moffett, who was determined to organize a bureau of aeronautics in the Navy Department and invited Wilson to join him in the project in Washington. The latter, however, had to complete a tour of sea duty, and through Moffett's intercession was assigned to commission the *Wright,* a new "kite balloon and seaplane tender." For a year and a half he cruised with the naval air force in the Caribbean. Then, in June 1922 Wilson was assigned to the United States International Rifle Team to participate in the international matches in Italy the following September. The team won the world championship. Commenting on this experience, Wilson says, "I learned here, however, that the last thing we can expect to accomplish from international sports competition is international friendship. Only the fear of spoiling the score prevented some of the competitors from wasting a few record shots on each other."

Two years after the Navy's Bureau of Aeronautics was created, Wilson in 1924 was appointed chief of the engine section by Moffett, now an admiral. He was called upon to do some writing for the Admiral, who, according to Wilson, "never did read any of the articles or speeches prepared for him but let us know that if it turned out all right that was one for him, but if it turned out wrong that would be too bad for us." During this period Wilson was instrumental in the development of the air-cooled radial engine, which had been considered by many an impossible task. But with Admiral Moffett's support, Wilson's program was carried through successfully, illustrating again, he believes, the effectiveness of competitive private industry. For several years Wilson had been anxious to train as a naval aviator, although he was beyond the age limit of twenty-eight. He finally requested sea duty, but, when such orders were issued, Admiral Moffett, instead of releasing him for this, granted him two months' leave in which to qualify as a pilot, with the provision that he remain in the Bureau afterward. In those two months in 1926 Wilson completed the nine months' course at the Naval Air Station at Pensacola, Florida, including over a hundred hours of student solo flying, and became a naval aviator at the age of thirty-nine.

Having earned his wings, he returned to the Bureau, to be put in charge of the design section. At this time the half-finished battle cruisers *Lexington* and *Saratoga*, which Moffett had "salvaged" from the Washington Disarmament Conference, were being converted into aircraft carriers. Wilson was responsible for developing new airplanes around new engines for these vessels. When the work was in progress he was appointed chief of staff to Admiral J. M. Reeves, commander of the battle fleet's aircraft squadrons. Wilson soon qualified for his deck landings and then proceeded to assist in the organization, training, and development of the carrier squadrons. Participating in broad naval operations, Wilson reports, "We were able to run the gantlet of the entire Atlantic and Pacific fleets with the *Saratoga* and attack the Panama Canal from one hundred and fifty miles at sea." This operation "represented the first application of the carrier-cruiser task force idea and the utilization of aircraft as the long-range striking force."

Wilson's next assignment came in May 1929, when he became aviation aide on the staff of the commander in chief of the battle fleet. The following fall Commander Wilson was offered the presidency of the Hamilton Standard Propellers Corporation, a subsidiary of the United Aircraft and Transport Corporation. Surprised by the offer, the naval officer was initially inclined to disregard it, but he says, "The more I thought about it the more I wondered if this lack of interest did not signify an unwillingness to give up the security of a naval career in exchange for the hazards of civil life." But he finally accepted the position, "more in a spirit of bravado than from rationalization," he admits, adding, "some of this may have come down from the pioneers." Upon assuming his new position with the Pittsburgh aircraft concern in January 1930, Wilson encountered "tough sledding" at the outset of the depression. He decided to undertake the development of a new propeller which had been patented by Hamilton's chief engineer, Frank W. Caldwell. Despite active opposition, this project was successful and won for Caldwell and the company the coveted Collier Trophy for achievement in aviation for the year 1933.

When Wilson accepted the presidency of another United subsidiary, the Sikorsky ⁴⁰ Aircraft Company, in the summer of 1930, he was again faced with a precarious industrial situation. The company suffered losses when it built the first three Clippers (S-40's) for Pan American Airways, and got in serious financial straits. Wilson suggested a study of a new high performance plane designed around the new controllable pitch propeller. Such a project was begun, and culminated in the S-42 Pan American Clippers which made pioneer Atlantic and Pacific crossings. With the death of the head of the Chance Vought Corporation, Wilson assumed leadership and was thus president of three of United's subsidiaries. When this last company was reorganized, it built the

first two-seat dive bomber and eventually produced the Corsair fighter-bomber. These aircraft, based on Wilson's fleet operating experiences, proved their value. By 1937 Wilson was senior vice-president of United Aircraft and had begun developing a research division. (In the April 1944 issue of *Aeronautical Engineering*, Caldwell, then United's director of research, discussed the vast engineering and technical work conducted under the company's four operating divisions [Pratt & Whitney, Hamilton, Chance Vought, and Sikorsky].) In 1945 Wilson considered that the organization period for the research division was practically at an end.

When the president of the company became ill in 1939 Wilson became acting chief executive, and with the death of the former the next year he was elected president. He was thus to head the aircraft concern during most of the period of acceleration brought about by the war, when the company reached its peak of production. Late in 1943 the executive relinquished the presidency to devote himself to the duties of vice-chairman. He foresaw probable threats to the aircraft industry with the end of the war, and in 1944 he and other leaders of the industry reconstituted the Aeronautical Chamber of Commerce and issued a statement of policy. As chairman of the organization's Board of Governors, the former naval man played a prominent part in the formulation of its policies. In April 1944 their recommendation for American air power policy was issued. The resolution states that "The United States should maintain an air power sufficient not only to win this war but also to keep the peace: 1) by maintaining adequate air forces at such strength and in such state of readiness as to preclude a successful assault upon our country or its possessions; 2) by acquiring and maintaining air bases essential to our security and that of overseas trade; 3) by facilitating the orderly and economic expansion of domestic and international air transport and of private flying; 4) by preserving a strong aircraft manufacturing industry." Wilson, in testifying before a subcommittee of the Senate Military Affairs Committee in July 1944, stressed the industry's desire for an air power policy, and recommended new legislation "restating as national policy the principle of advancing technological development of aviation through competitive private industry."

In response to what he termed "a crying need for a specific analysis of the role of air power in world affairs, based upon its history," the industrialist wrote *Air Power for Peace*, which was published in April 1945. Summarizing the history of American aviation between two wars, the work details the author's two major concepts: "One, the trinity of air power comprising air force, air commerce, and aircraft industry, and, two, the broad new concept of the economics of air power and its potentialities with respect to the peace." Pronounced in general by critics "a book of merit," the volume was called by the reviewer for *Aviation News* "delightful and solidly informative reading." In his review in the *Book-of-the-Month Club News*, Brigadier General Donald Armstrong wrote: "With notable economy of space, in a language intelligible to the layman, he [Wilson] describes the nature, purpose,

WILSON, EUGENE E.—*Continued*

and use of air power in war and peace. . . .His analysis . . . is a welcome example of objective thinking and reasoning in a field too often disturbed by excessive enthusiasm." Commander A. F. Bonnalie in *U. S. Air Services* commented: "For the first time it makes it possible for the layman to grasp an understanding of the most potent power of this age . . . it is not light reading; on the contrary it is strong medicine, vital thought-provoking comments abound in its pages." According to another critic, in *Air Power for Peace* Wilson "reaches beyond the horizons of most thinkers on the arts and problems of flight."

In May 1942 the executive delivered the commencement address at Trinity College, which awarded him an honorary Doctor of Science degree. In December 1943 he again served as a commencement speaker, this time at Rensselaer Polytechnic Institute, and was awarded an honorary Doctor of Engineering degree. Wilson's articles have been published in *Aviation, Popular Mechanics,* and *Flying.* His addresses to the Union League Club of Chicago and the Economic Club of New York have been reprinted in *Vital Speeches.* In a radio address on August 29, 1945 he predicted an 80 per cent reduction in the size of the aircraft industry and again called for "a definite public policy on production and development of research." Wilson has wide business connections; he is a director of the Hartford Electric Light Company, the Hartford National Bank and Trust Company, the Aetna Life Insurance Company, and the Southern New England Telephone Company. A Republican, the executive is president of the Aircraft Industries Association of America and the Navy Industrial Association. He is a fellow of the Royal Aeronautical Society of Great Britain, a member of the Institute of Aeronautical Sciences and the American Society of Naval Engineers. His clubs are the Army and Navy (Washington, D.C.), the Hartford Golf Club, Anglers', the Clove Valley Rod and Gun Club, and the New York Yacht Club.

Mrs. Wilson is the former Genevieve Speer of Illinois, whom he married on February 7, 1911. Still an eager photographer, Wilson uses principally 16mm kodachrome. He combined his out-of-doors interests with photography in 1942 when he wrote an article for the *National Geographic* about a favorite fishing haunt, illustrated by his pictures. Entitled "Anticostia Island, Nugget of the North," it is the story of a privately owned island at the mouth of the St. Lawrence River which has served in succession as "an explorer's reward, a pirate's stronghold, a rich man's social experiment, a pulpwood empire, and a sportsman's paradise." "I have found that I need to get in among the trees and relax in order to see the forest," he has said. In reflecting upon a career which has included revolutionary developments in aviation, Eugene Wilson asks, "What better pioneering could a man ask?"

References

Blue Book of American Aviation, 1940
Who's Who in America, 1944-45
Who's Who in Aviation, 1942-43

WITOS, WINCENTY (vě'tôs věn-tsěn'tǐ) 1874—Oct. 31, 1945 Polish statesman; considered a leader of Polish democratic elements; member of Galician Diet (1908-14); prime minister of Poland in 1920-21 and again from 1923 to 1926; lived in voluntary exile for thirteen years after 1926; vice-president of the Polish National Council; helped form the present Polish Provisional Government.

Obituary

N Y Times p23 N 1 '45 por

WOODHOUSE, (MARGARET) CHASE GOING 1890- United States Representative from Connecticut; economist; educator

Address: b. House of Representatives Old Office Bldg., Washington, D.C.; h. 751 Williams St., New London, Conn.

Of the three new women Representatives (all Democrats) whom the voters sent to the Seventy-ninth Congress of the United States, Chase Going Woodhouse of Connecticut's Second District is generally described as the most politically experienced. As a college professor on leave, she may also be said to have the greatest theoretical background. Her election, concurrent with that of Emily Taft Douglas [45] of Illinois, causes the Nutmeg State to share with Illinois the title of first state to have two women Representatives in Congress at the same time.

The only child of Harriet (Jackson) Going and Seymour Going, a prominent mining and railroad man of Alaska and the Canadian Northwest, Margaret Chase Going was born in 1890 on Canadian soil, in Victoria, British Columbia. After graduation in 1908 from Science Hill School at Shelbyville, Kentucky, Chase Going returned to Canada to study at McGill University, where she received her B.A. degree in 1912 and her M.A. the following year. After graduation she began her social work. The young economist went to Germany for advanced work at the University of Berlin (she has also studied in England), returning after the outbreak of the First World War to continue at the University of Chicago. When the United States entered the war in April 1917, Miss Going was a fellow in political economy at the university. That June she was married to Edward James Woodhouse, a professor of government.

While Professor Woodhouse was in the United States service his wife was an instructor at Smith College, where one of her students was a future Congressional colleague: Jessie Sumner [45] of Illinois. In 1918 Mrs. Woodhouse was advanced to assistant professor of economics, and in 1920 to associate professor. She also began to teach during the summer at the Smith School for Social Work. Her two children were born during this period: Noel Robert Seymour in September 1921, and Margaret Wark in January 1925. Later that year Mrs. Woodhouse joined the Department of Agriculture staff as senior economist in charge of the Bureau of Home Economics' Division of Economics. She continued her summer school work, and has taught at the universities of Oregon, Texas, and Iowa, the Vassar Institute of Euthenics, and the Teachers College of Columbia University, as well as at Smith.

After three years in the Civil Service, Mrs. Woodhouse became in 1928 the director of personnel at the Woman's College of the University of North Carolina. With Mrs. Jouett Shouse, formerly of the Department of Labor, she founded the Institute of Women's Professional Relations to study the status of working women and the needs of employers and to keep the students and colleges posted on curriculum needs. As managing director of the institute, Mrs. Woodhouse has had to meet a payroll every month since 1928, as her campaign posters were later to point out. She also edits the institute's various technical studies and survey results and the quarterly publication, *Women's Work and Education.*

In 1929 and 1930 the Canadian-born professor was also North Carolina State chairman of research for the Federation of Business and Professional Women's Clubs. In that year of 1930 a bibliography Mrs. Woodhouse had compiled was published, followed two years later by *After College—What?* and in 1934 by *Dentistry, Its Professional Opportunities.* From 1932 to 1933 Mrs. Woodhouse served as vice-president of the College Personnel Association, and from 1933 to 1937 she was the national president of Altrusa Clubs, in which connection she has twice made trips to Mexico. She was also active in the League of Women Voters, the American Home Economics Association, and the American Sociological Society, and contributed to various professional journals.

In 1934 Mrs. Woodhouse left the University of North Carolina to become professor of economics at Connecticut College. She continued her interest in the Southern Women's Educational Alliance, however, and became a board member as well as being elected to the board of the Carnegie Foundation's National Occupational Conference. In that year, too, she and Mrs. Shouse began the annual Institute of Women's Professional Relations conferences in Washington, at which employers and Government representatives meet with educators and students, and which have made her a familiar figure in the Capital. From 1936 to 1937, and again from 1938 to 1939, the economist was fellowship chairman of the Rhode Island-Connecticut Federation of the American Association of University Women. Her *Business Opportunities for the Home Economist* was published in 1938.

Two years later Mrs. Woodhouse, who was president of the Connecticut Federation of Democratic Women's Clubs, ran for Secretary of that State and was elected with the highest majority of any State official, assuming that office in 1941 for a two-year term. State secretaries keep the official records and are considered "nice guys who sign papers for everybody and make no enemies." The white-haired Madam Secretary added a new wrinkle: as the running of elections was one of her duties, she instituted "election law schools" in the interest of public information. She also became chairman of the New London Democratic Town Committee. When the National Roster of Scientific and Specialized Personnel was organized, Mrs. Woodhouse was named as consultant, to recruit and place women spe-

CHASE GOING WOODHOUSE

cialists in essential positions. She served in addition as State chairman of the Minimum Wage Board for the beauty industry, and was chosen to arbitrate a textile mill dispute. At the time when the first War Labor Board panel was set up in Connecticut, Chase Going Woodhouse was chosen to represent the public, and became panel chairman. She was also associate State administrator of the Treasury's War Finance Committee. These services the Professor continued on the expiration of her term as Secretary of Connecticut, when she was succeeded by a Republican woman, Frances B. Redick.

Mrs. Woodhouse resumed full-time work at Connecticut College, also preparing *The Big Store* for publication in 1943. In the year of 1944 she "made a bid for the Democratic Senatorial nomination, but was picked to stand for the House." Opposing the Republican incumbent, John D. McWilliams, in "a district the Republicans had counted as certain," she had the support of the Political Action Committee and the A.F. of L. The latter described the candidate as "one of the most liberal-minded women in Connecticut." "The main issue in this campaign," the nominee declared, "is how we shall set up some sort of a world organization that will make permanent peace possible." Other points she stressed were: that full employment could be maintained in peacetime "if we convert rapidly enough and keep wages up"; and "the necessity for a revision of the tax system; for working out allocation of fields between the state and the Federal Governments in the light of present-day conditions; the need for educational facilities, especially in the small towns; the need for further rural electrification." She stated her belief, moreover, that "the Congressman should be in the district every two weeks or so and available not only for private interviews but to conduct open forums on the bills before the Congress and upon matters of interest." And she won, in an election "upset," by 63,013 votes to 59,973.

(Continued next page)

WOODHOUSE, CHASE GOING—*Cont.*

Elected to the Congress from the Second Connecticut District, which includes sixty-four towns, the new Representative took a leave of absence from Connecticut College to join the lone woman on the Democratic side of the House, Mary Teresa Norton [44] of New Jersey. At this time her son Noel was an Army Air Force lieutenant (he had enlisted on the twenty-fifth anniversary of his father's enlistment in 1917); her daughter Margaret was studying, and her husband teaching at the University of North Carolina. (Also added to the Democratic roster were the two Mrs. Douglases: Helen Gahagan [44] of California and Emily Taft of Illinois.) At the Democratic caucus, the gentlewoman from Connecticut was appointed to a major standing committee, Banking and Currency, on which her former pupil Jessie Sumner was a minority member with three terms' seniority. "I have no illusions of what a new member of Congress can do the first year," she told reporters. "I'm going to evaluate every piece of legislation in terms of how many jobs there will be after the war. Feed them first and reform them later!" On the first roll-call votes of the new session, Mrs. Woodhouse said "Nay" to the Rankin [44] proposal to make the (Dies [40]) Committee on un-American Activities a permanent standing committee, and she voted with the majority for the May [41]-Bailey [45] bill, empowering local draft boards to order into essential industry all non-servicemen aged eighteen to forty-five; also for the bill to give insurance firms four years exemption from the Antitrust Act provisions; and against recommitting the George [43] bill, which action would have blocked the appointment of Henry Wallace [40] as Secretary of Commerce. Mrs. Woodhouse is said to be responsible in no small measure for Congressional implementation of the Bretton Woods plan for a world bank and world fund. She fought for it in committee, on the floor of the House, and before audiences throughout the country. She fought long and hard, also, for the retention of price control. In November she called a meeting of the Congressional Committee for the Protection of the Consumer, with Representative Aime Forand as chairman. She had visited London, Paris, Copenhagen, and Stockholm, observing the effects of inflation, and on her return in the fall reported, "Only the fighting is over. We have still got to win the war. And winning the war means working out a system of economic cooperation between nations." In a debate over OPA, when Republican Senator Kenneth S. Wherry displayed garments to illustrate his contention that the OPA was causing lowered quality, Mrs. Woodhouse reminded the audience that the Senator had voted against quality control, and also that low quality garments could not be attributed to high wages because the textile industry was one of the lowest-paid.

The Canadian-born Congresswoman was generally in favor of President Truman's [45] legislative program, but objected to the part of the Wyatt housing program intended to channel scarce materials into houses costing then not more than ten thousand dollars. She told reporters that the upper limit was too high for returning veterans. "What we need are houses to sell below sixty-five hundred dollars and to rent at fifty dollars or less," she asserted. She also warned against bringing American troops home too quickly and thus hindering policing of occupied territory, pointing out that her own son had been in the Pacific more than forty months: "Yet I am willing that he stay as long as necessary, rather than have his son sent there to fight twenty-five years from now." Without taking a position on peacetime conscription as such, she "debunked" the pro-conscription argument on health and educational grounds, stating that the age of eighteen was too late for that training, that what was needed were prenatal clinics, child welfare agencies, and more and better schools in all parts of the country; and that the best preparedness would be the elimination of Army rejections by developing physically fit men.

"As a long-time active campaigner," wrote one pre-election commentator, "Mrs. Woodhouse enjoys seniority in party activities and in association with legislative groups which should make her a valuable and effective Representative." No "glamour girl" like her Republican colleague from the Nutmeg State, Clare Boothe Luce [42], Mrs. Woodhouse is slight of frame; her hair is white, and her eyes are gray. Her religious affiliation is Episcopalian. Unable to find a suitable apartment in crowded Washington, the economist finally bought an old house in suburban Georgetown. Fortunately, her hobby is "doing over" old houses.

References

N Y Herald Tribune p11 N 9 '44; II p6 N 5 '44 por
N Y Times p42 N 12 '44
American Women, 1939-40
Congressional Directory, 1945
Leaders in Education (1941)
Who's Who in America, 1944-45

WOODLOCK, THOMAS FRANCIS

Sept. 1, 1866—Aug. 25, 1945 Contributing editor of the *Wall Street Journal*; member of the Interstate Commerce Commission from 1925 to 1930; last book, *The Catholic Pattern* (1942), awarded the Laetare Medal by the University of Notre Dame.

Obituary

N Y Times Ag 26 '45 por

WRIGHT, (SIR ROBERT ALDERSON WRIGHT), LORD

Oct. 15, 1869- Chairman of the United Nations War Crimes Commission; jurist

Address: b. House of Lords, London; h. 48 Hornton St., London

In January 1945 the sixteen-nation United Nations War Crimes Commission, which acts as a sort of international grand jury, elected the Right Honorable Lord Wright as its chairman. Lord Wright, more formally Baron Wright of Durley, is a distinguished lawyer, a member of the highest British tribunal, who is entitled to place after his name the initials K.C. (King's Counsel), P.C. (Privy Councillor), J.P. (Justice of the Peace), and F.B.A. (Fellow of the British Academy). Knighted in 1925 as Sir

Robert Alderson Wright, the jurist became in 1932 one of England's law lords, a life peer.

Lord Wright was born Robert Alderson Wright, the son of John and Elizabeth Middleton (Carr) Wright of South Shields, in England's North Country. The date was October 15, 1869. He was educated privately, and started his professional life, according to the British *Illustrated*, as a schoolmaster. Wright entered Trinity College of Cambridge University, receiving his B.A. in 1896, at the age of twenty-seven. In 1899 he was made a Fellow of the College, which he remained until 1905, meanwhile acquiring his M.A. in 1900. Wright had been studying law at the Inner Temple, perhaps the most famous of England's four inns of court (the combination law schools and bar associations to one of which all barristers must belong, and which alone possess the power of calling to the bar and disbarment). In 1900, when he was thirty-one, the future peer was called to the bar and entered the practice of law.

"There is no aspect of the law," to quote a British magazine, "in which Lord Wright's penetrating and analytical mind is not well versed." In 1917 he "took silk"—applied for and received letters patent from the Lord Chancellor as a King's Counsel, "one of His Majesty's counsel learned in the law," which made official his position as a leading barrister. Six years later he became a bencher of the Inner Temple; the benchers pass on the applicants for admission, and for sufficient cause, subject to appeal to the judiciary, may refuse to call offenders to the bar or may disbar or disbench them. In 1925 Wright was knighted and appointed a judge of the High Court of Justice, King's Bench Division. While in this post, Sir Robert was married to Margery Avis Bullows of Sutton Coldfield; this was in 1928, when he was fifty-nine.

In 1932 Sir Robert Wright was made a Lord of Appeal in Ordinary—a member of the highest judicial tribunal of the United Kingdom, and, as such, of the Judicial Committee of the Privy Council, which is the highest court of the British Commonwealth of Nations. The Lords of Appeal are made life peers (non-hereditary), with seats in the House of Lords, and Sir Robert was created Baron Wright of Durley in the county of Wiltshire. He continued to serve as a Lord of Appeal until 1935; then he became Master of the Rolls, a position ranking next after the Lord Chancellor and Lord Chief Justice, and also became chairman of a Royal Commission on Historical Monuments. Since 1937 Lord Wright has again been a Lord of Appeal. His *Legal Essays and Addresses* were published in 1939, and in 1940 he was elected a Fellow of the British Academy.

In July 1944 the High Commissioner appointed Lord Wright to represent Australia on the sixteen-member United Nations War Crimes Commission, a fact-gathering agency with no official authority to conduct trials or determine policy. In January 1945 the commission chairman, Sir Cecil Hurst, resigned, "partly for ill-health," in the words of John MacCormac in the New York *Times*, "and partly because he could get no cooperation from the Foreign Office"; the American member, Herbert C. Pell, was released by his Government; and Lord Wright was elected chairman. (Pell declared

British Official Photo.

LORD WRIGHT

that he had been dropped because certain State Department officials opposed his proposal to hold the Nazis criminally responsible for offenses against their own nationals on the grounds of race, creed, or political opinion, and he stated that Sir Cecil Hurst had a similar complaint.)

In Lord Wright's words: "When the United Nations War Crimes Commission was charged with investigating crimes . . . what it had to do was to 'investigate' the statements sent in to it in order to report whether a prima facie case of war crime was shown, and report it to the governments accordingly. . . .It was thus necessary to have some body or bodies to conduct the detailed detective inquiries in the appropriate localities. That duty was imposed on the National Offices . . . established and maintained by each of the United Nations. . . .The whole idea of the system was that the United Nations should each do its own work in bringing to justice those enemies who had committed offenses against its nationals. . . .The primary function of the military [in this connection] was to apprehend the criminals named in lists issued by the Commission. . . .The Commission has [also] power to act on its own initiative in listing offenders and has done so in its Seventh and Ninth Lists of Key Criminals. . . .It is also a central clearinghouse for the records and is thus able to classify and compare the cases and frame general charges of conspiracy in crime. . . .The Commission stands as the public embodiment of justice and of international law in the particular sphere of war crimes.

"The special feature of the Nazi or Fascist crimes is that they are not merely done on an unprecedented scale over the whole range of military operations and enemy occupation, but that they exhibit every trace of a general scheme; they all clearly emanated from a master criminal and his entourage and were carried out according to plan by elaborate organized agencies and instrumentalities—that is, by

WRIGHT, LORD—*Continued*

individuals acting under common direction and in common concert. This mass criminality has been forced on the attention of the Commission and has caused them to consider special methods of dealing with it. In particular, experience has made the Commission realize that membership in a particular organization which has systematically organized and effected the perpetration of atrocities is prima facie evidence of guilty complicity. I say prima facie, because it might be possible for an accused member to show that he was in no way implicated. . . . The Commission is acquiring the material to compare and classify, to point to common features, and to trace the crime from the actual perpetrators to the central mind or authority, such as Hitler '42 or Goering '41, right through the intermediate agencies, often by a chain of orders or directives passing down the line, and to analyze the element of common purpose or conspiracy. . . . They are all manifestly part of a systematic plan to crush and degrade and dehumanize the spirit of the peoples who are attacked, if not to exterminate them. . . . The Commission has positively declared its view that obedience to superior orders is not a defense and that heads of states are not immune. This last is a curious revival of the old bad idea of the divine right of kings."

Lord Wright also expressed his hope that the Commission would coordinate its work with that of the equivalent Soviet group, and in May 1945 the Commission submitted a proposal for an international tribunal to try the "arch-criminals" whose crimes affected nationals of many different countries. On August 8 the War Crimes Commission in London announced a pact, the Jackson agreement, establishing an International Military Tribunal to try the major European Axis war criminals. The Tribunal will consist of four members—one each from Britain, the United States, Russia, and France. Lord Wright published an article in the New York *Times Magazine* of October 28, 1945, in which he discussed the legal basis for bringing war criminals to justice.

The white-haired, beetle-browed judge is described as "a tower of strength in our [British] supreme legal tribunal." He has been awarded honorary LL.D.'s by the universities of London and Birmingham as well as Cambridge, of which he is Deputy High Steward; he also is an honorary Fellow of Trinity College. Since 1934 he has been a member of the Universities Committee of the Privy Council, and he is on the Visiting Committee of Harvard Law School in the United States, where he has often lectured on jurisprudence. Wright is a member of four clubs. "To his mental powers," it is said, "he can add physical prowess of which any man many years his junior might well be proud . . . is still a fine sportsman," and "performs without difficulty the acrobatics necessary when he has to search ceiling-high shelves for works on international jurisprudence." The Wrights, whose household includes eight assorted live dogs as well as many animal statuettes, are fond of horseback riding. (Lady Wright has won competitions in the United States and Canada.) The Baron is a believer in the public's right to information: "Secrecy,"

he has said, "is always undesirable if it can be avoided."

References

Burke's Peerage (1936)
Who's Who, 1945

WRIGHT, THEODORE P(AUL) May 25, 1895- United States Government official

Address: b. Civil Aeronautics Administration, Pentagon Bldg., Washington, D.C.; h. 2918 Glover Driveway, N.W., Washington, D.C.

Theodore P. Wright, head of the Civil Aeronautics Administration since 1944, has had a long career in the field of aviation. An aeronautical engineer as early as 1921, he was called to Washington a score of years later to aid in the defense program and, subsequently, after Pearl Harbor, was assigned an important part in the direction of the aircraft production program.

The son of Philip Green and Elizabeth Quincy (Sewall) Wright, Theodore Paul Wright was born on May 25, 1895. He spent the first twenty years of his life in his native town of Galesburg, Illinois, where he attended Lombard College. He received his Bachelor of Science degree from that college in 1915, and three years later was graduated from the Massachusetts Institute of Technology with a Bachelor of Science degree in architectural engineering. (In 1937 he was awarded the honorary degree of Doctor of Science by Knox College in Galesburg in recognition of his "distinguished services to aeronautics.")

His education completed, Wright was commissioned as ensign in the United States Naval Reserve Flying Corps shortly before the First World War ended and assigned to duty as an inspector of naval aircraft. Two years later he was promoted to the rank of lieutenant and appointed superintendent of construction of naval aircraft for the New York district. The Garden City (Long Island) and Buffalo plants of the Curtiss Aeroplane and Motor Company were included in the New York area, and Lieutenant Wright was responsible for the inspection of the Navy-Curtiss flying boats then under construction at the Garden City plant. (The Navy-Curtiss was the first plane to make a transatlantic flight.) There is a story told of Wright's devotion to his work in connection with this ship. Late one night, before the NC was finished, the general manager and chief engineer of the plant decided to have an undisturbed look at their history-making plane. When they arrived at the deserted factory, they were surprised to find a light burning in the hull of the plane. Suspecting the worst, they were therefore relieved when investigation disclosed not an intruder but the young Navy lieutenant busily examining some construction that he could not have inspected during the day without holding up production.

Wright's ability and zeal caused the company to offer him a position when the Navy project was completed and in 1921, after receiving his discharge from the Navy, he joined the Curtiss Aeroplane and Motor Company as an executive engineer. The next year he was the assistant manager of the Buffalo factory, and in 1923 he became the assistant to the chief engineer. Two years later he was promoted to chief engineer of the airplane division, a position he continued to hold after the company became known as the Curtiss-Wright Corporation in 1928. He became vice-president of the corporation in 1930 and was general manager and chief engineer of the Buffalo plant from that year until 1934, when he was transferred to New York to take the posts of director of engineering and chairman of the Engineering Policy and Planning Board. By 1941, when he severed his industrial ties in order to give his time to national defense, he had become the vice-president of the Curtiss-Wright Corporation, of the Reed Propeller Company, and of the Wright Aeronautical Corporation, which comprised the largest aircraft organization in the world.

While Wright was a chief engineer many of the best-known Curtiss planes were produced under his supervision. There were Pulitzer and Schneider cup winners, and such famous military designs as the Hawk, Falcon, Helldiver, Shrike, and Condor. From 1928 until 1930 his experimental laboratory concentrated on the development of civil aircraft, producing in 1929 the Tanager, the plane which won the hundred-thousand-dollar prize in the Guggenheim Safe Aircraft Competition of that year. Other commercial types were the Robin, Fledgling, Kingbird, and Commercial Condor. In 1931 the laboratory staff at Garden City was moved to Buffalo to combine with the research group functioning under Wright's direction. It was also during that period that he devised his "Project Engineer" system of aircraft design, development, and manufacture which has been adopted by almost every important aircraft organization in the United States as the standard method of production.

In the spring of 1940 Wright took a six months' leave of absence from his business duties to go to Washington as a consultant to the National Defense Commission at the request of William S. Knudsen '40, head of the commission. Working with the Army and Navy as well as with other industrial leaders, Wright helped lay the foundation for the orderly expansion of industry to meet war needs. When his leave expired he went back to Curtiss-Wright for a few months; then, shortly before Pearl Harbor, he resigned from his position and returned to Washington to work as assistant chief of the aircraft section of the Office of Production Management. When that agency became known as the War Production Board in December 1942, he organized the Aircraft Resources Control Office, of which he was made director on March 6, 1943. The ARCO served as executive agency of the Aircraft Production Board (of which he was also a member); coordinator of production of airframes, engines, and propellers; supervisory agency of the Aircraft Scheduling Unit at Dayton, Ohio; and liaison office between the Army and Navy Air Forces and the War Production Board. In an editorial in the April 1943 issue of *Aviation* Leslie E. Neville approved Wright's appointment by saying: "The Army, the Navy, the aviation industry, and the Nation have reason for a deeper feeling of confidence in the military aircraft production program than they have ever had before."

Wright was well prepared to solve the complicated problems involved in directing the

THEODORE P. WRIGHT

American aircraft production program during the Second World War. He was not only thoroughly familiar with airplane production in the United States, but he had made a careful study of conditions abroad, having visited factories in England, France, and Germany in the years 1934 through 1938. For his service during the war he received the War Department's highest award to civilians, the Medal for Exceptional Civilian Service, with a citation which reads: "In recognition of his outstanding contribution to the expansion of aircraft production by assisting in the equitable resolution of the many difficult and urgent problems of aircraft scheduling, standardization, and allocation. His development of useful methods for measuring manpower utilization and production efficiency has been of material assistance to the successful prosecution of the war."

On September 20, 1944, Wright's appointment as head of the Civil Aeronautics Administration, replacing Charles I. Stanton, was confirmed. Commenting on Wright's nomination, Scott Hershey, in an *Aviation News* article, said, "The fact that Wright is willing to leave his aircraft production post was taken in Washington as an indication that the plane production situation is well in hand. . . .It is known that Wright felt his job was not completed until the invasion of Europe was an assured success and that the production program was such that there would be ample aircraft for future Pacific operations." William A. M. Burden, then Assistant Secretary of Commerce, approved of the President's choice as "an outstanding step in preparing American civil aviation."

Among Wright's functions as administrator of the CAA is the encouragement of private flying, that is, the flying of planes by individuals as distinguished from commercial airlines. He feels that flying can be made feasible for a large number of people in the country if Federal agencies and private industry will cooperate. "Aviation cannot fly profitably and

WRIGHT, THEODORE P.—*Continued*

successfully without these two wings of support," said Wright in his article "Our Plan the development of civil aviation. It includes: April 1945 issue of *Flying*. In the article he outlined his own six-point program to facilitate the development of civil aviation. It includes: the mass production of a satisfactory personal airplane, safe and easy to fly; the construction of many simple and conveniently located airports; simplification of the regulations governing flying; an educational system similar to the old Civilian Pilot Training Program, to be sponsored by the Government; a campaign to make the general public airplane-conscious; and the development of a private airplane that will be superior to and cheaper than any yet built. Wright has organized an advisory group on nonscheduled flying to assist him in planning increased private flying.

Wright has contributed extensively to aeronautical literature on subjects ranging from aerodynamics to production problems and aviation's place in civilization. In 1930 the Society of Automotive Engineers, of which he is a member, awarded him the Wright Brothers Medal for his paper, "The Tanager—a Safe Airplane." "The Truth About Our National Defense Program," an article published in *Aviation* January 1941, sets forth America's need for defense measures, and methods for achieving them, and it won for the magazine the Industrial Marketing Award of Merit for the best article or editorial published in a business magazine during the period from August 1, 1940, to July 31, 1941. Another of his articles, "America's Answer," which appeared in *Aviation* in June 1939, was an answer to President Roosevelt's [42] request for the production of fifty thousand planes a year. In it Wright analyzed the capacity of the American aircraft industry to produce and showed how output might be increased to meet the needs of national defense. Some of his other articles are "Trends in Air Transport," "Winged Victory," and "50,000 Planes a Year," all of which were published in *Aviation*.

The aeronautical expert is well known in international aviation circles for his Wilbur Wright Memorial Lecture, "Aviation's Place in Civilization," which he delivered at the annual meeting of the Royal Aeronautical Society in London in May 1945, and for his participation in the United States Strategic Bombing Survey, which was formed to study the results of the strategic bombing of the Eighth Air Force in Europe during the war. In November 1944 he served as technical secretary of the International Civil Aviation Conference held in Chicago. After thirty-seven days and nights of work he produced a set of rules for safety in world air-transport operation which were adopted by the delegates to the conference.

Wright, who learned to fly in 1917, is a member of the Society of Automotive Engineers, former president and Fellow of the Institute of Aeronautical Sciences, and honorary Fellow of the Royal Aeronautical Society. He was married to Margaret McCarl in 1918; and their two sons are Douglas Lyman and Theodore Paul. Wright is of medium height, has graying light brown hair, and is described as "easy to talk to." When he was vice-president and general manager of the Curtiss plant in Buffalo,

he took orders from the blueprint boy—when the boy was captain of the basketball team and Wright was one of the players.

References

    Aviation 43 :217 O '44
    Aviation N 2:10-11 Ag 28 '44
    Bsns W p7 Ag 25 '44 por
    Collier's 115:8 Mr 3 '45 por
    Who's Who in America, 1944-45
    Who's Who in Aviation, 1942-43
    Who's Who in Commerce and Industry, 1940-41

WU YI-FANG (wōō yǐ-făng) Jan. 26, 1893- Chinese educator; religious leader; Government adviser

Address: Ginling College for Women, Nanking, China

The first and only woman college president in China, Dr. Wu Yi-fang has broken precedent in other ways. She is also the first woman to head the National Christian Council, having charge of all work by Christian bodies in the country; the first woman to be elected to the five-member presidium of the People's Political Council, making her the incumbent of the highest office held by any Chinese woman; and perhaps the leading worker for women's rights and education in all of China. Dr. Wu has represented her country abroad, having been a delegate to international conferences in Canada, England, India, and the United States, most recently at the San Francisco conference of April-June 1945.

Wu Yi-fang (the surname is placed first, Chinese fashion) was born on January 26, 1893, in Wuchang, Hupeh province, in northeastern China. Her father was a scholar and Government official, holding posts in Wuchang and northern Hupeh. A maternal uncle established one of the first girls' schools in China. As a young girl under the guidance of her older sister she read new books and pamphlets urging reforms, and in 1907, when the first schools for girls were authorized by imperial edict, she was enrolled in the newly established Hangchow Girls' School. During the next seven years she also attended the Laura Haygood Girls' School in Soochow and the Union Hangchow Girls' School. Then, in 1914-15, although only eighteen years old, Miss Wu became a teacher of English in the Girls' Normal School of Peking. Approximately a year later, in February 1916, however, she resigned the position to enter Ginling College for Women, a Protestant missionary school opened only half a year earlier and the first institution in the Yangtze Valley to offer work of college grade to women. A better than average student in all her subjects, and especially interested in science, she completed the course in three and a half years, receiving her B.A. in 1919 as a member of Ginling's first graduating class. While at college, in 1918, Miss Wu had been converted to Christianity.

Upon graduation Miss Wu had been offered an assistantship at Ginling, but she accepted instead the position of professor and head of the department of English at the Peking Higher Normal School for Girls. This she held until 1922, during a period marked by a literary renaissance, the beginning of Russian influence, and a rise in anti-Christian propaganda. Then, in the latter year, having been awarded a Barbour Scholarship to the University of Michigan, she left for the United States to pursue graduate studies in biology. In addition, she was active in American student affairs, being chairman of the Chinese Student Christian Association in the United States in 1924-25 and vice-chairman and acting chairman of the Chinese Student Alliance in North America in 1925-26. She had received her Master's degree from Michigan in 1924, and her Ph.D., for which she had written a dissertation entitled "A Contribution to the Biology of Simulium," was granted in 1928. That same year, abandoning her plans to teach biology when she returned to China, she accepted the presidency of Ginling College, becoming its first Chinese president when thirty-five years of age.

During the next nine years, the college underwent a "brilliant development." The enrollment doubled; new buildings were added to the campus; the curriculum was enlarged and modified to meet China's needs. Dr. Wu became known as a progressive Western-style educator and as the leading exponent in patriarchal China of the Occidental ideas of equal rights and education for women. (She has said, however, that she would be satisfied if women were given a fair chance in "a few special suitable fields," particularly education and social work.) In doing "man's work" she warned her girls against aping masculine styles and manners. To quote Delos Lovelace, "she approves of independence. She is glad that nowadays a girl in China may announce her own engagement to the boy friend of her own picking. But she holds that the announcement should have the feminine touch."

Miss Wu was also active in international goodwill and national Christian work. In 1929, 1931, and in 1933 she was one of the Chinese delegates to the Institute of Pacific Relations conferences, and in the latter year to the International Congress of Women in Chicago. Two years later, and again in 1937, she was elected chairman of the National Christian Council, China's coordinating body for Christian activities, with which she had been connected since 1928. During the years of the civil war and of Japanese aggression, which began in 1931, her position was "of tremendous responsibility, because of the intricacy of the problem involved." She also worked with Mme. Chiang Kai-shek [40], wife of the Generalissimo and a leader in her own right, in the New Life Movement, an organization devoted to national improvement through "courtesy, honesty, honor, service"—plus sanitation, social work, and the greater application of science. She and Mme. Chiang are also considered "mainly responsible for drawing China's women into their present widespread relief organization," the National Women's Association for War Relief.

When the official Sino-Japanese War began in 1937, Miss Wu was forced to flee, with her entire college, from the Japanese Army which was approaching the capital. From Nanking, Ginling moved some fifteen hundred miles to Chengtu, where three other refugee colleges had found quarters on the West China Union College campus. Despite "incredible difficul-

WU   YI-FANG

ties," Dr. Wu succeeded in organizing this exodus and reorganizing the college in temporary buildings. While a Japanese garrison was quartered on the Ginling campus, the students and teachers continued their work in Chengtu. They suffered from the loss of much equipment, and from the scarcity of books, materials, and even food and clothing; but the student body grew to an unprecedented three hundred (the percentage of women enrolled in all Chinese colleges and universities had jumped 10 to 20 per cent by 1943). Dr. Wu's girls used their studies in child welfare, rural sociology, adult education, and similar fields, by setting up nutrition, sanitation, and child-care projects in Szechuan Province.

"In Chengtu," to quote the Chinese News Service, "Dr. Wu is known to Government officials and kindergarten children alike. She sits on advisory boards, consults constantly with the Governor of the Province and with his economic and social welfare departments. In her office on the campus of Ginling College, she has a steady stream of visitors, only some of whom have to do with the administration of the college. Many of them are Government officials and war committee workers who seek her advice and support for their projects." In 1936 she represented Ginling at the Harvard Tercentenary, one of eighteen women at the ceremonies. In December 1938 she headed China's delegation to the International Missionary Congress at Tambaram, near Madras, India, probably the first woman, it is said, to lead a national deputation to a world convocation. That same year she was made a vice-chairman of the International Missionary Council and became a member of the Chinese People's Political Council, an advisory body to the Government; and in 1940 she was elected to its Presidium, becoming one of five presidents, the first woman so honored. This is described as the highest public office held by a woman in China. (Mme. Chiang had in the

WU YI-FANG—*Continued*

past headed the Air Force, and Mme. Sun [44] had also occupied an important post.)

In the spring of 1943 Miss Wu was the only woman member of a mission of educators and scholars sent to the United States to study various aspects of international relations and postwar reconstruction. "It is time to be thinking of the new world that lies ahead," said Dr. Wu, at a time when her country was in its sixth year of war. While in America she was awarded an honorary LL.D. by Smith College. Two years later she was similarly honored by Mills College and by the University of Southern California. This was when she was at the history-making United Nations Conference on International Organization, as the one woman in the ten-member Chinese delegation at San Francisco. (Some years earlier she had been the first woman to receive an honorary D. Sc. from St. John's University in Shanghai.) In 1940 she was co-editor of a symposium, *China Rediscovers Her West*.

The active Chinese educator is described as "small and thin and full of drive," "sharp-eyed behind spectacles but tactfully feminine amid so much masculinity." Like her countrywomen, Mmes. Chiang and Sun, she causes many western newspapermen to grow lyrical, the following description taken from the *Christian Science Monitor* being typical: "Miss Wu has the graces traditional to her countrymen: the impeccable courtesy, the disciplined composure, the nimbleness of wit and sagacity of heart," plus a "quality of vision, a vitality and steadfastness of spiritual conviction, that perpetually and incalculably marks the difference between intellectual and moral leadership. . . . Each phrase, each economical gesture, seemed margined with serenity, so that never, one felt, could she be jarred outside of the composure that she so luminously embodied."

References

C S Mon II p8 Je 8 '43; p10 Ap 30 '45
N Y Sun p6 My 19 '45
N Y Times p16 My 21 '43
China Handbook, 1937-43

WYETH N(EWELL) C(ONVERS) (wī′ĕth) Oct. 22, 1882—Oct. 19, 1945 American artist; illustrated twenty juvenile classics, including *Treasure Island* and *Robin Hood*; painted murals for public buildings, banks, churches, hotels; among them are those in the Federal Reserve Bank in Boston and the Missouri State Capitol.

Obituary

N Y Times p26 O 20 '45

WYNN, ED Nov. 9, 1886- Actor; producer; author

Address: h. Hollywood, Calif.

An "epic fellow of fabulous stature", "one of the ten most charming men in the world," "strangely sweet"—these are some of the words critics have used to describe comedian Ed Wynn. Besides a mastery of clowning, Wynn has a talent for writing and composing. He has written and produced the book, music, and lyrics of three of the eighteen Broadway shows in

which he has appeared; collaborated on several others; authored and produced seven complete vaudeville acts; and has written the words and music of some hundred published songs. His other accomplishments include crossword puzzle construction and the writing of a column which was syndicated for three years in one hundred and fifty newspapers. He is reportedly engaged in writing a book to be named "The Philosophy of a Fool," which will reveal the introspective side of this lisping, giggling stage figure, whose admirers range from Joseph Wood Krutch, erudite drama critic, to Earl Wilson, the self-styled "saloon" editor of the New York *Post*.

Born in Philadelphia, November 9, 1886, to Joseph and Minnie Leopold, Wynn was named Isaiah Edwin. (His stage name is derived from the two syllables of his middle name.) His father, then a moderately prosperous manufacturer and retailer of women's hats, was born near Prague; his mother was born in Constantinople (Istanbul), her father having been Rumanian and her mother Turkish. Apparently Wynn was born to comedy. As soon as he could walk he was trying on ladies' hats in his father's store, suspending all business with his droll mimicry of the customers. The first play he ever saw was that macabre study of a dual personality, *Dr. Jekyll and Mr. Hyde*. He loved it. After that, on days that he was to go to the theatre, his mother often found him sobbing, "I want eight o'clock."

Young Leopold attended Central High School in Philadelphia, but at fifteen ran away from home to join the Thurber-Nasher Repertoire Company as a general utility boy at twelve dollars a week. Between chores of taking care of trunks and passing out handbills, he played bits on the stage. His first role, described on the program as "an old retainer," was in *American Grit*. The company went broke in Maine, and young Ed crept home. His father put him to selling hats, which was not Ed's idea of congenial work.

When the youth ran away from home again he went to New York, teaming up with another aspirant, Jack Lewis, in an act called "Wynn and Lewis." They introduced this at a benefit show and were immediately engaged to play Broadway's then top vaudeville theater, the Colonial, at a salary of two hundred dollars a week. Their act played for ninety-eight weeks, and at the end of the run Wynn went on alone. At the age of nineteen he was a headliner in vaudeville, earning four hundred dollars a week. For eleven years he remained in vaudeville, except for a brief interlude in a Broadway musical, *The Deacon and the Lady* (1910). The producer and composer of the production was Alfred E. Aarons, father of a boyhood acquaintance of Wynn's who had persuaded the father to give the comedian a part in the show even though the elder Aarons, had thought Wynn was "not very funny." The play closed after sixteen performances, and Wynn returned to vaudeville, continuing as a headliner in acts he wrote himself.

In 1914 Ziegfeld put him in the *Follies*, where Broadway welcomed the comic. Cast in the 1915 edition of the *Follies*, Wynn found himself on the same bill with W. C. Fields. A feud developed between the two comedians. During his famous pool-table act Fields found his laughs coming at the wrong time. At last he discovered Wynn under the table happily catching flies. For several years after this these "epic fellows of fabulous statures," to quote Richard Watts, never spoke to each other. Finally, when Wynn defended his fellow troupers in an impassioned speech during the actors' strike of 1919, Fields publicly kissed Wynn on the brow—and peace between them was declared.

Beverly Smith says the strike almost broke Wynn's career, but ended by making his fortune. He "was making seventeen hundred dollars a week, but he threw down his tools—three hundred hats and fifty costumes—and walked out with the chorus girls and humbler sort of actors who were striking for better wages and working conditions. When the strike was won Wynn got a testimonial signed by 2,020 grateful actors and actresses." He was one of the few casualties of the strike which had included the Barrymores and almost all the leading stars of the day. Under contract to the Shuberts when he went on strike, Wynn was kept off the stage, first by an injunction, and later by a boycott from the Shuberts, who controlled the booking of New York theaters. The comedian brooded awhile, then closeted himself and wrote a whole show—songs, music, jokes. He drew his savings from the bank, picked up old scenery, and staged *Ed Wynn's Carnival* (1920), which ran for 116 weeks on Broadway. *The Perfect Fool* (1921) and *The Grab Bag* (1924) were also his creations. *The Perfect Fool,* his most successful role, played for 256 performances in New York, and then served Wynn as a road show until the season of 1924.

Although all of Wynn's Broadway roles did not win the acclaim that *The Perfect Fool* received, for twenty-five years every Wynn show was a box-office "honey" and there was not a single unfavorable notice. Joseph Wood Krutch, writing in the *Nation* of Wynn's power to send him into "paroxysms of mirth," said: "No one can exceed him in solid, impenetrable asininity, but no one can, at the same time, be more amiable, well-meaning, and attractive. Nature gave him a large and solemn face which seemed to promise an unending series of well-intentioned blunders, and his art succeeds, somehow, in giving the impression that his career has been more the result of following with an admirable consistency Polonius' excellent advice—'To thine own self be true.'"

In his radio work Wynn, contrary to custom, always works in costume. It has been said that his comedy make-up has more effect on his mood than upon his audiences. Unlike most comedians, Wynn uses entirely different voices on the stage and radio. On the stage the lisp is more pronounced, the treble always threatening, but never quite forthcoming; on the radio he shrieks in a hysterical falsetto. This change is all the result of a misapprehension on his part. Wynn had made his radio debut in the pioneer days of broadcasting, when he put his entire two-and-one-half-hour musical, *The Perfect Fool,* on a WJZ program, and his voice had then reached only New York audiences; his first experience on a national hook-up was in 1932 when he appeared as the Fire Chief for Texaco. Just before the première of this program Wynn was told that he had an audience of twenty-nine million, whereupon he shrieked anxiously into the microphone with

Bruno of Hollywood

ED WYNN

such comic effect that he continued to use the same pitch and volume on the radio. The Texaco program for three years (1932-35) was rated one of the most popular programs on the air. In it Wynn introduced the trick of combining his comedy with the sponsor's message. Wynn would break in on Graham McNamee's praises of the value of Texaco oil for automobile use with a quip, such as, "I'll stick to my horse—he doesn't have to be repainted every year."

In 1914 Wynn was married to Hilda Keenan, the actress-daughter of Frank Keenan, the Irish-American actor who for more than twenty years played leading roles in such well known productions as *The Girl of the Golden West, The Christian,* and *The Warrens of Virginia.* Their one child is Keenan, who has gained recognition as an actor in character roles in *See Here, Private Hargrove* and other films. He has been the absorbing interest in Wynn's life. When touring the comedian often traveled three hundred miles to see Keenan on Sundays. "On Sunday afternoons," says Wynn "my little friend and I would sit and talk things over. He was much steadier than I was, his judgment much more solid." (Early in 1945 Ed Wynn bought a home in Bel-Air, Hollywood, to be near his son.)

In 1937 Wynn was divorced by his wife, and a month later he was married to Frieda Mierse, a showgirl. The second marriage ended in divorce in 1939, and financial troubles followed the marital ones: a radio chain Wynn had backed failed with a loss of $300,000; and income tax difficulties reportedly brought his losses close to a million dollars. A nervous breakdown resulted in the retirement of America's Perfect Fool. "I can never be funny again," he told his son, who tried for seventeen months to bring the comedian out of his depression. (There have, in fact, always been two Ed Wynns—the giggling, befuddled clown of the stage, and the saddened, bedeviled, self-distrustful man who says in explanation of this off-stage Wynn, "Maybe I use all my

WYNN, ED—*Continued*

happiness on the stage.") One night Keenan persuaded his father to dine out with him. Some college boys at a table close by recognized Wynn and asked him when he was going to put on another show. Young Wynn saw his father give a smile in response—his first in many months.

When Wynn returned to Broadway in *Boys and Girls Together* (1940), critics who had hinted that the comedian was through were forced to admit that his new show was one of his best. "It is funny to the point of tears," said Brooks Atkinson[42]. "It is the peak of Ed's career." Highspots of comedy (Wynn wrote the book) were: the introduction of his cast as graduates from a showboat with, "I bred my cast upon the waters"; an exit line, "I'll be back in a flash with more trash"; the use of an eleven-foot pole for people he wouldn't touch with a ten-foot pole. This last is a veteran among the Wynn gags—he is not averse to repeating a good one.

Wynn's comeback as "King Bubbles" in the radio program *Happy Island* (September 1944), over the Blue Network, was not so fortunate as his stage reappearance. Harriet Van Horne, New York *World-Telegram* critic, called the program as "flimsy a piece of whimsey as ever tangled a major talent." *Variety* found Wynn's delivery "sure and deft," but feared that the "sponsor identification" in the entertainment part of the program would prove "short-sighted." It was discontinued after three months and Wynn went back to his Purple Heart circuit, visiting GI hospitals in the United States.

Wynn sees in television an opportunity for actors and actresses to realize the high point of their careers. In speaking before the Television Broadcasters Association in December 1944, he declared that the thought of television's future had made him "get serious for the first time in forty-three years on the stage and radio. . . .The new art can be a thing more dangerous than dynamite or the quintessence of good, depending upon how it is managed."

Ed Wynn has never used off-color jokes, his humor having been consistently free from any suggestion of obscenity. While Wynn has devoted most of his life since 1904 to dispensing humor he admits he does not know precisely what humor is. "It is too subtle to be pinned down," he once said in an interview with S. J. Woolf. "I can say that it differs from wit, which exaggerates the truth, while humor presents the truth in an original way." Wynn calls himself a "method comedian"—he does not so much depend upon his material as he does on the method of putting it over. His comedy costume—a collection of zany hats, misfit clothes, and an oversized pair of shoes—has become a Wynn trade-mark. The hats have been changed with the productions, but the shoes are the ones he bought in 1907 for three and a half dollars—but repatched until not a bit remains of the original leather, for Wynn is so superstitious about the footgear that he will not make any stage appearance without them. Between engagements they are kept in a safe, and the repair over the thirty-seven years he has worn them has cost about three thousand dollars. Although Wynn has a gift for

punning, he works hard over his gag lines. His library for the most part consists of joke books; when writing his comedy material he locks himself in a room and permits no one to disturb him. "It often takes hours," he says, "to think up something that is said in seconds."

Although Wynn has composed the score for three Broadway hits and has about a hundred songs to his credit, "his musicianship is rather circumscribed—he plays the piano in only one key, B-flat. However, Wynn creates the impression of a full, rich piano technique which fools some people into thinking that he is a thoroughly schooled musician."

The Wynn office is more like a museum than a business workshop. It is littered with wardrobe trunks, derelict costumes, and stage props. The walls are covered from floor to ceiling with testimonials, citations, awards of merit—and photographs of Wynn in his different roles from his sixteen Broadway shows, seven vaudeville acts, and two movies. (In 1933 Wynn, under contract to Metro-Goldwyn-Mayer, made *Follow the Leader* and *The Chief*.) There are mementoes and trophies, too: a gold cup for radio's finest performance in 1932; 127 firemen's badges as tribute to his radio character, the Fire Chief; and an autographed photograph from Woodrow Wilson for Wynn's work in the First World War. The star was the first to lead a Broadway company to Army camps in 1917. In the Second World War, Wynn made a tour of Army hospitals, while son Keenan went over "the hump" to entertain the armed forces in China and Burma. (In 1932 and 1933 Wynn's benefit broadcasts raised $82,000 for the relief of the unemployed.) The societies and clubs to which the comedian belongs are ASCAP, Authors' League of America, Dramatists, Actors Fund of America; and the Illinois State Board of Health elected him its honorary president.

Off the stage the comedian does not try to be waggish or witty. He talks seriously about his work, worries that his giggle may become too heavy (he speaks with a slight sibilance), while the well known curved eyebrows bob up and down "like waves on a sea" above his large shell-rimmed glasses. He is six feet tall and well built. His taste in clothes leans toward tweeds, red pajamas, and striped dressing gowns. Although he drinks moderately, he consumes five large black cigars during a rehearsal. His game of golf is fair, and he once owned an eighty-two-foot yacht. "I like boats," says Wynn. "When aboard I wear a captain's hat and a coat with brass buttons. It's marvelous how nautical I look. Without thinking a minute I can tell you the difference between the North Star and a movie star."

References

Am Mag 122:28-9+ O '36 por; 131:
  20-1+ F '41 il pors
N Y Herald Tribune VI p2 O 20 '40
N Y Post p4 D 3 '40 pors
N Y Sun p31 O 4 '40
N Y Times IX pl S 15 '40; IX pl O 13
  '40; IX p3 F 9 '41
N Y Times Mag p12+ Jl 5 '42 por
N Y World-Telegram p6 Jl 20 '40 por
Newsweek 24:86-8 Ag 21 '44

Who's Who in America, 1944-45
Who's Who in the Theatre (1939)

YEATS-BROWN, FRANCIS (yāts' broun')
Aug. 15, 1886—Dec. 19, 1944 British author,
soldier, and aviator; won the D.F.C. in First
World War; retired from the Army in 1925;
subject of his books were the British Army
and India; his autobiography *Bengal Lancer*
(1932) became a motion picture *Lives of a
Bengal Lancer* in 1935.

Obituary

N Y Times p21 D 21 '44 por

YOUNG, HUGH (HAMPTON) Sept. 18,
1870—Aug. 23, 1945 Internationally known
surgeon and urologist; professor of urology
at Johns Hopkins University; he and his associates are credited with the development in
1924 of mercurochrome; received a Francis
Amory Award from the American Academy of
Arts and Sciences in 1941.

Obituary

N Y Times p19 Ag 24 '45 por

YOUNG, OWEN D. Oct. 27, 1874- Corporation executive

Address: b. General Electric Co., Schenectady,
N.Y.; h. Van Hornesville, N.Y.

Known to the average student of history
as chairman of the committee which devised
the Young plan for the settlement of German
reparations after the First World War, Owen
D. Young has also served in the important
capacities of chairman of the boards of General Electric Company and Radio Corporation
of America, as well as of chairman or member of several Government committees. From
farm boy to lawyer, executive, and diplomat,
Young became one of America's foremost industrialists and public servants. He is recognized as one of the men responsible for his
country's rapid industrialization, and he has received international acclaim for his work in the
field of reparations.

Owen D. Young, the son of Jacob Smith and
Ida (Brandow) Young, was born in Van
Hornesville, New York, on October 27, 1874.
His first American ancestor was Peter Young,
a Protestant who had been driven from his
home in the Rhenish Palatinate in the late six-
teen-hundreds by French Catholics and had
come to America in 1710. Owen, the son of a
farmer, did his share of the chores in the home
and fields and attended the little district school.
Almost from the first, it is said, the boy was
an unusual pupil. "The teachers were not accustomed to having pupils absorb what they
gave them—soaking it in and asking for more—
and this child seemed to be of that sort." Thus,
after the boy's completion of grammar school
at the age of twelve, his parents, although their
means were relatively small, sent their son to
the Academy of East Springfield, about five
miles from Van Hornesville. Two years later
he was graduated, the valedictorian of his class.

In 1890, at the age of sixteen Young entered
St. Lawrence University, in Canton, New York,
to prepare for the study of law. He had decided on this future in his early teens when one
summer day he had gone to court to act as his
uncle's witness in a controversy over a horse
trade. "The cool of the courtroom, the appeal
of the books, and the witty exchange of ideas,"

OWEN D. YOUNG

says Young, "made me determined . . . this is
the life for me." At college he was described
as "mentally alert, reserved, and master of himself and his surroundings." He was a leader in
student activities, a business manager of the
college newspaper, and through his efforts funds
were raised for a college gymnasium. Much of
his free time was spent attending sessions at
the county court at Canton, where he observed
the law in practice. In June 1894, when he was
graduated from St. Lawrence, the prelaw student delivered the commencement address, voicing his thoughts on law and government: "The
state is more than a mere utilitarian machine
for the protection of life and property; it is a
moral organization founded on the eternal principle of right to establish justice as the end
for which it was created . . . right must be
substituted for narrow and selfish principles;
fairness and open-mindedness for senseless partisan abuse." At the university Young had met
Josephine Sheldon Edmonds, and four years
after his graduation they were married. They
had five children: Charles Jacob, John (deceased), Josephine, Philip, and Richard. (Mrs.
Young died in June 1935, and Young was married a second time, in February 1937, to Mrs.
Louise Powis Clark.)

Young entered Boston University Law School
in September 1894. He worked in the school
library to meet his tuition fee, the small allowance he received from his parents merely
covering his room and board expenses. Life
was sometimes hard for the young student but
he kept to his course. "I was doing the thing
I wanted to do," he recalls, "and was too excited to mind that sort of thing." The second
year, however, Young's financial problem was
solved when he became a tutor to a wealthy
law student. In 1896, having completed his
three-year course in two years, he received his
LL.B. degree *cum laude* and was again chosen
the orator of the class.

Soon after being admitted to the bar in Boston that July, Young obtained a job as a clerk
in the office of Charles H. Tyler, a lawyer who

YOUNG, OWEN D.—*Continued*

specialized in corporation and real estate cases. That same year he also secured a part-time position at the Boston University Law School as a teaching assistant to the lecturer on common-law pleading, a post he held until 1903. During his eleven years with Tyler his able handling of minutiae of trust estates, lease-holds, and property claims made him Tyler's right-hand man. Already in 1907 the law office of Charles H. Tyler had become the firm of Tyler and Young. With the large-scale developments of big business in the early nineteen-hundreds, the junior partner handled much of the legal work of electrical utility companies. Thus he became one of the best-informed advisers on utilities in the United States, skilled in adjusting disputes, in writing public utility contracts, and negotiating difficult transactions.

The year 1912 proved a turning point in the young lawyer's career. Young's defense of a client's rights to certain land contested by Bond and Share, then a General Electric subsidiary, brought him to the attention of Charles A. Coffin, president of General Electric. Impressed by the ability of the opposing counsel, Coffin invited Young to join the law department of his company, and Young, feeling that at General Electric he would have a chance to delve into "the no man's land of the law," accepted the offer. Accordingly, in January 1913 he became general counsel for the company. Shortly afterward he was put in charge of the law department, with the title of vice-president. He was particularly interested in the treatment of employees. Young has said: "I was shocked, outraged, when I found evidence that flimsy pretexts were being used for getting rid of workers when the real reason was that they were union men. I told the board I considered this the denial of man's constitutional right of association." Consequently, in 1918 he presented General Electric with a plan to effect closer cooperation between capital and labor.

In 1919, at the request of the United States Government, Young created the Radio Corporation of America in order to prevent American patents from falling into the hands of foreign companies. The Government was particularly concerned over the Alexander alternator, "a radio sending machine" invented in the General Electric laboratory, for which the British Marconi Wireless Company was negotiating. The sale of the alternator to the British company would have meant the supremacy of Great Britain in the radio field. In order to consolidate all electrical patents in the hands of one company, the newly formed RCA therefore took over the patents controlled by GE, United Fruit, American Telephone and Telegraph, Westinghouse, and General Motors, compensating these companies with shares in RCA commensurate with the value of their relinquished patents. Under Young's leadership RCA became known as the largest radio company in the world.

In 1919 the vice-president of General Electric first entered the field of public service. Upon President Wilson's request, Young joined the President's Second Industrial Conference to help formulate a plan to prevent industrial strife. One of the committee's important proposals was a national industrial board to handle all disputes that could not be settled by those immediately concerned. The chairman of the conference remarked that Young "seemed to be after the truth of things—no fear, no prejudice." In 1921, with a business depression in the offing, Young once again contributed his services to the Government, this time as a member of President Harding's Conference on Unemployment; and in 1922, at the suggestion of Herbert Hoover [43], President Harding appointed Young chairman of a committee to investigate the causes of business cycles. The following year the committee presented a report which was then considered the most thorough study on industrial stabilization yet made in the United States. In 1924 the economic adviser served as chairman of the American delegation to the international court of arbitration of trade disputes, a tribunal formed by the International Chamber of Commerce to facilitate the settlement of commercial controversies between firms of different countries. From 1925 to 1928 Young was also chairman of the International Chamber of Commerce.

In June 1922, upon Coffin's retirement, Young became chairman of the board of General Electric. A year and a half later General Electric gave him a temporary release when in December 1923 the Allied Reparations Commission, unable to cope with the German reparations problem, invited Young to join the newly formed Experts' Committee. Headed by an American, Charles G. Dawes, the commission was to determine Germany's capacity to pay reparations, and to devise a plan which would stabilize her rapidly depreciating currency and balance her budget. In May 1924, after six months of deliberation the committee's report, the Dawes plan, was completed, fixing the total sum of German reparations and method of payment. According to its framers, this plan was considered a temporary settlement. At the London Conference of Premiers in July Young's presence as a conciliator was thought largely responsible for the plan's acceptance by the Allied countries. Appointed Agent General ad interim the following month, Young set up an international bank which was to handle Germany's accounts and taxes. After the completion of this task in November Young returned to the United States to resume his business activities.

The Dawes plan worked successfully for more than three years and then was superseded by the Young plan. At the end of 1928 the Allied countries, agreeing to Germany's demand for a final settlement of the reparations problem, had appointed a new commission. Confident of Young's ability and fairness, the Allies drafted him to be chairman of the Second Committee of Experts, which convened in February of the following year. (The United States did not participate in this conference.) After much bitter wrangling among the representatives of Germany, France, England, Belgium, Italy, and Japan, in June the Young plan was launched. Germany's debt of twenty-five billion dollars was to be paid by 1988, payments to be made through the new Bank for International Settlements. Germany was to be free of Allied financial supervision and the Army of Occupation in the Rhineland was to be evacuated, beginning September 1929. The Allies floated a three-million-dollar loan to help finance her initial payment. ("In 1931 Hoover proposed a moratorium of one year for all payments on intergovernmental debts and reparations, and with some clarification the proposal was accepted. Since the expiration of this moratorium," states the *Columbia Encyclopedia* (1935), "no way has been found to secure satisfactory payments from Germany.") Of Young's part in the working out of this plan Thomas Lamont [40] has written, "His was a leadership that was never demanded by him, but was freely accorded to him by all his associates, because of their clear recognition of his fairness, his character, and his eminent capacity to be a leader of both affairs and men."

In 1929 Young relinquished his chairmanship of the board of RCA to become chairman of its executive committee (1929-33). A year later, when James G. Harbord [45] had become board chairman, the Supreme Court filed suit against RCA under the Sherman Antitrust Act, the charge being that it and other corporations had "created a patent combination . . . through which they exercise joint control over the radio industry." Young's viewpoint on government control, stated in 1931, was that "governmental organization is an inefficient and uneconomical instrument. . . .It is scarcely too much to say that the best of the publicly owned enterprises are comparable only with the worst of the privately owned concerns." In 1940, viewing the development of a decade and looking beyond the war, he declared: "The American system, having been through ten years of rapid change in which even dyed-in-the-wool conservatives of rapid change have learned to accommodate themselves to new conditions, is now newly supple and far more ready than ever before to cope with the confusions of war and its aftermath."

As an industrial leader, Young is seen as working continuously in the interest of labor. He is regarded as largely responsible for such innovations at General Electric as a system of employee stock plans, unemployment insurance, and a "cultural wage" (as opposed to a mere living wage). Young—of the opinion that "the world does not owe a man a living, but business, if it is to fulfill its ideal, owes men an opportunity to earn a living"—in 1931 presented Gerard Swope [41], president of General Electric, with a plan which "rather stunned" industry because of its "revolutionary features." The aim of the plan was to stabilize the entire electrical industry by uniting all its independent branches which employed fifty men or more into one unit. The whole industry was to operate according to rules established by a trade commission and was to be supervised by a Federal agency. An important feature of the plan was that "a uniform system of accounting, a free exchange of information, a balancing of production and consumption, and the insurance of workers in accident, sickness, and unemployment" were to be exercised by each firm in the association. Young pointed out that the stabilization of industry calls for the subordination of personal liberty to teamwork. "Too many people think that we can have an effective plan without paying anything for it," declared the industrialist.

The writers of the Swope plan, aware from the start that it would come into conflict with the Sherman Antitrust Act, hoped that the Supreme Court might sustain it if it were put into effect as a laboratory experiment under Federal supervision. However, the plan is still in its theoretical state. "The old notion," asserts Young, "that the heads of business are the paid attorneys of stockholders, to exploit labor and public in the stockholders' interest, is gone—I hope forever. Big business cannot be private business if it is to grow." "It is an institution," wrote Ida M. Tarbell, "of Young's conception."; its leaders are trustees . . . who have an obligation to everybody concerned in it, to the public which it must serve satisfactorily if it is to exist, to the workers from top to bottom who keep the institution not only going but growing, as well as to stockholders."

Interested also in youth and its problems, Young has devoted much time to the field of education. He believes that schools should place more emphasis on character and emotional development than on academic achievements. Among the findings of the American Youth Commission, of which he acted as chairman from 1936 to 1942, was this: "The community reaches its effectiveness in meeting the needs of young people in school and out, where there is some organization whose business it is to know and utilize all youth-serving resources, physical and organizational, at the community level." Young served also as a trustee of St. Lawrence University from 1912 to 1934, and was a member of the General Education Board and the International Education Board (1925-40), and in 1939 of the planning committee of the Conference on Children in a Democracy. He was also on the National Advisory Council of the National Youth Administration in 1940, and in 1945 is a member of the Board of Regents of the State of New York.

In April 1940 President Roosevelt [42] appointed Young, who had retired as chairman of General Electric in 1939, as head of a committee to survey the Nation's transportation problems. (The committee was supervised by the National Resources Planning Board.) After two years of study Young presented a report to the board on "the most economical and effective way of moving people and goods from one place to another." In 1941 he joined the National Patent Planning Commission, and the following year he became a member of the New York regional committee of the War Manpower Commission. After three years in retirement Young in 1942 resumed his duties as acting chairman of General Electric to supervise the manufacture of more than a billion dollars' worth of war orders held by the company. In the latter part of 1944 he retired once again, becoming honorary chairman of the board.

Young was awarded the gold medal of the National Institute of Social Sciences in 1925, and he also holds such foreign decorations as the Commander's Cross of the French Legion of Honor (1924), the Belgian Order of Leopold (1925), the First Order of the German Red Cross (1925), and the Order of the Rising Sun, fourth class, from Japan (1921). The executive has received the honorary degrees of LL.D., Litt.D., and D.C.S. (Doctor of Commercial Science) from more than twenty-five colleges in the United States. He is also an

YOUNG, OWEN D.—*Continued*
honorary member of several clubs and belongs
to various fraternities and organizations.

The industrialist is described as "lank,
dreamy, and gentle-spoken." He claims he is
a farmer at heart, spending most of his time
of late raising cows on his farm in Van
Hornesville and reading books and magazines
on agriculture. But he is a bibliophile, too,
and in 1941 he presented a collection of rare
books, autographed letters, and manuscripts to
the New York Public Library. One thing he
has shunned is politics, having continually refused to contest for a public office. More
than a decade ago he asserted, "Isolation
to America, either economic or political, is impossible. . . .Peace thrives in a world of contentment and mutual welfare. It cannot live
in a world or nation where there are inequalities and injustices caused by man-made barriers." In 1944 he described Lend-Lease as "an
invaluable factor in effecting successful economic settlement among nations after the
war. . . .There is no vast accumulation of
debt between the Allies. Lend-Lease has cared
for that. That I regard as one of the greatest
inventions of our time."

References

> Harper 163:275-83 Ag '31
> National Cyclopædia of American Biog-
> raphy Current vol A p81
> Tarbell, I. M. Owen D. Young (1932)
> Who's Who in America, 1944-45
> Who's Who in Commerce and Industry,
> 1940-41

ZULOAGA, IGNACIO (thoo͞o"lō-ä'gä ēg-
nä'thyō) July 26, 1870—Oct. 31, 1945 Spanish painter; prolific artist noted for his portraits and realistic portrayals of such Spanish
types as gypsies, beggars, and bull fighters;
first New York exhibition held in 1909; among
his works are *Doña Mercedes, Market Scene,
Gypsy Bull Fighter's Family,* and *Daniel Zuloaga and His Daughters.*

Obituary

> N Y Times p23 N 1 '45 por

BIOGRAPHICAL REFERENCES CONSULTED

The publication dates listed are those of volumes in CURRENT BIOGRAPHY's reference collection.

American Catholic Who's Who, 1942-43

American Medical Directory, 1942

American Men of Science (1938)

American Women, 1939-40

America's Young Men, 1938-39

Baker's Biographical Dictionary of Musicians (1940)

Baseball Register (1944)

Biographic Register of the Department of State, Sep 1, 1944

Blue Book of American Aviation, 1940

Burke, J. B. Genealogical and Heraldic History of the Peerage and Baronetage, the Privy Council and Knightage 1936 (Burke's Peerage)

Catholic Who's Who, 1941

Chavez, A. V. Contemporary Mexican Artists (1937)

Chemical Who's Who, 1937

Cheney, M. C. Modern Art in America (1939)

Chi è?, (1936)

China Handbook, 1937-1943

Congressional Directory (1945)

Dictionary of the American Hierarchy (1940)

Dictionnaire National des Contemporains (1936)

Directory of Medical Specialists, 1942

Ewen, D. ed. Composers of Today (1936)

Ewen, D. Dictators of the Baton (1943)

Ewen, D. ed. Living Musicians (1940)

International Motion Picture Almanac, 1943-44

International Press Who's Who; New Zealand, 1938

International Who's Who, 1942

Japan-Manchoukuo Year Book, 1940

Kunitz. S. J. and Haycraft, H. eds. Junior Book of Authors (1934)

Kunitz, S. J. and Haycraft, H. eds. Twentieth Century Authors (1942)

Leaders in Education (1941)

Mantle, B. Contemporary American Playwrights (1938)

Millett, F. B. Contemporary American Authors (1940)

National Cyclopædia of American Biography Current Volumes A-F (1924-42)

New Standard Encyclopedia of Art (1939)

Religious Leaders of America, 1941-42

Sobel, B. ed. Theatre Handbook (1940)

Streyckmans, F. B. Today's Young Men (1940)

Texian Who's Who (1937)

Thompson, O. ed. International Cyclopedia of Music and Musicians (1943)

Variety Radio Directory, 1940-41

Vodarsky-Shiraeff, A. comp. Russian Composers and Musicians (1940)

Webster's Biographical Dictionary (1943)

Wer ist Wer (1937)

Wer ist's? (1935)

Who is Who in Music, 1941

Who's Who, 1945

Who's Who Among North American Authors (1939)

Who's Who Among Physicians and Surgeons, 1938

Who's Who in America, 1944-45

Who's Who in American Art, 1940-41

Who's Who in American Education (1941-42)

Who's Who in American Jewry, 1938-39

Who's Who in Australia (1938)

Who's Who in Aviation, 1942-43

Who's Who in Canada, 1936-37

Who's Who in Central and East-Europe, 1935-36

Who's Who in China (1936)

Who's Who in Colored America, 1941-44

Who's Who in Commerce and Industry (1944)

Who's Who in Engineering, 1941

Who's Who in Japan, 1937

Who's Who in Latin America (1940)

Who's Who in Law, 1937

Who's Who in Library Service (1943)

Who's Who in the Nation's Capital, 1938-39

Who's Who in New York, 1938

Who's Who in Railroading, 1940

Who's Who in Polish America (1940)

Who's Who in the Clergy, 1935-36

Who's Who in the Theatre (1939)

Wier, A. E. ed. Macmillan Encyclopedia of Music and Musicians (1938)

Women of Achievement (1940)

PERIODICALS AND NEWSPAPERS CONSULTED

A. L. A. Bul—American Library Association Bulletin single copy 25c; free to members. American Library Assn, 520 N Michigan Ave, Chicago

Adult Ed J—Adult Education Journal $2. American Association for Adult Education, 525 W 120th St, New York
Formerly Journal of Adult Education

Adv & Selling—Advertising and Selling $3. Robbins Pub Co, Inc, 9 E 38th St, New York

Am Arch See Arch Rec

Am Artist—American Artist $3. Watson-Guptill Publications, Inc, 330 W 42nd St, New York
Formerly Art Instruction

Am Assn Univ Women J—Journal of the American Association of University Women $1. American Assn of University Women, 1634 I St, N W, Washington, D.C.

Am Federationist—American Federationist $2. American Federation of Labor, 901 Massachusetts Ave, Washington, D.C.

Am Hist R—American Historical Review $5; free to members of the American Historical Assn. Macmillan Co, 60 Fifth Ave, New York

Am Home—American Home $1.50. American Home Magazine Corp, 55 Fifth Ave, New York

Am Mag—American Magazine $3.00. Crowell-Collier Pub Co, Springfield, Ohio

Am Mag Art See Mag Art

Am Mercury—American Mercury $3. American Mercury, Inc, 570 Lexington Ave, New York

Am Photography—American Photography $2.50. American Photographic Pub Co, 353 Newbury St, Boston

Am Scand R—American Scandinavian Review $2; free to members. American Scandinavian Foundation, 116 E 64th St, New York

Am Scholar—American Scholar $2.50. United Chapters of Phi Beta Kappa, 12 E 44th St, New York

Am Soc R—American Sociological Review $4 (to libraries $3; to students $2.50). American Sociological Society, C. Taeuber, ed. U.S. Department of Agriculture, Washington, D.C.

Amerasia—Amerasia $2.50. Amerasia, 225 Fifth Ave, New York

Ann Am Acad—Annals of the American Academy of Political and Social Science $5; free to members. 3457 Walnut St, Philadelphia

Apollo—Apollo 35s. Field Press, Ltd, Field House, Bream's Bldgs, Chancery Lane, London, EC 4 ($7.50. 18 E 48th St, New York)

Arch Forum—Architectural Forum $4. Time, Inc, 330 E 22nd St, Chicago

Arch Rec—Architectural Record $3. F. W. Dodge Corp, 119 W 40th St, New York
American Architect and Architecture combined with Architectural Record March 1938.

Art Bul—Art Bulletin $10. College Art Assn, Inc, 625 Madison Ave, New York

Art Digest—Art Digest $3. Art Digest, Inc, 116 E 59th St, New York

Art N—Art News $5.50. Art Foundation, Inc, 136 E 57th St, New York

Arts & Arch—Arts and Architecture $3.50. John D. Entenza, 3305 Wilshire Blvd, Los Angeles
California Arts and Architecture until February 1944.

Arts & Dec—Arts and Decoration (discontinued)

Asia—Asia and the Americas $4. Asia Press, Inc, 40 E 49th St, New York

Asiatic R—Asiatic Review £1. East and West, Ltd. 3 Victoria St, London, SW 1

Atlan—Atlantic Monthly $5. Atlantic Monthly Co, 8 Arlington St, Boston

Bet Homes & Gard—Better Homes & Gardens $1.50. Meredith Pub Co, 1714 Locust St, Des Moines, Ia.

Book-of-the-Month Club N—Book-of-the-Month Club News Free to members. Book-of-the Month Club, Inc, 385 Madison Ave, New York

Bookm (London) See Life & Letters To-day

Books (N Y Herald Tribune) See N Y Herald Tribune Books

Books (N Y Times) See N Y Times Book R

Bul Bibliog—Bulletin of Bibliography and Dramatic Index $3. F. W. Faxon Co, 83 Francis St, Boston

Bul Museum Modern Art See New York City. Museum of Modern Art Bul

Bul Pan Am Union See Pan Am Union Bul

Business Week—Business Week $5. McGraw-Hill Pub Co, Inc, 330 W 42nd St, New York

Calif Arts & Arch—California Arts & Architecture. See Arts and Architecture

Canad Forum—Canadian Forum $2. Canadian Forum, Ltd, 28 Wellington St, W, Toronto 1, Canada

Canad Hist R—Canadian Historical Review $2. University of Toronto Press, Toronto

Cath Lib World—Catholic Library World $5; free to members. Catholic Library Assn, P.O. Box 631, Scranton, Pa.

Cath School J—Catholic School Journal $2.50. Bruce Pub Co, 540 N Milwaukee St, Milwaukee, Wis.

Cath World—Catholic World $4. Missionary Society of St Paul the Apostle, 401 W 59th St, New York

Christian Cent—Christian Century $4. Christian Century Press, 407 S Dearborn St, Chicago

Christian Sci Mon—Christian Science Monitor (Atlantic edition) $12. Christian Science Pub Society, 1 Norway St, Boston

Christian Sci Mon Mag—Christian Science Monitor Weekly Magazine Section $2.60. Christian Science Pub Society, 1 Norway St, Boston

Col Engl—College English $3. University of Chicago Press, 5750 Ellis Ave, Chicago
Formerly English Journal (college edition)

Collier's—Collier's $3. Crowell-Collier Pub Co, Springfield, Ohio

Commonweal—Commonweal $5. Commonweal Pub Co, Inc, 386 Fourth Ave, New York

Cong Digest—Congressional Digest $5. Congressional Digest, 726 Jackson Pl, Washington, D.C.

Connoisseur—Connoisseur 43s. Connoisseur, Ltd, 28 & 30 Grosvenor Gardens, London, SW 1 ($7.50. Connoisseur and International Studio, 572 Madison Ave, New York)
Published quarterly after September 1941

Contemp—Contemporary Review $9.50. British Periodicals Ltd, 46-47 Chancery Lane, London, WC 2

Coronet—Coronet $3. D. A. Smart 919 N Michigan Ave, Chicago

Cue—Cue (Manhattan edition) $3. Cue Publishing Co, Inc, 6 E 39th St, New York

Cur Hist See Cur Hist ns

Cur Hist & Forum See Cur Hist ns

Cur Hist ns—Current History $3. Events Pub Co, Inc, 5528 W Oxford St, Philadelphia
Forum and Century combined with Current History May 23, 1940 as Current History and Forum.
Current History and Forum combined with Events July 21, 1941 and the name Current History restored.

Cur Opinion—Current Opinion (discontinued)

Delin—Delineator (discontinued)

Design—Design $3. Design Pub Co, 131 E State St, Columbus. Ohio

Dram Mir—Dramatic Mirror (discontinued)

Dublin R—Dublin Review 15s. Burns Oates & Washbourne, Ltd, 28 Ashley Pl, London, SW 1 ($4 International News Co, 131 Varick St, New York)

Eccl R—Ecclesiastical Review $4. American Ecclesiastical Review, Catholic University of America, Washington, D.C.
Educa—Education $4. Palmer Co, 370 Atlantic Ave, Boston
El Engl R—Elementary English Review $2.50. Elementary English Review, National Council of Teachers of English, 211 W 68th St, Chicago
Engl J—English Journal $3. University of Chicago Press, 5750 Ellis Ave, Chicago
　　Formerly English Journal (high school edition)
Engl J (Col edition) See Col Engl
Engl J (H S ed) See Engl J
Engl R See Nat R
Esquire—Esquire $5. Esquire, Inc, 919 N Michigan Ave, Chicago
Etude—Etude $2.50. Theodore Presser Co, 1712 Chestnut St, Philadelphia

Facts on File—Facts on File $25. Person's Index, Facts on File, Inc, 516 Fifth Ave, New York
Flying—Flying $4. Ziff-Davis Publishing Co, 540 N Michigan Ave, Chicago
Foreign Affairs—Foreign Affairs $5. Council on Foreign Relations, Inc, 58 E 68th St, New York
Foreign Policy Rep—Foreign Policy Reports $5. (to libraries subscription includes Foreign Policy Bulletins and 6 headline books); $3 to F. P. A. members. Foreign Policy Assn, Inc, 22 E 38th St, New York
Fortnightly—Fortnightly $8.50. Fortnightly Review, Ltd, 13 Buckingham St, London, WC 2
Fortune—Fortune $10. Time, Inc, 330 E 22nd St, Chicago
Forum See Cur Hist ns
Free France—Free France (discontinued)

Good H—Good Housekeeping $3.50. Hearst Magazines, Inc, 959 Eighth Ave, New York

Harper—Harper's Magazine $4. Harper & Bros, 49 E 33rd St, New York
Harper's Bazaar—Harper's Bazaar $5. Hearst Magazines, Inc. 572 Madison Ave, New York
Home & F See House B
Horn Book—Horn Book $2.50. Horn Book, Inc, 248 Boylston St, Boston
House & Gard—House and Garden $4. Condé Nast Publications, Inc, Graybar Bldg, 420 Lexington Ave, New York
House B—House Beautiful combined with Home and Field $4. Hearst Magazines, Inc, 572 Madison Ave, New York

Illus Lond N—Illustrated London News £4 9s 6d. 1 New Oxford St, London, WC 1 (American edition $16. British edition $18. International News Co, 131 Varick St, New York)
Ind Woman—Independent Woman $1.50. National Federation of Business and Professional Women's Clubs, Inc, 1819 Broadway, New York
Inland Printer—Inland Printer $4. Maclean-Hunter Pub Corp, 309 W Jackson Blvd, Chicago

J Adult Ed See Adult Ed J
J Home Econ—Journal of Home Economics $2.50. American Home Economics Assn, 620 Mills Bldg, Washington, D.C.
J Negro Hist—Journal of Negro History $4. Association for the Study of Negro Life and History, 1538 Ninth St, N W, Washington, D.C.

Ladies' H J—Ladies' Home Journal $2. Curtis Pub Co, Independence Sq, Philadelphia
Liberty—Liberty $3.50. Liberty Magazine, Inc, 205 E 42nd St, New York
Library J—Library Journal $5. R. R. Bowker Co, 62 W 45th St, New York
Life—Life $4.50. Time, Inc, 330 E 22nd St, Chicago

Life & Letters To-day—Life and Letters To-day 14s. 430 Strand, London WC 2 ($3.50 International News Co, 131 Varick St, New York)
　　London Mercury absorbed Bookman January 1935
　　Life and Letters To-day absorbed London Mercury and Bookman May 1939
Lit Digest—Literary Digest (discontinued)
Liv Age—Living Age (discontinued)
London Mercury—London Mercury and Bookman See Life & Letters To-day
London Studio (Studio)—London Studio, American edition of the Studio $6. Studio Publications, Inc, 381 Fourth Ave, New York (28s; The Studio, Ltd, 66 Chandos Pl, London, WC 2)
Look—Look $2.50 Cowles Magazines, Inc, 511 Fifth Ave, New York

Mademoiselle—Mademoiselle $3. Street & Smith Publications, Inc, 153 W 15th St, New York
Mag Art—Magazine of Art $5; free to members. American Federation of Arts, Barr Bldg, Farragut Sq, Washington, D.C.
　　Formerly American Magazine of Art
Mo Labor R—Monthly Labor Review $3.50. Superintendent of Documents, Washington, D. C.
Motion Pict Classic—Motion Picture Classic (discontinued)
Movie Classic—Movie Classic (discontinued)
Musical Am—Musical America $4. Musical America Corp, 113 W 57th St, New York
Musical Courier—Musical Courier $3. Music Periodicals Corp, 119 W 57th St, New York
Musical Q—Musical Quarterly $3. G. Schirmer, Inc, 3 E 43rd St, New York
Musician—Musician $3. AMF Artists Service, Inc, 139 E 47th St, New York

N Y Dram—New York Dramatic Mirror (discontinued)
N Y Herald Tribune—New York Herald Tribune $17, including Sunday edition. New York Tribune, Inc, 230 W 41st St, New York
N Y Herald Tribune Books—New York Herald Tribune Books $1. New York Tribune, Inc, 230 W 41st St, New York
N Y Post—New York Post $16.50, including Saturday edition. New York Post, Inc, 75 West St, New York
N Y Sun—New York Sun $12. New York Sun, Inc, 280 Broadway, New York
N Y Times—New York Times $17, including Sunday edition. The New York Times Co, 229 W 43rd St, New York
N Y Times Book R—New York Times Book Review $2. The New York Times Co, 229 W 43rd St, New York
N Y World-Telegram—New York World-Telegram $12. New York World-Telegram Corp, 125 Barclay St, New York
Nat Educ Assn J—Journal of the National Education Association $2; free to members. National Education Assn, 1201 16th St, N W, Washington, D. C.
Nat R—National Review 36s. Rolls House, 2 Bream's Bldgs, London, EC 4 ($8.50 International News Co, 131 Varick St, New York)
　　Absorbed English Review August 1937
Nation—The Nation $5. The Nation Associates, Inc, 20 Vesey St, New York
Nation's Bus—Nation's Business $12 (3 years). Chamber of Commerce of the United States, 1615 H St, N W, Washington, D. C.
Natur Hist—Natural History $4. American Museum of Natural History, 79th St and Central Park West, New York
Nature—Nature Magazine $3. American Nature Assn, 1214 16th St, N W, Washington, D. C.
New England Q—New England Quarterly $4. New England Quarterly, 200 Stevens Hall, Orono, Me.
New Repub—New Republic $5. Editorial Publications, Inc, 40 E 49th St, New York
New Statesm & Nation—New Statesman and Nation—Week-end Review 32s. 6d 10 Great Turnstile, London, WC 1 ($7 International News Co, 131 Varick St, New York)
New York City. Museum of Modern Art Bul—Bulletin of the Museum of Modern Art. 10c a copy; free to members. Museum of Modern Art, 11 W 53rd St, New York

New Yorker—New Yorker $6. F-R. Pub Corp,
25 W 43rd St, New York

Newsweek—Newsweek $5. Weekly Publications,
Inc, Newsweek Bldg, 152 W 42nd St, New
York

19th Cent—Nineteenth Century and After $8.75.
Constable & Co, Ltd, 10 Orange St, London, WC 2

Opera N—Opera News $3; free to members.
Metropolitan Opera Guild, Inc, 654 Madison
Ave, New York

Pan Am Union Bul—Bulletin of the Pan American Union $1.50. Pan American Union, 17th
St and Constitution Ave, N W, Washington, D. C.

Parnassus—Parnassus (discontinued)

Pencil P—Pencil Points $3. Reinhold Pub Corp,
330 W 42nd St, New York

Photoplay—Photoplay $3.60 (two years). Macfadden Publications, Inc, 205 E 42nd St,
New York
　Combined with Movie Mirror

Pict R—Pictorial Review (discontinued)

PM—PM $15.50, including Sunday edition. Harry
C. Holden, Subscription Manager, P.O. Box
81, Times Square Station, New York

Poetry—Poetry $3. 232 E Erie St, Chicago

Pol Sci Q—Political Science Quarterly $5; free
to members. Academy of Political Science,
Columbia University, New York

Pop Mech—Popular Mechanics Magazine $2.50.
Popular Mechanics Co, 200 E Ontario St,
Chicago

Pop Sci—Popular Science Monthly $2.50. Popular Science Pub Co, Inc, 353 Fourth Ave,
New York

Progressive Educ—Progressive Education $3.
American Education Fellowship, 289 Fourth
Ave, New York

Prométhée—Prométhée L'Amour de l'Art (discontinued)

Pub W—Publishers' Weekly $5. R. R. Bowker
Co, 62 W 45th St, New York

Quar R—Quarterly Review 31s 4d. 50 Albermarle St, London, W 1. ($6.50 International
News Co, 131 Varick St, New York)

Queen's Q—Queen's Quarterly $2. Queen's University, Kingston, Canada

R of Rs—Review of Reviews (discontinued)

Read Digest—Reader's Digest $3. Reader's Digest Assn, Inc, Pleasantville, N. Y.

Ref Shelf—Reference Shelf $6 per volume of
ten bound numbers, published irregularly.
The H. W. Wilson Co, 950-972 University
Ave, New York

Rotarian—Rotarian $1.50. Rotary International,
35 E Wacker Drive, Chicago

Royal Inst Brit Arch J—Journal of the Royal
Institute of British Architects £1 16s postpaid. The Institute, 66 Portland Pl, London,
W 1

Sat Eve Post—Saturday Evening Post $5. The
Curtis Pub Co, Independence Sq, Philadelphia

Sat R Lit—Saturday Review of Literature $5.
Saturday Review Associates, Inc, 25 W 45th
St, New York

Sch & Soc—School and Society $5; free to
members of the Society for the Advancement of Education, Science Press, Lancaster, Pa.

Sch Arts—School Arts $4. School Arts, 44 Portland St, Worcester, Mass.

Sch R—School Review $2.50. Department of
Education, University of Chicago, 5835 Kimbark Ave, Chicago

Scholastic—Scholastic (high school teacher edition) $2.25 (combined, or teacher edition
only); school group rate (two or more subscriptions to one address) $1 for special
editions. $1.30 for combined edition. Scholastic Corp, 220 E 42nd St, New York

Sci Am—Scientific American $4. Munn & Co,
Inc, 24 W 40th St, New York

Sci Mo—Scientific Monthly $5. American Assn
for the Advancement of Science, Smithsonian Institution Bldg, Washington, D. C.

Sci N L—Science News Letter $5. Science
Service, Inc, 1719 N St, N W, Washington,
D. C.

Sci ns—Science (new series) $6. Science Press,
Lancaster, Pa.

Scrib Com—Scribner's Commentator (discontinued)

Scrib Mag—Scribner's Magazine (discontinued)

So Atlan Q—South Atlantic Quarterly $3. Duke
University Press, Durham, N. C.

Spec—Spectator 30s. 99 Gower St, London,
WC 1 ($7 International News Service, 131
Varick St, New York)

Studio (Am edition) See London Studio

Survey—Survey Mid-monthly $3. Survey Associates, Inc, 112 E 19th St, New York

Survey G—Survey Graphic $3. Survey Associates, Inc, 112 E 19th St, New York

Theatre Arts—Theatre Arts $3.50. Theatre Arts,
Inc, 130 W 56th St, New York
　Formerly Theatre Arts Monthly

Time—Time $5. Time Inc, 330 E 22nd St,
Chicago

Travel—Travel $4. Robert M. McBride & Co,
Inc, 116 E 16th St, New York

U S Bur Labor—Monthly Labor R See Mo Labor R

U S Bur Labor Bul—United States Bureau of
Labor Statistics, Bulletins. Free to libraries.
Bureau of Labor Statistics, Washington,
D. C. Purchase orders, Superintendent of
Documents, Washington, D. C.

U S News—United States News $4. United
States News Bldg, 22nd and M Sts, N W,
Washington, D. C.

U S Office Educ Bul—United States Office of
Education, Bulletins. Free to libraries. Office of Education, Washington, D. C. Purchase orders, Superintendent of Documents,
Washington, D. C.

Va Q R—Virginia Quarterly Review $3. University of Virginia, Charlottesville, Va.

Variety—Variety $10. Variety, Inc, 154 W 46th
St, New York

Victor Record R—Victor Record Review 60c.
RCA Victor div of Radio Corp of America,
Camden, N. J.

Vital Speeches—Vital Speeches of the Day
$3.50. City News Pub Co, 33 W 42nd St,
New York

Vogue—Vogue (Incorporating Vanity Fair) $6.
Conde Nast Publications Inc, Greenwich,
Conn.

Wilson Lib Bul—Wilson Library Bulletin $1.
The H. W. Wilson Co, 950-972 University
Ave, New York
　Formerly Wilson Bulletin

Woman's H C—Woman's Home Companion
$1.50. Crowell-Collier Pub Co, Springfield,
Ohio

Writer—The Writer $3. The Writer, Inc, 8
Arlington St, Boston

Yale R ns—Yale Review $3. 143 Elm St, New
Haven, Conn.

NECROLOGY—1945

This is an index to notices of deaths which occurred between November 10, 1944, and December 31, 1945. Deaths which occurred in late 1945 are recorded in early 1946 issues of CURRENT BIOGRAPHY; references to those issues are included in this index. See 1940-1944 Yearbooks for the necrologies for those years.

Abdullah, Achmed
Adams, Herbert
Albee, Fred H(oudlette) (biog 1943)
Alger, Ellice M(urdoch)
Allee, Marjorie (Hill)
Allee, Mrs. Warder Clyde See Allee, M. H.
Appleton, Robert
Argentinita (biog 1942)
Armetta, Henry
Asquith, Margot (Tennant), Countess of Oxford and Asquith See Oxford and Asquith, M. T. A.
Aston, Francis William See Jan 1946

Baker, S(ara) Josephine
Banning, Kendall
Barbier, George W.
Barnes, William R.
Bartók, Béla (biog 1940)
Beach, Amy Marcy See Beach, Mrs. H. H. A.
Beach, Mrs. H(enry) H(arris) A(ubrey)
Bellamann, Henry (biog 1942)
Benavides, Oscar (Raimundo)
Benchley, Robert (Charles) See Jan 1946 (biog 1941)
Bendix, Vincent
Berry, Edward Wilber
Bertram, Adolf, Cardinal
Bock, Fedor von (biog 1942)
Bogert, George H.
Bose, Subhas Chandra (biog 1944)
Brookhart, Smith W(ildman)
Browne, Edward E(verts) See Jan 1946 ..
Bryan, Charles W(ayland)
Buckner, Simon Bolivar, Jr. (biog 1942)
Bull, Johan
Burke, Thomas
Byas, Hugh (Fulton) (biog 1943)

Caillaux, Joseph
Calder, A(lexander) Stirling
Calder, William M.
Calles, Plutarco Elías
Cannon, Walter Bradford
Carlson, John F(abian)
Cassel, Karl Gustav
Chapman, Frank M(ichler) See Jan 1946
Charnwood, Godfrey Rathbone Benson, 1st Baron
Cheney, Russell

Chernyakhovsky, Ivan D(anilovich) (biog 1944)
Clarke, John Hessin
Clendening, Logan
Cole-Hamilton, J(ohn) B(eresford)
Colijn, Hendricus
Crabtree, James W(illiam)
Craig, Malin (biog 1944)
Craven, Frank
Cregar, Laird
Cret, Paul P(hilippe) (biog 1942)
Crewe, Robert Offley Ashburton Crewe-Milnes, 1st Marquis of
Crow, Carl (biog 1941)
Crownfield, Gertrude
Curtin, John (biog 1941)

Dallin, Cyrus Edwin
Dawson, Bertrand, 1st Viscount Dawson of Penn See Dawson of Penn, B. D., 1st Viscount
Dawson of Penn, Bertrand Dawson, 1st Viscount
De Casseres, Benjamin See Feb 1946
Deland, Margaret Wade (Campbell)
Dick, Charles
Dreiser, Theodore See Feb 1946
Dwyfor, David Lloyd George, 1st Earl of See Lloyd George of Dwyfor, D. L. G. 1st Earl (biog 1944)

Easley, Claudius M(iller)
Edwards, Gus
Edwards, John H(omer)
Eicher, Edward C(layton) (biog 1941)
Ekman, Carl Gustaf
Ertegun, Mehmet Munir

Fairfax, Beatrice See Jan 1946 (biog 1944)
Fall, Albert B(acon)
Ferris, Scott
Field, Sir Frederick Laurence
Fischer, Hans
Fleming, Sir (John) Ambrose
Flesch, Karl
Flexner, Bernard
Flexner, Jennie M(aas)
Flore, Edward F.
Fouilhoux, J(acques) Andre
Fraser, Leon

Gaffney, T(homas) St. John
Gasch, Marie Manning See Fairfax, B. Jan 1946

George, David Lloyd, 1st Earl Lloyd George of Dwyfor See Lloyd George of Dwyfor, D. L. G., 1st Earl (biog 1944)
Gibson, Charles Dana
Glasgow, Ellen (Anderson Gholson) See Jan 1946
Goddard, Robert H(utchings)
Grant, Heber J.
Green, Florence Topping
Green, Mrs. Howard See Green, F. T.
Guedalla, Philip

Hacha, Emil (biog 1942)
Halsey, Edwin A(lexander)
Harding, Nelson
Harmon, Millard F(illmore) (biog 1942)
Hay, Charles M(artin)
Herring, Clyde L(a Verne)
Hershey, Milton S(navely)
Hicks, Clarence J(ohn)
Himmler, Heinrich (biog 1941)
Holsti, (Eino) Rudolf (Woldemar)
Honjo, Shigerū, Baron See Jan 1946
Hopkins, Nevil Monroe
Howard, Alice Sturtevant
Howard, Mrs. Henry See Howard, A. S.
Howell, William H(enry)
Hughes, Hatcher
Hun, John Gale
Hunter, Glenn See Mar 1946

Igoe, Herbert A.
Ittner, Martin H(ill) (biog 1942)

James, W. Frank See Jan 1946
Jelliffe, Smith Ely
Johnson, Hiram (Warren) (biog 1941)
Johnson, William E(ugene)

Kandinsky, Wassily
Kan-in, Prince Kotohito
Keane, Doris See Jan 1946
Kelley, Edgar Stillman
Kemmerer, E(dwin) W(alter) See Feb 1946 (biog 1941)
Kern, Jerome (David) (biog 1942)
Knoblock, Edward
Konoye, Fumiraro, Prince See Feb 1946 (biog 1940)
Korngold, Julius

CLASSIFICATION BY PROFESSION—1945

Agriculture

Anderson, Clinton P(resba)
Goss, Albert S.
Patton, James G(eorge)

Architecture

Cret, Paul P(hilippe) obit
Ferriss, Hugh
Fouilhoux, J(acques) Andre obit
Kahn, Ely Jacques
Keck, George Fred
Shreve, R(ichard) H(arold)
Stokes, I(saac) N(ewton)
Phelps obit

Art

Adams, Herbert obit
Artzybasheff, Boris
Barnes, Albert C(oombs)
Bogert, George H. obit
Bull, Johan obit
Calder, A(lexander) Stirling obit
Carlson, John F(abian) obit
Charlot, Jean
Cheney, Russell obit
Dallin, Cyrus Edwin obit
Davidson, Jo
Epstein, Jacob
Ferriss, Hugh
Gibson, Charles Dana obit
Green, Florence Topping obit
Harding, Nelson obit
Hayter, William Stanley
Head, Edith
Igoe, Herbert A. obit
Kandinsky, Wassily obit
Kiam, Omar
McPharlin, Paul
Mauldin, Bill
Mydans, Carl M(ayer)
Partridge, Sir Bernard obit
Pippin, Horace
Ripley, Robert L(eroy)
Rockwell, Norman
Rosenthal, Joe
Rothenstein, Sir William obit
Roualt, Georges
Webster, H(arold) T(ucker)
Wyeth, N(ewell) C(onvers) obit
Zuloaga, Ignacio obit

Aviation

Bendix, Vincent obit
Cole-Hamilton, J(ohn) B(eresford) obit
Fitch, Aubrey (Wray)
Frye, Jack
Grumman, Leroy R(andle)
Harmon, Millard F(illmore) obit

Saint Exupéry, Antoine de obit
Smith, C(yrus) R(owlett)
Whittle, Frank
Wilson, Eugene E(dward)
Wright, Theodore P(aul)

Business

Appleton, Robert obit
Babson, Roger W(ard)
Baldwin, William H(enry)
Barnes, William R. obit
Benton, William (Burnett)
Dempsey, Jack
De Rochemont, Richard (Guertis)
Frye, Jack
Gannett, Frank E(rnest)
Head, Walter W(illiam)
Hicks, Clarence J(ohn) obit
Judson, Arthur (Leon)
Kiam, Omar
Knight, John S(hively)
Läuger, Paul
Melcher, Frederic G(ershom)
Mosher, Ira
Norton, W(illiam) W(arder) obit
Powers, John Robert
Rickey, Branch (Wesley)
Ringling, Robert E(dward)
Sloan, Samuel obit
Thackrey, Dorothy S(chiff)
Westmore, Perc

Dance

Argentinita obit
Astaire, Fred
Kelly, Gene
McCracken, Joan
Osato, Sono
Tudor, Antony

Diplomacy

Armour, Norman
Benavides, Oscar (Raimundo) obit
Bernadotte, Folke, Count
Bonnet, Henri
Braden, Spruille
Ertegun, Mehmet Munir obit
Gaffney, T(homas) St. John obit
Holmes, Julius C(ecil)
Holsti, (Eino) Rudolf (Woldemar) obit
Kirk, Alexander C(omstock)
Lattimore, Owen
Lindsay, Sir Ronald (Charles) obit
McCoy, Frank R(oss)
Matthews, H(arrison) Freeman
Oumansky, Constantine (Alexandrovich) obit

Paléologue, (Georges) Maurice obit
Prince, John Dyneley obit
Tatekawa, Yoshitsugu obit
Wang Shih-chieh
Waterlow, Sir Sydney P(hilip) obit
Watson, Edwin M(artin) obit

Education

Ackerman, Carl W(illiam)
Babson, Roger W(ard)
Barnes, Albert C(oombs)
Bartók, Béla obit
Benton, William (Burnett)
Bohr, Niels (Henrik David)
Bowman, Isaiah
Cassel, Karl Gustav obit
Chadwick, Sir James
Crabtree, James W(illiam) obit
Davis, Watson
Davison, F(rederick) Trubee
Dobie, J(ames) Frank
Dodds, Harold W(illis)
Evans, Luther H(arris)
Fischer, Hans obit
Flexner, Jennie M(aas) obit
Gannon, Robert I(gnatius), Rev.
Gauss, Christian
Gulick, Luther (Halsey)
Hansen, Alvin H(arvey)
Hayek, Friedrich A(ugust von)
Hickman, Emily (Gregory)
Hicks, Clarence J(ohn) obit
Hughes, Hatcher obit
Hun, John Gale obit
Laidler, Harry W(ellington)
Lattimore, Owen
Mays, Benjamin E(lijah)
Merriam, John Campbell obit
Milam, Carl H(astings)
Moley, Raymond (Charles)
Morrison, Henry Clinton obit
Norton, W(illiam) W(arder) obit
Nye, Russel B(laine)
Olmstead, Albert Ten Eyck obit
Oppenheimer, J. Robert
Peabody, Endicott, Rev. obit
Pratt, Frederic Bayley obit
Prince, John Dyneley obit
Roper, Elmo (Burns, Jr.)
Rothenstein, Sir William obit
Rowe, L(eo) S(tanton)
Russell, James Earl obit
Ryan, John (Augustine), Msgr. obit
Sabin, Florence R(ena)
Shaw, Lau
Shear, T(heodore) Leslie obit
Shellabarger, Samuel
Soule, George (Henry, Jr.)
Sproul, Robert Gordon
Tobias, Channing H(eggie)

Vail, Robert W(illiam) G(len-roie) obit
Villa-Lobos, Heitor
Wang Shih-chieh
White, Helen C(onstance)
Woodhouse, (Margaret) Chase Going
Wu Yi-fang
Young, Hugh (Hampton) obit

Engineering

Bailey, Sir Donald Coleman
Fleming, Sir (John) Ambrose obit
Howe, C(larence) D(ecatur)
Johnson, J(ohn) Monroe
Lake, Simon obit
Norden, Carl L(ucas)
Reybold, Eugene
Robinson, Holton D. obit
Sultan, Daniel I(som)
Taylor, A(lbert) Hoyt
Watson-Watt, Sir Robert (Alexander)

Finance

Babson, Roger W(ard)
Cassel, Karl Gustav obit
Dalton, Hugh
Fraser, Leon obit
Gulick, Luther (Halsey)
Hansen, Alvin H(arvey)
Head, Walter W(illiam)
Snyder, John W(esley)
Whitney, John Hay
Woodhouse, (Margaret) Chase Going
Woodlock, Thomas Francis obit

Government— International

Appleton, Sir Edward (Victor)
Benavides, Oscar (Raimundo) obit
Bidault, Georges
Bonnet, Henri
Bose, Subhas Chandra obit
Caillaux, Joseph obit
Calles, Plutarco Elías obit
Charnwood, Godfrey Rathbone Benson, 1st Baron obit
Chifley, Joseph B(enedict)
Colijn, Hendricus obit
Crewe, Robert Offley Ashburton Crewe-Milnes, 1st Marquis of obit
Curtin, John obit
Dalton, Hugh
Damaskinos, Archbishop
Ekman, Carl Gustaf obit
Ertegun, Mehmet Munir obit
Hacha, Emil obit
Himmler, Heinrich obit
Holsti, (Eino) Rudolf (Woldemar) obit
Howe, C(larence) D(ecatur)
Isaacs, George (Alfred)
Kan-in, Prince Kotohito obit
Laval, Pierre obit
Ley, Robert obit

Lindsay, Sir Ronald (Charles) obit
Lloyd George of Dwyfor, David Lloyd George, 1st Earl obit
Maher, Ahmed, Pasha obit
Marriott, Sir John (Arthur Ransome) obit
Mussolini, Benito (Amilcare Andrea) obit
Negrin, Juan
Oumansky, Constantine (Alexandrovich) obit
Paléologue, (Georges) Maurice obit
Parri, Ferruccio
Paul-Boncour, Joseph
Pueyrredon, Honorio obit
Renner, Karl
Salter, Alfred obit
Shawcross, Sir Hartley (William)
Smith, Sir Ben
Spaak, Paul-Henri
Sugiyama, Hajime obit
Suzuki, Kantaro, Baron
Tardieu, André obit
Tatekawa, Yoshitsugu obit
Terboven, Josef obit
Wake-Walker, Sir W(illiam) Frederick obit
Wang Ching-wei obit
Wang Shih-chieh
Waterlow, Sir Sydney P(hilip) obit
Watson-Watt, Sir Robert (Alexander)
Witos, Wincenty obit
Wright, (Sir Robert Alderson Wright) Lord
Wu Yi-fang

Government— United States

Anderson, Clinton P(resba)
Armour, Norman
Arnall, Ellis (Gibbs)
Bailey, Josiah W(illiam)
Baker, S(ara) Josephine obit
Benton, William (Burnett)
Bowman, Isaiah
Braden, Spruille
Brickell, (Henry) Herschel
Brookhart, Smith W(ildman) obit
Bryan, Charles W(ayland) obit
Burton, Harold H(itz)
Calder, William M. obit
Caraway, Hattie W(yatt)
Clark, Tom C(ampbell)
Clay, Lucius D(uBignon)
Davison, F(rederick) Trubee
Dawson, William L(evi)
Dick, Charles obit
Douglas, Emily Taft
Eaton, Charles A(ubrey)
Edge, Walter E(vans)
Edwards, John H(omer) obit
Eicher, Edward C(layton) obit
Evans, Luther H(arris)
Fall, Albert B(acon) obit
Ferris, Scott obit

Gaffney, T(homas) St. John obit
Goss, Albert S.
Gulick, Luther (Halsey)
Halsey, Edwin A(lexander) obit
Hay, Charles M(artin) obit
Herring, Clyde L(aVerne) obit
Herzog, Paul M(ax)
Hodgson, Joseph V(ernon)
Holmes, Julius C(ecil)
Izac, Ed(ouard) V(ictor Michel)
Johnson, Hiram (Warren) obit
Johnson, J(ohn) Monroe
Johnson, William E(ugene) obit
Kirk, Alexander C(omstock)
Lattimore, Owen
Lee, Blair obit
McCarthy, Frank
McCoy, Frank R(oss)
McMahon, (James O')Brien
Magnuson, Warren G(rant)
Maloney, Francis T. obit
March, Charles Hoyt obit
Martin, Edward
Martin, George Brown obit
Matthews, H(arrison) Freeman
Miller, Frieda S(egelke)
Moley, Raymond (Charles)
Moses, George Higgins obit
Moses, John obit
Mott, James W(heaton) obit
Murdock, Victor obit
Murray, James E(dward)
Newberry, Truman H(andy) obit
Newton, Cleveland Alexander obit
O'Connor, James Francis obit
O'Mahoney, Joseph C(hristopher)
Pasvolsky, Leo
Pauley, Edwin W(endell)
Porter, Paul A(ldermandt)
Reid, Frank R., Sr. obit
Roosevelt, Franklin D(elano) obit
Ross, Charles (Griffith)
Schwellenbach, Lewis B(axter)
Scrugham, James Graves obit
Smith, E(llison) DuRant obit
Smith, Margaret Chase
Snyder, John W(esley)
Speaks, John Charles obit
Sproul, Robert Gordon
Stanfield, Robert Nelson obit
Stokes, I(saac) N(ewton) Phelps
Sumner, Jessie
Symington, W(illiam) Stuart (3d)
Taft, Charles P(helps 2d)
Taylor, A(lbert) Hoyt
Thomas, John W. obit
Tisdel, Alton P. obit
Truman, Harry S.
Tydings, Millard E(velyn)
Waesche, Russell R(andolph)
Watt, Robert J.
Weaver, Arthur J. obit
Whitney, John Hay
Woodhouse, (Margaret) Chase Going
Wright, Theodore P(aul)

Industry

Barnard, Chester I(rving)
Bendix, Vincent obit
Braden, Spruille
Gifford, Walter S(herman)
Grumman, Leroy R(andle)
Harbord, James G(uthrie)
Hershey, Milton S(navely) obit
Mosher, Ira
Newberry, Truman H(andy)
  obit
Pauley, Edwin W(endell)
Rank, J(oseph) Arthur
Smith C(yrus) R(owlett)
Stanton, Frank
Symington, W(illiam) Stuart
  (3d)
Warner, Albert
Warner, Harry M(orris)
Warner, Jack L.
Weaver, Arthur J. obit
Weyerhaeuser, Frederick E(d-
  ward) obit
Wilcox, Herbert
Wilson, Eugene E(dward)
Wright, Theodore P(aul)
Young, Owen D.

Journalism

Ackerman, Carl W(illiam)
Arne, Sigrid
Banning, Kendall obit
Bonsal, Stephen
Boyle, Hal
Brickell (Henry) Herschel
Byas, Hugh (Fulton) obit
Canham, Erwin D(ain)
Chifley, Joseph B(enedict)
Crow, Carl obit
Davis, Watson
De Rochemont, Richard (Guer-
  tis)
Frick, Ford C(hristopher)
Gannett, Frank E(rnest)
Igoe, Herbert A. obit
Jensen, Oliver O(rmerod)
Knight, John S(hively)
Korngold, Julius obit
Laurence, William L(eonard)
MacGowan, Gault
Moley, Raymond (Charles)
Murdock, Victor obit
Mydans, Shelley Smith
Nathan, George Jean
Parri, Ferruccio
Pyle, Ernie obit
Ripley, Robert L(eroy)
Rosenthal, Joe
Ross, Charles (Griffith)
Seibold, Louis obit
Stark, Louis
Thackrey, Dorothy S(chiff)
Thompson, Oscar obit
Wilson, Edmund
Woodlock, Thomas Francis obit

Labor

Curran, Joseph E(dwin)
Flore, Edward F. obit
Foster, William Z(ebulon)

Frankensteen, Richard T(ruman)
Goss, Albert S.
Herzog, Paul M(ax)
Isaacs, George (Alfred)
Laidler, Harry W(ellington)
Miller, Frieda S(egelke)
Patton, James G(eorge)
Robins, Margaret Dreier obit
Schwellenbach, Lewis B(axter)
Smith, Sir Ben
Stark, Louis
Tobin, Daniel J(oseph)
Watt, Robert J.

Law

Clark, Tom C(ampbell)
Clarke, John Hessin obit
Eicher, Edward C(layton) obit
Flexner, Bernard obit
Fosdick, Raymond B(laine)
Hay, Charles M(artin) obit
Herzog, Paul M(ax)
Hodgson, Joseph V(ernon)
Kross, Anna M(oscowitz)
Landis, Kenesaw Mountain obit
Lerch, Archer L(ynn)
Newton, Cleveland Alexander
  obit
Paul-Boncour, Joseph
Porter, Paul A(ldermandt)
Reid, Frank R., Sr. obit
Schwellenbach, Lewis B(axter)
Shawcross, Sir Hartley (Wil-
  liam)
Spaak, Paul-Henri
Sykes, Eugene Octave obit
Taft, Charles P(helps 2d)
Wright, (Sir Robert Alderson
  Wright) Lord

Literature

Abdullah, Achmed obit
Allee, Marjorie (Hill) obit
Artzybasheff, Boris
Banning, Kendall obit
Bellamann, Henry obit
Bonsal, Stephen
Brickell (Henry) Herschel
Burke, Thomas obit
Chase, Mary (Coyle)
Crow, Carl obit
Crownfield, Gertrude obit
Deland, Margaret Wade
  (Campbell) obit
Dobie, J(ames) Frank
Gilder, Rosamond
Graham, Gwethalyn
Guedalla, Philip obit
Knoblock, Edward obit
Landon, Margaret (Dorothea
  Mortenson)
Langley, Adria Locke
McPharlin, Paul
Marriott, Sir John (Arthur Ran-
  some) obit
Melcher, Frederic G(ershom)
Mydans, Shelley Smith
Nathan, George Jean
Nock, Albert Jay obit
Norris, Charles G(ilman) obit
Nye, Russel B(laine)

Oxford and Asquith, Margot
  (Tennant) Asquith, Countess
  of obit
Paléologue, (Georges) Maurice
  obit
Papashvily, George
Papashvily, Helen (Waite)
Patten, Gilbert obit
Rama Rau, Santha
Robeson, Eslanda (Cardoza)
  Goode
Rolland, Romain obit
Saint Exupéry, Antoine de obit
Salten, Felix obit
Seabrook, William B(uehler)
  obit
Shaw, Lau
Shellabarger, Samuel
Smith, Lady Eleanor (Furneaux)
  obit
Symons, Arthur obit
Tolstoi, Aleksei Nikolaevich,
  Count obit
Troubetzkoy, Amélie (Rives)
  Princess obit
Ullman, James R(amsey)
Valéry, Paul Ambrose obit
Werfel, Franz obit
White, Helen C(onstance)
Wilson, Edmund
Yeats-Brown, Francis obit

Medicine

Albee, Fred H(oudlette) obit
Alger, Ellice M(urdoch) obit
Baker, S(ara) Josephine obit
Cannon, Walter Bradford obit
Clendening, Logan obit
Dawson of Penn, Bertrand Daw-
  son, 1st Viscount obit
Funk, Casimir
Gasser, Herbert S(pencer)
Howell, William H(enry) obit
Jelliffe, Smith Ely obit
McIntire, Ross T.
Menninger, William Claire
Sabin, Florence R(ena) obit
Salter, Alfred
Young, Hugh (Hampton) obit

Military

Allen, Frank A(lbert, Jr.)
Bailey, Sir Donald Coleman
Banning, Kendall obit
Benavides, Oscar (Raimundo)
  obit
Bock, Fedor von obit
Bolté, Charles G(uy)
Boyce, Westray Battle
Brunner, Jean Adam
Buckner, Simon Bolivar, Jr. obit
Calles, Plutarco Elías obit
Chernyakhovsky, Ivan D(anilo-
  vich) obit
Christison, Sir (Alexander
  Frank) Philip
Clay, Lucius D(uBignon)
Cole-Hamilton, J(ohn) B(eres-
  ford) obit
Craig, Malin obit
Crist, William E(arl)

Dobbie, Sir William (George Shedden)
Easley, Claudius M(iller) obit
Festing, Francis W(ogan)
Gavin, James M(aurice)
Geiger, Roy S(tanley)
Gerow, Leonard Townsend
Gregory, Edmund B(ristol)
Groninger, Homer M.
Groves, Leslie R(ichard)
Hansell, Haywood S(hepherd, Jr.)
Harbord, James G(uthrie)
Harmon, Millard F(illmore) obit
Hodge, John R(eed)
Hodgson, Joseph V(ernon)
Holmes, Julius C(ecil)
Horrocks, B(rian) G(wynne)
Kan-in, Prince Kotohito obit
Lattre de Tassigny, Jean (Joseph Marie Gabriel) de
Leigh-Mallory, Sir Trafford L(eigh) obit
Lerch, Archer L(ynn)
McCarthy, Frank
McCoy, Frank R(oss)
McCreery, Sir Richard L(oudon)
Mauldin, Bill
Menninger, William Claire
Porter, William N(ichols)
Price, Harrison J(ackson) obit
Reckord, Milton A(tchison)
Reybold, Eugene
Rose, Maurice obit
Rupertus, William H(enry) obit
Scobie, Ronald M(acKenzie)
Shaposhnikov, Boris (Mikhailovich) obit
Simpson, William H(ood)
Slim, Sir William Joseph
Smith, Holland M(cTyeire)
Stuart, Kenneth obit
Sugiyama, Hajime obit
Sultan, Daniel I(som)
Surles, Alexander D(ay)
Tatekawa, Yoshitsugu obit
Tolbukhin, Fedor I(vanovich)
Truscott, Lucian K(ing, Jr.)
Ulio, James A(lexander)
Vandenberg, Hoyt S(anford)
Wake-Walker, Sir W(illiam) Frederick obit
Watson, Edwin M(artin) obit
Wedemeyer, Albert C(oady)
Whittle, Frank
Wilby, Frances B(owditch)

Motion Pictures

Armetta, Henry obit
Arthur, Jean
Astaire, Fred
Barbier, George W. obit
Bergen, Edgar
Brown, Joe E(van)
Calloway, Cab
Christians, Mady
Colbert, Claudette
Craven, Frank obit
Cregar, Laird obit
Davis, Joan

De Rochemont, Richard (Guertis)
Dunne, Irene
Edwards, Gus obit
Fitzgerald, Barry
Gable, Clark
Gribble, Harry Wagstaff (Graham-)
Head, Edith
Johnson, Hall
Johnson, Van
Kelly, Gene
Langdon, Harry obit
Lillie, Beatrice
McCracken, Joan
Nazimova, Alla obit
Neagle, Anna
Pickford, Mary
Rank, J(oseph) Arthur
Romberg, Sigmund
Sheehan, Winfield R. obit
Temple, Shirley
Tucker, Sophie
Velez, Lupe obit
Warner, Albert
Warner, Harry M(orris)
Warner, Jack L.
Westmore, Perc
Whiteman, Paul
Whitney, John Hay
Whitty, Dame May
Wilcox, Herbert

Music

Bartók, Béla obit
Beach, Mrs. H(enry) H(arris) A(ubrey) obit
Bellamann, Henry obit
Calloway, Cab
Casadesus, Robert (Marcel)
Dunne, Irene
Edwards, Gus obit
Elman, Mischa
Fiedler, Arthur
Flesch, Karl obit
Goossens, Eugene
Gould, Morton
Johnson, Hall
Judson, Arthur (Leon)
Kelley, Edgar Stillman obit
Kern, Jerome (David) obit
Korngold, Julius obit
Landowska, Wanda
Lhevinne, Josef obit
Liebling, Leonard obit
Loesser, Frank (Henry)
McCormack, John obit
Martinelli, Giovanni
Mascagni, Pietro obit
Melton, James
Munsel, Patrice
Piatigorsky, Gregor
Ringling, Robert E(dward)
Romberg, Sigmund
Rubinstein, Artur
Sargent, (Harold) Malcolm (Watts)
Stebbins, George Coles obit
Szell, George
Teyte, Maggie
Thompson, Oscar obit
Tibbett, Lawrence
Tucker, Sophie

Villa-Lobos, Heitor
White, Portia
Whiteman, Paul

Naval

Barbey, Daniel E(dward)
Buckner, Simon Bolivar, Jr. obit
Field, Sir Frederick Laurence obit
Fitch, Aubrey (Wray)
Geiger, Roy S(tanley)
Jensen, Oliver O(rmerod)
Lee, Willis A(ugustus, Jr.) obit
McCain, John S(idney) obit
McIntire, Ross T.
Ramsay, Sir Bertram (Home) obit
Rawlings, Sir (Henry) Bernard (Hughes)
Royal, Forrest B. obit
Rupertus, William H(enry) obit
Smith, Holland M(cTyeire)
Suzuki, Kantaro, Baron
Tennant, William George
Waesche, Russell R(andolph)
Wilson, Eugene E(dward)

Politics

Anderson, Clinton P(resba)
Arnall, Ellis (Gibbs)
Bailey, Josiah W(illiam)
Benavides, Oscar (Raimundo) obit
Bidault, Georges
Bose, Subhas Chandra obit
Brookhart, Smith W(ildman) obit
Bryan, Charles W(ayland) obit
Burton, Harold H(itz)
Caillaux, Joseph obit
Calder, William M. obit
Calles, Plutarco Elías obit
Caraway, Hattie W(yatt)
Charnwood, Godfrey Rathbone Benson, 1st Baron obit
Chifley, Joseph B(enedict)
Colijn, Hendricus obit
Crewe, Robert Offley Ashburton Crewe-Milnes, 1st Marquis of obit
Curtin, John obit
Dalton, Hugh
Davidson, Jo
Dawson, William L(evi)
Dick, Charles obit
Douglas, Emily Taft
Eaton, Charles A(ubrey)
Edge, Walter E(vans)
Edwards, John H(omer) obit
Ekman, Carl Gustaf obit
Fall, Albert B(acon) obit
Foster, William Z(ebulon)
Frankensteen, Richard T(ruman)
Hacha, Emil obit
Hay, Charles M(artin) obit
Herring, Clyde L(aVerne) obit
Himmler, Heinrich obit
Holsti, (Eino) Rudolf (Woldemar) obit

Howe, C(larence) D(ecatur)
Isaacs, George (Alfred)
Izac, Ed(ouard) V(ictor Michel)
Johnson, Hiram (Warren) obit
Kross, Anna M(oskowitz)
Laidler, Harry W(ellington)
Laval, Pierre obit
Lee, Blair obit
Ley, Robert obit
Lloyd George of Dwyfor, David Lloyd George, 1st Earl obit
McMahon (James O') Brien
Magnuson, Warren G(rant)
Maher, Ahmed, Pasha obit
Maloney, Francis T. obit
March, Charles Hoyt obit
Marriott, Sir John (Arthur Ransome) obit
Martin, Edward
Martin, George Brown obit
Moses, George Higgins obit
Moses, John obit
Mott, James W(heaton) obit
Murdock, Victor obit
Murray, James E(dward)
Mussolini, Benito (Amilcare Andrea) obit
Negrin, Juan
Newberry, Truman H(andy) obit
Newton, Cleveland Alexander obit
O'Connor, James Francis obit
O'Mahoney, Joseph C(hristopher)
Parri, Ferruccio
Paul-Boncour, Joseph
Pauley, Edwin W(endell)
Pendergast, Thomas J(oseph) obit
Porter, Paul A(ldermandt)
Pueyrredon, Honorio obit
Reid, Frank, R., Sr. obit
Renner, Karl
Roosevelt, Franklin D(elano) obit
Salter, Alfred obit
Schwellenbach, Lewis B(axter)
Simms, Ruth Hanna McCormick obit
Smith, Sir Ben
Smith, E(llison) DuRant obit
Smith, Margaret Chase
Spaak, Paul-Henri
Speaks, John Charles obit
Stanfield, Robert Nelson obit
Sumner, Jessie
Suzuki, Kantaro, Baron
Taft, Charles P(helps 2d)
Tardieu, André obit
Terboven, Josef obit
Thomas, John W. obit
Truman, Harry S.
Tydings, Millard E(velyn)
Wang Ching-wei obit
Wang Shih-chieh
Waterlow, Sir Sidney P(hilip) obit
Weaver, Arthur J. obit
Woodhouse, (Margaret) Chase Going

Radio

Bergen, Edgar
Bonnell, John Sutherland, Rev.
Brown, Joe E(van)
Calloway, Cab
Davis, Joan
Fay, Frank
Gould, Morton
Harbord, James G(uthrie)
Kelly, Joe
Melton, James
Moley, Raymond (Charles)
Munsel, Patrice
Ripley, Robert L(eroy)
Sargent, (Harold) Malcolm (Watts)
Stanton, Frank
Tibbett, Lawrence
Whiteman, Paul
Wynn, Ed

Religion

Bertram, Adolf, Cardinal obit
Bonnell, John Sutherland, Rev.
Damaskinos, Archbishop
Eaton, Charles A(ubrey)
Fisher, Geoffrey Francis, Archbishop of Canterbury
Gannon, Robert I(gnatius), Rev.
Grant, Heber J. obit
Ironside, Henry Allan
Mays, Benjamin E(lijah)
O'Shea, William F(rancis), Bishop
Peabody, Endicott, Rev. obit
Pickett, Clarence E(van)
Pugmire, Ernest I(vison)
Ray, (Jackson Harvelle) Randolph, Rev.
Ryan, John (Augustine) Msgr. obit
Schleich, Michel, Rev. obit
Schrembs, Archbishop Joseph obit
Stebbins, George Coles obit
Szold, Henrietta obit
Tobias, Channing H(eggie)

Science

Appleton, Sir Edward (Victor)
Barnes, Albert C(oombs)
Berry, Edward Wilber obit
Bohr, Niels (Henrik David)
Bowman, Isaiah
Cannon, Walter Bradford obit
Chadwick, Sir James
Davis, Watson
Davison, F(rederick) Trubee
Fermi, Enrico
Fischer, Hans obit
Fleming, Sir (John) Ambrose obit
Funk, Casimir
Gasser, Herbert S(pencer)
Goddard, Robert H(utchings) obit
Groves, Leslie R(ichard)

Hopkins, Nevil Monroe obit
Ittner, Martin H(ill) obit
Jelliffe, Smith Ely obit
Lake, Simon obit
Läuger, Paul
Laurence, William L(eonard)
Meitner, Lise
Merriam, John Campbell obit
Müller, Paul (Herman)
Negrin, Juan
Oppenheimer, J. Robert
Porter, William N(ichols)
Robeson, Eslanda (Cardoza) Goode
Sabin, Florence R(ena)
Spearman, Charles E. obit
Taylor, A(lbert) Hoyt
Watson-Watt, Sir Robert (Alexander)

Social Science

Arne, Sigrid
Dodds, Harold W(illis)
Fosdick, Raymond B(laine)
Gulick, Luther (Halsey)
Hansen, Alvin H(arvey)
Hayek, Friedrich A(ugust von)
Hickman, Emily (Gregory)
Laidler, Harry W(ellington)
McCoy, Frank R(oss)
Olmstead, Albert Ten Eyck obit
Pasvolsky, Leo
Patton, James G(eorge)
Renner, Karl
Rolland, Romain obit
Roper, Elmo (Burns, Jr.)
Rowe, L(eo) S(tanton)
Ryan, John (Augustine), Msgr. obit
Schain, Josephine
Shear, T(heodore) Leslie obit
Soule, George (Henry, Jr.)
Stokes, I(saac) N(ewton) Phelps obit
Strauss, Anna Lord
Tardieu, André obit

Social Service

Baldwin, William H(enry)
Barnard, Chester I(rving)
Bernadotte, Folke, Count
Bolté, Charles G(uy)
Brunner, Jean Adam
Dickinson, Mrs. LaFell
Flexner, Bernard obit
Fosdick, Raymond B(laine)
Head, Walter W(illiam)
Hershey, Milton S(navely) obit
Howard, Alice Sturtevant obit
Johnson, William E(ugene) obit
Kross, Anna M(oskowitz)
McLean, Alice T(hrockmorton)
Pickett, Clarence E(van)
Pugmire, Ernest I(vison)
Robins, Margaret Dreier obit
Schain, Josephine
Szold, Henrietta obit
Thackrey, Dorothy S(chiff)
Tobias, Channing H(eggie)

Sports

Blaik, Earl (Henry)
Curtis, Ann
Dempsey, Jack
Frick, Ford C(hristopher)
Igoe, Herbert A. obit
Landis, Kenesaw Mountain obit
Little, Lou(is)
McKeever, Ed(ward Clark)
MacPhail, Larry
Nelson, (John) Byron (Jr.)
Rickey, Branch (Wesley)

Technology

Bendix, Vincent obit
Fleming, Sir (John) Ambrose obit
Garand, John C(antius)
Groves, Leslie R(ichard)

Hopkins, Nevil Monroe obit
Lake, Simon obit
Norden, Carl L(ukas)
Taylor, A(lbert) Hoyt
Whittle, Frank

Theater

Astaire, Fred
Barbier, George W. obit
Chase, Mary (Coyle)
Christians, Mady
Comden, Betty
Craven, Frank obit
Crawford, Cheryl
Edwards, Gus obit
Fay, Frank
Fitzgerald, Barry
Gilder, Rosamond
Green, Adolph

Gribble, Harry Wagstaff (Graham-)
Hill, Abram
Hughes, Hatcher obit
Johnson, Hall
Kern, Jerome (David) obit
Knoblock, Edward obit
Langdon, Harry obit
Lillie, Beatrice
McCracken, Joan
McPharlin, Paul
Nathan, George Jean
Nazimova, Alla obit
Neagle, Anna
Osato, Sono
Pemberton, Brock
Romberg, Sigmund
Taylor, Laurette
Tucker, Sophie
Ullman, James R(amsey)
Whitty, Dame May
Wynn, Ed

CUMULATED INDEX—1940 - 1945

This is a six-year cumulation of all names which have appeared in CURRENT BIOGRAPHY from 1940 through 1945. The date following each name indicates the monthly issue as well as the annual volume in which a biography or obituary is included. Please note that three of the 1940 references are not to monthly issues of CURRENT BIOGRAPHY: "Jan-Feb" refers to the combined number which covered the first two months of that year; and since the June and December numbers were not published in monthly form, "Jan-Jun" refers to June material contained in that six-month cumulation, and "Yrbk 40" refers to December material included in that Yearbook.

Abbott, Anthony See Oursler, F. Oct 42

Abbott, Berenice Jul 42

Abbott, Bud, and Costello, Lou Oct 41

Abbott, Edith Sep 41

Abbott, Edwin Milton obit Jan 41

Abbott, George Apr 40

Abbott, Robert Sengstacke obit Mar 40

Abdullah, Achmed obit Jun 45

Abend, Hallett (Edward) Sep 42

Aberhart, William C. obit Jul 43

Abetz, Otto Feb 41

Abul Kalam Azad, Maulana Jul 42

Acheson, Albert R(obert) obit Apr 41

Acheson, Dean (Gooderham) Mar 41

Ackerman, Carl W(illiam) Oct 45

Acland, Sir Richard (Thomas Dyke) Aug 44

Adamic, Louis Yrbk 40

Adamowski, Timothée obit May 43

Adams, Alva B(lanchard) obit Jan 42

Adams Franklin P(ierce) Jul 41

Adams, Herbert obit Jun 45

Adams, James Truslow Nov 41

Adams, Joseph H(enry) obit Apr 41

Adams, Randolph G(reenfield) Aug 43

Adams, Thomas obit Apr 40

Addams, Clifford Isaac obit Jan 43

Addington, Sarah obit Yrbk 40

Addis Ababa, Pietro Badoglio, Duca d' Oct 40

Additon, Henrietta Silvis Sep 40

Ade, George obit Jul 44

Adkins, Charles obit May 41

Adler, Cyrus obit May 40

Adler, Guido obit May 41

Adler, Harry Clay obit Apr 40

Adler, Larry Feb 44

Adler, Mortimer Jerome Apr 40

Adrian, (Gilbert) Feb 41

Agar, Herbert (Sebastian) Mar 44

Aguirre Cerda, Pedro biog Jan 41 obit Yrbk 41

Ahmed II, Sidi, Bey of Tunis obit Aug 42

Ainsworth, William Newman, Bishop obit Aug 42

Aitken, William Maxwell, 1st Baron Beaverbrook See Beaverbrook, W. M. A., 1st Baron Jul 40

Aked, Charles F(rederic), Rev. obit Oct 41

Alain, (Daniel A.) Sep 41

Alajálov, Constantin Jan 42

Albee, Fred H(oudlette) biog May 43 obit Apr 45

Albright, Ivan Le Lorraine Feb 44

Aldrich, Chester Holmes obit Feb 41

Aldrich, Richard S(teere) obit Feb 42

Aldrich, Winthrop Williams Oct 40

Aldridge, James Mar 43

Alegría, Ciro Dec 41

Alexander, Albert Victor Yrbk 40

Alexander, Franz Aug 42

Alexander, Sir Harold R(upert) L(eofric) G(eorge) Oct 42

Alexander, Harry Held obit Feb 41

Alexander, Ruth Mar 43

Alfonso XIII, Former King of Spain obit Apr 41

Alger, Ellice M(urdoch) obit Apr 45

Allee, Marjorie (Hill) obit Jun 45

Allee, Mrs. Warder Clyde See Allee, M. H. obit Jun 45

Allen, Edgar obit Mar 43

Allen, Florence (Ellinwood) Feb 41

Allen, Frank A(lbert, Jr.) Mar 45

Allen, Fred Feb 41

Allen, Gracie Jul 40

Allen, Jay (Cooke, Jr.) Oct 41

Allen, Joel Nott obit Mar 41

Allen, Larry Jul 42

Allen, Marion obit Feb 42

Allen, Robert Sharon See Pearson, D. A. R. and Allen, R. S. May 41

Allen, Terry (de la Mesa) Nov 43

Alley, Rewi Oct 43

Allyn, Lewis B. obit Jan-Jun 40

Almazán, Juan Andreu May 40

Alonso, José Ignacio Rivero y See Rivero (y Alonso), J. I. obit May 44

Alsberg, Carl Lucas obit Yrbk 40

Altenburg, Alexander obit Mar 40

Alter, George Elias obit Oct 40

Alvarez Quintero, Joaquín obit Aug 44

Alvear, Marcelo T. de See De Alvear, Marcelo T. de obit May 42

Amato, Pasquale obit Oct 42

Amedeo, Duke of Aosta obit Apr 42

Ameringer, Oscar obit Dec 43

Amery, L(eopold) Charles Maurice) S(tennett) Jul 42

Ames, Joseph S(weetman) obit Aug 43

Amherst, Alicia-Margaret, Baroness Rockley See Rockley, A.-M. A. Baroness obit Nov 41

Amsden, Charles (Avery) obit Apr 41

Amsterdam, Birdie Mar 40

Amulree, William Warrender Mackenzie, 1st Baron of Strathbraan obit Jun 42

Andersen, Hendrik Christian obit Feb 41

Anderson, Abraham Archibald obit Jan-Jun 40

Anderson, Alexander E. obit Feb 43

Anderson, Clinton P(resba) Jun 45

Anderson, Frederick L(ewis) May 44

Anderson, George Everett obit Apr 40

Anderson, Sir John Jul 41

Anderson, John Crawford obit Jan-Jun 40

Anderson, John (Hargis) obit Sep 43

Anderson, Judith Dec 41

Anderson, Sir Kenneth A(rthur) N(oel) Feb 43

Anderson, Marian May 40

Anderson, Mary Sep 40

Anderson, Mary See Navarro, M. de obit Jul 40

Anderson, Maxwell Nov 42

Anderson, Sherwood obit Apr 41

Andino, Tiburcio Carías See Carías Andino, T. Jun 42

Andrews, C(harles) M(cLean) obit Oct 43

Andrews, Frank M(axwell) biog Feb 42 obit Jun 43

Andrews, John B(ertram) obit Feb 43

Andrews, Roy Chapman Jan 41

Angarita, Isaías Medina See Medina Angarita, I. Mar 42

Angell, James Rowland Yrbk 40

Anthony, John J. Jan 42

Antoine, Josephine Aug 44

Antonescu, Ion Oct 40

Appleton, Edward Dale obit Mar 42

Appleton, Sir Edward (Victor) Sep 45

Appleton, Robert obit Mar 45

Appleyard, Rollo obit Apr 43

Aranha, Oswaldo Mar 42

Aras, Tevfik Rüstü Jun 42

Arco, Georg Wilhelm Alexander Hans, Graf von obit Jan-Jun 40

Argentinita biog Jun 42 obit Oct 45

Argeseanu, George obit Jan 41

Arias, Arnulfo May 41

Armetta, Henry obit Nov 45

Armfield, Anne Constance See Smedley, C. obit Apr 41

Armour, Allison V(incent) obit Apr 41

Armour, Norman Apr 45

Armstrong, Edwin Howard Apr 40

Armstrong, Louis Sep 44

Armstrong, Margaret (Neilson) obit Sep 44

Arnall, Ellis (Gibbs) Aug 45

Arne, Sigrid Oct 45

Arno, Peter Aug 42

Arnold, Bion J(oseph) obit Mar 42

Arnold, George Stanleigh obit Mar 42

Arnold, Henry H(arley) Feb 42

Arnold, Thurman Wesley Jan-Jun 40

Arnold, William Richard, Mgr. May 42

Arnstein, Daniel (G.) Mar 42

Aronson, Louis V. obit Yrbk 40

Aronson, Naoum obit Nov 43

Arrau, Claudio Jan 42

Arroyo del Río, Carlos Alberto Jun 42

Arsonval, Jacques Arsène d' obit Feb 41

Arthur, Jean Mar 45

Arthur, J(oseph) C(harles) obit Jun 42

Arthur William Patrick Albert, Duke of Connaught See Connaught, A. W. P. A., Duke of obit Mar 42

Artzybasheff, Boris Oct 45

Ascher, Leo obit Apr 42

Ashmun, Margaret Eliza obit Apr 40

Askwith, George Ranken Askwith, Ist Baron obit Jul 42

Asquith, Margot (Tennant), Countess of Oxford and Asquith See Oxford and Asquith, M.T.A. obit Sep 45

Astaire, Fred Sep 45

Astor, Nancy Witcher, Viscountess Nov 40

Atalena See Jabotinsky, V. E. obit Sep 40

Atherton, Gertrude Nov 40

Atherton, Warren H(endry) Dec 43

Atholl, John George Stewart-Murray, 8th Duke of obit May 42

Atkinson, Brooks Apr 42

Atkinson, Eleanor obit Jan 43

Atkinson, Justin Brooks See Atkinson, B. Apr 42

Attaway, William (Alexander) Dec 41

Attlee, Clement Richard May 40

Atwell, Wayne J(ason) obit May 41

Auchinleck, Sir Claude (John Eyre) Feb 42

Aughinbaugh, William (Edmund) obit Feb 41

August, John See De Voto, B. Sep 43

Aulaire, Edgar Parin d' See Aulaire, I. and Aulaire, E. P. d' Aug 40

Aulaire, Ingri d', and Aulaire, Edgar Parin d' Aug 40

Austin, F(rederick) Britten obit May 41

Austin, Herbert Austin, Ist Baron obit Jul 41

Austin, Warren R(obinson) Jan 44

Austin, William Lane Apr 40

Avenol, Joseph Louis Anne Jan-Feb 40

Avery, Sewell (Lee) Jun 44

Ayala, Eusebio obit Jul 42

Aydelotte, Frank Oct 41

Ayres, Agnes obit Feb 41

Ayres, Leonard Porter May 40

Azad, Abul Kalam, Maulana See Abul Kalam Azad, Maulana Jul 42

Azaña, Manuel obit Yrbk 40

Babson, Roger W(ard) Feb 45

Baca-Flor, Carlos obit Jul 41

Baccaloni, Salvatore Oct 44

Bach, Reginald obit Feb 41

Bache, Jules S(emon) obit May 44

Bachrach, Elise Wald obit Mar 40

Bacon, Charles R(eade) obit Jun 43

Bacon, George P(reston) obit Nov 41

Bacon, Leonard Jun 41

Bacon, Peggy Jan-Feb 40

Bada, Angelo obit May 41

Baden-Powell of Gilwell, Robert Stephenson Smyth Baden-Powell, Ist Baron obit Mar 41

Badoglio, Pietro See Addis Ababa, P. B., Duca d' Oct 40

Baehr, George May 42

Baekeland, Leo H(endrik) obit Apr 44

Baer, William J(acob) obit Nov 41

Bagramian, Ivan C(hristoforovich) Dec 44

Bailey, Sir Abe, Ist Baronet obit Sep 40

Bailey, Sir Donald Coleman Oct 45

Bailey, Guy Winfred obit Yrbk 40

Bailey, Josiah W(illiam) Apr 45

Bailey, Vernon obit Jun 42

Baird, John Lawrence, Ist Viscount Stonehaven See Stonehaven, J. L. B., Ist Viscount obit Oct 41

Baker, Asa George obit Oct 40

Baker, Charles Whiting obit Aug 41

Baker, Dorothy Dec 43

Baker, George Nov 44

Baker, Ray Stannard Jan-Jun 40

Baker, S(ara) Josephine obit Apr 45

Balanchine, Geoge Nov 42

Balbo, Italo obit Aug 40

Baldomir, Alfredo Jun 42

Baldwin, C(alvin) B(enham) Nov 43

Baldwin, Hanson W(eightman) Aug 42

Baldwin, Roger Nash Jan-Feb 40

Baldwin, William H(enry) Nov 45

Ball, Joseph H(urst) Oct 43

Ballantine, Stuart obit Jun 44

Bampton, Rose Mar 40

Bankhead, John H(ollis) May 43

Bankhead, Tallulah (Brockman) Jul 41

Bankhead, William Brockman biog Oct 40 obit Nov 40

Banning, Kendall obit Feb 45

Banning, Margaret Culkin May 40

Banting, Sir Frederick Grant obit Apr 41

Barber, Mary I(sabel) Jul 41

Barber, Red Jul 43

Barber, Samuel Sep 44

Barber, Walter Lanier See Barber, R. Jul 43

Barbey, Daniel E(dward) Jan 45

Barbier, George W. obit Aug 45

Barbirolli, John Yrbk 40

Barbour, Henry Gray obit Nov 43

Barbour, Ralph Henry obit Oct 44

Barbour, W. Warren obit Jan 44

Barclay, McClelland Sep 40

Barker, Lewellys Franklin obit Sep 43

Barkley, Alben W(illiam) May 41

Barlow, Howard Jan-Feb 40

Barlow, Reginald obit Aug 43

Barnard, Chester I(rving) Mar 45

Barnard, Elinor M. obit Apr 42

Barnard, James Lynn obit Oct 41

Barnes, Albert C(oombs) Mar 45

Barnes, Clifford W(ebster) obit Nov 44

Barnes, William R. obit Mar 45

Barnett, Eugene E(pperson) May 41

Barney, Samuel E. obit Mar 40

Barnouw, Erik Nov 40

Barr, Frank Stringfellow Aug 40

Barr, Norman B., Rev. obit May 43

Barratt, Sir Arthur Sheridan Jan 41

Barrère, Camille Eugène Pierre obit Yrbk 40

Barrère, Georges obit Aug 44

Barrett, Wilton Agnew obit Mar 40

Barringer, Emily Dunning Mar 40

Barringer, Paul Brandon obit Mar 41

Barrow, Joseph Louis See Louis J. Oct 40

Barton, William H(enry), Jr. obit Aug 44

Barry, Patrick Frank, Bishop obit Sep 40

Barrymore, Ethel Mar 41

Barrymore, John obit Jul 42

Barrymore, Lionel Jul 43

Barthé, Richmond Jul 40

Bartók, Béla biog Sep 40 obit Oct 45

Bartol, William Cyrus obit Yrbk 40

Barton, George obit Apr 40

Baruch, Bernard M(annes) Aug 41

Basie, Count Jun 42

Basie, William See Basie, C. Jun 42

Bates, Blanche obit Feb 42

Bates, Ernest Sutherland obit Jan-Feb 40

Bates, Granville obit Sep 40

Bates, H(erbert) E(rnest) Sep 44

Batista Y Zaldivar, Fulgencio Sep 40

Batt, William L(oren) Feb 42

Baudrillart, Henri Marie Alfred, Cardinal obit Jul 42

Baur, Bertha obit Nov 40

Baur, Harry obit May 43

Bausch, Edward obit Sep 44

Bausch, William obit Dec 44

Bax, Sir Arnold (Edward Trevor) Sep 43

Bayard, Thomas F(rancis) obit Sep 42

Beach, Amy Marcy See Beach, Mrs. H. H. A. obit Feb 45

Beach, Mrs. H(enry) H(arris) A(ubrey) obit Feb 45

Beals, Carleton Jun 41

Beard, Charles A(ustin), and Beard, Mary Mar 41

Beard, Daniel Carter obit Aug 41

Beard, James Thom obit Yrbk 42

Beard, Mary See Beard, C. A. and Beard, M. Mar 41

Bearden, Bessye J. obit Nov 43

Beaton, Cecil (Walter Hardy) Oct 44

Beatrice Marie Victoria Feodora, Princess of England obit Dec 44

Beatty, Arthur obit Apr 43

Beatty, Bessie Jan 44

Beauchamp, Mary Annette See Russell, M. A. R., Countess obit Mar 41

Beaux, Cecilia obit Nov 42

Beaverbrook, William Maxwell Aitken, 1st Baron Jul 40

Beck, Jozef obit Jul 44

Beck, Martin obit Jan 41

Becker, May Lamberton May 41

Becker, William Dee obit Sep 43

Bedaux, Charles E(ugene) obit Apr 44

Bede, J(ames) Adam obit Jun 42

Bedford, Herbrand Arthur Russell, 11th Duke of obit Oct 40

Beebe, Lucius Sep 40

Beebe, William Jul 41

Beecham, Sir Thomas, 2nd Baronet Dec 41

Beeding, Francis See Saunders, H. A. St. G. Jun 43

Beer, Thomas obit May 40

Beers, Clifford W(hittingham) obit Aug 43

Begg, Alexander Swanson obit Nov 40

Begg, Colin Luke obit Mar 41

Behrman, S(amuel) N(athaniel) Feb 43

Bei Tsung-hsi See Li Tsung-jen and Pai Tsung-hsi Nov 42

Bekessy, Jean See Habe, H. Feb 43

Bel Geddes, Norman See Geddes, N. B. May 40

Bell, Edward Price obit Nov 43

Bell, Lawrence D(ale) Jul 42

Bell, Thomas M(ontgomery) obit May 41

Bellamann, Henry biog Sep 42 obit Jul 45

Belmont, Mrs. August Jul 44

Belmont, Eleanor (Elise) Robson See Belmont, Mrs. A. Jul 44

Belmore, Alice obit Sep 43

Bemelmans, Ludwig Apr 41

Benavides, Oscar (Raimundo) obit Aug 45

Benchley, Belle Jennings Oct 40

Benchley, Robert (Charles) Sep 41

Bendix, Vincent obit May 45

Benedict, Ruth May 41

Beneš, Eduard Jan 42

Benét, Stephen Vincent obit Apr 43

Benjamin, William Evarts obit Mar 40

Bennett, Henry Gordon Mar 42

Bennett, James O'Donnell obit Mar 40

Bennett, John W(alter) F(rink) obit Oct 43

Bennett, Richard obit Dec 44

Bennett, Robert Russell See Bennett, Russell Apr 42

Bennett, Russell Apr 42

Benny, Jack Aug 41

Benrimo, J. Harry obit May 42

Benson, Allan Louis obit Oct 40

Benson, Edward Frederic obit Mar 40

Benson, Francis Colgate, Jr. obit Apr 41

Benson, John Apr 40

Benson, Sally Aug 41

Bentley, Irene obit Jul 40

Benton, Thomas Hart Oct 40

Benton, William (Burnett) Dec 45

Berg, Ernst J(ulius) obit Nov 41

Berg, Gertrude Jul 41

Berg, Hart O. obit Feb 42

Berg, Irving H(usted) obit Nov 41

Berg, Patricia Jane Sep 40

Bergen, Edgar May 45

Berger, Meyer Jan 43

Bergman, Ingrid Jan-Feb 40

Bergson, Henri (Louis) obit Feb 41

Beria, Lavrenti P(avlovitch) Dec 42

Berigan, Bunny obit Jul 42

Berle, Adolf Augustus, Jr. Jul 40

Berlin, Ellin (Mackay) Apr 44

Berlin, Irving May 42

Bernadotte, Folke, Count May 45

Bernard, Émile obit Jun 41

Bernays, Edward L. Feb 42

Bernheim, Bertram M(oses) Sep 43

Bernie, Ben biog Dec 41 obit Dec 43

Bernstein, Leonard Feb 44

Berry, Edward Wilber obit Oct 45

Berry, Martha McChesney biog Apr 40 obit Apr 42

Berry, William Ewert, 1st Viscount Camrose See Camrose, W. E. B., 1st Viscount Oct 41

Bertram, Adolf, Cardinal obit Aug 45

Bertrand, Louis (Marie Émile) obit Feb 42

Bess, Demaree (Caughey) Jan 43

Besteiro Y Fernandez, Julian obit Nov 40

Bestor, Arthur E(ugene) obit Mar 44

Bethe, Hans Albrecht Jan-Feb 40

Bethune, Mary McLeod Jan 42

Bevan, Aneurin May 43

Bevan, Arthur D(ean) obit Aug 43

Beveridge, Sir William (Henry) Jan 43

Bevier, Isabel obit May 42

Bevin, Ernest Sep 40

Bevis, Howard Landis Jan-Feb 40

Crewe, Robert Offley Ashburton Crewe-Milnes, 1st Marquis of obit Jul 45

Crews, Laura Hope obit Jan 43

Crile, George (Washington) obit Feb 43

Cripps, Charles Alfred, 1st Baron Parmoor See Parmoor, C. A. C., 1st Baron obit Aug 41

Cripps, Sir Stafford Jul 40

Crist, William E(arl) Nov 45

Croce, Benedetto Jan 44

Crompton, Rookes Evelyn Bell obit Mar 40

Cromwell, James H. R. Mar 40

Cronin, A(rchibald) J(oseph) Jul 42

Crosby, Bing Sep 41

Cross, Milton John Jan-Feb 40

Cross, Ronald H(ibbert), 1st Baronet Jun 41

Crossley, Archibald M(addock) Dec 41

Crouse, Russel Jun 41

Crow, Carl biog Oct 41 obit Jul 45

Crowell, T(homas) Irving obit Mar 42

Crowley, John J., Father obit Apr 40

Crowley, Leo T(homas) Jun 43

Crownfield, Gertrude obit Jul 45

Crumit, Frank obit Oct 43

Cruze, James obit Sep 42

Csáky, István, Count See Csáky, S., Count obit Mar 41

Csáky, Stephen, Count obit Mar 41

Cubberley, Ellwood P(atterson) obit Nov 41

Cudahy, John C(larence) obit Oct 43

Cugat, Xavier May 42

Cukor, George Apr 43

Culbertson, Ely May 40

Culkin, Francis D. obit Sep 43

Cullen, Glenn Ernest obit May 40

Cullen, Thomas H. obit Apr 44

Cullis, Winifred C(lara) Nov 43

Culver, Essae Martha Sep 40

Cunningham, Sir Andrew Browne May 41

Cunningham, William Francis obit Jan 41

Curie, Eve Mar 40

Curie, Irène See Joliot-Curie, I. Apr 40

Curran, Charles C(ourtney) obit Jan 43

Curran, Joseph E(dwin) Apr 45

Curran, Pearl Gildersleeve obit Jun 41

Currie, Lauchlin (Bernard) May 41

Curry, John Steuart Apr 41

Curtin, John biog July 41 obit Aug 45

Curtis, Ann Jun 45

Curtis, George Vaughan obit Oct 43

Curtis, Heber D(oust) obit Mar 42

Cushing, Charles C(yprian) S(trong) obit Apr 41

Cushing, Tom See Cushing, C. C. S. obit Apr 41

Czettel, Ladislas Mar 41

Daché, Lilly Jul 41

Dafoe, Allan (Roy) obit Jul 43

Dafoe, John Wesley obit Feb 44

Daladier, Edouard Apr 40

Dale, Benjamin J(ames) obit Sep 43

Dali, Salvador Sep 40

Dallin, Cyrus Edwin obit Jan 45

Dalton, Charles obit Aug 42

Dalton, Hugh Aug 45

Daly, Thomas A., Father obit Mar 41

Damaskinos, Archbishop Nov 45

Damerel, Donna obit Apr 41

Damon, Lindsay Todd obit Jan-Jun 40

Damrosch, Walter (Johannes) Mar 44

Dandurand, Raoul obit Apr 42

Danforth, William obit Jun 41

Daniell, (Francis) Raymond Mar 44

Daniels, Arthur Hill obit Apr 40

Daniels, Charles N. obit Mar 43

Daniels, Jonathan (Worth) Apr 42

Daniels, Josephus Oct 44

Dannay, Frederic See Queen, E. Jul 40

Danner, Louise Rutledge obit Nov 43

Dantchenko, Vladimir (Ivanovich), Nemirovich- obit Jun 43

Danvin, Mme. Charles See Radziwill, C., Princess obit Jul 41

Dardel, Nils von obit Jul 43

Dargan, E(dwin) Preston obit Feb 41

Darlan, Jean (Louis Xavier François) biog Mar 41 obit Feb 43

Darling, Jay Norwood Jul 42

Darré, R(ichard) Walther (Oskar) Nov 41

D'Arsonval, Jacques Arsène See Arsonval, J. A. d' obit Feb 41

Darwell, Jane Jun 41

Darwin, Leonard obit May 43

Dashiell, Willard obit Jun 43

Dashwood, Mrs. Edmée Elizabeth Monica (de la Pasture) See Delafield, E. M. obit Jan 44

Daudet, Léon obit Aug 42

Daugherty, Harry M(icajah) obit Dec 41

Daugherty, James Henry Jul 40

D'Aulaire, Ingri, and D'Aulaire, Edgar Parin See Aulaire, I. d' and Aulaire, E. P. d' Aug 40

Dauser, Sue S(ophia) Aug 44

Davenport, Charles B(enedict) obit Apr 44

Davenport, Eugene obit May 41

Davenport, Marcia Jan 44

Davenport, Russell W(heeler) Jan 44

Davidovitch, Ljuba obit Mar 40

Davidson, Jo Apr 45

Davies, Sir (Henry) Walford obit May 41

Davies, Joseph E(dward) Apr 42

Davies, William Henry obit Nov 40

Davis, Benjamin O(liver) Dec 42

Davis, Bette Oct 41

Davis, Chester Charles Jul 40

Davis, Elmer May 40

Davis, Herbert John Jan-Feb 40

Davis, J. Frank obit May 42

Davis, James Francis See Davis, J. Frank obit May 42

Davis, Joan Jun 45

Davis, Jonathan M(cMillan) obit Aug 43

Davis, Norman H(ezekiah) biog Jan-Feb 40 obit Aug 44

Davis, Robert C(ourtney) obit Oct 44

Davis, Robert H(obart) obit Dec 42

Davis, Stuart Aug 40

Davis, Watson Dec 45

Davis, Westmoreland obit Oct 42

Davis, William Ellsworth Apr 40

Davis, William H(ammatt) Jun 41

Davis, William Rhodes biog Mar 41 obit Sep 41

Davison, F(rederick) Trubee Dec 45

Dawes, Rufus Cutler obit Jan-Feb 40

Dawson, Bertrand, 1st Viscount Dawson of Penn See Dawson of Penn, B. D., 1st Viscount obit Apr 45

Dawson, William Apr 41

Dawson, William L(evi) Apr 45

Dawson of Penn, Bertrand Dawson, 1st Viscount obit Apr 45

Day-Lewis, Cecil Jan-Feb 40

De Alvear, Marcelo T. obit May 42

Dean, Vera Micheles May 43

Deane, Martha See McBride, M. M. Apr 41

Deane, Sidney N(orton) obit Jun 43

Deasy, Luere B. obit Apr 40

Déat, Marcel Jan 42

De Beck, William Morgan obit Jan 43

De Bono, Emilio (Giuseppe Gaspare Giovanni) See Bono, E. G. G. G. de obit Feb 44

De Castelnau, Edouard de Curieres See Castelnau, E. de C. de obit May 44

De Chappedelaine, Louis See Chappedelaine, L. de obit Jan-Feb 40

Fraser, Peter May 42
Fratellini, Paul obit Yrbk 40
Frazer, Sir James (George) obit Jul 41
Frazer, Spaulding obit Apr 40
Frazier, Edward Franklin Jul 40
Fredenthal, David Sep 42
Frederick, John T(ower) Jun 41
Fredman, Samuel, Rabbi obit Jun 41
Freedlander, Arthur R. obit Aug 40
Freeman, James Edward, Bishop obit Jul 43
Freeman, R(ichard) Austin obit Nov 43
Freeman-Thomas, Freeman, 1st Marquess of Willingdon See Willingdon, F. F.-T., 1st Marquess of obit Oct 41
Fremantle, Sir Francis Edward obit Oct 43
French, Hollis obit Jan 41
Freundlich, Herbert (Max Finlay) obit May 41
Freyberg, Bernard Cyril Oct 40
Frick, Ford C(hristopher) May 45
Frick, Wilhelm Aug 42
Frohman, Daniel obit Feb 41
Frost, Robert (Lee) Sep 42
Frye, Jack Apr 45
Fulbright, J(ames) W(illiam) Nov 43
Fuller, Clara Cornelia obit Yrbk 40
Fuller, George Washington obit Yrbk 40
Fuller, S(amuel) R(ichard), Jr. May 41
Fuller, Walter Deane Mar 41
Fulmer, Hampton Pitts obit Dec 44
Funk, Casimir May 45
Funk, Walther Oct 40
Fuqua, Stephen Ogden biog Feb 43 obit Jul 43
Fyfe, H. Hamilton Yrbk 40

Gabin, Jean Jun 41
Gable, Clark May 45
Gaffney, T(homas) St. John obit Mar 45
Gahagan, Helen (Mary) See Douglas, H. M. G. Sep 44
Gale, Henry Gordon obit Jan 43
Galindo, Carlos Blanco See Blanco Galindo, C. obit Nov 43
Galli, Rosina obit Jan-Jun 40
Gallup, George Horace Mar 40
Gamelin, Marie Gustave See Gamelin, M. G. Jan-Jun 40
Gamelin, Maurice Gustave Jan-Jun 40
Gandhi, Mohandas (Karamchand) Dec 42
Ganfield, William Arthur obit Yrbk 40
Gannett, Frank E(rnest) Mar 45
Gannett, Lewis (Stiles) Aug 41

Gannon, Robert I(gnatius), Rev. Mar 45
Ganso, Emil obit Jun 41
Garand, John C(antius) Aug 45
Gardner, Ed(ward Francis) Sep 43
Gardner, Erle Stanley Jun 44
Garfield, Harry A(ugustus) obit Feb 43
Garland, Hamlin obit Mar 40
Garland, Judy Nov 41
Garratt, Geoffrey Theodore obit Jun 42
Garrels, Arthur obit Aug 43
Garson, Greer Sep 42
Garvey, Marcus obit Aug 40
Gasch, Marie Manning See Fairfax, B. Aug 44
Gaselee, Sir Stephen obit Aug 43
Gasser, Herbert S(pencer) Oct 45
Gates, William obit Jan-Jun 40
Gatti-Casazza, Giulio obit Oct 40
Gaulle, Charles de See De Gaulle, C. Sep 40
Gauss, Christian Apr 45
Gauss, Clarence E(dward) Jan 41
Gauthier, Joseph Alexandre George, Archbishop obit Oct 40
Gavin, James M(aurice) Feb 45
Gayda, Virginio biog Sep 40 obit Sep 43
Gaylord, Robert (March) Mar 44
Geddes, Norman Bel May 40
Geer, Alpheus obit Oct 41
Gehrig, Lou biog Jan-Jun 40 obit July 41
Geiger, Roy S(tanley) Jul 45
Genêt See Flanner, J. May 43
Genthe, Arnold obit Oct 42
George VI, King of Great Britain Mar 42
George II, King of Greece Dec 43
George, Albert Bailey obit Apr 40
George, David Lloyd 1st Earl Lloyd George of Dwyfor See Lloyd George of Dwyfor, D. L. G., 1st Earl biog Nov 44 obit May 45
George, Harold L(ee) Dec 42
George, Walter F(ranklin) Jun 43
Géraud, André Sep 40
Gerow, Leonard Townsend Apr 45
Gervasi, Frank (Henry) Jun 42
Gesell, Arnold Nov 40
Gest, Morris obit Jul 42
Getman, F(rederick) H(utton) obit Jan 42
Ghormley, Robert L(ee) Oct 42
Gibbs, George obit Jul 40
Gibbs, William Francis Apr 44
Gibson, Charles Dana obit Feb 45
Gibson, Ernest Willard obit Aug 40

Gideonse, Harry David May 40
Giegengack, A(ugustus) E(dward) Nov 44
Gifford, Sanford R(obinson) obit Apr 44
Gifford, Walter S(herman) Jan 45
Gil Fortoul, José obit Aug 43
Gilbert, George obit May 43
Gilbreth, Lillian Evelyn May 40
Gilder, Robert Fletcher obit Mar 40
Gilder, Rosamond Nov 45
Gildersleeve, Virginia C(rocheron) Aug 41
Giles, Barney McKinney Jul 44
Gill, Eric obit Jan 41
Gillespie, Louis John obit Mar 41
Gillet, Louis obit Aug 43
Gillmore, Frank obit May 43
Gilmer, Elizabeth Meriwether See Dix, D. Jan-Jun 40
Gilmore, John Washington obit Aug 42
Gilmore, Melvin Randolph obit Sep 40
Gilmour, Sir John obit Apr 40
Ginsberg, Samuel See Krivitsky, W. G. obit Mar 41
Giraud, Henri Honoré Dec 42
Giraudoux, Jean obit Mar 44
Girdler, Tom M(ercer) Apr 44
Gish, Dorothy Aug 44
Gish, Lillian Aug 44
Glass, Carter Oct 41
Gleason, C(larence) W(illard) obit Dec 42
Glenn, Mary Wilcox obit Yrbk 40
Glicenstein, Enrico obit Feb 43
Glicenstein, Henryk See Glicenstein, E. obit Feb 43
Glyn, Elinor (Sutherland) obit Nov 43
Goddard, Robert H(utchings) obit Sep 45
Goebbels, Joseph Sep 41
Goering, Hermann (Wilhelm) Aug 41
Goetz, George See Calverton, V. F. obit Jan 41
Gogarty, Oliver (St. John) Jul 41
Golden, John Mar 44
Goldenweiser, Alexander A. obit Sep 40
Goldman, Edwin Franko Sep 42
Goldman, Emma obit Jan-Jun 40
Goldmark, Henry obit Mar 41
Goldmark, Peter Carl Nov 40
Goldsborough, John Byron obit May 43
Goldsmith, Lester Morris Apr 40
Goldthwaite, Anne obit Mar 44
Goldwater, S(igismund) S(chultz) obit Dec 42
Goldwyn, Samuel Jan 44
Goler, George Washington obit Nov 40
Golikov, Filip (Ivanovitch) Apr 43

Knickerbocker, Hubert Renfro Sep 40

Knight, Eric (Mowbray) biog Jul 42 obit Mar 43

Knight, John S(hively) Apr 45

Knight, Ruth Adams Aug 43

Knoblock, Edward obit Aug 45

Knopf, Alfred A. Jun 43

Knopf, Sigard Adolphus obit Sep 40

Knowlson, James S. Nov 42

Knox, Frank Aug 40

Knox, Jean Sep 42

Knox, Louise Chambers obit Mar 42

Knox (William) Frank(lin) biog Aug 40 obit Jun 44

Knudsen, William S. Jul 40

Koch, Frederick H(enry) obit Oct 44

Koch, Theodore Wesley obit May 41

Koenig, Joseph-Pierre Sep 44

Koestler, Arthur Apr 43

Koffka, Kurt obit Jan 42

Koga, Mineichi obit Oct 43

Kohler, Walter Jodok obit May 40

Kolb-Danvin, Mrs. Charles Louis See Radziwill, C., Princess obit Jul 41

Kolbe, Parke Rexford obit Apr 42

Kollontay, Alexandra (Mikhailovna) Oct 43

Konev, Ivan S(tepanovich) Oct 43

Konijnenburg, Willem Adriaan van obit Apr 43

Konoye, Fumimaro, Prince Sep 40

Koo, V(i) K(yuin) Wellington Jul 41

Korizis, Alexander biog Mar 41 obit Jun 41

Korngold, Erich Wolfgang Mar 43

Korngold, Julius obit Oct 45

Koslowski, Leon obit Jul 44

Kossak (-Szczucka), Zofia Jun 44

Kostelanetz, André Jul 42

Koussevitzky, Natalya obit Mar 42

Koussevitzky, Serge Nov 40

Koussevitzky, Mrs. Serge See Koussevitzky, N. obit Mar 42

Kozlenko, William Oct 41

Kramer, Edward Adam obit Feb 42

Kraus, René Jul 41

Krause, Allen K(ramer) obit Jul 41

Krebs, Richard Julius Herman See Valtin, J. Apr 41

Kreisler, Fritz Jul 44

Krenek, Ernst Jul 42

Kriebel, Hermann obit Apr 41

Krivitsky, Walter G. obit Mar 41

Krock, Arthur Feb 43

Kroll, Leon Mar 43

Kronenberger, Louis (Jr.) Aug 44

Kross, Anna M(oscowitz) Nov 45

Krueger, Maynard C. May 40

Krueger, Walter Apr 43

Krueger, Wilhelm obit Jun 43

Krug, J(ulius) A(lbert) Oct 44

Kruger-Gray, George (Edward) obit Jun 43

Kruif, Paul Henry de See De Kruif, P. May 42

Kubelik, Jan obit Jan 41

Küchler, George von Sep 43

Kuhlmann, Frederick obit Jun 41

Kulik, Grigory (Ivanovitch) Jul 42

Kung, H(siang) H(si) Mar 43

Kunitz, Stanley J(asspon) Mar 43

Kuniyoshi, Yasuo Jun 41

Kunz, Alfred A(ugustus) Dec 41

Kurenko, Maria Sep 44

Kurusu, Saburo Jan 42

Kuznetsov, Nikolai G(erasimovich) Nov 42

Kyser, Kay Apr 41

La Borde, Jean (Joseph Jules Noel) de Feb 43

La Cava, Gregory Dec 41

Ladd, Alan (Walbridge) Sep 43

LaFarge, John, Rev. Nov 42

Laffoon, Ruby obit Apr 41

La Follette, Robert M(arion, Jr.) May 44

La Fontaine, Henri obit Jul 43

Lagerlöf, Selma obit Apr 40

La Guardia, Fiorello Henry Oct 40

La Guardia, Ricardo Adolfo de See De La Guardia, R. A. May 42

Lahey, Frank H(oward) Mar 41

Laidlaw, Sir Patrick Playfair obit Apr 40

Laidler, Harry W(ellington) Feb 45

Lake, Simon obit Jul 45

Lambert, Sylvester Maxwell Oct 41

Lamberton, Robert Eneas obit Oct 41

Lamond, Felix obit Apr 40

Lamont, Thomas William Oct 40

Land, Emory S(cott) Sep 41

Landes, Bertha K(night) obit Jan 44

Landis, James M(cCauley) Mar 42

Landis, Kenesaw Mountain biog May 44 obit Jan 45

Landon, Alf(red Mossman) Feb 44

Landon, Margaret (Dorothea Mortenson) Feb 45

Landowska, Wanda Nov 45

Landsteiner, Karl obit Aug 43

Lane, Sir Arbuthnot obit Mar 43

Lane, Gertrude B(attles) obit Nov 41

Lane, Sir William Arbuthnot See Lane, Sir A. obit Mar 43

Lang, Cosmo Gordon, Archbishop of Canterbury Aug 41

Lang, Fritz Jun 43

Langdon, Harry obit Feb 45

Langley, Adria Locke Aug 45

Langmuir, Arthur Comings obit Jul 41

Langmuir, Irving Mar 40

Langner, Lawrence, and Helburn, Theresa Sep 44

Lanman, Charles Rockwell obit Apr 41

Lansbury, George obit Jan-Jun 40

Lapointe, Ernest obit Jan 42

Lasker, Emanuel obit Mar 41

Laski, Harold (Joseph) Sep 41

Latouche, John Treville Jan-Jun 40

Lattimore, Owen Dec 45

Lattre de Tassigny, Jean (Joseph Marie Gabriel) de Jan 45

Läuger, Paul, and Müller, Paul (Herman) Oct 45

Laughlin, Clara Elizabeth obit Apr 41

Laughlin, Irwin (Boyle) obit Jun 41

Laurence, William L(eonard) Oct 45

Laurent, Robert Jul 42

Lauri, Lorenzo, Cardinal obit Dec 41

Lauterbach, Jacob Zallel obit Jun 42

Laval, Pierre biog Sep 40 obit Nov 45

Lavery, Sir John obit Mar 41

Law, Richard K(idston) Feb 44

Lawes, Lewis E(dward) Oct 41

Lawford, Ernest obit Feb 41

Lawrence, Charles Edward obit Apr 40

Lawrence, David Dec 43

Lawrence, Ernest Orlando Jan-Feb 40

Lawrence, Gertrude Aug 40

Lawrence, Marjorie Apr 40

Lawrence, William, Bishop obit Jan 42

Lawson, Mary obit Jul 41

Lawson, Robert Oct 41

Lawson, Ted (W.) Dec 43

Laycock, Craven obit May 40

Laycock, R(obert) E(dward) May 44

Layton, Sir Geoffrey Feb 42

Lazareff, Pierre May 42

Leacock, Stephen (Butler) obit May 44

Leahy, Frank (William) Dec 41

Leahy, William D(aniel) Jan 41

Lear, Ben Jul 42

Leary, Herbert F(airfax) Aug 42

Leary, John Joseph, Jr. obit Feb 44

Leathers, Frederick James, 1st Baron Jun 41

Leblanc, Georgette obit Dec 41

Leblanc, Maurice obit Jan 42

Lecky, Prescott obit Jul 41

Leclerc, Jacques-Philippe Oct 44

Low, David Jan-Feb 40
Lowden, Frank O(rren) obit May 43
Lowell, A(bbott) Lawrence obit Feb 43
Lowry, Edward G(eorge) obit Sep 43
Lozovsky, S(olomon) A(bramovich) Nov 41
Lozowick, Louis Apr 42
Lubin, Isador Oct 41
Luce, Clare Boothe See Boothe, C. Nov 42
Luce, Henry R(obinson) Jul 41
Lucioni, Luigi Oct 43
Luckstone, Isidore obit May 41
Luhan, Mabel Dodge Jan-Feb 40
Luhring, Oscar Raymond obit Oct 44
Lukas, Paul Feb 42
Lumpkin, Alva M(oore) obit Sep 41
Lund, Wendell L(uther) Sep 42
Lundeen, Ernest obit Oct 40
Lunn, Katharine Fowler See Fowler-Billings, K. Jan-Feb 40
Lunt, Alfred, and Fontanne, Lynn Jun 41
Lupescu, Magda Oct 40
Lupino, Ida Sep 43
Lupino, Stanley obit Aug 42
Luquiens, Frederick Bliss obit May 40
Lutes, Della Thompson obit Sep 42
Lutyens, Sir Edwin L(andseer) biog Jun 42 obit Feb 44
Lutz, Frank E(ugene) obit Jan 44
Lydenberg, Harry Miller Sep 41
Lynch, William J(oseph) obit Aug 41
Lyndon, Edward obit Yrbk 40
Lyons, Eugene Jan 44
Lyttelton, Oliver Sep 41

McAdie, Alexander George obit Dec 43
McAdoo, William Gibbs obit Mar 41
McAfee, Mildred H(elen) Sep 42
MacArthur, Douglas Oct 41
Macartney, William Napier obit Aug 40
MacBride, Ernest William obit Jan 41
McBride, Katherine E(lizabeth) Feb 42
McBride, Mary Margaret Apr 41
McCain, John S(idney) biog Oct 43 obit Oct 45
MacCallum, William George obit Mar 44
McCarl, John Raymond obit Sep 40
McCarrens, John S. obit Sep 43
McCarthy, Clem Oct 41
McCarthy, Frank Sep 45
McCarthy, Leighton (Goldie) Oct 42
McClintic, Guthrie May 43

McCloskey, John Robert See McCloskey, R. Sep 42
McCloskey, Robert Sep 42
McCormack, Arthur Thomas obit Sep 43
McCormack, John obit Oct 45
McCormack, John W. Jun 43
McCormick, Anne O'Hare Mar 40
MacCormick, Austin H. May 40
McCormick, Jay (William) Apr 43
McCormick, Robert R(utherford) Aug 42
McCormick, William Patrick Glyn, Rev. obit Yrbk 40
McCoy, Frank R(oss) Nov 45
MacCracken, Henry Noble Sep 40
McCracken, Joan Jun 45
McCreery, Sir Richard L(oudon) May 45
McCullers, Carson Sep 40
McCune, Charles Andrew obit Yrbk 40
McCune, George S(hannon), Rev. obit Feb 42
McCurdy, William Albert, Rev. obit Feb 42
McDaniel, Hattie Sep 40
MacDonald, Cordelia Howard obit Oct 41
MacDonald, Duncan Black, Rev. obit Oct 43
MacDonald, Sir George obit Sep 40
MacDonald, Pirie obit Jun 42
MacEwen, Walter obit May 43
MacFarlane, F(rank) N(oel) Mason Feb 43
McGarry, William J(ames), Rev. obit Nov 41
McGeachy, Mary (Agnes) Craig Apr 44
McGee, Fibber, and McGee, Molly Nov 41
McGee, Molly See McGee, F. and McGee, M. Nov 41
McGillicuddy, Cornelius See Mack, C. Jun 44
McGinley, Phyllis Feb 41
MacGowan, Gault Jan 45
McGroarty, John Steven obit Sep 44
McGuire, Dorothy Sep 41
McGuire, William Anthony obit Nov 40
Machado, Bernardino (Luiz) obit Jun 44
McIntire, Ross T. Oct 45
McIntyre, Marvin H(unter) obit Feb 44
Mack, Connie Jun 44
Mack, Julian W(illiam) obit Oct 43
Mackay, Sir Iven Giffard Apr 41
McKeever, Ed(ward Clark) Nov 45
McKenna, Reginald obit Oct 43
McKenney, Eileen obit See West, N. obit Feb 41
McKenney, Ruth Aug 42

Mackenzie, Clinton obit Mar 40
McKenzie, Roderick Duncan obit Jan-Jun 40
McKenzie, William P. obit Oct 42
MacKenzie, William Warrender, 1st Baron Amulree of Strathbraan See Amulree, W. W. M., 1st Baron of Strathbraan obit Jun 42
McKittrick, Thomas H(arrington) Jul 44
McLean, Alice T(hrockmorton) Jul 45
McLean, Evalyn Walsh May 43
MacLean, Malcolm Shaw Jul 40
MacLeish, Archibald Oct 40
McMahon, (James O')Brien Dec 45
McManamy, Frank obit Nov 44
McMeekin, Clark See McMeekin, I. M. Sep 42
McMeekin, Isabel McLennan Sep 42
McMein, Neysa Feb 41
Macmillan, Harold Mar 43
Macmillan, Maurice Harold See Macmillan, H. Mar 43
McMurtrie, Douglas C(rawford) biog Jul 44 obit Nov 44
McNair, Lesley J(ames) biog Nov 42 obit Sep 44
McNamara, James Barnabas obit Apr 41
McNamee, Graham obit Jul 42
McNarney, Joseph T(aggart) Nov 44
McNary, Charles L(inza) biog Aug 40 obit Ap 44
McNaughton, Andrew (George Latta) Nov 42
MacNeil, Neil May 40
McNutt, Paul Vories Jan-Feb 40
MacPhail, Larry Mar 45
MacPhail, Leland Stanford See MacPhail, L. Mar '45
McPharlin, Paul Nov 45
McPherson, Aimee Semple obit Nov 44
Macrae, John obit Apr 44
MacRossie, Allan, Rev. obit Mar 40
MacVeagh, Lincoln Nov 41
McWilliams, Carey Oct 43
Madeleva, Sister Mary Feb 42
Magee, James C(arre) May 43
Maglione, Luigi, Cardinal obit Oct 44
Magnuson, Warren G(rant) Oct 45
Magoffin, Ralph Van Deman obit Jul 42
Maher, Ahmed, Pasha obit Apr 45
Mailhouse, Max obit Dec 41
Maillol, Aristide (Joseph Bonaventure) biog May 42 obit Nov 44
Main, Charles Thomas obit Apr 43
Mainbocher Feb 42
Maisky, Ivan (Mikhailovich) Sep 41

Otto of Austria, Archduke Jun 41

Oumansky, Constantine (Alexandrovitch) biog Feb 41 obit Mar 45

Oursler, Charles Fulton See Oursler, F. Oct 42

Oursler, Fulton Oct 42

Overman, Lynne obit Apr 43

Owen, Ruth Bryan Dec 44

Owens, Clarence Julian obit Apr 41

Owens, Robert Bowie obit Yrbk 40

Oxenham, John obit Mar 41

Oxford and Asquith, Margot (Tennant) Asquith, Countess of obit Sep 45

Oxnam, G(arfield) Bromley, Bishop Nov 44

Paasikivi, Juho Kusti May 44

Pacciardi, Randolfo Mar 44

Pace, Charles Ashford obit Feb 41

Pacelli, Eugenio See Pius XII, Pope Apr 41

Packard, Eleanor Apr 41

Packard, Frank L(ucius) obit Apr 42

Packard, Winthrop obit May 43

Paddock, Charles W(illiam) obit Sep 43

Paddon, Harry Locke obit Jan-Feb 40

Paderewski, Ignace Jan obit Aug 41

Padilla, Ezequiel Jul 42

Page, Marie Danforth obit Mar 40

Pagnanelli, George See Carlson, J. R. Oct 43

Pai Tsung-hsi See Li Tsung-jen and Pai Tsung-hsi Nov 42

Palencia, Isabel de May 41

Paléologue, (Georges) Maurice obit Jan 45

Paley, William Samuel Oct 40

Palmer, Albert deForest obit Jan-Feb 40

Palmer, James Lynwood obit Aug 41

Palmer, John Leslie obit Sep 44

Papandreou, George (Andreas) Dec 44

Papashvily, George, and Papashvily, Helen (Waite) Mar 45

Papashvily, Helen (Waite) See Papashvily, G. and Papashvily, H. W. Mar 45

Pape, William Jamieson Jan-Jun 40

Papen, Franz von Jun 41

Papi, Gennaro obit Jan 42

Paradise, N(athaniel) Burton obit Jun 42

Pardee, George C(ooper) obit Oct 41

Parke, William obit Sep 41

Parker, Barnett obit Oct 41

Parker, Louis N(apoleon) obit Nov 44

Parma, V. Valta obit Nov 41

Parmoor, Charles Alfred Cripps, 1st Baron obit Aug 41

Parr, A(lbert) E(ide) Jul 42

Parran, Thomas Aug 40

Parri, Ferruccio Nov 45

Parseval, August von obit Ap 42

Parsons, Elsie Worthington obit Feb 42

Parsons, Herbert Collins obit Jul 41

Parsons, Louella Oct 40

Partridge, Sir Bernard obit Sep 45

Partridge, Frank C(harles) obit Apr 43

Pascal, Gabriel Jan 42

Passos, John Dos See Dos Passos, J. Aug 40

Pasternack, Josef Alexander obit Jan-Jun 40

Pasvolsky, Leo May 45

Patch, Alexander M(cCarrell, Jr.) May 43

Patiño, Simón I(turi) Oct 42

Paton, Stewart obit Mar 42

Patri, Angelo Nov 40

Patrick, Mary Mills obit Mar 40

Patrick, Mason Mathews obit Mar 42

Pattee, Alida Frances obit May 42

Patten, Gilbert obit Mar 45

Patterson, Eleanor Medill Nov 40

Patterson, Joseph Medill Jan 42

Patterson, Robert P(orter) Oct 41

Patton, George S(mith), Jr. Jan 43

Patton, James G(eorge) Jan 45

Paul, Prince of Yugoslavia Apr 41

Paul, Eliot Jan-Feb 40

Paul-Boncour, Joseph Jun 45

Pauley, Edwin W(endell) Jun 45

Pavelić, Ante Aug 42

Pavolini, Paolo Emilio obit Nov 42

Paxinou, Katina Oct 43

Paxton, William McGregor obit Jul 41

Peabody, Endicott, Rev. biog May 40 obit Jan 45

Pearl, Raymond obit Jan 41

Pearson, Drew (Andrew Russell), and Allen, Robert (Sharon) May 41

Pearson, T(homas) Gilbert obit Oct 43

Pease, Charles G(iffin) obit Dec 41

Peattie, Donald Culross Oct 40

Peck, James L(incoln) H(olt) Aug 42

Peerce, Jan May 42

Pegler, Westbrook Mar 40

Peirce, Waldo Dec 44

Peirse, Sir R(ichard) E(dmund) C(harles) Sep 41

Peixotto, Ernest (Clifford) obit Jan 41

Pell, Edward Leigh obit Aug 43

Pellegrinetti, Ermenegildo, Cardinal obit May 43

Pelletier, Wilfred Dec 44

Pemberton, Brock Jan 45

Peña, Pedro obit Sep 43

Peñaranda, Enrique Jan-Jun 40

Pendergast, Thomas J(oseph) obit Mar 45

Penn, Arthur A. obit Apr 41

Pennell, Joseph Stanley Dec 44

Penner, Joe obit Mar 41

Penniman, Josiah H(armar) obit Jun 41

Pepper, Claude (Denson) Feb 41

Pepys, Mark Everard, 6th Earl of Cottenham See Cottenham, M. E. P., 6th Earl of obit Sep 43

Percy, William Alexander obit Mar 42

Péret, Raoul obit Sep 42

Perkins, Frances Yrbk 40

Perkins, Milo (Randolph) Jun 42

Perla, David biog Mar 40

Perón, Juan (Domingo) Jun 44

Peroni, Carlo obit May 44

Perret, Frank Alvord obit Mar 43

Pertinax See Géraud, A. Sep 40

Pétain, Henri Philippe Aug 40

Peter II, King of Yugoslavia Nov 43

Peter, Luther Crouse obit Jan 43

Peters, Le Roy S(amuel) obit Feb 42

Peterson, Reuben obit Jan 43

Petri, Egon Nov 42

Petrie, Sir William Matthew Flinders obit Sep 42

Petrillo, James Caesar Yrbk 40

Petroff, Eugene obit Aug 42

Petry, Lucile Apr 44

Pew, Joseph N(ewton), Jr. Sep 41

Peynado, Jacinto B. obit Mar 40

Peyrouton, Marcel Mar 43

Phelan, Michael F(rancis) obit Dec 41

Phelps, William Lyon biog Jan 43 obit Oct 43

Philip, André Aug 43

Phillips, Albert obit Mar 40

Phillips, Sir Frederick obit Oct 43

Phillips, H(arry) I(rving) Sep 43

Phillips, Irna Apr 43

Phillips, John C. obit Aug 43

Phillips, Theodore Evelyn Reece, Rev. obit Jul 42

Phillips, William Jul 40

Phillips, Ze Barney Thorne, Rev. obit Jul 42

Philoff, Bogdan (Dmitrov) Apr 41

Piatigorsky, Gregor Oct 45

Picard, Émile obit Feb 42

Picasso, Pablo Jan 43

Pick, Behrendt obit Jul 40

Pickett, Clarence E(van) Jun 45

Pickford, Mary Apr 45

Pidgeon, Walter Sep 42

Reeve, Sidney A(rmor) obit Aug 41

Reeves, Jesse S(iddal) obit Aug 42

Reich, Nathaniel Julius obit Nov 43

Reichenau, Walter von obit Mar 42

Reid, Frank R., Sr. obit Mar 45

Reid, Helen Rogers Feb 41

Reid, Mont R(ogers) obit Jun 43

Reid, Mrs. Ogden Mills See Reid, H. R. Feb 41

Reiner, Fritz Apr 41

Reinhardt, Aurelia Henry May 41

Reinhardt, Max obit Dec 43

Reisner, Christian Fichthorne, Rev. obit Sep 40

Reisner, George Andrew obit Jul 42

Reith, John Charles Walsham, 1st Baron Nov 40

Relander, Lauri Kristian obit Apr 42

Renault, Louis obit Dec 44

Renner, Karl Sep 45

Resnick, Louis obit May 41

Reston, James B(arrett) Mar 43

Reuter, Gabriele obit Jan 42

Reuther, Walter (Philip) Apr 41

Reventlow, Ernst, Graf zu obit Jan 44

Revueltas, Silvestro obit Yrbk 40

Reybold, Eugene Jun 45

Reynaud, Paul Apr 40

Reynolds, Helen Wilkinson obit Feb 43

Reynolds, James A. obit May 40

Reynolds, Quentin (James) Mar 41

Reynolds, Robert Rice Oct 40

Rhoades, Cornelia Harsen obit Jan 41

Rhodes, Edgar Nelson obit May 42

Riasanovsky, Antonina See Fedorova, N. Nov 40

Ribbentrop, Joachim von May 41

Rice, Alice Caldwell Hegan obit Apr 42

Rice, Elmer (L.) Apr 43

Rice, Grantland Sep 41

Rice, Gregory Dec 41

Rich, Louise Dickinson May 43

Richard, Louis obit Sep 40

Richards, C(harles) R(uss) obit Jun 41

Richards, John G(ardiner) obit Dec 41

Richards, Laura E(lizabeth) obit Mar 43

Richardson, Norval obit Yrbk 40

Richman, Charles J. obit Jan 41

Richmond, Charles Alexander, Rev. obit Sep 40

Richter, George Martin obit Jul 42

Rickenbacker, Edward Nov 40

Ricketts, Louis Davidson obit Mar 40

Rickey, Branch (Wesley) Oct 45

Rickey, James W(alter) obit Jun 43

Ridge, Lola obit Jul 41

Riesman, David obit Jul 40

Riggs, Austen Fox obit Mar 40

Riggs, T(homas) L(awrason), Rev. obit Jun 43

Rigling, Alfred obit Jan 41

Ring, Barbara T(aylor) obit Nov 41

Ringling, Robert E(dward) May 45

Río, Carlos Alberto Arroyo del See Arroyo del Río, C. A. Jun 42

Rios, Juan Antonio Apr 42

Ripley, Joseph obit Nov 40

Ripley, Robert L(eroy) Jul 45

Ripley, William Z(ebina) obit Oct 41

Rivero (y Alonso), José Ignacio obit May 44

Rives, Amélie. See Troubetzkoy, A. R. obit Jul 45

Riza Shah Pahlavi obit Sep 44

Robb, Hunter obit Jan-Jun 40

Robert, Georges (Achille Marie-Joseph) Jun 43

Roberts, Sir Charles G(eorge) D(ouglas) obit Jan 44

Roberts, Elizabeth Madox obit May 41

Roberts, Florence obit Jul 40

Roberts, George Lucas obit Apr 41

Roberts, Kate L(ouise) obit Oct 41

Roberts, Owen J(osephus) Oct 41

Robertson, Ben, Jr. Nov 42

Robeson, Eslanda (Cardoza) Goode Sep 45

Robeson, Mrs. Paul See Robeson, E.C.G. Sep 45

Robeson, Paul (Bustill) Mar 41

Robey, Ralph W(est) May 41

Robins, Edward obit Jul 43

Robins, Margaret Dreier obit Apr 45

Robins, Mrs. Raymond See Robins, M. D. obit Apr 45

Robinson, Bill Feb 41

Robinson, Boardman Dec 41

Robinson, Frederick B(ertrand) obit Dec 41

Robinson, Holton D. obit Jun 45

Robinson, Samuel M(urray) Feb 42

Robinson, William Heath obit Nov 44

Robson, May obit Dec 42

Roca, Julio A. obit Nov 42

Roche, Josephine (Aspinwall) Aug 41

Rockefeller, John D(avison), Jr. Jul 41

Rockefeller, Nelson (Aldrich) Mar 41

Rockley, Alicia-Margaret Amherst, Baroness obit Nov 41

Rockwell, Norman Jun 45

Rodgers, Richard, and Hart, Lorenz May 40

Rodriquez, Nicolas obit Sep 40

Rodzinski, Artur Aug 40

Roelofs, Henrietta obit Mar 42

Rogers, Edith Nourse Apr 42

Rogers, Ginger Apr 41

Rogers, Mark Homer obit Nov 41

Rogers, Norman McLeod obit Jul 40

Rogers, Robert Emmons obit Jul 41

Rohde, Ruth Bryan Owen See Owen, R. B. Dec 44

Rokossovsky, Konstantin Jan 44

Rolland, Romain obit Feb 45

Romano, Emanuel Mar 40

Romberg, Sigmund Mar 45

Rome, Harold J(acob) Apr 42

Rommel, Erwin biog Aug 42 obit Dec 44

Romulo, Carlos P(ena) Mar 43

Rood, Helen Martin obit Mar 43

Rooney, Mickey Feb 42

Roosevelt, Eleanor Nov 40

Roosevelt, Franklin D(elano) biog Mar 42 obit Apr 45

Roosevelt, Kermit obit Jul 43

Roosevelt, Sara Delano obit Oct 41

Roosevelt, Theodore, Jr. obit Sep 44

Root, Oren, Jr. Aug 40

Root, Waverley (Lewis) May 43

Roper, Daniel C(alhoun) obit May 43

Roper, Elmo (Burns, Jr.) Jan 45

Rosanoff, Aaron J(oshua) obit Feb 43

Rose, Billy Aug 40

Rose, Mary D. Swartz obit Mar 41

Rose, Maurice obit May 45

Rosenberg, Alfred Oct 41

Rosenberg, Anna M(arie) Jan 43

Rosenberg, Arthur obit Mar 43

Rosenfeld, Kurt obit Nov 43

Rosenman, Samuel I(rving) Aug 42

Rosenthal, Joe Jun 45

Rosett, Joshua obit May 40

Ross, Barnaby See Queen, E. Jul 40

Ross, Charles (Griffith) Jun 45

Ross, Sir Edward Denison obit Nov 40

Ross, Harold W(allace) May 43

Ross, Leonard Q. See Rosten, L. C. Oct 42

Ross, Malcolm Feb 44

Ross, Nellie Tayloe May 40

Rosten, Leo C(alvin) Oct 42

Rosten, Norman Apr 44

Rothenstein, Sir William obit Apr 45

Rothermere, Harold Sidney Harmsworth, 1st Viscount obit Jan 41

Rouault, Georges May 45

Rourke, Constance Mayfield obit May 41

Roussy de Sales, Raoul de See De Roussy de Sales, R. obit Jan 43

Rowan, Andrew S(ummers) obit Mar 43

Rowe, L(eo) S(tanton) Aug 45

Rowell, Chester H. Yrbk 40

Rowntree, Cecil obit Dec 43

Royal, Forrest B. obit Jul 45

Royden, A(gnes) Maude Apr 42

Royden, Maude See Royden, A. M. Apr 42

Royle, Edwin Milton obit Apr 42

Rubicam, Raymond Dec 43

Rubin, Reuven Apr 43

Rubinstein, Artur Dec 45

Rubinstein, Helena Jun 43

Ruckstull, F(rederick) Wellington obit Jul 42

Ruffing, Charles H(erbert) Nov 41

Rugg, Harold (Ordway) May 41

Ruiz Guiñazú, Enrique Apr 42

Rukeyser, Muriel Mar 43

Ruml, Beardsley May 43

Rumpler, Edmund obit Oct 40

Rundstedt, Gerd von See Rundstedt, K. R. G., von Nov 41

Rundstedt, Karl (Rudolf Gerd) von Nov 41

Runkle, Erwin W(illiam) obit Apr 41

Runyon, Alfred Damon See Runyon, D. Nov 42

Runyon, Damon Nov 42

Rupertus, William H(enry) obit May 45

Rusby, Henry H(urd) obit Jan 41

Rüshdi, Tevfik, Bey See Aras, T. R. Jun 42

Rushmore, David Barker obit Jul 40

Russell, Bertrand Arthur William, 3rd Earl Apr 40

Russell, Charles (Edward) obit Jun 41

Russell, Charles Ellsworth See Russell, P. W. Aug 44

Russell, Herbrand Arthur, 11th Duke of Bedford See Bedford, H. A. R., 11th Duke of obit Oct 40

Russell, James Earl obit Dec 45

Russell, Mary Annette Russell, Countess obit Mar 41

Russell, Pee Wee Aug 44

Russell, Rosalind Jan 43

Rust, Bernhard Jul 42

Rutenberg, Pinhas obit Mar 42

Ruth, Babe Aug 44

Ruth, George Herman See Ruth, B. Aug 44

Rutherford, Joseph Franklin biog Nov 40 obit Mar 42

Rutledge, Brett See Paul E. Jan-Feb 40

Rutledge, Wiley (Blount), Jr. May 43

Ryan, John (Augustine), Msgr. obit Oct 45

Ryan, T(ubal) Claude Jan 43

Ryti, Risto (Heikkie) Feb 41

Saarinen, Eliel Oct 42

Sabatier, Paul obit Oct 41

Sabin, Florence R(ena) Apr 45

Sabry, Hassan, Pasha obit Yrbk 40

Sachs, Bernard obit Mar 44

Sachs, Curt Aug 44

Sackett, Frederic M(oseley), Jr. obit Jul 41

Sadler, Sir Michael (Ernest) obit Dec 43

Saerchinger, César Apr 40

Sage, Dean obit Aug 43

Saint Exupéry, Antoine de Janbiog Feb 40 obit May 45

Saint-Gaudens, Homer (Schiff) Oct 41

St. George, Thomas R(ichard) Jan 44

St. John, Robert Jun 42

Saionji, Kimmochi, Prince obit Jan 41

Sakel, Manfred Jan 41

Salazar, Antonio de Oliveira May 41

Salten, Felix obit Nov 45

Salter, Alfred obit Sep 45

Salter, Andrew May 44

Salter, Sir (James) Arthur Mar 44

Saltonstall, Leverett Jun 44

Salvemini, Gaetano Dec 43

Sanborn, (John) Pitts obit Apr 41

Sandburg, Carl Jan-Jun 40

Sandefer, Jefferson Davis obit Apr 40

Sanders, George Jun 43

Sanders, Jared Young obit May 44

Sanger, Margaret (Higgins) Aug 44

San Martín, Ramón Grau See Grau San Martín, R. Oct 44

Santayana, George Apr 44

Saposs, David Nov 40

Saracoglu, Sükrü Jun 42

Sarajoglu Shukri, Bey See Saracoglu, S. Jun 42

Sarg, Tony obit Apr 42

Sargent, (Harold) Malcolm (Watts) Dec 45

Sargent, Porter (Edward) Jul 41

Sarnoff, David Nov 40

Sarojini, Nayadu See Naidu, S. May 43

Saroyan, William Jul 40

Sarton, George (Alfred Léon) Jul 42

Sauer, Emil von obit Jun 42

Saunders, Hilary A(idan) St. George Jun 43

Saunders, John Monk obit Apr 40

Savage, Augusta (Christine) Jan 41

Savage, John Lucian Apr 43

Savage, Michael Joseph obit Apr 40

Saxton, Alexander (Plaisted) Nov 43

Sayao, Bidu Feb 42

Sayles, R(obert) W(ilcox) obit Dec 42

Sayre, Francis Bowes Jan-Feb 40

Schacht, Hjalmar (Horace Greeley) Oct 44

Schain, Josephine Jul 45

Schechter, A(bel) A(lan) May 41

Scheiberling, Edward N(icholas) Dec 44

Schelling, Ernest Henry obit Jan-Feb 40

Scherer, Paul (Ehrman), Rev. May 41

Schereschewsky, Joseph Williams obit Sep 40

Scherman, Harry Sep 43

Schertzinger, Victor obit Dec 41

Schiaparelli, Elsa Jan-Feb 40

Schick, Béla Jul 44

Schilder, Paul Ferdinand obit Jan 41

Schillinger, Joseph obit May 43

Schlauch, Margaret Dec 42

Schleich, Michel, Rev. obit Jun 45

Schlesinger, Frank obit Aug 43

Schlink, Frederick John Mar 41

Schlosser, Alex L. obit Mar 43

Schmelkes, Franz C(arl) obit Feb 43

Schmidt, Fritz obit Aug 43

Schmitt, Bernadotte E(verly) Dec 42

Schmitt, Gladys (Leonore) Mar 43

Schnabel, Artur Jul 42

Schneider, Eugene obit Jan 43

Schneider, Hannes Mar 41

Schoen-René, Anna Eugéne obit Jan 43

Schoenberg, Arnold Apr 42

Schoff, Hannah Kent obit Feb 41

Schofield, Frank H(erman) obit Apr 42

Schönberg, Arnold See Schoenberg, A. Apr 42

Schoonmaker, Edwin Davies obit Jan-Jun 40

Schorr, Friedrich Jul 42

Schram, Emil Oct 41

Schratt, Katharina obit May 40

Schreiber, Georges May 43

Schrembs, Archbishop Joseph obit Dec 45

Schroeder, R(udolph) W(illiam) Jul 41

Schuchert, Charles obit Jan 43

Schulberg, Budd (Wilson) Jun 41

Schuller, Mary Craig McGeachy See McGeachy, M.A.C. Apr 44